England

written and researched by

Robert Andrews, Jules Brown, Phil Lee and Rob Humphreys

with additional contributions by

Emma Rees

NEW YORK • LONDON • DELHI

www.roughguides.com

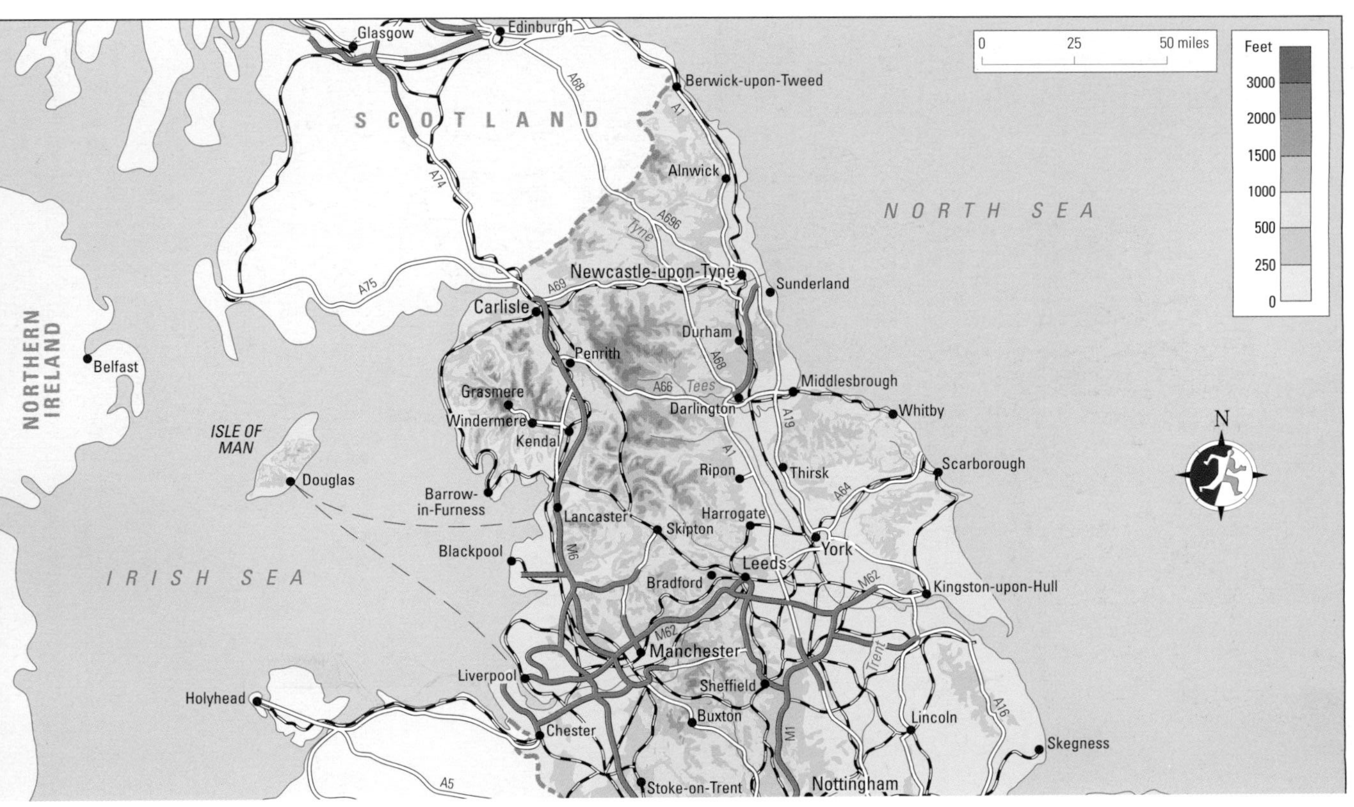

Glasgow
Edinburgh
0
25
50 miles
Feet
3000
2000
1500
1000
500
250
0
Berwick-upon-Tweed
S C O T L A N D
A68
A1
Alnwick
A74
NORTH SEA
A696
Tyne
Newcastle-upon-Tyne
Sunderland
A75
A69
Carlisle
Durham
NORTHERN IRELAND
Belfast
Penrith
A68
A66
Tees
Middlesbrough
Grasmere
Darlington
Whitby
A19
N
Windermere
ISLE OF MAN
Kendal
A1
Scarborough
Ripon
Thirsk
Douglas
Barrow-in-Furness
A64
Harrogate
Lancaster
Skipton
York
Blackpool
M6
Leeds
IRISH SEA
Bradford
M62
Kingston-upon-Hull
M62
Manchester
Trent
Liverpool
Sheffield
Holyhead
Buxton
A16
Lincoln
Chester
M1
Skegness
A5
Stoke-on-Trent
Nottingham

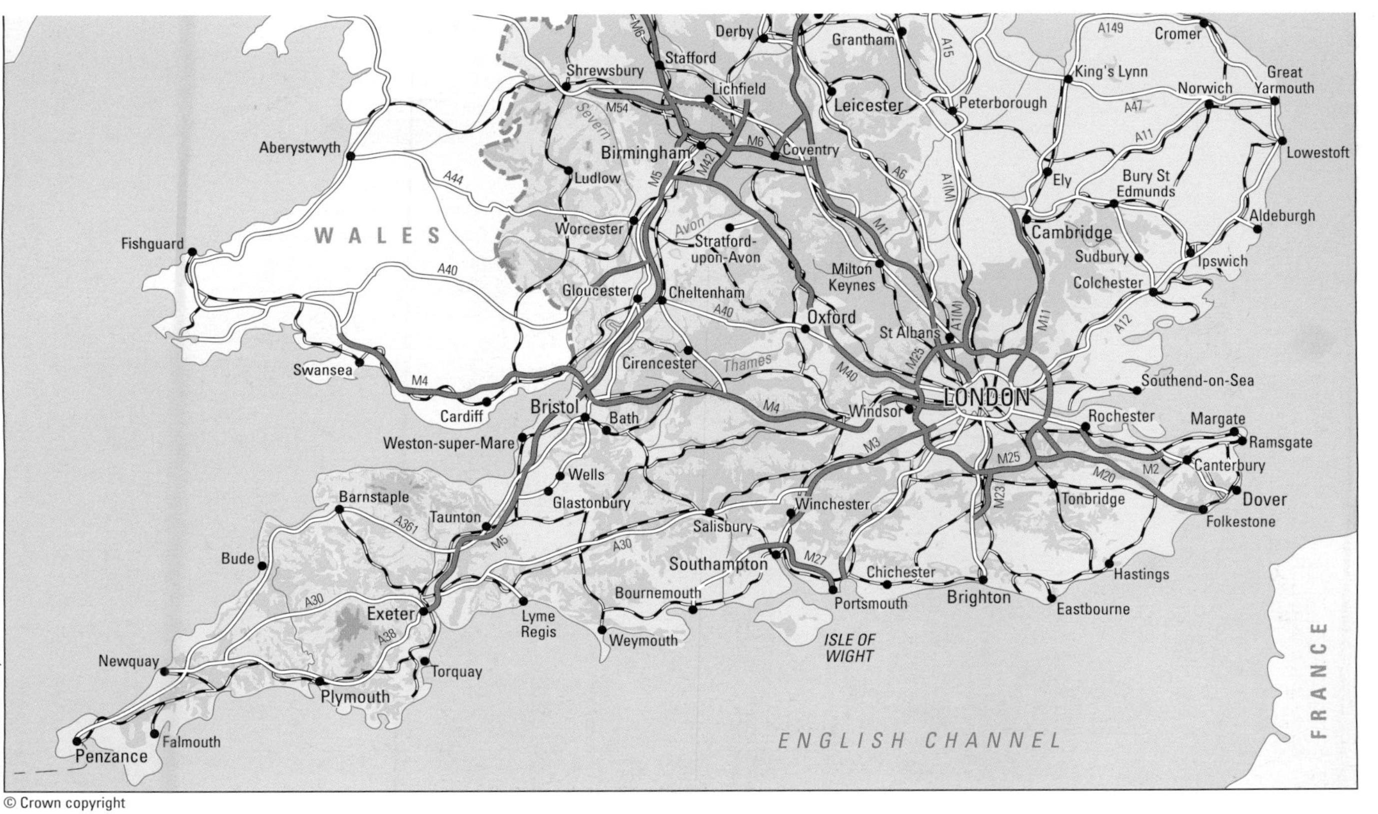
WALES
ENGLISH CHANNEL
FRANCE
ISLE OF WIGHT
The Isles of Scilly
LONDON
Derby
Grantham
Stafford
Shrewsbury
Lichfield
Leicester
Peterborough
King's Lynn
Cromer
Great Yarmouth
Norwich
Lowestoft
Aberystwyth
Birmingham
Coventry
Ludlow
Ely
Bury St Edmunds
Aldeburgh
Fishguard
Worcester
Stratford-upon-Avon
Cambridge
Sudbury
Ipswich
Milton Keynes
Colchester
Gloucester
Cheltenham
Oxford
St Albans
Swansea
Cirencester
Southend-on-Sea
Cardiff
Bristol
Bath
Windsor
Rochester
Margate
Ramsgate
Weston-super-Mare
Canterbury
Wells
Glastonbury
Tonbridge
Dover
Barnstaple
Taunton
Winchester
Folkestone
Salisbury
Southampton
Hastings
Bude
Chichester
Bournemouth
Portsmouth
Brighton
Eastbourne
Exeter
Lyme Regis
Weymouth
Newquay
Torquay
Plymouth
Penzance
Falmouth
Severn
Avon
Thames
M6
M54
M5
M42
M1
A6
A1(M)
A15
A149
A47
A11
M11
A12
M25
M40
M4
M3
M23
M20
M2
M27
A44
A40
A30
A361
A38
© Crown copyright

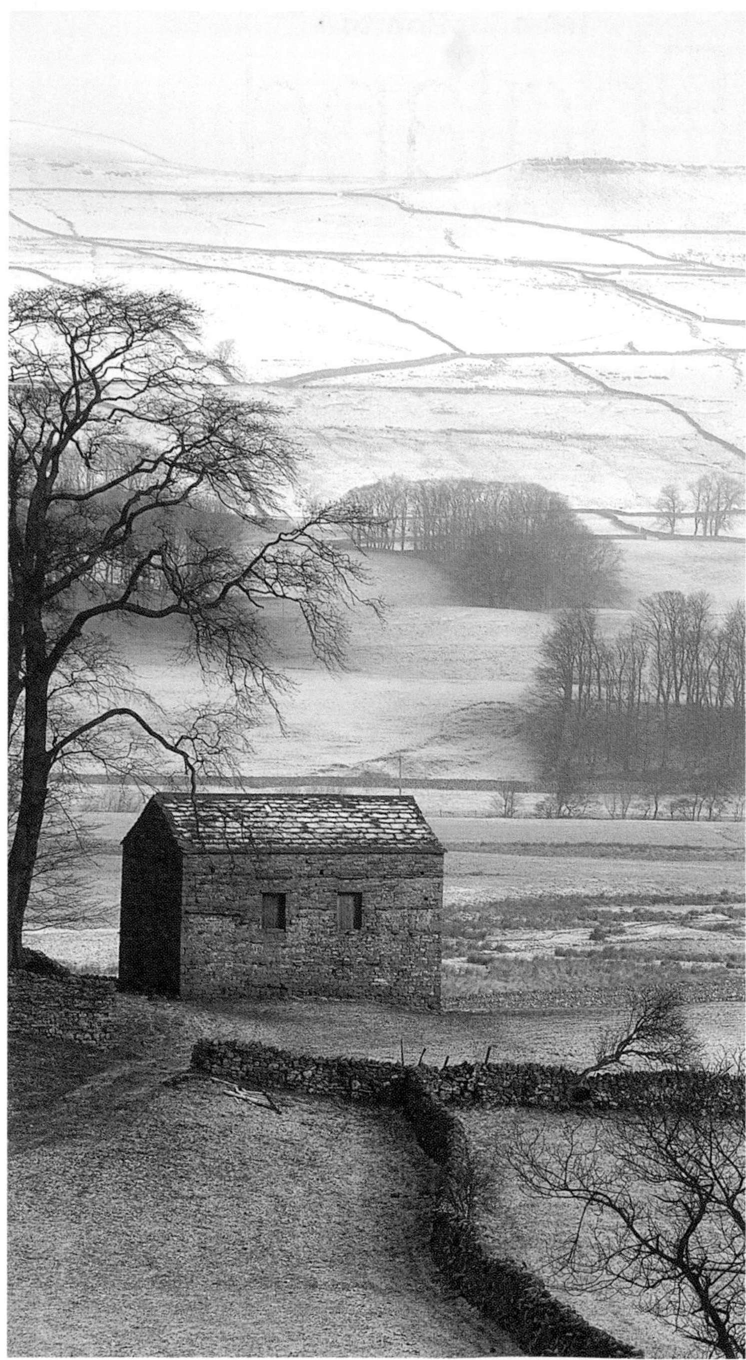

△ North Yorkshire Moors

Introduction to

England

Like an ageing cabaret star shuffling onto the stage, England really needs no introduction. When even the world's most remote communities are on first-name terms with its footballers, princes, pop stars and prime ministers, it's clear that everyone knows something about this crowded island nation, perched on the western fringe of Europe. Visitors can pick their favourite slice of "Englishness" and indulge themselves in a country with a notorious taste for nostalgia. The tales of King Arthur; the works of Shakespeare; the exploits of Drake; the intellect of Johnson; the invention of Brunel; the leadership of Churchill; the cult of Diana – all are endlessly recycled in England, providing a cultural backdrop to an unparalleled range of historic buildings, sites and monuments.

Of course, this isn't the whole story of England, or anything like it. For every tourist who wants to stand outside the gates of Buckingham Palace or visit Stratford-upon-Avon, there's another who makes a beeline for the latest Tracey Emin show or the contemporary cityscape of downtown Manchester. The difficulty is in saying which is the truer image of a country that flaunts proudly its many contradictions. Contemporary England is at the same time a deeply conservative place with a richly multi-ethnic culture. Famously, fish and chips has given way to chicken tikka masala as the country's favourite dish, and while the nation tends to distrust all things European, the English also increasingly embrace a continental lifestyle. Enjoy a fried English breakfast or a Devonshire cream tea by all means, but notice the locals at the next-door café-bar tucking into a croissant and a cappuccino.

Ask an English person to define their country in terms of what's worth seeing and you're most likely to have your attention drawn to the country's

Fact file

• As part of the United Kingdom of Great Britain and Northern Ireland, **England** is a parliamentary democracy, with Queen Elizabeth II as its head of state. Its traditional **industries** – fishing, farming, mining, engineering, shipbuilding – are all in decline, some terminal, and major contemporary income sources are banking and finance, communications technology, the production of steel, transport equipment, oil and gas, and tourism.

• Bordered by Scotland to the north and Wales to the west, England is the largest country in Great Britain, occupying an area of 50,085 sq miles (129,720 sq km). There's a diverse **terrain**, from plains to peaks, cliffs to beaches, though its superlatives are all modest on a world scale – the largest lake, Windermere, is 10 miles (16km) long, the highest mountain, Scafell, 3205ft (just 978m) above sea level.

• A **population** of approximately 50 million is dense for a country of its size, but settlement is concentrated in the southeast conurbations around the capital, London, and in the large industrial cities of the Midlands and the North.

• This is one of the world's most **multi-ethnic** countries, made up largely of people of Anglo-Saxon, Scots, Welsh and Irish descent, but with sizeable communities from the Caribbean, Africa, Bangladesh, Pakistan, India, China and Southeast Asia and Eastern Europe.

• The famous face of England has changed, not always for the best – red telephone boxes are hard to find and the police increasingly carry guns, but it's easier to get a drink after 11pm and shops are open on Sundays.

golden rural past. The classic images are found in every brochure – the village green, the duckpond, the country lane and the farmyard. And it's true that it's impossible to overstate the bucolic attractions of various English regions, from Cornwall to the Lake District, or the delights they provide – from walkers' trails and prehistoric stone circles to traditional pubs and obscure festivals. But despite celebrating their rural heritage, the modern-day English have an ambivalent attitude towards "the country". Farming today forms only a tiny proportion of the national income and there's a real dislocation between the urban population and the small rural communities badly hit by numerous crises in English farming.

△ Shaftesbury, Dorset

England isn't a simple destination, but rather a deeply engrained series of influences that ripple out into the world.

The national game

Football, soccer, call it what you will – the English invented it and subsequently appropriated it as an expression of (often misguided) national pride. The country has the oldest league and cup competitions in the world, the best-known club on the planet in Manchester United and players who are more famous than pop stars (or, like the incomparable David Beckham, are married to pop stars). For outsiders, though, the nuances of supporting a team can be difficult to unravel. The city of Manchester, like Liverpool or Sheffield, has two teams; London has thirteen (none of them called London). Supporters of geographically adjacent teams (Newcastle and Sunderland, say, or Southampton and Portsmouth) despise the other; while everyone despises Manchester United. And once you've got to the bottom of this, you still might never get to see a live game as tickets for the famous teams sell out a year in advance. You could watch it on TV (there's a game most nights between August and May), but for the real football experience you have to visit the unfashionable provincial clubs inhabiting the lower divisions. Huddersfield Town against Rochdale on a wet Tuesday night in February – that's a proper football match, everything else is entertainment.

So perhaps the heart of England is found in its towns and cities instead? The shift towards urban living and working has not been reversed since the Industrial Revolution, and industry – and the Empire it inspired – has provided a framework for much of what's on show. Virtually every English town bears a mark of former wealth and power, whether it be a magnificent Gothic cathedral financed from a monarch's treasury, a parish church funded by the tycoons of the medieval wool trade, or a triumphalist civic building raised on the back of the slave and sugar trade. In the south of England you'll find old dockyards from which the navy patrolled the oceans, while in the north there are mills that employed entire town populations. England's museums and galleries – several of them ranking among the world's finest – are full of treasures trawled from its imperial conquests. And in their grandiose stuccoed terraces and wide esplanades the old

△ Beachy Head

resorts bear testimony to the heyday of the English holiday towns, as fashionable once as any European spa.

In short, England isn't a simple destination, but rather a deeply engrained series of influences that ripple out into the world. Much of western history and culture is contained within its very fabric. Its inventions and creative momentum, from the Industrial Revolution to Cool Britannia, continue to inspire; while its idiosyncrasies and prejudices leave their mark across the English-speaking world. And the only certainty for visitors is that, however long you spend in the country and however much you see, it still won't be enough to understand England. After all, the English have lived here all their lives and they still can't agree whether the milk goes in before or after the tea.

Where to go

△ The Angel of the North, Gateshead

To begin to get to grips with England, **London** is the place to start. Nowhere else in the country can match the scope and innovation of the metropolis, a colossal, frenetic city, perhaps not as immediately attractive as its European counterparts, but with so much variety that lack of cash is the only obstacle to a great time. It's here that

Standing stones

Why the prehistoric peoples of England built dramatic circles of standing stones may never be fully known. The theories are as diverse as the sites themselves: perhaps they were places of sacrifice and celebration, or erected for an astronomical function. But two things remain obvious, even at a distance of five thousand years. Firstly, each series of standing stones represents a highly organized effort by ancient peoples once thought of as unsophisticated. And secondly, whatever their function, there's a powerful presence at work even today, recognized by the disparate bands of druids and New Age travellers who still seek solace in the stones. Mass tourism has dragged famous sites like Stonehenge into the embrace of the heritage industry, but there are other stone circles which retain their sense of mystery and isolation. At Castlerigg, near Keswick in the Lake District; or the site known as Long Meg and her Daughters near Penrith; or the circles on Bodmin Moor in the west country – here you can still wander alone, forming your own theories as the early morning mist rises above the stones.

you'll find England's best spread of nightlife, cultural events, museums, galleries, pubs and restaurants. However, each of the other large cities, such as **Birmingham**, **Newcastle**, **Leeds**, **Sheffield**, **Manchester** and **Liverpool**, makes its own claim for historic and cultural diversity, and you certainly won't have a representative urban view of the country if you venture no further than the capital. It's in these regional centres that, arguably, the most exciting architectural and social developments are taking place, though for many visitors they rank a long way behind ancient cities like **Lincoln**, **York**, **Salisbury**, **Durham** and **Winchester** – to name just those with the most celebrated of England's cathedrals. Most beguiling of all, though, are the long-established **villages** of England, hundreds of which amount to nothing more than a pub, a shop, a gaggle of cottages and a farmhouse offering bed and breakfast. Devon, Cornwall, the Cotswolds and the Yorkshire Dales harbour some especially picturesque specimens, but every county can boast a decent showing of photogenic hamlets.

Evidence of England's pedigree is scattered between its settlements as well. Wherever you're based, you're never more than a few miles from a **ruined castle**, a majestic **country house** or a **monastery**, and in some parts of the country you'll come across the sites of civilizations that thrived here before England existed as a nation. In the southwest there are remnants of a **Celtic** culture that elsewhere was all but eradicated by the

△ Notting Hill pub, London

Romans, and from the south coast to the northern border you can find traces of **prehistoric** settlers, the most famous being the megalithic circles of Stonehenge and Avebury.

Then of course there's the English **countryside**, an extraordinarily diverse terrain from which Constable, Turner, Wordsworth, Emily Brontë and a host of other native luminaries took inspiration. Most dramatic and best known are the moors and uplands – **Exmoor**, **Dartmoor**, **Bodmin Moor**, the **North York Moors** and the **Lake District** – each of which has its over-visited spots, though a brisk walk will usually take you out of the throng. Quieter areas are tucked away in every corner of England, from the lush vales of **Shropshire** near the border with Wales, to the flat waterlands of the eastern **Fens** and the chalk downland of **Sussex**. It's a similar story on the **coast**, where the finest sands and most rugged cliffs have long been discovered, and sizeable resorts have grown to exploit many of the choicest locations. But again, if it's peace you're after, you can find it by heading for the exposed strands of **Northumberland**, the pebbly flat horizons of **East Anglia** or the crumbling headlands of **Dorset**.

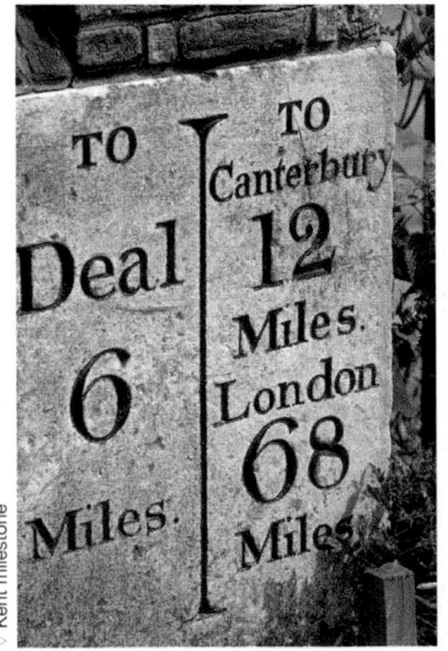

▽ Kent milestone

When to go

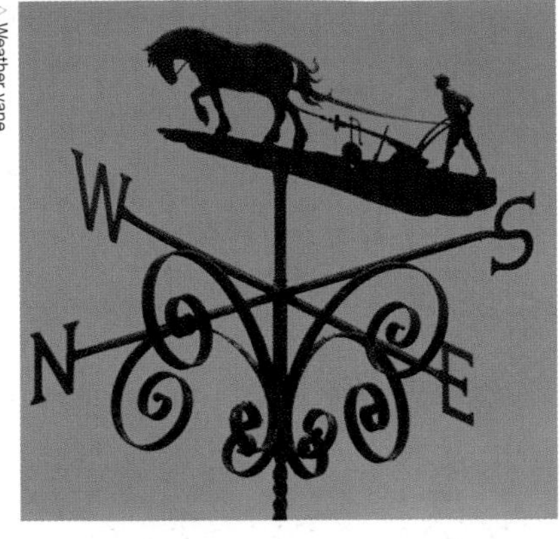

△ Weather vane

Considering the temperateness of the English **climate**, it's amazing how much mileage the locals get out of the subject – a two-day cold snap is discussed as if it were the onset of a new Ice Age, and a week in the upper 70s Fahrenheit starts rumours of drought. The fact is that English summers rarely get hot and the winters don't get very cold, and there's not a great deal of regional variation, as the chart shows. The average **summer temperature** in the landlocked Midlands is much the same as down on the southwest beaches, and within a degree or two of the average in the north. Summer rainfall is fairly even over all of England as well, though in general the south gets more **hours of sunshine** than the north. Differences between the regions are slightly more marked in **winter**, when the south tends to be appreciably milder and wetter than the north.

The bottom line is that it's impossible to say with any degree of certainty that the weather will be pleasant in any given month. May might be wet and grey one year and gloriously sunny the next, and the same goes for the autumnal months. November stands an equal chance of being crisp and clear or foggy and grim. Obviously, if you're planning to lie on a beach, or camp in the dry, you'll want to go between June and September – a period when you shouldn't go anywhere without booking your accommodation well in advance. Elsewhere, if you're balancing the likely fairness of the weather against the density of the crowds, the best time to get into the countryside or the towns would be between **April and early June** or in **September** or **October**.

▽ Deckchairs on Blackpool Beach

Considering the temperateness of the English climate, it's amazing how much mileage the locals get out of the subject

Average temperatures and rainfall

	Jan	Feb	Mar	Apr	May	June	July	Aug	Sept	Oct	Nov	Dec
Birmingham												
(°F)	42	43	48	54	60	66	68	68	63	55	48	44
(°C)	5	6	9	12	16	19	20	20	17	13	9	7
(inches)	3	2.1	2	2.1	2.5	2	2.7	2.7	2.4	2.7	3.3	2.6
(mm)	74	54	50	53	64	50	69	69	61	69	84	67
London												
°F)	43	44	50	56	62	69	71	71	65	58	50	45
(°C)	6	7	10	13	17	20	22	21	19	15	10	7
(inches)	2.1	1.6	1.5	1.5	1.8	1.8	2.2	2.3	1.9	2.2	2.5	1.9
(mm)	54	40	37	37	46	45	57	59	49	57	64	48
Plymouth												
(°F)	47	47	50	54	59	64	66	67	64	58	52	49
(°C)	8	8	10	12	15	18	19	19	18	15	11	10
(inches)	3.9	2.9	2.7	2.1	2.5	2.1	2.8	3	3.1	3.6	4.5	4.3
(mm)	99	74	69	53	63	53	70	77	78	91	113	110
York												
°F)	43	44	49	55	61	67	70	69	64	57	49	45
(°C)	6	7	10	13	16	19	21	20	18	14	10	7
(inches)	2.3	1.8	1.5	1.6	2	2	2.4	2.7	2.2	2.2	2.6	2
(mm)	59	46	37	41	50	50	62	68	55	55	65	50

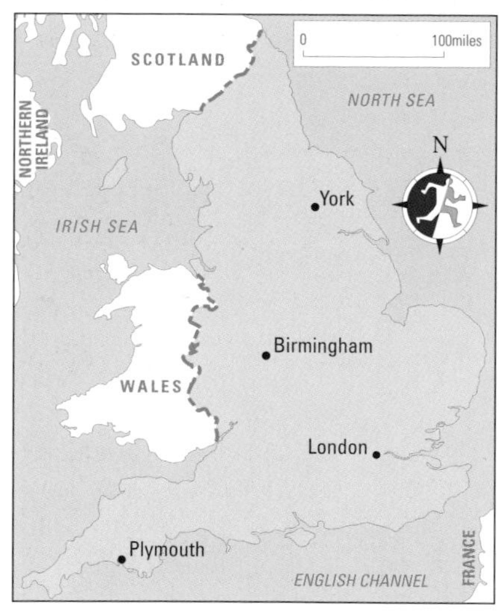

37 things not to miss

It's not possible to see everything England has to offer in one trip – and we don't suggest you try. What follows is a selective taste of the country's highlights – architecture, dramatic landscapes and even good things to eat and drink. Arranged in five colour-coded categories, you can browse through to find the very best things to see, do and experience. All highlights have a page reference to take you straight into the guide, where you can find out more.

01 Bath Page **408** • Visit the Roman baths, admire England's most elegant Georgian terrace or do some serious shopping in one of the country's most beautiful towns.

02 North York Moors Page **1014** • The North York Moors Railway steams along a dramatic course across the moors, providing access to some of the best hikes in this part of the country.

03 St Ives Tate, Cornwall Page **509** • The southwest's best arts collection occupies a superb site overlooking Porthmeor Beach, with a wonderful roof-top café.

04 Scafell and Scafell Pike Page **883** • The two highest peaks in England are on every serious hiker's hitlist though any reasonably fit person could tackle them too.

05 A pint down the pub Page **39** • From trendy micro-breweries to ancient coaching inns, England's pubs are an essential part of any visit to the country. The best brews to sample, and the best places to try them, are listed in the Guide.

06 Surfing, Newquay Page **522** • The beaches strung along the northern coast of Devon and Cornwall offer some great breaks, with Newquay the place to see and be seen.

07 The Royal Pavilion, Brighton Page **232** • George IV's pleasure dome, designed by Nash, is the supreme (and only) example of Oriental-Gothic architecture.

08 Notting Hill Carnival

Page **125** • Europe's biggest and loudest street carnival takes place every August Bank Holiday weekend in the streets of this west London district.

09 The Proms Page **159** • Running from July to September, this massive classical music festival is centred on the Royal Albert Hall and offers world-class performances and rock-bottom ticket prices.

10 Avebury stone circle

Page **320** • Stonehenge might get all the publicity, but the stones at nearby Avebury have a raw appeal and are far more accessible.

11 Afternoon tea Page **145** • The rooms may be out of most people's league, but London's top hotels serve upwickedly calorific afternoon teas to all and sundry.

12 Tate Modern Page **117** • Housed in a spectacular disused power station, London's modern-art gallery is simply awesome.

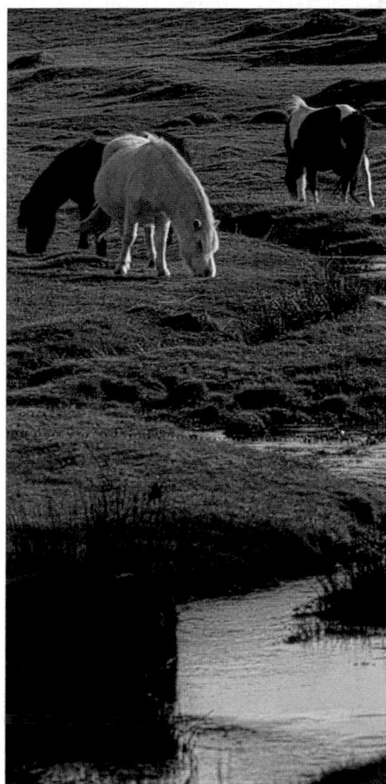

13 Hiking on Dartmoor Page **463** • Southern England's greatest expanse of wilderness offers solitude for experienced hikers and riders.

14 Books, Hay-on-Wye Page **651** • An outpost on the English-Welsh border, Hay-on-Wye may be remote, but it does cut a dash with the size and the variety of its second-hand bookshops.

15 **Oxford** Page **337** The famous old university town boasts a wealth of beautiful old buildings, many associated with well-known, former alumni.

16 **Blackpool Tower** Page **824** • The British seaside's best-known landmark provides a touch of grace to the Blackpool skyline, complemented perfectly by the autumn illuminations.

17 **Glastonbury** Page **424** • One of the oldest and biggest rock festivals still retains its authentic aura, less commercialized than most of the ilk, and still drawing an alternative crowd.

18 Newcastle nightlife Page **1073** • Lock up your inhibitions, leave your coat at home and hit the Toon.

19 York Minster Page **983** • Britain's biggest Gothic church has a thousand-year history and treasures to match, including the world's largest medieval stained-glass window.

20 Eden Project Page **492** • With its strong ecological thrust, the West Country's most spectacular attraction presents a refreshing alternative to the hard-sell, commercial edge of most of the region's crowd-pullers.

21 Punting on the Cam Page **602** • With every justification, Cambridge is an immensely popular tourist destination and punting on the River Cam is the best way to see some of the beautiful university buildings – even if you do get stuck in the mud.

22 Canterbury Cathedral Page **190** • Mother Church of the Church of England, this cathedral is famous for its shrine to the murdered Archbishop, Thomas à Becket, and the tales that Chaucer weaved round a fictitious pilgrimage to the martyr's tomb.

23 Bonfire Night (Nov 5) Page **742** • Most famous of the Gunpowder Plot conspirators, Guy Fawkes, was a native of York where they throw the country's most exuberant Bonfire Night celebrations.

24 Lizard Point, Cornwall Page **501** • This headland has none of the razzmatazz of Land's End, which is all to its favour, yet still has the views; there are some great beaches within a short coastal hike, too.

25 Fish and chips Page **38** • There's nothing better than fish and chips, nor any better way to eat them than wrapped in paper and eaten on the bracing North Yorkshire seafront in the little port of Whitby.

26 Ely Page **595** • An isolated Cambridgeshire town in the heart of the eerie fenland landscape, Ely is noted for its magnificent cathedral.

27 Appleby Horse Fair Page **903** • Britain's most important gathering of caravans, horse-drawn and otherwise, plus horse-trading, daredevil stunts and festivities in the usually quiet Eden Valley.

28 WOMAD Page **334** • This celebration of World Music, Arts and Dance is now held all over the world, but the first and the best is at Reading's Rivermead Leisure Complex each July.

29 The Peak District Page **686** • The Peak District offers great walking countryside and some of England's most appealing landscapes. Aim for the spa town of Buxton and head on out from there.

30 Windermere Page **861** • England's largest lake is also the gateway to the Lake District National Park. An easy day-trip from the conurbations of the northwest, Windermere is great for a waterside picnic, a gentle stroll or a slow cruise by steamer.

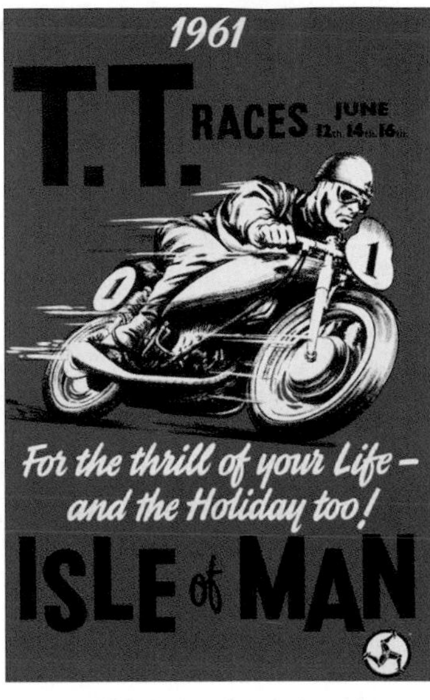

31 Isle of Man Page **835** • From Norse Crosses and ancient customs to stunning views and the TT Races, a visit to the Isle of Man is well worth the short boat trip or flight.

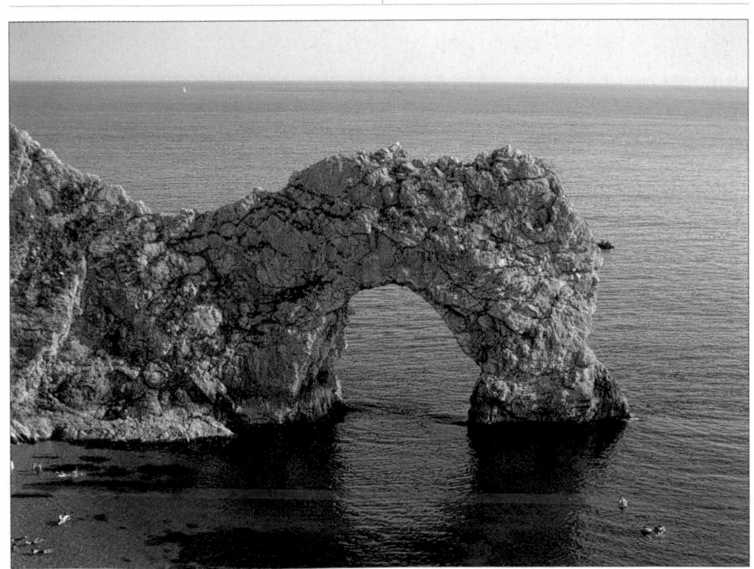

32 Durdle Door Page **299** • One of the highlights of the Dorset coast, this spectacular limestone arch has an immediate appeal, and is close to the marine wildlife reserve of Kimmeridge Bay as well as some choice beaches.

33
Stately homes and castles
Page **26** • For tangible and fascinating proof of England's long and often violent past, the country's many stately homes and castles – like Alnwick in Northumberland – can't be bettered.

34 A day at the races Page **244** • Once the sport of kings, these days everybody can enjoy a day at the races, with meetings across the country and throughout the year.

35 Curry Page **935** • This very English take on traditional Indian cuisine is now the country's favourite food. Birmingham, Bradford and Brick Lane in London are the best-known places to try it.

36 Wimbledon Page **45** • The only one of tennis's Grand Slam events to be staged on grass courts is a quintessentially English and – if you're prepared to queue – democratic event.

37 Hadrian's Wall Page **1084** • The most enduring and atmospheric reminder of the 350-year Roman period is this 76-mile long wall, stretching coast to coast through dramatic northern English countryside.

Contents

Using this Rough Guide

We've tried to make this Rough Guide a good read and easy to use. The book is divided into five main sections, and you should be able to find whatever you want in one of them.

Colour section

The front colour section offers a quick tour of England. The **introduction** aims to give you a feel for the place, with suggestions on where to go. We also tell you what the weather is like and include a basic country fact file. Next, our authors round up their favourite aspects of England in the **things not to miss** section – whether it's great food, amazing sights or a special hotel. Right after this comes a full **contents** list.

Basics

The Basics section covers all the **pre-departure** nitty-gritty to help you plan your trip. This is where to find out which airlines fly to your destination, what paperwork you'll need, what to do about money and insurance, about Internet access, food, security, public transport, car rental – in fact just about every piece of **general practical information** you might need.

Guide

This is the heart of the Rough Guide, divided into user-friendly chapters, each of which covers a specific region. Every chapter starts with a list of **highlights** and an **introduction** that helps you to decide where to go. Likewise, introductions to the various towns and smaller regions within each chapter should help you plan your itinerary. We start most town accounts with information on arrival and accommodation, followed by a tour of the sights, and finally reviews of places to eat and drink, and details of nightlife. Longer accounts also have a directory of practical listings. Each chapter concludes with **public transport** details for that region.

Contexts

Read Contexts to get a deeper understanding of what makes England tick. We include a brief history, articles about **wildlife, films** and **architecture**, and a detailed further reading section that reviews dozens of **books** relating to the country.

Index + small print

Apart from a **full index**, which includes maps as well as places, this section covers publishing information, credits and acknowledgements, and also has our contact details in case you want to send in updates and corrections to the book – or suggestions as to how we might improve it.

Map and chapter list

SCOTLAND

N

13

11

12

10

9

8

WALES

7

4

5

1

3

2

6

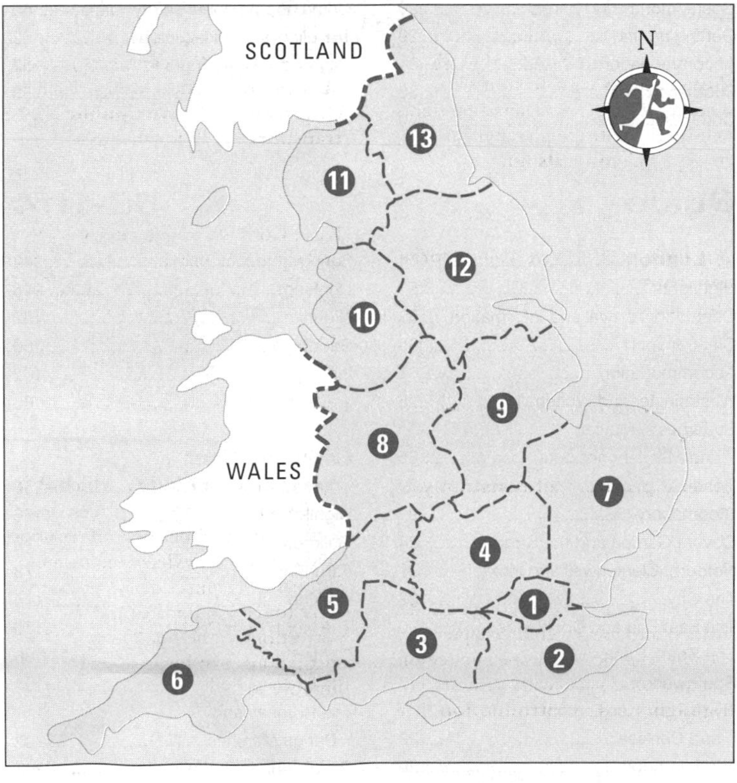

Contents

Colour section i–xxiv

Basics 9–53

Guide 56–1114

Contexts 1115–1171

Index + small print 1173–1192

Map symbols

maps are listed in the full index using coloured text

Motorway	Battlefield
Toll motorway	Abbey
Major road	Castle
Minor road	Church (regional maps)
Pedestrianized street	Gate
Path	Parking
Steps	London Underground station
Wall	Metro station
Railway	Motor racing circuit
Ferry route	Airport
River	Bus stop
National boundary	Internet access
County boundary	Tourist information
Chapter boundary	Post office
Mountain peak	Hospital
Hills	Accommodation
Waterfall	Restaurant
Lighthouse	Building
Caves	Church/cathedral
Point of interest	Park/national park
Ruin	Cemetery
Museum	Forest
Stately/historic house	Marshland
Public gardens	Beach

Basics

Basics

Getting there

London is one of the world's busiest transport hubs, and stiff competition between the airlines ensures a plethora of choice and good deals on flights. The city's Heathrow and Gatwick airports take the bulk of transatlantic and long-haul flights, but several airlines fly into Manchester, useful if you're heading for the north of the country. It's also possible to connect from London to many other regional airports, such as Birmingham, Bristol, Leeds/Bradford, Liverpool or Newcastle, on one of Britain's domestic carriers. London's other three airports – Stansted, Luton and City – are well served by low-cost flights from mainland Europe, as are Manchester and the country's other regional airports. Travelling from the Continent, drivers, foot and rail passengers can either cross the Channel by ferry or go under it via Eurotunnel (car) or the Eurostar (passenger train). If you really want to – or are on a very tight budget – you might consider picking up a bus from any of the major European cities. From Ireland, it's quickest to fly, but there are also plenty of ferry crossings.

Airfares always depend on the season, with the highest being around early June to mid-September, when the weather is best; fares drop during the "shoulder" seasons – mid-September to early November and mid-April to early June – and you'll get the best prices during the low season, November through to April (excluding Christmas and New Year, when prices are hiked up and seats are at a premium; it's wise to book at least two or three months ahead for this period). Note also that flying at weekends is generally more expensive; price ranges quoted below assume midweek travel.

You can often cut costs by going through a specialist flight agent – either a consolidator, who buys up blocks of tickets from the airlines and sells them at a discount, or a discount agent, who in addition to dealing with discounted flights may also offer special student and youth fares and a range of other travel-related services such as travel insurance, rail passes, car rentals, tours and the like. Some agents specialize in charter flights, which may be cheaper than anything available on a scheduled service, but departure dates are fixed and withdrawal penalties are high. Don't automatically assume that tickets purchased through a travel specialist will be cheapest, however – once you get a quote, check with the airlines and you may turn up an even better deal. A further possibility is to see if you can arrange a courier flight, although you'll need a flexible schedule, and preferably be travelling alone with very little luggage. In return for shepherding a parcel through customs, you can expect to get a deeply discounted ticket. You'll probably also be restricted in the duration of your stay.

If England is only one stop on a longer journey, you might want to consider buying a Round-the-World (RTW) ticket. Some travel agents can sell you an "off-the-shelf" RTW ticket that will have you touching down in about half a dozen cities (London is usually on the itinerary); others will assemble one for you, which can be tailored to your needs but is apt to be more expensive. Prices start from $1800 from Australia, $1200 from the US; for tailor-made itineraries and more flexible options such as Qantas/British Airways "Global Explorer", you'll be paying a lot more.

You might also consider the possibility of a package holiday to England, where all flights, accommodation and tour itineraries are arranged for you. However, though packages take a lot of the hassle out of travel, and can be ideal for those with a particular interest, they do tie you in to a group schedule, sometimes in the company of people you don't necessarily have much in common with.

Finally, if you're planning to see much of England (or Europe) by train, you may want to buy a rail pass (see p.30), which must be purchased in advance of your trip.

Booking flights online

Many airlines and discount travel websites offer you the opportunity to book your tickets online, cutting out the costs of agents and middlemen. Good deals can often be found through the discount or auction sites listed below, as well as through the airlines' own websites (see pp.14, 15 & 17).

Online booking agents

www.cheapflights.com Flight deals, travel agents, plus links to other travel sites; bookings from the US only – for Australia and New Zealand visit www.cheapflights.com.au; for Canada www.cheapflights.ca; and for Northern Ireland www.cheapflights.co.uk.

www.cheaptickets.com Discount flight specialists (US only).

www.expedia.com Discount airfares, all-airline search engine and daily deals.

www.hotwire.com Bookings from the US only. Last-minute savings of up to 40 percent on regular published fares. Travellers must be at least 18 and there are no refunds, transfers or changes allowed. Log-in required.

www.priceline.com Name-your-own-price website that has deals at around 40 percent off standard fares. You cannot specify flight times (although you do specify dates) and the tickets are non-refundable, non-transferable and non-changeable.

www.skyauction.com Bookings from the US only. Auctions tickets and travel packages using a "second bid" scheme. The best strategy is to bid the maximum you're willing to pay, since if you win you'll pay just enough to beat the runner-up regardless of your maximum bid.

www.travelocity.com Destination guides, hot Web fares and best deals for car rental and accommodation, as well as fares. Provides access to the Sabre travel network, the most comprehensive global reservations system.

www.travelshop.com.au Australian website offering discounted flights, packages, insurance and online bookings.

www.uniquetravel.com.au Australian site with a good range of packages and good-value flights.

travel.yahoo.com Incorporates a lot of Rough Guide material in its coverage of destination countries and cities across the world, with information about places to eat and sleep.

Package holidays and organized tours

Though you may want to see England at your own speed, you shouldn't dismiss the idea of a package deal out of hand. Many agents and airlines put together very flexible deals, sometimes amounting to nothing more restrictive than a flight plus accommodation and car or rail pass, and these can work out cheaper than the same arrangements made on arrival – especially car rental, which is fairly expensive in England. A package can also be great for your peace of mind, if only to ensure a worry-free first week while you're finding your feet for a longer tour. It's worth checking, too, for last-minute deals, especially out of season.

There's no shortage of operators specializing in tours of England. Most can do packages of the standard highlights, but of greater interest are the outfits that help you explore England's unique points: many organize walking or cycling trips through the countryside, boat trips along canals and any number of theme tours based around the country's literary heritage, history, pubs, gardens, theatre, golf – you name it. A few of the best operators are listed on p.13, and a travel agent will be able to point out others. (Companies offering walking holidays are listed on p.47, and those specializing in cycling on p.48.) Note that as opposed to fully inclusive package operators, the UK-based companies listed opposite do not arrange flights into England, but take care of itineraries, transport and accommodation once you've arrived. The advantage of booking with British tour operators is the greater range and flexibility of what's on offer, allowing you more freedom to join tours that fit your own schedule and interests. For a full listing of package and tour operators, contact Visit Britain (see p.22).

As a general rule, make sure that the tour operator belongs to an official association that guarantees minimum standards and the services offered, and be sure to examine the fine print of any deal, bearing in mind that everything in brochures always sounds great.

Tour operators in the UK

Acorn Activities ⓣ0870/740 5055, ⓦwww.acornactivities.co.uk. Diverse range of organized holidays for singles, couples and families, with the accent on activity breaks.
Capital Sport ⓣ01296/631671, ⓦwww.capital-sport.co.uk. Gentle cycling tours from the outskirts of London along the Thames as far as the Cotswolds, with stops at sights as well as all accommodation and luggage transfers arranged.
Cloudberry Holidays ⓣ01539/733522, ⓦwww.cloudberry.co.uk. Budget holidays based in YHA hostels in the Lake District.
Contiki Holidays ⓣ020/8290 6777, ⓦwww.contiki.com. Adventure trips and tours for 18–35s, going all over the country (and beyond to Scotland and Ireland).
Contours Walking Holidays ⓣ01768/867539, ⓦwww.contours.co.uk. England-wide walking holidays, including graded guided and self-guided hikes in Cornwall, the Cotswolds and Northumberland.
Country Lanes ⓣ01425/655022, ⓦwww.countrylanes.co.uk. Cycle tours and holidays, ranging from day-trips to week-long outings in the Cotswolds, Lake District and New Forest.
Discovery Travel ⓣ01904/766564, ⓦwww.discoverytravel.co.uk. Tailor-made cycling and walking holidays in the Lake District, Yorkshire Dales and North York Moors, as well as coast-to-coast itineraries. Transport to and within England can be arranged, too.
Drifters Club ⓣ020/7262 1292, ⓦwww.driftersclub.com. Adventure trips aimed at backpackers, offering good deals on flights to London.
Holiday Lakeland ⓣ01697/371871, ⓦwww.holiday-lakeland.co.uk. Offers 1-, 3- and 5-day cycle tours in the Lake District, Northumberland and the Pennines, including the Pennine Cycle Way.
Hoseasons Holidays ⓣ01502/502588, ⓦwww.hoseasons.co.uk. Self-catering holidays throughout the country, including cruises on the Norfolk Broads and Thames.
Outward Bound ⓣ0870/513 4227, ⓦwww.outwardbound-uk.org. Courses and activity holidays in the Lake District geared towards young people and families, including climbing, caving and canoeing.
Saddle Skedaddle ⓣ0191/265 1110, ⓦwww.skedaddle.co.uk. On- and off-road cycle tours in the Cotswolds, Northumberland and from coast to coast, from one day to a week.
Walking Women ⓣ0845/644 5335, ⓦwww.walkingwomen.co.uk. Women-only walking holidays and short breaks in the Lake District.
YHA ⓣ0870/770 8868, ⓦwww.yha.org.uk and ⓦwww.hostelholidays.com. Hostel-based holidays built around a range of activities, including walking, climbing, biking, kayaking and caving.

Tour operators in the US and Canada

BCT Scenic Walking ⓣ1-800/473-1210 or 760/944-4599, ⓦwww.bctwalk.com. Extensive line-up of walking trips of eight to sixteen days in the Cotswolds, Cornwall and from coast to coast.
British Airways Holidays ⓣ1-877/4-A-VACATION, ⓦwww.british-airways.com. Flight-inclusive vacations and customized itineraries.
British Travel International ⓣ1-800/327-6097, ⓦwww.britishtravel.com. Agent for all independent arrangements: rail and bus passes, hotels and a comprehensive B&B and vacation-homes reservation service.
English Experience ⓣ1-800/892-9317, ⓦwww.english-experience.com. Small-group guided tours in homestays or hotels, covering Sussex, Bath, the Cotswolds, the Lake District and the Yorkshire Dales.
English Lakeland Ramblers ⓣ1-800/724-8801 or 212/505-1020, ⓦwww.ramblers.com. Walking tours (usually seven or eight days) in the Lake District and the Cotswolds.
gaytravel.com ⓣ1-800/724-8801, ⓦwww.gaytravel.com. Gay and lesbian online travel agent and tour operator, offering a nine-day tour of "Haunted and Legendary England", including London, the Cotswolds, Glastonbury, Dartmoor and Cornwall.
Le Boat ⓣ1-800/922-0291 or 1-201/506-1941, ⓦwww.leboat.com. Specializes in canal trips in Cambridgeshire, Gloucestershire and on the River Thames.
Select Travel Service ⓣ1-800/752-6787, ⓦwww.selecttravel.com. Customized history, literature, theatre and horticulture tours.
Sterling Tours ⓣ1-800/727-4359, ⓦwww.sterlingtours.com. Variety of independent itineraries, packages, country-house hotels and activity holidays.
Virgin Atlantic Vacations ⓣ1-800/862-8621, ⓦwww.virgin-atlantic.com. Custom-made packages for independent travellers, including hotel, theatre and airfare deals.
Wilderness Travel ⓣ1-800/368-2794 or 510/558-2488, ⓦwww.wildernesstravel.com. Inn-to-inn hiking packages in the Lake District and from coast to coast.

Tour operators in Australia and New Zealand

Adventure World Australia ⓣ02/8913 0755, ⓦwww.adventureworld.com.au; New Zealand ⓣ09/524 5118, ⓦwww.adventureworld.co.nz. Wide variety of independent, customized and escorted excursions around England, including short tours to Stratford-upon-Avon and the Lake District.

Adventures Abroad Australia ⓣ1/800/147 827, New Zealand ⓣ0800/800 434, ⓦwww.adventures-abroad.com. Arranges trips of eight to fifteen days in the south of England, taking in London, the university towns, Salisbury, Stonehenge and the Isle of Wight.

Explore Holidays Australia ⓣ02/9857 6200 or 1300/731 000, ⓦwww.exploreholidays.com.au. Organizes customized "holidays for the independent traveller" that include accommodation, passes to sights and tours all over England.

YHA Travel Centre Australia ⓣ02/9261 1111 or 03/9670 9611, ⓦwww.yha.com.au; New Zealand ⓣ09/379 4224, ⓦwww.yha.co.nz. Organizes budget accommodation throughout Britain for YHA members.

Flights from the US and Canada

Figure on six and a half hours' flying time from New York to any of the British airports (it's an hour extra coming the other way, due to headwinds). Most eastbound flights cross the Atlantic overnight, depositing you at your destination the next morning without much sleep, but if you can manage to stay awake until after dinner on your night of arrival, you should be over the worst of the jet lag by the next morning. Some flights from the East Coast depart early in the morning, arriving late the same evening, but this lands you in London just as the city is shutting down – a recipe for a disorienting and possibly expensive first night.

Dozens of airlines fly from New York to London, and a few fly direct from other East Coast and Midwestern hubs. The best low-season fares from New York to London hover around $338 return with a similar price from Boston. In the same period you'll pay in the region of $410 from Washington DC, $450 from Chicago and $520 from Houston. You can pick up flights from Los Angeles and San Francisco for under $500, but for the West Coast cities you're looking at paying $100 or so more. For high-season fares, add $150–250 and bear in mind that travelling late on a Saturday can considerably reduce the fare.

Several airlines fly to Manchester from some of the above cities; Manchester and Birmingham are common rated with London, which means that the Apex fare should be the same. If you fly to London on a discounted ticket, expect to pay about $100 each way for an onward connection within England.

In Canada, you'll get the best deal flying to London from the big gateway cities of Toronto and Montréal, where low-season deals start from around CDN$770 return; direct flights from Ottawa and Halifax will probably cost only slightly more. From Edmonton, Calgary and Vancouver to London the equivalent fare is CDN$960. If you're travelling in high season, fares are likely to be about $300 higher.

Only Air Canada flies non-stop to Manchester (from Toronto), but you can pick up non-direct flights from many Canadian cities to Manchester, Birmingham and Newcastle (usually via London) and often at no extra cost over the fare to London.

Airlines in the US and Canada

Aer Lingus ⓣ1-800/474-7424, ⓦwww.aerlingus.com. Boston, Chicago, Los Angeles and New York to Dublin or Shannon with connections to many major British airports.

Air Canada ⓣ1-888/247-2262, ⓦwww.aircanada.ca. Calgary, Halifax, Montréal, Ottawa, Toronto and Vancouver to London; Toronto to Manchester.

American Airlines ⓣ1-800/433-7300, ⓦwww.aa.com. Chicago, Dallas/Fort Worth, Los Angeles, Miami, New York and Raleigh to London; Chicago to Manchester.

bmi/British Midland ⓣ1-800/788-0555, ⓦwww.flybmi.com. Washington and Chicago to Manchester.

British Airways ⓣ1-800/247-9297, ⓦwww.ba.com. Atlanta, Baltimore, Boston, Charlotte, Chicago, Dallas/Fort Worth, Denver, Detroit, Houston, Los Angeles, Miami, Montréal, New York, Orlando, Philadelphia, Phoenix, Pittsburgh, San Francisco, Seattle, Tampa, Toronto, Vancouver and Washington DC to London (with extensive connections on to other UK destinations); also New York to Manchester.

Continental Airlines ⓣ1-800/231-0856, ⓦwww.continental.com. Cleveland, Houston and Newark to London; Newark to Manchester.
Delta Air Lines ⓣ1-800/241-4141, ⓦwww.delta.com. Atlanta and Cincinnati to London; Atlanta to Manchester.
Northwest/KLM Airlines ⓣ1-800/447-4747, ⓦwww.nwa.com, ⓦwww.klm.com. Detroit and Minneapolis to London.
United Airlines ⓣ1-800/538-2929, ⓦwww.ual.com. Chicago, Los Angeles, Newark, New York, San Francisco and Washington DC to London.
Virgin Atlantic Airways ⓣ1-800/862-8621, ⓦwww.virgin-atlantic.com. Boston, Los Angeles, Miami, Newark, New York, Orlando, San Francisco and Washington DC to London.

Courier flights from the US and Canada

Air Courier Association ⓣ1-800/282-1202, ⓦwww.aircourier.org.
Now Voyager ⓣ212/459-1616, ⓦwww.nowvoyagertravel.com.

Discount flight agents in the US and Canada

Air Brokers International ⓣ1-800/883-3273 or 415/397-1383, ⓦwww.airbrokers.com. Consolidator and specialist in RTW packages.
Airtech ⓣ212/219-7000, ⓦwww.airtech.com. Standby seat broker. Also deals in consolidator fares and courier flights, mainly from northeastern US cities.
Educational Travel Center ⓣ1-800/747-5551 or 608/256-5551, ⓦwww.edtrav.com. Student/youth discount agent.
New Frontiers ⓣ1-800/677-0720 or 310/670-7318, ⓦwww.newfrontiers.com. French discount-travel firm based in Los Angeles.
STA Travel US ⓣ1-800/781-4040, Canada ⓣ1-888/427-5639, ⓦwww.sta-travel.com. Worldwide specialists in independent travel; also student IDs, travel insurance, car rental and rail passes.
TFI Tours International ⓣ1-800/745-8000 or 212/736-1140, ⓦwww.lowestairprice.com. Consolidator.
Travel Avenue ⓣ1-800/333 3335, ⓦwww.travelavenue.com. Full-service travel agent that offers discounts in the form of rebates.
Travel Cuts Canada ⓣ1-800/667-2887, US ⓣ1-866/246-9762, ⓦwww.travelcuts.com. Canadian student-travel organization.
Worldtek Travel ⓣ1-800/243-1723 or 203/772-0472, ⓦwww.worldtek.com. Discount travel agency.

Flights from Australia and New Zealand

Travel time from Australia and New Zealand to England is over twenty hours, and as long-haul flights can be very taxing you might want to consider taking advantage of a stopover and good night's sleep en route.

The route to London is a highly competitive one, with the lowest fares starting from around A$1520/NZ$2200 with such airlines as Royal Brunei and Emirates Air. More expensive, but worth it for the extras such as fly-drive, accommodation packages and onward travel to other European destinations, are carriers such as Singapore Airlines, Qantas, British Airways and Air New Zealand, whose fares start at around A$1700/NZ$2500.

The most direct flights from Australia are via Asia and Europe. In the low season, Qantas charges $1674 from Melbourne, $1694 from Sydney and $1681 from Perth, rising in high season to $2843, $2885 and $3151 respectively. Low/high season British Airways flights cost $1694/$3164 from Sydney, and $2613/$3153 from Perth, while Singapore Airlines flights cost $1714/$2864 from Sydney or $1691/$2601 from Perth. It's usually slower and considerably more expensive to travel via the Americas, involving the purchase of separate tickets; the return ticket from Sydney to Los Angeles alone costs around $2500.

The most direct route from New Zealand, however, is via North America, with United Airlines charging around $3350 year-round, while Air New Zealand's fares are around $2820/$3075 in low and high season respectively. British Airways charges roughly $2250/$3500, but this does include onward connections to other destinations in Britain. All three journeys involve stops in Los Angeles. Garuda, Korean Air and Thai Airways fly to London via Asia with either a transfer or stopover in their home city for around $2880; Qantas flies via Sydney and either Singapore or Bangkok from $2510.

Airlines in Australia and New Zealand

Air New Zealand ⓣ0800/737 000 or 09/357 3000, Australia ⓣ13/2476, ⓦwww.airnz.com. Daily flights to London from Brisbane, Melbourne and Sydney via Asia and from New Zealand via Los Angeles.

Britannia Airways Australia ⓣ02/9251 1299, New Zealand ⓣ0800/887 997, ⓦwww.britanniaairways.com. Several flights a month (Nov–March only) from Auckland, Brisbane, Cairns and Sydney to London, and once a week to Manchester via Bangkok and Abu Dhabi.

British Airways Australia ⓣ13/0076 7177, New Zealand ⓣ09/356 8690, ⓦwww.ba.com. Daily direct flights to London from Brisbane, Melbourne, Perth and Sydney. Code share with Qantas from other major cities to London via Los Angeles and Singapore, and twice weekly via Harare or Johannesburg from Sydney; daily from Auckland to London via Los Angeles. Onward connections to other destinations in Britain.

Cathay Pacific Australia ⓣ13/1747 or 02/9931 5500, New Zealand ⓣ09/379 0861, ⓦwww.cathaypacific.com. Several flights a week from Auckland, Brisbane, Cairns, Melbourne, Perth and Sydney to London and Manchester via Hong Kong.

Emirates Air ⓣ1800/7773999, ⓦwww.emirates.com. Daily flights from Auckland, Brisbane, Melbourne, Perth and Sydney via Dubai to London, Manchester and Birmingham.

Garuda Australia ⓣ13/1223 or 02/9334 9900, New Zealand ⓣ09/366 1862 or 1800/128 510, ⓦwww.garuda-indonesia.com. Several flights weekly from Adelaide, Auckland, Brisbane, Cairns, Darwin, Melbourne, Perth and Sydney to London via Denpasar or Jakarta.

KLM Australia ⓣ1300/303 747, New Zealand ⓣ09/309 1782, ⓦwww.klm.com. Daily flights from Sydney to London via Kuala Lumpur.

Malaysia Airlines Australia ⓣ13/2627, New Zealand ⓣ09/373 2741 or 0800/657 472, ⓦwww.malaysiaair.com. Several flights a week from Auckland, Melbourne, Perth and Sydney to London via Kuala Lumpur.

Qantas Australia ⓣ13/1313, New Zealand ⓣ09/357 8900 or 0800/808 767, ⓦwww.qantas.com.au. Daily flights from Adelaide, Auckland, Brisbane, Christchurch, Darwin, Melbourne, Perth, Sydney and Wellington to London via Bangkok or Singapore.

Royal Brunei Airlines Australia ⓣ07/3017 5000, New Zealand ⓣ09/977 2240, ⓦwww.bruneiair.com. Flights three or four times weekly from Auckland, Brisbane and Perth to London via Bandar Seri Begawan (Brunei).

Singapore Airlines Australia ⓣ13/1011 or 02/9350 0262, New Zealand ⓣ09/303 2129 or 0800/808 909, ⓦwww.singaporeair.com. Daily flights from Auckland, Brisbane, Christchurch, Melbourne, Perth and Sydney and several weekly from Adelaide and Cairns to London and Manchester via Singapore.

Thai Airways Australia ⓣ1300/651 960, New Zealand ⓣ09/377 3886, ⓦwww.thaiair.com. Several flights a week from Auckland, Brisbane, Melbourne, Perth and Sydney to London via Bangkok.

United Airlines Australia ⓣ13/1777, New Zealand ⓣ09/379 3800, ⓦwww.ual.com. Daily flights from Auckland to Melbourne and from Melbourne and Sydney to London via Los Angeles and San Francisco.

Virgin Atlantic Airways Australia ⓣ02/9244 2747, New Zealand ⓣ09/308 3377, ⓦwww.virgin-atlantic.com. Daily flights from Sydney to London via Kuala Lumpur. Code share with Malaysia Airlines for the first leg.

Travel agents in Australia and New Zealand

Flight Centres Australia ⓣ02/9235 3522, nearest branch on 13/1600, New Zealand ⓣ09/358 4310, ⓦwww.flightcentre.com.au. Concentrates on discounted air fares.

Holiday Shoppe New Zealand ⓣ0800/808 480, ⓦwww.holidayshoppe.co.nz. One of New Zealand's largest travel agencies, offering budget airfares and accommodation packages.

STA Travel Australia ⓣ13/1776 or 1300/360 960, New Zealand ⓣ09/309 0458 or 09/366 6673, ⓦwww.statravel.com.au. Fare discounts for students and under-25s as well as student cards, rail passes and accommodation.

Student Uni Travel Australia ⓣ02/9232 8444, ⓦwww.sut.com.au. Student/youth travel specialists offering discounted air fares.

Thomas Cook Australia ⓣ13/1771 or 1800/801 002, New Zealand ⓣ09/379 3920, ⓦwww.thomascook.com. Low-cost flights, tours and accommodation; also issues traveller's cheques.

Trailfinders Australia ⓣ02/9247 7666, ⓦwww.trailfinders.com.au. Discounted flights, car rental, tailor-made tours, rail passes and RTW tours.

Flights from Ireland

Stiff competition on routes between Ireland and England has kept the cost of flights relatively low, with airlines offering return tickets from Dublin for as little as €15 in off-peak seasons, though these will need to be booked well in advance. Ryanair flies to thirteen destinations in England from Cork, Kerry, Knock and Shannon as well as Dublin, and generally has the cheapest deals. If there are no special deals available, expect to pay around €50 for a return ticket to Stansted. Aer Lingus offers various deals from Dublin, Cork and Shannon, with fares from around €35 return, and British Airways often gives good discounts on their published fares from Dublin. Flying from Belfast, however, your best bet is with easyJet, whose return flights to Luton Airport start at £17.50 (excluding tax). Flights into Heathrow with bmi/British Midland cost from £64; BA is generally a little more expensive, with return fares from around £89.

Airlines in Ireland

Aer Lingus Northern Ireland ⓣ0845/084 4444, Republic of Ireland ⓣ0818/365 0000, ⓦwww.aerlingus.ie.
bmi/British Midland Northern Ireland ⓣ0870/607 0555, Republic of Ireland ⓣ01/407 3036, ⓦwww.flybmi.com.
British Airways Northern Ireland ⓣ0870/850 9850, Republic of Ireland ⓣ1-890/626747, ⓦwww.ba.com.
easyJet Northern Ireland ⓣ0870/600 0000, ⓦwww.easyjet.com.
Ryanair Ireland ⓣ0818/303030, ⓦwww.ryanair.com.

By rail

There are frequent through trains for passengers from Paris, Brussels and Lille to London run by Eurostar, which travel through the Channel Tunnel to Waterloo International in London via Ashford in Kent. The least expensive return fare (which must be booked 21–90 days in advance, or else – booked at shorter notice but with less availability – include a Saturday night away) is £59 from Paris and Brussels and £55 from Lille. Full fares with no restrictions are £298 from Paris and Brussels and £250 from Lille. Youth tickets (for under-26s) are fully flexible and cost £79 from Paris and Brussels and £75 from Lille. Eurail and Britrail pass holders qualify for a Passholder return which allows unrestricted journeys for £100 from Paris and Brussels and £80 from Lille.

Drivers from Europe have the option of using Eurotunnel, crossing underneath the Channel on freight trains which carry coaches, cars and motorbikes. The service runs every fifteen minutes at peak periods and takes 35 minutes to get between the loading terminals at Folkestone and Calais. You can just turn up, but booking is advised, especially at weekends; you should arrive at least thirty minutes before departure. A five-day fully flexible return for a car and passengers travelling off-peak costs £189, or £199 in high season.

From the Republic of Ireland, you can get rail/ferry deals from Iarnród Éireann (Irish Rail). If you're starting from the south or west, however, the best ferry crossings are the more expensive Cork–Swansea or Rosslare–Fishguard/Rosslare–Pembroke routes, which can bring the fare to around the same as a flight. If you're willing to travel overnight, the return fare from Dublin to London works out at £55; it rises to £73 during the day.

Useful rail contacts

Eurostar UK ⓣ0870/160 6600, France ⓣ08.36.35.33.39, ⓦwww.eurostar.com.
Eurotunnel UK ⓣ0870/535 3535, France ⓣ03.21.00.61.00, ⓦwww.eurotunnel.com.
Iarnród Éireann (Continental Rail Desk) ⓣ01/836 6222, ⓦwww.irishrail.ie.

By ferry

Tariffs on the ferries from mainland Europe are bewilderingly complex: prices vary with the month, day or even hour at certain times of the year, not to mention how long you're staying and the size of your car. Another thing to bear in mind is that some kind of sleeping accommodation is often obligatory on the longer crossings if made at night, pushing the price way above the basic rate. As an indication of cost, two people driving in a small car from Calais, Dieppe or Ostend to one of the English Channel ports by fast ferry or catamaran could expect to pay from £140 (the return fares are usually just twice the price); for a foot passenger the single fare is £24. On the Bergen–Newcastle route, one of the longest crossings, the one-way fare for four people and a car runs from £200 at off-peak periods to as much as £380 in high season, with foot passengers paying £60–£120. For a cabin supplement you can pay between £20 and £114. All current crossings, including foot-

Ferry connections

	Company	Frequency	Duration
From Belgium			
Ostend–Dover	Hoverspeed (SeaCat)	3 daily	2hr
Zeebrugge–Hull	P&O	1 daily	14hr 45min
From Denmark			
Esbjerg–Harwich	DFDS	3–4 weekly	20hr
From France			
Caen–Portsmouth	Brittany	2–3 daily	6hr
Calais–Dover	Hoverspeed (SeaCat)	6–10 daily	40min
Calais–Dover	P&O	30–35 daily	1hr 15min
Calais–Dover	SeaFrance	15–18 daily	90min
Cherbourg–Poole	Brittany	1–3 daily	2hr 15min–4hr 15min
Cherbourg–Portsmouth	P&O	1–4 daily	2hr 45min–9hr 30min
Dieppe–Newhaven	Hoverspeed (SeaCat/Super SeaCat)	3–5 daily	2hr
Le Havre–Portsmouth	P&O	2–3 daily	5hr 30min–9hr 30min
Roscoff–Plymouth	Brittany	6–12 weekly	6hr
St Malo–Poole (via Jersey or Guernsey)	Condor	late May–Sept 1 daily	4hr 45min
St Malo–Portsmouth	Brittany	1–2 daily	8hr 45min
From Germany			
Cuxhaven–Harwich (for Hamburg)	DFDS	3–4 weekly	19hr
From Holland			
Amsterdam–Newcastle	DFDS	1 daily Feb–Dec	16hr
Hook of Holland–Harwich	Stena	3 daily	3hr 40min–6hr 15min
Rotterdam–Hull	P&O	1 daily	12hr
From Ireland			
Cork–Swansea	Swansea–Cork Ferries	mid-March to Dec 4–6 weekly	10hr
Dun Laoghaire–Holyhead	Stena (Catamaran)	3 daily	1hr 40min
Dublin–Holyhead	Stena/Irish Ferries	2 daily	1hr 50min/3hr 50min
Dublin–Liverpool	Isle of Man Steam Packet (SeaCat)	April to early Nov 1 daily	3hr 45min
Dublin–Liverpool	Irish Sea	6 weekly	6hr 30min
Rosslare–Fishguard	Stena	May–Sept 2 daily	3hr 30min
Rosslare–Fishguard	Stena Lynx	May–Sept 2–4 daily	1hr 50min
Rosslare–Pembroke	Irish Ferries	2 daily	3hr 45min
From Norway			
Kristiansand–Newcastle	DFDS	2 weekly	18hr
Stavanger –Newcastle /Bergen	Fjord Line	2–3 weekly	20–27hr
From Spain			
Bilbao–Portsmouth	P&O	2 weekly	29hr
Santander–Plymouth	Brittany	2 weekly	24hr
From Sweden			
Gothenburg–Newcastle	DFDS	2 weekly	26hr

passenger, hovercraft and catamaran services, are listed opposite.

If you're travelling alone and can't split the fare, bringing your car from Ireland can be an expensive option. Fares fluctuate wildly depending on the time of year and the day of the week you travel, and also the length of your car, but expect to pay around €252 for a small vehicle and up to five adults on the ferry route between Dublin and Holyhead (€34–42 for a foot passenger), or €161–273 on the Cork–Swansea route (€35–50 foot passenger).

Ferry companies

Brittany Ferries UK ⓣ0870/366 5333, France ⓣ08.25.82.88.28, Spain ⓣ942.36.06.11, ⓦwww.brittanyferries.com.
Condor UK ⓣ0845/345 2000, France ⓣ02.99.20.03.00, ⓦwww.condorferries.co.uk.
DFDS Seaways UK ⓣ0875/333000, Holland ⓣ0255/534546, Sweden ⓣ031/650650, Germany ⓣ040/389 0371, Denmark ⓣ79.17.79.17, ⓦwww.dfdsseaways.co.uk.
Fjord Line UK ⓣ0191/296 1313, Norway ⓣ55/548711,ⓦwww.fjordline.com.
Hoverspeed UK ⓣ0870/524 0241, France ⓣ08.20.00.35.55, Belgium ⓣ059.53.99.55, ⓦwww.hoverspeed.co.uk.
Irish Ferries UK ⓣ0870/517 1717, Ireland ⓣ1890/313131, ⓦwww.irishferries.com.
Isle of Man Steam Packet UK ⓣ0870/552 3523, ⓦwww.seacat.co.uk.
P&O Ferries UK ⓣ0870/600 0611, Ireland ⓣ1-800/409049, Belgium ⓣ027.10.64.44, France ⓣ01.55.69.82.28, Germany ⓣ069.50.98.55.55, Holland ⓣ0202/013333, Spain ⓣ912.70.23.32, ⓦwww.poferries.com.
P&O Irish Sea UK ⓣ0870/242 4777, Ireland ⓣ1-800/409049, ⓦwww.poirishsea.com.
Sea France UK ⓣ0870/571 1711, France ⓣ08.03.04.40.45, ⓦwww.seafrance.com.
Stena Line UK ⓣ0870/570 7070, Ireland ⓣ01/204 7777, Holland ⓣ017/438 9333, ⓦwww.stenaline.co.uk.
Swansea Cork Ferries UK ⓣ01792/456116, Ireland ⓣ021/427 1166, ⓦwww.swansea-cork.ie.

By bus

You can catch buses from a long list of European countries to England. Given the low cost of air fares from many cities, however, you'd have to be a masochist to want to travel by bus from, say, Athens – a journey of two nights and three days that actually costs more than the price of a three-and-a-half-hour flight to London. Eurolines (ⓦwww.eurolines.com) is Britain's largest international coach company, with departures to London from 48 European cities, including Amsterdam, Brussels, Frankfurt, Hamburg, Madrid, Paris and Rome.

However, if you're coming from Ireland and want to keep costs to a minimum, take the coach. Eurolines (Northern Ireland ⓣ0870/514 3219 or 028/9033 7002, Republic of Ireland ⓣ01/836 6111, ⓦwww.eurolines.com) runs a service from Belfast (from £34 return) and Dublin (from €62) – with connections throughout Ireland – via Birmingham to London. You can also travel from Cork, Killarney, Limerick and Tralee to London via Fishguard and Bristol. Considering the distances involved, these fares are great value; the downside is that the trip, which can involve an overnight ferry crossing to Holyhead, takes around ten hours from Belfast, twelve hours from Dublin and up to fourteen hours from elsewhere.

Red tape and visas

Citizens of EU member countries have the right of free movement and residence throughout the European Economic Area (including the United Kingdom); there will be a brief passport/identity card check on arrival in the UK. Citizens of other European countries (with certain exceptions, mainly in the east and the former Soviet republics) can also enter Britain with just a passport, generally for up to three months. US, Canadian, Australian and New Zealand citizens don't need visas and can enter the country for up to six months with just a passport. All other nationalities require a visa, obtainable from the British Consular office in the country of application. Incidentally, the Channel Islands and the Isle of Man have their own immigration laws and policies, but UK visa offices can issue visas for these islands. For current details about entry and visa requirements, consult the UK's Foreign and Commonwealth Office's visa website ⓦwww.ukvisas.gov.uk.

Extending your stay

Citizens of EU countries who want to stay in the UK other than as a short-term visitor or tourist can apply for a residence permit, while others can also apply to extend their visas (though this must be done before the expiry date given in the passport). In both cases, you should first contact the Immigration and Nationality Directorate, Lunar House, 40 Wellesley Rd, Croydon CR9 2BY (ⓣ0870/606 7766, ⓦwww.ind.homeoffice.gov.uk), enclosing your passport or National Identity Card and all other relevant entry documents, as requested. US, Canadian, Australian and New Zealand citizens who want to stay longer than six months will need an entry clearance certificate, available from the British consular office at the embassy/high commission in your own country.

British embassies and high commissions abroad

Australia British High Commission, Commonwealth Ave, Yarralumla, Canberra, ACT 2600 ⓣ02/6270 6666, ⓦwww.britaus.net.
Canada British High Commission, 80 Elgin St, Ottawa, ON K1P 5K7 ⓣ613/237-1530, ⓦwww.britainincanada.org.
Ireland 29 Merrion Rd, Dublin 4 ⓣ01/205 3700, ⓦwww.britishembassy.ie.
New Zealand British High Commission, 44 Hill St, Wellington ⓣ04/924 2888, ⓦwww.britain.org.nz.
USA 3100 Massachusetts Ave, NW, Washington, DC 20008 ⓣ202/588-6500, ⓦwww.britainusa.com.

Overseas embassies and high commissions in England

American Embassy 24 Grosvenor Square, London W1A 1AE ⓣ020/7499 9000, ⓦwww.usembassy.org.uk.
Australian High Commission Australia House, Strand, London WC2B 4LA ⓣ020/7379 4334, ⓦwww.australia.org.uk.
Canadian High Commission 1 Grosvenor Square, London W1X 0AB ⓣ020/7250 6600, ⓦwww.canadianembassy.co.uk.
Irish Embassy 17 Grosvenor Place, London SW1X 7HR ⓣ020/7235 2171, ⓦireland.embassyhomepage.com.
New Zealand High Commission New Zealand House, 80 Haymarket, London SW1Y 4TQ ⓣ020/7930 8422, ⓦwww.nzembassy.com.

Customs

Travellers coming into Britain directly from another EU country do not have to make a declaration to Customs at their place of entry. In other words, you can bring almost as many cigarettes and as much French wine or German beer into the country as you can carry. The guidance levels are 10 litres of spirits, 90 litres of wine and 110 litres of beer, which should suffice for anyone's requirements – any more than this and you'll have to provide proof that it's for personal use only. The guidelines for tobacco are 800 cigarettes, 400 cigarillos, 200 cigars or 1kg of loose tobacco.

If you're travelling to or from a non-EU country, you can still buy duty-free goods, but within the EU, this perk no longer exists. The duty-free allowances are:

❑ Tobacco: 200 cigarettes; or 100 cigarillos; or 50 cigars; or 250 grammes of loose tobacco.

❑ Alcohol: 2 litres of still wine plus 1 litre of drink over 22 percent alcohol; or 2 litres of alcoholic drinks not over 22 percent.

❑ Perfumes: 60ml of perfume plus 250ml of toilet water.

❑ Other goods to the value of £145.

There are import restrictions on a variety of articles and substances, from firearms to furs derived from endangered species, none of which should bother the average tourist. However, if you need any clarification on British import regulations, contact the UK Customs and Excise (ⓣ0845/010 9000 or +4420/8929 0152 for international callers; ⓦwww.hmce.gov.uk).

Tax-free shopping

Most goods in Britain, with the chief exceptions of books and food, are subject to Value Added Tax (VAT), which increases the cost of an item by 17.5 percent (included in the marked price of goods). Visitors from non-EU countries can save a lot of money through the Retail Export Scheme (tax-free shopping), which allows a refund of VAT on goods to be taken out of the country. (Savings will usually be minimal for EU nationals because of the rates at which the goods will be taxed upon import to the home country.) Note that not all shops participate in this scheme (those doing so will display a sign to this effect), and that you cannot reclaim VAT charged on hotel bills or other services.

Information, maps and websites

If you want to do a bit of research before arriving in England, you can either contact the overall British tourist authority Visit Britain, which has offices worldwide, or one of the regional tourist boards in England, which concentrate on particular areas. The official tourist office websites are all pretty useful, covering everything from local accommodation to festival dates, but there is also an almost limitless supply of other sites dedicated to England and its ways. We've picked out some of the best below, and some of the more offbeat, and also provided a review of the most useful maps you can buy for navigating your way around England.

Tourist information

In England, tourist offices (usually called Tourist Information Centres, or "TICs" for short) exist in virtually every town. The average opening hours are much the same as standard shop hours, though they are also often open on Sundays, while hours are extended during the summer months and occasionally curtailed in the depths of winter, especially in more remote areas.

All centres offer information on local accommodation, public transport and attractions. Staff will nearly always be able to book accommodation for you (for a fee of around £3), reserve space on guided tours, and sell you guides, maps and walk leaflets. You can ask for lists of local cafés, restaurants and pubs, and though the staff aren't really supposed to recommend particular places, you'll often be able to get a feel for the best local places to eat. An increasing number of offices have Internet access for visitors, but don't count on being able to leave your bags at TICs while you scout around town – they don't usually have the space to act as left-luggage offices.

Areas designated as national parks (such as the Lake District, Yorkshire Dales, North York Moors and Dartmoor) tend to have their own information centres, which offer exactly the same services as TICs but are generally more expert in giving guidance on local walks and outdoor pursuits.

National tourist board

Britain and London Visitor Centre 1 Lower Regent St, Piccadilly Circus, London SW1Y 4XT ⓦwww.visitbritain.com. No telephone enquiries.

Regional tourist boards

Cumbria Tourist Board Ashleigh, Holly Rd, Windermere, Cumbria LA23 2AQ ⓣ01539/444444, ⓦwww.gocumbria.org. Cumbria.
East of England Tourist Board Toppesfield Hall, Hadleigh, Suffolk IP7 5DN ⓣ0870/225 4800, ⓦwww.eastofenglandtouristboard.com. Bedfordshire, Cambridgeshire, Hertfordshire, Essex, Norfolk and Suffolk.
North West Tourist Board Swan House, Swan Meadow Rd, Wigan Pier, Wigan WN3 5BB ⓣ01942/821222, ⓦwww.visitnorthwest.com. Cheshire, Greater Manchester, Merseyside, Lancashire, Derbyshire and the Peak District.
Northumbria Tourist Board Aykley Heads, Durham DH1 5UX ⓣ0191/375 3010, ⓦwww.visitnorthumbria.com. County Durham, Northumberland, Tees Valley, and Tyne and Wear.
South West Tourism Woodwater Park, Exeter, Devon EX2 5WT ⓣ0870/442 0880, ⓦwww.visitsouthwest.co.uk. Devon, Cornwall, Isles of Scilly, Dorset, Gloucestershire, Somerset and Wiltshire.
Tourism South East The Old Brew House, Warwick Park, Tunbridge Wells, Kent TN2 5TU ⓣ01892/540766; 40 Chamberlayne Rd, Eastleigh, Hampshire SO50 5JH ⓣ02380/625400; ⓦwww.southeastengland.uk.com. Sussex, Kent, Surrey, Berkshire, Hampshire, Oxfordshire, Buckinghamshire and Isle of Wight.
Visit Heart of England Larkhill Rd, Worcester WR5 2EZ ⓣ01905/761100; Apex Court, City Link, Nottingham NG2 4LA ⓣ0115/959 8383; ⓦwww.visitheartofengland.com. Herefordshire, Shropshire, Warwickshire, Staffordshire, Derbyshire, Lincolnshire, Nottinghamshire, Northamptonshire, Leicestershire and Rutland.
Visit London 1 Warwick Row, London SW1E 5ER ⓣ09068/663344, ⓦwww.visitlondon.com. Greater London.
Yorkshire Tourist Board 312 Tadcaster Rd, York YO24 1GS ⓣ01904/707961, ⓦwww.yorkshirevisitor.com. Yorkshire and north Lincolnshire.

Visit Britain offices overseas

Australia Level 2, 15 Blue St, North Sydney NSW 2060 ⓣ02/9021 4400 or 1300/858589, ⓦwww.visitbritain.com/au.
Canada 5915 Airport Rd, Suite 120, Mississauga, ON L4V 1T1 ⓣ1-888/847 4885, ⓦwww.visitbritain.com/ca.
Ireland 18–19 College Green, Dublin 2 ⓣ01/670 8000, ⓦwww.visitbritain.com/ie.
New Zealand Telephone enquiries only ⓣ0800/700 741, ⓦwww.visitbritain.com/nz.
USA 551 5th Ave, 7th Floor, New York, NY 10176 ⓣ1-800/462 2748, ⓦwww.travelbritain.org.

Websites

Throughout the guide, we've included websites for specific accommodation, museums, galleries, transport, entertainment venues and other attractions. If you're looking for more general information about England, or just a different take on things, then the list below is a useful starting point. However, it only scratches the surface of what's available online.

General

ⓦwww.craptowns.com England's "worst" towns, vitriolically reviewed by *The Idler* magazine, whose opinions are then attacked by outraged locals – good, knockabout fun.
ⓦwww.goodguides.com A combination of information from the *Good Britain Guide* and *Good Pub Guide*, both indispensable publications.
ⓦwww.information-britain.co.uk Comprehensive site with a county by county guide, as well as listings on every conceivable subject.
ⓦwww.knowhere.co.uk A self-styled user's guide to Britain incorporating scurrilous readers' comments, including best-of and worst-of sections.

News and current affairs

ⓦwww.bbc.co.uk The website of the world's most respected news organization, good for news, current affairs, sport and weather.
ⓦwww.guardian.co.uk Official website of the *Guardian*, the UK's main left-leaning broadsheet, particularly good for news and reviews.

ⓦwww.telegraph.co.uk The *Daily Telegraph* offers a right-leaning perspective on current affairs; its website has particularly strong travel and sports sections.

Maps, addresses and phone numbers

ⓦwww.multimap.com Town plans and area maps with scales up to 1:10,000, plus address search, traffic info and more.
ⓦwww.visitmap.com The Britain Visitor Atlas has a clickable A–Z of town and city maps.
ⓦwww.yell.com The Yellow Pages online – search for any UK business.

Miscellaneous

ⓦwww.clubconnexion.co.uk All the gen on the UK's club scene, what's hot and what's not.
ⓦwww.londontheatreguide.co.uk What's on in the West End, and how to get tickets.
ⓦwww.met-office.gov.uk England's favourite topic, the weather, discussed in detail with full regional forecasts.
ⓦwww.ngs.org.uk The National Gardens Scheme details gardens, many of them private, open throughout the year for charity.
ⓦwww.which.net Britain's biggest consumer organization provides reviews from its respected *Good Food Guide* alongside online access to its consumer reports on everything from electric toasters to holidays.

Maps

For an overview of the whole of England on one map, Estate Publications' *England and Wales* (1:650,000) is produced in cooperation with various local tourist boards and is designed to highlight places of interest. The *Geographers' A-Z* map has the London area on the reverse, while Collins' England map includes street plans of main cities.

Coverage of the country at scales around 1:250,000/1:200,000 is provided by the Ordnance Survey, AA, Geographers' A-Z, and Collins, either in a series of folded maps or combined into atlases for the whole of the UK. Ordnance Survey mapping is best at showing the country's topography with contours and altitude colouring. Collins covers a large area on each double-sided map, AA maps are very clear and easy to read, whilst Geographers' A-Z includes a fair amount of tourist information. Among other publishers, Michelin covers England on three maps at 1:400,000, which highlight scenic routes. Estate Publications has an extensive series of both regional and local maps at various scales, produced, like their general map, with the assistance of tourist boards and showing places of interest, recreational facilities, campsites, caravan parks and so forth. A similar series for popular holiday areas from Goldeneye includes additional altitude colouring, particularly useful for cyclists.

The National Cycle Network of cross-country routes along traffic-free roads is covered by a series of excellent waterproof maps (1:100,000) published by Sustrans. Ordnance Survey's new and expanding Touring series (also 1:100,000) can be disappointing, however: it's designed to carry plenty of tourist information, but the presentation of topography falls well short of the standard associated with the OS.

For hikers, Ordnance Survey's large-scale topographic maps, renowned for their accuracy and clarity, cover England on just over 100 sheets in their Landranger series at 1:50,000, or just under 200 in the more detailed Explorer series at 1:25,000. Although generally less detailed than their OS equivalent, Harvey's walking maps for popular hiking areas, at 1:40,000 and 1:25,000, are printed on waterproof paper.

Map outlets

USA

Adventurous Traveler.com US ⓣ1-800/282-3963, ⓦadventuroustraveler.com.
Book Passage 51 Tamal Vista Blvd, Corte Madera, CA 94925 ⓣ1-800/999-7909, ⓦwww.bookpassage.com.
Distant Lands 56 S Raymond Ave, Pasadena, CA 91105 ⓣ1-800/310-3220, ⓦwww.distantlands.com.
Elliot Bay Book Company 101 S Main St, Seattle, WA 98104 ⓣ1-800/962-5311, ⓦwww.elliotbaybook.com.
Globe Corner Bookstore 28 Church St, Cambridge, MA 02138 ⓣ1-800/358-6013, ⓦwww.globercorner.com.
Map Link 30 S La Patera Lane, Unit 5, Santa Barbara, CA 93117 ⓣ1-800/962-1394, ⓦwww.maplink.com.

Rand McNally US ⓣ1-800/333-0136, ⓦwww.randmcnally.com. Around thirty stores across the US; dial ext 2111 or check the website for the nearest location.

Canada

The Travel Bug Bookstore 2667 W Broadway, Vancouver V6K 2G2 ⓣ604/737-1122, ⓦwww.swifty.com/tbug.

World of Maps 1235 Wellington St, Ottawa, Ontario K1Y 3A3 ⓣ1-800/214-8524, ⓦwww.worldofmaps.com.

UK

Blackwell's Map and Travel Shop 50 Broad St, Oxford OX1 3BQ ⓣ01865/793550, ⓦmaps.blackwell.co.uk.

Heffers Map and Travel 20 Trinity St, Cambridge CB2 1TJ ⓣ01865/333536, ⓦwww.heffers.co.uk.

The Map Shop 30a Belvoir St, Leicester LE1 6QH ⓣ0116/247 1400, ⓦwww.mapshopleicester.co.uk.

National Map Centre 22–24 Caxton St, London SW1H 0QU ⓣ020/7222 2466, ⓦwww.mapsnmc.co.uk.

Newcastle Map Centre 55 Grey St, Newcastle-upon-Tyne NE1 6EF ⓣ0191/261 5622.

Stanfords 12–14 Long Acre, London WC2E 9LP ⓣ020/7836 1321; 29 Corn St, Bristol BS1 1HT ⓣ0117/929 9966; 39 Spring Gardens, Manchester M2 2BG ⓣ0161/831 0250; ⓦwww.stanfords.co.uk.

The Travel Bookshop 13–15 Blenheim Crescent, London W11 2EE ⓣ020/7229 5260, ⓦwww.thetravelbookshop.co.uk.

Ireland

Easons Bookshop 40 O'Connell St, Dublin 1 ⓣ01/858 3881, ⓦwww.eason.ie.

Hodges Figgis Bookshop 56–58 Dawson St, Dublin 2 ⓣ01/677 4754.

Australia

The Map Shop 6–10 Peel St, Adelaide, SA 5000 ⓣ08/8231 2033, ⓦwww.mapshop.net.au.

Mapland 372 Little Bourke St, Melbourne, Victoria 3000 ⓣ03/9670 4383, ⓦwww.mapland.com.au.

Perth Map Centre 900 Hay St, Perth, WA 6000 ⓣ08/9322 5733, ⓦwww.perthmap.com.au.

New Zealand

MapWorld 173 Gloucester St, Christchurch ⓣ0800/627 967 or 03/374 5399, ⓦwww.mapworld.co.nz.

Specialty Maps 46 Albert St, Auckland 1001 ⓣ09/307 2217, ⓦwww.specialtymaps.co.nz.

Health and insurance

No vaccinations are required for entry into Britain. Citizens of all EU countries and those with a reciprocal healthcare agreement with this country are entitled to free medical treatment at National Health Service hospitals. If you don't fall into either of these categories, you will be charged for all medical services, in which case health insurance is strongly advised. Even though EU healthcare privileges apply in England, visitors from elsewhere in the EU would do well to take out an insurance policy before travelling to cover against theft, loss and illness or injury.

Pharmacies and medical emergencies

Pharmacists (known as chemists in England) can dispense only a limited range of drugs without a doctor's prescription. Most pharmacies are open standard shop hours, though in large towns some may stay open as late as 10pm – local newspapers carry lists of late-opening "duty" pharmacies, and the information should also be posted on pharmacy doors. Doctor's surgeries tend to be open from about 9am to noon and then for a couple of hours in the afternoon or evening. For complaints that require immediate attention, you can turn up at the casualty (ER) department of the local hospital, though be prepared to wait unless it's an out-and-out emergency.

For medical advice by phone you can call NHS Direct (☎0845/4647, ⓦwww.nhsdirect.nhs.uk), which also runs an increasing number of walk-in centres (usually daily 7.30am–9pm) in the bigger towns and cities. In an emergency, call for an ambulance on ☎999.

Insurance policies

A typical travel insurance policy usually provides cover for the loss of baggage, tickets and – up to a certain limit – cash or cheques, as well as cancellation or curtailment of your journey. Most of them exclude so-called dangerous sports unless an extra premium is paid: in England this can mean most watersports, rock climbing and mountaineering, though probably not things like hiking, kayaking or jeep safaris. Many policies can be chopped and changed to exclude coverage you don't need – for example, sickness and accident benefits can often be excluded or included at will. If you do take medical coverage, ascertain whether benefits will be paid as treatment proceeds or only after you return home, and whether there is a 24-hour medical emergency number. When securing baggage cover, make sure that the per-article limit – typically under £500 – will cover your most valuable possession. If you need to make a claim, you should keep receipts for medicines and medical treatment, and in the event you have anything stolen, you must obtain an official statement from the police.

It's always best to contact a specialist travel insurance company, or you could consider the travel insurance deal we offer (see box below).

Rough Guides travel insurance

Rough Guides Ltd offers a low-cost travel insurance policy, especially customized for our statistically low-risk readers by a leading British broker, provided by the American International Group (AIG) and registered with the British regulatory body, GISC (the General Insurance Standards Council). There are five main Rough Guides insurance plans: **No Frills** for the bare minimum for secure travel; **Essential**, which provides decent all-round cover; **Premier** for comprehensive cover with a wide range of benefits; **Extended Stay** for cover lasting four months to a year; and **Annual multi-trip**, a cost-effective way of getting Premier cover if you travel more than once a year. Premier, Annual Multi-Trip and Extended Stay policies can be supplemented by a "Hazardous Pursuits Extension" if you plan to indulge in sports considered dangerous, such as scuba diving or trekking. For a **policy quote**, call the Rough Guide Insurance Line: toll-free in the UK ☎0800/015 0906 or ☎+44 1392/314665 from elsewhere. Alternatively, get an online quote at: www.roughguides.com/insurance

Costs, money and banks

England is an expensive place to visit. The minimum expenditure, if you're camping or hostelling, using public transport, buying picnic food and eating in pubs and cafés, would be in the region of £25 a day. Couples staying at budget B&Bs, eating at unpretentious restaurants and visiting a fair number of tourist attractions, are looking at around £45–55 per person per day, and if you're renting a car, staying in comfortable B&Bs or hotels and eating well, budget on at least £80 each per day. Single travellers should budget on spending around 60 percent of what a couple would spend (single rooms usually cost more than half that of a double), and on any visit to London, work on the basis that you'll need an extra £20 per day to get much pleasure out of the place.

Admission charges and discounts

Many of England's most important historic attractions – from castles and abbeys to stately homes and tracts of protected landscape – are owned and/or operated by either the National Trust (ⓦwww.nationaltrust.org.uk) or English Heritage (ⓦwww.english-heritage.org.uk), whose properties are denoted in the guide with "NT" or "EH". Both these organizations charge entry fees for the majority of their sites (usually £3–4), though some, especially the more grandiose National Trust estates, can be more expensive. If you think you'll be visiting more than half a dozen places owned by either, it's worth considering an annual membership. This allows free and unlimited entry to each organization's respective properties – and you can join at any of their properties. Both the NT's and EH's annual membership costs £34.

However, many stately homes remain in the hands of the landed gentry, who tend to charge in the region of £7 for admission to edited highlights of their domain – even more if, as at Longleat, they've added some theme-park attractions to the historic pile. Many other old buildings, albeit rarely the most momentous structures, are owned by the local authorities, which are generally more lenient with their admission charges, sometimes allowing free access. Municipal art galleries and museums are often free too, a situation that also holds with many of the great state museums, such as the British Museum and the National Gallery. On the other hand, several of the country's cathedrals charge admission – of around £3 – but the majority ask for voluntary donations, as do many churches. They usually suggest an appropriate fee – and again £3 mostly covers it. You will certainly have to pay to visit any of England's burgeoning heritage museums, which in some instances are large multi-building sites staffed by people in period costume, but more often consist of interactive displays, speaking dummies and atmospheric background noises or smells. Tickets for these can cost anywhere between £5 and £10, and expense is not necessarily an indication of quality.

Concessionary rates for senior citizens and children from 5 to 16 apply almost everywhere, from fee-paying attractions to sports classes and public transport; note that you'll often need official identification as proof of age. The unemployed and full-time students are often entitled to discounts too, and the under-5s are hardly ever charged at all. The entry charges given in the guide are the full adult rate – knock off up to fifty percent for concessions.

Various official and quasi-official ID cards also pay for themselves in savings. Full-time students are eligible for the International Student ID Card (ISIC; ⓦwww.isiccard.com), which entitles the bearer to special air, rail and bus fares and discounts at museums, theatres and other attractions. A university photo ID might open some doors, but is not as easily recognizable as the ISIC card. You only have to be 26 or younger to qualify for the International Youth Travel Card, which carries similar benefits to the ISIC card, while teachers qualify for the International Teacher Card. Several other travel organizations and accommodation groups (including the youth hostel organization, IYHF) also have their own cards, good for various discounts. Any specialist travel agency in your own country (including STA worldwide) can provide more information and application forms.

Currency

Britain has so far declined to adopt the euro, preferring instead its pound sterling (£), divided into 100 pence (p). Coins come in denominations of 1p, 2p, 5p, 10p, 20p, 50p and £1 and £2. Notes are in denominations of £5, £10, £20 and £50. Very occasionally you may receive Scottish banknotes: they're legal tender throughout Britain, but you may want to get rid of them sooner rather than later as some traders may be unwilling to accept them.

Banks, ATMs, cheques and cards

Banks or the larger post offices are the best places to change money. Every sizeable town (and many of the villages) has a branch of at least one of the main high-street banks: Barclays, Halifax, HSBC, Lloyds TSB and NatWest. Opening hours are generally Mon–Fri 9.30am–4.30pm, though many branches in larger towns open at 9am, close at 5.30pm and also remain open until 3 or 4/5pm on Saturdays.

The easiest way to get hold of cash is to use a bank's ATM; there's usually a daily withdrawal limit of around £250. You'll need a personal identification number (PIN) that's designed to work overseas – your bank's international banking department should be able to advise on this. You'll also find ATMs at all major points of arrival, train stations

England on a budget

Faced with another £2.50 pint, a £30 theatre ticket and a twenty-quid taxi ride back to your £100 a night hotel, England might seem like the most expensive country in Europe, but there are ways to stick to a **budget** and still live English life to the full.

- Entry is free to many of England's showpiece **museums and galleries**, including some of the world's finest art and historical collections in London, Leeds, Birmingham, Manchester, Liverpool and Bristol.
- **Beer** is cheaper in the north of the England, cheapest of all in Lancashire, according to the peerless *Good Pub Guide*.
- Take every **discount card/ID** you're entitled to, as students, young travellers, youth hostellers and seniors all get free or discounted entry to many sights and attractions.
- Go to the **cinema** during the day; it's nearly always cheaper before 5pm.
- Set lunches can be a real steal, even at the poshest of **restaurants**, where a limited-choice two- or three-course lunch might only cost 40 percent of what's charged in the evening.
- Book **transport** tickets as far in advance as possible, and always ask about day rovers and other special deals.
- Don't drive – **walk**. In places like the Yorkshire Dales, the Lake District, or along the Cornish coastal path, the easiest and most enjoyable way to get from village to village is on your own two feet.
- Give the big-ticket **festivals** (Glastonbury, Glyndebourne) a miss; there are thousands of others throughout the year that are free and fun, from Derbyshire well-dressing to the Notting Hill Carnival.
- Visit the **markets** – from grungy Camden to Northumberland farmers' markets, you can browse for free and pick up some bargains along the way.

and motorway service areas, as well as at most large supermarkets, some petrol stations and even in some pubs and village shops.

Some people still prefer traveller's cheques, available for a small commission from any major bank. The most commonly accepted are issued by American Express, followed by Visa and Thomas Cook. It's best to bring sterling cheques and it pays to get a selection of denominations. In the event that cheques are lost or stolen, the issuing company will expect you to report the loss immediately; most companies claim to replace lost or stolen cheques within 24 hours. Neither American Express nor Thomas Cook will charge commission if you exchange cheques at their own offices, but banks will charge around 1.5 percent commission. Note that in the UK you are unlikely to be able to use your traveller's cheques as cash – you'll always have to cash them first, making them less reliable a source of funds if you intend to get far off the beaten track.

Outside banking hours, you're best advised to change cheques or cash at either a post office (locations are detailed in the guide) or a bureau de change, the latter found in most city centres, and often at train stations and airports. The rates offered and commission charged at these tend to mirror that of the banks, though try to avoid changing money or cheques in hotels, where the rates are normally the poorest on offer.

Finally, credit cards can be used widely either in ATMs or over the counter. Mastercard, Visa, American Express and Diners Club are accepted in most hotels, shops and restaurants in England, but they're less useful in the most rural areas, and smaller establishments all over the country, such as B&Bs, will often accept cash only. Remember that cash advances from ATMs using your credit card are treated as loans, with interest accruing daily from the date of withdrawal.

Wiring money

Having money sent from home through a money-wiring company (Travelers Express Moneygram www.moneygram.com; Western Union www.westernunion.com) is rarely convenient or cheap and should be considered a last resort. Fees depend on the country, method of payment and amount being transferred, but as an example, wiring £500 to England from the US will cost £20–35. Both Thomas Cook and American express also have money-wiring services.

It's also possible to have money wired directly from a bank in your home country to a bank in England. Your home bank will need the address of the branch bank where you want to pick up the money and the address and telex number of the London head office, which will act as the clearing house; money wired this way normally takes at least two working days to arrive and costs around £25 per transaction.

Taxes and tipping

Value Added Tax (VAT). It's nearly always included in the price, though hotel bills and bills for other services are sometimes calculated with the tax added on separately.

Some restaurants – usually the fancier kind, though not always – levy a "discretionary" or "optional" **service charge** of 10 or 12.5 percent. If they've done this, it should be clearly stated on the menu and on the bill. However, you are not obliged to pay the charge, and certainly not if the food or service wasn't what you expected. Otherwise, although there are no fixed rules for **tipping**, a ten to fifteen percent tip is expected by taxi drivers and anticipated by restaurant waiters, except on those rare occasions when there is a service charge. It is not normal to leave tips in pubs, but the bar staff are sometimes offered drinks, which they may accept in the form of money (the assumption is they'll spend this on a drink after closing time). The only other occasions when you'll be expected to tip are in hairdressers, and in upmarket hotels where porters, bell boys and table waiters expect and usually get a pound or two.

Getting around

As you'd expect of such a small and densely populated country, just about every place in England is accessible by train or bus. However, costs are among the highest in Europe – London's commuters spend more on getting to work than any of their European counterparts – while cross-country travel can eat up a large part of your budget. It pays to plan ahead and make sure you're aware of all the passes and special deals on offer – note that some are only available outside England and must be purchased before you arrive. It's often cheaper to drive yourself around the country (certainly if you're sharing costs), though fuel and car rental tariffs again are among the highest in Europe and will seem prohibitive to North Americans. Congestion around the main cities can be bad, and even the motorways (notoriously the M25, London's orbital road) are liable to sporadic gridlocks, especially on public holidays when what seems like half the population takes to the roads. Given the congested state of the roads, cycling might not seem the most obvious (or safest) way to get around, but many people do bring bikes to England or rent once they arrive, and the country does have a growing network of cycleways and traffic-free routes. For more on cycling, see "Outdoor pursuits", p.47.

Trains

The British rail network has suffered a foolhardy privatization process and chronic under-investment, resulting in a severe decline in services. Ongoing track repairs and speed restrictions can still play havoc with official timetables, and you'll read endless horror stories in the papers about delayed services. However, it is fair to say that there are few major towns in England that cannot be reached by rail, while main-line routes out of London especially have fast and frequent services – York or Exeter, for instance, can be reached in two hours. Travelling across the country, on the other hand, can be a bit of a lengthy business, often involving connections with several different services.

In all instances, an essential first call for information on timetables, routes and services throughout the country is National Rail Enquiries' information line or website (see p.30). Credit-card reservations are made through the rail companies themselves (National Rail Enquiries can supply the necessary contact name and number), or online via ⓦwww.thetrainline.com (see p.30).

Given the huge variety of available options, it's almost impossible to give any meaningful advice about ticket types and costs, except to say that the earlier you book, the cheaper your ticket will be. Travelling on a Friday, or just turning up at the station and buying a ticket, are the most expensive ways to go. The various train-operating companies have different names for different tickets, all with byzantine restrictions and arcane rules (for instance, it's often cheaper to travel return from the north to London, rather than from London to the north). Basically, the cheapest tickets need to be booked fourteen or seven days in advance and, as only limited numbers are issued, they sell out fast. A seat reservation is usually included with the ticket – always ask, because if it isn't, you'll want one to ensure a seat and not a perch in the corridor next to the toilets. To give you an idea of the differing fares, using the London–Manchester service as an example, an open (ie, fully flexible) return fare can cost £175-plus. If you travel off-peak and accept certain restrictions, the fare is likely to drop to around £50 return, while booking at least two weeks in advance (no refund, no changes) can bring the return fare down as low as £20.

Children aged 5–15 inclusive pay half the adult fare on most journeys – but there are usually no discounts on advance-purchase tickets. Under-5s travel free, but are not entitled to a seat. At weekends and on public holidays, many long-distance services let you upgrade your ticket by buying a first-class supplement (£5–15), well worth paying if you're facing a five-hour journey on a popular route. If the station's ticket office is closed or does not have a vending machine, you may buy your ticket on the train. Otherwise, boarding without a ticket will render you liable to paying the full fare to your destination.

Useful rail contacts

National Rail Enquiries ⊕08457/484950, ⓦwww.rail.co.uk. Advice on timetables, routes and services throughout the country.

ⓦwww.seat61.com The world's finest train travel website. It's almost nerdishly detailed, with more than you ever wanted to know about train travel in the UK (and worldwide), but full of incredibly useful tips and links.

ⓦwww.thetrainline.com Ticket sales and seat reservations for any UK journey.

Rail passes

For foreign visitors who anticipate covering a lot of ground around Britain, a rail pass is a wise investment. For most this means either the BritRail or Eurail passes, either of which must be bought before you enter the country. Any good travel agent or specialist operator (see "Getting there", pp.13 & 16) can supply up-to-date information, or consult ⓦwww.eurail.com or ⓦwww.raileurope.com (North America), ⓦwww.railplus.com.au (Australia) or ⓦwww.railplus.co.nz (New Zealand).

The BritRail Classic Pass gives unlimited travel in England, Scotland and Wales, comes in either a first- or second-class version and is valid for four days (US$285/189), eight days (US$405/269), fifteen days (US$609/405), twenty-two days (US$769/515), or one month (US$915/609). Youth Pass (second-class only) and Senior Pass (first-class only) versions are also available, costing between twenty and thirty percent less than Classic Pass prices. In addition, you can buy a panoply of other BritRail passes, including a Flexi-Pass (good for travel on specified days in a time period), Family Pass, Party Pass (for three or four

UK rail passes

Some rail passes are available only in Britain itself, to locals and to visitors. These include the **Young Person's Railcard** (£18), available to full-time students and those aged between 16 and 25, and **Senior Citizens' Rail Card** for people over 60 (£18), both of which give a third off most fares. Families can make use of the **Family Railcard** (£20), which covers up to four adults who are entitled to a 33 percent discount, and up to four children who travel on a sixty percent reduction of the child's full fare. You can buy the passes at main stations – take along two passport photographs and proof of age or status.

adults travelling together) and Pass'n'Drive (train travel plus car rental). A particularly useful one for London-bound visitors is the London Visitor Travelcard (US$32 for three days, US$43 for four days, US$64 for a week), giving unlimited bus and Tube travel in the capital including the ride from Heathrow. For information on rail passes on sale in England, see the box above.

If you are planning to travel widely around Europe by train, then it may be worthwhile buying a Eurail pass, which allows unlimited free train travel in the UK and in sixteen other countries but is unlikely to pay for itself if you stick to England alone. The Eurail Youthpass (for under-26s) costs US$414 for fifteen days, US$534 for twenty-one days, or US$664 for one month; if you're 26 or over you'll have to buy a first-class Eurail Pass, available in fifteen-day (US$588), twenty-one-day (US$762), and one-month (US$946) versions. There are also two- and three-month versions of both. You may stand a better chance of getting your money's worth out of a Eurail Flexipass, which is valid for a certain number of travel days in a two-month period. This, too, comes in under-26/first-class versions: ten days costs US$488/694, and fifteen days US$642/914.

Buses

Long-distance bus services duplicate many rail routes, very often at half the price of the train or less. Services between major towns and cities are frequent and the buses – often referred to as coaches – are comfortable. Those plying longer routes often have drinks and sandwiches available on board. By far the biggest countrywide operator is National Express (see below), whose network extends to every corner of England. On busy routes, and on any route at weekends and during holidays, it's advisable to book ahead, rather than just turn up. UK residents in full-time education, or those under 25 or over 50, can buy a National Express Discount Coach Card (£10 for one year, £19 for three), which entitles the holder to a thirty percent discount on travel. Anyone else, including foreign travellers, of any age, can purchase a Tourist Trail Pass, which offers unlimited travel on the National Express network for two days within three (£49), five within thirty (£85), eight within thirty (£135), fifteen within thirty (£190) or fifteen within sixty (£205). Twenty percent discounts on these prices are available if you already hold a Discount Coach Card or (provided you would qualify for one) if you buy a Tourist Trail Pass from outside the UK. In England you can obtain passes from major travel agents, at Gatwick and Heathrow airports, or direct from National Express. Outside the UK either contact National Express or consult a specialist tour operator.

Local bus services are run by a bewildering array of companies. In many cases, timetables and routes are well integrated, but it's increasingly the case that private companies duplicate the busiest routes in an attempt to undercut the commercial opposition, leaving the farther-flung spots neglected. Thus, if you want to get from one end of a big English city to another, you'll probably have a choice of buses all offering cut-price fares, but to get out into the suburbs or to a satellite village, you may have to wait several hours. As a rule, the further away from urban areas you get, the less frequent and more expensive bus services become, but there are very few rural areas which aren't served by at least the occasional privately owned minibus.

In the summer, many national park areas support a network of weekend and bank holiday buses, taking visitors to beauty spots, villages, hiking trailheads and other out-of-the-way destinations. In addition, many rural areas not covered by other forms of public transport are served by the Postbus network (Ⓣ0845/774 0740, Ⓦwww.royalmail.com/postbus), which operates minibuses carrying mail and about eight fare-paying passengers. They set off in the morning – usually around 8am from the main post office – and collect mail from (or deliver it to) the outlying regions. It's a cheap way to travel (£2–4 a journey), and can be a convenient way of getting to hidden-away B&Bs, and even round the M25, although it is often excruciatingly slow.

Bus enquiries

National Express Ⓣ**0870/580 8080, +448705/808080 from outside the UK,** Ⓦ**www.nationalexpress.com.** For inter-town and city connections.

Traveline Ⓣ**0870/608 2608,** Ⓦ**www.traveline.org.uk.** Extremely useful service that can give you the latest details on all national and local services throughout the country. Phone lines are open daily 7am–9pm.

Minibus and bus tours

Backpackers and travellers on a budget often prefer the flexibility of touring England on Stray Travel's "jump-on-jump-off" minibus, where you'll get the chance to travel with like-minded folk and see some off-the-beaten-track destinations. The bus loops around the country (and into Wales and Scotland), calling at all the major destinations – Windsor, Bath, Liverpool, the Lakes, York, Stratford and Oxford – before heading back to the capital. You can arrange your own accommodation or have Stray Travel do it for you; either way, it's a good-natured, budget-orientated trip. Road Trip offers fully inclusive budget bus tours to a similar clientele, though you can't get on and off on their routes. If you're looking for something a bit more upmarket – escorted coach tours with an older target group – then any high street travel agency can provide brochures and recommend routes.

Bus tour operators

Road Trip Ⓣ**0845/200 6791,** Ⓦ**www.roadtrip.co.uk.** Three-day weekend tours (from £69) to destinations such as Cornwall, Liverpool and the Lakes, or York and Sherwood Forest; plus five-day tours of the south and southwest (from £129). An extra "kitty" paid on all tours covers accommodation, meals and entrance fees. Day-trips from London (£50–60) are also available.

Stray Travel ⓣ020/7373 7737, ⓦwww.straytravel.com. The All-Britain route (£159) takes a minimum of six days to complete, though the ticket is valid for four months. Other available routes include London to Liverpool (£109, three-day minimum) and Cornwall (£99, three-day), while a Get-a-fix Day Trip (Stonehenge, Oxford and Cotswolds; £34) is also offered.

Driving

In order to drive in England you need a current full driving licence. If you're bringing your own vehicle into the country you should also carry your vehicle registration or ownership document at all times. Furthermore, you must be adequately insured: check your existing insurance policy.

In England you drive on the left, a situation that can lead to a few tense days of acclimatization for overseas drivers. Motorways – "M" roads – and main "A" roads have four or six lanes, but you should still expect crowded roads and delays at peak travel times and around public holidays. In the country, on "B" roads and minor roads, there might only be one lane (single track), so you need to drive carefully – especially as locals (who know the roads) tend to assume there's nothing else coming. Also, don't underestimate the English weather – snow, ice, fog and wind cause havoc every year, and driving conditions on motorways as much as in rural areas can deteriorate quickly. Local radio stations and national Radio 5 (see p.43 for frequencies) feature constantly updated traffic bulletins.

Speed limits are 30–40mph (50–65kph) in built-up areas, 70mph (110kph) on motorways and dual carriageways (freeways) and 60mph (80kph) on most other roads. As a rule, assume that in any area with street lighting the speed limit is 30mph (50kph) unless otherwise stated. England has so far resisted toll roads (apart from one or two minor examples), but the principle has been broached by the success of congestion charging in London – if you intend to drive a car into central London, it will cost you (see p.67 for more).

Fuel is expensive compared to North American prices – unleaded petrol (gasoline) and diesel cost in the region of 80p per litre, a few pence more for leaded 4-star. The lowest prices of all are charged at out-of-town supermarkets; suburban service stations are usually fairly reasonable; and the highest prices are charged by motorway stations.

The AA (Automobile Association; ⓣ0870/600 0371, ⓦwww.theaa.com), RAC (Royal Automobile Club; ⓣ0870/572 2722, ⓦwww.rac.co.uk) and Green Flag (ⓣ0800/328 8772, ⓦwww.greenflag.com) all operate 24-hour emergency breakdown services, and also provide many other motoring and leisure services (including useful online route-planning tools). You may be entitled to free assistance through a reciprocal arrangement with overseas motoring organizations – check the situation with your own association before setting out. You can make use of these emergency services if you are not a member of the organizations, but you will be required to join at the roadside and you will incur a hefty surcharge as well.

Car parking in towns, cities and popular tourist spots can be a nightmare and will also cost you a small fortune. If you're in a tourist city for a day, look out for park-and-ride schemes where you can park your car on the outskirts and take a cheap or free bus to the centre. Parking in long- or short-stay car parks will be cheaper than using on-street meters, which restrict parking time to two or three hours at the most. As a rule, the smaller the town, the cheaper the parking. Some towns operate free disc-zone parking, which allows limited-hours town-centre parking in designated area: if that's what roadside signs indicate, you need to pick up a cardboard disc from any local shop and display it in your windscreen. A yellow line along the edge of the road indicates parking restrictions; check the nearest sign to see exactly what they are. A double-yellow line means no parking at any time, though you can stop briefly to unload or pick up people or goods (maximum stop two minutes), but if the lines are red, that means absolutely no stopping at all.

Vehicle rental

Compared to rates in North America, car rental in England is expensive, and you'll probably find it cheaper to arrange things from home through one of the multinational chains, or by opting for a fly/drive deal. If you do rent a car from a company in England, the least you can normally expect to pay is around £60 for a weekend or from £150 per week. Although easyCar (in London, Manchester, Liverpool and Birmingham) can provide a vehicle from around £10 per day, you'll need to book well in advance for the cheapest rates and be prepared for extra charges (like cleaning fees) if you bring the car back in an unacceptable state. Booking in England with one of the multinationals, reckon on paying around £35–40 per day, perhaps £10 or so less at a local firm. Rental agencies prefer you to pay by credit card and, you'll have to leave a deposit of £100 or more on top of the rental charge. There are very few automatics at the lower end of the price scale – if you want one, you should book well ahead. Few companies will rent to drivers with less than one year's experience and most will only rent to people between 21 and 75 years of age.

For camper van rental, contact Just Go (ⓣ0870/240 1918, ⓦwww.justgo.uk.com), which can supply quality vehicles sleeping four to six people, equipped with CD/DVD, full bathrooms and kitchen and bike racks. Rates range from £450 to £850 per week, depending on vehicle and season.

Car rental companies

In the US and Canada

Auto Europe US ⓣ1-800/223-5555, Canada ⓣ1-888/223-5555, ⓦwww.autoeurope.com.
Avis US ⓣ1-800/331-1084, Canada ⓣ1-800/272-5871, ⓦwww.avis.com.
Budget US ⓣ1-800/527-0700, ⓦwww.budgetrentacar.com.
Dollar US ⓣ1-800/800-4000, ⓦwww.dollar.com.
Enterprise Rent-a-Car US ⓣ1-800/325-8007, ⓦwww.enterprise.com.
Europcar US & Canada ⓣ1-877/940 6900, ⓦwww.europcar.com.
Europe by Car US ⓣ1-800/223-1516, ⓦwww.europebycar.com.
Hertz US ⓣ1-800/654-3001, Canada ⓣ1-800/263-0600, ⓦwww.hertz.com.
Holiday Autos US ⓣ1-800/422-7737, ⓦwww.holidayautos.com.
National ⓣ1-800/227-7362, ⓦwww.nationalcar.com.
Thrifty ⓣ1-800/367-2277, ⓦwww.thrifty.com.

In Australia

Avis ⓣ13/6333 or 02/9353 9000, ⓦwww.avis.com.au.
Budget ⓣ1300/362 848, ⓦwww.budget.com.au.
Dollar ⓣ02/9223 1444, ⓦwww.dollarcar.com.au.
Europcar ⓣ1300/131 390, ⓦwww.deltaeuropcar.com.au.
Hertz ⓣ13/3039 or 03/9698 2555, ⓦwww.hertz.com.au.
Holiday Autos ⓣ1300/554 432, ⓦwww.holidayautos.com.au.
National ⓣ13/1045, ⓦwww.nationalcar.com.au.
Thrifty ⓣ1300/367 227, ⓦwww.thrifty.com.au.

In New Zealand

Avis ⓣ09/526 2847 or 0800/655 111, ⓦwww.avis.co.nz.
Budget ⓣ09/976 2222, ⓦwww.budget.co.nz.
Hertz ⓣ0800/654 321, ⓦwww.hertz.co.nz.
Holiday Autos ⓣ0800/144 040, ⓦwww.holidayautos.co.nz.
National ⓣ0800/800 115, ⓦwww.nationalcar.co.nz.
Thrifty ⓣ09/309 0111, ⓦwww.thrifty.co.nz.

In England

Avis ⓣ0870/606 0100, ⓦwww.avis.co.uk.
Budget ⓣ0800/181181, ⓦwww.budget.co.uk.
easyCar ⓣ0906/333 3333, ⓦwww.easycar.com.
Europcar ⓣ0845/722 2525, ⓦwww.europcar.co.uk.
Hertz ⓣ0870/844 8844, ⓦwww.hertz.co.uk.
Holiday Autos ⓣ0870/400 0099, ⓦwww.holidayautos.co.uk.
National ⓣ0870/536 5365, ⓦwww.nationalcar.co.uk.
Suncars ⓣ0870/500 5566, ⓦwww.suncars.com.
Thrifty ⓣ01494/751600, ⓦwww.thrifty.co.uk.

In Ireland

Avis Northern Ireland ⓣ028/9024 0404, Republic of Ireland ⓣ01/605 7500, ⓦwww.avis.ie.
Budget Republic of Ireland ⓣ0903/27711, ⓦwww.budget.ie.
Europcar Northern Ireland ⓣ028/9442 3444, Republic of Ireland ⓣ01/614 2888, ⓦwww.europcar.ie.

Hertz Republic of Ireland ⓣ01/676 7476, ⓦwww.hertz.ie.
Holiday Autos Republic of Ireland ⓣ01/872 9366, ⓦwww.holidayautos.ie.
Thrifty Republic of Ireland ⓣ1-800/515 800, ⓦwww.thrifty.ie.

Taxis

It would be a rich tourist who got around exclusively by taxi, especially in London, but they are a useful option. In rural areas, there's often no alternative if you need to get to the next town in a hurry, and if you're with a group hiring a taxi can work out as cheap as taking a bus. Reckon on paying around £1.50 a mile in country districts. In towns and cities prices are higher for running shorter distances, but there are wide regional variations – a cab home after a night out in Manchester or Newcastle is far less of a wallet-emptying experience than in London. The famous black cabs are generally a little more expensive than minicabs, but are usually more reliable (the London cabbie's "knowledge" is such that he or she should know the location of every street in the capital – and if they don't they'll never admit it). You can hail a black cab on the street, but you must book minicabs by phone.

Useful contact

ⓦwww.traintaxi.co.uk. Useful online guide putting you in touch with taxi firms serving all Britain's train, tram, metro and tube stations.

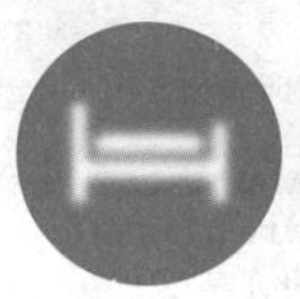

Accommodation

England has hundreds of hotels, ranging from motorway lodges to country retreats, as well as budget accommodation in B&Bs, guest houses and youth hostels. You'll want to stay in at least one nicely refurbished old building – the historic towns of England are full of former coaching inns and similarly ancient hostelries, while out in the countryside there are numerous converted mansions and manor houses, often with brilliant restaurants attached.

Nearly all tourist offices will book rooms for you, although the fee for this service can vary. In some areas you will pay a deposit that's deducted from your first night's bill (usually ten percent), in others the office will take a percentage or flat-rate commission – usually around £3. Another useful service operated by the majority of tourist offices is the "Book-a-bed-ahead" service, which locates accommodation in your next port of call – again for a charge of about £3, though the service is sometimes free.

Hotels and B&Bs

A nationwide system for grading hotels and B&Bs has been adopted in England, with hotels graded by stars (five stars is the top rank), and B&Bs by diamonds, with additional gold and silver awards for those that achieve distinction. Although there's not a hard and fast correlation between standards and price, you'll pay in the region of £60 per night for a double room at a one-star hotel (breakfast included), rising to around £100 in a three-star and from around £200 for a five-star – in London and some tourist hotspots, rates are twice that. In many towns and cities, larger hotels offer cut-price weekend rates to fill the rooms vacated by the weekday business trade. An increasing number of budget hotel chains – *Travel Inn*, *Travel Lodge*, *Holiday Inn Express*, *Ramada* and others – have properties usefully located in city centres across the country. The style at these tends towards the no-frills (with breakfast charged extra), but at £50–60 a room (often sleeping up to four), they're a good deal for families and people travelling in small groups.

Accommodation price codes

Throughout this guide, accommodation is graded on a scale of ❶ to ❾, the number indicating the lowest price you could expect to pay per night in that establishment for a **double room in high season**. Breakfast is included unless otherwise stated. Many places will also offer special weekend or seasonal rates – it's always worth asking. We've given the exact cost for **dorm accommodation** in youth and backpackers' hostels, and student halls of residence, as well price codes for those hostels that have private double rooms.

The prices indicated by the codes are as follows:

❶ under £40	❹ £61–70	❼ £111–150
❷ £41–50	❺ £71–90	❽ £151–200
❸ £51–60	❻ £91–110	❾ over £201

At its most basic, the typically English bed-and-breakfast (B&B) – often known as a guest house – is an ordinary private house with a couple of bedrooms set aside for paying guests, and a dining room for breakfast. At their best, however, B&Bs offer rooms as well furnished as those in hotels costing twice as much, plus delicious home-cooked breakfasts and an informal hospitality that a larger place couldn't match. The cheapest B&Bs are under £40 per night for a double or twin room, though at those prices you may be sharing bathroom facilities with other guests. In some traditional resorts, like Blackpool, competition is such that you'll be able to get a bed for the night for as little as £12. Further up the scale, you can pay £70 and upwards at a superior B&B, some of which have very definite boutique or gourmet pretensions. As many B&Bs, even the pricier ones, have a very small number of rooms, you should book as far in advance as possible. Single travellers shouldn't expect to pay half the price of a double room – as many B&Bs don't have single rooms, it's more usual to be charged £20–25 or so to occupy one of their doubles.

Finally, don't assume that a B&B is no good if it's ungraded. There are so many B&Bs in England that the inspectors can't possibly keep track of them all, and in the rural backwaters some of the most enjoyable accommodation is to be found in welcoming and beautifully set farmhouses and other properties whose facilities may technically fall short of official standards. In towns and villages, many pubs also offer B&B accommodation, again often not graded. Standards vary wildly – some are truly awful – but at best you'll be staying in a friendly spot with a sociable bar on hand, and you'll rarely pay more than £50 or so a double.

Useful contacts

Distinctly Different ⓣ**01225/866842**, ⓦ**www.distinctlydifferent.co.uk.** Consult the website or buy the guide (£3), and stay the night in converted buildings across the country, from old brothel to Baptist chapel, windmill to lighthouse.

Farm Stay UK ⓣ**0247/669 6909, free brochure on** ⓣ**01271/336141,** ⓦ**www.farmstay.co.uk.** The largest network of farm-based accommodation in the UK.

Hostels, camping barns and student halls

The Youth Hostels Association (YHA) has over 230 properties in England and Wales, offering bunk-bed accommodation in single-sex dormitories or smaller rooms of four to six beds. A few new hostels and many refurbished older ones also now have double and family rooms available, and in cities the facilities are often every bit as good as some budget hotels. Indeed, although a few places are spartan establishments of the sort traditionally associated with the wholesome, fresh-air ethic of the first hostels, most have moved well away from the old-fashioned, institutional ambience, and boast cafés, laundry facilities, Internet access, entertainment and bike rental.

Visitors who belong to any International Youth Hostel Federation (IYHF) association have automatic membership of the YHA; if you aren't a member of such an organization (see the list below), you can join the YHA in person at any affiliated hostel on your first night's stay. Membership costs £13.50 per year (£6.75 for under-18s). Bed prices at most English youth hostels are around £10.25 per night (£7 for under-18s), though in cities like York, Oxford and London the overnight price is more like £17–22 (under-18s £12–17). Students aged 18–25 can get a £1 reduction on production of a valid student card. Length of stay is normally unlimited and the hostel will provide a linen sleeping bag and bedding. Hostel meals – breakfast, packed lunch or dinner – are always good value (around a fiver), while nearly all hostels also have self-catering kitchen facilities.

It's best to book hostel beds well in advance, and it's essential to do so if you want to stay at Easter, from May to August and at Christmas. You can book online, and most hostels accept payment by Mastercard or Visa; with those that don't, you should confirm your booking in writing, with payment, at least seven days before arrival. If you're tempted to turn up on the spur of the moment, bear in mind that very few hostels are open year-round, many are closed at least one day a week, even in high season, and several have periods during which they take bookings from groups only. Always phone to check – we've given the number for every hostel mentioned. Most hostels are closed from 10am to 5pm, with an 11.30pm curfew, although all seven of the London hostels offer 24-hour access.

A growing number of independent backpacker hostels in town centres and resort areas offer similar facilities to the YHA at much the same prices. Facilities aren't always up to scratch (especially in London and the bigger cities), though some are of excellent quality – we've picked out the best in the guide. Many people prefer them to YHA hostels as they tend to attract a more youthful, backpacking (rather than family/hiker) crowd, and they usually don't have curfews; some even have their own bars. There's also no requirement to be a member of an organization to use the independent hostels. A useful publication to get hold of is the annually updated *Independent Hostel Guide* (Backpackers Press; ⓣ01629/580427, ⓦwww.backpackerspress.com). The website ⓦwww.backpackers.co.uk also gives the lowdown on independent hostels and budget accommodation.

In the wilder parts of England, such as the north Pennines, North Yorkshire, the Lake District, Peak District, Dartmoor and Exmoor, the YHA also administers some basic accommodation for walkers in camping barns. Holding up to twenty people, these agricultural outbuildings are often unheated and are very sparsely furnished, with wooden sleeping platforms – or bunks if you're lucky – a couple of tables, a toilet and a cold-water supply, but they are weatherproof, extremely good value (from £4/night) and perfectly situated for walking tours. You do not have to be a YHA member to stay in any of these. Similar barns, often called bunkhouses, are run by private individuals in many areas – the useful ones are mentioned in the guide and prices start at around £8 per night.

In England's university towns you should be able to find out-of-term accommodation (Easter & Christmas holidays, plus July to Sept) in student halls of residence, usually one-bedded rooms either with their own or shared bathrooms. Prices start at around £15 per night. In some instances (Durham, say) where there's no youth hostel, this may be the only budget accommodation on offer in the centre of town. All the useful university details are given in the guide, but if you want a list of everything that's on offer, contact the Summer Village (ⓣ0870/712 5002, ⓦwww.thesummervillage.com) or Venuemasters (ⓣ0114/249 3090, ⓦwww.venuemasters.co.uk).

Youth hostel associations

Australia Australian Youth Hostels Association ⓣ02/9565 1699, ⓦwww.yha.com.au.
Canada Hostelling International ⓣ613/237-7884, ⓦwww.hihostels.ca.
England and Wales Youth Hostel Association (YHA) ⓣ0870/770 8868, ⓦwww.yha.org.uk.
New Zealand Youth Hostels Association of New Zealand ⓣ03/379 9970, ⓦwww.yha.co.nz.com.
Northern Ireland Hostelling International Northern Ireland ⓣ028/9032 4733, ⓦwww.hini.org.

Republic of Ireland Irish Youth Hostel Association (An Oige) ⓣ01/830 4555, ⓦwww.irelandyha.org.
Scotland Scottish Youth Hostel Association ⓣ01786/891400, ⓦwww.syha.org.uk.
USA Hostelling International–American Youth Hostels (HI-AYH) ⓣ202/783-6161, ⓦwww.hiayh.org.

Camping and caravanning

There are hundreds of campsites in England, charging from £5 per tent per night to around £12 for the plushest sites, with amenities such as laundries, shops and sports facilities. Some YHA hostels have small campsites on their property, charging half the indoor overnight fee. In addition to these official sites, farmers may offer pitches for as little as £2 per night, but don't expect tiled bathrooms and hair dryers for that kind of money. Even farmers without a reserved camping area may let you pitch in a field if you ask first, possibly for free; setting up a tent without asking is an act of trespass, which will not be well received. Free camping is illegal in national parks and nature reserves.

The problem with many campsites in the most popular parts of rural England – especially the West Country coast – is that tents have to share the space with caravans. Every summer the country's byways are clogged by migrations of these cumbersome trailers, which are still far more numerous than camper vans in England. The great majority of caravans, however, are permanently moored at their sites, where they are rented out to families for self-catering holidays, and the ranks of nose-to-tail trailers in the vicinity of most of England's best beaches might make you think that half the population of Britain shacks up in a caravan for the midsummer break.

Detailed, annually revised guides to England's camping and caravan sites include the official *Caravan and Camping Parks in Britain*, available in all major bookshops.

Self-catering accommodation

There are thousands of properties for rent by the week in England, ranging from city penthouses to secluded cottages. The least you can expect to pay for self-catering accommodation sleeping four people in low season would be around £150 per week, but in summer for something attractive – such as a small house near the West Country moors or in the Lake District – you should budget for £400 or £500.

We've listed the main agencies below, but every regional tourist board has details of cottage rentals in its area. Alternatively, consult ⓦwww.visitbritain.com, which has an exhaustive list of (and links to) self-catering rental agencies in every region. Stilwell's (ⓣ01305/250151, ⓦwww.stilwell.co.uk) can send you their free annual guide, *Independent Holiday Cottages*, where you select your property and then book direct with the cottage owners. The weekend newspapers are another source of information on all types of self-catering accommodation, from canal boats to lighthouses; and of course most English travel agents can offer a range of self-catering holiday packages.

Property rental agencies

Country Holidays/English Country Cottages ⓣ08700/781200, ⓦwww.country-holidays.co.uk. More than three thousand properties all over England.
Hoseasons ⓣ01502/502588, ⓦwww.hoseasons.co.uk. Wide range of cottages and country lodges throughout the country.
Landmark Trust ⓣ01628/825925, ⓦwww.landmarktrust.co.uk. Their handbook (£9.50/US$25) lists over 160 converted historic properties, ranging from restored forts and Martello towers to a tiny radio shack used in World War II.
National Trust ⓣ0870/458 4422, ⓦwww.nationaltrust.org.uk. The NT owns around 300 cottages and farmhouses, most set in their own gardens or grounds.
Rural Retreats ⓣ01386/701177, ⓦwww.ruralretreats.co.uk. Upmarket accommodation in restored old buildings, many of them listed.

Food and drink

The English still tend to regard eating as a functional necessity rather than a sociable pleasure, but things are on the move and in the last decade changing tastes – and appetites – have spawned literally hundreds of good-to-excellent restaurants. As you might expect, London has been the epicentre of this gastronomic revolution, but today every major city and town has several very recommendable places. Modern British cuisine – in effect anything inventive – has been at the core of this change, though there's more than adequate back-up in the welter of restaurants established by England's various immigrant communities, primarily the Italians, the Chinese and the Indians. The other mainstay is the pub. Admittedly, city pubs have taken a beating from the arrival of the coffee house, whose slick modern furnishings have often made them look dowdy and dull, but the survivors have dusted themselves down and the pick now offer real ales and top-notch bar food. In the country, the pub has had an easier time and a drink (and a meal) in a traditional "local" remains the best introduction to village life.

Food

In many hotels and B&Bs you'll be offered what's termed an "English breakfast", which is usually sausage, bacon, tomatoes, mushrooms and eggs plus tea and toast – though the English actually switched over to cereals in their millions several decades ago. For most overseas visitors, the quintessential English meal is fish and chips, which can vary from the succulently fresh to the disgustingly greasy with (or without) lashings of salt and vinegar. The key is in the frying – or rather the freshness of the fat and, some would say, whether the fat contains lard or vegetable oils. If you ask the staff what's in the frying fat, don't be amazed if you get a hostile response – for some reason questions of this sort are regarded as rude. The classier fish-and-chip shops have tables, but more often than not they serve takeaway (takeout) food only with an (unappetizing) wooden fork thrown in. Fish-and-chip shops can be found on most high streets and main suburban thoroughfares, but in larger towns they often – and depressingly – play second fiddle to multinational pizza and burger joints. As an alternative, every town and city possesses at least a couple of cafés serving snacks and light meals during the day; the quality of the food varies markedly, but at their best these offer good, homemade traditional dishes. Incidentally, cafés are often dubbed tearooms in the more touristy areas.

Pub food varies enormously too. Some pubs take their food very seriously indeed, offering menus that can compete with any mid-range restaurant, but far too many places churn out very average stuff that conforms to every negative stereotype about English cooking; we have picked out many of the best in the guide. Common offerings include steak-and-kidney pie, chops or steaks, accompanied by boiled potatoes, carrots or some such vegetable. Pub kitchens often close in the afternoon – between about 2pm and 6pm – and on one or possibly two evenings per week, often Sunday; few serve after about 8.30/9pm. The better pubs can be counted on to have at least one vegetarian dish on their menus, as can many restaurants, but away from London and the Home Counties, specialist vegetarian places are invariably thin on the ground.

Restaurants

England's postwar immigrant communities have established literally hundreds of restaurants. The majority are in the inexpensive or moderate price brackets (see opposite) and the most common are Chinese, Indian and Thai, with the widest choice being in London

Restaurant prices

Restaurants listed in this guide have been assigned one of four **price categories**:

Inexpensive under £12.50

Moderate £12.50–20

Expensive £20–35

Very Expensive over £35

This is the price you can expect to pay per person for a three-course meal or equivalent, excluding drinks and service. Listed restaurants take credit cards unless otherwise stated.

and the industrial cities of the Midlands and the North. Indonesian, Japanese and North African places are now becoming more widespread, but are generally a shade more expensive, while farther up the economic scale there's no shortage of French and Italian restaurants, with the occasional Spanish tapas bar thrown in for good measure.

The ranks of England's gastronomic restaurants swell year on year, with cordon-bleu chefs producing high-class French-style dishes, California-influenced menus and internationalist hybrid creations to rival anything created across the English Channel. There's also been a revival of traditional English dishes, with the likes of shepherd's pie (basically mince meat and mashed potato) and hot pot (a stew) being trumpeted in many a fashionable restaurant. Inevitably, London has the highest concentration of top-flight places, but wherever you are in England you're never more than half an hour's drive from a really good meal – some of the very best dining rooms are to be found in country hotels. The problem is that fine food is expensive and if a place has any sort of reputation you're unlikely to be spending less than £15 per head for a main course, much more for the services of a top chef.

Our restaurant listings include a mix of high-quality and good-value establishments, but if you're intent on a culinary pilgrimage, you would do well to arm yourself with a copy of the *Which Good Food Guide*, which is updated annually and includes over a thousand detailed recommendations.

Drinking: cafés and pubs

Every city and town has a small selection of cafés, characteristically unassuming places offering non-alcoholic beverages and light meals. The majority are designed for shoppers and open in the daytime only, though London bucks the rule by having a slew of far more ambitious cafés, often in the grand European tradition. In the tourist towns, these cafés are often branded teashops, but there's little real difference. Added to this are the American-style coffee shops, serving lattes and so forth in crisp modern surroundings. These have really taken off and are to be found in numbers in every sizeable town.

Many city pubs were slow to react to the arrival of the coffee shop and hundreds have closed down, but nonetheless the pub remains the one great English social institution. Originating as wayfarers' hostelries and coaching inns, pubs have outlived the church and marketplace as the focal points of many an English town and village, and at their best they can be as welcoming as the full name – "public house" – suggests. Pubs are as varied as the country's townscapes: in larger market towns you'll find huge oak-beamed inns with open fires and polished brass fittings; in the remoter upland villages there are stone-built pubs no larger than a two-bedroomed cottage; and in the more inward-looking parts of industrial England you'll come across no-nonsense pubs where something of the old division of the sexes still holds sway – the "spit and sawdust" public bar is where working men can bond over a pint or two; the plusher saloon bar, with a separate entrance, is the preferred haunt of couples and unaccompanied women. Whatever the species of pub, its opening hours are daily 11am–11pm with or without an afternoon break from around 2.30pm or 3pm to 5.30pm or 6pm.

Beer

Many pubs are owned by large breweries who favour their own beers and lagers, as well as some "guest beers", all dispensed by the pint or half-pint. A pint costs anything from around £1.70 to £3.50, depending on the brew and the locale of the pub. The most widespread type of English beer is bitter, an uncarbonated, darkish beverage that should be pumped by hand from the cellar and served at room temperature. The sweeter, darker "mild" beer that once ruled the roost is now all but extinct. Lager, on the other hand, which was once a minor concern, is now consumed in greater quantities than bitter, largely on account of a prolonged advertising campaign by several of the major brewers. Every pub will have at least two brands of lager on offer, but rarely is it a patch on bitter – as CAMRA, the Campaign for Real Ale (®www.camra.org.uk) has long been at pains to point out. Some of the beer currently touted as good English ale is nothing of the sort – if the stuff comes out of an electric pump, it isn't the real thing – but the big breweries do distribute some excellent brews, including Directors, a very classy strong bitter.

Nonetheless, the real glory of English beer is in the local detail, and every really good pub – of which there is almost always one near at hand – sells the products of the innumerable small breweries that produce real ales to traditional recipes. Many of these pubs are so-called free houses, meaning independently run establishments that sell what they please, but this is by no means always the case. Our guide details lots of these first-rate pubs, but aficionados should consult the *Good Beer Guide*, published annually by CAMRA.

Cider and wine

In the West Country, cider, the fermented produce of apples, is the traditional drink. It comes in various forms, but perhaps the most authentic is scrumpy, a potent and cloudy beverage that is rarely sold in pubs outside of the southwest and Shropshire, though supermarkets everywhere frequently stock it. Incidentally, scrumpy has little in common with the fizzy and very sweet cider – principally Strongbow – sold in pubs all over England.

The English consume an enormous and ever increasing quantity of wine, but although restaurants (and supermarkets) commonly stock a good to excellent range, wine sold in pubs can vary enormously in quality, though standards are on the way up.

Communications

England has a competent and comprehensive postal system, with post boxes and post offices liberally distributed right across the country. Operated by Royal Mail, the postal system has thus far managed to avoid privatization – unlike the telephone network, though here one company, British Telecom (BT), still operates the bulk of the system and maintains thousands of public telephone boxes. Almost every major library in the country offers Internet access, as do many hotels; there are also Internet cafés in all the major cities.

Mail

Virtually all post offices are open from Monday to Friday from 9am to 5.30pm, and on Saturdays from 9am to 12.30 or 1pm. In small communities you'll find sub-post offices operating out of general stores, though note that the post office facilities are usually available only during the hours above even if the shop itself is open for longer. Stamps can be bought at supermarkets and newsagents as well as from post offices. A first-class stamp for letters and postcards to anywhere in the UK currently costs 28p and should – in theory at least – arrive the next day; second-class costs 20p and takes from two to three days. Letters and postcards weighing less than 20g

(0.7oz) sent by airmail cost 38p within Europe and either 47p (under 10g) or 68p (10–20g) to anywhere else in the world. For more information, check out ®www.royalmail.com.

Phones

You can make domestic and international telephone calls with equal ease from public (and private) phones. Public pay phones are plentiful and take coins from 10p upwards (minimum payment 20p); an increasing number also accept credit cards. Calling in peak periods (Mon–Fri 8am–6pm) is considerably more expensive than calling at the weekend or in the evening – and the same applies to international calls, though in both cases public pay phone tariffs are higher than those applied to private phones.

On private phones, BT operates a maze-like tariff structure, but on the most popular options all local and national calls are charged at the same rate – Mon–Fri 8am–6pm at 3p per minute, weekend and evenings 6p per hour. International call charges on private phones vary considerably. To Australia, BT currently charges 33p per minute at the weekend, 36p Monday to Friday from 6pm to 8am and 42p Monday to Friday 8am–6pm. To the USA charges are respectively 18p, 19p and 20p per minute. Note also that although the vast majority of hotel rooms have phones, there is almost always an exorbitant surcharge for their use.

Every English telephone number is prefixed by an area code, which is separated from the subscriber number by an oblique slash throughout this book. This area code can (but does not have to) be omitted when you are dialling a local number. However, some prefixes relate to the cost of calls rather than the location of the subscriber, and should never be omitted. These include ⓣ0800 and ⓣ0808 prefixes, which are free of charge to the caller, and ⓣ0845 and ⓣ0870 numbers, where callers are charged at local rates irrespective of where they call from – an important consideration if you are using a pay phone. Beware of premium-rate numbers, which are common for pre-recorded information services – and usually have the prefix ⓣ0906 or ⓣ0909; these are charged at anything up to £1.50 a minute. If you do call a premium line, there should be a pre-recorded warning announcement giving details of the cost per minute at the beginning of the call.

Phonecards, charge cards and credit-card calls

One of the most convenient ways of phoning home from abroad is via a telephone charge card from your phone company back home. Using a local access number and a PIN number, you can make calls from most hotel, public and private phones that will be charged to your own telephone account. Since most major charge cards are free to obtain, it's certainly worth getting one at least for emergencies; bear in mind, however, that rates aren't necessarily cheaper than making an ordinary call. Some international phone providers also allow you to route calls from England over their network, charging the cost to your credit card, which means dialling a local access number before the number you wish to call. Though convenient, this can be much more expensive than simply using coins or a charge card, so before going down this route you'll need to check the tariff with the company whose network you wish to use.

For inexpensive long-distance calls, you can buy an international phonecard, available in denominations of £5, £10 and upwards. As with charge cards, you dial the company's local access number, key in the pin number on the card and then dial your number. It's worth checking tariffs before you buy (posters detailing rates are displayed wherever the cards are sold): some companies are particularly cheap for North America, Africa or the Caribbean, while others concentrate on Europe. Bear in mind also that connections can sometimes be a bit slow or fuzzy.

Mobile phones

If you want to use your mobile phone in the UK, you'll need to check cellular access with your phone provider before you set out. Within Europe, this presents few problems as the GSM service frequencies – 900/1800 – are continent-wide, but North Americans will need a tri-band phone, as their frequency is different. As regards call charges, these can be excruciating, especially as you are likely to be charged extra for incoming calls when abroad (the people calling you will be paying the usual domestic rate). The same often applies to text messages, though in many cases these can now be received with the greatest of ease – no fiddly codes and so forth – and at ordinary rates. In England, mobile phone access is routine in all the major cities and in most of the countryside.

Operator services

UK operator ⓣ100
International operator ⓣ155
Directory assistance BT's domestic and international directory services were deregulated in 2003, with the former BT numbers replaced by numerous competing lines. BT's domestic service, on ⓣ118/500, is as good as any (30p per minute plus a basic fee of 25p from private phones; 60p per minute from pay phones); their international directory assistance number is ⓣ118/505 (£1.50 per minute).

International calls

To call England from overseas dial your international access code, then ⓣ44, followed by the number you require, omitting the initial zero.

To call overseas from England, begin with the dialling codes below, then dial the number you want, omitting the initial zero if present.

Australia ⓣ0061
Republic of Ireland ⓣ00353
New Zealand ⓣ0064
US and Canada ⓣ001

Email

One of the best ways to keep in touch while travelling is to sign up for a free Internet email address. YahooMail or Hotmail are perhaps the most popular, accessible via ⓦwww.yahoo.com and ⓦwww.hotmail.com. Once you've set up an account, you can use these sites to pick up and send mail from any Internet café, library or hotel with Internet access. ⓦwww.kropla.com is a useful website giving details of how to plug your laptop in when abroad, phone country codes around the world, and information about electrical systems in different countries.

The media

The English are fond of their daily newspapers and there are a lot to choose from, though the majority are drearily right-wing. An army of local titles – at least one in every major city – supplements the nationals, and newsagents' shelves are stacked high with magazines of every description. As regards TV, there are five universal channels. Three are commercial and two are state subsidized, operated by the British Broadcasting Company (BBC). Broadcasting standards are not as high as they used to be – though they still compare favourably with most of the rest of the world – at least in part because of the rise of satellite and cable channels. The BBC also runs an extensive network of radio stations, with the excellent Radio 4 serving as its political and contemporary affairs flagship.

Newspapers and magazines

From Monday to Saturday, four daily newspapers occupy the quality end of the market: the Rupert Murdoch-owned *Times*, the staunchly Conservative *Daily Telegraph*, the middle-of-the-road *Independent* and the left-of-centre *Guardian*. The *Guardian* probably offers the best international coverage, but the *Telegraph* tends to be the best written. Amongst the tabloids, the most popular is the *Sun*, a nasty right-wing Murdoch paper whose chief rival is the *Daily Mirror*, which can on occasion position itself well to the left of centre. The middle-brow daily tabloids – the *Daily Mail* and the *Daily Express* – are also noticeably right-wing. England's oldest Sunday newspaper, *The Observer*, is seen as a standard bearer for the soft left, but the quality of its articles is very variable. The *Observer* supplements the Sunday editions of the dailies, whose ranks are swelled by the amazingly popular *News of the World*, a Peeping Tom rag commonly known as "The News of the Screws".

When it comes to specialist periodicals, English newsagents offer a range covering just about every subject, with motoring, music, sport, computers, gardening and home improvements leading the way. One noticeably poor area is current events, though the *Economist*, which is essential reading in many a boardroom, does something to fill the gap; the socialist alternative is the weekly *New Statesman*. The satirical bi-weekly *Private Eye* is a much-loved institution that prides itself on printing the stories the rest of the press won't touch, and on riding the consequent stream of libel suits.

Australians and New Zealanders in London may be gratified by the weekly free magazine, *TNT*, which provides a resume of news from home as well as jobs, accommodation and events in the capital. *USA Today* and the *International Herald Tribune* are widely distributed, as are the magazines *Time* and *Newsweek*.

Television

In the UK, there are five universal television stations. These are divided between the state-owned BBC, with BBC1 and BBC2, and three independent commercial channels, ITV, Channel 4 and Channel 5. High broadcasting standards were once the hallmark of the BBC, but the quality of programming has slipped in recent years, the result being a rash of sloppy documentaries and numbskull quiz shows; however there's still (just) enough quality to keep the BBC in good repute both at home and abroad. Of the two BBC channels, BBC 2 is the more offbeat and heavyweight, BBC 1 more avowedly populist. Various regional companies together form the ITV network, but they're united by a more tabloid approach to programme making – necessarily so, because if they don't get the advertising they don't survive. Channel 4, once the most progressive of the bunch, now relies on US comedies and spurious documentaries – a recipe followed diligently by the newer Channel 5, though sustained mockery has recently obliged the latter to offer a better range of programmes.

These five channels are under pressure from the satellite and cable TV companies, whose dozens of channels offer all sorts of delights from porn to interactive shopping. However, neither the BBC nor the other commercial channels are taking things lying down, mounting their own ventures amongst which Film Four – from Channel 4 – has been especially well received. The proposed switch-over from the analogue to the digital broadcasting system promises a long battle for market share and, one assumes, a sustained attempt by the private sector to end the BBC's funding by an annual licence fee paid by all viewers.

Radio

The vanguard of the BBC's radio network is its five nationwide stations. These are Radio 1, which is almost exclusively devoted to pop music, with a chart-biased view of the rock world; Radio 2, a combination of easy listening and sassier jazz, rock and arts programmes; Radio 3, which focuses on classical music; Radio 4, a high-quality blend of current affairs, arts and drama; and Radio 5, a sports and news channel. For BBC radio frequencies, which vary up and down the country, visit ⓦwww.bbc.co.uk/radio. All have faced tough challenges for market share in recent years, the hardest hit being Radio 1, whose rivals include a plethora of local commercial stations, most notably London's Capital Radio (95.8 FM), though Radio 3 has had to struggle hard against classy Classic FM (visit ⓦwww.classicfm.com for frequencies). The BBC also operates a gaggle of local radio stations, mostly featuring local news, chat and mainstream pop; there are more details on the BBC website given above.

Radio Canada and Voice of America

The websites of Radio Canada (ⓦwww.rcinet.ca) and Voice of America (ⓦwww.voa.gov) list all the world service frequencies they broadcast on.

Opening hours, public holidays and festivals

Although most businesses, banks and offices remain firmly anchored to traditional opening hours (Mon–Fri 9am–5pm), supermarkets, petrol stations and department and convenience stores are often open until late in the evening from Monday through Saturday, with limited Sunday opening too. Some major tourist attractions also offer extended opening hours, but most don't, though few close on public holidays except Christmas. Full details of opening hours for every tourist attraction we've described are given in the guide.

Many of the biggest occasions in the English calendar have indelible associations with the ruling class – from the military pageant of the Trooping of the Colour to Ascot horse racing and the Henley Regatta – but these are well wide of the mark if you're after sampling contemporary England. Every major city has at least one prime event, some dating back centuries, others more recent concoctions, but everywhere there's a general willingness to revive the traditional and experiment with the new – from medieval jousting through to the performing arts.

Opening hours

General business hours are Monday to Saturday from 9am to 5.30 or 6pm, although you'll find late-night shopping (until 8 or 9pm) commonplace in the larger towns, with Wednesday and Thursday the favoured evenings. The big supermarkets also tend to stay open until 8 or 9pm from Monday to Saturday, some staying open round the clock. In addition, many major stores and supermarkets are open on Sundays, usually from 11am or noon to 4pm. By contrast, many provincial towns still retain an early-closing day, when shops close at 1pm; Wednesday is the favourite. Note also that not all service stations on motorways are open for 24 hours, although you can usually get fuel any time of the day or night in larger towns and cities.

Public holidays

Banks, businesses and most shops close down on public holidays, though large supermarkets and many tourist attractions do not. Confusingly, several of England's public holidays are usually referred to as bank holidays. Public/bank holidays are as follows:

January 1
Good Friday (late March or early April)
Easter Monday (late March or early April)
First Monday in May
Last Monday in May
Last Monday in August
December 25
December 26

Note that if January 1, December 25 or December 26 falls on a Saturday or Sunday, the next weekday becomes a public holiday.

Festivals and events

England has been accumulating festivals and special events from the time of the pre-Roman Druids to the 1970s hippies. For a taste of the country at its most idiosyncratic, steer towards one of the numerous local celebrations that perpetuate ancient customs, the origins and meanings of which have often been lost or conveniently misplaced. The sight of the entire population of a village scrambling around a field after a barrel, or chasing a cheese downhill, is not easily forgotten. From musical events to carnivals, England's festivals often illustrate the depth of the country's diversity, while others celebrate a particular skill or interest. The list below tries to touch all the bases, but it is very much an introduction rather than a comprehensive list. Also included below are the main sports finals, though as tickets are invariably hard to find, you may decide to settle for an ordinary league game instead. Football is the national pastime, with a wide programme of league matches taking place every Saturday afternoon from late August to mid-May, with some Sunday and mid-week fixtures too. Cricket is small beer by comparison, but an extensive summer programme, running from June to early September, includes four-day county matches, one-day limited-over matches and, best of the lot, five-day international Test matches.

Events calendar

Mid-Feb **Chinese New Year.** Festivities in the country's two main Chinatowns, in London and Manchester.

Mid-March **Cheltenham Gold Cup meeting.** The country's premier national hunt horse-racing event.

End of March or early April **University Boat Race.** Rowing contest on the Thames, between teams from Oxford and Cambridge universities. Once a big deal, it barely features on the news today.

Shrove Tuesday Traditional day for eating pancakes.

Maundy Thursday The Queen dispenses the Royal Maundy Money after attending church.

Good Friday **British and World Marbles Championship, Tinsley Green, near Crawley, Sussex.**

Easter Monday **Hare Pie Scramble and Bottle-Kicking, Hallaton, Leicestershire.** Barmy and chaotic village bottle-kicking contest.

Saturday in late March or early April **Grand National horse-racing meeting, Aintree, Liverpool.** Immensely – some would say cruelly – testing steeplechase that pulls most of Britain's population into the betting shops.

May 1 **Padstow Hobby Horse, Padstow, Cornwall.** Processions, music and dancing through the streets.

Early May **FA Cup Final.** A knock-out competition between all clubs in the English league and the cream of the country's semi-professional teams, the FA Cup is the biggest domestic football competition, though it has lost some of its allure with the increasing popularity of European cup football. With the closure of the national stadium at Wembley in London, it has also lost its home and, until the new London stadium is finished, the Final will be played at the Millennium Stadium in Cardiff in Wales.

Spring Bank Holiday Monday **Cheese Rolling, Brockworth, Gloucestershire.** Pursuit of a cheese wheel down a murderous incline – one of the weirdest knees-ups in England.

May–July **Glyndebourne Opera Festival, East Sussex.** One of the classiest arts festivals in the country.

Late May and early June **Bath International Festival.** International arts jamboree.

Last week of May **Chelsea Flower Show, Royal Hospital, Chelsea, London.** Essential event for England's green-fingered legions.

June **Aldeburgh Festival.** Jamboree of classical music, established by Benjamin Britten and held on the Suffolk coast.

First week in June **Derby week, Epsom racecourse, Surrey.** The world's most expensive horseflesh competing in the Derby, the Coronation Cup and the Oaks.

First or second Saturday in June **Trooping the Colour, Horse Guards Parade, London.** Equestrian pageantry for the Queen's Official Birthday.

Mid-June **Appleby Horse Fair, Appleby-in-Westmorland, Cumbria.**

Mid-June **Royal Ascot, Berkshire.** High-class horse-racing attended by the wealthy and well-connected; the best seats go to royalty and their disciples, while the proles mill around in the outfield.

End of June **World Worm-Charming Championships, Willaston, Cheshire.**

Last week of June **Glastonbury Festival, Somerset.** Hugely popular festival, with international bands, all genres of music and loads of hippies.

Last week of June and first week of July **Lawn Tennis Championships, Wimbledon, London.** Queues are phenomenal even for the early rounds, and you need to know an ex-champion to get in to the big games.

First week in July **Henley Royal Regatta, Oxfordshire.** Rowing event attended by much the same crew as populates the grandstands at Ascot.

Second week in July **York Early Music Festival.** The country's premier early music festival, lasting ten days.

Mid-July **British Open Golf Championship, variable venue.** The season's last Grand Slam golf tournament.

Third week in July **Swan Upping, River Thames from Sunbury to Pangbourne.** Ceremonial registering of the Thames cygnets.

Last week of July **Royal Tournament, Earl's Court Exhibition Centre, London.** Precision military displays.

Last week of July **Cambridge Folk Festival.** Biggest event of its kind in England.

Late July **WOMAD, Reading.** Three-day world music festival.

July to early September **The Promenade Concerts ("The Proms"), Royal Albert Hall, London.** Classical music concerts ending in the fervently patriotic Last Night of the Proms.

Early August **Sidmouth Folk Festival.** Folk and roots performers from around the world, plus theatre and dance.

August Bank Holiday Notting Hill Carnival, around Notting Hill, West London. Vivacious celebration led by London's Caribbean community but including everything from Punjabi drummers to Brazilian salsa – plenty of music, food and floats plus hundreds of thousands of spectators.
August Bank Holiday Reading Festival, Berkshire. Three-day hard rock jamboree.
Early September to early November Blackpool Illuminations, Lancashire. Five miles of extravagantly kitsch light displays.
First Monday after Sept 4 Abbots Bromley Horn Dance, Abbots Bromley, Staffordshire. Vaguely pagan mass dance in mock-medieval costume – one of the most famous of England's ancient customs.
First Sunday in November London to Brighton Veteran Car Rally. Ancient machines lumbering the 57 miles down the A23 to the seafront.
November 5 Guy Fawkes Night. Nationwide fireworks and bonfires commemorating the foiling of the Gunpowder Plot in 1605 – especially raucous celebrations at York (Fawkes' birthplace), Ottery St Mary in Devon and at Lewes, East Sussex.
Mid-November Lord Mayor's Procession and Show, the City of London. Cavalcade to mark the inauguration of the new mayor.
Dec 31 Tar Barrels Parade, Allendale Town, Northumberland. Unusual ceremony in which locals turn up with trays of burning pitch on their heads to parade round a large communal bonfire.

Outdoor pursuits

No matter where you are in England, you're never far from a stretch of countryside where you can cycle or walk. More energetically, the country is latticed with long-distance footpaths, and there are also lots of opportunities for anything from rock climbing and potholing (caving) through to running and swimming. On the coast, and at many of the country's inland lakes, you can follow the more urbane pursuits of sailing and windsurfing, and there are plenty of fine beaches to hone a tan – weather permitting.

Walking

England's finest walking areas are the granite moorlands and spectacular coastlines of Devon and Cornwall in the southwest, and the highlands of the north – the low limestone and millstone crags of the Peak District, between Sheffield and Manchester; the Yorkshire Dales, the stretch of the Pennines to the north of the Peak District; the North York Moors, a bleak, treeless upland to the east of the Pennines; and the glaciated Cumbrian Mountains, better known as the Lake District. On summer weekends the more accessible reaches of these regions can get very crowded with day-trippers, but at any time of the year you'll find yourself in relative isolation if you head out on one of the Long Distance Footpaths (LDPs). Defined as any route over twenty miles long, LDPs exist all over the country and are marked at frequent intervals with an acorn waymarker. Youth hostels are littered along most of these routes, though you may need a tent for some of the more heroic hikes – stretches of the Pennine Way, Britain's longest, at over 250 miles, for example. It goes without saying that for any kind of serious walking, and even for day hikes on high ground, you need to be properly equipped and prepared, follow local advice and listen out for the local weather reports. England's climate may be relatively benign, but the weather is changeable in any given season and people do die on the moors and mountains every year. There's also a useful government website, ⓦwww.nationaltrail.co.uk, which details all of England's long-distance footpaths as well as further contacts.

Walking-holiday specialists

Explore Britain ⓣ01740/650900, ⓦwww.xplorebritain.com. Guided or independent walking holidays countrywide with luggage transfer.
Footpath Holidays ⓣ01985/840049, ⓦwww.footpath-holidays.com. Packages to various hill and coastal districts in England with experienced group leaders.
HF Walking Holidays ⓣ020/8905 9556, ⓦwww.hfholidays.co.uk. A wide choice of locations and lodging in comfortable country houses.
Instep Walking Holidays ⓣ01903/766475, ⓦwww.instephols.co.uk. Self-guided holidays mainly in the south of England, with accommodation in small country hotels and guest houses.
Sherpa Expeditions ⓣ020/8577 2717, ⓦwww.sherpa-walking-holidays.co.uk. At-your-own-pace, self-guided walks between country pubs all over England.

Cycling

Although there has been a boom in the sale of mountain bikes and a rise in the number of towns and cities that have incorporated designated cycle routes into their traffic schemes, cyclists are still often given scant regard by the country's motorists. To prove the point, British cyclists are reckoned to be twelve times more likely to be killed or injured on the road (per miles cycled) than their counterparts in Denmark. Nevertheless, Sustrans (see p.48), a charitable trust devoted to the development of environmentally sustainable transport, is making gallant efforts to improve the situation.

Surprisingly, cycle helmets are not compulsory in Britain – but if you're hell-bent on tackling the congestion, pollution and aggression of city traffic, you're well advised to get one. You do have to have a rear reflector and front and back lights when riding at night, and are not allowed to carry children without a special child seat. It is also illegal to cycle on pavements (sidewalks), and in most public parks. A secure lock (preferably some kind of "D" lock) is also indispensable, and it's always a good idea to make a note of your frame number in case you have to report a theft to the police.

Bike rental is available at cycle shops in most large towns, and at villages within national parks and other scenic areas; the addresses and telephone numbers of these appear in the relevant sections of the guide. Expect to pay in the region of £10–20 per day for something sturdy, with discounts for longer periods.

Carrying your bike on public transport

The majority of airlines will carry bicycles as part of your luggage allowance on plane journeys, although protruding parts, such as pedals and handlebars, have to be removed, and the tyres deflated; some carriers also require you to stash the machine in a bike bag or cardboard cover. Check with your airline well in advance to find out exactly what their terms and conditions are, and bear in mind that you may have to pay excess baggage. Transporting cycles by ferry is also free, but a lot more straightforward; you just wheel them on and off, and reservations are not normally required.

Carrying your bike by train is a good way of getting to the interesting parts of England without a lot of boring pedalling, but the rail companies don't seem to want to play ball. Many express trains simply don't allow them, others insist on advance reservations and yet others levy a small surcharge. Contact the train company (or companies) concerned for specific advice; their details can be obtained from the National Rail Enquiries line (ⓣ08457/484950; ⓦwww.rail.co.uk).

Cycle routes

There are currently around six thousand miles of official cycle track in England, though plans to double this by 2010 are well in hand. A large chunk of the network is made up of quiet backroads, dubbed "Cycleways", but a goodly proportion runs along disused railways and canal towpaths, including a showpiece section connecting the cities of Bath and Bristol. If you do decide to cycle on the roads, try to avoid the busy "A" roads, where you stand a good chance of being mown down. Instead, stick to the quieter "B" roads, which generally have amiable gradients and a sufficient density of pubs and B&Bs to keep the days manageable. Cycles are not permitted on motorways ("M" roads) at all. Most good bookshops stock a range of cycling guides, featuring suggestions for rides of varying length, with coloured maps and detailed route descriptions. Also useful are the maps of the official cycle network produced by Sustrans (see below). In addition, the Cycle Touring Club, or CTC (see below), publishes maps of several of the challenging long-distance cycling routes that traverse the country. They also supply members with touring and technical advice as well as insurance. The classic cross-Britain route is Land's End, in the far southwest of England, to John O'Groats, on the northeast tip of Scotland – roughly a thousand miles that can be covered in two to three weeks, depending on which of the three CTC-recommended routes you choose. Another favourite coast-to-coast option is the journey from Lowestoft in East Anglia to the Ardnamurchan peninsula in northwest Scotland. The CTC suggests a ten-day itinerary, but you could easily spend twice that long scaling the English watershed. The same applies to the wonderful 130-mile Wye Valley route, which winds from the Severn Estuary through the forests and moorlands of the Welsh borders to the rough mountains of mid-Wales. Other tempting long-distance tours could take you around the Yorkshire Dales, Pennines, and Peak District, around Dartmoor and the Cornish coast, or across the austere North Yorkshire Moors.

Finally, off-road cycling is popular in the highland walking areas, but cyclists should remember to keep to rights of way designated on maps as Bridleways, BOATs ("Byways Open To All Traffic") or RUPFs ("Roads Used As Public Footpaths"), and to pass walkers at considerate speeds. Footpaths, unless otherwise marked, are for pedestrians only.

Useful cycling contacts

The Cycle Touring Club (CTC) ⓣ0870/873 0064, ⓦwww.ctc.org.uk.
Sustrans ⓣ0845/113 0065, ⓦwww.sustrans.org.uk.

Cycling holidays

For those who want a guaranteed hassle-free cycling holiday, there are various companies offering easy-going packages. These can take all sorts of forms, but generally include transport of your gear to each night's halt, pre-booked accommodation, detailed route instructions, a packed lunch and back-up support. Most companies offer budget cycling holidays, with hostels or B&Bs, as well as hotel packages.

Cycling holiday specialists

Acorn Activities ⓣ0870/740 5055, ⓦwww.acornactivities.co.uk. Weekend and one-week tours, with bikes, accommodation, luggage transportation and maps provided.
Compass Holidays ⓦwww.compass-holidays.com. Guided tours in the Cotswolds, Gloucestershire, the Lake District, Cornwall and Warwickshire.
Country Lanes ⓣ01590/622627, ⓦwww.countrylanes.co.uk. Tours in the New Forest, the Cotswolds and the Lake District.
Holiday Lakeland ⓣ016973/71871, ⓦwww.holiday-lakeland.co.uk. Guided and independent tours of two to five nights in the north of the country, focused on the Pennines and the Lake District.
Rough Tracks ⓣ0700/0560 749, ⓦwww.rough-tracks.co.uk. Mountain bike and road weekend tours across the country, as well as bike maintenance weekends.
Saddle Skedaddle ⓣ0191/265 1110, ⓦwww.skedaddle.co.uk. Highly recommended cycle specialist offering a wide range of cycling holidays from weekend trips to the Peak District to week-long coast-to-coast expeditions.

Beaches

England is ringed by fine beaches and bays, with many of the best being readily accessible by public transport – which means they tend to get crowded in high summer. For a combination of decent climate and good sand, the southwest is hard to beat, especially the northern coast of Cornwall and Devon. By comparison, the beaches of England's southern coast are not quite as appealing, and they become more pebbly as you approach the southeastern corner of the country. The East Anglian shoreline begins with the low cliffs and pebble beaches of the east coast, but then offers a string of wide sandy beaches on its northern shore from Cromer to Hunstanton. There are more wide strands in the northeast, though here the

North Sea breezes often require a degree of stoicism. Over in the northwest, the inland hills of Cumbria are a greater attraction than anything on the coast, but nevertheless Blackpool does have a certain appeal as the apotheosis of the "kiss-me-quick" holiday town, complete with a whopping, pancake-flat beach.

As regards cleanliness, English beaches have too often been below EU standards, though to be fair determined efforts have been made to improve the situation. For annually updated, detailed information on the condition of Britain's beaches, the definitive source is the annual *Good Beach Guide*, compiled by the Marine Conservation Society (Ⓣ01989/566017). Beach reviews are also given on their website, Ⓦwww.goodbeachguide.co.uk.

Surfing

For most people, surfing in England means surfing in Newquay, the country's undisputed surf centre, tucked away in the southwest in Cornwall. Visiting surfers are often amazed to see the hype surrounding this self-styled "surf city", where every other summer visitor seems to be a surfer sporting the regulation gear. The main break is Fistral, which regularly hosts international contests, but there are quieter spots both outside of town, primarily Perranporth and Polzeath, and beyond right along the north coast of Cornwall and Devon. The southwest has relatively mild waters (up to 18°C in summer), but even so you'll still need a wetsuit year round, with a thicker suit from October to May, plus boots and gloves, and maybe a hood (winter water temperatures get down to 9–10°C). There are plenty of places where you can rent or buy equipment, which means that prices are kept down to reasonable levels.

Alternatively, you might head for the northeast coast, from Yorkshire to Northumberland. This area has a growing population of hardy surfers willing to endure temperatures as low as 5°C in winter (and no higher than 14–15°C in summer), the reward being clean ground swells breaking over quality reef and beach breaks. The coastline here is often spectacular, especially in Northumberland, and although the more popular breaks, such as Cayton Bay and Saltburn, are now crowded, you can find greater isolation with ease.

Top ten English breaks

An asterisk (*) Indicates that the breaks are for experienced surfers only.

Fistral Newquay. Hype, crowds, but still a good wave if you can get one to yourself.

Staithes* Yorkshire. Excellent reef breaks, crowded and jealously guarded by locals.

Croyde Bay Devon. Good beach breaks, but again, crowds can be a problem.

Sennen Cove Cornwall. Picks up any swell going.

Woolacombe Devon. Two miles of fun beach breaks.

Kimmeridge* Dorset. A popular reef break that doesn't work that often, but is great when it does.

Saltburn Cleveland. Another good beach break, with atmosphere to match.

Bamburgh Northumberland. A wonderfully scenic quiet beach, with seals in the water and a spectacular castle as a backdrop.

Porthleven* Cornwall. A heavy reef break, and heavy locals.

Constantine Cornwall. Another southwest hot spot that picks up a lot of swell.

Crime and personal safety

Unless you're asking for directions, it's unlikely that you'll ever come into contact with the English police force. England is far from crime free, but statistically the vast majority of tourists never experience any problems, at least in part because they are unlikely to visit the inner-city estates where criminality flourishes. As far as personal safety goes, it's generally possible to walk around the larger cities without fear of harassment or assault. However, all the big conurbations have their edgy districts and it's always better to err on the side of caution late at night, when – for instance – badly lit streets and drunken males (a common sight) should be avoided.

The police

In recent years, the traditional image of the friendly and fair British "Bobby" has taken a battering from repeated – and often substantiated – allegations of racism and crooked dealings. Nonetheless, the police remain very approachable and characteristically helpful, though they can get (understandably) tetchy at football matches and at pub closing time. They wear blue uniforms of various types depending on duties, but officers on the streets always wear a distinctive domed hat with a silver tip. Most wear chest guards and they do not normally carry guns.

Emergencies

For Police, Fire Brigade, Ambulance and, in certain areas, Mountain Rescue or Coastguard, dial ⊕**999**.

Petty crime

Almost all the problems tourists encounter in England are to do with petty crime – pick-pocketing and bag-snatching – rather than more serious physical confrontations. If you are robbed, you need to go to the police to report it, not least because your insurance company will require a crime report number – don't leave the station without getting one. The ⊕999 number in the box opposite should only be used in emergencies.

Travellers with disabilities

In the last decade, the UK has made steady progress in improving its facilities for travellers with disabilities. There's still a long way to go, but all new public buildings – including museums and cinemas – are now obliged to provide wheelchair access, dropped kerbs are the rule in every city and town, and many buses have easy-access dropped boarding ramps. The railways have lagged behind, but are at least making moves in the right direction, and the number of accessible hotels and restaurants is increasing year on year. Reserved parking bays for blue-badge holders (ie people with disabilities) are available almost everywhere, from shopping malls to museums.

England has a number of specialist tour operators catering for travellers with disabilities, and the percentage of non-specialist operators who welcome clients with disabilities is on the up. Several useful organizations are listed below, but note in particular that RADAR produces an excellent and compendious annual *Holidays in Britain and Ireland* book for just £8.

Concessionary rates for travellers with disabilities are patchy, but one of the better deals is the Disabled Persons Railcard (ⓦwww.disabledpersons-railcard.co.uk), which knocks one third off the price of most railway tickets. The card costs £14 and is valid for one year. Applications must be made in writing to the Disabled Persons Railcard Office, PO Box 163, Newcastle upon Tyne NE12 8WX. As for the major car rental firms, Hertz is the leader in offering models with hand controls.

Contacts for travellers with disabilities

In the US and Canada

Access-Able ⓦwww.access-able.com. Online resource for travellers with disabilities.
Directions Unlimited 123 Green Lane, Bedford Hills, NY 10507 ⓣ1-800/533-5343 or 914/241-1700. Travel agency specializing in bookings for people with disabilities.
Mobility International USA 451 Broadway, Eugene, OR 97401 ⓣ541/343-1284, ⓦwww.miusa.org. Information and referral services, access guides, tours and exchange programmes. Annual membership $35 (includes quarterly newsletter).
Society for the Advancement of Travelers with Handicaps (SATH) 347 5th Ave, New York, NY 10016 ⓣ212/447-7284, ⓦwww.sath.org. Non-profit educational organization that has actively represented travellers with disabilities since 1976.
Wheels Up! ⓣ1-888/38-WHEELS, ⓦwww.wheelsup.com. Provides discounted airfare, tour and cruise prices for disabled travellers; also publishes a free monthly newsletter and has a comprehensive website.

In the UK and Ireland

All Go Here ⓣ01923/840463, ⓦwww.everybody.co.uk. Information on accommodation suitable for disabled travellers throughout the UK.
Holiday Care 2nd floor, Imperial Building, Victoria Rd, Horley, Surrey RH6 7PZ ⓣ0845/124 9971, minicom ⓣ0845/124 9976, ⓦwww.holidaycare.org.uk. Free lists of accessible accommodation and attractions in the UK. Information on financial help for holidays also available.
Irish Wheelchair Association Blackheath Drive, Clontarf, Dublin 3 ⓣ01/818 6400, ⓦwww.iwa.ie. Useful information provided about travelling abroad with a wheelchair.
RADAR (Royal Association for Disability and Rehabilitation) 12 City Forum, 250 City Rd, London EC1V 8AF ⓣ020/7250 3222, minicom ⓣ020/7250 4119, ⓦwww.radar.org.uk. A good source of advice on holidays and travel in the UK. They produce an annual holiday guide called *Holidays in Britain and Ireland* for £8 and have a dedicated accommodation website for Britain and Ireland, ⓦwww.radarsearch.org.
Tripscope Alexandra House, Albany Rd, Brentford, Middlesex TW8 0NE ⓣ0845/758 5641, ⓦwww.tripscope.org.uk. This registered charity provides a national telephone information service offering free advice on UK transport for those with a mobility problem.

In Australia and New Zealand

ACROD (Australian Council for Rehabilitation of the Disabled) PO Box 60, Curtin ACT 2605; Suite 103, 1st floor, 1–5 Commercial Rd, Kings Grove 2208; ⓣ02/6282 4333, TTY ⓣ02/6282 4333, ⓦwww.acrod.org.au. Provides lists of travel agencies and tour operators for people with disabilities.
Disabled Persons Assembly 4/173–175 Victoria St, Wellington, New Zealand ⓣ04/801 9100 (also TTY), ⓦwww.dpa.org.nz. Resource centre with lists of travel agencies and tour operators for people with disabilities.

Gay and lesbian England

England offers one of the most diverse and accessible lesbian and gay scenes to be found anywhere in Europe. Nearly every town of any size has some kind of organized gay life – pubs, clubs, community groups, campaigning organizations, shops and phone lines – with the major scenes being found in London, Manchester and Brighton. Many gay and lesbian venues are listed in this book, and you'll find a free local listings sheet in virtually every one of them.

Homosexual acts between consenting males were legalized in Britain in 1967, but the age of consent was only reduced from 21 to 18 – still two years older than that for heterosexuals – in 1994. Lesbianism has never specifically been outlawed, apocryphally because Queen Victoria refused to believe that such a thing existed. Attitudes are harder to gauge, but by and large the rest of society leaves the gay/lesbian scene to its own devices, a pragmatic tolerance – or intolerance soaked in indifference – that is occasionally rattled by the sensationalist trash published in the tabloid press.

Of the nationwide publications, the weekly *Pink Paper* provids an outstanding summary of ongoing campaigns along with limited listings. The best bet for a comprehensive national directory of pubs, clubs, groups, gay accommodation and local lesbian and gay switchboards is the glossy monthly *Gay Times*, available from many newsagents and alternative bookstores.

Contacts for gay and lesbian travellers

In the US and Canada

Damron ⓣ1-800/462-6654 or 415/255-0404, ⓦwww.damron.com. Publisher of the *Men's Travel Guide*, a pocket-sized yearbook full of listings of hotels, bars, clubs and resources for gay men; the *Women's Traveler*, which provides similar listings for lesbians; and *Damron Accommodations*, which provides detailed listings of over 1000 accommodations for gays and lesbians worldwide. All of these titles are offered at a discount on the website. No specific city guides – everything is incorporated in the yearbooks.

gaytravel.com ⓣ1-800/GAY-TRAVEL, ⓦwww.gaytravel.com. The premier site for trip planning, bookings, and general information about international gay and lesbian travel.

International Gay & Lesbian Travel Association ⓣ1-800/448-8550 or 954/776-2626, ⓦwww.iglta.org. Trade group that can provide a list of gay- and lesbian-owned or -friendly travel agents, accommodation and other travel businesses.

In the UK

Gay Britain Network ⓦwww.gaybritain.co.uk. Online information on events, restaurants and travel, with good links.

Gay Guide ⓦwww.gayguide.co.uk. Gay venues listed by location.

Gay Travel ⓦwww.gaytravel.co.uk. Online gay and lesbian travel agent, offering good deals on all types of holiday. Also lists gay- and lesbian-friendly hotels around the world.

Madison Travel ⓣ01273/202532, ⓦwww.madisontravel.co.uk. Established travel agents specializing in packages to gay- and lesbian-friendly mainstream destinations, and also to gay/lesbian destinations.

In Australia and New Zealand

Gay and Lesbian Tourism Australia ⓦwww.galta.com.au. Directory and links for gay and lesbian travel in Australia and worldwide.

New Zealand Gay and Lesbian Tourism Association ⓦwww.nzglta.org.nz. Organization devoted to enhancing the New Zealand travel experience for gay, lesbian and bisexual visitors.

Parkside Travel ⓣ08/8274 1222, ⓔparkside@herveyworld.com.au. Gay travel agent associated with local branch of Hervey World Travel; all aspects of gay and lesbian travel worldwide.

Silke's Travel ⓣ1800/807 860 or 02/8347 2000, ⓦwww.silkes.com.au. Long-established gay and lesbian specialist, with an emphasis on women's travel.

Tearaway Travel ⓣ1800/664 440 or 03/9510 6644, ⓦwww.tearaway.com. Gay-specific business dealing with international and domestic travel.

Directory

CHILDREN At almost every attraction in the land and on public transport, children are entitled to concessionary rates, and infants/babies go free. The only real hassle is that most licensed (ie alcohol-serving) premises will not allow children to enter, the main exception being restaurants.

CIGARETTES Smoking is banned from just about all public buildings and on public transport. Many restaurants have non-smoking sections, some forbid it altogether. Most hotels limit smoking in their public areas and have non-smoking rooms, but once again some operate a total ban. Pubs almost always allow smoking everywhere.

DRUGS Illegal drugs of one sort or another are consumed by thousands of Brits, especially on the weekend. If you are caught in possession of a small quantity of a "hard" drug – e.g. heroin – you can anticipate being held in a police cell; larger quantities lead to prosecution and imprisonment or deportation. "Soft" drugs – most commonly hashish (marijuana resin) and cannabis – are dealt with more leniently and being caught in possession of a small quantity will probably – but not always – result in either a police caution or a fine. If, on the other hand, the police suspect you are dealing, you can expect to be held in custody and ultimately prosecuted.

ELECTRICITY In England the current is 240V AC. North American appliances will need a transformer and adaptor; those from Australia and New Zealand only need an adaptor.

LAUNDRY Coin-operated laundries (launderettes) are commonplace in every large city and town, but they are often in out-of-the-way locations. Most operate extended opening hours – usually about twelve hours a day – and prices are very reasonable. At a small premium, many offer "service washes", with your laundry processed for you in just a few hours.

PHOTOGRAPHY Films manufactured by all the major international brands are widely available. They usually cost less at supermarkets and large chemists/pharmacies than on the high street, as does developing film.

PUBLIC TOILETS Almost every town and city centre has at least a couple of public toilets, and by law every train and bus station has to have them. A fee of 10p or 20p for their use is commonplace.

SENIOR TRAVELLERS Seniors (over 60 or 65 years old) are entitled to concessionary rates At almost every attraction and on public transport.

TIME Greenwich Mean Time (GMT) is used from late October to late March, when the clocks go forward an hour for British Summer Time (BST). GMT is five hours ahead of the US Eastern Standard Time and ten hours behind Australian Eastern Standard Time.

VIDEOS British videotapes (in what's called the PAL format) will not play back on North American VCRs (which are NTSC format). However, North American video cameras are compatible with blank tapes purchased in Britain – the camera will format the tape while it records.

Guide

Guide

London

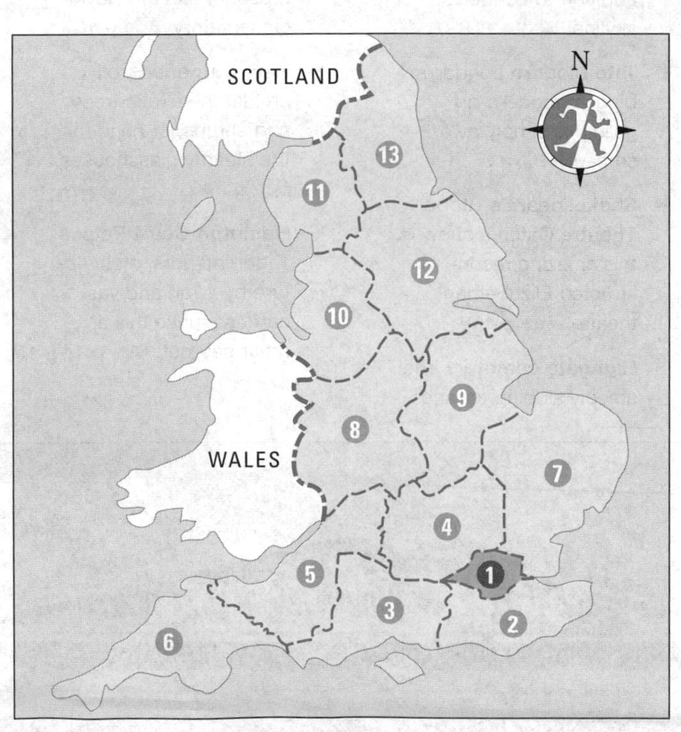

CHAPTER 1

Highlights

* **British Museum** For its 250th anniversary, the BM reinvented itself with a wonderful glass-covered courtyard. See p.91
* **London Eye** The universally loved observation wheel is a graceful addition to London's skyline. See p.115
* **Tate Modern** London's biggest modern-art gallery is simply awesome. See p.117
* **Shakespeare's Globe Theatre** Catch a show in this amazing reconstructed Elizabethan theatre. See p.118
* **Highgate cemetery** The steeply sloping terraces of the West Cemetery's overgrown graves are the last word in Victorian Gothic gloom. See p.132
* **Greenwich** Picturesque riverside spot, boasting a weekend market, the National Maritime Museum and old Royal Observatory. See p.133
* **Kew Gardens** Stroll amidst the exotic trees and shrubs, or head for the steamy glasshouses. See p.140
* **Hampton Court Palace** Tudor interiors, architecture by Wren and vast gardens make this a great day-out. See p.141

△ British Museum

1

London

What strikes visitors more than anything about **LONDON** is the sheer size of the place. With a population of just under eight million, it's Europe's largest city by far, stretching for more than thirty miles on either side of the **River Thames**. Ethnically, it's also Europe's most diverse metropolis, and for those without local roots the place can seem bafflingly diverse. Londoners tend to cope with all this by compartmentalizing the city, identifying with the neighbourhoods in which they work or live, and just making occasional forays into the "centre of town" or "up West" – to the West End, London's shopping and entertainment heartland.

Despite Scottish, Welsh and Northern Irish devolution, London still dominates the national horizon, too: this is where the country's news and money are made, it's where the central government resides and, as far as its inhabitants are concerned, provincial life begins beyond the circuit of the city's orbital motorway. Londoners' sense of superiority causes enormous resentment in the regions, yet it's undeniable that the capital has a unique aura of excitement and success – in most walks of British life, if you want to get on, you've got to do it in London.

For the visitor, too, London is a thrilling place and since the beginning of the new millennium, the city has also been in a relatively buoyant mood. Thanks to the national lottery and the millennium-oriented funding frenzy, virtually every one of London's **world-class museums**, galleries and institutions has been reinvented, from the Royal Opera House to the British Museum. With Tate Modern and the London Eye, the city can now boast the world's largest modern art gallery and observation wheel; as well as two new pedestrian bridges, the first to cross the central section of the Thames for over a hundred years. And after sixteen years of being the only major city in the world not to have its own governing body, London now has an elected assembly again, housed in an eye-catching building within sight of Tower Bridge, and a mayor who's determined to try and solve one of London's biggest problems – transport.

In the meantime, **traditional sights** – Big Ben, Westminster Abbey, Buckingham Palace, St Paul's Cathedral and the Tower of London – continue to draw in millions of tourists every year. Monuments from the capital's more glorious past are everywhere to be seen, from medieval banqueting halls and the great churches of Christopher Wren to the eclectic Victorian architecture of the triumphalist British Empire. There is also much enjoyment to be had from the city's quiet Georgian squares, the narrow alleyways of the City of London, the riverside walks, and the quirks of what is still identifiably a col-

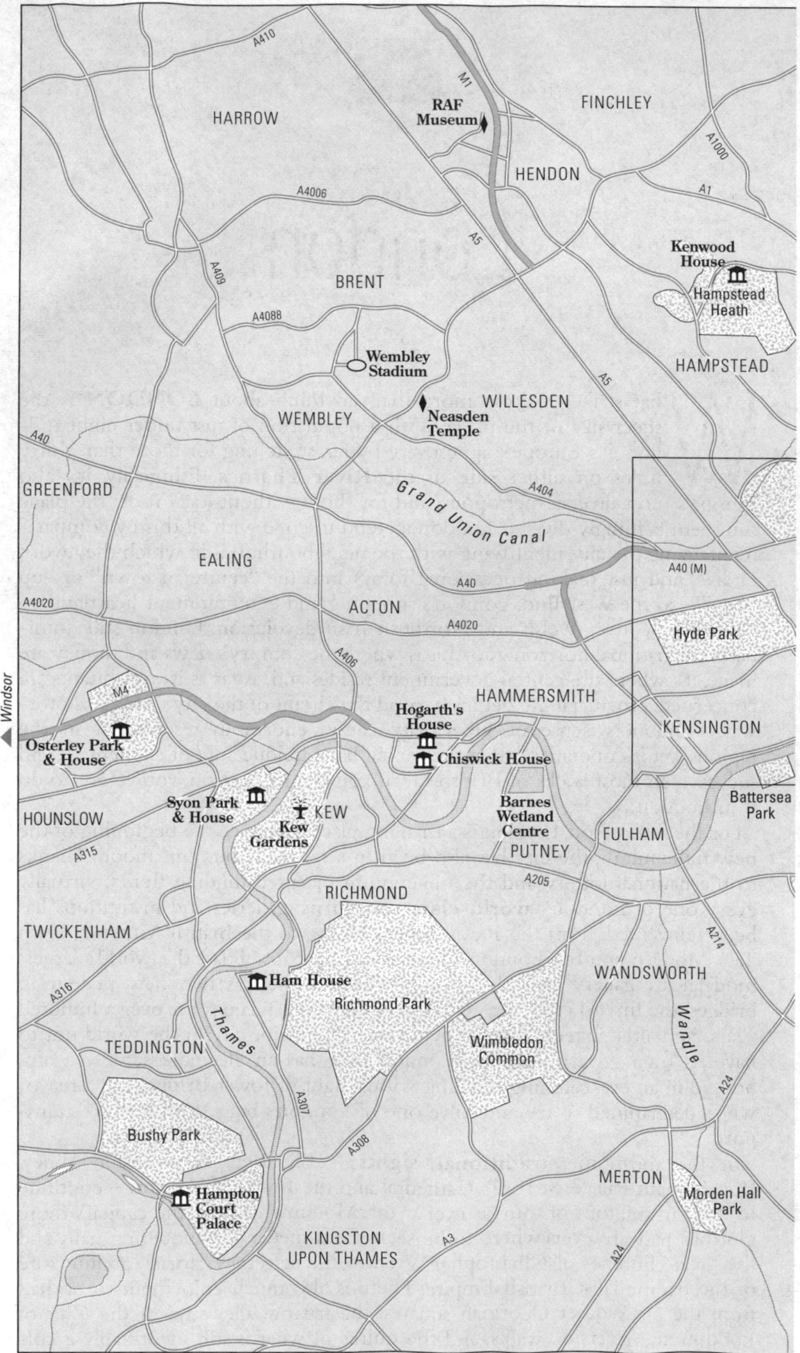

A410
M1
RAF Museum
FINCHLEY
HARROW
A1000
HENDON
A1
A4006
A5
Kenwood House
A409
BRENT
Hampstead Heath
A4088
Wembley Stadium
HAMPSTEAD
A5
WILLESDEN
WEMBLEY
Neasden Temple
A40
GREENFORD
Grand Union Canal
A404
EALING
A40 (M)
A40
A4020
ACTON
A4020
Hyde Park
A406
Windsor
M4
HAMMERSMITH
Hogarth's House
KENSINGTON
Osterley Park & House
Chiswick House
Syon Park & House
KEW
Kew Gardens
Barnes Wetland Centre
Battersea Park
HOUNSLOW
FULHAM
A315
PUTNEY
A205
RICHMOND
TWICKENHAM
A214
WANDSWORTH
Ham House
A316
Richmond Park
Wandle
Thames
TEDDINGTON
Wimbledon Common
A24
A307
Bushy Park
A308
MERTON
Morden Hall Park
Hampton Court Palace
KINGSTON UPON THAMES
A3
A24

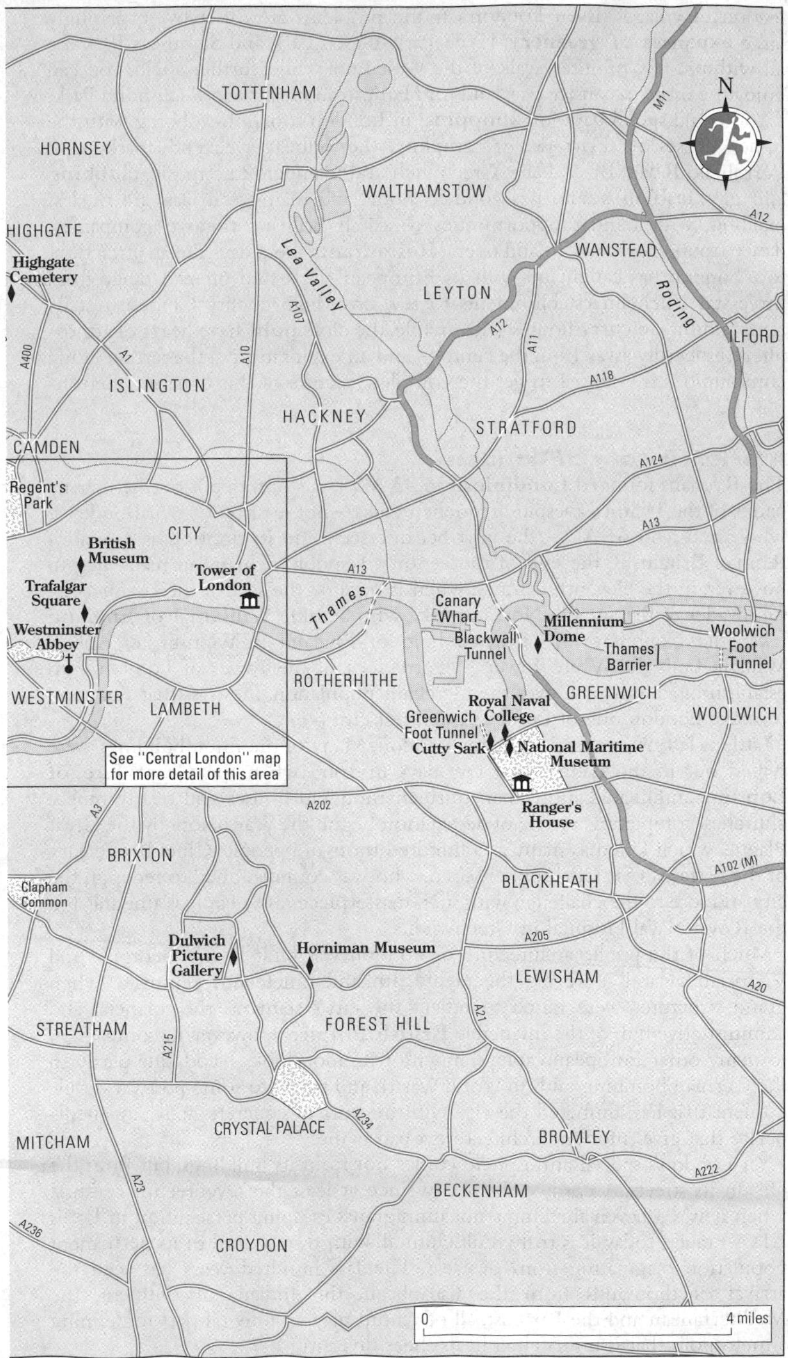
TOTTENHAM
HORNSEY
HIGHGATE
Highgate Cemetery
WALTHAMSTOW
WANSTEAD
LEYTON
Lea Valley
Roding
ILFORD
ISLINGTON
HACKNEY
STRATFORD
CAMDEN
Regent's Park
CITY
British Museum
Tower of London
Trafalgar Square
Westminster Abbey
Thames
Canary Wharf
Blackwall Tunnel
Millennium Dome
Thames Barrier
Woolwich Foot Tunnel
ROTHERHITHE
WESTMINSTER
LAMBETH
GREENWICH
Royal Naval College
Greenwich Foot Tunnel
Cutty Sark
National Maritime Museum
WOOLWICH
See "Central London" map for more detail of this area
Ranger's House
BRIXTON
Clapham Common
BLACKHEATH
Dulwich Picture Gallery
Horniman Museum
LEWISHAM
STREATHAM
FOREST HILL
CRYSTAL PALACE
MITCHAM
BROMLEY
BECKENHAM
CROYDON
M11
A12
A107
A10
A11
A1
A400
A118
A124
A13
A202
A3
A102 (M)
A205
A20
A21
A215
A234
A222
A23
A236
N
0
4 miles

lection of villages. Even London's traffic problems are offset by surprisingly large **expanses of greenery**: Hyde Park, Green Park and St James's Park are all within a few minutes' walk of the West End, while, further afield, you can enjoy the more expansive parklands of Hampstead Heath and Richmond Park.

You could spend days just **shopping** in London too, hob-nobbing with the upper classes in Harrods, or sampling the offbeat weekend markets of Portobello Road, Brick Lane, Greenwich and Camden. The music, **clubbing** and **gay/lesbian scene** is second to none, and mainstream arts are no less exciting, with regular opportunities to catch brilliant **theatre** companies, dance troupes, exhibitions and opera. **Restaurants** these days, are an attraction, too. London has caught up with its European rivals, and offers a range from three-star Michelin establishments to low-cost, high-quality Chinese restaurants and Indian curry houses. Meanwhile, the city's **pubs** have heaps of atmosphere, especially away from the centre – and an exploration of the farther-flung communities is essential to get the complete picture of this dynamic metropolis.

A brief history of London

The Romans founded **Londinium** in 43 AD as a stores depot on the marshy banks of the Thames. Despite frequent attacks – not least by Queen Boudicca, who razed it in 61 AD – the port became secure in its position as capital of Roman Britain by the end of the century. London's expansion really began, however, in the eleventh century, when it became the seat of the last successful invader of Britain, the Norman duke who became **William I of England** (aka "the Conqueror"). Crowned king of England in Westminster Abbey, William built the White Tower – centrepiece of the Tower of London – to establish his dominance over the merchant population, the class that was soon to make London one of Europe's mightiest cities.

Little is left of medieval or Tudor London. Many of the finest buildings were wiped out in the course of a few days in 1666 when the **Great Fire of London** annihilated more than thirteen thousand houses and nearly ninety churches, completing a cycle of destruction begun the year before by the Great Plague, which killed as many as a hundred thousand people. Chief beneficiary of the blaze was Sir Christopher Wren, who was commissioned to redesign the city and rose to the challenge with such masterpieces as St Paul's Cathedral and the Royal Naval Hospital in Greenwich.

Much of the public architecture of London was built in the Georgian and Victorian periods covering the eighteenth and nineteenth centuries, when grand structures were raised to reflect the city's status as the financial and administrative hub of the invincible **British Empire**. However, in comparison to many other European capitals, much of London looks bland, due partly to the German bombing raids in World War II, and partly to some postwar development that has lumbered the city with the sort of concrete-and-glass mediocrity that gives modern architecture a bad name.

Yet London's special atmosphere comes not from its buildings, but from the life on its streets. A cosmopolitan city since at least the seventeenth century, when it was a haven for Huguenot immigrants escaping persecution in Louis XIV's France, today it is truly multicultural, with over a third of its permanent population originating from overseas. The last hundred years has seen the arrival of thousands from the Caribbean, the Indian subcontinent, the Mediterranean and the Far East, all of whom play an integral part in defining a metropolis that is unmatched in its sheer diversity.

Orientation, arrival and information

Stretching for more than thirty miles at its broadest point, **London** is a big place. The majority of its sights are situated to the north of the **River Thames**, which loops through the city from west to east. However, there is no single predominant focus of interest, since London has grown not through centralized planning but by a process of agglomeration – villages and urban developments that once surrounded the core are now lost within the amorphous mass of Greater London.

One of the few areas which is manageable on foot is **Westminster** and **Whitehall**, the city's royal, political and ecclesiastical power base, where you'll find the **National Gallery** and a host of other London landmarks from **Buckingham Palace** to **Westminster Abbey**. The grand streets and squares of **St James's**, **Mayfair** and **Marylebone**, to the north of Westminster, have been the playground of the rich since the Restoration, and now contain the city's busiest shopping zones.

East of Piccadilly Circus, **Soho** and **Covent Garden** are also easy to walk around and form the heart of the West End entertainment district, containing the largest concentration of theatres, cinemas, clubs, flashy shops, cafés and restaurants. To the north lie the university quarter of **Bloomsbury**, home to the ever-popular British Museum, and the secluded quadrangles of **Holborn**'s Inns of Court, London's legal heartland.

The City – the City of London, to give it its full title – is both the most ancient and the most modern part of London. Settled since Roman times, it's now one of the world's great financial centres, yet retains its share of historic sights, notably the **Tower of London** and a fine cache of Wren churches that includes **St Paul's Cathedral**. Despite creeping trendification, the **East End**, to the east of the City, is not conventional tourist territory, but to ignore it entirely is to miss out a crucial element of contemporary London. **Docklands** is the converse of the down-at-heel East End, with the Canary Wharf tower, still the country's tallest building, epitomizing the pretensions of the Thatcherite dream.

A small slice of central London south of the Thames is definitely worth exploring. First off, there's the **South Bank Centre**, London's little-loved concrete culture bunker, which is enjoying a new lease of life thanks to inspired artistic direction and its proximity to the **London Eye**, the world's biggest observation wheel. Further east along the river in Bankside is **Tate Modern**, one of the world's greatest modern art museums, now linked to the City by the funky pedestrian-only Millennium Bridge.

The largest segment of greenery in central London is Hyde Park, which separates wealthy **Kensington and Chelsea** from the city centre. The **museums** of South Kensington – the Victoria and Albert Museum, the Science Museum and the Natural History Museum – are a must; and if you have shopping on your agenda, you'll want to check out the hive of plush stores in the vicinity of Harrods.

The capital's most hectic weekend market takes place around Camden Lock in **North London**. Further out, in the literary suburbs of Hampstead and Highgate, there are unbeatable views across the city from half-wild **Hampstead Heath**, the favourite parkland of thousands of Londoners. The glory of **South London** is **Greenwich**, with its nautical associations, royal park and observatory. Finally, there are plenty of rewarding day-trips along the Thames from **Chiswick** to **Windsor**, most notably to Hampton Court Palace and Windsor Castle.

Arrival

Flying into London, you'll arrive at one of the capital's five **international airports**: Heathrow, Gatwick, Stansted, Luton or City Airport, all of which are less than an hour from the city centre.

Heathrow (ⓣ08700/000123, ⓦwww.baa.co.uk), fifteen miles west of the centre, has four terminals, and two train/tube stations: one for terminals 1, 2 and 3, and a separate one for terminal 4. The high-speed **Heathrow Express** trains travel non-stop to Paddington Station (every 15min; 15–20min) for £13 each way or £23 return (less if you book online, more if you buy your ticket on board). A much cheaper alternative is to take the slow Piccadilly **Underground** line into central London (every 5–9min; 50min) for £3.70. If you plan to make several sightseeing journeys on your arrival day, buy a One-Day Travelcard (Zones 1–6) for £5.10 (see p.66). There is also a **National Express bus service** (ⓣ08705/808080, ⓦwww.nationalexpress.com) from Heathrow direct to Victoria Coach Station (daily 6am–9.30pm), which departs every thirty minutes, takes approximately an hour depending on the traffic, and costs £8 single, £11 return. **Airbus** #2, also runs from outside all four Heathrow terminals to several destinations in the city (every 30min; 1hr) and costs £8 single, £12 return. From midnight, you'll have to take **Night Bus #N9** to Trafalgar Square (every 30min; 1hr) for a bargain fare of £1. **Taxis** are plentiful, but cost at least £40 to central London, and take around an hour (longer in the rush hour).

Gatwick (ⓣ08700/002468, ⓦwww.baa.co.uk), thirty miles to the south, has two terminals, North and South, connected by a monorail. The non-stop **Gatwick Express** train runs between the South Terminal and Victoria Station (every 15–30min; 30min) for £11. Other options include the **South Central** services to Victoria (every 15–20min; 40min) for £8.20, or **Thameslink** to King's Cross (every 15–30min; 50min) for around £10.

Stansted (ⓣ08700/000303, ⓦwww.baa.co.uk), London's swankiest international airport, lies roughly 35 miles northeast of the capital, and is served by the **Stansted Express** to Liverpool Street (every 15min; 45min), which costs £13 single, £23 return. **Airbus #6** also runs 24 hours a day to Victoria Coach Station (every 30min; 1hr 30min), and costs £8 single, £12 return.

Luton airport (ⓣ01582/405100, ⓦwww.london-luton.com) is roughly thirty miles north of the city centre, and mostly handles charter flights. A **free shuttle bus** takes five minutes to transport passengers to Luton Airport Parkway station, connected by **rail** to King's Cross and other stations in central London, with **Thameslink** running trains every fifteen minutes, plus one or two throughout the night; the journey takes thirty to forty minutes and is £10 for a single fare. Alternatively, **Green Line** buses run from Luton to Victoria Station (every 30min; 1hr 30min), costing £8.50 single, £13.50 return.

London's smallest airport, **City Airport** (ⓣ020/7646 0000, ⓦwww.londoncityairport.com), is situated in Docklands, nine miles east of central London. It handles European flights only, and is connected by shuttle bus with Canning Town (every 5min; 5min; £2.50), Canary Wharf (every 10min; 10min; £3), and Liverpool Street (every 10min; 30min; £6) tube stations.

Eurostar trains arrive at the central **Waterloo International**, south of the river. Arriving by train (ⓣ08457/484950, ⓦwww.rail.co.uk) from elsewhere in Britain, you'll come into one of London's numerous main-line stations, all of which have adjacent Underground stations linking into the city centre's tube network. Coming into London **by coach** (ⓣ08705/808080,

The London Pass

If you're thinking of visiting a lot of fee-paying attractions in a short space of time, it's probably worth buying a **London Pass** (Ⓦwww.londonpass.com), which gives you entry to a mixed bag of attractions including Hampton Court Palace, Kensington Palace, London Aquarium, St Paul's Cathedral, the Tower of London and Windsor Castle, plus a whole host of lesser attractions, and various discounts at selected outlets. You can choose to buy the card with or without an All-Zone Travelcard thrown in; the saving is relatively small, but it does include free travel out to Windsor. The pass costs around £25 for one day (£16.50 for kids), rising to £70 for six days (£36.50 for kids); or £30 with a Travelcard (£19 for kids) rising to £107 (£56 for kids). The pass can be bought online or over the phone (Ⓣ08702/429988), or in person from Exchange International bureaux at Heathrow and Gatwick airports and London's mainline train or major Underground stations.

Ⓦwww.nationalexpress.com), you're most likely to arrive at **Victoria Coach Station**, a couple of hundred yards south down Buckingham Palace Road from the train and Underground stations of the same name.

Information

The chief British Tourist Authority (BTA) office in London is the **Britain Visitor Centre**, near Piccadilly Circus at 1 Regent Street (Mon–Fri 9am–6.30pm, Sat & Sun 10am–4pm; Aug & Sept same times except Sat 9am–5pm; Ⓦwww.visitbritain.com). London also has its very own **London Tourist Board** or LTB with information online at Ⓦwww.visitlondon.com. Individual boroughs also run tourist offices, the most central one is on the south side of St Paul's Cathedral (April–Sept daily 9.30am–5pm; Oct–March Mon–Fri 9.30am–5pm, Sat 9.30am–12.30pm; Ⓣ020/7332 1456, Ⓦwww.cityoflondon.gov.uk).

Most tourist offices hand out a basic reference **map** of central London, plus plans of the public transport systems, and the maps in this chapter should be enough for most exploring, but to find your way around every nook and cranny you need to invest in either an *A–Z Atlas* or a *Nicholson Streetfinder*, both of which have a street index covering every street in the capital; you can get them at most bookshops and newsagents for under £5. The two best, simple, fold-out maps are *London: The Rough Guide Map* – which also details hotels, restaurants, attraction opening hours and so on – and *Benson's London Mini Map*.

The only comprehensive and critical weekly **listings** magazine is *Time Out*, which costs £2.20 and comes out every Tuesday afternoon. In it you'll find details of all the latest exhibitions, shows, films, music, sport, guided walks and events in and around the capital.

City transport

London's transport network is among the most complex and expensive in the world. **Transport for London** (TfL) provides excellent free maps and details of bus and tube services from its **travel information** offices: the main one is at Piccadilly Circus tube station (daily 8.45am–6pm), and there are other desks at Heathrow and various tube and train stations. There's also a 24-hour phone line for information on all bus and tube services Ⓣ020/7222 1234 and a web-

Travelcards

To get the best value out of the transport system, buy a **Travelcard**. Available from machines and booths at all tube and train stations, and at some newsagents (look for the sign), these are valid for the bus, tube, Docklands Light Railway, Tramlink and suburban rail networks. **Day Travelcards** come in two varieties: Off-Peak – which are valid after 9.30am on weekdays and all day during the weekend – and Peak. A Day Travelcard (Off-Peak), costs £4.10 for the central zones 1 and 2, rising to £5.10 for zones 1–6 (including Heathrow); the Day Travelcard (Peak) starts at £5.10 for zones 1 and 2. **Weekend Travelcards**, for unlimited travel on Saturdays and Sundays, start at £6.10 for zones 1 and 2. **Weekly Travelcards** are even more economical, beginning at £19.60 for zones 1 and 2; these cards can only be bought by holders of a **Photocard**, which you can get, free of charge, from tube and train station ticket booths on presentation of a passport photo.

site ⓦwww.tfl.gov.uk. One word of warning – avoid travelling during the **rush hour** (Mon–Fri 8–9.30am & 5–7pm), when tubes become unbearably crowded (and the lack of air conditioning doesn't help), and some buses get so full they literally won't let you on.

Except for very short journeys, the fastest way of moving around the city is by **Underground** or tube (ⓦwww.thetube.com), as it's known to all Londoners. The eleven different tube lines cross much of the metropolis, although London south of the river is not very well covered. Each line has its own colour and name – all you need to know is which direction you're travelling in: northbound, eastbound, southbound or westbound. Services operate from around 5.30am Monday to Saturday, and from 7.30am on Sundays, and end just after midnight; you rarely have to wait more than five minutes for a train from central stations. **Tickets** must be bought in advance from the machines or booths in the station entrance hall; ticket inspectors operate throughout the system and if you cannot produce a valid ticket you'll be charged an on-the-spot Penalty Fare of £10. A single journey in the central zone costs an unbelievable £1.60, so if you're intending to travel about a bit, a Travelcard is a much better bet (see box above).

London's famous red **double-decker buses** are fun to ride on, but tend to get stuck in traffic jams, which prevent them running to a regular timetable. In central London, you must buy your ticket before boarding from one of the machines at the bus stop. Tickets for all bus journeys costs a flat fare of £1. In addition to the Travelcards mentioned above, a **One-Day Bus Pass** for zones 1–4, which can be used before 9.30am on weekdays costs £2 for adults and £1 for kids. Regular buses run between about 6am and midnight; **Night Buses** (prefixed with the letter "N") operate outside this period. Night bus routes radiate out from Trafalgar Square at approximately twenty to thirty-minute intervals, more frequently on some routes and on Friday and Saturday nights. Tickets are £1 and Travelcards (see box) are valid. All stops are treated as request stops.

Large areas of London's suburbs are best reached by the **suburban train** network (Travelcards valid). Wherever a sight can only be reached by overground train, we've indicated the nearest train station and the central terminus from which you must depart.

Boat services on the Thames do not form part of an integrated public transport system. Fares are expensive, and Travelcards currently only give the holders a 33 percent discount on tickets. All services are keenly affected by demand, tides and the weather, and tend to be drastically scaled down in the winter

Congestion charge

Given the traffic jams and the hassle, **driving in London** – especially central London – is by far the worst transport option available. The latest attempt to cut down on car usage in the capital is the controversial **congestion charge**, pioneered by Ken Livingstone in his first term as mayor of London. Since early 2003, all vehicles entering central London on weekdays between 7am and 6.30pm are liable to a congestion charge of £5 per vehicle. Drivers can pay for the charge online, over the phone and at garages and shops, and must do so before 10pm the same day or incur a £5 surcharge. The congestion-charging zone is bounded by Marylebone and Euston roads in the north, Commercial Street and Tower Bridge in the east, Kennington Lane and Elephant & Castle in the south and Edgware Road and Park Lane in the west.

months. **Timetables and services** are complex, and there are numerous companies and small charter operators – for a full list pick up the Thames River Services booklet from an LT travel information office, phone ⓣ020/7222 1234 or visit ⓦwww.tfl.gov.uk.

Compared to most capital cities, London's metered **black cabs** are an expensive option unless there are three or more of you – a ride from Euston to Victoria, for example, costs around £10, more at the weekend, and after 8pm on weekdays. A yellow light over the windscreen tells you if the cab is available – just stick your arm out to hail it. If you want to book one in advance, call ⓣ020/7272 0272.

Minicabs look just like regular cars and are considerably cheaper than black cabs, but they are a bit of a law unto themselves. There are hundreds of minicab firms in the phone book, but the best way to pick is to take the advice of the place you're at, unless you want to be certain of a woman driver, in which case call Ladycabs (ⓣ020/7254 3501), or a gay/lesbian-friendly driver, in which case call Freedom Cars (ⓣ020/7734 1313) or Liberty Cars (ⓣ020/7739 9080).

Accommodation

There's no getting away from the fact that **accommodation** in London is expensive and compared with most European cities, you pay over the odds in every category. Rates at the city's hostels are among the highest in the world, while venerable institutions such as the *Ritz*, the *Dorchester* and the *Savoy* charge guests the very top international prices – up to £300 and more per luxurious night.

The cheapest places to stay are the dorm beds of the city's numerous independent **hostels**, followed closely behind by the official YHA hostels. Even the most basic **B&Bs** struggle to bring their tariffs down to £45 for a double with shared facilities, and you're more likely to find yourself paying £60 or more.

If you want to avoid the hassle of contacting individual hotels and B&Bs, you could turn to one of the various **accommodation agencies**. The British Hotel Reservation Centre (BHRC) desks at Heathrow, Gatwick and Victoria train and coach stations, don't charge a fee for booking rooms, and most of their offices are open daily from 6am till midnight. You can also book for free via the 24-hour phone line (ⓣ020/7828 0601) or the Internet (ⓦwww.bhrc.co.uk).

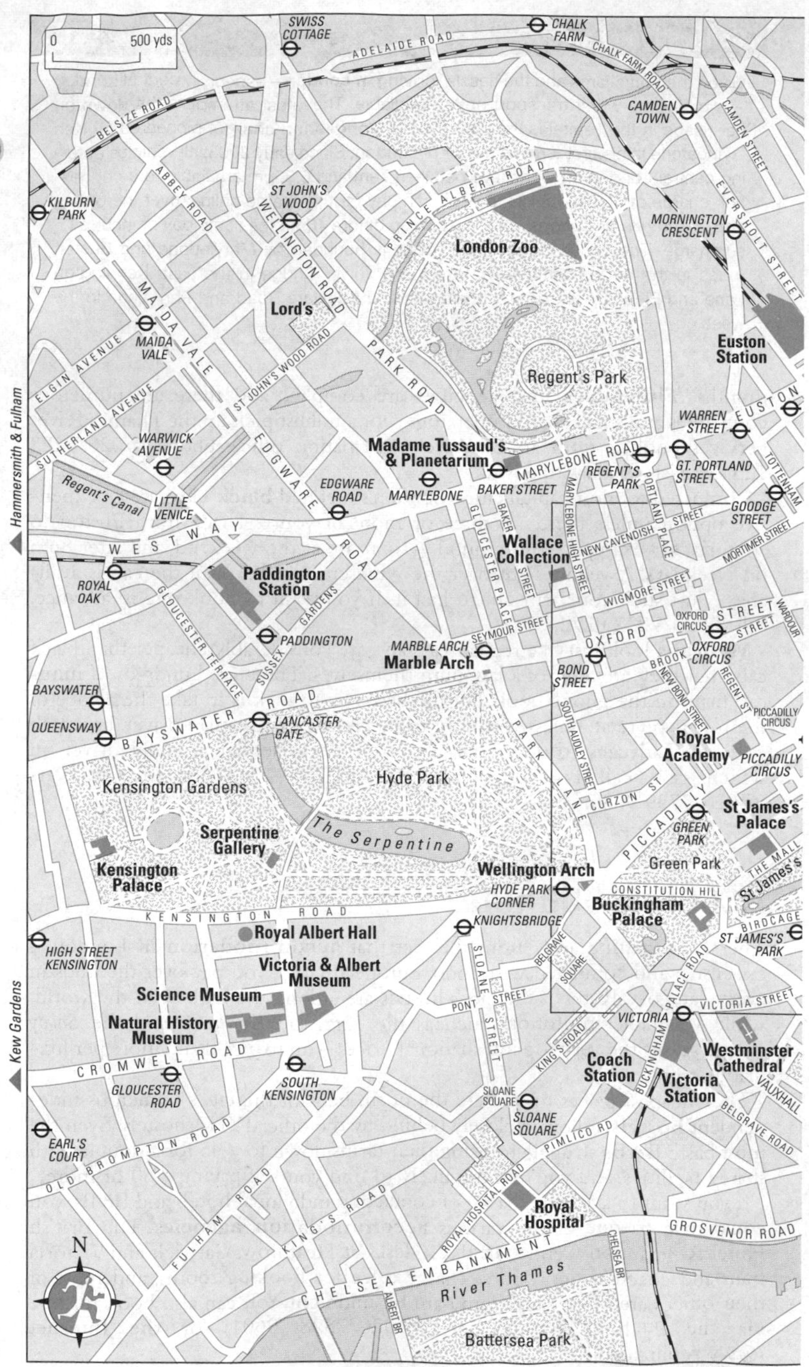
0 500 yds
SWISS COTTAGE
CHALK FARM
ADELAIDE ROAD
CHALK FARM ROAD
BELSIZE ROAD
CAMDEN TOWN
CAMDEN STREET
ABBEY ROAD
KILBURN PARK
ST JOHN'S WOOD
WELLINGTON ROAD
PRINCE ALBERT ROAD
London Zoo
EVERSHOLT STREET
MORNINGTON CRESCENT
MAIDA VALE
Lord's
ST JOHN'S WOOD ROAD
PARK ROAD
Euston Station
ELGIN AVENUE
Regent's Park
SUTHERLAND AVENUE
WARWICK AVENUE
EDGWARE ROAD
Madame Tussaud's & Planetarium
MARYLEBONE ROAD
WARREN STREET
EUSTON
Regent's Canal
LITTLE VENICE
MARYLEBONE
BAKER STREET
REGENT'S PARK
GT. PORTLAND STREET
TOTTENHAM
GOODGE STREET
WESTWAY
GLOUCESTER PLACE
BAKER STREET
MARYLEBONE HIGH STREET
PORTLAND PLACE
NEW CAVENDISH STREET
MORTIMER STREET
Wallace Collection
ROYAL OAK
GLOUCESTER TERRACE
Paddington Station
SUSSEX GARDENS
WIGMORE STREET
PADDINGTON
SEYMOUR STREET
OXFORD STREET
OXFORD CIRCUS
WARDOUR
MARBLE ARCH
Marble Arch
BOND STREET
BROOK
NEW BOND STREET
REGENT ST
BAYSWATER
QUEENSWAY
BAYSWATER ROAD
LANCASTER GATE
PARK LANE
SOUTH AUDLEY STREET
PICCADILLY CIRCUS
Royal Academy
Kensington Gardens
Hyde Park
CURZON ST
PICCADILLY
St James's Palace
GREEN PARK
Serpentine Gallery
The Serpentine
Green Park
THE MALL
Kensington Palace
Wellington Arch
HYDE PARK CORNER
CONSTITUTION HILL
St James's
Buckingham Palace
KENSINGTON ROAD
KNIGHTSBRIDGE
Royal Albert Hall
BIRDCAGE
ST JAMES'S PARK
HIGH STREET KENSINGTON
BELGRAVE SQUARE
SLOANE STREET
Victoria & Albert Museum
PALACE ROAD
Science Museum
PONT STREET
VICTORIA STREET
VICTORIA
Natural History Museum
KING'S ROAD
Westminster Cathedral
CROMWELL ROAD
BUCKINGHAM
Coach Station
Victoria Station
VAUXHALL
GLOUCESTER ROAD
SOUTH KENSINGTON
SLOANE SQUARE
BELGRAVE ROAD
EARL'S COURT
OLD BROMPTON ROAD
PIMLICO RD
FULHAM ROAD
KING'S ROAD
ROYAL HOSPITAL ROAD
Royal Hospital
GROSVENOR ROAD
CHELSEA BR
CHELSEA EMBANKMENT
River Thames
ALBERT BR
Battersea Park
N
Hammersmith & Fulham
Kew Gardens

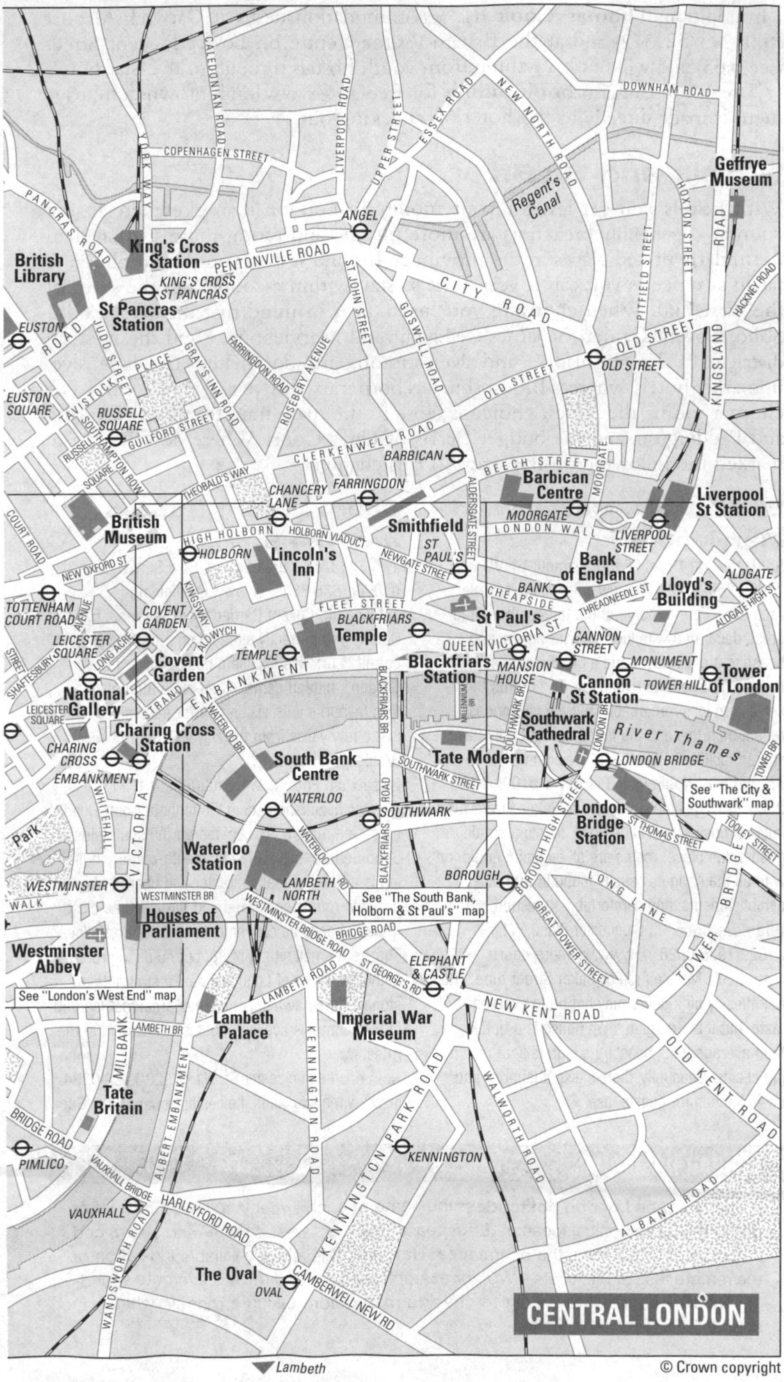

CENTRAL LONDON

Geffrye Museum
King's Cross Station
British Library
St Pancras Station
KING'S CROSS ST PANCRAS
EUSTON
EUSTON SQUARE
RUSSELL SQUARE
ANGEL
OLD STREET
BARBICAN
FARRINGDON
CHANCERY LANE
Barbican Centre
MOORGATE
Liverpool St Station
LIVERPOOL STREET
British Museum
HOLBORN
Lincoln's Inn
Smithfield
ST PAUL'S
Bank of England
BANK
Lloyd's Building
ALDGATE
TOTTENHAM COURT ROAD
COVENT GARDEN
BLACKFRIARS
Temple
St Paul's
LEICESTER SQUARE
Covent Garden
TEMPLE
Blackfriars Station
MANSION HOUSE
CANNON STREET
MONUMENT
TOWER HILL
Tower of London
Cannon St Station
National Gallery
Charing Cross Station
CHARING CROSS
EMBANKMENT
Southwark Cathedral
River Thames
South Bank Centre
Tate Modern
LONDON BRIDGE
London Bridge Station
WATERLOO
SOUTHWARK
Waterloo Station
WESTMINSTER
LAMBETH NORTH
BOROUGH
Houses of Parliament
Westminster Abbey
ELEPHANT & CASTLE
Lambeth Palace
Imperial War Museum
Tate Britain
KENNINGTON
PIMLICO
VAUXHALL
The Oval
OVAL
Park
Regent's Canal

CALEDONIAN ROAD
YORK WAY
LIVERPOOL ROAD
UPPER STREET
ESSEX ROAD
NEW NORTH ROAD
DOWNHAM ROAD
COPENHAGEN STREET
PANCRAS ROAD
PENTONVILLE ROAD
CITY ROAD
ST JOHN STREET
GOSWELL ROAD
HOXTON STREET
PITFIELD STREET
KINGSLAND ROAD
HACKNEY ROAD
OLD STREET
JUDD STREET
EUSTON ROAD
TAVISTOCK PLACE
GRAY'S INN ROAD
FARRINGDON ROAD
ROSEBERY AVENUE
SOUTHAMPTON ROW
RUSSELL SQUARE
GUILFORD STREET
CLERKENWELL ROAD
BEECH STREET
THEOBALD'S WAY
ALDERSGATE STREET
MOORGATE
COURT ROAD
HIGH HOLBORN
HOLBORN VIADUCT
LONDON WALL
NEWGATE STREET
NEW OXFORD ST
KINGSWAY
CHEAPSIDE
THREADNEEDLE ST
ALDGATE HIGH ST
FLEET STREET
QUEEN VICTORIA ST
ALDWYCH
LONG ACRE
SHAFTESBURY AVENUE
STRAND
EMBANKMENT
BLACKFRIARS BR
MILLENNIUM BR
SOUTHWARK BR
LONDON BR
WATERLOO BR
TOWER BR
SOUTHWARK STREET
WHITEHALL
VICTORIA
BLACKFRIARS ROAD
BOROUGH HIGH STREET
ST THOMAS STREET
TOOLEY STREET
WATERLOO RD
WESTMINSTER BR
WALK
LONG LANE
TOWER BRIDGE
WESTMINSTER BRIDGE ROAD
BRIDGE ROAD
GREAT DOVER STREET
LAMBETH ROAD
ST GEORGE'S RD
NEW KENT ROAD
OLD KENT ROAD
MILLBANK
LAMBETH BR
ALBERT EMBANKMENT
KENNINGTON ROAD
KENNINGTON PARK ROAD
WALWORTH ROAD
BRIDGE ROAD
VAUXHALL BRIDGE
HARLEYFORD ROAD
WANDSWORTH ROAD
CAMBERWELL NEW RD
ALBANY ROAD

See "The City & Southwark" map
See "The South Bank, Holborn & St Paul's" map
See "London's West End" map
Greenwich
Lambeth

In addition, **Thomas Cook** has accommodation desks at Gatwick Airport (Ⓣ01293/529372) and at the Britain Visitor Centre on Lower Regent Street (see p.65) and will book anything from youth hostels through to five-star hotels (£5 fee). You can also **book online** for free at Ⓦwww.londontown.com; payment is made directly to the hotel on checking out.

Hotels and B&Bs

With **hotels** you get less for your money in London than elsewhere in the country – generally breakfasts are more meagre and rooms more spartan than in similarly priced places in the provinces. In high season you should phone as far in advance as you can if you want to stay within a couple of tube stops of the West End. When choosing your **area**, bear in mind that the West End – Soho, Covent Garden, St James's, Mayfair and Marylebone – and the western districts of Knightsbridge and Kensington, are dominated by expensive, upmarket hotels, whereas Bloomsbury is both inexpensive and very central. For cheaper rooms, the widest choice is close to the main train termini of Victoria and Paddington, and the budget B&Bs of Earl's Court. Where possible, we've marked the following on the maps in this chapter.

St James's, Mayfair and Marylebone

Edward Lear Hotel 28–30 Seymour St, W1 Ⓣ020/7402 5401, Ⓦwww.edlear.com. Marble Arch tube. Former home of the famous poet and artist, decorated with lovely flower boxes, and boasting a plush foyer and a great location close to Oxford Street and Hyde Park. The rooms themselves are less remarkable, but the low prices reflect both this and the fact that most only have shared facilities. Kids free at weekends. ④

La Place 17 Nottingham Place, W1 Ⓣ020/7486 2323, Ⓦwww.hotellaplace.com. Baker Street tube. Just off busy Marylebone Road, this is a small, good-value place; rooms are all en suite, equipped with all the gadgets usually found in grander establishments, and comfortably furnished. ⑦

Wigmore Court 23 Gloucester Place, W1 Ⓣ020/7935 0928, Ⓦwww.wigmore-court-hotel.co.uk. Marble Arch or Baker Street tube. The relentlessly pink decor may not be to everyone's taste, but this Georgian town house is a better than average B&B, boasting a high tally of returning clients. Unusually, there's also a laundry and basic kitchen for guests' use. ⑤

Soho, Covent Garden and The Strand

The Fielding 4 Broad Court, Bow St, WC2 Ⓣ020/7836 8305, Ⓦwww.the-fielding-hotel.co.uk. Covent Garden tube. See map, p.76. Quietly and perfectly situated on a traffic-free and gas-lit court, this excellent hotel is one of Covent Garden's hidden gems. Its en-suite rooms are a firm favourite with visiting performers, since it's just a few yards from the Royal Opera House. Breakfast is extra. ⑥

Hazlitt's 6 Frith St, W1 Ⓣ020/7434 1771, Ⓦwww.hazlittshotel.com. Tottenham Court Road tube. See map, p.76. Located off the south side of Soho Square, this early-eighteenth-century building is a hotel of real character and charm, offering en-suite rooms decorated and furnished as close to period style as convenience and comfort allow. There's a small sitting room, but no dining room (although some of London's best restaurants are a stone's throw away); continental breakfast (served in the rooms) is available, but isn't included in the rates. ⑨

Manzi's 1–2 Leicester St, W1 Ⓣ020/7734 0224, Ⓦwww.manzis.co.uk. Leicester Square tube. See

London postcodes

A brief word on **London postcodes**: the name of each street is followed by a letter giving the geographical location (E for "east", WC for "west central" and so on) and a number that specifies the postal area. However, this is not a reliable indication of the remoteness of the locale – W5, for example, lies beyond the more remote sounding NW10 – so it's always best to check a map before taking a room in what may sound like a fairly central area.

map, p.76. Set over the Italian and seafood restaurant of the same name, *Manzi's* is one of very few central hotels in this price range. It's certainly right in the thick of the West End, just off Leicester Square, meaning noise might prove to be a nuisance. Continental breakfast is included in the price. ❺

St Martin's Lane 45 St Martin's Lane, WC2 ⓣ020/7300 5500 or ⓣ0800/634 5500, ⓦwww.ianschragerhotels.com. See map, p.76. Leicester Square tube. So cool you wouldn't know it was a hotel, this self-consciously chic "boutique hotel" from the New York-based Ian Schrager chain is a hit with the media crowd. From the fluorescent yellow and white minimalist lobby to the large Portuguese limestone bathrooms, the interior has been designed throughout by the mischievous Philippe Starck. Rooms currently start at around £250 a double, but rates come down at the weekend. ❾

Bloomsbury

Cavendish 75 Gower St, WC1 ⓣ020/7636 9079, ⓦwww.hotelcavendish.com. Goodge Street tube. See map, p.76. Gower Street is very busy with traffic, but get a room at the back of the property and you'll have a peaceful night, and a real bargain, too, with lovely owners, two beautiful overrun gardens and some quite well-preserved original features. All rooms have shared facilities, and there are some good-value family rooms, too. ❸

Crescent 49–50 Cartwright Gardens, WC1 ⓣ020/7387 1515, ⓦwww.crescenthoteloflondon.com. Euston or Russell Square tube. This very comfortable and tastefully decorated Regency B&B is definitely a cut above the rest. All doubles are en suite and have TVs, but there are a few bargain singles with shared facilities. Guests also have use of tennis courts in the nearby gardens. ❺

Garth 69 Gower St, WC1 ⓣ020/7636 5761, ⓦwww.garthhotel-london.com; Goodge Street tube. See map, p.76. Gay-friendly, small, Georgian town house hotel, which prides itself on its friendly atmosphere and features many original antiques in its mostly en-suite bedrooms. ❸

Jenkins 45 Cartwright Gardens, WC1 ⓣ020/7387 2067, ⓦwww.jenkinshotel.demon.co.uk. Euston or Russell Square tube. Smartly kept, family-run place in this fine Regency crescent, with just fourteen fairly small but well-equipped and very clean rooms, most of which are en suite. ❹

myhotel 11–13 Bayley St, WC1 ⓣ020/7667 6000, ⓦwww.myhotels.co.uk. Tottenham Court Road tube. See map, p.76.The aquarium in the lobby is the tell-tale sign that this is a feng shui hotel. Despite the positive vibes, and Conran-designed look, the double-glazed, air-conditioned rooms are on the small side for the price. Still, there's a gym, a very pleasant library, a restaurant attached and the location is great for the West End. ❽

Ridgemount 65–67 Gower St, WC1 ⓣ020/7636 1141, ⓦwww.ridgemounthotel.co.uk. Goodge Street tube. See map, p.76. Old-fashioned, very friendly family-run place, with small rooms, half with shared facilities, a garden, free hot-drinks machine and a laundry service. Cash only, but a reliable, basic bargain for Bloomsbury. ❸

Russell Russell Square, WC1 ⓣ020/7837 6470, ⓦwww.lemeridien.com. Russell Square tube. From its grand 1898 exterior to its opulent interiors of marble, wood and crystal, this late-Victorian landmark fully retains its period atmosphere in all its public areas. Thanks to a recent takeover – and makeover – by Le Meridien chain, the rooms now live up to the grandeur of the lobby, if not necessarily to its style. Expensive, but various deals are sometimes available. Breakfast not included. ❾

Clerkwenwell and the City

City 12 Osborn St, E1 ⓣ020/7247 3313, ⓦwww.cityhotellondon.co.uk. Aldgate East tube. See map, p.108. Spacious, clean and modern inside, this hotel stands on the eastern edge of the City, and in the heart of the Bengali East End at the bottom of Brick Lane. The plainly decorated rooms are all en suite, and many have kitchens, too; four-person rooms are a bargain for those in a small group. ❻

Great Eastern Liverpool St, EC2 ⓣ020/7618 5000, ⓦwww.great-eastern-hotel.co.uk. Liverpool Street tube. See map, p.108. Without doubt one of the best places to stay if you need or wish to be near the City. This venerable late-nineteenth-century station hotel has had a complete Conran makeover, yet manages to retain much of its club-by flavour. The rooms themselves are impeccably well appointed and tastefully furnished – to maximize your natural light, get a room facing out. Doubles start from around £200, but rates are cut at the weekend. ❾

Jurys Inn 60 Pentonville Rd, N1 ⓣ020/7282 5500, ⓦwww.jurys.com. Angel tube. This modern Irish chain hotel is decorated to a high, if bland, standard, and is geared up for business folk. Located on busy Pentonville Road, close to the tube, it's equally convenient for the City and for Islington and Clerkenwell's trendy bars and restaurants. Service is very friendly, and the fixed room-rate is a bargain for three adults sharing or for those with kids. ❺

The Rookery 12 Peter's Lane, Cowcross St, EC1 ⓣ020/7336 0931, ⓦwww.rookeryhotel.com. Farringdon tube. Rambling Georgian town house on the edge of the City in trendy Clerkenwell that makes a fantastically discreet little hideaway. The rooms start at around £265 a double; each one has been individually designed in a deliciously camp, modern take on the Baroque period, and all have super bathrooms with lots of character. ❽

South Bank & Southwark

London County Hall Travel Inn Belvedere Rd, SE1 ⓣ020/7902 1619, ⓦwww.travelinn.co.uk. Waterloo or Westminster tube. See map, p.98. Don't expect river views at these prices, but the location in County Hall itself is pretty good if you're up for a bit of sightseeing. Decor and ambience is functional, but for those with kids, the flat-rate rooms are a bargain. ❺

Mad Hatter 3–7 Stamford St, SE1 ⓣ020/7401 9222, ⓦwww.fullers.co.uk. Southwark or Blackfriars tube. See map, p.98. Situated above a Fuller's pub – where breakfast is served – on the corner of Blackfriars Road, this place has a great location, a short walk from the Tate Modern and the South Bank. Ask about the weekend deals. ❻

Victoria

Melbourne House 79 Belgrave Rd, SW1 ⓣ020/7828 3516, ⓦwww.melbournehousehotel.co.uk. Victoria or Pimlico tube. One of the best B&Bs along Belgrave Road: family run, well furnished, offering clean and bright rooms, excellent communal areas and friendly service. All doubles have en-suite facilities, but there are a couple of very cheap singles without. ❺

Oxford House 92–94 Cambridge St, SW1 ⓣ020/7834 6467, ⓕ020/7834 0225. Victoria tube. Probably the best-value rooms you can get in the vicinity of Victoria Station. Showers and toilets are shared, but kept pristine. Full English breakfast is included in the price. ❷

Sanctuary House 33 Tothill St, SW1 ⓣ020/7799 4044, ⓦwww.fullers.co.uk. St James's Park tube. See map, p.76. Situated above a Fuller's pub, and decked out like one, too, in smart, pseudo-Victoriana. Breakfast is extra, and is served in the pub, but the location right by St James's Park is very central. Ask about the weekend deals. ❻

Topham's 26 Ebury St, SW1 ⓣ020/7730 8147, ⓦwww.tophams.co.uk. Victoria tube. See map, p.122. Charming family-owned hotel in the English country-house style, just a couple of minutes' walk from Victoria mainline and tube station. Sumptuously furnished en-suite twins or doubles, including full English breakfast. ❼

Windermere 142–144 Warwick Way, SW1 ⓣ020/7834 5163, ⓦwww.windermere-hotel.co.uk. Sloane Square, Pimlico or Victoria tube. See map, p.122. Situated at the western end of Warwick Way, this is a tastefully decorated and quietly stylish place where most rooms are en suite. There's a tasty restaurant downstairs, too. ❻

Woodville House & Morgan House 107 & 120 Ebury St, SW1 ⓣ020/7730 1048, ⓦwww.woodvillehouse.co.uk. See map, p.122. Two above-average B&Bs, run by the same vivacious couple, with great breakfasts, patio gardens, and an iron and fridge for guests to use. All rooms at *Woodville* are with shared facilities; some at *Morgan* are en suite. Victoria tube. ❹

Paddington, Bayswater and Notting Hill

Columbia 95–99 Lancaster Gate, W2 ⓣ020/7402 0021, ⓦwww.columbiahotel.co.uk. Lancaster Gate tube. See map, p.122. The spacious public lounge, well-worn decor and useful 24-hour bar make this large white stucco hotel a rock-band favourite. The en-suite rooms themselves are actually very sober, and retain some original Victorian fittings. ❺

Garden Court 30–31 Kensington Garden Square, W2 ⓣ020/7229 2553, ⓦwww.gardencourthotel.co.uk. Queensway or Bayswater tube. See map, p.122. Presentable, family-run B&B on a quiet square close to Portobello Market; half the rooms are with shared facilities, half are en suite. Full English breakfast included. ❸

The Gresham 116 Sussex Gardens, W2 ⓣ020/7402 2920, ⓦwww.the-gresham-hotel.co.uk. Paddington tube. See map, p.122. B&B with a touch more class than many in the area. Rooms are small but tastefully kitted out, and all have TV. Continental breakfast included. ❺

Inverness Court 1 Inverness Terrace, W2 ⓣ020/7229 1444, ⓕ020/7229 3666. Bayswater or Queensway tube. See map, p.122. Late-Victorian facade, reception area, bar and lounges lend a charming ambience, even if most of the en-suite rooms are in an undistinguished modern style. Continental breakfast included. ❼

Pavilion 34–36 Sussex Gardens, W2 ⓣ020/7262 0905, ⓦwww.msi.com.mt/pavilion. Paddington tube. See map, p.122. The successful rock star's home-from-home, with outrageously over-the-top decor and every room individually themed. ❻

Pembridge Court 34 Pembridge Gardens, W11 ⓣ020/7229 9977, ⓦwww.pemct.co.uk. Notting Hill Gate or Holland Park tube. See map, p.122. Attractively converted town house close to Portobello Market, with spacious, fully equipped rooms. Two cats add to the homely feel, as does the lively *Caps Restaurant and Bar.* ❽

Knightsbridge, Kensington and Chelsea

Abbey House 11 Vicarage Gate, W8 ⓣ020/7727 2594, ⓦwww.abbeyhousekensington.com. High Street Kensington or Notting Hill tube. See map, p.122. Inexpensive Victorian B&B in a quiet street just north of Kensington High Street. Rooms are large and bright – prices are kept down by sharing facilities rather than fitting the usual cramped bathroom unit. Full English breakfast, with free tea and coffee available all day. Cash only. ❺

Aster House 3 Sumner Place, SW7 ⓣ020/7581 5888, ⓦwww.asterhouse.com. South Kensington tube. See map, p.122. Pleasant, non-smoking B&B in a luxurious white-stuccoed South Ken street; there's a lovely garden at the back and a large conservatory, where breakfast is served. ❼

Five Sumner Place 5 Sumner Place, SW7 ⓣ020/7584 7586, ⓦwww.sumnerplace.com. South Kensington tube. See map, p.122. Discreetly luxurious B&B in one of South Ken's prettiest white-stucco terraces. All rooms are en suite and breakfast is served in the house's lovely conservatory. ❼

The Gore 189 Queen's Gate, SW7 ⓣ020/7584 6601, ⓦwww.gorehotel.co.uk. South Kensington, Gloucester Road or High Street Kensington tube. See map, p.122. Popular, century-old hotel, awash with oriental rugs, rich mahogany, walnut panelling and other Victoriana. A pricey, but excellent bistro restaurant adds to its allure, and it's only a step away from Hyde Park. ❾

The Hempel 31–35 Craven Hill Gardens, W2 ⓣ020/7298 9000, ⓦwww.the-hempel.co.uk. Lancaster Gate or Queensway tube. See map, p.122. Deeply fashionable minimalist hotel, designed by the actress turned designer Anouska Hempel, with a huge and very empty atrium entrance, and white-on-white rooms. ❾

Hotel 167 167 Old Brompton Rd, SW5 ⓣ020/7373 3221, ⓦwww.hotel167.com. Gloucester Road tube. See map, p.122. Small, stylishly furnished B&B with en-suite facilities, double glazing and a fridge in all rooms. Continental buffet-style breakfast is served in the attractive morning room/reception. ❼

Vicarage 10 Vicarage Gate, W8 ⓣ020/7229 4030, ⓦwww.londonvicaragehotel.com. High Street Kensington or Notting Hill tube. See map, p.122. Ideally located B&B a step away from Hyde Park, with clean rooms – shared facilities – and a full English breakfast. Cash/traveller's cheques only. ❺

Earl's Court

Philbeach 30–31 Philbeach Gardens, SW5 ⓣ020/7373 1244, ⓦwww.philbeachhotel.freeserve.co.uk. Earl's Court tube. See map, p.122. Friendly, long-running gay/transvestite hotel, with basic and en-suite rooms, a pleasant TV lounge area, late bar and popular *Wilde About Oscar* garden restaurant. ❽

Rushmore 11 Trebovir Rd, SW5 ⓣ020/7370 3839, ⓕ020/7370 0274. Earl's Court tube. See map, p.122. A cut above the average, with its colourful murals, imaginative Italianate room decor and conservatory in this often dreary area. The attic rooms are especially spacious and comfortable. Full continental breakfast is included in the rates. ❺

Hampstead

Hampstead Village Guest House 2 Kemplay Rd, NW3 ⓣ020/7435 8679, ⓦwww.HampsteadGuesthouse.com. Lovely B&B in an old house set in a quiet backstreet between Hampstead village and the Heath. Rooms (some en suite, all non-smoking) have "lived-in" clutter, which makes a pleasant change from anodyne hotels and spartan B&Bs. Meals to order. Hampstead tube. ❺

La Gaffe 107–111 Heath St, NW3 ⓣ020/7435 4941, ⓦwww.lagaffe.co.uk. Hampstead tube. Small and warren-like but characterful hotel, situated over an Italian restaurant and bar in the heart of Hampstead village. All rooms are en suite and there's a roof terrace for use in fine weather. ❻

Hostels and student accommodation

London's official **Youth Hostel Association (YHA) hostels** are generally the cleanest, most efficiently run hostels in the capital. There's no age limit, and if you're not already a member, you can join on the spot. You can book a bed over the phone with a credit card by ringing individual hostels, or by logging on to their **website** at ⓦwww.yha.org.uk. **Independent hostels** are cheaper and more relaxed, but can be less reliable in terms of facilities. Typical of this laid-back brand is the Astor chain of five hostels, run exclusively for the 18–30 age group. A good **website** for booking independent places online is ⓦwww.hostellondon.com. Outside term time, you also have the option of staying in **student halls of residence**: the quality of the rooms varies enormously, but tends to be fairly basic and prices are slightly higher than hostels. London's **campsites** are all on the perimeter of the city, though they are without doubt the cheapest accommodation available.

Where possible we've marked the location of the following on one of the maps in this chapter.

YHA hostels

City of London 36 Carter Lane, EC4 ⓣ020/7236 4965, ⓔcity@yha.org.uk. St Paul's tube. See map, p.98. Two-hundred-bed hostel in a great location opposite St Paul's Cathedral; some twins too (❸), but mostly four- to eight-bed dorms for £24 per person. No groups.

Earl's Court 38 Bolton Gardens, SW5 ⓣ020/7373 7083, ⓔearlscourt@yha.org.uk. Earl's Court tube. See map, p.122. Better than a lot of accommodation in Earl's Court, but only offering dorms of mostly ten beds at £16.80 per person – the triple-bunks take some getting used to. Kitchen, café and patio garden. No groups.

Hampstead Heath 4 Wellgarth Rd, NW11 ⓣ020/8458 9054, ⓔhampstead@yha.org.uk. Golders Green tube. One of London's biggest and best-appointed YHA hostels, with its own garden and the wilds of Hampstead Heath nearby. Beds cost £20.40 per person; rooms have three to six beds and family rooms have two to five beds.

Holland House Holland Walk, W8 ⓣ020/7937 0748, ⓔhollandhouse@yha.org.uk. Holland Park or High Street Kensington tube. See map, p.122. Idyllically situated in the wooded expanse of Holland Park and fairly convenient for the centre of town, this extensive dorm-only hostel offers a decent kitchen, an inexpensive café and beds for £21. Popular with school groups.

Oxford Street 14 Noel St, W1 ⓣ020/7734 1618, ⓔoxfordst@yha.org.uk. Oxford Circus or Tottenham Court Road tube. See map, p.76. The West End location and modest size mean that this hostel tends to be full even out of high season. No children under 6, no groups, no café, but a large kitchen. Dorm bed £22 per person.

Rotherhithe Island Yard, Salter Rd, SE16 ⓣ020/7232 2114, ⓔrotherhithe@yha.org.uk. Rotherhithe or Canada Water tube. Large purpose-built hostel located in a Docklands area that has little going for it, though it's only a twenty-minute tube ride from the West End and often has space. Rooms have two, four, five or ten beds, and rates start at £15 per person.

St Pancras 79–81 Euston Rd, NW1 ⓣ020/7388 9998, ⓔstpancras@yha.org.uk. King's Cross or Euston tube. Big hostel situated opposite the British Library, on busy Euston Road. Rooms are very clean, bright, triple-glazed and air-conditioned – some even have en-suite facilities and beds cost £24. There are a few en-suite doubles (❸) and family rooms available with TVs.

Private hostels

Ashlee House 261–265 Gray's Inn Rd, WC1 ⓣ020/7833 9400, ⓦwww.ashleehouse.co.uk. King's Cross tube. Basic and a little cramped, but clean and friendly hostel in a converted office block near King's Cross Station. Laundry and kitchen facilities are provided. Dorms vary in size from four to sixteen beds, and there are also a few private rooms with bunk beds starting at £24 per person. Breakfast is included.

Generator Compton Place, off Tavistock Place, WC1 ⓣ020/7388 7666, ⓦwww.the-generator.co.uk. Russell Square or Euston tube. The neon- and UV-lighting and post-industrial decor may not be to everyone's taste, but with prices starting at just £12.50 a night for a dorm bed and breakfast, this is without doubt the best bargain in this part of town. Facilities include Internet access, a games rooms, movie nights, a bar open to residents only (till 2am) and a canteen.

Leinster Inn 7–12 Leinster Square, W2 ⓣ020/7229 9641, ⓦwww.astorhostels.com. Queensway or Notting Hill Gate tube. See map, p.122. The biggest and liveliest of the Astor hostels, with a party atmosphere, and two bars open until the small hours. Singles, doubles (❸) and dorm beds available from £15. Under 30s only.

Museum Inn 27 Montague St, WC1 ⓣ020/7580 5360, ⓦwww.astorhostels.com. Russell Square tube. See map, p.76. In a lovely Georgian house in Bloomsbury, this is the quietest of the Astor hostels. There's no bar, though it's still a sociable, laid-back place, and well situated. Small kitchen, TV lounge and Internet access. Under 30s only.

St Christopher's Village 161–165 Borough High St, SE1 ⓣ020/7407 1856, ⓦwww.st-christophers.co.uk. London Bridge tube. See map, p.108. Flagship of a chain of independent hostels, with no fewer than three properties on Borough High Street (and branches in Camden and Greenwich). The decor is upbeat and cheerful, the place is efficiently run and there's a party-animal ambience, fuelled by the neighbouring bar and the rooftop hot tub and sauna.

Student halls

Imperial College ⓣ020/7594 9507, ⓦwww.ic.ac.uk/conferences. Singles and twins available (with breakfast) in three halls of residence in South Kensington and Notting Hill. Open Easter & July to late Sept. ❸

International Student House 229 Great Portland St, W1 ⓣ020/7631 8300, ⓦwww.ish.org.uk. Great Portland Street tube. Hundreds of singles, twins (❸), quads and dorm beds in a vast complex at the southern end of Regent's Park. Open year round; rates from £12.

King's College ⓣ020/7848 1700, ⓦwww.kcl.ac.uk/kcvb. King's College has a wide range of accommodation available in Bankside, Victoria and Hampstead from July to September. You can either contact the Vacation Bureau by phone or book online. Central rooms tend to be en suite but without breakfast; further afield, it's shared facilities but breakfast included. Rooms are mostly singles from around £20 each; only Hampstead has twins (❷).

London School of Economics (LSE) ⓣ020/7955 7370, ⓦwww.lse.ac.uk/collections/vacations. The LSE offers singles, twins, triples and quads in five halls across London – en suite or with shared facilities. Singles start at £27, twins range from cheapies at Rosebery Hall in Clerkenwell (❶) to swanky en-suite affairs on Bankside (❹). To find out about availability, you can ring the central office, or visit the website and book online.

Campsites

Abbey Wood Federation Rd, Abbey Wood, SE2 ⓣ020/8311 7708. Train from Charing Cross or London Bridge to Abbey Wood. Enormous, and well-equipped Caravan Club site, east of Greenwich and ten miles southeast of central London. Open all year.

Crystal Palace Crystal Palace Parade, SE19 ⓣ020/8778 7155. Train from Victoria or London Bridge to Crystal Palace. Caravan Club site, with maximum stays of two weeks in summer, three weeks in winter. Open all year.

Lea Valley Leisure Centre Caravan Park Meridian Way, N9 ⓣ020/8803 6900. Train from Liverpool Street to Ponders End. Well-equipped site, situated behind the leisure centre at Pickett's Lock, backing on to a vast reservoir. Open all year.

Westminster and Whitehall

Political, religious and regal power has emanated from **Westminster** and **Whitehall** for almost a millennium. It was Edward the Confessor who first established Westminster as London's royal and ecclesiastical power base, some three miles west of the City of London. The embryonic English parliament met in the abbey in the fourteenth century and eventually took over the old royal palace of Westminster. In the nineteenth century, Whitehall became the "heart of the Empire", its ministries ruling over a quarter of the world's population. Even now, though the UK's world status has diminished, the institutions that run the country inhabit roughly the same geographical area: Westminster for the politicians, Whitehall for the civil servants.

The monuments and buildings in and around Whitehall and Westminster also span the millennium, and include some of London's most famous landmarks – **Nelson's Column**, **Big Ben** and the **Houses of Parliament**, **Westminster Abbey** and **Buckingham Palace**, plus two of the city's finest permanent art collections, the **National Gallery** and **Tate Britain**. This is a well-trodden tourist circuit since it's also one of the easiest parts of London to walk round, with all the major sights within a mere half-mile of each other, linked by two of London's most triumphant avenues, **Whitehall** and **The Mall**.

Trafalgar Square

Despite the pigeons and the traffic noise, **Trafalgar Square** is still one of London's grandest architectural set-pieces. John Nash designed the basic layout in the 1820s, but died long before the square took its present form. The Neoclassical National Gallery filled up the northern side of the square in 1838,

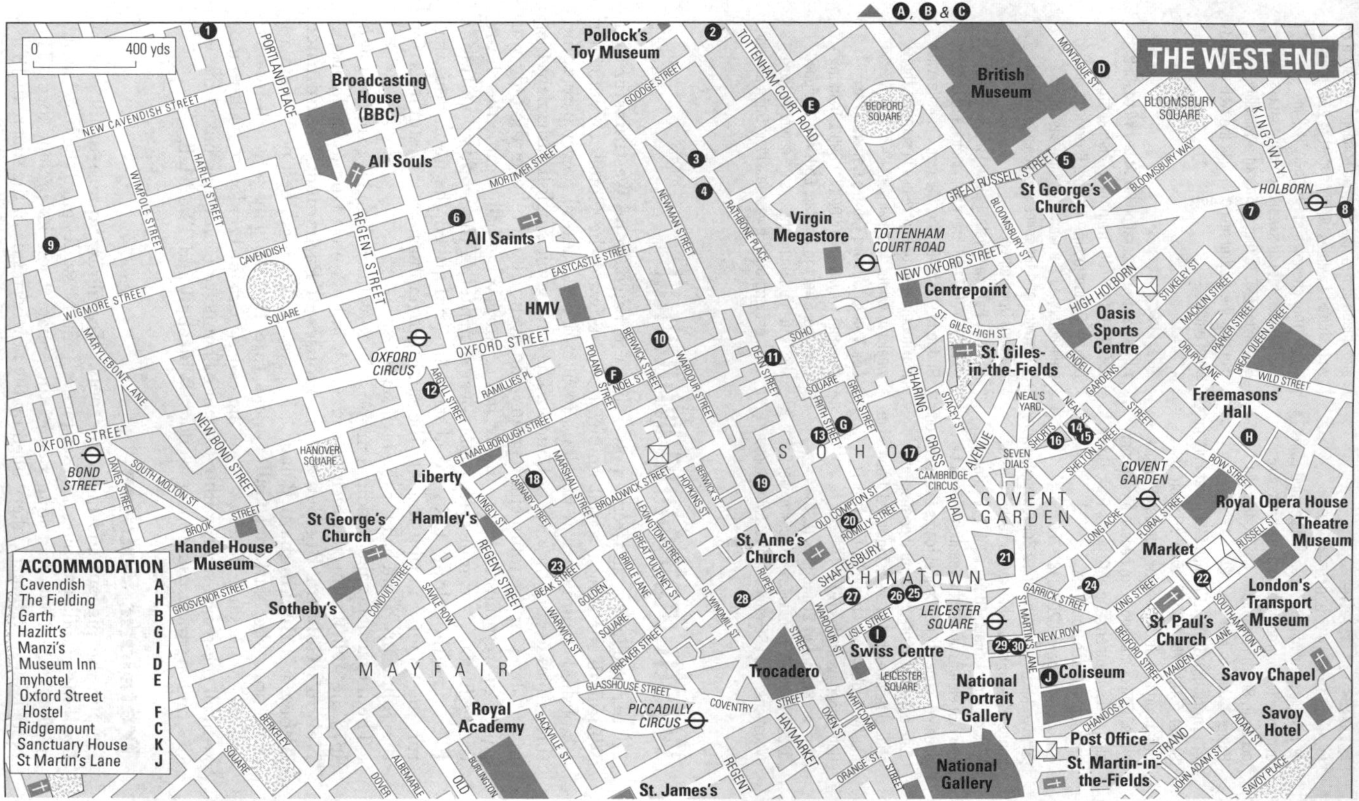

A, B & C

THE WEST END

0 400 yds

ACCOMMODATION

Cavendish	A
The Fielding	H
Garth	B
Hazlitt's	G
Manzi's	I
Museum Inn	D
myhotel	E
Oxford Street Hostel	F
Ridgemount	C
Sanctuary House	K
St Martin's Lane	J

Pollock's Toy Museum
Broadcasting House (BBC)
All Souls
All Saints
HMV
British Museum
St George's Church
Virgin Megastore
TOTTENHAM COURT ROAD
Centrepoint
Oasis Sports Centre
St. Giles-in-the-Fields
Freemasons' Hall
HOLBORN
OXFORD CIRCUS
Liberty
Hamley's
St George's Church
Handel House Museum
Sotheby's
BOND STREET
S O H O
COVENT GARDEN
COVENT GARDEN
Royal Opera House
Theatre Museum
Market
London's Transport Museum
St. Paul's Church
St. Anne's Church
CHINATOWN
LEICESTER SQUARE
Swiss Centre
Trocadero
National Portrait Gallery
Coliseum
Savoy Chapel
Savoy Hotel
Post Office
St. Martin-in-the-Fields
National Gallery
MAYFAIR
Royal Academy
PICCADILLY CIRCUS
St. James's
SEVEN DIALS
CAMBRIDGE CIRCUS
NEAL'S YARD
BLOOMSBURY SQUARE
BEDFORD SQUARE
CAVENDISH SQUARE
HANOVER SQUARE
SOHO SQUARE
GOLDEN SQUARE
LEICESTER SQUARE
BERKELEY SQUARE
PORTLAND PLACE
NEW CAVENDISH STREET
HARLEY STREET
WIMPOLE STREET
WIGMORE STREET
MARYLEBONE LANE
OXFORD STREET
NEW BOND STREET
DAVIES STREET
SOUTH MOLTON ST
BROOK STREET
GROSVENOR STREET
REGENT STREET
MORTIMER STREET
GOODGE STREET
TOTTENHAM COURT ROAD
NEWMAN STREET
RATHBONE PLACE
EASTCASTLE STREET
GREAT RUSSELL STREET
MONTAGUE ST
BLOOMSBURY WAY
BLOOMSBURY ST
KINGSWAY
NEW OXFORD STREET
HIGH HOLBORN
STUKELEY ST
MACKLIN STREET
PARKER STREET
GREAT QUEEN STREET
DRURY LANE
WILD STREET
ST. GILES HIGH ST
ENDELL STREET
GARDENS
NEAL ST
SHORTS GARDENS
SHELTON STREET
BOW STREET
FLORAL STREET
LONG ACRE
RUSSELL ST
KING STREET
SOUTHAMPTON ST
GARRICK STREET
BEDFORD STREET
MAIDEN LANE
CHANDOS PL
STRAND
ADAM ST
JOHN ADAM ST
SAVOY PLACE
NEW ROW
ST. MARTIN'S LANE
CHARING CROSS ROAD
STACEY ST
SHAFTESBURY AVENUE
OLD COMPTON ST
ROMILLY STREET
GREEK STREET
FRITH STREET
DEAN STREET
WARDOUR STREET
BERWICK STREET
POLAND STREET
NOEL ST
RAMILLIES PL
ARGYLL STREET
GT MARLBOROUGH STREET
MARSHALL STREET
CARNABY STREET
KINGLY ST
BROADWICK STREET
HOPKINS ST
BERWICK ST
LEXINGTON STREET
GREAT PULTENEY ST
BRIDLE LANE
BEAK STREET
WARWICK ST
GT WINDMILL ST
RUPERT STREET
LISLE STREET
BREWER STREET
GLASSHOUSE STREET
COVENTRY STREET
WHITCOMB STREET
OXEN ST
ORANGE ST
HAYMARKET
SAVILE ROW
CONDUIT STREET
SACKVILLE ST.
BURLINGTON
OLD
ALBEMARLE
DOVER

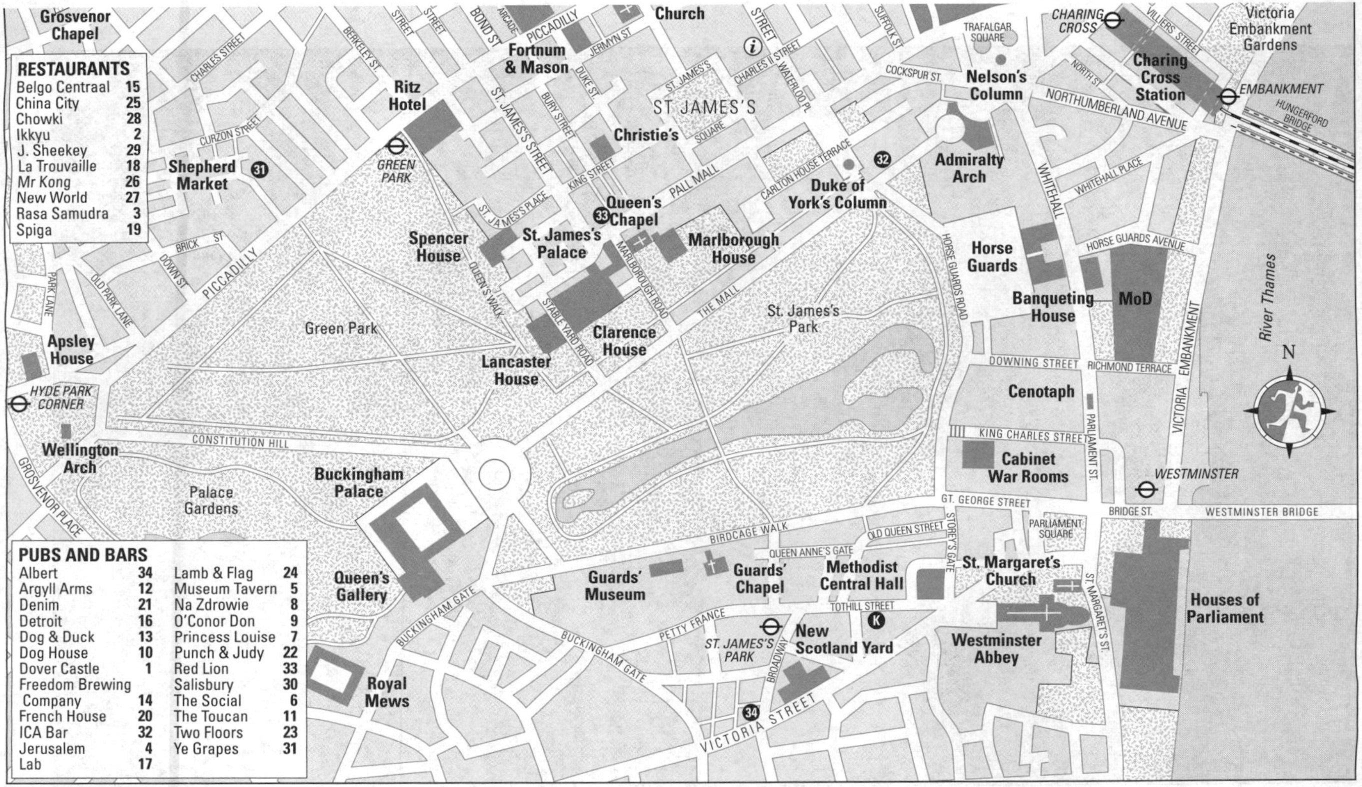

Grosvenor Chapel
Church
Fortnum & Mason
Ritz Hotel
ST JAMES'S
Christie's
Nelson's Column
Trafalgar Square
Charing Cross
Charing Cross Station
Embankment
Hungerford Bridge
Victoria Embankment Gardens
Shepherd Market
Green Park
Admiralty Arch
Duke of York's Column
Queen's Chapel
St. James's Palace
Spencer House
Marlborough House
Horse Guards
Banqueting House
MoD
River Thames
N
Green Park
St. James's Park
Clarence House
Lancaster House
Apsley House
Hyde Park Corner
Cenotaph
Wellington Arch
Cabinet War Rooms
Westminster
Buckingham Palace
Palace Gardens
Westminster Bridge
Parliament Square
Methodist Central Hall
St. Margaret's Church
Queen's Gallery
Guards' Museum
Guards' Chapel
Houses of Parliament
New Scotland Yard
St. James's Park
Westminster Abbey
Royal Mews
Piccadilly
Arcade
Bond St
Street
Berkeley St.
Charles Street
Curzon Street
Brick St
Down St
Park Lane
Old Park Lane
Jermyn St
Duke St.
Bury Street
St. James's Street
King Street
St. James's Place
Queen's Walk
Stable Yard Road
Marlborough Road
The Mall
Pall Mall
St. James's Square
Charles II Street
Waterloo Pl.
Suffolk St
Cockspur St.
Carlton House Terrace
Northumberland Avenue
North St.
Villiers Street
Whitehall
Whitehall Place
Horse Guards Avenue
Horse Guards Road
Victoria Embankment
Downing Street
Richmond Terrace
King Charles Street
Parliament St.
Gt. George Street
Bridge St.
Storey's Gate
Birdcage Walk
Old Queen Street
Queen Anne's Gate
Tothill Street
St. Margaret's St.
Petty France
Broadway
Victoria Street
Buckingham Gate
Constitution Hill
Grosvenor Place

RESTAURANTS

Belgo Centraal	15
China City	25
Chowki	28
Ikkyu	2
J. Sheekey	29
La Trouvaille	18
Mr Kong	26
New World	27
Rasa Samudra	3
Spiga	19

PUBS AND BARS

Albert	34	Lamb & Flag	24
Argyll Arms	12	Museum Tavern	5
Denim	21	Na Zdrowie	8
Detroit	16	O'Conor Don	9
Dog & Duck	13	Princess Louise	7
Dog House	10	Punch & Judy	22
Dover Castle	1	Red Lion	33
Freedom Brewing Company	14	Salisbury	30
French House	20	The Social	6
ICA Bar	32	The Toucan	11
Jerusalem	4	Two Floors	23
Lab	17	Ye Grapes	31

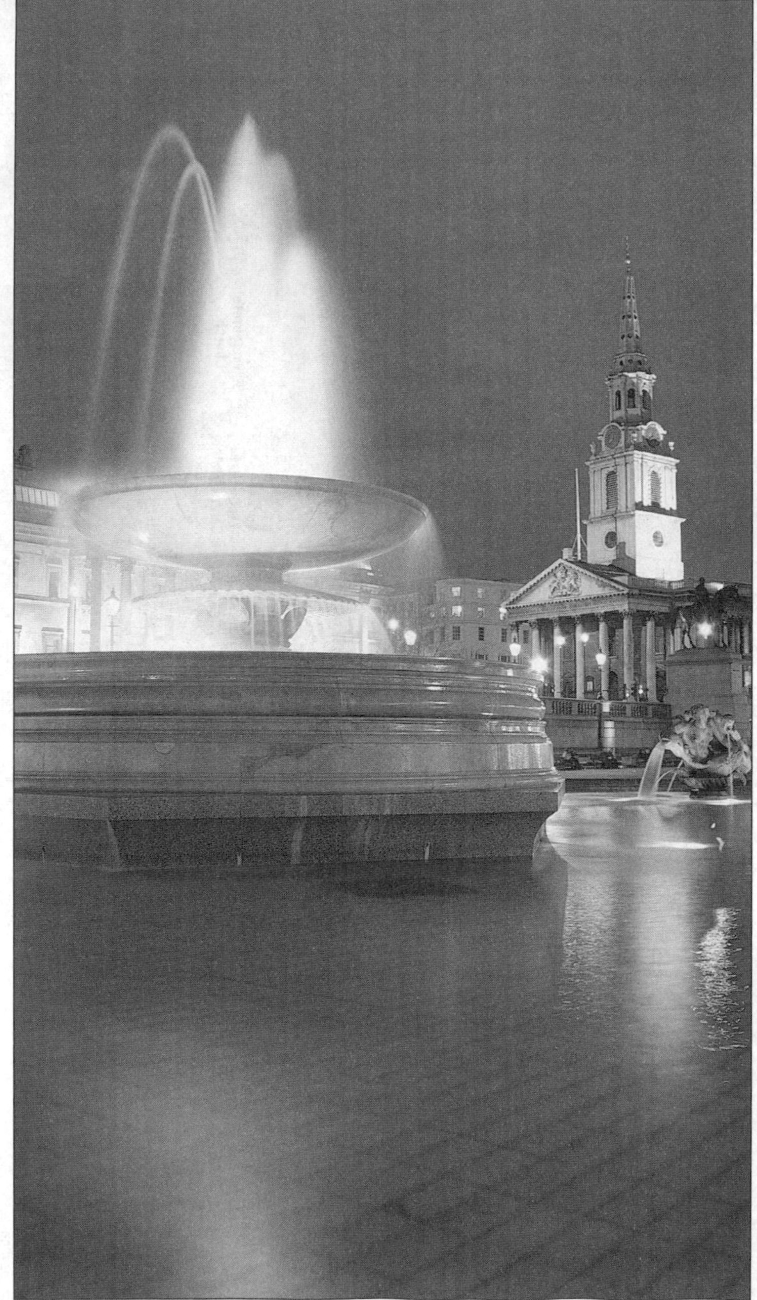

△ Trafalgar Square and St Martin-in-the-Fields

followed five years later by the square's central focal point, **Nelson's Column**, topped by the famous admiral; the very large bronze lions didn't arrive until 1868, and the fountains – a real rarity in a London square – didn't take their present shape until the late 1930s.

As one of the few large public squares in London, Trafalgar Square has been both a tourist attraction and a focus for **political demonstrations** since the Chartists assembled here in 1848 before marching to Kennington Common. On a more festive note, the square is graced each December with a giant Christmas tree, donated by Norway in thanks for liberation from the Nazis, and on **New Year's Eve**, thousands of inebriates sing in the New Year.

Stranded on a traffic island to the south of the column, and predating the entire square, is the **equestrian statue of Charles I**, erected shortly after the Restoration on the very spot where eight of those who had signed the king's death warrant were disembowelled. Charles's statue also marks the original site of the thirteenth-century **Charing Cross**, from where all distances from the capital are measured – a Victorian imitation now stands outside Charing Cross train station.

The northeastern corner of the square is occupied by James Gibbs's church of **St Martin-in-the-Fields** (Ⓦ www.stmartin-in-the-fields.org), fronted by a magnificent Corinthian portico and topped by an elaborate and distinctly unclassical tower and steeple. Completed in 1726, the interior is purposefully simple, though the Italian plasterwork on the barrel vaulting is exceptionally rich; it's best appreciated while listening to one of the church's free lunchtime concerts. There's a licensed café in the roomy **crypt**, not to mention a shop, gallery and brass-rubbing centre (Mon–Sat 10am–6pm, Sun noon–6pm).

The National Gallery

Unlike the Louvre or the Hermitage, the **National Gallery**, on the north side of Trafalgar Square (daily 10am–6pm, Wed until 8pm; free; Ⓦ www.nationalgallery.org.uk; Leicester Square or Charing Cross tube), is not based on a royal collection, but was begun as late as 1824 when the government bought 38 paintings belonging to a Russian emigre banker, John Julius Angerstein. The gallery's subsequent canny acquisition policy has resulted in more than 2300 paintings, but the collection's virtue is not so much its size, but the range, depth and sheer quality of its contents.

To view the collection chronologically, begin with the **Sainsbury Wing**, the softly-softly, postmodern 1980s adjunct that playfully imitates elements of the original gallery's Neoclassicism. However, with more than a thousand paintings on permanent display in the main galleries, you'll need real stamina to see everything in one day, so if time is tight your best bet is to home in on your areas of special interest, having picked up a gallery plan at one of the information desks. A welcome innovation is the **Gallery Guide Soundtrack**, with a brief audio commentary on a large selection of the paintings on display. The Soundtrack is available free of charge, though you're asked for a "voluntary contribution". Another possibility is to join up with one of the gallery's **free guided tours** (daily 11.30am & 2.30pm, plus Wed 6.30pm), which set off from the Sainsbury Wing foyer.

Among the National's **Italian** masterpieces are Leonardo's melancholic *Virgin of the Rocks*, Uccello's *Battle of San Romano*, Botticelli's *Venus and Mars* (inspired by a Dante sonnet) and Piero della Francesca's beautifully composed *Baptism of Christ*, one of his earliest works. The fine collection of Venetian works includes Titian's colourful early masterpiece *Bacchus and Ariadne*, his very late, much gloomier *Death of Acteon*, and Veronese's lustrous *Family of Darius before*

Alexander. Elsewhere, Bronzino's erotic *Venus, Cupid, Folly and Time* and Raphael's trenchant *Pope Julius II* keep company with Michelangelo's unfinished *Entombment*. Later Italian works to look out for include a couple by Caravaggio, a few splendid examples of Tiepolo's airy draughtsmanship and glittering vistas of Venice by Canaletto and Guardi.

From **Spain** there are dazzling pieces by El Greco, Goya, Murillo and Velázquez, among them the provocative *Rokeby Venus*. From the **Low Countries**, standouts include van Eyck's *Arnolfini Marriage*, Memlinc's perfectly poised *Donne Triptych*, and a couple of typically serene Vermeers. There are numerous genre paintings, such as Frans Hals' *Family Group in a Landscape*, and some superlative landscapes, most notably Hobbema's *Avenue, Middleharnis*. An array of Rembrandt paintings that features some of his most searching portraits – two of them self-portraits – is followed by abundant examples of Rubens' expansive, fleshy canvases.

Holbein's masterful *Ambassadors* and several of van Dyck's portraits were painted for the English court, and there's home-grown **British** art, too, represented by important works such as Hogarth's satirical *Marriage à la Mode*, Gainsborough's translucent *Morning Walk*, Constable's ever popular *Hay Wain*, and Turner's *Fighting Téméraire*. Highlights of the **French** contingent include superb works by Poussin, Claude, Fragonard, Boucher and Watteau, and the only two paintings in the country by David.

Finally, there's a particularly strong showing of **Impressionists** and **Post-Impressionists** in rooms 43–46 of the East Wing. Among the most famous works are Manet's unfinished *Execution of Maximilian*, Renoir's *Umbrellas*, Monet's *Thames below Westminster*, Van Gogh's *Sunflowers*, Seurat's pointillist *Bathers at Asnières*, a Rousseau junglescape, Cézanne's proto-Cubist *Bathers* and Picasso's Blue Period *Child with a Dove*.

The National Portrait Gallery

Around the east side of the National Gallery lurks the **National Portrait Gallery** (daily 10am–6pm, Thurs & Fri till 9pm; free; Ⓦwww.npg.org.uk; Leicester Square or Charing Cross tube), founded in 1856 to house uplifting depictions of the good and the great. Though it has some fine works in its collection, many of the studies are of less interest than their subjects, and the overall impression is of an overstuffed shrine to famous Brits rather than a museum offering any insight into the history of portraiture. However, it's fascinating to trace who has been deemed worthy of admiration at any moment: aristocrats and artists in previous centuries, warmongers and imperialists in the early decades of the twentieth century, writers and poets in the 1930s and 1940s, and, latterly, retired footballers, and film and pop stars.

The NPG's millennial extension has proved a great success, providing a bigger Tudor section, and a new contemporary gallery to expand the section that's by far the most popular. There's also a computer gallery, lecture theatre and rooftop café/restaurant with a view over the cityscape. The NPG's **Sound Guide**, which gives useful biographical background information to some of the pictures, is provided free of charge, though you're strongly invited to give a "voluntary contribution" of £3.

The Mall and St James's Park

The tree-lined sweep of **The Mall** is at its best on Sundays, when it's closed to traffic. It was laid out in the first decade of the twentieth century as a memorial to Queen Victoria, and runs from Trafalgar Square to Buckingham Palace.

The bombastic **Admiralty Arch** was erected to mark the entrance at the Trafalgar Square end of The Mall, while at the other end stands the ludicrous Victoria Memorial, Edward VII's overblown tribute to his mother.

Flanking nearly the whole length of the Mall, **St James's Park** is the oldest of the royal parks, having been drained and enclosed for hunting purposes by Henry VIII. It was landscaped by Nash in the 1820s, and today its tree-lined lake is a favourite picnic spot for the civil servants of Whitehall. Pelicans can still be seen at the eastern end of the lake, and there are ducks, swans and geese aplenty. From the bridge across the lake there's also a fine view over to Westminster and the jumble of domes and pinnacles along Whitehall.

Buckingham Palace

The graceless colossus of **Buckingham Palace** (Aug & Sept daily 9.30am–4.15pm; £12; Ⓦwww.royal.gov.uk; Green Park tube), popularly known as "Buck House", has served as the monarch's permanent London residence only since the accession of Victoria. It began its days in 1702 as the Duke of Buckingham's city residence, built on the site of a notorious brothel, and was sold by the duke's son to George III in 1762. The building was overhauled in the late 1820s by Nash and again in 1913, producing a palace that's as bland as it's possible to be.

For two months of the year, the hallowed portals are grudgingly nudged open; timed tickets are sold from the marquee-like box office in Green Park at the western end of The Mall – to avoid queuing, you must book in advance on Ⓣ020/7321 2233 or online. The interior, however, is a bit of an anticlimax: of the palace's 660 rooms you're permitted to see twenty or so, and there's little sign of life, as the Queen decamps to Scotland every summer. For the other

The Royal Family

Tourists may still flock to see London's royal palaces, but over the last decade the British public have become more critical of the huge tax bill that goes to support the **Royal Family** (Ⓦwww.royal.gov.uk) in the style to which they are accustomed. This creeping republicanism can be traced back to 1992, which the Queen herself, in one of her few memorable Christmas Day speeches, accurately described as her *annus horribilis*. This was the year that saw the marriage break-ups of Charles and Di, and Andrew and Fergie, and the second marriage of divorcee Princess Anne.

Matters came to a head, though, over who should pay the estimated £50 million costs of repairs after the fire at Windsor Castle (p.141). Misjudging the public mood, the Conservative government offered taxpayers' money to foot the entire bill. After a furore, it was agreed that some of the cost would be raised by opening up Buckingham Palace to the public for the first time (and by cranking up the admission charges on the rest of London's royal palaces). In addition, under pressure from the media, the Queen also reduced the number of royals paid out of the Civil List, and, for the first time in her life, agreed to pay taxes on her enormous personal fortune.

Given the mounting resentment of the Royal Family, it was hardly surprising that public opinion tended to side with Princess Diana rather than Prince Charles during their various disputes. Diana's subsequent death, and the huge outpouring of grief that accompanied her funeral, further damaged the reputation of the royals, though her demise has also meant the loss of the Royal Family's most vociferous critic. Despite the low poll ratings, none of the political parties currently advocates abolishing the monarchy, and public appetite for stories about the antics of the princes (and their potential girlfriends), or the latest on Charles and Camilla, shows few signs of abating.

ten months of the year there's little to do here – not that this deters the crowds who mill around the railings, and gather in some force to watch the **Changing of the Guard** (see below), in which a detachment of the Queen's Foot Guards marches to appropriate martial music from St James's Palace (unless it rains, that is).

The public can also pay through the nose to view a small portion of the Royal Collection, at the rebuilt **Queen's Gallery** (daily 10am–5.30pm; £6.50), on the south side of the palace. Exhibitions change regularly, drawn from a collection which is three times larger than the National Gallery, and includes masterpieces by Michelangelo, Reynolds, Gainsborough, Vermeer, van Dyck, Rubens, Rembrandt and Canaletto, as well as the odd Fabergé egg and heaps of Sèvres china.

There's more pageantry on show at the Nash-built **Royal Mews** (March–July & Oct daily 11am–4pm; Aug & Sept Mon–Sat 10am–5pm; £5; Victoria tube), further along Buckingham Palace Road. The royal carriages, lined up under a glass canopy in the courtyard, are the main attraction, in particular the Gold Carriage, made for George III in 1762, smothered in 22-carat gilding and weighing four tons, its axles supporting four life-size figures.

Whitehall

Whitehall, the broad avenue connecting Trafalgar Square to Parliament Square, is synonymous with the faceless, pinstriped bureaucracy charged with the day-to-day running of the country. Since the sixteenth century, nearly all the key governmental ministries and offices have migrated here, rehousing themselves on an ever-increasing scale. The statues dotted about Whitehall recall the days when this street stood at the centre of an empire on which the sun never set.

During the sixteenth and seventeenth centuries Whitehall was the permanent residence of the kings and queens of England, and was synonymous with royalty. The original **Whitehall Palace** was the London seat of the Archbishop of York, confiscated and greatly extended by Henry VIII after a fire at Westminster forced him to find alternative accommodation. The chief section of the old palace to survive the fire of 1698 was the **Banqueting House** (Mon–Sat 10am–5pm; £4; Ⓦ www.hrp.org.uk; Westminster tube), begun by Inigo Jones in 1619 and the first Palladian building to be built in England. The one room now open to the public has no original furnishings, but is well worth seeing

The Changing of the Guard

The Queen is colonel-in-chief of the seven **Household Regiments**: the Life Guards (who dress in red and white) and the Blues and Royals (who dress in blue and white) are the two Household Cavalry regiments; while the Grenadier, Coldstream, Scots, Irish and Welsh Guards make up the Foot Guards.

All these regiments still form part of the modern army as well as performing ceremonial functions such as the Changing of the Guard. If you're keen to find out more about the Foot Guards, pay a visit to the **Guards' Museum** (daily 10am–4pm; £2), in the Wellington Barracks on the south side of St James's Park.

The **Changing of the Guard** takes place at two separate locations in London: the two Household Cavalry regiments take it in turns to stand guard at Horse Guards on Whitehall (Mon–Sat 11am, Sun 10am, with inspection daily at 4pm), while the Foot Guards take care of Buckingham Palace (April–Aug daily 11.30am; Sept–March alternate days; no ceremony if it rains). A ceremony also takes place regularly at Windsor Castle (see p.141).

for the superlative Rubens ceiling paintings glorifying the Stuart dynasty, commissioned by Charles I in the 1630s. Charles himself walked through the room for the last time in 1649 when he stepped onto the executioner's scaffold from one of its windows.

Across the road, two mounted sentries of the Queen's Household Cavalry and two horseless colleagues, all in ceremonial uniform, are posted daily from 10am to 4pm. Ostensibly they are protecting the **Horse Guards** building, originally built as the old palace guard house, but now guarding nothing in particular. The mounted guards are changed hourly; those standing every two hours. Try to coincide your visit with the Changing of the Guard (see box opposite), when a squad of twelve mounted troops arrive in full livery.

Further down this west side of Whitehall is London's most famous address, **Number 10 Downing Street** (Ⓦwww.number-10.gov.uk; Westminster tube), the seventeenth-century terraced house that has been the residence of the prime minister since it was presented to Sir Robert Walpole, Britain's first PM, by George II in 1732. Facing the Downing Street gates, in the middle of the road, stands Edwin Lutyens' **Cenotaph**, eschewing any kind of Christian imagery, and inscribed simply with the words "The Glorious Dead". The memorial remains the focus of the Remembrance Sunday ceremony in November.

In 1938, in anticipation of Nazi air raids, the basements of the civil service buildings on the south side of King Charles Street, south of Downing Street, were converted into the **Cabinet War Rooms**, now open to the public (daily: April–Sept 9.30am–6pm; Oct–March 10am–6pm; £7; Ⓦwww.iwm.org.uk; Westminster tube). It was here that Winston Churchill directed operations and held Cabinet meetings for the duration of World War II and the rooms have been left pretty much as they were when they were finally abandoned on VJ Day 1945, making for an atmospheric underground trot through wartime London. The museum's free audioguide helps bring the place to life and includes various eyewitness accounts by folk who worked there.

The Houses of Parliament

Clearly visible at the south end of Whitehall is one of London's best-known monuments, the Palace of Westminster, better known as the **Houses of Parliament** (Ⓦwww.parliament.uk). The city's finest Victorian Gothic Revival building and symbol of a nation once confident of its place at the centre of the world, it's distinguished above all by the ornate, gilded clocktower popularly known as **Big Ben**, after the thirteen-ton main bell that strikes the hour (and is broadcast across the world by the BBC).

The original Westminster Palace was built by **Edward the Confessor** in the first half of the eleventh century, so that he could watch over the building of Westminster Abbey. It then served as the seat of all the English monarchs until a fire forced Henry VIII to decamp to Whitehall. The Lords have always convened at the palace, but it was only following Henry's death that the House of Commons moved from the abbey's Chapter House into the palace's St Stephen's Chapel, thus beginning the building's associations with parliament.

In 1834 the old palace burned down leaving the bare but impressive expanse of **Westminster Hall**, on the north side of the complex, as the chief relic of the medieval palace. Built by William Rufus in 1099, it's one of the most magnificent secular medieval halls in Europe – you get a glimpse of the hall en route to the public galleries. The **Jewel Tower** (daily: April–Sept 10am–6pm; Oct 10am–5pm; Nov–March 10am–4pm; £2; EH), across the road from parliament, is another remnant of the medieval palace, now housing an excellent exhibition on the history of parliament – worth visiting before you queue up to get into the Houses of Parliament.

To watch the proceedings in either the House of Commons or the Lords, simply join the queue for the **public galleries** (known as Strangers' Galleries) outside St Stephen's Gate. The public are let in slowly from about 4pm onwards on Mondays, from 1pm Tuesday to Thursday, and from 10am on Fridays; the security checks are very tight, and the whole procedure can take an hour or more. If you want to avoid the queues, turn up an hour or more later, when the crowds have usually thinned. Recesses (holiday closures) of both Houses occur at Christmas, Easter, and from August to the middle of October; phone ⓣ020/7219 4272 for more information.

To see **Question Time** (Mon 2.30–3.30pm, Tues–Thurs 11.30am–12.30pm) – when the House is at its most raucous and entertaining and the prime minister usually present – you really need to book a **ticket** several weeks in advance from your local MP (if you're a UK citizen) or your embassy in London (if you're not). For part of the summer recess (Aug & Sept), there are public **guided tours** of the building (Mon, Tues, Fri & Sat 9.15am–4.30pm, Wed & Thurs 1.15–4.30pm; £7), lasting an hour and fifteen minutes. Visitors can book in advance by phoning ⓣ08709/063773, or simply head for the ticket office on Abingdon Green, opposite Victoria Tower. The rest of the year, it's still possible to organize a tour of the building through your MP or embassy. It's also possible to arrange a free guided tour up **Big Ben** (Mon–Fri only; no under 11s; free), again through your MP or embassy; to find out more about access requirements, phone ⓣ020/7219 4862.

Westminster Abbey

The Houses of Parliament dwarf their much older neighbour, **Westminster Abbey** (Mon–Fri 9.30am–4.45pm, Wed also 6–7pm, Sat 9.30am–2.45pm; £6; ⓦwww.westminster-abbey.org; Westminster or St James's Park tube), yet this single building embodies much of the history of England: it has been the venue for all coronations since the time of William the Conqueror, and the site of more or less every royal burial for some five hundred years between the reigns of Henry III and George II. Scores of the nation's most famous citizens are honoured here, too (though many of the stones commemorate people buried elsewhere), and the interior is crammed with hundreds of monuments, reliefs and statues.

Entry is unfortunately via the north transept, cluttered with monuments to politicians and traditionally known as **Statesmen's Aisle**, shortly after which you come to the abbey's most dazzling architectural set-piece, the **Lady Chapel**, added by Henry VII in 1503 as his future resting place. With its intricately carved vaulting and fan-shaped gilded pendants, the chapel represents the final spectacular gasp of the English Perpendicular style. The public are no longer admitted to the **Shrine of Edward the Confessor**, the sacred heart of the building (except on a guided verger tour; £3) though you do get to inspect Edward I's **Coronation Chair**, a decrepit oak throne dating from around 1300 and still used for coronations.

Nowadays, the abbey's royal tombs are upstaged by **Poets' Corner**, in the south transept, though the first occupant, Geoffrey Chaucer, was in fact buried here not because he was a poet, but because he lived nearby. By the eighteenth century this zone had become an artistic pantheon, and since then, the transept has been filled with tributes to all shades of talent. From the south transept, you can view the central sanctuary, site of the coronations, and the wonderful **Cosmati floor mosaic**, constructed in the thirteenth century by Italian craftsmen, and often covered by a carpet to protect it.

Doors in the south choir aisle lead to the **Great Cloisters** (daily 8am–6pm), rebuilt after a fire in 1298 and now home to a café. At the eastern end of the cloisters lies the octagonal **Chapter House** (daily: April–Sept 9.30am–5pm; Oct 10am–5pm; Nov–March 10am–4pm; £1; EH), where the House of Commons met from 1257. The thirteenth-century decorative paving-tiles and wall-paintings have survived intact. Chapter House tickets include entry to the **Undercroft Museum** (daily 10.30am–4pm), filled with generations of bald royal death masks and wax effigies.

It's only after exploring the cloisters that you get to see the **nave** itself: narrow, light and, at over a hundred feet in height, by far the tallest in the country. The most famous monument in this section is the **Tomb of the Unknown Soldier**, by the west door, which now serves as the main exit.

Tate Britain

Tate Britain (daily 10am–5.50pm; free; Ⓦwww.tate.org.uk; Pimlico tube), the purpose-built gallery half a mile south of parliament, founded in 1897 with money from Henry Tate, inventor of the sugar cube, is now devoted exclusively to British art. As well as the collection covering from 1500 to the present and a whole wing devoted to Turner, Tate Britain also showcases contemporary British artists and continues to sponsor the Turner Prize, the country's most prestigious modern-art prize.

The galleries are rehung more or less annually, but always include a fair selection of works by British artists such as Hogarth, Constable, Gainsborough, Reynolds and Blake, plus foreign artists like van Dyck who spent much of their career over here. The ever-popular **Pre-Raphaelites** are always well represented, as are established twentieth-century greats such as Stanley Spencer and Francis Bacon alongside living artists such as David Hockney and Lucien Freud. Lastly, don't miss the Tate's outstanding **Turner collection**, displayed in the Clore Gallery.

Westminster Cathedral

Halfway down Victoria Street, which runs southwest from Westminster Abbey, you'll find one of London's most surprising churches, the stripey neo-Byzantine concoction of the Roman Catholic **Westminster Cathedral** (Mon–Fri & Sun 7am–7pm, Sat 8am–7pm; free; Ⓦwww.rcdow.org.uk; Victoria tube). Begun in 1895, and thus one of the last and wildest monuments to the Victorian era, it's constructed from more than twelve million terracotta-coloured bricks, decorated with hoops of Portland stone, and culminating in a magnificent tapered campanile which rises to 274 feet, served by a lift (April–Nov daily 9.30am–12.30pm & 1–5pm; Dec–March Thurs–Sun only; £2). The **interior** is only half finished, so to get an idea of what the place will look like when it's finally completed, explore the series of **side chapels** whose rich, multicoloured decor makes use of over one hundred different marbles from around the world.

St James's, Mayfair and Marylebone

St James's, **Mayfair** and **Marylebone** emerged in the late seventeenth century as London's first real suburbs, characterized by grid-plan streets feeding into grand, formal squares. This expansion set the westward trend for middle-class migration, and as London's wealthier consumers moved west, so too did the city's more upmarket shops and luxury hotels, which are still a feature of the area.

Aristocratic **St James's**, the rectangle of land to the north of St James's Park, was one of the first areas to be developed and remains the preserve of the seriously rich. **Piccadilly**, which forms the border between St James's and Mayfair, is no longer the fashionable promenade it once was, but a whiff of exclusivity still pervades **Bond Street** and its tributaries. **Regent Street** was created as a new "Royal Mile", a tangible borderline to shore up these new fashionable suburbs against the chaotic maze of Soho and the City, where the working population still lived. Now, along with **Oxford Street**, it has become London's busiest shopping district – it's here that Londoners mean when they talk of "going shopping up the West End".

Marylebone, which lies to the north of Oxford Street, is another grid-plan Georgian development, a couple of social and real-estate leagues below Mayfair, but a wealthy area nevertheless. It boasts a very fine art gallery, the **Wallace Collection**, and, in its northern fringes, one of London's biggest tourist attractions, **Madame Tussaud's**, the oldest and largest wax museum in the world.

St James's

St James's, the exclusive little enclave sandwiched between The Mall and Piccadilly, was laid out in the 1670s close to St James's Palace. Royal and aristocratic residences predominate along its southern border, gentlemen's clubs cluster along Pall Mall and St James's Street, while jacket-and-tie restaurants and expense-account gentlemen's outfitters line Jermyn Street. Hardly surprising then that most Londoners rarely stray into this area. St James's does, however, contain some interesting architectural set pieces, such as **Waterloo Place**, at the centre of which stands the Guards' Crimean Memorial, fashioned from captured Russian cannon and featuring a statue of Florence Nightingale. Clearly visible, beyond, is the "Grand Old" **Duke of York's Column**, erected in 1833, ten years before Nelson's more famous one in Trafalgar Square.

Cutting across Waterloo Place, **Pall Mall** – named after the croquet-like game of *paglio a maglio* (literally "ball and mallet") that was popular at the time – leads west to **St James's Palace**, whose main red-brick gate-tower is pretty much all that remains of the Tudor palace erected here by Henry VIII. When Whitehall Palace burned down in 1698, St James's became the principal royal residence and, in keeping with tradition, an ambassador to the UK is still known as "Ambassador to the Court of St James", even though the court moved down the road to Buckingham Palace when Queen Victoria ascended the throne. The rambling, crenellated complex is off limits to the public, with the exception of the **Chapel Royal** (Oct to Good Friday Sun 8.30am & 11.15am; Green Park tube), situated within the palace, and the **Queen's Chapel** (Easter–July Sun 8.30am & 11.15am; Green Park tube), on the other side of Marlborough Road; both are open for services only.

Clarence House, connected to the palace's southwest wing, was home to the Queen Mother, and now provides a bachelor pad for **Prince Charles** (Ⓦwww.princeofwales.gov.uk); the public was allowed to view the five rooms on the ground floor used for official receptions for the first time in the summer of 2003, so it's worth enquiring about further public openings. An even more palatial St James's residence is Princess Diana's ancestral home, **Spencer House** (Feb–July & Sept–Dec Sun 10.30am–5.45pm; £6), a superb Palladian mansion erected in the 1750s. Inside, tour guides take you through nine of the state rooms, the most outrageous of which is Lord Spencer's Room, with its astonishing gilded palm-tree columns. Note that children under 10 are not admitted.

Piccadilly Circus and Regent Street

Anonymous and congested it may be, but **Piccadilly Circus** is, for many Londoners, the nearest their city comes to having a centre. A much-altered product of Nash's grand 1812 Regent Street plan and now a major traffic bottleneck, it may not be a picturesque place, but thanks to its celebrated aluminium statue, popularly known as **Eros**, it's prime tourist territory. The fountain's archer is one of the city's top attractions, a status that baffles all who live here. Despite the bow and arrow, it's not the god of love at all but the *Angel of Christian Charity*, erected to commemorate the Earl of Shaftesbury, a bible-thumping social reformer who campaigned against child labour.

Regent Street, leading north off Piccadilly Circus, is reminiscent of one of Haussmann's Parisian boulevards without the trees. Drawn up by John Nash in 1812 as both a luxury shopping street and a triumphal way between George IV's Carlton House and Regent's Park, it was the city's earliest attempt at dealing with traffic congestion, and also the first stab at slum clearance and planned social segregation, which would later be perfected by the Victorians.

Despite the subsequent destruction of much of Nash's work in the 1920s, it's still possible to admire the stately intentions of his original Regent Street plan. The increase in the purchasing power of the city's middle classes in the last century brought the tone of the street "down" and heavyweight stores catering for the masses now predominate. Among the best known are **Hamley's**, reputedly the world's largest toyshop, and **Liberty**, the department store that popularized Arts and Crafts designs in the early 1900s.

Piccadilly

Piccadilly apparently got its name from the ruffs or "pickadills" worn by the dandies who used to promenade here in the late seventeenth century. Despite its fashionable pedigree, it's no place for promenading in its current state, with traffic careering down it nose to tail most of the day and night. Infinitely more pleasant places to window-shop are the **nineteenth-century arcades**, originally built to protect shoppers from the mud and horse-dung on the streets, but now equally useful for escaping exhaust fumes.

Piccadilly may not be the shopping heaven it once was, but there are still several old firms here that proudly display their royal warrants. One of the oldest institutions is the food emporium of **Fortnum & Mason** (Ⓦwww.fortnumandmason.com) at no. 181, established in the 1770s by one of George III's footmen, Charles Fortnum, and his partner, Hugh Mason. In a kitsch addition dating from 1964, the figures of Fortnum and Mason bow to each other on the hour every day as the clock over the main entrance clanks out the Eton school anthem.

Further along Piccadilly, with its best rooms overlooking Green Park, stands the **Ritz Hotel** (Ⓦwww.theritzhotel.co.uk), a byword for decadence since it first wowed Edwardian society in 1906; the hotel's design, with its two-storey French-style mansard roof and long arcade, was based on the buildings of Paris's Rue de Rivoli. For a prolonged look inside, you'll need to be in good appetite, dress appropriately, and book in advance, for the famous afternoon tea in the hotel's Palm Court.

Across the road from Fortnum & Mason, the **Royal Academy of Arts** (daily 10am–6pm, Fri until 10pm; £7–9; Ⓦwww.royalacademy.org.uk; Green Park or Piccadilly Circus tube) occupies the enormous Burlington House, one of the few survivors from the ranks of aristocratic mansions that once lined the north side of Piccadilly. The Academy itself was the country's first-ever formal art school, founded in 1768 by a group of English painters including Thomas Gainsborough and Joshua Reynolds. The Academy hosts a wide range of art exhibitions, and an annual **Summer Exhibition** that remains a stop on the social calendar of upper middle-class England. Anyone can enter paintings in any style, and the lucky winners get hung, in rather close proximity, and sold. Supposed gravitas is added by the RA "Academicians", who are allowed to display six of their own works – no matter how awful. The result is a bewildering display, which gets panned annually by highbrow critics.

Along the west side of the Royal Academy runs **Burlington Arcade**, built in 1819 and Piccadilly's longest and most expensive nineteenth-century arcade, lined with mahogany-fronted jewellers, gentlemen's outfitters and the like. Upholding Regency decorum, it is still illegal to whistle, sing, hum, hurry or carry large packages or open umbrellas on this small stretch, and the arcade's beadles (known as Burlington Berties), in their Edwardian frock-coats and gold-braided top hats, take the prevention of such criminality very seriously.

Bond Street

While Oxford Street, Regent Street and Piccadilly have all gone downmarket, **Bond Street**, which runs parallel with Regent Street, has carefully maintained its exclusivity. It is, in fact, two streets rolled into one: the southern half, laid out in the 1680s, is known as Old Bond Street; its northern extension, which followed less than fifty years later, is known as New Bond Street. They are both pretty unassuming streets architecturally, yet the shops that line them, and those of neighbouring Conduit Street and South Molton Street, are among the flashiest in London, dominated by perfumeries, **jewellers** and designer clothing stores, including Versace, Gucci, Nicole Farhi and Yves St-Laurent. In addition to fashion, Bond Street is also renowned for its fine art galleries and its **auction houses**, the oldest of which is Sotheby's, 34–35 New Bond St (Ⓦwww.sothebys.com), whose viewing galleries are open free of charge.

Handel House Museum

The German-born composer **George Frideric Handel** (1685–1759) spent the best part of his life in London, producing all the work for which he is now best known at 25 Brook Street, just west of New Bond Street, now the **Handel House Museum** (Tues–Sat 10am–6pm, Thurs till 8pm, Sun noon–6pm; £4.50; Ⓦwww.handelhouse.org). The composer used the ground floor as a sort of shop where subscribers could buy scores, while the first floor was employed as a rehearsal room. Although containing few original artefacts, the house has been painstakingly reconstructed and redecorated to show how it would have looked in Handel's day. Further atmosphere is provided by the harpsichord in the rehearsal room, which gets played by music students throughout the week, and with more formal performances on Thursday evenings from 6pm. Access to the house is via the chic, cobbled yard at the back.

Oxford Street and around

As wealthy Londoners began to move out of the City in the eighteenth century in favour of the newly developed West End, so **Oxford Street** (Ⓦwww.oxfordstreet.co.uk) – the old Roman road to Oxford – gradually became London's main shopping thoroughfare. Today, despite successive recessions and sky-high rents, this scruffy, two-mile hotchpotch of shops is still probably England's busiest street, and is home to (often several) flagship branches of Britain's major retailers (see p.161). The street's only real landmark store is Selfridge's, opened in 1909 with a facade featuring the Queen of Time riding the ship of commerce and supporting an Art Deco clock.

The Wallace Collection

Immediately north of Oxford Street, on Manchester Square, stands Hertford House, a miniature eighteenth-century French chateau which holds the splendid **Wallace Collection** (Mon–Sat 10am–5pm, Sun noon–5pm; free; ⓣ020/7563 9500, ⓦwww.wallacecollection.org), a museum-gallery best known for its eighteenth-century French paintings (especially Watteau), Franz Hals' *Laughing Cavalier*, Titian's *Perseus and Andromeda*, Velázquez's *Lady with a Fan* and Rembrandt's affectionate portrait of his teenage son, Titus. There's a modern café in the newly glassed-over courtyard, but at heart, the Wallace Collection remains an old-fashioned place, with exhibits piled high in glass cabinets, and paintings covering every inch of wall space. The fact that these exhibits are set amidst period fittings – and a bloody great armoury – makes the place even more remarkable. If you're here for the paintings, head for the Great Gallery on the first floor, where the best of the works are hung.

Madame Tussaud's and the Planetarium

Madame Tussaud's (Mon–Fri 10am–6pm, Sat & Sun 9am–6pm; school holidays daily 9am–6pm; tickets from £14.99; ⓣ08704/003000, ⓦwww.madame-tussauds.co.uk; Baker Street tube), just up Marylebone Road from Baker Street tube, has been pulling in the crowds ever since the good lady arrived in London from Paris in 1802 bearing the sculpted heads of guillotined aristocrats (she herself only just managed to escape the same fate – her uncle, who started the family business, was less fortunate). The entrance fee might be extortionate, the likenesses occasionally dubious and the automated dummies inept, but you can still rely on finding London's biggest queues here. The only way to avoid joining the line is to pay extra and book a timed entry ticket in advance over the phone or on the Internet.

As well as the usual parade of wax figures, the tour ends with a manic five-minute "ride" through the history of London in a miniaturized taxi. Tickets for Madame Tussaud's also cover entry to the adjoining and equally crowded **London Planetarium** (ⓦwww.london-planetarium.com), which features a twenty-minute high-tech presentation projected onto a giant dome; a quick romp through the cosmos accompanied by astro-babble commentary.

Soho

Soho gives you the best and worst of London: the porn joints that proliferated from the mid-1960s onwards still have a strong presence, but the area also boasts a lively fruit and vegetable market and a nightlife that has attracted writers and ravers of every sexual persuasion since the eighteenth century. The area's most recent transformation took place in the 1990s, when it became Europe's leading gay centre, with bars and cafés bursting out from the Old Compton Street area. Despite regeneration, it has retained an unorthodox and slightly raffish air, born of an immigrant history as rich as that of the East End (see p.110).

Bounded by Regent Street to the west, Oxford Street to the north and Charing Cross Road to the east, Soho remains very much the heart of London and one of the capital's most diverse and characterful areas. Conventional sights are few and far between, yet it's a great area to wander through, with probably more streetlife than anywhere else in London – whatever hour you wander through, there's always something going on. Most folk head here to visit one of the big movie houses on **Leicester Square**, to drink in the latest hip bar or to grab a bite to eat at the innumerable cafés and restaurants, ranging from the inexpensive Chinese places that pepper the tiny enclave of **Chinatown**, to exclusive, Michelin-starred establishments in the backstreets.

Leicester Square and Chinatown

By night, when the big cinemas and discos are doing good business, and the buskers are entertaining the crowds, **Leicester Square** is one of the most crowded places in London, particularly on a Friday or Saturday when huge numbers of tourists and half the youth of the suburbs seem to congregate here. It wasn't until the mid-nineteenth century that the square actually began to emerge as an entertainment zone; cinema moved in during the 1930s, a golden age evoked by the sleek black lines of the Odeon on the east side, and maintains its grip on the area. The Empire, on the north side, is the favourite for the big royal premieres and, in a rather half-hearted imitation of the Hollywood (and Cannes) tradition, there are hand prints visible in the pavement by the southwestern corner of the square.

Chinatown, hemmed in between Leicester Square and Shaftesbury Avenue, is a self-contained jumble of shops, cafés and restaurants that makes up one of London's most distinct and popular ethnic enclaves. **Gerrard Street**, Chinatown's main drag, has been endowed with ersatz touches – telephone kiosks rigged out as pagodas and fake oriental gates – though few of London's 60,000 Chinese actually live in the three small blocks of Chinatown. Nonetheless, it remains a focus for the community, a place to do business or the weekly shopping, celebrate a wedding, or just meet up for meals, particularly on Sundays, when the restaurants overflow with Chinese families tucking into *dim sum*.

Old Compton Street

If Soho has a main drag, it has to be **Old Compton Street**, which runs parallel with Shaftesbury Avenue. The corner shops, peep shows, boutiques and trendy cafés here are typical of the area and a good barometer of the latest fads. Soho has been a permanent fixture on the **gay scene** for the better part of a

Carnaby Street

Until the 1950s, **Carnaby Street** (Ⓦwww.carnaby.co.uk) was a backstreet on Soho's western fringe, occupied, for the most part, by sweatshop tailors who used to make up the suits for nearby Savile Row. Then, sometime in the mid-1950s, several trendy boutiques opened catering for the new market in flamboyant men's clothing. In 1964 – the year of the official birth of the Carnaby Street myth – Mods, West Indian Rude Boys and other "switched-on people", as the *Daily Telegraph* noted, began to hang out here. The area quickly became the epicentre of Swinging Sixties' London, and its street sign London's most popular postcard. A victim of its own hype, Carnaby Street declined equally quickly into an avenue of overpriced tack. More recently, the street has been smartened up, along with neighbouring Newburgh Street, where contemporary London fashion now has a firm foothold, and the whole area is enjoying a new lease of life, though it's never going to recapture the excitement of the 1960s.

century, but the approach is much more upfront nowadays, with gay bars, clubs and cafés jostling for position on Old Compton Street and round the corner in Wardour Street.

The streets round here are lined with Soho institutions past and present. One of the best known is London's longest-running jazz club, *Ronnie Scott's*, on Frith Street, founded in 1958 and still capable of pulling in the big names. Opposite is *Bar Italia*, an Italian café with late-night hours popular with Soho's clubbers. It was in this building, appropriately enough for such a media-saturated area, that John Logie Baird made the world's first public television transmission in 1926.

Bloomsbury

Bloomsbury gets its name from its medieval landowners, the Blemunds, though nothing was built here until the 1660s. Through marriage, the Russell family, the earls and later dukes of Bedford, acquired much of the land and established the many formal, bourgeois squares which are the main distinguishing feature of the area. The Russells named the grid-plan streets after their various titles and estates, and kept the pubs and shops to a minimum to maintain the tone of the neighbourhood.

In the twentieth century, Bloomsbury acquired a reputation as the city's most learned quarter, dominated by the dual institutions of the **British Museum** and **London University**, and home to many of London's chief book publishers, but perhaps best known for its literary inhabitants. Today, the British Museum is clearly the star attraction, but there are other sights, such as the **Dickens House Museum**, that are high on many people's itineraries.

In its northern fringes, the character of the area changes dramatically, becoming steadily seedier as you near the two big train stations of **Euston** and **King's Cross**, where cheap B&Bs and run-down council estates provide fertile territory for prostitutes and drug dealers, and an unlikely location for the new **British Library**.

The British Museum

The **British Museum** (Mon–Wed, Sat & Sun 10am–5.30pm, Thurs & Fri 10am–8.30pm; free; Ⓦwww.british-museum.ac.uk; Russell Square, Tottenham Court Road or Holborn tube) is one of the great museums of the world. With seventy thousand exhibits ranged over two and a half miles of galleries, the museum boasts one of the largest and most comprehensive collections of antiquities, prints and drawings to be housed under one roof – seven million at the last count (a number increasing daily with the stream of new acquisitions, discoveries and bequests). Its assortment of Roman and Greek art is unparalleled, its Egyptian collection is the most significant outside Egypt and, in addition, there are fabulous treasures from Anglo-Saxon and Roman Britain, from China, Japan, India and Mesopotamia – not to mention an enormous collection of prints and drawings, only a fraction of which can be displayed at any one time.

The building itself, begun in 1823, is the grandest of London's Greek Revival edifices, dominated by the giant Ionian colonnade and portico that forms the main entrance. The British Library's departure to St Pancras (see p.93) allowed the museum to open up and redevelop the building's **Great Court** (Mon–Wed, Sat & Sun 9am–6pm, Thurs & Fri 9am–11pm), which now features a remarkable, curving glass-and-steel roof, designed by Norman Foster.

At the centre stands the copper-domed former **Round Reading Room**, built in the 1850s to house the British Library. It was here, reputedly at desk O7, beneath one of the largest domes in the world, that Karl Marx penned *Das Kapital*. The building is now a public study area, and features a multimedia guide to the museum's displays.

You'll never manage to see everything in one visit, so the best advice is to concentrate on one or two areas of interest, or else sign up with one of the museum's **guided tours**. One place you could start is the BM's collection of **Roman and Greek antiquities**, perhaps most famous for the Parthenon sculptures, better known as the **Elgin Marbles**, after the British aristocrat who walked off with the reliefs in 1801. Amidst the plethora of Greek and Roman statuary and vases, the only other single item with a similarly high profile is the **Portland Vase**, made from cobalt-blue blown glass around the beginning of the first century, and decorated with opaque white cameos.

The **Egyptian collection** ranges from monumental sculptures, such as the colossal granite head of Amenophis III, to the ever-popular **mummies** and their ornate outer caskets. Also on display is the **Rosetta Stone**, which finally unlocked the secret of Egyptian hieroglyphs. Close by the Egyptian Hall, you'll find a splendid series of **Assyrian reliefs** from Nineveh, depicting events such as the royal lion hunts of Ashurbanipal, in which the king slaughters one of the cats with his bare hands. Among the most extraordinary artefacts from **Mesopotamia** are the enigmatic Ram in the Thicket (a lapis lazuli and shell statuette of a goat) and an equally mysterious box known as the Standard of Ur.

The leathery half-corpse of the 2000-year-old **Lindow Man**, discovered in a Cheshire bog, and the Anglo-Saxon treasure from the **Sutton Hoo** ship burial, are among the highlights of the prehistoric and Romano-British section. The medieval and modern collections, meanwhile, range from the twelfth-century Lewis chessmen, carved from walrus ivory, to twentieth-century exhibits such as a copper vase by Frank Lloyd Wright.

The dramatically lit Mexican and North American galleries, plus the African galleries in the basement, mark the beginning of the return of the museum's **ethnographic collection** (formerly housed in the Museum of Mankind), while select works from the BM's enormous collection of **prints and drawings** can be seen in special exhibitions. In addition, there are fabulous **Oriental treasures** in the north wing, closest to the back entrance on Montague Place. The displays include ancient Chinese porcelain, ornate snuffboxes, miniature landscapes, a bewildering array of Buddhist and Hindu gods, and – the showpiece of the collection – dazzling limestone reliefs from the second-century stupa of Amaravati in south India.

Dickens House

Despite the plethora of blue plaques marking the residences of local luminaries, **Dickens House** (Mon–Sat 10am–5pm, Sun 11am–5pm; £4; Ⓦ www.dickensmuseum.com), at 48 Doughty St, in Bloomsbury's eastern fringes, is the area's only literary museum. Dickens moved here in 1837 shortly after his marriage to Catherine Hogarth, and they lived here for two years, during which time he wrote *Nicholas Nickleby* and *Oliver Twist*. This is the only one of Dickens' fifteen London addresses to survive intact, but only the drawing room, in which Dickens entertained his literary friends, has been restored to its original Regency style. Letters, manuscripts and lots of memorabilia, including first editions, the earliest known portrait and the annotated books he used during extensive lecture tours, are the rewards for those with more than a passing interest in the novelist.

The University

London has more students than any other city in the world (over half a million at the last count), which isn't bad going for somewhere that only organized its own **University** in 1826 (Ⓦwww.lon.ac.uk; Russell Square, Euston Square or Goodge Street tube), more than six hundred years after the likes of Oxford and Cambridge. The university started life in Bloomsbury, but it wasn't until after World War I that the institution really began to take over the area.

The university's piecemeal development means that its departments are spread over a wide area, though the main focus is between the 1930s **Senate House** skyscraper, behind the British Museum, and the Neoclassical **University College** (UCL; Ⓦwww.ucl.ac.uk), near the top of Gower Street. UCL is home to London's most famous art school, the **Slade**, which puts on temporary exhibitions from its collection in the **Strang Print Room**, in the south cloister of the main quadrangle (term time Wed–Fri 1–5pm; free). Also on display in the south cloisters is the fully clothed skeleton of philosopher **Jeremy Bentham** (1748–1832), one of the university's founders, topped by a wax head and wide-brimmed hat.

The university also runs a couple of specialist museums. On the first floor of the D.M.S. Watson building on Malet Place, a tiny side street opposite Waterstone's bookshop on Torrington Place, the **Petrie Museum of Egyptian Archaeology** (Tues–Fri 1–5pm, Sat 10am–1pm; free; Ⓦwww.petrie.ucl.ac.uk) has a couple of rooms jam-packed with antiquities, including the world's oldest dress. Further east down Torrington Place, tucked away in the southeast corner of Gordon Square, at no. 53, the **Percival David Foundation of Chinese Art** (Mon–Fri 10.30am–5pm; free; Ⓦwww.pdfmuseum.org.uk) houses two floors of top-notch Chinese ceramics. Lastly, the temporary exhibitions of photography and art at the **Brunei Gallery** (Mon–Fri 10.30am–5pm; free), which is part of the School of Oriental and African Studies, east of Malet Street, are usually well worth visiting.

The British Library

The new **British Library** (Mon & Wed–Fri 9.30am–6pm, Tues 9.30am–8pm, Sat 9.30am–5pm, Sun 11am–5pm; free; Ⓦwww.bl.uk; King's Cross or Euston tube), located on the busy Euston Road on the northern fringes of Bloomsbury, opened to the public in 1998. As the country's most expensive public building it was hardly surprising that the place drew fierce criticism from all sides. Architecturally the charge was led, predictably enough, by Prince Charles, who compared it to an academy for secret policemen. Yet while it's true that the building's red-brick brutalism is horribly out of fashion, and compares unfavourably with its cathedralesque Victorian neighbour, the former *Midland Grand Hotel*, the interior of the library has met with general approval, and the high-tech exhibition galleries are superb.

With the exception of the reading rooms, the library is open to the general public. The three exhibition galleries are to the left as you enter; straight ahead is the spiritual heart of the BL, a multistorey glass-walled tower housing the vast **King's Library**, collected by George III, and donated to the museum by George IV in 1823; to the side of the King's Library are the pull-out draws of the **philatelic collection**. If you want to explore the parts of the building not normally open to the public, you must sign up for a **guided tour** (Mon, Wed

& Fri 3pm, Sat 10.30am & 3pm; £6; or Sun 11.30am & 3pm if you want to see the reading rooms; £7).

The first of the three exhibition galleries to head for is the dimly lit **John Ritblat Gallery**, where a superlative selection of the BL's ancient manuscripts, maps, documents and precious books, including the richly illustrated Lindisfarne Gospels, are displayed. One of the most appealing innovations is "**Turning the Pages**", a small room off the main gallery, where you can turn the pages of selected texts "virtually" on a computer terminal. The **Workshop of Words, Sounds and Images** is a hands-on exhibition of more universal appeal, where you can design your own literary publication, while the **Pearson Gallery of Living Words** puts on excellent temporary exhibitions, for which there is sometimes an admission charge.

Covent Garden and the Strand

Covent Garden's transformation from a workaday fruit and vegetable market into a fashion-conscious *quartier* is one of the most miraculous and enduring developments of the 1980s. More sanitized and brazenly commercial than neighbouring Soho, it's a far cry from the district's heyday when the piazza was the great playground (and red-light district) of eighteenth-century London. The buskers in front of St Paul's Church, the theatres round about, and the **Royal Opera House** on Bow Street are survivors in this tradition, and on a balmy summer evening, **Covent Garden Piazza** is still an undeniably lively place to be. Another positive side-effect of the market development has been the renovation of the run-down warehouses to the north of the piazza, especially around the Neal Street area, which now boasts some of the most fashionable shops in the West End, selling everything from shoes to skateboards.

As its name suggests, the **Strand**, just to the south of Covent Garden, once lay along the riverbank: it achieved its present-day form when the Victorians shored up the banks of the Thames to create the Embankment. The Strand's most intriguing sight is **Somerset House**, the sole survivor of the street's grandiose river palaces, which now houses several museums and galleries as well as a lovely new fountain courtyard.

Covent Garden Piazza

London's oldest planned square, laid out in the 1630s by Inigo Jones, **Covent Garden Piazza** was initially a great success, its novelty value alone attracting a rich and aristocratic clientele, but over the next century the tone of the place fell as the fruit and vegetable market expanded, and theatres and coffee houses began to take over the peripheral buildings. When the market closed in 1974, the piazza narrowly survived being turned into an office development. Instead, the elegant Victorian market hall and its environs were restored to house shops, restaurants and arts-and-crafts stalls.

Of Jones's original piazza, the only remaining parts are the two rebuilt sections of north-side arcading, and **St Paul's Church**, facing the west side of the market building. The proximity of so many theatres has earned it the nickname of the "Actors' Church", and it's filled with memorials to international thespians from Boris Karloff to Gracie Fields. The space in front of the church's Tuscan portico – where Eliza Doolittle was discovered selling violets by Henry Higgins in George Bernard Shaw's *Pygmalion* – is now a legalized venue for buskers and street performers, who must audition for a slot months in advance.

The piazza's museums

A former flower-market shed on the piazza's east side is now home to the **London Transport Museum** (Mon–Thurs, Sat & Sun 10am–6pm, Fri 11am–6pm; £5.95; Ⓦwww.ltmuseum.co.uk). A herd of old buses, trains and trams make up the bulk of the exhibits, though there's enough interactive fun – touch-screen computers and the odd costumed conductor and vehicles to climb on – to keep most children amused. There's usually a good smattering of London Transport's stylish maps and posters on display, too, and you can buy reproductions, plus countless other LT paraphernalia, at the shop on the way out.

The rest of the old flower market now houses the **Theatre Museum** (Tues–Sun 10am–6pm; free; Ⓦwww.theatremuseum.org; entrance on Russell Street), displaying three centuries of memorabilia from every conceivable area of the performing arts in the West. The corridors of glass cases cluttered with props, programmes and costumes are not especially exciting, but the special exhibitions and long-term "temporary" shows tend to be a lot more fun, and usually have a performance, workshop or hands-on element to them. The museum also runs a booking service for West End shows and has an unusually good selection of cards and posters.

The Royal Opera House

The arcading on the northeast side of the piazza was rebuilt as part of the recent redevelopment of the **Royal Opera House** (Ⓦwww.royaloperahouse.org), whose main Neoclassical facade dates from 1811 and opens onto Bow Street. Now, however, you can reach the opera house from a passageway in the corner of the arcading. The spectacular wrought-iron **Floral Hall** (daily 10am–3pm) serves as the opera house's main foyer, and is open to the public, as is the *Amphitheatre* bar/restaurant (from one and a half hours before performance to the end of the last interval), which has a glorious terrace overlooking the piazza. Backstage tours of the opera house take place from Monday to Saturday (10.30am, 12.30 & 2.30pm; £7).

Strand

Once famous for its riverside mansions, and later its music halls, the **Strand** – the main road connecting Westminster to the City – is a shadow of its former self. Nowadays, it's best known for the young homeless who shelter in the shop doorways at night.

One such doorway, at no. 440, belongs to what was once London's largest private bank, **Coutts & Co** (Ⓦwww.coutts.com), whose customers include the Queen herself. It was founded in 1692 by the Scottish goldsmith, John Campbell, a mock-up of whose original premises stands behind a screen in the bank's concrete and marble atrium. Today's male employees still sport anachronistic tail-coated suits, but the horse-drawn carriage which used to convey royal correspondence was sadly taken out of service in 1993.

Some way further east on the opposite side of the Strand, the blind side street of Savoy Court – the only street in the country where the traffic drives on the right – leads to **The Savoy**, London's grandest hotel, built in 1889 on the site of the medieval Savoy Palace. César Ritz was the original manager, Guccio Gucci started out as a dishwasher here, and the list of illustrious guests is endless: Monet painted the Thames from one of the south-facing rooms, Sarah Bernhardt nearly died here, and Strauss the Younger arrived with his own orchestra.

Victoria Embankment

The **Victoria Embankment**, built between 1868 and 1874, was the inspiration of French engineer Joseph Bazalgette, whose project simultaneously relieved congestion along the Strand, provided an extension to the underground railway and sewage systems, and created a new stretch of parkland with a riverside walk – no longer much fun due to the volume of traffic. The 1626 **York Watergate**, in the Victoria Embankment Gardens to the east of Villiers Street, gives you an idea of where the banks of the Thames used to be; the steps through the gateway once led down to the river.

London's oldest monument, **Cleopatra's Needle**, languishes little-noticed on the Thames side of the busy Victoria Embankment, guarded by two Victorian sphinxes. The 60-foot-high, 180-ton stick of granite in fact has nothing to do with Cleopatra – it's one of a pair erected in Heliopolis in 1475 BC (the other one is in New York's Central Park) and taken to Alexandria by the Emperor Augustus fifteen years after Cleopatra's suicide. This obelisk was presented to Britain in 1819 by the Turkish viceroy of Egypt, but nearly sixty years passed before it finally made its way to London.

The **Benjamin Franklin House** (Ⓦwww.rsa.org.uk/franklin), on the other side of Charing Cross Station at 36 Craven St, will probably attract more visitors than Cleopatra's Needle. Restored with the help of, among others, the nearby Royal Society of Arts, the museum should be open some time in 2005; for more information phone Ⓣ020/7930 9121. The tenth son of a candlemaker, Franklin (1706–1790) had "genteel lodgings" here more or less continuously from 1757 to 1775. Whilst Franklin was espousing the cause of the British colonies (as the US then was), the house served as the first de facto American Embassy; eventually, he returned to America to help draft the Declaration of Independence, negotiate the peace treaty with Britain and frame the Constitution.

Somerset House

Somerset House (Ⓦwww.somerset-house.org.uk) is the sole survivor of the grand edifices which once lined the riverfront, its four wings enclosing a large **courtyard** (daily 10am–11pm; free) rather like a Parisian hôtel. From March to October, the courtyard features a wonderful 55-jet fountain that spouts straight from the cobbles; in winter, an ice rink is set up in its place. The present building was begun in 1776 by William Chambers as a purpose-built governmental office development, but now also houses a series of museums and galleries.

The south wing, overlooking the Thames, is home to the **Hermitage Rooms** (daily 10am–6pm; ticket prices vary; Ⓦwww.hermitagerooms.com), featuring changing displays drawn from St Petersburg's Hermitage Museum, and the magnificent **Gilbert Collection** (daily 10am–6pm; £5; Ⓦwww.gilbert-collection.org.uk), a museum of decorative arts displaying European silver and gold, micro-mosaics, clocks, portrait miniatures and snuffboxes.

In the north wing are the **Courtauld Institute galleries** (daily 10am–6pm; £5; free Mon 10am–2pm; Ⓦwww.courtauld.ac.uk), chiefly known for their dazzling collection of Impressionist and Post-Impressionist paintings. Among the most celebrated works is a small-scale version of Manet's *Déjeuner sur l'herbe*, Renoir's *La Loge*, and Degas's *Two Dancers*, plus a whole heap of Cézanne's canvases, including one of his series of *Card Players*. The Courtauld also boasts a fine selection of works by the likes of Rubens, van Dyck, Tiepolo and Cranach the Elder. The collection has recently been augmented by the long-term loan of a hundred top-notch twentieth-century paintings and sculptures by, among others, Kandinksy, Matisse, Dufy, Derain, Rodin and Henry Moore.

Holborn, Clerkenwell and Hoxton

Holborn, **Clerkenwell** and **Hoxton** lie on the periphery of the financial district of the City. **Holborn** (pronounced "Ho-bun") has long been associated with the law, and its **Inns of Court** make for an interesting stroll, their archaic, cobbled precincts exuding the rarefied atmosphere of an Oxbridge college, and sheltering one of the city's oldest churches, the twelfth-century **Temple Church**. Close by the Inns, in Lincoln's Inn Fields, is the **Sir John Soane's Museum**, one of the most memorable and enjoyable of London's small museums, packed with architectural illusions and an eclectic array of curios.

Clerkenwell, further to the northeast, is definitely off the conventional tourist trail with just a few minor sights. Since the 1990s, however, parts of the area have been transformed and, to a certain extent, gentrified, by an influx of young, loft-living designer and media types, whose arrival has had a marked effect on the choice and style of bars and restaurants on offer.

Neighbouring **Hoxton** (aka Shoreditch) to the east, has also acquired a certain caché, due to the high density of artists and architects who currently live and work here. Visually, Hoxton, a slum area badly damaged in the Blitz, remains harsher on the eye than Clerkenwell, though it, too, has more than its fair share of trendy bars and restaurants. Several of London's contemporary art dealers now have Hoxton outlets, and there's the excellent **Geffrye Museum** of furniture design to aim for too.

Temple and the Royal Courts of Justice

Temple (Temple or Blackfriars tube) is the largest and most complex of the Inns of Court, where every barrister in England must study before being called to the Bar. Temple itself is comprised of two Inns – **Middle Temple** (Ⓦwww.middletemple.org.uk) and **Inner Temple** (Ⓦwww.innertemple.org.uk) – both of which lie to the south of the Strand, and, strictly speaking, just within the boundaries of the City of London. A few very old buildings survive here, but the overall scene is dominated by the soulless neo-Georgian reconstructions that followed the devastation of the Blitz. Still, the maze of courtyards and passageways is fun to explore – especially after dark, when Temple is gas-lit – and there are several points of access, simplest of which is Devereux Court.

Medieval students ate, attended lectures and slept in the **Middle Temple Hall** (Mon–Fri 10am–noon & 3–4pm), across the courtyard, still the Inn's main dining room. The present building was constructed in the 1560s and provided the setting for many great Elizabethan masques and plays – probably including Shakespeare's *Twelfth Night*, which is believed to have been premiered here in 1602. The hall is worth a visit for its fine hammerbeam roof, wooden panelling and decorative Elizabethan screen.

The two Temple Inns share use of the complex's oldest building, **Temple Church** (Wed–Sun 11am–4pm; Ⓦwww.templechurch.com), built in 1185 by the Knights Templar. An oblong chancel was added in the thirteenth century,

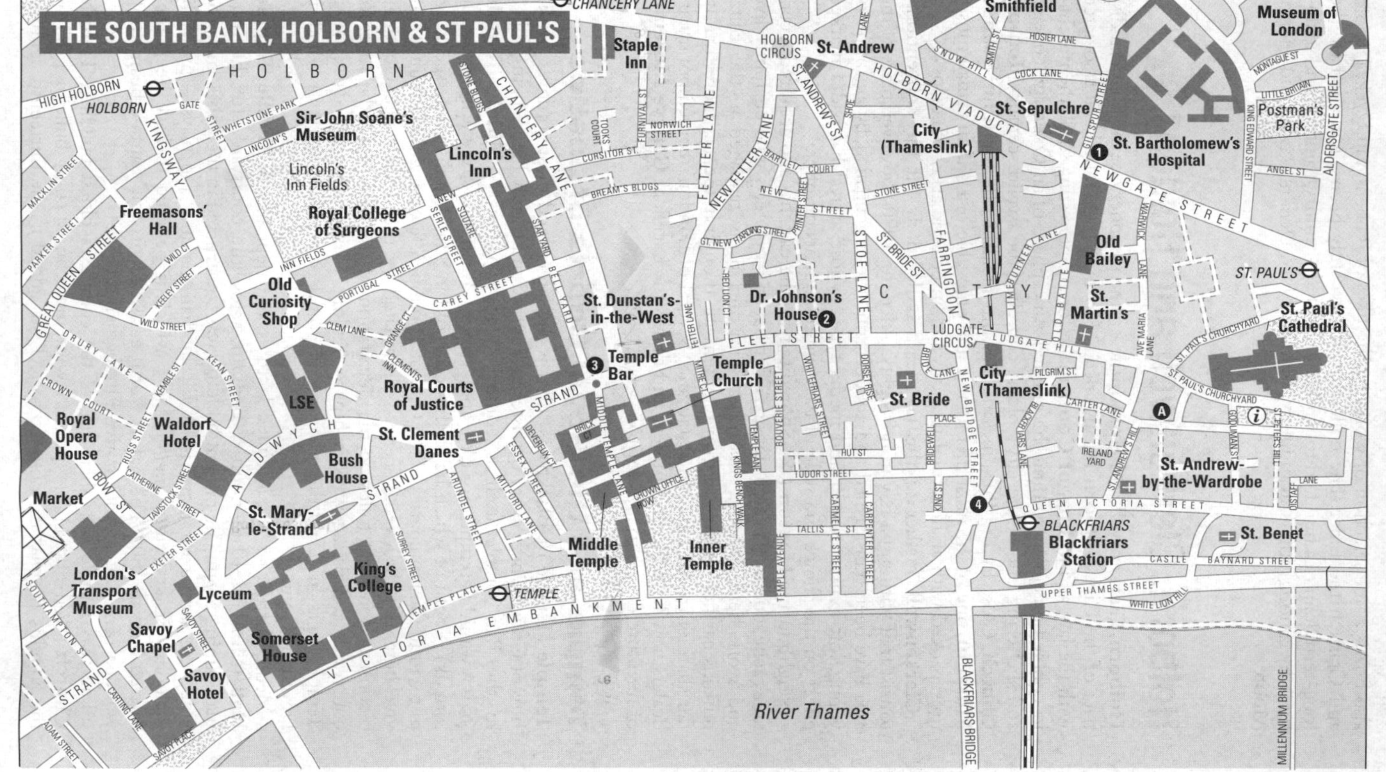
THE SOUTH BANK, HOLBORN & ST PAUL'S
CHANCERY LANE
HOLBORN
HIGH HOLBORN
KINGSWAY
Staple Inn
Sir John Soane's Museum
Lincoln's Inn
Lincoln's Inn Fields
Royal College of Surgeons
Freemasons' Hall
Old Curiosity Shop
St. Dunstan's-in-the-West
Temple Bar
Royal Courts of Justice
LSE
St. Clement Danes
Bush House
Royal Opera House
Waldorf Hotel
Market
St. Mary-le-Strand
London's Transport Museum
Lyceum
Savoy Chapel
Savoy Hotel
Somerset House
King's College
TEMPLE
VICTORIA EMBANKMENT
Middle Temple
Inner Temple
Temple Church
Dr. Johnson's House
FLEET STREET
STRAND
ALDWYCH
CITY
St. Bride
City (Thameslink)
LUDGATE CIRCUS
LUDGATE HILL
FARRINGDON
SHOE LANE
FETTER LANE
NEW FETTER LANE
HOLBORN CIRCUS
St. Andrew
HOLBORN VIADUCT
Smithfield
St. Sepulchre
St. Bartholomew's Hospital
NEWGATE STREET
Old Bailey
St. Martin's
ST. PAUL'S
St. Paul's Cathedral
Museum of London
Postman's Park
ALDERSGATE STREET
KING EDWARD STREET
St. Andrew-by-the-Wardrobe
QUEEN VICTORIA STREET
BLACKFRIARS
Blackfriars Station
St. Benet
UPPER THAMES STREET
NEW BRIDGE STREET
BLACKFRIARS BRIDGE
MILLENNIUM BRIDGE
River Thames

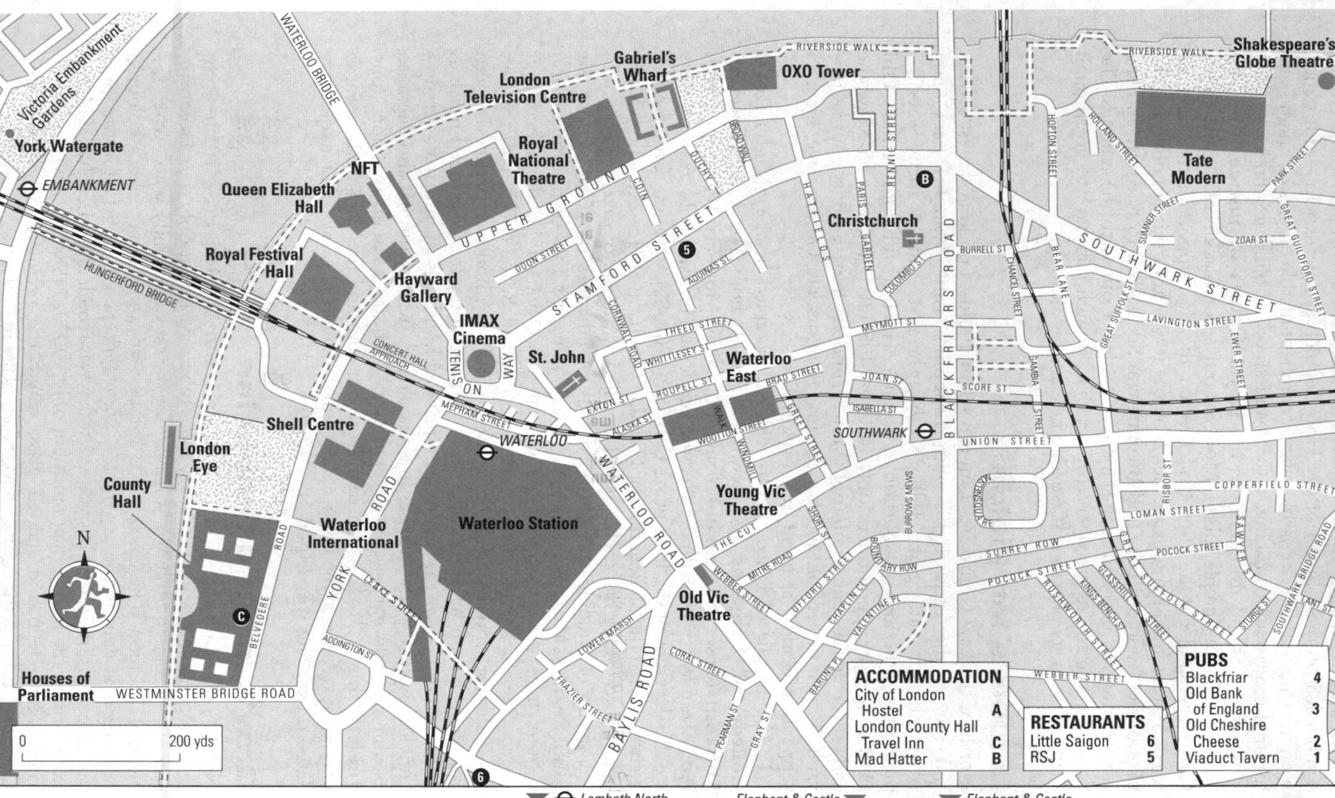
Victoria Embankment Gardens
York Watergate
EMBANKMENT
WATERLOO BRIDGE
HUNGERFORD BRIDGE
London Television Centre
Gabriel's Wharf
OXO Tower
RIVERSIDE WALK
Shakespeare's Globe Theatre
Tate Modern
NFT
Queen Elizabeth Hall
Royal National Theatre
Royal Festival Hall
Hayward Gallery
IMAX Cinema
St. John
Waterloo East
Christchurch
Shell Centre
London Eye
County Hall
Waterloo Station
Waterloo International
Young Vic Theatre
Old Vic Theatre
Houses of Parliament
WESTMINSTER BRIDGE ROAD
UPPER GROUND
STAMFORD STREET
SOUTHWARK STREET
BLACKFRIARS ROAD
UNION STREET
WATERLOO ROAD
YORK ROAD
BELVEDERE ROAD
BAYLIS ROAD
THE CUT
WATERLOO
SOUTHWARK
GREAT SUFFOLK STREET
SOUTHWARK BRIDGE ROAD
GREAT GUILDFORD STREET
HOPTON STREET
HOLLAND STREET
SUMNER STREET
BEAR LANE
CHANCEL STREET
HATFIELDS
CONCERT HALL APPROACH
TENISON WAY
CORNWALL ROAD
N
0 200 yds
ACCOMMODATION
City of London Hostel A
London County Hall C
Travel Inn C
Mad Hatter B
RESTAURANTS
Little Saigon 6
RSJ 5
PUBS
Blackfriar 4
Old Bank of England 3
Old Cheshire Cheese 2
Viaduct Tavern 1
Lambeth North
Elephant & Castle
Elephant & Castle

and the whole building was damaged in the Blitz, but the original round church – modelled on the Church of the Holy Sepulchre in Jerusalem – still stands, with its striking Purbeck marble piers, recumbent marble effigies of knights and tortured grotesques grimacing in the spandrels of the blind arcading.

Across the Strand from Temple, the **Royal Courts of Justice** (Mon–Fri 8.30am–4.30pm; Temple tube – Mon–Sat only – or Blackfriars), home to the Court of Appeal and the High Court, where the most important civil cases are tried. Appeals and libel suits are heard here – it was from this building that the likes of the Guildford Four and Birmingham Six walked to freedom, and it is where countless pop and soap stars have battled it out with the tabloids. The fifty-odd courtrooms are open to the public, though you have to go through stringent security checks first (strictly no cameras allowed).

Lincoln's Inn Fields

North of the Law Courts lies **Lincoln's Inn Fields**, London's largest square, laid out in the early 1640s with **Lincoln's Inn** (Mon–Fri 9am–6pm; Ⓦwww.lincolnsinn.org.uk; Holborn tube), the first – and in many ways the prettiest – of the Inns of Court on its east side. The Inn's fifteenth-century **Old Hall** is open by appointment only (Ⓣ020/7405 1393), but you can view the early seventeenth-century **chapel** (Mon–Fri noon–2pm), with its unusual fan-vaulted open undercroft and, on the first floor, its late Gothic nave, hit by a zeppelin in World War I and much restored since.

The south side of Lincoln's Inn Fields is occupied by the gigantic **Royal College of Surgeons** (Ⓦwww.rcseng.ac.uk), home to the **Hunterian Museum** (closed for refurbishment until 2005; Mon–Fri 10am–5pm; free; Holborn tube), a fascinating collection of pickled bits and bobs. Also on view are the skeletons of the Irish giant, O'Brien (1761–83), who was seven feet ten inches tall, and the Sicilian midget Caroline Crachami (1815–24), who was just one foot ten and a half inches when she died at the age of nine.

A group of buildings on the north side of Lincoln's Inn Fields house **Sir John Soane's Museum** (Tues–Sat 10am–5pm; first Tues of the month also 6–9pm; free; Ⓦwww.soane.org; Holborn tube), one of London's best-kept secrets. The chief architect of the Bank of England, Soane (1753–1837) was an avid collector who designed this house not only as a home and office, but also as a place to stash his large collection of art and antiquities. Arranged much as it was in his lifetime, the ingeniously planned house has an informal, treasure-hunt atmosphere, with surprises in every alcove; the museum has also begun to exhibit contemporary art. At 2.30pm every Saturday, a fascinating, hour-long **guided tour** (£3) takes you round the museum and the enormous research library, next door, containing architectural drawings, books and exquisitely detailed cork and wood models.

Gray's Inn and Staple Inn

North of Lincoln's Inn, **Gray's Inn** (Mon–Fri 10am–4pm; Ⓦwww.graysinn.org.uk; Chancery Lane tube – Mon–Sat only – or Holborn), entered from High Holborn, is named for the de Grey family, who owned the original mansion. The entrance is through an anonymous cream-coloured building next door to the venerable *Cittie of Yorke* pub. Established in the fourteenth century, most of what you see today was rebuilt after the Blitz, with the exception of the **hall** (by appointment only; Ⓣ020/7458 7822), with its fabulous Tudor screen and stained glass, where the premiere of Shakespeare's *Comedy of Errors* is thought to have taken place in 1594.

Heading east along High Holborn, it's worth pausing to admire **Staple Inn** on the right, not one of the Inns of Court, but one of the now defunct Inns of Chancery, which used to provide a sort of foundation course for those aspiring to the Bar. Its overhanging half-timbered facade and gables date from the sixteenth century and are the most extensive in the whole of London; they survived the Great Fire, which stopped just short of Holborn Circus, but had to be extensively rebuilt after the Blitz.

Clerkenwell

Poverty and overcrowding were the main features of nineteenth-century Clerkenwell, and **Clerkenwell Green** became known in the press as "the headquarters of republicanism, revolution and ultra-non-conformity". The green's connections with **radical politics** have continued and its oldest building, built as a Welsh Charity School in 1737, is now home to the **Marx Memorial Library** (Mon, Tues & Thurs 1–6pm, Wed 1–8pm, & Sat 10am–1pm; Ⓦwww.marxmemoriallibrary.sageweb.co.uk), at no. 37a. One-time headquarters of the Social Democratic Federation press, this is where **Lenin** edited seventeen editions of the Bolshevik paper *Iskra* in 1902–03. The poky little back room where he worked is maintained as it was then, as a kind of shrine – you can view it along with the workerist Hastings Mural from 1935.

Of Clerkenwell's three medieval religious establishments, remnants of two survive, hidden away to the southeast of Clerkenwell Green. The oldest is the priory of the Order of St John of Jerusalem; the sixteenth-century **St John's Gate** (Mon–Fri 10am–5pm, Sat 10am–4pm; free; Ⓦwww.sja.org.uk), on the south side of Clerkenwell Road, is the most visible survivor of the foundation. Today, the gatehouse forms part of a **museum**, which traces the development of the order before its dissolution in this country by Henry VIII, and its reestablishment in the nineteenth century. In 1877, the St John Ambulance was founded, to provide a voluntary first-aid service to the public. It's in this field that the order is now best known in Britain – a splendid interactive gallery is devoted to the history of the service. To get to see the rest of the gatehouse, and to visit the Norman crypt of the Grand Priory Church over the road, you must take a **guided tour** (Tues, Fri & Sat 11am & 2.30pm; £5 donation requested).

A little to the southeast of St John's, on the edge of Smithfield, lies **Charterhouse** (guided tours only April–Aug Wed 2.15pm; Ⓣ020/7251 5002; £5), founded in 1371 as a Carthusian monastery. The public school, with which the foundation is now most closely associated, moved out to Surrey in 1872, but forty-odd pensioners – known, in the monastic tradition, as "brothers" – continue to be cared for here. The only way to visit the site is to join one of the exhaustive two-hour **guided tours**, which start at the gatehouse on Charterhouse Square. Very little remains of the original monastic buildings, but there's plenty of Tudor architecture to admire, dating from after the Dissolution when Charterhouse was rebuilt as a private residence.

Hoxton

Until recently, Shoreditch, on the northeastern edge of the City, was a none-too-savoury slice of London, an unpleasant amalgam of wholesale clothes and shoe shops, striptease pubs and roaring traffic. Over the last few years, however, it has been colonized by artists, designers and architects and rejacketed: what was once Shoreditch is now **Hoxton**, previously a much smaller neighbourhood confined to the north of Old Street. Whatever its real name, the area is actually rich in literary and artistic associations. It was here that James Burbage established the country's first public theatre – called simply the Theatre – in 1576 (he subsequently took it down and reassembled it on Bankside as the Globe).

Just south of Old Street tube and roundabout – Hoxton's chief transport link with the rest of London – lie **Bunhill Fields**, the main burial ground for Dissenters or Nonconformists (practising Christians who were not members of the Church of England). The three most famous graves have been relocated in the central paved area: William Blake's simple tombstone stands next to a replica of Daniel Defoe's, while opposite lies John Bunyan's recumbent statue. Directly opposite Bunhill Fields on City Road stands the Georgian ensemble of **Wesley's Chapel and House** (Mon–Sat 10am–4pm; free). A place of pilgrimage for Methodists, the uncharacteristically ornate chapel, built in 1777, heralded the coming of age of Wesley's sect. Predictably enough, the **Museum of Methodism** in the basement has only a passing reference mention to the insanely jealous forty-year-old widow Wesley married, and who eventually left him. Wesley himself spent his last two years in the delightful Georgian house to the right of the main gates, and inside you can see his deathbed, plus an early shock-therapy machine he was particularly keen on.

The geographical focus of the area's current transformation is **Hoxton Square**, a strange and not altogether happy mixture of light industrial units and artists' studios arranged around a leafy, formal square. Despite the lack of aesthetic charm, the area has become an increasingly fashionable place to live and work and several leading West End **art galleries** have opened up premises here, among them Victoria Miro, Jay Jopling's White Cube and Sadie Coles' Hoxton House. Other than cruising the bars (listed on p.150), and art galleries, there are no real sights as such, though you might want to take a peek at the **Prince's Foundation** (Ⓦwww.princes-foundation.org), the institute of architecture set up by Prince Charles, which has its headquarters on Charlotte Road, with a gallery that puts on temporary exhibitions of contemporary artists, photographers and designers.

Hoxton's one conventional tourist sight is the **Geffrye Museum** (Tues–Sat 10am–5pm, Sun noon–5pm; free; Ⓦwww.geffrye-museum.org.uk), a museum of furniture design, set back from Kingsland Road in a peaceful little enclave of eighteenth-century ironmongers' almshouses. A series of period living rooms, ranging from the oak-panelled seventeenth century through refined Georgian and cluttered Victorian, leads to the state-of-the-art New Gallery Extension, housing the excellent twentieth-century section and a pleasant café/restaurant. To get to the museum, take bus #149 or #242 from Liverpool Street tube.

The City

The City is where London began. Long established as the financial district, it stretches from Temple Bar in the west to the Tower of London in the east – administrative boundaries that are only slightly larger than those marked by the Roman walls and their medieval successors. However, in this Square Mile (as the City is sometimes referred to), you'll find few leftovers of London's early days, since four-fifths of the area burnt down in the Great Fire of 1666. Rebuilt in brick and stone, the City gradually lost its centrality as London swelled westwards, though it has maintained its position as Britain's financial heartland.

The Corporation of London

The one unchanging aspect of the City is its special status, conferred on it by William the Conqueror and extended and reaffirmed by successive monarchs and governments ever since. Nowadays, with its Lord Mayor, its Beadles, Sheriffs and Aldermen, its separate police force and its select electorate of freemen and liverymen, the City is an anachronism of the worst kind. **The Corporation** (ⓦwww.corpoflondon.gov.uk), which runs the City like a one-party mini-state, is an unreconstructed old boys' network whose medievalist pageantry camouflages the very real power and wealth which it holds – the Corporation owns nearly a third of the Square Mile (and several tracts of land elsewhere in and around London). Its anomalous status is all the more baffling when you consider that the City was once the cradle of British democracy: it was the City that traditionally stood up to bullying sovereigns.

What you see on the ground is mostly the product of three fairly recent building phases: the Victorian construction boom of the latter half of the nineteenth century; the overzealous postwar reconstruction following the Blitz; and the building frenzy that began in the 1980s, during which nearly fifty percent of the City's office space has been rebuilt.

When you consider what has happened here, it's amazing that so much has survived to pay witness to the City's two-thousand-year history. Wren's spires still punctuate the skyline here and there and his masterpiece, **St Paul's Cathedral**, remains one of London's geographical pivots. At the eastern edge of the City, the **Tower of London** still stands protected by some of the best-preserved medieval fortifications in Europe. Other relics, such as the City's few surviving medieval alleyways, Wren's **Monument** to the Great Fire and London's oldest synagogue and church, are less conspicuous, and even locals have problems finding the more modern attractions of the **Museum of London** and the **Barbican** arts complex.

Perhaps the biggest change of all, though, has been in the City's population. Up until the eighteenth century the majority of Londoners lived and worked in or around the City; nowadays 300,000 commuters spend the best part of Monday to Friday here, but only 5000 people remain at night and at weekends. The result of this demographic shift is that the City is fully alive only during office hours. This means that weekdays are by far the best time to visit; many pubs, restaurants and even some tube stations and tourist sights close down at the weekend.

Fleet Street

In 1500 a certain Wynkyn de Worde, a pupil of William Caxton, moved the Caxton presses from Westminster to **Fleet Street**, to be close to the lawyers of the Inns of Court and to the clergy of St Paul's. However, the street really boomed two hundred years later when, in 1702, the now-defunct *Daily Courant*, Britain's first daily newspaper, was published here. By the nineteenth century all the major national and provincial dailies had their offices and printing presses in the Fleet Street district, a situation that prevailed until the 1980s, when the press barons relocated their operations elsewhere. The best source of information about the old-style Fleet Street is the so-called "journalists' and printers' cathedral", the church of **St Bride's** (Mon–Sat 9am–5pm; ⓦwww.stbrides.com; Blackfriars tube), which boasts Wren's tallest and most exquisite spire (said to be the inspiration for the tiered wedding cake), and whose crypt contains a little museum of Fleet Street history.

The City churches

The City of London boasts over forty churches (Ⓦwww.london-city-churches.org), the majority of them built or rebuilt by Wren after the Great Fire. As a general rule, weekday lunchtimes are the best time to visit these churches, many of which put on free lunchtime concerts for the local wage slaves.

On the surface, many of the City churches appear quite similar: plain, light-filled interiors, in white, gold and dark wood furnishings. Below is a list of six of the most varied and interesting churches within the Square Mile:

St Bartholomew-the-Great Cloth Fair; Barbican tube. The oldest surviving church in the City and by far the most atmospheric; a fascinating building. St Paul's aside, if you visit just one church in the City, it should be this one.

St Mary Abchurch Abchurch Lane, Cannon Street; Cannon Street or Bank tube. Uniquely for Wren's City churches, the interior features a huge painted domed ceiling, plus the only authenticated Gibbons reredos.

St Mary Aldermary Queen Victoria Street; Mansion House tube. Wren's most successful stab at Gothic, with fan vaulting in the aisles and a panelled ceiling in the nave.

St Mary Woolnoth Lombard Street; Bank tube. Hawksmoor's only City church, sporting an unusually broad, bulky tower and a Baroque clerestory that floods the church with light from its semicircular windows.

St Olave Hart Street; Tower Hill tube. Built in the fifteenth century, and one of the few pre-Fire Gothic churches in the City.

St Stephen Walbrook Walbrook; Bank tube. Wren's dress rehearsal for St Paul's, with a wonderful central dome and plenty of original woodcarving.

The western section of Fleet Street was spared the Great Fire, which stopped just short of **Prince Henry's Room** (Mon–Sat 11am–2pm; free; Ⓦwww.cityoflondon.gov.uk/phr), a fine Jacobean house with timber-framed bay windows. The first-floor room now contains material relating to the diarist **Samuel Pepys**, who was born nearby in Salisbury Court in 1633 and baptized in St Bride's. Even if you've no interest in Pepys, the wooden-panelled room is worth a look – it contains one of the finest Jacobean plasterwork ceilings in London, and a lot of original stained glass.

Numerous narrow alleyways lead off the north side of Fleet Street, two of which – Bolt Court and Hind Court – eventually open out into Gough Square, on which stands **Dr Johnson's House** (May–Sept Mon–Sat 11am–5.30pm; Oct–April Mon–Sat 11am–5pm; £4; Ⓦwww.drjh.dircon.co.uk). The great savant, writer and lexicographer lived here from 1747 to 1759, whilst compiling the 41,000 entries for the first dictionary of the English language, two first editions of which can be seen in the grey-panelled rooms of the house. You can also view the open-plan attic, in which Johnson and his six helpers put together the dictionary.

St Paul's Cathedral

St Paul's Cathedral (Mon–Sat 8.30am–5pm; £6; Ⓦwww.stpauls.co.uk; St Paul's tube), topped by an enormous lead-covered dome that's second in size only to St Peter's in Rome, has been a London icon since the Blitz, when it stood defiantly unscathed amid the carnage (as in the famous wartime propaganda photo). It remains a dominating presence in the City, despite the encroaching tower blocks – its showpiece west facade is particularly magnificent, and is at its most impressive at night when bathed in sea-green arc lights.

Westminster Abbey has the edge, however, when it comes to celebrity corpses, pre-Reformation sculpture, royal connections and sheer atmosphere. St Paul's, by contrast, is a soulless but perfectly calculated architectural set piece, a burial place for captains rather than kings, though it does contain more artists than Westminster Abbey. The cathedral's services, featuring the renowned St Paul's choir, are held from Monday to Saturday at 5pm and on Sunday at 10am, 11.30am and 3.15pm.

The best place from which to appreciate the glory of St Paul's is beneath the **dome**, decorated (against Wren's wishes) with Thornhill's trompe l'oeil frescoes. The most richly decorated section of the cathedral, however, is the Quire or **chancel**, where the mosaics of birds, fish, animals and greenery, dating from the 1890s, are particularly spectacular. The intricately carved oak and limewood **choir stalls**, and the imposing organ case, are the work of Wren's master carver, Grinling Gibbons. Meanwhile, in the south-choir aisle, is the only complete effigy to have survived from Old St Paul's (see below), the upstanding shroud of **John Donne**, poet, preacher and one-time dean of St Paul's.

A series of stairs, beginning in the south aisle, lead to the dome's three **galleries**, the first of which is the internal **Whispering Gallery**, so called because of its acoustic properties – words whispered to the wall on one side are distinctly audible over one hundred feet away on the other, though the place is often so busy you can't hear much above the hubbub. The other two galleries are exterior: the wide **Stone Gallery**, around the balustrade at the base of the dome, and ultimately the tiny **Golden Gallery**, below the golden ball and cross which top the cathedral.

Although the nave is crammed full of overblown monuments to military types, burials in St Paul's are confined to the **crypt**, reputedly the largest in Europe. The whitewashed walls and bright lighting, however, make this one of the least atmospheric mausoleums you could imagine. Immediately to your right is Artists' Corner, which boasts as many painters and architects as Westminster Abbey has poets, including Christopher Wren himself, who was commissioned to build the cathedral after its Gothic predecessor, Old St Paul's, was destroyed in the Great Fire. The crypt's two other star tombs are those of **Nelson** and **Wellington**, both occupying centre stage and both with more fanciful monuments upstairs.

Museum of London and the Barbican

Despite London's long pedigree, very few of its ancient structures are now standing. However, numerous Roman, Saxon and Elizabethan remains have been discovered during the City's various rebuildings, and many of these finds are now displayed at the **Museum of London** (Mon–Sat 10am–5.50pm, Sun noon–5.50pm; free; Ⓦwww.museumoflondon.org.uk; St Paul's or Barbican tube), hidden above the western end of London Wall, in the southwestern corner of the Barbican complex. The museum's permanent exhibition is basically an educational trot through London's past from prehistory to the present day. This is interesting enough (and understandably attracts a lot of school groups), but the real strength of the museum lies in the excellent temporary exhibitions, gallery tours, lectures, walks and videos it organizes throughout the year – visit the website or pick up a programme of exhibitions and events from the information desk before you set out.

The City's only large residential complex is the **Barbican**, a phenomenally ugly and expensive concrete ghetto built on the heavily bombed Cripplegate area. The zone's solitary pre-war building is the heavily restored sixteenth-century church of **St Giles Cripplegate** (Mon–Fri 11am–4pm), situated across from the infamously user-repellent **Barbican Arts Centre** (Ⓦwww.barbican.org.uk), London's supposed answer to Paris's Pompidou Centre, which was formally opened in 1982. The complex, which is at least traffic-free, serves as home to the London Symphony Orchestra and the London chapter of the Royal Shakespeare Company, and holds free gigs in the foyer area.

Guildhall

Situated at the geographical centre of the City, **Guildhall** (May–Sept daily 10am–5pm; Oct–April Mon–Sat 10am–5pm; free; Ⓦwww.cityoflondon.gov.uk; St Paul's or Bank tube) has been the ancient seat of the City administration for over eight hundred years. It remains the headquarters of the Corporation of London (see p.103), and is still used for many of the City's formal civic occasions. Architecturally, however, it is not quite the beauty it once was, having been badly damaged in both the Great Fire and the Blitz, and scarred by the addition of a grotesque 1970s concrete cloister and wing.

Nonetheless, the **Great Hall**, basically a postwar reconstruction of the fifteenth-century original, is worth a brief look, as is the **Clockmakers' Museum** (Mon–Fri 9.30am–4.30pm; free), a collection of over six hundred timepieces, including one of the clocks that won John Harrison the Longitude prize (see p.136). Also worth a visit is the purpose-built **Guildhall Art Gallery** (Mon–Sat 10am–5pm, Sun noon–4pm; £2.50), which contains one or two exceptional works, such as Rossetti's *La Ghirlandata*, and Holman Hunt's *The Eve of St Agnes*, plus a massive painting depicting the 1782 Siege of Gibraltar, commissioned by the Corporation.

The financial centre

Bank is the finest architectural arena in the City. Heart of the finance sector and the busy meeting point of eight streets, it's overlooked by a handsome collection of Neoclassical buildings – among them, the Bank of England, the Royal Exchange and Mansion House (the Lord Mayor's official residence) – each one faced in Portland Stone.

Sadly, only the **Bank of England** (Ⓦwww.bankofengland.co.uk), which stores the nation's vast gold reserves in its vaults, actually encourages visitors. Established in 1694 by William III to raise funds for the war against France, the so-called "Grand Old Lady of Threadneedle Street" wasn't erected on its present site until 1734. All that remains of the building on which Sir John Soane spent the best part of his career from 1788 onwards is the windowless, outer curtain wall, which wraps itself round the three-and-a-half-acre island site. However, you can view a reconstruction of Soane's Bank Stock Office, with its characteristic domed skylight, in the **museum** (Mon–Fri 10am–5pm; free; Bank tube), which has its entrance on Bartholomew Lane.

East of Bank, beyond Bishopsgate, stands Richard Rogers' glitzy **Lloyd's Building**, completed in 1984. A startling array of glass and blue steel pipes – a vertical version of Rogers' own Pompidou Centre – this is easily the most popular of the modern City buildings, at least with the general public. Its closest rival is Norman Foster's giant "erotic gherkin" building for **Swiss Re**, just completed to the north on the site of the old Baltic Exchange which was blown up by the IRA in the early 1990s.

Hidden away behind a modern red-brick office block in a little courtyard off Bevis Marks, north up St Mary Axe from the Lloyd's building, the **Bevis Marks Synagogue** (guided tours Mon–Wed, Fri & Sun noon; £2) was built in 1701 by Sephardic Jews who had fled the Inquisition in Spain and Portugal. This is the country's oldest surviving synagogue, and its roomy, rich interior gives an idea of just how wealthy the congregation was at the time. Nowadays, the Sephardic community has dispersed across London and the congregation has dwindled, though the magnificent array of chandeliers makes it popular for candle-lit Jewish weddings.

Just south of the Lloyd's building you'll find the picturesque **Leadenhall Market**, whose richly painted, graceful Victorian cast-ironwork dates from 1881. Inside, the traders cater mostly for the lunchtime City crowd, their barrows laden with exotic seafood and game, fine wines, champagne and caviar.

London Bridge and Monument

Until 1750, **London Bridge** was the only bridge across the Thames. The Romans were the first to build a permanent crossing here, but it was the medieval bridge that achieved world fame: built of stone and crowded with timber-framed houses, it became one of the great attractions of London – there's a model in the nearby church of St Magnus the Martyr (Tues–Fri 10am–4pm, Sun 10am–1pm). The houses were finally removed in the mid-eighteenth century, and a new stone bridge erected in 1831; that one now stands in the middle of the Arizona desert, having been bought for $2.4 million in the late 1960s by a gentleman who, so the story goes, was under the impression he had purchased Tower Bridge. The present concrete structure, without doubt the ugliest yet, dates from 1972.

The only reason to go anywhere near London Bridge is to see the **Monument** (daily 10am–6pm; £1.50), which was designed by Wren to commemorate the Great Fire of 1666. Crowned with spiky gilded flames, this plain Doric column stands 202 feet high, making it the tallest isolated stone column in the world; if it were laid out flat it would touch the bakery where the Fire started, east of Monument. The bas-relief on the base, now in very bad shape, depicts Charles II and the Duke of York in Roman garb conducting the emergency relief operation. The 311 steps to the viewing gallery once guaranteed an incredible view; nowadays it is somewhat dwarfed by the buildings around it.

The Tower of London

One of Britain's main tourist attractions, the **Tower of London** (March–Oct Mon–Sat 9am–6pm, Sun 10am–6pm; Nov–Feb Mon & Sun 10am–5pm, Tues–Sat 9am–5pm; £12; Ⓦ www.hrp.org.uk; Tower Hill tube), overlooks the river at the eastern boundary of the old city walls. Despite all the hype and heritage claptrap, it remains one of London's most remarkable buildings, site of some of the goriest events in the nation's history, and somewhere all visitors and Londoners should explore at least once. Chiefly famous as a place of imprisonment and death, it has variously been used as a royal residence, armoury, mint, menagerie, observatory and – a function it still serves – a safe-deposit box for the Crown Jewels.

Before you set off to explore the Tower complex, it's a good idea to get your bearings by taking one of the free **guided tours**, given every thirty minutes or so by one of the Tower's **Beefeaters** (officially known as Yeoman Warders). Visitors today enter the Tower along Water Lane, but in times gone by most prisoners were delivered through **Traitors' Gate**, on the waterfront. The nearby **Bloody Tower**, which forms the main entrance to the Inner Ward, is where the 12-year-old Edward V and his 10-year-old brother were accommodated

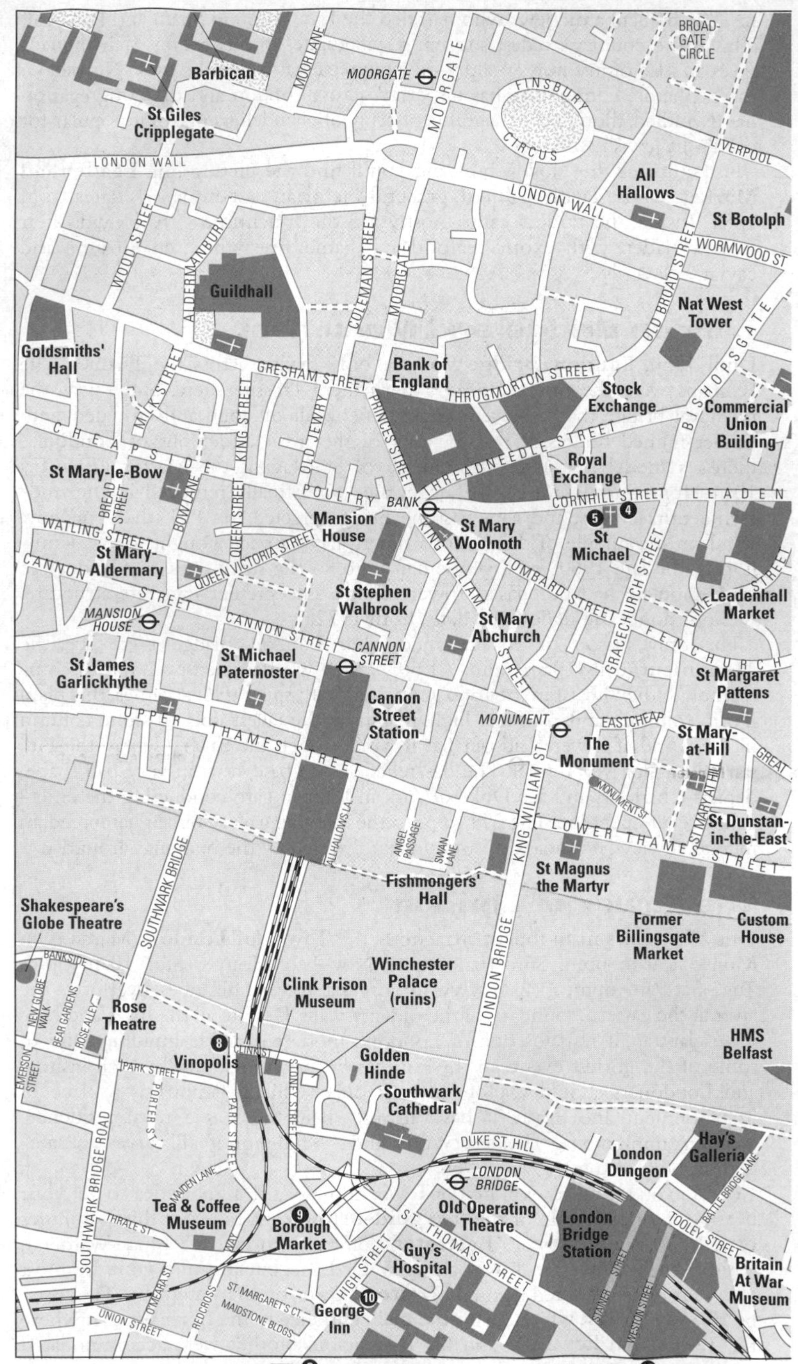

Barbican
BROAD-GATE CIRCLE
MOORGATE
MOOR LANE
FINSBURY CIRCUS
St Giles Cripplegate
LONDON WALL
LIVERPOOL
All Hallows
St Botolph
WORMWOOD ST
WOOD STREET
ALDERMANBURY
COLEMAN STREET
MOORGATE
Guildhall
OLD BROAD STREET
Nat West Tower
BISHOPSGATE
Goldsmiths' Hall
MILK STREET
KING STREET
GRESHAM STREET
Bank of England
THROGMORTON STREET
Stock Exchange
Commercial Union Building
CHEAPSIDE
OLD JEWRY
PRINCES STREET
THREADNEEDLE STREET
Royal Exchange
St Mary-le-Bow
BREAD STREET
BOW LANE
QUEEN STREET
POULTRY
BANK
CORNHILL STREET
LEADEN
Mansion House
St Mary Woolnoth
St Michael
WATLING STREET
St Mary-Aldermary
QUEEN VICTORIA STREET
KING WILLIAM
LOMBARD STREET
GRACECHURCH STREET
LIME STREET
Leadenhall Market
CANNON STREET
St Stephen Walbrook
MANSION HOUSE
CANNON STREET
St Mary Abchurch
FENCHURCH
CANNON STREET
St James Garlickhythe
St Michael Paternoster
Cannon Street Station
St Margaret Pattens
UPPER THAMES STREET
MONUMENT
EASTCHEAP
St Mary-at-Hill
The Monument
GREAT
MONUMENT ST
ST MARY AT HILL
St Dunstan-in-the-East
ALLHALLOWS LA.
ANGEL PASSAGE
SWAN LANE
KING WILLIAM ST
LOWER THAMES STREET
St Magnus the Martyr
SOUTHWARK BRIDGE
Fishmongers' Hall
Shakespeare's Globe Theatre
Former Billingsgate Market
Custom House
BANKSIDE
LONDON BRIDGE
Winchester Palace (ruins)
Clink Prison Museum
NEW GLOBE WALK
BEAR GARDENS
ROSE ALLEY
Rose Theatre
HMS Belfast
CLINK ST
Vinopolis
Golden Hinde
EMERSON STREET
PARK STREET
STONEY STREET
PORTER ST
Southwark Cathedral
SOUTHWARK BRIDGE ROAD
PARK STREET
DUKE ST. HILL
London Dungeon
Hay's Galleria
MAIDEN LANE
LONDON BRIDGE
BATTLE BRIDGE LANE
Tea & Coffee Museum
Borough Market
Old Operating Theatre
London Bridge Station
TOOLEY STREET
THRALE ST
WAY
ST. THOMAS STREET
Guy's Hospital
Britain At War Museum
O'MEARA ST
REDCROSS
ST. MARGARET'S CT.
MAIDSTONE BLDGS
HIGH STREET
George Inn
STAINER STREET
WESTON STREET
UNION STREET
4
5
8
9
10
C
12

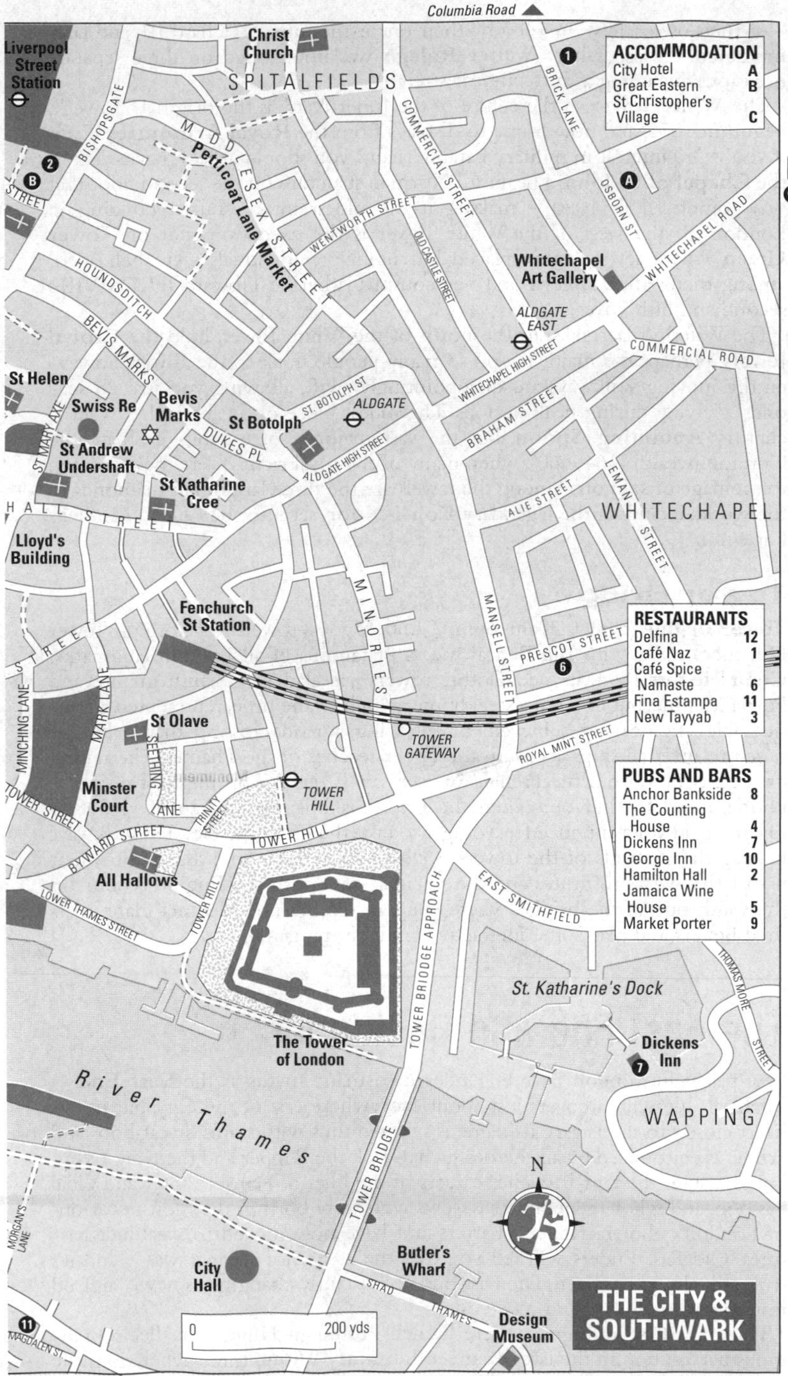

Columbia Road
ACCOMMODATION
City Hotel A
Great Eastern B
St Christopher's Village C
RESTAURANTS
Delfina 12
Café Naz 1
Café Spice Namaste 6
Fina Estampa 11
New Tayyab 3
PUBS AND BARS
Anchor Bankside 8
The Counting House 4
Dickens Inn 7
George Inn 10
Hamilton Hall 2
Jamaica Wine House 5
Market Porter 9
Liverpool Street Station
Christ Church
SPITALFIELDS
BRICK LANE
BISHOPSGATE
MIDDLESEX STREET
Petticoat Lane Market
COMMERCIAL STREET
OSBORN ST
WENTWORTH STREET
OLD CASTLE STREET
WHITECHAPEL ROAD
Whitechapel Art Gallery
HOUNDSDITCH
ALDGATE EAST
BEVIS MARKS
COMMERCIAL ROAD
WHITECHAPEL HIGH STREET
St Helen
Swiss Re
Bevis Marks
ST. BOTOLPH ST
ALDGATE
St Botolph
BRAHAM STREET
ST MARY AXE
St Andrew Undershaft
DUKES PL
ALDGATE HIGH STREET
LEMAN STREET
St Katharine Cree
ALIE STREET
WHITECHAPEL
HALL STREET
Lloyd's Building
MINORIES
MANSELL STREET
Fenchurch St Station
PRESCOT STREET
STREET
MINCHING LANE
MARK LANE
St Olave
SEETHING LANE
TOWER GATEWAY
ROYAL MINT STREET
Minster Court
TOWER HILL
TOWER STREET
TRINITY STREET
BYWARD STREET
TOWER HILL
All Hallows
LOWER THAMES STREET
TOWER HILL
TOWER BRIDGE APPROACH
EAST SMITHFIELD
St. Katharine's Dock
THOMAS MORE STREET
The Tower of London
Dickens Inn
River Thames
WAPPING
TOWER BRIDGE
N
MORGAN'S LANE
City Hall
Butler's Wharf
SHAD THAMES
Design Museum
0 200 yds
MAGDALEN ST.
THE CITY & SOUTHWARK

"for their own safety" in 1483 by their uncle, the future Richard III, and later murdered. It's also where **Walter Ralegh** was imprisoned on three separate occasions, including a thirteen-year stretch.

The **White Tower**, at the centre of the Inner Ward, is the original "Tower", begun in 1076, and now home to displays from the **Royal Armouries**. Even if you've no interest in military paraphernalia, you should at least pay a visit to the **Chapel of St John**, a beautiful Norman structure on the second floor that was completed in 1080 – making it the oldest intact church building in London. To the west of the White Tower is the execution spot on **Tower Green** where seven highly placed but unlucky individuals were beheaded, among them Anne Boleyn and her cousin Catherine Howard (Henry VIII's second and fifth wives).

The Waterloo Barracks, to the north of the White Tower, hold the **Crown Jewels**, perhaps the major reason so many people flock to the Tower; however, the moving walkways are disappointingly swift, allowing you just 28 seconds' viewing during peak periods. The oldest piece of regalia is the twelfth-century **Anointing Spoon**, but the vast majority of exhibits postdate the Commonwealth (1649–60), when many of the royal riches were melted down for coinage or sold off. Among the jewels are the three largest cut diamonds in the world, including the legendary **Koh-i-Noor**, set into the Queen Mother's Crown in 1937.

Tower Bridge

Tower Bridge (daily 9.30am–6pm; £4.50; Ⓦwww.towerbridge.org.uk; Tower Hill tube) ranks with Big Ben as the most famous of all London landmarks. Completed in 1894, its neo-Gothic towers are clad in Cornish granite and Portland stone, but conceal a steel frame, which, at the time, represented a considerable engineering achievement, allowing a road crossing that could be raised to give tall ships access to the upper reaches of the Thames. The raising of the bascules (from the French for "see-saw") remains an impressive sight – phone ahead to find out when the bridge is opening (Ⓣ020/7940 3984). Having paid your entrance fee, you get to take the lift to the elevated walkways linking the summits of the towers – closed from 1909 to 1982 due to their popularity with prostitutes and the suicidal – and visit the Engine Room, on the south side of the bridge, where you can see the now defunct giant coal-fired boilers and play some interactive engineering games.

The East End and Docklands

Few places in London have engendered so many myths as the **East End** (a catch-all title which covers just about everywhere east of the City, but has its heart closest to the latter). Its name is synonymous with slums, sweatshops and crime, as epitomized by antiheroes such as Jack the Ripper and the Kray Twins, but also with the rags-to-riches careers of the likes of Harold Pinter and Vidal Sassoon, and whole generations of Jews who were born in the most notorious of London's cholera-ridden quarters and have now moved to wealthier pastures. Old East Enders will tell you that the area's not what it was – and it's true, as it always has been. The East End is constantly changing as newly arrived immigrants assimilate and move out.

The area's first immigrants were French Protestant Huguenots, fleeing religious persecution in the late seventeenth century. Within three generations the

Huguenots were entirely assimilated, and the Irish became the new immigrant population, but it was the influx of Jews escaping pogroms in eastern Europe and Russia that defined the character of the East End in the second half of the nineteenth century. The area's Jewish population has now dispersed throughout London, though the East End remains at the bottom of the pile; even the millions poured into the **Docklands** development have failed to make much impression on local unemployment and housing problems. Unfortunately, racism is still rife, and is directed, for the most part, against the extensive Bengali community, who came here from the poor rural area of Sylhet in Bangladesh in the 1960s and 1970s.

As the area is not an obvious place for sightseeing, and certainly no beauty spot – Victorian slum clearances, Hitler's bombs and postwar tower blocks have all left their mark – most visitors to the East End come for its famous **Sunday markets**. However, there's plenty more to get out of a visit, including a trio of **Hawksmoor churches**, and the vast **Canary Wharf** redevelopment, which has to be seen to be believed.

Whitechapel and Spitalfields

The districts of **Whitechapel**, and in particular **Spitalfields**, within sight of the sleek tower blocks of the financial sector, represent the old heart of the East End, where the French Huguenots settled in the seventeenth century, where the Jewish community was at its strongest in the late nineteenth century, and where today's Bengali community eats, sleeps, works and prays. If you visit just one area in the East End, it should be this zone, which preserves mementos from each wave of immigration.

The easiest approach is from Liverpool Street Station, a short stroll west of **Spitalfields Market**, the red-brick and green-gabled market hall built in 1893, half of which was recently demolished in order to make way for yet more City offices. The dominant architectural presence in Spitalfields, however, is **Christ Church** (Mon–Fri 12.30–2.30pm), built in 1714–29 to a characteristically bold design by Nicholas Hawksmoor, and now facing the market hall. Best viewed from Brushfield Street, the church's main features are its huge 225-

East End Sunday markets

Most visitors to the East End come here for the **Sunday markets** (Ⓦwww.eastlondonmarkets.com). Approaching from Liverpool Street, the first one you come to, on the east side of Bishopsgate, is **Petticoat Lane** (Sun 9am–2pm; Liverpool Street or Aldgate East tube), not one of London's prettiest streets, but one of its longest-running Sunday markets, specializing in cheap (and often pretty tacky) clothing. The authorities renamed the street Middlesex Street in 1830 to avoid the mention of ladies' underwear, but the original name has stuck.

Two blocks north of Middlesex Street, down Brushfield Street, lies **Spitalfields Market** (organic market Fri & Sun 10am–5pm; general market Mon–Fri 11am–3pm & Sun 10am–5pm; Liverpool Street tube), once the capital's premier wholesale fruit and vegetable market, now specializing in organic food, plus clothes, crafts and jewellery. Further east lies **Brick Lane** (Sun 8am–1pm; Aldgate East, Shoreditch or Liverpool Street tube), heart of the Bengali community, famous for its bric-a-brac Sunday market, wonderful curry houses and non-stop bagel bakery, and now also something of a magnet for young designers. From Brick Lane's northernmost end, it's a short walk to **Columbia Road** (Sun 8am–1pm), the city's best market for flowers and plants, though you'll need to ask the way, or head in the direction of the folk bearing plants.

foot-high spire and a giant Tuscan portico, raised on steps and shaped like a Venetian window (a central arched opening flanked by two smaller rectangles), a motif repeated in the tower and doors.

Whitechapel Road – as Whitechapel High Street and the Mile End Road are collectively known – is still the East End's main street, shared by all the many races who live in the borough of Tower Hamlets. The East End institution that draws in more outsiders than any other here is the **Whitechapel Art Gallery** (Tues & Thurs–Sun 11am–6pm, Wed 11am–8pm; free; Ⓦwww.whitechapel.org), housed in a beautiful crenellated 1899 Arts and Crafts building by Charles Harrison Townsend, architect of the similarly audacious Horniman Museum (p.137). The gallery stages some of London's most innovative exhibitions of contemporary art, as well as hosting the biennial Whitechapel Open, a chance for local artists to get their work shown to a wider audience.

Bethnal Green Museum of Childhood

The East End's most popular museum is the **Bethnal Green Museum of Childhood** (daily except Fri 10am–5pm; free; Ⓦwww.museumofchildhood.org.uk), situated opposite Bethnal Green tube station. The open-plan, wrought-iron hall, originally part of (and still a branch of) the V&A museum (see p.126), was transported here in the 1860s to bring art to the East End. The variety of exhibits means that there's something here for everyone from 3 to 93, but the museum's most frequent visitors are children – that said, the displays are not very hands-on. The ground floor is best known for its unique collection of antique dolls' houses dating back to 1673. You'll need a pile of 20p pieces with you to work the automata – Wallace the Lion gobbling up Albert is always a favourite. Elsewhere, there are puppets, a jumble of toys, a vast doll collection and excellent temporary exhibitions.

Docklands

The architectural embodiment of Thatcherism, a symbol of 1980s smash-and-grab culture according to its critics, or a blueprint for inner-city regeneration to its free-market supporters – the **Docklands** redevelopment provokes extreme reactions. Despite its catch-all name, however, Docklands is far from homogeneous. Canary Wharf, with its Manhattan-style skyscrapers, is only its most visible landmark; industrial-estate sheds and riverside flats of dubious architectural merit are more indicative of the area. **Wapping**, the westernmost district, has retained much of its old Victorian warehouse architecture, while the **Royal Docks**, further east, are only just beginning to be transformed from an industrial wasteland.

The docks were originally built from 1802 onwards to relieve congestion on the Thames quays, and eventually became the largest enclosed cargo-dock system in the world. However, competition from the railways, and later, the development of container ships, forced the closure of most of the docks in the 1960s. Then, at the height of the recession in the 1980s, regeneration began in earnest. No one thought the old docks could ever be rejuvenated, but twenty years on, more has been achieved than many thought possible (though less than some had hoped). Travelling through on the overhead railway, Docklands comes over as an intriguing open-air design museum, not a place one would choose to live or work – most people stationed here still see it as a bleak business-oriented outpost – but a spectacular sight nevertheless.

Docklands transport

Although Canary Wharf is on the Jubilee line, the best way to view Docklands is either from one of the boats that course up and down the Thames (see p.66), or from the driverless, overhead **Docklands Light Railway** or DLR (Ⓦwww.tfl.gov.uk/dlr), which sets off from Bank, or from Tower Gateway, close to Tower Hill tube. Travelcards are valid on the DLR, or you can buy a variety of DLR-only day passes giving you unlimited travel on certain sections of the network. Tour guides give a free running commentary on DLR trains that set off on the hour from Tower Gateway (daily 10am–2pm) and Bank (Mon–Fri 11am–2pm, Sat & Sun 10am–2pm) as far as Cutty Sark; passengers and guides starting at Tower Gateway and heading for Canary Wharf or Greenwich must change at Westferry (except Sat & Sun 11am–5pm). If you're heading for Greenwich, and fancy taking a boat back into town, it might be worth considering a Rail River Rover ticket (£8.30), which gives you unlimited travel on the DLR and City Cruises services between Greenwich and Westminster.

Wapping to Limehouse

From the DLR overhead railway, you get a good view of two of Hawksmoor's landmark East End churches; the first one is **St George-in-the-East**, built in 1726 and visible to the south just before you reach Shadwell station. It's easy to spot thanks to its four domed corner towers and distinctive west-end tower topped by an octagonal lantern. You're missing nothing by staying on the train, though, as the interior was devastated in the Blitz. As the DLR leaves Limehouse station and skirts Limehouse Basin marina, Hawksmoor's **St Anne's Church** is visible to the north. Begun in 1714 and dominated again by a gargantuan west tower, the church is topped by an octagonal lantern and adorned with the highest church clock in London. Again, the interior isn't worth the effort as it was badly damaged by fire in 1850.

An alternative to the DLR is to walk from Wapping to Limehouse, along the Thames Path, which sticks to, or close to, the riverbank. You begin at **St Katharine's Dock**, immediately east of the Tower of London, and the first of the old docks to be renovated way back in the 1970s. St Katharine's redeeming qualities are the old swing bridges and the boats themselves, many of which are beautiful old sailing ships. Continue along **Wapping High Street**, lined with tall brick-built warehouses, most now tastefully converted into yuppie flats, and you will eventually find yourself in Limehouse, beyond which lies the Isle of Dogs (see below). The fairly well-signposted walk is about two miles in length, and will bring you eventually to Westferry DLR station.

The Isle of Dogs: Canary Wharf

The Thames begins a dramatic horseshoe bend at Limehouse, thus creating the **Isle of Dogs**, the geographical and ideological heart of the new Docklands. The area reaches its apotheosis in **Canary Wharf** (Ⓦwww.canarywharf.com), the strip of land in the middle of the former West India Docks, previously a destination for rum and mahogany, later tomatoes and bananas (from the Canary Islands – hence the name).

The only really busy bit of the new Docklands, Canary Wharf is best known as the home of Britain's tallest building, Cesar Pelli's landmark tower, officially known as **One Canada Square**. The world's first skyscraper to be clad in stainless steel, it's an undeniably impressive sight, both from a distance (its flashing pinnacle is a feature of the horizon at numerous points in London) and close up. However, it no longer stands alone, having been joined by several other skyscrapers that stop just short of Pelli's stumpy pinnacle.

The warehouses to the north of Canary Wharf have been converted into flats, bars, restaurants and the **Museum in Docklands** (daily 10am–6pm; £5; Ⓦwww.museumindocklands.org.uk), which charts the history of the area from Roman times to the development of Canary Wharf via interactive displays, a reconstructed sailor town and numerous paintings and photographs. Unless you're keen to visit the museum, there's little point in getting off the DLR as it cuts right through the middle of the Canary Wharf office buildings under a parabolic steel-and-glass canopy.

The South Bank

The **South Bank** (Ⓦwww.southbanklondon.com) – the area immediately opposite Victoria Embankment – is best known for the **London Eye**, the world's largest observation wheel and one of the capital's most popular millennium projects. The arrival of the eye helped kick-start the renovation of the **South Bank Centre**, London's much unloved concrete culture bunker of theatres and galleries, built, for the most part, in the 1960s. After decades in the doldrums, the centre is currently under inspired artistic direction and the whole area is enjoying something of a renaissance.

The wheel's success has rubbed off on the rest of the area too, prompting a major refurbishment programme beginning with the transformation of **Hungerford Bridge**, connecting the South Bank to Embankment, into a gleaming double suspension footbridge. What's more, you can now happily explore the whole area on foot, free from the traffic noise and fumes that blight so much of central London, thanks to the well-marked **Thames Path** which runs along the riverside.

Further afield, in what used to be the village of **Lambeth**, there are one or two places worth visiting, in particular the **Imperial War Museum**, which contains the most detailed exhibition on the Holocaust in Britain.

The South Bank Centre

The modern development of the South Bank dates back to the 1951 **Festival of Britain**, when the South Bank Exhibition was held on derelict land south of the Thames. The festival was a fairly successful attempt to revive postwar morale by celebrating the centenary of the Great Exhibition (when Britain really did rule over half the world). The most striking features of the site were the Royal Festival Hall (which still stands), the ferris wheel (inspiration for the current London Eye), the saucer-shaped Dome of Discovery (disastrously revisited in the guise of the Millennium Dome), and the cigar-shaped Skylon tower.

The Festival of Britain's success provided the impetus for the eventual creation of the **South Bank Centre** (Ⓦwww.sbc.org.uk), now home to artistic institutions such as the Royal Festival Hall (Ⓦwww.rfh.org.uk), the Hayward Gallery (Ⓦwww.hayward.org.uk), the National Film Theatre (NFT), the high-tech BFI London IMAX Cinema, and lastly Denys Lasdun's Royal National Theatre (Ⓦwww.nt-online.org), popularly known as "the National" or NT, which boasts three separate theatres. Its unprepossessing appearance is softened, too, by its riverside location, its avenue of trees, its fluttering banners, its occasional buskers and skateboarders and the secondhand bookstalls and café outside the National Film Theatre.

The London Eye and County Hall

South of the South Bank Centre proper, beside County Hall, is London's most prominent new landmark, the **London Eye** (daily: April–Sept 9.30am–10pm; Oct–March 9am–8pm; £11; Ⓣ08705/000600, Ⓦwww.ba-londoneye.com; Waterloo or Westminster tube), British Airways' magnificently graceful millennium wheel which spins slowly and silently over the Thames. Standing 443ft high, the wheel is the largest ever built, and it's constantly in slow motion – a full-circle "flight" in one of its 32 pods takes around thirty minutes, and lifts you high above the city. It's one of the few places (apart from a plane window) from which London looks a manageable size, as you can see right out to where the suburbs slip into the countryside. Ticket prices are outrageously high, and queues can be very bad at the weekend, so book in advance over the phone or online.

The colonnaded crescent of **County Hall** is the only truly monumental building in this part of town. Designed to house the LCC (London County Council), it was completed in 1933 and enjoyed its greatest moment of fame as the headquarters of the GLC (Greater London Council), abolished by Margaret Thatcher in 1986, leaving London as the only European city without an elected authority. In 2000, the former GLC leader Ken Livingstone was elected as Mayor of London, and moved into the new GLA (Greater London Authority) building near Tower Bridge (see p.120).

County Hall, meanwhile, is in the hands of a Japanese property company, and of the various attractions that have shaped the complex's redevelopment the most popular is the **London Aquarium** (daily 10am–6pm or later; £8.75; Ⓦwww.londonaquarium.co.uk; Waterloo or Westminster tube), laid out across three floors of the basement. With some super-large, multi-floor tanks, and everything from dog-face puffers to piranhas, this is somewhere that's pretty much guaranteed to please younger kids. The "**Beach**", where children can actually stroke the (non-sting) rays, is particularly popular. Though impressive in scale, the aquarium is fairly conservative in design, however, with no walk-through tanks and only the very briefest of information on any of the fish.

Three giant surrealist sculptures on the riverside walkway in front of County Hall advertise another of the building's attractions, **Dalí Universe** (daily 10am–6pm or later; £8.50; Ⓦwww.daliuniverse.com). There's no denying Salvador Dalí was an accomplished and prolific artist, but you'll be disappointed if you're expecting to see his "greatest hits" – those are scattered across the globe. Most of the works here are little-known bronze and glass sculptures, and various drawings from the many illustrated books that he published, ranging from works by Ovid to the Marquis de Sade. Aside from these, there's one of the numerous Lobster Telephones, which Edward James commissioned for his London home, a copy of his famous Mae West lips sofa, and the oil painting from the dream sequence in Hitchcock's movie *Spellbound*.

The latest recruit to the County Hall complex is the **Saatchi Gallery** (Mon–Thurs & Sun 10am–6pm, Fri & Sat 10am–10pm; £8.50; Ⓦwww.saatchi-gallery.co.uk) of contemporary art, which now occupies the imposing former council chamber on the first floor. Charles Saatchi, the Jewish Iraqi-born art collector behind the gallery, was, in fact, the man whose advertising for the Tory government helped topple County Hall's original incumbents, the GLC. Saatchi broke with the Tate in the 1980s, after he was accused of including too many items he owned in Tate exhibitions, and went on to help promote the Young British Artists of the 1980s and 1990s, snapping up such seminal Turner Prize-nominated works as Damien Hirst's pickled shark and Tracey Emin's soiled and crumpled bed. The gallery puts on exhibitions drawn from Saatchi's vast collection.

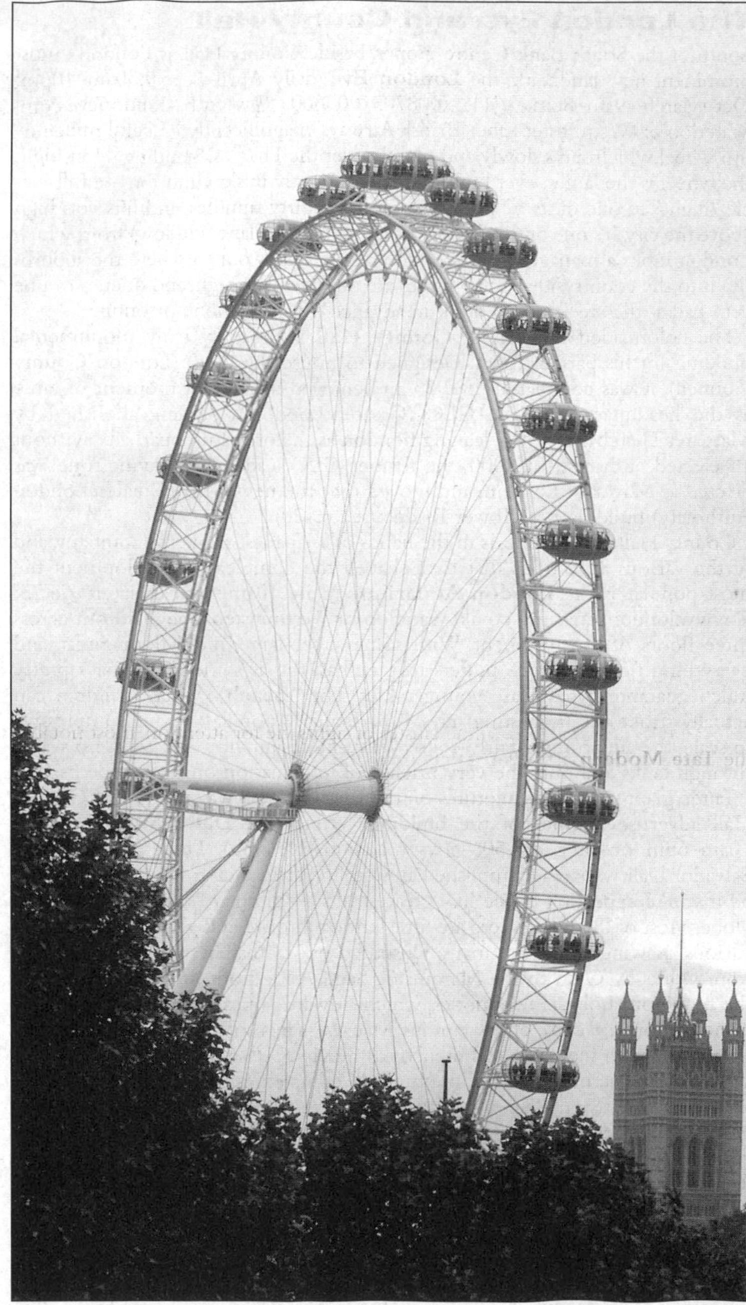

△ The London Eye

Imperial War Museum

The domed building at the east end of Lambeth Road, formerly the infamous lunatic asylum "Bedlam" is now the **Imperial War Museum** (daily 10am–6pm; free; ⓦwww.iwm.org.uk), by far the best military museum in the capital. The treatment of the subject is impressively wide-ranging and fairly sober, with the main hall's militaristic display offset by the lower-ground-floor array of documents and images attesting to the human damage of war. The museum also has a harrowing **Holocaust Exhibition** (not recommended for children under 14), which you enter from the third floor. The exhibition pulls few punches, and has made a valiant attempt to avoid depicting the victims of the Holocaust as nameless masses by focusing on individual cases, and interspersing the archive footage with eyewitness accounts from contemporary survivors.

Southwark

Until well into the seventeenth century, the only reason for north-bank residents to cross the Thames, to what is now **Southwark**, was to visit the infamous Bankside entertainment district around the south end of London Bridge, which lay outside the jurisdiction of the City. What started out as a red-light district under the Romans, reached its peak as the pleasure quarter of Tudor and Stuart London, where disreputable institutions banned in the City – most notably theatres – continued to flourish until the Puritan purges of the 1640s.

Thanks to wholesale regeneration in the last few years, Southwark's riverfront is once more somewhere to head for. The area is linked to St Paul's and the City by the fabulous new Norman Foster-designed **Millennium Bridge**, the first to cross the Thames for over a century, and London's first pedestrian-only bridge. At the end of the bridge, a whole cluster of sights vie for attention, most notably the **Tate Modern** art gallery, housed in a converted power station, and next to it, a reconstruction of Shakespeare's **Globe Theatre**. The **Thames Path** connects the district with the South Bank to the west, and allows you to walk east along Clink Street and Tooley Street, home to a further rash of popular sights such as the **London Dungeon**. Further east still, Butler's Wharf is a thriving little warehouse development centred on the excellent **Design Museum**.

Tate Modern

The masterful conversion of the austere Bankside power station into the **Tate Modern** (daily 10am–6pm; Fri & Sat open until 10pm; free; ⓦwww.tate.org.uk) has left plenty of the original, industrial feel, while providing wonderfully light and spacious galleries in which to show off the Tate's vast international twentieth-century art collection. The best way to enter is down the ramp from the west, so you get the full effect of the stupendously large turbine hall. It's easy enough to find your way around the galleries, with levels 3 and 5 displaying the permanent collection, level 4 used for fee-paying temporary exhibitions, and level 7 home to a café with a great view over the Thames.

Given that Tate Modern is the largest modern art gallery in the world, you need to spend the best part of a day here to do justice to the place, or be very selective. Pick up a plan (and, for an extra £1, an audioguide), and take the escalator to level 3. The curators have eschewed the usual chronological approach through the "isms", preferring to group works together thematically: Landscape/Matter/Environment, Still Life/Object/Real Life,

History/Memory/Society and Nude/Action/Body. On the whole this works very well, though the early twentieth-century canvases, in their gilded frames do struggle when made to compete with contemporary installations.

Although the displays change every six months or so, you're still pretty much guaranteed to see at least some works by **Monet** and Bonnard, Cubist pioneers **Picasso** and Braque, Surrealists such as **Dalí**, abstract artists like **Mondrian**, Bridget Riley and Pollock, and Pop supremos **Warhol** and Lichtenstein. There are seminal works such as a replica of **Duchamp**'s urinal, entitled *Fountain* and signed "R. Mutt", Yves Klein's totally blue paintings and Carl André's trademark piles of bricks. And such is the space here that several artists get whole rooms to themselves, among them the painter Francis Bacon, Joseph Beuys and his shamanistic wax and furs, and **Mark Rothko**, whose abstract "Seagram Murals", originally destined for a posh restaurant in New York, have their own shrine-like room in the heart of the collection.

From the Globe to the Cathedral

Seriously dwarfed by the Tate Modern but equally spectacular is **Shakespeare's Globe Theatre** (Ⓦwww.shakespeares-globe.org; Southwark or Blackfriars tube), a reconstruction of the polygonal playhouse where most of the Bard's later works were first performed, and which was originally erected on nearby Park Street in 1598. To find out more about Shakespeare and the history of Bankside, the Globe's pricey but stylish **exhibition** (daily: May–Sept 9am–noon & 12.30–4pm; Oct–April 10am–5pm; £8) is well worth a visit. It begins by detailing the long campaign by American actor Sam Wanamaker to have the Globe rebuilt, but it's the imaginative hands-on exhibits that really hit the spot. You can have a virtual play on medieval instruments such as the crumhorn or sackbut, prepare your own edition of Shakespeare, and feel the thatch, hazelnut-shell and daub used to build the theatre. Visitors also get taken on an informative **guided tour** round the theatre itself, except in the afternoons during the summer season, when you can only visit the exhibition (for a reduced entrance fee).

East of Bankside, beyond Southwark Bridge, lies **Vinopolis** (Mon, Fri & Sat noon–9pm, Tues–Thurs & Sun noon–6pm; £12.50; Ⓦwww.vinopolis.co.uk), discreetly housed in former wine vaults under the railway arches on Clink Street. The focus of the complex is the "**Wine Odyssey**", a light-hearted trot through the world's wine regions, equipped with an audioguide. There are plenty of visual gags – you get to tour round the Italian vineyards on a Vespa – but the most appealing and educative aspect of the tour is the **wine tasting**. Visitors get five generous samples – from champagne to vintage port – with the option of buying more if you've the head for it.

Further down the suitably gloomy confines of dark and narrow Clink Street is the **Clink Prison Museum** (daily 10am–6pm, until 9pm in summer; £4; Ⓦwww.clink.co.uk), built on the site of the former Clink Prison, origin of the expression "in the clink". The prison began as a dungeon for disobedient clerics, built under the Bishop of Winchester's Palace – the rose window of the palace's Great Hall survives just east of the museum – and later became a dumping ground for heretics, prostitutes and a motley assortment of Bankside lowlife. Today's exhibition features a handful of prison life tableaux, and dwells on the torture and grim conditions within, but, given the rich history of the place, this is a disappointingly lacklustre museum.

An exact replica of the **Golden Hinde** (phone for times Ⓣ08700/118700; £2.75; Ⓦwww.goldenhinde.co.uk), the galleon in which Francis Drake sailed around the world from 1577 to 1580, nestles in St Mary Overie Dock, at the eastern end of Clink Street. The ship is surprisingly small, and its original crew of eighty-plus must have been cramped to say the least. There's a refreshing lack of interpretive panels, so it's worth paying the little bit extra and getting a guided tour from one of the folk in period garb – ring ahead to check a group hasn't booked the place up.

Close by the *Golden Hinde* stands **Southwark Cathedral** (Mon–Sat 10am–6pm, Sun 11am–5pm; Ⓦwww.dswark.org/cathedral), built as the medieval Augustinian priory church of St Mary Overie, and given cathedral status only in 1905. Of the original thirteenth-century church, only the choir and retrochoir now remain, separated by a tall and beautiful stone Tudor screen, making them probably the oldest Gothic structures left in London. The nave was entirely rebuilt in the nineteenth century, but the cathedral contains numerous interesting monuments, from a thirteenth-century oak effigy of a knight to an early twentieth-century memorial to Shakespeare. If you're feeling peckish, the cathedral refectory serves tasty food, but the new multi-media **exhibition** (£3) that whizzes through Southwark's history can be happily skipped.

Borough Market (Ⓦwww.boroughmarket.org.uk), squeezed underneath the railway arches by the cathedral, is one of the few wholesale fruit and vegetable markets still trading under its original Victorian wrought-iron shed. It's recently undergone a transformation from scruffy obscurity to a small foodie haven, with permanent outlets such as Neal's Yard Dairy and Konditor & Cook, joined by gourmet market stalls on Fridays and, particularly, Saturdays.

The **Bramah Tea and Coffee Museum** has recently moved to 40 Southwark Street, a couple of blocks southwest of the cathedral. The place is endearingly ramshackle and well worth a visit. Founded in 1992 by Edward Bramah, who began his career on an African tea garden in 1950, the museum's emphasis is firmly on tea, though the café also serves a seriously good cup of coffee. There's an impressive array of teapots from Meissen to the world's largest, plus plenty of novelty ones, and coffee machines spanning the twentieth century, from huge percolator siphons to espresso machines.

From London Bridge to Butler's Wharf

The most educative and strangest of Southwark's museums, the **Old Operating Theatre, Museum and Herb Garret** on St Thomas Street (daily 10.30am–5pm; £4; Ⓦwww.thegarret.org.uk; London Bridge tube) is located to the east of the cathedral on St Thomas Street, on the other side of Borough High Street. Built in 1821 at the top of a church tower, where the hospital apothecary's herbs were stored, this women's operating theatre dates from the pre-anaesthetic era. Despite being entirely gore-free, the museum is as stomach-churning as the London Dungeon (see below). The surgeons who used this room would have concentrated on speed and accuracy (most amputations took less than a minute), but there was still a thirty percent mortality rate, with many patients simply dying of shock, and many more from bacterial infection, about which very little was known.

The vaults beneath the railway arches of London Bridge train station, on the south side of **Tooley Street**, are now occupied by two museums. Young teenagers and the credulous probably get the most out of the ever-popular **London Dungeon** (daily: March to mid-July, Sept & Oct 10am–5.30pm; mid-July to Aug 9.30am–7.30pm; Nov–Feb 10.30am–5pm; £12.95; Ⓦwww.thedungeons.com; London Bridge tube) – to avoid the inevitable queue, buy your ticket online. The life-sized waxwork tableaux inside include a man being hung, drawn and quartered and one being boiled alive, the general hysteria being boosted by actors, dressed as top-hatted Victorian vampires, pouncing out of the darkness. Visitors are then herded into a court room, condemned to the "River of Death" boat ride, and forced to endure the "Jack the Ripper Experience", an exploitative trawl through post-mortem photos and wax mock-ups of the victims, followed by the "Great Fire of London", in which you experience the heat and the smell of the plague-ridden city, before walking through a revolving tunnel of flames.

A little further east on Tooley Street is **Winston Churchill's Britain at War** (daily: April–Sept 10am–5.30pm; Oct–March 10am–4.30pm; £7.50; Ⓦwww.britainatwar.co.uk), an illuminating insight into the stiff-upper-lip London mentality during the Blitz. The museum contains hundreds of wartime artefacts, including an Anderson shelter, where you can hear the chilling sound of the V1 "doodlebugs" and tune in to contemporary radio broadcasts. The grand finale is a walk through the chaos of a just-bombed street.

There's more World War II history, from a more aggressive angle, at **HMS Belfast** (daily: March–Oct 10am–6pm; Nov–Feb 10am–5pm; £6; Ⓦwww.iwm.org.uk), a World War II cruiser, permanently moored between London Bridge and Tower Bridge. Armed with six torpedoes, and six-inch guns with a range of over fourteen miles, the *Belfast* spent over two years of the war in the Royal Naval shipyards after being hit by a mine in the Firth of Forth at the beginning of hostilities. It later saw action in the Barents Sea during World War II and during the Korean War, before being decommissioned. The maze of cabins is fun to explore but if you want to find out more about the *Belfast*, head for the exhibition rooms in zone 5.

A short stroll east of the *Belfast* is Norman Foster's startling glass-encased **City Hall** (Mon–Fri 8am–8pm; Ⓦwww.london.gov.uk), the new Greater London Authority headquarters that looks like a giant car headlight. Visitors are welcome to stroll around the building and watch the London Assembly proceedings from the second floor.

In contrast to the brash offices on Tooley Street, **Butler's Wharf**, east of Tower Bridge, has retained its historical character. **Shad Thames**, the narrow street at the back of Butler's Wharf, has kept the wrought-iron overhead gangways by which the porters used to transport goods from the wharves to the warehouses further back from the river, and is one of the most atmospheric alleyways in the whole of Bermondsey. The chief attraction of Butler's Wharf is the superb riverside **Design Museum** (daily 10am–5.45pm, Fri until 9pm; £6; Ⓦwww.designmuseum.org; Bermondsey or Tower Hill tube), a stylish, Bauhaus-like conversion of a 1950s warehouse at the eastern end of Shad Thames. The excellent temporary **exhibitions** on important designers, movements or single products are staged on the first floor, while the **galleries** on the top floor offer a brief overview of mass-produced industrial design from TVs to Tupperware. The small coffee bar in the foyer is a great place to relax, and there's a pricier restaurant on the top floor.

Hyde Park, Kensington and Chelsea

Hyde Park, together with its westerly extension, Kensington Gardens, covers a distance of two miles from Oxford Street in the northeast to Kensington Palace in the southwest. At the end of your journey, you've made it to one of London's most exclusive districts, the Royal Borough of **Kensington** and **Chelsea**, which makes up the bulk of this chapter. Other districts go in and out of fashion, but this area has been in vogue ever since royalty moved into **Kensington Palace** in the late seventeenth century.

Aside from the shops around Harrods in Knightsbridge, however, the popular tourist attractions lie in **South Kensington**, where three of London's top (and currently free) **museums** – the Victoria and Albert, Natural History and Science museums – stand on land bought with the proceeds of the Great Exhibition of 1851. Chelsea, to the south, has a slightly more bohemian pedigree. In the 1960s, the **King's Road** carved out its reputation as London's catwalk, while in the late 1970s it was the epicentre of the punk explosion. Nothing so rebellious goes on in Chelsea now, though its residents like to think of themselves as rather more artistic and intellectual than the purely moneyed types of Kensington.

Once slummy, now swanky, **Bayswater** and **Notting Hill**, to the north of Hyde Park, were the bad boys of the borough for many years, dens of vice and crime comparable to Soho. Despite gentrification over the last 25 years, they remain the borough's most cosmopolitan districts, with a strong Arab presence and vestiges of the African-Caribbean community who initiated and still run the city's (and Europe's) largest street **carnival**, which takes place every August Bank Holiday.

Hyde Park and Kensington Gardens

Seized from the Church by Henry VIII to satisfy his desire for yet more hunting grounds, **Hyde Park** (Ⓦwww.royalparks.gov.uk) was first opened to the public by James I, and soon became a fashionable gathering place for the beau monde, who rode round the circular drive known as the Ring, pausing to gossip and admire each other's *équipage*. Hangings, muggings and duels, the Great Exhibition of 1851 and numerous public events have all taken place in Hyde Park and even today it's still a popular gathering point or destination for political demonstrations. For most of the time, however, the park is simply a leisure ground – a wonderful open space that allows you to lose all sight of the city beyond a few persistent tower blocks.

Located at the treeless northeastern corner of the park, **Marble Arch** was originally erected in 1828 as a triumphal entry to Buckingham Palace, but is now stranded on a ferociously busy traffic island at the west end of Oxford Street. This is the most historically charged spot in Hyde Park as it marks the site of **Tyburn gallows**, the city's main public execution spot until 1783. It's also the location of **Speakers' Corner**, a peculiarly English Sunday morning tradition, featuring an assembly of ranters and hecklers.

A better place to enter the park is at **Hyde Park Corner**, the southeast corner, where the **Wellington Arch** (Wed–Sun: April–Sept 10am–6pm; Oct 10am–5pm; Nov–March 10am–4pm; £2.50) stands in the midst of another of London's busiest traffic interchanges. Erected in 1828 to commemorate Wellington's victories in the Napoleonic Wars, the arch was originally topped by an equestrian statue of the Duke himself, later replaced by Peace driving a four-horse chariot. Inside, you can view an exhibition on London's outdoor sculpture and take a lift to the top of the monument where the exterior balconies offer a bird's eye view of the swirling traffic.

Close by stands **Apsley House** (Tues–Sun 11am–5pm; £4.50; Ⓦwww.apsleyhouse.org.uk), Wellington's London residence and now a museum to the "Iron Duke". Unless you're a keen fan of the Duke (or the architect, Benjamin Wyatt), the highlight of the museum is the **art collection**, much of which used to belong to the King of Spain. Among the best pieces, displayed in the Waterloo

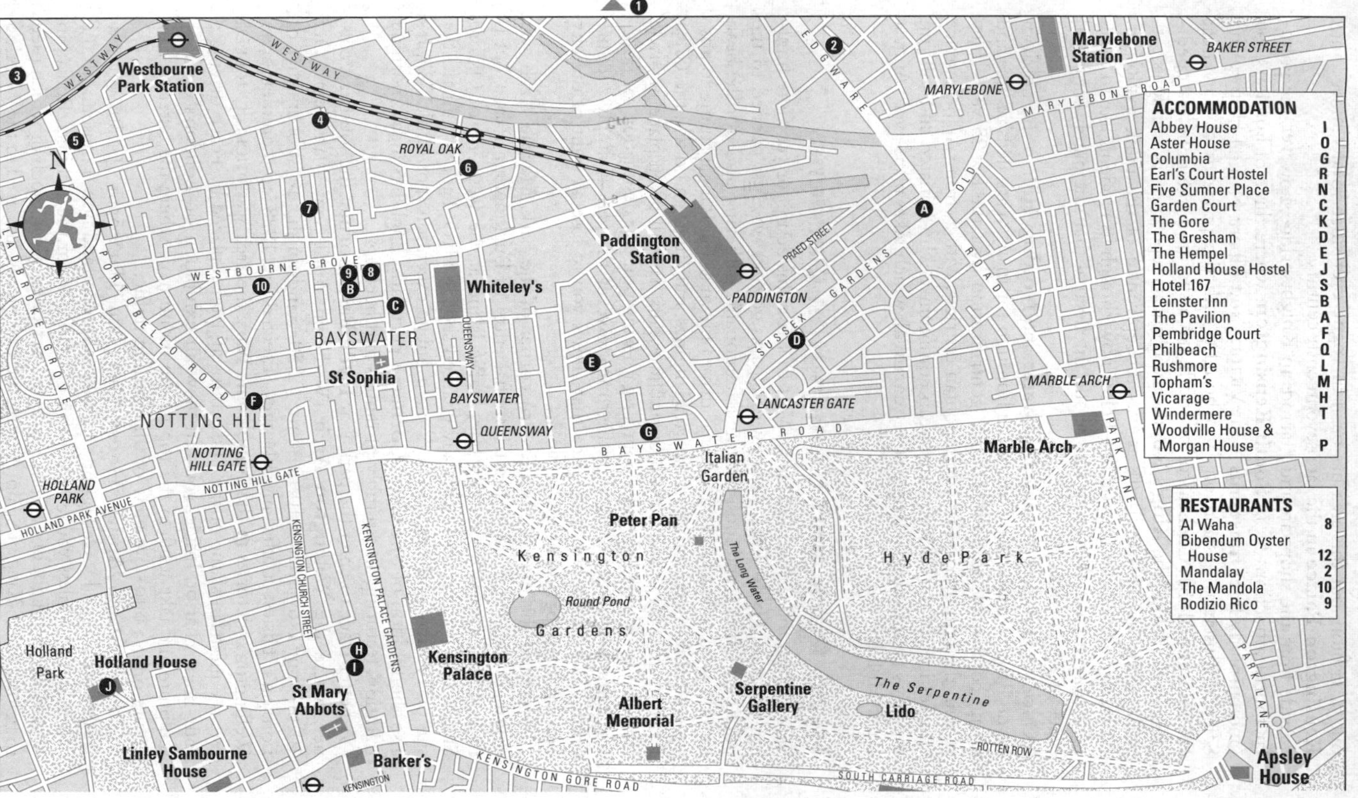
ACCOMMODATION
Abbey House I
Aster House O
Columbia G
Earl's Court Hostel R
Five Sumner Place N
Garden Court C
The Gore K
The Gresham D
The Hempel E
Holland House Hostel J
Hotel 167 S
Leinster Inn B
The Pavilion A
Pembridge Court F
Philbeach Q
Rushmore L
Topham's M
Vicarage H
Windermere T
Woodville House & Morgan House P
RESTAURANTS
Al Waha 8
Bibendum Oyster House 12
Mandalay 2
The Mandola 10
Rodizio Rico 9
Marylebone Station
BAKER STREET
MARYLEBONE
MARYLEBONE ROAD
Westbourne Park Station
WESTWAY
ROYAL OAK
EDGWARE ROAD
OLD ROAD
PRAED STREET
SUSSEX GARDENS
Paddington Station
PADDINGTON
Whiteley's
QUEENSWAY
BAYSWATER
St Sophia
WESTBOURNE GROVE
PORTOBELLO ROAD
LADBROKE GROVE
NOTTING HILL
NOTTING HILL GATE
HOLLAND PARK
HOLLAND PARK AVENUE
LANCASTER GATE
MARBLE ARCH
Marble Arch
BAYSWATER ROAD
PARK LANE
Italian Garden
Peter Pan
Kensington Gardens
Round Pond
The Long Water
Hyde Park
The Serpentine
Lido
Serpentine Gallery
Albert Memorial
Kensington Palace
KENSINGTON PALACE GARDENS
KENSINGTON CHURCH STREET
St Mary Abbots
Holland Park
Holland House
Linley Sambourne House
Barker's
KENSINGTON
KENSINGTON GORE ROAD
SOUTH CARRIAGE ROAD
ROTTEN ROW
Apsley House
N

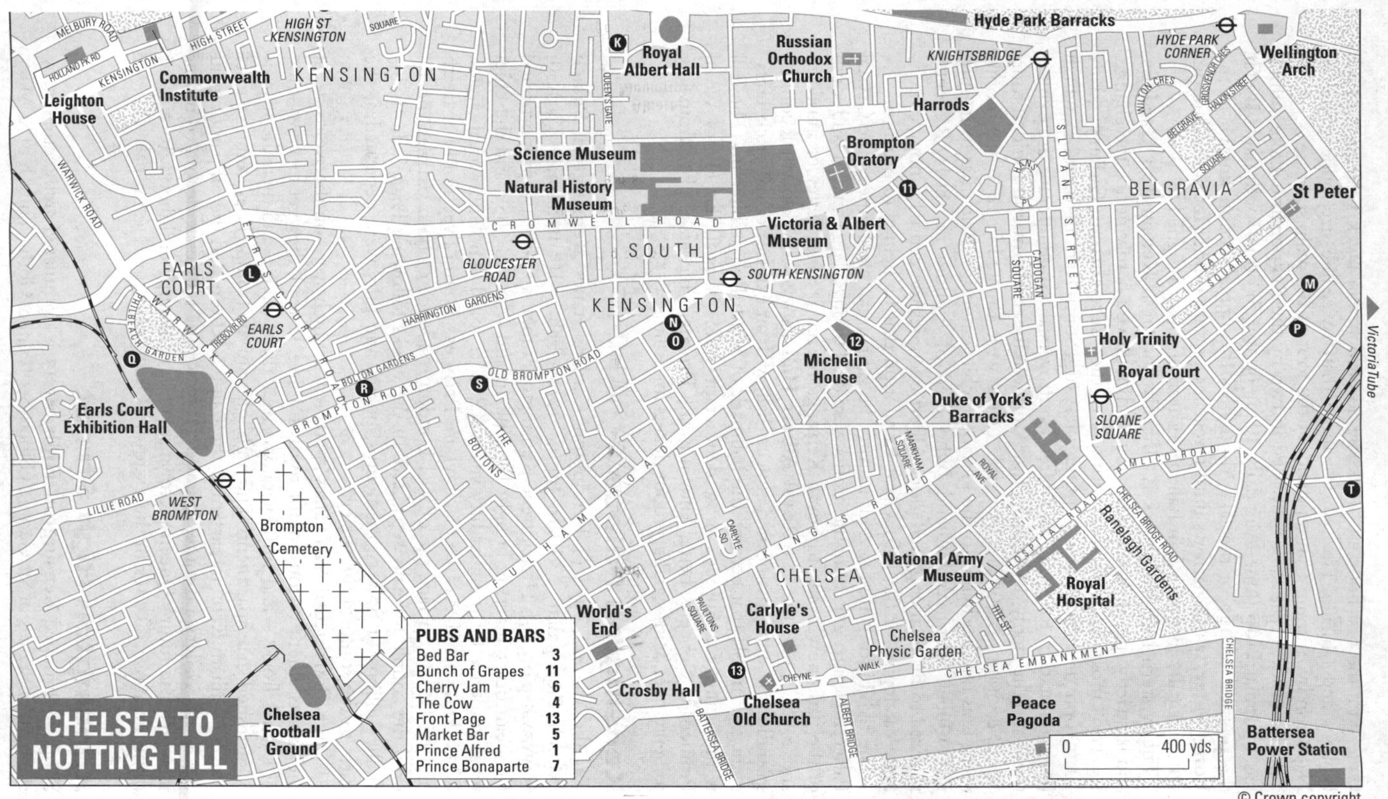
CHELSEA TO NOTTING HILL
PUBS AND BARS
Bed Bar 3
Bunch of Grapes 11
Cherry Jam 6
The Cow 4
Front Page 13
Market Bar 5
Prince Alfred 1
Prince Bonaparte 7
Hyde Park Barracks
Wellington Arch
HYDE PARK CORNER
KNIGHTSBRIDGE
Russian Orthodox Church
Royal Albert Hall
Commonwealth Institute
Leighton House
KENSINGTON
HIGH ST KENSINGTON
Harrods
Brompton Oratory
Science Museum
Natural History Museum
Victoria & Albert Museum
BELGRAVIA
St Peter
CROMWELL ROAD
SOUTH KENSINGTON
GLOUCESTER ROAD
EARLS COURT
Holy Trinity
Royal Court
SLOANE SQUARE
SLOANE STREET
CADOGAN SQUARE
EATON SQUARE
Michelin House
Duke of York's Barracks
Earls Court Exhibition Hall
WEST BROMPTON
Brompton Cemetery
OLD BROMPTON ROAD
BROMPTON ROAD
FULHAM ROAD
KING'S ROAD
PIMLICO ROAD
CHELSEA BRIDGE ROAD
Ranelagh Gardens
Royal Hospital
National Army Museum
CHELSEA
Carlyle's House
Chelsea Physic Garden
World's End
Crosby Hall
Chelsea Old Church
Chelsea Football Ground
CHELSEA EMBANKMENT
Peace Pagoda
Battersea Power Station
ALBERT BRIDGE
BATTERSEA BRIDGE
CHELSEA BRIDGE
Victoria Tube
0 400 yds
© Crown copyright

Gallery on the first floor, are works by de Hooch, van Dyck, Velázquez, Goya, Rubens and Murillo. The famous, more than twice life-size, nude statue of Napoleon by Antonio Canova stands at the foot of the main staircase.

Back outside, Hyde Park is divided in two by the **Serpentine Lake**, which has a popular **Lido** (June–Aug daily 10am–6pm; £3) on its south bank. By far the prettiest section of the lake, though, is the upper section known as the **Long Water**, which narrows until it reaches a group of four fountains, laid out symmetrically in front of an Italianate summerhouse designed by Wren.

The western half of the park is officially known as **Kensington Gardens**, and is, strictly speaking, a separate entity, though you hardly notice the change. Its two most popular attractions are the **Serpentine Gallery** (daily 10am–6pm; free; Ⓦwww.serpentinegallery.org; South Kensington tube), which has a reputation for lively, and often controversial, contemporary art exhibitions, and the richly decorated, High Gothic **Albert Memorial** (guided tours Sun 2 & 3pm; £3.50), clearly visible to the west. Erected in 1876, the monument is as much a hymn to the glorious achievements of Britain as to its subject, Queen Victoria's husband (who died of typhoid in 1861). Recently restored to his former gilded glory, Albert occupies the central canopy, clutching a catalogue for the 1851 Great Exhibition that he helped to organize.

The Exhibition's most famous feature, the gargantuan glasshouse of the Crystal Palace, no longer exists, but the profits were used to buy a large tract of land south of the park, now home to South Kensington's remarkable cluster of museums and colleges, plus the vast **Royal Albert Hall** (Ⓦwww.royalalberthall.com), a splendid iron-and-glass-domed concert hall, with an exterior of red brick, terracotta and marble that became the hallmark of South Ken architecture. The hall is the venue for Europe's most democratic music festival, the Henry Wood Promenade Concerts, better known as the **Proms**, which take place from July to September, with standing-room tickets for as little as £3.

Kensington Palace

On the western edge of Kensington Gardens stands **Kensington Palace** (March–Oct daily 10am–6pm; Nov–Feb 10am–5pm; £10.50; Ⓦwww.hrp.org.uk; High Street Kensington tube), a modestly proportioned Jacobean brick mansion bought by William and Mary in 1689, and the chief royal residence for the next fifty years. KP, as it's fondly known in royal circles, is best known today as the place where **Princess Diana** lived until her death in 1997. It was, in fact, the official London residence of both Charles and Di until the couple formally separated. In the weeks following Diana's death, literally millions of flowers, mementos, poems and gifts were deposited at the gates to the south of the palace.

Visitors don't get to see Diana's apartments, which were on the west side of the palace, where various minor royals still live. Instead, they get to view some of Diana's frocks – and also several worn by the Queen – and then the sparsely furnished state apartments. The highlights are the trompe l'oeil ceiling paintings by William Kent, in particular the Cupola Room, and the oil paintings in the King's Gallery. En route, you also get to see the tastelessly decorated rooms in which the future Queen Victoria spent her unhappy childhood. To recover from the above, take tea in the exquisite **Orangery** (times as for palace).

Kensington High Street

Shopper-thronged **Kensington High Street** is dominated architecturally by the twin presences of Sir George Gilbert Scott's neo-Gothic church of St Mary

Abbots, whose 250-foot spire makes it London's tallest parish church, and the Art Deco colossus of Barkers department store, remodelled in the 1930s.

Hidden away in the backstreets to the north of High Street Kensington is the densely wooded **Holland Park**, the former grounds of a Jacobean mansion (only the east wing still stands), where theatrical and musical performances are staged throughout the summer and several **formal gardens** surround the house – most notably the Japanese-style Kyoto Gardens – while the rest of the park is dotted with a series of abstract sculptures.

A number of wealthy Victorian artists rather self-consciously founded an artists' colony in the streets that lie between the High Street and Holland Park. It's possible to visit one of the most remarkable of these artist pads, **Leighton House**, at 12 Holland Park Rd (daily except Tues 11am–5.30pm; free; Ⓦwww.rbkc.gov.uk/leightonhousemuseum). "It will be opulence, it will be sincerity," Lord Leighton opined before starting work on the house in the 1860s – he later became President of the Royal Academy and was ennobled on his deathbed. The big attraction is the domed Arab Hall, decorated with Saracen tiles, gilded mosaics and woodwork drawn from all over the Islamic world. The other rooms are less spectacular but, in compensation, are hung with paintings by Lord Leighton and his Pre-Raphaelite chums.

Notting Hill

Epicentre of the country's first race riots, when bus-loads of whites attacked West Indian homes in the area, **Notting Hill** is now more famous for its annual **Carnival**, which began life in direct response to the riots. These days, it's the world's biggest street festival outside Rio, with an estimated two million revellers turning up on the last weekend of August for the two-day extravaganza of parades, steel bands and deafening sound systems.

The rest of the year, Notting Hill is a lot quieter, though its cafés and restaurants are cool enough places to pull in folk from all over. On Saturdays, big crowds of Londoners and tourists alike descend on the mile-long **Portobello Road Market**, which is lined with stalls selling everything from antiques to cheap second-hand clothes and fruit and vegetables.

Within easy walking distance of Portobello Road, on the other side of the railway tracks, gasworks and canal, is **Kensal Green Cemetery** (Ⓦwww.kensalgreen.co.uk; Kensal Green tube), opened in 1833 and still a functioning burial ground. Graves of the more famous incumbents – Thackeray, Trollope and Brunel – are less interesting architecturally than those arranged on either side of the Centre Avenue, which leads from the easternmost entrance on Harrow Road. Guided tours of the cemetery take place every Sunday at 2pm (£5); on the first and third Sunday of month, the tour includes a trip down the catacombs (bring a torch).

Knightsbridge and Harrods

South of Hyde Park lies the irredeemably snobbish **Knightsbridge**, revelling in its reputation as the swankiest shopping area in London, a status epitomized by **Harrods** (Mon–Sat 10am–7pm; Ⓦwww.harrods.com) on Brompton Road. London's most famous department store started out as a family-run grocery store in 1849, with a staff of two. The current 1905 terracotta building is owned by the Egyptian Mohammed Al Fayed and employs in excess of 3000 staff. Tourists flock to Harrods – it's thought to be one of the city's top-ranking tourist attractions – though if you can do without the Harrods carrier bag, you can buy most of what the shop stocks more cheaply elsewhere.

The store does, however, have a few sections that are architectural sights in their own right: the Food Hall, with its exquisite Arts and Crafts tiling, and the Egyptian Hall, with its pseudo-hieroglyphs and sphinxes, are particularly striking. Now that a fountain dedicated to Di and Dodi is in place, the Egyptian Escalators are an added attraction, and will whisk you to the first floor "luxury washrooms", where you can splash on free perfume after relieving yourself. Note, too, that the store has a draconian dress code: no shorts, no vest T-shirts and backpacks must be carried in the hand.

Victoria and Albert Museum (V&A)

In terms of sheer variety and scale, the **Victoria and Albert Museum**, on Cromwell Road (daily 10am–5.45pm, Wed & last Fri of month until 10pm; free; Ⓦ www.vam.ac.uk; South Kensington tube), popularly known as the V&A, is the greatest museum of applied arts in the world. The range of exhibits on display here means that, whatever your taste, there's bound to be something to grab your attention among the beautifully but haphazardly displayed seven miles of halls and corridors. With such a large collection, the V&A's treasures are impossible to survey in a single visit so a floor plan from the information desks is useful to help you decide which areas to concentrate on. If you're flagging, there's a restaurant in the basement of the Henry Cole Wing, or a more edifying, snacky café in the museum's period-piece **Poynter, Morris and Gamble** refreshment rooms.

The most celebrated of the V&A's numerous exhibits are the **Raphael Cartoons**, seven vast biblical paintings that served as designs for a set of tapestries destined for the Sistine Chapel. Close by, you can view highlights from the country's largest dress collection, and the world's largest collection of Indian art outside India. In addition, there are galleries devoted to British, Chinese, Islamic, Japanese and Korean art, as well as costume jewellery, glassware, metalwork and photography. Wading through the huge collection of European sculpture, you come to the surreal **Plaster Casts** gallery, filled with copies of European art's greatest hits, from Michelangelo's *David* to Trajan's Column (sawn in half to make it fit). There's even a gallery of twentieth-century objets d'art – everything from Bauhaus furniture to Swatch watches – to rival that of the Design Museum.

Over in the **Henry Cole Wing**, meanwhile, you'll find an entire office interior by Frank Lloyd Wright, a collection of sixteenth-century portrait miniatures, more Constable paintings than the Tate, and a goodly collection of sculptures by Rodin. As if all this were not enough, the V&A's temporary shows are among the best in Britain, ranging over vast areas of art, craft and technology.

If you've energy left after your visit, stop by London's most flamboyant Roman Catholic church, the **Brompton Oratory**, built in Neo-Baroque style in the 1880s, which lies just next door to the museum on Brompton Road.

Science Museum

Established as a technological counterpart to the V&A, the **Science Museum**, on Exhibition Road (daily 10am–6pm; free; Ⓦ www.sciencemuseum.org.uk; South Kensington tube), on Exhibition Road, is undeniably impressive, filling seven floors with items drawn from every conceivable area of science, including space travel, telecommunications, time measurement, chemistry, computing, photography and medicine. Keen to dispel the enduring image of museums devoted to its subject as boring and full of dusty glass cabinets, the Science Museum has been busy updating its galleries with more interactive displays, and puts on daily demonstrations to show that not all science teaching has to be deathly dry.

First off, head for the **information desk** in the Power Hall and find out what events and demonstrations are taking place; you can also sign up for a guided tour on a specific subject. Most people will want to head for the **Wellcome Wing**, full of state-of-the-art interactive computers and an IMAX cinema, and geared to appeal to even the most museum-phobic teenager. To get there, go past the info desk, and through the Space gallery, to the far side of the Making of the Modern World, a display of iconic inventions from Robert Stephenson's *Rocket* train of 1829 to the Ford Model T, the world's first mass-produced car.

The **Launch Pad**, one of the first hands-on displays aimed at kids, remains as popular and enjoyable as ever, as do the **Garden** and **Things** galleries all of which are in the basement. The **Materials** gallery, on the first floor, is aimed more at adults, and is an extremely stylish exhibition covering the use of materials ranging from aluminium to zerodur (used for making laser gyroscopes).

Natural History Museum

Alfred Waterhouse's purpose-built mock-Romanesque colossus ensures the **Natural History Museum** (Mon–Sat 10am–5.50pm, Sun 11am–5.50pm; free; Ⓦwww.nhm.ac.uk; South Kensington tube) its status as London's most handsome museum. Caught up, without huge public funds, in the current enthusiasm for museum redesign and accessibility, the contents are a mishmash of truly imaginative exhibits peppered amongst others little changed since the museum's opening in 1881. The museum is caught in a genuine conundrum, for its collections are important resources for serious zoologists, while its collection of real dinosaurs is a big hit with the kids.

The **main entrance**, in the middle of the 675-foot terracotta facade, leads to what are now known as the **Life Galleries**. Just off the vast Central Hall, dominated by an 85-foot-long plaster cast of a Diplodocus skeleton, you'll find the Dinosaur gallery, where a team of animatronic deinonychi feast on a half-dead tenontosaurus. Other popular sections include the Creepy-Crawlies Room, the Mammals gallery with its life-size model of a blue whale, and the high-tech Ecology Gallery, plus the somewhat ancient displays of stuffed creatures.

Visitors can view more of the museum's millions of zoological specimens in the collections store of the new **Darwin Centre**, Phase One of which opened in 2002. To see the rest of the building, however, you need to sign up for a **guided tour** (book ahead either online or by phone Ⓣ020/7942 6128; free). These set off roughly every half an hour and last about 35 minutes, allowing visitors to get a closer look at the specimens, including the larger ones which have to be preserved in tanks. You also get to see behind the scenes at the labs, and even talk to one of the museum's 350 scientists about their work.

If the queues for the museum are long (as they can be at weekends and during school holidays), you might be better off heading for the side entrance on Exhibition Road, which leads into the former Geology Museum, now known as the **Earth Galleries**, an expensively revamped and visually exciting romp through the earth's evolution. The most popular sections are the slightly tasteless Kobe earthquake simulator, and the spectacular display of gems and crystals in the Earth's Treasury.

Chelsea

It wasn't until the latter part of the nineteenth century that **Chelsea** began to earn its reputation as London's very own Left Bank. Its household fame, however, came through the **King's Road**'s role as the unofficial catwalk of the "Swinging Sixties". The road remained a fashion parade for hippies too, and in the Jubilee Year of 1977 it witnessed the birth of punk, masterminded from a shop called Sex, run by Vivienne Westwood and Malcolm McLaren. These days, the area is better known for its young, upper-class residents – the original Sloane Rangers – and is lined with the usual chain stores and interior design shops.

Among the most nattily attired of all those parading down the King's Road are the scarlet or navy-blue clad Chelsea Pensioners, army veterans from the nearby **Royal Hospital** (Mon–Fri 9am–noon & 2–4.30pm, Sat & Sun closes 3pm; free; Sloane Square tube), founded by Charles II in 1681. The hospital's majestic red-brick wings and grassy courtyards became a blueprint for institutional and collegiate architecture all over the English-speaking world. The public are allowed to view the austere hospital chapel, and the equally grand, wood-panelled dining hall, opposite, which has a vast allegorical mural of Charles II.

The concrete bunker next door to the Royal Hospital, on Royal Hospital Road, houses the **National Army Museum** (daily 10am–5.30pm; free; Ⓦwww.national-army-museum.ac.uk). The militarily obsessed are unlikely to be disappointed by the succession of uniforms and medals, but there's little here for non-enthusiasts. The temporary exhibitions staged on the ground floor are the museum's strong point, but it's rather disappointing overall – you're better off visiting the infinitely superior Imperial War Museum (see p.117).

Cheyne Walk and Cheyne Row

The quiet riverside locale of **Cheyne Walk** (pronounced "chainy") drew artists and writers in great numbers during the nineteenth century. Since the building of the Embankment and the increase in the volume of traffic, however, the character of this peaceful haven has been lost. Novelist Henry James, who lived at no. 21, used to take "beguiling drives" in his wheelchair along the Embankment; today, he'd be hospitalized in the process.

The chief reason to come here nowadays is to visit the **Chelsea Physic Garden** (April–Oct Wed noon–5pm, Sun 2–6pm; £4; Ⓦwww.chelseaphysicgarden.co.uk; Sloane Square tube), which marks the beginning of Cheyne Walk. Founded in 1673, this small walled garden is the second oldest botanic garden in the country. At the entrance (on Swan Walk) you can pick up a map of the garden with a list of the month's most interesting flowers and shrubs, whose labels are slightly more forthcoming than the usual terse Latinate tags. The garden also has an excellent teahouse, where you can get delicious home-made cakes.

It's also worth popping into the nearby **Chelsea Old Church** (daily 9.30am–1pm & 2–4.30pm; Sloane Square tube), halfway down Cheyne Walk, where Thomas More built his own private chapel in the south aisle. The church was badly bombed in the last war, but an impressive number of monuments were retrieved from the rubble and continue to adorn the church's interior.

A short distance inland from Cheyne Walk, at 24 Cheyne Row, is **Carlyle's House** (April–Oct Wed–Sun 11am–5pm; £3.50; NT; Sloane Square tube), where the historian Thomas Carlyle set up home, having moved down from his native Scotland in 1834. The house became a museum just fifteen years after Carlyle's death and is a typically dour Victorian abode, kept much as the Carlyles would have had it: the historian's hat still hanging in the hall, his socks in the chest of drawers.

North London

Almost all of **North London**'s suburbs are easily accessible by tube from the centre – indeed it was the expansion of the tube which encouraged the forward march of bricks and mortar into many of these areas – though just a handful of these satellite villages, now subsumed into the general mass of the city, are worth bothering with.

The first section covers one of London's finest parks, **Regent's Park**, framed by Nash-designed architecture and home of London Zoo. Close by is **Camden Town**, where the weekend market is one of the city's big attractions – a warren of stalls selling street fashion, books, records and ethnic goods.

The real highlights of north London, though, for visitors and residents alike, are **Hampstead** and **Highgate**, elegant, largely eighteenth-century developments which still reflect their village origins. They have the added advantage of proximity to one of London's wildest patches of greenery, **Hampstead Heath**, where you can enjoy stupendous views, kite flying and outdoor bathing, as well as outdoor concerts and high art in the setting of **Kenwood House**.

Regent's Park

As with almost all of London's royal parks, we have Henry VIII to thank for **Regent's Park** (ⓦwww.royalparks.org.uk; Regent's Park, Baker Street or Great Portland Street tube), which he confiscated from the Church for yet more hunting grounds. However, it wasn't until the reign of the Prince Regent (later George IV) that the park began to take its current form. According to the masterplan, devised by John Nash in 1811, the park was to be girded by a continuous belt of terraces, and sprinkled with a total of 56 villas, including a magnificent pleasure palace for the Prince himself, which would be linked by Regent Street to Carlton House in St James's. The plan was never fully realized, due to lack of funds, but enough was built to create something of the idealized garden city that Nash and the Prince Regent envisaged.

To appreciate the special quality of Regent's Park, take a closer look at the architecture, starting with the Nash terraces, which form a near-unbroken horseshoe of cream-coloured stucco around the Outer Circle. Within the Inner Circle is the **Open Air Theatre** (ⓦwww.openairtheatre.org), which puts on summer performances of Shakespeare, opera and ballet, and **Queen Mary's Gardens**, by far the prettiest section of the park. A large slice of the gardens is taken up with a glorious rose garden, featuring some four hundred varieties, surrounded by a ring of ramblers.

The northeastern corner of the park is occupied by **London Zoo** (March–Oct 10am–5.30pm; Nov–Feb 10am–4pm; £12; ⓦwww.londonzoo.co.uk; Camden tube), founded in 1826. It may not be the most uplifting place for animal lovers, but kids love it – smaller ones are particularly taken with the children's enclosure, where they can actually handle the animals, and the regular "Animals in Action" live shows. The zoo boasts some striking architectural features, too, most notably the modernist, spiral-ramped 1930s concrete penguin pool (where Penguin Books' original colophon was sketched); it was designed by the Tecton partnership, led by Russian emigre Berthold Lubetkin. Other zoo landmarks include the colossal tetrahedral aluminium-framed tent of the Snowdon Aviary, and the eco-conscious invertebrate-filled Web of Life.

Regent's canal by boat

Three companies run **boat services** on the Regent's Canal between Camden Lock (Camden Town tube) and Little Venice (Warwick Avenue tube), passing through the Maida Hill tunnel and stopping off at London Zoo on the way. The narrowboat *Jenny Wren* (ⓣ020/7485 4433) starts off at Camden Lock, at the top of Camden High Street, while Jason's narrowboats (ⓣ020/7286 3428, ⓦwww.jasons.co.uk) start off at Little Venice, opposite 60 Blomfield Rd; the London Waterbus Company (ⓣ020/7482 2660) sets off from both places. Jason's and the London Waterbus Company run all year round, though on weekends only during winter. Whichever you choose, you can board at either end; **tickets** cost around £5–6 one-way (and only a little more return) and journey time is 50 minutes one-way.

Camden Town

For all the gentrification of the last twenty years, **Camden Town** retains a gritty aspect, compounded by the various railway lines that plough through the area, the canal, and the large shelter for the homeless on Arlington Street. The market, however, gives the area a positive lift on the weekends, and is now the district's best-known attribute.

Having started out as a tiny crafts market in the cobbled courtyard by the lock, **Camden Market** has since mushroomed out of all proportion. More than 100,000 shoppers turn up here each weekend, and parts of the market now stay open week-long, alongside a similarly-oriented crop of shops, cafés and bistros. The sheer variety of what's on offer: from bootleg tapes to furniture, along with a mass of street fashion and clubwear, and plenty of foodstalls, is what makes Camden so special. To avoid the crowds, which can be overpowering on a summer Sunday afternoon, you'll need to get here by 10am – by 4pm many of the stalls will be packing up.

Despite having no significant Jewish associations, Camden is home to London's **Jewish Museum** (Mon–Thurs 10am–4pm, Sun 10am–5pm; £3.50; ⓦwww.jewishmuseum.org.uk), at 129 Albert St, just off Parkway. The purpose-built premises are smartly designed, but the conventional style and contents of the museum are disappointing: apart from the usual displays of Judaica, there's a video and exhibition explaining Jewish religious practices and the history of the Jewish community in Britain. More challenging temporary exhibitions are held in the museum's Finchley branch at 80 East End Rd, N3 (ⓣ020/8349 1143; Finchley Central tube).

Hampstead

Perched on a hill above Camden Town, **Hampstead** village developed into a fashionable spa in the eighteenth century, after a celebrated physician declared the waters of its spring as being of great medicinal value. Its sloping site, which deterred Victorian property speculators and put off the railway companies, saved much of the Georgian village from destruction, and it's little altered to this day. Later, it became one of the city's most celebrated literary *quartiers* and even now it retains its reputation as a bolt hole of the high-profile intelligentsia. You can get some idea of its tone from the fact that the local Labour MP is currently the actress-turned-politician Glenda Jackson.

Whichever route you take north of Hampstead tube, you'll probably end up at the small triangular green on Holly Bush Hill, on the north side of which stands the late-seventeenth-century **Fenton House** (mid-March to Oct

Wed–Fri 2–5pm, Sat & Sun 11am–5pm; £4.50; NT; Hampstead tube). As well as housing a collection of European and Oriental ceramics, this National Trust house contains the superb Benton-Fletcher collection of early musical instruments, chiefly displayed on the top floor. Among the many spinets, virginals and clavichords are the earliest extant English grand piano, and an Unverdorben lute from 1580 (one of only three in the world). For an extra £1, you can hire a tape of music played on the above instruments, to listen to while you walk round.

For a fascinating insight into the modernist mindset, take a look inside **2 Willow Road** (March & Nov Sat noon–5pm; April–Oct Thurs–Sat noon–5pm; £4.50; NT; Hampstead tube), an unassuming red-brick terraced house at the far end of Flask Walk, which leads east off the High Street. Built in the 1930s by the Hungarian-born architect Ernö Goldfinger, this was a state-of-the-art pad, its open-plan rooms flooded with natural light and much of the furniture designed by Goldfinger himself. Strangely for a modernist, Goldfinger changed little in the house in the following sixty years, so what you see is a 1930s avant-garde dwelling preserved in aspic, a house at once both modern and old-fashioned. An added bonus is that the rooms are packed with *objets trouvés* and works of art by the likes of Max Ernst, Marcel Duchamp, Henry Moore and Man Ray. Before 3pm, visits are by hour-long guided tour only (noon, 1 & 2pm), for which you must book in advance; after 3pm the public has unguided, unrestricted access.

Hampstead's most lustrous figure is celebrated at **Keats' House** (Tues–Sun: April–Oct noon–5pm; Nov–March noon–4pm; £3; Ⓦwww.cityoflondon.gov.uk/keats; Hampstead tube), an elegant, whitewashed Regency double villa on Keats Grove, a short walk south of Willow Road. Inspired by the peacefulness of Hampstead and by his passion for girl-next-door Fanny Brawne (whose house is also part of the museum), Keats wrote some of his most famous works here before leaving for Rome, where he died of consumption in 1821. The neat, rather staid interior contains books and letters, Fanny's engagement ring and the four-poster bed in which the poet first coughed up blood, confiding to his companion, Charles Brown, "that drop of blood is my death warrant".

One of the most poignant of London's house museums is the **Freud Museum** (Wed–Sun noon–5pm; £5; Ⓦwww.freud.org.uk; Finchley Road tube), hidden away in the leafy streets of south Hampstead at 20 Maresfield Gardens. Having lived in Vienna for his entire adult life, Freud, by now semi-disabled with only a year to live, was forced to flee the Nazis, arriving in London in the summer of 1938. The ground-floor study and library look exactly as they did when Freud lived here; the collection of erotic antiquities and the famous couch, sumptuously draped in Persian carpets, were all brought here from Vienna. Upstairs, home movies of family life in Vienna are shown continually, and a small room is dedicated to his daughter, Anna, herself an influential child analyst, who lived in the house until her death in 1982.

Hampstead Heath and Kenwood

North London's "green lung", **Hampstead Heath** is the city's most enjoyable public park. It may not have much of its original heathland left, but it packs a wonderful variety of bucolic scenery into its 800 acres. At its southern end are the rolling green pastures of **Parliament Hill**, north London's premier spot for kite flying. On either side are numerous ponds, three of which – one for men, one for women and one mixed – you can swim in for free. The thickest woodland is to be found in the **West Heath**, beyond Whitestone Pond, also the site of the most formal section, **Hill Garden**, a secretive and romantic little gem with eccentric balustraded terraces and a ruined pergola. Beyond lies **Golders Hill Park**, where you can gaze at pygmy goats and fallow deer, and inspect the impeccably maintained aviaries, home to flamingos, cranes and other exotic birds.

Finally, don't miss the landscaped grounds of Kenwood, in the north of the Heath, which are focused on the whitewashed Neoclassical mansion of **Kenwood House** (daily: April–Sept 10am–6pm; Oct 10am–5pm; Nov–March 10am–4pm; free; EH; Hampstead tube or bus #210 from Archway tube). The house is now home to the **Iveagh Bequest**, a collection of seventeenth- and eighteenth-century art, including a handful of real masterpieces by the likes of Vermeer, Rembrandt, Boucher, Gainsborough and Reynolds. Of the house's period interiors, the most spectacular is Robert Adam's sky-blue and gold **library**, its book-filled apses separated from the central entertaining area by paired columns. To the south of the house, a grassy amphitheatre slopes down to a lake where outdoor classical concerts are held on summer evenings.

Highgate

Northeast of the Heath, and fractionally lower than Hampstead (appearances notwithstanding), **Highgate** lacks the literary cachet of its neighbour, but makes up for it with London's most famous cemetery, resting place of Karl Marx. It also retains more of its village origins, especially around **The Grove**, Highgate's finest row of houses, the oldest dating as far back as 1685.

To get to the cemetery, head south down Highgate High Street and **Highgate Hill**, with its amazing views towards the City. When you get to the copper dome of "Holy Joe", the Roman Catholic Church which stands on Highgate Hill, pop into the pleasantly landscaped **Waterlow Park**, next door, with its fine café and restaurant.

The park provides a through route to **Highgate Cemetery** (Ⓦwww.highgate-cemetery.org), which is ranged on both sides of Swain's Lane. Highgate's most famous corpse, that of **Karl Marx**, lies in the **East Cemetery** (April–Oct Mon–Fri 10am–5pm, Sat & Sun 11am–5pm; Nov–March closes 4pm; £2). Marx himself asked for a simple grave topped by a headstone, but by 1954 the Communist movement decided to move his grave to a more prominent position and erect the vulgar bronze bust that now surmounts a granite plinth. Close by lies the much simpler grave of the author George Eliot.

What the East Cemetery lacks in atmosphere is in part compensated for by the fact that you can wander at will through its maze of circuitous paths, whereas to visit the more atmospheric and overgrown **West Cemetery**, with its spooky Egyptian Avenue and sunken catacombs, you must go round with a guided tour (March–Nov Mon–Fri 2pm, Sat & Sun hourly 11am–4pm; Dec–Feb Sat & Sun hourly 11am–3pm; £3). Among the prominent graves usually visited are those of artist Dante Gabriel Rossetti, and lesbian novelist Radclyffe Hall.

Hendon: The RAF Museum

A world-class assembly of historic military aircraft can be seen at the **RAF Museum** (daily 10am–6pm; free; Ⓦwww.rafmuseum.org.uk; Colindale tube), located in a godforsaken part of north London beside the M1 motorway. Enthusiasts won't be disappointed, but those looking for a balanced account of modern aerial warfare will – the overall tone is unashamedly militaristic, not to say jingoistic. Those with children should head for the hands-on Fun 'n'

Flight gallery; those without might prefer to explore the often overlooked display galleries, ranged around the edge of the Main Aircraft Hall, which contain an art gallery and an exhibition on the history of flight, accompanied by replicas of some of the death-traps of early aviation.

Neasden: the Shri Swaminarayan temple

Perhaps the most remarkable building in the whole of London lies just off the North Circular, in the glum suburb of **Neasden**. Here, rising majestically above the surrounding semi-detached houses like a mirage, is the **Shri Swaminarayan Mandir** (daily 9am–6pm; free, Ⓦwww.swaminarayan.org; Stonebridge Park or Neasden tube), a traditional Hindu temple topped with domes and shikharas, erected in 1995 in a style and scale unseen outside of India for more than a millennium. To reach the temple, you must enter through the adjacent Haveli, or cultural complex, with its carved wooden portico and balcony. After taking off your shoes, you can proceed to the **Mandir** (temple) itself, carved entirely out of Carrara marble, with every possible surface transformed into a honeycomb of arabesques, flowers and seated gods. Beneath the Mandir, an **exhibition** (£2) explains the basic tenets of Hinduism and details the life of Lord Swaminarayan, and includes a video about the history of the building.

South London

Now largely built-up into a patchwork of Victorian terraces, one area of **South London** stands head and shoulders above all the others in terms of sightseeing, and that is **Greenwich**, with its outstanding ensemble of the Royal Naval College and the Queen's House, courtesy of Christopher Wren and Inigo Jones respectively. Most visitors, it has to be said, come to see the National Maritime Museum, the Royal Observatory, and the beautifully landscaped royal park, though Greenwich also pulls in an ever-increasing volume of Londoners in search of bargains at its Sunday **market**.

Greenwich is, of course, also famous as the "home of time", thanks to its status as the **Prime Meridian of the World**, from where time all over the globe is measured. It's partly for this reason that Greenwich was chosen as the centrepiece of the country's millennium celebrations, though the **Dome** is, in fact, situated in the reclaimed industrial wasteland of North Greenwich, a mile or so northeast of Greenwich town centre.

The only other suburban sights that stand out are the **Dulwich Picture Gallery**, a public art gallery even older than the National Gallery, and the eclectic **Horniman Museum**, in neighbouring Forest Hill.

Greenwich

Greenwich is one of London's most beguiling spots, and the one place in southeast London that draws large numbers of visitors. At its heart stands one of the capital's finest architectural set pieces, the former Royal Naval College overlooking the Thames. To the west lies Greenwich town centre, while to the south, you'll find Greenwich's two prime tourist sights, the National Maritime Museum and the Royal Observatory.

If you're heading straight for the National Maritime Museum from central London, the quickest way to get there is to take the **train** from London Bridge (every 30min) to Maze Hill, on the eastern edge of Greenwich Park. Those wanting to start with the town or the *Cutty Sark* should alight at Greenwich station. A more scenic way of getting to Greenwich is to take a **boat** from one of the piers in central London. A third possible option is to take the **Docklands Light Railway** (DLR) to Cutty Sark station. For the best view of the Wren buildings, though, get off the DLR at Island Gardens, and then take the Greenwich Foot Tunnel under the Thames.

The town centre

Greenwich town centre, laid out in the 1820s with Nash-style terraces, is nowadays plagued with heavy traffic. To escape the busy streets, head for the old covered market, now at the centre of the weekend **Greenwich Market** (Thurs–Sun 9am–5pm), a lively place full of antiques, crafts and clothes stalls that have spilled out up the High Road, Stockwell Road and Royal Hill. A short distance in from the old covered market, on the opposite side of Greenwich Church Street, rises Nicholas Hawksmoor's **St Alfege's Church** (Mon–Sat 10am–4pm, Sun noon–4pm; Ⓦwww.st-alfege.org), built in 1712–18, flattened in the Blitz, but now magnificently restored to its former glory.

Wedged in a dry dock by the Greenwich Foot Tunnel is the majestic **Cutty Sark** (daily 10am–5pm; £3.95; Ⓦwww.cuttysark.org.uk), the world's last surviving tea clipper, built in 1869. The *Cutty Sark* spent just eight years in the China tea trade, and it was as a wool clipper that it actually made its name, making a return journey to Australia in just 72 days. Inside, there's little to see beyond the exhibition in the main hold which tells the ship's story from its inception to its arrival in Greenwich in 1954.

It's entirely appropriate that the one London building that makes the most of its riverbank location should be the **Old Royal Naval College** (daily 10am–5pm; free; Ⓦwww.greenwichfoundation.org.uk), Wren's beautifully symmetrical Baroque ensemble, initially built as a royal palace, but eventually converted into a hospital for disabled seamen. From 1873 until 1998 it was home to the Royal Naval College, but now houses the University of Greenwich and the Trinity College of Music. The two grandest rooms, situated underneath Wren's twin domes, are open to the public and well worth visiting. The **Chapel**, in the east wing, has exquisite pastel-shaded plasterwork and spectacular, decorative detailing on the ceiling, all designed by James "Athenian" Stuart after a fire in 1799 destroyed the original interior. From the chapel, you can take the underground Chalk Walk to gain access to the magnificent **Painted Hall** in the west wing, which is dominated by James Thornhill's gargantuan allegorical ceiling painting, and his trompe l'oeil fluted pilasters.

National Maritime Museum

The main entrance to the excellent **National Maritime Museum** (daily 10am–5pm; free; Ⓦwww.nmm.ac.uk), which occupies the old Naval Asylum, is on Romney Road. From here, you enter the spectacular glass-roofed central courtyard, which houses the museum's largest artefacts, among them the splendid 63-foot-long gilded **Royal Barge**, designed in Rococo style by William Kent for Prince Frederick, the much unloved eldest son of George II.

The various themed galleries are superbly designed to appeal to visitors of all ages. In **Explorers**, on Level 1, you get to view some of the museum's most highly prized relics, such as **Captain Cook**'s sextant and K1 marine clock, Shackleton's compass, and **Captain Scott**'s furry sleeping bag and sledging

Greenwich Mean Time

One of Greenwich's many claims to fame is as the home of **GMT** and the **Prime Meridian** – a meridian being any north–south line used as a basis for astronomical observations, and therefore also for the calculation of longitude and time. In 1852, Britain adopted "London time", which meant, in effect, Greenwich Mean Time (GMT), though, in fact, this wasn't formally acknowledged until 1880. Three years later the USA adopted Greenwich as the Prime Meridian, and in 1884 persuaded an international convention in Washington DC to agree to make Greenwich the Prime Meridian of the World – in other words, zero longitude. As a result, the entire world sets its clocks in relation to GMT.

The red strip in the main courtyard lies along the Greenwich Prime Meridian, which is still used as an absolute today. However, what the Royal Observatory don't tell you is that, as a result of communications problems encountered during the Vietnam War, the Americans starting using satellites to work out longitude in the 1980s. The global standard for air navigation, and used widely by the military, is now the **Global Positioning System** or GPS, which bases its calculations on the centre of the earth not the surface, and places the meridian approximately 336ft to the east of the red strip.

goggles. Sponsors P&O get to display their wares in **Passengers**, which traces the history of modern passenger liners, and **Cargoes**", which concentrates on containerization. On Level 2, there's a large maritime **art gallery**, a contemporary section on the future of the sea, and a gallery devoted to the legacy of the British Empire, warts and all.

Level 3 boasts two hands-on galleries: **The Bridge**, where you can attempt to navigate a catamaran, a paddle steamer and a rowing boat to shore; and **All Hands**, where children can have a go at radio transmission, loading miniature cargo, firing a cannon and so forth. Finally, you reach the **Nelson Gallery**, which contains the museum's vast collection of Nelson-related memorabilia, including Turner's *Battle of Trafalgar, 21st October, 1805*, his largest work and only royal commission.

Inigo Jones's **Queen's House**, originally built amidst a rambling Tudor royal palace, is now the focal point of the Greenwich ensemble, and is an integral part of the Maritime Museum. As royal residences go, it's an unassuming country house, but as the first Neoclassical building in the country, it has enormous architectural significance. The interior is currently used for temporary exhibitions. Nevertheless, one or two features survive (or have been reinstated) from Stuart times. Off the Great Hall, a perfect cube, lies the beautiful Tulip Staircase, Britain's earliest cantilevered spiral staircase – its name derives from the floral patterning in the wrought-iron balustrade.

Royal Observatory

Crowning the hill in Greenwich Park, behind the National Maritime Museum, the **Royal Observatory** (daily: April–Sept 10am–6pm; Oct–March 10am–5pm; free; Ⓦwww.rog.nmm.ac.uk) was established in 1675 by Charles II to house the first Astronomer Royal, John Flamsteed. Flamsteed's chief task was to study the night sky in order to discover an astronomical method of finding the longitude of a ship at sea, the lack of which was causing enormous problems for the emerging British Empire. Astronomers continued to work here at Greenwich until the postwar smog forced them to decamp to Herstmonceux Castle and the clearer skies of Sussex (they've since moved to the Pacific); the old observatory, meanwhile, is now a very popular museum.

The Dome

London's controversial **Millennium Dome** (North Greenwich tube) is clearly visible from the riverside at Greenwich and from the upper parts of Greenwich Park. Built at a cost approaching £800 million of public money, and designed by Richard Rogers (of Lloyd's Building and Pompidou Centre fame), it is by far the world's largest dome – over half a mile in circumference and 160ft in height – held up by a dozen, 300-foot-tall yellow steel masts. In 2000, for one year only, it housed the nation's chief millennium extravaganza: an array of high-tech themed zones set around a stage, on which a circus-style performance took place twice a day.

Like most grand projects, the Dome had a rough ride from the press right from the beginning. The hiccups and headaches continued into the new millennium, with bad reviews and over-optimistic estimates of visitor numbers. Nevertheless, millions paid up £20 each to visit the Dome, and millions went away happy.

With the empty Dome eating up £28 million of public money on maintenance costs in 2001 alone, the government were no doubt relieved the following year when entertainment giants, AEG, agreed to spend £135 million of their own money turning the Dome into a 26,000-seater venue.

The oldest part of the observatory is the Wren-built **Flamsteed House**, whose northeastern turret sports a bright red time-ball that climbs the mast at 12.58pm and drops at 1pm GMT precisely; it was added in 1833 to allow ships on the Thames to set their clocks. Passing through Flamsteed's restored apartments and the Octagon Room, where the king used to show off to his guests, you reach the Chronometer Gallery, which focuses on the search for the precise measurement of longitude, and displays four of the clocks designed by **John Harrison**, including "H4", which helped win the Longitude Prize in 1763.

The exhibition ends on a soothing note in the Telescope Dome of the octagonal **Great Equatorial Building**, home to Britain's largest telescope. In addition, there are regular presentations in the **Planetarium** (daily 2.30 & 3.30pm; £4), housed in the adjoining South Building.

The Ranger's House and the Fan Museum

Southwest of the observatory, and backing onto Greenwich Park's rose garden, is the **Ranger's House** (Wed–Sun: April–Sept 10am–6pm; Oct 10am–5pm; Nov, Dec & March 10am–4pm; closed Christmas to Feb; £4.50; EH), a red-brick Georgian villa that houses an art collection amassed by Julius Wernher, the German-born millionaire who made his money by exploiting the diamond deposits of South Africa. His taste in art is eclectic, ranging from medieval ivory miniatures to Iznik pottery, though he was definitely a man who placed technical virtuosity above artistic merit. The high points of the collection are Memlinc's *Virgin and Child*, the pair of sixteenth-century majolica dishes decorated with mythological scenes for Isabella d'Este, both located upstairs, and the Reynolds portraits and de Hooch interior, located downstairs.

Croom's Hill, running down the west side of the park, boasts some of Greenwich's finest Georgian buildings, one of which houses the **Fan Museum** at no. 12 (Tues–Sat 11am–5pm, Sun noon–5pm; £3.50; Ⓦwww.fan-museum.org). It's a fascinating little place (and an extremely beautiful house), revealing the importance of the fan as a social and political document. The permanent exhibition on the ground floor traces the history of the materials employed, from peacock feathers to straw, while temporary exhibitions on the first floor explore such subjects as techniques of production and changing fashion.

Dulwich Picture Gallery and the Horniman Museum

Dulwich Picture Gallery (Tues–Fri 10am–5pm, Sat & Sun 11am–5pm; £4, free on Fri; Ⓦwww.dulwichpicturegallery.org.uk; West Dulwich train station from Victoria), on College Road, is the nation's oldest public art gallery, designed by John Soane and opened in 1817. Soane created a beautifully spacious building, awash with natural light and crammed with superb paintings – elegiac landscapes by Cuyp, one of the world's finest Poussin series, and splendid works by Hogarth, Gainsborough, van Dyck, Canaletto and Rubens, plus **Rembrandt**'s tiny *Portrait of a Young Man*, a top-class portrait of poet, playwright and Royalist, the future Earl of Bristol. At the centre of the museum is a tiny mausoleum designed by Soane for the sarcophagi of the gallery's founders.

To the southeast of Dulwich Park, on the busy South Circular road, is the wacky **Horniman Museum** (daily 10.30am–5.30pm; free; Ⓦwww.horniman.ac.uk; Forest Hill train station from Victoria or London Bridge), purpose-built in 1901 by Frederick Horniman, a tea trader with a passion for collecting. The museum is principally a monument to its creator's freewheeling eclecticism: in addition to its small aquarium and its large collection of stuffed creatures, there's a wide-ranging anthropology section, and a musical department with more than 1500 instruments from Chinese gongs to electric guitars. The museum also has a lovely **park** (daily 8am–dusk), around the back, where you'll find turkeys, goats and rabbits, a sunken water garden, a bandstand and a graceful Victorian conservatory.

Out west: Chiswick to Windsor

Most people experience west London en route to or from Heathrow Airport, either from the confines of the train or tube (which runs overground at this point), or the motorway. The city and its satellites seem to continue unabated, with only fleeting glimpses of the countryside. However, in the five-mile stretch from Chiswick to Osterley there are several former country retreats, now surrounded by suburbia, which are definitely worth digging out.

The Palladian villa of **Chiswick House** is perhaps the best known of these attractions. However, it draws nothing like as many visitors as **Syon House**, most of whom come for the gardening centre rather than for the **house** itself, a showcase for the talents of Robert Adam, who also worked at **Osterley House**, another Elizabethan conversion, now owned by the National Trust.

Running through much of the area is the **River Thames**, once known as the "Great Highway of London" and still the most pleasant way to travel in these parts during the summer. Boats plough up the Thames all the way from central London via the **Royal Botanic Gardens** at **Kew** and the picturesque riverside at **Richmond**, as far as **Hampton Court**, home of the country's largest royal residence and the famous maze. To reach the heavily touristed royal outpost of **Windsor Castle**, however, you need to take the train.

Chiswick

Chiswick House (daily: April–Sept 10am–6pm; Oct 10am–5pm; £3.50; EH; Chiswick train station from Waterloo), is a perfect little Neoclassical villa, designed in the 1720s by the Earl of Burlington, and set in one of the most beautifully landscaped gardens in London. Like its prototype, Palladio's Villa Rotonda near Vicenza, the house was purpose-built as a "temple to the arts" where, amid his fine-art collection, Burlington could entertain artistic friends such as Swift, Handel and Pope. Visitors enter via the **lower floor**, where you can pick up an audio guide, before heading to the **upper floor**, a series of cleverly interconnecting rooms, each enjoying a wonderful view out onto the gardens – all, that is, except the Tribunal, the central octagonal hall, where the earl's finest paintings and sculptures would have been displayed.

If you leave Chiswick House gardens by the northernmost exit, beyond the Italian garden, it's just a short walk along the thunderous A4 road to **Hogarth's House** (April–Oct Tues–Fri 1–5pm, Sat & Sun 1–6pm; Nov–March Tues–Fri 1–4pm, Sat & Sun 1–5pm; closed Jan; free), where the artist spent each summer with his wife, sister and mother-in-law from 1749 until his death in 1764. Nowadays it's difficult to believe Hogarth came here for "peace and quiet", but in the eighteenth century the house was almost entirely surrounded by countryside. In addition to scores of Hogarth's engravings, you can see copies of his satirical series *An Election*, *Marriage à la Mode* and *A Harlot's Progress*, and compare the modern view from the parlour with the more idyllic scene in *Mr Ranby's House*.

Barnes: the Wetland Centre

For anyone even remotely interested in wildlife, the **Wetland Centre** (Mon–Sat: summer 9.30am–6pm; winter 9.30am–5pm; £6.75; Ⓦwww.wwt.org.uk; bus #283 from Hammersmith tube, or walk from Barnes train station) in well-to-do Barnes, across the river from Chiswick, is something of an unexpected boon. On the site of four disused reservoirs, the Wildfowl & Wetland Trust (WWT) has created a high-tech, 105-acre mosaic of wetland habitats. Heading north from the visitor centre, you enter **World Wetlands**, where a variety of extremely rare wildfowl – from White-faced Whistling Ducks to Blue Ducks – are breeding in captivity in miniature versions of their own endangered wetland habitats. Beyond, in the **Wildside**, are the reedbeds and pools that attract native species, such as lapwing, tufted ducks, grebes and even the odd bittern. **Waterlife**, east of the visitor centre, includes a chance for younger children to get near some domesticated wildfowl, and, best of all, do some pond-dipping. At the far end is the mother of all hides: a triple-decker octagonal one with a lift, allowing views over the whole of the reserve.

Around Kew Bridge

Difficult to miss thanks to its stylish Italianate standpipe tower, **Kew Bridge Steam Museum** (daily 11am–5pm; Mon–Fri £3.50, Sat & Sun £4.60; Ⓦwww.kbsm.org; Kew Bridge train station from Waterloo; or bus #237 or #267 from Gunnersbury tube) occupies a former pumping station, on the corner of Kew Bridge Road and Green Dragon Lane, 100m west of the bridge itself. At the heart of the museum is the Steam Hall, which contains a triple expansion steam engine and four gigantic nineteenth-century Cornish beam engines. The museum also has a hands-on **Water for Life** gallery in the basement, devoted to the history of the capital's water supply. The best time to visit is at weekends, when each of the museum's industrial dinosaurs is put through its paces, and the small narrow-gauge steam railway runs back and forth round the yard.

Just west of the Steam Museum along Kew Bridge Road and Brentford High Street is the superb **Musical Museum** (Ⓦwww.musicalmuseum.co.uk),

River transport

Westminster Passenger Services (Ⓣ020/7930 2062, Ⓦwww.wpsa.co.uk) runs four boats from Westminster Pier to Kew, and two boats to Richmond and Hampton Court daily from April to September. The full trip takes 3hr 30min one way, and costs £12 single, £18 return. In addition, Turks (Ⓣ020/8546 2434, Ⓦwww.turks.co.uk) runs a regular service from Richmond to Hampton Court (April to mid-Sept) which costs £5.50 single or £7 return.

packed with musical automata and run by wildly enthusiastic and engaging volunteers. The museum has recently moved into new purpose-built premises and is due to re-open sometime in 2004. When it does, it will definitely be worth a visit for the noisy ninety-minute demonstrations, during which you get to hear every kind of mechanical music-making machine, from cleverly crafted music boxes to the huge orchestrions that were once a feature of London's swish cafés. The museum also boasts one of the world's finest collections of player-pianos, and an enormous Art Deco Wurlitzer cinema organ.

Syon House

Across the water from Kew stands **Syon Park** (Ⓦwww.syonpark.co.uk), seat of the Duke of Northumberland since Elizabethan times, now as much a working commercial concern as a family home, embracing a garden centre, a wholefood shop, an aquatic centre stocked with tropical fish, a mini-zoo and a butterfly house, as well as the old aristocratic mansion and its gardens.

From its rather plain castellated exterior, you'd never guess that **Syon House** (April–Oct Wed, Thurs & Sun 11am–5pm; £6.95, including entry to the gardens; bus #237 or #267 from Gunnersbury tube or Kew Bridge train station) contains the most opulent eighteenth-century interiors in the whole of London. The splendour of Robert Adam's refurbishment is immediately revealed, however, in the pristine **Great Hall**, an apsed double cube with a screen of Doric columns at one end and classical statuary dotted around the edges. There are several more Adam-designed rooms to admire in the house, plus a smattering of works by van Dyck, Lely, Gainsborough and Reynolds.

While Adam beautified Syon House, Capability Brown laid out its **gardens** (daily 10.30am–5.30pm; £3.50) around an artificial lake, surrounding it with oaks, beeches, limes and cedars. The gardens' chief focus now, however, is the crescent-shaped **Great Conservatory**, an early-nineteenth-century addition which is said to have inspired Joseph Paxton, architect of the Crystal Palace. Those with young children will be compelled to make use of the **miniature steam train**, which runs through the park at weekends from April to October, and on Wednesdays during the school holidays.

Another plus point for kids is Syon's **Butterfly House** (daily: May–Sept 10am–5pm; Oct–April 10am–3pm; £3.50; Ⓦwww.butterflies.org.uk), a small, mesh-covered hothouse, where you can walk amid hundreds of exotic butterflies from all over the world, as they flit about the foliage. If your kids show more enthusiasm for life-threatening reptiles than delicate insects, then you could skip the butterflies and go instead for the adjacent **London Aquatic Experience** (daily: April–Sept 10am–6pm; Oct–March 10am–5pm; £4; Ⓦwww.aquatic-experience.org), a purpose-built centre with a mixed range of aquatic creatures from the mysterious basilisk, which can walk on water, to the perennially popular piranhas.

Osterley Park and House

Robert Adam redesigned another colossal Elizabethan mansion three miles northwest of Syon at **Osterley Park** (daily 9am–7.30pm or dusk; free), which maintains the impression of being in the middle of the countryside, despite the presence of the M4 to the north of the house. The park itself is well worth exploring, and there's a great café in the Tudor stables, but anyone with a passing interest in Adam's work should pay a visit to **Osterley House** (March Sat & Sun 1–4.30pm; April–Oct Wed–Sun 1–4.30pm; £4.50; NT; Osterley tube). From the outside, Osterley bears some similarity to Syon, the big difference being Adam's grand entrance portico, with its tall, Ionic colonnade. From here, you enter a characteristically cool **Entrance Hall**, followed by the so-called State Rooms of the south wing. Highlights include the **Drawing Room**, with Reynolds portraits on the damask walls and a coffered ceiling centred on a giant marigold, and the **Etruscan Dressing Room**, in which every surface is covered in delicate painted trelliswork, sphinxes and urns, a style that Adam (and Wedgwood) dubbed "Etruscan", though it is in fact derived from Greek vases found at Pompeii.

Kew Gardens

Established in 1759, the **Royal Botanic Gardens** (daily 9.30am–7.30pm or dusk; £7.50; Ⓦ www.kew.org; Kew Gardens tube) have grown from their original eight acres into a three-hundred-acre site in which more than 33,000 species are grown in plantations and glasshouses, a display that attracts over a million visitors every year, most of them with no specialist interest at all. There's always something to see, whatever the season, but to get the most out of the place, come sometime between spring and autumn, bring a picnic and stay for the day. The only drawback to Kew is that it lies on a frequently used (and very noisy) flight path to Heathrow. Of all the glasshouses, by far the most celebrated is the **Palm House**, a curvaceous mound of glass and wrought-iron, designed by Decimus Burton in the 1840s. Its drippingly humid atmosphere nurtures most of the known palm species, while in the basement there's a small but excellent tropical aquarium. Kew's origins as an eighteenth-century royal pleasure garden are evident in the numerous follies dotted about Kew, the most conspicuous of which is the ten-storey, 163-foot-high **Pagoda**.

Richmond Park and Ham House

Richmond, upriver from Kew, basked for centuries in the glow of royal patronage, with Plantagenet kings and Tudor monarchs frequenting the riverside palace. Although most of the courtiers and aristocrats have gone, **Richmond** is still a wealthy district, with two theatres and highbrow pretensions. Richmond's greatest attraction though, is the enormous **Richmond Park** (daily: March–Sept 7am–dusk; Oct–Feb 7.30am–dusk; free; Ⓦ www.royalparks.gov.uk), at the top of Richmond Hill – 2500 acres of undulating grassland and bracken, dotted with coppiced woodland and as wild as anything in London. Eight miles across at its widest point, this is Europe's largest city park, famed for its red and fallow deer, which roam freely, and for its ancient oaks. For the most part untamed, the park does have a couple of deliberately landscaped plantations that feature splendid springtime azaleas and rhododendrons, in particular the Isabella Plantation.

Back down the hill, if you continue along the towpath beyond Richmond Bridge, after a mile or so, you leave the rest of London far behind and arrive at **Ham House** (April–Oct Mon–Wed, Sat & Sun 1–5pm; £7; NT; bus #371 or walk from Richmond tube), home to the earls of Dysart for nearly three hundred years. Expensively furnished in the seventeenth century, but little altered since then, the house boasts one of the finest Stuart interiors in the country, from the stupendously ornate Great Staircase to the Long Gallery, featuring six "Court Beauties" by Peter Lely. Elsewhere, there are several fine Verrio ceiling paintings, some exquisite parquet flooring and works by van Dyck and Reynolds. Another bonus are the formal seventeenth-century **gardens** (Mon–Wed, Sat & Sun 10.30am–6pm; £3), especially the Cherry Garden, laid out with a pungent lavender parterre, surrounded by yew hedges and pleached hornbeam arbours. The Orangery, overlooking the original kitchen garden, currently serves as a tearoom.

Hampton Court

Hampton Court Palace (April–Oct Mon 10.15am–6pm, Tues–Sun 9.30am–6pm; Nov–March closes 4.30pm; £11.50; Ⓦwww.hrp.org.uk; Hampton Court train station from Waterloo), a sprawling red-brick ensemble on the banks of the Thames, thirteen miles southwest of London, is the finest of England's royal abodes. Built in 1516 by the upwardly mobile **Cardinal Wolsey**, Henry VIII's Lord Chancellor, it was purloined by Henry himself after Wolsey fell from favour. In the second half of the seventeenth century, Charles II laid out the gardens, inspired by what he had seen at Versailles, while William and Mary had large sections of the palace remodelled by Wren a few years later.

The **Royal Apartments** are divided into six thematic walking tours. There's not a lot of information in any of the rooms, but guided tours, each lasting 45 minutes, are available at no extra charge for Henry VIII's and the King's apartments; all are led by period-costumed historians, who do a fine job of bringing the place to life. If your energy is lacking – and Hampton Court is huge – the most rewarding sections are: **Henry VIII's State Apartments**, which feature the glorious double hammerbeamed Great Hall; the **King's Apartments** (remodelled by William III); and the vast **Tudor Kitchens**. The last two are also served by audio tours. Part of the Royal Collection is housed in the **Renaissance Picture Gallery** and is chock-full of treasures, among them paintings by Tintoretto, Lotto, Titian, Cranach, Bruegel and Holbein.

Tickets to the Royal Apartments cover entry to the rest of the sites in the grounds. Those who don't wish to visit the apartments are free to wander around the gardens, but have to pay extra to visit the curious **Royal Tennis Courts** (50p), the palace's famously tricky yew-hedge **Maze** (£3), and the **Privy Garden** (£3), where you can view Andrea Mantegna's colourful, heroic canvases, *The Triumphs of Caesar*, housed in the Lower Orangery, and the celebrated **Great Vine**, whose grapes are sold at the palace each year in September.

Windsor and Eton

Every weekend trains from Waterloo and Paddington are packed with people heading for **WINDSOR**, the royal enclave 21 miles west of London, where they join the human conveyor belt round **Windsor Castle** (March–Oct 9.45am–5.15pm; Nov–Feb 9.45am–4.15pm; £11.50; Ⓦwww.royal.gov.uk; Paddington to Windsor & Eton Central via Slough, or Waterloo to Windsor & Eton Riverside – note that you must arrive and depart from the same station, as tickets are not interchangeable). Towering above the town on a steep chalk bluff, the castle is an undeniably awesome sight, its chilly grey walls, punctuated by mighty medieval bastions, continuing as far as the eye can see. Inside, most visitors just gape in awe at the monotonous, gilded grandeur of the **State Apartments**, while the real highlights – the paintings from the Royal Collection that line the walls – are rarely given a second glance. More impressive is **St George's Chapel** (Mon–Sat 10am–4pm), a glorious Perpendicular structure ranking with Henry VII's chapel in Westminster Abbey (see p.84), and the second most important resting place for royal corpses after the Abbey. On a fine day, it pays to put aside some time for exploring Windsor Great Park, which stretches for several miles to the south of the castle.

Crossing the bridge at the end of Thames Avenue in Windsor town brings you to **ETON**, a one-street village lined with bookshops and antique dealers, but famous all over the world for **Eton College** (Easter, July & Aug daily 10.30am–4.30pm; after Easter to June & Sept daily 2–4.30pm; £3.50; guided tours daily 2.15pm & 3.15pm; £4.50; Ⓦwww.etoncollege.com), a ten-minute walk from the river. When the school was founded in 1440, its aim was to give free education to seventy poor scholars and choristers; how times have changed. The original fifteenth-century **schoolroom**, gnarled with centuries of graffiti, survives, but the real highlight is the **College Chapel**, completed in 1482, a wonderful example of English Perpendicular architecture. The self-congratulatory **Museum of Eton Life**, where you're deposited at the end of the tour, is well worth missing unless you have a fascination with flogging, fagging and bragging about the school's facilities and alumni – Percy Bysshe Shelley is a rare rebellious figure in the roll call of Establishment greats.

Among younger kids, the attractions of Windsor Castle are overshadowed by the town's **Legoland** (daily 10am–5pm, later in school holidays; adults £18.95, under 15s £15.95, under 3s free; Ⓦwww.legoland.co.uk) theme park aimed at pre-teenage children (the perfect age is around 5 to 8). Whatever you do, though, try not to go at the weekend or during the school holidays, when the queues for the various rides become grievously long and the tickets cost £4 more. On arrival, a funicular railway takes visitors down into the park, disgorging them close to Miniland, with its miniature Lego depictions of various European landmarks. The rest of the park is really just a series of rides, most of them very gentle. There are numerous places to eat, though it makes sense to take a picnic and save yourself some money.

Eating

London is an exciting (though often expensive) place in which to eat out. It's home to people from all over the globe, and you can pretty much sample any kind of cuisine here, from Georgian to Peruvian. Indeed, London is now home to some of the best **Cantonese** restaurants in the whole of Europe, is a noted centre for **Indian** and **Bangladeshi** food, and has numerous French, Greek, Italian, Japanese, Spanish and Thai restaurants; and within all these cuisines, you can choose anything from simple meals to gourmet spreads. Traditional and modern **British** food is available all over town, and some of the best venues are reviewed below.

Cafés and snacks

There are plenty of **cafés** and small, basic restaurants all over London that can fill you up for under £10, including tea or coffee. A huge number of them are run by Anglo-Italians, which means you're guaranteed proper coffee and decent sandwiches. Several of the places listed are also open in the evening, but the turnover is fast, so don't expect to linger; they're best seen as fuel stops before – or in a few cases, after – a night out. It's worth bearing in mind that most **pubs** (which are covered in the following section) serve meals, and some take their food quite seriously.

Mayfair and Marylebone

Mô 25 Heddon St, W1. Piccadilly Circus tube. The ultimate Arabic pastiche. The adjacent restaurant is pricey, but the tearoom serves delicious snacks and is a great place to hangout, with tables and hookahs spilling out onto the pavement of this little alleyway off Regent Street. Closed Sun.

Patisserie Valerie at Sagne 105 Marylebone High St, W1. Bond Street tube. Founded as *Maison Sagne* in the 1920s, and preserving its wonderful decor from those days, this café is Marylebone's finest without doubt.

Soho

Bar Italia 22 Frith St, W1. Leicester Square tube. A tiny café that's a Soho institution, serving coffee, croissants and sandwiches more or less around the clock – as it has done since 1949.

Bar du Marché 19 Berwick St, W1. Tottenham Court Road, Piccadilly Circus or Leicester Square tube. A weird find in the middle of raucous Berwick Street market: a licensed French café serving brasserie staples for under £10. Closed Sun.

Beatroot 92 Berwick St, W1. Piccadilly Circus tube. Great little veggie café by the market, doling out hot savoury bakes, stews and salads (plus delicious cakes) in boxes of varying sizes – all under £5. Closed Sun.

Centrale 16 Moor St, W1. Leicester Square tube. Tiny, friendly Italian café that serves up huge plates of steaming, garlicky pasta, as well as omelettes, chicken and chops for around £5. Closed Sun.

Maison Bertaux 28 Greek St, W1. Leicester Square tube. Long-standing, old-fashioned and downbeat Soho patisserie, with tables on two floors (and one or two outside) and a loyal clientele that keeps things busy.

Patisserie Valerie 44 Old Compton St, W1. Leicester Square or Piccadilly Circus tube. Popular 1920s coffee, croissant and cake emporium attracting a loud-talking, arty Soho crowd.

Red Veg 95 Dean St, W1. Tottenham Court Rd tube. Simple veggie junk food outlet, which doles out a short list of cheap, classic munchie-fodder: veggie burgers, noodles and felafel.

Chinatown

Lee Ho Fook 4 Macclesfield St, W1. Leicester Square tube. Difficult to find, but a genuine Chinese barbecue house – small, spartan and cheap.

Kopi-Tiam 9 Wardour St, W1. Leicester Square tube. Bright, cheap Malaysian café serving up curries, coconut rice, juices and "herbal soups" to local Malays, all for around a fiver.

Tokyo Diner 2 Newport Place, WC2. Leicester Square tube. Friendly place on the edge of Chinatown that shuns elaboration for fast food, Tokyo style. Minimalist decor lets the sushi and sumo do the talking.

Covent Garden and Bloomsbury

Café in the Crypt St Martin-in-the-Fields, Duncannon St, WC2. Charing Cross tube. The self-service buffet food is nothing special, but there are regular veggie dishes, and the handy location makes this an ideal spot to fill up before hitting the West End.

Food for Thought 31 Neal St, WC2. Covent Garden tube. Long-established but minuscule, bargain veggie restaurant and takeaway counter – the food is good, with the menu changing twice daily. Expect to queue and don't expect to linger at peak times.

Gaby's 30 Charing Cross Rd, WC2. Leicester Square tube. Busy café and takeaway joint serving a wide range of home-cooked veggie and Middle Eastern specialities.

Monmouth Coffee Company 27 Monmouth St, WC2. Covent Garden or Leicester Square tube. The marvellous aroma is the first thing you notice here, while the cramped wooden booths and daily newspapers on hand evoke an eighteenth-century coffee-house atmosphere. No smoking. Closed Sun.

Paul 29 Bedford St, WC2. Covent Garden tube. Seriously French, classy boulangerie with a wood-panelled café at the back. Try one of the chewy *fougasses*, quiches or tarts, before launching into the exquisite patisserie.

Rock & Sole Plaice 47 Endell St, WC2. Covent Garden tube. A rare survivor: a no-nonsense traditional fish and chip shop in central London. Takeaway, eat in or out at one of the pavement tables.

Wagamama 4 Streatham St, WC1. Tottenham Court Road tube. Much copied since, *Wagamama* was the pioneer when it comes to austere, minimalist, canteen-style noodle bars. Branches around central London.

London for veggies

Most cafés and restaurants in London will make some attempt to cater for **vegetarians**. Below is a list of exclusively vegetarian places recommended in the "Eating" section.

Beatroot 92 Berwick St, W1 (see p.143)
Food for Thought 31 Neal St, WC2 (see p.143)
The Gate 51 Queen Caroline St, W4 (see p.148)
The Gate 2 72 Belsize Lane, NW3 (see p.147)
Manna 4 Erskine Rd, NW3 (see p.148)
The Place Below Church of St Mary-le-Bow, Cheapside, EC2 (see p.144)
Rasa 6 Dering St, W1 (see p.146)
Red Veg 95 Dean St, W1 (see p.143)
World Food Café 14 Neal's Yard, WC2 (see p.144)

World Food Café 14 Neal's Yard, WC2. Covent Garden tube. First-floor veggie café that comes into its own in summer, when the windows are flung open and you can gaze down upon trendy humanity as you tuck into pricey but tasty dishes from all corners of the globe.

Clerkenwell & Hoxton

Clark & Sons 46 Exmouth Market, EC1. Angel or Farringdon tube. Exmouth Market is currently undergoing something of a transformation, so it's all the more surprising to find this genuine eel and pie shop still going strong. Closed Sun.

Feast 86 St John St, 7 EC1. Farringdon or Barbican tube. Delicious tortilla-wrapped sandwiches made to order; takeaway or eat-in in this small, trendy, designer Clerkenwell café. Closed Sat & Sun.

Ktchn 35 Charlotte Rd, EC2. Old Street tube. Tiny, vowel-free Hoxton/Shoreditch café with just four stools, serving delicious upmarket lunch options: big soups, grilled tuna, rare-roast beef, exotic salads and great pastries all freshly prepared. Closed Sat & Sun.

The City and the East End

Arkansas Café Unit 12, Old Spitalfields Market, E1. Liverpool Street tube. American barbecue fuel stop, using only the very best free-range ingredients.

Brick Lane Beigel Bake 159 Brick Lane, E1. Shoreditch or Whitechapel tube. The bagels at this no-frills 24-hour takeaway in the heart of the East End are freshly made and unbelievably cheap, even when stuffed with smoked salmon and cream cheese.

Café 1001 1 Dray's Lane, E1. Whitechapel tube. Off Brick Lane, tucked in by the Truman Brewery, this smoky café has a beaten-up studenty look, with lots of sofas to crash in, and dishes out simple sandwiches and delicious cakes.

The Place Below St Mary-le-Bow, Cheapside, EC2. St Paul's or Bank tube. City café serving imaginative (albeit slightly pricey) vegetarian dishes in a wonderful Norman crypt. Closed Sat & Sun.

The South Bank & Southwark

Konditor & Cook 22 Cornwall Rd, SE1. Waterloo tube. A cut above your average bakery, *Konditor & Cook* makes wonderful cakes and biscuits, as well as offering a choice of sandwiches and coffee and tea. There are branches elsewhere on the south side of the Thames at 10 Stoney St by Borough Market, in the Design Museum and in the Young Vic Theatre. Closed Sun.

Kensington, Chelsea and Notting Hill

Books for Cooks 4 Blenheim Crescent, W11. Ladbroke Grove or Notting Hill Gate tube. Tiny café/restaurant within London's top cookery bookshop – just wander in and have a coffee while browsing, or get there in time to grab a table for the set menu lunch. No smoking.

Daquise 20 Thurloe St, SW7. South Kensington tube. This old-fashioned Polish café right by the tube is something of a South Ken institution, serving Polish home cooking or simple coffee, tea and cakes depending on the time of day.

Gloriette 128 Brompton Rd, SW7. South Kensington or Knightsbridge tube. Long-established Viennese café that makes a perfect post-museum halt for coffee and outrageous cakes; also serves sandwiches, Wiener Schnitzel, pasta dishes, goulash and fish and chips.

Lisboa Patisserie 57 Golborne Rd, W10. Ladbroke Grove tube. Authentic and friendly Portuguese pastelaria, with coffee and cakes including the best custard tarts this side of Lisbon. The *Oporto*, at 62a Golborne Rd, is a good fallback if this place is full.

Afternoon tea

The classic English **afternoon tea** – assorted sandwiches, scones and cream, cakes and tarts and, of course, lashings of tea – is available all over London. The best venues are the capital's top hotels and most fashionable department stores; a selection of the best is picked out below. To avoid disappointment it's best to book ahead. Expect to spend £15–25 a head, and leave your jeans and trainers at home – most hotels will expect men to wear a jacket of some sort, though only the *Ritz* insists on jacket and tie.

Brown's 33–34 Albemarle St, W1 ⓣ020/7493 6020, ⓦwww.brownshotel.com. Green Park tube. Daily 2–6pm.
Claridge's Brook St, W1 ⓣ020/7629 8860, ⓦwww.savoy-group.co.uk. Bond Street tube. Daily 3–5.30pm.
The Dorchester 54 Park Lane, W1 ⓣ020/7629 8888, ⓦwww.dorchesterhotel.co.uk. Hyde Park Corner tube. Daily 3–6pm.
Fortnum & Mason 181 Piccadilly, W1 ⓣ020/7734 8040, ⓦwww.fortnumandmason.com. Green Park or Piccadilly Circus tube. Daily 3–5.45pm.
Lanesborough Hyde Park Corner, SW1 ⓣ020/7259 5599, ⓦwww.lanesborough.com. Hyde Park Corner tube. Daily 3.30–6pm.
The Ritz Piccadilly, W1 ⓣ020/7493 8181, ⓦwww.theritzhotel.co.uk. Green Park tube. Daily 1.30, 3.30 & 5.30pm.
The Savoy Strand, WC2 ⓣ020/7836 4343, ⓦwww.savoy-group.co.uk. Charing Cross tube. Daily 3–5.30pm.

Camden and Hampstead

Brew House Kenwood, Hampstead Lane, NW3. Bus #210 from Archway tube or a walk across the Heath. Everything from full English breakfast to lunches, cakes and teas, all served in the old laundry at Kenwood, or enjoyed on the terrace overlooking the lake.
Café Mozart 17 Swains Lane, N6. Gospel Oak train station or bus #C2 from Kentish Town tube. Viennese café that's usefully close to the southeast side of Hampstead Heath, and also serves a few hearty Austrian dishes.
Louis Patisserie 32 Heath St, NW3. Hampstead tube. Popular central-European tearoom in Hampstead village serving sticky cakes to a mix of Heath-bound hordes and elderly locals.
Marine Ices 8 Haverstock Hill, NW3. Chalk Farm tube. Situated halfway between Camden and Hampstead, this is a splendid and justly famous old-fashioned Italian ice-cream parlour; pizza and pasta are served in the adjacent restaurant.

Greenwich

Pistachio's Café 15 Nelson Rd, SE10. Cutty Sark DLR or Greenwich DLR and train station. Just about the only decent sandwich café in the centre of Greenwich, serving excellent coffee, and with a small garden out back.
Tai Won Mein 39 Greenwich Church St, SE10. Cutty Sark DLR or Greenwich DLR and train station. Good quality fast-food noodle bar that gets very busy at weekends. Decor is functional and minimalist; choose between rice, soup or various fried noodles, all for under a fiver.

Restaurants

Many of the restaurants we've listed will be busy on most nights of the week, particularly on Thursday, Friday and Saturday, and it's best to **reserve a table**. As for **prices**, you can pay an awful lot for a meal in London, and if you're used to North American portions, you're not going to be particularly impressed by the volume in most places. For cheaper eats, see the section above. For an explanation of the pricing system, see Basics, p.39. Where possible we've marked the following options on the maps in this chapter.

St James's, Mayfair and Marylebone

Fairuz 3 Blandford St, W1 ⓣ020/7486 8108. Bond Street tube. One of London's more accessible Middle Eastern restaurants, with an epic list of mezze, a selection of charcoal grills and one or two oven-baked dishes. Moderate.

La Galette 56 Paddington St, W1 ⓣ020/7935 1554. Baker Street tube. Bright modern pancake place. The hors d'oeuvres are very simple and very French and the savoury and sweet buckwheat galettes are generous. Inexpensive.
Mandalay 444 Edgware Rd, W2 ⓣ020/7258 3696. Edgware Road tube. See map, p.122. Small non-smoking restaurant that serves Burmese cuisine – a *melange* of Thai, Malaysian, a lot of Indian and a few things that are unique. The portions are huge and the flavours hit the mark. Closed Sun. Inexpensive.
The Providores 109 Marylebone High St, W1 ⓣ020/7935 6175. Green Park tube. Outstanding fusion restaurant run by amiable New Zealander and split into two: snacky tapas bar downstairs and full-on restaurant upstairs. The food at both is original and wholly satisfying. Inexpensive to Moderate.

Soho and Chinatown

China City White Bear Yard, WC2 ⓣ020/7734 3388. Leicester Square tube. See map, p.76. Large restaurant tucked into a little courtyard off Lisle Street; fresh and bright, with *dim sum* that's up there with the best, service that's "Chinatown brusque". Moderate.
Chowki 2–3 Denman St, W1 ⓣ020/7439 1330. Piccadilly Circus tube. See map, p.76. Large, cheap Indian restaurant serving authentic food in stylish surroundings. The menu changes every month in order to feature three different regions of India – the regional feast for around £10 is great value. Inexpensive.
La Trouvaille 12a Newburgh St, W1 ⓣ020/7287 8488. Oxford Circus tube. See map, p.76. Here, they understand the English need for really French Frenchness and if you hanker after a "dangerously French" dish, try the tripe terrine. Closed Sun lunch. Moderate.
Mr Kong 21 Lisle St, WC2 ⓣ020/7437 7923. Leicester Square tube. See map, p.76. One of Chinatown's finest. To sample the restaurant's more unusual dishes order from the "Today's" and "Chef's Specials" menu, and don't miss the mussels in black-bean sauce or the fresh razor clam with garlic. Moderate.
New World 1 Gerrard Place, W1 ⓣ020/7734 0396. Leicester Square tube. See map, p.76. Another reasonable stab at an overblown Hong Kong dining palace – all red, gold and dragons. Best deal here is the lunchtime *dim sum*, served by indefatigable trolley-pushers. Inexpensive.
Spiga 84–86 Wardour St, W1 ⓣ020/7734 3444. Leicester Square tube. See map, p.76. A pleasantly casual Italian affair, with a lively atmosphere, a serious wood-fired oven and a cool look about it. Moderate.

Covent Garden & Bloomsbury

Belgo Centraal 50 Earlham St, WC2 ⓣ020/7813 2233. Covent Garden tube. See map, p.76. Massive metal-minimalist cavern off Neal Street, serving excellent kilo buckets of *moules marinière*, with frites and mayonnaise, a bewildering array of Belgian beers to choose from, and waffles for dessert. The lunchtime specials are a bargain for central London. Inexpensive to Moderate.
Ikkyu 67a Tottenham Court Rd, W1 ⓣ020/7636 9280. Goodge Street tube. See map, p.76. Busy, basic basement Japanese restaurant, good enough for a quick lunch or a more elaborate dinner. Be warned, however: it's hard to find and, when you do, shockingly popular. Closed all Sat & Sun lunch. Moderate.
J. Sheekey 28–32 St Martin's Court, WC2 ⓣ020/7240 2565. Leicester Square tube. See map, p.76. Long-established stylish place whose menu is focused on fish, from traditional fare such as grilled Dover sole, to modernist dishes like grilled cuttlefish with creamed brandade. Expensive.
Rasa Samudra 5 Charlotte St, W1 ⓣ020/7637 0222. Goodge Street tube. See map, p.76. Sophisticated Southern Indian fish dishes that are a million miles from the usual London curry-house staples. *Rasa* also has an exclusively vegetarian branch at 6 Dering St, W1 (ⓣ020/7629 1346; Bond Street tube). Closed Sun. Moderate to Expensive.

Clerkenwell & Hoxton

Cicada 132 St John St, EC1 ⓣ020/7608 1550. Farringdon tube. Bar-restaurant set back from the street with alfresco eating and an unusual Thai-based menu. Closed Sat lunch & Sun. Moderate.
Real Greek 15 Hoxton Market, N1 ⓣ020/7739 8212. Old Street tube. Small, modern and comfortable place where the menu has authentic Greek dishes, and the service is excellent. Set lunch and early doors dinner are a bargain. Closed Sun. Moderate.
St John 26 St John St, EC1 ⓣ020/7251 0848. Farringdon tube. A genuinely English restaurant, specializing in all those strange and unfashionable cuts of meat that were once commonplace in rural England – brains, bone marrow. Closed Sat lunch & Sun. Expensive.
Viet Hoa Café 72 Kingsland Rd, E2 ⓣ020/7729 8293. Old Street tube. Large, light and airy Vietnamese café not far from the Geffrye Museum,

serving splendid "meals in a bowl" – soups and noodle dishes with everything from spring rolls to tofu.

East End

Café Naz 46–48 Brick Lane, E1 ⓣ020/7247 0234. Aldgate East tube. See map, p.108. Self-proclaimed contemporary Bangladeshi restaurant with an open-plan kitchen offering all the standards plus a load of "baltis". Inexpensive.

Café Spice Namaste 16 Prescott St, E1 ⓣ020/7488 9242. Tower Hill tube. See map, p.108. Very popular Indian on the fringe of the City that is definitely not your average curry house. Parsee delicacies rub shoulders with dishes from Goa, Hyderabad and Kashmir, and the tandoori specialities are awesome. Closed Sat lunch & Sun. Moderate.

New Tayyab 83 Fieldgate St, E1 ⓣ020/7247 9543. Aldgate East or Whitechapel tube. See map, p.108. Smart, designer restaurant serving straightforward Pakistani fare: good, freshly cooked and served without pretension. Booking is essential and service is speedy and slick. Cash or cheque only. Inexpensive.

South Bank and Southwark

Delfina 50 Bermondsey St, SE1 ⓣ020/7357 0244. London Bridge tube. See map, p.108. This adjunct to the Delfina art gallery is a serious Modern British restaurant and a great place to go for lunch if you're in the area. The prices have moved well beyond café norms, but the quality justifies a bit of a splurge. Closed Sat & Sun. Expensive.

Fina Estampa 150 Tooley St, SE1 ⓣ020/7403 1342. London Bridge tube. See map, p.108. One of London's few Peruvian restaurants, that also happens to be very good, bringing a little of downtown Lima to London Bridge. The menu is traditional Peruvian, with a big emphasis on seafood. Closed Sat lunch & all Sun. Moderate.

Little Saigon 139 Westminster Bridge Rd, SE1 ⓣ020/7207 9747. Waterloo tube. See map, p.98. Great Vietnamese spring rolls, grilled squid-cake and crystal pancakes, all served with a wonderful array of sauces, plus crispy fried noodles. Closed Sat & Sun lunch. Moderate.

RSJ 13a Coin St, SE1 ⓣ020/7928 4554, ⓦwww.rsj.uk.com. Waterloo tube. Regularly high standards of Anglo-French cooking make this a good spot for a meal after or before an evening at a South Bank theatre or concert hall. The set meals for around £15 are particularly popular. Closed Sat lunch & Sun. Expensive.

Kensington and Chelsea

Bibendum Oyster House Michelin House, 81 Fulham Rd, SW3 ⓣ020/7589 1480, ⓦwww.bibendum.co.uk. South Kensington tube. See map, p.122. A glorious tiled affair built in 1911, this former garage is one of the prettiest places to eat shellfish in London – if you're really hungry, go for the "Plateau de Fruits de Mer". Moderate.

Boisdale 15 Ecclestone St, SW1 ⓣ020/7730 6922, ⓦwww.boisdale.co.uk. Victoria tube. Owned by Ranald MacDonald, son of the Chief of Clanranald, this is a very Scottish place, strong on hospitality, and fresh Scottish produce. Closed Sun. Moderate to Expensive.

Hunan 51 Pimlico Rd, SW1 ⓣ020/7730 5712. Sloane Square tube. Probably England's only restaurant serving Hunan food, a relative of Sichuan cuisine, with the same spicy kick to most dishes. Closed Sun. Expensive.

Bayswater and Notting Hill

Al Waha 75 Westbourne Grove, W2 ⓣ020/7229 0806. Queensway or Bayswater tube. See map, p.122. Arguably London's best Lebanese restaurant; mezze-obsessed, but also painstaking in its preparation of the main-course dishes, where spanking fresh and accurately cooked grills predominate. Moderate.

The Mandola 139–141 Westbourne Grove, W11 ⓣ020/7229 4734. Notting Hill Gate tube. See map, p.122. Small, seriously informal, supremely popular, unlicensed neighbourhood restaurant serving strikingly delicious "urban Sudanese" food at sensible prices. Closed Mon lunch. Moderate.

Rodizio Rico 111 Westbourne Grove, W11 ⓣ020/7792 4035. Notting Hill Gate or Queensway tube. See map, p.122. No menu, no prices, but no problem either as this Brazilian eatery specializes in smoky, grilled meat. Carvers come round and lop off chunks of freshly grilled meats, while you help yourself from the salad bar and hot buffet to prime your plate. Closed Mon–Fri lunch. Moderate.

Camden and Hampstead

Cucina 45a South End Rd, NW3 ⓣ020/7435 7814. Belsize Park tube. Brightly painted, wooden-floored, modern British restaurant that's very contemporary, very fashionable and very Hampstead. Expensive.

The Gate 2 72 Belsize Lane, NW3 ⓣ020/7435 7733. Belsize Park tube. The modern, minimalist *Gate 2* serves excellent and original veggie dishes with intense and satisfying tastes and textures, ranging from wild mushroom terrine to root vegetable tagine. Moderate.

Manna 4 Erskine Rd, NW3 ⓣ020/7722 8028. Chalk Farm tube. Old-fashioned, casual vegetarian restaurant with 1970s decor, serving large portions of very good veggie food. Don't show up here in a hurry or without a serious appetite. Closed Mon–Fri lunch & Sat & Sun eve. Moderate.

Chiswick to Richmond

Chez Lindsay 11 Hill Rise, Richmond ⓣ020/8948 7473. Richmond tube. Small, bright, authentic Breton creperie, offering galettes, crepes or more formal French main courses, including lots of fresh fish and shellfish, all washed down with Breton cider in traditional earthenware *bolées*. Inexpensive to Moderate.

The Gate 51 Queen Caroline St, W4 ⓣ020/8748 6932. Hammersmith tube. Tucked away behind the Hammersmith Apollo, this is a vegetarian restaurant that eschews healthy, wholefood eating. It's as rich, colourful, calorific and naughty as anywhere in town, just without meat. Moderate.

Drinking

London's **drinking** establishments run the whole gamut from grand Victorian gin palaces to funky modern bars with resident DJs catering to a pre-club crowd. The emergence in the last decade or so of gastropubs, where the food is as important as the drink, has had a huge impact on the rest of the pub trade.

Where possible we've marked the places below on the maps in this chapter.

Whitehall and Westminster

Albert 52 Victoria St, SW1. St James's Park or Victoria tube. See map, p.76. Roomy High-Victorian pub with big bay windows, glass partitions, good bar food and an excellent carvery upstairs.

ICA Bar 94 The Mall, SW1. Piccadilly Circus or Charing Cross tube. See map, p.76. You have to be a member (or be visiting an exhibition or cinema/theatre/talk event) to drink at the late-opening *ICA Bar* – but anyone can join on the door (Mon–Fri £1.50; Sat & Sun £2.50). It's a cool drinking venue, with a *noir* dress code observed by the arty crowd and staff, but beware the weekend DJ nights.

Paviour's Arms Page St, SW1. Pimlico tube. A unique survivor, this large, stylish 1930s Art Deco pub, in the backstreets close to the Tate Gallery, has much of its original decor intact; you can also get decent Thai food with your beer. Closed Sat & Sun.

St James's, Mayfair and Marylebone

Dover Castle 43 Weymouth Mews, W1. Regent's Park or Oxford Circus tube. See map, p.76. A traditional, quiet boozer hidden away down a labyrinthine Marylebone mews. Green upholstery, dark wood and a nicotine-stained lincrusta ceiling add to the ambience. Closed Sun.

O'Conor Don 88 Marylebone Lane, W1. Bond Street tube. See map, p.76. A stripped bare, anti-theme Irish pub that's a cut above the average, with excellent Guinness, a pleasantly measured pace and Irish food on offer. Closed Sat & Sun.

Red Lion 23 Crown Passage, SW1. Green Park tube. See map, p.76. Not to be confused with the nearby pub of the same name, this is a small, local, wood-panelled place hidden away in a passageway off Pall Mall. Closed Sun.

The Social 5 Little Portland St, W1. Oxford Circus tube. See map, p.76. Industrial club-bar with great DJs playing everything from rock to rap, a truly hedonistic-cum-alcoholic crowd and the ultimate snacks – beans on toast and soup in a mug. Closed Sun.

Ye Grapes 16 Shepherd Market, W1. Green Park or Hyde Park Corner tube. See map, p.76. A great local in the heart of Mayfair, this busy Victorian free house has a good selection of real ales and an open fire.

Soho

Argyll Arms 18 Argyll St, W1. Oxford Circus tube. See map, p.76. A stone's throw from Oxford Circus, this is a great Victorian pub, which has preserved many of its original features and serves good real ales.

Dog & Duck 18 Bateman St, W1. Leicester Square or Tottenham Court Road tube. See map, p.76. Tiny Soho pub that retains much of its old character, beautiful Victorian tiling and mosaics, and a loyal clientele. Closed Sat & Sun lunch.

Dog House 187 Wardour St, W1. Leicester Square or Tottenham Court Road tube. See map, p.76. Colourful basement bar, popular for hip-hop, funk and acid jazz, that draws a friendly mix of office types, students and film runners. Mon–Sat eve only.

French House 49 Dean St, W1. Leicester Square tube. See map, p.76. Soho institution since before World War I. Free French and literary associations galore, half pints only at the bar and a fine little restaurant upstairs (book ahead on ⓣ020/7437 2799).

Lab 12 Old Compton St, W1. Tottenham Court Road or Leicester Square tube. See map, p.76. Chic, multicoloured former strip joint that stirs up some of the best cocktails in town for its style-conscious crowd of beautiful Soho-ites.

The Toucan 19 Carlisle St. Tottenham Court Road tube. See map, p.76. Small bar serving excellent Guinness and a wide range of Irish whiskeys, plus cheap, wholesome and filling food. So popular it can get mobbed. Closed Sun.

Two Floors 3 Kingly St, W1. Oxford Circus or Piccadilly Circus tube. See map, p.76. Laid-back, designer-style Soho bar, laid out, unsurprisingly, on two floors, attracting a mixed media crowd. Closed Sun.

Covent Garden

Denim 4a Upper St Martin's Lane, WC2. Leicester Square tube. See map, p.76. The retro orange and purple decor goes down a treat with the young after-work punters, who don't seem to flinch at the outrageous bar prices. Eve only.

Detroit 35 Earlham St, WC2. Covent Garden tube. See map, p.76. Cavernous underground venue with an open-plan bar area, secluded Gaudíesque booths and a huge range of spirits. DJs take over at the weekends. Closed Sun.

Freedom Brewing Company 41 Earlham St, WC2. Covent Garden tube. See map, p.76. Busy, brick-vaulted basement brewery bar with wrought-iron pillars, lots of brushed steel and pricey, strong brews, made on the premises – in particular, there's a very fine organic honey wheat beer.

Lamb & Flag 33 Rose St, WC2. Leicester Square tube. See map, p.76. Busy, tiny and highly atmospheric pub, tucked away down an alley between Garrick Street and Floral Street, where John Dryden was attacked in 1679 for writing scurrilous verses about one of Charles II's mistresses.

Punch & Judy 40 The Market, WC2. Covent Garden tube. See map, p.76. Horribly mobbed and loud, but this Covent Garden Market pub does boast an unbeatable location with a very popular balcony overlooking the Piazza.

Salisbury 90 St Martin's Lane, WC2. Leicester Square tube. See map, p.76. Easily one of the most beautifully preserved Victorian pubs in the capital – and certainly the most central – with cut, etched and engraved windows, bronze figures, red velvet seating and a fine lincrusta ceiling.

Bloomsbury & Holborn

Jerusalem 33–34 Rathbone Place, W1. Tottenham Court Road tube. See map, p.76. Chandeliers and velvet drapes set the tone, and there's an especially good mix of music on Thursday nights, though it does attract a large proportion of local office workers. Closed Sun.

Lamb 94 Lamb's Conduit St, WC1. Russell Square tube. Pleasant pub with a marvellously well-preserved Victorian interior of mirrors, old wood and snob screens.

Museum Tavern 49 Great Russell St, WC1. Tottenham Court Road or Russell Square tube. See map, p.76. Large and characterful old pub, right opposite the British Museum, erstwhile drinking hole of Karl Marx.

Na Zdrowie 11 Little Turnstile, WC1. Holborn tube. See map, p.76. Great Polish bar hidden in an alleyway behind Holborn tube, with a wicked selection of flavoured vodkas and cheap Polish food.

Princess Louise 208 High Holborn, WC1. Holborn tube. See map, p.76. Old-fashioned place, with highly decorated ceilings, lots of glass, brass and mahogany, and a good range of real ales. Closed Sun.

Clerkenwell

Café Kick 43 Exmouth Market, EC1. Farringdon or Angel tube. Stylish take on a local French-style café-bar in the heart of fashionable Exmouth Market, with table football to complete the retro theme. Closed Sun.

Clerkenwell House 23–27 Hatton Wall, EC1. Farringdon tube. The Med food is good, there are four American pool tables in the basement bar and the retro 1970s furniture includes some seriously comfy semi-circular sofas. Closed Sat lunch.

Eagle 159 Farringdon Rd, EC1. Farringdon tube. The first of London's pubs to go foody, this place is heaving at lunch and dinnertimes, as *Guardian* workers tuck into Med dishes, but you should be able to find a seat at other times. Closed Sun eve.

Fox & Anchor 115 Charterhouse St, EC1. Farringdon or Barbican tube. Handsome Smithfield market pub famous for its early opening hours (from 7am) and huge breakfasts. Closed Sat & Sun.

Jerusalem Tavern 55 Britton St, EC1. Farringdon tube. Cosy converted Georgian parlour, stripped bare and slightly "distressed", serving tasty food along with an excellent range of draught beers from St Peter's Brewery in Suffolk. Closed Sat & Sun.

Lifthouse 85 Charterhouse St, EC1. Farringdon tube. Next door to *Fabric*, this three-floored New York style club-bar-restaurant houses a cocktail bar and club space upstairs.

Hoxton

Bricklayer's Arms 63 Charlotte Rd, EC2. Old Street tube. An appealingly ramshackle Shoreditch pub (serving Thai food) that predates the area's trendification, and is therefore all the more popular with its new arty residents. Closed Sun.

Dragon 5 Leonard St, EC2. Old Street tube. Discreetly signed clubby pub with bare-brick walls and crumbling leather sofas, that attracts a mixed crowd happy to listen to whatever takes the resident DJ's fancy.

Shoreditch Electricity Showrooms 39a Hoxton Square, N1. Old Street tube. The upstairs bar mixes kitsch artwork with digital boards flashing ironic weather and text messages, while the intimate club downstairs hosts weekend parties. Good Modern European food available too. Closed Mon.

The City: Fleet Street to St Paul's

Blackfriar 174 Queen Victoria St, EC4. Blackfriars tube. See map, p.98. A gorgeous, utterly original pub, with Art Nouveau marble friezes of boozy monks and a wonderful highly decorated alcove, all dating from 1905. Closed Sat & Sun.

Old Bank of England 194 Fleet St, EC4. Temple or Chancery Lane tube. See map, p.98. Not the actual Bank of England, but the former Law Courts' branch, this imposing High Victorian banking hall is now a magnificently opulent ale and pie pub. Closed Sat & Sun.

Old Cheshire Cheese Wine Office Court, 145 Fleet St, EC4. Blackfriars tube. See map, p.98. A famous seventeenth-century watering hole, with several snug, dark panelled bars and real fires. Popular with tourists, but by no means exclusively so. Closed Sun eve.

Viaduct Tavern 126 Newgate St, EC1. St Paul's tube. See map, p.98. Glorious gin palace built in 1869 opposite what was then Newgate Prison and is now the Old Bailey. Ask to see the old cells now used for storing beer. The walls are adorned with oils of faded ladies representing Commerce, Agriculture and the Arts.

The City: Bank to Bishopsgate

The Counting House 50 Cornhill, EC2. Bank tube. See map, p.108. Another City bank conversion, with fantastic high ceilings a glass dome, chandeliers and a central oval bar. Naturally enough, given the location, it's wall-to-wall suits. Closed Sat & Sun.

Hamilton Hall Liverpool Street Station, EC2. Liverpool Street tube. See map, p.108. Cavernous, gilded, former ballroom of the *Great Eastern* hotel, adorned with nudes and chandeliers. Packed out with City commuters tanking up before the train home, but a great place nonetheless.

Jamaica Wine House St Michael's Alley, EC3. Bank tube. See map, p.108. An old City institution tucked away down a narrow alleyway. Despite the name, this is really just a pub, divided into four large snugs by high wood-panelled partitions. Closed Sat & Sun.

East End and Docklands

Dickens Inn St Katharine's Way, E1. Tower Hill tube. See map, p.108. Eighteenth-century timber-framed warehouse transported on wheels from its original site, with a great view over the docks, but very firmly on the tourist trail.

The Gun 27 Cold Harbour, E14. South Quay or Blackwall DLR, or Canary Wharf tube. An old dockers' pub with lots of maritime memorabilia, and – the main attraction – an unrivalled view of the Millennium Dome.

Prospect of Whitby 57 Wapping Wall, E1. Wapping tube. London's most famous riverside pub with a flagstone floor, a cobbled courtyard and great views over the Thames.

Town of Ramsgate 62 Wapping High St, E1. Wapping tube. Dark, narrow medieval pub located by Wapping Old Stairs, which once led down to Execution Dock. Captain Blood was discovered here with the crown jewels under his cloak, and Admiral Bligh and Fletcher Christian were regular drinking partners in pre-mutiny days.

South Bank and Southwark

Anchor Bankside 34 Park St, SE1. London Bridge, Southwark or Blackfriars tube. See map, p.108. While the rest of Bankside has changed almost beyond all recognition, this pub still looks much as it did when first built in 1770 (on the inside, at least). Good for alfresco drinking by the river.

George Inn 77 Borough High St, SE1. Borough or London Bridge tube. See map, p.108. London's only surviving coaching inn – dating from the seventeenth century and now owned by the National Trust – serving a good range of real ales.

Market Porter 9 Stoney St, SE1. London Bridge tube. See map, p.108. Handsome semicircular pub with early opening hours for workers at the Borough Market, and a seriously huge range of real ales.

Kensington & Chelsea

Bed Bar 310 Portobello Rd, W10. Westbourne Park tube. See map, p.122. Despite Moroccan-theme, low-level lighting and cushioned seating areas *Bed Bar* is crammed with hedonistic locals Wed–Sun, standing on the sofas, arms aloft while the DJs spin funky house and Latin-tinged beats.

Bunch of Grapes 207 Brompton Rd, SW3. South Kensington tube. See map, p.122. This popular High-Victorian pub, complete with snob screens, is the perfect place for a post-V&A (or post-Harrods) pint, pie and chips.

Front Page 35 Old Church St, SW3. Sloane Square tube. See map, p.122. Tucked away in the centre of villagey, bohemian Chelsea and infinitely preferable to anything on offer on the King's Road, the *Front Page* is small and snug, and serves very good Mediterranean food.

Notting Hill

Cherry Jam 52 Porchester Rd, W2. Royal Oak tube. See map, p.122. Owned by Ben Watt (house DJ and half of pop group Everything But The Girl), this smart intimate basement place mixes a decadent cocktail bar with top-end West London DJs. Eve only.

The Cow 89 Westbourne Park Rd, W2. Westbourne Park or Royal Oak tube. See map, p.122. Vaguely Irish-themed pub that pulls in the beautiful W11 types thanks to its spectacular food, including a daily supply of fresh oysters, and excellent Guinness.

Market Bar 240a Portobello Rd, W11. Ladbroke Grove tube. See map, p.122. Self-consciously bohemian pub divided by gilded mirrors and ruched curtains and scattered with weird *objets* – all very Portobello Road. Occasional live music and DJs.

Prince Bonaparte 80 Chepstow Rd, W2. Royal Oak tube. See map, p.122. Pared-down, minimalist pub, with acres of space for sitting and supping or enjoying the excellent Mediterranean food. Notting Hill Gate or Royal Oak tube.

St John's Wood and Maida Vale

Prince Alfred 9 Formosa St, W9. Warwick Avenue tube. See map, p.122. A fantastic period-piece Victorian pub with all its original 1862 fittings intact, right down to the glazed snob screens that divide the bar into a series of snugs, and a surprisingly young and funky clientele.

Warrington Hotel 93 Warrington Crescent, W9. Warwick Avenue or Maida Vale tube. Yet another architectural gem – this time flamboyant Art Nouveau – in an area replete with them. The interior is rich and satisfying, as are the draught beers and the Thai restaurant upstairs.

Camden Town

Bar Vinyl 6 Inverness St, NW1. Camden Town tube. Tiny, funky glass-bricked place with a breakbeat and trip-hop vibe, and a record shop downstairs.

Bartok 78–79 Chalk Farm Rd, NW1. Chalk Farm or Camden Town tube. Unusual bar where punters sink into the sofas and sup beer or wine while listening to classical music and live jazz instead of the usual muzak. Closed Mon–Fri lunch.

The Engineer 65 Gloucester Ave, NW1. Chalk Farm tube. One of a number of gastropubs in the much sought-after residential area of Primrose Hill, *The Engineer* is a smart, grandiose place which serves exceptional but pricey Modern Brit/Med food.

Hampstead and Highgate

The Flask 14 Flask Walk, NW3. Hampstead tube. Convivial Hampstead local, hidden away along the pedestrianized Flask Walk, that retains its original Victorian snob screen and serves above-average food and Young's ale.

The Flask 77 Highgate West Hill, N6. Highgate tube. Ideally situated at the heart of Highgate village green, with a rambling low-ceilinged interior and a summer terrace. The range of beers is good, but the food is nothing special.

Freemason's Arms 32 Downshire Hill, NW3. Hampstead tube. Big, smart pub close to the Heath, popular on sunny days primarily for its large beer garden; also does comfort pub food, has a basement skittle alley, and an outdoor pell mell pitch.

Holly Bush 22 Holly Mount, NW3. Hampstead tube. A lovely old wood-panelled, gas-lit pub, tucked away in the steep backstreets of Hampstead village. Mobbed on the weekend.

Dulwich and Greenwich

Crown & Greyhound 73 Dulwich Village, SE21. West Dulwich train station from Victoria. Grand, spacious Victorian pub with an ornate plasterwork ceiling and a nice summer beer garden. Convenient for the Picture Gallery, but be prepared for the Sunday lunchtime crowds.

Cutty Sark Ballast Quay, off Lassell St, SE10. Cutty Sark DLR or Maze Hill train station. The nicest riverside pub in Greenwich, spacious, more of a local and much less touristy than the more famous *Trafalgar Tavern* (it's a couple of minutes' walk further east, following the river). The views are great, as is the draught beer, and the bar food is a cut above the norm.

Trafalgar Tavern 5 Park Row, SE10. Cutty Sark DLR or Maze Hill train station. A great riverside position and a mention in Dickens' *Our Mutual Friend* have made this Regency-style inn a firm tourist favourite, which is fair enough really, as it's a convivial period piece, and serves good food.

Chiswick to Richmond

Dove 19 Upper Mall, W6. Ravenscourt Park tube. A short walk from Hammersmith Bridge this old riverside pub is known for its literary associations and the smallest back bar in the UK (4ft by 7ft).

White Cross Hotel Water Lane, Richmond. Richmond tube. With a longer pedigree and more character than its clinical chain rivals nearby, the *White Cross* is also much closer to the river (its front garden regularly gets flooded).

White Swan Riverside, Twickenham. Twickenham train station from Waterloo. Filling pub food, draught beer and a quiet riverside location – with a beer pontoon on the Thames if you want to get even closer to the water – make this a good halt on any towpath ramble.

Nightlife

On any night of the week London offers a bewildering range of things to do after dark, ranging from top-flight opera and theatre to clubs with a life span of a couple of nights. The **listings magazine** *Time Out*, which comes out every Tuesday afternoon, is essential if you want to get the most out of this city, giving full details of prices and access, plus previews and reviews.

Live music venues

Over the past five years London has established itself as the music capital of not just Europe, but the world. Rio may be sunnier, Paris prettier and Madrid madder but for sheer range and diversity there's nowhere to beat London. The **live music** scene remains extremely diverse, encompassing all variations of rock, blues, roots and world music; and although London's jazz clubs aren't on a par with those in the big American cities, there's a highly individual scene of home-based artists, supplemented by top-name visiting players.

Rock and blues clubs and pubs

Astoria 157 Charing Cross Rd, WC2 Ⓦwww.meanfiddler.com. Tottenham Court Road tube. This central, large, balconied one-time theatre tends to host slightly alternative bands, with club nights on Fri & Sat.

Borderline Orange Yard, off Manette St, W1 Ⓦwww.borderline.co.uk. Tottenham Court Road tube. Intimate basement joint and a good place to catch new bands, although big names sometimes turn up under a pseudonym.

Brixton Academy 211 Stockwell Rd, SW9. Brixton tube. This refurbished Victorian hall, complete with Neoclassical decorations, can hold 4000 but still manages to seem small and friendly.

Forum 9–17 Highgate Rd, NW5 Ⓦwww.meanfiddler.com. Kentish Town tube. The Forum is North London's best medium-sized venue, and is still a frequent stop-off point for established jazz-funk and rock bands.

Mean Fiddler 24–28a Harlesden High St, NW10 Ⓦwww.meanfiddler.com. Willesden Junction tube. An excellent – if inconveniently located – small venue with a main hall and smaller acoustic room. The bands veer from rock to world to folk.

Orange 3 North End Crescent, North End Rd W14. West Kensington tube. Pub-like venue for serious-minded jazz-funkers. There are also varying club nights (call ahead on Ⓣ020/7371 4317).

Roadhouse Jubilee Hall, 35 The Piazza, WC2 Ⓦwww.roadhouse.co.uk. Covent Garden tube. American food, 1950s US-style decor and a line-up of mainly blues and rock 'n' roll bands performing to a mature, nostalgic crowd.

Shepherd's Bush Empire Shepherds Bush Green, W12 Ⓦwww.shepherds-bush-empire.co.uk. Shepherd's Bush tube. Grand old West London theatre that regularly draws the cream of the crop of non-stadium-rocking bands.

Station Tavern 41 Bramley Rd, W10. Latimer Road tube. Arguably London's best blues venue, with free – and occasionally great – blues six nights a week.

Subterania 12 Acklam Rd, W10 Ⓦwww.meanfiddler.com. Ladbroke Grove tube. One of the original live music/club crossover venues, set in an arch under a bridge. The crowd is as clued up as the music, which is often dance-oriented.

Underworld 174 Camden High St, NW1 ⓦ www.theunderworldcamden.co.uk. Camden Town tube. Labyrinthine venue that's good for new bands, and has sporadic club nights.

Jazz, world music and roots

100 Club 100 Oxford St, W1. Tottenham Court Road tube. Unpretentious and inexpensive jazz venue – in a very central location.

606 Club 90 Lots Rd, SW10. Fulham Broadway tube. A rare all-jazz venue, located just off the less trendy end of King's Road.

Africa Centre 38 King St, WC2 ⓦ www.africacentre.org.uk. Covent Garden tube. Small place hosting African bands and nights like Saturday's P-funk-heavy Funkin Pussy, drawing a vibrantly enthusiastic crowd.

Cargo 83 Rivington St, EC2 ⓦ www.cargo-london.com. Old St tube. Great live music venue for modern genre mix ups that blend jazz with Brazilian, Latin and African music, from young, vibrant bands, often complemented by DJs.

Jazz Café 5 Parkway, NW1 ⓦ www.jazzcafe.co.uk. Camden Town tube. Futuristic, white-walled venue with an adventurous booking policy exploring Latin, rap, funk, hip-hop and musical fusions. Diehard trad-jazz fans won't be happy, despite the fact that there's a rather good restaurant upstairs with a few prime view tables overlooking the stage.

Pizza Express 10 Dean St, W1. Oxford Street tube. Enjoy a good pizza, then listen to the resident band or highly skilled guest players – late-night session on Saturdays.

Ronnie Scott's 47 Frith St, W1 ⓦ www.ronniescotts.co.uk. Leicester Square tube. The most famous jazz club in London: small and smoky and still going strong. Top-line names play two sets – one at around 10pm, the other after midnight. Book a table, or you'll have to stand.

Clubs

More than fifteen years after acid-house irreversibly shook up British clubs, London remains *the* place to come if you want to party after dark. The sheer diversity of dance music has enabled the city to maintain its status as **Europe's dance capital** – and it's still a port of call for DJs from around the globe. Nearly all of London's **dance clubs** open their doors between 10pm and midnight. Some are open six or seven nights a week, some keep irregular days, others just open at the weekend – and very often a venue will host a different club on each night of the week; for up-to-the-minute listings, pop into one of Soho's many record shops to pick up flyers or check *Time Out*.

Admission charges vary wildly, with small midweek sessions starting at around £3 and large weekend events charging as much as £15; around £10 is the average for a Friday or Saturday night, but bear in mind that profit margins at the bar are often more outrageous than at live music venues.

Clubs

333 333 Old St, EC1. Old Street tube. Three floors of drum'n'bass, twisted disco and breakbeat madness.

93 Feet East 150 Brick Lane, E2 ⓦ www.93feeteast.co.uk. Old St tube. An old East End brewery with four rooms across two levels, as well as an excellent rooftop balcony and outdoor space that's well worth a visit in the summer.

Bagley's Studios King's Cross Goods Yard, off York Way, N1. King's Cross tube. Vast warehouse-style venue, making it the perfect place for enormous raves, with a different DJ in each of the three rooms, and a chill-out bar complete with sofas.

Bar Rumba 36 Shaftesbury Ave, W1 ⓦ www.barrumba.co.uk. Piccadilly Circus tube. Fun, smallish West End venue with an adventurous mix of nights ranging from the future-jazz to top-notch house and R&B at weekends.

Café de Paris 3 Coventry St, W1. Leicester Square tube. Elegantly restored ballroom that plays house, garage and disco to a smartly dressed crowd of wannabes – no jeans or trainers.

Camden Palace 1 Camden High St, NW1 ⓦ www.camdenpalace.com. Camden Town tube. Home to popular Saturday garage nights with great lights, great sounds and heaving crowds.

The Cross Goods Way Depot, off York Way, N1 ⓦ www.the-cross.co.uk. King's Cross tube. House and garage club hidden underneath railway arches, that's bigger than you imagine, but always crammed with Balearic clubby types.

Cuba 11–13 Kensington High St, W8. Kensington High Street tube. Grab a cocktail upstairs in the sociable bar before heading below for club nights that focus around Latin, salsa and Brazilian bossa-nova.

Electric Ballroom 184 Camden High St, NW1 Ⓦwww.electricballroom.co.uk. Camden Town tube. This place attracts a truly mixed crowd of Camden regulars from punks to b-boys who come for the wide range of sounds: rock, hip-hop, jazz and house.

The End 18 West Central St, WC1 Ⓦwww.the-end.co.uk. Tottenham Court Road or Holborn tube. Designed for clubbers by clubbers, *The End* is large and spacious, with chrome minimalist decor and a devastating sound system.

Fabric 77a Charterhouse St, EC1 Ⓦwww.fabriclondon.com. Farringdon tube. If you're a serious dance music fan then there really isn't a better weekend venue in London than *Fabric*, a cavernous, underground brewery-like space with three rooms, holding 2500 people. Get there early to avoid a night of queuing.

Fridge Town Hall Parade, Brixton Hill, SW2 Ⓦwww.fridge.co.uk. Brixton tube. Weekends alternate between pumping mixed/gay nights, and nights with a psychedelic, trancey vibe.

Gardening Club 4 The Piazza, WC2 Ⓦwww.rockgarden.co.uk. Covent Garden tube. A popular choice for house and garage, but be warned – you could well find yourself sharing the dancefloor with beer-boys and bemused tourists.

Gossips 69 Dean St, W1 Ⓦwww.gossips.co.uk. Tottenham Court Road tube. Cave-like basement club that seems to have been around for aeons. Located deep in the heart of Soho, it's a popular stop for swing and hip-hop fans.

Herbal 12–14 Kingsland Rd, E2 Ⓦwww.herbaluk.com. Old Street tube. An intimate two-floored venue that's often home to big name DJs for the entrance price of a packet of cigarettes.

HQs West Yard, Camden Lock, NW1. Camden Town tube. Smallish venue by the canal with a range of nights, though the emphasis is on hip-hop and jazz-fusion. Friendly vibe, good cocktails and free entry if you arrive early on weekdays.

ICA The Mall, SW1 Ⓦwww.ica.org.uk. Piccadilly Circus or Charing Cross tube. Weekends at the ICA play host to some of the most cutting-edge audio-visual collaborations in town.

Ministry of Sound 103 Gaunt St, SE1 Ⓦwww.ministryofsound.co.uk. Elephant & Castle tube. A vast, state-of-the-art club based on New York's legendary *Paradise Garage*, with an exceptional sound system. Corporate clubbing and full of tourists, but it still draws the top talent.

Notting Hill Arts Club 21 Notting Hill Gate, W11. Notting Hill Gate tube. Basement club that's popular for everything from Latin-inspired funk, jazz and disco through to soul, house and garage, and famed for Ben Watt's Sunday night deep house session, Lazy Dog.

Office 3–5 Rathbone Place W1. Tottenham Court Road tube. Various music styles, often focusing on swing and hip-hop, but best known as home to a midweek session where you can play silly board games like Ker-Plunk. Booking a table in advance is advised.

Salsa! 96 Charing Cross Rd, WC2. Leicester Square tube. Funky and fun salsa-based club-cum-restaurant that's a popular choice for group birthday bookings; you can book a table to eat as you mambo.

Scala 278 Pentonville Rd, N1 Ⓦwww.scala-london.co.uk. King's Cross tube. One of London's best clubs, holding unusual and multi-faceted nights that take in film, live bands and music ranging from quirky hip-hop to drum'n'bass and deep house.

Subterania 12 Acklam Rd, W10 Ⓦwww.meanfiddler.com. Ladbroke Grove tube. Worth a visit for its diverse club nights at weekends, including the superior hip-hop and R&B-heavy Rotation every Friday.

Turnmills 63 Clerkenwell Rd, EC1 Ⓦwww.turnmills.com. Farringdon tube. The place to come if you want to sweat to trance and house from dusk till dawn, with an alien-invasion-style bar and funky split-level dancefloor in the main room.

Gay and lesbian London

London's **lesbian and gay scene** is so huge, diverse and well established that it's easy to forget just how much – and how fast – it has grown over the last few years. **Soho** is the obvious place to start exploring, with a mix of traditional gay pubs, designer café-bars and a range of gay-run services. Details of most events appear in *Time Out*, while another excellent source of information is the London **Lesbian and Gay Switchboard** (Ⓣ020/7837 7324, Ⓦwww.llgs.org.uk), which operates around the clock. The **outdoor event** of the year is **Mardi Gras** (Ⓦ www.londonmardigras.com) in July, a colourful, whistleblowing march through the city streets followed by a huge, ticketed party in a central London park.

Bars and clubs

There are loads of lesbian and gay **cafés**, **bars and pubs** in London, many of which have been around for years while some pop up and disappear within months, such is the fickle nature of the scene. Our list is by no means exhaustive as every corner of London has its own gay local. Many cafés and bars transform themselves into **drinking dens** at night and, as some open beyond licensing hours, they can be a cheap alternative to some **clubs**, which open up and shut down with surreal frequency – it's a good idea to check the gay press and listings mags before you set out. Bear in mind that although more and more lesbian bars admit gay men, mixed, as ever, tends to mean mostly men.

Mixed bars

Bar Aquda 13–14 Maiden Lane, WC2. Leicester Square or Covent Garden tube. Bright, modern and fashionable café-bar with good food. Mixed, but mostly boys.

The Black Cap 171 Camden High St, NW1. Camden Town tube. Venerable North London institution offering cabaret of wildly varying quality almost every night. Laugh, sing and lip-synch along, and then dance to 80s tunes until the early hours.

The Box 32–34 Monmouth St, WC2. Covent Garden or Leicester Square tube. Popular, bright café/bar serving good food for a mixed gay/straight crowd during the day, and becoming queerer as the night draws in.

The Edge 11 Soho Square, W1. Tottenham Court Road tube. Busy, style-conscious and pricey Soho café/bar spread over several floors, and (in summer) onto the pavement. Food daily, good art exhibitions and DJs most nights.

First Out 52 St Giles High St, WC2. Tottenham Court Road tube. The West End's original gay café/bar, and still permanently packed, serving good veggie food at reasonable prices. *Girl Friday* is a busy pre-club Friday session for girls; gay men are welcome as guests.

Freedom 60–66 Wardour St, W1. Piccadilly Circus tube. Hip, busy, late-opening café/bar, popular with a mixed straight/gay Soho crowd. Great juices and healthy food in the daytime, cocktails and overpriced beer in the evening.

Old Compton Café 34 Old Compton St, W1. Tottenham Court Road or Leicester Square tube. This enduringly busy Soho institution never closes. Strong coffee and a cosmopolitan range of cakes and snacks make it the obvious solution to sudden mid- or post-party wooziness.

Ted's Place 305a North End Rd, W14. West Kensington or West Brompton tube. Friendly, late-opening local with a gay/lesbian/bi and TV/TS clientele, long-running lesbian Blind Date contest and assorted outbreaks of frivolity.

The Yard 57 Rupert St, W1. Piccadilly Circus tube. Attractive café/bar with courtyard and loft areas. Good food, weekly cabaret and regular fortune tellers.

Lesbian bars

Candy Bar 4 Carlisle St, WC2. Tottenham Court Road tube. Now re-established at its original venue but still with the same crucial, cruisey vibe that made it the hottest girl bar in central London.

The Glass Bar West Lodge, Euston Square Gardens, 190 Euston Rd, NW1. Euston tube. Difficult to find (and hard to forget), you knock on the door and become a member to enter this friendly and intimate late-opening women-only bar. Closed Sun.

Vespa Lounge The Conservatory, Centrepoint House, 15 St Giles High St, WC1. Tottenham Court Road tube. This centrally located girls bar gets super busy at weekends. Pool table, video screen, cute bar staff and a predominantly young crowd. Gay men welcome as guests.

Gay men's bars

79CXR 79 Charing Cross Rd, WC2. Leicester Square tube. Busy, cruisey men's den on two floors, with industrial decor, late licence and a no-messing atmosphere.

Central Station 37 Wharfdale Rd, N1. King's Cross tube. Award-winning, late-opening community pub on three floors, offering cabaret, cruisey club nights, and the UK's only gay sports bar. Not strictly men-only, but mostly so.

Compton's of Soho 53 Old Compton St, W1. Leicester Square or Piccadilly tube. This large, traditional-style pub is a Soho institution, always busy with a youngish crowd, but still a relaxed place to cruise or just hang out.

Site 41–43 St Martin's Lane, WC2. Leicester Square tube. Formerly *Brief Encounter*, this is one of the oldest men's bars in London and still hard at it. A popular pre-*Heaven* or post-opera hangout; the front bar is bright, the back bar dark, both are busy.

Clubs

Crash 66 Goding St, SE11. Vauxhall tube. Four bars, two dancefloors, chill-out areas and hard bodies make this weekly Saturday club night busy, buzzy, sexy and mostly boyzy.

DTPM *Fabric*, 77a Charterhouse St, EC1 Ⓦwww.dtpm-online.net. Farringdon Road tube. This long-running Sunday-nighter can now be found in *Fabric*'s chic surroundings, with three dancefloors offering soul, jazz, funk, R&B, hip-hop, Latino house and progressive to hard house.

Duckie *The Royal Vauxhall Tavern*, 372 Kennington Lane, SE11 Ⓦwww.duckie.co.uk. Vauxhall tube. Modern, rock-based hurdy gurdy provides a creative and cheerfully ridiculous antidote to the dreary forces of gay house domination.

Exilio Latino 229 Great Portland St, W1. Great Portland Street tube. Every Saturday night, *Exilio* erupts in a lesbian & gay Latin frenzy, spinning salsa, cumbias and merengue, and also featuring live acts.

G.A.Y. *The Astoria*, 157 Charing Cross Rd, WC2. Tottenham Court Road tube. Widely considered as the launch venue for new (and ailing) boy and girl bands, this huge, unpretentious and fun-loving dance night is where the young crowd gathers.

Heaven under The Arches Villiers St, WC2. Charing Cross or Embankment tube. Widely regarded as the UK's most popular gay club, this legendary, 2000-capacity venue continues to reign supreme. More Muscle Mary than Diesel Doris.

Popstarz *Scala*, 27 Pentonville Rd, N1. King's Cross tube. A groundbreaking Friday night indie club, *Popstarz* has had to enforce a gay and lesbian majority door policy as its winning formula of alternative toons, 70s and 80s trash, cheap beer and no attitude attracts a growing straight, student-y crowd.

Queer Nation *Substation South*, 9 Brighton Terrace, SW9. Brixton tube. Long-running and popular New York-style house and garage weekly Saturday night club for funksters.

Trade *Turnmills*, 63b Clerkenwell Rd, EC1, Ⓦwww.turnmills.com. Farringdon tube. Legendary techno and hard house Saturday all-nighter (4am to Sunday lunchtime) that features some of the best DJs in the country, plus lots of lasers and special effects.

Theatre

The **West End** is the heart of London's "Theatreland", with Shaftesbury Avenue its most congested drag, but the term is more of a conceptual pigeonhole than a geographical term. West End theatres tend to be dominated by tourist-magnet musicals (more often than not by Andrew Lloyd Webber) or similarly unchallenging shows, but others offer more intriguing productions. The government-subsidized **Royal Shakespeare Company** and the **National Theatre** often put on extremely original productions of mainstream masterpieces, while some of the most exciting work is performed in what have become known as the **Off-West End** theatres, which consistently stage interesting and often challenging productions. Further down the financial ladder still are the **Fringe** theatres, more often than not pub venues, where ticket prices are low, and quality variable.

Tickets under £10 are restricted to the Fringe; the box-office average is closer to £15–25, with £30–40 the usual top whack. Ticket agencies such as Ticketmaster (Ⓣ020/7344 4444, Ⓦwww.ticketmaster.co.uk) or First Call (Ⓣ020/7497 9977, Ⓦwww.firstcalltickets.com), can get seats for most West End shows, but add up to ten percent on the ticket price. The cheapest way to buy your ticket is to go to the theatre box office in person; if you book over the phone, you're likely to be charged a booking fee. Students, senior citizens and the unemployed can get **concessionary rates** on tickets for many shows, and several theatres offer reductions on standby tickets to these groups. Whatever you do, avoid the touts and the dodgy-looking ticket agencies that abound in the West End – there's no guarantee that the tickets are genuine.

The Society of London Theatre (Ⓦwww.officiallondontheatre.co.uk) runs the **tkts ticket booth** in Leicester Square (Mon–Sat 10am–7pm, Sun noon–3pm), which sells on-the-day tickets for all the West End shows at discounts of up to fifty percent, though they tend to be in the top end of the price range, are limited to four per person, and carry a service charge of £2.50 per ticket.

Venues

What follows is a list of those West End theatres that offer a changing roster of good plays, along with the most consistent of the Off-West End and Fringe venues. This by no means represents the full tally of London's stages, as there are scores of fringe places that present work on an intermittent basis – the weekly listings mag *Time Out* provides the most comprehensive and detailed up-to-the-minute survey.

Almeida Almeida St, N1 ⓣ020/7359 4404, ⓦwww.almeida.co.uk. Angel or Highbury & Islington tube. A deservedly popular Off-West End venue in Islington, which premieres excellent new plays and excitingly reworked classics, attracting some big Hollywood names in the process.

Barbican Centre Silk St, EC2 ⓣ020/7638 8891, ⓦwww.barbican.org.uk. Barbican or Moorgate tube. The Barbican's two venues – the excellently designed Barbican Theatre and the much smaller Pit – put on a wide variety of theatrical spectacles from puppetry and musicals to new drama works, and, of course Shakespeare, courtesy of the Royal Shakespeare Company who perform here (and elsewhere in London) on and off from autumn to spring each year.

Battersea Arts Centre 176 Lavender Hill, SW11 ⓣ020/7223 2223, ⓦwww.bac.org.uk. Clapham Junction train station from Victoria or Waterloo. The BAC is a triple-stage building, housed in an old town hall in south London, and has acquired a reputation for excellent fringe productions, from straight theatre to comedy and cabaret.

Bush Shepherd's Bush Green, W12 ⓣ020/7610 4224. Goldhawk Road or Shepherd's Bush tube. This minuscule above-pub theatre is London's most reliable venue for new writing after the Royal Court, and it has turned out some real crackers.

Donmar Warehouse Thomas Neal's, Earlham St, WC2 ⓣ020/7369 1732, ⓦwww.donmar-warehouse.com. Covent Garden tube. A performance space that's noted for new plays and top-quality reappraisals of the classics, and whose former artistic director, Sam Mendes, managed to entice several Hollywood stars to take to the stage.

Drill Hall 16 Chenies St, WC1 ⓣ020/7307 5060, ⓦwww.drillhall.co.uk. Goodge Street tube. This studio-style venue specializes in gay, lesbian, feminist and all-round politically correct new work. Monday evenings are women only; Thursdays are no smoking.

ICA Nash House, The Mall, SW1 ⓣ020/7930 3647, ⓦwww.ica.org.uk. Piccadilly Circus or Charing Cross tube. The Institute of Contemporary Arts attracts the most innovative practitioners in all areas of performance. It also attracts a fair quantity of modish junk, but the hits generally outweigh the misses.

National Theatre South Bank Centre, South Bank, SE1 ⓣ020/7452 3000, ⓦwww.nationaltheatre.org.uk. Waterloo tube. National Theatre, as it's now officially known, consists of three separate theatres: the 1100-seater Olivier, the proscenium-arched Lyttelton and the experimental Cottesloe. Standards set by the late Laurence Olivier, founding artistic director, are maintained by the country's top actors and directors in a programme ranging from Greek tragedies to Broadway musicals. Some productions sell out months in advance, but 20–30 of the cheapest tickets go on sale on the morning of each performance – get there by 8am for the popular shows.

Open Air Theatre Regent's Park, Inner Circle, NW1 ⓣ020/7486 2431, ⓦwww.openairtheatre.org. Baker Street tube. If the weather's good, there's nothing quite like a dose of alfresco drama. This beautiful space in Regent's Park hosts a tourist-friendly summer programme of Shakespeare, musicals, plays and concerts.

Royal Court Sloane Square, SW1 ⓣ020/7565 5000, ⓦwww.royalcourttheatre.com. Sloane Square tube. The refurbished Royal Court is one of the best places in London to catch radical new writing, either in the proscenium arch Theatre Downstairs, or the smaller-scale Theatre Upstairs studio space.

The Royal Hampstead Theatre Eton Avenue, NW3 ⓣ020/7722 9301, ⓦwww.hampstead-theatre.co.uk. Swiss Cottage tube. A spanking new zinc and glass-fronted theatre in Swiss Cottage (not in Hampstead proper) whose productions often move on to the West End. Such is its prestige that the likes of John Malkovich have been seduced into performing here.

Shakespeare's Globe New Globe Walk, SE1 ⓣ020/7902 1400, ⓦwww.shakespeares-globe.org.

London Bridge, Blackfriars or Southwark tube. This thatch-roofed replica Elizabethan theatre uses only natural light and the minimum of scenery, and currently puts on Shakespearean shows and other period pieces from mid-May to mid-September, with "groundling" tickets (standing only) for around £5.

Tricycle Theatre & Cinema 269 Kilburn High Rd, NW6 ⓣ020/7328 1000, ⓦwww.tricycle.co.uk. Kilburn tube. One of London's most dynamic fringe venues, showcasing a mixed bag of new plays, with an emphasis on black and Irish issues, and international productions of the core repertoire.

Young Vic The Cut, SE1 ⓣ020/7928 6363, ⓦwww.youngvic.org. Waterloo tube. A large "in-the-round" space, perfect for Shakespeare, which is something of a speciality, as well as a studio for variable Fringe productions. Big names have appeared at the main stage over the years – Vanessa Redgrave's version of Ibsen's *Ghosts* is near-legendary.

Comedy and cabaret

London's **comedy scene** continues to live up to its status as the new rock-'n'roll with the leading comedians catapulted to unlikely stardom on both stage and screen. The Comedy Store is the best-known and most central venue on the circuit, but just about every London suburb has a venue giving a platform to young hopefuls (full listings appear on ⓦwww.chortle.co.uk, and in the weekly *Time Out*). Note that many venues operate only on Friday and Saturday nights, and that August is a lean month, as much of London's talent heads north for the Edinburgh Festival. **Tickets** at smaller venues can be had for around £5, but in the more established places, you're looking at £10 or more.

Venues

Backyard Comedy Club 231 Cambridge Heath Rd, E2 ⓣ020/7739 3122, ⓦwww.leehurst.com. Bethnal Green tube. Purpose-built club in Bethnal Green established by comedian Lee Hurst, who has successfully managed to attract a consistently strong line-up. Fri & Sat.

Banana Cabaret *The Bedford*, 77 Bedford Hill, SW12 ⓣ020/8673 8904, ⓦwww.bananacabaret.co.uk. Balham tube. This double-stage pub has become one of London's most welcoming comedy venues – well worth the trip out from the centre of town. Fri & Sat from 9pm, followed by a DJ.

Canal Café Theatre *The Bridge House*, Delamere Terrace, W2 ⓣ020/7289 6054, ⓦwww.chortle.co.uk/venues/canal.html. Warwick Avenue tube. Perched on the water's edge in Little Venice, this venue is good for improvisation acts and is home to the Newsrevue team of topical gagsters; there's usually something going on from Thursday to Sunday.

Comedy Café 66 Rivington St, EC2 ⓣ020/7739 5706, ⓦwww.comedycafe.co.uk. Old Street tube. Long-established, purpose-built club in Shoreditch/Hoxton, often with impressive line-ups, and free admission for the new-acts slot on Wednesday nights. Wed–Sat.

Comedy Store Haymarket House, 1a Oxendon St, SW1 ⓣ020/7344 0234, ⓦwww.thecomedystore.co.uk. Piccadilly Circus tube. Widely regarded as the birthplace of alternative comedy, though no longer in its original venue, the Comedy Store has catapulted many a stand-up onto primetime TV. Improvisation by in-house comics on Wednesdays and Sundays, in addition to a stand-up bill; Friday and Saturday are the busiest nights, with two shows, at 8pm and midnight – book ahead.

Jongleurs Camden Lock, Dingwalls Building, 36 Camden Lock Place, Chalk Farm Road, NW1; box office ⓣ020/7564 2500, information ⓣ08707/870707, ⓦwww.jongleurs.com. Camden tube. Jongleurs is the chain store of comedy, doling out high quality stand-up and post-revelry disco-dancing nightly on Fridays. Book well in advance.

Meccano Club Dove Regent, 65 Graham St, N1 ⓣ020/7813 4478, ⓦwww.themeccanoclub.co.uk. Angel tube. Popular, intimate, pub-based Islington venue that features consistently strong line-ups. Fri & Sat.

Cinema

There are an awful lot of **cinemas** in the West End, but very few places committed to independent films, and even fewer repertory cinemas programming serious movies from the back catalogue. November's **London Film Festival**

(Ⓦwww.lff.org.uk), which occupies half a dozen West End cinemas, is now a huge event, and so popular that many of the films sell out soon after publication of the festival's programme. Below is a selection of the cinemas that put on the most interesting programmes.

Cinemas

BFI London Imax Centre South Bank, SE1 Ⓣ020/7902 1234, Ⓦwww.bfi.org.uk/imax. Waterloo tube. The British Film Institute's remarkable glazed drum has the largest screen in Europe. It's stunning, state-of-the-art stuff alright, showing 2D and 3D films on a massive screen, but like all IMAX cinemas, it suffers from the paucity of good material that's been shot in the format.

Ciné Lumière 17 Queensberry Place, SW7 Ⓣ020/7073 1350, Ⓦwww.institut-francais.org.uk. South Kensington tube. Predominantly, but by no means exclusively, French films, both old and new (sometimes with subtitles), put on by the Institut Français.

Electric 191 Portobello Rd, W11 Ⓣ20/7299 8688, Ⓦwww.the-electric.co.uk. Notting Hill Gate or Ladbroke Grove tube. One of the oldest cinemas in the country (opened 1910), the Electric has been restored and refurbished as the most luxurious cinema in London with leather armchairs and sofas, and a bar.

ICA Cinema Nash House, The Mall, SW1 Ⓣ020/7930 3647, Ⓦwww.ica.org.uk. Piccadilly Circus or Charing Cross tube. Vintage and underground movies shown on one of two tiny screens in the avant-garde HQ of the Institute of Contemporary Arts.

National Film Theatre South Bank, SE1 Ⓣ020/7928 3232, Ⓦwww.bfi.org.uk/nft. Waterloo tube. Known for its attentive audiences and an exhaustive, eclectic programme that includes directors' seasons and thematic series. Around six films daily are shown in the vast NFT1 and the smaller NFT2.

Prince Charles 2–7 Leicester Place, WC2 Ⓣ020/7494 3654, Ⓦwww.princecharlescinema.com. Leicester Square or Piccadilly Circus tube. The bargain basement of London's cinemas (entry for most shows is just £3.50), with a programme of new movies, classics and cult favourites – the *Sing-Along-A-Sound-of-Music* (as well as other participatory romps) is a regular.

Classical music, opera and dance

London is spoilt for choice when it comes to **orchestras**. On most days you'll be able to catch a concert by either the London Symphony Orchestra, the London Philharmonic, the Royal Philharmonic, the Philharmonia or the BBC Symphony Orchestra, or a smaller-scale performance from the English Chamber Orchestra, London Sinfonietta or the Academy of St Martin-in-the-Fields. During the week, there are also **free lunchtime concerts** by students or professionals in many of London's churches, particularly in the City; performances in the Royal College of Music and Royal Academy of Music are of an amazingly high standard, and the choice of work a lot riskier than the commercial venues can manage.

The principal **large-scale venue** is the South Bank Centre (Ⓣ020/7960 4242, Ⓦwww.sbc.org.uk), where the biggest names appear at the Royal Festival Hall, with more specialized programmes staged in the Queen Elizabeth Hall and Purcell Room. With the outstanding London Symphony Orchestra as its resident orchestra, and with top foreign orchestras and big-name soloists in regular attendance, the Barbican (Ⓣ020/7638 8891, Ⓦwww.barbican.org.uk) is one of the capital's best arenas for classical music. Programming is much more adventurous than it was, and free music in the foyer is often very good. For **chamber music**, the intimate and elegant Wigmore Hall, 36 Wigmore St, W1 (Ⓣ020/7935 2141, Ⓦwww.wigmore-hall.org.uk), is many a Londoner's favourite.

From July to September each year, **the Proms** at the Royal Albert Hall (Ⓣ020/7589 8212, Ⓦwww.bbc.co.uk/proms) feature at least one concert daily, with hundreds of standing tickets sold for just £3 on the night. The acoustics aren't the world's best, but the calibre of the performers is unbeatable and the programme is a fascinating mix of standards and new or obscure works. The hall is so vast that if you turn up half an hour before the show starts there should be little risk of being turned away.

Despite its elitist image, **opera** in the capital continues to attract new audiences. Of the two main companies, the **Royal Opera House** (Ⓣ020/7304 4000, Ⓦwww.royaloperahouse.org), is undergoing a new lease of life since its refurbishment and the appointment of a new music director. Meanwhile **English National Opera** at the Coliseum on St Martin's Lane (Ⓣ020/7632 8300, Ⓦwww.eno.org), has started renovating its theatre, the vast London Coliseum, while continuing to show what can be achieved with young, home-grown talent and lively, radical productions.

From the time-honoured showpieces of the **Royal Ballet** (Ⓣ020/7304 4000, Ⓦwww.royaloperahouse.org) to the diverse and exciting range of British and international dance that goes on at the newly rebuilt Sadler's Wells (Ⓣ020/7863 8000, Ⓦwww.sadlers-wells.com), and at the much smaller venue, The Place (Ⓣ020/7387 0031, Ⓦwww.theplace.org.uk), there's always a **dance performance** of some kind afoot in London, and the city also has a good reputation for international dance festivals showcasing the work of a spread of ensembles. The biggest of the annual events is the **Dance Umbrella** (Ⓣ020/8741 5881, Ⓦwww.danceumbrella.co.uk), a six-week season (Sept–Nov) of new work from bright young choreographers and performance artists at venues across the city.

Shopping

Whether it's time or money you've got to burn, London is one big shoppers' playground, and although chains and superstores predominate along the high streets, you're still never too far from the kind of oddball, one-off establishment that makes shopping an adventure rather than a chore. From the *folie de grandeur* that is Harrods to the frantic street markets of the East End, there's nothing you can't find in some corner of the capital.

In the centre of town, **Oxford Street** is the city's most frantic chain store mecca, and together with **Regent Street**, which crosses it halfway, offers pretty much every mainstream clothing label you could wish for. Just off Oxford Street, high-end designer outlets line **St Christopher's Place** and **South Molton Street**, and you'll find even pricier designers and jewellers along the very chic **Bond Street**.

Tottenham Court Road, which heads north from the east end of Oxford Street, is the place to go for electrical goods and furniture and design shops. **Charing Cross Road**, heading south, is the centre of London's book trade, both new and second-hand. At its north end, and particularly on **Denmark Street**, you can find music shops selling everything from instruments to sound equipment and sheet music. **Soho** offers an offbeat mix of sex boutiques, records and silks, while the streets surrounding **Covent Garden** yield art and design shops, mainstream fashion stores, designer wear and outdoor pursuits gear.

Just off Piccadilly, **St James's** is the natural habitat of the quintessential English gentleman, with **Jermyn Street** in particular harbouring shops dedicated to his grooming. **Knightsbridge**, further west, is home to Harrods and Harvey Nichols, and the big-name fashion stores of **Sloane Street** and **Brompton Road**.

Books

The biggest bookstore in the capital is Waterstones' Piccadilly branch (Piccadilly Circus tube), but the largest choice of bookshops is still on **Charing Cross Road**, where you'll not only find all the **chain stores** – Borders at no. 120, and Blackwell's at no. 100 – but also Foyles at no. 113–119, and other smaller **independent shops** such as Islamic bookshop Al-hoda at no. 76–78, art specialists Zwemmer at no. 80, crime specialists Murder One at no. 71–73 and numerous **second-hand stores**, including Any Amount of Books at no. 62.

Department stores

Fortnum & Mason, 181 Piccadilly (Green Park or Piccadilly Circus tube), is the place to go for fabulous, gorgeously presented and pricey food, plus upmarket clothes, furniture and stationery. **Harrods**, Knightsbridge (Knightsbridge tube), is famous for its fantastic Art Nouveau tiled food hall, obscenely huge toy department and supremely tasteless memorial to Diana and Dodi; beware the draconian dress code (see p.125). Nearby, **Harvey Nichols**, 109–125 Knightsbridge, offers all the latest designer collections and famously frivolous and pricey luxury foods. Over at Oxford Circus, several major stores are close at hand, among them: **John Lewis**, 278–306 Oxford St (Oxford Circus tube), which offers everything from buttons to stockings to furniture and household goods; **Liberty**, 210–220 Regent St (Oxford Circus tube), founded as a retail outlet for the Victorian Arts and Crafts Movement, and still the place to go for regal fabrics and decorative household goods; and **Selfridge's**, 400 Oxford St (Bond Street tube), London's first great department store, which has a wide range of clothing, food and furnishings.

Markets

Camden, running from Camden High Street to Chalk Farm Road (daily; Camden Town tube), is top of the list for market shopping on most tourist itineraries; the atmosphere is a studenty mix of clubby and grungey and the stuff on sale is mainly cheap clothes and jewellery, though the stalls around Camden Lock are generally more interesting; weekends are the best – and busiest – times to visit. **Spitalfields**, Commercial Street (Sun; Liverpool Street tube), is an arty-crafty market similar to Camden, but on a much smaller scale, which also offers organic fruit and veg. Nearby, **Brick Lane** (Sun; Aldgate East, Shoreditch or Liverpool Street tube) has everything from sofas and antiques to cheap junk; and **Petticoat Lane**, Middlesex Street and Goulston Street (Sun; Aldgate East or Liverpool Street tube), offers cheap and cheerful clothes. **Bermondsey** (New Caledonian) Market, Bermondsey Square (Fri; Borough, London Bridge or Bermondsey tube), is a huge, unglamorous but highly regarded antique market that kicks off at 5am; while **Portobello**, Portobello Rd (Fri–Sun; Notting Hill or Ladbroke Grove tube), is mostly boho-chic clothes and (Sat only) portable antiques. South of the river, **Greenwich**, Market Square (Sat & Sun; Cutty Sark DLR or Greenwich train station), is another small arty-crafty market, with second-hand clothing and antiques on sale, too.

Music

The **megastores** are: HMV, 150 Oxford St (Oxford Circus tube); Tower Records, 1 Piccadilly Circus (Piccadilly Circus tube); Virgin Megastore, 14–16 Oxford St (Tottenham Court Road tube). For **jazz**, try Ray's on the first floor of Foyles, 113–119 Charing Cross Rd (Tottenham Court Road tube). For

indie music, there's Sister Ray, 94 Berwick St (Oxford Circus or Piccadilly Circus tube). For **reggae**, **ragga** and **drum'n'bass**, head to Daddy Kool, 12 Berwick St (Oxford Circus or Tottenham Court Road tube). **Hip-hop** is available at Mr Bongo 44 Poland St (Oxford Circus tube). For **house**, **techno** and **trance** go to Eukatech, 49 Endell St (Covent Garden tube).

Listings

Airport enquiries Gatwick ⓣ08700/002468, ⓦwww.baa.co.uk; Heathrow ⓣ08700/000123, ⓦwww.baa.co.uk; London City Airport ⓣ020/7646 0000, ⓦwww.londoncityairport.com; Luton ⓣ01582/405100, ⓦwww.london-luton.com; Stansted ⓣ08700/000303, ⓦwww.baa.co.uk.

American Express 30–31 Haymarket, SW1 ⓣ020/7484 9600 (and other branches); ⓦwww.americanexpress.com. Mon–Sat 9am–6pm, Sun 10am–5pm. Piccadilly Circus tube.

Bike rental On Your Bike, 52–54 Tooley St, SE1 ⓣ020/7378 6669, ⓦwww.onyourbike.net. Mon–Fri 8am–7pm, Sat 9.30am–5.30pm. London Bridge tube.

Car rental For the most competitive rates, ring round a few local firms from the Yellow Pages (ⓦwww.yell.com) before you try your luck with the usual suspects. Europcar ⓣ020/7259 1600, ⓦwww.europcar.co.uk and at Heathrow, Gatwick, Stansted and City airports; Hertz ⓣ020/7278 1588, ⓦwww.hertz.co.uk and at Heathrow, Gatwick and City airports; Easycar ⓣ09063/333333, ⓦwww.easycar.com.

Cricket Two Test matches are played in London each summer: one at Lord's (ⓣ020/7432 1000, ⓦwww.lords.org), the home of English cricket, in St John's Wood; the other at The Oval (ⓣ020/7582 6660, ⓦwww.surreycricket.com), in Kennington. In tandem with the full-blown five-day Tests, there's also a series of one-day internationals, two of which are usually held in London.

Consulates and embassies Australia, Australia House, Strand, WC2 ⓣ020/7379 4334, ⓦwww.australia.org.uk; Canada, Canada House, Trafalgar Square, WC2 ⓣ020/7528 6533 ⓦwww.canada.org.uk; Ireland, 17 Grosvenor Place, SW1 ⓣ020/7235 2171; New Zealand, New Zealand House, 80 Haymarket, SW1 ⓣ020/7930 8422, ⓦwww.nzembassy.com; South Africa, South Africa House, Trafalgar Square, WC2 ⓣ020/7451 7299, ⓦwww.southafricahouse.com; USA, 24 Grosvenor Square, W1 ⓣ020/7499 9000, ⓦwww.usembassy.org.uk.

Dentist Emergency treatment: Guy's Hospital, St Thomas St, SE1 ⓣ020/7955 4317 (Mon–Fri 9am–3pm).

Football London's top club at the moment is Arsenal (ⓣ020/7704 4000, ⓦwww.arsenal.com); their closest rivals (geographically) are Tottenham Hotspur (ⓣ08700/112222, ⓦwww.spurs.co.uk). Meanwhile, in west London, Chelsea (ⓣ020/7915 2951, ⓦwww.chelseafc.co.uk) have recently had millions pumped into them by a Russian billionaire. Tickets for most Premiership games start at £20–25 and are virtually impossible to get hold of on a casual basis: you need to book in advance, or try and see one of the European or knock-out cup fixtures.

Hospitals For 24hr accident and emergency: St Mary's Hospital, Praed St, W2 ⓣ020/7886 6666; University College Hospital, Grafton Way, WC1 ⓣ020/7387 9300.

Internet cafés easyInternetcafe (ⓦwww.easy.everything.com) has 24hr branches at 456 Strand, off Trafalgar Square (Charing Cross tube), 9–16 Tottenham Court Rd (Tottenham Court Road tube) and 9–13 Wilton Rd (Victoria tube).

Left luggage AIRPORTS Gatwick: North Terminal (daily 6am–10pm); South Terminal (24hr). Heathrow: Terminal 1 (daily 6am–11pm); Terminal 2 (daily 5.30am–11pm); Terminal 3 (daily 5am–11pm); Terminal 4 (daily 5.30am–11pm). London City Airport (daily 5.30am–9.30pm). Stansted Airport (24hr).

TRAIN STATIONS Charing Cross (daily 7am–11pm); Euston (Mon–Sat 6.45am–11.15pm, Sun 7.15am–11pm); Victoria (daily 7am–10.15pm); Waterloo International (daily 7am–10pm).

Lost property AIRPORTS Gatwick ⓣ01293/503162 (Mon–Sat 8am–7pm, Sun 8am–4pm); Heathrow ⓣ020/8745 7727 (daily 8am–4pm); London City Airport ⓣ020/7646 0000 (Mon–Fri 5.30am–10pm, Sat 5.30am–1am, Sun 10am–10pm); Stansted ⓣ01279/680500 (daily 6am–midnight).

BUSES ⓣ020/7222 1234 (24hr).

HEATHROW EXPRESS ⓣ020/8745 7727, ⓦwww.heathrowexpress.co.uk (daily 8am–4pm).

TAXIS (black cabs only) ⓣ07918/2000 (Mon–Fri 9am–4pm).

TRAIN STATIONS Euston ⓣ 20/7387 8699 (Mon–Fri 9am–5.30pm); King's Cross ⓣ 020/7278 3310 (Mon–Fri 9am–5.30pm); Liverpool Street ⓣ 020/7247 4297 (Mon–Fri 9am–5.30pm); Paddington ⓣ 020/7313 1514 (Mon–Fri 9am–5.30pm); Victoria ⓣ 020/7922 9887 (daily 7am–midnight); Waterloo ⓣ 020/7401 7861 (Mon–Fri 7.30am–8pm).
TUBE TRAINS Transport for London ⓣ 020/7486 2496, ⓦ www.tfl.gov.uk.

Police Central police stations include: Charing Cross, Agar St, WC2 ⓣ 020/7240 1212; Holborn, 70 Theobalds Rd, WC1 ⓣ 020/7404 1212; King's Cross, 76 King's Cross Rd, WC1 ⓣ 020/7704 1212; West End Central, 10 Vine St, W1 ⓣ 020/7437 1212; City of London Police, Bishopsgate, EC2 ⓣ 020/7601 2222.

Post offices The only (vaguely) late-opening post office is the Trafalgar Square branch at 24–28 William IV St, WC2 4DL ⓣ 020/7484 9304 (Mon–Fri 8.30am–6.30pm, Sat 9am–5.30pm); it's also the city's poste restante collection point. For general postal enquiries phone ⓣ 08457/740740 (Mon–Fri 8am–7.30pm, Sat 8am–6pm), or visit the website ⓦ www.royalmail.co.uk.

Tennis Tennis in England is synonymous with Wimbledon (ⓣ 020/8946 2244, ⓦ www.wimbledon.com), the only Grand Slam tournament in the world to be played on grass, and for many players the ultimate goal of their careers. To buy tickets on the day, you must arrive by around 7am for tickets on Centre and No. 1 courts, or by around 9am for the outside courts (and avoid the middle Saturday of the tournament).

Train stations and information As a rough guide, Euston handles services to northwest England and Glasgow; King's Cross northeast England and Edinburgh; Liverpool Street eastern England; Paddington western England; Victoria and Waterloo southeast England. For information, contact national rail enquiries ⓣ 08457/484950, ⓦ www.rail.co.uk.

Travel agents STA Travel, 33 Bedford St, WC1 ⓣ 020/7240 9821, ⓦ www.statravel.co.uk; Trailfinders, Lower Ground Floor Waterstone's, 203–205 Piccadilly, W1 ⓣ 020/7292 1888, ⓦ www.trailfinders.co.uk.

Travel details

Buses

For information on all local and national bus services, contact Traveline ⓣ 08706/082608 (daily 7am–9pm), ⓦ www.traveline.org.uk.

London Victoria Coach Station to: Bath (every 1–2hr; 3hr 15min); Birmingham (hourly; 2hr 40min); Brighton (every 30min; 2hr); Bristol (hourly; 2hr 30min); Cambridge (every 30min; 2hr); Canterbury (hourly; 1hr 50min); Dover (hourly; 2hr 25min); Exeter (every 1–2hr; 4hr 10min); Gloucester (hourly; 3hr 15min); Liverpool (5 daily; 4hr 30min–5hr); Manchester (8 daily; 4hr 30min–5hr); Newcastle (4 daily; 6hr 30min–7hr); Oxford (every 20min; 1hr 40min); Plymouth (8 daily; 4hr 50min–5hr 15min); Stratford (3 daily; 3hr).

Trains

For information on all local and national rail services, contact National Rail Enquiries ⓣ 08457/484950, ⓦ www.rail.co.uk.

London Charing Cross to: Canterbury (hourly; 1hr 25min); Dover Priory (every 30min; 1hr 45min).

London Euston to: Birmingham New St (every 30min; 1hr 45min); Carlisle (every 2hr; 4hr); Lancaster (hourly; 3hr–3hr 20min); Liverpool Lime St (hourly; 3hr); Manchester Piccadilly (hourly; 2hr 30min).

London King's Cross to: Brighton (Thameslink; every 15–30min; 1hr 15min); Cambridge (every 30min; 45min–1hr); Durham (every 1–2hr; 2hr 40min–3hr); Leeds (hourly; 2hr 20min); Newcastle (every 30min; 3hr); Peterborough (every 30min; 45min); York (every 30min; 2hr).

London Liverpool Street to: Cambridge (Mon–Sat every 30min; 1hr 20min); Norwich (every 30min–hourly; 1hr 50min); Stansted Airport (every 15–30min; 45min).

London Paddington to: Bath (every 30min–hourly; 1hr 30min); Bristol (every 30–45min; 1hr 20min); Cheltenham (every 2hr; 2hr); Exeter (every 1–2hr; 2hr 5min); Gloucester (every 2hr; 1hr 45min); Oxford (every 30min–hourly; 1hr); Penzance (8–9 daily; 5hr); Plymouth (hourly; 3hr–3hr 40min); Windsor (change at Slough; Mon–Fri every 20min; Sat & Sun every 30min; journey time 30–40min); Worcester (hourly; 2hr 20min).

London St Pancras to: Leicester (every 30min; 1hr 30min); Nottingham (hourly; 2hr 10min); Sheffield (hourly; 2hr 20min).
London Victoria to: Brighton (every 30min; 1hr); Gatwick (every 15min; 30min).

London Waterloo to: Portsmouth Harbour (every 30min; 1hr 30min); Southampton Central (every 30min; 1hr 15min); Winchester (every 30min; 1hr 10min); Windsor (Mon–Sat every 30min, Sun hourly; 50min).

2

Surrey, Kent and Sussex

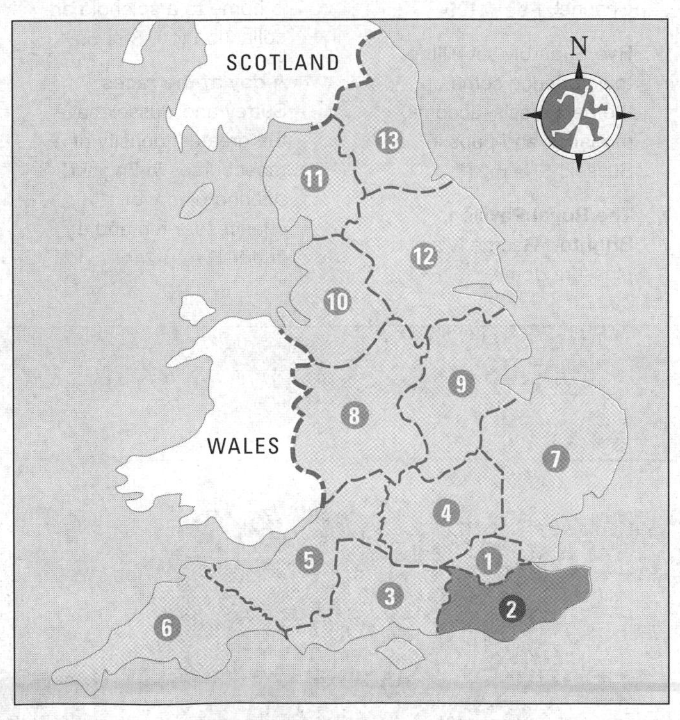

CHAPTER 2

Highlights

* **Canterbury Cathedral** An essential, tourist stop that lives up to the hype. See p.190

* **The white cliffs of Dover** Best seen from a boat, the famed chalky cliffs also offer walks and vistas over the Channel. See p.199

* **Rye** Superbly set hilltop town offering some of the best meals, accommodation and pubs in Sussex. See p.218

* **The Royal Pavilion, Brighton** George IV's pleasure dome, designed by Nash, is the supreme (and only) example of Oriental-Gothic architecture. See p.232

* **Petworth House** As well as being one of the country's most attractive stately homes, this place is home to a splendid art collection too. See p.243

* **A day at the races** Surrey and Sussex have the greatest density of racecourses in England, offering plenty of chances for fun and a flutter. See p.244

△ Brighton's Palace Pier

2

Surrey, Kent and Sussex

The southeast corner of England was traditionally where London went on holiday. In the past, trainloads of Eastenders were shuttled to the hop fields and orchards of **Kent** for a working break from the city; boats ferried people down the Thames to the beach at Margate; and everyone from royalty to cuckolding couples enjoyed the seaside at Brighton, a blot of decadence in the otherwise sedate county of **Sussex**. **Surrey** is the least pastoral and historically significant of the three counties – the home of wealthy metropolitan professionals prepared to commute from what has become known as the "stockbroker belt".

The late twentieth century brought big changes to the southeast region. In purely administrative terms the three counties have become four, since local government reorganization split Sussex into East and West. More significantly, many of the old seaside resorts struggled to keep their tourist custom in the face of ever more accessible foreign destinations combined with the vagaries of the English weather. To make matters worse, **Brighton**, long known as "London beside the sea", now matches the capital with one of the highest proportions of homeless people in the country. On the positive side, there has been something of a renaissance in recent years, with various celebrities and other big-city refugees choosing to settle in more congenial surroundings away from the metropolitan hubbub, while the whole region has maintained consistently high standards of both accommodation and gourmet dining. Narrow country lanes and verdant meadows preserve their picturesque charm, and there are even pockets of comparative wilderness, not to mention the miles of bleak and cliffy coastline.

The proximity of Kent and Sussex to the continent has dictated the history of this region, which has served as a gateway for an array of invaders, both rapacious and benign. **Roman** remains dot the coastal area – most spectacularly at **Bignor** in Sussex and **Lullingstone** in Kent – and many roads, including the main A2 London to Dover road, follow the arrow-straight tracks laid by the legionaries. When **Christianity** spread through Europe, it arrived in Britain on the **Isle of Thanet** – the northeast tip of Kent, since rejoined to the mainland by silting and subsiding sea levels. In 597 AD Augustine moved inland and established a monastery at **Canterbury**, still the home of the Church of England and the county's prime historic attraction. (Surprisingly, Sussex was

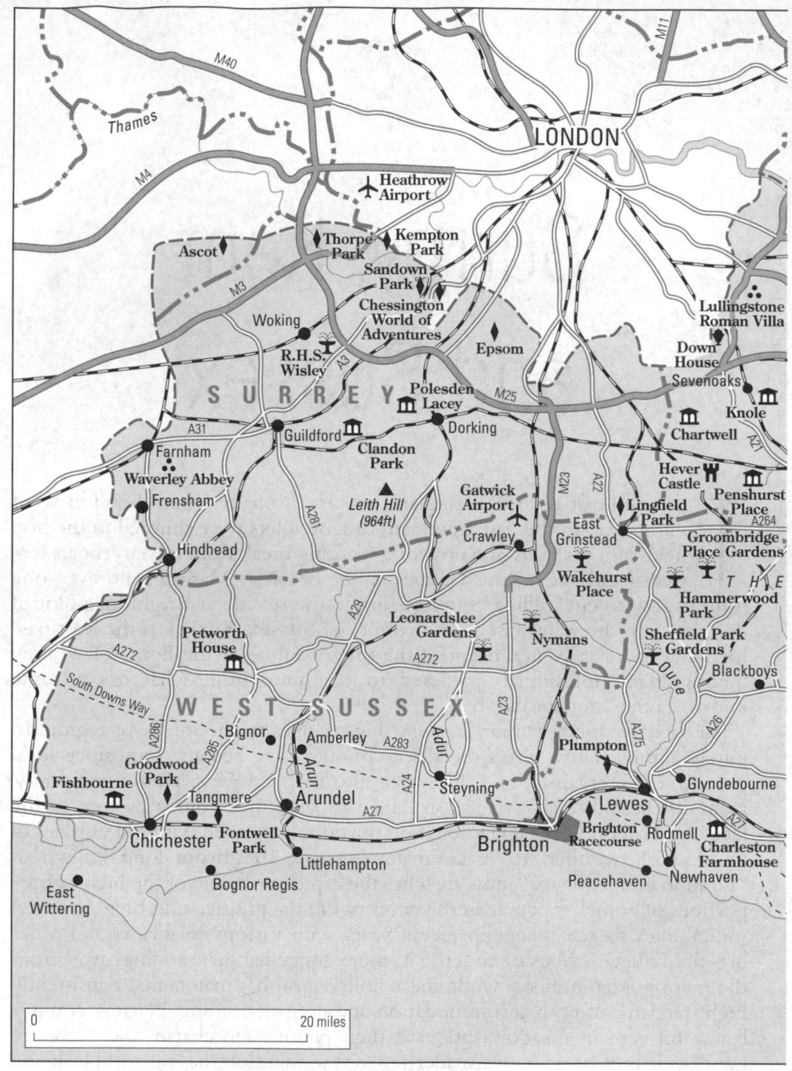

among the last counties to accept the Cross – due more to the region's then impenetrable forest than to its innate ungodliness.)

The last successful invasion of England took place in 1066, when the **Normans** overran King Harold's army near **Hastings**, on a site now marked by **Battle Abbey**. The Normans left their mark all over this corner of the kingdom, and Kent remains unmatched in its profusion of medieval castles, among them **Dover**'s sprawling cliff-top fortress guarding against continental invasion and **Rochester**'s huge, box-like citadel, close to the old dockyards of **Chatham**, power-base of the formerly invincible British navy.

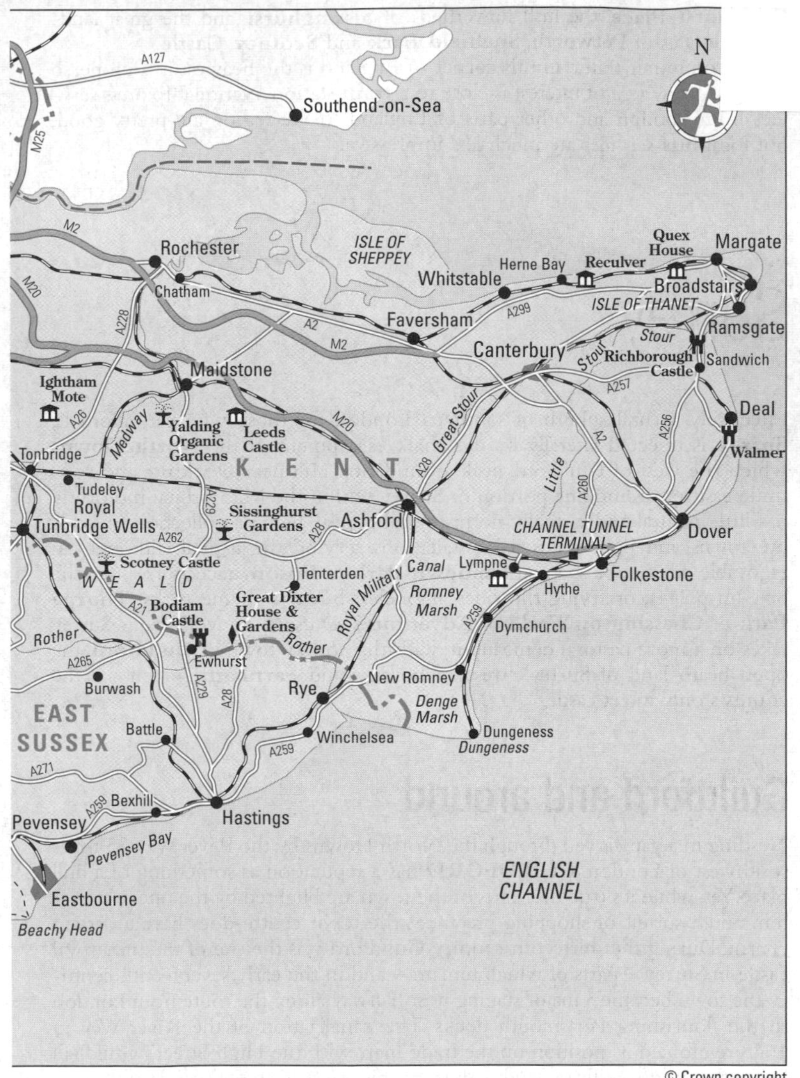

Away from the great historic sites, you can spend unhurried days in elegant old towns such as **Royal Tunbridge Wells**, **Rye** and **Lewes**, or enjoy the less-elevated charms of the traditional resorts, of which **Brighton** is far and away the best, combining the buzz of a university town with a blowsy good-time atmosphere and an excellent range of eating options. Dramatic scenery may be in short supply, but in places the **South Downs Way** offers an expanse of rolling chalk uplands that, as much as anywhere in the crowded southeast, gets you away from it all. And of course Kent, Sussex and Surrey harbour some of the country's finest **gardens**, ranging from Kew Gardens' country home at

Wakehurst Place, the lush flowerbeds of **Sissinghurst** and the great landscaped estates of **Petworth**, **Sheffield Park** and **Scotney Castle**.

The commuter traffic in this corner of England is the heaviest in Europe, so almost everywhere of interest is close to a **train** station. National Express services from London and other parts of England to the region are pretty good, but local **bus** services are much less impressive.

Surrey

Effectively a rural suburb of southern London for those who can afford it, **Surrey** is bisected laterally by the chalk escarpment of the **North Downs** which rise west of Guildford, peak around Box Hill near **Dorking**, and continue east into Kent. The portion of Surrey within the M25 orbital motorway has little natural and virtually no historical appeal, being a collection of satellite towns and light industrial installations serving the capital, although an enjoyable day can be spent at **Sandown Park** or **Epsom** racecourses (see the box on p.244), or trying the rides at one of Surrey's theme parks, **Thorpe Park** or **Chessington World of Adventures**. Outside the M25's ring, Surrey takes on a more pastoral demeanour, with the county town of **Guildford**, the open heath land of Surrey's western borders and **Farnham**, which has the county's only intact castle.

Guildford and around

Nestling in a gap carved through the North Downs by the River Wey, 35 miles southwest of London, **GUILDFORD** has a reputation as something of a dull place. Yet, while it's true that parts of the town are blighted by the one-way system and a surfeit of shopping precincts, the town centre does have a certain charm. During the thirteenth century Guildford was the site of the only royal castle in Surrey – parts of which remain – and in the early seventeenth century the town became a major staging post halfway along the route from London to the flourishing Portsmouth docks. The canalization of the River Wey in 1648 reinforced its position on the trade map, with the High Street's Guildhall being the most significant landmark from this era. Within easy reach of the city are two National Trust properties, **Clandon Park** and **Hatchlands Park**, as well as the Royal Horticultural Society's gardens at **Wisley**.

Arrival, information and accommodation

Guildford's main **train station**, with regular trains from London Waterloo and Portsmouth, lies just over the river to the west of the town centre. Between the town centre and the train station, at the western end of North Street, the **bus station** has regular connections to London, Dorking, Portsmouth and Winchester. The county's main **tourist office** is at 14 Tunsgate (May–Sept Mon–Sat 9am–5.30pm, Sun 10am–4.30pm; Oct–April Mon–Sat

9.30am–5.30pm; ⓣ01483/444333, ⓦwww.guildford.gov.uk), just off the High Street near the Guildhall. Free guided **tours** of the town leave from Tunsgate Arch, just below the tourist office (May–Sept Mon 11.30am & 2.30pm, Wed & Sun 2.30pm; Thurs, May–Aug only 7.30pm). There's **Internet** access at *Quark's* in Jeffries Passage at the top of the High Street (Mon–Fri 9.30am–9pm, Sat 10am–9pm, Sun 10am–8pm).

Guildford's less expensive **accommodation** options are all some distance from the town centre and include the homely *Atkinsons Guest House*, 129 Stoke Rd (ⓣ01483/538260, ⓦwww.s-h-systems.co.uk; ❷), with four rooms, ten minutes' walk up the A320 Woking road. Plusher lodgings can be found at the *Jarvis Guildford Hotel*, 253 Upper High St (ⓣ01483/564511, ⓦwww.jarvis.co.uk; ❻) and at the timber-beamed, 500-year-old *Angel Posting House and Livery*, 91 High St (ⓣ01483/564555, ⓦwww.johansens.com; ❼). The nearest **youth hostel** is in the village of Holmbury St Mary, eight miles southeast of Guildford (see p.175).

The Town

Guildford's sloping **High Street** retains a great deal of architectural interest and several picturesque narrow lanes and courts lead off it to the adjoining North Street, and south towards the castle. As you look up the cobbled High Street you can't fail to spot the wonderful gilded clock projecting over the street that has marked the town's time for more than three hundred years. The clock belongs to the **Guildhall** (guided tours Tues & Thurs 2pm & 3pm; free; ⓦwww.guildford.gov.uk) with its elaborate Restoration facade disguising Tudor foundations. A little further up the High Street is the **Archbishop Abbot's Hospital**, a hospice built for the elderly in 1619 fronted by a palatial red-brick Tudor gateway. You can take a peek at the pretty courtyard, but if you want to inspect the Flemish stained glass and oak beams that characterize the interior you must join a guided tour. Back down towards the river, on the left at no. 72 is the **Undercroft** (also viewable on a guided tour), a well-preserved thirteenth-century basement of vaulted arches.

Guildford **Castle**'s Norman keep (due to reopen in 2004 after extensive renovation; for the latest information, ask at the tourist office or check ⓦwww.guildford.gov.uk) sits on its motte behind the High Street, surrounded by flower-filled gardens. Frequently used as a palace by King John – he might have departed from here to Runnymede to sign the Magna Carta in 1215 – the castle was enlarged and improved during Henry III's reign, after which it was left to crumble into its present state. Beneath the castle, **Guildford Museum**, in Castle Arch on Quarry Street (Mon–Sat 11am–5pm; free), gives an account of the region's pre-Christian culture and displays cases of ceramic relics as well as some exquisite Saxon jewellery. Upstairs are mementoes of the writer Lewis Carroll (aka the Reverend Charles Dodgson), author of the children's classics, *Alice's Adventures in Wonderland* and *Alice through the Looking Glass*. An imaginative sculpture of Alice passing through the looking glass is to be found in the Castle Gardens, and Dodgson's grave can be visited in the cemetery off the Mount, on the other side of the river.

At the bottom of the High Street runs the **River Wey**, a rather neglected feature of the town, although the once-crucial River Wey and Godalming Navigation Canal has been restored into a picturesque waterway. From Easter to October, you can **rent canoes** (swimmers only) and **rowing boats** (Mon–Sat 9am–5.30pm, Sun 10am–6pm; canoes £4/hour; rowing boats £6/hour; £20 deposit) from Guildford Boat House, based in the Millbrook car park, and in summer take the same company's **pleasure cruises** up the river from the town wharf, at the bottom of the High Street (ⓣ01483/504494 or

536186 for timetable information; Ⓦwww.guildfordboats.co.uk). Half a mile further north up the river is **Dapdune Wharf** (March–Oct Mon & Thurs–Sun 11am–5pm; £3; NT), whose buildings house an interactive museum recounting the story of what is claimed to be Britain's oldest working waterway, while outside you can visit the restored barge *Reliance*.

Ostentatiously perched on Stag Hill by the university, a mile northwest of the centre, is Guildford's monumentally unremarkable red-brick **Cathedral** (daily 8.30am–5.30pm; Ⓦwww.guildford-cathedral.org), one of only four Anglican cathedrals built in England in the twentieth century, topped by a gaudy gilded angel. Resembling an outsized crematorium and consecrated in 1961 following wartime delays, the cathedral's plain, bright interior, with its concrete vaulting, has all the spirituality of a concert hall, but without the acoustics. Its most notable claim to fame is having been a location in the film *The Omen*.

Eating, drinking and entertainment

For **eating** options, it's best to head off the High Street down South Hill, where the stylish Italian-run *Cambio* at no. 2–4 (Ⓣ01483/577702; closed Sun eve) offers a set two-course lunch for £12, or to the more expensive *Zinfandel*, at no. 4–5 Chapel St (Ⓣ01483/455155; closed Sun), which dishes up Californian and Pacific-rim cooking plus good-value pizzas. Just around the corner, the *Café de Paris* at 35 Castle St (Ⓣ01483/534896; closed Sun) is a busy French-style brasserie in a listed building, offering three-course meals from around £16.50, while *Olivo*, at 53 Quarry St (Ⓣ01483/303535; closed Sun), housed in the town's sixteenth-century dispensary, specializes in delicious regional Italian dishes and has a roof-terrace. Virtually next door is one of Guildford's better **pubs**, the *King's Head*, also with a terrace, serving real ales and inexpensive meals. Guildford's oldest hostelry, *Ye Olde Ship Inn,* is on Portsmouth Road and boasts open fires; alternatively, try the *Weyside,* a pleasant riverside pub with gardens where you can sample daily home-made specials. Also on Millbrook is one of the most well-known **theatres** outside London, the Yvonne Arnaud Theatre (Ⓣ01483/440000, Ⓦwww.yvonne-arnaud.co.uk), which often stages plays before they reach London's West End. Alternatively, in more ways than one, The Electric Theatre (Ⓣ01483/444789, Ⓦwww.electrictheatre.co.uk), based in the former electric works on Onslow Street, is an innovative riverside venue for both music and theatre and houses an excellent café.

Clandon Park, Hatchlands Park and Wisley

Five miles east of Guildford, the Palladian **Clandon Park** (April–Oct Tues–Thurs & Sun 11am–5pm; £6; NT) was built in the 1730s by Venetian architect Giacomo Leoni, for the second Lord Onslow. The two-storey Marble Hall is particularly impressive as is the Gubbay collection of porcelain, furniture, needlework and carpets and the Ivo Forde collection of Meissenware Italian comedy figures, also housed here. Within the extensive grounds, landscaped by Capability Brown, there's an outsized souvenir in the form of a Maori meeting house brought back from New Zealand by the fourth Lord Onslow, who had been governor there.

If you're up for another National Trust stately home, buy a combined ticket (£9) to get you into **Hatchlands Park** (house April–July, Sept & Oct Tues–Thurs & Sun 2–5.30pm; Aug also Fri 2–5.30pm; grounds April to early Nov daily 11am–6pm; house £6, park & gardens £2.50; NT), a mile or two further along the A246. The grounds are reason enough to come here, with woodland walks and a small Gertrude Jekyll garden, while the **house** itself is a splendid red-brick Palladian pile with richly ornate Robert Adam interiors, a stunning collection of eighteenth- and nineteenth-century keyboard instruments played by the likes of Mozart, Chopin and Mahler, and an exhibition on Admiral Edward Boscowen, who built the house in 1758. Outside, an additional dummy set of windows on the south side of the house adds grandeur, making it look as if there's a third floor, though in fact there are only two.

Five miles northeast of Guildford, signposted off the A3, the Royal Horticultural Society's gardens at **Wisley** (March–Oct Mon–Fri 10am–6pm, Sat & Sun 9am–6pm; Nov–Feb daily 10am–4.30pm; £6; Ⓦ www.rhs.org.uk) are a research establishment and a gardeners' garden, with staff on hand to offer advice and solve horticultural queries. The greenhouses contain a vast array of fragile specimens, including orchids and fuchsias; late spring is the best time to visit. The best way to get there by public transport is to pick up the hourly #515 bus from Guildford (less frequent Sun), alternatively catch a train to Woking, from where there is a special bus to Wisley (May–Sept Mon–Fri 11am, returning at 4.30pm; £5).

Farnham and around

Tucked into Surrey's southwestern corner, ten miles west of Guildford along the exposed ridge-top of the Hog's Back, lies **FARNHAM**. Smaller and, in parts, more charming than Guildford, the town moves at a slower pace – though, despite its bypass, the town centre is often clogged by traffic. Notwithstanding its thousand-year history, the majority of Farnham's architecture dates from the eighteenth century, when it enjoyed a boom period based on hop farming.

Yet Farnham is also home to Surrey's only intact **castle**, built around 1138 by Henry de Blois, Bishop of Winchester, as a convenient residence halfway between his diocese and London. The castle was continuously occupied until 1927, but now houses a conference venue. The **keep** (April–Sept daily 10am–6pm; Oct daily 10am–5pm; £2.50; EH), from where there are good views over the rooftops to the downs beyond, is the only part of the castle that is open to the public.

Farnham's refined Georgian dwellings are at their best along the broad **Castle Street**, which links the town centre with the castle, but you can actually step inside one of the smart Georgian houses at 38 West St. Once home to one of Farnham's wealthy hop merchants and now containing the **Museum of Farnham** (Tues–Sat 11am–5pm; free), the house contains a refreshingly succinct rundown on the town's history, its local hero, the late eighteenth-century journalist and social reformer William Cobbett, and the highly regarded local art school. On the same street, the town's library is housed in **Vernon House**, where Charles I spent the night in 1648 en route to his trial and eventual execution in London.

Farnham **train station**, with frequent connections to London Waterloo, is five minutes from the centre, over the river on the southern edge of town, down South Street and over the bypass. You'll find the **tourist office** in the council offices on South Street, midway between the station and the centre (Mon–Thurs 9.30am–5.15pm, Fri 9.30am–4.45pm, Sat 9am–noon; Ⓣ 01252/715109, Ⓦ www.waverley.gov.uk). For **accommodation**, *The Bush Hotel*, a former seventeenth-century coaching inn, is slap bang in the centre of town on The Borough (Ⓣ01252/715237, Ⓦwww.macdonaldhotels.co.uk; ❽), while vying for lavishness and age is *The Bishop's Table Hotel*, West St (Ⓣ01252/710222, Ⓦwww.bishopstable.com; ❼); both offer much-reduced weekend deals. Alternatively, there's comfortable town-house accommodation at *Meads Guest House*, 48 West St (Ⓣ01252/715298; no credit cards; ❸), or try the excellent *Stafford House Hotel*, 22 Firgrove Hill (Ⓣ01252/724336; ❸), close to the station. Out of town, you'll need to book ahead for the best of the **B&B** options, the peaceful *High Wray*, 73 Lodge Hill Rd (Ⓣ01252/715589, Ⓔcrawford@highway73.co.uk; no credit cards; ❸), which lies about a mile south of Farnham Station off the Tilford Road, and close to the start of the North Downs Way; it's a little off the beaten track, so ask for clear directions, or get a cab from the station. Back in town, the French-style brasserie *Café Rouge* in Town Hall Buildings on The Borough (Ⓣ01252/733688; closed Sun) does decent **food**, while the oak-beamed *Nelson Arms* on Castle Street offers reasonable bar meals. For Italian, the best bet is the friendly *Caffe Piccolo*, 84 West St (Ⓣ01252/723277) while the more upmarket *Vienna Stuberl* at 112 West St (Ⓣ01252/722978; closed Sun) is good for seafood.

Waverley Abbey, Frensham and Hindhead

From Farnham Station, the B3001 leads two miles southeast to the evocative riverside ruins of **Waverley Abbey** (open access) the first of many Cistercian bases on British soil. Much of the stone was removed from the abbey after the Dissolution to construct Tudor houses in the area, a common fate of many such monastic establishments.

Three miles south of Farnham, **FRENSHAM** is set among the heather-covered heath lands that typify the Surrey/Hampshire borders. **Frensham Ponds**, established in medieval times as fish repositories and now popular with anglers, lies just south of town; the land hereabouts is as wild as Surrey gets. Five miles south of here on the A287 lies the village of **HINDHEAD**, whose most famous former resident was Arthur Conan Doyle, creator of Sherlock Holmes. Fans of Conan Doyle might be interested in staying in his Edwardian home, now the *Undershaw Hotel* (Ⓣ01428/604039; no credit cards; ❶), which overlooks Hindhead's main junction. On the northeastern edge of town, the curious depression known as the **Devil's Punchbowl** is crisscrossed with walking trails and bridle-paths. Local legends tell of witches, abductions and satanic rituals in the Punchbowl area, but perpetrators of these stories were most likely cattle thieves and highwaymen preying on the Portsmouth-bound stages. Yak-like Highland cattle graze in the area and the nearby Gibbet Hill, a former site of executions a mile east of the village, gives the best views of the vicinity.

There's a tiny **youth hostel** (Ⓣ0870/770 6113; dorm bed £8), on the rim of the Punchbowl, one mile north of Hindhead, signposted off the A3. This secluded hostel, converted from National Trust cottages, makes an idyllic base from which to explore the Punchbowl's trails.

Dorking and around

Set at the mouth of a gap carved by the River Mole through the North Downs, **DORKING**, 25 miles from London (frequent trains from London Victoria), lies at the intersection of the former Roman Stane Street and the medieval byway known as the **Pilgrim's Way**, which linked Winchester with

North Surrey Theme Parks

Less than an hour's drive southwest of central London lie two popular **theme parks** – **Chessington** and **Thorpe Park**. Both primarily appeal to the 8–14 age group, and can become extremely crowded during school holidays; an early arrival on summer weekends will avoid long queues for the more popular rides. If it's action you're after, Chessington has the edge, but both easily return their seemingly pricey entrance fees with activities that fill the best part of a day.

Thorpe Park

Purpose-built and water-oriented **Thorpe Park** (April–Oct daily, times vary, call to check on ⓣ08704/444466; £19 off-peak, £25 peak, less by advanced booking; ⓦwww.thorpepark.co.uk) is well signposted off the A320 south of Staines and easily reached by train from London's Waterloo Station to Staines or Chertsey stations, with buses taking you on to the park itself. Set in an old gravel pit, the park continues to develop new attractions, such as the volcanic Nemesis Inferno, and Colossus, the world's first ten-looping roller coaster. It's advisable to bring swimwear for small children, who are excluded from the more exhilarating rides for safety reasons, but can have fun on the smaller slides and in the pools at Neptune's Beach.

Chessington World of Adventures

Smaller and more animated, but marginally tackier than Thorpe Park, is **Chessington World of Adventures** (mid-April to Oct daily, times vary, call to check on ⓣ08704/447777, last admission 2hr before closing; £19 off-peak, £25 peak; ⓦwww.chessington.co.uk). The park is signposted off the A243, twelve miles southwest of London, and reached from London's Waterloo train station (to Chessington South) or bus #467 from Epsom. Located in a former zoo, the park's yellow Safari Skyway monorail introduces you to the few remaining animals while the Chessington Railroad circulates around the rest of the park. The better rides tend to be fun rather than frightening. Seastorm is a watery favourite, as is Rameses' Revenge, though it's slightly scarier.

Canterbury. There's nothing much to see in Dorking itself, but it makes a convenient base for exploring the surrounding countryside. If you want to **stay**, try *The White Horse Hotel* (ⓣ0870/400 8282, ⓦwww.macdonaldhotels.co.uk; ❺) on the High Street, an oak-beamed former coaching inn dating from the seventeenth century that is also the town's best **food** option.

Box Hill, on the northern edge of town, is a popular draw for suburban weekenders and a staple of school trips during the week, when the intricacies of the River Mole's contrary flow through the chalk downs are explained. It's a three-hour climb to the top, but the snack-bar (daily 11am–4pm) and the view south over the town and the Weald's sandstone ridges reward the effort. You'll also find the grave of the eccentric local resident Major Peter Labilliere here; the major was famously buried head first, so that, in a topsy-turvy world, he would be the only one to "face his Maker the right way up". Though walkable from Dorking (around 45min), the nearest **train station** to Box Hill is at Westhumble, on the Dorking–London line.

Box Hill is situated on the 151-mile **North Downs Way**, a tame long-distance footpath, stretching from Farnham to Dover and at its best around here, with two **youth hostels** nearby. In the village of **HOLMBURY ST MARY**, six miles southwest of Dorking (Gomshall train station), the purpose-built hostel (ⓣ0870/770 5868, ⓔholmbury@yha.org.uk; dorm bed £10.25; ❶) is about an hour's walk to **Leith Hill**, southeastern England's highest point, offering views south to the Channel and north across London. Former local resident Richard Hull built a tower at the hill's summit in 1764, bringing its height up to 1029ft, and is now buried beneath it. You can look through a telescope from the top of the **tower** (April–Sept Wed, Sat & Sun 10am–5pm; Oct–March Sat & Sun 10am–3.30pm; £1.50; NT). There's a kiosk nearby, selling light refreshments and open the same times as the tower, or you could head for the *Plough* in neighbouring Coldharbour, for real ales and bar meals.

Tanners Hatch youth hostel, a basic cottage at the end of a muddy track, two and a half miles northwest of Dorking (Ⓣ0870/770 6060, Ⓔtanners@yha.org.uk; dorm bed £9), lies just a mile away from **Polesden Lacey** (April–Oct Wed–Sun 11–5pm; grounds daily 11am–6pm or dusk; £7, grounds only £4; NT), a Regency-era villa built by Thomas Cubitt in 1824. Renovated in Edwardian times, it houses an assortment of silver, Chinese porcelain, French furniture and paintings, including works by Reynolds and has a delightful Edwardian rose garden.

Kent

Not so long ago Kent's tourist industry was focused chiefly on the resorts of its northern coast and the **Isle of Thanet**, the northeastern tip of the county. Nowadays these seaside towns have lost much of their gloss, but the county still boasts one of the most popular destinations in the entire country – the county town of **Canterbury**, site of one of the great English cathedrals. Furthermore, Kent can also boast its fair share of alluring castles and gardens, the best known of which are the estate of **Knole**, on the edge of Sevenoaks, **Leeds Castle**, to the west of Maidstone, and **Sissinghurst Gardens**, in the heart of the Weald and an inspiration to thousands of amateur horticulturalists. Exploration of the county's other scattered attractions – such as **Scotney Castle**, Winston Churchill's home at **Chartwell**, **Penshurst Place**, **Hever Castle** or the remnants of the Roman villa at Lullingstone – could fill a long and pleasurable weekend.

Transport links from London are good: the A2, M2 and M20 link the Channel ports of Ramsgate, Dover and Folkestone with the capital and rail connections to the county's key towns from London's Charing Cross, London Bridge and Victoria stations are reliable. Sevenoaks, Maidstone, Tunbridge Wells and Canterbury are well served by daily National Express bus services too, but local rail and bus links are slow.

The North Kent coast

It's a commonly held view that the northern part of Kent is a scenic and cultural wasteland, a prejudice that stems partly from the fact that most visitors only glimpse the area as they race to or from the Channel ports. However, the region has its fair share of attractions, all of which are easily accessible from London. There is a knot of historic sites at **Rochester** and **Chatham**, two of the five "Medway towns" – so-called because they are grouped around River Medway (the others are Strood, Gillingham and Rainham) – while the seaside resorts of **Whitstable**, **Margate** and **Broadstairs** ranging from genteel to seedy, have a growing cachet among weekenders from the capital.

Rochester and around

ROCHESTER, the most pleasant of the Medway towns, was first settled by the Romans, who built a fortress on the site of the present **castle** (daily: April–Sept 10am–6pm; Oct–March 10am–4pm; £3.90; Ⓦwww.medway.gov.uk), at the northwest end of the High Street; some kind of fortification has remained here ever since. In 1077, William I gave Gundulf – architect of the White Tower at the Tower of London – the See of Rochester and the job of improving the defences on the River Medway's northernmost bridge on Watling Street. The resulting castle remains one of the best-preserved examples of a Norman fortress in England, with the stark hundred-foot-high keep glowering over the town, while the interior is all the better for having lost its floors, allowing clear views up and down the dank interior. It has three square towers and a cylindrical one, the southwest tower, which was rebuilt following its collapse during the siege of 1215, when the bankrupt King John eventually wrested the castle from its archbishop. The outer walls and two of the towers retain their corridors and spiral stairwells, allowing access to the uppermost battlements.

The foundations of the adjacent **cathedral** (daily 7.30am–6pm; suggested donation £3; Ⓦwww.rochester.anglican.org/cathedral) were also Gundulf's work, but the building has been much modified over the past nine hundred years. Plenty of Norman touches have endured, however, particularly in the cathedral's west front, with its pencil-shaped towers, blind arcading and richly carved portal and tympanum above the doorway. Norman round arches, decorated with zigzags and made from lovely honey-coloured Caen stone, also line the nave. Some fine paintings survived the Dissolution, most notably the thirteenth-century depiction of the Wheel of Fortune on the walls of the choir (only half of which survives); shown as a treadmill, it's a trenchant image of medieval life's relentless slog. The cathedral once enshrined the remains of St William of Perth, a pious baker from Scotland, who in 1201 embarked on a pilgrimage to the Holy Land, but got only as far as Rochester, where he was robbed and murdered. The monks of Rochester, envying the popular appeal of St Thomas à Becket's shrine at nearby Canterbury, used William's demise as an opportunity to establish a rival shrine – indeed substantial additions to the cathedral were financed by donations from pilgrims paying their respects to the canonized baker's tomb, which has long since disappeared.

Rochester's long, semi-pedestrianized **High Street** is a handsome affair, lined with antique shops, cafés and pubs, many of which are housed within appealingly old half-timbered and weatherboarded buildings. Rochester's most famous son **Charles Dickens** spent his youth here, but would seem to have been less than impressed by the place – it appears as "Mudfog" in *The Mudfog Papers*, and "Dullborough" in *The Uncommercial Traveller*. Many of the buildings feature in his novels: the *Royal Victoria and Bull Hotel*, at the top of the High Street, became the *Bull* in *Pickwick Papers* and the *Blue Boar* in *Great Expectations*, while most of his last book, the unfinished *Mystery of Edwin Drood*, was set in the town.

A gritty picture of Victorian life is conjured up by the tableaux at the **Charles Dickens Centre** in the distinctive red-brick and timber-framed Eastgate House at the southeast end of the High Street (daily: April–Sept

10am–6pm; Oct–March 10am–4pm; £3.90; Ⓦwww.medway.gov.uk). High-tech audio-visual displays, including the "Dickens' Dream" sequence, depict key scenes and characters from his well-known books, and the whole place is entertaining and informative whether you're a Dickens enthusiast or not. Even if you've no intention of visiting the centre, it's worth taking a look round the back of the building where **Dickens' Chalet** now stands, having been removed from his house at Gad Hill Place. A pretty little two-storey wooden structure with sky-blue gables, balcony and shutters, this Swiss-style chalet was used by Dickens as his summer study and it was here that he was working on *The Mystery of Edwin Drood* just before he died in 1870.

Back up the High Street, past the French Huguenot Hospital, **La Providence**, which moved into this peaceful early Victorian cul-de-sac in 1960, stands **Watts' Charity** (March–Oct Tues–Sat 2–5pm; free), a sixteenth-century almshouse founded by the philanthropist, Richard Watts, for passing travellers and immortalized in Dickens' short story *The Seven Poor Travellers*. The building was used for its original purpose until as late as 1940, and, behind the eighteenth-century stone facade, with its trio of triangular gables, it still boasts a series of galleried Elizabethan bedrooms.

Lastly, it's worth giving Rochester's excellent **Guildhall Museum** at the northwest end of the High Street (daily 10am–4.30pm; free; Ⓦwww.medway.gov.uk) a look. Inside this splendid building, built in 1687, is a vivid model of King John's siege of the castle and a chilling exhibition on the prison ships or hulks. Following American Independence in 1776, England was stuck for a place to transport her growing numbers of convicts – an increase caused as much by desperate poverty and draconian sentencing as any wave of criminality. Until the penal colony of Botany Bay was established a decade or so later, criminals were housed in appalling and overcrowded conditions inside decommissioned naval vessels moored in the Thames. With the clever use of mirrors, the exhibit replicates the grim conditions inside these floating prisons.

Practicalities

Rochester **train station**, served by regular trains from London's Charing Cross, London Bridge and Victoria, is at the southeastern end of the High Street. The **tourist office** is halfway along the High Street, opposite the cathedral at no. 95 (Mon–Sat 10am–5pm, Sun 10.30am–5pm; Ⓣ01634/843666, Ⓦwww.medway.gov.uk). From here you can join a free guided tour of the town (Easter–Sept Wed, Sat, Sun & public holidays at 2.15pm).

As for **accommodation**, you can spend the night with some Dickensian ghosts at the ancient *Royal Victoria and Bull Hotel*, 16–18 High St (Ⓣ01634/846266, Ⓦwww.rvandb.co.uk; ❸), or at the plush *Gordon House Hotel* at no. 91 (Ⓣ01634/831000, Ⓦwww.gordonhousehotel.net; ❹). Decent B&Bs include the *Grayling House*, 54 St Margaret's St (Ⓣ01634/826593, Ⓔgraylinghouse@aol.com; no credit cards; ❷), further up the hill behind the castle. The nearest **youth hostel** (Ⓣ0870/770 5964, Ⓔmedway@yha.org.uk; dorm bed £11.50, ❶*)* is at Capstone Farm, Gillingham, two miles southeast of Chatham; to get there by bus, take the #114 from Chatham bus station and get off at the *Waggon at Hale* pub.

Rochester has a varied, if unremarkable selection of cafés and **restaurants**. On the High Street you'll find Italian either at the modest, family-run *Casa Lina,* at no. 146 (Ⓣ01634/844993; closed Sun & Mon), or the more expensive *Don Vincenzo* (Ⓣ01634/408373) at no. 108, while at no. 188 the *Cumin Club* (Ⓣ01634/400880) offers contemporary Indian cuisine in modern surroundings. As for **pubs**, the *Coopers Arms* on St Margaret's Street, which runs uphill between the castle and cathedral, serves good lunches in its small beer garden. The trendier *City Wall Bar*, 122 High St, has a good lunchtime menu, while traditionalists might prefer Wetherspoon's *Golden Lion* at 149 High St. *Amadeus* (Ⓣ01634/723370), one of the biggest **nightclubs** in the southeast, is part of the Medway Valley Park, a big entertainment complex a couple of miles west of the centre.

Chatham

CHATHAM, less than two miles east of Rochester, has none of the charms of its neighbour and is, in truth, rather a grim place. Its chief attraction is its dockyards, originally founded by Henry VIII and once the major base of the Royal Navy, many of whose vessels were built, stationed and victualled here and which commanded worldwide supremacy from the Tudor era until the end of the Victorian age. Well sheltered, yet close to London and the sea, and lined with tidal mud flats that helped support ships' keels during construction, the port expanded quickly and by the time of Charles II it had become England's largest naval base. This era of shipbuilding came to an ignominious end when the dockyards were closed in 1984, re-opening soon afterwards as a tourist attraction.

The **Historic Dockyard** (mid-Feb to Oct daily 10am–6pm or dusk; Nov Sat & Sun 10am–dusk, last entry 2 hours before closing; £9.50; Ⓦwww.chdt.org.uk) occupies a vast eighty-acre site about one mile north of the town centre along the Dock Road; it's a not very pleasant fifteen-minute walk from Chatham town centre, or a short bus ride (ask at the tourist office in Rochester for the latest timetable). Once there, take advantage of the free vintage-bus service to take you around. Behind the stern brick wall you'll find an array of historically and architecturally fascinating buildings dating back to the early eighteenth century. In addition to an impressive display of fifteen historic RNLI lifeboats, there's the "Wooden Walls" gallery, where you can experience life as an apprentice in the eighteenth-century dockyards. Here too lies the Ocelot Submarine, the last warship built at Chatham, whose crew endured unbelievably cramped conditions – a major deterrent to visiting claustrophobes – and a newly restored Victorian sloop, the *Gannet*. The main part of the exhibition, however, consists of the Ropery complex including the former rope-making room – at a quarter of a mile long, it's the longest room in the country.

Signposted to the east of the dockyards, up Wood Street, the **Royal Engineers Museum** (Mon–Thurs 10am–5pm, Sat, Sun & public holidays 11.30am–5pm; £5; Ⓦwww.royalengineers.com) is devoted to the army's all-purpose construction corps, nicknamed the "sappers", who were responsible for building London's Royal Albert Hall as well as numerous temporary wartime structures. Over the years the museum has acquired several artefacts from the sappers' campaigns, including Wellington's map of Waterloo and General Gordon's silk robes.

Less interesting by far is **Fort Amherst**, back towards the town centre at the bottom of Dock Road (March–Easter & mid-Sept to early Dec Sat & Sun 10.30am–4.30pm; Easter to late July Wed–Sun 10.30am–5pm; late July to mid-Sept daily 10.30am–5pm, last admission 1hr before closing; £5; Ⓦwww.fortamherst.com). Built to defend the dockyard in the mid-eighteenth century but never actually put to the test, the fort was extended by prisoners-of-war during the Napoleonic era. The fort's honeycomb of tunnels has been restored and includes a reconstruction of the World War II Civil Defence control room. The best time to come is on Sundays during the summer, when there's usually some costumed military re-enactment to help bring the place alive.

Boat trips run along the River Medway throughout the summer from the Historic Dockyard (£8) on Britain's last working coal-fired paddle steamer, the *Kingswear Castle*, built in 1924 (ⓣ01634/827648, ⓦwww.pskc.freeserve.co.uk). The cruise takes you past **Upnor Castle** (April–Sept daily 10am–6pm; Oct daily 10am–4pm; £3.90; EH), an atmospheric sixteenth-century gun fort built on the river to protect Elizabeth I's fleet.

Whitstable

Peculiarities of silt and salinity have made **WHITSTABLE** an oyster-friendly environment since classical times, when the Romans feasted on the region's marine delicacies. Indeed, production grew to such levels during the Middle Ages that **oysters** were exported all over Europe, and they were so cheap and plentiful that they became regarded as poor people's food – as Dickens observed, "where there are oysters, there's poverty". However, the whole industry collapsed during the twentieth century, the result of pollution and, in particular, a destructive storm in the 1950s which wrecked all the farms. Though oysters are once more farmed in the area – mostly the faster-growing Pacific oysters, which have displaced the original native oysters – Whitstable is now more dependent on its commercial port, fishing and seaside tourism, while small-scale boat-building and a mildly bohemian ambience make this one of the few pleasant spots along the north Kent coast and a popular day-trip destination for Londoners.

Walking along Whitstable's busy High Street, you'd never guess that you're just a stone's throw from the sea. There's no promenade or bandstand – for that you have to go to Tankerton, Whitstable's easternmost suburb, or Herne Bay, six miles further east. Follow the signs at the top of the High Street to reach the seafront, a very pleasant, quiet shingle beach, backed onto by some pretty weatherboard cottages. Most folk come to Whitstable, to eat the local oysters; you can see one of Whitstable's last surviving wooden oyster yawls *The Favourite* – built in 1890 when there were around one hundred and fifty working out of the harbour – along Island Wall, a ten-minute walk west at the end of Harbour Street. For more maritime history, head for the **Whitstable Museum and Gallery** (July & Aug Mon–Sat 10am–4pm, Sun 1–4pm; Sept–June closed Sun; free; ⓦwww.whitstable-museum.co.uk), housed in the former Foresters' Hall, heralded by its eye-catching entrance on Oxford Street, with displays on diving and some good photographs and old film footage of the town's heyday. Back in 1830, Whitstable became the northern terminus for one of Britain's first steam-powered passenger railway services – the so-called "Crab & Winkle Line" which linked the town via a half-mile tunnel (the world's longest at that time) with Canterbury, ten miles to the south. Relics of this line still survive today.

Whitstable's current **train station** is five minutes' walk along Cromwell Road, east of Oxford Street, the southern continuation of the High Street, while the **tourist office** is next to the museum at 7 Oxford St (July & Aug Mon–Sat 10am–5pm; Sept–June Mon–Sat 10am–4pm; ⓣ01227/275482, ⓦwww.canterbury.co.uk). For **accommodation** along the seafront, try *Copeland House*, 4 Island Wall (ⓣ01227/266207, ⓦwww.copelandhouse.co.uk; no credit cards; ❷), west of the High Street, with a garden that backs onto the beach; the art deco *Hotel Continental*, 29 Beach Walk (ⓣ01227/280280, ⓦwww.hotelcontinental.co.uk; ❺), off the northern tip of Harbour Street, which also has accommodation in wooden fishermen's huts in the centre of town; or *The Cherry Garden*, 62 Joy Lane (ⓣ01227/266497; no credit cards; ❷), a homely B&B with a delightful garden ten minutes' stroll along Seasalter Road. For **campsites**, you're best off heading to *Seaview Caravan Park* (☎01227/792246; closed Nov–March), which backs onto the beach towards Herne Bay.

Whitstable's fishing background is reflected in its **eating** places, from any number of fish-and-chip outlets along the High Street and Harbour Street to the very popular *Royal Native Oyster Stores,* The Horsebridge (☎01227/276856; closed Sun eve & Mon), one of the town's best restaurants, with main fish dishes starting at £14, and half a dozen oysters costing £12.50. A good alternative is *Pearson's Crab and Oyster House*, opposite (☎01227/272005), which offers bar meals downstairs and has a pricier restaurant upstairs. On the way into town *Giovanni's*, 49–55 Canterbury Rd (☎01227/273034: closed Sun eve & all Mon), is deservedly reckoned to be one of the best Italian restaurants in the county. *Tea and Times*, 36 High St, serves a decent English breakfast with real coffee. For a **drink** and excellent atmosphere check out the *Old Neptune*, standing alone in its white weatherboards on the shore, while another excellent locals' pub is the *Wall Tavern*, 82 Middle Wall. Whitstable is at its most lively during its **Oyster Festival**, held annually in the last two weeks of July, featuring not only lots of crustacean crunching, but also jazz and parades.

Herne Bay and Reculver

Six miles east of Whitstable is the drab seaside resort of **HERNE BAY** which, like its storm-severed pier, is something of a relic from a bygone age when holiday-makers believed that sitting on a wind-blasted patch of shingle and sand was something to look forward to. Certain temperaments may find something stirring in moribund resorts like this, but overall Herne Bay has neither the energetic tackiness nor the discreet refinement of the larger resorts further east. Indeed, thanks to its large numbers of retired senior citizens, the town is often disparagingly referred to as Hernia Bay. The handsome Neoclassical clocktower on the seafront, and the King's Hall, further east, with its slender wrought-iron colonnade, hint at Herne Bay's halcyon days, but even the prom's new modern Sculpture Trail can't really hide the fact that the resort's glory days are over.

You'll find the **tourist office** at the Bandstand, Central Parade, between the pier and the clocktower (Jan–March & Sept–Dec Mon–Sat 10am–4pm; April–June Mon–Sat 10am–4pm & Sun noon–4pm; July & Aug Mon–Sat 10am–5pm & Sun noon–5pm; ☎01227/361911, Ⓦwww.canterbury.co.uk). Herne Bay's decline as a holiday resort has left just a few **B&Bs**, clustered together on the seafront. A better alternative is *Foxden*, 5 Landen Rd (☎01227/363514, Ⓦwww.foxden-hernebay.co.uk; no smoking; no credit cards; ❸), offering en-suite accommodation and a pretty garden, fifteen minutes from the centre off Beltinge Road. Greasy-spoon **cafés** are plentiful in Herne Bay, but for superior fish and chips head for *Andrews Fish Bar*, 76–77 Central Parade, by the clocktower. *The Ship*, at the junction of East Street and Central Parade, has more character than most Herne Bay **pubs**, and serves a good range of real ales.

One good reason to come to Herne Bay is to go on a **boat trip** with Wildlife Sailing (April–Sept; ☎01227/366712 or ☎07771/714563, Ⓦwww.wildlifesailing.com) to an offshore sandbank, home to a large herd of seals; the trip, in a lovely open yacht, takes five hours and costs from £12 per person, depending on the size of the group. This and other shorter trips depart from Neptune's Arm (part of the harbour). For most visitors, though, Herne

Bay's main value lies in its proximity to the ruined **Roman Fort** situated inside Reculver Country Park (always open; free), which occupies an isolated headland two miles east of Herne Bay; to get there, either walk along the coast or catch one of the local buses from the train station. The original fort, built around 280 AD by Carausis, self-styled Emperor of Britain, was used to guard the Wantsum Channel which separated the Isle of Thanet from the mainland and made an easily defended harbour for the Roman fleet. In the seventh century the Saxon **Church of St Mary** was built within the fort's walls, surviving until 1809, when coastal erosion brought about its collapse. Trinity House – the government's maritime navigation authority – bought the ruins the following year, rebuilding the twin twelfth-century **Reculver Towers** in order to render them "sufficiently conspicuous to be useful to navigation". An **interpretation centre** (April–Aug Tues–Sun 11am–5pm; Sept Wed–Sun 11am–5pm; Oct–March Sun 11am–3pm; free) near the car park tells the full story and provides details on ecological aspects of this part of the coast. The *King Ethelbert* **pub**, close to the towers, provides an important refuelling function for passing tourists.

The Thanet resorts

The **Isle of Thanet**, a featureless plain fringed by low chalk cliffs and the odd sandy bay, became part of the mainland when the navigable Wantsum Channel began silting up around the time of the first Roman invasion. In 43 AD, nearly a century after Julius Caesar's exploratory visit, the Romans got into their stride when they landed near Pegwell Bay and established Richborough port in preparation for the march inland. The Saxons followed them four hundred years later – the island is named after the "tenets", or fire beacons, which used to warn local residents of the Saxons' raids – and Augustine arrived here in 597 on a divine mission to end Anglo-Saxon paganism. The evangelist is supposed to have met King Ethelbert of Kent and preached his first sermon at a spot three miles west of Ramsgate – a cross marks the location at Ebbsfleet, next to St Augustine's Golf Club.

Over the next thousand years or so, civilization advanced to the point at which, in 1751, a resident of Margate, one Mr Benjamin Beale, invented the bathing machine, a wheeled cubicle that enabled people to slip into the sea without undue exhibitionism. It heralded the birth of sea bathing as a recreational and recuperative activity, and led to the growth of **seaside resorts**. By the mid-twentieth century the Isle's intermittent expanses of sand had become fully colonized as the "bucket and spade" resorts of the capital's leisure-seeking proletariat. That heyday has passed, but these earliest of resorts still cling to their traditional attractions to varying degrees.

Getting to the Thanet resorts is straightforward: **trains** and **buses** make the two-hour journey from London Victoria to Margate, Ramsgate and Broadstairs several times a day, and there are local rail and bus services from Canterbury and Dover. Once there, one easy way to visit Thanet in the summer is to take the **open-top bus service** which plies a clockwise circuit from Ramsgate and allows for time to visit both Margate and Broadstairs (late May to early Sept; day ticket £5.50; Ⓦ www.city-sightseeing.com).

Margate and around

MARGATE – memorably summarized by Oscar Wilde as "the nom-de-plume of Ramsgate" – is a ragged assortment of cafés, shops and amusement arcades wrapped around a broad bay, a rather less elegant place than the one with which it's been twinned, the Black Sea resort of Yalta. Yet more than two centuries of tourism are embodied in Margate: at its peak thousands of Londoners were ferried down the Thames every summer's day, to be disgorged at the pier – the functional precursor of all such seaside structures. Even today, on a fine summer weekend, the place is heaving with day-trippers enjoying the traditional fish and chips, candyfloss and donkey rides.

Other than the agreeable, if small, sandy beach, and the amusement arcades on the tacky seafront, the main attraction is the intriguing and intricately decorated **Shell Grotto** on Grotto Hill, off Northdown Road (Easter–Oct daily 10am–5pm; Nov–Easter Sat & Sun 11am–4pm; £2), claiming to be the world's only underground shell temple. It has been open to the public since it was discovered by some schoolkids in 1835, but its origin is open to continued dispute. Less interesting are **Margate Caves** further down Northdown Road (daily: July & Aug 10am–5pm; April–June, Sept & Oct daily 10am–4pm; £2), man-made chalk caverns that were discovered by a gardener in 1798 – if nothing else, a good place to cool off on a hot day. The narrow streets of Margate's old town, centred on the Market Place, have potential, but many of the shopfronts are now boarded up, having been superseded by the town's ugly out-of-town shopping centres. Still, you can take a trip down memory lane in the **Margate Museum** on the Market Place (April–Sept Tues–Sun 10am–5pm; Oct–March Thurs–Sun 11am–4.30pm; £1; Ⓦwww.ekmt.fsnet.co.uk); the building also served as the town's police station from 1858 to 1959 and there are several surviving police cells on the ground floor. A new centre for the visual arts to be located on the pier, the Turner Centre (Ⓦwww.turnercentre.org), is promised for 2007.

Practicalities

The **tourist office** is at 12–13 The Parade (Easter–Sept Mon–Fri 9am–5pm, Sat 9am–4pm, Sun 10am–4pm; Oct–Easter Mon–Sat 9am–4pm; Ⓣ01843/583333, Ⓦwww.tourism.thanet.gov.uk) and the **train station** is on All Saints' Avenue. Margate has plenty of **B&Bs**, the better ones lining the Regency squares and crescents of the Cliftonville area – try the family-run *Malvern Hotel*, 29 Eastern Esplanade (Ⓣ01843/290192, Ⓦwww.malvern-hotel.co.uk; ❸), or the welcoming *Innsbruck Hotel*, Dalby Square (Ⓣ01843/298946; no credit cards; ❶). Alternatively, there's the grand 1920s-style *Walpole Bay Hotel*, Fifth Avenue (Ⓣ01843/221703, Ⓦwww.walpolebayhotel.co.uk; ❹) styled a "living museum", which cordially invites browsers to wander its corridors and investigate its exhibits (free). Margate's YHA **hostel** (Ⓣ0870/770 5956, Ⓔmargate@yha.org.uk; dorm bed £11.50; ❶) is situated in the former Beachcomber Hotel, 3–4 Royal Esplanade, by Westbrook Bay to the west of the train station. Prosaic seaside **food** is on offer at all of the seafront greasy spoons and fish-and-chip outlets, but you can dine well at *Greenfields Bistro* (Ⓣ01843/224347; closed Sun & Mon) at 4 Hawley Square, near the Regency theatre, and get fine **pastries** and snacks from *Batchelor's Patisserie*, at 246 Northdown Rd in Cliftonville. The *Walpole Bay Hotel* is the place for afternoon tea or a Sunday lunch with piano accompaniment; book for lunches. Most of Margate's **pubs** are a bit rough round the edges, so it's worth steering away from the seafront: try the tiny Victorian *Rose in June* on Trinity Square, or for real ales (and pizzas), the *Spread Eagle*, at the top of Victoria Road.

Quex House

If you have time to explore the surrounding area, you could spend a rewarding afternoon at **Quex House**, a rambling Regency stately home set in its own gardens in the village of Birchington, four miles from Margate. The building houses the **Powell-Cotton Museum** (April–Oct Tues–Thurs, Sun & public holidays 11am–5pm; Nov, Dec & March Sun 11am–4pm; £4), a collection of trophies and artefacts amassed by Major Powell-Cotton, a nineteenth-century big-game hunter, from his 28 expeditions to the African bush. The major built special galleries to house the dioramas in which over five hundred stuffed animals have been arranged, and there's also a wonderful collection of early photographs documenting the expeditions, along with displays of ethnographic material. In the nearby village of Birchington, the graveyard holds the tomb of Dante Gabriel Rossetti, the Victorian painter and poet, and the village also has a memorial garden to him at Sandles Road, right by the train station.

Broadstairs

Said to have been established on the profits of shipbuilding and smuggling, today **BROADSTAIRS** is the smallest, quietest and, undoubtedly, the most pleasant of Thanet's resort towns, overlooking the pretty little Viking Bay from its cliff-top setting. The town's charm lies in its quiet self-sufficiency: there are no big hotels to dominate and tourism seems to have endured without spoiling the place. If you're staying at the weekend, book ahead as it's a popular spot.

Viking Bay is just one of several **sandy coves** which punctuate Thanet's eastern shore; between Broadstairs and Margate you'll find Stone, Joss, Kingsgate and Botany bays with Louisa Bay to the south – all quiet and undeveloped gems that make a good antidote to the busier resort areas. However, Broadstairs' main claim to fame is as Dickens' holiday retreat – he described it as "one of the freest and freshest little places in the world". Throughout his most productive years he stayed in various hostelries here, and eventually rented an "airy nest" overlooking Viking Bay from Fort Road, since renamed **Bleak House** (daily: July & Aug 10am–9pm; Sept to mid-Dec & mid-Feb to June 10am–6pm; mid-Dec to mid-Jan 11am–4pm; £3; Ⓦwww.bleakhouse.ndo.co.uk) and opened to the public. It was here that he planned the eponymous novel as well as finishing *David Copperfield*, and three rooms in the house have been preserved as the author would have known them. There's more of the same on the main cliff-top seafront at the **Dickens House Museum**, 2 Victoria Parade (daily: Easter to mid-June and Sept & Oct 2–5pm; mid-June to Aug daily 10.30am–5pm; £2; Ⓦwww.dickenshouse.co.uk), in the house Dickens used as a model for Betsy Trotwood's House. The town's **Dickens Festival**, held annually since 1937, takes place during the third week in June and features lectures, dramatizations of the author's works and a nightly Victorian music hall.

If you're in search of further diversions, pay a visit to the **Crampton Tower Museum** (Easter–Oct Mon, Tues, Thurs & Fri, plus Sun 2.30–5pm on public holiday weekends; £2), on the other side of the road and railway tracks from the train station. Named after local-born Victorian engineer, Thomas Crampton, who built the town's first water system, it's the museum's buildings rather than its contents that are intriguing: the flint-studded tower, the pumping-engine shed and the nearby "beehive" building are all relics of Crampton's sophisticated water system.

Practicalities

It's a ten-minute walk from the **train station** to Broadstairs' seafront along the High Street, where you'll find the **tourist office** at no. 6b (April–Sept daily 9am–5pm; Oct–March Mon–Sat 9am–4.30pm; Ⓣ01843/583334,

Ⓦwww.tourism.thanet.gov.uk). Many **hotels**, restaurants and other establishments cash in on the Dickens angle; he wrote part of *Nicholas Nickleby* at the family-run *Royal Albion Hotel*, 6–12 Albion St (Ⓣ01843/868071, Ⓦwww.marchesi.co.uk; ❻), a comfortable treat for Dickens fans – ask about the special offer that includes a meal in the excellent *Marchesi Brothers* restaurant, two doors down (see below). Alternatively, try the *East Horndon Hotel*, 4 Eastern Esplanade (Ⓣ01843/868306, Ⓦwww.easthorndonhotel.com; ❸), or the *Devonhurst Hotel*, also on the Eastern Esplanade (Ⓣ01843/863010, Ⓦwww.devonhurst.co.uk; ❸). There are several ivy-covered Georgian establishments in Belvedere Road, behind the High Street: the *Dundonald House* at no. 43 (Ⓣ01843/862236, Ⓦwww.dundonaldhousehotel.co.uk; ❸) and the *Hanson Hotel* next door (Ⓣ01843/868936, Ⓔhotelhanson@aol.com; ❷) may lack sea views, but both are good value. There is also a **youth hostel** at 3 Osborne Rd just two minutes' walk south from the train station (Ⓣ0870/770 5730, Ⓔbroadstairs@yha.org.uk; dorm bed £10.25; ❶); it's housed in a Victorian villa and has a pleasant family atmosphere.

For **food**, there are plenty of fish-and-chip outlets and cafés along Albion Street and down Harbour Street. For a more congenial setting, head for *Harpers Wine Bar*, also on Harbour Street (Ⓣ01843/602494; eve only), which serves moderately priced fish and seafood dishes. Broadstairs' top restaurant is the aforementioned Swiss-run *Marchesi Brothers* restaurant, 18 Albion St (Ⓣ01843/862481), where a main course will set you back at least £10; alternatively, the less expensive *Osteria Pizzeria Posillipo*, next door (Ⓣ01843/601133; closed Tues in winter), does excellent pizzas, pasta and other Italian standards, and has a balcony overlooking the bay. As for **pubs**, *Ballard's Lounge* at the *Royal Albion Hotel* also has bay views from its garden, while the popular and friendly *Neptune's Hall*, at the top of Harbour Street, serves great beer. The *Tartar Frigate,* also on Harbour Street, with it own seafood restaurant upstairs, and the *Lord Nelson*, round the corner in Nelson Place, are solid sociable English pubs. The Broadstairs **Folk Week**, held in the middle of August, is one of England's longest-standing folk music events and features singers, bands and dancing in locations around the town, both indoor and alfresco (Ⓦwww.broadstairsfolkweek.com).

Ramsgate

If Thanet had a capital, it would be **RAMSGATE**, a handsome resort, rich in robust Victorian red brick. Most of the town is set high on a cliff linked to the seafront and harbour by broad, sweeping ramps, with the villas on the seaward side displaying wrought-iron verandas and bricked-in windows – a legacy of the tax on glazed windows. Overall the port has avoided Margate's vulgarity while retaining some of Broadstairs' class, and the large-scale regeneration project in the harbour and along the seafront by the Maritime Museum is breathing some new life into the area.

Currently, the most entertaining sight in Ramsgate is the subterranean **Motor Museum** at West Cliff Hall, on The Paragon just by the ferry terminal (April–Oct daily 10.30am–5.30pm; Nov–Easter Sun 10am–5pm; £3.50), which spices up its eclectic collection of cars and motorbikes by placing each vehicle in historical context. A 1905 Rex pushbike is on show alongside a newspaper proclaiming the increase of third-class steamer fares to the USA to £6, and a 1904 De Dion Bouton is displayed along with details of events from the same year – the founding of Rolls-Royce and the arrest of a New York woman for the heinous crime of smoking in public.

A predictable chronicle of municipal life from Roman times onwards is presented at the **Ramsgate Maritime Museum**, in the harbour's nineteenth-century Clock House (Easter–Sept Tues–Sun 10am–5pm; Oct–Easter Thurs–Sun 11am–4pm; £1.50; Ⓦwww.ekmt.fsnet.co.uk); the display is brightened by an illuminating section on the Goodwin Sands sandbanks – six miles southeast of Ramsgate – the occasional playing field of the eccentric Goodwin Sands Cricket Club.

Practicalities

Ramsgate's **train station** is about a mile northwest of the centre, at the end of Wilfred Road, at the top of the High Street. The **tourist office** is at 17 Albert Court, York St (daily 9.30am–4.30pm; Ⓣ01843/583333, Ⓦwww.tourism.thanet.gov.uk). For an overnight **stay**, the *Spencer Court Hotel*, 37 Spencer Square (Ⓣ01843/594582, Ⓦwww.s-h-systems.co.uk; ❶), offers comfortable accommodation in a listed Regency building, directly above the ferry terminal; while, just east of the harbour, the Victorian *Eastwood Guest House*, 28 Augusta Rd (Ⓣ01843/591505; no credit cards; ❷), has some rooms with balconies. *The Crescent*, 19 Wellington Crescent (Ⓣ01843/591419, Ⓦwww.ramsgate-uk.com; ❷), is an attractive seafront option in a Georgian terrace originally built to house the duke's officers. The nearest **campsite** is *Nethercourt Touring Park*, just two miles southwest of the town centre (Ⓣ01843/595485; closed Nov–March). For **food** the reasonably priced *Surin Thai* at 30 Harbour St (Ⓣ01843/592001; closed Mon) specializes in quality Cambodian, Lao as well as Thai food. The relaxed *Ocean Lounge Bar* at 62 Harbour Parade serves Mediterranean snacks all day. Best for fish and chips is the gaudy *Peter's Fish Factory* at 96 Harbour Parade. For traditional **pubs** try the ornately tiled *Queen's Head* on Harbour Parade and for cliff-top views, real ales and live music (Sun), head for the *Churchill Tavern* on The Paragon, overlooking the harbour.

Canterbury

One of England's most venerable cities, **CANTERBURY** offers a rich slice through two thousand years of history, with Roman and early Christian ruins, a Norman castle and a famous cathedral that dominates a medieval warren of time-skewed Tudor dwellings. The city began as a Belgic settlement that was overrun by the Romans and renamed **Durovernum**, which they established as a garrison and supply base and from where they went on to build a system of roads that was to reach as far as the Scottish borders. With the empire's collapse came the Saxons, who renamed the town **Cantwarabyrig**; it was a Saxon king, Ethelbert, who in 597 welcomed Augustine, despatched by the pope to convert the British Isles to Christianity. By the time of his death, Augustine had founded two Benedictine monasteries, one of which – Christ Church, raised on the site of the Roman basilica – was to become the first cathedral in England.

At the turn of the first millennium Canterbury suffered repeated sackings by the Danes until Canute, a recent Christian convert, restored the ruined Christ Church, only for it to be destroyed by fire a year before the Norman invasion. As Christianity became a tool of control, a struggle for power developed between the archbishops, the abbots from the nearby Benedictine abbey and King Henry II, culminating in the assassination of Archbishop Thomas à Becket in 1170, a martyrdom that effectively established the autonomy of the

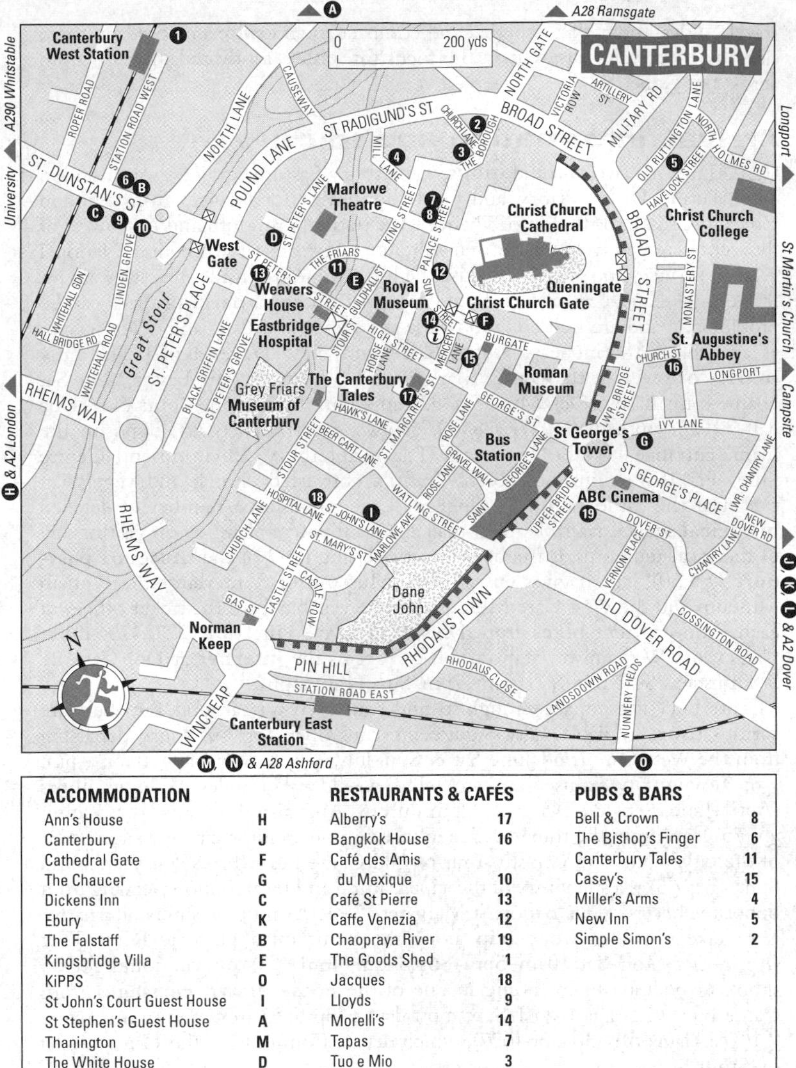

ACCOMMODATION	
Ann's House	H
Canterbury	J
Cathedral Gate	F
The Chaucer	G
Dickens Inn	C
Ebury	K
The Falstaff	B
Kingsbridge Villa	E
KiPPS	O
St John's Court Guest House	I
St Stephen's Guest House	A
Thanington	M
The White House	D
Wincheap Guest House	N
Youth Hostel	L

RESTAURANTS & CAFÉS	
Alberry's	17
Bangkok House	16
Café des Amis du Mexique	10
Café St Pierre	13
Caffe Venezia	12
Chaopraya River	19
The Goods Shed	1
Jacques	18
Lloyds	9
Morelli's	14
Tapas	7
Tuo e Mio	3

PUBS & BARS	
Bell & Crown	8
The Bishop's Finger	6
Canterbury Tales	11
Casey's	15
Miller's Arms	4
New Inn	5
Simple Simon's	2

archbishops and made this one of Christendom's greatest shrines. Geoffrey Chaucer's *Canterbury Tales*, written towards the end of the fourteenth century, portrays the unexpectedly festive nature of pilgrimages to Becket's tomb, which was later plundered and destroyed on the orders of Henry VIII.

In 1830 a pioneering passenger railway service linked Canterbury to the sea and prosperity grew until the city suffered extensive German bombing on June 1, 1942, in one of the notorious **Baedeker Raids** – the Nazi plan to destroy Britain's most treasured historic sites as described in the eponymous German travel guides. Today the cathedral and compact town centre, enclosed on three sides by medieval walls, remain the focus for leisure-motivated pilgrims from across the globe.

Arrival, information and tours

Canterbury has two **train stations**, Canterbury East for services from London Victoria and Dover Priory, and Canterbury West for services from London Charing Cross and the Isle of Thanet – the stations are south and northwest of the centre respectively, each a ten-minute walk from the cathedral. National Express services and local **buses** use the bus station just inside the city walls on St George's Lane. Car drivers should note that finding a **parking** space can be problematic and are best advised to use the signposted Park-and-Ride services available on Wincheap, Sturry Road and New Dover Road. The busy **tourist office** is at the Butter Market at 12–13 Sun St (Jan–Easter Mon–Sat 10am–4pm; Easter–Oct Mon–Sat 9.30am–5pm, Sun 10am–4pm; Nov–Dec daily 10am–4pm; ⓣ01227/378100, ⓦwww.canterbury.co.uk), opposite the main entrance to the cathedral. The Canterbury Environment Centre (Tues–Fri 10am–5pm, Sun 10am–4pm), a converted church and vegetarian café near the cathedral on St Alphege's Lane, publishes a number of detailed **historical walks**, available for a small charge. If you're planning on visiting any of the local museums, it might be worth getting hold of the **museum passport** (£5.50), which gives entry to the Museum of Canterbury, the Roman Museum and the West Gate Museum and is available from the ticket offices of each. You can rent **bikes** from Downland Cycle Hire (ⓣ01227/479643) at Canterbury West railway station. You can access the **internet** at Dot Café, 21 St Dunstan's St (Mon–Sat 10am–7pm, Sun 11am–7pm).

Canterbury is compact enough to find your own way around, but there are various **tours** available. City Sightseeing runs open-top bus tours, departing from the West Gate (mid-June Sat & Sun; July, Aug & Sept daily 10am–4pm; £6; ⓦwww.city-sightseeing.com). The Guild of Guides Walking Tours (April–June, Sept & Oct daily 2pm; July & Aug also 11.30am; 1hr 30min; £3.75) leave from the tourist office to take you on an informative walking tour of the city, while The Ghostly Tour of Old Canterbury (Fri & Sat year round 8pm; 1hr; £5) is a spicy mix of the supernatural and local folklore, leaving from opposite *Alberry's Wine Bar* on St Margaret's Street. A more leisurely alternative is to take a guided **boat trip** along the Stour on a Historic River Tour (April–Oct Mon–Sat 10am–5pm, Sun 11am–4pm; £5), or you could cock a snook to pedestrians by riding in one of the **horse-drawn carriages** from Canterbury Carriage (April–Sept most days 1–5pm; 25 min; minimum charge £10/carriage; ⓣ01304/364027), which depart from outside the *County Hotel* on Stour Street.

Accommodation

Accommodation consists mostly of B&Bs and small hotels and can be difficult to secure in July and August. In the town centre, some old hotels offer all the creaking, authentic antiquity you could ask for, while there's a host of B&Bs to be found just outside the city walls. The tourist office can help you find a place to stay, though they charge £2.50 for the service. Alternatively, both the University of Kent (ⓣ01227/828000, ⓦwww.ukc.ac.uk/hospitality), a mile or so north of town, and Christ Church University College, North Holmes Rd (ⓣ01227/782225; ⓦwww.canterbury.ac.uk), behind St. Augustine's Abbey, offer bed and breakfast in student accommodation (single and double) during the Easter and Summer vacations (from £21–35 per person).

Hotels and B&Bs

Ann's House 63 London Rd ⓣ01227/768767. Traditional Victorian villa offering comfortable rooms, most of which are en suite, a ten-minute walk from the centre. ❸

Canterbury 71 New Dover Rd ⓣ01227/450551, ⓦwww.canterbury-hotel-apartments.co.uk. Fifteen minutes' walk from the town centre with a French restaurant and friendly service. ❻

Cathedral Gate 36 Burgate ⓣ01227/464381, ⓦwww.cathgate.co.uk. Built in 1438 and set in the city's medieval heart, this venerable pilgrims' hostelry features crooked floors and exposed timber beams alongside more modern amenities. ❸

The Chaucer 63 Ivy Lane ⓣ01227/464427, ⓦwww.macdonaldhotels.co.uk. Large hotel just beyond the city walls, fully refurbished with modern comforts but retaining some of its early Georgian charm. ❽

The Dickens Inn 71 St Dunstan's St ⓣ01227/472185, ⓦwww.dickens-inn.co.uk. Originally a thirteenth-century yeoman's house, this black and white timbered inn has cosy and colourful rooms and a pleasant walled garden. ❸

Ebury 65–67 New Dover Rd ⓣ01227/768433, ⓦwww.eburyhotel.co.uk. Very comfortable and spacious family-owned Victorian hotel, fifteen minutes' walk from the centre; indoor pool and well-appointed rooms. ❺

The Falstaff 8–10 St Dunstan's St ⓣ01227/462138, ⓦwww.corushotels.co.uk/thefalstaff. Popular fifteenth-century coaching inn by the West Gate, with four-poster beds and an award-winning restaurant. ❺

Kingsbridge Villa 15 Best Lane ⓣ01227/766415, ⓦwww.canterburykingsbridgevilla.co.uk. Rooms 2 and 4 of this very central and well-furnished Victorian house have views of the cathedral. Vegan and vegetarian breakfasts on offer too. ❷

St John's Court Guest House St John's Lane ⓣ01227/456425, ⓔnigelnrw@aol.com. Obliging and good-value guest house, offering B&B in a quiet but central location, just south of the old town. No credit cards. ❶

St Stephen's Guest House 100 St Stephen's Rd ⓣ01227/767644, ⓦwww.st-stephens.fsnet.co.uk. A mock-Tudor house on the northern side of the city, ten minutes' walk along the Stour and handily placed for the university, offering excellent-value en-suite accommodation. No credit cards. ❸

Thanington 140 Wincheap ⓣ01227/453227, ⓦwww.thanington-hotel.co.uk. Comfortably converted Georgian building, ten minutes' walk from the centre with an indoor pool, games room and friendly, attentive service. ❺

The White House 6 St Peter's Lane ⓣ01227/761836, ⓦwww.sh-systems.co.uk. Small and friendly guest house offering en-suite accommodation in a fine Regency building, midway between the cathedral and Canterbury West Station. ❸

Wincheap Guest House 94 Wincheap ⓣ01227/762309, ⓦwww.wincheapguesthouse.co.uk. Good-value Victorian B&B, with shared facilities, close to Canterbury East Station. ❶

Hostels and campsites

The Caravan and Camping Club Site Bekesbourne Lane ⓣ01227/463216. Large year-round caravan park, one and a half miles east of the city off the A257 road to Sandwich.

KiPPS 40 Nunnery Fields ⓣ01227/786121, ⓦwww.kipps-hostel.com. Self-catering hostel offering single and double rooms (❶) and dormitory (£12) accommodation a few minutes' walk from Canterbury East Station.

Youth Hostel 54 New Dover Rd ⓣ0870/770 5744 ⓔcanterbury@yha.org.uk. Half a mile out of town, and 15min on foot from Canterbury East Station, this friendly hostel is set in a Victorian villa. Dorm bed £14.50. Closed Jan. ❶

The City

Despite the presence of a university and art and teacher-training college, England's second most visited city is a surprisingly small place with a population of just 40,000. The town centre, partly ringed by ancient walls, is virtually car free, but this doesn't stop the High Street seizing up all too frequently with tourists, two and a half million of whom visit the city each year. Having said that, the very reason for the city's popularity is its rich tapestry of historical sites, combined with a good selection of places to stay, eat and drink, and no visit to south-east England would be complete without, at the very least, a quick stop here.

The Cathedral

Mother Church of the Church of England and seat of the Primate of All England, **Canterbury Cathedral** (Mon–Sat 9am–6.30pm, Sun 12.30–2.30pm & 4.30–5.30pm; closes Mon–Sat 5pm in winter; also closed on some days in mid-July for university graduation ceremonies; £4, free on Sun; Ⓦwww.canterbury-cathedral.org) fills the northeast quadrant of the city with a befitting sense of authority, even if architecturally it's perhaps not among the country's most impressive. A cathedral has stood here since 602, but in 1070 the first Norman archbishop, Lanfranc, levelled the original Saxon structure to build a new cathedral. Over successive centuries the masterpiece was heavily modified, and with the puritanical lines of the Perpendicular style gaining ascendancy in late medieval times, the cathedral now derives its distinctiveness from the thrust of the 235-foot-high Bell Harry Tower, completed in 1505. The precincts (daily 7am–9pm) are entered through the superbly ornate early-sixteenth-century **Christ Church Gate**, where Burgate and St Margaret's Street meet. This junction, the city's medieval core, is known as the Butter market, where religious relics were once sold to pilgrims hoping to prevent an eternity in damnation. Having paid your entrance fee, you pass through the gatehouse and get one of the finest views of the cathedral, foreshortened and crowned with soaring towers and pinnacles.

Once in the magnificent **interior**, look for the tomb of Henry IV and his wife, Joan of Navarre, and for the gilded effigy of Edward III's son, the Black Prince, all of them to be found in the Trinity Chapel, behind the main altar. Also here, until demolished by Henry VIII's act of ecclesiastical vandalism in 1538, was the shrine of Thomas à Becket; the actual spot where he died is marked by the **Altar of the Sword's Point**, in the "Martyrdom" in the northwest transept, where a jagged sculpture of the assassins' weapons are suspended on the wall. Steps from here descend to the low, Romanesque arches of the **crypt**, one of the few remaining relics of the Norman cathedral and considered the finest such structure in the country, with some amazingly well-preserved carvings on the capitals of the columns. Particularly vivid is the medieval **stained glass**, much of which dates back to the twelfth and thirteenth centuries, notably in the Trinity Chapel, where the life and miraculous works of Thomas à Becket are depicted. Look out too for Adam delving, girt about with an animal skin, in the west window and Jonah and the whale in the Corona (beyond the Trinity Chapel). Contemporary with the windows (1220) is the white marble **St Augustine's Chair** on which all archbishops of Canterbury are enthroned; it's located in the choir at the top of the steps beyond the high altar.

On the cathedral's north flank are the fan-vaulted colonnades of the **Great Cloister**, from where you enter the **Chapter House**, with its intricate web of fourteenth-century tracery supporting the roof and a wall of stained glass. In 1935 it was a fitting venue for the inaugural performance of T.S. Eliot's *Murder in the Cathedral.*

St Augustine's Abbey and St Martin's Church

Passing through the cathedral grounds and out through the city walls at the (exit-only) Queningate, you come to the vestigial remains of **St Augustine's Abbey** (daily: April–Sept 10am–6pm; Oct 10am–5pm; Nov–March 10am–4pm; £3; EH), occupying the site of the church founded by Augustine in 598. It was built outside the city because of a Christian tradition that forbade burials within the walls, and became the final resting place of Augustine, Ethelbert and successive archbishops and kings of Kent, although no trace

Thomas à Becket and the Canterbury Tales

Appointed Archbishop of Canterbury in 1162 by his good friend and drinking partner Henry II, **Thomas à Becket** fell out with the king when the latter attempted to impose his jurisdiction over that of the church. After a six-year spell in France, Becket was reconciled with Henry and returned home in 1170 – only to incur the king's wrath once more by refusing to absolve two bishops whom he had previously excommunicated, provoking Henry to utter the well-known words, "Will no one rid me of this turbulent priest?" Four knights took it upon themselves to seek out Becket and, finding him at prayer in the cathedral, murdered him on the spot. Almost immediately miracles were said to occur at his tomb, and Becket was canonized in 1173, by which time a steady stream of pilgrims had already begun to arrive at the shrine.

One such pilgrimage provided the setting for Geoffrey Chaucer's **Canterbury Tales**. Written between 1387 and 1400, the *Tales* are a collection of stories within a story, in which a group of thirty pilgrims exchange a series of fantastic yarns to while away the time as they journey. The group is a colourful cross-section of medieval society, including a knight, a monk, a miller, a squire and the oft-widowed wife of Bath. Chaucer chose to write their earthy and often raunchy stories in English – at a time when French was very much the language of literature – and this, combined with their universal themes, has ensured their continuing popularity today, as witnessed by the regular film and television treatments. The narrator of the best tale was promised a free meal at Canterbury's *Tabard Inn* – though as Chaucer died before he could complete his work, the winner was never announced.

remains either of them or of the original Saxon church. Shortly after the Normans arrived, the church was demolished in the same building frenzy that saw the creation of the cathedral. It was replaced by a much larger abbey, most of which was destroyed in the Dissolution so that today only the ruins and foundations remain. To help bring the site to life, pick up an audio tour from the abbey's excellent interpretive centre.

Nearby, on the corner of North Holmes Road and St Martin's Lane is **St Martin's Church** (Tues & Thurs 10am–3pm, Sat 10am–1pm ; free), one of England's oldest churches, built on the site of a Roman villa or temple and used by the earliest Christians. Although medieval additions obscure the original Saxon structure, this is perhaps the earliest Christian site in Canterbury – it was here that Queen Bertha welcomed St Augustine in 597, and her husband King Ethelbert was baptized.

Along the High Street

For the most part, the **High Street** is lined with picturesque and ancient buildings – the view up Mercery Lane towards Christ Church Gate is one of the most photographed views in the city: a narrow, medieval street of crooked, overhanging houses behind which loom the turreted gatehouse and the cathedral's towers.

Just before High Street becomes St Peter's Street, you come to the **Royal Museum and Art Gallery** (Mon–Sat 10am–5pm; free), housed on the first floor of an awesome mock-Tudor building, with big wooden gables and a mosaic infilling between its timbers. There's lots of military memorabilia in the Buffs regimental gallery, which traces the history of the local regiment raised in Tudor times and merged in 1967. The art gallery is worth a quick perusal, with the odd Henry Moore and Gainsborough hidden among the local artists, and interesting temporary exhibitions in the Slater Gallery.

Where the street passes over a branch of the River Stour, stands **Eastbridge Hospital** (Mon–Sat 10am–4.45pm; £1; Ⓦwww.eastbridgehospital.org.uk), founded in the twelfth century to provide poor pilgrims with shelter. Downstairs is an exhibition on Chaucer's life, while storytellers in feudal garb recite parts of his book. Over the road is the wonky, half-timbered **Weavers' House** – built around 1500 and now a café – that was once inhabited by Huguenot textile workers who had been offered religious asylum in post-Reformation England.

St Peter's Street terminates at the two massive crenellated towers of the medieval **West Gate**, between which local buses just manage to squeeze. The only one of the town's seven city gates to have survived intact, its prison cells and guard chambers house a small **museum** (Mon–Sat 11am–12.30pm & 1.30–3.30pm; £1; Ⓦwww.canterbury-museums.co.uk), which displays contemporary armaments and weaponry used by the medieval city guard, as well as giving access to the battlements. In fine weather, you can take a forty-minute trip on a **chauffeured punt** (Ⓣ01227/768915; £6/person; minimum charge £15/boat) along the gentle River Stour from the nearby bridge.

The Roman Museum, The Canterbury Tales and the Museum of Canterbury

The redevelopment of the Longmarket area (situated between Burgate and the High St) in the early 1990s exposed Roman foundations and mosaics that are now part of the **Roman Museum** (June–Oct Mon–Sat 10am–5pm, Sun 1.30–5pm; Nov–May closed Sun; £2.70; Ⓦwww.canterbury-museums.co.uk). The extant remnants of the larger building are pretty dull, and better mosaics can be seen at Lullingstone (see p.211), but the display of recovered artefacts and general design of the museum are tasteful, with Roman domestic scenes re-created, as well as a computer-generated view of Durovernum.

Turning in the other direction down St Margaret's Street leads to the former church that's now **The Canterbury Tales** (daily: mid-Feb to June 10am–5pm; July–Oct 9.30am–5.30pm; Nov to mid-Feb 10am–4.30pm; £6.75; Ⓦwww.canterburytales.org.uk), a quasi-educational show based on Geoffrey Chaucer's book, which lays claim to being the first original work of English literature ever to be printed. Equipped with a headset, visitors set off on a wander through mildly odour-enhanced galleries in which mannequins occupy idealized fourteenth-century tableaux and recount five of Chaucer's tales.

Genuinely educational and better value is the **Museum of Canterbury**, round the corner in Stour Street (June–Oct Mon–Sat 10.30am–5pm, Sun 1.30–5pm; Nov–May Mon–Sat 10.30am–5pm; £3; Ⓦwww.canterbury-museums.co.uk), an interactive exhibition spanning local history from the splendour of Durovernum through to the more recent literary figures of Joseph Conrad (buried in the cemetery on London Road) and Oliver Postgate, originator of *Bagpuss* and *The Clangers*. The check-trousered philanthropist Rupert Bear, created by local-born Mary Tourtel, merits a museum of his own within the main museum. An excellent thirty-minute video on the Becket story details the intriguing personalities and events that led up to his assassination, presenting Becket as an overbearing and unpopular figure whose genuine piety was only recognized after his death.

Eating and drinking

The combination of a large student population and the tourist trade means Canterbury has a good selection of places to eat and drink, with many **restau-**

rants and **pubs** in genuinely old settings. However, the Church, which owns much of the city within the walls, keeps a tight rein on any wanton revelry and, bar the occasional yelp of an over-intoxicated student, at night all is as quiet as Becket's tomb.

Cafés

Café St Pierre 40 St Peter's St. Excellent French patisserie and bakery with tables on the pavement and in the garden when the weather's fine.

Caffe Venezia 60–61 Palace St. Spacious self-service Italian café with decent sandwiches, pasta dishes, pizza slices and good coffee.

Morelli's 11 Sun St. Neapolitan-coloured ice-cream parlour next to the tourist office serving snacks and coffees as well as ice creams.

Restaurants

Alberry's St Margaret's St ⓣ01227/452378. This lively wine bar has good snacks and a range of more substantial meals, including various pastas, fish and meat dishes. Moderate.

Bangkok House 13 Church St ⓣ01227/471141. Excellent, well-presented Thai fare with spices adjusted to suit every palate in this small restaurant near St Augustine's Abbey. Good selection of cocktails and rum too. Closed Mon. Moderate.

Café des Amis du Mexique 95 St Dunstan's St ⓣ01227/464390. Very popular, authentic Mexican place close to Westgate; try the sizzling chicken *fajitas* or the delicious paella followed by a bubbling chocolate *fondido*. "Phenomenally hot" habanero chilis are only for the brave. Moderate.

Chaopraya River 2 Dover St ⓣ01227/462876. The refined delights of Thai cuisine at a reasonable price – the *Nua pud naman hoy*, beef marinated in oyster sauce and served sizzling with mushrooms and baby corn, is delicious. Closed Mon. Inexpensive.

The Goods Shed Canterbury West Station ⓣ01227/459153. Everything from a bowl of soup or sandwich to a first-class full meal, guaranteed super-fresh as it comes from the adjacent farmers' market. Closed Sun eve & all day Mon. Inexpensive to moderate.

Jacques 71 Castle St ⓣ01227/781000. Homely little French bistro offering *moules, frites* and a jazz pianist Tues–Sat. Closed Sun eve. Moderate to Expensive.

Lloyds 89–90 St Dunstans St ⓣ01227/768222. Beamed barn setting, but contemporary in style and food. The three-course set dinner £17.50 (Sun–Thurs) is good value. Expensive.

Tapas 13 Palace St ⓣ01227/762637. Tasty Spanish tapas in three sizes from £4 to £8 a dish. Occasional live music. Inexpensive.

Tuo e Mio 16 The Borough ⓣ01227/761471. Long-established restaurant offering classy Italian dishes, a range of pizzas and some delicious, homemade desserts. Closed Mon & Tues lunch. Moderate.

Pubs and bars

Bell & Crown 10 Palace St. Authentic and cramped medieval hostelry.

The Bishop's Finger 13 St Dunstan's St. Popular wood-panelled bar just through the West Gate with a fine range of ales and a patio suntrap.

Canterbury Tales 12 The Friars. Marble-top bar and lots of polished wood in this tidy little pub opposite the Marlowe Theatre. Nachos and BLTs on the bar menu.

Casey's 5 Butchery Lane. Cosy, low-ceilinged Irish pub serving soda bread, pies and other pub grub, with occasional live folk music.

Miller's Arms Mill Lane. A pleasant weir-side spot for a summertime pint whose splendid bar snacks and meals ensure its continued popularity.

New Inn 19 Havelock St. One of Canterbury's tiniest pubs, this converted terrace house is popular with students and locals and offers a decent selection of real ale.

Simple Simon's Radigund's Hall, 3 Church Lane. Old hostelry that's popular with the university and King's School crowd; live music Tues–Sat.

Nightlife

Nightlife in Canterbury keeps a low profile – check out what's happening in the free *What, Where and When* **listings magazine** available at the tourist office. Opposite Canterbury East Station at 15 Station Rd East there are three **nightclubs** in the same building: *BaaBars*, also open during the day, the *Works*, good for party pop and R&B, and the more civilized *Bizz* (for all three ⓣ01227/462520, ⓦwww.baabarsnightclub.co.uk). On the other side of town, the university puts on a good range of arty **films** at Cinema 3 (ⓦwww.kent.ac

.uk/gulbenkian) and has the best **live music**. There are more commercial celluloid offerings at the Odeon, a two-screen cinema on St George's Place by the ring road. The university also houses the **Gulbenkian Theatre** (Ⓣ01227/769075, Ⓦwww.kent.ac.uk/gulbenkian), a venue that shares the city's more edifying cultural events with the **Marlowe Theatre** (Ⓣ01227/787787, Ⓦwww.marlowetheatre.com) – named after the sixteenth-century Canterbury-born playwright – in The Friars. In Northgate, the Penny Theatre presents local and global **live music**. Finally, there's the **Canterbury Festival** (Ⓣ01227/452853, Ⓦwwwcanterburyfestival.co.uk), an international potpourri of music, theatre and arts worth catching if you're in the area in the middle two weeks of October.

The Channel Ports: Sandwich to Folkestone

Dover, just 21 miles from mainland Europe (Calais' low cliffs are visible on a clear day), is the southeast's principal cross-Channel port. As a town it is not immensely appealing, even though its key position has left it with a clutch of historic attractions. To the north lie **Sandwich**, once the most important of the Cinque Ports but now no longer even on the coast, and the pleasant resort towns of **Deal** and **Walmer**, each with its own set of distinctive fortifications as well as a smattering of traditional seaside B&Bs. **Folkestone**, Kent's second major port, seven miles southwest of Dover, is even more forlorn than its neighbour.

There are frequent **train** and **bus** connections to both the main Channel ports during the day – trains leave from London Victoria and Charing Cross, buses from Victoria Coach Station. A useful branch-line offers train connections from Dover up the coast to Walmer, Deal and Sandwich and on to Ramsgate. If you arrive by ferry at Dover late in the evening, the last train service leaves for London at 11pm, and the last (much faster) direct service an hour earlier.

Sandwich and around

SANDWICH, situated on the River Stour four miles north of Deal, is best known nowadays for giving rise to England's favourite culinary contribution when, in 1762, the Fourth Earl of Sandwich, passionately absorbed in a game of cards, ate his meat between two bits of bread for a quick snack. Aside from this incident, the town's main interest lies in its maritime connections – it was chief among the Cinque Ports (see box opposite) until the Stour silted up. Unlike other former harbour inlets, however, the Stour hasn't silted up completely and still flows through town, its grassy willow-lined banks adding to the once great medieval port's present charm.

By the bridge over the Stour stands Sandwich's best-known feature, the sixteenth-century **Barbican**, a stone gateway decorated with chequerwork, where tolls were once collected. Running parallel to the river is **Strand Street**, whose crooked half-timbered facades front antique shops and private homes while, back in the town centre, another fine sixteenth-century edifice, the **Guildhall**, houses both the tourist office (see opposite) and a small **museum** recounting the town's history (April–Sept Tues, Wed & Fri 10.30am–12.30pm & 2–4pm, Thurs & Sat 10.30am–4pm, Sun 2–4pm; Oct to

The Cinque Ports

In 1278 Dover, Hythe, Sandwich, New Romney and Hastings – already part of a long-established but unofficial confederation of defensive coastal settlements – were formalized under Edward I's charter as the **Cinque Ports** (pronounced "sink", despite its French origin). In return for providing England with maritime support when necessary, chiefly in the transportation of troops and supplies to the Continent during times of war, the five ports were given trading privileges and other liberties, which enabled them to prosper while neighbouring ports struggled to survive. Some took advantage of this during peacetime, boosting their wealth by various nefarious activities such as piracy and the smuggling of tax-free contraband.

Later, Rye and Winchelsea were added to the confederation along with several other "limb" ports on the southeast coast which joined up at various times. The confederation continued until 1685, when the ports' privileges were revoked. Their maritime services had become increasingly unnecessary after Henry VIII had founded a professional navy and, due to a shifting coastline, several of the ports' harbours had silted up anyway, leaving some of them several miles inland. Nowadays, only Dover is still a major working port, though the post of Lord Warden of the Cinque Ports still exists as an honorary title, bestowed by the presiding monarch.

mid-Dec & March Tues, Wed, Fri & Sun 2–4pm, Thurs & Sat 10.30am–4pm; £1). The genteel town is separated from the sandy beaches of Sandwich Bay by the **Royal St George Golf Course** – frequent venue of the British Open tournament – and a mile of nature reserves. The reserve that most ornithologists make for is the **Gazen Salts Nature Reserve** – renowned for its diversity of seabirds – three miles north of town, across the Stour.

Overlooking the doleful expanse of Pegwell Bay, two miles northwest of Sandwich, is **Richborough Fort** (April–Sept daily 10am–6pm; Oct daily 10am–5pm; Nov–Feb Sat & Sun 10am–4pm; March Wed–Sun 10am–4pm; £3; EH), one of the earliest coastal strongholds built by the Romans along what later became known as the Saxon Shore on account of the frequent raids by the Germanic tribe. Like Reculver (see p.181), it guarded the southern entrance to the Wantsum Channel, which then isolated the Isle of Thanet from the mainland. Rumour has it that Emperor Claudius, on his way to London, once rode on an elephant through a triumphal arch erected inside the castle, but all that remains within the well-preserved Roman walls are the relics of an early Saxon church. Richborough's historical significance far outshines its present appearance, especially as Pegwell Bay is now blighted by an ugly chemical works. The nicest way of reaching the fort is to take the **river bus** up the Stour from Sandwich Quay (ⓣ07958/376183; £3).

Finding **accommodation** in Sandwich shouldn't be much of a problem – the local **tourist office**, housed in the Guildhall (April–Oct daily 10am–4pm; ⓣ01304/613565, ⓦwww.whitecliffscountry.org.uk), will provide you with a list of local **hotels** and **guest houses**. The golfers' choice, the *Bell Hotel* on The Quay by the Barbican (ⓣ01304/613388, ⓦwww.princes-leisure.co.uk; ❻) is out of a lot of people's range, but its weekend deals are good value; the en-suite rooms at the old coaching inn, the *Fleur de Lis*, near the Guildhall at 6–8 Delf St (ⓣ01304/611131, ⓦwww.verinitaverns.co.uk; ❹), are more affordable; or opt for the modest *Le Trayas* bungalow, 10 Poulders Rd (ⓣ01304/611056, ⓦwww.letrayas.co.uk; closed Oct; no credit cards; ❶), a ten-minute walk from The Quay. If you don't mind being a bit further out of town, try the *St Crispin Inn*, an attractive fifteenth-century pub in the village of Worth, a couple of miles southeast of Sandwich (Ⓣ01304/612081; ❹). Your best choice for top-class **food** is the pricey *Fishermans Wharf* on the quayside (Ⓣ01304/613636), which serves excellent seafood. For something less expensive try one of the pubs by the Barbican or *The Haven*, 20a King St, for good coffee, snacks and light meals. For the definitive Sandwich sandwich, head for the twee *Little Cottage Tearooms*, on The Quay.

Deal and around

One of the most unusual of Henry VIII's forts is the diminutive castle at **DEAL**, six miles southeast of Sandwich and site of Julius Caesar's first successful landfall in Britain in 55 BC. The **castle** (April–Sept daily 10am–6pm; Oct daily 10am–5pm; Nov–March Wed–Sun 10am–4pm; £3.50; EH) is situated off the Strand at the south end of town. Its unusual shape – viewed from the air it looks like a Tudor rose – is as much an affectation as a defensive design, though the premise was that the rounded walls would be better at deflecting missiles; inside, the comprehensive display on the other similar forts built during Henry VIII's reign is well worth a visit. Much more recently, the town was the focal point of Kent's small-scale coal industry, until the pits were closed during the bitterly fought downsizing of the 1980s.

Another aspect of Deal's history is reflected by the **Maritime Museum** (April–Sept Mon–Sat 2–5pm; £1.50) in St George's Road, just around the corner from the tourist office. A mildly interesting look at the town's seafaring past, the museum contains both real and model boats, relics from ships and tales of the destructive powers of the Goodwin Sands. Out on the seafront, at the corner with Sondes Road, stands a real oddity, the **Timeball Tower** (Easter–Sept daily 10am–5pm; £2), a four-storey pink-faced building that began life as a shutter telegraph during the Napoleonic Wars. Following the Wars' end in 1815 it was reconstructed as a semaphore tower aimed at catching smugglers. Yet again, in 1853, the tower was converted to house a giant timeball surmounted by a cross, large enough to be visible from ships at sea, which dropped from the roof at exactly 1pm in summer, so providing an accurate time check in the days before radio. The ball still drops regularly and the building also houses a small museum of horology and telegraphy.

Deal's **tourist office** is situated in the library on Broad Street near the Quarterdeck car park (Mon, Tues & Thurs–Sat 9.30am–5pm, Wed 9.30am–1pm; Ⓣ01304/369576, Ⓦwww.whitecliffscountry.org.uk). There's a whole host of places offering **accommodation** on Beach Street: try the winsome *King's Head* pub at no. 9 (Ⓣ01304/368194, Ⓦwww.kingsheaddeal.co.uk; ❸), or the nearby town house of *Channel View* at no. 17 (Ⓣ01304/368194; ❸), run by the same proprietor. Another option is *Dunkerley's*, next door at no. 19 (Ⓣ01304/375016, Ⓦwww.dunkerleys.co.uk; ❻), whose **restaurant** is possibly Deal's finest (and priciest). For more affordable seafood try the *Lobster Pot* (Ⓣ01304/374713), 81–83 Beach St, opposite the pier.

Walmer Castle

A mile south of Deal **Walmer Castle** (April–Sept daily 10am–6pm; Oct daily 10am–5pm; Nov, Dec & March Wed–Sun 10am–4pm; Jan & Feb Sat & Sun 10am–4pm; £5.50; EH) is another rotund Tudor-rose-shaped affair, commissioned when the castle became the official residence of the Lord Warden of the Cinque Ports in 1730. Now it resembles a heavily fortified stately home more than a military stronghold. The best-known resident was the Duke of Wellington, who died here in 1842, and not surprisingly, the house is devoted primarily to his life and times. Busts and portraits of the Iron Duke crowd the rooms and corridors, where you'll also find the armchair in which he expired and the original Wellington boots in which he triumphed at Waterloo. The castle's terraced gardens, overlooking the channel, are a good spot for a picnic, or you can have afternoon tea in The Lord Warden's Tearooms (April–Oct daily; Nov–March Sun).

To get to Walmer Castle from Deal, you can either catch one of the hourly buses or, if the weather's good, make the pleasant walk along the seafront (45min).

Dover

Badly bombed during the war, **DOVER**'s town centre and seafront just don't have what it takes to induce many travellers to linger. That said, the town authorities have put a lot of effort and money into sprucing the place up, particularly the early Victorian New Bridge development along the Esplanade. Despite such valiant attempts, **Dover Castle** is still by far the most interesting of the numerous attractions that plug the port's defensive history. Entertainment of a saltier nature is offered by Dover's legendary **White Cliffs**, which dominate the town and have long been a source of inspiration for lovers, travellers and soldiers sailing off to war.

Arrival and information

There are frequent train services from both Charing Cross and Victoria stations in London to Dover Priory **train station**, situated off Folkestone Road, a ten-minute walk west of the centre; there are regular shuttle buses to the Eastern and Western Docks. Buses from London (hourly; 2hr 30min) run to the Eastern Docks and the town-centre **bus station** on Pencester Road.

The **tourist office**, situated in the Town Hall in Biggin Street (June–Aug daily 9am–5.30pm; Sept–May Mon–Fri 9am–5.30pm & Sat 10am–4pm; ⓣ01304/205108, ⓦwww.whitecliffscountry.org.uk), has a free *White Cliffs Trails* pamphlet that outlines many good walks near Dover, both coastal and inland. *Café En-route* provides **Internet** access at 8 Bench St (Mon–Sat 9am–9pm, Sun 11am–9pm), near Market Square.

Accommodation

Accommodation in Dover is plentiful. The biggest concentration of small **hotels and B&Bs** is to be found on the Folkestone Road, close to the train station, but the ones around the base of Castle Hill Road on the other side of town are generally nicer. *Hubert House*, 9 Castle Hill Rd (ⓣ01304/202253, ⓦwww.huberthouse.co.uk; ❷), is a friendly B&B, convenient for the Eastern Dock, as is the good-value *Number One Guesthouse*, opposite, at 1 Castle St (ⓣ01304/202007, ⓦwww.number1guesthouse.co.uk; ❷). *Blakes of Dover*, further along Castle Street at no. 52 (ⓣ01304/202194, ⓦwww.blakesofdover.co.uk; ❷), is a small, comfortable B&B with a very genial owner; the non-smoking *St Albans*, at no. 71 (ⓣ01304/206308, ⓦwww.accommodation-dover.co.uk; ❷), is one of the better B&Bs along the Folkestone Road. There's a very busy **youth hostel** in a listed Georgian house at 306 London Rd (ⓣ0870/770 5798, ⓔdover@yha.org.uk; £14.50 dorm bed; ❶), a mile up the High Street from Dover Priory Station. The most convenient **campsite** is *Hawthorn Farm* (ⓣ01304/852658; closed Dec–Feb) close to Martin Mill train station, one stop up the line towards Ramsgate.

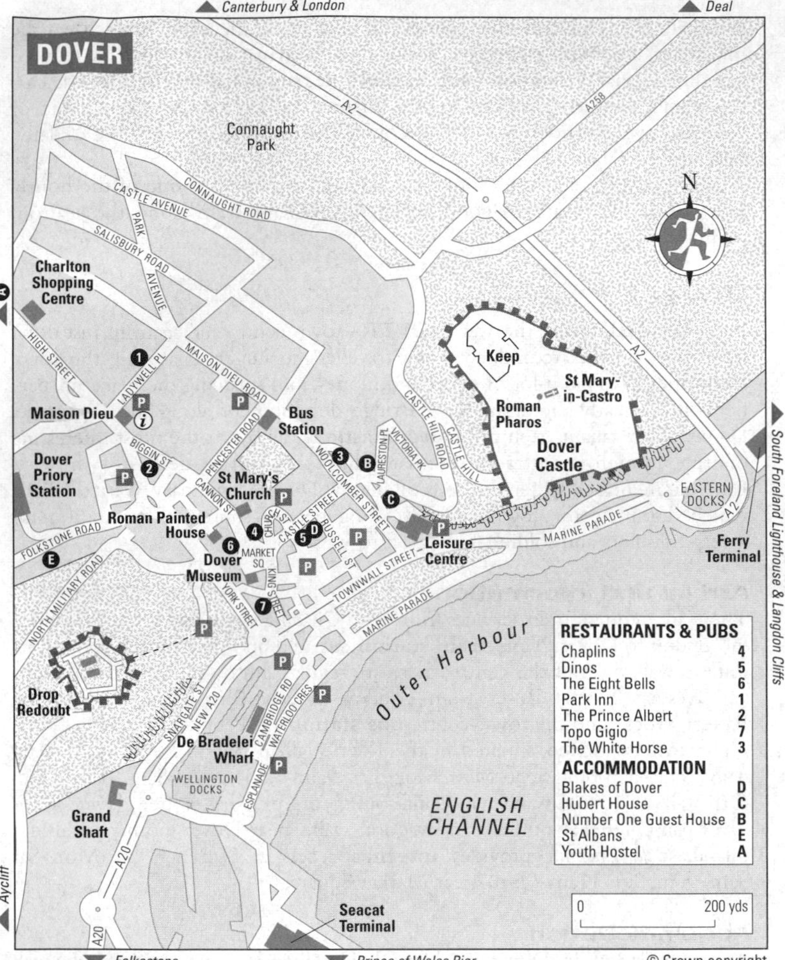

Dover Castle

It was in 1168, a century after the Conquest, that the Normans constructed the keep that now presides over the bulk of **Dover Castle** (daily: April–Sept 10am–6pm; Oct 10am–5pm; Nov–March 10am–4pm; £8; EH), a superbly positioned defensive complex that was in continuous use as some sort of military installation from then right up to the 1980s. The castle's a stiff climb from the town centre, and there's a lot to see – including a Roman lighthouse, a multi-media re-creation of the French siege of the castle in 1216 and a tour of its warren of tunnels – so allow up to half a day for a thorough visit.

Much earlier, the Romans had put Dover on the map when they chose the harbour as the base for their northern fleet, and erected a **lighthouse** (*pharos*) here to guide the ships into the river mouth. Beside the chunky hexagonal remains of the Roman *pharos* stands a Saxon-built church, **St Mary-in-Castro**, dating from the seventh century, with motifs graffitied by irreverent

Crusaders still visible near the pulpit. Further up the hill is the impressive, well-preserved **Norman Keep**, built by Henry II as a palace. Inside, there's an interactive exhibition on spying, and you can also climb its spiral stairs to the lofty battlements for views over the sea to France.

The castle's other main attraction is its network of **Secret Wartime Tunnels** dug during the Napoleonic war. Extended during World War II, you can tour "Hellfire Corner" – the tunnels' wartime nickname – on a fifty-minute guided tour (leaving every 20min). During World War II, the tunnels were used as a headquarters to plan the Dunkirk evacuation, which successfully brought back three hundred and thirty thousand stranded British and French troops from the continent in a flotilla of local fishing and pleasure boats. The tour is spiced up with a little gore, and reveals the quaintly low-tech communications systems and war rooms of the navy's command post.

The Town

Postwar rebuilding has made Dover town centre a rather unprepossessing place which most people passing through aren't tempted to explore. There is, however, a handful of low-key attractions which merit a glance. The **Roman Painted House** (April–Sept Tues–Sun 10am–5pm; £2), once a hotel for official guests, possesses some reasonable Roman wall paintings, the remains of an underground Roman heating system and some mosaics. The nearby **Dover Museum** on the Market Square (April–Oct Mon–Sat 10am–6pm; Nov–March 10am–5.30pm; £2; Ⓦwww.dovermuseum.co.uk) has three floors packed with informative displays on Dover's past, including a restored Bronze Age boat discovered in the town in 1992 – and a stuffed polar bear.

As you walk along pedestrianized Cannon Street, the main shopping street, you pass **St Mary's Church**, Victorian for the most part, but of Norman origin as the tower makes clear. Further up the road in Biggin Street, there's another very ancient building, the **Maison Dieu**, founded in the thirteenth century as a place for pilgrims en route to Canterbury. After the Reformation, it was turned into a naval storehouse, and in the last century became part of the town hall. The Stone Hall, with its fine timber roof, dates from 1253; the neighbouring neo-Gothic Connaught Hall and the Council Chamber upstairs are the work of the great Victorian architects Poynter and Burges.

The high ground to the west of town, originally the site of a Napoleonic-era fortress, retains one interesting oddity, the **Grand Shaft** (for opening times contact Dover Museum Ⓣ01304/201066 or see Ⓦwww.dover-westernheights.org), a 140-foot triple staircase, entered on Snargate Street, by which troops could go down at speed to defend the port in case of attack. Looming above the Grand Shaft is the formidable **Drop Redoubt** (as above for opening information), a sunken fortress built in 1808, from which guns could fire in all directions.

Dover's cliffs

As the first and last sight of England for travellers throughout the centuries, the **white cliffs of Dover** hold a complex role in the English psyche. Matthew Arnold invoked their massive grandeur in his famous elegy for a lost time, *Dover Beach*, written in the 1860s. Today, the beach has little of the romance invested in the spot by Arnold, but the cliffs flanking the town retain their majesty, even if pollution has taken some of the edge off their whiteness. The best views, of course, are to be had from several miles out to sea and **boats** leave hourly from De Bradelei Wharf in Dover Marina (hourly; £5), but an alternative vantage point on land is the Prince of Wales Pier in the harbour.

There are some great **walks** to be had along the cliffs themselves. To reach **Shakespeare Cliff**, catch bus #D2A from Worthington Street towards Aycliff. Alternatively, there's a steep two-and-a-half-mile climb to Shakespeare Cliff from North Military Road, off York Street, taking you by the **Western Heights**, a series of defensive battlements built into the cliff in the nineteenth century. From here there's a sweeping panorama of the Straits of Dover – the world's busiest shipping lanes – and a bird's-eye view of the harbour and the surrounding cliffs. It's even possible to catch a glimpse of France on a clear day.

At Langdon Cliffs, a couple of miles east of town, is the **Gateway to the White Cliffs** (daily: March–Oct 10am–5pm; Nov–Feb 11am–4pm; free; NT), a purpose-built centre whose excellent displays explain the ecology and history of the local coast and countryside. There's a coffee shop here too and regular countryside events and guided walks (Ⓣ01304/202756). A further two-mile walk northeast from here takes you to St Margaret's Bay and the **South Foreland Lighthouse** (March–Oct Mon & Thurs–Sun 11am–5.30pm; £2; NT). This Victorian construction, that looks somewhat like a minaret, was built to warn shipping off the dangerous Goodwin Sands; it was also where Marconi conducted his first ship-to-shore radio experiments in 1898.

Eating and drinking

Given the town's uninspiring appearance, Dover's **pubs** are surprisingly characterful, although the town gets a rather rough reputation from its shift-workers servicing the docks and ferries. There are two decent pubs near the town hall: *Park Inn*, a big revamped old boozer at 1–2 Park Place, Ladywell, with plenty of real ales, and the *Prince Albert*, 83 Biggin St, on the corner with Priory

Road. *The White Horse* on St James Street is a nice old eighteenth-century pub at the foot of the castle. Dover's culinary offerings are poor, though *Blakes* (see "Accommodation", p.197) has a lovely wood-panelled wine bar and restaurant, good for fresh fish and malt whiskies, and *Chaplins*, 2 Church St, serves excellent-value **breakfasts** and **lunches**. Alternatively, there's **pub food** at *The Eight Bells*, a big Wetherspoon's pub on Cannon St. Despite its garish exterior, *Topo Gigio*, 1–2 King St (ⓣ01304/201048), offers acceptable and inexpensive Italian food, as does *Dino's*, 58 Castle St (ⓣ01304/204678).

Folkestone

Seven miles down the coast from Dover, **FOLKESTONE** started life as a fishing village and rose to prominence as a resort in the nineteenth century, when the grandiose terraces which still dominate the town were built. In theory, Folkestone, with its narrow cobbled streets and cliff-top marine promenade, should be a more appealing place than, say, Dover, but the truth is that the good times, like the Channel Tunnel, have passed Folkestone by. In 2003 the town asserted itself by carving a new white horse on Cheriton Hill (viewable from the M20) at the entrance to the Channel Tunnel. The project has evoked controversy, however, being located on a site of special scientific interest, and its future is uncertain.

The **Folkestone Museum and Sassoon Gallery** on Grace Hill (Mon, Tues & Thurs 9.30am–6pm; Wed & Sat 9.30am–5pm, Fri 9.30am–7pm; free; ⓦwww.kent-museums.org.uk) gives an overview of the town. More exciting is the Victorian **Leas Lift**, to the west along the run-down Marine Parade (Easter–Sept daily 9am–6pm; Oct–Easter Sun 9am–5pm; 60p), which will

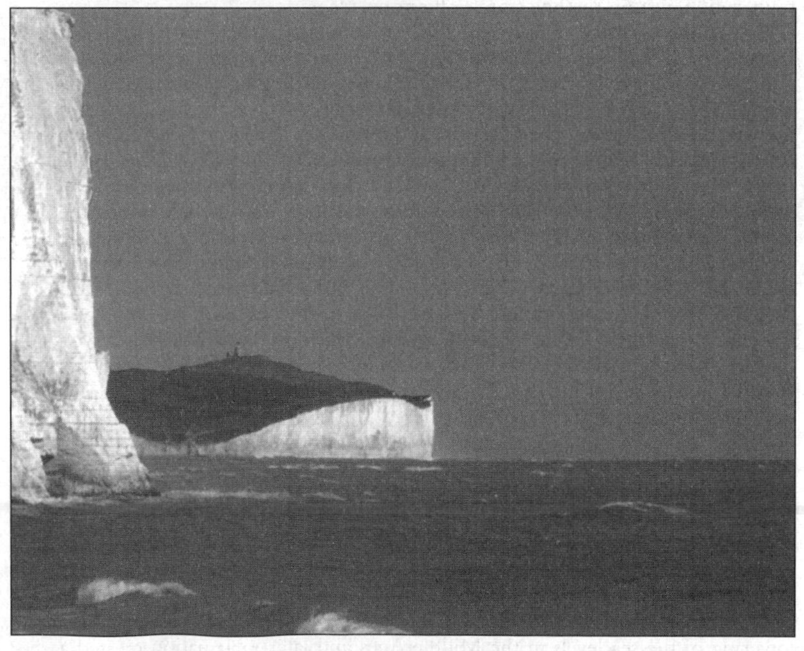

△ The White Cliffs of Dover

transport you to **The Leas**, the town's justly famous marine promenade which was once patrolled by the local Lord Radnor's own police force. It's worth persevering to the far end of the Leas to admire the fantastically ornate red-brick and terracotta Metropole Hotel building, and its architectural cousin and neighbour, the Grand – sadly neither function as hotels any more, though the Metropole now houses an **arts centre and gallery** (April–Oct Mon–Sat 10am–5pm, Sun noon–5pm).

Up on Folkestone's East Cliff is **Martello Tower No. 3** (May–Sept daily 10.30am–12.30pm & 1.30–5pm; £1), one of 74 similar towers along this stretch of coast, about which you can learn more from the tower's small exhibition. Further east along the cliffs, at Capel-le-Ferne on the B2011, you should be able to spot the new **Battle of Britain Memorial**, a giant seated figure of an RAF pilot gazing out to sea, with the various squadron badges carved onto the sandstone base. Those with a further interest in the subject should head three miles inland on the A260 to the **Kent Battle of Britain Museum** (Easter–Sept Tues–Sun 10am–5pm; £3.50; ⓦwww.kbobm.org), at Hawkinge airfield, where several hangars house World War II memorabilia, including a crashed Messerschmitt and replica Spitfires and Hurricanes.

Practicalities

Folkestone Central **train station** is fifteen minutes' walk northwest of Folkestone town centre, off Cheriton Road; buses and coaches arrive at the **bus station** on Bouverie Square, a short distance west of the pedestrianized shopping streets. Thanks to competition from the Channel Tunnel, passenger ferries no longer run from Folkestone harbour; Eurostar passengers for Paris and Brussels can climb aboard at the pompously named Ashford International train station, just up the line from Folkestone.

The **tourist office** (May–Sept daily 10am–5pm; Oct–April Mon–Sat 10am–5pm & Sun noon–3pm; ⓣ01303/258594, ⓦwww.shepway.gov.uk) is in a public car park at Harbour Street, at the junction of Tontine Street and The Tram Road, near the quayside. For **overnight** stays, the nicest part of town is to the west along The Leas. The red-brick and terracotta *Burlington Hotel*, Earls Ave (ⓣ01303/255301, ⓦwww.theburlingtonhotel.com; ❺), and the *Chilton House Hotel*, 14–15 Marine Parade (ⓣ01303/249786, ⓦwww.chiltonhousehotel.co.uk; ❷), with very reasonably priced en-suite rooms, are the best among the scores of hotels and B&Bs. If you want a peaceful countryside setting opt for *Pigeonwood House* at Arpinge (ⓣ01303/891111, ⓦwww.pigeonwood.com; no credit cards; ❷), four miles northwest of Folkestone and close to the North Downs Way and Channel Tunnel. The *Guildhall*, in the old town on The Bayle, is a pleasant **pub** to relax in; for **food**, head to Bouverie Road West, where you can try the reasonably priced Italian, *Giovanni's*, at no. 18 (ⓣ01303/850962; closed Sun eve), or for modern British cuisine sample the expensive but exquisite *Paul's*, at no. 2a (ⓣ01303/259697; closed Sun eve).

Hythe to Dungeness: the Romney and Denge marshes

In Roman times, the **Romney and Denge marshes** – now the southernmost part of Kent – were submerged beneath the English Channel. The lowering of the sea levels in the Middle Ages and later reclamation created a forty-square-mile area of shingle and marshland which, until the nineteenth century, was afflicted by malaria and various other malaises. Contrasting strongly with the wooded pastures of Kent's interior, the sheep-speckled marshes have an eerie, forlorn appearance, as if still unassimilated with the mainland and haunted by their maritime origins. The ancient town of **Hythe** is on the eastern edge of the reclaimed marshes and is linked with Rye in East Sussex (see p.218), on the marsh's western edge, by the arc of the twenty-three-mile Napoleonic-era **Royal Military Canal**.

Hythe and Lympne

Separated from Folkestone by the massive earthworks of the Channel Tunnel, **HYTHE** is a sedate seaside resort bisected by the disused waterway of the Royal Military Canal, which was built as a defensive obstacle during the perceived threat of Napoleonic invasion. Hythe's receding shoreline reduced its usefulness as a port and the nearby coast is now just a sweep of beach punctuated by **Martello towers**, part of the chain of 74 such towers built along the south and east coasts in the early nineteenth century as a defence against potential French invasion.

The nicest part of Hythe is not the seafront, but the old town, and in particular the quiet back alleys to the north of the High Street. To give purpose to your wandering, follow the signs to the macabre collection of various ancient bones and skulls in the **crypt** (May–Sept Mon–Sat 10.30am–noon & 2.30–4pm, Sun noon–4.30pm; 50p) of the eleventh-century St Leonard's Church. A ride on the world's largest toy train – or smallest public railway – the **Romney, Hythe and Dymchurch Railway** (R, H & DR), a fifteen-inch-gauge line which runs the fourteen miles from Hythe to Dungeness (April–Sept daily; March & Oct Sat & Sun; plus school holidays throughout the year; ⓣ01797/362353, ⓦwww.rhdr.demon.co.uk), is also a must. Built in the 1920s as a tourist attraction linking the resorts along the shore, its fleet of steam locomotives – mainly one-third scale models from the Twenties and Thirties – are now maintained by volunteers. The station is to the west of the town centre, on the south bank of the canal by Station Bridge. The price of a return ticket from Hythe to Dungeness is £9.60.

LYMPNE (pronounced "lim"), set on top of a rise that was once lapped by the sea, three and a half miles inland from Hythe, was the site of the Roman **Portus Lemanis**, which continued to be an important harbour until the Channel receded and stranded the settlement at its present location. Little remains of the Roman port, bar some stonework scattered at the foot of the hill, but on top of the hill, offering fine views over the marshes, is a small Norman church and the much modified **Lympne Castle**, now a wedding and conference venue, both built by Archbishop Lanfranc, the Norman architect of Canterbury's cathedral. The castle served as a residence for later archbishops, and retains its fourteenth-century Grand Hall. Two miles west of the castle, the overpriced **Howletts and Port Lympne Wild Animal Park** (daily: May–Sept 10am–6pm; Oct–April 10am–4pm, last admission 1hr 30min before closing; £11.95, £9.50 by advanced online booking; ⓦwww.howletts.net) houses more than five hundred beasts, including gorillas, elephants, wolves, lions, tigers and black rhinos.

Practicalities

Hythe is easily accessible by frequent **buses** from Folkestone. The **tourist office** is, bizarrely, situated in the old public toilets in Red Lion Square (Mon–Fri 9am–5.30pm Sat 9am–5pm; ⓣ01303/267799, ⓦwww.shepway.gov.uk). For **accommodation** check out the Tudor-style *Seabrook House*

(Ⓣ01303/269282; ❸), with pleasing light and airy rooms; the *Swan Hotel*, a friendly pub on the High Street (Ⓣ01303/266236, Ⓦwww.theswanhotelhythe.co.uk; ❷), which has a Nepalese restaurant; the Edwardian *Fern Lodge*, a mile east of the town centre at 87 Seabrook Rd (Ⓣ01303/267315; no credit cards; ❸), or if you've got more money to spend, the very superior *Hythe Imperial*, Prince's Parade (Ⓣ01303/267441, Ⓦwww.marstonhotels.com; ❼). For **food** there's high-class fish and chips, eat-in or takeaway at *Torbay of Hythe*, 81 High St (closed Sun & Mon); alternatively, there's sensibly priced home cooking at the *King's Head*, 117 High St (Ⓣ01303/266283; closed Sun eve), which serves quality meat and fish dishes.

Along the coast to Dungeness

The Romney, Hythe and Dymchurch Railway stops at five stations along the bleak stretch of coastline en route to Dungeness, the first of which is Dymchurch, a tacky seaside resort worth passing over in favour of the sandy strand of **St Mary's Bay**, an easy walk from the next station, **St Mary-in-the-Marsh**; if you need to stop for lunch, head for the excellent *Star* pub opposite the village church, not far from the station.

Next stop on the railway is one of the original Cinque Ports, **NEW ROMNEY**, nine miles southwest of Hythe. It's now really only of interest to connoisseurs of miniature railways, who will be enthralled by the R, H & DR's **Toy and Model Train Museum** (same days as the railway; 10am–5pm; £1.20) at New Romney Station, halfway between the town and the seafront. There's a **tourist office** on Church Approach, just off the High Street (Tues–Sat 9am–12.30pm & 1.30–4.45pm, closes 4.30pm Sat; Ⓣ01797/364044, Ⓦwww.shepway.gov.uk), where you'll also find the sixteenth-century *Cinque Ports Arms* (Ⓣ01797/361894; ❷), a nice-looking pub with inexpensive rooms. For something a bit more special, head for *Romney Bay House* (Ⓣ01797/364747; ❺), a wonderfully secluded place designed by the quirky architect Clough Williams-Ellis, by the beach in neighbouring **LITTLESTONE-ON-SEA**.

Dungeness

DUNGENESS, six miles south of Romney and the southern terminus for the R, H & DR, is set in the sort of wasteland normally used as an army firing range, but in this case the former Atomic Energy Authority grabbed the tip of the Denge Marsh site and built a nuclear power station here in the 1960s. Another landmark, right by the station, is the **Old Lighthouse** (May–Oct Sat & Sun 11am–5pm, call ahead for winter hours; £2.50; Ⓣ01797/321300, Ⓦwww.dungenesslighthouse.com), built in 1904 and the fourth one on the site since 1615 – the present one is visible half a mile away.

The spooky, shingle-swathed expanse of Dungeness has become the abode of eccentric and reclusive characters living in basic fishermen's cabins or disused railway carriages, apparently relishing the area's bleak austerity and carcinogenic threat. The barren environment of the Denge Marsh also supports a unique floral ecology and all around you'll see tiny communities of wildflowers struggling against the unrelenting breeze. If you follow the road back towards Lydd, past the two lighthouses, you will eventually come to **Prospect Cottage**, where the avant-garde director, writer and artist, Derek Jarman, spent much of his time until his death in 1995. The cottage is still privately owned and not a tourist attraction as such, but a steady trickle of pilgrims come by to pay their respects. The flotsam sculptures and the flora in the shingle garden make an eye-catching sight and were the subject of one of Jarman's last books, *The Garden* (1995).

A few houses up the road from Prospect Cottage, there's a traditional oak-fired smokery, for the curing of fish, where you can buy delicious picnic fodder, as well as smoked fish; alternatively, you can refuel at the unprepossessing but welcoming *Britannia* **pub**, which lies between the two lighthouses. The Dungeness shingle bank also attracts huge colonies of gulls and terns, as well as smews and gadwalls – if you're interested in finding out more, pop into the **RSPB visitor centre** (daily: March–Oct 10am–5pm; Nov–Feb 10am–4pm; £3), off the road from Dungeness to Lydd.

The Kent Weald

The Weald is usually taken to refer to the region around the spa town of **Royal Tunbridge Wells**, but in fact it stretches across a much larger area between the North and South Downs and includes parts of both Kent and Sussex, though the majority of its attractions are just inside Kent. We've taken the wider definition to include the medieval manor at **Penshurst** and nearby **Hever Castle**, just northwest of Tunbridge Wells, as well as the towns of **Sevenoaks** and **Maidstone**, on the edge of the North Downs.

During Saxon times, much of the Weald was covered in thick forest – the word itself derives from the Germanic word *Wald*, meaning forest, and the suffixes -hurst (meaning wood) and -den (meaning clearing) are commonly found in Wealden village names. Now, however, the region is epitomized by gentle hills, sunken country lanes and somnolent villages as well as some of England's most beautiful gardens – **Sissinghurst**, fifteen miles east of Tunbridge Wells, being the best known.

Public transport to the area is good, but in order to explore the Wealden countryside in any depth, you'll need your own vehicle. If you are driving or on a bicycle, you may want to follow the signs indicating the **High Weald Country Tour**, a seventy-mile back-country loop stretching through the best of the Kentish Weald, from Penshurst in the west to Tenterden in the east. Ask for the leaflet and map at tourist offices in the area.

Regular **trains** from London run to Sevenoaks, Maidstone and Tunbridge Wells, taking under an hour. National Express operates several **bus** services daily to the above towns from Victoria Coach Station. Regional bus companies also run regular services from Victoria to the major Wealden towns as well as providing an adequate service between the major towns in Kent.

Royal Tunbridge Wells and around

ROYAL TUNBRIDGE WELLS – not to be confused with the more mundane Tonbridge, a few miles to the north – is the home of the mythical whingeing right-wing letter-writer known as "Disgusted of Tunbridge Wells". Most British people, therefore, view it with derision, but don't be misled – this prosperous spa town, surrounded by gorgeous countryside, is an elegant and diverting place, meriting a few hours' visit.

In 1606 Lord North discovered a bubbling spring while riding through the Waterdown Forest, which covered the area at that time. From the claim that this spring had curative properties a spa resort evolved: Charles I's wife camped out here for several weeks after giving birth to the future Charles II, whose own wife later came here in an attempt to cure her infertility. The spa reached its height of popularity during the Regency period when such restorative cures were in vogue. The distinctively well-mannered architecture of that period, generously surrounded by parklands in which the rejuvenated gentry exercised, gives the southern and western part of town its special character. The architecture also has an effect on the locals. If you turn up in late July, you'll find that many of the townsfolk have taken to the streets in eighteenth-century garb for the five-day **Georgian Festivities**.

Tunbridge Wells is also a good base for several interesting places in the local area, including two country piles with strong Tudor associations, **Penshurst Place** and **Hever Castle**, and one, **Sissinghurst**, from the same period, but more famous for its twentieth-century gardens. There are more horticultural delights at **Groombridge Place Gardens**, while **Hammerwood Park** offers a new angle on the construction, upkeep and restoration of rural mansions.

The spa and the town

The icon of those genteel times, and the best place to start your wanderings, is the **Pantiles**, an elegant colonnaded parade of shops, ten minutes' walk south of the train station, where the fashionable once gathered to promenade and take the waters. The name stems from the chunky Kent tiles made of baked clay, which were put down as paving during Queen Anne's reign. Hub of the Pantiles is the original **Chalybeate Spring** (pronounced with the emphasis on the "be") in the Bath House (Easter–Sept daily 10am–5pm), where a "Dipper" has been employed since the late eighteenth century to serve the ferrous waters. A period-dressed incumbent will fetch you a glass from the cool spring for 40p – or, if you bring your own cup, you can help yourself for free from the adjacent source. The Bath House itself was built in 1804, but failed as an enterprise as the water turns a nasty colour when heated; it closed in 1847 and now houses a pharmacy.

You can view one of the original Pantiles in the exhibition, **A Day at the Wells** (daily: April–Oct 10am–5pm; Nov–March 10am–4pm; £5.50; Ⓦ www.heritageattractions.co.uk), situated in the basement of the nearby Corn Exchange. An audio tour, narrated as if by Richard "Beau" Nash – self-appointed arbiter of good taste (see box on p.412) – attempts to re-create, with the help of various historical tableaux, spa life in the eighteenth century. In bad weather, a stroll along the museum's reconstruction of the Pantiles might seem preferable to the real thing.

Apart from tiles, Tunbridge also produced domestic ceramics, on view with other local relics and historical artefacts in the **Museum and Art Gallery** built in the 1950s at the top of Mount Pleasant Road (Mon–Sat 9.30am–5pm; free; Ⓦ www.tunbridgewells.gov.uk/museum), a fifteen-minute walk up the old-fashioned High Street, from the Pantiles. The museum's main attraction is a superb collection of locally made wooden boxes, known as "Tunbridge Ware", introduced in the 1830s, whose "mosaic-style" inlaid lids are decorated with rural scenes and ornamental borders. The gallery also puts on excellent temporary exhibitions in its one-room art gallery.

On the east side of the High Street, the Grove and, to the north, Calverley Grounds are havens of urban tranquillity, while **The Common**, spreading out on the west side of town, is laced with pathways carved by the original visitors to the spa. You can trace the course of the old horse-racing track, or simply sit among the strange sandstone formations of Wellington Rocks. If you fancy a more energetic scramble, head three miles west of Tunbridge Wells to **High Rocks** (daily 9am–6pm or dusk; £2), another fissured outcrop of towering rocks linked by stairways and bridges and bursting with rhododendrons; traces of a Neolithic settlement are also visible here.

Four miles north of Tunbridge Wells at Tudeley, the modest church of **All Saints** (daily 9am–6pm or dusk; free) basks in the reflected light of the blue and yellow hues of twelve windows by Marc Chagall. They are a poignant reminder of the life and death of a young girl who drowned in a sailing accident in 1963.

Practicalities

The Tunbridge Wells **tourist office** is housed in the Old Fish Market, in the Pantiles (June–August Mon–Sat 9am–6pm, Sun 10am–5pm; Sept–May Mon–Sat 9am–5pm, Sun 10am–4pm; ⓣ01892/515675, ⓦwww.visittunbridgewells.com) and will hand out a map of the town. The **train station**, on the London Charing Cross to Hastings line, is south of the town centre, where High Street becomes Mount Pleasant Road. There's free **Internet** access in the library on Mount Pleasant Road (Mon 9.30am–6pm, Tues–Fri 9.30am–7pm, Sat 9.30am–5pm, Sun 10am–4pm).

Tunbridge Wells has a fair number of very plush **hotels**, relics of the good old days, such as the exemplary *Royal Wells Inn*, overlooking the Common from Mount Ephraim (ⓣ01892/511188, ⓦwww.royalwells.co.uk; ❻), the chic *Hotel du Vin* in Crescent Road (ⓣ01892/526455, ⓦwww.hotelduvin.com; ❻), which has an excellent bistro, and *The Swan Hotel*, a worthwhile splurge in the Pantiles itself (ⓣ01892/543319, ⓦwww.the-swan-hotel.com; ❺). For **B&B** the elegant *Ephraim Lodge* on The Common (ⓣ01892/523053, ⓔjohnandglyn@freenet.co.uk; no credit cards; ❹), and the nearby *Clarken Guest House*, a large Victorian house with gardens at 61 Frant Rd (ⓣ01892/533397, ⓔbarry.kench@virgin.net; no credit cards; ❷), are both good value.

The town has a good selection of **restaurants**, one of the best being *Thackeray's House*, one-time home of the writer, at 85 London Rd (ⓣ01892/511921, ⓦwww.thackeraysrestaurant.com; closed Sun eve & Mon); it's expensive but there's a bargain three-course lunch for £12.50. At the other end of the gastronomic and cultural spectrum, there's *Gracelands Palace*, a Chinese restaurant on Cumberland Walk (ⓣ01892/540754; closed Sun), with a live Chinese Elvis show. For top-notch seafood try *Sankey's* at 39 Mount Ephraim (ⓣ01892/511422, ⓦwww.sankeys.co.uk; main restaurant closed Sun) which also has a great selection of specialist beers in its cosy cellar wine bar; a two-course lunch here will set you back £7.50. Less expensive are *Zapata's*, a Tex-Mex specialist on Union Square, at the southern end of the Pantiles, and *Thai and Shanghai Cuisine* (ⓣ01892/511370) at 71 Calverley Rd, off Mount Pleasant, while *Flippers*, 9 High St (closed Sun), fry superior fish and chips. There are great veggie options both at the *Trinity Arts Centre Café* in a converted church on Church Road (lunch & pre-theatre deals only; closed Sun) and at *Continental Flavour*, 14 Mount Pleasant, a wholefood restaurant and shop (open daytime only; closed Sun).

One **pub** you're unlikely to miss is the popular *Opera House*, a Wetherspoon's conversion in the town's former 1902 theatre on Mount Pleasant Road – you can sit in the foyer, the stalls or even on stage and gaze up at the balconies. *Chaplins*, in the Pantiles, is much smaller and snug, as is the pleasant *Grape Vine* wine bar at 8 Chapel Place, which has weekend DJs. For a cocktail or beer, check out the curiously named *Orson Welles* on Grove Hill Road or *Bar Zia* at the bottom of High St.

Groombridge Place Gardens and Hammerwood Park

Four miles due west of Tunbridge Wells, **Groombridge Place Gardens** (daily April–Oct 9am–6pm or dusk if earlier; £8.30; Ⓦwww.groombridge.co.uk) makes a great place to amuse kids. The inventively designed gardens include treetop walkways and swings, "plesiosaur nests" and mazes, and are complemented by the formal gardens, which were a haunt of a former neighbour Arthur Conan Doyle. There's an hourly #291 bus service (not Sun) from Tunbridge Wells.

A further six miles west, signposted off the A264, **Hammerwood Park** (June–Sept Wed, Sat & public holidays, guided tours 2–5.30pm; £5; Ⓦwww.mistral.co.uk/hammerwood), built in 1792, is the first work of Greek revivalist architect Benjamin Latrobe, who conceived the house as a Temple to Apollo. After emigrating to America, Latrobe was responsible for the Capitol and portico of the White House in Washington. Idiosyncratic tours, given by the owners are fascinating as much for the accounts of the difficulties encountered in the ongoing and painstaking restoration (witness the derelict dining room) as for the anecdotes and history of the house. Since its rescue in 1982 from Led Zeppelin – whose plans for a music studio and accommodation for the band failed to materialize – and with the aid of a dedicated group of craftsmen and volunteers, the present owners have turned a derelict and dry-rot-ridden shell of a building into a family home. After the tour you can take tea and scones beneath a copy of the Elgin marbles.

If you can afford it, this is also a wonderful place to **spend the night**: there's a huge Victorian bedroom replete with a stunning antique four-poster bed, with an equally generous bathroom; a couple of smaller rooms are also available (Ⓣ01342/850594; no credit cards; ❻–❼). The #291 bus (not Sun) from Tunbridge Wells stops on the main road, from where it's a ten-minute walk.

Penshurst Place and Hever Castle

Tudor timber-framed houses and shops line the high street of the attractive village of **PENSHURST**, five miles northwest of Tunbridge Wells (bus #231 or #233; not Sun). Its village church, **St John the Baptist**, is capped by an unusual four-spired tower and is entered under a beamed archway that conceals a rustic post office. However, the main reason for coming here is to visit **Penshurst Place** (March Sat & Sun noon–5.30pm; April–Oct daily noon–5.30pm; grounds same days 10.30am–6pm; £6.50, grounds only £5; Ⓦwww.penshurstplace.com), home to the Sidney family since 1552 and birthplace of the Elizabethan soldier and poet, Sir Philip Sidney. The fourteenth-century Barons Hall, built for Sir John de Pulteney, four times Mayor of London, is the chief glory of the interior, with its sixty-foot-high chestnut roof still in place. The ten acres of grounds include a formal Italian garden with clipped box hedges, and double herbaceous borders mixed with an abundance of yew hedges.

The moated and much-altered **Hever Castle**, three miles further west (daily: March–Nov noon–5pm; £8.40, gardens only £6.70; Ⓦwww.hevercastle.co.uk), is where Anne Boleyn, second wife of Henry VIII, grew up, and where Anne of Cleves, Henry's fourth wife, lived after their divorce. In 1903, having fallen into disrepair, the castle was bought by William Waldorf-Astor, American millionaire owner of *The Times*, who had the house assiduously restored, panelling the rooms with worthy reproductions of Tudor woodcarvings. In the Inner Hall hangs a fine portrait of Henry VIII by Holbein; a further Holbein painting of Elizabeth I has recently been restored and is hanging on the middle floor. Upstairs, in Anne Boleyn's room, you can see her book of prayers which she carried with her to the executioner's block, but more impressive is the Anne of Cleves room, which houses an unusually well-preserved tapestry, illustrating the marriage of Henry's sister to King Louis XII of France, with Anne Boleyn as one of the ladies-in-waiting.

Outside in the grounds, next to the gift shop, is the absorbing **Guthrie Miniature Model Houses Collection**, showing the development of aristocratic seats from feudal times on. However, the best feature of the grounds is Waldorf-Astor's beautiful **Italian Garden**, built on reclaimed marshland and decorated with Roman statuary. For kids (and adults) there's a traditional **yew hedge maze** to figure out, an adventure playground and a **water maze**. Also in the grounds is a twenty-bedroom mock-Tudor annexe, built by Waldorf-Astor, who decided that the castle didn't have enough rooms to accommodate the guests of a thrusting newspaper magnate in style; it's now used solely as a conference venue.

Scotney Castle and Sissinghurst

Picturesque **Scotney Castle**, eight miles southeast of Tunbridge Wells (March to early Nov Wed–Sun and public holidays 11am–6pm or dusk if earlier; £4.40; NT), sits half-ruined within romantically landscaped gardens on the edge of a small lake (bus #256 then a mile's walk southeast; not Sun). The only part of the small castle still intact is the Jacobean wing (open May to late Sept only), which houses artefacts from the sixteenth century, but the real reason to visit is to admire the castle's delightful setting and its superb grounds.

Sissinghurst, twelve miles east of Tunbridge Wells (late March to Oct Mon, Tues & Fri 11am–6.30pm or dusk, Sat & Sun 10am–6.30pm or dusk; £6.50; NT), was described by Vita Sackville-West as "a garden crying out for rescue" when she and her husband took it over in the 1920s. Over the following years they transformed the five-acre plot into one of England's greatest and most popular modern gardens.

Spread over the site of a medieval moated manor (which was rebuilt into an Elizabethan mansion of which only one wing remains today), the gardens were designed around the linear pattern of the former buildings' walls. A major part of Sissinghurst's appeal derives from the way that the flowers are allowed to spill over onto the narrow walkways, defying the classical formality of the great gardens that preceded it. The brick tower that Vita had restored and used as her study acts as a focal point and offers the best views of the walled gardens. Most impressive are the **White Garden**, composed solely of white flowers and silvery-grey foliage, and the **Cottage Garden**, featuring flora in shades of orange, yellow and red.

The reputation of the gardens, as well as its limited capacity for visitors, is such that Sissinghurst gets extremely busy in summer when timed tickets for half-hourly visits are issued. Food options in the gardens are limited and overpriced – your best bet is to bring a picnic. **Bus** #297 from Royal Tunbridge Wells takes you within two miles of the gardens, and buses #4 and #5 run between Maidstone and Hastings, stopping in Sissinghurst village en route.

Sevenoaks and around

Set among the green sand ridges of west Kent, 25 miles from London, **SEVENOAKS** was once a small Kent village but is now a very popular commuter town, with trains reaching London in under an hour. Sadly, the place lost all but one of the ageing oaks from which it derives its name in a freakish storm that struck southern England in October 1987. With mere saplings having taken their place, the only real reason to come to the town is to visit the immense baronial estate of **Knole**, or to use it as a base for seeing the mosaics at **Lullingstone Roman Villa**, memorabilia relating to Charles Darwin and Winston Churchill, at their homes of **Down House** and **Chartwell** respectively, and **Ightham Mote**, a winning blend of architectural styles in a lovely rural setting.

Knole (late March to Oct Wed–Sun 11am–4pm; garden May–Sept first Wed of month 11am–4pm; £5.50, garden £2; NT) is entered from the south end of Sevenoaks High Street, making it very nearly half an hour's walk from the train station, fifteen minutes from the bus station. The house was created in 1456 by Archbishop Thomas Bourchier, who transformed the existing dwelling into a palace for himself and succeeding archbishops of Canterbury. The palace, numerically designed to match the calendar with 365 rooms, 7 courtyards and 52 staircases, was appropriated by Henry VIII, who lavished further expense on it and hunted in the thousand acres of **parkland** (free access throughout the year), still home to several hundred deer. Henry's daughter, Elizabeth I, passed the estate on to her cousin, Thomas Sackville, who remodelled the house in 1605. Part of Knole's allure is that it has preserved its Jacobean exterior and remained in the family's hands ever since. Vita Sackville-West, who in 1923 penned a definitive history of her family entitled *Knole and the Sackvilles*, was brought up here, and her one-time lover Virginia Woolf derived inspiration for her novel *Orlando* from her frequent visits to the house. Only thirteen rooms are open to the public, featuring an array of fine, if well-worn, furnishings and tapestries. Paintings by Gainsborough and Van Dyck are on display, as are Reynolds's depictions of George III and of Queen Charlotte – between them hangs a painting of their strutting, dandified progeny, George IV, one of the fifteen children she bore the king.

Sevenoaks' **tourist office** is in the library building (April–Sept Mon–Sat 9.30am–5pm; Oct–March Mon–Fri 9.30am–5pm, Sat 9.30am–4.30pm; Ⓣ01732/450305, Ⓦwww.heartofkent.org.uk), just beyond the **bus station** in Buckhurst Lane; the **train station** is fifteen minutes' walk north of the town centre on London Road. The town's priciest and smartest **accommodation** is at the excellent *Royal Oak Hotel*, a seventeenth-century coaching inn at the south end of the High Street (Ⓣ01732/451109, Ⓦwww.brook-hotels.co.uk/royaloak.html; ❺), beyond the entrance to Knole. In most people's range is the spacious family room at *Burley Lodge*, Rockdale Road (Ⓣ01732/455761; no credit cards; ❷), close to the entrance to Knole, or you can have a timber-clad cottage to yourself at *4 Old Timber Top Cottages*, Bethel Road (Ⓣ01732/460506, Ⓔanthony@ruddassociates.ndo.co.uk; ❹); breakfast is included in the nightly rate, though the cottage also has basic self-catering facilities. The nearest **youth hostel** (Ⓣ0870/770 5890; dorm bed £10.25) is an imposing Victorian vicarage set in its own grounds in Kemsing, four miles northeast of Sevenoaks; it's a two-mile hike from Kemsing Station or you can take bus #425/6 or #433 from Sevenoaks to Kemsing post office, which is close by – note that no public transport runs to Kemsing on Sundays.

For inexpensive filling **food**, you can't fault *Pizza Express*, 146 High St, but for something more snackish (and a really good coffee), pop into *Coffee Call* on Dorset St. The menu at the nearby *Dorset Arms* is better than your average **pub**, as is also *The Black Boy*, Bank St, but for some truly delicious (and expensive) food, you need to go to *No. 5* (Ⓣ01732/455555), the restaurant at the *Royal Oak Hotel*; for an inexpensive evening meal, head for the hotel's bistro (in other words the bar), which is also good – and half the price.

Lullingstone Roman Villa

Lullingstone Roman Villa, seven miles north of Sevenoaks and three quarters of a mile along the river west of the village of Eynsford (daily: April–Sept 10am–6pm; Oct 10am–5pm; Nov–March 10am–4pm; £3; EH), has some of the best-preserved Roman mosaics in southeast England on show, in a pleasant location alongside the trickle of the River Darent. Believed to have been the first-century residence of a farmer, the site has yielded some fine marble busts – these are now on display in the British Museum in London, but a superb floor remains depicting the killing of the Chimera, a mythical fire-breathing beast with a lion's head, goat's body and a serpent's tail. Excavation in a nearby chamber has revealed early Christian iconography, which suggests that the villa may have become a Romano-Christian chapel in the third century, pre-empting the official arrival of that religion by three hundred years and making Lullingstone one of the earliest sites of clandestine Christian worship in England. From Sevenoaks there are hourly trains to Eynsford, from where it's a fifteen-minute walk.

Down House

Down House (Wed–Sun: April–Sept 10am–6pm; Oct 10am–5pm; Nov, Dec, Feb & March 10am–4pm; £6; EH), home of the scientist Charles Darwin, is situated ten miles northwest of Sevenoaks in the village of Downe, overlooking the southeastern suburbs of London. Born in Shrewsbury in 1809, Darwin showed little academic promise at Cambridge. It was only after returning from his five-year tour of South America aboard the HMS *Beagle* – in which he stopped off at the Galapagos Islands – that he began work on the theory he would eventually publish in 1859 as *On the Origin of Species*. Darwin moved to Down House in 1842, shortly after his marriage to his cousin Emma Wedgwood, who nursed the hypochondriac scientist here until his death forty years later. The house itself is set in lovely grounds, and is stuffed with Darwin memorabilia, though there's no sign (nor smell) of the barnacles which Darwin spent eight years dissecting – he later moved on to the study of orchids, to the relief, no doubt, of his wife and children. Note that parking is very limited, so English Heritage is trying to encourage folk arriving by car to **pre-book** timed-entry tickets. Trains connect Sevenoaks with Orpington station, from where bus #R2 runs twice hourly (not Sun).

Chartwell

The residence of Winston Churchill from 1924 until his death in 1965, **Chartwell**, six miles west of Sevenoaks (late March to June & Sept to early Nov Wed–Sun 11am–5pm; July & Aug Tues–Sun 11am–5pm; £6.50; NT), is one of the most visited of the National Trust's properties. It's an unremarkable, heavily restored Tudor building whose main appeal is the wartime premier's memorabilia, including his paintings, which show an unexpectedly contemplative side to the famously gruff statesman. Entry to the house is by timed ticket at peak times – expect long queues. A direct bus service runs to Chartwell from Sevenoaks bus station four times daily on Sundays and public holidays.

Ightham Mote

The secluded, moated manor house of **Ightham Mote** (pronounced "I-tam"), six miles southeast of Sevenoaks just off the A227 (late March to early Nov Mon, Wed–Fri, Sun & public holidays 10.30am–5pm; £6; NT), originates from the fourteenth century and is one of the southeast's most picturesque National Trust properties, though the original defensive appearance of this half-timbered ragstone building has been muted by Tudor alterations. A tour of the interior reveals a mixture of architectural styles ranging from the fourteenth-century Old Chapel and crypt, through a barrel-vaulted Tudor chapel with a painted ceiling to an eighteenth-century Palladian window. This idyllically situated medieval dwelling is being restored by the National Trust, whose efforts are described in a small exhibition on the ground floor. Ightham is tricky to get to by bus, with only the infrequent #404 from Sevenoaks (not Sun) making the trip.

Maidstone and around

If on your travels you missed out **Maidstone**, you wouldn't be missing much, though the somewhat prosaic town offers a trio of enticements in the vicinity, namely the magnificently sited **Leeds Castle**, the **Museum of Kent Life**, devoted to the local rural culture, and **Yalding Gardens**, where the mysteries of organic gardening are revealed.

A minor Roman and later a Saxon settlement, **MAIDSTONE** is Kent's principal commercial, industrial and agricultural centre, but the only bit of town that holds any interest at all to the visitor is the cluster of ancient buildings south of the High Street down Mill Street, by the banks of the River Medway, a spot whose charm is somewhat tempered by the fact that it lies right by a six-lane highway.

Of most interest is the **Archbishop's Palace** (daily 10.30am–5pm; free), built around 1348 and formerly used as a stopping-off point for the Archbishop of Canterbury on journeys to London. Although the building is now used as a registry office, with a café upstairs, it's worth checking out the impressive oak-panelled function rooms. Close by is **All Saints' Church**, a good example of late-fourteenth-century Perpendicular architecture. Standing on its very own traffic island, opposite the Archbishop's Palace, is a wonderful old red-brick, ragstone and timber building, originally the archbishop's stables, and now appropriately enough the **Tyrwhitt-Drake Museum of Carriages** (daily 10.30am–5pm; £2), housing every type of carriage from infant perambulators to royal wagons. If you've time to spare, it's worth paying a visit to **Maidstone Museum and Bentlif Art Gallery** (Mon–Sat 10am–5.15pm, Sun 11am–4pm; free; Ⓦwww.museum.maidstone.gov.uk), which occupies a grandiose red-brick Elizabethan mansion built by a former local MP on St Faith's Street, two blocks north of High St. The highlights of the museum's vast collection are a half-unravelled Egyptian mummy, a statue of Lady Godiva and a whole cabinet of curiosities brought back from around the Pacific Ocean by the local-born Victorian explorer, Julius Brenchley.

Maidstone's **tourist office** is situated in the Town Hall in the High Street (daily: Mon–Sat 9am–5pm, Sun 10am–4pm; Ⓣ01622/602169, Ⓦwww.tour-maidstone.co.uk). The town has no fewer than three **train stations**: Maidstone East, served by trains from London Victoria, is ten minutes' walk north of the High Street up pedestrianized Week Street; while Maidstone Barracks and Maidstone West, both on the west bank of the Medway and less than ten minutes' walk from the High Street, are served by local trains from Tonbridge and Strood.

Thanks to its proximity to the motorways, Maidstone's **accommodation** has seen much recent development, especially at the top end of the scale. Options include the large new *Hilton Hotel* on Bearsted Road (Ⓣ01622/734322, Ⓦwww.hilton.com; ❺), close to the M20 access point and the elegant *Best Western-Russell Hotel*, 136 Boxley Rd (Ⓣ01622/692221,

Ⓦwww.bestwestern.co.uk; ❼), northeast of the town centre. For something more affordable, try the *Rock House Hotel*, 102 Tonbridge Rd (Ⓣ01622/751616, Ⓦwww.s-h-systems.co.uk; ❷), west of the centre, or, if you have your own transport, head for the characterful converted oast house (originally used for drying hops) *Goldings* at Elphicks Farm in Hunton (Ⓣ01622/820758; Ⓦwww.s-h-systems.co.uk; no smoking; no credit cards; ❷), seven miles southwest of Maidstone. **Food** options in town include the *Paramount*, Middle Row (Ⓣ01622/606941), which has a tasty and moderately priced daytime menu, and the funkier *Frobishers*, 57 High St (Ⓣ01622/678628; closed Sun), with a restaurant upstairs and a lively bar and cheaper food downstairs. The cool and modern *Mediterrano* (Ⓣ01622/690069; closed Sun eve) at 37 High St concentrates on organic produce and is certainly worth the expense. Otherwise, there's reliable **pub grub** and real ales at the *Muggleton Inn*, a big Wetherspoon's pub on High Street, and a branch of *Pizza Express* in the old Conservative Club on Earl Street. If you're in the mood for a pricey gastronomic treat, head for *Le Soufflé*, on The Green in Bearsted (Ⓣ01622/737065; closed Sat lunch, Sun eve & Mon), two miles east of Maidstone on the A20, which specializes in classic French dishes.

Museum of Kent Life

Though too close to the M20 to re-create any rural idyll, the **Museum of Kent Life**, two miles north of Maidstone at Cobtree (late Feb to early Nov daily 10am–5.30pm, last admission 4pm; £5.50), offers a fascinating account of rural life in the county over the last hundred years or so. The farm was bought in 1904 by local bigwigs, the Tyrwhitt-Drakes, and was at one time a zoo – today, the animals are purely livestock. The section on hop-picking in the traditional oast house (the distinctive conical building where the hops were dried) is particularly fascinating. Nearby, you can view a series of hopper huts, in which East Enders from London used to spend their hop-picking "holidays". To get to the museum from Maidstone, you can take **bus** #155 (not Sun), or in summer catch a **boat** from the Archbishop's Palace (daily: April–Sept 11.30am–4.30pm; £4 return).

Leeds Castle

Leeds Castle, five miles east of Maidstone, off the A20 (daily: April–Oct 10am–5pm; Nov–March 10am–3pm; grounds close 2hr later; castle, park & gardens £12; park & gardens £9.50; Ⓦwww.leeds-castle.com), more closely resembles a fairytale palace than a defensively efficient fortress. Named after the local village, work on the castle began around 1120. Set half on an island in the middle of a lake and half on the mainland surrounded by landscaped parkland, following centuries of regal and noble ownership (and, less glamorously, service as a prison) the castle is now run as a commercial concern, hosting conferences as well as sporting and cultural events. Its interior fails to match the castle's stunning, much-photographed external appearance and, in places, twentieth-century renovations have quashed any of its historical charm; possibly the most unusual feature inside is the dog collar museum in the gatehouse. In the grounds, there's a fine aviary with some superb and colourful exotic specimens, as well as manicured gardens and a mildly challenging maze. The easiest way to get to Leeds Castle by public transport is to buy an all-inclusive ticket; you can travel either by rail to Bearsted Station from London Victoria via Maidstone East, or by coach from Victoria Coach Station, and a shuttle service and entry to the castle are included.

Yalding Organic Gardens

Vegetable-growers and other garden fans will find much to appreciate at the compact **Yalding Organic Gardens** (May–Sept Wed–Sun 10am–5pm; £3; Ⓦ www.hdra.org.uk), on the edge of the village of Yalding, six miles southwest of Maidstone on the B2010. The series of sample gardens from different periods makes a charming and informative introduction to gardens and their history from the thirteenth century to the 1950s allotment, and there are practical displays on organic gardening. Bus #23 from Maidstone (not Sun) stops here, while #26 stops in Yalding village, which is also served by train.

Sussex

Although now separated into two counties, East and West, **Sussex** (deriving from "land of the south Saxons") retains a unified identity. Most of the region was covered in dense forest until the Tudor era, when the huge demand for timber and charcoal began its deforestation. However, large areas of woodland still exist in inland parts of the counties and contribute to Sussex's bucolic character. Nowhere is this rural atmosphere more evident than on the southeast's main long-distance footpath, the **South Downs Way**, which runs along the grassy ridge of the South Downs, giving dramatic views over some fine countryside as well as over the coast, where the Downs meet the sea at the chalk cliffs of **Beachy Head** and **Seven Sisters**.

However, Sussex also has its fair share of urban centres, many of which are populated by London commuters. The best known is the traditional seaside resort of **Brighton**, the counties' biggest and brashest town, while a few miles inland more sedate **Lewes**, the county town of East Sussex, is famed for its bonfire night celebrations. **Hastings**, farther east, is renowned for its historical connections, although the eponymous fight actually took place six miles away at **Battle**. Farther east still, on the edge of the Romney Marshes, the former Cinque Port of **Rye** exemplifies rustic English tweeness. In West Sussex, the main centres of interest are the attractive hilltop town of **Arundel**, surrounded by unspoilt countryside, and the county town of **Chichester**.

Hastings and around

During the twelfth and thirteenth centuries, **Hastings** flourished as an influential Cinque Port (see p.195). In 1287 its harbour creek was silted up by the same storm that washed away nearby **Winchelsea**, forcing the settlement to be temporarily abandoned. These days, Hastings is a curious mixture of unpretentious fishing port, traditional seaside resort and arty retreat popular with painters (there's even a street and quarter named Bohemia). In 1066, William, Duke of Normandy, landed at Pevensey Bay, a few miles west of town, and made Hastings his base, but his forces met Harold's army – exhausted after quelling a Nordic invasion near York – at **Battle**, six miles northwest of

Hastings. Battle today boasts a magnificent abbey built by William in thanks for his victory, which makes a good afternoon's excursion from Hastings. Farther north, **Batemans**, once the home of Rudyard Kipling, and the classic **Bodiam Castle** are both easily reached from Hastings in a day-trip.

Arrival, information and accommodation

Hasting's **train station**, served by regular trains from both London's Charing Cross (via Ashford International) and Victoria (via Lewes) stations, is a ten-minute walk from the seafront along Havelock Road; National Express **bus** services operate from the station at the junction of Havelock and Queen's roads. The **tourist office** is located within the Town Hall on Queen's Road (Mon–Fri 8.30–6.15pm, Sat 9am–5pm, Sun 10am–4.30pm; ⓣ01424/781111, ⓦwww.hastings.gov.uk); there's also a smaller seafront office (Easter–Oct daily 10am–5pm, Nov–Easter Sat & Sun 11am–4pm; ⓣ01424/781120) near the Boating Lake on East Parade by the old town. You'll find **Internet** access at *Revolver Internet Café*, 26 George St (ⓣ01424/439899), and **bikes** can be rented from Hastings Cycles (ⓣ01424/444013) in St Andrews Market off Queens Road.

As for **accommodation**, Hastings has a preponderance of drab hotels and chintzy B&Bs, but you can still find some more upbeat places, with the best choices in the old town.

Hotels, guest houses and B&Bs

Argyle Guest House 32 Cambridge Gardens ⓣ01424/421294, ⓦwww.argyleguesthouse.com. Good-value rooms in a street near the station. Continental breakfast. No credit cards. ❶

Bryn-y-mor 12 Godwin Rd ⓣ01424/722744, ⓦwww.s-h-systems.co.uk. A Victorian pile overlooking the town, with four-posters in every room, sea views, terraced gardens and heated swimming pool in July and August. No kids under 12. ❺

Lavender and Lace 106 All Saints St ⓣ01424/716290. Popular, cosy, timber-framed guest house right in the middle of the old town. Closed Jan & Feb. No credit cards. ❷

Lionsdown House 116 High St ⓣ01424/420802, ⓦwww.lionsdownhouse.co.uk. This authentic Wealden house has ingelnook fireplaces, exposed beams, and homemade bread and organic produce for breakfast. Vegans and vegetarians catered for. No smoking. ❷

Hostels and campsites

Shear Barn Holiday Park Barley Lane ⓣ01424/423583, ⓦwww.shearbarn.co.uk. The nearest campsite is situated next to the seafront Hastings Country Park, a mile east of the town centre off All Saints Street.

Youth Hostel Guestling Hall ⓣ0870/770 5850. This large manor house, set in its own grounds, is three miles east of Hastings on the road to Rye. Camping possible. Take bus #711 from the main tourist office. Dorm bed £10.25.

The Town

Hastings **old town**, east of the pier, holds most of the appeal of this part tacky, part pretty seaside resort. With the exception of the oddly neglected Regency architecture of **Pelham Crescent**, directly beneath the castle ruins, **All Saints Street** is by far the most evocative thoroughfare, punctuated with the odd, rickety, timber-framed dwelling from the fifteenth century. The thirteenth-century **St Clement's Church** stands in the High Street, which runs parallel to All Saints Street, on the other side of The Bourne. By a louvred window at the top of the church's tower rests a cannonball that was lodged there by a Dutch galleon in the 1600s – its poignancy rather dispelled by a companion fitted in the eighteenth century for the sake of symmetry. On the right as you walk up the High Street, you'll see **Starr's Cottages**, one of which is wedge-shaped and painted to resemble a piece of cheese, while the **Old Town Hall**

Museum on High Street (daily: April–Sept 10am–4.45pm; Oct–March 11am–3.45pm; free) offers the customary spread on local history. Also on High Street at no. 58a is the tiny working **Flower-makers Museum** (Mon–Sat 9.30am–5pm; £1) where petals and leaves for weddings, television, theatre and film sets (including 100,000 rose petals for *Gladiator*) are made using original Victorian tools and moulds.

Down by the seafront, the area known as **The Stade** is characterized by its tall, black weatherboard **net shops**, most dating from the mid-nineteenth century (and still in use), but which first appeared here in Tudor times. To raise Hastings' tone, the town council attempted to shift the fishermen and their malodorously drying nets from the beach by increasing rents per square foot, and these sinister-looking towers were their response. Somewhat remarkably, Hastings still boasts a working fishing fleet, the boats being dragged up onto the shingle, and you can still buy fresh fish from several of the net shops.

There's a trio of nautical attractions on nearby Rock-a-Nore Road. The **Fisherman's Museum** (daily: April–Oct 10am–5pm; Nov–March 11am–4pm; free), a converted seaman's chapel, offers an account of the port's commercial activities and displays one of Hastings' last clinker-built luggers – exceptionally stout trawlers able to withstand being winched up and down the shingle beach. The neighbouring **Shipwreck Heritage Centre** (daily: 10.30am–5pm; free) details the dramas of unfortunate mariners, focusing on the wreck of the *Amsterdam*, beached in 1749 and now embedded in the sand three miles west of town awaiting excavation. Opposite is **Underwater World** (daily: Easter–Sept 10am–5.30pm; Oct–Easter 11am–4pm £5.75; Ⓦwww.discoverhastings.co.uk), a series of aquariums with walk-through tunnels, magnified tanks housing marine creatures and an excellent and sympathetic film on sharks.

Castle Hill, separating the old town from the visually less-interesting modern quarter, can be ascended by the **West Hill Cliff Railway**, from George Street, off Marine Parade, one of two Victorian funicular railways in Hastings (daily: April–Oct 10.30am–5.30pm; Nov–March 11am–4.30pm; 90p), the other being the **East Cliff Railway**, on Rock-a-Nore Road (same times and price). Castle Hill is where William the Conqueror erected his first **Castle** in 1066, one of several prefabricated wooden structures brought over from Normandy in sections. Built on the site of an existing fort, probably of Saxon origins, it was soon replaced by a more permanent stone structure, but in the thirteenth century storms caused the cliffs to subside, tipping most of the castle into the sea; the surviving ruins, however, offer an excellent prospect of the town. The castle is home to **The 1066 Story** (daily: Easter–Sept 10am–5pm; Oct–Easter 11am–3pm; £3.20; Ⓦwww.discoverhastings.co.uk), in which the events of the last successful invasion of the British mainland are described inside a mock-up of a siege tent. The twenty-minute audiovisual details the history of the castle and corrects a few myths about the famous battle.

More fun is the **Smugglers' Adventure**, over the hill (daily: Easter–Sept 10am–5.30pm; Oct–Easter 11am–4.30pm; £5.75; Ⓦwww.discoverhastings.co.uk). Here the labyrinthine St Clement's caves, named after a carving resembling St Clement but probably predating Christianity, have been converted to house a number of amusing and educational dioramas depicting the town's long history of duty dodging. During the eighteenth century, smuggling – especially of alcohol and tobacco – was the region's biggest source of income after agriculture and a farm worker could earn more than a week's wages with one night's contraband. Large-scale smuggling waned in the 1830s when a more efficient coastguard and diminishing taxes reduced its viability.

Hastings also has its fair share of traditional English seaside activities – mini-golf, boating, go-karts and **Hastings Pier**, west of the old town, where bingo and palm-reading are on offer, along with the usual video games and slot machines.

Eating

Hastings has a good range of affordable places for a meal, most very central. For something more special, head out to St Leonard's-on-Sea.

Bonaparte's 64 Eversfield Place, St. Leonard's-on-Sea ☎01424/712218. A classy option specializing in fish. On the seafront in St Leonards-on-Sea, a short walk west of central Hastings. Closed Sun & Mon. Expensive.

Gannets Bistro 45 High St. Nice place offering a wide daytime range of food and good afternoon teas. Inexpensive.

Harris 58 High St ☎01424/437221. Wood-panelled walls and potted plants enhance the ambience of this specialist in tapas. Closed Sun and Mon. Moderate.

The Hastings Arms 3 George St. A fine pub, noted for its imaginative fish and meat dishes. Inexpensive.

Mermaid 2 Rock-a-Nore. The best fish and chips in town are at this eat-in restaurant, right by the beach; jellied eels can be sampled from the adjacent net shop. Inexpensive.

Pissarro's 10 South Terrace ☎01424/421363. Good variety of bistro food; you can graze or have a full meal while listening to regular live jazz and blues. Moderate.

Drinking and nightlife

There are more than thirty **pubs** to choose from in Hastings: the local fishermen's favourite is the *Lord Nelson* right by the front on The Bourne; others to check out are the ever-popular *First In Last Out,* 15 High St in the old town, the creaky-beamed hostelry, *Ye Olde Pump House*, 64 George St, or the trendy clubby bar, *The Street*, 53 Robertson St, accessible via a tiny entrance on Cambridge Road in the new town centre.

For **entertainment**, *The Hastings Arms* has a longstanding blues night every Monday with jazz at *The Anchor* further up George Street on Tuesdays; *Pissarro's* (Ⓦwww.pissarros.co.uk) has regular jazz and blues nights. *The Stag Inn*, 14 All Saints St, has a folk session on Wednesdays and bluegrass the following night. For **clubs**, *The Crypt*, on Havelock Road, is popular with students from the town's thirty-odd language schools. Look out too for events at the innovative arts venue, *St. Mary-in-the Castle* on Pelham Crescent. For comprehensive **listings** of what's on, get the free *Ultimate Alternative*, available in pubs, clubs and record shops and at Ⓦwww.ua1066.co.uk.

Battle

The town of **BATTLE** – a ten-minute train ride inland from Hastings – occupies the site of the most famous land battle in British history. Here, on October 14, 1066, the invading Normans swarmed up the hillside from Senlac Moor and overcame the Anglo-Saxon army of King Harold, who is thought to have been killed not by an arrow through the eye – a myth resulting from the misinterpretation of the Bayeux Tapestry – but by a workaday clubbing about the head. Before the battle took place, William vowed that, should he win the engagement, he would build a religious foundation on the very spot of Harold's slaying to atone for the bloodshed, and, true to his word, **Battle Abbey** (daily: April–Sept 10am–6pm; Oct 10am–5pm; Nov–March 10am–4pm; £5; EH) was built four years later and subsequently occupied by a fraternity of Benedictines. The magnificent structure, though partially destroyed in the Dissolution and much rebuilt and revised over the centuries, still dominates the town, with the huge gatehouse, added in 1338, containing a good audiovisual exhibition on the battle. You can also wander through the ruins of the abbey to the spot where Harold was killed – the site of the high altar of William's abbey, now marked by a memorial stone.

Though nothing can match the resonance of the abbey, the rest of the town is worth a stroll. **St Mary's Church** on High Street, has a fine Norman font and nave and the churchyard contains the grave of one Isaac Ingall who, according to the inscription on his tomb, was 120 years old when he died in 1798. At the far end of High Street is the fourteenth-century **almonry** – the present town hall – at the back of which is a **museum** (April–Oct Mon–Sat 10am–4.30pm, Sun 2–5pm; £1; Ⓦ www.battlemuseum.co.uk) that contains the only battle axe discovered at Battle and the oldest Guy Fawkes in the country. Every year, on the Saturday nearest to November 5, this 300-year-old effigy is paraded along High Street at the head of a torch-lit procession culminating at a huge bonfire in front of the abbey gates – similar celebrations occur in Lewes (see p.225).

Wealden Hall House, just past the tourist office, houses a more modern diversion, though one still firmly rooted in the past. **Buckleys Yesterday's World** (daily 9.30am–6pm; closes 5pm in winter; last entry 1hr 15min before closing; £4.75; Ⓦ www.yesterdaysworld.co.uk) is a must for nostalgia buffs consisting of thirty re-created rooms and shop settings stocked with original materials and goods. Highlights include a Bakelite-crammed 1930s wireless shop and a Victorian kitchen replete with authentic accessories. The grounds outside include a country garage and railway station, a café and play areas for children and toddlers.

Practicalities

The **tourist office** is situated in the Gatehouse at Battle Abbey (daily: April–Sept 9.30am–5.30pm; Oct 9am–5pm; Nov–March 10am–4pm; Ⓣ 01424/773721, Ⓦ www.battletown.co.uk). Battle's **accommodation** tends to be agreeable but expensive, as at the *George Hotel*, an old coaching inn at 23 High St (Ⓣ 01424/774466; ❹), and at the luxurious country house, *Powdermills Hotel*, Powdermill Lane (Ⓣ 01424/775511, Ⓦ www.powdermillshotel.co.uk; ❼). For less pricey B&B deals try the obliging *High Hedges*, 28 North Trade Road (Ⓣ 01424/774140, Ⓔ gloria.jones@btinternet.com; no credit cards; ❷), a few minutes walk north of High Street, or the en-suite rooms above the *Gateway Café*, 78 High St (Ⓣ 01424/772856; ❷). The excellent *Food Rooms* delicatessen and **restaurant** at 53–55 High St (daytime only) serves locally sourced food, and they also supply the more expensive *Pilgrims*, a fifteenth-century hall next to the Abbey, 1 High St (Ⓣ 01424/772314) – also an ideal spot for afternoon tea. For town-centre **pubs** in Battle, serving decent meals, try the fifteenth-century *Old King's Head* on Mount St or the *Chequers Inn* at Lower Lake, on High St.

Rye and Winchelsea

Perched on a hill overlooking the Romney Marshes, ten miles east of Hastings, sits the ancient town of **RYE**. Added as a "limb" to the original Cinque Ports (see p.195), the town then became marooned two miles inland with the retreat of the sea and the silting-up of the River Rother. It is now one of the most popular places in East Sussex – half-timbered, skew-roofed and quintessentially English, but also very commercialized.

From Strand Quay, head up The Deals to Rye's most picturesque street, the sloping cobbled lane of **Mermaid Street**, which will bring you eventually to the peaceful oasis of Church Square. Henry James, who strangely suggested that "Rye would … remind you of Granada", lived from 1898 until his death in 1916 in **Lamb House** at the east end of Mermaid Street (April–Oct Wed & Sat 2pm–6pm; £2.60; NT). The house's three rooms and garden are of interest chiefly to fans of James's novels, or to admirers of E.F. Benson, who lived here after James. A blue plaque in High Street also testifies that Radclyffe Hall, author of the seminal lesbian novel, *The Well of Loneliness*, was also once a resident of the town. At the centre of Church Square stands **St Mary's Church**, boasting the oldest functioning pendulum clock in the country; the ascent of the church tower – whose bells were looted by French raiders in 1377 and then retrieved with similar audacity – offers fine views over the clay-tiled roofs and grid of narrow lanes. In the far corner of the square stands the **Ypres Tower** (April–Oct Mon, Thurs & Fri 10am–1pm & 2–5pm, Sat & Sun 10.30am–1pm & 2–5pm; Nov–March Sat & Sun 10.30am–3.30pm; £1.90), formerly used to keep watch for cross-Channel invaders, and now a part of the **Rye Castle Museum** on nearby East Street (April–Oct Mon, Thurs & Fri 10am–1pm & 2–5pm, Sat & Sun 10.30am–1pm & 2–5pm; £1.90; combined ticket for both sites £2.90). Both sites house a number of relics from Rye's past, including an eighteenth-century fire engine. Also worth seeking out are the **Rye Art Galleries** (daily 10.30am–5pm; free), located in two lovely houses: the Easton Rooms, 107 High St, stages exhibitions by local contemporary artists, while the Stormont Studio, around the corner in Ockman Lane, off East St, has a small permanent collection, including works by artists associated with Rye, such as Burra and Nash. Rye's **festival** (Ⓣ01797/224442, Ⓦwww.ryefestival.co.uk), one of the best-known literary festivals in the country, takes place over the first two weeks in September and also features a wide range of musical and visual arts events.

WINCHELSEA, perched on a hill two miles southwest of Rye and easily reached by train, bus, foot or bike, shares Rye's indignity of having become detached from the sea, but has a very different character. Rye gets all the visitors, whereas Winchelsea feels positively deserted, an impression augmented as you pass through the medieval Strand Gate and see the ghostly ruined **Church of St Thomas à Becket**. The original settlement was washed away in the great storm in 1287, after which Edward I planned a new port with a chequerboard pattern of streets. Even at the height of Winchelsea's economic activity, however, not all the plots on the grid were used. The town also suffered from incursions by the French in the fourteenth and fifteenth centuries, at which time the church was pillaged; the remains of the church constitute Sussex's finest example of the Decorated style. Head south for a mile and a half and you get to **Winchelsea beach**, a long expanse of pebbly sand. Three miles further east, **Camber Sands** is a two-mile stretch of sandy beach that has become a renowned centre of wind and water sports.

Practicalities

Hourly **trains** run to Rye and Winchelsea from Hastings; Rye's station is at the bottom of Station Approach, off Cinque Ports Street, while Winchelsea's is a mile north of the town. **Bus** #711 runs into the centre of both towns from Hastings. Rye's **tourist office**, on Strand Quay (April–Oct Mon–Sat 10am–5pm, Sun 10am–4pm; Nov–March Mon–Sat 10am–4pm; Ⓣ01797/226696, Ⓦwww.visitrye.co.uk), has masses of information on local attractions. The same building houses Rye's **Heritage Centre** (same hours) with an interesting twenty-minute audiovisual (£2.50) about the town and a scaled-down model of Rye on show – they also rent out audio tours to take you round the town itself (£2.50).

The town's popularity with weekending Londoners gives it an excellent choice of **accommodation**. The most luxurious option is *The Mermaid* (Ⓣ01797/223065, Ⓔmermaidinnrye@btclick.com; ❼), a fifteenth-century inn on Mermaid Street; the handsomely furnished rooms in *Jeake's House* are also on Mermaid Street (Ⓣ01797/222828, Ⓦwww.jeakeshouse.com; ❺). Both are deservedly popular. Alternatively, there's *Old Vicarage*, 66 Church Square (Ⓣ01797/222119, Ⓦwww.oldvicaragerye.co.uk; ❺), a lovely pink Georgian house next to the church; the *Durrant House Hotel*, 2 Market St (Ⓣ01797/223182, Ⓦwww.durranthouse.com; ❹), is another friendly and well-equipped Georgian house with a garden looking out towards Dungeness and the marshes. At Camber Sands, three miles east of Rye, *The Place* (Ⓣ01797/225057, Ⓦwww.theplacecambersands.co.uk; ❹) has stylish, contemporary rooms and a brasserie, and in Winchelsea the best accommodation option is the fourteenth-century *Strand House* (Ⓣ01797/226276, Ⓦwww.s-h-systems.co.uk; ❸), at the foot of the cliff below Strand Gate. The *Mermaid* (see above) is by far Rye's most atmospheric **pub**, with heavy exposed timbers throughout, though an excellent alternative is the *Ypres Castle* in Gun Gardens (down the steps behind the Ypres Tower), an unspoiled place often used for film locations; a younger crowd frequents the more laid-back *Strand Quay*, at the bottom of Mermaid St.

Rye's best **restaurant** is the pricey *Landgate Bistro* at 5–6 Landgate (Ⓣ01797/222829; Tues–Sat eve only), which serves good game and lamb but if you want something a touch less expensive in Rye, try the seafood at the *Old Forge*, 24 Wish St (Ⓣ01797/223227), or the small and intimate *Gatehouse Restaurant*, 1 Tower St (Ⓣ01797/222327; closed Mon lunch). For more excellent seafood dishes, head for the *Flushing Inn* on Market Street (Ⓣ01797/223292; closed Mon eve & all Tues). *The Peacock*, 8 Lion St (Ⓣ01797/226702), serves up everything from snacks to moderately priced fresh Rye Bay plaice in a suitably ancient setting – it's also a good place for delicious cream teas.

Bodiam Castle and Great Dixter

Ask a child to draw a castle and the outline of **Bodiam Castle**, nine miles north of Hastings (late Feb to Oct daily 10am–6pm or dusk; Nov–Feb Sat & Sun 10am–4pm or dusk; £4; NT), would be the result: a classically stout square block with rounded corner turrets, battlements and a wide moat. When it was built in 1385 to guard what were the lower reaches of the River Rother, Bodiam was state-of-the-art military architecture, but during the Civil War a company of Roundheads breached the fortress and removed its roof to reduce its effectiveness as a possible stronghold for the king. Over the next 250 years Bodiam fell into neglect until restoration earlier last century by Lord Curzon. The extremely steep spiral staircases, leading to the crenellated battlements, will test all but the strongest of thighs. An absorbing fifteen-minute video portrays medieval life in a castle. You can get here from Hastings by regular buses #4 and #5.

If you've got children to entertain, it's worth knowing about the **Kent and East Sussex Railway** (Ⓣ01580/765155; £9, Ⓦwww.kesr.org.uk), which runs full-scale steam trains from Bodiam to Tenterden, ten miles to the north-east.

There's a lush display of colourful borders, topiary and meadow flowers at **Great Dixter House and Gardens** (April–Oct Tues–Sun & public holidays 2–5pm; £6.50, Ⓦwww.greatdixter.co.uk), three miles east of Bodiam, and just north of Northiam. The fifteenth-century "hall house", family home of the garden writer Christopher Lloyd, was enlarged and restored by Edwin Lutyens and contains a mixture of antique and specially commissioned contemporary furniture.

The best **accommodation** and **food** options are a couple of miles west of Northiam, in the lovely village of Ewhurst, which houses a quaint country pub, the *White Dog Inn* (Ⓣ01580/830264; ❷).

Burwash and Bateman's

Fifteen miles northwest of Hastings on the A265, halfway to Tunbridge Wells, **BURWASH**, with its red-brick and weatherboarded cottages and Norman church tower, exemplifies the pastoral idyll of inland Sussex. Half a mile south of the village lies the main attraction, **Bateman's** (house & garden: April–Oct Mon–Wed, Sat, Sun & public holidays 11am–5pm; £5.20; garden only March Sat & Sun 11am–4pm; £2.60; NT), home of the Nobel Prize-winning writer and journalist Rudyard Kipling from 1902 until his death in 1936. Built by a local ironmaster in the seventeenth century and set amid attractive gardens, the house features a working watermill converted by Kipling to generate electricity, and which now grinds corn every Saturday at 2pm. Inside, the house is laid out as Kipling left it, with letters, early editions of his work and mementoes from his travels on display. Next to the house, a garage houses the last of Kipling's Rolls-Royces, one of the many that he owned during his lifetime, although he never actually drove them himself, preferring the services of a chauffeur. Getting here without your own transport involves a three-mile walk from Etchingham Station, which is served by regular trains from Hastings.

Eastbourne and around

Like so many of the southeast's seaside resorts, **EASTBOURNE** was kick-started into life in the 1840s, when the Brighton, Lewes and Hastings Rail Company built a branch line from Lewes to the sea. The Seventh Duke of Devonshire, William Cavendish, promptly developed the resort, an achievement zealously commemorated in the town's Devonshire Park, Devonshire swimming baths and Devonshire Place, where a self-satisfied statue of the duke stands. Past holiday-makers include George Orwell, the composer Claude Debussy, who finished writing *La Mer* here, as well as Marx and Engels. Nowadays Eastbourne has a solid reputation as a retirement town – albeit one that's a touch livelier than the nearby custom-built Peacehaven. Eastbourne's elegant three-mile seafront consists of houses and hotels and is barely tainted by a shop, but the greatest draw is the South Downs, which the sea has ground into a series of dramatic chalk cliffs around **Beachy Head**, just southwest of town.

Conforming to tradition, the **Pier** is the focal point of the seafront: opened in 1872, it was intended to match the best on the south coast, which it certainly does. To the west, along the Grand Parade, is the ever-popular sunken **Bandstand**, with its regular (frequently military) band concerts. Further west along the promenade, the **Wish Tower** – whose name derives from an old Sussex word meaning "marsh" – is the first of the prom's two prominent red-

The South Downs Way

Following the undulating crest of the South Downs, between the city of Winchester and the spectacular cliffs at Beachy Head, the **South Downs Way** rises and dips over eighty miles along the chalk uplands, offering the southeast's finest walks. If undertaken in its entirety, the bridle-path is best traversed from west to east, taking advantage of the prevailing wind, Eastbourne's better transport services and accommodation, and the psychological appeal of ending at the sea. **Steyning**, the halfway-point, marks a transition between predominantly wooded sections and more exposed chalk uplands – to the east of here you'll pass the modern **youth hostel** at Truleigh Hill (Ⓣ0870/770 6078, Ⓔtruleigh@yha.org.uk; dorm bed £10.25; ❶). Other hostels along the way are at Telscombe and at Alfriston, where a southern loop can be taken which brings you to Eastbourne along the cliffs of the Seven Sisters, and there's a bunkhouse at an old bothy (a small, stone-built outhouse) at Gumber Farm (Ⓣ01243/814484; closed Nov–Easter), near Bignor Hill.

The OS Landranger **maps** #198 and #199 cover the eastern end of the route; you'll need #185 and #197 as well to cover the lot. Half a dozen guides are available, the best being *South Downs Way* by Miles Jebb (Cicerone Press), or the more detailed *South Downs Way* by Paul Millmore (Aurum Press). You can also check the website Ⓦwww.nationaltrails.gov.uk.

brick Martello towers, and has been transformed into a **puppet museum** (mid-July to Sept daily 11am–5pm; April to mid-July & Oct–Nov Sat & Sun 11am–5pm; £1.80; Ⓦwww.puppets.co.uk), while the **Redoubt Fortress**, half a mile east of the pier, now houses a military museum (April to early Nov daily 9.30am–5.30pm; £1.50; Ⓦwww.eastbournemuseums.co.uk) and is the venue for evening classical music concerts (mid-June to Sept Wed & Fri) – often the *1812 Overture* – with accompanying firework displays.

One bright spark in sedate Eastbourne is the **Towner Art Gallery and Museum** (Tues–Sat noon–5pm, Sun 2–5pm; Nov–March Tues–Sat noon–4pm, Sun 2–5pm; free; Ⓦwww.eastbournemuseums.co.uk), a ten-minute walk northwest of the train station; it shows a refreshingly contemporary and ever-changing range of work. This is complemented by the **"How We Lived Then" Museum of Shops** at 20 Cornfield Terrace (daily 10am–5.30pm; £3.50), just down from the tourist office. The amount of artefacts – old packages, coronation cups, toys – from the last hundred years of consumerism is just staggering, all crammed into mock-up shops spread over several floors. Finally, a more serious attempt to tackle the history of the town is made at the **Eastbourne Heritage Centre** (May–Sept Mon–Fri & Sun 2–5pm; £1), in a distinctive corner house opposite the Winter Gardens.

Practicalities

Eastbourne is served by hourly trains from London Victoria (via Lewes), with the **train station**, a splendid Italianate terminus, ten minutes' walk from the seafront up Terminus Road; there are also frequent services between here and Hastings (see p.214) and Brighton (see p.228). The **bus station**, on Cavendish Place right by the pier, receives daily services from London and has hourly services to Brighton via Newhaven. The **tourist office** is at 3 Cornfield Rd, just off Terminus Road (July to early Sept Mon–Sat 9.30am–5.30pm, Sun 10am–1pm; rest of year closed Sun; Ⓣ01323/411400, Ⓦwww.eastbourne.org. The town's trackless **Dotto trains** ply up and down the sea front and into the centre from Easter to October and a day ticket (daily 10am–5.30pm; £5.25) allows visitors to hop on or off at a series of designated stops.

There are hundreds of places to **stay** here: a couple of good choices are *Sea Breeze Guest House*, 6 Marine Rd (Ⓣ01323/725440, Ⓦwww.seabreezeguesthouse.co.uk; no credit cards; ❷), a cheap and cheerful place just a hundred yards from the sea, and *Sea Beach House Hotel*, 39–40 Marine Parade (Ⓣ01323/410458, Ⓦwww.seabeachhousehotel.com; ❸), on the seafront. A mile and a half west along the A259 to East Dean there's a **youth hostel** (Ⓣ0870/770 5806, Ⓔeastbourne@yha.org.uk; dorm bed £10.25) with spectacular views across Eastbourne; take buses #710, #712, #713 from the train station. You can camp right by a sandy beach at the secluded *Bay View* **campsite** (Ⓣ01323/768688; closed Oct–March), off the A259 east to Pevensey.

The best **restaurant** option is the *Café Belge* on the seafront at 11–23 Grand Parade, good for *moules et frites* and snack lunches. Otherwise head for the concentration of moderately priced restaurants in the Terminus Road area, between the train station and the sea, for example the Italian *Mediterraneo* at no. 72 (Ⓣ01323/736994; closed Sun eve). If you're in need of a large ice-cream sundae, go to *Fusciardi's* opposite the Winter Gardens on Carlyle Road.

The best **pubs** are some distance from the seafront: the capacious Wetherspoon's bar at 21–23 Cornfield Rd; the *Hurst Arms* at 76 Willingdon Rd, a ten-minute walk inland from the station up Upperton Road, has Harvey's locally brewed beers on tap, with the same brew also available at the *Lamb*, a slightly over-enthusiastic but very pleasant version of a traditional English inn situated in nearby High Street. Slightly out of the centre at 220 Seaside is the ornate Victorian *Black Horse* pub (along the A259 to Bexhill), one of Eastbourne's least touristy places.

Beachy Head, Seven Sisters and the Cuckmere

A short walk west from Eastbourne takes you out along the most dramatic stretch of coastline in Sussex, where the chalk uplands of the Sussex Downs are cut by the sea into a sequence of splendid cliffs. The most spectacular of all, **Beachy Head**, is 575ft high, with a diminutive-looking lighthouse, but no beach – the headland's name derives from the French *beau chef* meaning "beautiful head". The beauty certainly went to Friedrich Engels' head; he insisted his ashes be scattered here, and depressed individuals regularly try to join him by leaping to their doom from this well-known suicide spot. An open top bus runs half-hourly (late May to Sept; £6) from Eastbourne Pier to the top of Beachy Head.

West of the headland the scenery softens into a diminishing series of cliffs, a landmark known as the **Seven Sisters**. The eponymous country park provides some of the most impressive walks in the county, taking in the cliff-top path and the lower valley of the meandering River Cuckmere, into which the Seven Sisters subside. At **LITLINGTON**, five miles up the Cuckmere, the idyllic *Litlington Tea Gardens* provides a beautiful refreshment halt. On the opposite bank of the river in **ALFRISTON** is the wonderfully ancient timber-framed and thatched **Clergy House** (early to mid-March Sat & Sun 11am–4pm; late March to early Nov Mon, Wed, Thurs, Sat & Sun 10am–5pm; early Nov to late Dec Wed–Sun 11am–4pm £2.80; NT), built in the fourteenth century and the first property to be acquired by the National Trust in 1896. Less edifying, but potentially more fun for kids, a mile or so up the valley, is **Drusillas Park** (daily: April–Sept 10am–5pm; Oct–March 10am–4pm; £9.49; Ⓦwww.drusillas.co.uk), where visitors can get to look at penguins and meerkats, milk a cow, touch snakes, and lark about on the adventure playground and miniature railway.

If you'd rather stay round this neck of the woods than in Eastbourne, check in at the *Birling Gap Hotel* (ⓣ01323/423197; ❸), a Victorian villa overlooking the dramatic cliffs between Seven Sisters and Beachy Head, or bed down at the Frog Firle **youth hostel** (ⓣ0870/770 5666, ⓔalfriston@yha.org.uk; dorm bed £10.25) in a traditional Sussex flint building a couple of miles south of Alfriston, wonderfully set in the Cuckmere Valley.

Herstmonceux

Twelve miles northeast of Eastbourne is the huge partially moated, castellated castle of **Herstmonceux** (tours only; call ahead to confirm times ⓣ01323/833816; gardens mid-April to Oct daily 10am–6pm; tours £2.50, gardens £4.50; ⓦwww.herstmonceux-castle.com), whose Elizabethan grounds, featuring a formal walled garden and extensive woodland, make an ideal picnic spot. Tours are of a restricted area of the house only, as most of it forms part of Queen's University of Canada. Highlights include the Ballroom, Medieval Room and a stunning staircase – claimed to be one of the finest in the country – from the Elizabethan era, though most of the building has been extensively renovated and is very plain. Also in the grounds is the **Science Centre** (mid-April to Sept daily 10am–6pm; Oct daily 10am–5pm; £5.40; combined ticket with castle grounds £8.90; ⓦwww.science-project.org), former home of the Royal Observatory, which moved here from Greenwich in the 1950s to escape the postwar smog and light pollution, only to be forced to leave for the clearer skies over the Pacific Ocean in the 1980s. The observatory's domes and telescopes are now open to the public and make an enjoyable day's outing for budding astronomers.

Lewes and around

East Sussex's county town, **LEWES** straddles the River Ouse as it carves a gap through the South Downs on its final stretch to the sea. Though there's been some rebuilding in the riverside Cliffe area (the place where Lewes started), and new housing estates are spreading from the town's fringes, the core of Lewes remains remarkably good-looking: Georgian and crooked older dwellings still line the High Street and the narrow lanes – or "Twittens" – lead off this main street and its continuations, with views onto the downs. With some of England's most appealing chalkland right on its doorstep, and numerous traces of a history that stretches back to the Saxons, Lewes is a worthwhile stopover on any tour of the southeast – and an easy one, with good rail connections with London and along the coast.

Following the Norman Conquest, William's son-in-law, William de Warenne, built a priory and castle here, the latter still dominating the High Street. In 1264 Henry III's incompetence caused a baronial revolt led by Simon de Montfort which culminated in the king's surrender at the Battle of Lewes, although de Montfort and his reduced force were annihilated within a year at the Battle of Evesham. De Montfort's name crops up all over the town, as do references to the Lewes Martyrs, the seventeen Protestants burned here in 1556, at the height of Mary Tudor's militant revival of Catholicism – an event commemorated in spectacular fashion every November 5 (see box opposite). Intellectual non-conformity is something of a Lewes trademark, its roll call of free-thinkers featuring pioneer paleontologist Gideon Mantell and the radical humanist Tom Paine, whose *Common Sense* and *The Rights of Man* inspired or

The bonfire societies

Each November 5, while the rest of Britain lights small domestic bonfires or attends municipal firework displays to commemorate the 1605 foiling of a Catholic plot to blow up the Houses of Parliament (see p.83), Lewes puts on a more dramatic show, whose origins lie in the deaths of the town's Protestant martyrs. By the end of the eighteenth century, Lewes' **Bonfire Boys** had become notorious for the boisterousness of their anti-Catholic demonstrations, in which they set off fireworks indiscriminately and dragged rolling tar barrels through the streets – a tradition still practised today, although with a little more caution. In 1845 events came to a head when the incorrigible pyromaniacs of Lewes had to be read the Riot Act, instigating a night of violence between the police and Bonfire Boys. Lewes' first **bonfire societies** were established soon afterwards, to try to get a bit more discipline into the proceedings, and in the early part of the last century they were persuaded to move their street fires to the town's perimeters.

Today's tightly knit bonfire societies, each with its quasi-militaristic motto ("Death or Glory", "True to Each Other", etc), spend much of the year organizing the Bonfire Night shenanigans, when their members dress up in traditional costumes and parade through the town carrying flaming torches, before marching off onto the downs for their society's big fire. At each of the fires, effigies of Guy Fawkes and the pope are burned alongside contemporary, but equally reviled, figures – chancellors of the exchequer and prime ministers are popular choices.

supported the revolutions in France and America. The conservative spirit triumphed in 1914, however, after a pair of local enthusiasts commissioned a version of Rodin's majestic sculpture *The Kiss*, depicting Paolo and Francesca – lovers from Dante's *Inferno* – clinched in a full-on embrace. Local sentiment was outraged when the piece was unveiled in Lewes town hall, leading to its rapid removal amid a flurry of controversy (the sculpture was re-exhibited in the town hall in 1999, 85 years after the scandal).

Within a few miles of Lewes lies a trio of places worth visiting: two houses associated with the Bloomsbury group – **Rodmell** and **Charleston** – and the mecca for picnicking opera lovers, **Glyndebourne**.

The Town

The best way to begin a tour of the town from the train station is to walk up Station Road, then left down the High Street. Lewes's **Castle** (Mon–Sat 10am–5.30pm, Sun 11am–5.30pm; closed Mon in Jan; winter closes at dusk; £4.20; Ⓦwww.sussexpast.co.uk) is hidden from view behind the houses on your right. Inside the castle complex – unusual for being built on two mottes, or mounds – the shell of the eleventh-century keep remains, and both the towers can be climbed for excellent views over the town to the surrounding downs. Tickets for the castle include admission to the **museum** (same hours as castle), by the castle entrance, which is much better than the usual stuffy town museum.

A few minutes' walk further west along the High Street, past St Michael's Church with its unusual twin towers, one wooden and the other flint, brings you to the steep cobbled and much photographed **Keere Street**, down which the reckless Prince Regent is alleged to have driven his carriage. Keere Street leads to **Southover Grange** (Mon–Sat 8am–dusk, Sun 9am–dusk; free), with its lovely gardens. Built in 1572 from the priory's remains, the Grange was also the childhood home of the diarist John Evelyn and now houses the local

Registry Office. Past the gardens, a right turn down Southover High Street leads to the Tudor-built **Anne of Cleves House** (Tues–Sat 10am–5pm, Mon, Sun & public holidays 11–5pm; Nov–Feb closed Mon; £2.80; combined ticket with the castle £5.80; Ⓦ www.sussexpast.co.uk), given to her in settlement after her divorce from Henry VIII – though she never actually lived there. The magnificent oak-beamed Tudor bedroom is impressive, with its cumbersome "bed wagon", a bed-warming brazier which would fail the slackest of fire regulations and which the 400-year-old Flemish four-poster has managed to survive. The house's decor dates from the sixteenth century when the Wealden iron industry was flourishing and Sussex produced most of England's iron, with Lewes being a centre of cannon manufacture.

On the opposite side of the road and closer to the train station is the church of **St John the Baptist**, with its squat, brick tower capped by a six-foot shark for a weather vane; inside there's some superb stained glass and a tiny chapel with the lead coffins of William de Warenne and his wife Gundrada, William I's daughter. De Warenne was one of the six barons presiding over the new administrative provinces – known as the **Rapes of Sussex** – created by the Normans soon after the Conquest. Behind the church are the ruins of de Warenne's **St Pancras Priory**, once one of Europe's principal Cluniac institutions, with a church the size of Westminster Abbey. Sadly it was dismantled to build town houses following the Dissolution and is now an evocative ruin surrounded by playing fields.

Back in the town centre, the **Star Brewery Studio** off Fisher St, north of the High Street, displays the creative talents of a collective of artists, bookbinders, carpenters and other artisans; the attached **Star Gallery** (Mon–Sat 10.30am–5.30pm; free) presents a changing series of exhibitions. At the east end of the High Street, School Hill descends towards **Cliffe Bridge**, built in 1727 and entrance to the commercial centre of the medieval settlement. For the energetic, a path leads up onto the downs from the end of Cliffe High Street – site of England's worst avalanche disaster in 1836, when a bank of snow slid onto Cliffe village, killing eight people. The path passes close to an obelisk, commemorating the town's seventeen Protestant martyrs.

Practicalities

The **train station**, south of High Street down Station Road, has regular services from London Victoria and along the coast to Brighton, Eastbourne, Hastings. Buses leave from the **bus station** on Eastgate Street near the foot of School Hill. The **tourist office** is at the junction of the High Street and Fisher Street (April–Sept Mon–Fri 9am–5pm, Sat 10am–5pm, Sun 10am–2pm; Oct–March Mon–Fri 9am–5pm, Sat 10am–2pm; Ⓣ 01273/483448, Ⓦ www.lewes.gov.uk). While there, pick up a copy of the free monthly **listings magazine**, *Lewes News*, for details of events in the town.

For **accommodation** try *Castle Banks Cottage*, 4 Castle Banks (Ⓣ 01273/476291, Ⓦ www.s-h-systems.co.uk; no smoking; no credit cards; ❸), a beamed period house with great views, tucked away off West Street. The *Crown Inn*, 191 High St, close to the tourist office (Ⓣ 01273/480670, Ⓦ www.s-h-systems.co.uk; ❸), is a reasonable fallback. The nearest **youth hostel** is in the village of Telscombe, six miles south of Lewes (see opposite); there's another – a rustic wooden cabin with basic facilities – eleven miles northeast of town at Blackboys, near Uckfield (Ⓣ 0870/770 5698; dorm bed £10.25; ❶).

Lewes is home of the excellent Harvey's brewery and most of the pubs serve its wares – try the *Brewers' Arms*, opposite St John the Baptist or the *Lewes Arms* tucked behind the Star Brewery Studio. The lively *Snowdrop Inn* on the outskirts of the town at South Street also serves excellent **food** including vegetarian and vegan options. Other alternatives are the inexpensive Indian *Dilraj,* 12 Fisher St (ⓣ01273/479279) and *Pailin Thai* restaurant, at 19–20 Station St (ⓣ01273/473906), while opposite at no. 13 *Stoyan* (ⓣ01273/476707; closed Sun and Mon lunch), offers moderately priced Mediterranean food. If you go for the more upmarket and very contemporary *Circa* (ⓣ01273/471777; closed Mon) at 145 High St, a two-course lunch will set you back £11.75 and a three-course dinner £27.50. A snack in the gardens at *Southover Grange* (March–Oct daily 9am–5pm), however, will cost a fraction of that.

Glyndebourne

Glyndebourne, Britain's only unsubsidized opera house, is situated near the village of Glynde, three miles east of Lewes. Founded in 1934, the Glyndebourne season (mid-May to Aug) is an indispensable part of the high-society calendar, with ticket prices and a distribution system that excludes all but the most devoted opera-lovers. On one level, Glyndebourne is a repellent spectacle, its lawns thronged with gentry and corporate bigwigs ingesting champagne and smoked salmon – the productions have massive intervals to allow an unhurried repast. On the other hand, the musical values are the highest in the country, using young talent rather than expensive star names, and taking the sort of risks Covent Garden wouldn't dream of taking – for example, *Porgy and Bess* is now taken seriously as an opera largely as a result of a great Glyndebourne production. The recent arrival of a new, award-winning theatre (seating 1200) has broadened the appeal of this exclusive venue to a wider audience. There are tickets available at reduced prices for dress rehearsals or for standing-room-only tickets; call ⓣ01273/813813 for details or check the website at ⓦwww.glyndebourne.com.

Rodmell and around

Three miles south of Lewes lies the village of **RODMELL**, whose main source of interest is the **Monk's House** (April–Oct Wed & Sat 2–5.30pm; £2.60; NT), former home of Virginia Woolf, a leading figure of the Bloomsbury Group (see box p.228). She and her husband, Leonard, moved to the weatherboarded cottage in 1919 and Leonard stayed there until his death in 1969; both Virginia's and Leonard's remains are interred in the gardens. Nearby, you can see the River Ouse where Virginia killed herself in 1941 by walking into the water with her pockets full of stones. The house's interior is nothing special and will only really be of interest to ardent Bloomsbury fans; admirers can look round the study where Virginia wrote several of her novels, and her bedroom which is laid out with period editions of her work. To get there, catch a train to Southease, from where it's a mile northwest to Rodmell village, across the river.

Three miles south of Rodmell, in the village of **TELSCOMBE**, is a quiet **youth hostel** (ⓣ0870/770 6062; £10.25), whose simple accommodation is in 200-year-old cottages; take bus #123 from Lewes.

Charleston Farmhouse

Six miles east of Lewes, off the A27, is another Bloomsbury Group shrine, **Charleston Farmhouse** (March–June, Sept & Oct Wed–Sun and public holidays 2–6pm; July & Aug Wed–Sat 11am–6pm, Sun & public holidays 2–6pm; £6; guided tours Wed–Sat; last entry 5pm; ⓦwww.charleston.org.uk), home to Virginia Woolf's sister Vanessa Bell, Vanessa's husband, Clive Bell, and her lover,

The Bloomsbury Group

The **Bloomsbury Group** were essentially a bevy of upper-middle-class friends, who took their name from the Bloomsbury area of London, where most of them lived before acquiring houses in the Sussex countryside. The group revolved around Virginia, Vanessa, Thoby and Adrian Stephen, who lived at 46 Gordon Square, the London base of the Bloomsbury Group. Thoby's Thursday evening gatherings and Vanessa's Friday Club for painters attracted a whole host of Cambridge-educated snobs who subscribed to Oscar Wilde's theory that "aesthetics are higher than ethics". Their diet of "human intercourse and the enjoyment of beautiful things" was hardly revolutionary, but their behaviour, particularly that of the two sisters (unmarried, unchaperoned, intellectual and artistic), succeeded in shocking London society, especially through their louche sexual practices (most of the group swung both ways).

All this, though interesting, would be forgotten were it not for their individual work. In 1922 Virginia declared, without too much exaggeration, "Everyone in Gordon Square has become famous": Lytton Strachey had been the first to make his name with *Eminent Victorians*, a series of unprecedentedly frank biographies; Vanessa, now married to the art critic Clive Bell, had become involved in Roger Fry's prolific design firm, Omega Workshop; and the economist John Maynard Keynes had become an adviser to the Treasury (he later went on to become the leading economic theorist of his day). The group's most celebrated figure, Virginia, married Leonard Woolf and became an established novelist; she and Leonard also founded the Hogarth Press, which published T.S. Eliot's *Waste Land* in 1922.

Eliot was just one of a number of writers, such as Aldous Huxley, Bertrand Russell and E.M. Forster, who were drawn to the interwar Bloomsbury set, but others, notably D.H. Lawrence, were repelled by the clan's narcissism and snobbish narrow-mindedness. Whatever their limitations, the Bloomsbury Group were Britain's most influential intellectual coterie of the interwar years, and their appeal shows little sign of waning – even now, scarcely a year goes by without the publication of the biography or memoirs of some Bloomsbury peripheral.

Duncan Grant. As conscientious objectors, the trio moved here during World War I so that the men could work on local farms (farm labourers were exempted from military service). The farmhouse became a gathering point for other members of the Bloomsbury Group, including the biographer Lytton Strachey, the economist Maynard Keynes and the novelist E.M. Forster. Duncan Grant continued to live in the house until his death in 1978. Unless it's a Sunday, you have to join a fifty-minute guided tour in order to view the interior of the farmhouse, where almost every surface is painted and the walls are hung with paintings by Picasso, Renoir and Augustus John, alongside the work of the markedly less talented residents. Many of the fabrics, lampshades and other artefacts bear the unmistakable mark of the Omega Workshop, the Bloomsbury equivalent of William Morris's artistic movement.

Brighton

Recorded as the tiny fishing village of Brithelmeston in the Domesday Book, **BRIGHTON** seems to have slipped unnoticed through history until the mid-eighteenth-century sea-bathing trend established it as a resort that has never looked back since. The fad received royal approval in the 1780s when the decadent Prince of Wales (the future George IV) began patronizing the town in the company of his mistress, thus setting a precedent for the "dirty weekend", Brighton's major contribution to the English collective consciousness. Trying to shake off this blowsy reputation, Brighton now highlights its Georgian charm, its upmarket shops and classy restaurants, and its thriving conference industry. Yet, however much it tries to present itself as a comfortable middle-class town (granted city status in 2000), the essence of Brighton's appeal is its faintly bohemian vitality, a buzz that comes from a mix of English holiday-makers, thousands of young foreign students from the town's innumerable language schools, a thriving gay community and an energetic local student population from the art college and two universities.

Arrival and information

Brighton is served by numerous trains from London's Victoria, London Bridge and King's Cross Thameslink stations. There are also regular services along the coast from Hastings, Eastbourne via Lewes, and from Portsmouth via Chichester. The **train station** is at the head of Queen's Road, which descends to the Clock Tower and then becomes West Street which eventually leads to the seafront – a distance of about half a mile. National Express and Southdown **bus services** arrive at Pool Valley **bus station**, tucked just in from the seafront on the south side of the Old Steine. Open-top **bus tours** (April–Oct; £6.50) operate on a circular route around the town and up and down the sea front, passing both the train station and tourist office – tickets are valid all day. If you're coming by car, make use of the car parks; vouchers, available from the tourist office and newsagents are required for on-street parking in the centre.

The **tourist office** is at 10 Bartholomew Square (June–Sept Mon–Fri 9am–5.30pm, Sat 10am–5pm, Sun 10am–4pm; Oct–May Mon–Sat 9am–5pm, Sun 10am–4pm, closed Sun Nov–Feb; ⓣ0906/7112255, ⓦwww.visitbrighton.com), behind the town hall on the southern side of the Lanes – the maze of narrow alleyways marking Brighton's old town.

Accommodation

You'll find most budget **accommodation** clustered around the **Kemp Town** district, to the east of the Palace Pier, with the more elegant and expensive hotels west of the town centre around Regency Square, opposite the West Pier. Many places offer reductions for stays of two nights or more and at weekends there's often a two-night stay minimum required. Brighton's official **campsite** is the *Sheepcote Valley* site (ⓣ01273/626546), just north of Brighton Marina; take bus #1 or #7 to Wilson Ave, or take the Volks railway and walk up Arundel Road to Wilson Avenue.

Hotels, B&Bs and guest houses

Adelaide 51 Regency Square ⓣ01273/205286, ⓦwww.s-h-systems.co.uk. Top-notch guest house in the fancier part of town. ❹

Ainsley House 28 New Steine ⓣ01273/605310, ⓦwww.ainsleyhotel.com. Friendly, upmarket guest house in an attractive Regency terrace. ❸

Arlanda 20 New Steine ⓣ01273/699300, ⓦwww.arlandahotel.co.uk. Plusher than average choice in New Steine, with wide price range depending on the room; the cheapest are on the top floor and quite poky. ❹

Ascott House 21 New Steine ⓣ01273/688085, ⓦwww.ascotthousehotel.com. Very comfortable traditional and bright guest house near the sea front. ❹

Cavalaire House 34 Upper Rock Gardens ⓣ01273/696899, ⓦwww.cavalaire.co.uk. Just off Marine Parade, with contemporary iron beds and triples and quads. No smoking. ❹

Four Seasons 3 Upper Rock Gardens ⓣ01273/673574, ⓦwww.hotel4seasons.co.uk. Bright and light B&B in the Kemp Town area, offering good vegetarian breakfast options. No smoking. ❹

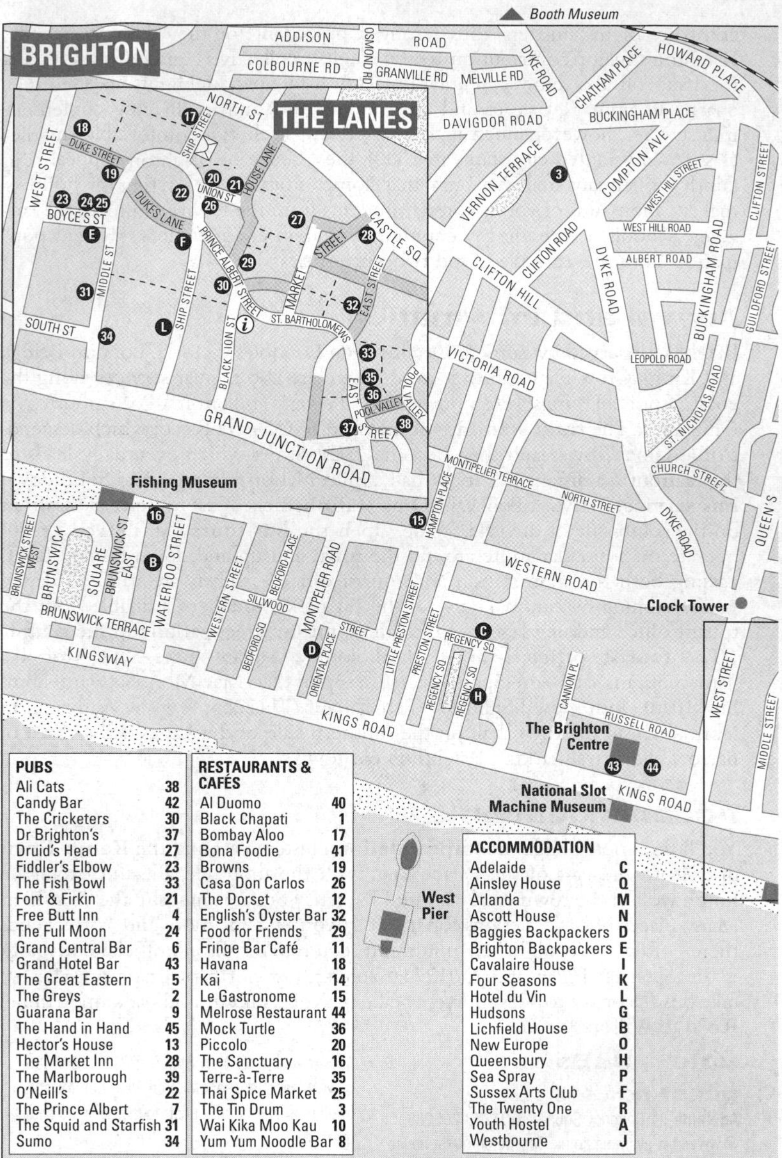

Hotel du Vin Ship St ⓣ01273/718588, ⓦwww.hotelduvin.com. A Gothic revival building in a contemporary style, luxuriously furnished in subtle seaside colours with an excellent bar and bistro. 7

Hudsons 22 Devonshire Place ⓣ01273/683642, ⓦwww.hudsonshotel.demon.co.uk. Relaxed and exclusively gay and lesbian guest house east of the centre off St James St. 4

Lichfield House 30 Waterloo St ⓣ01273/777740, ⓦwww.lichfieldhouse.freeserve.co.uk. Stylishly and colourfully furnished town house. 3

New Europe 31–32 Marine Parade ⓣ01273/624462, ⓦwww.neweuropehotel.co.uk.

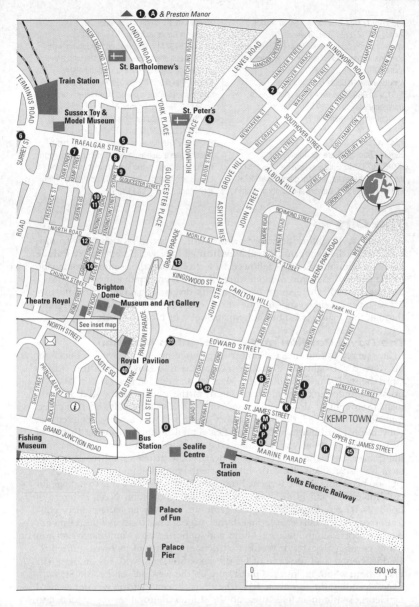

Large, buzzing, gay hotel on the seafront, with late bar and regular cabaret nights. ❹

Queensbury 58 Regency Square ⓣ01273/325558. Comfortable guest house in Brighton's definitive Georgian district. ❹

Sea Spray 25 New Steine ⓣ01273/680332, ⓦwww.seaspraybrighton.co.uk. Boutique hotel with themed rooms, breakfast in bed, and veggie and vegan options. ❺

Sussex Arts Club 7 Ship St ⓣ01273/727371, ⓦwww.sussexarts.com. Laid-back and lively hotel, though with just seven rooms, in a Regency house right in the centre of town. There's a pub on the ground floor and a club in the basement. ❺

The Twenty One 21 Charlotte St, off Marine Parade ⓣ01273/686450, ⓦwww.s-h-systems.co.uk. Classy Kemp Town B&B with very comfortable rooms in an ornate, early Victorian house. ❹

Westbourne 46 Upper Rock Gardens ⓣ01273/686920, ⓦwww.s-h-systems.co.uk. Traditional well-appointed B&B close to the seafront and all amenities. ❸

Hostels

Baggies Backpackers 33 Oriental Place ⓣ01273/733740. Spacious house a little west of the West Pier with large bright dorms, starting at £12 a night, decent showers and plenty of room to spread out. No credit cards. ❶

Brighton Backpackers 75 Middle St ⓣ01273/777717, ⓦwww.brightonbackpackers.com. Established independent hostel with a lively, easy-going atmosphere and vivid murals. An annexe just round the corner overlooks the seafront and offers a quieter alternative; dorm beds £11. No credit cards. ❶

Youth Hostel Patcham Place, London Rd ⓣ0870/770 5724, ⓔbrighton@yha.org.uk. Brighton's YHA hostel is housed in a splendid Queen Anne mansion, in parkland four miles north of the sea, close to the junction of the roads to Lewes and London. Take bus #5 or #5A from the town centre. Dorm bed £13.25.

The City

Any visit to Brighton inevitably begins with a visit to its two most famous landmarks – the exuberant **Royal Pavilion** and the wonderfully tacky **Palace Pier**, a few minutes away – followed by a stroll along the seafront promenade or the pebbly beach. Just as interesting, though, is an exploration of Brighton's car-free **Lanes**, where some of the town's diverse restaurants, bars and tiny bric-a-brac, jewellery and antique shops can be found, or an idle meander through the quaint, but more bohemian streets of **North Laine**.

The Royal Pavilion and the Brighton Museum

In any survey to find England's most loved building, there's always a bucketful of votes for Brighton's exotic extravaganza, the **Royal Pavilion** (daily: April–Sept 10am–5.45pm; Oct–March 10am–5.15pm; £5.80; ⓦwww.royalpavilion.org.uk), which flaunts itself in the middle of the Old Steine, a main thoroughfare along which most of the seafront-bound road traffic gets funnelled. Until 1787, the building that stood here was a well-appointed but conventional farmhouse, which was first rented by the fun-loving Prince of Wales in the previous year. He then commissioned its conversion into something more regal, and for a couple of decades the prince's south-coast pied-à-terre was a Palladian villa, with mildly oriental embellishments.

Upon becoming Prince Regent, however, George was fully able to indulge his taste for excess, and in 1815 his patronage fell upon John Nash, architect of London's Regent Street. What Nash came up with was an extraordinary confection of slender minarets, twirling domes, pagodas, balconies and miscellaneous motifs imported from India and China and supported on an innovative cast-iron frame, creating an exterior profile that defines a genre of its own – Oriental-Gothic. George had the time of his life here, frolicking with his mistress, Mrs Fitzherbert, whom he installed in a house on the west side of the Old Steine.

On ascending the throne in 1837 the dour Queen Victoria was not amused by George's taste in architecture, and she shifted the royal seaside residence to the Isle of Wight. All the Pavilion's valuable fittings were carted off to Buckingham and Kensington palaces and Victoria sold the gutted building to the town. The Pavilion was then pressed into a series of humdrum roles – tea room, hospital, concert hall, radar station, ration office – but has now been brilliantly restored, completely eradicating damage caused by an arson attack in 1975, and by the storm in October 1987, which hurled a dislodged minaret through the roof and floor of the nearly completed Music Room.

Inside the Pavilion the exuberant compendium of Regency exotica has been enhanced by the return of many of the objects that Victoria had taken away. One of the highlights – approached via the restrained Long Gallery – is the **Banqueting Room**, which erupts with ornate splendour and is dominated by a one-ton chandelier hung from the jaws of a massive dragon cowering in a plantain tree. Next door, the huge, high-ceilinged kitchen, fitted with the most modern appliances of its time, has iron columns disguised as palm trees.

Nearby, the stunning **Music Room**, the first sight of which reduced George to tears of joy, has a huge dome lined with more than twenty-six thousand individually gilded scales and hung with exquisite umbrella-like glass lamps. After climbing the famous cast-iron staircase with its bamboo-look banisters, you can go into Victoria's sober and seldom-used bedroom and the North Gallery where the king's portrait hangs, along with a selection of satirical cartoons. More notable, though, is the **South Gallery**, decorated in sky blue with trompe l'oeil bamboo trellises and a carpet that appears to be strewn with flowers.

Across the gardens from the Pavilion stands the **Dome**, once the royal stables and now the town's main concert hall. Adjoining it is the refurbished **Brighton Museum and Art Gallery** (Tues 10am–7pm, Wed–Sat & public holidays 10am–5pm, Sun 2–5pm; free; Ⓦwww.brighton.virtualmuseum.info), which is entered just around the corner on Church Street. It houses an eclectic mix of modern fashion and design, archeology, painting and local history, including a large collection of pottery from basic Neolithic earthenware to delicate porcelain figurines popular in the eighteenth century. The collection of classic Art Deco and Art Nouveau furniture stands out, the highlight being Dalí's famous sofa based on Mae West's lips. The *Balcony Café* is the perfect setting for a coffee or tea, perched above a sea of exhibits from which you can enjoy the lines of this lovingly restored Victorian building.

The Lanes and North Laine

Tucked between the Pavilion and the seafront is a warren of narrow, pedestrianized thoroughfares known as **the Lanes** – the core of the old fishing village from which Brighton evolved. Long-established antiques shops, designer outlets and several bars, pubs and restaurants generate a lively and intimate atmosphere in this part of town. **North Laine** – "laine" was the local term for a strip of land – which spreads north of North Street along Kensington, Sydney, Gardner and Bond streets, is more bohemian with its hub along pedestrianized Kensington Gardens. Here the shops are more eclectic, selling second-hand records, clothes, bric-a-brac and New Age objects, and mingle with earthy coffee shops and downbeat cafés. Slightly to the north of here is the **Sussex Toy and Model Museum** (Tues–Fri 10am–5pm, Sat 11am–5pm; £3.50; Ⓦwww.brightontoymuseum.co.uk), housed in an old stables underneath the train station. The collection is impressive, ranging from an entire cabinet full of Smurfs to a set of Pelham puppets, but it's the working model railways that are likely to be the focus of most children's attention.

The seafront

Although its western end holds appealing Georgian terraces and squares, much of Brighton's seafront is an ugly mix of shops, entertainment complexes and hotels, ranging from the impressively pompous plasterwork of the *Grand Hotel* – scene of the IRA's attempted assassination of the Conservative Cabinet in October 1984 – to the green-glass monstrosity of the *Brighton Thistle Hotel*. To appreciate fully the tackier side of Brighton, take a stroll along the **Palace Pier**, completed in 1899, whose every inch is devoted to fun and money-

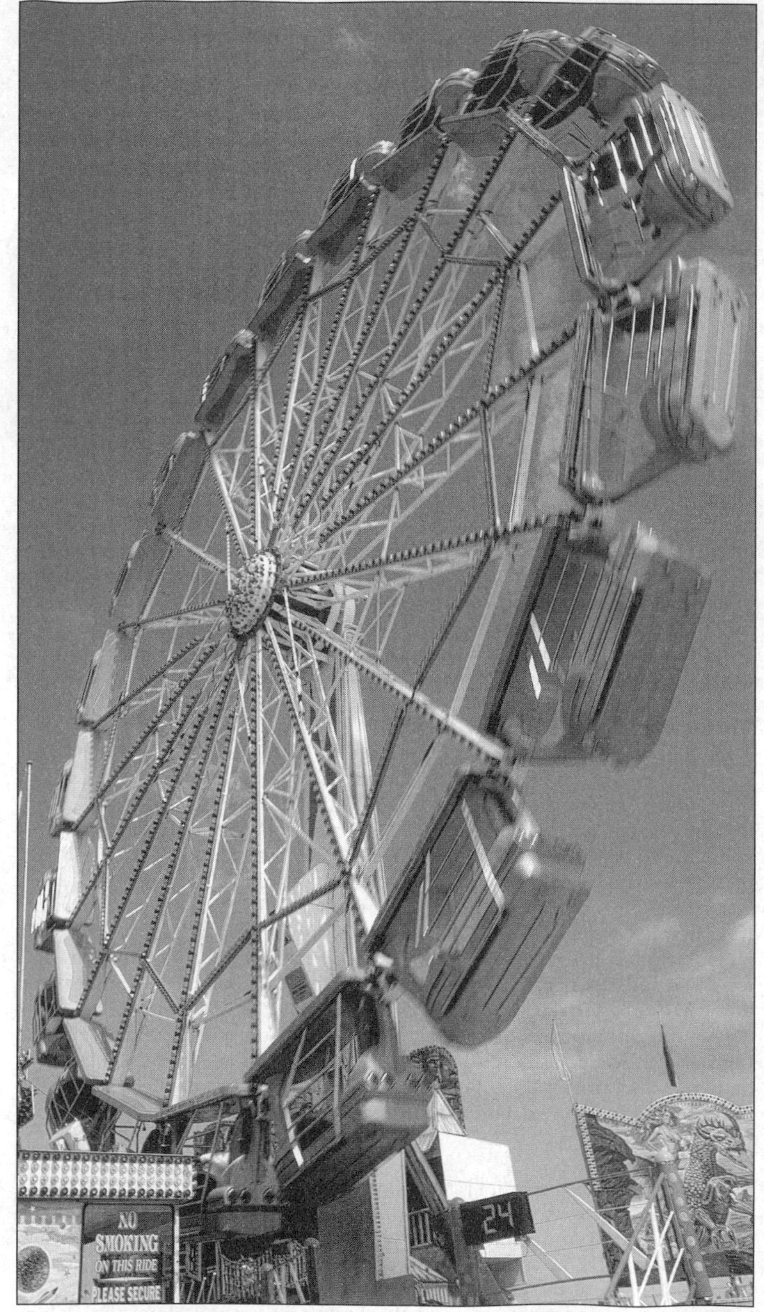

△ Funfair, Brighton

making, embracing the cacophonous Palace of Fun and the Pleasure Dome to the state-of-the-art video games and the fairground rides and karaoke sessions at the end of the pier. Brighton's architecturally superior West Pier, built in 1866 half a mile west along the seafront, was damaged in World War II and then fell into disrepair, suffering partial collapse in 2002 and a fire a year later, though it is still on course to be restored to its former glory by 2006.

Underneath the arches between the Palace and West piers, there are two small museums: the **National Museum of Penny Slot Machines** (Easter–Oct Sat, Sun & school holidays noon–6pm; also during school holidays daily 11am–6pm; free), which houses decrepit antique slot machines which struggle to function; and the **Brighton Fishing Museum** (May–Oct daily 10am–5pm; free), which has old photos and video footage of the golden days of the local fishing industry and shelters a large Sussex clinker, once a common boat on Brighton beach.

Across the road from the Palace Pier, on Marine Parade, is the **Sea-Life Centre** (daily 10am–5pm; £7.25; ⓦ www.sealife.co.uk), one of the best marine life displays of its kind, with a transparent tunnel passing through a huge aquarium – a walk along the bottom of the sea with sharks and rays gliding overhead. Nearby, the antiquated locomotives of **Volk's Electric Railway** (Easter to mid-Sept Mon–Fri 11am–5pm, Sat & Sun 11am–6pm; £2.40 return) – the first electric train in the country – run eastward towards the Marina and the nudist beach, usually the preserve of just a few thick-skinned souls. En route, you pass the **Madeira Lift** (Easter to mid-Sept 9.45am–7.15pm; free), a pagoda-like Victorian tower built in 1890 from which you can enjoy a great view over Brighton and out to sea.

St Bartholomew's, Booth Museum and Preston Manor

Towering above Anne Street (Mon–Sat 10am–1pm & 2–4.30pm), just east of the train station, the biggest brick church in Europe, **St Bartholomew's** (known locally as the Ark) deserves a brief inspection. Completed in 1894 and undivided by side aisles or chancel, the soaring nave contains a 45-foot-high marble baldacchino, dazzling figurative mosaics and intricate Art Nouveau metalwork.

In the north of Brighton's suburbs there are two museums worth a look. The big municipal museum, the **Booth Museum of Natural History** (Mon–Wed, Fri & Sat 10am–5pm, Sun 2–5pm; free; ⓦ www.booth.virtualmuseum.info), is a mile up Dyke Road from the centre of town (bus #26 or #26A). Purpose-built to house Mr E.T. Booth's prodigious collection of stuffed birds, this is a wonderfully fusty old Victorian museum with beetles, butterflies and animal skeletons galore, but which also displays very imaginative temporary shows.

The delightful **Preston Manor** (Mon 1–5pm, Tues–Sat 10am–5pm, Sun 2–5pm; £3.30; ⓦ www.prestonmanor.virtualmuseum.info) was originally built in 1250, though the present building dates from 1738 and 1905. Inside, a series of period interiors evokes the life of the Edwardian gentry, from the servants' quarters downstairs to the luxury nursery upstairs. The house is two miles north of Brighton on the A23, but only a short walk from Preston Park train station.

Eating, drinking and nightlife

Brighton has the greatest concentration of **restaurants** anywhere in the southeast, outside London. Around North Laine are some great, inexpensive cafés, while for classier establishments head to the Lanes and out towards neighbouring Hove. Many of the cheaper places fight hard to attract the large student market with discounted deals of around ten percent, so if you have student ID, use it.

Nightlife is hectic and compulsively pursued throughout the year, making Brighton unique in the sedate southeast. As well as the mainstream **theatre** and **concert** venues, there are myriad **clubs**, lots of **live music** and plenty of cinemas. Midweek entry into the clubs can cost just a couple of pounds and cinema seats are similarly priced before 6pm.

Every May the three-week-long **Brighton Festival** (ⓣ01273/709709, ⓦwww.brighton-festival.org.uk) takes place in various venues around town. This arty celebration includes funfairs, exhibitions, street theatre and concerts from classical to jazz. Running at the same time is the **Brighton and Hove Fringe Festival** (ⓣ01273/709709), which also stages live music and drama, literature readings and tons of club nights.

Brighton has one of the longest established and most thriving **gay communities** in Britain, with a variety of lively clubs and bars drawing people from all over the southeast. It also hosts a number of gay events including the annual **Gay Pride Festival**, held over two weeks at the beginning of July. It's a great excuse for a party with loads going on from performing arts to exhibitions, not to mention the **Brighton Parade**, a day-and-night-long jamboree. For details check out ⓦwww.gay.brighton.co.uk.

For up-to-date details of **what's on**, there's a an array of free listings magazines: the monthly *Insight* (ⓦwww.theinsight.co.uk), *What's On* (ⓦwww.getasociallife.co.uk) and *Source* or the more comprehensive *This is Brighton* are all available from the tourist office as is the similarly free *3Sixty* which covers gay events. If you've access to the Internet check out the highly praised **website** ⓦwww.brighton.co.uk. See "Listings" (p.239) for details of Brighton's Internet cafés.

Cafés

Bona Foodie 21 St James's St, Kemp Town. Delicatessen with colourful, cosy café at the back, serving excellent baguettes; choose from the speciality patés and cheeses or come early for lunching in.

The Dorset corner of Gardner St and North Rd. Bar, café and restaurant rolled into one, with delicious international vegetarian dishes. They also do real cream teas.

Fringe Bar Café 10 Kensington Gardens. Small, smart bar, with a terrace for watching life in the North Laine go by, serving good breakfasts, home-made burgers and salads. There's a restaurant below as well.

Kai 52 Gardner St. Fully organic café offering both wheat- and gluten-free options. No smoking.

Mock Turtle 4 Pool Valley. Old-fashioned teashop crammed with bric-a-brac and inexpensive home-made cakes. Closed Sun & Mon.

The Sanctuary 51–55 Brunswick St East, Hove ⓣ01273/770002. Cool and arty vegetarian café with a cosy, relaxed ambience and cellar performance venue. Deservedly popular, despite its not-very-central location.

Restaurants

Al Duomo 7 Pavilion Buildings ⓣ01273/326741. Brilliant pizzeria, with a genuine wood-burning oven. There's a more intimate sister restaurant, *Al Forno*, at 36 East St (ⓣ01273/324905). Inexpensive.

Black Chapati 12 Circus Parade ⓣ01273/699011. Innovative Asian cooking with Japanese and Thai influences as well as more conventional Indian dishes, which are brilliantly executed. Something of a Brighton landmark despite its out-of-the-way location, more than a mile inland, at the point where the London road enters town. Moderate.

Bombay Aloo 39 Ship St ⓣ01273/776038. No flock wallpaper and an all-you-can-eat veggie buffet for a fiver – what more could you ask for? Inexpensive.

Browns 3–4 Duke St ⓣ01273/323501. A mixture of meat, seafood and pasta dishes as well as traditional favourites like Guinness-marinated steak-and-mushroom pie, served in a sophisticated continental setting. Moderate.

Casa Don Carlos 5 Union St ⓣ01273/327177. Small, long-established tapas bar in the Lanes with outdoor seating and daily specials. Also serves more substantial Spanish dishes and drinks. Inexpensive.

English's Oyster Bar 29–31 East St ☎01273/327980. Three fishermen's cottages knocked together to house a marble and brass oyster bar and a red velvet dining room. Seafood's the speciality with a mouth-watering menu and better value than you might expect, especially the set menus. Expensive.

Food for Friends 17 Prince Albert St ☎01273/202310. Brighton's ever-popular wholefood veggie eatery is imaginative enough to please die-hard meat-eaters too. It's usually busy, but well worth the squeeze. Moderate.

Le Gastronome 3 Hampton Place ☎01273/777399. Well known for its good-value classic French cuisine, friendly service and outstanding selection of wines; a set dinner costs £22.95. Closed Sun & Mon. Moderate.

Havana 32 Duke St ☎01273/773388. Very stylish continental brasserie with just a hint of colonial ambience – palms and rattan chairs – to evoke tropical luxury and a feeling of being pampered. The menu is French influenced – the lunchtime deal is particularly good value. Expensive.

Melrose Restaurant 132 King's Rd ☎01273/326520. Traditional and decent seafront establishment that has been serving seafood, roasts and custard-covered puddings for over forty years. The *Regency Restaurant* next door is a similar and smaller option. Inexpensive.

Piccolo 56 Ship St ☎01273/380380. Informal Italian restaurant with pizza and pasta dishes from around £5 and special deals for students. Inexpensive.

Terre-à-Terre 71 East St ☎01273/729051. Imaginative, global, veggie cuisine in a modern arty setting. Closed Mon lunch. Moderate–Expensive.

Thai Spice Market 13 Boyce's St ☎01273/325195. Classical Thai interior and cuisine, serving meat, seafood and vegetarian varieties. Inexpensive to moderate. Closed Mon.

The Tin Drum 95–97 Dyke Rd ☎01273/777575. Buzzing continental-style café-bar and restaurant with a taste for Baltic-rim cooking and a blend of Eastern European influences; fresh seasonal ingredients and speciality vodkas. Moderate.

Wai Kika Moo Kau 11 Kensington Gardens ☎01273/671117. Slightly distressed decor at this funky global veggie café/restaurant with everything from Thai curry to aubergine bake – all for around £5. Inexpensive.

Yum Yum Noodle Bar 22–23 Sydney St ☎01273/606777. Serves anything Southeast Asian – Chinese, Thai, Indonesian and Malaysian noodle dishes at good-value prices – situated above a Chinese supermarket. Lunch only. Inexpensive.

Pubs and bars

Ali Cats 80 East St. Subterranean bar near the pier, serving good-value drinks and showing free films at 6pm.

Candy Bar 33 St James's St. Stylish lesbian hangout on two floors. Gay or straight men are welcomed as guests.

The Cricketers 15 Black Lion St. Just west of the Lanes, this is Brighton's oldest pub and it looks it too; very popular with good daytime pub grub served in the pleasant setting of its Courtyard Bar.

Dr Brighton's 16 King's Rd. Popular gay venue.

Druid's Head 9 Brighton Place. Great, old pub in the heart of the Lanes with a flagstone floor and local art on the walls.

Fiddler's Elbow 11 Boyce's St. Irish pub with traditional music on Wed nights.

The Fish Bowl 74 East St. A popular pre-club choice for its range of music – sometimes better than the clubs themselves – and a good daytime menu.

Font & Firkin Union St. Spacious converted chapel with a bar in place of the altar and occasional live music.

Free Butt Inn 1 Phoenix Place. Busy pub with a full calendar of live music.

The Full Moon 8 Boyce's St. A garish yellow and blue facade hides an airy interior where you can pick from a menu consisting of almost entirely organic food and beer.

Grand Central Bar 29–30 Surrey St. Cool, light and comfy bar opposite the station. Exemplary, well-priced breakfasts and snacks; live jazz and funk at weekends.

Grand Hotel Bar King's Rd. Swish surroundings for afternoon tea or (pricey) evening cocktail.

The Great Eastern 103 Trafalgar St. Relaxing pub with bare boards and bookshelves, lots of real ales and malt whiskies, and no fruit machines or TV.

The Greys 105 Southover St. Old-fashioned pub with an open fire, stone floors and wooden benches, plus good food and Belgian beers. Frequent live bands.

Guarana Bar 36 Sydney St. Brazilian-style daytime bar serving herbal cocktails and shakes made with guarana (extract of Amazonian vine).

The Hand in Hand 33 Upper St James St. An agreeable pub with its own brewery out the back.

Hector's House 52 Grand Parade. Big bare-boards-and-sofa student pub that has nightly pre-club music (except Mon) with in-house DJs.

The Market Inn 1 Market St. Old-fashioned real ale pub offering reasonably priced lunches and evening meals.
The Marlborough 4 Prince's St. Friendly pub with good food, just off Old Steine, popular with a gay and mixed crowd.
O'Neill's 27 Ship St. Big, popular Irish-themed pub with occasional live music.
The Prince Albert 48 Trafalgar St. A listed building, right by the train station, popular with students. Live rock upstairs, real ale downstairs; regular theme nights.
The Squid and Starfish 78 Middle St. A self-styled pre-club bar in pink and grey, with drinks from £1.90 a shot to fire you up for the night.
Sumo 8–12 Middle St. Designer-cool Pacific-rim bar with DJs spinning R&B and hip-hop plus Internet access too.

Clubs and live music venues

The Beach King's Road Arches ⓣ01273/722272, ⓦwww.thebeachbrighton.co.uk. House, anthems, Seventies funk and disco.
Brighton Gloucester 27 Gloucester Place ⓣ01273/688010, ⓦwww.thebrightongloucester.co.uk. Indie, classic pop and rock and school disco.
Casablanca 2 Middle St ⓣ01273/321817. Basement venue featuring live bands and all types of funk, including latin and jazz.
Club New York 11 Dyke Rd ⓣ01273/208678. Salsa seven nights a week upstairs and a mixture of everything from Sixties nights to highlife downstairs.
Concorde 2 Madeira Shelter, Madeira Drive ⓣ01273/772770, ⓦwww.concorde2.co.uk. Live music venue, with an admirable booking policy featuring everyone from Bert Jansch to Lemon Jelly; also has club nights at the weekend and regular early shows for young teenagers.
Escape 10 Marine Parade ⓣ01273/606906, ⓦwww.theescapeclub.co.uk. Brighton's trendiest nightclub packs them in night after night, specializing in funk and house.
Funky Buddha Lounge 169 King's Rd Arches ⓣ01273/725541. Tiny venue renowned for progressive house, breakbeats and soul.
Hanbury Ballroom St George's Rd, ⓣ01273/605789. Kemp Town's answer to mainstream clubs – anything from Japanese manga music to jamming on laptops, plus party nights.
Honey Club 214 King's Rd Arches ⓣ01273/202807, ⓦwww.thehoneyclub.co.uk. Garage, trance, house and hip-hop – and big name DJs.
The Jazz Place *Smugglers Inn*, 10 Ship St ⓣ01273/328439. Popular weekend jazz venue in the basement, with the livelier *Enigma* upstairs catering for active ravers.
The Joint 37 West St ⓣ01273/321692. Indie and disco sounds and a pole for dancing round.
Pool 8–9 Marine Parade ⓣ01273/624091. Small, smart gay club that puts on special nights and cabaret. Women's night on first and third Fri of month.
The Pressure Point 33 Richmond Place ⓣ01273/888846. Live bands, hip-hop and jungle, and comedy nights.
Revenge 32 Old Steine ⓣ01273/606064, ⓦwww.revenge.co.uk. The south's largest gay club with Mon night cabarets plus upfront dance and retro boogie on two floors.
Secrets 5 Steine St ⓣ01273/609672. This place pulls in the older gay crowd who don't merely want to dance all night.
Volks Tavern 3 The Colonnade, Madeira Drive ⓣ01273/682828, ⓦwww.volksclub.co.uk. Under the arches on Marine Parade you'll find a groovy crowd with live bands, reggae revival nights, hip-hop and breakbeats.
The Zap 180–192 Kings Rd Arches ⓣ01273/202407. Brighton's most durable club, right on the seafront spanning Seventies and Eighties disco and funky house; dress up.

Arts centres, theatres and comedy clubs

Brighton Dome 29 New Rd ⓣ01273/709709, ⓦwww.brighton-dome.org.uk. Three venues under one roof – Pavilion Theatre, Dome Auditorium and Corn Exchange – offering mainstream theatre, concerts, ballet and even Viennese tea dances.
Cinematheque 9–12 Middle St ⓣ01273/384300. Art-house cinema and exhibition space, with Internet facilities available.
Gardner Arts Centre University of Sussex, Falmer ⓣ01273/685861, ⓦwww.gardnerarts.co.uk. Performing and visual arts; theatre, cinema, workshops, exhibition space and café.
Komedia Gardner St, North Laine ⓣ01273/647100, ⓦwww.komedia.co.uk. Lively alternative theatre-café notable for its regular roll call of stand-up comedy and live music. Late bar.
Sussex Arts Club 7 Ship St ⓣ01273/727371, ⓦwww.sussexarts.com. Live bands, theatre and performance, plus exhibition space. The building includes a late bar and hotel too.
Theatre Royal New Rd ⓣ01273/328488. Mixture of mainstream and progressive plays, opera, musicals and one-man shows.

Listings

Banks and exchange There are branches of all the major high-street banks in the main shopping streets leading away from the Clock Tower. Exchanges include: American Express, 82 North St ☎01273/712901; Streetwise, Castle Square ☎01273/729948; and Thomas Cook, 58 North St ☎01273/367700.
Bike rental Freedom Bikes, 45 George St ☎01273/681698; Planet Cycle Hire, Madeira Drive ☎01273/695755; Sunrise Cycle Hire, West Pier, King's Rd Arches ☎01273/748881.
Books Borders, Churchill Square ☎01273/731122; Waterstone's, 71–74 North St ☎01273/327867.
Buses One Stop Travel, 16 Old Steine ☎01273/886200, Ⓦwww.buses.co.uk; and in the train station; National Express ☎08705/808080; Traveline ☎08706/082608
Car rental Affordable Car Hire, 1–2 Victoria Terrace, Kingsway, Hove ☎01273/724464; Hertz, 47 Trafalgar St ☎01273/738227.
Cinemas Duke of York's Picturehouse, Preston Circus ☎01273/602503; Odeon, West St ☎08705/505000; UCG Multiplex, Brighton Marina ☎08701/551145.
Dentist ☎01273/625691.
Hospital For emergencies Royal Sussex County, Eastern Rd ☎01273/696955.
Internet Curve 45 Gardner St, ☎01273/603031; Sumo 8–12 Middle St ☎01273/749465; Brighton Reference Library, Church St ☎01273/296968; Foobar, 37 Preston St ☎01273/227185; Internet Junction, 109 Western Rd ☎01273/772272 & 101 St George St ☎01273/607650.
Laundry Wash-a-Rama, 12 Elm Grove; Bubbles, 75 Preston St; KG Launderette, 116 St George's Rd.
Lesbian and Gay Switchboard Daily 5–11pm ☎01273/204050.
Pharmacies Ashton's, 98 Dyke Rd ☎01273/325020. Daily till 10pm.
Police John St, off Edward St, near the Pavilion ☎01273/607 0999.
Post offices 51 Ship St (Mon–Sat 9am–5.30pm).
Taxis ☎01273/205205, 204060 or 747474.
Travel agents Going Places, 34 West Mall, Churchill Square Shopping Centre ☎01273/329176 ; STA Travel, 38 North St ☎01273/728282; Thomas Cook, 58 North St ☎01273/367700.

Mid-Sussex

The principal attraction of **Mid-Sussex** is its wealth of fine gardens, ranging from the majestic **Sheffield Park** and the tree plantations of **Wakehurst**, to the luscious flowerbeds of **Nymans** and the landscaped lakes of **Leonardslee**. Exploring this region by public transport isn't really feasible unless you take your bike on the train; tourist information is thin on the ground too – it's best to get clued up at Brighton's tourist office beforehand, if you're interested in doing a thorough tour.

Sheffield Park and the Bluebell Railway

Around twenty miles northeast of Brighton lies the country estate of **Sheffield Park**, its centrepiece a Gothic mansion built for Lord Sheffield by James Wyatt. The house is closed to the public, but you can roam around the hundred-acre **gardens** (Jan & Feb Sat & Sun 10.30am–4pm; March–Oct Tues–Sun & public holidays 10.30am–6pm; Nov & Dec Tues–Sun 10.30am–4pm; £5; combined ticket with Bluebell Railway £11; NT), which were laid out by Capability Brown, the Christopher Wren of the grassy knoll. The gardens and pathways are based around a series of five landscaped ponds – vestiges of Sussex's industrial iron-smelting days. At their best in spring and autumn, the gardens feature a wide range of exotic plants and trees, with the taller conifers mimicking the house's spires.

A mile southwest of the gardens lies the southern terminus of the **Bluebell Railway** (May–Sept daily; Oct–April Sat, Sun & school holidays; day ticket

£8.50; Ⓣ01825/722370 24hr information line; Ⓦwww.bluebellrailway.co.uk), whose vintage steam locomotives chuff nine miles north via Horsted Keynes to Kingscote. Although the service gets extremely crowded at weekends – especially in May, when the bluebells blossom in the woods through which the line passes – it's an entertaining and nostalgic way of travelling through the Sussex countryside and your day ticket lets you go to and fro as often as you like. A vintage bus service connects the northern terminus of Kingscote (no car access) with East Grinstead train station (hourly trains from London Victoria), though this will be unnecessary when the remaining two miles of track have been extended and link the Bluebell directly with East Grinstead.

Wakehurst Place and Nymans

Wakehurst Place, eighteen miles north of Brighton (daily: Feb & Oct 10am–5pm; March 10am–6pm; April–Sept 10am–7pm; Nov–Jan 10am–4pm; £7; NT), is the country home of Kew Royal Botanic Gardens (Ⓦwww.kew.org). Guided tours take place at 11.30am throughout the year and at 2.30pm (2pm in winter) at weekends. The 180-acre site is given over mainly to trees and shrubs but, like many gardens in the area, was badly hit by the 1987 storm when it lost more than fifteen thousand trees. However, the collection has been gradually replenished and now features a variety of horticultural environments, including a Himalayan Glade and an Asian Heath Garden. The gardens spread down from the Jacobean mansion to beyond Westwood lake, from where paths then lead back to the house, making a pleasant hour-and-a-half's round walk. Wakehurst's newest development is the Millennium Seed Bank whose aim is to safeguard some 24,000 plant species by cleaning and then freezing the seeds in underground vaults. The nearest station is Haywards Heath, on the London–Brighton line, from where you can catch daily buses #81 or #82.

For one of the southeast's greatest gardens, head five miles southwest of Wakehurst Place to **Nymans** (March to early Nov Wed–Sun 11am–6pm; £6.20; early Nov to Feb Sat & Sun 11am–4pm; NT), near the village of Handcross; bus #273 from Brighton to Crawley can drop you off on the A23 beside the village. Created by Ludwig Messel, an inspired gardener and plant collector, the gardens contain a valuable collection of exotic trees and shrubs as well as more everyday plants, of which the colourful rhododendrons are particularly prolific. Nymans consists of a series of different enclosures and gardens, the highlight of which is the large, romantic walled garden, almost hidden from sight by an abundance of climbing plants and housing a collection of rare Himalayan magnolia trees. The gardens are centred on the picturesque ruins of a mock-Tudor manor house, now covered in wisteria, roses and honeysuckle, and are laced with gently sloping paths linking the huge beds of rhododendrons, azaleas and roses.

Leonardslee Gardens

The most picturesque of all the mid-Sussex gardens are those at **Leonardslee** (daily: April–Oct 9.30am–6pm, last admission 4.30pm; £5, £7/£8 in May; Ⓦwww.leonardslee.com), four miles southwest of Nymans, near the village of Crabtree; bus #107 from Brighton to Horsham passes by the garden gates. Set in a wooded valley, the seventy-acre gardens are crisscrossed by steep paths, which link six lakes created – like those at Sheffield Park – in the sixteenth century to power waterwheels for iron foundries. The range of flora is especially impressive here, featuring many hybrid species of rhododendron that were created specifically for this garden and are at their best in May. Wallabies, sika and fallow deer roam freely, adding to the Edenic atmosphere. There are also exhibitions of a miniature country estate and full-size motor cars, both from the Victorian era.

Arundel and around

The hilltop town of **ARUNDEL**, eighteen miles west of Brighton, has for seven centuries been the seat of the dukes of Norfolk, whose fine castle looks over the valley of the River Arun. The medieval town's well-preserved appearance and picturesque setting draws in the crowds on summer weekends, but at any other time a visit reveals one of West Sussex's least spoilt old towns. Arundel also has a unique place in English cricket: traditionally, the first match of every touring side is played against the Duke of Norfolk's XI on the ground beneath the castle and other matches are played regularly throughout the summer. North of here lie two contrasting sites: **Bignor Roman Villa**, containing some of the best Roman mosaics in the country, and the grand seventeenth-century **Petworth House**, replete with an impressive collection of paintings.

The Town

Arundel Castle, towering over the High Street (April–Oct Mon–Fri & Sun noon–5pm; castle, grounds & chapel £9; grounds & chapel £3.50; Ⓦ www.arundelcastle.org), is what first catches the eye and, despite its medieval appearance, most of what you see is little more than a century old. The structure dates from Norman times, but was ruined during the Civil War, then lavishly reconstructed from 1718 onwards by the eighth, eleventh and fifteenth dukes. From the top of the keep, you can see the current duke's spacious residence and the pristine castle grounds. Inside the castle, the renovated quarters include the impressive **Barons Hall** and the **library**, which boasts paintings by Gainsborough, Holbein and Van Dyck. On the edge of the castle grounds, the fourteenth-century **Fitzalan Chapel** houses tombs of past dukes of Norfolk including twin effigies of the seventh duke – one as he looked when he died and, underneath, one of his emaciated corpse. The Catholic chapel belongs to the Norfolk estate, but is actually physically joined to the **Church of St Nicholas**, the parish church, whose entrance is in London Road. It is separated from the altar of the main Anglican church by an iron grille and a glass screen. Although traditionally Catholics, the dukes of Norfolk have shrewdly played down their papal allegiance in sensitive times – such as during the Tudor era when two of the third duke's nieces, Anne Boleyn and Catherine Howard, became Henry VIII's wives.

West of the parish church, further along London Road, is Arundel's other major landmark, the towering Gothic bulk of **Arundel Cathedral** (April–Oct daily 9am–6pm; Nov–March 9am–dusk; Ⓦ www.arundelcathedral.org). Constructed in the 1870s by the fifteenth duke of Norfolk over the town's former Catholic church, the cathedral's spire was designed by John Hansom, inventor of the hansom cab, the earliest taxi. Inside are the enshrined remains of St Philip Howard, the fourth duke's son, exhumed from the Fitzalan Chapel after his canonization in 1970. Following his wayward youth, Howard returned to the Catholic fold at a time when the Armada's defeat saw anti-Catholic feelings soar. Caught fleeing overseas and sentenced to death for praying for Spanish victory, he spent the next decade in the Tower of London, where he died. The cathedral's impressive outline is more appealing than the interior, but it fits in well with the townscape of the medieval seaport.

The rest of Arundel is pleasant to wander round, with the antique-shop-lined Maltravers and Arun streets being the most attractive thoroughfares. Halfway up the High Street, in the same building as the tourist office, is the **Arundel Heritage Museum** (April–Sept Mon–Sat 10am–4pm, Sun 10am–2pm; Oct Sat 10am–4pm & Sun 10am–2pm; £1), a surprisingly interesting local museum with a history of medicine on the ground floor and lots of information on Arundel's days as a busy port, once connected by canal to Weybridge on the Thames.

Practicalities

Arundel is served by regular trains from London Victoria, Portsmouth, Brighton and Chichester. The **train station** is half a mile south of the town centre over the river on the A27, with **buses** arriving either on High Street or River Road. The **tourist office** is at 61 High St (April–Oct Mon–Sat 10am–6pm, Sun 10am–4pm; Nov–March daily 10am–3pm; ⓣ01903/882268, ⓦwww.sussexbythesea.com). **Boat rental** and riverboat **cruises** upstream to the village of Amberley, with its impressive castle (now a hotel, see below) are available from *Skylark Cruises* (ⓣ01903/717337) by the bridge.

In the centre of town, the best **accommodation** options are the ornate rooms of the genial Georgian *Town House*, 65 High St (ⓣ01903/883847, ⓦwww.thetownhouse.co.uk; ❹) or the elegant eighteenth-century *Byass House*, 59 Maltravers St (ⓣ01903/882129, ⓦwww.byasshouse.co.uk; no credit cards; ❹) further up the hill. Less expensive is *Woodpeckers*, 15 Dallaway Rd (ⓣ01903/883948; no smoking; no credit cards; ❷) a modern house on the outskirts of town. For a real splurge, head for Amberley, four miles north, where you can get a luxury double room at the 600-year-old *Amberley Castle* (ⓣ01798/831992, ⓦwww.amberleycastle.co.uk; ❼). Arundel's **youth hostel** (ⓣ0870/770 5676; dorm bed £11.50) is in a large Georgian house by the river at Warningcamp, a mile and a half northeast of town. You can **camp** at the hostel, or try the *Maynards* site (ⓣ01903/882075) at the top of the hill on the A27 two miles southeast of town.

If your pocket is up to it, first choice for **food** is the *Town House* (see above; closed Mon) where you dine under a spectacular Italian gilded ceiling. Otherwise try *The Muse* (ⓣ01903/883477; closed Sun eve & Mon) at 2–8 Castle Mews, or the restaurant attached to the *White Hart* pub over the river at 3 Queen St (ⓣ01903/882374). The *Red Lion*, on High St has solid pub grub and real ales, *Butlers Wine Bar*, 25 Tarrant St (ⓣ01903/882222; closed Sun eve), complete with an indoor vine, is a popular choice for steak-lovers, while further down the same road at no. 41, *The Eagle* is the best real-ale **pub** in town. A ten-minute stroll from the bridge along Mill Road takes you to the very popular *Black Rabbit* set right beside the River Arun. Arundel's **festival** takes place throughout the last week in August in a variety of locations around the town and features everything from open air theatre to salsa bands. For details see ⓦwww.arundelfestival.co.uk.

Bignor and Petworth

Six miles north of Arundel, the excavated second-century ruins of the **Bignor Roman Villa** (March & April Tues–Sun 10am–5pm; May & Oct daily 10am–5pm; June–Sept daily 10am–6pm; £3.50) include some well-preserved mosaics, of which the Ganymede is the most outstanding. The site, first excavated between 1811 and 1819, is superbly situated at the base of the South Downs and features the longest extant section of mosaic in England, as well as the remains of a hypocaust, the underfloor heating system developed by the Romans.

Adjoining the pretty little village of **PETWORTH**, replete with antiques shops, eleven miles north of Arundel, is **Petworth House** (April–Oct Mon–Wed, Sat & Sun 11–5.30pm; park daily 8am–dusk; £7, park free; NT), one of the southeast's most impressive stately homes. Built in the late seventeenth century, the house contains an outstanding art collection, with paintings by Van Dyck, Titian, Gainsborough, Bosch, Reynolds, Blake and Turner – the last a frequent guest here. Highlights of the interior decor are Louis Laguerre's murals around the **Grand Staircase** and the **Carved Room**, where work by Grinling Gibbons and Holbein's full-length portrait of Henry VIII can be seen. The seven-hundred-acre grounds were landscaped by Capability Brown and are considered one of his finest achievements. The extensive **Servants' Quarters**, connected by a tunnel to the main house, contain an impressive series of kitchens bearing the latest technological kitchen-ware of the 1870s. For an alternative and intriguing view of the life of one of the house's former employees, **Petworth Cottage Museum**, 346 High St (April–Oct Wed–Sun 2–4.30pm; £2.50), is well worth a call. This gas-lit abode was the home of Mary Cummings, erstwhile seamstress, and re-creates her home, using her own possessions, as it must have looked in 1910.

To get to Petworth by **public transport** from Arundel involves a train journey to Pulborough Station from where you can pick up the regular Stagecoach Coastline #1 bus. Petworth's **tourist office** is on the Market Square (April–Sept Mon–Sat 10am–5pm, Sun 11am–4pm; March & Oct Mon–Sat 10am–4pm; Nov & Dec Wed–Sat 10am–3pm; Jan & Feb Fri–Sat 10am–4pm; ⓣ01798/343523, ⓦwww.chichester.gov.uk). For a memorable night's **stay**, book in at the converted *Old Railway Station* (ⓣ01798/342346, ⓦwww.old-station.co.uk; ❺), two miles south of Petworth on the A285 Chichester road.

Chichester and around

The county town of West Sussex and its only city, **CHICHESTER** is an attractive, if stuffy, market town, which began life as a Roman settlement – the Roman cruciform street plan is still evident in the four-quadrant symmetry of the town centre, spread around the Market Cross. The city has built itself up as one of southern England's cultural centres, hosting the **Chichester Festival** (ⓦwww.chifest.org.uk) for two weeks in July; its focus is a fairly safe programme of middlebrow plays, though the studio theatre is a bit more adventurous; for the latest details check their website. The racecourse at **Goodwood Park**, north of the city, hosts one of England's most fashionable racing events at the same time (see box p.244). The Gothic cathedral is the chief permanent attraction in the city, but two miles west of the town are the restored Roman ruins of **Fishbourne**, one of the most visited ancient sites in the county. To the south is the flat headland of Selsey Bill, a dull section of coast, fringed with retirement estates for the well-to-do; if you want some fresh sea air, your best bet is to make for the inlets of **Chichester Harbour** or the Witterings, east of the harbour mouth, though there's little here of interest other than the sandy expanses of beach.

Horse racing in the southeast

A popular way to spend a day out in southeast England is to go to the races at one of the many tracks in the region. **Glorious Goodwood** and the **Derby week** are the fashionable meetings to attend, as is **Royal Ascot**, in Berkshire, but the less well-known courses, such as Brighton, Fontwell Park and Kempton Park, offer equally entertaining meetings throughout the year. For course locations, see the map on pp.168–9. Generally it'll cost you £5–10 to get into a "basic" enclosure, but you can pay much higher prices for admission into the grandstand and more exclusive enclosures, where the social event often takes precedence over the racing.

Ascot ⓣ01344/622211, ⓦwww.ascot.co.uk. Ten minutes' walk from Ascot train station. No account of racing in southeast England would be complete without Ascot, the jewel in the crown of English racecourses. Admission is rather expensive, but the facilities and atmosphere make it worth the price. The week-long Royal Meeting in mid-June is the one to attend, and to dress up for, with a selection of outrageous hats, outfits and royals on display, especially on Ladies' Day. The racecourse hosts less glamorous meetings throughout the rest of the year.

Brighton ⓣ01273/603580, ⓦwww.brightonracecourse.co.uk. Brighton train station with free connecting buses on race days; or local services #2, #21 or #22. Overlooking Brighton Marina at the east end of town, Brighton's racecourse has a U-shaped track and is one of the few courses in England that doesn't form a complete circuit; binoculars are useful and can be rented. The racecourse's situation, on top of the South Downs overlooking the English Channel, makes it particularly appealing for a day out. Up to twenty meetings take place from May to October every year with the three-day meeting in early August providing the best action.

Epsom Downs ⓣ01372/726311, ⓦwww.epsomderby.co.uk. Epsom Downs or Tattenham Corner train station with connecting buses on race days. Home of two of England's most famous races, the Derby and the Oaks, both of which take place during Derby week, the first week in June. The Derby has been run for nearly two hundred years and is the time when Epsom really comes alive – a fun day out for all. There are very few meetings at other times: evening meetings at the end of June and July and a two-day event at the end of August.

Fontwell Park ⓣ01243/543335, ⓦwww.fontwellpark.co.uk. Barnham train station with connecting buses on race days. Midway between Arundel and Chichester, Fontwell Park, which held its first meeting in the 1920s, is a lesser known racecourse

The City

The main streets lead off to the compass's cardinal points from the Gothic **Market Cross**, a bulky octagonal rotunda topped by ornate finials and a crown lantern spire, and built in 1501 to provide shelter for the market traders, although it appears far too small for its function.

A short stroll down West Street brings you to the neat form of the **Cathedral** (daily: Easter to mid-Sept 7.30am–7pm; mid-Sept to Easter 7.30am–5pm; ⓦwww.chichestercathedral.org.uk), whose slender spire – a nineteenth-century addition – is visible out at sea. Building began in the 1070s, but the church was extensively rebuilt following a fire a century later and has been only minimally modified since about 1300, except for the spire and the unique, free-standing fifteenth-century bell tower, which now houses the cathedral shop. The **interior** is renowned for its contemporary devotional art, which includes a stained-glass window by Marc Chagall and an enormous altar-screen tapestry by John Piper. Other points of interest are the sixteenth-century painting in the north transept of the past bishops of Chichester, and the fourteenth-

which makes it a friendly and welcoming venue for first-time race-goers. It's one of only two figure-of-eight racecourses in Britain. One-day meetings take place once or twice a month in May and from August to December, with around a dozen fixtures a year.

Goodwood Park ⓣ01243/774107, ⓦwww.goodwood.co.uk. Four miles from Chichester train station, with connecting buses on race days. Goodwood boasts a wonderful location, on a lush green hill overlooking Chichester with the South Downs as a backdrop. Even if you have only the mildest interest in the sport, and no interest in betting, it's worth a visit for the main meeting, Goodwood Week – or "Glorious Goodwood" to its fans; held in late July, it's second only to Ascot in its social cachet. There are plenty of other meetings from May to October.

Kempton Park ⓣ01932/782292, ⓦwww.kempton.co.uk. Five minutes' walk from Kempton Park train station. Just fifteen miles from London, this popular course has excellent facilities, including covered enclosures for inclement meetings; the majority of the fixtures are run on the flat. Racing takes place all year with evening meetings in April and from June to August. A highlight is the very popular two-day Christmas Festival which starts on Boxing Day.

Lingfield Park ⓣ01342/834800, ⓦwww.lingfield-racecourse.co.uk. Ten minutes' walk from Lingfield train station. This place has an all-weather synthetic track so races can be run here when they would have to be abandoned elsewhere, but unfortunately this hasn't really caught on with the public, and crowds are poor. If you want a lively atmosphere, stick to the turf (grass) events – especially the Turf National Hunt at the beginning of December and the Turf Flat in early May.

Plumpton ⓣ01273/890383, ⓦwww.plumptonracecourse.co.uk. A short walk from Plumpton train station. Eight miles out of Brighton, this course has one of the sharpest tracks in the country (leading to its being nicknamed the "Wall of Death"), with extremely tight bends and a downhill back straight. Facilities here are good and races take place from late September to April.

Sandown Park ⓣ01372/470047, ⓦwww.sandown.co.uk. Ten minutes' walk from Esher train station. Only fourteen miles from Central London, this hugely popular venue near Esher has been frequently voted "Racecourse of the Year". Atmosphere, an excellent location and superb facilities all add up to a great day's racing, with the "attheraces" Gold Cup towards the end of April and the Coral-Eurobet Stakes in early July bringing out the crowds and being well worth attending.

century Fitzalan tomb which inspired a poem by Philip Larkin, *An Arundel Tomb*. However, the highlight is a pair of reliefs in the south aisle, close to the tapestry – created around 1140, they show the raising of Lazarus and Christ at the gate of Bethany. Originally highly coloured, the reliefs once featured semi-precious stones set in the figures' eyes and are among the finest Romanesque stone carvings in England.

There are several fine buildings up **North Street**, including a dinky little Market House, built by Nash in 1807 and fronted by a Doric colonnade and a tiny flint Saxon church – now an ecclesiastical bookshop – with a diminutive wooden shingled spire. Finally, you come to the appealingly dumpy red-brick **Council House**, built in 1731, with Ionic columns and delightful intersecting tracery on its street facade, and crowned by a wonderful stone lion. East off South Street, in the well-preserved Georgian quadrant of the city known as the Pallants, you'll find **Pallant House Gallery**, 9 North Pallant (Tues–Sat 10am–5pm, Sun & public holidays 12.30–5pm; £4; ⓦwww.pallant.org.uk). Stone dodos stand guard over the gates of this fine mansion, which houses artefacts and furniture from the early eighteenth century. Modern works of art are also included, among them pieces by Henry Moore and Barbara Hepworth and Graham Sutherland's portrait of Walter Hussey, the former Dean of Chichester, who commissioned much of the cathedral's contemporary art.

Continuing in an anticlockwise direction around the town and crossing East Street to head north up Little London brings you to the **Chichester District Museum** (Tues–Sat 10am–5.30pm; free), housed in an old white weather-boarded corn store. Inside, the modest but entertaining display on local life includes a portable oven carried by Joe Faro, the city pieman, as well as the portable stocks used for the ritual humiliation of petty criminals. The **Guildhall** (June to mid-Sept Sat noon–4pm; free), a branch museum within a thirteenth-century Franciscan church in the middle of Priory Park, at the north end of Little London, has some well-preserved medieval frescoes. It was formerly a town hall and court of law, and the poet, painter and visionary William Blake was tried here for sedition in 1804.

If you're keen on exploring the harbour, take a **boat trip** with Chichester Harbour Water Tours (Ⓣ01243/786418, Ⓦwww.chichesterharbourwatertours.co.uk; £6).

Practicalities

A regular service runs from London Victoria to Chichester's **train station** on Stockbridge Road, with the **bus station** across the road at South Street. From either station it's a ten-minute walk north to the Market Cross, passing the **tourist office** at 29a South St (April–Sept Mon–Sat 9.15am–5.15pm, Sun 10am–4pm; Oct–March closed Sun; Ⓣ01243/775888, Ⓦwww.chichester.gov.uk). There's **Internet** access at the *Internet Junction*, a café at 2 Southdown Buildings next to the bus station.

Every other house on the main roads out of Chichester seems to offer B&B **accommodation**, so there's no problem finding a place to stay other than during the festival. If you want to splash out, try *The Ship Hotel*, North St (Ⓣ01243/778000, Ⓦwww.shiphotel.com; ❻), a comfortable and characterful inn in the centre of town. Less expensive central B&B options include the brick and flint *Riverside Lodge*, 7 Market Ave, outside the Pallants quarter (Ⓣ01243/783164, Ⓦwww.riverside-lodge-chichester.co.uk; no smoking; no credit cards; ❷), or the 200-year-old *Friary Close*, Friary Lane (Ⓣ01243/527294, Ⓦwww.tuckedup.com; ❸), just inside the city wall. You can **camp** at the *Red House Farm*, Brookers Lane, Earnley (Ⓣ01243/512959; closed Nov–Easter), six miles southwest of town, a mile or so from the beach.

As well as offering excellent accommodation, *The Ship* is a good place for a **drink**, or you could try *The Park Tavern*, a convivial pub, serving excellent Gale's ales on Priory Lane, overlooking Priory Park. *The Fountain Inn*, a fourteenth-century pub at the top of Southgate, makes an excellent alternative. For something to **eat**, both the *Toad* pub, formerly a church in West Street and a lively spot for snacks and meals, and the intimate but more expensive *Café Coco*, 13 South St (Ⓣ01243/786989; closed Sun), specializing in French cuisine, are close to the cathedral. Chichester's best Indian is the aptly named *Little London Indian Restaurant*, 38 Little London, off East St (Ⓣ01243/537550), and further east, *Sadlers Wine Bar and Restaurant* (Ⓣ01243/774765) at 42 East St offers innovative modern English cooking. *Purchase's Wine* Bar, 31 North St (Ⓣ01243/537532; closed Sun), serves a good selection of Danish open sandwiches, patés and salads.

Fishbourne Roman Palace

Fishbourne, two miles west of Chichester (March–July, Sept & Oct daily 10am–5pm; Aug daily 10am–6pm; Nov, Dec & Feb Sat & Sun 10am–4pm; £5; Ⓦ www.sussexpast.co.uk), is the largest and best-preserved Roman palace in the country. Roman relics have long been turning up in Fishbourne and in 1960 a workman unearthed their source – the site of a depot used by the invading Romans in 43 AD which is thought later to have become the vast, hundred-room palace of the Romanized Celtic aristocrat, Cogidubnus. A pavilion has been built over the north wing of the excavated remains, where floor mosaics depict Fishbourne's famous dolphin-riding cupid as well as the more usual geometric patterns.

Like the more evocative remains at Bignor (see p.242), only the residential wing of the former quadrangle has been excavated – other parts of the dwelling fulfilled mundane service roles and probably lacked the mosaics that give both sites their singular appeal. The underfloor heating system has also been well restored and an audiovisual programme gives a fuller picture of the palace as it was in Roman times. The extensive gardens attempt to re-create the appearance of the palace grounds as they would have been then.

To get to Fishbourne take the train from Chichester to Fishbourne Station, turn right as you leave the station and the palace is a few minutes' walk away.

Tangmere Military Aviation Museum

Three miles east of Chichester, signposted off the A27, is **Tangmere Military Aviation Museum** (Feb & Nov daily 10am–4.30pm; March–Oct daily 10am–5.30pm; £4; Ⓦ www.tangmere-museum.org.uk), sited at one of England's earliest airfields, which was established in 1917 and closed in 1970. On display are a number of aircraft including replicas of the legendary Hurricane and Spitfire fighters that took off from Tangmere airfield during the Battle of Britain. Early supersonic jets are also housed, with a display about Neville Duke whose Hawker Hunter reached 727mph along the nearby coast in the early 1950s. Up the road the *Bader Arms* is a reasonable **pub**, which commemorates the famous Battle of Britain pilot Douglas Bader who lost both his legs in a 1931 stunt accident, yet fought in the war, survived being shot down, and continued flying afterwards. To get to Tangmere, take bus #58 from Chichester.

Goodwood House and Sculpture at Goodwood

Three miles north of Chichester lies **Goodwood House** (April–July, Sept & Oct Sun & Mon 1–5pm; Aug Mon–Thurs & Sun 1–5pm; closed on racing days; £7; Ⓦ www.goodwood.co.uk), an imposing Regency mansion set in the heart of a 12,000-acre estate and home to the dukes of Richmond for three hundred years. In addition to collections of furniture and porcelain, the house's highlights include Canaletto's views from the family's London home and paintings of the family's horses by Stubbs. Just to the east of Goodwood House, **Sculpture at Goodwood** (April–Oct Thurs–Sat 10.30am–4.30pm; £10; Ⓦ www.sculpture.org.uk) is an absolute must for anyone interested in contemporary art – the entry fee appears deliberately designed to put off casual punters. Since 1994 Wilfred and Jeanette Cass, long-time collectors of sculpture, have created a unique woodland environment for more than forty large-scale works, some of which have been specially commissioned and each of which is sited to allow you to appreciate it in isolation. The selection of pieces on display changes from year to year, but has been known to include Turner Prize winners.

Weald and Downland Open-Air Museum

Five miles north of Chichester, the **Weald and Downland Open-Air Museum** (March–Oct daily 10.30am–6pm; Nov–Feb Sat & Sun 10.30am–4pm; £7; ⓣ01243/811363, ⓦwww.wealddown.co.uk), just outside the village of Singleton, is one the best rural museums in the southeast. More than forty old buildings – from a Tudor market hall to a medieval farmstead – have been saved from destruction and reconstructed at the fifty-acre museum site. There's a daily guided tour at 1.30pm of the latest building, the innovative timber Downland Grishell, the museum's workshop and store. Besides a whole range of livestock there are also numerous special events and activities, particularly in July and August, so it's worth calling ahead for details. There's a half-hourly bus from Chichester (#60), which will drop you off in Singleton; a Weald and Downland ticket (£7) combines a day's unlimited travel on Stagecoach Coastline buses and museum entry.

Travel details

Buses

For information on all local and national bus services, contact Traveline ⓣ0870/608 2608 (daily 7am–9pm), ⓦwww.traveline.org.uk.

Arundel to: Chichester (Mon–Sat, hourly; 1hr 5min); Brighton (Mon–Sat every 30min, 1hr 55min).

Battle to: Hastings (Mon–Sat hourly; 30min); Maidstone (Mon–Sat hourly; 1hr 30min).

Brighton to: Chichester (Mon–Sat every 30min, Sun hourly; 2hr 30min); Eastbourne (Mon–Sat every 20min, Sun every 30min; 1hr 20min–1hr 30min); Lewes (Mon–Sat every 15min, Sun hourly; 30–40min); London Victoria (hourly; 2hr 5min); Portsmouth (Mon–Sat every 30min, Sun hourly; 3hr 30min); Tunbridge Wells Mon–Sat hourly, Sun 7; 1hr 45min).

Broadstairs to: Dover (Mon–Sat hourly; 40min); Margate (Mon–Fri 8 daily; 1hr); Ramsgate (every 20–30min; 15min).

Canterbury to: Deal (Mon–Sat hourly, Sun 4; 1hr 5min); Dover (Mon–Sat hourly; 40min); Herne Bay (Mon–Sat every 15min, Sun hourly; 30min); London Victoria (hourly; 2hr); Margate (Mon–Sat hourly; 1hr 25min); Ramsgate Mon–Sat hourly; 40min); Sandwich (Mon–Sat hourly, Sun 4; 45min); Whitstable (Mon–Sat every 15min, Sun hourly; 35min).

Chatham to: Rochester (every 10min; 5min).

Chichester to: Arundel (Mon–Sat hourly; 1hr 55min), Brighton (Mon–Sat every 30min, Sun hourly; 2hr 30min); Portsmouth (Mon–Sat every 30min, Sun hourly; 1hr 5min).

Deal to: Canterbury (Mon–Sat hourly, Sun 4; 1hr 5min); Dover (Mon–Sat hourly, Sun 6; 30min); Sandwich (Mon–Sat hourly, Sun 4; 25min).

Dorking to: Guildford (Mon–Sat every 30min, Sun every 2hr; 15min).

Dover to: Canterbury (Mon–Sat hourly; 40min); Deal Mon–Sat hourly, Sun 6; 30min); Folkestone (Mon–Sat hourly, Sun 6; 30min); Hastings (Mon–Sat hourly, Sun 6; 2hr 40min); London Victoria (hourly; 2hr 40min–3hr 20min); Sandwich (Mon–Sat 8 daily; 55min).

Eastbourne to: Brighton (Mon–Sat every 20min, Sun every 30min; 1hr 20min–1hr 30min); Hastings (Mon–Sat every 30min, Sun hourly; 1hr 10min–1hr 55min).

Farnham to: Guildford (Mon–Sat 1–2 hourly, Sun hourly; 35min).

Folkestone to: Dover (Mon–Sat hourly, Sun 6; 30min); London Victoria (5 daily; 2hr 30min–2hr 55min); Hastings (Mon–Sat hourly, Sun 6; 2hr 15min); Hythe (Mon–Sat hourly, Sun 6; 30min); Rye (Mon–Sat hourly, Sun 6; 1hr 35min).

Gatwick Airport to: Brighton (every 30min; 45min); London Victoria (hourly; 1hr 20min).

Guildford to: Farnham (Mon–Sat 1–2 hourly, Sun hourly; 35min); London Victoria (6 daily; 1hr).

Hastings to: Eastbourne (Mon–Sat every 30min, Sun hourly; 1hr 10min–1hr 55min); Dover

(Mon–Sat hourly, Sun 6; 2hr 40min); Folkestone (Mon–Sat hourly, Sun 6; 2hr 15min); London Victoria (2 daily; 2hr 50min–3hr 50min); New Romney (Mon–Sat hourly, Sun 6; 1hr 25min); Rye (Mon–Sat hourly, Sun 6; 45 min).

Herne Bay to: Canterbury (Mon–Sat every 15 min, Sun hourly; 30min); Margate (Mon–Sat hourly, Sun 5; 45min); Ramsgate (Mon–Sat 5 daily; 45min); Whitstable (Mon–Sat every 15min, Sun hourly; 20min).

Hythe to: Folkestone (Mon–Sat hourly, Sun 6; 30min); New Romney (Mon–Sat hourly, Sun 6; 20min); Rye (Mon–Sat hourly, Sun 6; 1hr 10min).

Lewes to: Brighton (Mon–Sat every 15min, Sun hourly; 30–40min); Tunbridge Wells (Mon–Sat hourly, Sun 7; 1hr 30min).

Maidstone to: London Victoria (Mon–Sat 13 daily, Sun 7; 1hr 45min–2hr); Rochester (Mon–Sat 9 daily; 45min); Tunbridge Wells (Mon–Sat 2 hourly; 1hr 20min–1hr 55min).

Margate to: Broadstairs (Mon–Fri 8 daily; 1hr); Canterbury (Mon–Sat hourly; 1hr 25min); Herne Bay (Mon–Sat hourly, Sun 5; 45min); London Victoria (5 daily; 2hr 30min); Ramsgate (Mon–Sat every 30min; 40min).

Ramsgate to: Broadstairs (every 20–30min; 15min); Canterbury (Mon–Sat hourly; 40min); London Victoria (5 daily; 3hr); Margate (Mon–Sat every 30min; 40min).

Rochester to: Chatham (every 10min; 5min); Maidstone (Mon–Sat 9 daily; 45min).

Rye to: Hastings Mon–Sat hourly, Sun 6; 45min); Hythe (Mon–Sat hourly, Sun 6; 1hr 10min); New Romney (Mon–Sat hourly, Sun 6; 40min).

Sandwich to: Canterbury (Mon–Sat hourly, Sun 4; 45min); Deal (Mon–Sat hourly, Sun 4; 25min); Dover (Mon–Sat 8 daily; 55min).

Sevenoaks to: Tunbridge Wells (Mon–Sat hourly; 50min).

Tunbridge Wells to: Brighton Mon–Sat hourly, Sun 7; 1hr 45min); Lewes (Mon–Sat hourly, Sun 7; 1hr 30min); Maidstone (Mon–Sat 2 hourly; 1hr 20min–1hr 55min); Sevenoaks (Mon–Sat hourly; 50min).

Whitstable to: Canterbury (Mon–Sat every 15min, Sun hourly; 30min); Herne Bay (Mon–Sat every 15min, Sun hourly; 20min).

Trains

For information on all local and national rail services, contact National Rail Enquiries: ⓣ08457/484950, ⓦwww.rail.co.uk.

Arundel to: London Victoria (Mon–Sat every 30min, Sun hourly; 1hr 20min).

Battle to: Hastings (Mon–Sat every 30min, Sun hourly; 15min); London Charing Cross (every 30min; 1hr 20min); Sevenoaks (Mon–Sat every 30min, Sun hourly; 45min); Tunbridge Wells (Mon–Sat every 30min, Sun hourly; 30min).

Brighton to: Chichester (Mon–Sat every 30min, Sun hourly; 50min); Gatwick Airport (every 15min; 25–40min); Hastings (Mon–Sat every 30min, Sun hourly; 1hr 10min); Lewes (Mon–Sat every 15min, Sun every 30min; 15min); London Victoria (every 30min; 1hr–1hr 20min); London King's Cross (Mon–Sat every 15min, Sun every 30min; 1hr 15min); London Bridge (Mon–Sat every 15min, Sun every 30min; 1hr); Oxford (1 daily; 2hr 40min); Portsmouth Harbour (hourly; 1hr 30min).

Broadstairs to: London Victoria (Mon–Sat every 30min, Sun hourly; 1hr 50min); Ramsgate (every 20–30min; 5min).

Canterbury East to: Dover Priory (Mon–Fri every 30min, Sat & Sun hourly; 40min); London Victoria (Mon–Sat every 30min, Sun hourly; 1hr 20min).

Canterbury West to: London Charing Cross (hourly; 1hr 40min); Ramsgate (hourly; 20min).

Chatham to: Dover Priory (Mon–Sat every 30min, Sun hourly; 1hr 10min); London Victoria (every 30min; 1hr).

Chichester to: London Victoria (Mon–Sat every 30min, Sun hourly; 1hr 45min); Portsmouth Harbour (Mon–Sat every 30min, Sun hourly; 40min).

Dorking to: Farnham (hourly; 1hr); London Waterloo (Mon–Sat every 30min; 50min).

Dover Priory to: Folkestone Central (Mon–Sat every 30min, Sun hourly; 10min); London Charing Cross (Mon–Fri every 30min, Sat & Sun hourly; 1hr 40min); London Victoria (Mon–Fri every 30min, Sat & Sun hourly; 1hr 50min).

Eastbourne to: Gatwick Airport (every 30min; 1hr); Hastings (Mon–Sat every 30min, Sun hourly; 30min); Lewes (Mon–Sat every 20min, Sun hourly; 20min); London Victoria (Mon–Sat every 30min, Sun hourly; 1hr 35min).

Farnham to: Aldershot (for connections to London Waterloo; Mon–Sat 1–2 hourly, Sun hourly; 10min); Guildford (Mon–Sat 1–2 hourly, Sun hourly; 35min).

Folkestone Central to: London Charing Cross (Mon–Sat every 30min, Sun hourly; 1hr 30min).

Folkestone West to: London Charing Cross (Mon–Sat every 30min; Sun hourly; 1hr 30min).

Gatwick Airport to: Brighton (every 15min; 30min); London Victoria (very frequent; 30min).

Guildford to: Farnham (Mon–Sat 1–2 hourly, Sun hourly; 35min); London Waterloo (Mon–Sat every 20min, Sun hourly; 35min).

Hastings to: Gatwick Airport (hourly; 1hr 30min); London Victoria (hourly; 2hr); Rye (hourly; 30min).

Herne Bay to: London Victoria (Mon–Sat every 30min, Sun hourly; 1hr 30min); Ramsgate (Mon–Sat every 30min, Sun hourly; 30min).
Lewes to: Brighton (Mon–Sat every 15min, Sun every 30min; 15min); London Victoria (Mon–Sat every 30min, Sun hourly; 1hr 10min).
Maidstone East to: London Victoria (Mon–Sat every 30min, Sun hourly; 1hr).
Margate to: Canterbury West (hourly; 30min); London Victoria (Mon–Sat every 30min, Sun hourly; 1hr 50min).
Ramsgate to: London Victoria (Mon–Sat every 30min, Sun hourly; 1hr 50min).
Rochester to: Dover Priory (Mon–Sat every 30min, Sun hourly; 1hr 10min); Herne Bay (Mon–Sat every 30min; Sun hourly; 45min); London Charing Cross (every 30min; 1hr 15min); London Victoria (Mon–Sat every 15–20min, Sun every 30min; 45min).
Rye to: Hastings (hourly; 20min).
Sandwich to: Dover Priory (hourly; 30min); Ramsgate (hourly; 15min).
Sevenoaks to: London Charing Cross (Mon–Sat every 20min; 30min);
Tunbridge Wells to: London Charing Cross (Mon–Sat every 30min, Sun hourly; 55min).
Whitstable to: London Victoria (hourly; 1hr 20min); Ramsgate (Mon–Sat every 30min, Sun hourly; 30min).
Woking to: London Waterloo (every 20–30min; 35min).

Hampshire, Dorset and Wiltshire

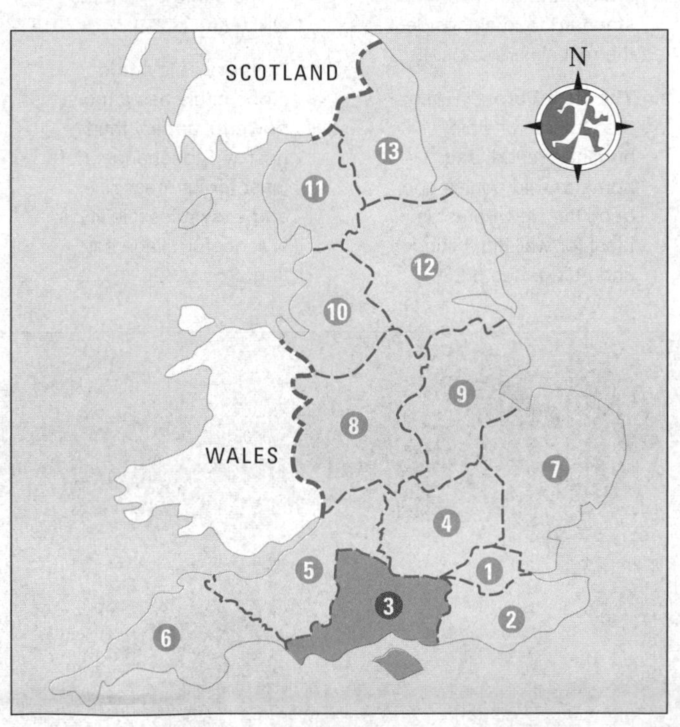

CHAPTER 3

Highlights

* **Cowes Week, Isle of Wight** This yachting jamboree draws thousands, infecting even the staunchest landlubbers. See p.276

* **Wykeham Arms, Winchester** Ancient tavern serving gourmet-standard food alongside the real ales. See p.283

* **The New Forest** William the Conqueror's old hunting ground, and home to wild ponies and deer, the New Forest is ideal for walking, biking and riding. See p.286

* **Corfe Castle** Picturesque ruins with a weathered, romantic charm. See p.297

* **Durdle Door** This crumbling natural arch stands at the end of a splendid beach – a great place for walkers and swimmers alike. See p.299

* **Avebury** This crude stone circle has a more powerful appeal than nearby Stonehenge, not least for its great size and easy accessibility, in a peaceful village setting. See p.320

△ New Forest ponies

3

Hampshire, Dorset and Wiltshire

The distant past is perhaps more tangible in **Hampshire** (often abbreviated to "Hants"), **Dorset** and **Wiltshire** than in any other part of England. Predominantly rural, these three counties overlap substantially with the ancient kingdom of **Wessex**, whose most famous ruler, Alfred, repulsed the Danes in the ninth century and came close to establishing the first unified state in England. Before Wessex came into being, however, many earlier civilizations had left their stamp on the region. The chalky uplands of Wiltshire boast several of Europe's greatest Neolithic sites, including **Stonehenge** and **Avebury**, while in Dorset you'll find **Maiden Castle**, the most striking Iron Age hill fort in the country, and the **Cerne Abbas Giant**, source of many a legend. The Romans tramped all over these southern counties, leaving the most conspicuous signs of their occupation at the amphitheatre of **Dorchester** – though that town is more closely associated with the novels of Thomas Hardy and his distinctively gloomy vision of Wessex.

None of the landscapes of this region could be described as grand or wild, but the countryside is consistently seductive, its appeal exemplified by the crumbling fossil-bearing cliffs around **Lyme Regis**, the managed woodlands of the **New Forest** and the gentle, open curves of **Salisbury Plain**. Its towns are also generally modest and slow-paced, with the notable exceptions of the two great maritime bases of **Portsmouth** and, to a lesser extent, **Southampton**, a fair proportion of whose visitors are simply passing through on their way to the more genteel pleasures of the **Isle of Wight**. This is something of an injustice, though neither place can compete with the two most interesting cities in this part of England – **Salisbury** and **Winchester**, each of which possesses a stupendous cathedral amid an array of other historic sights. Of the region's great houses, **Wilton**, **Stourhead**, **Longleat** and **Kingston Lacy** are the ones that attract the crowds, but every cranny has its medieval church, manor house or unspoilt country inn – there are few parts of England in which an aimless meander can be so rewarding. If it's straightforward seaside fun you're after, **Bournemouth** leads the way, with Weymouth and Lyme Regis heading the ranks of the minor resorts, along with the yachties' havens over on the Isle of Wight.

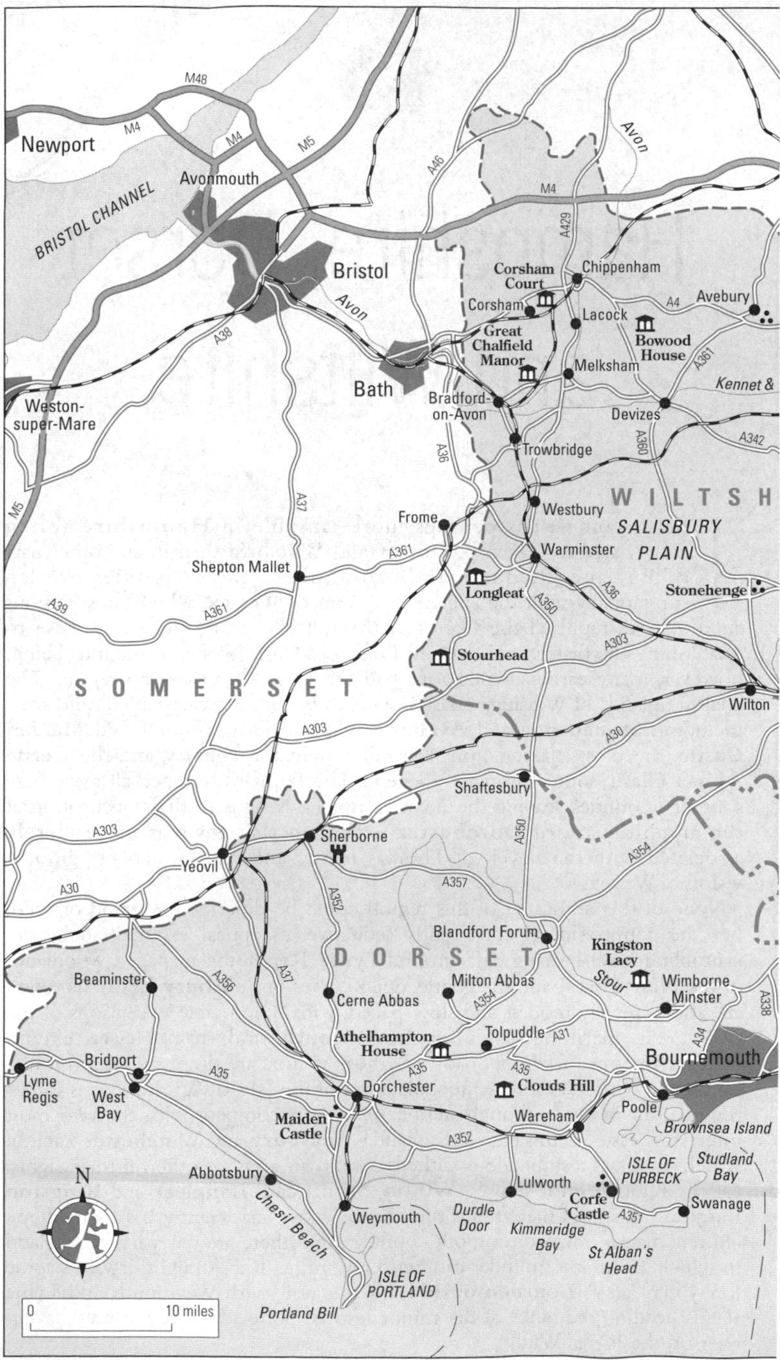

Newport
M48
M4
M5
Avonmouth
BRISTOL CHANNEL
Bristol
Avon
A38
Bath
Weston-super-Mare
A46
M4
Avon
A429
Corsham Court
Chippenham
Corsham
Lacock
A4
Avebury
Great Chalfield Manor
Bowood House
Melksham
A361
Kennet &
Bradford-on-Avon
Devizes
A36
Trowbridge
A360
A342
W I L T S H
Westbury
SALISBURY PLAIN
A37
Frome
Warminster
A361
Shepton Mallet
Longleat
A36
Stonehenge
A350
A39
A361
A303
Stourhead
S O M E R S E T
Wilton
A303
A30
Shaftesbury
A303
Sherborne
A350
Yeovil
A354
A30
A352
A357
Blandford Forum
D O R S E T
Kingston Lacy
Beaminster
A356
A37
Milton Abbas
Stour
Wimborne Minster
A338
Cerne Abbas
A354
Athelhampton House
Tolpuddle
A31
A34
Bournemouth
Bridport
A35
A35
A35
Lyme Regis
West Bay
Dorchester
Clouds Hill
Poole
Maiden Castle
Wareham
Brownsea Island
A352
ISLE OF PURBECK
Studland Bay
Abbotsbury
Lulworth
Corfe Castle
Swanage
Chesil Beach
Weymouth
Durdle Door
A351
Kimmeridge Bay
St Alban's Head
ISLE OF PORTLAND
0
10 miles
Portland Bill
N
Channel Islands
Channel Islands & Cherbourg

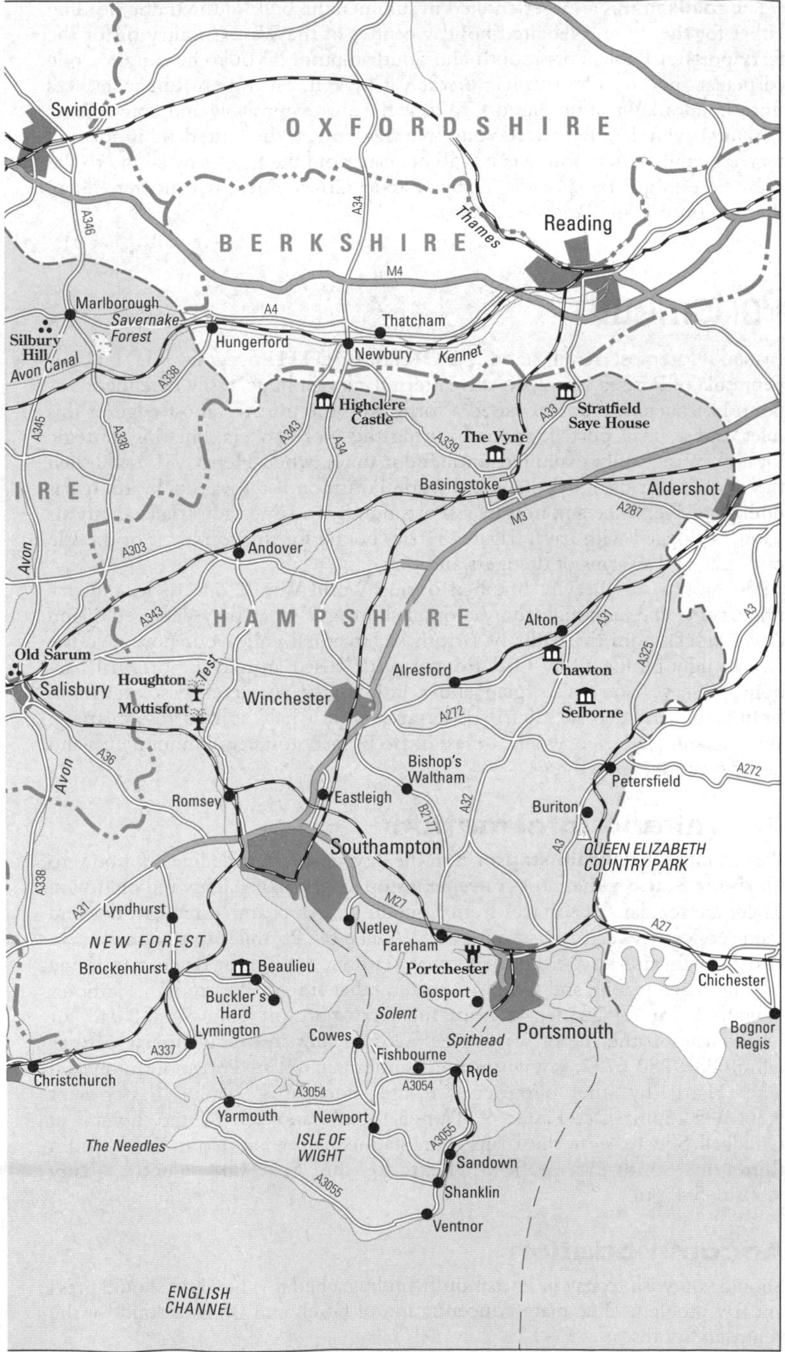
Swindon
OXFORDSHIRE
BERKSHIRE
Thames
Reading
M4
A346
A34
Marlborough
Savernake Forest
A4
Silbury Hill
Avon Canal
Hungerford
Thatcham
Newbury
Kennet
A338
A345
A343
Highclere Castle
A33
Stratfield Saye House
The Vyne
A339
IRE
Basingstoke
Aldershot
A287
M3
A303
Andover
Avon
A343
HAMPSHIRE
Alton
A31
A3
A325
Old Sarum
Houghton
Test
Salisbury
Mottisfont
Winchester
Alresford
Chawton
Selborne
A272
A36
Avon
Bishop's Waltham
Petersfield
A272
Romsey
Eastleigh
B2177
A32
Buriton
Southampton
A3
QUEEN ELIZABETH COUNTRY PARK
A338
A31
Lyndhurst
M27
Netley
A27
NEW FOREST
Fareham
Brockenhurst
Beaulieu
Portchester
Chichester
Buckler's Hard
Gosport
Lymington
Solent
Portsmouth
Bognor Regis
Cowes
Spithead
A337
Fishbourne
Christchurch
A3054
Ryde
A3054
Yarmouth
Newport
A3055
The Needles
ISLE OF WIGHT
Sandown
A3055
Shanklin
Ventnor
ENGLISH CHANNEL
Caen, St Malo, Bilbao, Cherbourg & Le Havre
© Crown copyright

The **roads** in this area get choked in summer, the bulk of the traffic heading either for the more celebrated holiday centres of the West Country or for the ferry ports of Poole, Portsmouth and Southampton. If you're heading for one particular spot, it's often easier to reach it by **rail**, on the fast direct services from London's Waterloo Station. To tour the area extensively and conveniently, though, you definitely need your own transport, as the hinterland is not well served by public transport. Keen **walkers** can avoid the hordes by taking to the New Forest's quieter spots or to the **Dorset Coast Path**, which stretches all the way from Lyme Regis to Poole.

Portsmouth

Britain's foremost naval station, **PORTSMOUTH** occupies the bulbous peninsula of Portsea Island, on the eastern flank of a huge, easily defended harbour. The ancient Romans raised a fortress on the northernmost edge of this inlet, and a small port developed during the Norman era, but this strategic location wasn't fully exploited until Tudor times, when Henry VII established the world's first dry dock here and made Portsmouth a royal dockyard. It has flourished ever since and nowadays Portsmouth is a large industrialized city, its harbour clogged with naval frigates, ferries bound for the continent or the Isle of Wight, and swarms of dredgers and tugs.

Portsmouth was heavily bombed during World War II due to its military importance and, although the Victorian slums got what they deserved, bland tower blocks from the nadir of British architectural endeavour now give the city an ugly profile. Only **Old Portsmouth**, based around the original harbour, preserves some Georgian and a little Tudor character. East of here is **Southsea**, a residential suburb of terraces with a half-hearted resort strewn along its shingle beach, where a mass of B&Bs face stoic naval monuments and tawdry seaside amusements.

Arrival and information

Portsmouth's main **train station** is in the city centre, but the line continues to **Harbour Station**, the most convenient stop for the main sights and old town. There are regular fast services from London Waterloo, and a frequent bus and train service between Portsmouth and Winchester, 25 miles to the northwest. Passenger **ferries** leave from the jetty at Harbour Station for Ryde, on the Isle of Wight (see p.265), and Gosport, on the other side of Portsmouth Harbour. Wightlink car ferries depart from the ferry port off Gunwharf Road for Fishbourne on the Isle of Wight (see p.265). There are three **tourist offices** (all ⓣ023/9282 6722, ⓦwww.visitportsmouth.co.uk) in Portsmouth, one on The Hard, by the entrance to the dockyards (daily: Easter–Sept 9.30am–5.45pm; Oct–Easter 9.30am–5.15pm); another in the library at Guildhall Square, near the main train station (Mon–Sat 10am–5pm); and a third on Southsea's seafront, next to the Sea Life Centre (daily 9.30am–5.45pm).

Accommodation

Should you wish to stay in Portsmouth, finding a bed for the night should present few problems. The main concentration of hotels and B&Bs is south of the centre in Southsea.

Hotels and guest houses

Albatross Guest House 51 Waverley Rd, Southsea ⓣ023/9282 8325. One of many good-value B&Bs in this part of Southsea, this one dating from the 1860s has nautically themed rooms and some parking space. No smoking. No credit cards. ❶

Dorcliffe Guest House 42 Waverley Rd, Southsea ⓣ023/9282 8283, ⓔdorcliffe@supanet.com. Family-run guest house overlooking a small park, close to restaurants and seafront. En-suite rooms are available. No credit cards. ❶

Fortitude Cottage 51 Broad St, Old Portsmouth ⓣ023/9282 3748, ⓦwww.fortitudecottage.co.uk. Comfortable cottage overlooking the quayside with three comfortable en-suite rooms, and a beamed breakfast room with views of the boats. No smoking. ❷

Sailmakers Loft 5 Bath Square, Old Portsmouth ⓣ023/9282 3045, ⓔsailmakersloft@aol.com. Spithead views from this small B&B in a quiet location next to the *Spice Island Inn*. Most rooms are en suite. ❷

The Sally Port 57–58 High St, Old Portsmouth ⓣ023/9282 1860. Opposite the cathedral, this historic inn has sloping floors and extremely comfortable bedrooms, some with en-suite showers. ❹

Spitbank Fort ⓣ023/9250 4207, ⓦwww.spitbankfort.co.uk. One mile from Portsmouth Harbour and accessible by ferry, this man-made island in the middle of the Solent has two very basic rooms – the Sergeants' Room and the Officers' Room – available when the weather permits between April and September. No credit cards. ❷

Hostels and campsites

Portsmouth and Southsea Backpackers 4 Florence Rd, Southsea ⓣ023/9283 2495 or 9282 2963, ⓦwww.portsmouthbackpackers.co.uk. Fifty-bed hostel with full facilities, including a large kitchen, at the east end of Clarence Esplanade. Dorm beds go for £12, and there are en-suite doubles, and discounts for longer stays. A forty-minute walk from the city centre, or catch bus #5, #6 or #7 from Harbour Station, or any bus to South Parade Pier. ❶

Southsea Leisure Park Melville Rd, Southsea ⓣ023/9273 5070, ⓔinfo@southsea-caravans-ltd.co.uk. Well-appointed campsite right at the east end of Southsea Esplanade (bus #15 from the Harbour station to Ferry Road, from where it's a short walk).

Youth Hostel Wymering Manor, Old Wymering Lane, Cosham ⓣ023/9237 5661, ⓔportsmouth@yha.org.uk. Housed in an attractive Tudor manor, ten minutes west of Cosham train station. Alternatively, take bus #5 or #57 from Harbour Station as far as Cosham Health Centre (from where it's the first left). Dorm beds £10.25.

The Royal Naval Base

For most visitors, a trip to Portsmouth begins and ends at the **Historic Ships**, in the **Royal Naval Base** (ⓦwww.historicdockyard.co.uk) at the end of Queen Street (daily: April–Oct 10am–5.30pm; Nov–March 10am–5pm; last entry 1hr before closing). The complex comprises three ships and as many museums, with each ship visitable separately, though most people opt for an all-inclusive ticket (£14.85). The main attractions are *HMS Victory*, *HMS Warrior* (including the Royal Naval Museum), Action Stations (an interactive simulation of life aboard a modern naval frigate), the Mary Rose Museum, and a harbour tour. If you don't manage to do everything in one day, your ticket allows for return visits. Note that visits to the *Victory* are guided, with limited numbers at set times, so it's worth booking early to ensure a place, and even then you may have to wait up to two hours for your turn. Also, visitors with disabilities will have a hard time moving between decks on the two complete ships; a virtual tour by video (call ⓣ023/9272 2562 for details) is a good alternative.

Nearest the entrance to the complex is the youngest ship, **HMS Warrior** (£9.50), dating from 1860. It was Britain's first armoured, or "iron-clad" battleship, complete with sails and steam engines, and was the pride of the fleet in its day. Longer and faster than any previous naval vessel, and the first to be fitted with washing machines, the *Warrior* was described by Napoleon III as a "black snake amongst the rabbits". You can wander around its main deck and see where 18 seamen ate, slept and relaxed in the tiny spaces between each of the ship's 36 cannons. Not surprisingly, the captain's cabin, at the stern of the

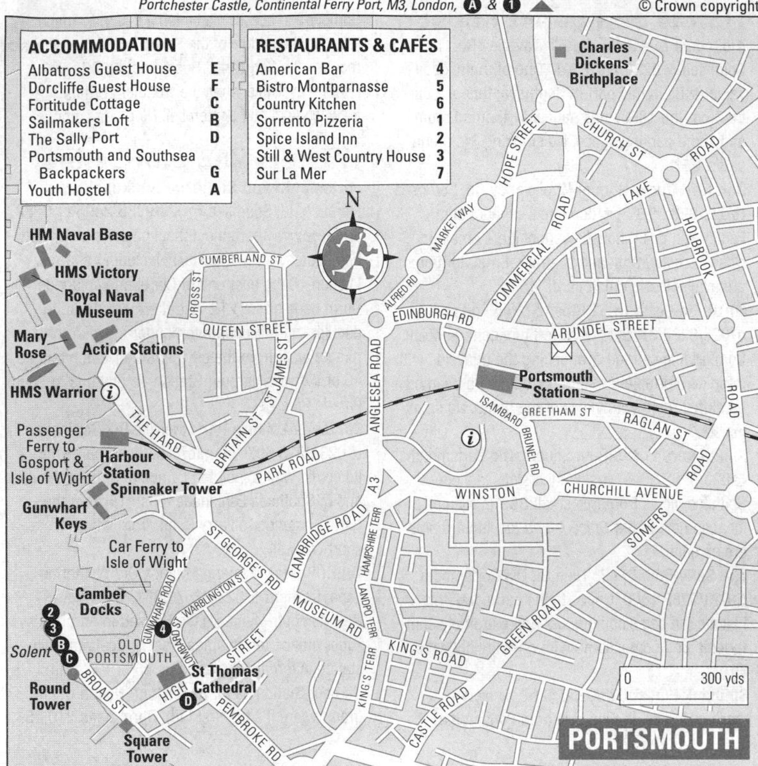

ship, resembles a sumptuous four-star suite, while the navigator also had a cabin to himself, although he shared it with a massive cannon. Other weaponry, including rifles, pistols and sabres, is all neatly stowed, but the *Warrior* was never challenged nor even fired a cannon in her 22 years at sea.

HMS Victory (£9.50) was already forty years old when she set sail from Portsmouth for Trafalgar on September 14, 1805, returning in triumph three months later, but bearing the corpse of Admiral Nelson. Shot by a sniper from a French ship at the height of the battle, Nelson expired below decks three hours later, having been assured that victory was in sight. The usual fate of casualties at sea was to be sewn into their hammocks with a cannon ball and thrown overboard, but Nelson didn't wish to be buried at sea, so his body was preserved in a huge vat of brandy pending his eventual burial in St Paul's Cathedral. Although badly damaged during the battle, the *Victory* continued in service for a further twenty years, before being retired to the dry dock where she rests today.

Opposite the *Victory*, various buildings house the exhaustive **Royal Naval Museum** (same ticket as *Warrior*). Tracing naval history from Alfred the Great's fleet to the present day, this is the most resistible attraction in the complex. One building contains a collection of jolly figureheads, Nelson memorabilia and numerous nautical models, but coverage of a more recent conflict, the Falklands War of 1982, is treated very lightly.

In a shed behind the *Victory* are the remains of the **Mary Rose** (£9.50), Henry VIII's flagship, which capsized before his eyes off Spithead in 1545 while engaging French intruders. Whether she was top-heavy (she was certainly overloaded at the time) or took in water through her lower gunports having reeled from a broadside, is uncertain, but the *Mary Rose*, named after Henry's daughter and the Tudor rose, sank swiftly with almost all her 700-strong crew. In 1982 a massive conservation project successfully raised the remains of the hull, which silt had preserved beneath the seabed, and it was moved to its present position. This may be a sterling bit of history and the successful culmination of a painstaking archeological recovery, but you can't help feeling it's the techniques of retrieval and preservation that are being celebrated here, rather than the ship itself. Many of the thousands of objects that were found near the wreck are now displayed in a rather more absorbing exhibition close to the *Warrior*. Videos of the recovery operation are shown, as well as depictions of life aboard a sixteenth-century warship.

From the harbour

The naval theme is continued at the **Submarine Museum** on Haslar Jetty in Gosport (daily: April–Oct 10am–5.30pm; Nov–March 10am–4.30pm; last tour 1hr before closing; £4, or £7.20 with Explosion Museum), reached by taking the passenger ferry from Harbour train station jetty (daily 5.30am–midnight; £1.60 return), just south of the entrance to the Royal Naval Base, or, from the same place, the water-bus, which gives you a half-hour tour of the harbour before dropping you in Gosport (Easter–Oct 10.30am–5pm; £4). Allow yourself a couple of hours to explore these slightly creepy vessels – a guided tour inside *HMS Alliance* gives you an insight into life on board and the museum elaborates evocatively on the long history of submersible craft. Nearby, housed in the old armaments depot at Priddy's Hard, **Explosion! The Museum of Naval Firepower** (April–Oct daily 10am–5.30pm; Nov–March Thurs, Sat & Sun 10am–4.30pm; £5, or £7.20 with Submarine Museum) tells the story of naval warfare from the days of gunpowder to the present, much helped by computer animations.

From the pontoon beside *HMS Warrior*, ferries depart (Sun 2.45pm; £8, including entry to the fort) for the mile-long ride to **Spitbank Fort**, an offshore bastion of granite, iron and brick little altered since its construction in the 1860s. With over fifty rooms linked by passages and steps on two floors, the complex includes a 400-foot-deep well, which still draws fresh water from below the seafloor, and an inner courtyard complete with a café and sheltered terrace. The artificial island hosts pub nights (Wed & Thurs), parties (Fri & Sat) and Sunday lunches, for all of which transport is provided in the form of water-taxis from the Gosport and Hard ferry pontoons (fares included in the price of entry tickets); call ☎01329/664286 or ask at the tourist office for details. Accommodation is also available at the fort (see p.257).

The rest of the city

Back at the Harbour train station in Portsmouth, it's a well-signposted twenty-minute walk south to what remains of **Old Portsmouth**. Along the way, you pass the simple **Cathedral of St Thomas** on the High Street, whose original twelfth-century features have been obscured by rebuilding after the Civil War and again in the twentieth century. The High Street ends at a maze of cobbled Georgian streets huddling behind a fifteenth-century wall protecting the **Camber**, or old port, where Walter Raleigh landed the first potatoes and tobacco from the New World. Nearby, the Round and Square Towers, which punctuate the Tudor fortifications, are popular vantage points for observing nautical activities. There's also a couple of lively shoreside pubs, the *Still & West Country House* and *Spice Island* (see p.261), with seats outside for viewing the comings and goings in the Solent.

Stretching along the historic waterfront, the sleek **Gunwharf Quays** development hosts myriad stylish cafés, restaurants and nightspots alongside the retail outlets. It's also the site of Portsmouth's newest attraction, the **Spinnaker Tower**, due to be completed by the end of 2004. The tower will rise a full 165 metres above the harbour, offering views over Portsmouth and up to twenty miles beyond from three viewing decks. Although the design was voted for by the local population, the tower still excites continuing controversy due to its dominance of the historic harbour.

South of Old Portsmouth, **Southsea**'s main attraction is the **D-Day Museum** on Clarence Esplanade (daily: April–Sept 10am–5.30pm; Oct–March 10am–5pm; last entry 1hr before closing; £5; Ⓦwww.ddaymuseum.co.uk), which relates how Portsmouth avenged its wartime bombing by being the main assembly point for the D-Day invasion, code-named "Operation Overlord". The museum's most striking exhibit is the 270-foot-long *Overlord Embroidery*, which tells the tale of the Normandy landings. Next door to the museum, the squat profile of **Southsea Castle** (April–Oct daily 10am–5pm; £2.50), built from the remains of Beaulieu Abbey (see p.289), may have been the spot from where Henry VIII watched the *Mary Rose* sink in 1545. A mile further along the shoreside South Parade, just past South Parade pier, the **Royal Marines Museum** (daily: June–Sept 10am–5pm; Oct–May 10am–4.30pm; last entry 1hr before closing; £4.75; Ⓦwww.royalmarinesmuseum.co.uk) describes the origins

Naval vernacular

Many phrases in today's English language owe their origins to the country's seafaring heritage. Below are some of the more familiar expressions whose daily use has blurred their naval ancestry:

- "Three square meals a day". Sailors aboard the *Victory* were served a meagre trio of daily meals on square wooden plates.
- "Let the cat out of the bag" and "Not enough room to swing a cat". Both refer to the cat-o'-nine-tails, a nine-thonged whip with knots at the end of each thong. Taking the "cat" out of its baize bag made subsequent intentions obvious, and floggings were carried out on the upper deck where the bosun could get a good swing at the wrongdoer.
- "Limeys". This nickname for Brits derives from the casks of lime juice ships carried to prevent scurvy.
- "Grog". Slang for alcohol still current in Australia. In Nelson's time sailors were allocated a gallon of beer or a pint of rum per day; in the early 1700s, Admiral Vernon, noted for his coat made of grogram and so nicknamed "Old Grog", became notorious for diluting the daily servings with water, producing an insipid brew akin to some Australian beers.
- "Turn a blind eye". Part of Nelson's early reputation was made on his irreverent attitude to authority. At the Battle of Copenhagen, the arrogant second-in-command thought he knew best and "ignored" unnecessary signals from other ships by holding the telescope to his blind eye.
- "Son of a gun". A scoundrel. Women unfortunate enough to give birth on ship did so between the cannons to keep the gangways clear.

and greatest campaigns of the navy's elite fighting force. Outside, a junior assault course gives aspirant young commandos a chance to get in shape.

The only other point of interest in Portsmouth itself is **Charles Dickens' Birthplace** at 393 Old Commercial Rd (daily: April–Sept 10am–5pm; £2.50), half a mile north of the town centre, where the writer was born in 1812. A couple of rooms have been fitted out as they were during his lifetime, but for true fans there's far more of interest in Rochester (see p.177) and, to a lesser extent, Broadstairs (see p.184), where Dickens wrote many of his greatest books.

More compelling is **Portchester Castle** (daily: April–Sept 10am–6pm; Oct 10am–5pm; Nov–March 10am–4pm; £3.50; EH), six miles out of the centre, just past the marina development at Port Solent. Built by the Romans in the third century this fortification boasts the finest surviving example of Roman walls in northern Europe – still over twenty feet high and incorporating some twenty bastions. The Normans felt no need to make any substantial alterations when they moved in, but a castle was later built within Portchester's precincts by Henry II, which Richard II extended and Henry V used as his garrison when assembling the army that was to fight the Battle of Agincourt. Today its grassy enclosure makes a sheltered spot for a congenial game of cricket or a kickabout with a football.

Eating and drinking

Portsmouth has a small and fairly unremarkable range of restaurants, though you'll find more choice in Southsea. In Old Portsmouth, your best bet is one of the old seafaring pubs, where snacks and full meals are generally available.

American Bar 52 Whitehart Rd ☎023/9281 1585. Stylish bar/restaurant adjacent to the Wightlink ferry terminal, where quality, mainly Modern British fare is served at highly reasonable prices. There's pavement seating and a leafy terrace with wrought-iron tables. Inexpensive to Moderate.

Bistro Montparnasse 103 Palmerston Rd, Southsea ☎023/9281 6754. This place stands out from the many restaurants in this part of Southsea for its good-quality French and seafood dishes. Closed Sun & Mon. Moderate.

Country Kitchen 59 Marmion Rd, Southsea ☎023/9281 1425. Vegetarian and vegan restaurant, open daytime only, with newspapers on hand and free coffee refills. Closed Sun. Inexpensive.

Sorrento Pizzeria Port Solent ☎023/9220 1473. Swish Italian restaurant in Portsmouth's prestigious marina development, six miles north of the city centre, near Portchester Castle. Moderate.

Spice Island Inn Bath Square, Old Portsmouth ☎023/9282 4293. Old hostelry in a quiet location in the oldest part of town, boasting a handsome front and cosy interior; serves a great range of hot and cold dishes. Inexpensive.

Still & West Country House 2 Bath Square, Old Portsmouth. Adjacent pub to the *Spice Island*, and of similar age, with an innovative seafood menu and a range of Gale's beers, as well as tables outside overlooking the Solent. Inexpensive.

Sur La Mer 69 Palmerston Rd, Southsea ☎023 9287 6678. A good-value French and seafood restaurant with set-price three-course meals for around £7 and £12. Closed Sun. Inexpensive.

Southampton and around

A glance at the map gives some idea of the strategic maritime importance of **SOUTHAMPTON**, which stands on a triangular peninsula formed at the place where the rivers Itchen and Test flow into Southampton Water, an eight-mile inlet from the Solent. Sure enough, Southampton has figured in numerous stirring events: it witnessed the exodus of Henry V's Agincourt-bound army, the Pilgrim Fathers' departure in the *Mayflower* in 1620 and the maiden voyages of such ships as the *Queen Mary* and the *Titanic*. Unfortunately, since its pummelling by the Luftwaffe and some disastrous postwar planning, the thousand-year-old city has changed beyond recognition. Now a sprawling conurbation easily bypassed by motorways, it'll be pretty low on your list of places to visit in southern England, but you may pass through on your way to the Isle of Wight, and it has enough of interest to occupy a couple of hours while you wait for the ferry.

King Knut is alleged to have commanded the waves to retreat at Southampton – not, as legend has it, from a misguided sense of his kingly powers, but to rebuke his obsequious courtiers. Whatever his motive, the task would have been especially difficult here, for Southampton, like other Solent ports, enjoys the phenomenon of "double tides" – a prolonged period of high water as the Channel first swirls up the westerly side of the Solent, then, two hours later, backs up round Spithead. This means that exceptionally large vessels can berth here and, even though ocean-going liners are pretty much a rarity nowadays, there'll certainly be some sort of large-scale vessels floating by, either to the **Eastern Docks** at the tip of the promontory, or in the **Western Docks**, which has the largest commercial dry dock in England.

Core of the modern town is the **Civic Centre**, a short walk east of the train station. Its clocktower is the most distinctive feature of the skyline, and it houses an excellent **art gallery** that's particularly strong on twentieth-century British artists such as Sutherland, Piper and Spencer (Tues–Sat 10am–5pm, Sun 1–4pm; free). The **Western Esplanade**, curving southward from the station, runs alongside the best remaining bits of the old city **walls**. Rebuilt after a French attack in 1338, they feature towers with evocatively chilly names – Windwhistle, Catchcold and **God's House Tower** – the last of these, at the southern end of the old town in Winkle Street, houses a **Museum of Archeology** (Tues–Fri 10am–5pm, Sat 10am–4pm, Sun 2–5pm; free). Best preserved of the city's seven gates is **Bargate**, at the opposite end of the old town, at the head of the High Street; an elaborate structure, cluttered with lions, classical figures and machicolations (defensive apertures through which missiles could be dropped), it was formerly the guildhall and court house.

Other ancient buildings survive amid the piecemeal redevelopment of the High Street area. The oldest church is **St Michael's**, to the west of the High Street, with a twelfth-century font of black Tournai marble. The nearby **Tudor House Museum**, in Bugle Street, is an impressive fifteenth-century timber-framed building, its grand banqueting hall and reconstructed Tudor garden outshining the sundry exhibits of Georgian, Victorian and early twentieth-century social history, which include a 680cc Ackland motorbike from 1923 (the site is due to re-open after refurbishment in 2004: call ⓣ023/8063 5904 for opening times). On the opposite side of the High Street, the ruined **Holy Rood** church, bomb-damaged in World War II, stands as a monument to the merchant navy men killed in that war; it also has a memorial fountain to the crew of the *Titanic*, many of whom came from Southampton. Down at the south-west corner of the old town, by the seafront, the **Wool House** is a fine fourteenth-century stone warehouse; formerly used as a jail for Napoleonic prisoners, it now houses a **Maritime Museum** (Tues–Fri 10am–5pm, Sat 10am–4pm, Sun 2–5pm; free) with accounts of the heyday of ocean liners, and includes a huge model of the *Queen Mary* and various mementoes from the *Titanic*. The museum also offers the opportunity to listen to the recorded voices of various survivors of the *Titanic* tragedy relating their experiences, while *Titanic* obsessives can follow a "*Titanic* Trail" walking tour around Southampton – ask for the free pamphlet at the tourist office.

If you're an aviation enthusiast you should visit the **Hall of Aviation** in Albert Road South, by the car ferry terminal (Tues–Fri 10am–5pm, Sat 10am–4pm, Sun noon–5pm; also Mon 10am–5pm during school holidays; last entry 1hr before closing; £4). Dedicated to local aviation designer R.J. Mitchell, it has sixteen of his aircraft on display, including a Spitfire, the Sandringham Flying Boat and the Supermarine seaplane, which in 1931 won the Schneider Trophy by whizzing round the Isle of Wight at an average speed of 340mph. Check first with the tourist office if you're planning to visit, as plans are afoot to transfer the exhibits to new premises in Marchwood, on the western side of Southampton Water off the A326.

Practicalities

Services from London Waterloo arrive twice-hourly at the central **train station** in Blechynden Terrace, west of the Civic Centre; the **bus** and **coach stations** are immediately south and north of the Civic Centre. The **tourist office** is at 9 Civic Centre Rd (Mon, Tues & Thurs–Sat 8.30am–5.30pm, Wed 10am–5.30pm; ⓣ023/8083 3333, ⓦwww.southampton.gov.uk).

Southampton isn't a wildly attractive **place to stay**, but there are plenty of business hotels and commercial guest houses in the centre, including the large and solid *Elizabeth House* 42–44 The Avenue (ⓣ023/8022 4327, ⓦwww.elizabethhousehotel.com; ❸), and *Linden*, just north of the train station on the Polygon (ⓣ023/8022 5653; no credit cards; ❶), which has more modest but still bright, good-value rooms. In the same bracket, try *Argyle Lodge*, 13 Landguard Rd (ⓣ023/8022 4063; ❶), a family-run B&B in a quiet road close to the station, where evening meals are available. For a grander atmosphere, try the four-hundred-year-old *Star* (ⓣ023/8033 9939, ⓦwww.thestarhotel.com; ❺) or the slightly younger *Dolphin* (ⓣ023/8033 9955, ⓔenquiries@thedolphin.co.uk; ❹); both hotels are halfway down the High Street, newly refurbished and provide accommodation with all the antique trimmings.

There's not a great choice of original **eating** places in town either. Near the art gallery you could try *Buon Gusto,* 1 Commercial Rd, an attractive and inexpensive Italian restaurant (ⓣ023/8033 1543; closed Sun), but you'll find more choice and character among the eateries clustered on Oxford Street, off Bernard Street from the High Street. *The Olive Tree* at no. 29 (ⓣ023/8034 3333, ⓦwww.olivetree.co.uk), serving moderately priced Mediterranean dishes in an airy setting with pavement seating, and live music on Sundays; the *Oxford Brasserie* at no. 35 (ⓣ023/8063 5043), a relaxed place for baguettes, salads, pastas and fuller evening meals, and *Charlie Chan's* at no. 59 (ⓣ023/8023 3360), which offers fine Chinese food at moderate prices. As for **pubs**, the tiny old *Platform Tavern* in Winkle Street, at the south end of the High Street, and the twelfth-century *Red Lion*, complete with minstrels' gallery at 55 High St, are more charismatic alternatives to the bars at the *Star* and *Dolphin* hotels.

Around Southampton

There are a few places in the immediate vicinity of Southampton which are well worth a visit, and all are easily accessible by bus. **NETLEY**, three miles southeast on Southampton Water, has a picturesquely ruined Cistercian abbey (open during daylight; free; EH), a Solent fortress and the Royal Victoria Country Park, which makes a good picnic spot overlooking the water. Ten miles east of Southampton (reachable on bus #7), you can roam among the remains of the medieval seat of the bishops of Winchester at **Bishop's Waltham Palace** (April–Sept daily 10am–6pm; Oct daily 10am–5pm; £2.50;

EH), a grassy, ruined site just outside the village of Bishop's Waltham. There's an exhibition on Winchester's bishops – most of them extravagantly rich – on the first floor. **ROMSEY**, ten miles northwest (bus #8 or #15 from Southampton), offers a largely original Norman **abbey church** (daily 8.30am–5.30pm; free), completed in 1150 and bought by the townsfolk a few years after the Dissolution. Just south of the town is the stately home of **Broadlands**, a Palladian mansion on the River Test which was the birthplace and country residence of Lord Palmerston (his statue adorns Romsey's main square) and former home of Lord Mountbatten (mid-June to Sept daily noon–5.30pm, last admission 4pm; £5.95), who lies buried in the abbey and whose family still live in the house.

Four miles north of Romsey, **Mottisfont Abbey House and Garden** (mid-March to early June & late June to Sept Mon–Wed, Sat & Sun 11am–6pm or dusk; middle two weeks June daily 11am–8.30pm; last entry 1hr before closing; £6; NT) enjoy a lovely location right by the Test. The house of this former twelfth-century Augustinian priory (daily 1–5pm) is noted for the drawing room decorated by Whistler and the medieval cellarium, but it's the gardens that are the real draw, particularly for their old-fashioned rose collection, at its best in June. Mottisfont is accessible by train from Southampton – get off at Dunbridge, from where it's a fifteen-minute walk – or by bus from Romsey. Horticultural fans will also be interested in Houghton Lodge, five miles north of Mottisfont (see p.283).

The Isle of Wight

A separate county since 1974, the lozenge-shaped **ISLE OF WIGHT** still has difficulty shaking off its image as a mere adjunct of rural southern England – comfortably off, scrupulously tidy and desperately unadventurous. However, despite the high density of retirement homes and golf clubs, this bastion of Victorian values offers much more than strait-laced provincialism and quirky nostalgia. The island's mild climate is well suited to outdoor amusements, both inland and coastal, while the yachting regatta for which the island is most famous, **Cowes Week**, has grown in recent years to encompass a rather livelier scene than a mere gathering of the blue-blazer brigade.

Measuring less than 23 miles at its widest point and divided fairly neatly by a chalk spine that runs east to west across its centre, the Isle of Wight packs a surprising variety of landscapes and coastal scenery within its bounds. North of the ridge is a terrain of low-lying woodland and pasture, deeply cut by meandering rivers; southwards lies open chalky downland fringed by high cliffs. Two **Heritage Coast** paths follow the best of the shoreline, one running from Totland to St Lawrence on the south coast, the other from east of Yarmouth to west of Cowes along the north coast. Blending into this background is a splendid array of well-preserved Victoriana clad in fretted bargeboards and pseudo-Gothic gables, often grandiose but also charming and elegant too. The Victorian character of the Isle of Wight is scarcely surprising, for the founding Victorian herself felt most at home here – **Osborne House**, near Cowes, originally designed as a summer retreat for the royal family, became Queen Victoria's permanent home after Albert died. Several other great Victorians also had close associations with the island: Tennyson lived at Freshwater in a frowsty old mausoleum that is now a hotel, Dickens stayed and wrote in Winterbourne House (now also a hotel) in Bonchurch – the town

Sea routes to the Isle of Wight

Hovertravel ⓣ023/9281 1000 or 01983/811000, ⓦwww.hovertravel.co.uk. Year-round hovercraft service from Southsea to Ryde Mon–Fri 7.10am–8.45pm, Sat & Sun 8.15am–8.45pm (early Oct to early April last sailing at 8.10pm); every 15–30min; 10min; £11.60 for foot passengers only.

Red Funnel ⓣ023/8033 4010, ⓦwww.redfunnel.co.uk. Year-round ferries on two routes, one of them a high-speed service: **Southampton–East Cowes** 2 hourly; 55min; £9.80 for foot passengers; £69.50 for car and driver plus £9.80 per passenger. **Southampton–West Cowes** high-speed service daily 5.50am–11pm (Mon–Wed & Sun) or 11.40pm (Thurs–Sat); every 30min; 22min; £14 for foot passengers only.

Wightlink Ferries ⓣ0870/582 7744, ⓦwww.wightlink.co.uk. Three year-round ferry routes, including a faster but more expensive catamaran service to Ryde: **Portsmouth–Ryde** catamaran; 1–2 hourly; 15min; £13 for foot passengers only. **Portsmouth–Fishbourne** ferry runs once or twice every two hours; 35min; £10.60 for foot passengers; £71.90–93.80 according to season and day for car and driver, plus £10.60 per passenger. **Lymington–Yarmouth** ferry (June–Dec) midnight–10.15pm; 2 hourly; 30min; £10.60 for foot passengers; £71.90–93.80 according to season and day for car and driver plus £10.60 per passenger.

All the prices quoted are for a ninety-day (Wightlink and Red Funnel) or one-year (Hovertravel) standard return ticket. Wightlink and Red Funnel offer day and half-day returns as well as a range of other short-break deals for cars, with discounts of around 35 percent.

where the poet and critic Swinburne grew up and is now buried – while Julia Margaret Cameron resided at Dimbola Lodge, where a museum commemorates her photographic work. The island's history extends beyond this fashionable coterie, as attested by such older remains as the castles at **Yarmouth** and **Carisbrooke**, and the partly ruined eighteenth-century **Appuldurcombe House**. Along with a scattering of less monumental attractions, these sights would justify more than a day or two's sojourn on the island, not least in view of the relatively high ferry fares to get here.

Information and getting around

If you're dependent upon **public transport**, pick up the Southern Vectis bus route map and timetable (50p) from the tourist office, ferry office or bus station at your point of arrival. The company's hourly Island Explorer buses (routes #7 and #7A) run all round the island in about four hours. The **rail line** is a short east-coast stretch linking Ryde, Brading, Sandown and Shanklin. A Rover Ticket allows you unlimited travel on the bus and train networks, costing £7.50 for a Day Rover, £13 for a Two-Day Rover and £30 for a Weekly Rover; tickets are available from any bus or train station or tourist office.

Cycling is a very popular way of getting around the Isle of Wight, especially as bikes are carried free on all ferry services, but beware that in summer the narrow lanes can get very busy. For **bike rental**, you can expect to pay around £12 a day; ask at any tourist office for the four trail leaflets with recommended off-road cycling routes (£1) – best used in conjunction with a good map – and the free leaflet giving the best on-road routes round the island, which are all clearly signposted. If you're planning to do a lot of cycling, it may be worth getting hold of Ron Crick's detailed *Cyclist's Guide to the Isle of Wight* (£2.95), and off-road cyclists should check out the routes described in *Cycling Wight 1* and *2* (£2.95 each) by John Goodwin and Ian Williams, sold by Offshore Sports, Orchardleigh Rd, Shanklin (☎01983/866269), and 2–4 Birmingham Rd, Cowes (☎01983/290514); both outlets rent out mountain bikes (deposit and ID required). Tourist offices can supply a full list of bike rental shops.

For **information about the whole island**, call ☎01983/813818, consult Ⓦwww.islandbreaks.co.uk, or call in at the tourist offices detailed below.

Ryde and around

As a major ferry terminal, **RYDE** is the first landfall many visitors make on the island, but one where few choose to linger. A working town that came to prominence as a resort in the Victorian era, Ryde offers some grand nineteenth-century architecture and decent beach amusements, but is unexceptional by island standards.

Reaching out over the shallows of Ryde Sands, the functional half-mile-long **pier** is where the ferries dock and former London Underground rolling stock carries the seasonal throngs inland. Union Street rises steeply from the pier's base to the town centre and at its crest sits All Saints' Church whose spire acts as a landmark from vantage points all across the east of the island and even from parts of the mainland. The **Esplanade** extends eastwards from the pier, and along it are found traditional diversions: Ryde Arena and Ice Rink, the Eastern Pavilion (mimicking Brighton's original) and boating lake, all backed by sandy beaches. At the Esplanade's far end is the small Gothic Revival folly of Appley Tower, celebrating the sailing of the First Fleet to Botany Bay from Mother Bank, off Ryde, in 1787. It was once part of Appley House (now an expensive country hotel) built in the 1720s on the vast ill-gotten gains of arch-smuggler Daniel Boyce. Successful in bribing witnesses, sheriffs and juries at his many trials, he was finally convicted in 1733 when the law introduced the random appointment of jurors.

Practicalities

Ryde's **tourist office** (March–Oct Mon–Sat 9am–5.30pm, Sun 9am–5pm; Nov–Feb daily 9am–4.30pm; ☎01983/813818), **bus station**, **hovercraft terminal** and **Esplanade train station** (the northern terminus of the Island Line train line, which runs south to Shanklin) are all located near the base of the pier; there's also a **taxi** rank close by. **Boat trips** to the Solent forts leave from Ryde jetty; for details contact Solent & Wight Line Cruises (☎01983/564602).

Accommodation is available just over the road from the jetty in St Thomas Street, where the popular *Biskra House Hotel and Restaurant* at no. 17 (☎01983/567913; ⑤) offers balconied rooms and a terrace looking out to sea as well as a fine restaurant. *Yelf's Hotel* on Union Street (☎01983/564062, Ⓦwww.yelfshotel.com; ④) is one of Ryde's oldest hotels, right in the town centre, but is mainly geared up for business travellers. Inexpensive **B&Bs** don't exactly jump out at you in Ryde, but the *Trentham Guest House*, 38 The Strand (☎01983/563418; no credit cards; ①), offers great value, as does the similar *Vine Guest House*, 16 Castle St (☎01983/566633; ①; closed Nov & Dec) – both are just south of the Esplanade. The nearest **campsites** are the *Pondwell Caravan Park* two miles east of town on the way to Seaview (☎01983/612330), and *Beaper Farm*, three miles south on the Sandown road (☎01983/615210).

The area around Union Street offers the best **eating** opportunities. *Joe Daflo's Café Bar* at no. 24 has full restaurant meals and an appealing continental air, while just off it, on Castle Street, the *Blue Moon* has a cool sophistication and

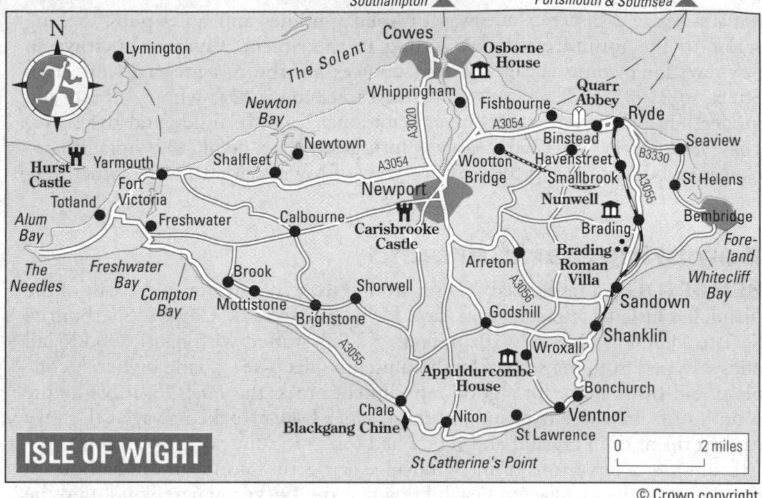

© Crown copyright

good fish and meat dishes (closed lunch, plus all Sun & Mon); both are moderately priced. On the Esplanade, the *Seafood Cabin* has seafood and sandwiches in plainer surroundings (closed Nov–Easter). The *Redan* at no. 76–7 is a traditional **pub** with bar meals and live bands on Thursday and Saturday nights.

Around Ryde

As elsewhere on the island, just a couple of miles can remove you from an undistinguished urban setting into one of idyllic rusticity. Just outside the village of Binstead, two miles west of Ryde's centre, lies one of the island's earliest Christian relics. In 1132 **Quarr Abbey** was founded by Richard de Redvers for Savigny monks; its name was derived from the quarries nearby, where stone was mined for use in the construction of Winchester and Chichester cathedrals. Subsequently the abbey was occupied by Benedictine and, later, Cistercian monks. Only stunted ruins survived the Dissolution and ensuing plunder of ready-cut stone, although an ivy-clad archway still hangs picturesquely over a farm track. In 1907 a new abbey was founded just west of the ruins – it's a striking rose-brick building with Byzantine overtones, and is open to the public (daily 9am–9pm; vespers 5pm).

Two miles south of Binstead, the village of **HAVENSTREET** houses the **Brickfields Horse Country** (daily 10am–5pm; £5.50), a centre for all things equine. Its attractions include a horse museum with a carriage collection, saddlery and blacksmith and wagon rides pulled by huge, docile Shires.

Three miles west of Havenstreet, **Wootton Bridge** is the end-stop of the **Isle of Wight Steam Railway** (late May to Oct 10.30am–4.15pm; £7.50, valid all day; ⓣ01983/882204, ⓦwww.iwsteamrailway.co.uk), which starts its delightful ten-mile round trip at Smallbrook on the main Ryde–Shanklin line to the east. The impeccably restored carriages in traditional green livery pass through lovely unspoilt countryside, and the ride makes a nostalgic way of spending an afternoon.

Two miles east of Ryde's centre, the quiet village of **SEAVIEW** used to be dominated by maritime industries, before the popularity of sea bathing elevated it to a select resort in the middle of the nineteenth century. And so it remains today, a discreet hideaway of holiday homes and quiet pubs, looking across to the rotund naval forts sitting in the Solent. **Overnight stays** in Seaview don't come cheap: the best choices are the *Seaview Hotel* on High Street (Ⓣ01983/612711, Ⓦwww.seaviewhotel.co.uk; ❻), whose superb and moderately priced restaurant serves traditional English dishes, and the *Spring Vale Hotel* (Ⓣ01983/612533, Ⓦwww.springvale-hotel.co.uk; ❻), a grand late-Georgian building along the seafront west of town, with a lovely garden terrace.

Bembridge and around

BEMBRIDGE, a residential area set around its own harbour in the east of the island, has little to attract visitors, save for its **Shipwreck Centre**, Sherbourne St (late March to Oct daily 10am–5pm; £2.95), stuffed with nautical odds and ends salvaged from the seabed by the museum's deep-sea-diving owner. A couple of old **pubs** make for a good refreshment break: the *Pilots' Boat Inn* by the mouth of Bembridge harbour and the *Crab & Lobster*, tucked away at the very eastern tip of the Foreland and renowned for its locally caught seafood.

In summer a ferry runs from Bembridge across the mouth of the harbour to the spit of land and adjacent beach known as the **Duver**, where you'll find the seasonal *Baywatch Café*. At the Duver's northern edge are the buttressed remains of St Helens Church, built by the Normans on the site where Hildila, an early Saxon missionary, set about converting the islanders to Christianity. From the church, follow the path southwest, which curls round the harbour past an old mill and returns to Bembridge along the boat-lined Embankment, built to reclaim from the sea the former inlet which once extended all the way to Brading (see below).

The island's easternmost tip, the **Foreland**, is a rather dreary corner, although the tidal beach at **Whitecliff Bay**, to the south, lightens the pallid air. From Whitecliff Bay a path gradually ascends towards the chalk cliffs of Culver and then onto **Bembridge Down**. A monument to Lord Yarborough, first commodore of the Royal Yacht Squadron at Cowes, caps the down, with refreshments available at the adjacent *Culver Haven Inn*. If you don't feel like walking up the steep two-mile path, you can drive to the top of the down (there's no bus service) and then stroll around up there; leave Bembridge on the Sandown road, the B3395, and soon after the airport a sharp left turn leads steeply upwards past a mid-nineteenth-century fort (currently occupied by an electronics company). The road ends in a warren of World War II emplacements – now colonized by rabbits – with island-wide views.

Brading

On the busy Ryde to Sandown road (A3055; bus #7, #7A, or #7B), the ancient village of **Brading** boasts a surprisingly disparate collection of ancient and modern sites. Just south of the village are the remains of **Brading Roman Villa** on Morton Old Road (April–Oct daily 9.30am–5pm; £2.95), one of two such villas on the island (the other is in Newport; see p.278), both of which were probably sites of bacchanalian worship. The Brading site is renowned for its superbly preserved mosaics, including intact images of Medusa and depictions of Orpheus – associated with the cult of Bacchus – as well as the mysterious and unique man with a cockerel's head.

In the centre of Brading, what is believed to be the island's oldest intact dwelling – dating from 1228 – now houses the **Isle of Wight Wax Works** (daily: mid-May to mid-Sept 10am–10pm; mid-Sept to mid-May 10am–5pm;

last entry 1hr before closing; £5.25). Inside, various dioramas portray island celebrities from Vespasian, the conqueror of Vectis (the Roman name of the island), to Tennyson. The Chamber of Horrors is as gruesome as you'd expect, with Animal World offering a little relief until you get to the "freaks of nature" section. Next door is the **Old Town Hall**, which still has the original stocks and whipping post once used to immobilize miscreants. For breakfasts, light lunches and teas, try *Penny Plain*, across the road at 44 High St (closed Nov–Easter), or *The Secret Garden*, 60–61 High St; both with charming, secluded gardens, while at 56 High St, the *Bugle Inn*, formerly a smugglers' rendezvous, has bar snacks. From behind the pub, a path leads to Brading Haven, once an inlet connected to the sea, where the smugglers used to land their contraband.

Nunwell House (July to early Sept Mon–Wed 1–5pm; £4), signposted off the A3055 less than a mile northwest of Brading, was where, in 1647, Charles I spent his last night of freedom before being taken to Carisbrooke Castle (see p.278) and thence to his eventual execution in Whitehall. The house has been in the Oglander family for nearly nine hundred years, with the present building being a mix of Jacobean and Georgian styles with Victorian additions. It sits in five acres of lovely gardens and remains very much the family home of the present owners, whose military legacy is reflected inside in a small exhibition commemorating the Home Guard, the voluntary defence force recruited during the early years of World War II when the island prepared to resist Nazi occupation. Guided tours of the house take place at 1.30pm, 2.30pm and 3.30pm, and the entry ticket includes a free guide booklet.

Sandown and Shanklin

The two eastern resorts of Sandown and Shanklin merge into each other across the sandy reach of Sandown Bay, representing the island's holiday-making epicentre. Frequently recorded as among Britain's sunniest spots, Sandown is a relic of a traditional Sixties bucket-and-spade resort, while Shanklin, with its auburn cliffs, Old Village and scenic Chine, has a marginally more sophisticated aura.

Appropriately, **SANDOWN** possesses the island's only surviving pleasure **pier**, bedecked with amusement arcades, cafeterias, dodgems and a large theatre with nightly entertainment in season – but out of season the town becomes rather desolate. The main distractions here lie next to each other at the northern end of the Esplanade. **Dinosaur Isle** on Culver Parade (daily: summer 10am–6pm, winter 10am–4pm; £4.60) is a lively exhibition of locally excavated dinosaur bones, with an animatronic model and working laboratory, and incorporating an illuminating **geological collection**, displaying some massive ammonites recovered locally. The adjacent **Tiger and Big Cat Sanctuary and Isle of Wight Zoological Gardens** (April–Sept daily 10am–6pm; March & Oct daily 10am–4pm; Nov open weekends weather permitting, call ⓣ01983/403883; £5.95) contains several species of tigers, panthers and other big cats, some of which are heading for extinction in the wild, as well as some frisky lemurs and monkeys. The zoo's reptile house has an exhaustive selection of spiders and snakes, and in summer there are snake-handling displays and talks.

Possibly being separated from the shore by hundred-foot cliffs has preserved **SHANKLIN** from the tawdry excesses of its northern neighbour – though it hasn't stopped the promotion of the **Old Village**'s rose-clad, thatched charm with the same zeal as Sandown's pier. The real thing can be found in any number of inland villages, but with the adjacent **Shanklin Chine** (daily: late March to May & Oct 10am–5pm; June–Sept 10am–10pm; £3.50), a twisting pathway descending a mossy ravine and decorated on summer nights with fairy lights, it all adds up to a picturesque spot, popular since early Victorian times when local resident John Keats drew his Romantic imagery from the environs.

Arrival and information

Sandown's **tourist office** is located at 8 High St (Easter–Oct Mon–Sat 9am–5.30pm, Sun 9am–5pm; Nov–Easter irregular hours, alternating with Shanklin tourist office; ⓣ01983/813818); Shanklin's is at 67 High St (same hours and telephone number). Both towns have Island Line train stations about half a mile inland from their beachfront centres.

Accommodation

As perennially popular resorts, Sandown and Shanklin have numerous accommodation options, mostly open year-round, though availability often dwindles to nothing in summer.

Hotels and B&Bs

Grange Hall 2 Grange Rd, Sandown ⓣ01983/403531, ⓔgrangehall@C4.com. Good-value Victorian cliff-top hotel in its own grounds, with all rooms en suite. ❸

Holliers 3 Church Rd, Shanklin Old Village ⓣ01983/862764, ⓦwww.holliers-hotel.com. Well-appointed seventeenth-century hotel in the Old Village equipped with indoor and outdoor swimming pools as well as a good restaurant and two bars. ❺

Luccombe Hall Luccombe Rd, Shanklin ⓣ01983/862719, ⓦwww.luccombehall.co.uk. Originally built as the summer palace for the Bishop of Portsmouth, this is now a secluded and finely situated hotel with two pools and an array of sporting facilities, a mile from the Old Village. ❺

Mount Brocas 15 Beachfield Rd, Sandown ⓣ01983/406276, ⓔbrocas@netguides.co.uk. Good-value B&B at the west end of High Street, very close to the beach. ❷

Pink Beach 20 Esplanade, Shanklin ⓣ01983/862501, ⓦwww.pink-beach-hotel.co.uk. Shocking-pink Victorian hotel, fronted by lawns, a stone's throw from the beach. All rooms are en suite. ❸

Ryedale Private Hotel 3 Atherley Rd ⓣ01983/862375, ⓦwww.ryedale-hotel.co.uk. Agreeably cluttered, family-run B&B just steps from Sandown train station; it's a short downhill walk to the beach. ❷

St Catherine's 1 Winchester Park Rd, Sandown, ⓣ01983/402392, ⓔstcatherines@wight-hotels.co.uk. Comfortable B&B with all rooms en suite, just five minutes' walk from the beach. ❸

Hostels and campsites

Cheverton Copse Holiday Park Sandown ⓣ01983/403161, ⓦwww.cheverton-copse.co.uk. Spacious park set among woodland, less than two miles from the beach, mainly for caravans but with some tent pitches. Signposted off the A3056 road. Closed Oct–March.

Landguard Camping Park Landguard Manor Rd, Shanklin ⓣ01983/867028, ⓦwww.landguard-camping.co.uk. Inexpensive and well-equipped campsite, a ten-minute walk north of the train station. Closed Oct–Easter.

Sandown Youth Hostel Fitzroy St, Sandown ⓣ0870/770 6020, ⓔsandown@yha.org.uk. Converted house right in the town centre, but only a few minutes' walk from the beach. Check for opening days as they vary. Dorm beds £11.50 per night.

Restaurants and cafés

Don't expect much in the way of gourmet cuisine in Shanklin or Sandown, though you'll find low prices for the straightforward seaside fare, and generally friendly service.

Barnaby's 4 Pier St, Sandown. Good-looking licensed eatery, close to the pier with meals and snacks under £5. Inexpensive.

Cottage Restaurant 8 East Cliff Rd, Shanklin Old Village ⓣ01983/862504. Olde-worlde restaurant serving traditional English dishes. Closed lunchtime & Mon. Moderate.

Fisherman's Cottage Free House Esplanade, Shanklin. Atmospheric seafaring pub at the southern end of the Esplanade, on Appley Beach, serv-

ing wholesome food. Closed Nov–Feb. No credit cards. Moderate.
Francine's 16 High St, Sandown ☎01983/403289. Licensed restaurant with a good variety of English and seafood dishes. No smoking. Closed Dec–Easter. Inexpensive to Moderate.
King's House Café 43 High St, Sandown. Continental-style licensed café with great views over the sea; snacks plus a dish of the day available from noon to 2pm. No credit cards. Moderate.
Ocean Deck Inn Esplanade, Sandown. Free house with an outdoor patio. Hot and cold meals are served all day as well as teas and coffees. Inexpensive to Moderate.

Ventnor and around

The seaside resort of **VENTNOR** and its two village suburbs of **Bonchurch** and **St Lawrence** sit at the foot of St Boniface Down, the island's highest point at 787ft. The down periodically disintegrates into landslides, creating the jumbled terraces known locally as the **Undercliff**, whose sheltered, south-facing aspect, mild winter temperatures and thick carpet of undergrowth have contributed to the former fishing village becoming a fashionable health spa. Thanks to these unique factors, the town possesses rather more character than the island's other resorts, its Gothic Revival buildings clinging dizzily to zigzagging bends.

The floral terraces of the **Cascade** curve down to the slender Esplanade and narrow beach, where former boat builders' cottages now provide more recreational services. Among them the **Longshoreman's Museum** (Easter–Christmas daily 9.30am–5pm; £1) offers a peep into Ventnor's bygone days with a collection of nautical objects, models and old photographs. From the shoreside *Spyglass Inn* (see below) on the Esplanade, it's a pleasant mile-long stroll to Ventnor's famous **Botanical Gardens**, where 22 landscaped acres of subtropical vegetation flourish. Displays are divided thematically, including the South African and Australian banks, the Culinary Herb and the Medicinal Gardens. There's also a **Smuggling Museum** inside the gardens (April–Sept daily 10am–5pm; £2.80), which capitalizes on Ventnor's long history of "owling", as the nefarious nocturnal activity was once known.

To the east of Ventnor, the ancient village of **BONCHURCH** exudes an alluring rustic charm with its duck pond and rows of quaint cottages set on the Undercliff's wooded slopes. Behind high stone walls loom grand Victorian country houses where writers such as Dickens, Thackeray and Swinburne once stayed. At Bonchurch's east end is the spartan, towerless edifice of the eleventh-century **Old Church of St Boniface** with its wreath of skewed gravestones and mature trees further enhancing the village. Above the village the **Landslip Footpath** descends the Undercliff. It's occasionally closed due to subsidence, so it's worth checking with the tourist office before you set off on an exploration.

Heading west from Ventnor, the road, still prone to subsidence, winds its way along the wooded hillside where the village of **St Lawrence** appears lost in the tumbling Undercliff. The studios of **Isle of Wight Glass** in the Old Park (Mon–Fri 9am–5pm, also Sat in summer 10am–4pm; 70p) give a rare chance to observe the process of glassblowing.

Practicalities

Ventnor's **tourist office** is at 34 High St (Easter–Oct Mon–Sat 9.30am–5.30pm, Sun 10am–3pm; ☎01983/813818). For **accommodation**, try the *Spyglass Inn* on Ventnor's Esplanade (☎01983/855338; ❸), which has a few self-contained rooms and balconies, with discounts for longer stays. A few doors down is *St Martin's* (☎01983/852345; no credit cards; ❸), with comfortable rooms and sea views, right next to the little wooden cottage where, in

1860, Turgenev started his novel *Fathers and Sons*. Some of the area's best choices are in Bonchurch, however, where the *Horseshoe Bay House Café*, Horseshoe Bay, offers B&B accommodation right on the beach (ⓣ01983/856800, ⓔhoward@horseshoebayhouse.com; ❷), and the small Georgian *Under Rock Country House* on Shore Road (ⓣ01983/855274; no credit cards; ❷) has light rooms and a subtropical rock garden. Off Shore Road, the classy, good-value *Winterbourne Hotel* (ⓣ01983/852535; ❷), right by St Boniface Church, has a pool and a private path leading to a small beach; most rooms have sea views and all are en suite. Lastly, on the main A3055, at Undercliff Drive, *Lisle Combe* (ⓣ01983/852582, ⓦwww.lislecombe.co.uk; no credit cards; ❷) offers B&B accommodation in a beautifully preserved early Victorian villa that was once the home of poet Alfred Noyes.

Apart from *St Martin's* – which does do cream teas and snacks – and *Lisle Combe*, you can eat at any of the above accommodation choices, and the excellent *Horseshoe Bay House Café* is worth exploring in any case, boasting 180-degree views from its outdoor tables, and crab salad, sea bass and lobster on the menu, as well as baguettes (closed eve & weekdays in winter; no credit cards). In Ventnor town centre, *Merlin's Bistro* (ⓣ01983/731173) on Blackgang Road serves tasty and inexpensive home-cooked snacks in a mellow atmosphere.

Appuldurcombe House and Godshill

Follow the B3327 for a couple of miles inland, over St Boniface Down, through arable farmland and past market gardens, to Wroxall, where a track leads left for half a mile to the ruins of **Appuldurcombe House** (ⓣ01983/852484 daily: May–Sept 10am–5pm; mid-Feb to April & Oct to mid-Dec 10am–4pm; £2.50; EH), the island's grandest pre-Victorian house. The present mansion was built in the late eighteenth century in the Palladian style on the site of an eleventh-century priory and an Elizabethan manor. Its gardens landscaped by Capability Brown (which included the erection of a "scenic" castle ruin – since dismantled – across the valley), the house was the home of Lord Yarborough before impecuniousness and neglect led to its semi-abandonment in the early twentieth century. What makes Appuldurcombe unusual is that it has been preserved in this state of decay, a partially roofed but intact shell where the evidence of a former owner's extravagant raising of all floor levels and doorways can clearly be seen. The house's stately eastern facade, spring-fed fountain and impressive situation, overlooking a fold in the downs, make for an illuminating visit. Back down the track, *Appuldurcombe Holiday Park* (ⓣ01983/852597, ⓦwww.appuldurcombegardens.co.uk; closed Nov–March) offers facilities for **campers**.

Pass through Freemantle Gate, an Ionic triumphal arch reputedly designed by James Wyatt and formerly the entrance to Appuldurcombe House, then follow the old carriage drive across the fields for a couple of miles and you'll come out opposite the village car park in **GODSHILL**. By road it's twice the distance to this "tourist village", jammed with summertime day-trippers come to appreciate the fairy-tale cuteness of its old core where the square-towered **Church of the Lily Cross** overlooks a cluster of thatched cottages and high-walled lanes. The church contains a very rare fifteenth-century painting, rediscovered in 1857, depicting Christ crucified on a triple-branched lily, as well as effigies of past owners of Appuldurcombe House, the Leighs and the Worsleys.

Other attractions have sprung up to capitalize on Godshill's enduring popularity. **Godshill Model Village** (April to late July & Sept daily 10am–5pm; late July to Aug 10am–6pm; March & Oct daily 10.30am–4pm; £2.95) is just what it says; and there's an Old Smithy, antique shops and a brace of quaint teashops on site, too.

St Catherine's Point to the Needles

The western Undercliff begins to recede at the village of Niton, where a footpath continues to the most southerly tip of the island, **St Catherine's Point**, marked by a modern lighthouse. A prominent landmark on the downs behind is **St Catherine's Oratory**, known locally as the "Pepper Pot". In fact it's a medieval lighthouse, reputedly built in 1325 as an act of expiation by Walter de Goditon who had attempted to pilfer a cargo of wine owned by a monastic community whose ship was wrecked off Atherfield Point in 1313. An adjacent oratory was also constructed but demolished during the Dissolution, although the crude lighthouse remained in use for over three hundred years.

A short distance west, **Blackgang Chine** (daily: end March to June & early Sept to Oct 10am–5pm; July to early Sept 10am–10pm; £7.50) opened as a landscaped garden in 1843 and gradually evolved into a theme park – possibly the world's first – that now offers a half-dozen exhibits from Cowboy Town to Jungleland, a giant maze, a rendition of a Victorian Quay and a high-speed water ride.

From Chale, Military Road continues west along the coast, a flat windswept drive with occasional turn-offs to small bays – though swimming is too dangerous on this stretch – and chines of which **Hanover Point** is the most impressive. Several old buildings in the area – including the *Wight Mouse Inn* – were once extended using timber salvaged from wrecks which foundered here.

At the village of Brook, where the impressive Brook House overlooks the valley, Military Road ascends the flank of Compton Down before descending into Freshwater Bay. If you're walking this way, you might stop off at the National Trust-owned **Compton Bay,** a splendid spot for a swim or a picnic, frequented by local surfers and accessed by a steep path leading down from the dark red cliffs.

Accommodation on the southwestern coast includes the very popular *Clarendon Hotel and Wight Mouse Inn*, Newport Road, Chale (ⓣ01983/730431, ⓦwww.wightmouseinns.co.uk; ⑤), a cluttered, family-run combination of pub, restaurant and hotel which welcomes children and puts on nightly live entertainment, located half a mile from Blackgang Chine. There are **campsites** at *Chine Farm*, Atherfield Bay (ⓣ01983/740228, ⓦwww.chine-farm.co.uk; closed Oct–April), *Grange Farm*, Brighstone Bay (ⓣ01983/740296, ⓦwww.brighstonebay.fsnet.co.uk; closed Nov–Feb) and *Compton Farm*, Brook (ⓣ01983/740215; closed Oct–April) – the last two working farms with free-range hens, ducks and milking cows (*Grange Farm* even has llamas and water buffalos).

Inland to Shorwell, Brighstone and Calbourne

A leisurely and rewarding inland detour northwards can fill a half-day or more and passes through many of the island's prettiest villages, containing nothing more than picturesque, typically English village greens, ancient churches and country pubs. **SHORWELL**, for example, has its terrace of thatched cottages, the *Crown Inn*'s delectable ales and a fine walk through the woodlands up onto Chillerton Downs, signposted near the wooden footbridge on the village's northern exit. For an overnight stay in the village, try *North Court*

(Ⓣ01983/740415; no credit cards; ❷), an impressive mansion with six bedrooms, all en suite, a music room, snooker, lovely gardens, and a croquet lawn.

The pretty village of **BRIGHSTONE**, a couple of miles west of Shorwell, has a fine pub, the *Three Bishops,* while three miles north of Brighstone, **CALBOURNE**'s quaint Winkle Street makes a much photographed rural, thatched scene. *Swainston Manor Hotel*, a mile and a half east of Calbourne (Ⓣ01983/521121, Ⓔswainstonmanor@aol.com; ❼), can provide a memorably grand overnight stay.

Dimbola Lodge, Alum Bay and the Needles

The western tip of the Isle of Wight holds sundry traces of some of the venerable Victorians who were drawn to the area. On the coastal road at Freshwater Bay, on the corner with Terrace Lane, **Dimbola Lodge** (Tues–Sun 10am–5pm, also Mon during school holidays; £3.50; Ⓦwww.dimbola.co.uk) was the home of pioneer photographer Julia Margaret Cameron. After visiting local resident Tennyson in 1860, Cameron immediately bought adjacent land on the nearby coast, joining two cottages to make a substantial home for herself and her family, where she practised her art until moving to Ceylon in 1875. The building now houses a gallery of her work, including an impressive range of portraits of some of the foremost society figures of her day, and also features changing exhibitions. There's a bookshop, tearoom and vegetarian restaurant on the premises too. If you want **accommodation** around here and are prepared to fork out, book into *Farringford Hotel*, on Bedbury Lane (Ⓣ01983/752500, Ⓦwww.farringford.co.uk; ❻), Tennyson's former home, where the facilities now include an outdoor pool, putting green and tennis courts as well as several cottage suites. On the way, you'll pass Freshwater's unusual ninety-year-old thatched Church of St Agnes; Tennyson's wife is buried in the churchyard. Inside, there are memorials to Tennyson as well as Thackeray's daughter, Lady Ritchie.

Between Freshwater Bay and the Needles, the breezy four-mile ridge of **Tennyson Down** is one of the island's most satisfying walks, with yet another monument to the poet at its 485-foot summit and vistas onto rolling downs and vales. There's a **youth hostel** a short walk northeast from the Needles, at Totland Bay (Ⓣ0870/770 6070, Ⓔtotland@yha.org.uk; closed Sun in winter), where beds are available for £11.50 a night; take bus #7A, #7B (both from just about anywhere on the island), #12 or #42 (both from Newport), alighting at Totland War Memorial, and walk a quarter-mile up Weston Road and Hurst Hill.

The focal points of the isle's western tip are **Alum Bay**'s multichrome cliffs and the chalk stacks of the Needles where Tennyson Down slips into the Channel. The road ends at **The Needles Pleasure Park** (April to early Nov daily 10am–5pm; free; buses #7, #7A, #7B, #42), a collection of fairground amusements, a glass studio and companies running boat trips out around the Needles. There's a plinth commemorating Marconi's first telegraph messages to a tug moored in the bay in 1898. A chair lift (£3.50 return) runs down to the foot of the cliffs of Alum Bay whose ochre-hued sands, used as pigments for painting local landscapes in the Victorian era, contrast brightly with the chalk face of the Needles headland.

From the Pleasure Park, it's a twenty-minute walk to the lookout on top of the three tall chalk stacks known as **The Needles**, best seen from a boat trip leaving from Alum Bay (Needles Pleasure Cruises; Ⓣ01983/754477; 25min), or from the tunnel by the **Old Battery**, a fort built 250ft above the sea dating from 1862 (April to June, Sept & Oct Mon–Thurs & Sun 10.30am–5pm; July

& Aug daily 10.30am–5pm; last entry 1hr before closing; £3; NT; bus #42 from Newport). During the 1950s the fort was a military establishment where rockets were strapped down and their engines tested. You can see the original gun tunnels, one of which, 250ft long, holds an exhibition. The fort is sometimes closed in bad weather; call to check on ☎01983/754772.

Yarmouth and around

Situated at the mouth of the River Yar, the pleasant town of **YARMOUTH** was the island's first purpose-built port. Although razed by the French in 1377 on their way to Newtown and Carisbrooke, the port began to prosper again after **Yarmouth Castle** (April–Sept daily 10am–6pm; Oct 10am–5pm; £2.50; EH), tucked between the quay and the pier, was built in the sixteenth century by the command of Henry VIII. The castle today holds exhibitions of paintings and photography relating to the Isle of Wight. Although there's little more to see in town, Yarmouth, linked to Lymington in the New Forest by car ferry, makes an appealing arrival or departure point (for details of ferry departures, see p.265).

The **tourist office** is on Yarmouth Quay (Easter–Oct Mon–Sat 9am–5.30pm, Sun 9am–5pm; Nov–Easter daily 10am–4pm; ☎01983/813818). There's a decent range of affordable **accommodation** in town including *Jireh House* in St James's Square (☎01983/760513; ❸), a pretty seventeenth-century stone guest house and tearoom, which serves evening meals in summer. *Wavell's*, a grocer's shop also on the square (☎01983/760738; ❷), offers bright, contemporary-style rooms and huge breakfasts, while opposite is the cosy *Bugle Hotel* (☎01983/760272; ❸), which has a range of rooms (all non-smoking) and also holds one of the town's many good **pubs**. There are bar meals in the *Bugle*'s pub and more sophisticated fare at its moderately priced *Poacher's Restaurant*. Alternatively, try the less expensive *Fender's Bistro* – its ceiling plastered with board games – in Bridge Road.

Two miles west of town **Fort Victoria Country Park** (free access) is a Palmerston-era fort looking out to Hurst Castle on the mainland, less than a mile away. Besides footpaths through the woodlands and along the coast, there's an **aquarium** (April–Oct daily 10am–6pm; £1.90), a **planetarium** (during school holidays daily 10am–5pm; last ticket 1hr before closing; at other times, call to check; £2.50; ☎0800/195 8295), a **Maritime Heritage Exhibition** (April–Oct daily 10am–5pm; £1.50), focusing on the work of marine archeologists, and a **model railway**, claimed to be the largest in England (April–Sept daily 10am–5pm; Oct Sat & Sun 10am–5pm; £3.50).

Newtown and Shalfleet

At the time of the fourteenth-century raids on the island, **NEWTOWN**, sitting on an inlet of the eponymous estuary on the northwest coast, had been the Isle of Wight's capital for 150 years. This purpose-built medieval settlement never fully recovered from the French sacking in 1377 and nothing remains of the ancient town, bar a trace of its gridded street pattern and an incongruously stranded Jacobean **town hall** (April–June & Sept–Nov Mon, Wed & Sun 2–5pm; July & Aug Mon–Thurs & Sun 2–5pm; £1.60; NT). North of the town, a jetty leads out around a nature reserve, past the disintegrating quays of Newtown's former harbour, where curlews, geese and other waterfowl nest.

Just a mile's walk away, at the head of one of the estuary's inlets, **SHALFLEET**'s position on the Newport road makes it livelier than Newtown. The *New Inn*, just opposite the largely unrestored Norman church, serves delicious seafood dishes (book in the evenings: ☎01983/531314); while over the road the *Old Malthouse* (ⓣ01983/531329, ⓔb&b@oldmalthouse.demon.co.uk; no credit cards; ❷) is a quiet and comfortable **B&B**. Heading north up Mill Road, you'll pass the old watermill and the stunted remains of the quays that once lined the inlet. At the end of Mill Road a boatyard looks out onto the tidal creeks, another popular spot for birdwatchers.

Cowes and around

COWES, at the island's northern tip, is inextricably associated with sailing craft and boat building: Henry VIII built a castle here to defend the Solent's expanding naval dockyards from the French and Spanish, and in the 1950s the world's first hovercraft made its test runs here. In 1820 the Prince Regent's patronage of the yacht club gave the port its cachet with the Royal Yacht Squadron, now one of the world's most exclusive sailing clubs, permitted to fly the St George's Ensign guaranteeing free entry to all foreign ports. Only its three hundred members and their guests are permitted within the hallowed precincts of the club house in the remains of Henry VIII's castle, and the club's landing stage is sacrosanct. The first week of August sees the international yachting festival known as **Cowes Week**, which visiting royalty turns into a high-society gala, although the presence of serious sailors helps to lift the event above the merely ceremonial. In fact, it's a great opportunity to view some extraordinary craft and immerse yourself in yachting lore among the cognoscenti, while the glitzy element helps to invest the proceedings with a bit of glamour and frivolity. There are dozens of organized events, including a spectacular fireworks display on the Friday night, and a great party atmosphere. You don't need to be in Cowes during Cowes Week to sample the nautical vibe, however, as most summer weekends there's some form of yachting or powerboat racing.

The town is bisected by the River Medina, with West Cowes being the older and more interesting half, its High Street meandering up from the waterfront Parade. Along the High Street you'll find shops reflecting the town's gentrified heritage, with boatyards, chandlers and Beken's famous yachting gallery – a photo by Beken of your yacht is considered as prestigious as a family portrait by Lord Snowdon.

Practicalities

The Cowes **tourist office** is at the Arcade, Fountain Quay, West Cowes (April–Oct Mon–Sat 9am–5pm, Sun 10am–4pm, with extended hours during Cowes Week; Nov–March Tues–Sat 9.30am–4.30pm; ⓣ01983/813818). **Boat trips** upriver and around the harbour leave from the Parade; for details contact Solent & Wight Line Cruises (ⓣ01983/564602, ⓦwww.solentcruises.co.uk).

The more affordable **accommodation** options include the *Union Inn* in Watch House Lane, off High Street (ⓣ01983/293163; ❸), and *Halcyone Villa*, Grove Road, up Mill Hill Road from the east end of the High Street (ⓣ01983/291334, ⓔhalcyonevilla@bigfoot.com; ❷), and in East Cowes, there's the *Doghouse* (ⓣ01983/293677; no credit cards; ❸), Crossways Rd, opposite Osborne House, and, nearby, the *Crossways House Hotel* (ⓣ01983/298282; ❸). Prices rise steeply during Cowes Week, and most places are booked up well in advance.

The town has a decent selection of places to **eat**: the *Octopus's Garden*, 63 High St, is a café and bistro filled with Beatles memorabilia and serving all-day breakfasts as well as baguettes and pies. *Cats*, 15 Shooters' Hill (ⓣ01983/298754), offers an eclectic and innovative menu and has *The Kitten*

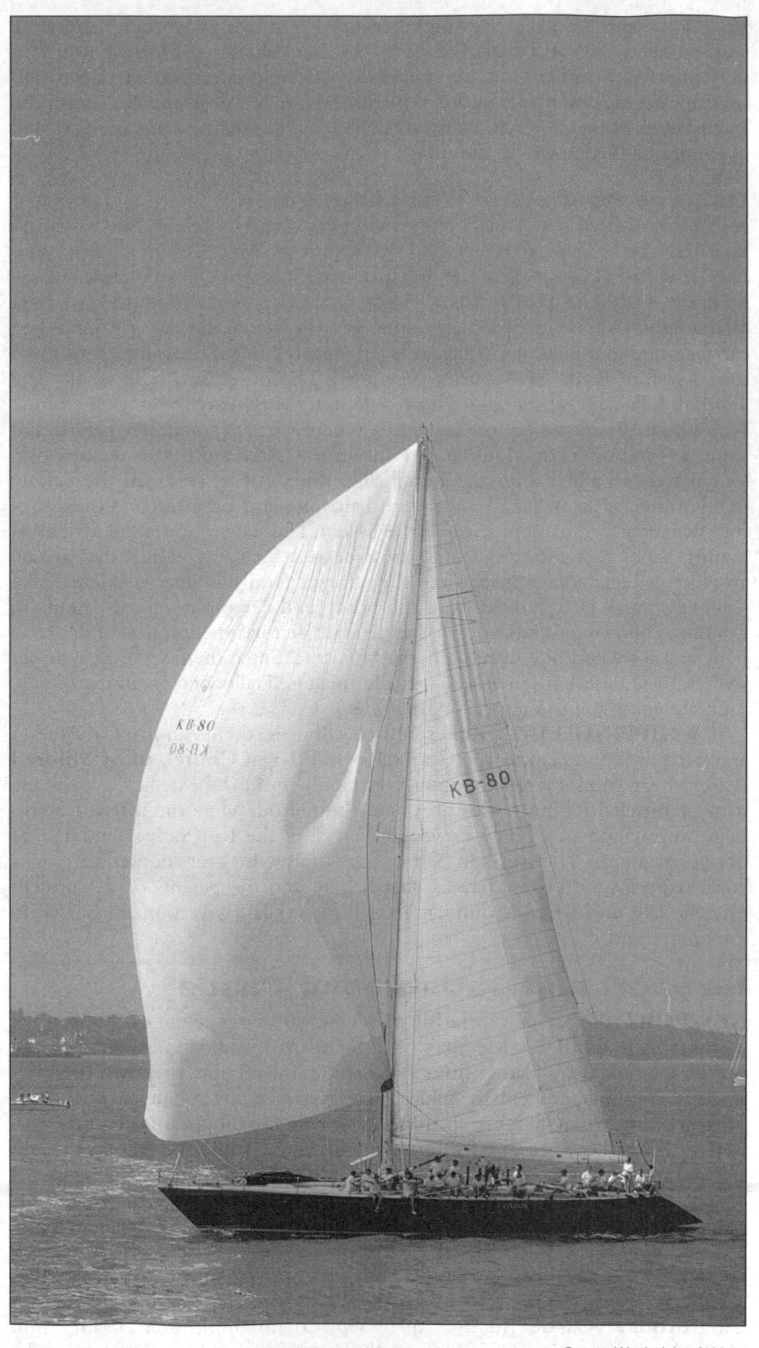

△ Cowes Week, Isle of Wight

Club downstairs, good for late-night drinking and lounging. Under the same management, *DB's* at 3 Bath Rd (☎01983/291714; closed Mon, Tues & Sun in winter) is a more intimate restaurant, offering international dishes and mouthwatering desserts. Traditional **pub** meals are served at the *Anchor* on the High Street, which also has rooms (☎01983/292823; ❷) and a garden, as well as live music Wednesday to Saturday.

Osborne House and Whippingham

A "floating bridge", or chain ferry (Mon–Sat 5am–midnight, Sun 6.35am–midnight; pedestrians free, cars £1.30) connects West Cowes to the more industrial East Cowes, where the only place of interest is Queen Victoria's family home, **Osborne House** (daily: April–Oct 10am–5pm; grounds April–Sept 10am–6pm; Oct 10am–5pm; last admission 1hr before closing; £8 including carriage ride to the Swiss Cottage; EH), signposted one mile southeast of town (bus #4 from Ryde or #5 from Newport). The house was built in the late 1840s by Prince Albert and Thomas Cubitt, with extensions such as the Household Wing, the Swiss Cottage – where Victoria's children played and studied – and the exotic Durbar Room with its elaborate Indian plasterwork, which were all added over the next half-century. Albert designed the private family home as an Italianate villa, with balconies and large terraces overlooking the landscaped gardens towards the Solent. The state rooms, used for entertaining visiting dignitaries, exude an expected formality, while the private apartments feel more homely, like the affluent family holiday residence that Osborne was – far removed from the pomp and ceremony of state affairs in London. Following Albert's death, the desolate Victoria spent much of her time here, and it's where she eventually died in 1901. Since then, according to her wishes, the house has remained virtually unaltered, allowing an unexpectedly intimate glimpse into Victoria's family life.

At **WHIPPINGHAM**, a mile south of Osborne, there's another of Albert's architectural extravaganzas, the Gothic Revival **Royal Church of St Mildred** (Easter–Sept Mon–Fri 10am–5pm; Oct closes 4pm). Its exterior evokes the many-pinnacled Rhine castles of Albert's homeland, while the interior boasts huge rose windows, a finely carved altarpiece of the Last Supper and a large octagonal lantern. The German Battenberg family, who later adopted the anglicized name Mountbatten, have a chapel here and the parents of the present Queen's late uncle, Earl Mountbatten, the island's last governor, are buried in the churchyard.

Newport and Carisbrooke Castle

NEWPORT, the capital of the Isle of Wight, sits at the centre of the island at a point where the River Medina's commercial navigability ends. Apart from a few pleasant old quays dating from its days as an inland port, the town isn't particularly engaging, content to fulfil its role as the island's municipal and commercial centre, where familiar chain stores draw in the shoppers. Newport offers little of cultural interest apart from a cinema, the Medina and Apollo theatres and the remains of the **Roman villa** in Cypress Road (April–Nov Mon–Sat 10am–4.30pm, July & Aug also Sun noon–4pm; £2). A well-signposted ten-minute walk southeast of the town centre, a few rudimentary foundations of the third-century villa are on show, as well as some excavated artefacts in the museum, but frankly you'd be better off visiting its sister villa in Brading (see p.268).

The town's main attraction, however, lies in the hilltop fortress of **Carisbrooke Castle** (daily: April–Sept 10am–6pm; Oct 10am–5pm; Nov–March 10am–4pm; £5; EH), on the southwest outskirts (buses #7, #7A or #7B from Newport). The austere Norman keep was greatly extended over the years, first in the thirteenth century by the imperious Countess Isabella who inherited much of the island and ruled it as a petty kingdom. Having tolerated her excesses, the Crown bought her estates as she lay dying in 1293 and appointed governors to defend the island, rather than risking its security to the vagaries of birthright. This precaution proved timely as the following century saw repeated French raids right across the island.

Carisbrooke's most famous visitor was Charles I, detained here (and caught one night ignominiously jammed between his room's bars while attempting escape) prior to his execution in London. The **museum** in the centre of the castle features many relics from his incarceration, as well as those of the last royal resident, Princess Beatrice, Queen Victoria's youngest daughter. The castle's other notable curiosity is the sixteenth-century well-house, where donkeys still trudge inside a huge treadmill to raise a barrel 160ft up the well shaft. A stroll around the battlements provides several lofty perspectives of the castle's interior as well as sweeping views across the centre of the island.

Newport's **tourist office** is in the centre of town at the Guildhall, High Street (Mon–Sat 9am–5.30pm, Sun 10am–4pm; ⓣ01983/813818). Your best option for a meal or a drink is to stick around Carisbrooke: try the *Eight Bells* **pub**, near the castle, serving food all day until 10.30pm or the ever-popular, moderately priced *Valentino's* Italian **restaurant** (ⓣ01983/522458; closed Sun), both on Carisbrooke High Street, at the top of the hill.

Winchester and around

Nowadays a tranquil, handsome market town, set amid docile hay-meadows and watercress beds, **WINCHESTER** was once one of the mightiest settlements in England. Under the Romans it was Venta Belgarum, the fifth largest town in Britain, but it was **Alfred the Great** who really put Winchester on the map when he made it the capital of his Wessex kingdom in the ninth century. For the next couple of centuries Winchester ranked alongside London, its status affirmed by William the Conqueror's coronation in both cities and by his commissioning of the local monks to prepare the **Domesday Book**. As the shrine of St Swithun, King Alfred's tutor, Winchester attracted innumerable pilgrims, and throughout the medieval era the city continued to command enormous ecclesiastical and political influence – Bishop **William of Wykeham**, founder of Winchester College and Oxford's New College, was twice chancellor of England. It wasn't until after the Battle of Naseby in 1645, when Cromwell took the city, that Winchester began its decline into provinciality.

Hampshire's county town now has a scholarly and slightly anachronistic air, embodied by the ancient almshouses that still provide shelter for senior citizens of "noble poverty" – the pensioners can be seen wandering round the town in medieval black or mulberry-coloured gowns with silver badges. A trip to this secluded old city is a must – not only for the magnificent **cathedral**, chief relic of Winchester's medieval glory, but for the all-round, well-preserved ambience of England's one-time capital.

Arrival and information

Winchester **train station** is about a mile northwest of the cathedral on Stockbridge Road. If you arrive by **bus**, you'll find yourself on the Broadway, conveniently opposite the **tourist office** in the imposing Guildhall (May–Sept

Mon–Sat 9.30am–5.30pm, Sun 11am–4pm; Oct–April Mon–Sat 10am–5pm; ⓣ01962/840500, ⓦwww.visitwinchester.co.uk). The tourist office has plenty of information about the city and its environs, and distributes excellent visitors' guides. Ask here about the daily, **guided walks** of the city (1hr 30min; £3), or pick up the free "Winchester Walk" leaflet which allows you to take in all the sights at your own pace. You can also find here literature on the eighty-mile South Downs Way, which runs for eighty miles between Winchester and Beachy Head, Sussex (see p.223).

Accommodation

Winchester has a range of attractive hotels and B&Bs, though you'll be paying fairly high rates to stay in the most central area. Ask about reductions for stays of more than a couple of nights.

Hotels and guest houses

9 St Faith's Road ⓣ01962/877522 or 07811/952618. Not very central and there's only one twin room available, but this B&B makes a highly pleasant stop. Breakfast overlooking the garden is all organic, with veggie food a speciality. No credit cards. ❷

12 Christchurch Rd ⓣ01962/854272. There are just two rooms at this neat and homely B&B with a conservatory and garden. No credit cards. ❶

Dawn Cottage 99 Romsey Rd ⓣ01962/869956, ⓔdawncottage@hotmail.com. Classy non-smoking B&B about a mile west of the centre and connected by frequent bus services. The comfortable rooms – one with a spa bath at a slightly higher rate – have great views over the Itchen Valley. ❸

East View 16 Clifton Hill ⓣ01962/862986. Small Victorian town house overlooking the city and surrounding countryside. ❸

The Farrells 5 Ranelagh Rd ⓣ01962/869555. Small, inexpensive B&B in a Victorian house off St Cross Road. No smoking. No credit cards. ❷

Portland House 63 Tower St ⓣ01962/865195, ⓔtony@knightworld.com. Georgian house in a quiet mews between the cathedral and train station. All rooms are en suite and fully equipped, and there's a guests' lounge. No credit cards. ❸

Stratton House Stratton Rd, St Giles Hill ⓣ01962/863919, ⓔStrattongroup@btinternet.com. Hundred-year-old house in its own grounds with good views of the city. Large gardens and car park. Free collection from bus or train stations. ❹

Sullivans 29 Stockbridge Rd ⓣ01962/862027, ⓔsullivans_bandb@amserve.net. Victorian town cottage a few minutes' walk from the train station, with shared bathrooms, low rates and multilingual owners. No credit cards. ❶

Wykeham Arms 75 Kingsgate St ⓣ01962/853834. Fine old hostelry where the art of classy inn-keeping has not yet vanished. Quirkily shaped rooms with beams and assorted antiques enhance the atmosphere. ❺

Hostels and campsites

Folly Farm Touring Caravan Park Crawley ⓣ01962/776486. Flat site with full facilities, four miles west of town towards Stockbridge off the B3049. Take any bus towards Salisbury (#7, #25, #26 and #28 are most frequent) – there's a stop right outside the back gate. Closed Nov–Feb.

Youth Hostel City Mill, 1 Water Lane ⓣ0870/770 6092, ⓔwinchester@yha.org.uk. One of the original YHA hostels is housed in a lovely National Trust-owned eighteenth-century mill. It's very popular, so book ahead. Beds cost £10.25.

The City

The first minster to be built in Winchester was raised by Cenwalh, the Saxon king of Wessex in the mid-seventh century and traces of this building have been unearthed near the present **cathedral** (daily 8.30am–6pm; £3.50 donation requested), which was begun in 1079 and completed some three hundred years later, producing a church whose elements range from early Norman to Perpendicular styles. The exterior is not its best feature – squat and massive, the cathedral crouches stumpily over the tidy lawns of the Cathedral Close. The interior is rich and complex, however, and its 556-foot **nave** makes this Europe's longest medieval church. Outstanding features include its carved

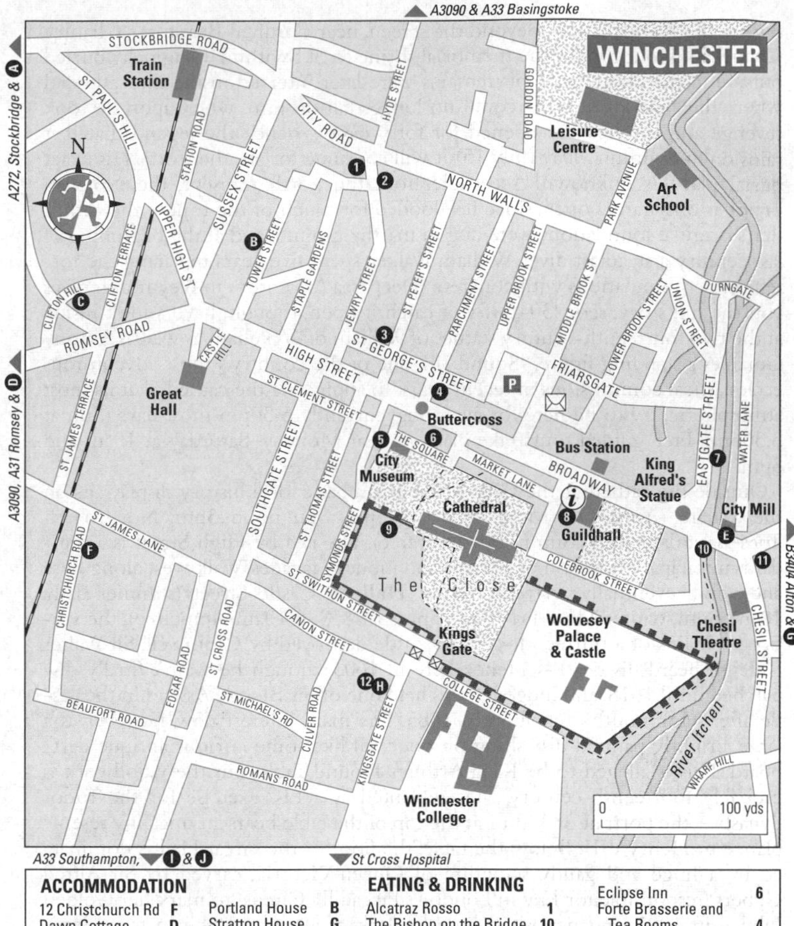

ACCOMMODATION

12 Christchurch Rd	F	Portland House	B
Dawn Cottage	D	Stratton House	G
East View	C	Sullivans	A
The Farrells	J	Wykeham Arms	H
9 St Faith's Road	I	Youth Hostel	E

EATING & DRINKING

Alcatraz Rosso	1
The Bishop on the Bridge	10
La Bodega	5
Cathedral Refectory	9
Courtyard Café	8
Dilse	3
Eclipse Inn	6
Forte Brasserie and Tea Rooms	4
The Mash Tun	7
Loch Fyne	2
Old Chesil Rectory	11
Wykeham Arms	12

Norman font of black Tournai marble, the fourteenth-century misericords (the choir stalls are the oldest complete set in the country) and some amazing monuments – **William of Wykeham's Chantry**, halfway down the nave on the right, is one of the best. Jane Austen, who died in Winchester, is commemorated close to the font by a memorial brass and slab beneath which she's interred, though she's recorded simply as the daughter of a local clergyman. Above the high altar lie the mortuary chests of pre-Conquest kings, including Knut (though the bones were mixed up after Cromwell's Roundheads broke up the chests in 1645); William Rufus, killed while hunting in the New Forest in 1100, lies in the presbytery. The statuary on the impressive screen at the end of the presbytery, showing Queen Victoria and Alfred the Great among many others, was added in the Victorian era, to replace the original images destroyed during the Reformation. Beyond the screen, near Cardinal Beaufort's Chantry Chapel, look out too for the memorial shrine to St Swithun. Originally buried outside in the churchyard, his remains were later interred inside the cathedral where the "rain of heaven" could no longer fall on him, whereupon he took revenge and the heavens opened for forty days – hence the legend that if it rains on St Swithun's Day (July 15) it will continue for another forty. His exact burial place is unknown. Accessible from the north transept, the Norman **crypt** is only rarely open, since it's flooded for much of the time – the cathedral's original foundations were dug in marshy ground, and at the beginning of last century a steadfast diver, William Walker, spent five years replacing the rotten timber foundations with concrete (Deep Sea Adventure in Weymouth gives you the full story; see p.304). If you catch it open, though, have a look inside at the two fourteenth-century statues of William of Wykeham as well as Antony Gormley's standing figure, "Sound II", one of the country's most adventurous ecclesiastical commissions in recent years. To appreciate the cathedral at its most atmospheric, try to be here for evensong, currently 5.30pm most days (Sun at 3.30pm). Free guided tours take place all year Monday–Saturday at 10am and 3pm.

Outside the cathedral, the **City Museum**, a basic local history display, sits on the Square (April–Oct Mon–Sat 10am–5pm, Sun noon–5pm; Nov–March Tues–Sat 10am–4pm, Sun noon–4pm; free). The nearby High Street is a standard municipal mishmash of ancient and modern facades. Walk west along here and you'll eventually arrive at **Great Hall** on Castle Street (summer daily 10am–5pm; winter Mon–Fri 10am–5pm, Sat & Sun 10am–4pm; free), the vestigial remains of a thirteenth-century castle destroyed by Cromwell. Sir Walter Raleigh heard his death sentence here in 1603, though he wasn't finally dispatched until 1618, and Judge Jeffreys held one of his Bloody Assizes in the castle after Monmouth's rebellion in 1685. The main interest now, however, is a large, brightly painted disc slung on one wall like some curious antique dartboard. This is alleged to be King Arthur's Round Table, but the woodwork is probably fourteenth-century, later repainted as a PR exercise for the Tudor dynasty – the portrait of Arthur at the top of the table bears an uncanny resemblance to Henry VIII. Below the table, the floor of the Great Hall is dominated by a huge and gaudy sculpture of Queen Victoria, carved by Sir Alfred Gilbert (responsible for *Eros* in London's Piccadilly Circus) to mark her Golden Jubilee in 1887, and deposited here for lack of anywhere else in town large enough to hold it. Adjoining the Great Hall, an illuminating exhibition relates the history of the Norman castle and Great Hall, and you can also take a brief wander in Queen Eleanor's Medieval Garden – a re-creation of a noblewoman's shady retreat.

Head east along the High Street, past the striking, neo-Gothic Guildhall and the august bronze statue of King Alfred on the Broadway, to reach the River Itchen and the **City Mill** (March Sat & Sun 11am–5pm; April–June, Sept & Oct Wed–Sun 11am–5pm; July & Aug daily 11am–5pm; £2; NT), where you can see restored mill machinery; the building is now part-occupied by a youth hostel (see p.280). Turning right before the bridge you pass what remains of the Saxon walls, which bracket the ruins of the twelfth-century **Wolvesey Castle** (April–Sept daily 10am–6pm; Oct daily 10am–5pm; £2.20; EH) and the Bishop's Palace, built by Christopher Wren. Immediately to the west up College Street stand the buildings of **Winchester College**, the oldest public school in England – established in 1382 by William of Wykeham for "poor scholars", it now educates few but the wealthy and privileged. The cloisters and chantry are open during term time and the chapel is open all year. Jane Austen moved to the house at 8 College St from Chawton in 1817, when she was already ill with Addison's Disease, dying there later the same year. The thirteenth-century **Kings Gate**, at the top of College Street, is one of the city's original medieval gateways, housing the tiny St Swithun's Church.

About a mile south of College Walk, reached by a pleasant stroll across the watermeadows of the Itchen, lies **St Cross Hospital** (Easter–Sept Mon–Sat 9.30am–5pm; Oct–Easter 10.30am–3.30pm; £2). Founded in 1136 as a hostel for poor brethren, it boasts a fine church, begun in that year and completed a century or so later, where you can see a triptych by the Flemish painter Mabuse. Needy wayfarers may still apply for the "dole" at the Porter's Lodge – a tiny portion of bread and beer.

Eating and drinking

Winchester's restaurants and pubs offer fairly traditional fare on the whole, though choice has widened in recent years, and there are a handful of places worth going out of your way for.

Alcatraz Rosso Jewry St ☎01962/860047. Cool, modern Italian eaterie, with a reliable menu of pizzas and pastas. Moderate.

The Bishop on the Bridge 1 High Street. Spacious modern bar with nice riverside terrace and standard pub food. Inexpensive.

La Bodega 9 The Square ☎01962/864004. Lively wine bar with tapas downstairs, restaurant upstairs with Spanish and Italian dishes, and views across to the cathedral. Inexpensive to Moderate.

Cathedral Refectory Inner Close. Good-value lunch-spot run by the Friends of Winchester Cathedral, where you can sample "trenchers", thick bread soaked in juices, used in medieval times as plates. Inexpensive.

Courtyard Café The Guildhall, Broadway. Casual café with gallery attached and outdoor eating; more substantial food and ales are served at the indoor bistro. Also accessed from the tourist office. Closed evenings. Inexpensive.

Dilse 8 St George Street ☎01962/862838. Welcome antidote to traditional Indian restaurants, with bright colours and modern canvases on walls. North Indian and Bengali cuisine predominates. Moderate.

Eclipse Inn 25 The Square. Picturesque sixteenth-century inn with some pavement seating, occupying the former rectory of Saint Lawrence's Church. Specializes in pies and casseroles. Inexpensive.

Forte Brasserie and Tea Rooms 78 Parchment St ☎01962/856840. Animated spot in the heart of the shopping area. Buffalo burgers and Moroccan lamb with couscous are on the menu, as well as a range of snacks, including renowned scones. Open daytime and Thurs & Fri eves only. Closed Sun. Inexpensive to Moderate.

Loch Fyne 18 Jewry St ☎01962/872930. Converted jailhouse retaining its galleries and beams. It specializes in fish flown in direct from Scotland's Loch Fyne, but also serves up excellent meat and vegetarian dishes. Moderate.

The Mash Tun 60 Eastgate St. Riverside alehouse catering to a largely student population, with a secluded terrace. Snacks served until 7pm, and there are DJs and live music, plus discounts for students. Inexpensive.

Old Chesil Rectory 1 Chesil St ☎01962/851555. Fifteenth-century oak-beamed restaurant serving traditional English cooking. Moderate.

Wykeham Arms 75 Kingsgate St ☎01962/853838. Winchester's best pub is somewhat unprepossessing from the outside, but inside it's a maze of characterful, intimate spaces where gourmet-standard food is served daily. Moderate.

Houghton Lodge

Eight miles west of Winchester and one and a half miles south of Stockbridge, **Houghton Lodge** (March–Sept Mon, Tues, Thurs & Fri 2–5pm, Sat & Sun 10am–5pm; £5) is a rare example of an eighteenth-century cottage orné, or rural retreat for rich townsfolk. The main attraction, though, is the surrounding gardens that sweep down to the River Test at a choice trout-fishing spot. Admission also includes a tour of the Hydroponicum and a talk on the art of hydroponics (a system of growing plants in water).

Central and northern Hampshire

Aside from a few centres of population of little interest to the visitor, such as Petersfield and Basingstoke, central and northern Hampshire is a relatively rural region. It holds a few points of interest, such as the village of **Chawton**, where Jane Austen wrote most of her books, and **Alton**, the jumping-off point for the Mid-Hants Watercress Railway Line. Hampshire's northern reaches are most notable for their stately homes: **Stratfield Saye**, Wellington's reward for winning at Waterloo; the superbly preserved Tudor manor house, **the Vyne**; and the outstanding excess of **Highclere Castle** in the county's northwest corner. Although Alton, Petersfield and Basingstoke are all easily accessible by train from Waterloo, getting to the sites described below is far more easily accomplished with your own transport.

Queen Elizabeth Country Park

Petersfield, situated on the Portsmouth to London road, originally grew up as a staging post on the old coach road and today is an unassuming provincial town with little appeal for tourists. Its main attraction lies three miles south of town where the A3 cuts through the South Downs. The **Queen Elizabeth Country Park** (free access; information centre April–Oct daily 10am–5.30pm; Nov & Dec daily 10am–4.30pm; Jan–March Sat & Sun 10am–dusk; ⓣ023/9259 5040), although the path actually continues another quarter of a mile to Buriton. A mixture of chalk downland and managed forest, the park is crisscrossed with marked trails which you can explore on foot, horse or mountain bike; the more adventurous can try hang- and para-gliding from Butser Hill on the other side of the A3.

Local information is available from Petersfield's **tourist office,** housed in the library on Petersfield Square and keeping the same hours (April–Sept Mon, Wed & Fri 9.30am–5pm, Sat 9.30am–1pm; Oct–March Mon–Wed & Fri 9.30am–5pm, Sat 9.30am–1pm; ⓣ01730/268829), and **mountain bikes** can be rented from Owen Cycles, Lavant St, Petersfield (£10/day; ⓣ01730/260446) – phone first to make sure of availability. Bed and breakfast **accommodation** is available at the nearby village of Buriton, on the north side of the park; try the eighteenth-century farmhouse *Nursted Farm* (ⓣ01730/264278; no credit cards; ❶) a few minutes' drive northeast of the village off the B2146. Alternatively, in the pretty village of East Meon, three miles west of Buriton, *Mizzards Farm* (ⓣ01730/821656; no credit cards; ❹) offers B&B rooms in a lovely, five-hundred-year-old building.

Alton, Chawton and Selborne

Thirteen miles north of Petersfield and accessible hourly by train from London Waterloo or bus from Winchester, **ALTON** is an attractive town, whose major point of interest is the fifteenth-century **Church of St Lawrence** (daily 9am–6pm; free), notable for its austere Perpendicular style. Its south door still bears the marks of the shot which killed Royalist commander Colonel Boles, who had been chased by Roundheads through the streets of Alton and into the church during the Civil War. Buried in the church's cemetery is Fanny Adams, a little girl brutally hacked to death in 1867, whose name gave rise to the expression "sweet Fanny Adams" – meaning something negligible or without value; sailors at that time used the murder victim's name to describe the recent issue of tinned mutton, whose nutritional value they doubted.

Alton is the terminus for the **Mid-Hants Watercress Line** (March, April & Oct Sat & Sun; May–Sept & school holidays daily; ⓣ01962/733810, ⓦwww.watercressline.co.uk; £9), a jolly, steam-powered train, so named because it passes through the former watercress beds that once flourished here. The train chuffs ten miles to Alresford, east of Winchester, with gourmet dinners served on board on Saturday evenings and traditional Sunday lunches too.

A mile southwest of Alton lies the village of **CHAWTON**, where Jane Austen lived from 1809 to 1817, during the last and most prolific years of her life, and where she wrote or revised almost all her six books, including *Sense and Sensibility* and *Pride and Prejudice*. **Jane Austen's House** (March–Nov daily 11am–4pm; Dec–Feb Sat & Sun 11am–4pm; £4), in the centre of the village, is a plain red-brick building, containing first editions of some of her greatest works.

Four miles south of Chawton is the little village of **SELBORNE** where the eighteenth-century naturalist Gilbert White wrote his ecological treatise, *The Natural History and Antiquities of Selborne*. In the High Street his house, **The Wakes** (daily 11am–5pm; £4), is preserved as a memorial to his work and contains the original manuscript. White constructed the Zig Zag Path with his brother and made many of his observations on Selborne Hill, just southwest of the village. The house also contains a museum commemorating Captain Oates, a member of Scott's ill-fated Antarctic expedition in 1912 – though Oates had no connection with the house or even the locality. From here, it's a pleasant hour's walk up to the top of the hill.

The Vyne

A couple of miles north of Basingstoke, just outside the village of Sherborne St John, **the Vyne** is a distinguished country house dating from several different periods (April–Oct Mon–Wed, Sat & Sun 11am–5pm; grounds Feb–March Sat & Sun 11am–5pm; £6.50; NT). The original Tudor building was started in 1520, and the classical portico, supposedly the oldest in England, was added in 1645. Inside the superbly preserved rooms, some featuring their original oak panelling, are many unusual antiques, among them two late-seventeenth-century maps of London and England, a camera obscura and a portrait of a dashing young Isaac Newton. The Chute family owned the house for two hundred years (ancestral portraits decorate many walls) until an heirless Charles Chute bequeathed the house to the National Trust in the 1950s.

Outside the sombre Tudor chapel, which features its original Flemish glass and tiles, a row of truncheons inscribed with the letter "P" line one wall. These are a relic from the civil unrest which took place in protest at the Corn Laws. The weapons were securely stored here at the Vyne in order to arm local officers in the event of trouble. The "P" refers to Robert Peel, founder of the Metropolitan Police, whose officers were commissioned to suppress any popular discontent. Ironically, as prime minister, Peel repealed the Corn Laws in 1846.

Stratfield Saye

Stratfield Saye House, five miles northeast of the Vyne (guided tours June–Aug Wed–Sun 11.30am–5pm; last entry at 3pm; £5.75), was given to the Duke of Wellington as a reward for victory at Waterloo in 1815. The house, still home of the current duke, contains a plethora of "Wellingtonia" as well as copious Regency ornaments, many originating from dispossessed French aristocrats. The mosaics in the entrance hall were taken from the Roman ruins at nearby Silchester. In the former stables is an absorbing exhibition of Wellington's life and times, ending in the Gothic monstrosity of his funeral carriage which bore him to his final resting place at St Paul's, where his nautical counterpart Admiral Nelson already lay.

Highclere Castle

The "Gothic" profile of **Highclere Castle**, four miles south of Newbury off the A34 Winchester road (July to early Sept Mon–Fri & Sun 11am–5pm, Sat 11am–3.30pm; last admission 1hr before closing; £7), results from its lavish remodelling by Sir Charles Barry, co-architect of the Houses of Parliament. Formerly a Georgian mansion set in parkland designed by Capability Brown, this ancestral home of the earls of Carnarvon was completely refurbished inside and out by Barry and others in the 1840s. Inside the house, the ostentatious style continues unbridled, from the Gothic "Saloon" or entrance hall to the adjacent state rooms, one of them in the Rococo style – all examples of the excessive opulence so beloved of the Victorian aristocracy. The house also contains a collection of personal mementoes of the Fifth Earl of Carnarvon who, along with Howard Carter, unearthed Tutankhamun's tomb near Luxor in 1922. There are artefacts from that excavation as well as his earlier Egyptian treasures, which were discovered after the Earl's death in Egypt in 1923. His tomb is situated atop Beacon Hill, a mile southeast of the house. Also on view here is Napoleon's desk and chair and a collection of old master paintings, including works by Reynolds and Van Dyck.

Sandham Memorial Chapel

Four miles east of Highclere on the A34, the **Sandham Memorial Chapel** at Burghclere (April–Oct Wed–Sun 11am–5pm; March & Nov Sat & Sun 11am–4pm; £2.80; NT) houses murals by the artist Stanley Spencer, inspired by his experiences as a medical orderly in Macedonia during World War I. Working for over four years here *in situ*, on what he described as "a mixture of real and spiritual fact", Spencer abandoned his initial decision to paint in fresco in imitation of Giotto – whose Scrovegni chapel in Padua was the model for this one – in favour of his usual medium of oils on canvas. Above the altar, the dominating central *Resurrection of the Soldiers*, with its jumble of white crosses, is flanked by scenes of a soldier's daily routine – scrubbing floors, making sandwiches, shaving under mosquito nets and scraping the dead skin off frost-bitten feet. It's best to come here on a sunny day if you can, as only natural light illuminates Spencer's subdued tones.

The New Forest

Covering about 144 square miles – a third now in private ownership, the rest administered by the Forestry Commission – the **NEW FOREST** is one of southern England's main rural playgrounds, and about eight million visitors flock here annually to enjoy a breath of fresh air, often after spending hours in traffic jams.

The name itself is misleading, for much of this region's woodland was cleared for agriculture and settlement long before the Normans arrived, and its poor sandy soils support only a meagre covering of heather and gorse in many areas. The forest was requisitioned by William the Conqueror in 1079 as a game reserve, and the rights of its inhabitants soon became subservient to those of his precious deer. Fences to impede their progress were forbidden and terrible punishments were meted out to those who disturbed the animals – hands were lopped off, eyes put out. Later monarchs less passionate about hunting than the Normans gradually restored the forest-dwellers' rights, and today the New Forest enjoys a unique patchwork of ancient laws and privileges, enveloped in an arcane vocabulary dating from feudal times. The forest boundary is the "perambulation", and owner-occupiers of forest land have common rights to obscure practices such as "turbary" (peat-cutting), "estover" (firewood collecting) and "mast" (letting pigs forage for acorns and beech nuts), as well as the more readily comprehensible right of pasture, permitting domestic animals to graze freely.

The **trees** of the forest are now much more varied than they were in pre-Norman times, with birch, holly, yew, Scots pine and other conifers interspersed with the ancient oaks and beeches. One of the most venerable trees is the much-visited **Knightwood Oak**, just a few hundred yards north of the A35 three miles southwest of Lyndhurst, which measures about 22ft in circumference at shoulder height. The most obvious species of New Forest **fauna** are the New Forest **ponies** (reputedly descendants of the Armada's small Spanish horses that survived the battle), now thoroughly domesticated – you'll see them grazing nonchalantly by the roadsides and ambling through some villages. The local deer are less likely to be seen now that some of the faster roads are fenced, although several species still roam the woods, including the tiny **sika deer**, descendants of a pair that escaped from nearby Beaulieu in 1904. Deer numbers are carefully surveyed and an annual cull keeps numbers at a steady 2000, helping to prevent damage to the woodland and the habitats of other New Forest species.

To get the best from the region, you need to **walk** or **ride** through it, avoiding the places cars can reach. There are 150 miles of car-free gravel roads in the forest, making cycling an appealing prospect – pick up a book of route maps from tourist offices or bike rental shops (£4). The Ordnance Survey Leisure Map 22 of the New Forest is worth getting if you want to explore in any detail, and in Lyndhurst you can pick up numerous specialist walking books and natural history guides. **Trains** from London Waterloo serve Brockenhurst once or twice hourly; for Lyndhurst you have to alight at Lyndhurst Road Station, a couple of miles east of the town proper. Lyndhurst and nearby Brockenhurst are centres of County Bus routes to most parts of the forest, and both have plenty of reasonably priced accommodation, though there are also several expensive country house hotels and restaurants scattered in isolated settings. The forest has ten **campsites** run by the Forestry Commission, most closed between October and Easter – to get the full list, write to 231 Corstorphine Rd, Edinburgh EH12 7AT (Ⓣ0131/334 0066) – and there's a **youth hostel** in Cottesmore House, Cott Lane, Burley, in the west of the Forest (Ⓣ0870/770 5734, Ⓔburley@yha.org.uk; closed early Oct–March, limited opening April & Sept to early Oct), which offers beds for £10.25 a night. The hostel's not directly accessible on public transport; it's a quarter-mile walk from Durmast Corner (buses #X34/35), and half a mile from Burley (buses #105 or #126). Note that the path leading through the forest is unlit.

The main wooded areas are around **Lyndhurst**, the "capital" of the New Forest, though **Brockenhurst** makes a pleasant alternative stopover. On the edge of the region lies the stately home and motor vehicle museum of **Beaulieu**, while on the coast, **Lymington** is a charming seaside resort, popular with weekending city types.

Lyndhurst and Brockenhurst

LYNDHURST, its town centre skewered by an agonizing one-way system, isn't a particularly interesting place, though the brick **parish church** is worth a glance for its William Morris glass, a fresco by Lord Leighton and the grave of one Mrs Reginald Hargreaves, better known as Alice Liddell, Lewis Carroll's model for Alice. The town is of most interest to visitors for the **New Forest Museum and Visitor Centre** in the central car park off the High Street (March–Oct daily 10am–5pm; Nov–Feb Mon–Fri 10am–4pm, Sat & Sun 10am–5pm; ⓣ023/8028 2269, ⓦwww.thenewforest.co.uk), where you can buy Explorer bus passes and maps for cycling and riding. There's also a **museum** here focusing on the forest, its history, wildlife and industries (same times as tourist office; £2.75). Nearby in Gosport Lane, AA Bike Hire (ⓣ023/8028 3349) rents **bikes**. For **accommodation** try the clean and airy *Clarendon Villa*, also in Gosport Lane (ⓣ023/8028 2803, ⓦwww.clarendonvilla.i12.com; no smoking; ❷); *Forest Cottage*, at the west end of the High Street (ⓣ023/8028 3461, ⓦwww.forestcottage.co.uk; no credit cards; no smoking; ❷), where you can consult a natural history library; or *Burwood Lodge*, 27 Romsey Rd (ⓣ023/8028 2445, ⓦwww.burwoodlodge.co.uk; ❸), a large old house a few minutes from the High Street. *Le Café Parisien* at 64 High St sells **snacks** that you can eat in its small garden in summer; for larger **meals**, head for the nearby *Crown Hotel*.

The forest's most visited site, the **Rufus Stone**, stands a few hundred yards from the M27 motorway, three miles northwest of Lyndhurst. Erected in 1745, the monument marks the putative spot where the Conqueror's ghastly son and heir, **William II** – aka William Rufus after his ruddy complexion – was killed in 1100. The official version is that a crossbow bolt fired by a member of the royal hunting party glanced off a stag and struck the king in the heart. Sir William Tyrrell took the rap for the "accident" and fled incriminatingly to France, though he later swore on his deathbed that he had not fired the fatal arrow. As William II was a tyrant with many enemies, his death was probably a political assassination – a strong suspect was William's brother Henry, also in the shooting party, who promptly raced to Winchester to claim the crown, leaving Rufus to be carted ignominiously to the cathedral by a passing charcoal burner. The stone is remarkably unimpressive for such a landmark: the Victorians encased it in a protective layer of metal to deter vandals, and now it can't be seen at all clearly.

Three miles southwest of Lyndhurst you'll find the popular **Ornamental Drives** of Bolderwood and Rhinefield, Victorian plantations of exotic trees, which are suggestive of overgrown ancient woodland. If you fancy a guided woodland hike, ask at the visitor centre in Lyndhurst about the ranger-led walks organized by the Forestry Commission, or call ⓣ023/8028 3141.

BROCKENHURST, four miles to the south of Lyndhurst, is a useful centre for visitors without their own transport. There's a train station right in town and **bikes for rent** by the level-crossing at New Forest Cycle Experience (ⓣ01590/624204). The town also has some decent places to **stay**; try the *Cottage Hotel* on Sway Road (ⓣ01590/622296; ⓔterry_eisner@compuserve.com; ❺; closed Dec–Feb) with evening meals on request. A short distance farther south in Sway, there's a quiet B&B at *Little Purley Farm* in Chapel Lane (ⓣ01590/682707; no credit cards; no smoking; ❶), with views over to the Isle of Wight. The *Snakecatcher* on Lyndhurst Road is a good **pub** that also serves terrific bar food.

Beaulieu and Buckler's Hard

The village of **BEAULIEU** (whose name originates from the French meaning "Beautiful Place", but is pronounced "Bewley"), in the southeast corner of the New Forest, was the site of one of England's most influential monasteries, a Cistercian house founded in 1204 by King John – in remorse, it is said, for ordering a group of supplicating Cistercian monks to be trampled to death. Built using stone ferried from Caen in northern France and Quarr on the Isle of Wight, the **abbey** managed a self-sufficient estate of ten thousand acres and became a famous sanctuary, offering shelter to Queen Margaret of Anjou among many others. The abbey was dismantled soon after the Dissolution, and its refectory now forms the parish church, which, like everything else in Beaulieu, has been subsumed by the Montagu family who have owned a large chunk of the New Forest since one of Charles II's illegitimate progeny was created duke of the estate.

The estate has been transformed with a prodigious commercial vigour into **Beaulieu** (daily: May–Sept 10am–6pm; Oct–April 10am–5pm; £13; Ⓦwww.beaulieu.co.uk), a tourist complex comprising **Palace House**, the attractive if unexceptional family home, the abbey and the main attraction, Lord Montagu's **National Motor Museum**. An undersized monorail and an old London bus ease the ten-minute walk between the entry point and Palace House. The home, formerly the abbey's gatehouse, contains masses of Montagu-related memorabilia while the undercroft of the adjacent abbey houses an exhibition depicting medieval monastic life. Inside the celebrated Motor Museum, a collection of 250 cars and motorcycles includes a £650,000 McLaren F1, spindly antiques and recent classics, as well as a couple of svelte land-speed racers, including the record-breaking *Bluebird*. The entertaining "Wheels", a dizzying ride-through display, takes you on a trip through the history of motoring. You can also **rent bikes** from the museum (April–Sept; Ⓣ01590/611029).

If Beaulieu amply deserves its name, **Buckler's Hard**, a couple of miles downstream on the River Beaulieu (daily: Easter–Sept 10.30am–5pm; Oct–Easter 11am–4pm; £5), has an even more wonderful setting. It doesn't look much like a shipyard now, but from Elizabethan times onwards dozens of men o' war were assembled here from giant New Forest oaks. Several of Nelson's ships, including *HMS Agamemnon*, were launched here, to be towed carefully by rowing boats past the sandbanks and across the Solent to Portsmouth. The largest house in this hamlet of shipwrights' cottages, which forms part of the Montagu estate, belonged to Henry Adams, the master builder responsible for most of the Trafalgar fleet; it's now an upmarket **hotel** and **restaurant**, the *Master Builder's House Hotel* (Ⓣ01590/616253, Ⓦwww.themasterbuilders.co.uk; ❼). At the top of the village, the **Maritime Museum** traces the history of the great ships and incorporates a labourer's cottage as it was in the 1790s, as well as the New Inn, shipwright's cottage and chapel – all preserved in their eighteenth-century form.

Lymington

The most pleasant point of access for the Isle of Wight (for ferry details, see p.265) is **LYMINGTON**, a sheltered haven that's linked by ferry to Yarmouth and has become one of the busiest leisure harbours on the south coast. Rising from the quay area, the old town is full of cobbled streets and Georgian houses and has one unusual building – the partly thirteenth-century church of **St Thomas the Apostle**, with a cupola-topped tower built in 1670.

Information is available in summer from the local **visitor centre** in New Street, off the High Street (May–Sept Mon–Sat 10am–5pm, Sun 2–5pm; Oct–April Mon–Sat 10am–4pm; ⓣ01590/689000). Places to **stay** in town include *The Monks Pool*, 22 Waterford Lane (ⓣ01590/678850, ⓦwww.camandjohn.com; ❸), a pleasant family home with a private lake; *Dolphins*, 6 Emsworth Rd (ⓣ01590/676108, ⓦwww.dolphinsnewforestbandb.co.uk; ❷), which rents out bikes and offers use of a chalet by the beach, and *Durlston House*, Gosport Street (ⓣ01590/677364, ⓔdurlstonhouse@aol.com; ❹), a smart and clean town house with six guest rooms and bike rental. For **snacks**, try the cheap and cheerful *Coffee Mill*, opposite the visitor centre on New Street. Lymington's best **pubs** are the *Chequers* on Ridgeway Lane, on the west side of town, the *Bosun's Chair*, on Station Road, and the harbourfront *Ship Inn*, on the quayside, with seats outside looking over the water.

Signposted two miles east of Lymington, the **Sammy Miller Museum**, in New Milton (daily 10am–4.30pm; £3.50), gives classic motorcycles the "Beaulieu" treatment. Many of the once-eminent British marques from Ariel to Vincent are displayed, as well as exotica from MV, NSU and several acclaimed trials bikes ridden by Sammy Miller himself, one of Britain's most successful trials riders.

Bournemouth and around

Renowned for its clean sandy beaches, the resort of **Bournemouth** is the nucleus of Europe's largest non-industrial conurbation stretching between Lymington and Poole harbour. The resort has a single-minded holiday-making atmosphere, though neighbouring **Poole** and **Christchurch** are more interesting historically. North of this coastal sprawl, the pleasant old market town of **Wimborne** has one of the area's most striking churches, while the stately home of **Kingston Lacy** contains an outstanding collection of old masters and other paintings.

Arrival, information and accommodation

Trains from London Waterloo stop just under a mile east of the centre, but frequent **buses** run into town from the bus station opposite. The **tourist office**, right in the centre of town on Westover Road (mid-July to mid-Sept Mon–Sat 9.30am–7pm, Sun 10.30am–5pm; mid-Sept to mid-July Mon–Sat 9.30am–5.30pm; ⓣ0906/8020234, ⓦwww.bournemouth.co.uk), exchanges money and books National Express tickets.

There's no shortage of **accommodation** in the Bournemouth area – the town has more than four hundred hotels and guest houses covering all budget ranges. There are no central **campsites**, however; the nearest is just north of Christchurch (see p.293).

Bournemouth Backpackers 3 Frances Rd ⓣ01202/299491, ⓦwww.bournemouthbackpackers.co.uk. Small, friendly hostel, three minutes from train and bus stations; dorm beds cost up to £16 in peak season, as low as £9 at other periods or for two nights or more. Also has doubles. ❷

Connaught West Hill Rd, West Cliff ⓣ01202/298020, ⓦwww.theconnaught.co.uk. Well-equipped three-star hotel, five minutes' walk from the town centre and beach, with excellent leisure facilities and restaurant, and discounts on longer stays. ❼

Earlham Lodge 91 Alumhurst Rd, Alum Chine ⓣ01202/761943, ⓦwww.earlhamlodge.com. Friendly guest house near the beach, with all rooms en suite and some with four-posters. Parking available. ❸

Grove 2 Grove Rd, East Cliff ⓣ01202/552233,

Ⓦ www.grovehotel.net. Well-positioned family-run hotel set in its own grounds. ❺

Langtry Manor 26 Derby Rd, East Cliff Ⓣ01202/553887, Ⓦ www.langtrymanor.com. Former hideaway of Edward VII and his mistress, Lillie Langtry, this comfortable, well-equipped hotel has Edwardian furnishings and hosts period-style banquets on Saturday evenings. ❼

Royal Bath Bath Rd Ⓣ01202/555555, Ⓦ www.devereonline.co.uk. This grand, late-Victorian hotel is among the town's finest, and also one of the most expensive, but it's right in the centre with excellent sea views. Guests can use the fully equipped leisure complex, which includes a pool and gym. ❽

Tudor Grange 31 Gervis Rd, East Cliff Ⓣ01202/291472. Tudor-style house with attractive interior and gardens, situated on the east side of town. ❹

The City

BOURNEMOUTH dates only from 1811, when a local squire, Louis Tregonwell, built a summer house on the wild, unpopulated heathland that once occupied this stretch of coast, and planted the first of the pine trees that now characterize the area. By the end of the century Bournemouth's mild climate, sheltered site and glorious sandy beach had attracted nearly sixty thousand inhabitants. Today the resort has twice that number of residents, and an unshakably genteel, elderly image, though its geriatric nursing homes are counterbalanced by burgeoning numbers of language schools and a nightclub scene fuelled by a transient youthful population.

The blandly modern town that you see today has little to remind you of Bournemouth's Victorian heyday, though the River Bourne still runs down through a park to the town's centre, which consists of a network of one-way streets running around the Square and down to **Bournemouth Pier**. Other than sunbathing along the pristine sandy beach – one of southern England's cleanest – the town's greatest attraction is its unusually high proportion of green space, set aside during the boom years at the end of the nineteenth century. As well as having more than three million pine trees, a sixth of the town – around two thousand acres – is given over to horticultural displays, and exploring Bournemouth's **public gardens** can easily fill a day.

The most enthralling experience in Bournemouth, however, is one of the region's best collections of Victoriana, the excellent **Russell-Cotes Art Gallery and Museum** on East Cliff Promenade (Tues–Sun 10am–5pm; free) which houses a motley assortment of artworks and oriental souvenirs gathered from around the world by the Russell-Cotes family, hoteliers who grew wealthy during Bournemouth's late-Victorian tourist boom. The benefactors' lavishly decorated former home, featuring unusual stained glass and ornate painted ceilings, is jam-packed with their eclectic collections, of which the Japanese artefacts are especially interesting. There are some good examples of Pre-Raphaelite and other British art downstairs, period decor throughout and a cliff-top landscaped garden.

In the centre of town, you might visit the graveyard of **St Peter's Church**, just east of the Square, where Mary Shelley, author of the Gothic horror tale *Frankenstein*, is buried, together with the heart belonging to her husband, the Romantic poet Percy Bysshe Shelley, former resident of Boscombe. The tombs of Mary's parents – radical thinker William Godwin and early feminist Mary Wollstonecraft – are also here.

Eating and drinking

With ubiquitous fast-food joints, Bournemouth has few noteworthy places for a **meal**, though it's still possible to unearth a decent seafood dish in congenial surroundings. Likewise, the town is awash with big booze halls, but you'll need to venture off the beaten track to find a decent pub with both ale and atmosphere.

Bistro on the Beach Esplanade, Southbourne end ☎01202/431473. Situated right on the beach and specializing in freshly prepared steak and seafood. Often booked weeks ahead. Closed Mon, Tues & Sun. Moderate.

Brass House 8 Westover Rd. One of Bournemouth's most popular café-bars, also serving meals. Can be rowdy.

CH2 37 Exeter Rd ☎01202/296296. Elegantly modern restaurant specializing in steaks and mussels with a variety of sauces, and with a good fish selection. Closed Sun & Mon. Moderate.

Chez Fred 10 Seamoor Rd, Westbourne. Well-known fish-and-chips outlet offering deals such as a bread roll, mushy peas and a glass of wine to accompany your meal. Inexpensive.

Goat and Tricycle 27 West Hill Rd. Worth a trek up the hill for the real ales and homemade food in this quiet and unpretentious pub. Inexpensive to moderate.

Salathai 1066 Christchurch Rd, Boscombe. Authentically spicy Thai dishes, including chilli-laced chicken and fried noodles. Closed Sun. Moderate.

West Beach Pier Approach ☎01202/587785. Good seafood restaurant that's also a takeaway (in summer), centrally located on the Promenade by the pier. Live jazz every Thurs eve. Moderate.

Nightlife and entertainment

The university, foreign-language students and young holiday-makers have helped liven up Bournemouth's **nightlife** – though the traditional entertainment scene continues to throw up a steady stream of dire pier-end comedians well past their prime. The chief established venues lie just north of the pier – the Pavilion Theatre, with its own ballroom; the Winter Gardens, home of Bournemouth's symphony orchestra; a multiplex cinema; and an ice-skating rink. Pick up a copy of the free monthly listings magazine *Live Wire* for news of gigs in the town.

Of the **nightclubs**, the biggest and best known is *Elements*, right in the centre of town on Firvale Road (currently Mon, Wed, Fri & Sat). Mainstream club and house sounds predominate, along with R&B and revival evenings, and there's an adjoining pub/club, *Circo*, which takes in the pre-club crowds. Next door on Firvale Road, the *Slam Bar* plays mainstream dance on the ground floor, R&B and hip-hop in the basement. On Terrace Road, the *K-Bar*, also a bar and restaurant, offers a nightly diet of R&B, garage, funk and house, with comedy on Sundays. The *Triangle Club*, Bournemouth's biggest **gay** club, is located at the top of Commercial Road from The Square. *Bumbles* on Poole Hill (Wed, Fri & Sat) reverberates to dance and Seventies and Eighties music. In Boscombe, the flamboyant *Opera House*, 570 Christchurch Rd, is a well-attended venue open Fridays and Saturdays as a mainstream club, while Thursday is students' night and Sunday has the primarily gay Bolts.

On a more sedate note, the fortnight at the end of June and the beginning of July sees the **Bournemouth International Festival** draw performers of every musical genre. There's also a buskers' festival that takes place around the second weekend of May – check at the tourist office for further details.

Christchurch

CHRISTCHURCH, five miles east of Bournemouth, is best known for its colossal parish church, **Christchurch Priory** (Mon–Sat 10am–5pm, Sun 2.15–5.30pm; £1 donation requested), bigger than most cathedrals. Built on the site of a Saxon minster dating from 650 AD, but exhibiting chiefly Norman and Perpendicular features, the church is the longest in England, at 311ft, and its fan-vaulted North Porch is the country's biggest. Legend tells of how the building materials were moved overnight to the present location and of the hand of a mysterious carpenter who assisted in the work, hence the priory's name. The choir, beautifully lit by huge, clear-glass windows and separated from the nave by a finely carved Jesse Screen, contains what is probably the oldest misericord in England, dating from 1210, and complemented by a 1960s mural by Hans Feibush above the stone reredos. Fine views can be gained from the top of the 120-foot tower (ask at desk; £1).

The area round the old town quay has a carefully preserved charm. The **Red House Museum and Gardens** on Quay Road (Tues–Sat 10am–5pm, Sun 2–5pm; £1.50) contain an affectionate collection of local memorabilia, and **boat trips** (Easter to mid-Oct daily; ⓣ01202/429119) can be taken from the grassy banks of the riverside quay east to Mudeford (30min; £4.50 return) or up the river to the Tuckton Tea Rooms outside Bournemouth (15 min; £2 return).

The **tourist office**, 23 High St (June–Sept Mon–Fri 9.30am–5.30pm, Sat 9.30am–5pm; July & Aug also Sun 10am–2pm; Oct–May Mon–Fri 9.30am–5pm, Sat 9.30am–4.30pm; ⓣ01202/471780, ⓦwww.resort-guide.co.uk/christchurch), can supply you with a town map and a Visitor's Guide. Good **accommodation** options in or around town can be fairly pricey, though *The Three Gables*, 11 Wickfield Avenue (ⓣ01202/481166, ⓦwww.3gables-christchurch.co.uk; ❷), offers a convenient overnight stop close to the centre and beaches, with abundant continental or English breakfasts. A few minutes northwest of the centre, Barrack and Stour roads are lined with a selection of unexciting but reliable guest houses such as *Grosvenor Lodge*, 53 Stour Rd (ⓣ01202/499008, ⓦwww.grosvenorlodge.co.uk; ❸). In the centre, try the *King's Arms Toby Hotel*, 18 Castle St (ⓣ01202/484117; ❺); eastwards lie more exclusive choices, such as the *Avonmouth Hotel*, 95 Mudeford (ⓣ0870/4008120, ⓦwww.avonmouth-hotel.co.uk; ❼), and *Waterford Lodge*, 87 Bure Lane, Friars Cliff, Highcliffe (ⓣ01425/278801; ❻), two miles east of the town centre. **Campers** should head out to *Mount Pleasant Touring Park*, Matchams Lane, Hurn, Christchurch (ⓣ01202/475474; closed Nov–Feb), five miles northeast of town on the road to Ringwood.

For something **to eat**, try *La Mamma*, 51 Bridge St (ⓣ01202/471608; closed Sun lunch & Mon in winter), where you can enjoy candle-lit Italian classics (including pizzas) at moderate prices, with alfresco eating in summer; or the *Bistro on the Bridge*, 3 Bridge St (ⓣ01202/482522; closed Mon & Tues), where you can have inexpensive Bistro Express lunches, afternoon tea, or pricier evening meals, and there's riverside seating on a veranda. Recommended **pubs** include the *King's Arms Hotel*, right by the priory, with a nice garden area; or check out Christchurch's oldest pub, *Ye Olde George Inn*, 2a Castle St, which has a beer garden and serves meals at lunchtime.

Poole

Five miles west of Bournemouth's centre – though effectively joined to the town – **POOLE** is an ancient seaport on a huge, almost landlocked harbour. The port developed in the thirteenth century and was successively colonized by pirates, fishermen and timber traders, more recently replaced by companies prospecting for oil in the shallow waters – the harbour's environmental significance ensures that the extraction process is carefully disguised. The old quarter by the quayside is worth exploring: the old Custom House, Scaplen's Court and Guildhall are the most striking of over a hundred historic buildings within a fifteen-acre site.

At the bottom of Old High Street, near the Poole Pottery showroom and crafts centre, **Scaplen's Court** (Aug Mon–Sat 10am–5pm, Sun noon–5pm; free) is a late medieval building where Cromwell's troops were once billeted (you can see their graffiti around the fireplace). It has now been restored as an educational centre, with reconstructions of a Victorian kitchen, pharmacy and school room and displays of old-time toys and games. Over the road, local history is more accessibly elaborated at the **Waterfront Museum** (April–Oct Mon–Sat 10am–5pm, Sun noon–5pm; Nov–March Mon–Sat 10am–3pm, Sun noon–3pm; free), tracing Poole's development over the centuries and featuring well-displayed local ceramics and tiles and a rare Iron Age log boat, as well as changing exhibitions.

In the middle of the harbour between Poole and the Isle of Purbeck, **Brownsea Island** (daily: April–June & Sept to early Oct 10am–5pm; July & Aug 10am–6pm; £3.70; NT) is linked by regular boats ferrying visitors over from Poole's quayside (about 25min; two hourly; £5.50 return). Now a National Trust property, this five-hundred-acre island is famed for its red squirrels, wading birds and other wildlife, which you can spot along themed trails that reveal a surprisingly diverse landscape – including heath, woodland and fine beaches – and good views. One shore holds a grand pile of a castle, rebuilt after the original was gutted by fire in 1896; it's now leased to a large retail group for staff holidays. But the most regular visitors to Brownsea are scouts and guides: the Boy Scout movement was formed in the wake of a camping expedition to the island led by Lord Baden-Powell in 1907, and scouts are now the only people allowed to camp here.

From Poole Quay, you can also join a **cruise** to the Isle of Wight (April–Oct Mon, Wed & Sat at 9.15am, irregular winter sailings, call to check; £16 return; ⓣ01202/558550), allowing excellent views over Poole Bay to Bournemouth and Christchurch, and a four-hour stop in Yarmouth (see p.275).

One of the area's most famous gardens lies on the outskirts of Poole, **Compton Acres** (March–Oct daily 10am–6pm; £5.95; ⓦwww.comptonacres.co.uk), signposted off the A35 Poole Road, towards Bournemouth. Here you'll find seven gardens, each with a different international theme, the best of which, the elegantly understated Japanese Garden, contrasts with the more familiar classical symmetry of the Italian Garden. Buses #150 and #151 between Poole and Bournemouth, and in summer the open-top coastal #12 service stop outside.

Practicalities

Poole's **tourist office** is in the Waterfront Museum (April, May & Oct Mon–Sat 10am–5pm, Sun noon–5pm; June, July & Sept Mon–Fri 10am–5.30pm, Sat & Sun 10am–5pm; Aug daily 10am–6pm; Nov–March Mon–Fri 10am–5pm, Sat 10am–3pm, Sun noon–3pm; ⓣ01202/253253, ⓦwww.pooletourism.com). Best choice for **accommodation** is the *Antelope Hotel* at 8 High St (ⓣ01202/672029; ❻), a handsome old hostelry in the old town centre; if you fancy a stay in a former mayoral residence, try the eighteenth-century *Mansion House*, Thames Street (ⓣ01202/685666, ⓦthemansionhouse.co.uk; ❻). Further out, at Canford Cliffs, smaller hotels worth trying include the *Sea Witch*, 47 Haven Rd (ⓣ01202/707697, ⓔseawitch@eurolink.ltd.net; ❹), and *Norfolk Lodge*, 1 Flaghead Rd (ⓣ01202/708614, ⓦwww.norfolklodge.activehotels.com; ❹), both of which are convenient for the Sandbanks beaches south of the centre. A mile or so north of the centre, the more economical *Harbour Lights Hotel*, 121 North Rd, Parkstone (ⓣ01202/748417; no credit cards; ❷) has basic but comfortable rooms with shared bathrooms.

There's a collection of good **restaurants** at the southern end of the High Street; look out for *Storm*, a moderately priced seafood restaurant at no. 16 (☎01202/674970; closed lunchtime), right next to *Hardy's* (closed Sun), which is good for light lunches and sandwiches. Just around the corner, on Sarum Street, *Cranberries* has an extensive bar menu as well as more elaborate evening fare including such rarities as ostrich and crocodile. At the top end of the High Street, *Alcatraz* is a lively Italian brasserie with outdoor tables, while, at the other end, on the Quayside, *Corkers* has a café and bar downstairs and a restaurant above, serving traditional English dishes and seafood; it also has five en-suite rooms available (☎01202/681393; no smoking in bedrooms; ❸). For **pubs** try the medieval hall in the *King Charles* on Thames Street, with its leather armchairs and big screen, or, on the quayside, the green tile-fronted *Poole Arms*, which serves inexpensive pub grub.

Wimborne Minster and Kingston Lacy

An ancient town on the banks of the Stour, just a few minutes' drive north from the suburbs of Bournemouth, **WIMBORNE MINSTER**, as the name suggests, is mainly of interest for its great church, the **Minster of St Cuthberga** (Mon–Sat 9.30am–5.30pm). Built on the site of an eighth-century monastery, its massive twin towers of mottled grey and tawny stone dwarf the rest of the town, and at one time the church was even more imposing – its spire crashed down during morning service in 1602, though amazingly no one was injured, and since then Wimborne has not risked heavenly ire by replacing it. What remains today is basically Norman with later features added such as the Perpendicular west tower, which bears a figure dressed as a grenadier of the Napoleonic era, who strikes every quarter-hour with a hammer. Inside, the church is crowded with memorials and eye-catching details – look out for the orrery clock inside the west tower, with the sun marking the hours and the moon marking the days of the month, and for the organ with trumpets pointing out towards the congregation instead of pipes. The **Chained Library** above the choir vestry (Easter–Oct Mon–Thurs 10.30am–12.30pm & 2–4pm, Fri 10.30am–12.30pm), dating from 1686, is Wimborne's most prized possession and one of the oldest public libraries in the country.

Wimborne's older buildings stand around the main square near the minster, and are mostly from the late eighteenth or early nineteenth century. The **Priest's House** on the High Street started life as lodgings for the clergy, then became a stationer's shop. Now it is an award-winning **museum** (April–Nov 10am–4.30pm; also open two weeks after Christmas; £2.70), each room furnished in the style of a different period. A working Victorian kitchen, a Georgian parlour and an ironmonger's shop are among its exhibits, and there's a display of items relating to local archeology and history; a walled garden at the rear provides an excellent place for summer teas.

Kingston Lacy (house: late March to Oct Wed–Sun 11am–5pm; grounds: Feb to mid-March Sat & Sun 10.30am–4pm; late March to Oct daily 10.30am–6pm or dusk if earlier; Nov–Dec Fri & Sun 10.30am–4pm, Sat 10am–12.30pm; house & grounds £6.80, grounds only £3.50; NT), one of the country's finest seventeenth-century country houses, lies two miles northwest of Wimborne Minster, in 250 acres of parkland grazed by a herd of Red Devon cattle. Designed for the Bankes family, who were exiled from Corfe Castle (see p.297) after the Roundheads reduced it to rubble, the brick building was clad in grey stone during the nineteenth century by Sir Charles Barry, co-architect of the Houses of Parliament. William Bankes, then owner of the house, was a great traveller and collector, and the **Spanish Room** is a superb scrapbook of his Grand Tour souvenirs, lined with gilded leather and surmounted by a Venetian ceiling. Kingston Lacy's **picture collection** is also outstanding, featuring Titian, Rubens, Velázquez and many other old masters. Be warned, though, that this place gets so swamped with visitors that the National Trust has to issue timed tickets on busy weekends.

You'll find Wimborne's **tourist office** at 29 High St (Mon–Sat: April–Sept 9.30am–5.30pm; Oct–March 9.30am–4.30pm; ⓣ01202/886116, ⓦwww.visiteastdorset.com). This is a place that is unlikely to hold your attention for longer than half a day, but if you want to **stay**, try *Homestay* at 22 West Borough (ⓣ01202/849015, ⓔjulietridg@onetel.com; no credit cards; ❷), a friendly place with en-suite facilities, or the *King's Head* on The Square, which offers more character but steeper rates (ⓣ01202/880101, ⓔkingshead.wimborne@oldenglishinns.co.uk; ❺). For bistro **lunches** or suppers try *Primizia* (ⓣ01202/883513; closed Sun & Mon) on West Borough, or *Cloisters* at 40 East St, which also serves teas, coffees and snacks (closed eve & Sun afternoon).

The Isle of Purbeck

Though not actually an island, the **ISLE OF PURBECK** – a promontory of low hills and heathland jutting out beyond Poole Harbour – does have an insular and distinctive feel. Reached from the east by the **ferry from Sandbanks**, at the narrow mouth of Poole harbour, or by a long and congested landward journey via the bottleneck of **Wareham**, Purbeck can be a difficult destination to reach, but its villages are immensely pretty, none more so than **Corfe Castle**, with its majestic ruins. **Swanage**, a low-key seaside resort, is flanked by more exciting coastlines, all accessible on the Dorset Coast Path: to one side the chalk stacks and soft dunes of Studland Bay, to the other the cliffs of Durlston Head and Dancing Ledge, leading to the oily shales of Kimmeridge Bay, the spectacular cove at Lulworth and the much-photographed natural arch of **Durdle Door**. Like Portland, further west, the area is pockmarked with stone quarries – Purbeck marble is the finest grade of the local oolitic limestone.

Wareham and around

The grid pattern of its streets indicates the Saxon origins of **WAREHAM**, and the town is surrounded by even older earth ramparts known as the Walls. A riverside setting adds greatly to its charms, though the major road junction at its heart causes horrible traffic queues in summer, and the scenic stretch along the Quay also gets fairly overrun. Nearby lies an oasis of quaint houses around **Lady St Mary's Church**, which contains the marble coffin of Edward the Martyr, murdered at Corfe Castle in 978 by his stepmother, to make way for her unready son Ethelred. **St Martin's Church**, at the north end of town, dates from Saxon times and the chancel contains a faded twelfth-century mural of St Martin offering his cloak to a beggar, but the church's most striking feature is a romantic effigy of T.E. Lawrence in Arab dress, which was originally destined for Salisbury Cathedral, but was rejected by the dean there who disapproved of Lawrence's sexual proclivities. Lawrence was killed in 1935 in a motorbike accident on the road from Bovington (6 miles west), after returning to Dorset from his Middle Eastern adventures. His simply furnished cottage is at **Clouds Hill**, seven miles northwest of Wareham (April–Oct Thurs–Sun noon–5pm or dusk; £2.90; NT). Back in Wareham itself the small **museum** next to the town hall in East Street (Easter–Oct Mon–Sat 11am–1pm & 2–4pm; free) displays some of Lawrence's memorabilia, as does the absorbing but over-priced **Tank Museum** in Bovington Camp, five miles west of town (daily 10am–5pm; £7.50; Ⓦwww.tankmuseum.co.uk). The 150 vehicles here include tanks from many of the conflicts from World War I onwards, including British Challenger I and Challenger II tanks and captured Iraqi tanks from both Gulf Wars. You can also walk through a replica trench of the Somme, and watch a mock tank battle complete with pyrotechnics (July & Sept Thurs at noon; Aug Thurs & Fri at noon).

A much-advertised local tourist honeypot is the **Blue Pool**, an intensely coloured clay-pit lake near Furzebrook, some three miles south of Wareham. A small museum (Easter to early Oct daily 10.30am–6pm; £3.20) gives the background to the local clay industry, and there are cream teas, nature trails and other amenities for less studious customers.

Holy Trinity Church, on South Street, contains Wareham's **tourist office** (June to mid-Sept Mon–Sat 9.30am–5pm, Sun 10am–1pm; mid-Sept to May Mon–Sat 9.30am–1pm & 1.45–5pm; Ⓣ01929/552740). From the nearby Quay, row- and motor-boats are available to rent (£8–12 an hour). The best **accommodation** options are *Anglebury House*, 15 North St (Ⓣ01929/552988; ❸), whose previous guests have included Thomas Hardy and T.E. Lawrence, and the pleasant *Belle Vue*, West Street (Ⓣ01929/552056; no credit cards; ❷), with all rooms en suite. The *Old Granary* **restaurant** on the Quay (Ⓣ01929/552010; ❷) also has rooms, with views over the river and the meadows beyond. *Kemps*, one and a half miles west of town in East Stoke, serves imaginative but unpretentious food and is particularly good value at lunchtime – rooms are also available here (Ⓣ01929/462563, Ⓔkemps.hotel@lineone.net; ❻).

Corfe Castle

The romantic ruins crowning the hill behind the village of **CORFE CASTLE** (daily: March 10am–5pm; April–Oct 10am–6pm; Nov–Feb 10am–4pm; £4.40; NT) are perhaps the most evocative in England. The family seat of Sir John Bankes, Attorney General to Charles I, this Royalist stronghold withstood a Cromwellian siege for six weeks, gallantly defended by Lady Bankes. One of her own men, Colonel Pitman, eventually betrayed the castle to the Roundheads, after which it was reduced to its present gap-toothed state by gunpowder. Apparently the victorious Roundheads were so impressed by Lady Bankes's courage that they allowed her to take the keys to the castle with her – they can still be seen in the library at the Bankes's subsequent home, Kingston Lacy (see p.295).

The village is well stocked with tearooms and gift shops and has a couple of good **pubs** too: the *Fox* on West Street, where you can drink or have lunch in a large garden with views to the castle, and, below the castle ramparts, the *Greyhound*. If you can't afford the high **room** rates and expensive dinners at the Elizabethan *Mortons House Hotel* on East Street (Ⓣ01929/480988, Ⓦwww.mortonshouse.co.uk; ❻), you can still enjoy a reasonably priced bar meal or tea. For more moderately priced accommodation, head for *The Old Curatage*, 30 East St (Ⓣ01929/481441, Ⓔoldcuratage@aol.com; no smoking; no credit cards; ❷), or the *Bankes Arms Hotel* (Ⓣ01929/480206, Ⓦwww.dorset-hotel.co.uk; ❷), an old inn outside the castle entrance, also serving pub lunches in its beer garden.

Shell Bay to St Alban's Head

Purbeck's most northerly coastal stretch, **Shell Bay**, is a magnificent beach of icing-sugar sand backed by a remarkable heathland ecosystem that's home to all six British species of reptile – adders are quite common, so be careful. At the top end of the beach a chain **ferry** (daily 7am–11pm every 20min; pedestrians 90p, bikes 80p, cars £2.20) crosses the mouth of Poole harbour connecting the Isle of Purbeck with Sandbanks in Poole.

To the south, beyond the broad sweep of Studland Bay, is **SWANAGE**, a traditional seaside resort with a pleasant sandy beach and an ornate town hall, the facade of which once adorned the Mercers' Hall in the City of London and was brought back here as ballast on a cargo ship. The town's station is the southern terminus of the **Swanage Steam Railway** (April–Oct daily; Nov, Dec & late Feb to March Sat & Sun; £7 return), which is slowly being restored to run as far as Wareham, but has currently only reached Norden (on the A351). For timetables, call ⓣ01929/425800, check at ⓦswanagerailway.co.uk or pick up a leaflet from the tourist office.

Swanage's **tourist office** is by the beach on Shore Road (Easter–Oct daily 10am–5pm; Nov–Easter Mon–Thurs 10am–5pm, Fri 10am–4pm; ⓣ01929/420680, ⓦwww.swanage.gov.uk), and there's a **youth hostel**, with good views across the bay, on Cluny Crescent (ⓣ0870/770 6058, ⓔswanage@yha.org.uk; open Fri–Sun during school terms and daily during school holidays). Beds cost £11.50 and should be booked 48 hours in advance. There are scores of **B&B**s in Swanage; try the *Purbeck Hotel*, 19 High St (ⓣ01929/425160, ⓦwww.purbeckhotel.co.uk; ❷), which also has a decent pub; alternatively, there's a handy trio on King's Road near the train station, and a cluster along Park Road, just off the High Street. Swanage has a wide variety of places **to eat**, ranging from fish-and-chip shops to upmarket restaurants, the best of which is the cosy *Trattoria*, 12 High St (ⓣ01929/423784; closed daytime), a moderately priced family-run Italian place that gets extremely busy; during the day, cappuccinos and baguettes are served next door at *Forte's Caffè Tratt*, under the same management. If you're interested in exploring the Purbeck Cycleway (map available from the tourist office), **rent bikes** from Bikeabout, 71 High St (ⓣ01929/425050), opposite the town hall, open daily.

Highlights of the coast beyond Swanage are the cliffs of **Durlstone Head**, topped by a lighthouse. Nearby stands a vast stone globe weighing forty tonnes, installed by George Burt, an eccentric Victorian building contractor from Swanage, who also erected the local folly castle. The cliffs continue to **St Alban's Head**, their ledges crowded with seabirds and rare wildflowers in spring. Paths lead inland to the attractive villages of **Langton Matravers**, where the **Coach House Museum** interprets the local stone-quarrying industry (April–Sept Mon–Sat 10am–noon & 2–4pm; 60p), and **Worth Matravers**, where there's a fine Norman church and a great **pub,** the *Square & Compass,* full of nooks and crannies, and with outdoor seating to enjoy the views; homemade pies are available.

Kimmeridge Bay to Durdle Door

Beyond St Alban's Head the coastal geology suddenly changes as the grey-white chalk and limestone give way to darker beds of shale. **Kimmeridge Bay** may not have a sandy beach but it does have a remarkable marine wildlife reserve much appreciated by divers – there's a Dorset Wildlife Trust **informa-**

tion centre by the slipway (daily 10am–5pm; ⓣ01929/481044). The amazing range of species is all the more surprising because the bay has been the site of small-scale industry for centuries. The Saxons crafted amulets from the shale and the extraction of alum (for glassmaking) and coal followed. Today a low-tech "nodding donkey" oil well fits unobtrusively into the landscape. In the village, the sixteenth-century *Kimmeridge Farmhouse* (ⓣ01929/480990; no credit cards; ❷) is a quiet and scenic spot for an overnight **stay**.

The Lulworth artillery ranges west of Kimmeridge are inaccessible during weekdays but generally open at weekends and in school holidays – watch out for the red warning flags and notices and always stick to the path. Roads in this area have similar restrictions, but generally open before 9am and after 5pm to allow commuters through. The coastal path passes close to the deserted village of **Tyneham**, whose residents were summarily evicted by the army in 1943; the abandoned stone cottages have an eerie fascination, and an exhibition in the church explains the history of the village. Ironically, the army's presence has actually helped to preserve the local habitat which plays host to many species of flora and fauna long since vanished from farmed or otherwise developed areas.

The quaint thatch-and-stone villages of East and West Lulworth form a prelude to **Lulworth Cove**, a perfect shell-shaped bite formed when the sea broke through a weakness in the cliffs and then gnawed away at them from behind, forming a circular cave which eventually collapsed to leave a bay enclosed by sandstone cliffs. Lulworth's scenic charms are well known, and as you descend the hill through West Lulworth in summer the sun glints off the metal of a thousand car roofs in the parking lot behind the cove. At the **Lulworth Heritage Centre** the mysteries of the local geology are explained (daily: March–Oct 10am–6pm, Nov–Feb 10am–4pm; free; parking £2.50/2hr, £5/day).

Immediately west of the cove you come to **Stair Hole**, a roofless sea cave riddled with arches that will eventually collapse to form another Lulworth, and a couple of miles west is **Durdle Door**, a famous limestone arch that appeals to serious geologist and casual sightseer alike. Most people take the uphill route to the arch which starts from the car park at Lulworth Cove but, if you want to avoid the steep climb, you can drive a mile from West Lulworth towards East Chaldon and park at the *Durdle Door Holiday Park* for a small fee. An alternative, if tide-dependent, route goes up the private drive from the Heritage Centre and down into the secluded St Oswald's Bay which separates Lulworth from Durdle Door. If you've timed it right you can slip round the headland and climb up to the arch although you may prefer to stay on the more agreeable St Oswald's Beach.

WEST LULWORTH is the obvious **place to stay** or eat on this section of coast. The *Castle Inn* (ⓣ01929/400311, ⓦwww.thecastleinn-lulworthcove.co.uk; ❸), *Cromwell House Hotel* (ⓣ01929/400253, ⓦwww.lulworthcove.co.uk; ❹), right on the coast path and sporting a heated pool, and *Ivy Cottage* (ⓣ01929/400509; no credit cards; ❶), a seventeenth-century cottage with inglenook fireplace, all make for good stop-offs. You'll find a **youth hostel** at the end of School Lane West (ⓣ0870/770 5940, ⓔlulworth@yha.org.uk; sporadic opening in winter; dorm beds £10.25); a plain chalet with small rooms, it's a stone's throw from the Dorset Coast Path. **Campers** can find a pitch at the above-mentioned *Durdle Door Holiday Park* (ⓣ01929/400200; closed Nov–Feb). In East Lulworth, the *Weld Arms* also has rooms (ⓣ01929/400211; ❷), while in East Chaldon, four miles northwest of Lulworth Cove, the easily overlooked *Sailor's Return* is unsurpassed locally for its mouthwatering **pub food**.

Dorchester and around

The county town of Dorset, **DORCHESTER** still functions as the main agricultural centre for the region, and if you catch it on a Wednesday when the market is in full swing you'll find it livelier than usual. For the local tourist authorities, however, this is essentially **Thomas Hardy**'s town; he was born at Higher Bockhampton, three miles east of here, his heart is buried in Stinsford, a couple of miles northeast (the rest of him is in Westminster Abbey), and he spent much of his life in Dorchester itself, where his statue now stands on High West Street. Even without the Hardy connection, Dorchester makes an attractive stop, with its pleasant central core of mostly seventeenth-century and Georgian buildings, and the prehistoric Maumbury Rings on the outskirts. To the southwest of town looms the massive hill fort of **Maiden Castle**, the most impressive of Dorset's many pre-Roman antiquities, and the Tudor **Athelhampton House**, near the village of Puddletown, six miles east of Dorchester, stands out because of its decorative gardens.

The Town

Dorchester was Durnovaria to the Romans, who founded the town in about 70 AD. The original Roman walls were replaced in the eighteenth century by tree-lined avenues called "Walks" (Bowling Alley Walk, West Walk and Colliton Walk), but some traces of the Roman period have survived. At the back of County Hall excavations have uncovered a fine Roman villa with a well-preserved mosaic floor, and on the southeast edge of town you'll find **Maumbury Rings**, where the Romans held vast gladiatorial combats in an amphitheatre adapted from a Stone Age site. The gruesome traditions continued into the Middle Ages, when gladiators were replaced by bear-baiting and public executions or "hanging fairs".

Continuing the sanguinary theme, after the ill-fated rebellion of the Duke of Monmouth (another of Charles II's illegitimate offspring) against James II, Judge Jeffreys was appointed to punish the rebels. His "Bloody Assizes" of 1685, held in the Oak Room of the **Antelope Hotel** on Cornhill, sentenced 292 men to death. In the event, 74 were hung, drawn and quartered, and their heads then stuck on pikes throughout Dorset and Somerset; the luckier suspects were merely flogged and transported to the West Indies. Judge Jeffreys lodged just round the corner from the *Antelope* in High West Street, where a half-timbered restaurant now capitalizes on the lurid association.

In 1834 the **Shire Hall**, further down High West Street, witnessed another *cause célèbre*, when six men from the nearby village of Tolpuddle were sentenced to transportation for banding together to form the Friendly Society of Agricultural Labourers, in order to present a request for a small wage increase on the grounds that their families were starving. After a public outcry the men were pardoned, and the **Tolpuddle Martyrs** passed into history as founders of the trade union movement. The room in which they were tried is preserved as a memorial to the martyrs, and you can find out more about them in Tolpuddle itself, eight miles east on the A35, where there's a fine little **museum** (April–Oct Tues–Sat 10am–5.30pm, Sun 11am–5.30pm; Nov–March closes at 4pm; free).

The best place to find out about Dorchester's history is the engrossing **Dorset County Museum** on High West Street (May–Oct daily 10am–5pm; Nov–April Mon–Sat 10am–5pm; £3.90), where archeological and geological displays trace Celtic and Roman history, including a section on Maiden Castle.

Hardy's Wessex

Thomas Hardy (1840–1928) resurrected the old name of **Wessex** to describe the region in which he set most of his fiction. In his books, the area stretched from Devon and Somerset ("Lower" and "Outer Wessex") to Berkshire and Oxfordshire ("North Wessex"), though its central core was Dorset ("South Wessex"), the county where Hardy spent most of his life. His books richly depict the life and appearance of the towns and countryside of the area, often thinly disguised under fictional names. Thus Salisbury makes an appearance as "Melchester", Weymouth (where he briefly lived) as "Budmouth Regis", and Bournemouth as "Sandbourne" – described as "a fairy palace suddenly created by the stroke of a wand, and allowed to get a little dusty" in *Tess of the d'Urbervilles*. But it is **Dorchester**, the "Casterbridge" of his novels, which is portrayed in most detail, to the extent that many of the town's buildings and landmarks that still remain can be identified in the books (especially *The Mayor of Casterbridge* and *Far From the Madding Crowd*). Hardy knew the town well; he attended school here (walking daily from the family home at Higher Bockhampton) and set up as an architect (his father and grandfather were both stonemasons), a profession which he later practised in Cornwall and London. He returned to Dorchester in 1885, spending the rest of his life in a house built to his own designs at Max Gate, on the Wareham Road.

Today, the Hardy industry takes two forms; the bookish and low-profile activities of the **Thomas Hardy Society**, whose diehard zealots help to preserve the relics and places with which the author is associated, and the high-profile overkill of the tourist mandarins who have made sure that some reminder of Hardy and his works greets the visitor to Dorchester at every turn. The Thomas Hardy Society (Box 1438, Dorchester, Dorset DT1 1YH ⓣ01305/251501) can provide plenty of material for enthusiasts to pore over, and organizes walks and tours, including a fifteen-mile hike which follows in the steps of Tess on her Sunday mission to her father-in-law, Parson Clare of Beauminster, in an attempt to rescue her failed marriage. If this sounds ambitious, content yourself with one of the walking itineraries outlined in the leaflets sold by the Society (and also available in the museum and tourist office) at 30p each.

Alternatively, you could read the books. Recommended reading includes *Under the Greenwood Tree* (1872) for an evocation of Hardy's childhood in and around Higher Bockhampton; *Tess of the d'Urbervilles* (1891), for elegiac descriptions of the Frome Valley; *The Return of the Native* (1878), for wild Egdon Heath and the eerie yew forest of Cranborne Chase; and *The Mayor of Casterbridge* (1886) for Dorchester and Maumbury Rings.

Pride of place goes to the re-creation of Thomas Hardy's study, where his pens are inscribed with the names of the books he wrote with them. Other museums in town include the formidably turreted **Keep Military Museum** (July & Aug Mon–Sat 9.30am–5pm, Sun 10am–4pm; rest of year closed Sun; £3; ⓦwww.keepmilitarymuseum.org), at the top of High West Street, which traces the fortunes of the Dorset and Devonshire regiments over three hundred years and offers sweeping views over the town; and a small **Dinosaur Museum** off High East Street on Icen Way (daily: April–Sept 9.30am–5.30pm; Oct–March 10am–4.30pm; £5.50), chiefly geared to children. Best of all is **Tutankhamun: The Exhibition** on the High Street (daily 9.30am–5.30pm; £5.50), a fascinating and thorough exploration of the young pharaoh's life and afterlife through to the eventual discovery of his tomb in 1922. Everything from the mummified remains, complete burial chamber and the celebrated golden mask has been carefully and atmospherically re-created with painstaking detail.

If you're on the Hardy trail, you'll want to visit **Thomas Hardy's Cottage** (April–Oct Mon & Thurs–Sun 11am–5pm or dusk; £2.80; NT) in Higher

Bockhampton, about three miles northeast of Dorchester, where the writer was born and lived from 1840 to 1862 and from 1867 to 1870, and his last and longest abode, **Max Gate** (April–Sept Mon, Wed & Sun 2–5pm; £2.40; NT), a twenty-minute walk east from the centre on the Wareham road (A352) – though you may be disappointed by the paucity of what there is to see. The nearer of the two, Max Gate, where the writer completed *Tess of the D'Urbervilles, Jude the Obscure* and much of his poetry, has only the garden and dining and drawing rooms open to the public, while Thomas Hardy's Cottage has even less on offer: bits of period furniture and some original manuscripts. Infrequent buses (#184–189) all pass within half a mile of the latter – otherwise you can walk (on the A35 and Bockhampton Road) or take a taxi.

Practicalities

Dorchester has two **train stations**, both of them to the south of the centre: trains from Weymouth and London arrive at Dorchester South, while Bath and Bristol trains use the Dorchester West station. Most **buses** stop around the car park on Acland Road, to the east of South Street; there are about four services daily from Poole and Salisbury, and several times hourly from Weymouth. There are also two daily bus connections with London, operated by National Express and First Southern National (☎01305/783645) – the latter is one of two main bus operators in the region, the other being Wilts & Dorset (☎01202/673555). The **tourist office** is in Antelope Walk (April & Oct Mon–Sat 9am–5pm; May–Sept Mon–Sat 9am–5pm, Sun 10am–3pm; Nov–March Mon–Sat 9am–4pm; ☎01305/267992, Ⓦwww.westdorset.com). **Bikes for rent** are available at Dorchester Cycles, 31 Great Western Rd (☎01305/268787), as well as helmets, panniers and locks (deposit or ID required).

Dorchester has a good selection of **accommodation**, including top of the range *Casterbridge Hotel*, 49 High East St (☎01305/264043, Ⓦwww.casterbridgehotel.co.uk; ❺), a superior Georgian guest house; and the best budget option, *Maumbury Cottage*, 9 Maumbury Rd (☎01305/266726; no credit cards; ❶), a small, friendly B&B just a few minutes' walk from the centre of town. The *King's Arms*, High East St (☎01305/265353; ❷), a historic local landmark, also serves good food, including vegetarian dishes. Out of town, try the *Old Rectory* in Winterbourne Steepleton, three miles to the west (☎01305/889468, Ⓦwww.trees.eurobell.co.uk; no smoking; no credit cards; ❸), surrounded by lawns, or, two miles north of town in Charminster, *Slades Farm*, North Street (☎01305/265614; no credit cards; ❷), a converted barn with en-suite rooms. There's a **youth hostel** at Litton Cheney (☎0870/770 5922; closed Sept–March; dorm beds £10.25), halfway between Dorchester and Bridport: take bus #31 to Whiteway, then follow directions for a mile and a half. The closest **campsite** is the *Giant's Head Caravan and Camping Park*, Old Sherborne Rd (☎01300/341242; closed Nov–Easter), about five miles north of town, above the Cerne Abbas giant (see p.310).

When it comes to **food**, your best bet is a pub meal; try the *Royal Oak*, which has a large beer garden, or the *Old Ship Inn*, both on High West Street and both highly recommended. Near the tourist office at 19 Durngate St, the *Potter's Bistro* has wholesome snacks and bistro food at weekends, while the famous *Judge Jeffreys Restaurant*, at 6 High West St (☎01305/264369), is inevitably touristy, but offers fair value. Further up at 34 High West St, *Sienna* (☎01305/250022; closed Sun & Mon) offers quality but moderately priced English cuisine with a Mediterranean twist. It's right across the road from the seventeenth-century *Old*

Tea House, good for teas and snacks. Dorchester's **nightlife** is limited, but *Paul's Nightclub* at 33 Trinity St and *Liberty's* at the top of High West Street lay on comedy and live-music nights, as well as club sounds at weekends.

Maiden Castle and Athelhampton House

One of southern England's finest prehistoric sites, **Maiden Castle** (free access) stands on a hill two miles or so southwest of Dorchester. Covering about 115 acres, it was first developed around 3000 BC by a Stone Age farming community and then used during the Bronze Age as a funeral mound. Iron Age dwellers expanded it into a populous settlement and fortified it with a daunting series of ramparts and ditches, just in time for the arrival of Vespasian's Second Legion. The ancient Britons' slingstones were no match for the more sophisticated weapons of the Roman invaders, and Maiden Castle was stormed in a bloody massacre in 43 AD.

What you see today is a massive series of grassy concentric ridges about sixty feet high, creasing the surface of the hill. The site is best visited early or late in the day, when the low-angled sun casts the earthworks in shadow, showing them up more clearly. The main finds from the site are displayed in the Dorset County Museum (see p.300).

Five miles east of Dorchester on the A35, just past the village of Puddletown, lies **Athelhampton House** (March–Oct Mon–Fri & Sun 10.30am–5pm; Nov–Feb Sun 10.30am–5pm; £7, or £4.95 gardens only), a fine fifteenth-century house surrounded by walled gardens resplendent with fountains and unusual topiary pyramids of yew. Inside, the oak-panelled Great Hall is Athelhampton's most outstanding feature, with its hammer-beam ceiling, original fireplace and oriel window. Other rooms don't quite live up to the Hall's Tudor grandeur, but feature an interesting collection of antiques which the house was bought to display.

Weymouth to Bridport

Whether George III's passion for sea bathing was a symptom of his eventual madness is uncertain, but it was at the bay of **Weymouth** that in 1789 he became the first reigning monarch to follow the craze. Sycophantic gentry rushed into the waves behind him, and soon the town, formerly a workaday harbour, took on the elegant Georgian stamp which it bears today. A likeness of the monarch on horseback is even carved into the chalk downs northwest of the town, like some guardian spirit. Weymouth nowadays plays second fiddle to the vast resort of Bournemouth to the east, but it's still a lively family holiday destination, with several costly new attractions to augment its more sedate charms.

Just south of the town stretch the giant arms of Portland Harbour, and a long causeway links Weymouth to the strange five-mile-long excrescence of the **Isle of Portland**. West of the causeway, the eighteen-mile bank of pebbles known as **Chesil Beach** runs northwest in the direction of **Bridport**.

Weymouth

WEYMOUTH had long been a port before the Georgians popularized it as a resort. It's possible that a ship unloading a cargo here in 1348 first brought the Black Death to English shores – and on a happier note it was from

Weymouth that John Endicott sailed in 1628 to found Salem in Massachusetts. A few buildings survive from these pre-Georgian times: the restored **Tudor House** on Trinity Street (June–Sept Tues–Fri 1pm–3.45pm; Oct–May first Sun of month 2–4pm; £2.50) and the ruins of **Sandsfoot Castle** (free access), built by Henry VIII, overlooking Portland Harbour. But Weymouth's most imposing architectural heritage stands along the Esplanade, a dignified range of bow-fronted and porticoed buildings gazing out across the graceful bay, an ensemble rather disrupted by the garish **Clocktower** commemorating Victoria's jubilee. The more intimate quayside of the Old Harbour, linked to the Esplanade by the main pedestrianized thoroughfare St Mary's Street, is lined with waterfront pubs from where you can view the passing yachts, trawlers and ferries.

Like most British seaside resorts, Weymouth has had to supply more than sand and saucy postcards to its clientele in recent years. Its slightly faded gentility is now counterbalanced by a number of "all-weather" attractions, the most high-profile of which is the **Sea Life Park** in Lodmoor Country Park, east of the Esplanade (daily: 10am–5pm; winter weekdays closes at 4pm; last admission 1hr before closing; £8.95, £6.50 from tourist office; ⓣ01305/761070), where you can get close to sharks and rays and wander among multichrome birds in the tropical house. Other attractions include the **Deep Sea Adventure** at the Old Harbour (daily 9.30am–7pm; last entry 90min before closing; £3.75), which describes the origins of modern diving and the sobering story of the *Titanic* disaster. Over the river on Hope Square, **The Timewalk**, housed in Brewer's Quay (Mon–Sat 10am–5.30pm, Sun 11am–4.30pm; school holidays open until 9pm; last entry 1hr before closing; £4.25), contains an entertaining and educational walk-through exhibition of Weymouth's maritime and brewing past. A fifteen-minute walk southwards leads to **Nothe Fort** (May to mid-Sept daily 10.30am–5.30pm; rest of year hours are variable; ⓣ01305/766626; £3.50), built 1860–72 to defend Portland Harbour, where there are displays on military themes and a museum describing garrison life and the castle's role in coastal defence. If you're interested in exploring the bay, check out the glass-bottomed *Fleet Observer*, which sails from the *Ferrybridge* pub near Abbotsbury Oysters on the A354 Portland Road (June–Sept 5 daily; 1hr 30min; £6; ⓣ01305/759692).

Practicalities

Weymouth is easily reached by public transport: there's a regular **train** service from London, Bournemouth and Poole, and less frequent services from Bristol and Bath. There are also good **bus** services between Weymouth and Dorchester, eight miles north, a hub for many other routes. Condor Ferries (ⓣ0845/345 2000, ⓦwww.condorferries.co.uk) operates a daily **catamaran** service to the Channel Islands between April and October, leaving at 7.15am from Weymouth's harbour; sailings are irregular in winter, contact Condor directly for details. The town's **tourist office** is at King's Statue, the Esplanade (daily: April–Sept 9.30am–5pm; Oct–March 10.30am–3pm; ⓣ01305/785747, ⓦwww.weymouth.gov.uk).

A cluster of the town's **accommodation** options lies at the south end of the Esplanade, between the bay and harbour, for instance *Chatsworth*, 14 The Esplanade (ⓣ01305/785012, ⓦwww.thechatsworth.co.uk; ❺), which has a garden terrace, and the good-value *Cavendish House*, 5 The Esplanade (ⓣ01305/782039; no credit cards; ❷), in a detached Georgian terrace overlooking the bay with harbour views at the back. Nearer the train station but just a few steps from the seafront, the *Wilton Guest House* (ⓣ01305/783317, ⓦwww.weymouthwilton-gh.co.uk; ❶) and *Melcombe Villa* (ⓣ01305/783026;

no credit cards; ❶), both on Gloucester Street, have friendly management and clean, comfortable rooms; those at the *Wilton* are slightly larger. At the quieter northern end of the Esplanade, *Bay Lodge*, at 27 Greenhill (☎01305/782419, ⓦwww.baylodge.co.uk; ❺), is a better-than-average B&B with good sea views and a car park.

Weymouth is also well served by its refreshment outlets and **restaurants**. If it's seafood you're after, you can't do better than *Perry's*, a moderately priced place overlooking the quayside at 4 Trinity Rd (☎01305/785799; closed Sat lunch & Mon lunch, also Sun eve in winter). Other cheaper places include *Criterion* at 63 The Esplanade (behind the statue of George III), a useful self-service restaurant near the beach with all-day breakfasts, and the *Seagull Café*, 10 Trinity St, a family-run chippie with fresh fish and lashings of chips (closed Sun & Mon). At the *Statue House*, 109 St Mary's St, you can gaze out to sea through the large windows of this popular and inexpensive tapas bar in a wooden-floored Georgian building. On the corner of St Nicholas Street and Commercial Road, the *Sailor's Return* is one of a number of amenable **pubs** in town, a harbourside tavern with in-your-face angling paraphernalia and fresh fish on the menu; others include the *Old Rooms Inn*, at the northern end of Trinity Road, an inexpensive lunch venue, again with a strong maritime theme, and the *Nothe Tavern*, buried among Nothe Gardens (south of the harbour on Barrack Road), which offers bar meals and Eldridge Pope beer and has views from the garden. For a rowdier time, head for the *Rendezvous*, by the Town Bridge, a bar/restaurant/nightclub open until 2am.

Portland

Stark, wind-battered and treeless, the **Isle of Portland** is famed above all for its hard white limestone, which has been quarried here for centuries – Wren used it for St Paul's Cathedral, and it clads the UN headquarters in New York. It was also used for the six-thousand-foot breakwater that protects Portland Harbour – the largest artificial harbour in Britain, which was built by convicts in the mid-nineteenth century. The quarries are prominent and unlovely features of the island today.

By public transport, you can reach the Isle of Portland from Weymouth on the frequent #1 and #1A buses (not Sun in winter). The causeway road by which the Isle is approached stands on the easternmost section of the Chesil shingle. To the east you get a good view of the harbour, a naval base since 1872, but now jeopardized by the post-Cold War rundown of Britain's defences. The first settlement you come to, **FORTUNESWELL**, overlooks the huge harbour and is itself surveyed by a 460-year-old Tudor fortress, **Portland Castle** (April–Sept daily 10am–6pm; Oct daily 10am–5pm; Nov–March Fri–Sun 10am–4pm; £3.50; EH), commissioned by Henry VIII. The craggy limestone of the isle rises to 496 feet at Verne Hill, to the southeast of here. South of **EASTON**, the main village on the island, Wakeham Road holds **Pennsylvania Castle** (now a private house), built in 1800 for John Penn, governor of the island and a grandson of the founder of Pennsylvania. A couple of hundred yards beyond the house, the seventeenth-century **Avice's Cottage**, a gift of Marie Stopes, the pioneer of birth control, is home to a small **museum** (Easter–July, Sept & Oct Mon, Tues & Fri–Sun 10.30am–1pm & 1.30–5pm; Aug & school holidays daily 10.30am–1pm & 1.30–5pm; £2), with exhibitions on local shipwrecks, smuggling and quarrying. The cottage owes its name to Thomas Hardy, who described it in his novel, *The Well-Beloved*. Nearby, in **Church Ope Cove**, you can see the ruins of St Andrew's Church and those of Rufus Castle, associated with William II (William Rufus, son of William the Conqueror), though there is evidence of an older Saxon fortification here, while the visible remains probably belong to a reconstruction after the Norman castle was destroyed in 1142.

At **Portland Bill**, the southern tip of the island, a lighthouse has guarded the promontory since the eighteenth century. You can climb the 153 steps of the present one, dating from 1906, for the views (Easter–Sept Mon–Fri & Sun 11am–5pm; tours £2), and it also houses Portland's **tourist office** (Easter–Sept Mon, Tues & Thurs–Sun 10am–4pm, Wed 11am–4pm; ⓣ01305/861233), which can supply leaflets on the area's special features, including geology and wildlife. **Accommodation** options in the area include *Sturt Corner* (ⓣ01305/822846; no credit cards; ❶) and the *Pulpit Inn* (ⓣ01305/821237; ❷), both nearby on Portland Bill, and there's a **youth hostel** just south of Portland Castle, on Castle Road (ⓣ0870/770 6000; closed Oct to mid-April; dorm beds £11.50); it's left off Victory Square onto Victory Road, then left again. If you want to stay in a lighthouse, the *Old Higher Lighthouse* (ⓣ01305/822300, ⓦwww.oldhigherlighthouse.co.uk; no smoking) offers **self-catering** facilities for which you'll pay £300–600 per week, depending on season; book well in advance.

Chesil Beach to Bridport

Chesil Beach is the strangest feature of the Dorset coast, a two-hundred-yard-wide, fifty-foot-high bank of pebbles that extends for eighteen miles, its component stones gradually decreasing in size from fist-like pebbles at Portland to "pea gravel" at Burton Bradstock in the west. This sorting is an effect of the powerful coastal currents, which make this one of the most dangerous beaches in Europe – churchyards in the local villages display plenty of evidence of wrecks and drownings. Though not a swimming beach, Chesil is popular with sea anglers, and its wild, uncommercialized atmosphere makes an appealing antidote to the south coast resorts. To explore it, you need your own transport or plenty of time – infrequent bus services connect the main villages, and the Dorset Coast Path runs close to the shore for most of the way.

Chesil Beach encloses a brackish lagoon called **The Fleet** for much of its length – it was the setting for J. Meade Faulkner's classic smuggling tale, *Moonfleet*. Overlooking the lagoon, *Moonfleet Manor* (ⓣ01305/786948; ❽), a **hotel** and large sports resort three miles west of Weymouth, capitalizes on the Faulkner connection. At the point where the shingle beach attaches itself to the shore is the pretty village of **ABBOTSBURY**, all tawny ironstone and thatch. Its Tithe Barn is a fifteenth-century building, the last remnant of the village's Benedictine abbey, and today, as the **Smuggler's Barn** (daily: Easter–Oct 10am–6pm; Nov–Easter Sat & Sun 11am–dusk; last admissions 1hr before closing; £4.80), it features the ins and outs of contrabanding and is the venue for occasional exhibitions. The village **Swannery** (mid-March to Sept daily 10am–6pm; Oct daily 10am–5pm; last admission 1hr before closing; £5.80), a wetland reserve for mute swans, dates back to medieval times, when presumably it formed part of the abbot's larder. The eel-grass reeds through which the swans paddle were once harvested to thatch roofs throughout the region. Other attractions are the hilltop **Chapel of St Catherine**, also dating from the fifteenth century, and the **Subtropical Gardens** (daily: March–Oct 10am–6pm; Nov–Feb 10am–dusk; last admission 1hr before closing; £5.80), where delicate species thrive in the micro-climate created by Chesil's stones, which act as a giant radiator to keep out all but the worst frosts. Up on the downs a couple of miles inland from Abbotsbury is a monument to Thomas

Hardy, not the usual one associated with Dorset, but the flag captain in whose arms Admiral Nelson expired.

If you want to **stay** in Abbotsbury try *Swan Lodge*, 1 Rodden Row, for good B&B accommodation (Ⓣ01305/871249; ❸), which has fully equipped rooms, some en suite, or the *Ilchester Arms* in the village centre, a handsome stone inn with comfortable facilities and fine food (Ⓣ01305/871243, Ⓦwww.ilchesterarms.co.uk; ❷). West of the village three miles along the coast at **West Bexington**, the *Manor Hotel* is an excellent unpretentious hostelry offering accommodation and a sumptuous range of food (Ⓣ01308/897616, Ⓔthemanorhotel@bt.connect.com; ❻); while inland and further west, in the lovely village of **Shipton Gorge**, *Innsacre Farmhouse* (Ⓣ01308/456137, Ⓔinnsacre.farmhouse@btinternet.com; closed Nov; ❺) provides similar services.

BRIDPORT, just beyond the far end of Chesil Beach, is a pleasant old town of brick rather than stone, with unusually wide streets, a hangover from its rope-making days when cords made of locally grown hemp and flax were stretched between the houses. Bridport has several fine buildings: a medieval church, a Georgian town hall, a fourteenth-century chantry and a Tudor building housing the local **museum** (April–Oct Mon–Sat 10am–5pm; £2). If you want to know about the rope and net industry head for the fishing resort of **West Bay**, Bridport's access to the sea, where majestic red cliffs rear up above the sea. The **Harbour Life Exhibition** (April–Oct daily 10am–5pm; £1) will fill you in about "Bridport daggers" (hangmen's nooses) and more besides. West Bay also has the area's best place to **eat**, the *Riverside Restaurant*, a renowned but informal fish place with good views over the river, worth booking ahead (Ⓣ01308/422011; moderate–expensive). Across the harbour, the *Bridport Arms Hotel* (Ⓣ01308/422994; ❹) offers good **accommodation** near the beach; also worth trying is *Britmead House*, 154 West Bay Rd (Ⓣ01308/422941, Ⓦwww.britmeadhouse.co.uk; ❸), on the road back to Bridport. In the centre of Bridport, try *Cranston Cottage*, 27 Church St (Ⓣ01308/456240; no credit cards; ❶), which has three rooms with and without bathroom. Bridport's **tourist office** is at 32 South St (April–Oct Mon–Sat 9am–5pm; Nov–March Mon–Sat 10am–3pm; Ⓣ01308/424901, Ⓦwww.bridportandwestbay.co.uk), and there's a seasonal office at West Bay sharing the same premises with the Harbour Life Exhibition (April–Oct daily 10am–5pm; Ⓣ01308/422807).

Lyme Regis and around

From the end of Chesil Beach an ever more dramatic sequence of cliffs runs westward, followed as closely as possible by the **Dorset Coast Path**, which has to deviate inland in a few places to avoid areas of landslip. The most prominent feature along this coast is **Golden Cap**, an outcrop of sandstone close to west Dorset's main resort, **Lyme Regis**. On summer days it can seem that tourism is threatening to choke the life out of Lyme – but you can quickly find refuge inland, where **Beaminster** makes a good base for exploring picturesque Dorset villages of golden stone and thatched cottages.

Lyme Regis

LYME REGIS, Dorset's most westerly town, shelters snugly between steep hills, just before the grey, fossil-filled cliffs lurch into Devon. Its intimate size and undeniable photogenic qualities make Lyme so popular that in high summer car-borne crowds jostle with pedestrians for the limited space along its narrow streets. For all that, the town lives up to the classy impression created by its regal name, which it owes to a royal charter granted by Edward I in 1284. It has some upmarket literary associations to further bolster its self-esteem – Jane Austen summered in a seafront cottage and set part of *Persuasion* here (and the town appears in the 1995 film adaptation), while novelist John Fowles is Lyme's most famous current resident. It was the film adaptation of Fowles' book, *The French Lieutenant's Woman*, shot on location here, that did more than any tourist board production ever could to place the resort firmly on the map.

Though Lyme Regis now relies mostly on holiday-makers for its keep, it was for centuries a port for the wool traders of Somerset, and shipbuilding thrived here until Victorian times. Colourwashed cottages and elegant Regency and Victorian villas line its seafront and flanking streets, but Lyme's best-known feature is a briskly practical reminder of its commercial origins. **The Cobb**, the curving harbour wall, was first constructed in the thirteenth century but has suffered many alterations since, most notably in the nineteenth century, when its massive boulders were clad in neater blocks of Portland stone.

As you walk along the seafront and out towards The Cobb, look for the outlines of ammonites in the walls and paving stones. The cliffs around Lyme are made up of a complex layer of limestone, greensand and unstable clay, a perfect medium for preserving fossils, which are exposed by landslips of the waterlogged clays. One of the most famous landslides occurred in 1839, when a large block of land, complete with a crop of turnips, was severed from its neighbouring fields by a chasm so dramatic that Queen Victoria came to inspect the scene from her yacht. In 1811, after a fierce storm caused parts of the cliffs to collapse, 12-year-old Mary Anning, a keen fossil-hunter, discovered an almost complete dinosaur skeleton, a thirty-foot ichthyosaurus now displayed in London's Natural History Museum (see p.127).

Hammering fossils out of the cliffs is frowned on by today's conservationists, and in any case is rather hazardous. Hands-off inspection of the area's complex geology can be enjoyed on both sides of town: to the west lies the **Undercliff**, a fascinating jumble of overgrown landslips, now a nature reserve. East of Lyme, the Dorset Coast Path is closed as far as jaded **Charmouth** (Jane Austen's favourite resort), but at low tide you can walk for two miles along the beach, then, just past Charmouth, rejoin the coastal path to the headland of **Golden Cap**, whose brilliant outcrop of auburn sandstone is crowned with gorse. One good way of exploring the area would be on a **guided walk**, of which several are available that focus on the fossil heritage, tides permitting. For details, contact the tourist office or the Philpott Museum, or call ⊕01297/443370 or 01297/443758. Tours generaly last two or three hours and cost £5–10.

Lyme's excellent **Philpot Museum** on Bridge Street (April–Oct Mon–Sat 10am–5pm, Sun 11am–5pm; Nov–March Sat 10am–5pm, Sun 11am–5pm, also open Christmas & school half-terms at same times; £2) provides a crash course in local history and geology, while **Dinosaurland** on Coombe Street (daily 10am–5pm, Aug until 6pm; £4) fills out the story on ammonites and other local fossils. Also worth seeing is the small **marine aquarium** on The Cobb (Easter–Oct 10am–5pm, with later closing in July & Aug; £2), where local fishermen bring unusual catches, and the fifteenth-century **parish church** of St Michael the Archangel, up Church Street, which contains a seventeenth-century pulpit and a massive chained Bible.

Practicalities

Lyme's nearest **train station** is in Axminster, five miles north; the #31 **bus** runs from here to Lyme Regis; a **taxi** will cost around £9. National Express runs a daily service from Exeter (see p.439). The **tourist office** is on Church Street (May–Oct Mon–Sat 10am–5am, Sun 10am–4pm; Nov–April Mon–Sat 10am–2pm; ⓣ01297/442138, ⓦwww.lymeregistourism.co.uk).

Lyme's sole seafront hotel is the pricey *Bay Hotel* on Marine Parade (ⓣ01297/442059; ❻), but you don't have to walk far for more moderately priced accommodation. The *Old Monmouth Hotel* is centrally located at 12 Church St (ⓣ01297/442456, ⓦwww.lyme-regis-hotel.co.uk; ❷), while *Cliff Cottage* on Cobb Road (ⓣ01297/443334; no credit cards; closed Nov–March; ❶) has harbour views, a garden chalet and a fish restaurant; the *Red House*, a ten-minute walk out of town on Sidmouth Road (ⓣ01297/442055; ❸; closed mid-Nov to mid-March), offers an especially warm welcome as well as fabulous views. Other good choices include *Coombe House,* 41 Coombe St (ⓣ01297/443849; no credit cards; ❷), a friendly, central place, with large rooms and a self-catering studio; the *New Haven*, 1 Pound St (ⓣ01297/442499; ❶), which has one standard room on the ground floor, more expensive rooms upstairs, and the *Cobb Arms*, Marine Parade (ⓣ01297/443242; ❷).

For a crowded but cheerful atmosphere and inexpensive daytime **meals**, try the *Bell Cliff Restaurant* at 5–6 Broad St, where salmon fishcakes are on the menu; it occasionally stays open on summer evenings. Alternatively, head for *Café Clemence*, Mill Lane (ⓣ01297/445757; closed Mon daytime), a Mediterranean-style bistro serving good pasta and fish dishes in a pleasant courtyard. The best **pubs** are the *Royal Standard* on Ozone Parade, and the *Pilot Boat* on Bridge Street, which also does smashing seafood and vegetarian meals.

Inland Dorset and southern Wiltshire

The main pleasures of inland Dorset come from unscheduled meandering through its ancient landscapes and tiny rural settlements, many of which boast preposterously winsome names such as Ryme Intrinseca, Piddletrenthide, Up Sydling and Plush. Two of the most interesting of these villages are **Milton Abbas** and **Cerne Abbas**, the former attractive on account of its curious artificiality, the latter for its rumbustious chalk-carved giant. The major tourist honeypots, though, are the towns of **Blandford Forum**, **Shaftesbury** and **Sherborne**, the landscaped garden at **Stourhead** across the county boundary in Wiltshire, and the brasher stately home at **Longleat**, an unlikely hybrid of safari park and historic monument.

Blandford Forum

BLANDFORD FORUM, the gateway into mid-Dorset from Bournemouth, owes its latinate name not to the Romans but to medieval pedantry – the original Saxon name Cheping, meaning "market", was translated as Forum by Latin-speaking tax officials in the thirteenth century. The Romans weren't far away, however – their main route from Old Sarum (see p.317) to Dorchester ran through the Iron Age fortification of Badbury Rings, just east of the town, where it made an uncharacteristic bend.

In 1731 Blandford was all but destroyed by fire, the fourth such conflagration since the end of the sixteenth century. The phoenix that rose from these ashes – as the Fire Monument near the church puts it – was designed by the unfortunately named Bastard brothers, John and William, whose "Blandford School" produced buildings characterized by mellow dapplings of brick and stone. Sleepy Blandford still boasts one of the most harmonious and complete

Georgian townscapes in England, with its centrepieces being the **Town Hall** and the **Church of St Peter and St Paul**, built in 1739. Outside, the church's distinguishing feature is the cupola perched on its handsome square tower; inside, it has fine box pews and huge Ionic columns. It doesn't quite look as John Bastard intended, though: the church was daringly altered at the end of the nineteenth century, when the chancel was sawn off the nave, stuck on wheels, rolled out of the way so that a new section could be built in the gap, and then stuck back onto the extension. The town **museum** in Bere's Yard, opposite the church (Easter–Sept daily 10am–4pm; £1.50), offers a pithy account of local history, while **Mrs Penny's Cavalcade of Costume** at Lime Tree House, The Plocks (Easter–Sept Mon & Thurs–Sun 11am–5pm; Oct–Easter same days 11am–4pm; £3.40), presents over five hundred items of costume and accoutrements from 1730 to the 1950s, collected throughout the lifetime of a local woman, Mrs Penny.

You can reach Blandford on the regular #184 **bus** from Weymouth, Dorchester or Salisbury, or the hourly #311 from Dorchester. The town's **tourist office** is in the car park on West Street (Mon–Sat: April–Oct 10am–5pm; Nov–March 10am–1pm; ⓣ01258/454770, ⓦwww.ruraldorset.com). There are numerous **B&B**s along Whitecliff Mill Street to choose from, or try *Gone Walkabout*, at 3 Alexandra St (ⓣ01258/455699, ⓔgonewalkabout@talk21.com; no smoking; no credit cards; ❶), a Georgian house close to the town centre and welcoming to walkers and cyclists. The local Hall & Woodhouse brewery supplies many local **hostelries** – the *Greyhound*, in quiet Greyhound Place (off Market Place), is a good-looking pub with outdoor seating and great food. Other eating options include the moderately priced *Ottoman* Turkish restaurant, at 65 East St.

Milton Abbas and Cerne Abbas

The village of **MILTON ABBAS**, six miles southwest of Blandford (and reachable on buses #184 and #311), is an unusual English rural idyll. It owes its model-like neatness to the First Earl of Dorchester who, in the eighteenth century, found the medieval squalor of former "Middleton" a blot on the landscape of his estate. Although some see the earl as an enlightened advocate of modern town planning, the more likely truth is that he simply wanted to beautify his land, so he had the village razed and rebuilt in its present location as thirty semi-detached, whitewashed and thatched cottages on wide grassy verges. No trace remains of the old village which once surrounded the fourteenth-century **abbey church** (dawn–dusk; small charge during school holidays), a mile's walk away near the lake at the bottom of the village. Delayed by the Black Death and cut short by the Dissolution, the abbey church lacks much internal decoration, and instead retains a spacious, uncluttered feel.

Not far from the village, the brick and flint cottage *Dunbury Heights* (ⓣ01258/880445; no smoking; no credit cards; ❷), about a mile towards Blandford, offers comfortable B&B **accommodation**. The *Dorset Tea Rooms* provides light lunches and the *Hambro Arms* **pub** at the top of the hill is the best bet for more substantial evening meals.

The most visited site in Dorset lies a further ten miles west, just off the A352, on the regular bus route between Dorchester and Sherborne (#216). **CERNE ABBAS** has bags of charm in its own right, with gorgeous Tudor cottages and abbey ruins, not to mention a clutch of decent pubs. Its main attraction, however, is the enormously priapic **giant** carved in the chalk hillside, standing 180-feet high and flourishing a club over his disproportionately small head. The age of the monument is disputed, some authorities believing it to be pre-Roman, others thinking it might be a Romano-British figure of Hercules, but in view of his prominent feature it's probable that the giant originated as some primeval fertility symbol. Folklore has it that lying on the outsize member will induce conception, but the National Trust, which now owns the site, does its best to stop people wandering over it and eroding the two-foot trenches that form the outlines.

Shaftesbury

Ten miles north of Blandford, **SHAFTESBURY** perches on a spur of lumpy green-gold hills, with severe gradients on three sides of the town. On a clear day, views from the town are terrific – one of the best vantage points is **Gold Hill**, quaint, cobbled and very steep. The local history **museum** at the top of Gold Hill (Mon–Tues & Thurs–Sun 10.30am–4.30pm; £1) is worth a glance – its contents include a collection of locally made buttons, for which the area was once renowned.

Pilgrims used to flock to Shaftesbury to pay homage to the bones of Edward the Martyr, which were brought to the **Abbey** in 978, though now only the footings of the abbey church survive, just off the main street (April–Nov daily 10am–5pm; £2). **St Peter's Church** on the market place is one of the few reminders of Shaftesbury's medieval grandeur, when it boasted a castle, twelve churches and four market crosses.

You can reach Shaftesbury on **bus** #40 from Dorchester or #182/183 from Bournemouth. The helpful **tourist office** on Bell Street (April–Sept daily 10am–5pm; Oct–March Mon–Sat 10am–3pm, ⓣ01747/853514, ⓦwww.ruraldorset.com) can provide a full list of available **accommodation**. *Maple Lodge* on Christy's Lane has modern, fully equipped rooms in a purpose-built house (ⓣ01747/853945, ⓦwww.maplelodgebb.com; no credit cards; ❸), while the *Knoll* in Bleke Street (ⓣ01747/855243, ⓦwww.pick-art.org.uk; ❸) boasts views over three counties. Three miles south of town in the village of **Compton Abbas**, on the scenic A350 to Blandford, the *Old Forge*, on Chapel Hill (ⓣ01747/811881, ⓔtheoldforge@hotmail.com; no credit cards; ❷), offers B&B in an eighteenth-century cottage with log fires. For a **snack** or main **meal** in Shaftesbury, the *Salt Cellar* at the top of Gold Hill makes a great place to sit, without suffering from over-quaintness.

Stourhead

Landscape gardening – the creation of an artificially improved version of nature – was a favoured mode of display among the grandest eighteenth-century landowners, and **Stourhead**, ten miles northwest of Shaftesbury, is one of the most accomplished survivors of the genre (April–Oct Mon, Tues & Fri–Sun 11am–5pm or dusk; garden: daily 9am–7pm or dusk; house & garden £8.90; house £5.10; garden £5.10 or £3.95 in winter; NT). The Stourton estate was bought in 1717 by Henry Hoare, who commissioned Colen Campbell to build a new villa in the Palladian style. Hoare's heir, another Henry, returned from his Grand Tour in 1741 with his head full of the paintings of Claude and Poussin, and determined to translate their images of well-ordered, wistful classicism into real life. He dammed the Stour to create a lake, then planted the terrain with blocks of trees, domed temples, stone bridges, grottoes and statues, all mirrored vividly in the water. In 1772 the folly of **King Alfred's Tower** (April–Nov daily noon–5pm or dusk; £1.85) was added and today affords fine views across the estate and into neighbouring counties. The rhododendrons and azaleas that now make such a splash in early summer are a later addition to this dream landscape. The house, in contrast, is fairly run-of-the-mill, though it has some good Chippendale furniture. To get here **by bus**, your best option is to catch the #25/26 from Salisbury (4–6 daily).

A mile to the southeast, in the showpiece village of **STOURTON**, also now owned by the National Trust, the *Spread Eagle Inn* has five en-suite **rooms** available (☎01747/840587; ⑤) with prices halving in winter – it's also a good place to have **lunch**. However, Stourton is difficult to reach without your own transport – the nearest train station is at Gillingham, over six miles away.

Longleat

If Stourhead is an unexpected outcrop of Italy in Wiltshire, the African savannah intrudes even more bizarrely at **Longleat** (house April–Sept daily 10am–5.30pm; Oct–March guided tours at set times 10am–3pm, check at ☎01985/844400 or ⓦwww.longleat.co.uk; safari park Easter–Oct Mon–Fri 10am–4pm, Sat, Sun & school holidays 10am–5pm; house £9; safari park £9; combined ticket £16), two and a half miles south of the road from Warminster to Frome. In 1946 the sixth marquess of Bath raised eyebrows among his peers as the first stately-home owner to open his house to the paying public on a regular basis to help make ends meet. In 1966 he caused even more amazement when Longleat's Capability Brown landscapes were turned into a drive-through **safari park** – the first in the country. (The car-less visitor can survey the lions, tigers, giraffes, elephants, zebras and hippos from a safari bus for an extra £3.) Once committed to such commercial enterprise, the bosses of Longleat knew no limits: other attractions now include the world's largest hedge maze, a Doctor Who exhibition, a hi-tech simulation of the world's most dangerous modes of travel and the seventh marquess's steamy murals encapsulating his interpretation of life and the universe (children may not be admitted). Beyond the brazen razzmatazz, though, there's an exquisitely furnished Elizabethan house, built for Sir John Thynne, Elizabeth's High Treasurer, with the largest private library in Britain and a fine collection of pictures, including Titian's *Holy Family*.

Longleat is about four miles from the train stations of Frome and Warminster and is currently served by a Lion-Link bus (Easter–Oct only) that leaves Warminster train station at 11.10am and returns from the Information Centre at Longleat at 5.15pm – the service is provided free to coach- and rail-ticket holders, and otherwise costs £1.50. Alternatively, there's the #53 bus (Mon–Sat) which shuttles roughly every hour between Warminster and Frome train stations – though be prepared to walk the two and a half miles from the entrance of the house to its grounds.

Sherborne

Tucked away in the northwest corner of Dorset, the pretty town of **SHERBORNE** was once the capital of Wessex, its church having cathedral status until Old Sarum (see p.317) usurped the bishopric in 1075. This former glory is embodied by the magnificent **Abbey Church** (daily: April–Oct 8.30am–6pm; Nov–March 8.30am–4pm), which was founded in 705, later becoming a Benedictine abbey. Most of its extant parts date from a rebuilding in the fifteenth century, and it is one of the best examples of Perpendicular architecture in Britain, particularly noted for its outstanding **fan vaulting**. The church also has a famously weighty peal of bells, led by "Great Tom", a tenor bell presented to the abbey by Cardinal Wolsey. Among the abbey church's many tombs are those of Alfred the Great's two brothers, Ethelred and

Ethelbert, and the Elizabethan poet Thomas Wyatt, all located in the northeast corner. The **almshouse** on the opposite side of the Abbey Close was built in 1437 and is a rare example of a medieval hospital; another wing provides accommodation for Sherborne's well-known public school.

The town also has two "castles", both associated with Sir Walter Raleigh. Queen Elizabeth I first leased, then gave, Raleigh the twelfth-century **Old Castle** (April–Sept daily 10am–6pm; Oct daily 10am–1pm & 2–5pm; £2; EH), but it seems that he despaired of feudal accommodation and built himself a more comfortably domesticated house, **Sherborne Castle**, in adjacent parkland (April–Oct Tues, Thurs & Sun 11am–4.30pm, Sat 2.30–5pm; gardens closed Sat; castle & gardens £6, gardens only £3.25). When Sir Walter fell from the queen's favour by seducing her maid of honour, the Digby family acquired the house and have lived there ever since; portraits, furniture and books are displayed in a whimsically Gothic interior, remodelled in the nineteenth century. The Old Castle fared less happily, and was pulverized by Cromwellian cannonfire for the obstinately Royalist leanings of its occupants. The **museum** near the abbey on Church Lane (April–Oct Tues, & Thurs–Sat 10.30am–4.30pm, Sun 2.30–4.30pm; last admission 4pm; £1) includes a model of the Old Castle and photographs of parts of the fifteenth-century Sherborne Missal, a richly illuminated tome weighing nearly fifty pounds, now housed in the British Library.

Buses #36, #46 and #58 run between Shaftesbury and Sherborne. The **tourist office** is at 3 Tilton Court, Digby Rd (Mon–Sat: Easter–Oct 9am–5pm; Nov–Easter 10am–3pm; ⓣ01935/815341). For an **overnight stay** try the *Half Moon*, Half Moon St (ⓣ01935/812017; ❹), the *Britannia Inn*, on Westbury, just down from the abbey (ⓣ01935/813300; ❷), or the *Cross Keys Hotel*, 88 Cheap St (ⓣ01935/812492; ❷), a cosy **pub** which has a few tables out front for drinks and meals. *Oliver's*, 19 Cheap St, and the *Church House Gallery*, close to the abbey on Half Moon Street, are both good for teas and light lunches.

Salisbury

SALISBURY, huddled below Wiltshire's chalky plain in the converging valleys of the Avon and Nadder, looks from a distance very much as it did when Constable painted his celebrated view of it from across the water meadows, even though traffic may clog its centre and military jets scream overhead from local air bases. Prosperous and well kept, Wiltshire's only city is designed on a pleasantly human scale, with no sprawling suburbs or high-rise buildings to challenge the supremacy of the cathedral's immense spire – unusually, the local planners have imposed a height limit on new construction.

The town sprang into existence in the early thirteenth century, when the bishopric was moved from **Old Sarum**, an ancient Iron Age hillfort settled by the Romans and their successors. The deserted remnant of Salisbury's precursor now stands on the northern fringe of the town, just a bit closer in than **Wilton House** to the west, one of Wiltshire's great houses.

The City

Begun in 1220, **Salisbury Cathedral** (June–Aug Mon–Sat 7.15am–7.15pm, Sun 7.15am–6.15pm; Sept–May daily 7am–6.15pm; £3.80 suggested donation) was mostly completed within forty years and is thus unusually consistent in its style, with one extremely prominent exception – the **spire**, which was added a century later and at 404ft is the highest in England. Its survival is some-

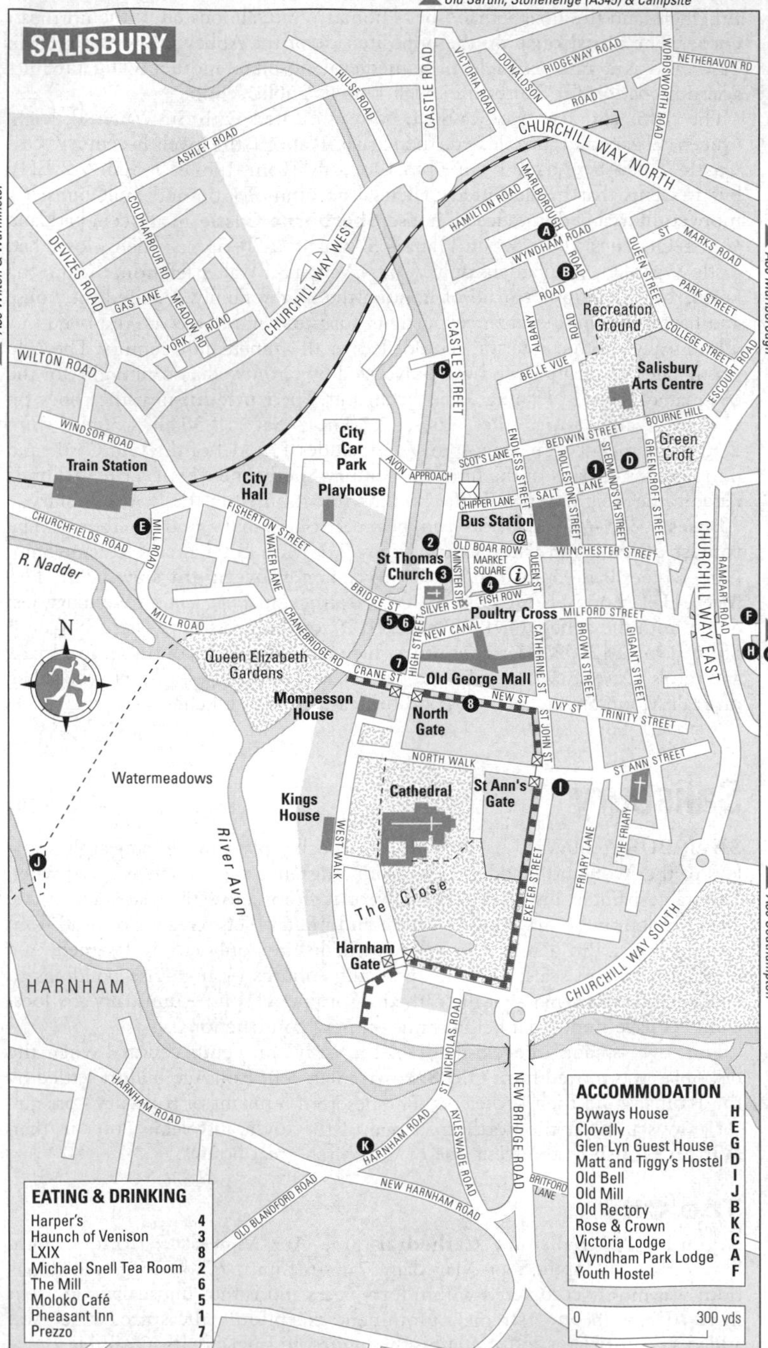
SALISBURY
Old Sarum, Stonehenge (A345) & Campsite
A36 Wilton & Warminster
A30 Marlborough
A36 Southampton
A338 Bournemouth
Train Station
City Hall
Playhouse
City Car Park
Bus Station
St Thomas Church
Market Square
Poultry Cross
Old George Mall
Recreation Ground
Salisbury Arts Centre
Green Croft
Queen Elizabeth Gardens
Mompesson House
North Gate
St Ann's Gate
Cathedral
Kings House
The Close
Harnham Gate
Watermeadows
HARNHAM
R. Nadder
River Avon
Churchill Way North
Churchill Way West
Churchill Way East
Churchill Way South
Castle Street
Fisherton Street
Bridge St
High Street
New Canal
Crane St
New St
Milford Street
Winchester Street
Exeter Street
St John St
St Ann Street
New Bridge Road
Harnham Road
New Harnham Road
Old Blandford Road
Wilton Road
Devizes Road
Ashley Road
Mill Road
Churchfields Road
Windsor Road
EATING & DRINKING
Harper's 4
Haunch of Venison 3
LXIX 8
Michael Snell Tea Room 2
The Mill 6
Moloko Café 5
Pheasant Inn 1
Prezzo 7
ACCOMMODATION
Byways House H
Clovelly E
Glen Lyn Guest House G
Matt and Tiggy's Hostel D
Old Bell I
Old Mill J
Old Rectory B
Rose & Crown K
Victoria Lodge C
Wyndham Park Lodge A
Youth Hostel F
0 300 yds
© Crown copyright

thing of a miracle, for the foundations penetrate only about six feet into marshy ground, and when Christopher Wren surveyed it he found the spire to be leaning almost two and a half feet out of true. He added further tie-rods, which finally arrested the movement.

The interior is over-austere after James Wyatt's brisk eighteenth-century tidying, but there's an amazing sense of space and light in its high nave, despite the sombre pillars of grey Purbeck marble, which are visibly bowing beneath the weight they bear. Monuments and carved tombs line the walls, where they were neatly placed by Wyatt, and in the north aisle there's a fascinating clock dating from 1386, one of the oldest functioning clock mechanisms in Europe. Other features not to miss are the vaulted colonnades of the **cloisters**, and the octagonal **chapter house** (June–Aug Mon–Sat 9.30am–6.45pm, Sun noon–5.30pm; Sept–May Mon–Sat 9.30am–5.30pm, Sun noon–5.30pm), which displays a rare original copy of the Magna Carta, and whose walls are decorated with a frieze of scenes from the Old Testament. On most days, you can join a free 45-minute tour of the church leaving two or more times a day, and there are also tours to the roof and spires (variable times; £4).

Surrounding the cathedral is the **Close**, the largest and most impressive in the country, a peaceful precinct of lawns and mellow old buildings. Most of the houses have seemly Georgian facades, though some, like the Bishop's Palace and the deanery, date from the thirteenth century. **Mompesson House** (April–Oct Mon–Wed, Sat & Sun 11am–5.30pm, last entry 4.30pm; £3.90, garden only 80p; NT), built by a wealthy merchant in 1701, contains some beautifully furnished eighteenth-century rooms and a superbly carved staircase, as displayed to great effect in the film *Sense and Sensibility*; the entry price includes a thirty-minute guided tour. The other building to head for in the Close is the **King's House**, in which you'll find the **Salisbury and South Wiltshire Museum** (July & Aug Mon–Sat 10am–5pm, Sun 2–5pm; rest of year closed Sun; £3.50) – an absorbing account of local history. It includes a good section on Stonehenge and also focuses on the life and times of General Pitt-Rivers, the father of modern archeology, who excavated many of Wiltshire's prehistoric sites, including Avebury (see p.320).

The Close's **North Gate** opens onto the centre's older streets, where narrow pedestrianized alleyways bear names like Fish Row and Salt Lane, indicative of their trading origin. Many half-timbered houses and inns have survived all over the centre, and the last of four market crosses, **Poultry Cross**, stands on stilts in Silver Street, near the Market Square. The market, held on Tuesdays and Saturdays, still serves a large agricultural area, as it did in earlier times when the city grew wealthy on wool. Nearby, the church of **St Thomas** – named after Thomas à Becket – is worth a look inside for its carved timber roof and "Doom painting" over the chancel arch, depicting Christ presiding over the Last Judgment. Dating from 1475, it's the largest of its kind in England. Opposite the church, *Snell's* sells memorable chocolates and cakes.

Lastly, to best appreciate the city's inspiring silhouette – the view made famous by Constable – take a twenty-minute walk through the water meadows southwest of the centre to **HARNHAM**; the *Old Mill* here serves drinks and modestly priced meals.

Practicalities

Salisbury is a major transport hub, with regular **trains** from London, Exeter, Bristol, Southampton and Portsmouth; National Express **bus** services from London; and local buses to such sights as Stonehenge and Avebury. Trains arrive

half a mile west of the centre, on South Western Road; the bus station is a short way north of the Market Place, on Endless Street, with an adjacent office (Mon–Fri 8.15am–5.15pm, Sat 8.45am–4.45pm; ⓣ01722/336855) providing details of services throughout the region, including tours to Stonehenge and around. For details on all Wiltshire bus routes, ring ⓣ08457/090899. For a **taxi**, call ⓣ01722/505050.

The **tourist office** is on Fish Row, just off the Market Square (May Mon–Sat 9.30am–5pm, Sun 10.30am–4.30pm; June–Sept Mon–Sat 9.30am–6pm, Sun 10.30am–4.30pm; Oct–April Mon–Sat 9.30am–5pm; ⓣ01722/334956, ⓦwww.visitsalisbury.com) and is the starting point for informative and inexpensive **guided walks** of the city (May–Sept daily 11am, also Mon & Thurs–Sun 8pm; 1hr 30min; £2.50); the tourist office also has details of the Cathedral Walk (summer only) and Ghost Walk, costing about the same. A.S. Tours (ⓣ01980/862931) runs frequent minibus **tours** to Stonehenge and Old Sarum (£12); to Stonehenge and Avebury (£20); and to Wells, Glastonbury and "King Arthur Country" (£22). If you want to **rent a bike**, go to Hayball's Cycle Shop, 30 Winchester St (ⓣ01722/411378), which charges a £25 cash deposit. There's a dedicated Cycling and Walking Hotline which provides information on itineraries around Salisbury (Mon–Fri 9am–5pm; ⓣ01980/623255). There's **Internet access** at Starlight Internet Café, 1a Endless Street (ⓣ01722/328043; Mon–Sat 9.30am–8pm, Sun 11am–5pm; £4/hour).

Accommodation

With its year-round stream of visitors, Salisbury offers numerous accommodation possibilities, mostly in or within a short walk of the centre. All the same, make sure you phone early to be sure of a place.

Hotels and B&Bs

Byways House 31 Fowlers Rd ⓣ01722/328364, ⓦwww.bed-breakfast-salisbury.co.uk. Victorian house in a quiet location, offering rooms with or without bath. Two rooms have a view of the cathedral. ❸

Clovelly 17 Mill Rd ⓣ01722/322055, ⓦwww.clovellyhotel.co.uk. Useful choice close to the train station, with traditionally furnished rooms and delicious homemade yoghurt for breakfast. No smoking. ❹

Glen Lyn Guest House 6 Bellamy Lane, Milford Hill ⓣ01722/327880, ⓦwww.glenlynbandbatsalisbury.co.uk. Elegant Victorian house in a quiet lane, a ten-minute walk east of the centre. ❸

Old Bell 2 St Ann St ⓣ01722/327958, ⓔoldbellinn@hotels.activebooking.com. Attractive fourteenth-century inn right opposite St Ann's Gate, near the cathedral. ❸

Old Mill Town Path, Harnham ⓣ01722/327517. Great views across the meadows to the cathedral from the fully equipped rooms of this riverside pub about a mile from the centre. Real ales are on tap in the bar, and there's an adjoining 800-year-old restaurant. ❺

Old Rectory 75 Belle Vue Rd ⓣ01722/502702, ⓦwww.theoldrectory-bb.co.uk. Light and modern conversion of a 1920s building, with lots of pale greens and blues, and an airy breakfast room overlooking the garden. Quiet, friendly and very clean. No smoking. No credit cards. ❸

Rose & Crown Harnham Rd ⓣ01722/399955, ⓦwww.corushotels.com/roseandcrown. Riverside hostelry dating from the thirteenth century. Enticements include traditional oak beaming, grand four-poster beds and a huge pavilion restaurant. ❼

Victoria Lodge 61 Castle Rd ⓣ01722/320586, ⓦwww.viclodge.co.uk. One of several good-value B&Bs along this main road to Stonehenge. All rooms with bath, and there's a good restaurant (meals by pre-arrangement). ❸

Wyndham Park Lodge 51 Wyndham Rd ⓣ01722/416517, ⓦwww.wyndhamparklodge.co.uk. Victorian B&B in a quiet part of town (off Castle St), full of period furniture, wallpaper and hangings. One room has its own patio. No smoking. ❷

Hostels and campsites

Matt and Tiggy's Hostel 51 Salt Lane ⓣ01722/327443. Friendly and clean independent hostel close to the bus station, though there are just seven beds available, at £12 each. Discounted breakfasts are available at a local restaurant.

Salisbury Camping and Caravanning Club Site Hudson's Field ⓣ01722/320713. Well-appointed campsite a mile and a half north of Salisbury close to Old Sarum. Closed Oct to mid-March.

Youth Hostel Milford Hill ⓣ0870/770 6018, ⓔsalisbury@yha.org.uk. A 220-year-old building in its own spacious grounds, ten-minutes' walk east of the cathedral. Bed and breakfast costs £14.50. Separate lodges accommodate couples or smaller groups at £16 per person.

Eating and drinking

You don't need to search far for food in Salisbury, with its good mix of traditional and contemporary outlets. The centre also has a good sprinkling of pubs, many of which serve meals.

Harper's Market Square ⓣ01722/333118. Serves good-value, traditional English lunches and evening meals. Closed Sun eve in winter. Inexpensive to Moderate.

Haunch of Venison Minster St. One of the city's most atmospheric pubs which also serves good food. Look out for the mummified hand of a nineteenth-century card player still clutching his cards. Inexpensive.

LXIX 69 New St ⓣ01722/340000. Very close to the cathedral, this has an elegant, modern style and upmarket local cooking, such as smoked river eel. Closed Sun. Moderate to Expensive.

Michael Snell Tea Room 8 St Thomas's Square. Established and popular patisserie in the city centre, with outdoor tables. Closed Sun.

The Mill Bridge St. Popular pub with riverside seating, right in the city centre. Abbot and Greene King IPA on tap, and food, tea and coffee available until 7pm.

Moloko Café 5 Bridge St. Cool café and vodka bar, open til late.

Pheasant Inn 19 Salt Lane. This atmospheric fifteenth-century inn serves sandwiches as well as traditional pub food and decent vegetarian dishes. Inexpensive.

Prezzo 52–54 High St ⓣ01722/341333. Steps from the cathedral, and housed in one of Salisbury's wonkiest buildings – all sagging timbers – this straightforward Italian trattoria is usually packed out, and offers a good selection of pastas, pizzas and mozzarella salads, plus daily specials. Inexpensive to Moderate.

Old Sarum and Wilton

The ruins of **Old Sarum** (daily: April–June & Sept 10am–6pm; July & Aug 9am–6pm; Oct 10am–5pm; Nov–March 10am–4pm; £2.20; EH) occupy a bleak hilltop site two miles north of the city centre – an easy walk, but there are plenty of buses: #5, #6, #8 and #9 running every fifteen minutes or so (less frequent on Sun). Possibly occupied up to five thousand years ago, then developed as an Iron Age fort whose double protective ditches remain, it was settled by Romans and Saxons before the Norman bishopric of Sherborne was moved here in the 1070s. Within a couple of decades a new cathedral had been consecrated at Old Sarum, and a large religious community was living alongside the soldiers in the central castle. Old Sarum was an uncomfortable place, parched and windswept, and in 1220 the dissatisfied clergy – additionally at loggerheads with the castle's occupants – appealed to the pope for permission to decamp to Salisbury (still known officially as New Sarum). When permission was granted, the stone from the cathedral was commandeered for Salisbury's gateways, and once the church had gone the population waned. By the nineteenth century Old Sarum was deserted, but it continued to exist as a political constituency – William Pitt was one of its representatives. The most notorious of the "rotten boroughs", it returned two MPs at a time to Westminster up until the 1832 Reform Act put a stop to it. Huge earthworks, banks and ditches are the dominant features of the site today, with a broad trench encircling the promontory, on which lie the rudimentary remains of the Norman palace, castle and cathedral.

WILTON, five miles west of Salisbury, is renowned for its carpet industry and the splendid **Wilton House** (mid-April to Oct daily 10.30am–5.30pm;

last entry 1hr before closing; £9.25, grounds only £4.75; ⓦwww.wiltonhouse.com), of which Daniel Defoe wrote: "One cannot be said to have seen any thing that a man of curiosity would think worth seeing in this county, and not have been at Wilton House." The Tudor house, built for the First Earl of Pembroke on the site of a dissolved Benedictine abbey, was ruined by fire in 1647 and rebuilt by Inigo Jones, whose classic hallmarks can be seen in the sumptuous Single Cube and Double Cube rooms, so called because of their precise dimensions. Sir Philip Sidney, illustrious Elizabethan courtier and poet, wrote part of his magnum opus *Arcadia* here – the dado round the Single Cube Room illustrates scenes from the book – and the Double Cube room was the setting for the ballroom scene in Ang Lee's film, *Sense and Sensibility*. The easel **paintings** are what makes Wilton really special, however – the collection includes paintings by Van Dyck, Rembrandt, two of the Brueghel family, Poussin, Andrea del Sarto and Tintoretto. In the grounds, the famous **Palladian Bridge** has been joined by ancillary attractions including an adventure playground, garden centre and an audiovisual show on the colourful earls of Pembroke, all designed to subsidize a massive programme of structural renovation.

Salisbury Plain and northwards

The Ministry of Defence is the landlord of much of **Salisbury Plain**, the hundred thousand acres of chalky upland to the north of Salisbury. Flags warn casual trespassers away from MoD firing ranges and tank training grounds, while rather stricter security cordons off such secretive establishments as the research centre at Porton Down, Britain's centre for chemical and biological warfare. As elsewhere, the army's presence has ironically saved much of the plain from modern agricultural chemicals, thereby inadvertently nurturing species that are all but extinct in more trampled landscapes.

Though now largely deserted except by forces families living in ugly, temporary-looking barracks quarters, Salisbury Plain once positively throbbed with communities. Stone Age, Bronze Age and Iron Age settlements left hundreds of burial mounds scattered over the chalklands, as well as major complexes at Danebury, Badbury, Figsbury, Old Sarum, and, of course, the great circle of **Stonehenge**. North of Salisbury Plain, beyond the A342 Andover–Devizes road, lies the softer Vale of Pewsey, traversed by the Kennet canal. **Marlborough**, to the north of the Vale, is the centre for another cluster of ancient sites, including the huge stone circle of **Avebury**, the mysterious grassy mound of **Silbury Hill** and the chamber graves of **West Kennet**. Malmesbury, though in Wiltshire, is covered in Chapter 5 (see p.380), as it feels more closely allied to the Cotswolds area than to the rest of its county, from which it's cut off by the M4 and the rail line.

Stonehenge

No ancient structure in England arouses more controversy than **Stonehenge** (daily: mid-March to May & Sept to mid-Oct 9.30am–6pm; June–Aug 9am–7pm; mid-Oct to end Oct 9.30am–5pm; end Oct to mid-March 9.30am–4pm; £5; NT & EH; ⓦwww.stonehengemasterplan.org), a mysterious ring of monoliths nine miles north of Salisbury. While archeologists argue over whether it was a place of ritual sacrifice and sun-worship, an astronomical cal-

culator or a royal palace, the guardians of the site struggle to accommodate its year-round crowds who are resentful at no longer being able to walk among the stones; it is, however, possible to make a supervised tour of the stones by calling ahead on ⓣ01980/626267. Annual battles between the police and gatherings of druids and New Age travellers trying to celebrate the summer solstice are a thing of the past since the passage of the draconian Criminal Justice Act in 1994 – though low-key solstice celebrations are now permitted.

Conservation of Stonehenge, one of UNESCO's designated World Heritage Sites, is obviously an urgent priority, and the current custodians are trying to address the dissatisfaction that many feel on visiting this landmark. A new visitors' centre is planned two miles east of the stones at the Amesbury roundabout (scheduled to open 2005), and a re-routing of the nearby roads is projected. In the meantime, visitors are issued with handsets programmed to dispense a range of information on the site – some of the soundtrack is interesting, but much is misleading and patronizing.

What exists today is only a small part of the original prehistoric complex, as many of the outlying stones were probably plundered by medieval and later farmers for building materials. The **construction** of Stonehenge is thought to have taken place in several stages. In about 3000 BC the outer circular bank and ditch were constructed, just inside which was dug a ring of 56 pits, which at a later date were filled with a mixture of earth and human ash. Around 2500 BC the first stones were raised within the earthworks, comprising approximately forty great blocks of dolerite (bluestone), whose ultimate source was Preseli in Wales. Some archeologists have suggested that these monoliths were found lying on Salisbury Plain, having been borne down from the Welsh mountains by a glacier in the last Ice Age, but the lack of any other glacial debris on the plain would seem to disprove this theory. It really does seem to be the case that the stones were cut from quarries in Preseli and dragged or floated here on rafts, a prodigious task which has defeated recent attempts to emulate it.

The crucial phase in the creation of the site came during the next six hundred years, when the incomplete bluestone circle was transformed by the construction of a circle of twenty-five **trilithons** (two uprights crossed by a lintel) and an inner horseshoe formation of five trilithons. Hewn from Marlborough Downs sandstone, these colossal stones (called sarsens), ranging from 13ft to 21ft in height and weighing up to thirty tons, were carefully dressed and worked – for example, to compensate for perspectival distortion the uprights have a slight swelling in the middle, the same trick as the builders of the Parthenon were to employ hundreds of years later. More bluestones were arranged in various patterns within the outer circle over this period. The purpose of all this work remains baffling, however. The symmetry and location of the site (a slight rise in a flat valley with even views of the horizon in all directions) as well as its alignment towards the points of sunrise and sunset on the summer and winter solstices tend to support the supposition that it was some sort of observatory or time-measuring device. The site ceased to be used at around 1600 BC, and by the Middle Ages it had already become a "landmark".

There's a lot less charisma about the reputedly significant Bronze Age site of **Woodhenge** (dawn–dusk; free), two miles northeast of Stonehenge. The site consists of a circular bank about 220ft in diameter enclosing a ditch and six concentric rings of post holes, which would originally have held timber uprights, possibly supporting a roofed building of some kind. The holes are now marked more durably if less romantically by concrete pillars. A child's grave was found at the centre of the rings, suggesting that it may have been a place of ritual sacrifice.

Marlborough

An obvious base from which to explore Salisbury Plain is **MARLBOROUGH**, a peaceful spot now that the M4 deflects traffic from the old stagecoach route passing through the town. It's a handsome place too: the wide High Street, a dignified assembly of Georgian buildings, has a fine Perpendicular church standing at each end and half-timbered cottages rambling up the alleyways behind. The famous public school is not especially old – it was established in 1843 – but incorporates an ancient coaching inn among its red-brick buildings.

Marlborough **tourist office** is in the car park on George Lane, accessible from the High Street via Hilliers Yard (Easter–Oct Mon–Sat 10am–5pm; Nov–Easter Mon–Sat 10am–4.30pm; ⓣ01672/513989, ⓦwww.kennet.gov.uk) and there are several inns and guest houses offering **accommodation** along the High Street. Top of the range are *Ivy House* at no. 43 (ⓣ01672/515333, ⓦwww.ivyhousemarlborough.co.uk; ❺), the antique *Castle and Ball* (ⓣ01672/515201, ⓔcastleball@oldenglish.co.uk; no credit cards; ❺) and the *Merlin* pub at no. 36–39 (ⓣ01672/512151; ❹). Less expensive central options include the B&B at 63 George Lane (ⓣ01672/512771; no credit cards; ❶), which overlooks water meadows, while with your own transport you could stay at *Clench Farmhouse* (ⓣ01672/810264; no credit cards; ❸), an eighteenth-century farmhouse equipped with a tennis court and pool four miles south near Wootton Rivers. **Eating** options in central Marlborough include the reasonable bistro food at *Ivy House*, while *Polly Tea Rooms* serves good snacks and ice cream.

If you fancy a woodland walk or picnic, head out southeast of town into **Savernake Forest**, an ancient royal forest of oak and beech, crossed by eight long avenues that converge at its centre. You can walk there in less than thirty minutes, or else take a bus to Great Bedwyn from Marlborough (roughly hourly), asking the driver to let you off en route.

Silbury Hill, West Kennet and Avebury

The neat green mound of **Silbury Hill**, five miles west of Marlborough, is probably overlooked by the majority of drivers whizzing by on the A4. At 130ft it's no great height, but when you realize it's the largest prehistoric artificial mound in Europe, and was made by a people using nothing more than primitive spades, it commands more respect. It was probably constructed around 2600 BC, but like so many of the sites of Salisbury Plain, no one knows quite what it was for, though the likelihood is that it was a burial mound. You can't actually walk on the hill – so having admired it briefly from the car park, cross the road to the footpath that leads half a mile to the **West Kennet Long Barrow** (free access; NT & EH). Dating from about 3250 BC, this was definitely a chamber tomb – nearly fifty burials have been discovered at West Kennet.

Immediately to the west, the village of **AVEBURY** stands in the midst of a **stone circle** (free access; NT & EH) that rivals Stonehenge – the individual stones are generally smaller, but the circle itself is much wider and more complex. A massive earthwork 20ft high and 1400ft across encloses the main circle, which is approached by four causeways across the inner ditch, two of them leading into wide avenues stretching over a mile beyond the circle. The best guess is that it was built soon after 2500 BC, and presumably had a similar ritual or religious function to Stonehenge. The structure of Avebury's diffuse circle is

quite difficult to grasp, but there are plans on the site, and you can get an excellent overview at the **Alexander Keiller Museum**, at the western entrance to the site (daily: April–Oct 10am–6pm or dusk if earlier; Nov–March 10am–4pm; £4 also for Barn Gallery; NT & EH), which displays excavated material and explanatory information. Nearby, the **Barn Gallery** (same times and prices) holds a permanent exhibition of Avebury and the surrounding country, and shows clips from recently discovered home-movies of Keiller excavating the stones aided by a bevy of nubile assistants. Having absorbed the contents of the various collections, you can wander round the peaceful circle, accompanied by sheep and cattle grazing unconcernedly among the stones. To the southeast, an avenue of standing stones leads half a mile beyond West Kennet towards a spot known as the Sanctuary, though there is little left to see here.

Back in the placid **village** of Avebury, you might drop into **Avebury Manor** (April–Oct Tues, Wed & Sun 2–4.40pm; gardens April–Oct Tues, Wed & Fri–Sun 11am–5.30pm; £3.70, garden only £2.80; NT), behind the Alexander Keiller Museum. This sixteenth-century house – incorporating later alterations – has four or five panelled and plastered rooms, for which you are issued with over-shoes to protect the wooden floors from the chalk dust, and a **garden** with topiary and medieval walls. House and garden are distinctly low-key attractions, however, and little to do with the spirit of Avebury; you might find it more satisfying poking around the small village, half inside the circle, and having a **snack** or cream tea at *The Circles* vegetarian restaurant, or a drink in the *Red Lion* **pub** which also serves reasonable **meals** as well as providing a few en-suite rooms should you wish to **stay** over (☎01672/539266; ❸), though these can be a bit seedy. A preferable choice might be *The Lodge* (☎01672/539023, ⓔavebury@email.com; no smoking; ❺) on the High Street, a charming Georgian B&B with discounts for longer stays and late arrivals; the strictly vegetarian or vegan breakfasts can be taken in the garden, with views towards the stones. There's a **tourist office** (daily: summer 10am–5.30pm; winter 10am–4.30pm; ☎01672/539425) in the Avebury Chapel Centre on Green Street. Good bus routes connect Avebury with Salisbury, Marlborough and Devizes, and A.S.Tours runs regular guided trips here from Salisbury (see p.316).

Devizes

DEVIZES, seven miles down the A361 from Avebury at the mouth of the Vale of Pewsey, is a pleasant place, with some attractive eighteenth-century houses, a stately semicircular market place and a couple of fine churches, St Mary's and St John's. It's chiefly worth a stop, however, for the excellent **Museum** at 41 Long St (Mon–Sat 10am–5pm, Sun noon–4pm; £3, free Sun & Mon), housing an exceptional collection of prehistoric finds from barrows and henges throughout the county. Star exhibit is the so-called Marlborough Bucket, decorated with bronze reliefs from the first century BC.

The town offers some appealing nooks to explore: seek out the timbered and jettied row of Elizabethan-era houses on the cobbled St John's Alley, tucked away behind St John's Street. Out of town, you can enjoy a pleasant canalside stroll along the **Kennet and Avon Canal** which boasts 29 locks at Caen Hill, roughly an hour-and-a-half's walk westwards, but easily cyclable too.

Devizes has a very helpful **tourist office** at Cromwell House, Market Place (Mon–Sat 9.30am–5pm; ☎01380/729408). The best place **to stay** is the *Castle Hotel*, on New Park Street, a former coaching inn with a bar, a restaurant and a patio (☎01380/729300; ❹); less expensive are the *Craven House* B&B, Station Rd (☎01380/723514; no credit cards; ❶), with bathrooms en suite or shared;

and the *White Bear Inn*, Monday Market St (Ⓣ01380/727588; no credit cards; ❷). For **eating**, try *Quintessence*, St John's St, which serves light lunches and snacks at lace-draped tables (closed eves), while *The Bistro* on The Little Brittox, a quiet lane off the High Street, specializes in organically prepared dishes with fantastic vegetarian options (closed daytime & Mon; moderate). In Market Place, you'll find *The Market Plaice,* a fish-and-chip takeaway that also provides more substantial sit-down meals at cheap prices.

Lacock and around

LACOCK, ten miles northwest of Devizes, is the perfect English feudal village, albeit one gentrified by the National Trust to within a hair's breadth of natural life, and besieged by tourists all summer. Appropriately for so photogenic a spot, it has a fascinating museum dedicated to the founding father of photography, Henry Fox Talbot, a member of the dynasty which has lived in the local **abbey** since it passed to Sir William Sharington on the Dissolution of the Monasteries in 1539. Ten years later Sharington was arrested for colluding with Thomas Seymour, Treasurer of the Mint, in a plot to subvert the coinage: he narrowly escaped with his life by shopping his partner in crime – who was beheaded – and after a period of disgrace managed to buy back his estates. His descendant, William Henry Fox Talbot, was the first to produce a photographic negative, and the **Fox Talbot Museum**, in a sixteenth-century barn by the abbey gates (March–Oct daily 11am–5.30pm; £4.20; NT), captures something of the excitement he must have experienced as the dim outline of an oriel window in the abbey steadily imprinted itself on a piece of silver nitrate paper. A copy of the postage-stamp-sized result is on display in the museum (the original is in Bradford's National Museum of Photography, Film and Television, see p.934). The **abbey** itself (April–Oct Mon & Wed–Sun 1–5.30pm; £5.30; £6.50 including museum; NT) preserves a few monastic fragments amid the eighteenth-century Gothic, while the church of **St Cyriac** (free access) contains the opulent tomb of the nefarious Sir William Sharington, buried beneath a splendid barrel-vaulted roof.

The village's delightfully Chaucerian-sounding hostelry, *At the Sign of the Angel*, is a good, if expensive, **hotel** and **restaurant** (Ⓣ01249/730230, Ⓦwww.lacock.co.uk; ❼).

Corsham Court and Bowood House

The main sight within a short drive of Lacock is **Corsham Court** (mid-March to Oct Sat, Sun & Tues–Thurs 2–5.30pm; Nov to mid-March Sat & Sun 2–4.30pm; £5, garden only £2), three miles west. It dates from Elizabethan times, though what you see now bears the Georgian stamp of Nash and Capability Brown, and the house, furnished by Robert Adam and Thomas Chippendale among others, contains a fine collection of art, including pieces by Caravaggio, Rubens, Reynolds and Michelangelo. The village of **CORSHAM** is another dignified little cloth-making town of Bath stone, riddled with underground limestone quarries and a long railway tunnel engineered by Brunel.

Ten miles east of Corsham, off the A342 Chippenham–Devizes road and just outside the village of Calne, **Bowood House** (April–Oct daily 11am–5.30pm; £6.25) was designed in the eighteenth century by the likes of Henry Keene, Charles Barry and – again – Robert Adam. Adam was primarily responsible for the great south front and the Orangery, and, inside the house, the library – though the present appearance of this owes more to Charles Robert Cockerell,

architect of Oxford's Ashmolean Museum, who also built the Neoclassical chapel. But it is the magnificent grounds of Bowood that are the real draw, with rhododendron gardens, a Doric temple on the banks of its placid lake and a waterfall in the woods; there's also an adventure playground for kids, and a restaurant.

Bradford-on-Avon and around

With its buildings of mellow auburn stone, reminiscent of the townscapes just over the county border in Bath and the Cotswolds, **BRADFORD-ON-AVON** is the most appealing town in the northwest corner of Wiltshire, offering far more than the dull county town of Trowbridge, or the slightly more distant Chippenham and Warminster. Sheltering against a steep wooded slope, it takes its name from its "broad ford" across the Avon, though the original fording place was replaced in the thirteenth century by a **bridge** that was in turn largely rebuilt in the seventeenth century. The domed structure at one end is a quaint old jail converted from a chapel.

The local industry, based on textiles like that of its Yorkshire namesake, was revolutionized with the arrival of Flemish weavers in 1659, and many of the town's handsome buildings reflect the prosperity of this period. Yet Bradford's most significant building is the tiny **St Lawrence Church** on Church Street, an outstanding example of Saxon architecture dating from about 700 AD. Wrecked by Viking invaders, and later used as a school and a simple dwelling, it was rehabilitated by a local vicar in 1856. Its distinctive features are the carved angels over the chancel arch.

Trains call regularly at Bradford from Weymouth, Dorchester, Bath and Bristol; the **train station** is on St Margaret's Street close to the town centre, while regular **bus** services from Bath, Trowbridge and Frome arrive at the town bridge. **Bike rental** is available at *Lock Inn Cottage*, 48 Frome Rd (Ⓣ01225/867187). The well-equipped **tourist office** is at 50 St Margaret's St (daily: April–Dec 10am–5pm; Jan–March 10am–4pm; Ⓣ01225/865797, Ⓦwww.bradfordonavontown.com). Bradford has a good range of **accommodation**, none more characterful than *Bradford Old Windmill*, a B&B up the hill at 4 Mason's Lane (Ⓣ01225/866842, Ⓔtic@bradfordoldwindmill.co.uk; ❸), where an imaginative vegetarian menu is served house-party style (evening meals currently on Mon, Thurs & Sat). The lowest rates are given for anyone arriving after 6pm (assuming there's space); winter opening is irregular. *Priory Steps*, closer to the centre on Newtown (Ⓣ01225/862230, Ⓦwww.priorysteps.co.uk; ❺), is a family home with bags of personality, well-prepared dinners and excellent views over the rooftops of weavers' cottages. The *Riverside Inn,* 49 St Margaret's St (Ⓣ01225/863526; ❷), lives up to its name, with private facilities in all rooms. For light lunches or cakes, try the *Bridge Tea Rooms* on Bridge Street, or the excellent *Scribbling Horse* at 34 Silver St or *The Cottage Cooperative,* just around the corner at no. 33, which serves good coffee and light vegetarian meals in a secluded garden setting (**Internet access** is also available here). For alcohol or more substantial food, head for the *Bunch of Grapes* **pub** on Silver Street, also a venue for jazz, folk and blues every other Tuesday.

Great Chalfield

Great Chalfield Manor (guided tours: April–Oct Tues–Thurs 12.15pm, 2.15pm, 3pm, 3.45pm & 4.30pm; £4.20; NT), two and a half miles northeast of Bradford, is a splendid moated complex of house, church and outbuildings

dating from about 1470, sensitively restored at the beginning of the twentieth century as a family home. The exterior looks like a typical Cotswold manor, all gables and mullions; inside, the Great Hall is overlooked by a minstrels' gallery from which three gargoyle-like masks gaze down into the hall, the eyes cut away so that the womenfolk could inspect the proceedings below without jeopardizing their modesty. The interior of the church features some fifteenth-century wall paintings.

Travel details

Buses

Details of minor and seasonal local bus services are frequently given in the text. For information on all other local and national bus services, contact Traveline ⓣ0870/608 2608 (daily 7am–9pm), ⓦwww.traveline.org.uk.

Bournemouth to: Dorchester (3 daily; 1hr 15min–1hr 35min); London (every 30min; 2hr 35min–4hr 10min); Southampton (10 daily; 45min–2hr); Weymouth (3 daily; 1hr 15min–1hr 30min); Winchester (6 daily; 1hr 15min–2hr).
Dorchester to: Bournemouth (3 daily; 1hr 10min–1hr 40min); London (1 daily; 4hr); Weymouth (every 20–30min; 20min–1hr).
Portsmouth to: London (13 daily; 2hr 20min–3hr 45min); Salisbury (1 daily; 1hr 25min); Southampton (9 daily; 40min–1hr); Winchester (hourly; 1hr 10min–2hr).
Salisbury to: London (3 daily; 2hr 45min–3hr 40min); Portsmouth (1 daily; 1hr 30min); Southampton (every 30min; 35min–1hr 30min).
Southampton to: Bournemouth (10 daily; 50min–1hr 30min); Bristol (1 daily; 2hr 40min), London (every 30min; 2hr 20min–3hr); Portsmouth (10 daily; 40min–55min); Salisbury (every 30min; 35–1hr 30min); Weymouth (2 daily; 3hr–3hr 15min); Winchester (every 30min; 25min–1hr).
Winchester to: Bournemouth (5 daily; 1hr 15 min–2hr); London (11 daily; 2hr–2hr 35min); Portsmouth (every 30min; 1hr 15min–2hr); Southampton (every 30min; 25min–1hr).

Trains

For information on all local and national rail services, contact National Rail Enquiries ⓣ08457/484950, ⓦwww.rail.co.uk.

Bournemouth to: Brockenhurst (every 20min; 15–25min); Dorchester (hourly; 45min); London (every 30min; 1hr 45min–2hr); Poole (1–4 hourly; 10–15min); Southampton (every 20min; 30min–1hr 20min); Weymouth (hourly; 55min); Winchester (1–3 hourly; 45min–1hr 15min).
Dorchester to: Bournemouth (hourly; 40min); Brockenhurst (hourly; 1hr); London (hourly; 2hr 30min); Weymouth (1–2 hourly; 10–15min).
Portsmouth to: London (every 20min; 1hr 35min–1hr 50min); Salisbury (hourly; 1hr 15min); Southampton (every 30min; 40–55min); Winchester (hourly; 1hr).
Ryde (Isle of Wight) to: Shanklin (every 30min; 20–25min).
Salisbury to: Exeter (every 2hr; 1hr 45min–2hr); London (every 20–30min; 1hr 25min); Portsmouth (hourly; 1hr 25min); Southampton (1–2 hourly; 30–40min).
Southampton to: Bournemouth (every 20min; 35–50min); Bristol (1–2hourly; 1hr 35–1hr 55min); Brockenhurst (every 15min; 20–45min); London (every 15min; 1hr 15min–1hr 30min); Portsmouth (every 30min; 40min–1hr); Salisbury (every 30min; 30–40min); Weymouth (hourly; 1hr 30min); Winchester (every 15min; 20min).
Winchester to: Bournemouth (every 20min; 45min–1hr); London (every 15–30min; 1hr–1hr 10min); Portsmouth (hourly; 55min); Southampton (every 15min; 15–20min).

Ferries and hovercraft

Lymington to: Yarmouth, Isle of Wight (1–2 hourly; 30min).
Portsmouth to: Fishbourne, Isle of Wight (1–2 hourly; 35min); Ryde, Isle of Wight (1–2 hourly; 15min).
Southampton to: East Cowes, Isle of Wight (hourly; 55min); West Cowes, Isle of Wight (hourly; 22min).
Southsea to: Ryde, Isle Of Wight (2–3 hourly; 10min).

Oxford and around

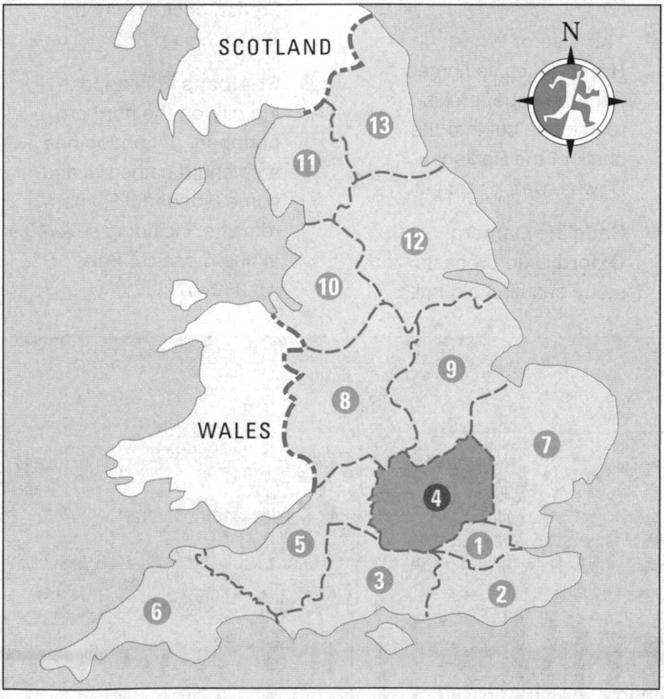

CHAPTER 4

Highlights

* **Chiltern Hills** Stretching southwest from Luton to the River Thames near Reading, the Chiltern Hills offer lovely wooded scenery. Henley-on-Thames, site of the famous Henley Regatta, is the best base for further explorations. See pp.329–334

* **The Vale of White Horse** Takes its name from the huge, prehistoric horse cut into the chalk of the Berkshire Downs. See pp.334–336

* **Radcliffe Camera, Oxford** Oxford boasts many beautiful old buildings, but the most imposing is the Italianate rotunda, Radcliffe Camera. See p.347

* **Le Petit Blanc restaurant, Oxford** Oxford has several excellent restaurants, but the pick is *Le Petit Blanc*, creation of the French chef, Raymond Blanc. See p.352

* **St Albans** This appealing city on the northern periphery of London has a splendid cathedral and some wonderful Roman remains, including several fine mosaics. See pp.360–62

△ Oxford's dreaming spires

Oxford and around

Arching around the peripheries of London, beyond the orbital M25, the "Home Counties" of England form London's commuter-belt. Beyond the suburban sprawl, however, there is plenty to entice. The north-western Home Counties – **Berkshire**, **Buckinghamshire** and **Hertfordshire** – are at their most appealing amidst the **Chiltern Hills**, a picturesque band of chalk uplands whose wooded ridges rise near Luton, beside the M1, and stretch southwest, petering out beside the River Thames near Reading. The hills provide an exclusive setting for many of the capital's wealthiest commuters, but for the casual visitor the obvious target is **Henley-on-Thames**, a good-looking old town famous for its Regatta and with a good supply of accommodation. Henley is also a handy base for further explorations, with the village of **Cookham** – and its Stanley Spencer gallery – leading the way, though **Reading** is also of interest as the host of two of Europe's most prestigious music festivals.

The Chilterns are traversed by the **Ridgeway**, a prehistoric track – and now a national trail – that offers excellent hiking, though its finest portion is further to the west, across the Thames, on **the downs** straddling the Berkshire-Oxfordshire border. Here, the Ridgeway visits a string of prehistoric sites, the most extraordinary being the gigantic chalk horse that gives the **Vale of White Horse** its name. The Vale is dotted with pleasant little villages, and both **Woolstone** and plainer **Uffington** have places to stay; but neither is it far to the university city of **Oxford**, which, with its superb architecture, museums and lively student population, can keep you busy for several days. Oxford is this region's star turn and it's also close to **Woodstock**, the handsome little town abutting one of England's most imposing country homes, **Blenheim Palace**.

To the northeast of Oxford, well beyond the Chilterns, the plain landscapes of north Buckinghamshire hardly fire the soul, though modest **Buckingham** is pleasant enough and it is also within easy striking distance of **Stowe Gardens**, which holds a remarkable collection of outdoor sculptures, monuments and follies. Travel east from Buckingham and you soon reach **Woburn**, home to another whopping stately home, **Woburn Abbey**, as well as **Woburn Safari Park**. It's another short hop from here over into Bedfordshire, mostly flat agricultural land with a hint of industrial Midlands. It is not a county you'd cross England to visit, but **Bedford** is of interest for its John Bunyan connection and possibly useful for its hotels and restaurants.

Hit Bedfordshire and you're on the edge of the East Midlands (see Chapter 9), but travel back towards London and you'll cross Hertfordshire. The prime target here is **St Albans**, an ancient and dignified town with Roman remains and a superb cathedral – but marooned amidst a knot of motorways and new

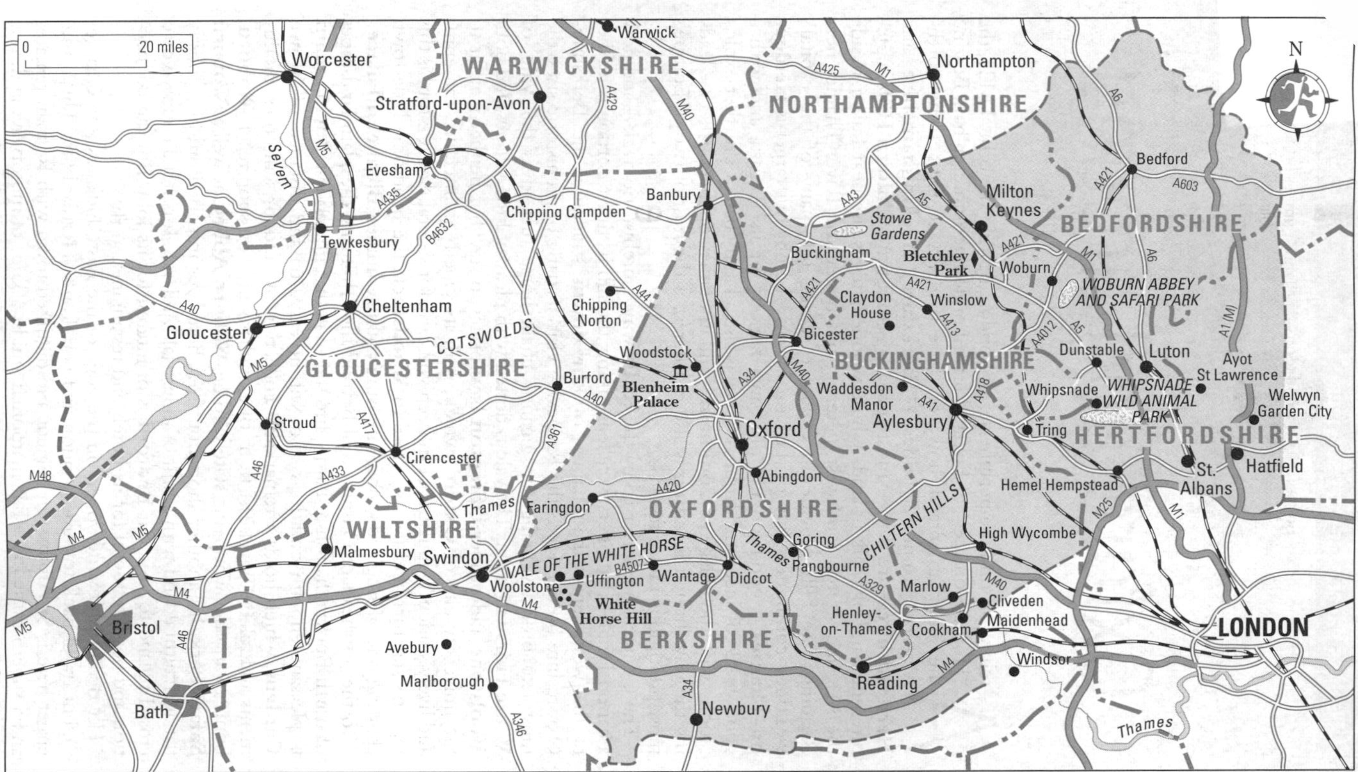
N
0 20 miles
WARWICKSHIRE
NORTHAMPTONSHIRE
BEDFORDSHIRE
GLOUCESTERSHIRE
BUCKINGHAMSHIRE
HERTFORDSHIRE
OXFORDSHIRE
WILTSHIRE
BERKSHIRE
COTSWOLDS
CHILTERN HILLS
VALE OF THE WHITE HORSE
Warwick
Worcester
Stratford-upon-Avon
Northampton
Evesham
Severn
Banbury
Bedford
Milton Keynes
Chipping Campden
Tewkesbury
Stowe Gardens
Buckingham
Bletchley Park
Woburn
WOBURN ABBEY AND SAFARI PARK
Cheltenham
Chipping Norton
Claydon House
Winslow
Gloucester
Bicester
Dunstable
Luton
Ayot St Lawrence
Woodstock
Whipsnade
WHIPSNADE WILD ANIMAL PARK
Welwyn Garden City
Burford
Blenheim Palace
Waddesdon Manor
Aylesbury
Tring
Stroud
Oxford
Cirencester
Abingdon
Hemel Hempstead
St. Albans
Hatfield
Thames
Faringdon
Goring
Pangbourne
High Wycombe
Malmesbury
Swindon
Uffington
Wantage
Didcot
Woolstone
White Horse Hill
Marlow
Cliveden
Henley-on-Thames
Cookham
Maidenhead
LONDON
Bristol
Avebury
Reading
Windsor
Marlborough
Bath
Newbury
M1
M4
M5
M25
M40
M48
A1 (M)
A5
A6
A34
A40
A41
A43
A44
A46
A346
A361
A413
A417
A418
A420
A421
A425
A429
A433
A435
A603
A4012
A329
B4507
B4632

Thames passenger boat services

Salter's Steamers runs **passenger boats** along the River Thames from mid-May to late September. There are services between Oxford and Abingdon, Reading and Henley, Henley and Marlow, and between Marlow, Cookham and Windsor. Prices are reasonable – Oxford to Abingdon costs £7.60, Henley to Marlow £7.50 – and there are one or two boats daily on the more popular routes, three weekly on others. Further details from local tourist offices or direct from Salter Brothers on ⓣ01865/243421, ⓦwww.saltersteamers.co.uk.

towns on the fringes of London. These new towns – among them Welwyn Garden City and Hemel Hempstead – have little obvious appeal, but there are a few surprises hereabouts, principally **Hatfield House**, one of the country's finest ancestral homes.

The area covered in this chapter is threaded by five **motorways**, the M25, M4, M40, M1 and A1(M). These give swift access from all directions, though drivers will need a detailed map to explore successfully the rural nooks and crannies. Long-distance **buses** mostly stick to the motorways, too, providing an efficient service to all the larger towns, but local services between the villages are patchy, sometimes non-existent. There are mainline **train** services from London's Paddington Station to Oxford, Henley-on-Thames and Reading, and from London's St Pancras to St Albans and Bedford. These main routes are supplemented by a number of branch lines, the most useful of which links Henley-on-Thames with Cookham.

The Chiltern Hills and the Vale of White Horse

The **Chiltern Hills** extend southwest from the workaday town of Luton, beside the M1, bumping across Buckinghamshire and Oxfordshire as far as the River Thames, just to the west of Reading. At their best, the hills offer handsome countryside, comprising a band of forested chalk hills with steep ridges and deep valleys interrupted by easy, rolling farmland. The Chilterns are also one of the country's wealthiest areas, liberally sprinkled with exclusive commuter hideaways-cum-country homes – though there are unappetizing suburban blotches too. For non-residents, the obvious target is **Henley-on-Thames**, a pleasant riverside town within easy striking distance of the area's key attractions and with a reasonable range of accommodation. Nearby highlights include the sumptuous Victorian mansion of **Cliveden** and the village of **Cookham**, home to the fascinating Stanley Spencer gallery. Spare a thought also for Thameside **Reading**, not so much for itself (it's brusquely modern), but for its two big **music festivals**, Reading Rock Festival and the World Music extravaganza, WOMAD.

Crossing the Chilterns to the north and west of Henley, the **Ridgeway National Trail** (see box on p.330) offers splendid hiking, though the most diverting part of the trail is further to the west, beyond the Chilterns and the Thames, amongst the more open scenery of the Berkshire and Oxfordshire downs. Here, on the edge of the **Vale of White Horse**, the trail sticks to a chalky ridge that provides magnificent views of the surrounding countryside and skirts the giant prehistoric figure after which the Vale is named. Here, you

The Ridgeway

The Iron Age inhabitants of Britain developed the **Ridgeway** as a major thoroughfare, a fast route that beetled across the chalky downs of modern-day Berkshire and Oxfordshire, negotiated the Thames and then traversed the Chiltern Hills. It was probably part of a longer route extending from the Dorset coast to the Wash in Norfolk, but this is conjecture. Today, the Ridgeway is one of England's fourteen national trails, running from **Overton Hill**, near Avebury in Wiltshire, to **Ivinghoe Beacon**, 85 miles to the northeast near Tring, which is itself just a few miles southwest of Luton. Crossing five counties, the trail avoids densely populated areas, keeping to the hills, except where the Thames slices through the trail at **Goring Gap** and marks the transition from the wooded valleys of the Chilterns to the more open Berkshire–Oxfordshire downs. By and large, the Ridgeway is fairly easy hiking and over half of it is accessible to cyclists and RVs. The prevailing winds mean that it is best walked in a northeasterly direction. The Ridgeway is strewn with prehistoric monuments of one description or another, though easily the finest archeological remains are on the downs edging the **Vale of White Horse** and around **Avebury** (see p.320). There are several youth hostels within reach of the Ridgeway – most notably the *Ridgeway Centre Youth Hostel* near Wantage – and numerous B&Bs. The *Ridgeway National Trail Companion*, available from the National Trails Office (Cultural Services, Holton, Oxford OX33 1QQ ⓣ01865/810224), gives the low-down and also includes details of local accommodation. There's also a useful website: ⓦwww.nationaltrails.gov.uk.

might opt to stay locally in the attractive YHA hostel on the ridge above **Wantage**, in the humdrum town itself or in one of the Vale's quaint villages – tiny **Woolstone** is perhaps the most appealing – though the Vale most readily lends itself to day-trips.

As regards public transport, Henley and Reading are easy to reach by **train** and **bus**, but for the smaller towns and the Vale of White Horse you will, for the most part, have to cope with intermittent local bus services. The only good news is the **Ridgeway Explorer bus**, which links Reading and Swindon via Wantage and the Vale of White Horse on Saturdays and Sundays from mid-April to late October; there are four buses daily in each direction and the journey time from Reading to Swindon is a little over two hours (timetable details on ⓣ0870/608 2608). A day pass costs £5.

Henley-on-Thames

Three counties – Oxfordshire, Berkshire and Buckinghamshire – meet at **HENLEY-ON-THAMES**, a long-established stopping place for travellers between London and Oxford. Henley is a good-looking, affluent commuter town that is at its prettiest among the old brick and stone buildings that flank the short main drag, **Hart Street**. At one end of Hart Street is the Market Place and its large and fetching **Town Hall**, at the other stands the easy Georgian curves of **Henley Bridge**. Overlooking the bridge is the **parish church of St Mary**, whose sturdy square tower sports a set of little turrets worked in chequerboard flint and stone, a popular decorative motif in the fifteenth and sixteenth centuries. Several operators run **boat trips** out along the Thames from the jetties just south of the bridge, including Hobbs & Sons (ⓣ01491/572035, ⓦwww.hobbs-of-henley.com), who offer frequent, hour-long jaunts from April to September for £4.75. There is also an imaginative **River and Rowing Museum** (daily 10am–5pm; £4.95), a ten-minute walk south along the river bank from the foot of Hart Street via Thames Side. This focuses on three main themes: the history of the town, the development of rowing from the Greeks onwards, and the Thames both as a wildlife habitat and as a trading link.

Henley is, however, best known for its **Royal Regatta**, the world's most important amateur rowing tournament, when the town gets all puffed up. Established in 1839, the regatta is the boating equivalent of the Ascot races (see p.244), a quintessentially English parade ground for the rich, aristocratic and aspiring, whose champagne-swilling antics are inexplicably found thrilling by larger numbers of the hoi polloi. The regatta, featuring past and potential Olympic rowers, begins on the Wednesday before the first weekend in July and runs for five days. Further information is available from the Regatta Headquarters on the east side of the Henley Bridge (Ⓣ01491/572153, Ⓦwww.hrr.co.uk).

Practicalities

Two or three times daily a direct train runs from London's Paddington Station to Henley, but mostly you have to change at Twyford. From Henley **train station**, it's a five-minute walk north to Hart Street, along Station Road and its continuation Thames Side. Henley is easy to reach by bus, too, with regular services from Oxford, Reading and London. **Buses** from Reading and points south and west mostly pull in on Hart Street, while those from the north and east – including Marlow and Cookham – stop on Bell Street, immediately to the north of Hart Street. The **tourist office** (Mon–Sat 9.30am–5pm, Sun 11am–4pm; Ⓣ01491/578034, Ⓦwww.visit-henley.org.uk) is located in a refurbished old barn, in a courtyard across from the Town Hall – it's clearly signed.

Henley has several first-rate **B&Bs**. One especially good option is the smart and tastefully furnished *Alftrudis*, 8 Norman Ave (Ⓣ01491/573099, Ⓦwww.alftrudis.co.uk; no credit cards; ❸), which occupies a handsome Victorian town house in a quiet, leafy residential street. There are three guest rooms here, all en suite. Another excellent choice is *Lenwade*, 3 Western Rd (Ⓣ01491/573468, Ⓔlenwadeuk@aol.com; no credit cards; ❹), an attractive Edwardian house with three en-suite guest rooms, comfortable furnishings and fittings and an unusual stained glass window in the hallway. **Hotels** are thin on the ground here, but pick of the bunch is the delightful, wisteria-clad old coaching inn, the *Red Lion*, beside Henley Bridge, with over twenty well-appointed bedrooms, individually decorated in period style (Ⓣ01491/572161, Ⓦwww.redlionhenley.co.uk; ❼).

The *Red Lion* has the best **restaurant** in town, but there are other more informal – and less expensive – places on Hart Street, including the *Thai Orchard* at no. 8 (Ⓣ01491/412227). **Pubs** line up on Hart Street, but the *Angel*, by the bridge, has the advantage of an outside deck overlooking the river. Within easy striking distance of Henley are several outstanding **country pubs**. *Horns* (Ⓣ01189/401416), some three miles to the southeast off the A321, in the hamlet of Crazies Hill, is an ancient place with open fires and low-beamed ceilings, Brakspear beers and excellent, moderately priced food (not Sun eve). Alternatively, the *Stag & Huntsman* (Ⓣ01491/571227), in Hambleden, some three miles to the northeast off the Marlow Road, the A4155, has a short but delicious menu – and the village itself is a pretty spot on the edge of the Chilterns. And finally, there's the *Crooked Billet* (Ⓣ01491/681048), in Stoke Row, five miles west of Henley off the B481, which is more a restaurant than a pub – a much lauded place dating from the 1640s and offering exquisite food from a creative menu.

Marlow

Heading north and then east out of Henley along the A4155, it's eight leafy miles to bustling **MARLOW**, another pleasant Thames-side town, its centre dotted with comely Georgian buildings. Here, you can while away an hour or two watching boats go through the lock, or tracing Marlow's literary connections. In 1817 Shelley and his wife Mary moved to a cottage on West Street just along from the Sir William Borlase School and stayed for a year – just long enough for him to compose the *Revolt of Islam* and for her to write *Frankenstein*. T.S. Eliot lived down the road at no. 31 in 1918, and Jerome K. Jerome wrote a chunk of *Three Men in a Boat* in the *Two Brewers* on St Peter's St, Marlow's best pub.

There are regular **buses** from Henley to Marlow; they are also linked by **train** – though you do have to change twice and it takes about an hour. Buses drop passengers close to Marlow High Street, a couple of minutes' walk from the **tourist office**, at no. 31 (Mon–Fri 9am–5pm, Sat 9.30am–5pm; winter closes 4pm; ⓣ01628/483597). From the train station, it's a short walk west along Station Road to the tourist office.

Cookham

Tiny **COOKHAM**, on the other side of the Thames just three miles south-east of Marlow – and not to be confused with neighbouring Cookham Dean and Cookham Rise – is noteworthy as the former home of **Stanley Spencer** (1891–1959), one of Britain's greatest – and most eccentric – artists. The Bible fired Spencer's imagination and many of his paintings depict biblical tales transposed into his Cookham surroundings – remarkable, visionary works in which the village is turned into a sort of earthly paradise. Spencer made his artistic name in the 1920s, firstly as an official war artist and then for his *Resurrection: Cookham*, which attracted rave reviews when it was exhibited in London in 1927. No-one minded much that his brand of Christianity was extremely unorthodox – he called his religious system the "Church of Me" – but in the 1930s his reputation temporarily dipped and he took endless critical flak when his work took an erotic turn. In part, this reflected his own changing circumstances; in 1937, he divorced his first wife, Hilda, in order to marry his mistress, Patricia Preece, but the latter exploited him financially and, so most contemporaries thought, regularly humiliated him. Perhaps surprisingly, Spencer continued writing to Hilda throughout his troubled second marriage, a passionate correspondence that – bizarrely – continued after her death in 1950.

Much of Spencer's most acclaimed work is displayed at Tate Britain, in London (see p.85), but there's a fine sample here at the **Stanley Spencer Gallery** (Easter–Oct daily 10.30am–5.30pm; Nov–Easter Sat & Sun 11am–5pm; £1), which occupies the old Methodist Chapel on the High Street. Three prime exhibits are *The Last Supper*, *Christ Preaching at Cookham Regatta: Listening from Punts* and another wonderful (but unfinished) *Christ Preaching at Cookham Regatta*. The permanent collection is enhanced by regular exhibitions of Spencer paintings and the gallery also contains incidental Spencer letters, documents and memorabilia, including the pram in which he used to wheel his artist's clobber around the village. As a boy, Spencer worshipped in the chapel, and his home, *Fernlea* (no access), is on the High Street. The gallery has a leaflet detailing an hour-long walk round Cookham, visiting all those places with which he is associated.

There's an hourly **train** service from Marlow to Cookham and from the station it's a pleasant ten-minute walk east across the common to the Spencer

Gallery. Cookham's *Bel & Dragon* **pub**, directly opposite the gallery, has ancient beams and ample leather chairs, pulls a good pint and serves decent home-made food.

Cliveden

Perched on a ridge across the Thames just to the east of Cookham, **Cliveden** is a grand Victorian mansion, whose sweeping Neoclassical lines were designed by Sir Charles Barry, architect of the Houses of Parliament. Its most famous occupant was **Nancy Astor**, the first woman to sit in the House of Commons and, together with her husband, the second Viscount Astor, a leading light of the "**Cliveden set**" – a weekly gathering of influential politicians who came here at weekends in the run up to World War II. Reactionary to the core, their ability to appreciate the difficulties faced by Hitler was not readily understood by many of their compatriots, but this didn't stop Churchill appointing Astor a minister in his wartime cabinet. The second Viscount died in 1952, but the family scandals didn't end there, with the third Viscount outdoing his predecessor by getting enmeshed in the Profumo affair, which transfixed Britain in the early 1960s (see box below).

The National Trust owns Cliveden today and leases the house as a luxury **hotel** (ⓣ01628/668561, ⓦwww.clivedonhouse.co.uk; ⑨) – doubles cost from £255 a night – which boasts an extraordinarily lavish interior. Acres of wood panelling, portraits of past owners and fancy chimneypieces culminate in the French Dining Room, containing the complete fittings and furnishings of Madame de Pompadour's eighteenth-century dining room, bought as a job lot in Paris by one of the Astors. Most of the hotel is only open to guests, but visitors are permitted into the **west wing** to gawp at all the baubles (April–Oct Thurs & Sun 3–5.30pm; £1). Note, however, that the number of visitors allowed into the house is limited: timed tickets are issued on a first-come, first-

The Profumo affair

The **Profumo affair** was a complicated tale of sex and spies, but the lynchpin was **Stephen Ward**, a well-connected osteopath who acted as a sort of middleman, introducing women to the high and mighty. At the third Viscount Astor's invitation, Ward spent many a weekend at a cottage on Astor's Cliveden estate in the company of **Christine Keeler** who, at one of the many parties, was introduced to **John Profumo**, the Conservative government's Secretary of State for War. They proceeded to have an affair, but unluckily for the minister Keeler was also sleeping with a Russian naval attaché at the Soviet embassy – and this at the height of the Cold War. It's long been a matter of debate as to whether Keeler passed information from pillow to pillow and if, for that matter, Profumo spilt any secret beans, but Keeler's autobiography certainly insists that Ward was a Soviet spy. Whatever the truth, when the story broke in 1962, it created the most intense of scandals. Initially, Profumo denied the affair, but eventually he had to come clean, thereby polishing off his own political career and fatally undermining the credibility of the Harold Macmillan government. Perhaps inevitably, the fall guy was Ward, who was prosecuted for living off immoral earnings, but committed suicide on the very last day of the trial, before the jury reached their verdict; Profumo withdrew from public life and dedicated himself to charitable works. From the whole debacle, one quote has echoed down the years. At Ward's trial, the prosecution alleged that one of Keeler's friends, **Mandy Rice-Davies**, had received money from Viscount Astor for sex. Astor denied ever having relations with her, prompting Rice-Davies to respond "He would say that, wouldn't he?"

served basis at the ticket office from 11am, so get there early to avoid disappointment. More satisfying are the **grounds** (daily: mid-March to Oct 11am–6pm; Nov & Dec 11am–4pm; £6), which comprise a series of themed gardens – roses, topiary, water gardens and so forth – and offer fine views of the Thames. The gardens teem with tourists at the weekend, but you can find peace and quiet in the woods along the river.

Reading

READING is a modern, prosperous town on the south bank of the River Thames, ten miles south of Henley. Guarding the western approaches to the capital, it has always been important, long a stopping-off point for kings and queens and once home to one of the country's richest abbeys. Henry VIII took care of the abbey, seizing its lands and hanging the abbot from the main gate, and today almost nothing remains of the old town except the shattered remains of the aforementioned abbey, a short walk to the east of the pedestrianized shopping centre.

There is a flourishing **arts scene** in the town, with both the Reading Film Theatre (Ⓣ0118/986 8497, Ⓦwww.readingfilmtheatre.co.uk) and the Hexagon Theatre (Ⓣ0118/960 6060, Ⓦwww.readingarts.com) offering a good programme of shows, but you wouldn't make a beeline for the place were it not for its two big summertime **music festivals**. The first, the three-day **WOMAD** festival (Ⓦwww.womad.org; tickets Ⓣ0118/939 0930), held each July, is a celebration of World Music, Arts and Dance, originally inspired by Peter Gabriel. Since the first WOMAD in 1982, there have been about a hundred spin-off events in twenty countries, but the Reading festival remains the focus, held at the Rivermead Leisure Complex, Richfield Avenue, just to the north of the town centre. At the same venue, but a little later in the summer, the **Reading Festival** (Ⓦwww.readingfestival.com) is a three-day event featuring many of the big names of contemporary music. Details of who is performing are published in the music press at least a couple of months in advance and tickets are available from record shops and ticket outlets across the country. The vast majority of festival-goers **camp on site** and special buses run there in their hundreds, or you can walk from Reading train station – it only takes fifteen minutes.

Reading can be reached by train from London Paddington and Waterloo. The **tourist office**, in the town centre in Church House, on Chain Street (Mon–Fri 10am–5pm, Sat 9.30am–4pm; Ⓣ0118/956 6226, Ⓦwww.readingtourism.org.uk), operates an accommodation-booking service; be sure to reserve a room months in advance if you're planning on being here for either festival.

The Vale of White Horse

The **Vale of White Horse**, falling between Wantage, a modest market town about thirty miles west of Henley, and Faringdon, seventeen miles southwest of Oxford, is a shallow valley, whose fertile farmland is studded with tiny villages. It takes its name from the prehistoric figure cut into the chalk downs above two of its smaller hamlets – **Uffington** and **Woolstone**. Carved in the first century BC, the horse is the most conspicuous of a string of prehistoric remains that punctuates the downs and includes burial mounds and Iron Age forts. The **Ridgeway National Trail** (see box on p.330), running along – or near – the top of the downs, links several of these sites and offers wonderful, breezy views over the vale. Originally a prehistoric footpath, the Ridgeway was long used as a drove road, with sheep taken over the downs to market. Nowadays, horses are more common, the well-drained turf providing an ideal training ground for racehorses.

Wantage

Workaday **WANTAGE** is an unassuming, somewhat care-worn market town, whose crowded Market Place is overseen by a statue of its most famous son, Alfred the Great (849–99), the most distinguished of England's Saxon kings. Unveiled in 1877, the statue doesn't do Alfred any favours – though he must have been very strong to stand any chance of lifting his over-large axe. From the south side of the Market Place – which is where long-distance buses pull in – a couple of alleys lead through to Church Street. This is the location of the **tourist office** (Ⓣ01235/760176), which shares its premises – and times – with the modest **Vale and Downland Museum** (Mon–Sat 10am–4.30pm, Sun 2.30–5pm; £1.50).

Wantage is handy for the finest portion of the **Ridgeway** and the tourist office is the place to pick up local hiking maps and bus timetables. The quickest way to reach the Ridgeway direct from Wantage is to take bus #38 (Mon–Sat only, hourly; 20min) from the Market Place to **Letcombe Bassett**, less than a mile from the path, but be aware that not all of these buses follow the same route – so check with the driver. Excellent walking along the Ridgeway takes you westwards from Letcombe Bassett to the White Horse (see below), a distance of about seven miles.

There's no strong reason to stay in Wantage, but there are several **B&Bs**, the most recommendable of which is the well-kept *Alfred's Lodge*, in a detached Victorian house about five minutes' walk southeast of the centre at 23 Ormond Rd (Ⓣ01235/762409; no credit cards; ❶). To get there from the east end of the Market Place, take Newbury Street and watch for Ormond on the left. Alternatively, the **Ridgeway youth hostel** (Ⓣ0870/770 6064, Ⓔridgeway@yha.org.uk; dorm beds £11.50) occupies a prime position just off the A338 a couple of miles south of Wantage – watch for the sign. The hostel consists of several sympathetically converted old timber barns set around a courtyard with the Ridgeway a stone's throw away. The hostel has sixty beds in four- to thirteen-bedded rooms and advance reservations are required from September to June at least 48hr ahead; this does not apply in July and August. Facilities include a self-catering kitchen, a café, drying room and cycle store. On weekdays, the nearest you'll get by public transport is **bus #38** (Mon–Sat only, hourly; 20min) from Wantage to Letcombe Regis, from where it's a mile or so uphill to the hostel. On the weekend, **The Ridgeway Explorer** bus (mid-April to late Oct Sat & Sun 4 daily; timetable details Ⓣ0870/608 2608) stops right outside.

Wantage has one excellent **restaurant**, *Thyme and Plaice*, near the east end of the Market Place at 8 Newbury St (Ⓣ01235/760568). This serves a changing menu of imaginatively prepared contemporary dishes featuring local ingredients, but it's expensive, with a two-course set meal costing around £20. For a much less pricey deal, try the *Cornucopia Coffee Shop*, which serves tasty snacks and lunches from its premises at Unit 13, Post Office Vaults, at the east end of the Market Place. For a **drink**, head northwest from the Market Place to *The Lamb*, a revamped seventeenth-century inn at the foot of Mill Street.

White Horse Hill

White Horse Hill, six miles west of Wantage along the B4507, follows close behind Stonehenge (see p.318) and Avebury (see p.320) in the hierarchy of

Britain's ancient sites, though it attracts nothing like the same number of visitors. Carved into the north-facing slope of the downs above the villages of Uffington and Woolstone, the 374-foot-long **horse** looks like something created with a few swift strokes of an immense brush, and there's been no lack of weird and wonderful theories as to its origins. Some have suggested it was a glorified signpost, created to show travellers where to join the Ridgeway; others that it represented the horse (or even the dragon) of St George; and in Victorian times, the best-loved legend – popularized in a ballad by G.K. Chesterton – claimed that it was cut by King Alfred to celebrate his victory over the Danes at the battle of Ashdown, fought around here in 871 AD. In fact, burial sites excavated in the surrounding area point to the horse having some kind of sacred function, though frankly no one knows quite what. The first written record of the horse's existence dates from the time of Henry II, but it was cut much earlier, probably in the first century BC, making it one of the oldest chalk figures in Britain. A detailed 1994 study showed that its creators dug out the soil to a depth of a metre and then filled the hollow with clear white chalk taken from a nearby hilltop.

Just below the horse is **Dragon Hill**, a small flat-topped hillock that has its own legend. Locals long asserted that this was where St George killed and buried the dragon, a theory proved, so they argued, by the bare patch at the top and the channel down the side, where blood trickled from the creature's wounds. Here also, at the top of the hill, is the Iron Age earthwork of **Uffington Castle**, which provides wonderful views over the vale.

The Ridgeway runs alongside the horse and continues west to reach, after one-and-a-half miles, **Wayland's Smithy**, a 5000-year-old burial mound encircled by trees. It is one of the best Neolithic remains along the Ridgeway, though heavy restoration has rather detracted from its mystery. In ignorance of its original function, the invading Saxons named it after Wayland Smith, an invisible smith who, according to their legends, made invincible armour and shoed horses without ever being seen.

Travelling west from Wantage, the **B4507** passes the narrow lane that leads - after 500 yards - to the car park just below the White Horse. Getting here by public transport can be difficult: the only **bus**, the Ridgeway Explorer, linking Wantage and Swindon via the B4507, only runs four times daily on Saturdays, Sundays and bank holidays between mid-April and late October (timetable details on ⓣ0870/608 2608).

Woolstone and Uffington

About three quarters of a mile below the White Horse car park, on the north side of the B4057, is the minuscule hamlet of **WOOLSTONE**. Here, the attractive *White Horse Inn* (ⓣ01367/820726; ❸) occupies a rickety, half-timbered, partly thatched old building and offers both good-quality pub food and **accommodation**, mostly in a modern annexe. A second option is the *Hickory House* (ⓣ01367/820303; no credit cards; ❷), offering two en-suite guest rooms in a spick-and-span modern house close to the pub. A mile or two to the north of Woolstone, the much larger (and plainer) village of **UFFINGTON** has a couple of **B&Bs**, notably the well-kept and unassuming *Norton House*, next to the post office on the main street (ⓣ01367/820230; no credit cards; ❷). Uffington's most famous son was Thomas Hughes (1823–96), the author of *Tom Brown's School Days* – hence the pocket-sized Tom Brown's School Museum.

Oxford

When they think of **OXFORD**, visitors almost always think of its **university**, revered as one of the world's great academic institutions, inhabiting honey-coloured stone buildings set around ivy-clad quadrangles. Much of this is accurate enough, but although the university dominates central Oxford both physically and mentally, the wider city has an entirely different character, its economy built on the **car plants** of Cowley to the south of the centre. It was here that Britain's first mass-produced cars were produced in the 1920s and, although there have been more downs than ups in recent years, the plants are still vitally important to the area.

Oxford started late, in Anglo-Saxon times, and blossomed even later, under the Normans, when the cathedral was constructed and Oxford was chosen as a royal residence. The origins of the university are obscure, but it seems that the reputation of **Henry I**, the so-called "Scholar King", helped attract students in the early twelfth century, their numbers increasing with the expulsion of English students from the Sorbonne in 1167. The first colleges, founded mostly by rich bishops, were essentially ecclesiastical institutions and this was reflected in collegiate rules and regulations – until 1877 lecturers were not allowed to marry and women were not granted degrees until 1920. There are common architectural features, too, with the private rooms of the students arranged around quadrangles (quads), as are most of the communal rooms – the chapels, halls (dining rooms) and libraries.

Though they share a similar history, each of the university's 35 colleges has its own character and often a particular label, whether it's the richest (St John's), most left-wing (Wadham and Balliol) or most public-school-dominated (Christ Church). Collegiate rivalries are long established, usually revolving around sports, and tension between the university and the city – "Town" and "Gown" – has existed as long as the university itself. Relations became especially fractious during the **Civil War**, when the colleges sided with Charles I (who turned Oxford into a Royalist stronghold) while the city backed the Parliamentarians. The privileges enjoyed by the colleges – until 1950 the university had two MPs of its own – have also stoked resentment and this still flares into the occasional confrontation, but a non-communicative coexistence is more typical. Given that thousands of tourists and foreign-language students also invade the city throughout the year, it is no surprise that Oxford's 120,000 permanent inhabitants often choose to keep themselves to themselves.

Despite – indeed, partly because of – its idiosyncrasies, Oxford should be high on anyone's itinerary, and can keep you occupied for several days. The university buildings include some of England's finest architecture, and the city can also boast some excellent museums and numerous bars and restaurants. Getting there is easy, too: from London the journey takes just an hour by train, and around two hours by bus.

Arrival

From Oxford **train station**, it's a five- to ten-minute walk east to the centre along Park End Street and then Hythe Bridge Street. Long-distance and many county-wide buses terminate at the Gloucester Green **bus station**, in the centre adjoining George Street. The Oxford Bus Company (Ⓣ01865/785400) operates most local and city buses, many of which pull in on the High Street and St Giles. They also run the city's **Park-and-Ride** scheme, with buses (daily Mon–Sat 5.30am–11pm, Sun 8.30am–6.30pm) travelling into the centre every

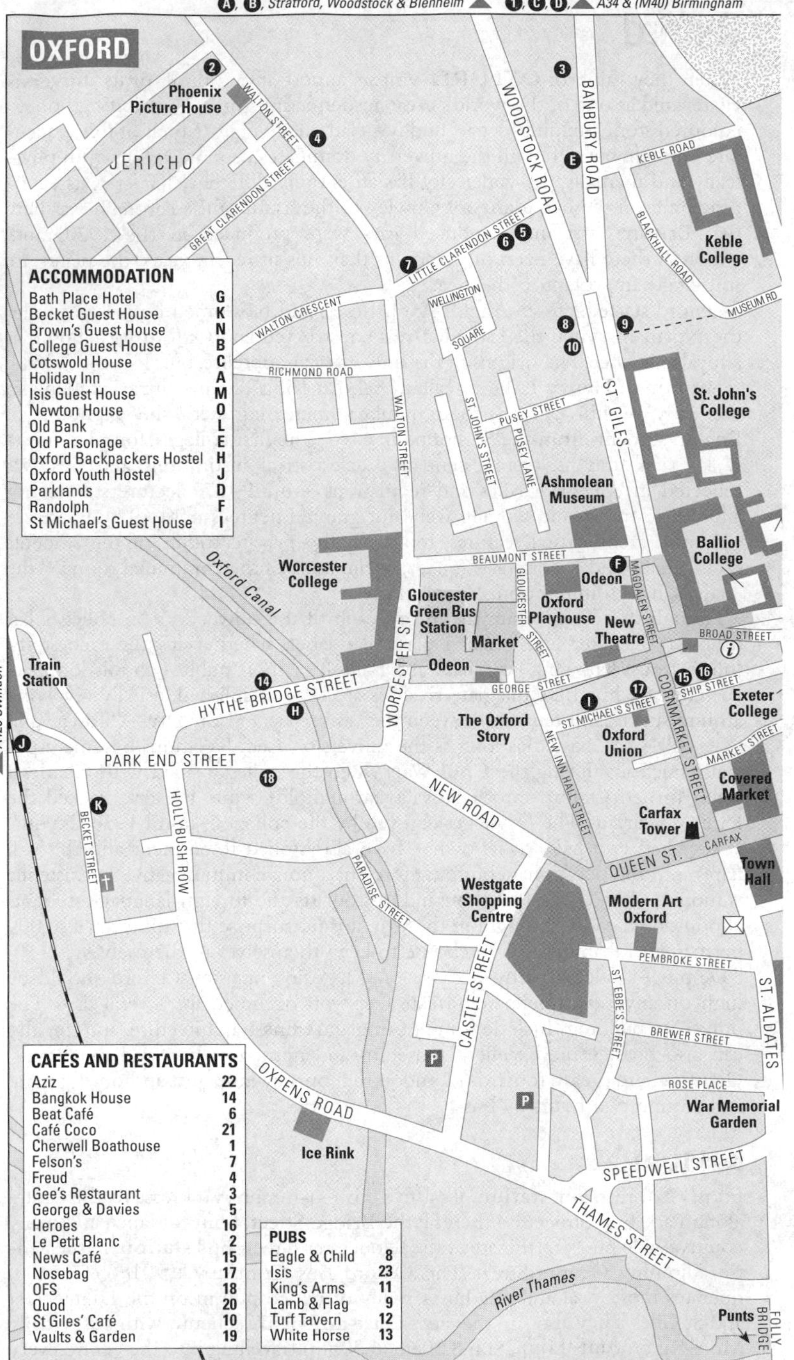
A, B, Stratford, Woodstock & Blenheim
1, C, D, A34 & (M40) Birmingham
OXFORD
Phoenix Picture House
JERICHO
WALTON STREET
GREAT CLARENDON STREET
WOODSTOCK ROAD
BANBURY ROAD
KEBLE ROAD
BLACKHALL ROAD
Keble College
MUSEUM RD
LITTLE CLARENDON STREET
WALTON CRESCENT
WELLINGTON SQUARE
RICHMOND ROAD
ST. GILES
St. John's College
PUSEY STREET
ST. JOHN'S STREET
PUSEY LANE
Ashmolean Museum
ACCOMMODATION
Bath Place Hotel G
Becket Guest House K
Brown's Guest House N
College Guest House B
Cotswold House C
Holiday Inn A
Isis Guest House M
Newton House O
Old Bank L
Old Parsonage E
Oxford Backpackers Hostel H
Oxford Youth Hostel J
Parklands D
Randolph F
St Michael's Guest House I
Oxford Canal
Worcester College
BEAUMONT STREET
GLOUCESTER STREET
MAGDALEN STREET
Balliol College
Odeon
Oxford Playhouse
New Theatre
Gloucester Green Bus Station
Market
WORCESTER ST
BROAD STREET
Odeon
GEORGE STREET
SHIP STREET
Exeter College
Train Station
HYTHE BRIDGE STREET
A420 Swindon
The Oxford Story
ST. MICHAEL'S STREET
CORNMARKET STREET
Oxford Union
MARKET STREET
Covered Market
PARK END STREET
NEW ROAD
NEW INN HALL STREET
Carfax Tower
CARFAX
BECKET STREET
HOLLYBUSH ROW
PARADISE STREET
QUEEN ST.
Town Hall
Westgate Shopping Centre
Modern Art Oxford
CASTLE STREET
PEMBROKE STREET
ST. EBBE'S STREET
ST. ALDATES
BREWER STREET
CAFÉS AND RESTAURANTS
Aziz 22
Bangkok House 14
Beat Café 6
Café Coco 21
Cherwell Boathouse 1
Felson's 7
Freud 4
Gee's Restaurant 3
George & Davies 5
Heroes 16
Le Petit Blanc 2
News Café 15
Nosebag 17
OFS 18
Quod 20
St Giles' Café 10
Vaults & Garden 19
OXPENS ROAD
ROSE PLACE
War Memorial Garden
Ice Rink
SPEEDWELL STREET
THAMES STREET
PUBS
Eagle & Child 8
Isis 23
King's Arms 11
Lamb & Flag 9
Turf Tavern 12
White Horse 13
River Thames
Punts
FOLLY BRIDGE

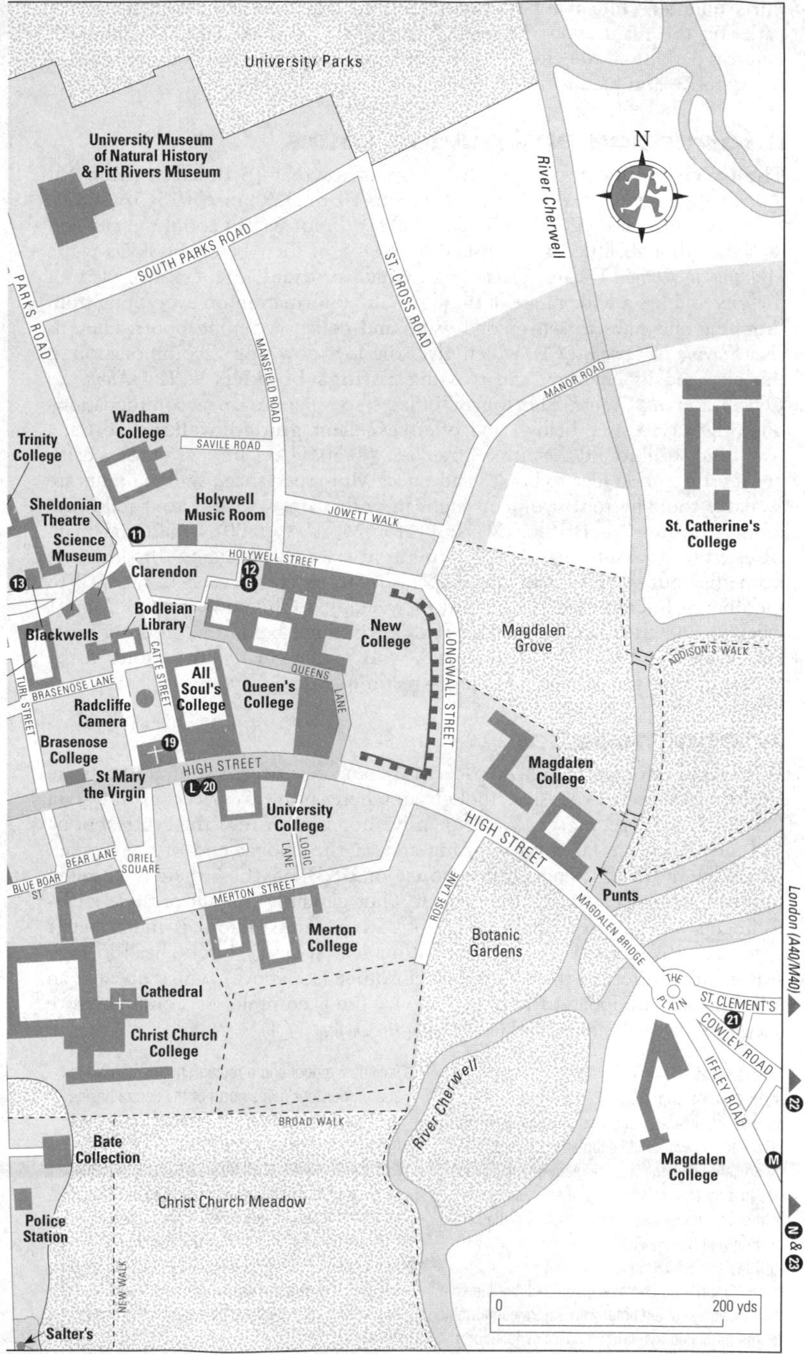

4 OXFORD AND AROUND | Oxford

thirty minutes – fifteen at peak periods – from four large and clearly signed car parks on the main approach roads into the city. Parking costs are minimal, whereas parking in the city centre is – by municipal design – both inordinately expensive and hard to find.

Information and guided tours

The **tourist office** is plum in the centre of town at 15 Broad St (Mon–Sat 9.30am–5pm, plus late April to late Oct Sun 10am–3.30pm; ⓣ01865/726871, ⓦwww.visitoxford.org). They have a wealth of information about the city and its sights, though little of it is issued free. One of their better booklets is the *Welcome to Oxford Visitors' Guide* (£1), which provides a general overview of the city and has a wide range of more specific information on everything from shopping and pubs to self-guided walks and college opening hours. There is also *Staying in Oxford* (£1), which gives the low-down on accommodation in the city and its environs, and two free **listings booklets** – *This Month in Oxford* and *In Oxford*. The tourist office also operates an accommodation-booking service (see below) and offers excellent **guided walking tours**; a two-hour stroll round the city centre costs £6.50. There are several tours daily, but it's still a good idea to book in advance. More specialized walking tours are available too. The tourist office weighs in with a once-weekly tour following in the footsteps of British TV's Inspector Morse (£6.50), whilst the main Blackwell's bookshop (ⓣ01865/333606), just along and across Broad Street from the tourist office, runs three specialist tours at £6 each from April to October: a Literary Tour of Oxford (3 weekly); a Children's Writers Tour (1 weekly); and an Inklings Tour (1 weekly) – Inklings being the group of writers, Tolkien and C. S. Lewis included, who met regularly in Oxford in the 1930s. In all cases, advance booking is recommended.

Accommodation

With supply struggling to keep pace with demand, Oxford's central **hotels** are almost invariably expensive, though nowhere near as pricey as those in London. There are one or two inexpensive hotels in or near the centre, but by and large they are far from inspiring and, at the budget end of the market, you're better off choosing a **guest house** or **B&B**, of which there is a healthy supply. The problem is that the majority (but certainly not all) of these establishments are scattered on the edge of town – and Oxford is much better appreciated if you stay in the centre. Wherever you stay, book ahead in high season either direct or through the tourist office (see above), which operates an efficient accommodation-booking service and compiles a comprehensive accommodation listings booklet, *Staying in Oxford* (£1).

Hotels

Bath Place Hotel 4 Bath Place ⓣ01865/791812, ⓦwww.bathplace.co.uk. This unusual, pink and blue hotel, down an old cobbled courtyard flanked by ancient buildings with higgledy-piggledy roofs, has just thirteen rooms, all of them reasonably attractive. The location is excellent – in the centre, off Holywell Street. ❻

Holiday Inn Pear Tree Roundabout ⓣ0870/4009086, ⓦwww.oxford.holiday-inn.com. Well-designed chain hotel with smart, comfortable rooms furnished in a crisp modern style. Sports facilities, a pool and a restaurant are all provided. Just under four miles north of the centre beside the Pear Tree Roundabout – the second one out from the centre along the Woodstock Road. ❻

Old Bank Hotel 92 High St ⓣ01865/799599, ⓦwww.oxford-hotels-restaurants.co.uk. Great location for a first-rate hotel, a slick, glistening conversion of an old bank. Over twenty immaculate bedrooms decorated in smart, modern style. Some of the rooms have great views over All Souls college. The *Quod* bistro is on the ground floor. ❽

Old Parsonage Hotel 1 Banbury Rd ⓣ01865/310210, ⓦwww.oxford-hotels-restaurants.co.uk. Arguably the best hotel in town, this lovely little place occupies a charming, wisteria-clad stone former-parsonage by the church at the top of St Giles. The twenty-odd rooms are tastefully furnished. ❽

Parklands Hotel 100 Banbury Rd ⓣ01865/554374, ⓔtheparklands@freenet.co.uk. Pleasant fourteen-room hotel in a Victorian house with a garden, licensed restaurant and bar. North of the centre, but connected to it by a frequent bus service. Good value. ❺

Randolph Hotel 1 Beaumont St ⓣ0870/4008200, ⓦwww.therandolph.com. The most famous hotel in the city, long the favoured choice of the well-heeled, the *Randolph* is a large and well-proportioned brick building with a distinctive neo-Gothic interior. It has lost much of its allure since it was swallowed into a chain – it's now a Macdonald hotel – but it is bang in the centre of town. Scenes from the *Inspector Morse* TV series were shot here. ❽

Guest houses and B&Bs

Becket Guest House 5 Becket St ⓣ01865/724675. Modest but proficient bay-windowed guest house in a plain terrace close to the train station. Most rooms en suite. ❸

Brown's Guest House 281 Iffley Rd ⓣ01865/246822, ⓦwww.brownsguesthouse.co.uk. Well-maintained and recently revamped guest house in a pleasing Victorian property with ten rooms, all en suite. ❸

College Guest House 103 Woodstock Rd ⓣ01865/552579, ⓦwww.oxfordcity.co.uk. About ten minutes' walk north of the centre, this pleasant guest house occupies a distinctive older, high-gabled building. There are eight rooms, four en suite. ❸

Cotswold House 363 Banbury Rd ⓣ01865/310558, ⓦwww.house363.freeserve.co.uk. This top-notch B&B, about two miles north of the centre, occupies a bright and breezy modern brick house on the busy Banbury Road. Excellent breakfasts and comfortable, well-appointed en-suite rooms. ❹

Isis Guest House 45–53 Iffley Rd ⓣ01865/248894, ⓔisis@herald.ox.ac.uk. From July to September, this college hall becomes a guest house with around thirty single and double rooms, about half of which are en suite. Located within easy walking distance of Magdalen Bridge. Good value, but spartan. ❷

Newton House 82–84 Abingdon Rd ⓣ01865/240561, ⓦwww.oxfordcity.co.uk. Appealing, family-run guest house in two good-looking and well-kept Victorian town houses about ten minutes' walk south of the centre – well placed for evening strolls along the Thames. The guest rooms are decorated in a smart rendition of traditional style. No singles. ❸

St Michael's Guest House 26 St Michael's St ⓣ01865/242101. Often full, this friendly, well-kept B&B, in a cosy three-storey terrace house, has unsurprising furnishings and fittings, but a charming, central location. A real snip. ❸

Hostels

Oxford Backpackers Hostel 9a Hythe Bridge St ⓣ01865/721761, ⓣoxford@hostels.co.uk. Independent hostel with quads and dorms, holding up to eighteen people each. Fully equipped kitchen and laundry plus Internet facilities. Handy location between the train station and the centre; 24-hour access. Dorm beds £13.

Oxford Youth Hostel 2a Botley Rd ⓣ0870/770 5970, ⓔoxford@yha.org.uk. Next door to the train station, this popular YHA hostel has 184 beds divided up into two-, four- and six-bedded rooms. There's 24-hour access, good self-catering facilities and an inexpensive café. Dorm beds including breakfast £19.50.

The City

The compact centre of Oxford is wedged in between the rivers Thames and the Cherwell, just to the north of the point where they join. In theory, and on most maps, the Thames is known within the city as the "Isis", but few locals actually use the term. Central Oxford's principal point of reference is **Carfax**, a busy junction from where three of the city's main thoroughfares begin: the **High Street** runs east to Magdalen Bridge and the Cherwell; **St Aldates** south to the Thames; and **Cornmarket** north to the broad avenue of St Giles. Many of the oldest **colleges** face onto the High Street or the side streets adjoining it, their mellow stonework combining to create one of the most beautiful parts of Oxford, though the most stunning college of them all is **Christ Church**. Here, as elsewhere in the city, all of the more visited colleges have restricted opening

On the river

Punting is a favourite summer pastime among both students and visitors, but handling a punt – a flat-bottomed boat ideal for the shallow waters of the Thames and Cherwell rivers – requires some practice. The punt is propelled and steered with a long pole, which beginners inevitably get stuck in riverbed mud: if this happens, let go and paddle back, otherwise you're likely to be pulled overboard. The Cherwell, though much narrower than the Thames and therefore trickier to navigate, provides more opportunities for pulling to the side for a picnic, an essential part of the punting experience.

As regards **boat rental**, there are two fairly central places. The first is the Magdalen Bridge boathouse (Ⓣ01865/202643), beside the Cherwell at the east end of the High Street; the second is the Thames boat station at Folly Bridge (Ⓣ01865/243421), a five- to ten-minute stroll south of the centre along St Aldates. However, in summer the queues soon build up at both, so either get there early in the morning – at around 10am – or head off to the Cherwell Boat House (Ⓣ01865/515978), a mile or so north of the centre: to get there, head out of the centre on Banbury Road, turn right along Linton Road and the boat house is at the end, behind Wolfson College. At all three boathouses, expect **to pay** about £12 per hour for a boat plus a £30 deposit, and remember that sometimes ID is required. Punts can take a maximum of five passengers – four sitting and one punting. Call the boathouses for opening times – which vary – or if there are any doubts about the weather.

If you're determined not to do any actual punting yourself, you might consider hiring a **chauffeured punt** (£25 for 30min). The boathouses also rent out pedaloes, which cost less, but aren't as much fun. In addition, Salter's Steamers (Ⓣ01865/243421, Ⓦwww.salterssteamers.co.uk) runs **passenger boats** along the River Thames from Oxford's Folly Bridge to Abingdon between mid-May and late September. There is one boat daily in each direction, a one-way cruise takes two hours and a return ticket costs £12.

The other boats most commonly seen on the Thames belong to the university's **rowing clubs**, which started up in the early nineteenth century, when top hats were *de rigueur*. The first Oxford versus Cambridge boat race – now staged in Putney, London – took place in 1829. Rowers mostly practise along the wide stretch of river to the south of Folly Bridge, which is also used for college races – the **Torpids** held in March and the **Eights** at the end of May. The latter are the more important and therefore attract the larger crowds.

hours and some impose an admission charge, while others permit no regular public access at all. Of those that do open their doors, **college opening times** are fairly consistent throughout the year, but there are sporadic term-time variations, especially at weekends. It's also worth noting that during the exam season, which stretches from late April to early June, all the colleges have periods when they are closed to the public. For more specific information, call the relevant college – the **phone numbers** are given in the text below.

South from Carfax to Modern Art Oxford

Too busy to be comfortable and too modern to be pretty, the **Carfax** is not a place to hang around, but it is overlooked by an interesting remnant of the medieval town, a chunky fourteenth-century **tower**, adorned by a pair of clocktower jacks dressed in vaguely Roman gear. The tower is all that remains of St Martin's church, where legend asserts that William Shakespeare stood sponsor at the baptism of one of his friend's children. You can climb the **tower** (daily: April–Oct 10am–5.30pm; Nov–March 10am–3.30pm; £1.40) for wide views over the centre, though other vantage points have the edge.

Spreading down St Aldates from the Carfax, Oxford's **Town Hall** is an ostentatious Victorian confection that reflects a municipal determination not to be overwhelmed by the university. A staircase on its south side gives access to the **Museum of Oxford** (Tues–Fri 10am–4pm, Sat 10am–5pm, Sun noon–4pm; £2), which makes good use of photographs to tell the history of the city. In the face of tough competition this museum often gets ignored, but you'll discover far more here than at the "Oxford Story" in Broad Street (see p.349).

From the Town Hall, cross St Aldates and it's a few paces to Pembroke Street, which possesses the city's best contemporary art gallery, **Modern Art Oxford** (Tues–Sat 10am–5pm, Sun noon–5pm; free; Ⓦ www.modernartoxford.org.uk). The gallery has an excellent programme of temporary exhibitions, featuring international contemporary art in a wide variety of media, along with lectures, films, workshops and multimedia performances (not all of which are free).

Christ Church College

Doubling back along Pembroke Street, turn right down St Aldates for the main facade of **Christ Church College** (Mon–Sat 9.30am–5.30pm, Sun noon–5.30pm; £4; Ⓣ 01865/276492), whose distinctive Tom Tower was added by Christopher Wren in 1681 to house the weighty "Great Tom" bell. The tower lords it over the main entrance of what is Oxford's largest and arguably most prestigious college, but visitors have to enter from the south, a signed five-minute walk away – just past the tiny War Memorial Garden and from the top of Christ Church Meadow (see p.344). Albert Einstein, William Gladstone and no fewer than twelve other British prime ministers were educated here and the college also claims the distinction of having been founded three times, firstly by Cardinal Wolsey in 1525, then by Henry VIII after the cardinal's fall from favour and finally, after the Reformation – when the second college was suppressed – in 1545, when it assumed its present name.

Entering the college from the south, it's a short step to the striking **Tom Quad**, the largest quad in Oxford, so large in fact that the Royalists penned up their mobile larder of cattle here during the Civil War. Guarded by the Tom Tower, the Quad's soft, honey-coloured stone makes a harmonious whole, but it was built in two main phases with the southern side dating back to Wolsey, the north finally finished in the 1660s. A wide stone staircase in the southeast corner of the Quad leads up to the **Dining Hall**, the grandest refectory in Oxford with a fanciful hammer-beam roof and a set of stern portraits of past scholars by a roll-call of well-known artists, including Reynolds, Gainsborough and Millais. Charles I held court here when the Parliamentarians were in control of London and, in one of those snippets of information beloved of academics, Lewis Carroll, former student and author of *Alice's Adventures in Wonderland*, ate eight thousand meals in this very hall.

Just to the rear of the Tom Quad stands the **Cathedral**, which is also – in a most unusual arrangement – the college chapel. The Anglo-Saxons built a church on this site in the seventh century as part of St Frideswide Priory. The priory was suppressed in 1524, but the church survived, becoming a cathedral forty years later, though in between Wolsey knocked down the west end to make space for the Tom Quad. It's an unusually discordant church, with all sorts of bits and bobs from different periods, but it's fascinating all the same. The dominant feature is the sturdy circular columns and rounded arches of the Normans, but there are also early Gothic pointed arches and the chancel ceiling is a particularly fine example of fifteenth-century stone vaulting. The battered **shrine of St Frideswide**, in the Latin Chapel – to the far right of the entrance – was destroyed during the Dissolution, but the pieces were found down an old well and gamely assembled by the Victorians. Today, it exhibits some of the earliest natural foliage in English sculpture, a splendid confection of leaves dating from around 1290. The shrine is overlooked by an equally rare, two-storey, stone and timber **watching loft**, from where custodians would keep a close eye on the tomb of the saint, and by a cluttered but deeply coloured **stained-glass window** by Edward Burne-Jones. The window, crammed with Biblical bodies, was completed in 1858, long before Jones got into his Pre-Raphaelite stride, but there are three examples from this later period along the back of the chancel, with the **St Catherine Window**, in the near right-hand corner of the church, being the prime example.

A passage at the northeast corner of the Tom Quad leads through to the **Peckwater Quad**, whose pleasantries are overwhelmed by the whopping Neoclassical library. A few paces more and you're in the pocket-sized **Canterbury Quad**, where the **Picture Gallery** (Mon–Sat 10.30am–5.30pm, Sun 2–5pm; £2) is home to works by many of Italy's finest artists from the fifteenth to eighteenth centuries, including Leonardo da Vinci and Michelangelo. There's also a good showing by the Dutch – Van Dyck, Frans Hals and so forth. The Canterbury Quad abuts Oriel Square and Merton College (see below), or you can return to the college's south entrance for Christ Church Meadow.

Christ Church Meadow and the Bate Collection

Christ Church Meadow fills in the tapering gap between the rivers Cherwell and Thames. Emerging from Christ Church, head east along Broad Walk for the Cherwell or keep straight down tree-lined (and more appealing) New Walk for the Thames. Alternatively, return to St Aldates and turn left for the **Bate Collection** (Mon–Fri 2–5pm; free), which contains England's most comprehensive collection of European woodwind instruments. Though only music buffs will make sense of some of the explanatory notes, you don't have to be an expert to enjoy the displays. In addition to rows of flutes and clarinets, there are all sorts of other instruments on show, from medieval crumhorns, looking like rejected walking sticks, to the country's finest example of a gamelan.

Merton College

Next door to Christ Church, **Merton College** (Mon–Fri 2–4pm, Sat & Sun 10am–4pm; free; ⓣ01865/276310) is historically the city's most important college. Balliol and University colleges may have been founded earlier, but it was Merton – opened in 1264 – which set the model for colleges in both Oxford and Cambridge, being the first to gather its students and tutors together in one place. Furthermore, unlike the other two, Merton retains some of its original medieval buildings, with the best of the thirteenth-century architecture clustered around **Mob Quad**, a charming courtyard with mullioned windows and Gothic doorways to the right of the Front Quad. The quad's **Library** is of interest too, built in the 1370s and the first library in England to store books upright on shelves as distinct from in piles. Much of the woodwork, including the panelling, screens and bookcases, dates from the Tudor period, but some fittings are original and there's a small display on one of the college's most distinguished alumni, Max Beerbohm. From the Mob Quad, an archway leads through to the **Chapel**, which dates from 1290. This has never had a nave, leaving the choir as the main body of the church and the transepts as ante-chapels. In the latter is the curious funerary plaque of Thomas Bodley – founder of Oxford's most important library – his bust surrounded by ungainly, boyish-looking women in classical garb. The windows of the choir were donated by Henry de Mamesfeld, an egocentric who appears as a kneeling figure no less than 24 times. Apart from Bodley, famous Merton alumni include T.S. Eliot, Angus Wilson, Louis MacNeice and Kris Kristofferson.

University and Queen's colleges

From Merton, narrow Logic Lane threads to the east end of **University College** (no set opening times; ⓣ01865/276602), whose long curved facade and twin gateway towers spread along the High Street. Known as "Univ", the college claims Alfred the Great as its founder, but things really got going with a formal endowment in 1249, making it Oxford's oldest college – though nothing of that period survives. A year the college may prefer to forget is 1811, when it expelled **Percy Bysshe Shelley** for distributing a paper called *The Necessity of Atheism*. Guilt later induced Univ to accept a memorial to the poet, who drowned in Italy in 1822: the white marble monument, showing the limp body of the poet borne by winged lions and mourned by the Muse of Poetry, occupies a shrine-like domed chamber in the northeast corner of the Front Quad. The college's most famous recent alumnus was Bill Clinton, the non-inhaling Rhodes Scholar; former Australian premier Bob Hawke also studied here.

Across the High Street from Univ stands **Queen's College** (no set opening times; ⓣ01865/279120), whose handsome Baroque buildings cut an impressive dash. The only Oxford college to have been built in one period (1682–1765), Queen's benefited from the skills of several talented architects, most notably Nicholas Hawksmoor and Christopher Wren. Wren designed (or at least influenced the design of) the college's most diverting building, the **Chapel**, whose ceiling is filled with cherubs amidst dense foliage.

St Mary the Virgin

From Queen's, it's a couple of minutes' walk west along the High Street to **St Mary the Virgin** (daily 9am–5pm; free), a hotchpotch of architectural styles, but mostly dating from the fifteenth century. The church's saving graces are its elaborate, thirteenth-century pinnacled spire and its distinctive Baroque porch, flanked by chunky corkscrewed pillars – and paid for by one of Archbishop Laud's friends in 1637. Curiously, the House of Commons cited the porch when they tried Laud, the Archbishop of Canterbury and religious adviser to Charles I, for high treason in 1640, the objection being that the porch was idolatrous, or at least too "Catholic". The real beef was Laud's sustained persecution of the Puritans and, although the trial dragged on and on, he was finally executed at the height of the Civil War in 1644. The church's interior is disappointingly mundane, though the carved poppy heads on the choir stalls are of some historical interest: the tips were brusquely flattened off when a platform was installed here in 1554 to stage the heresy trial of Cranmer, Latimer and Ridley, leading Protestants who had run foul of Queen Mary. The other diversion is the church **tower** (same times; £2), with wonderful views across to the Radcliffe Camera (see p.347) and east over **All Souls College** (Mon–Fri 2–4pm; free; ⓣ01865/279379), with its twin mock-Gothic towers (the work of Hawksmoor) and conspicuous, brightly decorated sundial designed by Wren. The tower can also be entered round the back of the church.

Magdalen College and the University Botanic Gardens

Heading east along the High Street, it's a short walk to **Magdalen College** (pronounced "Maudlin"; Mon–Fri noon–6pm, Sat & Sun 2–6pm; £3; ⓣ01865/276000), whose gaggle of stone buildings is overshadowed by its chunky medieval bell tower. Steer right from the entrance and you soon reach the **Chapel**, which has a handsome reredos – though you have to admire it from a distance, through the windows of an ungainly stone screen. The adjacent **cloisters**, arguably the finest in Oxford, are adorned by standing figures, some of which are biblical and others folkloric – most notably the cacophony of bizarre grotesques. Magdalen also boasts better **grounds** than most other colleges, with a bridge – at the back of the cloisters – spanning the River Cherwell to join **Addison's Walk**, which you can follow along the river and around a water meadow; rare wild fritillaries flower there in spring. Magdalen has a fine choir, whose annual duties include singing madrigals from the top of the bell tower at 6am on May 1. Pubs open especially for this May Day event and the din made by drunken students often drowns out the singing. Magdalen's alumni include Oscar Wilde, C.S. Lewis, John Betjeman, Julian Barnes, A.J.P. Taylor and Dudley Moore.

Across the High Street from Magdalen lie the **University of Oxford Botanic Gardens** (daily: April–Sept 9am–5pm; Oct–March 9am–4.30pm; £2.50), whose greenery is bounded by a graceful curve of the Cherwell. First planted in 1621, the gardens comprise several different zones, from a lily pond, a bog garden and a rock garden through to borders of bearded irises and variegated plants. There are also eight large **glasshouses** featuring tropical and desert species (daily: April–Sept 10am–4.30pm; Oct–March 10–4pm; no extra charge).

The gardens are next to **Magdalen Bridge**, where you can rent punts (see box on p.342).

New College

Retracing your steps back along the High Street to Queen's, cut up **Queen's Lane** and you'll dog-leg your way north to **New College** (daily: April–Oct 11am–5pm; Nov–March 2–4pm; £2; ⓣ01865/279555). Founded in 1379, the college kicks off with an attractive **Front Quad**, though the splendid Perpendicular Gothic architecture of the original was spoiled by the addition of an extra storey in 1674. The adjoining **Chapel** has been mucked about, too, yet it can still lay claim to being the finest in Oxford, not so much for its design as its contents. The ante-chapel contains some superb fourteenth-century stained glass and the west window – of 1778 – holds an intriguing (if somewhat unsuccessful) Nativity scene based on a design by Sir Joshua Reynolds. Beneath it stands the wonderful *Lazarus* by Jacob Epstein; Khrushchev, after a visit to the college, claimed that the memory of this haunting sculpture kept him awake at night. The entire east wall of the main chapel is occupied by a magnificent nineteenth-century stone reredos, consisting of about fifty canopied figures, mostly saints and apostles, with Christ Crucified for a centrepiece. An archway on the east side of the Front Quad leads through to the modest **Garden Quad**, with the thick flower beds of the **College Garden** beckoning beyond. The north side of the garden is flanked by the largest and best-preserved section of Oxford's medieval **city wall**, but the conspicuous earthen **mound** in the middle is a later decorative addition and not, disappointingly, medieval at all. Notable New College alumni include the Labour Party leader Hugh Gaitskell, Tony Benn and the author John Fowles.

From the entrance to New College, it's the briefest of walks to the east end of Broad Street.

The Sheldonian Theatre and the Bodleian Library

The east end of Broad Street abuts some of Oxford's most monumental architecture, beginning with the **Sheldonian Theatre** (Mon–Sat 10am–12.30pm

& 2–4.30pm; winter closes 3.30pm; £1.50), ringed by a series of glum-looking, pop-eyed classical heads. The Sheldonian was Christopher Wren's first major work, a reworking of the Theatre of Marcellus in Rome, semi-circular at the back and rectangular at the front. It was conceived in 1663, when the 31-year-old Wren's main job was as professor of astronomy. Designed as a stage for university ceremonies, nowadays it also functions as a concert hall, but the interior lacks any sense of drama, and even the views from the cupola are disappointing.

Wren's colleague, Nicholas Hawksmoor, designed the **Clarendon Building**, a domineering, solidly symmetrical edifice topped by allegorical figures that is set at right angles to – and lies immediately east of – the Sheldonian. The Clarendon was erected to house the University Press, but is now part of the **Bodleian Library** – the UK's largest after the British Library in London – which has an estimated eighty miles of shelves distributed among various buildings. The heart of the Bodleian is located straight across from the Clarendon in the **Old Library**, which inhabits the beautifully proportioned **Old Schools Quadrangle**, built in the early seventeenth century in the ornate Jacobean-Gothic style that distinguishes many of the city's finest buildings. On the quad's east side is the handsome **Tower of the Five Orders**, which gives a lesson in architectural design, with tiers of columns built according to the five classical styles – Tuscan, Doric, Ionic, Corinthian and Composite. On the west side is the library's main entrance and, although most of the complex is out of bounds to the general public, you can pop into the **Divinity School** (Mon–Fri 9am–4.45pm, Sat 9am–12.30pm; free), one large room where, until the nineteenth century, degree candidates were questioned in detail about their subject by two interlocutors, with a professor acting as umpire. Begun in 1424, and sixty years in the making, the Divinity School boasts an extravagant vaulted ceiling, a riot of pendants and decorative bosses that comprises an exquisite example of late Gothic architecture. However, this elaborate design was never carried right through – funding was a constant problem – and parts of the school were finished off in a much plainer style with the change being especially pronounced on the south wall.

You can also sign up for an hour-long **guided tour** (mid-March to Oct Mon–Fri 10.30am, 1.30pm, 2pm & 3pm, Sat 10.30am & 11.30am; Nov to mid-March Mon–Fri 2pm & 3pm; £4) of **Convocation House**, adjacent to the Divinity School, and **Duke Humfrey's Library**, immediately above. The former is a sombre wood-panelled chamber graced by a fancy fan-vaulted ceiling, completed in 1759 but designed to look much older. The latter is distinguished by its painted beams and carved corbels, dating from the fifteenth century, but restored and remodelled by Thomas Bodley at the turn of the seventeenth century.

The Radcliffe Camera

Behind the Old Schools Quadrangle rises Oxford's most imposing – or vainglorious – building, the Bodleian's **Radcliffe Camera** (formerly the Radcliffe Library; no public access), a mighty rotunda, built between 1737 and 1748 by James Gibbs, architect of London's St Martin-in-the-Fields church. There's no false modesty here. Dr John Radcliffe was, according to a contemporary diarist, "very ambitious of glory" and when he died in 1714 he bequeathed a mountain of money for the construction of a library – the "Radcliffe Mausoleum" as one wag termed it. Gibbs was one of the few British architects of the period to have been trained in Rome and his rotunda was thoroughly Italian in style, its limestone columns ascending to a delicate balustrade, decorated with

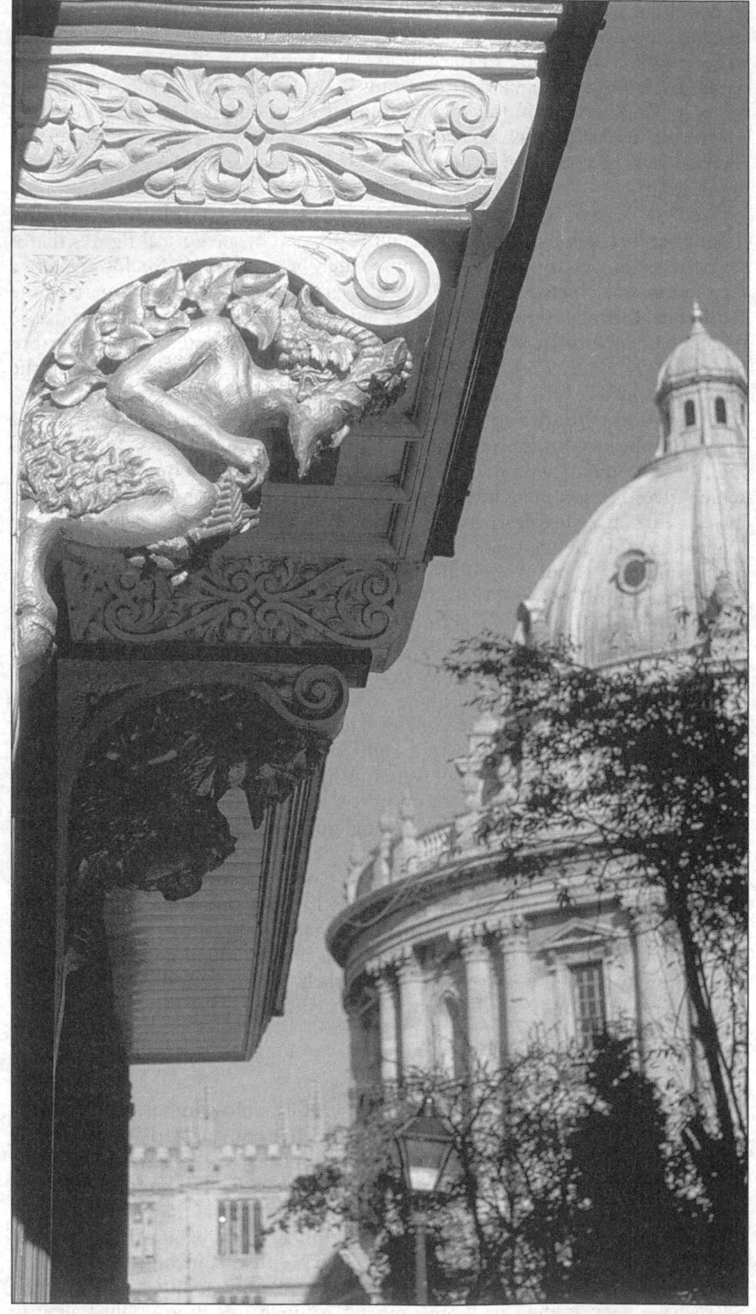

△ Radcliffe Camera, Oxford

pin-prick urns and encircling a lead-sheathed dome. For a less overpowering perspective, climb the tower of the church of St Mary the Virgin (see p.345) to the rear of the rotunda – from where there's also a charming view of All Souls College (see p.345).

Trinity, Balliol and Exeter colleges

Back on Broad Street, the classical heads that shield the Sheldonian continue along the front of the modest **History of Science Museum** (Tues–Sat noon–4pm, Sun 2–5pm; free), where microscopes and early calculators are immaculately displayed alongside Islamic and European astrolabes. Across and along the street, **Trinity College** (Mon–Sat 10.30am–noon & 2–4pm, Sun 2–4pm; £1; ⓣ01865/279900) is fronted by a pair of dinky lodge cottages. Behind them the manicured lawn of the Front Quad stretches back to the cosy **Durham Quad**, an attractive ensemble of old stone buildings begun at the end of the seventeenth century. Separating the two quads is the college's architectural pride and joy, its dark but richly decorated **Chapel**, awash with Baroque stucco work, the high altar flanked by an exquisite example of the work of Grinling Gibbons – a distinctive performance, with cherubs' heads peering out from delicate foliage. Recent alumni include Richard Burton, Terence Rattigan and the Labour Party politician, Anthony Crosland.

Next door, **Balliol College** (daily 2–5pm; £1; ⓣ01865/277777) is Trinity's arch rival, the collegiate antipathy ritualized in the tradition of Gordouli, when Balliol students chant abuse at their adversaries across the wall, usually at unsociable hours of the night. It's historically appropriate: the Balliol family of Scotland founded Balliol in the 1260s as a penance after one of the family insulted the Bishop of Durham – and the Durham bishops had associations with Trinity. Nevertheless, despite its antiquity, Balliol has little to offer: remodelled and rebuilt in the nineteenth century, it now presents an unexceptional assembly of buildings, haphazardly gathered around two quads. Amongst many notable alumni are Adam Smith, Hilaire Belloc, Graham Greene and Aldous Huxley, plus a raft of politicians, including Harold Macmillan, Edward Heath, Denis Healey and Roy Jenkins.

From the south side of Broad Street, take Turl Street and you'll soon reach – on the left – the entrance to **Exeter College** (daily: term time 2–5pm; otherwise 10am–5pm; free; ⓣ01865/279600), another medieval foundation whose original buildings were chopped about in the nineteenth century. On this occasion, however, the Victorians did create something of interest in the elaborate, neo-Gothic **Chapel**, whose intricate, almost fussy detail was conceived by Sir Gilbert Scott in the 1850s. The chapel contains a fine set of stained glass windows illustrating scores of Biblical stories – St Paul on the Road to Damascus and Samson bringing down the pillars of the Philistine temple for example – but their deep colours put the nave in permanent shade. The chapel also holds a superb Pre-Raphaelite tapestry, the *Adoration of the Magi*, a fine collaboration between William Morris and Edward Burne-Jones. Morris and Burne-Jones were both students here, as were J.R.R. Tolkien, Alan Bennett and Imogen Stubbs.

Near the west end of Broad Street, the **Oxford Story** (Jan–June & Sept-Dec Mon–Sat 10am–4.30pm, Sun 11am–4.30pm; July & Aug daily 9.30am–5pm; £6.75) is a purpose-built tourist attraction devoted to the history of the city and its university. It begins with an audio-visual display on university life and thereafter you hop on a "time-car", which moves through a series of historical dioramas.

Cornmarket and the Oxford Union

Broad Street leads into the **Cornmarket**, a busy shopping strip lined by major stores. There's precious little here to fire the imagination, but **St Michael's Street** – the first turning on the right – is a pleasant residential street and the location of the **Oxford Union** (no public access), which occupies an inconsequential Victorian pile that belies its political importance. The Union is home to the university debating society, where scores of budding British politicians have flexed their oratorical muscles. The Union has also hosted a mixed bag of internationally famous celebrity speakers, among them Yasser Arafat, Archbishop Desmond Tutu, Ronald Reagan, Mother Theresa and Diego Maradona. The original debating hall, shaped rather like an upturned boat and now the union library, is decorated with Pre-Raphaelite murals illustrating the Arthurian legend, created (but never completed) in the 1850s by William Morris, Rossetti, Burne-Jones and a few like-minded friends.

The Ashmolean

The **Ashmolean** (Tues–Sat 10am–5pm, Sun 2–5pm, plus late opening one evening a week in summer; free) is the university's principal museum and it occupies a mammoth Neoclassical building on the corner of Beaumont Street and St Giles. The museum grew up around the collections of the magpie-like **John Tradescant**, gardener to Charles I and an energetic traveller. During his wanderings, Tradescant built up a huge assortment of artefacts and natural specimens, which became known as Tradescant's Ark. He bequeathed all this to his friend and sponsor, the lawyer Elias Ashmole, who in turn gave it to the university. Tradescant's Ark has been added to ever since – though parts were hived off to the Pitt-Rivers Museum (see p.351) years ago – and today the Ashmolean is far too large to absorb in one visit, so either allow for several or stick to the highlights. Plans are available at reception and the museum shop sells a useful introductory guide.

Beginning on the ground floor, the **Egyptian** rooms should not be missed: in addition to well-preserved mummies and sarcophagi, there are unusual frescoes, rare textiles from the Roman and Byzantine periods and several fine examples of relief carving, such as on the shrine of Taharqa. Nearby, the **Islamic Art** room includes superb Islamic ceramics, while the six **Chinese Art** rooms contain some remarkable early Chinese pottery with the simple monochrome pots of the Sung dynasty (960–1279) looking surprisingly modern.

On the first floor, a selection from Tradescant's Ark is gathered together in **Room 27**. Amongst the assorted curiosities, a particular highlight is Powhatan's mantle, a handsome garment made of deerskin and decorated with shells. Powhatan was the father of Pocahontas, and this mantle therefore dates back to the earliest contacts between English colonists and the Native Americans of modern-day Virginia. In this room also are Guy Fawkes' lantern, Oliver Cromwell's death mask and the peculiar armour-plated hat that Bradshaw, the president of the board of regicides, thought it prudent to wear when he condemned Charles I to death.

Moving on, the archeologist Arthur Evans had close ties with the museum and he gifted it a stunning collection of Minoan finds from his years working at Knossos in Crete (1900–06). These artefacts are displayed in the **Ancient Crete & Aegean Room** and pride of place goes to the storage jars, sumptuously decorated with sea creatures and marine plants. Close by, in **Room 35**, is the extraordinary Alfred Jewel, a tiny gold, enamel and rock crystal piece of uncertain purpose. The inscription reads "Alfred ordered me to be made" – almost certainly a reference to King Alfred the Great. Most of the rest of the first floor is devoted to European painting from the Italian Renaissance to the early twentieth century with a series of clearly labelled galleries arranged in roughly chronological order. Amongst the **Italian** works, look out for Piero di Cosimo's *Forest Fire* and Paolo Uccello's *Hunt in the Forest*, though Tintoretto, Veronese and Bellini are all well represented too. There's also a strong showing of **French paintings**, with Pissarro, Monet, Manet and Renoir featuring alongside Cézanne and Bonnard.

Up on the second floor, one room each is devoted to eighteenth- and nineteenth-century **British art**: Samuel Palmer's visionary paintings run rings around the rest, though there are lashings of Pre-Raphaelite stuff from Rossetti and Holman Hunt to assorted cohorts.

St John's College and University and Pitt-Rivers museums

Across St Giles from the Ashmolean, the sturdy stone walls of **St John's College** (daily 1–5pm; ⓣ01865/277300; free) shield four immaculate quads. The first – the Front Quad – is the oldest, but the second – the **Canterbury Quad** – is the most enjoyable, decorated with Baroque gargoyles and dainty statues of Charles I and his wife, Henrietta Maria.

Back outside, it's a brief walk up St Giles to the *Lamb & Flag* pub, beside which an alley cuts through to the **University Museum of Natural History** (daily noon–5pm; free), opposite the mottled brick facade of Keble College on Parks Road. The building, constructed under the guidance of John Ruskin, looks like a cross between a railway station and a church – and the same applies inside, where a high Victorian–Gothic fusion of cast iron and glass features soaring columns and capitals decorated with animal and plant motifs. Exhibits include a working beehive and some impressive fossil dinosaurs, though the museum's natural history displays are outdone by the **Pitt-Rivers Museum** (Mon–Sat noon–4.30pm, Sun 2–4.30pm; free), reached through a door at the far end. Founded in 1884 from the bequest of grenadier guard turned archeologist Augustus Henry Lane Fox Pitt-Rivers, this is one of the world's finest ethnographic museums and an extraordinary relic of the Victorian Age, arranged like an exotic junk shop with each bulging cabinet labelled meticulously by hand. The exhibits, brought to England by several explorers, Captain Cook among them, range from totem poles and mummified crocodiles to African fetishes and gruesome shrunken heads from Ecuador.

Eating and drinking

With so many students and tourists to cater for, Oxford has developed a wide choice of places to eat and drink. For a midday bite, the numerous **sandwich bars** are ideal – some of the best are listed below and you'll find several others in the **Covered Market**, between the High Street and Cornmarket, an Oxford institution as essential to local shoppers as the Bodleian is to academics. There's also a sprinkling of first-rate (and pricey) **restaurants**, but the majority cater for the less expensive end of the market with varying degrees of success – again some of the better options are listed below. Reasonable food is served at most **pubs**, but those listed have been singled out for their ambience or selection of beers rather than for their menus.

Snacks and cafés

Beat Café Little Clarendon St. Hippified café with fancy decor and stained-glass windows. Good, inexpensive sandwiches, salads and smoothies.

Café Coco 23 Cowley Rd. Café-brasserie offering a wide selection of aperitifs, delicious coffee and reasonably priced food with a Mediterranean slant. Lively atmosphere too.

Felson's 32 Little Clarendon St. Another hot contender for Oxford's best sandwich bar, this tiny, friendly place has a huge range of fillings for its baguettes and rolls.

George & Davies Little Clarendon St. An established ice-cream parlour that stays open well after the pubs and cinemas. The cow mural is good fun too.

Heroes 8 Ship St. Sandwich bar with some of the best (and most adventurous) fillings in town.

News Café 1 Ship St. Breakfasts, bagels and daily specials offered here, plus beers and wines and, as the name suggests, newspapers and TVs tuned to news broadcasts.

Nosebag 6 St Michael's St. A civilized but unassuming place, with chintzy decor and classical background music. The hot and cold food attracts queues at lunchtime; not so in the evening, when it is a good place for a quick but wholesome meal. Good selection of veggie food.

St Giles' Café 52 St Giles. Oxford's favourite greasy spoon. The huge fry-ups and strong coffee pull an interesting mix of people, from poets to punks.

Vaults & Garden Radcliffe Square. Attached to the church of St Mary the Virgin, this inexpensive café occupies an atmospheric stone-vaulted room and serves up good-quality coffee and cake and quiche-and-salad lunches. There's a small outside area, but it's a little glum. Daily 10am–6pm.

Restaurants

Aziz 228–230 Cowley Rd ⓣ01865/794945. Spacious and brightly decorated Bangladeshi restaurant, with bamboo furniture and rugs. The food's delicious, and they do an exceptional range of vegetarian dishes. Reservations recommended at weekends. Inexpensive.

Bangkok House 42a Hythe Bridge St ⓣ01865/200705. Best Oriental restaurant in town, with superb Thai food and excellent service. The mixed starter and the coconut-milk curries are particularly good. Moderate.

Cherwell Boathouse Bardwell Rd, off Banbury Rd ⓣ01865/552746. The decor is a tad too traditional for some tastes, but there's no doubting the quality of the food at this deservedly popular riverside spot about a mile north of town. The menu features local ingredients and the wine cellar is first rate. Reservations advisable in summer. Moderate.

Freud Walton St ⓣ01865/311171. Occupying a grand building in the style of a Roman temple, this fashionable café-bar serves Italian food with a twist. Located about five minutes' walk north of Worcester College, opposite Great Clarendon St. Open Mon & Tues 11am–midnight, Wed–Sat 11am–2am, Sun 11am–10.30pm.

Gee's Restaurant 61 Banbury Rd ⓣ01865/553540. Chic conservatory setting, but not as expensive as it looks. The inventive menu includes such items as chargrilled vegetables with polenta, roasted beetroot, a variety of steaks and a wide choice of breads. Strong on fish, too, with seafood main courses for around £15. Open daily for lunch and dinner plus brunch at weekends. Moderate.

Le Petit Blanc 71–72 Walton St ⓣ01865/510999. Renowned French chef Raymond Blanc's affordable, and much praised, alternative to his famous *Manoir aux Quat' Saisons* in Great Milton, some seven miles east of Oxford (ⓣ01844/278881). The food is a refreshing mix of French gourmet (corn-fed quail with lime leaf and ginger) and traditional English (pan-fried Gloucester old spot pork). If you want to splash out, this is the place to do it; main courses are a very reasonable £15–18.

Quod 92 High St ⓣ01865/202505. Part of the *Old Bank Hotel*, this slick restaurant-cum-bar, all angular furnishings and fittings, serves a good line in Italian food – from pizzas and pastas through to chargrilled meats and seafood. A popular spot with moderate prices.

Pubs

Eagle & Child 49 St Giles. Known variously as the "Bird & Baby", "Bird & Brat" or "Bird & Bastard", this pub was once the haunt of J.R.R. Tolkien and C.S. Lewis, and still attracts a comparatively genteel mix of professionals and academics.

Isis By Iffley Lock. Agreeable pub in a lovely setting, amid the flood meadows just under two miles southeast of Folly Bridge at the west edge of Iffley village. The best way to get there is along the Thames Path, which runs along the river from Folly Bridge.

King's Arms 40 Holywell St. Prone to student overkill on term-time weekends, but otherwise very pleasant, with snug rooms at the back and a reasonably good choice of beers.

Lamb & Flag St Giles. Generations of university students have hung out in this old pub, which comes complete with low-beamed ceilings and a series of cramped but cosy rooms. Good range of ales.

Turf Tavern Bath Place, off Holywell St. Small, extraordinarily atmospheric seventeenth-century pub with a fine range of beers, and mulled wine in winter. Abundant seating outside.

White Horse 52 Broad St. A tiny, old pub with snug rooms, pictures of old university sports teams on the walls and real ales. It was used as a set for the *Inspector Morse* TV series.

Entertainment and nightlife

Having spawned both Supergrass and Radiohead, you'd think Oxford would be hot on popular music, but the star quality of its local heroes is not reflected in either the **live-music** or **club scene** which, aside from a couple of noteworthy venues, is comparatively lame. Part of the reason for this is that the city's students tend to fall back on college music dos, an option closed to the rest. By comparison, devotees of **classical music** are well catered for, with the city's main concert halls and certain college chapels – primarily Christ Church, Merton and New College – offering a wide-ranging programme of concerts and recitals. As regards **theatre**, student productions dominate the city repertoire, but the quality of acting varies, particularly when they tackle Shakespeare, the favourite for the open-air college productions put on for tourists during the summer.

For jazz, classical music and theatre **listings**, consult either *This Month in Oxford* or *In Oxford*, both free and available at the tourist office. The daily *Oxford Mail* newspaper and the weekly *Oxford Times* also both carry information on up-coming gigs and events. For more adventurous stuff – special club nights etc – watch out for wall-posted flyers.

Live music and clubs

Old Fire Station (OFS) 40 George St. Multi-purpose venue with musicals and theatre (box office ⓣ01865/297170), plus a separate café-bar featuring one-off DJ club nights.

Park End Club Cantay House, 37 Park End St ⓣ01865/250181. A slick outfit, currently the most popular mainstream club in Oxford, with heavies on the door and a cattle-market atmosphere at weekends.

Zodiac 190 Cowley Rd ⓣ01865/420042, ⓦwww.thezodiac.co.uk. Far and away Oxford's most respected indie and dance venue, with a fast-moving programme of live bands and guest DJs.

Classical music and theatre

Holywell Music Room 32 Holywell St. This small, plain, Georgian building was opened in 1748 as the first public music hall in England. It offers a varied programme, from straight classical to experimental, with occasional bouts of jazz. Programme details are posted outside and are available at the Oxford Playhouse (see below), which also sells its tickets.

New Theatre George St ⓣ0870/606 3500. Popular – and populist – programme of theatre, dance, pop music, musicals and opera. Formerly the Apollo.

Oxford Playhouse Beaumont St ⓣ01865/305305, ⓦwww.oxfordplayhouse.com. Professional touring companies perform a mixture of plays, opera and concerts at what is generally regarded as the city's best theatre.

Pegasus Theatre Magdalen Rd ⓣ01865/722851, ⓦwww.pegasustheatre.org.uk. Low-budget, avant-garde productions dominate the programme of this east Oxford theatre.

Sheldonian Theatre Broad St ⓣ01865/277299. Some have criticized the acoustics here, but this is still Oxford's top concert hall and its resident symphony orchestra is the Oxford Philomusica (ⓣ01865/798600, ⓦwww.oxfordphil.com).

Listings

Banks and exchanges All the major banks have branches on or near Cornmarket.

Bike rental Bikezone, 6 Lincoln House, Market St, off Cornmarket ⓣ01865/728877.

Bookshops The leading university bookshop is Blackwells. They have several outlets including three shops a stone's throw from each other on Broad St: Blackwells Music, Blackwells Art & Posters and the main bookshop, at 50 Broad St (ⓣ01865/792792).

Buses Most local buses, including Park-and-Ride, are operated by the Oxford Bus Company (ⓣ01865/785400), which also – amongst several companies – offers fast and frequent services to London and Gatwick and Heathrow airports. Most other long-distance services are in the hands of National Express (ⓣ08705/808080).

Car rental Avis ⓣ01865/249000; National ⓣ01865/240471.

Cinema The Odeon cinemas on Magdalen and

George streets (both ⓣ0870/505 0007) show the latest blockbusters, while the best arts cinema is the Ultimate Picture Palace (UPP) on Jeune St, off Cowley Rd (ⓣ01865/245288, ⓦwww.ultimatepicturepalace.com). The Phoenix Picture House, 57 Walton St (ⓣ01865/554909, ⓦwww.picturehouses.co.uk), shows mainstream and arts films, and regularly screens foreign-language films too.

Internet & email Mices, Gloucester Green and 118 High St (both Mon–Sat 9am–11pm, Sun 10am–11pm).

Pharmacies Boots, 6 Cornmarket (Mon–Sat 9am–6pm, Sun 11am–5pm; ⓣ01865/247461).

Police St Aldates ⓣ01865/266000.

Post office At the top of St Aldates, near the corner with High St.

Taxis Ranks are liberally distributed across the city centre, including at the train station and on the High St and St Giles. Alternatively, call City Taxis ⓣ01865/201201.

Around Oxford

As a base for exploring some of the more delightful parts of central England, Oxford is hard to beat. It's a short drive west to the Cotswolds (see pp.369–387) and near at hand also are the Vale of White Horse (see p.334) and the Chiltern Hills (see pp.329–334). If, on the other hand, you're using public transport, the options are much more limited, the best choice being the short and easy bus ride north to the charming little town of **Woodstock** and its imperious neighbour, **Blenheim Palace**.

Woodstock

WOODSTOCK, eight miles north of Oxford, has royal associations going back to Saxon times, with a string of kings attracted by its excellent hunting. Henry I built a royal lodge here and his successor, Henry II, enlarged it to create a grand manor house-cum-palace, where, incidentally, the Black Prince was born in 1330. The Royalists used Woodstock as a base during the Civil War, but, after their defeat, Cromwell never got round to destroying either the town or the palace; the latter was ultimately given to (and flattened by) the Duke of Marlborough, in 1704. Long dependent on royal and then ducal patronage, Woodstock is now both a well-heeled commuter town for Oxford and a provider of food, drink and beds for visitors to Blenheim. It is also an extremely pretty little place, its handsome stone buildings gathered around the main square, at the junction of Market and High streets. It is here that you'll find the town's one specific sight, the **Oxfordshire Museum** (Tues–Sat 10am–5pm, Sun 2–5pm; £2.50), a well-composed review of the archeology, social history and industry of the county.

The museum shares its premises with the town's **tourist office** (March–Oct Mon–Sat 9.30am–5.30pm, Sun 1–5pm; Nov–Feb Mon–Sat 10am–5pm; ⓣ01993/813276, ⓦwww.oxfordshirecotswolds.org), which has a useful range of information on the nearby Cotswolds. Woodstock has several good **pubs**, the best being the *Bear*, a delightful old coaching inn across from the museum with low-beamed ceilings and antique furnishings; it offers a varied menu and serves a good range of beers. **Buses** from Oxford run every thirty minutes or so (reduced service on Sun), with some continuing on to Stratford-upon-Avon.

Blenheim Palace

Nowadays, successful British commanders get medals and titles, but in 1704, as a thank-you for his victory over the French at the battle of Blenheim, Queen Anne gave **John Churchill**, **Duke of Marlborough** (1650–1722), the royal estate of Woodstock, along with the promise of enough cash to build himself a gargantuan palace. Marlborough was an exceptionally brilliant general –

undoubtedly, one of Britain's all-time military greats – and this was but one of his victories. Nonetheless, the largesse shown him had more to do with the queen's fear of Louis XIV – and the relief she felt after the battle – than it did to a recognition of his genius, as events were to prove.

Work started promptly on **Blenheim Palace** (mid-March to Oct daily 10.30am–4.45pm; £10.50 including park & gardens) with the principal architect being Sir John Vanbrugh, who was also responsible for Castle Howard in Yorkshire (see p.993). All seemed set fair, but things went downhill fast. The duke's formidable wife, Sarah Jennings, who had wanted Christopher Wren as architect, was soon at loggerheads with Vanbrugh, while Queen Anne had second thoughts, stifling the flow of money. Construction work was halted and the house was only finished after the duke's death at the instigation of his widow, who ended up paying most of the bills and designing much of the interior herself. The end result is the country's grandest example of Baroque civic architecture, an Italianate palace that is more a monument than a house – just as Vanbrugh intended.

The **interior** is stuffed with paintings and tapestries, plus all manner of objets d'art, including furniture from Versailles, and stone and marble carvings by Grinling Gibbons. The ceiling of the Great Hall sports painted allegories celebrating Marlborough's martial skills and the Dining Saloon holds murals by Louis Laguerre, but frankly it's hard to warm to all this conspicuous consumption. Horace Walpole, the eighteenth-century wit and social commentator, had it about right when he wrote that Blenheim resembled "the palace of an auctioneer who had been chosen King of Poland". As for the Marlboroughs, John Churchill was one of the few members of the clan to have made anything but a poor impression, the spectacular exception being **Sir Winston Churchill**, born here in 1874. Several rooms are dedicated to the wartime prime minister, who is buried with his wife in the graveyard of **Bladon Church**, visible from the palace.

Formal **gardens** (same times; £3.50 gardens only) flank the house, but the open **parkland** (daily 9am–4.45pm; £2.50 pedestrians, £7.50 for cars, including passengers) is more enticing, especially just north of the house, where the ground falls away dramatically to an exquisite artificial lake, Queen Pool. It's said that Capability Brown, who landscaped the grounds, laid out the trees and avenues to represent the battle of Blenheim. Whatever the truth of the tale, fine vistas fan out in every direction, including one from Vanbrugh's Grand Bridge, over the main lake, up to the **Column of Victory**, erected by Sarah Jennings and topped by a statue of her husband posing heroically in a toga.

There are two entrances to Blenheim, one just south of Woodstock on the Oxford road and another through the Triumphal Arch at the end of Park Street in Woodstock itself.

North Buckinghamshire and Bedfordshire

The untidy landscapes of **north Buckinghamshire** and **Bedfordshire** herald a transition between the satellite towns of London and the Midlands. Since the war, the character of the region has been transformed by the attempt to solve London's overcrowding. Sprawling suburbs now festoon many of the small country towns of yesteryear and, in the 1960s, Milton Keynes swallowed thirteen existing villages to become the country's largest new town. Nonetheless, there are several interesting targets. North Buckinghamshire weighs in with three National Trust properties – two country houses and, pick of the bunch, **Stowe Gardens**, dotted with a remarkable assortment of outdoor sculptures and follies. Over in Bedfordshire, the county's most distinctive feature is the wriggling **River Ouse**, whose banks were once lined with dozens of watermills, though these were not nearly as important as the brickworks that long underpinned the local economy. For the casual visitor, the county might not warrant a major detour, but **Woburn Abbey**, a whopping country mansion, and neighbouring **Woburn Safari Park** together comprise one of the country's premier tourist attractions. In addition, **Bedford** itself deserves more than just a sideward glance, if for no other reason than for its links with John Bunyan.

As regards public transport, local **buses** link all the larger towns and there is a fast and frequent **train** service from London to Bedford and Milton Keynes.

Buckingham and around

Unassuming **BUCKINGHAM** is tucked into a sharp bend in the River Ouse about 25 miles northeast of Oxford. It became the county town of Buckinghamshire in the tenth century and flourished during medieval times, but it was bypassed by the Industrial Revolution and remained a forgotten backwater until a recent wave of incomers created the modern suburbs that surround it today. The town centre is at its prettiest along the wide, sloping Market Hill, standing in the middle of which is the **Old Gaol**, a chunky, stone structure that is home to the tourist office (see below) and a modest, local history **museum** (Mon–Sat 10am–4pm; £1.50). Otherwise, Buckingham is short on sights, though you might take a peek inside the sombre **Church of St Peter and St Paul**, which perches on the hill where the castle once stood – take Castle Street from the west end of Market Hill and you can't miss it.

There's no train service to Buckingham, but there are **bus** links from neighbouring towns, principally Milton Keynes. Buses stop on the High Street a few yards from the **tourist office** in the Old Gaol (July & Aug Mon–Sat 10am–4pm, Sun noon–4pm; rest of year closed Sun; ⓣ01280/823020). They have a small supply of **B&Bs**, which they will book on your behalf, or you can target Buckingham's best **hotel**, the *Villiers*, which occupies an imaginatively modernized old inn bang in the centre of town at 3 Castle St (ⓣ01280/822444; ❼). Most of the rooms flank the courtyard to the rear of the main building and each is decorated in smart modern style. The best spot for **food** is the *Dipalee Indian Restaurant* (ⓣ01280/813151), just along Castle Street from the hotel and with a good range of dishes; main courses average about £8.

Stowe Gardens

Just three miles northwest of Buckingham off the A422, the extensive **Stowe Landscape Gardens** (Wed–Sun: March–Oct 10am–5.30pm; Nov–Dec 10am–4pm; £5; NT) contain an extraordinary collection of outdoor sculptures, monuments and decorative buildings by some of the greatest designers and architects of the eighteenth century. They worked at the behest of the prodigiously wealthy Temple and Grenville families, and later the dukes of Buckingham and Chandos. The thirty-odd structures that comprise this ornamental miscellany are spread over a sequence of separate, carefully planned landscapes, from the lake views of the Western and Eastern gardens to the wooded delights of the Elysian Fields and the gentle folds of the Grecian Valley, Capability Brown's first large-scale design. The gardens were planned in detail, but the romantic rural idyll they represented was a fundamental break with the strictly formal garden tradition that had dominated Europe for decades. There was a political agenda too: the owners were Whigs, proudly committed to the constitutional monarchy and liberal, albeit class-based notions of political liberty, their bête-noirs being the absolutist Stuarts, whom they had helped depose in the Glorious Revolution of 1688. Several of the monuments hammer home the Whig agenda, especially **The Temple of British Worthies**, whose fourteen busts represent a selection of those leading figures of whom the family approved. As for the architecture, several buildings are of particular interest, most memorably the neo-Romanesque **Hermitage**, the eccentric **Gothic Temple**, and the beautifully composed **Palladian Bridge**, one of only three such bridges in the country.

Finally, at the heart of the gardens, the **main house**, with its whopping Neoclassical facade, is separate from the gardens, as it is used by Stowe school, which offers fairly regular guided tours (£3) – ring ⓣ01280/818282 for the schedule.

Claydon House and Waddesdon Manor

The plain Neoclassical facade of **Claydon House** (April–Oct Mon–Wed, Sat & Sun 1–5pm; £4.50; NT), five miles south of Buckingham in tiny Middle Claydon, conceals an exuberant, stunningly persuasive Rococo interior, commissioned in the middle of the eighteenth century by the second earl Verney. The intricacy of the woodcarving peaks in the Chinese rooms, probably the finest example of **chinoiserie** in Britain with the delicate ornamentation dripping like icing.

Heading south from Claydon House, a network of obscure country lanes eventually reaches the A41 at Waddesdon, on the southern edge of which is the extraordinarily flashy **Waddesdon Manor** (April–Oct Wed–Sun 11am–4pm; house £7 timed ticket, grounds £4; NT). From 1874 to 1889, minions of Baron Ferdinand de Rothschild laboured to transform this dreary slice of Buckinghamshire into a palatial country estate, with the main house built in the style of a French chateau. The end result is too pompous for many tastes, but there's no denying the magnificence of the contents. The interior holds a vast collection of French eighteenth-century decorative arts including Savonnerie carpets, some of the finest examples of Sèvres porcelain in England, Beauvais tapestries and furniture once owned by the French royal family. There are also paintings by early Dutch and Flemish masters and portraits by major English artists including Gainsborough and Reynolds. The extravagance is overwhelming – even the cast-iron aviary in the **grounds** (March–Dec Wed–Sun 10am–5pm) is a work of art.

Bletchley Park

Nowadays, **Bletchley Park** (Feb–Dec Mon–Fri 12.30–6pm, last admission 2.30pm, Sat & Sun 10.30am–5pm, last admission 3.30pm; £8; ⓣ01908/640404, ⓦwww.bletchleypark.org.uk) is marooned on the edge of new town **Milton Keynes** thirteen miles east of Buckingham via the A421 and the B4034, but in World War II it was "**Station X**", the home of Britain's leading code breakers. It was here that the British built the first program computer – Colossus – and it was here that they famously broke the German "enigma" code, the enigma machine being the main encoder for all communications within Hitler's armed forces. Much of Station X has survived, its scattering of missen huts spread over a leafy parcel of land that surrounds the original Victorian mansion. Inside are a variety of displays explaining and exploring the workings of Station X as well as the stolen enigma machine that was crucial in deciphering the German code. At the **weekend** visitors can explore Station X under their own steam, but it's better to join one of the informative and frequent, ninety-minute **guided tours**, especially as there is no extra charge. On **weekdays** visitors are not permitted to wander around on their own and have to join a guided tour (Mon–Fri 2pm; 2hr 30min) – though again there's no extra fee. Advance bookings are not essential, but are a good idea.

Woburn and Woburn Abbey and Safari Park

About sixteen miles east of Buckingham, on the peripheries of Milton Keynes, the little village of **WOBURN** makes a healthy living from its location beside Woburn Abbey and Safari Park. Little more than one main street lined with some sterling Georgian buildings, the village's most interesting feature is **St Mary's Church**, whose cumbersome stonework is guarded by a couple of peculiar – and peculiarly large – gargoyles, one of which looks like a prototype Tolkien hobgoblin. The interior is less distinctive but certainly impressive, refitted in fancy Gothic style by the Duke of Bedford in the 1860s and supplemented with an elaborate reredos a few years later. Woburn has several good **restaurants**, where you can prime up for – or unwind after – an excursion into the Abbey and the Safari Park. Amongst several options, the *Nicholls Brasserie* (Ⓣ01525/290896) is a chic establishment with an imaginative menu that ranges from guinea fowl to fish cakes, with main courses averaging £12. Alternatively, try the *Black Horse*, which sells top-notch pub food.

Woburn Abbey and Safari Park

The grandiloquent Georgian facade of **Woburn Abbey** (April–Sept Mon–Sat 11am–4pm, Sun 11am–5pm; Oct & Jan–March Sat & Sun 11am–4pm; £8.50) overlooks a huge area of parkland just to the east of the eponymous village. Called an "abbey" since it was built on the site of a Cistercian foundation, the house is the ancestral pile of the dukes of Bedford, whom Queen Victoria once dismissed as a dull lot. Judging from the family's penchant for canine portraits, she may have had a point, but the lavish state rooms also contain some fine paintings, including an exquisite set of **Tudor portraits** hanging in the Long Gallery, most notably the famous *Armada Portrait* of Elizabeth I by George Gower. Elsewhere are works by Van Dyck, Velázquez, Gainsborough and Rembrandt, whilst Reynolds and Canaletto each have a room to themselves. The surrounding parkland, with its rolling hills and trees, was landscaped by Humphry Repton and supports nine species of deer.

Another part of the duke's enormous estate is given over to **Woburn Safari Park** (mid-March to Oct daily 10am–5pm or dusk; Nov to mid March Sat & Sun 10am–5pm or dusk; £13; Ⓦwww.woburnsafari.co.uk), the largest drive-through wildlife reserve in Britain – which means that you have to have your own car to enter. The animals include endangered species such as the African white rhino and bongo antelope, and appear to be in excellent health. A posse of guards tours about looking for drivers in distress, but the main danger is an overheated engine rather than an attack by an enraged animal – the Safari Park is extraordinarily popular and in high season the traffic can achieve rush-hour congestion, so turn up as early as possible for a quieter experience.

Bedford

BEDFORD, some fourteen miles northeast of Woburn, has struggled to retain a modicum of character in the face of redevelopment, but the end result is pleasant enough, the town's neat and tidy centre hugging the north bank of the River Ouse. Bedford also makes the most of its connections with **John Bunyan** (1628–88), a blaspheming tinker turned Nonconformist preacher, who lived most of his life in and around the town. Bunyan fought for Parliament in the Civil War and became a well-known public speaker during Cromwell's Protectorate, but the Restoration proved disastrous for him. In 1660, he was arrested for breaking Charles II's new religious legislation, which restricted the activities of Nonconformist preachers, and he spent most of the next seventeen years in Bedford prison. During his incarceration, he wrote *The Pilgrim's Progress*, a seminal text whose simple language and powerful allegories were to have a profound influence on generations of Nonconformists – and it was they who championed a raft of progressive causes, most notably the campaign for the abolition of slavery.

Built in 1850 on the spot where Bunyan founded his first Independent Congregation, the **Bunyan Meeting Free Church** (Tues–Sat 10am–4pm), just east of the High Street on Mill Street, is still a Nonconformist church. It bears several memorials to Bunyan, beginning with the splendid bronze doors, decorated with ten finely worked panels depicting scenes from *Pilgrim's Progress*. Inside, the stained-glass windows develop the theme, again depicting scenes from the book, plus one showing Bunyan scribbling away in prison. Next door, the homely **Bunyan Museum** (March–Nov Tues–Sat 11am–4pm; free) features extracts from his book and tracks through the author's life and times – including his notably insignificant military exploits. Bunyan spent the war on garrison duty at nearby Newport Pagnell, where he never saw a shot fired in anger, though he did suffer the indignities of being poorly supplied – at one point, the garrison only had one pair of breeches for every two men.

Bedford's other noteworthy attraction is the **Cecil Higgins Art Gallery**, just to the south of Mill Street on Castle Lane (Tues–Sat 11am–5pm & Sun 2–5pm; £2.20, free on Fri). The gallery holds strong collections of ceramics, glass and local lace as well as a competent range of watercolours and prints, though these are not always on display due to their sensitivity to light. There are also several period rooms, done out in high Victorian style, and it's here you'll find the eccentric **Burges Room**, a colourful fantasy of ersatz classical and medieval decoration created by William Burges (1827–81), one of the leading figures in the Gothic Revival movement. Burges's main interest was French Gothic, but he was a playful soul – witness the bookcase painted with the signs of the zodiac in a vaguely Assyrian manner and the wardrobe featuring Adam trying on different clothes after his ejection from the Garden of Eden. The gallery's admission charge covers the adjacent **Bedford Museum** (same hours), a ponderous trawl through the city's history.

Practicalities

Bedford is on the London St Pancras–Sheffield rail line with **trains** arriving at Midland Station, from where it's a ten-minute walk east to the centre – just follow the signs. The **bus station** is on All Hallows and from here it's a couple of minutes' walk east to the short High Street, which runs north–south and spans the River Ouse. The **tourist office** (Mon–Sat 9.30am–5pm; ⓣ01234/215226, ⓦwww.bedford.gov.uk/tourism) is in the old Town Hall, just off the High Street on St Paul's Square.

The town's best **hotel** is *The Swan* (ⓣ01234/346565, ⓦwww.bedfordswanhotel.co.uk; ❼), whose Georgian stonework conceals a lavish and tastefully modernized interior; it's down by the river on The Embankment at the foot of the High Street. As a second choice, the *Embankment Hotel* (ⓣ01234/261332, ⓦwww.embankmenthotelbedford.co.uk; ❸), just along the river from the Swan, has twenty comfortable en-suite rooms behind an extravagant mock-Tudor facade; it shares its premises with a real ale pub. Alternatively, the tourist office has a small cachet of **B&Bs**.

Bedford's large Italian community adds a bit of zip to the local **restaurant** scene. Pick of the bunch, serving the tastiest pizzas and pastas in town, is *Pizzeria Santaniello*, 9 Newnham St, immediately to the east of Mill Street's Bunyan Meeting Free Church. Further down Newnham Street, at no. 36, *Bar Cappuccino* chips in with authentic coffee, ice cream, pizzas and snacks. In between the two, *The Castle* has bar food and real ales, and occupies ancient (but heavily modernized) premises.

St Albans and around

ST ALBANS is one of the most appealing towns on the peripheries of London, its well-blended medley of medieval and modern features grafted onto the site of Verulamium, the town founded by the Romans soon after their successful invasion of 43 AD. Boudicca and her followers burned this settlement to the ground eighteen years later, but reconstruction was swift and the town grew into a major administrative base. It was here, in 209 AD, that a Roman soldier by the name of Alban became the country's first Christian martyr, when he was beheaded for giving shelter to a priest. Pilgrims later flocked to the town that had come to bear his name, with the place of execution marked by a hilltop cathedral that was once one of the largest churches in the Christian world.

Not just a religious centre, St Albans also flourished as a trading town and a staging post on the route to London from the north, its economy further buttressed by two local industries, brewing and straw-hat-making. In the nineteenth century, the coaching trade faded away with the coming of the railways, but when St Albans was connected to London by train in 1868, it rapidly reinvented itself as a prosperous and pleasant commuter town, a description that fits well today.

St Albans' best-known attraction is its **cathedral**, but the town also possesses the outstanding **Verulamium Museum**, home to several breathtaking Roman mosaics, as well as a likeable riverside park and a number of charming old streets. All the town's main sights are within easy walking distance of each other, making St Albans an ideal day out, but if you do decide to stay the night be sure to try out some of the excellent pubs.

The City

One good way to start a tour of the city is by climbing to the top of the fifteenth-century **Clocktower**, plumb in the centre of town where the High Street and Market Place meet (Easter–Oct Sat & Sun 10.30am–5pm; 30p). The climb is a tight squeeze, but worth it for the view over the **Cathedral** (daily 8am–5.45pm; donation requested), a vast brick and flint edifice immediately to the south – and reached down a narrow passageway across from the foot of the tower. An abbey was constructed here in 1077, on the site of a Saxon abbey founded by King Offa of Mercia, and despite subsequent alterations – including the ugly nineteenth-century west front – the legacy of the Normans remains the most impressive aspect. The sheer scale of their design is breathtaking: the **nave**, almost 300-feet long, is the longest medieval nave in Britain, even if it isn't the most harmonious – the massive Norman **pillars** on the north side stand out from those in the later Early English style opposite. Some of the Norman pillars retain thirteenth- and fourteenth-century paintings, the detail clear though the ochre colours are much faded. Two- and three-tone geometric designs decorate the Norman **arches** in the nave and at the central crossing, where the impact of the original design reaches its peak with the mighty Norman tower.

Behind the high altar an elaborate stone **reredos** (a clumsy construction compared with the splendid Gothic rood screen) hides the fourteenth-century **shrine** of St Alban. The tomb was smashed up during the Dissolution, but the Victorians discovered the pieces and gamely put them all together again. Some of the carving on the Purbeck marble is now remarkably clear – look out for the scene on the west end depicting the saint's martyrdom.

A few yards to the west of the cathedral's main entrance, the **abbey gateway** is the only other part of the original complex to have survived the Dissolution.

Verulamium

From the abbey gateway, Abbey Mill Lane leads down past the *Fighting Cocks* (one of the oldest pubs in the country) and across the trickle of the River Ver to **Verulamium Park**, whose sloping lawns and duck-happy ponds occupy the site of the Roman city. The park holds a scattering of Roman remains, including fragments of the old city wall and the foundations of a town house complete with an in situ mosaic and the original underfloor heating system or **hypocaust** of the bath suite. However, this is small beer in comparison with the **Verulamium Museum** (Mon–Sat 10am–5.30pm, Sun 2–5.30pm; £3.30), which occupies an attractive circular building on the northern edge of the park. Inside, a series of well-conceived displays illustrate and explain life in Roman Britain, but these are eclipsed by the **mosaics**, five wonderful floor mosaics exhibited in one gallery and unearthed hereabouts in the 1930s and 1950s. Dated to about 200 AD, the Sea God Mosaic has created its share of academic debate, with some arguing it depicts a god of nature with stag antler horns rather than a sea god with lobster claws, but there's no disputing the subject of the Lion Mosaic, in which a lion carries the bloodied head of a stag in its jaws. The most beautiful of the five is the Shell Mosaic, a gorgeous work of art whose semicircular design depicts a beautifully crafted scallop shell within a border made up of rolling waves.

Just to the west, across busy Bluehouse Hill, the **Roman Theatre of Verulamium** (daily: March–Oct 10am–5pm; Nov–April 10am–4pm; £1.50) was built around 140 AD, but was reduced to the status of a municipal rubbish dump by the fifth century. Little more than a small hollow now, the site is still impressive enough and gives a real sense of how these theatres would once have looked. Further excavation is underway nearby, revealing a house and several workshops.

From the theatre, you can walk back to the centre along **St Michael's Street**, over one of the prettier stretches of the Ver, past a sixteenth-century **watermill**, now a museum and café (Easter–Oct Mon–Sat 10am–6pm, Sun 11am–6pm; Nov–Easter closes 5pm; £1.10). At the end of St Michael's Street, steer right up the gently curving **Fishpool Street**, a quiet road lined with medieval inns and handsome Georgian houses and leading back to the Clocktower.

Practicalities

Trains on the Bedford to London King's Cross line call at **St Albans Station**, from where it's a ten-minute walk west up the hill along Victoria Street to the main drag – at a point just north of the Clocktower. Trains from Watford Junction (for London Euston and the north) serve the small **St Albans Abbey Station**, a similar distance from the centre, but this time to the south at the bottom of Holywell Hill. Almost all **buses** pull in on the main street, again to the north of the Clocktower, and some continue on to St Albans Station.

The **main street** comprises Chequer Street, which begins at the Clocktower, and its northern continuation St Peter's Street. At the intersection of the two is the Market Place, home of the **tourist office**, in the Town Hall (Easter–Oct Mon–Sat 9.30am–5.30pm, Sun 10am–4pm; Nov–Easter Mon–Sat 10am–4pm; ⓣ01727/864511, ⓦwww.stalbans.gov.uk).

St Albans has a good supply of **B&Bs** with several clustered near St Albans Station, including the first-rate *Wren Lodge*, 24 Beaconsfield Rd (ⓣ01727/855540; no credit cards; ❸), a well-maintained Edwardian house with four comfortable and attractively furnished bedrooms – two en suite. Fishpool Street is, however, a much prettier spot to head for and it's here you'll find the splendid *St Michael's Manor Hotel* (ⓣ01727/864444, ⓦwww.stmichaelsmanor.com; ❽), a family-run establishment in a handsome Georgian house down by the river. Each of the hotel's 22 rooms is tastefully decorated in appropriate style and the hotel sits in its own splendid grounds on whose terraces guests can take breakfast, weather permitting.

When it comes to **food**, the *St Michael's Manor Hotel* (see above) has a first-class restaurant featuring modern British cuisine, but it's pricey. Less expensively, several pubs serve up tasty bar food, with *The Goat*, on Sopwell Lane off Holywell Hill (ⓣ01727/833934), leading the way. St Albans is the headquarters of CAMRA, the real ale campaigners, so it's gratifying to see the excellent quality of the local **pubs**. The *Blue Anchor*, on Fishpool Street, is a good, solid old pub with an open fire in winter and garden seating in summer, whilst the *Farmer's Boy*, a short stroll east of the Clock Tower at 134 London Rd, brews its own beers on site and also stocks a superb range of German and Belgian bottled beers. Finally, the antique *Fighting Cocks*, on Abbey Mill Lane, has been chopped around a bit and does get mightily crowded on sunny summer days, but still has lots of enjoyable nooks and crannies in which to nurse a pint.

Around St Albans

St Albans lies just five minutes' drive outside the M25 and midway between the two main routes to the Midlands and the North – the M1 and A1(M). The best day-trips take you north away from the traffic into (what's left of) rural Hertfordshire, with the obvious target being the hamlet of **Ayot St Lawrence**, site of George Bernard Shaw's old home, Shaw's Corner. There's no avoiding the congestion if you travel east, but neighbouring **Hatfield** boasts Hatfield House, a splendid Jacobean manor house; while to the northwest of the city is one of the country's best zoos, **Whipsnade Wild Animal Park**.

Ayot St Lawrence and Shaw's Corner

The tiny village of **AYOT ST LAWRENCE**, hiding among gentle hills in one of the prettiest corners of Hertfordshire, was the home of **George Bernard Shaw** from 1906 until his death in 1950. He lived in a trim

Edwardian villa known as **Shaw's Corner** (April–Oct Wed–Sun 1–5pm; £3.60; NT), which has been left pretty much as it was at the time of his demise, packed with literary bits and pieces, his personal effects and various press releases. Not one to mince his words, one of these releases implores his readers not to send him birthday cards as the "arrival of thousands of them together is a calamity that is not the less dreaded because it occurs but once a year". There's also the **shed** at the bottom of the garden where Shaw used to write, but this is little more than a cell, the only luxuries being a telephone and the hut's ability to revolve in order to maximize the available sunlight.

The village's other point of interest is the Greek Revival **Church of St Lawrence**, built in the 1770s on the instructions of the local bigwig, Lyonel Lyde, who simultaneously turned the existing medieval church into a picturesque ruin to make the village more "romantic". When the bishop heard of these antics, he threw a fit, but it was too late. The ruined church is hidden among the trees opposite the village's excellent **pub**, the *Brocket Arms* (Ⓣ01438/820250, Ⓦwww.brocketarms.com; ❺), a cosy, half-timbered old place with low-beamed ceilings and a walled garden. They serve real ales here, the food is excellent – daily specials cover the full range of meat and seafood dishes – and there are six bedrooms decorated in a crisp modern style.

Ayot St Lawrence is eight miles north of St Albans, accessible along narrow country lanes. There's no **public transport**, but the nearest train station is Welwyn Garden City, from where it's a four-mile taxi ride.

Hatfield House and Hatfield town

Hatfield House (April–Sept daily noon–4pm; house, park & gardens £7.50), six miles east of St Albans, is an impressive Jacobean structure, which was built at the beginning of the seventeenth century for the powerful royal adviser Sir Robert Cecil. Cecil's mansion replaced an earlier manor house that Henry VIII had used as a country retreat – though his Catholic daughter, Queen Mary, used it more as a prison, confining her Protestant half-sister, Elizabeth, here during her brief reign. James I, on succeeding to the throne in 1603, took an instant dislike to Hatfield and did a house-swap with the Cecils, who gutted the existing building and had it remodelled in true Jacobean style by the architect Robert Lyminge. The commission made Lyminge's name and he went on to design Norfolk's Blickling Hall (see p.582).

E-shaped, Hatfield House boasts an imposing red-brick and stone-trimmed exterior, its south facade equipped with a dainty clocktower and loggia. Inside, amidst oodles of dark wood panelling, there are some magnificent Tudor and Jacobean portraits, a roll call of the great, the good and the not-so-good. Elizabeth I provides a central theme, her memorabilia including a hat, gloves and a pair of silk stockings, as well as an extraordinary genealogical tree tracing her descent from Adam and Eve via Noah and King Lear. The banqueting hall is the main survivor from the earlier building, but it is rarely open, being used for "Elizabethan banquets" and so forth. The splendid oak staircase bears a relief of John Tradescant, the royal gardener and collector who kick-started Oxford's Ashmolean Museum (see p.350). Tradescant planned Hatfield's original garden, the flavour of which is provided by today's knot garden.

Hatfield House is easy to reach by **train** – its entrance is opposite Hatfield town train station, on the King's Cross–Cambridge line. As for **HATFIELD town**, it's mostly a suburban sprawl, but the old centre is worth exploring. To get there from the station, take North Street south to the roundabout, turn left along Broadway and steep Fore Street is on the right – a five- to ten-minute walk in total. Climb the steep Fore Street to the **Church of St Etheldreda**, which has a window by the Pre-Raphaelite artist Edward Burne-Jones and the tomb of Sir Robert Cecil, a macabre affair with Cecil's effigy resting over a skeleton. The *Eight Bells* pub at the bottom of Fore Street serves a good pint and a reasonable lunch.

Whipsnade Wild Animal Park

Whipsnade Wild Animal Park (March–Sept Mon–Sat 10am–6pm, Sun 10am–7pm; Oct–Feb daily 10am–4pm; £12.50; Ⓦ www.whipsnade.co.uk), the free-range menagerie of the Zoological Society of London, perches high up on the downs about eleven miles northwest of St Albans – and six miles southwest of Luton. Whipsnade takes its educational role seriously and runs a number of major breeding programmes – there's a flourishing cheetah population, and the rare Burmese elephant has also been bred here successfully. Most animals, from tigers to wallabies, are kept in large enclosures, separated from the public by a fence or a ditch. You can drive around the zoo (an additional £9 per car), but it's possible to see everything perfectly well on foot. Alternatively, you could hop on the free Safari bus that stops at the main enclosures, or take a ride in the little steam train (Easter–Sept; £2.30), which offers an "Asian Railway Safari" as it pulls past herds of elephants and one-horned rhinos.

To reach Whipsnade by **car**, leave the M1 at Junction #9 (approaching from the south) or #12 (from the north) and follow the signs. The nearest **train station** is at Luton Parkway, from where there are regular **buses** to the zoo; call the zoo on Ⓣ01582/872171 for schedule details.

Travel details

Buses

For information on all local and national bus services, contact Traveline: Ⓣ0870/608 2608, Ⓦ www.traveline.org.uk.

The Ridgeway Explorer bus service operates on Saturdays, Sundays and bank holidays from mid-April to late October. It links Swindon bus station with Reading rail station (4 daily; 2hr 15min) via Woolstone, the Ridgeway Centre YHA and Wantage. A one-day Rover ticket costs £5.

Bedford to: Buckingham (hourly; 2hr 30min).

Buckingham to: Bedford (hourly; 2hr 30min); Oxford (hourly; 1hr 30min).

Henley to: Oxford (hourly; 50min); Reading (hourly; 20min); Wantage (hourly; 1hr 40min).

Oxford to: Buckingham (hourly; 1hr 30min); Henley (hourly; 50min); Reading (every 2hr; 1hr 30min); Wantage (hourly; 1hr).

Reading to: Henley (hourly; 20min); Oxford (every 2hr; 1hr 30min).

Wantage to: Henley (hourly; 1hr 40min); Oxford (hourly; 1hr).

Trains

For information on all local and national rail services, contact **National Rail Enquiries** Ⓣ08457/48 4950, Ⓦ www.rail.co.uk.

Bedford to: London (1–2 hourly; 30min–1hr); Oxford (hourly; 2hr 30min); St Albans (1–2 hourly; 40min).

Hatfield to: London (1–2 hourly; 20min).

Henley to: London (3 daily; 1hr).

Oxford to: Bedford (hourly; 2hr 30min); Birmingham (hourly; 1hr 30min); London (1–2 hourly; 1hr); Worcester (hourly; 1hr 10min).

St Albans to: Bedford (1–2 hourly; 40min); London (14 daily; 20–40min).

The Cotswolds and Somerset

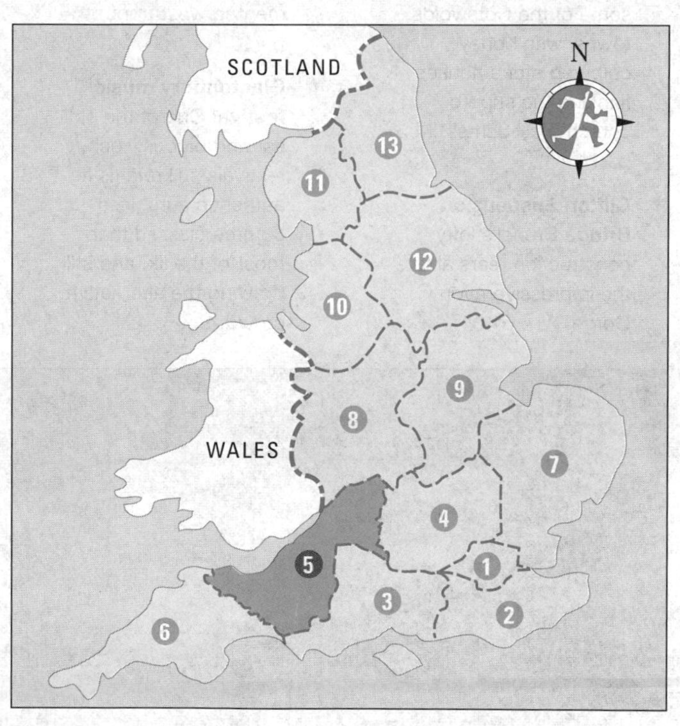

CHAPTER 5

Highlights

* **Falkland Arms, Great Tew** Wonderful pub in the most charming of hamlets, deep in the heart of the Cotswolds. See p.372

* **Chipping Campden, Gloucestershire** Perhaps the most handsome of the Cotswolds towns, with honey-coloured stone houses flanking the superb church of St James. See p.374

* **Clifton Suspension Bridge** Brunel's lofty construction rears above the impressive Avon Gorge. See p.404

* **Bath** Beautifully preserved Roman baths and wonderful Georgian architecture make a visit to Bath a must. See p.408

* **Wells Cathedral** A gem of medieval masonry, not least for its richly ornamented west front. See p.418

* **Glastonbury music festival** One of the oldest and biggest rock festivals still retains its authentic aura, less commercialized than most of the ilk, and still drawing the alternative crowd. See p.424

△ Royal Crescent, Bath

5

The Cotswolds and Somerset

The rolling green swards of **Gloucestershire** and **Somerset**, a wedge of land linking the Midlands with the West Country, encapsulate a vision of rural England that has very largely survived the inroads of modern urban culture. The relatively remote settlements may not, for the most part, be peopled by shepherds and farmers, but the landscape has preserved its slumberous charm, and wears a mellow tranquillity which has even seeped into the towns which grew rich on its wealth. Occupying the eastern side of Gloucestershire, the **Cotswolds**, in particular, show plenty of evidence of past prosperity, not least in the beautiful old mansions and churches endowed from the fortunes made through the medieval wool trade. Moreover, the remarkable continuity of Cotswold architecture has created villages as picturesque as any in England, though the resulting tourist deluge makes some spots nightmarish in summer. Tourism is less of a nuisance in the south of this region, around the busy market town of **Cirencester**, once an important Roman stronghold and still a major transport hub.

To the west, the land drops sharply from the Cotswold escarpment down to **Cheltenham**, an elegant Regency spa town most famous these days for its horse racing. The town's reputation as a bastion of blue-stockinged conservatism is fairly passé now, and it has developed a more sophisticated veneer in recent years, boasting some of the best restaurants and nightlife in the region. Cheltenham would also make a good base for visits to **Gloucester**, with its superb cathedral and rejuvenated harbour area, and **Stroud**, where the much-praised Museum in the Park has recently opened. The Vale of Gloucester follows the route of the **River Severn** northeast towards Worcestershire, the stone cottages of the Cotswolds giving way to the thatched, half-timbered and red-brick houses which are characteristic of **Tewkesbury**, a solidly provincial town with a magnificent abbey.

South down the M5, **Bristol** is the biggest city in these parts, and one of the most go-ahead, cosmopolitan places outside London. Its dynamism and flare have saddled it with dense traffic and some pretty hideous postwar architecture, but all is compensated for by its surviving traces of every phase in its long maritime history. Bristol is within reach of old-fashioned seaside resorts – more

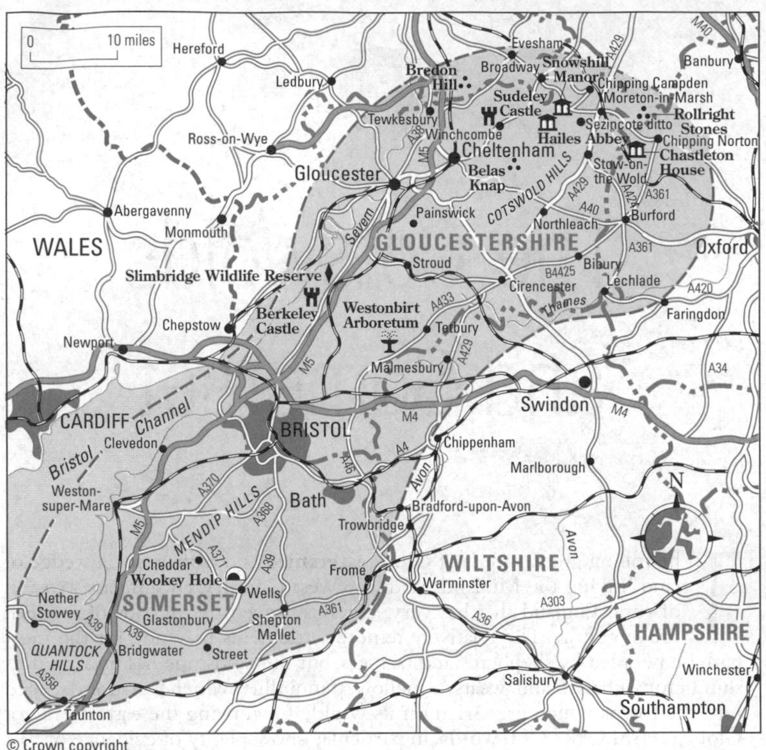

alluring for their nostalgic atmosphere than for their swimming possibilities – and only a few miles from Georgian **Bath**, whose symmetrical honey-toned terraces contribute to its operatic setting. The proximity of urban grace to panoramic splendour is characteristic of much of **Somerset**, as in the exquisite cathedral city of **Wells**, lying on the edge of the Mendip Hills. The landscape assumes more dramatic lines west of here, where the hills are pocked by cave systems, as at **Wookey Hole**, and sliced through by the **Cheddar Gorge**. The ancient town of **Glastonbury** lies close at hand, a site steeped in Christian lore and Arthurian legend, and popular with New Age mystics. To the west, **Bridgwater** and **Taunton** lie at the southern end of the **Quantock Hills**, where Coleridge and Wordsworth roamed, a time recalled in Coleridge's old house at **Nether Stowey**.

The line between London's Paddington Station and Bristol provides the backbone of the **rail network** through this region, though you could also make use of the London–Oxford–Worcester line which runs through Moreton-in-Marsh, in the middle of the Cotswolds. There are also direct lines to Cheltenham and Gloucester, and these towns form the hubs of **bus routes** which connect nearly all the places covered here – though beware that services in the Cotswolds can be extremely sketchy, with little running at all on a Sunday. Your own transport would be ideal for exploring this area, while the M4 and M5 motorways are useful through-routes for longer-distance jaunts.

The Cotswolds

The limestone hills of the **Cotswolds** are preposterously photogenic, s
with countless picture-book villages built by wealthy cloth merchants. W
was important here as far back as the Roman era, but the greatest fortunes w
made between the fourteenth and sixteenth centuries, and it was at this time that many of the region's fine manors and churches were built. Largely bypassed by the Industrial Revolution, which heralded the area's commercial decline, much of the Cotswolds is technically speaking a relic, its architecture preserved in often immaculate condition. Numerous churches are decorated with beautiful Norman carving, for which the local limestone was ideal: soft and easy to carve when first quarried, but hardening after long exposure to the sunlight. The use of this local stone is a strong unifying characteristic, though its colour modulates as subtly as the shape of the hills, ranging from a deep golden tone in **Chipping Campden** to a silvery grey in **Painswick**.

The consequence is that the Cotswolds have become one of the country's main tourist attractions, with many towns afflicted by plagues of tearooms and souvenir and antiques shops – this is Morris Dancing country. To see the Cotswolds at their best, you should visit off-season or perhaps avoid the most popular towns and instead escape into the hills themselves, though really it's churlish to avoid the charms of Chipping Campden and **Northleach** at any time of the year. As for walking, this might be a tamed landscape, but there's good scope for exploring the byways, either in the gentler valleys that are most typical of the Cotswolds or along the dramatic escarpment that marks the boundary with the Severn Valley. A long-distance path called the **Cotswold Way** runs along the top of the ridge, stretching about one hundred miles from Chipping Campden past Cheltenham, Gloucester and Stroud as far as Bath. A number of prehistoric sites provide added interest along the route, with some – such as **Belas Knap** near Winchcombe – being well worth a diversion.

There are a few large settlements in this region, the biggest true Cotswold town being **Cirencester**, a buzzing community dating back to the Romans. On the western edge, **Cheltenham** has a very different feel, predominantly Regency in tone and well supplied with bars and restaurants, while **Stroud**'s no-nonsense style is a world away from Cotswold gentility, though the old wool town is within easy reach of attractive countryside as well as the wildfowl sanctuary of **Slimbridge** and **Berkeley Castle**.

Lechlade and around

Marking the westernmost navigable point of the Thames, **LECHLADE**, some twenty miles west of Oxford, teems with pleasure boats, but for most people it's handier as a springboard for exploring the southern fringe of the Cotswolds. For **overnight stops** easily the best place is the modern and stylish *Cambrai Lodge* (ⓣ01367/253173; no credit cards; ❸) in Oak Street. You can pitch a tent either at the St John's Priory **campsite** (ⓣ01367/252360), a mile southeast along the A417 (follow the signs for Faringdon), or in the field by the *Trout* pub (ⓣ01367/252313) next door. The *Trout*, reachable by footpath across the meadow by the church, is a real anglers' pub, with stuffed fish on the wall, and on Tuesday and Sunday there's live jazz. From Easter to October the *Trout* rents out **rowing boats** (£10/hour) and motors boats (£15/hour).

There's lots to see around Lechlade, the nearest sight being the tiny, disused church at **INGLESHAM**, by a farm about a mile south. Its oldest parts are late Saxon, from which period comes the carved Madonna and Child on the south

William Morris and the Pre-Raphaelites

William Morris (1834–1896), the socialist, writer and craftsman, had a profound influence on his contemporaries and on subsequent generations. In some respects he was an ally of Karl Marx, railing against the iniquities of private property and the squalor of industrialized society. Where he differed from Marx, however, was in his belief that machines necessarily enslave the individual, and in his vision of a world in which each person would be liberated through a sort of communistic, crafts-based economy. His prose/poem story *News from Nowhere* vaguely described his Utopian society, but his main legacy was the **Arts and Crafts Movement**, a direct offshoot of his work and a lasting influence on British crafts.

His career as an artist began at Oxford, where he met **Edward Burne-Jones**, who shared his admiration for the arts of the Middle Ages. After graduating they both ended up in London, painting under the direction of Dante Gabriel Rossetti, the leading light of the **Pre-Raphaelites** – a loose grouping of artists intent on regaining the spiritual purity characteristic of art before Raphael and the Renaissance "tainted" the world with humanism. In 1861 Morris founded **Morris & Co** ("The Firm"), whose designs came to embody the ideas of the Arts and Crafts Movement, one of whose basic tenets was formulated by its founder: "Have nothing in your houses that you do not know to be useful or believe to be beautiful." Rossetti and Burne-Jones were among the designers, though the former remains better known for his paintings of Jane Morris, his friend's wife and his own mistress, whom he turned into the archetypal Pre-Raphaelite woman. Morris's own designs for fabrics, wallpapers and numerous other products were to prove a massive – some would say negative – influence in Britain, as evidenced by the success of the Laura Ashley aesthetic, a lineal descendant of Morris's rustic nostalgia.

Morris's energy was not exhausted by his work for The Firm. In 1890 he set up the **Kelmscott Press**, named after but not located at his summer home, whose masterpiece was the so-called *Kelmscott Chaucer*, the collected poems of one of the Pre-Raphaelites' great heroes, with woodcuts by Burne-Jones. Morris also pioneered interest in the architecture of the Cotswolds – it was in response to hideous restoration work in this region that Morris instigated the **Society for the Protection of Ancient Buildings**, still an active force in preserving the country's architectural heritage.

wall; the colourful fragments of wall paintings date from the fourteenth century. You can walk to the church along the east bank of the Thames, though you must rejoin the A361 for a short distance at the end. Also intriguing is the **church of St Mary** at **FAIRFORD**, some four miles to the west, which is renowned for its complete set of narrative medieval stained-glass windows. The choir stalls reveal an entertaining set of secular scenes on their polished misericords, including various incidents and altercations such as a dog stealing food from a cooking pot.

Isolated among fields just three miles east of Lechlade, **KELMSCOTT** has become a place of pilgrimage for devotees of **William Morris** (see box above), who used the Tudor manor as a summer home from 1871 to his death in 1896. The simple beauty of the **house** (April–Sept Wed & third Sat of month 11am–5pm; July & Aug also first Sat of month 11am–5pm; £7; ⓣ01367/252486, ⓦwww.kelmscottmanor.co.uk) is enhanced by the furniture, fabrics, wallpapers and tapestries – some rescued from dog baskets – that were created by Morris and his Pre-Raphaelite friends, including Burne-Jones and Rossetti. Entry is by timed ticket and it's wise to call first to confirm the opening hours, which are erratic. You can't reach Kelmscott on public transport, but it's a pleasant stroll along the north bank of the Thames from Lechlade, and, should you need **to stay**, there are eight en-suite rooms in the modernized *Plough Inn* (☎01367/253543; ⑤), which dates from the seventeenth century and also serves **meals**.

Burford and the Windrush Valley

Eight miles north of Lechlade you get your first real taste of the Cotswolds at **BURFORD**, where the magnificent High Street, which slopes down to the bridge over the **River Windrush**, holds every variety of golden Cotswold stone. Try to avoid visiting the town in summer, when cars battle for space and tourists fight it out on the pavements and in the antique shops, though the huge **parish church of St John**, originally Norman but remodelled in the fifteenth century, is a delight at any time. An unusual monument to Henry VIII's barber, Edmund Harman, shows four Amazonian Indians, said to be the first representation of Native Americans in Britain.

Spare a morning to follow the footpath along the Windrush through **WIDBROOK**, a hamlet with an idyllic medieval chapel built in the middle of a field on the site of a Roman villa, and on to **SWINBROOK**, just under three miles east of Burford. The church of St Mary in this immaculate village holds a monument showing six members of the Fettiplace family reclining comically on their elbows: the Tudor effigies rigid and stony-faced, their Stuart counterparts stylish and rather camp. The best place for lunch or a drink in Swinbrook is the *Swan Inn*.

Burford straddles several main Cotswold routes. **Buses** along the A40 between Oxford and Cheltenham stop several times a day; buses along other routes are mostly once-a-week market-day services. The **tourist office** is situated in Sheep Street (April–Sept Mon–Sat 9.30am–5.30pm, Sun 10am–3pm; Oct–March Mon–Sat 10am–4.30pm; ☎01993/823558, Ⓦwww.oxfordshirecotswolds.org). Many of Burford's old inns have metamorphozed into expensive **hotels**, but the unassuming *Highway Hotel* at 117 High St (☎01993/822136; ③) is good value. There are several **B&Bs**, including the discreetly signed *Tudor Cottage* at 40 Witney St, off the main High Street, beautifully furnished with antiques (☎01993/823251, Ⓔbunkered@compuserve.com; no credit cards; ③). For good **food** *The Angel Brasserie* (☎01993/822714, Ⓦwww.theangel-uk.com; closed Sun & Mon eve, plus late Jan to early Feb) at 14 Witney St should satisfy; there are three themed bedrooms as well (⑤). For the obligatory tea and cakes, head for *Huffkins*, on the High Street.

Chipping Norton and around

The bustling market town of **CHIPPING NORTON**, eleven miles north of Burford, presides over one of the least explored, but most scenic, corners of the Cotswolds – a region of rambling limestone uplands latticed by long dry-stone walls and dotted with picturesque villages. The western approach to the town, via the A44 from Moreton-in-Marsh, is dominated by the extraordinary chimneystack of the **Bliss Tweed Mill**, mounted on a domed tower and the quirkiest of a crop of monuments dating from the boom of the textile trade. Granted a charter in the twelfth century by King John to hold a wool fair, Chipping Norton reached its peak three hundred years later, when it acquired most of the stalwart stone houses and half-timber-framed coaching inns that now line up along the market square. Also paid for by wealthy wool merchants, **St Mary's Parish Church**, just below the square in Church Street, harbours a fine fifteenth-century Perpendicular nave, in addition to some well-preserved brasses and tombs. More remnants of the town's former prominence are housed

…mall **museum** at the top of the square above the Westgate Centre … Oct Tues–Sun 2–4pm; £1). Among the exhibits is a carved head of a … river god unearthed by a local farmer, equipment salvaged from the … wool mill, and a display on Fred Lewis, who founded the English Baseball Club in 1920.

Buses to Chipping Norton drop passengers in front of the town hall, at the opposite end of the square to the **tourist office** (March–Oct Mon–Sat 9.30am–5.30pm; Nov–Feb Mon–Sat 10am–3pm; ⓣ01608/644379), which is good for local information. **Accommodation** is thin on the ground, but there are pleasant rooms behind the imposing facade of the *Crown and Cushion* (ⓣ01608/642533, ⓦwww.thecrownandcushion.com; ❸), which is handily located on the High Street – and was once owned by Keith Moon of The Who. Three miles southwest of town along the B4450 in the hamlet of **Churchill**, there's also *The Forge* (ⓣ01608/658173, ⓦwww.cotswolds-accommodation.com), an excellent country house B&B offering en-suite rooms in tastefully converted old stone premises.

The best **pubs** are both in Goddards Lane, on the square: the stone-tiled *Blue Boar* serves imaginative bar food and real ales, as does the *Chequers* close by. If you prefer a **café-bar** atmosphere, try *Whistlers* (ⓣ01608/643363; closed Sun eve) just along from the tourist office at 9 Middle Row, where a set lunch will cost £12.

Great Tew and the Rollright Stones

A labyrinth of country lanes spreads east of Chipping Norton through a string of well-manicured villages and valleys to tiny **GREAT TEW**, the perfect target for a pub walk. Hidden deep amid woodland, this hamlet of honey-coloured thatched houses contains one of England's most idyllic pubs, the **Falkland Arms**, which rotates half a dozen guest beers (including the legendary local bitter, Hook Norton), and sells a fine selection of single malts, herbal wines, snuff, and clay pipes you can fill with tobacco for a smoke in the flower-filled garden. Little has changed in the flagstone-floored bar since the sixteenth century, although the adjacent snug was recently converted into a small restaurant serving snacks and evening meals. It's also a popular place to stay (ⓣ01608/683653; ⓦwww.falklandarms.org.uk; ❹), but at weekends is booked up months ahead.

Another local expedition takes in the **Rollright Stones**, high up on the wolds about five miles northwest of Chipping Norton, and the third most important **stone circle** in Britain after Stonehenge and Avebury. Legend recounts that these gnarled Bronze Age rocks are a king and his army (of unknown identity), petrified by a witch while on a campaign to conquer England.

Moreton-in-Marsh and around

MORETON-IN-MARSH, eight miles northwest of Chipping Norton, has more of a buzz than most Cotswold towns, particularly on Tuesdays, when the High Street disappears beneath a huge market. But the thing not to miss is the **Batsford Arboretum** (March to mid-Nov daily 10am–5pm; mid-Nov to Feb Sat & Sun 10am–4pm; £4, joint ticket with Falconry Centre £6.50; ⓦwww.batsford-arboretum.co.uk), a fifteen-minute walk from the High Street. The largest private collection of rare trees in the country, it was planted in the 1880s by Lord Redesdale following his return from a posting in Tokyo. The hilly gardens have a distinctly Japanese flavour, and you can sit here amid magnolias and Chinese pocket-handkerchief trees enjoying wonderful views. Beside the entrance to the arboretum is the **Cotswold Falconry Centre** (March–Nov daily 10.30am–5pm; £4, joint ticket £6.50; ⓦwww.cotswold-falconry.co.uk) which, in addition to a substantial collection of birds of prey, gives regular flying displays against a backdrop of the sweeping Evenlode Valley.

Moreton has better **public transport** services than most other towns in the region, with daily **buses** (except Sun) to Stow-on-the-Wold, Chipping Campden, Evesham, Malvern, Stratford and Cheltenham. In addition, Moreton is on the London–Oxford–Worcester **train** line. There's a useful **tourist office** in the High Street (Mon 8.45am–5pm, Tues–Thurs 8.45am–5.15pm, Fri 8.45am–4.45pm, Sat 10am–12.30pm; ⓣ01608/650881, ⓦwww.cotswold.gov.uk) and **bike rental** is available from the toyshop on the High Street (ⓣ01608/650756). Best value of the **hotels** is the lively *Bell Inn*, ⓣ01608/652195, ⓦwww.bellinncotswold.com; ❸), also on the High Street. For **B&B**, try *Acacia*, in a fetching stone terrace house at 2 New Rd, on the way to the station (ⓣ01608/650130; no credit cards; ❶); or the luxurious *Windy Ridge* (ⓣ01451/832328, ⓦwww.windy-ridge.co.uk; ❺), in an attractive thatched house a couple of miles southwest of town towards Longborough and with its own arboretum and indoor pool.

Places to eat line the High Street, but the pick of the bunch is the *Redesdale Arms*, whose forte is game and seafood – all at affordable prices.

Sezincote

Follow the A44 west from Moreton and take the signed turning just before you reach Bourton-on-the-Hill to get to the blue onion domes and miniature minarets of **Sezincote** (May–July & Sept Thurs & Fri 2.30–5.30pm; garden Jan–Nov Thurs & Fri 2pm–dusk; £5, garden only £3.50). Tucked gracefully if incongruously among the Cotswold hills, this extraordinary house was built in the early nineteenth century, the result of a collaboration between two old India hands, the architect Samuel Pepys Cockerell (a distant relative of the diarist) and the artist Thomas Daniell, both of whom had been inspired by Moghul architecture. The end result so impressed the Prince Regent on a visit in 1806 that he ordered the designs for Brighton Pavilion to be changed along these exotic lines. Inside, a curious classical-cum-Chinese style takes precedence; outside, temples, statues and unusual trees and shrubs are scattered about the small but exquisite garden – and in the early months of the year the snowdrops make a glorious display.

Chastleton House

The other stately home well worth a visit hereabouts is **Chastleton House**, three miles southeast of Moreton off the A44 (April–Sept Wed–Sat 1–5pm, Oct Wed–Sat 1–4pm; £5.60; timed tickets, pre-bookable on ⓣ01494/755585; NT). Built between 1605 and 1612 by Walter Jones, a wealthy Welsh wool merchant, this ranks among the most splendid Jacobean properties in the country, set amid ornamental gardens that include England's first-ever croquet lawn (the rules of this most eccentric of games were codified here in 1865). Inside, the house looks as if it's been in a time warp for four hundred years, with unwashed upholstery, unpolished wood panelling and miscellaneous clutter clogging some of the corners. This disheveled air partly derives from the previous owners, the Jones family, who lost their fortune in the aftermath of the Civil War – they were Royalists – and never had enough cash to modernize thereafter. It's also a credit to the National Trust, who took on the property in 1991, but wisely decided to stick to the "lived-in look". It's the general flavour of the house that is of most appeal, but there are several highlights, notably the huge barrel-vaulted long gallery, oodles of elaborate plasterwork and panelling, tapestries and exquisite glassware, and, in the beer cellar, the longest ladder (dated 1805) you're ever likely to come across. There's also a topiary garden, where the hedges are clipped into bulbous shapes reminiscent of squirrels and tortoises.

Chipping Campden

CHIPPING CAMPDEN, six miles northwest of Moreton-in-Marsh, gives a better idea than anywhere else in the Cotswolds as to what a prosperous wool town might have looked like in the Middle Ages. The houses have undulating, weather-beaten roofs and many retain their original mullioned windows, while the fine Perpendicular **Church of St James** (March–Oct Mon–Sat 10am–5pm, Sun 2–5pm; Nov–Feb Mon–Sat 11am–3pm, Sun 2–4pm; free) dates from the fifteenth century, the zenith of the town's wool-trading days. Inside, an ostentatious monument commemorates the family of Sir Baptist Hicks, a local benefactor who built the nearby almshouses and the market hall in the High Street. His own home was burnt down during the Civil War, but you can glimpse the ruins over the wall beside the church.

A fine panoramic view rewards those who make the short but severe hike up the Cotswold Way northwest to **Dover's Hill** (follow Hoo Lane north off the High Street). Since 1610 this natural amphitheatre has been the stage for an Olympics of rural sports, though the event was suspended last century when games such as shin-kicking became little more than licensed thuggery. A more civilized version, the **Cotswold Olimpick Games**, has been staged each June since 1951: no shin-kicking, but still the odd bit of hammer-throwing and tug-of-war pulling.

Such a museum-piece as Chipping Campden must inevitably cope with a bevy of visitors in summer. Try to stay overnight and explore in the evening or at dawn, when the streets are empty and the golden hues of the stone at their richest. **Public transport** to the area is good, with frequent bus services to Moreton, Evesham and Stratford. You can't move for **guest houses** along the High Street and most of them can be booked through the **tourist office** (daily 10am–5.30pm; ⓣ01386/841206, ⓦwww.chipping-campden.net). Recommendable places include the *Dragon House*, on the High Street (ⓣ01386/840734, ⓦwww.dragonhouse-chipping-campden.co.uk; no credit cards; ❸), a tastefully converted former coaching inn with delightful gardens whose various old stone buildings are mostly given over to self-catering, though there's B&B in two neat and trim, en-suite rooms as well. Most of the **pubs** have rooms with one of the classiest establishments being the *Noel Arms*, which occupies a handsome old stone building on the High Street (ⓣ01386/840317, ⓦwww.cotswold-inns-hotels.co.uk; ❼). The *Noel* is good for a pint as well, but the best **pub** in town is the *Eight Bells Inn*, a particularly cosy spot around the corner from the church. Curiously, there's a window in the floor showing the passage once used by Catholic priests escaping from the church.

Winchcombe and around

The journey to **WINCHCOMBE**, twelve miles southwest of Chipping Campden, is stunning, an exhilarating ride down the B4632, which weaves along the lower folds of the escarpment. Winchcombe was an important Saxon town, one-time capital of the kingdom of **Mercia**, and the possessor of a large Saxon abbey. The town lost its importance centuries ago – and the abbey didn't

Short walks from Winchcombe

Drained by the sinuous River Isbourne, the scenic valley around Winchcombe is riddled with rewarding and well-marked trails, one of the finest being the **Cotswold Way** (see p.369), which cuts through the town before climbing to Belas Knap and the plateau of Cleve Common and West Down. From the edge of the escarpment, reached after a stiff one- to two-hour hike, the views over Cheltenham and the Severn Valley to the distant Malverns are superb.

A less strenuous, but equally inspiring, option is the three-and-a-half-hour round route to **Spoonley Farm**, just over two miles southeast of town, which takes in a ruined Roman villa where you can see a beautifully preserved **mosaic** *in situ*. The villa's existence was a well-kept secret until the American travel writer Bill Bryson featured it in his chart-topping *Notes From A Small Island*. Since then, the tourist office has been inundated with requests for its *Country Walks Around Winchcombe* booklet, which describes the route in detail. If you can't get hold of one of these, check OS Outdoor Leisure Map 45. The footpath to Spoonley Farm starts in the same place as the Cotswold Way, opposite the church at the south end of the main street, but shortly after peels left towards Sudeley Castle. After crossing the castle grounds, it follows the contour of the hill to Waterhatch Woods, site of the old villa; the mosaic is covered in sheets of plastic held down with stones, which you have to remove yourself (be sure to replace them afterwards). From the ruin, strike uphill as far as a farm track, which you can follow southwest, turning right at Cole's Hill towards Waterhatch Farm. The path then drops gently down to river level and eventually back to Winchcombe.

survive the Dissolution – but it's a pleasant spot all the same, even if its fetching blend of stone and half-timbered buildings play second fiddle to a quartet of neighbouring attractions – Sudeley Castle, Hailes Abbey, Snowshill Manor and Belas Knap. These, together with some of the finest scenery in the region and Tewkesbury only a short hop away, make Winchcombe a useful and enjoyable base, quieter than Cheltenham and less touristy than the likes of Burford.

Winchcombe is easy to reach by **bus** from Cheltenham, though services are spasmodic on Sundays. The **tourist office** (April–Oct Mon–Sat 10am–1pm & 2–5pm, Sun 10am–1pm & 2–4pm; Nov–March Sat & Sun 10am–1pm & 2–4pm; ⓣ01242/602925, ⓦwww.visitcotswoldsandsevernvale.gov.uk) is in the Town Hall, next to the modest **Police and Folk Museum** (April–Oct Mon–Sat 10am–5pm; £1), which displays examples of 1829 Peeler, Japanese and Nazi uniforms. Of the many **B&Bs**, one of the best is the Jacobean *Great House* on Castle Street (ⓣ01242/602490; no credit cards; ❷), full of old family furniture and one lovely four-poster room. Alternatively, the excellent *Gower House*, 16 North St (ⓣ01242/602616; no credit cards; ❷), offers three extremely comfortable en-suite rooms, whilst the unassuming *Cleevely*, three miles south of the village on Corndean Lane (ⓣ01242/602059; no credit cards; ❷), is the least expensive option in the area.

There's little to choose between the town's two main **pubs**, the *White Hart* and the *Plaisterers Arms*, which are both on the main street and serve food, though the former always has Scandinavian fare on offer (specials on Wed eve).

Sudeley Castle

A short walk east of Winchcombe, **Sudeley Castle** (April–Oct daily 11am–5pm; gardens March–Oct daily 10.30am–5.30pm; £6.70, gardens only £5; ⓦwww.sudeleycastle.co.uk) was once a favourite country retreat of Tudor and Stuart monarchs, though it never actually belonged to the royal family. It cularly strong connection with Catherine Parr, the sixth wife of I, who came to live here with her second husband, Thomas ord of Sudeley, shortly after the king's death. During the Civil War ecame a base for the Royalists and suffered the consequences when odel Army smashed the place up. What remained stood empty until 1830, when the ruins were bought by the Dent family, who restored much – but not all – of the exterior. Inside, the uneven collection includes paintings by Turner and Constable, a bed Charles I once slept in and one of Catherine Parr's teeth – her tomb is in the chapel. The real joy of Sudeley lies outside: in the **Queen's Garden**, with its huge yew hedges cut like masonry; in the creeper-covered ruins of the banqueting hall; and, above all, in the setting, with the green slopes of the escarpment behind.

Hailes Abbey and Snowshill Manor

Hailes Abbey (April–Sept daily 10am–6pm; Oct daily 10am–5pm; £3; EH), a two-mile stroll northeast of Winchcombe, was once one of England's great Cistercian monasteries. Pilgrims came here from all over the country to pray before the abbey's phial of Christ's blood, a relic shown to be a fake at the time of the Dissolution, when the thirteenth-century monastery was demolished. Not much of the original complex remains beyond the foundations, but some cloister arches survive, worn by wind and rain. The ruins may lack drama, but Hailes is still worth visiting for its **museum**, where you can examine thirteenth-century bosses at close quarters, and for the nearby **church**, which is older than the abbey and contains beautiful wall paintings dating from around 1300. The cartoon-like hunting scene was probably a warning to Sabbath-breakers.

Three miles northeast of Hailes Abbey, **Snowshill Manor** is a good-looking Cotswold manor house that invites a detour (April–June & Sept–Oct Wed–Sun noon–5pm; July & Aug Mon & Wed–Sun noon–5pm; garden same months & days 11am–5.30pm; £6.40, gardens only £3.60; NT). Inspired as a boy by his grandmother's "wonderful" Chinese cabinet (now in the Zenith room of the house), the architect, craftsman and poet Charles Paget Wade (1883–1956) spent decades hunting down objects which were not "rare or valuable" but "of interest as records of various vanished handicrafts". The results of his forays – model carts, boneshaker bicycles, children's prams, wooden toys, beds, beetles, all kinds of musical instruments – were crammed into the house, while he himself lived in a cottage in the garden. It's an endlessly diverting collection, a veritable trove of exotic curiosities. Most dramatic is the arrangement of 26 Samurai warriors dating from the seventeenth to the nineteenth centuries in the Green Room. Note that there is a ten-minute walk to the house from the entrance to the grounds.

Belas Knap

Up on the ridge overlooking Winchcombe to the south, the Neolithic long barrow of **Belas Knap** occupies one of the most breathtaking spots in the Cotswolds. Dating from around 3000 BC, this is the best-preserved burial chamber in England, stretching out like a strange sleeping beast cloaked in green velvet. The two-mile climb up the Cotswold Way from Winchcombe contributes to the fun, giving good views back over Sudeley Castle. The path strikes off to the right near the entrance to Sudeley; when you reach the road at the top, turn right and then left up into the woods, from where it's a ten-minute hike to Belas Knap.

Stow-on-the-Wold

Straddling eight roads, including the Roman Fosse Way (now the A429) some eleven miles east of Winchcombe – and four miles south of Moreton-in-Marsh – windswept **STOW-ON-THE-WOLD** sucks in a disproportionate number of visitors for its size and attractions, which essentially comprise an old marketplace surrounded by brassy pubs, antiques shops and souvenir boutiques. The narrow walled alleyways, or "tunes", running into the square were designed for funnelling sheep into the market, which is itself dominated by an imposing Victorian hall and, just to the south, a medieval cross allegedly raised to instill honesty among the traders.

Stow is the logical springboard for trips deeper into the region with its good bus connections to Moreton-in-Marsh and Cheltenham, and its healthy supply of hotels and B&Bs. The **tourist office** on the Market Square (April–Oct Mon–Sat 9.30am–5.30pm; Nov–March Mon–Sat 9.30am–4.30pm; Ⓣ01451/831082, Ⓦwww.cotswold.gov.uk), sells National Express bus tickets and keeps a list of local accommodation. Among the **B&Bs**, one very recommendable spot is the secluded and pretty *Honeysuckle Cottage* (Ⓣ01451/830973; no credit cards; closed Nov & Jan; ❸), which is tucked away on Union St – take the short cut passage through the *King's Arms* pub from the square; or you could try *Tall Trees* (Ⓣ01451/831296; no credit cards; ❸), on the edge of town off the Oddington road (A436), which has sweeping views and a cosy wood burner in its modern sitting room annexe. Close to the tourist office stands the popular **youth hostel** (Ⓣ0870/770 6050, Ⓔstow@yha.org.uk; restricted opening Oct–March; £13), which has fifty beds in four- to eight-bedded rooms. Also central, on the corner of Park and Digbeth streets, is *The Royalist* (Ⓣ01451/830670, Ⓦwww.theroyalisthotel.co.uk; ❼), an upmarket hotel that bills itself as England's oldest inn, a claim partly substantiated by wooden beams carbon-dated at around one thousand years old.

For **food**, *The Royalist* offers tasty light meals in its *Eagle & Child* bar and also possesses the more formal but extremely good *947AD* restaurant, where a three-course meal will relieve you of about £30. Alternatively, the *Cotswold Garden Tearoom*, next to the church on Sheep Street, offers mouth-watering homemade cakes and snacks in a delightful walled garden.

Northleach

NORTHLEACH, secluded in a shallow depression nine miles south of Stow, is one of the most appealing and least developed villages in the Cotswolds. This, together with its location at the heart of the plateau, within easy reach of Oxford, Stratford and the picturesque Windrush Valley, makes it a perfect base from which to explore the region. Rows of immaculate late-medieval cottages cluster around the village's spacious central square, but the most outstanding feature is its handsome Perpendicular **Church of St Peter and St Paul**, erected in the fifteenth century at the height of the wool boom, when the surrounding fields of rich limestone grasses supported a vast population of sheep. The local breed, known as the Cotswold Lion, was a descendant of flocks introduced by the Romans, and by the thirteenth century had become the largest in the country, producing heavy fleeces that were exported to the Flemish weaving towns. The income from this lucrative trade, initially controlled by the clergy but later by a handful of wealthy merchants, financed the construction of three major churches in the region, of which the one at Northleach is arguably the most impressive (the others are in Cirencester and Chipping Campden). Inside, the floor of the beautifully proportioned nave, lit by wide clerestory windows, is inlaid with an exceptional collection of **memorial brasses** marking the tombs of the merchants whose endowments paid for the church. On several, you can make out the woolsacks laid out beneath the corpse's feet – a symbol of wealth and power that features to this day in the House of Lords, where a woolsack is placed on the Lord Chancellor's seat.

Two minutes' walk up the main street from the village square, **Keith Harding's World of Mechanical Music** (daily 10am–6pm; £5) is Northleach's other main attraction, comprising a bewildering collection of antique musical boxes, automata, barrel organs and mechanical instruments all stuffed into one room. For your money you get an hour-long demonstration tour of the collection, of which the highlight is hearing the likes of Rachmaninov, Gershwin or Paderewski playing their own masterpieces on piano rolls.

Excellent **accommodation** can be enjoyed right in the centre of the village at the *Cotteswold House*, a wonderfully well-preserved Tudor cottage with exposed stone arches and antique oak panelling on the Market Place (Ⓣ01451/860493, Ⓦwww.cotteswoldhouse.com; ❸). A recommendable second choice is the *Wheatsheaf Hotel* (Ⓣ01451/860244, Ⓦwww.wheatsheafatnorthleach.com; ❸), a former coaching inn just down from the square on West End with eight, spick-and-span, en-suite modern rooms. The best **restaurant** in Northleach is the *Old Woolhouse*, on the Market Place (Ⓣ01451/860366; reservations recommended), where you can expect to spend around £40 per head for top-notch French cuisine; the wine list is as good as the food. Less expensively, the *Wheatsheaf* offers restaurant meals and the *Sherborne Arms*, on the Market Place, supplies good bar food.

Cirencester

Ten miles from Northleach, on the southern fringes of the Cotswolds, **CIRENCESTER** makes a refreshing change from its more gentrified neighbours. Here, the "olde-worlde" image in which many Cotswold towns indulge has been exchanged for an endearingly old-fashioned atmosphere, generated partly by shops that haven't changed for decades. Under the **Romans**, the town was called Corinium and ranked second only to Londinium in size and importance. A provincial capital and a centre of trade, it flourished for three centuries and had one of the largest forums north of the Alps. However, the Saxons destroyed almost all of the Roman city and the town's prosperity was only restored with the wool boom of the Middle Ages. Nowadays, Cirencester, with its handsome stone buildings, is one of the most affluent towns in the area and lays claim to be the "Capital of the Cotswolds".

Cirencester's heart is the delightful swirling **Market Place**, on Mondays and Fridays packed with traders' stalls. An irregular line of eighteenth-century facades along the north side contrasts with the heavier Victorian structures opposite, but the parish church of **St John the Baptist**, built in stages during the fifteenth century, dominates. The extraordinary flying buttresses that support the tower had to be added when it transpired that the church had been constructed upon a filled-in ditch. Its grand three-tiered south porch, the largest in England – big enough to function as the one-time town hall – leads to the nave, where slender piers and soaring arches create a superb sense of space, enhanced by clerestory windows that bathe the nave in a warm light. The church contains much of interest, including a colourful wineglass **pulpit**, carved in stone around 1450 and one of the few pre-Reformation pulpits to have survived in Britain. North of the chancel, superb fan vaulting hangs overhead in the **chapel of St Catherine**, who appears in a still vivid fragment of a fifteenth-century wall painting. In the adjacent **Lady Chapel** are two good seventeenth-century monuments, to Humphrey Bridges and his family and to the dandified Sir William Master. Outside, one of the best views of the church is from the **Abbey Grounds**; site of the Saxon abbey, it's now a small park skirted by the modest river Churn and a fragment of the Roman city wall.

Few medieval buildings other than the church have survived in Cirencester. The houses along the town's most handsome streets – Park, Thomas and Coxwell – date mostly from the seventeenth and eighteenth centuries. One of those on Park Street houses the **Corinium Museum** (closed till July 2004), which mostly devotes itself to Roman and Saxon artefacts, including several wonderful **mosaic pavements**. A yew hedge the height of telegraph poles runs along Park Street, concealing **Cirencester House**, the home of the Earl of Bathurst. At no point can you see the building (it's rather plain anyway), but the attached three-thousand-acre park is open to the public: you enter it from Cecily Hill, a lovely street except for the eccentric Victorian barracks. Although the avenues in the park restrict the scope for walks, you can still enjoy a pleasant stroll. The polo pitches here attract some of the country's top players, with games held almost daily between May and September.

Finally, the **Brewery Arts Centre** (Mon–Sat 10am–5pm; free; ⓣ01285/657181), off Cricklade Street, is occupied by more than a dozen resident artists, whose studios you can visit and whose work you can buy in the shop. The centre's theatre hosts high-calibre plays and concerts (from jazz to classical), and there is a buzzing café on the first floor.

Practicalities

Despite nine roads radiating from Cirencester – five of them Roman – **bus** services to the town could be better, though there are at least daily connections from Swindon, fourteen miles southeast, and Cheltenham, fifteen miles north. All services stop in the Market Place. The **tourist office** (April–Dec Mon–Sat 9.30am–5.30pm; Jan–March Mon–Sat 9.30am–5pm; ⓣ01285/654180, ⓦwww.thecotswolds.org), in the Corn Hall on the Market Place, covers the whole of the Cotswolds and has a list of local **accommodation** pinned outside. A string of **B&Bs** lines Victoria Road, a short walk east: two good options here are *The Ivy House*, in high-gabled Victorian premises at no. 2 (ⓣ01285/656626, ⓦwww.ivyhousecotswolds.com; ❷), and similarly appointed *The Leauses*, at no. 101 (ⓣ01285/653643, ⓦwww.theleauses.co.uk; no credit cards; ❷). For a little more luxury, stay at the *Crown of Crucis Hotel* in Ampney Crucis (ⓣ01285/851806, ⓦwww.thecrownofcrucis.co.uk; ❺), a sixteenth-century former coaching inn with riverside gardens, a good restaurant and a no-smoking rule; to reach it, head two and a half miles east on the A417. The most accessible **campsite** is at the *Mayfield Touring Park* at Perrotts Brook (ⓣ01285/831301), two miles north on the A435; any Cheltenham-bound bus will drop you there.

For **snacks** you can't do much better than *Keith's Coffee Shop* on Blackjack Street, which also serves the best coffee in town. The *Café Bar* **restaurant**, next to the Brewery Centre, is inexpensive and goes out of its way to make its vegetarian dishes interesting (no credit cards; closed Sun). The best choice for a relaxing evening meal, however, is *Harry Hare's* at 3 Gosditch St (ⓣ01285/652375), just behind the church, which specializes in classy renditions of down-to-earth English dishes for under £20. If you're splashing out and have transport, the *Crown of Crucis* (see accommodation above) is another option also worth considering.

Cirencester has plenty of **pubs**, their clientele swollen by tweedy students from the nearby Royal Agricultural College. Try the *Kings Head* on the Market Place or, for **bar meals**, the *Waggon & Horses* on London Road, and the *Butcher's Arms* in Ampney Crucis.

Malmesbury

The striking half-ruin of a Norman abbey presides over the small hilltown of **MALMESBURY**, one of the oldest boroughs in England. Lying twelve miles south of Cirencester (and only five miles north off the M4 motorway), it's not part of the Cotswolds geologically, though the town's early wealth was based on wool. Malmesbury certainly lacks the tweeness of the Cotswold towns to the north, with new housing estates encircling the centre, and modern developments marring views over the Avon. But none of this can detract from the splendour of the abbey, a majestic structure with some of the finest Romanesque sculpture in the country.

The High Street begins at the bottom of the hill by the old silk mills and heads north across the river and up past a jagged row of ancient cottages on its way to the octagonal **Market Cross**, built in around 1490 to provide shelter from the rain. Nearby, the eighteenth-century **Tolsey Gate** leads through to the **abbey** (daily: April–Oct 10am–5pm; Nov–March 10am–4pm; free), which was once a rich and powerful Benedictine monastery. The first abbey burnt down in about 1050, the second was roughed up during the Dissolution, but the beautiful Norman **nave** has survived, its south porch sporting a multitude of exquisite if badly worn figures. Three bands of figures surround the doorway, depicting scenes from the Creation, the Old Testament and the life of Christ, while inside the porch the apostles and Christ are carved in a fine deep relief – stately figures in flowing folds surmounted by a flying angel. The tympanum shows Christ on a rainbow, supported by gracefully gymnastic angels. Within the main body of the church, the pale stone brings a dramatic freshness, particularly to the carving of the nave arches (look out for the Norman beak-heads) and of the clerestory. To the left of the high altar, the pulpit virtually hides the **tomb of King Athelstan**, grandson of Alfred the Great and the first Saxon to be recognized as king of England; the tomb, however, is empty, the location of the king's remains unknown. The abbey's greatest surviving treasures are housed in the parvise (room above the porch), reached via a narrow spiral staircase right of the main doorway, where pride of place is given to four Flemish **medieval Bibles**, written on parchment and sumptuously illuminated with gilt ink and exquisite miniature paintings.

Malmesbury was also the birthplace of **Thomas Hobbes** (1588–1679), the moral and political philosopher who believed in the separation of theology and philosophy and the subordination of the church to the state – beliefs that got him into all sorts of hot water with the Puritans. Most contentious of all, however, was Hobbes's assertion that the power of the state is absolute as against the individual, a view he expounded in his most influential work, *Leviathan*. Another local celebrity is **Elmer the Monk**, who in 1005 attempted to fly from the abbey tower with the aid of wings: he limped for the rest of his life, but won immortal fame as the "flying monk".

Practicalities

Buses to Malmesbury – including services from Cirencester and Chippenham – pull into the Market Place, a short walk from the **tourist office**, in the town hall off Cross Hayes car park (Mon–Thurs 9am–4.50pm, Fri 9am–4.20pm, Sat

banned in recent years, but it has been reinstated by popular demand, and now there are four races run, three for men and one for women.

Arrival, information and accommodation

All long-distance **buses** arrive at the station in Royal Well Road, just west off the Promenade. The **train station** is on Queen's Road, southwest of the centre; buses #D and #E run into town every fifteen minutes, otherwise it's a twenty-minute walk. Among the many leaflets and brochures handed out at the **tourist office**, at 77 Promenade (Mon–Sat 9.30am–5.15pm; ⓣ01242/522878, ⓦwww.visitcheltenham.com), is one giving a rundown of bus services to and from most destinations in the area. They also sell tickets for walking **tours** of the town (late June to mid-Sept Mon–Fri at 11am; £2.50), and for guided bus tours stopping at several destinations in the Cotswolds that are otherwise difficult to reach on public transport (late June to mid-Sept Tues & Thurs; £22); they're popular, so book in advance.

Cheltenham makes an excellent base for exploring the Cotswolds by **bike** if you can face the hills: they're available to rent from Compass Holidays, who operate at the train station (book on ⓣ01242/250642, ⓦwww.compass-holidays.com). They also arrange cycling holidays.

Hotels and **guest houses** abound, many of them in fine Regency houses, and rooms are easy to come by – except during the races and festivals, when you should book weeks in advance. There are several B&Bs on or near Bath Road, east of the promenade.

Hotels & B&Bs

Abbey 14–16 Bath Parade ⓣ01242/516053, ⓦwww.abbeyhotel-cheltenham.com. Rooms here are attractively and individually furnished and wholesome breakfasts are taken overlooking the garden. Friendly service. ④

Brennan 21 St Luke's Rd ⓣ01242/525904. This is a good-value option in a small Regency building, on a quiet square. Non-smoking dining room. ②

Crossways 57 Bath Rd ⓣ01242/527683, ⓦwww.crosswaysguesthouse.com. This comfortable, non-smoking Regency house makes a good base, only two minutes' walk from the centre. ③

Kandinsky Bayshill Rd ⓣ01242/527788, ⓦwww.aliashotels.com. With colourful and stylish bedrooms, Chinese and Indonesian decoration, and 1950s-style disco (residents and members only), this hotel is not at all bad value for the price. ⑥

Lawn 5 Pittville Lawn ⓣ01242/526638. In a quiet location near the park, and with an art gallery *in situ*, this well-decorated hotel caters for vegetarians and vegans only. No credit cards. No smoking. ④

Lypiatt House Lypiatt Rd ⓣ01242/224994, ⓦwww.lypiatt.co.uk. Set in its own grounds, this place rates highly for comfort and personal attention. Open fires and a conservatory with a small bar set the tone. ⑤

Willoughby 1 Suffolk Square ⓣ01242/522798, ⓦwww.willoughbyhouse.com. South of the centre, this smart place has high-class home comforts at fairly steep prices. Self-catering available. ⑥

Hostels and camping

Briarfields Touring Park Gloucester Road ⓣ01242/235324. The nearest campsite is one mile west on the B4063, off the M5 (junction 11). It's accessible by bus #94 from the Promenade.

YMCA 6 Victoria Walk ⓣ01242/524024. Cheltenham's cheapest central option is a short walk from the town hall. There are also extremely good-value lunches on offer. Private room £16.

The Town

The focus of Cheltenham, the broad **Promenade**, sweeps majestically south from the High Street, lined with the town's grandest houses, smartest shops and most genteel public gardens. A short walk north of the High Street brings you to **Pittville**, which, planned as a spa town to rival Cheltenham, was never completed and is now mostly parkland. All you can do here these days, apart from strolling along a few solitary Regency avenues and visiting the grandest spa building, the domed **Pump Room** (Mon & Wed–Sun 11am–4pm), whose

10am–4pm; ⓣ01666/823748, ⓦwww.wiltshiretourism.co.uk). There's no strong reason to stay the night here, but the *Old Bell* (ⓣ01666/822344, ⓦwww.oldbellhotel.com; ⑥), in Abbey Row, originally built as a guest house for the abbey, has plush and extremely comfortable rooms. For **food**, stick to either the *Whole Hog*, a stone-walled tearoom-cum-pub overlooking the Market Place, or the *Summer Café* on the High Street, which does a good line in sandwiches.

Cheltenham

Until the eighteenth century **CHELTENHAM** was like any other Cotswold town, but then the discovery of a spring in 1716 transformed it into Britain's most popular **spa**. During Cheltenham's prime, a century or so later, the royal, the rich and the famous descended in hordes to take the waters, which were said to cure anything from constipation to worms. These days, while a fair proportion of Cheltenham's hundred thousand-odd inhabitants are undoubtedly well heeled, of Conservative persuasion (true of the Cotswolds in general) and above retirement age, the town saves itself from too smug an image by a lively and increasingly cosmopolitan atmosphere. It's by far the best spot around for nightlife and makes a convenient base for touring the area.

Cheltenham is a natural stopping-off place en route to the Severn Valley, and the haughty elegance of the Regency architecture, characterized by fancy ironwork and Greek columns, can be a pleasant change after the folksy Cotswolds. The town is also a thriving arts centre, famous for its festivals of **folk** (Feb), **jazz** (April), **science** (June), **classical music** (July) and **literature** (October) – and then, of course, there are the races (see box below). In addition, Coopers' Hill, six miles southwest on the A46, is the venue for the region's most bizarre, and established, competition. On the second bank holiday in May, a steep section of the Cotswold escarpment hosts the village's annual **Cheese Rolling Festival**, when a large Double Gloucester cheese is rolled down the one-in-two incline and chased by dozens of drunken folk; the first person to get down the hill is the winner. The damage to life and limb has resulted in the race being

Cheltenham races

Cheltenham racecourse, a ten-minute walk north of Pittville Park at the foot of Cleeve Hill, is Britain's main steeplechasing venue. The principal event of the season, the three-day **National Hunt Festival** in March, attracts forty thousand people each day. A fair proportion of them come from Ireland, the birthplace of some of the greatest horses to have raced here, including the supreme steeplechaser, **Arkle**. Other meetings take place in January, April, October, November and December: a list of fixtures is posted up at the tourist office. For the cheapest but arguably the best view, pay £5 (rising to £15 during the Festival) for entry to the Courage Best Enclosure, as the pen in the middle is known. For schedules and other information, call ⓣ01242/513014 or access the website at ⓦwww.cheltenham.co.uk. For the National Hunt Festival it's essential to buy tickets in advance.

A popular pre-meet watering hole is the *King's Arms*, a short walk east of the racecourse in **Prestbury**, an old Cotswold village with a reputation for being the most haunted village in England, and which has now been subsumed into the town. **Fred Archer**, considered by many to have been the finest Flat jockey of all time, was brought up here, and he features prominently among the pub's racing memorabilia. Sadly, the pub has lost much of its character since becoming part of a chain, and you might find the nearby *Royal Oak* more congenial.

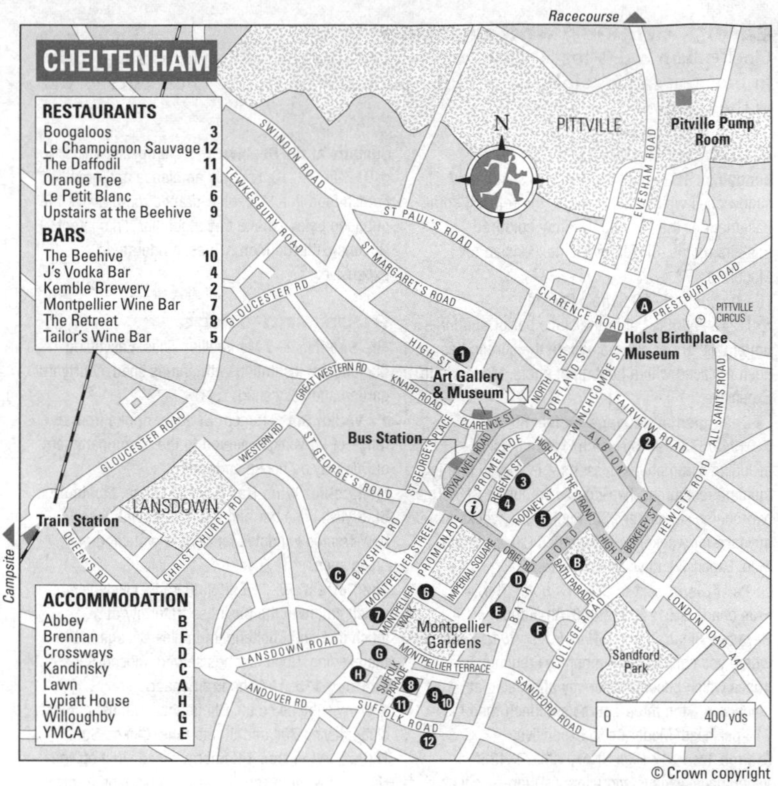

chief function nowadays is as a concert hall, is sample England's only naturally alkaline water for free. On your return route, the **Holst Birthplace Museum** is worth a glance, at 4 Clarence Rd (Tues–Sat 10am–4pm; £2.50). Once the home of the composer of *The Planets*, the intimate rooms hold plenty of Holst memorabilia – including his piano – and also give a good insight into Victorian family life. Back in the centre, the well-set-out **Art Gallery and Museum** on Clarence St (Mon–Sat 10am–5.20pm, Sun 2–4.20pm; free; Ⓦwww.cheltenhammuseum.org.uk) marks the high point of Cheltenham. It's very good on social history, with different eras represented by table displays of personal belongings and a typical dinner of the time. There's also a fine room dedicated to the Arts and Crafts Movement, containing several pieces by Charles Voysey and Ernest Gimson, two of the period's most graceful designers. Also on display is an array of rare Chinese ceramics, works by Cotswold artists such as Stanley Spencer and Vanessa Bell, and a section devoted to Edward Wilson, a local man who died on Scott's ill-fated expedition to the Antarctic.

For a matchless view over the town, catch bus #606 out to Southam, one mile north of Prestbury village on the B4632, and follow the public footpath east up the sheer face of the Cotswold escarpment to the top of **Cleeve Common**. The summit, known as Cleeve Cloud and topped by a cluster of radio masts, is the highest point along the Cotswold escarpment (1083ft). To round off the walk, head north along the ridge to Cleeve Hill, from where you can pick up buses back into town via the main road.

Eating, drinking and nightlife

Cheltenham caters for all tastes and pockets, has the best style bars and **pubs** in the area, and its **clubs** draw in the punters from nearby Gloucester as well as the Cotswolds.

Restaurants

Boogaloos 16 Regent St. Good for salads and sandwiches while chilling out in the relaxed sofa basement or the buzzing, brightly coloured upstairs rooms. Closed eves. Inexpensive to Moderate.

The Daffodil 18–20 Suffolk Parade ⓣ01242/700060. Eat in the circle bar or auditorium of this former cinema, where the screen has been replaced with a hubbub of chefs. Moderate to Expensive.

Le Champignon Sauvage Suffolk Rd ⓣ01242/573449. Top-notch French cuisine – including scrumptious desserts – is served in this intimate restaurant. Two-course set lunch £16.50, two-course set dinner £35. Book three weeks in advance for weekends in summer. Closed Sun & Mon. Expensive to Very Expensive.

Le Petit Blanc next to *Queen's Hotel*, The Promenade ⓣ01242/266800. An outpost of Raymond Blanc's famed *Manoir Aux Quat' Saisons* where you can eat contemporary French cuisine at prices which become distinctly affordable at lunchtime – the three-course set lunch menu is £16 per head. Moderate to Expensive.

Orange Tree 317 High St ⓣ01242/234232. Vegetarians, vegans and allergy sufferers will appreciate the wide range of dishes on offer here. There's a pleasant courtyard, and breakfasts, organic wines and beers are all available too. Closed Mon eve & all Sun. Moderate.

Upstairs at the Beehive 1–3 Montpellier Villas ⓣ01242/702270. Friendly ambience and great French food in a lofty, blue-draped room above the pub (see below) make this a popular dining spot. No lunch. Closed Mon & Tues. Moderate to Expensive.

Pubs and clubs

The Beehive 1–3 Montpellier Villas. Easygoing Cheltenham institution with games shed, courtyard garden and cosy snug.

J's Vodka Bar 6 Regent St. Killer drinks from a range of 24 vodkas, served to the accompaniment of DJs playing house and funk.

Montpellier Wine Bar Bayshill Lodge, Montpellier St. Stylish wine bar and restaurant, with lovely bow-fronted windows for people-watching or being seen.

The Retreat 10–11 Suffolk Parade. Lively venue which caters to the business fraternity at lunchtime and Cheltenham Ladies College set in the evening. Good lunches served. Closed Sun.

Subtone 115–117 The Promenade ⓦwww.subtone.co.uk. Cheltenham's most popular club, playing 70s and 80s to funk. Closed Sun.

Tailor's Wine Bar 4 Cambray Place. Just off the High Street, here you can relax in old leather armchairs, watch sport on a big screen or sit in the pavement courtyard.

Time 33–35 Albion St ⓣ01242/570583. Large dance club, playing mainstream sounds.

Stroud and around

Five heavily populated valleys converge at **STROUD**, twelve miles west of Cirencester, creating an exhausting jumble of hills and a sense of high activity atypical of the Cotswolds. The bustle is not a new phenomenon. During the heyday of the wool trade the Frome River powered 150 mills, turning Stroud into the centre of the local cloth industry. Even now, the town is very much a working place, and one that doesn't need to peddle its heritage to the tourists in order to survive. While some of the old mills have been converted into flats, others contain factories, but only two continue to make cloth – no longer the so-called Stroudwater Scarlet used for military uniforms, but high-quality felt for tennis balls and snooker tables. In recent years, Stroud has become a thriving alternative centre, and contains one of the country's first eco-housing projects. You'll see mountains of organic food and sustainable goods for sale in the centre, while the nearby valleys are home to a community of artists and New Agers. Sadly, however, in spite of its scenic setting, the town remains the dowdiest of the region.

For visitors, the main point of interest is the excellent and family-friendly **Museum in the Park**, housed in an eighteenth-century mansion in Stratford Park, half a mile from the centre of town on the Gloucester road (April–Sept Tues–Fri 10am–5pm, Sat & Sun 11am–5pm; Oct–March Tues–Fri 10am–5pm, Sat & Sun 11am–4.30pm; free). Beautifully laid out, the collection demonstrates the history of the town through imaginatively themed rooms such as "Clean, Fit and Tidy" and "Industry and Invention", which are complemented by numerous questions and quotations. You can hear the voice of local author Laurie Lee and see the world's first lawnmower invented in 1830 by another local, Edward Budding, who took his inspiration from the machines which cut the nap on cloth. Look out for the lovely eighteenth-century paintings showing the tentering (hanging out) of the scarlet cloth on the hillsides.

Industrial archeology is strewn the length of the Frome Valley – the so-called Golden Valley. Council offices occupy one of the valley's finest mills, **Ebley Mill**, a twenty-minute walk west of the centre along the old Stroudwater Canal – for the best view you should then walk south across the field to the village of **Selsley**.

The unused **Severn and Thames Canal** east of Stroud cuts a more picturesque route, particularly beyond Chalford, three miles east, where houses perch precariously on the hillside. Walk thirty minutes along the towpath from here and you'll end up at the mouth of the **Sapperton tunnel**, more than two miles long and a great feat of eighteenth-century engineering. It's unsafe to go inside, so seek sustenance at the nearby *Daneway Inn* instead, or head for the hilltop village of Sapperton, a world away from the hurly-burly of the Frome Valley.

Trains on the London–Gloucester rail line stop at Stroud, which is also well served by **buses** from Cirencester. These and other bus services arrive at the station on Merrywalks. The **tourist office** is in the Subscription Rooms on Kendrick Street (Mon–Sat 10am–5pm; ⓣ01453/760960, ⓦwww.visitthecotswolds.co.uk). The most central place to **stay** is the *London Hotel*, 30–31 London Rd (ⓣ01453/759992, ⓦwww.s-h-systems.co.uk; ③), otherwise head for the *Downfield Hotel* at 134 Cainscross Rd (ⓣ01453/764496, ⓦwww.downfieldhotel.co.uk; ③), in a Georgian building five minutes from the High Street, or for the rambling Cotswold stone *Clothiers Arms* at 1 Bath Rd (ⓣ01453/763801, ⓦwww.clothiersarms.co.uk; ③), a mile from the town centre on the A46. You'll find the nearest **youth hostel** and **campsite** at Slimbridge (see p.386).

For **food** in the daytime go straight to *Mills Café* in Withey's Yard off High Street, which sells delicious cakes, homemade soups and other wholesome concoctions. In the evenings, the choice narrows down to Indian or Chinese as Stroud's nightlife gives over to laddish pub culture. Its saving grace, however, is the *Retreat* wine bar in Church Street, which is smartish, but only serves food during the day.

Uley

The B4066 cuts a glorious route along the valley ridge southwest of Stroud, passing through **ULEY**, six miles from town. Boasting one of the best settings in the region, the village **church** lords it over the small green and the *Old Crown* pub, where the local brews include one called Pig's Ear. **Uley Bury**, among the largest hill forts in Britain, extends along the ridge above the village. The path from the church takes you up the shortest and steepest route, though motorists can opt to drive up to the car park right by the fort. Fences prevent you from clambering on top of the bury, but you can walk around the edge – a distance of about two miles altogether – and take in some staggering views. The atmosphere peaks on a winter's day, when bracing winds blow across the ridge while mist gathers in the valley below.

Slimbridge

Eight miles southwest of Stroud, out of the Cotswolds, **SLIMBRIDGE** sits in a narrow corridor between the M5 and the Severn – a surprising location for the **Slimbridge Wildfowl and Wetlands Centre** (daily: April–Oct 9.30am–6pm; Nov–March 9.30am–5pm; last entry 1hr before closing; £6.40; Ⓦwww.wwt.org.uk), covering 120 acres between Sharpness Canal and the river. Since ornithologist Sir Peter Scott created it in 1946, the centre has become Britain's largest **wildfowl sanctuary**, and a breeding ground with an important conservation role. Geese, swans, ducks and a huge gathering of flamingos make up the bulk of the birdlife. While some birds are resident all year round, many are migratory: the greatest numbers congregate in the winter months, when Bewick swans, for example, migrate from Russia. There's an extensive network of trails around the sanctuary, with hides for observation.

Slimbridge has a comfortable, purpose-built **youth hostel** (Ⓣ0870/770 6036, Ⓔslimbridge@yha.org.uk), with beds for £10.25, accessible from a lane opposite the *Tudor Arms* pub in the village, and a **campsite**, the *Tudor Caravan Park* (Ⓣ01453/890483, Ⓦwww.tudorcaravanpark.co.uk), midway between the village and the wildfowl centre, about half a mile from each. The only **buses** to go anywhere near Slimbridge are those between Gloucester and Bristol or Dursley, which stop by the turn-off on the A38, just over a mile east of the village.

Berkeley

Though quite secluded within a swathe of meadows and neat gardens, **Berkeley Castle** (April–Aug Tues–Sat 11am–4pm, Sun 2–5pm; Sept Wed–Sat 11am–4pm, Sun 2–5pm; Oct Sun 2–5pm; £6.25, grounds only £3) dominates the little village of **BERKELEY**, five miles southwest of Slimbridge on the A38. The fortress has an agreeably turreted medieval look, the robust twelfth-century walls softened by later accretions acquired in its gradual transformation into a family home. The interior is packed with mementoes of its long history, including its grisliest moment in 1327, when Edward II was murdered here – apparently by a red-hot iron thrust into his bowels. You can view the cell where the event took place, along with dungeons, dining room, kitchen, picture gallery and the Great Hall. Outside, the grounds include an Elizabethan terraced garden and a Butterfly Farm (£2), and within easy walking distance, in the village itself, is the **Jenner Museum** (April–Sept Tues–Sat 12.30–5.30pm, Sun 1–5.30pm; Oct Sun 1–5.30pm; £3), dedicated to Edward Jenner, son of a local vicar and discoverer of the principle of vaccination. After studying in London, he returned here to practise as a doctor and conduct his experiments; the house's garden holds the thatched hut where he treated needy locals for free.

For a lunchtime stop near Berkeley, follow the narrow High Street out of the centre of the village for about a mile to reach the *Salutation*, an unpretentious country **pub** with a garden; it serves up bacon sandwiches and the like at lunchtimes. To reach Berkeley by public transport, Beaumont Travel operates coaches from Gloucester (Mon–Sat 5 daily, Sun 3; Ⓣ01452/309770, Ⓦwww.beaumont-travel.com).

Painswick

The A46 and the B4070 are equally attractive routes linking Stroud and Cheltenham, but the former has the edge because after four miles you reach the old wool town of **PAINSWICK**, where ancient buildings jostle for space on narrow streets running downhill off the busy main street. The fame of Painswick's **church** stems not so much from the building itself as from the surrounding **graveyard**, where 99 yew trees, cut into bizarre bulbous shapes resembling lollipops, surround a collection of eighteenth-century table-tombs unrivalled in the Cotswolds. However, it's the **Rococo Garden** (mid-Jan to Oct daily 11am–5pm; £3.60), about half a mile north up the Gloucester road and attached to Painswick House (not open to the public), that ranks as the town's main attraction. Created in the early eighteenth century and later abandoned, the garden has been restored to its original form with the aid of a painting dated 1748. Although there's usually some restoration in progress, it's a beautiful example – and the country's only one – of Rococo garden design, a short-lived fashion typified by a mix of formal geometrical shapes and more naturalistic, curving lines. With a vegetable patch as an unusual centrepiece, the Painswick garden spreads across a sheltered gully – for the best vistas, walk around anticlockwise. In February and March people flock to see the snowdrops that smother the slopes beneath the pond.

The best **bus** service to Painswick is the #46 between Stroud and Cheltenham, which runs hourly during the week and three times on Sundays. The number of **guest houses** and **hotels** attests to the amount of people who find Painswick a more congenial place than Stroud, and the **tourist office**, housed in the library on the main street (April–Oct Tues–Fri 10am–4pm, Sat 10am–1pm; ⓣ01452/813552), can help you find somewhere at the right price if the following places are booked: *Thorne Guest House* on Friday Street (ⓣ01452/812476; no credit cards; closed Dec & Jan; ❸), one of the oldest houses in the village, or *Cardynham House* on St Mary's Street (ⓣ01452/814006, ⓦwww.cardynham.co.uk; ❺), where all rooms are beautifully themed, and one has a lounge and private pool (£135 a night). In the evenings, there's a set meal on offer in the attached *March Hare* Thai **restaurant** for £24.50 (ⓣ01452/813452; closed Sun & Mon), which is almost the only place to eat in the village – not counting the nearby *Royal Oak*, reckoned to be the best **pub** hereabouts. Alternatively, you might consider heading out of Painswick, to the village of Edge, half a mile west, where *Upper Dorey's Mill* (ⓣ01452/812459, ⓦwww.doreys.co.uk; non-smoking; ❸) offers plenty of rural atmosphere in a converted eighteenth-century cloth mill by the riverside.

Gloucester

For centuries life was good for **GLOUCESTER**. The Romans chose the spot for a garrison to guard the Severn and spy on Wales, and later for a *colonia* or home for retired soldiers – the highest status a provincial Roman town could dream of. Commercial prestige came with trade up the River Severn, which developed into one of the busiest trade routes in Europe. The city's political importance hit its peak under the Normans, when William the Conqueror met here frequently with his council of nobles. The Middle Ages saw Gloucester's rise as a religious centre, and the construction of what is now the cathedral, but also witnessed its political and economic decline: navigating the Severn as far up as Gloucester was so difficult that most trade gradually shifted south to Bristol. In a brave attempt to reverse the city's decline, a canal was opened in 1827 to link Gloucester to Sharpness, on a broader stretch of the Severn further south. Trade picked up for a time, but it was only a temporary stay of execution.

Today, the canal is busy once again, though this time with pleasure boats. The Victorian dockyards too have undergone a facelift, the warehouses now given over to offices, apartments, a large antiques centre and a fine museum. Gloucester's most magnificent possession, however, is the **cathedral**, its tower visible for miles around. Few other buildings in the city have survived the ravages of history and the twentieth century, with the centre a mish-mash of medieval ruins swallowed up by ugly new buildings. Gloucester is solidly downmarket, discount stores taking the place of the boutiques that characterize nearby Cheltenham. Yet this comes almost as a relief: Gloucester is without airs, and as variegated culturally as it is architecturally; the Guildhall on Eastgate Street, a buzzing arts centre, has a cinema, regular exhibitions and a full and varied programme of concerts.

A web of roads engulfs Gloucester, surrounding the city like the tentacles of an octopus. If you're **driving**, head for the docks (well signposted) and park there. National Express runs **buses** from all neighbouring cities and beyond, and there are frequent local services from Cheltenham. **Trains** arrive every one or two hours from London, Cheltenham, Cardiff, Worcester and Bristol.

The City

Gloucester lies on the east bank of the Severn, its centre spread around a curve in the river. **The Cross**, once the entrance to the Roman forum, marks the heart of the city and the meeting-point of Northgate, Southgate, Eastgate and Westgate streets, all Roman roads. **St Michael's Tower**, the remains of an old church, overlooks it. The main shopping area lies east of the Northgate–Southgate axis, with the **cathedral** and the **docks**, the focus of interest, to the west of it.

Southgate and Westgate streets

The most interesting parish church in Gloucester is **St Mary de Crypt** on Southgate Street, mostly late medieval but with some of its original Norman features; fragments of a sixteenth-century wall painting of the Adoration of the Magi in the chancel shows unusual detail for work of that period. The church is kept locked, but you can get the key from the tourist office across the road. Greyfriars runs alongside St Mary's, past the ruins of a Franciscan church and the Eastgate Market to the **City Museum** on Brunswick Road (Tues–Sat 10am–5pm; £2; combined ticket with Folk Museum £3; ⓦwww.mylife.gloucester.gov.uk), with a good archeological collection including the decorative bronze Birdlip mirror and what's claimed to be the world's oldest complete backgammon set (1100 AD), carved from bone and amber. A fragment of the Roman city wall, preserved *in situ* below ground level, can be viewed from the museum on summer Saturdays only, or at any time from Eastgate Street. Westgate Street, quieter and many times more pleasant than its three Roman counterparts, retains several medieval buildings. One of them, a creaking timber-framed house at the bottom of the street, contains the **Folk Museum** (Tues–Sat 10am–5pm; £2; combined ticket with City Museum £3; ⓦwww.mylife.gloucester.gov.uk), which illustrates the social history of the Gloucester area using an impressive collection of objects, from huge wrought-iron cheese presses to salt-filled rolling pins used to scare off witches. College Court Alley leads from Westgate Street to the haven of the cathedral, passing the Beatrix Potter shop and museum – the house sketched by the children's artist and author while she was on holiday here in 1897 and subsequently appearing in every copy of *The Tailor of Gloucester*.

GLOUCESTER

ACCOMMODATION

Albert	A
Edward	B
Lulworth	E
New County	C
Spalite	D

RESTAURANTS & PUBS

Café René	7
Cellars	5
Fountain Inn	3
New Inn	4
Orchids at the Undercroft	1
Pizza Piazza	6
Ye Olde Fish Shoppe	2

Cheltenham
Nature in Art & Tewkesbury
Stroud
E, A430 & M5 South to Bristol
Ross & Ledbury

Cheltenham Rd
Hillfield Court
Alexandra Road
The Firs
Heathville Road
Hyde Lane
Newland St
London Road
Henry St
Oxford Road
Claremont Rd
Columbia Ct
Oxford Street
Wellington Place
Union St
Alvin Street
Worcester Parade
Great Western Road
Metz Way
Train Station
Bruton Way
Black Dog Way
Worcester Street
Skinner St
St Catherine St
Hare Lane
Park Lane
Gouda Way
Pitt Street
Priory Rd
Cathedral
St John's Ln
College Court
College St
St Mary's Sq
Archdeacon Street
Mount St
Clare St
St Oswald's Road
Royal Oak Road
Folk Museum
Lower Quay St
Upper Quay St
Quay Street
Westgate Street
Berkeley St
Bearland
Police Station
Bull Ln
Cross Keys
The Cross
St Michael's Tower
Northgate Street
The Oxbode
Kings Walk
Kings Square
Bus Station
Market Parade
Station Road
Bedford St
St Kilda
Russell Street
Clarence St
Eastgate Street
Queens St
Market Way
Bell Walk
Southgate Street
St Mary de Crypt
Brunswick Road
Greyfriars
City Museum
Longsmith Street
Blackfriars
Ladybellgate St
Barbican Rd
Commercial Rd
Regiments of Gloucester Museum
Docks
The Quay
River Severn
Castle Meads
Footbridge
Severn Road
Llanthony Road
National Waterways Museum
Parliament Street
St Michaels Square
Hampden Way
Wellington Street
Barton Kings Square
Arthur Street
Trier Way
Midland Road
All Saints Road
Barton Street
Park Road
Montpellier
Brunswick Road
Brunswick Square
Albion St
Norfolk Street
Spa Road

© Crown copyright

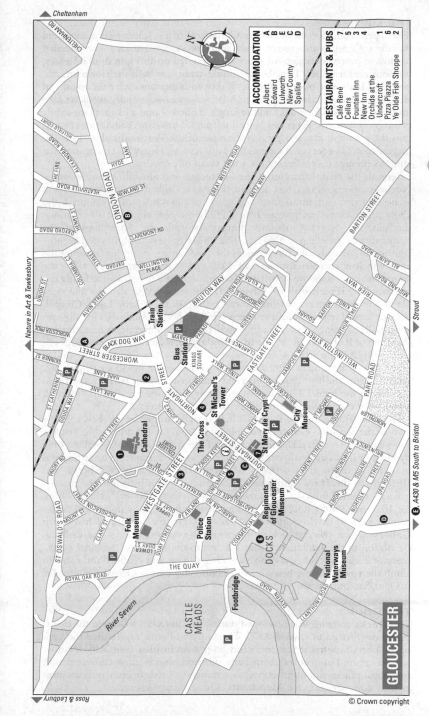

The Cathedral

The superb condition of Gloucester **Cathedral** (daily 7.30am–6pm; suggested donation £2.50; ⓦwww.gloucestercathedral.uk.com) is striking in a city that has lost so much of its past. An abbey was founded on this spot by the Saxons, but four centuries later Benedictine monks came and built their own church, begun in 1069. As a place of worship it shot to importance after the murder at Berkeley Castle of Edward II in 1327: Bristol and Malmesbury wouldn't take his body, but Gloucester did, and the king's shrine became a major place of pilgrimage. The money generated helped to finance the conversion of the church into the country's first and greatest example of the **Perpendicular style**: the magnificent 225-foot tower crowns the achievement. Henry VIII recognized the church's prestige by conferring on it the status of cathedral.

Beneath the reconstructions of the fourteenth and fifteenth centuries, some Norman aspects remain, best seen in the **nave**, flanked by sturdy pillars and arches adorned with immaculate zigzag mouldings. Only when you reach the choir and transepts can you see how skilfully the new church was built inside the old, the Norman masonry hidden beneath the finer lines of the Perpendicular panelling and tracery. The **choir** has extraordinary fourteenth-century misericords, and also provides the best vantage point for admiring the **east window** completed in around 1350 and – at almost 80 feet tall – the largest medieval window in Britain. Beneath it, to the left (as you're facing the east window) is the **tomb of Edward II**, immortalized in alabaster and marble and in good fettle apart from some graffiti. In the nearby **Lady Chapel**, delicate carved tracery holds a staggering patchwork of windows, virtually creating walls of stained glass. There are well-preserved monuments here, too, but the tomb of Robert II, in the **south ambulatory**, is far more unusual. Robert, eldest son of William the Conqueror, died in 1134, but the painted wooden effigy dates from around 1290. Dressed as a crusader, he lies in a curious pose, with his arms and legs crossed, his right hand gripping his sword ready to do battle with the infidel. The modern, vibrantly blue glass installed in the south ambulatory chapel works surprisingly well in the context.

The innovative nature of the cathedral's design can perhaps be best appreciated in the beautiful **cloisters**, completed in 1367 and featuring the first fan vaulting in the country. The fine quality of the work is outdone perhaps only by Henry VII's Chapel in Westminster Abbey, which it inspired. The setting was used to represent the corridors of Hogwart's School of Witchcraft and Wizardry in the *Harry Potter* films. Back inside, an **exhibition** in the upstairs galleries, reached from the north transept (April–Oct Mon–Fri 10.30am–4pm, Sat 10.30am–3pm; £1.50) gives the low-down on the east window and allows you to view it at close quarters. Here, you can try out the **Whispering Gallery**, where you can pick up the tiniest sounds from across the vaulting. Admission to the exhibition includes access to the **treasury**, the usual assortment of ecclesiastical bric-a-brac, including flagons and chalices. You can also climb the **tower** for the best views of Gloucester (April–Oct Wed, Thurs, Fri 2.30pm, Sat 2pm & 3pm; £2.50).

The Docks

The **Docks** complex was developed during the fifty years following the opening of the Sharpness canal in 1827. The import of corn represented the bulk of the port's business at that time, and huge **warehouses** were built for storing the grain. Fourteen of them have survived, mostly now converted into municipal offices and shops as well as a museum, a redevelopment at its most crudely commercial in the **Merchants' Quay** shopping centre.

The **National Waterways Museum** (daily 10am–5pm, last admission 4pm; £5; ⓦwww.nwm.org.uk), in the southernmost Llanthony Warehouse, completely immerses you in the canal mania that swept Britain in the eighteenth and nineteenth centuries, touching on everything from the engineering of the locks to the lives of the horses that trod the towpaths. The three floors contain plenty of atmospheric noises off, videos, accessible information and interactive displays. Out from the main building you can practise "walking the wall" in the time-honoured manner of boatmen, who propelled their narrowboats through the tunnels by their feet, and explore the boats themselves along the quayside. In the old customs house, the **Regiments of Gloucestershire Museum** (June–Sept daily 10am–5pm; Oct–May Tues–Sun 10am–5pm; £4.25) does an award-winning job of making a potentially dull or alienating subject fascinating. It doesn't rely on the displays of uniforms and miscellaneous memorabilia used in most military museums, but concentrates on all aspects of life as a soldier, both in war and during peacetime.

Nature in Art Museum and Art Gallery

Housed in a Georgian mansion two miles north of Gloucester on the A38 Tewkesbury road, the **Nature in Art Museum and Art Gallery** (Tues–Sun 10am–5pm; £3.35) shows a wide range of paintings, sculpture, ceramics and other applied arts inspired by nature, by such artists as Picasso, Henry Moore, René Lalique and David Shepherd. With exhibits arranged inside and outdoors, it's an engaging collection, complemented by a good programme of temporary exhibitions and artists in residence. Buses #71 and #371 running between Gloucester and Tewkesbury stop at Orchard Park, Twigworth (not Sun), from where it's a half-mile walk.

Practicalities

Gloucester's bus and train stations are opposite one another across Bruton Way, five minutes' walk east of the Cross. The **tourist office** is at 28 Southgate St (Mon–Sat 10am–5pm, also Sun in July & Aug 11am–3pm; ⓣ01452/396572, ⓦwww.gloucester.gov.uk/tourism). Daily walking **tours** (£2.50) of the city leave from the tourist office at 2.30pm from mid-June to mid-September. Judging from the amount of **accommodation** in the city centre, Gloucester doesn't expect many visitors to stay overnight. Of the few **hotels** within easy walking distance of the train station and centre, the *Albert* at 56–60 Worcester St (ⓣ01452/502081, ⓦwww.alberthotel.com; ❷), a listed red-brick building from the 1830s, and the Victorian *Edward* at 88–92 London Rd (ⓣ01452/525865, ⓦwww.edwardhotel-gloucester.co.uk; ❸) offer the best value. Also very central, and with more comforts but fairly bland, is the *New County Hotel* at 44 Southgate St (ⓣ01452/307000, ⓦwww.thenewcounty.com; ❺). Among the central, inexpensive B&Bs is *Spalite* (ⓣ01452/380828, ⓦwww.spalitehotel.com; ❷), at the bottom of Southgate Street near the docks, although it's right on the main road and a bit prone to traffic noise, and the four-storey *Lulworth* at 12 Midland Rd (ⓣ01452/521881, ⓦwww.s-h-systems.co.uk; ❷), in a quiet location behind the park.

The selection of **restaurants** is no more remarkable than the hotels, and many places are open only during the day. You'll find reliable if rather unimaginative fare in the *Orchids at the Undercroft* restaurant in the cathedral, open until 5pm, and at the café-bar in the Guildhall on Eastgate Street – open until 11pm and always lively. *Ye Olde Fish Shoppe* on Hare Lane, even more of a Gloucester institution, occupies a sixteenth-century building and is the fanciest take-away for miles; it serves excellent crispy fish until 6.30pm, though the attached restaurant stays open later (Ⓣ01452/255502; no credit cards; closed all Sun & Mon eve). In the evenings, choice extends to the vaulted *Cellars* (closed Sun & Mon) in Longsmith Street, with a set-price menu at £11.95 for two courses, or the *Café René*, Greyfriars, Southgate Street, where walls and ceilings are smothered with bottles. For pizzas go to *Pizza Piazza* at Merchants' Quay – the only reason to venture to the docks in the evening.

There isn't a huge choice of **pubs** either, though the best are all within spitting distance of the Cross. The rambling fifteenth-century *New Inn* in Northgate Street has a good atmosphere, a splendid galleried courtyard and cheap meals, but for really tasty hot food at rock-bottom prices go to the *Fountain Inn*, down a narrow alley off Westgate Street; this pub pulls a sublime pint of Abbot ale and has tables in an olde-worlde adjacent courtyard – ideal for a sunny day. For **clubbers**, *Innteraction* on Bruton Way (Wed–Sat; Ⓣ01452/302222, Ⓦwww.innteraction.com) covers most tastes and has theme nights.

Tewkesbury and around

The small market town of **TEWKESBURY**, ten miles north of Gloucester, stands hemmed in by the Avon and Severn rivers, which converge nearby, and the threat of floods has curbed expansion more efficiently than any conservation-conscious planning office could. Pressure of space accounts for the narrow alleys and courts leading off from the main streets, of which thirty of the original ninety still survive. The comparatively unchanging face of Tewkesbury is also due to the fact that it almost completely missed out on the Industrial Revolution. Elegant Georgian houses and medieval timber-framed buildings still line several of the town's main streets – especially Church Street – and the Norman **abbey** has survived as one of the greatest in England. Some old buildings inevitably fell to postwar bulldozers, however, particularly along the High Street, and recent years haven't been kind to the town's economy.

The constant rumble of traffic through Tewkesbury can be troublesome, but the fact that four main roads meet here (Gloucester, Worcester, Evesham and Ledbury are all within fifteen miles) means that getting to the town is fairly easy. Stagecoach, Swanbrook and Midland Red operate most **buses** to Tewkesbury, running from Gloucester, Cheltenham, Worcester and Evesham; for current timetable information, call Ⓣ0870/608 2608, or visit Ⓦwww.traveline.org.uk.

Tewkesbury Abbey

The site of **Tewkesbury Abbey** (daily 7.30am–6pm; suggested donation £2) was first selected for a Benedictine monastery in the eighth century, but virtually nothing of the Saxon complex survived a sacking by the Danes, and a new abbey was founded by a Norman nobleman in 1092. The work took about sixty years to complete, with some additions made in the fourteenth century. Two hundred years later the Dissolution brought about the destruction of most of the monastic buildings, but the abbey itself survived thanks to a buy-out in which the local people paid Henry VIII £453 for the property.

The sheer scale of the abbey's exterior makes a lasting impact: its colossal **tower** is the largest Norman tower in the world, while the west front's soaring recessed arch – 65 feet high – is the only exterior arch in the country to boast such impressive proportions. In the nave, fourteen stout Norman pillars steal the show, graceful despite their size, and topped by a fourteenth-century ribbed and vaulted ceiling, studded with gilded bosses (look for the musical angels). On the blue and scarlet **choir** roof the bosses include a ring of shining suns (emblem of the Yorkist cause), said to have been put there by Edward IV after the defeat of the Lancastrians at Tewkesbury in 1471, the last important battle of the Wars of the Roses. (The battlefield, known as Bloody Meadow, is off Lincoln Green Lane, southwest of the abbey.) The best way to appreciate the bosses is to look in the mirror trolley from the west door. South of the choir is the **Milton Organ**, played by the poet when he was secretary to Oliver Cromwell at Hampton Court and bought by the townspeople in 1727. The abbey's medieval tombs celebrate Tewkesbury's greatest patrons, the Fitzhamons, De Clares, Beauchamps and Despensers, who turned the building into something of a mausoleum for themselves. The Despensers have the best monuments, particularly Sir Edward, standard-bearer to the Black Prince, who died in 1375 and is shown as a kneeling figure on the roof of the **Trinity Chapel** to the right of the high altar: you can see it best from beside the Warwick Chantry Chapel in the north aisle. Nearby, in the ambulatory, the macabre so-called **Wakeman Cenotaph**, carved in the fifteenth century but of otherwise uncertain origin, represents a decaying corpse being consumed by snakes and other creatures.

Practicalities

Tewkesbury's **tourist office** at 64 Barton St (April–Oct Mon–Sat 9.30am–5pm, Sun 10am–4pm; Nov–March closed Sun; ⓣ01684/295027, ⓦwww.visitcotswoldsandsevernvale.gov.uk) has inexpensive town and walking maps, plus a small museum (£1) upstairs, which includes two good models, one of the Battle of Tewkesbury of 1471 and the other a delightful, miniature fairground completed in 1958 by Mr Salt, a local resident. You won't have to look far to find a **room**: almost opposite the abbey at 62 Church St, *Abbey Antiques Guest House* (ⓣ01684/298145; no credit cards; ❸) is colourfully furnished with antiques, and offers rooms with plenty of character, while *Barton House*, 5 Barton Rd (ⓣ01684/292049 or 07946/460601, ⓦwww.s-h-systems.co.uk; no credit cards; ❷) has an eclectic mix of furniture, and plain rooms. More genteel are the *Two Back of Avon*, a beautiful period building on Riverside Walk, left off Quay Street (ⓣ01684/298935, ⓦwww.s-h-systems.co.uk; no smoking; no credit cards; ❷), and the quiet *Carrant Brook House* on Rope Walk (ⓣ01684/290355; no credit cards; ❸). Most of Tewkesbury's old **hotels** are run by chains; best are the *Royal Hop Pole*, Church Street (ⓣ01684/293236, ⓦwww.regalhotels.co.uk; ❺), whose annexe has a loggia facing the garden, and the black and white *Tudor House*, High Street (ⓣ01684/297755; ❹), which has capacious rooms and a priest's hole in the seventeenth-century Mayor's Parlour lounge. There are no fewer than five **campsites** within striking distance of the city, the most easily accessible being the *Abbey Caravan Club* in the park at the bottom of Gander Lane (ⓣ01684/294035).

For daytime **snacks** or **lunches**, there are plenty of places on Church Street: choose between the chrome of the *Aubergine* café-bar (closed Sun) at no. 25 for good salads and sandwiches, *My Great Grandfathers* (closed Mon) at no. 84, which is excellent for traditional puddings such as Spotted Dick, and the ancient *Berkeley Arms* **pub** at no. 8, popular with pensioners and serving astoundingly cheap but fairly basic food. At the top of the High Street, *Ye Olde Black Bear* also pulls some of the best pints in town. In the evenings, the blue and oak-furnished *Rendezvous* at 78 Church St (☎01684/290357; closed Mon) concentrates on moderately priced Mediterranean-style fish and meat dishes and has a cellar bar for snacks; it also opens for Sunday lunch.

Deerhurst

Before the construction of Tewkesbury's Norman abbey, **Deerhurst**, just south of the town, was the most prestigious religious centre in the area. As the chief monastery in the Saxon kingdom of Hwicce, it was considered a suitable venue for the meeting in 1016 between the English king Edmund Ironside and Knut (Canute) the Dane, at which the partition of England was agreed. Deerhurst's importance declined after 1100, but two outstanding buildings date back to the village's heyday.

The monastery church of **St Mary's** is a chronological jumble: some masonry dates back to the eighth century, but the Saxon work was done mainly in the tenth. The Normans then chopped the insides about a bit (they knocked arches into the nave walls, which somehow didn't collapse), and other additions came later. The interior remains remarkably simple considering, and contains several very rare features, none more so than the series of curious **windows and holes** that puncture the nave walls: these small triangular piercings, cut by the Saxons, are said to represent the eyes of God. There's a ninth-century **font** of golden Cotswold stone in the north aisle, with intricate spiral decoration unique for that period, and, above the inner doorway, look out for the very fine, almost abstract Saxon sculpture of the Virgin Mary, unusually with the child in her womb and not her arms; its flat surface would originally have been brightly painted. Outside, a sign directs you to a stylized carved angel high up on the wall of the ruined apse; though also Saxon, the relief looks more Celtic in inspiration. The adjoining house once formed part of the monastery's cloister.

The nearby **Odda's Chapel**, which also clings to another building (in this case a half-timbered cottage), lay neglected until last century, its Saxon masonry smothered underneath plaster. It's only slightly younger than St Mary's, having been built in 1056 by Odda in honour of his brother Aelfric, both relatives of the king. The small chapel, just forty feet long, has survived in good condition apart from a few damp patches. The original dedicatory inscription is in the Ashmolean Museum in Oxford, but a copy has been put in its original place.

Deerhurst is four miles south of Tewkesbury by road, but only two miles on foot across the fields or along the Severn. Alternatively, you can catch the #71 or #372 **bus** (not Sun) from Tewkesbury to Gloucester, which stops within a mile of Deerhurst.

Bredon Hill

The most important Iron Age fort in the area once crowned **Bredon Hill**, six miles northeast of Tewkesbury and visible for miles around in the flat Severn Vale. Excavation of the site revealed more than fifty bodies, all hacked to pieces, seemingly the victims of a final assault by unknown attackers in the first century AD. Inside the rampart, a huge expanse covering eleven acres, an eighteenth-century tower called Parson's Folly is an incongruous centrepiece, but the views are supreme, with deer often grazing on the slopes.

Bredon Hill can be approached from various places around the southern foot of the hill. From **Overbury**, one of the prettier villages, the climb takes less than an hour. If you're relying on public transport, buses bound for Evesham from Tewkesbury pass through the village of **Bredon** (except Sun), from where you should allow about three hours to walk to the hill and back.

Bristol and around

On the borders of Gloucestershire and Somerset, **BRISTOL** has harmoniously blended its mercantile roots with a slick, modern culture, fuelled in recent years by fast money, new technology and a large student population. As a centre for the arts and media, the city has a vibrant youth culture and can boast some of the region's best restaurants and nightlife, while its sights range from medieval churches to cutting-edge attractions that highlight its scientific achievements.

Weaving through its centre, the River Avon forms part of a system of waterways that made Bristol a great inland port, in later years booming on the transatlantic trafficking of such goods as rum, tobacco and slaves. In the nineteenth century the illustrious **Isambard Kingdom Brunel** laid the foundations of a tradition of engineering, creating two of Bristol's greatest monuments – the *SS Great Britain* and the lofty Clifton Suspension Bridge. More recently, spin-offs from the aerospace industry have placed the city at the forefront of the fields of communications, computing, design and finance. Though the ports have long since fallen into decline, the old docks area has benefitted from a massive renewal programme, and now forms the heart of an extensive leisure and entertainment scheme which includes a pedestrian- and cycle-way linking the redeveloped train station at Temple Meads with the docks as far as the *SS Great Britain*, taking in St Mary Redcliffe and Queen Square.

Beneath the prosperous surface, Bristol has its negative aspects – one of England's highest populations of homeless people, some of the most notorious housing estates and the highest proportion of cars to inhabitants. Nonetheless, it remains an attractive city, predominantly hilly, and surrounded by rolling countryside. It's also just a short ride from the sea, where you might spend a day at the Victorian resorts of **Clevedon** and the much grander **Weston-super-Mare**, though be warned that the Bristol Channel is not the most inspiring place to swim, the sea reduced at low tide to a distant ribbon on the horizon.

Arrival, information and accommodation

Bristol is an easy place to get to. Twice-hourly **trains** from London Paddington arrive at either Bristol Parkway or Bristol Temple Meads. The latter, a twenty-minute walk from the centre, is used by services to and from the west, and served by frequent buses #8 and #9, which pass through the centre on their way to Cotham (#9 only) and Clifton. Parkway is too far out of town to walk from: take bus #73 (on Sundays, #73, #82, #573 or #584). The **bus station**, where National Express coaches from London arrive hourly, is in Marlborough Street, near Broadmead, the modern shopping centre. Cheaper Bakers Dolphin Coaches (Ⓣ01934/413000) also connect Bristol with London's Marble Arch, with stops at the bus station and Clifton.

The **tourist office** is in the at-Bristol complex, on Wildscreen Walk, Harbourside (March–Oct daily 10am–6pm; Nov–Feb Mon–Sat 10am–5pm, Sun 11am–4pm; Ⓣ0906/586 2313, Ⓦwww.visitbristol.co.uk); they offer a booking service for rooms in hotels and B&Bs (£3). Most of Bristol's **accommodation** is in the leafy Georgian areas of Cotham and Clifton, which are also the districts where the majority of the city's students live.

Hotels and B&Bs

Arches 132 Cotham Brow Ⓣ0117/924 7398, Ⓦwww.arches-hotel.co.uk. In an attractive area of town, though a bus ride from the centre. Small but comfortable rooms with or without bath, and vegetarian breakfasts. Non-smoking. ❷

Downs View 38 Upper Belgrave Rd Ⓣ0117/973 7046, Ⓦwww.downsviewguesthouse.co.uk. As the name implies, this B&B enjoys a good view over Clifton Downs, though the views over the city from the back are even better. Rooms are plain, but adequate, some with shared bathrooms. ❸

Naseby House 105 Pembroke Rd ⓣ0117/973 7859, ⓦwww.nasebyhousehotel.co.uk. Located in Clifton a short walk from the downs, this plush Victorian building is beautifully furnished in period style. ❹

Oakfield 52 Oakfield Rd ⓣ0117/973 5556. In Clifton, about a mile from the city centre; the public rooms are gloomy, though the bedrooms are fine, all with basins; bathrooms are shared. ❷

St Michael's Guest House 145 St Michael's Hill ⓣ0117/907 7820. Simple accommodation situated over one of Cotham's most popular cafés, near the university. Tea- and coffee-making facilities, plus cable-linked TVs in all rooms, but no en-suite bathrooms. ❷

Sunderland Guest House 4 Sunderland Place ⓣ0117/973 7249 or 0797/624 9108, ⓔsunderland.gh@blueyonder.co.uk. This is the only budget lodging in this part of town, Lower Clifton, very near the centre. Rooms are fairly small and basic, but quiet, clean and adequate for a night or two. No credit cards. ❷

Victoria Square Victoria Square ⓣ0117/973 9058, ⓦwww.vicsquare.com. With a choice location near Clifton Village, this Georgian hotel has smart, light rooms, though some are on the small side. Breakfast (included in price) is taken overlooking the leafy square. ❻

Hostels, student halls and campsites

Baltic Wharf Cumberland Rd ⓣ0117/926 8030. The prime riverside location of this campsite in the centre of town compensates for the cramped space, which is dominated by caravans. Unless you bag one of the eight grass pitches, you'll have to cope with unforgiving stone chippings. There is no space for campers' cars on site.

Bristol Backpackers 17 St Stephen's St ⓣ0117/925 7900, ⓦwww.bristolbackpackers.co.uk. Very central, this friendly independent hostel housed in a lovely old building has a late-drinking bar, washing facilities and first-class showers. Kitchen and cheap Internet access too, but can be noisy. Dorm beds cost £14.

Bristol YHA Hayman House, 14 Narrow Quay ⓣ0870/770 5726, ⓔbristol@yha.org.uk. Modern and central, located in a refurbished warehouse on the quayside; most dorms have four beds at £16 each (including breakfast), though there are also some twin rooms. Kitchen, laundry, games room and bike storage available. ❶

Brook Lodge Farm Cowslip Green, Redhill ⓣ01934/862311, ⓔbrooklodgefarm@aol.com. Nine miles southwest of Bristol, this is the nearest rural campsite to town, a mile southwest of the village of Redhill off the A38. Bikes can be rented, and an outdoor pool is open in summer. Closed Nov–Feb.

University of Bristol The Hawthorns Woodland Road, Clifton, ⓣ0117/954 5555, ⓦwww.bris.ac.uk/depts/hawthorns. The university's main hall of residence opens its doors to non-students during the summer vacations (usually late June to late Sept), renting out singles at £8.50 per night, or £10 en suite, with self-catering facilities. The only snag is the week minimum stay (and no arrivals at weekends). A restaurant, bar and laundrette are available on weekdays. Rooms must be prior booked.

The City

A good place to start exploring, **the Centre** was once a quay-lined dock but is now the traffic-ridden nucleus of the city, with cars swirling round the statues of Edmund Burke, MP for Bristol from 1774 to 1780, and local merchant and benefactor Edward Colston (1636–1721). The Centre is just a few steps from the cathedral and the oldest quarter of town, and is linked by water-taxi to the sights around the Floating Harbour, the waterway network that runs through the southern part of town and connects with the River Avon. You could cover Bristol's other central attractions on foot without too much sweat, but there are enough steep hills to make it worthwhile using the bus network for more distant sights, especially in the Clifton district, at the highest part of town, on the edge of the Avon Gorge.

From the Cathedral to the City Museum

A short walk west of the Centre, the grassy expanse of College Green is dominated by the crescent-shaped Council House from 1956, and, facing it, by the contrastingly medieval lines of **Bristol Cathedral** (daily 8am–6pm; suggested donation £2). Founded around 1140 as an abbey on the supposed spot of St Augustine's convocation with Celtic Christians in 603, this became a cathedral church with the Dissolution of the Monasteries. Among the many additions in subsequent centuries are the two towers on the west front, erected in the nineteenth century in a faithful act of homage to Edmund Knowle, architect and abbot at the start of the fourteenth century. The cathedral's interior offers a unique example among Britain's cathedrals of a German-style hall church, in which the aisles rise to the same height as the central area. Abbot Knowle's **choir** offers one of the country's most exquisite illustrations of the early Decorated style of Gothic, while the adjoining **Elder Lady Chapel**, dating from the early thirteenth century, contains some fine tombs and eccentric carvings of animals, including a monkey playing the bagpipes accompanied by a ram on the violin. The ornate **Eastern Lady Chapel** has some of England's finest examples of heraldic glass. From the south transept, a door leads through to the **Chapter House**, a richly carved piece of late Norman architecture.

Opposite the cathedral's west front, take a look at the Norman **Abbey Gateway**, which blends harmoniously with the cathedral on one side and the city library – constructed at the beginning of this century – on the other. The northeast side of the green has one more vestige from the Middle Ages: the **Lord Mayor's Chapel** (Tues–Sat 10am–noon & 1–4pm), conspicuous by its large Perpendicular window – the interior has some lovely French and Flemish stained glass, and striking effigies of the thirteenth-century founders of the hospital of which the church once formed a part.

Elegant Georgian streets lead off the shop-lined **Park Street** climbing steeply up from College Green. On Great George Street, the **Georgian House** (April–Oct Mon–Wed, Sat & Sun 10am–5pm; free), is the faithfully restored former home of a local sugar merchant, its spacious rooms filled with examples of period furniture – sumptuous cabinets, divans and armchairs. The basement kitchens are fitted with equipment that would have been used in the early eighteenth century, and there's even an indoor pool, or rather a plunge bath, for morning dips. In one of the upstairs rooms, illustrated panels put it all into context, and tell the engrossing story of the family's dealings in the West Indies, including their involvement in slaving. From Great George Street, or from Berkeley Square further up the hill, you can gain access to **Brandon Hill Park**, a sequestered pocket of greenery that is home to the landmark **Cabot Tower** (open daily until dusk; free), built in 1897 to commemorate the 400th anniversary of John Cabot's voyage to America. You can climb up the 105-foot tower for the city's best panorama.

At the top of Park Street stands central Bristol's other chief landmark, the **Wills Memorial Tower**, erected in the 1920s to lend some stature to the newly opened university. One of the last great neo-Gothic buildings in England, the tower was the gift of the local Wills tobacco dynasty, the university's main benefactors.

Next to the tower, on Queen's Road, the **City Museum and Art Gallery** (daily 10am–5pm; free) occupies another building donated by the Wills family, this time neo-Classical. The ground-floor sections on local archeology, geology and natural history are pretty well what you'd expect, but the scope of the museum is occasionally surprising – it has an important collection of Chinese porcelain, glassware, stoneware and ivory, and some magnificent Assyrian reliefs carved in the eighth century BC. The second-floor gallery of paintings and sculptures includes work by English Pre-Raphaelites and French Impressionists, as well as a few choice older pieces, among them a portrait of Martin Luther by Cranach and Giovanni Bellini's unusual *Descent into Limbo*.

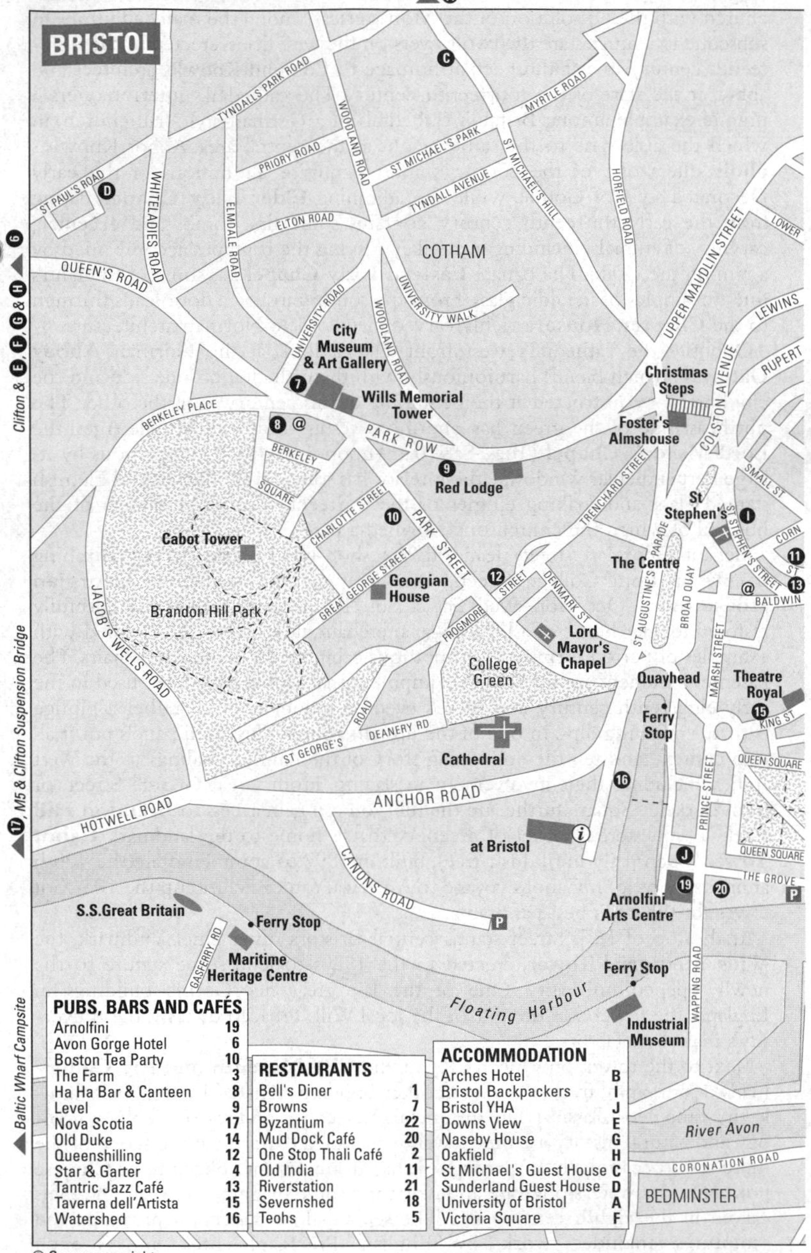
BRISTOL
A
C
D
TYNDALLS PARK ROAD
MYRTLE ROAD
WOODLAND ROAD
ST MICHAEL'S PARK
PRIORY ROAD
ST MICHAEL'S HILL
ST PAUL'S ROAD
WHITELADIES ROAD
ELMDALE ROAD
TYNDALL AVENUE
HORFIELD ROAD
ELTON ROAD
COTHAM
LOWER
UPPER MAUDLIN STREET
QUEEN'S ROAD
UNIVERSITY ROAD
UNIVERSITY WALK
LEWINS
City Museum & Art Gallery
7
Wills Memorial Tower
RUPERT
Christmas Steps
COLSTON AVENUE
BERKELEY PLACE
8 @
PARK ROW
Foster's Almshouse
BERKELEY SQUARE
9
Red Lodge
TRENCHARD STREET
SMALL ST
CHARLOTTE STREET
10
PARK STREET
St Stephen's
I
ST STEPHEN'S ST
CORN ST
11
Cabot Tower
12
STREET
DENMARK ST
The Centre
13
@
BALDWIN
GREAT GEORGE STREET
Georgian House
ST AUGUSTINE'S PARADE
BROAD QUAY
JACOB'S WELLS ROAD
Brandon Hill Park
FROGMORE
MARSH STREET
Lord Mayor's Chapel
College Green
Quayhead
Theatre Royal
15
KING ST
Ferry Stop
ROAD
DEANERY RD
ST GEORGE'S
Cathedral
QUEEN SQUARE
PRINCE STREET
16
ANCHOR ROAD
HOTWELL ROAD
at Bristol
i
J
QUEEN SQUARE
CANONS ROAD
19
20
THE GROVE
P
S.S.Great Britain
Ferry Stop
P
Arnolfini Arts Centre
GASFERRY RD
Maritime Heritage Centre
Ferry Stop
Floating Harbour
WAPPING ROAD
Industrial Museum
River Avon
CORONATION ROAD
BEDMINSTER
Clifton & E, F, G & H ▲ 6
▲ 17, M5 & Clifton Suspension Bridge
▲ Baltic Wharf Campsite
PUBS, BARS AND CAFÉS
Arnolfini 19
Avon Gorge Hotel 6
Boston Tea Party 10
The Farm 3
Ha Ha Bar & Canteen 8
Level 9
Nova Scotia 17
Old Duke 14
Queenshilling 12
Star & Garter 4
Tantric Jazz Café 13
Taverna dell'Artista 15
Watershed 16
RESTAURANTS
Bell's Diner 1
Browns 7
Byzantium 22
Mud Dock Café 20
One Stop Thali Café 2
Old India 11
Riverstation 21
Severnshed 18
Teohs 5
ACCOMMODATION
Arches Hotel B
Bristol Backpackers I
Bristol YHA J
Downs View E
Naseby House G
Oakfield H
St Michael's Guest House C
Sunderland Guest House D
University of Bristol A
Victoria Square F

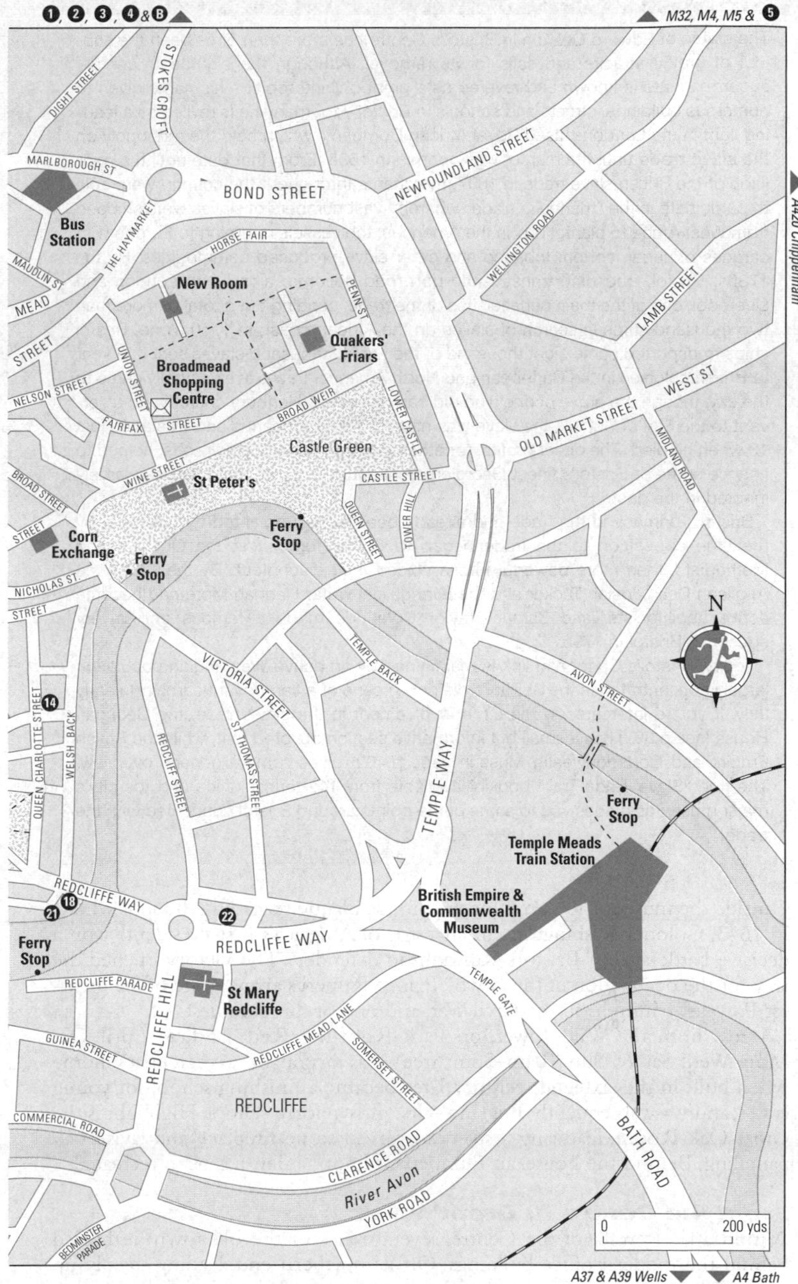
❶, ❷, ❸, ❹ & Ⓑ
M32, M4, M5 & ❺
A420 Chippenham
A37 & A39 Wells
A4 Bath
DIGHT STREET
STOKES CROFT
MARLBOROUGH ST
BOND STREET
NEWFOUNDLAND STREET
Bus Station
THE HAYMARKET
HORSE FAIR
MAUDLIN ST
MEAD
New Room
WELLINGTON ROAD
LAMB STREET
PENN ST
Quakers' Friars
STREET
UNION STREET
Broadmead Shopping Centre
NELSON STREET
BROAD WEIR
LOWER CASTLE
WEST ST
OLD MARKET STREET
FAIRFAX
STREET
Castle Green
MIDLAND ROAD
WINE STREET
St Peter's
CASTLE STREET
BROAD STREET
STREET
Corn Exchange
Ferry Stop
QUEEN STREET
TOWER HILL
NICHOLAS ST.
STREET
N
VICTORIA STREET
TEMPLE BACK
AVON STREET
QUEEN CHARLOTTE STREET
WELSH BACK
REDCLIFF STREET
ST THOMAS STREET
TEMPLE WAY
Temple Meads Train Station
REDCLIFFE WAY
British Empire & Commonwealth Museum
REDCLIFFE PARADE
REDCLIFFE HILL
St Mary Redcliffe
TEMPLE GATE
GUINEA STREET
REDCLIFFE MEAD LANE
SOMERSET STREET
REDCLIFFE
COMMERCIAL ROAD
BATH ROAD
CLARENCE ROAD
River Avon
YORK ROAD
BEDMINSTER PARADE
0
200 yds
14
18
21
22

5

THE COTSWOLDS AND SOMERSET | Bristol

The slave trade in Bristol

The statue of Edward Colston in Bristol's Centre has more than once been the subject of graffiti attacks and calls for its removal. Although the eighteenth-century sugar magnate is known and revered as a great philanthropist – his name given to numerous buildings, streets and schools in Bristol – for many he is reviled as a leading light in the London-based Royal African Company, which held the monopoly on the **slave trade** until the market was opened in 1698. From that date until the abolition of the British slave trade in 1807, merchants throughout the country were able to participate in the "triangular trade" whereby vast numbers of slaves were shipped from West Africa to plantations in the Americas, the vessels returning to Europe with cargoes of sugar, cotton, tobacco and other slave-produced commodities. By the 1730s, Bristol, a leading transatlantic port, had become, along with London and Liverpool, one of the main beneficiaries of the trade, sending out a total of more than two thousand ships in search of slaves on the African coast; in 1750 alone, Bristol ships transported some eight thousand of the twenty thousand slaves sent that year to British colonies in the Caribbean and North America. Few slaves actually came to the city, though the grave of one who did can be seen in Henbury churchyard: a servant to the Earl of Suffolk, the slave was named Scipio Africanus and was aged just 18 when he died. The direct profits, together with the numerous spin-offs, helped to finance some of Bristol's finest Georgian architecture – a fact that has been largely ignored in the past.

Bristol's primacy in the trade had already been long supplanted by Liverpool by the time opposition to the trade began to gather force: first the Quakers and Methodists, then more powerful forces voiced their discontent. By the 1780s the Anglican Dean Josiah Tucker and the Evangelical writer Hannah More had become active abolitionists, and Samuel Taylor Coleridge made a famous anti-slavery speech in Bristol in 1795.

Today, Bristol's Caribbean link is maintained by an active West Indian population largely concentrated in the St Paul's district – scene of a flamboyant carnival in early July. If you're interested in the city's involvement in the slave trade, the Georgian House (see p.397) has a small but informative section devoted to it, while the British Empire and Commonwealth Museum (see p.402) gives a more general overview. The free "Slave Trade Trail" booklet available from the tourist office and the city's major museums guides you to some of the points around Bristol connected with the trade.

Outside the museum, look out for the bronze plaque recording the spot where, in 1643, Colonel Washington (an ancestor of America's first president) won a decisive battle against Bristol's Roundhead defenders. The victory opened the way for the occupation of the city by Prince Rupert's army – one of the greatest Royalist triumphs in the Civil War, and one of the bloodiest.

Across from the Wills Tower, on Park Row, the **Red Lodge** (April–Oct Mon–Wed, Sat & Sun 10am–5pm; free) was originally a merchant's home when built in the sixteenth century, later became a finishing school for young ladies, and was subsequently England's first girls' reform school. Highlight is the Great Oak Room, featuring a splendid carved stone fireplace and lavish oak panelling. Behind the house, an Elizabethan knot garden has been recreated.

From the Centre to Broadmead

Within a short walk of the Centre, several relics of the old town lie buried behind the modern office buildings. Off its northern end, leading steeply up from Colston Avenue, **Christmas Steps** is a stepped shop-lined alley with a cramped, timeworn flavour, though none of the present buildings dates further back than the eighteenth century. At the top stands **Foster's Almshouse**, a red-brick, gabled and turreted affair built in 1481 but remodelled in the nineteenth century on a Burgundian Gothic pattern. Founder of the almshouse was Bristol merchant and mayor John Foster, also responsible for the adjacent **Chapel of the Three Kings of Cologne**, a tiny church named after a chapel in Cologne Cathedral, which was no doubt admired on Foster's Rhineland journeys. The three kings carved on the facade were added in the 1960s.

One of Bristol's oldest churches, **St Stephen's**, stands on the opposite side of the Centre. Established in the thirteenth century, rebuilt in the fifteenth and thoroughly restored with plenty of neo-Gothic trimmings in 1875, the parish church has some flamboyant tombs inside, mainly of various members of the merchant class who were the church's main patrons. Especially good are those of Justice Snygge and Edmund Blanket, a fourteenth-century cloth merchant.

On nearby **Corn Street**, in the city's financial quarter, you'll find the Georgian Corn Exchange, designed by John Wood of Bath, and now holding the covered St Nicholas markets, good for all kinds of bric-a-brac, including records and books, as well as cafés. Outside the entrance stand four engraved bronze pillars, dating from the sixteenth and seventeenth centuries and transferred from a nearby arcade where they served as trading tables – thought to be the "nails" from which the expression "pay on the nail" is derived.

Beyond the market, Wine Street runs along the site of the old **Bristol Castle**, an eleventh-century structure that was completely dismantled at the end of the Civil War. The site is now a park, with the hollow shell of the fourteenth-century **St Peter's Church** – gutted during World War II – the only thing still standing, though the castle's moat is still visible. The park, which runs alongside a stretch of Bristol waterways, attracts lunchers from the surrounding shops and offices, and is the occasional venue for summer concerts and fairs.

North of Castle Green extends Bristol's **Broadmead** shopping centre, an uninspiring development laid out on the ruins left by wartime bombing. Two older buildings miraculously survived the devastation however. Accessible from both the central strip of Broadmead and the Horsefair, **the New Room** (Mon–Sat 10am–4pm; free) was the country's first Methodist chapel, established by John Wesley in 1739. Looking very much as Wesley left it, the chapel has a double-deck pulpit beneath a hidden upstairs window, from which the evangelist could observe the progress of his trainee preachers. Tours of the chapel and some of the rooms used by Wesley and his acolytes are available by prior arrangement (☎0117/926 4740; £2.80), and include an entertaining introduction by the man himself – or rather, by an actor kitted out in Wesleyan garb. Outside the chapel is an equestrian statue of Wesley, and, in the main courtyard, another one representing John's brother Charles, also a leading Methodist and hymn-writer. Nearby, another testimony to Bristol's close links with nonconformist sects has also survived: **Quakers' Friars**, a thirteenth-century construction whose name derives from the Dominican friars who first used the building, and the Quakers who took it over from the sixteenth century. William Penn, founder of Pennsylvania, was married here, as was the Quaker founder George Fox.

King Street to St Mary Redcliffe

King Street, a short walk east from the Centre, was laid out in 1633 and still holds some fine seventeenth-century buildings, among them the **Merchant Venturers' Almshouses** for retired seamen, founded in the fifteenth century but restored in 1699 by Edward Colston. Further down, the **Theatre Royal** is the oldest working theatre in the country, opened in 1766 and preserving many of its original Georgian features. The theatre hosted most of the famous names of its time, including Sarah Siddons, whose ghost is said to stalk the building.

In a different architectural style, one of King Street's most prominent buildings is the timber-framed **Llandoger Trow** pub, its name taken from the flat-bottomed boats that traded between Bristol and the Welsh coast. Traditionally the haunt of seafarers, it is reputed to have been the meeting place of Daniel Defoe and Alexander Selkirk, the model for Robinson Crusoe. The area around here bristles with pubs, restaurants and nightclubs, getting pretty lively at weekends and on summer evenings.

South of King Street, **Queen Square** is an elegant grassy area with a statue of William III by Rysbrack at its centre, reckoned to be the best equestrian statue in the country. The square was the site of some of the worst civil disturbances ever seen in England when the Bristolians rioted in support of the Reform Bill of 1832, burning houses on two sides of the square; among the survivors was no. 37, where the first American consulate was established in 1792. The square has a decent pub at its southeastern corner, the *Hole in the Wall*, so-called after the narrow window at the back of the building used to keep watch for press gangs – it was reputedly the model for the *Spyglass Inn* in Robert Louis Stevenson's *Treasure Island*.

The southeast corner of the square leads to Redcliffe Bridge and the Redcliffe district, where the spire of **St Mary Redcliffe** (Mon–Sat 9am–5pm, or 9am–4pm in winter, Sun 8am–8pm; requested donation £1) provides one of the distinctive features of the city's skyline. Described by Elizabeth I as "the goodliest, fairest, and most famous parish church in England", the church was largely paid for and used by merchants and mariners who prayed here for a safe voyage. The present building was begun at the end of the thirteenth century, though it was added to in subsequent centuries and the spire was constructed in 1872. Inside, memorials and tombs recall some of the figures associated with the building, including the arms and armour of Sir William Penn, admiral and father of the founder of Pennsylvania, on the north wall of the nave, and the Handel Window in the North Choir aisle, installed in 1859 on the centenary of the death of Handel, who composed on the organ here. The whale bone above the entrance to the Chapel of St John the Baptist is thought to have been brought back from Newfoundland by John Cabot. The poets Samuel Taylor Coleridge and Robert Southey were both married in St Mary, within six weeks of each other in 1795.

Above the church's north porch is the muniment room, where **Thomas Chatterton** claimed to have found a trove of medieval manuscripts; the poems, distributed as the work of a fifteenth-century monk named Thomas Rowley, were in fact dazzling fakes. The young poet committed suicide when his forgery was exposed, thereby supplying English literature with one of its most glamorous stories of self-destructive genius. The "Marvellous Boy" is remembered by a memorial stone in the south transept, and there is another one to his family, who were long associated with the church, in the churchyard. Chatterton's birthplace is just across the busy Redcliffe Way, administered by the city museum and viewable only on application there – though there's precious little to see inside.

A few minutes' walk away, Bristol's **Old Station** stands outside Temple Meads Station, the original terminus of the Great Western Railway linking London and Bristol. The terminus, like the line itself, was designed by Brunel in 1840, and was the first great piece of railway architecture. Part of the original building now houses the **British Empire and Commonwealth Museum** (daily 10am–5pm; £5.95; Ⓦ www.empiremuseum.co.uk), which focuses on the history of the empire and the Commonwealth that succeeded it, covering trade, slavery, and various of the cultures which it encompassed. Film, photographs and sound recordings help to fill out the picture, and there are exhibitions throughout the year on such themes as aboriginal art.

Around Bristol's waterways

At the southern end of the Centre, the River Frome disappears underground at the **Quayhead**, a spot marked by a statue of Neptune and a memorial plaque to Samuel Plimsoll, inventor of the eponymous line that's painted on the hulls of merchant ships. **St Augustine's Reach**, the central part of the Floating Harbour, is flanked by the **Arnolfini** and **Watershed** arts centres, bastions of Bristol's cultural scene and both housed in refurbished Victorian warehouses. Outside the Arnolfini is a statue of **John Cabot**, the Genoan-born explorer licensed by Henry VII to sail from Bristol in 1497; his landing at Newfoundland formed the basis of England's later claims on the New World (he disappeared on his second expedition the following year). Moored onto the adjacent quays are several boats converted into pubs, restaurants and music venues.

Beyond the Watershed, Bristol's newly developed Harbourside is the home of **at-Bristol** (daily 10am–6pm; Explore £7.50, Wildwalk £6.50, Imax £6.50, or £16.50 for all three, valid for a week; Ⓦwww.at-bristol.org.uk), a complex made up of three principal attractions: Explore, an interactive science centre; Wildwalk, a multimedia wildlife complex, including an indoor "tropical forest"; and an IMAX cinema (film screenings need to be booked in advance). Although chiefly aimed at families and schoolkids, there's enough here to occupy everyone for a whole day or more. The wildlife displays and scientific wizardry are most impressive, and subsidiary attractions include the Imaginarium (£2), a metal-clad spherical planetarium.

To explore further afield, take advantage of the **ferry service**, which connects the various parts of the Floating Harbour, and which leaves every forty minutes from near Neptune's statue at the Quayhead (10.30am–5.50pm; £1.20 single fare; £3.50 forty-minute round trip; £4 one-hour round trip; £5 all-day ticket; Ⓣ0117/927 3416, Ⓦwww.bristolferryboat.co.uk). The first stop is the **Industrial Museum**, featuring a diverse collection of vehicles, mostly with Bristol connections, and a display of maritime models and reconstructions (Mon–Wed, Sat & Sun 10am–5pm; free). On weekends between March and October, you can take a thirty-minute **harbour cruise** from here (£3), on either a motor tug, a fireboat or what is claimed to be the oldest steam tug in the world (built in 1861), and when one of these isn't operating, there's the **Bristol Harbour Railway** (Sat & Sun noon–5pm; every 15min; £1 return; Ⓣ0117/925 1470), a steam train which runs along the quayside. Call to find out which of these is operating on a particular weekend.

From the Industrial Museum, you could use the Bristol Harbour Railway, catch the ferry or walk the 500 yards along the quayside to visit the **SS Great Britain**. Built in 1843 by Brunel, the *SS Great Britain* was the first propeller-driven, ocean-going iron ship, used initially between Liverpool and New York, then between Liverpool and Melbourne, circumnavigating the globe 32 times over a period of 26 years. Her ocean-going days ended in 1886 when she was caught in a storm off Cape Horn, and abandoned in the Falkland Islands; she was recovered from there and returned to Bristol in 1968. Now berthed in the same dry dock where she was constructed, the *Great Britain* is still undergoing restoration work, but is **open to visitors** (daily: April–Oct 10am–5.30pm; Nov–March 10am–4.30pm; £6.25). Some cabins have been restored, the bunks occupied by eerily breathing mannequins, and you can peer into the immense engine room. Alongside is docked a much smaller affair: a replica of the **Matthew** (same times as the *Great Britain*; entry covered by same ticket), the vessel in which John Cabot sailed to America in 1497, rebuilt in time for the voyage to be re-enacted on the 500th anniversary. The adjoining **Maritime Heritage Centre** (same times as the *Great Britain*; entry covered by same ticket) gives the full history of both the *Great Britain* and the *Matthew*, and the few facts that are known about Cabot and his exploits. The museum also illustrates the port's long shipbuilding history from the eighteenth century, when it was second only to London, to its decline in the last century, when Bristol's inability to berth the increasingly large vessels led to its decline.

Clifton

North and west of the Wills Tower (see p.397) extends **Clifton**, once an aloof spa resort, now Bristol's most elegant quarter. Clifton Village, its select enclave, is centred on the Mall, close to **Royal York Crescent**, the longest Georgian crescent in the country, offering splendid views over the steep drop to the River Avon below.

A few minutes' walk behind the Crescent is Bristol's most famous symbol, **Clifton Suspension Bridge**, 702ft long and poised 245ft above high water. Money was first put forward for a bridge to span the Avon Gorge by a Bristol wine merchant in 1753, though it was not until 1829 that a competition was held for a design, won by Isambard Brunel on a second round, and not until 1864 that the bridge was completed, five years after Brunel's death. Hampered by financial difficulties, the bridge never quite matched the engineer's original ambitious design, which included Egyptian-style towers topped by sphinxes on each end. The original drawings of Brunel's designs are in the university's Brunel Collection and can be viewed on application, but you can see copies in the **Visitor Centre**, due to reopen right next to the bridge in late 2004 (check for opening hours at ⓣ0117/974 4664, ⓦwww.clifton-suspension-bridge.org.uk), alongside the other designs proposed by Brunel's rivals, some of them frankly bizarre. Display boards give the full background on the various competitions and the vicissitudes that accompanied the bridge's construction, and there are models and photographs too.

Just above the bridge in Clifton, a small **Observatory** sits on an arm of Clifton Downs overlooking the gorge, and contains a working camera obscura (daily: summer 11am–5pm; rest of year noon–4pm; £1). You can also buy a ticket (£1) for the 190-foot tunnel leading from here to the "Giant's Cave" set in the cliffs overlooking the gorge; it housed a Roman Catholic chapel in the fifteenth century. Both attractions may be closed in bad weather, however. Adjoining the downs is **Bristol Zoo** (daily: June–Aug 9am–5.30pm; Sept–May 9am–4.30pm; £8.90), renowned for its animal conservation work, and also featuring a collection of rare trees and shrubs.

Cross the bridge for the view, and continue over to reach the thick Leigh Woods, and Bristol's widest expanse of parkland, **Ashton Court**, scene of a free music festival held each July.

Eating, drinking and nightlife

Bristol's numerous **pubs** and **restaurants** are nearly always buzzing – especially those around King Street. Nightlife is equally lively; if you want to check out the **clubs**, look for the music that suits your tastes rather than simply turning up at a venue – and be prepared to queue. You can usually find something happening every night until late; pick up a copy of *Venue*, the Bristol and Bath weekly listings magazine (£1.20), or look up the website ⓦwww.thisisbristol .com, for details of what's on where.

Restaurants

Bell's Diner 1 York Rd ⓣ0117/924 0357. In the villagey Montpelier quarter (ten minutes from the bus station up Stokes Croft), this corner bistro offers an inventive menu with award-winning food – though portions can be small. No smoking in dining area. Closed Sat & Mon lunch, plus all day Sun. Moderate.

Browns 38 Queen's Rd ⓣ0117/930 4777. Spacious and relaxed place for a cocktail, hamburger or delicious fisherman's pie; it's housed in the former university refectory, a Venetian-style structure next to the City Museum. Moderate.

Byzantium 2 Portwall Lane ⓣ0117/922 1883. Opposite St Mary Redcliffe, a warehouse that's been transformed into a highly theatrical dining area, themed along the lines of a Beirut hotel circa 1930. The food is superb, with a good-value set-price menu, and there's an equally exotic bar downstairs that stays open late. Closed Sun. Expensive.

Mud Dock Café 40 The Grove. A winning if unlikely combination of bike shop and café-bar/restaurant by the river. There's good food and a barbecue on the balcony in summer. Moderate.

Old India 34 St Nicholas St ⓣ0117/922 1136. Housed in the old Stock Exchange building, this Indian restaurant has classy dishes to match the sumptuous surroundings. Moderate.

One Stop Thali Café 12 York Rd ⓣ0117/942 6687. Dhaba-style Asian food in soothing surroundings in the heart of Montpelier. There's no menu, but a combination of dishes are served on a steel plate. Live music currently on Wed. Closed Mon. Inexpensive.

riverstation The Grove ⓣ0117/914 4424. A former river-police station that has been artfully transformed into two great restaurants: downstairs you can chew on deli-type snacks or just have a drink at *The Deck*, while the more formal upstairs restaurant offers a range of international dishes. Try to bag a table by the window, for the views over the river. Inexpensive to Moderate.

Severnshed The Grove ⓣ0117/925 1212. Right next to *riverstation* in a harbour setting with a waterside terrace, this serves light, tasty food, ranging from fish and chips "with Yorkshire caviar" (mushy peas) to vegetarian risotto. There's a good-value £7.77 two-course meal available (Mon–Fri noon–7pm). Inexpensive to Moderate.

Teohs 28–34 Lower Ashley Rd ⓣ0117/907 1191. On the edge of the St Paul's area, this oriental bistro is well worth tracking down for its relaxed atmosphere and extremely low prices, offering thirty-odd dishes from China, Thailand, Malaysia and Japan, all at £5.50. Bottled beers and house wine at £12 a carafe. Closed Sun. Inexpensive.

Pubs, bars and cafés

Arnolfini Narrow Quay. This art centre serves excellent vegetarian and meat dishes, plus drinks at the bar. There are communal wooden benches, and the crowd spills onto the the cobbled quayside.

Avon Gorge Hotel Sion Hill. On the edge of the Gorge in Clifton Village, this mediocre bar has a broad terrace with tables from which to contemplate the magnificent views. Snacks available.

Boston Tea Party 75 Park St. Cosy place in the centre of town for teas and coffees as well as soups and pies, with seating on two floors and a heated terrace garden.

The Farm Hopetoun Rd, St Werburgh's. A country pub in the city, off Ashley Hill to the northeast of the centre; vegetarian cooking, baguettes and DJs at weekends make this a popular spot, especially in summer when the beer garden is usually buzzing.

Ha! Ha! Bar & Canteen Berkeley Square. Sofas, a mellow vibe and cool sounds, with a chilled-out DJ on Sun. Food served until 10pm, and there's courtyard seating.

Level 24 Park Row. Late bar with a 1960s airport feel and good city views. Drum'n'bass and hip-hop predominate on the turntables.

Nova Scotia Cumberland Basin. Traditional dockside pub with seats by the nineteenth-century lock. Inexpensive food available.

Old Duke King St. Jolly, trad jazz pub with live bands nightly and tables outside.

Queenshilling 9 Frogmore St. Gay pub and club near the centre, with regular live music.

Star & Garter 33 Brook Rd, Montpelier. Smoky, loud and cramped – an excellent reggae pub, with a coffin to sit around in the back room and a late lock-in.

Tantric Jazz Café 39–41 St Nicholas St ⓣ0117/940 2304. Relaxed coffee stop that offers full Mediterranean-style meals in the evenings, when there are live jazz and blues performances until late. Closed Sun.

Taverna dell'Artista King St. A haunt of theatrical folk as well as a rowdy bunch of regulars, this is a successful Anglo-Italian dive with a late licence. Pizzas, pastas and salads are served in the main bar, and there's a restaurant upstairs. Closed Sun & Mon.

Watershed 1 Canons Rd, St Augustine's Reach. A great bar and café in the arts complex overlooking the boats, with food available until 9pm.

Clubs and venues

The Academy Frogmore St ⓣ0117/927 9227, ⓦwww.bristol-academy.co.uk. Near the Centre, this spacious, popular place stages live gigs as well as mainstream and hard-house parties. Thursday is student night.
Bierkeller All Saints St, off Broadmead ⓣ0117/926 8514, ⓦwww.bristolbierkeller.co.uk. Live music from thrash metal to revival bands in this sweaty cellar venue.
Blue Mountain Stokes Croft ⓣ0117/942 0341. Excellent non-mainstream club with a relaxed feel, and the best funk, hip-hop and drum'n'bass in town.
Colston Hall Colston Ave ⓣ0117/922 3686, ⓦwww.colstonhall.org. Major names appear in this stalwart of mainstream venues. Most of the events in the classical Proms Festival, at the end of May, take place here.
Creation 13–21 Baldwin St ⓣ0117/922 7177. Central clubbers' club, for banging house tunes from top-flight DJs. Dress up, and expect a crowd.
Fiddlers Willway St, Bedminster ⓣ0117/987 3403, ⓦwww.fiddlers.co.uk. Mainly live folk and world music at this relaxed and well-run club on the south side of the river, off Bedminster Parade.
Fleece and Firkin 12 St Thomas St ⓣ0117/945 0996. Stone-flagged ex-wool warehouse, now a loud and sweaty pub putting on live rock and comedy six nights a week.
Lakota 6 Upper York St ⓣ0117/942 6208. Bristol's most celebrated club has seen better days, but can still muster a good old-skool atmosphere, specializing in hard house, trance and techno, with occasional live bands.
St George's Great George St ⓣ0117/923 0359. This elegant Georgian church has regular lunchtime and evening concerts of classical music, jazz and world, with near-perfect acoustics.
The Station Silver St ⓣ0117/904 3336, ⓦwww.screamtheclub.co.uk. Central, multi-storey club in an old fire station, better than most mainstream places and with occasional live music (usually Tues or Thurs).
Thekla Phoenix Wharf, off Queen Square ⓣ0117/929 3301, ⓦwww.thekla.co.uk. A riverboat venue staging regular club nights and occasional live shows, popular with students. Food available.
Vibes 3 Frog Lane ⓣ0117/934 9076. Friendly gay club with two bars and comfy seating on two floors. Wednesday is cabaret night.

Listings

Airport Lulsgate Airport ⓣ0870/121 2747. Eight miles southwest of the centre on the A38. National and international flights. Coach service to centre every 30min.
Banks and exchange Barclays, 40 Corn St; Lloyds, 15 Queen St; HSBC, 24 College Green; NatWest, 32 Corn St; American Express 74 Queen's Rd.
Bike rental Bristol Bicycle Hire, Smeaton Rd ⓣ0117/965 5192 or 0780/365 1945. City bikes and mountain bikes available, right on the National Cycle Route, near the Create Centre; £25 deposit and ID required. Always phone first.
Buses Local services ⓣ0870/608 2608; National Express ⓣ08705/808080, ⓦwww.nationalexpress.co.uk.
Car rental Avis, Rupert St and airport ⓣ0870/606 0100; Speedway, 654 Fishponds Rd ⓣ0117/965 5555; Victoria Car Hire, 155 Victoria St, near train station ⓣ0117/927 6909.
Hospital Bristol Royal Infirmary, Marlborough St ⓣ0117/923 0000.
Internet Internet Exchange, 25 Queen's Rd ⓣ0117/929 8026; Bristol Life, 27 Baldwin St ⓣ0117/945 9926.
Laundry 78 Alma Rd, Clifton; 34 Princess Victoria St, Clifton.
Left luggage Temple Meads Station, in the subway (Mon–Sat 9am–4pm, Sun 10am–4pm).
Pharmacy Boots, 19 St Augustine's Parade, the Centre (Mon–Fri 8am–7pm, Sat 8.30am–5pm).
Police Broad St ⓣ0117/927 7777.
Post office The Galleries, Wine St (Mon–Sat 9am–5.30pm).
Taxis Bristol Hackney Cabs ⓣ0117/953 8638; Streamline Black & White Taxis ⓣ0117/926 4001.
Travel agents STA Travel, 43 Queen's Rd ⓣ08701/676777; Usit CAMPUS, 39 Queen's Rd ⓣ0117/929 2494.

Clevedon

Fifteen miles south of Bristol, **CLEVEDON** is centred on hills inland from the sea, but its handsome beach promenade invites a stroll, with wind-bent trees and views across to Wales. Focal point is the **pier** (Mon–Wed 10am–5pm,

Thurs–Sun 9am–5pm; £1), from where, between Easter and October, you can take cruises to Bristol, Gloucester, Lundy Island, along the coast to Devon and over to Wales; tickets can be obtained from the pier's Tollhouse (☎01275/878846). Here, you can pick up a leaflet on the **Poet's Walk**, an easy stroll you can make round the headland just south of the beach. The path, which was supposed to have provided inspiration for Tennyson and Coleridge, winds round Church Hill, passing St Andrew's churchyard and climbing Wain's Hill, taking in some bracing views en route – about a mile in all. Two hundred yards south of the pier on the seafront, you might also drop in to the **Clevedon Heritage Centre** (April–Oct daily 10.30am–4pm; Nov–March closed Wed; 75p), which offers some historical background on the locality, including the local picture house, claimed to be the oldest continuously used cinema in Europe – it's located close by on Old Church Road if you want to see it.

Clevedon is also the site of **Clevedon Court** (April–Oct Wed, Thurs & Sun 2–5pm; £4.70; NT), a fourteenth- and fifteenth-century manor house a couple of miles inland. Since 1709 it has been the property of the Elton family, among whose offspring were Sir Arthur Hallam Elton – inspiration for Tennyson's elegy *In Memoriam* – and his son Edmund, whose internationally known pottery is displayed here. You'll also find a fascinating collection of glassware, some fine specimens of furniture spanning three hundred years and portraits of and drawings by William Makepeace Thackeray, who wrote much of *Vanity Fair* here, as well as making it the setting of *Henry Esmond*. The chapel is worth a look for its fine tracery, and the terraced gardens give good views seaward.

There's a **tourist office** in the town library, three quarters of a mile inland at 37 Old Church Rd (Mon, Thurs & Sat 9.30am–5pm, Tues & Fri 9.30am–7pm; ☎01275/873498, ⓦwww.somersetcoast.com). It's easy to get here from Bristol – **buses** run at least hourly, and as well as services exclusively for Clevedon, you can take many of the buses bound for Weston-super-Mare. There are a few **pubs and restaurants** on or around Clevedon's seafront, including *Il Giardino* (☎01275/878832; closed Sun & Mon). For **accommodation**, *Fairview* is a comfortable B&B with some rooms overlooking the sea at 20 Lea Grove Rd (☎01275/872176; no credit cards; ❶); bathrooms are shared.

Weston-super-Mare

Buses and trains from Bristol – and a regular bus service from Clevedon – run frequently to the major resort on this coast, **WESTON-SUPER-MARE**, eight miles south of Clevedon. A tiny fishing village at the beginning of the nineteenth century, Weston boomed to become one of the chief West Country seaside towns of the Edwardian era. It's rather moth-eaten today, though its sandy beaches and seafront amusements still attract busloads of trippers. If the crowds get you down, you can always climb up into Weston Woods, rising to the north of the main beach and reachable just around the point on Kewstoke Road. Beyond the point lies **Sand Bay**, a less-developed beach zone bounded to the north by Sand Point, a headland maintained by the National Trust. More adventurously, you can cross to the southern end of Weston – walk or bus to Uphill (#5a to Links Rd) – to join the **West Mendip Way** footpath, following the Mendip hills for thirty miles to Wells and beyond.

Trains arrive at Neva Road, a ten-minute walk from the seafront; the **bus station** is nearer, on Beach Road, though some buses stop in the streets around. The **tourist office** is on Beach Lawns, a traffic island between Beach Road and Marine Parade (Easter–Sept daily 9.30am–5.15pm; Oct–Easter Mon–Fri

10am–5pm, Sat 9.30am–1pm & 1.30–4.15pm; ⓣ01934/888800, ⓦwww.somersetcoast.com). If you want to stay in Weston, you can take your pick from a good selection of **B&Bs**: try *Jamesfield*, very near to the seafront at 1a Ellenborough Park North (ⓣ01934/642898; ❷), or else *Edelweiss* at 24 Clevedon Rd (ⓣ01934/624705; no credit cards; ❷); both have en-suite doubles and are non-smoking. There's a **campsite** north of town in Sand Bay: *Country View* (ⓣ01934/627595; closed Nov–Feb), 200m from the bus stop and beach.

Bath and around

Though only twelve miles from Bristol, **BATH** has a very different feel from its neighbour – more harmonious, compact, leisurely and complacent. Jane Austen set *Persuasion* and *Northanger Abbey* here, it is where Gainsborough established himself as a portraitist and landscape painter, and the city's elegant crescents and Georgian buildings are studded with plaques naming Bath's eminent inhabitants from its heyday as a spa resort. Nowadays Bath ranks as one of Britain's top ten tourist cities – the Roman Baths are the busiest fee-charging historic site outside London – yet the place has never lost the exclusive air those names evoke.

Bath owes its name and fame to its **hot springs** – the only ones in the country – which made it a place of reverence for the local Celtic population, though it had to wait for Roman technology to create a fully fledged bathing establishment. The baths fell into decline with the departure of the Romans, but the town later regained its importance under the Saxons, its abbey seeing the coronation of the **first king of all England**, Edgar, in 973. A new bathing complex was built in the sixteenth century, popularized by the visit of Elizabeth I in 1574, and the city reached its fashionable zenith in the eighteenth century, when **Beau Nash** ruled the town's social scene. It was at this time that Bath acquired its ranks of Palladian mansions and town houses, all of them built in the local **Bath stone**, which is still the city's leitmotif today.

The swathes of parkland between the Georgian developments lend modern Bath a spacious feel, but the sheer weight of traffic pouring through the central streets can often counteract the pleasures of these open spaces. Drivers are advised to use one of the **Park-and-Ride** car parks around the periphery – and if you're coming from Bristol, note that you can **cycle** all the way along a cycle-path that follows the route of a disused railway line and the course of the Avon. You can easily experience the verdant hilly country outside town on brief excursions to **Claverton**, where a handsome mansion houses an absorbing museum of Americana, **Dyrham Park**, for panoramic views and period furnishings, and the unspoiled village of **Frome**.

Arrival, information and accommodation

Bath Spa **train station** and the city's **bus station** are both on Manvers Street, a short walk from the centre. The **tourist office** is right next to the abbey on Abbey Churchyard (May–Sept Mon–Sat 9.30am–6pm, Sun 10am–4pm; Oct–May Mon–Sat 9.30am–5pm, Sun 10am–4pm; ⓣ0906/711 2000, ⓦwww.visitbath.co.uk). Here you can find a detailed list of **accommodation**, of which Bath has an abundant choice. All the same, places fill quickly, and most establishments are small, so it's always wise to book early. Note that most places demand a two-night minimum stay at weekends in high season.

Hotels and B&Bs

Belmont 7 Belmont, Lansdown Rd ⓣ01225/423082. Huge rooms – though the single's a bit poky – some with en-suite shower in a house designed by John Wood, very near to the Assembly Rooms, Circus and Royal Crescent. No credit cards. ❷

Cranleigh 159 Newbridge Hill ⓣ01225/310197, ⓦwww.cranleighgguesthouse.com. A mile or so west of the centre, this period Victorian house has fine views from the back rooms, some four-posters and seven breakfast options. Buses #17, #319 and #332 (#632 Sun). No smoking. ❺

Henry Guest House 6 Henry St ⓣ01225/424052, ⓦwww.thehenry.com. Excellent budget choice just round the corner from the abbey, with large rooms (none en suite) and friendly owners, but its central location means that availability is limited. No credit cards. ❸

Holly Villa 14 Pulteney Gardens ⓣ01225/310331, ⓦwww.hollyvilla.com. Neat and friendly B&B, close to the Kennet and Avon Canal, a small, flower-filled front garden and six rooms with floral wallpaper and en-suite or private facilities, including a triple. No smoking and no credit cards. Closed 2 weeks in March & in Nov. ❹

Koryu 7 Pulteney Gardens ⓣ01225/337642, ⓔjapanesekoryu.@aol.com. The name means "Sunshine" in Japanese – the mother-tongue of the landlady, who offers brightly painted rooms, small but clean. No shoes inside and no smoking. No credit cards. ❸

Paradise House 88 Holloway ⓣ01225/317723, ⓦwww.paradise-house.co.uk. The wonderful view justifies the ten-minute uphill trudge from the centre to this lovely Georgian villa. Croquet or boules in the lush garden and open fires in the winter are other attractions. All rooms are en suite, three have four-posters and two open straight onto the garden. No smoking. ❻

Tasburgh House Warminster Rd ⓣ01225/425096, ⓦwww.bathtasburgh.co.uk. This Victorian country house about one mile east of the centre is decidedly posh, but the views and location are excellent, with access to the Kennet and Avon Canal at the bottom of seven acres of gardens and meadows. Gourmet meals and picnics are provided. ❻

Hostels and campsite

Bath Backpackers Hostel 13 Pierrepoint St ⓣ01225/446787, ⓦwww.hostels.co.uk. Aussie-run place right in the centre of things. There's no curfew, no lockout, a kitchen, bar, pool room and Internet access, but no breakfast. Dorm beds are £12, doubles with bath ❶

Bath YHA Bathwick Hill ⓣ0870/770 5688, ⓔbath@yha.org.uk. An Italianate mansion a mile from the centre, with gardens and panoramic views. Dorm beds (£11.50 each) and double rooms with evening snacks also available. Take buses #18 or #418 from the station. ❶

Newton Mill Touring Centre ⓣ01225/333909, ⓦwww.campinginbath.co.uk. The nearest campsite, three miles west of the centre at Newton St Loe (bus #5 to Newton Mill). The site holds a laundry, restaurant (closed weekdays in winter) and shop, and the price includes use of hot showers, and the Bristol–Bath cycleway lies nearby.

White Hart Widcombe Hill ⓣ01225/313985, ⓦwww.whitehartbath.co.uk. The comfiest of Bath's hostels has a kitchen, a licensed café and a sunny courtyard. Dorms mainly have four beds (at £12.50 each), and doubles and twins are available. ❶

YMCA International House, Broad St ⓣ01225/460471, ⓦwww.bathymca.co.uk. Clean, central, with lots of room and convenient prices, this place is a good option, charging £10–12 for dorm beds, £20–24 for singles, £32 for doubles, and with reductions for weekly stays; all prices include breakfast (but there's no kitchen). ❶

The City

Although Bath could easily be seen on a day-trip from Bristol, it really deserves a stay of a couple of days, particularly if you want to explore some of the out-of-town attractions. The city itself is chock-full of museums, but some of the greatest enjoyment comes simply from the streets, with their pale gold architecture and sweeping vistas. With limited time you might consider viewing these on a walking or open-top bus tour (see "Listings", p.416).

The Baths and the Abbey

Bath's focal point is the pedestrianized Abbey Church Yard, two interlocking squares usually milling with buskers, tourists and traders, and site of both the Baths and the Abbey. Although ticket prices are high for the **Roman Baths**

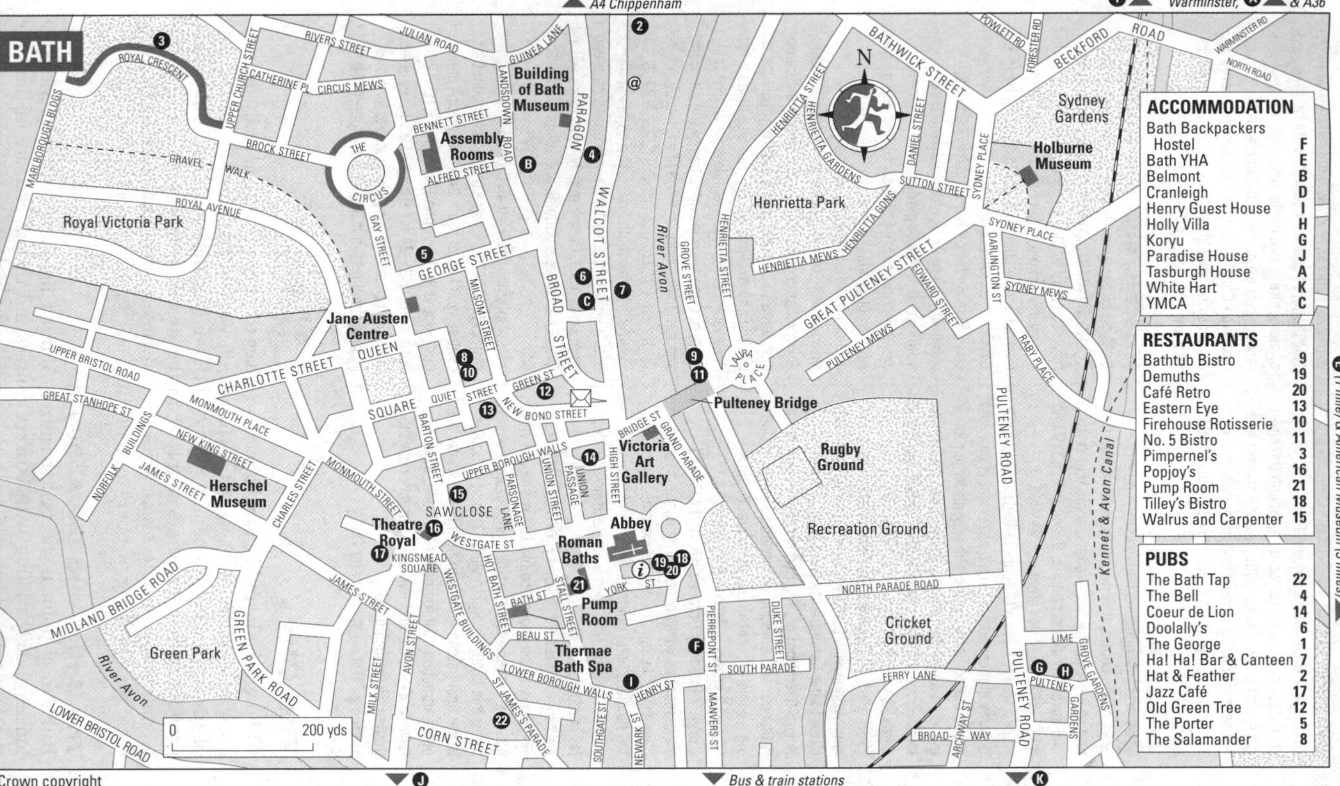
BATH
ACCOMMODATION
Bath Backpackers Hostel F
Bath YHA E
Belmont B
Cranleigh D
Henry Guest House I
Holly Villa H
Koryu G
Paradise House J
Tasburgh House A
White Hart K
YMCA C
RESTAURANTS
Bathtub Bistro 9
Demuths 19
Café Retro 20
Eastern Eye 13
Firehouse Rotisserie 10
No. 5 Bistro 11
Pimpernel's 3
Popjoy's 16
Pump Room 21
Tilley's Bistro 18
Walrus and Carpenter 15
PUBS
The Bath Tap 22
The Bell 4
Coeur de Lion 14
Doolally's 6
The George 1
Ha! Ha! Bar & Canteen 7
Hat & Feather 2
Jazz Café 17
Old Green Tree 12
The Porter 5
The Salamander 8
A4 Chippenham
Warminster, A & A36
E (1 mile) & American Museum (3 miles)
D & A4 Bristol
A36 Tiverton
J
Bus & train stations
K
Royal Victoria Park
Building of Bath Museum
Assembly Rooms
Jane Austen Centre
Herschel Museum
Theatre Royal
Roman Baths
Pump Room
Thermae Bath Spa
Abbey
Victoria Art Gallery
Pulteney Bridge
Henrietta Park
Sydney Gardens
Holburne Museum
Rugby Ground
Recreation Ground
Cricket Ground
Green Park
River Avon
Kennet & Avon Canal
0 200 yds
© Crown copyright

(daily: March–June, Sept & Oct 9am–6pm; July & Aug 9am–10pm; Nov–Feb 9.30am–5.30pm; £7.50, £9.50 combined ticket with Museum of Costume), there's two or three hours' worth of well-balanced, informative entertainment here, with a taped commentary provided on handsets allowing you to wander at your own pace around the temple and bathing complex, where a spring still issues water at a constant 46.5°C. Highlights of the remains are the open-air (but originally covered) Great Bath, its vaporous waters surrounded by nineteenth-century pillars, terraces and statues of famous Romans; the Circular Bath, where bathers cooled off; the Norman King's Bath; and part of the temple of Minerva. Among a quantity of coins, jewellery and sculpture exhibited are the gilt bronze head of Sulis Minerva, the local deity, and a grand, Celtic-inspired gorgon's head from the temple's pediment. Models of the complex at its greatest extent give some idea of the awe which it must have inspired, while the graffiti salvaged from the Roman era – mainly curses and boasts – give a nice personal slant on this antique leisure centre. You can get a free glimpse into the baths from the next-door **Pump Room**, the social hub of the Georgian spa community and still redolent of that era, housing an excellent tearoom and restaurant.

Although there has been a church on the site since the seventh century, **Bath Abbey** (daily 9am–6pm; closes 4pm in winter; requested donation £2.50) did not take its present form until the end of the fifteenth century, when Bishop Oliver King began work on the ruins of the previous Norman building, some of which were incorporated into the new church. The bishop was said to have been inspired by a vision of angels ascending and descending a ladder to heaven, which the present facade recalls on the turrets flanking the central window. The west front also features the founder's signature in the form of carvings of olive trees surmounted by crowns, a play on his name.

Much of the building underwent restoration following the destruction that took place under Henry VIII; his daughter, Queen Elizabeth, played a large part in the repairs. The interior is in a restrained Perpendicular style, and boasts splendid fan vaulting on the ceiling, which was not properly completed until the nineteenth century. The floor and walls are crammed with elaborate monuments and memorials, and traces of the grander Norman building are visible in the Norman Chapel.

To the Circus and the Royal Crescent

Present-day visitors to Bath can take the waters at the city's newest attraction, **Thermae Bath Spa**, a state-of-the-art spa complex at the bottom of the elegantly colonnaded Bath Street, leading west from Abbey Church Yard (daily 7am–10pm; ⓣ01225/331234, ⓦwww.thermaebathspa.com). Utilizing the city's thermal waters (also used for heating), the spa offers everything from massages to dry flotation, in three separate settings: the Hot Bath, designed by the younger John Wood and incorporating treatment rooms; the Cross Bath, site of a Celtic place of worship, now housing an open air thermal pool, and the centrepiece, New Royal Bath, Nicholas Grimshaw's sleekly futuristic "glass cube", with steam rooms and a rooftop pool with magnificent views. No membership is required to use the facilities: tickets are available for the Cross Bath pool (£10 for 1hr 30min) and the New Royal Bath (£17 for 2hr, £23 for 4hr, £35 full day), and a range of other services is also offered. Towels, robes and slippers can be rented, but you'll need a bathing costume. There's also a visitor centre with displays relating to Bath's thermal waters and a fountain where you can taste the stuff.

North of Hot Bath Street, Westgate Street and Sawclose are presided over by the **Theatre Royal**, opened in 1805 and one of the country's finest surviving

Beau Nash and Bath's Golden Age

Bath's golden age was played out according to a strictly defined set of rules, both in architecture and social style. Among the arbiters of etiquette, none enjoyed greater prestige than **Richard "Beau" Nash**, an ex-army officer, ex-lawyer, dandy and gambler, who became Bath's Master of Ceremonies in 1704, conducting public balls of an unprecedented splendour. Wielding dictatorial powers over dress and behaviour, Nash orchestrated the social manners of the city and even extended his influence to cover road improvements and the design of buildings. In an early example of health awareness, he banned smoking in Bath's public rooms at a time when pipe-smoking was a general pastime among men, women and children. Less philanthropically, he also encouraged gambling and even took a percentage of the bank's takings. Nonetheless, he was generally held in high esteem and succeeded in establishing rules such as the setting of specific hours and procedure for all social functions. Balls were to begin at six and end at eleven and every ball had to open with a minuet "danced by two persons of the highest distinction present". White aprons were banned, gossipers and scandalmongers were shunned, and, most radical of all, the wearing of swords in public places was forbidden, a ruling referred to in Sheridan's play *The Rivals*, in which Captain Absolute declares, "A sword seen in the streets of Bath would raise as great an alarm as a mad dog." By such measures, Nash presided over the city's greatest period, during the first four decades of the eighteenth century. He lived in Bath until his death at the age of 87, by which time he had been reduced to comparative poverty.

As for Bath's distinctive Georgian style of architecture, this was largely the work of **John Wood** ("the elder", c. 1704–54) and his son, also called John Wood ("the younger", 1727–81), both champions of the neo-Classical Palladianism that originated in Renaissance Italy. Their "speculative developments", designed to cater to the seasonal floods of fashionable visitors, were constructed in the soft oolitic limestone from local quarries belonging to **Ralph Allen** (c. 1694–1764), another prominent figure of the period. A deputy postmaster who made a fortune by improving England's postal routes, and later from Bath's building boom, Allen was nicknamed "the man of Bath", and is best remembered for Prior Park, the mansion he built outside the city based on the elder Wood's designs, and for his association with Pope, Fielding and other luminaries who were frequent visitors.

Next to the innovations of Nash and the creations of Allen and the two John Woods, the name of **William Oliver** should not be forgotten in the story of Georgian Bath. A physician and philanthropist, Oliver did more than anyone to boost the city's profile as a therapeutic centre, thanks to publications such as his *Practical Essay on the Use and Abuse of Warm Bathing in Gouty Cases* (1751), and by founding the Bath General Hospital to enable the poor to make use of the waters. He is remembered today by the Bath Oliver biscuit, which he invented, and by the use of Olivers as the exchange currency in a local community bartering scheme.

Georgian theatres. Next door is the house where Beau Nash spent his last years, now a restaurant. Up from the Theatre Royal, off Barton Street, the gracious **Queen Square** was the first Bath venture of the architect **John Wood**, who with his son (see box above) was chiefly responsible for the Roman-inspired developments of the areas outside the confines of the medieval city. Wood himself lived at no. 24, giving him a vista of the northern terrace's palatial facade.

Just north of the square, at 40 Gay St, the **Jane Austen Centre** (Mon–Sat 10am–5.30pm, Sun 10.30am–5.30pm; £4.45) allows you to tie the various Austen threads together with an overview of the author's connections with the city, illustrated by extracts from her writings, contemporary costumes, furnishings and household items. However, a lot of the displays have only a tangential link to Austen, so even die-hard fans may find it disappointing. Austen herself, who wasn't entirely enamoured of the city, lived just down the road at 25 Gay St – one of a number of places the author inhabited while in Bath.

West of Queen Square, at 19 New King St, another typical Bath townhouse was where the musician and astronomer Sir William Herschel, in collaboration with his sister Caroline, discovered the planet Uranus in 1781. You can take a brisk whirl around the small **Herschel Museum** here (mid-Feb to Nov Mon, Tues, Thurs & Fri 2–5pm; Sat & Sun 11am–5pm; £3.50), showing contemporary furnishings, musical instruments, a replica of the telescope with which Uranus was identified and various knick-knacks from the Herschels' life. In the basement, the Star Vault auditorium screens a short film relating the lustrous careers of the siblings.

Up from Queen Square, at the end of Gay Street, is the elder John Wood's masterpiece, **The Circus**, consisting of three crescents arranged in a tight circle of three-storey houses, with a carved frieze running round the entire circle. Wood died soon after laying the foundation stone for this enterprise, and the job was finished by his son. The painter Thomas Gainsborough lived at no. 17 from 1760 to 1774.

The Circus is connected by Brock Street to the **Royal Crescent**, grandest of Bath's crescents, begun by the younger John Wood in 1767. The stately arc of thirty houses is set off by a spacious sloping lawn from which a magnificent vista extends to green hills and distant ribbons of honey-coloured stone. The interior of **No. 1 Royal Crescent**, on the corner with Brock Street, has been restored to reflect as nearly as possible its original Georgian appearance at the end of the eighteenth century (mid-Feb to Oct Tues–Sun 10.30am–5pm; Nov Tues–Sun 10.30am–4pm; last entry 30min before closing; £4). The furnishings, drapes and Laura Ashley-style wallpaper are all authentic or else faithful recreations, as explained by the attendants providing commentaries in each room.

At the bottom of the Crescent, Royal Avenue leads onto **Royal Victoria Park**, the city's largest open space, containing an aviary and botanical gardens.

The Assembly Rooms, the Paragon and Milsom Street

The younger John Wood's **Assembly Rooms**, east of the Circus on Bennett Street, were, with the Pump Room, the centre of Bath's social scene. A fire virtually destroyed the building in 1942, but it has now been perfectly restored and houses a **Museum of Costume** (daily 10am–5pm; £4.20, or £9.50 with Baths), an entertaining collection of clothing from the Stuart era to the latest Japanese designs.

From the Assembly Rooms, Alfred Street leads to the area known as the **Paragon**. Here, accessed from the raised pavement, the Georgian-Gothic Countess of Huntingdon's Chapel houses the **Building of Bath Museum** (mid-Feb to Nov Tues–Sun 10.30am–5pm; £4), a fascinating explanation of the construction and architecture of Bath. This should ideally be an early stop in your explorations around the city, both focusing on such specific features as the styles of doors, windows and interior decoration that you'll see on your wanderings, and allowing you to view Bath in long-shot by means of a huge 1:500 scale model of the city. At the bottom of the Paragon, off George Street, lies **Milsom Street**, a wide shopping strand designed by the elder Wood as the main thoroughfare of Georgian Bath.

… and Great Pulteney Street

…bbey, Grand Parade looks down onto the formal Parade Gardens …er Avon. At the top of Grand Parade, the **Victoria Art Gallery** …)am–5.30pm, Sat 10am–5pm; free) has an impressive exhibition …s where you can see works by artists who worked locally, includ-…rough, while subjects of the numerous portraits include Beau Nash; the ground-floor rooms are used for temporary exhibitions. Across the road, the flow of the river – a crucial ingredient in the city's charm – is interrupted by a graceful V-shaped weir just below the shop-lined **Pulteney Bridge**, an Italianate structure designed by the eighteenth-century Scottish architect Robert Adam. The bridge was intended to link the city centre with **Great Pulteney Street**, a handsome avenue originally planned as the nucleus of a large residential quarter on the eastern bank. The work ran into financial difficulties, however, so the roads running off it now stop short after a few yards, though there is a lengthy vista to the imposing classical facade of the **Holburne Museum** at the end of the street (Feb to mid-Dec Tues–Sat 10am–5pm, Sun 2.30–5.30pm; £4.50). The three-storey building contains an impressive range of decorative and fine art, mostly furniture, silverware, porcelain and paintings, including work by Stubbs and the famous *Byam Family* by Gainsborough, his biggest portrait. Behind Holburne House, **Sydney Gardens** make a delightful place to take a breather. When Holburne House was a bustling hotel, the pleasure gardens were the venue for concerts and fireworks, as witnessed by Jane Austen, a frequent visitor here – the family had lodgings across the street at 4 Sydney Place in the autumn of 1801. As well as entertainments, breakfasts and dinners were served at the hotel, as described by Austen in a letter: "There is a public breakfast in Sydney Gardens every morning, so we shall not be wholly starved." Today, the slopes are cut through by the railway and the Kennet and Avon Canal. From here, it's a pleasant one-and-a-half mile saunter along the canal to the *George* pub (see opposite).

If you want to explore the river itself, rent a skiff, punt or canoe in summer from the **Victorian Bath Boating Station** at the end of Forester Road, behind the Holburne Museum (April–Sept; £5 per person per hour). Organized river trips can be made from Pulteney Bridge and weir, and there are cruises on the Kennet and Avon Canal from Sydney Wharf, near Bathwick Bridge. A two-mile **nature trail** winds along the banks of the restored canal, which itself extends east as far as Reading.

Eating and drinking

Bath has a reputation for gourmet cuisine, even if too many of the town's **restaurants** do over-exploit the period trappings. In the less exalted regions of the price scale, there are several decent, inexpensive places to eat, and coffee shops and snack bars are ubiquitous in the centre, as are pubs offering lunchtime fare.

Restaurants

Bathtub Bistro 2 Grove St ☎01225/460593. Round the corner from Argyle Street, off Pulteney Bridge, this place looks tiny from the outside but reveals several eating areas on three levels. The menu is international, and includes one hundred percent beef hamburgers and innovative vegetarian dishes. BYO Mon & Tues. Inexpensive to Moderate.

Café Retro 18 York St. A laid-back place near the abbey for a cappuccino break during the day, or inventive international dishes in the evenings, all to mellow sounds. There's also the *Retro-to-Go* takeaway next door. Moderate.

Demuths 2 North Parade Passage ☎01225/446059. Bath's favourite eating place for veggies and vegans, offering original and delicious dishes, as well as organic beers, wines and coffees. Decor is bright and modern. No smoking. Booking advisable on Fri, Sat & Sun. Moderate to Expensive.

Eastern Eye 8 Quiet St ☎01225/422323. Just off Milsom Street, this designer curry house occupies a Georgian bank, with a spectacular vaulted ceiling. The food's good too, impeccably presented and briskly served. Moderate.

Firehouse Rotisserie 2 John St ☎01225/482070. Delicious, outsized Californian pizzas and grills are the main items in this busy place with a pleasant woody interior on two floors. Booking essential. Closed Sun. Moderate.

No. 5 Bistro 5 Argyle St ☎01225/444499. Candles on the tables and French posters on the walls set the tone here, just off Pulteney Bridge. BYO Mon & Tues; Wed is fish night, and the desserts are always good. No smoking. Expensive.

Pimpernel's *Royal Crescent Hotel*, 16 Royal Crescent ☎01225/823333. English-based classics with Mediterranean influences make this the best restaurant in Bath, all in sumptuous surroundings. Meat and vegetarian set menus are available. No smoking. Very Expensive.

Popjoy's Sawclose ☎01225/460494. Though somewhat touristy and twee, this restaurant is still worth sampling for its prime location next to the Theatre Royal, and for the curiosity value of being Beau Nash's house (it's named after his mistress). The food is high-quality Modern British, with great desserts, and there's a good-value pre-theatre menu. Closed Sun. Expensive.

Pump Room Abbey Church Yard ☎01225/444477. If you don't want to splash out on an Eggs Benedict brunch, you might succumb to a Bath bun here in the morning, the bewildering range of cream teas in the afternoon, or the excellent lunch-time menu, all to the accompaniment of a pianist or a classical trio. You get a good view of the baths, and a chance to sample the waters, though be prepared to queue for a table. Open daytime only, plus evenings during the Bath Festival, Aug and Christmas. Inexpensive to Moderate.

Tilley's Bistro 3 North Parade Passage ☎01225/484200. Informal, rather cramped French restaurant with starter-sized and -priced portions to allow more samplings, good set-price lunchtime menus and a separate vegetarian menu. Closed Sun. Moderate.

Walrus and Carpenter 28 Barton St ☎01225/314864. Popular spot near the Theatre Royal, serving steaks, burgers, poultry dishes and a full vegetarian menu in a warren of small rooms. Moderate.

Pubs and cafés

The Bath Tap 19–20 St James's Parade. Home of Bath's gay and lesbian scene, though without so much of the "scene". It's lively but relaxed, with a mixed crowd enjoying the regular cabaret as well as late-closing club nights (see p.416).

The Bell 103 Walcot St. Excellent, easy-going pub with atmosphere, a beer garden, live music three times a week (Mon & Wed eve, plus Sun lunchtime) and bar billiards.

Coeur de Lion Northumberland Place, off High St. Centrally located tavern on a flagstoned shopping alley. It's Bath's smallest boozer and a regular tourist stop, but you should persevere for the good lunchtime food, and there are a few tables outside.

Doolally's 51 Walcot St. Friendly place to extend a coffee or lunch break. Spicy teas, mochas and lassis are specialities. Dinner is available Thurs–Sat for the live music evenings, usually world or folk.

The George Mill Lane, Bathampton. Popular canal-side pub twenty minutes' walk from the centre and with better than average bar food.

Ha! Ha! Bar & Canteen Beehive Yard, Walcot St. Drinks, nibbles and full meals in this modern lounge and outdoor terrace, also a great breakfast stop.

Hat & Feather 14 London St. At the top of Walcot Street, this grungy drinking hole continues the quarter's alternative theme, with table football, a pool table and regular DJs and live music. Evenings are packed, but it's a haven of calm by day.

Jazz Café 1 Kingsmead Square. Big breakfasts and other snack fodder, and first-class lattes are served at this boho-style greasy spoon. Newspapers are on hand, and there's some outside seating. Open Mon–Sat 8am–9pm, Sun 10.30am–4pm.

Old Green Tree Green St. Wood panelling, low ceilings and real ales make this a popular stop among beer connoisseurs and others. It's the departure-point for a guided pub crawl (8pm Mon–Wed & Sun).

The Porter Miles Buildings, George St. Part of *Moles* club (see p.416), serving good beer and veggie food in a funky setting. There are tables outside and pool and table football in the Cellar Bar, where, in the evenings, there's free live music (Mon–Thurs), DJs (Fri & Sat) and comedy (Sun).

The Salamander 3 John St. Real ale pub with a woody decor, a laid-back atmosphere and good food available (currently Tues–Sat only) at the bar or in the renowned upstairs restaurant. The pub has a no-smoking area.

Bath's festivals

Bath has a great range of festivals throughout the year, offering talks, gigs and other events in often sumptuous surroundings. If you're visiting during one of these occasions, you'll find the city's mellow pace livened up a notch or two, though you should be aware that accommodation gets very scarce. Best of the bunch are: the **Bath International Music Festival** (ⓦwww.bathmusicfest.org.uk), held between mid-May and June and featuring jazz, classical and world music; the **Bath Fringe Festival** (ⓦwww.bathfringe.co.uk), running from late May to early June, with the accent on art and performance; and **Bath Literature Festival** (ⓦwww.bathlitfest.org.uk), taking place over ten days in Feb/March. There's also an international guitar festival in July/August, a Jane Austen festival in late September and a film festival in October. For further information on each, call ⓣ01225/463362, ⓦwww.bathfestivals.org.uk, or check out the individual websites above.

Nightlife and entertainment

First and foremost of town-centre **clubs** is *Moles* (ⓣ01225/404445, ⓦwww.moles.co.uk) on George Street, a Bath institution which has live music for half the week and DJs playing club sounds the rest of the time. Other places include *Babylon* on Kingston Road (ⓣ01225/400404), large and generally packed; *T's*, a sweaty dive right under Pulteney Bridge that's popular with students and younger clubbers (ⓣ01225/425360); the Moroccan-style *Fez Club*, The Paragon (ⓣ01225/444162), playing funk, trance and old skool, and *Po Na Na*, 8 North Parade (ⓣ01225/401115), also Moroccan-themed, with a largely student crowd. The best gay and lesbian venue is the *Bath Tap Bar and Nightclub* (see p.415) at 19 St James's Parade, open on Thursdays, Fridays and Saturdays until 2am. There are three floors in all, including a chill-out zone. For **live music**, head for *Moles* or the Cellar Bar in the next-door *Porter*, or try the *Porter Butt* pub on London Road (ⓣ01225/425084), which has live bands most weekends embracing roots, punk and ska.

Theatre and ballet fans should check out what's showing at the Theatre Royal on Sawclose (ⓣ01225/448844), which stages more experimental productions in the Ustinov Studio. If you're in Bath in early summer, look out for the **Bath International Music Festival** (see box above), which features big names in classical music, jazz, folk and blues, with a plethora of fringe events accompanying the official programme, plus fireworks, literary and art events and lots of busking. For concerts, gigs and other events during the rest of the year, refer to *Venue*, the weekly listings magazine (£1.20), or to *This Month in Bath*, a free monthly listings guide available from the tourist office.

Listings

Banks and exchange Nat West, bottom of High Street; American Express, 5 Bridge S. There is also a bureau de change in Bath's tourist office.

Buses Local services ⓣ0870/608 2608; National Express ⓣ08705/808080, ⓦwww.nationalexpress.co.uk.

Car rental Avis, Unit 4b, Riverside Business Park, Lower Bristol Rd ⓣ01225/446680.

Internet Click Internet Café, 13 Manvers St; MCCM, 128 Walcot St. Both charge around £1.50 for 30min and are open until late.

Left luggage You can leave bags at *Bath Backpackers* (see p.409), for £2 per item per day.

Taxis Abbey Radio Taxis ⓣ01225/444444; DC Travel ⓣ01225/425678.

Tours Free walking tours of Bath daily except Sat at 2pm (more frequent departures in summer), leaving from Abbey Churchyard. Bizarre Bath offers nightly "comedy walks" around Bath every evening at 8pm in summer, lasting 90min; meet outside the *Huntsman Inn* on North Parade Passage

(☎01225/335124). A plethora of open-top bus tours are available, leaving from Grand Parade or the bus station, with all-day tickets. Outside Bath, Mad Max Tours offers full-day excursions to Lacock, Castle Combe, Stonehenge and Avebury: contact the YMCA for details (☎01225/325900, ⓦwww.madmaxtours.com).

Claverton, Frome and Dyrham Park

For a quick sample of the lovely countryside around Bath you could make an easy excursion to **CLAVERTON**, on the eastern edge of Bath, where the **American Museum** (late March to July & Sept–Nov Tues–Sun 2–5pm, Aug daily 2–5pm; grounds Tues–Thurs 1–6pm, Fri–Sun noon–6pm; £6, grounds only £3.50) merits at least half a day. Occupying the early nineteenth-century Claverton Manor, where Winston Churchill made his maiden political speech in 1897, this was the first museum of Americana to be established outside the US, and consists of a series of reconstructed rooms illustrating life in the New World from the seventeenth to the nineteenth centuries, as well as special sections devoted to textiles, whaling, the opening of the West, Native Americans and Hispano-American culture. The glorious **grounds** contain a replica of George Washington's garden, an arboretum and assorted relics resembling items from a movie set. University buses #18 and #418 run throughout the year to the Avenue (the stop before the campus), from where it's a ten-minute walk to the museum.

Fifteen miles south of Bath, at the eastern end of the Mendip Hills, the town of **FROME** (pronounced "Froom") is a picturesque ensemble of steep cobbled streets, yellow-stone weavers' cottages, Georgian rows and some dusty old shops. You could spend a pleasant hour or two roaming Frome's nooks and crannies, such as Gentle Street, or perusing the old gravestones in the churchyard of St John's. Bus #267 connects Bath with Frome at least hourly (4 on Sun on service #767). From here, it's only five miles across the Wiltshire border to Longleat (see p.312).

A visit to **Dyrham Park**, seven miles north of Bath (daily 11am–5.30pm or dusk; house April–Oct Mon, Tues & Fri–Sun noon–5pm; grounds & house £7.90, grounds £3, park only, on days when house closed, £2; NT), is almost worth it for the journey alone, which takes in a far-reaching panorama at the top of Tog Hill, where the A420 intersects with the A46. Standing on the site of a calamitous defeat of the Britons by the Saxons in 677, the house is a late seventeenth-century Baroque mansion, finely decorated and panelled in oak, cedar and walnut. Alongside furniture used by the diarists Pepys and Evelyn, many of the contents reflect the career of the first owner William Blathwayt, a diplomat who collected pieces from Holland and North America. The name Dyrham means "deer enclosure", and the surrounding 268 acres of parkland are still grazed by fallow deer – the deer park gives views as far as the Welsh hills.

Bus connections are limited to two daily from Bath on #X56 (Mon–Fri only), currently leaving the bus station at 10.40am and 1.40pm, returning at 2.40pm and 5.30pm (20-minute journey): the route passes through Dyrham village, half a mile from the park.

Wells, the Mendips and Glastonbury

Wells, twenty miles south of Bristol across the Somerset border and the same distance southwest from Bath, is a miniature cathedral city that has not significantly altered in eight hundred years. You could spend a good half-day kicking around here, and you might decide to make it an accommodation stop for visiting nearby attractions in the **Mendip Hills**, such as the **Wookey Hole** caves and the **Cheddar Gorge**. On the southern edge of the range, and just a jump away from Wells, the town of **Glastonbury** has for centuries been one of the main Arthurian sites of the West Country, and is now the country's most enthusiastic centre of New Age cults.

Wells

Technically England's smallest city, **WELLS** owes its celebrity entirely to its **Cathedral** (daily: April–Sept 7am–7pm; Oct–March 7am–6pm; suggested donation £4.50). Hidden from sight until you pass into its spacious close from the central Market Place, the building presents a majestic spectacle, the broad lawn of the former graveyard providing a perfect foreground. The west front teems with some three hundred thirteenth-century figures of saints and kings, once brightly painted and gilded, though their present honey tint has a subtle splendour of its own. Close up, the impact is slightly lessened, as most of the statuary is badly eroded and many figures were damaged by Puritans in the seventeenth century. The facade was constructed about fifty years after work on the main building was begun in 1180. The **interior** is a supreme example of early English Gothic, the long nave punctuated by a dramatic "scissor arch", one of three that were constructed in 1338 to take the extra weight of the newly built tower. Though some wax enthusiastic about the ingenuity of these so-called "strainer" arches, others argue that they're "grotesque intrusions" from an artistic point of view.

Other features worth scrutinizing are the narrative carvings on the **capitals and corbels** in the transepts – including men with toothache and an old man caught pilfering an orchard. In the north transept, don't miss the 24-hour astronomical clock, dating from 1390, whose jousting knights charge each other every quarter-hour, as announced by a figure known as Jack Blandiver, who kicks a couple of bells from his seat high up on the right – on the hour he strikes the bell in front of him. Opposite the clock, a doorway leads to a graceful, much-worn flight of steps rising to the **Chapter House** (closes 4.30pm), an octagonal room elaborately ribbed in the Decorated style. There are some gnarled old tombs to be seen in the aisles of the **Quire**, at the end of which is the richly coloured stained glass of the fourteenth-century **Lady Chapel**. The best way to see it all is on one of the **free guided tours**, which take place up to five times daily (twice daily in winter; none on Sun). If you want to take pictures, you have to buy a photographic permit (£2); the use of flashes is banned in the Quire. Evensong takes place at 5.15pm (3pm on Sun).

The row of clerical houses on the north side of the cathedral green are mainly seventeenth- and eighteenth-century, though one, the **Old Deanery**, shows traces of its fifteenth-century origins. The chancellor's house is now a **museum** (Easter–July & mid-Sept to Oct Mon–Sat 10am–5.30pm, Sun 10am–4pm; Aug to mid-Sept daily 10am–8pm; Nov–Easter Mon & Wed–Sun 11am–4pm; £2.50), displaying, among other items, some of the cathedral's original statuary, placed here for conservation reasons (and replaced by replicas), as well as a good geological section with fossils from the surrounding area, including Wookey Hole.

Beyond the arch, a little further along the street, the cobbled medieval **Vicars' Close** holds more clerical dwellings, linked to the cathedral by the Chain Gate and fronted by small gardens. The cottages were built in the mid-fourteenth century – though only no. 22 has not undergone outward alterations – and have been continuously occupied by members of the cathedral clergy ever since.

On the other side of the cathedral – and accessible through the cathedral shop – are the cloisters, from which you can enter the tranquil grounds of the **Bishop's Palace** (April–July, Sept & Oct Mon–Fri 10.30am–6pm, Sun 1–6pm; Aug daily 10.30am–6pm, though occasionally closed for functions; last entry at 5pm; £3.50), also reachable from Market Place through the Bishop's Eye archway. The residence of the Bishop of Bath and Wells, the palace was walled and moated as a result of a rift with the borough in the fourteenth century, and the imposing gatehouse still displays the grooves of the portcullis and a chute for pouring oil and molten lead on would-be assailants. On a less warlike note, look out for the bell attached to the side of the gatehouse, which swans and their cygnets have learned to ring when they're hungry. Within, the tranquil gardens contain the springs from which the city takes its name – and which still feed the moat as well as the streams flowing along the gutters of Wells's High Street – and the scanty but impressive remains of the **Great Hall**, built at the end of the thirteenth century and despoiled during the Reformation. Across the lawn, which is used for regular croquet matches in summer, stands the square **Bishop's Chapel** and the **Undercroft**, holding displays relating to the history of the site, state rooms and a café. Outside, a stroll along the rampart walk reveals glimpses of Glastonbury Tor to the south.

Practicalities

Wells is not connected to the rail network, but its **bus station**, off Market Street, receives hourly buses from Bristol and Bath (less frequent on Sun). The **tourist office** is on Market Place (daily: April–Oct 9.30am–5.30pm; Nov–March 10am–4pm; ⓣ01749/672552, ⓦwww.wells-uk.com).

There are several central choices of **accommodation**: of the B&Bs, try *Canon Grange*, right on the Cathedral Green, its spacious rooms facing the west front (ⓣ01749/671800, ⓦwww.canongrange.co.uk; ❷); or *Bekynton House*, at 7 St Thomas St (ⓣ01749/672222, ⓦwww.bekynton-house.co.uk; no smoking; ❸), with four rooms available, all en suite, or, slightly cheaper, with a private bathroom. A little further out, but still within a ten-minute walk of the centre, the *Bay Tree* is a simple but comfortable B&B at 85 Portway, the Cheddar road (ⓣ01749/677933; no credit cards; ❷), run by an Italian ex-hotelier and his wife. Alternatively, soak up the authentically antique flavour in either of the old coaching inns in the centre of town: the *Crown Hotel*, Market Place (ⓣ01749/673457, ⓦcrownatwells.co.uk; ❹), where William Penn was arrested in 1695 for illegal preaching, and the *Swan*, on Sadler Street (ⓣ01749/836300; ❻), with limited views of the cathedral.

Wells offers the full gamut of eating possibilities. Close to the cathedral on Market Place, *Crofter's* (closed eves) offers coffees and **snacks**, as does the *Bekynton Brasserie*, which also serves moderately priced full **evening meals** of British and Continental dishes (ⓣ01749/675993; closed Mon–Wed eves). Round the corner on Sadler Street, the Italian-run *Ancient Gate House* (ⓣ01749/672029) and *Ritcher's* (ⓣ01749/679085) are more formal places with quality fare and fairly expensive prices. The latter also has a downstairs bar/patisserie selling a range of coffees, panini, baguettes and salads. Excellent wholefood is on hand at the *Good Earth* on Priory Rd, near the bus station (closed daytime & Sun), with pizzas, flans and "real" ice cream, plus delicious takeaway items. For a **drink**, head for the *City Arms* on Cuthbert Street, formerly the city jail, with a flower-filled courtyard and meals in the upstairs restaurant.

The area around Wells makes good cycling country: you can **rent bikes** at *Bike City*, 31 Broad St, at the bottom of the High St (☎01749/671711), though, with few available, it's a good idea to reserve one as far ahead as possible.

The Mendips

The **Mendip Hills**, rising to the north of Wells, are chiefly famous for Wookey Hole – the most impressive of many caves in this narrow limestone chain – and for the **Cheddar Gorge**, where a walk through the narrow cleft might make a starting point for more adventurous trips across the Mendips. From Wells, there are hourly buses to Wookey Hole from Monday to Saturday (#172 or #670), and four departures on Sunday (#972), while the #126 and #826 run to the gorge hourly, or every two hours on Sunday.

Wookey Hole

Hollowed out by the River Axe a couple of miles outside Wells, **Wookey Hole** is an impressive cave complex of deep pools and intricate rock formations, but it's folklore rather than geology that takes precedence on the guided tours (daily: April–Oct 10am–5pm; Nov–March 10.30am–4.30pm; closed Dec 17–25; £8.80). Highlight of the tour is the alleged petrified remains of the Witch of Wookey, a "blear-eyed hag" who was said to turn her evil eye on crops, young lovers and local farmers until the Abbot of Glastonbury intervened; he dispatched a monk who drove the witch into the inner cave, sprinkled her with holy water and turned her into stone. Some substance was lent to the legend when an ancient skeleton – in fact Romano-British – was unearthed here in 1912, together with a dagger, sacrificial knife and a big rounded ball of pure stalagmite, the so-called witch's ball. Beside her were found two skeletons, the remains of goats tied to a stake. The guides point out several other fancied resemblances to people and things during the hour-long tour, at the end of which you can use your ticket to visit a functioning Victorian paper mill by the river, and rooms containing speleological exhibits. On a less earnest note, the range of amusements includes a collection of gaudy, sometimes ghoulish, Edwardian fairground pieces.

A walkable couple of miles uphill west of Wookey Hole, **Ebbor Gorge** offers a wilder alternative to the more famous Cheddar Gorge, with tranquillity guaranteed on the wooded trails that follow the ravine up to the Mendip plateau.

Cheddar Gorge

Six miles west of Wookey on the A371, Cheddar has given its name to Britain's best-known cheese – most of it now mass-produced far from here – and is also renowned as a centre for strawberry-growing. However, the biggest selling point of this rather plain village is the **Cheddar Gorge**, lying beyond the neighbourhood of Tweentown about a mile to the north.

Cutting a jagged gash across the Mendip Hills, the limestone gorge is an impressive geological phenomenon, though its natural beauty is undermined by the minor road running through it and by the Lower Gorge's mile of shops, coach park and **tourist office** (June–Sept daily 10am–5pm; Oct daily 10.30am–4.30pm; Nov–March Sun 11am–4pm; ☎01934/744071, Ⓦwww.somersetbythesea.co.uk). Few trippers venture further than the first few curves of the gorge, beyond the shops, which admittedly holds its most dramatic scenery, though each turn of the two-mile length presents new, sometimes startling vistas. At its narrowest the path squeezes between cliffs towering almost five hundred feet above, and if you don't want to follow the road as far as **Priddy**, the highest village in the Mendips, you can reach more dramatic destinations by branching off onto marked paths to such secluded spots as **Black Rock**, just two miles from Cheddar, or **Black Down**, at 1067ft the Mendips' highest peak. Cliff-top paths winding along the rim of the gorge provide an alternative to walking next to the road. The tourist office can give you details of a two-and-a-half-hour circular walk and of the **West Mendip Way**, a forty-mile route extending from Uphill, near Weston-super-Mare, to Wells and Shepton Mallet.

Beneath the gorge, the **Cheddar Caves** (daily: July & Aug 10am–5pm; Sept–June 10.30am–4.30pm; £9.50) were scooped out by underground rivers in the wake of the Ice Age, and subsequently occupied by primitive communities. The bigger of the two main groups, **Gough's Caves**, is a sequence of chambers with names such as Solomon's Temple, Aladdin's Cave and the Swiss Village, all arrayed with tortuous rock formations that resemble organ pipes, waterfalls and giant birds. **Cox's Caves** (same ticket), entered lower down the main drag, have floodlighting that picks out subtle pinks, greys, greens and whites in the rock, and a set of lime blocks known as "the Bells", which produce a range of tones when struck. The Crystal Quest, attached to Cox's Caves, is the kids' favourite, with high-tech light and laser effects playing on its gushing waterfall.

Outside again, close to Cox's Caves, the 274 steps of **Jacob's Ladder** (same ticket as caves) lead to a cliff-top viewpoint looking towards Glastonbury Tor, Exmoor and the sea. It's a muscle-wrenching climb – anyone not in a state of honed fitness can reach the same spot with a great deal more ease via the narrow lane winding up behind the cliffs. You can also survey the panorama from **Pavey's Lookout Tower** nearby, and there's a circular three-mile clifftop Gorge Walk accessible from here.

Practicalities

Among Cheddar's handful of **B&Bs**, there's *Chedwell Cottage*, Redcliffe St (☎01934/743268; no credit cards; ❷), which has two en-suite rooms and a garden; and, on the outskirts, *Wossells House*, Upper New Rd (☎01934/744317; no credit cards; ❷), where huge breakfasts are served; both are non-smoking. Other options include the **youth hostel**, opposite the fire station, off the Hayes (☎0870/770 5760; closed Jan & very limited opening mid-Nov to Dec & Feb; beds £11.50). There are three **campsites**, two near the centre of Cheddar – *Froglands* (☎01934/742058; closed mid-Oct to Easter), a hundred yards past the church, and *Cheddar Bridge Park,* a five-star camping and caravan complex opposite (☎01934/743048; no children except during summer holiday) – and the fully equipped *Broadway House* on the northwestern outskirts of the village off the A371 to Axbridge (☎01934/742610; closed Dec–Feb). If you want to stay in the heart of the Mendips, there's a fourth site to consider: *Mendip Heights* (☎01749/870241, Ⓦwww.mendipheights.co.uk; closed mid-Nov to Feb), outside the village of Priddy lies east along the B3135 road through the gorge to Priddy, from which it's a signposted five hundred yards.

Glastonbury

Six miles south of Wells, and reachable from there in twenty minutes on frequent buses, **GLASTONBURY** lies at the centre of the so-called **Isle of Avalon**, a region rich with mystical associations. At the heart of it all is the early Christian legend that the young Christ once visited this site, a story that is not as far-fetched as it sounds. The Romans had a heavy presence in the area, mining lead in the Mendips, and one of these mines was owned by **Joseph of Arimathea**, a well-to-do merchant said to have been related to Mary. It's not completely impossible that the merchant took his kinsman on one of his many visits to his property, in a period of Christ's life of which nothing is recorded. It was this possibility to which William Blake referred in his *Glastonbury Hymn*, better known as *Jerusalem*: – "And did those feet in ancient times/Walk upon England's mountains green?"

Another legend relates how Joseph was imprisoned for twelve years after the Crucifixion, miraculously kept alive by the **Holy Grail**, the chalice of the Last Supper, in which the blood was gathered from the wound in Christ's side. The Grail, along with the spear which had caused the wound, were later taken by Joseph to Glastonbury, where he founded the abbey and commenced the conversion of Britain.

According to the official version, however, **Glastonbury Abbey** (daily: Feb 10am–5pm; March 9.30am–5.30pm; April–Sept 9.30am–6pm; Oct 9.30am–5pm; Nov 9.30am–4.30pm; Dec & Jan 10am–4.30pm; £4; Ⓦwww.glastonburyabbey.com) was a Celtic monastery founded in the fourth or fifth century – making this the oldest Christian foundation in England – and enlarged by St Dunstan, under whom it became the richest Benedictine abbey in the country. Three Anglo-Saxon kings (Edmund, Edgar and Edmund Ironside) were buried here, the library had a far-reaching fame, and the church had the longest known nave of any monastic church at the time of the Dissolution (580ft – Wells Cathedral's nave reaches 415ft). The original building was destroyed by fire in 1184 and the ruins are the rather scanty remains of what took its place, reduced to their present state at the Dissolution. Hidden behind walls at the centre of town, surrounded by grassy parkland and shaded by trees, the ruins only hint at the extent of the building, which was financed largely by a constant procession of medieval pilgrims. Most prominent and photogenic remains are the transept piers and the shell of the Lady Chapel, with its carved figures of the Annunciation, the Magi and Herod.

The abbey's **choir** introduces another strand to the Glastonbury story, for it holds what is alleged to be the tomb of **Arthur and Guinevere**. As told by William of Malmesbury and Thomas Malory, the story relates how, after being mortally wounded in battle, King Arthur sailed to Avalon where he was buried alongside his queen. The discovery of two bodies in an ancient cemetery outside the abbey in 1191 – from which they were transferred here in 1278 – was taken to confirm the popular identification of Glastonbury with Avalon. In the grounds, the fourteenth-century abbot's kitchen is the only monastic building to survive intact, with four huge corner fireplaces and a great central lantern above. Behind the main entrance to the grounds, look out for the thorn-tree that is supposedly from the original **Glastonbury Thorn** said to have sprouted from the staff of Joseph of Arimathea when he landed here to convert the country. The plant grew for centuries on a nearby hill known as Wyrral, or Weary-All, and despite being hacked down by Puritans, lived long enough to provide numerous cuttings whose descendants still bloom twice a year (Easter & Dec). Only at Glastonbury do they flourish, it is claimed – anywhere else they die after a couple of years.

On the edge of the abbey grounds, the medieval **Abbey Barn** forms the centrepiece of the engaging **Somerset Rural Life Museum** (April–Oct Tues–Fri 10am–5pm, Sat & Sun 2–6pm; Nov–March Tues–Sat 10am–5pm; free), illustrating a range of local rural occupations, from cheese- and cider-making to peat-digging, thatching and farming. A collection of heavy-duty farm machinery is on show in the barn, a fourteenth-century tithe farm that originally held

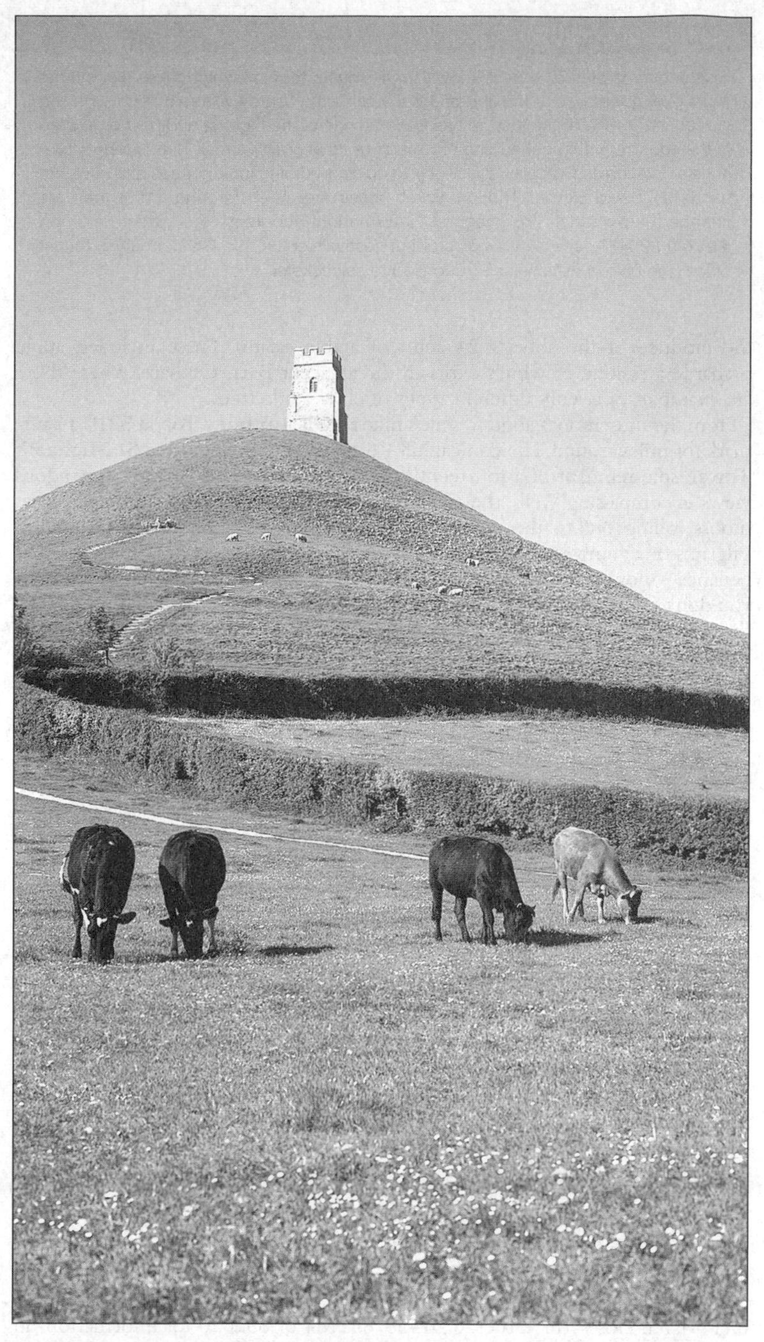

△ Glastonbury Tor

Glastonbury Festival

Glastonbury is of course best known for its **music festival** which takes place most years over three days at the end of June outside the nearby village of Pilton. Having started in the 1970s, the festival has become one of the biggest and best organized in the country, without shedding too much of its alternative feel. Bands range from huge acts such as Coldplay and Moby to up-and-coming indie groups and such old hands as David Bowie. Though ticket prices are steep (around £105) they are snapped up early: for general information, contact the promoters on ⓣ01749/890470, see ⓦwww.glastonburyfestivals.co.uk, or Glastonbury's tourist office (see below), which is also licensed to sell tickets.

the produce of the abbey's 24 acres of arable estates. These included apple orchards, a residue of which exists in the adjacent Barn Orchard, where there are examples of twenty different types of cider apple trees.

From the museum it's about a mile's hike to **Glastonbury Tor**, at 521ft a landmark for miles around. The conical hill – topped by the dilapidated **St Michael's Tower**, sole remnant of a fourteenth-century church – commands stupendous views encompassing Wells, the Quantocks, the Mendips, the once-marshy peat moors rolling out to the sea, and, on very clear days, the Welsh mountains. Pilgrims once embarked on the stiff climb here with hard peas in their shoes as penance – nowadays people come to feel the vibrations of crossing ley-lines. If you don't fancy the steep ascent, take the easier path farther up Wellhouse Lane, the road that leads to the Tor Park from the centre of town. You can also save some legwork by taking advantage of the **Glastonbury Tor Bus**, a summer service (May to mid-Sept) which ferries people from the High Street to the base of the Tor every thirty minutes; your £1 ticket can be used all day.

At the bottom of Wellhouse Lane, in the middle of a lush garden intended for quiet contemplation, the **Chalice Well** (daily: Feb, March & Nov 11am–5pm; April–Oct 10am–6pm; Dec & Jan noon–4pm; £2.70) is alleged to be the hiding-place of the Holy Grail. The iron-red waters were considered to have curative properties, making the town a spa for a brief period in the eighteenth century, and they are still prized – there's a tap in Wellhouse Lane.

Back in town, you might take a glance at the fifteenth-century church of **St John the Baptist**, halfway along the High Street. The tower is reckoned to be one of Somerset's finest, and the **interior** has a fine oak roof and stained glass illustrating the legend of St Joseph of Arimathea, both from the period of the church's construction. The Glastonbury thorn in the churchyard is the biggest in town.

Further down the street, the fourteenth-century **Tribunal** was where the abbots presided over legal cases; it later became a hotel for pilgrims, and now holds the small **Glastonbury Lake Village Museum** of finds from the Iron Age lake villages that once fringed the marshland below the Tor (April–Sept Mon–Thurs & Sun 10am–5pm, Fri & Sat 10am–5.30pm; Oct–March closes 1hr earlier; £2).

Practicalities

Buses #376 and #377 (on Sun #977 and #929) run once or twice an hour from Wells. Glastonbury's **tourist office** is housed in the Tribunal on the High St (April–Sept Mon–Thurs & Sun 10am–5pm, Fri & Sat 10am–5.30pm; Oct–March closes 1hr earlier; ⓣ01458/832954 or 832020 for information on tickets for the festival, ⓦwww.glastonburytic.co.uk).

Accommodation

Glastonbury has a rich assortment of good-value **accommodation** ranging from medieval hostelries to hostels. Most places are within a brief walk of the Tor and town centre.

Hotels and guest houses

1 Park Terrace Street Road ⓣ01458/835845, ⓦwww.no1parkterrace.co.uk. Large Victorian house, five minutes' walk from the centre, where all rooms are en suite or have private facilities. ❷

3 Magdalene St ⓣ01458/832129. Beautifully furnished bedrooms make for a stylish stay in this listed Georgian house with a large walled garden, right next to the abbey. ❻

George & Pilgrims High Street ⓣ01458/831146, ⓦwww.georgeandpilgrims.activehotels.com. This atmospheric fifteenth-century oak-panelled inn is the place to head for a medieval atmosphere. ❸

Glastonbury Backpackers 4 Market Place ⓣ01458/833353, ⓦwww.backpackers-online.com/Glastonbury. Very centrally located old coaching inn with café, restaurant, pool room and no curfew, plus occasional bands playing in the bar. Dorm beds £12, doubles ❶

Isle of Avalon Campsite ⓣ01458/833618. Decent campsite within sight of the Tor, ten minutes' walk up Northload Street on Godney Road.

Little Orchard Ashwell Lane ⓣ01458/831620. At the foot of the Tor, on the A361 Shepton Mallet road, this good-value B&B offers panoramic views. No credit cards. ❷

Meadow Barn Middlewick Farm, Wick Lane ⓣ01458/832351. A mile and a half north of town, this place offers peace and quiet in rural surroundings, with nice views and an indoor heated pool. No smoking. ❷

Shambhala Healing Retreat Coursing Batch, near the Tor ⓣ01458/831797, ⓔfindyourself@shambhala.co.uk. Recharge your spiritual batteries in one of the retreat's Tibetan, Egyptian and Chinese guest rooms. There's also a water garden and eight types of massage on offer. Three-day minimum stay. No smoking. ❺

YHA hostel Ivythorn Hill, Street ⓣ0870/770 6056. The nearest YHA lies a couple of miles south of Glastonbury but is easily accessed by bus (#376 or #377, on Sun #977; alight at Marshalls Elm crossroads and follow signs). Open Wed & Thurs only Oct–March; £10.25).

Eating, drinking and entertainment

Wedged between the esoteric shops of Glastonbury's High Street are several decent **cafés** serving inexpensive meals, including the *Blue Note Café* at no. 4, a good place to hang out over coffees and cakes with outside seating in the courtyard at the back, and open for evening meals on Fridays and Saturdays, when there's live music, and *Olly's Café/Bar* at no. 52, opposite the post office, which has wooden tables and some meat dishes among the predominantly vegetarian choices, and also stays open on Friday and Saturday evenings, for which booking is recommended (ⓣ01458/834521). Just off Market Place, *Mocha Berry* has a buzzy feel and serves up organic sausages and mash and Homity Pie. Almost opposite the abbey entrance, the *Market House Inn* has snacks, a garden and occasional bands – and also offers basic accommodation with and without private bathrooms (ⓣ01458/832220; ❷) – while *Glastonbury Backpackers* is usually fairly lively for drinks, snacks and entertainment. Halfway up the High Street, the Assembly Rooms has a wholefood café, but is better known as the venue for talks and musical and theatrical **performances**, including an international **dance festival** which takes place over a week between July and August. You can also buy tickets for concerts and miracle plays staged within the abbey grounds between mid-June and mid-September – call ⓣ01458/832267 for details, or view the abbey's website (see p.422).

Bridgwater, Taunton and the Quantocks

Travelling west through the Somerset Levels, your route could take you through both **Bridgwater** and **Taunton**, each of which would make a handy starting point for excursions into the gently undulating **Quantock Hills**, a mellow landscape of snug villages set in scenic wooded valleys or "combes". Public transport is fairly minimal round here, but you can see quite a lot on the **West Somerset Railway** between Bishops Lydeard and the coastal resort of Minehead, with stops at some of the thatched, typically English villages along the west flank of the Quantocks; and there are **horse-riding** facilities at many local farms.

Bridgwater

Sedate **BRIDGWATER** has seen little excitement since it was embroiled in the Civil War and its aftermath, in particular the events surrounding the **Monmouth Rebellion** of 1685. Having landed from his base in Holland, the Protestant Duke of Monmouth, an illegitimate son of Charles II, was enthusiastically proclaimed king at Taunton, and was only prevented from taking Bristol by the encampment of the Catholic James II's army there. Monmouth turned round and attempted to surprise the king's forces on **Sedgemoor**, three miles outside Bridgwater. The disorganized rebel army was mown down by the royal artillery, Monmouth himself was captured and later beheaded, and a period of repression was unleashed under the infamous Judge Jeffreys, whose Bloody Assizes created a folk-memory in Somerset of gibbets and gutted carcasses displayed around the county.

The town was once one of Somerset's major ports and, despite some ugly outskirts, still has some handsome red-brick buildings around its centre. Northgate leads to the River Parrett and King's Square, which occupies the site of the keep of Bridgwater Castle, built in the thirteenth century but fallen into decay after the Civil War. A few traces remain above ground: part of the main wall is visible on West Quay, and a lesser wall on Queen Street – much of the original material was recycled for the construction of other houses in town. The thirteenth- to fourteenth-century **St Mary's Church** (Tues–Sun 10.30am–noon; free), immediately identifiable by its polygonal, acutely angled steeple that soars over the town centre, has an oak pulpit and a seventeenth-century Italian altarpiece. The church is starkly contrasted by the Neoclassical Baptist church opposite, dating from 1600 but rebuilt in 1837. Just round the corner from the red-brick Christ Church, where Coleridge preached in 1797 and 1798, Bridgwater's **Blake Museum**, by the River Parrett on Blake Street (Tues–Sat 10am–4pm; free) shows relics, models and a video-documentary relating to the Battle of Sedgemoor. The sixteenth-century building is reputedly the birthplace of local hero Robert Blake, admiral under Oliver Cromwell, whose swashbuckling career against Royalists, Dutch and Spanish is chronicled and illustrated here. There's also an archeology section, and a room devoted to local merchant, cartoonist and anti-slavery campaigner John Chubb, a friend of Coleridge.

You can spend a rewarding hour or two here and the surrounding area: equip yourself with the Bridgwater Castle Trail pamphlet from the **tourist office**, beyond the tall white Town Hall on High Street (Easter–Oct Mon–Fri 10am–5pm Sat 10am–4.30pm; Nov–Easter Mon, Wed & Fri 10am–1pm & 1.45–4pm; ⓣ01278/427652, ⓦwww.somersetbythesea.co.uk), which can also tell you about available **accommodation** hereabouts. A central choice would be the green and white *Old Vicarage* right opposite St Mary's Church (ⓣ01278/458891, ⓔoldvicaragehotel@aol.com; ❹), which calls itself one of Bridgwater's oldest buildings – and you can still see some of the wattle and daub of the original walls on the left of the gateway into the courtyard. On

West Quay, the *Castle Bar* (☎01278/423847; no smoking; ❸) has nine fairly basic rooms, all en suite, the best ones overlooking the river; or try the *Acorns*, 61 Taunton Rd (☎01278/445577; no credit cards; ❷), on the banks of the Bridgwater–Taunton Canal south of the centre, which has twenty rooms, mostly en suite. For **snacks** head for the *Nutmeg House* in Angel Crescent, behind the shopping centre off the High Street, offering good pastas, soups and grills at outdoor tables (closed Sun), or the nearby *Great Escape* **pub**, also with tables outside, and with a full bar menu and DJs on Fridays and Saturdays. Alternatively, pick up a bag of fish and chips at the *West Quay Fish Bar*, by the river at the bottom of Castle Street; they also dish out takeaway breakfasts. Also on Castle Street, the Bridgwater Arts Centre (☎01278/422700) has concerts, plays, comedy and a bar. At the far end of St Mary Street, you can while away an evening in more boisterous style at the *Rock Garden*, a café-bar with live local bands (usually Thurs, Fri or Sat) and club nights, with late closing.

A good time to be in Bridgwater would be for the **carnival** celebrations, which usually take place on the nearest Thursday or Friday to Bonfire Night (one of the Catholic conspirators of the Gunpowder Plot hailed from nearby Nether Stowey; see p.429). Grandly festooned floats of the local carnival clubs roll through town, before heading off to do the same in various other Somerset towns and villages, including North Petherton, Glastonbury, Wells and Shepton Mallet.

If you're spending a few days in the area, think about renting a **bike**; cycling is an ideal way of getting around the Somerset Levels – the area of reclaimed marshes between Bridgwater and Glastonbury. In the village of Burtle, about ten miles northeast of Bridgwater, Bluebell Cycle Hire (☎01278/722123) provides bikes and a leaflet outlining a twelve-mile circular route around the Levels. The shop is based at the *Old Burtle Inn*, which also does good bar food and offers a **camping** field.

Taunton

Twelve miles from Bridgwater, Somerset's county town of **TAUNTON** lies in the fertile Vale of Taunton, wedged between the Quantock, Brendon and Blackdown hills. The region is famed for its production of cider and scrumpy (cider's less refined cousin), while Taunton itself is host to one of the country's biggest cattle markets.

Taunton's **Castle**, started in the twelfth century, staged the trial of royal claimant Perkin Warbeck, who in 1490 declared himself to be the Duke of York, the younger of the "Princes in the Tower" – the sons of Edward IV, who had been murdered seven years earlier. Most of the castle was pulled down in 1662, but a part of it now houses the **County Museum** (Tues–Sat 10am–5pm; free), which includes a portrait of Judge Jeffreys among other memorabilia of local interest. Overlooking the county cricket ground are the pinnacled and battlemented towers of the town's two most important churches: **St James** and **St Mary Magdalene**, both fifteenth-century though remodelled by the Victorians. St Mary's is worth a look inside for its roof-bosses carved with medieval masks.

Otherwise Taunton should only detain you as a base to visit the Quantock villages or Exmoor. Information is on hand at the **tourist office** on Paul Street (April–Oct Mon–Thurs 9.30am–5.30pm, Fri 9.30am–7pm, Sat 9.30am–5pm; Nov–March Mon–Fri 9.30am–5.30pm, Sat 9.30am–5pm; ☎01823/336344, Ⓦwww.heartofsomerset.com), in the library building. If you want to stay here, head for Wellington Road at the centre of town, where there are three **B&Bs** within a few steps of each other: *Brookfield* at no. 16 (Ⓣ01823/272786; no credit cards; ❷), *Beaufort Lodge* at no. 18 (Ⓣ01823/326420; no credit cards; ❷) – both with all rooms en suite and non-smoking – and *Acorn Lodge* at no. 22 (Ⓣ01823/337613; no credit cards; ❶) with shared bathrooms for its two single and three twin rooms, all of which have TVs. The most atmospheric place in town is next to the museum: the *Castle*, Castle Green (Ⓣ01823/272671, Ⓦwww.the-castle-hotel.com; ❽), a wisteria-clad, three-hundred-year-old hotel exuding old-fashioned good taste – the place to stop for a cup of tea if nothing else. On a more down-to-earth note, *Prockters Farm*, a couple of miles outside town, near the village of West Monkton (Ⓣ01823/412269; no smoking; ❷), is a comfortable old country retreat with brass beds and antiques plus a large garden, offering rooms with or without private bathroom. For a snack or **meal**, head down East Street from Fore Street to *Brettons*, a congenial wine bar and restaurant at 49 East Reach (closed lunchtime Sat & Mon, and all day Sun). Vegetarian dishes are served at the *Brewhouse Theatre and Arts Centre* on Coal Orchard, by the cricket ground, a good place to come in the evening, when there's usually something going on.

The Quantock Hills

Geologically closer to Devon than Somerset, the **Quantock Hills** are a cultivated outpost of Exmoor, similarly crossed by clear streams and grazed by red deer. Just twelve miles in length and mostly between 800 and 900 feet high, the range is enclosed by a triangle of roads leading up from Bridgwater and Taunton, within which snake a tangle of narrow lanes connecting secluded hamlets, reached by local buses from Taunton and Bridgwater. Along the western edge of the range, a restored steam railway is also a useful transport link, originally built to serve the harbour of Watchet, now used by tourists, bird-watchers and trekkers.

Bishops Lydeard and north

North of Taunton, the first villages you pass through on the A358 give you an immediate introduction to the flavour of the Quantocks. **BISHOPS LYDEARD**, four miles up, has a splendid church tower in the Perpendicular style; the church's interior is also worth a look for its carved bench-ends, one of them illustrating the allegory of a pelican feeding its young with blood from its own breast – a symbol of the redemptive power of Christ's blood. The village is the terminus of the **West Somerset Railway**, linked by buses #28 and, on Sunday, #928 from Taunton's train station (from which you can save money by buying a combined bus-and-rail ticket to Minehead). From mid-March to the first week of November (plus some dates in Dec & Jan) steam and diesel trains depart up to seven times daily, stopping at renovated stations on the way to Minehead, some twenty miles away (see p.483). For a talking timetable call Ⓣ01643/707650, for other enquiries call Ⓣ01643/704996, or log on at Ⓦwww.west-somerset-railway.co.uk.

A couple of miles north, **COMBE FLOREY** is almost exclusively built of the pink-red sandstone characteristic of Quantock villages. For over fifteen years (1829–45), the local rector was the unconventional cleric Sydney Smith, called "the greatest master of ridicule since Swift" by Macaulay; more recently it's been home to Evelyn Waugh. A little over three miles further or so along the A358, and the first stop on the West Somerset Railway (though the station lies around four miles west of the village), **CROWCOMBE** is another typical cob-and-thatch Quantock village, with a well-preserved Church House from

1515. Opposite, the parish church has some pagan-looking carved bench-ends from around the same time that are worth a look. There's a **youth hostel** signposted southeast of the village, half a mile from the station (☎0870/770 5782; closed Oct to mid-March), with beds at £10.25 and evening meals available. **Mountain bikes** can be rented from the *Quantock Orchard Caravan Park* (☎01984/618618), between Crowcombe and Triscombe. The cycle, hike or drive across the Quantocks from Crowcombe to Nether Stowey (see below) takes in some lovely wooded scenery.

Nether Stowey and around

Eight miles west of Bridgwater on the A39, on the edge of the hills, the pretty village of **NETHER STOWEY** is best known for its association with **Samuel Taylor Coleridge**, who walked here from Bristol at the end of 1796, to join his wife and child at their new home. This "miserable cottage", as Sara Coleridge called it, was visited six months later by William Wordsworth and his sister Dorothy, who soon afterwards moved into Alfoxden House, near Holford, a couple of miles down the road. The year that Coleridge and Wordsworth spent as neighbours was extraordinarily productive – Coleridge composed some of his best poetry at this time, including *The Rime of the Ancient Mariner* and *Kubla Khan*, and the two poets in collaboration produced the *Lyrical Ballads*, the poetic manifesto of early English Romanticism. Many of the greatest figures of the age made the trek down to visit the pair, among them Charles Lamb, Thomas De Quincey, Robert Southey, Humphry Davy and William Hazlitt, and it was the coming and going of these intellectuals that stirred the suspicions of the local authorities in a period when England was at war with France. Spies were sent to track them and Wordsworth was finally given notice to leave in June 1798, shortly before *Lyrical Ballads* rolled off the press. In **Coleridge Cottage** (April–Sept Thurs–Sun 2–5pm; £3; NT), not such an "old hovel" now, you can see the man's parlour and reading room, and, upstairs, his bedroom and an exhibition room containing various letters and first editions.

The village library in nearby Castle Street has a **Quantock Information Centre** (Mon, Wed & Fri 10am–12.30pm & 2–5pm, Sat 10am–1pm & 2–4pm; ☎01278/732845, Ⓦwww.quantockhills.com), which can provide walking itineraries and some local information. As for **accommodation**, the best choices locally are *Stowey Brooke House*, 18 Castle St (☎01278/733356, Ⓦwww.stoweybrookehouse.co.uk; ❷), handsomely furnished with all rooms en suite (one has its own sitting area), and, across the street, the *Old Cider House* at no. 25 (☎01278/732228, Ⓦwww.theoldciderhouse.co.uk; ❷), which also serves evening meals. The *Rose & Crown* on St Mary Street has standard inn accommodation (☎01278/732265; ❶). This and the tile-fronted *George* next door also provide sustenance in the form of ales and bar meals – and the *George* has pool, table football and occasional live bands. **Campers** should head for *Mill Farm* (☎01278/732286), a couple of miles east of Nether Stowey on the A39, outside the village of Fiddington. There's also a stables here, and two pools – one outdoor – are laid on for campers and riders.

Five miles further west along the A39, the village of **HOLFORD**, a stop on the #15 Bridgwater–Minehead bus route, has the *Plough Inn*, where Virginia and Leonard Woolf spent their honeymoon, today serving simple **snacks**. Signposted two miles west of the village, there's also a **youth hostel** (☎0870/770 6006; closed early Sept to mid-April), where you can **camp** in the grounds. Beds cost £10.25 each.

From Nether Stowey, a minor road winds south off the A39 to the highest point on the Quantocks at **Wills Neck** (1260ft); park at Triscombe Stone, on the edge of Quantock Forest, from where a footpath leads to the summit about a mile distant. Stretching between the Wills Neck and the village of Aisholt, the bracken- and heather-grown moorland plateau of **Aisholt Common** is the heart of the Quantocks – the best place to begin exploring this central tract is near **West Bagborough**, where a five-mile path starts at Birches Corner. Lower down the slopes, outside the village of Aisholt, the banks of **Hawkridge Reservoir** make a lovely picnic stop.

The Quantocks are notorious for confrontations between hunting parties and anti-hunt activists, but if you want to indulge in less contentious **pony trekking**, contact *Mill Farm* at Fiddington, near Nether Stowey (see p.429).

Kilve, Watchet and Cleeve Abbey

The Quantock seaboard can be seen at its best at **Kilve Beach**, signposted off the A39 below Holford. Not so much a beach as a grand shale-studded foreshore, it's perfect for messing about in the rock pools and roaming the seaweedy shore.

Six miles to the west, **WATCHET** is Somerset's only port of any consequence, and the place from which Coleridge's Ancient Mariner set sail. Having made a halt at the harbour, the quiet heart of the village, you can get a good all-round view from **St Decuman's Church** above it, built on the site of the saint's martyrdom. Decuman, who floated over the sea from Wales, was decapitated by a Danish invader who was instantly converted when the saint picked up his bleeding head, washed it in a stream, and gently placed it next to him as he lay down to die. Watchet is only a stop away on the West Somerset Railway from **Washford**, from where it's a ten-minute walk to **Cleeve Abbey** (daily: April–Sept 10am–6pm; Oct 10am–5pm; Nov–March 10am–1pm & 2–4pm; £3; EH), a Cistercian house founded in 1198. Although the church itself has been mostly destroyed, the convent buildings are in excellent condition, providing the country's most complete collection of domestic buildings belonging to this austere order. An exhibition on the premises illustrates how the monks lived and how the local population unsuccessfully pleaded with Henry VIII for the abbey's survival.

Travel details

Buses

For information on all local and national bus services, contact Traveline ☎0870/608 2608 (daily 7am–9pm), www.traveline.org.uk.

Bath to: Bradford-on-Avon (Mon–Sat every 30min, Sun every 2hr; 30min); Bristol (every 15–30min; 50min); London (11 daily; 2hr 50min–3hr 50min); Salisbury (1 daily; 1hr 25min); Wells (Mon–Sat hourly, Sun 7; 1hr 15min).

Bridgwater to: Glastonbury (Mon–Sat hourly, 1hr 10min); Minehead (4–6 daily; 1hr 30min); Taunton (Mon–Sat every 30min, Sun every 2hr; 45min); Wells (Mon–Sat hourly; 1hr 25min).

Bristol to: Bath (every 15–30min; 50min); Birmingham (5–8 daily; 2hr–2hr 30min); Cheltenham (3–5 daily; 1hr–1hr 25min); Exeter (4–5 daily; 1hr 45min–2hr); Gloucester (3–5 daily; 1hr–1hr 25min); London (hourly; 2hr 30min); Wells (hourly; 1hr).

Burford to: Chipping Norton (4 daily; 2hr); Cirencester (4 daily; 1hr 30min); Lechlade (2 daily; 1hr); Oxford (hourly; 30min).

Cheltenham to: Gloucester (Mon–Sat every 20min, Sun hourly; 40min); London (11 daily; 2hr 50min–3hr 20min); Painswick (Mon–Sat hourly; Sun 3 daily; 30min); Stroud (Mon–Sat hourly, Sun 3 daily; 45min); Tewkesbury (Mon–Sat every 20min, Sun 6 daily; 30min).

Chipping Campden to Moreton-in-Marsh (3 daily; 30min).

Chipping Norton to: Burford (4 daily; 2hr); Cirencester (every 2–3hr; 2hr); Lechlade (every 3hr; 2hr 30min); Oxford (hourly; 50min).

Cirencester to: Burford (4 daily; 1hr 30min); Chipping Norton (every 2–3hr; 2hr); Lechlade (every 2–3hr; 1hr); Moreton-in-Marsh (every 2hr; 1hr); Oxford (every 2hr; 2hr).
Glastonbury to: Bridgwater (Mon–Sat hourly, 1hr 10min); Taunton (5–6 daily; 50min); Wells (1–2 hourly; 15min).
Gloucester to: Bristol (3–5 daily; 50min–1hr); Cheltenham (Mon–Sat every 20min, Sun hourly; 40min); Tewkesbury (Mon–Sat hourly, Sun 5 daily 20min); London (11 daily; 3hr 20min).
Lechlade to: Burford (2 daily; 1hr); Chipping Norton (every 3hr; 2hr 30min); Cirencester (every 2–3hr; 1hr); Oxford (hourly; 1hr 40min).
Moreton-in-Marsh to: Chipping Campden (3 daily; 30min); Cirencester (every 2hr; 1hr).
Oxford to: Burford (hourly; 30min); Chipping Norton (hourly; 50min); Cirencester (every 2hr; 2hr); Lechlade (hourly; 1hr 40min).
Taunton to: Bridgwater (Mon–Sat every 30min, Sun every 2hr; 45min); Exeter (Mon–Sat 5 daily; 1hr 20min); Glastonbury (5–6 daily; 50min); Minehead (Mon–Sat hourly, Sun 9; 1hr 10min).
Tewkesbury to: Cheltenham (Mon–Sat every 20min, Sun 6; 30min); Gloucester (Mon–Sat hourly, Sun 5; 20min).
Wells to: Bath (Mon–Sat hourly, Sun 7 daily; 1hr 15min); Bridgwater (Mon–Sat hourly, 1hr 25min); Bristol (hourly; 1hr); Glastonbury (1–2 hourly; 15min).

Trains

For information on all local and national rail services, contact National Rail Enquiries ⓣ08457/484950, ⓦwww.rail.co.uk.
Bath to: Bristol (every 20min; 20min); Dorchester (Mon–Sat 6–7 daily, Sun 1 daily; 2hr); London (1–2 hourly; 1hr 30min); Salisbury (hourly; 1hr); Southampton (hourly; 1hr 30min).
Bristol to: Bath (every 20min; 20min); Birmingham (every 30min; 1hr 30min); Cheltenham (2 hourly; 50min); Exeter (1–2 hourly; 1hr 15min–1hr 45min); Gloucester (1–2 hourly; 50min–1hr 20min); London (2 hourly; 1hr 45min); Penzance (5 daily; 4hr–4hr 30min); Plymouth (1–2 hourly; 2hr–2hr 30min); Truro (5 daily; 3hr 15min–4hr 15min).
Cheltenham to: Bristol (2 hourly; 45min); Gloucester (1–2 hourly; 10min); London (1–2 hourly; 2hr–2hr 40min); Worcester (hourly; 30min).
Gloucester to: Bristol (1–2 hourly; 50min–1hr 20min); Cheltenham (1–2 hourly; 10min); London (1–2 hourly; 1hr 50min–2hr 15min); Stroud (hourly; 15–20min).

6

Devon and Cornwall

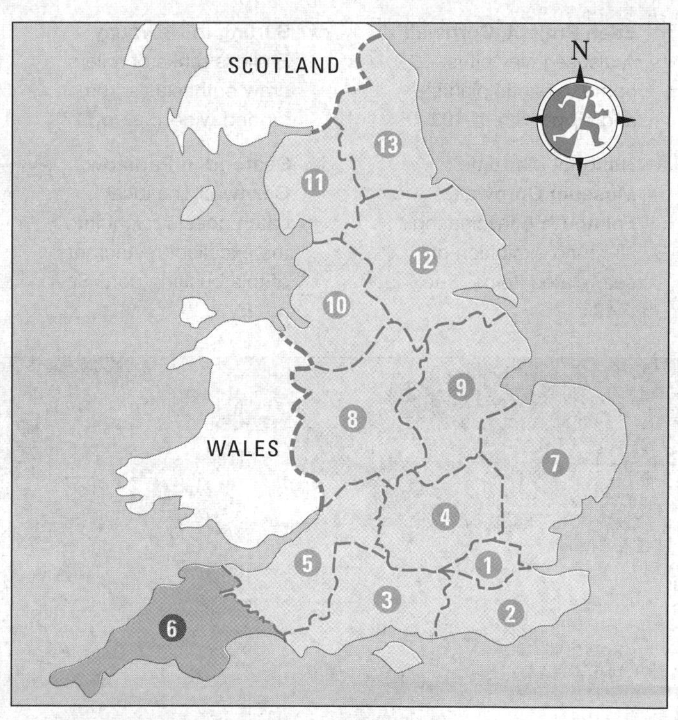

CHAPTER 6 # Highlights

* **Clovelly** Impossibly picturesque village on North Devon coast. See p.477

* **South West Coast Path** The ever-changing vistas ensure constant variety on Britain's longest way-marked path. See p.483

* **Eden Project, Cornwall** A disused clay pit is home to exotic plants and crops. See p.492

* **National Maritime Museum Cornwall, Falmouth** A fascinating, all-round exhibition of sea-related items. See p.496

* **Lizard Point, Cornwall** This unspoiled headland is the starting point for some inspiring walks. See p.501

* **St Ives Tate, Cornwall** This modern gallery showcases local artists. See p.511

* **Surfing in Newquay** Endless ranks of rollers draw enthusiasts from far and wide. See p.520

* **Seafood in Padstow, Cornwall** The local catch goes straight into the excellent restaurants of this bustling port. See p.525

△ Clovelly

6

Devon and Cornwall

At the western extremity of England, the counties of **Devon and Cornwall** encompass everything from genteel, cosy villages to vast Atlantic-facing strands of golden sand and wild expanses of granite moorland. The combination of rural peace and first-class beaches has made the peninsula perennially popular with tourists, so much so that tourism has replaced the traditional occupations of fishing and farming as the main source of employment and income. Enough remains of these beleaguered communities to preserve the region's authentic character, however – even if this can be occasionally obscured during the summer season. Avoid the peak periods and you'll be seduced by the genuine appeal of this region, which beckons ever westwards into rural backwaters where increasingly exotic place names and idiosyncratic pronunciations recall that this was once England's last bastion of Celtic culture.

Although the human history of the region has left its stamp, it's the natural landscape which exerts the strongest pull, and not just in the beauty of the long, deeply indented seaboard. Straddling the border between Devon and Somerset, **Exmoor** is one of the peninsula's three great moors, its heathery slopes much favoured by hunting parties as well as by hikers. For wilderness, however, nothing can beat the remoter tracts of **Dartmoor**, which takes up much of the southern half of inland Devon. The greatest of the West Country's granite massifs, most of Dartmoor retains its solitude in spite of its proximity to the only major cities at this end of the country, either of which would make a good touring base. Of the two, **Exeter** is by far the more interesting, dominated by the twin towers of its medieval cathedral and offering a rich selection of restaurants and nightlife. Much of the city was destroyed by bombing during World War II, though the largest city of Devon and Cornwall, **Plymouth**, suffered far worse, the consequence of its historic role as a great naval port. Bland postwar development inflicted almost as much damage as the Luftwaffe, although enough of Plymouth's Elizabethan core has survived to merit a visit, and the city, by capitalizing on its maritime associations, has succeeded in reviving its port area.

The coastline on either side of Exeter and Plymouth is within easy reach. Warmed by the Gulf Stream, and enjoying more hours of sunshine than virtually anywhere else in England, this part of the country can sometimes come fairly close to the atmosphere of the Mediterranean, and indeed Devon's principal resort, **Torquay**, styles itself the capital of the "English Riviera". St Tropez it ain't, but there's no denying a certain glamour, far removed from the old-fashioned charm of the seaside towns of **East Devon**, or the cliff-backed resorts of the county's northern littoral.

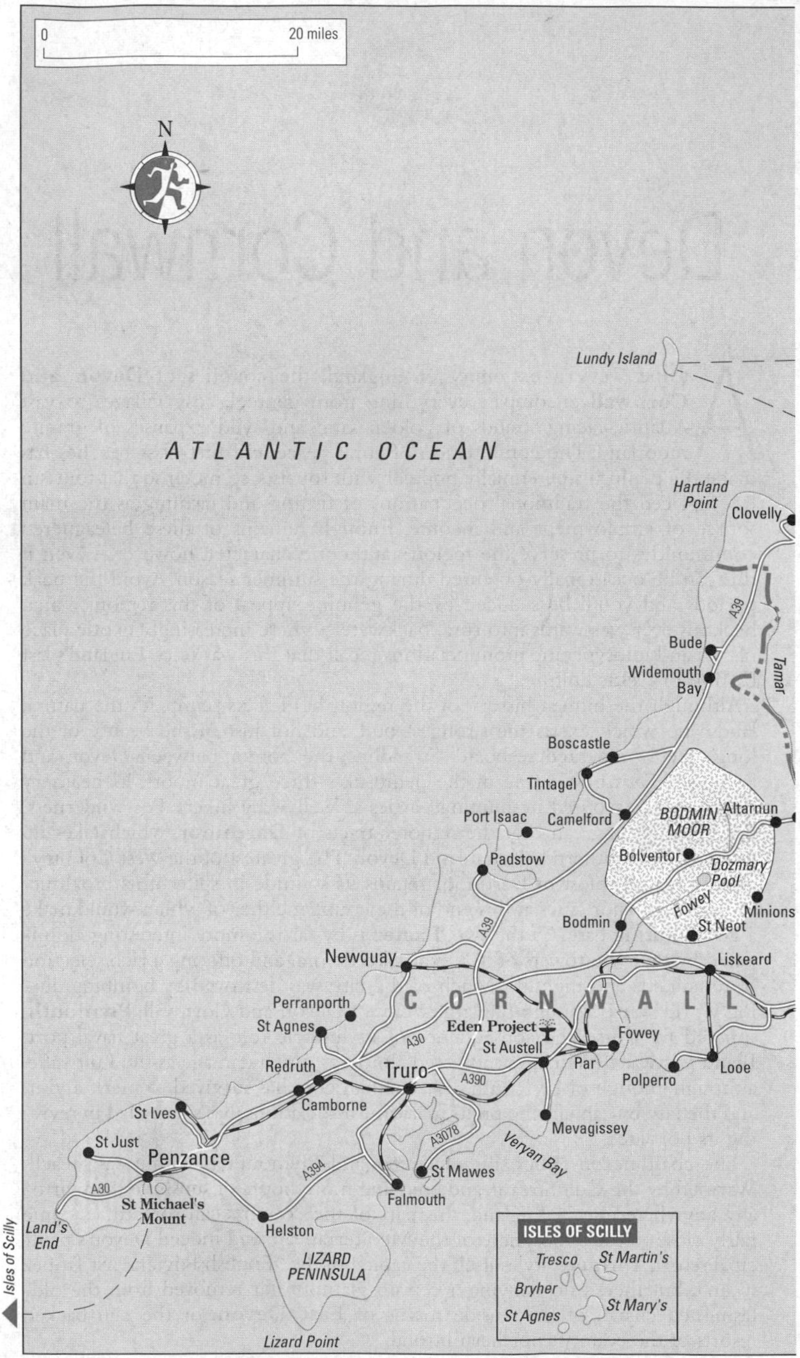
0
20 miles
N
ATLANTIC OCEAN
Lundy Island
Hartland Point
Clovelly
A39
Bude
Widemouth Bay
Tamar
Boscastle
Tintagel
Port Isaac
Camelford
BODMIN MOOR
Altarnun
Bolventor
Dozmary Pool
Fowey
Minions
Padstow
A39
Bodmin
St Neot
Newquay
Liskeard
CORNWALL
Perranporth
St Agnes
Eden Project
St Austell
Fowey
A30
Par
Polperro
Looe
Redruth
Truro
A390
Camborne
St Ives
Mevagissey
A3078
Veryan Bay
St Just
Penzance
A394
St Mawes
A30
St Michael's Mount
Falmouth
Land's End
Helston
LIZARD PENINSULA
Lizard Point
Isles of Scilly
ISLES OF SCILLY
Tresco
St Martin's
Bryher
St Mary's
St Agnes

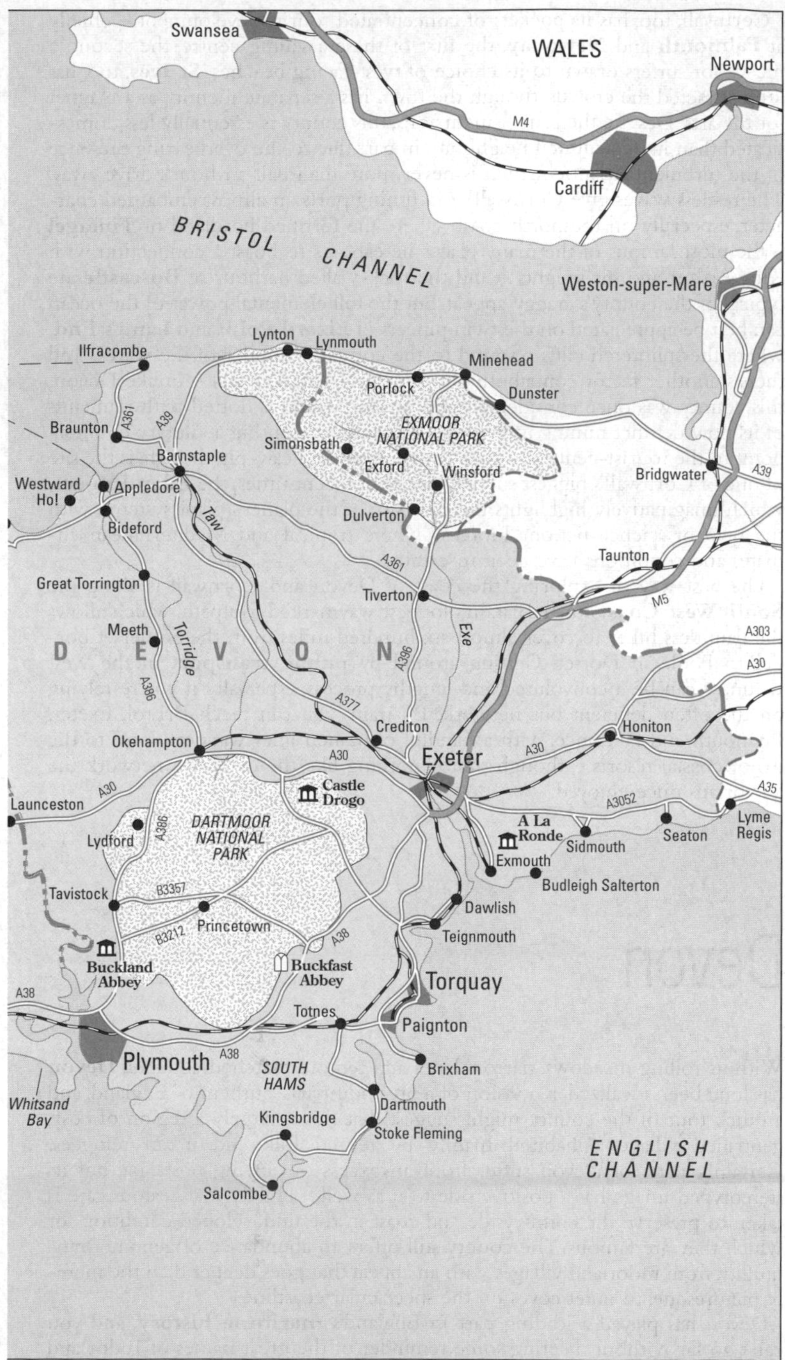

© Crown copyright

6 DEVON AND CORNWALL

Cornwall, too, has its pockets of concentrated tourist development – chiefly at **Falmouth** and **Newquay**, the first of these a sailing centre, the second a mecca for surfers drawn to its choice of west-facing beaches. **St Ives**, too, has long attracted the crowds, though the town has a separate identity as a magnet for the arts. Despite the tourist incursions, this county is essentially less domesticated than its agricultural neighbour, in part due to the overbearing presence of the turbulent Atlantic, which is never more than half an hour's drive away. The restless waves give Cornwall's old fishing ports an almost embattled character, especially on the north coast, where the fortified headland of **Tintagel** – the most famous of the many places hereabouts to boast a connection with King Arthur and his knights – and the rock-walled harbour of **Boscastle** are typical of the county's craggy appeal, but the full elemental power of the ocean can best be appreciated on the twin pincers of **Lizard Point** and **Land's End**, where the splintered cliffs resound to the constant thunder of the waves. And there's another factor contributing to Cornwall's starker feel – unlike Devon, this county was once considerably industrialized, and is dotted with remnants of its now defunct mining industries, their ruins presenting a salutary counterpoint to the tourist-centred seaside towns. A disused clay-pit, though, is the site of one of Cornwall's biggest success stories of recent times, the **Eden Project**, which imaginatively highlights the diversity of the planet's plant systems, with the help of science-fiction "biomes" where tropical and Mediterranean climates and conditions have been re-created.

The best way of exploring the coast of Devon and Cornwall is along the **South West Coast Path**, Britain's longest waymarked footpath, which allows the dauntless hiker to cover almost six hundred miles from the Somerset border to Poole in Dorset. Getting around by **public transport** in the West Country can be a convoluted and lengthy process, especially if you're relying on the often deficient bus network. By train, you can reach Bristol, Exeter, Plymouth and Penzance, with a handful of branch lines wandering off to the major coastal resorts – though there's nothing like the extensive network the Victorians once enjoyed.

Devon

With its rolling meadows, narrow lanes and remote thatched cottages, **Devon** has long been idealized as a vision of a pre-industrial, "authentic" England, and a quick tour of the county might suggest that this is largely a region of cosy, gentrified villages inhabited mainly by retired folk and urban refugees. Certainly parts of Devon suffer from an excess of cloying nostalgia, but its stereotyped image has a positive side to it as well – chiefly that zealous care is taken to preserve the countryside and coast in the undeveloped condition for which they are famous. The county still offers an abundance of genuine tranquillity, from moorland villages with an appeal that goes deeper than the merely picturesque, to quiet coves on the spectacular coastline.

Devon has played a leading part in England's **maritime history**, and you can't go far without meeting some reminder of the great names of Tudor and

Stuart seafaring, particularly in the two cities of **Exeter** and **Plymouth**. These days the nautical tradition is perpetuated on a domesticated scale by yachtspeople taking advantage of Devon's numerous creeks and bays, especially on its southern coast, where ports such as Dartmouth and Salcombe are awash with amateur sailors. Land-bound tourists flock to the sandy beaches and seaside resorts, of which **Torquay**, on the south coast, and **Ilfracombe**, on the north, are the busiest – though the most attractive are those which have retained something of their nineteenth-century elegance, such as **Sidmouth**, in East Devon. Other seaside villages retain a low level of fishing activity but otherwise live on a stilted olde worlde image, of which **Clovelly** is the supreme example. **Inland**, Devon is characterized by swards of lush pasture and a scattering of sheltered villages, the county's low population density dropping to almost zero on **Dartmoor**, the wildest and bleakest of the West's moors, and **Exmoor**, whose seaboard constitutes one of the West Country's most scenic littorals.

Exeter and Plymouth are on the main **rail** lines from London and the Midlands, with branch lines from Exeter linking the north coast at Barnstaple and the south-coast towns of Exmouth and Torquay. **Buses** from the chief stations fan out along the coasts and into the interior, though the service can be extremely rudimentary for the smaller villages.

Exeter

EXETER's sights are richer than those of any other town in Devon or Cornwall, the legacy of an eventful history since its Celtic foundation and the establishment here of the most westerly Roman outpost. After the Roman withdrawal, Exeter was refounded by Alfred the Great and by the time of the Norman Conquest had become one of the largest towns in England, profiting from its position on the banks of the River Exe. The expansion of the wool trade in the Tudor period sustained the city until the eighteenth century, and Exeter has maintained its status as commercial centre and county town, despite having much of its ancient centre gutted by World War II bombing.

You're likely to pass through this transport hub for Devon at least once on your West Country travels, and Exeter's sturdy cathedral and the remnants of its compact old quarter would repay an overnight stay. The city is also the obvious starting point for forays to the shingly beaches and crumbly, red cliffs of east Devon, where a scattering of towns and villages preserve a genteel, old-fashioned flavour.

Arrival, information and accommodation

Exeter has two **train stations**, Exeter Central and St David's, the latter a little further out from the centre of town, though connected by frequent city buses. South West trains on the London Waterloo–Salisbury line stop at both, as do trains on the Tarka Line to Barnstaple (see p.472) and those to Exmouth, though Exeter Central is not served by most other long-distance trains. **Buses** stop at the station on Paris Street, where there are **left-luggage** lockers, and it's right across from the **tourist office** (July & Aug Mon–Sat 9am–5pm, Sun 10am–4pm; Sept–June Mon–Sat 9am–5pm; ⓣ01392/265700, ⓦwww.exeter.gov.uk). There's a second visitor centre in The Quay House on Exeter's Quayside (Easter–Oct daily 10am–4pm; ⓣ01392/265213). There are **Internet points** in the library on Castle Street (ⓣ01392/384206) and at the St Sidwell Centre, Sidwell Street (ⓣ01392/666222). The city is best negotiated on foot,

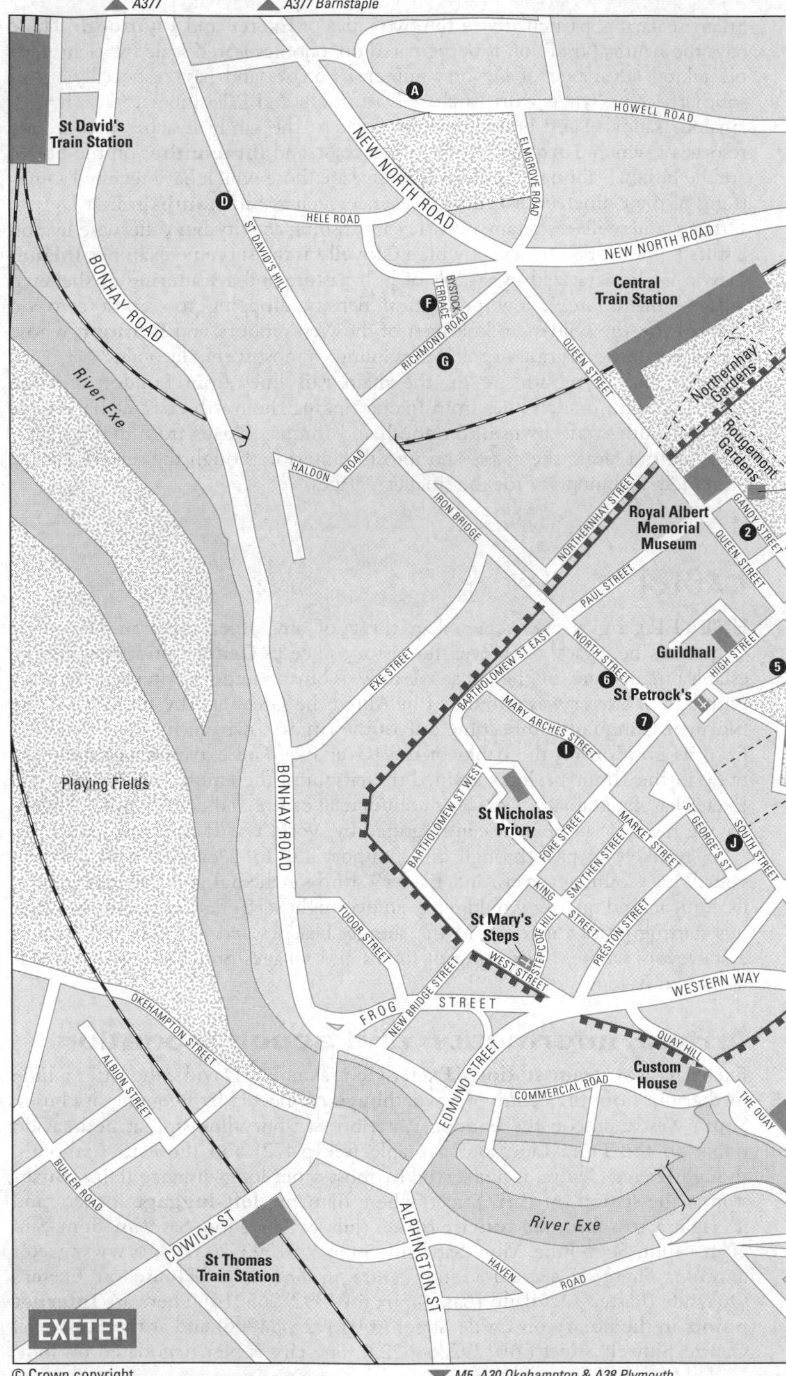
A377
A377 Barnstaple
St David's Train Station
HOWELL ROAD
NEW NORTH ROAD
ELMGROVE ROAD
HELE ROAD
NEW NORTH ROAD
ST DAVID'S HILL
BONHAY ROAD
BYSTOCK TERRACE
RICHMOND ROAD
Central Train Station
QUEEN STREET
Northernhay Gardens
Rougemont Gardens
River Exe
HALDON ROAD
IRON BRIDGE
NORTHERNHAY STREET
Royal Albert Memorial Museum
GANDY STREET
QUEEN STREET
PAUL STREET
EXE STREET
NORTH STREET
BARTHOLOMEW ST EAST
Guildhall
HIGH STREET
St Petrock's
MARY ARCHES STREET
Playing Fields
BONHAY ROAD
BARTHOLOMEW ST WEST
St Nicholas Priory
FORE STREET
SMYTHEN STREET
MARKET STREET
ST GEORGE'S ST
SOUTH STREET
KING STREET
STEPCOTE HILL
PRESTON STREET
St Mary's Steps
TUDOR STREET
WEST STREET
NEW BRIDGE STREET
FROG STREET
WESTERN WAY
OKEHAMPTON STREET
QUAY HILL
Custom House
EDMUND STREET
COMMERCIAL ROAD
ALBION STREET
THE QUAY
BULLER ROAD
River Exe
COWICK ST
St Thomas Train Station
ALPHINGTON ST
HAVEN ROAD
EXETER
M5, A30 Okehampton & A38 Plymouth

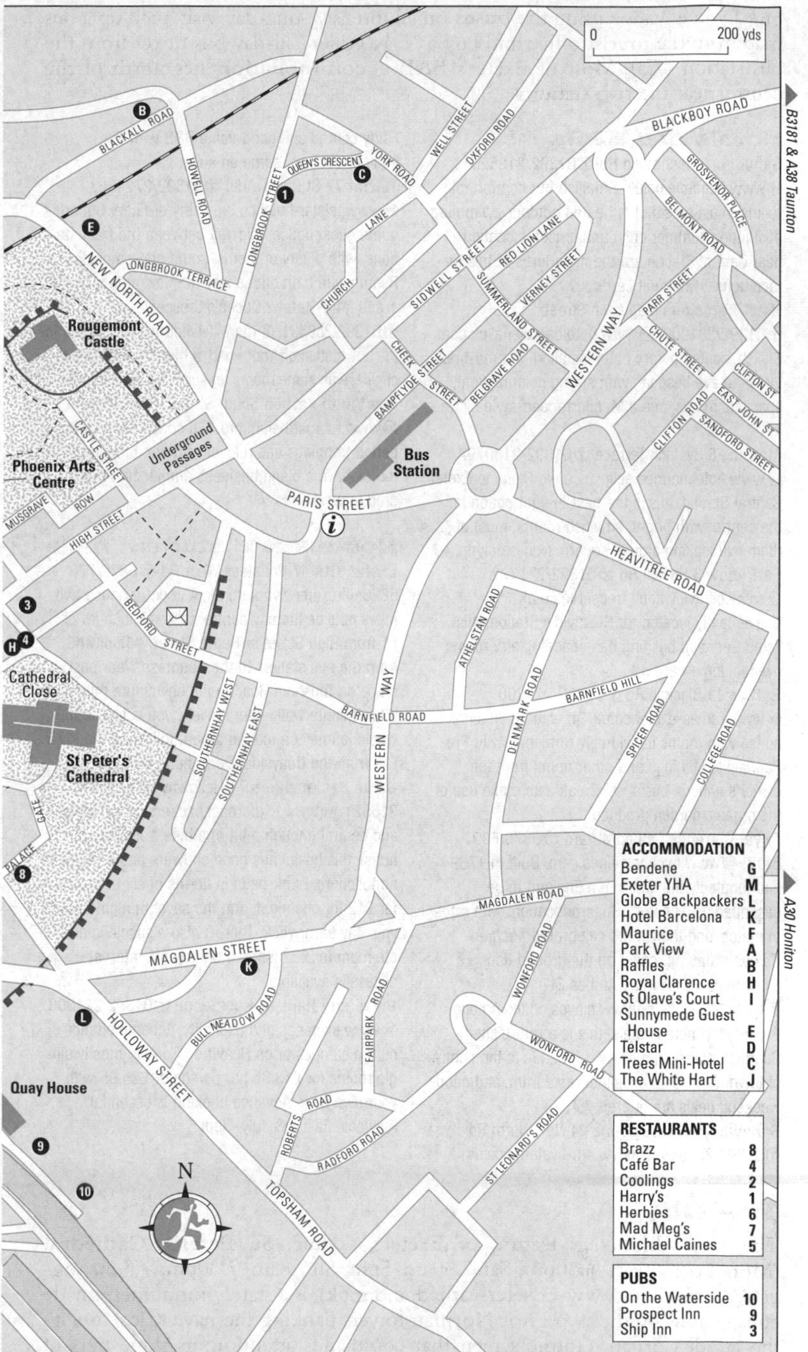

ACCOMMODATION

Bendene	G
Exeter YHA	M
Globe Backpackers	L
Hotel Barcelona	K
Maurice	F
Park View	A
Raffles	B
Royal Clarence	H
St Olave's Court	I
Sunnymede Guest House	E
Telstar	D
Trees Mini-Hotel	C
The White Hart	J

RESTAURANTS

Brazz	8
Café Bar	4
Coolings	2
Harry's	1
Herbies	6
Mad Meg's	7
Michael Caines	5

PUBS

On the Waterside	10
Prospect Inn	9
Ship Inn	3

but if you envisage using the **buses** on an intensive one-day visit, pick up a bus map from the tourist office and buy a "Day Rider" all-day bus ticket from the bus station (£3). Most of Exeter's B&B **accommodation** lies north of the centre, near the two stations.

Hotels and B&Bs

Bendene 15 Richmond Rd ⓣ01392/213526, ⓦwww.bendene.co.uk. Smallish but comfortable rooms (most en suite), a heated outdoor swimming pool (open summer only) and a useful location near Central Station are the main lures of this terrace house. No credit cards. ❷

Hotel Barcelona Magdalen Street ⓣ01392/281000, ⓦwww.hotelbarcelona-uk.com. Stylish, contemporary hotel installed in a red-brick Victorian eye hospital, with strong colours, light, spacious rooms, and a Mediterranean-style bistro. ❻

Maurice 5 Bystock Terrace ⓣ01392/213079, ⓦwww.hotelmaurice.eclipse.co.uk. Close to Exeter Central Station, this is the best budget option in the centre, with bright, smallish rooms, most of them overlooking a quiet square. Non-smoking. ❶

Park View 8 Howell Rd ⓣ01392/271772, ⓦwww.parkviewhotel.freeserve.co.uk. Conveniently located for St David's Station, this listed Georgian building has peaceful, airy rooms overlooking a park. ❷

Raffles 11 Blackall Rd ⓣ01392/270200, ⓦwww.raffles-exeter.co.uk. An elegant Victorian house with rooms individually furnished with Pre-Raphaelite etchings and other items from the owner's antique business. Breakfasts make use of the organic garden produce. ❸

Royal Clarence Cathedral Yard ⓣ0870/609 6117, ⓦwww.michaelcaines.com. Built in 1769 and reputedly the first inn in England to be described as a "hotel". Superb location, with rates to match, and there's the celebrated *Michael Caines* restaurant chain on the ground floor. ❼

St Olave's Court Mary Arches St ⓣ01392/217736, ⓦwww.olaves.co.uk. Among Exeter's top-notch hotels, this is a refurbished Georgian mansion in its own grounds in the centre of town. There's an excellent restaurant, and good weekend deals are offered. ❼

Sunnymede Guest House 24 New North Rd ⓣ01392/273844, ⓦwww.s-h-systems.co.uk. Fairly central and good-value B&B with TV-equipped rooms, some en suite. ❷

Telstar 77 St David's Hill ⓣ01392/272466, ⓦwww.telstar-hotel.co.uk. Fairly ordinary but adequate guest house, midway between the train stations, with plenty of rooms, some non-smoking. Rooms with bath nudge into the next category. ❷

Trees Mini-Hotel 2 Queen's Crescent ⓣ01392/259531, ⓔrnorfolk@hotmail.com. Close to the bus station off York Road, a friendly and reliable choice, with some rooms en suite. No smoking. ❷

The White Hart 65 South St ⓣ01392/279897, ⓦwww.roomattheinn.info. Old coaching inn with period trappings and a lovely old bar, though rooms have a bland business ambience. Prices drop at weekends. ❹

Hostels and student halls

Exeter YHA 47 Countess Wear Rd ⓣ0870/770 5826, ⓔexeter@yha.org.uk. A country house two miles outside the city centre; take minibus #K or #T from High Street or South Street, #57 or #85 from the bus station, to the Countess Wear post office on Topsham Road, a fifteen-minute ride, plus a ten-minute walk. Alternatively, you could do the whole journey on foot on a path following the River Exe from the Quayside. Dorm beds cost £11.50.

Globe Backpackers 71 Holloway St ⓣ01392/215521, ⓦwww.exeterbackpackers.co.uk. Clean and central (though a bit of a hike from the stations), this hostel has good showers and an upbeat atmosphere. Bunk-beds in dorms of six to ten go for £12 for one night, and the seventh night free if you stay for a week. There's also a spacious double room for £32 (shared bathroom). Internet access is available.

University Halls of Residence ⓣ01392/211500, ⓦwww.exeter.ac.uk/hospitality. Accommodation on the campus or on Heavitree Road in mostly single rooms for £13.95 per person or £25.95 with your own bath. Advance booking is essential. Available Easter & July–Sept.

The City

The most distinctive feature of Exeter's skyline, **St Peter's Cathedral** (Mon–Fri 7.30am–6.30pm, Sat 7.30am–5pm, Sun 8am–7.30pm; £3.50 suggested donation; ⓦwww.exeter-cathedral.org.uk), is a stately monument made conspicuous by the two great Norman towers flanking the nave. Close up, it's the facade's ornate Gothic screen that commands attention: its three tiers of sculpted (and very weathered) figures – including Alfred, Athelstan, Canute, William the Conqueror and Richard II – were begun around 1360, part of a rebuilding programme which left only the Norman towers from the original construction.

Entering the cathedral, you're confronted by the longest unbroken **Gothic ceiling** in the world, its **bosses** vividly painted – one, towards the west front, shows the murder of Thomas à Becket. The **Lady Chapel** and **Chapter House** – respectively at the far end of the building and off the right transept – are thirteenth-century, but the main part of the nave, including the lavish rib-vaulting, dates from the full flowering of the English Decorated style, a century later. There are many fine examples of sculpture from this period, including, in the minstrels' gallery high up on the left side, angels playing musical instruments, and, below them, figures of Edward III and Queen Philippa.

Dominating the cathedral's central space are the organ pipes installed in the seventeenth century and harmonizing perfectly with the linear patterns of the roof and arches. In the **Choir** don't miss the sixty-foot **bishop's throne** or the **misericords** – decorated with mythological figures around 1260, they are thought to be the oldest in the country. Near the entrance stands a comparatively recent addition to the many medieval tombs and memorials lining the cathedral's walls: a monument to R.D. Blackmore, author of *Lorna Doone*. If you want to make sure you don't miss a thing, take one of the **tours** (April–Oct daily 11am & 2.30pm; Nov–March Thurs 11am; £2.50 suggested donation). Photo permits cost £1.

Outside, a graceful statue of the theologian Richard Hooker surveys the **Cathedral Close**, a motley mixture of architectural styles from Tudor to Regency, though most display Exeter's trademark red-brick work. One of the finest buildings is the Elizabethan **Mol's Coffee House**, impressively timbered and gabled, now a map shop.

Some older buildings are still standing amid the banal concrete of the modern town centre, including Exeter's finest civic building, the fourteenth-century **Guildhall** – claimed to be England's oldest municipal building in regular use. Standing not far from the cathedral on the pedestrianized **High Street**, it's fronted by an elegant Renaissance portico, and the main chamber merits a glance for its arched roof timbers, which rest on carved bears holding staves, symbols of the Yorkist cause during the Wars of the Roses. The Guildhall is usually **open to visitors** on weekdays from 10.30am to 1pm and 2pm to 4pm, and on Saturdays from 10am to noon (but may be closed for functions, call ⓣ01392/265500 to check), and when things are quiet the doorman will give you a brief tour. Just down from here, opposite **St Petrock's** – one of Exeter's six surviving medieval churches in the central area – you'll find the impossibly narrow Parliament Street, just 25 inches wide at this end.

On the west side of Fore Street, the continuation of the High Street, a turning leads to **St Nicholas Priory** (Easter–Oct Mon, Wed & Sat 2–4.30pm; 50p), part of a small Benedictine foundation that became a merchant's home after the Dissolution; the interior has been restored to what it might have looked like in the Tudor era. On the other side of Fore Street, trailing down towards the river, cobbled **Stepcote Hill** was once the main road into Exeter from the west, though it is difficult to imagine this steep and narrow lane as a main thoroughfare. Another of central Exeter's ancient churches, **St Mary Steps**, stands surrounded by mainly Tudor houses at the bottom, with a fine seventeenth-century clock on its tower and a late Gothic nave inside.

Exeter's centre is bounded to the southwest by the River Exe, where the port area is now mostly devoted to leisure activities, particularly around the old

Quayside. Pubs, shops and cafés share the space with handsomely restored nineteenth-century warehouses and the smart **Custom House**, built in 1681, its opulence reflecting the former importance of the cloth trade. Next door, the Quay House from the same period has an information desk and, upstairs, a video on Exeter's history (Easter–Oct). The area comes into its own at night, but is worth a wander at any time, and you can **rent bikes** and **canoes** at Saddles & Paddles on the quayside (Ⓣ01392/424241, Ⓦwww.saddlepaddle.co.uk) to explore the **Exeter Canal**, which runs five miles to Topsham and beyond.

Back at the north end of the High Street, Romansgate Passage (next to Boots) holds the entrance to a network of **underground passages** first excavated in the thirteenth century to bring water to the cathedral precincts. The passages can be visited as part of a fascinating fifty-minute guided **tour** (June–Sept & school holidays Mon–Sat 10am–noon & 2–5pm; Oct–May Tues–Fri noon–5pm, Sat 10am–5pm; last tour at 4.30pm; June–Sept £3.75, rest of year £3) – not recommended to claustrophobes, however. Nearby, Castle Street leads to what remains of **Rougemont Castle**, now little more than a perimeter of red-stone walls that are best appreciated from the surrounding Rougemont and Northernhay Gardens. Following the path through this park, exit at Queen Street to drop in at the excellent **Royal Albert Memorial Museum** (Mon–Sat 10am–5pm; free), the closest thing in Devon to a county museum. Exuding the Victorian spirit of wide-ranging curiosity, this motley assortment includes everything from a menagerie of stuffed animals to mock-ups of the various building styles used at different periods in the city. The collections of silverware, watches and clocks contrast nicely with the colourful ethnography section, and the picture gallery has some good specimens of West Country art alongside work by other artists associated with Devon.

Eating and drinking

The cafés inside the Royal Albert Memorial Museum and the Phoenix Arts Centre, behind the museum, are handy and congenial for wholesome **snacks**, while round the corner from the museum, in medieval Gandy Street, *Coolings* is a popular wine bar and bistro serving tasty lunches and is also open until late evening with DJs on Tuesdays and Wednesdays and a cellar bar open Fridays and Saturdays. Opposite the cathedral, the *Café Bar* is a casually modish spot for a coffee or lunch, serving toasties, salads, burgers and pastas, and full meals in the evenings, with themed nights and live jazz on Fridays (for which booking is advised; Ⓣ01392/310130). It's part of the next-door *Michael Caines* (Ⓣ01392/31003; closed Sun), one of Exeter's classiest **restaurants** where you'll find sophisticated modern European cuisine in sleek surroundings; prices are fairly high, though there are reasonable fixed-price menus at lunchtime. In total contrast, the olde worlde atmosphere is laid on thickly at *Mad Meg's* (closed Mon–Wed lunch & Sun eve; Ⓣ01392/221225) – once a nunnery, now staffed by waitresses in wench costume – but there are some good-value traditional dishes here; it's tucked away near the top of Fore Street, below a bike shop. Nearby *Herbie's,* 15 North St (Ⓣ01392/258473; closed all day Sun & Mon eve), is the only wholefood restaurant in town, and has organic ice cream on the menu, while good-value Mexican, Italian and American staples are on the menu at *Harry's*, in a converted church at 86 Longbrook St (Ⓣ01392/202234). Near the cathedral, *Brazz*, at 10–12 Palace Gate, off South Street, is a stylish bar/bistro with a sparkly ceiling and an aquarium.

Among the **pubs** the *Ship Inn*, in St Martin's Lane (between the High Street and the cathedral), serves reasonably priced lunches and prides itself on the claim that it was once Francis Drake's local. The pubs and clubs on Exeter's Quay make this a lively spot to while away an evening. You can eat and drink sitting outside at the seventeenth-century *Prospect Inn* and the more contemporary *On the Waterside*.

Nightlife and entertainment

You'll find Exeter's two biggest **club complexes** facing each other on the Quay: the *Warehouse*, *Boxes* and *Boogies*, and *Volts* and *Hothouse*, all open in various combinations and play mainstream dance and retro sounds. In the centre, the *Timepiece*, Little Castle Street, occupies a former prison and has a good daytime bar with a garden. Try also *Bar Bomba*, a cool pre-club lounge beneath *Fruta Bomba* on Queen Street (closed Sun). For **live music**, especially post-punk bands, head for the *Cavern Club* (Ⓣ01392/495370, Ⓦwww.cavernclub.co.uk), with entrances in Queen and Gandy streets (also open 10.30am–4pm for snacks), the university's *Lemon Grove* (term time only; Ⓣ01392/263528), in Cornwall House on the campus, and *St George's Hall*, with entrances on Fore Street and Market Street (Ⓣ01392/265866), which attracts occasional big names (and has club nights and comedy).

Off Gandy Street, the **Phoenix Arts Centre** (Ⓣ01392/667080, Ⓦwww.exeterphoenix.org.uk) is the focus of a medley of cultural pursuits, including regular non-mainstream films, exhibitions, gigs and various workshops. Of the town's theatres, the **Northcott**, near the university on Stocker Road (Ⓣ01392/493493), and the Barnfield, on Barnfield Road (Ⓣ01392/271808), have the best productions, with the former also staging ballet and opera performances. The **Exeter Festival** (Ⓣ01392/265198) takes place during the first three weeks of July, and features jazz and blues concerts as well as classical performances and cabaret, at various venues around town.

Around Exeter

The coast south and east of Exeter holds an architectural oddity, **A La Ronde**, and a string of old-fashioned seaside resorts, none of them over-commercialized, though still best seen outside the summer peak. **Sidmouth** would be a good choice for an overnight stop, as would the neighbouring villages of **Beer** and **Seaton**.

A La Ronde, Exmouth and Budleigh Salterton are all served by **bus** #57 running every ten minutes from Exeter's bus station, while #52, #52A and #52B are best for Sidmouth (some #57 buses also connect Exmouth with Sidmouth). The #899 service connects Sidmouth with Beer and Seaton; it runs six–seven times daily on weekdays, three times on Saturday and not at all on Sunday (in summer the #378 operates a Sunday service). You can also get to Exmouth by **train**, and from the train station at **Honiton**, eight miles inland, #340 runs every couple of hours to Sidmouth (not Sun).

A La Ronde

The Gothic folly of **A La Ronde** (April–Oct Mon–Thurs & Sun 11am–5.30pm; £3.80; NT), a couple of miles outside Exmouth off the A376, was the creation of two cousins, Jane and Mary Parminter, who in the 1790s were inspired by their European Grand Tour to construct a sixteen-sided house possibly based on the Byzantine basilica of San Vitale in Ravenna. The end product is filled with mementoes of the Parminters' tour as well as a number of their more offbeat creations, such as a frieze made of feathers culled from game birds and chickens. In the upper rooms are a gallery and staircase completely covered in shells, too fragile to be visited, though part can be glimpsed from the completely enclosed octagonal room on the first floor – a closed-circuit TV system enables visitors to home in on details.

The women intended that the house should be inherited only by female descendants, though the conditions of Mary Parminter's will (she died in 1849) were broken at the end of the nineteenth century when the building was inherited by the Reverend Oswald Reichel, the only male owner of the house in its history. Reichel's refurbishment improved the building, with the addition of dormer windows on the second floor, which had previously not enjoyed any natural light, let alone the superb views which it now enjoys over the Exe Estuary to Haldon Hill and Dawlish Warren.

Exmouth and Budleigh Salterton

EXMOUTH started as a Roman port and went on to become the first of the county's resorts to be popularized by holiday-makers in the late eighteenth century. Overlooking lawns, rock pools and a respectable two miles of beach, Exmouth's Georgian terraces once accommodated such folk as the wives of Nelson and Byron – installed at nos. 6 and 19 The Beacon respectively (on a rise overlooking the seafront, above the public gardens). The town's still unhurried air contrasts sharply with the cranes and warehouses of the docks beyond the Esplanade. From April to October, Exmouth is linked by **ferry** to Starcross, on the other side of the Exe estuary (hourly service; £3 single fare), where you can pick up a bus route to Dawlish and Teignmouth (see p.448). **Staying** here is a good option, with plenty of choice: near the tourist office and the beach, try the non-smoking *Blenheim Guest House*, 39 Morton Rd (Ⓣ01395/223123, Ⓦwww.come.to/freesunshine; no credit cards; ❷), which offers spacious rooms in an easy-going atmosphere, though there's a two-night minimum stay in summer. Spending a bit more, you can enjoy wonderful panoramic views from the rooms at the *Manor Hotel*, The Beacon (Ⓣ01395/274477, Ⓦwww.manorexmouth.co.uk; ❹). The **tourist office** is on Alexandra Terrace (mid-March to June, Sept & Oct Mon–Sat 9.30am–5pm; July & Aug Mon–Sat 9.30am–5pm, Sun 10am–3pm; Nov to mid-March Mon–Sat 9.30am–2pm; Ⓣ01395/222299, Ⓦwww.exmouthguide.co.uk).

Four miles east of Exmouth, bounded on each side by red sandstone cliffs, **BUDLEIGH SALTERTON** continues the genteel theme – its thatched and whitewashed cottages attracted such figures as Noël Coward and P.G. Wodehouse, and John Millais painted his famous *Boyhood of Raleigh* on the shingle beach here. (Sir Walter Raleigh was born in pretty East Budleigh, a couple of miles inland.) Three miles east, **Ladram Bay** is a popular pebbly beach sheltered by woods and beautiful eroded cliffs. If you want to stay in the area, contact the **tourist office** on Fore Street (Easter–June, Sept & Oct Mon–Sat 10am–5pm; July & Aug Mon–Sat 10am–5pm, Sun 11am–5pm; Nov–Easter Mon–Sat 10am–12.30pm; Ⓣ01395/445275, Ⓦwww.eastdevon.net/tourism).

Sidmouth

Set amidst a shelf of crumbling red sandstone, cream-and-white **SIDMOUTH** is the chief resort on this stretch of coast and boasts nearly five hundred buildings listed as having special historic or architectural interest, among them the stately Georgian homes of **York Terrace** behind the Esplanade. Moreover, the **beaches** are better tended than many along this stretch, not only the mile-long main town beach but also Jacob's Ladder, a cliff-backed shingle-and-sand strip beyond Connaught Gardens to the west of town. To the east, the South Devon

Coast Path (part of the South West Coast Path) climbs steep Salcombe Hill to follow cliffs that give sanctuary to a range of birdlife including yellowhammers and green woodpeckers, as well as the rarer grasshopper warbler. Further on, the path descends to meet one of the most isolated and attractive beaches in the area, **Weston Mouth**.

The **tourist office** is on Ham Lane, off the eastern end of the Esplanade (March & April Mon–Thurs 10am–4pm, Fri & Sat 10am–5pm, Sun 10am–1pm; May–July & Sept–Oct Mon–Sat 10am–5pm, Sun 10am–4pm; Aug Mon–Sat 10am–6pm, Sun 10am–5pm; Nov–Feb Mon–Sat 10am–1.30pm; ⓣ01395/516441, ⓦwww.visitsidmouth.co.uk). Of the B&Bs, *Rock Cottage* on Peak Hill Road (ⓣ01395/514253; no smoking; ④) offers unrivalled sea views from its spacious rooms and access to the beach at the quieter, western end of the Esplanade. Further from the seafront, the *Old Farmhouse*, on Hillside Road (ⓣ01395/512284; no smoking; no credit cards; ④; closed Nov–Jan), offers plenty of atmosphere, and delicious meals on request. There's more choice in the string of decent guest houses along Salcombe Road, including *Berwick Guest House* at 4 Albert Terrace (ⓣ01395/513621, ⓦwww.berwick-house.co.uk; no under-12s; no smoking; no credit cards; ③). For **meals** in town, try the seafood at *Mocha Restaurant* on The Esplanade (daytime only, eves in summer), and the daily specials (including vegetarian dishes) at *Brown's Wine Bar & Bistro* at 33 Fore St (closed Sun). On Old Fore Street, two hundred yards from the seafront, the *Old Ship* and *Anchor* **pubs** provide excellent bar meals and suppers as well as a good range of ales.

Sidmouth hosts what many consider to be the country's best **folk festival** over eight days at the beginning of August. Folk and roots artists from around the world as well as dance and theatre companies take over various venues including the Arena Theatre and various pubs and parks. A campsite is laid on outside Sidmouth with shuttle buses to the centre, and tickets can be bought for specific days, for the weekend or the entire week. For detailed information, contact the tourist office, call ⓣ01629/827010 or check out the website at ⓦwww.sidmouthfestival.com. Book early for the main acts.

Beer and Seaton

Eight miles east along the coast, the fishing village of **BEER** lies huddled within a small sheltered cove between gleaming white headlands. A stream rushes along a deep channel dug into Beer's main street, and if you can ignore the crowds in high summer much of the village looks unchanged since the time when it was a smugglers' eyrie, its inlets used by such characters as Jack Rattenbury, who published his *Memoirs of a Smuggler* in 1837. The village is best known for its quarries, which were worked from Roman times until the nineteenth century: **Beer Stone** was used in many of Devon's churches and houses, and also went into the construction of some London buildings. You can visit the complex of **underground quarries** (Easter–Sept 10am–5pm; Oct 11am–4pm; last entry 1hr before closing; £4.25) a mile or so west of the village on a guided tour, along with a small exhibition of pieces carved by medieval masons, among others. Take something warm to wear. *Bay View* (ⓣ01297/20489; no credit cards; ①; closed Nov–Easter), overlooking the sea on Fore Street, is easily the best of the **B&Bs**, and Beer's **youth hostel** is half a mile northwest, at Bovey Combe, Townsend (ⓣ0870/770 5690, ⓔbeer@yha.org.uk; closed Wed–Sun Nov–Feb; £11.50). For **food**, head straight to the *Barrel of Beer* pub, on the main street, where the superb menu includes local delicacies such as Devon oysters and home-smoked fish; there are imaginative vegetarian options, too.

SEATON, a smooth stroll less than a mile eastwards, has a steep, pebbly beach like Beer's, but this is a much more developed resort, mutating from a placid, slow-moving haven at its western end to a much gaudier affair to the east. One of the main attractions is the open-top **tramway** (Easter–Oct daily 10am–5pm; Nov–Christmas Sat & Sun 10am–4pm; every 20min; £5.40) which follows the path of the old railway line to the inland village of Colyton. Seaton's **tourist office** is on the Underfleet, in the main car park on Harbour Road (Easter–June, Sept & Oct Mon–Sat 10am–5pm; July & Aug Mon–Sat 10am–5pm, Sun 10am–2pm; Nov–Easter Mon–Sat 10am–2pm; ⓣ01297/21660, ⓦwww.eastdevon.net/tourism). On Trevelyan Road, at the far end of the Esplanade on the eastern edge of town, you'll find *Beach End* (ⓣ01297/23388; no credit cards; ❸; closed Nov–March), a bright and roomy Edwardian **B&B**; or, just across from the tourist office, the friendly *Beaumont* on Castle Hill (ⓣ01297/20832, ⓔjane@lymebay.demon.co.uk; no credit cards; ❸), on the west side – both have sea views.

The "English Riviera" region

The wedge of land between Dartmoor and the sea contains some of Devon's most fertile pastures, backing onto some of the West's most popular coastal resorts. Chief of these is **Torbay**, an amalgam of **Torquay**, **Paignton** and **Brixham**, together forming the nucleus of an area optimistically known as "**The English Riviera**". To the north of the Torbay conurbation lie small-scale **Teignmouth** and **Dawlish**, while to the south the port of **Dartmouth** offers another calmer alternative, linked by riverboat to historic and almost unspoiled **Totnes**. West of the River Dart, the rich agricultural district of **South Hams** extends as far as Plymouth, cleft by a web of rivers flowing off Dartmoor. The main town here is **Kingsbridge**, at the head of an estuary down which you can ferry to the sailing resort of **Salcombe**.

Trains from Exeter to Plymouth run down the coast as far as Teignmouth before striking inland for Totnes – to get to Torbay, change at Newton Abbot. The hourly #X46 **bus** connects Exeter and Torquay in an hour, while the #85 and #85A serve Teignmouth and Dawlish. For the hinterland and points south and west along the coast, you can rely on a network of buses from Torquay, and travellers to Totnes and Dartmouth could make use of the **South Devon Railway** and **boats** along the River Dart.

Teignmouth and Dawlish

The estuary town of **TEIGNMOUTH** (pronounced "Tinmuth"), once a terminus for shipments of Dartmoor granite, still has a thriving harbour along the banks of the Teign, and fishing boats are still hauled up onto the pebble beach from which juts a pier that formerly segregated male and female bathers. The town began to attract holiday-makers at the end of the eighteenth century – Fanny Burney and John Keats both stayed – and some dainty Georgian and Victorian villas adorn Powderham Terrace and the Den. Behind the town centre, the lanes hold some interesting old pubs, while the estuary crossing to **Shaldon**, either by road bridge or by passenger ferry (last one at around dusk; £1.20, bikes free), deposits you in a smaller version of Teignmouth, relatively unscathed by the seasonal crowds.

Teignmouth's **tourist office** is near the pier (May–Sept daily 9am–5pm; Oct–April Mon–Sat 9am–1pm & 2–5pm; ⓣ01626/215666). *Riverbeach House*

(☎01626/772198; no credit cards; ❶; closed Nov–Easter)) provides plain but great-value **accommodation** at 3 Ivy Lane, near the seafront and just a few steps from the river, while the much posher *Thomas Luny House*, a white, Regency villa on Teign Street (☎01626/772976, ⓦwww.thomas-luny-house.co.uk; no under-12s; no smoking; ❺), provides spacious, well-equipped rooms in the former home of a local artist. For **food and drink**, Teignmouth's backstreets and alleys unearth some choice pubs, notably the *Ship Inn* on Queen Street, overlooking the water, or try the *Ferryboat Inn* on Shaldon's Strand, which has a terrace with views.

North of Teignmouth, **DAWLISH** is a smaller, more sedate resort, known to Jane Austen and Charles Dickens, whose character Nicholas Nickleby was born here. The seafront, a mile from the older inland centre, is spanned by a granite railway viaduct built by Brunel, under which you pass to reach a beach of sand and shingle. A better beach lies a little further south, at Coryton Cove, though most people head a couple of miles north to **Dawlish Warren**, a sandy area backed by dunes and caravan parks and also holding a nature reserve. If you want to **stay**, make for the *Walton Guest House*, a Georgian building five minutes from the seafront on Plantation Terrace (☎01626/862760; no credit cards; closed Dec–March; ❸), with all rooms en suite.

Torquay

Five miles south of Teignmouth, the coast is heavily urbanized around **Torbay**, a tourist conglomeration entirely dedicated to the exploitation of the bay's sheltered climate and exuberant vegetation. **TORQUAY**, the largest component of the super-resort, comes closest to living up to the self-penned "English Riviera" sobriquet, sporting a mini-corniche and promenades landscaped with flowerbeds. The much-vaunted palm trees (actually New Zealand cabbage trees) and the coloured lights that festoon the harbour by night contribute to the town's unique flavour, a slightly frayed combination of the exotic and the classically English. Torquay's transformation from a fishing village began with its establishment as a fashionable haven for invalids, among them the consumptive Elizabeth Barrett Browning, who spent three years here. In more recent years the most famous figures associated with Torquay – crimewriter Agatha Christie and traveller Freya Stark – have been joined by the fictional TV hotelier Basil Fawlty, whose jingoism and injured pride perfectly encapsulate the town's adaptation to the demands of mass tourism.

Arrival, information and accommodation

The **train station** is off Rathmore Road, next to the Torre Abbey gardens; most **buses** leave from outside the Pavilion, including the #X80 to Totnes and Plymouth, and the frequent #12 and #12B service linking Torquay with Paignton and Brixham. Torquay's **tourist office** is on Vaughan Parade, near the Pavilion (late May to Sept Mon–Sat 9.30am–6pm, Sun 10am–6pm; Oct to late May Mon–Sat 9.30am–5pm; ☎0906/680 1268, ⓦwww.theenglishriviera.co.uk).

Torquay has plenty of **accommodation**, but you'll need to book in advance during peak season. Most of the budget choices lie along Belgrave Road and, slightly further out, Avenue Road, though you'll do better looking in the side streets.

Hotels, guest houses and hostels

Allerdale Croft Road ☎01803/292667, ⓦwww.allerdalehotel.co.uk. The place to come for views and stately surroundings, with a long, lawned garden sloping below it and all en-suite rooms. ❹

The Exton 12 Bridge Rd ☎01803/293561, ⓦwww.extonhotel.co.uk. Small, clean and quiet hotel, very close to Belgrave Road and a ten-minute walk from the train station. ❷

Lanscombe House ⓣ01803/606938, ⓦwww.lanscombehouse.co.uk. A couple of miles west and connected by frequent buses, this elegant choice offers a pleasant rural retreat in the touristy village of Cockington. ❸

Morningside Hotel Babbacombe Downs ⓣ01803/327025. Another out-of-town option, ideally placed for Babbacombe Beach, with views over the bay. The village is linked to Torquay's centre by buses #32, #33, #34 and #12d. ❸

Mulberry House 1 Scarborough Rd ⓣ01803/213639. Non-smokers with a yen for antique pine furnishings and crisp bed linen should head for this place, with showers in the attached bathrooms and a rated wholefood restaurant on the premises (see below). ❹

Torquay Backpackers 119 Abbey Rd ⓣ01803/299924, ⓦwww.torquaybackpackers.co.uk. If you're looking for cheap and friendly hostel accommodation, make a beeline for this very central place. Dorm beds £12 a night, less in winter, and doubles are avilable too (shared bathroom). Ten-minute walk from the station or a free pick-up service. ❶

The Town

Torquay is focused on the small **harbour** and marina, where the mingling crowds can seem almost Mediterranean, especially at night. To one side stands the copper-domed **Pavilion**, an Edwardian building that originally housed a ballroom and assembly hall and is now refurbished with shops. Behind the Pavilion, limestone cliffs sprouting white high-rise hotels and apartment blocks separate the harbour area from Torquay's main beach, **Abbey Sands**. Good for chucking a frisbee about but too busy for serious relaxation, it takes its name from **Torre Abbey**, sited in ornamental gardens behind the beachside road. The Norman church that once stood here was razed by Henry VIII, though a gatehouse, tithe barn, chapter house and tower escaped demolition. The present **Abbey Mansion** (Easter–Oct daily 9.30am–6pm, last entry 5pm; £3) is a seventeenth- and eighteenth-century construction, now containing the mayor's office, a suite of period rooms with collections of paintings, silver and glass, and one devoted to Agatha Christie, who was born and raised in Torquay. There's more material relating to the Mistress of Murder at the main **Torquay Museum**, 529 Babbacombe Rd (Mon–Sat 10am–5pm, also Sun in summer 1.30–5pm; £3), but most of the space is given over to the local history and natural history collections. Buses #32 and #33 stop outside.

You'll probably find the walk round the promontory at Torbay's north end more stimulating, as it leads to some good sand beaches. To reach the nearest, follow the pretty half-mile coastal walk that takes you through Daddyhole Plain, a large chasm in the cliff caused by a landslide locally attributed to the devil ("Daddy"). The path descends to meet the seawall at **Meadfoot Beach**, where boats and pedalos can be rented. If you're searching for something a little more low-key, continue round the point to where a string of beaches extends along the coast as far as the cliff-backed coves of **Watcombe** and **Maidencombe**.

Eating, drinking and nightlife

There is a surprisingly high standard of cuisine in Torquay's restaurants, one of the best being the *Mulberry House Restaurant*, 1 Scarborough Rd (ⓣ01803/213639; open lunchtime Fri & Sat, eves Wed–Sat, also Mon & Tues to residents), where the English and Continental menu uses mainly organic ingredients and is colour-coded according to its cholesterol content; prices are in the expensive category, and booking is advised. Alternatively, the *Orange Tree Restaurant*, 14 Parkhill Rd (ⓣ01803/213936; eve only; closed Sun) serves up elegant but fairly expensive English and European dishes. Cheaper places are thick on the ground: on the harbourside, try the *Sea Spray* at 8 Victoria Parade (closed Mon–Wed eves), offering everything from toasties to ostrich and swordfish steaks, while the *Bombay Express* at 98 Belgrave Rd claims to be the southwest's "first and only original Balti House"; it's also good for takeaways. Strong on atmosphere, the cobbled *Hole in the Wall* **pub** on Park Lane serves some vegetarian dishes and has sing-songs round the piano – it was the Irish playwright Sean O'Casey's boozer when he lived in Torquay.

Torquay has the hottest and rowdiest **nightlife** in Devon; the main clubs include *The Venue* on Torwood Street (⊕01803/213903) and *Claire's* at 41 Torwood Ave (⊕01803/292079), while *Valbonne's* on Higher Union Street (⊕01803/290458) caters to a slightly older and smarter crowd. By the harbour, *Café Mambo* on The Strand (⊕01803/291112) has three floors including a patio, and *Smove*, playing garage and R'n'B, at the top. *Rocky's* (⊕01803/292279), near the Pavilion on Rock Road (off Abbey Road), is a long-established gay club.

Paignton

Not so much a rival to Torquay as its complement, **PAIGNTON** lacks the gloss of its neighbour, but also its pretensions. Activity is concentrated at the southern end of the wide town beach, around the small harbour that nestles in the lee of the appropriately named Redcliffe headland. Otherwise, diversion-seekers could wander over to **Paignton Zoo** (daily summer 10am–6pm, last entry 5pm, winter 10am–5pm or dusk if earlier, last entry 3pm; £8.25), a mile out on Totnes Road, or board the **Paignton & Dartmouth Steam Railway** at Paignton's Queen's Park train station near the harbour (⊕01803/555872, ⓦwww.paignton-steamrailway.co.uk). Running daily from June to September, with a patchy service in April, May, October and December, the line connects with Paignton's other main beach – **Goodrington Sands** – before trundling alongside the Dart estuary to Kingswear, seven miles away. The accent is on Victorian nostalgia, with railway personnel in period uniforms, but it's a pleasant way to view the scenic countryside, and you could make a day of it by taking the ferry connection from Kingswear to Dartmouth (see p.454), then taking a river boat up the Dart to Totnes, from where you can take any bus back to Paignton – a "Round Robin" ticket (£12) lets you do this.

Paignton's bus and train stations are next to each other off Sands Road. Five minutes away, the seafront has a **tourist office** (late May to Sept Mon–Sat 9.30am–6pm, Sun 10am–6pm; Oct to late May Mon–Sat 9.30am–1 & 2–5pm; ⊕0906/680 1268). Torquay has a far better selection of **accommodation**, though if you'd like to stay in Paignton, you could do worse than *St Weonard's Hotel*, 12 Kernou Rd (⊕01803/558842; no smoking; ❶), a couple of minutes' walk from the seafront; en-suite rooms are in the next price category. The harbour area has a few pubs and restaurants, including the *Harbour Light* (open daily in summer, only Fri eve, Sat eve & Sun lunch in winter), and the nearby *Pier Inn*.

Brixham

From Paignton, it's a fifteen-minute bus ride down to **BRIXHAM**, the prettiest of the Torbay towns. Fishing was for centuries Brixham's lifeblood, its harbour extending some way farther inland than it does now to afford a safe anchorage – a function performed today by an extensive breakwater. Indeed, at the beginning of the nineteenth century, this was the major fish market in the West Country, and it still supplies fish to restaurants as far away as London. Among the trawlers on Brixham's quayside is moored a full-size reconstruction of the **Golden Hind** (daily: July–Aug 9am–10pm, Sept–June 10am–5pm;

£2.50), the surprisingly small vessel in which Francis Drake circumnavigated the world – it has no real connection with the port, however. Below decks you can see the extremely cramped surgeon's and carpenter's cabins, and the only slightly grander captain's quarters. The harbour is overlooked by an unflattering statue of William III, a reminder of his landing in Brixham to claim the crown of England in 1688. From here, steep lanes and stairways thread up to the older centre around Fore Street, where the bus from Torquay pulls in.

From the harbour, you can reach the promontory of **Berry Head** along a path winding up from the *Berry Head House Hotel*. Fortifications built during the Napoleonic wars are still standing on this southern limit of Torbay, which is now a conservation area, attracting colonies of nesting seabirds and affording fabulous views.

The town's **tourist office** (June to Sept daily 9.30am–6pm, Sun 10am–6pm; Oct Mon–Sat 9.30am–5pm; Nov–May Mon–Fri 9.30am–5pm; ⓣ0906/680 1268) is on the quayside, next to William's statue. **Accommodation** is listed on the door when the office is closed. The places on King Street, overlooking the harbour, have the best views – for example the *Harbour View Hotel*, at no. 65 (ⓣ01803/853052, ⓦwww.s-h-systems.co.uk; ❷), with all rooms en suite, and two doors down the classier *Quayside Hotel* (ⓣ01803/855751, ⓦwww.quaysidehotel.co.uk; ❺), which has two bars and a restaurant. Away from the harbour, the reputedly ghost-ridden *Smugglers' Haunt* on Church Hill (ⓣ01803/853050, ⓦwww.smugglershaunt-hotel-devon.co.uk; ❸) is creaky and cramped, but useful if everywhere else is full; all rooms are en suite. The nearest YHA **hostel** is four miles away outside the village of Galmpton, on the banks of the Dart (ⓣ0870/770 5962, ⓔmaypool@yha.org.uk; closed Nov to mid-Feb; £10.25), a two-mile walk from Churston Bridge, accessible on bus #12 or #12A (every 15min) – you can also get there on the Paignton & Dartmouth Steam Railway (see p.451), which passes right through the hostel's grounds.

When it comes to **eating options**, Brixham offers fish and more fish – from the stalls selling cockles, whelks and mussels on the harbourside to the moderately expensive *YardArms* (ⓣ01803/858266; closed lunch & all Mon, plus all Tues in winter; no kids), on Beach Approach off the quayside, one of Brixham's top choices for seafood; there's also a wine bar here for cheaper lunchtime eats. By the harbour, the *Sprat & Mackerel* offers staple **pub** snacks. For a more relaxed pint, try the *Blue Anchor* on Fore Street, with coal fires and low beams.

Totnes

Most of the Plymouth buses from Paignton and Torquay make a stop at **TOTNES**, on the west bank of the River Dart. The town has an ancient pedigree, its period of greatest prosperity occurring in the sixteenth century when this inland port exported cloth to France and brought back wine. Some handsome structures from that era remain, and there is still a working port down on the river, but these days Totnes has mellowed into a residential market town, enjoying an esoteric fame as a centre of the New Age arts-and-crafts crowd. With its arcaded High Street and secretive flowery lanes, Totnes has its syrupy side, partly the result of its proximity to the Torbay tourist hive, but so far its allure has survived more or less intact.

Totnes centres on the long main street that starts off as Fore Street, site of the town's **museum** (mid-March to Oct Mon–Fri 10.30am–5pm; £1.50), which occupies a four-storey Elizabethan house at no. 70. Showing how wealthy clothiers lived at the peak of Totnes's fortunes, it's packed with domestic objects and furniture, and also has a room devoted to local mathematician Charles Babbage, whose "analytical engine" was the forerunner of the computer. There are a number of other houses along Fore and High streets in an equally good state of preservation: the late-eighteenth-century, mustard-yellow "Gothic House", a hundred yards up Fore Street on the left; 28 High St, overhung by some curious grotesque masks; and 16 High St, a house built by pilchard merchant Nicholas Ball, whose initials are carved outside. His wealth, inherited by his widow, was eventually bequeathed by her second husband, Thomas Bodley, to found Oxford's Bodleian Library.

Fore Street becomes the **High Street** at the East Gate, a much retouched medieval arch. Beneath it, Rampart Walk trails off along the old city walls, curling round the fifteenth-century church of **St Mary**. Inside, an exquisitely carved roodscreen stretches across the full width of the red sandstone building. Behind the church, the eleventh-century **Guildhall** (April–Sept Mon–Wed 10.30am–3.30pm; £1) was originally the refectory and kitchen of a Benedictine priory. Granted to the city corporation in 1553, the building still houses the town's Council Chamber, which you can see together with the former jail cells, used until the end of the nineteenth century, and the courtroom, which ceased to function only in 1974.

Totnes **Castle** (April–Sept daily 10am–6pm; Oct daily 10am–5pm; £1.80; EH) on Castle Street – leading off the High Street – is a classic Norman structure of the motte and bailey design, its simple crenellated keep atop a grassy mound offering wide views of the town and Dart valley. Totnes assumes a much livelier air at the bottom of Fore Street, at river level. This is the highest navigable point on the **River Dart** for seagoing vessels, and there's constant activity around the craft arriving from and leaving for European destinations. More locally, there are also cruises to Dartmouth between Easter and October, leaving from Steamer Quay, on the other side of the Dart. Riverside walks in either direction pass some congenial pubs, and near the railway bridge you can board a steam train of the **South Devon Railway** on its run along the course of the Dart to Buckfastleigh, adjacent to Buckfast Abbey (see p.467).

A walkable couple of miles out of Totnes, both rail and river pass near the estate of **Dartington Hall**, the arts and education centre set up in 1925 by US millionairess Dorothy Elmhirst and her husband. A constant programme of films, plays, concerts, dance and workshops is run here, but you can walk through the sculpture-strewn gardens and – when it's not in use – visit the fourteenth-century Great Hall, rescued from dereliction by the Elmhirsts. For details of events here, call ⓣ01803/847870, or log on to ⓦwww.dartingtonarts.org.uk.

Practicalities

Totnes's **tourist office** is in the Town Mill, signposted off the Plains near the Safeway car park (Mon–Sat 9.30am–5pm; ⓣ01803/863168, ⓦwww.totnesinformation.co.uk). You'll find a range of **accommodation** in and around town. Opposite the castle car park on North Street, the *Elbow Room* (ⓣ01803/863480, ⓔelbowroomtotnes@aol.com; no smoking; no credit cards; ❸) occupies a 200-year-old converted cottage and cider press. For a bit extra, pamper yourself at the atmospheric *Royal Seven Stars Hotel* on The Plains (ⓣ01803/862125, ⓦwww.s-h-systems.co.uk; ❹) or, just over the river in Seymour Place, at the *Old Forge* (ⓣ01803/862174; non-smoking; ❸) – a medieval former forge with comfortably modernized rooms and a secluded walled garden. Above the centre, next to a field at 7 Cherry Cross, *Acacias* (ⓣ01803/867306; no smoking; no credit cards; ❷), offers good B&B with views, a ten-minute walk from the centre, and serves organic, vegetarian and vegan breakfasts. If you want to stay nearer to Dartington, try the *Cott Inn*,

Shinner's Bridge, (ⓣ01803/863777, ⓦwww.thecottinn.co.uk; ⑤) – two miles west of Totnes on the A385 – outwardly almost unchanged since its construction in 1320, with snug bedrooms under the eaves. The local **youth hostel** (ⓣ0870/770 5788; closed Sept to mid-April; £10.25), in a sixteenth-century cottage, lies next to the River Bidwell two miles from Totnes and half a mile from Shinner's Bridge, a stop on the #X80 Torquay–Plymouth bus route. There's a **campsite** at Rattery, five miles west of Totnes, where *Edeswell Farm* lies just south of the A385 with an indoor pool and bike rental (ⓣ01364/72177, ⓦwww.edeswellfarm.co.uk).

You don't need to stray off the Fore Street/High Street axis to find a good place to **eat** in Totnes. *Willow*, 87 High St (ⓣ01803/862605; closed Sun), has inexpensive vegetarian snacks, evening meals (Wed, Fri & Sat) and live music (Fri). Indonesian food is on offer at *Rickshaws*, 98 High St (ⓣ01803/866171; closed Tues eve, plus all Sun & Mon), while *Rumour*, 30 High St, serves coffees, snacks and good-value full meals including homemade pizzas (ⓣ01803/864682; closed Sun lunch; no credit cards). There are also several decent **pubs**: the lively *Castle Inn* on Fore Street, the *Bull Inn* at the top of the High Street and the *Kingsbridge Inn* on Leechwell Street (off Kingsbridge Hill) – all have a warm atmosphere, bar snacks and good ale. By the riverside, the *Steampacket* on St Peter's Quay is also good for evening meals, reached by walking west along The Plains. **Bike rental** is available from *Hot Pursuit*, 26 The Stables, Ford Road, on Totnes Industrial Estate, just a few minutes from the train station (ⓣ01803/865174).

Dartmouth

South of Torbay, and eight miles downstream from Totnes, **DARTMOUTH** has thrived since the Normans recognized the potential of this deepwater port for trading with their home country. Today its activities embrace fishing, freight and a booming leisure industry, as well as the education of the senior service's officer class at the Royal Naval College, built at the start of this century on a hill overlooking the port. Coming from Torbay, visitors to Dartmouth can save time and a long detour through Totnes by using the frequent ferries crossing over the Dart's estuary from Kingswear (75p, £2.50 for cars), the last one at around 10.45pm (11.45pm Fri–Sun).

Behind the enclosed boat basin at the heart of town stands Dartmouth's most photographed building, the four-storey **Butterwalk**, built in the seventeenth century for a local merchant. Richly decorated with wood carvings, the timber-framed construction was restored after bombing in World War II, though still looks precarious as it overhangs the street on eleven granite columns. This arcade now holds shops and Dartmouth's small **museum** (Mon–Sat: April–Sept 11am–4.30pm; Oct–March noon–3pm; £1.50), mainly devoted to maritime curios, including old maps, prints and models of ships. Nearby **St Saviour's**, rebuilt in the 1630s from a fourteenth-century church, has long been a landmark for boats sailing upriver. The building stands at the head of Higher Street, the old town's central thoroughfare and the site of another tottering medieval structure, the *Cherub* inn. More impressive is **Agincourt House** on the parallel Lower Street, built by a merchant after the battle for which it is named, then restored in the seventeenth century and again in the twentieth.

Lower Street leads down to **Bayard's Cove**, a short cobbled quay lined with well-restored eighteenth-century houses, where the Pilgrim Fathers stopped en route to the New World. A twenty-minute walk from here along the river takes you to **Dartmouth Castle** (April–Sept daily 10am–6pm; Oct daily 10am–5pm; Nov–March Wed–Sun 10am–1pm & 2–4pm; £3.20; EH), one of two fortifications on opposite sides of the estuary. The site includes coastal defence works from the nineteenth century and from World War II, though the main interest is in the fifteenth-century castle, the first in England to be constructed specifically to withstand artillery. The castle was never actually tested in action, and consequently is excellently preserved. If you don't relish the return walk, you can take advantage of a ferry back to town, leaving roughly every fifteen minutes from Easter to October (£1).

Continuing south along the coastal path brings you through the pretty hill-top village of **Stoke Fleming** to **Blackpool Sands** (45min from the castle), the best and most popular beach in the area. The unspoilt cove, flanked by steep, wooded cliffs, was the site of a battle in 1404 in which Devon archers repulsed a Breton invasion force sent to punish the privateers of Dartmouth for their raiding across the Channel.

From Dartmouth there are regular ferries across the river to **Kingswear**, terminus of the **Paignton & Dartmouth Steam Railway** (see p.451). There are also various **cruises** from Dartmouth's quay up the River Dart to Totnes (1hr 15min; £7 return; ⓣ01803/834488, ⓦwww.riverlink.co.uk); this is the best way to see the river's deep creeks and the various houses overlooking the river, among them the **Royal Naval College** and **Greenway House**, birth-place of Walter Raleigh's three seafaring half-brothers, the Gilberts, and later rebuilt for Agatha Christie.

Practicalities

Dartmouth's **tourist office** is opposite the car park at Mayor's Avenue (Jan & Feb Mon–Sat 9.30am–4pm; March–June & Sept to mid-Oct Mon–Sat 9.30am–5.30pm; July & Aug Mon–Sat 9.30am–5.30pm, Sun 10am–2pm; mid-Oct to Dec Mon–Sat 9.30am–5pm; ⓣ01803/834224, ⓦwww.dartmouth-information.co.uk). The less expensive **accommodation** is either at the top of steep hills or strung along Victoria Road, a continuation of Duke Street. The hill-top choices are preferable for their views, such as the spacious and elegant *Avondale* at 5 Vicarage Hill (ⓣ01803/835831, ⓦwww.avondaledartmouth.co.uk; no credit cards; ❸), while good choices lower down include *Sunnybanks* at 1 Vicarage Hill (ⓣ01803/832766, ⓦwww.sunnybanks.com; no credit cards; ❷), and, more centrally, *Café Caché*, 24 Duke St (ⓣ01803/833804, ⓦwww.cafecache.co.uk; ❸), which offers three light and airy en-suite rooms above a café/restaurant. Alternatively, you can splurge on the *Royal Castle Hotel* (ⓣ01803/833033, ⓦwww.royalcastle.co.uk; ❼), right on the central quay, converted from two seventeenth-century merchants' houses. For something a little different, book a berth on the *Res Nova Inn* (ⓣ07770/628967, ⓦwww.res-nova.co.uk; closed Nov–Easter), a barge moored in mid-river run by a friendly couple who will ferry guests to and from town. Comfy cabins – one en suite – can sleep up to three, costing £25 for a single berth, £45 for a double (£55 en suite), £60 for three (no credit cards).

As for eating, the *Café Alf Resco* on Lower Street is good for breakfasts and coffees and has outdoor tables; it's open daytime only, and evenings in summer (closed Mon & Tues). For full meals, take your pick among Dartmouth's wide range of **restaurants**, ranging from the relaxed *Café Caché* on Duke Street (see above), which has light, moderately priced Mediterranean meals, and the more formal (and expensive) *Taylor's*, 8 The Quay (ⓣ01803/832748), where you can tuck into quality seafood while enjoying great harbourside views. Also with views, the most famous place in town is the *Carved Angel*, at 2 South Embankment (ⓣ01803/832465; closed Sun eve, Mon lunch), a high-class fish restaurant that also excels in game in winter (very expensive). If you're put off by the prices and ambience, drop into its inexpensive offshoot at 7 Foss St, the *Carved Angel Café* (Ⓣ01803/834842; no smoking; closed Mon–Wed eve & all Sun). The menu may lack the sparkle of its parent, but it offers some great soups and puddings. The *Res Nova Inn* (see p.455) also offers excellent fish suppers, including fresh lobster: call to be picked up (closed Nov–Easter).

The South Hams

The area between the Dart and Plym estuaries, the **South Hams**, holds some of Devon's comeliest villages and most striking coastline. The "capital" of the region, **KINGSBRIDGE**, is easily accessible by hourly buses from Dartmouth or Totnes, and is the hub of local services to the South Hams villages. Fine Tudor and Georgian buildings distinguish this busy market town, especially along the steep Fore Street, where the colonnaded Shambles is largely Elizabethan on the ground floor, its granite pillars supporting an upper floor added at the end of the eighteenth century. The town hall hosts a craft **market** on Tuesdays and Fridays (Tues only in winter), and there are also regular markets on the Quay, right by the **tourist office**, where you can pick up information on the whole region (Easter–Sept Mon–Sat 9am–5.30pm, Sun 10am–4pm; Oct–Easter Mon–Sat 9am–5pm; Ⓣ01548/853195, Ⓦwww.kingsbridgeinfo.co.uk). For a snack or full **meal**, drop in to the boldly coloured *Pig Finca Café*, The Quay (closed Sun & Mon), which has Mediterranean dishes, a courtyard and a sofa-filled lounge. There's also weekly live jazz, funk and roots music.

Salcombe

A summer ferry runs from Kingsbridge to Devon's southernmost resort of **SALCOMBE**, almost at the mouth of the Kingsbridge estuary. Once a nondescript fishing village, Salcombe is now a full-blown sailing and holiday resort, its calm waters strewn with small craft and the steep streets overflowing with leisurewear. There's still some fishing activity here, and a few working boatyards, but a certain serenity prevails, with the ruined Fort Charles at the entrance to the harbour injecting a touch of romance amid the villas and hotels. You can bone up on boating and local history at **Salcombe Maritime Museum** on Market Street, off the north end of the central Fore Street (Easter–Oct 10.30am–12.30pm & 2.30–4.30pm; £1).

The **tourist office** is housed in the Council Hall on Market Street (Easter to mid-July, Sept & Oct daily 10am–5pm; mid-July to Aug Mon–Sat 9am–5pm, Sun 10am–5pm; Nov–March Mon–Thurs 10am–3pm, Fri & Sat 10am–5pm; Ⓣ01548/843927, Ⓦwww.salcombeinformation.co.uk). Most of the **B&Bs** are above Fore Street, enjoying excellent estuary views, for example *Rocarno* on Grenville Road (Ⓣ01548/842732, Ⓔrocarno@aol.com; no credit cards; ❷). Near the car park on Shadycombe Road, there's the lovely timber-framed *Old Tree House* (Ⓣ01548/843670, Ⓔsuehobbs1@aol.com; ❸) and *The Old Porch House* (Ⓣ01548/842157; ❸), which dates back to 1660, making it the oldest house in Salcombe – though it has full modern facilities amid the brass ornaments and hanging tankards. **Campers** have a good choice in the area, the nearest sites being *Ilton Farm* (Ⓣ01548/842858; closed Nov–Easter) and *Alston Farm* (Ⓣ01548/561260, Ⓦwww.welcome.to/alstonfarm), both signposted off the A381 Malborough road, while *Sun Park* at Soar Mill Cove (Ⓣ01548/561378, Ⓦwww.sun-park.co.uk) and *Higher Rew* at Rew Cross, south of Salcombe (Ⓣ01548/842681, Ⓦwww.higherrew.co.uk), are both within good walks of two of the area's finest beaches. Back in town, fish is top of the menu at *Restaurant Forty-Two*, a moderately priced place that shares a building with the *Salcombe Hotel* on Fore Street, looking out over the river (Ⓣ01548/843408; eves only, closed Sun & Mon).

From a quay off Fore Street, you can take a **ferry** down to the beach at South Sands (Easter–Oct every 30min; £2.20), while there's a year-round ferry (Easter–Oct every 15 or 30min 8am–7pm; Nov–Easter hourly 8am–5.30pm; £1) across the narrow channel to **East Portlemouth**, from where you can follow the coastal path to the craggily photogenic **Gammon Point**. Half a mile southeast of here, you can reach Devon's most southerly tip at **Prawle Point**, where a broken-backed freighter is a reminder of the hazards of this stretch of coast. A couple of miles inland from Lannacombe Bay, which links Prawle Point with Start Point – the headland at the top of Start Bay – you can find a quiet nook to **stay** at *South Allington House* (Ⓣ01548/511272, Ⓦwww.sthallingtonbnb.demon.co.uk; non-smoking; no under-4s; no credit cards; ❹); call for directions.

Sharpitor

At **SHARPITOR**, a couple of miles south of Salcombe, the National Trust runs **Overbecks Museum** (April–July & Sept Mon–Fri & Sun 11am–5.30pm; Aug daily 11am–5.30pm; Oct Mon–Thurs & Sun 11am–5pm; garden open daily all year 10am–7pm; £4.40; NT), which is mainly given over to natural history and houses a capacious **youth hostel** (Ⓣ0870/770 6016; closed Nov to mid-April; £11.50) in its grounds. You can reach the site from Salcombe on the ferry to South Sands (see above), from which it's a fifteen-minute walk. South of here, the six-mile hike from Bolt Head to Bolt Tail takes you along a ragged coast where shags, cormorants and other marine birds swoop over the rocks, and wild thyme and sea thrift grow underfoot.

Thurlestone and Bigbury-on-Sea

West of Kingsbridge, **THURLESTONE** is a chocolate-box village of pink-washed thatched cottages, with a splendid undeveloped sandy beach backed by rolling farmland. Surfers prefer the extensive sands to the opposite side of the Avon estuary at **BIGBURY-ON-SEA**, reachable in summer by a ferry between the hamlets of Bantham and Cockleridge – or by wading the river at low tide. A special tractor-like vehicle ferries visitors the short distance from Bigbury's Beach to Burgh Island, where a grand Art Deco hotel and the atmospheric *Pilchard Inn* are the main attractions. For an **overnight stay** in the area, Bantham's *Sloop Inn* (Ⓣ01548/560489, Ⓕ01548/561940; no credit cards; ❺) has several rooms overlooking the sea and estuary, and a restaurant serving good seafood.

Plymouth

PLYMOUTH's predominantly bland and modern face belies its great historic role as a naval base, a role assured in the sixteenth century by the patronage of such national heroes as John Hawkins and Francis Drake. It was from here that the latter sailed to defeat the Spanish Armada in 1588, and 32 years later the port was the last embarkation point for the Pilgrim Fathers, whose New Plymouth colony became the nucleus for the English settlement of North America. The sustained prominence of the city's Devonport dockyards as a shipbuilding and military base made it a target in World War II, when the Luftwaffe reduced the old centre to rubble, apart from the compact area around the Barbican. Subsequent reconstruction, spurred on by growth that has made Plymouth by far Devon's biggest town, has done nothing to enhance the place. That said, it would be difficult to spoil the glorious vista over **Plymouth Sound**, the basin of calm water at the mouth of the combined Plym, Tavy and Tamar estuaries, which has remained largely unchanged since Drake played his famous game of bowls on the Hoe before joining battle with the Armada. This alone makes a visit to Plymouth a memorable one, and you could also spend a couple of hours wandering around the Elizabethan warehouses and inns of the **Barbican**. The latter is the focus of occasionally raucous nightlife, and a gamut of excellent restaurants specializing in freshly caught seafood. Although this area is easy to stroll around, you could also make use of the regular and frequent circular **bus** service (#25a) for getting around the town, which stops at the train station, Sutton Harbour, the Hoe and the Citadel. Plymouth makes a good starting point for forays onto Dartmoor, and a base for visiting a trio of elegant country houses with both aesthetic appeal and historical resonance, though transport connections are not always easy.

Arrival, information and accommodation

Plymouth's **train station** is off Saltash Road, from where bus #25a leaves every twenty minutes (hourly on Sun) for the central Royal Parade, Sutton Harbour and the Hoe. The **bus station** is just over St Andrew's Cross from Royal Parade, at Bretonside, and holds **left-luggage lockers**. The **tourist office** is off Sutton Harbour at 9 The Barbican (April–Oct Mon–Sat 9am–5pm, Sun 10am–4pm; Nov–March Mon–Fri 9am–5pm, Sat 10am–4pm; ⓣ0870/225 4950, ⓦwww.visitplymouth.co.uk). Ask here about guided tours, a useful way to get an informed view of the city and surrounding areas. **Internet** access is available from the Carp Internet Café, 32 Franfort Gate (Mon–Sat 9am–5pm; ⓣ01752/221777).

Plymouth has plenty of choice when it comes to **accommodation**: try first the row of B&Bs edging the Hoe on Citadel Road if you want to be near the sights, though you won't be more than a twenty-minute walk from the Hoe and Barbican areas if you prefer to stay close to the train station. Ferry passengers might want to be nearer the docks in the Millbay district, on the western side of town.

Hotels, B&Bs and hostels

Acorns and Lawns 171 Citadel Rd ⓣ01752/229474. One of a terrace of competitively priced B&Bs off the eastern side of Plymouth Hoe, this one offering superb-value accommodation and a choice of rooms with shared bathrooms, en-suite shower or full private facilities. No credit cards. ❶

The Beeches 175 Citadel Rd ⓣ01752/266475. A good choice on this row close to the Barbican, with access at all times to the well-equipped rooms, most of which are en suite. No credit cards. ❶

Bowling Green 9–10 Osborne Place, Lockyer St ⓣ01752/209090, ⓦwww.bowlingreenhotel.com. Smart establishment overlooking Francis Drake's fabled haunt on the west side of the Hoe. ❸

Brittany Guest House 28 Athenaeum St ⓣ01752/262247, ⓦwww.brittanyguesthouse.co.uk. More stylish than the similar establishments in the area, this easy-going place offers kippers for breakfast and use of a private car park (a bonus around here). ❷

Georgian House 51 Citadel Rd ⓣ01752/663237, ⓦwww.georgianhousehotelonline.co.uk. Small hotel with all rooms en suite, and facilities for bike storage. ❷

Grosvenor Park 114 North Road East ⓣ01752/229312, ⓦwww.grosvenorparkhotel.co.uk. Convenient stop for the train station, off the North Cross roundabout. Excellent value, and evening meals available on request. ❷

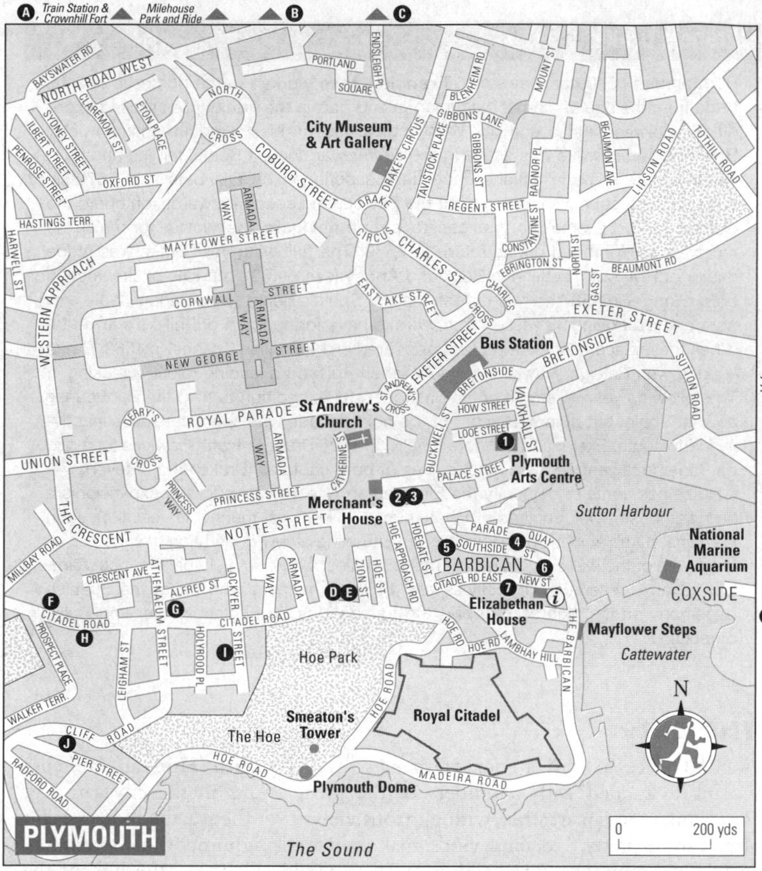

ACCOMMODATION

Acorns and Lawns	D	Oliver's	C
The Beeches	E	Osmond Guest House	J
Bowling Green	I	Phantele	A
Brittany Guest House	G	Plymouth Backpackers	H
Georgian House	F		
Grosvenor Park	B		

RESTAURANTS

Barbican Revival	3
Pasta Bar	5
Piermaster's	4
Plymouth Arts Centre	1
Tropical Sensation	2
Tudor Rose	7

PUBS

Dolphin	6
Mount Batten Bar	8

Oliver's 33 Sutherland Rd ⓣ01752/663923. A few minutes from the train station, with a good restaurant. ❷

Osmond Guest House 42 Pier St ⓣ01752/229705, ⓔmike@osmondgh.freeserve.co.uk. Comfortable choice between the Hoe and the Great Western Docks, with bright red walls and offering a pick-up service from the bus and train stations. No smoking. ❷

Phantele 176 Devonport Rd ⓣ01752/561506. Unpretentious budget place towards the Torpoint ferry on the west side of town; useful if everywhere central is booked up. No credit cards. ❶

Plymouth Backpackers 172 Citadel Rd ⓣ01752/225158, ⓦwww.backpackers.co.uk/plymouth. Relaxed place in a convenient location on the hotel strip near the Hoe and Royal Parade. Call ahead, as beds fill up quickly. Dorm beds £10, double rooms £25.

Francis Drake

Born around 1540 near Tavistock, **Francis Drake** worked in the domestic coastal trade from the age of 13, but was soon taking part in the first English slaving expeditions between Africa and the West Indies, led by his Plymouth kinsman John Hawkins. Later, Drake was active in the secret war against Spain, raiding and looting merchant ships in actions unofficially sanctioned by Elizabeth I. In 1572 he became the first Englishman to sight the Pacific, and soon afterwards, on board the *Golden Hind*, became the first one to **circumnavigate the world**, for which he received a knighthood on his return in 1580. The following year Drake was made mayor of Plymouth, settling in Buckland Abbey (see p.463), but was back in action before long – in 1587 he "singed the king of Spain's beard" by entering Cadiz harbour and destroying 33 vessels that were to have formed part of Philip II's **armada**. When the replacement invasion fleet appeared in the English Channel in 1588, Drake – along with Raleigh, Hawkins and Frobisher – played a leading role in wrecking it. The following year he set off on an unsuccessful expedition to help the Portuguese against Spain, but otherwise most of the next decade was spent in relative inactivity in Plymouth, Exeter and London. Finally, in 1596 Drake left with Hawkins for a raid on Panama, a venture that cost the lives of both captains (Drake died of fever).

Drake has come to personify the Elizabethan Age's swashbuckling expansionism and patriotism, but England's naval triumphs were as much the result of John Hawkins' humbler work in building and maintaining a new generation of warships as they were of the skill and bravery of their captains. Drake was simply the most flamboyant of a generation of reckless and brilliant mariners who broke the Spanish hegemony on the high seas, laying the foundations for England's later imperialist pursuits.

The City

A good place to start a tour of the city is **Plymouth Hoe**, an immense esplanade studded with reminders of the great events in the city's history. Resplendent in fair weather, with glorious views over the sea, the Hoe can also attract some pretty ferocious winds, making it well-nigh impossible to explore in wintry conditions. Approaching from the Civic Centre – the hub of the town centre – the most distinctive landmark is a tall white naval war memorial, standing alongside smaller monuments to the defeat of the Spanish Armada and to the airmen who defended the city during the wartime blitz, and a rather portly statue of Sir Francis Drake, gazing grandly out to the sea. Appropriately, there's a bowling green back from the brow.

In front of the memorials the red-and-white-striped **Smeaton's Tower** (Easter–Sept 10.30am–4.30pm; £2, combined ticket with Plymouth Dome £6) was erected in 1759 by John Smeaton on the treacherous Eddystone Rocks, fourteen miles out to sea. When replaced by a larger lighthouse in 1882, it was reassembled here, where it gives the loftiest view over Plymouth Sound. Below Smeaton's Tower is the **Plymouth Dome** complex (April–Oct daily 10am–5pm, Nov–March Tues–Sat 10am–4pm; last entry 1hr before closing; £4.50, combined ticket with Smeaton's Tower £6), which includes audiovisual exhibitions on Plymouth's history and the lives of Drake, the Mayflower Pilgrims and Captain Cook. On the seafront, Plymouth's **Royal Citadel** (June–Sept tours at 2.30pm lasting 1hr 15min; £3; EH) is an uncompromising fortress constructed in 1666 to intimidate the populace of the only town in the southwest to be held by the Parliamentarians in the Civil War. The stronghold is still used by the military, though there are guided tours through some of its older parts, including the seventeenth-century Governor's House and the Royal Chapel of St Katherine; tickets for tours are available from the Plymouth Dome and the tourist office.

Round the corner, the old town's quay at **Sutton Harbour** is still used by the trawler fleet and is the scene of a boisterous early-morning fish market. The **Mayflower Steps** here commemorate the sailing of the Pilgrim Fathers and a nearby plaque lists the names and professions of the 102 Puritans on board. All three of Captain Cook's voyages to the South Seas, Australia and the Antarctic also started from here, as did the nineteenth-century transport ships to Australia, carrying thousands of convicts and colonists. Nowadays, the harbour is the starting point for cruises, ranging from one-hour tours around the Sound and the Devonport naval dockyard, to longer sea trips and the four-hour cruise up the Tamar to the Cornish village of Calstock.

The **Barbican** district, which edges the harbour, is the heart of old Plymouth. Most of the buildings are now shops and restaurants, but off the quayside, New Street holds most of the oldest buildings, among them the **Elizabethan House** (April–Sept Wed–Sun 10am–5pm; £1.10), a captain's dwelling retaining most of the original architectural features, including a lovely old pole staircase. The Pilgrim Fathers are thought to have spent their last night in England in Island House, at the end of the parallel Southside Street, now home to the tourist office.

Cross the bridge over Sutton Harbour to reach Plymouth's newest exhibit, the grand **National Marine Aquarium** (daily: April–Oct 10am–6pm; Nov–March 10am–5pm; last entry 1hr before closing; £8). On three levels, the complex represents a range of marine environments from moorland stream to coral reef and deep-sea ocean, including sharks and Europe's largest collection of seahorse species. Talks and presentations take place throughout the day, and the feeding times – carried out by divers – are among the highlights. Back in the centre of town, the handsome timber-framed, mainly seventeenth-century **Merchant's House Museum**, 33 St Andrew's St (April–Sept Tues–Fri 10am–1pm & 2–5.30pm, Sat 10am–1pm & 2–5pm; £1.10) goes into various aspects of Plymouth's history. Behind it, off Royal Parade, stands the city's chief place of worship, **St Andrew's**, a reconstruction of a fifteenth-century building that was almost completely gutted by a bomb in 1941. The entrails of the navigator Martin Frobisher are buried here, as are those of Admiral Blake, the Parliamentarian who died as his ship entered Plymouth after destroying a Spanish treasure fleet off Tenerife. Local boy William Bligh, of *Mutiny on the Bounty* fame, was baptized here.

Eating and drinking

You'll find a wildly eclectic range of **restaurants** in and around Plymouth's Barbican area. One of the best fish restaurants is *Piermaster's*, at 3 Southside St (Ⓣ01752/229345; closed Sun), whose kitchen is supplied straight from the nearby harbour; it's plain but elegant, with a good fixed-price menu offered for lunch. Across the road, tasty Italian dishes draw the crowds at the more casual *Pasta Bar*, while if you hanker for simple English fast food, head for the *Tudor Rose*, 36 New St, which is good for cottage pies and teas and opens its garden in summer. Notte Street, at the top of Southside, has the inexpensive *Barbican Revival*, a Mexican/Italian/American diner with lots of jazzy ambience, and, four doors down, *Tropical Sensation*, which offers Caribbean and African cuisine (closed Sun). *Plymouth Arts Centre*, 38 Looe St, has a vegetarian restaurant (closed all Sun & Mon eve), useful for anyone coming here for its exhibitions, films and live performances (Ⓣ01752/206114, Ⓦwww.plymouthac.org.uk).

The *Dolphin* **pub** on Southside Street is a landmark in the Barbican, and is crowded with fishermen in the morning and locals and boisterous boozers at night; it also serves simple lunchtime snacks. In the Mount Batten area, reachable by water taxi from the Mayflower Steps, the *Mount Batten Bar*, Lawrence Road, has wrought-iron pillars and a good choice of snacks and meals, with **live bands** on Saturdays. You can also hear live bands and club sounds at *The Cooperage*, 134 Vauxhall St (Ⓣ01752/229275, Ⓦwww.thecooperage.co.uk).

Around Plymouth

One of the best local day excursions from Plymouth is to **Mount Edgcumbe**, where woods and meadows provide a welcome antidote to the urban bustle, and are within easy reach of some fabulous sand. East of Plymouth, the aristocratic opulence of **Saltram House** includes some fine art and furniture, while to the north of town you can visit Drake's old residence at **Buckland Abbey**.

Mount Edgcumbe

Lying on the Cornish side of Plymouth Sound and visible from the Hoe, **Mount Edgcumbe** features a Tudor house, landscaped gardens and acres of rolling parkland and coastal paths. The **house** (April to Sept Mon–Thurs & Sun 11am–4.30pm; £4.50) is a reconstruction of the bomb-damaged Tudor original, though inside the predominant note is eighteenth century, the rooms elegantly restored with authentic Regency furniture. The house alone, however, would not merit the expedition here: far more enticing are the **grounds**, which include impeccable gardens divided into French, Italian and English sections – the first two a blaze of flowerbeds adorned with classical statuary, the last an acre of sweeping lawn shaded by exotic trees. The **park**, which is free and open all year, covers the whole of the peninsula facing the estuary and the sea, including a part of the Cornish Coastal Path. From the peninsula's two headlands, Rame Head and Penlee Point, extensive views show Plymouth in its best light.

You can reach the house by the passenger **ferry** to Cremyll, leaving at least hourly from Admiral's Hard, a small mooring in the Stonehouse district of town, reachable on bus #34 from outside the Guildhall; in summer there's also a direct motor launch (4 daily) between the Mayflower Steps and the village of **Cawsand**, an old smugglers' haunt two hours' walk from the house. Cawsand itself is just a mile from the southern tip of the huge **Whitsand Bay**, the best bathing beach for miles around.

Saltram House

The remodelled Tudor mansion **Saltram House** (Mon–Thurs, Sat & Sun: April–Sept noon–4.30pm: Oct 11.30am–3.30pm; garden same days April–Sept 11am–5pm; Nov–March 11am–4pm; £6.30, garden only £3.30, less in winter; NT), two miles east of Plymouth off the A38, is Devon's largest country house, featuring work by the great architect Robert Adam and fourteen portraits by **Joshua Reynolds**, who was born nearby in Plympton. Showpiece is the Saloon, a fussy but exquisitely furnished room dripping with gilt and plaster, and set off by a huge Axminster carpet especially woven for it in 1770. Saltram's landscaped park provides a breather from this riot of interior design, though it's marred by the proximity of the road. You can get here on the hourly #22 bus (not Sun) from Royal Parade to Merafield Road, from where it's a fifteen-minute signposted walk.

Buckland Abbey

Six miles north of Plymouth, close to the River Tavy and on the edge of Dartmoor, stands **Buckland Abbey** (mid-April to Oct Mon–Wed & Fri–Sun 10.30am–5.30pm; Nov to late Dec & mid-Feb to March Sat & Sun 2–5pm; £5, grounds only £2.70; NT), once the most westerly of England's Cistercian abbeys. After its dissolution Buckland was converted to a family home by the privateer Richard Grenville (cousin of Walter Raleigh), from whom the estate was acquired by Sir Francis Drake in 1582, the year after he became mayor of Plymouth. It remained his home until his death, but the house reveals few traces of Drake's residence, as he spent most of his retirement years plundering on the Spanish main. There are, however, numerous maps, portraits and mementoes of his buccaneering exploits on show, most famous of which is Drake's Drum, which was said to beat a supernatural warning of impending danger to the country. Apart from Drake's knick-knacks, the collection includes some stirring relics of the Elizabethan era of seafaring, as well as model ships, including the *Golden Hind*. The house stands in majestic grounds which contain a fine fourteenth-century **Great Barn**, buttressed and gabled and larger than the abbey itself. To get here, take bus #84, #85 or #86 from Plymouth to Tavistock, changing at Yelverton for the hourly #55a minibus (not Sun).

Dartmoor

The longer one stays here the more does the spirit of the moor sink into one's soul, its vastness, and also its grim charm. When you are once out upon its bosom you have left all traces of modern England behind you, but on the other hand you are conscious everywhere of the homes and the work of the prehistoric people... If you were to see a skin-clad, hairy man crawl out from the low door, fitting a flint-tipped arrow on to the string of his bow, you would feel that his presence there was more natural than your own.

Arthur Conan Doyle, *The Hound of the Baskervilles*

Occupying the main part of the county between Exeter and Plymouth, **DARTMOOR** is southern England's greatest expanse of wilderness, some 365 square miles of raw granite, barren bogland, sparse grass and heather-grown moor. It was not always so desolate, as testified by the remnants of scattered Stone Age settlements and the ruined relics of the area's nineteenth-century tin-mining industry. Today desultory flocks of sheep and groups of ponies are virtually the only living creatures to be seen wandering over the central fastnesses of the National Park, with solitary birds – buzzards, kestrels, pipits, stonechats and wagtails – wheeling and hovering high above.

The core of Dartmoor, characterized by tumbling streams and high tors chiselled by the elements, is **Dartmoor Forest**, which has belonged to the Duchy of Cornwall since 1307, though there is almost unlimited public access as long as certain guidelines are followed – for instance, you are not allowed to park overnight in unauthorized places, and no vehicles are allowed farther than fifteen yards from the road. Camping is permitted out of sight of houses and roads, but fires are strictly forbidden. Though networks of signposts or painted stones do exist to guide **walkers**, map-reading abilities are a prerequisite for any but the shortest walks, and a good deal of experience is essential for longer distances – it's not uncommon for search parties to have to look for hikers gone

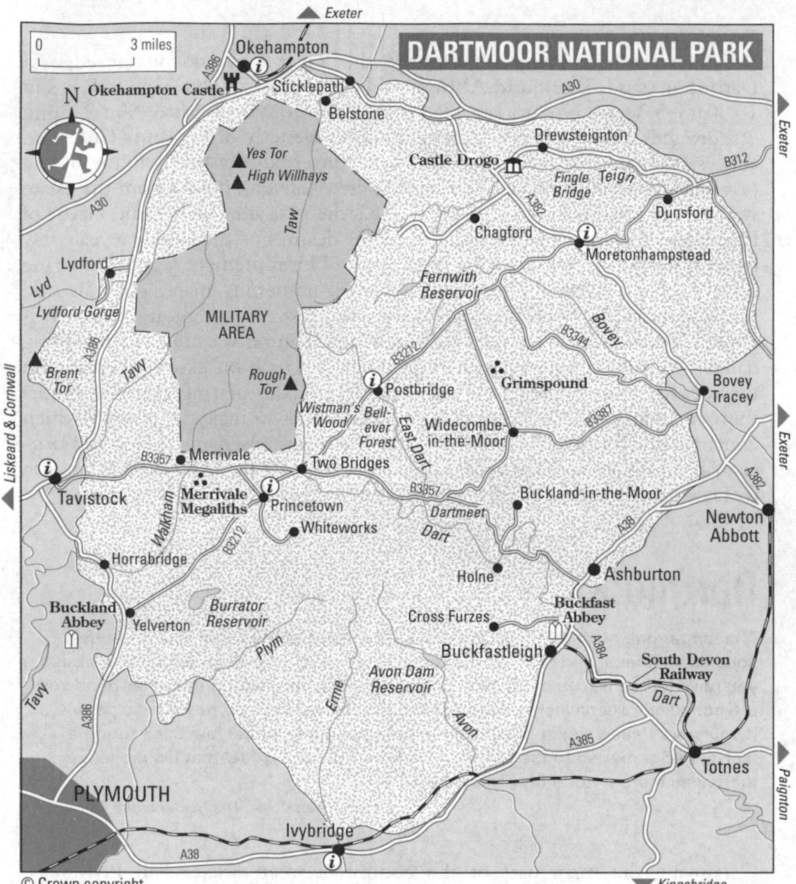

astray. Two- to six-hour guided walks are listed in the *Dartmoor Visitor* newspaper, available free from National Park Visitor Centres in Dartmoor's major towns and villages, and from information points in smaller villages. The *Dartmoor Visitor* also has info on camping and other accommodation, events, facilities for disabled travellers, and military firing-range schedules (see p.465); ask at visitor centres about **riding** facilities on the moor.

Princetown, at the heart of the moor, has the Dartmoor National Park's main information centre and a selection of stores, pubs and places to stay. A few other villages, such as **Postbridge** and **Widecombe**, have B&Bs and shops, though for the widest choice of accommodation you have to go to the towns and villages circling the moor – chief of them **Tavistock**, **Lydford** and **Okehampton**. It would not be impossible to base yourself in Exeter or Plymouth, neither more than an hour's ride from the central **Two Bridges**, at the intersection of the B3212 and B3357, which gives access to some of the wildest tracts of Dartmoor. Always plan ahead and book places to stay – availability can be extremely restricted in high season.

Much to the irritation of locals and visitors alike, the **Ministry of Defence** has appropriated a significant portion of northern Dartmoor, an area that contains Dartmoor's highest tors and some of its most famous beauty spots. The MoD firing ranges are marked by red and white posts; when firing is in progress, red flags or red lights signify that entry is prohibited. As a general rule, you can assume that if no warning flags are flying by 9am between April and September, or by 10am from October to March, there is to be no firing on that day; alternatively, check at ⓣ0800/458 4868 or ⓦwww.dartmoor-ranges.co.uk.

Getting around

In summer, a Transmoor **bus** service (#82) operates between Exeter and Plymouth, with stops at Two Bridges and Princetown – for most of the year it runs on weekends only, but there are at least three daily services from late May to late September. Also from Exeter, the regular #173 runs to Castle Drogo and nearby Chagford (not Sun), on the northeast side of the moor. Okehampton is served by National Express coaches between Cornwall and Exeter, as well as #X9 and #X10 between Bude, Boscastle and Exeter, and #171 from Exeter (not Sun); #86, connecting Plymouth and Barnstaple and taking in Tavistock and Lydford; and #118 (a classic red double-decker operating on Sundays in summer only), running between Plymouth, Tavistock, Lydford and Okehampton. Bus #98 connects Princetown with Tavistock five or six times daily from Monday to Saturday, and buses run from Tavistock to Plymouth roughly every couple of hours. Apart from these, there's little except once-weekly runs to remote villages. There are also a couple of **train** services, one, along an old goods line, linking Okehampton with Exeter via Crediton in about forty minutes on summer Sundays, while the Tamar Valley Line runs along the Tamar river between Plymouth and Gunnislake, five miles southeast of Tavistock, just over the Cornish side of the River Tamar. The *Discovery Guide to Dartmoor by Bus and Train* (free from bus stations and some tourist offices) gives all timetables for transport on the moor, and has helpful advice on combining walks with bus and train routes; you can also call DevonBus at ⓣ01392/382800 or consult ⓦwww.devon.gov.uk/devonbus. The Sunday Rover ticket (£6) covers all transport on the moor, including the Exeter–Okehampton and Tamar Valley rail lines.

Princetown and the central moor

PRINCETOWN owes its growth to the proximity of Dartmoor Prison, a high-security jail originally constructed for POWs captured in the Napoleonic wars. The grim presence seeps into the village, which has a somewhat oppressed air and functional grey stone houses, some of them – like the parish church of St Michael – built by French and American prisoners. What Princetown lacks in beauty is amply compensated for by the surrounding countryside, the best of which lies immediately to the north.

Information on all of Dartmoor is given by the main **National Park information centre**, on the village's central green (daily: Easter–Oct 10am–5pm; Nov–March 10am–4pm; ⓣ01822/890414, ⓦwww.dartmoor-npa.gov.uk). One of the best places to stay is the non-smoking *Duchy House*, 200 yards from the centre, on Tavistock Road (ⓣ01822/890552, ⓔduchyhouse@aol.com; ❸; closed Nov), which has rooms with and without private bath. Two pubs in Princetown's central square also offer accommodation, the *Railway Inn* (ⓣ01822/890232; ❷) and the *Plume of Feathers* (ⓣ01822/890240; ❶); the latter claims to be the oldest building in town, and also has dormitory accommodation in two bunkhouses as well as a convenient **campsite** – standard bar food is always available.

Northeast of Princetown, two miles north of the crossroads at Two Bridges, the dwarfed and misshapen oaks of **Wistman's Wood** are an evocative relic of the original Dartmoor Forest, cluttered with lichen-covered boulders and a dense undergrowth of ferns. The gnarled old trees are alleged to have been the site of druidic gatherings, a story unsupported by any evidence but quite plausible in this solitary spot.

Three miles northeast of Two Bridges, the largest and best preserved of Dartmoor's **clapper bridges** crosses the East Dart river at **POSTBRIDGE**. Used by tin-miners and farmers since medieval times, these simple structures consist of huge slabs of granite supported by piers of the same material; another more basic example is at Two Bridges. The tiny settlement has a useful tourist office in the car park near the bridge (Easter–Oct 10am–5pm, Nov & Dec Sat & Sun 10am–4pm; ⓣ01822/880213), which can point out local walks. If you're not content with strolling up and down the river, you might decide to venture south through **Bellever Forest** to the open moor where **Bellever Tor** (1453ft) affords outstanding views. On the edge of the forest, a couple of miles south of Postbridge on the banks of the East Dart river, lies one of Dartmoor's three **youth hostels** (ⓣ0870/770 5692, ⓔbellever@yha.org.uk; closed Nov–Feb; £10.25) – it's on a minor road from Postbridge, accessible on Plymouth Citybus #98 from Tavistock, or else walk the mile from Postbridge. There's also a **camping barn** close to Bellever Forest at Runnage Farm with a bunkhouse and outdoor camping facilities alongside, and bikes available for rent – for this and any of Dartmoor's other camping barns, it's wise to book ahead, particularly at weekends: ⓣ0870/770 6113, ⓔcampingbarns@yha.org.uk. You'll find a lot more luxury in the riverside *Lydgate House Hotel*, signposted off the main road half a mile southwest of Postbridge and offering easy access to Bellever Forest and the moor (ⓣ01822/880209, ⓦwww.lydgatehouse.co.uk; no under-12s and no smoking; ➎). Two miles northeast of Postbridge, the solitary *Warren House Inn* offers warm, firelit comfort and **meals** in an unutterably bleak tract of moorland.

To the east of the B3212, reachable on a right turn towards Widecombe-in-the-Moor, the Bronze Age village of **Grimspound** lies below Hameldown Tor, about a mile off the road. Inhabited some three thousand years ago, when Dartmoor was fully forested and enjoyed a considerably warmer climate than it does today, this is the most complete example of Dartmoor's prehistoric settlements, consisting of 24 circular huts scattered within a four-acre enclosure. A stone wall nine-feet thick surrounds the huts, several of which have raised bed-places, and you can see how the villagers ensured a constant water supply by enclosing part of a stream with a wall. Grimspound itself is thought to have been the model for the Stone Age settlement in which Sherlock Holmes camped in *The Hound of the Baskervilles*, while **Hound Tor**, an outcrop three miles to the southwest, was the inspiration for Conan Doyle's tale – according to local legend, phantom hounds were sighted racing across the moor to hurl themselves on the tomb of a hated squire following his death in 1677. There's a **camping barn** here, *Great Houndtor*, with two upstairs sleeping areas, a cooking area and showers (ⓣ0870/770 6113 or ⓣ01647/221202).

Buckland-in-the-Moor and the southeastern moor

Four miles east of the crossroads at Two Bridges, **Dartmeet** marks the place where the East and West Dart rivers merge after tortuous journeys from their remote sources. Crowds home in on this beauty spot, but the valley is memorably lush and you don't need to walk far to leave the car park and ice-cream vans behind. From here the Dart pursues a more leisurely course, joined by the River Webburn near the pretty moorland village of **BUCKLAND-IN-THE-MOOR**, one of a cluster of moorstone-and-thatched hamlets on this southeastern side of the moor.

Four miles north is another candidate for most popular Dartmoor village, **WIDECOMBE-IN-THE-MOOR**, set in a hollow amid high granite-strewn ridges. Its church of **St Pancras** provides a famous local landmark, its pinnacled tower dwarfing the fourteenth-century main building, whose interior boasts a beautiful painted rood screen. Look out here too for the carved one-eared rabbits above the communion rail. The nearby **Church House** was built in the fifteenth century for weary churchgoers from outlying districts, and was later converted into almshouses. Widecombe's other claim to fame is the traditional song, *Widdicombe Fair*: the **fair** is still held annually on the second Tuesday of September, but is now primarily a tourist attraction. You could **stay** in Widecombe in the elegant *Old Rectory* (Ⓣ01364/621231, Ⓔrachel.belgrave@care4free.net; no credit cards; ❷), opposite the post office and set in a lovely garden; or try *Manor Cottage* (Ⓣ01364/621218; no credit cards; ❷), next to the post office, which has an inglenook fireplace in the dining room and a garden; packed lunches are also available. Half a mile out, *Higher Venton Farm* (Ⓣ01364/621235; no credit cards; ❷) is a peaceful thatched longhouse close to a couple of good pubs. You can **camp** at *Cockingford Farm*, one and a half miles south of Widecombe (Ⓣ01364/621258; closed mid-Nov to mid-March). There's also the *Dartmoor Riding* **pony-trekking** centre a mile outside the village at Shilstone Rocks (Ⓣ01364/621281), for tuition and excursions.

South of Buckland, the village of **HOLNE** is another rustic idyll surrounded on three sides by wooded valleys. The vicarage here was the birthplace of Charles Kingsley, author of *The Water Babies* and such Devon-based tales as *Westward Ho!*. A window commemorates him in the village church, which also has a whimsical epitaph on the grave of Edward Collins, landlord of the next-door *Church House* inn until 1780. The pub itself was built three hundred years before that, and offers excellent **meals** and some **accommodation** (Ⓣ01364/631208, Ⓦwww.churchhouse-holne.co.uk; ❸). Oliver Cromwell is said to have stayed here. On the edge of Holne, on the route of the Two Moors Way, there's a **camping barn** at Stone Barn, with good facilities (Ⓣ01364/631544), backing onto a small camping field.

A couple of miles east, the Dart weaves through a wooded green valley to enter the grounds of **Buckfast Abbey** (daily: May–Oct 9am–5.30pm; Nov–April 10am–4pm; free), a modern monastic complex occupying the site of an abbey founded in the eleventh century by Canute, abandoned two hundred years later, refounded, and finally dissolved by Henry VIII. The present buildings were the work of a handful of French Benedictine monks who consecrated their new abbey in 1932, though work on the other monastic buildings has continued until recently. The church itself is in a traditional Anglo-Norman style, following the design of the Cistercian building razed in 1535, and shows examples of the monks' dexterity in making stained-glass windows – which, along with honey, handicrafts and tonic wine, help to keep the community funded. An exhibition covers the abbey's history and displays its treasures.

Dartmoor's northern tors

A seven-mile, three-hour walk from Okehampton skirts the east of the MoD's Okehampton Range, brings you within view of the highest points on the moor, then plunges you into the recesses of the East Okement River, before rounding Belstone Common and returning north to Okehampton via the village of Belstone. From Okehampton, follow signs for Ball Hill and the East Okement Valley from the Mill Street car park near the centre, passing under the graceful arches of the **Fatherford Viaduct**, which carries the Exeter–Okehampton railway. Follow a well-defined path for about a mile through Halstock Wood, sloping down diagonally until meeting the East Okement River, which you can cross at **Chapel Ford** – a good spot for a pause. Walk up the eastern bank of the East Okement for five hundred yards before passing through an opening in the hedge, leaving the valley to head towards **Winter Tor**, a little more than a mile due south of the ford. At the tor, carry on up to the top of the ridge, from which a splendid panorama unfolds, with Dartmoor's highest peaks of **Yes Tor** (2028ft) and **High Willhays Tor** (2039ft) about three miles southwest. To the east the great bowl of Taw Marsh can be seen.

Follow the rock-strewn ridge northwards, to the rocky pinnacles of **Belstone Common**. Between **Higher Tor** and **Belstone Tor** you'll pass **Irishman's Wall**, the vestige of an attempt to enclose part of the moor against the wishes of the locals, who waited until the wall was nearly complete before gathering to push the structure down. Carry on heading north, descending sharply towards the **Nine Stones** cairn circle, seven hundred yards below Belstone Tor. This Bronze Age burial ground was popularly held to be the petrified remains of nine maidens turned to stone for dancing on Sunday (there are in fact twelve stones). A little way north, a track brings you northeast to the village of Belstone, half a mile away.

From Belstone, follow the road signed "Okehampton Indirect" for about half a mile northwest; you can then either turn left to Cleave House, descend to the river and return northwards up the East Okement to Okehampton, or continue along the road.

The northeastern moor

The essentially unspoilt market town of **MORETONHAMPSTEAD**, lying on the northeastern edge of the moor, makes an attractive entry point from Exeter – and, incidentally, shares with Woolfardisworthy (near Bideford) the honour of having the longest single-word place name in England. Local **information** is handled by a Visitor Information Point at 10 The Square (Easter–Oct daily 10am–5pm; Nov–Easter Fri–Sun 10am–5pm; ⓣ01647/440043). There's classy **accommodation** on the western edge of the village in the *Old Post House* in Court Street (ⓣ01647/440900, ⓦwww.theoldposthouse.com; no credit cards; non-smoking; ❷), a friendly B&B which welcomes walkers and will set you up with a packed lunch if required, and at *Cookshayes*, a little further out at 33 Court St (ⓣ01647/440374, ⓦwww.cookshayes.co.uk; ❷; closed Nov–Feb), offering good home cooking. The village also has a first-rate, centrally located independent **hostel**, *Sparrowhawk Backpackers*, at 45 Ford St (ⓣ01647/440318, ⓦwww.sparrowhawkbackpackers.co.uk), with dorm beds (£11) and private rooms sleeping four (❶). There's another hostel nearby: the *Steps Bridge* youth hostel (ⓣ0870/770 6048, ⓔbellever@yha.org.uk; closed Sept–March; dorm beds £9) is on the outskirts of **Dunsford**, three miles northeast of Moretonhampstead and right on the boundary of the National Park – buses #359 (between Exeter and Moretonhampstead, not Sun) and #82 stop nearby. Its woodland setting overlooking the Teign Gorge makes it a popular overnight stop for hikers.

Moretonhampstead has a historic rivalry with neighbouring **CHAGFORD**, a Stannary town (a chartered centre of the tin trade) that also enjoyed prosperity as a centre of the wool industry. It stands on a hillside overlooking the River Teign, with a fine fifteenth-century church on its edge and enough attractions within and around to keep its pubs and hotels in business. The ancient *Three Crowns Hotel* (ⓣ01647/433444, ⓦwww.chagford-accom.co.uk; ❹), facing the church, is one of a number of decent pubs in the village, and offers **accommodation**, though subject to noise from the church clock. A quieter alternative is the sixteenth-century *Cyprian's Cot*, 47 New St (ⓣ01647/432256, ⓦwww.dartmooraccommodation.co.uk; no credit cards; no smoking; ❸), where you can warm your bones at a log fire in an inglenook fireplace. There's also a renowned and very expensive **restaurant** in the village, the non-smoking *22 Mill Street* (ⓣ01647/432244, ⓦwww.22millstreet.co.uk; closed Sun and lunchtime Mon & Tues), which offers pricey, but top-quality modern cuisine. For diners only, there are also two en-suite rooms available (❸).

There are numerous **walks** to be made in the immediate vicinity, for instance to Fernworthy Reservoir, four miles to the southwest along signposted narrow lanes, or downstream along the Teign to the twentieth-century extravaganza of **Castle Drogo** (April–Oct Mon & Wed–Sun 11am–5.30pm; grounds daily 10.30am–dusk; £5.90, grounds only £3; NT), which occupies a stupendous site overlooking the Teign Gorge. Having retired at the age of 33, grocery magnate Julius Drewe unearthed a link that suggested his descent from a Norman baron, and set about creating a castle befitting his pedigree. Begun in 1910, to a design by **Sir Edwin Lutyens**, it was not completed until 1930, but the result was an unsurpassed synthesis of medieval and modern elements. The croquet lawn is available for use, with mallets for rent.

Paths lead from Drogo east to **Fingle Bridge**, one of Dartmoor's most noted beauty spots, where shaded green pools hold trout and the occasional salmon. The *Fingle Bridge Inn* here has an adjoining **restaurant**.

The north and northwestern moor

The main centre on the northern fringes of Dartmoor, **OKEHAMPTON** grew prosperous as a market town for the medieval wool trade, and some fine old buildings survive between the two branches of the River Okement that meet here, among them the prominent fifteenth-century tower of the **Chapel of St James**. Across the road from the seventeenth-century town hall, a granite archway leads into the **Museum of Dartmoor Life** (Easter–Sept Mon–Sat 10am–5pm, Sun 10am–4.30pm; Oct–Easter Mon–Sat 10am–5pm; £2.50; ⓦwww.museumofdartmoorlife.eclipse.co.uk), an excellent overview of habitation on the moor since earliest times. Four miles east of Okehampton at Sticklepath (bus #X9, #X10 or #171), **Finch Foundry** (April–Oct Mon & Wed–Sun 11am–5.30pm; £3; NT) is a Victorian forge with working machinery and demonstrations. Loftily perched above the West Okement on the other side of town, **Okehampton Castle** (April–Sept daily 10am–6pm; Oct daily 10am–5pm; £2.60; EH) is the shattered hulk of a stronghold laid waste by Henry VIII; its ruins include a gatehouse, Norman keep and the remains of the Great Hall, buttery and kitchens.

Okehampton's station, which provides a useful Sunday **rail** connection from Exeter between late May and late September) lies a fifteen-minute walk up Station Road from Fore Street in Okehampton's centre, where the **tourist office** (April, May & mid-Sept to Oct Mon–Sat 10am–4.30pm; June to mid-Sept daily 10am–5pm; Nov–March Mon, Fri & Sat 10am–4.30pm; ⓣ01837/53020, ⓦwww.okehamptondevon.co.uk) sits next to the museum.

Nearby on Fore Street the beamed *Fountain Hotel* (☎01837/53900; no smoking; ❹), an old coaching inn, offers very central **accommodation** in rooms with character, though cheaper B&B can be found a short walk north of here towards the station at *Meadowlea*, 65 Station Rd (☎01837/53200; no credit cards; ❷). If you prefer rural surroundings, you'll find the comfortable and spacious *Upcott House* on Upcott Hill, half a mile north of the centre (☎01837/53743, Ⓦwww.upcotthouse.com; no credit cards; ❷), while six miles north of Okehampton on the Hatherleigh Road, *Higher Cadham Farm* (☎01837/851647, Ⓦwww.highercadham.co.uk; closed 3 weeks Dec–Jan; ❸) is located right on the Tarka Trail, and offers oak-beamed ambience (with some rooms in a refurbished cowshed) and evening meals; it's signposted past the church at **Jacobstowe**. Okehampton's **youth hostel** (☎0870/770 5978, Ⓔokehampton@yha.org.uk; closed Dec & Jan; £13) provides four- and six-bed bunkrooms in a converted goods shed at the station, and offers a range of outdoor activities including rock climbing and pony trekking, as well as bikes for rent. The nicest **campsites** in the vicinity are the small *Yertiz* (☎01837/52281), three-quarters of a mile east of Okehampton on the B3260, and *Olditch Caravan and Camping Park*, Sticklepath (☎01837/840734, Ⓦwww.olditch.co.uk; closed mid-Nov to mid-March), which has walking access to the moor.

Okehampton has no great choice when it comes to **eating**, though the *Coffee Pot*, tucked away behind the museum in Fairplace Terrace, can be relied upon for breakfasts, coffees and meals (closed eve & Mon); *Le Café Noir* (closed Sun), across West Street in Red Lion Yard, is good for inexpensive lunches, and *Cellars Bistro*, a candlelit basement beside the river at 25 Fore St (☎01837/54242; no smoking; closed Sun & Mon), offers light lunches and moderately priced evening meals, with Mediterranean specialities. For **riding** on the moor, contact Skaigh Riding Stables (☎01837/840917) or Eastlake (☎01837/52513), both east of town in the Belstone/Sticklepath area.

Lydford

Five miles southwest of Okehampton, the village of **LYDFORD** boasts the sturdy but small-scale Lydford Castle, a Saxon outpost, then a Norman keep and later used as a prison. The chief attraction here, though, is **Lydford Gorge** (April–Sept 10am–5.30pm; Oct 10am–4pm; Nov–March 10.30am–3pm; £3.80; NT), whose main entrance is a five-minute walk downhill. Two routes – one above, one along the banks – follow the ravine burrowed through by the River Lyd as far as the hundred-foot White Lady Waterfall, coming back on the opposite bank. Overgrown with thick woods, the one-and-a-half-mile gorge is alive with butterflies, spotted woodpeckers, dippers, herons and clouds of insects. The full course would take you roughly two hours at a leisurely pace, though there is a separate entrance at the south end of the gorge if you only want to visit the waterfall. In winter months, when the river can flood, the waterfall is the only part of the gorge open.

Back in the village, the picturesque *Castle Inn* sits right next to the castle, and provides a fire-lit sixteenth-century bar where you can drink and snack, and also has an extensive beer garden. The inn offers en-suite **accommodation** in low-ceilinged oak-beamed rooms (☎01822/820242, Ⓔcastleinnlyd@aol.com; ❹), and there is a rather pricey but first-rate **restaurant** too, in a back room cluttered with curios and memorabilia; cheaper rooms are available at the family-run *Moorlands* (☎01822/820229; no credit cards; ❸), 300yd from the A386 on the Lydford turning. **Horse riding** in the area is on offer at the *Lydford House Hotel* (☎01822/820347, Ⓦwww.s-h-systems.co.uk; ❺).

The western moor

Southwest from Princetown, walkers can trace the grassy path of the defunct rail line to **Burrator Reservoir**, four miles away; flooded in the 1890s to provide water for Plymouth, this is the biggest stretch of water on Dartmoor. The wooded lakeside teems with wildlife, and the boulder-strewn slopes are overlooked by the craggy peaks of **Sharpitor** (1312ft) and **Sheep's Tor** (1150ft). From here, the best walk is to strike northwest to meet the valley of the **River Walkham**, which rises in a peat bog at Walkham Head, five miles north of Princetown, then scurries through moorland and woods to join the River Tavy at Double Waters, two miles south of Tavistock. The fast-flowing water attracts herons, kingfishers and other colourful birdlife, to be seen darting in and out of dense woods of alder, ash and sycamore.

The river crosses the B3357 Tavistock road at **MERRIVALE**, a tiny village with a decent **pub** (the *Dartmoor Arms*), four miles west of Princetown. Merrivale makes another good starting point for moorland walks – there's decent **camping** at *Higher Longford Caravan and Camping Park*, Moorshop, less than a mile out of Merrivale on the Tavistock Road (Ⓣ01822/613360, Ⓦwww.higherlongford.co.uk) – and it's only half a mile west of the most spectacular of Dartmoor's stone rows, the **Merrivale Megaliths**. Just a few yards from the B3357, the upright stones form a stately procession, stretching 850ft across the bare landscape. Dating from between 2500 BC and 750 BC, and probably connected with burial rites, the rows are known locally as "Potato Market" or "Plague Market" in memory of the time when provisions for plague-stricken Tavistock were deposited here. A mile to the southwest, on the western slopes of the Walkham valley, the sphinx-like pinnacle of **Vixen Tor** looms over the barren moor.

Tavistock

The main town of the western moor, **TAVISTOCK** owes its distinctive Victorian appearance to the building boom that followed the discovery of copper deposits here in 1844. Originally, however, this market and Stannary town on the River Tavy grew around what was once the West Country's most important Benedictine abbey, established in the eleventh century and, at the time of its dissolution, owning land as distant as the Isles of Scilly. Some scant remnants survive in the churchyard of **St Eustace**, a mainly fifteenth-century building with stained glass from William Morris's studio in the south aisle.

Half a mile south of Tavistock, on the Plymouth Road, stands a statue of Francis Drake, who was born and raised on Crowndale Farm, a mile south of town; the statue on Plymouth Hoe is a replica of this one.

Tavistock's **tourist office**, in the town hall on Bedford Square (Easter to late July & early Sept to Oct Mon–Sat 9.30am–5pm; late July to early Sept daily 9.30am–5pm; Nov–Easter Mon, Tues, Fri & Sat 10am–4.30pm; Ⓣ01822/612938), can supply you with information on the western moor, for which the town would make an ideal base. There's a good range of **accommodation** choices, including *Kingfisher Cottage*, Mount Tavy Road (Ⓣ01822/613801, Ⓔkingfisher.cott@btopenworld.com; no smoking; no credit cards; ❷), and, about half a mile east of Tavistock off the B3357 Princetown Road, *Mount Tavy Cottage* (Ⓣ01822/614253, Ⓦwww.mounttavy.freeserve.co.uk; ❸), set in a lush garden and offering organic breakfasts; self-catering accommodation is also offered here. There's a **campsite** two miles east of Tavistock on the B3357 near Merrivale (see above). **Bikes** can be rented from Tavistock Cycles, Paddons Row, Brook St (Ⓣ01822/617630), and Dartmoor Cycles, 6 Atlas House, West Devon Business Park, next to Safeway supermarket (Ⓣ01837/618718).

North of Tavistock, a four-mile lane wanders up to **Brent Tor**, 1130ft high and dominating Dartmoor's western fringes. Access to its conical summit is easiest along a path gently ascending through gorse on its southwestern side, leading to the small church of St Michael at the top. Bleak, treeless moorland extends in every direction, wrapped in silence that's occasionally pierced by the shrill cries of stonechats and wheatears. A couple of miles eastwards, **Gibbet Hill** looms over Black Down and the ruined stack of the abandoned Wheal Betsy silver and lead mine.

North Devon

From Exeter the A377 runs alongside the scenic Tarka Line railway to **North Devon**'s major town, **Barnstaple**. Within easy reach of here, the resorts of **Ilfracombe** and **Woolacombe** draw the crowds, though the fine sandy beaches surrounding the latter give ample opportunity to find your own space. The river port of **Bideford** gives its name to a long bay that holds another beach resort, **Westward Ho!**, as well as the precipitous village of **Clovelly**, perhaps Devon's most famous beauty spot. Inspiring coastal walks follow the bay, particularly to the stormy **Hartland Point** and beyond. Away from the coast, there is plenty of scope for walking and cycling along the Tarka Trail long-distance path, passing through some of the region's loveliest countryside, while for a complete break, the tiny island of **Lundy** provides further opportunities for stretching the legs and clearing the lungs.

Barnstaple

BARNSTAPLE, at the head of the Taw estuary, makes an excellent North Devon base, being well connected to the resorts of Bideford Bay, Ilfracombe and Woolacombe, as well as to the western fringes of Exmoor. The town's centuries-old role as a marketplace is perpetuated in the daily bustle around the huge timber-framed **Pannier Market** off the High Street, alongside which runs **Butchers Row**, its 33 archways now converted to a variety of uses. Also off the High Street, in the pedestrianized area, lies Barnstaple's **parish church**, itself worth a look, and the fourteenth-century **St Anne's Chapel**, converted into a grammar school in 1549 and later numbering among its pupils John Gay, author of *The Beggar's Opera*; it's now closed to the public (though you can apply at the tourist office for the key). At the end of Boutport Street, make time to visit the **Museum of North Devon** (Tues–Sat 10am–4.30pm; free), a lively miscellany including wildlife displays and a collection of eighteenth-century pottery for which the region was famous. The museum lies alongside the Taw, where footpaths make for a pleasant riverside stroll, with the colonnaded eighteenth-century **Queen Anne's Walk** – built as a merchants' exchange – providing some architectural interest and housing the **Barnstaple Heritage Centre** (April–Oct Mon–Sat 10am–5pm; Nov–March Mon–Fri 10am–4.30pm, Sat 10am–3.30pm; £2.50), which traces the town's social history by means of reconstructions and touch-screen computers.

Barnstaple's well-equipped **tourist office** lies within the Museum of North Devon (Mon–Sat 9.30am–5pm; ⓣ01271/375000, ⓦwww.staynorthdevon.co.uk). There are plenty of **places to stay** in town, one of them five hundred yards south of Long Bridge, at the bottom of the High Street: *Ivy House*, Victoria Road, off Newport Road (ⓣ01271/325167, ⓔivy.grundy@btopenworld.com; no smoking; no credit cards; ❷), an elegant B&B with some rooms en suite.

The Tarka Line and the Tarka Trail

Henry Williamson's *Tarka the Otter* (1927), rated by some as one of the finest pieces of nature writing in the English language, has been appropriated as a promotional device by the Devon tourist industry. As parts of the book are set in the Taw valley, it was inevitable that the Exeter to Barnstaple rail route – which follows the Taw for half of its length – should be dubbed the **Tarka Line**. Leaving almost hourly from Exeter St David's Station, trains on this branch line cut through the sparsely populated heart of Devon, the biggest town en route being **Crediton**, ancient birthplace of St Boniface (patron saint of Germany and the Netherlands) and site of the bishopric before its transfer to Exeter in the eleventh century.

Barnstaple forms the centre of the figure-of-eight traced by the **Tarka Trail**, which tracks the otter's wanderings for a distance of over 180 miles. To the north, the trail penetrates Exmoor then follows the coast back, passing through Williamson's home village of **Georgeham** on its return to Barnstaple. South, the path takes in Bideford (see p.475), following a disused rail line to Meeth, and continuing as far as Okehampton (see p.469), before swooping up via Eggesford, the point at which the Tarka Line joins the Taw valley.

Twenty-three miles of the trail follow a former rail line that's ideally suited to **bicycles**, and there are rental shops at Barnstaple (near the train station), and Bideford (see p.476). Sculptures have been placed along the route to mark its inclusion in the National Cycle Network. A good ride from Barnstaple is to **Torrington** (fifteen miles south), where you can eat at the *Puffing Billy* pub, formerly the train station.

Tourist offices give out leaflets on individual sections of the trail, but the best overall book is *The Tarka Trail: A Walker's Guide* (Devon Books; £4.95), available from tourist offices or bookshops.

A little further out, on Landkey Road – a continuation of Newport Road – is the first-rate *Mount Sandford* (☎01271/342354; no credit cards; ❷), a Regency building with a beautiful garden. Convenient for the station, *Herton* (☎01271/323302; no credit cards; ❷) is a semi-rural B&B out on Lake Road (left onto Sticklepath Terrace, then left again) that boasts its own tennis court, a twenty-minute walk from the centre. On a plusher note, the Victorian *Royal & Fortescue Hotel* off the square on Boutport Street (☎01271/342289, Ⓦwww.royalfortescue.co.uk; ❺) is a rather formal place with a decent café-bistro on the ground floor. With your own transport, you could spend less and have a more interesting stay at *Broomhill Art Hotel*, Muddiford, signposted two miles north of Barnstaple off the A39, a striking combination of gallery, restaurant and hotel (☎01271/850262, Ⓦwww.broomhillart.co.uk; no credit cards; ❹), where the en-suite rooms overlook a sculpture garden, and there's a pool and tennis court.

You can pick up coffees and **snacks** at the *Old School Coffee House*, a building dating from 1659 on Church Lane, near St Anne's Chapel, and the coolly modern *PV*, 70 Boutport St (closed Sun), has a moderately priced upstairs **restaurant** and the ground floor becomes a wine bar in the evening. On Butchers Row, *Jan's Kitchen* at no. 14 (closed Sun) serves baguettes and lamb and mint pasties and breakfasts, while *Marshford Organic Produce* sells pies, breads and other wholefoods to take away. Out of town, the moderately priced *Broomhill Restaurant*, part of the *Broomhill Art Hotel* (see above), lays on delicious Mediterranean-style meals (closed all Sun, Mon & Tues, also Wed in winter, and eves Mon–Thurs & Sun). For a **drink**, the *Corner House* pub on the corner of Joy Street and Boutport Street has a 1930s feel, with wooden panelling, guest beers and homemade food. At the top end of the High Street, conveniently placed for the northern section of the Tarka Trail towards Braunton, the *Rolle Quay Inn* on Rolle Street can provide lunches to eat in or take as a picnic, and also has accommodation (❷). Cyclists can **rent bikes** from Tarka Trail Cycle Hire at the train station (⊕01271/324202).

Ilfracombe and around

The most popular resort on Devon's northern coast, **ILFRACOMBE** is essentially little changed since its evolution into a Victorian and Edwardian tourist centre, large-scale development having been restricted by the surrounding cliffs. Nonetheless, the relentless pressure to have fun and the ubiquitous smell of chips can become oppressive, though in summer you can always pop down to the small harbour and escape on a coastal tour, a cruise to Lundy Island (see p.478) or a fishing trip. An attractive stretch of coast runs east out of Ilfracombe, beyond the grassy cliffs of Hillsborough, where a succession of undeveloped coves and inlets is surrounded by jagged slanting rocks and heather-covered hills. Three miles to the east, above the almost enclosed Watermouth Bay, lies **Watermouth Castle** (Mon–Fri & Sun: Easter–June & Oct 10am–4pm; July & Sept 10am–6pm; last admission 1hr before closing; £8.50), an imposing nineteenth-century mansion, best admired from the outside unless you have kids, who will appreciate the water shows, dungeons and carousel.

The pick of the **beaches** in the area – indeed the best on Devon's northern coast – are round **Morte Point**, five miles west of Ilfracombe, from which the view takes in the island of Lundy, fifteen miles out to sea. Below the promontory stretches a rocky shore whose menacing sunken reef inspired the Normans to give it the name Morte Stone. A break in the rocks makes space for the pocket-sized **Barricane Beach**, famous for the tropical shells washed here from the Caribbean by the Atlantic currents, and a popular swimming spot. Luckily there's room for everyone on the two miles of **Woolacombe Sands**, a broad, west-facing expanse much favoured by surfers and families alike. The beach can get crowded towards its northern end, where a cluster of hotels, villas and retirement homes makes up the summer resort of **WOOLACOMBE**. At the quieter southern end, **Putsborough Sands** is a choice swimming spot bracketed by **Baggy Point**, where from September to November the air is a swirl of gannets, shags, cormorants and shearwaters. South of this promontory, **Croyde Bay** is another surfers' delight, more compact than Woolacombe, with stalls on the sand renting surfboards and wet-suits, while **Saunton Sands** is a magnificent long stretch of coast pummelled by endless ranks of classic breakers.

Practicalities

From Barnstaple, First Red Bus #3 and #30 (not Sun) runs daily several times an hour to Ilfracombe, and the frequent #303 (not Sun) runs to Woolacombe. From Minehead and Lynton, take the three-times-daily "Exmoor Coastlink" #300. You can reach Woolacombe from Ilfracombe on First Red Bus #31 and #31a, while DevonBus #308 travels from Barnstaple to Croyde, via Saunton. There's no service between Woolacombe and Croyde. The Ilfracombe **tourist office** is at the Landmark on the seafront (Easter–July & Oct Mon–Sat 10am–5pm, Sun 10am–4pm; Aug & Sept daily 10am–5.30pm; Nov–Easter Mon–Sat 10am–5pm, Sat 10am–4pm; ⊕01271/863001, Ⓦwww.ilfracombe-tourism.co.uk).

Ilfracombe has a good range of **accommodation**, including inexpensive **B&Bs** such as the Victorian *Wentworth House*, at the top of Church Hill on Belmont Road (⊕01271/863048; no credit cards; ❷), which has gardens and rooms with and without bathrooms, and hotels, among them the *Sherborne Lodge Hotel*, Torrs Park (Ⓣ01271/862297; ❷), a roomy Victorian villa with a bar and dining room in a quiet area of town west of the centre. There's also an excellent independent **hostel**, *Ocean Backpackers*, near the bus station and harbour at 29 St James Place (Ⓣ01271/867835, Ⓦwww.oceanbackpackers.co.uk), offering dorm beds at £11 and double rooms (❶). The area's best **campsites** are around Morte Point – good choices are *North Morte Farm* (Ⓣ01271/870381, Ⓦwww.northmortefarm.co.uk; closed Oct–Easter), unsheltered, but with panoramic views and 500yds from the beach and also offering caravans for rent, or try the *Little Meadow* site at Lydford Farm (Ⓣ01271/862222; closed Oct–Easter), connected by footpath to Watermouth Castle and the beach – bus #30 goes there. Not yet open at the time of writing but already Ilfracombe's most famous **restaurant**, *No. 11, The Quay*, promises to be a quality seafood eaterie owned by artist Damien Hirst. Prices in the first-floor dining area start at around £35 a head, though the more relaxed *Colonial Bar* on the ground floor serves Mediterranean food at more affordable prices. A very different atmosphere is offered at the *Atlantis*, a friendly international restaurant run by *Ocean Backpackers* (see above), with ambient, world and jazz musical background (closed Oct–Easter); *Swivel*, 155 High St, is a modern **bar** with cocktails and a laid-back atmosphere, and a dance area downstairs (closed Sun).

In **Woolacombe**, *Sandunes* is one of a number of B&Bs on Beach Road (Ⓣ01271/870661; no smoking; no credit cards; ❷), minutes from the beach and with views; two rooms have large balconies. Surfers and others gather at the *Red Barn*, a popular **bar** and **restaurant** just behind the beach (closed Sun eve). In **Croyde**, *Parminter*, at 16 St Mary's Rd (Ⓣ01271/890030; no credit cards; ❸), has large rooms in two converted barns and friendly owners; the *Thatch* pub is the local hangout. Woolacombe's **tourist office** is on the Esplanade (Easter–Oct Mon–Sat 10am–5pm, Sun 10am–3pm; Nov–Easter Mon–Sat 10am–4pm; Ⓣ01271/870553, Ⓦwww.woolacombetourism.co.uk).

Bideford Bay

BIDEFORD BAY (sometimes called Barnstaple Bay) encapsulates the variety of Devon, encompassing the downmarket beach resort of **Westward Ho!**, the savage windlashed rocks of **Hartland Point** and the photogenic village of **Clovelly**. **Instow** and **Appledore**, sheltered towns in the mouth of the Torridge estuary, have a lower-key attraction, while **Bideford** itself is mainly a transit centre, with some decent accommodation and bus connections to all the towns on the bay, and regular boats for Lundy.

Bideford

Like Barnstaple, nine miles to the east, the estuary town of **BIDEFORD** formed an important link in the north Devon trade network, mainly due to its **bridge**, which still straddles the River Torridge. First built in 1300, the bridge was reconstructed in stone in the following century, and subsequently reinforced and widened, hence the irregularity of its 24 arches, no two of which have the same span. Bideford's greatest prosperity arose in the seventeenth and eighteenth centuries, when it enjoyed a flourishing trade with the New World, and today the tree-lined quay along the west riverbank is still the focal point for the knot of narrow shop-lined streets.

From the Norman era until the eighteenth century, the port was the property of the Grenville family, whose most celebrated scion was **Richard Grenville**, commander of the ships that carried the first settlers to Virginia, and later a major player in the defeat of the Spanish Armada. Grenville also featured in *Westward Ho!*, the historical romance by **Charles Kingsley** who wrote part of the book in Bideford and is thus commemorated by a statue at the quay's northern end. Behind, **Victoria Park** extends up the riverbank, containing guns captured from the Spanish in 1588.

Alongside the park is the **tourist office** (Easter–June & Sept Mon–Sat 10am–5pm, Sun 10am–1pm; July & Aug Mon–Sat 10am–5pm, Sun 10am–4pm; Oct–Easter Mon, Tues, Thurs & Fri 10am–4.30pm, Wed & Sat 10am–1pm; ⓣ01237/477676, ⓦwww.torridge.gov.uk), from which you can pick up an accommodation list as well as information on coastal cruises and the boat to Lundy (see p.478) – tickets from here or the booths along the quayside. A useful **B&B** nearby is the *Cornerhouse*, 14 The Strand, two minutes from Victoria Park (ⓣ01237/473722, ⓦwww.cornerhouse-guesthouse.co.uk; no credit cards; ❷), or opt for the attractive *Mount* (ⓣ01237/473748, ⓦwww.themount1.cjb.net; ❸), further out on Northdown Road, but linked to the centre by a footpath, and set in its own walled garden; both are non-smoking. The swanky *Royal Hotel* (ⓣ01237/472005, ⓦwww.royalbideford.co.uk; ❹), just over the old bridge on Barnstaple Street, whose oak-panelled Kingsley Room is named after Charles Kingsley who penned much of his novel *Westward Ho!* at the hotel. For a **meal** or a drink, head up Bridge Street from Bideford's bridge to Market Place, where the porticoed *Old Coach Inn* provides ales and hearty snacks, while the more up-to-date *Praxis II* across the square has French sticks, quiches and lasagne during the day (closed Wed pm & all Sun; no credit cards).

For exploring the Tarka Trail by **bike**, there's Bideford Bicycle Hire, Torrington St (ⓣ01237/424123), 200yd south of the bridge on the far riverbank.

Appledore and Instow

The old shipbuilding port of **APPLEDORE**, near the confluence of the Taw and Torridge rivers, still has several operating boatyards and a small sailing fleet moored in the river, but the peaceful pastel-coloured Georgian houses give little hint of the extent of the industry in earlier times. Take time to explore West Appledore and walk along Irsha Street where you can stop for a pint and enjoy the view at the *Royal George* or *Beaver Inn*. There are a few **B&Bs** overlooking the estuary on Marine Parade, including *Regency House* at no. 2 (ⓣ01237/473689; ❷); further along the Quay, there's the plain *Seagate Hotel* (ⓣ01237/472589; ❸), where you'll be charged extra for a room with a view. Pub **meals** are also available here.

In summer, foot passengers can take the five-minute **ferry** journey (late May to mid-Oct; every 15min during high tide; £1.80, plus £1 for bikes) across to **INSTOW**, whose sandy beach stretches in a long line, broadening to a muddy flat at low tide. There's little more than a couple of pubs serving snacks here, and a cosy **B&B**: *Lovistone*, 3 Lyndale Terrace (ⓣ01271/860676; no credit cards; no smoking; ❷), at the southern end of the village.

Westward Ho!

WESTWARD HO!, three miles northwest of Bideford, is the only English town to be named after a book. After the publication of Kingsley's historical romance in 1855, speculators recognized the tourist potential of what was then an empty expanse of sand and mud pounded by Atlantic rollers, and the town's first villa was built within a decade. Rudyard Kipling spent four years of his youth here, as described by him in *Stalky and Co*, and his presence is recalled in Kipling Terrace – the site of his school – and **Kipling Tors**, the heights at the west end of the three-mile sand and pebble beach, affording excellent views.

Kingsley didn't think much of the new resort when he paid a visit, and he certainly wouldn't care for it now, with its spawning amusement arcades, caravan sites and holiday chalets, and its substandard sea water. You might content yourself with the **walk** along the magnificent beach, however, or else across **Northam Burrows** extending behind it – a flat, marshy expanse of dunes and meadows rich in flora and attracting plenty of migratory birds.

Clovelly

The impossibly picturesque village of **CLOVELLY**, which must have featured on more calendars, biscuit boxes and tourist posters than anywhere else in the West Country, was put on the map in the second half of the nineteenth century by two books: Charles Dickens' *A Message From the Sea* and, inevitably, *Westward Ho!* – Charles Kingsley's father was rector here for six years. To an extent, the tone of the village has been preserved since then by limiting hotel accommodation and precluding holiday homes, but on summer days it's impossible to see past the artifice. Although the strict commercial control has meant that the presence of coach parties has been contained, there's still a fairly regular stream of visitors.

The first hurdle to surmount is the **visitor centre** (daily: April–Oct 9am–5pm; Nov–March 10am–4pm; ⓦwww.clovelly.co.uk), where you are charged £4 for access to shops, snack bars and an audiovisual show, and also for use of the car park (there's nowhere else to leave your motor). Walkers, cyclists and users of public transport have free right of way to the village (there's a separate entrance to the right of the visitor centre). Below the centre, the cobbled, traffic-free main street plunges down past neat, flower-smothered cottages where sledges are tethered for transporting goods – the only way to carry supplies since the use of donkeys ceased.

At the bottom lies Clovelly's stony beach and tiny harbour, snuggled under a cleft in the cliff wall. A lifeboat operates from here, and a handful of fishing boats are the only remnants of a fleet that provided the village's main business before the herring stocks became depleted. The jetty was built in the fourteenth century to shelter the coast's only safe harbour between Appledore and Boscastle in Cornwall. If you can't face the return climb, take the Land Rover, which leaves about every fifteen minutes from behind the *Red Lion* (Easter–Oct 9am–5.30pm; £2, or £3 return) back to the top of the village. It is here, immediately below the visitor centre, that Hobby Drive begins, a three-mile **walk** you can make along the cliffs through woods of sycamore, oak, beech, rowan and the occasional holly, with grand views over the village.

You can reach Clovelly by Western National **bus** #319, which traces a route from Barnstaple to Hartland, also passing through Bideford. There are just two **hotels** in the village, both pricey: the *New Inn* halfway down the High Street (ⓣ01237/431303, ⓔnewinn@clovelly.co.uk; ❼), and, enjoying a superb position, the *Red Lion* at the harbour (ⓣ01237/431237, ⓔredlion@clovelly.co.uk; ❽). Below the *New Inn* is a small **B&B**, *Donkey Shoe Cottage* (ⓣ01237/431601; no credit cards; ❷), which you should book a long way in advance. There's a greater selection of guest houses a twenty-minute walk up from the visitor centre in Higher Clovelly: try *Boat House Cottage*, on the main road (ⓣ01237/431209; no credit cards; ❷) or, further out – but just ten minutes' walk from lower Clovelly along a track through fields – *Fuchsia Cottage* on Burscott Lane (ⓣ01237/431398; no smoking; no credit cards; ❷), a modern house with views from its first-floor rooms. Clovelly's best **eating** option is the *Red Lion*, which offers a two-course dinner for £20.

Hartland Point and around

You could drive along minor roads to **Hartland Point**, ten miles west of Clovelly, but the best approach is on foot along the coastal path. Shortly before arriving, the path touches at the only sandy beach between Westward Ho! and the Cornish border, **Shipload Bay**. The headland presents one of Devon's most dramatic sights, its jagged black rocks battered by the sea and overlooked by a solitary lighthouse 350ft up. South of Hartland Point, the saw-toothed rocks and near-vertical escarpments defiantly confront the waves, with spectacular waterfalls tumbling over the cliffs. This sheer stretch of coast has seen dozens of shipwrecks over the centuries, though many must have been prevented by the sight of the tower of fourteenth-century **St Nectan's** – a couple of miles south of the point in the village of **STOKE** – which acted as a landmark to sailors before the construction of the lighthouse. At 128ft, it is the tallest church tower in north Devon, and overlooks a weathered old graveyard containing memorials to various members of the Lane family – of the Bodley Head and Penguin publishing empire – who were associated with the area; inside, the church boasts a finely carved rood screen and a Norman font, all covered by a repainted wagon-type roof. Tea and homemade scones are served at *Stoke Barton Farm*, just opposite (Easter–Sept Tues–Thurs, Sat & Sun).

Half a mile east of the church, gardens and lush woodland surround **Hartland Abbey** (May, June & Sept Wed, Thurs & Sun 2–5.30pm; July & Aug also Tues 2–5.30pm; gardens April–Sept daily except Sat 2–5.30pm; £6), an eighteenth-century country house incorporating the ruins of an abbey dissolved in 1539, and displaying fine furniture, old photographs and recently uncovered frescoes. There's a nice walk through grounds to the beach here. **HARTLAND** itself, further inland, holds little appeal beyond its three pubs and café, but on the coast, **Hartland Quay** deserves a linger: once a busy port, financed in part by the mariners Raleigh, Drake and Hawkins, it was mostly destroyed by storms in the nineteenth century, and now holds a solitary pub and hotel, surrounded by beautiful slate cliffs. About one mile south of here, **Speke's Mill Mouth** is a select surfers' beach.

Accommodation options in the area are scattered, and you'll need your own transport unless you stay in Hartland itself, where you'll find a small, friendly B&B, at 2 Harton Manor, North St, off Fore St (☎01237/441670; no credit cards; ❷). For proximity to the sea, you can't do better than the *Hartland Quay Hotel*, Hartland Quay (☎01237/441218; ❸), but if you want to be nearer Shipload Bay and Hartland Point, try *West Titchberry Farm* (☎01237/441287; no credit cards; ❷), for which you should follow signs for Hartland Lighthouse. In nearby Stoke, *Stoke Barton Farm* (see above) also provides basic **camping** facilities (☎01237/441238), while further south, at Elmscott, at the end of a three-and-a-half-mile signposted footpath from Hartland, and about half a mile from the sea, there's a **youth hostel** in a converted Victorian schoolhouse (☎0870/770 5814; closed mid-Sept to mid-April; £10.25). The only public transport is bus #319 from Barnstaple; alight at Hartland.

Lundy Island

There are fewer than twenty full-time residents on **Lundy**, a tiny windswept island twelve miles north of Hartland Point. Now a refuge for thousands of marine birds, Lundy has no cars, just one pub and one shop – indeed little has changed since the Marisco family established itself here in the twelfth century, making use of the shingle beaches and coves to terrorize shipping along the Bristol Channel. The family's fortunes only fell in 1242 when one of their number, William de Marisco, was found to be plotting against the king, whereupon he was hung, drawn and quartered at Tower Hill in London.

After the Mariscos, Lundy's most famous inhabitants were Thomas Benson, MP for Barnstaple in the eighteenth century – who was discovered using slave labour to work the granite quarries, and later found guilty of a massive insurance fraud – and **William Hudson Heaven**, who bought the island in 1834 and established what became known as the "Kingdom of Heaven". His home, **Millcombe House**, an incongruous piece of Georgian architecture in the desolate surroundings, is one of many relics of former habitation scattered around the island, though a recent addition compared with the castle standing on Lundy's southern end, which was erected by Henry III following the downfall of the Mariscos.

Today the island is managed by the Landmark Trust. **Walking** is really the only thing to do here, along the interweaving tracks and footpaths. Inland, the grass, heather and bog is crossed by dry-stone walls and grazed by ponies, goats, deer and the rare soay sheep. The shores – mainly cliffy on the west, softer and undulating on the east – shelter a rich variety of **birdlife**, including kittiwakes, fulmars, shags and Manx shearwaters, which often nest in rabbit burrows. The most famous birds, though, are the **puffins** after which Lundy is named – from the Norse *Lunde* (puffin) and *ey* (island). They can only be sighted in April and May, when they come ashore to mate. Offshore, **grey seals** can be seen all the year round.

Practicalities

The *MS Oldenburg* sails to Lundy up to six times a week from Bideford or Ilfracombe between March and October, taking around two hours from both places. Day return tickets cost around £25, period returns £42; to reserve a place, call ⓣ01271/863636 (day returns can also be booked from local tourist offices). Between November and March, a helicopter service from Hartland Point (see opposite) takes over, taking just seven minutes (currently Mon & Fri at midday, £69 return).

Accommodation on the island can be booked up months in advance, and B&B is only available in houses that have not already been taken for weekly rentals. Since B&B bookings can only be made within two weeks of the proposed visit, this limits the options, though outside the holiday season it is still possible to find a double room for under £50 per night. **Bookings** must be made through the Landmark Trust's office in Maidenhead (ⓣ01628/825925). Options range from the remote *Admiralty Lookout* (lacking electricity and with only hand-pumped water), through the two-storey granite *Barn*, a hostel sleeping fourteen, to the comfortable *Old House*, where Charles Kingsley stayed in 1849, and the *Old Light*, a lighthouse built in 1820 by the architect of Dartmoor Prison. A single person might find the *Radio Room* cosy; it once housed the radio transmitter that was the island's only link with the outside world. There's also a **campsite** on the island open throughout the year, though it can get pretty rainy and windswept in winter. More information on transport and accommodation can be found on the island's website, ⓦwww.lundyisland.co.uk.

Exmoor

A high bare plateau sliced by wooded combes and splashing rivers, **EXMOOR** can be one of the most forbidding landscapes in England, especially when its sea mists fall. When it's clear, though, the moorland of this National Park reveals rich swathes of colour and an amazing diversity of wildlife, from buzzards to the unique **Exmoor ponies**, a species closely related to prehistoric horses. In the treeless heartland of the moor around **Simonsbath**, in particular, it's not difficult to spot these short and stocky animals, though fewer than twelve hundred are registered, and of these only about two hundred are free-living on the moor. Much more elusive are the **red deer**, England's largest native wild animal, of which Exmoor supports England's only wild population. The effect of hunting through the centuries has accounted for a drastic depletion in numbers, though they have a strong recovery rate, and about two and half thousand are thought to inhabit the moor today, their annual culling is a regular point of issue among conservationists and nature-lovers.

Endless permutations of **walking routes** are possible along a network of some six hundred miles of footpaths and bridleways. In addition, the National Park Authority and other local organizations have put together a programme of guided walks, graded according to distance, speed and duration and costing £3–5 per person. Contact any of the visitor centres or else contact the National Park base at Dulverton (ⓣ01398/323841, ⓦwww.exmoor-nationalpark.gov.uk) for details. **Horseback** is another option for getting the most out of Exmoor's desolate beauty, and stables are dotted throughout the area – the most convenient are mentioned below; expect to pay around £12 an hour. Whether walking or riding, bear in mind that over seventy percent of the National Park is privately owned and that access is theoretically restricted to public rights of way; special permission should certainly be sought before camping, canoeing, fishing or similar.

There are four obvious bases for inland walks, all on the Somerset side of the county border: **Dulverton** in the southeast, site of the main information facilities and useful also for excursions into the neighbouring Brendon Hills; **Simonsbath** in the centre; **Exford**, near Exmoor's highest point of Dunkery Beacon; and the attractive village of **Winsford**, close to the A396 on the east of the moor. Exmoor's coastline offers an alluring alternative to the open moorland, all of it accessible via the **South West Coast Path**, which embarks on its long coastal journey at **Minehead**, though there is more charm to be found farther west at the sister-villages of **Lynmouth** and **Lynton**, just over the Devon border.

Getting around

Minehead stands at the end of the **West Somerset Railway**, but otherwise you have to rely on infrequent local **buses** for public transport. The main lines are run in the summer only. Looping between Minehead, Dunster, Wheddon Cross, Exford and Porlock, the #285 (Mon, Wed & Fri from late July to late Aug; Mon–Fri from late May to late July and late Aug to late Sept), and the #400 Exmoor Explorer vintage bus service, which is open-top in fine weather (Sat & Sun between Easter and the end of Sept, also Tues & Thurs from late July to late Aug). Services #307, connecting Dulverton with Taunton and Barnstaple, and #398, between Minehead, Dunster, Wheddon Cross, Dulverton and Tiverton, run throughout the year (not Sun). In winter there are also a few once- or twice-weekly community buses connecting Dulverton, Minehead and Lynton. On the coast, the most useful route is the #300 (three times daily: Easter–Oct daily; Nov–Easter Sat & Sun only) connecting Minehead with Lynton and Ilfracombe, extending as far as Taunton on one of its journeys; while the #38 runs nine times daily between Minehead and Porlock (not Sun). If you're planning to make good use of the buses, purchase a money-saving "First Day Southwest" ticket (£5), valid for one day's travel, available from the bus driver.

Dulverton

The village of **DULVERTON**, on the southern edge of the National Park, is the Park Authority's headquarters and so makes a good introduction to Exmoor. Information on the whole moor is available at the **visitor centre**, 7 Fore St (daily: April–Oct 10am–1.15pm & 1.45–5pm; Nov–March 11am–3pm; ⓣ01398/323841). Dulverton's best **accommodation** choice is *Town Mills* (ⓣ01398/323124; ❸), an old mill house in the centre of the village. If the handful of other options are full, or you hanker after beams and four-posters, try the equally central but slightly more expensive *Lion Hotel* in Bank Square (ⓣ01398/323444; ❹), or the relaxed *Crispin's*, off 26 High St (ⓣ01398/323397; ❷), which has one double and a suite with a sitting room and kitchenette. With its small garden, this is also the place to come for moderately priced snacks and full evening **meals**, while further down the High Street, *Lewis's Tea Rooms* serves teas and snacks. Moorland **horse riding** and tuition at all levels is offered at West Anstey Farm (ⓣ01398/341354), a couple of miles west of Dulverton; there's also a **camping barn** here.

Winsford

Just west of the A396 five miles north of Dulverton, **WINSFORD** – birthplace of the renowned Labour politician Ernest Bevin – lays good claim to being the moor's prettiest village. A scattering of thatched cottages ranged around a sleepy green, it is watered by a confluence of streams and rivers – one of them the Exe – giving it no fewer than seven bridges. *Larcombe Foot* (ⓣ01643/851306; no credit cards; ❷; closed Dec–Feb), one mile to the north, offers excellent **B&B** overlooking the Exe, and there's a well-equipped **campsite** a mile southwest of the village at *Halse Farm* (ⓣ01643/851259, ⓦwww.halsefarm.co.uk; closed Nov to mid-March). The *Royal Oak*, a thatched and

Walks from Dulverton and Tarr Steps

The most popular short walk from Dulverton goes along the east bank of the Barle to the seventeen-span medieval bridge at **Tarr Steps**, five miles to the northwest. You could combine this walk with a hike up **Winsford Hill**, a circular walk of less than four hours from Tarr Steps. Follow the riverside path upstream from Tarr Steps, turning right after about half a mile along Watery Lane, a rocky track that deteriorates into a muddy lane near Knaplock Farm. Stay on the track until you reach a cattle-grid, on open moorland. Turn left here, cross a small stream and climb up Winsford Hill, a heather moor whose 1400-foot summit is invisible until you are almost there. At the top, from where there are views as far as Dartmoor, you can see the **Wambarrows**, three Bronze Age burial mounds. If you want a refreshment stop, descend the hill on the other side to the village of Winsford.

A quarter-mile due east of the barrows, the ground drops sharply by more than two hundred feet to the Punchbowl, a bracken-grown depression resembling an amphitheatre. Keep on the east side of the B3223 which runs up Winsford Hill, following it south for a mile, until you come across the **Caractacus Stone**, an inscribed stone just by Spire Cross. The stone is thought to date from between 450 and 650, the damaged inscription reading "Carataci Nepos" – that is, "kinsman of Caractacus", the first-century British king.

Continue south on the east side of the road, cross it after about a mile, and pass over the cattle grid on the Tarr Steps road, from which a footpath takes you west another one and a half miles back to Tarr Steps. The *Tarr Farm* café here provides food and refreshment.

rambling old inn on the village green, can offer you drinks, snacks and full restaurant **meals** (restaurant closed Sun & Mon, but bar meals always available), though the room rates are high – cheapest in the modern annexe and more expensive Friday and Saturday (Ⓣ01643/851455, Ⓦwww.royaloak-somerset.co.uk; ❻).

Exford and Dunkery Beacon

The hamlet of **EXFORD**, an ancient crossing-point on the River Exe, is popular with hunting folk as well as with walkers here for the four-mile hike to **Dunkery Beacon**, Exmoor's highest point at 1700ft. There's a good range of **accommodation**, including *Exmoor Lodge*, a friendly B&B on Chapel Street (Ⓣ01643/831694, Ⓦwww.smoothhound.co.uk; no smoking; ❷), and the village also holds Exmoor's main **youth hostel**, a rambling Victorian house in the centre (Ⓣ0870/770 5820; limited opening Nov–Feb; £11.50). Two and a half miles northwest of Exford off the Porlock Road, *Westermill Farm* (Ⓣ01643/831238, Ⓦwww.exmoorcamping.co.uk) provides a tranquil **campsite** on the banks of the Exe.

Exmoor Forest and Simonsbath

At the heart of the National Park stands **Exmoor Forest**, the barest part of the moor, scarcely populated except by roaming sheep and a few red deer – the word "forest" denotes simply that it was a hunting reserve. In the middle of it stands the village of **SIMONSBATH** (pronounced "Simmonsbath"), at a crossroads between Lynton, Barnstaple and Minehead on the River Barle. The village was home to the Knight family, who bought the forest in 1818 and, by introducing tenant farmers, building roads and importing sheep, brought systematic agriculture to an area that had never before produced any income. The Knights also built a wall round their land – parts of which can still be seen – as well as the intriguing Pinkworthy (pronounced "Pinkery") Pond, four miles to the northwest, whose exact function remains unexplained.

Simonsbath would make a useful base for hikes on the moor, but there are only two **accommodation** possibilities: the *Exmoor Forest Hotel* (Ⓣ01643/831341; ❹; closed Jan), which has numerous hunting trophies and old-fashioned rooms, and the *Simonsbath House Hotel* (Ⓣ01643/831259, Ⓦwww.simonsbathhouse.co.uk; ❺), former home of the Knights and now a cosy bolt-hole offering seven agreeably gnarled rooms, all en suite, and a good, if fairly expensive non-smoking **restaurant**. In a converted barn next to the hotel, *Boevey's* offers coffees and snack lunches, while a couple of miles outside the village on the Brayford Road is the *Poltimore Arms* at **Yarde Down**, a classic country **pub** serving excellent **food**, including vegetarian dishes.

The Brendon Hills

Sandwiched between the Quantocks and Exmoor, the **Brendon Hills** are effectively an extension of the moor, separated from it by the rivers Avill and Exe. The A396, which runs alongside the rivers, offers opportunities to take woodland paths rising to such scenic spots as **Wimbleball Lake**, accessible from the village of **Brompton Regis**. Exmoor's major reservoir, the lake is the habitat of herons and kingfishers, and footpaths lead from its southern shores up **Haddon Hill**, enjoying sweeping panoramas from its 1164-foot summit.

Overlooking Wimbleball Lake, *Holworthy Farm* offers comfortable en-suite **accommodation** and traditional farmhouse evening meals (£14) to its guests

The South West Coast Path

The South West Coast Path, the longest footpath in Britain, starts at Minehead and tracks the coastline as closely as it possibly can along Devon's northern seaboard, round Cornwall, back into Devon, and on to Dorset, where it finishes close to the entrance to Poole Harbour. The path was conceived in the 1940s, but it was just over 25 years ago that – barring a few significant gaps – the full **630-mile route** opened, much of it on land owned by the National Trust, and all of it well signposted with the acorn symbol of the Countryside Agency.

Some degree of **planning** is essential for any long walk along the South West Coast Path, in particular on the south Devon stretch, where there are six ferries to negotiate and one ford to cross between Plymouth and Exmouth. **Accommodation** needs to be considered too: don't expect to arrive late in the day at a holiday town in season and immediately find a bed. Even campsites can fill to capacity, though campers have the flexibility of asking farmers for permission to pitch in a corner of a field.

The relevant Ordnance Survey **maps** can be found at most village shops on the route, while many newsagents, bookshops and tourist offices will stock books or pamphlets containing route plans and details of local flora and fauna. Aurum Press (Ⓦwww.aurumpress.co.uk) publishes four National Trail Guides books using Ordnance Survey maps and describing different parts of the path, while the **South West Coast Path Association** publishes an annual guide (£7) to the whole path, including accommodation lists, ferry timetables and transport details; there's also a supplement, the *Other Way Round* (£3.50), for those travelling in the Poole-to-Minehead direction. You can contact the Association at Windlestraw, Penquit, Devon PL21 0LU (Ⓣ01752/896237, Ⓦwww.swcp.org.uk).

(Ⓣ01398/371244, Ⓦwww.holworthyfarm.co.uk; no credit cards; ❸). Further north, **Wheddon Cross** has the excellent *Rest and Be Thankful* inn, with a beer garden, good food and several rooms (Ⓣ01643/841222, Ⓦwww.restandbethankful.co.uk; ❹). There's also a **riding stables** nearby at Huntscott House Stables (Ⓣ01643/841272), which caters for experienced adult riders.

Minehead and around

A chief port on the Somerset coast, **MINEHEAD** quickly became a favourite Victorian watering-hole with the arrival of the railway, and it has preserved an upbeat holiday-town atmosphere ever since. Steep lanes link the two quarters of **Higher Town**, on North Hill, containing some of the oldest houses, and **Quay Town**, the harbour area. It's in Quay Town that the **Hobby Horse** performs its dance in the town's three-day May Day celebrations, snaring maidens under its prancing skirt and tail in a fertility ritual resembling the more famous festivities at the Cornish port of Padstow (see p.523).

The **tourist office** is midway between Higher Town and Quay Town at 17 Friday St, off the Parade (April–June, Sept & Oct Mon–Sat 9.30am–5pm; July & Aug Mon–Sat 9.30am–5.30pm, Sun 10am–1pm; Nov–March Mon–Sat 10am–4pm; Ⓣ01643/702624). If you want to **stay** in Minehead, try the *Old Ship Aground* right by the harbour on Quay Road (Ⓣ01643/702087; ❷), or, nearer the centre, a few minutes' walk up from the tourist office, *Kildare Lodge* on Tudor Road (Ⓣ01643/702009; ❹), a comfortable, reconstructed Tudor inn designed by a pupil of Lutyens. There's a **youth hostel** a couple of miles southeast, outside the village of Alcombe (Ⓣ0870/770 5968; £10.25 limited opening Sept–March), in a secluded combe on the edge of Exmoor. Minehead is crammed with **places to eat**, mostly very mediocre. However, you could do a lot worse than an evening at the *Queen's Head*, on Holloway Street, off the Parade and near the tourist office, a free house with a range of ales and menu selections, as well as darts and pool.

Dunster

As well as being the start of the South West Coast Path (see box p.483), Minehead is a terminus for the **West Somerset Railway**, which curves eastwards into the Quantocks as far as Bishops Lydeard (see p.428). The Minehead area's major attraction, the old village of **DUNSTER**, is about a mile from the line's first stop, three miles inland. Dunster's main street is dominated by the towers and turrets of its **castle** (April–Sept Mon–Wed, Sat & Sun 11am–5pm; Oct Mon–Wed, Sat & Sun 11am–4pm; grounds daily: April–Oct 10am–5pm; Nov–March 11am–4pm; £6.40, grounds only £3.50; NT). Most of its fortifications were demolished after the Civil War, after which time the castle became something of an architectural showpiece, and Victorian restoration has made it more like a Rhineland *schloss* than a Norman stronghold.

On a tour of the castle you can see various portraits of the Luttrells, owners of the house for six hundred years before the National Trust took over in the 1970s; a bedroom once occupied by Charles I; a fine seventeenth-century carved staircase; and a richly decorated banqueting hall. The grounds include terraced gardens and riverside walks – and drama productions and other events are regularly staged here in the summer (call ⓣ01985/843601 for details). The nearby hilltop tower is a folly, **Conygar Tower**, dating from 1776.

Despite the influx of seasonal visitors, Dunster village preserves relics of its wool-making heyday; the octagonal **Yarn Market**, in the High Street below the castle, dates from 1609, while the three-hundred-year-old **water mill** at the end of Mill Lane is still used commercially for milling the various grains which go to make the flour and muesli sold in the shop (April, May & Oct daily except Fri 10.30am–5pm; June–Sept daily 10.30am–5pm; £2.30; NT) – the café, overlooking its riverside garden, is a good spot for lunch. For somewhere to **stay**, try the traditional *Yarn Market Hotel*, 25–31 High St (ⓣ01643/821425, ⓦwww.yarnmarkethotel.co.uk; ❹), which has rooms overlooking the Yarn Market and a restaurant. There's a **visitor centre** at the top of Dunster Steep by the main car park (Easter–Oct daily 10am–5pm; Nov–Easter some weekends 11am–3pm; ⓣ01643/821835).

Porlock

The real enticement of **PORLOCK**, six miles west of Minehead, is its extraordinary position in a deep hollow, cupped on three sides by the hogbacked hills of Exmoor. The thatch-and-cob houses and dripping charm of the village's long main street have led to invasions of tourists, some of whom are also drawn by the place's literary links. According to Coleridge's own less than reliable testimony, it was a "man from Porlock" who broke the opium trance in which he was composing *Kubla Khan*, while the High Street's beamed *Ship Inn* prides itself on featuring prominently in the Exmoor romance *Lorna Doone* and, in real life, having sheltered the poet Robert Southey, who staggered in rain-soaked after an Exmoor ramble. There's little specific to do in Porlock, but the **Dovery Manor Museum** (Easter & May–Oct Mon–Fri 10am–1pm & 2–5pm, Sat 10am–noon & 2.30–4.30pm; free), in a fifteenth-century house at the eastern end of the High Street, holds a degree of interest, with a couple of cramped rooms showing traditional domestic and agricultural tools of Exmoor – including a man-trap – together with some material on the local wildlife. The most impressive items here though are the beautiful window and huge fireplace on the ground floor.

Porlock's **tourist office** is at West End, High St (Easter–Oct Mon–Fri 10am–1pm & 2–5pm, Sat 10am–5pm, Sun 10am–1pm; Nov–Easter Mon–Fri 10am–1pm, Sat 10am–2pm; ⓣ01643/863150, ⓦwww.porlock.co.uk). The best **accommodation** in town is on the High Street, where the Victorian *Lorna Doone Hotel* (ⓣ01643/862404; ❷) offers three sizes of rooms, all with private bath and TV. Further down, *The Cottage* is smaller and quainter, but a little pricier (ⓣ01643/862996; ❸). Both *The Cottage* and the *Lorna Doone* serve snacks, meals and teas – as does the *Whortleberry Tearoom* (closed Mon), also on the High Street. Porlock has a central **campsite**, *Sparkhayes Farm* (ⓣ01643/862470; closed Jan & Feb), signposted off the main road near the *Lorna Doone*.

Two miles west over the reclaimed marshland, the tiny harbour of **PORLOCK WEIR** gives little inkling of its former role as a hard-working port trafficking with Wales. It's a peaceful spot, giving onto a bay that enjoys the mildest climate on Exmoor, and there's a top-notch – and very expensive – **restaurant**, *Andrews on the Weir* (ⓣ01643/863300, ⓦwww.andrewsontheweir.co.uk), which cooks up local lamb and seafood to perfection, and also offers **accommodation** in five luxury rooms (❺). An easy two-mile stroll west from Porlock Weir along the South West Coast Path brings you to **St Culbone**, a tiny church – claimed to be the country's smallest – sheltered within woods once inhabited by a leper colony.

Lynton and Lynmouth

West from Porlock, the road climbs 1350ft in less than three miles, though cyclists and drivers might prefer the gentler and more scenic toll-road alternative to the direct uphill trawl (cars £2). Nine miles along the coast, on the Devon side of the county line, the Victorian resort of **LYNTON** perches above a lofty gorge with splendid views over the sea. Almost completely cut off from the rest of the country for most of its history, the village struck lucky during the Napoleonic wars, when frustrated Grand Tourists – unable to visit their usual continental haunts – discovered in Lynton a domestic piece of Swiss landscape. Coleridge and Hazlitt trudged over to Lynton from the Quantocks,

Walks from Lynton and Lynmouth

As well as the draws of the coastal path, there are several popular walks inland in this region. The one-and-a-half-mile tramp to **Watersmeet**, for example, follows the East Lyn River to where it's joined by Hoar Oak Water, a tranquil spot transformed into a roaring torrent after a bout of rain. From the fishing lodge here – now owned by the National Trust and open as a café and shop in summer – you can branch off on a range of less-trodden paths, such as the three-quarters-of-a-mile route south to **Hillsford Bridge**, the confluence of Hoar Oak and Farley Water.

North of Watersmeet, a path climbs up **Countisbury Hill** and the higher **Butter Hill** (nearly 1000ft) giving riveting views of Lynton, Lynmouth and the north Devon coast, and there's also a track leading to the lighthouse at **Foreland Point**, close to the coastal path. East from Lynmouth you can reach the point via a fine sheltered shingle beach at the foot of Countisbury Hill – one of a number of tiny coves that are easily accessible on either side of the estuary.

From Lynton, an undemanding expedition takes you west along the North Walk, a mile-long path leading to the **Valley of the Rocks**, a steeply curved heathland dominated by rugged rock formations. At the far end of the valley, herds of wild goats range free, as they have done here for centuries.

but the greatest spur to the village's popularity came with the publication in 1869 of R.D. Blackmore's Exmoor melodrama *Lorna Doone*, a book based on the outlaw clans who inhabited these parts in the seventeenth century. Since then the area has become indelibly associated with the swashbuckling romance.

Opposite the school on Market Street, one of the oldest houses in the village houses the **Lyn and Exmoor Museum** (Easter–Oct Mon–Fri 10am–12.30pm & 2–5pm, Sun 2–5pm; £1), holding a motley selection of relics from the locality and a reconstructed Exmoor kitchen c.1800. Lynton's imposing **town hall** on Lee Road epitomizes the Victorian–Edwardian accent of the village. It was the gift of publisher George Newnes, who also donated the nearby **cliff railway** connecting Lynton with Lynmouth (March to mid-July & mid-Sept to Nov daily 9am–7pm; mid-July to mid-Sept daily 9am–9pm; £2.75 return). The device is an ingenious hydraulic system, its two carriages counterbalanced by water tanks, which fill up at the top, descend, and empty their load at the bottom.

Five hundred feet below, **LYNMOUTH** lies at the junction and estuary of the East and West Lyn rivers, in a spot described by Gainsborough as "the most delightful place for a landscape painter this country can boast". The picturesque scene was shattered in August 1952 when Lynmouth was almost washed away by floodwaters coming off Exmoor, a disaster of which there are many reminders around the village. Having recovered its calm, Lynmouth is only ruffled now by the summer crowds, though nothing could compromise the village's unique location. Shelley spent his honeymoon here with his 16-year-old bride Harriet Westbrook, making time in his nine-week sojourn to write his polemical *Queen Mab* – two different houses claim to have been the Shelleys' love-nest. R.D. Blackmore, author of *Lorna Doone*, stayed in **Mars Hill**, the oldest part of the town, its creeper-covered cottages framing the cliffs behind the Esplanade. In summer, the harbour offers boat trips and fishing expeditions, and you can explore the **Glen Lyn Gorge** up the wooded valley with its walks and waterfalls and displays of the uses and dangers of waterpower (daily 10am–dusk; exhibition Easter–Oct 10am–dusk; £3, gorge only £2) – this was the course taken by the destructive floods of 1952.

You can also ask at the gorge about **boat trips** from Lynmouth harbour with Exmoor Coast Boat Cruises (April–Sept; ⓣ01598/753207); excursions range from a forty-minute trip west to Lee Bay (£5) to a four-hour sail to Porlock Weir and back (£10), but between April and July, the most popular trip is to the view the abundant birdlife on the cliffs between Woody Bay and Heddon's Mouth, west of Lee Bay (£9).

Practicalities

Lynton's **tourist office** is in the town hall (Easter–Oct Mon–Sat 9.30am–5.30pm, Sun 10am–4pm; Nov–Easter Mon–Sat 10am–4pm, Sun 10am–2pm; ⓣ01598/752225 or 0845/660 3232, ⓦwww.lyntourism.co.uk), while Lynmouth has a **National Park Visitor Centre** on the seafront (Easter–Oct daily 10am–5pm; Nov, Dec & Feb–Easter Sat & Sun 11am–4pm; ⓣ01598/752509).

Lynton has the better choice of **B&Bs** at the cheaper end of the market, among them the friendly, Victorian *The Turret*, 33 Lee Rd (ⓣ01598/753284, ⓦwww.turrethotel.co.uk; no smoking; no under-14s; ❷), one of a row of guest houses lining this street, this one built by the same engineer who built the cliff railway; all six spacious rooms are en suite or have private facilities. A more central choice is *St Vincent House* (ⓣ01598/752244, ⓔstvincenthotel@aol.com; no smoking; ❸), a whitewashed, Georgian house on Castle Hill with spacious, beautifully furnished bedrooms and a garden. There's a **youth hostel** (☎0870/770 5942; limited opening Nov–Easter; £10.25) in a homely Victorian house about one mile inland from Lynton's centre, and signposted off Lynbridge Road. Intimate **evening meals** are served at the *Mad Hatter's* bistro (☎01598/753614; eves only, closed mid-Dec to mid-March, Sun, also Mon–Thurs Nov to mid-Dec) where the menu includes curries and good vegetarian choices, and, in summer, *Lily May's*, 1 Castle Hill (☎01598/753591; closed all day Wed, also eves in winter); both are non-smoking.

In **Lynmouth**, central choices include *Riverside Cottage*, above a busy tea-shop, on Riverside Road (☎01598/752390, Ⓦwww.riversidecottage.co.uk; ❸), which has en-suite rooms with river views, and the posh *Shelley's*, right next to the Glen Lyn Gorge (☎01598/753219, Ⓦwww.shelleyshotel.co.uk; ❹), where you can sleep in the room supposed to have been occupied by the poet – he apparently left without paying his bill. Splendidly sited across the river at the harbour entrance, the *Rock House Hotel* (☎01598/753508, Ⓦwww.rock-house.co.uk; ❹) has chintzy, non-smoking rooms with views. There's also a tea-garden, snacks at the bar and meals in its **restaurant**. There's more atmosphere, however, at the traditional and fairly expensive *Rising Sun* inn, on Harbourside, while the restaurant at the *Bath Hotel* (opposite the *Rock House*) charges £17.50 for a three-course dinner; both are non-smoking.

Cornwall

When D.H. Lawrence wrote that being in **Cornwall** was "like being at a window and looking out of England", he wasn't just thinking of its geographical extremity. Virtually unaffected by the Roman conquest, Cornwall was for centuries the last haven for a **Celtic culture** elsewhere eradicated by the Saxons – a land where princes communed with Breton troubadours, where chroniclers and scribes composed the epic tales of Arthurian heroism, and where itinerant monks from Welsh and Irish monasteries disseminated an elemental and visionary Christianity. Primitive granite crosses and a crop of Celtic saints remain as traces of this formative period, and though the Cornish language had ebbed away by the eighteenth century, it is recalled in Celtic place names that in many cases have grown more exotic as they have become corrupted over time.

Another strand of Cornwall's folkloric character comes from the **smugglers** who thrived here right up until the nineteenth century, exploiting the sheltered creeks and hidden anchorages of the southern coasts. For many fishing villages, such as Polperro and Mousehole, contraband provided an important secondary income, as did the looting of the ships that regularly came to grief on the reefs and rocks. Further distinguishing it from its neighbour, Cornwall has also had a strong **industrial economy**, based mainly on the mining of **copper** and **tin** in the north, centred on the towns of Redruth and St Agnes, and in the south on the deposits of **china clay**, which are still being mined in the area around St Austell.

Nowadays, of course, Cornwall's most flourishing industry is tourism. The repercussions of the holiday business on Cornwall have been uneven, for instance cluttering **Land's End** with a tacky leisure complex but leaving

Cornwall's other great promontory, **Lizard Point**, undeveloped. All the stops are pulled out in the thronged resorts of **Falmouth**, site of a new and impressive National Maritime Museum, and **Newquay**, the West's chief surfing centre, though the effects of mass tourism have been more destructive in smaller, quainter places, such as **Mevagissey**, **Polperro** and **Padstow**, whose genuine charms can be hard to make out in full season. Other villages, such as **Charlestown, Port Isaac** and **Boscastle**, are hardly touched, however, and you couldn't wish for anything more remote than **Bodmin Moor**, a tract of wilderness in the heart of Cornwall – and even **Tintagel**, site of what is fondly known as King Arthur's castle, has preserved its sense of desolation. Near **St Austell**, the spectacular and high-profile **Eden Project**, located in an abandoned clay pit, has pointed the way to a less destructive and exploitative form of crowd-pulling, while other places – such as **St Ives**, **Fowey** and **Bude** – have reached a happy compromise with the seasonal influx, or else are saved from saturation by sheer distance, as is the case with the **Isles of Scilly**. Throughout the county, though, it only requires a shift of a few miles to escape the crowds, and there are enough good beaches around for everyone to find a space.

The best way to reach the quietest spots is along the **South West Coast Path** (see box on p.483), but a car is almost indispensable for anyone wanting to see a lot in a short time, as the system of public transport is limited to a couple of **rail** branch lines off the main line to Penzance and a thin network of local bus services.

From Looe to Veryan Bay

The southeast strip of the Cornish coast from Looe to Veryan Bay holds a string of medieval harbour towns tarnished by various degrees of commercialization, but there are also a few spots where you can experience the best of Cornwall, including some wonderful coastline. The main rail stop is **St Austell**, the capital of Cornwall's china clay industry, though there is a branch line connecting nearby **Par** with the north coast at Newquay. To the east of St Austell Bay, the touristy **Polperro** and **Looe** are easily accessible by bus from Plymouth, and there's a rail link to Looe from Liskeard. The estuary town of **Fowey**, in a niche of Cornwall closely associated with the author Daphne Du Maurier, is most easily reached by bus from St Austell and Par, as is **Mevagissey**, to the west.

Looe and Polperro

LOOE was drawing crowds as early as 1800, when the first "bathing-machines" were wheeled out, but the arrival of the railway in 1879 was what really packed its beaches. Though Looe now touts itself as something of a shark-fishing centre, most people come here for the sand, the handiest stretch being the beach in front of East Looe – the busier half of the river-divided town. Away from the river mouth, you'll find a cleaner spot to swim a mile eastwards at **Millendreath**. Most of Looe's attractions are in boating and bathing, and in summer, you'll find a range of **boating and fishing trips** advertised on the long quayside, spread along the river parallel to the main Fore Street. If the weather's bad, you could always shelter in the **Old Guildhall Museum** (Easter & late May to Sept Mon–Fri & Sun 11.30am–4.30pm; £1.50), a diverse collection of maritime models and exhibits, though none so interesting as the building itself, a fifteenth-century construction preserving its prisoners' cells and raised magistrates' benches.

East Looe's **tourist office** is at the New Guildhall, on Fore Street (Easter & May to mid-Sept daily 10am–5pm; April & mid-Sept to Oct daily 10am–2pm; ⓣ01503/262072, ⓦwww.looecornwall.com). There's plenty of **accommodation** here: **in East Looe**, try the old-fashioned *Dolphin Hotel* (ⓣ01503/262578, ⓦwww.looedirectory.co.uk/dolphin.htm; ❸) for estuary views, or the chintzier *Sea Breeze*, a three-storey B&B very close to the beach and harbour in Lower Chapel Street (ⓣ01503/263131, ⓦwww.cornwallexplore.co.uk/seabreeze; ❶). **In West Looe**, the non-smoking *St Aubyn's* stands away from the bustle on Marine Drive (ⓣ01503/264351, ⓦwww.staubyns.co.uk; no under-5s; ❸; closed Nov–March), a mile west of the centre in the Hannafore district; three of the rooms have balconies with great sea views and there's a garden. The town has nothing special in the way of **restaurants**, though the oak-beamed *Old Sail Loft* (ⓣ01503/262131; closed lunchtime in winter) on the harbourside and *Trawlers* (ⓣ01503/263593; eves only; closed Sun & Mon) are good places to sample fresh local seafood, at expensive prices. For plainer food, try the inexpensive *Golden Guinea* on Fore Street, a seventeenth-century building that does a brisk trade in staple seaside meals as well as cream teas.

Looe is linked by hourly buses (less frequent on Sun & in winter) with neighbouring **POLPERRO**, a smaller and quainter place, but with a similar feel. From the bus stop and car park at the top of the village, it's a five- or ten-minute walk alongside the River Pol to the pretty harbour. The surrounding cliffs and the tightly packed houses rising on each side of the stream have an undeniable charm, and the tangle of lanes is little changed since the village's heyday of smuggling and pilchard fishing, but the "discovery" of Polperro has almost ruined it, and its straggling main street – the Coombes – is now an unbroken row of tourist shops and fast-food outlets.

Polperro's best places to **stay** include *The House on Props*, Talland Street (ⓣ01503/272310; no credit cards; ❹), which, as the name suggests, is propped up over the river and has superb harbour views, and the central but relatively secluded *Old Mill House*, an agreeable old pub on Mill Hill offering eight comfortable rooms (ⓣ01503/272362, ⓦwww.oldmillhouse.i12.com; ❸).

There's a separate **restaurant** at the *Old Mill*, though you'll find better-quality fare at the non-smoking *Kitchen* on the Coombes (ⓣ01503/272780; eves only; closed Oct–Easter), especially if you're a vegetarian or seafood fan. Also on the main road, *The Plantation* (ⓣ01503/272223; closed Nov–Easter) provides cream teas and snacks by day, full meals in the evenings, and it has some outdoor seating.

Fowey and around

The ten miles west from Polperro to Polruan are among the best stretches of the coastal path in south Cornwall, giving access to some beautiful secluded sand beaches. There are frequent ferries across the River Fowey from Polruan, giving a fine view of the quintessential Cornish port of **FOWEY** (pronounced "Foy"), a cascade of neat, pale terraces at the mouth of one of the peninsula's greatest rivers. The major port on the county's south coast in the fourteenth century, Fowey finally became so ambitious that it provoked Edward IV to strip the town of its military capability, though it continued to thrive commercially, coming into its own as the leading port for china clay shipments in the nineteenth century. In addition to the bulkier freighters sailing from wharves north of the town, the harbour today is crowded with trawlers and yachts, giving the town a brisk, purposeful character lacking in many of Cornwall's south-coast ports.

Fowey's steep layout centres on the church of **St Fimbarrus**, a distinctive fifteenth-century construction replacing a church that was sacked by the French. The church marks the traditional end of the ancient **Saints' Way footpath** from Padstow, linking the north and south Cornish coasts (see p.524). Beside St Fimbarrus, the **Literary Centre** on South Street is a small exhibition including a twelve-minute video of Daphne Du Maurier's life and work (daily summer 10.30am–5pm, closes 7.30pm in Aug, winter 10.30am–4pm; free). The centre sells tickets for the Daphne Du Maurier Festival of Arts and Literature, taking place over ten days in May (Ⓣ01726/223535, Ⓦwww.dumaurier.org). Behind the church stands **Place House**, an extravagance belonging to the local Treffry family, with a Victorian Gothic tower grafted onto the fifteenth- and sixteenth-century fortified building. Below the church, the **Ship Inn**, sporting some fine Elizabethan panelling and plaster ceilings, was originally home to the Rashleighs – a recurring name in the annals of this region – and held the local Roundhead HQ during the Civil War. From here, Fore Street, Lostwithiel Street and the Esplanade fan out, the **Esplanade** leading to a footpath that gives access to some splendid walks around the coast. Past the remains of a blockhouse that once supported a defensive chain hung across the river's mouth, the small beach of **Readymoney Cove** is soon reached – so-called either because it was where smugglers buried their ill-gotten gains, or because it was where the flotsam of shipwrecks came ashore. Close by stand the ruins of **St Catherine's Castle**, built by Thomas Treffry on the orders of Henry VIII, and offering fine views across the estuary.

You don't have to take on the entire thirty miles of the Saints' Way to get the flavour of this trail, while if you prefer a circular route you can try the **Hall Walk**, a scenic four-mile hike north of Fowey. More details are available from the tourist office, though it's simple enough: cross the river on the car ferry (at the car park north of town) to **Bodinnick**, walk downstream on the other side, crossing the footbridge over the narrow creek of Pont Pill, then take the passenger ferry back from Polruan. The route passes a memorial to "Q", alias Sir Arthur Quiller-Couch, who lived on Fowey's Esplanade between 1892 and 1944, and whose writings helped popularize the place he called "Troy Town". Fans of Daphne Du Maurier can join a guided walk around scenes described in her books – contact the tourist office for details.

Beyond the west bank ferry stage you come to **Golant**, a riverside hamlet a little more than a mile from the Iron Age fort of **Castle Dore**, which features in Arthurian romance as the residence of King Mark of Cornwall, husband of Iseult. You can also get to the fort from Fowey on bus #24, though there is still a ten-minute walk from the stop on the crossroads.

LOSTWITHIEL, three miles further upriver (train from Par, or bus or train from St Austell), is an old market town on the lowest bridging point of the Fowey. It's an appealing mixture of Georgian houses and medieval passageways, with a peculiar, Breton-inspired octagonal spire on St Bartholomew's Church. The town lies below the watchful eye of **Restormel Castle** (April–Sept daily 10am–6pm; Oct daily 10am–5pm; £2; EH), a shale-built shell of a circular keep that crowns a hill a mile or so north. It's a peaceful, panoramic spot, which last saw service when Royalist forces prised it out of the hands of the Earl of Essex's Parliamentarian army in 1644.

Practicalities

Separated from eastern routes by its river, Fowey is most accessible by twice-hourly #24 **buses** from St Austell (hourly on Sun). Travellers to or from the west might make use of the **ferry** linking Fowey with Mevagissey (see p.493), which operates several times daily between May and September, (35min; £9 return). There is a small **tourist office** in the town's post office on Custom House Hill (Easter–Oct Mon–Fri 9am–5.30pm, Sat & Sun 9am–5pm; Nov–Easter Mon–Fri 9am–5.30pm, Sat 9am–5pm, Sun 9am–1pm; ⓣ01726/833616, ⓦwww.fowey.co.uk). All of the central pubs offer **B&B**; on Lostwithiel Street, try the *Ship* (ⓣ01726/832230; ❷) or the *Safe Harbour* (ⓣ01726/833379; ❸), both offering en-suite rooms and parking. From the top of Lostwithiel Street, climb up New Road Gill to 11 Park Rd, where *Pendower* (ⓣ01726/833559; no smoking; no credit cards; ❷) has two en-suite rooms with Laura Ashley decor and river views. Outside Fowey, the *Old Ferry Inn*, Bodinnick, also has river views, bars and a restaurant (ⓣ01726/870237, ⓦwww.oldferryinn.co.uk; ❸), and *Coombe Farm* (ⓣ01726/833123, ⓔtessapaull@hotmail.com; no under-12s; no credit cards; ❸) provides perfect rural isolation just twenty minutes' walk from town, at the end of a lane off the B3269 – and there's a bathing area just 300yd away. There's a **youth hostel** outside Golant at *Penquite House*, a Georgian mansion with views over the valley (ⓣ0870/770 5832, ⓔgolant@yha.org.uk; closed Dec & Jan; £13). The nearest **campsite** is at *Yeate Farm* (ⓣ01726/870256; closed Nov–Feb), on the eastern bank of the river, three-quarters of a mile up from the Bodinnick ferry crossing.

Fowey has some good seafood **restaurants**; among the best is the elegant but relaxed Q, by the waterside at the sumptuous *Old Quay House Hotel* at 28 Fore St (ⓣ01726/83302; expensive), specializing in Mediterranean takes on meat and seafood dishes, and *Food For Thought* on the Quay, which offers a three-course fixed-price menu for around £20 on weekdays (ⓣ01726/832221; eves only, also lunchtime June–Aug; closed Sun & Dec–March), also quite expensive. The area is also well provided with good **pubs** such as Golant's *Fisherman's Arms*, the *Old Ferry Inn* at Bodinnick and Polruan's excellent *Lugger Inn*. The *Old Ferry* also has comfortable rooms (ⓣ01726/870237, ⓦwww.oldferryinn.co.uk; ❸).

St Austell and around

It was the discovery of china clay, or kaolin, in the downs to the north of **ST AUSTELL** that spurred the town's growth in the eighteenth century. An essential ingredient in the production of porcelain, kaolin had until then only been produced in northern China, where a high ridge, or *kao-lin*, was the sole known source of the raw material. Still a vital part of Cornwall's economy, the clay is now mostly exported for use in the manufacture of paper, as well as paint and medicines. The conical spoil heaps left by the mines are a feature of the local landscape, especially on Hensbarrow Downs to the north, the great green and white mounds making an eerie sight.

St Austell itself is fairly unexciting, but makes a useful stop for trips in the surrounding area. The town's nearest link to the sea is at **CHARLESTOWN**, an easy downhill walk from the centre of town. This unassuming and unspoilt port is named after the entrepreneur Charles Rashleigh, who in 1791 began work on the harbour in what was then a small fishing community two miles south of St Austell, widening its streets to accommodate the clay wagons daily passing through. The wharves are still used, loading clay onto vessels that appear oversized beside the tiny jetties, and also providing a backdrop for the location filming that frequently takes place here. Behind the harbour, the **Shipwreck & Heritage Centre** (March–Oct daily 10am–5pm, closes 6pm in peak season; £5) is entered through tunnels once used to convey the clay to the docks, and shows a good collection of photos and relics as well as tableaux of historical scenes.

On each side of the dock the coarse sand and stone **beaches** have small rock pools, above which cliff walks lead around St Austell Bay. Eastwards, you soon arrive at overdeveloped **Carlyon Bay**, whose main resort is **Par**. The beaches here get clogged with clay – the best swimming is to be found by pressing on to the sheltered crescent of **Polkerris**. The easternmost limit of St Austell Bay is marked by **Gribbin Head**, near which stands Menabilly House, where Daphne Du Maurier lived for 24 years – it was the model for the "Manderley" of *Rebecca*. The house is not open to the public, but you can walk down to Polridmouth Cove, where Rebecca met her watery end.

Eden Project

A disused clay pit four miles northeast of St Austell holds the newest and highest-profile of Cornwall's attractions, the **Eden Project** (daily: April–Oct 10am–6pm, closes 8pm Tues–Thurs late July to early Sept; Nov–March 10am–4.30pm; last entry 90min before closing; £11; Ⓦwww.edenproject.com), reachable on bus #T9 from St Austell Station and #T10 from Newquay, and signposted on most roads in the area. Occupying a 160-foot-deep crater whose awesome scale only reveals itself once you have passed the entrance at its lip, the project showcases the diversity of the planet's plant life in an imaginative, sometimes wacky, but refreshingly ungimmicky style. The whole site is stunningly landscaped with an array of various crops and flower beds, but at centre stage are the vast geodesic "biomes", or conservatories made up of eco-friendly, Teflon-coated, hexagonal panels. One cluster holds groves of olive and citrus trees, cacti and other plants more usually found in the warm, temperate zones of the Mediterranean, southern Africa and southwestern USA, while the larger group contains plants from the tropics, including teak and mahogany trees, and there's a waterfall and river gushing through – things can get pretty steamy here, and you can take cool refuge in an air-conditioned bunker halfway along the course. Equally impressive are the external grounds (described as "Picasso meeting the Aztecs"), where plantations of bamboo, tea, hops, hemp and tobacco are interspersed with brilliant swathes of flowers. The whole "living theatre" presents a constantly changing spectacle, and should ideally be visited in different seasons. Allow at least half a day for a full exploration, but arrive early – or take advantage of the extended opening in summer – to avoid congestion. There are timed "story-telling" sessions, a lawn-carpeted arena where world, jazz and other music is performed, and abundant good food on hand – consult the website for events.

Note that anyone arriving at the site by bike or on foot is entitled to a £3 discount and can skip the queues by going straight to the fast-track ticket window. See below for bike rental and accommodation in the area.

Practicalities

Trains on the main London–Penzance line serve St Austell, with most services stopping at Par, which is also connected to Newquay on the north coast. Western National runs the half-hourly to hourly **bus** service #24 linking St Austell, Charlestown, Par and Polkerris.

Accommodation options around the Eden Project include *Treberthan*, Bodelva, a farmhouse halfway between Par and the site and just fifteen minutes from Eden via a footpath (Ⓣ01726/817711; no smoking; ❸). Charlestown also has two really attractive places to stay: *T'Gallants* (Ⓣ01726/70203; ❸), a smart Georgian B&B at the back of the harbour where cream teas are served in the garden, and *Broad Meadow House*, behind the Shipwreck Centre on Quay Road (Ⓣ01726/76636, Ⓔbest.tribe@btopenworld.com; no credit cards; ❸), which has one beautifully furnished bedroom, a large sitting room and choice breakfasts, and also offers "tent and breakfast" (£15 per person), with family-size tents provided in a meadow by the sea, to which breakfast is brought in the mornng. Behind *T'Gallants*, the *Rashleigh Arms* offers real ale and a range of **food**, though the most highly commended **pub** in the area is the *Rashleigh Inn* at Polkerris. The best **campsite** in St Austell Bay is *Carlyon Bay* (ⓣ01726/812735, ⓦwww.chycor.co.uk; closed Nov–March), at Bethesda, near the beach at Carlyon Bay, and just a mile and a half from the Eden Project.

To **rent a bike** locally, contact Bugle Bike Hire in the village of Bugle, five miles north of St Austell on the A391 and a little less than that west of the Eden Project (Easter–Oct; ⓣ01726/852285, ⓦwww.buglecyclehire.co.uk), while Happy Trails Bike Rides (ⓣ01726/852058, ⓦwww.happytrailsbikerides.com) arranges accompanied bike rides to the Eden Project from surrounding villages between April and September (£15 including Eden entry).

Mevagissey to Veryan Bay

MEVAGISSEY was once known for the construction of fast vessels, used for carrying contraband as well as pilchards. Today the tiny port might display a few stacks of lobster pots, but the real business is tourism, and in summer the maze of back streets is saturated with day-trippers, converging on the inner harbour and overflowing onto the large sand beach at **Pentewan** a mile to the north, despite the poor water quality.

A couple of miles north of Mevagissey lie the **Lost Gardens of Heligan** (daily: April–Oct 10am–6pm, last entry 4.30pm; Nov–March 10am–5pm, last entry 3.30pm; £6; ⓦwww.heligan.com), a fascinating resurrection of a Victorian garden which had fallen into neglect and was rescued from a ten-foot covering of brambles by Tim Smit, the visionary instigator of the Eden Project (see opposite). The abundant palm trees, giant Himalayan rhododendrons, immaculate vinery and glasshouses scattered about all look as if they've been transplanted from warmer climes; a boardwalk takes you past interconnecting ponds, through a jungle and under a canopy of bamboo and ferns down to the Lost Valley, where there are lakes, wild flower meadows and leafy oak, beech and chestnut rides. You can get here on Western Greyhound #526 buses from St Austell and Mevagissey.

Past the headland to the south of Mevagissey, the small sandy cove of **Portmellon** retains little of its boat-building activities but is freer of tourists. Further still, **GORRAN HAVEN** was formerly a crab-fishing village but now looks merely suburban, though it has a neat rock-and-sand beach, and a footpath that winds round to the even more attractive **Vault Beach**, half a mile south. South of here juts the most striking headland on Cornwall's southern coast, **Dodman Point**, cause of many a wreck and topped by a stark granite cross built by a local parson as a seamark in 1896. The promontory holds the substantial remains of an Iron Age fort, with an earthwork bulwark cutting right across the point.

Curving away to the west, the elegant parabola of **Veryan Bay** is barely touched by commercialism. Just west of Dodman Point lies one of Cornwall's most beautiful coves, **Hemmick Beach**, an excellent swimming spot with rocky outcrops affording a measure of privacy. Visually even more impressive is **Porthluney Cove**, a crescent of sand whose centrepiece is the battlemented **Caerhays Castle** (mid-March to May Mon–Fri 1–4pm; gardens mid-Feb to May daily 10am–5.30pm, last entry 4.30pm; house £5.50, garden £5.50, combined ticket £9.50), built in 1808 by John Nash and surrounded by beautiful gardens which are open in spring and on occasional charity days only.

A little further on, the minuscule and whitewashed **Portloe** is fronted by jagged black rocks that throw up fountains of seaspray, giving it a good, end-of-the-road kind of atmosphere. Sequestered inland, **VERYAN** has a pretty village green and pond, but is best known for its curious circular white houses built in the 19th century by one Reverend Jeremiah Trist. A lane from Veryan leads down to one of the cleanest swimming spots on Cornwall's southern coast, **Pendower Beach**. Two-thirds of a mile long and backed by dunes, Pendower joins with the neighbouring **Carne Beach** at low tide to create a long sandy continuum.

Practicalities

From St Austell's train station or Trinity Street, **buses** #25 and #526 leave for Mevagissey and Heligan (less frequent #526 service on Sun), with some #526 buses continuing to Gorran Haven. Veryan and Portloe are reachable on #51 from Truro. Right in the heart of Mevagissey, the best **accommodation** option is the fifteenth-century *Fountain Inn* (ⓣ01726/842320, ⓦwww.fountain.inn.cwc.net; ❷), on Cliff Street, off East Quay; alternatively try *Lawn House*, set back from the harbour at 1 Church Lane (ⓣ01726/842754; no credit cards; ❹; phone ahead Nov–Easter), a lovely, spacious Queen Anne construction with chandeliers and brass beds. You might appreciate the coast better by staying in Portmellon, where the weathered old *Rising Sun Inn* (ⓣ01726/843235, ⓦwww.risingsunportmellon.co.uk; ❹; closed Nov–Feb) confronts the sea. In Gorran Haven, the well-situated *Llawnroc Inn* (ⓣ01726/843461; ❺) is pricey but has tasteful and comfortable sea-facing rooms, and offers good short-break rates. The nearest **youth hostel** (ⓣ0870/770 5712; closed Nov–March; £11.50) is in a former farmhouse at **Boswinger**, a remote spot half a mile from Hemmick Beach. Difficult to reach without your own transport, it's about a mile from the bus stop at Gorran Church Town, served infrequently by some #526 buses. Boswinger also has a **campsite**, *Seaview* (ⓣ01726/843425, ⓦwww.seaviewinternational.com; closed Oct–March), with, as the name implies, a panoramic position overlooking Veryan Bay; with a heated outdoor pool, it's popular, so you'd be advised to book ahead in July and August. If you want to stay in **Veryan**, head for the *Elerkey Guest House* (ⓣ01872/501261, ⓦwww.elerkey-guest-house.co.uk; ❸), an ex-farmhouse with a spacious garden and adjoining art gallery; it's the first on the left after the church. The *New Inn* serves pub meals and also provides B&B (ⓣ01872/501362; ❸).

There's no shortage of **restaurants** in Mevagissey, most specializing in fish – for location you might try the large harbour-front *Sharksfin Hotel*, where fish is the main dish (ⓣ01726/843241). The dainty *Alvorada* (closed daytime, all day Sun, also Mon & Tues Nov–Feb; ⓣ01726/842055), one street back from West Quay at 2 Polkirt Hill, has seafood with a Portuguese slant, while the *Fountain Inn* and the *Ship Inn* on Fore Street both offer pub grub, and Portmellon's *Rising Sun* serves Cornish sausages as well as fresh seafood.

Truro, Falmouth and St Mawes

Lush tranquillity collides with frantic tourist activity around **Carrick Roads**, the complex estuary basin to the south of **Truro**, a stop on the main line to Penzance and the region's main centre for transport and accommodation. At the end of a branch line from Truro and at the mouth of the Carrick Roads, **Falmouth** is the major resort around here, and the site of one of Cornwall's mightiest castles, Pendennis. Its sister fort lies across the Carrick Roads in **St Mawes**, the main settlement on the **Roseland** peninsula, a luxuriant backwater of woods and sheltered creeks between the River Fal and the sea.

Truro

TRURO, seat of Cornwall's law courts and other county bureaucracies, has a distinctly small-scale provincial feel, even if its Georgian houses do reflect the prosperity that came with the tin-mining boom of the 1800s. Blurring the town's overall identity, its modern shopping centre stands alongside the powerful but chronologically confused **Cathedral** (daily 7.30am–6pm; £4 donation requested), at the bottom of Pydar Street. Completed in 1910, this was the first Anglican cathedral to be built in England since St Paul's in London, but it incorporates part of the fabric of the old parish church that previously occupied the site. The airy interior's best feature is its neo-Gothic baptistry, complete with emphatically pointed arches and elaborate roof vaulting. To the right of the choir, St Mary's aisle is a relic of the original Perpendicular building, other fragments of which adorn the walls, including – in the north transept – a colourful Jacobean memorial to local Parliamentarian John Robartes and his wife. Free **guided tours** of the cathedral take place at 11.30am between April and October, with an additional tour during school holidays at 2pm.

Truro's other unmissable attraction is the **Royal Cornwall Museum** (Mon–Sat 10am–5pm; £4), housed in an elegant Georgian building on River Street. The exhibits include minerals, Celtic inscriptions and paintings by Cornish artists. Between Easter and October, Enterprise Boats runs scenic **river cruises** to Falmouth up to five times daily from the quayside (about £7.25 return; ⓣ01326/374241, ⓦwww.enterprise-boats.co.uk).

Practicalities

Truro's **tourist office** is on Boscawen Street (April–May & Sept Mon–Fri 9am–5.30pm, Sat 9am–1pm; June–Aug Mon–Fri 9am–5.30pm, Sat 9am–5pm; Oct Mon–Fri 9am–5pm, Sat 9am–1pm; Nov–March Mon–Fri 9am–5pm; ⓣ01872/274555, ⓦwww.truro.gov.uk). Buses stop nearby at Lemon Quay, or near the train station on Richmond Hill. Best **accommodation** near the train station is the *Gables*, at the bottom of Station Road at 49 Treyew Rd (ⓣ01872/242318; no credit cards; ❶), where all rooms have showers and shared WC; near the centre of town, the *Bay Tree* is a restored Georgian house halfway between the station and the centre at 28 Ferris Town (ⓣ01872/240274; ❶). Among the cluster of B&Bs on or around the pleasant Lemon Street: try *Patmos*, 8 Burley Close, off Barrack Lane, where Lemon Street meets Falmouth Road, with views over the river (ⓣ01872/278018; no smoking; no credit cards; ❷). At the bottom of Lemon Street, the very central *Royal Hotel* (ⓣ01872/270345, ⓦwww.royalhotelcornwall.co.uk; ❺) has eschewed traditional trappings in favour of a bright, modern feel, and it has a good, informal brasserie. The nearest **campsite** is *Carnon Downs*, three miles outside Truro on the A39 Falmouth Road (ⓣ01872/862283; closed Nov–March).

A good selection of Truro's **restaurants** lie on or around Kenwyn Street, including *Number Ten* at no. 10, where you can choose wholesome dishes from around the world at inexpensive prices (ⓣ01872/272363); teas, coffees and healthy fruit drinks are on the menu, or bring your own booze; smoking is permitted in the garden only. There's also an outdoor eating area at the *Feast*, 15 Kenwyn St, which cooks up excellent wholefood to eat in or take away, and offers a choice of organic wines and Belgian beers (ⓣ01872/272546; daytime only, but open last Fri & Sat of month for themed evenings; closed Sun).

Elsewhere in town, the non-smoking *Saffron* at 5 Quay St offers inexpensive brunches and an especially good-value early-evening menu (☎01872/263771; closed Sun), while *Pizza Express* on Boscawen Street is housed in the imposing old Coinage Hall, which sports carpets on the walls alongside portraits of George II and other notables. On the corner of Frances and Castle streets, the *Wig and Pen* is a decent **pub** with bar food, real ale and patio seating; next door, the *Globe Inn* also serves hot meals as well as a range of coffees.

Falmouth

The construction of Pendennis Castle on the southern point of Carrick Roads in the sixteenth century prepared the ground for the growth of **FALMOUTH**, then no more than a fishing village. The building of its deepwater harbour was proposed a century later by Sir John Killigrew, and Falmouth's prosperity was assured when in 1689 it became chief base of the fast Falmouth Packets, which sped mail to the Americas. The port has maintained its allure for sailors but its character has become submerged beneath the waves of tourist traffic, attracted to the lush beaches to the south of town. Recent years have seen the growth of a local arts scene, however, and the castle alone is reason enough to brave the hard sell.

The long **High Street** and its continuations Market and Church streets are crammed with humdrum bars and cafés, though at the southern end, Arwenack Street does have the Tudor remains of the Killigrews' **Arwenack House** (closed to the public). The peculiar granite pyramid standing opposite the house, built in 1737, is probably intended to commemorate the local family, though its exact significance has never been clear. The dynasty's most eminent member was Thomas Killigrew, an indifferent Restoration dramatist who was also manager of the king's company of actors. The founder of London's Theatre Royal in Drury Lane, Charles II's former companion-in-exile obtained permission to use female actors for the first time on stage – thereby introducing Nell Gwyn to the king's notice.

Falmouth's newest attraction, the **National Maritime Museum Cornwall**, stands on the seafront opposite Arwenack House (Feb–Dec daily 10am–5pm; £6; ⓦwww.nmmc.co.uk). The large, purpose-built exhibition centre holds diverse examples of vessels from all over the world, many of them suspended in mid-air in the Flotilla Gallery, the cavernous centrepiece of the museum. The exhibits here, which can be viewed from three different levels, are re-hung annually to illustrate different maritime themes; panels on the walkways explain the finer points of boat design. In addition, there are numerous smaller galleries that focus on boat-building and repairing skills, seafaring history, Falmouth's packet ships and Cornwall's various other links with the sea, including fishing. There's plenty of interactive gadgetry, and at one end of the museum, a lighthouse-like look-out tower offers excellent views over the harbour and estuary.

A few minutes' walk west of the museum, **Pendennis Castle** stands sentinel at the tip of the promontory that separates Carrick Roads from Falmouth Bay (daily: April–Sept 10am–6pm; Oct 10am–5pm; Nov–March 10am–4pm; £4.20; EH). The extensive fortification shows little evidence of its five-month siege by the Parliamentarians during the Civil War, which ended only when half its defenders had died and the rest had been starved into submission. Though this is a less-refined contemporary of the castle at St Mawes (see p.498), its site wins hands down, facing right out to sea on its own pointed peninsula, the stout ramparts offering the best all-round views of Carrick Roads and Falmouth Bay. In July and August, the castle grounds stay open late for concerts and other events – call ☎01326/316594 for details of these and other more sporadic events during the rest of the year.

You can view the castle from the sea on one of the numerous **ferries** departing from the Prince of Wales Pier, below the Moor in the centre of town. The service to St Mawes is year-round, but there are many more options offered in summer, including tours of the Carrick Roads and a river cruise to Truro (see p.495). Between Easter and September, the pier is also the embarkation point for ferries to Discovery Quay, site of the Maritime Museum (every 20min; £4 return). If you want to swim in the area, head for the long sandy bay round Pendennis Point, south of the centre, where a succession of sheltered **beaches** are backed by expensive hotels. From the popular **Gyllyngvase Beach**, you can reach the more attractive **Swanpool Beach** by cliff path, or walk a couple of miles further on to **Maenporth**, from where there are some fine cliff-top walks.

Practicalities

Falmouth's **tourist office** is off the Moor, on Killigrew Street (April–Sept Mon–Sat 9.30am–5.30pm; July & Aug also Sun 10am–2pm; Oct–March Mon–Fri 9.30am–4.30pm, Sat 10am–4pm; ⓣ01326/312300, ⓦwww.go-cornwall.com). Most of the town's **accommodation** is south, near the train station and beach area: try the Victorian *Melvill House Hotel*, 52 Melvill Rd (ⓣ01326/316645, ⓦwww.melvill-house-falmouth.co.uk; no smoking; ❸), a few minutes' walk from the beach, and with sea or harbour views from its en-suite rooms. If you prefer to be in the centre, you can't do better than the *Arwenack Hotel* at 27 Arwenack St (ⓣ01326/311185; no credit cards; ❷), where the top room enjoys a great view. Expect to pay more for places nearer the beaches: *Gyllyngvase House Hotel* is a staid but comfortable choice on Gyllyngvase Road (ⓣ01326/312956; ❹), two minutes from the sea, with views from two of its rooms, and *Chellowdene* (ⓣ01326/314950; no credit cards; ❸; closed Oct–April) on the parallel Gyllyngvase Hill has very similar rates, its well-equipped, non-smoking rooms just 50yd from the sea. The very clean and friendly *Falmouth Lodge* backpacker's **hostel** is also near the beach at 9 Gyllyngvase Terrace (ⓣ01326/319996, ⓦwww.falmouthbackpackers.co.uk; no smoking; £12), with use of kitchen and Internet access. Among the overdeveloped caravan parks on the coast south of Falmouth, the **campsite** at *Tregedna Farm* is more tent-friendly, two and a half miles from town and half a mile from Maenporth Beach and the coast path (ⓣ01326/250529; closed Oct–April).

For a coffee and a snack away from the bustle, the *Cinnamon Girl* wholefood **café** in Brewery Yard, off the High Street, provides a pleasant ambience during the day (closed Sun), while the *Harbour Lights* at Custom House Quay provides fast food at outdoor tables with harbour views in the thick of things off Arwenack Street. On the same street are two very cool and contemporary **café/restaurants**, *Blue South* at no. 35–37 (ⓣ01326/212122), offering everything from burgers to Thai red chicken curry, and *Hunky Dory* at no. 46 (ⓣ01326/212997), with excellent seafood and vegetarian dishes. Both get very busy. The best fish in town is to be found across the main drag at the *Seafood Bar*, Lower Quay Hill (ⓣ01326/315129; closed lunch, plus all Sun & Mon Oct–June), where thick crab soup is a speciality. Right on Gyllyngvase Beach, you can tuck in to grills and pizzas at the *Gyllyngvase Beach Café-Bar*, which has a lively feel and is open in the evenings in summer (with live music on Tuesday). The *Quayside Inn*, on Arwenack Street, is the pick of the **pubs**, with outdoor tables overlooking the harbour. Drivers or boaters might venture out of town to the *Pandora Inn* at Restronguet, four miles north of Falmouth, where you can drink by the waterside; superior bar food is available at lunchtime, or you can eat in the upstairs restaurant – good for fresh seafood (ⓣ01326/372678).

St Mawes and the Roseland peninsula

Stuck at the very end of a prong of land at the bottom of Carrick Roads, the secluded, unhurried town of **ST MAWES** has an attractive walled seafront lying below a hillside of villas and abundant gardens. Just out of sight at the end of the seafront stands the small and pristine **St Mawes Castle** (April–Sept daily 10am–6pm; Oct daily 10am–5pm; Nov–March Wed–Sun 10am–1pm & 2–4pm; £3; EH). Built during the reign of Henry VIII, the castle owes its excellent condition to its early surrender during the Civil War when it was placed under siege by Parliamentary forces in 1646, a move which hastened the bloody occupation of Pendennis Castle over in Falmouth. Both castles adhere to the same cloverleaf design, with a round central keep surrounded by robust gun emplacements, but this is the more attractive of the pair. The dungeons and gun installations contain various artillery exhibits as well as some background on local social history.

Moving away from St Mawes, you could spend a pleasant afternoon poking around the Roseland peninsula between the Percuil River and the eastern shore of Carrick Roads. It's only two and a half miles north to the scattered hamlet of **ST JUST-IN-ROSELAND**, where the strikingly picturesque church of St Just stands right next to the creek, surrounded by palms and sub-tropical shrubbery, its gravestones tumbling down to the water's edge.

The fastest road route to Truro, Falmouth and west Cornwall involves crossing the River Fal on the chain-driven **King Harry Ferry** (May–Sept Mon–Fri 7.50am–9.30pm, Sat 7.50am–10.30pm, Sun 9.50am–9.30pm; Oct–April Mon–Sat 7.50am–7.20pm, Sun 9.50am–6.20pm; £3.50/car, 50p/bike, foot passengers 20p; ⓣ01872/862312, ⓦwww.kingharry-info.co.uk), which crosses every twenty minutes, docking close to **Trelissick Garden** (mid-Feb to Oct Mon–Sat 10.30am–5.30pm, Sun 12.30–5.30pm; £4.80; NT), which is celebrated for its hydrangeas and other Mediterranean species, and has a splendid woodland walk along the Fal (free access all year). Take bus #T16 (not Sun) from Truro to get here.

In summer, there's a **ferry** from St Mawes to the southern arm of the Roseland peninsula, which holds the twelfth- to thirteenth-century church of **St Anthony-in-Roseland** and the **lighthouse** on St Anthony's Head, marking the entry into Carrick Roads. There's also a ferry crossing from St Mawes to Falmouth (every 30min–1hr in summer, less frequent in winter; ⓣ01326/313201, ⓦwww.stmawes-ferry.co.uk; £5 day return).

Practicalities

Though lacking Falmouth's range of accommodation, St Mawes makes an attractive – if pricey – place **to stay**. The best budget choices are a ten-minute walk up from the seafront on Newton Road: *Little Newton* (ⓣ01326/270664; ❸) and *Newton Farm*, next door (ⓣ01326/270427; ❸), both are non-smoking establishments, with spacious rooms and friendly hosts. For location – and steep rates – book in at the upmarket *St Mawes Hotel*, located right on the seafront with glorious views over the estuary (ⓣ01326/270266, ⓦwww.stmaweshotel.co.uk; ❻; closed Jan). There's a decent **campsite** at Trethem Mill, three miles north, outside St-Just-in-Roseland (ⓣ01872/580504; closed mid-Oct to March). Back in St Mawes, you can enjoy the views from the bar and brasserie of the *St Mawes Hotel*, while the *Victory Inn* is a fine old oak-beamed **pub** just off the seafront, which also serves seafood meals.

The Lizard peninsula

The **Lizard peninsula** – from the Celtic *lys ardh*, or "high point" – preserves a thankfully undeveloped appearance in contrast to many other areas of Cornwall. If this flat and treeless expanse can be said to have a centre, it is **Helston**, a junction for buses running from Falmouth and Truro to the spartan villages of the peninsula's interior and the tiny fishing ports on its coast. From Truro, Truronian's **bus** #T1 takes 40–55 minutes to reach Helston – which is linked to Penzance by the frequent First Western National #2 – and goes on via **Mullion** to the village of **The Lizard**. Truronian's #T2 connects Helston with the east-coast villages of **St Keverne** and **Coverack**, and #T3 "Lizard Rambler" links all the villages two or three times daily (neither service runs on Sun in winter).

The east coast to Lizard Point

To the north of the peninsula, the snug hamlets sprinkled in the valley of the **River Helford** are a complete contrast to the rugged character of most of the Lizard. At the river's mouth stands **MAWNAN**, whose granite church of St Mawnan-in-Meneage is dedicated to the sixth-century Welsh missionary St Maunanus – Meneage (rhyming with "vague"), means "land of monks". Upstream, outside the village of Gweek, the **Gweek Seal Sanctuary** (daily: summer 10am–5pm, winter 10am–4pm; £7.50), a rehabilitation and release centre for the increasing number of injured seals being rescued from around Cornwall and beyond. Most entertaining are the seal pups, which can be seen during the winter months; other creatures, such as sea lions, otters, ponies and goats, are also cared for here. On the south side of the estuary, **Frenchman's Creek**, one of a splay of creeks and arcane inlets running off the river, was the inspiration for Daphne Du Maurier's novel of the same name – her evocation of it holds true: "still and soundless, surrounded by the trees, hidden from the eyes of men".

You can get over to the south bank by the seasonal ferry (Easter–Oct hourly) from Helford Passage to **Helford**, an agreeable old smugglers' haunt worth a snack-stop – *Rose Cottage* provides teas and light meals, or you can eat pub lunches in the garden of the *Shipwright's Arms*, overlooking the river. South of here, on the B3293, the broad, windswept plateau of Goonhilly Downs is interrupted by the futuristic saucers of Goonhilly Satellite Station, and the nearby ranks of wind turbines. East, the road splits: left to **ST KEVERNE**, an inland village whose tidy square is flanked by two pubs and a church, right to meet the sea at **COVERACK**, a fishing port at one end of a sheltered bay. Three miles offshore lurk the dreaded Manacles rocks, the cause of numerous shipwrecks over the centuries, many of which were gleefully claimed by the local wreckers. Coverack has a few decent **places to stay**, including the pleasant and friendly *Fernleigh* (☎01326/280626; no credit cards; ❸), on Chymbloth Way, a turn-off from Harbour Road, which has three rooms – including one spacious one at the front with en-suite bathroom and wonderful bay views – and amiable proprietors who can cook up a good three-course meal for £15. Alternatively, try the smaller *Bakery Cottage* (☎01326/280474; no credit cards; ❶), where two rooms share a bathroom, right by the seafront. Five minutes from the harbour, on the coast path, *Tamarisk Cottage* offers good-value B&B in a quaint, eighteenth-century house with shared bathrooms (☎01326/280638; no credit cards; ❶; closed Nov–Easter). There's a **youth hostel** just west of Coverack's centre overlooking the bay (☎0870/770 5780;

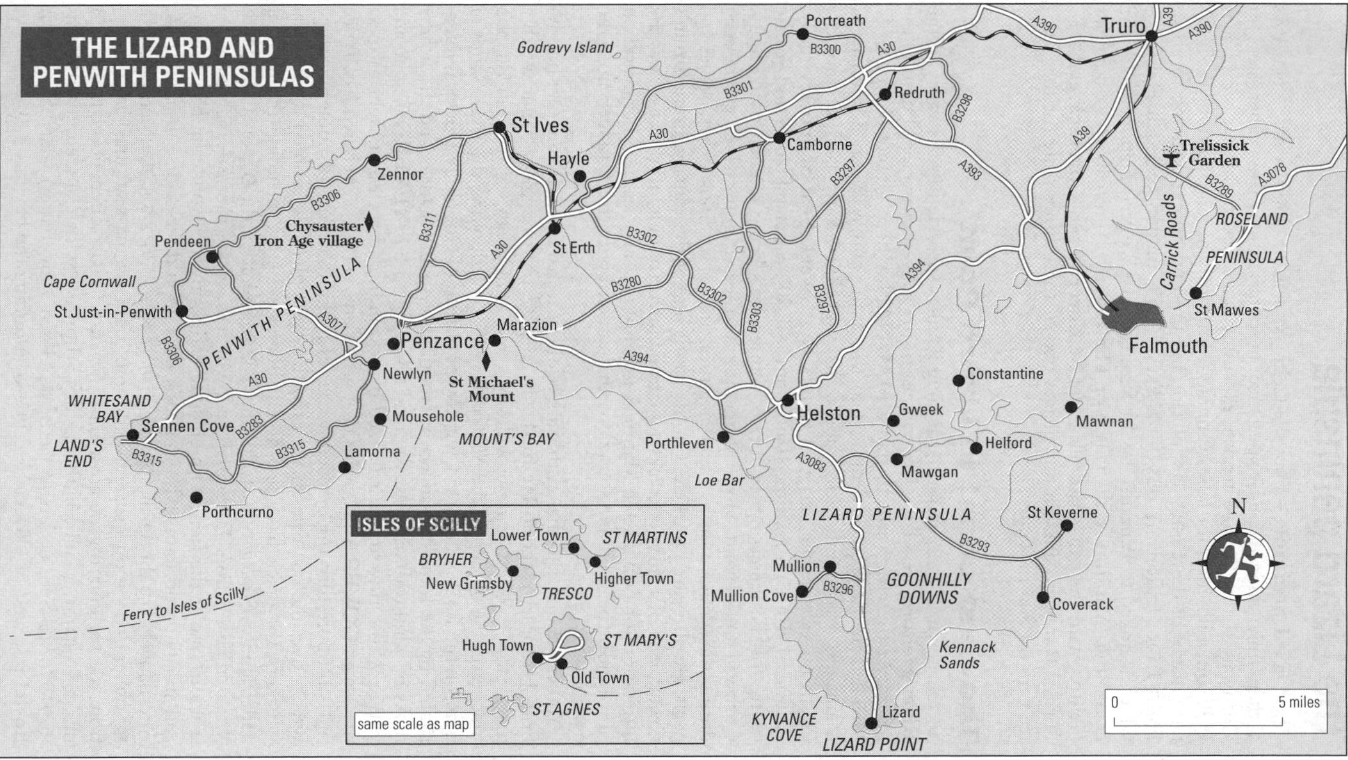
THE LIZARD AND PENWITH PENINSULAS
Truro
Portreath
Godrevy Island
Redruth
Camborne
St Ives
Hayle
Zennor
Chysauster Iron Age village
Pendeen
Cape Cornwall
St Just-in-Penwith
PENWITH PENINSULA
St Erth
Marazion
Penzance
Newlyn
St Michael's Mount
Mousehole
MOUNT'S BAY
WHITESAND BAY
Sennen Cove
LAND'S END
Lamorna
Porthcurno
Ferry to Isles of Scilly
Trelissick Garden
Carrick Roads
ROSELAND PENINSULA
St Mawes
Falmouth
Constantine
Mawnan
Helston
Gweek
Helford
Mawgan
Porthleven
Loe Bar
LIZARD PENINSULA
St Keverne
Mullion
Mullion Cove
GOONHILLY DOWNS
Coverack
Kennack Sands
KYNANCE COVE
Lizard
LIZARD POINT
ISLES OF SCILLY
Lower Town
ST MARTINS
BRYHER
New Grimsby
TRESCO
Higher Town
Hugh Town
ST MARY'S
Old Town
ST AGNES
same scale as map
N
0
5 miles
A39
A390
A30
A393
A394
A3071
A3078
A3083
B3300
B3301
B3298
B3297
B3302
B3280
B3303
B3306
B3311
B3315
B3283
B3289
B3293
B3296

closed Nov–Feb; £10.25), and a campsite outside the village, *Little Trevothan* (ⓣ01326/280260, ⓦwww.littletrevothan.com; closed Oct–Easter). For eating, the *Lifeboat House Seafood Restaurant* (ⓣ01326/280899; closed Mon & Oct–Easter) is pricey and often fully booked, but the fish is superb, and you can pick up first-class fish and chips from the attached takeaway. Ask at the Coverack Windsurfing Centre, below the post office, about windsurfing courses (Easter–Oct; ⓣ01326/280939, ⓦwww.coverack.co.uk).

Beyond the safe and clean swimming spot of **Kennack Sands**, the south tip of the promontory and mainland Britian's southernmost point, **Lizard Point**, is marked by a plain lighthouse and a couple of low-key cafés and gift shops. Sheltered from the ceaselessly churning sea, a tiny cove holds a disused lifeboat station. Behind the point, a road and footpath lead a mile inland to the nondescript village called simply **THE LIZARD**, holding a handful of places to sleep and eat: the non-smoking *Caerthillian* is a comfortable Victorian **B&B** in the centre of the village (ⓣ01326/290019; no credit cards; ❷), while Penmenner Road has several possibilities, including *Parc Brawse House* (ⓣ01326/290466, ⓦwww.cornwall-online.co.uk/parcbrawsehouse; ❷) and the non-smoking *Penmenner House* (ⓣ01326/290370; ❸), both a twenty-minute walk from Lizard Point and forty minutes from Kynance Cove. One of the country's newest **youth hostel**s is housed in a classic Victorian villa right on the coast, with majestic views, signposted from the village (ⓣ0870/770 6120, ⓔcoverack@yha.org.uk; closed Nov–March; £11.50). *The Witchball Restaurant* in the village provides evening **meals**, and you can pick up snacks and pub grub at the *Top House* in the village centre.

A mile westward lies the peninsula's best-known beach, **Kynance Cove**. With its sheer hundred-foot cliffs, its stacks and arches of serpentine rock and its offshore islands, the beach has a wild grandeur, and the water quality is excellent – but take care not to be stranded on the islands by the tide, which submerges the entire beach at its flood.

The west coast

Four miles north of Kynance Cove, the inland village of **MULLION** has a fifteenth- to sixteenth-century church dedicated to the Breton **St Mellane** (or Malo), with a dog-door for canine churchgoers. In the centre of the village, behind an enclosed garden at the top of Nansmellyon Road, *The Old Vicarage* (ⓣ01326/240898, ⓦwww.s-h-systems.co.uk; no credit cards; ❹) provides elegant **accommodation** in four spacious rooms with en-suite or private bathrooms; a brief distance outside Mullion, try *Campden House*, a friendly B&B with a fuchsia-filled garden (ⓣ01326/240365; no credit cards; ❶), less than ten minutes' walk from the sea; snacks and evening meals are also available. In the village, *Stock's* is a tearoom and **restaurant** serving local meat and seafood (ⓣ01326/240727; closed Mon Easter–Oct, Wed, Sun & lunchtime Nov–Easter), while the shop across the road offers sandwiches and a glorious range of dairy ice cream.

There's a small beach at tiny **Mullion Cove**, sheltered behind a lovely harbour and more rock stacks, though the neighbouring sands at **Polurrian** and **Poldhu**, to the north, are better and attract surfers. At the cliff edge, the Marconi Monument marks the spot from which the first transatlantic radio transmission was made in 1901. Three miles further north, strong currents make it unsafe to swim at the beautiful beach at **Loe Bar**, a strip of shingle which separates the freshwater **Loe Pool** from the sea. The elongated pool is one of two places claiming to be where the sword Excalibur was restored to its watery source (the other is on Bodmin Moor), and there's a path running along its western shore as far as Helston, five miles north, making a nice **walk**.

Another three or four miles up the coast, **PORTHLEVEN** is a sizeable port that once served to export tin ore from the inland Stannary town of **HELSTON**, the main transport junction and centre for the Lizard peninsula. The town is best known for its **Furry Dance** (or Flora Dance), which dates from the seventeenth century. Held on May 8 (unless this falls on a Sun or Mon, when the procession takes place on the nearest Sat), it's a stately procession of top-hatted men and summer-frocked women performing a solemn dance through the town's streets and gardens. You can learn something about it and absorb plenty of other local history and lore in the eclectic **Helston Folk Museum** (Mon–Sat 10am–1pm, closes 4pm school holidays; £2), housed in former market buildings behind the Guildhall on Church Street. The quiet attractions on display are a world away from the garish **Flambards Theme Park**, just west of town off the A394 (Easter & June to late July daily 10am–5pm; Easter–May, Sept & Oct daily 10.30am–5pm; late July to Aug daily 10am–5.30pm; sometimes closes Mon & Fri in Oct, call to check ⓣ0845/601 8684, ⓦwww.flambards.co.uk; £12.25), which combines a costumed nostalgia theme park with white-knuckle rides. Helston has the peninsula's only **tourist office** at 79 Meneage St (Aug Mon–Fri 10am–1pm & 2–4.30pm, Sat 10am–4pm; rest of year closes 1pm on Sat; ⓣ01326/565431). Just along from the tourist office at 95 Meneage St is *Hutchinson's*, an award-winning fish-and-chip shop. For a drink or a **pub** snack, check out the *Blue Anchor*, 50 Coinagehall St, a fifteenth-century monastery rest house, now a cramped pub with flagstone floors and mellow Spingo beer brewed on the premises in three strengths. Next door to the pub, the **B&B** at 52 Coinagehall St makes a smart night-stop, with solid old furnishings (ⓣ01326/569334; no credit cards; ❷). For those wanting to explore the Lizard peninsula **by bike** – a great way to get the best out of the network of tiny lanes connecting the villages and coastal tracts – apply to Helston's Bike Services on Meneage Road (ⓣ01326/564564), which rents out mountain bikes, provides a repair service and supplies accessories.

The Penwith peninsula

Though more densely populated than the Lizard, the **Penwith peninsula** is a more rugged landscape, with a raw appeal that is still encapsulated by **Land's End**, despite the commercial paraphernalia superimposed on that headland. The seascapes, the quality of the light and the slow tempo of the local fishing communities made this area a hotbed of artistic activity towards the end of the nineteenth century, when the painters of **Newlyn**, near **Penzance**, established a distinctive school of painting. More innovative figures – among them Ben Nicholson, Barbara Hepworth and Naum Gabo – were soon afterwards to make **St Ives** one of England's liveliest cultural communities, and their enduring influence is illustrated in the St Ives branch of the Tate Gallery, showcasing the modern artists associated with the locality.

Penwith is far more easily toured than the Lizard, with a road circling its coastline and a better network of public transport from the two main towns, St Ives and Penzance, which have most of the accommodation. From Penzance – the terminus for **rail** services from London and Birmingham – **buses** #1, #1A and #1B go straight to Land's End, whereas the #6, #345 and #346 take in Newlyn and Mousehole (#345 and #346 also go to Lamorna, not Sun). North of Land's End, the headland of Cape Cornwall is served by the twice-daily circular #345 (not Sun), otherwise walk from St Just, reachable on the #345, the #10 service from Penzance (not Sun) and the summer-only #300, which circles the peninsula five times daily, taking in Penzance, Marazion, St Ives, Zennor, Sennen Cove and Land's End. St Ives can be reached by branch rail line or numerous buses from Penzance and Truro. **Hikers** might consider walking the eight miles separating Penzance from St Ives along the old St Michael's Way, a waymarked pilgrim's route for which the tourist office in both these towns can provide a free route map.

Penzance and around

Occupying a sheltered position at the northwest corner of Mount's Bay, **PENZANCE** has always been a major port, but most traces of the medieval town were obliterated at the end of the sixteenth century by a Spanish raiding party. Today the dominant style of Penzance is Georgian, particularly at the top of **Market Jew Street** (from *Marghas Jew*, meaning "Thursday Market"), which climbs from the harbour and the train and bus stations. At the top of the street stands the green-domed Victorian **Market House** before which stands a statue of **Humphry Davy** (1778–1829), the local woodcarver's son who pioneered the science of electrochemistry and invented the life-saving miners' safety-lamp which his statue holds.

Turn left here into **Chapel Street**, which has some of the town's finest buildings, including the flamboyant **Egyptian House**, built in 1835 to contain a geological museum but subsequently abandoned until its restoration 25 years ago. Across the street, the **Union Hotel** dates from the seventeenth century, and originally housed the town's assembly rooms: the news of Admiral Nelson's victory at Trafalgar and the death of Nelson himself were first announced from the minstrels' gallery here in 1805.

On the seafront, opposite the harbour, the **Lighthouse Centre** (Easter–Oct daily 10am–4.30pm; £3) recalls a time when lighthouses were staffed and inhabited, and gathers together a collection of items relating to the keeper's job and lonely existence, illustrating the various methods, devices and navigation aids used from earliest times to alert shipping to danger. Just south of here, bulging out of the Promenade into Mount's Bay, the Art Deco **Jubilee Pool** (mid-May to mid-Sept daily 10am–6pm; £2.25) is a tidal, salt-water (though chlorinated) open-air swimming pool, built to mark the Silver Jubilee of George V in 1935. It's a classic example of the style, and non-swimmers can stroll around (60p) to get a closer view of the pool and bay.

If your interest is roused by the art scene that flourished hereabouts at the turn of the nineteenth century, head up Morrab Road from the Promenade (you can also reach it from Alverton Street, a continuation of Market Jew Street), where the **Penlee House Gallery and Museum** (Mon–Sat: May–Sept 10am–5pm; Oct–April 10.30am–4.30pm; £2, free on Sat) holds the biggest collection of the works of the Newlyn School – impressionistic harbour scenes, frequently sentimentalized but often bathed in an evocatively luminous light. There are frequent exhibitions, and also displays on local history.

NEWLYN itself, Cornwall's biggest fishing port, lies immediately south of Penzance, protected behind two long piers. The colony of artists who gathered here around the Irish painter Stanhope Forbes is represented in the collection in Penzance, but Newlyn's **art gallery**, near the harbour at 24 New Rd (Mon–Sat 10am–5pm; free), which concentrates on contemporary art, gives an often stimulating insight into how that tradition has evolved. The port also has the absorbing **Pilchard Works** on Tolcarne (Easter–October Mon–Fri 10am–6pm; £3.25), an insight into what was once the basis of one of

Cornwall's greatest industries. The museum incorporates a working salt pilchard factory, from which you can buy fresh pilchards – which are actually mature sardines – in summer.

Practicalities

Penzance's **tourist office** (May–Sept Mon–Fri 9.30am–5pm, Sat 9am–5pm, Sun 10am–1pm; Oct–April Mon–Fri 9am–5pm, Sat 10am–1pm; ⓣ01736/362207, ⓦwww.go-cornwall.com) is right next to the train and bus stations on the seafront. Drivers can deposit their vehicles during excursions to the Isles of Scilly at Avalon **car park** near the harbour with entrances at 33 Regent Terrace and South Place (ⓣ01736/364622), for £3.50 per day. For **bike rental** head for Pedals on the seafront in the Wharfside shopping centre (ⓣ01736/360600). Penzance Computer Centre, 76 Market Jew St, provides **Internet access**.

Guest houses nearest the bus and train stations include *Honeydew* at 3 Leskinnick St (ⓣ01736/364206; no smoking; no credit cards; ❷), at the bottom of Market Jew Street, though you should venture further afield for a bit more character. On Chapel Street, you could soak up the atmosphere in the *Union Hotel* (ⓣ01736/362319; ❸) or, further down, sample the Bohemian ambience of the *Penzance Arts Club* (ⓣ01736/363761, ⓦwww.penzanceartsclub.co.uk; ❺), where you can sleep in one of the seven tasteful rooms of what was once the Portuguese embassy; there's a good café/restaurant in the basement too. Off Chapel Street on Abbey Street, the seventeenth-century *Abbey Hotel* is a top-of-the-league treat, owned by former model Jean Shrimpton and her husband, where you'll be pampered with lashings of old-fashioned comfort, superb views and an excellent restaurant (ⓣ01736/366906, ⓦwww.theabbeyonline.com; ❻). Most cheaper B&Bs are along Morrab and Alexandra roads to the west of the centre: on Morrab Road, try *Kimberley House* at no. 10 (ⓣ01736/362727, ⓦwww.s-h-systems.co.uk; no smoking; no credit cards; ❸), where there are large rooms and croissants for breakfast; on Alexandra Road, *Holbein House* (ⓣ01736/332625; no credit cards; ❶) is a cheerful and spacious B&B, with breakfast served in the bright-painted rooms. On the seafront, the non-smoking *Camilla House Hotel* is useful for the harbour at 12 Regent Terrace, on a parallel road to the Promenade (ⓣ01736/363771, ⓦwww.camillahouse-hotel.co.uk; ❸); most rooms have sea views (the top rooms are cosiest), and the owners can help with local travel, including trips to the Isles of Scilly. Alexandra Road is also the location of the tidy and friendly *Penzance Backpackers* **hostel** (ⓣ01736/363836, ⓦwww.pzbackpack.com), where dorm beds are £10 and there are doubles (❶). The YHA hostel is out of town, housed in a Georgian mansion at Castle Horneck, Alverton (ⓣ0870/770 5992, ⓔpenzance@yha.org.uk; closed Jan; £11.50), a two-mile hike from the station up Market Jew Street into Alverton Road, then turn right at the *Pirate Inn*, or take bus #5 or #6 from Penzance Station as far as the *Pirate Inn*.

Penzance does not have a great choice of **restaurants**, though *Bar Coco's* on Chapel Street is good for coffees and cakes as well as beers and tapas. Quality cuisine can be had at the formal *Harris's* nearby at 46 New St (ⓣ01736/364408; closed Sun, plus Mon in winter), and the contrastingly ultra-modern *Abbey Restaurant* in Abbey Street (ⓣ01736/330680; closed Sun & Mon, plus lunchtime Tues–Thurs, and all Jan), both expensive. Vegetarians and wholefoodies will feel at home in the spacious and relaxed *Brown's*, above a health shop in Bread Street, off the pedestrianized Causeway Head, currently open on Friday evenings for a buffet, otherwise open daytime only and closed all day Sunday. There are also a few congenial café-bars serving ciabattas, salads, wraps and evening meals: the *Blue Snappa*, 18 Market Place (at the top of Chapel Street), the *Boatshed*, facing the harbour on the Promenade, and *The Renaissance Café*, in the Wharfside centre on the Promenade, which has a lively feel and an outdoor terrace with views over to St Michael's Mount. At street level below it, *The Olive Farm* is the place for delicious rolls and other takeaway snacks.

Chapel Street has a couple of characterful **pubs**, the *Admiral Benbow*, crammed with gaudy ships' figureheads and other nautical items, and the *Turk's Head*, the town's oldest inn, reputed to date back to the thirteenth century, with a garden and the remains of a contrabanders' tunnel to the harbour.

St Michael's Mount

Buses from Penzance bus station leave every thirty minutes for Marazion, five miles east, from where the medieval chimneys and towers of **St Michael's Mount** (April–Oct Mon–Fri 10.30am–5.30pm, plus most weekends; Nov–March guided tours Mon, Wed & Fri, phone for times ⓣ01736/710507; £4.80; NT) can be seen a couple of hundred yards offshore. A vision of the archangel Michael led to the building of a church on this granite pile around the fifth century, and within three centuries a Celtic monastery had been founded here. The present building derives from a chapel raised in the eleventh century by Edward the Confessor, who handed over the abbey to the Benedictine monks of Brittany's Mont St Michel, whose island abbey – also founded after a vision of St Michael – was the model for this one. The complex was appropriated by Henry V during the Hundred Years War, and it became a fortress after its dissolution a century later. After the Civil War, when it was used to store arms for the Royalist forces, it became the residence of the St Aubyn family, who still inhabit the castle.

The fortress-isle has a milder, more pedestrian feel than its prototype off the Breton coast, but there's no doubting its eye-catching site, which demands a first-hand inspection from anyone travelling along this part of the Cornish littoral. A good number of its buildings date from the twelfth century, but the later additions are more interesting, such as the battlemented **chapel** and the seventeenth-century decorations of the Chevy Chase Room, the former refectory. Other rooms are crowded with paintings of the castle, portraits of various St Aubyns and general memorabilia.

At low tide the promontory can be approached on foot via a cobbled causeway; at high tide there are boats from Marazion (£1).

Mousehole to Land's End

Accounts vary as to the derivation of the name of **MOUSEHOLE** (pronounced "Mowzle"), though it may be from a smugglers' cave just south of town. In any case, the name evokes perfectly this minuscule harbour, cradled in the arms of a granite breakwater three miles south of Penzance. The village attracts more visitors than it can handle, so hang around until the crowds have departed before you walk through its tight tangle of lanes to take in Mousehole's oldest house, the fourteenth-century Keigwin House (a survival of the 1595 attack when the village was burned by the Spaniards), and a drink at the *Ship Inn*, which also has **rooms** (ⓣ01736/731234; ❸) – those with a view are slightly more expensive. Half a mile inland, the churchyard wall at **Paul** holds a monument to Dolly Pentreath, a resident of Mousehole who died in 1777 and was reputed to have been the last person to speak the Cornish language. The inscription includes a Cornish translation of a verse from the Bible.

Three miles south round the coast, **Lamorna Cove** is squeezed between granite headlands, linked by a flower-bordered lane to the tiny village of **LAMORNA**, where you can see an old flour mill and drink at the comfortable old *Lamorna Wink* pub – as the sign shows, it was the wink that signified that contraband spirits were available. The spot makes a nice starting point for exploring the coastpath: following it westwards brings you round Boscawen Point to **St Loy's Cove**, a hike of a couple of miles, where *Cove Cottage* serves up teas, delicious cakes or savoury snacks, and also offers **B&B** in a huge double room with a fabulous panorama (Ⓣ01736/810010; ❹).

Five miles west of Lamorna lies one of the best beaches on Penwith, at **PORTHCURNO**. The name means "Port Cornwall", but its beach of tiny white shells suggests privacy and isolation rather than the movement of ships. Steep steps lead up from here to the cliff-hewn **Minack Theatre**, created in the 1930s and since enlarged to hold 750 seats, though the basic Greek-inspired design has remained intact. The spectacular backdrop of Porthcurno Bay makes this one of the country's most inspiring theatres – providing the weather holds. The summer season lasts seventeen weeks from May to September, presenting a gamut of plays, opera and musicals, with tickets costing just £5.50 for afternoon performances, £7 for evening ones (box office Mon–Fri from 9.30am; Ⓣ01736/810181, Ⓦwww.minack.com). Bring a cushion and a rug. You can also visit the **Exhibition Centre** (daily: April–Sept 9.30am–5.30pm; Oct–March 10am–4pm; closed during performances; £2.50), which allows you to see the theatre and follow the story of its creation through photographs and audiovisual displays.

The peculiar white pyramid on the shore to the east of Porthcurno marks the spot where the first transatlantic cables were laid in 1880. On the headland beyond lies an Iron Age fort, **Treryn Dinas**, close to the famous rocking stone called **Logan's Rock**, a seventy-ton monster that was knocked off its perch by a nephew of playwright Oliver Goldsmith and a gang of sailors in 1824. Somehow they replaced the stone, but it never rocked again.

The best way to approach **Land's End** is unarguably on foot along the coastal path. Although nothing can completely destroy the potency of this, the extreme western tip of England, the colossal theme park built behind this majestic headland in 1987 comes close to violating irreparably the spirit of the place. The trivializing **Land's End Experience** (daily: Easter–Oct 10am–6pm; Oct–Easter 10am–5pm, or earlier at quiet times; Ⓣ0870/458 0099; £10) substitutes a tawdry panoply of lasers and unconvincing sound effects for the real open-air experience, but the location is still a public right of way (though you'll have to pay to use the car park; £3), and once past the paraphernalia, nature takes over. Turf-covered cliffs sixty feet high provide a platform to view the Irish Lady, the Armed Knight, Dr Syntax Head and the rest of the Land's End outcrops, beyond which you can spot the Longships lighthouse, a mile and a half out to sea, and sometimes the Wolf Rock lighthouse, nine miles southwest, or even the Isles of Scilly, twenty-eight miles away.

Whitesand Bay to Zennor

To the north of Land's End the rounded granite cliffs fall away at **Whitesand Bay** to reveal a glistening mile-long shelf of beach that offers the best swimming on the Penwith peninsula. The rollers make for good surfing and boards can be rented at **Sennen Cove**, the more popular southern end of the beach. There are a few places to **stay** around the southern end of the strand, including *Myrtle Cottage* (Ⓣ01736/871698; no credit cards; ❷), which also has a cosy café open to non-residents, and the nearby *Polwyn Cottage*, tucked away on Old

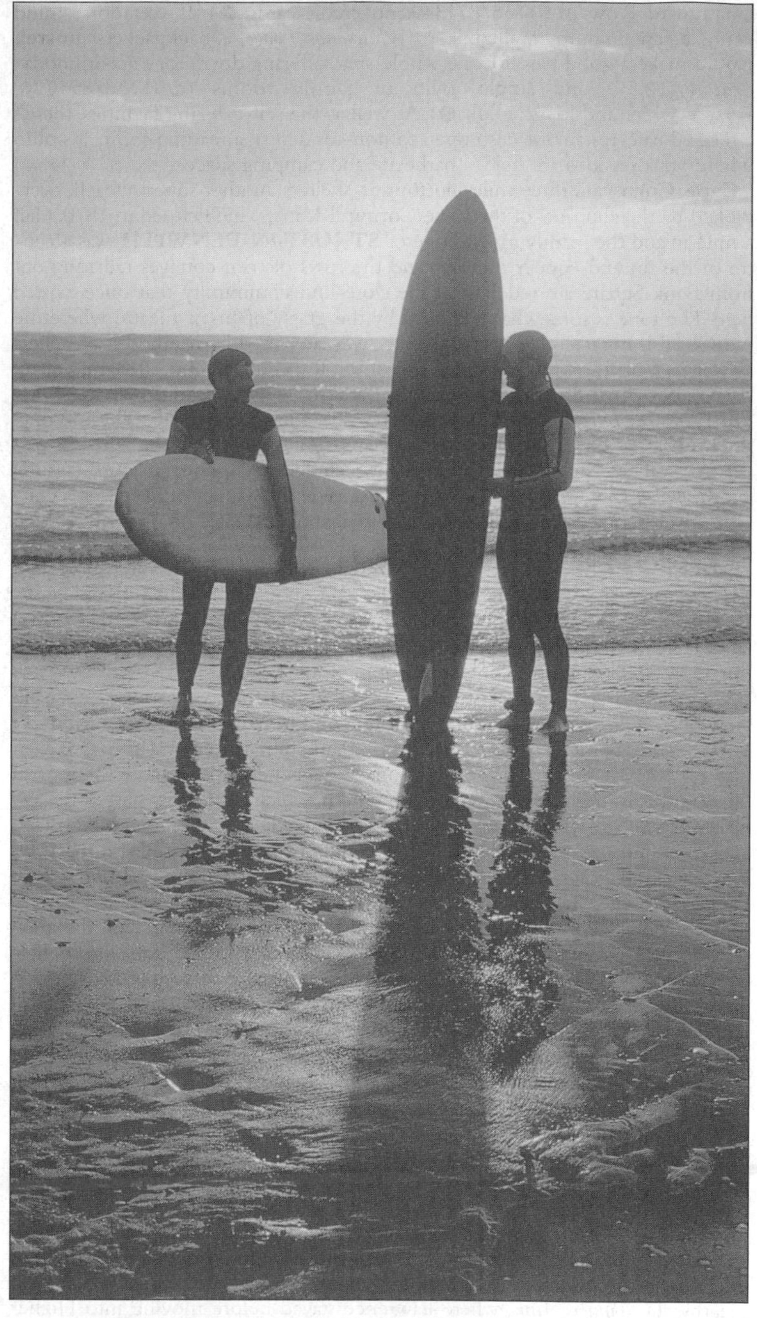

△ Surfing in Cornwall

Coastguard Row (☎01736/871349; no credit cards; ❷). If you don't mind being a few minutes' walk inland, *Whitesands Lodge*, a backpackers' **hostel**, would make a good base for the whole area, offering dormitory accommodation (£12.50) and single, twin or family rooms (☎01736/871776, Ⓦwww.whitesandslodge.co.uk; ❷). As well as the self-catering facilities, there's a relaxed café-restaurant (also open to non-residents), a reading room, a studio where yoga sessions are held, a barbecue and camping space.

Cape Cornwall, three miles northward, shelters another superb beach, overlooked by the chimney of the Cape Cornwall Mine, which closed in 1870. Half a mile inland the grimly grey village of **ST JUST-IN-PENWITH** was a centre of the tin and copper industry, and the rows of trim cottages radiating out from Bank Square are redolent of the close-knit community that once existed here. The tone is somewhat lightened by the grassy open-air theatre where the old Cornish miracle plays were staged; it was later used by Methodist preachers as well as Cornish wrestlers. Three out of the four pubs in and off Bank Square have **accommodation**, the best of them is the traditional *Star Inn* (☎01736/788767; no credit cards; ❷). The village has a **youth hostel** on its outskirts (☎0870/770 5906; closed Nov–March; £11.50) – take the left fork past the post office – and there's an excellent secluded **campsite**, *Kelynack Caravan and Camping Park* (☎01736/787633), just outside the hamlet of Kelynack a couple of miles south of St Just, one of the few sheltered sites on Penwith, which also has bunks in small dorms (£8). For good coffees, teas and **lunches** *The Cook Book*, 3 Cape Cornwall Rd, should satisfy, with soups and homemade cakes, tables outside and second-hand books for sale upstairs (closed Mon; no smoking), or step into *Kegen Teg*, 12 Market Square, which offers fish pie, rich chocolate cake and wonderful Kelly's ice creams, as well as moderately priced **dinners** (☎01736/788562; no smoking at lunchtime; closed Sun).

A couple of miles north of St Just, outside **PENDEEN**, you can get a close-up view of the Cornish mining industry at **Geevor Tin Mine** (Easter–Oct Mon–Fri & Sun 10am–5pm; Nov–Easter Mon–Fri 10am–4pm; last entry 1hr before closing; £6.50), where you can tour the surface machinery and explore the innards of an underground mine and visit the museum, which is the only part of the site open for visits in winter (£2). East of here, the landscape is all rolling moorland and an abundance of granite, the chief building material of **ZENNOR**. D.H. Lawrence and Frieda came to live here in 1916: "It is a most beautiful place," Lawrence wrote, "lovelier even than the Mediterranean." The Lawrences were soon joined by John Middleton Murry and Katherine Mansfield, with the hope of forming a writers' community, but the new arrivals soon left for a more sheltered haven near Falmouth. Lawrence stayed on to write *Women in Love*, spending in all a year and a half in Zennor before being given notice to quit by the local constabulary, who suspected Lawrence and his German wife of unpatriotic sympathies. His Cornish experiences were later described in *Kangaroo*.

At the bottom of the village, the **Wayside Museum** is dedicated to Cornish life from prehistoric times (April to late July, Sept & Oct daily 11am–5pm; late July to Aug daily 10.30am–5.30pm; £2.75). Note the "plague stone" on the road outside the building, where a hole containing vinegar was used to disinfect visiting merchants' money during cholera outbreaks in the nineteenth century. At the top of the lane, the church of **St Sennen** displays a sixteenth-century bench-carving of a mermaid who, according to local legend, was so entranced by the singing of a chorister that she lured him down to the sea, from where he never returned – though his singing can still occasionally be heard. Nearby, the *Tinners Arms*, where Lawrence stayed before moving into Higher Tregerthen, is a cosy place to **drink** and **eat**. If you don't mind sleeping up to six to a room, the *Old Chapel Backpackers Hostel* makes a fun place **to stay**, right next to the Wayside Museum (ⓣ01736/798307, ⓦwww.backpackers.co.uk /zennor); dorm beds go for £12 each, there's a family room (❷) too, and a café provides breakfast and evening meals.

The Iron Age village of **Chysauster** (April–Sept daily 10am–6pm; Oct daily 10am–5pm; £2; EH), located on a windy hillside a couple of miles inland from Zennor, off the minor road to Penzance, is the best-preserved ancient settlement in the southwest. Dating from about the first century BC, it contains two rows of four buildings, each consisting of a courtyard with small chambers leading off it, and a garden that was presumably used for growing vegetables.

St Ives

East of Zennor, the road runs four hilly miles on to the steeply built town of **ST IVES**, a place that has smoothly undergone the transition to holiday haunt from its previous role as a centre of the fishing industry. So productive were the offshore waters that a record sixteen and a half million fish were caught in one net on a single day in 1868, and the diarist Francis Kilvert was told by the local vicar that the smell was sometimes so great as to stop the church clock. Virginia Woolf, who spent every summer here to the age of 12, described St Ives as "a windy, noisy, fishy, vociferous, narrow-streeted town; the colour of a mussel or a limpet; like a bunch of rough shell fish clustered on a grey wall together." By the time the pilchard reserves dried up around the early years of the last century, the town was beginning to attract a vibrant **artists' colony**, precursors of the wave later headed by Ben Nicholson, Barbara Hepworth (second of Nicholson's three wives), Naum Gabo and the potter Bernard Leach, who in the 1960s were followed by a third wave including Terry Frost, Peter Lanyon, Patrick Heron, Bryan Wynter and Roger Hilton.

Arrival and information

To reach St Ives by **train**, change at St Erth on the main line to Penzance or there are direct services from Penzance. Regular and frequent **buses** connect Penzance with St Ives, which you can reach from Truro on #X14 and National Express buses. The train station is off Porthminster Beach, just north of the bus station on Station Hill. The **tourist office** is in the Guildhall, in the narrow Street-an-Pol, two minutes' walk away (mid-May to June Mon–Sat 9.30am–5.30pm, Sun 10am–1pm; July & Aug Mon–Sat 9am–6pm, Sun 10am–4pm; Sept Mon–Fri 9.30am–5pm, Sat 9am–1pm; Oct to mid-May Mon–Fri 9am–5pm, Sat 10am–1pm; ⓣ01736/796297, ⓦwww.go-cornwall.com). Among the places where you can rent **surfing equipment** are Porthmeor Beach and the surf specialists on Fore Street and by the harbour. The St Ives **Festival** of folk, jazz and blues, also taking in classical music and theatre, takes place over two weeks in mid-September.

Accommodation

Even with West Cornwall's greatest concentration of hotels and guest houses, St Ives can still run short of available **accommodation** in peak season, and advance booking is essential. Most of the following choices are central, and most offer one or two parking spaces.

Hotels and B&Bs

Allamanda 83 Back Rd East ⓣ01736/793548, ⓦwww.allamanda.co.uk. Superior Georgian conversion in the cobbled heart of St Ives, with two small but elegant rooms with en-suite or private bathrooms. No smoking, no under-12s and no credit cards. Closed Nov–Feb. ❻

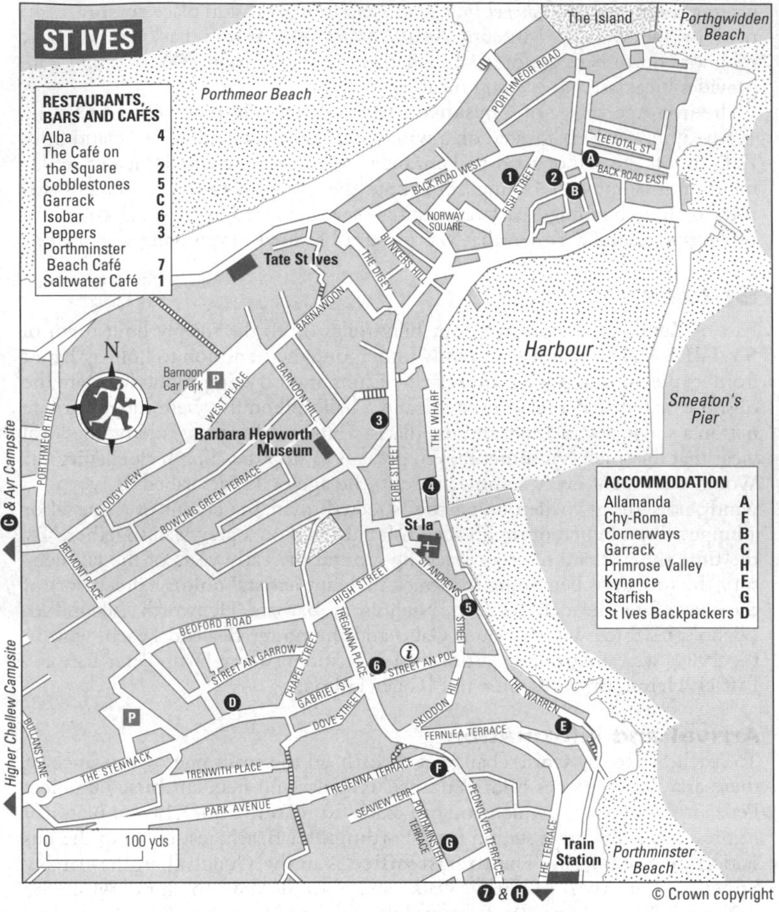

Chy-Roma 2 Seaview Terrace ⓣ01736/797539, ⓦwww.connexions.co.uk/chyroma. Convenient for the bus and train stations, among a cluster of similar lodgings, this one offers homemade muesli, yoghurt, bread and jam for breakfast and boasts great panoramic views. One-week minimum stay in summer. No credit cards. 2

Cornerways The Square ⓣ01736/796706. Daphne Du Maurier once stayed in this tastefully modern cottage conversion, which has friendly management and lovely, airy rooms – ask for the top room (no. 6). No credit cards. 3

Garrack Burthallan Lane ⓣ01736/796199, ⓦwww.garrack.com. One of the best hotels in the area, outside the town's bustle, but within walking distance of Porthmeor Beach. Family-run, the hotel has an indoor pool, gym and sauna, and an excellent restaurant (see p.512); the atmosphere is polite but friendly. 7

Kynance 24 The Warren ⓣ01736/796636, ⓦwww.kynance.com. A good choice among the many B&Bs in this area of town near Porthminster Beach. The top-floor rooms have good views but get booked up early. No smoking. Closed Nov to March. 3

Primrose Valley Porthminster Beach ⓣ01736/794939, ⓦwww.primroseonline.co.uk. Lovely Edwardian villa just above Porthminster Beach. Rooms, some with balconies, are fresh and light. There's a week's minimum stay in July and August. 5

Starfish 6 Porthminster Terrace ⓣ01736/799575, ⓦwww.starfishbandb.co.uk. Near Porthminster Beach and the stations, this quiet B&B run by a young family offers soft colours in airy, en-suite rooms, including a more spacious one with sea views, in the next price category up. No smoking. No credit cards. ❷

Campsites and hostels

Ayr Higher Ayr ⓣ01736/795855, ⓦwww.ayrholidaypark.co.uk. St Ives has no campsites right on the seafront but this large complex with caravans and holiday homes, half a mile west of the centre above Porthmeor Beach, has a good sea prospect. It's near to the coast path, and buses #8B and the summer-only #300 to Land's End pass close by.

Higher Chellew Nancledra ⓣ01736/364532. Good out-of-town alternative to the *Ayr*, and much cheaper. Facilities are basic but clean and include washing machines. Located on the B3311 road, equidistant between St Ives and Penzance. Closed Oct–Easter.

St Ives Backpackers The Stennack ⓣ01736/799444, ⓦwww.backpackers.co.uk/st-ives. Restored Wesleyan chapel school from 1845, usefully located in the centre of St Ives opposite the cinema. Comfortable and clean, with barbecues and free tours around the area. Dorms have four, six or eight beds for £14 per night and there are double and twin rooms (❶). Rates drop in winter.

The Town

Sunday painters dominate the dozens of galleries sandwiched between the town's restaurants and bars; the place to view the best work created in St Ives is the **St Ives Tate Gallery**, overlooking Porthmeor Beach on the north side of town (March–Oct daily 10am–5:30pm; Nov–Feb Tues–Sun 10am–4:30pm; £4.75; combined ticket with Barbara Hepworth Museum £7.50; ⓦwww.tate.org.uk/stives). The sights and sounds of the beachfront are a constant presence inside the airy, gleaming-white building, creating a dialogue with the gallery's paintings, sculptures and ceramics, most of which date from the period 1925 to 1975. Apart from these, the Tate has some specially commissioned contemporary works on view. The museum's rooftop **café** is one the best places in town for tea and cake.

A short distance away on Barnoon Hill, the **Barbara Hepworth Museum** (March–Oct daily 10am–5.30pm; Nov–Feb Tues–Sun 10am–4.30pm or dusk; £4.25; combined ticket with the Tate £7.50) gives another insight into the local arts scene. One of the foremost non-figurative sculptors of her time, Hepworth lived in the building from 1949 until her death in a studio fire in 1975. Apart from the sculptures, which are arranged in positions chosen by Hepworth in the house and garden, the museum has masses of background on her art, from photos and letters to catalogues and reviews. A few Hepworths are scattered around the town, including a tender *Madonna* in the harbourside church of **St Ia** – a fifteenth-century building dedicated to the female missionary who was said to have floated over from Ireland on an ivy leaf.

Devotees of Bernard Leach's Japanese-inspired ceramics can visit his former studio, the **Leach Pottery** (Mon–Sat 10am–5pm; £2.50), in the Higher Stennack neighbourhood, three-quarters of a mile outside St Ives on the Zennor road. Some examples of Leach's work are on display here, alongside that of his wife, Janet Leach, as well as pieces by Shoji Hamada, Michael Cardew and other more contemporary artworks.

The wide expanse of **Porthmeor Beach** dominates the northern side of St Ives, the stone houses tumbling almost onto the yellow sands. Unusually for a town beach, the water quality is excellent, and the rollers make it popular with surfers (boards available for rent below the Tate); there's also a good open-air café here. South of the station, the broader, usually less crowded **Porthminster Beach** is another favourite spot for sunbathing and swimming, while, heading east out of town, you'll find a string of magnificent golden beaches lining **St Ives Bay** – the strand is especially fine on the far side of the port of Hayle, at the mouth of the eponymous river.

Restaurants, bars and cafés

The year-round tourist industry has given St Ives a dazzling range of **restaurants**, mostly concentrating on seafood, and including the inevitable array of fast-food outlets. **Bar life** is fairly low-level, however, with little in the way of café culture.

Alba The Wharf ☎01736/797222. Sleekly modern harbourside restaurant in a converted lifeboat house. There are fixed-price menus, on which mullet, brill and sea bass rub shoulders with Cornish beef and free-range roast chicken. Downstairs, the cheaper *Harbour Kitchen* café has some of the same dishes. Closed Sun eve & all Mon in winter. Moderate–Expensive.

The Café on the Square Island Square ☎01736/793621. Lunches and intimate evening meals are served in this tiny place with a Mediterranean feel, along with a good range of coffees. Closed Sun. Moderate.

Cobblestones 5 St Andrews St. Basic English seaside nosh, or just tea and cakes, with a plain modern interior and some outdoor tables with a view over the harbour. Late opening till 10pm in summer, daytime only for the rest of the year. Inexpensive.

Garrack Burthallan Lane ☎01736/796199. A bit out of the way, but worth the detour. The kitchen excels at fish, but meat dishes are also excellent, and there are some astounding desserts. Expensive.

Isobar Tregenna Place ☎01736/799199. Cocktail and tapas bar serving coffees, chunky ciabattas, salads and seafood. DJs play most evenings downstairs and there's a club upstairs (July & Aug Mon–Sat; rest of year Wed–Sat) playing dance music from 1970s to the present day.

Peppers 22 Fore St ☎01736/794014. Mellow pizza and pasta parlour, also serving fish and steaks. Inexpensive.

Porthminster Beach Café Porthminster Beach ☎01736/795352. With its sun deck and fantastic beach location, this makes a superb spot for coffees, lunches, cream teas and full evening meals. Under the same management, the *Porthgwidden Beach Café* in the Downalong area of town offers a smaller range of similar fare. Closed Nov to mid-March. Moderate–Expensive.

Saltwater Café Fish Street ☎01736/794928. Bright, beachy paintings on the walls and a good choice of seafood, from swordfish to pan-fried scallops wrapped in pancetta. Desserts include homemade ice cream. Eves only. Closed Sun & Mon (except July–Sept). Moderate.

The Isles of Scilly

The **Isles of Scilly** are a compact archipelago of about a hundred islands 28 miles southwest of Land's End, none of them bigger than three miles across, and only five of them inhabited – **St Mary's**, **Tresco**, **Bryher**, **St Martin's** and **St Agnes**. In the annals of folklore, the Scillies are the peaks of the submerged land of Lyonesse, a fertile plain that extended west from Penwith before the ocean broke in, drowning the land and leaving only one survivor to tell the tale. In fact they form part of the same granite mass as Land's End, Bodmin Moor and Dartmoor, and despite rarely rising above a hundred feet, they possess a remarkable variety of landscape. All are swept by an energizing briny air filled with the cries of seabirds, and though the water is cold the beaches are well-nigh irresistible, ranging from small coves to vast untrammelled strands. Other points of interest include Cornwall's greatest concentration of prehistoric remains, some fabulous rock formations, and masses of **flowers**. Along with tourism, the main source of income here is flower-growing, for which the equable climate and the long hours of sunshine – their name means "Sun Isles" – make the islands ideal. The profusion of wild flowers is even more noticeable than the fields of narcissi and daffodils, and the heaths and pathways are often dense with marigolds, gorse, sea thrift, trefoil and poppies, not to mention a host of more exotic varieties introduced by visiting foreign vessels.

Getting to the islands

The islands are accessible by sea or air. **Boats from Penzance to St Mary's** operated by the Isles of Scilly Steamship Group (☎0845/710 5555, ⓦwww.ios-travel.co.uk) depart from the South Pier, where there's a ticket office. Sailings, which can be nauseatingly rough, take place daily between April and October and last about two and three-quarter hours; single tickets cost £38, day returns £32, short-break returns (travelling on Mon, Tues or Wed) £60, and period returns £78, with discounts for children. There are ferries between each of the inhabited islands (about £6.50 return fare), though these are sporadic in winter.

The main departure points for **flights** (also operated by the Isles of Scilly Steamship Company) are **Land's End**, near St Just (Mon–Sat; 15min; £80–103 return), **Newquay** (Mon–Sat; 30min; £100–125 return), **Exeter** (Mon–Sat; 50min; £199 return), **Bristol** (Mon–Sat; 1hr 10min; £245 return) and **Southampton** (Mon–Wed & Fri; 90min; £260 return). In winter, there are departures only from Land's End and Newquay. British International also runs **helicopter** flights (☎01736/363871, ⓦwww.scillyhelicopter.co.uk) from the heliport a mile east of Penzance to St Mary's (not Sun) and Tresco (not Sun) taking twenty minutes, with return fares currently at £117 – though you can get discounted day returns, advance returns and short-break returns.

Free of traffic, theme parks and amusement arcades, the Scillies are a welcome respite from the tourist trail, the main drawbacks being the high cost of reaching the islands and the shortage of accommodation – making advance booking essential at any time. Note that most places offer, and often insist on, a dinner, bed and breakfast package, and this option should not be automatically rejected, considering the tiny choice of places to eat (Hugh Town in St Mary's is better supplied), though basic groceries are always available. If you're coming between May and September, try to time your visit to be here on a Wednesday or Friday evening to witness the **gig races**, the most popular sport on the Scillies, performed by six-oared vessels some thirty feet in length. Some of the boats used are over a hundred years old, built originally to carry pilots to passing ships.

St Mary's

The island of **ST MARY'S** holds the overwhelming majority of the archipelago's population and most of its tourist accommodation. From the airport there are buses to shuttle passengers the mile to **HUGH TOWN**, straddling a neck of land at the southwestern end of the island. Ferries from Penzance dock on the north side of town, under a knob of land still known as the Garrison, where the eight-pointed **Star Castle**, built in Elizabeth I's reign after the scare of the Spanish Armada, has been converted into a hotel. The rampart walk hereabout is a good place to get your bearings, affording views over all the islands and the myriad rocky fragments around them.

Hugh Town itself has a limited appeal, and once you've exhausted the pubs and shops there's little to occupy your time apart from the engaging **Isles of Scilly Museum** on Church Street, well worth an hour or two's wander (April–Oct daily 10am–noon, 1.30–4.30pm & 7.30–9pm; Nov–March Mon–Sat 10am–noon; £1.50). Most of the exhibits are relics salvaged from the many ships which foundered on or around the islands, including the happy miscellany of finds recovered from the most recent wreck, the *Cita*, which sank off St Mary's Porth Hellick in March 1997 en route from Southampton to Belfast, much of its cargo, ranging from trainers to tobacco, finding its way into the islanders' homes.

Hugh Town's best bathing **beach** is in the sheltered bay of Porthcressa, from which a path wanders south to skirt the **Peninnis Headland**, passing some impressive sea-sculpted granite rocks. Other weathered boulders stand behind the Peninnis Lighthouse, notably the formation known as the **Kettle and Pans**, where a rock said to resemble a kettle stands close to some massive rounded basins. The path follows the coast to **Old Town Bay**, around which the modern houses of **OLD TOWN** give little hint of its former role as the island's chief port. The town has cafés and a sheltered south-facing beach, where Underwater Diving Safari offers diving trips and rents out equipment (Ⓣ01720/422732; closed Nov–Easter).

Three-quarters of a mile east, **Porth Hellick** is the next major inlet on the island's southern coast, marked by a rugged quartz monument to the fantastically named Sir Cloudesley Shovell, who in 1707 was washed up here from a shipwreck which claimed four ships and nearly 1700 lives. On one side of the bay is another rock shape, the **Loaded Camel**; near it a gate leads to a 4000-year-old **barrow**, probably used by Bronze Age people from the Iberian peninsula who were the Scillies' first colonists.

Pelistry Bay, on the northeastern side of St Mary's, less than two miles from Hugh Town, is one of the most secluded spots on the island, its sandy beach and crystal-clear waters sheltered by the outlying **Toll's Island**. The latter, joined to St Mary's at low tide by a slender strand, holds the remains of an old battery known as Pellow's Redoubt as well as several pits in which kelp was burned to produce a substance used for the manufacture of soap and glass. Grey seals are a common sight here.

The best remnants of early human settlement on the Scillies are to be found at **Halangy Down**, a mile or so north of Hugh Town, overlooking the sea. Dating from around 200 BC, it's an extensive complex of stone huts, chief of them a structure built around a courtyard with interconnecting buildings. Most complete is **Bant's Carn**, part of a much earlier site, probably contemporaneous with the one at Porth Hellick, comprising a long rectangular roofed chamber where cremations were carried out.

Practicalities

Hugh Town's **tourist office**, on Hugh Street (Easter to Oct Mon–Fri 8.30am–5.30pm, Sat 8.30am–5pm; Nov–Easter Mon–Fri 9am–5pm; Ⓣ01720/422536, Ⓦwww.simplyscilly.co.uk), has information on available accommodation for all the Scillies. On The Strand, Buccabu Bike Hire (Ⓣ01720/422289) offers a good way to get around the island. Alternatively, you can take advantage of the circular **bus** service leaving from The Parade (summer every 90min, reduced service rest of year), or of one of the island's four **tour buses** – one of them open-top, one a vintage bus from 1948 – which circle the island in about 90 minutes daily in summer. Neither bike nor bus, though, is ideal for exploring the remoter coastal sections of St Mary's.

Though rooms can be fairly scarce in peak season, the town is relatively well supplied with **B&Bs**: The Strand has the friendly, non-smoking *Lyonesse Guest House* (Ⓣ01720/422458; no credit cards; ❸; closed Nov–March), right on the harbourfront, while *The Boathouse*, on the Thoroughfare, also enjoys a good view over the harbour (Ⓣ01720/422688; ❸; closed Nov to mid-April). If you're loaded, you might consider the island's most atmospheric hotel, the *Star Castle* (Ⓣ01720/422317, Ⓦwww.starcastlescilly.demon.co.uk; ❽; closed 6 weeks Jan–Feb), high up on the Garrison. In the same area is the more modest *Veronica Lodge*, The Garrison (Ⓣ01720/422585; no credit cards; ❸), a comfortably solid house with a spacious garden and excellent views. There is much to be said for staying outside Hugh Town, for example at *Atlantic View* (☎01720/422684; no credit cards; ❸; closed Nov–March), in the centre of the island on High Lanes (right off Telegraph Road heading north), which also offers **bike rental**. The island's **campsite** is *Garrison Campsite*, near the playing field at the top of the eponymous promontory in Hugh Town (☎01720/422670). Camping elsewhere is not allowed.

There are plenty of **places to eat** in Hugh Town. The *Pilot's Gig* is a basement restaurant below the Garrison Gate at the end of Hugh Street, specializing in fish but also offering simple snacks at lunchtime (closed Oct–Easter). In the middle of the main street, the *Kavorna Bakery* is a handy spot for daytime refreshment (closed Oct–Easter), while the *Star Castle Hotel* in the Garrison has two quality restaurants, both fairly formal – the modern, seafood-based *Conservatory* and the more traditional *Castle Dining Room*. Out of town, *Juliet's* serves light meals and moderately priced dinners indoors or in its garden between Porthmellon and Porthloo beaches; phone to check evening opening (☎01720/422228; closed Dec–Feb).

Tresco

After St Mary's, **TRESCO** is the most visited island of the Scillies, yet the boatloads of visitors somehow manage to lose themselves on the two-miles-by-one island, the second largest in the group. Once the private estate of Devon's Tavistock Abbey, Tresco still retains a cloistered, slightly privileged air, and it has none of St Mary's short-term budget accommodation.

According to the tide, boats pull in at **New Grimsby**, halfway up the west coast, or the smaller quay at Old Grimsby, on the east coast, or the southernmost point of Carn Near. Whichever the case, it's only a few minutes' walk to the entrance to **Abbey Gardens** (daily 10am–4pm; £6.50), featuring a few ruins from the priory amid subtropical gardens first laid out in 1834. Many of the plants were grown from seeds taken from London's Kew Gardens, others were brought here from Africa, South America and the Antipodes. The entry ticket also admits you to a collection of figureheads and name plates taken from the numerous vessels that have come to grief around here.

You don't need to walk far to find alluring sandy beaches: one of the best – **Appletree Bay** – is only a few steps from the southern ferry landing at Carn Near. **Old Grimsby**, on the island's eastern side, has another couple of sand beaches, looking out to a submarine-shaped rock offshore, though the wide strands south of here are the island's best, and good for shell hunting.

There's another gorgeous sandy bay around the cluster of cottages that make up **New Grimsby**, on the island's western shore. North of here, Tresco's tidy fields give way to an untended heathland of heather and gorse, while a narrow path traces the coast to **Charles' Castle**, built in the 1550s. Strategically positioned on a height to cover the lagoon-like channel separating Tresco from Bryher, the castle was in fact badly designed, its guns unable to depress far enough to be effective, and it was superseded in 1651 by the much better-preserved **Cromwell's Castle**, actually no more than a gun tower, built at sea level next to a pretty sandy cove.

The shore path winds northwest from here, round to **Piper's Hole**, a deep underground cave accessible from the cliff edge on the northern coast. The entrance can be a little difficult to negotiate but it's worth pressing ahead to its freshwater pool. A torch is essential.

Practicalities

Apart from the exclusive *Island Hotel* at the centre of the island (ⓣ01720/422883, ⓦwww.tresco.co.uk; ❾; closed Nov to mid-March), and the *New Inn* at New Grimsby (ⓣ01720/422844, ⓦwww.tresco.co.uk; ❽), the only **accommodation** on the island comprises self-catering homes, usually available for weekly rent only, though it's worth asking if you want a place for less time (there's usually no availability in July and August). Prices for a two-bedroom property run from around £400 to £800 a week: contact *Borough Farm* (ⓣ01720/422843 or ⓣ01720/422840; closed Dec–Feb) or Tresco Estate Office (ⓣ01720/422849, ⓦwww.tresco.co.uk; closed Jan) for bookings and further details. The *New Inn* has a **restaurant** with an expensive four-course set menu, and you can eat quality pub snacks in its bar and garden. For gourmet cuisine, head for the restaurant at the *Island Hotel*, where fresh fish is the speciality.

Bryher and Samson

Covered with a thick carpet of bracken, heather and bramble, **BRYHER** is the wildest of the inhabited islands, but the seventy-odd inhabitants have introduced some pockets of order in the form of flower plantations, mostly confined to the small settlement around the quay and climbing up the slopes of **Watch Hill** on Bryher's eastern side, from which you can enjoy a grand panorama of the whole group of islands.

It's the exposed western seaboard that takes the full brunt of the Atlantic, and nowhere more spectacularly so than at the aptly named **Hell Bay**, cupped by a limb of land on the northwestern shore, and worth catching when the wind's up. In contrast to this sound and fury, peace reigns in the southern cove of **Rushy Bay**, one of the best beaches on the island.

From the quay, there's a daily boat service to the other islands, and frequent tours to seal and bird colonies as well as fishing expeditions. You could make a quick hop to the small isle of **SAMSON**, deserted since 1855 when the last impoverished inhabitants were ordered off by the island's proprietor. Most of the abandoned cottages are on the **South Hill**, site of several primitive burial chambers dating from the second millennium BC. The North Hill has a stone coffin from the same period, thought to be the sepulchre of a tribal chief. Most of the famous **gig races** start off from Nut Rock, to the east of Samson, finishing at St Mary's quay.

Practicalities

Bryher has a tiny choice of **B&Bs**, the best of which are *Soleil D'Or*, on the eastern side of the island with views over to Tresco (ⓣ01720/422003; ❷; closed Nov–Feb), and *Bank Cottage*, on the western side near Gweal Pool (ⓣ01720/422612; ❺; closed Nov–March), where half-board is the rule – and *Soleil D'Or* also offers meals. There's a **campsite** at Jenford Farm on Watch Hill (ⓣ01720/422886; closed Nov–March). For refreshment, the island's one hotel, the *Hell Bay* (ⓣ01720/422947; ❽; closed Nov–Feb) – actually a safe distance away from Hell Bay, near the pool below Gweal Hill – has a **bar** and **restaurant**. You can also eat inexpensively at the *Vine Café*, below Watch Hill (no credit cards; closed Nov–Feb, Fri eve & Sat eve), and the *Fraggle Rock*, near the post office, which has an upstairs restaurant – Friday is fish-and-chips night.

St Martin's

The main landing stage at **ST MARTIN'S** is on the southern promontory, at the head of the majestic sweep of **Par Beach** – a fitting entry to the island that boasts the best of the Scillies' beaches. From the quay, a road leads up past a public tennis court (rackets and balls for rent) to **HIGHER TOWN**, the main concentration of houses and location of the only shop. Here you can also find St Martin's Diving Centre (Ⓣ01720/422848, Ⓦwww.scillydiving.com), giving tuition at all levels. The water here is among the clearest in Britain, and is much favoured by scuba enthusiasts.

Beyond the church, follow the road westwards along the island's long, narrow ridge to **LOWER TOWN**, little more than a cluster of cottages on the western extremity, where there's a second quay for coming and going. The town overlooks the uninhabited isles of **Teän** and **St Helen's**, the latter holding the remains of a tenth-century oratory, monks' dwellings and a chapel, as well as a pest house, erected in 1756 to house plague-carriers entering British waters.

Along the southern shore, the gentler side of the island, you'll find the long strand of **Lawrence's Bay** and large areas of flowerbeds. On the northern side, the coast is rougher, with the exception of **Great Bay**, a beautiful half-mile recess of sand, utterly secluded and ideal for swimming. From its western end, you can climb across boulders at low tide to the hilly and wild **White Island**, on the northeastern side of which is a vast cave, **Underland Girt**, accessible at low tide.

At **St Martin's Head** on the northeastern tip of the main island lies the red and white Daymark erected in 1683 (not 1637 as inscribed) as a warning to shipping. On a clear day you can see the foam breaking against the Seven Stones Reef seven miles distant, where the tanker *Torrey Canyon* was wrecked in 1967, causing one of the world's worst oil spills. Below St Martin's Head, on the southeastern shore, lies another fine beach, **Perpitch**, looking out to the scattered Eastern Isles, slivers of rock to which boats take trippers to view puffins and grey seals.

Practicalities

St Martin's has just one **B&B**: *Polreath* (Ⓣ01720/422046, Ⓦwww.polreath.com; ❺; closed Nov to mid-March), in Higher Town, where the two comfortable en-suite rooms have all-round views, and there's a restaurant, conservatory and an extensive garden. You can find out about other possibilities by looking at the notice board in the post office in Higher Town. There's also a choice **hotel**, *St Martin's on the Isle* in Lower Town (Ⓣ01720/422092; ❽; closed Nov–Feb), consisting of a cluster of cottages with modern rooms looking onto a sandy beach. In Middletown, between Higher Town and Lower Town, you'll find a **campsite** (Ⓣ01720/422888, Ⓦwww.stmartinscampsite.co.uk; closed mid-Oct to March), just off the road near Lawrence's Bay – the only Scillies' campsite enjoying some degree of shelter. Book early. *Polreath* also has a simple **café** serving light meals and home-made cakes during the day, which opens in the evening for non-guests on two evenings a week. Otherwise, you could venture down the valley south of Higher Town to the wholefood café and restaurant at *Little Arthur Farm* for a range of delicious home-baked cakes and organic salads (April–Sept; closed Sat & Sun). The only **pub** on the island is the *Seven Stones* in Lower Town, where snacks are available.

St Agnes

Visitors to the southernmost inhabited island of the Scillies, **ST AGNES**, disembark at **Porth Conger**, from where a road leads to the western side of the island, on the way passing the disused **Old Lighthouse**, one of the oldest in the country – dating from 1680 – and the most significant landmark on St

Agnes. From here the right-hand fork leads to **Periglis Cove**, a mooring for boats on the western side of the island, while the left-hand fork goes to **St Warna's Cove**, where the patron saint of shipwrecks is reputed to have landed from Ireland, the exact spot being marked by a holy well. Between the two coves is a fine coastal path which passes the miniature **Troy Town Maze**, thought to have been created a couple of centuries ago, but possibly much older. Beyond St Warna's Cove, the path continues down over Wingletang Down to the southern headland of **Horse Point**, where there are some tortuous wind-eroded rocks. **Beady Pool**, an inlet on the eastern side of the headland, gained its name from the trove of beads washed ashore from the wreck of a seventeenth-century Dutch trader; some of the reddish-brown stones still occasionally turn up. The eastern side of St Agnes has one of the best beaches, the small, sheltered **Covean** (accessible from the path opposite *Covean Cottage*). Between here and Porth Conger a sand bar appears at low tide to connect the smaller isle of **Gugh**, the strand creating another lovely sheltered beach. You can walk across the bar to see a scattering of untended Bronze Age remains, and there's a good panorama of the islands from the hill at Gugh's northern end; take care not to be marooned by the incoming tide, which is extremely fierce.

St Agnes's western side looks out onto the **Western Rocks**, a horseshoe of islets that can be explored on boat tours. Biggest of them is Annet, a nesting place for a variety of birds such as the stormy petrel and Manx shearwater, as well as colonies of puffins and shags, though many have been chased out or killed in recent years by the predatory great black-beaked gull – largest of the gull family. The islands forming the western arm of the group are the best place to see grey seals. The island of **Rosevean** has the remains of houses used by the builders of the Bishop Rock Lighthouse, five miles out – at 175ft the tallest in Britain and the westernmost one on this side of the Atlantic.

Practicalities

Good **B&B**s on St Agnes include the *Coastguards*, one of a smart row of cottages past the Old Lighthouse and post office on the island's western side (☎01720/422373; ❸; closed Nov–March), and *Covean Cottage*, above Porth Conger (☎01720/422620; ❸; closed Oct–Easter). Both have cafés and **restaurants** open to all. There's a good **campsite** at *Troy Town Farm* above Periglis Cove (☎01720/422360; closed Nov–Feb), enjoying first-rate views over to the Western Rocks. Just above the jetty at Porth Conger, the *Turk's Head* serves superb St Agnes pasties to go with its beer.

Redruth to Bude

Though generally harsher than the county's southern seaboard, the north Cornish coast is punctuated by some of the finest beaches in England, the most popular of which are to be found around **Newquay**, the surfers' capital. Other major holiday centres are to be found down the coast at the ex-mining town of **St Agnes** and north around the Camel estuary, where the port of **Padstow** makes a good base for some remarkable beaches as well as a fine inland walk. North of the Camel, the coast is an almost unbroken line of cliffs as far as the Devon border, the gaunt, exposed terrain making a melodramatic setting for **Tintagel**, though the wide strand at **Bude** attracts legions of surfers and family holiday-makers.

Offsetting the beaches and caravan parks, parts of the more westerly stretches are littered with the derelict stacks and castle-like ruins of the engine-houses that once powered the region's **copper** and **tin mines**, industries that at one time led the world. Also prominent are the grey nonconformist chapels that reflect the impact of John Wesley on Cornwall's mining communities. His open-air meetings attracted thousands of listeners in such places as Gwennap Pit outside **Redruth**, the centre of the industry.

North Cornwall's network of public transport leaves a lot to be desired. Newquay is the terminus for the cross-peninsula **train** route from Par, while the main line to Penzance stops at Redruth and Camborne, which are connected to Truro on the #40 **bus** route, and to Falmouth on #41. Truronian's #T1 plies between Perranporth, St Agnes, Truro, Helston and The Lizard, while First Western National's #X85 links Perranporth with Truro, and #86, #87, #87B, #X89, #X90 and #592 run between Newquay and Truro (#87 and #87B also taking in Perranporth, and #X89 and #X90 going on to Falmouth). In July and August, service #301 starts in Penzance and continues on to St Ives, Perranporth and Newquay. Western Greyhound #556 runs along the coast between Newquay and Padstow, the latter also served by the regular #55 from St Austell and Bodmin. Services #522 and #524 link Port Isaac, Boscastle, Tintagel and Bude (not Sun in winter). Finally, Okehampton and Exeter are linked to Bude by #X9, and to Newquay by the #X10 (not Sun).

Redruth and around

In the 1850s **REDRUTH** and neighbouring **CAMBORNE**, with which it is now amalgamated, accounted for two-thirds of the world's copper production, the 350 pits employing some fifty thousand workers, many of whom were forced to emigrate when cheaper deposits of tin and copper were discovered overseas at the turn of the century. The simple granite mine buildings bear a resemblance to the numerous Methodist chapels in the area – testimony to the success enjoyed by the nonconformist sects in Cornwall. Between 1762 and 1786 the grassy hollow of Gwennap Pit, outside **St Day**, a mile southeast of Redruth, was the scene of huge gatherings of miners and their families to hear John Wesley preach. The first visits to Cornwall by the founder of Methodism were met with derision and violence, but he later won over the tough mining communities who could find little comfort in the gentrified established church. At one time Wesley estimated that the congregation at Gwennap Pit exceeded thirty thousand, noting in his diary, "I shall scarce see a larger congregation till we meet in the air." The present tiered amphitheatre was created in 1805, and is today the venue of Methodist meetings for the annual Whit Monday service.

The town's former harbour lies two and a half miles away at **PORTREATH**, a surfing beach that enjoys the cleanest water on this stretch. The village is within walking distance of the awe-inspiring **Hell's Mouth**, a cauldron of waves and black rocks at the base of two-hundred-foot cliffs five miles down the coast at the top of St Ives Bay; it's also just three miles south of **Porthtowan**, another popular surfing beach.

You can find a good selection of **B&Bs** in Redruth, among them the attractive *Lansdowne House*, five minutes from the bus and train stations at 42 Clinton Rd (ⓣ01209/216002, ⓦwww.s-h-systems.co.uk; ❷), which has rooms with and without private facilities. Portreath has the light and airy *Cliff House*, a 200-year-old cottage just off the harbourside on The Square (ⓣ01209/843847, ⓔcliffhouse@portreathr164lb.freeserve.co.uk; no under-12s; no credit cards; ❸), or venture a little further out to the charmingly old-fashioned restored

Georgian mansion *Fountain Springs*, Glenfeadon House, Glenfeadon Terrace (☎01209/842650; no credit cards; ❸; closed Nov–Feb), about a quarter-mile from the sea – take the second left turning after the school on the B3300.

St Agnes and around

Though the village is surrounded by ruined engine houses, **ST AGNES** today gives little hint of the conditions in which its population once lived, the straggling streets of uniform grey cottages now housing retired people, whose immaculate flower-filled gardens are admired by the troops of holiday-makers striding up and down the steep terrace called Stippy-Stappy.

Well connected by bus to Truro, St Ives, Redruth and Newquay, St Agnes makes a useful stopover for exploring the coast in the area. At the end of a steep valley below St Agnes, **Trevaunance Cove** is the site of several failed attempts to create a harbour for the town. Its fine sandy beach is a favourite with surfers and other bathing enthusiasts, despite the poor water quality. West of St Agnes lies one of Cornwall's most famous vantage points, **St Agnes Beacon**, 630ft high, from which views extend inland to Bodmin Moor and even across the peninsula to St Michael's Mount. A short distance away, the headland of **St Agnes Head** has the area's largest colony of breeding kittiwakes, and the nearby cliffs also shelter fulmars and guillemots, while grey seals are a common sight offshore.

Past the old World War II airfield three miles north of St Agnes, the resort of **PERRANPORTH** lies at the southern end of Perran Beach, a three-mile expanse of sand enhanced by caves and natural rock arches, very popular with surfers – boards and equipment are available to rent from Surf Shack, Beach Road.

There's a good choice of **accommodation** in and around St Agnes, including the eighteenth-century *Malthouse*, Peterville, the lower part of the village, a former brewing-house where you'll find a relaxed and bohemian atmosphere (☎01872/553318; no credit cards; ❶). Near the centre on Penwinnick Road, *Penkerris* (☎01872/552262, Ⓦwww.penkerris.co.uk; ❷) is a spacious creeper-clad house, with log fires in winter, a big garden, and good home-cooked dinners. If you want to be near the beach, head down to Trevaunance Cove, where the whitewashed *Driftwood Spars* (☎01872/552428, Ⓦwww.driftwoodspars.com; ❺) occupies a seventeenth-century tin miners' warehouse. Right next to the beach at Perranporth, the *Seiners' Arms* is a huge pub and restaurant where you can sit outside and also sleep (☎01872/573118, Ⓦwww.seinersarms.com; ❹). The small *Tides Reach Hotel* is also close to the beach at Ponsmere Road (☎01872/572188, Ⓦwww.tidesreachhotel.com; ❸), and offers bright en-suite rooms, a pool table and *Tidy's Bistro and Restaurant* (Thurs–Sat eves; closed late Dec to mid-Feb). On the cliff-top outside Perranporth, the **youth hostel** (☎ & Ⓕ0870/770 5994; closed Oct to mid-April; £10.25), in a former coastguard station, enjoys great views towards Ligger Point at the north end of the beach. Back in St Agnes, the most interesting **pub** is the *Railway Inn* on Vicarage Road; decorated with an idiosyncratic collection of shoes, horsebrasses and naval memorabilia, it also has a good selection of ales and snacks.

Newquay

It is difficult to imagine a lineage for **NEWQUAY** that extends more than a few decades, but the "new quay" was built in the fifteenth century in what was already a long-established fishing port. Up to then it had been more colourfully known as Towan Blistra, and was concentrated in the sheltered west end of the bay. The town was given a boost in the nineteenth century when its harbour was expanded for coal import and a railway was constructed across the peninsula for china clay shipments. With the trains came a swelling stream of seasonal visitors, drawn to the town's superb position on a knuckle of cliffs overlooking fine golden sands and Atlantic rollers, natural advantages which have made Newquay the premier resort of north Cornwall.

Aside from the sea's allure, however, there's little specific to see in Newquay. The centre of town is a somewhat tacky parade of shops and restaurants, partly pedestrianized, from which lanes lead to ornamental gardens and sloping lawns on the cliff-tops. At the bottom of Beach Road, adjacent to the small harbour, the **Blue Reef Aquarium** (daily 10am–5pm; £5.50) provides some distraction, allowing you to admire tropical fish from an underwater tunnel. There are tours, talks and various feeding sessions. Below the aquarium, in the crook of the massive Towan Head, **Towan Beach** is the most central of the seven miles of firm sandy beaches that follow in an almost unbroken succession. You can reach all of them on foot, though for some of the further ones, such as **Porth Beach**, with its grassy headland, or the extensive **Watergate Bay**, you might prefer to make use of bus #556 to Padstow (not Sun in winter). The beaches can all be unbearably crowded in full season, and all are popular with surfers, particularly Watergate and – west of Towan Head – **Fistral Bay**, the largest of the town beaches. On the other side of East Pentire Head from Fistral, **Crantock Beach** – reachable over the Gannel River by ferry or upstream footbridge – is usually less crowded, and has a lovely backdrop of dunes and undulating grassland. Try to coincide your visit to Newquay with one of the **surfing competitions** and events that run right through the summer – contact the tourist office for details.

Practicalities

Newquay's **train station** is off Cliff Road, a couple of hundred yards from the **bus station** on East Street. All buses for the beaches stop on Cliff Road and its extension Narrowcliff. The **tourist office** lies opposite the bus station at Marcus Hill (mid-May to mid-Sept Mon–Sat 9.30am–5.30pm, Sun 9.30am–1pm; Oct–April Mon–Fri 9.30am–4.30pm, Sat 9.30am–12.30pm; ⓣ01637/854020, ⓦwww.newquay.co.uk). There's an **Internet** café, *Tad & Nick's*, at 72 Fore St.

Accommodation

There's loads of **accommodation** in Newquay, though rooms can still be at a premium in July and August. Two of the nicest **B&Bs** are the beautifully furnished *Rockpool Cottage*, 92 Fore St (ⓣ07971/594485, ⓦwww.rockpoolcottage.co.uk; ❷; closed Jan–Easter), convenient for Fistral Beach, and the equally tasteful and non-smoking *Trewinda Lodge*, 17 Eliot Gardens (ⓣ01637/877533, ⓦwww.trewindalodge.co.uk; ❷), a few minutes' walk from Tolcarne Beach; both can give informed advice to surfers, and neither accepts credit cards. Newquay has a plethora of independent **hostels** offering beds in small dorms and some double rooms, with varying standards and seasonal rates. Best of the bunch are the fully equipped *Escape Hotel*, near the tourist office at 1 Mount Wise (ⓣ01637/851736, ⓦwww.escape2newquay.co.uk; £18–20); *St Christopher's*, with a great location overlooking the harbour, above *Belushi's* bar at 35 Fore St (ⓣ01637/859111, ⓦwww.st-christophers.co.uk/newquay_hostel; £18–25), and *Safi*, Narrowcliff Seafront (ⓣ01637/872800, ⓦwww.mysafi.com; £15–30), a gigantic place facing Tolcarne Beach, with small, plain and clean en-suite bunkrooms and a 24-hour bar. All hostels have TVs, kitchens, and places to store your surfboard.

Surfing and other outdoor activities

You can rent or buy **surfing equipment** from beach stalls, or else try Tunnel Vision, 6 Alma Place, off Fore Street (ⓣ01637/879033, ⓦwww.tvsurfshop.com), or Fistral Surf Co, 1 Beacon Rd, on the harbour side of the headland, with other outlets on Central Square and Cliff Road (ⓣ01637/850378). Boards cost £5–10 a day, wet suits about the same. A number of outfits provide **tuition**, usually between April and October, with all equipment provided. The British Surfing Association (ⓣ01736/876474, ⓦwww.britsurf.co.uk) offers courses at both Fistral and Tolcarne beaches; Dolphin Surf School (ⓣ01637/873707, ⓦwww.surfschool.co.uk) also provides B&B accommodation, while Reef Surf School (ⓣ01637/879058, ⓦwww.reefsurfschool.com) is open all year round and arranges three-day surfing holidays including hostel accommodation. The UK's first women-only surf school, Hibiscus (ⓣ01637/879374, ⓦwww.hibiscussurfschool.co.uk), offers three-hour sessions for £20, a full day for £35. For **kite-surfing**, **land yachting**, **wave-skiing** and **paragliding**, head for The Extreme Academy on Watergate Bay (ⓣ01637/860840, ⓦwww.watergatebay.co.uk); a two-hour wave-skiing session will cost £30.

If you're more interested in **biking**, head for Bike Spec on Tor Road, just round the corner from *Bertie's* (ⓣ01637/877575), or Shoreline, 7 Fore St (ⓣ01637/879165).

The **campsites** in the area are all mega-complexes, many of which will only take families. The most convenient site, *Porth Beach* (ⓣ01637/876531, ⓦwww.porthbeach.co.uk; closed Nov–Feb), behind the beach of the same name to the east of town, falls into this category, and a little further back, on Trevelgue Road, *Trevelgue* (ⓣ01637/851851, ⓦwww.trevelgue.co.uk; closed Nov–Easter) separates families from groups. The next-door *Smugglers Haven* (ⓣ01637/852000, ⓦwww.smugglershaven.co.uk; closed Sept–June), however, run by the same management, has a more relaxed attitude towards same-sex groups, while the *Sunnyside* on Quintrell Downs (ⓣ01637/873338, ⓦwww.sunnyside.co.uk) goes out of its way to attract the 18-to-30 singles crowd – it's a couple of miles inland, close to a stop on the train line or reached on bus #567.

Eating, drinking and nightlife

Although most of Newquay's numerous **eateries** are pretty bland, recent years have seen an influx of more stylish places, and its gastronomic profile is soon to be raised even higher with the completion of a new quality waterfront restaurant belonging to Rick Stein of Padstow (see p.525). There's no need to wait to enjoy inspiring views and top-notch seafood, however – drop in at *Finn's*, Newquay Harbour (ⓣ01637/874062; closed Mon & Tues), where you can watch the fish being landed just yards away, and cooked at the outdoor kitchen (expensive); all wines are organic. The town also has a good choice of **cafés**, including *The Chy*, a sleekly modern place on Beach Road, with a spacious terrace for seafood lunches by day, and DJs in the evenings. Just across from here, the Aussie-themed *Walkabout Inn* on Beachfield Avenue is large and comfortable by day, loud and crowded every evening, again with great waterside views. At 38 Fore St, the laid-back *Café Irie* serves snacks, teas and evening meals accompanied by world music sounds and live folk on Mondays (closed Tues & Wed), while on Tower Road, the *Lifebuoy Café* serves fresh juices, smoothies and all-day breakfasts (also vegetarian). At **Watergate Bay**, *The Beach Hut* provides surf food and fish specials all day.

Newquay has become Cornwall's biggest centre for **nightclubbing**: the town's current hot spots are *Berties* on East Street (Ⓣ01637/872255, Ⓦwww.bertiesclub.com), *Sailors* on Fore Street (Ⓣ01637/872838), *The Beach* on Beach Road (Ⓣ01637/872194, Ⓦwww.beachclubnewquay.com) and *Tall Trees* on Tolcarne Road (Ⓣ01637/850313, Ⓦwww.talltreesclub.co.uk), though these mainstream places tend to be fairly glittery and overwhelmed in summer. You can sometimes hear more underground sounds at the *Koola Club* on Beach Road (Ⓣ01637/870240, Ⓦwww.thekoola.com), the *Springbok Club*, 27–29 Cliff Rd (Ⓣ01637/875800), and *Foster's* pub in Narrowcliff; otherwise ask around and watch the posters for the current venues.

Padstow and around

The small fishing port of **PADSTOW** is nearly as popular as Newquay, but has a very different feel. Enclosed within the estuary of the Camel – the only river of any size that empties on Cornwall's north coast – the town long retained its position as the principal fishing port on this coast, and still has something of the atmosphere of a medieval town. Its chief annual festival is also a hangover from times past, the **Obby Oss**, a May Day romp when one of the locals garbs himself as a horse and prances through the town preceded by a masked and club-wielding "teaser" – a spirited if rather institutionalized re-enactment of old fertility rites.

On the hill overlooking Padstow, the church of **St Petroc** is dedicated to Cornwall's most important saint, a Welsh or Irish monk who landed here in the sixth century, died in the area and gave his name to the town – "Petrock's Stow". The building has a fine fifteenth-century font, an Elizabethan pulpit and some amusing carved bench-ends. The walls are lined with monuments to the local Prideaux family, who still occupy nearby **Prideaux Place**, an Elizabethan manor house with grand staircases, richly furnished rooms full of portraits, fantastically ornate ceilings and formal gardens (Easter & mid-May to early Oct Mon–Thurs & Sun 1.30–5pm, last tour at 4pm; £6, grounds only £2), all of which have been used as settings for a plethora of films, such as *Twelfth Night* and *Oscar and Lucinda*. The grounds contain an ancient deer park, and give good views over the Camel estuary.

The harbour is jammed with launches and boats offering cruises in Padstow Bay, while a regular **ferry** (summer daily 8am–7.30pm; winter Mon–Sat 8am–4.30pm; £2 return) carries people across the river to **ROCK** – close to the low-slung church of **St Enodoc** (John Betjeman's burial place) and to the good beaches around Polzeath. The ferry leaves from the harbour's North Pier except at low water when it goes from near the war memorial downstream.

The coast on the **south side** of the estuary also offers some good **beach** country, which you can reach on bus #556, though walking would enable you to view some terrific coastline. Out of Padstow, the rivermouth is clogged by **Doom Bar**, a sand bar that was allegedly the curse of a mermaid who had been mortally wounded by a fisherman who mistook her for a seal. Apart from thwarting the growth of Padstow as a busy commercial port, the bar has scuppered some three hundred vessels, with great loss of life. Round **Stepper Point** you can reach the sandy and secluded Harlyn Bay and, turning the corner southwards, **Constantine Bay**, the area's best surfing beach. The dunes backing the beach and the rock pools skirting it make this one of the most appealing bays on this coast; moreover it boasts the best water quality, though the tides can be treacherous and bathing hazardous near the rocks. Surfers are attracted to other beaches in the neighbourhood, too, but the surrounding caravan sites can make these claustrophobic in summer – the sands around **Porthcothan** are worth exploring.

The Saints' Way

Padstow's St Petroc Church is the traditional starting point for one of Cornwall's oldest walking routes, the **Saints' Way**. Extending for some thirty miles between Cornwall's north and south coasts, and connecting the principal ports of Padstow and Fowey, the path originates from the Bronze Age when traders preferred the cross-country hike to making the perilous sea journey round Land's End. The route was later travelled by Irish and Welsh missionaries crossing the peninsula between the fifth and eighth centuries, on pilgrimage to the principal shrines of Cornwall's Celtic culture.

Skirting Bodmin Moor, the reconstructed Saints' Way is rarely dramatic, though it passes a variety of scenery and several points of interest along the way, from Neolithic burial chambers to medieval churches and the more austere lines of Wesleyan chapels. The route is well marked and can be walked in stages, the country paths that constitute it stretching for two to six miles each; although it crosses several trunk roads, these do not impinge too much. You can pick up **guides and leaflets** giving detailed directions in Padstow, Bodmin and Fowey tourist offices.

From St Petroc's, follow Hill Street, crossing New Street, and continue along Dennis Lane to the lake at Dennis Cove, from where the path climbs through fields to the monument to Queen Victoria, the point at which most people stop. If you choose to continue, you'll find that seven or eight miles out of Padstow, the route crosses the **St Breock Downs** with views stretching from the Camel estuary to the white clay mountains around St Austell. From here the path veers southeast to pass through **Lanivet**, the halfway point of the Way lying a couple of miles outside Bodmin. Here, the *Lanivet Inn* provides welcome refreshment; for **B&Bs**, see accommodation for Bodmin, p.532.

South of here, **Helman Tor** (674ft) holds the trail's most impressive scenery, studded with bare boulders and wind-eroded rocks and flanked by acres of gorse. At Helman Tor Gate, the path divides, giving you the choice of reaching Fowey via **Lanlivery** – home of St Brevita's Church with one of Cornwall's landmark towers – or **Luxulyan**, which boasts a lush gorge crossed by a viaduct and aqueduct built in 1842 and a holy well below the fifteenth-century church. The eastern route through Lanlivery takes you through the wooded estuary of the River Fowey – legendary meeting place of Tristan and Iseult – to the port. The longer western route follows an old cobbled causeway for part of the way, and passes through **Tywardreath**, which once marked the inland extent of the sea before the port of Par was built by industrialist Joseph Treffry (builder of the viaduct at Luxulyan). Tywardreath means "house on the strand", and was described by Daphne Du Maurier in her novel of that name. Fowey is four miles southeast of here. The end of the route is the church of St Fimbarrus in Fowey; see p.491 for accommodation hereabouts.

Three or four miles further south lies one of Cornwall's most dramatic beaches, **Bedruthan Steps**. Traditionally held to be the stepping stones of a giant called Bedruthan (a legendary figure conjured into existence in the nineteenth century), these slate outcrops can be readily viewed from the cliff-top path, at a point which drivers can reach on the B3276. Steps lead down to the broad beach below (closed in winter), which has dangerous tides and thunderous waves and is not advised for swimming.

Padstow is also the start of an excellent **cycle track** converted from the old railway line between Wadebridge and Padstow, forming part of the **Camel Trail**, a fifteen-mile traffic-free path that follows the river up as far as Wenfordbridge, on the edge of Bodmin Moor, with a turn-off for Bodmin. The five-mile Padstow–Wadebridge stretch offers glimpses of a variety of birdlife, especially around the small **Pinkson Creek**, habitat of terns, herons, curlews and egrets. You can **rent bikes** from Brinham's (☎01841/532594) and Padstow Cycle Hire (☎01841/533533), both on South Quay, by the start of the Camel Trail. Further up the trail, at the top of the estuary outside Wadebridge, Bridge Bike Hire has a greater stock, though it's still advisable to book (☎01208/813050). **Walkers** can set out from Padstow on the thirty-mile **Saints' Way** across the peninsula to Fowey (see box opposite).

Practicalities

Padstow's **tourist office** is on the harbour (Easter–Oct daily 9.30am–5pm; Nov–Easter Mon–Fri 9am–4pm; ☎01841/533449, Ⓦwww.padstowlive.com). Central **accommodation** includes the B&B at 4 Riverside (☎01841/532383; no credit cards; ❷), a three-storey building right on the harbour; the top bedroom has a French window leading onto a balcony. A few minutes away, *Armside*, 10 Cross St (☎01841/532271; ❸), is an elegant eighteenth-century town house, while the posher *Old Ship* on Mill Square (☎01841/532357; ❺) has plenty of character, strewn with antique furnishings and stacked with paintings, and all rooms are equipped with double showers. The nearest **youth hostel** has stunning views and is excellently sited almost on the beach at Treyarnon Bay (☎0870/770 6076, Ⓔtreyarnon@yha.org.uk; closed Nov–March; £10.25); to get there, take a bus to Constantine (#556, also from Newquay) then walk for half a mile. The nearest congenial **campsites** to Padstow are *Trerethern Touring Park* (☎01841/532061; closed Oct–March), a mile southwest, and *Dennis Cove* (☎01841/532349; closed Oct–Easter), picturesquely situated alongside the estuary about a ten-minute walk south of town.

Padstow's quayside is lined with snack bars and pasty shops as well as pubs where you can sit outside, such as the *Shipwright's* on the harbour's north side. But foodies know the town best for its high-class **restaurants**, particularly those associated with star chef Rick Stein, whose *Seafood Restaurant*, at Riverside (☎01841/532700), is one of England's top fish restaurants – and expensive, with most main courses around £27 (though cod, chips and mushy peas cost a more reasonable £17.50). Nevertheless, the waiting list for a table here can be months long, though a reservation on a weekday out of season can mean booking only a day or two ahead, and there's always the chance of a cancellation if you turn up on spec. The TV chef has responded to the demand by opening up another couple of places in town, *St Petroc's Bistro* at 4 New St (☎01841/532700), which has a lighter, slightly cheaper but more restricted version of the *Seafood Restaurant's* menu, and the casual *Rick Stein's Café* nearby at 10 Middle St, whose small tables lend it the style of a Milanese bar (except that you can't smoke), and which serves snacks at lunch and moderate meals at night (closed Sun). All three establishments also offer attractive accommodation (❺–❻, ; no smoking in any).

Rick Stein doesn't have a monopoly of classy restaurants in Padstow; *No. 6*, at 6 Middle St (☎01841/532093; closed lunchtime and all Mon & Tues), is an excellent but quite pricey Mediterranean-style place which uses organic produce whenever possible (no smoking except in the courtyard). For cheaper eats, the *Old Custom House* on the harbourside serves pub snacks (and also has an adjoining fine seafood restaurant, *Pescadou*; ☎01841/532359), while *Rojano's* on Mill Square dishes up pizza and pasta (☎01841/532796; closed Sun and all Dec & Jan). Otherwise, the *London Inn* on Lanadwell Street, adorned with hanging baskets outside and wood panelling within, does sandwiches, pasties and more substantial meals, as does the *Old Ship*, where you can eat outside. And if you really can't leave Padstow without sampling some of Rick Stein's creations, you could always feast on a gourmet picnic, supplied by the master's **delicatessen** on South Quay.

Polzeath to Port Isaac

Facing west into Padstow Bay, the beaches of and around **POLZEATH** are the finest in the vicinity, pelted by rollers which make this one of the best surfing sites in the West Country; Daymer Bay is more popular with the windsurfing crowd. The *Seascape Hotel* offers about the only solid-walled **accommodation** around here, beautifully situated a few yards up from Polzeath's beach (ⓣ01208/863638, ⓦwww.seascapehotel.co.uk; ❺), while the popular *Tristram* **campsite** (ⓣ01208/862215; closed Nov–Feb) also occupies a prime position, on a cliff overlooking the beach. In recent years, Polzeath campsites, like those in Newquay, have barred same-sex groups of young people owing to past fracas, though *Trenant Steading* (ⓣ01208/862407; closed Nov–Easter) between Polzeath and New Polzeath currently admits small groups. On the beach, the *Galleon* does various snacks and takeaways, and *Finn's* does full meals as well as cream teas. *Granny's Grotto*, just up from the beach, offers very cheap fast food, and the *Oyster Catcher* bar is a lively evening hangout. *Surf's Up* at 21 Trenant Close (ⓣ01208/862003, ⓦwww.surfsupsurfschool.com) and on the beach offers **surfing** tuition; the gear can be rented from shops.

Heading east, the coastal path brings you through cliff-top growths of feathery tamarisk, which flower spectacularly in July and August. From the headland of **Pentire Point**, views unfold for miles over the offshore islets of **The Mouls** and **Newland**, with their populations of grey seals and puffins. Half a mile east, the scanty remains of an Iron Age fort stand on the humpy back of **Rump's Point**, from where the path descends a mile or so to **Lundy Bay**, a pleasant sandy cove surrounded by green fields. Climbing again, you pass the shafts of an old antimony mine on the way to **Doyden Point**, which is picturesquely ornamented with a nineteenth-century castle folly once used for gambling parties.

The inlet of **Port Quin** has a few cottages but no shops – the next settlement of any size is **PORT ISAAC**, wedged in a gap in the precipitous cliff-wall and dedicated to the crab and lobster trade. Only seasonal trippers ruffle the surface of life in this cramped harbour town, whose narrow lanes focus on a couple of pubs at the seafront, where a pebble beach and rock pools are exposed by the low tide. The village offers a range of **accommodation**, best of all the *Slipway Hotel* (ⓣ01208/880264, ⓦwww.portisaac.com; ❺), a sixteenth-century building right opposite the harbour, with friendly management. Higher up on Fore Street, the *Old School Hotel* enjoys wonderful views from its tastefully decorated rooms (ⓣ01208/880721, ⓦwww.cornwall-online.co.uk/old-school-hotel; ❸), as does the elegant, Victorian *Bay Hotel*, 1 The Terrace (ⓣ01208/880380, ⓦwww.bayhotelportisaac.co.uk; ❹), and *Anchorage Guest House*, 12 The Terrace (ⓣ01208/880629; non-smoking; no credit cards; ❷), the latter with a prospect of both Port Isaac Bay and neighbouring Port Gaverne Bay.

Food-wise, Port Isaac is most famous for crab, which you can sample from stalls at the harbour or from either of the excellent **restaurants** at the *Slipway Hotel* and the *Old School* (closed Tues in winter), which is also open for snacks and teas. Across from the *Old School*, you might be tempted by the fresh fish and chips at the *Old Drugstore*. The *Golden Lion* is Port Isaac's most cheerful **pub** and has an adjoining bistro and balcony seating overlooking the harbour; the bar at the *Slipway* is another amenable place for a pint.

At the main car park at the top of the village, a kiosk which alternates between Port Isaac and Tintagel provides information on **walking along the heritage coast** on either side of the town. **Port Gaverne**, the next cove to the east, is a serene cluster of houses, with a snug bar at the *Port Gaverne Inn*, where you can eat bar food or quality fare in the expensive restaurant – quaint but pricey rooms are also available here (Ⓣ01208/880244, Ⓦwww.chycor.co.uk/hotels/port-gaverne; ❻).

Tintagel

East of Port Isaac, the coast is wild and unspoiled, making for some steep and strenuous walking, and interspersed with some stupendous strands of sandy beaches such as that at **Trebarwith**. A few miles further north, the rocky littoral provides an appropriate backdrop for the black, forsaken ruins of **Tintagel Castle** (daily: April to mid-July & late Aug to Sept 10am–6pm; mid-July to late Aug 10am–7pm; Oct 10am–5pm; Nov–March 10am–4pm; £3.20; EH). It was the twelfth-century chronicler Geoffrey of Monmouth who first popularized the notion that this was the **birthplace of King Arthur**, son of Uther Pendragon and Ygrayne, but by that time local folklore was already saturated with tales of King Mark of Cornwall, Tristan and Iseult, Arthur and the knights of Camelot. Twin influences were at work in Geoffrey's story, which merges the historic figure of Arthur with a separate body of legend centring on the missionary activity of the Celtic monastery that occupied this site in the sixth century. Tintagel is certainly a plausibly resonant candidate for the abode of the Once and Future King, but the **castle** ruins in fact belong to a Norman stronghold occupied by the earls of Cornwall, who after sporadic spurts of rebuilding allowed it to decay, most of it having been washed into the sea by the sixteenth century. The remains of the **Celtic monastery** are still visible on the headland and are an important source of knowledge of how the country's earliest monastic houses were organized. Recent digs on the eastern side of the island have also revealed glass fragments dating from the sixth or seventh centuries believed to originate in Malaga, as well as a 1500-year-old section of slate bearing two Latin inscriptions, one of them attributing authorship to one "Artognou, father of Coll's descendant". You can find out more at the storytelling events held at the castle in summer (currently Wed at 6pm & some weekends at noon); there are occasionally musical evenings as well – call Ⓣ01840/770328 for information.

The best approach to the site is from **Glebe Cliff** to the west, where the parish church of **St Materiana** sits in isolation; the South West Coast Path passes the church, and for drivers it's a good place to park before descending to the castle. From the village of **TINTAGEL** the shortest access is from the signposted path, a well-trodden route. The only item of note in this dreary collection of cafés and B&Bs is the **Old Post Office** (April–Sept daily 11am–5.30pm; Oct daily 11am–4pm; £2.40; NT), a rickety-roofed, slate-built construction dating from the fourteenth century, now restored to its appearance in the Victorian era when it was used as a post office.

Buses stop on the main Fore Street close to the octagonal **tourist office** (daily: March–Oct 10am–5pm; Nov–Feb 10.30am–4pm; Ⓣ01840/779084), sited in the council car park on the road from Camelford. The village has plenty of **accommodation**, most of it fairly basic. The best B&Bs are a few minutes' walk along Atlantic Road: *Pendrin House* (Ⓣ01840/770560, Ⓦwww.pendrinhouse.co.uk; ❷; closed Nov–Feb) and the non-smoking *Bosayne* (Ⓣ01840/770514, Ⓦwww.bosayne.co.uk; ❸). Nearer the castle, and within sight of it, is *Castle View*, 2 King Arthur's Terrace (Ⓣ01840/770421, Ⓔcastleviewbandb@aol.com; no smoking; no credit cards; ❶), which has small, plain rooms and a no-breakfast option. Near here, two pubs on Fore Street also

King Arthur in Cornwall

Did **King Arthur** really exist? If he did, it's likely that he was an amalgam of two people; a sixth-century Celtic warlord who united the local tribes in a series of successful battles against the invading Anglo-Saxons, and a local Cornish saint. Whatever his origins, his role was recounted and inflated by poets and troubadours in later centuries (particularly in Welsh poems, the earliest of which is *Gododdin*). Though there is no mention of him in the ninth- to twelth-century *Anglo-Saxon Chronicle*, his exploits were elaborated later by the unreliable medieval chronicler Geoffrey of Monmouth, who made Arthur the conqueror of western Europe, and was the first to record the belief that **Tintagel** was his birthplace. Twelfth-century chronicler William of Malmesbury narrated the story of Glastonbury, including the popular legend that, after being mortally wounded in battle, Arthur sailed to Avalon (Glastonbury), where he was buried alongside Guinevere. The Arthurian legends were crystallized in Thomas Malory's epic, *Morte d'Arthur* (1485), further romanticized in Tennyson's *Idylls of the King* (1859–85) and resurrected in T.H. White's saga, *The Once and Future King* (1937–58).

Although there are places throughout Britain and Europe which claim some association with Arthur, it's England's West Country, and **Cornwall** in particular, that has the greatest concentration of places boasting a link. Relatively untouched by the Saxon invasions, Cornwall has practically appropriated the hero as its own, a far more authentic bond than the efforts of the county's tourist industry might suggest. Here, the legends (fertilized by fellow Celts from Brittany and Wales) have established deep roots, so that, for example, the spirit of Arthur is said to be embodied in the Cornish chough – a bird now almost extinct. Cornwall's most famous Arthurian site is **Tintagel**, which is said to be his birthplace. Meanwhile, Merlin is thought to have lived in a cave under the castle – and also on a rock near Mousehole, south of Penzance. Nearby Bodmin Moor is full of places with associated names such as "King Arthur's Bed" and "King Arthur's Downs", while Camlan, the battlefield where Arthur was mortally wounded fighting against his nephew Mordred, is thought to lie on the northern reaches of the moor at Slaughterbridge, near Camelford (which is also sometimes identified as Camelot itself). Nearby, at Dozmary Pool, the knight Bedivere was dispatched by the dying Arthur to return the sword Excalibur to the mysterious hand emerging from the water – though Loe Pool in Mount's Bay also claims this honour. According to some, Arthur's body was transported after the battle to Boscastle, on Cornwall's northern coast, from where a funeral barge transported the body to Avalon. Cornwall is also the presumed home of King Mark, at the centre of a separate cycle of myths which later became interwoven with the Arthurian one. It was Mark who sent the knight Tristan to Ireland to fetch his betrothed, Iseult; his headquarters is supposed to have been at Castle Dore, north of Fowey. Out beyond Land's End, the fabled, vanished country of Lyonesse is also said to be the original home of Arthur, as well as being (according to Spenser's *Faerie Queene*) the birthplace of Tristan.

Much of the Cornish tourist office's celebration of the Arthurian sagas has the same cynical basis as the more ancient desire to claim Arthur by the various villages and sites throughout England and Wales: the cachet and hence profit to be had from the veneration of a secular saint. Witness the "discovery" of the tomb of Arthur and Guinevere by the Benedictine monks of Glastonbury in the twelfth century, which helped to boost the profile of this powerful abbey. Today in Tintagel you find Arthurian tack galore, including every kind of Merlin-esque hogwash (crystal balls, sugar-coated wands, etc), and even Excaliburgers.

offer rooms: the *Old Malt House* (☎01840/770461; ❸) and the *Wharncliffe Arms* (☎01840/770393; ❷). Three-quarters of a mile outside the village at Dunderhole Point, past St Materiana, the offices of a former slate quarry now house a **youth hostel** with great views of the coastline (ⓣ0870/770 6068; closed Nov to mid-April; £10.25). At the end of Atlantic Road, the *Headland* site offers scenic **camping** (ⓣ01840/770239, ⓦwww.headland caravanpark.co.uk; closed Oct–Easter). There's no shortage of cafés and tea-rooms in Tintagel, and both the *Old Malt House* and the *Tintagel Arms Hotel* on Fore Street have decent **restaurants**.

Boscastle

Three miles east of Tintagel, the port of **BOSCASTLE** lies compressed within a narrow ravine drilled by the rivers Jordan and Valency, its tidy riverfront bordered by thatched and lime-washed houses giving on to the twisty harbour. Above and behind, a collection of seventeenth- and eighteenth-century cottages can be seen on a circular walk, starting either from Fore Street or the main car park, where there is a local map. The walk traces the valley of the Valency for about a mile to reach Boscastle's graceful **parish church**, tucked away in a peaceful glen. A mile and a half further up the valley lies another church, **St Juliot's**, restored by Thomas Hardy when he was plying his trade as a young architect. It was while he was working here that he met Emma Gifford, whom he married in 1874, a year after the publication of *A Pair of Blue Eyes*, the book that kicked off Hardy's literary career. It opens with an architect arriving in a Cornish village to restore its church, and is full of descriptions of the country around Boscastle.

Boscastle's **tourist office** is situated in the car park at the bottom of the main road into the village (daily: March–Oct 10am–5pm; Nov–Feb 10.30am–4pm; ⓣ01840/250010). One of the most appealing **places to stay** is *St Christopher's Hotel* (ⓣ01840/250412, ⓦwww.stchristophershotel.co.uk; ❷; closed Dec–Feb), a restored Georgian manor house at the top of the High Street, but for a real Hardy experience, head for the *Old Rectory*, on the road to St Juliot (ⓣ01840/250225, ⓦwww.stjuliot.com; no smoking; no under-12s; ❸; closed Dec–March), where you can stay in Hardy's or Emma's bedroom, or in a converted stable, and roam the extensive grounds. The lovely old **youth hostel** on the harbour (ⓣ0870/770 5710; closed mid-Oct to mid-March; £10.25) is also housed in a former stables. Nearby, you can eat at the *Harbour Restaurant* (ⓣ01840/250380; closed Nov to Easter, also eves Easter–May & Oct), which serves moderately priced organic, Asian-influenced food at wooden kitchen tables, as well as sandwiches and teas; it's worth booking ahead at weekends. By the youth hostel, pick up an ice cream from the *Harbour Light* (closed Nov–Easter), whose splendidly saggy roof marks it out as one of Boscastle's oldest buildings. The village has three good **pubs**: in the upper part of town, the *Napoleon* has the advantage of a good seafood bistro and a spacious lawned garden, while the *Cobweb* down near the harbour rates highly on atmosphere and has bar food; both have live music evenings.

Bude and around

There is little distinctively Cornish in Cornwall's northernmost town of **BUDE**, four miles west of the Devon border. Built around an estuary surrounded by a fine expanse of sands, the town has sprouted a crop of holiday homes and hotels, though these have not unduly spoilt the place nor the magnificent cliffy coast surrounding it.

Of the excellent beaches hereabouts, the central **Summerleaze** is clean and wide, growing to such immense proportions when the tide is out that a seawater swimming pool has been provided near the cliffs. The mile-long

Widemouth Bay, two and a half miles **south** of Bude, is the main focus of the holiday hordes – it has the cleanest water monitored between Bude and Polzeath, though bathing can be dangerous near the rocks at low tide. Surfers also congregate five miles down the coast at **Crackington Haven**, wonderfully situated between 430-foot crags at the mouth of a lush valley, though the water quality is poor. The cliffs on this stretch are characterized by remarkable zigzagging strata of shale, limestone and sandstone, a mixture which erodes into vividly contorted detached formations.

To the **north** of Bude, acres-wide **Crooklets** is the scene of **surfing** and life-saving demonstrations and competitions. A couple of miles further on, **Sandy Mouth** holds a pristine expanse of sand with rock pools beneath the encircling cliffs. The water quality is up to EU standards despite the seaborne litter, and myriad wildflowers dot the country around. It's a short walk from here to another surfers' delight, **Duckpool**, a tiny sandy cove flanked by jagged reefs at low tide. The beach is dominated by the three-hundred-foot **Steeple Point**, at the mouth of a stream that flows through the **Coombe valley**. Once the estate of the master Elizabethan mariner Sir Richard Grenville, the valley is now managed by the National Trust, which has laid out a one-and-a-half-mile nature trail alongside the wooded stream, half a mile inland.

Between Duckpool and the Devon border stretch five miles of strenuous but exhilarating coast. The only village along here is **Morwenstow**, just south of **Henna Cliff**, at 450ft the highest sheer drop of any sea cliff in England after Beachy Head, affording magnificent views along the coast and beyond Lundy to the Welsh coast.

Practicalities

Bude's **tourist office** is in the car park off the Crescent (April–Sept Mon–Fri 9.30am–5pm, Sat & Sun 10am–4pm; Oct–March Mon–Fri 10am–4pm, Sat 10am–2pm; ⓣ01288/354240, ⓦwww.visitbude.info). The town's cheaper **accommodation** lies fairly central but away from the sea, with a cluster of B&Bs overlooking the golf course on Burn View, among them *Sunrise* at no. 6 (ⓣ01288/353214; no credit cards; ❷), with a friendly landlady and all rooms en suite, and *Palms* at no. 17 (ⓣ01288/353962; no credit cards; ❷), which has some rooms with shared facilities. Near Summerleaze Beach, the *Falcon Hotel* on Breakwater Road is a much fancier affair (ⓣ01288/352005, ⓦwww.falconhotel.com; ❻), supposed to be the oldest coaching house in north Cornwall. If you don't mind being further from the beaches, head a mile inland to Cot Hill, Stratton, where the *Stratton Gardens Hotel* (ⓣ01288/352500, ⓦwww.s-h-systems.co.uk; no smoking; ❸) provides all the comforts in a small, whitewashed, sixteenth-century building; there's a great restaurant, too. There's a friendly backpacker's **hostel** not far from the beaches at 57 Killerton Rd (ⓣ01288/354256, ⓦwww.northshorebude.com; £12), with a large garden, Internet access and some double rooms (❶). The nearest of the numerous **campsites** around Bude are *Upper Lynstone Caravan and Camping Park* (ⓣ01288/352017, ⓦwww.upperlynstone.co.uk; closed Nov–Easter), three-quarters of a mile south of the centre on the coastal road to Widemouth Bay, and *Wooda Park* (ⓣ01288/352069, ⓦwww.wooda.co.uk; closed Nov–March), away from the sea at Poughill (pronounced "Poffil"), two miles north of Bude.

For style, location and cuisine, Bude's best **restaurant** is *Life's a Beach*, right on Summerleaze Beach, a café by day and a romantic (and expensive) bistro in the evening, worth reserving ahead for (ⓣ01288/355222); fish features strongly on the menu. In town, try out the *Atlantic Diner*, 5–7 Belle Vue (closed Mon, also eves Tues–Thurs & Sun in winter; inexpensive–moderate), popular with shoppers and surfers alike for its burgers, steaks, curries and ice creams. The *Falcon Hotel* (see opposite) offers abundant portions at its bar and has a more formal and expensive restaurant, which specializes in seafood. A mile inland from Bude, the village of **Stratton** offers two good possibilities: the *Stratton Gardens Hotel* (see opposite) and the *Tree Inn*, which was used as the Royalist headquarters during the battle of Stamford Hill – an engagement re-enacted annually on the nearest weekend to May 16. The pub was the home of the "Cornish Giant" Anthony Paine, manservant of Lord Grenville, who commanded the king's forces at their victory. There's a choice of **surfing equipment rental** outlets, including Zuma Jay on Belle Vue Lane. On a different note, the **Bude Jazz Festival** attracts a range of stomping sounds from around the world for a week in August/September (Ⓦ www.budejazzfestival.co.uk).

Bodmin and Bodmin Moor

Bodmin Moor, the smallest, mildest and most accessible of the West Country's great moors, has some beautiful tors, torrents and rock formations, but much of its fascination lies in the strong human imprint, particularly the wealth of relics left behind by its **Bronze Age** population, including such important sites as Trethevy Quoit and the stone circles of the Hurlers. Separated from these by some three millennia, the churches in the villages of St Neot's, Blisland and Altarnun are among the region's finest examples of fifteenth-century art and architecture.

The biggest centre in the area, **Bodmin**, stands outside the moor but can provide information on walking routes and on the Camel Trail, which touches here. With the north moor village of **Camelford**, Bodmin has the area's widest choice of accommodation, and is the most accessible town, sitting on the main A30 and within reach of the main rail line. Thanks to its central position, Bodmin is also well connected on bus routes, but the only services onto the moor are the twice-daily #78 (not Sat or Sun) and five-times-daily #264 (not Sun) to St Neot from Liskeard (a train stop); Tilley's Coaches #225, running four times daily on weekdays between Launceston and Altarnun, and the hourly #267 and #269 plying between Liskeard and Callington via St Cleer and Darite (not Sun). Camelford is connected to Newquay, Okehampton and Exeter on the #X10 route, to Bude on the #X11, and to Truro, Polzeath and Port Isaac on the #524 route (no Sun service for any). On summer weekdays, Camelford is also a stop on the once-daily #523 that runs from Truro to Bude, taking in Bodmin, Tintagel and Boscastle en route.

Bodmin

The town of **BODMIN** lies on the western edge of Bodmin Moor, equidistant from the north and south Cornish coasts and the Fowey and Camel rivers, a position that encouraged its growth as a trading town. It was also an important ecclesiastical centre after the establishment of a priory by St Petroc, who moved here from Padstow in the sixth century. The priory disappeared but Bodmin retained its prestige through its church of St Petroc, built in the fifteenth century and still the largest in Cornwall (April–Sept daily 10am–3pm; at other times call Ⓣ 01208/73867). Though officially the county town, Bodmin sacrificed much of its administrative role by refusing access to the Great Western Railway in the 1870s, as a result of which much local business transferred down the road to Truro. Nonetheless, though lying three miles outside town, **Bodmin**

Parkway Station makes the town quickly accessible from Penzance, Plymouth and Exeter, and there's a regular bus connection to the centre. Penzance, Plymouth and Newquay are also linked to Bodmin on four-times-daily National Express coaches. Otherwise, you can reach the town from Padstow, Wadebridge and St Austell on the hourly First Western National #55 **bus** service.

Bodmin's most prominent landmark is the **Gilbert Memorial**, a 144-foot obelisk honouring a descendant of Walter Raleigh and occupying a commanding location on Bodmin Beacon, a high area of moorland near the centre of town. Below, at the end of Fore Street, stands **St Petroc's Church**; inside, there's an extravagantly carved twelfth-century font and an ivory casket that once held the bones of the saint, while the southwest corner of the churchyard holds a sacred well. Close by, the notorious **Bodmin Jail** (Mon–Fri & Sun 10am–6pm, Sat 11am–5pm; £4.25) glowers darkly on Berrycombe Road, redolent of the public executions that were guaranteed crowd-pullers until 1862, from which time the hangings continued behind closed doors until 1909. You can visit part of the original eighteenth-century structure, including the condemned cell and some grisly exhibits chronicling the lives of the inmates. The jail finally closed in 1927.

Further up Berrycombe Road begins a section of the **Camel Trail** (see p.524), linking the town by cycle- and footpath to the main route along the Camel River at Boscarne Junction a mile up, which is itself connected by steam locomotives of the **Bodmin & Wenford Railway** to the restored station on St Nicholas Street and beyond to Bodmin Parkway (April–Sept 4–7 daily; £6–8 return; ⓣ0845/125 9678, ⓦwww.bodminandwenfordrailway.co.uk). The trains make a stop at Colesloggett, a good place to get off to explore **Cardinham Woods**, an excellent place for a day's rambling.

From Parkway it's less than two miles' walk to one of Cornwall's most celebrated country houses, **Lanhydrock** (April–Sept Tues–Sun 11am–5.30pm; Oct Tues–Sun 11am–5pm; garden open daily 10am–6pm or dusk; £7.20, grounds only £3.90; NT), originally seventeenth-century but totally rebuilt after a fire in 1881. The granite exterior remains true to its original form, but the 42 rooms show a very different style, including a long picture gallery with a plaster ceiling depicting scenes from the Old Testament, and – most illuminating of all – servants' quarters that reveal the daily workings of a Victorian manor house. The grounds have magnificent beds of magnolias, azaleas and rhododendrons, and a huge area of wooded parkland bordering onto the River Fowey.

Practicalities

Bodmin's **tourist office** (Easter–Sept Mon–Sat 10am–5pm; Oct–Easter Mon–Fri 10am–5pm; ⓣ01208/76616) is near the main car park at the bottom of St Nicholas Street. Comfortable **B&B** is available at *Higher Windsor Cottage*, 18 Castle St (ⓣ01208/76474, ⓦwww.higherwindsorcottage.co.uk; no credit cards; ❷), and the beflowered and lattice-windowed *Priory Cottage*, near St Petroc's Church at 34 Rhind St (ⓣ01208/73064, ⓦwww.stayanite.com; no smoking; no credit cards; ❷), which dates from the seventeenth century. There are a couple of good **B&Bs** three miles south of town near Lanivet and well located for the Saints' Way (see p.524): *Tremorvah* (ⓣ01208/831379, ⓔwendy@tremorvah.fsnet.co.uk; no credit cards; ❷), a ten-minute walk from the village located on Rosehill (the Bodmin Road), and *Bokiddick Farm*, two miles east of Lanivet, towards the Lanhydrock estate (ⓣ01208/831481, ⓦwww.bokiddickfarm.co.uk; ❸); both boast magnificent views and are non-smoking. There's a decent **campsite** on Old Callywith Road, a fifteen-minute walk from Castle Street in the centre (ⓣ01208/73834; closed Nov–Feb).

Off Fore Street, the *Hole in the Wall* **pub** in Crockwell Street has a pleasant backroom bar in what used to be the debtors' prison, with exposed fourteenth-century walls enclosing a collection of antiquities and bric-a-brac. There are bar lunches available, and in summer you can drink in the courtyard; for fuller meals there's an upstairs **restaurant**. Wholesome snacks are also served at the *Maple Leaf*, a tiny café just across from St Petroc's at 14 Honey St (closed Sun).

Bodmin Moor

Just ten miles in diameter, **BODMIN MOOR** is a wilderness on a small scale, its highest tor rising to just 1375ft from a platform of 1000ft. Yet the moor conveys a sense of loneliness quite out of proportion to its size, with scattered ancient remains providing in places the only distraction from an empty horizon. Aside from its tors, the main attractions of the landscape are the small Dozmary Pool, a site steeped in myth, and a quartet of rivers – the Fowey, Lynher, Camel and De Lank – that rise from remote moorland springs and effectively bound the moor to the north, east and south.

Blisland and the western moor

BLISLAND stands in the Camel valley on the western slopes of Bodmin Moor, three miles northeast of Bodmin. Georgian and Victorian houses cluster around a village green and a church whose well-restored interior has an Italianate altar and a startlingly painted screen. On **Pendrift Common** above the village, the gigantic **Jubilee Rock** is inscribed with various patriotic insignia commemorating the jubilee of George III's coronation in 1809. From this seven-hundred-foot vantage point you look eastward over the De Lank gorge and the boulder-crowned knoll of **Hawk's Tor**, three miles away. On the shoulder of the tor stand the Neolithic **Stripple Stones**, a circular platform once holding 28 standing stones, of which just four are still upright.

Blisland lies just a couple of miles east of the **Merry Meeting** crossroads, a point near the end of the Camel Trail. There's a really nice **place to stay** in the area, *Lavethan* (Ⓣ01208/850487, Ⓦwww.cornwall-online.co.uk/lavethan; no credit cards; ⑤), a beautiful sixteenth-century manor house set in thirty acres of park-like fields and gardens sloping to a small river; it's ten minutes' walk from the village towards St Mabyn. One and half miles north of Blisland on the St Breward Road, the small *South Penquite* **campsite** (Ⓣ01208/850491, Ⓦwww.southpenquite.co.uk) is a good option, closed to tents November–March, though the cosy, fully equipped Mongolian yurt sleeping six is available all year; it's heated by a woodburner. On Blisland's village green, you can sample good **ales and food** at the *Blisland Inn*, with outdoor tables.

Bolventor and Dozmary Pool

The village of **BOLVENTOR**, lying at the centre of the moor midway between Bodmin and Launceston, is an uninspiring place close to one of the moor's chief focuses for walkers and sightseers alike – **Jamaica Inn** (Ⓣ01566/86250, Ⓦwww.jamaicainn.co.uk; ④). A staging-post even before the precursor of the A30 road was laid here in 1769, the inn was described by Daphne Du Maurier as being "alone in glory, four square to the winds", and the combination of its convenient position and its association with her has led to its growth into a hotel and restaurant complex. One corner exhibits the room where the author stayed in 1930, soaking up inspiration for her smugglers' yarn. Adjacent to the hotel, the **Smuggler's Museum** (daily 10am–5pm; £2.50) shows the diverse ruses used for concealing contraband.

Bolventor is not on any public transport route. If you're driving, the inn's car park is a useful place to leave your vehicle and venture forth on foot. Just a mile away, along what must be the most travelled path on the moor, **Dozmary Pool** is another link in the West Country's Arthurian mythologies – after Arthur's death Sir Bedevere hurled Excalibur, the king's sword, into the pool, where it was seized by an arm raised from the depths. Loe Pool, near Porthleven on the Lizard, also claims the honour. Despite its proximity to the A30, the diamond-shaped lake usually preserves an ethereal air, though it's been known to run dry in summer, dealing a bit of a blow to the legend that the pool is bottomless.

The lake is also the source of another, more obviously Cornish legend, that of John Tregeagle, a steward at Lanhydrock, whose unjust dealings with the local tenant farmers in the seventeenth century brought upon his spirit the curse of endlessly baling out the pool with a perforated limpet shell. As if this were not enough, his ghost is further tormented by a swarm of devils pursuing him as he flies across the moor in search of sanctuary; their infernal howling is sometimes audible on windy nights.

Liskeard and St Neot

LISKEARD, a bus and rail junction just off the southern limits of the moor, makes a decent overnight stop, with **accommodation** at two reliable B&Bs: *Elnor*, 1 Russell St (ⓣ01579/342472; no credit cards; ❷), located on the way to the train station, and the immaculately kept *Hyvue* just north of the centre at Barras Cross (ⓣ01579/348175; non-smoking; no credit cards; ❶). From here, buses go on to **ST NEOT**, one of Bodmin Moor's prettiest villages, approached through a lush wooded valley. Its fifteenth-century **church** contains some of the most impressive stained-glass windows of any parish church in the country, the oldest glass being the fifteenth-century **Creation Window**, at the east end of the south aisle. Next along, **Noah's Window** continues the sequence, but the narration soon dissolves into windows portraying patrons and local bigwigs, while others present cameos of the ordinary men and women of the village. Among the best of St Neot's **accommodation** options is the seventeenth-century *Dye Cottage* (ⓣ01579/321394, ⓦwww.cornwall-info.co.uk/dye-cottage; no credit cards; ❶), which has a suite sleeping up to four, a guests' lounge, and a garden that slopes down to a stream; breakfast includes home-grown produce and homemade bread.

This southern edge of the moor is far greener and more thickly wooded than the northern reaches, due to the confluence of a web of rivers into the Fowey. One of the moor's best-known beauty spots is a couple of miles east, below Draynes Bridge, where the Fowey tumbles through the **Golitha Falls**, less a waterfall than a series of rapids. Dippers and wagtails flit through the trees, and there's a pleasant woodland walk you can take to the dam at the Siblyback Lake reservoir just over a mile away: follow the river up to Draynes Bridge, then walk north up a minor road until a path branches off on the right after a half-mile, leading down to the water's edge.

Camelford and the northern tors

The northern half of Bodmin Moor is dominated by its two highest tors, both of them easily accessible from **CAMELFORD**, a town once associated with King Arthur's Camelot, while Slaughterbridge, which crosses the River Camel north of town, is one of the contenders for his last battleground. The town has resisted trading on the Arthurian myths, but does have a couple of museums providing some diversion: the **British Cycling Museum** (daily: Mon–Thurs

& Sun 10am–5pm, phone ahead for Fri & Sat ⓣ01840/212811; £2.90), housed in the old station one mile north of town on the Boscastle Road, is a cyclophile's dream, containing some four hundred examples of bikes through the ages and a library of books and manuals. The collection may be of special interest to bikers on Route 3 on the National Cycle Way, which runs through Camelford. Meanwhile, the more conventional **North Cornwall Museum** (April–Sept Mon–Sat 10am–5pm; £2) in Camelford's centre contains domestic items and exhibits showing the development of the local slate industry, and also has a **tourist office** (same hours; ⓣ01840/212954).

Although it lacks excitement, Camelford makes a useful touring base. Among its **accommodation** is the central *Mason's Arms* on Market Place (ⓣ01840/213309; no credit cards; ❶) and the thirteenth-century, slate-hung *Darlington Inn* on Fore Street (ⓣ01840/213314; ❶). The *Countryman Hotel*, at 7 Victoria Rd (ⓣ01840/212250, ⓦwww.cornwall-online.co.uk/countryman; ❷), lies close to the National Cycle Way and is favoured by bikers, while *King's Acre* (ⓣ01840/213561; ❷), on the B3266 between Camelford's centre and the cycling museum, provides both B&B and **camping** (campsite closed Nov–Easter). Campers will find more facilities at the larger *Lakefield Caravan Park*, Lower Pendavey Farm (ⓣ01840/213279, ⓦwww.lakefieldcaravanpark.co.uk; closed Oct–March), which also offers **horse riding**. Both the *Mason's Arms*, which has a beer garden, and the *Darlington Inn* make good **refreshment** pit-stops.

Rough Tor, the second highest peak on Bodmin Moor at 1311ft, is four miles' walk southeast from Camelford. The hill presents a different aspect from every angle: from the south an ungainly mass, from the west a nobly proportioned mountain. A short distance to the east stand the Little Rough Tor, where there are the remains of an Iron Age camp, and Showery Tor, capped by a prominent formation of piled rocks.

Easily visible to the southeast, **Brown Willy** is, at 1375ft, the highest peak in Cornwall, as its original name signified – Bronewhella, or "highest hill". Like Rough Tor, Brown Willy shows various faces, its sugarloaf appearance from the north sharpening into a long multi-peaked crest as you approach. The tor is accessible by continuing from the summit of Rough Tor across the valley of the De Lank, or, from the south, by footpath from Bolventor. The easiest ascent is by the worn path which climbs steeply up from the northern end of the hill.

Altarnun and the eastern moor

ALTARNUN is a pleasant, granite-grey village snugly sheltered beneath the eastern heights of the moor. Its prominent **church**, dedicated to St Nonna, mother of David, patron saint of Wales, contains a fine Norman font and 79 bench-ends carved at the beginning of the sixteenth century, depicting saints, musicians and clowns. The village also has a Methodist chapel, over the door of which there is an effigy of John Wesley – a regular visitor to the neighbourhood – by Nevill Northey Burnard (1818–78), a local sculptor who, despite the praise of his contemporaries, ended his days in a Redruth poorhouse. Accessed by a private gate from St Nonna's (and also from the road), *Penhallow Manor* (ⓣ01566/86206, ⓦwww.penhallow-manor.co.uk; no smoking; ❺), originally the vicarage, now offers tasteful **accommodation** in spacious, old-fashioned rooms. Cheaper rooms can be found 500yd towards the A30, where the *King's Head* (ⓣ01566/86241; no credit cards; ❷) has beams, saggy ceilings and **meals** from around a fiver.

South of Altarnun, **Withey Brook** tumbles 400ft in less than a mile of gushing cascades before meeting up with the River Lynher, which bounds Bodmin

Moor to the east. Beyond the brook, on **Twelve Men's Moor**, lie some of Bodmin Moor's grandest landscapes. The quite modest elevations of Hawk's Tor (1079ft) and the lower Trewartha Tor appear enormous from the north, though they are overtopped by **Kilmar**, highest of the hills on the moor's eastern flank at 1280ft.

Withey Brook starts life about six miles from Altarnun on **Stowe's Hill**, site of the moor's most famous stone pile, **The Cheesewring**, a precarious pillar of balancing granite slabs, marvellously eroded by the wind. Gouged out of the hillside nearby, the disused Cheesewring Quarry is a centre of rock climbing. A mile or so south down Stowe's Hill stands an artificial rock phenomenon, **The Hurlers**, a wide complex of three circles dating from about 1500 BC. The purpose of these stark upright stones is not known, though they owe their name to the legend that they were men turned to stone for playing the Celtic game of hurling on the Sabbath.

The Hurlers are easily accessible just outside **MINIONS**, Cornwall's highest village, three miles south of which stands another Stone Age survival, **Trethevy Quoit**, a chamber tomb nearly nine feet high, surmounted by a massive capstone. Originally enclosed in earth, the stones have been stripped by centuries of weathering to create Cornwall's most impressive megalithic monument. Buses #267 and #269 from Liskeard call at St Cleer and Darite (not Sun), both of which are close to Trethevy Quoit; alternatively, it's a three-mile walk from Liskeard.

Travel details

Buses

For information on all local and national bus services, contact Traveline ⊕0870/608 2 608 (daily 7am–9pm), ⊛www.traveline.org.uk.

Bodmin to: Newquay (1–2 daily; 30–45min); Plymouth (2 daily; 1hr); St Austell (hourly; 50min–1hr); Truro (Mon–Sat 5 daily; 1hr 30min).

Exeter to: Bristol (4 daily; 1hr 45min–2hr); Falmouth (1 daily; 3hr 50min); Newquay (Mon–Sat 6 daily; 3hr); Plymouth (hourly; 1hr 15min); Sidmouth (Mon–Sat 2 hourly, Sun hourly; 45min); St Austell (1 daily; 2hr 25min); Torquay (hourly; 1hr–1hr 20min); Truro (1 daily; 3hr).

Falmouth to: Exeter (1 daily; 4hr); Helston (Mon–Sat 2 hourly, Sun in summer 4 daily; 35min); Penzance (Mon–Sat hourly; 1hr 5min); Plymouth (1–2 daily; 2hr 30min); St Austell (Mon–Sat hourly; 1hr 10min); Truro (Mon–Sat 1–2 hourly; 30min–1hr 15min).

Newquay to: Bodmin (2 daily; 50min); Exeter (Mon–Sat 7 daily; 3hr); Plymouth (2–3 daily; 1hr 30min–2hr); St Austell (hourly; 1hr).

Penzance to: Falmouth (Mon–Sat hourly; 1hr 10min); Helston (Mon–Sat 2 hourly, Sun hourly; 45min); Plymouth (5 daily; 3hr 30min); St Austell (Mon–Sat hourly, Sun 3 daily; 2hr 15min); St Ives (every 20–30min; 35–45min); Truro (1–2 hourly, Sun 8 daily; 1hr 35min).

Plymouth to: Bodmin (2 daily; 1hr); Exeter (hourly; 1hr 15min); Falmouth (2 daily; 2hr 15min); Newquay (2–3 daily; 1hr 20min–1hr 45min); Penzance (5 daily; 3hr–3hr 20min); St Austell (4 daily; 1hr 15min); St Ives (3 daily; 2hr 40min–3hr); Torquay (hourly; 1hr 45min); Truro (4 daily; 1hr 50min).

St Austell to: Bodmin (hourly; 50min); Exeter (1 daily; 2hr 35min); Falmouth (Mon–Sat hourly; 1hr 10min); Newquay (hourly; 1hr); Penzance (Mon–Sat hourly, Sun 3 daily; 2hr–2hr 15min); Plymouth (4 daily; 1hr 20min); St Ives (2 daily; 1hr 30min); Truro (1–2 hourly; 30–40min).

St Ives to: Penzance (2–3 hourly; 35min); Plymouth (3 daily; 3hr–3hr 20min); St Austell (1 daily; 1hr 50min); Truro (Mon–Sat hourly, Sun 1 daily; 1hr 25min).

Torquay to: Exeter (hourly; 1hr–1hr 20min); Plymouth (hourly; 1hr 45min).

Truro to: Bodmin (Mon–Sat 6 daily; 1hr 30min); Exeter (1 daily; 3hr 35min); Falmouth (Mon–Sat 1–2 hourly; 25min); Penzance (Mon–Sat every 30min, Sun 9 daily; 1hr 30min); Plymouth (1–2 daily; 2hr); St Austell (1–2 hourly; 35min); St Ives (Mon–Sat hourly, Sun 1 daily; 1hr–1hr 25min).

Trains

For information on all local and national rail services, contact National Rail Enquiries ⓣ08457/484950, ⓦwww.rail.co.uk.

Barnstaple to: Exeter (Mon–Sat 9–14 daily, Sun 4–5 daily; 1hr–1hr 15min).

Bodmin to: Exeter (1–2 hourly; 1hr 35min–1hr 50min); London (8–10 daily; 4hr); Penzance (1–2 hourly; 1hr 25min); Plymouth (1–2 hourly; 40min–1hr 15min).

Exeter to: Barnstaple (Mon–Sat 9–14 daily, Sun 4–5 daily; 1hr–1hr 10min); Birmingham (hourly; 2hr 45min); Bodmin (1–2 hourly; 1hr 45min); Bristol (1–2 hourly; 1hr 10min–1hr 25min); Exmouth (Mon–Sat every 30min, Sun 7–13 daily; 25min); Honiton (every 1–2hr; 25min); Liskeard (1–2 hourly; 1hr 30min); London (8–10 daily; 2hr 30min); Par (hourly; 2hr); Penzance (hourly; 3hr 15min); Plymouth (1–2 hourly; 1hr–1hr 20min); Salisbury (every 2hr; 2hr); Torquay (hourly; 45min); Totnes (1–2 hourly; 40min); Truro (hourly; 2hr 15min).

Falmouth to: Truro (10–12 daily; 25min).

Honiton to: Exeter (hourly; 30min); Salisbury (every 1–2hr; 1hr 20min).

Liskeard to: Exeter (1–2 hourly; 1hr 30min); London (9–11 daily; 3hr 45min–4hr 20min); Looe (8–10 daily, not Sun in winter; 30min); Penzance (hourly; 1hr 30min); Plymouth (1–2 hourly; 25min); Truro (hourly; 1hr 30min).

Newquay to: Par (4–6 daily, not Sun in winter; 50min).

Par to: Exeter (hourly; 1hr 50min); Newquay (4–6 daily, not Sun in winter; 50min); Penzance (hourly; 1hr 15min); Plymouth (1–2 hourly; 50min).

Penzance to: Bodmin (hourly; 1hr 20min); Bristol (5 daily; 4hr); Exeter (hourly; 3hr); Liskeard (hourly; 1hr 30min); London (7 daily; 5–6hr); Par (hourly; 1hr 10min); Plymouth (hourly; 2hr); St Ives (4–6 daily, not Sun in winter; 20min); Truro (1–2 hourly; 40min).

Plymouth to: Birmingham (11 daily; 3hr 45min); Bodmin (1–2 hourly; 40min); Bristol (8 daily; 2hr–2hr 45min); Exeter (2 hourly; 1hr); Liskeard (1–2 hourly; 30min); London (8 daily; 3–4hr); Par (1–2 hourly; 45min–1hr); Penzance (hourly; 2hr); St Erth (hourly; 1hr 50min); Truro (hourly; 1hr 15min).

St Ives to: Penzance (4–6 daily, not Sun in winter; 20min); St Erth (every 30min; 15min).

Torquay to: Exeter (hourly; 45min).

Truro to: Bristol (5 daily; 3–4hr); Exeter (hourly; 2hr 15min); Falmouth (10–12 daily; 25min); Liskeard (hourly; 50min); London (9 daily; 4hr 40min); Penzance (1–2 hourly; 40min); Plymouth (hourly; 1hr 15min).

7

East Anglia

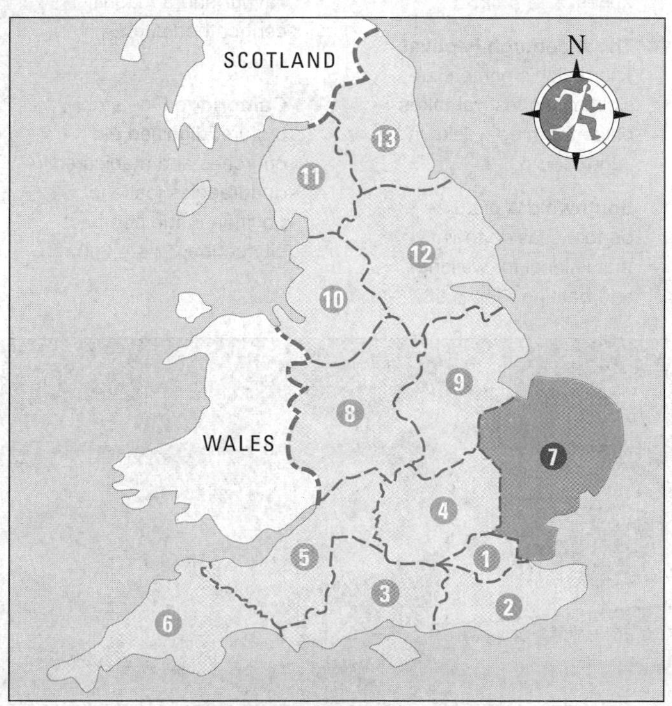

CHAPTER 7 Highlights

- **Orford** Remote and peaceful hamlet making for a wonderful weekend away. See p.564
- **Holkham Bay and beach** This wide bay holds Norfolk's finest beach, acres of golden sand set against hilly dunes. See p.586
- **The Aldeburgh Festival** The region's prime classical music festival takes place for three weeks in June. See p.566
- **Southwold** A picture-perfect seaside town that is ideal for walking and bathing. See p.567
- **Norwich Market** This open-air market is the region's biggest and best for everything from whelks to wellies. See p.575
- **Ely** Isolated Cambridgeshire town, with a true fenland flavour and a magnificent cathedral. See p.595
- **Cambridge** Fine architecture, dignified old churches and manicured quadrangles jostle for position in the compact city centre. See p.600

△ Southwold, Suffolk

East Anglia

Strictly speaking, **East Anglia** is made up of just three counties – Suffolk, Norfolk and Cambridgeshire – which were settled by Angles from Holstein in the fifth century, though in more recent times it's come to be loosely applied to parts of Essex too. As a region it's renowned for its wide skies and flat landscapes, and of course such generalizations always contain more than a grain of truth – if you're looking for mountains, you've come to the wrong place. That said, East Anglia often fails to conform to its stereotype: parts of Suffolk are positively hilly, and its coastline can induce vertigo; the north Norfolk coast holds steep cliffs as well as wide sandy beaches; and even the pancake-flat fenlands are broken by wide, muddy rivers and hilly mounds, on one of which perches Ely's magnificent cathedral. Indeed, the whole region is sprinkled with fine medieval churches, the legacy of the days when this was England's most progressive and prosperous region.

Of all the region's counties, **Suffolk** is the most varied. Its undulating southern reaches, straddling the River Stour, are home to a string of picturesque, well-preserved little towns – **Lavenham** and **Kersey** are two excellent examples – which enjoyed immense prosperity during the thirteenth to sixteenth centuries, the heyday of the wool trade. Elsewhere, **Bury St Edmunds** can boast not just the ruins of its once-prestigious abbey, but also some fine Georgian architecture on its grid-plan streets, while even the much maligned county town of **Ipswich** has more to offer than it's generally given credit for. Nevertheless, for many visitors it's the north Suffolk coast that steals the local show. In **Southwold**, with its comely Georgian high street, Suffolk possesses a delightful seaside resort, elegant and relaxing in equal measure, and neighbouring **Aldeburgh** hosts one of the best music festivals in the country.

Norfolk, as everyone knows thanks to Noël Coward, is very flat. It's also one of the most sparsely populated and tranquil counties in England, a remarkable turnaround from the days when it was an economic and political powerhouse – until, that is, the Industrial Revolution simply passed it by. Its capital, **Norwich**, is still East Anglia's largest city, renowned for its Norman cathedral and castle, and for its high-tech Sainsbury Centre, exhibiting a challenging collection of twentieth-century art. The most visited part of Norfolk is, however, the **Broads**, a unique landscape of reed-ridden waterways that has been intensively exploited by boat-rental companies for the last twenty years. Similarly popular, the **Norfolk coast** holds a string of busy, very English seaside resorts – **Great Yarmouth**, **Cromer**, **Sheringham** and **Hunstanton** to name but four – but for the most part it's a charmingly unspoilt region of tiny flintstone villages with **Blakeney Point** and the surrounding marshes among the country's top nature reserves. Meanwhile, sheltering inland, are two outstanding

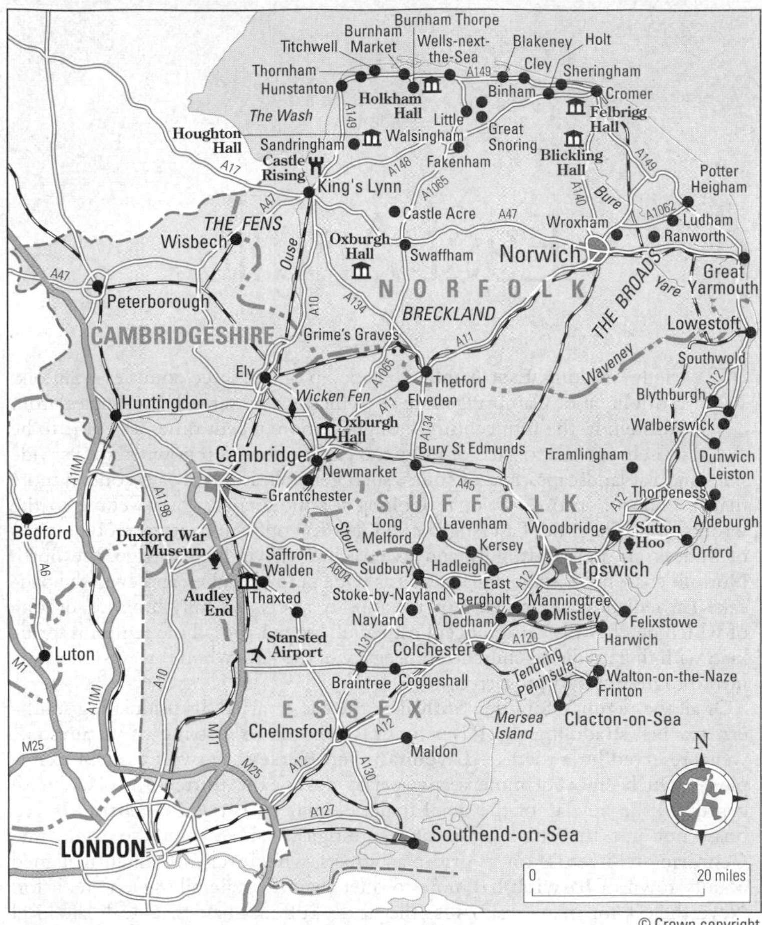

© Crown copyright

stately homes – **Blickling Hall** and **Holkham** – with several more within easy striking distance of **King's Lynn**, a strange, almost disconcerting mixture of fenland town and ancient seaport.

Cambridge is the one place in East Anglia everyone visits, largely on account of its world-renowned university, whose ancient colleges boast some of the finest medieval and early modern architecture in the country. The rest of Cambridgeshire is dominated by the landscape of the **Fens**, for centuries an inhospitable marshland, which was eventually drained to provide rich alluvial farming land. The one star turn here is the cathedral town of **Ely**, settled on one of the few areas of raised ground in the fens and an easy and popular day-trip from Cambridge – as is burgeoning **Peterborough**'s magnificent cathedral.

Heading into the region from the south almost inevitably takes you through **Essex**, though there's little here to divert you. Not properly part of East Anglia, but generally lumped together with the region, Essex's proximity to London has turned much of the county into an unappetizing commuter strip, while its inhabitants – "Essex man and woman" – are typically dubbed brash, conservative and uncultured by a fair slice of England's middle class. The county capital, Chelmsford, is no great shakes and instead it's best to aim for the historic town of **Colchester** and, at a pinch, the kiss-me-quick seaside resort of **Southend-on-Sea**.

Getting around

The **train** network is at its best to and from London, with quick and frequent services from the capital to all of East Anglia's major towns. One main line service links Colchester, Ipswich and Norwich, another Cambridge, Ely and Peterborough, which means it is relatively easy to move from one major town to another. However, once you get away from the major towns, you're going to have to rely on local **buses**, whose services, run by a multitude of companies, are very patchy – especially on Sundays and in winter. Indeed, in parts of north Norfolk and inland Suffolk, you may find the only way to get about is by your own transport. The largest regional bus operator is **First Eastern Counties**, which sells Ranger tickets (£7) providing unlimited travel for one day or more on their buses. These are available either in advance or from their drivers. Most tourist offices carry details of local buses and some of the more useful services are listed in the text and in Travel details at the end of the chapter.

Hiking, naturally enough, is less strenuous here than in most English regions, and there are several **long-distance footpaths**. The main routes run through Norfolk, starting with the **Peddars Way**, from Knettishall near Thetford and heading north to the coast at Hunstanton. The route then continues east as the **Norfolk Coast Path** as far as Cromer, from where the **Weaver's Way** then wends through the Broads to Great Yarmouth. Most local tourist offices can provide trail guides.

Southend-on-Sea

SOUTHEND-ON-SEA owes its existence to the Prince Regent, who in 1809 decided that the village of Prittlewell (now a suburb of Southend) would provide a healthier atmosphere for his wife, Princess Caroline, than London, forty miles to the west. Caroline lodged at Prittlewell's "south end", which henceforth became the town's official name. As the nearest sandy beach to London, Southend has doggedly maintained the popularity that followed from its royal patronage, though nowadays it has come to epitomize the downmarket English seaside resort of fish and chips, candyfloss and slot machines.

With a population of over a hundred and fifty thousand, Southend today incorporates many of the neighbouring towns along a seven-mile stretch of sand, which faces south onto the muddy Thames estuary. It's a rather dull geographical backdrop, with little in the town itself to raise the spirits and nothing on the promenade that isn't repeated up and down the English coast in dozens of comparable resorts. Nothing, that is, save for Southend's **pier** (April–Sept daily 8am–10pm; Oct–March Mon–Fri 8am–5pm, Sat & Sun till 7pm), which, at one and a third miles, is reputedly the longest in the world. Paul Theroux finished his grumpy circuit of Britain here, recounted in *The Kingdom By The Sea*, and to emulate him you can either walk or take the special pier shuttle train. Gazing out over the Thames estuary is not perhaps the most enticing of scenic experiences, but it's pleasant enough and afterwards you can wander the seafront, with its amusement arcades, brash pubs and fast-food joints. Just west of the pier, the resort's early days are recalled by the

Georgian **Royal Terrace**, with its distinctive wrought-iron verandas, on the embankment above the seafront; Princess Caroline stayed here, at nos. 7 and 9.

Two other seafront attractions are worth pointing out, beginning with **Sea Life Adventure** (daily 10am–5pm; £5.25; Ⓦwww.sealifeadventure.co.uk), about half a mile east of the pier, where, if there's nothing hanging about the estuary, you can gawp through the glass at the usual suspects from sharks and starfish to spiky spider crabs; note that the complex often opens until 7pm, call Ⓣ01702/442201 to check before you visit. A short walk beyond is the **Marine Activity Centre** (no set hours, call Ⓣ01702/612770 to check; Ⓦwww.local-life.co.uk/southendmarine), which offers sailing, windsurfing and canoeing. Needless to say, Southend has its share of **amusement parks**, the two major ones being Adventure Island (Ⓦwww.adventureisland.co.uk) and the tiny tots' Never Never Land (Ⓣ01702/460618), both of which are near the pier on the Western Esplanade. And then there's the **beach** – crowded near the arcades and amusement parks, but more secluded to the east towards Shoeburyness.

Practicalities

Trains from London's Fenchurch Street Station take just under an hour to reach Southend Central Station, which lies at the top of the pedestrianized High Street, a good ten minutes' walk from the pier: head down the High Street onto Pier Hill and you can't miss it. Services from Liverpool Street arrive a little further out of the centre at Southend Victoria. The **bus station** is at the junction of High Street and Heygate Avenue, opposite the Royals Shopping Centre – the best place for drivers to aim for, since it has a large multi-storey **car park**. The **tourist office** is located about five minutes' walk from the pier at 19 High St (July & Aug Mon–Sat 9.30am–5.30pm, Sun 11am–4pm; Sept–June closed Sun; Ⓣ01702/215120, Ⓦwww.southend.gov.uk).

The bulk of Southend's visitors are day-trippers and it's difficult to conceive of a reason to buck the trend. Nevertheless, if you're determined to find **accommodation**, you should have few problems as Southend abounds in inexpensive B&Bs, many along the Eastern Esplanade, though by far the nicest places to stay are the few Georgian properties on Royal Terrace, off the High Street. Here, the trim *Terrace Hotel*, at no. 8 (Ⓣ01702/348143, Ⓦwww.s-h-systems.co.uk/hotels/terracehotel.html; ❶), festooned with flowers and overlooking the more pleasant end of the seafront, has neat and well-kept rooms. Alternatively, ten minutes' walk east at Eastern Esplanade 190, away from much of the hustle and bustle, is the *Pebbles Guest House* (Ⓣ01702/582329, Ⓦwww.s-h-systems.co.uk/hotels/pebblesg.html; ❸), which holds five immaculate en-suite rooms and a pleasant roof terrace. The nearest **campsite** is the *East Beach Caravan and Camping Park* (Ⓣ01702/292466; closed Nov–Feb), which overlooks an undeveloped slice of the coast in Shoeburyness, the easternmost suburb of Southend.

Southend's proximity to London has had a beneficial effect on the quality of its **restaurants**. One of the best places to eat is the *Fleur de Provence*, just west of the High Street at 52 Alexandra St (Ⓣ01702/352987; closed Sun), where the Provençal food is delicious and a main course will set you back a reasonable £8–12. Alternatively, for a cheap fill-up, there's *G. R. Bailey & Son*, a traditional Southend chippy on the Eastern Esplanade.

Various **festivals** add more focus to a visit. One of the best is the annual summer jazz festival (dates vary, check with the tourist office), followed by carnival week in August, complete with processions and a fireworks display. The biggest event each year, though, is the **Air Show** held over the May bank holiday weekend, with aerial displays and fly-overs along the Thames estuary.

Colchester

If you visit anywhere in Essex, it should be **COLCHESTER**, an agreeable town with a castle, a university and a large army base, fifty miles or so north-east of London. More than anything else, Colchester prides itself on being England's oldest town and there is indeed documentary evidence of a settlement here as early as the fifth century BC. By the first century AD, the town was the region's capital under **King Cunobelin** – better known as Shakespeare's Cymbeline – and when the **Romans** invaded Britain in 43 AD they chose Colchester (Camulodunum) as their new capital, though it was soon eclipsed by London, becoming a retirement colony for legionaries instead. The first Roman temple in the country was erected here, and in 60 AD the colony was the target of Boudicca's abortive revolt (see box p.545). A millennium later, the conquering Normans built one of their mightiest strongholds in Colchester, but the conflict that most marked the town was the **Civil War**. In 1648, Colchester was subjected to a gruelling siege by the Parliamentarian army led by Lord Fairfax; after three months, during which the population ate every living creature within the walls, the town finally surrendered and the Royalist leaders were promptly executed for their pains.

Today, Colchester makes a potential base for further explorations of the surrounding countryside – particularly the Stour valley towns of Constable country (see pp.552–555), within easy reach to the north, and the handsome little village of **Coggeshall** a few miles to the west.

Arrival, information and accommodation

Colchester has two **train stations**. Services from London, Ipswich and Harwich arrive at the mainline Colchester North Station, from where it's a fifteen-minute walk south into town – follow North Station Road and its continuation North Hill until you reach the west end of the High Street. Trains from Frinton, Walton and Clacton-on-Sea arrive at Colchester Town Station,

Boudicca

Boudicca – aka Boadicea – was the wife of Prasutagus, chief of the Iceni tribe of Norfolk, who allied himself to the Romans during the conquest of Britain in 43 AD. Five years later, when the Iceni were no longer useful, the Romans attempted to disarm them and, although the Iceni rebelled, they were soon brought to heel. On Prasutagus's death, the Romans ignored his will and confiscated his property and when Boudicca protested, the Romans flogged her and raped her daughters. Enraged, Boudicca determined to take her revenge, quickly rallying the Iceni and their allies before setting off on a rampage across southern Britain in 60 AD.

As the ultimate symbol of Roman oppression, the Temple of the Deified Claudius in Colchester was the initial focus of hatred, but, once Colchester had been demolished, Boudicca soon turned her sights elsewhere. She laid waste to London and St Albans, massacring over seventy thousand citizens and inflicting crushing defeats on the Roman units stationed there. She was far from squeamish, ripping traitors' arms out of their sockets and torturing every Roman and Roman collaborator in sight. The Roman governor Suetonius Paulinus eventually defeated her in a pitched battle, which cost the Romans just four hundred lives and the Britons untold thousands. Boudicca knew what to expect from the Romans, so she opted for suicide, thereby ensuring her later reputation as a patriotic Englishwoman, who died fighting for liberty and freedom – claims which Boudicca would have found incomprehensible.

to the south of the centre at the bottom of St Botolph's Street. The **bus station** is off Queen Street, the northerly continuation of St Botolph's Street, and a couple of minutes' walk from the east end of High Street. You can get bus timetables here from the First Eastern National office (Mon–Fri 9am–5pm, Sat 9am–1pm; ⓣ01206/572478), which also sells Bus Ranger tickets (£7) valid for a day's travel throughout much of East Anglia.

The **tourist office** is at 1 Queen St (April–Oct Mon–Sat 9.30am–6pm, Sun 10am–5pm; Nov–March Mon–Sat 10am–5pm; ⓣ01206/282920, ⓦwww.colchesterwhatson.co.uk), at the east end of High Street, just behind the castle. As well as helping with accommodation, they sell leaflets detailing local walks and co-ordinate daily **guided walks** around town (May–Sept; £2.50). You can rent a **bike** from Action Bikes, beside the Odeon Cinema on Crouch Street (ⓣ01206/541744) – one way of getting out to see the nearby "Constable Country" (see pp.552–555).

For **accommodation**, Colchester has more than its fair share of old hotels as well as a scattering of pleasant, well-located B&Bs. The *Rose & Crown Hotel*, East Street (ⓣ01206/866677, ⓦwww.rose-and-crown.com; ❹), occupies an old, tastefully refurbished Tudor inn – the oldest inn in town – while the *George Hotel*, 116 High St (ⓣ01206/578494, ⓦwww.bestwestern.co.uk; ❺), is an attractive old coaching inn, whose rooms come with all mod cons. The *Red Lion*, 43 High St (ⓣ01206/577986, ⓦwww.brook-hotels.co.uk; ❺), is another old-timer, a fifteenth-century timber building containing 24 modernized en-suite rooms. The *Old Manse*, 15 Roman Rd (ⓣ01206/545154, ⓦwww.doveuk.com/oldmanse; ❸), is the best of the many B&B options along Roman Road, with three pleasant guest rooms; Roman Road is on the east side of the castle.

The Town

Most visitors start off at the town's rugged, honey-coloured **castle** (Mon–Sat 10am–5pm, Sun 11–5pm; £4.25), the perfect introduction to Colchester's long history, set in attractive parkland, which stretches down to the River Colne. Begun less than ten years after the Battle of Hastings, it boasts a phenomenally large keep – the largest in Europe at the time – built on the site of the defunct Roman temple. The castle's **museum** contains the best of the region's Romano-British archeological finds, although, apart from a fine bronze of Mercury, the messenger of the gods, this amounts to little more than a smattering of coins, tombstones, statues and mosaics. Perhaps the most impressive mosaic – depicting sea beasts pursuing dolphins – is on display at the castle entrance, next to the castle well. The museum also covers the Boudicca revolt and the 1648 siege, and you can sign up for a **guided tour** of the underground tunnels (45min; £1.50), which give access to the foundations of the Roman temple and the Norman chapel and walls – parts not otherwise accessible to regular visitors. Outside, down towards the river in Castle Park is a section of the old **Roman walls**, whose battered remains are still visible around much of the town centre. They were erected after Boudicca had sacked the city in 60 AD and, as such, are a case of too little too late.

The castle stands at the eastern end of the wide and largely pedestrianized **High Street**, which lies pretty much along the same route as it did in Roman times. The most arresting building here is the flamboyant **Town Hall**, built in 1902 and topped by a statue of St Helena, mother of Constantine the Great and daughter of "Old King Cole" of nursery-rhyme fame – after whom, some say, the town was named. Immediately north of the High Street is the so-called **Dutch Quarter**, where Flemish refugees settled in the sixteenth century giving a boost to the town's ailing cloth trade. The area's lofty buildings still make this a pleasant place to stroll, particularly along West and East Stockwell streets. South of the High Street, much of the medieval street plan has been subsumed within a vast shopping precinct and an open-air **market** held every Friday and Saturday in Vineyard Street. Nearby, narrow Trinity Street is home to the **Tymperleys Clock Museum** (April–Oct Tues–Sat 10am–1pm & 2–5pm; free), featuring a large collection of eighteenth- and nineteenth-century clocks, all wonderfully ornate and all made in Colchester. The museum itself occupies a good-looking and very old timber-framed building with its own little garden with scented lavender and rosemary.

Looming above the western end of the High Street is the town landmark, "**Jumbo**", a disused nineteenth-century water tower, considerably more imposing than the nearby **Balkerne Gate**, which marked the western entrance to Roman Colchester. Built in 50 AD, this is the largest surviving Roman gateway in the country, though with the remains at only a touch over six feet in height, it's far from spectacular. The gate is joined to another section of the town's **Roman Walls**, though here the effect is spoiled by the adjacent ring road.

With a little time to spare, it's worth strolling down **East Hill**, a continuation of the High Street east of the castle. Splendid Georgian houses line the top end of the hill, one of which – opposite the tourist office – is now the **Hollytrees Museum** (Mon–Sat 10am–5pm, Sun 11am–5pm; free), containing a modest collection of costumes, toys, domestic items, trade implements and decorative arts from the eighteenth to the twentieth century. Over the road at the **Minories** (April–Sept Mon–Sat 10am–5pm, Sun 11am–5pm; Oct–March closed Sun; free) another Georgian exterior conceals a contemporary arts centre, with a changing exhibition programme, a garden and a great café.

Doubling back, Queen Street heads south, becoming St Botolph's Street before it reaches Colchester Town Station. Just before the station are the ruins of **St Botolph's Priory**, beside the squat, quasi-fortified church of the same name. As the first Augustinian priory built in England, St Botolph's became head of the black-clad order until the Dissolution. It was reduced to rubble, like so much of the town, in 1648, though the twelfth-century western doorway and the thick piers of the nave give some idea of its Romanesque glories.

Eating, drinking and nightlife

Colchester's **oysters** have been highly prized since Roman times and the local vineyards have an equally long heritage, so it's no surprise to find the town has a good choice of first-rate **restaurants**. Pickings are slim on Sundays, however, when most places are closed. Probably the best place in town is *The Hub*, 19 Head St (ⓣ01206/564977), which offers tasty dishes at moderate prices from a contemporary, broadly Mediterranean menu. Alternatively, try *Ruan Thai*, 82a East Hill (ⓣ01206/870770), an excellent and moderately priced Thai restaurant near the top of East Hill; *Tilly's*, 22 Trinity St (closed Sun), a Victorian tearoom that serves snacks and full English meals; or the garden café at the Minories (closed Sun in winter), where the lunches are delicious. *The Lemon Tree*, 48 St John's St (ⓣ01206/767337; closed Sun), is a moderately priced option, popular for its lunch specials and sunny courtyard seating. To get top-quality oysters you do, however, have to venture out of town to the oyster fisheries at **West Mersea**, home of *The Company Shed*, 129 Coast Rd, **West Mersea** (ⓣ01206/382700), where the freshest of oysters are served without any frills at rickety tables. Mersea Island, home to both West and East Merseas, is located about six miles south of Colchester; the season runs from September to May.

Colchester's town centre is crowded with **pubs**, with three of the best being the *Red Lion*, 43 High St; the *Foresters Arms*, a nice backstreet local on Castle Rd; and the *Goat & Boot*, just one of several lively spots down East Hill. And, as you'd expect in a university town, the town rates reasonably well when it comes to the **arts and nightlife**. The Colchester Arts Centre, on Church Street next to the Balkerne Gate (Ⓣ01206/500900, Ⓦwww.colchesterartscentre.com), puts on a good programme of rock, folk, jazz, theatre and dance, plus some club nights – all in a converted Victorian church. Nearby is the Mercury Theatre (Ⓣ01206/573948, Ⓦwww.mercurytheatre.co.uk), the town's main drama venue. In term time it's also worth checking what's on at the university's Lakeside Theatre (Ⓣ01206/873261, Ⓦwww.essex.ac.uk/arts/office/theatre.htm), a mile or so east of the centre, where they provide a varied programme of theatre and music.

Around Colchester: Coggeshall

COGGESHALL, eight miles west of Colchester, boasts a plethora of sixteenth- and seventeenth-century timber-framed housing, the legacy of its days as a prosperous lace town. The most interesting buildings sport fine decorative **pargeting**, a once-fashionable style in which the faults of any building could be concealed by plasterwork with incised patterns – the more ornate the pattern, the wealthier the householder. This makes for some enjoyable viewing, as does the Victorian **clocktower**, faced with deep-blue weatherboarding and surmounted by a dinky white belfry, which lords it over the main square.

The village also contains two National Trust properties. The first, **Paycocke's House** on West Street (April to early Oct Tues, Thurs & Sun 2–5.30pm; £2.30; combined ticket for Grange Barn £3.40), is a rambling, cloth merchant's house dating from around 1500. The half-timbered facade, with its oriel windows and woodcarvings, is charming, but the interior is even more appealing, containing a wide variety of decorative carving – look for the detail in the linen-fold panelling of the dining room and over the main fireplace. A small sample of locally made lace is on display here too. The second property, **Grange Barn** (same details), a thirteenth-century timber-framed barn, the oldest in Europe, lies half a mile south of the village centre across the River Blackwater.

For **lunch**, head for any one of Coggeshall's antique pubs, the oldest of which is the medieval *Woolpack Inn* at the far end of Church Street.

There's no direct **bus** to Coggleshall from Colchester, but First in Essex operates a half-hourly service between the two with a change at Marks Tey; journey time is fifty minutes

The Tendring Peninsula

East of Colchester a thick nub of land juts out into the North Sea to form the **Tendring Peninsula**. The clean sandy beaches strung along the peninsula's southeast shore, the so-called "Essex Sunshine Coast," have been thoroughly developed over the last hundred years, resulting in a series of brash resorts, the most famous of which is **Clacton-on-Sea**. All are accessible by train from Colchester (or London's Liverpool Street), but in truth, none stands out, with the flat hinterland providing little visual relief from the dull seascape. By contrast, the attractive old quarter of **Harwich**, the international ferry terminal at the northeastern tip of the peninsula, is worth at least an hour or two of anyone's time.

It's disappointing that Tendring's most alluring historical sight, the privately owned medieval remains and gardens of **St Osyth Priory**, just west of Clacton, are closed to the public. The priory is associated with the gruesome legend of Osyth, daughter of Frithwald, the first king of East Anglia, who, as the story goes, refused to renounce her Christianity when asked to do so by Viking raiders. In response they lopped off her head, which she then carried to the church (that then stood here) before collapsing.

Clacton-on-Sea

CLACTON-ON-SEA, the Tendring's chief town, is a tad more polished than Southend-on-Sea (see p.543) and immediately more attractive, with its floral promenade gardens and broad sands. Attempts to lure you onto its pier with precisely phrased promises – the "largest" (as opposed to Southend's "longest") pleasure pier in the UK – and to "the new shopping experience at Clacton Common" are a tad desperate, but actually the town has little need of such bolstering. Clacton is a pleasant, unassuming family resort – it's as straightforward as that.

The **train station** is a couple of blocks east of the resort's main drag, Pier Avenue. **Buses** mostly stop near the seafront promenade. The **tourist office** at 23 Pier Ave (June to mid-Sept daily 9.30am–4.30pm; mid-Sept to May closed Sun; ⓣ01255/423400) can dish out details on local attractions, accommodation and campsites. As you might expect, there are plenty of **places to stay** with two good options being the bright and breezy, green and white seafront *Parade Hotel*, on Marine Parade East (ⓣ01255/222020, ⓦwww.paradehotel.com; ❸), and the well-kept *Dingle Dolphin Guest House*, 46 Wellesley Rd (ⓣ01255/474312; ❶), painted pink and bedecked with hanging baskets.

Frinton and Walton

FRINTON-ON-SEA, seven miles up the coast from Clacton, is a smaller, slightly snootier resort, sporting manicured lawns, sea views, a string of handsome Art Deco houses and a clutch of sedate-looking hotels and B&Bs. There's nothing so downmarket as an amusement arcade here, though fortunately you can still buy plastic buckets and spades to play with in the sand. The main street, **Connaught Avenue**, was once pronounced the "Bond Street of East Anglia" – though this claim seems more than a little far-fetched today.

Nearby **WALTON-ON-THE-NAZE** is a quiet place with a garish pier and a rather forlorn air. Its most appealing aspect is **The Naze** itself, a spatulate promontory which pokes north of the resort to form the eastern perimeter of **Hamford Water**, a large area of muddy creeks and salt marshes that produces the tastiest of oysters. It's also a major wintering area for wildfowl, and thousands of migrating birds pause here during spring and autumn. A few footpaths nudge into the area from the nearest minor roads – the B1034 to the south, the B1414 in the west – enabling visitors to get a closer look at the birdlife.

To reach Frinton and Walton-on-The-Naze by **train**, change at Thorpe-le-Soken on the Colchester–Clacton line – both resorts are on a tiny branch line. Neither place has a tourist office, but finding your way around is hardly problematic and there are lots of reasonably priced **B&Bs** to choose from. In Frinton an especially good choice is the *Uplands Guest House*, 41 Hadleigh Rd (ⓣ01255/674889, ⓦwww.uplandsguesthouse.com; ❸), a pleasant 1920s dwelling with eight attractively furnished bedrooms; it's located in a quiet residential area, just a couple of hundred yards from the beach. Walton's best hotel – not perhaps a zealously fought-for title – is the seafront *Regency Hotel*, 45 The

Parade (Ⓣ01255/676300, Ⓦwww.regency-hotel-uk.com; ❸), an amiable seaside guest house with its own bar – ask for a room with sea views.

Harwich

HARWICH, at the northeastern tip of the Tendring Peninsula, has a long history as a sea and river port. It equipped Elizabethan mariners such as Drake and Hawkins and provided the dockyards that built the *Mayflower*, the ship that took the Pilgrim Fathers to America. Sitting beside the estuary of the rivers Stour and Orwell, it also prospered from the proceeds of the Essex wool trade, slipping into prolonged decline when the focus of English trade moved from Europe to the Americas in the eighteenth century. Today, it's Britain's main North Sea ferry terminal, though since ferry traffic goes no further than Parkeston Quay, this has left the old town, a mile or so to the east, relatively undisturbed – and all the more appealing for that – save perhaps for the forest of container cranes that crowds the horizon.

The most interesting sites of old Harwich are conveniently clustered on the east side of a stumpy little headland. Starting at the train station, turn right along Main Road and you'll soon reach the entrance to **Harwich Redoubt** (June–Sept daily 10am–4pm; £1), an especially well-preserved circular fort constructed in 1808 as part of the coastal defences against Napoleon's expected invasion. Doubling back along Main Road, turn right down Harbour Crescent for both the **Low Lighthouse**, which holds the local maritime museum (June–Sept daily 10am–4pm; 50p), and, just across the green, the slender **High Lighthouse**, home to the National Wireless and Television Museum (April–Sept Sat & Sun 1.30–4.30pm; £1). In between the two is the only surviving **Treadwheel Crane** in the world, a seventeenth-century wooden structure that looks like a large garden shed. The crane's two large wheels were operated by men walking inside them – an unenviable job if ever there was one.

Pushing on north, it's a short walk to King's Quay Street's **Electric Palace**, a purpose-built cinema in the Edwardian Baroque style and dating from 1911 – and still going strong – and another short hoof to England's last manned **lightship**, which is scheduled to be turned into a floating museum by late 2004. The museum will be devoted to the pirate radio stations that flourished offshore in the 1960s, when the government was dead set against commercial radio broadcasting.

Practicalities

Harwich has three **train stations**: Harwich International Port Station by the Parkeston Quay ferry terminal; Dovercourt Bay Station on the edge of Harwich; and Harwich Town Station just off Main Rd, near Harwich Green. The **bus** service from Colchester to Parkeston Quay and Harwich old town is fast and frequent. Harwich **tourist office** is at the Safeway supermarket store, off the A120 between Parkeston Quay and Harwich old town (April–Sept Mon–Fri 9am–5pm, Sat & Sun 9am–4pm; Oct–Mar closed Sun; Ⓣ01255/506139, Ⓦwww.harwich.net/tic.htm). For **accommodation**, Harwich has about a dozen hotels and B&Bs, but stick to the old town, where the best bet is *The Pier*, down on The Quay (Ⓣ01255/241212, Ⓦwww.pieratharwich.com; ❹). This pleasant hotel has fourteen en-suite rooms, each of which is decorated in a broadly nautical style. Downstairs, the eponymous **restaurant** is an outstanding but moderately priced place specializing in the freshest of seafood.

The Stour Valley and the old wool towns of south Suffolk

Five miles or so north of Colchester, the **Stour River Valley** forms the border between Essex and Suffolk, and signals the beginning of East Anglia proper. Compared with much of the region it is positively hilly, a handsome landscape of farms and woodland latticed by dense, well-kept hedges and thick grassy banks that once kept the Stour in check. The valley is dotted with lovely little villages, where rickety, half-timbered Tudor houses and elegant Georgian dwellings cluster around medieval churches, proud buildings with square, self-confident towers. The Stour's prettiest villages are concentrated along its lower reaches – to the east of the A134 – in Dedham Vale, with **Stoke-by-Nayland** and **Dedham** arguably the most appealing of them all. The vale is also known as "**Constable Country**", as it was the home of John Constable (1776–1837), one of England's greatest artists, and the subject of his most famous works. Inevitably, there's a Constable shrine – the much-visited complex of old buildings down by the river at **Flatford Mill**.

The villages along the River Stour and its tributaries were once busy little places at the heart of East Anglia's weaving trade, which boomed from the thirteenth to the fifteenth century. By the 1490s, the region produced more cloth than any other part of the country, but in Tudor times production shifted to Colchester, Ipswich and Norwich and, although most of the smaller settlements continued spinning cloth for the next three hundred years, their importance slowly dwindled. Bypassed by the Industrial Revolution, south Suffolk had, by the late nineteenth century, become a remote rural backwater, an impoverished area whose decline had one unforeseen consequence. With few exceptions, the towns and villages were never well enough off to modernize, and the architectural legacy of medieval and Tudor times survived. The two best-preserved villages are **Lavenham** and **Kersey**, both of which heave with sightseers on summer weekends, but there are other attractive spots too, notably **Long Melford** and **Sudbury**. The latter boasts an excellent museum devoted to the work of Thomas Gainsborough, another great English artist and a native of the town who spent much of his time painting the local landscape.

Seeing the region by **public transport** is problematic – distances are small (Dedham Vale is only about ten miles long), but buses between the villages are infrequent and you'll find it difficult to get away from the towns. Several rail lines cross south Suffolk, the most useful being the London–Colchester–Sudbury route. More positively, the area is crisscrossed by **footpaths**, some of the most enjoyable of which are in the vicinity of Dedham village. All the local tourist offices sell easy-to-use walking leaflets.

Manningtree and Mistley

At the turn of the eighteenth century, work was undertaken to make the **River Stour** navigable between Manningtree, where the river suddenly narrows, and Sudbury about fifteen miles inland. All manner of goods were to be transported into the Essex and Suffolk hinterland by this route over the next two centuries, including regular supplies of grindstones supplied to the mills which lined the river. One of the beneficiaries of the scheme was **MANNINGTREE**, around eight miles northeast of Colchester (and connected by a regular train service), whose largely Georgian High Street is evidence of its heyday as a river port. Only a small quay has survived, but a much larger working dockyard exists a mile or so to the east at **MISTLEY**, where the air is pungent with malt from the local maltings. The B1352 between the two forms a pleasant riverside promenade, passing by the incongruous Neoclassical **Mistley Towers**, Robert Adam's only foray into church architecture. Built as embellishments to the local church, which was later demolished, the towers were paid for by a local bigwig, a certain Richard Rigby. Rigby's pet idea was to turn Mistley into a fashionable spa resort, but his grandiose plans never got off the ground – all that's left is an unusual swan fountain with an oval basin just beyond the towers on the main road.

With much prettier places close at hand, there's really no need to stay hereabouts, but *The Crown* pub, 51 High St (ⓣ01206/396333; ❸), offers simple, en-suite accommodation as well as a pleasant spot for a drink.

East Bergholt, Flatford Mill – and John Constable

"I associate my careless boyhood to all that lies on the banks of the Stour," wrote **John Constable**, who was born the son of a miller in **EAST BERGHOLT**, nine miles northeast of Colchester in 1776. The house in which he was born has long since disappeared, so it has been left to **Flatford Mill**, a mile or so to the south, to take up the painter's cause. The mill was owned by his father and was where Constable painted his most famous canvas, *The Hay Wain* (now in the National Gallery, London), which created a sensation when it was exhibited in 1824. To the chagrin of many of his contemporaries, Constable turned away from the landscape-painting conventions of the day, rendering his scenery with a realistic directness that harked back to the Dutch landscape painters of the seventeenth century. Typically, he justified this approach in unpretentious terms, observing that, after all "no two days are alike, nor even two hours; neither were there ever two leaves of a tree alike since the creation of the world." The mill itself – not the one he painted, but a Victorian replacement – is not open to the public, but the sixteenth-century thatched **Bridge Cottage** (March & April Wed–Sun 11am–5.30pm; May–Sept daily 10am–5.30pm; Oct daily 11am–4.30pm; Nov & Dec Wed–Sun 11am–3.30pm; Jan & Feb Sat & Sun 11am–3.30pm; free, but parking £1.50; NT), which overlooks the scene, has been painstakingly restored and stuffed full of Constabilia. Unfortunately, none of the artist's paintings are displayed here, but there's a pleasant riverside tearoom to take in the view. Beyond stands **Willy Lott's Cottage** (also closed to the public), which does actually feature in *The Hay Wain*.

In summer, the National Trust organizes **guided walks** around the sites of Constable's paintings (call ⓣ01206/298260 for details), but there are many other pleasant walks to be had along this deeply rural bend in the Stour. One footpath connects the mill to the **train station** at Manningtree, two miles to the east, and another runs over to the village of Dedham, a mile and a half to the west. (You can buy leaflets detailing the routes from local tourist offices.) It's also possible to rent a **rowing boat** (£5 per hour) from beside the bridge and potter peacefully along the river. There's a **B&B** here too, the *Flatford Granary* (ⓣ01206/298111; ❷), where the comfortable rooms, with their beamed ceilings, are pleasant, and the views idyllic.

Dedham

Constable went to school in **DEDHAM**, just upriver from Flatford Mill and one of the region's most attractive villages, with a scattering of ancient timber-framed houses strung along the wide main street. The only sights as such are

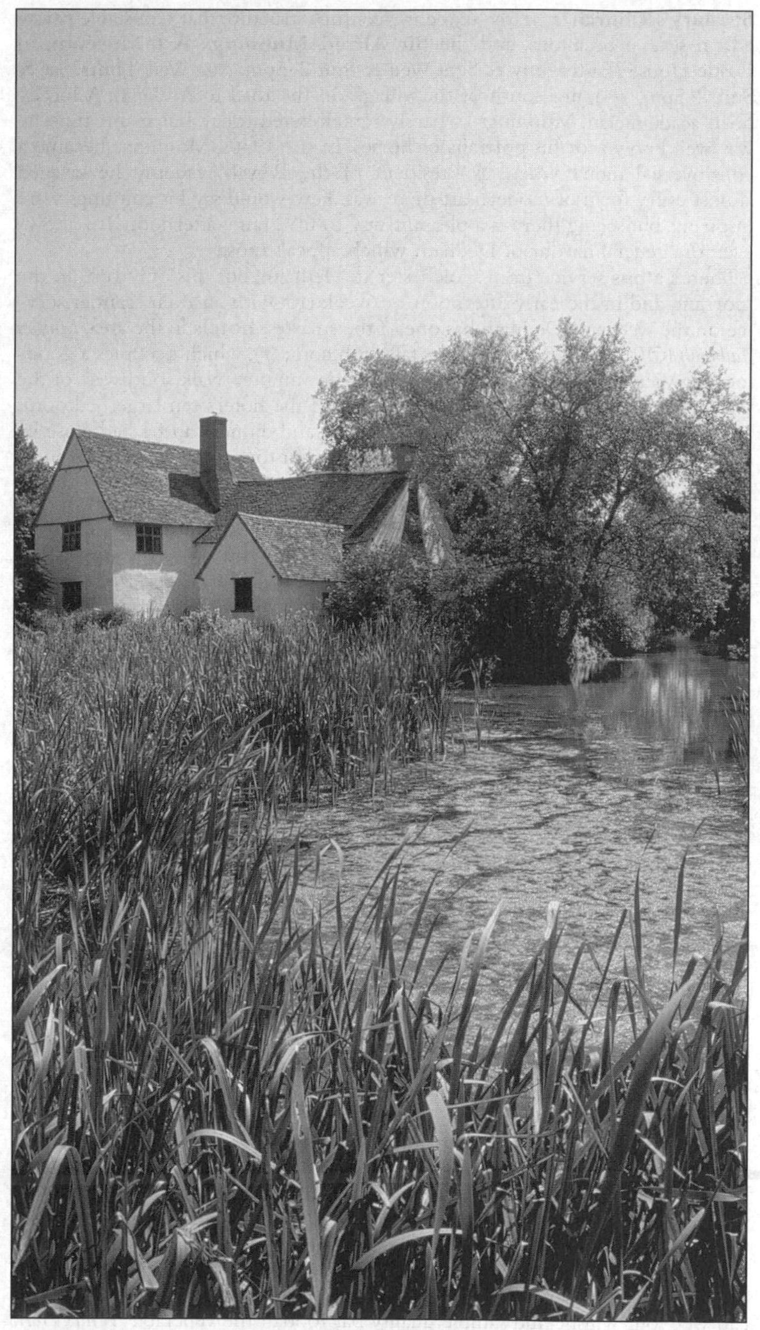

△ Flatford Mill, Suffolk

St Mary's Church, an early-sixteenth-century structure that Constable painted on several occasions, and the **Sir Alfred Munnings Art Museum**, in Castle House (Easter–July & Sept Wed & Sun 2–5pm; Aug Wed, Thurs, Sat & Sun 2–5pm; £4), just south of the village on the road to Ardleigh. A locally born academician, Munnings is barely remembered today, but in his time he was well known for his portraits of horses. In the 1940s, Munnings became a controversial figure when, as President of the Royal Academy, he savaged almost every form of modern art there was. Few would say his paintings were inspiring, but seeing them is a pleasant way to fill a rainy afternoon. It is, however, the general flavour of Dedham which appeals most.

There's a **bus** service from Colchester to Dedham, but this only runs in the morning and in the early afternoon on weekdays with an even scantier service on the weekend. Dedham has one of the smartest **hotels** in the area, *Maison Talbooth* (Ⓣ01206/322367, Ⓦwww.talbooth.com; ❽), which occupies a good-looking Victorian country house about fifteen minutes' walk southwest of the village on the road to Stratford St Mary. All of the hotel's ten large bedrooms are individually decorated in sumptuous style and dinner can be had close by at *Le Talbooth* (Ⓣ01206/323150), an expensive, but top-notch **restaurant** in an ancient timber-framed house down by the River Stour. Alternatively, there's *Dedham Hall* (Ⓣ01206/323027, Ⓦwww.dedhamhall.demon.co.uk; ❺), an old manor house set in its own grounds on the east side of the village off Brook Street – be sure to ask for a room in the house itself. The restaurant here is very good too (closed Mon). You can also stay in the heart of Dedham itself at the *Marlborough Head* pub (Ⓣ01206/323250; ❹), where a handful of very pleasant rooms are available above the bar, and excellent, moderately priced **food** can be had from an inventive and wide-ranging menu.

Stoke-by-Nayland and Nayland

Heading northwest from Dedham, the B1029 dips beneath the A12 to reach the byroad to Higham, an unremarkable hamlet where you pick up the road to **STOKE-BY-NAYLAND**, four miles to the west. This is the most picturesque of villages, where a knot of half-timbered, pastel-painted cottages snuggles up to **St Mary's Church** (daily 9am–5pm; free), which, with its pretty brick and stone-trimmed tower, was one of Constable's favourite subjects. The doors of the south porch are sumptuously covered by the carved figures of a medieval Jesse Tree and although the interior is sombre and severe, it does boast a magnificent, soaring tower arch. The village also has a great old **pub**, the *Angel Inn* (Ⓣ01206/263245; ❹), known for its adventurous food (eat in the bar or book for the restaurant) and cosy **rooms**. There are several other good places to stay in and near the village, including *Thorington Hall* (Ⓣ01206/337329; ❸), which offers four bedrooms in a seventeenth-century house. The hall is located a little over a mile east of the village on the road to Higham; note that it's open from Easter to September only.

Southwest from here, it's two miles back to the River Stour at **NAYLAND**, a workaday little place that is chiefly remarkable for its church's altar painting, *Christ Blessing the Bread and Wine*. It's one of only two attempts by Constable at a religious theme – and, dated to 1809, it was completed long before he found his artistic rhythm. There's also the fine, largely Norman church of St Mary a mile or so to the west at tiny **WISSINGTON**, where the nave is decorated with a rare series of thirteenth-century frescoes. Back in Nayland, you can wet your whistle and sample quality bar food at the venerable *White Hart*, 11 High St. Local **accommodation** is available at *Hill House*, Gravel Hill

(Ⓣ01206/262782; ❷), on the edge of the village, and at *Gladwins Farm*, Harper's Hill (Ⓣ01206/262261, Ⓦwww.gladwinsfarm.co.uk; ❹), a secluded timber-framed farmhouse with its own indoor pool.

Sudbury

SUDBURY – the fictional "Eatanswill" of Dickens' *Pickwick Papers* – has doubled in size in the last thirty years, to become easily the most important town in this part of the Stour Valley. A handful of timber-framed houses harks back to its days of wool-trade prosperity, but its three Perpendicular churches were underwritten by another local industry, **silk weaving**, which survives on a small scale to this day. Sudbury's most famous export, however, is **Thomas Gainsborough** (1727–1788), the leading English portraitist of the eighteenth century, whose statue, with brush and palette, stands on Market Hill, the town's predominantly Victorian market place. A superb collection of the artist's work is on display a few yards away in the house where he was born – **Gainsborough's House**, at 46 Gainsborough St (April–Oct Tues–Sat 10am–5pm, Sun 2–5pm; Nov–March Tues–Sat 10am–4pm, Sun 2–4pm; £3.50). Gainsborough left Sudbury when he was just 13, moving to London where he was apprenticed to an engraver, but it seems he was soon moonlighting and the earliest of his surviving portrait paintings – his *Boy and Girl*, a remarkably self-assured work dated to 1744 – is displayed here. In 1752, Gainsborough moved on to Ipswich, where he quickly established himself as a portrait painter to the Suffolk gentry with one of his specialities being wonderful "conversation pieces", so-called because the sitters engage in polite chitchat – or genteel activity – with a landscape as the backdrop. Seven years in Ipswich was followed by a move upmarket to Bath, where he painted high-society figures, as he did when he moved back to London in 1774. During his years in Bath, Gainsborough developed a fluid, flatteringly easy style that was ideal for his aristocratic subjects, who posed in becoming postures painted in soft, evanescent colours. Examples of Gainsborough's later work exhibited here include the *Portrait of Harriet, Viscountess Tracy* (1763) and the particularly striking *Portrait of Abel Moysey, MP* (1771). In his later years, the artist also dabbled with romantic paintings of country scenes – as in *A Wooded Landscape with Cattle by a Pool* – a playful variation of the serious landscaping painting he loved to do best; the rest, he often said, just earned him money. Gainsborough never bothered with assistants, with one exception, his nephew **Gainsborough Dupont**, and there's a room devoted to his work on the top floor. Finally, don't forget the agreeable tearoom in the garden.

Sudbury is just seven miles northwest of Nayland – and twice that from Colchester – along the A134. It's accessible by **train** from Colchester (for some services, change at Marks Tey) and is the hub of **bus** services to and from neighbouring towns and villages including Colchester and Ipswich. Once you've seen Gainsborough's house, though, there's little reason to hang around. If you do decide to stay, the **tourist office** in the town hall on Market Hill (April–Sept Mon–Fri 9am–5pm & Sat 10am–4.45pm; Oct–March Mon–Fri 9am–5pm & Sat 10am–2.45pm; Ⓣ01787/881320, Ⓦwww.visit-suffolk.org.uk) can provide **accommodation** details.

Long Melford

True to its name, **LONG MELFORD**, just four miles north of Sudbury, has possibly the longest main street in the country. That in itself is not much of a recommendation, but more to the point, for much of its two miles the street is lined with handsome timber-framed houses. At its northern end, it opens up into a wide sloping **green**, beyond which stands a collection of sixteenth-century almshouses presided over by the mighty stone and flint **Holy Trinity Church** (daily 10am–5pm; free). Built in the fifteenth century, around the same time as Lavenham's (see below), it's one of the most majestic of the so-called wool churches, with huge windows which flood the nave with light. For centuries, rich benefactors have left their legacy here in the form of brightly coloured stained glass, including one window decorated with three rabbits representing the Holy Trinity.

To the east of the green, behind a high brick wall, is **Melford Hall** (April & Oct Sat & Sun 2–5.30pm; May–Sept Wed–Sun 2–5.30pm; £4.50; NT), a turreted red-brick Tudor mansion that was once a country retreat for the abbots of nearby Bury St Edmunds. The exterior has changed little since its construction in the 1570s, but the interior has been remodelled on several occasions – witness the Regency library and the Victorian bedrooms.

If you want to **stay** in Long Melford, the *George & Dragon* (☎01787/371285; ④), on Hall Street, a continuation of High Street, is the best option with eight comfortable, en-suite rooms and a garden. As for **food and drink**, *The Bull*, on the same stretch of road, is a real heavyweight among old inns, shouting its Elizabethan credentials throughout and serving decent, moderately priced food in its public bar. There's a reasonably frequent **bus** service from Sudbury to Long Melford (not Sun).

Lavenham

Four miles northeast of Long Melford, off the A134, lies **LAVENHAM**, formerly a centre of the region's wool trade and today one of the most visited villages in Suffolk, thanks to its unrivalled ensemble of perfectly preserved half-timbered houses. The whole place has changed little since the demise of the wool industry, owing in part to a zealous local preservation society that has carefully maintained the village's antique appearance by banning from view such modern frivolities as advertising hoardings and TV aerials.

The village is at its most beguiling in the triangular **Market Place**, an airy spot flanked by pastel-painted, medieval dwellings whose beams have been bent into all sorts of wonky angles by the passing of the years. It's here you'll find Lavenham's most celebrated building, the pale-white, timber-framed **Corpus Christi Guildhall** (March & Nov Sat & Sun 11am–4pm; April Wed–Sun 11am–5pm; May–Oct daily 11am–5pm; £3; NT), erected in the sixteenth century as the headquarters of one of Lavenham's four guilds. In the much-altered interior (used successively as a prison and workhouse), there's an exhibition on the wool industry, but most visitors quickly reach the walled garden and the teashop. Just to the east across the square is the mostly fifteenth-century **Little Hall** (April–Oct Wed, Thurs, Sat & Sun 2–5.30pm; £1.50), which contains a modest collection of furniture and objets d'art, but the view down Prentice Street from beside the neighbouring *Angel Hotel* is much more arresting – a line of creaky timber-framed dwellings dipping into the deep green countryside beyond. The other building worthy of special notice is the Perpendicular **church of St Peter and St Paul** (daily: May–Sept 8.30am–5.30pm; Oct–April 8.30am–3.30pm; free), though it's sited a short walk southwest of the centre, at the top of Church Street. Local merchants endowed the church with a nave of majestic proportions and a mighty flint tower, at 141ft the highest for miles around, partly to celebrate the Tudor victory at the Battle of Bosworth in 1485 (see p.1123), but mainly to show off their wealth.

Practicalities

There are fairly frequent **buses** to Lavenham from Colchester via Sudbury and Long Melford, with the service continuing on to Bury St Edmunds. The **tourist office** is located on Lady Street (April–Oct daily 10am–5pm; Nov–March Sat & Sun 11am–4pm; ⓣ01787/248207, ⓦwww.visit-suffolk.org.uk), just south off Market Place. They can help with **accommodation** and sell a detailed, street-by-street walking guide. Rooms at the *Swan Hotel* (ⓣ0870/400 8116, ⓦwww.macdonald-hotels.co.uk; ❻), a splendid old inn on High Street, are some of the most comfortable in town; the building incorporates part of the Elizabethan Wool Hall and is a warren of cosy lounges and courtyard gardens. There's more luxurious accommodation at *Lavenham Priory*, on Water Street (ⓣ01787/247404, ⓦwww.lavenhampriory.co.uk; ❺), where four immaculate rooms are contained within the old Benedictine priory. Less expensive options on the Market Place include the ancient *Angel Hotel* (ⓣ01787/247388, ⓦwww.lavenham.co.uk/angel; ❹), which has eight pleasant rooms above its bar, and the dinky *Angel Gallery* (ⓣ01787/248417, ⓦwww.lavenham.co.uk/angel-gallery; ❸), where the three guest rooms are situated above a pocket-sized art shop. For cheaper B&B options, you'll probably end up staying outside Lavenham itself; the tourist office can provide details.

For **food**, the *Angel Hotel* serves up excellent, moderately priced bar meals, as does the *Swan*. The other choice in Market Place is the *Great House* (ⓣ01787/247431; closed Sun & Mon), whose outstanding restaurant serves reasonably priced food on both its à la carte and set menus.

Kersey and Hadleigh

Seven miles southeast off the A1141, **KERSEY** vies with Lavenham as the most photographed village in Suffolk. Another old wool town, Kersey seems to have dodged just about every historical bullet since the seventeenth century and now comprises little more than one exquisite street of timber-framed houses, which dips in the middle to cross a ford that's inhabited by a family of fearless ducks. Prime real estate today, Kersey's more populous past is recalled by its large and austere parish **church**, visible for miles around, perched on high ground above the village. There's nowhere to stay, but there is one good **pub**, the *White Horse*, which serves good, reasonably priced bar food.

Another couple of miles southeast, the market town of **HADLEIGH** is a positive metropolis compared to Kersey, but nonetheless everything of interest is within a stone's throw of the **Parish Church of St Mary's** (daily: May–Sept 9am–5.30pm, Oct–April 9am–3.30pm). The church, one block west of the elongated High Street, is mainly fifteenth century, a good-looking replacement for several earlier versions. Legend asserts that Guthrum, the Danish chieftain and arch-rival of **Alfred the Great**, was buried underneath the south aisle in 889, but his remains have never been definitively identified. Opposite the church, across the graveyard, is the half-timbered **Guildhall** (guided tours June–Sept Thurs & Sun 2–4.30pm; donation), every bit as immaculate as Lavenham's, with the earliest sections dating from 1438 – and offering very-English cream teas in the garden from June to September (Mon–Fri & Sun 2.30–5pm). At the back of the church is the extravagantly ornate **Deanery Tower**, a fifteenth-century gatehouse whose palace was never completed. In the garret room at the top of the tower, the Oxford Movement, which opposed liberal tendencies within the Anglican Church and sought to promote Anglo-Catholicism, was founded in 1833 by local rector Hugh Rose.

Hadleigh is easy to reach by **bus** with regular services from Sudbury, Lavenham, Ipswich and Colchester, though Sundays can be a bit tricky. Several Hadleigh-bound buses pass through Kersey too. For a bite to **eat**, *Ferguson's Delicatessen*, 48 High St (closed Sun), sells delicious sandwiches.

Bury St Edmunds

Appealing **BURY ST EDMUNDS** started out as a Benedictine monastery, founded to house the remains of Edmund, the last Saxon king of East Anglia, who was tortured and beheaded by the marauding Danes in 869. Almost two centuries later, England was briefly ruled by the kings of Denmark and the shrewdest of them, **King Canute**, made a gesture of reconciliation to his Saxon subjects by conferring on the monastery the status of abbey. It was a popular move and the abbey prospered, so much so that before its dissolution in 1539, it had become the richest religious house in the country. Most of the abbey disappeared long ago, and nowadays Bury is better known for its graceful Georgian streets, its flower gardens and its sugar-beet plant than for its ancient monuments. Nonetheless, it's an amiable, eminently likeable place, one of the prettiest towns in Suffolk, and, with good transport connections on to Cambridge, Colchester, Ipswich and Norwich, it demands at least half a day of anyone's time.

The Town

The town centre has preserved its Norman street plan, a gridiron in which Churchgate was aligned with – and sloped up from – the abbey's high altar. It was the first planned town of Norman Britain and, for that matter, the first example of urban planning in England since the departure of the Romans. Beside the abbey grounds is **Angel Hill**, a broad, spacious square partly framed by Georgian buildings, the most distinguished being the ivy-covered **Angel Hotel**, which features in Dickens' *Pickwick Papers*. Dickens also gave readings of his work in the **Athenaeum**, the Georgian assembly rooms at the far end of the square. A twelfth-century wall runs along the east side of Angel Hill, with the bulky fourteenth-century **Abbey Gate** forming the entrance to the abbey gardens and ruins.

The **abbey ruins** themselves (open access) are like nothing so much as petrified porridge, with little to remind you of the grandiose Norman complex that dominated the town. Thousands of medieval pilgrims once sought solace at St Edmund's altar and the cult was of such significance that the barons of England gathered here to swear that they would make King John sign their petition – the Magna Carta of 1215. Today, the only significant remnants are on the far side of the abbey gardens, behind the more modern cathedral (see below), and they comprise the rubbled remains of a small part of the old **abbey church** integrated into a set of unusual Georgian houses. In front, across the green, is the imposing **Norman Tower**, once the main gateway into the abbey and now a solitary monument with dragon gargoyles and fancily decorated capitals.

Incongruously, the tower is next to the front part of Bury's Anglican **Cathedral of St James** (daily: 8.30am–6pm; £2 donation requested), with chancel and transepts added as recently as the 1960s. That its thousand-odd kneelers (the cushions in the pews used when the congregation pray) are often cited as one of its major highlights gives an idea of the paucity of the interior – notwithstanding the hammer-beam roof and a couple of quality stained-glass windows. In fact, it was a toss-up between this place and **St Mary's Church** (Mon–Sat 10am–4pm, 3pm in winter; free), further down Crown Street, as to which would be given cathedral status in 1914. The presence of the tomb of the resolutely Catholic Mary Tudor in the latter was probably the clinching factor.

Round the corner from St Mary's, just off Crown Street on Honey Hill, the **Manor House Museum** (Wed–Sun 11am–4pm; £3) occupies a grand Georgian mansion built by the wife of the First Earl of Bristol as a pied-à-terre party house. An enjoyable assortment of clocks and watches forms the core of the museum's collection, which is supplemented by a modest sample of portrait and landscape paintings. The museum also mounts extremely popular temporary exhibitions on art and textiles, often based on TV and film costume dramas. At the far end of Crown Street stands Bury's most important industrial concern, the pungent **Greene King Brewery** (tours: Mon–Fri 3 daily, Sat 2 daily; £7; reservations on ⓣ01284/714382), whose powerful Abbot Ale is an intense bittersweet beer to be quaffed with caution. The brewery and the National Trust are joint owners of the neighbouring Regency **Theatre Royal**, at the junction of Crown and Westgate streets, built in 1819 by William Wilkins and still staging plays.

The town's main **commercial area** is on the west side of the centre, a five-minute walk up Abbeygate Street from Angel Hill. There's been some intrusive modern planning here, but dignified Victorian buildings flank both **Cornhill** and **Buttermarket**, the two short main streets, as well as the narrower streets in between. Also in between the two is **Bury St Edmunds Art Gallery** (Tues–Sat 10am–5pm; £1; ⓦwww.burystedmundsartgallery.org), which features a lively programme of temporary exhibitions focusing on contemporary fine and applied art. Older still is the Cornhill's flint-walled **Moyse's Hall**, one of the few surviving Norman houses in England, while the streets to the south are lined by an attractive medley of architectural styles, from elegant Georgian town houses to Victorian brick terraces. You'll see the best by strolling along Guildhall Street and turning left down Churchgate, which brings you back to Angel Hill.

Practicalities

From Bury St Edmunds' **train station**, it's ten minutes' walk south to Angel Hill via Northgate Street. The **bus station** is on St Andrew Street North, near Cornhill. The town's **tourist office**, at 6 Angel Hill (Easter–Sept Mon–Sat 9.30am–5.30pm, Sun 10am–3pm; Oct–Easter Mon–Fri 10am–4pm, Sat 10am–1pm; ⓣ01284/764667, ⓦwww.stedmundsbury.gov.uk), provides free town maps and has a useful range of leaflets.

The pick of the town's **hotels** is the *Angel*, on Angel Hill (ⓣ01284/714000, ⓦwww.theangel.co.uk; ❻), an immaculately maintained hotel with thick carpets, oodles of wood panelling and suitably luxurious rooms. A good alternative is the *Chantry Hotel*, 8 Sparhawk St (ⓣ01284/767427; ❹), which has sixteen comfortable rooms in a converted Georgian building near the Manor House Museum. The town has a good supply of **B&Bs**, including the excellent *South Hill House*, 43 Southgate St (ⓣ01284/755650, ⓦwww.southhill.freeserve.co.uk; ❷), a handsome old town house with many Georgian features and three large en-suite bedrooms.

For **restaurants**, *Maison Bleue*, 31 Churchgate St (ⓣ01284/760623; closed Sun & Mon), serves wonderfully fresh seafood at moderate prices. *The Vaults*, inside the medieval undercroft at the *Angel Hotel*, is also first-rate, with tasty main dishes from £8. Otherwise, aim for coffee, cakes and **snacks** in either the Cathedral *Refectory* (closed Sun) or the *Scandinavia Coffee House*, 30 Abbeygate

St. Of the **pubs**, the one you shouldn't miss is the *Nutshell* (closed Sun), on The Traverse at the top of Abbeygate, which, at sixteen feet by seven and a half, claims to be Britain's smallest. The Greene King brewery's pub is the ancient-looking *Dog & Partridge*, 29 Crown St. For entertainment, there's a year-round programme of cultural events held at the **Theatre Royal**, on Westgate Street (Ⓣ01284/755127, Ⓦwww.theatreroyal.org).

Ipswich

Situated at the head of the Orwell estuary, **IPSWICH** was a rich trading port in the Middle Ages, but its appearance today is mainly the result of a revival of fortunes in the Victorian era – give or take some clumsy postwar development. The two surviving reminders of old Ipswich – **Christchurch Mansion** and the splendid **Ancient House** – plus the recently renovated quayside are all reason enough to spend at least an afternoon here. Ipswich also boasts a wealth of medieval flint churches, some now locked and slowly rusting away, but others sympathetically restored. One now houses the tourist office, from where **guided walks** depart a couple of times a week during the season (May–Sept Tues & Thurs 2.15pm; £2) – perhaps the best way to see the town on a short visit.

The Town

The ancient Saxon market place, **Cornhill**, is still the town's focal point, a likeable urban space flanked by a bevy of imposing Victorian edifices – the Italianate town hall, the old Neoclassical Post Office and the pseudo-Jacobean Lloyds building. From here, it's just a couple of minutes' walk to the Buttermarket and Ipswich's most famous building, the **Ancient House**, whose exterior was decorated around 1670 in extravagant style, a riot of pargeting and stucco work that together make one of the finest examples of Restoration artistry in the country. There are plasterwork reliefs of pelicans and nymphs as well as representations of the four continents known at the time. Europe is symbolized by a Gothic church, America a tobacco pipe, Asia an Oriental dome and Africa, eccentrically enough, by an African astride a crocodile. Since the house is now a shop, you're free to take a peek inside to view yet more of the decor, including the hammer-beam roof on the first floor.

From the Ancient House, head up Dial Lane past the fifteenth-century church of **St Lawrence** and you're soon on Tavern Street, where two wonderful mock-Tudor shops, built in the 1930s, face the **Great White Horse Hotel**, the "overgrown tavern" which appears in Dickens' *Pickwick Papers*. Heading north from here up Northgate Street takes you past the much-restored sixteenth-century, half-timbered **Oak House**, once an inn and now housing office space, to busy St Margaret's Plain and the gates of **Christchurch Mansion** (Tues–Sat 10am–5pm, 4pm Nov–March, Sun 2.30–4.30pm; free). This handsome, if much-restored Tudor building, sporting seventeenth-century Dutch gables, is set in 65 acres of parkland, an area larger than the town centre itself. The mansion's labyrinthine interior is well worth exploring, with period furnishings and a good collection of paintings by Constable and Gainsborough, as well as more contemporary art exhibitions.

Back in the town centre, the western half of old Ipswich has been transformed by some fairly hideous, postwar development along **Civic Drive**, but there is one modern building which puts the rest to shame. It's the **Willis**

Corroon Building, designed by Norman Foster in the 1970s, whose smoked glass exterior snakes its way along Princes Street at Franciscan Way, reflecting the older buildings around it by day but allowing a startling X-ray vision of the illuminated interior after dusk. From here, it's a short stroll east to College Street, named after the college that Cardinal Wolsey, a native of Ipswich, established here in 1528, but failed to complete before his fall from grace. All that remains of Cardinal College now is the solitary **Wolsey's Gateway**, next to the fourteenth-century St Peter's Church.

Pressing on, head east along College Street and, after rounding **St-Mary-at-Quay**, another medieval church, follow Key Street and you'll soon reach the Neptune Quay marking the northern edge of the **Wet Dock**, the largest in Europe when it opened in 1845 and looking much as it did then, apart from the rash of yachts in the marina. The smell of malt and barley still wafts across the quayside, and several of the granaries continue to function, though other warehouses have been turned into pubs, restaurants and offices. Halfway along the Neptune Quay stands the proud Neoclassical **Customs House**, built for the opening of the dock.

Practicalities

Ipswich **train station** is on the south bank of the river, ten minutes' walk from Cornhill along Princes Street. The **bus station** is more central, occupying part of the old cattle market, a short walk south of Cornhill and close to the **tourist office** (Mon–Sat 9am–5pm; ⓣ01473/258070, ⓦwww.suffolk.org.uk/tourism), in the converted St Stephen's Church off St Stephen's Lane. The town is compact enough to walk around, though you might consider using **City Sightseeing** (ⓣ01473/232600, ⓦwww.city-sightseeing.com), whose hop-on, hop-off, open-topped double-decker buses cruise round the town daily from mid-April to August; buses turn up hourly between 10.45am and 3.45pm and a 24-hour ticket costs £5.

There's no overriding reason **to stay**, especially with the Suffolk coast so close, but a full list of B&Bs is available from the tourist office. One of the best is *Burlington Lodge*, 30 Burlington Rd (ⓣ01473/251868, ⓔburlingtonlodge@bigfoot.com; no cards; ❷), an attractive Victorian detached house with five comfortable en-suite bedrooms, ten minutes' walk west of Cornhill. Alternatively, try the ultra-modern *Novotel Hotel*, in the centre near Wolsey's Gateway, on Grey Friars Rd (ⓣ01473/232400, ⓦwww.novotel.com; ❸) or, even better, the newly converted *Salthouse Harbour Hotel*, 82 Fore St (ⓣ01473/257677, ⓦwww.salthouseharbour.com; ❼), with views over the harbour and slick and stylish rooms.

There are several good **restaurants** down by the Wet Dock. *Il Punto*, on Neptune Quay (ⓣ01473/289748), offers good-quality French cuisine at moderate prices – and it also has the most distinctive premises, on board a Dutch pleasure boat. Opposite, there's also the more expensive *Bistro On The Quay* (ⓣ01473/286677; closed Sun), located in one of the old red-brick quayside warehouses and specializing in seafood. **Cafés** in town include *Pickwick's*, 1 Dial Lane, with courtyard seating next to St Lawrence's Church.

For a **drink**, try either the *Black Horse* on Black Horse Lane, near the Civic Centre, or the *Glasshouse* on the Buttermarket. For **entertainment**, head for the Ipswich Film Theatre, in the Corn Exchange complex (ⓣ01473/433100, ⓦwww.ipswich-ents.co.uk), behind the town hall on King Street, which shows mainstream and art movies.

Woodbridge, Sutton Hoo and Framlingham

Beyond Ipswich, the obvious destination is the Suffolk coast (see pp.563–570), but on the way it's worth considering a short stop at the breezy little town of **Woodbridge** along with neighbouring **Sutton Hoo**, where a National Trust visitor centre has been built beside an Anglo-Saxon burial site unearthed in 1939. Near here also, a short detour to the north, is the tranquil village of **Framlingham**, a delightful place with a gaunt, ruined castle.

Woodbridge

Stringing along the banks of the River Deben eight miles northeast of Ipswich, **WOODBRIDGE** is a pleasant if somewhat unremarkable town whose easy access to the sea – along the river's long and sheltered estuary – once nourished a thriving seaport and shipbuilding industry. From the lazy waterfront of today, it's an easy five-minute walk up Quay and Church streets to **Market Hill**, the heart of the town since the Middle Ages. Here you'll find the unusual **Suffolk Punch Horse Museum** (Easter–Sept Tues–Sun 2–5pm; £2), housed in the eye-catching, sixteenth-century Shire Hall and featuring paintings, photographs and exhibits celebrating the Suffolk Punch breed, heavy working horses bred in the town since time immemorial.

Woodbridge **train station** is handily located at the foot of Quay Street, beside the waterfront. **Buses** pull in here too. The **tourist office** is at the train station (Easter–Sept Mon–Sat 9am–5.30pm, Sun 9.30am–5pm; Oct–Easter Mon–Fri 9am–5.30pm, Sat 10am–4pm & Sun 10am–1pm; ☎01394/382240) and can help with accommodation as well as providing sketch maps of the town. There's no strong reason to overnight here, but among several **hotels** and **B&Bs** perhaps the most appealing is the *Station Hotel*, at the station (☎01394/384831; ④), which has pleasant en-suite rooms and river views. The town has several first-rate **restaurants**, but the pick is *Spice*, 17 The Thoroughfare (☎01394/382557; closed Sun), which serves delicious Malaysian and Mediterranean-influenced dishes at moderate prices; it also has a **bar** with a buzz.

Sutton Hoo

In the fearful summer of 1939, at **SUTTON HOO**, a couple of miles east of Woodbridge on the opposite side of the River Deben, a local landowner stumbled across an Anglo-Saxon royal burial site belonging to Raedwald, king of East Anglia, who died around 625 AD. It was the richest single archeological find in Britain, comprising a forty-oar open ship containing a wooden tomb stuffed with gold and jewelled ornaments. Further archeological research was conducted on the site in the 1980s, and in November 1991 a second undisturbed grave was uncovered. Most of the artefacts are displayed in London's British Museum, but some (along with replicas of others) have been returned to Sutton Hoo, where the National Trust has an immaculate **exhibition hall** (late March to May & Oct Wed–Sun 10am–5pm; June–Sept daily 10am–5pm; Nov–Feb Sat & Sun 11am–4pm; £4; NT). The latter holds a full-size reconstruction of the burial chamber and explains the history and significance of the finds – with vim and gusto. Afterwards, you can wander out onto the burial site itself, about 500 yards away.

There's no public transport to Sutton Hoo; if you don't have a car, you'll need to take a taxi. Otherwise take the Melton Road – the B1438 – out of Woodbridge, turn right onto the A1152 and watch for the signs.

Framlingham

FRAMLINGHAM, ten miles north of Woodbridge, boasts a magnificent **castle** (daily: April–Oct 10am–6pm; Nov–March 10am–4pm; £4; EH), whose severe, turreted walls date from the twelfth century. The original seat of the dukes of Norfolk, the fortress is little more than a shell inside, but the curtain-wall, with its thirteen towers, has survived almost intact, a splendid example of medieval military architecture topped by ornamental Tudor chimney stacks. Footpaths crisscross the earthen banks encircling the castle, and from the internal wall walkways there are sweeping views across town to the imposing red-brick mass of Framlingham College. Unfortunately nothing remains of the castle's Great Hall where Mary Tudor was proclaimed Queen of England in 1553.

The drowsy little village next to the castle is a real pleasure, its elongated main street, **Market Hill**, flanked by a harmonious ensemble of sedate old buildings, including the *Crown Hotel* (ⓣ01728/723521, ⓦwww.framlingham-crown.com; ❺), a traditional seventeenth-century inn with roaring fires, wood panelling and snug bedrooms. The parish **Church of St Michael** is also intriguing, its finely crafted hammer-beam roof sheltering several wonderful, sixteenth-century tombs belonging to the Howard family, who owned the castle at the time. They were a turbulent clan. During the reign of Henry VIII, both Thomas Howard, the Duke of Norfolk and his son Henry Howard, the Earl of Surrey, schemed away, determined to be the leading nobles of their day. They brought down the powerful Chancellor of the Exchequer, Thomas Cromwell, in 1540 and their position seemed secure when the king married one of their kin, Catherine, later the same year. But the Howards had over-reached themselves. In 1542, the king had Catherine beheaded for adultery and, from his deathbed in 1547, he ordered that Henry Howard should be executed. The same fate would have befallen Howard's father had the king lived a few days longer.

Dennington

In the hamlet of **DENNINGTON**, a couple of miles to the north of Framlingham along the B1116, stands another interesting church. This is **St Mary's** (daily 10am–5pm; free), a sturdy, medieval edifice, whose benches and pews sport a fantastical series of carvings – wild and folkloric figures and beasts. In particular, there is a rare representation of a **sciapod**, a mythical creature that avoided sunlight by shading itself with its one, large foot. The sciapod died if it smelt contaminated air, so it carried sniffable fresh fruit everywhere it went. Equally unusual is a rare pyx canopy over the altar (the pyx was the vessel in which the Holy Sacrament was kept) – one of only two such surviving canopies in Europe.

The district is also a centre of East Anglia's developing wine industry and several local vineyards offer tours and tastings. The well-established **Shawsgate Vineyard** (March–Sept 10am–4pm; ⓣ01728/724060, ⓦwww.shawsgate.co.uk; £4) is situated one mile north of Framlingham along the B1120.

The Suffolk coast

The **Suffolk coast** feels detached from the rest of the county: the road and rail lines from Ipswich to Lowestoft funnel traffic five miles inland for most of the way, and patches of marsh and woodland make the separation still more complete. The coast has long been plagued by erosion and this has contributed to the virtual extinction of the local fishing industry, and, in the case of **Dunwich**, destroyed virtually the entire town. What is left, however, is undoubtedly one of the most unspoilt shorelines in the country – if, that is, you set aside the **Sizewell** nuclear power station. Highlights include the sleepy isolation of minuscule **Orford** and several genteel resorts, most notably **Southwold**, which has evaded the lurid fate of so many English seaside towns. There are scores of delightful **walks** hereabouts, easy routes along the coast that are best followed with either OS map #156 or #0169, or the simplified *Footpath Maps* available at most tourist offices. The Suffolk coast is also host to East Anglia's most compelling cultural gathering, the three-week-long **Aldeburgh Festival**, which takes place each June.

Orford and Orford Ness

Twelve miles east of Woodbridge, on the far side of Rendlesham Forest, the tiny village of **ORFORD** is dominated by two buildings, both of them medieval. The more impressive is the twelfth-century **Castle** (April–Oct daily 10am–6pm; Nov–March Wed–Sun 10am–1pm & 2–4pm; £4; EH), built on high ground to the southwest of the village by Henry II, and under siege within months of its completion from Henry's rebellious sons. Most of the castle disappeared centuries ago, but the lofty keep remains, its impressive stature hinting at the scale of the original fortifications. Orford's other medieval edifice, on the far side of the main square, is **St Bartholomew's Church**, where Benjamin Britten premiered his most successful children's work, *Noye's Fludde*, as part of the 1958 Aldeburgh Festival (see box on p.566).

From the top of the castle keep, there's a great view across **Orford Ness**, a six-mile-long shingle spit that has all but blocked off Orford from the sea since Tudor times. Its mud flats and marshes harbour sea lavender beds, which act as feeding and roosting areas for wildfowl and waders. The National Trust offers **boat trips** (July–Sept Tues–Sat outward boats between 10am–2pm, last ferry back 5pm; mid-April to June & Oct Sat only; £5.70; NT members £3.70; ⓣ01394/450057) across to the Ness from Orford Quay, four hundred yards down the road from the church, and a five-mile hiking trail threads its way along the spit. En route, the trail passes the occasional, abandoned **military building**. Some of the pioneer research on radar was carried out here, but the radar station was closed at the beginning of World War II because of the threat of German bombing – though the military stayed on until the 1980s. There are also plenty of **walks** to be had around Orford itself. One of the best is the five-mile hike north along the river wall that guards the west bank of the River Alde, returning via Ferry Road, a narrow country lane.

Orford's gentle, unhurried air is best experienced on a night's stay. **Rooms** are available at the *Crown & Castle* (ⓣ01394/450205, ⓦwww.crownandcastlehotel.co.uk; ⑤), an attractive inn across from the castle with chic bedrooms kitted out with all mod cons, and at the marginally less enticing *King's Head* (ⓣ01394/450271; ③), on Market Hill, the main square. For **meals**, don't miss the *Butley Orford Oysterage* (ⓣ01394/450277; closed Oct–April) also on Market Hill. This has a very reasonably priced café/restaurant, whose menu focuses on fresh oysters and oak-wood smoked fish. Its main rival is the top-notch restaurant at the *Crown & Castle*, which again features local produce – traditional food served with style and panache; main courses average around £12. For a **pint**, it's the *Crown & Castle* again or the *Jolly Sailor Inn*, down near the quay.

Aldeburgh and around

ALDEBURGH is best known for its annual arts festival, the brainchild of composer **Benjamin Britten** (1913–76), who is buried in the village churchyard alongside the tenor Peter Pears, his lover and musical collaborator. They lived by the seafront in Crag House on Crabbe Street – the street named for the poet who provided Britten with his greatest inspiration (see box p.566). Outside of June, when the festival takes place, and November, when the three-day international poetry festival fills the town, Aldeburgh is the quietest of places, with just a small fishing fleet selling its daily catch from wooden shacks along the pebbled shore.

The wide **High Street** and its narrow sidestreets run close to the beach, but this was not always the case – hence their garbled appearance. The sea swallowed most of what was once an extensive medieval town long ago and today Aldeburgh's oldest remaining building, the sixteenth-century **Moot Hall** (Easter–May & Oct Sat & Sun 2.30–5pm; June & Sept daily 2.30–5pm; July & Aug daily 10.30am–12.30pm & 2.30–5pm; £1), which began its days in the centre of town, now finds itself on the seashore. It's a handsome building made out of a mixture of red brick, flint and timber and the interior accommodates a modest museum of local finds and history. One of Aldeburgh's newest buildings, the **RNLI Lifeboat Station**, is situated bang in the middle of the seafront opposite the Jubilee Hall. From the public viewing deck you can look at the town's lifeboat and inspect the tractor used to drag it out to sea.

Several **footpaths** radiate out from Aldeburgh, with the most obvious trail leading north along the seashore to Thorpeness (see p.566), with others leading southwest to the winding estuary of the **River Alde**, an area rich in wildfowl.

Practicalities

Aldeburgh's festival box office (see box, p.566) shares its High Street premises with the local **tourist office** (daily 9am–5.30pm, till 5.15pm in winter; ⓣ01728/453637, ⓦwww.suffolkcoastal.gov.uk/leisure), which has a useful range of local leaflets. They will also book **accommodation** on your behalf, though things get very tight during the main festival and leading events when you should book months in advance. The town boasts several splendidly sited **hotels**, including the comfortable *Wentworth* (ⓣ01728/452312, ⓦwww.wentworth-aldeburgh.com; ❻), a family-owned hotel along the seafront from the Moot Hall. Of the **B&Bs**, the *Ocean House*, 25 Crag Path (ⓣ01728/452094; ❹), is probably the best. An immaculately maintained Victorian dwelling right on the seafront in the centre of town, it's decorated in period style, with two of its three guest rooms overlooking the beach; dinner is available by prior arrangement. Also in the town centre is *East Cottage*, 55 King St (ⓣ01728/453010; ❷; closed Sept–April), a brightly painted Victorian cottage a block back from the sea. Another option is *Wateringfield*, on Golf Lane (ⓣ01728/453163; ❷), a spacious 1930s house overlooking the golf course on the edge of town. There's also a forty-bed YHA **youth hostel** on Heath Walk in the hamlet of Blaxhall (ⓣ0870/770 5702, ⓔblaxhall@yha.org.uk; closed Nov–Feb; dorm beds £11.50), a couple of miles west of the concert facilities at Snape Maltings.

There are tearooms and fish-and-chip shops on the High Street, but Aldeburgh does much better than that with the town's highbrow leanings sustaining a glut of terrific **restaurants**. *152 Aldeburgh*, 152 High St (ⓣ01728/454594), is one of the best, offering reasonably priced and stylishly

Benjamin Britten and the Aldeburgh Festival

Benjamin Britten was born in Lowestoft in 1913, and was closely associated with Suffolk for most of his life. The main break was during World War II when, as a conscientious objector, Britten exiled himself to the USA. Ironically enough, it was here that Britten first read the work of the nineteenth-century Suffolk poet, George Crabbe, whose *The Borough*, a grisly portrait of the life of the fishermen of Aldeburgh, was the basis of the libretto of Britten's best-known opera, *Peter Grimes*. The latter was premiered in London in 1945 to great acclaim.

In 1947 Britten founded the English Opera Group and the following year launched the **Aldeburgh Festival** as a showpiece for his own works and those of his contemporaries. He lived in the town for the next ten years and it was during this period that he completed much of his best work as a conductor and pianist. For the rest of his life he composed many works specifically for the festival, including his masterpiece for children, *Noye's Fludde* and the last of his fifteen operas, *Death in Venice*.

By the mid-1960s, the festival had outgrown the parish churches in which it began, and moved into a collection of disused malthouses, five miles west of Aldeburgh on the River Alde, just south of the small village of **Snape** along the B1069. **Snape Maltings** were subsequently converted into one of the finest concert venues in the country. In addition to the concert hall, there's now a recording studio, a music school, various craft shops and galleries, a tearoom, and a nice pub, the *Plough & Sail*, so even if there's nothing specific on, it's worth calling into the complex to nose around.

For more information on the Aldeburgh Festival, contact the **festival box office**, 152 Aldeburgh High St (April–Sept Mon–Sat 9.30am–4.30pm, Oct–March Mon–Sat 10am–1pm & 2–4pm; ⓣ01728/687110, ⓦwww.aldeburgh.co.uk). Tickets for the concerts, talks, exhibitions and other special events go on sale to the public towards the end of March, and usually sell out fast for the big-name recitals; prices range from £9 to £50. There are all sorts of concerts and performances at other times of the year too – again details are available from the booking office – with showcase events including the Proms season in August and the three-day Britten Festival in late October.

prepared fresh fish served in elegant but simple surroundings. There are more Mediterranean flavours and adventurous use of local ingredients at both the *Lighthouse*, 77 High St (ⓣ01728/453377), and the *Regatta*, 171–173 High St (ⓣ01728/452011; closed Mon & Tues in winter), each moderately priced and the latter open to the pavement in summer. For **drinks**, head for the *White Lion Hotel*, just along the seafront from the Moot Hall.

Thorpeness, Sizewell and Leiston

THORPENESS, two miles up the coast from Aldeburgh, is a strange little resort, planned as a "fantasy" holiday village in 1910 by local landowner Stuart Ogilvie "for people who want to experience life as it was in Merrie England". This eccentricity explains the mock-Tudor style of much of the architecture – eye-catching follies such as the watertower-shaped *House in the Clouds* – and, less tangibly, the sense of keep-out privacy that pervades the place. The large pleasure lake at the centre of the village, the "Meare", has its islets named after characters from *Peter Pan*, whose author, J.M. Barrie, was an Ogilvie family friend. For further details on the history of Thorpeness, head for the **windmill** (March Mon & Fri–Sun 11am–1pm & 2–5pm; April–June & Sept Sat & Sun 11am–1pm & 2–5pm; July & Aug Mon–Fri 2–5pm, Sat & Sun 11am–1pm & 2–5pm; free), a few hundred yards back from the sea and signposted down a lane from the main street, The Whinlands.

Two miles beyond Thorpeness it's impossible to miss the ominous presence of the **Sizewell nuclear power station**, whose superstructure is topped by what looks like a giant golf ball. The gas-cooled reactor, Sizewell A, has been producing electricity since 1966, and will continue to do so for the foreseeable future. A second pressurized-water reactor (PWR), **Sizewell B** – the first of its kind in the UK – provoked one of the longest public enquiries in the country's history, lasting 340 days. Work began shortly after the disaster at Chernobyl, and the reactor was completed in the early part of 1995.

A couple of miles inland from Sizewell, the small town of **LEISTON** was synonymous with the agricultural engineering firm Garretts for over two centuries, until the company closed in 1980. Much of the original plant has been removed, but the main iron- and timber-framed factory building, built in 1852 and nicknamed "the cathedral", now forms part of the **Long Shop Museum** on Main Street (April–Oct Mon–Sat 10am–5pm, Sun 11am–5pm; £3). Here, you can view a selection of Garretts finest products from steamrollers and trolleybuses to baker's ovens and dry-cleaning machines.

Dunwich

Seat of the kings of East Anglia, a bishopric and once the largest port on the Suffolk coast, the ancient city of **DUNWICH**, about twelve miles up the coast from Aldeburgh, reached its peak of prosperity in the twelfth century. Over the last millennium, however, something like a mile of land has been lost to the sea, a process that continues at the rate of about a yard a year. As a result, the whole of the medieval city now lies underwater, including all twelve churches, the last of which toppled over the cliffs in 1919. All that survives today are fragments of the Greyfriars monastery, which originally lay to the west of the city and now dangles at the sea's edge. For a potted history of the lost city, head for the **museum** (April–Sept daily 11.30am–4.30pm; Oct daily noon–4pm; free) in what's left of Dunwich – little more than one small street of terraced houses built by the local landowner in the nineteenth century.

A sprawling, coastline **car park** gives ready access to this part of the seashore and is also where fishing boats still sell their daily catch off the shingle beach. From the car park, it's a short stroll west to the village and south to Greyfriars. Or you can hike further south, out along the beach to **Dunwich Heath**, where the coastguard cottages have been turned into a National Trust shop and tearoom (mid-July to mid-Sept daily 10am–5pm; rest of year varies, but always open Sat & Sun from 10am; ⓣ01728/648505). The heath is itself next to the **Minsmere RSPB Nature Reserve**, whose star turn is a colony of avocets. You can rent binoculars from the RSPB **visitor centre** (for times, call ⓣ01728/648281) and strike out on the trails to the birdwatching hides.

The coastline and its heaths have an eerie quality – P.D. James distils this perfectly in her *Unnatural Causes*, portraying the coast as the "battlefield where for nearly nine centuries the land had waged its losing fight against the sea." This atmosphere is best appreciated by **staying** at Dunwich's one and only pub, the *Ship Inn* (ⓣ01728/648219; ❸). With its low wooden beams and open fire, the bar here is a great place for a drink and the **food** is both moderately priced and very tasty with seafood the main event.

Southwold

Perched on robust cliffs just to the north of the River Blyth, **SOUTHWOLD** gained what Dunwich lost, and by the sixteenth century it had overtaken all its local rivals. Its days as a busy fishing port are, however, long gone – though a small fleet still brings in herring, sprats and cod – and today it's a genteel seaside resort, an eminently appealing little town with none of the crassness of many of its competitors. There are fine old buildings, a long sandy beach, open heathland, a dinky harbour and even a little industry – in the shape of the Adnams brewery – but no burger bars and certainly no amusement arcades. This gentility was not to the liking of **George Orwell**, who lived for a time at his parents' house at 36 High St (a plaque marks the spot). Orwell heartily disliked the town's airs and graces, and has left no trace of his time here – apart from disguised slights in a couple of early novels.

The Town

Southwold's breezy **High Street** is framed by attractive, mainly Georgian buildings, which culminate in the pocket-sized Market Place. From here, it's a brief stroll along East Street to the curious **Sailors' Reading Room** (daily 9am–5pm; free), decked out with model ships and nautical texts, and the bluff above the **beach**, where row upon row of candy-coloured huts march across the sands. Queen Street begins at the Market Place too, quickly leading to **South Green**, the prettiest of several greens dotted across town. In 1659, a calamitous fire razed much of Southwold and when the town was rebuilt the greens were left to act as firebreaks. Beyond, both Ferry Road and the ferry footpath lead down to the **harbour**, at the mouth of the River Blyth, an idyllic spot, where fishing smacks rest against old wooden jetties and nets are spread out along the banks to dry. There's a footpath along the harbourside that leads to a tiny **ferry** (Easter–May Sat & Sun 10am–12.30pm & 2–4.30pm; June–Aug daily 10am–12.30pm & 2–4.30pm; 40p), which pops across the river to Walberswick (see opposite). Turn right after the Harbour Inn and right again to walk back into town across **Southwold Common**. The whole circular walk takes about thirty minutes.

Back on the Market Place, it's a couple of hundred yards north along Church Street to East Green, with Adnams Brewery on one side and the stumpy lighthouse on another. Close by is Southwold's architectural pride and joy, the **Church of St Edmund** (daily: June–Aug 9am–6pm; Sept–May 9am–4pm; free), a handsome fifteenth-century structure whose solid symmetries are balanced by its long and elegantly carved windows. Inside, the slender, beautifully proportioned nave is distinguished by its panelled roof, embellished with praying angels, and its intricate rood screen. The latter carries paintings of the apostles and the prophets, though Protestants defaced them during the Reformation. Beyond the screen, the choir stalls carry finely carved human and animal heads as well as grotesques – look out for the man in the throes of toothache. Look out also for "**Southwold Jack**", a brightly painted, medieval effigy of a man in armour nailed to the wall beside the font. No one knows when or why this very military carving was moved into the church – it certainly doesn't fit in – but the betting is that he was once part of a clock, nodding belligerently as he struck the hours. From the church, it's a short walk north to the **pier**, the latest incarnation of a structure that dates from 1899. Built as a landing stage for passenger ferries, the pier has had a troubled history: it has been repeatedly damaged by storms, was hit by a sea-mine and then partly chopped up by the army as a protection against German invasion in World War II.

Practicalities

With frequent services from other towns along the coast, Southwold is easy to reach by **bus**. These stop on the Market Place, yards from the **tourist office**, at 69 High St (April–Sept Mon–Fri 10am–5pm, Sat 10am–5.30pm, Sun

11am–4pm; Oct–March Mon–Fri 10.30am–3.30pm, Sat 10am–4.30pm; ⓣ01502/724729, ⓦwww.visit-southwold.co.uk), which has details of local attractions and sells walking maps. The town has two well-known **hotels** beside the Market Place, both owned and operated by Adnams. The smarter of the two is *The Swan* (ⓣ01502/722186, ⓦwww.adnams.co.uk; ⑥), which occupies a splendid Georgian building with lovely period rooms, though the bedrooms – in the main house and in a garden annexe behind – are a little on the small side. *The Crown,* just along the High Street (ⓣ01502/722275, ⓦwww.adnams.co.uk; ⑤), has just twelve simple bedrooms, all of which are en suite. The best **B&B** in town is the delightful *Acton Lodge*, 18 South Green (ⓣ01502/723217; no credit cards; ⑤), which occupies a grand Victorian house complete with its own neo-Gothic tower. The interior is decorated in period style and the three comfortable bedrooms are all en suite. Breakfasts are delicious, too. Alternatively, there's a string of **guest houses** down along the seafront on North Parade: try the *North Parade*, at no. 21 (ⓣ01502/722573; ②), a well-tended Victorian house with sprucely decorated bedrooms; or the attractive *Dunburgh*, at no. 28 (ⓣ01502/723253, ⓦwww.southwold.ws/dunburgh/; ③), housed in a rambling building with its own mini-tower.

Southwold has two outstanding **places to eat**. The *Crown*'s front bar provides superb informal meals, encompassing daily fish and meat specials combined with an enlightened wine list where all the choices are available by the glass. Turn up, wait for a table and expect to pay £15 or so for two courses; you'll have to make a booking if you want to eat in the adjacent restaurant, which is pricier, slightly more adventurous and just as terrific. The *Swan*'s more formal dining room is the place for a gourmet blow-out, offering a choice of set dinners at £20–30 a head. For a **drink**, sample Adnams' brews in the *Crown*'s wood-panelled back-bar or stroll along to the *Red Lion* on South Green.

Around Southwold: Walberswick and Blythburgh

Just across the River Blyth from Southwold lies the leafy little village of **WALBERSWICK**, another once-prosperous port now fallen into peaceful decline. For many years, it was the home of the English Impressionist painter, Philip Wilson Steer (1860–1942), and is now a seaside escape popular with well-heeled holiday-makers, who consider its larger neighbour too boisterous. As such, there's not much to see and most visitors make a bee-line for the *Bell*, an old village pub close to the riverfront which offers tasty bar food and Adnams beer. There are two ways for walkers to get here from Southwold – either via the ferry (see p.568) or over the Bailey bridge about a mile further inland. The footpath to the bridge begins on Station Road, a continuation of Southwold's High Street.

Up until the sixteenth century, **BLYTHBURGH**, five miles west of Southwold, was a thriving port at the head of a wide estuary, but the silting up of the River Blyth slowly strangled the town, reducing it to an inconsequential hamlet. The **Church of the Holy Trinity**, a handsome flint and stone structure dating from the 1440s, recalls the village's previous prosperity – its sheer bulk earning it the title, "Cathedral of the Marshes". Inside, the light and airy nave is decorated with carved angels and brightly painted flower patterns similar to St Edmund's in Southwold. The bench-ends depict the Seven Deadly Sins with gusto and, in another echo of Southwold, there's a "Jack-o'-the-Clock" here, too.

Lowestoft

LOWESTOFT, the easternmost point in the British Isles, is a world apart from the likes of Southwold and Aldeburgh. It's a fishing port and has been since the railway arrived here in 1847 and Lowestoft began seriously to challenge its

Norfolk neighbour, Great Yarmouth (see p.579). The town is bisected by its **Inner Harbour** with the older part to the north. Here, the narrow alleyways, known locally as "scores", once lined with fishermen's huts and smokehouses, run east off the High Street towards the giant Bird's Eye frozen food factory, destination of much of the trawlers' haul. If you've an interest in Lowestoft's history, visit the **Maritime Museum** on Whapload Road (May–Oct daily 10am–5pm; 75p), near the lighthouse on the north side of town. The **tourist office** is at East Point Pavilion (April–Sept daily 9.30am–5.30pm; Oct–March Mon–Fri 10.30am–5pm, Sat & Sun 10am–5pm; Ⓣ01502/533600, Ⓦwww.visit-lowestoft.co.uk), on the south side of the harbour.

Norwich

One of the five largest cities in Norman England, **NORWICH** once served a vast hinterland of East Anglian cloth producers, whose work was brought here by river and exported to the Continent. Its isolated position beyond the Fens meant that it enjoyed closer links with the Low Countries than with the rest of England – it was, after all, quicker to cross the North Sea than to go cross-country to London. The local textile industry, based on worsted cloth (named after the nearby village of Worstead), was further enhanced by an influx of Flemish and Huguenot weavers, who made up more than a third of the population in Tudor times. By 1700, Norwich was the second-richest city in the country after London.

With the onset of the Industrial Revolution, however, Norwich lost ground to the northern manufacturing towns – the city's famous mustard company, Colman's, is one of its few industrial success stories – and this, together with its continuing geographical isolation, has helped preserve much of the ancient street plan and many of the city's older buildings. Pride of place goes to the beautiful cathedral and the castle, but the city's hallmark is its medieval **churches**, thirty or so squat flintstone structures with sturdy towers and sinuous stone tracery round the windows. Isolation has also meant that the population has never swelled to any great extent and today, with just 170,000 inhabitants, Norwich remains an easy and enjoyable city to negotiate. Yet Norwich is no provincial backwater. In the 1960s, the foundation of the University of East Anglia (UEA) made it more **cosmopolitan** and bolstered its arts scene, while in the 1980s it attracted new high-tech companies, who created something of a mini-boom, making the city again one of England's wealthiest. As East Anglia's unofficial capital, Norwich also lies at the hub of the region's **transport** network and serves as a useful base for visiting the Broads, and even as a springboard for the north Norfolk coast.

Arrival and information

Norwich's grandiose **train station** is on the east bank of the River Wensum, ten minutes' walk from the city centre along Prince of Wales Road. Long distance **buses** terminate at the Surrey Street Station, also little more than ten minutes' walk from the town centre, but this time to the South off Surrey Street (though some stop in the centre on Castle Meadow too). Information on local and regional bus services is provided by **NORBIC**, 17–19 Castle Meadow (Mon–Sat 8.30am–5pm; Ⓣ08453/006116). The First Eastern Counties' Bus Tourist Ticket (£7), valid for a day's unlimited travel on most East Anglian bus routes, is available here, as is the three-day ticket for unlimited travel on three

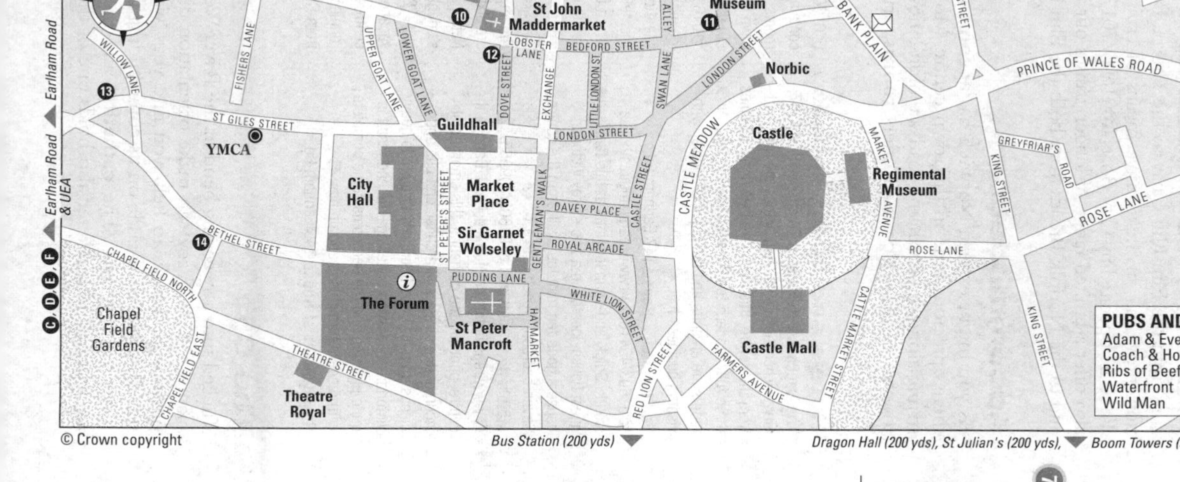
NORWICH
0 200 yds
Broads Authority Office (100 yds)
A1151 Wroxham & 1
Bishopsgate
Bishopsgate & 2
Dereham Road & A47
Earlham Road
Earlham Road & UEA
C, D, E, F
Pulls Ferry & River
Train Station (50 yds), B & A47 Great Yarmouth
Bus Station (200 yds)
Dragon Hall (200 yds), St Julian's (200 yds), Boom Towers (800 yds) & 15
Cathedral
Canary Chapel
Edith Cavell's Grave
Wrights Court
Riverbus
River Wensum
Erpingham Gate
St Andrew's & Blackfriars' Hall
St Peter Hungate
Ethelbert's Gate
Cinema City
Bridewell Museum
Maddermarket Theatre
St John Maddermarket
Norbic
Guildhall
Castle
Regimental Museum
City Hall
Market Place
Sir Garnet Wolseley
The Forum
St Peter Mancroft
Castle Mall
YMCA
Chapel Field Gardens
Theatre Royal
WENSUM STREET
PALACE STREET
ELM HILL
ELM HILL QUAY
TOMBLAND
UPPER CLOSE
LOWER CLOSE
HOOK'S WALK
PRINCES STREET
ST GEORGE'S STREET
DUKE STREET
OAK STREET
WESTWICK STREET
ST BENEDICT'S STREET
CHARING CROSS
ST ANDREW'S STREET
ST ANDREWS PLAIN
QUEEN STREET
KING STREET
ST FAITH'S LANE
BANK PLAIN
BRIDEWELL ALLEY
TEN BELLS LANE
POTTERGATE
FISHERS LANE
WILLOW LANE
UPPER GOAT LANE
LOWER GOAT LANE
DOVE STREET
LOBSTER LANE
BEDFORD STREET
EXCHANGE STREET
LITTLE LONDON ST
SWAN LANE
LONDON STREET
PRINCE OF WALES ROAD
ST GILES STREET
CASTLE MEADOW
MARKET AVENUE
GREYFRIAR'S ROAD
ST VEDAST ST
ROSE LANE
CASTLE STREET
DAVEY PLACE
ROYAL ARCADE
GENTLEMAN'S WALK
ST PETER'S STREET
PUDDING LANE
WHITE LION STREET
HAYMARKET
BETHEL STREET
CHAPEL FIELD NORTH
CHAPEL FIELD EAST
THEATRE STREET
RED LION STREET
FARMERS AVENUE
CATTLE MARKET STREET
ACCOMMODATION
The Beeches E
Earlham Guest House D
Maid's Head A
Rosedale Guest House C
Swallow Nelson B
University of East Anglia F
RESTAURANTS AND CAFÉS
Adlard's 13
Belgian Monk 10
Britons Arms 5
Brummell's 1
The Last Wine Bar 4
Pinocchio's 8
St Andrew's Hall Crypt Coffee Bar 7
Tatler's 6
Take 5 9
Tree House 12
PUBS AND BARS
Adam & Eve 2
Coach & Horses 14
Ribs of Beef 3
Waterfront 15
Wild Man 11

days in seven (£16). The **tourist office** is in the gleamingly new, glassy Forum building beside the Market Place (June–Sept Mon–Sat 10am–6pm & Sun 10.30am-4.30pm; Oct–May Mon–Sat 10am–5.30pm; ⓣ01603/666071, ⓦwww.norwich.gov.uk). The **Broads Authority Office**, 18 Colegate (Mon–Fri 9.30am–5pm; ⓣ01603/610734, ⓦwww.broads-authority.gov.uk), is a useful source of information for those heading for the Broads (see p.578).

The best way to see the city is on **foot** and the tourist office's **city walking tours** (April, May & Oct Sat 1 daily; June & Sept 4 weekly; July & Aug Mon–Sat 1–2 daily; 1hr 30min; £2.50) are a good way of getting the lie of the land. It's also worth bearing in mind the **riverbus** (May–Oct 5 daily; 15min; £1.50), which runs from the Elm Hill Quay to the Thorpe Road Quay, opposite the train station, providing an inexpensive means of cruising Norwich's central waterway. They are operated by City Boats (ⓣ01603/701701, ⓦwww.cityboats.co.uk), who also offer a limited range of longer cruises out into the surrounding countryside and to the Norfolk Broads from both the Elm Hill and Thorpe Road quays.

Accommodation

As you might expect, Norwich has **accommodation** to suit all budgets, but there's precious little in the town centre. Most **B&Bs** and **guest houses** are strung along the Earlham Road, a tedious, mostly Victorian street running west towards UEA, which itself offers **rooms**, primarily during the summer and Easter vacations.

Hotels and guest houses

The Beeches 2–6 Earlham Rd ⓣ01603/621167, ⓦwww.beeches.co.uk. Just across the ring road from the centre, this medium-sized hotel occupies three fully modernized Victorian townhouses. All 36 rooms are en suite and the place is popular with visiting business folk. ⑤

Earlham Guest House 147 Earlham Rd ⓣ01603/454169, ⓦwww.earlhamguesthouse.co.uk. Spick-and-span lodgings at this family-run guest house, located in a two-storey Victorian house a good ten minutes' walk from the centre. Seven bedrooms, each with a TV. ②

Maid's Head Tombland ⓣ01603/209955, ⓦwww.regalhotels.co.uk/maidshead. Bang in the centre, opposite the cathedral, this smart hotel incorporates all sorts of architectural bits and pieces from Art Deco flourishes through to heavy Victorian-style wood panelling. The end result is quite pleasing and the bedrooms come complete with modern furnishings and fittings. ⑥

Rosedale Guest House 145 Earlham Rd ⓣ01603/453743. Typical Victorian guest house containing six frugal but perfectly adequate bedrooms, each with a TV. A ten-minute walk from the town centre. ②

Swallow Nelson Prince of Wales Rd ⓣ01603/760260, ⓦwww.swallownelsonhotel.co.uk. This modern, riverside hotel, directly opposite the train station, caters to a mainly business clientele. It offers spick-and-span rooms, some of which overlook the water, an indoor pool and a health club. ⑦

Student halls

University of East Anglia ⓣ01603/593297. There are sixty en-suite rooms available year-round in Nelson Court (£52.50 per double), and also single student rooms with shared bathrooms (£25) and en suite (£35) available during Easter and summer vacations. The campus is four miles west of the centre along Earlham Road; of the many buses running here from the centre, #25, #26 and #27 from Castle Meadow are the most frequent.

The City

Tucked into a sweeping bend of the River Wensum, Norwich's irregular street plan, a Saxon legacy, can make orientation difficult. There are, however, three obvious landmarks to help you find your way – the cathedral with its giant spire, the Norman castle on its commanding mound and the distinctive clock-tower of City Hall. The **cathedral** and the **castle** are the town's premier attractions and the latter also holds one of the region's most satisfying collections of fine art. Finally, note that **Sunday** can be a disastrous day to visit if you want to see anything other than the cathedral: most museums and attractions are closed, not to mention most restaurants.

The Cathedral

Norwich **Cathedral** (daily: May–Sept 7.30am–7pm; Oct–April 7.30am–6pm; free tours Mon–Sat; £3 donation requested) is distinguished by its prickly octagonal spire which rises to a height of 315ft, second only to Salisbury. It's best viewed from the Lower Close (see below) to the west, where the thick curves of the flying buttresses, the rounded excrescences of the ambulatory chapels – unusual in an English cathedral – and the straight symmetries of the main trunk can all be seen to perfection.

The **interior** is pleasantly light thanks to a creamy tint in the stone and the clear glass windows of much of the nave, where the thick pillars are a powerful legacy of the Norman builders who began the cathedral in 1096. Look up to spy the nave's fan vaulting, delicate and geometrically precise carving adorned by several hundred roof **bosses** recounting – from east to west – the story of the Old and New Testaments from the Creation to the Last Judgement. Moving on down the south side of the ambulatory, you reach **St Luke's Chapel** where the cathedral's finest work of art, the *Despenser Reredos*, is a superb painted panel commissioned to celebrate the crushing of the Peasants' Revolt of 1381. Across the aisle, encased by the choir, is the **bishop's throne**, a sturdy stone structure placed directly behind the high altar. Norman bishops were barons as much as religious leaders, and to emphasize their direct relationship with Almighty God they usually put their thrones behind the high altar. Most were later relocated, but this one occupies its original position. Here in Norwich, the bishop also had a spiritual prop: a flue runs down from the back of the throne to a reliquary recess behind in the ambulatory, the idea being that divine essences would be transported up to him.

Accessible from the south aisle of the nave are the cathedral's unique **cloisters**. Built between 1297 and 1450, and the only two-storey cloisters left standing in England, they contain a remarkable set of sculpted **bosses**, similar to the ones in the main nave, but here they are close enough to be scrutinized without binoculars. The carving is fabulously intricate and the dominant theme is the **Apocalypse**, but look out also for the bosses depicting green men, pagan fertility symbols. A computer screen by the main entrance gives the low-down on all of them.

The cathedral precincts

Outside, beside the main entrance, stands the medieval **Canary Chapel**. This is the original building of Norwich School, whose blue-blazered pupils are often visible during term time – the rambling school buildings are adjacent. A statue of the school's most famous boy, Horatio Nelson, faces the chapel, standing on the green of the **Upper Close**, which is guarded by two ornate and imposing medieval gates, **Erpingham** and, a few yards to the south, **Ethelbert**. Beside the Erpingham gate is a memorial to **Edith Cavell**, a local woman who was a nurse in occupied Brussels during World War I. She was shot by the Germans in 1915 for helping allied prisoners to escape, a fate that made her an instant folk hero; her grave is beside the cathedral ambulatory. Both gates lead onto the old Saxon market place, **Tombland**, a wide and busy thoroughfare whose name derives from the Saxon word for an open space.

Tombland is a convenient place to start an exploration of the rest of the city centre, but instead you might prefer to wander pedestrianized **Cathedral**

Close, which extends east to the river from – and including – the Upper Close. Just beyond the Upper Close is the **Lower Close**, where a scattering of silver birches is flanked by attractive Georgian and Victorian houses. Keeping straight, the footpath continues east to **Pull's Ferry**, a landing stage at the city's medieval watergate, named after the last ferryman to work this stretch of the river. It's a picturesque spot and from here you can wander along the riverbank either south to the railway station or north to Bishopgate, by means of which you can regain Tombland.

From Tombland to Elm Hill and Bridewell

At the north end of Tombland, fork left into Wensum Street and cobbled **Elm Hill**, more a gentle slope than a hill, soon appears on the left. Priestley, in his *English Journey* of 1933, thought this part of Norwich to be overbearingly Dickensian, proclaiming "it difficult to believe that behind those bowed and twisted fronts there did not live an assortment of misers, mad spinsters, saintly clergymen, eccentric comic clerks, and lunatic sextons." Since then, the tourist crowds have sucked the atmosphere, but the quirky half-timbered houses still appeal and while you're here take a look at **Wright's Court**, down a passageway at no. 43, one of the few remaining enclosed courtyards which were once a feature of the city. Elm Hill quickly opens out into a triangular square centred on a plane tree, planted on the spot where the eponymous elm tree from Henry VIII's time once stood. It then veers left up to **St Peter Hungate**, a good-looking, fifteenth-century flint church equipped with a solid square tower and gentle stone tracery round its windows.

Turn right at the church and it's just a few yards to **St Andrew's Hall** and **Blackfriars Hall**, two adjoining buildings that were originally the nave and chancel, respectively, of a Dominican monastery church. Imaginatively recycled, the two halls are now used for a variety of public events, including concerts, weddings and antique fairs; the crypt of the former now serves as a café (Mon–Sat 10am–4.30pm). South of here, off St Andrews Street and along Bridewell Alley, stands the **Bridewell Museum** (April–Sept Mon–Sat 10am–4.30pm, but closed Mon during school terms; £2), one of the city's more enjoyable museums. Formerly the city jail, the Bridewell holds a pot-pourri of old machines, adverts, signs, and reconstructed shops celebrating Norwich's old trades and industry. Inevitably, there's a lot on the all-important mustard industry, which did much to keep the city's economy afloat in its more troubled times.

Maddermarket

From the top of Bridewell Alley, Bedford Street and then Lobster Lane lead west to Pottergate's **St John Maddermarket** (June–Sept Tues–Sat 10.30am–5pm; free), one of thirty medieval churches standing within the boundaries of the old city walls. Most are redundant and are rarely open to the public, but this is one of the more accessible, courtesy of dedicated volunteers. Apart from the stone trimmings, the church is almost entirely composed of flint rubble, the traditional building material of east Norfolk, an area chronically short of decent stone. It's a good example of the Perpendicular style, a sub-division of English Gothic which flourished from the middle of the fourteenth to the early sixteenth century and is characterized by straight vertical lines – as you might expect from the name – and large windows framed by flowing, but plain, tracery. By comparison, the interior is something of a disappointment, its furnishings and fittings thoroughly remodelled at the start of the twentieth century. It's from this period that the heavy-duty oak altar canopy and the extensive wood panelling date. The church also has a good selection of **brasses** and the volunteers will kit you out so you can rub away to your heart's content. Back outside, the arch under the church tower leads through to the **Maddermarket Theatre**, built in 1921 in the style of an Elizabethan playhouse. Incidentally, Maddermarket is named after the yellow flower that the weavers used to make red vegetable dye, or madder.

The Market Place

From Pottergate, several narrow alleys lead through to the city's **Market Place**, site of one of the country's largest open-air markets (closed Sun), with stalls selling everything from bargain-basement clothes to local mussels and whelks. Four very different but equally distinctive buildings oversee the market's stripy awnings, the oldest of them being the fifteenth-century **Guildhall**, an attractive flint and stone structure begun in 1407. Opposite, commanding the heights of the market place, are the austere **City Hall**, a lumbering brick pile with a landmark clocktower built in the 1930s in a Scandinavian style – it bears a striking resemblance to Oslo's city hall – and **The Forum**, a flashy, glassy structure completed in 2001. The latter is home to the tourist office and the three-floor, interactive **Origins** exhibition (Mon–Sat 10am–6pm, Sun 10.30am–4.30pm; £4.95; Ⓦwww.theforumnorfolk.com/visiting/origins), exploring everything to do with Norwich and Norfolk from its history to a feature on the local accent. On the south side of the Market Place is the finest of the four buildings, **St Peter Mancroft** (Mon–Fri 9.30am–4.30pm, Sat 10am–3pm; free), whose long and graceful nave leads to a mighty stone tower, an intricately carved affair surmounted by a spiky little spire. The church once delighted John Wesley, who declared "I scarcely ever remember to have seen a more beautiful parish church," a fair description of what remains an exquisite example of the Perpendicular style with the slender columns of the nave reaching up towards the delicate groining of the roof. Completed in 1455, the open design of the nave was meant to express the mystery of the Christian faith with light filtering in through the stained-glass windows in a kaleidoscope of colours. Some of the original glass has survived, most notably in the east window which boasts a cartoon strip of biblical scenes from the Virgin nursing the baby Jesus, through to the Crucifixion and Resurrection.

Back outside and just below the church is the **Sir Garnet Wolseley** pub, sole survivor of the 44 ale houses that once crowded the Market Place – and stirred the local bourgeoisie into endless discussions about the drunken fecklessness of the working class. Opposite the pub, across **Gentlemen's Walk**, the town's main promenade, which runs along the bottom of the market place, is the **Royal Arcade**, an Art Nouveau extravagance from 1899. The arcade has been beautifully restored to reveal the swirl and blob of the tiling, ironwork and stained glass, though it's actually the eastern entrance, further from Gentlemen's Walk, which is the most appealing section.

The Castle

Perched high on a grassy mound in the centre of town, and imaginatively tailored into a modern shopping mall down below, the stern walls of **Norwich Castle**, replete with blind arcading and dating from the twelfth century, were built to intimidate the local population. To begin with they were a reminder of Norman power and then, when the castle was turned into a prison, they served as a grim warning to potential law-breakers. Recently refurbished in lavish style, the castle now holds an excellent **Museum and Art Gallery** (July & Aug Mon–Sat 10am–6pm, Sun 1–5pm; Sept–June Mon–Sat 10.30am–4.30pm, Sun 1–5pm; £4.95 all zones), which is divided into three colour-coded zones –

yellow for Art and Exhibitions, green for Natural History, and pink for the Castle Keep. The **Natural History** section holds a fairly routine collection of stuffed and mounted wildlife, but **Art and Exhibitions** scores well with its temporary displays and boasts an outstanding selection of work by the **Norwich School**. Founded in 1803, and in existence for just thirty years, this school of landscape painters produced – for the most part at least – richly coloured, formally composed land- and seascapes in oil and watercolour, paintings whose realism harked back to the Dutch landscape painters of the seventeenth century. The leading figures were John Crome – aka "Old Crome" – and more particularly John Sell Cotman, who is generally acknowledged as one of England's finest watercolourists. Both have a gallery to themselves and, helpfully, there's also a gallery given over to those Dutch painters who influenced them.

Moving on, the **Castle Keep** is no more than a shell, its gloomy walls towering above a scattering of local archeological finds and exhibits that illustrate traditional forms of punishment. The gibbet and its instruments of torture attract most attention, but more unusual is a bloated model **dragon**, known as Snap, which was paraded round town on the annual guilds' day procession – a folkloric hand-me-down from the dragon St George had so much trouble finishing off. To see more of the keep, join one of the regular **guided tours** (an extra £2.50) that explore the battlements and the dungeons.

Finally, a long and dark (and one-way) tunnel leads down from the Castle Museum to the **Royal Norfolk Regimental Museum** (Mon–Sat 10am–4.30pm, closed Mon during school terms), which tracks through the history of the regiment with remarkable candour – including an even-handed account of the Norfolks' police-keeping role in Northern Ireland. The exit leaves you below the castle on Market Avenue.

King Street and the river

East of the castle, **King Street** possesses one or two surprises, beginning with the **Dragon Hall**, at no. 115–123 (April–Oct Mon–Sat 10am–4pm; Nov–March Mon–Fri 10am–4pm; £2.50), an extraordinarily long, half-timbered showroom built for the cloth merchant Robert Toppes in the fifteenth century. Bowed and bent by age, you get a good impression of the building from the outside, but enthusiasts can pop in to have a closer look at the roof – there's nothing else to see. A right turn opposite the hall up St Julian's Alley leads to **St Julian's Church** (daily 7.30am–6pm; free) and an adjoining monastic cell, thatched and standing in open countryside as late as the mid-nineteenth century. One of the smallest of the city's religious foundations, this was the retreat of St Julian, a Norwich woman who took to living here after experiencing visions of Christ in 1373. Her mystical *Revelations of Divine Love* – written after twenty years' meditation on her visions – was the first widely distributed book written by a woman in the English language, and has been in print ever since.

Still further down King Street, at Carrow Bridge near the football ground, are the ruins of two medieval **boom towers**, which formed part of the city's defences. From here, a **riverside walk** – initially on the east bank – follows the Wensum around the city centre to Bishopgate, switching to the inner (west) bank at Foundry Bridge, beside the train station. The walk is at its most appealing between Pull's Ferry (see p.574) and **Cow Tower**, a fifty-foot-high watchtower where the bishop's retainers collected river tolls. This is one of the few survivors of Norwich's **fortified walls**, which once stretched for over two miles, surrounding the city and incorporating thirty such circular towers and ten defensive gates. Up until the 1790s, the gates were closed at dusk and all day on Sundays.

The University

The **University of East Anglia** (UEA) occupies a sprawling campus on the western outskirts of the city beside the B1108. Its buildings are resolutely modern concrete-and-glass blocks of varying designs – some quite ordinary, others like the prize-winning "ziggurat" halls of residence, designed by Denys Lasdun, eminently memorable. The main reason to visit is the flashy, high-tech **Sainsbury Centre for Visual Arts** (Tues–Sun 11am–5pm, plus Wed till 8pm mid-May to mid-Sept; £2; Ⓦ www.uea.ac.uk/scva), built by Norman Foster in the 1970s. The interior houses one of the most varied collections of sculpture and painting in the country, donated by the family which founded the Sainsbury supermarket chain, in which the likes of Degas, Seurat, Picasso, Giacometti, Bacon and Henry Moore rub shoulders with Mayan and Egyptian antiquities. The centre also runs a first-rate programme of temporary exhibitions (call ⓣ01603/593199 for further details). **Buses** #25, #26 and #27 run frequently to UEA from Castle Meadow.

Eating and drinking

There are plenty of **cafés and restaurants** in the city centre – most of them very good value. Decent **pubs**, though, are harder to find, maybe because previously serviceable places have been turned into ersatz "traditional" drinking dens for students.

Cafés and restaurants

Adlard's 79 Upper Giles St ⓣ01603/633522. Engaging modern-British restaurant with accomplished seasonal cooking from a brief but enticing menu. Closed all Sun & Mon lunch. Expensive.

Belgian Monk 7 Pottergate ⓣ01603/767222. Perhaps too theme-ish for some tastes, this bar and restaurant specializes in all-things Flemish – from beers through to soup and, of course, mussels and chips. Moderate.

Britons Arms 9 Elm Hill. Homemade quiches, tarts, cakes and scones plus pies and salads in a quaint Elm Hill thatched house with a terraced garden. Mon–Sat 9.30am–5pm. Inexpensive.

Brummell's 7 Magdalen St ⓣ01603/625555. Serving the best seafood in town, a fish-fest in stylishly rustic surroundings. Expensive.

The Last Wine Bar 70–76 St George's St ⓣ01603/626626. Converted factory building holding a smart wine bar, which serves up tasty bistro-style dishes. A couple of minutes' walk north of the river. Closed Sun. Moderate.

Pinocchio's 11 St Benedict's St ⓣ01603/613318. Relaxed Italian restaurant in a pleasantly converted old general store, with inventive food combinations and live music a couple of times a week. Closed Sun. Moderate.

St Andrew's Hall Crypt Coffee Bar St Andrew's Plain at St George's St. Bargain spot for budget meals or just a coffee and cake. Mon–Sat 9am–4.30pm. Inexpensive.

Tatler's 21 Tombland ⓣ01603/766670. Brasserie in an elegantly converted Georgian town house with modern French cooking and an excellent wine list. Moderate.

Take 5 Cinema City, St Andrew's Plain. Imaginative, budget bistro food served in amenable surroundings. A student favourite. Mon–Sat 11am–11pm. Inexpensive.

Tree House 14 Dove St, above the Rainbow wholefood shop. Vegetarian wholefood café-restaurant offering a daily changing menu of soups, salads and main courses, plus organic wines and beers. Closed Sun. Inexpensive.

Pubs, bars and clubs

Adam & Eve Bishopgate. There's been a pub on this site for seven hundred years and it's still the top spot in town for the discerning drinker with a changing range of real ales and an eclectic wine list supplied by Adnams.

Coach & Horses Bethel St. Pleasant city-centre pub – across the street from City Hall – with lived-in furnishings and fittings. Good for a quiet drink.

Ribs of Beef Wensum St. Boisterous riverside drinking haunt popular with students and townies alike. Well-kept ales and inexpensive bar food.

Waterfront 139–41 King's St ⓣ01603/632717. Norwich's principal club and alternative music venue, with gigs and DJs most nights. Sponsored by UEA.

Wild Man Bedford St. Long-established, popular city-centre watering hole that has greased many a student wheel.

Entertainment

Predictably, Norwich has its fair share of multi-screen **cinemas** showing Hollywood blockbusters, but it also has the excellent art-house **Cinema City**, in Suckling House on St Andrew's Plain (Ⓣ01603/622047, Ⓦwww.cinemacity.co.uk). The **arts scene** here is perhaps a tad self-conscious, but the city does possess several first-rate **theatres**. The Theatre Royal, on Theatre Street (Ⓣ01603/630000, Ⓦwww.theatreroyalnorwich.co.uk), has a wide-ranging programme of mainstream and more adventurous plays and dance, while the amateur Maddermarket, St John's Alley, off Pottergate (Ⓣ01603/620917, Ⓦwww.maddermarket.co.uk), offers an interesting range of modern theatre. Predictably enough, **UEA** is a major source of entertainment for students and locals alike, with gigs at the Union and classical concerts at the Music Centre. The annual **Norfolk and Norwich Festival** each October (Ⓣ01603/766400, Ⓦwww.n-joy.org) features music, film, theatre, comedy, dance, walks and talks at venues all over the city.

The Norfolk Broads

Three rivers – the Yare, Waveney and Bure – meander across the flatlands to the east of Norwich, converging on Breydon Water before flowing into the sea at Great Yarmouth. In places these rivers swell into wide expanses of water known as "broads", which for years were thought to be natural lakes. In fact they're the result of extensive peat cutting, several centuries of accumulated diggings made in a region where wood was scarce and peat a valuable source of energy. The pits flooded when sea levels rose in the thirteenth and fourteenth centuries to create the **Norfolk Broads**, now one of the most important wetlands in Europe – a haven for many birds such as kingfishers, grebes and warblers – and the county's major tourist attraction.

The Broads' delicate ecological balance suffered badly during the 1970s and 1980s. The careless use of fertilizers poisoned the water with phosphates and nitrates encouraging the spread of algae; the decline in reed cutting – previously in great demand for thatching – made the broads partly unnavigable; and the enormous increase in pleasure-boat traffic began to erode the banks. National Park status was, however, accorded to the area in 1988, and efforts are now under way to clear the waters and protect the ecosystem. Co-ordinating the clean up is the **Broads Authority** (Ⓣ01603/610734, Ⓦwww.broads-authority.gov.uk), which maintains a series of information centres throughout the region. At any of these, you can pick up a free copy of the *Broadcaster*, a useful newspaper guide to the Broads as a whole.

The region is crossed by several **train** lines, with connections from Norwich to Wroxham, Acle and Reedham, as well as Berney Arms, near Breydon Water, one of the few places in England that can be reached by rail but not road. However, the best – really the only – way to see the Broads themselves is **by boat**, and you could happily spend a week or so exploring the 125 miles of lock-free navigable waterways, visiting the various churches, pubs and windmills en route. Among many **boat rental** companies, two of the more established are Blakes Holiday Boating (Ⓣ01603/739400, Ⓦwww.blakes.co.uk) and Broads Tours Ltd (Ⓣ01603/782207, Ⓦwww.broads.co.uk), both of whom operate out of Wroxham (see p.579). Prices for cruisers start at around £700 a week for four people in peak season, but less expensive, short-term rentals are widely available too. Houseboats are much cheaper than cruisers, but they are, of course, static.

Trying to explore the Broads by car is pretty much a waste of time, but cyclists and walkers have it much better, taking advantage of the region's network of footpaths and cycling trails. There are eight Broads Authority **bike rental** points dotted around (Ⓣ01603/782281). **Walkers** might consider the 56-mile Weavers' Way, a long-distance footpath that winds through the best parts of the Broads on its way from Cromer to Great Yarmouth, though there are many shorter options too.

Wroxham and Ludham

The easiest boating centre to reach from Norwich is **WROXHAM**, seven miles to the northeast and accessible by train, bus and car. Wroxham is itself short on charm, but it has a useful **information centre**, on Station Road (Easter–Oct daily 9am–1pm & 2–5pm; Ⓣ01603/782281), and plenty of places where you can stock up with food before heading out on a cruise.

Some six miles east of Wroxham, the village of **LUDHAM** straggles along the roadside at the tip of the Womack Water, an offshoot of the River Thurne. Just north of the village is How Hill, where the Broads Authority maintains **Toad Hole Cottage** (June–Sept daily 10am–6pm; April, May & Oct Mon–Fri 11am–1pm & 1.30–5pm; free), an old eel catcher's cottage housing a small exhibit on the history of the trade, which was common hereabouts until the 1940s. Behind the cottage is the narrow River Ant, where there are hour-long, wildlife-viewing boat trips in the *Electric Eel* from Easter to October – call Ⓣ01692/678763 for schedule and reservations; trips cost £4.

Potter Heigham and Ranworth

A couple of miles east of Ludham, **POTTER HEIGHAM** is the nominal capital of the Broads, taking its name from the pottery which once stood here on the River Thurne and from the Saxon lord of Heacham who founded the first settlement. Again, there's not much to keep your attention, though you can watch boaters struggling with the village's fourteenth-century bridge, regarded as one of the most difficult passages in the Broads. All the major boat rental companies have outlets here and there's also an **information centre** (Easter–Oct daily 9am–1pm & 2–5pm; Ⓣ01692/670779). The only public transport to Potter Heigham is by bus from Great Yarmouth.

Tiny **RANWORTH**, around twelve miles east of Norwich via the B1140, is a quieter spot altogether, though in the evening the place does fill up with boaters, who moor up in Ranworth Staithe and then pop into the local for a pint. There's no point in coming here if you're after renting a boat, but the village does have its own **information office** (Easter–Oct daily 9am–5pm; Ⓣ01603/270453), with stacks of stuff on local walking and wildlife. Ranworth also possesses a good-looking **church**, which is graced by a much-admired fifteenth-century rood screen, and there are regular **boat trips** to the isolated ruins of **St Benet's Abbey**, a couple of miles downstream along the River Bure (April–Oct Mon–Sat 1 daily; £5.50). There's also a **ferry** (April–Oct 2–4 daily; 30min; 80p) service to the **Broadland Conservation Centre**, a floating information centre and nature reserve just across Ranworth Staithe.

Great Yarmouth

First and foremost, **GREAT YARMOUTH** is a seaside resort, its promenade a parade of amusement arcades and rainy-day attractions, deserted in winter, heaving in summer. But it's also a port with a long history and, despite extensive wartime bomb damage, it retains a handful of sights that give some idea of the place Daniel Defoe thought "far superior to Norwich".

Yarmouth was a major trading port by the fourteenth century, its economy underpinned by its control of the waterways leading inland to Norwich. It also benefited from **fishing**, especially during the nineteenth century when there was a spectacular boom in the herring industry. The fishing finally fizzled out in the 1960s, but the timely discovery of **gas and oil** deposits off the Norfolk coast helped mitigate the effects and have since made the town a major base for the offshore gas industry, second only to Aberdeen for North Sea oil.

The Town

Arriving by train or car from Norwich, initial impressions are favourable thanks to the appealing silhouette of the church of **St Nicholas**, which boasts one of the widest naves in the country and, consequently, an impressive west front. The church stands at the northern end of the broad **Market Place**, which served as the centre of medieval Yarmouth, but is now mostly undistinguished. The one exception, at the square's northeast corner, is the **Hospital for Decayed Fishermen**, almshouses built in 1702 and opening out into a lovely little courtyard flanked by Dutch gables, the central cupola topped by a chilly looking statue of the fishermen's friend himself, St Peter. Just beyond, in Prior Plain and now a teashop, is Sewell House, the childhood home of Anna Sewell, author of *Black Beauty*.

One especially interesting feature of the old town is the narrow parallel alleys – locally "**rows**" – which were built to connect South Quay, running beside the River Yare, with the town centre just to the east. Sixty-nine rows have survived, and English Heritage maintains two seventeenth-century row houses, the **Old Merchant's House** in Row 117 and a **Row 111 House** (guided tours only, departing the Row 111 House April–Oct 4 times daily; £3; reservations ⓣ01493/857900; EH). Each holds furnishings and fittings illustrating the life of local folk between the 1870s and the 1940s and tours also drop by the remains of a Franciscan monastery, the **Greyfriars' Cloisters**. Of the town's several other museums, the most interesting is the **Norfolk Nelson Museum**, near Row 111 at 26 South Quay (April–Oct Mon–Fri 10am–5pm, Sat & Sun 2–5pm; £2), devoted to the eponymous admiral, who was a regular visitor to Yarmouth, and with a particularly good feature on Nelson's early life in Norfolk. The town is also developing a brand new **Maritime Museum**, which, with extensive displays on all things nautical from deep-sea fishing through to inland waterways, will be housed in a renovated herring curing tower on Blackfriars Road; it's due to be opened towards the end of 2004.

Row houses or not, the vast majority of visitors make a beeline for the wide sandy **beach** and the gimcrackery of **Marine Parade**, the seafront promenade where you'll find the usual suspects – gardens, huts, waxworks, crazy golf, an aquarium and a pier. The beach was also the unlikely setting for many of the most dramatic events in Dickens' *David Copperfield*.

Practicalities

It's a ten-minute walk east from Great Yarmouth's **train station** to the central Market Place – cross the river by the footbridge and you'll find yourself on North Quay, from where The Conge leads straight through to the square. **Buses** terminate one block from the sea on Wellesley Road and about 600 yards to the northeast of Market Place. There are two **tourist offices**, one in the town hall on South Quay (Mon–Fri 9am–5pm; ⓣ01493/846345,

Ⓦ www.great-yarmouth.co.uk), and a seasonal office on Marine Parade (June–Sept Mon–Sat 9.30am–5.30pm, Sun 10am–5pm; April, May & Oct daily 10am–1pm & 2–5pm; Ⓣ01493/842195). There's also a useful **Broads Information Centre** in the Yacht Station, Tar Works Road, just off North Quay (April–Oct daily 9am–8pm; Ⓣ01493/842794).

B&Bs line every street, with price a fair indication of quality, but if you don't have much luck, call in at the tourist office, which operates an accommodation booking service. Among many options, the *Willow Guest House*, 26 Trafalgar Rd (Ⓣ01493/332355; ❶), offers sea views from some of its nine bedrooms and has a top location just off Marine Parade. There's also *Senglea Lodge*, 7 Euston Rd (Ⓣ01493/859632; ❶), a cosy, well-maintained terraced house with seven pleasant bedrooms a short walk from Marine Parade. Yarmouth's YHA **youth hostel**, with self-catering facilities, is in a large Victorian house near the bus station at 2 Sandown Rd (Ⓣ0870/770 5840, Ⓔgtyarmouth@yha.org.uk; closed Sept–May plus limited opening in June; dorm beds £10.25).

Far and away the best **restaurant** in town is the reasonably priced *Seafood Restaurant*, 85 North Quay (Ⓣ01493/856009; closed Sun), which does a superb fish soup and Mediterranean-influenced seafood dishes.

The north Norfolk coast

Beyond Yarmouth, the first thirty miles of the **north Norfolk coast** is preoccupied by its beach, with barely a village, never mind an estuary or a harbour, in sight. The first place of any note is **Cromer**, a workaday seaside town whose bleak and blustery cliffs have drawn tourists for over a century. A few miles to the west is another well-established resort, **Sheringham**, but thereafter the shoreline becomes a ragged patchwork of salt marshes, dunes and shingle spits which form an almost unbroken series of nature reserves, supporting a fascinating range of flora and fauna. It's a lovely stretch of coast and the villages bordering it, principally **Cley**, **Blakeney** and **Wells-next-the-Sea** are prime targets for an overnight stay. The other major attractions hereabouts are the string of stately homes that lie a short distance inland – some, such as **Felbrigg** and **Holkham Hall**, are among the finest in the region.

Cromer and Sheringham are the only places reachable by **train**, with an hourly service from Norwich on the Bittern Line. Local **bus** services fill in (most of) the gaps, connecting all of the towns and many of the villages. There's also the **Coasthopper bus** (June–Sept Mon–Sat hourly, Sun 4 daily; Ⓣ08453/006116), which provides regular services along the whole length of the coast from Cromer to Hunstanton, with some buses continuing to Great Yarmouth and King's Lynn. The Coasthopper Rover ticket (£5) gives a day's unlimited travel on the route. For **walkers**, there's the **Norfolk Coast Path**, which runs from Hunstanton to Cromer (where it joins the Weavers' Way), an exhilarating route through the dunes and salt marshes; a National Trail Guide covers the route in detail, otherwise you'll need OS Landranger maps 132 and 133.

Cromer and around

Dramatically poised on a high bluff, **CROMER** should be the most memorable of the Norfolk coastal resorts, but its fine aspect is partly undermined by a shabbiness in the streets and shopfronts – an "atrophied charm" as Paul Theroux called it. The tower of **St Peter and St Paul**, at 160ft the tallest in Norfolk, attests to the port's medieval wealth, but it was the advent of the railway in the 1880s that heralded the most frenetic flurry of building activity. A bevy of grand Edwardian hotels was constructed along the seafront and for a moment Cromer became the most fashionable of resorts, but the gloss soon wore off and only the dishevelled **Hotel de Paris** has survived. While you're here, be sure to take a stroll out onto the **pier**, which was badly damaged in a storm in November 1993, but has since been repaired and struggles gamely on, and, of course, don't forget to grab a **crab** – J.W.H. Jonas, 7 New St has some fine specimens.

Somewhat miraculously Cromer has managed to retain its rail link with Norwich; the **train station** is a five-minute walk west of the centre. **Buses** terminate on Cadogan Road, next to the **tourist office** (April to late July, Sept & Oct Mon–Sat 10am–5pm & Sun 10am–4pm; late July to Aug daily 9.30am–5pm; Nov–March daily 10am–1pm & 2–4pm; ⓣ0870/225 4853), which is just 200 yards from the cliff-top promenade. An hour or two in Cromer is probably enough, though the **beach** is first-rate and the cliff-top walk exhilarating. There's no shortage of inexpensive **accommodation** – the tourist office has all the details – but it's hard to beat the enticing *Beachcomber B&B*, a cosy place with six en-suite rooms conveniently located near the centre at 17 Macdonald Rd (ⓣ01263/513398, ⓦwww.beachcomber-guesthouse.co.uk; no cards; ❷).

Felbrigg Hall

Just a couple of miles southwest of Cromer off the A148, **Felbrigg Hall** (April–Oct Mon–Wed, Sat & Sun 1–5pm; £6; NT) is a charming Jacobean mansion. The main facade is particularly appealing, the soft hues of the ageing limestone and brick intercepted by three bay windows, which together sport a large, cleverly carved inscription – Gloria Deo in Excelsis – in celebration of the reviving fortunes of the family who then owned the place, the Windhams. The interior is splendid too, with the studied informality of both the dining room and the drawing room enlivened by some magnificent seventeenth-century plasterwork ceilings and sundry objets d'art. Many of the **paintings** in Felbrigg were purchased by William Windham II, who did his Grand Tour in the 1740s. In the drawing room, for instance, are several marine scenes, notably two paintings of the Battle of the Texel by Willem van de Velde the Elder, hung just as William had arranged them. Pride of place here goes to the six oils and twenty-odd gouaches of Rome and southern Italy by Giovanni Battista Busiri.

The surrounding **parkland** (daily dawn to dusk) divides into two, with woods to the north and open pasture to the south. Footpaths crisscross the park and a popular spot to head for is the medieval church of **St Margaret's** in the southeastern corner, which contains a fine set of brasses and a fancy memorial to William Windham I and his wife by Grinling Gibbons. Nearer the house there's the extensive **walled garden**, which features flowering borders and an octagonal dove house, and the **stables**, which have been converted into very pleasant **tearooms**.

Blickling Hall

Blickling Hall (April–Sept Wed–Sun 1–5pm; Oct 1–4pm; house & gardens £6.90, gardens only £3.90; NT), set in a sheltered, wooded valley ten miles south of Cromer via the A140, is another grand Jacobean pile. Built for Sir Henry Hobart, a Lord Chief Justice, the hall dates from the 1620s and although it was extensively remodelled over a century later, the modifications respected the integrity of the earlier design. Consequently, the long facade, with its slender chimneys, high gables and towers, is the apotheosis of Jacobean design.

Inside, highlights include a superb plasterwork ceiling in the Long Gallery and an extraordinarily grand main staircase. There's also a gargantuan tapestry depicting Peter the Great defeating the Swedes, given to one of the family by Catherine the Great.

The surrounding **parkland** (daily dawn to dusk) incorporates a mile-long lake and a weird pyramidal mausoleum holding the earthly remains of the last of the male Hobarts.

Sheringham

SHERINGHAM, a popular seaside town four miles west of Cromer, has an amiable, easy-going air and makes a reasonable overnight stop, though frankly you're still only marking time until you hit the more appealing places further west. One of the distinctive features of the town is the smooth local beach pebbles that face and decorate the houses, a **flinting technique** used frequently in this part of Norfolk – the best examples here are off the High Street. The downside is that the power of the waves which makes the pebbles smooth has also forced the local council to spend thousands rebuilding the sea defences. The resultant mass of reinforced concrete makes for a less than pleasing seafront – all the more reason to head, instead, for **Sheringham Park**, the 770-acre woodland park a couple of miles southwest of the town, laid out by Humphry Repton in the early 1800s. The park boasts a wonderful array of rhododendrons and azaleas, at their best in late May to early June, and a series of look-out posts from which you can admire the view down to the coast. The other out-of-town jaunt is on the **North Norfolk Railway**, whose steam trains operate along the five miles of track southwest from Sheringham to the modest market town of Holt (May–Sept daily, frequent services in April & Oct; all-day ticket £8; ⓣ01263/820800, ⓦwww.nnrailway.co.uk).

Sheringham's two **train stations** are opposite each other on either side of Station Road. The main station, the terminus of the Bittern Line from Norwich, is just to the east, the North Norfolk Railway station to the west. The **tourist office** (April–Oct Mon–Sat 10am–5pm, Sun 10am–4pm; ⓣ0870/255 4854) is in between them on Station Approach. From the tourist office, it's a five-minute walk north to the seafront, straight down Station Road and its continuation, the High Street.

There are plenty of **B&B** options, with one of the best being *Oak Lodge* at 2 Morris St (ⓣ01263/823158, ⓦwww.oak-lodge.co.uk; ③), a smart Edwardian house with four attractive bedrooms right in the centre of town. A reasonable alternative is the unassuming *Two Lifeboats*, 2 High St (ⓣ01263/822401, ⓦwww.twolifeboats.co.uk; ④), a small hotel on the promenade offering sea views from most of its bedrooms. The YHA **youth hostel** is a short, five-minute walk south of the main train station at 1 Cremer's Drift (ⓣ0870/770 6024, ⓔsheringham@yha.org.uk; closed Dec–Jan; £11.50), set in its own grounds just off Cromer Road.

For a bite to **eat**, *Dave's*, 50 High St, serves the best fish chips for miles around and afterwards you can wash it down with one of *Ronaldo's*, 14 High St, home-made ice creams with flavours ranging from chocolate and ginger to cinnamon and lavender.

Cley and Blakeney Point

Travelling west from Sheringham, the **A149** meanders through a pretty rural landscape offering occasional glimpses of the sea and a shoreline protected by a giant shingle barrier erected after the catastrophic flood of 1953, a disaster which claimed over one thousand lives. After seven miles you reach **CLEY**, once a busy wool port but now little more than a row of flint cottages and Georgian mansions set beside a narrow, marshy inlet that (just) gives access to the sea. The original village was destroyed in a fire in 1612, which explains why Cley's fine medieval **Church of St Margaret** is located half a mile inland at the very southern edge of the current village, overlooking the green. The Black Death brought church construction to a sudden halt, hence the contrast between the stunted, unfinished chancel and the splendid nave, which boasts several fine medieval brasses and some folksy fifteenth-century bench-ends depicting animals and grotesques. Cley's other great draw – housed in an old forge on the main street – is the excellent **Cley Smoke House**, selling local smoked fish and other delicacies, while nearby **Picnic Fayre** has long been one of the finest delis in East Anglia.

It's about 400 yards east from the village to the mile-long byroad that leads to the shingle mounds of **Cley beach**. This is the starting point for the four-mile hike west out along the spit to **Blakeney Point**, a nature reserve famed for its colonies of terns and seals. The seal colony is made up of several hundred common and grey seals, and the old lifeboat house, at the end of the spit, is now a National Trust information centre. The shifting shingle can, however, make the going difficult, so keep to the low-water mark – which also means that you won't accidentally trample any nests. The easier alternative is to take one of the boat trips to the point from Blakeney or Morston (see p.585). The Norfolk Coast Path passes close to the beach too and then continues along the edge of the **Cley Marshes**, which attract a bewildering variety of waders – and, of course, "twitchers".

As for a **place to stay**, Cley holds the outstanding *Cley Mill B&B* (Ⓣ01263/740209, Ⓦwww.cleymill.co.uk; ⑤), housed in a converted windmill complete with sails and a balcony offering wonderful views over the surrounding salt marshes and seashore. Another very recommendable place is the *Three Swallows* pub (Ⓣ01263/740526; ③), on the green by the church, which has several pleasant en-suite rooms. For **food**, *The Café at Whalebone House* (Ⓣ01263/740336, Ⓦwww.thecafe.org.uk), on the main street, is an intimate vegetarian restaurant offering an innovative menu at affordable prices. They also have a couple of stylish **rooms** (⑤) for stays of two nights or more.

Blakeney

BLAKENEY is delightful. Once a bustling port exporting fish, corn and salt, it's now a lovely little place of pebble-covered cottages sloping up from a narrow harbour just a mile west of Cley. Crab sandwiches are sold from stalls at the quayside, the meandering high street is flanked by family-run shops, and footpaths stretch out along the sea wall to east and west, allowing long, lingering looks over the salt marshes. The only sight as such is the **Church of St Nicholas**, beside the A149 at the south end of the village, whose sturdy tower and nave are made of flint rubble with stone trimmings, the traditional building materials of north Norfolk. Curiously, the church has a second, much smaller tower at the back. In the nineteenth century this was used as a lighthouse to guide ships into harbour, but its original function is unknown. Inside, the oak and chestnut hammer-beam roof and the delicate rood screen are the most enjoyable features of the nave, which is attached to a late thirteenth-century chancel, the only survivor from the original Carmelite friary church. With its seven stepped lancet windows, the east window is a rare example of Early English design, though the stained glass is much later.

Blakeney **harbour** is linked to the sea by a narrow channel, which wriggles its way through the salt marshes. The channel is, however, only navigable for a few hours at high tide – at low tide the harbour is no more than a muddy creek (ideal for a bit of quayside crabbing). Depending on the tides, there are **boat trips** from Blakeney or **Morston quay**, a mile or two to the west, to both Blakeney Point (see opposite) – where passengers have a couple of hours at the point before being ferried back – and to the seal colony just off the point. The main operators advertise departure times on blackboards by the quayside or you can reserve in advance with Beans Boats (ⓣ01263/740505) or Bishop's Boats (ⓣ01263/740753). Both the seal trips and those to Blakeney Point cost about £6.

For **accommodation**, the quayside *Blakeney Hotel* (ⓣ01263/740797, ⓦwww.blakeney-hotel.co.uk; ❼) is one of the most charming hotels in Norfolk, a rambling building with high-pitched gables and pebble-covered walls. The hotel has a heated indoor swimming pool, a secluded garden, cosy lounges decorated in soft pastel colours and sea views, and serves outstanding **food**. The cheaper rooms can be poky and somewhat airless, but pay a little more and you'll be rewarded with splendid views across the harbour and the marshes. There are discounts for longer stays with full board. A good alternative is the *Manor Hotel* (ⓣ01263/740376, ⓦwww.blakeneymanor.co.uk; ❺), which occupies a low-lying courtyard complex a few yards to the east of the harbour; or you might try the excellent *King's Arms*, just back from the quay on Westgate (ⓣ01263/740341; ❹), a traditional pub, with low, beamed ceilings and seven en-suite bedrooms. The latter also serves up delicious, reasonably priced **bar food**. For longer stays, contact *Quayside Cottages* (ⓣ01462/768627, ⓦwww.blakeneycottages.co.uk), which rents some charming local cottages. Finally, *Morston Hall*, a couple of miles west of Blakeney on the A149 (ⓣ01263/741041, ⓦwww.morstonhall.com; ❻), occupies an attractive old house with beautiful gardens and tastefully decorated rooms; they also have a top-flight but relaxed restaurant where the emphasis is on seafood.

Wells-next-the-Sea and around

Despite its name, **WELLS-NEXT-THE-SEA**, some eight miles west of Blakeney, is situated a good mile or so from open water. In Tudor times, when it enjoyed much easier access to the North Sea, it was one of the great ports of eastern England, a major player in the trade with the Netherlands. Those heady days are long gone and although today it's the only commercially viable port on the north Norfolk coast, this is hardly a huge advantage. More importantly, Wells is also one of the county's more attractive towns, and even though there are no specific sights among its narrow lanes, it does make a very good base for exploring the surrounding coastline.

The town divides into three distinct areas, starting with **The Buttlands**, a broad rectangular green on the south side of town, lined with oak and beech trees and framed by a string of fine Georgian houses; it takes its unusual name from the years it was used for archery practice (a butt being the earthen mound behind the target). North from here, across Station Road, lie the narrow lanes of the town centre with **Staithe Street**, the minuscule main drag, flanked by quaint old-fashioned shops. Staithe Street leads down to the **quay**, a somewhat forlorn affair inhabited by a couple of amusement arcades and fish-and-chip shops, and the mile-long byroad that scuttles north to the **beach**, a handsome sandy tract backed by pine-clad dunes. The beach road is shadowed by a high flood defence and a tiny narrow-gauge **railway**, which scoots down to the beach every twenty minutes or so from 10.30am, Easter to October (90p each way).

Buses to Wells stop on The Buttlands, a short stroll from the **tourist office** at the foot of Staithe Street (April–Oct Mon–Sat 10am–5pm, Sun 10am–4pm; ⓣ0870/225 4857). Several of the best **guest houses** are along Standard Road, which runs up from the eastern end of the quayside. First choice should be the elegant *Normans* (ⓣ01328/710657; ❸), whose five spacious and tastefully decorated rooms are all en suite; the TV lounge has a log fire and racks of games and the first-floor look-out window provides a wide view over the marshes – binoculars are provided. Other recommendable options include *Mill House*, a dignified old millowner's home on Northfield Lane (ⓣ01328/710739, ⓦwww.broadland.com/millhouse; ❸), and *Ilex House* on Bases Lane (ⓣ01328/710556, ⓦwww.broadland.com/ilexhouse; ❸). The last is a good-looking Georgian villa with three guest rooms that sits in its own grounds, just to the west of the centre. There's also a **campsite**, the sprawling *Pinewoods Caravan and Camping Park*, by the beach (ⓣ01328/710439; closed Nov to mid-March).

For **pub food**, head straight for the *Crown* on The Buttlands, the best pub in town. Alternatively, *Nelson's*, 21 Staithe St, is a pleasant tea and coffee shop that serves inexpensive meals.

Holkham Hall

One of the most popular outings from Wells is to **Holkham Hall** (June–Sept Mon & Thurs–Sun 1–5pm; £6.50; ⓦwww.holkham.co.uk), three miles to the west and a stop on the Coasthopper bus (see p.581). This grand and self-assured stately home was designed by the eighteenth-century architect William Kent for the first earl of Leicester and is still owned by the family. The severe sandy-coloured Palladian exterior belies the warmth and richness of the interior, which retains much of its original decoration, notably the admired marble hall, with its fluted columns and intricate reliefs. The rich colours of the state rooms are an appropriate backdrop for a fabulous selection of **paintings**, including canvases by Van Dyck, Rubens, Gainsborough and Gaspar Poussin. One real treat is the Landscape Room where around twenty landscape paintings are displayed in the cabinet style of the eighteenth century. Most depict classical stories or landscapes, a poetic view of the past that enthralled the English aristocracy for decades.

The **grounds** (dawn to dusk; free) are laid out on sandy, saline land, much of it originally salt marsh. The focal point is an eighty-foot-high obelisk, atop a grassy knoll, from where you can view both the hall to the north and the triumphal arch to the south. In common with the rest of the north Norfolk coast, there's plenty of **birdlife** to observe in and around the park – Holkham's lake attracts Canada geese, heron and grebes and several hundred deer graze the open pastures.

The footpaths latticing the estate stretch as far as the A149, from where a half-mile byroad – Lady Anne's Drive – leads north across the marshes from opposite the *Victoria Hotel* to **Holkham Bay**, which boasts one of the finest sandy beaches on this stretch of coast, golden sand flexed against pine-studded sand dunes. Warblers, flycatchers and redstarts inhabit the drier coastal reaches, while waders paddle about the mud and salt flats.

Little Walsingham and Binham Priory

For centuries **LITTLE WALSINGHAM**, five miles south of Wells (and not to be confused with adjoining Great Walsingham), rivalled Bury St Edmunds and Canterbury as the foremost pilgrimage site in England. It all began in 1061 when the Lady of the Manor, a certain Richeldis de Faverches, was prompted to build a replica of the **Santa Casa** (Mary's home in Nazareth) here – inspired, it is said, by visions of the Virgin Mary. Whatever the reason for her actions, it brought instant fame and fortune to this little Norfolk village and every medieval king from Henry III onwards made at least one trip, walking the last mile barefoot. Both the Augustinians and the Franciscans established themselves here and all seemed set fair when Henry VIII followed in his predecessors' footsteps in 1511. However, pilgrim or not, it didn't stop Henry from destroying the shrine in the Dissolution of the 1530s, and at a stroke the village's principal trade came to an abrupt halt. Pilgrimages resumed in earnest after 1922, when the local vicar, one Alfred Hope Patten, organized an Anglo-Catholic pilgrimage, the prelude to the building of an Anglican shrine in the 1930s to the chagrin of the diocesan authorities. Today the village does good business out of its holy connections and the narrow-gauge **steam railway** from Wells (Easter–Oct daily 4–5 daily each way; 30min; £6 return; ⓣ01328/710631).

Little Walsingham now has a number of **shrines** catering to a variety of denominations – there's even a Russian Orthodox Church – though the main one is the **Anglican shrine**, beside the road from Holt, a few yards from the main square, **Common Place**. It's a strange-looking building – a cross between an English village hall and an Orthodox church – and inside the candle-lit Santa Casa contains the statue of Our Lady of Walsingham.

Shrines apart, Little Walsingham has an attractive centre, beginning with the Common Place, whose half-timbered buildings surround a quaint octagonal structure built to protect the village **pump** in the sixteenth century. The **High Street** extends south from here, overlooked by handsome Georgian and half-timbered houses, several of which are given over to shrine shops and religious bookstores. The High Street is also flanked by the impressive fifteenth-century **Abbey gatehouse** of the old Augustinian Priory – look up and you'll spy Christ peering out from a window – though the **ruins** beyond (April–Oct daily 10am–4.30pm; March, Nov & Dec Sat & Sun 10am–4pm; Feb daily 10am–4pm for snowdrop walks; closed Jan; £3 including Shirehall Museum), whose landscaped grounds stretch east to the River Stiffkey, are inconsequential. Footsteps from the south end of the High Street is the town's second square, **Friday Market Place**, which backs onto the village's second set of ecclesiastical **ruins** – those of the old Franciscan Friary (unrestricted access; free).

Much more substantial are the remains of **Binham Priory** (open access; free; EH), in a handsome rural setting about three miles northeast of Walsingham, on the edge of the hamlet of Binham. The Benedictines established a priory here in the late eleventh century, but long before it was suppressed at the Dissolution in 1540, it had a bad reputation, its priors renowned for their irresponsibility. One of the worst was William de Somerton, a fourteenth-century prior who funded his dabblings in alchemy by selling the church silverware and even the vestments. Neither were the monks a picture of contentment – one became insane through excessive meditation, so the prior had him flogged and then kept in solitary confinement until his death. Today, the ruins focus on the **priory church**, whose nave was turned into the parish church during the Reformation. Inside, the nave arcades are a handsome illustration of the transition between the Norman and Early English styles, a triple bank of windows that sheds light on the bare interior. Among the fittings, look out for the delicately carved font and the remains of the former rood screen kept at the back of the church. The Protestants whitewashed the screen and then covered it with biblical texts, but the paint is wearing thin and the saints they were keen to conceal have started to appear again.

Practicalities

The Coasthopper **bus** – as well as the fairly frequent Wells to Fakenham (for Norwich) bus – stops outside the Anglican shrine. The **train station** (for the steam train from Wells, see p.585) is a five-minute walk from Common Place: from the station, turn left along Egmere Road and take the second major right down Bridewell Street. The **tourist office** is on Common Place (April–Oct daily 10am–4.30pm; ⓣ01328/820510). It's difficult to find accommodation during major **pilgrimages** – the main ones are the national pilgrimage on the late May Bank Holiday and the pilgrimage for the sick and disabled on August 30. That said, the *Black Lion Hotel* on Friday Market (ⓣ01328/820235; ❺) has comfortable en-suite rooms and a restaurant, as does the more modest *Bull Inn* on Common Place (ⓣ01328/820333; ❹). Even better is *The Manor House*, on Barsham Road in the neighbouring hamlet of **Great Snoring** (ⓣ01328/820597, ⓦwww.norfolkcountryhouse.co.uk; ❻). This family-run hotel occupies a very distinctive house, whose towers and turrets date back to the fifteenth century. The gardens are splendid and each of the six en-suite rooms is pleasantly furnished in homely style; dinners are by prior arrangement only.

Burnham Market, Burnham Thorpe and Burnham Deepdale

A quick diversion off the A149 five miles west of Wells takes you to the picturesque village of **BURNHAM MARKET**, whose Georgian houses are ranged around an appealing green. The target here is the *Hoste Arms* (ⓣ01328/738777, ⓦwww.hostearms.co.uk; ❺), an old coaching inn which offers some of the best restaurant and bar **food** on the coast – and attracts a well-heeled crew to match. The same people also own the village's *Railway Inn*, in the old station on Creake Road (ⓣ01328/730505, same website; ❹). There's nothing specially fancy about the **rooms** at either, but they are perfectly adequate, neat and trim.

A mile or so to the southeast, **BURNHAM THORPE** was the birthplace of **Horatio Nelson**, who began life in the parsonage on September 29, 1758. Nelson joined the navy at the tender age of 12, and was sent to the West Indies, where he met and married Frances Nisbet, retiring to Burnham Thorpe in 1787. Back in action by 1793, his bravery cost him first the sight of his right eye, and shortly afterwards his right arm. His personal life was equally eventful – famously, his infatuation with Emma Hamilton, wife of the ambassador to Naples, caused the eventual break-up of his marriage. His finest hour was during the Battle of Trafalgar in 1805, when he led the British navy to victory against the combined French and Spanish fleets, a crucial engagement that set the scene for Britain's century-long domination of the high seas. The victory, as everyone knows, didn't do Nelson much good – he was shot in the chest during the battle and even the kisses of Hardy failed to revive him. Thereafter, Nelson was placed in a barrel of brandy and the pickled body shipped back to England, where he was laid in state at Greenwich and then buried at St Paul's (see p.104).

The Burnham Thorpe parsonage was demolished years ago, but Nelson is celebrated in **All Saints Parish Church**, where the lectern is made out of timbers taken from the *Victory*, the chancel sports a Nelson bust, and the south aisle has a small exhibition on his life and times. It was actually Nelson's express wish that he should be buried here, but to no avail. The other place to head for here is the **village pub** (no prizes for guessing the name) where Nelson held a farewell party for the locals in 1793.

Back on the A149, it's a couple of miles more to the hamlet of **BURNHAM DEEPDALE**, where *Deepdale Farm* (Ⓣ01485/210156, Ⓦwww.deepdale-farm.co.uk; dorm beds £10.50, ❶), situated just off the road, is a lively and very friendly set-up, operating a combined campsite, café and hostel, which occupy inventively renovated former stables.

Titchwell Marsh and Thornham

Beyond Burnham Market there's more rich marshland swimming with wildfowl, especially at **Titchwell Marsh** where the RSPB maintains a reserve based around reed beds and fresh and saltwater lagoons. **TITCHWELL** itself is insignificant, but it does have the *Titchwell Manor Hotel* (Ⓣ01485/210221, Ⓦwww.titchwellmanor.co.uk; ❺), beside the A149, where the bar offers great seafood from grilled oysters and mussels to monkfish and plaice. Lunch can easily be had for under a tenner and there are good-value dinner, bed and breakfast deals as well. **THORNHAM**, a mile further west, has three more likely looking pubs, including the splendid *Lifeboat Inn* on Ship Lane (Ⓣ01485/512236, Ⓦwww.lifeboatinn.co.uk; ❹), again with great food and good all-in deals. All the fourteen bedrooms here are en suite and most have sea views.

Hunstanton

The Norfolk coast pretty much ends at **HUNSTANTON**, a Victorian seaside resort that grew up to the southwest of the original fishing village – now **Old Hunstanton**. Like Great Yarmouth, it has its fair share of amusement arcades, crazy golf, and entertainment complexes, but it has also hung on to its genteel origins – and its sandy beaches, backed by stripy gateau-like cliffs, are among the cleanest in the county. Incidentally, in "The World of Fun" on Greevegate, Hunstanton possesses the self-proclaimed largest joke shop in Britain with more whoopee cushions and Dracula fangs than even the most unpleasant 10-year-old could want.

The **tourist office** is in the town hall (daily: April–Sept 9.30am–5pm; Oct–March 10.30am–4pm; Ⓣ01485/532610) on the wide sloping green, which serves as the focal point of the town. They can help out with **accommodation**, though it's easy enough to find. The nicest and priciest places are among the cottages of Old Hunstanton. One particular recommendation is *Le Strange Arms*, Golf Course Rd (Ⓣ01485/534411, Ⓦwww.abacushotels.co.uk; ❻), a large mansion dating from the nineteenth century and with gardens running down to the beach. At the other end of the market, the **youth hostel** occupies a pair of Victorian town houses at 15 Avenue Rd (Ⓣ0870/770 5872, Ⓔhunstanton@yha.org.uk; closed Nov–Easter; dorm beds £10.25), south of Hunstanton green.

King's Lynn and around

An ancient port, **KING'S LYNN** straddles the mouth of the Great Ouse, a mile or so before it flows into The Wash. It occupies an improbably marshy location, but was strategically placed for easy access to seven English counties. Consequently, the town's merchants grew rich, importing fish from Scandinavia, timber from the Baltic and wine from France, while exporting wool, salt and corn to the Hanseatic ports. The good times came to an end when the focus of maritime trade moved to the Atlantic seaboard, but its port struggled on until it was reinvigorated in the 1970s by the burgeoning trade between the UK and its EU partners. Much of the old centre was demolished during the 1950s and 1960s to make way for commercial development and, as a result, Lynn lacks the concentrated historic charm of towns such as Bury St Edmunds. That said, it does have a number of well-preserved buildings, including the oldest guildhall in the country, and taken together they are well worth a couple of hours. In addition, a handful of stately homes and medieval castle ruins are within easy reach.

Arrival, information and accommodation

From the **train station** it's a short walk west along Waterloo Street to Railway Road, the principal thoroughfare, which borders the eastern edge of the town centre. The **bus station** is nearer the centre, a few yards to the west of Railway Road. The **tourist office** is by the river, bang in the centre in the Custom House on Purfleet Quay (April–Oct Mon–Sat 9.30am–5pm, Sun 10am–4.30pm; Nov–March daily 10.30am–4pm; ⓣ01553/763044, ⓦwww.visitwestnorfolk.com).

Accommodation presents few problems. Most of the budget **B&Bs** lie southeast of the train station on Tennyson Road and Goodwins Road, its continuation to the south. To get to Tennyson Road on foot from the train station, take St John's Walk across the park. Options on Goodwins Road include the *Old Rectory*, at no. 33 (ⓣ01553/768544, ⓦwww.theoldrectory-kingslynn.com; no cards; ❷), with four, smart en-suite guest rooms in a good-looking nineteenth-century villa. Here also, at no. 79, is *Fairlight Lodge*, (ⓣ01533/762234, ⓦwww.fairlightlodge-online.co.uk; no cards; ❶), a trim Victorian brick house holding seven guest rooms, most en suite. Of Lynn's **hotels**, the pick is the *Tudor Rose*, which occupies a stylishly modernized fifteenth-century building right in the centre on St Nicholas Street (ⓣ01553/762824, ⓦwww.tudorrose-hotel.co.uk; ❹). The town's YHA **youth hostel** enjoys a central location in the converted Thorseby College on College Lane (ⓣ0870/770 5902, ⓔkingslynn@yha.org.uk; closed Oct to Easter; dorm beds £10.25).

The Town

Lynn's historic core lies in the two blocks between the High Street and the quayside. A good place to begin is the **Saturday Market Place**, the older and smaller of the town's two marketplaces, presided over by the hybrid **Church of St Margaret**, which contains two of the most fanciful medieval brasses in East Anglia. These are the Walsoken brass, adorned with country scenes, and the Braunche brass, named after a certain Robert Braunche and depicting the lavish feast he laid on for Edward III. Across the square is Lynn's prettiest building, the **Trinity Guildhall**, its wonderful chequered flint and stone facade dating to 1421 and repeated in both the Elizabethan addition to the left and in the adjoining Victorian Town Hall. Next door to the Guildhall is the entrance to the **Tales of the Old Gaol House** (Easter–Oct daily 10am–5pm; Nov–Easter Mon, Tues & Fri–Sun 10am–5pm; last admission 4.15pm; £2.50), which incorporates a series of eighteenth-century cells within a small museum on local baddies. There's also access to the Guildhall undercroft, which displays an exhibition on the town's rich collection of civic regalia. This is actually more stimulating than you might think, since the treasures include King John's cup and sword, which were gifted to the town prior to the king's ill-fated and ill-timed dash across The Wash. The king and his retinue were caught by the incoming waters and, although they saved themselves, they lost the crown jewels – and people have been looking for them ever since.

Of the medieval warehouses which survive along the quayside, the most evocative is the former **Hanseatic Warehouse**, built around 1475, whose half-timbered upper floor juts unevenly over the cobbles of St Margaret's Lane. The other architectural highlight is a short stroll north, at the end of the gentle Georgian curve of Queen Street. It's here you'll find the splendid **Custom House**, erected in 1683 in a style clearly influenced by the Dutch. There are classical pilasters, petite dormer windows and a roof-top balustrade, but it's the dinky little cupola that catches the eye. The Custom House holds the tourist office (see above) and overlooks **Purfleet Quay**, a short and stumpy harbour once packed with merchant ships.

Beyond the Custom House, King Street, with its much wider berth, continues where Queen Street left off. On the left, just after Ferry Lane, stands Lynn's most precious building, **St George's Guildhall** (Mon–Fri 10am–4pm, Sat 10am–1pm & 2–3.30pm; free), dating from 1410 and one of the oldest surviving guildhalls in England. It was a theatre in Elizabethan times and is now part of the King's Lynn Arts Centre (see below). Beyond the Guildhall is the later and much larger **Tuesday Market Place**, with the pastel-pink *Duke's Head Hotel*, dating from 1689, and the Neoclassical **Corn Exchange** – imaginatively converted into a second arts centre for the town – standing out against an otherwise unspectacular assemblage.

Eating, drinking and entertainment

There's a good **café**, *Crofter's* (Mon–Sat 9.30am–5pm), in the undercroft of St George's Guildhall, at the King's Lynn Arts Centre, and one highly recommendable, if comparatively expensive, **restaurant** – the *Riverside*, 27 King St (Ⓣ01553/773134; closed Sun), in an old fifteenth-century warehouse round the back of the same arts centre. The food – light lunches and dinner – is excellent and you get river views and tables outside in decent weather too. Alternatively, there's moderately priced *Rembrandt's*, a homely restaurant offering traditional English food with a twist just off the Tuesday Market Place at 19 Chapel Street, and tasty **pub meals** at the *Tudor Rose* on St Nicholas Street close by. The latter is also the best place for a **drink**.

Entertainment in Lynn revolves around the **King's Lynn Arts Centre** (Ⓣ01553/764864, Ⓦwww.kingslynnarts.co.uk). Its galleries, cinema and theatre stage much of the town's annual festival, held in July. The **Corn Exchange**, on the Tuesday Market Place (same number), adds to the programme, chipping in with a wide-ranging programme from theatre and music to comedy and dance. As for **markets**, which still attract large fenland crowds, there's one on the Saturday Market Place every Saturday and two others on the Tuesday Market Place – on Tuesdays and Fridays.

Around King's Lynn

Within a ten-mile radius of King's Lynn are several notable attractions. The architectural highlight is **Houghton Hall**, a splendid Palladian mansion with Baroque flourishes, but it's **Sandringham**, one of the Queen's country residences, that pulls in the crowds. The area also holds some fine Norman ruins at **Castle Rising** and, a little further afield, **Castle Acre**.

Castle Rising

Situated at the centre of extensive earthworks five miles north of Lynn via the A149, the shell of the twelfth-century keep of **Castle Rising** (April–Oct daily 10am–6pm; Nov–March Wed–Sun 10am–4pm; £3.75; EH) is in remarkably good condition. Towering over the surrounding flatlands, it's a powerful, imposing structure and some of its finer architectural details have survived as well – from the blind arcading and ox-eye windows on the outside to the vaulted ceilings and ornamented fireplaces within. The nearby village is laid out on a grid plan and contains a quadrangle of beautiful seventeenth-century **almshouses**, whose elderly inhabitants still go to church in red cloaks and pointed black hats, the colours of the original benefactor, the Earl of Northampton. First Eastern Counties **buses** #410 and #411 (hourly) from King's Lynn to Hunstanton stop off at the *Black Horse* pub in the village.

Sandringham House

From Castle Rising, it's a couple of miles north on the A149 to the turnings that lead into the seven-thousand-acre estate of **Sandringham House** (mid-April to Oct daily 11am–4.45pm; closed for two weeks late-July or early Aug; £6.50; Ⓦwww.sandringhamestate.co.uk), bought in 1861 by Queen Victoria for her son, the future Edward VII. The house is billed as a private home, but few families have a drawing room crammed with Russian silver and Chinese jade. The **museum**, housed in the old coach and stable block, contains an exhibition of royal memorabilia from dolls to cars, but much more arresting are the beautifully maintained **grounds** (10.30am–5pm), a mass of rhododendrons and azaleas in spring and early summer. The estate's sandy soil is also ideal for game birds, which was the attraction of the place for the terminally bored Edward, whose tradition of posh shooting parties is still followed by the royals. Local **buses** #410 and #411 make the journey from King's Lynn, as does the summer Coasthopper service (see p.581).

Houghton Hall

Located five miles due east of Sandringham, along narrow country lanes, **Houghton Hall** (late April to Sept Wed, Thurs & Sun 2–5.30pm; £6.50; Ⓦwww.houghtonhall.com) is an early Palladian extravagance dating from the 1720s. It was built for Sir Robert Walpole, a leading Whig politician whose roller-coaster career included a couple of terms as prime minister and a period of imprisonment for corruption. As at Holkham Hall (see p.586), the exterior, with its classical portico, is formal and severe, though the four corner domes do add a touch of frivolity. Inside, the lavishness of the state rooms is at its most overpowering in the stone hall and saloon, the ceilings dripping with fancy plasterwork. Look out also for the overmantels in the parlour, the work of Grinling Gibbons. The original Walpole art collection was sold to Catherine the Great of Russia in 1779 to pay off family debts, but there are still plenty of objets d'art on display, notably Sèvres porcelain and Mortlake tapestries.

There's no bus service to the hall – the nearest you'll get is the village of **Harpley**, a mile or so to the south just off the A148.

Castle Acre

The remote hamlet of **CASTLE ACRE** stands in the shadow of one of the few hilltops in Norfolk, twenty miles east of King's Lynn and reached via the A47. Taking advantage of the terrain, one of William I's most trusted lieutenants, a certain William Warenne, built a fortified manor house here shortly after the Conquest. The site was refortified as a stone **castle** (open access; free; EH) in the 1140s, but little remains from either period – except, that is, for the Norman earthworks. These are some of the most complete in the whole of England, with the mound of the keep and the circular bailey easy to discern. To the west, on the banks of the River Nar, there are more medieval ruins, those of the Cluniac **priory** (April–Sept daily 10am–6pm; Oct daily 10am–5pm; Nov–March Wed–Sun 10am–4pm; £4; EH) founded by Warenne's son in 1090. The most significant remains are the gatehouse, with its chequered flint and stone facade, and the west front of the priory church, an excellent illustration of the way different medieval styles were blended together, with the Norman doorway and delicate blind arcading set beneath an arching Early English window.

The *Ostrich* **pub** (Ⓣ01760/755398) on the village green makes a great target for lunch, not so much for the food as for its ancient atmosphere and good location. There's a **bus** service linking Castle Acre with King's Lynn, but it runs infrequently; check at the tourist office for details.

Breckland

Until the late eighteenth century, the **Breckland**, a chunky slab of land running south from Swaffham to Thetford, was a sparsely populated district characterized by open heaths and pastureland grazed by thousands of sheep. The animals had to contend with frequent sandstorms as the wind whipped the dry, sandy soils and travellers had the added problem of the highwaymen who plagued the area. The next century saw some hard-won agricultural gains, but it was the work of the Forestry Commission that changed the character of the area in the 1920s when they launched a vast tree-planting programme, covering much of the heathland with the assorted conifers of **Thetford Forest**. Further dramatic change came during World War II when the establishment of a mock "battle area" destroyed five villages and thousands of acres of farmland. The end result was the largest concentration of military bases in the country. All of this hardly makes the area seem alluring, but in **Thetford** the district has a pleasant market town with one or two historical curiosities and there are lots of woodland walks to be enjoyed nearby. In addition, Thetford is within easy striking distance of a diverting medieval manor house, **Oxburgh Hall**, and, oddly enough, the tomb of the last Sikh Maharajah in **Elveden**.

Thetford

The Breckland's most interesting town is **THETFORD**, birthplace of the radical eighteenth-century ideologue **Thomas Paine**, and, way back in the eleventh century, seat of the kings and bishops of East Anglia. It's a pleasant place, with riverside walks and gardens, though the remains of the Cluniac priory and the giant earthworks of Castle Hill – at opposite ends of the town centre – are the only reminders of the town's former importance. On **King Street**, the partly pedestrianized main drag, there's a striking gilt **statue** of Paine, paid for by the Thomas Paine Foundation of America. For years disowned by his native town, Paine was the chief British apologist for the French Revolution, and a prominent theorist for the American one, publishing his most famous tract, *The Rights of Man*, in 1791. In this, he advocated, among other things, the abolition of the monarchy and the establishment of a social welfare system to succour the poor. His books were subsequently banned and his effigy burned in many towns, and then, accused of sedition, he was forced to flee the country, going first to France and then to America. Paine's birthplace, on White Hart Street, was pulled down long ago – the Thomas Paine Hotel now stands on the site – but the timber-framed **Ancient House**

Elveden

The tiny village of **Elveden**, strung out along the A11 three miles southwest of Thetford, is – strange though it may seem – a place of pilgrimage for Britain's 250,000-strong Sikh community. The pilgrims come to pay homage to the last Sikh Maharajah, **Prince Duleep Singh**, who is buried beside his wife and son in the local churchyard. Having been forced to sign away his Punjab kingdom and the famous Koh-i-Noor diamond to the British, he was sent to England and handed as compensation the 17,000-acre estate at Elveden in 1863. He became a favourite of Queen Victoria, who thought him "extremely handsome", and with his state pension he transformed Elveden Hall (no public access) into an oriental extravaganza.

Museum, close by at 21 White Hart St (Mon–Sat 10am–5pm, plus June–Aug Sun 2–5pm; £1 in July & Aug, free rest of year), has an interesting display on the man. It also possesses replicas of the Thetford treasure of Roman gold and silverwork unearthed in 1979 (the originals are in the British Museum) and a herb garden.

From Thetford **train station**, it's about half a mile south to King Street – follow Station Road and veer right at the end over Thomas Paine Avenue and onto White Hart Street. The **bus station** is closer to King Street – to get there, cross the bridge and proceed up Bridge Street. There's no **tourist office** as such, but information is available from St Peter's Church, at the foot of White Hart Street (daily 9am–5pm). Thetford's most promising **hotel** is *The Bell*, a smartly updated fifteenth-century inn with over forty comfortable rooms decorated in modern style on King Street (Ⓣ01842/754455, Ⓦwww.oldenglish.co.uk; ❺). There's also the pleasantly appointed *Thomas Paine Hotel* on White Hart Street (Ⓣ01842/755631, Ⓦwww.thomaspainehotel.activehotels.com; ❹). For **food**, the *Albion*, in a row of flint cottages at 93 Castle St, is an attractive old pub that offers good-quality bar food.

Thetford Forest and Grime's Graves

The biggest change affecting the Breckland has been the creation of **Thetford Forest**, eighty thousand acres planted with unerring regularity in the 1920s immediately to the west of Thetford town. Realizing the error of their ways, the Forestry Commission (FC) is currently engaged in more imaginative replanting, and has laid out several **forest walks**, wildlife hides and other recreational facilities to try and entice people to come here. Call in at **High Lodge Forest Centre**, five miles west of Thetford on the B1107 (Easter–Oct Mon–Fri 9am–5pm, Sat & Sun 9am–6pm; Nov–Easter Sat & Sun 11am–4pm; Ⓣ01842/810271), for trail maps or to rent a bike.

A mile or so to the west of High Lodge, the B1107 leaves the forest as it approaches the outskirts of Brandon. From here, it's about three miles north via the A1065 to **Grime's Graves** (April–Oct daily 10am–1pm & 2–6pm, Nov–March Wed–Sun 10am–1pm & 2–4pm; £2.50; EH), where the open heathland is pocked by dozens of shallow indentations, the results – remarkably enough – of Stone Age flint mining. The earliest significant industrial site in Europe, dated to around 2000 BC, the mines were not identified as such until they were excavated in the 1870s, though they owe their collective name to the Anglo-Saxons, who called them after one of their gods, Grim. English Heritage has opened one of the shafts and visitors can descend no less than thirty feet by ladder.

Oxburgh Hall

From Grime's Graves, it's about ten miles north to **Oxburgh Hall** (April–Oct Mon–Wed, Sat & Sun 1–5pm; gardens open 11am; £5.50, gardens only £2.80; NT), a medieval manor house of postcard prettiness, whose dappled brickwork overlooks a reed-choked moat. The hall was built in 1482 for the Bedingfeld family, staunch Catholics whose religious sympathies gave them all sorts of trouble from the Reformation onwards. The approach to the hall is via an eighty-foot-high ceremonial gateway, matched by the main gate tower of the house itself, but the interior is something of a disappointment. Aside from the tapestries executed by the imprisoned Mary Queen of Scots, the rooms are routinely Victorian, the product of extensive renovations in the middle of the nineteenth century. The most exquisite Bedingfeld legacy – a set of terracotta tombs – is just outside the grounds of the hall in the chapel.

Ely and around

Perched on a mound of clay above the River Great Ouse, **ELY** – literally "eel island" – was to all intents and purposes a true island until the draining of the fens in the seventeenth century. Up until then, the town was encircled by treacherous marshland, which could only be crossed with the help of the local "fen-slodgers" who knew the firm tussock paths. In 1070, **Hereward the Wake** turned this inaccessibility to military advantage, holding out against the Normans and forcing William the Conqueror to undertake a prolonged siege – and finally to build an improvised road floated on bundles of sticks. Centuries later, the Victorian writer Charles Kingsley resurrected this obscure conflict in his novel *Hereward the Wake*. He presented the protagonist as the Last of the English who "never really bent their necks to the Norman yoke and . . . kept alive those free institutions which were the germs of our British liberty" – a heady mixture of nationalism and historical poppycock that went down a storm.

Since then, Ely has always been associated with Hereward, which is really rather ridiculous as Ely is, above all else, an ecclesiastical town and a Norman one to boot. The Normans built the **cathedral**, a towering structure visible for miles across the flat landscape and Ely's only significant sight. It's easy to see the town on a day-trip from Cambridge, but Ely does make a pleasant night's stop in its own right. It's also close to a couple of Cambridgeshire's other historic sights – namely the cathedral at **Peterborough** and the small town of **Wisbech** – not to mention the undrained and unmolested **Wicken Fen** (see box on p.597).

The Town

Ely **Cathedral** (June–Sept daily 7am–7pm; Oct–May Mon–Sat 7.30am–6pm, Sun 7.30am–5pm; Mon–Sat £4.80, free on Sun) is seen to best advantage from the south, the crenellated towers of the west side perfectly balanced by the prickly finials to the east with the distinctive timber lantern rising above them both. To approach from this direction, follow the footpath leading up the hill into the cathedral precincts from **Broad Street** – also the second turning on the right as you walk up Station Road from the train station. At the top of the footpath, pass through the medieval **Porta**, once the principal entrance to the monastery complex, and turn right to reach the main entrance on the lopsided **west front** – one of the transepts collapsed in a storm in 1701.

The first things to strike you as you enter the **nave** are the sheer length of the building and the lively nineteenth-century painted ceiling, largely the work of amateur volunteers. The nave's procession of plain late-Norman arches, built around the same time as those at Peterborough, leads to the architectural feature that makes Ely so special, the **octagon** – the only one of its kind in England – built in 1322 to replace the collapsed central tower. Its construction, employing the largest oaks available in England to support some four hundred tons of glass and lead, remains one of the wonders of the medieval world, and the effect, as you look up into this Gothic dome, is simply breathtaking. From March to October, **Octagon tours** (£3; reservations & schedule ⓣ01353/667735) depart two to four times daily from the desk at the entrance, venturing up into the octagon itself.

When the central tower collapsed, it fell eastwards, onto the **choir**, the first three bays of which were rebuilt at the same time as the octagon in the Decorated style – in contrast to the plainer Early English of the choir bays beyond. Further east still is the thirteenth-century **presbytery**, which houses the relics of **St Ethelreda**, founder of the abbey in 673, who, despite being twice married, is honoured liturgically as a virgin. Also at the east end are three **chantry chapels**, the most charming of which (on the left) is an elaborate Renaissance affair dated to 1533. The other marvel at Ely is the **Lady Chapel**, a separate building accessible via the north transept. It lost its sculpture and its stained glass during the Reformation, but its fan vaulting remains, an exquisite example of English Gothic. Retracing your steps, the south triforium near the main entrance holds the **Stained Glass Museum** (Easter–Oct Mon–Sat 10.30am–5pm, Sun noon–6pm; Nov–Easter Mon–Sat 10.30am–4.30pm, Sun noon–4.30pm; £3.50), an Anglican money-spinner exhibiting examples of this applied art from 1240 to the present day.

The cathedral precincts

The **precincts** of the cathedral boast a fine ensemble of medieval domestic architecture, a higgledy-piggledy assortment of old stone, brick and half-timbered buildings that runs south from the Infirmary complex, abutting the presbytery, to the Prior's buildings near the Porta gate. Many of the buildings are used by the King's boarding school – where the cathedral's choristers are trained – others by the clergy, but although you can't go in any of them, it's still a pleasant area to stroll; a free map and brochure are available from the cathedral.

The rest of the town

The rest of Ely is pretty enough, but hardly compelling after the wonders of the cathedral. To the north, the **High Street**, with its Georgian buildings and old-fashioned shops, makes for an enjoyable browse and, if you push on past the Market Place down Forehill and then Waterside, you'll soon reach the **Babylon Gallery** (Tues–Sun 10am–4pm; free), where an imaginative programme of temporary exhibitions featuring contemporary art and craft is displayed in an attractively renovated old brewery warehouse. Alternatively, head west from the cathedral entrance across the Palace Green, to **Oliver Cromwell's House** at 29 St Mary's St (April–Oct daily 10am–5.30pm; Nov–March Mon–Fri & Sun 11am–4pm, Sat 10am–5pm; £3.50), a timber-framed former vicarage, which holds a small exhibition on the Protector's ten-year sojourn in Ely, when he was employed as a tithe collector.

Practicalities

Ely lies on a major rail intersection, with direct **trains** from as far afield as Liverpool, Norwich and London, as well as from Cambridge, just twenty minutes to the south. The **train station** is a ten-minute walk from the cathedral straight up Station Road and its continuation Back Hill. **Buses** (from King's Lynn and Cambridge) stop on Market Street immediately to the north of the cathedral. The **tourist office** is in Oliver Cromwell's House (April–Oct daily 10am–5.30pm; Nov–March Mon–Fri & Sun 11am–4pm, Sat 10am–5pm; ⓣ01353/662062, ⓦwww.eastcambs.gov.uk) and they issue free town maps and will help with accommodation.

Ely has several appealing **B&Bs**, the best being the handy *Cathedral House*, 17 St Mary's St (ⓣ01353/662124, ⓦwww.cathedralhouse.co.uk; no cards; ❸), an attractive Georgian town house with three comfortable, en-suite bedrooms. Several other good options are concentrated along Egremont Street, about five minutes' walk north from the cathedral via Lynn Road. Possibilities here include the spacious *Old Egremont House* at no. 31 (ⓣ01353/663118; no cards; ❸), with cathedral views and a walled garden, and the more modern, spick and span *Posthouse* at no. 12a (ⓣ01353/667184; no cards; ❷).

Of the numerous **tearooms** in town, *The Almonry* (daily 10am–5pm), in the grounds on the north side of the cathedral, is by far the best sited, with garden seats granting great views of the octagon. A good reserve is the *Steeplegate Tea*

The Fens – and Wicken Fen

One of the strangest of all English landscapes, the **Fens** cover a vast area from just north of Cambridge right up to Boston in Lincolnshire. For centuries, they were an inhospitable wilderness of quaking bogs and marshland, punctuated by clay islands on which small communities eked out a livelihood cutting peat for fuel, using reeds for thatching and living on a diet of fish and wildfowl. Piecemeal land reclamation took place throughout the Middle Ages, but it wasn't until the seventeenth century that the systematic draining of the fens was undertaken – amid fierce local opposition – by the Dutch engineer **Cornelius Vermuyden**. This wholesale draining had unforeseen consequences: as it dried out, the peaty soil shrank to below the level of the rivers, causing frequent flooding, and the region's **windmills**, which had previously been vital in keeping the waters at bay, compounded the problem by causing further shrinkage. The engineers had to back-track and although much of the fenland was drained, the task was only completed in the 1820s following the introduction of **steam-driven pumps**, leviathans which could control water levels with much greater precision. Drained, the fens now comprise some of the most fertile agricultural land in the country.

At **Wicken Fen National Nature Reserve** (daily dawn to dusk; ⓣ01353/720274; £3.80; NT), nine miles south of Ely via the A142, you can visit one of the few remaining areas of undrained fenland. Its survival is thanks to a group of Victorian entomologists who donated the land to the National Trust in 1899, making it the oldest nature reserve in the UK. The seven hundred acres are undrained but not uncultivated – sedge and reed cutting are still carried out to preserve the landscape as it is – and they are readily explored by means of three easy and clearly marked **footpaths**, one of which – the easiest – is a fifteen-minute stroll along a boardwalk. The boardwalk trail passes one of the last surviving fenland wind pumps and the reserve holds about ten bird-watching hides. At the main entrance, there's a **visitor centre** (Tues–Sun 10am–5pm) and an antique fenland thatched **cottage** (April–Oct Sun only 2–5pm; £1.50). The visitor centre organizes a variety of events and guided walks – call ahead for details.

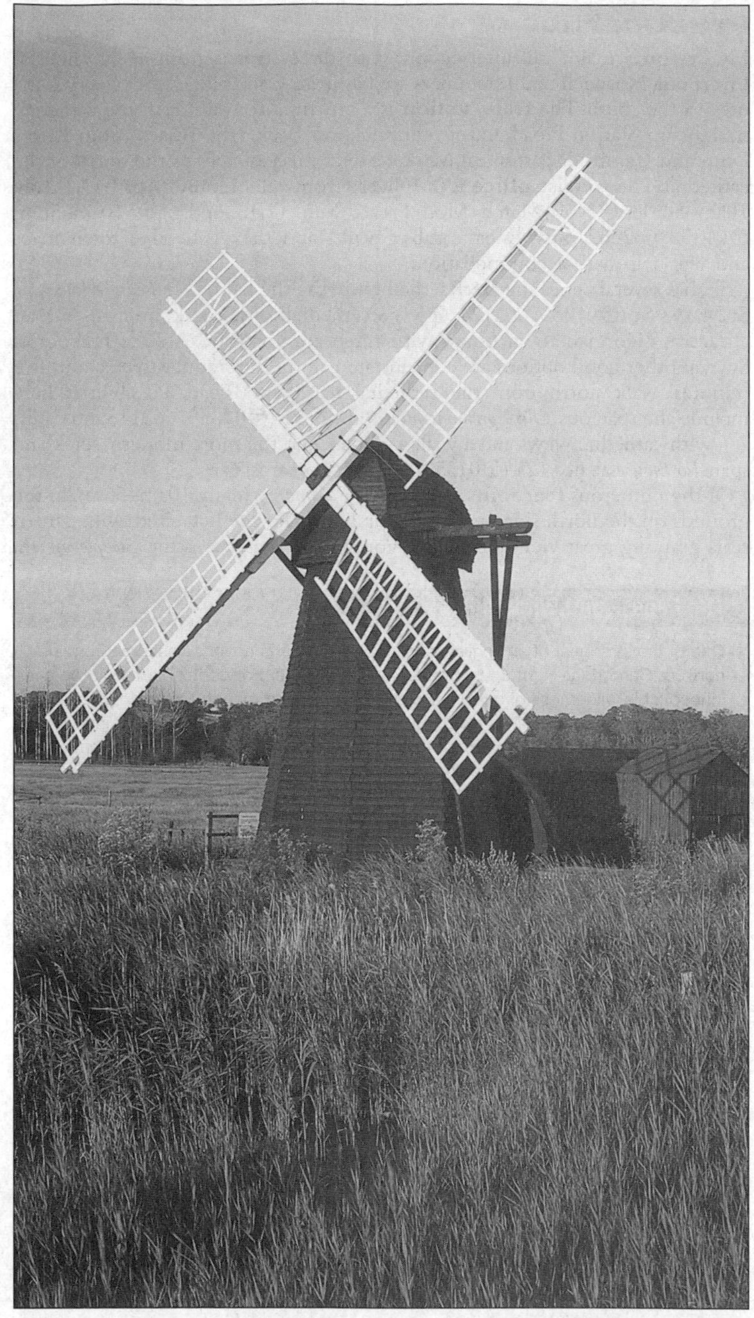

△ East Anglian windmill

Rooms at 16–18 High St (closed Sun), backing onto the cathedral grounds. The pick of the town's **restaurants** is the *Old Fire Engine House*, 25 St Mary's St (☎01353/662582; closes 9pm, 5pm on Sun), a gourmet English restaurant of some local repute with main courses averaging £9. Ely has two excellent **pubs** and both are on Silver Street, just south of the cathedral along The Gallery. These are the relaxed and welcoming *Fountain* at no. 1, which comes complete with a goodly set of stuffed animals, and the *Prince Albert*, at no. 62, which squeezes in a little book-selling to help you with your pint. For **entertainment**, the riverside *Maltings*, on Ship Lane, has a cinema (☎01353/666388) as well as a brasserie and bar.

Around Ely: Wisbech

The small town of **WISBECH** sits in the middle of agricultural flatlands some 25 miles north of Ely. The town first developed as Peterborough's seaport, but the silting up of The Wash has slowly pushed it back from the coast, which is now ten miles away along the navigable River Nene. The Nene slices through the heart of old Wisbech with the town's most interesting buildings to either side on the "brink". The North Brink has the architectural edge, thanks partly to **Peckover House** (April–Oct Wed, Sat & Sun 1.30–4.30pm, plus May–Aug Thurs same hours; £4, gardens only £2.50; NT), a substantial Georgian property which was purchased by Jonathan Peckover, a wealthy local banker, in the late eighteenth century. The exterior of the house is typically plain, and the interior is only sparsely furnished, but the Rococo woodwork and fancy plaster decorations make the trip worthwhile, not to mention the Victorian garden with its orangery, summerhouses, reed barn and herbaceous borders.

It's an easy drive to Wisbech from Ely, though rather more complicated by **public transport**: take the train to March (20min) and catch a local bus on to Wisbech, but note that services are infrequent so check times at the tourist office before you depart. Wisbech is only twelve miles west of King's Lynn and daily buses make the onward journey from there.

Peterborough

Some thirty-odd miles northwest of Ely, booming **PETERBOROUGH** has shaken off its dusty history as a brick-making town, attracting a raft of high-tech industries, whose employees now occupy the sprawling, leafy suburbs that surround its compact centre. But, whatever the merits of Peterborough as a place to live and work, for the casual visitor it has but one distinct – and unmissable – attraction, its superb Norman **Cathedral** (Mon–Sat 9am–5.15pm, Sun noon–5.15pm; £3.50 suggested donation). A site of Christian worship since the seventh century, the first two churches here were destroyed – the original Saxon monastery by the Danes in 870, its replacement by fire in 1116. Work on the present structure began a year after the fire and was largely completed within the century. The one significant later addition is the thirteenth-century **west facade**, one of the most magnificent in England, made up of three grandiloquent, deeply recessed arches, though the purity of the design is marred slightly by an incongruous central porch added in 1370.

The **interior** is a wonderful example of Norman architecture. Round-arched rib vaults and shallow blind arcades line the nave, while up above the painted wooden ceiling, dating from 1220, is an exquisite example of medieval art, one of the most important in Europe. There are several notable tombs in the cathedral, too, beginning with that of **Catherine of Aragon**, who is buried in the north aisle of the presbytery under a slab of black Irish marble. Catherine was

Henry VIII's first wife and the king's determination to divorce her in favour of Anne Boleyn precipitated the English Reformation. The marriage was finally declared void in 1533, but much to the king's chagrin, Catherine insisted till her death (in 1536) that she remained Henry's lawful wife. Mary Queen of Scots was also interred here, in the south aisle, after her execution in 1587, but 25 years later she was transferred to Westminster Abbey.

With frequent connections in all directions – including Ely – Peterborough is easy to reach by rail. The **train station** is a short, signposted walk across the pedestrianized town centre from the cathedral. The **tourist office** is in the lovely little close that surrounds the cathedral at no. 3–5 (July–Sept Mon & Wed–Fri 9am–5pm, Tues & Sat 10am–5pm, Sun noon–4pm; Oct–June Mon–Sat 10am–4pm; ⓣ01733/452336, ⓦwww.peterborough.gov.uk). Predictably, there are lots of **cafés** and bars in the town centre with one of the more recommendable being *Beckett's*, which serves tasty snacks from its premises on Cathedral square.

Cambridge

On the whole, **CAMBRIDGE** is a much quieter and more secluded place than Oxford, though for the visitor what really sets it apart from its scholarly rival is "**the Backs**" – the green swathe of land that straddles the languid River Cam, providing exquisite views over the backs of the old colleges. At the front, the handsome facades of these same colleges dominate the layout of the town centre, lining up along the main streets. Most of the older colleges date back to the late thirteenth and early fourteenth centuries and are designed to a **similar plan** with the main gate leading through to a series of "courts," typically a carefully manicured slab of lawn surrounded on all four sides by college residences or offices. Many of the buildings are extraordinarily beautiful, but the most famous is **King's College**, whose magnificent **King's College Chapel** is one of the great statements of late Gothic architecture. There are 31 university colleges in total, each an independent, self-governing body, proud of its achievements and attracting – for the most part at least – a close loyalty from its students, amongst whom privately educated boys remain hopelessly over-represented despite decades of perfectly adequate state education. This intrinsic elitism is amplified by all sorts of eccentric (some say charming) rules and regulations and by an arcane vocabulary unfamiliar to ordinary mortals. "Heads of house" are heads of college – whether they be "Masters", "Provosts", "Principals", "Presidents" or "Wardens" – and most of them are elected by the "Fellows", graduates or senior members with teaching responsibilities. "The Other Place" is Oxford, "bedders" are college domestics and "porters" wear bowler hats and keep good order. There are **three terms** – Michaelmas (Oct–Dec), Lent (Jan–March) and Easter (April–June) – and the students' biggest annual knees-up, the "May balls", are held in June.

Cambridge is an extremely compact place, and you can **walk** round the centre, visiting the most interesting colleges, in an afternoon. A more thorough exploration, covering more of the colleges, a visit to the fine art of the Fitzwilliam Museum and a leisurely afternoon on a **punt**, will however take at least a couple of days. If possible, avoid coming in high summer, when the students are replaced by hordes of sightseers and posses of foreign-language students, though you can still miss the crowds by getting up early – the tourists only start to appear in numbers from around 10am. Faced with such crowds, the more popular colleges have restricted their opening times and several have introduced admission charges. Bear in mind, too, that during the exam period (late April to early June), most colleges close their doors to the public at least some of the time.

Some history

Tradition has it that Cambridge was founded in the late 1220s by scholastic refugees from Oxford, who fled the town after one of their number was lynched by hostile townsfolk – though the first proper college wasn't founded until 1271. Rivalry has existed between the two institutions ever since – epitomized by the annual Boat Race on the River Thames (see p.602) – while internal tensions between "**town and gown**" have inevitably plagued a place where, from the late fourteenth century onwards, the university has tended to control local life. The first (but by no means the last) rebellion against the scholars occurred during the Peasants' Revolt of 1381, and had to be put down with armed troops by the Bishop of Norwich.

In the sixteenth century, Cambridge became a centre of **church reformism**, educating some of the most famous Protestant preachers in the country, including Cranmer, Latimer and Ridley, all of whom were martyred in Oxford by Mary Tudor. Later, during the Civil War, Cambridge once again found itself at the centre of events: **Oliver Cromwell** was both a graduate of Sidney Sussex and the local MP, though the university itself was largely Royalist. After the Restoration, the university regained most of its privileges, but by the eighteenth century it was in the doldrums, better known, as Byron put it, for its "din and drunkenness" than for its academic record.

In Victorian times, the university finally lost its ancient **privileges** over the town, which was expanding rapidly thanks to the arrival of the railway. The town's population quadrupled between 1800 and 1900 and meanwhile the university expanded too, with the number of students increasing by leaps and bounds following the broadening of the curriculum to include new subjects such as natural science and history. More recently, change has been much slower in coming, particularly when it comes to **equality of the sexes**. The first two women's colleges were founded in the 1870s, but it was only in 1947 that women were actually awarded degrees, and one or two colleges held out against accepting women students until the 1980s. In the meantime, the city and university had been acquiring a reputation as a **high-tech centre** of excellence, what locals refer to half-seriously as "Silicon Fen". Cambridge has always been in the vanguard of scientific research – its alumni have garnered no less than ninety Nobel prizes – and it has now become a major international player in the lucrative electronic communications industry.

Arrival

Cambridge **train station** is a mile or so southeast of the city centre, off Hills Road. It's an easy but tedious twenty-minute walk into the centre, or take shuttle bus #3, which runs to downtown Emmanuel Road every ten minutes or so (less frequently on Sun). The **bus station** is centrally located on Drummer Street, right by Christ's Pieces – and Emmanuel Road. **Stansted**, London's third airport, is just thirty miles south of Cambridge on the M11; there are hourly trains from the airport to the city, and regular bus services too. Arriving by **car**, you'll find much of the city centre closed to traffic and on-street parking well-nigh impossible – for a day-trip, at least, the best option is a **Park-and-Ride** car park; they are signposted on all major approaches.

Messing about on the water

Punting is the quintessential Cambridge activity, though it's a good deal harder than it looks. First-timers find themselves zigzagging across the water and "punt jams" are very common on the stretch of the Cam beside the Backs in summer. **Punt rental** is available at several points, including the boatyard at Mill Lane (beside the Silver Street bridge), at Magdalene Bridge, and at the Garret Hostel Lane bridge at the back of Trinity College. It costs around £10 an hour (and most places charge a deposit), with up to six people in each punt. If you find it all too daunting you can always hire a **chauffeur punt** from any of the rental places; this works out at about a fiver a head.

Cambridge is also famous for its **rowing clubs**, which are clustered along the north bank of the river across from Midsummer Common. For their convenience, this stretch of water is punt-free. The most important inter-college races are the **May Bumps**, which, confusingly, take place in June.

Information and getting around

Cambridge **tourist office** is conveniently situated in the ornate former public library on Wheeler Street, off King's Parade (April–Oct Mon–Fri 10am–5.30pm, Sat 10am–5pm, Sun 11am–4pm; Nov–March Mon–Fri 10am–5.30pm, Sat 10am–5pm; information ⓣ09065/862526 premium line; accommodation bookings ⓣ01223/457581, ⓦwww.tourismcambridge.com). They issue city maps, have lots of leaflets on local attractions and sell an in-depth guide to the city (£5) as well as a mini-guide for just 50p. They can also help with accommodation (see below). Currently, the best source of **information** on entertainment is the *Cambridge Agenda*, a free bi-monthly magazine with details of upcoming events; it's available at the tourist office and larger bookshops. There are, however, plans to launch a much more detailed listings magazine.

The city centre is small enough to walk round comfortably, so apart from getting to and from the train station, you shouldn't have to use the city's buses. On the other hand, cycling is an enjoyable way of getting around and has long been extremely popular with locals and students alike. **Bike rental** outlets are dotted all over town (see p.614), including a couple of places handy for the train station. When and wherever you leave your bike, padlock it to something immovable as bike theft is commonplace. For a more focused direction to your roamings, the tourist office runs very popular **walking tours** of the centre (1–4 daily; 2hr; £7.85; guided tours number ⓣ01223/457574). Admittedly, they're expensive but they do include entrance to at least one college that normally charges for the privilege. Book well in advance in summer. The other high-profile tour is operated by **City Sightseeing** (ⓣ01708/866000, ⓦwww.city-sightseeing.com), whose hop-on, hop-off, open-topped double-decker buses cruise round the town daily between 10am and 4pm; buses turn up every thirty minutes in winter, fifteen in the summer and a 24-hour ticket costs £7.50. Tickets are on sale from the driver, selected hotels and from the City Sightseeing Tourism Centre in the train station.

Accommodation

Cambridge is short of central accommodation and those few **hotels** that do occupy prime locations are expensive. That said, Chesterton Lane and its continuation, Chesterton Road, the busy street running east from the top of

Magdalene Street, has several reasonably priced hotels and guest houses. There are lots of **B&Bs** on the outskirts of town, with several in the vicinity of the train station, and it's here you'll also find the **youth hostel**. In high season, when vacant rooms are often thin on the ground, the tourist office's efficient **accommodation booking service** can be very useful (Ⓣ01223/457581, Ⓔaccommodationbookings@cambridge.gov.uk).

Hotels, guest houses and B&Bs

Arundel House 53 Chesterton Rd Ⓣ01223/367701, Ⓦwww.arundelhousehotels.co.uk. A converted row of late-Victorian houses overlooking the river and Jesus Green makes for one of the better mid-range B&B choices. Neat and tidy rooms with mundanely modern furnishings. Breakfasts are good. ⑥

Benson House 24 Huntingdon Rd Ⓣ01223/311594, Ⓔbensonhouse@btconnect.com. Pleasant, well-kept guest house in a demure brick house about five minutes' walk north from the Magdalene Bridge near New Hall College. Five rooms, three en suite. ③

Cambridge Garden House Moat House Granta Place, Mill Lane Ⓣ01223/259988, Ⓦwww.moathousehotels.com. Disregard the clumsy name, for this is arguably Cambridge's best central hotel, set in its own gardens with a fine riverside location, rooms with balconies, indoor pool and health club. ⑧

Crowne Plaza Cambridge Downing St Ⓣ01223/464466, Ⓦwww.cambridge.crowneplaza.com. Immaculately tailored behind a dignified facade, this sleek and slick hotel is first-rate. The foyer is adventurously designed and the rooms are resolutely modern in efficient chain-hotel style. Great central location too. ⑥

De Vere University Arms Regent St Ⓣ01223/351241, Ⓦwww.devereonline.co.uk. This chain hotel is a bit of a mixed bag with a brutal modern wing glued onto an older, grander brick mansion of Victorian provenance. Standard issue furnishings and fittings, but handy location, overlooking Parker's Piece, on the south side of the city centre. ⑨

Lensfield 53 Lensfield Rd Ⓣ01223/355017, Ⓦwww.lensfieldhotel.co.uk. Well-kept, family-owned hotel on the ring road, just round the corner from the Fitzwilliam Museum, with thirty unassuming rooms. ⑥

Netley Lodge 112 Chesterton Rd Ⓣ01223/363845. Cosy B&B in a Victorian town house, a manageable one-mile walk from the centre. Three attractively furnished bedrooms, one en suite. No credit cards. ②

Regent 41 Regent St Ⓣ01223/351470, Ⓦwww.regenthotel.co.uk. Small-scale, recently refurbished hotel in an old brick town house within easy walking distance of the centre, beside Parker's Piece. The thirty-odd rooms are decorated in an efficient modern style. ⑥

Royal Cambridge Trumpington St Ⓣ01223/351631, Ⓦwww.forestdale.com. One of the city's more polished hotels, occupying a rehashed Georgian terrace. The conversion is rather heavy-handed, and the furniture and fittings look too chain-like to be at ease, but no quibbles about the location, just down from the Fitzwilliam Museum. ⑥

Sleeperz Station Rd Ⓣ01223/304050, Ⓦwww.sleeperz.com. This popular hotel is in an imaginatively converted granary warehouse, right outside the train station. Most of the rooms are bunk-style affairs done out in the manner of a ship's cabin, and there are a few doubles too. All rooms are en suite, with shower and TV. ②

Worth House 152 Chesterton Rd Ⓣ01223/316074, Ⓦwww.worth-house.co.uk. Pleasant B&B in a tastefully upgraded Victorian house, about twenty minutes' walk from the centre. Two bedrooms only, both en suite. Very recommendable. ③

Hostels and campsites

Cambridge YHA 97 Tenison Rd Ⓣ0870/770 5742, Ⓔcambridge@yha.org.uk. This well-equipped hostel has laundry and self-catering facilities, a cycle store, a games room and a small courtyard garden. It's close to the train station – Tenison Road is a right turn a couple of hundred yards down Station Road. Dorm beds £16.

Cherry Hinton Caravan Club Site Lime Kiln Road, Cherry Hinton Ⓣ01223/244088. Three miles east of the city centre in the village of Cherry Hinton, this pleasantly landscaped camping and caravan site spreads over five acres. Closed Jan & Feb.

YMCA Queen Anne House, Gonville Place Ⓣ01223/356998. Central location on the south side of Parker's Piece – turn right a quarter of a mile east from the junction of Drummer Street and Emmanuel Road. Offers singles (£23) and twins (£37), with breakfast included in the price, but very busy during summer – book well in advance. ①

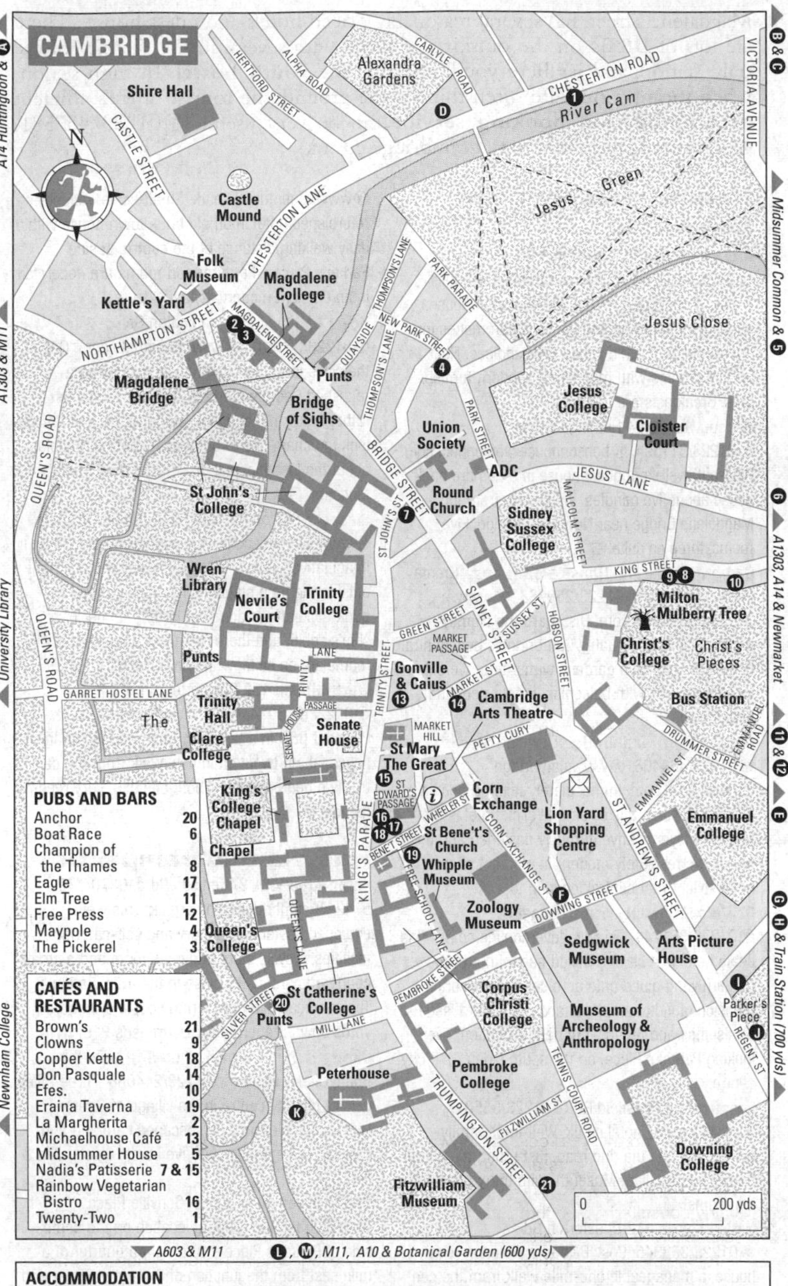

ACCOMMODATION

Arundel House Hotel	D	Crown Plaza Cambridge	F	Lensfield	L	Sleeperz	H
Benson House	A	De Vere University Arms	I	Netley Lodge	B	Worth House	C
Cambridge Garden House	K			Regent	J	YMCA	E
Cambridge YHA	G			Royal Cambridge	M		

The City

Cambridge's main shopping street is Bridge Street, which becomes Sidney Street, St Andrew's Street and finally Regent Street; the other main thoroughfare is the procession of St John's Street, Trinity Street, King's Parade and Trumpington Street. The university developed on the land west of this latter route along the banks of the Cam, and now forms a continuous half-mile parade of **colleges** from Magdalene to Peterhouse, with sundry others scattered about the periphery. The **Fitzwilliam Museum**, with easily the city's finest art collection, is just along Trumpington Street south of Peterhouse. The account below starts with **King's College**, whose chapel is the university's most celebrated attraction, and covers the rest of the town in a broadly clockwise direction.

King's College

Henry VI founded **King's College** (ⓣ01223/331212) in 1441, but he was disappointed with his initial efforts, so four years later he cleared away half of medieval Cambridge to make room for a much grander foundation. His plans were ambitious, but the Wars of the Roses – and bouts of royal insanity – intervened and by the time of his death in 1471 very little had been finished. Indeed, work on Henry's **Great Court** hadn't even started and the site remained empty for three hundred years. The present complex – facing King's Parade from behind a long stone screen – is largely neo-Gothic, built in the 1820s to a design by William Wilkins. However, Henry's workmen did start on the college's finest building, the much celebrated **King's College Chapel** (term time Mon–Fri 9.30am–3.30pm, Sat 9.30am–3.15pm, Sun 1.15–2.15pm; rest of year Mon–Sat 9.30am–4.30pm, Sun 10am–5pm; £3.50), on the north side of today's Great Court. Committed to canvas by Turner and Canaletto, and eulogized in three sonnets by Wordsworth, it's now best known for its **boys' choir**, whose members process across the college grounds during term time in their antiquated garb to sing evensong (Tues–Sat at 5.30pm) and carols on Christmas Eve. Begun in 1446 and over sixty years in the making, the chapel is an extraordinary building. **From the outside**, it seems impossibly slender, its streamlined buttresses channelling up to a dainty balustrade and four spiky turrets, but the exterior was, in a sense at least, a happy accident – its design predicated by the carefully composed interior. Here, in the final flowering of the Gothic style, the mystery of the Christian faith was expressed by a long, uninterrupted **nave** flooded with kaleidoscopic patterns of light filtering in through copious stained-glass windows. Paid for by Henry VIII, the **stained glass** was largely the work of Flemish glaziers, with the lower windows portraying scenes from the New Testament and the Apocrypha, and the upper

College admission charges and opening times

All of the more visited colleges now impose an **admission charge**, partly to control the number of tourists and partly to raise cash. It is, however, a creeping trend, so don't be surprised if other, lesser known colleges follow suit. **Opening times** are fairly consistent throughout the year, though there are sporadic term-time variations especially at the weekend. It's also worth noting that during the exam season, which stretches from late April to early June, all the colleges have periods when they are closed to the public. Where no opening hours are given, you're usually free to tour the grounds at any time during the day. For more specific information, call the relevant college; **phone numbers** are given in the text.

windows displaying the Old Testament. Henry VIII also paid for the intricately carved wooden **choir screen**, one of the earliest examples of Italian Renaissance woodcarving in England, but the **choir stalls** beyond date from the 1670s. Above the **altar** hangs Rubens' *Adoration of the Magi*. Finally, an exhibition in the **chantries** puts more historical flesh on Henry's grand plans.

Like Oxford's New College, King's enjoyed an exclusive supply of students from one of the country's public schools – in this case, Eton – and until 1851 claimed the right to award its students degrees without taking any examinations. The first non-Etonians were only accepted in 1873. Times have changed since those days, and, if anything, King's is now one of the more progressive colleges, having been one of the first to admit women in 1972. Among its most famous alumni are E.M. Forster, who described his experiences in *Maurice*, film director Derek Jarman, poet Rupert Brooke and John Maynard Keynes, whose economic theories did much to improve the college's finances when he became the college bursar.

From King's Parade to Clare College

King's Parade, originally the medieval High Street, is inevitably dominated by King's College and Chapel, but the higgledy-piggledy shops opposite are an attractive foil to William Wilkins's architectural screen. At the northern end of King's Parade is **St Mary the Great** (daily 9am–6pm except during services; free), the university's pet church, a sturdy Gothic structure dating from the fifteenth century. Its tower (Mon–Sat 9.30am–4.30pm, Sun 12–4.30pm; £2) offers a good overall view of the colleges and a bird's-eye view of **Market Hill**, east of the church, where food and bric-a-brac stalls are set out daily. Opposite the church stands **Senate House**, an exercise in Palladian classicism by James Gibbs, and the scene of graduation ceremonies on the last Saturday in June, when champagne corks fly around the rabbit-fur collars and black gowns. It's not usually open to the public, though you can wander around the quad if the gate is open.

The northern continuation of King's Parade is Trinity Street, a short way along which, on the left, is the main entrance to **Gonville and Caius College** (Ⓣ01223/332400), known simply as Caius (pronounced "keys"), after the sixteenth-century co-founder John Keys, who latinized his name, as was then the custom with men of learning. The design of the college owes much to Keys, who placed a gate on three sides of two adjoining courts, each representing a different stage on the path to academic enlightenment: the **Gate of Humility**, through which the student entered the college, now stands in the Fellows' Garden; the **Gate of Virtue**, sporting the female figures of Fame and Wealth, marks the entrance to Caius Court; while the exquisite **Gate of Honour**, capped with sundials and decorated with classical motifs, leads to Senate House Passage and on to Senate House.

Senate House Passage continues west beyond the Gate of Honour to Trinity Lane and **Trinity Hall** (Ⓣ01223/332500) – not to be confused with Trinity College – where the Elizabethan library retains several of its original chains, designed to prevent students from purloining the texts. A few metres to the south is the much more diverting **Clare College** (daily 10am–5pm; £2; Ⓣ01223/333200). One of seven colleges founded, rather surprisingly, by women, its plain period-piece courtyards, completed in the early eighteenth century, lead to one of the most picturesque of all the bridges over the Cam, **Clare Bridge**. Beyond lies the Fellows' Garden, one of the loveliest college gardens open to the public (times as college). Back at the entrance to Clare, it's a few metres more to the North Gate of King's College, beside the chapel (see previous page).

Trinity

Trinity College, on Trinity Street (daily 10am–4.30pm; £2; ☎01223/338400), is the largest of the Cambridge colleges and to ram home the point it also has the largest courtyard. It comes as little surprise then that its list of famous alumni is longer than any other college: literary greats, including Dryden, Byron, Tennyson and Vladimir Nabokov; the Cambridge spies Blunt, Burgess and Philby; two prime ministers, Balfour and Baldwin; William Thackeray, Isaac Newton, Lord Rutherford, Vaughan Williams, Pandit Nehru, Bertrand Russell and Ludwig Wittgenstein, not to mention a trio of (much less talented) royals, Edward VII, George VI and Prince Charles.

A statue of Henry VIII, who founded the college in 1546, sits in majesty over Trinity's **Great Gate**, his sceptre replaced with a chair leg by a student wit. Beyond lies the vast asymmetrical expanse of **Great Court**, which displays a fine range of Tudor buildings, the oldest of which is the fifteenth-century clocktower – the annual race against its midnight chimes is now common currency thanks to the film *Chariots of Fire*. The centrepiece of the court is the delicate fountain, in which, legend has it, Lord Byron used to bathe naked with his pet bear – the college forbade students from keeping dogs.

To get through to **Nevile's Court** – where Newton first calculated the speed of sound – you must pass through "the screens", a passage separating the Hall from the kitchens, a common feature of Oxbridge colleges. The west end of Nevile's Court is enclosed by the university's most famous building after King's College Chapel, the **Wren Library** (term time Mon–Fri noon–2pm, Sat 10.30am–12.30pm; rest of year Mon–Fri noon–2pm; free). Viewed from the outside, it's impossible to appreciate the scale of the interior thanks to Wren's clever device of concealing the internal floor level. In contrast to many modern libraries, natural light pours into the white stuccoed interior, which contrasts wonderfully with the dark lime-wood bookcases, also Wren-designed and housing numerous valuable manuscripts including Milton's *Lycidas*, Wittgenstein's journals and A.A. Milne's *Winnie the Pooh*.

St John's

Next door, **St John's College**, on St John's Street (daily 10am–5pm; £2; ☎01223/338600), sports a grandiloquent Tudor gatehouse, distinguished by the coat of arms of the founder, Lady Margaret Beaufort, the mother of Henry VII, held aloft by two spotted, mythical beasts. Beyond, three successive courts lead to the river, but there's an excess of dull reddish brickwork here – enough for Wordsworth, who lived above the kitchens on F staircase, to describe the place as "gloomy". The arcade on the far side of Third Court leads through to the **Bridge of Sighs**, a chunky, covered bridge built in 1831 but in most respects very unlike its Venetian namesake. The bridge is best viewed either from a punt or from the much older, more stylish Wren-designed bridge a few metres to the south. The Bridge of Sighs links the old college with the fanciful nineteenth-century **New Court**, a crenellated neo-Gothic extravaganza topped by a feast of pinnacles and a central tower – hence its nickname "the wedding cake".

From the Round Church to Magdalene

Back on St John's Street, it's a few seconds' walk to Bridge Street and the **Round Church** (June–Sept Tues–Sat 10am–5pm, Sun & Mon 1–5pm; Oct–May daily 1–4pm; free), built in the twelfth century on the model of the Holy Sepulchre in Jerusalem. It's a curious-looking structure, squat with an ill-considered late medieval extension to the rear, but the Norman pillars of the original church remain, overseen by sturdy arcading and a ring of finely carved faces. The church is also the starting point for Christian heritage walks around the city (Feb–Nov Wed 11am, Sun 2.30pm; £3 recommended donation; ⓣ01223/311602).

Set back from the road, down a footpath beside the church, is the **Union Society**, a bastion of male-dominated debating culture, founded in 1815 and finally opened to women in the 1960s. The society likes to think of itself as a miniature House of Commons – its debating chamber is designed as such – and its debates continue to attract many of the leading politicians and speakers of the day. These are presided over by the Union's officers, who tend to be made up of the university's more ambitious, conservative elements. In the normal scheme of things, election to the Union presidency leads about twenty years later to a place in Cabinet – the last Tory administration barely contained a minister who hadn't been Union president.

Saving nearby Jesus College till later (see below), it only takes a minute or two to stroll up from the Round Church to **Magdalene Bridge**, the site of the old Roman ford. Just beyond is **Magdalene College** (ⓣ01223/332100) – pronounced "maudlin" – which was founded as a hostel by the Benedictines, became a university college in 1542 and was the last of the colleges to admit women, finally succumbing in 1988. Here, the main focus of attention is the **Pepys Building** (Nov & mid-Jan to mid-March Mon–Sat 2.30–3.30pm; late April to Aug Mon–Sat 11.30am–12.30pm & 2.30–3.30pm; free), in the second of the college's ancient courtyards. Samuel Pepys, a Magdalene student, bequeathed his entire library to the college, where it has been displayed ever since in its original red-oak bookshelves – though his famous diary, which also now resides here, was only discovered in the nineteenth century.

Castle Street

Cross busy Chesterton Lane at the top of Magdalene Street and you'll reach two of the city's less visited attractions, sandwiched together at the foot of **Castle Street**. These are the **Folk Museum**, 2–3 Castle St (April–Aug Tues–Sun 1.30am–4.30pm; Sept–March Tues–Sun 2–4pm; £2.50), with a collection of domestic items from the seventeenth century onwards, and **Kettle's Yard** (gallery Tues–Sun 11.30–5pm; house Tues-Sun 1.30–4.30pm; free), a deceptively spacious open-plan conversion of some old slum dwellings, originally owned by the art critic Jim Ede. The gallery here holds an enjoyable collection of paintings, including many by the St Ives primitivist Alfred Wallis, and has an imaginative programme of exhibitions featuring contemporary artists.

A little further up Castle Street, a short, signposted footpath leads to the grassy mound which is all that remains of **Cambridge Castle**. Climb it for the view over the city centre.

Jesus

Back down Magdalene Street and Bridge Street, the first left after the Round Church takes you to **Jesus College** (ⓣ01223/339339), whose intimate cloisters are reminiscent of a monastery. This is not too surprising as the Bishop of Ely founded the college on the grounds of a suppressed Benedictine nunnery in 1496. The main red-brick gateway is approached via a distinctive walled walkway strewn with bicycles and known as "the Chimney". Beyond, much of the ground plan of the nunnery has been preserved, especially around **Cloister Court**, the prettiest of the college's courtyards, dripping with ivy and overflowing hanging baskets. Entered from the court, the college **chapel** occupies the former priory chancel and looks like a medieval parish church; it was imaginatively restored in the nineteenth century, using ceiling designs by William Morris and Pre-Raphaelite stained glass. The poet Samuel Taylor Coleridge was the college's most famously bad student, absconding in his first year to join the Light Dragoons, and returning only to be kicked out for a combination of bad debts and unconventional opinions.

Sidney Sussex and Christ's College

Near Jesus, Malcolm Street cuts off Jesus Lane to reach King Street, from where it's a short stroll through to **Sidney Sussex College** (☎01223/338800), whose sombre, mostly mock-Gothic facade glowers over Sidney Street. Oliver Cromwell studied here and, in 1960, his skull was brought to the college and buried in a secret location in the pint-sized ante-chapel. The adjacent **chapel** is long and slender with a fancy marble floor, a hooped roof and oodles of Baroque wood panelling.

Just to the south of Sidney Sussex, on St Andrew's Street, you hit the hustle and bustle of the town's central shopping area, dominated by the **Lion Yard** shopping centre. This was one of the few town-planning mistakes in the centre of Cambridge, a clumsy modern structure that rumbles along **Petty Cury**, formerly a cobbled curve of leaning half-timbered houses. Aesthetic relief is, however, close at hand, just opposite Lion Yard, in the turreted gateway of **Christ's College** (☎01223/334900), which features the coat of arms of the founder, Lady Margaret Beaufort, who also founded St John's. Passing through First Court you come to the Fellows' Building, attributed to Inigo Jones, whose central arch gives access to the **Fellows' Garden** (Mon–Fri 10am–noon; free). The poet John Milton is said to have either painted or composed beneath the garden's elderly mulberry tree, though there's no definite proof that he did either; Christ's other famous undergraduate was Charles Darwin, who showed little academic promise and spent most of his time hunting. If you continue walking through the college, you come to its modern adjunct, Denys Lasdun's concrete pyramidal accommodation block, dubbed "the typewriter".

Emmanuel College

A little further along St Andrew's Street is **Emmanuel College** (☎01223/334200), whose stolid Neoclassical facade hides a neat and trim Front Court, where the college **chapel** was designed by Wren in a simple Classical style, its wood-panelled nave set beneath a fancy stucco ceiling. The college was founded in 1584 to train a new generation of Protestant clergy following the Reformation. Emmanuel men were numbered among the Pilgrims who settled New England, which not only explains the derivation of the place name Cambridge in Massachusetts but also accounts for Harvard University – **John Harvard**, another alumnus, is remembered by a memorial window in the chapel.

Downing Street and the museums

Opposite Emmanuel, **Downing Street** and its continuation **Pembroke Street** link St Andrew's and Trumpington streets. To either side is a rambling assortment of large, mostly Victorian buildings, in parts of which are a group of scientific and specialist museums. Each museum is connected to one of the university faculties and forms an important resource for students, but is also open to the public. First up, on the left, is the **Sedgwick Geology Museum** (Mon–Fri 9am–1pm & 2–5pm, Sat 10am–1pm; free), which displays fossils and skeletons of dinosaurs, reptiles and mammals, plus the oldest geological collection in the world. In the same complex is the **Museum of Archeology and Anthropology** (Tues–Sat 2–4.30pm; free), which is probably the pick of the bunch for the non-specialist, covering the development of the city from prehistoric times to the nineteenth century and, better still, holding a superb ethnographical gallery. This is centred on a soaring fifty-foot native totem pole and many of the exhibits derive from the "cabinets of curiosities" collected by eighteenth-century explorers. Several pieces were gathered on Captain Cook's first voyage to the South Pacific between 1768 and 1771.

A little further down – and on the opposite side of – Downing Street is the **Museum of Zoology** (Mon–Fri 10am–4.45pm; free), some of whose exhibits were donated by Darwin. Next up, with its entrance round the corner on Free School Lane, is the **Whipple Museum of the History of Science** (Mon–Fri 1.30–4.30pm; free), crammed with hundreds of scientific instruments from the fourteenth century onwards.

St Catherine's and Corpus Christi

There are four more town-centre colleges clustered at the west end of Pembroke Street, around the foot of King's Parade and the top of Trumpington Street. On the west side of King's Parade is **St Catherine's College** (☎01223/338300) – popularly known as "Catz" – which was founded by the provost of King's in 1473. In contrast to King's, its glamorous neighbour, the Principal Court here is a cheerless affair, whose dour, heavy-duty brick buildings mirror the college's relative impecuniousness – in 1880 St Catherine's was so broke that it was nearly forced to close. Much more enticing is **Corpus Christi College** (☎01223/338000), just across King's Parade, founded by two of the town's guilds in 1352. Ignore the first court and instead head north into **Old Court**, which dates from the foundation of the college and is where Christopher Marlowe wrote *Tamburlaine* before graduating in 1587. The college library, on the south side, contains a priceless collection of Anglo-Saxon manuscripts, while the north side is linked by a gallery to **St Bene't's Church**, which served as the college chapel, but is of much earlier Saxon origin. Inside, Thomas Hobson's Bible is exhibited in a glass case; Hobson was the owner of a Cambridge livery stable, where he would only allow customers to take the horse nearest the door – hence "Hobson's choice".

Queens'

Nearby **Queens' College** (daily 10am–4.30pm; £1.30; ☎01223/335511), accessed through the gate on Queens' Lane, just off Silver Street, is the most popular college with university applicants, and it's not difficult to see why. In the **Old Court** and the **Cloister Court**, Queens' possesses two fairy-tale Tudor courtyards, with the first of the two the perfect illustration of the original collegiate ideal with kitchens, library, chapel, hall and rooms all set around a tiny green. Cloister Court is flanked by the Long Gallery of the President's Lodge, the last remaining half-timbered building in the university, and, in its southeast corner, by the tower where Erasmus is thought to have beavered away during his four years here, probably from 1510 to 1514. Be sure to pay a visit to the college **Hall**, off the screens passage between the two courts, which holds mantel tiles by William Morris, and portraits of Erasmus and one of the college's co-founders, Elizabeth Woodville, wife of Edward IV. Equally eye-catching is the wooden **Mathematical Bridge** over the Cam (visible for free from the Silver Street Bridge), a copy of the mid-eighteenth-century original which, it was claimed, would stay in place even if the nuts and bolts were removed.

Pembroke and Peterhouse

Doubling back to Trumpington Street, **Pembroke College** (☎01223/338100) contains Wren's first ever commission, the college **chapel**, paid for by his Royalist uncle, erstwhile Bishop of Ely and a college fellow, in thanks for his deliverance from the Tower of London after seventeen years' imprisonment. It holds a particularly fine, though modern, stained-glass east window and a delicate fifteenth-century marble relief of St Michael and the Virgin, the product of an unusually skilled early English workshop. Outside the library there's a statue of a toga-clad William Pitt the Younger, who entered the college at 15 and was prime minister ten years later. Pitt is just one of a long list of college alumni, which includes poets Edmund Spenser, Thomas Gray and Ted Hughes.

Across the street and just along from Pembroke is the oldest and smallest of the colleges, **Peterhouse** (☎01223/338200), founded in 1284. Few of the original buildings have survived, the principal exception being the thirteenth-century **Hall**, entered from the main court, whose interior was remodelled by William Morris. As at Corpus Christi, Peterhouse used the church next door – in this case Little St Mary's – as the college chapel, until the present one, a sterling, somewhat overblown structure, was plonked in the main court in 1632.

The Fitzwilliam Museum

Of all the museums in Cambridge, the **Fitzwilliam Museum**, on Trumpington Street (Tues–Sat 10am–5pm, Sun 2.15–5pm; free), stands head and shoulders above the rest. The building itself is a splendidly grandiloquent interpretation of Neoclassicism, built in the mid-nineteenth century to house the vast collection bequeathed by Viscount Fitzwilliam in 1816. Since then, the museum has been bequeathed a string of private collections, most of which are focused on a particular specialism. Consequently, the Fitzwilliam says much about the changing tastes of the British upper class. The **Lower Galleries** contain a wealth of antiquities including Egyptian sarcophagi and mummies, fifth-century BC black- and red-figure Greek vases, plus a bewildering display of European ceramics. Further on, there are sections dedicated to armour, glass and pewterware, medals, portrait miniatures and illuminated manuscripts, and – right at the far end – galleries devoted to Far Eastern applied arts and Korean ceramics.

The **Upper Galleries** concentrate on painting and sculpture with three of the first five rooms containing an eclectic assortment of mostly nineteenth- and early twentieth-century European paintings. Among many, there are works by Picasso, Matisse, Monet, Renoir, Delacroix, Cézanne and Degas. The other two rooms feature British painting, with works by William Blake, Constable and Turner, Hogarth, Reynolds, Gainsborough and Stubbs. Moving on, the Italian section displays paintings by Fra Filippo Lippi and Simone Martini, Titian and Veronese, while Frans Hals and Ruisdael feature in the Flemish section. The post-1945 gallery is packed with a fascinating selection including pieces by the likes of Lucian Freud, David Hockney, Henry Moore, Ben Nicholson and Barbara Hepworth.

To the University Botanic Gardens

Past the Fitzwilliam Museum, turn left along busy Lensfield Road for the **Scott Polar Research Institute** (Tues–Sat 2.30–4pm; free), founded in 1920 in memory of the explorer, Captain Robert Falcon Scott (1868–1912), with displays from the expeditions of various polar adventurers, plus exhibitions on native cultures of the Arctic. There's more general interest near at hand in the shape of the **University Botanic Gardens** (daily: Feb–Oct gardens 10am–6pm, glasshouses 10am–4.30pm; Nov–Jan gardens 10am–4pm, glasshouses 10am–3.30pm; £2.50), whose entrance is on Bateman Street, about 500 yards to the south of Lensfield Road via Panton Street. Founded in 1760 and covering forty acres, the gardens are second only to Kew with glasshouses as well as bountiful outdoor displays. The outdoor beds are mostly arranged by natural order, but there's also a particularly unusual series of chronological beds, showing when different plants were introduced into Britain.

Eating and drinking

Even at Cambridge, students are not the world's greatest restaurant goers, so although the downtown **takeaway** and **café** scene is fine, decent **restaurants** are a little thin on the ground. On any kind of budget, the myriad Italian places – courtesy of Cambridge's large Italian population – will stand you in good stead; otherwise, choose carefully, particularly in the more touristy areas, where quality isn't always all it should be. Happily, Cambridge abounds in excellent **pubs**, and our list rounds up some of the best traditional student and local drinking haunts.

Cafés and restaurants

Brown's 23 Trumpington St. Breezy brasserie with a competent, fairly wide-ranging menu housed in a former hospital outpatients department (the rest of the hospital has become a management institute). The grand setting – all plants and fans – sets the meal off a treat. Inordinately popular, but no reservations – wait in line or at the bar. Moderate.

Clowns 54 King St. Italian-style cappuccino and cakes, sandwiches and snacks, plus newspapers to browse. Off the tourist route and not part of a chain – bonuses in anyone's books.

Copper Kettle 4 King's Parade. Generations of students have whiled away the hours in this resolutely old-fashioned café opposite King's College, sipping coffee, eating pastries and putting the world to rights.

Don Pasquale 12 Market Hill. Great marketside location, with seats on the square for lunchtime diners. Tasty food and an especially good place for a quick pick-me-up espresso and slice of pizza. Inexpensive.

Efes 80 King St ⓣ01223/350491. Intimate Turkish restaurant, with chargrilled meats prepared under your nose and a decent meze selection. Moderate.

Eraina Taverna 2 Free School Lane ⓣ01223/368786. Packed Greek taverna, which satisfies the hungry hordes with huge platefuls of stews and grills, as well as pizzas, curries and a whole host of other menu madness. Try to avoid getting stuck in the basement, though at weekends (when you'll probably have to queue) you'll be lucky to get a seat anywhere. Inexpensive.

La Margherita 15 Magdalene St ⓣ01223/315232. Cheapish and cheerful Italian outfit offering pizzas and pastas as well as standard meat and fish dishes. Inexpensive to moderate.

Michaelhouse Café Trinity St. Vegetarian café serving homemade snacks, salads and sandwiches in the converted St Michael's church, opposite Caius College. Inexpensive.

Midsummer House Midsummer Common ⓣ01223/369299. Lovely riverside restaurant with conservatory, specializing in top-notch French-Mediterranean cuisine. On the south side of the river, beside the footbridge just to the east of Victoria Avenue. Reservations essential. Expensive.

Nadia's Patisserie 11 St John's St. Good sandwich and cake takeaway in the centre, opposite St John's. One of several outlets – there's another at 20 King's Parade.

Rainbow Vegetarian Bistro 9a King's Parade ⓣ01223/321551. Vegetarian restaurant with main courses – ranging from couscous to lasagne and Indonesian *gado-gado* – all for around £7. Good-value breakfasts, and organic wines served with meals. Great location, opposite King's College. Closed Sun. Inexpensive.

Twenty-Two 22 Chesterton Rd ⓣ01223/351880. Consistently the best restaurant in Cambridge, a candlelit town house in which the good-value, fixed-price menu (at around £25) touches all the modern bases. Closed Sun & Mon. Expensive.

Pubs and bars

Anchor Silver St. Very popular riverside tourist haunt with views of the Backs, adjacent punt rental and an outdoor deck.

Champion of the Thames 68 King St. Gratifyingly old-fashioned central pub with decent beer and a student/academic clientele.

Eagle Bene't St. An ancient inn with a cobbled courtyard where Crick and Watson sought inspiration in the 1950s, at the time of their discovery of DNA. It's been tarted up since and gets horribly crowded, but is still worth a pint of anyone's time.

Elm Tree 42 Orchard St. Cosy local with frequent live music, mainly jazz. Just to the north of Parker's Piece and full of furiously smoking refugees from the nearby *Free Press* (see below). Well worth seeking out: to get there, follow Emmanuel Road north off Drummer Street, near the bus station, and take the third turning on the right – it's on the corner with Eden Street.

Free Press 7 Prospect Row. Classic, superbly maintained backstreet local with an admirable no-smoking policy, good beer and fine food. It's located a few yards along the street from the *Elm Tree* – for directions, see opposite.

Maypole 20a Park St. Small, well-kept pub with an invigorating atmosphere. In the centre near the Round Church.

The Pickerel 30 Magdalene St. Once a brothel and one of several pubs competing for the title of the oldest pub in town, the *Pickerel* has a lively atmosphere and offers a good range of beers beneath its low beams.

Entertainment

The **performing arts** scene is at its best during term time, with numerous student **drama** productions, **classical concerts** and **gigs** culminating in the traditional whizzerama of excess following the exam season. That said, the more firmly town-based venues, such as the Corn Exchange, do put on events throughout the year. Apart from the places highlighted below, each college and several churches contribute to the performing arts scene too, with the **King's College choir** being, of course, the most famous attraction (see p.605), though the choral scholars who perform at the chapels of St John's and Trinity are also exceptionally good. For upcoming events, ask for details at the tourist office (see p.602), which issues various listings leaflets and also stocks the *Cambridge Agenda*, a free bi-monthly listings magazine. For advance tickets for most events, pop into the Corn Exchange (see below).

June and July are the busiest times in Cambridge's calendar of **events**. The fortnight of post-exam celebrations, which take place in the first two weeks of June – and are confusingly known as **May Week** – herald the ball and garden-party season, and include boat races, known as the "May Bumps", on the Cam by Midsummer Common. The vaguely hippified **Midsummer Fair**, descendant of the town's famous medieval Stourbridge Fair, discontinued in 1934, takes place in mid-June on Midsummer Common, with bands, theatre and much more besides – all for free. By contrast, you'll have to pay out around £50 for a tent pitch and entry into the three-day **Cambridge Folk Festival** (Ⓦ www.cam-folkfest.co.uk), held annually at the end of July at neighbouring Cherry Hinton, and attracting a wide variety of loosely folk-based acts.

Arts Picture House 38–39 St Andrew's St Ⓣ01223/504444, Ⓦwww.picturehouses.co.uk. Art-house cinema with an excellent, wide-ranging programme.

Boat Race 170 East Rd Ⓣ01223/508533, Ⓦwww.boatrace.co.uk. Lively pub venue for all kinds of music, with gigs every night.

Cambridge Arts Theatre 6 St Edward's Passage, off King's Parade Ⓣ01223/503333, Ⓦwww.cambridgeartstheatre.com. The city's main repertory theatre, founded by John Maynard Keynes, and launching pad of a thousand-and-one famous careers, offers a top-notch range of cutting-edge and classic productions.

Cambridge Corn Exchange Wheeler St Ⓣ01223/357851, Ⓦwww.cornex.co.uk. Revamped nineteenth-century trading hall, now the main city-centre venue for opera, ballet, musicals and comedy as well as regular rock and folk gigs.

Cambridge Modern Jazz Club at Sophbeck Sessions, 14 Tredgold Lane, Napier St Ⓣ01223/722811, Ⓦwww.cambridgejazz.org. East of the city centre, near the Grafton Centre shopping mall, off Newmarket Road, this place attracts top-ranking artists from around the world.

Junction Clifton Rd Ⓣ01223/511511, Ⓦwww.junction.co.uk. Rock, indie, jazz, reggae or soul gigs, plus occasional comedy acts and dance groups at this popular arts and entertainments venue.

Listings

Airport London Stansted Airport ⓣ0870/000 0303, ⓦwww.stansted.co.uk.

Banks and exchanges There are banks all over the city centre, and you can also exchange traveller's cheques at the main post office (see below); at American Express, 25 Sidney St ⓣ01223/345201; and Thomas Cook, in the Grafton Centre ⓣ01223/543000, and at 23 St Andrew's St ⓣ01223/543100.

Bike rental Station Cycles, outside the train station (Mon–Fri 8.30am–6pm, Sat 9am–5pm, Sun 10am–4pm; ⓣ01223/307125); Mikes Bikes, 28 Mill Rd (Mon–Sat 9am–6pm, Sun 10am–4pm; ⓣ01223/312591); and H. Drake, near the train station at 56–60 Hills Rd (Mon–Fri 8.30am–5.30pm; ⓣ01223/363468).

Bookshops Heffers has several outlets with its main branch at 20 Trinity St; Cambridge University Press has a shop at 1 Trinity St; Borders is at 12–13 Market St; and Waterstones at 22 Sidney St. For second-hand books try the shops down St Edward's Passage off King's Parade: G. David, at no.3, is an antiquarian's and hard-back hunter's paradise; the Haunted Bookshop, at no. 9, is better for first editions, travel and illustrated books.

Buses Most city buses pull in at – and depart from – the stops along Emmanuel Street. Close by, at the top of Emmanuel Street, the Drummer Street bus station is for long-distance services. For information on Cambridgeshire bus services, call the information line (ⓣ0870/608 2608), or drop by the Premier Travel Agency, beside the Drummer Street station (ⓣ01223/572300). In addition, Airlinks (ⓣ0870/574 7777) operates direct services to the London airports; and National Express (ⓣ0870/580 8080) runs services to London and other major cities.

Car rental Avis ⓣ01223/212551; Budget ⓣ01223/323838; Europcar ⓣ01223/233644; National ⓣ01223/365438.

Internet Internet Exchange, opposite St Mary the Great church.

Left luggage 24-hour lockers at the train station.

Pharmacies Boots, 28 Petty Cury ⓣ01223/350213; Lloyds, 30 Trumpington St ⓣ01223/359449.

Post office The main office is at 9–11 St Andrew's St (Mon–Sat 9am–5.30pm).

Taxis There are ranks at the train and bus stations. To book, call Diamond ⓣ01223/523523; or Panther ⓣ01223/715715.

Around Cambridge

Within easy reach of Cambridge, across the flat fen landscape, are several absorbing, day-trip destinations. Just south of the city is **Grantchester**, a smart little place that's typical of the villages hereabouts – though the real draw is that you can cycle or punt there through open countryside. To the northeast is **Anglesey Abbey**, a handsome old mansion that holds an outstanding collection of fine and applied art, and, a little further afield, south along the M11, stands the extensive **Duxford Imperial War Museum** with the straggling market town of **Saffron Walden** lying beyond, among the rolling hills of northwest Essex. Horse-racing aficionados will, however, have little truck with all of this, heading straight for **Newmarket**, just thirteen miles to the east of Cambridge.

Grantchester

The pretty little village of **GRANTCHESTER**, replete with thatched cottages and chestnut trees, is just a couple of miles up the River Cam from Cambridge. It's a popular destination on sunny days since it's an easy bike or punt ride away through **Grantchester Meadows** – the signposted cycle route starts at the southern end of Newnham Road. The poet Rupert Brooke, who died in World War I, lodged in the old vicarage here as an undergraduate, penning the much-quoted lines "Stands the Church clock at ten to three? And is there honey still for tea?" The clock in the pub named after Brooke stands permanently at ten to three, though of the three village **pubs**, you're better off heading for the *Red Lion* or the *Green Man*, both sited where the path from Cambridge emerges on the village's main street.

Anglesey Abbey

Anglesey Abbey (house: April–Oct Wed–Sun 1–5pm; gardens: April–June & Sept–Oct Wed–Sun 10.30am–5.30pm, July–Aug daily 10.30am–5.30pm; £6.40, garden only £4; NT), six miles northeast of Cambridge near the village of **Lode**, was actually never an abbey at all, but a priory that suffered the same fate as all such institutions during the Dissolution hammered through by Henry VIII. In its place was built the good-looking mansion-cum-manor house of today whose mullion windows, rough stonework and attenuated chimneys date back to 1600. The house is, however, of less interest than its contents, which feature the Fairhaven collection of paintings and furniture. There's everything here from an Egyptian bronze cat to Ming vases, works by Lorrain, Constable, Cuyp and Gainsborough, all gathered together by the house's last, very wealthy owner, Lord Fairhaven. Fairhaven also transformed the surrounding fenland into a glorious hundred-acre **garden**, dotted with sculptures and urns from his collection.

To get to the abbey from Cambridge, take Stagecoach **bus** #111 or #122.

Duxford Imperial War Museum

Eight miles south of Cambridge, and visible from the M11 – it's next to junction #10 – are the giant hangars of the **Imperial War Museum** (daily: mid-March to late Oct 10am–6pm; late Oct to mid-March 10am–4pm; £8.50; Ⓦwww.iwm.org.uk/duxford), based at Duxford airfield. Throughout World War II, East Anglia was a centre of operations for the RAF and the USAF, with the flat, unobstructed landscape dotted by dozens of airfields. Duxford itself was a Battle of Britain station, equipped with Spitfires, and there's a reconstructed Operations Room in one of the control towers. In total, the museum holds over 150 historic aircraft, a wide-ranging collection of civil and military planes from the Sunderland flying boat to Concorde and the Vulcan B2 bombers, which were used for the first and last time in the 1982 Falklands conflict; the Spitfires remain the most enduringly popular. Most of the planes are kept in full working order and are taken out for a spin several times a year at **Duxford Air Shows**, which attract thousands of visitors. There are usually four air shows a year and tickets cost from £18 to £22.50; advance bookings are strongly recommended (Ⓣ01223/499353).

For details of the free courtesy bus service linking Duxford with Cambridge, call Ⓣ01223/835000.

Saffron Walden

Some twelve miles south of Cambridge, the fenlands are left behind for the hillier landscapes of Uttlesford, the district council's euphemism for the north-west corner of Essex. The main event here is **SAFFRON WALDEN**, a good-looking town that possesses dozens of antique timber-framed houses. There are several particularly fine examples on the main road, but the nicest areas of town to explore are away from the thundering traffic, in the network of alleyways around the **Market Place** and the book and antique shops of **Church Street** just to the north. Many of these old houses sport fancy decorative plasterwork, known as pargeting – the last word on which is provided by the stepped gables of the **Old Sun Inn**, on Church Street and once used by Cromwell as his headquarters. The town's prefix was coined in medieval times when saffron crocuses were cultivated here for their dye and medicinal qualities. You can learn more about this and other aspects of the town's history at the **museum** on Museum Street, off Church Street (March–Oct Mon–Sat 10am–5pm, Sun 2–5pm; Nov–Feb Mon–Sat 10am–4.30pm, Sun 2–4.30pm; £1). Behind the museum are the scant ruins of the twelfth-century **castle**.

The nearest **train station** is Audley End, a couple of miles to the southwest of town off the B1383 (and a good mile from Audley End village). **Buses** are much more convenient, stopping close to the Market Place, where the **tourist office** (April–Oct Mon–Sat 9.30am–5.30pm; Nov–March Mon–Sat 10am–5pm; ⓣ01799/510444, ⓦwww.uttlesford.gov.uk) issues free maps and has plenty of leaflets on local attractions. Saffron Walden is best enjoyed as a day-trip, but there are several **B&Bs**, with one of the best being the *Archway Guest House*, Church Street (ⓣ01799/501500; no cards; ❸), which possesses a large collection of pop memorabilia from the 1960s' jukebox in the entrance hall through to a sports bag signed by none other than Andy Warhol. The forty-bed **youth hostel**, 1 Myddylton Place (ⓣ0870/770 6014, ⓔsaffron@yha.org.uk; closed Nov to mid-April; £10.25), occupies a converted, half-timbered medieval maltings, footsteps from the junction of Bridge and Castle streets. The best **pub** in town is the ancient *Eight Bells*, on Bridge Street.

Audley End House

A mile or so to the west of Saffron Walden – and beyond the village that bears its name – the palatial Jacobean mansion of **Audley End House** (April–Sept Wed–Sun noon–5pm; Oct Sat & Sun 11am–4pm; house & grounds £8, grounds only £4; EH) was built for the Earl of Suffolk at the start of the seventeenth century. A spectacularly lavish building, it was soon the talk of the aristocracy, so much so that Charles II purchased it in 1668, staying here whenever he went to the races at Newmarket. Returned to the Suffolks after the king's death, Audley End was modified on several later occasions, most notably when one of the Suffolks demolished the east wing in 1735 to reduce his overheads. Highlights include the striking wood panelling and plasterwork of the Great Hall and, less ostentatiously, the subtle elegance of Robert Adam's two drawing rooms. English Heritage has worked hard on renovating the **grounds**, which were first laid out by Capability Brown and contain a river, a lake and a splendid flower garden.

To get to Audley End House from Saffron Walden, take the signed byroad that leads west through Audley End village. Confusingly, Audley End train station is about a mile southwest of the village, off the B1383.

Thaxted

THAXTED, eight miles southeast of Saffron Walden, enjoyed its heyday in the fourteenth and fifteenth centuries, when it prospered on the profits of the local cutlery industry. It was during this period that the town's splendid three-tiered, half-timbered **Guildhall** was erected on the marketplace, its beams now twisted with age and leaning at an alarming angle. There are more half-timbered buildings on nearby Stony Lane, which leads to the town's gargantuan **parish church of St John the Baptist**, completed in 1500, its landmark spire reaching 181ft. Gustav Holst (1874–1934) was organist here during his twelve-year stay in Thaxted and it was then that he wrote much of *The Planets* as well as initiating the town's annual music festival, held from mid-June to mid-July (call ⓣ01371/831421 for details).

There's a reasonably regular **bus** service from Saffron Walden to Thaxted (not Sun).

Newmarket

NEWMARKET, thirteen miles east of Cambridge, on springy heathland just over the county border in Suffolk, is famous for just one thing – **horse racing**. According to legend, Boudicca's Iceni were keen on Ben-Hur style chariot-racing, but history gives James I the honour of founding modern horse racing here. James may have started it off, but Charles II brought the sport to prominence, visiting twice a year and bringing the entire royal court – and Nell Gwyn – with him. Two of the country's five flat-racing classics are held at Newmarket, the One Thousand Guineas and the Two Thousand Guineas, both held early in the season, which runs from the middle of April to October.

Coming in from Cambridge, you pass the Rowley Mile Course, named after one of Charles's own steeds. This, as well as the other approach roads, are flanked by bridleways, and in the morning dozens of racehorses exercise along them. Newmarket itself is a one-horse town, with the Georgian Jockey Club, founded in 1752, occupying pride of place on the High Street. Next door is the **National Horse Racing Museum** (mid-April to June, Sept & Oct Tues–Sun 11am–5pm; July & Aug daily 11am–5pm; £4.50), telling you more than you'll ever want to know about the sport. It also offers a variety of guided tours, including trips to the equine pool, a stud and a couple of horse-training yards (for further details, call Ⓣ01638/667333, Ⓦwww.nhrm.co.uk). There are also tours of the prestigious National Stud, a couple of miles southwest of town at the junction of the A1304 and A1303 (March–Sept 1–2 daily; £4.50; reservations on Ⓣ01638/666789, Ⓦwww.nationalstud.co.uk).

Four **buses** an hour make the thirty-minute journey to town from Cambridge and there's also a regular **train** service.

Travel details

Buses

For information on all local and national bus services, contact Traveline Ⓣ0870/608 2608, Ⓦwww.traveline.org.uk.

Cambridge to: Birmingham (3 daily; 3hr 45min); Bury St Edmunds (hourly; 55min); Colchester (7 daily; 2hr 30min); Ely (every 30min; 45 min); Ipswich (daily; 2hr); King's Lynn (2 daily; 1hr 45min); London (hourly; 2hr); Manchester (2 daily; 2hr 20min); Newmarket (every 15min; 20min); Norwich (1 daily; 2hr 50min); Peterborough (hourly; 2hr 20min); Stansted Airport (hourly; 50 min).

Colchester to: Bury St Edmunds (7 daily; 1hr 30min); Cambridge (7 daily; 2hr 30min); Clacton-on-Sea (4 daily; 35 min) Ipswich (hourly; 1 hour); London (3 daily; 2hr 20 min).

Ely to: Cambridge (every 30min; 45 min); King's Lynn (7 daily; 1hr); Newmarket (hourly; 35min); Peterborough (hourly; 1hr 40).

Ipswich to: Aldeburgh (hourly; 1hr 30min); Bury St Edmunds (2 daily; 1hr 30min); Colchester (hourly; 1hr); London (2 daily; 3hr); Peterborough (4 daily; 3hr); Woodbridge (4 hourly; 30min).

Norwich to: Bury St Edmunds (5 daily; 1hr 30min); Cambridge (1 daily; 2hr 50min); Great Yarmouth (every 15min; 30 min); London (5 daily; 3 hr); Peterborough (hourly; 2hr 50min); King's Lynn (hourly; 1hr 45min); Sheringham (every 30min; 1hr 20min); Thetford (every 30min; 1 hr).

Peterborough to: Bury St Edmunds (1 daily; 2hr 25min); Cambridge (hourly; 2hr 20min); Ely (hourly; 1hr 40min); Ipswich (1 daily; 3hr); King's Lynn (hourly; 1hr 10min); London (5 daily; 2hr 20min); Norwich (hourly; 2hr 50min); Nottingham (2 daily; 1hr 40min).

The Norfolk Coasthopper runs from Cromer to King's Lynn – or Hunstanton – via a whole gaggle of towns and villages, including Blakeney, Sheringham, Wells and the Burnhams. Frequencies vary on different stretches of the route and there are more buses in the summer than in the winter, but on the more popular stretches are mostly every half-hour or hour. The operator is Norfolk Green Ⓣ01553/776980.

Trains

For information on all local and national rail services, contact National Rail Enquiries ⓣ08457/484950, ⓦwww.rail.co.uk.

Cambridge to: Audley End (2 hourly; 15min); Bury St Edmunds (8 daily; 40min); Ely (hourly; 15min); Ipswich (6 daily; 1hr 20min); King's Lynn (hourly; 45min); London (every 30min; 1hr); Newmarket (8 daily; 20min); Norwich (hourly; 1hr); Peterborough (hourly; 50min); Stansted Airport (10 daily; 40min); Thetford (hourly; 20–30min).

Colchester to: Clacton-on-Sea (hourly; 40min); Ipswich (2 hourly; 25min); London (2 hourly; 50min); Norwich (hourly; 1hr).

Ely to: King's Lynn (hourly; 30min); Manchester (hourly; 3hr 30min); Nottingham (hourly 1hr 45min); Peterborough (hourly; 30min); Thetford (hourly; 30min).

Ipswich to: Bury St Edmunds (10 daily; 30min); Ely (7 daily; 1hr); Felixstowe (every 1–2hr; 25min); London (every 30min; 1hr 10min); Lowestoft (every 1–2hr; 1hr 30min); Norwich (hourly; 45min); Peterborough (7 daily; 1hr 50min); Woodbridge (every 1–2hr; 15min).

Norwich to: Cromer (every 1–2hr; 50min); Ely (hourly; 50min); Great Yarmouth (hourly; 30min); London (hourly; 2hr); Lowestoft (hourly; 30–45min); Manchester (hourly; 4hr 30min); Nottingham (hourly; 2hr 30min); Peterborough (hourly; 1hr 30min); Sheringham (every 1–2hr; 1hr); Thetford (hourly; 30min).

Peterborough to: Bury St Edmunds (6 daily; 1hr); Cambridge (hourly; 50min); London (2 hourly; 1hr); Manchester (hourly; 3hr); Norwich (hourly; 1hr 30min); Nottingham (hourly; 1hr 10min).

8

The West Midlands and the Peak District

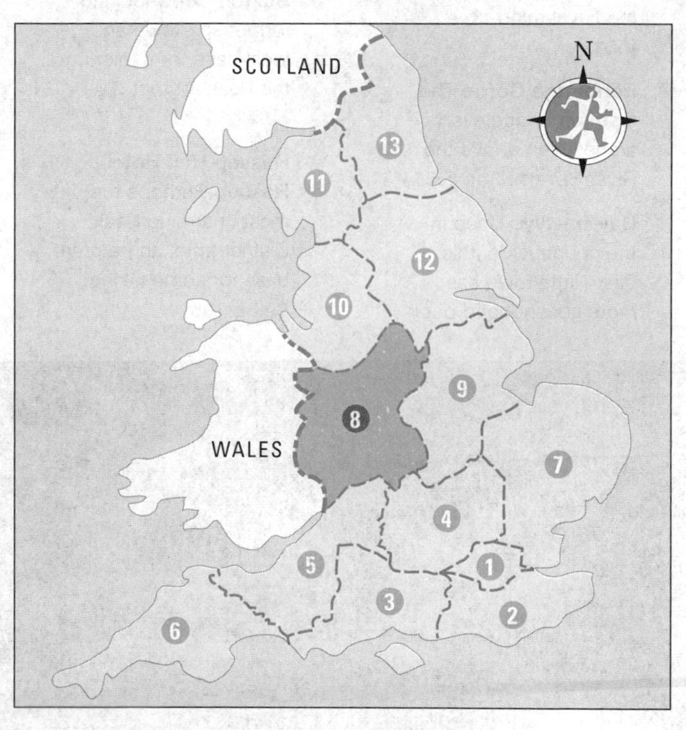

CHAPTER 8

Highlights

* **The theatres, Stratford-upon-Avon** *The* place to see Shakespeare's plays. See p.629

* **Mappa Mundi, Hereford Cathedral** This antique map, dating to around 1300, provides a powerful insight into the medieval mind. See p.643

* **Ironbridge Gorge** The first iron bridge ever arches high above the River Severn. See p.653

* **Hay-on-Wye** Deep in the countryside, this dinky little town has more secondhand bookshops than anywhere else in the world. See p.650

* **Ludlow** A postcard-pretty country town with half-timbered houses and a gaggle of restaurants. See p.665

* **Buxton** Good-looking former spa town and ideal base for exploring the Peak District. See p.692

* **Hassop Hall Hotel, Hassop** Perhaps the most charming Peak District hotel and a great base for some hiking. See p.706

△ Hassop Hall

8

The West Midlands and the Peak District

With justification, the small country towns and untrammelled scenery of the **West Midlands** are the apple of the tourist eye, but there's no disputing the urban epicentre of the region – **Birmingham**, Britain's second city, once the world's greatest industrial metropolis with a slew of factories that powered the Industrial Revolution. Long saddled with a reputation as a culture-hating, car-loving backwater, Birmingham has redefined its image in recent years, initiating some ambitious architectural and environmental schemes, jazzing up its museums and industrial heritage sites and giving itself a higher profile on the nation's cultural map than it's ever had before. It's not an especially good-looking city, it must be admitted, but it does hold several excellent attractions and it's certainly lively, with nightlife encompassing everything from Royal Ballet productions to all-night grooves, and a great spread of restaurants and pubs in between. To some extent change was forced on Birmingham by the decline in its manufacturing base – it lost over a third of its manufacturing jobs between 1974 and 1983 – but things were even worse in the **Black Country**, that knot of industrial towns clinging to the western side of the city. This area has found it difficult to re-route itself through the maze of post-industrialization and more amply fulfils the negative stereotypes once attached to Birmingham. Nonetheless, even here you'll find a few pleasant surprises, in the shape of several excellent museums and galleries.

The **counties** to the south and west of Birmingham and beyond the Black Country – Warwickshire, Worcestershire, Herefordshire and Shropshire – comprise a rural stronghold that maintains an emotional and political distance from the conurbation. The left-wing politics of the big city seem remote indeed when you're in Shrewsbury, but in fact it's only seventy miles from one to the other. For the most part, the four counties constitute a quiet, unassuming stretch of pastoral England whose beauty is rarely dramatic, but whose charms become more evident the longer you stay. Of the four counties, **Warwickshire** is the least obviously scenic, but draws by far the largest number of visitors, for – as the road signs declare at every entry point – this is "Shakespeare Country". The prime target is, of course, **Stratford-upon-Avon**, with its handful of Shakespeare-related sites and world-class theatre, but spare time also for the diverting town of **Warwick**, which has a superb church and a whopping castle, and there's also the magnificent modernity of **Coventry Cathedral**.

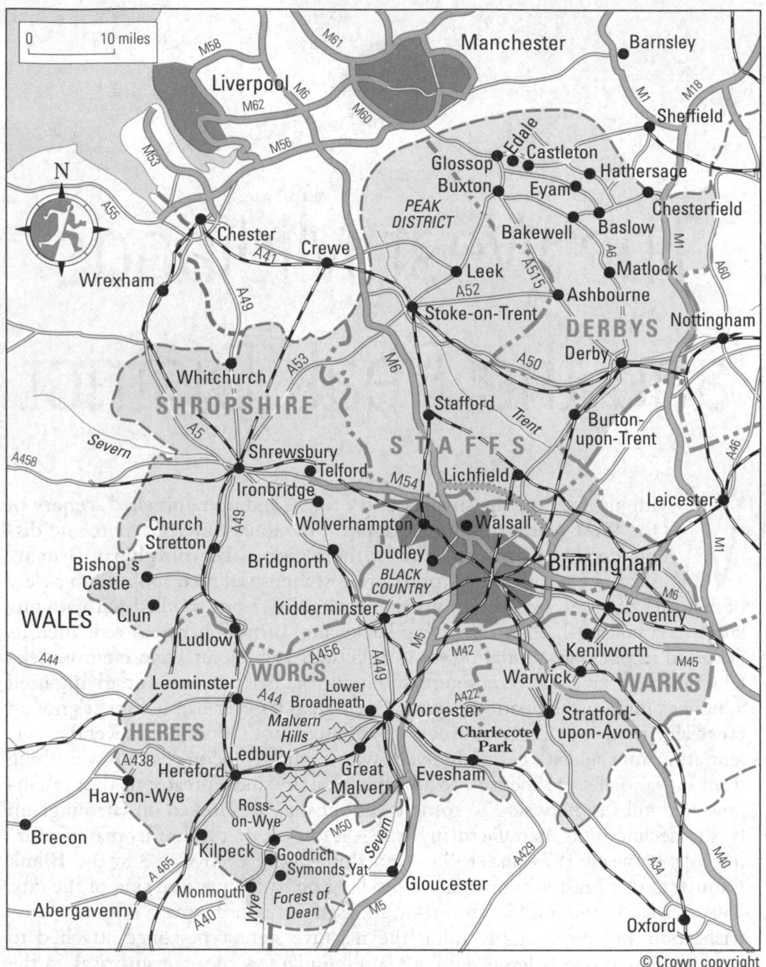

Neighbouring **Worcestershire**, which stretches southwest from the urban fringes of the West Midlands, holds two principal places of interest, **Worcester**, which is graced by a mighty cathedral, and **Great Malvern**, a mannered inland resort spread along the rolling contours of the **Malvern Hills** – prime walking territory. From here, it's west again for **Herefordshire**, a large and sparsely populated county that's home to several charming market towns, most notably picture-postcard **Ledbury** and **Hay-on-Wye**; the latter has the largest concentration of second-hand bookshops in the world. There's also **Hereford**, where the remarkable medieval Mappa Mundi map is displayed, and pocket-sized **Ross-on-Wye**, which is within easy striking distance of an especially scenic stretch of the **Wye River Valley**. Next door, to the north, rural **Shropshire** weighs in with **Ludlow**, one of the region's prettiest towns, awash with antique half-timbered buildings, and the amiable county town of **Shrewsbury**, which is also close to the hiking trails of the **Long Mynd**.

Shropshire has a fascinating industrial history, too, for it was here in the **Ironbridge Gorge** that British industrialists built the world's first iron bridge and pioneered the use of coal as a smelting fuel. These were two key events in the Industrial Revolution and, appropriately, the gorge's industrial heyday is recalled by a phalanx of museums.

To the east of Shropshire, sprawling north of the Birmingham conurbation, is **Staffordshire**, where **Lichfield** makes a good hand of its links with **Samuel Johnson**, while **Stoke-on-Trent** remembers the good times, when its potteries dominated the world market, in an excellent museum and several heritage sites – and factory shops. Beyond lies **Derbyshire**, whose northern reaches incorporate the region's finest scenery in the rough landscapes of the **Peak District National Park**. The latter offers great opportunities for moderately strenuous walks, as well as the diversions of the comely former spa town of **Buxton**, the limestone caverns of **Castleton** and the so-called "Plague Village" of **Eyam**. In addition, there's the grandiose stately pile of **Chatsworth House** and **Haddon Hall**, an exceptionally intact old manor house.

Birmingham, the region's **public transport hub**, is easily accessible by **train** from London Euston, Liverpool, Manchester, Leeds, York and a score of other towns. It is also well served by the National Express **bus** network, with dozens of buses leaving every hour for destinations all over Britain. Local **bus** services are excellent around the West Midlands conurbation and very good in the Peak District, but fade away badly in amongst the villages of Herefordshire and Shropshire.

Stratford-upon-Avon and around

Despite its worldwide fame, **STRATFORD-UPON-AVON** is, at heart, an unassuming market town with an unexceptional pedigree. Its first settlers forded, and later bridged, the River Avon, and developed commercial links with the farmers who tilled the surrounding flatlands. A charter for Stratford's weekly market was granted in the twelfth century, a tradition continued to this day, and the town later became an important stopping-off point for stagecoaches between London, Oxford and the north. Like all such places, Stratford had its clearly defined class system and within this typical milieu John and Mary **Shakespeare** occupied the middle rank, and would have been forgotten long ago had their first son, **William**, not turned out to be the greatest writer ever to use the English language. A consequence of their good fortune is that this ordinary little town is nowadays all but smothered by package-tourist hype and, in the summer at least, its central streets groan under the weight of thousands of tourists. Don't let that deter you: the **Royal Shakespeare Company** offers superb theatre and dodging the multitudes is possible by avoiding the busiest attractions – principally the Birthplace Museum. Moreover, Stratford still has the ability to surprise and delight, whether in the excellence of some of its restaurants or by the gentle river views beside the lovely **Holy Trinity Church**. It is also within easy striking distance of the pleasant house and gardens of **Charlecote Park**.

Arrival, information and getting around

Stratford's **train station** is on the northwestern edge of town, ten minutes' walk from the centre. Now the end of the line, it receives hourly services from Birmingham (Moor Street and Snow Hill stations) and fairly frequent trains from Warwick (for London Paddington and London Marylebone). Local **bus**

services arrive and depart from the central Bridge Street; National Express services and most other long-distance and regional buses pull into the Riverside station on the east side of the town centre, off Bridgeway.

The **tourist office** (Mon–Sat 9.30am–5pm, Sun 10.30am–4.30pm; ⓣ01789/293127, ⓦwww.shakespeare-country.co.uk) is located a couple of minutes' walk from the bus station by the bridge at the junction of Bridgeway and Bridgefoot. They have oodles of information on local attractions and operate an accommodation-booking service (see below), which is very useful during the height of the summer when rooms can be in very short supply. They also issue bus timetables and sell bus tickets and, in addition, sell the all-in ticket for all five **Shakespeare Birthplace Trust** properties (£13), or a **Three In-Town Shakespeare Property Ticket** (£9) for the three Trust properties in the town centre; both tickets are also available from the sites themselves.

The best way to see Stratford is on **foot**, but **City Sightseeing** (ⓣ01789/294466) runs open-topped, double-decker buses around the major sights, a hop-on, hop-off service that costs £7.50 per day.

Accommodation

As one of the most popular tourist destinations in England, Stratford's **accommodation** is a tad pricey and gets booked up well in advance. In peak months, and during the Shakespeare birthday celebrations around April 23, it's pretty much essential to book ahead. The town has a couple of dozen **hotels**, the pick of which occupy old half-timbered buildings right in the centre of town, but most visitors choose to stay in a **B&B**. These have sprung up in every part of Stratford, but there's a particular concentration to the southwest of the centre around Grove Road, Evesham Place and Broad Walk. The tourist office operates an efficient and extremely useful **Accommodation Booking Hotline** (ⓣ01789/293127, ⓦwww.shakespeare-country.co.uk; £3).

Hotels

Falcon Chapel St ⓣ01789/279953, ⓦwww.regalhotels.co.uk/thefalcon. Handily situated in the middle of town, this place has a half-timbered facade dating from the sixteenth century, though most of the rest is an unremarkable modern rebuild. ❺

Grosvenor Warwick Rd ⓣ01789/269213, ⓦwww.groshotelstratford.co.uk. Close to the canal, just a couple of minutes' walk from the town centre, the *Grosvenor* occupies a row of pleasant, two-storey Georgian houses. The interior is crisp and modern and there's ample parking at the back. Discounted short break deals available. ❹

Marlyn 3 Chestnut Walk ⓣ01789/293752, ⓦwww.marlynhotel.co.uk. In a pleasant two-storey brick house with sash windows, this small hotel is good value and has comfortable rooms. Convenient for the town centre, too. ❸

Payton 6 John St ⓣ01789/266442, ⓦwww.payton.co.uk. On the north side of the town centre, a couple of minutes' walk from the Birthplace Museum, this comfortable hotel occupies an attractive Georgian town house on a quiet residential street. Family-run, the hotel has five comfortable rooms, all en suite. A good bet and very affordable. ❸

The Shakespeare Chapel St ⓣ0870/400 8182, ⓦwww.shakespearehotel.net. Now part of a chain, this old hotel, with its mullion windows and half-timbered facade, is one of Stratford's best known. The interior has low beams and open fires and represents a fairly successful amalgamation of the old and new. Right in the centre of town. ❽

Guest houses and B&Bs

Chadwyns Guest House 6 Broad Walk ⓣ01789/269077, ⓦwww.chadwyns.co.uk. Just off Evesham Place, this unassuming guest house occupies a two-storey Victorian terrace house and offers seven en-suite rooms. Great breakfasts with vegetarian options. ❷

Heron Lodge B&B 260 Alcester Rd ⓣ01789/299169, ⓦwww.heronlodge.com. Bright and cheerful B&B about a mile from the town centre. Occupies a well-maintained detached family home and all the rooms, which are decorated in pleasant modern style are en suite. Tasty breakfasts too. ❸

Parkfield Guest House 3 Broad Walk ⓣ01789/293313, ⓦwww.parkfieldbandb.co.uk.

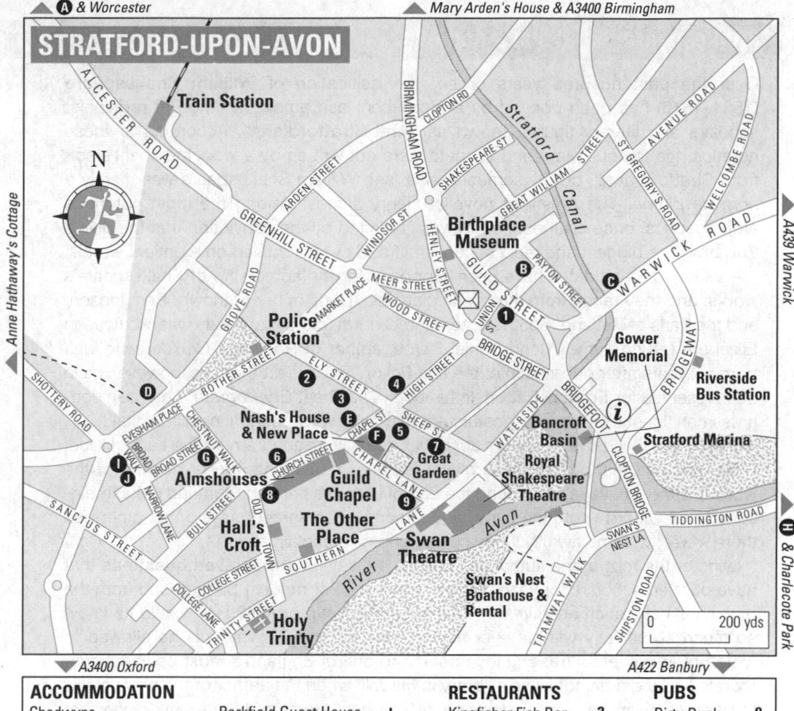

ACCOMMODATION				RESTAURANTS		PUBS	
Chadwyns Guest House	I	Parkfield Guest House	J	Kingfisher Fish Bar	2	Dirty Duck	9
Falcon	E	Payton Hotel	B	Lamb's Restaurant	5	Garrick Inn	4
Grosvenor	C	The Shakespeare	F	Restaurant Margaux	1	Windmill Inn	8
Heron Lodge B & B	A	Woodstock Guest House	D	Russons	6		
Marlyn	G	Youth Hostel	H	The Opposition	7		
				Sorrento	3		

Very pleasant B&B in a rambling Victorian house in a residential street off Evesham Place. There's a private car park – a useful facility in crowded Stratford – and most rooms are en suite. Under ten minutes' walk from the centre. ❷

Woodstock Guest House 30 Grove Rd ⓣ01789/299881, ⓔwoodstockhouse@compuserve.com. A smart and neatly kept B&B five minutes' walk from the centre, by the start of the path to Anne Hathaway's Cottage (see p.630). It has five extremely comfortable bedrooms, all en suite. No credit cards. ❷

Hostels and camping

Stratford-on-Avon Racecourse Camp Site Luddington Rd ⓣ01789/267949. Well-equipped camping and caravan site one mile or so to the southwest of the town centre. Regular buses into town (not Sun). Closed Oct–March. Tent pitches from £5, caravans from £9.

Stratford-upon-Avon Youth Hostel Hemmingford House, Alveston ⓣ0870/770 6052, ⓦwww.yha.org.uk. This hostel occupies a rambling Georgian mansion on the edge of the pretty village of Alveston. There are dormitories and family rooms, some of which are en suite, plus laundry, Internet access, car parking and self-catering facilities. Breakfasts and evening meals are on offer too. It's located two miles east of the town centre on the B4086 and served by regular bus from Stratford's Riverside bus station. Open all year. Dorm beds £16.

The Town

Spreading back from the River Avon, Stratford's **town centre** is flat and compact, its mostly modern buildings filling out a simple gridiron just two blocks

Shakespeare: What's in a name?

Over the past hundred years or so, the deification of **William Shakespeare** (1564–1616) has been dogged by a loony backlash among a fringe of revisionist scholars and literary figures known as "**Anti-Stratfordians**". According to these heretics, the famous plays and sonnets were not written by a wool merchant's son from Stratford at all, but by someone else, and William Shakespeare was merely a *nom de plume*. The American novelist Henry James, among the most notorious arch-sceptics, once claimed that he was "haunted by the conviction that the divine William is the biggest and most successful fraud ever practised on a patient world."

A variety of candidates have been proposed for the authorship of Shakespeare's works, and they range from the faintly plausible (Christopher Marlowe, Ben Jonson, and the Earls of Rutland, Southampton and Oxford) to the manifestly whacko (Queen Elizabeth I, King James I and Daniel Defoe, author of *Robinson Crusoe*, who was born six years after publication of the first Folio). The wildest theories, however, have been reserved for **Francis Bacon**. In his book *The Great Cryptogram*, American congressman Ignatius Donnelly postulated that the word "honorificabilitudinitatibus", which crops up in *Love's Labours Lost*, was actually an anagram for the Latin "Hi ludi F Baconis nati tuiti orbi" ("These plays, F. Bacon's offspring, are preserved for the world"). Others have rallied around the Earl of Oxford's banner; Sigmund Freud maintained that Oxford wrote the plays, and Orson Welles agreed, saying that otherwise there were "... some awfully funny coincidences to explain away".

Lying at the root of the authorship debate are several **unresolved questions** that have puzzled scholars for years. How could a man of modest background from the provinces have such an intimate knowledge of royal protocol? How could he know so much about Italy without ever having travelled there? Why was he allowed to write potentially embarrassing love poems to one of England's most powerful aristocrats? Why did he not leave a library in his will, when the author of the plays clearly possessed an intimate knowledge of classical literature? And why, given that Shakespeare was supposedly a well-known dramatist, did no death notice or obituary appear in publications of the day?

The speculation surrounding Shakespeare's work stems from the lack of definite information about his life. The few details that have been preserved come mostly from official archives – birth, marriage and death certificates and court records. From these we know that on April 22 or 23, 1564, a certain John Shakespeare, variously

deep and four blocks long. Running along the northern edge of the centre is **Bridge Street**, the main thoroughfare lined with shops and chock-a-block with local buses. At its west end Bridge Street divides into Henley Street, home of the **Birthplace Museum**, and Wood Street, which leads up to the market place. It also intersects with High Street. This, and its continuation Chapel and Church streets, cuts south to pass most of the old buildings that the town still possesses, most notably **Nash's House** and, on neighbouring Old Town Street, **Hall's Croft**. From here, it's a short hop to the charming **Holy Trinity Church**, where Shakespeare lies buried, and then only a few minutes back along the river past the **theatres** to the foot of Bridge Street. In itself, this circular walk only takes about fifteen minutes, but it takes all day if you potter around the attractions. In addition, there are two outlying Shakespearean properties, **Anne Hathaway's Cottage** in Shottery and **Mary Arden's House** in Wilmcote – though you have to be a really serious sightseer to want to see them all.

The Birthplace Museum

Top of everyone's Bardic itinerary is the **Birthplace Museum**, on Henley Street (June–Aug Mon–Sat 9am–5pm, Sun 9.30am–5pm; April–May &

described as a glove-maker, butcher, wool merchant and corn trader, and his wife, Mary, had their first son, William. We also know that the boy attended a local grammar school until financial problems forced him into his father's business, and that, at the age of 18, he married a local woman, **Anne Hathaway**, seven years his senior, who five months later bore a daughter, Susanna, the first of three children. Several years later, probably around 1587, the young Shakespeare was forced to flee Stratford after being caught poaching on the estate of Sir Thomas Lucy at nearby Charlecote (see p.631). Five companies of players passed through the town on tour that year, and it is believed he **absconded** with one of them to London, where a theatre boom was in full swing. *Henry VI*, Shakespeare's first play, appeared soon after, followed by the hugely successful *Richard III*. Over the next decade, Shakespeare's output was prodigious. Thirty-eight plays appeared, most of them performed by his own theatre troupes based in the **Globe** (see p.118), a large timber-framed theatre overlooking the south bank of the River Thames, in which he had a one-tenth share.

Success secured Shakespeare the patronage of London's fashionable set, among them the dashing young courtier, Henry Wriothesley, Earl of Southampton, with whom the playwright is believed to have had a passionate affair (Southampton is thought to have been the "golden youth" of the Sonnets). The ageing Queen Elizabeth I, bewigged and decked in opulent jewellery, regularly attended the Globe, as did her successor, James I, whose Scottish ancestry and fascination with the occult partly explain the subject matter of *Macbeth* – Shakespeare knew the commercial value of appealing to the rich and powerful. This, as much as his extraordinary talent, ensured his plays were the most acclaimed of the day, earning him enough money to **retire** comfortably to Stratford, where he largely abandoned literature in the last years of his life to concentrate on business and family affairs.

Ultimately, the sketchy details of Shakespeare's life are of far less importance than the **plays**, **sonnets and songs** he left behind. Whoever wrote them – and despite all the conjecture, William Shakespeare almost certainly did – the body of work attributed to this shadowy historical figure comprises some of the most inspired and exquisite English ever written. The greatest irony is not that *King Lear* and *The Tempest* were penned by a provincial middle-class merchant's son, but that of all the millions of visitors who pass through Stratford each year, the majority appear to be more interested in the writer himself than in what he wrote.

Sept–Oct Mon–Sat 10am–5pm, Sun 10.30am–5pm; Nov–March Mon–Sat 10am–4pm, Sun 10.30am–4pm; £6.50), comprising an ugly modern visitor centre and the heavily-restored half-timbered building where the great man was born. The visitor centre pokes into every corner of Shakespeare's life and times, making the most of what little hard evidence there is. His will is interesting in so far as he passed all sorts of goodies to his daughter, but precious little to his wife – the museum commentary tries to gainsay this apparent meanness, but fails to convince. Next door, the half-timbered dwelling is actually two buildings knocked into one. The northern half, now fitted out in the style of a sixteenth-century domestic interior, was the business premises of the poet's father, who is thought to have worked as a glover, though some argue that he was a wool merchant or a butcher. Neither is it certain that Shakespeare was born in this building nor that he was born on April 23, 1564 – it's just known that he was baptized on April 26, and it's an irresistible temptation to place the birth of the national poet three days earlier, on St George's Day. The south half of the building – bought by John Shakespeare in 1556 – displays a modest range of period artefacts designed to illuminate a life which remains distinctly enigmatic.

Nash's House and New Place

Follow **High Street** south from the junction of Bridge and Henley streets, and you'll soon come to another Birthplace Trust property, **Nash's House** on Chapel Street (June–Aug Mon–Sat 9.30am–5pm, Sun 10am–5pm; April–May & Sept–Oct daily 11am–5pm; Nov–March daily 11am–4pm; £3.50). Once the property of Thomas Nash, first husband of Shakespeare's granddaughter, Elizabeth Hall, the house's ground floor is now kitted out with a pleasant assortment of period furnishings. Upstairs, one display provides a potted history of Stratford, including a scattering of archeological bits and pieces, and another focuses on the house with a cabinet of woodcarvings made from the **mulberry tree** that once stood outside. Reputedly planted by Shakespeare, the tree was chopped down in the 1750s by the owner, a certain Reverend Francis Gastrell, because he was fed up with all the pilgrims. An enterprising woodcarver bought the wood and carved Shakespearean mementoes from it – hence the carvings in the cabinet.

The adjacent gardens contain the bare foundations of **New Place** (same hours), Shakespeare's last residence, which was demolished by the same Reverend Gastrell, but for different reasons – Gastrell was in bitter dispute with the town council over taxation. A replacement mulberry tree has been planted beside the foundations of New Place and there are others in the adjacent **Great Garden** (March–Oct Mon–Sat 9am–dusk, Sun 10am–dusk; Nov–Feb Mon–Sat 9am–4pm, Sun noon–4pm; free), a formal affair of topiary, lawns and flowerbeds. A path leads into the Great Garden from New Place, but the main entrance is on Chapel Lane. One of the mulberries – it's got a plaque – was planted by Dame Peggy Ashcroft.

On the other side of Chapel Lane stands the **Guild Chapel**, whose chunky tower and sturdy stonework shelter a plain interior enlivened by some rather crude stained-glass windows and a faded mural above the triumphal arch. The adjoining King Edward VI **Grammar School**, where it's assumed Shakespeare was educated, incorporates a creaky line of fifteenth-century **almshouses** running along Church Street.

Hall's Croft

Chapel Street continues south as Church Street. At the end, turn left along Old Town Street for Stratford's most impressive medieval house, the Birthplace Trust's **Hall's Croft** (June–Aug Mon–Sat 9.30am–5pm, Sun 10am–5pm; April–May & Sept–Oct daily 11am–5pm; Nov–March daily 11am–4pm; £3.50). The former home of Shakespeare's elder daughter, Susanna, and her doctor husband, John Hall, the immaculately maintained Croft, with its creaking wooden floors, beamed ceilings and fine kitchen range, holds a good-looking medley of period furniture and – mostly upstairs – a fascinating display on **Elizabethan medicine**. Hall established something of a reputation for his medical know-how and after his death some of his case notes were published in a volume entitled *Select Observations upon English Bodies*. You can peruse extracts from Hall's book – noting that Joan Chidkin of Southam "gave two vomits and two stools" after being "troubled with trembling of the arms and thighs" – and then suffer vicariously at the displays of eye-watering forceps and other implements. The best view of the building itself is at the back, in the neat walled garden.

Holy Trinity Church

Beyond Hall's Croft, Old Town Street steers right to reach the handsome **Holy Trinity Church** (April–Sept Mon–Sat 8.30am–6pm & Sun 12.15–5pm;

March & Oct Mon–Sat 9am–5pm & Sun 12.15–5pm; Nov–Feb Mon–Sat 9am–4pm & Sun 12.15pm–5pm; free), whose mellow, honey-coloured stonework dates from the thirteenth century. Enhanced by its riverside setting and flanked by the yews and weeping willows of its graveyard, the dignified proportions of this quintessentially English church are the result of several centuries of chopping and changing, culminating in the replacement of the original wooden spire with today's stone version in 1763. At the entrance, on the second set of doors, the **Sanctuary Knocker** is a reminder of medieval times when local criminals could seek refuge from the law here, but only for 37 days. This, so local custom dictated, was long enough for them to negotiate a deal with their persecutors. Inside, the nave is bathed in light from the clerestory **windows**, some of whose stained glass dates back to the fourteenth century. Quite unusually, you'll see that the nave is built on a slight skew from the line of the chancel – supposedly to represent Christ's inclined head on the cross. In the north aisle, beside the transept, is the **Clopton Chapel**, where the large wall-tomb of George Carew is a Renaissance extravagance decorated with military insignia appropriate to George's job as master of ordnance to James I. But poor old George is long forgotten, unlike William Shakespeare, who lies buried in the **chancel** (£1), his remains overseen by a sedate and studious memorial plaque and effigy added just seven years after his death.

The theatres and the Gower Memorial

Doubling back from the church, turn right along Southern Lane and its continuation, Waterside, to reach the town's two Royal Shakespeare Company **theatres** – the Swan Theatre and the Royal Shakespeare Theatre. There was no theatre in Stratford in Shakespeare's day and indeed the first home-town festival in his honour was only held in 1769 at the behest of London-based David Garrick. Thereafter, the idea of building a permanent home in which to perform Shakespeare's works slowly gained momentum, and finally, in 1879, the first Memorial Theatre was opened on land donated by local beer baron Charles Flower. A fire in 1926 necessitated the construction of a new theatre, and the ensuing architectural competition, won by Elisabeth Scott, produced today's **Royal Shakespeare Theatre**. In the 1980s, the burnt-out original theatre round the back was turned into a replica "in-the-round" Elizabethan

Tickets for the RSC

As the **Royal Shakespeare Company** (information: ⓣ01789/403444, ⓦwww.rsc.org.uk) works on a repertory system, you could stay in Stratford for a few days and see three or four different plays. Tickets for the **Royal Shakespeare Theatre** start at £5 for standing room and a restricted view, rising to £40 for the best seats in the house, but note that the more popular shows often get booked up months in advance. **Swan** tickets are generally between £5 and £36. The Royal Shakespeare Theatre's foyer **box office** (Mon–Sat 9.30am–6pm, till 8pm when there is an evening performance; ⓣ0870/609 1110, ⓦwww.rsc.org.uk) serves as the central booking agent for both houses.

At the Royal Shakespeare Theatre, twenty tickets are kept back for that evening's performance and sold – from 9.30am onwards – at between £16 and £25 each; for a real blockbuster, arriving to queue at 5am will not be too early. Stand-by tickets (for unsold seats) are also available on the day of performance, but only concessionary groups (OAPs, students, etc) are eligible. If all else fails, turn up about an hour before the performance and try your luck, though last-minute **returns** are quite rare.

stage – the **Swan**. A third RSC auditorium, **The Other Place**, on Southern Lane, is currently closed except for special events. The RSC organizes a number of behind-the-scenes **tours** (£4) – ask at the desk in the foyer of the Royal Shakespeare Theatre for details.

In front of the Royal Shakespeare Theatre, the manicured lawns of a small riverside park stretch north as far as **Bancroft Basin**, where the Stratford canal meets the river. The basin is usually packed with narrowboats and in the parklet on the far side, over the little hump-backed pedestrian bridge, is the finely sculpted **Gower Memorial** of 1888 in which a seated Shakespeare is surrounded by figures from his plays.

Anne Hathaway's Cottage and Mary Arden's House

Anne Hathaway's Cottage (June–Aug Mon–Sat 9am–5pm, Sun 9.30am–5pm; April, May, Sept & Oct Mon–Sat 9.30am–5pm, Sun 10am–5pm; Nov–March daily 10am–4pm; £5), also operated by the Birthplace Trust, is located just over a mile west of the centre in the well-heeled suburb of Shottery. The cottage – actually an old farmhouse – is an immaculately maintained, half-timbered affair with a thatched roof and dinky little chimneys. This was the home of Anne Hathaway before she married Shakespeare in 1582, and the interior now holds a comely combination of period furniture, including a superb, finely carved four-poster bed. The garden is splendid too, crowded with bursting blooms in the summertime, and the adjacent **Shakespeare Tree Garden** and orchard features a scattering of modern sculptures and over forty trees, shrubs and roses mentioned in the plays, with each bearing the appropriate quotation inscribed on a plaque. The most agreeable way to get to the cottage from the town centre is on the signposted **footpath** from Evesham Place, at the south end of Rother Street.

The Birthplace Trust also keeps **Mary Arden's House** (June–Aug Mon–Sat 9.30am–5pm, Sun 10am–5pm; April, May, Sept & Oct Mon–Sat 10am–5pm, Sun 10.30am–5pm; Nov–March daily 10am–4pm; £5.50), three miles northwest of the town centre in the village of Wilmcote. Mary was Shakespeare's mother and, at the time of his death in 1556, the only unmarried daughter of her father, Robert. Unusually for the time, Mary inherited the house and land, thus becoming one of the neighbourhood's most eligible women – John Shakespeare, eager for self-improvement, married her within a year. The house is a well-furnished example of an Elizabethan farmhouse and, though the labelling is rather scant, a platoon of guides fills in the details of family life and traditions.

Eating and drinking

Stratford is used to feeding and watering thousands of visitors, so finding refreshment is never difficult. The problem is that many places are geared to serving the day-tripper as rapidly as possible – not a recipe for much gastronomic delight. That said, there is a scattering of very good **restaurants**, several of which have been catering to theatre-goers for many years, and a handful of **pubs** and **cafés** offering good food, too. The best restaurants are concentrated along Sheep Street, running up from Waterside near the theatres.

Restaurants and cafés

Kingfisher Fish Bar 13 Ely St. The best fish-and-chip shop in town. Takeaway and sit-down. A five-minute walk from the theatres. Closed Sun.

Lamb's Restaurant 12 Sheep St ☎01789/292554. Smart restaurant serving a mouth-watering range of stylish English and continental dishes in antique premises – beamed ceilings and so forth. Expensive.

The Opposition 13 Sheep St ⓣ01789/269980. Top-quality, imaginative international cuisine in a busy but amiable atmosphere. The dishes of the day, chalked up on a board inside, are excellent value. Moderate.

Restaurant Margaux 6 Union St ⓣ01789/269106. Smart and intimate restaurant serving top-quality seafood and meat dishes, often with a Mediterranean slant. Expensive.

Russons 8 Church St ⓣ01789/268822. Excellent but good-value cuisine, featuring interesting meat and vegetarian dishes on the main menu and an extensive blackboard of seafood specials. Closed Sun & Mon. Moderate

Sorrento 8 Ely St ⓣ01789/297999. Smart-verging-on-the-formal Italian restaurant offering great meat and seafood along with pizzas and pastas. Expensive.

Pubs

Dirty Duck 53 Waterside. The archetypal actors' pub, stuffed to the gunwales every night with a vocal entourage of RSC employees and hangers-on. Traditional beers in traditional premises with an appealing terrace.

The Garrick Inn 25 High St. Arguably the town's most photogenic and best-preserved old ale house: exposed beams, real ales and good bar food.

Windmill Inn Church St. Popular pub of cosy little rooms with low-beamed ceilings. A good range of Flowers beers too.

Listings

Banks and exchange There are lots of banks in the town centre and all of them will change foreign currency and traveller's cheques. Lloyds is at 22 Bridge St; HSBC at 13 Chapel St.

Bike rental Clarke's Cycles, 3 Guild St ⓣ01789/205057.

Boat rental and cruises Avon Boating, Swan's Nest Boathouse, Swan's Nest Lane (Easter–Oct 9am to dusk; ⓣ01789/267073, ⓦwww.avon-boating.co.uk) offers 30min town cruises at £3 per person. Also does rowing boat and punt rental.

Books Waterstones, 8 High St ⓣ01789/414418.

Buses National Express ⓣ0870/575 7747; Stagecoach ⓣ08456/001314; West Midlands Centro Hotline ⓣ024/7655 9559.

Car rental Hertz, at the train station ⓣ01789/298827.

Laundry Sparklean, 74 Bull St, off Old Town ⓣ01789/269075.

Pharmacy Boots, 11 Bridge St ⓣ01789/292173 (Mon–Sat 9am–5.30pm; late opening roster posted on the door).

Police Rother Street near the junction with Ely Street ⓣ01789/414111.

Post office Henley Street (Mon–Fri 9am–5.30pm, Sat 9am–6pm).

Taxis Stratford Taxis ⓣ01789/415888.

Around Stratford: Charlecote Park

Some five miles east of Stratford off the B4086, **Charlecote Park house** (early March to Oct Mon, Tues & Fri–Sun noon–5pm; £6; NT) is an ornate Tudor mansion at the heart of an expansive country estate. The house, refurbished in a rather heavy Victorian interpretation of Elizabethan style, is awash with souvenirs of the British empire, paintings of the estate and portraits of the Lucy family, who have lived here since 1247. An exploration takes a good hour and afterwards you can stroll the formal **gardens** (early March to Oct Mon, Tues & Fri–Sun 11am–6pm; Nov–Dec Sat & Sun 11am–4pm; £3), which feature borders of plants and flowers from Shakespeare's plays as well as a croquet lawn – you can rent equipment at the house. The gardens are a preamble to the surrounding **deer park** (same details), which is watered by the rivers Avon and Dene and provides wide views over the Warwickshire countryside. Grazing the estate are herds of fallow deer, whose ancestors are supposed to have been poached by the young William Shakespeare.

Stagecoach Midland Red **buses** #18 and #X18 run to Charlecote village on the edge of the park (not Sun).

Warwick

WARWICK, just eight miles northeast of Stratford and easily reached by bus and train, is famous for its massive castle, but it also possesses several charming streetscapes erected in the aftermath of a great fire in 1694, as well as an especially fine church chancel. An hour or two is quite enough time to nose around the town centre, though you'll need the whole day if, braving the crowds and the medieval musicians, you're also set on exploring the castle and its extensive grounds thoroughly. Either way, Warwick is the perfect day-trip from Stratford, although you may well decide to stay here if you plan to visit the sprawling ruins of nearby **Kenilworth Castle** and maybe drop by Coventry (see p.634) to see its magnificent cathedral, too.

The Castle

Towering above the River Avon at the foot of the town centre, **Warwick Castle** (daily: April–Sept 10am–6pm; Oct–March 10am–5pm; £13.50; parking £2.50) is locally proclaimed the "greatest medieval castle in Britain" and, if bulk equals greatness, then the claim is certainly valid, though much of the existing structure is the result of extensive nineteenth-century restoration. It's likely that the first fortress here was raised by Ethelfleda, daughter of Alfred the Great, in about 915 AD, but things really took off with the Normans, who built a large motte and bailey towards the end of the eleventh century. Almost three hundred years later, the eleventh Earl of Warwick turned the stronghold into a formidable stone castle, complete with elaborate gatehouses, multiple turrets and a keep. The earl and his descendants played a prominent part in the Hundred Years' War. One of their number was the executioner of Joan of Arc and they all brought prisoners back to Warwick and incarcerated them in the dingy dungeons of Caesar's Tower pending ransom negotiations.

The **entrance** to the castle is through the old stable block, beyond which a footpath leads round to the imposing moated and mounded **East Gate**. Over the footbridge – and beyond the protective towers – is the main **courtyard**. You can stroll along the ramparts and climb the towers, but most visitors head straight for one or other of the special displays installed inside by the present owners, Madame Tussauds. The most popular of these displays is the "Royal Weekend Party, 1898", an extravaganza of waxwork nobility hobnobbing in the private apartments which were rebuilt in the 1870s after fire damage. Another display, "Kingmaker – a preparation for Battle", adds smells and atmospheric sounds to waxwork scenes detailing the preparations for Richard Earl of Warwick's – as in "Warwick the Kingmaker" – final battle in 1471. Rather less obviously commercial are the **Great Hall** and neighbouring **Chapel**, though both are drably Victorian, the only saving grace being the former's assorted suits of armour. The **grounds** are much more enjoyable, acres of woodland and lawn inhabited by peacocks and including a large glass **conservatory**. A footbridge leads over the River Avon to **River Island**, the site of jousting tournaments and other such medieval hoopla.

The town centre

Re-emerging from the castle at the stables, **Castle Street** leads up the hill for a few yards to its junction with the High Street. Turn left and it's a brief stroll to another outstanding building, the **Lord Leycester Hospital** (April–Oct Tues–Sat 10am–5pm & Sun 11am–5pm; Nov–March Tues–Sun 10am–4pm; £3.20), a tangle of half-timbered buildings that lean at fairy-tale angles against

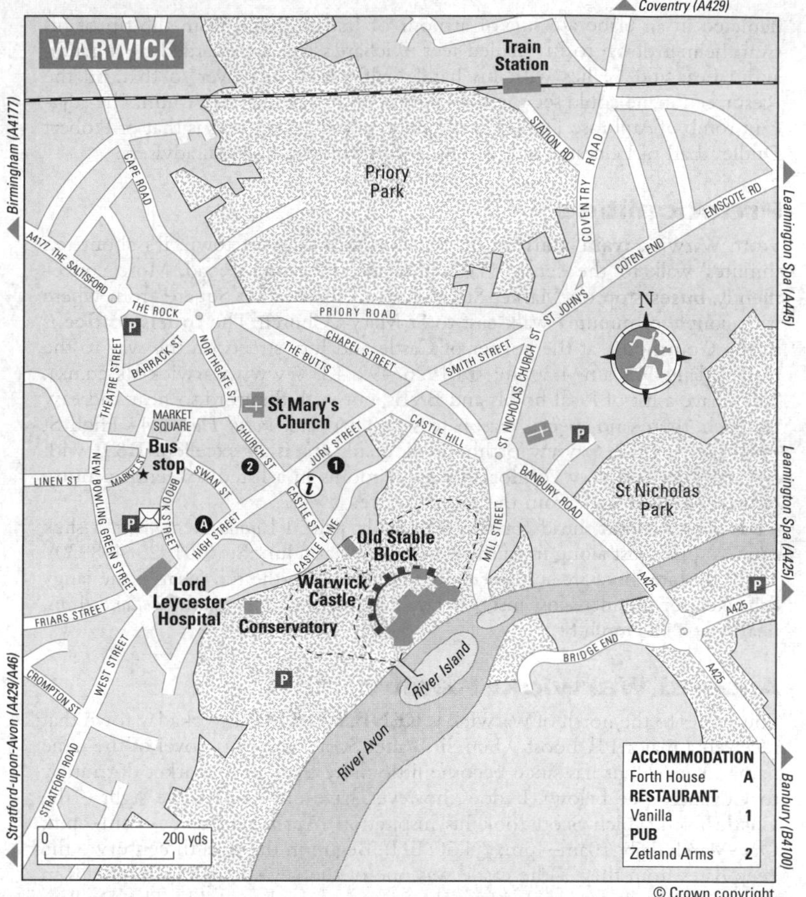

the old West Gate. The complex represents one of Britain's best-preserved examples of domestic Elizabethan architecture. It was established as a hostel for old soldiers by the Earl of Leicester, a favourite of Queen Elizabeth I, and incorporates several beamed buildings, principally in the Great Hall and the Guildhall, as well as a wonderful galleried courtyard and an intimate chantry chapel. There's a modest regimental museum here, too – appropriately enough as retired servicemen (and their wives) still live here. Known as "Brethren", the veterans are distinguished by their black cloaks and silver boar pendants, which they don for ceremonial occasions.

Doubling back along the High Street, turn left up Church Street – opposite Castle Street – for **St Mary's Church** (daily 10am–5pm, 4pm in winter; £1 donation suggested), which was rebuilt in a weird Gothic-Renaissance amalgam after the fire of 1694. One part remained untouched, however – the **chancel**, a glorious illustration of the Perpendicular style with a splendid vaulted ceiling of flying and fronded ribs. On the right-hand side of the chancel, the **Beauchamp Chapel** contains several beautiful tombs, exquisite works of art beginning with that of Richard Beauchamp, Earl of Warwick, who is depicted in an elaborate suit of armour of Italian design from the tip of his swan helmet down to his mailed feet. Richard's feet are guarded by a griffin and a bear and he lies with his hands half joined in prayer so that, on the Resurrection, he could see the holy figures on the ceiling above him. The adjacent tomb of Ambrose Dudley is of finely carved alabaster, as is that of Robert Dudley, Earl of Leicester, one of Elizabeth I's most influential advisers.

Practicalities

From Warwick **train station**, on the northern edge of town, it's about ten minutes' walk to the centre via Station and Coventry Road. More conveniently, **buses** stop on Market Street, just off the Market Square, from where it's a couple of minutes' walk east to St Mary's Church. The **tourist office** is in the Courthouse at the corner of Castle and Jury streets on the way to the castle (daily 9.30am–4.30pm; ⓣ01926/492212, ⓦwww.warwick-uk.co.uk). They have a list of local hotels and B&Bs, but with Stratford so near and easy to reach, there's no special reason to stay. That said, *Forth House*, 44 High St (ⓣ01926/401512, ⓦwww.forthhouseuk.co.uk; ④), is an excellent **B&B** with two en-suite and very comfortable guest rooms in a listed sixteenth-century property a short walk from the tourist office.

For a bite to **eat**, head for the reasonably priced *Vanilla Restaurant*, a slick modern place just along from the tourist office at 6 Jury St (ⓣ01926/498930). The light bites here are actually more tempting than the full meals – the tangy fishcakes, for instance, cost just £6. For a **drink**, try the amiable *Zetland Arms*, nearby at 11 Church St.

Around Warwick: Kenilworth

Four miles to the north of Warwick is **KENILWORTH**, a workaday town that received a major PR boost when Sir Walter Scott wrote his novel of the same name in 1862, but has since become little more than an upmarket dormitory to Coventry (see below). It does, however, have one remarkable sight – the **Castle** from which Scott took his inspiration (April–Sept daily 10am–6pm; Oct–March daily 10am–4pm; £4.50; EH). Begun in the twelfth century – the keep dates from then – the castle was one of the key strategic strongholds in the Midlands, alternately held by the king or a leading noble. The Dudleys acquired the castle in the sixteenth century and one of the family, Robert, Earl of Leicester, pleased Elizabeth I no end by turning the draughty fortress into an elegant palace in preparation for her visit. Kenilworth then became one of England's most fashionable country houses, hosting spectacular pageants and entertainments, but following Dudley's death the castle fell into decline, a process hastened by the attentions of Cromwell's troops in the Civil War. Today, the substantial sandstone ruins, approached across a long causeway that once damned an artificial lake, still maintain a tremendous presence, with large chunks of masonry drawn from each era still decipherable.

Coventry

In medieval times, **COVENTRY**, twenty miles east of Birmingham and eleven miles north of Warwick, was one of England's most prosperous cities. Its wealth was founded on the cloth, thread and dyeing industries, precursors of the engineering plants that were to become the staple of the local economy during the nineteenth century. It was here, in 1898, that the Daimler Company manufactured the first **British motor car**, and thereafter the city rapidly became a major centre of car production. As a sign of the good times, the population quadrupled between 1900 and 1930 – from 70,000 to 250,000 – and the future looked rosy. However, Coventry's industrial success attracted the attentions of the Luftwaffe and, on November 14, 1940, in one of the biggest bombing raids of World War II, the Germans destroyed most of the city. The postwar period has not been easy for Coventry. Heavy industry has been on the skids and the motor production lines have waned to near-extinction. Neither has the new Coventry built to replace the old been an architectural success and – with the exception of the splendid **cathedral** – the city is lumbered with more than its fair share of unsightly buildings.

The City

The city's pride and joy is Basil Spence's **St Michael's Cathedral** (daily: Easter–Oct 8.30am–6pm; Nov–Easter 8.30am–5.30pm; £3 donation requested), raised alongside the shell of the blitzed old cathedral and dedicated with a performance of Benjamin Britten's specially written *War Requiem* in 1962. Easily the most successful of Coventry's postwar buildings, the cathedral's pink sandstone is light and graceful, the main entrance adorned by a stunningly forceful *St Michael Defeating the Devil* by Jacob Epstein. Inside, Spence's high and slender nave is bathed in light from the soaring stained-glass windows, a perfect setting for the magnificent and immense **tapestry** of *Christ in Glory* by Graham Sutherland. The choice of artist could not have been more appropriate. A painter, graphic artist and designer, Sutherland (1903–80) had been one of Britain's official war artists, his particular job being to record the effects of German bombing. A canopied walkway links the new cathedral with the old, whose shattered nave flanks the church tower and spire that somehow eluded the bombs – and hint at the building's former magnificence for this was once one of the country's finest Gothic cathedrals.

A stone's throw southeast of the cathedral on Jordan Well stands the **Herbert Art Gallery and Museum** (Mon–Sat 10am–5.30pm, Sun noon–5pm; free). On Floor 1, the most outstanding exhibits are Luca Giordano's seventeenth-century *Bacchus and Ariadne*, which fills an entire wall, and a room on Lady Godiva that includes John Collier's much photographed pre-Raphaelite version. Also of interest on this floor are Sutherland's sketch studies for the cathedral tapestry, followed up with a trial piece made by French weavers. Downstairs, on the ground floor, the go-ahead *Godiva City* exhibition covers one thousand years of local history with a succession of lively displays. Among the original artefacts on display are a large bronze Saxon bowl, known as the Bagington Bowl, sundry items of pristine medieval leatherwork, and lots of ornate ribbons, whose manufacture was long a Coventry speciality.

Coventry has been home to dozens of car makers, including such almost-forgotten names as Singer, Riley, Humber and Hillman. These connections are celebrated at the **Coventry Transport Museum** (daily 10am–5pm; free), a short stroll northwest of the cathedral on Hales Street and containing the world's largest collection of British vehicles. Inevitably, the older vehicles attract most of the attention – there's a 1908 Riley, a bull-nosed Morris of 1922 and lots more – but there are more modern cars, too, including the XJ6 Jaguar and the phallus-like *Thrust 2*, in which Richard Noble set the world land speed record of 633.468mph. The museum also has a display devoted to the Coventry Blitz and a gift shop selling motor memorabilia.

Lady Godiva

The story of **Lady Godiva** riding naked on horseback through the streets of Coventry is one of England's favourite folk tales – and the city makes the most of the connection with postcards, key rings and statues. According to the most popular version of the story, Lady Godiva, the beautiful wife of the local lord, Leofric, the earl of Mercia, was appalled by the poverty she saw around her, and begged her husband to abolish the crippling taxes he levied on his people. Wearying of his wife's philanthropy, Leofric said he would do as she asked on condition that she ride naked through the town, never suspecting that a woman of her rank would agree to such a proposal. Lady Godiva, however, got around the dilemma by ordering the townsfolk to lock themselves in their houses and bolt their windows on the appointed day. Only one local lad, the original **"Peeping Tom"**, dared disobey the Countess's command, and he was struck blind before he had a chance to see Godiva, her long hair covering her body like a cape as she rode through the city, eyes lowered. The ordeal over, Godiva returned to her husband, who kept his word and repealed the taxes.

The story first appeared in 1188, but the historical figures it depicted lived nearly a century and a half before. **Leofric** was the Anglo-Saxon earl who, in 1043, built the Benedictine priory that helped transform Coventry from a small settlement into medieval England's fourth-largest town. His wife, **Godgifu**, outlived him by ten years, and may have been a powerful ruler in her own right after her husband's death; she was also pious and donated land and money to the Church. Beyond this, little is known about the couple. The Godiva story probably evolved from some kind of pagan fertility ritual, and was popularized in the writings of the Norman chronicler, Roger of Wendover, during the thirteenth century. "Peeping Tom" was a later embellishment, seemingly inspired by a particularly odd chain of events. In 1586, Coventry council asked a certain Adam van Noort (1562–1641) to paint the Godiva legend. He did so, but he placed Leofric in a window looking down at Godiva on her horse. For reasons that remain obscure, the city fathers exhibited the painting on Coventry's main square and, mistakenly, the populace took the figure to be a peeper – and the sub-plot stuck. Researchers in the Herbert Art Gallery (where this painting now hangs) have sorted all this out and also believe that the notion of Godiva's nudity may have been a fanciful elaboration too. It seems more likely that Leofric, if he challenged his wife at all, dared her to ride through the city stripped of her jewellery and finery.

Whatever the truth of the matter, locals kept the story going and **"Godiva Processions"** kicked off Coventry's annual summer fair from its introduction in the seventeenth century until the 1800s, when all this public flaunting proved too much for the Victorians. More recently, the tradition has been revived in the form of a canny PR exercise to mark the start of the Godiva Festival in June, when a local woman rides through the streets dressed in a body stocking.

From the Road Transport Museum, it's a short walk west along Corporation Street to the squat, red-stone church of **St John's**, beside the roundabout. It's not much to look at, but the church has played an interesting part in linguistic history. During the English Civil War, Puritan Coventry sided squarely with Parliament, and Royalist prisoners from the surrounding districts were rounded up and incarcerated here in the church – hence the expression "**sent to Coventry**", meaning shunned or ostracized. But not everyone goes along with this version of events. Some claim the phrase derives from Shakespeare's Henry IV Part I, when Falstaff says of his motley band of foot soldiers: "I'll not march through Coventry with them". Church and roundabout are at the foot of truncated **Spon Street**, which has several restored medieval houses, mostly moved here from other parts of the city. It's hardly an inspiring streetscape, but it is one of the more agreeable parts of the city and it does have several good places to eat and drink.

Practicalities

Coventry is an important rail junction and its **train station** has direct services to and from London, Birmingham and many major British cities. It's located just south of the central ring road, a ten- to fifteen-minute walk from the cathedral – take Warwick Road north, cross the ring road and keep going straight – or catch the shuttle bus. Rather more conveniently, the Pool Meadow **bus station** lies a short way north of the cathedral – just follow the signs. The bus station has good connections with many major cities and is also the hub of the local bus network, with regular services to Warwick, Warwick University and Stratford.

For free town maps and local brochures, head for the **tourist office** on Bayley Lane, right in the centre of town opposite the old cathedral (June–Aug Mon–Fri 9.30am–5pm, Sat & Sun 10am–4.30pm; rest of year Mon–Fri 9.30am–4.30pm, Sat & Sun 10am–4.30pm; ⓣ02476/227264, ⓦwww.visitcoventry.co.uk). Their main city guidebook has a list of all the town's **accommodation** and they will book a room on your behalf at no cost – though, frankly, with other more enticing towns so near at hand, there's no real reason to stay here. That said, one particularly pleasant **B&B** is the *Crest Guest House*, 39 Friars Rd (ⓣ02476/227822; ③), whose four spick-and-span guest rooms, two of which are en suite, occupy a comfortable modern house near the ring road, about ten minutes' walk from the centre.

Coventry hardly heaves with great places to **eat**, but *Pizza Express*, near the cathedral at 10a Hay Lane, is a safe bet for moderately priced pizza and pasta, and they have a congenial rear terrace opening onto Castle Yard too. Alternatively, *Tête à Tête*, at 188 Spon St (Mon–Fri 8am–3pm, Sat 8am–4pm), is a flowery tearoom, and the *Old Windmill*, at 22 Spon St, with its attractive interior of flagstones and exposed wooden beams, serves a good range of **brews** and provides inexpensive bar food. Otherwise, Coventry's pub scene is rather too rough and ready for most tastes – and many retreat to the campus of Warwick University, three miles to the south of the city. Here, the **Warwick Arts Centre** is a large arts complex, with two theatres, a cinema, art gallery, a bar and restaurant. For details of what's on, telephone the box office (ⓣ02476/524524, ⓦwww.warwickartscentre.co.uk).

Worcestershire

In geographical terms, **Worcestershire** can be compared to a huge saucer, with the low-lying plains of the Severn Valley and the Vale of Evesham, Britain's foremost fruit-growing area, rising to a lip of hills, principally the Malverns in the west and the Cotswolds to the south (see pp.369–387). In character, the county divides into two broad belts. To the north lie the industrial and overspill towns – Droitwich and Redditch for instance – that have much in common with the Birmingham conurbation, while the south is predominantly rural. Marking the transition between the two is **Worcester** itself, whose main claim to fame is its splendid cathedral. The south holds the county's finest scenery in the **Malvern Hills**, excellent walking territory and home to the amiable former spa town of **Great Malvern**. South Worcestershire's rural lifestyle is famously portrayed in *The Archers*, the BBC's long-running radio soap, which attracts a massive and extraordinarily dedicated audience. Steam train enthusiasts will be keen to ride the **Severn Valley Railway**, which chugs north from Worcestershire's Kidderminster terminus to Bridgnorth (see p.658) in Shropshire.

The proximity of Birmingham ensures Worcestershire has a good network of **trains** and **buses**, though services are spasmodic amongst the villages in the south of the county. There's an excellent regional public transport information line covering all of the West Midlands – Centro Hotline (☎024/7655 9559) – or you can resort to the usual national numbers for bus (☎0870/608 2608) and rail (☎0845/748 4950).

Worcester and around

Right at the geographical heart of the county **WORCESTER** is something of an architectural hotchpotch, its half-timbered Tudor and stone Georgian buildings standing cheek by jowl with some fairly charmless modern developments. Postwar clumsiness apart, the biggest single influence on the city has always been the **River Severn**, which flows along Worcester's west flank. It was the river that drew the Romans here and river trade that made it an important settlement as early as Saxon times. The river's major drawback is its propensity to breach its banks, inundating parts of the city in murky water, though this has at least limited development along the riverside, where a leafy footpath passes below the mighty bulk of the **cathedral**, Worcester's star turn.

The Cathedral

Worcester's riverside is dominated by the sandstone bulk of the **Cathedral** (daily 8.30am–5.30pm; free), a rich stew of architectural styles dating from 1084. The bulk of the church is firmly medieval, from the Norman transepts through to the late Gothic cloister, though the Victorians did have a good old hack at the exterior. Inside, the cavernous **nave** is unexceptional except for its two west bays, which are an unusual – and unusually fine – example of the transitional period, when the rounded Norman arch was being supplanted by the pointed arches of Early English Gothic. They date to the 1160s. The pillars of the nave are decorated with bunches of fruit, initially carved by stonemasons from Lincoln, most of whom succumbed to the Black Death, leaving inferior successors to finish the job.

Moving on, the **choir**, built between 1220 and 1260, is a beautiful illustration of the Early English style, with a forest of slender pillars soaring over the intricately worked choir stalls. Here also, in front of the high altar, is the **table-tomb** of England's most reviled monarch, **King John**, who died in 1216. Much-loathed, perhaps rightly so, but John certainly would not have appreciated the lion that lies at his feet biting the end of his sword – a reference to the curbing of his power by the barons when they obliged him to sign the Magna Carta (see p.1121). Just beyond the tomb – on the right – is **Prince Arthur's Chantry**, a delicate lacy confection of carved stonework built in 1504 to commemorate Arthur, King Henry VII's son, who died at the age of 15 in Ludlow. He was on his honeymoon with Catherine of Aragon, who was soon passed on – with such momentous consequences – to his younger brother, Henry. The chantry is liberally plastered with heraldic and symbolic depictions of the houses of York and Lancaster, united by the Lancastrian Henry VII after his victory at Bosworth Field (see p.731) and subsequent marriage to Elizabeth, daughter of the Yorkist king Edward IV.

A stairway beside the chantry leads down to the **crypt**, the oldest part of the cathedral and the largest Norman crypt in the country. In addition, a doorway on the south side of the nave leads to the **Cloisters**, with their delightful roof bosses, and the circular, largely Norman **Chapter House**, which has the distinction of being the first such building constructed with the use of a central supporting pillar.

The rest of the city centre

Tucked away behind the cathedral on Severn Street, the **Royal Worcester Porcelain** complex (Mon–Sat 9am–5.30pm, Sun 11am–5pm) contains factory shops, a visitor centre, a substantial porcelain museum (same times; £3.50), and the factory itself (tours Mon–Fri only, reservations required on ⓣ01905/746000; £5.50). Beginning in the mid-eighteenth century, porcelain manufacture was long the city's main industry and Royal Worcester its leading light. Traditionally, the company's wares were ornate to a fault, but they also kept abreast of fashions – as they continue to do today. Among the pieces exhibited in the museum, keep an eye out for Dorothy Doughtey's bird pieces and an extravagant vase celebrating Wellington and his Prussian ally Blucher, whose timely help proved crucial at the battle of Waterloo.

From the Royal Worcester complex, it's a brief walk north via Severn Street to the **Commandery** (Mon–Sat 10am–5pm & Sun 1.30–5pm; £3.95), on the far side of the busy Sidbury dual carriageway. This is the oldest building in the city, a rambling, half-timbered and smartly panelled structure dating from the early sixteenth century. Its moment of fame came when **King Charles II** used the building as his headquarters during the battle-cum-siege of Worcester in 1651. Charles II's father – King Charles I – had been executed in 1649 and England had become a Commonwealth, run by Parliament. Two years later Charles II landed in Scotland, raised an army and then marched south bent on seizing the English crown. In the event, Oliver Cromwell, Parliament's leading general, outwitted and trapped Charles and his army here in Worcester. However, much to Cromwell's chagrin, Charles managed to escape Parliament's clutches and reach safety in France by fleeing in disguise – no mean feat considering the would-be king was six feet and two inches tall, about ten inches more than the average. To celebrate the Charles II connection, the Commandery holds the large and detailed **Civil War Exhibition**, but over the years this has become rather bedraggled and there are plans to revamp the place. Whatever happens, the small **painted chamber** should receive more attention, its walls covered with intriguing cameos recalling the Commandery's original use as a monastery hospital. Each of the cameos relates to a saint with healing powers – for starters St Roch nursing plague victims and St Erasmus, the patron saint of stomach diseases, having his bowels winched out by his tormentors. There's also a painting of St Thomas à Beckett being stabbed in the head by a group of knights, enough to make him the saint who specialized in headaches.

Friar Street and Greyfriars

It's a short step northwest from the Commandery along the dual carriageway to **Friar Street**, whose pedestrianized upper reaches – beyond some pretty awful modern stuff – hold an attractive sequence of antique half-timbered buildings. Amongst them is **Greyfriars** (April–Oct Wed–Fri 2–5pm, Sat 1–5pm; £3.10; NT), a largely fifteenth-century town house, whose wonky timbers and dark-stained panelling shelter a charming collection of antiques bequeathed to the National Trust by the last owner-occupiers, the Moores, in the 1980s. Particular highlights include several superb Flemish tapestries and a finely carved four-poster bed.

Greyfriars is about five minutes' walk from the cathedral and the bottom of the **High Street**, where there's a quizzical-looking **statue** of the composer Edward Elgar, for more on whom see below. From the statue, it's a few paces more to the tourist office (see below), which is housed in the extravagant **Guildhall**, built in the 1720s and complete with trumpeting cherubs, allegorical figures and niche statues of Charles I, Charles II and Queen Anne.

Practicalities

Worcester has two **train stations**. The handiest for the city centre is Foregate Street, from where it's about half a mile south to the cathedral along Foregate Street and its continuation The Cross and the High Street. The other train station, Shrub Hill, is located further out, about a mile to the northeast of the cathedral. The **bus station** is at the back of the sprawling Crowngate shopping mall, on The Butts, about 600 yards northwest of the cathedral. The **tourist office** (Mon–Sat 9.30am–5pm; ⓣ01905/726311, ⓦwww.visitworcester.com) is in the Guildhall towards the cathedral end of the High Street.

There's no overriding reason to overnight in Worcester, but one of the city's most appealing **hotels** is the likeable *Diglis House Hotel*, in an attractive Georgian building beside the river just behind the cathedral on Severn Street (ⓣ01905/353518, ⓦwww.diglishousehotel.co.uk; ⑤). The hotel has a vaguely old-fashioned air – and is not the worse for that – and each of the twenty-odd rooms is very comfortable. Amongst several central **B&Bs**, the pick is *Burgage House*, 4 College Precincts (ⓣ01905/25396, ⓦwww.burgagehouse.co.uk; no credit cards; ③), which occupies a narrow Georgian town house on a cobbled lane beside the cathedral.

For **food**, there are several recommendable cafés and restaurants dotted along Friar Street and its northerly continuation, New Street. These include *Puccini's*, opposite Greyfriars at 12 Friar St, a moderately priced restaurant serving pastas and pizzas from £5. Rather better is the pastel-painted *Saffron's Bistro*, 15 New St (ⓣ01905/610505), where an imaginative menu features such delights as monkfish and tiger prawns in a wine sauce; main courses here average £14, less for the vegetarian dishes. Friar Street possesses a cosy, traditional **pub** too, the *Cardinal's Hat*, near the foot of the street at no. 23.

Around Worcester: Lower Broadheath

One of Worcestershire's most famous sons was **Sir Edward Elgar** (1857–1934), the first internationally acclaimed English composer for almost two hundred years. Elgar built his reputation on a series of lyrical works celebrating his abiding love of the Worcestershire countryside, quintessentially English pieces amongst which the most famous is the *Enigma Variations*. Elgar was born in **LOWER BROADHEATH**, a hamlet just four miles west of Worcester off the A44, and it's here you'll find the **Elgar Birthplace Museum** (daily 11am–5pm, last admission 4.15pm; £4.50). This comprises a modern **visitor centre**, exploring Elgar's life and times with the assistance of some fascinating old photographs, and – just behind at the end of the path – the modest brick **cottage** where he was born. Inside the cottage, the cramped rooms contain several of Elgar's musical scores, personal correspondence in his spidery handwriting, press cuttings, and miscellaneous mementoes. The museum also organizes an imaginative programme of special events from illustrated talks to Elgar concerts and recitals. Lower Broadheath is not, however, of any scenic interest and if you want to see the green, quilted landscapes which inspired Elgar you'll have to push on to The Malverns.

Great Malvern and the Malvern Hills

One of the most exclusive and prosperous areas of the Midlands, **The Malverns** is the generic name for a string of towns and villages stretched along the eastern lower slopes of the **Malvern Hills**, which rise spectacularly out of the flat plains a few miles to the southwest of Worcester. About nine miles from north to south – between the A44 and the M50 – and never more than five miles wide, the hills straddle the Worcestershire–Herefordshire boundary. Of ancient granite rock, the hills are punctuated by over twenty summits, mostly around 1000 feet high, and in between lie innumerable dips and hollows. Nonetheless, it's easy if energetic walking country, with great views, and there's an excellent network of hiking trails, most of which can be completed in a day or half-day.

Amongst The Malverns, it's **GREAT MALVERN** which grabs the attention, its pocket-sized centre clambering up the hillside with the crags of North Hill beckoning beyond. The Benedictines chose this hilly setting for one of their abbeys and although Henry VIII closed the place down in 1538, the **Priory Church** (daily: April–Sept 9am–6.30pm; Oct–March 9am–4.30pm) has survived, the crisp symmetries and elaborate decoration of its exterior witnessing the priory's former wealth. Inside, the high and mighty nave is sternly Norman and it sweeps down to the chancel, which came later, a fine example of the Perpendicular, its sinuous tracery serving to frame a simply fabulous set of **stained-glass windows** dating from the end of the fifteenth century. Amongst them, pride of place goes to the great east window, a giant flash of colour with several easily decipherable Biblical scenes, such as Palm Sunday and the Crucifixion. The north transept window is also of special interest as it holds both a portrait of Prince Arthur, Henry VII's son – the same Arthur who is commemorated in Worcester Cathedral (see p.638) – and a rare Coronation of Mary set against a blue sky background. These coronation windows were once a common feature of English monastery churches, but the Protestants, inflamed by such idolatry, hunted almost all of them down.

A couple of minutes' walk away, hard by the top of Church Street, the modest **Malvern Museum** (Easter–Oct daily 10.30am–5pm; £1) is housed in the delicately proportioned Priory Gatehouse, but it concentrates on Great Malvern's days as a spa town. The spring waters hereabouts became popular at the end of the eighteenth century, but it was to be the Victorians who packed the place out – and built the grand stone houses that still line the town's streets. The museum has a goodly selection of old cartoons showing patients packed into cold wet sheets before hopping gaily away from their crutches and wheelchairs – exaggerated claims perhaps, but poor hygiene did bring on a multitude of skin complaints and the relief the spa waters brought was real enough. You can still sample the waters at **St Ann's Well** (Sat & Sun 10am–5pm, plus Easter–Sept Mon–Fri 10am–5pm or dusk), a cosy Victorian building (and café) situated a steep fifteen-minute walk up the wooded hillside from the top of town; the signposted path begins on the far side of the main road across from the *Foley Arms Hotel*.

Back at the museum, it's a short walk down the hill to Grange Road, where the **Malvern Theatres** (Ⓣ01684/892277 Ⓦwww.malvern-theatres.co.uk) is the key venue for the wide range of special events the town puts on each year.

Hiking The Malverns

Great Malvern tourist office (see p.642) sells hiking maps and issues half a dozen free **Trail Guide leaflets**, which describe circular routes up to and along the hills that rise behind the town. The shortest trail is just one and a half miles, the longest four. One of the most appealing is the 2.5-mile hoof up to the top – and back – of **North Hill** (1307ft), from where there are panoramic views over the surrounding countryside; this hike takes in St Ann's Well (see p.641). Alternatively, the one-way hike along the top of the ridge is a sterner test that takes all day and is ten miles long. On the way, you'll pass through the vague remains of a brace of Iron Age hill forts. It's best to start at the southern end – at **Chase End Hill** – and work your way north.

Practicalities

With its dainty ironwork and quaint chimneys, Great Malvern's infinitely rustic **train station** has fast and frequent connections with Birmingham and Worcester. It's located half a mile or so from the town centre via Avenue Road and then **Church Street**, the steeply sloping main drag. The **tourist office**, is at the top of Church Street, across from the Priory Church (daily 10am–5pm; ⓣ01684/892289, ⓦwww.malvernhills.gov.uk).

Accommodation is plentiful. Amongst the **hotels**, the pick is *The Abbey* (ⓣ01684/892332, ⓦwww.sarova.com; ❼), a rambling, creeper-clad Victorian hotel with mock-Tudor timbering, handsome stone doorways and plush rooms, all set behind the Priory Church on Abbey Road – but note that the modern wing is rather unappetizing. A second good bet is the *Foley Arms Hotel*, footsteps from the top of Church Street at 14 Worcester Rd (ⓣ01684/573397, ⓦwww.foleyarmshotel.com; ❻), though the bedrooms here can't help but seem a tad dowdy after the attractive Georgian facade with its fancy wrought-iron balcony. One very recommendable **B&B** is the *Wyche Keep*, an impressive Edwardian house with garden access to the Malvern Hills. It's located one mile south from the top of Church Street along the A449 at 22 Wyche Rd (ⓣ01684/567018; no credit cards; ❹). A more central choice is *The Red Gate B&B*, in a large Victorian house near the train station at 32 Avenue Rd (ⓣ01684/565013; ❹) and offering a handful of well-appointed en-suite rooms. The **youth hostel**, 18 Peachfield Rd, (ⓣ0870/770 5948, ⓦwww.yha.org.uk; dorm beds £10.25), occupies a rambling Edwardian house just one mile south of the train station in neighbouring Malvern Wells; days and dates of opening vary, so be sure to book ahead.

With most visitors apparently eating where they sleep, the **restaurant** scene in Great Malvern is not perhaps as varied as you might expect. Nonetheless, *The Abbey Hotel* has a very competent if pricey restaurant, or you could try the *White Season Restaurant*, at the top of Church St (ⓣ01684/575954; closed Sun), a crisply decorated modern place with a good line in seafood. The town also possesses the curious *Lady Foley's Tea Room* (Mon–Sat 9am–6pm), a **café** with character – in a converted waiting room down at the train station. Snacks here cost just £2–4.

Herefordshire

Over the Malvern Hills from Worcestershire, the rolling agricultural landscapes of **Herefordshire** have an easy-going charm, but the finest scenery hereabouts is along the banks of the **River Wye**, which wriggles and worms its way across the county linking most of the places of interest. Plonked in the middle of the county on the Wye is **Hereford**, a sleepy, rather old-fashioned sort of place whose proudest possession, the cathedral's remarkable Mappa Mundi map, was almost flogged off in a round of ecclesiastical budget cuts, back in the 1980s. Hereford is also close to the superb Norman church of tiny **Kilpeck**, to the southwest, and, to the east, the delightful little town of **Ledbury**, sitting on the edge of the Malvern Hills and distinguished by its Tudor and Stuart half-timbered buildings – sometimes called "Black and Whites". Moving on, the southeast corner of the county has one attractive town, **Ross-on-Wye**, a genial little place with a picturesque river setting. Ross is also an ideal base for explorations into one of the wilder portions of the **Wye River Valley**, with the tamer landscapes of the **Forest of Dean**, nestling in between the rivers Wye and Severn over in Gloucestershire, beckoning beyond. To the west of Hereford, hard by the Welsh border, the key attraction is **Hay-on-Wye**, which – thanks to the purposeful industry of Richard Booth (see p.650) – has become the world's largest repository of second-hand books, on sale in around thirty bookshops.

Herefordshire possesses one **rail line**, linking Ledbury, Hereford and Leominster and running north to Shrewsbury and east to Great Malvern and Worcester. Otherwise, you'll be restricted to the tender mercies of the county's **buses**, which provide a reasonable service between the villages and towns, except on Sundays when there's almost nothing at all. All the local tourist offices have bus timetables and there's **bus information** on ⓣ0870/608 2608.

Hereford

Founded by the Saxons in the seventh century, **HEREFORD** – literally "army ford" – was long a border garrison town against the Welsh, its military importance guaranteed by its strategic position beside the River Wye. It also became a religious centre after the Welsh murdered the Saxon king Ethelbert near here in 794. These were bloody times, so in itself the murder was pretty routine, but legend asserts that Ethelbert's ghost kept on turning up to insist his remains be interred here in Hereford – and eventually it got its way. Ethelbert's posthumous antics made him a military martyr and a Saxon cult soon grew up around his name, prompting the construction of the town's first cathedral. The Welsh were, however, having none of this and, in 1055, they attacked Hereford and burnt the cathedral to the ground.

Today, with the fortifications that once girdled the city all but vanished, it's the second **cathedral**, dating from the eleventh century, which forms the main focus of architectural interest. It lies just to the north of the River Wye at the heart of the city centre, whose compact tangle of narrow streets and squares is clumsily boxed in by the ring road. Taken as a whole, Hereford makes for a pleasant – if not exactly riveting – overnight stay and is also within easy striking distance of **Kilpeck**, with its exquisite Norman church, and pocket-sized **Ledbury**, one of the county's prettiest towns.

The Cathedral and the Mappa Mundi

Hereford **Cathedral** (daily 8.30am–5.30pm; £2 donation suggested) is a curious building, an uncomfortable amalgamation of architectural styles, with bits and pieces added to the eleventh-century original by a string of bishops and culminating in an extensive – and not especially sympathetic – Victorian refit. From the outside, the sandstone **tower** is the dominant feature, constructed in the early fourteenth century to eclipse the Norman western tower, which subsequently collapsed under its own weight in 1786. The tumbling masonry mauled the **nave** and its replacement lacks the grandeur of most other English cathedrals, though the forceful symmetries of the long rank of surviving Norman arches and piers more than hints at what went before. The **north**

transept is, however, a flawless exercise in thirteenth-century taste, its soaring windows a classic example of Early English architecture and a handsome home for the delicately carved table-tomb of St Thomas Cantilupe. Across the church, the **south transept** is largely Norman, its chunky stonework interrupted by an old fireplace, one of the few still surviving within an English church, and decorated by an intricately carved *Adoration of the Magi*, a sixteenth-century, bas-relief triptych from Germany.

In the 1980s, financial difficulties prompted the cathedral authorities to plan the sale of one of their most treasured possessions, the **Mappa Mundi**. There was an awful lot of cultural huffing and puffing about this controversial proposal, but the government and John Paul Getty Jnr rode to the rescue, with the oil tycoon stumping up a million pounds to keep the map here and install it in a brand new building. Made of sandstone, this New Library – located next to the cathedral at the west end of the cloisters – blends in seamlessly with the other, older buildings close by. It contains the immaculate **Mappa Mundi and Chained Library Exhibition** (April–Sept Mon–Sat 10am–5pm, Sun 11am–4pm; Oct–March Mon–Sat 11am–4pm; last admission 45min before closing; £4.50), which begins with a series of interpretative panels that lead to the Mappa, displayed in a dimly lit room. Dating to about 1300, and 62 by 52 inches in size, the map is quite simply remarkable – and it provides an extraordinary insight into the medieval mind. It is indeed a map (as we know it) in so far as it suggests the general geography of the world – with Asia at the top and Europe and Africa below, to left and right respectively – but it also squeezes in history, mythology and theology. At the top of the map, Christ sits in judgement with the saved on one side, the damned on the other – hell is represented by the jaws of a dragon. The rest of the border contains representations of the twelve winds and the repeated monogram "MORS" – for death. Inside the border, at the top of the earth, is the Garden of Eden, shown as an island, and in the centre is the walled city of Jerusalem. Britain is at the bottom on the left with Hereford – and several other cathedral cities – labelled in Latin, as are almost all the other inscriptions. In total, the three continents are adorned by over five hundred drawings, some signifying towns and cities, others biblical events, plants, birds and animals as well as a menagerie of mythological creatures – from the manticoras (man-headed-lions) and the essedones (cannibals), through to the blemyae (who have heads in their chests). As if this wasn't enough, the New Library also holds the **Chained Library**, a remarkably extensive collection of books and manuscripts dating from the eighth to the eighteenth century. A selection is always on display. The cathedral also owns a copy of the **Magna Carta** – or, to be exact, one of the revised versions drawn up after the original of 1215 with clauses revised in the king's favour – and this is frequently on display in the Chained Library too.

The rest of the city

After the Mappa, Hereford's other attractions can't help but seem rather pedestrian. Nonetheless, the **Hereford Museum and Art Gallery**, in a flamboyant Victorian building opposite the cathedral on Broad Street (April–Sept Tues–Sat 10am–5pm, Sun 10am–4pm; rest of year Tues–Sat 10am–5pm; free), does hold a mildly diverting collection of geological remains, local history and Victorian art. From the gallery, Broad Street continues up and round into the main square, **High Town**, which is fringed by several good-looking Georgian buildings.

Set amidst rolling countryside, Hereford's economy is still largely dependent on its agricultural base and the local **cider** industry is one of the city's biggest trades. Cider enthusiasts should make their way to the **Cider Museum and King Offa Distillery**, 21 Ryelands St (April–Oct daily 10am–5.30pm; Nov–March Tues–Sun 11am–3pm; £2.70), which tracks through the history of cider-making, provides views of the distillation process and offers samples of King Offa ciders, including a particularly tasty Cider Brandy. The museum is, however, a dull fifteen-minute walk west of the centre, off the A438. To get there, take Eign Gate west from High Town, cross the ring road onto Eign Street and watch for Ryelands Street on the left.

Practicalities

From Hereford **train station**, it's about half a mile southwest to the main square, High Town – via Station Approach, Commercial Road and its continuation Commercial Street. The long-distance **bus station** is just off Commercial Road, but most local buses stop in St Peter's Square, at the east end of High Town. The **tourist office** is directly opposite the cathedral, at 1 King St (Mon–Sat 9am–5pm; ⓣ01432/268430, ⓦwww.visitorlinks.com). They stock oodles of local leaflets and issue the free Herefordshire Visitor Guide, which has comprehensive accommodation listings.

Easily the best **hotel** in town is the *Castle House*, a truly immaculate hotel in an elegantly refurbished Georgian mansion just a couple of minutes' walk from the cathedral on Castle St (ⓣ01432/356321, ⓦwww.castlehse.co.uk; ❽). The hotel has a chic waterside terrace at the rear and each of the rooms is decorated in plush modern style. Hereford also has a substantial number of **B&Bs**, the pick of which is *Charades*, 34 Southbank Rd (ⓣ01432/269444; ❷), with six comfortable, mostly en-suite guest rooms in a large Victorian house a ten- to fifteen-minute walk northeast from the centre. To get there, take Commercial Street and then Commercial Road, cross the railway bridge and Southbank is the second on the right.

As regards **eating**, there are several appealing places near the cathedral on pedestrianized Church Street. Options here include two very good and inexpensive cafés, *Rendez-vous* (Mon–Tues 9.30am–5pm & Wed–Sat 9.30am–5pm & 7–10pm), which is strong on everything from salads and baguettes through to tortillas, and *Nutters* (Mon–Sat 9am–5pm), a vegetarian place just off Church St on Capuchin Yard. There's also *Cafe@allsaints*, in the old church at the top of Broad St (Mon–Sat 8.30am–5.30pm), where they serve a tasty range of well-conceived dishes – ricotta pie with salad leaves for instance – at around £6. The best restaurant in town is *La Rive*, at the *Castle House Hotel* (see above), but although this smart and polished place offers French cuisine at its finest, it's very expensive – set meals weigh in at around £37.

When it comes to **drinking**, don't leave town without sampling the favourite local tipple, **cider**. Every pub in town serves the stuff with one of the most enjoyable being *The Barrels*, a traditional kind of place, five minutes' walk southeast of High Town, on St Owen's Street. *The Barrels* is also the home pub of the local Wye Valley Brewery, whose trademark **bitters** are much acclaimed.

Around Hereford: Kilpeck

The lonely hamlet of **KILPECK**, nine miles southwest of Hereford off the A465, boasts the red sandstone **Church of St Mary and St David**, arguably the most perfectly preserved Norman church in Britain. Here, the full vitality of Saxon-Norman sculpture is revealed, principally around the south door where Oriental warriors gaze out from the shafts and the tympanum's Tree of Life is hooped by birds, dragons, green men, a phoenix and all sorts of mythical monsters. Up above, running right round the church, a superb set of no less than ninety tiny **corbel** sculptures features all manner of curiosities from grotesques and animal heads to musicians and acrobats, with barely a saint or religious figure in sight. The sculptors, who may or may not have had some sort of decorative plan, seem to have been inspired by pagan Viking carving, reminders of the Normans' Scandinavian ancestry – William the Conqueror was the descendant of a Viking chief who seized Normandy in the tenth century. The Victorians restored the corbel sculptures, but removed the more sexually explicit, with the exception of the genital-splaying **sheila-na-gig** on the apse to the right of the south doorway – food for thought. Inside, the church is plain and frugal, but there are several exquisite carvings here too, much more serene than the corbels and at their finest in the pious saints decorating the chancel arch.

Kilpeck was originally a frontier settlement, but the old village disappeared ages ago as did the **castle**, now no more than an overgrown hump at the top of the church graveyard.

Ledbury

Heading east from Hereford, it's an easy fifteen miles along the A438 to **LEDBURY**, a good-looking little town glued to the western edge of the Malvern Hills. The focus of the town is the Market Place, home to the dinky **Market House**, a Tudor beamed building raised on oak columns and with herringbone pattern beams. From beside it, narrow **Church Lane** – not to be confused with adjacent Church Street – runs up the slope framed by an especially fine ensemble of half-timbered Tudor and Stuart buildings. Among them is the Butcher Row House Museum and, pick of the bunch, the so-called **Painted Room** (Easter–Sept Mon–Fri 11am–3pm; free), in the town council offices, featuring a set of bold symmetrical floral frescoes painted on wattle-and-daub walls sometime in the sixteenth century. At the far end of the lane stands **St Michael's parish church**, whose strong and angular detached spire pokes high into the sky. The nucleus of the adjacent church is Norman – note the sturdy round pillars and the chancel's porthole windows – but there are early Gothic flourishes too, most importantly the nave's long and slender windows. Otherwise, the most interesting features are the funerary monuments, including the spectacular seventeenth-century **Skynner Tomb**, where five sons and five daughters kneel in honour of their parents, beneath the canopied slab on which their parents also kneel, she in a hat that looks fancy enough to wear at Ascot.

Ledbury **train station** is inconveniently situated on the northern edge of town, about three-quarters of a mile from the Market Place – straight down the A438. **Buses** stop on the Market Place, across from the **tourist office** (March to mid-July & mid-Sept to Nov Mon–Sat 10am–5pm; mid-July to mid-Sept daily 10am–5pm; ⓣ01531/636147). **Accommodation** is thin on the ground, but the *Feathers Hotel* (ⓣ01531/635266, ⓦwww.feathers-ledbury.co.uk; ⑥) occupies a smashing "Black and White" on the High Street, footsteps from the Market Place – and has just nineteen very comfortable rooms along with a health and leisure spa. As for **food**, the *Malthouse Restaurant*, on Church Lane (ⓣ01531/634443; closed Sun), is exemplary, with a creative menu featuring local ingredients – main courses average around £15 in the evening, lunches cost around £7. Also on Church Lane, the charming *Prince of Wales* **pub** is a great place to sink a beer amidst its snug, low-beamed rooms.

Ross-on-Wye

Pocket-sized **ROSS-ON-WYE**, perched above a loop in the river sixteen miles southeast of Hereford, is a relaxed, easy-going town with an artsy/New Age undertow. It's also the obvious base for exploring one of the more dramatic sections of the Wye River Valley and the Forest of Dean (see p.649).

Ross's jumble of narrow streets zeroes in on the **Market Place**, which is shadowed by the seventeenth-century **Market House**, a sturdy two-storey sandstone structure that now accommodates a modest **Heritage Centre** (April–Oct Mon–Sat 10am–5pm, Sun 10.30am–4pm; Nov–March Mon–Sat 10am–4pm; free), exploring the town's history. The Market House sports a medallion bust of a bewigged Charles II, placed here at the instigation of the pioneering seventeenth-century town planner, John Kyrle. A local man, Kyrle did much to improve the town's amenities and his reputation was such that the poet Alexander Pope singled him out for praise in one of his *Moral Essays*.

Veer right at the top of the Market Place, then turn left up Church Street to reach Ross's other noteworthy building, the mostly thirteenth-century **St Mary's Church**, whose sturdy stonework culminates in a slender, tapering spire. In front of the church, at the foot of the graveyard, is a plain but rare **Plague Cross**, commemorating the three hundred or so townsfolk who were buried here by night without coffins during a savage outbreak of the plague in 1637. Inside, the church holds two distinctive **table-tombs**, one of which – that of a certain William Rudhall (d.1530) – is a late example of the wonderful alabaster sculptures created by the specialist masons of Nottingham, whose work was prized right across medieval Europe. Beside the church, to the right of the entrance, **The Prospect** is a neat public garden offering pleasant views over the river.

If you've strolled long enough around town but still have time to spare, strike out along one of the many well-defined **footpaths** that thread their way through the riverine fields and woods bordering the Wye. A collection of leaflets giving detailed descriptions of several circular routes is available at the tourist office (see below).

Practicalities

There are no trains to Ross, but the **bus station** is handily located on Cantilupe Road, from where it's a couple of minutes' walk west to the Market Place. The **tourist office** is equally convenient, located a few yards west of the Market Place on the corner of High and Edde Cross streets (Mon–Sat 9.30am–5pm, plus mid-July to mid-Sept Sun 10am–4pm; ⓣ01989/562768). **Bikes** can be rented from Revolutions on Broad Street (ⓣ01989/562639). The main cultural event is the **Ross International Festival** (ⓣ01989/562562, ⓦwww.rossonwye-intfestival.co.uk), a mixed bag of music, theatre and dance held over two weeks in August.

Ross is strong on **B&Bs** with one of the best being the *Linden House*, in a fetching, three-storey Georgian building opposite St Mary's at 14 Church St (ⓣ01989/565373, ⓦwww.lindenguesthouse.com; ❷). The seven guest rooms, half of which are en suite, are cosily decorated in a modern style and the breakfasts are delicious – both traditional and vegetarian. Another excellent if pricier choice is the *Old Court House*, across from the tourist office at 53 High St (ⓣ01989/762275, ⓦwww.visitorlinks.com; ❸). This is sited in a sympathetically modernized, half-timbered town house with grand fireplaces and an idiosyncratic, warren-like lay-out – all in all, quite a treat.

For **food**, *Oat Cuisine*, a daytime café at 41 Broad St, sells an unusual range of whole- and health foods, everything from salads and soups through to dandelion coffee and beyond. Alternatively – and this is something of a gastronomic surprise in rural Herefordshire – there's *Meaders Hungarian Restaurant* (☎01989/562803; closed Sun), just along the High Street from the Market Place and offering delicious Hungarian dishes at moderate prices. Of the **pubs**, the *Crown & Spectre,* on Broad Street, offers a goodly range of brews, but the traditional *Man of Ross*, at the top of Wye Street across from the tourist office, wins on atmosphere.

The Wye River Valley

Heading **south from Ross** along the B4234, it's just five miles to the sullen sandstone mass of **Goodrich Castle** (April–Oct daily 10am–6pm; Nov–March Wed–Sun 10am–1pm & 2–4pm; £3.70; EH), which commands wide views over the hills and woods of the **Wye River Valley**. Dating from the twelfth century, the castle's strategic location beside a busy river crossing point guaranteed its importance as a border stronghold from the twelfth century onwards. Today, the substantial ruins incorporate a Norman keep, a maze of later rooms and passageways and walkable ramparts, complete with murder holes, the slits through which boiling oil or water was poured onto the attackers down below. During the Civil War, a determined Royalist garrison held on until the Parliamentarians built themselves a special cannon, "Roaring Meg", which soon brought victory – a great achievement considering the unreliability of the technology: large cannons had the unfortunate habit of blowing up as soon as anyone fired them.

The castle stands next to tiny **GOODRICH VILLAGE**, which is on the Ross to Monmouth bus route – Stagecoach **bus** #34 (every 2hr, not Sun). From the village, it's around a mile and half southeast along narrow country lanes to the solitary **Welsh Bicknor hostel** (☎0870/770 6086, Ⓦwww.yha.org.uk; £11.50; restricted opening Sept–March; closed 10am–5pm), in a Victorian riverside rectory. The hostel, in 25-acre grounds, has 76 beds in anything from two-bed to ten-bed rooms, and provides evening meals on request; you can just show up and hope for a berth, but given the hostel's seclusion booking ahead is strongly recommended.

Symonds Yat Rock and Symonds Yat East

From Goodrich – and beyond all hope of a bus – it's a couple of miles south along narrow roads to the signposted turning that wriggles its way up to the top of **Symonds Yat Rock**, rising high above a wooded, hilly loop in the Wye. This is one of the region's most celebrated views and you'll probably share it with the birdwatchers who come here to spy the raptors gliding the valley below. At the foot of the rock – a two-mile drive away – is **SYMONDS YAT EAST**, a pretty little hamlet that straggles along the east bank of the river. It's a popular spot, with canoe rental and forty-minute cruises operated by Kingfisher (☎01600/891063; March–Oct only), and there are several places to stay. The most appealing **hotel** is the bright and cheerful *Forest View* (☎01600/890210; ❺).

The road to the village is a dead end, so you have to double back to regain the **B4432**. This continues south towards Coleford – and the Forest of Dean (see opposite) – with the **B4228** pressing on thereafter to loop round to St Briavels, not far from the Wye, and passing the Clearwell Caves (see p.650) on the way.

St Briavels

Over the border in Gloucestershire, **ST BRIAVELS** is a pleasant rose-stone village with a small but forbidding Norman **castle** (April–Sept daily 1–4pm; free; EH) plonked right in the middle on a grassy knoll. Formerly used by King John as a hunting lodge, and the region's administrative centre during medieval times, the castle now accommodates one of England's more impressive **youth hostels** (ⓣ0870/770 6040, ⓦwww.yha.org.uk; variable days of opening; dorm beds £11.50) with 76 beds distributed between two- to ten-bedded rooms. Beneath the keep extends a network of **tunnels** (no access) originally excavated in the thirteenth century by local miners. As a reward for their work, men over the age of 21 born within the St Briavels district were granted the right to mine for coal and iron ore anywhere in the Forest of Dean for free. This law is still in place, and within living memory a significant number of foresters made their living as "**Free Miners**", just paying a nominal royalty each year from their earnings to the Crown.

If you're tempted to **stay**, the hostel is the obvious choice, though there are also a handful of spick-and-span, en-suite rooms upstairs in *The George*, a friendly old pub beside the castle (ⓣ01594/530228, ⓦwww.thegeorgeinn.info; ③). The pub also serves good **food** – including tasty local meat and game – both inside and outside on its garden terrace. One other advantage is that the village is within comfortable walking distance of the River Wye – and the Offa's Dyke Path (see p.665), which itself leads north in a few miles to **The Kymin** in Monmouthshire (house: April–Oct Sun & Mon 11am–4pm, £2.10; grounds: daily dawn to dusk, free; NT). This Georgian country home is a small, circular affair attached to a temple dedicated to the Royal Navy. The grounds offer commanding views across the Wye.

The Forest of Dean

Wedged between the Severn estuary and the River Wye to the south of Ross-on-Wye (and Goodrich), Gloucestershire's **Forest of Dean** is an extensive tract of woodland, whose excellent hunting long attracted royal attention – and protection – beginning with King Edward the Confessor in the eleventh century. Later, the forest's oak trees were much in demand for the construction of Royal Navy ships and there was also large-scale iron- and coal-mining, as recalled by the names of the two largest towns hereabouts – **Coleford** and **Cinderford**. The Forestry Commission took over the running of the forest in the 1930s and in recent years they have developed a number of tourist attractions as well as a network of cycling and hiking trails. With so many large towns and cities less than an hour away by road, it's not surprising that tens of thousands of visitors congregate here every year, but however good the forest may be for family holidays, the scenery isn't all that special and neither are the purpose-built attractions. Just over half of the forest is made up of conifers, and the remainder is broadleaf woodland with oak the most common tree.

The best way to sample the forest is to take the six-mile-long **B4226** from Coleford to Cinderford. First up, after about half a mile, is **Hopewell Colliery Museum** (March–Oct daily 10am–4pm; free), where you can amble through a shallow, surface mine. Thereafter, it's another short trip to both the picnic sites and playgrounds of **Beechenhurst Lodge** and the **Sculpture Trail**, the most interesting attraction in the forest. Three and a half miles long – allow about three hours – the trail is an energetic hike up into the forested hills and it leads past twelve pieces of contemporary artwork and sculpture, including a giant chair on the crest of a hill. This part of the forest is also popular with cyclists; **bicycle rental** is available from Pedalabikeaway (ⓣ01594/860065,

Ⓦ www.pedalabikeaway.com), located about half a mile from the B4226 just to the west of the Beechenhurst/Sculpture Trail turning – follow the signs; they also hand out maps showing the best cycle routes.

Finally, just south of Coleford, off the B4228 St Briavels road, the **Clearwell Caves** (March–Oct daily 10am–5pm; £3.50) comprise a natural cave system enlarged by generations of iron-ore miners. Nine caverns can be explored on foot and without a guide; you can also don a boiler suit, lamp and hard hat for trips to the deeper parts of the mines, still worked to supply tinted pigments to the cosmetics and paints industries.

Hay-on-Wye

Straddling the Anglo-Welsh border some twenty miles west of Hereford, the hilly little town of **HAY-ON-WYE** is known to most people for one thing – **books**. Hay saw its first bookshop open in 1961 and has since become a bibliophile's paradise, with just about every spare inch of the town being given over to the trade, including the old cinema and the ramshackle stone castle. As a consequence, many of Hay's inhabitants are now outsiders, which means that it has little indigenous feel, but there again when the hill farmers come into town on the razzle Hay gets a bit of a (welcome) jolt.

Hay has an attractive setting, amidst rolling forested hills, and its narrow, bendy streets are lined with a particularly engaging assortment of old stone houses. In summer, the town plays host to a succession of riverside parties and travelling fairs, the pick of which is the **Hay Festival of Literature and the Arts** (Ⓣ01497/821066, Ⓦ www.hayfestival.co.uk), held over ten days at the back end of May, when London's literary world decamps here.

Before you start ambling round the town, visit the tourist office (see p.651) to pick up the free leaflet that gives the low-down on all of Hay's bookshops together with a street plan. Across the street from the tourist office, a signed

The King of Hay

Richard Booth, whose family originates from the area, opened the first of his Hay-on-Wye second-hand bookshops in 1961. Since then, he has built an astonishing empire and attracted other booksellers to the town, turning it into the greatest market of used books in the world. There are now over thirty such shops in this minuscule town, the largest of which – Booth's own – contains around half a million volumes.

Whereas many of the region's country towns have seen their populations ebb in recent decades, Hay has **boomed** on the strength of its bibliophilic connections. Booth regards this success as a prototype for other endangered communities, placing the emphasis firmly on local initiatives and unusual specialisms. He is unequivocal in his condemnation of government regeneration programmes, which, he asserts, have done little to stem the flow of jobs and people out of the region. This healthy distaste for bureaucracy, coupled with Booth's self-promotional skills and Hay's geographical location slap bang on the Anglo–Welsh border, led him to declare Hay independent of the UK in 1977, with himself, naturally enough, as **King**. In a flurry of activity, he appointed his own ministers and offered "official" government scrolls, passports and car stickers to bewitched visitors. Although this proclamation of independence carried no official weight, most of the locals rallied behind King Richard and were delighted with the publicity – and the visitors. With Hay's success now assured, Booth no longer has to be so publicity-hungry, but he remains an important and popular local figure.

footpath leads up the slope to the **castle**, a careworn Jacobean mansion built into the walls of an earlier medieval fortress. Richard Booth lives in part of the castle, but its southern extremities are given over to a pair of bookshops: **Castle Drive Books** (daily 10.30am–5pm; ⓣ01568/780707), which has a large stock of remaindered books, and **Hay Castle Bookshop** (daily 9.30am–5.30pm; ⓣ01497/820503 ⓦwww.boothbooks.co.uk), a trusty collection focused on fine art, cinema, antiquarian and photography. From here, the footpath twists its way round the western flank of the castle to meet the steps that lead down to Castle Street, home to **Bookends**, at no. 9 (April–Oct Sun–Wed 11am–5.30pm, Thurs–Sat 9am–8pm; Nov–March daily 9am–5.30pm; ⓣ01497/821341, ⓦwww.bookspostfree.com), where all the books cost £1.

Castle Street slopes up to the main square, High Town, from where it's straight on for Lion Street, where **Booth Books**, at no. 44 (April–Oct Mon–Sat 9am–8pm, Sun 11.30am–5.30pm, Nov–March Mon–Sat 9am–5.30pm, Sun 11.30am–5.30pm; ⓣ01497/820322, ⓦwww.richardbooth.demon.co.uk) is a huge, draughty warehouse of almost unlimited browsing potential. At the foot of Lion Street is the town's Victorian **clocktower**.

Practicalities

Buses to Hay stop in the centre of town on Oxford Road beside the main car park. The adjacent **tourist office** (daily: Easter–Oct 10am–1pm & 2–5pm; Nov–Easter 11am–1pm & 2–4pm; ⓣ01497/820144, ⓦwww.hay-on-wye.co.uk) stocks an exhaustive range of hiking books and maps, and will arrange accommodation.

Accommodation in town is plentiful, though things get booked up long in advance for the Hay Festival of Literature. Amongst the town's many **B&Bs** and **guest houses**, one excellent option is the *Seven Stars*, plum in the centre across from the clocktower at 11 Broad St (ⓣ01497/820886, ⓦwww.hay-on-wye.co.uk/sevenstars; no cards; ❸). A family-run place, this B&B occupies an attractive ivy-clad stone house with beamed ceilings, and the six en-suite guest rooms are immaculate; breakfasts – kippers, haddock – are smashing too. Another good bet is the *Belmont House*, Belmont Rd (ⓣ01497/820718; no credit cards; ❷), a well-kept B&B with three commodious guest rooms in a good-looking Georgian villa near the junction of Castle Street. There's also *20 Lion Street B&B*, a cosy and carefully tended little stone cottage on the east side of the centre at – you guessed it – 20 Lion St (ⓣ01497/821901; no cards; ❶). Outside of Hay, the *Old Post Office*, **Llanigon** (ⓣ01497/820008, ⓦwww.old-post-office.co.uk; no cards; ❶), is a first-rate B&B in a seventeenth-century former post office, complete with wood floors and beamed ceilings. There are

Canoeing in Hay-on-Wye

Scores of visitors come to Hay-on-Wye to hike and cycle, but the district is just as pleasantly explored by kayak or canoe on the River Wye. In four to six days, it's possible to paddle your way downriver from Hay to Ross-on-Wye (see p.647), overnighting in tents on isolated stretches of river bank, or holing up in comfortable B&Bs and pubs along the way. As regards kayak and canoe rental, Paddles & Peddles, 15 Castle St (ⓣ01497/820604, ⓦwww.canoehire.co.uk), is a reputable outfit, full of good ideas and advice. Rental of life jackets and other essential equipment (such as waterproof canisters to carry your gear) is included in the price, which works out at around £40 per canoe for a full 24 hours, with discounts for longer trips. In addition, Paddles & Peddles will transport their customers to the departure and from the finishing points by minibus.

three rooms, two en suite, and the entirely vegetarian breakfasts are outstanding. Llanigon is a couple of miles south of Hay within easy hiking distance of Offa's Dyke Path (see p.665), which also cuts across the west end of Hay. The nearest **campsite** to Hay is *Radnors End* (☎01497/820780), in a pleasant setting five minutes' walk from the town centre across the Wye bridge on the Clyro road; washing and toilet facilities here are simple, but pitches are inexpensive (£3.50).

As regards **food**, *Shepherds*, 9 High Town (Mon–Sat 9.30am–5.30pm, Sun 11am–5.30pm), is an appealing café with a good line in snacks and mouth-watering, locally made ice cream. There's also the hard-to-beat *Granary* (daily till 9pm; ☎01497/820790), a combined café, bar and restaurant opposite the clocktower on Broad Street. Here they serve delicious wholefood snacks and soups as well as filling main meals (£6–8) with the emphasis on local organic produce; they have a roadside terrace, too, where hikers can kick off their boots and sink a leisurely pint. For a more formal meal, head for the *Famous Old Black Lion*, Lion St (☎01497/820841), an antique inn serving first-rate food with main courses kicking off at around £9.

Shropshire

One of England's largest and least populated counties, **Shropshire** stretches from its long and winding border with Wales to the very edge of the urban Black Country. Its most unique attraction is industrial: it was here that the Industrial Revolution made a huge stride forward with the spanning of the River Severn by the very first **iron bridge**. The assorted industries that subsequently squeezed into the gorge are long gone, but a series of **museums** celebrate their craftsmanship – from tiles and iron through to porcelain. The River Severn also flows through the county town of **Shrewsbury**, whose antique centre holds dozens of old half-timbered buildings, though **Ludlow**, further to the south, has the edge when it comes to handsome Tudor and Jacobean architecture. In between the two lie some of the most beautiful parts of Shropshire, namely the twin ridges of **Wenlock Edge** and the **Long Mynd**, both of which are prime hiking areas, best explored from the attractive little town of **Church Stretton**. Out west, the hills become increasingly barren and dramatic as they approach the Welsh border. This is one of the most remote parts of England, a solitary landscape dusted with tiny hamlets and the occasional town, amongst which **Bishop's Castle** and **Clun** are perhaps the most appealing.

Yet, for all its attractions, Shropshire remains well off the main tourist routes, one factor protecting the county's isolation being the paucity of its **public transport**. Shrewsbury and Telford are connected to Birmingham, whilst Ludlow, Craven Arms and Church Stretton are connected to Shrewsbury on the Hereford line, but that's about the limit of the **train** services, whilst rural **buses** tend to connect outlying villages on just a few days of the week. One recent step forward has been the creation of the **Shropshire Hills Shuttle bus** service (Ⓦwww.shropshirehillsshuttles.co.uk) aimed at the tourist market and operating every weekend from April to November. The shuttle has five main routes with one nosing around the Long Mynd, another Wenlock Edge. There are buses every hour or two and an Adult Day Rover ticket, valid on the whole caboodle, costs just £3. Bus timetables are available at most Shropshire tourist offices.

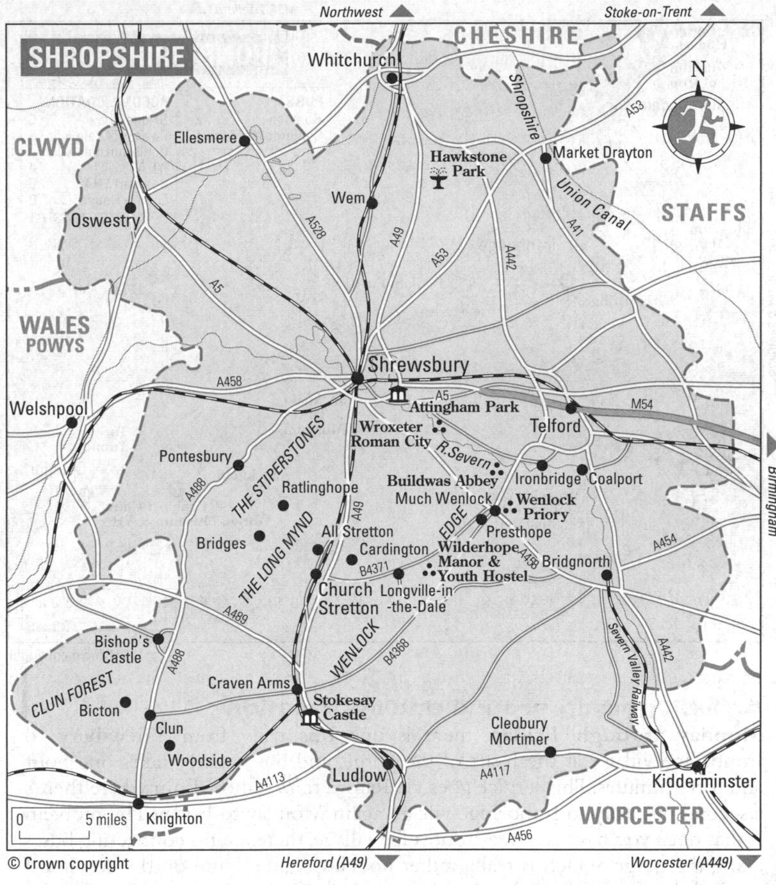

Ironbridge Gorge

Both geographically and culturally, **Ironbridge Gorge**, the collective title for a cluster of small villages huddled in the wooded Severn Valley to the south of new-town Telford, looks to the cities of the West Midlands conurbation rather than rural Shropshire. Ironbridge Gorge was the crucible of the Industrial Revolution, a process encapsulated by its famous span across the Severn – the world's first **iron bridge**, engineered by Abraham Darby and opened on New Year's Day, 1781. Darby was the third innovative industrialist of that name – the first Abraham Darby started iron-smelting here back in 1709 and the second invented the forging process that made it possible to produce massive single beams in iron. Under the guidance of such creative figures as the Darbys and Thomas Telford, the area's factories once churned out engines, rails, wheels and other heavy-duty iron pieces in quantities unmatched anywhere else in the world. Manufacturing has now all but vanished, but the surviving monuments make the gorge the most extensive industrial heritage sight in England – and one that has been granted World Heritage Site status by UNESCO.

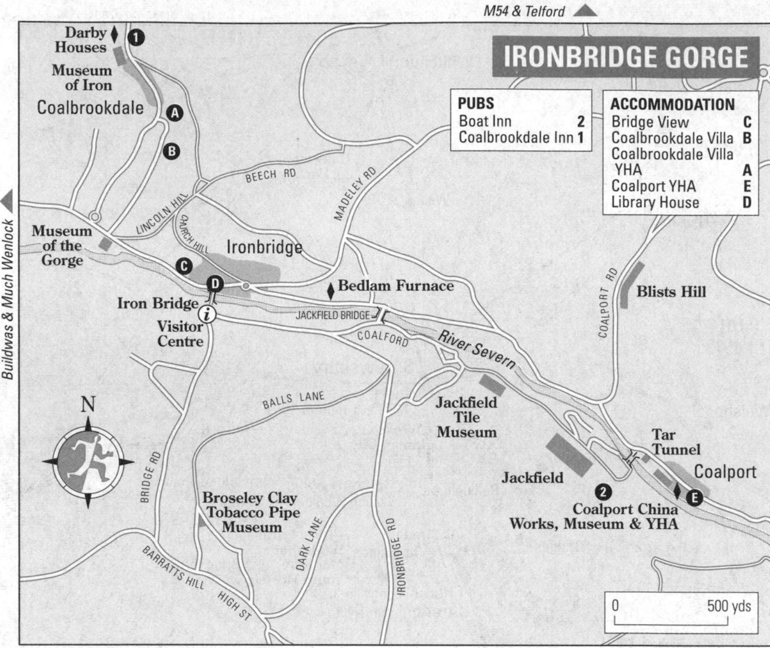

Arrival, getting around and information

Monday through Friday, there is one **bus** daily from Shrewsbury to Ironbridge village, at the heart of the gorge, and the journey takes one hour and forty minutes. This service goes via Telford train station, from where there's a second bus daily to Ironbridge village, again Monday to Friday. The problem is that once you have reached Ironbridge village, there are no connecting buses along the gorge, which is really rather hopeless. The picture on the **weekend** is a little rosier. On Saturdays and Sundays, the **Gorge Connect bus** shuttles along the gorge from Coalbrookdale in the west to Coalport in the east every half hour or so, but again there are still only a couple of buses a day linking Telford train station (and Shrewsbury) with Ironbridge village. On the plus side, the Gorge Connect does run from Ironbridge village to Buildwas Abbey (see p.657) and Much Wenlock (see p.657) four times on both Saturday and Sunday. A Day Rover ticket, valid on all Gorge Connect services, costs just £3. Finally, although there's currently no **bike** rental in the gorge, it's possible this service may be resumed – ring the tourist office (see below) for news.

Ironbridge Gorge contains four museums and an assortment of other industrial attractions spread along a four-mile stretch of the River Severn Valley. A thorough exploration takes a couple of days, but the **highlights** – the Museum of Iron and the Coalport China works and Museum – are easily manageable on a day-trip. Each museum and attraction charges its own admission fee, but if you're intending to visit several, then buy a **passport ticket** (£13), which allows access to each of them once in any calendar year. Passport tickets are available at all the main sights. **Parking** is free at most of the sights, but not in Ironbridge village itself. Pick up local maps and information from the **Ironbridge Visitor Information Centre** (Mon–Fri 9am–5pm, Sat & Sun

10am–5pm; ⓣ01952/432166, ⓦwww.ironbridge.org.uk), in the old toll house at the south end of the iron bridge in Ironbridge village.

Accommodation

Most visitors to the gorge come for the day, but there are several pleasant **B&Bs** in Ironbridge village, which is where you want to be. Two of the best are *The Library House*, which occupies a charming Georgian villa just yards from the iron bridge at 11 Severn Bank (ⓣ01952/432299, ⓦwww.libraryhouse.com; no credit cards; ❸); and *Bridge View*, whose neat and trim rooms are also a stone's throw from the bridge at 10 Tontine Hill (ⓣ01952/432541, ⓦwww.ironbridgeview.co.uk; ❷). Alternatively, *Coalbrookdale Villa* occupies an attractive Victorian ironmasters' house about half a mile up the hill from the west end of Ironbridge village in tiny Paradise, close to Coalbrookdale iron foundry (ⓣ01952/433450, ⓦwww.coalbrookdalevilla.co.uk; no credit cards; ❸). The villa is a splendid neo-Gothic affair, all towers and turrets, and it stands in splendid gardens. It's also metres from one of the gorge's two **youth hostels**, *Coalbrookdale*, in the old Literary and Scientific Institute building, a Victorian whopper with eighty beds parcelled up into two- to eight-bedded rooms (ⓣ0870/770 5882, ⓦwww.yha.org.uk; dorm beds £11.50). Breakfasts and evening meals are provided here, but pre-booking is required. The hostel is open during school holidays and on Fridays and Saturdays in term time – as is the second hostel, *Coalport* (same details), three miles east along the gorge in the former Coalport China factory. Coalport hostel also provides breakfasts and evening meals, has 85 beds, in two- to eleven-bedded rooms, but does not require advance booking.

Ironbridge village

There must have been an awful lot of nervous sweat during the construction of the **iron bridge** over the River Severn in the late 1770s. The first of its kind, no one was quite sure how the new material would wear and although the single-span design looked sound, many feared the bridge would simply tumble into the river. To compensate, Abraham Darby used more iron than was strictly necessary, but the end result still manages to appear stunningly graceful, arching between the steep banks with the river far below. The settlement at the north end of the span was promptly renamed **IRONBRIDGE**, and today its brown-brick houses climb prettily up the hill from the bridge. The village is also home to the **Museum of the Gorge** (daily 10am–5pm; £2.10), located in a church-like, neo-Gothic old riverside warehouse about 500yd west of the bridge along the main road. This provides an introduction to the industrial history of the gorge and provides a few environmental pointers too.

Coalbrookdale iron foundry

At the roundabout just to the west of the Museum of the Gorge, turn right for the half-mile trip up to what was once the gorge's big industrial deal, the **COALBROOKDALE iron foundry**, which boomed throughout the eighteenth and in the early nineteenth century, employing up to four thousand men and boys. The foundry has been imaginatively converted into the **Museum of Iron** (daily 10am–5pm; £5.15, including Darby Houses), with a wide range of displays on iron-making in general and the history of the company in particular. There are superb examples of Victorian and Edwardian ironwork here, including the art castings – stags, dogs and even camels – that became the house speciality. Also in the complex, across from the foundry beneath a protective canopy, are the ruins of the **furnace** where Abraham Darby pioneered the use of coke as a smelting fuel in place of charcoal.

From the foundry, it's about 100yd up to the **Darby Houses** (daily 10am–5pm; £3) – Dale House and Rosehill – a pair of attractively restored, old ironmasters' homes with Georgian period rooms and a scattering of items that once belonged to the Darby family.

Jackfield and Coalport

Heading east from the iron bridge, it's a third of a mile along the river to the battered brick-and-stone remains of the **Bedlam furnace** (open access; free), one of the first furnaces to use coke rather than charcoal. It was kept alight round-the-clock and at night its fiery silhouette scared passers-by half to death – hence the name. From here, it's a mile to the turning for Blists Hill (see below) and another 500yd or so to the **Tar Tunnel** (April–Oct daily 10am–5pm; £1.15), built to transport coal from one part of the gorge to another, but named for the bitumen that oozes naturally from its walls.

Beside the tunnel, a footbridge crosses the river to reach **JACKFIELD**, a sleepy little place that once hummed to the tune of its tile factory, about half a mile west from the footbridge along the river. The factory has now been turned into the **Jackfield Tile Museum** (daily 10am–5pm; £4.50), which features an excellent collection of brightly coloured tiles, from the fancy, flowery patterns of washstand splash-backs through to intricate Victorian fireplace tiles and a folksy *Punch and Judy* panel from the 1920s.

Back at the tunnel, a canal towpath leads east in a couple of minutes to **COALPORT China works**, a large brick complex holding a youth hostel (see p.655) and the **Coalport China Museum** (daily 10am–5pm; £4.30). The museum kicks off with a couple of rooms crammed full with Coalport wares, the particular highlight being the gaudy and ornate pieces manufactured in the company's Victorian heyday, from around 1820 to 1890 – the company moved production to Stoke-on-Trent in 1926. There's also a workshop, where potters demonstrate their skills, and a Social History Gallery, which explores the hard life of the factory's workers, whose health was constantly at risk from the factory's lead-dosed dust. The museum also includes two **bottle-kilns**, those distinctive conical structures that were long the hallmark of the pottery industry. In the base of one is a small display of fine Coalport pieces, whilst the other explains how the kilns worked – though quite how the firers survived the conditions defies the imagination.

Blists Hill Victorian Town

Doubling back along the river, it's a third of a mile west from Coalport to the clearly signed, mile-long road that cuts up to the gorge's most popular attraction, the rambling **Blists Hill Victorian Town** (daily 10am–5pm; £8.25). This encloses a substantial number of reconstructed Victorian buildings, most notably a school, a candle-makers, a doctor's surgery complete with horrific instruments, a gas-lit pub, and a wrought-iron works. Jam-packed on most summer days, it's especially popular with school parties, who keep the period-dressed employees very busy.

The Broseley Clay Tobacco Pipe Museum

During the late seventeenth and early eighteenth centuries, the satellite settlement of **BROSELEY**, across the river directly south of Ironbridge village, became a boom town in its own right, producing **clay pipes** for the swelling ranks of tobacco smokers in Britain. There were all sorts of clay pipes from the simple and unadorned to the fancily embossed and the extraordinary, arm-length pipes known as "Church Wardens", and many smokers even had their own special pipe cases. The decline in the popularity of the clay pipe was a long, drawn-out process but by the 1920s working-class smokers had mostly switched to cigarettes, the middle class to wood pipes. Nevertheless, one of the Broseley clay pipe companies held out until 1957 and the factory has now been turned into the **Broseley Clay Tobacco Pipe Museum** (April–Oct daily 1–5pm; £3), though "turned" is something of an exaggeration as well-nigh everything has been left untouched since its closure. Spread over three floors are the assorted work benches, cutting machines, racks and mini-furnace of the old works, looking suitably dusty and illustrated by a series of informative panels. Nevertheless, somehow you can't help but feel the museum should be more interesting than it actually is, despite the best efforts of the pipe-making demonstrators.

The Broseley Museum is a circuitous two and a half miles from the iron bridge – just follow the signs.

Eating and drinking

There are two excellent **pubs** in the gorge – the *Boat Inn*, a cosy little place with a riverside setting across the footbridge from the Tar Tunnel, and the *Coalbrookdale Inn*, a smashing traditional pub on the main road above the Museum of Iron. Both serve inexpensive **food,** but the *Coalbrookdale Inn* does it much better.

Buildwas Abbey and Much Wenlock

Heading west from Ironbridge village along the northern bank of the River Severn, it's only a couple of miles to the A4169 and **Buildwas Abbey** (April–Sept daily 11am–5pm; £2.20; EH), whose scattered ruins, dating from the twelfth century, stand in woodland above the river. The old abbey church is the main event here, roofless but otherwise well preserved with a long line of sturdy Norman arches surviving from the nave.

From Buildwas, it's just three miles more to **MUCH WENLOCK**, a tiny little town where a medley of Tudor, Jacobean and Georgian buildings dots the High Street – and pulls in the day-trippers by the score. At the foot of the High street is the **Guildhall**, sitting pretty on sturdy oak columns, but the town's architectural high point is **Wenlock Priory** (April–Oct daily 10am–6pm, Nov–March Wed–Sun 10am–1pm & 2–4pm; £3; EH) a short stroll away – turn left at the Guildhall and then first right along the Bull Ring. The Saxons built a monastery at Much Wenlock in the seventh century, but today's remains mostly stem from the thirteenth and fourteenth centuries when the Cluniac monastery established here in the 1080s was at its height. Set amidst immaculate gardens and fringed by woodland, the ruins are particularly picturesque, from the peeling stonework of the old priory church's transepts to the shattered bulk of St Michael's chapel next to the bare foundations of the church's west door. Of special note also is the Chapter House, where a trio of immaculately preserved, dog-tooth decorated Norman arches have survived along with some delicate false arcading on the inside walls – the Cluniacs were particularly fond of this decorative design. Next to the Chapter House are the cloisters, not especially interesting in themselves, but holding a rare example of a free-standing lavabo (wash stand) – to be precise the base – with carved panels on the side.

It only takes an hour or so to look round the town, but the **tourist office**, at the foot of the High Street (June–Aug daily 10.30am–5pm; April–May &

Sept–Oct Mon–Sat 10.30am–1pm & 2–5pm; ☎01952/727679), does have a small cachet of **B&Bs** and **hotels**. One recommendable option is the *Talbot Inn*, High St (☎01952/727077, Ⓦwww.the-talbot-inn.com; ⑤), an old coaching inn with exposed beams, fresh flowers in summer and open fires during the winter; the guest rooms are in the converted malthouse overlooking the courtyard at the back of the inn. For **food**, the *Talbot Inn* has a very competent restaurant, where the emphasis is on local produce and the house speciality is bread and butter pudding. Main courses average about £13 in the evening, half that at lunch times. Alternatively, *The Deli*, close by on the High Street, offers a good line in takeaway sandwiches and baguettes.

Wenlock Edge

Attracting hikers from all over the region, the beautiful and deeply rural **Wenlock Edge** is a limestone escarpment that runs twenty-odd miles southwest from Much Wenlock to the A49. On its south side is a gently shelving slope of open farmland, while the thickly wooded north side scarps steeply down to the Shropshire plains. Much of the Edge is owned by the National Trust, and a network of waymarked **trails**, graded by colour according to length and difficulty, winds through the woodland from a string of car parks along the **B4371**, which hugs the ridge from Much Wenlock to **LONGVILLE-IN-THE-DALE**. The paths are easy to follow, but it's still a good idea to pick up the appropriate OS map and a copy of the National Trust's very helpful and free "Walks along Wenlock Edge" leaflet. The latter is available from Much Wenlock tourist office (see p.657) and Wilderhope Manor (see p.664). For the most part, these NT escarpment walks provide only limited views – the trees get in the way – but this is not the case on the red walk (3km; 1hr; medium difficulty) beginning at the **Presthope car park**, about two and a half miles from the start of the B4371, heading south from Much Wenlock. This hike affords superb views over Shropshire's sea of patchwork fields with the hills of the Welsh border beckoning beyond.

Normal **buses** along all or parts of the Edge are few and far between, but the **Wenlock Wanderer**, linking Church Stretton (see p.663) and Much Wenlock along the B4371 (April–Nov Sat & Sun only, every 2hr; Day Rover £3), does something to fill the gap. As for **accommodation**, there are one or two B&Bs dotted along the B4371, but all in all you're probably better off either hunkering down in Ironbridge village (see p.655) or aiming for one of the YHA's most distinctive **hostels**, *Wilderhope Manor* (☎0870/770 6090; Ⓦwww.yha.org.uk; call ahead for opening dates & reservations; dorm beds £11.50). The hostel occupies a remote Elizabethan mansion next to a farm about one mile off the B4371 – the turning is clearly signed on the north edge of Longville-in-the-Dale. Facilities include a self-catering kitchen and a cycle store and breakfasts and evening meals are on offer; there are seventy beds in four- to fourteen-bedded rooms.

Bridgnorth

BRIDGNORTH, nine miles southeast of Much Wenlock along the A458, may be in Shropshire, but – with Wolverhampton just twenty minutes' drive away – it has all the bustle of the West Midlands. Spilling down a sheer-sided bluff beside the River Severn, the town prospered throughout the medieval era as a bridging point for the river, but was badly mauled and its economy dislocated by the Parliamentary army during the Civil War. Today, Bridgnorth is at its prettiest on top of the bluff in the **High Town**, where the High Street is interrupted by the seventeenth-century **Town Hall**, a half-timbered building perched on an arcaded base. At its southern end, High Street runs into West Castle Street. This soon leads to the domed **St Mary's Church**, a solemn-looking edifice designed by Thomas Telford, and the shattered thirty-foot **tower** which is all that remains of the medieval castle: the ruin leans at a precarious angle of seventeen degrees. From here, a short but pleasant walkway tracks along the bluff above the river, ending up at the century-old **cliff railway** (April–Sept Mon–Sat 8am–8pm, Sun noon–8pm; rest of year closes 6.30pm; 70p), which clanks up and down the steepest rail gradient in Britain to connect Bank Street (off West Castle Street) to the Low Town below.

Bridgnorth is also the northern terminus of the **Severn Valley Railway** (Ⓣ01299/403816, Ⓦwww.svr.co.uk), whose trains steam down the valley to Kidderminster, some thirteen miles away. Trains operate all year, daily from May to September. It takes a little over an hour for the train to travel from Bridgnorth to Kidderminster with the return fare costing from £10.50. In Bridgnorth, the SVR station is in High Town a short walk from West Castle Street.

It only takes an hour or two to look round Bridgnorth and there are regular **bus** services on to Shrewsbury and Ludlow amongst many possible destinations. Most countywide services arrive and depart from the bus stops on the High Street. If you do decide to stay, the **tourist office**, on Listley Street, off the south end of High Street (April–Oct Mon–Wed, Fri–Sun 9.30am–5pm, Thurs 10am–1pm & 2–5pm; Nov–March Mon–Wed, Fri & Sat 9.30am–5pm; Ⓣ01746/763257, Ⓦwww.bridgnorthshropshire.com), can help you out with a list of local **B&Bs**.

Shrewsbury and around

SHREWSBURY, the county town of Shropshire, sits in a narrow loop of the River Severn, a three-hundred-yard spit of land being all that keeps the town centre from becoming an island. It would be difficult to design a better defensive site and the Britons were quick to erect a fort here once the Roman legions had hot-footed it out of their colony in the fifth century. Later, the Normans built a stone castle, which Edward I decided to strengthen and expand, though by then the local economy owed as much to the Welsh wool trade as it did to all this military hoopla. In Georgian times, Shrewsbury became a fashionable staging post on the busy London to Holyhead route, boasting a lively social season, patronized by the sort of people who could afford to send their offspring to the famous Shrewsbury School. However, those heady days are long gone and nowadays Shrewsbury is an easy-going, middling market town, whose jingle and jangle of narrow lanes, courtyards and alleys fills out the hilly neck of land that comprises the centre. It's the overall feel of the place that is its main appeal, though **St Mary's Church** and its immediate environs are particularly pleasing. Shrewsbury is also within easy striking distance of two enjoyable attractions, the ruins of **Wroxeter Roman City** and the grottoes and follies of **Hawkstone Historic Park** – though you'll need your own transport to get to either easily.

Arrival, information and orientation

Shrewsbury is well connected by **train** to the rest of the country, and its station lies at the northeast edge of the centre off Castle Gates. **Buses** from London, Birmingham and beyond pull into the National Express stand at the Raven Meadows bus station, off the Smithfield Road, five minutes' walk west of the train station. The **tourist office** is a five-minute walk south up the hill from the train station, on The Square (May–Sept Mon–Sat 9.30am–5.30pm, Sun 10am–4pm; Oct–April Mon–Sat 10am–5pm; ⓣ01743/281200, ⓦwww.shrewsburytourism.co.uk).

The labyrinthine streets of the centre can be baffling, but fortunately it's too small an area to be lost for long. As a general guide, Castle Gates/Castle Street runs from the train station up to Pride Hill, a short pedestrianized street that meets St Mary's Street/Dogpole at one end and High Street/Wyle Cop at the other. The Square off the High Street is at the heart of the town centre.

Accommodation

Shrewsbury has one particularly good **hotel**, the *Prince Rupert*, which occupies a cannily converted old building, right in the centre of town off Pride Hill on Butcher Row (ⓣ01743/499955, ⓦwww.prince-rupert-hotel.co.uk; ❻). There are over seventy bedrooms here and although some are a tad too fancy for some tastes – ornate bed-head canopies and so forth – each is undeniably comfortable. A second recommendable town-centre hotel is *The Lion*, an uneven former coaching inn on the Wyle Cop (ⓣ0870/609 6167, ⓦwww.regalhotels.co.uk/the lion; ❻). The pick of the central **B&Bs** is the *College Hill Guest House*, in a well-maintained Georgian town house at 11 College Hill, just south of The Square (ⓣ01743/365744; no credit cards; ❷). Further afield, one mile east of the centre across the English Bridge, is another quality B&B, the *Fieldside*, in a large Victorian property with eight neat and trim mostly en suite guest rooms, next to St Giles's Church at 38 London Rd (ⓣ01743/353143, ⓦwww.fieldsideguesthouse.co.uk; no cards; ❸). The B&B is also yards from Lord Hill's Column, a whopping monument raised in memory of Wellington's sidekick at the Battle of Waterloo – and there's even another column at Hawkstone Park (see p.662). A final good choice is the comfortable and most agreeable *Trevellion Guest House* (ⓣ01743/249582; ❷), less than a mile from the centre just off Monkmoor Road at 1 Bradford St; the breakfasts here are memorably sustaining.

The Town

Poking up above the mansion-like train station, the careworn ramparts of Shrewsbury **castle** are but a pale reminder of the mighty medieval fortress that once dominated the town, largely because the illustrious Thomas Telford turned the castle into the private home of a local bigwig in the 1780s. **Castle Gates** winds up the hill from the station into the heart of the river loop where the medieval town took root. Here, off Pride Hill, several half-timbered buildings are dotted along **Butcher Row**, which leads into the quiet precincts of **St Alkmund's Church**, from where there's a charming view of the fine old buildings of **Fish Street**. Close by is the most interesting of the town's churches, **St Mary the Virgin** (Mon–Fri 10am–5pm, Sat 10am–4pm; free), whose sombre exterior is partly redeemed by its slender spire. Inside, the church is unusual in so far as it exhibits both the rounded arches beloved of the Normans in the nave and the pointed arches of Early English Gothic in the choir and the transepts. The nave also boasts a splendid panelled roof, featuring angels with musical instruments, while the east window of the chancel, with its filigree tracery rising above the high altar, represents the apogee of the Decorated style and dates to the 1330s. The stained glass of this east window comprises a superlative **Tree of Jesse**, one of the finest in the country with Jesse – the supposed father of David, King of the Israelites – at the bottom with his genealogical tree rising above him, its branches inhabited by Biblical characters. Look out also – in the chapel off the north transept – for the funerary plaque commemorating a bewigged **Admiral John Benbow** (1653–1702), who rose through the ranks to become one of Britain's finest admirals – hence the plaque's ship-of-the-line.

Doubling back, it's the briefest of walks from St Mary's to the High Street, on the far side of which, in the narrow confines of The Square, is the **Old Market House**, a heavy-duty stone structure built in 1596. From here, it's a couple of minutes' stroll north to Barker Street and the pick of the town's museums, the **Shrewsbury Museum and Art Gallery** (Oct to late May Tues–Sat 10am–4pm; late May to Sept Tues–Sat 10am–5pm, Sun & Mon 10am–4pm; free), which occupies an antique merchants' mansion and warehouse. The museum contains a wide range of displays relating to local life, with some of the more interesting exhibits coming from the nearby Roman city of Wroxeter (see p.662), including a rare silver mirror from the third century AD. There are also modest displays on two of the town's most illustrious sons, Charles Darwin (1809–82) and **Robert Clive of India** (1725–74). Largely forgotten today, Clive was the conqueror of a vast chunk of India, but his meteoric rise was followed by an equally dramatic fall. Elevated to the peerage following his defeat of the ruler of Bengal, Clive was later the subject of a full-scale parliamentary enquiry into his conduct and, although he was acquitted of corruption, he ended up committing suicide shortly afterwards.

St Chad's Church and Quarry Park

Pushing on from the museum, it's a pleasant stroll west along Claremont Hill to **St Chad's Church** (daily: April–Oct 8am–5pm; Nov–March 8am–1pm; free), a handsome structure built in a fulsome rendition of the classical style in the 1790s. A segment of the old city wall was demolished to make way for the church, which looks out over **Quarry Park**, whose trim gardens and lawns run gently down to the river via a miniature lake and bandstand. It's a pretty spot and the park is guarded to the west by a pair of good-looking River Severn bridges. From either bridge, it's about half a mile back to the centre.

Wyle Cop and the Abbey Church

Back on The Square, High Street snakes down the hill to become **Wyle Cop**, lined with higgledy-piggledy ancient buildings and leading to the **English Bridge**, which sweeps across the Severn in grand Georgian style. Beyond the bridge, on Abbey Foregate, is the stumpy redstone mass of the **Abbey Church** (daily: April–Oct 9.30am–5.30pm; Nov–March 10.30am–3pm; free), all that remains of the Benedictine abbey that was a major political and religious force hereabouts until the Dissolution. The **church** is still in use as a place of worship, hence its good condition, but the interior is fairly pedestrian, the best features being the doughty Norman columns of the nave and the soaring triumphal arch.

Eating and drinking

For **daytime food**, try the inexpensive *Goodlife Wholefood Restaurant* (Mon–Fri 9.30am–3.30pm & Sat 9.30am–4.30pm), on Barracks Passage, just off – and about halfway along – Wyle Cop; they specialize in salads and vegetarian dishes. Another good bet is *Philpotts Quality Sandwiches*, which deserves its name and is located at 15 Butcher Row. In the **evening**, there's tasty tandoori at *Shalimar*, by the Abbey Church at 23 Abbey Foregate, and a wide range of snacks and meals – including some surprises, wild boar sausages for one – just along the street in the modern and inexpensive *Peach Tree* café-bar at 21 Abbey Foregate (daily 9am–10pm). Another good bet is the authentic Asian cuisine of *Thai Orchids* (☎01743/353117) right in the centre of town, off Pride Hill on Butchers Row; main courses here average £8. However, many locals think that the best restaurant in town is *Osteria da Paolo*, a homely Italian place offering mouth-watering cuisine from its premises down a narrow alley off Hills Lane near the Welsh Bridge (☎01743/243336); main courses here average around £9.

Amongst Shrewsbury's many **pubs**, one of the most distinctive is the *Loggerheads*, an ancient place – perhaps a little too authentically so – with four small rooms and great real ales; it's located near St Alkmund's Place at 1 Church St. Other recommendable **pubs** include the smoke-free *Three Fishes*, in an ancient building on Fish Street, and the cosy *Coach & Horses*, on Swan Hill just south of The Square.

North of Shrewsbury: Hawkstone Park and Follies

Cocooned by servants, the landed gentry of the eighteenth and nineteenth centuries had time to fill, and many of them took to converting their estates into pleasure parks for strolling, hunting and contemplating nature. **Hawkstone Park and Follies** (Jan–March Sat & Sun 10am–2.30pm; April to mid-May & Sept–Oct Wed–Sun 10am–3pm; late May to Aug daily 10am–4pm; £5.50; ⓦwww.hawkstone.co.uk), which lies about ten miles north of Shrewsbury off the A49, is one such, the creation of the Hill family in the late eighteenth century. The Hills were major local landowners and the most famous member of the clan served with Wellington at Waterloo and had two protuberant columns erected in his honour – one back in town (see p.660) and one here. The park, with its maze of tree-lined avenues, makes good use of the lie of the land, in which rocky outcrops and two roughly parallel ridges bubble up from the surrounding flatland. On one ridge is a whopping tower whose 150 spiral steps lead to a windswept balcony, and other features – or follies – include the White Tower, Swiss Bridge, two tree trunks spanning a deep gully, a hermit's cave and a curious set of dim and eerie grottoes on Grotto Hill. From this hill top, the views stretch for miles across the plains to the Welsh hills.

The park is readily explored on a couple of one- to two-hour circular footpaths, straightforward hiking for the most part, though sections can be a little tricky underfoot, especially towards Foxes Knob, a sandstone outcrop reached via dark passageways snaking through the rock.

East of Shrewsbury: Attingham Park and Wroxeter Roman City

Heading east from the Shrewsbury ring road, it's a couple of miles along the B4380 to **Attingham Park** (hall: April–Oct Mon, Tues & Fri–Sun 1–4.30pm; park: March–Oct daily 9am–8pm; Nov–Feb daily 9am–5pm; £5, grounds only £2.30; NT), a sprawling estate set close to the looping River Severn. At the heart of the estate is the **hall**, a colossal Georgian mansion with a massive Neoclassical facade, incorporating four imperious pillars and a colossal portico, all to a 1782 design by George Stuart, with later additions by John Nash. The interior is similarly over-blown, crammed with luxurious furniture and souvenirs from successive Grand Tours – and typical of the Regency predilection for all things French and Italian. Thomas Hill, the second lord, was a particularly avid collector and he added the picture gallery for his collection of Renaissance art in 1805. However, today's paintings are a poor reflection of the original collection as Thomas over-reached himself and, faced with bankruptcy, was forced to sell off his finest works. Interestingly, the picture gallery is spanned by the world's first cast-iron-rib ceiling, a product of the Coalbrookdale foundry (see p.655). The surrounding deer **park and grounds** offer pleasant riverside and woodland walks.

Wroxeter Roman City

Heading east from the turning for Attingham Park, the B4380 follows the course of **Watling Street**, the former Roman military road that linked the wild Welsh borders with St Albans, London, Canterbury and Dover. After a couple of miles, the B4380 reaches the signed turning to **Wroxeter Roman City** (daily: April–Oct 10am–6pm; Nov–March 10am–1pm & 2–4pm; £3.70; EH), originally Roman Britain's fourth largest city, **Viroconium**, occupying a key strategic location where Watling Street crossed the River Severn. The site was first settled by the Cornovii, but it was the Emperor Nero who really got things going in 58 AD as part of his drive to conquer Wales. In the event, the Welsh proved intractable and, when there was a second imperial visit sixty years later, the Emperor Hadrian focused on security, doubling the size of the Viroconium garrison. Hadrian also ordered the construction of a grand set of municipal buildings and today the ruins of his civic centre are still impressive, particularly the large chunk of masonry that once enclosed part of the main baths. You will, however, need a vivid imagination to picture the ruins as a teeming Roman metropolis, even though the site's modest museum helps fill in the gaps.

Church Stretton – and the Long Mynd

Beginning about ten miles south of Shrewsbury, the upland heaths of the **Long Mynd**, some ten miles long and between two and four miles wide, run parallel to and just to the west of the A49. This is prime walking territory and the heathlands are latticed with footpaths, the pick of which offer sweeping views over the border to the Black Mountains of Wales. Nestled at the foot of the Mynd beside the A49 is **CHURCH STRETTON**, a tidy little village and popular day-trippers' destination that makes it the ideal base for hiking the area. The village also possesses the dinky parish **church of St Laurence**, parts of which – especially the nave and transepts – are Norman. Look out also for the fertility symbol over the side door, just to the left of the entrance – it's a (badly weathered) sheila-na-gig comparable to the one in Kilpeck (see p.645).

As for practicalities, Church Stretton is easy to reach from Shrewsbury and Ludlow by **train** and **bus**. Most buses stop in the centre of the village along the High Street, but some pull in beside the train station, close to the A49 – and about 600yd east of the High Street. The **tourist office**, on Church St (Easter–Sept Mon–Sat 10am–1pm & 2–5pm; ⓣ01694/723133), is yards from St Laurence, one street to the west of the High Street. They stock an excellent range of local hiking leaflets and booklets, have information on off-road cycle routes and will book accommodation on your behalf. Of the many **hikes** beginning in the village, a selection is described in Ian Jones's excellent *Twenty Church Stretton Walks*, which is available at the tourist office. One good choice is the six-mile circular hike to the top of **Caer Caradoc**, the steep hill to the northeast of the village, and back again. The hill is crowned by the scant remains of an Iron Age fort and affords superb views. The most popular hikers' target is, however, **Carding Mill Valley**, a gently sloping valley from where several trails lead up to the Mynd. The valley is owned by the National Trust and it starts about half a mile to the north of Church Stretton.

There's no shortage of good-value **accommodation** in and around Church Stretton. One particularly recommendable **B&B** is *Acton Scott Farm* (ⓣ01694/781260, ⓦwww.actonscottfarm.co.uk; no credit cards; ❷; closed Nov–Jan), a seventeenth-century farmhouse with log fires and a choice of three well-appointed rooms; it's located some three miles south of Church Stretton, just east off the A49 in the hamlet of Acton Scott. There's also the first-rate *Jinlye Guest House* (ⓣ01694/723243, ⓦwww.jinlye.co.uk; ❹), in an attractively modernized and extended stone cottage on Castle Hill in All Stretton, one mile north of Church Stretton. **Campers** have a choice of several sites, including *Ley Hill Farm* (ⓣ01694/771366; tents £6), deep in the countryside a couple of miles to the northeast of Church Stretton, along narrow country lanes near the hamlet of Cardington. **Hostellers** have choices too – between **Wilderhope Manor** (see p.664), in Longville-in-the-Dale, about six miles east of Church Stretton along the B4371, and **Bridges Long Mynd** (ⓣ01588/650656, ⓕ650531; Mon–Sat only; dorm beds £9), five miles west from Church Stretton near Ratlinghope. Both are splendid bases for hiking, the first for Wenlock Edge (see p.658), the second for either the Long Mynd or the **Stiperstones**, a remote range of boggy heather dotted with ancient cairns and earthworks.

Stokesay Castle near Craven Arms

Inconsequential **Craven Arms**, the next stop along the rail line south of Church Stretton, lies a mile or so to the north of the hamlet of **STOKESAY**, the site of one of England's most appealing manor houses. **Stokesay Castle** (April–Oct daily 10am–6pm; Nov–March Wed–Sun 10am–4pm; £4.50; EH), as it's known, comprises a collection of leaning, half-timbered buildings that span a range of over three hundred years, gathered around a neat grassy courtyard. The main block is a thirteenth-century fortified manor house, originally built by a prosperous wool merchant for the princely price of a sparrowhawk. Beautifully restored by English Heritage, it contains an expansive banqueting hall that retains its central fireplace, vaulted timbers and large windows. The size of the windows is actually very significant: Edward I's suppression of the Welsh had made border life a good deal more secure for the English, so they could afford to weaken the walls to let more light in. Across the central courtyard is the black and yellow gatehouse, built three hundred years after the manor house yet forming a harmonious group with the main building as well as the tiny parish church next door. The church was largely rebuilt in the mid-seventeenth century, but some of the original Norman features remain.

Bishop's Castle

BISHOP'S CASTLE, some eleven miles from Craven Arms near the Welsh border, is a real treat – uncluttered, very pretty and full of intriguing second-hand bookshops and junk stores. Its short **High Street** winds up a hill past half-timbered frontages to the Market Square, home to the lurching **House on Crutches** and a miniature Georgian **Town Hall** – this was England's smallest borough until 1967. Stroll up past the town hall and veer to the right to reach the seventeenth-century **Three Tuns brewery** and its delightful, time-warped **pub** in Salop Street, which serves up traditional home-brew – a pale, cider-coloured concoction that's deceptively potent – as well as excellent and imaginative bar meals. The eccentric **tourist office** is housed in a second-hand shop called *Old Time*, at 29 High St (Mon–Sat 10am–10pm, Sun 10am–2pm; ⓣ01588/638467, ⓦwww.bishopscastle.co.uk); they have the full list of local accommodation, and offer two en-suite rooms of their own (no credit cards; ❷). **Buses**, linking Bishop's Castle with Shrewsbury, Ludlow and Clun, drop passengers near the foot of the High Street.

Clun

Just five miles south of Bishop's Castle, the modest pocket-sized village of **CLUN** holds the battered ruins of a medieval **castle** (dawn–dusk; free), built by the Normans but abandoned in the sixteenth century. The castle's only noteworthy feature is the chunky masonry of the ruined keep, but the setting more than compensates – the keep is raised on an earthen mound cradled by the river below. Clun also makes an excellent base for jaunts out across the surrounding hills that roll west over into Wales. These hills are crisscrossed with footpaths, including a stretch of the **Offa's Dyke Path**, a long-distance hiking trail, which runs north/south along – or near – the Welsh–English border, from Prestatyn to Chepstow, both of which are in Wales. Some 180 miles long, the path takes its name from the ditch King Offa of Mercia (broadly central England) had dug along the Anglo–Welsh frontier in the eighth century. Unlike Hadrian's Wall, it was never guarded or patrolled, acting as a boundary marker, not a defensive work. For all that, it was an extraordinary enterprise, though there's precious little to actually see today – the dyke merged with its surroundings centuries ago. The path cuts a varied course, traversing open moorland and agricultural land but also weaving through deep wooded valleys; three miles west of Clun, it crosses the **B4368** and this is as good a place as any to join it – or, more realistically, to walk a section.

In and around Clun are several excellent **B&Bs**. One of the most enjoyable is the *Old Farmhouse* (ⓣ01588/640695, ⓦwww.vuan1.freeserve.co.uk; no credit cards; ❷;), whose handful of simple guest rooms are in a sympathetically updated old farmhouse half a mile southeast from – and 300 feet above – Clun in Woodside. There's also the delightful *Birches Mill B&B*, which occupies a lovely old stone cottage deep in the countryside, about a mile north of Clun, near Bicton, just off the A488 (ⓣ01588/640409; no cards; open April–Oct; ❸). They have three guest rooms here, all en suite, the extensive gardens amble down to the river, and the breakfasts are a treat; evening meals are available by prior arrangement. Clun also possesses a small **youth hostel** (ⓣ0870/770 5766, ⓦwww.yha.org.uk; closed Sept–March; dorm beds £10.25), in a converted watermill on the northeastern edge of the village – about ten minutes' walk from the B4368. The hostel has 24 beds in five- to eleven-bedded rooms; it's self-catering only.

As regards **pubs**, Clun has two good ones – the *Buffalo Inn* (ⓣ01588/640225), which offers excellent bar food, and the *Sun Inn* (ⓣ01588/640277), whose a la carte restaurant is first-rate. There are **buses** to Clun from Shrewsbury, Ludlow and Bishop's Castle; they stop in the centre of the village.

Ludlow

LUDLOW, perched on a hill nearly thirty miles south of Shrewsbury, is one of the most picturesque towns in the West Midlands, if not in England – a cluster of beautifully preserved black-and-white half-timbered buildings packed around a craggy stone castle, with rural Shropshire forming a drowsy backdrop. Close to the Welsh border, the Saxons were the first to recognize the site's defensive qualities, but it was the Normans who got down to business when Roger Montgomery turned up here with his men in 1085. Over the next few decades, Montgomery's fortifications were elaborated into an immense **Castle** (Jan Sat & Sun 10am–4pm; Feb, March & Oct–Dec daily 10am–4pm; April–July & Sept daily 10am–5pm; Aug daily 10am–7pm; £3.50), strong enough to keep the Welsh at bay and the seat of the Lord President of the Council of the Marches, as the borders were then known. Surviving the attentions of the Parliamentary troops in the Civil War, the rambling and imposing ruins that remain today include towers and turrets, gatehouses and concentric walls as well as the remains of the 110-foot Norman **keep** and an unusual **Round Chapel** built in 1120. With its spectacular setting above the rivers Teme and Corve, the castle also makes a fine open-air auditorium during the **Ludlow Festival** (Ⓣ01584/872150, Ⓦwww.ludlowfestival.co.uk), three weeks of assorted musical and theatrical fun running from the end of June to early July.

The castle gates open out onto **Castle Square**, an airy rectangle, whose eastern side abuts four narrow lanes – take the one on the left, Church Street and then King Street, to reach the gracefully proportioned **Church of St Laurence** (daily 10am–5.30pm; £1 suggested donation), whose interior is distinguished by its stained-glass windows. Amongst them, two of the most exquisite are the fifteenth-century Annunciation window in the north wall and the east window, where the men in blue are members of the Palmer's Guild. Founded in the middle of the thirteenth century, and dissolved in 1551, the guild dominated the economy of medieval Ludlow and its members often undertook pilgrimages to Jerusalem. Thus, one window panel shows the Palmers on their pilgrimage, another the enthusiastic welcome they receive on their return. The church also holds an especially fine set of misericords. Carved in oak, they run the gamut from royal emblems and religious scenes to the folkloric and seemingly profane – green men, devils, a fox preaching to geese, a witch, a mermaid and a woman disappearing into the mouth of hell bottom first. More serene are the church's several table-tombs, including, in the south transept, the delicately carved alabaster memorial to a certain Dame Mary Evre (d.1612), complete with intricate ruff and bodice. Back outside the church, King Street leads into the **Bull Ring**, home of the **Feathers Hotel** (see p.667), a beautiful Jacobean building with the fanciest wooden facade imaginable.

To the south of Castle Square, the gridiron of streets laid out by the Normans has survived intact, though most of the buildings date from the eighteenth century. It's the general appearance that appeals rather than any special sight, but steeply sloping **Broad Street** is particularly attractive, flanked by many of Ludlow's five hundred half-timbered Tudor and red-brick Georgian listed buildings, its north end framed by the high and mighty **Butter Cross**, a Neoclassical extravagance from 1744. At the foot of Broad Street is Ludlow's only surviving medieval **gate**, which was turned into a house in the eighteenth century.

Practicalities

From Ludlow **train station**, on the Shrewsbury–Hereford line, it's a five- to ten-minute walk southwest to the castle – just follow the signs. Most **buses** stop on Mill Street, just off Castle Square. Ludlow's **tourist office**, on Castle Square (April–Sept Mon–Sat 10am–5pm, Sun 10.30am–5pm; rest of year Mon–Sat 10am–5pm; Ⓣ01584/875053, Ⓦwww.ludlow.org.uk), has a wide range of maps and books for walkers, as well as a selection of inexpensive leaflets detailing day hikes in the area. **Accommodation** is plentiful, though rooms can get scarce during the festival. First choice, if you can afford it, has to be the beautiful *Feathers Hotel* on the Bull Ring (Ⓣ01584/875261, Ⓦwww.feathersatludlow.co.uk; ❻), an intricately decorated Jacobean town house with luxury rooms and period furnishings to match. Two other, less expensive options in the town centre are the *Wheatsheaf Inn*, a quaint little pub next to the old town gate at the foot of Broad Street (Ⓣ01584/872980; ❷), and, just beyond at 28 Lower Broad St, the excellent *Number Twenty Eight B&B*, in an attractive Georgian house with four smart en-suite guest rooms (Ⓣ01584/875466, Ⓦwww.ludlowno28.com; ❺). The people from no. 28 also operate 4 Lower Broad St as a B&B (same details) – and to the same high standards, but this time the property is Victorian.

Ludlow has a string of fine **restaurants** with one of the best being the *Merchant House* (Ⓣ01584/875438; closed Sun & Mon), in a good-looking half-timbered building about half a mile from the centre on Corve Street, a northerly continuation of the Bull Ring. There are just seven tables here, an intimate environment for the most superb of four-course meals (£30–35) taken from a short menu featuring such delights as scallops with a lentil and coriander sauce. Note that getting there can be a bit tricky – to the north of the centre, Corve Street appears to veer to the left, but this is in fact Coronation Avenue and you need to keep straight. A second outstanding restaurant is the *Hibiscus*, much closer to the centre at 17 Corve St (Ⓣ01584/872325; closed Sun), where they serve classic French cuisine with vim and gusto; again a four-course meal will rush you £30–35. If all that sounds too wallet-wilting, head for the popular *Olive Branch*, on the Bull Ring (daily 10am–3pm), whose speciality is inexpensive light meals and salads, or the *Ego Café-Bar*, just north off Castle Square on Quality Square, which serves everything from snacks to filling meals at moderate prices.

Birmingham

If anywhere can be described as the first purely industrial conurbation, it has to be **BIRMINGHAM**. Unlike the more specialist industrial towns that grew up across the north and Midlands, "Brum" – and its "Brummies" – turned its hand to every kind of manufacturing, gaining the epithet "the city of 1001 trades". It was here also that the pioneers of the Industrial Revolution – James Watt, Matthew Boulton, William Murdock, Josiah Wedgwood, Joseph Priestley and Erasmus Darwin (grandfather of Charles) – formed the **Lunar Society**, an extraordinary melting-pot of scientific and industrial ideas. They conceived the world's first purpose-built factory, invented gas lighting and pioneered both the distillation of oxygen and the mass production of the steam engine. Thus, a modest Midlands market town mushroomed into the nation's economic dynamo – in the fifty years up to 1830 the population more than trebled to 130,000.

Now the second largest city in Britain, with a population of over one million, Birmingham has long outgrown the squalor and misery of its boom years and today its industrial supremacy is recalled in a crop of excellent **heritage museums** and an extensive network of **canals**. It also boasts a thoroughly multiracial population that makes this one of Britain's most cosmopolitan cities. The shift to a post-manufacturing economy has been symbolized by an intelligent and far-reaching revamp of the city centre that has included the construction of a glitzy **Convention Centre**, while the enormous **National Exhibition Centre** (NEC) now inhabits the outskirts near the international

BIRMINGHAM

RESTAURANTS	
Brasserie Malmaison	11
Canalside Café	9
Chez Jules	5
Chung Ying	13
Grand Tandoori	16
Kushi	17
Mongolian Bar	2
Le Petit Blanc	7
Punjab Paradise	18
Royal Nain	19
Warehouse Café	10
Zizzi	12

ACCOMMODATION	
Ashdale House	H
Burlington Hotel	B
Copthorne Birmingham	A
Days Inn	F
Ibis Centre Hotel	G
Malmaison	E
Novotel Birmingham Centre	C
Paragon Hotel	I
Travelodge	D

PUBS	
Fiddle & Bone	6
Green Room	14
Medicine Bar	20
Old Fox	15
Old Joint Stock	3
Prince of Wales	4
Red Lion	1
Tap & Spile	8

1 & Museum of the Jewellery Quarter
Aston, M6 & A38 Lichfield
Custard Factory, Birmingham Intl. Airport & NEC, M42, M6 & A45 Coventry, 16, 17, 18, 19, 20, H & I
M5
A456 Kidderminster
M5, A38

JEWELLERY QUARTER
RBSA
St Paul's
St Chad's Catholic Cathedral
General Hospital
Police Station
Snow Hill Train Station
Victoria Law Courts
St Philip's Anglican Cathedral
Think Tank
Birmingham Museum & Art Gallery
Library
Council House
Town Hall
CHAMBERLAIN SQUARE
VICTORIA SQUARE
Repertory Theatre
War Memorial
CENTENARY SQUARE
National Indoor Arena
Sea Life Centre
International Convention Centre
Ikon Gallery
BRINDLEY PLACE
Boat Trips
Gas Street Basin
Crescent Theatre
FIVE WAYS
Rotunda
Bull Ring
Moor Street Station
EASTSIDE
New Street Station
St Martin's Church
Market Halls
Coach Station
Old Rep.
Alexandra Theatre
The Mailbox
Antique & Craft Market
CHINESE QUARTER
Hippodrome Theatre
Arcadian Centre
Glee Club

Birmingham & Fazeley Canal
Birmingham Main Line Canal
Farmer's Bridge Locks

ST PAUL'S SQUARE, JAMES ST, BROOK ST, VITTORIA ST, GRAHAM STREET, FREDERICK STREET, GEORGE STREET, CHARLOTTE STREET, FLEET STREET, LIONEL STREET, NEWHALL STREET, LUDGATE HILL, LIVERY STREET, GREAT CHARLES ST Q'WAY, CORNWALL STREET, CHURCH STREET, EDMUND STREET, COLMORE ROW, COLMORE CIRCUS, SNOW HILL Q'WAY, ST CHAD'S CIRCUS, SHADWELL ST, ST CHAD'S QUEENSWAY, WHITTALL STREET, STEELHOUSE LANE, CORPORATION STREET, JAMES WATT QUEENSWAY, ASTON STREET, JENNENS ROAD, FOX STREET, ALBERT STREET, FAZELEY STREET, NEW CANAL STREET, BORDESLEY ST, OLD SQUARE, PRIORY Q'WAY, DALE END, BULL STREET, TEMPLE ROW, HIGH STREET, MOOR STREET QUEENSWAY, WATERLOO STREET, TEMPLE ST, CANNON STREET, NEW STREET, STEPHENSON STREET, HILL STREET, NAVIGATION STREET, JOHN BRIGHT ST, STATION STREET, SUFFOLK STREET QUEENSWAY, SMALLBROOK Q'WAY, HURST STREET, HOLLOWAY CIRCUS, EDGBASTON STREET, PERSHORE STREET, UPPER DEAN ST, MOAT LANE, DIGBETH, BRADFORD STREET, ALLISON STREET, MERIDEN STREET, SUMMER ROW, CLEMENT ST, EDWARD STREET, KING EDWARD'S ROAD, CAMBRIDGE STREET, PARADISE CIRCUS, QUEENSWAY, BROAD STREET, BRIDGE STREET, HOLLIDAY STREET, SEVERN STREET, GOUGH STREET, BLUCHER STREET, COMMERCIAL STREET, GRANVILLE STREET, GAS STREET, BERKLEY STREET, TENNANT ST, SHEEPCOTE STREET, SHERBORNE STREET, RYLAND STREET, RUSTON ST, GROSVENOR STREET WEST

0 — 400 yds

airport. In addition, Birmingham has launched a veritable raft of cultural initiatives, enticing a division of the **Royal Ballet** to take up residence here, and building a fabulous new concert hall for the City of **Birmingham Symphony Orchestra**. Nonetheless, there's no pretending that Birmingham is packed with interesting sights – it isn't – though along with its first-rate restaurant scene and nightlife, it's well worth at least a day or two.

Arrival, information and city transport

Birmingham's **international airport** is eight miles east of the city centre off the A45 and near the M42 (Junction 6); the main terminal is beside Birmingham International train station, from where there are regular services into the centre. **New Street train station**, to which all InterCity and the vast majority of local services go, is right in the heart of the city. However, trains on the Stratford-upon-Avon, Warwick, Worcester and Malvern lines usually use **Snow Hill** and **Moor Street stations**, both about ten minutes' signposted walk from New Street. National Express **coach** travellers are dumped in the grim surroundings of **Digbeth coach station**, from where it's a ten-minute uphill walk to the centre.

Maps, loads of local leaflets and transport information are provided by all the city's **tourist offices**. The main office is located in the city centre in the base of the Rotunda at the east end of New Street (Mon–Sat 9.30am–5.30pm & Sun 10.30am–4.30pm; ⓣ0121/202 5099, ⓦwww.birmingham.org.uk). A second, smaller office occupies a large glass kiosk also in New Street (Mon–Sat 9.30am–5.30pm; same number). In addition, there are tourist offices at the International Convention Centre, Centenary Square (ICC; same number), and next to the airport in the National Exhibition Centre (NEC; same number). All of the tourist offices operate a hotel bed booking service at no charge.

To see Birmingham at its best, you really need to stay in the centre, but most of the less expensive accommodation is scattered around the suburbs. This may mean you'll be dealing with Birmingham's excellent local transport system, whose **trains**, **metro** and **buses** delve into almost every urban nook and cranny. Various companies provide these services, but they are co-ordinated by **Centro**, which operates a regional public transport information line, **Centro Hotline** (ⓣ0121/200 2700, ⓦwww.centro.org.uk). A one-day **Centrocard**, valid on all services, can be purchased from bus drivers and at train and metro stations; it costs £5 (£4 after 9.30am and at the weekend).

One thing that may confuse is the name of the **inner ring road**: it's called the Queensway, but individual stretches keep their other names too, for example: Great Charles St, Queensway.

Accommodation

As you might expect, Birmingham has a wide range of **accommodation**, from tower-block chains out near the airport and family-run hotels in the leafier suburbs through to gritty inner-city B&Bs. All of the city's tourist offices have the full details and there's a selection of hotels in both their *Pocket Guide to Birmingham* (free) and the *Night & Day Essential Visitor Guide* (£1.25). All the tourist offices operate a **hotel room booking service** at no charge and, even better, they are often aware of special deals and discounts, which can slash costs considerably, especially on the weekend. The best bet is to stay in the vicinity of the ICC – you'll almost certainly pay more than in the rest of the city, but it's well worth it.

Ashdale House Hotel 39 Broad Rd, Acocks Green ⓣ0121/706 3598, ⓦwww.ashdalehouse.co.uk. Well-situated hotel in a pleasant Victorian town house with nine smartly furnished, mostly en-suite guest rooms. Full English or vegetarian breakfasts. Acocks Green is a couple of miles southeast of the centre. There are buses from the centre, but you're probably best off taking the train from Moor Street to Spring Road Station and walking the half mile or so from there. ❷

Burlington Hotel 6 Burlington Arcade, 126 New St ⓣ0121/643 9191, ⓦwww.burlingtonhotel.com. Handsomely refurbished Victorian red-brick hotel with over one hundred bright and well-appointed rooms. Fitness facilities, too. ❽

Copthorne Birmingham Paradise Circus ⓣ0121/200 2727, ⓦwww.millenniumhotels.com. It may look rather like a Rubik cube from the outside, but this is a great hotel, partly because its 212 modern bedrooms are neat and trim, and partly because its location – plum in the centre beside Centenary Square – can't be bettered. It's expensive during the week, but weekends bring prices down to more reasonable levels. ❽, ❺ at weekends.

Days Inn 160 Wharfside St, The Mailbox ⓣ0121/643 9344, ⓦwww.daysinn.com. Modest chain hotel in a trendy setting – the newly developed Mailbox complex has über cool shops, restaurants and bars. ❹

Ibis Centre Hotel Ladywell Walk, Arcadian Centre ⓣ0121/622 6010, ⓦwww.ibishotel.com. Rather characterless, but well-situated chain hotel, bang in the Chinese Quarter, near the major theatres and nightclubs. ❸

Malmaison Hotel The Mailbox, Royal Mail St ⓣ0121/246 5000, ⓦwww.malmaison.com. This impeccably stylish, designer hotel offers first-class accommodation of wit and substance – no wonder it's next door to Harvey Nichols. Every convenience and a central location. ❼

Novotel Birmingham Centre 70 Broad St ⓣ0121/643 2000, ⓦwww.novotel.com. Great location for this smart and well-run chain hotel. Over 140 bedrooms decorated in crisp modern style. Good fitness facilities too. ❼

Paragon Hotel 145 Alcester St ⓣ0121/627 0627, ⓦwww.paragonhotel.net. Splendid conversion of a magnificent Victorian workhouse about fifteen minutes' walk from New Street Station out along Digbeth and its continuation High Street. Alcester Street is a turning on the right. Excellent-value doubles, though the surrounding area hardly inspires confidence. ❸

Travelodge 230 Broad St ⓣ0121/644 5266, ⓦwww.travelodge.com. Workaday central chain hotel, but prices are very reasonable and it's within easy walking distance of lots of restaurants, bars and clubs. ❸

The City Centre

Many visitors get their first taste of central Birmingham at **New Street Station**, whose unreconstructed ugliness – piles of modern concrete – makes a dispiriting start, though there are plans afoot to give the place a thoroughgoing face lift. Things do, however, soon get better if you stroll west along pedestrianized **New Street**, one of the city's principal shopping streets, to the elegantly revamped **Victoria Square**, with its tumbling water fountain. The adjacent **Chamberlain Square** has been refurbished too, but here pride of place goes to the **Birmingham Museum and Art Gallery**, the city's finest museum, complete with a fabulous collection of Pre-Raphaelite art. Beyond, further west still, is the glossy **International Convention Centre**, from where it's another short hop to the **Gas Street Basin**, the prettiest part of the city's serpentine canal system. Close by is canalside **Brindley Place**, a smart, brick and glass complex with slick cafés and bars and the enterprising **Ikon Gallery** of contemporary art.

From Brindley Place, it's a short walk southeast to the **Mailbox**, the immaculately rehabilitated former postal sorting office with yet more chic bars and restaurants, or you can head north along the old tow path of the **Birmingham and Fazeley canal** as far as Newhall Street. The latter is within easy walking distance of both **St Philip's Cathedral**, back in the centre on Colmore Row, and – in the opposite direction – the **Jewellery Quarter**, which holds an excellent museum and scores of workshops and retail outlets. Finally, the **Bullring**, at the east end of New Street, has been redeveloped with panache, while the nearby **Eastside** district is in the throes of a massive regeneration, the first fruits of which are the **Think Tank** museum of science and discovery

Victoria and Chamberlain squares

At its west end, New Street opens out into the handsomely refurbished **Victoria Square**, whose centrepiece is a large and particularly engaging water fountain designed by Dhruva Mistry. The fountain's large and distinctive female figure is affectionately known as "the floozy in the jacuzzi" by the locals – but there's no such term of endearment for Anthony Gormley's rusting *Iron Man* lurking nearby, and leaning at a precarious angle like a Saturday-night drunk. The waterfall outdoes poor old Queen Victoria, whose **statue** is glum and uninspired, though the thrusting self-confidence of her bourgeoisie is very apparent in the flamboyant buildings that frame the adjacent **Chamberlain Square**. Amongst the assorted ornate gables and cupolas, columns and towers, the **Council House** is the most impressive edifice, opened in 1879 and complete with a pair of proud lions.

Very different is Chamberlain Square's **Town Hall** of 1834, whose classical design – by Joseph Hansom, who went on to design Hansom cabs – was based on the Roman temple in Nîmes. The building's simple, flowing lines contrast with much of its surroundings, but it's an appealing structure all the same, erected to house public meetings and musical events in a flush of municipal pride. It's currently undergoing a long-term refurbishment, but you can pop inside for a peek (Mon–Fri 10am–4pm; free), though at present there's nothing much to see. In the middle of the square is a dinky neo-Gothic memorial in honour of **Joseph Chamberlain** (1836–1914), who made himself immensely popular by taking the city's gas and water supplies into public ownership. His political career ultimately took him from the Birmingham mayor's office to national prominence as leader of the Liberal Unionists and figurehead of the resistance to Irish home rule. Close by, on the steps, is a second political statue, this one to the city's first MP, **Thomas Attwood**, his coat-tails tumbling down the concrete.

The Birmingham Museum and Art Gallery

The **Birmingham Museum and Art Gallery** occupies a rambling, Edwardian building on Chamberlain Square (Mon–Thurs & Sat 10am–5pm, Fri 10.30am–5pm, Sun 12.30–5pm; free). Its several sections are spread over Floors 2 and 3, but the pick is the **art section**, which contains one of the world's most comprehensive collections of **Pre-Raphaelite** work, concentrated on Floor 2, in Rooms 14 and 17–19. Founded in 1848, the Pre-Raphaelite Brotherhood consisted of seven young artists, of whom Rossetti, Holman Hunt, Millais and Madox Brown are best known. The name of the group was selected to express their commitment to honest observation, which they thought had been lost with the Renaissance. Many of the Brotherhood's most important paintings are displayed here, including **Dante Gabriel Rossetti**'s (1828–82) seminal *First Anniversary of the Death of Beatrice* (1849), inspired by Dante, and **Ford Madox Brown**'s (1821–93) powerful image of emigration, *The Last of England* (1855). There's actually a lot more going on in Brown's painting than first meets the eye. On one level, it is a sentimental portrayal of a migrant family, but to Brown they also symbolized the yeomen of England – as evidenced by their possessions – whose enforced emigration was a result of poor government, and thus a national outrage. Political sub-texts aside, the group's dedication to realism (as they conceived it) was unyielding and **Hunt**, for example, visited the Holy Land to prepare a series of religious paintings including his extravagant *The Finding of the Saviour in the Temple*. By 1853, the Brotherhood had effectively disbanded, but a second wave of artists carried on in its footsteps. The most prominent of them was **Edward Burne-Jones** (1833–98), who has an entire room to himself (Room 14); there, you'll find a remarkable sample of his work, though it's his *Star of Bethlehem* which catches the eye, one of the largest watercolours ever painted, a mysterious, almost magical piece with earnest Magi and a film-star-like Virgin Mary.

The rest of the art section, though not quite as memorable, contains a first-rate collection of eighteenth- to twentieth-century British art, including an extensive collection of **watercolour** landscapes as well as some especially fine, bucolic paintings by **David Cox**, Constable's Birmingham contemporary. There's also a significant sample of **European** paintings from the likes of Jan van Scorel and Lucas Cranach through to the Impressionists. Look out also for Sir Peter Lely's iconic portrait of a thoughtful and determined *Oliver Cromwell* in Room 24.

Sharing Floor 2 is the **industrial art section**, which kicks off with the **Industrial Gallery**, set around an expansive atrium whose wrought-iron columns and balconies clamber up towards fancy skylights. This section holds a superb sample of locally produced stained glass, ceramics, metalwork – especially silver – and jewellery that amply illustrates the city's industrial prowess. Here also is the **Edwardian Tea Room**, one of the more pleasant places in Birmingham for a cuppa.

Moving on, Floor 1's cavernous **Gas Hall** is an impressive venue for touring art exhibitions, while the newly opened **Waterhall Gallery** (same times), just across Chamberlain Square from the main museum building, showcases modern and contemporary art including the likes of Francis Bacon and Bridget Riley.

To Gas Street Basin

From the north side of Chamberlain Square, walk through the hideously kitsch **Paradise Forum** shopping and fast-food complex to get to **Centenary Square**, where there's an unusual World War I war memorial. The square has been entirely revamped to complement the showpiece **International Convention Centre** (ICC) and the **Birmingham Repertory Theatre**, but the sculpture that was designed as the centre piece – *Forward* by Raymond Mason – has recently been burnt down

From the square, it's a brief stroll along Broad Street to the bridge over – and steps down to – **Gas Street Basin**, the hub of Birmingham's intricate **canal system**. There are eight canals within the city's boundaries, comprising no less than 32 miles of canal. The highpoint of canal construction was the late eighteenth century, when almost all heavy goods were transported by water. In the middle of the nineteenth century, the railways made the canals uneconomic, but they struggled on until the 1970s when tourism – and narrow boats – gave them a new lease of life. Much of Birmingham's surviving canal network slices through the city's grimy, industrial bowels, but certain sections have been immaculately restored with Gas Street Basin leading the way. At the junction of the Worcester and Birmingham and Birmingham Main Line canals, the Basin, with its herd of brightly painted narrow boats, is edged by a delightful medley of old brick buildings. There's a good pub here – the *Tap & Spile* – and regular **boat trips** leave to explore the prettier parts of the system. There are several operators, but Second City Canal Cruises is as good as any (☎0121/236 9811; £3 per person). In summer, there's also a **water taxi** service between several stops along the central part of the canal system (July & Aug daily 10am–5pm; May, June & Sept Sat & Sun 10am–5pm; every 45min; day pass £3.50).

Brindley Place and the Ikon Gallery

From the Basin, it's a short walk north along the canal towpath to the bars, shops and clubs of waterside **Brindley Place**, named after James Brindley the eighteenth-century engineer who was responsible for many of Britain's early canals. It's an extraordinarily successful – and aesthetically pleasing – development and here you'll also find the city's celebrated **Ikon Gallery** (Tues–Sun 11am–6pm; free; ⓦwww.ikon-gallery.co.uk), housed in a lovely old Victorian building and one of the country's most imaginative venues for touring exhibitions of contemporary art.

Along the Birmingham & Fazeley canal to St Paul's Square

Just beyond Brindley Place, in front of the huge dome of the National Indoor Arena (NIA), the **canal forks**: the Birmingham & Fazeley leads northeast (to the right) and the Birmingham Main Line canal cuts west (to the left), though to complicate matters the latter has a spur loop here, going under Sheepcote Street. Also beside the main canal junction is the shell-like **National Sea Life Centre** (daily 10am–5pm, last admission 1hr before closing; £9; ⓣ0121/633 4700, ⓦwww.sealife.co.uk), which can't help but raise a few eyebrows, given the city's inland location. Nevertheless, it's an enterprising educational venture, offering Birmingham's landlubbers an opportunity to view and even touch many unusual varieties of fish and sea life – it's so popular with kids that bookings are advised during school holidays.

Beyond the main canal fork, the first part of the **Birmingham & Fazeley canal** has been attractively restored, its antique brick buildings cleaned of accumulated grime and leading to the quaint **Farmer's Bridge Locks**. Further on, however, things take a grittier aspect as the canal bores beneath the city centre amidst its industrial tangle. Emerging at **Newhall Street** (it's signed), about half a mile from the main canal junction, you're a stone's throw from **St Paul's Square**, flanked by sturdy Georgian buildings and one of the more agreeable parts of the centre. Here, beside the square in Dakota House, on Brook Street, the **Royal Birmingham Society of Artists** (RBSA; Mon–Wed & Fri 10.30am–5.30pm, Thurs 10.30am–7pm, Sat 10.30am–5pm; donation), offers an inventive range of fine art exhibitions.

St Philip's Cathedral

Also near at hand is **Colmore Row**, a busy shopping strip where pride of architectural place goes to **St Philip's Cathedral** (Mon–Fri 7am–7pm, Sat & Sun 9am–5pm; free), a bijou example of English Baroque. Consecrated in 1715, St Philips was initially a parish church that served as an overspill for St Martin's (see p.674). It was, however, in a more genteel location than the older church and when, in 1905, the Church of England decided to establish a new diocese in Birmingham, they made St Philip's the cathedral. The church was extended in the 1880s, when four new stained-glass windows were commissioned from local boy **Edward Burne-Jones**, a leading light of the Pre-Raphaelite movement (see p.671). The windows are typical of his style – intensely coloured, fastidiously detailed and distinctly sentimental. Three – the *Nativity*, *Crucifixion* and *Ascension* – are at the far end of the church beyond the high altar, the fourth – the *Last Judgement* – is at the opposite end of the church.

The Bullring – and the new Selfridges

Colmore Row lies just to the west of the city centre's pedestrianized core with chain stores and shopping precincts lining up along Corporation, New and

High streets. At the intersection of New and High streets is the distinctive modernism of the whopping **Rotunda**, but mercifully its neighbour, the notorious **Bullring** indoor shopping centre, which fulfilled every miserable cliché of 1960s town planning, has been demolished. The new Bullring shopping centre that has sprung up in its place would be a textbook example of safe yet uninspiring contemporary planning were it not for the billowing organic swell of **Selfridges** protruding from its east side. Reminiscent of an inside-out octopus, Selfridges shimmers with an architectural chain mail of thousands of silver discs, altogether a bold and hugely successful attempt to create a popular city landmark. It was designed by Future Systems (responsible for the media centre at Lord's cricket ground in London) to resemble a sequinned dress, hence its nickname – the "Bobbles Building".

Nestling at the foot of the Bullring, **St. Martin's Church** has recently been cleared of its accumulated grime and now reveals itself to be a rather fetching amalgamation of the Gothic and the neo-Gothic, with fancifully carved decoration and a delightful Burne-Jones stained-glass window. Just to the south are the **Market Halls** (daily 7.30am–4pm), jam-packed with every conceivable knick-knack, all sold at bargain basement prices and supplemented by a **Rag Market** on Tuesdays, Thursdays and Saturdays (same times).

Digbeth's Custard Factory

From the Bullring, **Digbeth** – once the main thoroughfare through medieval Birmingham – falls away to the southeast. Jammed with traffic and jostled by decrepit industrial buildings, there are only two reasons to venture out here – the first is the bus station on the right, the second – on the left just along and off Gibb Street – is the arts complex that occupies the old **Alfred Bird Custard Factory**. The factory is a homely affair set around a friendly little courtyard and the **arts complex** offers a variety of workshops and has gallery space for temporary exhibitions of modern art. There are a couple of cafés and bars here, too (see p.679).

Eastside

Long a neglected corner of the city, **Eastside**, the grid of streets to the east of Moor Street Queensway – and north of Digbeth – is currently undergoing a major, pedestrian-friendly regeneration. First off the blocks has been the **Think Tank** (daily 10am–5pm; £6.95; ⓣ0121/202 2222, ⓦwww.thinktank.ac), a brand new museum of science and discovery at the Millennium Point complex on Curzon Street. The museum rambles over four floors and is everything a discovery museum should be – there are hands-on exhibits for all ages, a Lego robotics lab, and an imaginative exploration of the history of Birmingham. It's an excellent museum and it's made even more appealing by its neighbour, the **Imax theatre** (show times on ⓣ0121/202 2222, ⓦwww.imax.ac; £6.00), where you can explore away in 3-D. Also in the offing for Eastside are a £250-million Richard Rogers library, scheduled for 2007 and said to resemble a giant floating leaf, a large park and a multi-religious public venue, **The Shrine**, a place for religious contemplation and appropriate musical performances. Finally, an £18-million **needle** is on the bill for 2008, redefining the city's skyline as it soars up into the heavens.

The Jewellery Quarter

Birmingham's long-established **Jewellery Quarter** lies just to the northwest of the city centre, about half a mile from Colmore Row via Newhall Street. Buckle-makers and toy-makers first colonized the area in the 1750s, opening

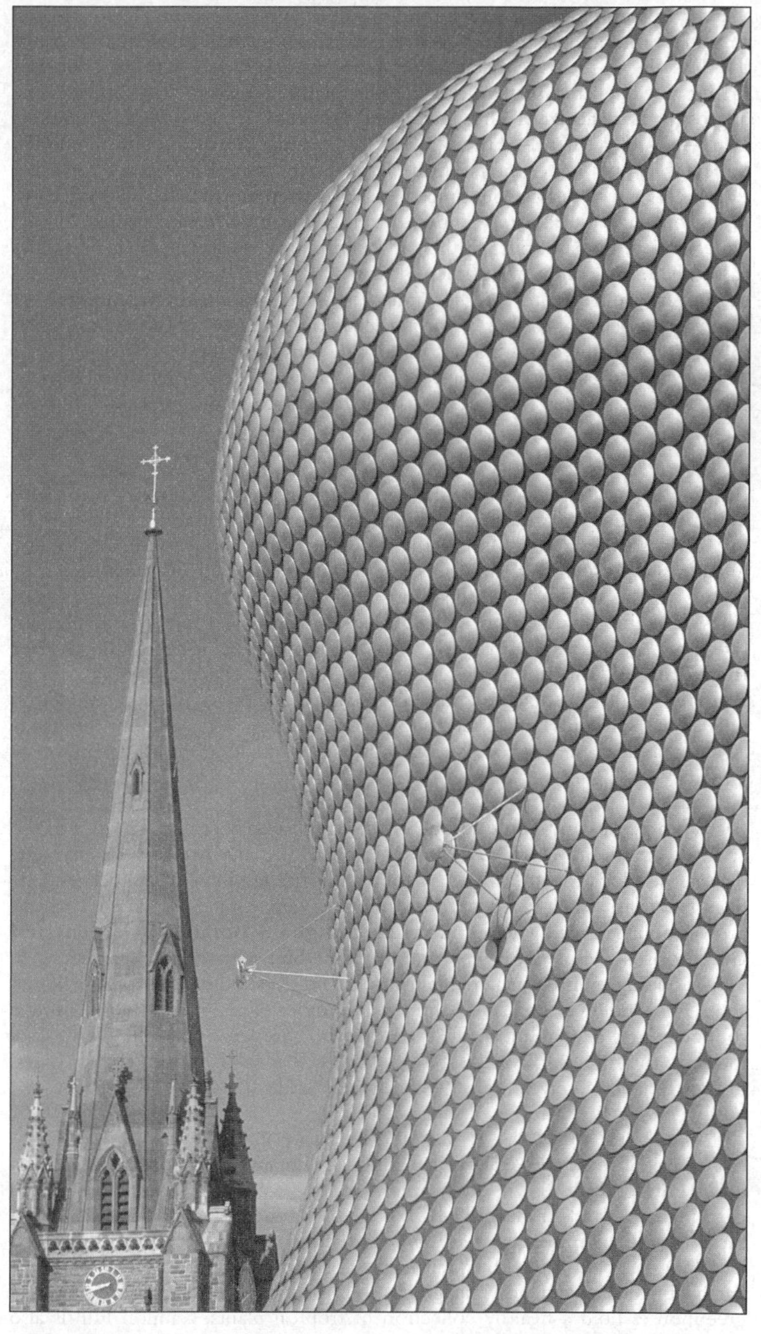

△ Selfridges, Birmingham

the way for hundreds of silversmiths, jewellers and goldsmiths. There are still around five hundred jewellery-related companies in the district with most of the **jewellery shops** concentrated along Vittoria Street and the adjacent Frederick Street and Warstone Lane. The prime attraction hereabouts is the engrossing **Museum of the Jewellery Quarter**, 75–79 Vyse St (Mon–Fri 10am–4pm, Sat 11am–5pm; £3), a short walk north of the Frederick Street/Warstone Lane intersection. It is built around a factory that has remained virtually unchanged since the 1950s, though it was in use until 1980. A visitor centre starts proceedings, detailing the growth and decline of the trade in Birmingham, but it's the old factory that steals the show. Here, the atmosphere and conditions of the old works are superbly re-created – the jewellers were wedged into tiny, hot and noisy spaces to churn out hundreds of earrings, brooches and rings. Their modern counterparts use the old machines to show how some of the most common designs were produced.

From the museum, it's a couple of minutes' walk back along Vyse Street to the Jewellery Quarter **train station** and **metro stop**, on the Snow Hill line.

The suburbs

Birmingham's suburbs fan out from the centre in every direction, a mammoth industrial – and post-industrial – sprawl intermittently relieved by the municipal parks so much favoured by the Victorians. Inevitably, some districts are much more prosperous than others, and it's in well-heeled **Edgbaston**, a mile or two to the southwest of the centre, you'll find a trio of engaging sights. These are the **Birmingham Botanical Gardens**, the green and pleasant lake-studded **Cannon Hill Park** and the European paintings of the **Barber Institute** on Birmingham University's campus. Further south still is **Bournville**, the planned workers' village laid out by the Cadburys in Victorian times. The main pull here is **Cadbury World**, where displays about the history and manufacture of chocolate are a prelude to tucking into the stuff.

Edgbaston

Leafy, prosperous and home to one of the most famous cricket grounds in the country, the suburb of **EDGBASTON**, just to the southwest of the city centre, was developed in the 1790s by the Calthorpe family as a genteel residential estate from which industry and commerce were explicitly banned. It's here, on Westbourne Road, you'll find the **Birmingham Botanical Gardens and Glasshouses** (Mon–Sat 9am–7pm or dusk, Sun 10am–7pm or dusk; £5, £5.50 on Sun), whose ornamental gardens and glasshouses extend over fifteen acres. The gardens are parcelled up into a number of distinct areas, including a rhododendron garden and brilliant herbaceous borders, while the glasshouses focus on the tropics. Buses #21, #22, #23, #29 and #103 from Broad Street, in the city centre, travel along Westbourne Road.

Cannon Hill Park and the Midland Arts Centre

Arguably the most agreeable of Birmingham's many public parks is **Cannon Hill Park** (daily dawn–dusk; free), about two miles south of central Birmingham – and a mile and a half or so east of the Botanical Gardens. To get there from the centre, take the A441 onto the Pershore Road and then turn left along Edgbaston Road, which marks the park's northern perimeter. There are boating lakes and bowling greens, tennis courts and woodland, and the greenhouses hold a healthy collection of tropical plants. Cannon Hill is also home to the excellent **Midland Arts Centre** (mac; ☎0121/440 3838,

Ⓦwww.mac-birmingham.org.uk), which has a popular bar and café, two cinemas, three theatres and a bookshop. The centre also hosts an imaginative programme of art, craft and photography exhibitions. It's located opposite the cricket ground on Edgbaston Road.

Buses #45 and #47, departing from Corporation Street, in the city centre, travel along Pershore Road, from where it's a short amble along Edgbaston Road to both the northern edge of the park and the Midland Arts Centre.

Birmingham University's Barber Institute of Fine Arts

For the casual visitor, the campus of **Birmingham University**, on the southern fringe of Edgbaston, has one big draw, the **Barber Institute of Fine Arts**, at the east gate off Edgbaston Park Road (Mon–Sat 10am–5pm, Sun noon–5pm; free; Ⓦwww.barber.org.uk). Opened in 1939, the gallery contains a small but eclectic collection of European paintings from the thirteenth century onwards. Notable pieces include an unusual Rubens – *Landscape near Malines* – and Degas' eccentric *Jockeys Before the Race*, a characteristically audacious piece of off-centre composition. Other artists featured include Monet, Magritte, Bellini, Whistler, Gainsborough, Van Gogh, Gauguin and Turner.

The campus has its own train station – University, two stops along the line from New Street – and can also be reached by bus #44 from Hill Street, in the centre.

Bournville

A purpose-built factory community founded by the Cadbury family in 1879, **BOURNVILLE** is the most distinctive of Birmingham's suburbs, located just beyond the university, some four miles southwest of the city centre. The first of this Quaker dynasty, **John Cadbury**, opened a grocery store in Birmingham in 1824 and from it he sold his home-produced "Cocoa Nibs", part soothing (non-alcoholic) nightcap, part a way of weaning the working class from alcohol by providing a cheap and tempting alternative to beer. The popularity of this sweet concoction exceeded John's wildest dreams and just over fifty years later his sons, George and Richard, were able to move the family business out of their cramped premises in the city centre to Bournville – a so-called "factory in a garden". Much influenced by the utopian ideas of William Morris and the Arts and Crafts movement, the Cadburys' Bournville scheme included gardens for every worker's house, a village green and a half-timbered parade of shops. The Bournville Village Trust still operates today, laying down basic rules (no unkempt gardens, for example) to which all inhabitants, even those who own their property, are expected to subscribe. Despite its unusual history, Bournville village doesn't have much in the way of sights, though the **Village Green**, bounded by Linden Road (the A4040) and Sycamore Road, is pleasant enough and it backs onto Maple Road, where the Cadburys plonked a pair of Tudor buildings that were threatened with demolition. These two timber-framed structures, **Selly Manor** and **Minworth Greaves** (April–Sept Tues–Fri 10am–5pm, Sat & Sun 2–5pm; Oct–March Tues–Fri 10am–5pm; £2) – the first a manor house, the second a hall – are furnished in period style and are flanked by pretty "Tudor" gardens.

However, in terms of popularity, these two buildings are as nothing when compared with the excellent **Cadbury World** (phone for times Ⓣ0121/451 4159, Ⓦwww.cadburyworld.co.uk; £8.50), just to the south off Linden Road, adjoining Cadbury's Bournville Works. Billed as "The Ultimate Chocolate Experience", this attraction tells you all you could ever want to know about the cocoa bean, the manufacture of chocolate and the history of Cadbury's itself – the display on the company's adverts is especially interesting. But for chocoholics the point of the tour is the opportunity to gorge on free samples from the production line and stock up on the cut-price finished product. Needless to say, it's very popular, so reservations are advised.

The easiest way to get to Bournville is by **train** from New Street. Bournville Station, the fourth stop along the line, is about half a mile from Cadbury World – follow the trademark Cadbury's people signs west along Bournville Lane and then right up Linden Road.

Eating and drinking

Central Birmingham has a bevy of first-rate **restaurants** with a string of smart, new venues springing up in the slipstream of the burgeoning conference- and trade-fair business, particularly along Broad Street, near the ICC. There's also a concentration of decent, reasonably priced restaurants in the Chinese Quarter, just south of New Street Station, on and around Hurst Street. Birmingham's gastronomic speciality is the **balti**, a delicious and astoundingly inexpensive Kashmiri stew cooked and served in a small wok-like dish called a *karahi*, with nan bread instead of cutlery. Although balti houses have opened up within the city centre, the original and arguably the best balti houses are in the gritty suburbs of **Balsall Heath**, a couple of miles to the south of the centre, and **Sparkhill**, about three miles to the southeast. Some of these are listed here – but note that many are unlicensed, so you may want to take your own booze.

City centre **pubs** vary as much as you'd expect. The liveliest, catering for a mixed bag of conference delegates and Brummies-out-on-the-ale, are liberally sprinkled along Broad Street, in the immediate vicinity of the Convention Centre, and in Brindley Place. Most of these are decorated in sharp, modern style, but there are one or two more traditional places here as well – as there are in other parts of the city centre.

Cafés and restaurants

Brasserie de Malmaison The Mailbox, Royal Mail St ☎0121/246 5000. Delicious French cuisine with a menu that concentrates on a particular – and changing – region of France. Part of the *Malmaison Hotel* (see p.670). Moderate.

Canalside Café Gas St ☎0121/248 7979. Cosy café on the Gas Street Basin serving homemade snacks, cakes and fantastic cherry pies. Inexpensive.

Chez Jules 5a Ethel St, off New Street ☎0121/633 4664. Recommendable medium-priced French restaurant in the city centre, with especially good lunchtime deals. Moderate.

Chung Ying 16–18 Wrottesley St ☎0121/622 1793. Arguably the best Cantonese dishes in the Chinese Quarter, and always busy. Moderate.

Grand Tandoori 343 Stratford Rd, Sparkhill ☎0121/773 9244. Extensive balti menu in a concentration of other balti houses. Buses #4, #31 and #41 from the centre. Inexpensive.

Kushi 558 Moseley Rd, Balsall Heath ☎0121/449 2311. Excellent, award-winning balti house that's unlicensed, very inexpensive, and deservedly popular. Bus #50 from the centre.

Mongolian Bar 24 Ludgate Hill ☎0121/236 3842. Lively and enjoyable curry house, where you choose your ingredients and see them flash-fried before you. Just off the inner ring road. Moderate.

Le Petit Blanc 9 Brindley Place ☎0121/633 7333. Directly opposite the Ikon Gallery, this swish restaurant, with its slick modern furnishings and fittings, offers first-rate French cuisine with a touch of Asia thrown in for good measure. Reservations advised. Expensive.

Punjab Paradise 377 Ladypool Rd, Balsall Heath ☎0121/449 4110. One of the city's classic balti houses, specializing in milder dishes. Inexpensive.

Royal Nain 417 Stratford Rd, Sparkhill ☎0121/766 7849. Twice named Brum's best balti house – as good as it gets. Bus #6 from Corporation St. Inexpensive.

Warehouse Café 54 Allison St, Digbeth ☎0121/633 0261. Imaginative vegan and vegetarian café; ring for times. Bring your own wine. Just below the Bull Ring, near the start of Digbeth – Allison St is a turning on the left. Inexpensive.

Zizzi The Mailbox, Royal Mail St ☎0121/632

1333. Canalside restaurant, part of a chain, with great stone-baked pizzas. Good spot to nurse a drink too. Moderate.

Pubs and bars

Fiddle and Bone 4 Sheepcote St ⓣ0121/200 2223. Canalside pub-cum-restaurant with good old-fashioned decor and regular live music, often to a very high standard.

The Green Room Hurst St. Busy and very amenable bar opposite the Hippodrome. A good range of ales.

Medicine Bar Custard Factory, Gibb Street, off Digbeth. Great bar located in a laid-back arts complex that was once a custard factory. Turns into a club late at night – see *Medicine Bar* below.

The Old Fox Arcadian Centre, Hurst Street. Over-modernized but popular pub, with an excellent selection of beers and a boisterous atmosphere.

Old Joint Stock 4 Temple Row West. Lively bar in an attractively re-worked old bank. A stone's throw from St Philips Cathedral.

Prince of Wales 84 Cambridge St. Old-fashioned haunt with long-standing custom from the Repertory Theatre, now pulling them in from the neighbouring ICC too. Very recommendable.

Red Lion 94 Warstone Lane. Appealing, traditional Brummie pub in the Jewellery Quarter.

Tap & Spile 10 Gas St. Charming traditional pub with rickety rooms and low-beamed ceilings beside the canal on Gas Street Basin. Once the hangout of weathered canal men, it now attracts tourists and locals in equal measure.

Nightlife and entertainment

Nightlife in Birmingham is thriving, and the **club scene** is recognized as one of Britain's best, spanning everything from word-of-mouth underground parties to meat-market mainstream clubs. There's a particular emphasis on special nights with leading DJs turning up at different venues on different nights. **Live music** is strong in the city, too, with big-name concerts at several major venues and other, often local bands appearing at some clubs and pubs (see above). Birmingham's showpiece **Symphony Orchestra** and **Royal Ballet** are the spearheads of the city's resurgent classical scene. The social calendar also gets an added fillip from a wide range of upmarket **festivals**, including the **Film and TV Festival** (ⓣ0121/212 0999, ⓦwww.film-tv-festival.org.uk) in March, the **Jazz Festival** (ⓣ0121/454 7020, ⓦwww.bigbearmusic.com) in the first two weeks of July and the three-day **Artsfest** (ⓦwww.artsfest.org.uk) of film, dance, theatre and music in September.

For current **information** on all events, performances and exhibitions, pick up a free copy of the excellent, fortnightly **What's On**, Birmingham's definitive listings guide. It's available at all of the tourist offices and many public venues.

Clubs

Air Heath Mill Lane, off Digbeth ⓣ0121/693 2633, ⓦwww.godskitchen.com. Shiny, hi-tech superclub host to God's Kitchen and hundreds of house- and trance-hungry clubbers.

Baker's 162 Broad St ⓣ0121/633 3839. Intimate and energetic hard house venue.

Bobby Brown's 52 Gas St ⓣ0121/643 2573. Chart sounds plus speciality nights. Popular with students.

House of God Various venues monthly. Birmingham's ever-popular techno night is still going strong and loud. This is the sound of the city.

The Jam House 1 St Paul's Square ⓣ0121/200 3030, ⓦwww.thejamhouse.co.uk. With Jools Holland as the musical director, there's nightly piano jams and a bluesy-jazz focus at this fashionable restaurant-club.

Medicine Bar Custard Factory, Gibb St, off Digbeth ⓣ0121/604 7777, ⓦwww.medicinebarbirmingham.co.uk. Eclectic and frequently impeccable music policy, plus juicy live events. One of the best nights out in town. Part of the arts complex that inhabits the old Alfred Bird Custard Factory (see p.674).

The Nightingale Essex House, Kent St ⓣ0121/622 1718, ⓦwww.nightingaleclub.co.uk. The king of Brum's gay clubs, but popular with straights too. Five bars, three levels, two discos, a café bar and even a garden. About ten minutes' walk south of New Street Station, out along Hurst Street.

Snob's 30 Paradise Circle ⓣ0121/643 5551, ⓦwww.snobsnightclub.co.uk. Unashamed mosh pit heaving with indie and rock fans; abandonment galore.

Waterworks Jazz Club Gough St ⓣ0121/354

6059. Specialist jazz joint just off the inner ring road near Holloway Circus.

Classical music, theatre, comedy and dance

Alexandra Theatre Suffolk Street, Queensway ⓣ0870/607 7544. Mainstream pop concerts, musicals and plays.

Birmingham Repertory Theatre Broad St ⓣ0121/236 4455, ⓦwww.birmingham-rep.co.uk. Mixed diet of classics and new work, featuring local and experimental writing.

The Crescent Theatre Sheepcote Street, Brindley Place ⓣ0121/643 5858, ⓦwww.crescent-theatre.co.uk. Adventurous theatre group and venue for visiting companies.

Glee Club Arcadian Centre, Hurst St ⓣ0121/693 2248, ⓦwww.glee.co.uk. Dedicated comedy club, with top national names and up-and-coming stars.

Hippodrome Theatre Hurst St ⓣ0870/730 1234, ⓦwww.birmingham-hippodrome.co.uk. Lavishly refurbished, the Hippodrome is home to the Birmingham Royal Ballet and regularly hosts the Welsh National Opera. Also features touring plays and big pre- and post-West End productions, plus a splendiferous Christmas pantomime.

National Exhibition Centre (NEC) Bickenhill Parkway ⓣ0870/909 4133, ⓦwww.necgroup.co.uk. The NEC's arena hosts major pop concerts. Ten miles east of the centre beside the M42; train from New Street to Birmingham International Station.

Old Rep Theatre Station St ⓣ0121/236 5622. Britain's oldest repertory theatre, with regular performances by the imaginative Birmingham Stage Company.

Symphony Hall International Convention Centre, Broad St ⓣ0121/780 3333, ⓦwww.symphonyhall.co.uk. Acoustically one of the most advanced concert halls in Europe, home of the acclaimed City of Birmingham Symphony Orchestra (CBSO), as well as a venue for touring music and opera.

Listings

Airport information desk ⓣ0121/7677799.

Banks Lloyds, 125 Colmore Row; HSBC, 130 New St; Royal Bank of Scotland, 79 Colmore Row.

Bike rental On Yer Bike, 98 Corporation St ⓣ0121/236 4118.

Bookshops Waterstone's, 24 High St and 128 New St.

Bus enquiries Centro Hotline ⓣ0121/200 2700, ⓦwww.centro.org.uk.

Car rental Avis ⓣ0121/622 5666 and at the airport ⓣ0121/782 6183; Europcar, at the airport ⓣ0121/782 6507; National ⓣ0121/622 6131 and at the airport ⓣ0121/782 5481.

Cricket Warwickshire County Cricket Club, Edgbaston Rd, Edgbaston ⓣ0121/446 4422, ⓦwww.warwickccc.org.uk.

Football Aston Villa is the city's big club; they're based at Villa Park, just north of the centre in Aston (ⓣ0121/327 2299, ⓦwww.avfc.co.uk). One-time equal, Birmingham City, is based at St Andrew's, Small Heath (ⓣ0121/772 0101, ⓦwww.blues.premiumtv.co.uk).

Internet At the main library, in the city centre on Chamberlain Square. Free access for the first hour.

Laundry Clean & Care, 758 Alum Rock Rd.

Pharmacy Boots, 65 High St ⓣ0121/212 1631. Late-night opening roster posted in the window here and at the tourist office.

Police Steelhouse Lane ⓣ0845/113 5000.

Post office 1 Pinfold St, on the corner with Victoria Square (Mon–Fri 9am–5.30pm, Sat 9am–6pm).

Taxis Toa Taxis ⓣ0121/427 8888, Radio Taxis ⓣ0121/764 6464.

The Black Country

To outsiders the area known as the **Black Country** appears to be an undifferentiated mass sprawling away from the western side of Birmingham, but in fact it's composed of several tightly knit industrial communities, which have gradually expanded until each is touching its neighbours. The region earned its name in the mid-nineteenth century, when smoke from hundreds of ironworkings choked the air and sooted the buildings – and it's stuck even though the environment is much cleaner today. Some of these towns grew on the basis of one or two staple products – leather in Walsall, locks in Willenhall, glass in Stourbridge – whilst the rest exploited the abundant local resources (chiefly coal and limestone) to develop a range of industries, with heavy engineering predominant. Although many of the older trades have long gone, this is still an area where manufacturing is regarded as the only real work. Consequently, it's hardly surprising that the Black Country's industrial heritage is the main reason for visiting the area. The Black Country Museum in **Dudley** is the chief tourist attraction, though the modern art of **Walsall**'s New Art Gallery is not to be sniffed at. In addition, factories producing decorative goods – such as the glassworks in Brierley Hill – are often open to shoppers. The region is best dipped into by day-tripping from Birmingham, from where there are frequent **buses** and **trains**.

Dudley

Some eight miles west of Birmingham, **DUDLEY** (from Birmingham's Corporation Street take bus #126) lays fair claim to being the capital of the Black Country as it was here in the seventeenth century that coal was first used for smelting iron. The town is actually much older, the main evidence being its ruined Norman **castle**, perched on the hill above the workaday town centre and with grounds that now contain a zoo (daily: Easter to mid-Sept 10am–4pm; mid-Sept to Easter 10am–3pm; £7.50). However, Dudley's main attraction is the **Black Country Living Museum** on the Tipton Road, over the far side of Castle Hill, about a mile from the town centre (March–Oct daily 10am–5pm; Nov–Feb Wed–Sun 10am–4pm; £9.60). Buildings from the surrounding district – shops, a chapel, a pub, workshops, forges and homes – have been re-erected here and populated with local people in period costume, mimicking forms of labour that once employed thousands in these parts. For added authenticity you can take a trip down an underground coal seam, watch a silent movie in a 1920s cinema, or enjoy a canal trip into a tunnel under Castle Hill, through some floodlit limestone caverns.

Walsall

About ten miles northwest of Birmingham, and readily reached by train or bus, **WALSALL** is a pleasantly stoic town, now attempting to diversify into tourism after years as a centre of the leather industry. Its prime attraction is the downtown **New Art Gallery Walsall** (Tues–Sat 10am–5pm, Sun noon–5pm; free; Ⓦwww.artatwalsall.org.uk), on Gallery Square, at the junction of Wolverhampton and Park streets – near the train and bus stations as well as the Walsall canal. The gallery contains a wide-ranging collection of paintings, drawings, prints and sculpture assembled by Kathleen Epstein, the widow of Jacob Epstein, and her friend Sally Ryan. Among the paintings, there are works by Blake, Degas, Modigliani, Van Gogh, Picasso, Ruskin, Turner and – of course – Jacob Epstein. American-born, Epstein (1880–1959) was a controversial figure whose bold and audacious public sculptures were regularly criticized for indecency. In Paris, his *Tomb of Oscar Wilde* created such a stink that a bronze plaque was eventually fixed over the angel's genitals, whilst the aggressiveness of his robot-like *Rock Drill* of 1913 had the art establishment howling with horror. The museum displays Epstein's original drawings for both – and one of his most impressive sculptures adorns Coventry Cathedral (see p.635).

Of more local significance, the **Walsall Leather Museum**, on Littleton Street West (April–Oct Tues–Sat 10am–5pm, Sun noon–5pm; Nov–March Tues–Sat 10am–4pm, Sun noon–4pm; free), provides a surprisingly interesting look at the industry's development and its effect on the town. In particular, there are excellent displays examining the relentless working conditions of the early leather workers, and practical demonstrations of traditional skills. There's also a shop selling locally made leather goods. Littleton Street West is part of the ring road – the A4148 – a short walk to the north of the Art Gallery.

Finally, Walsall was the birthplace of **Jerome K. Jerome**, the author of *Three Men in a Boat*. His family moved away in 1861, when he was just 2, but the town makes something of the connection at the tiny **Birthplace Museum**, in Belsize House, Bradford Place (admission by prior arrangement on ⓣ01922/653116), in the centre, a brief walk south of the art gallery.

Wolverhampton

WOLVERHAMPTON, around fourteen miles northwest of Birmingham – and again easily reached by bus or train – doesn't win any beauty contests, but it does possess a very distinct sense of itself as represented by the illustrious history of its football team, Wolves, or more properly Wolverhampton Wanderers. The town also has the excellent **Wolverhampton Art Gallery and Museum**, bang in the middle of town on Lichfield Street (Mon–Sat 10am–5pm; free). There's a healthy sample of English paintings here, featuring the likes of Gainsborough, Paul Nash, Stanley Spencer and Landseer, but the gallery is best known for its extensive collection of American and British Pop Art. Amongst many, Hamilton, Hockney, Warhol, Allen Jones and Lichtenstein are all featured, and there are also temporary exhibitions plus an eclectic selection of contemporary art.

Staffordshire

Spreading north from the Birmingham conurbation, the miscellaneous and low-key landscapes of **Staffordshire** don't enthral too many people. Nonetheless, the county packs in coachloads of visitors on account of **Alton Towers** (ⓣ0870/444 4455, ⓦwww.altontowers.com; closed Nov–March; day pass £26, under-12s £21), the nation's most popular amusement park, with several million visitors annually howling and screaming on rides with names that include *Nemesis* and *Ripsaw*. The white-knuckle rides take much more money than do the hoteliers in the cathedral city of **Lichfield**, at the southern end of Staffordshire, both the main historic attraction and the county's most agreeable town. Lichfield also makes a handy base for visiting **Stoke-on-Trent**, not much to look at, perhaps, but world-famous for its pottery and with the museums – and factory shops – to match.

Both Lichfield and Stoke are easy to reach by **rail** and **bus** from Birmingham and other major cities.

Lichfield

Some eighteen miles to the north of Birmingham, the pocket-sized town of **LICHFIELD** is a slow-moving, amiable kind of place that demands a visit for one reason – its magnificent sandstone **Cathedral** (daily 8am–6.30pm; £3 donation requested). Begun in 1085, but substantially rebuilt in the thirteenth and fourteenth centuries, the cathedral is unique in possessing three spires – an appropriate distinction for a bishopric that once extended over virtually all of the Midlands. The church stands on the site of a shrine built for the relics of St Chad, a much-venerated English bishop noted for his humility, who died here in Lichfield in 672.

The cathedral's **west front** is adorned by over one hundred statues of biblical figures, English kings and the supposed ancestors of Christ, some of them dating back to the thirteenth century, but mostly Victorian replacements of originals destroyed by Cromwell's troops. Even the central spire was demolished during the skirmishes – Lichfield suffered more damage in the Civil War than any other cathedral. Extensive and painstaking rebuilding and restoration work began immediately after the Restoration in 1660 and has gone on ever since, although the bulk of the work was only completed at the end of the nineteenth century.

Inside, the **nave** is graced by a long line of slender pointed arches, whose decorated capitals are set beneath an elaborately carved clerestory and a soaring vaulted roof that, taken together, resemble the rib-cage of a giant beast – a distinctly eerie experience. The adjoining **south transept** is earlier than the nave, dating to the 1220s, but the main item of interest here is unreservedly Victorian and imperialist. The transept's **St Michael's Chapel** is dedicated to the Staffordshire Regiment and its railings are decorated with replica Zulu shields to celebrate their involvement in the Zulu War; the sphinx does the same for another vainglorious campaign in Egypt, the 1882 suppression of the proto-nationalist uprising of Arabi Pasha. Beyond the transepts, the first three bays of the **choir** are the oldest part of the church, completed in the Early English style of the twelfth century, but thereafter the choir is resolutely middle Gothic. On the south side of the choir a narrow stone stairway leads up to a fine **minstrels' gallery** and the **St Chad's Head Chapel**, where the head of the saint was once displayed to cheer up the faithful. Most impressive of all, however, is the **Lady Chapel**, at the far end of the choir, which boasts a set of magnificent sixteenth-century windows, purchased from the Cistercian abbey at Herkenrode in Belgium in 1802.

The cathedral's greatest treasure, the **Lichfield Gospels**, is displayed in the **chapter house**, off the north side of the choir. A rare and exquisite example of Anglo-Saxon artistry dating to the eighth century, this illuminated manuscript contains the complete gospels of Matthew and Mark, and a fragment of the gospel of Luke, written in Latin and embellished with elaborate decoration. No one knows who wrote it, but it's likely it was produced locally and records certainly show it was stolen in a raid and carried off to Wales, from where it was eventually returned in medieval times. Different pages are exhibited at different times, but a particular favourite is the gorgeous Carpet Page, showing a decorative cross whose blend of Coptic, Celtic and Oriental influences make it the equal of the more famous Irish Book of Kells and Lindisfarne Gospels (see p.1109). The fact that the book ends midway through St Luke means it's almost certainly one of a pair – and rare book specialists have long been on the look-out for the other volume.

The rest of the town centre

The cathedral is flanked by **The Close**, which, with its good-looking medley of Tudor, Georgian and Victorian buildings, is the prettiest place in town. From the Close, it's a short walk along **Dam Street** – past the gloomy waters of the Minster Pool – to the **Market Place**, where there's a peculiar little statue of a puck-nosed Boswell and a much better one honouring **Samuel Johnson**, who looks suitably intellectual. The plinth below the statue is carved with three key scenes from Johnson's life. The most revealing shows Johnson making a public penance in Uttoxeter Market Place for the sin – as he saw it – of refusing to work on his father's Uttoxeter book stall fifty years before.

Samuel Johnson

Eighteenth-century England's most celebrated wit and critic, **Samuel Johnson**, was born above his father's bookshop in Lichfield's Market Place in 1709. From Lichfield he went to Pembroke College, Oxford, which he left in 1731 without having completed his degree. Disgruntled with academia, Johnson returned to Staffordshire as a teacher, before settling in Birmingham for three years, a period that saw his first pieces published in the *Birmingham Journal*.

In 1735 Johnson married Elizabeth Porter, a Birmingham friend's widow twenty years his senior, returning to his home district to open a private school in the village of Edial, just outside Lichfield. The school was no great success, so after two years the Johnsons abandoned the project and went to London with the young **David Garrick**, their star pupil. Journalism and essays were the mainstay of the Johnsons' penurious existence until publisher Robert Dodsley asked Samuel to consider compiling a **Dictionary of the English Language**, a project that nobody had undertaken before, and which was to occupy him for eight years prior to its publication in 1755. Massively learned and full of mordant wit ("lexicographer: a writer of dictionaries; a harmless drudge"), the Dictionary is one of Johnson's greatest legacies, although he was financially and emotionally stretched to breaking point by the workload it imposed. The dictionary was widely acclaimed, but, despite his increasing celebrity, money problems continued to dog him – in 1759 he wrote the novel *Rasselas* in one week, in order to raise money for his mother's funeral. Nevertheless, Johnson's financial bacon was saved shortly afterward when, in the early 1760s, the new king, George III, granted him a bursary of £300 per year.

In 1763 Johnson met James Boswell, a pushy young Scot who clung tenaciously to the cantankerous older man until he learned to like him. Their journey to Scotland resulted in one of the finest travel books ever written, **A Journey to the Western Isles of Scotland** (1775), in which Johnson's fascinated incredulity at the native way of life makes for utterly absorbing reading. Other publications from his final decade included a preface to Shakespeare's plays, a series of political tracts and the magnificent **Lives of the English Poets**. However, the work by which he is now best known is not one that he wrote himself – it's Boswell's **Life of Johnson**, commenced on its subject's death in 1784, published in 1791 and arguably still the English language's most full-blooded biography. Johnson was buried in Westminster Abbey.

At the back of the Market Place stands **St Mary's Church**, unremarkable in itself and now home to the **Lichfield Heritage Centre** (Mon–Sat 10am–5pm, Sun 10.30am–5pm; £3.50), which tracks through the city's history, with an illuminating section on the Civil War. On the outside wall of the church several **plaques** commemorate noteworthy incidents. One of them is a memorial to the unfortunate Edward Wightman, who was burnt at the stake for heresy on this very spot in 1612 – the last Englishman to be so punished for this particular crime.

Also on the Market Place, is the **Samuel Johnson Birthplace Museum** (April–Sept daily 10.30am–4.30pm; Oct–March daily noon–4.30pm; £2.20). The great man's father – Michael – was a bookseller and this house, a narrow four-storey affair, was both the family home and a bookshop. The museum's ground floor still serves as a bookshop – with copies of Boswell's biography and many of Johnson's works – whilst up above, on the first floor, a video provides a well-considered potted introduction to its subject. Thereafter, a series of modest displays explore Johnson's life and times. Of particular interest is the biting letter he sent to a certain Lord Chesterfield, after the latter falsely claimed credit for sponsoring Johnson's dictionary. The top floor holds a small collection of personal memorabilia, including Johnson's favourite armchair, his chocolate pot (chocolate was a real Georgian delicacy), bib holder, shoe buckles and ivory writing tablets.

Practicalities

Lichfield has two **train stations**: Lichfield City, with regular connections to and from Birmingham, is about five minutes' walk south of the centre, while Lichfield Trent Valley, served by mainline trains from London Euston, is on the eastern fringe of the city, about twenty minutes' walk from the centre. The **bus station** is opposite Lichfield City Station. Clearly signed from all three stations, the city centre is dominated by the sprawling Three Spires Shopping Mall. The **tourist office** is currently on Bore Street, just off the Market Place, though there are plans to move to the west edge of Minster Pool, on Bird Street (April–Sept Mon–Sat 9am–5pm; Oct–March Mon–Fri 9am–4.45pm & Sat 9am–2pm; ⓣ01543/308209, ⓦwww.lichfield-tourist.co.uk).

Once you've seen the sights, there's no strong reason to hang around, but Lichfield does have a reasonable supply of affordable **B&Bs**. The pick is *Mrs Taylor's B&B*, with just one twin room, in an appealing and well-kept, two-storey old town house beside the cathedral at 23 The Close (ⓣ01543/306142; ❷).

Lichfield has a healthy selection of **cafés** and **restaurants** within easy walking distance of the cathedral. The *Cathedral Coffee Shop*, on the south side of the cathedral at 19 The Close (Mon–Sat 9.30am–5pm, Sun noon–5pm), is an old-fashioned café with a pleasant atmosphere and inexpensive homemade food; or you could try the *Garrick Coffee Shop*, just beyond the Minster Pool at 14 Dam St, another inexpensive café, occupying old beamed premises and serving a tasty line in pies. Bird Street, a brief walk west of the Market Place, holds a string of recommendable restaurants. These include *Don Paco*, a Spanish place at no. 28 (ⓣ01543/300789; closed Sun), and a smart, modern Mongolian joint, the *Llama Palor*, at no.17 (ⓣ01543/411911), where you select what you want to eat and it's cooked on the spot. The centre of Lichfield has also received a real fillip with the opening in 2003 of the **Lichfield Garrick Theatre** (ⓣ01543/412121, ⓦwww.lichfieldgarrick.com), right in the centre on Castle Dyke and promising a lively contemporary programme.

Stoke-on-Trent

The inhabitants of **STOKE-ON-TRENT**, some thirty miles northwest of Lichfield, have been making pottery since Roman times, but mass production only began in the eighteenth century. Then, in the space of forty years, the development of local coalfields, the securing of a regular supply of fine-quality clay from Devon and Cornwall and the digging of the Trent–Mersey canal transformed the town and its environs into the biggest centre of pottery production in the world – known, logically enough, as **The Potteries**. It was all a terrible eyesore and the district, with its belching smoke stacks and fuming bottle kilns, became synonymous with industrial squalor, but the profits were enormous – quite enough to attract a string of talented entrepreneur-designers. The first of them, and still the most renowned, was **Josiah Wedgwood**, who opened a factory here in 1769. More recently, the industry has been in decline, hit hard by cheap foreign imports, but Britain's department stores are still stacked with The Potteries' products and local companies – such as Royal Doulton, Spode, Royal Worcester and Wedgwood – are making a fight of it. All this industrial activity doesn't spell much in the way of tourist delight, but Stoke-on-Trent's heritage museums and factory shops are enough to keep most visitors happy for a few hours at least.

The city of Stoke-on-Trent is actually an amalgam of **six towns** – confusing for fans of locally born Arnold Bennett (1867–1931), who wrote about the five towns in novels such as *Clayhanger* and *Anna of the Five Towns*, ignoring the smallest of the six, **Fenton**. Of the other five, the major two are **Stoke** itself, which feels as if it has been left to wither to the benefit of **Hanley**, a mile to the north, which has all the main shops and the main civic museum. **Tunstall** – hometown of Robbie Williams no less – and **Burslem** to the north and **Longton** to the southeast are the remaining Stoke towns, all largely autonomous communities. Trains arrive at **Stoke** Station, whereas most buses use the **Lichfield Street bus station** in central Hanley.

Potteries museums and factory tours

The **Potteries Museum and Art Gallery** on Bethesda Street in Hanley (March–Oct Mon–Sat 10am–5pm, Sun 2–5pm; Nov–Feb Mon–Sat 10am–4pm, Sun 1–4pm; free), occupies an unappetizing modern building, but it holds a magnificent and colossal collection of English pottery and ceramics. The museum tracks through the industry's eighteenth-century artistic heyday and the boom of the nineteenth with examples from all the leading manufacturers. There is also a section of Art Deco pieces – look out for the work of Clarice Cliff – and examples of present-day production. An excellent social history department includes a poignant **coal sculpture** commemorating the two colliers who died on picket duty in the 1984–85 miners' strike as well as the 20,000 who were injured, the 200 imprisoned and the 966 men who were sacked. For an introduction to the pottery industry itself, head for the excellent **Gladstone Pottery Museum** in Uttoxeter Road, Longton (daily 10am–5pm; £4.95). Distinguished by pristine examples of the conical bottle-kilns that used to dominate the entire city, the museum employs craftspeople to demonstrate the skills of pottery production, and details the evolution of the six towns and the social conditions of their people.

These two museums are the pick of the bunch, but there are several others focusing on different aspects of pottery manufacture and, in addition, there are over twenty **factory shops** open to the public. The **tourist office**, in the Potteries Shopping Centre on Quadrant Road in Hanley (Mon–Sat 9.15am–5.15pm; ⓣ01782/236000, ⓦwww.visitstoke.co.uk), issues a free leaflet giving the low-down and has local bus timetables too. One of the better known companies is **Royal Doulton**, which has a visitor-cum-display centre at its Nile Street Works, in Burslem (Mon–Sat 9am–5.30pm, Sun 10.30am–4.30pm; £3). They also offer factory tours by prior arrangement from Monday through Friday except during the factory's annual two-week holiday (ⓣ01782/292451, ⓦwww.royaldoulton.com; £6.50).

Derby and the Peak District

In 1951, the hills and dales of the **Peak District**, at the southern tip of the Pennine range, became Britain's first National Park. Wedged between **Derby**, Manchester and Sheffield, it is effectively the backyard for the fifteen million people who live within an hour's drive of its boundaries, though somehow it accommodates the huge influx with minimum fuss.

Landscapes in the Peak District come in two forms. The brooding high moorland tops of **Dark Peak**, fifteen miles east of central Manchester, take their name from the underlying gritstone, known as millstone grit for its former use – a function commemorated in the millstones demarcating the park boundary. Windswept, mist-shrouded and inhospitable, the flat tops of these peaks are nevertheless a firm favourite with walkers on the **Pennine Way**, which meanders north from the tiny village of **Edale** to the Scottish border (see box, p.698). Altogether more forgiving, the southern limestone hills of the **White Peak** have been eroded into deep forested dales populated by small stone villages and often threaded by walking trails, some of which follow former rail routes. The limestone is riddled with complex cave systems around **Castleton** and under the region's largest centre, **Buxton**, a charming former spa town just outside the park's boundaries and at the end of an industrialized corridor that reaches out from Manchester. Two of the country's most distinctive manorial piles, **Chatsworth House** and **Haddon Hall**, stand near **Bakewell**, a town famed locally not just for its cakes but also for its **well-dressing**, a possibly pagan ritual of thanksgiving for fresh water that takes place in about thirty local villages each summer. The well-dressing season starts in early and continues through to mid-September; a specialist leaflet, available at most tourist offices, gives the low-down on when and where.

There's no obvious **route** around the Peaks, but the one outlined below comes in from the south – from Derby – and then cuts up to Buxton before looping round in a clockwise direction to Castleton, Hathersage, Baslow, Bakewell and points in between. The nearest motorway is the **M1** – come off at either junction 29 or 30 and you're within easy striking distance of Baslow, on the way to which you'll pass **Chesterfield**, a workaday town famous for the conspicuous **crooked spire** of the church of Our Lady and All Saints. To Midlanders, the spire announces the start of the Peak District and although Chesterfield doesn't have much else of immediate appeal, it does have a smashing Thursday morning open-air flea market. The town tourist office, opposite the spire (Mon–Sat 9am–5.30pm; ⓣ01246/345777), is also a good place to stock up on Peak District information.

As for a **base**, you're spoiled for choice, but Buxton probably wins out with Eyam and Castleton coming a close second.

Public transport

As regards public transport, there are frequent **trains** south from Manchester to end-of-the-line Buxton and Manchester–Sheffield trains cut through Edale and Hathersage. The main **bus access** is via the Trent Barton bus company's TransPeak service from Nottingham to Manchester via Derby, Matlock, Bakewell and Buxton; otherwise First Mainline's bus #272 runs regularly from Sheffield to Castleton, via Hathersage and Hope, and Stagecoach's bus #65 connects Sheffield to Buxton every hour or so. If you're not planning on walking or driving between towns and villages, you'll need the essential, encyclopedic **Peak District Bus Timetable** (60p) as well as the free **Derbyshire Train Times booklet**, both of which are available at local tourist and National Park information offices. Buses are more widespread than you might imagine, though there are limited winter and Sunday services, and often only sporadic links between the smaller villages. Various one-day **bus passes** allow unlimited travel to and within specified zones. It's a complicated system, but broadly speaking the South Yorkshire Peak Explorer (£5.25) covers the chunk of the park in Yorkshire, the Wayfarer (£7), and the Derbyshire Wayfarer (£7.50) covers the rest. For all Peak District bus **timetable information** call ⓣ0870/608 2608.

The Peaks has a wide network of dedicated cycle lanes, tracks and old railway lines – and the National Park Authority provides a series of **cycle rental** outlets from which to make use of them (10 percent discount for YHA

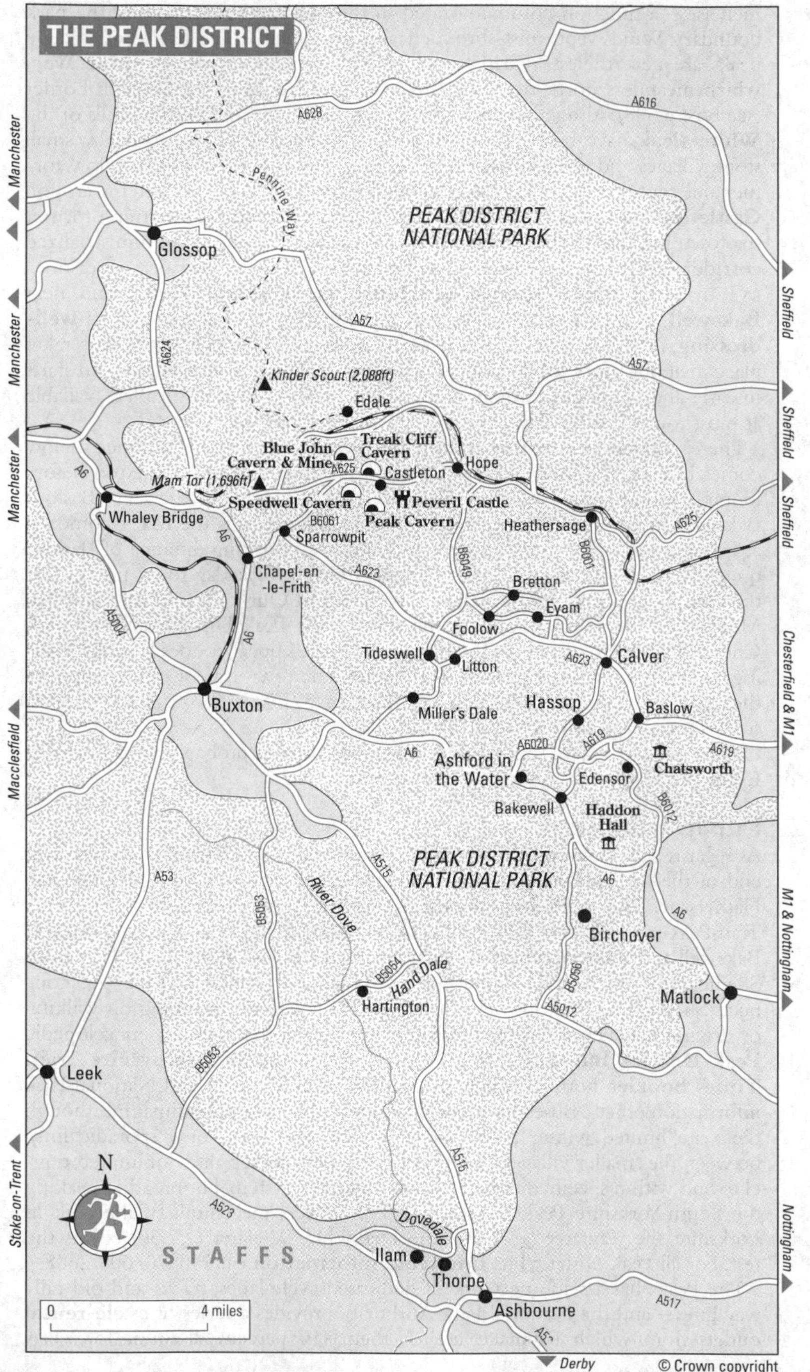
THE PEAK DISTRICT
PEAK DISTRICT NATIONAL PARK
PEAK DISTRICT NATIONAL PARK
Glossop
Pennine Way
Kinder Scout (2,088ft)
Edale
Blue John Cavern & Mine
Treak Cliff Cavern
Castleton
Hope
Mam Tor (1,696ft)
Speedwell Cavern
Peveril Castle
Peak Cavern
Whaley Bridge
Sparrowpit
Chapel-en-le-Frith
Heathersage
Bretton
Eyam
Foolow
Tideswell
Litton
Calver
Buxton
Miller's Dale
Hassop
Baslow
Ashford in the Water
Edensor
Chatsworth
Bakewell
Haddon Hall
Birchover
Matlock
River Dove
Hand Dale
Hartington
Leek
STAFFS
Dovedale
Ilam
Thorpe
Ashbourne
A628
A616
A57
A57
A624
A6
A625
B6061
A6
A623
B6049
B6001
A625
A5004
A6
A623
A6
A6020
A619
A619
B6012
A53
A515
B5053
A6
A6
B5054
B5056
A5012
B5053
A515
A523
A517
A52
Manchester
Manchester
Manchester
Macclesfield
Stoke-on-Trent
Sheffield
Sheffield
Sheffield
Chesterfield & M1
M1 & Nottingham
Nottingham
Derby
N
0
4 miles
© Crown copyright

members). The centres are located at Ashbourne (☎01335/343156); Derwent (☎01433/651261); Hayfield (☎01663/746222); Middleton Top (☎01629/823204); Parsley Hay, Buxton (☎01298/84493); and Waterhouses (☎01538/308609).

Information

The main **Peak District National Park Authority office** is at Aldern House, Baslow Road, Bakewell DE45 1AE (☎01629/816200, ⓦwww.peakdistrict.org). They operate a string of **information centres**, whose services supplement a host of town and village tourist offices. A variety of **maps** and **trail guides** are widely available, but for the non-specialist it's hard to beat the **Grate Little Guides**, a series of leaflets which provide hiking suggestions and trail descriptions for a dozen or so localities in a clear and straightforward style. They cost £1.80 each and are on sale at almost every tourist office and information centres, but note that the maps printed on the leaflets are best used in conjunction with an OS map. Finally, be sure to pick up a copy of the free and official **Peak District paper**, crammed with useful information and local news.

Accommodation

There's plenty of **accommodation** in and around the National Park, mostly in B&Bs, though one of the area's distinctive features is the quality of its **country hotels** – like the ones in Ashford in the Water (see p.706), Baslow (see p.703) and Hassop (see p.706). The greatest concentration of first-rate hotels and B&Bs is, however, in the town of Buxton. The Peak District also holds numerous campsites and a dozen or so youth hostels as well as a network of YHA-operated **camping barns**. These are located in converted farm buildings and provide simple and inexpensive self-catering accommodation for between six and twenty-four people. For further details, contact the YHA Camping Barns Reservation Office on ☎0870/770 6113 or ⓔcampingbarns@yha.org.uk.

Derby

The proximity of the Peak District might lead you to think that **DERBY**, 25 miles northeast of Lichfield, could prove to be an interesting stopping-off point. Sadly, the city – a status conferred as recently as 1977 – is an unexciting place, though its workaday centre is partly redeemed by several long and handsome nineteenth-century stone terraces. There's also a fine **Cathedral** (daily 8.30am–6pm; free), whose pinnacled tower soars high above its modest, mostly Victorian surroundings on Queen Street – just north along Irongate from the spacious, central Market Place. The church's interior is of equal appeal, the wide and graceful Georgian nave sweeping down to a splendidly ornate wrought-iron rood screen. Here also, south of the chancel, is the magnificent table-tomb of Bess of Hardwick, her calm and neutral face presiding over the most intricate of alabaster carving; for more on Bess, see p.720.

Of the city's several museums, easily the best is the attractively laid-out **Derby Museum and Art Gallery** at the top of the Strand (Mon 11am–5pm, Tues–Sat 10am–5pm, Sun 2–5pm; free), a couple of minutes' walk west from the cathedral via Irongate and Sadlergate. Amongst a string of separate displays, the museum exhibits a splendid collection of Derby **porcelain**, several hundred pieces tracking through the different phases and styles from the mid-eighteenth century until today. Of particular appeal is the painted pottery of the

Duesbury II & Kean period (1786–1811), featuring the exquisite flowers of one William Billingsley. Royal Crown Derby, founded in 1878, is still in production and the museum holds a healthy sample of their fancifully ornate ware – but really this is something of an acquired taste. Upstairs, there's a period room devoted to and a small display on Charles Edward Stuart – aka **Bonnie Prince Charlie** – who attempted to seize the throne from George II in the Jacobite Rebellion of 1745. Advancing south from Scotland, Charles and his army got as far as Derby, spreading panic in London, but, unable to press their advantage, it was here they turned round for the long and dismal retreat that ended with their defeat at the bloody battle of Culloden.

In addition, the museum possesses a first-rate collection of the work of **Joseph Wright** (1734–97), a local artist generally regarded as one of the most talented English painters of his generation. Wright's bread and butter came from portraiture, though his attempt to fill the boots of Gainsborough, when the latter moved from Bath to London, came unstuck – his more forceful style did not satisfy his genteel customers and Wright soon hightailed it back to Derby. Typical of his style is his portrait of *Sir Richard Arkwright*, looking uncompromising and very porky. Wright was one of the few artists of his period to find inspiration in technology and his depictions of the scientific world were hugely influential – as in his *The Alchemist Discovering Phosphorus* and *A Philosopher Lecturing on the Orrery*.

Practicalities

With fast and frequent connections to many major cities – including Sheffield and Birmingham – Derby **train station** is a mile to the southeast of the city centre: follow Midland Road and turn right onto London Road at the end, though it's a dreary walk, so best advice is to take a taxi. The **bus station** is more convenient, just off the inner ring road about five minutes' walk southeast of the Market Place, which is where you'll find the **tourist office** (Mon–Fri 9.30am–5.30pm, Sat 9.30am–5pm, Sun 10.30am–2.30pm; ⓣ01332/255802, ⓦwww.visitderby.co.uk). For a bite to **eat**, there are several good places on Sadler Gate including *Café B*, across from the Derby Museum and serving the best coffee in town.

Ashbourne

Sitting pretty on the edge of the Peaks twelve miles northwest of Derby, **ASHBOURNE** is an amiable little town, whose stubby, cobbled **Market Place** is flanked by a happy ensemble of old stone buildings. Hikers tramp into town from the neighbouring dales to hang around the square's cafés and pubs, and stroll down the hill to take a peek at the suspended wooden beam spanning Church Street. Once a common feature of English towns, but now a rarity, these **gallows** were not warnings to malcontents, but advertising hoardings. Walk west along Church Street from here and you soon leave the bustling centre for a quieter part of town, all set beneath the soaring spire of **St Oswald's Church**, an imposing lime- and ironstone structure dating from the thirteenth century. Something of an architectural muddle, the interior of the church is intriguing nonetheless, its columns decorated with all sorts of weathered sculptures and graced by handsome stained-glass windows, the best of which are exquisite examples of early-twentieth-century Arts and Crafts design. In the east aisle of the north transept, the **Cockayne Chapel** is named after the eponymous clan of local landowners who lie buried here. Of the five main table tombs in and just outside the chapel the earliest dates from 1483, the latest from 1592 and taken together they illustrate changing fashions culminating in the elaborate ruffs and hats popular with the Elizabethans. The most striking tomb is that of Sir John (d.1447) and his son, Edmund, with delicately carved alabaster figures – John in his suit of armour, Edmund in a fancy cloak and belted doublet.

Practicalities

There are no trains to Ashbourne, but the town is easy to reach by bus from Derby, Buxton and Manchester. From Ashbourne **bus station**, it's a short walk to the Market Place – turn right out of the station, left at the T-junction and follow Dig Street over the river. The **tourist office**, on the Market Place (March–June, Sept & Oct Mon–Sat 9.30am–5pm; July & Aug Mon–Sat 9.30am–5pm, Sun 10am–4pm; Nov–Feb Mon–Sat 10am–4pm; ⓣ01335/343666), has oodles of hiking maps and guides, including the first-rate *Grate Little Guide to Dovedale* (£1.80). They can also advise on **accommodation**, though Ashbourne is perhaps best regarded as a pit-stop rather than as a base for further wanderings. For **food**, *Ye Olde Vaults*, on the Market Place, serves competent bar meals, whilst the *Patrick & Brooksbank* delicatessen, 22 Market Place, has a superb selection of takeaway food, including local cheeses and hams.

Dovedale and Ilam

The **River Dove** wriggles its way across the Peak District, cutting a circuitous course from the high hills of Derbyshire to the flatlands southwest of Derby, where it joins the River Trent. The Dove is at its scenic best just four miles north of Ashbourne in the stirring two-mile gorge that comprises **Dovedale** – confusingly, other parts of the river are situated in different dales. To get to Dovedale, head north from Ashbourne along the A515 and then follow the signs to the car park, which is on a narrow country road just beyond the hamlet of Thorpe – and a mile or so before you reach minuscule Ilam (see below). The **hike** along the gorge is a real pleasure and easy to boot, the only problem being the bogginess of the valley after rain, but be warned that the place simply heaves with visitors on summer weekends and bank holidays. If you do decide to hike here, be sure to pick up a map and trail guide from Ashbourne tourist office (see above).

ILAM is itself a pleasant little spot, a scramble of country cottages abutting **Ilam Park** (daily dawn to dusk; free; NT), whose immaculate lawns and woods fall either side of the River Manifold. At the heart of the park is **Ilam Hall**, a rambling neo-Gothic Victorian mansion that has been recycled as a **youth hostel** (ⓣ0870/770 5876, ⓦwww.yha.org.uk; ring for opening times & bookings; dorm beds £11.50). It's a large hostel, with nearly 150 beds distributed in two- to fourteen-bedded rooms, and it's well equipped with a self-catering kitchen, lounge, games room, laundry facilities, cycle store and café. Furthermore, it only takes twenty minutes or so to hike over to Dovedale.

Hartington

Best approached from the east, through the boisterous scenery of Hand Dale, **HARTINGTON**, thirteen miles north of Ashbourne via the A515, is one of the prettiest villages in the Peaks, its easy ramble of stone houses zeroing in on a tiny duck pond. The village is also within easy walking distance of the River Dove as well as a sequence of handsome limestone dales – Biggin Dale is perhaps the pick. In addition, Hartington has several **B&Bs**, the most recommendable of which is the *Bank House Guest House*, in an attractive old building on the Market Place (Ⓣ01298/84465; no cards; ❷). There's also a **youth hostel** (Ⓣ0870/770 5848, Ⓦwww.yha.org.uk; dorm beds £14), whose 120 beds – in two- to nine-bedded rooms – are squeezed into a seventeenth-century manor house, Hartington Hall. The hostel is about 300yd from the centre of the village and is very well equipped. Facilities include a self-catering kitchen, a café, an adventure playground and Internet access.

Buxton

BUXTON, twenty miles north of Ashbourne, may have had its doldrums, but is now on its way up, its centre revamped and reconfigured with imagination and flair. Buxton also holds a string of excellent hotels and B&Bs, which makes it a perfect base for exploring much of the Peaks National Park, and boasts the outstanding **Buxton Festival** (brochure line Ⓣ01298/70395, tickets Ⓣ0845/1272190; Ⓦwww.buxtonfestival.co.uk), running for two weeks in July. This features a full programme of classical music, opera and literary readings, and it has spawned the first-rate **Buxton Festival Fringe** (Ⓦwww.buxtonfringe.com), with the emphasis on contemporary music, theatre and film. The biggest festival is, however, the **Gilbert & Sullivan Festival** (Ⓦwww.gs-festival.co.uk), a three-week affair in August that attracts an international audience.

Buxton has a long history as a **spa**, beginning with the Romans, who happened upon a spring from which 1500 gallons of pure water gushed every hour at a constant 28°C. Impressed by the recuperative qualities of the water, the Romans came here by the chariot load, setting a trend that was to last hundreds of years. One of the most famous visitors was Mary, Queen of Scots, who was allowed by her captors to visit Buxton for the treatment of her rheumatism, another was Daniel Defoe, who loved the place. The spa's salad days came at the end of the eighteenth century with the **fifth Duke of Devonshire**'s grand design to create a northern answer to Bath or Cheltenham, a plan ultimately thwarted by the climate, but not before some distinguished buildings had been erected, most memorably The Crescent. Neither was Victorian Buxton a laggard for although it may not have had quite the elan of its more southerly rivals, it still flourished, creating the raft of handsome stone houses that edge the town centre today. The stickiest years came after the town's thermal baths were closed for lack of custom in 1972, but Buxton hung on to emerge as the most appealing town in the Peaks.

Arrival and information

There's an hourly train service from Manchester Piccadilly to Buxton, terminating two minutes' walk from The Crescent at the **train station** on Station Road. The **TransPeak bus**, running every two hours between Manchester (Chorlton Street Coach Station) and Nottingham, stops in Buxton's Market Place, as do the regular buses from Sheffield. Buxton **tourist office** is in The Crescent (March–Oct daily 9.30am–5pm; Nov–Feb daily 10am–4pm; Ⓣ01298/25106, Ⓦwww.visitbuxton.co.uk) in what used to be the old Mineral Baths – hence the small display on Buxton's mineral water. They operate an accommodation booking service and have oodles of information on the town in particular and the Peaks in general.

Accommodation

The town centre is liberally sprinkled with first-rate **B&Bs** and **hotels**. Several of the best choices are located on the pedestrianized Broad Walk, where a string of distinguished Edwardian and Victorian stone houses face out onto the

BUXTON
ACCOMMODATION
Buxton's Victorian Guest House D
Grosvenor House Hotel C
Old Hall Hotel B
Palace Hotel A
Roseleigh Hotel E
RESTAURANTS, BARS & CAFÉS
Columbine 1
Café Nathaniels 3
Sun Inn 4
Watsons 2
0
200 yds
N
Bakewell
Ashbourne
Manchester
Leek
River Wye
BAKEWELL ROAD
LONDON ROAD
MOSLEY ROAD
COMPTON ROAD
BYRON STREET
WEST ROAD
SPENCER ROAD
TEMPLE ROAD
ERRWOOD AVENUE
ECCLESBOURNE DRIVE
MILLDALE AVENUE
GREEN LANE
Poole's Cavern
MACCLESFIELD ROAD
ST JOHNS ROAD
LISMORE RD
BURLINGTON ROAD
HARTINGTON ROAD
BROAD WALK
Pavilion Gardens
HIGH STREET
DALE ROAD
MARKET ST
CATTLE MARKET
SOUTH ST
SOUTH AVENUE
DARWIN AVENUE
PEVRIL ROAD
SOLOMONS VIEW
SILVERLANDS
HOLKER ROAD
HARDWICK SQ E
Museum & Art Gallery
MARKET PLACE
Bus Stop
HALL BANK
The Slopes
The Pump Room
TERRACE ROAD
H'WICK MT
HARDWICK ST
SPRING GDNS
THE QUADRANT
STATION APPROACH
STATION ROAD
Train Station
The Crescent
St Ann's Well
THE SQUARE
Opera House
Pavilion Gardens
Derby University Dome
DEVONSHIRE ROAD
PARK RD
PARK ROAD
The Park
CARLISLE ROAD
WATFORD ROAD
© Crown copyright

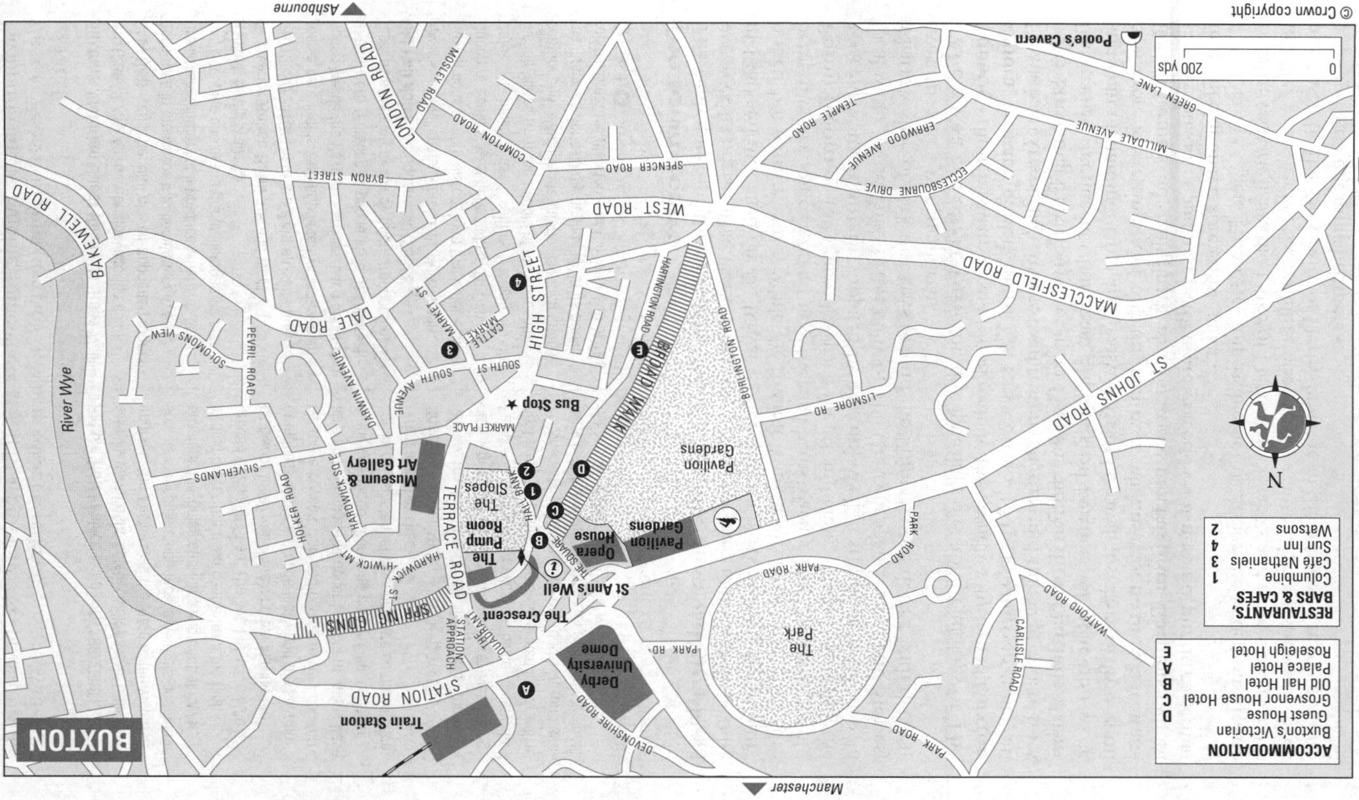

Pavilion Gardens. Finding somewhere is rarely a problem, except during the Buxton Festival in July (see p.692), when advance reservations are well-nigh essential.

Buxton's Victorian Guest House 3a Broad Walk ⓣ01298/78759, ⓦwww.buxtonvictorian.co.uk. Cosy B&B with a handful of well-appointed rooms decorated in crossover traditional/modern style. Breakfasts feature local produce wherever feasible. Occupies one of the grand Victorian houses flanking Broad Walk. ❹

Grosvenor House Hotel 1 Broad Walk ⓣ01298/72439. There are eight en-suite guest rooms here in this well-appointed Victorian town house beside the Pavilion Gardens, each decorated in a modern rendition of period style. Tasty breakfasts plus evening meals by prior arrangement. ❸

Old Hall Hotel The Square ⓣ01298/22841, ⓦwww. oldhallhotelbuxton.co.uk. Nowhere in Buxton boasts more history than this hotel – Mary, Queen of Scots stayed here and so did Daniel Defoe. The building itself, with its fetching, ivy-clad facade, dates from the middle of the sixteenth century and, although the interior is much later, it maintains an appealingly antique air in its public rooms. Great location too – at the west end of The Crescent. ❻

Palace Hotel Palace Road ⓣ01298/22001, ⓦwww.paramount-hotels.co.uk/palace. Built to impress, the *Palace* was the pride of the Victorian spa, its sweeping stone facade, with its pediments, pilasters, balconies and imposing central tower, lording it over the town centre from the high ground of Palace Road. The hotel is just a little careworn today, but there's no gainsaying the grandness of the entrance lobby and the soaring staircase beyond. The bedrooms are very comfortable and although the decor is modern, many have a quirky antique charm, as do the long, echoing corridors. Substantial discounts are commonplace – ring ahead to check. ❼

Roseleigh Hotel 19 Broad Walk ⓣ01298/24904, ⓦwww.roseleighhotel.co.uk. This classic three-storey gritstone Victorian town house, overlooking Pavilion Gardens, is an excellent place to stay, its neat and trim public rooms decorated in attractive Victorian style, the en-suite bedrooms beyond similarly well appointed. Family-run and very competitively priced. ❸

The town centre

The centrepiece of Buxton's hilly, compact centre is **The Crescent**, a broad sweep of Georgian stonework commissioned by the fifth Duke of Devonshire in 1780 and modelled on the Royal Crescent in Bath. It's recently been refurbished, but remains empty while the townsfolk discuss its future, one good idea being the creation of a brand new thermal baths. Facing The Crescent, the old **Pump Room** of 1894 provides space for art and crafts exhibitions, while the adjacent water **fountain**, supplied by St Ann's Well, is still used to fill many a local water bottle. For a better view of The Crescent, clamber up **The Slopes**, a narrow slice of park that rises behind the Pump Room dotted with decorative urns and a war memorial.

At the west end of The Crescent, the appealing old stone buildings of **The Square** – though square it isn't – nudge up to the grandly refurbished **Buxton Opera House** (guided tours £3; ring ⓣ0845/127 2190 for schedule), an Edwardian extravagance whose twin towers, cherubs and tiffany glass date from 1903. Stretching back from the Opera House is the **Pavilion Gardens**, a slender string of connected buildings distinguished by their wrought-iron work and culminating in a large and glassy dome. The pavilions are actually a good deal more interesting from outside than from within, reason enough to wander off into the adjoining park, also known as the **Pavilion Gardens**, whose immaculate lawns and neat borders are graced by a bandstand, ponds, dinky little footbridges and fountains.

Back at the Opera House, it's impossible not to notice the enormous **dome** of what was originally the Duke of Devonshire's stables and riding school, built in 1789. For decades, the building was used as a hospital, but it's recently been purchased by the University of Derby, who are in the process of turning it into a leisure and educational complex.

The Market Place and the Museum and Art Gallery

From the south end of The Square, the fetching stone terrace that comprises **Hall Bank** scuttles up to the wide and breezy but traffic-choked **Market Place**. There's nothing much here to hold the eye, but it's only a few yards back down the hill along Terrace Road to the first-rate **Buxton Museum and Art Gallery** (Tues–Fri 9.30am–5.30pm, Sat 9.30am–5pm & Easter–Sept Sun 10.30am–5pm; free). The museum begins well with its ground floor largely devoted to enterprising temporary displays featuring the work of local contemporary artists. There's also a period room dedicated to two Victorian archeologists-cum-geologists – William Boyd Dawkins (1837–1929) and Wilfred Jackson (1880–1978) – who spent decades exploring and explaining the Peaks. Upstairs, the large and extremely proficient "Wonders of the Peak" display tracks through the history of the region from its geological construction through the Romans and on to the Victorians. One of the most diverting sections looks at the prehistoric hilltop forts that lie dotted over the Peaks, another examines the relics left by the Anglo-Saxons, most notably the incised Crosses at Eyam (see p.701) and Bakewell (see p.705). Best of all, however, is the section dealing with the **petrifactioners**, who turned local semi-precious stones into ornaments and jewellery designed to tickle the fancy of the visitors who arrived here in numbers after the duke had put Buxton on the tourist map. By the 1840s, Buxton had no less than fourteen petrifactioners' shops, selling every stone trinket imaginable from plates and stone eggs to vases and obelisks. A variety of materials were used, but the two favourites were Blue John fluorspar (for more on which, see p.696) and Ashford black marble, actually a dark limestone – and the museum displays a superb collection of both.

Poole's Cavern

The Peaks are riddled with cave systems and around half a dozen have become popular tourist attractions. One is **Poole's Cavern** (mid-Feb to Oct daily 10am–5pm; £5.40), whose impressively large chambers are home to a host of orange and blue-grey stalactites and stalagmites. The cavern is located about a mile to the southwest of the centre just off Green Lane. To get there by car, follow Macclesfield Road from the top of Broad Walk and watch for the signs; on foot, take Temple Road from the top of Broad Walk, turn left onto Milldale Avenue and then hang a right when you reach Green Lane.

Eating and drinking

Buxton has several great places to eat, with one of the best **restaurants** in town being the *Columbine*, a small and intimate place in the centre at 7 Hall Bank (☎01298/78752; closed Sun & Tues in winter). The menu here is short but imaginative with main courses averaging £12. An excellent second choice is the *Sun Inn*, a fine old pub with antique beamed rooms just south of the Market Place at 33 High St. They offer fine ales and first-rate bar food – beef in ale, for instance, at £7.50, chicken, ham & meat pies £8. A third very recommendable spot is *Café Nathaniel's*, just off the Market Place at 11 Market St, where, amidst the stripped wood interior, they serve an excellent range of seafood with main courses averaging around £7.50, seafood salads £5. The best place for a **pint** is the *Sun Inn* (see above), but you could also check out *Watsons Café Bar None*, on Hall Bank, a bar-cum-café with a laidback atmosphere, inviting decor and frequent live music, especially jazz. The most studenty place is *The George*, right in the centre of town on The Square.

Castleton

The agreeable little village of **CASTLETON**, ten miles northeast of Buxton, lies on the northern edge of the White Peak, its huddle of old stone cottages ringed by hills and set beside a babbling brook. As a base for local walks, the place is hard to beat and the hikers resting up in the quiet Market Place, just off the main drag behind the church, have the choice of a healthy spread of local accommodation and services. Overseeing the whole ensemble is **Peveril Castle** (April–Oct daily 10am–6pm; Nov–March Wed–Sun 10am–4pm; £2.50; EH), from which the village takes its name. William the Conqueror's illegitimate son William Peveril raised the first fortifications here to protect the king's rights to the forest that then covered the district, but most of the remains – principally the ruinous square keep – date to the 1170s. After a stiff climb up to the keep, you can trace much of the surviving curtain wall, which commands great views of the Hope Valley down below with the swollen mass of Mam Tor (see box opposite) rising to the west.

The Peak and Speedwell caverns

The limestone hills pressing in on Castleton are riddled with water-worn **cave systems** and four of them have been developed as tourist attractions. They can all be reached by car or on foot – a three-and-a-half mile circular trail that begins in the village and takes two hours; the tourist office (see p.697) has the leaflet and sells the maps. **Peak Cavern** is the handiest (April–Oct daily 10am–5pm; Nov–March Sat & Sun 10am–5pm; £5.50; ☎01433/620285), tucked in a gully at the back of the village, its gaping mouth once providing shelter for a rope factory and a small village. Daniel Defoe, visiting in the eighteenth century, noted the cavern's colourful local name, the **Devil's Arse**, after the fiendish fashion in which the interior contours twisted and turned – hence the signs of today. Most visitors settle for just one set of caves – and either the Peak or the Treak Cliff Cavern (see below) will do very nicely – but it's only 600yd or so west from the village along the main road to **Speedwell Cavern** (daily: April–Oct 9.30am–6pm; Nov–March 10am–4.30pm; last entry 1hr before closing; £6; ☎01433/620512). At 600 feet below ground, this is the deepest of the four cave systems, but the main drama comes with the means of access – down a hundred dripping steps and then by boat through a quarter-mile-long claustrophobic tunnel that was blasted out in search of lead. At the end lies the Bottomless Pit, a pool where 40,000 tons of mining rubble were dumped without raising the water level one iota.

The Treak Cliff and Blue John caverns

The other two caves are the world's only source of the sparkling fluorspar known as **Blue John**. Highly prized for ornaments and jewellery since Georgian times, this semi-precious stone comes in a multitude of hues from blue through deep red to yellow, depending on its hydrocarbon impurities. Before being cut and polished, it is soaked in pine resin, a process originally carried out in France, where the term *bleu et jaune* (after its primary colours) provided its English name. The **Treak Cliff Cavern** (daily: March–Oct 10am–5pm; Nov–Feb 10am–4pm; last entry 40min before closing; £5.60; ☎01433/ 620571), across the main road some four hundred yards from Speedwell, contains the best examples of the stone *in situ* and a good deal more in the shop. This is also the best cave to visit in its own right, dripping – literally – with stalactites (some up to 100,000 years old), flowstone and bizarre rock formations, all visible on an entertaining forty-minute walking tour

Walks around Castleton

Several **walking routes** take you up from Castleton to the swollen hill tops ringing the village. Most are easy to follow in good weather, but you will need an appropriate OS map and one of the trail leaflets issued by the tourist office. The obvious and most appealing target is the National Trust-owned **Mam Tor** (3km from Castleton; 1hr 30min), at 1696ft the Peak District's second-highest peak and the NT's most tramped-upon outdoor site, attracting over 250,000 visitors a year – hence the flagstoned path up to the top and along the ridge. This channels the summer crowds along something of a hikers' motorway, but it has allowed the hillside to regenerate itself and the nesting birds to return. The views – to Kinder Scout, Castleton, Edale and down the Hope Valley – remain unsurpassed and you also get a look at the plunging gorge that comprises **Winnats Pass**, which you have to pass through if you're approaching Castleton from the west.

From the Mam Tor peak, the ridge rolls along to the northeast and there are opportunities to drop back down to Castleton at either Hollins Cross, Back Tor or from Losehill Pike, making the complete walk anything from three to six hours. Hollins Cross is also the lowest crossing-point on the two- to three-hour walk from Castleton to Edale, which could also form part of a circuit involving scaling Mam Tor.

through the main cave system. Water collected in one of the caves is used to make tea in the café at the entrance – it's much purer than the stuff that pours from local taps.

Further afield, just two miles or so west of Castleton off the B6061, tours of **Blue John Cavern** (daily: April–Oct 9.30am–5.30pm; Nov–March 9.30am–dusk; £6.50; ⓣ01433/620638) dive deep into the rock, with narrow steps and sloping paths following an ancient watercourse. The tour leads through whirlpool-hollowed chambers to Lord Mulgrave's Dining Room, a cavern where the eponymous lord and owner once put on a banquet for his miners. A goodly sample of Blue John is on sale at the cavern gift shop.

Practicalities

Easily the most scenic approach to Castleton is from the west, either along the A625 or the A623/B6061, though they merge just to the west of the village to wiggle through the dramatic Winnats Pass. However, the principal **bus** service to Castleton arrives from the east – from Sheffield and Hathersage. It's First Mainline's bus #272 and it runs hourly. The only bus from Buxton to Castleton is Stagecoach's bus #203, but this only operates on summer weekends and even then only once daily. The nearest **train station** is at Hope, a couple of miles or so to the east of Castleton along the valley. The station is on the Manchester Piccadilly, Hope Valley and Sheffield line and there are trains every hour or two; bus #272 links Hope Station with Castleton. The brand new **Castleton Centre** (daily: April–Sept 9.30am–5.30pm, Oct–March 10am–5pm; ⓣ01433/621656), a combined museum, visitor centre and tourist office, stands beside the car park on the west side of the village, just off the main street, which dog-legs through Castleton doubling as the A625. They sell hiking leaflets and maps and operate an accommodation booking service.

Accommodation is plentiful, but should be booked in advance at holiday times. Cream of the **B&B** crop is *Bargate Cottage*, in a modernized old cottage at the top end of the Market Place (ⓣ01433/620201, ⓦwww.bargatecottage.co.uk; no credit cards; ❷). They have three, well-kept en-suite rooms, each kitted out in frilly modern style, and the breakfasts are first-rate. Another inexpensive option is the *Cryer House*, just off the Market Place opposite the church on Castle St (Ⓣ01433/620244; no credit cards; ❷). This B&B occupies an older building as well and has just two guest rooms – plus a pleasant conservatory. The best pub lodgings are at *Ye Olde Nag's Head* (Ⓣ01433/620248; ❺), a heavily revamped old coaching inn on the main street. Finally, the lively **youth hostel** (Ⓣ0870/770 5758, Ⓦwww.yha.org.uk; closed Jan; dorm beds £11.50) is housed in Castleton Hall, a capacious old stone mansion on the Market Place. The hostel is well equipped with a self-catering kitchen, a café, cycle store and drying room, and its 150 beds are parcelled up between two- to eight-bedded rooms, many of which are en suite.

For **food**, Castleton's pubs are its gastronomic mainstay and there's nowhere better than the *Castle*, opposite the church on Castle Street, which offers tasty bar food at very affordable prices. Alternatively, *Ye Olde Nag's Head*, on the main street, offers more-than-competent bar food (6–9pm), including home-made steak and Guinness pies, and also holds the *Stables Tearoom* (daily 9am–5.30pm), good for snacks and light meals.

Edale village

There's almost nothing to **EDALE village**, some seven miles by road from Castleton, except for a slender, half-mile trail of stone houses, which march up the main street from the train station with a couple of pubs, an old stone church and a scattering of B&Bs on the way – and it's this somnambulant air that is of immediate appeal. Walkers arrive in droves throughout the year to set off on the 250-mile **Pennine Way** (see box below) across England's backbone to Kirk Yetholm on the Scottish border; the route's starting-point is signposted from outside the *Old Nag's Head* at the head of the village.

The Pennine Way

The 250-mile-long **Pennine Way** was the country's first long-distance footpath, officially opened in 1965. It stretches north from the boggy plateau of the Peak District's Kinder Scout, through the Yorkshire Dales and Teesdale, crossing Hadrian's Wall and the Northumberland National Park, before entering Scotland to fizzle out at the village of Kirk Yetholm. People had been using a similar route for over thirty years before the official opening, inspired by Tom Stephenson, secretary of the Ramblers' Association, who had first identified the need for such a long-distance path in the 1930s. His idea was to stick to the crest of the Pennines where practicable and link up existing tracks, bridleways and footpaths, only descending to the valleys for overnight accommodation and services. The problem was that much of the route lay on private land, so years of negotiation and re-routing were necessary before the Pennine Way could be officially declared open.

Now it's one of the most popular walks in the country, either taken in sections or completed in two to three weeks, depending on your level of fitness and experience. It's a challenge in the best of weather, since it passes through some of the most remote countryside in England. You must certainly be properly equipped, able to use a map and compass and be prepared to follow local advice about current diversions and re-routing; changes are often made to avoid erosion of the existing trail. The National Trail Guides, *Pennine Way: South* and *Pennine Way: North*, are essential, though some still prefer to stick to Wainwright's *Pennine Way Companion*. Peak National Park **information centres** along the route – like the one at Edale village – stock a selection of guides and associated trail leaflets and can offer advice. Finally, on reaching the end, you can get your certificate stamped at Edale's *Old Nag's Head* in the south or Kirk Yetholm's *Border Hotel* in the north.

An excellent **circular walk** (9 miles; 5hr) uses the first part of the Pennine Way, leading up onto the bleak gritstone, table-top of **Kinder Scout** (2088ft), below which Edale cowers. The route cuts west from the *Old Nag's Head* along a packhorse route once used by Cheshire's salt exporters to reach the campsite and **camping barn** at Upper Booth Farm (Ⓣ0870/770 6113). From here, you climb the path called Jacob's Ladder and then continue half a mile west to the carved medieval **Edale Cross**. Backtracking a couple of hundred yards, the Pennine Way branches north along the broken edge of the plateau to **Kinder Downfall**, Derbyshire's highest cascade. This was the site of the Kinder Scout Trespass of 1932, when dozens of protesters walked onto unused but private land, five subsequently receiving prison sentences. It was the turning-point in the fight for public access to open moorland, leading, three years later, to the formation of the Ramblers' Association. At Kinder Downfall turn east then southeast across the often boggy peat towards the wind-sculpted **Wool Pack** rocks, then across to the eastern rim, where a path to the south along Grindslow Knoll and down into Edale avoids Grindsbrook Clough, the highly eroded route of the original Pennine Way. It can be extremely wet up here among the bare furrows of peat – as long-distance walker John Hillaby recorded on his *Journey Through Britain*. Hillaby had to resort to removing his footwear to make his way across the sodden top of Kinder Scout, which to his appalled mind looked as if it was "entirely covered in the droppings of dinosaurs".

Practicalities

Edale village is about five miles northwest of Castleton by road, slightly more by footpath. Hourly **trains** from Manchester, Sheffield and Hathersage provide surprisingly easy access. **Buses** #200 and #260 supplement the trains with a reasonably frequent service from Castleton. From Edale train station, it's 400yd or so up the road to the **Peak National Park Information Centre** (daily 9am–1pm & 2–5pm; Ⓣ01433/670207). They sell all manner of trail leaflets and hiking guides and can advise about local accommodation. The nearest **youth hostel**, the extremely popular *Edale YHA Activity Centre* (Ⓣ0870/770 5808, Ⓦwww.yha.org.uk; dorm beds £11.50), lies two miles east of Edale Station, in an old country house at Rowland Cote, Nether Booth. It's clearly signed from the road into Edale or you can hoof it there across the fields from behind the information centre. There are 150 beds in two- to twelve-bedded rooms and a good range of facilities from a laundry and a café through to a self-catering kitchen. They also offer an extensive programme of outdoor pursuits, but these need to be booked in advance. Naturally enough, the hostel is popular with Pennine Way walkers – as is the YHA **camping barn** at Cotefield Farm, Ollerbrook (Ⓣ0870/770 6113), which lies on the path from the village to the hostel. There are two village **campsites**, *Fieldhead* (Ⓣ01433/670386), behind the information centre, and *Cooper's* at Newfold Farm (Ⓣ01433/670372), in the centre of Edale near the *Old Nag's Head*.

Those without hair shirts, or with more money, will do better at Edale's **B&Bs**, starting with *Stonecroft*, a detached Victorian house with two pleasantly comfortable guest rooms in the village near the church (Ⓣ01433/670262, Ⓦwww.stonecroftguesthouse. co.uk; ❸). Nearby, in another old stone house, is *Mam Tor B&B* (Ⓣ01433/670253, Ⓦwww.edale-valley.co.uk/mamtor.htm; no credit cards; ❶), which offers three pleasant guest rooms. As for **food**, there are only two options – the *Rambler*, yards from the train station at the bottom of the village, and the *Old Nag's Head*, at the top. Both are hiker-friendly and both serve bar food, though the *Rambler* has the edge.

Hathersage

Hilly **HATHERSAGE**, five miles east of Castleton and just eleven from Sheffield on the A625, has a hard time persuading people not to pass straight through into the heart of the Peaks. This little town is, however, worth at least an hour of anyone's time, the prime target being the much restored **Church of St Michael and All Angels**, a good-looking stone structure perched high on the hill on its eastern edge. The views out over the surrounding countryside are delightful and, enclosed within a miniature iron fence in the churchyard opposite the porch, is the grave – or at least what legend asserts to be the grave – of Robin Hood's old sparring partner, **Little John**. In typically English style, Little John wasn't "little" at all and, although no one can be sure if he actually existed, one of the church's Georgian vicars couldn't resist opening up the tomb to check it out. He unearthed the skeleton of a giant of a man, over 7ft tall, quite enough encouragement for the vicar to display a green cap, longbow and arrows in the church, though sadly there is no sign of them today; for more on Robin and his Merry Men, see p.722. Hathersage's other claim to fame is its association with Charlotte Brontë's **Jane Eyre**. The title of the book was borrowed from a certain James Eyre, a former landlord of the *George Hotel*, and the book's "Morton" takes its name from the landlord – James Morton – who met Charlotte off the stagecoach from Haworth when she came to stay here in 1845. Charlotte was visiting a friend, whose brother was the local vicar, and Charlotte was doubtless shown the Eyre brasses, inside the church beside the table-tomb of Robert Eyre (d.1459) – another prompt for the title. Charlotte also used several other local names and buildings for her novel, notably North Lees Hall (Rochester's Thornfield Hall) and Moorseats (St John Rivers' Moor House).

In the 1800s, Hathersage became a needle-making centre with a string of factories billowing out dust and dirt. The needle grinders were the best paid factory workers, but most of them didn't last very long – the metallic dust simply killed them off. Those dangerous days are long gone, but the metalworking tradition has been revived by the Sheffield designer David Mellor, who has set up his factory in the distinctive **Round Building**, a comely gritstone edifice with a sweeping lead roof. The attached Country Shop (Mon–Sat 10am–5pm, Sun 11am–5pm; ⓣ01433/650220, ⓦwww.davidmellordesign.com) sells the full range of Mellor cutlery, tableware and kitchenware – but you do pay for the quality. The factory is about half a mile south of town on the B6001, beyond the train station.

Practicalities

Hathersage is on the Manchester–Sheffield rail line and from the town **train station** it's about 500yd north to the scattering of shops, banks and pubs that comprise the centre, strung along the main street, which doubles as the A625. Among several **buses** to Hathersage, one of the most useful is the frequent First Mainline bus #272 linking Sheffield and Castleton. In Hathersage, it stops on the main street outside the *Best Western George Hotel* (ⓣ0845/456 0581, ⓦwww.george-hotel.net; ❼), a one-time coaching inn with an immaculate interior that remains very much *the* place to stay – don't be deterred by the discordant stone facade. Brontë fans will be delighted to know that the beautifully restored *North Lees Hall* can be rented – contact the Vivat Trust (ⓣ0845/0900194, ⓦwww.vivat.org.uk) to make a booking. At the other end of the price range, Hathersage **youth hostel** (ⓣ0870/770 5852, ⓦwww.yha.org.uk; dorm beds £10.25) occupies a rambling Victorian house on the main road just to the west of the *George*. It has forty beds, in two- to six-bedded rooms, and a good range of facilities, including a self-catering kitchen.

The *George* has a first-rate **restaurant** featuring a canny amalgamation of traditional and modern dishes with main courses averaging around £14. A second good choice is the inexpensive *Longland's Eating House* (Mon 11am–5pm, Tues–Fri 10am–5pm, Sat & Sun 9am–6pm), a laid-back, vegetarian café above a hiking/outdoors shop across from the *George*.

Eyam

Within a year of September 7, 1665, the lonely lead-mining settlement of **EYAM** (pronounced "Eem"), five miles south of Hathersage, had lost almost half of its population of 750 to the bubonic plague, a calamity that earned it the enduring epithet "The Plague Village". The first victim was one George Vicars, a journeyman tailor who is said to have released some infected fleas into his lodgings from a package of cloth he had brought here from London. Acutely conscious of the danger to neighbouring villages, William Mompesson, the village rector, speedily organized a self-imposed quarantine, arranging for food to be left at places on the parish boundary. Payment was made with coins left in pools of disinfecting vinegar in holes chiselled into the old boundary stones – and these can still be seen at **Mompesson's Well**, half a mile up the hill to the north of the village and accessible by footpath. The rector closed the church and held services in the open air at a natural rock arch to the south of the village – and every year since 1906, on the last Sunday in August, a commemorative service has been held here, at Cucklet Delph. Mompesson himself survived the plague, though his wife did not – poor reward for a man whose endeavours prevented the plague from spreading across the Peaks.

Long, thin and hilly, Eyam is little more than one main street – Church and then Main Street – which trails west up from **The Square**, which is really no more than a crossroads overlooked by a few old stone houses. First up of interest along Church Street is the comely **Church of St Lawrence** (Easter–Sept Mon–Sat 9am–6pm, Sun 1–5.30pm; Oct–Easter Mon–Sat 9am–4pm, Sun 1–5.30pm; free), of medieval foundation but extensively revamped in the nineteenth century. In the church graveyard a few feet from the entrance stands a conspicuous, eighth-century carved **Celtic cross** and close by is the distinctive **table-tomb** of Mompesson's wife, whose sterling work nursing sick villagers is recalled every Remembrance Day when red roses are left beside her tomb. Rather more cheerful is the grave of one Harry Bagshawe (d. 1927), a local cricketer whose tombstone shows a ball breaking his wicket with the umpire's finger raised above, presumably – on this occasion – to heaven. Bagshawe lies buried round the back of the church on the right-hand side of this part of the graveyard. Inside the church, informative panels reveal more of the village's plague history, highlighting a number of associated sites in and around the village. The most harrowing of these is the **Riley Graves**, in open country half a mile east of The Square, where a certain Elizabeth Hancock buried her husband, three sons and three daughters within the space of six days in 1666.

Much nearer at hand, immediately to the west of the church, are the so-called **plague cottages**, where plaques explain who died where and when – it was here that Vicars met his maker. Another short hop brings you to **Eyam Hall** (guided tours late May to Aug Wed, Thurs & Sun 11am–4pm; £4.50), which was built for Thomas Wright a few years after the plague ended, possibly in an

The plague

As the residents of Eyam began to drop like flies from **the plague** in the autumn of 1665, they resorted to home remedies and desperate snatches from folkloric memory to stave off the inevitable. There was little understanding in the seventeenth century of why or how the disease spread: Daniel Defoe, in his later journal of London's plague, recorded how the lord mayor ordered the destruction of all the city's pets, believing them to be responsible. Others, thinking it to be a miasma, kept coal braziers alight day and night in the hope that the smoke would push the infection back into the sky from where it was thought to have come. In isolated Eyam, with the plague among them and no way out through the self-imposed cordon, the locals improvised with great invention but little effect. Applications of cold water, herb infusions and draughts of brine or lemon juice were tried; poultices applied; bleeding by leeches was commonplace; and when all else failed, charms and spells were wheeled out – the plucked tail of a pigeon laid against the sore supposedly drew out the poison. All, of course, had no effect and the death toll mounted, though occasionally there was coincidental success: one 14-year-old girl mistakenly drank a pitcher of discarded bacon fat, left by her bedside; the fever passed and she recovered.

The horrors of plague-ridden England were recorded in a children's **nursery rhyme**, whose gruesome verse has been popular ever since:

Ring a ring o' roses
A pocket full of posies
Atishoo, atishoo
We all fall down

The "roses" are the patches which developed on the victim's chest soon after contracting the disease; the "posies" are herbs or flowers, carried as charms; as the fever took hold, sneezing ("atishoo, atishoo") was a common symptom; until, chillingly, at death's door, "we all fall down".

attempt to secure his position as the squire of the depleted village. Wright's heirs have lived in it ever since, building up a mildly diverting collection of furnishings, family portraits, tapestries, costumes and incidental bygones. Some of the adjacent farm buildings have been turned into a **Craft Centre** (Tues–Sun 10.30am–5pm; free) with a restaurant and gift shop.

From the hall, it's a few minutes' walk along Main Street and up Hawkhill Road – follow the signs – to the modest Methodist chapel that now houses the **Eyam Museum** (April–Oct Tues–Sun 10am–4.30pm; £1.50). This tracks through the history of the village and has a good section on the bubonic plague – its transmission, symptoms and social aftermath.

Practicalities

Buses to Eyam – from Sheffield, Manchester, Buxton, Hathersage, Bakewell and Baslow – all stop on The Square, and one or two also run along Main/Church Street. Amongst a handful of **B&Bs**, the pick is the *Delf View House* (Ⓣ01433/631533, Ⓦwww.delfviewhouse.co.uk; no credit cards; ❺), a beautifully kept Georgian villa set in its own grounds just along and across the street from the church; breakfast is served in a superb old dining room with its flagstone floor, imposing fireplace and beamed ceiling. A second choice is the *Miner's Arms*, in antique premises just off The Square on Water Lane (Ⓣ01433/630853; ❹), which has seven perfectly adequate, en-suite rooms of a modern disposition. Finally, there's the well-equipped **youth hostel** (Ⓣ0870/770 5830, Ⓦww.yha.org.uk; £11.50), which occupies an idiosyncratic Victorian house, whose ersatz medieval towers and turrets overlook Eyam from amidst wooded grounds on Hawkhill Road, a stiff, half-mile ramble up from the museum. There are sixty beds here in two- to eight-bedded rooms, but note that opening days and dates vary – ring ahead for details.

The best place **to eat** is the *Miner's Arms*, which serves delicious bar meals as well as very enjoyable and moderately priced, traditional British dinners in its restaurant every evening except Sunday and Monday.

Around Eyam: Foolow, Bretton and Tideswell

Keep going west out of Eyam along Main Street and you're soon into open countryside, a quick flash of scenery before you reach – after almost two miles – the pretty little hamlet of **FOOLOW** with a village green, duck pond and cross.

From Foolow, a mile-long country lane cuts north, climbing up to a windswept ridge, where **BRETTON** is little more than a pub – the appealing *Barrel Inn* (☎01433/630856; ❹), a low-slung old stone building with beamed ceilings, good ales, top-quality bar food and panoramic views. The inn also offers a handful of unassuming but perfectly comfortable rooms. Hikers can reach Bretton direct from Eyam, but it's a stiff and steep two-mile hoof; there are no buses.

Heading west from Bretton along narrow country roads, it's a couple of miles to the B6049, where you turn left for the two-mile zip down to **TIDESWELL**, a substantial stone village that was long a centre of the local lead-mining industry. Nowadays, the village is noteworthy for the church of St John the Baptist, known as **The Cathedral of the Peak** (dawn to dusk; free), whose strong, square tower dominates its surroundings. The interior is largely fourteenth-century, the wide and airy nave stomping down to the chancel, where the ends of the choir stalls sport intricately carved saints performing the deeds with which they are associated.

Tideswell is just south of the A623, which runs from Baslow (see p.703) to Sparrowpit (for Castleton, see p.696) and the A6. In the other direction, the B6049 wriggles its way south over the hills to isolated **Miller's Dale** en route to the A6 east of Buxton (see p.692).

Baslow

BASLOW, on the north edge of the Chatsworth estate (see p.704) some four miles southeast of Eyam, is an inconclusive little village, whose oldest stone cottages string prettily along the River Derwent. The only building of note is the **Church of St Anne's**, whose stone spire pokes up above the Victorian castellations of its nave in between the river and the busy junction of the A623/A619. Baslow may be inconsequential, but it is a handy base for exploring this portion of the Peaks – especially if you're travelling by bus – and it possesses several **B&Bs**. The most recommendable of these is *The Old School House*, in attractive Victorian premises in the centre on School Lane (☎01246/582488; ❹). Even better – and one of the Peak's greatest luxuries – is *Fischer's Baslow Hall* (☎01246/583259, ⓦwww.fischers-baslowhall.co.uk; ❼), a mile or so out the village back towards Eyam along the A623. In its own grounds, the hall is picture-postcard perfect, a handsome Edwardian building made of local stone with matching gables and a dinky canopy over the front door. The interior is suitably lavish and the service attentive with rooms both in the main building and in the Garden House annexe next door. The **restaurant** is superb too, and has won several awards for its imaginative cuisine – or you can pop back into Baslow for a bite at the excellent *Avant Garde Café* (daily 9am–5pm), where they serve a delicious range of salads and light meals in bright, modern surroundings; the café is opposite St Anne's Church.

Chatsworth House

Fantastically popular, **Chatsworth House** (April to late Dec daily 11am–5.30pm, last admission 4.30pm; gardens till 6pm, last admission 5pm; house & gardens £8.50, gardens only £5), just south of Baslow via the A619, was built in the seventeenth century by the first duke of Devonshire. It has been owned by the family ever since and several of them have done a bit of tinkering – the sixth duke, for instance, added the north wing in the 1820s – but the end result is remarkably harmonious. The house is seen to best advantage from the **B6012**, which meanders across the estate to the west of the house, giving a full view of its vast Palladian frontage, whose clean lines are perfectly balanced by the undulating partly wooded **parkland**, which rolls in from the south and west. The B6012 also gives access to the immaculately maintained estate village of **EDENSOR**, whose sturdy stone houses are well worth a look in their own right, and a signed turning off it leads to the house itself.

Many visitors forgo the house altogether, concentrating on the gardens instead, and this is understandable given the predictability of the assorted baubles accumulated by the family over the centuries. Nonetheless, amongst the maze of grand staircases and grandiose rooms, there are several noteworthy highlights, including the ornate ceilings of the **State Apartments**, daubed with strikingly energetic cherubs. In the apartments is the **State Bedroom**, where pride of place goes to the four-poster in which King George II breathed his last, and the anachronistic **Oak Room**, kitted out with overpoweringly heavy oak panelling in the 1840s. There's also the showpiece **Great Dining Room**, which has its table set as it was for the visit of George V and Queen Mary in 1933. And then there are the paintings. Amongst many, Frans Hals, Tintoretto, Veronese and Van Dyck all have a showing and there's even a Rembrandt – *A Portrait of an Old Man* – hanging in the chapel. The sixth duke also added a **Sculpture Gallery** to show all the tackle he had acquired on his travels, mostly large-scale Italian sculptures, but here also is the Chatsworth tazza, probably the largest Blue John vase in the world; for more on this semi-precious stone, see p.696.

Back outside, the **gardens** are a real treat and owe much to the combined efforts of Capability Brown, who designed them in the 1750s, and Joseph Paxton (designer of London's Crystal Palace), who had a bash seventy years later. Amongst all sorts of fripperies, there are water fountains, a rock garden, an artificial waterfall, a grotto and a folly as well as a nursery and greenhouses. Afterwards, you can wend your way to the **café** in the handsomely converted former Stables.

The best way to get to Chatsworth House is **on foot** along one of the footpaths that lattice the estate. It's easy walking and the obvious departure point is Baslow on the northern edge of the estate. The "Grate Little Guide" (see p.689) to Chatsworth describes an especially pleasant four-mile loop through the estate, taking in the house and beginning and ending in Baslow. By **bus**, take any Bakewell–Baslow bus and ask to be put off at Edensor, from where it's about one mile east across the park to the house.

Bakewell

BAKEWELL, flanking the banks of the River Wye four miles southwest of Baslow – and twelve miles east of Buxton – is famous for its **Bakewell Pudding**. Known throughout the rest of the country as a Bakewell Tart, this is a wonderful slippery, flaky, almond-flavoured confection – now with a dab of jam – invented here around 1860 when a cook botched a recipe for strawberry tart. Almost a century before this fortuitous mishap, the Duke of Rutland set out to turn what was then a remote village into a prestigious spa, thereby trumping the work of his rival, the Duke of Devonshire, in Buxton. The frigidity of the water made failure inevitable, leaving only the prettiness of **Bath Gardens** at the heart of the town centre, beside the crossroads Rutland Square, as a reminder of the venture.

Famous tart apart, Bakewell is an undemanding place today, its main streets too crowded by traffic – and tourists – to be much fun, though it is within easy striking distance of several first-rate attractions. In town, there is some interest in the web of narrow shopping streets around **Water Street**, just off the main drag near Rutland Square, as well as in the nearby **riverside walkway**, but the most agreeable part of Bakewell trails up the hill at the west end of the centre. Here, strolling up North Church Street, with its line of comely stone cottages, you soon reach **All Saints Church**, the result of centuries of architectural fiddling from the Normans onwards. Outside, in the churchyard, is a rare **Saxon cross**, carved with decorative circles and scrolls, and inside in the south transept's Vernon Chapel are the **tombs** of the Vernons/Manners, local bigwigs who long ruled the Bakewell roost. The finest is that of George Manners (d.1623), whose alabaster effigy is set above his kneeling children plus the baby he lost at birth, all wrapped up in swaddling clothes.

Bakewell is a popular starting point for short **hikes** into the easy landscapes that make up the town's surroundings with one of the most relaxing excursions being a four-mile loop along the banks of the River Wye to the south of the centre. Chatsworth (see opposite) is within easy hiking distance too – about seven miles there and back – and so is Ashford-in-the-Water, a brief hike away to the northwest along the Wye. Rather more ambitious – and one of the best-known hikes in the National Park – is the **Monsal Trail**, which cuts eight miles north and then west through some of Derbyshire's finest limestone dales using part of the old Midland Railway line. The trail begins at Coombs viaduct, one mile southeast of Bakewell, and ends at Blackwell Mill Junction, three miles east of Buxton; for more on Buxton, see p.692.

Practicalities

Bakewell doesn't have a train station, but there are regular **buses** from a string of towns and villages including Baslow, Buxton, Manchester, Derby, Sheffield and Nottingham. All services stop on – or very close to – central Rutland Square. The **tourist office** is just a couple of hundred yards along the main drag – Bridge Street – from the square in the recycled Old Market Hall (daily: Easter–Oct 9.30am–5.30pm; Nov–Easter 10am–5pm; ⓣ01629/813227). They are very well equipped with public transport timetables as well as local biking and hiking leaflets and guides.

There's no overriding reason to stay the night in Bakewell, but there are several appealing **B&Bs**. One good choice is *Avenue House*, whose three attractively furnished, en suite rooms are in a spacious Victorian building just south of the centre on Haddon Road (ⓣ01629/812467; no credit cards; ❷); Haddon Road doubles as the A6. A second option is the homely *Castle Inn*

(Ⓣ01629/812103; ❸), a sympathetically modernized old inn set plum in the centre at the foot of busy Castle Street, yards from the main bridge into town and with four straightforward, comfortable rooms. The **youth hostel**, with just 28 beds in two- to six-bedded rooms, is in a modest, modern building on Fly Hill (Ⓣ0870/770 5682, Ⓦwww.yha.org.uk; dorm beds £10.25; call for days & dates of opening). It has self-catering facilities and serves evening meals. Fly Hill is near the church – just follow North Church Street round and you'll hit it. There's also pedestrian-only access up a steep lane from Buxton Road – the A6 – just north of the centre.

Bakeries all over town claim to make Bakewell Pudding to the original recipe, but arguably the most authentic is the *Old Original Bakewell Pudding Shop*, on the main street a few yards from Rutland Square. They sell the pudding in several sizes, from the small and handy to the gargantuan version, enough to keep the average family going for a whole day. Alternatively, *Bloomer's*, just off the main drag on Water Street, is an excellent café, deli and bakery with a special line in homemade sweet and savoury pies. There are several good **restaurants** too, most notably *Renaissance*, on Bath St immediately north of the main street (Ⓣ01629/812687), where the emphasis is on French cuisine with a la carte and set meals – a three-courser costs about £20. Bakewell is also a ten-minute drive from one of the area's most popular restaurants, *The Druid Inn* (Ⓣ01629/650302; closed Mon), an unpretentious, laid-back place occupying an ivy-clad stone building dating from the 1840s in the village of **BIRCHOVER**. The menu here is quite simply outstanding and consistently receives rave reviews – two recent offerings are, for example, lemon apricot casserole with rice (£9) and pheasant with port and redcurrant sauce (£14). Needless to say, reservations are strongly advised. To get to the *Druid* from Bakewell, take the A6 south past Haddon Hall (see opposite) and shortly afterwards turn right along the B5056, following the signs to Birchover thereafter.

Around Bakewell: Hassop and Ashford in the Water

Hidden away in the heart of the Peaks, about three miles north of Bakewell on the B6001, the tiny hamlet of **HASSOP** has a rugged, solitary feeling. It is also home to one of the region's finest **hotels**, the wonderful *Hassop Hall* (Ⓣ01629/640488; ❺), a handsome Neoclassical manor house whose long stone facade ripples with elegant bay windows. The interior has kept faith with the Georgian architecture too – modernization has been kept to a subtle minimum – and the views out over the surrounding parkland are perfectly delightful. Nor should you leave the hotel to eat as the **restaurant** (closed Sun eve) is first class with a two-course set meal costing £21, considerably more on Saturday.

Tiny **ASHFORD IN THE WATER**, just over a mile to the west of Bakewell along the River Wye, is one of the prettiest and wealthiest villages in the Peaks, its old stone cottages nuzzling up to a quaint medieval church. It was not always so. Ashford was once a poor lead-mining settlement with sidelines in milling and agriculture, hence the impossibly picturesque Sheepwash Bridge. There was, however, a bit of a boom when locals took to polishing the dark limestone found on the edge of the village (and nowhere else), turning it into so-called Ashford black marble – much to the delight of Buxton's petrifactioners (see p.692). Ashford also possesses an outstanding **hotel**, the plush *Riverside House* (Ⓣ01629/814275, Ⓦwww.riversidehousehotel.co.uk; ❽), which occupies a handsome Georgian building by the banks of the Wye. There are fifteen extremely well-appointed rooms here and the hotel takes justifiable pride in both its gardens and its restaurant.

Haddon Hall

Haddon Hall (April–Sept daily 10.30am–5pm; Oct Thurs–Sun 10.30am–4.30pm; £7.25, plus £1 parking), perched on a hill above the River Wye two miles south of Bakewell along the A6, is one of the finest medieval manor houses in the Midlands. The original Norman manor house passed to the Vernons in the middle of the twelfth century and they held on to it until 1558 when the sole heir, one **Dorothy Vernon**, married John Manners, scion of another powerful family, who were later ennobled as the dukes of Rutland. All might have been well, but for antics of the Devonshires whose construction of Chatsworth in the eighteenth century made neighbouring Haddon Hall look very paltry indeed. Partly as a consequence, the Rutlands left the hall to its own devices, preferring to live elsewhere – and thereby sparing it from Georgian and Victorian meddling.

A Lord Manners still owns the place and today the hall is immaculately maintained, the soft yellow stonework of its main buildings set around a wonky, paved courtyard. Inside, a veritable rabbit warren of ancient rooms incorporates an appealing hotch-potch of architectural features dating from the fourteenth to the seventeenth century. The kitchen is one of the oldest parts of the complex, a rare survivor of a typical medieval kitchen complete with its original fireplace and mullion windows. The Dining Room is also of special interest for its splendid painted chequer-board ceiling, while the Long Gallery, built by John Manners himself, is encased by rich oak panelling with walnut inlays. Even more fascinating is the **chapel**, whose murals sport a jungle of foliage and a herd of exotic animals as well as pictures of the saints – most strikingly St Christopher fording a stream. The paintings were plastered over at the Reformation and only uncovered at the beginning of the twentieth century. The chapel also holds an exquisite alabaster **reredos** depicting nine finely detailed scenes from the life of Christ. It was carved in Nottingham in the fifteenth century – a time when the work of the city's alabaster masons was famous across the whole of Europe. After you've finished in the house, be sure to allow time for the terraced **gardens**, which tumble down towards the river.

Haddon Hall is on the TransPeak **bus** route, but be sure to ask the driver to put you off.

Travel details

Buses

For information on all local and national bus services, contact Traveline ⓣ0870/608 2608, ⓦwww.traveline.org.uk.

The TransPeak

Operated by the Trent Barton bus company, the TransPeak bus service runs from Nottingham to Manchester via Derby, Matlock, Bakewell and Buxton 5 times daily. The whole journey takes 3 hours.

Birmingham to: Buxton (2 daily; 4hr); Cambridge (3 daily; 3hr 25min); Coventry (every 20min; 1hr); Great Malvern (2 daily; 1hr 30min); Hereford (2 daily; 2hr 20min); Liverpool (6 daily: 3hr); London (hourly; 3hr); Ludlow (hourly; 2hr 10min); Manchester (hourly; 2hr 30min); Nottingham (6 daily; 1hr 30min); Oxford (5 daily; 1hr 30min); Ross-on-Wye (2 daily; 1hr 30min); Shrewsbury (2 daily; 1hr 20min); Stratford-upon-Avon (every 2 hr; 1hr); Walsall (every 5min; 40min); Wolverhampton (every 10min; 1hr 20min); Worcester (hourly; 1hr 30min).

Buxton to: Ashbourne (4 daily; 2hr); Birmingham (2 daily; 4hr); Derby (3 daily; 1hr 30min).
Derby to: Buxton (3 daily; 1hr 30min).
Great Malvern to: Birmingham (2 daily; 1hr 30min); Hereford (1 daily; 40min); Stratford-upon-Avon (5 daily; 3hr 50min); Worcester (7 daily; 35min).
Hay-on-Wye to: Hereford (4 daily; 1hr); Ross-on-Wye (5 daily; 2hr).
Hereford to: Birmingham (2 daily; 2hr 20min); Great Malvern (1 daily; 40min); Hay-on-Wye (4 daily; 1hr); Ludlow (4 daily; 4hr); Ross-on-Wye (hourly; 40min); Shrewsbury (2 daily; 3hr 30min); Worcester (2 daily; 1hr).
Ludlow to: Birmingham (hourly; 2hr 10min); Hereford (4 daily; 4hr); Shrewsbury (6 daily; 1hr 20min); Worcester (2 daily; 2hr 15min).
Ross-on-Wye to: Birmingham (2 daily; 1hr 30min); Hay-on-Wye (5 daily; 2hr); Hereford (hourly; 40min).
Shrewsbury to: Birmingham (2 daily; 1hr 20min); Hereford (2 daily; 3hr 30min); Ludlow (6 daily; 1hr 20min); Stratford-upon-Avon (2 daily; 2hr 30min).
Stratford-upon-Avon to: Birmingham (every 2 hr; 1hr); Great Malvern (5 daily; 3hr 50min); Shrewsbury (2 daily; 2hr 30min).
Worcester to: Birmingham (hourly; 1hr 30min); Great Malvern (7 daily; 35min); Hereford (2 daily; 1hr); Ludlow (2 daily; 2hr 15min).

Trains

For information on all local and national rail services, contact National Rail Enquiries ⓣ08457/484950, ⓦwww.rail.co.uk.

Birmingham New Street to: Birmingham International (every 15–30min; 15min); Coventry (every 15–30min; 30min); Derby (hourly; 45min); Great Malvern (every 30min; 1hr); Hereford (10 daily; 1hr 50min); Kidderminster (every 30min; 30min); Leicester (hourly; 50min); Lichfield (every 15min; 45min); London (every 30min; 1hr 40min); Shrewsbury (hourly; 1hr 20min); Stoke-on-Trent (hourly; 1hr); Worcester (every 30min; 1hr).
Birmingham Snow Hill to: Stratford-upon-Avon (Mon–Sat hourly; 50min); Warwick (Mon–Sat hourly; 40min).
Derby to: Birmingham (every 20min; 45min); Leicester (hourly; 30min); London (hourly; 1hr 50min); Nottingham (every 20min; 35min).
Hereford to: Birmingham (hourly; 1hr 40min); Great Malvern (hourly; 30min); London (5 daily; 2hr 45min); Ludlow (hourly; 30min); Shrewsbury (hourly; 1hr); Worcester (every 1hr 30min; 40min).
Shrewsbury to: Birmingham (2–4 hourly; 1hr 10min); Church Stretton (every 30min; 15min); Craven Arms (hourly; 30min); Hereford (2–3 hourly; 1hr); Ludlow (hourly; 30min); Telford (every 30min; 20min).
Stoke-on-Trent to: Birmingham (hourly; 1hr).
Stratford-upon-Avon to: Birmingham (Mon–Sat hourly; 1hr); Oxford (4 daily; 1hr 10min); Warwick (Mon–Sat 8 daily; 30min).
Worcester to: Birmingham (every 30min; 40min–1hr); Hereford (13 daily; 40min).

9

The East Midlands

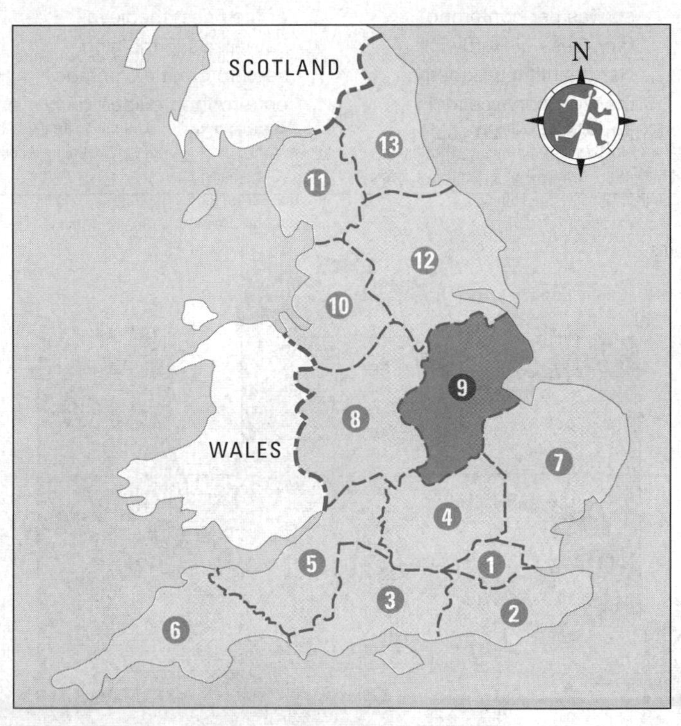

CHAPTER 9 Highlights

* **The Bomb, Nottingham** Nottingham is proud of its nightclubs, with good reason – it's cutting edge stuff and *The Bomb* continues the story. **See p.719**

* **Hardwick Hall** Elizabeth I was formidable – and so was her contemporary, Bess of Hardwick. Her beautiful Elizabethan mansion survives in fine fettle. **See p.720**

* **Rufford Country Park** Well off the usual tourist track, Rufford offers a ceramic gallery, a bird sanctuary, a mill and a sculpture garden with lots of relaxed strolling in between. **See p.722**

* **Lincoln Cathedral** One of the finest medieval cathedrals in the land, seen to great advantage on a rooftop guided tour. **See p.750**

△ Hardwick Hall

9

The East Midlands

Many tourists bypass the four major counties of the **East Midlands** – Nottinghamshire, Leicestershire, Northamptonshire and Lincolnshire – on their way to more obvious destinations, an understandable mistake given that the region is short on star attractions. The most obvious targets are **Nottingham**, **Leicester** and **Northampton** – three of the four county towns – but although they share a long and eventful history, all have been badly bruised by postwar town planning and industrial development. Nevertheless, embedded in the modernity are a few historical landmarks – an especially fine church in Northampton, the castle in Nottingham, and traces of Roman baths in Leicester – and even though these are the frills rather than the substance, Nottingham does have enough character to give it an aesthetic edge. Furthermore, if few would actually describe this trio of towns as especially good-looking, the countryside surrounding them can be delightful, with rolling farmland punctuated by wooded ridges and flowing hills, all sprinkled with prestigious country homes, pretty villages and old market towns. In Nottinghamshire, Byron's **Newstead Abbey** is intriguing, though **Hardwick Hall**, just over the border in Derbyshire, is even better, an especially beautiful Elizabethan country home built by the redoubtable Bess of Hardwick. In addition, the eastern reaches of Nottinghamshire hold two appealing market towns – **Southwell** and **Newark** – whilst west Leicestershire weighs in with the fascinating mansion of **Calke Abbey**. East of Leicestershire, the easy countryside rolls over into **Rutland**, the region's fifth and smallest county, and here you'll find two more pleasant country towns, **Oakham** and **Uppingham**, though tiny **Lyddington** is even more picturesque. Rutland benefits from the use of limestone as the traditional building material, as does **Northamptonshire**. Here, the rural parts of the county are studded with handsome, old stone villages and small towns – most notably **Fotheringhay** and **Oundle** – plus large country estates, the best known of which is **Althorp**, the final resting place of Princess Diana.

Lincolnshire is very different in character from the rest of the region, an agricultural backwater that remains surprisingly remote – locals sometimes call it the "forgotten" county. This was not always the case: throughout medieval times the county flourished as a centre of the wool trade with Flanders, its merchants and landowners becoming some of the wealthiest in England. Reminders of the high times are legion, beginning with the majestic cathedral that graces **Lincoln**, a dignified old city which, with its cobbled lanes and ancient buildings, well deserves an overnight stay. Equally enticing is the splendidly intact stone town of **Stamford**, but the county's urban attractions pretty much end

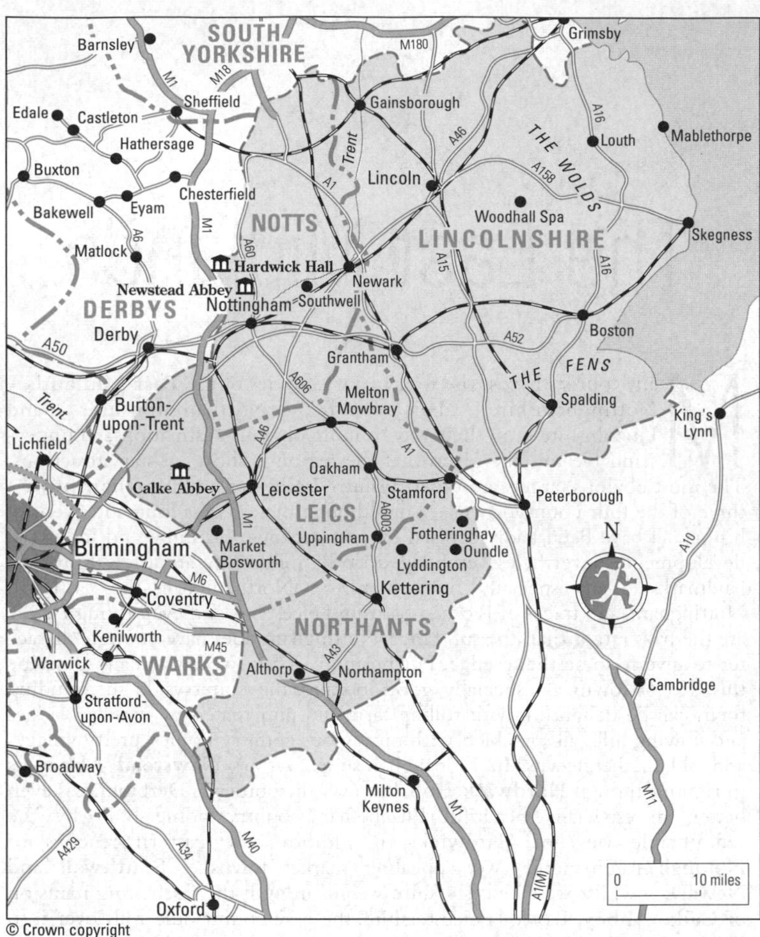

there. Out in the sticks, the most distinctive feature is **The Fens**, whose pancake-flat fields, filling out much of the south of the county and extending deep into East Anglia (see Chapter 7), have been regained from the marshes and the sea. Fenland villages are generally short of charm, but the **parish churches**, whose spires regularly interrupt the wide-skied landscape, are simply stunning, the most impressive of the lot being St Botolph's in **Boston**.

In north Lincolnshire, the gentle chalky hills of the **Lincolnshire Wolds** contain the county's most diverse scenery, including woodland clustered round **Woodhall Spa**, and a string of sheltered valleys concentrated in the vicinity of **Louth**, an especially fetching country town. To the east of the Wolds is the **coast**, whose long sandy beach extends, with a few marshy interruptions, from Mablethorpe to **Skegness**, the main resort. The coast has long attracted thousands of holiday-makers from the big cities of the East Midlands and Yorkshire, hence its trail of bungalows, campsites and caravan parks – though, to be fair, significant chunks of the seashore are now protected as nature reserves.

As for public transport, travelling between the cities of the East Midlands by **train** or **bus** is simple and most of the larger towns have good regional links, too; but things are very different in the country with bus services very patchy.

Nottinghamshire

With a population of 270,000, **Nottingham** is one of England's big cities, a long-time manufacturing centre for bikes, cigarettes, pharmaceuticals and lace. It is, however, more famous for Nottingham Forest football team (or rather, for its mercurial ex-manager, Brian Clough), for the Trent Bridge cricket ground and for its association with **Robin Hood**, the legendary thirteenth-century outlaw. Hood's bitter enemy was, of course, the Sheriff of Nottingham, but unfortunately his home and lair – the city's imposing medieval castle – is long gone, and today Nottingham is at its most diverting in the Lace Market, whose cramped streets are crowded with the mansion-like warehouses of the Victorian lacemakers.

The county town is flanked to the south by the commuter villages of the Nottinghamshire Wolds and to the north by the gritty towns and villages of what was, until Thatcher and her cronies decimated it in the late 1980s, the Nottinghamshire coalfield. Both are unremarkable, but encrusted within the old coalfield are the thin remains of **Sherwood Forest**, the bulk of which is contained within **The Dukeries**, named after the five dukes who owned most of this area and preserved at least part of the ancient broad-leaved forest. Three of the four remaining estates – Worksop, Welbeck and Thoresby – are still in private hands, though **Welbeck** does hold the pleasing Harley Art Gallery and Thoresby Hall has recently been turned into a Warner resort hotel. The fourth estate, **Clumber Park**, is very different, now owned by the National Trust and offering charming woodland walks. Also within the confines of the former coalfield are two fascinating country houses, **Newstead Abbey**, one-time home of Byron, and, even better, the wonderful Elizabethan extravagance of **Hardwick Hall**. Moving on, eastern Nottinghamshire is agricultural, its most important town being **Newark**, an agreeable, low-key kind of place straddling the River Trent. Newark has a castle, but the main attraction hereabouts is the fine Norman church at nearby **Southwell**.

Fast and frequent **trains** connect Nottingham with, among many destinations, London, Birmingham, Newark, Lincoln and Leicester. County-wide **bus** services radiate out from the city, too, making Nottingham the obvious base for a visit.

Nottingham and around

Controlling a strategic crossing point over the River Trent, the Saxon town of **NOTTINGHAM** was built on one of a pair of sandstone hills whose 130-foot cliffs looked out over the river valley. In 1068, William the Conqueror built a castle on the other hill, and the Saxons and Normans traded on the low ground in between, the **Market Square**. The castle was a military stronghold

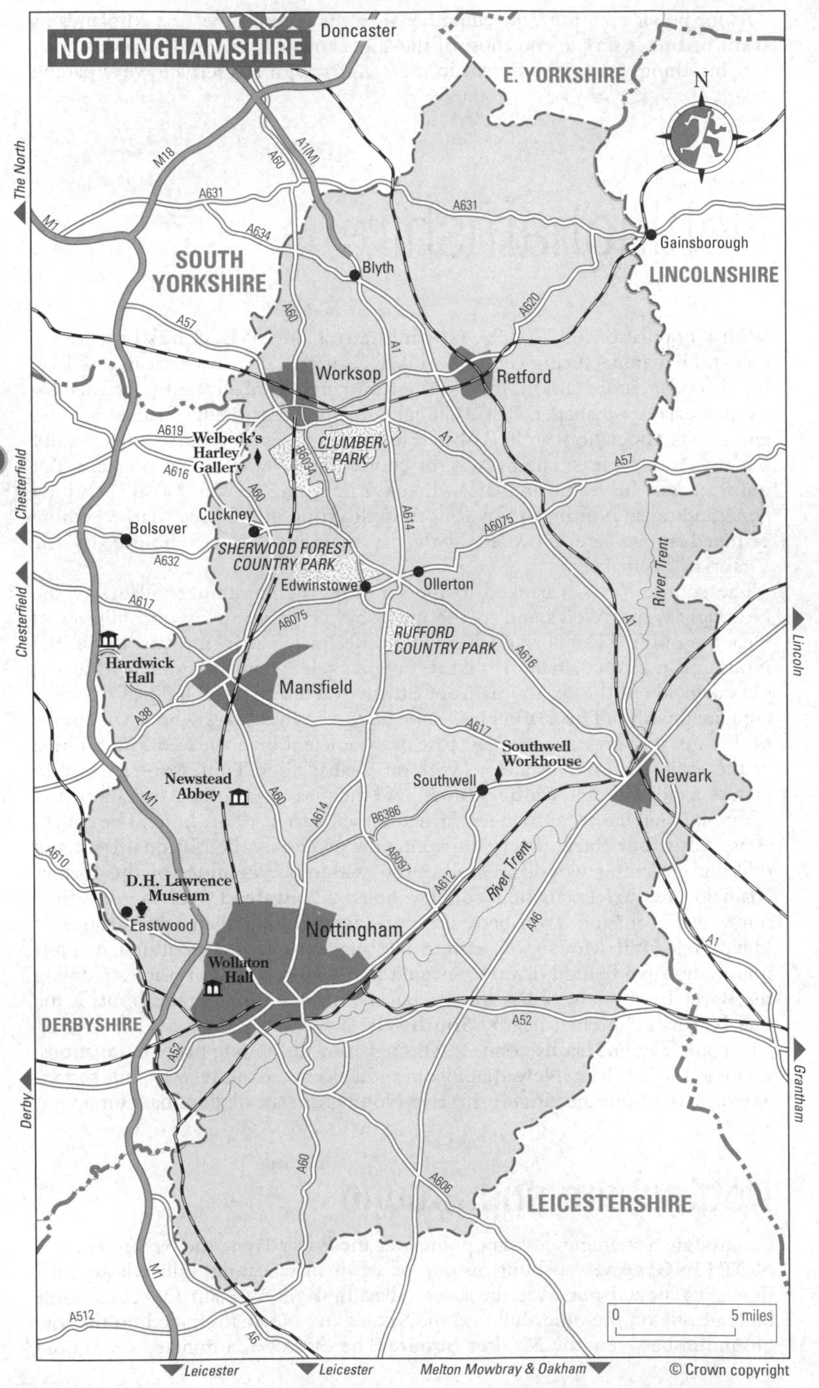
NOTTINGHAMSHIRE
Doncaster
E. YORKSHIRE
N
The North
M18
A1(M)
A60
A631
M1
A634
SOUTH YORKSHIRE
Blyth
Gainsborough
LINCOLNSHIRE
A620
A57
A1
Worksop
Retford
A619
Welbeck's Harley Gallery
CLUMBER PARK
B6034
A616
Chesterfield
A614
Cuckney
A6075
Bolsover
SHERWOOD FOREST COUNTRY PARK
A632
River Trent
Edwinstowe
Ollerton
A617
RUFFORD COUNTRY PARK
Lincoln
Hardwick Hall
Mansfield
A38
Southwell Workhouse
Newstead Abbey
Southwell
Newark
B6386
A610
A6097
A612
D.H. Lawrence Museum
A46
Eastwood
Nottingham
Wollaton Hall
DERBYSHIRE
A52
Grantham
Derby
A606
LEICESTERSHIRE
A512
A6
0
5 miles
Leicester
Leicester
Melton Mowbray & Oakham
© Crown copyright

and royal palace, the equal of the great castles of Windsor and Dover, and every medieval king of England paid regular visits. In August 1642, **Charles I** stayed here, too, riding out of the castle to raise his standard and start the Civil War – not that the locals were overly sympathetic. Hardly anyone joined up, even though the king had the ceremony repeated on the next three days.

After the Civil War, the Parliamentarians slighted the castle and, in the 1670s, the ruins were cleared by the duke of Newcastle to make way for a **palace**, whose continental – and, in English terms, novel – design he chose from a pattern book, probably by Rubens. Beneath the castle lay a market town which, according to contemporaries, was handsome and well kept – "One of the most beautiful towns in England," commented Daniel Defoe. But in the second half of the eighteenth century, it was transformed by the expansion of the lace and hosiery industries, and within the space of fifty years, Nottingham's population increased from ten thousand to fifty thousand, the resulting slum becoming a hotbed of radicalism. In the 1810s, a recession provoked the hard-pressed workers into action. They struck against the employers and, calling themselves **Luddites**, after an apprentice-protester by the name of Ned Ludd, raided the factories to smash the knitting machines. The Luddites were beaten into submission, but this was but the first of several troubled periods, the most dramatic of which came during the **Reform Bill** riots of 1831, when the workers set fire to the duke's palace in response to his opposition to parliamentary reform.

The worst of Nottingham's slums were cleared in the late nineteenth century, when the city centre assumed its present structure, with the main commercial area ringed by alternating industrial and residential districts. Crass **postwar development**, adding tower blocks, shopping centres and a ring road has, however, ensconced the remnants of the city's past in a townscape that will be dishearteningly familiar if you've seen a few other English commercial centres. The flavour of this postwar industrial city was described by Nottingham's own **Alan Sillitoe** in his perceptive and forceful novel, *Saturday Night, Sunday Morning*.

Arrival and information

Nottingham **train station** is on the south side of the city centre, a five- to ten-minute walk from the Market Square – just follow the signs. Most long-distance buses arrive at the Broad Marsh **Bus Station**, down the street from the train station on the way to the centre, but some – including services to north Nottinghamshire – pull in at the Victoria Bus Station, a five-minute walk north of the Market Square. If you spend any time in the centre, you can't miss the new **tram**, but it serves the suburbs rather than any of the city's attractions. The city's **tourist office** is on the Market Square, on the ground floor of the Council House, 1 Smithy Row (Easter–July Mon–Fri 9am–5.30pm, Sat 9am–5pm; Sept &Oct Mon–Fri 9am–5.30pm, Sat 9am–5pm, Sun 10am–3pm; Nov–Easter Mon–Sat 9am–5.30pm; ⓣ0115/9155330, ⓦwww.nottinghamcity.gov.uk).

Accommodation

As you might expect of a big city, Nottingham has a good range of accommodation, with the more expensive **hotels** concentrated in the centre, the cheaper places and the **B&Bs** mostly located on the outskirts and the main approach roads. Finding a room is rarely difficult, but the tourist office can always help out.

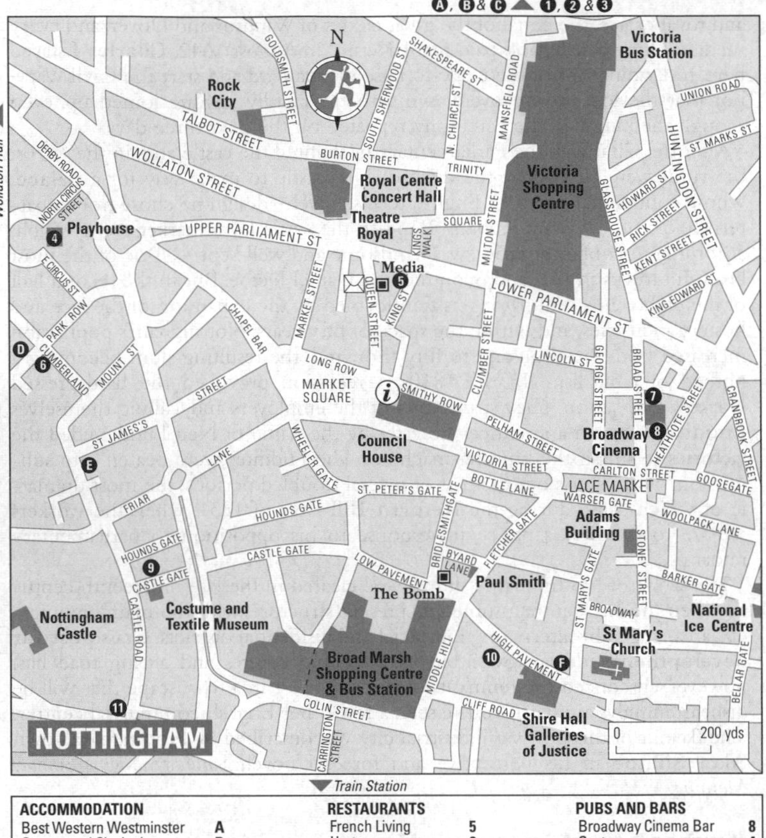

ACCOMMODATION		RESTAURANTS		PUBS AND BARS	
Best Western Westminster	A	French Living	5	Broadway Cinema Bar	8
Greenwood City Lodge	B	Harts	6	Cast	4
Harts	D	La Cappanna	1	Lincolnshire Poacher	3
Igloo Tourist Hsotel	C	Saagar Tandoori	2	Pitcher & Piano	10
Lace Market Hotel	F	Shaw 's	7	Ye Olde Trip to Jerusalem Inn	11
Rutland Square Hotel	E	World Service	9		

Hotels and guest houses

Best Western Westminster Hotel 312 Mansfield Rd ⓣ0115/955 5000, ⓦwww.westminster-hotel.co.uk. Comfortable, popular mid-range hotel in a big old red-brick mansion complete with turret and high gables. On a main road about one mile north of the city centre. ❺

Greenwood City Lodge 5 Third Ave, off Sherwood Rise ⓣ0115/962 1206, ⓦwww.greenwoodlodgecityguesthouse.co.uk. Attractive guest house in a quiet corner of the city, down a narrow lane about a mile north of the city centre. Six bedrooms decorated in smart Victorian style. Highly recommended. ❼

Harts Hotel Standard Hill Park Row ⓣ0115/988 1900, ⓦwww.hartshotel.co.uk. A new addition to the Nottingham scene, this chic hotel has comfort and style in equal measure: ultra modern fixtures and fittings, Egyptian cotton bed linen and so forth. It's quite pricey – expense account material perhaps – but first rate. ❼

Lace Market Hotel 29 High Pavement ⓣ0115/852 3232, ⓦwww.lacemarkethotel.co.uk. Great location, footsteps from St Mary's Church, this smart hotel has thirty individually decorated rooms within a tastefully modernized Georgian house. ❻

Rutland Square Hotel Rutland St, off St James' St ⓣ0115/941 1114, ⓦwww.forestdale.com. Enticing and tastefully furnished modern hotel in a good location, just by the castle. Ninety-odd rooms. ❻

Hostels

Igloo Tourist Hostel 110 Mansfield Rd ⓣ0115/947 5250, ⓦwww.igloohostel.co.uk. Backpackers' haven in a large Victorian house in the town centre, opposite the *Golden Fleece* pub, with a convivial atmosphere, good showers and free tea and coffee. Bunk-beds in mixed or single-sex dorms for £13 per person.

The Market Square and the Castle

The old **Market Square** is still the heart of the city, an airy open plaza whose shops, offices and fountains are watched over by the grand neo-Baroque **Council House**, completed as part of a make-work scheme in 1928. From here, it's a five-minute walk west up Friar Lane to **Nottingham Castle** (daily 10am–5pm, grounds daily 9am–dusk; Sat & Sun £2, free at other times), whose heavily restored gateway stands above a folkloric bronze of Robin Hood, with plaques depicting legendary scenes from his life on the wall behind. Beyond the gateway, lawns slope up to the squat ducal **palace**, which – after remaining a charred shell for forty years – was opened as the country's first provincial museum in 1878. The mansion occupies the site of the castle's upper bailey; round the back, just outside the main entrance, two sets of steps lead down into the maze of ancient caves that honeycomb the cliff beneath. One set is currently open for guided tours only (1–2 daily; call ⓣ0115/915 3700; £2), and this leads into **Mortimer's Hole**, a three-hundred-foot shaft along which, so the story goes, the young Edward III and his chums crept in October 1330 to capture the queen mother, Isabella, and her lover, Roger Mortimer. The couple had already polished off Edward III's father, the hapless Edward II, and were intent on usurping the crown, but the young Edward proved too shrewd for them – however although the incident certainly took place, it's unlikely that this was the secret tunnel Edward used.

The interior of the ducal mansion holds the **Castle Museum and Art Gallery**, which makes a dull start on the ground floor with a series of small, piecemeal exhibitions. Much better is the "Story of Nottingham" on the lower level, a lively, well-presented and entertaining account of the city's development. In particular, look out for a small but exquisite collection of late medieval **alabaster carvings**, an art form for which Nottingham once had an international reputation. It's worth walking up to the top floor, too, for a turn round the main **picture gallery**, a handsome and spacious room which has a curious assortment of mostly English nineteenth-century romantic paintings. The works are regularly rotated, but look out for the especially evocative canvases of Nottingham's own Richard Parkes Bonington (1801–1828) and Laslett John Pott's (1837–98) melodramatic *Mary Queen of Scots being led to her Execution*. One surprise is a typical industrial scene by Lowry (see p.786), entitled *Industrial Panorama*.

A couple of minutes' walk east of the castle is the **Costume and Textile Museum**, 51 Castle Gate (Wed–Sun 10am–4pm; free), one of the city's best, but sadly threatened with closure by the local council. In the 1760s, Nottingham saw the earliest experiments to produce machine-made lace, but it was not until the 1840s that the city produced the world's first fully machined lace garments. Thereafter the industry boomed until its collapse after World War I when lace, a symbol of an old and discredited order, suddenly had no place in the wardrobe of most women. The museum's lace-trimmed dresses, accessories and underclothes are displayed on two floors, the changing fashions illustrated by a sequence of dioramas. There's also an intriguing collection of **samplers**, try-outs made on linen scraps before work on the handmade garments began.

The Lace Market

A few minutes' walk away, on the east side of the Market Square up along Victoria Street, is the **Lace Market**, whose narrow lanes and alleys are flanked by an attractive assortment of Victorian factories and warehouses. **Stoney Street**, for one, holds the imposing Adams Building, with its handsome stone and brick facade, whilst adjoining **Broadway** chips in with a line of especially homogeneous red-brick and sandstone-trimmed buildings that perform a neat swerve halfway along the street. One feature that many of the buildings share is long attic windows designed to light what were once the mending and inspection rooms. Intruding into the Lace Market is the **National Ice Centre** (Ⓦwww.wayahead.com/icecentre), a whopping spaceship-like structure that's both the home of the Panthers ice-skating team and a trainee skaters' paradise. Daytime and evening skating sessions take place daily (2hr 30min; £3.20–3.70), and there's also "disco" sessions (Fri–Sun, same prices); to arrange lessons (£13 per half-hour), call Ⓣ0115/853 3036. At the heart of the Lace Market is the church of **St Mary**, a good-looking, mostly fifteenth-century structure built on top of the hill that was once the Saxon town. The church abuts High Pavement, the administrative centre of Nottingham in Georgian times, and here you'll find **Shire Hall**, whose Neoclassical columns, pilasters and dome date from 1770. The facade also bears the marks of a real Georgian cock-up: to the left of the entrance, at street level, the mason carved the word "Goal" onto an arch and then had to have a second bash, turning it into "Gaol"; both are clearly visible. Now accommodating the **Galleries of Justice** (Tues–Sat 10am–5pm, plus Mon 10am–5pm in school holidays; £6.95), the Shire Hall boasts two superbly preserved Victorian courtrooms as well as an Edwardian police station, some spectacularly unpleasant old cells, a women's prison with bath house and a prisoners' exercise yard. Most visitors opt for the "Crime and Punishment" tour, which includes role play – on arrival you are issued with a criminal identity number, and so it continues – but it is possible to wander round under your own steam, which takes about an hour.

Nearby, on Byard Lane, is the first shop of local lad **Paul Smith**, a major success story of recent British fashion.

Eating

Nottingham's **restaurant** scene has improved immeasurably in the last decade, and the city now boasts at least a dozen first-rate places. Most of the smarter restaurants feature fairly elaborate menus which attempt to balance unusual ingredients, but there are more straightforward joints too – primarily French, Italian and Asian. Like every other city in the UK, Nottingham is now awash with **cafés** and **café-bars**. Almost without exception, they've adopted the same formula – angular and ultra-modern furnishings and fittings – but the vast majority stick to coffees and snacks rather than more substantial offerings.

French Living 27 King St Ⓣ0115/958 5885. Authentic French cuisine served in cosy basement surroundings. Daytime snacks and baguettes on the ground floor too. Moderate.

Harts Standard Court, Park Row Ⓣ0115/911 0666. One of the city's most acclaimed restaurants, occupying part of the old general hospital and serving an international menu of carefully presented (and expensive) meals. Attractive pastel/modernist decor and attentive service. Expensive.

La Cappanna 596 Mansfield Rd Ⓣ0115/985 7411. Outstanding, family-run Italian restaurant with all the usual dishes – supplemented by daily specials – as well as a great line in seafood – the mussels are, so some Nottinghamians say, the best in England. The decor is very ordinary, but don't let that put you off. It's located a mile or so north of the city centre. Moderate.

Saagar Tandoori Restaurant 473 Mansfield Rd Ⓣ0115/962 2014. Excellent Indian restaurant, a mile or so north of the city centre. The decor is very homely – you feel as if you're in someone's living room – but it's a very popular spot. Moderate.

Shaw's 20 Broad St ⓣ0115/950 0009. Informal, pleasantly decorated basement restaurant serving an imaginative, well-considered menu supplemented by an outstanding selection of daily specials – the sardines, when they're on, are simply superb. Customers can eat in the ground-floor bar too. Very reasonable prices; highly recommended. Moderate.

World Service Newdigate House, Castle Gate ⓣ0115/847 5587. Chic restaurant with bags of flair in charming premises up near the castle. An international menu done with imagination. Expensive.

Pubs and nightlife

Nottingham's **nightclub** scene is boisterous, with places moving in and out of cool all the time. The **pubs** around Market Square have a tough edge to them, especially on the weekend, but within a few minutes' walk there's a selection of equally lively and more enjoyable drinking-holes. For **live music**, both popular and classical, most big names play at the Royal Centre Concert Hall on Wollaton Street (ⓣ0115/989 5555, ⓦwww.royalcentre-nottingham.co.uk; nearby *Rock City* (see below) also pulls in some star turns. The Broadway, in the Lace Market at 14 Broad St (ⓣ0115/952 6611, ⓦwww.broadway.org.uk), is far and away the best **cinema** in town, featuring the pick of mainstream and avant-garde films.

Pubs and bars

Broadway Cinema Bar Broadway Cinema, 14 Broad St. Informal, fashionable bar serving an eclectic assortment of bottled beers to a cinema-keen clientele. Can get too smoky for comfort, so they have a smaller, smoke-free café-bar upstairs.

Cast Wellington Circus. The bar of the Nottingham Playhouse is a popular, easy-going spot with courtyard seating on summer nights. Good supply of real ales.

Lincolnshire Poacher 161 Mansfield Rd. Very popular and relaxed pub, with a wide selection of bottled and real ales. An older clientele than in the (very youthful) city centre – a five- to ten-minute walk away.

Pitcher & Piano High Pavement. Lively, fashionable pub in an imaginatively converted Victorian church on the edge of the Lace Market. Good fun; very young.

Ye Olde Trip to Jerusalem Inn Below the castle in Brewhouse Yard. Carved into the castle rock, this ancient inn may well have been a meeting point for soldiers gathering for the Third Crusade. Its cave-like bars, with their rough sandstone ceilings, are delightfully secretive.

Clubs

The Bomb 45 Bridlesmith Gate ⓣ0115/950 6667, ⓦwww.thebomb.twelveten.com. A front-runner in the club scene with regular house, techno and garage nights.

Media Queen St ⓣ0115/910 1101, ⓦwww.meanfiddler.com. One of the grooviest places in town with grand decor and great sounds. Leading DJs are its forte.

Rock City 8 Talbot St ⓣ0115/958 8484, ⓦwww.rock-city.co.uk. Giant-sized, crowded nightclub/music venue, with different sounds and crowds each night, from Goth to metal to indie. Regularly hosts name bands on UK tours.

Around Nottingham: Wollaton Hall and Eastwood

Some four miles west of central Nottingham, **Wollaton Hall** is a flamboyant Elizabethan mansion built for Sir Francis Willoughby in the 1580s by the architect of Longleat, Robert Smythson. Perched on top of a grassy knoll, the hall presents a grand facade of chimneys, turrets and tiers to the surrounding **parkland** (daily dawn–dusk; free), but the interior, clumsily refashioned in the nineteenth century, can only muster a workaday **natural history museum** (April–Oct daily 11am–5pm, Nov–March daily 11am–4pm; £1.50 at weekends, otherwise free). Many visitors – and there are a lot of them – prefer to stroll the woodland around the park's lake. Buses #35 #36 and #38, leaving from outside John Lewis, in the city centre on Milton Street, pass the park's Derby Road entrance gates, a short stroll from the house; buses depart every twenty minutes or so.

D.H. Lawrence was born in the coal mining village of **EASTWOOD**, about eight miles west of Nottingham. The mine closed years ago, and Eastwood is something of a post-industrial eyesore, but Lawrence's childhood home, a tiny terraced house, has survived, refurbished as the **D.H. Lawrence Birthplace Museum**, 8a Victoria St, off Nottingham Road (daily: April–Oct 10am–5pm; Nov–March closes 4pm; Mon–Fri free, Sat & Sun £2). None of the furnishings and fittings are Lawrence originals, which isn't too surprising considering the family moved out when he was 2, but it's an appealing evocation of the period interlaced with biographical insights into the author's early life. Afterwards, enthusiasts can follow the Blue Line Walk round those parts of Eastwood with Lawrence associations – a mention in a book here, a comment in a letter there. The walk is three miles long and takes an hour or two; a brochure is available at the museum. Interestingly, few locals thought well of Lawrence – and the sexual scandals hardly helped. Famously, he ran off with Freda, the wife of a Nottingham professor, and then there was the *Lady Chatterley's Lover* obscenity trail, but equally unpopular was the author's move to the political right until, eventually, he espoused a cranky and unpleasant form of elitism.

Buses leave Nottingham's Victoria Centre bus station for Eastwood every twenty minutes or so; the journey takes about half an hour.

Northern Nottinghamshire

Rural **northern Nottinghamshire**, with its easy rolling landscapes and large ducal estates, was transformed in the nineteenth century by **coal** – deep, wide seams of the stuff that spawned dozens of collieries, and colliery towns, stretching north across the county and on into Yorkshire. Almost without exception, the mines have closed, their passing marked only by the old pit-head winding wheels left, bleak and solitary, to commemorate the thousands of men who laboured here. The suddenness of the pit closure programme imposed by the Conservative government in the 1980s knocked the stuffing out of the area and only now is it beginning to revive. One prop has been the tourist industry, for the countryside in between these mining communities holds several enjoyable attractions, the best-known of which is **Sherwood Forest** – or at least the patchy remains of it – one-time haunt (allegedly) of Robin Hood. Byron is a pip-squeak in the celebrity stakes by comparison, but his family home – **Newstead Abbey** – is here too, there are some pleasant woodland walks in the NT's **Clumber Park** and, last but certainly not least, there's **Hardwick Hall**, a stunningly handsome Elizabethan mansion.

Reaching this quartet of attractions by **bus** from Nottingham is easy enough – with the exception of Hardwick Hall, for which you'll need your own transport.

Hardwick Hall

Born the daughter of a minor Derbyshire squire, Elizabeth, Countess of Shrewsbury (1527–1608) – aka **Bess of Hardwick** – became one of the leading figures of Elizabethan England, renowned for her political and business acumen. She also had a penchant for building and her major achievement, **Hardwick Hall** (April–Oct Wed, Thurs, Sat & Sun 12.30–5pm; plus July & Aug Mon 12.30–5pm; gardens same months daily 11am–5.30pm; house & gardens £6.60, gardens only £3.50; NT), begun when she was 62, has survived in amazingly good condition. The house was the epitome of fashionable taste, a balance of symmetry and ingenious detail in which the rectangular lines of the building are offset by line upon line of window – there's actually more glass than stone – whilst up above her giant-sized initials – E.S. – hog every roof line. Inside, the ground floor is relatively routine, but it's here that Hardwick's extensive collection of sixteenth- and seventeenth-century needlework is displayed, including several pieces by Mary, Queen of Scots, who was held in custody by the Earl of Shrewsbury for years. He moaned about the expense incessantly, one of the reasons for the souring of his relationship with Bess, a deterioration that prompted their estrangement.

On the top floor, the **High Great Chamber**, where Bess received her most distinguished guests, boasts an extraordinary plaster frieze, a brightly painted, finely worked affair celebrating the goddess Diana, the virgin huntress – it was, of course, designed to please the virgin queen herself. Next door, the **Long Gallery** is simply breathtaking, like an indoor cricket pitch only with exquisite furnishings and fittings from the splendid chimneypieces and tapestries through to a set of portraits, including one each of the queen and Bess. The gallery was where Bess and her chums could exercise – and keep out of the sun at a time when any hint of a tan was considered peasant-plebeian.

Outside, the **garden** makes for a pleasant wander and, beyond the ha ha (the animal-excluding ditch and low wall), rare breeds of cattle and sheep graze the surrounding **parkland** (daily 8am–6pm; free). Finally – and rather confusingly – Hardwick Hall is next to **Hardwick Old Hall** (April–Oct Mon, Wed, Thurs, Sat & Sun 11am–6pm; £3; EH), Bess's previous home, but now little more than a broken-down if substantial ruin.

The easiest way to reach Hardwick is along the M1; come off at Junction #29 and follow the signs from the roundabout at the top of the slip road – a three-mile trip. Note, however, that Hardwick is not signed from the motorway itself.

Newstead Abbey

In 1539, Henry VIII granted **Newstead Abbey** (house April–Sept daily noon–5pm; grounds daily 9am–dusk; £5, grounds only £2.50), ten miles north of Nottingham on the A60, to Sir John Byron, who demolished most of the church and converted the monastic buildings into a family home. In 1798, **Lord Byron** inherited Newstead, then little more than a ruin. He restored part of the complex during his six-year residence (1808–14), but most of the present structure dates from later renovations, which maintained much of the shape and feel of the medieval original while creating the warren-like mansion that exists today. **Inside**, a string of intriguing period rooms includes everything from a neo-Gothic Great Hall to the Henry VII bedroom, fitted with carved panels and painted house screens imported from Japan. Some of the rooms are pretty much as they were when Byron lived here – notably his bedroom and dressing room – and in the library is a small collection of the poet's possessions, from letters and manuscripts through to his pistols and boxing gloves. In the west gallery, look out also for the painting of Byron's favourite dog, Boatswain, a perky beast who was buried just outside the house – the conspicuous memorial, with its absurdly extravagant inscription, marks the spot. The surrounding **gardens** are delightful, a secretive and subtle combination of walled garden, lake, Gothic waterfalls, yew tunnels and Japanese-style rockeries, complete with eccentric pagodas.

There's a fast and frequent **bus** service leaving every twenty minutes or so from Nottingham's Victoria Centre bus station to the gates of Newstead Abbey, a mile from the house; the journey takes about 25 minutes.

Rufford Country Park

Council-run country parks may be ten-a-penny, but **Rufford Country Park** (daily dawn–dusk; main facilities daily 10.30am–5pm; free) shows just how things should be done. The remains of the original twelfth-century Cistercian abbey and the country house built in its stead – but largely demolished in 1956 – are neither very substantial nor especially interesting, but the old buildings are all pleasantly maintained and the former stable block now holds a café, a better-than-average craft shop and a first-rate ceramics gallery. At the back of the stables are the gardens, both informal and formal, and an outstanding **Sculpture Garden**, which manages to be both very accessible and very contemporary. Further afield is a lake and a mill, a bird sanctuary and a wetland area, all reachable via a footpath. There's a lively programme of special events and temporary art exhibitions too.

Rufford is right beside the A614 about eighteen miles north of Nottingham and reached on hourly Stagecoach **bus** #33 from Nottingham's Victoria Centre bus station.

Robin Hood – and Sherwood Forest Country Park

Most of **Sherwood Forest**, once a vast royal woodland of oak, birch and bracken covering all of northern Nottinghamshire, was cleared in the eighteenth century – nowadays it's difficult to imagine the protection it provided for generations of outlaws, the most famous of whom was **Robin Hood**. There's no "true story" of Robin's life – the earliest reference to him, in Langland's *Piers Plowman* of 1377, treats him as a fiction – but to the balladeers of fifteenth-century England, who invented most of the folklore, this was hardly the point. For them, Robin was a symbol of yeoman decency, a semi-mythological opponent of corrupt clergymen and evil officers of the law; in the early tales, although Robin shows sympathy for the peasant, he has rather more respect for the decent nobleman, and he's never credited with robbing the rich to give to the poor. This and other parts of the legend, such as Maid Marion and Friar Tuck, were added later.

Robin Hood may lack historical authenticity, but it hasn't discouraged the county council from spending thousands of pounds sustaining the **Major Oak**, the creaky tree where Maid Marion and Robin are supposed to have "plighted their troth". The Major Oak is on a pleasant one-mile trail that begins beside the visitor centre at the main entrance to **Sherwood Forest Country Park** (daily dawn–dusk; free), which comprises 450 acres of oak and silver birch crisscrossed with footpaths. The visitor centre is half a mile north of the village of Edwinstowe, itself just two miles northwest of Rufford Park and twenty-odd miles north of Nottingham via the A614.

There's a regular **bus** service on Stagecoach bus #33 from Nottingham's Victoria Centre bus station to Edwinstowe via Rufford.

Clumber Park

North of Ollerton, Edwinstowe's immediate neighbour, the A614 trims the edge of Thoresby Park, to reach, after six miles, the eastern entrance to the NT's **Clumber Park** (daily dawn–dusk; free, but parking for non-NT members £3.60), four thousand acres of park and woodland lying to the south of industrial Worksop. The estate was once the country seat of the dukes of Newcastle, and it was here in the 1770s that they constructed a grand mansion overlooking Clumber Lake. The house was dismantled in 1938, when the duke sold the estate, and today the most interesting survivor of the lakeside buildings – located about two and a half miles from the A614 – is the Gothic Revival **Chapel** (daily: April–Sept 10.30am–5.30pm; Oct–March 10.30am–4pm; free; NT), an imposing edifice with a soaring spire and an intricately carved interior built for the seventh duke in the 1880s. Close by, the old **stable block** now houses a National Trust office, shop and **café** (daily: April–Sept 10.30am–5.30pm; Oct–March 10.30am–4pm), and there's **bike rental** (April–Sept) immediately behind the chapel. The woods around the lake offer some delightful strolls and rides through planted woodland interspersed with the occasional patch of original forest.

Departing Nottingham's Victoria Centre bus station, Stagecoach East Midlands hourly **bus** #33 runs to Rufford and Edwinstowe, from where it travels on up the west side of Clumber Park en route to Worksop; get off at Carburton for the 2.5-mile walk to the Clumber Park NT office. The excursion is best done as a day-trip from Nottingham, but there is a **campsite** (ⓣ01909/482303; closed Nov–April) in Clumber Park's walled garden, a few minutes' walk north of the chapel.

Welbeck Abbey's Harley Gallery

To the west of Clumber Park lies **Welbeck Abbey estate**, most of which is leased by the Ministry of Defence. The remainder is still in ducal hands, and the old gas works, built on the edge of the estate in the 1870s, has been imaginatively turned into the **Harley Gallery** (Tues–Sun 10am–5pm; free). The gallery is mainly devoted to temporary exhibitions featuring the work of local living artists, all well presented and intelligently arranged, but there's also a permanent exhibition on the ducal family, variously named Cavendish, Portland and Newcastle. It's a small display – just one room – but includes an appealing assortment of family knick-knacks, from portraits, timepieces and rare books through to silverware. Locally at least, the most famous of the line was the Fifth Duke of Portland (1800–1879), known as the "burrowing duke" for the maze of gaslight tunnels he built underneath his estate. Naturally enough, many thought he was bonkers, but the truth may well be far more complex – an issue cleverly explored in Mick Jackson's novel *The Underground Man*, wherein the duke is portrayed as a shy man haunted by his obsessions. Another school of thought puts his burrowing down to the disfiguring effects of a skin disease. The tunnels are not, however, open to the public.

The entrance to Welbeck Abbey is on the A60, two miles north of the hamlet of Cuckney and about seven miles from the west entrance to Clumber Park. There are no **buses** between Clumber Park and Welbeck, but there is an hourly service from Nottingham's Victoria bus station to Welbeck (Stagecoach bus #757; Mon–Sat only); the bus stop is a couple of hundred yards from the Harley Gallery.

Eastern Nottinghamshire

Without coal, **eastern Nottinghamshire** escaped the heavy-duty industrialization that fell upon its county neighbours in the late nineteenth century. It remains a largely rural area, its undulating farmland, punctuated by dozens of pint-sized villages, rolling seamlessly over to the River Trent, the boundary with Lincolnshire. By and large, it's a prosperous part of the county and by no means unpleasant, but for the casual visitor the attractions are distinctly low-key, being essentially confined to **Southwell** and **Newark**, both of which are easy to reach by public transport from Nottingham.

Southwell

SOUTHWELL, some fourteen miles northeast of Nottingham, is a sedate backwater distinguished by **Southwell Minster** (April–Sept Mon–Sat 8am–7pm; Oct–March Mon–Sat 8am–dusk; Sun year-round same hours, depending on services; free but £3 donation suggested), whose twin towers are visible for miles around, and the fine Georgian mansions facing it along Church Street. The Normans built the minster at the beginning of the twelfth century and, although some elements were added later, their design predominates, from the imposing west towers through to the dog-tooth-decorated doorways. Inside, the proud and forceful arcaded **nave**, with its sturdy columns, marches up to the **north transept**, where there is a remarkably fine alabaster tomb of a long forgotten churchman, one Archbishop Sandys, who died in 1588. The red-flecked alabaster effigy of Sandys is so precise that you can make out the furrows on his brow and the crows' feet round his eyes; his children are depicted kneeling below and it's assumed that Sandys was one of the first bishops to marry – and beget – after the break with Rome changed the rules. The nave's stonework ends abruptly at the transepts with the inelegance of the fourteenth-century rood screen, beyond which lies the Early English **choir** and the extraordinary **chapter house**. The latter is embellished with naturalistic foliage dating from the late thirteenth century, some of the earliest carving of its type in England. About a mile from the minster, out on the road to Newark, stands **The Southwell Workhouse** (April–July & Sept–Oct Mon & Thurs–Sun noon–5pm; Aug Mon & Thurs–Sun 11am–5pm; £4.20; NT), a rare survivor of the Victorian workhouses that once dotted every corner of the country. They were built as result of the New Poor Law of 1834, which made a laudable attempt to provide shelter for the destitute. However, the middle classes were concerned that the workers would take advantage of free shelter, so conditions were made – as a matter of policy – hard and dull, and the "workhouses" were much feared. Most were knocked down or redeveloped years ago, but Southwell remained almost untouched, though the bare rooms and barred windows of the building end up making a surprisingly dull visit.

For a bite to **eat**, the daytime *Deli* (Mon–Sat 9am–5pm), a five-minute walk from the minster on the main drag through the village at 85a King St, sells a tasty range of baguettes and paninis. Alternatively, the *Saracen's Head*, across from the minster, does a good line in afternoon teas – scones, jam and cream and so forth.

There are regular **buses** from Queen Street in the centre of Nottingham to Southwell and Newark.

Newark

From Southwell, it's eight miles east to **NEWARK**, an amiable, low-key river port and market town that was once a major staging point on the Great North Road. Fronting the town as you approach from the west are the gaunt riverside ruins of **Newark Castle** (daily dawn–dusk; free), all that's left of the mighty medieval fortress that was pounded to pieces during the Civil War. Opposite, just across the street to the north, is **The Ossington**, a flashy structure whose Tudor appearance is entirely fraudulent – it was built in the 1880s as a temperance hotel by a local bigwig, in an effort to save drinkers from themselves. In the opposite direction, the town council have laid out a brief but pleasant riverside walk that leads past ancient houses to the old town lock, and from here it's just five minutes east to the expansive **Market Place**. This square, surrounded by a network of narrow and ancient alleys, is framed by a sequence of attractive Georgian and Victorian facades, as well as the mostly thirteenth-century church of **St Mary Magdalene** (Mon–Sat 8.30am–4.30pm), whose massive spire, at 236ft, towers over the town centre. It's a handsome church, its well-proportioned nave cheered by some brightly restored roof paintings and a fancy reredos. Look out also for a pair of medieval Dance of Death panel paintings behind the reredos in the choir's Markham Chantry Chapel. One panel has a well-to-do man holding a plate, the other shows a carnation-carrying skeleton pointing to the grave – an obvious reminder to the observer of his or her mortality.

There's a regular **bus** service from Nottingham to Newark via Southwell, and Newark is also on the Nottingham–Lincoln **train** line. The Newark Castle **train station** (there is another, so be sure to get off at the right one) is on the west side of the River Trent, a five-minute walk from both the castle and the adjacent **tourist office**, on Castlegate (daily 9am–5pm; ⓣ01636/655765). The **bus station** is on Lombard Street, a couple of minutes' walk south from the tourist office along Castlegate. Newark has a small supply of **hotels** and **B&Bs**, which the tourist office will book on your behalf at no extra charge, but remember that rooms are well-nigh impossible to find during the Newark International Antiques Fair, Europe's biggest such event, held six times a year. For **food**, make for the excellent *Gannets*, 35 Castlegate (Mon–Fri 9am–4pm, Sat 9am–5pm, Sun 9.30am–4pm), an astoundingly good coffee bar serving daytime snacks and meals, or the simply superb *Café Bleu*, opposite at 14 Castlegate (ⓣ01636/610141), a brilliant French restaurant serving top-class meals from an inventive menu. It's one of the best restaurants in the county, with an outside terrace and live jazz; the decor – all pastel-painted cheerfulness – is appealing too.

Leicestershire and Rutland

The compact county of **Leicestershire** is one of the more anonymous of the English shires, though **Leicester** itself is saved from mediocrity by its role as a focal point for Britain's Asian community. West Leicestershire has rather more to offer, for although its rolling landscape is blemished by a series of industrial settlements, things pick up markedly at **Ashby-de-la-Zouch**, a pleasing little town graced by the substantial remains of its medieval castle. Near here too are **Calke Abbey**, a dishevelled country house set in its own estate just over the border in Derbyshire, and the trim charms of **Market Bosworth**, the site of the Battle of Bosworth Field, the climactic engagement of the Wars of the Roses. In east Leicestershire, the farmland is studded with long-established market towns. None of them are particularly enthralling, but genial **Market Harborough** holds several attractive old buildings and an interesting museum, whilst **Melton Mowbray** is the pork pie capital of the world.

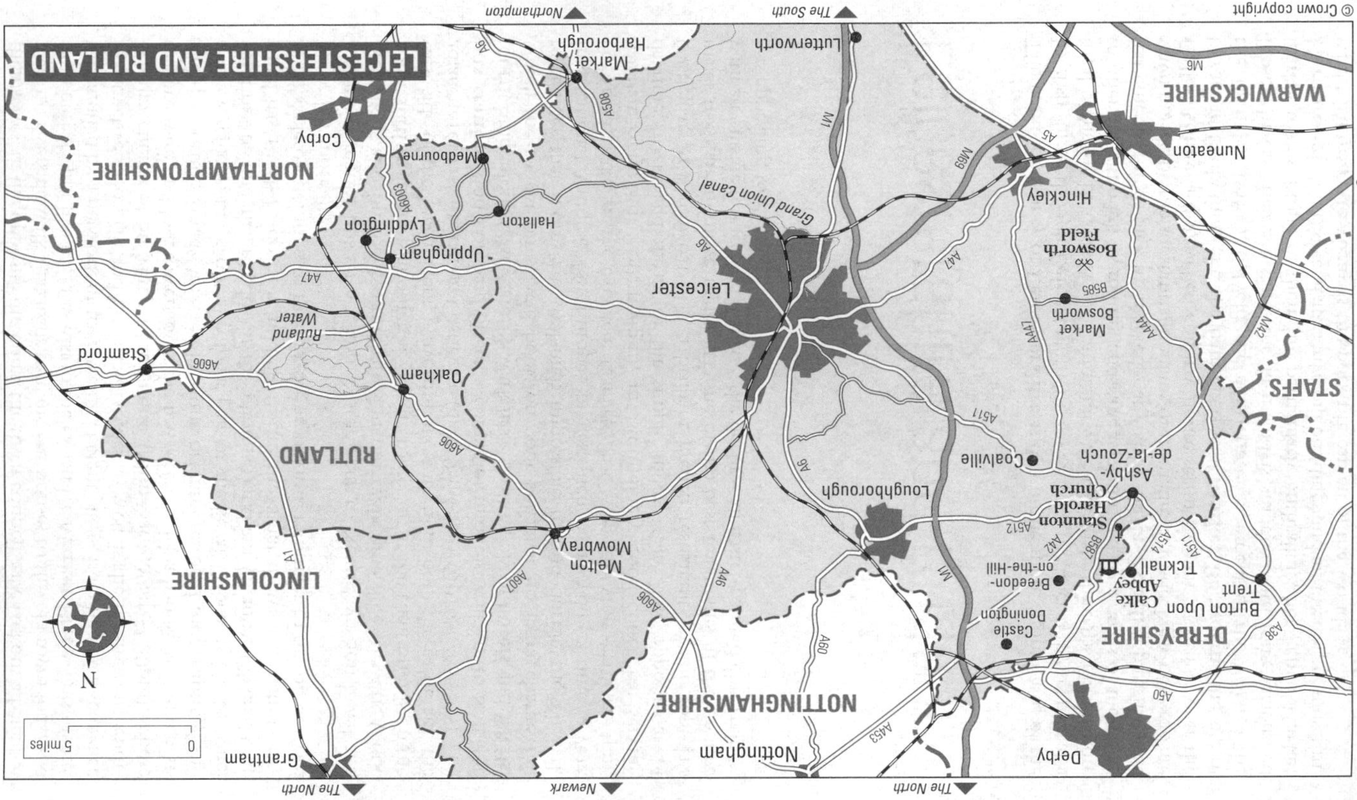

LEICESTERSHIRE AND RUTLAND

NORTHAMPTONSHIRE
LINCOLNSHIRE
RUTLAND
NOTTINGHAMSHIRE
DERBYSHIRE
STAFFS
WARWICKSHIRE

Peterborough
The South
The North
Newark
The North
Northampton
The South
Birmingham

Grantham
Stamford
Rutland Water
Oakham
Uppingham
Lyddington
Corby
Medbourne
Hallaton
Market Harborough
Melton Mowbray
Leicester
Grand Union Canal
Lutterworth
Nottingham
Loughborough
Coalville
Derby
Castle Donington
Breedon-on-the-Hill
Staunton Harold Church
Ashby-de-la-Zouch
Calke Abbey
Ticknall
Burton Upon Trent
Market Bosworth
Bosworth Field
Hinckley
Nuneaton

A1
A606
A47
A6003
A508
A6
A607
A46
A60
A453
M1
A512
A511
A42
B587
A514
A50
A38
A444
A447
B585
M69
A5
M6
M42

0 5 miles
N

To the east of Leicestershire lies England's smallest county, **Rutland**, reinstated in 1997 following 23 unpopular years of merger with its larger neighbour. As part of their spirited publicity campaign to revive their ancient county, Rutland's well-heeled burghers issued "passports" to locals and created quite a stir, breaking through the profound apathy which characterizes the English attitude to local government. Rutland has three places of note, beginning with **Oakham**, the county town, and **Uppingham**, both rural centres with some elegant Georgian architecture. Even prettier is the tiny stone hamlet of **Lyddington**.

Getting around Leicestershire and Rutland can be problematic. **Train** lines radiate out from Leicester, most usefully to Market Harborough and Oakham, and there's a good network of **bus** services between the market towns, but these fade away in the villages where, if there is a bus at all, it only runs once or twice a day.

Leicester

On first impression, **LEICESTER** is a resolutely modern city, but further inspection reveals traces of its medieval and Roman past, situated immediately to the west of the downtown shopping area near the River Soar. The Romans, choosing this site in the middle of the rebellious Coritani, developed Leicester's precursor, Ratae Coritanorum, as a fortified town on the Fosse Way, the military road running from Lincoln to Cirencester, and **Emperor Hadrian** kitted it out with huge public buildings. Subsequently, in the eighth century, the Danes colonized the town and later still its medieval castle became the base of the earls of Leicester, the most distinguished of whom was **Simon de Montfort**, who forced Henry III to convene the first English Parliament in 1265. Since the late seventeenth century, Leicester has been a centre of the hosiery trade and it was this industry that attracted hundreds of Asian immigrants to settle here in the 1950s and 1960s. Today, about one third of Leicester's population is **Asian** and the city elected the country's first Asian MP, Keith Vaz, in 1987. Leicester's Hindus put on two massive and internationally famous festivals in October and November, **Navrati** and **Diwali**, the Festival of Light (Ⓦ www.discoverleicester.com). In addition, the city's sizeable Afro-Caribbean community celebrates its culture in a whirl of colour and music on the first weekend in August. This, the **Leicester Caribbean Carnival** (Ⓦ www.lccarnival.org.uk), is the country's second biggest street festival after the Notting Hill Carnival (see p.125).

Arrival, information and accommodation

On the northern line from London's St Pancras Station, Leicester **train station** is situated on London Road just to the southeast of the city centre. The **bus station** is on the north side of the centre, just off Gravel Street. The centre is signed from both – the large Haymarket Shopping Centre in between the two is an easy landmark. The **tourist office** is a short walk to the south of the Haymarket at 7–9 Every St, on Town Hall Square (Mon–Wed & Fri 9am–5.30pm, Thurs 10am–5.30pm, Sat 9am–5pm; premium-rate line Ⓣ 0906/294 1113, Ⓦ www.discoverleicester.com).

With other more enticing cities near at hand – Nottingham being a case in point – there's no strong reason to overnight here, but Leicester does have a good crop of business **hotels** close to the centre, within walking distance of the train station. The tourist office also has a substantial list of competitively priced **B&Bs**, though most are out of the centre. They will help fix you up with somewhere to stay, but things rarely get tight except during Navrati and Diwali.

Accommodation

Best Western Belmont House Hotel De Montfort St ⓣ0116/254 4773, ⓦwww.belmonthotel.co.uk. Proficient chain hotel in an efficiently modernized and extended Georgian property about 300 yards south of the train station via London Rd. Popular with business folk. ❺

Holiday Inn 129 St Nicholas Circle ⓣ0116/253 1161, ⓦwww.leicester.holiday-inn.com. Plush chain hotel which manages to counteract its motorized setting – in the middle of the ring road – by creating a relaxed and self-enclosed environment. Comfortable rooms, indoor pool and extensive fitness facilities. ❺

Leicestershire Backpacker's Hostel 157 Wanlip Lane Birstall ⓣ0116/267 3107. On the northern edge of town, this is an unusual self-styled backpackers' hostel in a suburban semi, with patio and summerhouse. It has just five beds and costs £10 per person for the first night, £8 for two nights or more. Self-catering facilities. Several local buses link Birstall with the centre, but services vary with the day of the week – call ahead for details and to make reservations.

Spindle Lodge Hotel 2 West Walk ⓣ0116/233 8801. Well-maintained, medium-sized place in a pleasantly converted, three-storey, ivy-clad Victorian town house on a quiet residential street. Ten minutes' walk from the train station – head south on London Rd, turn right onto De Montfort St and then left onto Regent Rd; *Spindle Lodge* is at the junction of Regent Rd and West Walk. ❸

The city centre

The most conspicuous building in Leicester's crowded centre is undoubtedly the modern Haymarket Shopping Centre, but the proper landmark is the Victorian **clocktower** of 1868, standing in front of the Haymarket and marking the spot where seven streets meet. One of the seven is Cheapside, which leads south in a few yards to Leicester's open-air produce **market** (Mon–Sat), arguably the best in the land. Alternatively, from back at the clocktower, East Gates and then the old High Street run west with Silver Street (subsequently Guildhall Lane), soon branching off to reach **St Martin's Cathedral**, a much modified eleventh-century structure that incorporates a fine, ornately carved medieval wooden entrance porch. Next door is the **Guildhall** (Mon–Sat 10am–5pm & Sun 1–5pm, Oct–March till 4pm; free), a half-timbered building that has served, variously, as the town hall, prison and police station. The highlight of a visit is the rickety Great Hall, its beams bent with age, but there are a couple of old cells too, plus the town gibbet in which the bodies of the hanged were publicly displayed until the 1840s.

From the Guildhall, it's a short walk west to St Nicholas Place and then St Nicholas Circle, a large roundabout that is part of the ring road. Go round it to the right – there's a walkway – and on the right behind the church is the **Jewry Wall**, a chunk of Roman masonry some 18ft high and 73ft long that was originally part of Hadrian's public baths. The project was a real irritation to the emperor. Hadrian's grand scheme was spoilt by the engineers, who miscalculated the line of the aqueduct that was to pipe in the water, and so bathers had to rely on a hand-filled cistern replenished from the river – which wasn't what he had in mind at all. The adjacent **Jewry Wall Museum** (April–Sept Mon–Sat 10am–5pm, Sun 1–5pm; Oct–March Mon–Sat 10am–4pm, Sun 1–4pm; free) charts Leicester's history from prehistoric to medieval times. The most interesting artefacts are Roman, a hotchpotch of archeological finds from Fosse Way milestones to two splendid mosaics.

To St Mary de Castro and the Jain Centre

From the museum, keep on going round St Nicholas Circle – with the *Holiday Inn* on the left – then veer down the first street on the right and opposite you'll spy the entrance to **Castle Gardens**, a narrow strip of a park that runs alongside a canalized portion of the Soar. The gardens are a pleasant spot, incorporating the overgrown mound where Leicester's Norman castle motte once stood. At the far end, you emerge on The Newarke; turn left and follow the road round, and in a minute or two you'll reach Castle View, a narrow lane spanned by the **Turret Gateway**, a rare survivor of the city's medieval castle. Just beyond the gateway is **St Mary de Castro** (Easter–Oct Sat 2–5pm), a dignified old church with a dainty crocketted spire and a harmonious mix of architectural styles below, including several Norman features such as the dog-tooth decorated doorways and a five-seater sedilia in the chancel. Interestingly enough, this was probably where Chaucer got married.

Doubling back to The Newarke, it's a few paces more to the **Newarke Houses Museum** (April–Sept Mon–Sat 10am–5pm, Sun 1–5pm; Oct–March Mon–Sat 10am–4pm, Sun 1–4pm; free), two adjoining Jacobean houses that make a pleasant setting for an exploration of the city's social history, including a feature on Thomas Cook (1808–92), who organized his first travel jaunt here in Leicester in 1841. It was an excursion by train to a Temperance Society meeting in nearby Loughborough and it proved so successful that Cook was soon planning more, taking – for example – over 150,000 people to the Great Exhibition in London's Hyde Park. At the east end of The Newarke, ignominiously stranded between the carriageways of the ring road, stands the distinctive and substantial **Magazine Gateway** (no access), once a medieval entrance into the city and arsenal – hence the name.

Take the underpass under the ring road, veer right along Oxford Road and you'll soon reach the **Jain Centre** (Ⓦwww.jaincentre.com), which occupies a remodelled Congregational chapel dating from the nineteenth century. The rites and beliefs of the Jains, a long-established Indian religious sect, focus on an extreme reverence for all living things – traditional customs include the wearing of gauze masks to prevent the inhalation of passing insects. The temple, the only one of its kind in western Europe, has a splendidly garish white marble facade, and visitors may enter the lobby – or, better, view the interior by prior appointment – call Ⓣ0116/254 3091.

New Walk Museum and Art Gallery

From the Jain Centre, it's about ten minutes' walk east to the **New Walk Museum and Art Gallery** (April–Sept Mon–Sat 10am–5pm, Sun 1–5pm; Oct–March Mon–Sat 10am–4pm, Sun 1–4pm; free), easily the best of the city's museums. To get there from the Jain temple, go back to the beginning of Oxford Street, turn right onto Newarke Street and keep going straight until you intersect with – and turn right onto – **New Walk**, a pedestrianized promenade that runs out from the centre to leafy Victoria Park. On the museum's ground floor is a real surprise – an outstanding collection of work by German Expressionists, mostly sketches, woodcuts and lithographs by the likes of Otto Dix and George Grosz. In particular, look out for the latter's 1919 rallying-call sketch of the coffins of the two murdered leftists, Rosa Luxembourg and Karl Liebknecht. The Germans share the ground floor with the Ancient Egypt Gallery, featuring mummies and hieroglyphic tablets brought from Egypt as souvenirs in the 1880s. The Victorian Gallery is fascinating too, dominated by extravagant, often mawkish romantic paintings, amongst which is Charles Green's iconic *The Girl I left behind Me* of 1880.

From the museum, it takes about ten minutes to walk back to the Haymarket.

Belgrave and The National Space Centre

Beginning about a mile to the northeast of the centre, the gritty **Belgrave** neighbourhood is the focus of Leicester's Asian community. Both Belgrave Road and its northerly continuation, Melton Road, are lined with Indian and Pakistani goldsmiths and jewellers, sari shops, Hindi music stores and curry houses. It's never dull down here, but Sunday afternoons are particularly enjoyable, when locals have time to stroll the streets in their finest gear. Belgrave celebrates two major Hindu festivals: **Diwali**, the Festival of Light, held in October or November, when six thousand lamps are strung out along the Belgrave Road and 20,000 come to watch the switch-on alone; and **Navrati**, an eight-day celebration in October held in honour of the goddess Ambaji.

On the edge of Belgrave, just off the A6 two miles north of the city centre, the gleaming new **National Space Centre** (school term time Tues–Fri 10am–3.30pm, Sat & Sun 10am–4.30pm; school holidays Mon noon–4.30pm, Tues–Sun 10am–4.30pm; £8.95, children (4–16) £6.95; ⓣ0870/607 7223, ⓦwww.spacecentre.co.uk) is devoted to space science and astronomy, with five themed galleries exploring everything from the planets to orbiting earth. The emphasis is on the interactive, which makes the place very popular with children. Bus #54 links the train station and the Haymarket with Abbey Lane, a five-minute walk from the centre.

Eating, drinking, nightlife and entertainment

People come from miles around to eat at the **Indian restaurants** along Belgrave Road. The pick are clustered at the beginning of Belgrave Road, just beyond the flyover to the northeast of the centre, and it's here you'll find the most famous, *Bobby's*, at no. 154–156 (ⓣ0116/266 0106). Run by Gujaratis, this moderately priced, unassuming place is strictly vegetarian and uses no garlic or onions; try their delicious house speciality, *undhyu*, or the multi-flavoured Bobby's Special Chaat. Excellent alternatives include the *Sayonara Thali*, at no. 49 (ⓣ0116/266 5888), which specializes in set thali meals, where several different dishes, breads and pickles are served together on large steel plates, and the *Chaat House* (ⓣ0116/266 0513), south of *Bobby's* on the same side of the road at no. 108. The latter does wonderful masala dosas and other south Indian snacks – legendary cricket captain Kapil Dev and his Indian team ate here when they were on tour. In the city centre, and diversifying from the Asian restaurants, the cream of the crop is the *Opera House*, 10 Guildhall Lane (ⓣ0116/223 6666), in lovely old premises and with an imaginative, wide-ranging menu – ravioli with wild mushrooms and the like.

The city's **pubs** have taken a pounding from the boom in cafés and café-bars, but *The Globe*, 43 Silver St, supplies a goodly range of ales in traditional surroundings, while the much slicker *Watsons Restaurant & Bar*, 5 Upper Brown St, is – with its crisply modern furnishings and fittings – one of the most popular places in town.

The **performing arts** come up trumps in Leicester at the excellent Phoenix Arts Centre, Newarke St (ⓣ0116/255 4854, ⓦwww.phoenix.org.uk), which features a first-rate mix of comedy, music, theatre and dance, whilst doubling up as an independent cinema. The city's main concert arena is De Montfort

Hall, on Granville Road (ⓣ0116/233 3111, ⓦwww.demontforthall.co.uk) – adjoining Victoria Park at the far end of New Walk.

West Leicestershire

Give or take the odd industrial blip, most of **west Leicestershire** – to the west of the A6 – is rural, its small towns and villages dotted over undulating countryside. The key attractions here are best visited as day-trips, beginning with **Calke Abbey**, technically over the boundary in Derbyshire and not an abbey at all, but an intriguing country house whose faded charms witness the declining fortunes of the landed gentry. There's also **Market Bosworth**, a pleasant little spot near the site of **Bosworth Field**, where Richard III came an unpleasant cropper – not before time according to Shakespeare; a good castle, at **Ashby-de-la-Zouch**; and a fine church, perched on top of one of the few hills hereabouts at **Breedon-on-the-Hill**.

With the notable exception of Calke Abbey, all the places mentioned above are easy to reach by **bus** from Leicester – and Ashby can readily be reached by bus from Nottingham, too.

Market Bosworth

The thatched cottages and Georgian houses of tiny **MARKET BOSWORTH**, some twelve miles west of Leicester, fan out from a dinky market square that was an important trading centre throughout the Middle Ages. From the sixteenth to the nineteenth century, the dominant family hereabouts was the Dixies, merchant-landlords who mostly ended up at the local church of **St Peter**, a good-looking edifice with a castellated nave and a sturdy square tower. Heavily revamped by the Victorians, the church's interior is fairly routine, but the chancel does hold the charming early-eighteenth-century tomb of John Dixie, one-time rector, who is honoured by a long hagiographic plaque and the effigy of his weeping sister. John apparently apart, the Dixies were not universally admired. The young Samuel Johnson taught at the **Dixie Grammar School** – whose elongated facade still abuts the Market Place – but disliked the founder, Sir Wolstan Dixie, so much that he recollected his time there "with the strongest aversion and even a sense of horror".

Market Bosworth is, however, best known for the **Battle of Bosworth Field**, fought on hilly countryside a couple of miles south of town in 1485. This was the last and decisive battle of the Wars of the Roses, an interminably long-winded and bitterly violent conflict amongst the nobility for control of the English crown. The victor was Henry Tudor, subsequently Henry VII, the vanquished Richard III, who famously died on the battlefield. In desperation, Shakespeare's villainous Richard cried out "A horse, a horse, my kingdom for a horse," but in fact the defeated king seems to have been a much more phlegmatic character. Taking a glass of water before the fighting started, he actually said "I live a king: if I die, I die a king." The battlefield is now organized as a tourist attraction, beginning with the **visitor centre** (March Sat & Sun 11am–5pm; April–Oct daily 11am–5pm; Nov & Dec Sun 11am–dusk; £3), where a fifteen-minute video provides a lively account of the battle and its historical context. From here, a two-mile circular trail explores the battlefield with explanatory plaques filling out the details on the way – and good fun it is, too.

There are hourly **buses** from Leicester to Market Bosworth, from where it's a three-mile walk to the visitor centre along country roads. There are two signed routes – the Shenton route is the more pleasant. There's supposed to be a footpath and it's supposed to be shorter, but it isn't signed, so you'll need the appropriate Ordnance Survey map (Landranger 140). Afterwards, take a **pint** at the traditional *Dixie Arms Hotel*, on the Market Place.

Ashby-de-la-Zouch

ASHBY-DE-LA-ZOUCH, fourteen miles northwest of Leicester, takes its fanciful name from two sources – the town's first Norman overlord was Alain de Parrhoet la Souche and the rest means "place by the ash trees". Nowadays, Ashby is far from rustic, but it's an amiable little place. A short walk off main drag Market Street stands its principal attraction, the **Castle** (April–Oct daily 10am–6pm; Nov–March Wed–Sun 10am–4pm; £3.20; EH). Originally a Norman manor house, the stronghold was the work of Edward IV's chancellor, Lord Hastings, who received his "licence to crenellate" in 1474. But Hastings didn't enjoy his new home for long. Just nine years later, he was dragged from a Privy Council meeting to have his head hacked off on a log by the order of Richard III, his crime being his lacklustre support for the Yorkist cause. Today, the rambling ruins include substantial left-overs from the old fortifications, as well as the shattered remains of the great hall, solar and chapel, but the star turn is the hundred-foot-high **Hastings Tower**, a self-contained four-storey stronghold which has survived in reasonably good nick. This tower house represented the latest thinking in castle design. It provided a secure inner fastness for Hastings and his retinue both against any outside enemy and his own mercenaries – who, experience had shown elsewhere, were often a threat to their employer – and it also provided much better accommodation than was previously available. Improved living quarters reflecting the power and pride of the nobility were built all over England at this time and this is a rare survivor – witness the large windows on the upper floors, accessible via the tower's well-worn spiral staircase.

There are fast and frequent **buses** from Leicester and Nottingham to Ashby and they pull in along Market Street.

Breedon-on-the-Hill

It's five miles northeast from Ashby to the village of **BREEDON-ON-THE-HILL**, which sits in the shadow of the large but partly quarried hill from which it takes its name. A steep footpath and a winding, half-mile lane lead up from the village to the summit, where the fascinating church of **St Mary and St Hardulph** (daily 9.30am–6.30pm or dusk; free) occupies the site of an Iron Age hillfort and an eighth-century Anglo-Saxon monastery. Mostly dating from the thirteenth century, the church is kitted out with Georgian pulpit and pews as well as a large and distinctly rickety box pew. Much rarer are a number of **Anglo-Saxon carvings**, both individual saints and prophets and wall friezes, where a dense foliage of vines is inhabited by a tangle of animals and humans. The friezes are quite extraordinary, and the fact that the figures look Byzantine rather than Anglo-Saxon has fuelled much academic debate. The church has something else too, in the form of a set of fine alabaster tombs occupied by members of the Shirley family, who long ruled the local roost. One is an especially imposing affair with the kneeling family up above and a skeleton down below.

Calke Abbey and Staunton Harold Church

The eighteenth-century facade of **Calke Abbey house** (April–Oct Mon–Wed, Sat & Sun 1–5.30pm; garden same days 11am–5.30pm; £5.60, garden only £3.20; NT) is all self-confidence, its acres of dressed stone and three long lines of windows polished off with an imposing Victorian Greek Revival portico. This all cost oodles of money and the Harpurs and then the Harpur-Crewes, who owned the estate, were doing very well until the economics of the English country estate changed after World War I. Then, at a time when country houses were being demolished by the score, the Harpur-Crewes simply hung on, becoming the epitome of faded gentility and refusing to make all but the smallest of changes to the house – though they did finally plump for electricity in 1962. The last Harpur-Crewe to live here, Charles, died in 1981 and the estate passed in its entirety to the National Trust. Very much to their credit, the Trust decided not to bring in the restorers and have kept the house in its dishevelled state – and this is its real charm.

A visit starts in one of the old agricultural outbuildings, from where it's a short stroll to the **house**, whose Entrance Hall adroitly sets the scene, its walls decorated with ancient and distinctly mothy stuffed heads from the family's herd of prize cattle. Beyond is the Caricature Room, whose walls are lined (up to three or four deep) with satirical cartoons, some of which were executed by the leading cartoonists of their day, including Gillray and Cruikshank. Further on, there are more animal heads and glass cabinets of stuffed birds in the capacious Saloon; an intensely cluttered Miss Havisham-like Drawing Room; a chaotic at-home School Room and, seeming to indicate that eccentricity was a family trait, a state bed given to the Harpurs by the daughter of George II in 1734 and then left packed until the National Trust arrived. It's displayed on its own in one of the first-floor rooms viewable towards the end of the self-guided tour. After you've finished in the house, you can wander out into the **gardens** and pop into the Victorian estate **church**.

There's no public transport to Calke Abbey, and motorists must follow a long-winded one-way system: to get there from Ashby, take the B587 Melbourne Road and follow the signs – the entrance is at the village of Ticknall to the north of the house; the exit is to the south. Back towards Ashby on the B587, spare a little time for **Staunton Harold Church** (April–Sept Wed–Sun 1–5pm; Oct Sat & Sun 1–5pm only; free, but £1 donation requested; NT), a political rant of a building in which the local lord, the reactionary Robert Shirley, expressed his hatred of Oliver Cromwell. There's no missing Shirley's intentions, as he carved them above the church door: "In the year 1653 when all things sacred were throughout the nation either demolished or profaned…" and so he goes on. Whatever the politics, it was certainly an audacious – probably foolhardy – gesture, and sure enough Cromwell had the last laugh when an unrepentant Shirley died in prison three years later. The church itself is a good-looking affair, largely in the Perpendicular style with delightful painted ceilings and wood panelling.

East Leicestershire and Rutland

For the casual visitor at least, there's nothing compelling about **east Leicestershire**, though the scenery is pleasant enough, with open farmland broken up by hills and ridges. Two middling towns are worth a pit-stop here,

Melton Mowbray and **Market Harborough**. Things improve over in neighbouring **Rutland** with a pair of pleasant country towns – **Oakham** and **Uppingham** – and get even better at the postcard-pretty hamlet of **Lyddington**.

Both Melton Mowbray and Stamford are on the Leicester–Peterborough branch line, whilst Market Harborough is on the Leicester–London main line. There are reasonably frequent **buses** to and between all the destinations mentioned above, except Lyddington.

Market Harborough

MARKET HARBOROUGH, fifteen miles southeast of Leicester, is an unassuming provincial town that once prospered from its position at the junction of the turnpike roads to Leicester, Nottingham and London. Consequently, the predominantly Georgian High Street's *Three Swans* and *Angel* hotels were originally coaching inns, and the square and solid old **Town Hall**, opposite the *Three Swans*, was designed to help local traders sell their wares, with butchers on the ground floor and cloth merchants up above. Just off the High Street, the triangular **Market Place** is overlooked by the church of **St Dionysius**, whose striking tower is in stark contrast to the dumpy ironstone nave down below. Here, also, is the **Old Grammar School**, an early-seventeenth-century, half-timbered structure mounted on stilts to protect locals from the rain. From 1908 to 1974, the large Victorian building standing directly behind the grammar school on Adam & Eve Street was a factory owned by the Symington family, who designed the world's best-selling corsets. The factory has been redeveloped and now houses both the council offices and the **town museum** (Mon–Sat 10am–4.30pm, Sun 2–5pm; free), which has a small but intriguing display on Symington corsetry. In particular, look out for the adverts attempting to sell bodices to kids and the 1937 poster advertising the full range of Avro corsets – a mind-boggling selection designed to cover every occasion and eventuality. Market Harborough's **tourist office** (Mon–Fri 9am–5pm & Sat 9.30am–12.30pm; ⓣ01858/821270) is here too.

There are frequent services from Nottingham, London and Leicester to Market Harborough's **train station**, fifteen minutes' walk east of the town centre. More conveniently, **buses** – including services from Melton Mowbray – stop a couple of minutes' walk from the Market Place at the top of Northampton Road, a southerly continuation of the High Street. For **food**, *Aldin's Tea Rooms*, across from St Dionysius, is a spick-and-span café serving tasty homemade food at reasonable prices – main courses average around £3.

Melton Mowbray

MELTON MOWBRAY, some fifteen miles northeast of Leicester, is famous for **pork pies**, an unaccountably popular English snack made (with some honourable exceptions – see below) of compressed balls of meat and gristle encased in wobbly jelly and thick pastry. The pie is the traditional repast of the fox-hunting fraternity, for whom the town of Melton, lying on the boundary of the region's most important hunts – Belvoir, Cottesmore and Quorn – has long been a favourite spot. The antics of some of the aristocratic huntsmen are legend – in 1837 the Marquis of Waterford literally painted the town's buildings red, hence the saying – but with legislation banning blood sports looking imminent, the days of the tally-ho brigade may well be numbered. If you want to sample the genuine traditional hunters' pie, it is available in Melton only at **Dickinson & Morris** (closed Sun), just off the pedestrianized Market Place on Nottingham Street – and a superior product it is too, as are the sausages the same company sells next door.

Most of Melton Mowbray is Victorian or modern red brick, but a brief walk south from the central Market Place stands the medieval church of **St Mary**, distinguished by its impressive size (150ft long, with a tower soaring to over 100ft) and by some of its detail. The clerestory is an especially fine illustration of the Perpendicular style, its 48 windows encircling the church and bathing the interior with a gentle light. The **town museum** (daily 10am–4.30pm; free), five minutes' walk from the Market Place along Sherrard Street, holds small displays on items of local interest: fox hunting, pork pies and so forth. The museum also owns half a dozen paintings by **John Ferneley** (1815–1862), a local artist who made a small fortune selling hunting scenes to the gentry, but unfortunately only one (and it's not his best) is currently on view.

Central **trains** runs frequent services from Leicester to Oakham and Stamford via Melton Mowbray; there are also regular **bus** links between Nottingham, Melton and Oakham. From Melton train station, it's a five-minute walk north to the Market Place, from where the bus station is 300 yards north on St Mary's Way.

Oakham

Some twenty miles east from Leicester and ten southeast of Melton Mowbray, well-heeled **OAKHAM**, Rutland's county town, has a long history as a commercial centre, its prosperity bolstered by Oakham School, a late-sixteenth-century foundation that's become one of the country's more exclusive private schools. The town's stone terraces and Georgian villas are too often interrupted by the mundanely modern to assume much grace, but Oakham does have its architectural moments – particularly in the L-shaped **Market Place**, where a brace of sturdy awnings shelter the old water pump and town stocks. Footsteps from the north side of the Market Place stands **Oakham Castle** (Mon–Sat 10.30am–1pm & 1.30–5pm, Sun 1–5pm; free), comprising a banqueting hall that was originally part of a fortified house dating back to 1191. The hall is a good example of Norman domestic architecture, and inside the whitewashed walls are covered with horseshoes, the result of an ancient custom by which every lord or lady, king or queen, is obliged to present an ornamental horseshoe when they first set foot in the town.

Oakham School is housed in a series of impressive ironstone buildings that frame the west edge of the Market Place. On the right-hand side of the school, a narrow lane allows you to see a little more of the buildings on the way to **All Saints'** church, whose heavy tower and spire rise high above the town. Dating from the thirteenth century, the church is an architectural hybrid, but the airy interior is distinguished by the intense medieval carvings along the columns of the nave and choir, with Christian scenes and symbols set alongside dragons, grotesques, devils and demons. Finally, you could also spare a few minutes for the sizeable **Rutland County Museum**, on Catmose Street (Mon–Sat 10.30am–5pm, Sun 2–4pm; free), a brief signposted walk from the Market Place via the High Street. Here, an assortment of agricultural tools and Rutland County mementoes is enlivened by a lithograph of a disconcertingly huge prize-winning heifer.

Practicalities

With regular services from Leicester, Melton Mowbray and Peterborough, Oakham **train station** lies on the west side of town, five minutes' walk from the Market Place. **Buses** connect the town with – amongst many places – Leicester, Nottingham and Melton Mowbray, and these pull in on John Street, close to – and also west of – the Market Place, just behind the Somerfield supermarket. A thorough exploration of Oakham only takes a couple of hours, but if you do decide to stay the **tourist office** in Victoria Hall, 41 High St (Tues–Sat 11am–3pm; ⓣ01572/724329, ⓦwww.rutnet.co.uk), will help you find **accommodation**. Options include the *Whipper-In Hotel*, on the Market Place (ⓣ01572/756971, ⓦwww.brook-hotels.co.uk; ⑤), whose smartly decorated modern rooms are set behind an attractive old facade, and the more distinctive *Lord Nelson's House Hotel*, just along the street (ⓣ01572/723199, ⓦwww.nelsons-house.com; ⑥), which has a handful of elegant bedrooms, each with its own decorative theme. For **food**, stick to the excellent and affordably priced *Nicks Restaurant*, part of the *Lord Nelson Hotel*, where they serve a tasty modern menu featuring local ingredients. For a **drink**, head off to the *Wheatsheaf*, a traditional pub with a good range of brews across from All Saints' church at 2–4 Northgate.

9 Uppingham

The town of **UPPINGHAM**, six miles south of Oakham, has the uniformity of style Oakham lacks, its narrow, meandering High Street flanked by bow-fronted shops and ironstone houses, mostly dating from the eighteenth century. It's the general appearance that pleases, rather than any individual sight, but the town is famous as the home of **Uppingham School**, a bastion of privilege whose imposing fortress-like building stands at the west end of the High Street. Founded in 1587, the school was distinctly second-rate until the middle of the nineteenth century, when a dynamic headmaster, the Reverend Edward Thring, grabbed enough land to lay out some of the biggest playing-fields in England – fitness being, of course, an essential attribute of the rulers of the British Empire.

Uppingham has one especially good **hotel**, the *Lake Isle*, in a tastefully modernized eighteenth-century town house at 16 High St East (ⓣ01572/822951, ⓦwww.lakeislehotel.com; ⑤). The hotel **restaurant** is outstanding, offering a superb and varied menu from guinea fowl to local venison, with main courses averaging around £14. For a **drink**, head for *The Vaults*, on the minuscule Market Place.

Lyddington

Two miles southeast of Uppingham, **LYDDINGTON** is a sleepy village of honey-hued cottages straggling along a meandering main street, set against a backdrop of plump hills and broken broadleaf woodland. Early in the twelfth century, the Bishop of Lincoln, whose lands once extended south as far as the Thames, chose this as the site of a small palace – one of thirteen he erected to accommodate himself and his retinue while away on episcopal business. Confiscated during the Reformation, **Lyddington Bede House**, overlooked by the ironstone bulk of the church of St Andrew on Church Lane (April–Oct daily 10am–6pm; £3.20; EH), was later converted into almshouses by Lord Burghley and has since been beautifully restored by English Heritage. The highlight is the light and airy Great Chamber, with its exquisitely carved oak cornices, but the attic is intriguing too, its careful lighting setting off the building's sturdy medieval timber frame to best advantage. Look out also for the tiny ground-floor rooms that were occupied by local pensioners and the poor for centuries, and don't forget the immaculate gardens.

Of the village's **pubs**, easily the most convivial is *The Old White Hart* on Main Street (Ⓣ01572/821703), whose beamed ceilings and stone walls date back to the 1600s. There's delicious bar food, and the **restaurant** has main courses averaging around £12 – but note that no food is available on Sunday evenings. Finally, the pub has five en-suite **rooms** (❺), each pleasantly decorated in modern style.

Hallaton

Leicestershire's **HALLATON**, some five miles southwest of Uppingham along winding country lanes, is a pleasant little village, whose High Street is flanked by a fetching medley of buildings, including antique ironstone houses and thatched cottages. However, every Easter Monday the **Hare Pie Scramble and Bottle Kicking** contest disturbs this peaceful scene, when the inhabitants of Hallaton and nearby Medbourne fight for pieces of pie before proceeding to kick small barrels of ale around a hill and across a stream, as has been the custom for several hundred years – though no one has the faintest idea why. The village **museum** (May–Oct Sat & Sun 2.30–5pm; free), on Hog Lane near the minuscule green, does its best to shed some light on the business. For a **pint** and a ploughman's, head for the *Bewicke Arms* beside the green.

Northamptonshire

Northamptonshire is one of the region's most diverse counties – so diverse in fact that even many Midlanders can't recall what is actually in it and what isn't. With justification, its superabundance of stately homes and historic churches enables it to style itself as the "County of Spires and Squires". It also holds a scattering of charming villages, the most picturesque of which, untouched by all but the vaguest sniff of the twentieth century, are built of local limestone. By contrast, however, three of the county's four big towns – Wellingborough, Corby and Kettering – are primarily industrial and whatever charms they offer to their inhabitants, there's not much to attract the regular tourist. Yet the fourth town, **Northampton**, does something to bridge the gap, its busy centre possessed of several fine old buildings and an excellent museum devoted to shoe-making, the industry that has long made the place tick.

Gentle hills, farmland and patchy woodland stretch right across the county with the **A508** forming an easy if arbitrary dividing line between west and east Northamptonshire. The prime target in the former is **Althorp**, family home of the Spencers and the burial place of Diana, Princess of Wales. Runners-up by a long chalk are the Anglo-Saxon church at **Brixworth** and the canalside village of **Stoke Bruerne**. East Northamptonshire's star turn is the good-looking country town of **Oundle**, which makes the best base for visiting the delightful hamlet of **Fotheringhay** and, at a pinch, the overbearing pomp and circumstance of **Boughton House**. The county also has a notable **long-distance footpath**, the seventy-mile Nene Way, which follows the looping course of the river right across the county. Nene Way brochures are available at or from Northampton Tourist Office.

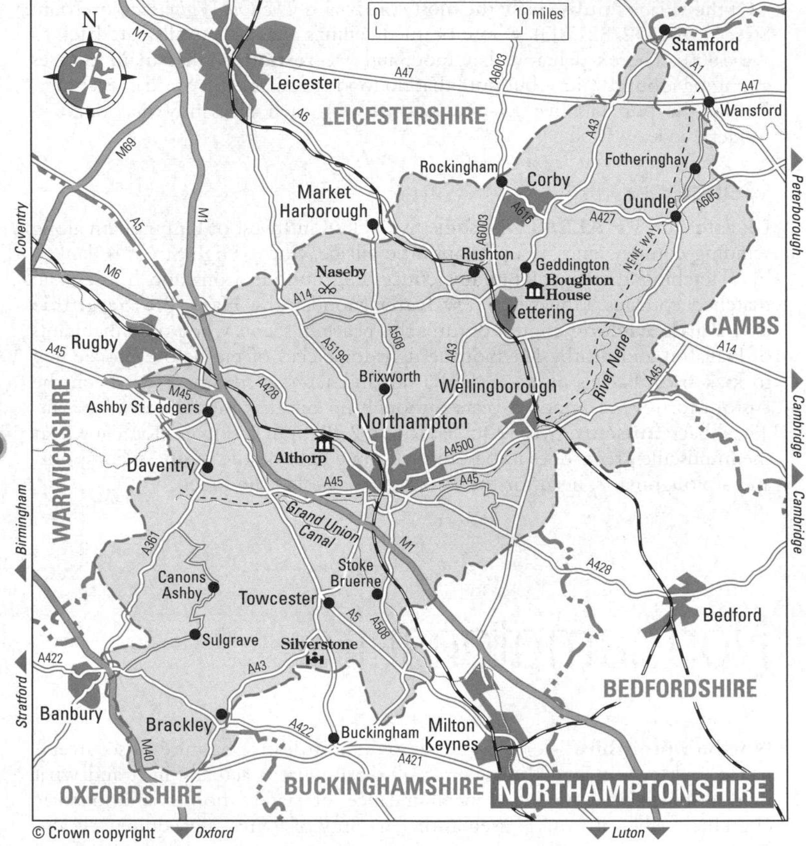

Getting to Northampton by **public transport** is no problem, but to reach the villages and stately homes, you'll mostly need your own vehicle – or some careful planning around patchy bus services.

Northampton

Spreading north from the banks of the River Nene, **NORTHAMPTON** is a workaday modern town whose appearance largely belies its ancient past. Throughout the Middle Ages, this was one of central England's most important towns, a flourishing commercial centre whose now demolished castle was a popular stopping-off point for travelling royalty. A fire in 1675 burnt most of the medieval city to a cinder, and the Georgian town that grew up in its stead was itself swamped by the industrial revolution, when Northampton swarmed with boot- and shoemakers. Their products shod almost everyone in the Empire – from Australia to Canada – as well as the British army, though things did go badly awry during the Crimea War. The army ordered two boat-loads of Northampton boots in preparation for the Russian winter, but – for reasons that remain obscure – insisted that all the left boots be shipped in one vessel, the right ones in another. Unfortunately, one of the boats sank en route – and the soldiers were left perplexed by the ways of the army commissariat. Equally perplexed were the Northampton tailors who had put clothes on the back of Errol Flynn, after he got a start here in repertory in 1933. Always a charmer, Flynn dressed well, but he hightailed it out of town after just a year, leaving a whopping tailor's debt behind him.

Northampton's compact **centre** is at its most appealing on and around its main plaza, Market Square, which is where you'll find the town's finest buildings, notably All Saints' Church and the Guildhall. Half a day is enough for a quick gambol round the sights, but if you're tempted to stay the night there's a reasonable supply of hotel accommodation and a scattering of B&Bs. The only times of the year when finding a room can be difficult are during the annual **Balloon Festival** in August, which attracts thousands of visitors, and over the weekend of the British Grand Prix, held in July at the nearby **Silverstone** race track.

The Town

Northampton's expansive, cobbled **Market Square** has a busy, self-confident air, its sides flanked by a comparatively harmonious mixture of the old and the new. From here, either of a couple of narrow lanes leads through to the church of **All Saints** (Mon–Sat 9am–2pm; free), whose unusually secular appearance stems from its finely proportioned, pillared portico as well as its towered cupola. A statue of a bewigged Charles II in Roman attire surmounts the portico, a (flattering) thank you for his donation of a thousand tons of timber after the Great Fire of 1675 had incinerated the earlier church. Inside, the elegant interior looks more like a ballroom than a church, from the sweep of its timber galleries through to its Neoclassical pillars and a ceiling coated in delicately sculpted plasterwork.

Behind the church is one of Lutyens's less inspiring monuments, a plain, blunt **war memorial** dating from 1926, and, just beyond that, in St Giles' Square, is the **Guildhall**, a flamboyant Victorian edifice constructed in the 1860s to a design by Edward Godwin. Godwin was one of the period's most inventive architects and his Gothic exterior, with its high-pointed windows and dinky turrets and towers, sports kings and queens plus scenes central to the county's history – look out for Mary, Queen of Scots' execution, the Great Fire and the battle of Naseby. Fought a few miles to the north of town in 1645, Naseby was a crucial engagement in the Civil War. It pretty much sealed the fate of King Charles and blooded Parliament's (later Cromwell's) New Model Army, a volunteer force driven by religious conviction (rather than money) that was soon to be the scourge of the Lord Protector's enemies.

The **Northampton Museum and Art Gallery** (Mon–Sat 10am–5pm, Sun 2–5pm; free), a few yards south on Guildhall Road, celebrates the town's industrial heritage with a fabulous collection of **shoes**. Along with silk slippers, clogs and high-heeled nineteenth-century court shoes, there's one of the four boots worn by an elephant during the British Expedition of 1959, which retraced Hannibal's putative route over the Alps into Italy. There's celebrity footwear too – almost inevitably, a pair of Elton John shoes (the giant DMs he wore in *Tommy*) – plus whole cabinets of heavy-duty riding boots, pearl-inlaid raised wooden sandals from Ottoman Turkey and a couple of cabinets showing just how long high heels have been in fashion. Moving on, the next floor up focuses on ceramics, glass and fine art, whilst the top floor is given over to an excellent display charting the town's history from its Roman days to the present, paying particular attention to the significance of the shoe industry, which employed no less than half the town's population in 1920.

Practicalities

From Northampton **train station**, which has regular services to London Euston and Birmingham, it's a ten-minute walk east to the Market Square – just follow the signs. Buses pull into the **bus station** on Lady's Lane, behind the hideous Grosvenor Shopping Centre, immediately to the north of the Market Square; motorists aiming for the centre, should follow the signs for – and park in – the Grosvenor. The **tourist office** (Mon–Sat 10am–5pm, Sun 2–5pm; ⓣ01604/622677, ⓦwww.northampton.gov.uk/tourism) shares premises with the Northampton museum (see above). Staff operate an accommodation-booking service, have oodles of information on the county and issue bus timetables.

Amongst a light scattering of downtown **hotels**, the *Northampton Moat House* is a dependable chain hotel in a large modern block on Silver Street (ⓣ01604/739988, ⓦwww.moathousehotels.com; ❼). More distinctive is the *Lime Trees Hotel*, 8 Langham Place, Barrack Road (ⓣ01604/632188, ⓦwww.limetreeshotel.co.uk; ❺), in pleasant Georgian premises half a mile north from the centre. The pick of the more central **B&Bs** is the *St George's Private Hotel*, 128 St George's Ave (ⓣ01604/792755, ⓦwww.stgeorgeshotel.co.uk; ❷). This attractive place has ten spacious, comfortable en-suite guest rooms and occupies a large Victorian house about a mile and a half from the centre, overlooking Racecourse Park.

A good spot for daytime **snacks** and coffee is *Ask*, opposite the Guildhall on St Giles Square, where you can get pizzas (£5–8) as well as more substantial Italian meals averaging around £7.

West Northamptonshire

The slice of easy countryside that comprises **west Northamptonshire**, falling to the west of the A508, is dotted with stately homes, amongst which the most diverting are **Althorp**, the last resting place of Diana, Princess of Wales, and **Sulgrave Manor**, which has family links with the USA's own George Washington. The area also possesses the canal locks and narrowboats of tiny **Stoke Bruerne**, on the Grand Union Canal, and a rare and fine Saxon church at **Brixworth**. The best of the county's limestone villages lie further to the east, but there is a sprinkling here too, with **Ashby St Ledgers**, not far from Althorp, being an especially picturesque spot.

Brixworth

Located just six miles north of Northampton off the A508, **BRIXWORTH** would be an inconsequential village were it not for **All Saints' Church** (usually open daily 10am–5pm), one of England's finest surviving Anglo-Saxon churches, dating from around 680 AD. From a distance, its most striking feature is its unusual cylindrical stair-turret, added to the western tower in the ninth century as part of a plan to fortify the church against Viking raids. Closer inspection, however, reveals something even rarer. The church is mostly limestone, but scores of Roman tiles, probably salvaged from a nearby villa, frame the windows and doorways, often mortared in at irregular angles. Inside, the uncluttered **nave** is whitewashed except for certain key features, including the **great arch** spanning the nave. Built around 1400, this arch replaced a Saxon wall with three arches that had previously separated the nave from the chancel; look carefully at each end of the later arch and you'll spot the remains of the Saxon stonework. At the far end of the church, the rounded **apse**, modelled on a Roman basilica, was once encased by an ambulatory, but this was closed off during restoration work in the nineteenth century – note the two small and blocked doorways low down on either side of the apse arch. During the refurbishment, the Victorians found fragments of bone, thought to be St Boniface's larynx, buried under the apse. The bones were Brixworth's most important reliquary and they may well have been hidden here for safekeeping when Viking raids were at their peak. On the south side of the chancel, a brightly painted wooden screen guards the **Lady Chapel**, built in the thirteenth century by a local baron, Sir John de Verdun. His badly weathered stone effigy lies in a recess in the south wall, with legs crossed and his suit of chain mail just about decipherable.

Althorp

Some six miles northwest of Northampton off the A428, the ritzy mansion of **Althorp** is the focus of the Spencer estate. The Spencers have lived here for centuries, but this was no big deal until one of the tribe, **Diana**, married Prince Charles in 1981. The disintegration of the marriage and Diana's elevation to sainthood is a story known to millions – and most perceptively analysed by B. Campbell in her book, *Diana, Princess of Wales: How Sexual Politics Shook the Monarchy*. The public outpouring of grief following Diana's death in 1997 was quite astounding, and Althorp became the focus of massive media attention as the coffin was brought up the M1 motorway from London to be buried on an island in the grounds of the family estate. Today, visitors troop round the **Diana exhibition**, in the old stable block, as well as the adjacent Althorp house, where there's a large collection of priceless paintings, including works by Gainsborough, Van Dyck and Rubens. From the house, a footpath leads round a lake in the middle of which is the islet (no access) on which Diana is buried. The estate is open from July to September (daily 10am–2pm & 1–5pm, last admission 4pm; £10.50 in advance, £11.50 on the gate; ⓣ0870/167 9000, ⓦwwww.visitalthorp.com) and advance reservations are strongly advised.

There are no scheduled **buses** from Northampton to Althorp, but there are sometimes special coaches – contact Northampton tourist office for details.

Ashby St Ledgers

The Gunpowder Plot, which so dismally failed to blow the Houses of Parliament to smithereens in 1605, was hatched in **ASHBY ST LEDGERS**, immediately to the west of the M1 off the A361, about seven miles northwest of Althorp. Since those heated conversations, nothing much seems to have happened here, and the village's one and only street, flanked by handsome limestone cottages and a patch of ancient grazing land, still leads to the conspiratorial **manor house** (no access), a beautiful Elizabethan complex set around a wide courtyard. The adjacent **church**, dedicated to St Mary and St Leodegarius (hence Ledger), looks a little stodgy, but its modest fourteenth-century stonework holds some wonderful, if faded, medieval **murals**. Those above and to the side of the rood loft depict the Passion of Christ, from Palm Sunday onwards, but the clearest is the large painting in the nave of St

The Gunpowder Plot

Born in York, **Guy Fawkes** (1570–1606) was a young convert to Catholicism, and his enthusiasm for the old faith induced him to leave Elizabeth I's Protestant England to fight in the Spanish army – against the "heretics" of the Netherlands – in 1593. There he established a reputation as a brave and determined soldier, catching the eye of leading Catholics back home. Cowed by Elizabeth for decades, these same Catholics viewed the queen's death, in 1603, and the accession of **James I** with some optimism, but their hopes were dashed when the new king proved unsympathetic to the Catholic cause. A small group, under the leadership of one **Robert Catesby**, decided that this called for desperate measures and, keen to recruit a military man, one of them popped over to the Netherlands to seek out Fawkes, who signed up and returned to England like a shot. The plan was simple – almost amazingly so: first the conspirators rented a cellar under Parliament and then Fawkes filled it with barrels of gunpowder, enough to blow Parliament sky high. But on November 4, 1605, the eve of the planned attack, the authorities discovered this so-called **Gunpowder Plot** and poor old Fawkes was promptly tortured into giving away the names of his co-conspirators. Fawkes was tried and executed in January 1606, but he is burnt in effigy all over the country on **Bonfire Night**, November 5.

Christopher carrying the infant Jesus. Tradition asserts that St Christopher was a giant of a man, who earned his living carrying travellers across a river. He did, however, fail in his attempt to carry Jesus, who became impossibly heavy – as in Jesus taking on the sins of the world; Christopher became a Christian and was later installed as the patron saint of travellers.

For a **drink**, the *Olde Coach Inn*, at the start of the village, is a delightful country **pub** with a good range of ales and food.

Canons Ashby and Sulgrave

Heading south from Ashby St Ledgers on the A361, follow the road round **Daventry** and then, after a few miles more, watch for the signed turning that leads east along narrow country lanes to the pleasant little limestone village of **CANONS ASHBY**. This is another quiet spot, deep in the country, and it possesses one of the region's finest Elizabethan manor houses, **Canons Ashby House** (April–Oct Mon–Wed, Sat & Sun 1–5.30pm; £5.40; NT). The Drydens (as in John Dryden) have owned the property since its construction, and by and large they have respected its architectural integrity, though one of the clan did muck up the exterior by adding an incongruous peel tower. The main event is, however, the interior, which sports rare Elizabethan wall paintings and decorative Jacobean plasterwork of extraordinarily florid design. The neighbouring **church** is all that remains of the twelfth-century Augustinian priory after which the house is named.

As the crow flies, it's only a couple of miles south from Canons Ashby to tiny **SULGRAVE**, but the route is positively baffling, cutting between a maze of country lanes – so be sure to follow the signs carefully. Sulgrave itself hardly sets the pulse racing, but it is home to **Sulgrave Manor**, a neat stone country house built by an ancestor of George Washington – his seven times great-grandfather to be precise (guided tours: April–Oct Tues–Thurs, Sat & Sun 2–5.30pm, last admission 4.30pm; £5). The house remained in the family until 1656, when Colonel John, great-grandfather of the American president, set sail for the New World and settled in Virginia. George Washington never visited Sulgrave, but nevertheless the place has taken on the air of a shrine to American democracy and the interior holds a small museum charting George's remarkable career. The best features of the building are the Great Hall, with its low-beamed ceiling, flagstones and huge fireplace, and the kitchen, set around an ancient hearth hung with copper pots and pans.

Stoke Bruerne

Heading south out of Northampton on the A508, it's about seven miles to the village of **STOKE BRUERNE**, which profits from its location beside a flight of seven locks on the Grand Union Canal. By water at least, the village is also very close to England's longest navigable tunnel, the one and three quarter miles' long Blisworth Tunnel, constructed at the beginning of the nineteenth century. Before the advent of steam tugs in the 1870s, boats were pushed through the tunnel by "legging" – two or more men would push with their legs against the tunnel walls until they emerged to hand over to waiting teams of horses. This exhausting task is fully explained in the village's excellent **Canal Museum** (daily: Easter–Oct 10am–5pm; Nov–Easter Tues–Sun 10am–4pm; £3), housed in a converted canalside corn mill. The museum records two hundred years of canal history with models, exhibits of canal art and spit-and-polish engines. It also houses the cabin of a butty boat, a showcase for the painted crockery and embroidery of canal families.

There are two good places to **eat** near the museum – the moderately priced *Bruernes Lock Restaurant* and the *Old Chapel Tea Rooms*, the latter featuring snacks and meals with a Mediterranean slant as well as displays of local art work. Over the canal bridge, there's also the *Boat Inn* **pub**, well stocked with narrowboat trinkets. Finally, both the Stoke Bruerne Boat Company (ⓣ01604/862107) and the Indian Chief (ⓣ01604/862428) offer **narrowboat cruises** through the tunnel (2hr; £5) as well as longer excursions. It is best to book ahead, but you can turn up on spec, and in the summertime there are several departures weekly.

East Northamptonshire

The River Nene wriggles and worms its way across **east Northamptonshire** – that part of the county east of the A508 – passing through a string of little villages and towns, amongst which **Oundle** is by far the most diverting. Within easy striking distance of Oundle is the historic hamlet of **Fotheringhay** and several country houses – hilltop **Rockingham Castle** is the most dramatic, **Boughton House** the richest. Spare time also for the eccentric Catholicism of the Triangular Lodge in **Rushton**.

Oundle

Arguably Northamptonshire's prettiest town, pocket-sized **OUNDLE** slopes up gently from the River Nene, its congregation of old limestone houses zeroing in on the congenial **Market Place**. Preserving much of its medieval layout, Oundle boasts some of the finest seventeenth- and eighteenth-century streetscapes in the Midlands, and is a suitably exclusive setting for one of England's better-known private schools, **Oundle School**, which has been running since 1556 and owns many of the town's most prized buildings. Above all it's the general appearance of the place that appeals rather than anything in particular, the exception being the parish church of **St Peter**, whose magnificent two-hundred-foot Decorated spire soars high above the centre, though the interior – give or take the odd stained-glass window – is unremarkable.

Buses from Peterborough and Northampton stop on the Market Place, a short walk from the **tourist office**, at 14 West St (Easter–Aug Mon–Sat 9am–5pm, Sun 1–4pm; Sept–Easter closed Sun; Ⓣ01832/274333). They issue maps and bus timetables, have comprehensive details of local attractions and operate an **accommodation** service. One recommendable place to stay is the *Talbot Hotel*, just along from the Market Place on New Street (Ⓣ01832/273621, Ⓦwww.oldenglish.co.uk; ❻). This hotel dates from 1626 and comes complete with what is thought to be the very oak staircase Mary, Queen of Scots used on her way to her execution at Fotheringhay Castle (see below). Apparently the queen's executioner stayed at the *Talbot* and both his and Mary's ghost are said to wander the upper floor. For somewhere less expensive, head for the immaculate *Ashworth House*, a modest little stone house with two en-suite guest rooms, five minutes' walk from the Market Place at 75 West St (Ⓣ01832/275312, Ⓦwww.ashworthhouse.co.uk; ❷). The best place to **eat** is at the *Talbot*, unless you want a takeaway or picnic, in which case *Trendalls* (closed Sun), on the Market Place, is just dandy for baguettes and sandwiches of all descriptions.

Fotheringhay

Nestling by the River Nene just four miles northeast of Oundle, the tiny hamlet of **FOTHERINGHAY** has long been left to its own devices, but its medieval heyday is recalled by its magnificent church of **St Mary and All Saints** (dawn–dusk; free), rising mirage-like above the green riverine meadows. Begun in 1411 and a hundred and fifty years in the making, the church is a paradigm of the Perpendicular, its exterior sporting wonderful arching buttresses, its nave lit by soaring windows and the whole caboodle topped by a splendid octagonal lantern tower. The interior is a tad bare, but there are two fancily carved medieval pieces to look for – a painted pulpit and a sturdy stone font. On either side of the altar are the tombs of Elizabeth I's ancestors, the dukes of York, Edward and Richard. Elizabeth found the tombs in disarray in 1573 and promptly had them rebuilt in a smooth white limestone that still looks like new.

Fotheringhay **castle** witnessed two key events – the birth of Richard III in 1452 and the beheading of Mary, Queen of Scots in 1587. On the orders of Elizabeth I, Mary was executed in the castle's Great Hall with no one to stand in her defence – apart, that is, from her dog, who is said to have rushed from beneath her skirts as her head dropped off. Not long afterwards, the castle fell into disrepair and nowadays only a grassy **mound** and ditch remain to mark its position; it's signposted down a short and narrow lane on the bend of the road as you come into the village from Oundle.

Fotheringhay has an excellent **pub-restaurant**, *The Falcon* (Ⓣ01832/226254), in a neat stone building with modern patio, and offering a delicious and imaginative menu – lamp chump and artichoke for example – with main courses averaging around £10.

Rockingham Castle

It's only eleven miles west from Oundle, but the best approach to **ROCKINGHAM** village is actually from the north with the A6003 (from Oakham, see p.735) shooting up the hill, limestone cottages to either side and the castle looming up above. The original **Rockingham Castle** (April, May, June &

Sept Sun 1–5pm, July & Aug Tues, Thurs & Sun 1–5pm; £6) was built by William the Conqueror and it remained in royal hands for five centuries, substantially redesigned on several occasions. A long line of Watsons has owned the place ever since, turning it into an opulent private residence. Today, the castle incorporates bits and pieces from several periods – including Edward I's gatehouse – but is mostly Tudor, a handsome, honey-coloured brick-and-stone complex whose highlight is the timber-beamed **Great Hall**, with grand fireplaces and trellised windows.

Geddington and Boughton House

When Queen Eleanor, cherished wife of Edward I, died in 1290 at Harby, near Lincoln, her embalmed body was carried in state to Westminster Abbey, and a memorial built at each resting point of the cortège. The most complete of the three surviving monuments graces the centre of **GEDDINGTON**, a sprawling village about twelve miles southwest of Oundle beside the A43 between Corby and Kettering. Mounted on a stepped platform, this sumptuously carved **Eleanor Cross** stands like a spire, culminating in a cluster of points above three figures of Eleanor, overlooking the village she had stayed in when accompanying Edward on his royal hunting trips.

From Geddington, a country road leads the one mile southeast to the grandest of Northamptonshire's stately homes, **Boughton House** (Aug daily 2–4.30pm; grounds May–July Mon–Thurs, Sat & Sun 1–5pm, Aug daily 1–5pm; house & grounds £6; grounds only £1.50, free for disabled visitors). This pompous pile is the centre of an eleven-thousand-acre estate that incorporates five villages and has been owned by the dukes of Buccleuch and their ancestors, the Montagus, for five hundred years. The core of the house was originally a monastery, bought by Sir Edward Montagu in 1528 and enlarged by successive generations. Ralph, First Duke of Montagu, who claimed descent from William the Conqueror, made the grandest extensions in the 1690s when he added the arcaded north front. Ambassador to France, Ralph borrowed freely from French design and employed French artists and architects to glorify his mansion, earning the house the nickname "the English Versailles"; he also bought London's Mortlake tapestry factory so he could have the best works for his home.

The house is stuffed with the baubles and bangles of the landed aristocracy. Highlights include paintings by Gainsborough, Raphael and El Greco, a wonderful set of Baroque painted ceilings by Louis Chéron, no less than forty delicate oil sketches by Van Dyck, an extensive collection of swords, pistols and armour, and fine silverware, antique furniture, tapestries and porcelain.

Kettering–Corby **buses** pass through Geddington every couple of hours (not Sun).

Rushton

Five miles west of Geddington, reached along country roads and occupying a solitary location just to the west of the village of **RUSHTON**, is the weird and wonderful **Triangular Lodge** of 1597 (April–Oct daily 10am–6pm; £2; EH). It was built by Thomas Tresham, a determined Catholic whose refusal to accept England's Protestant reforms got him fined and banged up in prison. After his release, Tresham expressed his religious fervour architecturally with this ingenious building, whose triangular construction celebrates the Trinity – Father, Son and Holy Ghost. Made of limestone and ironstone to give a striped effect, each of the three sides is 33ft long, with three windows and three gables, and even the central chimney topping the three storeys is triangular. Only two of the six date stones around the lodge are "true" – his release from prison in 1593, and the construction of the lodge in 1595. The rest form an outlandish arithmetical puzzle: subtracting 1593 from the other figures gives the dates of the Crucifixion, the Virgin Mary's death, the Great Flood and the traditional date of the world's creation, 3962 BC. The entrance on "God's" side leads inside, where the whitewashed walls are only interrupted by incised crosses and triangular windows.

Lincolnshire

The obvious place to start a visit to **Lincolnshire** is **Lincoln** itself, an old and easy-paced city where the cathedral, the third largest church in England, remains the county's outstanding attraction. Northeast and east of here, the Lincolnshire **Wolds** band the county, their gentle green hills harbouring the pleasant market town of **Louth**, where conscientious objectors were sent to dig potatoes during World War II. In this vicinity also is **Woodhall Spa**, a former Edwardian resort of studied gentility that served as the base of the Dambusters as they prepared for their Ruhr raid in 1943. The Wolds are flanked by the coast, so different from the rest of Lincolnshire, its brashness encapsulated by the mega resort of **Skegness**, though there are unspoilt stretches, too, most notably at the **Gibraltar Point Nature Reserve**.

Beguiling **Stamford**, in the southwest corner of the county, is an alternative base, an attractive town where the narrow streets are flanked by a handsome ensemble of antique stone buildings, and next door stands one of the great monuments of Elizabethan England, **Burghley House**. From Stamford, it's a short hop east into **The Fens**, whose most diverting villages lie along the A17, a road that runs close to the old fenland port of **Boston**, now Lincolnshire's second town. On any tour of the Fens you'll pass some of the county's most imposing medieval **churches**. Several are worth a special visit, especially **St Botolph's** in Boston, **St Andrew's** in Heckington and **St Mary Magdalen's** in Gedney – seen to best advantage, like all the other churches of this area, in the pale, watery sunlight of the fenland evening. The other chief town of southern Lincolnshire is careworn **Grantham**, birthplace of Margaret Thatcher and the site of its own splendid medieval church.

Getting around Lincolnshire by public transport can be difficult. Lincoln is the hub of the county's limited **rail** network, with regular services south to Sleaford and Spalding and east via Sleaford to Heckington, Boston and Skegness. There are also links northwest to Gainsborough and west to Grantham and Newark, in Nottinghamshire, both of which are on the main line from London to the Northeast. In addition, there are reasonable **bus** services between Lincoln and the county's larger market towns, like Louth and Boston, but amongst the villages you'll be struggling without your own transport. This is especially true as many of these villages are long and straggly, built along slight ridges as a precaution against flooding.

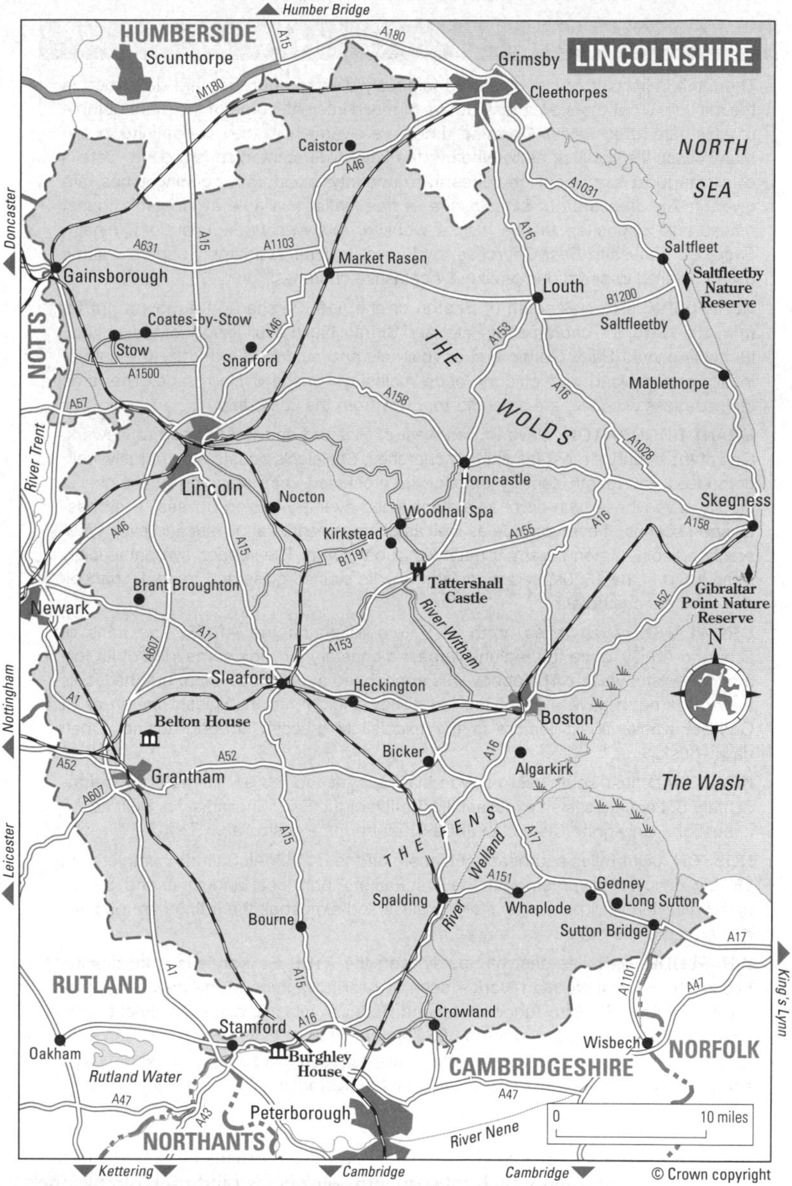

Humber Bridge
HUMBERSIDE
Scunthorpe
LINCOLNSHIRE
Grimsby
Cleethorpes
A180
A15
M180
Caistor
A46
NORTH
SEA
A1031
A16
Doncaster
A631
A1103
Market Rasen
Saltfleet
Saltfleetby Nature Reserve
Gainsborough
Louth
B1200
Saltfleetby
NOTTS
Coates-by-Stow
Stow
Snarford
A1500
THE
WOLDS
A153
Mablethorpe
A57
A158
River Trent
A1028
Horncastle
Lincoln
Nocton
Woodhall Spa
Skegness
Kirkstead
A155
A158
A46
A15
B1191
Tattershall Castle
Gibraltar Point Nature Reserve
Brant Broughton
Newark
River Witham
A52
A17
A607
A153
N
Nottingham
Sleaford
Heckington
A1
Belton House
Boston
Bicker
A52
A16
Algarkirk
Grantham
The Wash
A607
THE FENS
A15
Leicester
River Welland
A17
A151
Gedney
Long Sutton
Spalding
Whaplode
Bourne
Sutton Bridge
A17
King's Lynn
A1101
A47
RUTLAND
A1
A15
Crowland
A16
Stamford
Wisbech
NORFOLK
Oakham
Burghley House
CAMBRIDGESHIRE
Rutland Water
A47
A47
A43
Peterborough
0
10 miles
NORTHANTS
River Nene
Kettering
Cambridge
Cambridge
© Crown copyright

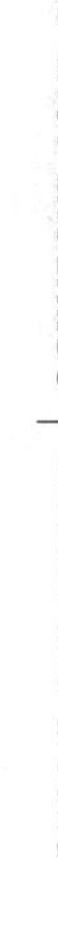

Lincoln and around

Reaching high into the sky from the top of a steep hill, the triple towers of the mighty cathedral of **LINCOLN** are visible for miles across the flatlands. This conspicuous spot was first fortified by the Celts, who called their settlement Lindon, "hillfort by the lake", a reference to the pools formed by the River

Lincolnshire churches

The most important of Lincolnshire's famously diverse **churches** are described in the main text, but there are many others of much interest, some of the more notable of which are listed below. **Opening times** are given where they are definite, but in many cases it's pot luck as to whether the key holder/custodian is around. Details of all the most significant churches in the county, along with opening times, are given in *The Treasures of Lincolnshire*, a free leaflet available at Lincoln's tourist offices (see opposite); there's also a website, ⓦwww.churchtourism.org. Finally, *England's Thousand Best Churches*, by Simon Jenkins, is a simply superb volume giving detailed descriptions of sixty Lincolnshire churches.

ALGARKIRK, six miles south of Boston on the A16. Perched on a mound not far from The Wash, the church of St Peter and St Paul has the full flavour of the fenland, its richly carved Early Gothic arches, capitals and arcades funded by the sale of locally grown woad and chicory, once mainstays of the dyeing trade. The large stained-glass windows are splendid too. Key from the custodian.

BRANT BROUGHTON, eleven miles west of Sleaford on the A17 road to Newark. One of the county's most fascinating churches, St Helen's boasts a supremely well-composed, fourteenth-century exterior, its crocketed spire standing guard over a stocky nave whose twin porches are enlivened by finely carved bosses. The bosses sport scenes of everyday life as well as phantasmagorical beasts and even irreverent cameos – among them, a man with a bare bum. The interior, sympathetically remodelled in the 1870s, is distinguished by its stained glass and tranquil chancel. Key from the custodian.

CROWLAND, seven miles north of Peterborough on the A1073. The ruins of Croyland Abbey, once the region's largest monastery, provide some idea of its former power and wealth. The abbey was abandoned at the Dissolution, but the locals turned the north nave aisle of the old abbey church into the parish church of St Guthlac, whose finest feature is the exquisitely graceful ribbed vaulting. Open dawn–dusk.

KIRKSTEAD, just southwest of Woodhall Spa off the B1191. Remote thirteenth-century St Leonard's is an excellent illustration of the Early English style. Built as the chapel of a long-gone Cistercian abbey. Key from the custodian.

NOCTON, eight miles southeast of Lincoln off the B1188. All Saints', completed in 1872, was built to commemorate the First Earl of Ripon, local landowner and, briefly, prime minister. Wall paintings, stained glass and almost all the fittings are original. Key from the custodian.

WHAPLODE, six miles east of Spalding on the A151. St Mary's is a fascinating hybrid, the original Norman work - seen at best advantage in the nave - supplemented by Early English, Tudor, Stuart and Georgian bits and pieces. Its finest monument is the brightly painted tomb of Sir Anthony Irby, a local MP and Puritan supporter of Oliver Cromwell. The five mourners represent his sons, all of whom did a stretch in the Parliamentary army. Key from the custodian.

Witham in the marshy ground below. In 47 AD the Romans occupied Lindon and built a fortified town which subsequently became, as Lindum Colonia, one of the four regional capitals of Roman Britain.

Today, only fragments of the Roman city survive, mostly pieces of the third-century town wall, and these are outdone by reminders of Lincoln's medieval heyday, which began during the reign of William the Conqueror with the building of the **castle** and **cathedral**. Lincoln flourished, first as a Norman power-base and then as a centre of the wool trade with Flanders, until 1369, when the wool market was transferred to neighbouring Boston. It was almost five hundred years before the town revived, the recovery based upon its manufacture of agricultural machinery and drainage equipment for the fenlands. As the nineteenth-century town spread south down the hill and out along the old Roman road – the Fosse Way – so Lincoln became a place of precise class distinctions: the "**Uphill**" area, spreading north from the cathedral, became synonymous with middle-class respectability, "**Downhill**" with the proletariat. It's a distinction that remains – locals selling anything from second-hand cars to settees still put "Uphill" in brackets to signify a better quality of merchandise.

For the visitor, almost everything of interest is confined to the "Uphill" part of town, and it's here also you'll find the best **pubs** and **restaurants**. In addition, within easy striking distance of Lincoln by car stand several fascinating **churches**: to the northeast, there's Snarford church, to the northwest two more, one at Coates-by-Stow, the other at Stow. In this direction too is the rare **Old Hall** at Gainsborough.

Arrival and information

Both Lincoln's **train station**, on St Mary's Street, and its **bus station**, close by off Norman Street, are located "Downhill" in the city centre. From either, it's a very steep, twenty-minute walk to the cathedral, which can also be reached on the city's **Walk & Ride bus** service (Mon–Sat 10am–5pm & Sun noon–5pm; 3 hourly; 70p each way) – the nearest stop to the bus and train stations is at the junction of Mint and Silver streets. There are two **tourist offices**. One is in the shopping centre on Cornhill, close to the train and bus stations (Mon–Thurs 9.30am–5.30pm, Fri 9.30am–5pm, Sat 10am–5pm; ⓣ01522/873256, ⓦwww.lincoln.gov.uk); the other is at 9 Castle Hill, between the cathedral and the castle (Mon–Thurs 9.30am–5.30pm, Fri 9.30am–5pm, Sat & Sun 10am–5pm; ⓣ01522/873213, same website). Both have a useful range of literature on Lincoln and its surroundings, take bookings for guided tours of the city, and operate an accommodation-booking service.

Accommodation

Lincoln has a good supply of competitively priced **hotels** and **B&Bs**, though surprisingly few of them are in the vicinity of the cathedral – "Uphill" – and this is precisely where you want to be. All the places below are "Uphill," unless otherwise indicated. On occasion, demand can exceed supply, in which case head for the tourist office.

Hotels, guest houses and B&Bs

Carline Guest House 1–3 Carline Rd ⓣ01522/530422, ⓦwww.carlineguesthouse.co.uk. One of the best B&Bs in the city, *Carline* occupies a spick-and-span Edwardian house about ten minutes' walk down from the cathedral – take Drury Lane from in front of the castle and keep going. Breakfasts are first-rate, and the rooms smart and tastefully furnished. No credit cards. ❷

D'Isney Place Hotel Eastgate ⓣ01522/538881, ⓦwww.disneyplacehotel.co.uk. This delightful hotel occupies a lovely eighteenth-century building close to the cathedral. Breakfast is served in the bedrooms, some of which have four-poster beds and spa baths. Highly recommended. ❺

Edward King House The Old Palace, Minster Yard ⓣ01522/528778, ⓦekhs.org.uk. For something a little different, head for this unusual B&B in a former residence of the bishops of Lincoln, immediately below the cathedral. The exterior is a good bit grander than the rooms, but these are perfectly adequate and some have fine views over the city. ❷

Hillcrest Hotel 15 Lindum Terrace ⓣ01522/510182, ⓦwww.hillcrest-hotel.com. Traditional, very English hotel in a large red-brick house that was originally a Victorian rectory. Sixteen comfortable rooms with all mod cons plus a large, sloping garden. The owner, who is often in attendance, has loads of ideas about what to visit. About ten minutes' walk from the cathedral: go

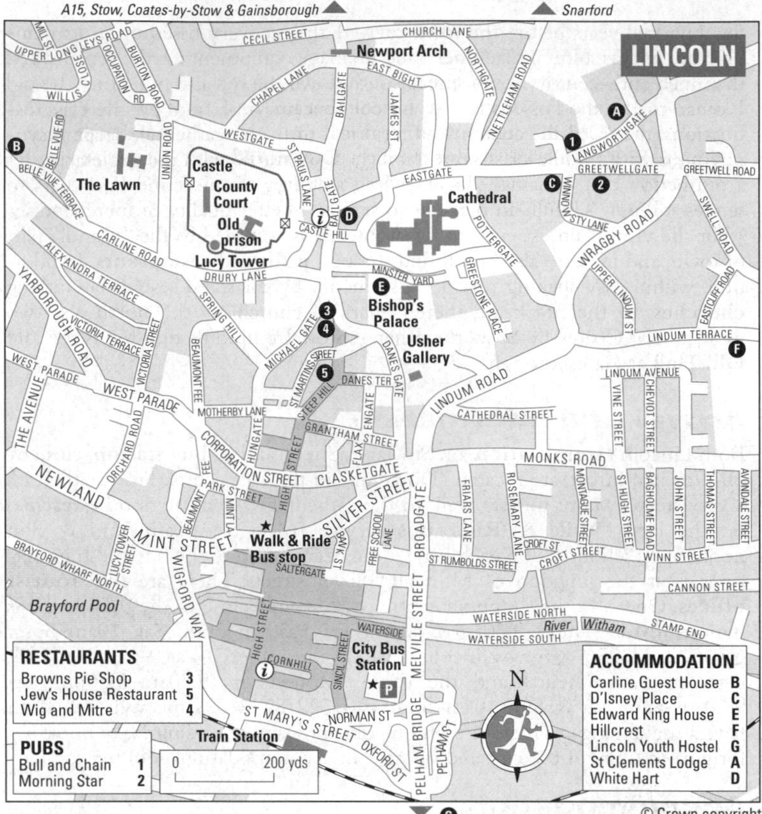

down Pottergate, turn right onto Wragby Rd and then almost immediately turn left onto Lindum Terrace. 5

St Clements Lodge 21 Langworth Gate ☎01522/521532. In a brisk, modern house a short walk from the cathedral, this comfortable B&B offers a handful of pleasant, en-suite guest rooms. To get there, follow Eastgate east from beside the cathedral. No credit cards. 3

White Hart Hotel Bailgate ☎0870/400 8117, www.macdonaldhotels.co.uk. Antique former coaching inn with charming public rooms, all hidden nooks and crannies. The bedrooms beyond are not as distinctive, but they're comfortable enough and many of them overlook the cathedral. Great Uphill location. One of the Macdonald chain. Weekend deals can slash the normal price. 7

Hostel

Lincoln Youth Hostel 77 South Park ☎0870/770 5918, lincoln@yha.org.uk. The town's YHA hostel occupies a Victorian house beside South Common park, one mile south of the train station. There are 46 rooms that sleep two (1), as well as dorms with up to eight beds (£10.25 per bed). To get there from the centre, head south along Canwick Rd and South Park is on the right opposite the cemetery. Closed Nov–Jan.

The Cathedral

Not a hill at all, **Castle Hill** is a wide, short and level cobbled street that links Lincoln's castle and cathedral. It's a charming spot and its east end is marked by the arch of the medieval **Exchequergate**, beyond which soars the glorious west front of **Lincoln Cathedral** (daily: May–Sept 7.15am–8pm, Oct–April

Guided tours of Lincoln cathedral

Monday through Saturday, the cathedral offers two sorts of **guided tour** free with the price of admission. The first – the **Floor Tour** (Mon–Sat 1–2 daily) – is a quick gambol round the cathedral's salient features, while the second, the **Roof Tour** (Mon–Sat 2–3 daily), takes in parts of the church otherwise out of bounds. Both are very popular, so it's a good idea to book in advance – call ⓣ01522/544544 or see ⓦwww.lincolncathedral.com.

7am–6pm, except during services when access is restricted; £4 including guided tour – see box above), a sheer cliff-face of blind arcading mobbed by decorative carving. Most striking of all is the extraordinary band of twelfth-century carved panels which depict biblical themes with passionate intimacy, their inspiration being a similar frieze at Modena cathedral in Italy. The west front's apparent homogeneity is, however, deceptive, and further inspection reveals two phases of construction – the small stones and thick mortar of much of the facade belong to the original church, completed in 1092, whereas the longer stones and finer courses date from the early thirteenth century. These were enforced modifications, for in 1185 an earthquake shattered much of the Norman church, which was then rebuilt under the auspices of **Bishop Hugh of Avalon**, the man responsible for most of the present cathedral, with the notable exception of the (largely) fourteenth-century central tower.

The cavernous **interior** is a fine example of Early English architecture, with the nave's pillars conforming to the same general design yet differing slightly, their varied columns and bands of dark Purbeck marble contrasting with the oolitic limestone that is the building's main material. Looking back up the nave from beneath the central tower, you can also observe a major medieval cock-up: Bishop Hugh's roof is out of alignment with the earlier west front, and the point where they meet has all the wrong angles. It's possible to pick out other irregularities, too – the pillars have bases of different heights, and there are ten windows in the nave's north wall and nine in the south – but these are deliberate features, reflecting a medieval aversion to the vanity of symmetry. Also medieval is the use of pre-Christian imagery, especially on and around the rood screen at the top of the nave, where there's a veritable menagerie of demons and gargoyles peering out of the foliage.

Beyond the rood screen lies **St Hugh's Choir**, its fourteenth-century misericords carrying an eccentric range of carvings, with scenes from the life of Alexander the Great and King Arthur mixed up with biblical characters and folkloric parables. Further on is the open and airy Gothic **Angel Choir**, completed in 1280, dotted with stone table-tombs and its roof embellished by dozens of finely carved statuettes, including the tiny Lincoln Imp (see p.754). Finally, a corridor off the choir's north aisle leads to the wooden-roofed **cloisters** and the polygonal **chapter house**, where Edward I and Edward II convened gatherings that pre-figured the creation of the English Parliament.

Hidden behind a wall immediately below (and to the south of) the cathedral on Minster Yard are the ruins of what would, in its day, have been the city's most impressive building. This, the medieval **Bishop's Palace** (April–Oct daily 10am–6pm; Nov–March Sat & Sun 10am–4pm; £3.20; EH), once consisted of two grand halls, a lavish chapel, kitchens and ritzy private chambers, but today the most coherent survivor is the battered and bruised Alnwick Tower – where the entrance is. The damage was done during the Civil War when a troupe of Roundheads occupied the palace until they themselves had to evacuate the

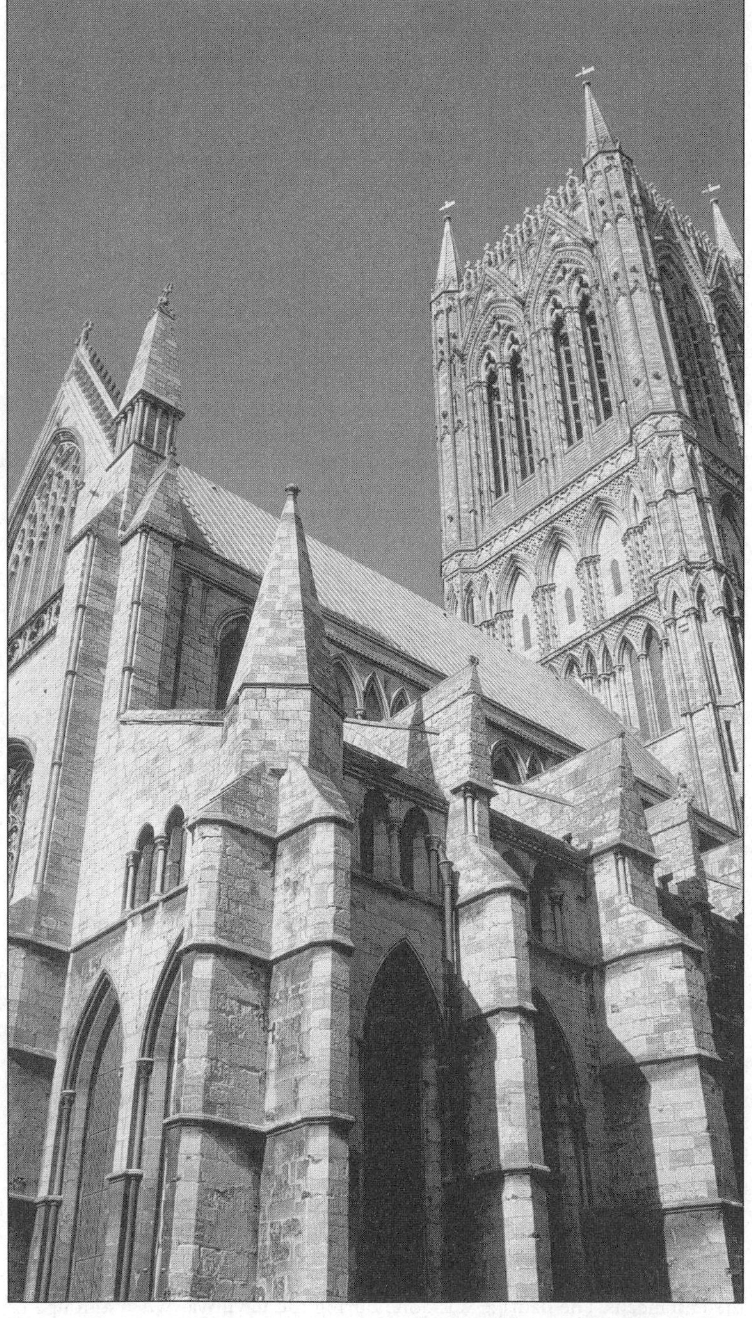

△ Lincoln Cathedral

place after a fierce fire. Nonetheless, the ruins are suitably fetching, with wide views over the surrounding flatlands. The adjoining gardens are immaculate, and abut an elevated terrace holding one of Europe's most northern vineyards.

The Castle

From the west front of the cathedral, it's a quick stroll across Castle Hill to **Lincoln Castle** (April–Sept Mon–Sat 9.30am–5.30pm, Sun 11am–5.30pm; Oct–March Mon–Sat 9.30am–4pm, Sun 11am–4pm; £3.50). Intact and forbidding, the castle walls incorporate bits and pieces from the twelfth to the nineteenth century and the wall walkway offers great views over town. The earliest remains are those of the **Lucy Tower**, built on the steep grassy mound to the left of the main entrance and once the site of one of the two original Norman mottes. The castle was turned into a prison in the 1820s and some of the prisoners were unceremoniously buried here at the top of the mound – a sad and lonely spot if ever there was one, especially as the tombs were only allowed to carry the prisoners' initials. The spacious grounds enclosed by the castle walls hold the old **prison**, a dour red-brick structure with multiple turrets that holds one of the four surviving copies of the **Magna Carta** (see p.1121) as well as a truly remarkable **prison chapel**. Here, the prisoners were locked in high-sided cubicles, where they could see the preacher and his pulpit but not their fellow internees. Neither was this approach just applied to chapel visits: the prisoners were kept in perpetual solitary confinement, and were compelled to wear masks when they took to the exercise yard. This system was founded on the pseudo-scientific theory that defined crime as a contagious disease, but unfortunately for the theorists, their so-called Pentonville System of "Separation and Silence", which was introduced here in 1846, drove many prisoners crazy, and it had to be abandoned thirty years later; nobody ever bothered to dismantle the chapel.

Leaving the castle via the west gate, you reach **The Lawn**, formerly a lunatic asylum and now a leisure complex incorporating – among several modest attractions – the **Sir Joseph Banks Conservatory** (April–Sept Mon–Fri 9am–5pm, Sat & Sun 10am–4pm; Oct–Easter daily 10am–4pm; free). This is a large tropical glasshouse named after a local botanist who travelled with Cook on his first voyage to Australia.

The rest of the city

As for the rest of "**Uphill**" **Lincoln**, it's scattered with historic remains, notably several chunks of Roman wall, the most prominent of which is the second-century **Newport Arch** straddling Bailgate and once the main north gate into the city. There's also a bevy of medieval stone houses, at their best on and around the aptly named **Steep Hill** as it cuts down to the city centre. In particular, look out for the tidily restored twelfth-century **Jew's House**, a reminder of the Jewish community that flourished in medieval Lincoln. A rare and superb example of domestic Norman architecture, it now houses the *Jew's House Restaurant* (see p.754).

The **Usher Gallery**, Lindum Rd (Tues–Sat 10am–5.30pm, Sun 2.30–5pm; £2), is on the hillside too, its well-presented displays featuring some fine paintings of the cathedral and its environs, the best being those of William Logsdail (1859–1944). There's also a *Lincoln* view by Lowry as well as memorabilia celebrating Lincolnshire's own Alfred Tennyson (1809–1892), one of Victorian England's favourite poets. In addition, the gallery holds an eclectic collection of coins, porcelain, and watches and clocks dating from the seventeenth century. The timepieces were given to the gallery by its benefactor, James Ward Usher, a local jeweller and watchmaker who made a fortune by devising the legend of the **Lincoln Imp**, which he turned into the city's emblem in the 1880s. His story has a couple of imps hopping around the cathedral, until one of them is turned to stone for trying to talk to the angels carved into the roof of the Angel Choir. His chum made a hasty exit on the back of a witch, but the wind is still supposed to haunt the cathedral awaiting their return.

Eating and drinking

Lincoln's **café** and **restaurant** scene is a little patchy – with lots of places offering mundane food geared to the day-tripping trade – but there are excellent places too, mostly within shouting distance of the cathedral. First stop must be *Browns Pie Shop*, 33 Steep Hill – at the top – which has a creative menu where the emphasis is on British ingredients; a main course here will cost you about £10. Next door, and similarly enticing, is the *Wig and Mitre*, with a restaurant upstairs and a bar-restaurant below. They offer a wide-ranging menu covering everything from sandwiches with salad (£5) through to fillet steak and fish (£12). Another recommendable spot on Steep Hill is the more expensive – and more formal – *The Restaurant in the Jew's House* (☎01522/524851), where again much emphasis is placed on local ingredients.

As for **pubs**, there are a pair of amiable and traditional locals near the cathedral – the *Bull & Chain*, on Langworthgate, and the *Morning Star*, close by on Greetwellgate. The former has a garden.

Around Lincoln: Snarford, Stow and Gainsborough

Half-hidden by a clump of trees, the solitary, square-towered church of **St Lawrence** (daily dawn–dusk) stands half a mile down a country lane off the A46, about nine miles northeast of Lincoln on the edge of minuscule **SNARFORD**. St Lawrence's is dedicated to a Roman saint who was roasted to death on a gridiron, a fate that's made him the patron saint of cooks. For several centuries, the church stood next to the long-gone manor house of the St Pauls, the local lords, who used it as the family mausoleum. Today, its cramped interior is dominated by the Elizabethan tomb of Sir Thomas and his wife, Faith, whose alabaster figures lie on an elaborately carved six-poster bed. The brightly painted carving is superb, with finely crafted detail such as the flower-embroidered cushion at Sir Thomas's feet, Faith's ruff and open gown and the figures of the couple's eight kneeling children carved round the canopy. Opposite is the tomb of their son, Sir George, and his wife Frances, who lie propped up on their elbows looking back towards Sir Thomas. Once again, the carving is magnificent, with Frances decked out in Jacobean finery, a dark gown and a wide ruff beneath the frizzed hairstyle then fashionable. Behind the couple and the effigy of their child are the emblems of death – coffins and gravediggers' tools – together with the lily of purity and the rose of eternity.

Coates-by-Stow and Stow

A series of obscure byroads lead the eleven miles west from Snarford to the remote farmstead and adjacent church of **St Edith** (dawn–dusk) that together constitute **COATES-BY-STOW**. Entered through a narrow Norman doorway, this tiny church boasts a rare and delicately carved wooden rood screen dating from the fifteenth century. Round about are the residue of several hundred years of worship: medieval pews and pulpit and a Norman font.

The village of **STOW**, two miles west of St Edith, embraces the fortress-like church of **St Mary** (daily 9am–dusk), whose austere rubble walls date from the beginning of the eleventh century. Inside, the outstanding feature is the magnificent Saxon arches of the central tower, the tallest of their period in England, whose simple elegance contrasts with the sturdy arches inserted in front of them by the Normans. There's more Norman work in the ornate vaulted ribbing of the chancel and the dogtooth carving around the doorways. Look out also for a vague (but labelled) drawing of a Viking longship scratched into a wall and some crude thirteenth-century wall paintings devoted to Thomas à Beckett. Beckett, the Archbishop of Canterbury, was murdered in 1170 on the orders of King Henry II after the former friends became estranged. Beckett was a popular medieval saint, but Henry VIII suppressed the cult with great vigour – just in case anyone else decided to get ideas about standing up against the king.

Gainsborough

From Stow, it's just seven miles north to the old river-port of **GAINSBOROUGH**, a dreary place but for two outstanding buildings. These are the church of **All Saints** (Mon, Tues, Thurs & Fri 10am–4pm, Sat 10am–noon), whose spacious pastel-painted interior is a fine example of Georgian style, and **Gainsborough Old Hall** (Mon–Sat 10am–5pm, plus Easter–Oct Sun 2–5.30pm; £2.50; EH), a sprawling manor house with a magnificent Great Hall. Built in the 1460s, the timber-framed hall, bending and buckling from the contractions of the oak, has a huge hoop-shaped roof where the grain of the wood skilfully follows the lines of the arches. At the back of the hall, tiny doors lead to the well-preserved kitchen, and the timbered bedrooms of the first floor are worth inspecting, too. Gainsborough is thought to have been the setting for St Oggs in George Eliot's *Mill on the Floss*, whose tragic events result from a particularly ferocious tidal bore. Fortunately for the locals, the bore – or eagre – which rolls up the River Trent through Gainsborough fifty minutes after high tide in the Humber estuary doesn't often do much damage, but it still raises the river level between eight and thirteen feet; times are given in the local press.

The Wolds and the coast

The rolling hills and gentle valleys of the **Lincolnshire Wolds**, a narrow band of chalky land running southeast from Caistor to just outside Skegness, stand out amidst the more mundane agricultural landscapes of north Lincolnshire. A string of particularly appealing valleys is concentrated in the vicinity of **Louth**, which, with its striking church and antique centre, is easily the most enticing of the region's towns – with the added advantage of being fairly close to the coast. A few miles to the south of Louth, the Wolds dip down to the wooded heathland surrounding the once fashionable hamlet of **Woodhall Spa**, and it's south again to the imposing red-brick **Tattershall Castle**, north Lincolnshire's main historical attraction. Beyond the castle, all is fenland, pancake-flat and creating a wide and deep arch around the intrusive stump of The Wash. In the other direction, east of the Wolds, lies the coast, whose bungalows, campsites and caravans are parked beside a sandy beach that extends, with a few marshy interruptions, north from **Skegness**, the main resort, to Mablethorpe and ultimately Cleethorpes. Near Skegness, the **Gibraltar Point Nature Reserve** is a welcome diversion from the bucket-and-spade/amusement-arcade commercialism.

Louth and around

Henry VIII described the county of Lincolnshire as "one of the most brutal and beestlie of the whole realm", his contempt based on the events of 1536, when thousands of northern peasants rebelled against his religious reforms. In Lincolnshire, this insurrection, the **Pilgrimage of Grace**, began in the north-east of the county at **LOUTH**, 23 miles from Lincoln, under the leadership of the local vicar, who was subsequently hung, drawn and quartered. There's a commemorative plaque in honour of the rebels beside Louth's church of **St James** (Easter to mid-Dec Mon–Sat 10.30am–4pm; free), which is the town's one outstanding building, its soaring Perpendicular spire, buttresses, battlements and pinnacles set on a grassy knoll just to the west of the centre. The interior is delightful too, the sweeping symmetries of the nave illuminated by slender windows and capped by a handsome Georgian wooden roof decorated with dinky little angels. The roof of the tower vault is, if anything, even finer, its intricate stonework an exercise in geometrical precision. St James also owns a collection of old chests, or "hutches", used as portable cupboards for holding plate. One of them, the curious Sudbury Hutch, stored in the vestry (ask one of the wardens to let you in) bears a portrait of Henry VII and Elizabeth of York, but although it purports to be medieval, it may well be a fake. Finally, don't forget the café and its homemade cakes – locals set out early to get a slice of lemon-drizzle.

Next to the church, the well-tended gardens and Georgian houses of **Westgate** make it one of Louth's prettiest streets; you can grab a drink here at the antique *Wheatsheaf Inn*. Afterwards, it doesn't take long to explore the rest of the town centre, whose cramped lanes and alleys – focusing on the **Cornmarket** – are flanked by red-brick buildings mostly dating from the nineteenth century.

Practicalities

With reasonably regular weekday services from Boston and Lincoln, Louth's **bus station** is at the east end of Queen Street, a couple of minutes' walk from the Cornmarket – walk west along Queen Street and turn right onto the Market Place. The **tourist office**, in the Market Hall off Cornmarket (Mon–Sat 9am–5pm; ⓣ01507/609289), has a competent range of local information including accommodation details. The best **hotel** is the *Priory*, on Eastgate (ⓣ01507/602930, ⓦwww.theprioryhotel.com; ④), an excellent family-run place in a Georgian villa of 1818 with an idiosyncratic neo-Gothic facade and extensive gardens; it's located at the east end of the centre, about ten minutes' walk from the Cornmarket.

For **food**, the antique *Ye Olde Whyte Swanne*, at 45 Eastgate on the corner of Market Place, sells tasty bar snacks, including homemade game and pork pies as well as the illustrious (and extremely large) Lincolnshire sausage.

Around Louth: the Saltfleetby-Theddlethorpe dunes

An enjoyable short excursion from Louth takes you east along the **B1200** across about nine miles of fen farmland to the coast. This byroad is built on an old Roman road that was used to transport salt inland from the seashore salt pans, once a lucrative source of income for local traders. At the coast, at the end of the B1200, turn right along the main A1031 and, after about half a mile, take the (poorly signed) gravel track on the left through the dunes of the **Saltfleetby-Theddlethorpe Dunes National Nature Reserve**. Comprising over five miles of sand dune, salt and freshwater marsh, the reserve is at its prettiest in midsummer, when the dunes sprout buckthorn bushes and sea heather flowers, forming a carpet of violet spreading down towards the ocean. A network of trails navigates the dunes and lagoons, with the latter attracting hundreds of migratory wildfowl in spring and autumn.

Woodhall Spa

Heading south from Louth along the A153, it's thirteen miles to **HORNCASTLE**, which was once famous for its horse fairs – as described in George Borrow's *Romany Rye* – and seven more along the B1191 to **WOODHALL SPA**, an elongated village surrounded by a generous chunk of woodland. Here, the main street – **The Broadway** – is lined with Victorian and Edwardian villas, reminders of the time when the spring water of this isolated place, rich in iodine and bromine, was a favourite tipple of the great and the good. The tiny **Cottage Museum** (Easter–Oct Mon–Sat 10am–5pm, Sun 11am–4.30pm; £1), on Iddesleigh Road off the Broadway, outlines the development of the spa and has a section on the Dambusters (see below). It also doubles as the **tourist office** (same times; ⓣ01526/353775). The last spa treatment centre closed down in the 1930s and today the village can't help but feel a little marooned, even though it does boast one of Britain's most famous golf courses, whose speciality is its huge bunkers.

Woodhall Spa also possesses a particularly interesting hotel, the **Petwood**, Stixwould Rd (ⓣ01526/352411, ⓦwww.petwood.co.uk; ❼) – coming in on the B1191, keep on going to the end of The Broadway and turn right at Woodhall's one and only major intersection. Surrounded by immaculate gardens, the hotel's half-timbered gables and stone facades shelter a fine panelled interior, built in 1905 for the furniture millionaires, the Maples. In World War II, long after the family had moved out, the house was requisitioned by the RAF and turned into the Officers' Mess of 617 Squadron, the **Dambusters**, famous for their bombing raid of May 16, 1943. The raid was planned to deprive German industry of water and electricity by breaching several Ruhrland dams, a mission made possible by Barnes Wallis's **bouncing bomb**. A rusting specimen stands outside the hotel, which also contains the old **Officers' Bar**, kitted out with memorabilia from bits of aircraft engines to newspaper cuttings. Another unexpected delight is Woodhall's **Kinema**, deep in the woods, yet only five minutes' walk from The Broadway – just follow the signs. Opened in 1922, the Kinema is one of England's few remaining picture houses that projects a film from behind the screen, and at weekend showings a 1930s organ rises in front of the screen to play you through the ice-cream break. For details of what's on at the Kinema, call ⓣ01526/352166 or consult ⓦwww.thekinemainthewoods.co.uk. Incidentally, if you fancy staying in Woodhall but don't want to stump up the cost of the *Petwood*, the *Oglee Guest House*, in Edwardian premises off the Broadway at 16 Stanhope Ave (ⓣ01526/353512; ❷), is a pleasant alternative; all its rooms are en suite and the breakfasts are delicious.

Tattershall Castle

From Woodhall Spa, it's about four miles southeast to **Tattershall Castle** (April–Sept Mon–Wed & Sat–Sun 11am–5.30pm; Oct same days 11am–4pm, March & Nov to mid-Dec Sat & Sun noon–4pm; £3.40; NT), whose massive, moated red-brick keep dominates the fenland from beside the main road between Sleaford and Skegness. There's been a castle here since Norman times, but it was Ralph Cromwell, the Lord High Treasurer, who built the present quadrangled tower in the 1440s. A veteran of Agincourt, Cromwell was familiar with contemporary French architecture and it was to France that he looked for his basic design – in England, keeps had been out of fashion since the thirteenth century. Cromwell's quest for style explains Tattershall's contradictions. The castle walls are sixteen feet thick and rise to a height of one hundred feet, but there are no fewer than three ground-floor doorways with low-level windows to match. It's a medieval keep as fashion accessory, a theatricality that's continued inside the castle with the grand chimney-pieces, the only highlight of the bare interior – give or take the occasional Flemish tapestry. The adjacent church of the **Holy Trinity** (April–Sept daily 10am–5pm; free) is a high and mighty fifteenth-century structure, whose soaring nave, with its slender columns and pointed windows, is bright but bare of decoration. The church makes a rather austere home for a volunteer-run café – but don't miss their homemade cakes.

Skegness and around

SKEGNESS, some 26 miles east of Tattershall, has been a busy resort ever since the railways reached the Lincolnshire coast in 1875. Its heyday was before the 1960s, when the Brits began to take themselves off to sunnier climes, but it still attracts tens of thousands of city-dwellers who come for the wide, sandy beaches and for a host of attractions ranging from nightclubs to bowling greens. Every inch the traditional English seaside town, Skegness gets the edge over many of its rivals by keeping its beaches sparklingly clean and its parks spick-and-span, whilst a massive leisure complex in neighbouring Ingoldmells has a whopping indoor "fun pool". Indeed, Skegness has a tradition of keeping ahead of its competitors: in 1908 it came up with the ground-breaking "Skegness is So Bracing" slogan beneath a picture of a "Jolly Fisherman", and it was here in 1936 that ex-showman Billy Butlin opened the first Butlin's Holiday Camp. All that said, the seafront, with its rows of souvenir shops and amusement arcades, can be dismal, especially on rainy days, and you may well decide to sidestep the whole caboodle by heading south three miles along the coastal road to the **Gibraltar Point National Nature Reserve** (daily dawn–dusk). Here, a network of clearly signed footpaths patterns a narrow strip of salt and freshwater marsh, sand dune and beach that attracts an inordinate number of birds, both resident and migratory.

As for practicalities, Skegness **bus** and **train stations** are next door to each other about ten minutes' walk from the seashore – cut across Lumley Square and go straight up the High Street to the landmark clocktower. The **tourist office** (daily: April–Sept 9.30am–5pm; Oct–March 10am–4pm; ⓣ01754/899887, ⓦwww.funcoast.co.uk) is yards from the clocktower, opposite the Embassy Centre on Grand Parade. They can provide a colossal list of accommodation, including scores of **hotels**, **B&Bs** and **guest houses**. Several good ones are strung along South Parade, which runs south from the clocktower, behind the large park that fronts onto the beach. Options here include the unassuming *Palm Court Hotel* (ⓣ01754/767711; ❷), a tidy little place in a modern building, and the comparable *South Parade Hotel* (ⓣ01754/764113; ❷). Moving upmarket, the *Best Western Vine Hotel*, Vine Road (ⓣ01754/763018, ⓦwww.bestwestern.co.uk; ❻), is located on a quiet residential street about three quarters of a mile from the clocktower, and occupies a rambling, ivy-clad old house set in its own grounds.

The Lincolnshire Fens

The Lincolnshire section of **The Fens**, the great chunk of eastern England extending from Boston to Cambridge, encompasses some of the most productive farmland in Europe. With the exception of the occasional hillock, this pancake-flat, treeless terrain has been painstakingly reclaimed from the marshes and swamps that once drained into the Wash, a process that has taken almost two thousand years. In earlier times, outsiders were often amazed by the dreadful conditions hereabouts – as one medieval chronicler put it: "There is in the middle part of Britain a hideous fen which [is] oft times clouded with moist and dark vapours having within it divers islands and woods as also crooked and winding rivers." These dire conditions spawned the distinctive culture of the so-called **fen slodgers**, who embanked small portions of marsh to create pastureland and fields, supplementing their diets by catching fish and fowl, and gathering reed and sedge for thatching and fuel. Their economy was threatened by the large-scale land reclamation schemes of the late fifteenth and sixteenth centuries, and time and again the fenlanders sabotaged progress by breaking down the banks and dams. But the odds were stacked against the saboteurs, and a succession of great landowners eventually drained huge tracts of the fenland; by the end of the eighteenth century the fen slodgers' way of life had all but disappeared. Nonetheless, the Lincolnshire Fens remain a distinctive area of introverted little villages, with just one major settlement, the old port of **Boston**.

Boston

As it nears The Wash, the muddy River Witham weaves its way through **BOSTON** (a corruption of Botolf's stone, or Botolph's town), which was named after the Anglo-Saxon monk-saint who first established a monastery here, overlooking the main river crossing point in 645 AD. In the thirteenth and fourteenth centuries, the settlement expanded to become England's second largest seaport, its flourishing economy dependent on the wool trade with Flanders. Local merchants, revelling in their success, decided to build a church that demonstrated their wealth, the result being the magnificent medieval church of St Botolph, whose 272-foot tower still presides over the town and surrounding fenland. The church was completed in the early sixteenth century, but by then Boston was in decline as trade drifted west towards the Atlantic and the Witham silted up. The town's fortunes only revived in the late eighteenth century when, after the nearby fens had been drained, it became a minor agricultural centre with a modest port that has, in recent times, been modernized for trade with the EU. A singular mix of fenland town and seaport, Boston is an unusual little place that is at its liveliest on **market days** – Wednesday and Saturday.

The Town

Mostly edged by Victorian red-brick buildings, the mazy streets of Boston's cramped and compact centre, on the east side of the Witham, radiate out from the **Market Place**, a dishevelled square of irregular shape. Just to the west looms the massive bulk of **St Botolph's** (daily 8.30am–4.30pm, Sun 8.30am–12.30pm; free), whose exterior masonry is embellished by the high-pointed windows and elaborate tracery of the Decorated style. Most of the structure dates from the fourteenth century, but the huge and distinctive **tower**, whose lack of a spire earned the church the nickname the "Boston Stump", is of later construction. The octagonal lantern is later still, added in the sixteenth century and graced by flying buttresses and pointy pinnacles. Visible from twenty miles away, it once sheltered a beacon that guided travellers in from the fens and the North Sea. A tortuous 365-step spiral staircase (closed on Sun) leads to a balcony near the top, from where the panoramic views over Boston and the fens amply repay both the price of the ticket (£2) and the effort of the climb. Down below, St Botolph's light and airy **nave** is an exercise in the Perpendicular, all soaring columns and high windows. The sheer purity of design is stunning, its virtuosity heightened by the narrowness of the annexe-like chancel and the elegance of the Decorated arch that partly screens it from view. Indeed, the chancel is comparatively dowdy, though it does boast some intriguing fourteenth-century **misericords**, bearing a lively mixture of vernacular scenes such as organ-playing bears, a pair of medieval jesters squeezing cats in imitation of bagpipes and a schoolmaster birching a boy, watched by three more awaiting the same fate.

The church's most famous vicar was **John Cotton** (1584–1652), who helped stir the Puritan stew during his twenty-year tenure, encouraging a stream of Lincolnshire dissidents to head off to the colonies of New England to found their "New Jerusalem". Cotton emigrated himself in 1633 and soon became the leading light among the Puritans of Boston, Massachusetts. The Cotton connection was finally commemorated here in the Stump by the creation of the **Cotton Chapel**, at the west end of the nave, in 1857. Curiously enough, some of the locals wanted to paint the chapel ceiling with the Stars and Stripes, but the Church of England resisted. The most interesting relic from Cotton's sojourn here is not in the chapel at all, but in the nave in the form of the ornate **pulpit** from which he pounded out his three-hour sermons.

Boston had been alive to religious dissent before Cotton arrived and, in 1607, several of the **Pilgrim Fathers** were incarcerated here after their failed attempt to escape religious persecution by slipping across to Holland. They were imprisoned for thirty days in the old **Guildhall** on South Street, a brief walk south from St Botolph's back through the Market Place. It was closed for refurbishment at the time of writing; call the tourist office on ⓣ01205/356656 to check reopening dates. A creaky affair, the Guildhall spreads over three levels and incorporates an antique Council Chamber, the court where the Pilgrim Fathers were tried and sentenced, as well as the cells where they were locked up. Part of the redevelopment will involve sorting out the 5000-plus historical artefacts held here – a fascinating hotchpotch including some spectacularly ferocious anti-poacher traps and mementoes of locally born John Fox (1516–87), whose *Book of Martyrs* whipped up an anti-Catholic storm.

Practicalities

It's ten minutes' walk east from Boston **train station** to the town centre – head straight out of the station along Station Street and keep going until you hit the river. The **bus station** is also to the west of the centre, just five minutes' walk away on Lincoln Lane. The **tourist office** (Mon–Sat 9am–5pm; ⓣ01205/356656, ⓦwww.boston.gov.uk) is in the Market Place beneath the Assembly Rooms. Staff have oodles of local information and a list of **B&Bs**, among which one good option is the *Bramley House* (ⓣ01205/354538; no cards; ❷), in an attractively converted eighteenth-century farmhouse about one mile west of town beyond the train station at 267 Sleaford Rd. Another good choice is *Fairfield Guest House*, in a much enlarged Victorian property about three miles to the south of the centre at 101 London Rd (ⓣ01205/362869; no cards; ❷). There are fifteen guest rooms here (seven en suite), each is decorated in bright and cheerful style. Town-centre accommodation is limited and the best you'll do is the *New England Hotel*, Wide Bargate (Ⓣ01205/365255, Ⓦwww.thenewengland.co.uk; ⑤), an unassuming mid-range place of thirty bedrooms with modern furnishings and fittings.

For **food**, cosy *Goodbarns Yard*, just to the north of the Stump on Wormgate, serves copious pub meals inside or out in a back garden overlooking the river. Vegetarians should make a beeline for *Maud's Tea Rooms*, inside the Maud Foster Windmill, on Willoughby Road (open 3 to 5 days a week, 10am or 11am–5pm; Ⓣ01205/352188). Built to grind corn in 1819, the windmill, with its five whopping sails, is still in full working order. You can inspect its grinding gears and/or buy the (organic) flour it churns out at the tearoom, which serves a range of vegetarian and vegan meals and a good selection of delicious cakes. The windmill is about ten minutes' walk northeast of the Market Place, beside the road to Horncastle.

Heckington

The village of **HECKINGTON**, thirteen miles west of Boston and five east of Sleaford, has a tidy little centre that drapes around the church of **St Andrew** (Mon–Sat 9am–5pm or dusk in winter; free), a splendid example of the Decorated style, with a pinnacled spire and elaborate canopied buttresses framing the flowing tracery of the windows. Inside, the original fourteenth-century chancel fittings have survived, including the battered tomb of the founder, Richard de Potesgrave, and an **Easter Sepulchre**, whose folksy and energetic carved figures are set against a dense undergrowth of foliage. The sepulchre, one of the finest in England, was built to accommodate the host between Good Friday and Easter morning. The **sedilia** is intriguing, too, boasting a cartoon strip of domestic scenes on the subject of food – a man eating fruit, a woman feeding the birds and suchlike. Heckington has one other attraction, its unique eight-sailed **windmill**, located a short stroll from the church and worth visiting when it's in operation (call Ⓣ01529/461919 for times). In between the windmill and the church, on the High Street, the village's best pub is the *Nag's Head*.

On the Skegness–Grantham line, Heckington **train station** is in the centre opposite the windmill.

Spalding

Built beside the treacle-like banks of the River Welland fourteen miles south of Boston, pocket-sized **SPALDING** is every inch an agricultural town, marooned amidst a great chunk of fen farmland. Its centre has few pretensions, but the wealthy merchants who once controlled things around here did build a string of portentous riverside mansions. One of them, **Ayscoughfee Hall** (pronounced "Ascuffee"; closed for refurbishment until 2005; check on Ⓣ01775/725468), on the east side of the river – on Churchgate – is a much modified medieval wool merchant's house that will, when work is complete, accommodate a museum devoted to the history of the Fens and the culture of its people.

It's unlikely you'll want to stay in Spalding, but the *Bedford Court Guest House* is first-rate, occupying a handsome mullioned villa just set back from the street – and the west bank of the Welland – at 10 London Rd (Ⓣ01775/722377; no credit cards; ③); all four of the commodious guest rooms are en suite.

Gedney to Sutton Bridge

Travelling east from Spalding (possibly on the way to Norfolk, see Chapter 7), it's eleven miles to the scattered hamlet of **GEDNEY**, where the massive tower of **St Mary Magdalene** (daily dawn–dusk; free) intercepts the fenland landscape. Seen from a distance, the church seems almost magical, or at least mystical, its imposing lines so much in contrast with its fen-flat surroundings. Close up, the nave is simply beautiful, its blend of Early English and Perpendicular features culminating in a phalanx of elongated windows. Locals keep the church in fine fettle and buff the Renaissance alabaster effigies of Adlard and Cassandra Welby, facing each other on the south wall near the chancel.

There's more ecclesiastical excitement just a mile or two to the east in **LONG SUTTON**, a modest farming centre that limps along the road until it reaches its trim Market Place. Here, the church of **St Mary** (daily dawn–dusk; free) has preserved many of its Norman features, with its arcaded tower supporting the oldest lead spire in the country, dating from around 1200. Look out also for the striking medieval stained glass in the chancel aisle. Long Sutton once lay on the edge of the five-mile-wide mouth of the **River Nene**, where it emptied into The Wash. This was the most treacherous part of the road from Lincoln to Norfolk, and locals had to guide travellers across the obstacle on horseback, though not always without mishap. In 1205, **King John** was caught by the rising tide, losing his jewels and baggage train in the quicksands somewhere between Long Sutton and Terrington St Clement in Norfolk. In 1831, the River Nene was embanked and then spanned with a wooden bridge at **SUTTON BRIDGE**, a hamlet just two miles east of Long Sutton. The present swing bridge, with its nifty central tower, was completed in 1894.

The marshy shores of **The Wash** remain wild and desolate. There are several access points, but the best is near Sutton Bridge – from the car park on the east side of the mouth of the Nene. This marks the start of the Peter Scott Walk running east along – or near – the seashore to King's Lynn (see p.589). You'll need proper maps and hiking tackle. Incidentally, the walk is named after the famous naturalist, who spent long periods in a renovated lighthouse near the mouth of the Nene.

Stamford

STAMFORD is delightful, a handsome little limestone town of yellow-grey seventeenth- and eighteenth-century buildings edging narrow streets that slope up from the River Welland. It was here that the Romans forded this important river, establishing a fortified outpost that the Danes subsequently selected for one of their regional capitals. Later the town became a centre of the medieval wool and cloth trade, its wealthy merchants funding a series of almshouses known as "**callises**" – after Calais, the English-occupied port through which most of them traded. Indeed, Stamford **cloth** became famous throughout Europe for its quality and durability, a reputation confirmed when Cardinal Wolsey used it for the tents of the "Field of the Cloth of Gold", the grand conference between Henry VIII and Francis I of France held outside Calais in 1520. Stamford was also the home of **William Cecil**, Elizabeth's chief minister, who built his splendid mansion, Burghley House, close by. The town survived the collapse of the wool trade, prospering as an inland port after the Welland was made navigable to the sea in 1570, and, in the eighteenth century, as a staging point on the Great North Road from London. More recently, Stamford escaped the three main threats to old English towns – the Industrial Revolution, wartime bombing and postwar development – and was designated the country's first Conservation Area in 1967. Thanks to this, its unspoilt streets readily lend themselves to period drama- and film-making.

The town centre

Above all, it's the harmony of Stamford's architecture that pleases, rather than any specific sight. There are, nevertheless, a handful of buildings of some special interest amongst the web of narrow streets that make up the town's compact centre, beginning with the church of **St Mary** (no regular opening hours), set beside a pristine close of proud Georgian buildings on St Mary's Place. The church, with its splendid spire, has a small, airy interior, which incorporates the Corpus Christi chapel, whose intricately embossed, painted and panelled roof dates from the 1480s.

Across the street from St Mary's, several lanes thread through to the carefully preserved **High Street**, from where Ironmonger Street leads north again to the wide and handsome Broad Street, the site of the **Stamford Museum** (April–Sept Mon–Sat 10am–5pm, Sun 2–5pm; Oct–March Mon–Sat 10am–5pm; free). This features a tasteless exhibit comparing the American midget Tom Thumb with **Daniel Lambert**, the Leicester fat man who died at Stamford in 1809, aged 39 and weighing 52st 11lb (336kg). After Lambert's death his clothes were displayed in a local inn, which Tom Thumb, otherwise Charles Stratton, visited several times to perform a few party tricks, such as standing in Lambert's waistcoat armhole.

Nearby, also on Broad Street, is **Browne's Hospital** (May–Sept Sat & Sun 11am–4pm; £2.50), the most extensive of the town's almshouses, dating from the late fifteenth century. Not all of the complex is open to the public, but it's still worth visiting with the first room – the old dormitory – capped by a splendid wood-panelled ceiling. The adjacent chapel holds some delightfully folksy misericords, and upstairs, the audit room is illuminated by a handsome set of stained-glass windows. Here also is a small feature on one of the inmates, a certain George Spencer, who lived here from 1945 until his death in 1963. After his demise, Spencer was found to have stuffed a cake tin with his savings – enough to refurbish a goodly slice of the hospital.

From Browne's, it's a few paces more to Red Lion Square, which is overlooked by **All Saints'** (daily dawn–dusk; free). Several centuries in the making, this church is a happy amalgamation of Early English and Perpendicular features that takes full advantage of its position, perched on a small hillock. Entry is via the south porch, itself an ornate structure with a fine – if badly weathered – crocketted gable, and, although most of the interior is routinely Victorian, the carved capitals are of great delicacy. There's also an engaging folkloric carving of the Last Supper behind the high altar.

High Street St Martin's

Down the slope from St Mary's, across the reedy River Welland on High Street St Martin's, is the **George Hotel**, a splendid old coaching inn whose Georgian facade supports one end of the gallows that span the street – not a warning to criminals, but an advertising hoarding. Just along – and across – the street, the plain and sombre, late-fifteenth-century church of **St Martin** (daily 9.30am–4pm; free) shelters the magnificent tombs of the lords Burghley, with a recumbent William Cecil carved beneath twin canopies, holding his rod of office and with a lion at his feet. Just behind, the early eighteenth-century effigies of John Cecil and his wife show the couple as Roman aristocrats, propped up on their elbows, she to gaze at him, John to stare across the nave commandingly.

Burghley House

Burghley House (April–Oct daily 11am–4.30pm; viewing by guided tours only every 10–20min, except Sat & Sun pm; £7.50; Ⓦwww.burghley.co.uk), an extravagant Elizabethan mansion standing in parkland landscaped by Capability Brown, is located a mile and a half or so to the east of Stamford, out along the Barnack Road from High Street St Martin's. Completed in 1587 after 22 years' work, the house sports a mellow-yellow ragstone exterior, embellished by dainty cupolas, a pyramidal clocktower and skeletal balustrading, all to a plan by **William Cecil**, the long-serving adviser to Elizabeth I. A shrewd and cautious man, Cecil steered his queen through all sorts of difficulties, from the wars against Spain to the execution of Mary, Queen of Scots, vindicating Elizabeth's assessment of his character when she appointed him secretary of state in 1558: "You will not be corrupted with any manner of gifts, and will be faithful to the state."

With the notable exception of the Tudor kitchen, little remains of Burghley's Elizabethan interior. Instead, the house bears the heavy hand of John, fifth Lord Burghley, who toured France and Italy in the late seventeenth century, commissioning furniture, statuary and tapestries, as well as buying up old Florentine and Venetian paintings, such as Paolo Veronese's *Zebedee's Wife Petitioning our Lord*. To provide a suitable setting for his old masters, John brought in Antonio Verrio and his assistant Louis Laguerre, who between them covered many of Burghley's walls and ceilings with frolicking gods and goddesses. These gaudy and gargantuan murals are at their most engulfing in the **Heaven Room**, an artfully painted classical temple that adjoins the **Hell Staircase**, where the entrance to the inferno is through the gaping mouth of a cat. Have a close look also at the fine portraits in the **Pagoda Room**, in particular the querulous Elizabeth I and a sublimely self-confident Henry VIII by Joos van Cleve.

Practicalities

With frequent services from Peterborough and Oakham, Stamford **train station** is five minutes' walk from the town centre, which lies just to the north across the river. The **bus station** is on the west side of the centre, on Sheepmarket, off All Saints' Street. The **tourist office** is in the centre inside Stamford Arts Centre at 27 St Mary's St (April–Oct Mon–Sat 9.30am–5pm, Sun 10am–4pm; Nov–March closed Sun; Ⓣ01780/755611, Ⓦwww.stamfordonline.co.uk).

Stamford has several charming **hotels**, the most celebrated of which is the beguiling *George*, 71 High Street St Martin's (Ⓣ01780/750750, Ⓦwww.georgehotelofstamford.com; ❻), an old and cleverly remodelled coaching inn with flagstone floors and antique furnishings, where the most appealing rooms overlook the cobbled courtyard. Just along the street is the attractive *Garden House* (Ⓣ01780/763359, Ⓦwww.gardenhousehotel.com; ❻), which occupies a tastefully modernized eighteenth-century building with twenty smart bedrooms. Stamford also possesses a clutch of **B&Bs** and as ever the tourist office has the full list, but the majority are on the town's outskirts.

For **food**, it has to be the *George Hotel* – either in the formal and expensive restaurant, where the emphasis is on British ingredients served in imaginative ways, or in the moderately priced and informal *Garden Lounge*. There's delicious and inexpensive bar food, too, served in the *York Bar* at lunchtimes.

As for summer festivals, the **Stamford Shakespeare Company** (Ⓣ01780/756133, Ⓦwww.stamfordshakespeare.co.uk) spends June, July and

August performing out at Tolethorpe Hall, a graceful Elizabethan mansion not far from town. The troupe performs out in the open, but the audience is safely covered by a vast open-fronted marquee.

Grantham

GRANTHAM, midway between Stamford and Lincoln, was once a major staging point on the Great North Road from London, but today its lengthy main street is no more than a provincial thoroughfare flanked by an unappetizing combination of modern blocks and Victorian red brick. The town's more successful days are recalled by two ancient inns towards the north end of the main street. These are the stone-fronted **Angel & Royal**, founded by the Knights Templar in the twelfth century, and the nearby **George**, where Charles Dickens' Nicholas Nickleby stopped on his way to Dotheboys Hall – and now guzzled up into a shopping centre. Close by, the **Market Place** is a pleasant open square – or at least it would be were it not for the traffic – but this pales into insignificance when compared with Grantham's pride and joy, the church of **St Wulfram** (Mon–Fri 9am–4pm, Sat 10am–4pm; free), set within its own close across the main drag just east of the Market Place. St Wulfram's most obvious feature is its 282-foot central spire, a fourteenth-century, crocketted construction whose angular lines are emphasized by pointed blind arcading, slim window openings and narrow buttresses. Many reckon this to be the most perfect steeple in the country. The interior of the church was mucked up by the Victorians, but highlights include the timber ceiling with its angel corbels, the sinuous window tracery and the late-sixteenth-century, 150-volume **chained library** (May–Sept Mon 10am–noon & 2–4pm, Thurs & Fri 2–4pm) above the south porch. The high altar is of interest, too, not for itself, but because its position prompted a bitter wrangle in 1627. Believing the altar should be more conspicuous, the High Church party turned it round to look down the nave, but the Puritans objected and came to move it back again. The resulting brawl, something of a cause célèbre, hardened attitudes in the run-up to the Civil War.

Beside the church, on narrow Church Street, is the original sixteenth-century **classroom** in which **Isaac Newton** received his initial education in the 1650s – there's a plaque. In addition, there's a statue of the great physicist and mathematician in the parklet outside the **Guildhall**, an elaborate Victorian confection a short walk to the south along Castlegate, which runs behind St Wulfram's. While you're here, you might as well pop into the adjacent **Grantham Museum** (Mon–Sat 10am–5pm; free), which has a small feature on Newton, including a plaster-cast of his death mask, and another on **Margaret Thatcher**, the former prime minister who was born in Grantham in 1925. In a moment of gay abandon, Mrs Thatcher gave several of her dresses to the museum, though her absurdist handbags and threatening hairstyle were always more memorable. Her childhood home, now a chiropractic clinic, is up at the top of the main street at 2 North Street, on the corner with Broad Street.

Practicalities

Grantham **train station** is half a mile from the Market Place: follow Station Road north to the roundabout, veer second right along Westgate and keep going. The **bus station** is also to the south of the Market Place, but a little nearer, just off the main drag on Wharf Road. The **tourist office** (Mon–Fri 9.30am–4.30pm, Sat 9.30am–1pm; ⓣ01476/406166) is in the Guildhall, on the main street south of the Market Place. They have a list of **B&Bs**, though frankly there's precious little reason to hang around. For **food**, *Ask*, 58 High St, does a good line in reasonably priced Italian meals in pleasantly modern surrounding. For a **drink**, the *Beehive Inn*, 11 Castlegate, has a good range of beers and also boasts its own hive of South African bees, fixed to the tree outside.

Around Grantham: Belton House

The honey-coloured limestone facade of **Belton House** (April–Oct Wed–Sun 12.30–5pm, garden from 11am; park daily dawn–dusk; £5.80; NT), three miles northeast of Grantham beside the A607, is Restoration design at its finest, its delicate symmetry enhanced by formal gardens and surrounded by rolling parkland. Belton was built in the 1680s for a local family of lawyer-landowners, the Brownlows, whose subsequent climb up the aristocratic ladder prompted them to remodel the interior of their home in the sumptuous Neoclassical style of the late eighteenth century. Entry is through the Marble Hall, where the intricate **limewood carvings** that remain Belton's most distinctive feature frame a sequence of (mostly family) portraits, including three by Reynolds. One of the picture frames and several more carvings in the adjacent **saloon** are thought to be the work of **Grinling Gibbons**, the great Rotterdam-born woodcarver and sculptor. Belton is also noted for its pastel-shaded, Adam-style plasterwork ceilings and, on display in the Chapel Drawing Room, a pair of splendid tapestries, which, despite their Indian and Japanese themes, were made in John Vanderbank's workshop in Soho, London. The surrounding **park**, dotted with aristocratic bits and pieces – from a Gothic wilderness ruin to a boathouse – is noted for its woodland walks.

It's easy to reach Belton by **bus** from Grantham on weekdays, with service #601 making the ten-minute trip every hour or two.

Travel details

Buses

For information on all local and national bus services, contact Traveline ⓣ0870/608 2608, ⓦwww.traveline.org.uk.

Grantham to: Lincoln (every 30min; 1hr 20min); Nottingham (every 1–2hr; 1hr 10min); Stamford (2 daily; 30min).

Leicester to: Lincoln (hourly; 1hr 40min); Market Harborough (every 15min; 40min); Northampton (hourly; 1hr); Nottingham (every 30min; 1hr 40min); Oakham (hourly; 1hr 10min); Stamford (hourly; 2hr).

Lincoln to: Boston (hourly; 1hr 30min); Grantham (every 30min; 1hr 20min); Leicester (hourly; 1hr 30min); Louth (every 1–2hr; 40min); Northampton (hourly; 3hr); Nottingham (hourly; 2hr 30min); Oakham (hourly; 2hr 20min); Skegness (hourly; 1hr 45min).

Northampton to: Leicester (hourly; 1hr); Lincoln (hourly; 3hr); Nottingham (hourly; 2hr+); Stamford (hourly; 2hr 30–50min).

Nottingham to: Grantham (every 1–2hr; 1hr 10min); Leicester (every 30min; 1hr 40min); Lincoln (hourly; 2hr 30min); Newark (hourly; 30min); Northampton (hourly; 2hr+);.

Oakham to: Leicester (hourly; 1hr 10min); Lincoln (hourly; 2hr 20min); Stamford (every 30min; 20min).

Stamford to: Grantham (2 daily; 30min); Leicester (hourly; 2hr); Northampton (hourly; 2hr 30–50min); Oakham (every 30min; 20min).

Trains

For information on all local and national rail services, contact National Rail Enquiries ⓣ08457/484950, ⓦwww.rail.co.uk.

Grantham to: Derby (hourly; 1hr); Lincoln (every 30min; 45min); London (hourly; 1hr 15min); Nottingham (every 30min; 35min); Skegness (hourly; 1hr 20min).
Leicester to: Birmingham (every 30min; 1hr); Coventry (hourly; 45min); Derby (hourly; 35min); Lincoln (hourly; 1hr 40min); London (every 30min; 1hr 30min); Market Harborough (every 1–2hr; 15min); Melton Mowbray (hourly; 15min); Nottingham (every 30min; 20min); Oakham (hourly; 30min); Stamford (hourly; 50min).
Lincoln to: Birmingham (hourly; 3hr); Boston (hourly; 1hr); Cambridge (hourly; 1hr); Gainsborough (hourly; 20min); Grantham (every 30min; 45min); London (hourly; 2hr 15min); Leicester (hourly; 1hr 30min); London (hourly; 2hr 15min); Newark (hourly; 25min); Nottingham (hourly; 45min); Peterborough (hourly; 1hr 20min); Skegness (hourly; 1hr 40min); Spalding (every 1–2 hours; 1hr).
Northampton to: Birmingham (every 30min; 1hr); Coventry (hourly; 40min); London Euston (every 30min; 1hr 10min–1hr 40min).
Nottingham to: Leicester (every 30min; 30min); Lincoln (hourly; 1hr 15min); London (hourly; 1hr 40min); Newark (hourly; 30min).
Stamford to: Cambridge (hourly; 1hr 20min); Leicester (hourly; 40min); Oakham (hourly; 10min); Peterborough (hourly; 15min).

The Northwest

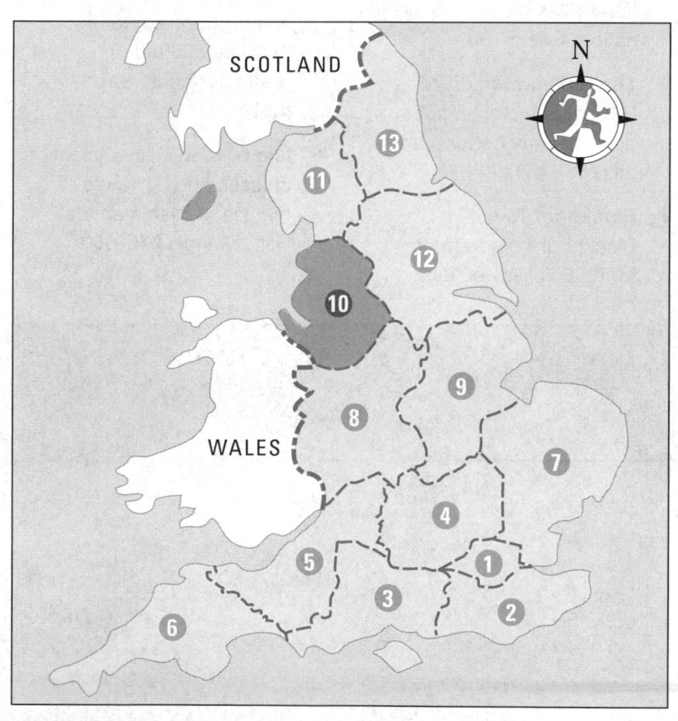

CHAPTER 10

Highlights

* **Café society, Manchester** Manchester's café-bars set the tone for this happening city. See p.789

* **City walls, Chester** The ancient walls of Chester make a great introduction to this historic destination. See p.798

* **The Philharmonic, Liverpool** Victorian pubs don't get any better than this. See p.819

* **Blackpool Tower** Blackpool's bold answer to the Eiffel Tower lights up the skyline of the UK's favourite resort. See p.824

* **Lancaster Castle** From the dungeons to the ornate court rooms, the castle tour is a historical tour-de-force. See p.832

* **Heysham village** Spend an afternoon exploring the Saxon church and pretty cottages. See p.834

* **Isle of Man** With ancient crosses and TT races, the Isle of Man merits a visit. See pp.835–850

△ Blackpool Tower and Beach

10

The Northwest

Within the **northwest** of England lie some of the ugliest and some of the most beautiful parts of the country. The least attractive zones are to be found in the sprawl connecting the country's third and sixth largest conurbations, Manchester and Liverpool, but even here the picture isn't unrelievedly bleak, as the cities themselves have an ingratiating appeal. **Manchester**, in particular, surprises many who don't expect to see beyond its dour, industrial heritage. Where once only a handful of Victorian Gothic buildings lent any grace to the cityscape, Manchester today has been completely transformed by a rebuilding programme that puts it in the vanguard of modern British urban design. Quite apart from a clutch of top-class visitor attractions – including The Lowry and the new Imperial War Museum North – where Manchester really scores is in the buzz of its thriving café and club scene, which places it at the leading edge of the country's youth culture. **Liverpool**, set on the Mersey estuary, is perhaps less appealing at first glance, though Georgian town houses, grand civic buildings, its twin cathedrals and a burgeoning café scene soon change perceptions. At the redundant docks that once made the city's fortune, many of the old warehouses and buildings have been redeveloped as part of the Albert Dock scheme, housing a fine swathe of museums, including the northern outpost of the Tate Gallery.

The hills, which form the southern tip of the Pennine range, melt away to the west into undulating, pastoral **Cheshire**, a county of rolling green countryside and country manor houses, interspersed with dairy farms from whose churns emerge tons of crumbly white Cheshire cheese. The county town, **Chester**, with its complete circuit of town walls and partly Tudor centre, is as alluring as any of the country's northern towns, capturing the essence of what has always been one of England's wealthiest rural counties. It's easily the main place of interest in the region, though the villages of the **Cheshire Plain** are set in a landscape that conjures archetypal images of pastoral England.

Lancashire, which historically lay directly to the north of Cheshire, reached industrial prominence in the nineteenth century primarily due to the cotton-mill towns around Manchester and to the thriving port of Liverpool. Today, neither of those cities is part of the county, having been excised when England's first substantial county boundary changes since the Domesday Book were enacted in 1974. The urban counties of Merseyside and Greater Manchester chopped off the southern section of Lancashire while Cumbria grabbed a substantial northern chunk leaving the county little more than half its former size. Its oldest town, and major commercial and administrative centre, is **Preston** – home of the national museum of England's national game,

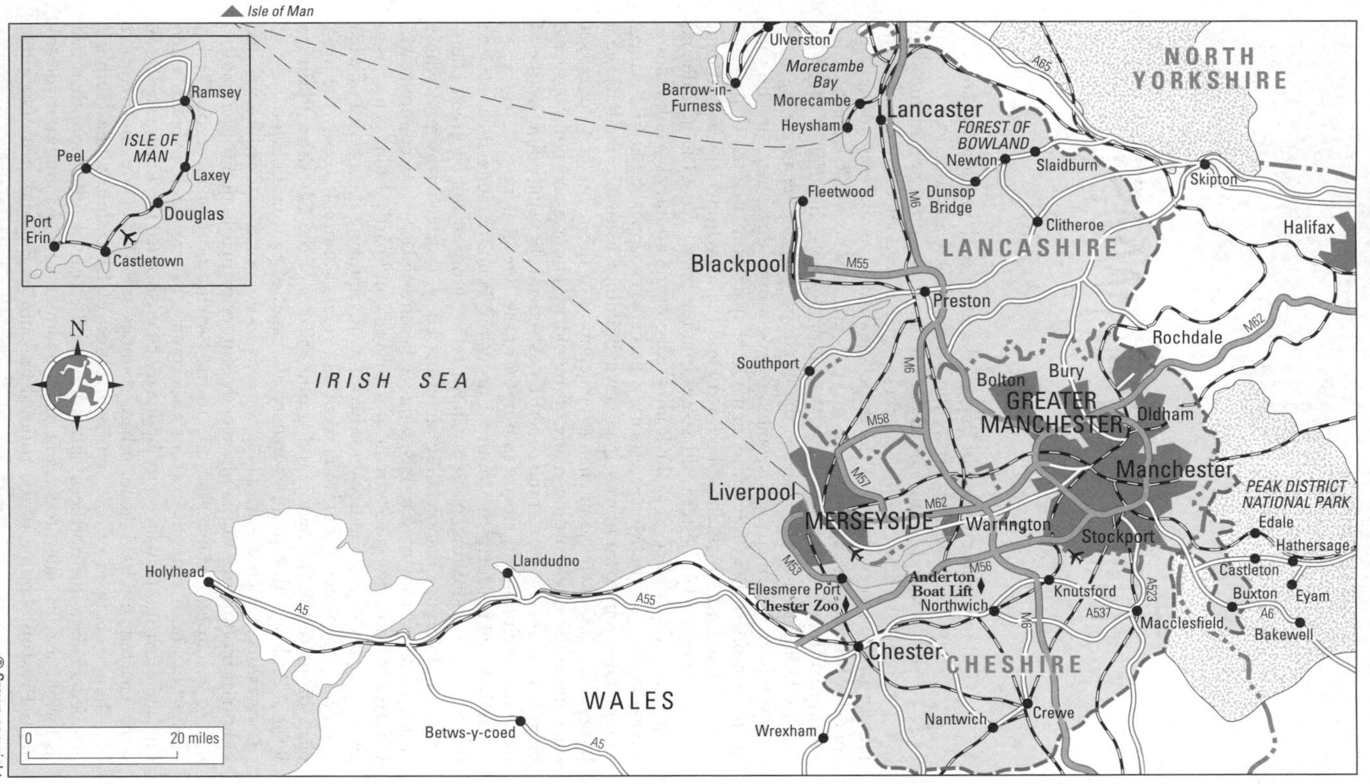
Isle of Man
ISLE OF MAN
Ramsey
Peel
Laxey
Douglas
Port Erin
Castletown
N
IRISH SEA
NORTH YORKSHIRE
LANCASHIRE
GREATER MANCHESTER
MERSEYSIDE
CHESHIRE
WALES
PEAK DISTRICT NATIONAL PARK
FOREST OF BOWLAND
Morecambe Bay
Ulverston
Barrow-in-Furness
Morecambe
Heysham
Lancaster
Newton
Slaidburn
Dunsop Bridge
Clitheroe
Skipton
Halifax
Fleetwood
Blackpool
Preston
Rochdale
Southport
Bolton
Bury
Oldham
Manchester
Liverpool
Warrington
Stockport
Edale
Hathersage
Castleton
Buxton
Eyam
Bakewell
Macclesfield
Knutsford
Northwich
Anderton Boat Lift
Ellesmere Port
Chester Zoo
Chester
Crewe
Nantwich
Wrexham
Holyhead
Llandudno
Betws-y-coed
A65
M6
M55
M62
M58
M57
M53
M56
A523
A537
A6
A5
A55
0
20 miles
© Crown copyright

football – though tourists are perhaps more inclined to linger in the charming towns and villages of the nearby **Ribble Valley**. Meanwhile, along the coast to the west and north of the major cities stretches a line of **resorts** – from Southport to **Morecambe** – which once formed the mainstay of the northern British holiday trade before their client base disappeared on cheaper, sunnier holidays to Florida and the Mediterranean. Only **Blackpool** is really worth visiting for its own sake, a rip-roaring resort which has stayed at the top of its game by supplying undemanding entertainment with more panache than its neighbours. For anything more culturally invigorating you'll have to continue north to the historically important city of **Lancaster**, with its Tudor castle. Finally, the semi-autonomous **Isle of Man**, only 25 miles off the coast and served by ferries from Liverpool and Heysham (or short flights from various regional airports), provides a terrain almost as rewarding as that of the Lake District but without the seasonal overcrowding.

Getting around

Manchester's international **airport** picks the city out as a major UK point of arrival, and there are direct train services from the airport to Liverpool, Blackpool, Lancaster, Leeds and York, as well as to Manchester itself. Both Manchester and Liverpool are well served by **trains**, with plentiful connections to the Midlands and London, and up the west coast to Scotland. There's also a frequent rail and bus service between both cities, and from each to Chester, allowing an easy triangular loop between Greater Manchester, Merseyside and Cheshire. The major east–west rail lines in the region are the direct routes between Manchester, Leeds and York, and between Blackpool, Bradford, Leeds and York. In addition, the Morecambe/Lancaster–Leeds line slips through the Yorkshire Dales (with possible connections at Skipton for the famous Settle–Carlisle line; see p.952); further south, the Manchester–Sheffield line provides a rail approach to the Peak District. Regional **rover tickets** are available for a week's unlimited travel in the northwest or in the "coast and peaks" region (basically between Liverpool, Manchester, the Peak District and North Wales).

Manchester

Few cities in the world have embraced social change so heartily as **MANCHESTER**. From engine of the Industrial Revolution to test-bed of contemporary urban design, the city has no realistic provincial English rival. Its domestic dominance expresses itself in various ways, most swaggeringly in the success of Manchester United, the richest football club in Britain, but also in a thriving music and cultural scene that has given birth to world-beaters as diverse as the Hallé Orchestra and Oasis. Moreover, the city's cutting-edge concert halls, theatres, clubs and café society are boosted by one of England's largest student populations and a blooming gay community, whose spending power has created a pioneering **Gay Village**. For inspiration, Manchester's planners look to Barcelona – another revitalized industrial powerhouse – and scoff at many of their northern rivals.

Despite a **history** stretching back to Roman times, and pockets of surviving medieval and Georgian architecture, Manchester is first and foremost a Victorian manufacturing city with the imposing streets and buildings to match. Its rapid growth was the equal of any flowering of the Industrial Revolution –

from little more than a village in 1750 to the world's major cotton-milling centre in only a hundred years. The spectacular rise of **Cottonopolis**, as it became known, came from the production of vast quantities of competitively priced imitations of expensive Indian calicoes, using machines evolved from Arkwright's first steam-powered cotton mill, which opened in 1783. The rapid industrialization of the area brought prosperity for a few but a life of misery for the majority. The discontent this engendered amongst the working class came to a head in 1819 when eleven people were killed at **Peterloo**, in what began as a peaceful demonstration against the oppressive Corn Laws. Things were, however, even worse when the 23-year-old Friedrich Engels came here in 1842 to work in his father's cotton plant, and the suffering he witnessed – recorded in his *Condition of the Working Class in England* – was a seminal influence on his later collaboration with Karl Marx in the *Communist Manifesto*.

Waterways and railway viaducts form the matrix into which the city's principal buildings have been bedded – as early as 1772 the Duke of Bridgewater had a canal cut to connect the city to the coal mines at Worsley, and in 1830 the Manchester–Liverpool railway opened. The **Manchester Ship Canal**, constructed to entice ocean-going vessels into Manchester and away from burgeoning Liverpool, was completed in 1894, and played a crucial part in sustaining Manchester's competitiveness. Within sixty years, though, the city was in trouble, with the docks, mills and canals in dangerous decline. The traditional image of the struggling post-industrial city was of empty mills and factories, and rows of back-to-back houses whose slate roofs and cobbled back alleys glistened in the seemingly ever-present rain – an image perpetuated, to an extent, by the popularity of Britain's longest-running TV soap opera, *Coronation Street*. Sporadic efforts were made to pull Manchester out of the economic doldrums of the 1960s and 1970s, but the main engine of change turned out to be the devastating **IRA bomb**, which exploded in June 1996 and wiped out much of the city's commercial infrastructure. The largest explosion on the mainland since World War II devastated the area around the Arndale Centre and the Royal Exchange. Rather than simply patch up the buildings, the planning authorities embarked on an ambitious rebuilding scheme, which also came to embrace the **Commonwealth Games**' facilities – the games were held here in 2002. Entire new districts have taken shape as once-blighted areas along the canals are reclaimed for retail and residential use – the downtown areas have seen a surge in population as city-centre living in converted warehouses has become the rage. Meanwhile inner-city suburbs such as Hulme and Moss Side, often scarred by gang violence and drug dealing, are at last giving tenants a say in the design of new housing estates and shopping centres, and encouraging the development of local businesses.

Arrival and information

A direct rail link into the city makes **Manchester Airport**, ten miles south of the city, an increasingly popular point of entry into Britain. Trains to Piccadilly (every 10min 5.15am–10.15pm, reduced service through the night; 25min) cost £2.35, £2.80 on weekdays before 9.30am. A taxi from the airport to the centre costs £12–15. There are tourist information offices in the arrivals halls of Terminal 1 (daily 8am–9pm; ⓣ0161/436 3344) and Terminal 2 (daily 7.30am–12.30am; same number); and a Travel Shop for public-transport enquiries in Terminal 1 (Mon–Sat 5.30am–9pm, Sun 7am–9pm).

Manchester's three main **train stations** form the points of a triangle that encloses much of the city centre. National mainline trains all pull into

Piccadilly Station, facing London Road, on the east side, from where you can walk a few hundred yards west into the city's core, via Piccadilly Gardens (or catch the free Centreline bus #4 from outside the station, every 10min, not Sunday, to all main city-centre locations).

Regional train routes to points south, east and west call both at Piccadilly and at **Oxford Road Station**, south of the centre, while **Victoria Station**, in the north, services the northern hinterland and Bradford. The city's Metrolink **tram** service connects Piccadilly Station (the platform is underneath the train station) to Victoria and G-Mex – the latter being the best stop if you're heading straight for Castlefield. National Express and most long-distance buses use **Chorlton Street Coach Station**, a few hundred yards west of Piccadilly train station. Local and some regional buses might drop you instead in nearby Piccadilly Gardens.

The **Manchester Visitor Centre** in the town hall extension on Lloyd Street, facing central St Peter's Square (Mon–Sat 10am–5.30pm, Sun 10.30am–4.30pm; ⓣ0161/234 3157, ⓦwww.manchester.gov.uk/visitorcentre/), offers a free map of the city centre, the handy *City Guide* and various other useful leaflets and brochures. You can also buy National Express bus tickets, check rail timetables, and book guided tours. They book accommodation too and are often knowledgeable about special deals and discounts; for more on accommodation, see p.778. There are direct trams to the Visitor Centre (St Peter's Square stop) from Piccadilly and Victoria stations. To find out **what's on** in the city, buy the weekly *City Life* listings and reviews magazine (ⓦwww.citylife.co.uk), from any newsstand, or check out the Friday edition of the *Manchester Evening News* (ⓦwww.manchesteronline.co.uk).

City transport

The city centre is compact enough to cover on **foot**, though buses will be needed for Oxford Road and its continuation Wilmslow Road – which runs to the curry restaurants of Rusholme – and you'll have to take the tram out to Salford Quays. **Piccadilly Gardens Bus Station** is the hub of the urban bus network, though a new transport interchange at **Shudehill** (north of the Arndale Centre; due for completion by 2006) may affect some routes. For Oxford and Wilmslow roads, use the stops at the top of Oxford Road by the *Palace Hotel*. **Information** about all services is available from the Travel Shop in Piccadilly Gardens (Mon–Sat 7am–6pm, Sun 10am–6pm); or call the GMPTE Travel Line (ⓣ0161/228 7811, ⓦwww.gmpte.gov.uk; daily 8am–8pm). Various bus companies ply the city-centre and suburban routes, though they are all accessible with a **Day Saver** ticket (£3.30), which gives unlimited travel on any city bus. There's also a seven-day Mega-Rider (£7.80) for travel on the network of Stagecoach city and local buses, or the Wayfarer (£7.50), which allows 24 hours' unlimited travel throughout Greater Manchester and into the Peak District.

Metrolink (ⓣ0161/205 2000) – the electric tram service – whisks through the city centre and out to the suburbs, linking Manchester with Bury, Salford Quays, Eccles and Altrincham (every 6–15min 6am–11.30pm). New stations are planned for the Shudehill transport interchange and the airport. Tickets for short hops cost from 50p to £1.90, though (trips to Salford Quays aside) you're unlikely to use the system for getting around unless you simply fancy the ride. There are stations at Piccadilly Station, Piccadilly Gardens, St Peter's Square, G-Mex, Market Street and Victoria Station.

MANCHESTER

ACCOMMODATION	
Castlefield	G
Didsbury House	P
Elton Bank	N
Grafton	O
Holiday Inn Express	H
Jury's Inn	K
The Lowry	B
Malmaison	C
Manchester Backpackers Hostel	M
Manchester YHA	F
Midland Crowne Plaza	D
The Ox	I
Premier Lodge	A & E
The Palace	L
Travel Inn Metro	J

PUBS	
The Beer House	3
Britons Protection	36
Circus Tavern	27
Dukes '92	41
The Lass o' Gowrie	42
Marble Arch	2
The Mark Addy	13
Mr Thomas' Chop House	14
Peveril of the Peak	34
Pot of Beer	1
Rain Bar	37
Sinclair's Oyster Bar	5
Temple of Convenience	33

A56 & M62
A664 Rochdale
Salford Quays
N
Manchester Evening News Arena
Victoria Station
Urbis
Chetham's Hospital School
Printworks
Corn Exchange
Cathedral
Cathedral Visitor Centre
Exchange Square
Craft & Design Centre
Northern Quarter
Arndale Centre
Royal Exchange
Easyeverything
Salford Station
People's History Museum
John Rylands Library
Opera House
Museum of Science & Industry
Town Hall
Central Library
City Art Gallery
China Town
Albert Square
Piccadilly Gardens
Piccadilly Gardens Bus Station
Chorlton Street Coach Station
Gay Village
River Irwell
Trinity Way
Great Ducie St
Cheetham Hill Road
Miller Street
Angel Street
Rochdale Road
Swan Street
Oldham Road
George Leigh Street
Blossom Street
Jersey Street
Great Ancoats Street
Shude Hill
Thomas Street
Oak Street
High Street
Withy Grove
Corporation Street
Cannon Street
Church St
Tib Street
Oldham Street
Lever Street
Dale Street
Newton Street
Tariff Street
Ducie Street
Store Street
Station Approach
Piccadilly
Hope St
Chatham St
Aytoun Street
Auburn St
Portland Street
Chorlton
Faulkner Street
Nicholas St
George St
Charlotte St
Mosley Street
York St
Spring Gardens
Market Street
Brown Street
King Street
Cross Street
St Ann's St
St Ann's Square
St Mary's Gate
New Cathedral St
Victoria Street
Victoria Bridge St
Blackfriars Road
Blackfriars Street
Chapel Street
Deansgate
Bridge Street
New Bailey St
Irwell Street
John Dalton St
Brazenose St
Princess Street
Hardman St
Lloyd St
Jacksons Row
Quay Street
Peter Street
Water Street

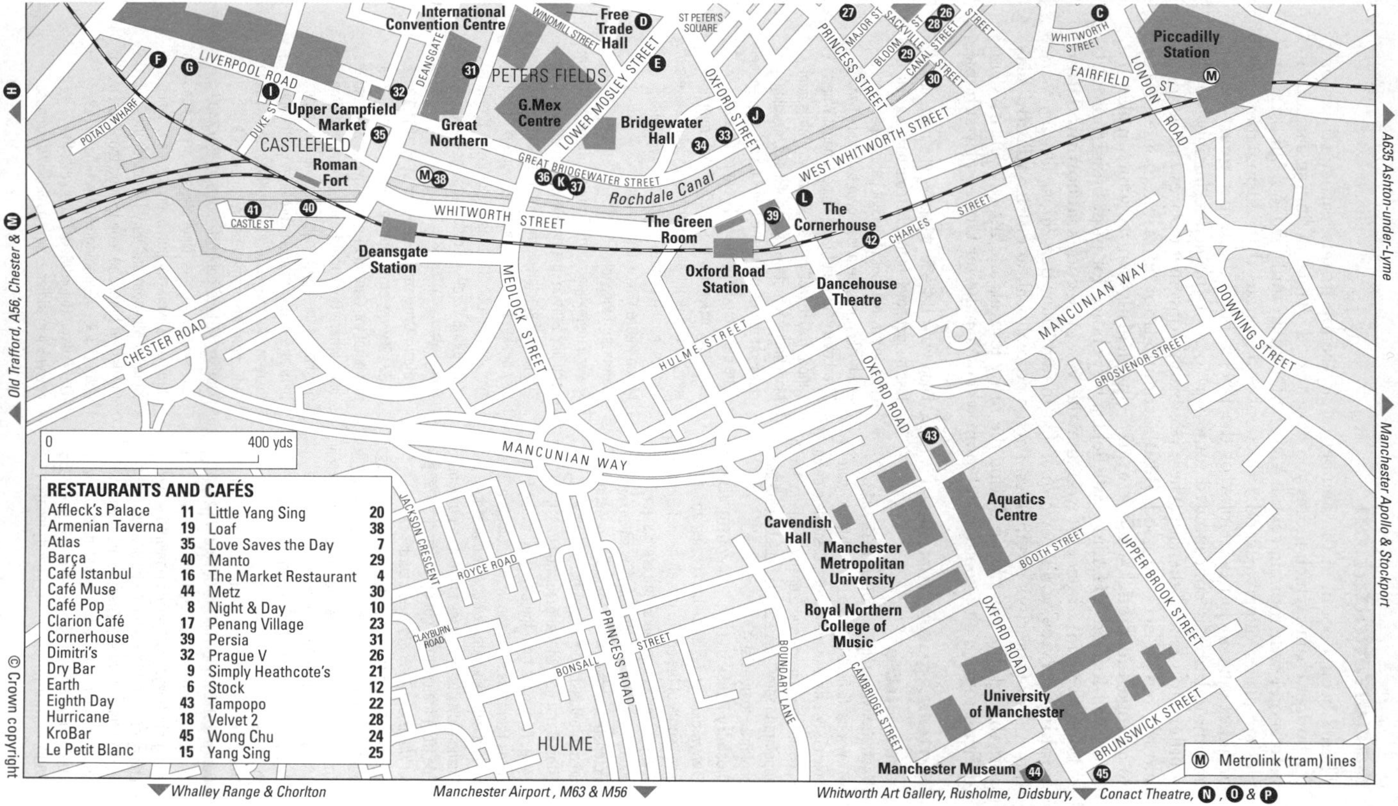

A635 Ashton-under-Lyme
Manchester Apollo & Stockport
Whitworth Art Gallery, Rusholme, Didsbury, Conact Theatre, N, O & P
Manchester Airport, M63 & M56
Whalley Range & Chorlton
Old Trafford, A56, Chester & M
H

Piccadilly Station
International Convention Centre
Free Trade Hall
PETERS FIELDS
G.Mex Centre
Bridgewater Hall
Upper Campfield Market
Great Northern
CASTLEFIELD
Roman Fort
The Green Room
The Cornerhouse
Deansgate Station
Oxford Road Station
Dancehouse Theatre
Cavendish Hall
Manchester Metropolitan University
Aquatics Centre
Royal Northern College of Music
University of Manchester
Manchester Museum
HULME
Rochdale Canal
LIVERPOOL ROAD
POTATO WHARF
DUKE ST
CASTLE ST
DEANSGATE
WINDMILL STREET
LOWER MOSLEY STREET
ST PETER'S SQUARE
OXFORD STREET
PRINCESS STREET
MAJOR ST
SACKVILLE ST
BLOOM ST
CANAL STREET
WHITWORTH STREET
FAIRFIELD ST
LONDON ROAD
GREAT BRIDGEWATER STREET
WEST WHITWORTH STREET
WHITWORTH STREET
CHARLES STREET
MEDLOCK STREET
CHESTER ROAD
HULME STREET
MANCUNIAN WAY
DOWNING STREET
GROSVENOR STREET
OXFORD ROAD
BOOTH STREET
UPPER BROOK STREET
BRUNSWICK STREET
CAMBRIDGE STREET
BOUNDARY LANE
PRINCESS ROAD
BONSALL STREET
JACKSON CRESCENT
ROYCE ROAD
CLAYBURN ROAD

0 400 yds

Ⓜ Metrolink (tram) lines

RESTAURANTS AND CAFÉS

Affleck's Palace	11	Little Yang Sing	20
Armenian Taverna	19	Loaf	38
Atlas	35	Love Saves the Day	7
Barça	40	Manto	29
Café Istanbul	16	The Market Restaurant	4
Café Muse	44	Metz	30
Café Pop	8	Night & Day	10
Clarion Café	17	Penang Village	23
Cornerhouse	39	Persia	31
Dimitri's	32	Prague V	26
Dry Bar	9	Simply Heathcote's	21
Earth	6	Stock	12
Eighth Day	43	Tampopo	22
Hurricane	18	Velvet 2	28
KroBar	45	Wong Chu	24
Le Petit Blanc	15	Yang Sing	25

Accommodation

There's been a boom in the number of city-centre **hotels**, particularly among the budget chains, which means you have a good chance of finding a smart, en-suite, motel-style room in central Manchester for around £50–60. Almost all the plusher places offer weekend reductions too – note that, during the week, breakfast isn't included at most of the pricier hotels. Cheaper **guest-house** accommodation is concentrated some way out of the centre, mainly on the southern routes into the city, where reasonably convenient places can be found and the bus services are good. **B&B** accommodation in private houses is easy to arrange, too, though again it won't be particularly central, which makes the city's well-located **YHA**, in Castlefield, a first choice for most budget travellers – book well in advance. If you use the Visitor Centre's **accommodation booking service**, you'll pay a small fee, though their free *Accommodation Guide* lists most of the city's possibilities. There's no real peak **accommodation season**, though the city fills up during the many festivals and major events; it's also difficult to get a city-centre hotel room when Manchester United play at home.

Hotels, guest houses and B&Bs

Castlefield Liverpool Rd ⓣ0161/832 7073, ⓦwww.castlefield-hotel.co.uk. Red-brick, warehouse-style development in the Castlefield basin, opposite the Science and Industry Museum. Nicely appointed rooms, and attached leisure club and pool (free to guests). ❹

Didsbury House Didsbury Park ⓣ0161/448 2200, ⓦwww.didsburyhouse.co.uk. Located about four miles south of the centre in well-heeled Didsbury Village – buses into the centre are fast and frequent – this is a slick and stylish conversion of Victorian premises with immaculate guest rooms. Great breakfasts too; pricey, but well worth it. ❼

Elton Bank 62 Platt Lane, Rusholme ⓣ0161/224 6449. Two miles from the city, overlooking Platt Fields Park, this small family-run hotel is a bit floral and old-fashioned, but is convenient for Rusholme's currry houses and only a quick bus ride from the centre – get off at *Hardy's Well* pub on Wilmslow Road. No credit cards. ❷

Grafton 56–58 Grafton St, Rusholme ⓣ0161/273 3092, ⓦwww.graftonhotelmanchester.co.uk. Six knocked-through terraced houses by the medical school, off Oxford Road, with simple rooms. Regular buses make the short trip into town; and there's a bar. No credit cards. ❷

Holiday Inn Express Waterfront Quay, Salford Quays ⓣ0161/868 1000 or 0800/897121, ⓦwww.hiexpress.co.uk. Reasonably sized rooms in a great Quays location, convenient for The Lowry or even Old Trafford – book ahead for a view of the "Theatre of Dreams" from your window. Continental breakfast included. ❹

Jury's Inn 56 Great Bridgewater St ⓣ0161/953 8888, ⓦwww.jurys.com. Very handy location – by Bridgewater Hall – for this large, 265-room, no-fuss budget hotel. Rates are room only, but you're close to any number of decent cafés; special week-end deals bring the price down a code or two. ❺

The Lowry 50 Dearman's Place, Chapel Wharf, Salford ⓣ0161/827 4000, ⓦwww.rfhotels.com. Manchester's first five-star hotel sits, exuding class, on the banks of the River Irwell, resplendent in its contemporary finery. Room rates are hideously expensive (up to £500 for a riverside view), but you get all mod cons, excellent levels of service, health centre, sauna and gym, and a Marco Pierre White dining room. ❾

Malmaison Piccadilly ⓣ0161/278 1000, ⓦwww.malmaison.com. A couple of minutes from Piccadilly Station, the ornate Edwardian facade of this place hides sleek interior lines and contemporary design from the Malmaison group. There's a gym, sauna, bar and brasserie, though breakfast costs extra. Weekend discounts depend on availability. ❼

Midland Crowne Plaza Peter St ⓣ0161/236 3333, ⓦwww.crowneplaza.com. Once the terminus hotel for Central Station (now G-Mex) and the place where Rolls met Royce for the first time, this building is the apotheosis of Edwardian style. The bars and public rooms impress most, though there's a full raft of leisure facilities and weekend reductions are sometimes available. ❽

The Ox 71 Liverpool Rd ⓣ0161/839 7740, ⓦwww.theox.co.uk. Nine pleasant rooms above a traditional, well-run pub opposite the Science and Industry Museum and very handy for the Castlefield bars. The food is good too; breakfast is extra (£3–6, depending what you have). ❷

The Palace Oxford St ⓣ0800/282840, ⓦwww.lemeridien.com. An Alfred Waterhouse glazed-tile extravaganza (formerly the Refuge Assurance HQ), with an equally magnificent interior, opposite the Cornerhouse arts centre. It's a business visitors' stalwart with no leisure facilities apart from the bar and restaurant. Good weekend discounts (when breakfast is included in the price). ❼

Premier Lodge 7–11 Lower Mosley St ⓣ0870/700 1476; and North Tower, Victoria Bridge St, Salford, ⓣ0870/700 1488; both ⓦwww.premierlodge.com. Good-value, city-centre, motel-style rooms and comfort from the Premier Lodge chain. The first is near G-Mex, the second near Deansgate, and there are several other lodges scattered about Greater Manchester, including one at the airport. ❷

Travel Inn Metro The Circus, 112 Portland St ⓣ0870/238 3315, ⓦwww.travelinn.co.uk. New city-centre location for the budget *Travel Inn*, offering decently equipped rooms (2 adults plus 2 children) at great rates, though breakfast is not included. ❷

Hostels and student halls

Manchester Backpackers Hostel 64 Cromwell Rd, Stretford ⓣ0161/865 9296 or 07711/556157. Attractive Victorian terrace house two miles out of the centre, with walled garden backing onto a park; take Metrolink to Stretford, or it's a ten-minute walk from leafy Chorlton which has regular buses into the city. Laundry facilities, kitchen, TV lounge and pool table. The small dorm provides the cheapest accommodation at £15; en-suite twins/doubles also available. No credit cards. ❶

Manchester YHA Potato Wharf, Castlefield ⓣ0870/770 5950, ⓦwww.yhamanchester.org.uk. Excellent hostel, overlooking the canal, opposite the Museum of Science and Industry. The en-suite rooms sleep one to four people (you can pay more to have the room to yourself) and the bunks convert into double beds; facilities for disabled people are available. Dorm beds £19, twins ❷

University accommodation University of Manchester/UMIST Central Accommodation Office, ⓣ0161/275 2888. Call for information about vacancies at the various university hostels (available during summer vacations). Office open Mon–Fri 9am–5pm. ❶–❷

The City

If Manchester can be said to have a centre, it's **St Peter's Square** and the cluster of buildings focused on it – the Town Hall (with the Visitor Centre in its modern extension), Central Library and the *Midland Crowne Plaza Hotel*, originally built in the railway age for visitors to Britain's greatest industrial city. South of here, the former Central Station now functions as the **G-Mex** exhibition centre, with the Hallé Orchestra's home, **Bridgewater Hall**, opposite; **Chinatown** (Britain's largest) and the **Gay Village** are just a short walk to the east; while to the northeast, the revamped **Piccadilly Gardens** provides access to the so-called **Northern Quarter**, the funkiest of the regenerated inner-city areas. To the southwest is the **Castlefield** district, site of the **Museum of Science and Industry**. Central spine of the city is **Deansgate**, which runs from Castlefield to the cathedral and, in its northern environs, displays the most dramatic core of urban regeneration in the country, centred on **Exchange Square**. Other city-centre diversions – including the Manchester Museum and Whitworth Art Gallery – string out along the main southern artery **Oxford Road**. Southwest of the centre, trams run out to **Salford Quays** where the renovated docks and quays now maintain two high-profile visitor attractions, **The Lowry** arts centre and the **Imperial War Museum North**; and no soccer fan will want to miss the tour of nearby **Old Trafford**, home of Manchester United.

Year-round, two-hour **guided walks** (£4) can be booked at the Visitor Centre in St Peter's Square. There are usually two or three departures a week, concentrating on various themes – from city burial grounds and industrial archeology to pub walks and music.

St Peter's Square and around

Manchester could claim little architectural merit without its Victorian neo-Gothic buildings. One of its boldest, Alfred Waterhouse's Town Hall, finished in 1877, divides the plain expanse of **St Peter's Square** from the more harmonious **Albert Square** to the north (whose memorial to Prince Albert is flanked by statues of John Bright and a perky William Gladstone). You're free to wander inside the **Town Hall** (Mon–Fri 9am–5pm; free) – enter from Albert Square or Lloyd Street into the echoing stone-vaulted interior and climb one of the grand staircases to the **Great Hall**, with its iron candelabras, stained-glass windows, double hammer-beam roof and paintings by Ford Madox Brown depicting decisive moments from Manchester's past. Elsewhere in the building, the mosaic floors are littered with statues and busts of civic worthies, from Anti Corn-Law leaders to Sir Charles Hallé. **Guided tours** of the building set off from the Visitor Centre (Easter–Dec every other Sat & each Thurs, usually at 2pm, though times can vary; £4).

On the south side of the Town Hall, the circular **Central Library** (Mon–Thurs 10am–8pm, Fri & Sat 10am–5pm) faces St Peter's Square. Built in 1934 as the largest municipal library in the world, it's an elegant classical construction with a domed reading room. The library building is still an impressive sight, but modern construction work has dwarfed adjacent landmarks: Lutyens' **Cenotaph** in St Peter's Square passes virtually unnoticed these days amid the swooshing trams; while around the back of the library (head through Library Walk), on Mount Street, the historic **Friends Meeting House** has managed to see off various attempts to knock it down.

Over on Peter Street, the late-Victorian **Midland Hotel** has worn well, and might tempt you in for tea and cakes in its lavish Edwardian interior. The exterior is no less beguiling: witness the exterior dragon-relief tiling. The hotel's earlier visitors ventured out for an evening's entertainment at the **Free Trade Hall** further to the west up Peter Street, which sponsored concerts by the city's own Hallé Orchestra for over a century, until Bridgewater Hall was completed in

Peterloo

Agitation for social and parliamentary reform in the early nineteenth century was concentrated in the booming industrial cities, led by radical orators, among them Henry Hunt, who addressed massed rallies of working men and women. Such a meeting was planned for **St Peter's Fields** in Manchester for August 16, 1819, with Hunt as main speaker, and though rumours spread throughout the city about the possibility of trouble, the local magistrates seemed content to let the rally take place. In the weeks before the event, many local people practised marching in orderly file so as to look respectable on the day – and on the day itself, a crowd of almost 80,000 turned up in its Sunday best, with women and children much in evidence – hardly the revolutionary rabble feared by the government critics of the reform movement. But as Hunt began to speak the magistrates had a change of heart, sending in their special constables (mostly recruited from the ranks of local businessmen) to arrest him. As pandemonium erupted, Hunt gave himself up to avoid further trouble, but with the special constables now under siege from the crowd, the soldiers were sent in.

Panic broke out as people tried to escape from the swords of the mounted soldiers, who cleared the fields in ten minutes. In what the press dubbed "**Peterloo**", 400 people were wounded, over a hundred by sword cuts, the rest by the stampeding crowd, and the final reckoning saw eleven dead, including two women and one child. Home Secretary Lord Sidmouth later congratulated the Manchester authorities on their handling of the situation and the government passed the draconian Six Acts, restricting the right of public meeting. Protests were widespread, even among the government's own supporters, and Peterloo became the catalyst for yet more agitation, culminating in the 1832 Reform Act and the subsequent rise of the Chartist movement.

1996. The Italianate facade survived wartime bombing and will be retained as part of any future development on the site. The Free Trade Hall was originally built on St Peter's Fields, the site of the "Peterloo Massacre" (see box opposite).

South of St Peter's Square, Lower Mosley Street runs past the **G-Mex** exhibition and conference centre, in use as a train station until 1969; pop your head into the huge vaulted interior for a quick goggle at its proportions. Adjacent is the **International Convention Centre**, while on the other side of G-Mex rises the **Bridgewater Hall**, at the junction of Bridgewater Street. This – Britain's finest purpose-built concert hall – is, uniquely, balanced on shock-absorbing springs to guarantee clarity of sound. The *Stalls* café-bar inside makes a good drinks stop. Moving on, the flashy apartment block at the corner of Lower Mosley Street and Whitworth Street West bears the name of the site's previous occupant, the fabulously famous – and musically seminal – **Hacienda** club, the spiritual home of Factory Records which opened in 1982 and finally closed in 1997. In its 1980s heyday, the club showcased live performances by an army of important bands, many from Manchester, including the likes of the Happy Mondays, Oasis and The Smiths, and pioneered and popularized a new dance craze – "House"; the rest is, as they say, is history.

The City Art Gallery and around

The other way up Mosley Street, north of St Peter's Square, rises Charles Barry's porticoed **City Art Gallery** (Tues–Sun 10am–5pm; free Ⓦwww.manchestergalleries.org), where a comprehensive collection of high Victorian art includes the country's finest public collection of works by the Pre-Raphaelite Brotherhood and possibly the best decorative art collection outside London. Following extensive refurbishment, the gallery has doubled in size and has a new extension linked by a glass public area to the original gallery. A top-floor space for special exhibitions concentrates on visual art and design, while the separate Gallery of Craft and Design provides space to display many items from the permanent collection for the first time. The Manchester Gallery is devoted to the visual history of the city and there's also a dedicated children's gallery, plus a theatre for decorative arts, a café and restaurant.

Around the corner from here, the grid of streets between Princess and Charlotte streets marks the boundaries of Britain's largest **Chinatown**, heralded by the inevitable Dragon Arch, focus of the city's annual Chinese New Year celebrations. To the southeast, the roads off Portland Street lead down to the Rochdale Canal, where Canal Street is the heart of Manchester's thriving **Gay Village**. The pink pound has transformed this part of the city and canalside cafés, clubs, bars and businesses have turned a formerly abandoned warehouse district into something with the verve of San Francisco.

Castlefield - and the Museum of Science and Industry

Fifteen minutes' walk southwest of St Peter's Square lies **Castlefield**. The country's first man-made canal, the Bridgewater Canal, brought coal and other goods to the warehouses here in the eighteenth century; the railway followed fifty years later, cementing Castlefield's pre-eminent position, which only declined after World War II. Since the early 1980s, an influx of money allied to a fair amount of speculative vision has resulted in a cobbled canalside, cleaned-up water, outdoor events arena and some attractive café-bars. It was Britain's first "urban heritage park" and it hosts various festivals and activities, notably the September carnival, bank-holiday street markets and canal cruises.

The castle-in-the-field itself is a **Roman fort** – finally abandoned around 410 AD – whose reconstructed north gate and the foundations of a few houses can be seen on Liverpool Road. This is just a hundred yards from the **Museum of Science and Industry** (daily 10am–5pm; last admission 4pm; free, admission charge for special exhibitions; ⓣ0161/832 2244; ⓦwww.msim.org.uk), one of the most impressive museums of its type in the country, set in various connected buildings and mixing technological displays and special blockbuster exhibitions with trenchant analysis of the social impact of industrialization. With Manchester at the forefront of the Industrial Revolution, it's hardly surprising that the museum trumpets the region's massive technological contribution – starting with the Lancashire-made steam engines, some of which are fired daily in the **Power Hall**. Pride of place goes to a working replica of Robert Stephenson's *Planet* – for which his father George's *Rocket* was the prototype. Built in 1830, the *Planet* reliably attained a scorching 30mph but had no brakes; the museum's version does, and uses them at weekends (call for times), dropping passengers a quarter-mile away at the **world's oldest passenger railway station**. It was here that the *Rocket* arrived on a rainy September 15, 1830, after fatally injuring Liverpool MP William Huskisson at the start of the inaugural passenger journey from Liverpool.

A reconstructed Victorian **sewer** below the station illustrates the problems of sanitation in the 1870s, when poor areas were still using street-end standpipes. The improvements brought about by domestic electrification are brought home in a suite of rooms that includes a wonderfully kitsch Fifties' living room. There's also a hands-on science centre and interactive gallery, where the kids hog all the best experiments, and displays dealing with fibres, fabrics and fashion, while the museum's comprehensive selection of carding machines, bobbin threaders and cotton looms crash into action at weekends in the **Textile Gallery**. Another glimpse into the past is provided by **Warehouse for the World**, a sound-and-light show (free) which delves into the history of the warehouses whose goods fuelled Manchester's early wealth. By way of contrast, the **Air and Space Hall** is something of an anomaly in that it barely touches on Manchester at all, though the cutaway engines, passenger-carrying kite and lightweight treatment of space exploration are bolstered by the popular attraction of a flight simulator (for which there's a charge).

Along Deansgate

Central **Deansgate** cuts through the city from the canal to the cathedral, its architectural reference points ranging from Victorian industrialism to post-millennium posturing. South of Peter Street, the **Peter's Fields** development has transformed a magnificent sweep of late-nineteenth-century warehousing into the **Great Northern** commercial and leisure complex, offset by glass walls, a campanile, open-air amphitheatre and grassy lawn. The inevitable café-bars, restaurants and shops provide a social focus; a pattern repeated a few minutes' further south down Deansgate where **Deansgate Locks** (stretching along Whitworth St) house a run of café-bars in the old railway arches along a section of the Rochdale Canal.

North along Deansgate, past Peter Street, keep an eye out for modern **Lincoln Square** (tucked between Queen and Brazenose streets), named after its standing statue of the American President. Manchester refused to break the embargo on using cotton from the Southern states during the Civil War, which led to unemployment among the city's workers – a sacrifice recognized by Lincoln himself, whose grateful letter to the city is quoted on the statue.

Across Deansgate, opposite Brazenose Street, is the beautifully detailed **John Rylands Library** (closed for refurbishment till 2005), the city's supreme example of Victorian Gothic. It was founded in 1890 by Enriqueta Ryland to house the theological works collected by her late husband, and has in the past displayed Bibles in more than three hundred languages among its million-strong general collection. Books are sure to be the main focus when the library reopens, but it's the interior detail that catches the eye – all carved and burnished wood, Art Nouveau metalwork, delicately crafted stone and stained glass.

From the library, continue up Deansgate and left into Bridge Street to reach the **People's History Museum** (Tues–Sun 11am–4.30pm; £1, free on Fri; Ⓦwww.peopleshistorymuseum.org.uk), an exhibition recording the lives and protests of England's working class over the last two hundred years. Posters, press reports, charters and anti-Government cartoons show the struggles of suffragettes, reformers and radicals, fighting for equal representation, votes and fair pay. Trade unionism is also well documented, with one of the country's best historic collections of marching banners, and there are displays devoted to social and cultural life, including coverage of local football and music.

St Ann's Square is tucked away off the eastern side of Deansgate, a couple of blocks up from John Dalton Street. Squat **St Ann's Church** (daily 9.30am–5pm) – baptismal church of Thomas De Quincey – flanks its southern side. Built in 1712, its lovely Renaissance interior was restored under the masterful direction of Alfred Waterhouse at the end of the nineteenth century, from when the striking stained glass dates. The church is fronted by a statue of nineteenth-century Free Trader Richard Cobden, joint-leader with John Bright of the Anti-Corn-Law League, which finally forced the repeal in 1846 of the restrictive Corn Laws. On the western side of the square, keep an eye out for the entrance to the **Barton Arcade**, a stunning Victorian glass-domed shopping gallery that runs through to Deansgate.

Crowning glory of St Ann's Square is the **Royal Exchange**, which houses the famous **Royal Exchange Theatre**, the country's largest theatre-in-the-round, whose steel-and-glass cat's cradle sits plonked under the building's immense glass-vaulted roof. Formerly the Cotton Exchange, this building employed seven thousand people until trading finished on December 31, 1968 – the old trading board still shows the last day's prices for American and Egyptian cotton. Also inside there's a good bookshop and crafts gallery, a café/restaurant plus bar, while the associated Royal Exchange Shopping Centre – three floors of shops and cafés – wraps around the building.

The Cathedral and Chetham's Library

At the far end of Deansgate stands the small, Perpendicular **Cathedral** (daily 8am–5.30pm; free), the third church on this site since its foundation in the ninth century. A fragment of stone by the choir and a fourteenth-century arch by the tower are all that remain of the earlier structures, and in truth it's been hacked about too much to have any real coherence. Indeed, the famed widest nave in England (114ft, as opposed to York Minster's 106ft) is entirely a result of rich families adding side chapels to the fifteenth-century church, which were later opened out to provide space for Manchester's burgeoning nineteenth-century church-goers. Actually, it's surprising it's still here at all: in 1940, a 1000lb bomb all but destroyed the interior, knocked out most of the stained glass (which is why it's so light inside) and necessitated the complete restoration of the fine misericords, which depict dragon-slaying as well as more mundane scenes – backgammon players and a calf butcher among them.

The cathedral's choristers are trained in **Chetham's Hospital School** (Ⓦwww.chethams.org.uk), across the way on Long Millgate (ask at the porter's lodge for entrance). This fifteenth-century manor house became a school and a free public library in 1653, then was transformed into a music school in 1969. There are free recitals (usually Mon–Fri 1.30pm) during term time and a half-hour tour following the concert on Wednesdays. The oak-panelled **library** (Mon–Fri 9am–12.30pm & 1.30–4.30pm) itself – with its carved eighteenth-century bookcases – is a real delight. Someone is usually on hand to show you the restored reading room, with the windowed alcove where, it's claimed, Marx and Engels used to study.

The area around the cathedral is being refashioned as the city's **Millennium Quarter**, with the six-storey **Urbis** (daily 10am–6pm; £5; Ⓦwww.urbis.org.uk) at its core. This hi-tech visitor centre explores the experience of six of the planet's cities – Manchester, naturally, claimed as the world's first industrial city – through a whole series of interactive exhibits; the other cities are Sao Paulo, Los Angeles, Tokyo, Paris and Singapore. If that doesn't draw you in, perhaps the SkyGlide indoor funicular (apparently the world's first) will, or you might be tempted by the top-floor restaurant, which offers splendid city views.

Exchange Square and around

Just to the north of St Ann's Square, **Exchange Square** sits at the heart of the ambitious city-centre rebuilding programme launched following the devastating bomb of 1996. A pedestrian boulevard – **New Cathedral Street** – runs from St Ann's Square to the cathedral, skirting the flanks of the flagship **Marks & Spencer** store whose gigantic glazed facade makes up the south side of Exchange Square. The landscaped square, with its water features and public sculpture, plus Selfridges and Harvey Nichols stores, has quickly become a much-frequented, if not exactly loved, urban space, buzzed by skateboarders. Two historic pubs, the *Old Wellington Inn* and *Sinclair's Oyster Bar*, both moved brick-by-brick to this new site, mop up some of the foot traffic at their outdoor tables.

To the east, the Sixties' eyesore that was the **Arndale Centre** has been enlarged, modernized and clad in glass. To the north, the old **Corn Exchange** has been refurbished completely, while retaining its historic facade and glass dome. Relaunched as the **Triangle** (reflecting the unusual shape of its interior), this is a rare wrong foot in the brave new Manchester: gone is any sense of the building's tradition, replaced by yet another batch of retail outlets selling expensive shoes and Japanese rice bowls. Across Withy Grove, meanwhile, the former Mirror Building contains the futuristic **Printworks**, an adult "entertainment centre", complete with IMAX screen, cinema megaplex and various themed bars and restaurants. Step inside and you're confronted by a theme-park style recreation of a New York street, though some of the building's original features have survived.

Piccadilly Gardens and the Northern Quarter

For years, the bleak expanse of **Piccadilly Gardens** divided rather than united the city, though a recent beautification project has dramatically enhanced its character. Japanese architects have re-styled the area, adding groves of trees, a fountain and water jets, and a pavilion at one end to screen off the traffic. Piccadilly Plaza, comprising the ugly Sixties' buildings on the southwest side, is also due a facelift, while a new shopping arcade is planned to link the gardens with Chinatown.

The gardens remain a major local transport hub and gateway to the still shabby but improving Oldham Street, which has been adopted by "alternative" entrepreneurs who have dubbed it the **Northern Quarter**. Traditionally, this is Manchester's garment district and you'll still find shops and wholesalers selling high-street fashions, shop fittings, mannequins and hosiery, but there are also new design outlets, lots of music stores, and some funky bars and cafés. The nineteenth-century, red-brick Fish Wholesale Market on High Street is now just a shell, though it retains its marvellous sculpted pediments; for off-beat contemporary shopping, look in Affleck's Palace (52 Church St), and in the Coliseum (18–24 Church St). Loft-style apartments change hands around here for serious money these days; the renovated **Smithfield Buildings** are an example of what can be done with Oldham Street's fine old buildings – in this case, a former department store. There are more skills and crafts on display in the excellent **Manchester Craft and Design Centre**, 17 Oak St (Mon–Sat 10am–5.30pm; free; Ⓦ www.craftanddesign.com) – a great place to pick up ceramics, fabrics, earthenware, jewellery and decorative art, or just sip a drink in the cosy café.

Oxford Road and points south

From St Peter's Square, **Oxford Road** – initially Oxford Street – stretches through a ragged mile of faculty buildings to Rusholme and the leafy suburbs beyond. Oxford Road Station lurks behind the **Cornerhouse**, the dynamo of the Manchester arts scene. In addition to screening art-house films, the Cornerhouse has three floors of gallery space (Tues–Sat 11am–6pm, Sun 2–6pm; free) devoted to contemporary and local artists' work. The café and bar are popular, too. Across the road, Alfred Waterhouse's majestic **Refuge Assurance** building of 1891 is one of Manchester's joys, its soaring clock-tower, dome and terracotta facade now hiding the bulk of the *Palace Hotel*. An endless stream of buses runs down Oxford Road from here, passing the buildings and sights detailed below.

The Manchester Aquatics Centre and the Manchester Museum

Built with the Commonwealth Games in mind, the **Manchester Aquatics Centre** (Mon–Fri 6.30am–10pm, Sat & Sun 7am–6pm; £2.50), at Booth Street, about ten minutes' walk from the Cornerhouse, holds two fifty-metre pools under a wave-shaped roof. From here, it's another ten-minute hoof along Oxford Road to the Gothic Revival home of the **Manchester Museum** (Mon–Sat 10am–5pm; free; Ⓦ www.museum.man.ac.uk), one of the city's great unsung treats. At the centre of the Egyptology world since the 1890s, the museum has done pioneering work on mummy dissection and captivating displays enlarge upon the burial practices and techniques that their work has revealed. Rocks, minerals, fossils and natural history also get their own exhibition space, while the top-floor Science for Life section concentrates on the human body and biomedical research – and zeroes in on Mancunian health pioneers who led the way in developing treatments for cancer, test-tube babies, hip replacements, colour blindness and so forth. A vivarium and an aquarium complete the list of attractions, and an excellent café tops it all off.

The Whitworth Gallery and Rusholme

Another half-mile away is the city's modern art collection, housed in the red-brick **Whitworth Gallery** (Mon–Sat 10am–5pm, Sun 2–5pm; free; Ⓦ www.whitworth.man.ac.uk). The gallery forms two distinct halves, pre-1880s and modern, with the former collection incorporating a strong assembly of watercolours by Turner, Constable, Cox and Blake as well as Gillray engravings, and Hogarth prints. There are also several diverting oddities, most notably Ford Madox Brown's *Execution of Mary Queen of Scots* – his first, and not entirely successful, attempt at a large-scale historical work. The modern collection concentrates on post-1880 British staples, with Moore, Frink and Hepworth setting off contributions from lesser-known artists. Look for works by Paul Nash (one of the organizers of the London Surrealist exhibition of 1936), the World War II artist John Piper and those of Stephen Conroy, a contemporary figurative painter whose subjects resonate with Victorian images. With Manchester's cotton connections it is perhaps not surprising that the gallery also displays the country's widest range of textiles outside London's Victoria and Albert Museum.

Walk just two hundred yards south of the Whitworth Gallery and you'll catch the pungent spicy smell of **Rusholme**'s Wilmslow Road, a "golden mile" of curry houses, sari shops and grocers stocked with all manner of exotic vegetables, halal meats and sticky sweets. In **Platt Fields Park**, at the south end of the curry mile (just past *Hardy's Well* pub), the **Gallery of Costume** (last Sat of the month 10am–5pm; pre-booked visits Tues–Fri 10am–5pm; ⓣ0161/224 5217; free) fills Georgian Platt Hall. Its collection spans fashion through the ages, giving particular emphasis to Manchester's former role as a textile centre, its large Asian population and the clothes of the working class – you're just as likely to see Indian wedding outfits or contemporary street fashion as designer shoes and silk jackets.

Didsbury and Chorlton Green

Most of the buses that head down Oxford Road continue through Rusholme and the student areas of Fallowfield and Withington to **Didsbury Village**, Manchester's most prestigious and leafy suburb. There are some great pubs and restaurants here – and in nearby **West Didsbury** – plus a large park containing **Didsbury Botanical Gardens** (dawn–dusk; free), a landscaped patch of ponds, shrubs, rare pines and firs and an imaginative array of cacti and flowers. A pleasant hour's walk follows the river from Didsbury to **Chorlton Water Park** (daily 8am–dusk; free), where water sports are available between April and September; in the winter, ducks and other wildfowl visit the lake. From the park, a short walk will take you to Barlow Moor Road, served by frequent buses returning to the city centre. Or you can walk up to **Chorlton Green**, another attractive suburb with its own village green, where there are a couple of great pubs (the *Horse and Jockey* and *Trevor Arms*).

Salford Quays – The Lowry and the Imperial War Museum North

The Metrolink extension to **Salford Quays** provides easy access to one of the city's first urban development projects. For ninety years, from 1894 when the Manchester Ship Canal opened, the Salford docks turned the city into one of Britain's busiest ports. Trade declined in the 1970s and the docks eventually closed in 1982, since which time the Salford Quays development has transformed the run-down quays on the western edge of the city centre into a hugely popular waterfront residential and leisure complex, with its own watersports centre and new outlet mall.

Various Metrolink stations serve the area: for the **Salford Quays tourist information office** (Mon–Fri 8.30am–4.30pm, Sun 10am–4pm; ⓣ0161/848 8601, ⓦwww.visitsalford.com) get off at Salford Quays Station. You can pick up a map here and wander down the Centenary Walkway quayside, studded with commemorative discs whose engraved words and snippets reflect the area's history. This ends at the promontory taken up by **The Lowry** (daily from 9.30am; free; ⓦwww.thelowry.com), the Quays' striking, shining steel arts centre whose theatres, galleries (Sun–Wed 11am–5pm, Thurs–Sat 11am–8pm; free)

△ Imperial War Museum North

and creative ArtWorks exhibition (Mon–Fri 10am–3pm, Sat & Sun 10am–4pm; suggested donation £3) have quickly become one of Manchester's leading attractions; to travel straight here, stay on the Metrolink until Broadway. The building itself is a great piece of art and you're free to wander around or take a guided tour (3 daily; £4), popping into the galleries and exhibitions at will, or grabbing a bite to eat in the café or restaurant. The centre, of course, takes its name from L.S. Lowry and no artist is more closely linked with an English city than Lowry is with Manchester. There's always a selection of **Lowry paintings** on show for free, illustrating both his early views on the desolation and sadness of Manchester's mill workers and his changing outlook in later life when he repeated earlier paintings changing the greys and sullen browns for lively reds and pinks. Lowry also expanded his repertoire as he grew older, capturing mountain scenes and seascapes in broad sweeps of his brush, and painting full-bodied realistic portraits that are far less known than his matchstick crowds.

A footbridge runs from The Lowry across to the Trafford side of the docks where the startling new **Imperial War Museum North** (daily 10am–6pm; free; Ⓦwww.iwm.org.uk/north) raises a giant steel fin into the air, all to the design of Daniel Libeskind. The museum's three steel "shards" represent war on land and sea and in the air. The interior is just as striking, its angular lines serving as a dramatic backdrop to the displays, which kick off with the Big Picture, when the walls of the main hall are transformed into giant screens to show three rotated, fifteen-minute, surround-sound films. Among the hundreds of artefacts displayed in the main hall are five so-called "iconic objects", including the artillery piece that fired the first British shell in World War I and a fire pump used when Manchester was blitzed in World War II. In addition, there are all sorts of themed displays in six separate exhibition areas – the Silos – focusing on everything from women's work in the two world wars to war reporting and the build up to the Iraq conflict of 2003. It's an ambitious and carefully conceived museum with a mixture of the personal and the general that is nothing less than superb.

Old Trafford

Looming in the near distance from the Salford Quays is **Old Trafford**, the self-styled "Theatre of Dreams" and home of **Manchester United**, arguably the most famous football team in the world. The club's following is such that only season-ticket holders can ever attend games, but **tours** of Old Trafford and its museum (daily 9.30am–5pm; museum & tour £8.50, museum only £5.50; advance booking essential, Ⓣ0870/442 1994, Ⓦwww.manutd.com) placate out-of-town fans who want to gawp at the silverware, sit in the dug-out and visit the *Red Café*. To get here, take the Metrolink to Old Trafford Station and walk up Warwick Road to Sir Matt Busby Way. Incidentally, the city's poorer soccer cousins, **Manchester City** (Ⓦwww.mcfc.co.uk), who have been almost entirely overshadowed by their neighbour's success for years, have finally evacuated their old inner-city ground, Maine Road – the "Theatre of Base Comedy", according to soccer commentator Stuart Hall – and moved to the spanking new City of Manchester stadium on the east side of the city.

Eating and drinking

Second only to London in the breadth and scope of its **cafés** and **restaurants**, Manchester has something to suit everyone, from a cheap curry to a night out in a celebrity-chef hotspot. Moreover, at both ends of the market, your money goes a lot further than it does in London, while smart in Manchester doesn't always mean snobby. The bulk of Manchester's eating and drinking places are scattered around the city centre, while out at Rusholme you'll find the best range of curries this side of the Pennines. Most city **pubs** dish up something filling at lunchtime, but for a more modish snack or drink, European-style **café-bars** are everywhere, especially in the new city-centre developments, in the Northern Quarter, and in the Gay Village on the Rochdale Canal.

Daytime cafés

The coffee-bar and sandwich chains have moved swiftly into the city, so if you want a *Starbuck's*, a *Coffee Republic*, a *Caffé Nero* or a *Prêt à Manger* you won't have far to look. Mancunians, though, favour the local *Java* outlets (8a Oxford Rd, 95 Piccadilly and Victoria Station), which serve up all the usual coffee variants, plus biscotti, croissants and sandwiches, and the half-dozen, city-wide *Feed The Five Thousand* sandwich bars. The places listed below usually open daily from around 10am to 6 or 7pm, unless otherwise stated.

Affleck's Palace 52 Church St, at Oldham Street. Five floors of boutiques, with the best of the cafés on the top floor, where you can grab a coffee and a grilled sandwich. Closed Sun.

Café Muse Manchester Museum, Oxford Rd. First-rate, inventive snacks at this light and airy museum café. Popular in equal measure with university lecturers and museum goers. Mon–Sat 10am–5pm.

Café Pop 34–36 Oldham St. Retro café full of 1970s' kitsch and pop collectables, with the emphasis on veggie fry-ups, hefty sandwiches (including the famous triple-decker Scooby Snax), omelettes and the like. Service can be a bit chaotic but portions are enormous and prices very fair. Closed Sun.

Clarion Café Left Bank, Bridge St. The café at the People's History Museum serves a good-value daily lunch (noon–2pm), plus drinks and snacks, and there's outdoor seating in the summer. Closes at 4pm and all day Mon.

Cornerhouse 70 Oxford St. The place to sip a cappuccino after viewing the galleries or catching a movie. The first-floor café (daily until 11pm) dishes up mezze and pizzas, and there's also a good bar downstairs.

Earth 16–20 Turner St. Gourmet vegan and organic food in a stylish Northern Quarter pit-stop with Buddhist leanings – stuffed pancakes, pies, bakes, juices and deli delights. Closes 5pm on Sat & all day Sun.

Eighth Day 107–111 Oxford Rd. Manchester's oldest organic-vegetarian café has got spanking new premises on its old Oxford Road site – shop, takeaway and juice bar upstairs, café/restaurant downstairs.

Love Saves the Day Smithfield Building, Tib St. New York style and sass in this Northern Quarter deli-café, where a daily changing menu of platters, salads, pasta and sandwiches keep the locals happy. And there's very good coffee too. Closed Sun.

Café-bars

Manchester's **café-bar** scene is its pride and joy, with most of the places below fielding a very definite crowd and atmosphere. Many of those in the Gay Village, the Northern Quarter and Castlefield are reasonably laidback, though evenings always see the atmosphere ratcheted up a notch; while at the half-dozen places along Deansgate Locks (Whitworth St West) or in the Printworks (Withy Grove) the emphasis is more on serious partying. Lots of café-bars have outdoor seating, and take advantage of relaxed licensing laws to offer drinks without food. As a general rule, those listed below are open daily from 11am or noon until around midnight, often later at the weekend or if there's music.

Atlas 376 Deansgate. Wood-panel the inside of an old railway arch, add bamboo thickets to a large urban patio and you've got one of the best café-bars in the city. Justly known for its quality focaccia sandwiches, it's also the place for Sunday brunch, a bottle of beer or a decent glass of wine – and don't forget to browse in the associated deli next door.

Barça Arch 8 & 9, Catalan Square. Trendy Castlefield bar/restaurant tucked into the restored railway arches, with a lovely canalside terrace, cosy lounge with fire, and upstairs dining room and deck for fashionable Mediterranean flavours.

Dry Bar 28–30 Oldham St. The earliest of the designer café-bars on the scene, started by Factory records and the catalyst for much of what has happened since in the Northern Quarter. *Dry* is still as cool as they come.

KroBar 325 Oxford Rd, opposite Manchester University Students' Union. Half the students in Manchester crowd into this huge good-natured café-bar, sited in a former men-only teetotalers' club. Offers value-for-money food, caffeine and a vast range of on-tap beers; on a sunny day, you'll struggle to find table space outside. One of the city's best, with another branch further up Oxford Road towards the city centre.

Loaf Deansgate Locks, Whitworth St West. Large queues at the weekend for this designer-industrial café-bar, not nearly so crowded during the day when you can grab an outdoor table underneath the arches and soak up the weak Manchester sun.

Manto 46 Canal St. Gay Village stalwart whose chic crowd laps up the cool sounds and club nights. A canalside Sunday brunch is a treat here, or hop upstairs to *Sarasota*, for fusion cooking and the city's only retractable roof for alfresco dining.

Metz 3 Brazil St. Classy converted warehouse bar and restaurant. It's great for a pre-club drink or two and its Eastern European food's not bad either.

Night & Day 26 Oldham St. Unpretentious café-bar with a late licence and live music – jazz, blues, Latin and funk – most nights from local musicians. Closed Sun.

Persia Great Northern Warehouse, Peter's Fields, Peter St. Manchester meets the Arabian Nights. Lurk at the funky bar; marvel at the brick ovens, pillars and tiles; or lounge under parasols, grazing on flat-bread pizzas (house special: langoustine, artichoke and fontina), dips, wraps, tagines and salads.

Prague V 40 Chorlton St. Gay-friendly hangout on the Canal Street corner, with Czech beer, Mediterranean-inspired meals and snacks, and a late weekend drinks licence.

Velvet 2 Canal St. The red-brick facade hides a stylish, laid-back basement cavern, with good food, outrageous staff, campy clientele and late-night sounds.

Restaurants

There's been a revolution in Manchester's dining scene in recent years, with the long-standing city-centre **restaurants** being joined by a host of trendy brasseries and celebrity-chef ventures. Paul Heathcote (the only vaguely local boy), Gary Rhodes, Raymond Blanc and Marco Pierre White are all associated with various Manchester restaurants (ie they don't necessarily do the cooking) and if you've got the cash and are in the city for any length of time, you should go to at least one of them to see what all the fuss is about. **Chinatown** in the city centre can always be counted upon for a budget lunch or a late-night meal; otherwise, most city-centre restaurants congregate along and off Deansgate. It also pays to visit the **suburbs**, particularly those of south Manchester, where Asian (Rusholme) and Mediterranean/Modern-British (Didsbury Village and West Didsbury) restaurants are all the rage. Taxis aren't particularly expensive to any of these places, or you can easily take a bus.

City centre

Armenian Taverna Albert Square ☎0161/834 9025. Filling meze platters (for vegetarians too) bring in many, who then find they wish they'd plumped for a halibut kebab or grilled spring chicken, or one of a dozen other mighty main courses. Closed Mon. Moderate.

Café Istanbul 79 Bridge St ☎0161/833 9942. Delicious Turkish dishes, including a great meze selection, and an extensive wine list (including a powerful Turkish red). Closed Sun. Inexpensive to Moderate.

Dimitri's 1 Campfield Arcade, Deansgate ☎0161/839 3319. Pick and mix from the Greek/Spanish/Italian menu (particularly good for vegetarians), or grab a sandwich, an arcade table and sip a drink (Greek coffee to Lebanese wine). Moderate.

Hurricane King St, Spring Gardens ☎0161/839 9966. The city's great and good have adopted this former haunt of the Reform Club as their pet restaurant, revelling in its oh-so-glamorous Venetian-Gothic exterior and spiffing French-inspired food. Closed Sun. Expensive.

Le Petit Blanc 55 King St ☎0161/832 1001. Best place in the city for reasonably priced classic and regional French cooking is Raymond Blanc's mid-range brasserie operation – fish soup to a roast poussin off the a la carte menu or good-value, three-course, *prix fixe* for around £18. Real food for children too. Moderate.

Little Yang Sing 17 George St ☎0161/228 7722.

Celebrated basement restaurant (forerunner to the larger *Yang Sing*) where the emphasis is on *dim sum*, rice or noodle dishes, and down-to-earth Cantonese cooking, with lots of choice under £8. Moderate.

The Market Restaurant 104 High St ☎0161/834 3743. One of the city's hidden treasures, this is a very relaxing spot for dinner. The regularly changing menu throws its Modern-British weight around in adventurous, eclectic fashion. Also a very good wine and beer list. Reservations essential. Open Wed–Sat dinner only. Expensive.

Penang Village 56 Faulkner St ☎0161/236 2650. You soon get the idea – Malay village scenes on the wall, a traditional fishing boat as centrepiece – but this friendly Malaysian joint backs up the decor with tasty, authentic dishes. *Ayam percik* (barbecued chicken with a mild curry sauce), beef rendang, veg curry, and the good *roti* bread are all recommended. Closed Mon. Moderate.

Simply Heathcote's Jackson Row ☎0161/835 3536. Massive, minimalist dining rooms operated by Lancastrian chef Paul Heathcote. Mixes Mediterranean and local flavours, so expect updated working-class dishes alongside the parmesan shavings. The set lunch/early-bird menu is one of the city's best deals for food of this stature. Expensive.

Stock 4 Norfolk St ☎0161/839 6644. Superior Italian cooking – the fish is renowned – accompanied by a wine list of serious intent. It's housed In the city's old stock exchange, hence the name. Closed Sun. Expensive.

Tampopo 16 Albert Square ☎0161/819 1966. Basement noodle bar with long benches and a fast turnover. Noodle dishes are Japanese, Thai, Malaysian or Indonesian with most dishes under £7. Inexpensive.

Wong Chu 63 Faulkner St ☎0161/236 2346. Simply the best of the budget Chinatown eateries, this no-frills, paper-tablecloth joint serves up enormous portions of Cantonese staples. Highlights are the deep-bowl noodle soups or piled-high rice-and-meat plates, at bargain prices. Inexpensive.

Yang Sing 34 Princess St ☎0161/236 2200. The *Yang Sing* is one of the best Cantonese restaurants in the country, with thoroughly authentic food, from a lunchtime plate of fried noodles to the full works. Stray from the printed menu for the most interesting dishes; ask the friendly staff for advice. Moderate to Expensive.

Rusholme

Darbar 65–67 Wilmslow Rd ☎0161/224 4392. Award-winning Asian food in plain but friendly surroundings. The chef's special (he's been voted Manchester's Curry Chef of the Year twice) is *nihari*, a slow-cooked lamb dish, while other homestyle choices appear on Sundays. Take your own booze. Inexpensive.

Sanam 145–151 Wilmslow Rd, Rusholme ☎0161/224 8824. One of Rusholme's earliest arrivals, now thirty years old, the *Sanam* serves all the usual dishes plus award-winning *gulab juman*. Drop by the take-away sweet and snack centre on the way home. No alcohol allowed. Inexpensive to Moderate.

Shere Khan IFCO Centre, 52 Wilmslow Rd, Rusholme ☎0161/256 2624. A Rusholme standard-bearer, this big Indian brasserie gets packed at the weekends, but always maintains its high standards. The open grill dispenses marvellous kebabs, and the wide-ranging menu is also strong on *karahi* and *biryani* dishes. A celebrity favourite – hence the Gallagher brothers on the walls. Inexpensive to Moderate.

Didsbury and West Didsbury

Chiang Rai 762 Wilmslow Rd, Didsbury Village ☎0161/448 2277. Manchester's best – and most elegant – Thai restaurant specializes in cuisine from the north, including fine steamed fish and flavourful Thai sausage. Good lunch deals. Moderate.

Greens 43 Lapwing Lane, West Didsbury ☎0161/434 4259. Imaginative gourmet vegetarian meals in stripped-down surroundings. Early-bird and Sunday specials get you three courses for around a tenner – and you can bring your own wine. Closed Mon & Sat lunch. Moderate.

Lime Tree 8 Lapwing Lane, West Didsbury ☎0161/445 1217. Bundles of Modern-British joy, with a menu that chargrills and oven-roasts as if its life depended on it. Organic salmon is a signature dish, or else you could be chowing down on such delights as crispy duckling or courgette and leek cheesecake. Very fashionable, and reservations recommended. Closed Mon & Sat lunch, & Sun dinner; early bird, three-course meals for just £15. Moderate to Expensive.

Peppers 4 Warburton St, Didsbury Village ☎0161/445 0448. Tucked away off the main road, this cottage-style bolt-hole from the Didsbury chain restaurants and bars is an oasis of charm. Two floors of intimate dining, with a window onto the kitchen, where omelettes and open sandwiches at lunch (around £5) give way to seasonally changing Modern-British dinners. Moderate to Expensive.

Salford and Trafford

Rhodes and Co Waters Reach, Trafford Park ☎0161/868 1900. Gary Rhodes' sleek brasserie is a bit out of the way for everything except Old Trafford (but then Gary's a Reds' fan). Good deals at lunch can keep the cost down. Expensive.

Steven Saunders at The Lowry The Lowry, Salford Quays ☎0161/876 2121. The Lowry's flagship restaurant has a seasonally changing Modern-British menu. Set lunches for around a tenner and pre-theatre menus take the edge off the bill, and you get the high-tech designer Lowry surroundings for free. Expensive.

Pubs

As you might expect, Manchester has a full complement of **pubs**, from Victorian classics to modern designer bars and pubs which occupy imaginatively recycled older buildings. Inevitably, there are also the off-the-shelf contemporary chains – Irish theme-bars and the like – but these are easy to avoid. As far as **beer** goes, Boddington's is the big deal hereabouts, though independent local brewers Hydes, Holts and Robinson's all have their adherents.

The Beer House 6 Angel St. The best place for ale tasting, with a constant stock of more than thirty brews.

Britons Protection 50 Great Bridgewater St. Elegantly decorated traditional pub opposite Bridgewater Hall, with a couple of cosy, smoky rooms and a brickyard beer garden. The home-made pies are good, and there are comedy nights.

Circus Tavern 86 Portland St. Manchester's smallest pub – a Victorian drinking-hole that's many people's favourite city-centre pit-stop. You may have to knock on the door to get in; once you do, you're confronted by the landlord in the corridor pulling pints.

Dukes '92 Castle St. Classily revamped former stable block (for canal horses) with art on the walls, terrace seating and a fine selection of beers. Serves great-value food too, including a wide range of pâtés and cheeses.

The Lass o' Gowrie 1 Charles St. Outside, glazed tiles and Victorian styling; inside, stripped floors and a micro-brewery.

Marble Arch 73 Rochdale Rd. Curious real ale house with a sloping floor, whose in-house Marble Brewery produces some fine brews – the seasonal "Ginger Marble" or the strong "Chocolate Heavy" among them.

The Mark Addy 2 Stanley St. Mainly known for its food, the Mark Addy – named after a local Victorian character – serves a choice of fifty cheeses and eight pâtés (including vegetarian). Eat inside, or outside by the River Irwell.

Mr Thomas' Chop House 52 Cross St. Victorian classic with a Dickensian feel to its nooks and crannies. Office workers, hardcore daytime drinkers, old goats and students all call it home. There's good-value, traditional English "chop-house" food (oysters, bubble and squeak, etc) served in the ornate dining-and-drinking room at the rear – and old-fashioned table service for anyone who can't make their own way to the bar.

Peveril of the Peak 127 Great Bridgewater St. The pub that time forgot – one of Manchester's best real ale houses, with a youthful crowd and some superb Victorian glazed tilework outside.

Pot of Beer 36 New Mount St. Nicely restored real ale pub with a secondary line in Polish bar meals; on the northern fringes of the city centre but worth the hike.

Rain Bar 80 Great Bridgewater St. Pub or bar? Experience both, drinking inside the stripped-wood pubby interior, up in the swish bar, or out on the sweeping canalside terraces. Good range of beers, a decent menu and summer barbecue nights.

Sinclair's Oyster Bar Cathedral Gates, top of New Cathedral St. This well-loved eighteenth-century hostelry was moved to its new site lock, stock and barrel after the Arndale bomb. It shares outdoor seating with the equally venerable *Wellington* pub, for ringside views of Exchange Square.

Temple of Convenience Great Bridgewater St. A tiny converted public toilet – yes that's right – stocking a wide selection of Belgian beers.

Nightlife

For the last twenty years Manchester has been vying with London as Britain's capital of **youth culture**, spearheaded by the success of its musical exports, from the saintly Morrissey to Badly Drawn Boy, Joy Division to Oasis. Banks of fly posters advertise what's going on in the numerous **clubs** which, as elsewhere, frequently change names and styles on different nights of the week,

The gay scene

Manchester has one of Britain's most vibrant gay scenes, centred on the Rochdale Canal between Princess and Sackville streets, in the so-called **Gay Village** – focus of Channel 4's gay-soap "Queer As Folk". The café-bars and clubs here are among the city's best, though some claim that the area's increased popularity – with straight as well as gay visitors – has somewhat diluted its essence. Amongst gay-specific events, one of the best is **Gayfest**, held every August bank holiday in and around the village. Other events, including an annual arts festival every May/June, are co-ordinated by **queerupnorth** (information on ⓣ0161/833 2288, ⓦwww.queerupnorth.com).

Out on the town, early evenings kick off by the lock at one of the **café-bars** along Canal Street – *Manto*, *Metz*, *Baby Cream*, *Spirit* or *Velvet* – at the extravagant *Via Fossa* pub or at the more macho *New Union*, 111 Princess St, just off Canal Street. An older crowd drinks in the *Rembrandt Hotel* on Sackville Street (which also has gay-friendly accommodation available; ⓦwww.rembrandtmanchester.com), while *Vanilla* on Richmond Street is a good-natured women's café-bar with club nights. Meanwhile, a camp neon Liberty beckons you into *New York, New York*, 98 Bloom St. **Clubs** include the state-of-the-art *Essential*, 8 Minshull St (ⓣ0161/237 5445); old favourite *Cruz*, 101 Princess St (ⓣ0161/237 1554); the over-the-top *Hollywood Showbar*, 100 Bloom St (ⓣ0161/236 6151); and *Follies*, 6 Whitworth St (ⓣ0161/236 8149), a lesbian favourite.

For further **information**, try the Lesbian and Gay Foundation (daily 4–10pm; ⓣ0161/235 8035, ⓦwww.lgfoundation.org.uk) which can put you in touch with the dozens of other organizations and services operating out of the Gay Village.

though it has to be said that clubbing is not quite what it was. The gang-related violence that precipitated the implosion of the "Madchester" scene in the early 1990s left a bitter taste and only now is the air beginning to clear. The most enduring clubs are listed below and you can expect to pay £3–15 cover depending on what's on. Many of the city's grooviest café-bars also host regular club nights. Manchester also has an excellent **live music** scene in pubs and clubs, with tickets for local bands usually under £5, more like £10–15 for someone you've heard of. Mega-star gigs take place either at the G-Mex Centre or one of the major stadiums, all listed below. For the broadest coverage of Manchester's musical happenings, check the weekly *City Life* magazine or Friday's *Manchester Evening News*.

Smaller live-music and club venues

The Attic above the *Thirsty Scholar*, 50 New Wakefield St ⓣ0161/236 6071. Regular weekend blasts of funk, soul and dance for a student crowd.

Band on the Wall 25 Swan St ⓣ0161/834 1786, ⓦwww.bandonthewall.org. Cosy Northern Quarter joint with a great reputation for its live bands – from world and folk to jazz and reggae – and club nights.

The Brickhouse 6 Whitworth St West ⓣ0161/236 4418. Rotating Indie and pop in a relaxed atmosphere geared up for an older crowd.

Havana Bar 42 Blackfriars St ⓣ0161/832 8900. Best place for Latin and world sounds, with dance classes some nights.

Manchester Academy 269 Oxford Rd, on the university campus ⓣ0161/275 2930, ⓦwww.umu.man.ac.uk. Popular student venue for new and established bands.

Manchester Roadhouse 8–10 Newton St ⓣ0161/237 9789, ⓦwww.theroadhouse.u-net.com. Regular and varied gigs by local bands plus a succession of fine club nights.

The Music Box 65 Oxford St ⓣ0161/236 9971, ⓦwww.jillys.co.uk/musicbox. The astute clubber's venue of choice, host to the wildly popular monthly Electric Chair with Mr Scruff keeping it unreal on many a night. Recommended.

Paradise Factory 112–116 Princess St ⓣ0161/273 5422, ⓦwww.paradisefactory.com. One of the hottest clubs on the scene, featuring a varied diet of DJ nights with soulfunk a speciality.

The Ritz Whitworth St West ⓣ0161/236 4355. A one-time ballroom where they still spread talc on the floor some nights of the week. Suits and stilettos disco Fri & Sat; student nights Mon & Wed; tea dances Wed afternoon.

Sankey's Soap Beehive Mill, Jersey St, Ancoats ⓣ0161/661 9668, ⓦwww.tribalgathering.co.uk. Many people's favourite night out, brought to you by the legendary Tribal Gathering crew – Friday's Tribal Sessions and Saturday's The Red Light, playing sleazy house music – in newly revamped premises.

South 4a South King St ⓣ0161/831 7756, ⓦwww.south-club.co.uk. Eclectic music, depending on the night, from funk, 70s disco and house to punk or Northern Soul. Closed Sun and Mon.

Star & Garter 18–20 Fairfield St ⓣ0161/273 6726, ⓦwww.starandgarter.co.uk. Thrash/punk pub venue for loud, young bands and Saturday club nights; late bar until 2am.

Stadium venues

G-Mex Centre Windmill St ⓣ0161/834 2700, ⓦwww.g-mex.co.uk. Mid-sized city-centre indoor stadium.

The Manchester Apollo Stockport Rd, Ardwick Green ⓣ0161/242 2560, ⓦwww.alive.co.uk/apollo. Huge theatre auditorium for all kinds of concerts.

Manchester Evening News Arena Victoria Station, 21 Hunts Bank ⓣ0161/950 5000, ⓦwww.men-arena.com. Indoor stadium that seats 20,000 and hosts all the big names.

Arts and culture

Manchester is blessed with the North's most highly regarded **orchestra**, the Hallé, which is resident at Bridgewater Hall. Other acclaimed names include the BBC Philharmonic, the Manchester Camerata chamber orchestra, and The Lindsays (classical string quartet), who perform **concerts** at a variety of venues across the city. The Cornerhouse is the local **arts** mainstay, while a full range of mainstream and fringe **theatres** produce a year-round programme of events, and there's a decent selection of **comedy** on offer in the city too. For **film**, the **Printworks** entertainment complex contains the twenty-screen **Filmworks** cinema as well as an IMAX cinema, though there are plenty of other places to catch movies, too, including art-house screenings at the Cornerhouse. The biggest annual event is August's **Manchester Festival** (ⓦwww.festivalmanchester.com), an arts and TV extravaganza with events in the city's clubs, theatres and open spaces. October's **x.traxonthestreets** (ⓦwww.xtrax.org.uk) festival, showcasing live street theatre, music and entertainment, is the other highlight of a varied festival programme – the tourist office has the full low-down.

Concerts and music

Bridgewater Hall Lower Mosley St ⓣ0161/907 9000, ⓦwww.bridgewater-hall.co.uk. Home of the Hallé (founded 1857) and the Manchester Camerata; also sponsors a full programme of chamber, classical and jazz concerts.

The Lowry Pier 8, Salford Quays ⓣ0161/876 2000, ⓦwww.thelowry.com. Full, year-round programme of music events, from opera to country.

Manchester Cathedral Victoria St ⓣ0161/833 2220. Concert season runs September to June, for concerts by the Cantata Choir and other soloists, ensembles and orchestras.

Royal Northern College of Music (RNCM) 124 Oxford Rd ⓣ0161/907 5278, ⓦwww.rncm.ac.uk. Stages top-quality classical and modern-jazz concerts, including performances by Manchester Camerata.

Opera House Quay St ⓣ0161/242 2509, ⓦwww.manchestertheatres.co.uk. Major venue for touring West End musicals, drama and concerts.

Theatre and the arts

Contact Theatre 15 Oxford Rd ⓣ0161/274 0600, ⓦwww.contact-theatre.org. One of the most innovative theatre companies in town, housed in provocatively designed premises and putting on predominantly modern works.

Cornerhouse 70 Oxford St ⓣ0161/200 1500, ⓦwww.cornerhouse.org. Engaging centre for contemporary arts, with three cinema screens, changing art exhibitions, recitals, talks, bookshop, café and bar.

Dancehouse Theatre 10 Oxford Rd ⓣ0161/237 9753, ⓦwww.thedancehouse.co.uk. Home of the Northern Ballet School, and venue for dance, drama and comedy.

Green Room 54–56 Whitworth St West ⓣ0161/950 5900, ⓦwww.u-net.com/set/greenroom. Rapidly changing fringe programme that includes theatre, dance, mime and cabaret.
Library Theatre St Peter's Square ⓣ0161/236 7110, ⓦwww.librarytheatre.com. Classic drama and new writing in an intimate theatre beneath the Central Library.
Royal Exchange Theatre St Ann's Square ⓣ0161/833 9833, ⓦwww.royalexchange.co.uk. The theatre-in-the-round in the Royal Exchange is the most famous stage in the city; and there's a Studio Theatre (for works by new writers) alongside the main stage.

Stand-up comedy

The Buzz The Southern, Nell Lane, Chorlton ⓣ0161/440 8662, ⓦwww.buzzcomedy.co.uk. The city's longest-running comedy club has pay-on-the-door shows every Thursday night.
The Comedy Store Deansgate Locks, Whitworth St West ⓣ08705/932932, ⓦwww.thecomedystore.co.uk. Showcase for the best in nationwide stand-up comedy talent, with gigs every Wed–Sat. Bar and brasserie too.
Frog & Bucket 102 Oldham St ⓣ0161/228 6335, ⓦwww.frogandbucket.com. Pub venue for regular stand-up comedy gigs. Shows Mon & Thurs–Sat

Cinemas

Cornerhouse 70 Oxford St ⓣ0161/200 1500, ⓦwww.cornerhouse.org. The three screens at the Cornerhouse are your best bet for art-house releases, special screenings and cinema-related talks and events.
The Filmworks Printworks, Exchange Square ⓣ08700/102030, ⓦwww.thefilmworks.co.uk. State-of-the-art cinema-going with twenty screens, IMAX movies, digital projection and comfortable seating.
Odeon 1 Oxford St ⓣ0870/505 0007, ⓦwww.odeon.co.uk. Seven-screen city-centre cinema showing mainstream movies at cut-price rates.

Listings

Airport General enquiries ⓣ0161/489 3000; flight enquiries ⓣ0901/010 1000.
Banks and exchange The city centre and the student areas along Oxford and Wilmslow roads are strewn with banks and ATMs are commonplace. Piccadilly Station and the airport also have cashpoints.
Bookshops The main chains have outlets on Deansgate and around St Ann's Square. Blackwell's academic bookshop is in the Precinct Centre, Oxford Rd; Sportspages, the sports specialist, is in Barton Square, off St Ann's Square; and Gibb's Bookshop, 10 Charlotte St, is great for second-hand books and classical music.
Bus information For all city services, call GMPTE on ⓣ0161/228 7811 or visit ⓦwww.gmpte.gov.uk; for intercity services, call National Express on ⓣ08705/808080.
Car rental Avis ⓣ0161/236 6716 and at the airport ⓣ0161/436 2020; Europcar ⓣ0161/236 0311 and at the airport ⓣ0161/436 2200; Hertz ⓣ0161/236 2747 and at the airport ⓣ0161/437 8208.
Internet easyEverything, 18 Exchange St, St Ann's Square; Net-Works Centre at the Central Library.
Laundry Several along Wilmslow Road in Rusholme, or you could use the facilities at the YHA hostel (see p.779).
Left luggage Chorlton Street coach station (daily 9.30am–5.30pm); or Piccadilly train station, platform 10 (Mon–Fri 8am–10pm, Sat 9am–9pm, Sun 10am–8pm).
Pharmacy Boots, 11–13 Piccadilly Gardens (ⓣ0161/834 8244) and 20 St Ann's St (ⓣ0161/839 1798).
Post office 29 Spring Gardens; 63 Newton St.
Taxis Mantax ⓣ0161/230 3333; Taxifone ⓣ0161/236 9974. Airtax (for the airport) ⓣ0161/499 9000.

Chester and around

In 1779 Boswell wrote to Samuel Johnson: "Chester pleases me more than any town I ever saw" – and although **CHESTER**, forty miles southwest of Manchester, has changed since then, it's not by much. A glorious two-mile ring of medieval and Roman walls encircles a neat kernel of Tudor and Victorian buildings, including the unique raised arcades called the "Rows". Very much the commercial hub of its county, Chester has enough in the way of sights, restaurants and atmosphere to make it an enjoyable base for a couple of days, though admittedly it can get very crowded.

The fabric of the town is riddled with two thousand years of history. In 79 AD the Romans built Deva Castra here, their largest known fortress in Britain. Later, Ethelfleda, the daughter of King Alfred the Great, extended and refortified the place, only for it to be brutally sacked by William the Conqueror. Trade routes to Ireland made Chester the most prosperous port in the northwest, a status it recovered after the English Civil War, during which its enthusiasm for Charles I saw it subjected to a two-year siege by the Parliamentarians. By the middle of the eighteenth century, however, silting of the port had forced the Irish trade to be re-routed first through Parkgate on the Dee estuary, and then to Liverpool. Things improved a little with the Industrial Revolution, as the canal and railway networks made Chester an important regional trading centre, a function it still retains.

Arrival and information

National Express and most regional bus services (including the hourly bus from Liverpool) arrive at **Chester bus station**, between Delamere and George streets. Close by are the northern city walls and Northgate Street. Most other local buses use the **bus exchange** just behind the town hall, off Princess Street. Merseyrail **trains** from Liverpool (every 20–30min 6am–11pm; 45min) and all other regional and national services call at the **train station**, northeast of the centre, from where it's a ten-minute walk down City Road and along Foregate Street to the central Eastgate Clock. The City-Rail Link bus from the station to the centre (every 12min, 30min on Sun) is free to anyone with a valid train ticket.

There's a **tourist office** in the Town Hall (April–Sept Mon–Sat 9.30am–5.30pm, Sun 10am–4pm; Oct–March Mon–Sat 10am–5pm) and also the **Chester Visitor Centre**, on Vicars Lane opposite the amphitheatre (May–Oct Mon–Sat 9am–5.30pm, Sun 10am–4pm; Nov–April Mon–Sat 10am–5pm, Sun 10am–4pm), both with the same telephone enquiries number and website (Ⓣ01244/402111, Ⓦwww.chestertourism.com). At either, you can book accommodation and guided tours, and pick up a copy of the *Chester Visitor Guide*. The upper-storey houses of the Chester Visitor Centre also have a mock-nineteenth-century street with period shops, where locally made crafts are on sale, and there's a café here too. Central city **parking** is scarce, so drivers should use the Park and Ride scheme, catching a bus from one of the car parks scattered around the ring road.

Accommodation

Chester's popularity is apparent as soon as you arrive, and in high summer **B&B accommodation** can be in short supply, as can space in the more characterful old inns. The places reviewed below are the best of the central choices: if you arrive late, or strike out in the centre, there are lots of budget-rated B&Bs along Brook Street, just a couple of minutes from the train station, and several moderate hotels down City Road, also near the station.

Hotels and B&Bs

10 The Groves Ⓣ01244/317907. There's just one double (en suite) in this riverside B&B, so get your booking in early. There's TV, tea- and coffee-making facilities, and parking available. No credit cards. ❷

Blossom's St John St Ⓣ01244/346433, Ⓦwww.macdonaldhotels.co.uk. Seventeenth-century town house with a variety of rooms, including one with a four-poster bed. Good full-board rates available. ❼

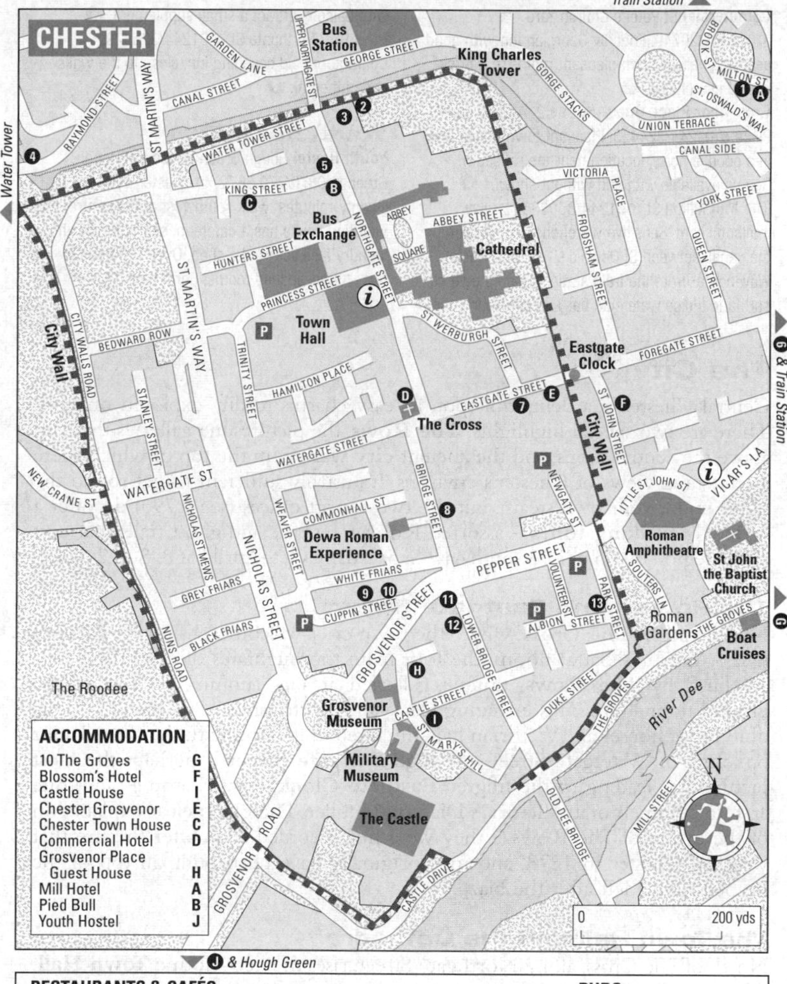

RESTAURANTS & CAFÉS				PUBS	
Alexander's Jazz Theatre and Café Bar	2	Francs	9	Albion Inn	13
Boulevard de la Bastille	8	The Mediterranean Restaurant	3	Falcon	11
La Brasserie	7	Ruan Orchid	12	Mill Hotel	1
Chez Jules	5	La Tasca	10	Old Harkers Arms	6
				Telford's Warehouse	4

Castle House 23 Castle St ⓣ01244/350354. B&B in a sixteenth-century house with good facilities; bang in the centre and excellent value for money. No credit cards. ②

The Chester Grosvenor Eastgate St ⓣ01244/324024, ⓦwww.chestergrosvenor.co.uk. Superbly appointed luxury hotel bristling with liveried staff, very comfortable bedrooms and a whole host of facilities, not least two fine restaurants. Parking available. One price code less at weekends. ⑨

Chester Town House 23 King St ⓣ01244/350021, ⓦwww.chestertownhouse.co.uk. A very high-standard B&B in a comfortably furnished seventeenth-century town house, on a curving, cobbled central street off Northgate Street. There are five en-suite rooms and private parking. ③

Commercial St Peter's Church Yard ⓣ01244/320749. Friendly Georgian inn with good beer and half-a-dozen pleasant rooms in a brick-walled churchyard. ❷

Grosvenor Place Guest House 2–4 Grosvenor Place ⓣ01244/324455. Pleasant town house B&B in a good, if noisy, location near the museum. Rooms available with and without shower. ❷

The Mill Milton St ⓣ01244/350035, ⓦwww.millhotel.com. Sensitive warehouse conversion on the canal, between St Oswald's Way and Hooley Way, not far from the train station. Has its own car park and a nice waterside bar and café-bar; rooms with balcony attract a small supplement. ❺

Pied Bull Northgate St ⓣ01244/325829. Characterful old coaching inn, close to the walls and cathedral. ❷

Youth hostel

Youth Hostel Hough Green House, 40 Hough Green ⓣ0870/770 5672, ⓔ chester@yha.org.uk. Twenty-minutes' walk southwest of the centre, this Victorian house has a cafeteria, self-catering and laundry facilities, and a shop. Over 100 beds in two- to ten-bedded rooms; dorm beds £15.

The City

Central Chester is a delightful spot, its easy charms readily explored on foot. There are two special highlights, **The Rows**, the picturesque galleries that run above the central shops, and the ancient **city wall**, from the top of which there are fetching views of Chester's environs. It's usually sufficient to get round the sights under your own steam, but the two tourist offices (see p.796) do offer a variety of **walking tours** – assorted Roman, historic and ghost trails that cost in the region of £3 per person (May–Sept 2 daily, Oct–April Sat & Sun 2 daily).

The Rows – and Eastgate Street

Intersecting at **The Cross**, where the town crier welcomes visitors to the city (May–Aug Tues–Sat at noon), the four main thoroughfares of central Chester are lined by **The Rows**, unique galleried arcades running on top of the ground-floor shops. This engaging black-and-white tableau is a blend of genuine Tudor houses and Victorian half-timbered imitations, with the finest Tudor buildings on Watergate Street – though **Eastgate Street** is perhaps the most picturesque, leading to the filigree **Eastgate Clock**, erected atop a sandstone arch to commemorate Victoria's Diamond Jubilee. There's no clear explanation of the origin of The Rows – they were first recorded soon after the fire that wrecked Chester in 1278, and may originally have been built on top of the heaped rubble left after the blaze.

The Town Hall and the Cathedral

North of The Cross, along Northgate Street, rises the neo-Gothic **Town Hall**, whose acres of red and grey sandstone look over to the **Cathedral** (daily 7.30am–6pm; free tours Mon–Sat at 2.30pm, donation requested), a much modified structure dating back to the Normans, but dedicated to St Werburgh, an Anglo-Saxon princess who became Chester's patron saint. Parts of the original eleventh-century structure can still be seen in the north transept, but the highlight of an otherwise simple interior is the fourteenth-century choir stalls, with their intricately carved misericords. Doors in the north wall of the nave lead into the shady sixteenth-century cloisters, encircling a small garden whose focal point is an imaginative and striking bronze sculpture by Stephen Broadbent of the Woman of Samaria offering Jesus water at the well.

Around the walls

East of the cathedral, steps provide access to the top of the two-mile girdle of the medieval and Roman **city walls** – the most complete in Britain, though in places the wall is barely above street level. You can walk past all its towers, turrets and gateways in an hour or two, and most have a tale to tell. The fifteenth-century **King Charles Tower** in the northeast corner is so named because Charles I is said to have stood here in 1645 watching his troops being beaten on Rowton Moor, two miles to the southeast. The earlier **Water Tower** at the northwest corner, meanwhile, once stood in the river – evidence of the changes brought about by the gradual silting of the River Dee. South from the Water Tower you'll see the **Roodee**, England's oldest racecourse, laid out on a silted tidal pool where Roman ships once unloaded wine, figs and olive oil from the Mediterranean and slate, lead and silver from their mines in North Wales. Races are still held here in May, June and July; the tourist office has the details.

The Grosvenor Museum and Chester Castle

Scores of sculpted tomb panels and engraved headstones once propped up the wall to either side of the Water Tower, evidence of some nervous repair work undertaken when the Roman Empire was in retreat. Much of this stonework was retrieved by the Victorians and is now on display at the **Grosvenor Museum**, at 27 Grosvenor St (Mon–Sat 10.30am–5pm, Sun 2–5pm; free). This is the best investigation of Roman Chester, with good displays about the legionary system, city buildings, grave sites, defences, daily life and culture. The tombstones themselves form the largest collection from a single Roman site in Britain, the finest being the carving of a wounded barbarian – the surviving piece of a memorial to a Roman cavalryman. The back of the museum opens into a preserved Georgian house complete with furnished kitchen, parlour, bedrooms, rickety floors and sloping stairs.

Close by, on Castle Street, the **Cheshire Military Museum** (daily 10am–4.30pm; £2) inhabits part of the same complex as **Chester Castle** (no public access), built by William the Conqueror, though most of what you see today is resolutely Georgian and used as courts and offices. From the castle, it's an easy stroll east to the Roman Amphithetre (see below), or you can make a brief detour north to the mildly diverting **Dewa Roman Experience** tucked away up Pierpoint Lane, off Bridge Street (daily 9am–5pm; £3.95). This features a reconstruction of a Roman street and gives access to some underground Roman remains.

The Roman Amphitheatre and around

East of the castle, the city wall is buried under the street, but it rises again alongside the **Roman Gardens** (open access) on Souters Lane at Little John Street, where Roman foundations and columns dug up during redevelopment are on display. Across the road stands the half-excavated remains of the **Roman Amphitheatre** (open access); it is estimated to have held seven thousand spectators, making it the largest amphitheatre in Britain, but the stonework is barely head-high now. The garrison at Roman Deva was 6000 strong in its heyday, and the amphitheatre was used by soldiers of the Twentieth Legion for weapons training as well as for entertainment.

The partly ruined pink-stone **Church of St John the Baptist** (daily 9.15am–6pm; free), a little to the east in Grosvenor Park, was founded by the Saxon king Ethelred in 689 and briefly served as the cathedral of Mercia. Rebuilt in its entirety by the Normans, it's an impressive structure, the solid Norman pillars of the nave rising to a Transitional triforium and Early English clerestory. The east portion of the church was abandoned at the Reformation and left to crumble, creating the romantic ruins of today – look out for what purports to be a thirteenth-century coffin emblazoned with the inscription "Dust to Dust" set into an arch.

Steps lead down from the church gardens to the tree-shaded **Groves**, stretched along the River Dee and complete with bandstand, slender iron footbridge, willows and good-looking villas. Bithells Boats (Ⓣ01244/325394, Ⓦwww.showboatsofchester.co.uk) runs half-hour **cruises** on the river (every 30min; April–Oct 11am–5pm; Nov–March Sat & Sun 11am–4pm; £5) and two-hour trips in the summer (daily at noon; £10).

Eating, drinking and entertainment

You can't walk more than a few paces in downtown Chester without coming across somewhere to **eat and drink**, as often as not housed in a medieval crypt or Tudor building. Given the number of day-trippers, it's not surprising that some places serve up some pretty mediocre stuff, but standards are generally high and several of the **pubs** are delightful. The cafés and restaurants listed below are open for lunch and dinner unless otherwise stated.

A batch of annual **festivals** keeps the town's concert halls and churches busy. The most renowned is the **Summer Music Festival** (Ⓦwww.chesterfestivals.co.uk), held every July, which sees outdoor concerts and fireworks in Grosvenor Park, as well as a simultaneous Fringe Festival.

Cafés and restaurants

Alexander's Jazz Theatre and Café Bar 2 Rufus Court Ⓣ01244/340005. Continental-style café-bar with tapas and live music or comedy nightly. Inexpensive.
Boulevard de la Bastille Bridge St Row. One of the nicest of the arcade cafés, with tables looking over the street, doing a roaring trade in breakfasts, pastries and sandwiches. Inexpensive.
Chez Jules 69 Northgate St Ⓣ01244/400014. Classic brasserie menu (salad niçoise to vegetable cassoulet, Toulouse sausage to rib-eye steak, all served with dauphinois potatoes) including a terrific value two-course lunch. Inexpensive.
Francs 14 Cuppin St Ⓣ01244/317952. An excellent and very French bistro with good-value set meals. You can also just drop in for a coffee and cake. Moderate.
Hattie's Tea Shop 5 Rufus Court. Pleasant café with homemade soups, sandwiches and cakes. Inexpensive.
La Brasserie *Chester Grosvenor Hotel*, Eastgate St Ⓣ01244/324024. The *Grosvenor*'s informal brasserie is a great place for a coffee and pastry, or inventive French and fusion cooking. Moderate.
La Tasca 6–12 Cuppin St Ⓣ01244/400887. Huge tapas selection – Spanish cheeses to grilled prawns – and paella too. Nice spot in the summer when they throw the windows wide open. Inexpensive to Moderate.
The Mediterranean Restaurant 1 Rufus Court, off Northgate St Ⓣ01244/320004. Georgian house by the walls, with a sunny courtyard garden, serving tapas, pasta, fish, paella and meze. Moderate.
Ruan Orchid 14 Lower Bridge St Ⓣ01244/400661. This place's huge menu ranges across all the Thai regions – good for red and green curries, duck dishes and noodles. Moderate.

Pubs and bars

Albion Inn corner of Albion and Park streets. A true English Victorian terraced pub in the shadow of the city wall – no fruit machines or muzak. Good bar food and a great range of ales.
The Falcon Lower Bridge St. This half-timbered pub was once a town house built by the Grosvenor family by enclosing part of a Row.
Mill Hotel Milton St. Ale lovers flock to this converted Victorian corn mill to sample an excellent range of brews in a lively atmosphere.
Old Harkers Arms 1 Russell St, below the City Road bridge. Canalside real ale pub imaginatively sited in a former warehouse.
Telford's Warehouse Tower Wharf, Raymond St. Warehouse-style wine-bar pub with regular live music. It's just off the city walls by the Water Tower, built partly over the turning basin of the Shropshire Union Canal.

Around Chester

The two main attractions in the environs of Chester are the **zoo** and the **boat museum** at Ellesmere Port, both easily reached by public transport from the city.

Chester Zoo

Chester's most popular attraction, **Chester Zoo** (daily: April–Sept 10am–5.30pm; Oct–March 10am–4pm; last admission 2hr before closing; £11; ⓦwww.chesterzoo.org), is one of the best in Europe. It is also the second-largest in Britain (after London's), spreading over 110 landscaped acres, with new attractions opening all the time. The zoo is well known for its conservation projects and has had notable success with its Asiatic lions, while other additions include the giant komodo dragons – Chester is the only British zoo to support these creatures – and a jaguar enclosure. Animals are grouped by region in large paddocks viewed from a maze of pathways or from the creeping monorail, with main attractions being the baby animals (elephants, giraffes and orang-utans), the rainforest habitat, the Twilight Zone bat cave and the Chimpanzee Forest with the biggest climbing frame in the country. Kids enjoy the Animal Discovery Centre, where they're encouraged by the staff to touch and learn. The zoo entrance is signposted off the A41 to the north of town and reached by bus #1 (Mon–Sat every 20min, Sun hourly) from Chester's bus exchange.

Ellesmere Port Boat Museum

It's claimed that the **Ellesmere Port Boat Museum** (April–Oct daily 10am–5pm; Nov–March Mon–Wed, Sat & Sun 11am–4pm; £5.50; ⓦwww.boatmuseum.org.uk), seven miles north of Chester, has Britain's largest collection of floating canal vessels, a contention that seems completely plausible when you see the flotilla. Scores of barges are scattered throughout the canal basin and staircase of locks where the Shropshire Union Canal meets the refinery-lined River Mersey at the head of the Manchester Ship Canal. Indoor exhibits trace the history of canals and their construction, and in summer you can take a thirty-minute ride on a narrow boat (£2.50). The museum is ten minutes' walk from Ellesmere Port **train station** (change at Hooton from Chester) or take the half-hourly bus (hourly on Sun) from Chester bus exchange.

The Cheshire Plain

The bustle of Chester is no measure of the rest of the county, a region of lush pastureland and unflustered little towns strung together by hedgerowed lanes. Perhaps because of the familiarity of the landscape, the Danes took a liking to the **Cheshire Plain**, leaving the names of the River Dane and **Knutsford** (Canute's ford) as evidence of their occupation. Since that time farming has continued to be the mainstay of the county's economy, but salt mining around **Northwich** and silk manufacturing in **Macclesfield** have contributed in their day. These three towns are the highlights of the Cheshire Plain and they are best visited on day-trips from Manchester or, at a pinch, Chester – or even better on the journey between the two. As for **public transport**, Northwich and Knutsford are on the Chester–Manchester rail line and there are regular trains from Manchester to Macclesfield with connections to and from Knutsford via Stockport. Call the Cheshire Travel Line (ⓣ01244/602666; daily 8am–8pm) for all timetable enquiries.

Northwich and around

Most of the interest in **NORTHWICH**, seventeen miles east of Chester, lies in its pretty, town-centre conservation area, which nestles by the confluence of the rivers Weaver and Dane. Like several towns on the Cheshire Plain,

Northwich owes its existence to the pockets of rock salt that lie beneath it, deposited when the area was an inland sea. Salt was a crucial commodity to the Romans, who began sluicing it to the surface as brine, then evaporating it in lead pans. Methods of salt extraction changed little until well into the last century, but brine is now pumped from under the town to chemical plants on the Mersey as the raw material for chlorine and alkali manufacture.

Over the centuries, the extraction of the underlying strata caused considerable subsidence in Northwich – and this worried the Victorians no end. The result was a novel construction method in which many new buildings were erected on liftable timber frames, enabling them to be shifted intact in the event of further danger. It worked a treat and the town was largely rebuilt during the 1890s in an homogeneous **mock-Tudor** style, and the best of the buildings can be viewed on an enjoyable, hour-long, self-guided walking tour – pick up the trail leaflet from the tourist office (see below). The largest timber-framed building in town, the striking former post office on Witton Street, is now *The Penny Black* pub.

The town trail starts down at the **Salt Museum**, 162 London Rd (Tues–Fri 10am–5pm, Sat & Sun 2–5pm; Aug also Mon noon–5pm; £2.25), housed in a former workhouse, half a mile south of the town centre. This fills you in on the background to the town's industrial past, though if you want to see salt in production you'll have to head off to the nineteenth-century **Lion Salt Works** (Mon–Fri & Sun 1.30–4.30pm; donation requested; ⓦ www.lionsaltworkstrust.co.uk), beside the Trent and Mersey Canal, on Ollershaw Lane in Marston a couple of miles north of the town, off the A559. This maintains a series of traditional open salt pans, and has its own exhibitions about the industry. Salt was shipped from here to Liverpool and Manchester for export via the nearby **Anderton Boat Lift**, a marvel of Victorian engineering built in 1875 to link the canal with the River Weaver. A **visitor centre** (April–Oct daily 9.45am–5pm; £2.50; ⓣ01606/786777; ⓦ www.andertonboatlift.co.uk) is attached to the Boat Lift and this explores the historical background and explains the engineering. They also take bookings for **rides** on the Boat Lift (6 daily; £6.50 including visitor centre) – and good fun they are too. Both salt works and Boat Lift are linked by a six-mile circular walk, along the canal banks and through the attractive local village of **Great Budworth**. A final option is a two-hour Canal Explorer **boat trip** departing from the Boat Lift throughout the summer (April–Oct Tues–Sun 2–3 daily; £5)

With regular services from Manchester and Chester, Northwich **train station** is about twenty minutes' walk from the town centre – follow the ring road, Chester Way, in past the parish church. The **tourist office** is at 1 The Arcade, opposite the County Council building (June–Aug Mon–Fri 9am–5pm, Sat 10am–2pm; Sept–May Mon–Fri 9am–5pm, Sat 9.30am–12.30pm; ⓣ01606/353534).

Knutsford

An energetic ruler, King Knut (Canute) pieced together a large Anglo-Scandinavian empire in the early eleventh century and, on one of his trips to the northwest, he crossed a local stream at what became known as **KNUTSFORD**, some six miles from Northwich. The settlement prospered and it soon established itself as an important trading centre and, later, as a major stopping point on the coach road to Chester. Nowadays, it's a quiet, well-heeled market town of winding streets and antique houses that makes much of its role as the model for Cranford in the book of the same name by **Elizabeth**

Gaskell. Gaskell spent her childhood years here, living for a while in Heathwaite House, 18 Gaskell Ave (not open to the public), and getting married in **St John's** parish church. A small permanent exhibition in the **Knutsford Heritage Centre**, 90a King St (Jan–March Mon–Fri 1.30–4pm, Sat noon–4pm, Sun 2–4.30pm; April–Dec Mon–Sat 11am–4pm & Sun 2–4.30pm; free), explains more about her connection with the town. Admirers will want to complete their Gaskell tour by visiting the **Unitarian** church, behind the train station, where she is buried. A map posted outside the tourist office can help you track down all these sights.

Even without the lure of Mrs Gaskell, Knutsford makes an enjoyable place for a stroll with narrow **King Street** lined with old inns, antique shops, boutiques and cafés, and still featuring several cobbled yards and side-alleys. The buildings raised by Manchester glove-maker and philanthropist **Richard Watt** also catch the eye, though their loosely Mediterranean style may not be to everyone's taste. The most diverting of these is the **King's Coffee House**, 60 King St, which now houses the *Belle Epoque* brasserie (see below), all done up in its Art Nouveau finery.

Knutsford is on the Chester–Manchester **train** line. The **tourist office** is opposite the train station in the council offices on Toft Road (Mon–Thurs 8.45am–5pm, Fri 8.45am–4.30pm, Sat 9am–1pm; ⓣ01565/632611). To reach King Street, walk along Toft Road from the tourist office and turn right down Church Hill at the parish church. A few hours takes care of the sights and the well-regarded *Belle Epoque* offers tasty light and full meals (closed Sun).

Macclesfield

The original silk mill was established in **MACCLESFIELD** in 1743, rapidly changing the character of this erstwhile market town some twelve miles east of Knutsford – and eighteen south of central Manchester. By 1804 there were thirteen mills and, by the 1820s, over seventy, trade having boomed when French silks became unavailable during the Napoleonic Wars. Silk of all kinds was produced here, with silk and mohair buttons a particular speciality. The demand for parachute material and service badges during World War II provided another boost, though from the late 1940s, with artificial fibres becoming widely available, the mills fell into decline. However, silk is still made in the town (and the industry has provided a nickname – the "Silk Men" – for the local football team), while many of the old mills have found new leases of life following redevelopment as shops, offices and housing.

The first of the town's two **Silk Museums** is in the Heritage Centre, a former Sunday School on Roe Street (Mon–Sat 11am–5pm, Sun 1pm–5pm; £3.10, joint ticket with Paradise Mill & second Silk Museum £6.20). This tracks the history of the industry in entertaining style and displays a pleasing collection of silk costumes and clothes. From here, it's a short stroll to the second **Silk Museum**, on Park Lane (Mon–Sat 11am–5pm, Sun 1–5pm; £3.10), where the emphasis is on the material's properties – its versatility emphasized by a World War II silk map of northern Europe. This museum occupies what was formerly the Macclesfield School of Art, where many of the silk designers picked up their skills. Next door is **Paradise Mill** (Mon–Sat 11am–5pm, Sun 1-5pm; £3.10), whose top floor is devoted to rows of ageing Jacquard looms and spinning machines that are set in action by the staff.

It's a five-minute walk from both the **train station** on Sunderland Street (frequent services from Manchester Piccadilly) and the **bus station**, across the road from the train station, up the hill to the central Market Place. The **tourist**

office is in the town hall (Mon–Thurs 9am–5pm, Fri 9am–4.30pm, Sat 9am–4pm; ⓣ01625/504114). The rest of the compact shopping centre is close at hand; for the museums, follow pedestrianized Mill Street downhill from Market Place. For a bite to **eat**, try the *Cheshire Gap*, 37 Mill St, a deli with smashing sandwiches and snacks.

Liverpool and around

Once the empire's second city, **LIVERPOOL** spent too many of the twentieth-century postwar years struggling against adversity. Things are looking up at last, as economic and social regeneration brightens the centre and old docks, while the city's successful bid to be European Capital of Culture for 2008 promises to transform the way outsiders see the city. Some may sneer at the very concept of Liverpudlian "culture", but this is already a city with a Tate Gallery of its own, as well as a series of stand-out museums that traces its fascinating social history. Indeed, acerbic wit and loyalty to one of the city's two football teams (Liverpool and Everton) are the linchpins of Scouse culture, although Liverpool also makes great play of its musical heritage, which is reasonable enough from the city that produced The Beatles.

Although it gained its charter from King John in 1207, Liverpool remained a humble fishing village for half a millennium until the silting-up of Chester and the booming slave trade prompted the building of the first dock in 1715. From then until the abolition of slavery in Britain in 1807, Liverpool was the apex of the **slaving triangle** in which firearms, alcohol and textiles were traded for African slaves, who were then shipped to the Caribbean and America. The holds were filled with tobacco, raw cotton and sugar for the return journey. After the abolition of the trade, the port continued to grow into a seven-mile chain of docks, not only for freight but also to cope with wholesale European **emigration**, which saw nine million people from half of Europe leave for the Americas and Australasia between 1830 and 1930. Some never made it further than Liverpool and contributed to a five-fold increase in population in fifty years. An even larger boost came with immigration from the Caribbean, China and especially Ireland in the wake of the potato famine in 1845. The resulting mix became one of Britain's earliest multi-ethnic communities, described by Carl Jung as "the pool of life".

The docks lost their pre-eminence by the middle of the twentieth century and, although the arrival of car manufacturing plants in the 1960s stemmed the decline for a while, during the 1970s and 1980s Liverpool became a byword for British economic malaise. However, over the last decade there's been a concerted effort to transform Liverpool's economy and reputation, with major investment by blue-chip companies, plus a move away from traditional industries into financial services, information technology and biotechnology. Liverpool is also the most filmed British city outside London, doubling as locations as diverse as St Petersburg and Venice. Ford is still building cars here too, while the Port of Liverpool now handles more cargo than at any time in its history – and it's still the largest British port for trade with the east-coast USA.

There's a welcome new confidence about the city, as plans are laid to redevelop the waterfront, rebuild parts of the city centre and refurbish its magnificent municipal and industrial buildings. Visitors, meanwhile, have to plan ahead if they are to get around the sights in two or three days. The **River Mersey** provides one focus, whether crossing on the famous ferry to the **Wirral** peninsula or on a tour of the attractions in the rejuvenated warehouses of **Albert Dock**. The associated **Beatles'** sights – former homes to song inspirations – can easily occupy another day. In addition, the city's mercantile past and aspects of its recent history are well covered in a number of fine **museums**; if you want a **cathedral**, they've "got one to spare" as the song goes; plus there's a fine showing of British art in the celebrated **Walker Art Gallery**, and a revitalized arts and nightlife urban quarter centred on **FACT**, Liverpool's showcase for film and the media arts. You'll also want to make time to drop into one of Liverpool's many excellent pubs or bars, perhaps the surest way to get the feel of the place and the people.

Arrival and information

Mainline trains pull in to **Lime Street Station**, while the suburban **Merseyrail** system (for trains from Chester) calls at four underground stations in the city, including Lime Street, Central (under the main post office on Ranelagh Street) and James Street (for Pier Head and the Albert Dock). National Express **buses** use the station on Norton Street, just northeast of Lime Street. Local buses depart from a variety of terminals: Queen Square (for city centre, Pier Head and Chester services); Paradise Street Bus Station (southbound and a few northbound services); and St Thomas Street (eastbound and cross-river).

Liverpool **airport** – officially named after John Lennon – is eight miles southeast of the city centre. From outside the main entrance, the **Airport Express #500 bus** (every 30min; 5.15am–1.35am; £2) runs directly into the city centre, stopping at all major bus terminals and at Lime Street. The slower, cheaper local bus #80A (every 15–30min; 6am–11pm) makes the same journey, or a **taxi** to Lime Street costs around £12. Most **ferry** arrivals – from the Isle of Man, Dublin and Belfast – dock at the terminals just north of Pier Head, not far from James Street Merseyrail station, though Norse Merchant arrivals are over the water on the Wirral at Twelve Quays, near Woodside ferry terminal (ferry or Merseyrail to Liverpool). For all **departure details** and travel enquiry numbers, see "Listings" on p.820.

Tourist information – including timetables, maps and the comprehensive *Liverpool and Merseyside Visitor Guide* – is available from two handy offices: the **Queen's Square Centre** centrally located in Queen Square (Mon–Sat 9am–5.30pm, Sun 10.30am–4.30pm) and the **Albert Dock Centre** at the Atlantic Pavilion (daily 10am–5.30pm), which both share the same telephone enquiries number and website (Ⓣ09066/806886, Ⓦwww.visitliverpool.com).

City transport

Liverpool city centre is surprisingly compact and you'll easily be able to get around on foot, though the odd bus route may come in useful and everyone should take a ferry across the Mersey at some point, if only to be able to say that they've sung *that* song in its proper environment. **Mersey ferry** ticket information is given on p.813.

The local transport authority is **Merseytravel** (Ⓦwww.merseytravel.gov.uk), which co-ordinates all buses, trains and ferries. There's a telephone enquiry line (Ⓣ0151/236 7676; daily 8am–8pm) or visit one of the Merseytravel information centres to pick up timetables, located at 24 Hatton Gardens, at the Queen's Square Centre, at Paradise Street Bus Station and Pier Head. Daily off-peak, zonal **Saveaway tickets** (£2–3.50) for unlimited use on most city buses, trains and ferries are available from post offices, newsagents and the Merseytravel offices. Useful bus routes include Smart buses #1 (linking Queen Square and

Albert Dock), #4 (Albert Dock, Paradise Street and the cathedrals) and #5 (Queen Square and Albert Dock on evenings and Sundays). The #222/224 links Pier Head, Albert Dock and Queen Square.

The most bizarre addition to the city's fleet is the amphibious half-truck-half-boat **Yellow Duckmarine** (mid-Feb to Christmas, daily every hour from 11am; £9.95; ⓣ0151/708 7799, ⓦwww.theyellowduckmarine.co.uk), which departs from Gower Street, in front of Albert Dock, and trundles around the city centre before splashing down into the docks themselves for a spot of aquatic sightseeing.

Accommodation

Central accommodation has improved over recent years and there's a fair choice, from budget chains and small-scale guest houses to boutique hotels and business-oriented four-stars (with a waterfront *SAS Radisson* and *Malmaison* to come). There's also a wide range of hostels and halls of residence. If you prefer, you can opt for a B&B in the surrounding suburbs – the tourist offices can help with specific recommendations – but you're unlikely to beat the prices at the budget chains in the centre. There's no useful campsite. Both tourist offices will book rooms for you for free; call ⓣ0845/601 1125 for their details of special-offer weekend breaks and packages. It's also always worth asking about weekend rates at the bigger hotels, which can turn up some surprising deals.

Hotels and guest houses

Aachen 89–91 Mount Pleasant ⓣ0151/709 3477, ⓦwww.aachenhotel.co.uk. The best and most popular of the Mount Pleasant budget choices, with friendly staff, a range of value-for-money rooms (with and without en-suite showers), big "eat-as-much-as-you-like" breakfasts, a late bar and parking. ❸

Alicia 3 Aigburth Drive, Sefton Park ⓣ0151/727 4411, ⓦwww.feathers.uk.com. Restored town house – a former cotton merchant's home – with park views and a variety of inviting rooms, plus Edwardian-style bar, restaurant, conservatory and garden. ❺

Britannia Adelphi Ranelagh Place ⓣ0151/709 7200, ⓦwww.britannia-hotels.co.uk. Liverpool's enormous (400-room) *Adelphi* catered to passenger-liner customers in its heyday, but it's lost its lustre since then. For its location, one block from Lime Street Station, it remains a relatively good deal, though there's a bit of a package-tour ambience and breakfast isn't included. Weekend discounts and special-break rates always available. ❺

Campanile Wapping and Chaloner St ⓣ0151/709 8104. Purpose-built, budget, motel-style property near Albert Dock, overlooking the Mersey, and offering all-one-price rooms, plus parking, bistro and bar. ❸

Crowne Plaza Liverpool St Nicholas Place, Princes Dock, Pier Head ⓣ0151/243 8000, ⓦwww.cpliverpool.com. Great dockside location and brimful of facilities, including pool, sauna and gym, brasserie and bar. Family rooms have two double beds, and under-12s stay free in the room. Good weekend rates. ❺–❼

Express by Holiday Inn Britannia Pavilion, Albert Dock ⓣ0151/709 1133, ⓦwww.hiexpress.com. Red-brick warehouse with river views. All of the en-suite dockside rooms go for the same bargain price, with continental buffet breakfast and parking included. ❹

Feathers 117–125 Mount Pleasant ⓣ0151/709 9655, ⓦwww.feathers.uk.com. A converted, modernized terrace of Georgian houses, with a variety of rooms in warm crimson tones, all en suite, some with plenty of space. Late bar, 24hr reception, and help-yourself hot-and-cold buffet breakfast included in the price. ❺

Hope Street 40 Hope St (entrance on Hope Place) ⓣ0151/709 3000, ⓦwww.hopestreethotel.co.uk. Victorian warehouse given a contemporary makeover – hardwood floors, huge beds, widescreen TVs and in-room broadband. It's a very good-looking building, retaining the old brickwork and cast-iron columns, and there's a sharp restaurant and bar. Breakfast not included. ❼

Liverpool Moat House Paradise St ⓣ0151/471 9988, ⓦwww.moathousehotels.com. Well-equipped, modern hotel a short walk from the Albert Dock, with comfortable rooms and good sports facilities including a fine indoor pool and spa. The midweek rate doesn't include breakfast. ❻–❼

Marriott 1 Queen Square ⓣ0151/476 8000, ⓦwww.marriott.com. Stylish city-centre hotel, handy for Lime Street and the museums, and featuring a leisure club (with indoor pool and hot tub), restaurant and bar, with more bars and restaurants outside in revamped Queen Square. The midweek rate doesn't include breakfast. ❻–❼

Premier Lodge 45 Victoria St ⓣ8709/906584, ⓦwww.premierlodge.co.uk. Motel-style comfort near the Cavern Quarter at pretty much unbeatable prices. Family rooms available. Breakfast not included. ❸

Racquet Club Hargreaves Building, 5 Chapel St ⓣ0151/236 6676, ⓦwww.racquetclub.org.uk. Boutique-style town-house hotel with just eight rooms, each individually and artfully furnished, mixing good linen and traditional furniture with contemporary art and all mod cons. Breakfast isn't included in the price, but it is provided (£6–10) courtesy of *Ziba*, the hotel's cutting-edge Modern British restaurant. ❻

Travel Inn Vernon St ⓣ08702/383323, ⓦwww.travelinn.co.uk. Bang in the city centre, offering decent-sized en-suite rooms with big beds; a good deal for families. Breakfast not included. ❸

Trials 56 Castle St ⓣ0151/227 1021, ⓦwww.trialshotel.com. Classy nineteenth-century building with Victorian-styled public areas and modernized rooms, or rather "suites" – just twenty of them with Jacuzzi bathroom, Internet hook-ups, valet service, 24hr room service and parking. ❼

Hostels and halls of residence

International Inn 4 South Hunter St, off Hardman St ⓣ0151/709 8135, ⓦwww.internationalinn.co.uk. Converted Victorian warehouse in a great location, with modern accommodation for 100 in heated, en-suite rooms sleeping two to ten people. Really helpful staff, and information-packed noticeboards, plus lounge, kitchen, laundry and baggage storage, bedding provided and no curfew. Adjacent café has Internet access. Dorm £15, twin rooms ❶

John Moores University ⓣ0151/231 3511, ⓦwww.livjm.ac.uk. Self-catering accommodation, either in Cathedral Park, in the shadow of the metropolitan cathedral, or at North Western Hall, next to Lime Street. Single rooms available with or without continental breakfast. Mid-June to early Sept only. Room-only £17.50, B&B £19.50.

Liverpool YHA Wapping ⓣ0870/770 5924, ⓔliverpool@yha.org.uk. One of the YHA's best, just south of Albert Dock, purpose-built and decorated with Beatles' memorabilia. Accommodation (the price includes breakfast) is in smart two-, three-, four- or six-bed rooms (with private bathroom and heated towel rail). There's also a kitchen, licensed café, luggage storage, laundry facilities and 24hr reception. Premium twin rooms (small surcharge) come with a TV and tea/coffee facilities. £19.

University of Liverpool Halls of Residence, Greenbank House, Greenbank Lane ⓣ0151/794 6402. Hundreds of single rooms available, with continental breakfast, set in private parkland, three miles out of the centre (bus #80). Open mid-April to early May & mid-June to mid-Sept. £17.50.

The City

The main sights are fairly widely scattered throughout the centre of Liverpool but you can easily walk between most of them, through cityscapes ranging from revamped shopping arcades and restyled city squares to the surviving regal Georgian terraces around Rodney and Hope streets. Even the walk from the Anglican cathedral through the shops to Albert Dock will only take half an hour or so. The tourist offices can book you onto a variety of **guided walks and tours** (from £3), or make your own way using the themed trail leaflets on sale in the offices. **Public sculpture** abounds, from the statues of Victoria, Albert, Disraeli and Gladstone around St George's Hall to contemporary groupings like the assortment of suitcases and trunks at the Hope Street end of Mount Street.

Lime Street and St George's Hall

Emerging from **Lime Street Station** – whose cast-iron train shed was the largest in the world on its completion in 1867 – you can't miss **St George's Hall** (ⓦwww.stgeorgeshall.com), one of Britain's finest Greek Revival buildings and a testament to the wealth generated from transatlantic trade. Once Liverpool's concert hall and crown courts, its tunnel-vaulted Great Hall features an exquisite floor, tiled with thirty thousand precious Minton tiles, while the Willis organ is the third largest in Europe. The hall is currently under

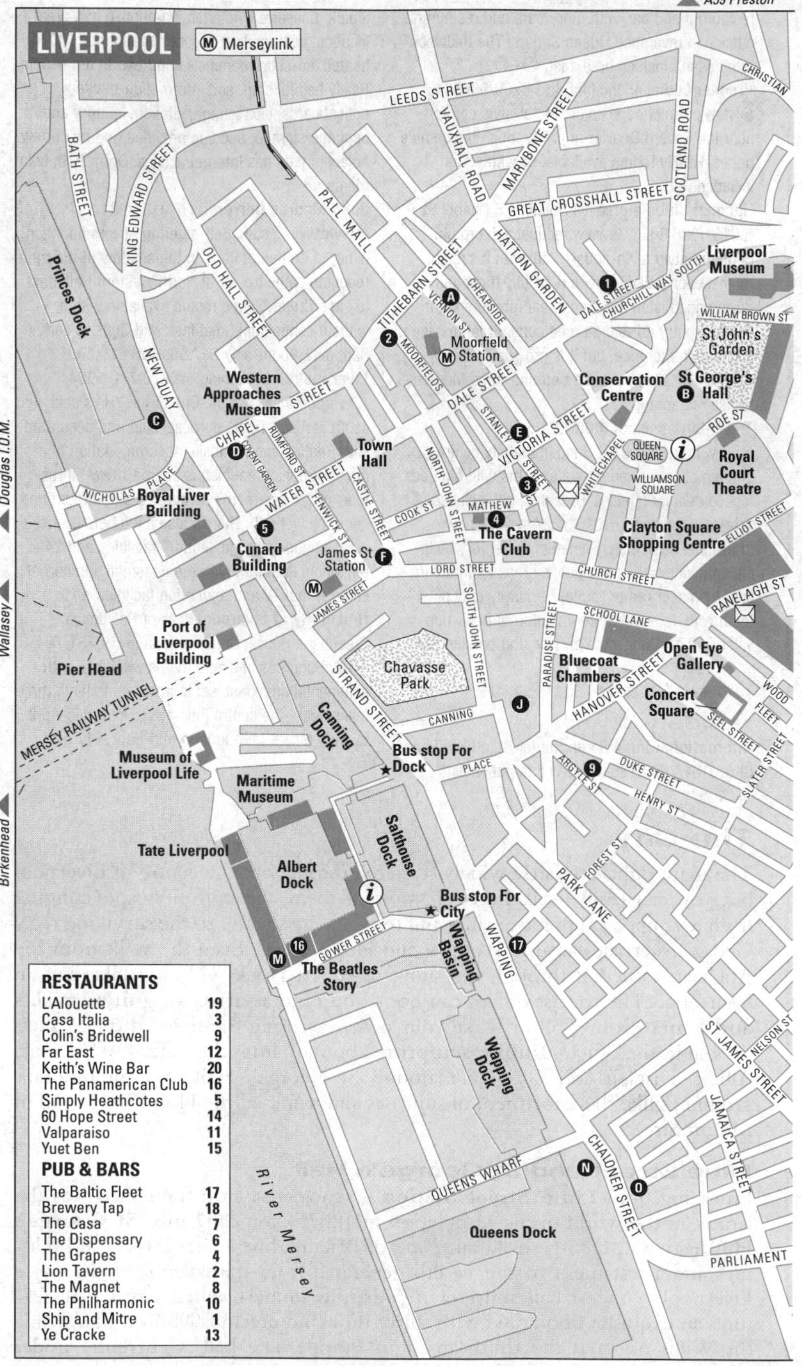
LIVERPOOL
M Merseylink
A59 Preston
LEEDS STREET
CHRISTIAN
VAUXHALL ROAD
MARYBONE STREET
SCOTLAND ROAD
BATH STREET
KING EDWARD STREET
PALL MALL
GREAT CROSSHALL STREET
HATTON GARDEN
Liverpool Museum
OLD HALL STREET
TITHEBARN STREET
CHEAPSIDE
VERNON ST
DALE STREET
CHURCHILL WAY SOUTH
WILLIAM BROWN ST
Princes Dock
MOORFIELDS
Moorfield Station
St John's Garden
Western Approaches Museum
STREET
DALE STREET
Conservation Centre
St George's Hall
NEW QUAY
STANLEY
VICTORIA STREET
ROE ST
CHAPEL
RUMFORD ST
COVENT GARDEN
Town Hall
NORTH JOHN STREET
QUEEN SQUARE
WHITECHAPEL
Royal Court Theatre
STREET
WILLIAMSON SQUARE
Douglas I.O.M.
NICHOLAS PLACE
Royal Liver Building
WATER STREET
CASTLE STREET
FENWICK ST
COOK ST
MATHEW ST
The Cavern Club
Clayton Square Shopping Centre
ELLIOT STREET
Cunard Building
James St Station
LORD STREET
CHURCH STREET
Wallasey
JAMES STREET
RANELAGH ST
SCHOOL LANE
Port of Liverpool Building
PARADISE STREET
SOUTH JOHN STREET
Open Eye Gallery
Pier Head
Chavasse Park
Bluecoat Chambers
MERSEY RAILWAY TUNNEL
STRAND STREET
HANOVER STREET
Concert Square
WOOD
FLEET
Canning Dock
CANNING
SEEL STREET
Museum of Liverpool Life
Bus stop For Dock
PLACE
ARGYLE ST
DUKE STREET
SLATER STREET
Maritime Museum
HENRY ST
Salthouse Dock
Tate Liverpool
FOREST ST
Birkenhead
Albert Dock
PARK LANE
Bus stop For City
GOWER STREET
The Beatles Story
Wapping Basin
WAPPING
NELSON ST
ST JAMES STREET
Wapping Dock
JAMAICA STREET
River Mersey
QUEENS WHARF
CHALONER STREET
Queens Dock
PARLIAMENT
RESTAURANTS
L'Alouette 19
Casa Italia 3
Colin's Bridewell 9
Far East 12
Keith's Wine Bar 20
The Panamerican Club 16
Simply Heathcotes 5
60 Hope Street 14
Valparaiso 11
Yuet Ben 15
PUB & BARS
The Baltic Fleet 17
Brewery Tap 18
The Casa 7
The Dispensary 6
The Grapes 4
Lion Tavern 2
The Magnet 8
The Philharmonic 10
Ship and Mitre 1
Ye Cracke 13

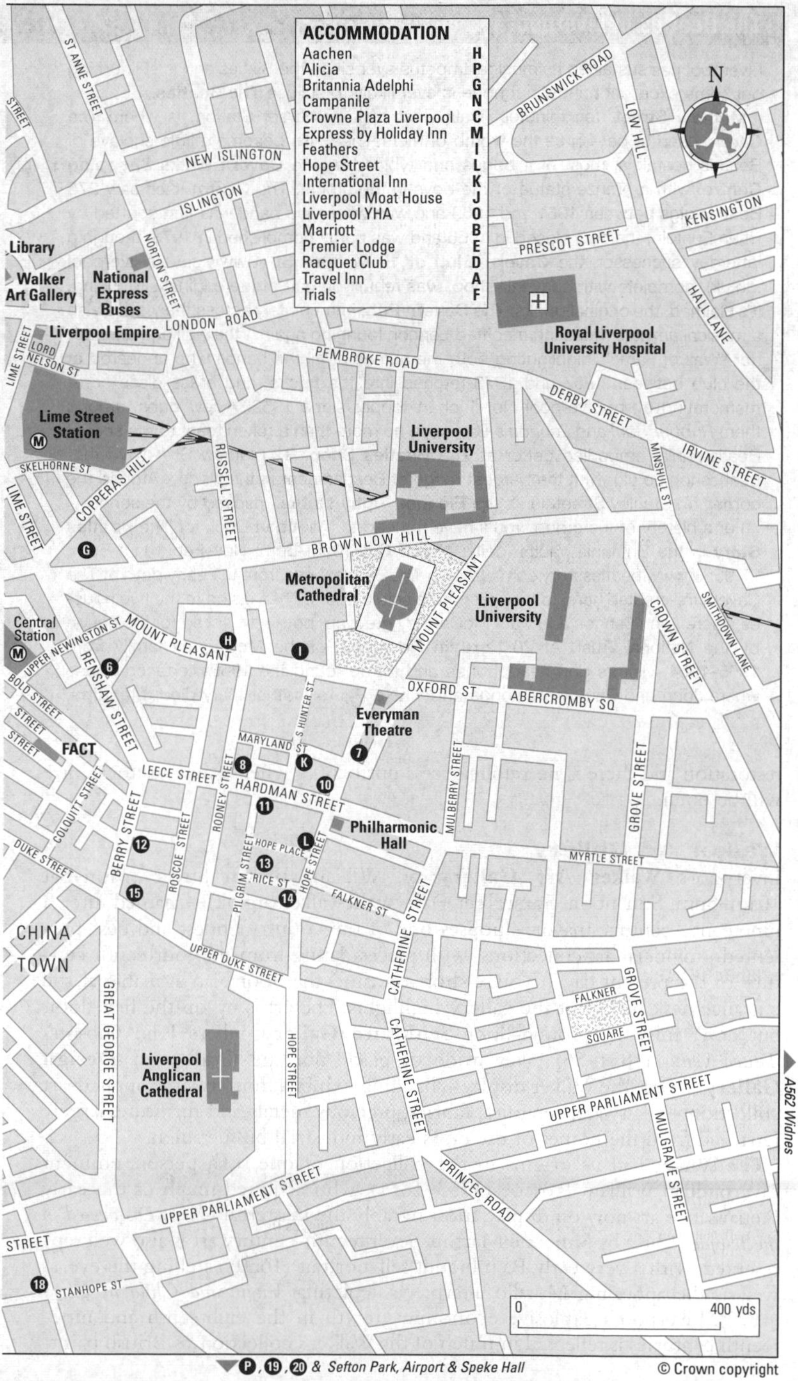

ACCOMMODATION

Aachen	H
Alicia	P
Britannia Adelphi	G
Campanile	N
Crowne Plaza Liverpool	C
Express by Holiday Inn	M
Feathers	I
Hope Street	L
International Inn	K
Liverpool Moat House	J
Liverpool YHA	O
Marriott	B
Premier Lodge	E
Racquet Club	D
Travel Inn	A
Trials	F

ST ANNE STREET
STREET
NEW ISLINGTON
ISLINGTON
BRUNSWICK ROAD
LOW HILL
N
KENSINGTON
PRESCOT STREET
HALL LANE
Library
Walker Art Gallery
National Express Buses
NORTON STREET
LONDON ROAD
Royal Liverpool University Hospital
Liverpool Empire
LORD NELSON ST
LIME STREET
PEMBROKE ROAD
DERBY STREET
IRVINE STREET
Lime Street Station
SKELHORNE ST
COPPERAS HILL
RUSSELL STREET
Liverpool University
MINSHULL ST
LIME STREET
BROWNLOW HILL
G
Metropolitan Cathedral
MOUNT PLEASANT
Liverpool University
CROWN STREET
SMITHDOWN LANE
Central Station
UPPER NEWINGTON ST
MOUNT PLEASANT
H
I
RENSHAW STREET
6
BOLD STREET
STREET
STREET
FACT
S HUNTER ST
OXFORD ST
ABERCROMBY SQ
Everyman Theatre
MARYLAND ST
7
8
K
10
LEECE STREET
HARDMAN STREET
11
COLQUITT STREET
BERRY STREET
RODNEY STREET
ROSCOE STREET
MULBERRY STREET
GROVE STREET
Philharmonic Hall
L
HOPE PLACE
HOPE STREET
12
PILGRIM STREET
13
MYRTLE STREET
DUKE STREET
RICE ST
15
14
FALKNER ST
CATHERINE STREET
CHINA TOWN
UPPER DUKE STREET
GREAT GEORGE STREET
FALKNER SQUARE
GROVE STREET
HOPE STREET
Liverpool Anglican Cathedral
CATHERINE STREET
UPPER PARLIAMENT STREET
MULGRAVE STREET
A562 Widnes
PRINCES ROAD
UPPER PARLIAMENT STREET
STREET
18
STANHOPE ST
0 400 yds

P, 19, 20 & *Sefton Park, Airport & Speke Hall*

The Beatles in Liverpool

Liverpool has sustained its musical impetus ever since the Sixties and is still turning out some excellent bands, but none is ever likely to eclipse **The Beatles**.

Mathew Street, ten minutes' walk west of Lime Street Station, is where *The Cavern* used to be – once the womb of Merseybeat, it's become a little enclave of Beatles nostalgia, most of it bogus and typified by the **Cavern Walks Shopping Centre**, with a bronze statue of the boys in the atrium. *The Cavern* itself saw 275 Beatles gigs between 1961 and 1963 and was where the band was first spotted by Brian Epstein; the club closed in 1966 and was partly demolished in 1973, though a latterday successor, the **Cavern Club** at 10 Mathew St (ⓦwww.cavern-liverpool.co.uk), complete with souvenir shop, was rebuilt on half of the original site, using, it's claimed, the original bricks. The **Cavern Pub**, immediately across the way, is also a musical *arriviste*, boasting a coiffed Lennon lounging against the wall and an exterior "Wall of Fame", highlighting both the names of all the bands who appeared at the club between 1957 and 1973 (etched into the bricks) and brass discs commemorating every Liverpool No. 1 chart-topper since 1952. A few pubs, among them *Rubber Soul* and *Lennon's Bar*, raise no more than a token toast to the soul of Beatlemania, embodied better at **The Beatles Shop**, 31 Mathew St (ⓦwww.thebeatleshop.co.uk), with the "largest range of Beatles gear in the world". Around the corner, on Stanley Street, lurks the **Eleanor Rigby statue**, inspired by the song.

For a history of the group, you'll have to head to the Albert Dock for **The Beatles Story** in the Britannia Vaults (daily: March–Oct 10am–6pm; Nov–Feb 10am–5pm; £7.95; ⓦwww.beatlesstory.com), tracing The Beatles' rise from the early days at *The Cavern* (re-created here) to their disparate solo careers. Then it's on to the two houses where John Lennon and Paul McCartney grew up, both now saved for the nation by the National Trust. At **20 Forthlin Rd**, home of the McCartney family from 1955–1964, visitors don headphones and tramp round the 1950s terraced house where John and Paul wrote songs and where Paul's mother Mary died. **Mendips**,

restoration and there is no public access until 2005, when a new visitor centre will be open.

Walker Art Gallery

Liverpool's **Walker Art Gallery** on William Brown Street (Mon–Sat 10am–5pm, Sun noon–5pm; free; ⓦwww.thewalker.org.uk) – named after a nineteenth-century mayor – houses one of the country's finest and best-presented provincial art collections, with pieces dating from the fourteenth century to the present day. If you're short on time, the floor plan available at the entrance desk picks out the gallery highlights. The art is up on the first floor, but don't miss the ground-floor **Sculpture Gallery**, where John Gibson's *Tinted Venus* (1851–56) takes pride of place, nor the **Craft and Design Gallery**, where the Walker displays changing exhibits from its large applied-art collection – glassware, ceramics, fabrics, precious metals and furniture, largely retrieved from the homes of the city's early industrial businessmen.

The Walker had its origins in the collection of one such person, eminent Liverpudlian William Roscoe (1753–1831), who acquired much of the early Renaissance art now on display, most notably the masterful *Christ Discovered in the Temple* (1342) by Simeone Martini. Seventeenth-century art is also well represented, with a very early Rembrandt self-portrait (1630) catching the eye, as well as the appealing Murillo altarpiece depicting *Virgin and Child in Glory* (1673). Liverpool's explosive economic growth in the eighteenth and nineteenth centuries is reflected in much of the Walker's collection, as British paint-the rather more genteel house where John Lennon lived between 1945 and 1963 with his Aunt Mimi and Uncle George, was bought by Yoko Ono and presented to the National Trust. It's been similarly preserved, its rooms and environs the source of inspiration for some of Lennon's finest early songs. The houses are only accessible on a pre-booked minibus tour (Easter–Oct Wed–Sun; booking essential; £10; NT members £5), departing at 10.30am and 11.20am from Albert Dock (Ⓣ0151/708 8574) and at 1.50pm and 3.55pm from Speke Hall (Ⓣ0151/427 7231; see p.815). The price also includes free access to Speke Hall garden and grounds.

Dedicated pilgrims will undoubtedly want to see both homes and all the other famous Beatles' landmarks, like Strawberry Fields (a Salvation Army home) and Penny Lane (an ordinary suburban street). This is best done on an **organized Beatles tour**, and the two best options are listed below, though note that these tours only show you the exteriors of the Lennon and McCartney homes. Finally, Beatlemania is wholeheartedly celebrated on August Bank Holiday Monday (the last Monday of the month) at the culmination of the annual **International Beatles Week** and **Mathew Street Festival**, filling the town centre with wannabe moptops, jiving to the sounds of tunes that have been hummed and strummed in Liverpool since the first concert rocked *The Cavern*.

Beatles Tours

Phil Hughes Ⓣ0151/228 4565 or 07961/511223, Ⓦwww.tourliverpool.co.uk. Small (8-seater) minibus tours with a guide well versed in The Beatles and Liverpool life. Three-and-a-half hour tours daily on demand, £11 per person (private tour £65); city-centre pick-ups/drop-offs, plus free refreshments.

Magical Mystery Tour Book through Cavern City Tours Ⓣ08712/221967, Ⓦwww.cavern-liverpool.co.uk, or Mersey Tourism Ⓣ0151/709 3285. Two-hour tours (£10.95 or £15 with the Beatles Story) on board a multi-coloured Mystery Bus, departing daily throughout the year from Queen Square and Albert Dock.

ing begins to occupy centre stage – George Stubbs, England's greatest animal painter (and native Liverpudlian) shows off his preoccupation with horse anatomy in his paintings of *Molly Longlegs* (1762) and *A Horse Frightened by a Lion* (1770), while J.M.W. Turner's maturing style is captured in various works. With Victorian art the Walker shifts up another gear, with John Everett Millais' *Isabella* (1848) one of the first Pre-Raphaelite works, followed by a succession of splendid classical pieces by the likes of Dante Gabriel Rossetti, William Holman Hunt, Edward Burne-Jones and Henry Holiday. Victorian taste also ran to melodrama, encapsulated perfectly in a work by W.F. Yeames whose English Civil War subject might not be immediately familiar but whose title undoubtedly is – *And when did you last see your father?* (1878). A group of Impressionists and post-Impressionists, including Degas, Sickert, Cézanne and Monet, drag the collection into more modern times and tastes, before the Walker embarks on its final round of galleries of contemporary British art. Paul Nash, Lucian Freud, Ben Nicholson, David Hockney and John Hoyland all have work here, much of it first displayed (and subsequently purchased from) the Walker's biennial **John Moores Exhibition** (usually held from October of odd-numbered years to the following January).

Liverpool Museum

Further along William Brown Street the **Liverpool Museum** (Mon–Sat 10am–5pm, Sun noon–5pm; free; Ⓦwww.liverpoolmuseum.org.uk) is undergoing a major overhaul and certain sections may still be closed during your visit. Planned additions include a six-storey glass atrium, new café, aquarium, Bug House, and natural history and discovery centre – apposite since the museum had its origins in the natural history collections bequeathed by the Earl of Derby in the mid-nineteenth century. These have subsequently been augmented by some superior fossil, natural habitat and geological collections, while another handy benefactor was Henry Blundell, eighteenth-century gentleman-collector, who gathered together Roman antiquities, busts, sculpture and funerary monuments and then built a replica of the Parthenon to house them. The result is a museum collection that's eclectic to say the least, from tarantulas to space rockets. There's also a full dinosaur section, starring a set of dinosaur footprints found on the Wirral, and ethnographical collections from the Americas, Egypt, the Pacific Islands and West Africa. Make time too for the Planetarium (schedule posted at entrance desk; £1).

The cathedrals

On the hill behind Lime Street, off Mount Pleasant, rises the funnel-shaped Catholic **Metropolitan Cathedral** of Christ the King (Mon–Sat 8am–6pm, Sun 8am–5pm; free), denigratingly known as "Paddy's Wigwam" and the "Mersey Funnel". Built in the 1960s in the wake of the revitalizing Second Vatican Council, it was raised on top of the tentative beginnings of Sir Edwin Lutyens's grandiose project to outdo St Peter's in Rome. Bits of Lutyens's cathedral can be seen in the crypt. At the other end of the aptly named Hope Street, the Anglican **Liverpool Cathedral** (daily 8am–6pm; donation requested) looks much more ancient but was actually completed eleven years later, in 1978, after 74 years in construction. The last of the great neo-Gothic structures, Sir Giles Gilbert Scott's masterwork claims a smattering of superlatives: Britain's largest and the world's fifth-largest cathedral, the world's tallest Gothic arches and the highest and heaviest bells. Not enough important people have died to fill out the stark pillarless interior, but a visit to see the beautiful stone tracery in the finely detailed Lady Chapel – the first part of the cathedral to be completed, in 1910 – and a look at Elizabeth Frink's last work, a bronze of Christ, pad out the free **guided tours** (times vary, call ⓣ0151/709 6271 for details). On a clear day, a trip up the 330-foot **tower** (11am–4pm; £2) through the cavernous belfry is rewarded by views to the Welsh hills. In the southern arcade the **Elizabeth Hoare Embroidery Collection** (included in tower ticket) contains a manageable display of sumptuous ecclesiastical vestments and traces the art's history from the thirteenth century.

The city centre

After years of neglect, the rest of the city centre is slowly being rebuilt or refashioned, often to quite dramatic effect. Some of the most strident changes have been made in the former warehouse and factory district between **Bold Street** and **Duke Street** (sometimes called the Ropewalks), where new apartments, urban spaces, café-bars and shops have sprouted in recent years. There's an increasing number of places in which you can sip a latte, or shop for punk records and vintage clothing, while **Concert Square**, just off Bold Street occupies space once taken up by a factory which was levelled to provide room for warehouse-style bar developments. **FACT** at 88 Wood St (ⓦwww.fact.co.uk) – that's "Film, Art and Creative Technology" – provides a cultural anchor for the neighbourhood with its galleries for art, video and new media exhibitions (Tues & Wed 11am–6pm, Thurs–Sat 11am–8pm, Sun noon–5pm; free), community projects, cinema screens, café and bar. Further down Wood Street, the **Open Eye Gallery**, at nos. 28–32 (Tues–Fri

10.30am–5.30pm, Sat 10.30am–5pm; free; Ⓦ www.openeye.org.uk), features several temporary exhibitions a year, concentrating on photography, installation and video work.

Bold Street ends at Hanover Street, with the pedestrianized shopping street, Church Street continuing beyond. To the left, School Lane throws up the beautifully proportioned **Bluecoat Chambers**, built in 1717 as an Anglican boarding school for orphans and now a contemporary art gallery (Tues–Sat 9.30am–5.30pm; free) with a decent café, bookstore and crafts centre (Mon–Sat 9.30am–5pm; Ⓦ www.bluecoatdisplaycentre.com). The **Quiggins Centre** (Mon–Sat 10am–6pm), a bit further along at 12–16 School Lane, is a converted warehouse packed with shoplets hawking records, posters, jewellery, clubwear and skateboards.

From School Lane turn right on Paradise Street and walk down Whitechapel towards **Queen Square**, where one of the neighbourhood's surviving Victorian warehouses, on the corner of Whitechapel and Queen Square, is occupied by the **Conservation Centre** (Mon–Sat 10am–5pm, Sun noon–5pm; free, tours £2 on Wed at 2pm & 3pm, Sat 2pm; Ⓦ www.conservationcentre.org.uk). This is where Merseyside's museums and galleries undertake their restoration work and give visitors a hands-on, behind-the-scenes look, so you soon learn to identify fabrics and furniture beetles and how to get the rust off a gold disc.

Heading west towards Pier Head, **Mathew Street and the Cavern Quarter** (see box on p.810) loom large, but rather than taking the most direct route to the ferry, don't pass up the opportunity to walk down Water Street. The Georgian **Town Hall** is a beauty and is open to the public (by appointment, call Ⓣ 0151/225 5530, or on August open days), while behind here, at 1 Rumford St, the **Western Approaches Museum** (Easter–Oct Mon–Thurs & Sat 10.30am–4.30pm, last admission 3.30pm; £4.75) fills about a third of the hundred-room underground complex where, from spring 1941 until the end of the war, the Anglo-American air-sea campaign was orchestrated. Sticking with **Water Street** for the final approach to Pier Head gives you a flavour of the city's nineteenth- and early-twentieth-century mercantile heyday, passing gems such as the Martins Bank Building (now Barclays) with its lavish lobby, and the deeply resonant India Buildings and West Africa House.

Pier Head, Mersey Ferry and the Graces

Though the tumult of shipping which once fought the current here has gone, the **Pier Head** landing stage remains the embarkation point for the **Mersey Ferry** (Ⓣ 0151/330 1444, Ⓦ www.merseyferries.co.uk) to Woodside (for Birkenhead) and Seacombe (Wallasey). Straightforward ferry shuttles (£2 return) operate during the morning and evening rush hours, but at other times the boats run circular fifty-minute **cruises** (hourly: Mon–Fri 10am–3pm, Sat & Sun 10am–6pm; £4.30). You can stop off on the Wirral side of the river (see p.815) for the Birkenhead sights; and if you're planning on going to Seacombe Aquarium, buy the joint ticket (£5.20). It's all a long way from the simple rowboat crossing pioneered by medieval Benedictine monks who first wanted to cross the Mersey at this point. Even when Daniel Defoe visited Liverpool in the eighteenth century – when the city was first booming – he was taken by the rusticity of the river crossing "over the Mersee": having reached the city side he was surprised to find himself hoisted "on the shoulders of some honest Lancashire clown" and bundled through the shallows to the shore.

The view back across the Mersey to the Liverpool skyline is one of the city's glories. Dominating the waterfront are the so-called **Three Graces** – namely the Port of Liverpool Building (1907), Cunard Building (1913) and, most prominently, the 322-feet-high **Royal Liver Building** (1910), topped by the "Liver Birds", a couple of cormorants which have become the symbol of the city. A "Fourth Grace" – Will Alsop's controversial "Cloud" building – is due to be completed by 2007, the centrepiece of a planned Seventy-mile-long Mersey Waterfront Regional Park.

Albert Dock

Albert Dock, five minutes' walk south of Pier Head, was built in 1846 when Liverpool's port was a world leader. It started to decline at the beginning of the twentieth century, as the new deep-draught ships were unable to berth here, and last saw service in 1972. A decade later the site was given a complete refit, emerging as a type of rescued urban heritage that's been copied throughout the country, but rarely as successfully as here – fashionable bars and restaurants continue to thrive, while the dock's major maritime and city **museum** collections are bolstered by the high-profile Beatles Story (see p.810) and the art at Tate Liverpool. There's free **parking** – follow the city-centre signs – and **buses** every twenty minutes during the day from Queen Square bus station.

Merseyside Maritime Museum

The **Merseyside Maritime Museum** (daily 10am–5pm; free; Ⓦwww.liverpoolmuseums.org.uk) fills one wing of the Albert Dock and in summer also takes over part of neighbouring Canning Dock for floating displays. A trip through the museum can easily take two hours. Spread over four floors, it has sections on the history of Liverpool's evolution as a port and shipbuilding centre, plus an illuminating display detailing Liverpool's pivotal role as a springboard for over nine million emigrants. The Irish potato famine and a multiplicity of European wars, combined with the lure of gold and free land, brought people scurrying here to buy their passage to North America or Australia, and to cater for them, short-stay lodging houses sprang up all over the centre, as illustrated in an 1854 street scene. On board the ships – there's a walk-through example – people were packed into dark, noisy ranks of bunks where they "puffed, groaned, swore, vomited, prayed, moaned and cried". Meanwhile, the **HM Customs and Excise Museum**, inside the Maritime Museum, gives the lowdown on smuggling and revenue collection.

The Maritime Museum is at its best, however, in its "Transatlantic Slavery" exhibit, which manages to be enlightening, shocking and refreshingly honest. The slave trade continued for four hundred years up to 1900, with the number of slaves shipped to sugar plantations in the Americas running into millions. The conditions they endured on the transatlantic voyage are illustrated by a reconstruction of a slave ship, echoing with haunting voices reading from diaries of slaves and slavers, telling of rape, torture and death. The exhibition winds up with a video of Africans resident in Britain airing their views on the impact of slavery and the legacy of racism, after which you'll probably be ready to mull over what you've seen in the museum's top-floor café.

The Tate and Elvis in Liverpool

Tate Liverpool (Tues–Sun 10am–6pm; free, special exhibitions usually £3–5; Ⓦwww.tate.org.uk/liverpool) is the country's national collection of modern art in the north. Popular retrospectives and an ever-changing display of individual works are its bread and butter, and there's also a full programme of events, talks and tours – the daily half-hour gallery talk at 2pm is free. Break up visits with espressos in the Tate's dockside café-bar.

There couldn't be a bigger contrast between the Tate and the dock's latest attraction, **Fingerprints of Elvis** (daily 10–6pm; £7.95; Ⓦwww.fingerprintsofelvis.com), which does indeed display the only known set of the King's fingerprints (taken for his gun licence) alongside other Elvis-related ephemera and memorabilia. True fans are going to relish the chance to view his favourite Harley, plus stage outfits, guitars, karate belts, army insignia and jewellery; others might baulk at the entrance price and stick with The Beatles.

Museum of Liverpool Life

The **Museum of Liverpool Life** (daily 10am–5pm; free; Ⓦwww.museumofliverpoollife.org.uk) is particularly revealing about the hardships that have moulded the resilient Scouse character. It has excellent sections on the city's traditional work, with investigations of the lives of ordinary shipwrights, stevedores, carters and seamen. The role of trade unions is covered, and there's space too for coverage of topics as diverse as the women's suffrage movement and the social unrest that led to the Toxteth riots in the 1980s. "City Lives", meanwhile, hones in on Liverpool's cultural diversity, examining the experiences of immigrants and the former living conditions of ordinary Scousers. This might all sound a bit worthy, but it's utterly engrossing, with other equally illuminating sections spreading light on the history of the River Mersey and on the city's own King's Regiment – the last section heralded by a big-screen cacophonous blood-and-guts Napoleonic battle. In the popular culture sections, Merseyside football gets good coverage (though there's no mention of poor old Tranmere Rovers), as does Aintree's Grand National. There's also an overview of music from the Sixties to the present day (with a working jukebox), plus information about local writers, including Alan Bleasdale, Willy Russell, Beryl Bainbridge and Carla Lane.

Speke Hall

Located near Liverpool's airport, six miles southeast of the centre, **Speke Hall** (Easter–Oct Wed–Sun 1–5.30pm; Nov to mid-Dec Sat & Sun 1–4.30pm; gardens Easter–Oct daily 11am–5.30pm, Nov–Easter daily 11am–4.30pm; house & gardens £5.50, gardens only £2.50; NT) is one of the country's finest examples of Elizabethan timbered architecture. Dating from 1530, and sitting in an oasis of rhododendrons, the house encloses a beautifully proportioned courtyard overlooked by myriad diamond panes. Highlights of the interior are the Jacobean plasterwork in the Great Parlour and the Great Hall's carved oak panel. There are ornamental gardens and woodland walks, a model Victorian farm, and horse-drawn carriage rides through the estate most Sundays. Any bus to the airport from Paradise Street in the city centre runs within half a mile of the entrance; parking at the hall costs an extra £3.

The Wirral

Across the Mersey lies the **Wirral**, the peninsula that sits between Liverpool and Chester, flanked by the Irish Sea and the River Dee. There's plenty to tempt you off the Mersey Ferry from Liverpool, particularly in **Birkenhead** (get off at Woodside ferry terminal), while Merseyrail trains run under the river and out as far as the garden village of **Port Sunlight** and the **Lady Lever Art Gallery**. Local information is available from **Birkenhead tourist office**, inside Woodside ferry terminal (daily 10am–5pm; Ⓣ0151/647 6780, Ⓦwww.wirral.gov.uk).

Birkenhead

Hop off the ferry at Woodside and it's a ten-minute walk (or bus #E1 from the ferry terminal) to **Birkenhead Priory** (Easter–Oct Tues–Sun 1–5pm; Nov–Easter Tues–Sun noon–4pm; free), dating from 1150, the oldest building on Merseyside. The Benedictine foundation is a peaceful haven, and there are magnificent river views from the church tower. You can walk back to the ferry via **Hamilton Square**, entirely surrounded by listed buildings, one of which houses the local **Wirral Museum** of applied art and historical artefacts (Tues–Sun 10am–5pm; free). Back at Woodside ferry, catch one of the **vintage trams** (weekends only: Easter–Oct 1–5pm; Nov–Easter noon–4pm; £1 return) which run as far as the depot, where you can get out and look around the rest of the transport collection, which includes an old Hong Kong tram as well as the gleamingly restored open-top Birkenhead Number 20.

However, if you've just got time for one side trip, apart from the priory, it should be to Birkenhead's **Historic Warships**, moored at the East Float Dock on Dock Road (Easter–Oct daily 10am–5pm, Nov–Easter closes at 4pm, and closed weekdays Jan & Feb; £5.50; ⓦ www.warships.freeserve.co.uk); bus #401 runs there from Woodside ferry terminal. Both the Type 12 frigate HMS Plymouth and the O-class sub HMS Onyx saw action in the Falklands War – indeed, the surrender of South Georgia was signed in the Plymouth's wardroom. A self-guided tour takes you through both vessels, clambering around bunkrooms, cabins, galleys, engine rooms and bomb bays. It seems impossible, given the space constraints, but the Onyx carried 74 crew, including SAS and SBS special forces who slept for weeks at a time on the torpedo gantries. A separate tour (adults only; booking essential; £8; call ⓣ0151/650 1573) investigates the rust-caked U534, the only World War II German submarine to be raised from the seabed – she was sunk at the end of the war in May 1945 and retrieved in 1996.

Port Sunlight and Lady Lever Art Gallery

For a glimpse of one of the more benign aspects of Merseyside's industrial past, take the Merseyrail under the river to **Port Sunlight**, a garden village created

This sporting life

Liverpool's most popular recreational activity, bar none, is football. **Liverpool** football club has never quite recovered its glory days of the Seventies and Eighties, though it's still one of England's top clubs. The team plays at **Anfield** (ticket office ⓣ08702/202345, ⓦwww.liverpoolfc.net) in front of some of the nation's most loyal supporters. You're unlikely to get a ticket for a game, but there's a popular tour around the well-stocked museum, trophy room and dressing rooms (daily 10am–5pm; museum and tour £8.50, museum only £5; booking essential ⓣ0151/260 6677). **Everton**, the city's less glamorous side, command equally intense devotion at **Goodison Park** (ticket office ⓣ0151/330 2300; tours Mon, Wed, Fri & Sun 11am & 2pm; £6.50; booking advised on ⓣ0151/330 2277; ⓦwww.evertonfc.com).

The first Saturday in April is **Grand National Day** at **Aintree** – the "World's Greatest Steeplechase" and a must for horse-racing fans. The race is the culmination of a meeting that starts on the previous Thursday, with prices for entry into the grounds ranging from £7 to £65. Catch the Merseyrail to Aintree and buy a ticket on the gate or book on ⓣ0151/523 2600. The "Grand National Experience" (May–Oct Tues–Fri 11am–2pm; £7, booking advised on ⓣ0151/522 2921, ⓦwww.aintree.co.uk) shows you the stables, weighing room and museum, before letting you ride the National on a race simulator.

in 1888 by industrialist William Hesketh Lever for the workers at his soap factory. The project, similar in scope to those of Titus Salt at Saltaire near Bradford and John Cadbury at Bournville in Birmingham, is explained at the **Port Sunlight Heritage Centre**, 95 Greendale Rd (April–Oct daily 10am–4pm; Nov–March Sat & Sun 11am–4pm; 70p; ⓦwww.portsunlightvillage.com), from where a self-guided trail runs through the housing estates. Off Greendale Road, a little further from Port Sunlight Station, the **Lady Lever Art Gallery** (Mon–Sat 10am–5pm, Sun noon–5pm; free; ⓦwww.ladyleverartgallery.org.uk) houses a small collection of English eighteenth-century furniture, Pre-Raphaelite paintings by artists such as Rossetti and Ford Madox Brown, Wedgwood china, porcelain and assorted Greek and Roman artefacts. There's also a nice café.

Eating, drinking and nightlife

Liverpool's dining scene is slowly shifting up a gear and there's now a good choice of classy **restaurants** alongside a fine selection of cafés and budget places to eat. Most are around Hardman and Bold streets, at Albert Dock, and along Nelson Street, heart of Liverpool's **Chinatown**, which stretches around the corner onto Berry Street. Or take a short taxi ride out to **Lark Lane** in Aigburth, close to Sefton Park, where a dozen great eating and drinking spots pack into one short street.

Fashionable **café-bars** are muscling in on the action and you won't want for a decent cup of coffee these days in most parts of the city. Liverpool's **pubs and bars** stay open later than most, with many serving until 1am or 2am. Fleet Street, Slater Street and Wood Street have seen most development, with the action centred on Concert Square, where drinkers spill out on to the terraces until the small hours from a variety of cafés, dance bars and theme pubs. Victoria Street in the business district is another fast-developing area for bars and nightlife.

You'll catch regular gigs at any of the **live music** venues detailed below, and Liverpool has some excellent annual **music festivals and events**, namely the Summer Pops (July) and the Party at the Pier (August) for big-name pop and rock, and Liverpool Now (October) which sees local bands playing in various venues around the city. The city's dance **clubs** are mainly notable for their lack of pretence, fashion playing second string to dancing and drinking. The evening paper, the *Liverpool Echo*, has **listings** of what's going on, or pick up flyers in the shops, bars and cafés.

Cafés

Bluecoat Café Bar Bluecoat Chambers, School Lane. Mainly vegetarian food – salad bar, baked potatoes and dips – served throughout the day. Closed Sun.

Café Eros Conservation Centre, Whitechapel Rd. The best of the museum and gallery cafés is a light-filled space with nice food, also used for temporary art and photography exhibitions.

Caffe Latte.net 4 South Hunter St. Nice place with fast Internet access, good coffee, big sandwiches, cheap café food, and friendly service. Closes at 9pm, weekends at 5.30pm.

Cavern Walks Shopping Centre Mathew St. Lunch or snack with the lovable moptops. Both *Chantilly* and *Lucy in the Sky with Diamonds* offer daytime drinks and meals right by the Fab Four statue.

Espresso Exchange 6 Victoria St. Locally owned espresso bar with great coffee, a patisserie, snacks and sandwiches. Open until 8pm, Thurs–Sat until 1am; closed Sun.

Number Seven Café 7 Falkner St. Daytime deli and coffee shop, between the two cathedrals, with some seats outside on the Georgian terrace. Great for coffee and cake and a browse around the deli counter. Closed Sun.

The Refectory Liverpool Anglican Cathedral, St James' Mount. Appetizing snacks and lunches under the Gothic arches, and with terrace seating, too.

Café-bars

Beluga Bar 40 Wood St. Hip basement space that's great for just a drink, or come to eat – there's a changing, seasonal menu. Opens at 5pm.

Blue Bar Edward Pavilion, Albert Dock. Brick-vaulted café-bar with dockside tables, big sofas and upstairs grill – the Liverpool soccerati drop by now and again, and it's a useful stop for cappuccino, lunch, dinner or a late-night drink.

Everyman Bistro and Bar 9–11 Hope St. Long-standing theatre-basement hangout with home-made quiche, pies and bakes, pizza and salad-type meals, at around a tenner for two courses. It's known for its range of beers and wines by the glass, and the bar closes at midnight or 2am at weekends. Closed Sun.

The Living Room 15 Victoria St. Classy piano bar ambience and a fusion menu, plus a simply huge range of cocktails.

Modo Concert Square. Indoor and outdoor hi-jinks at night, though quieter during the day, when you can stop by for a meal or a coffee.

Newz New Zealand House, 18 Water St. Thoroughly OTT bar and brasserie aimed at a city, soccer, soap star crowd; bagels and coffee to cocktails and dinner. Closed Sun.

The Platinum Lounge Beetham Plaza, 25 The Strand. Feeling smooth? Come right on in to the Liverpool lounge scene where you'll need a bulging wallet and a taste for cocktails.

Tabac 126 Bold St. Contemporary café-bar, serving a wide-ranging menu from breakfast onwards. The food is excellent (all the bread is homemade for starters), with Thai curry, risotto and Italian-style pot-roasts particular favourites, and is served until 10pm, drinks until 11pm.

Tea Factory 79 Wood St. Very cool, very chic "bar and kitchen" in the Ropewalks neighbourhood, with a wide range of beers.

Restaurants

60 Hope Street 60 Hope St ⓣ0151/707 6060. Currently Liverpool's best, with inventive salads, gourmet sandwiches and bistro-style dishes in the café-bar (open all day; closed Sun), and Modern British food of distinction in the restaurant (closed Sat lunch and all Sun). A fashionable feed, but one that doesn't forget its roots – witness Goosnargh chicken with Lancastrian mash or lamb served with bubble and squeak. Café Moderate, restaurant Expensive.

Casa Italia 40 Stanley St ⓣ0151/227 5774. There's no stand-out Italian in the city, but this lively family-run trattoria dishes up reliable pasta and pizza dishes. Moderate.

Colin's Bridewell Campbell St, off Duke St ⓣ0151/707 8003. Drink and dine in the cells of the old police lock-up. Big banquettes along the brick walls fill up with a lunch and after-work crowd, while the gastropub-style upstairs room concentrates on Modern British food. Lunch Moderate, dinner Expensive.

Far East 27–35 Berry St ⓣ0151/709 6072. One of the longest-serving and most reliable of Liverpool's Cantonese eating houses: a fairly no-frills operation, but with authentic *dim sum* (noon–6pm), superb roast duck, plus noodles, casseroles, rice plates and other classics. Moderate.

Keith's Wine Bar 107 Lark Lane ⓣ0151/728 7688. An old favourite, as much for its good-value bistro food as its wine selection. Inexpensive.

L'Alouette 2 Lark Lane ⓣ0151/727 2142. Contemporary French cuisine in intimate surroundings, with the bonus of a nice open fire in winter. Closed Sat lunch and all Mon. Moderate.

The Panamerican Club Britannia Pavilion, Albert Dock ⓣ0151/709 7097. Extraordinarily handsome warehouse conversion that brings snappy North American style and service to its cavernous bar and restaurant. Food ranges from sushi to gourmet pizza, and there are killer cocktails and drinking until 2am at weekends, when a DJ plays. Expensive.

Simply Heathcotes Beetham Plaza, 25 The Strand ⓣ0151/236 3536. Lancastrian magic under a glass canopy – roast lamb and Goosnargh duckling feature among other delights from Paul Heathcote, in many people's favourite Liverpool restaurant. Come Fri–Sun lunch, and before 7pm Fri & Sat, and you'll get a three-course meal for £15. Expensive.

Valparaiso 4 Hardman St ⓣ0151/708 6036. Latin-American dishes, with wines to match, including a Chilean-style *bouillabaisse* and serious steaks. There's a good vegetarian selection too. Closed Sun & Mon. Moderate.

Yuet Ben 1 Upper Duke St ⓣ0151/709 5772. Specialist in Beijing-style food, with a superb range of dishes including barbecued ribs that experts drool over. Dinner only; closed Mon. Moderate.

Pubs and bars

The Baltic Fleet 33a Wapping. Restored pub with age-old shipping connections, opposite Albert Dock. It's got a great period feel and is known for its fine food and local beer.

Brewery Tap Stanhope St. Enjoyable Victorian brewery pub where you can sample Liverpool's own Cains beers. There are brewery tours if you're interested in the process (call ⓣ0151/709 8734, ⓦwww.cainsbeer.com; £3.75), and seats inside and out if you're just interested in the product.

The Casa 29 Hope St. Community-based project, with input from Liverpool's dockers, which provides a good, cheap meeting place for drinks (until 2am at weekends) and bistro food (Mon–Wed noon–3pm, Thurs & Fri noon–7pm).

The Dispensary 87 Renshaw St. Entirely synthetic but highly sympathetic re-creation of a Victorian pub using rescued and antique wood, glass and tiles. A real-ale choice.

The Grapes 25 Mathew St. Busy city-centre pub in the Cavern Quarter, where John, Paul, George and Ringo once downed pints between sets at *The Cavern*.

Lion Tavern 67 Moorfields. Real ale in superbly restored Victorian surroundings, from the tiles to the stained-glass rotunda. Also excellent cheese and pate lunches (Mon–Fri).

The Magnet 45 Hardman St. Booth seating, blood-red decor, a bit of Barry White – it's groovy all right, plus there's a funky club downstairs and a great diner next door that stays open until 2am for well-priced bistro food.

The Philharmonic 36 Hope St. A superb, traditional watering-hole where the main attractions – the beer aside – are the mosaic floors, tiling, gilded wrought-iron gates and the marble decor in the gents.

Ship and Mitre 133 Dale St. For the biggest real ale choice in Liverpool – ten guest beers, plus ciders and imported lagers – visit this renowned Art Deco free house.

Ye Cracke 13 Rice St. Crusty backstreet pub off Hope Street, much loved by the young Lennon, and with a great jukebox.

Clubs, live music and comedy

The Cavern Club 10 Mathew St ⓣ08712/221957, ⓦwww.cavern-liverpool.co.uk. The self-styled "most famous club in the world" puts on live bands Thurs to Sun.

Liverpool Academy 160 Mount Pleasant ⓣ0151/794 6868, ⓦwww.liverpoolacademy.co.uk. Three music venues in one, with local bands, touring acts and club nights playing to a mostly student audience, though open to all.

Masque Venue 90 Seel St ⓣ0151/708 8708, ⓦwww.masquevenue.fsnet.co.uk. Varied club nights and live bands in the theatre or Loft, and a bar-bistro (open until 2am Thurs–Sat). Closed Sun & Mon.

The Picket 24 Hardman St ⓣ0151/708 5318, ⓦwww.thepicket.co.uk. One of the best venues for local bands (usually Thurs–Sat nights), with two bars, a beer garden and a friendly local (*The Flying Picket*) attached, tucked in behind the Trade Union centre.

Rawhide *Baby Blue*, Edward Pavilion, Albert Dock ⓣ0151/726 0077. Comedy shows every Thurs, Fri and Sat at this lounge bar.

Arts, concerts and entertainment

The Royal Liverpool Philharmonic Orchestra, ranked with Manchester's Hallé as the northwest's best, dominates the city's **classical music** scene and often plays at the Philharmonic Hall and the Everyman Theatre. Liverpool Cathedral is also a favourite spot for classical concerts, with its good acoustics and inexpensive tickets. **Theatre** is well entrenched in the city, at a variety of venues, while independent **cinema** has found a home at FACT, the city's creative technology centre. Annual **festivals** include the Hope Street Festival (June); ship visits and events at the Mersey Maritime Festival (June); a celebration of African arts and music in Africa Oye (June); the Summer Pops (July), when the Royal Philharmonic and top pop names perform beneath a huge marquee on King's Dock; the **Merseyside International Street Festival** (August; ⓦwww.brouhaha.uk.com), which involves performances by a host of European theatre groups; and the **Mathew Street Festival** (August; ⓦwww.mathewstreetfestival.com), a free shindig, with local and national street performers playing the best of The Beatles.

Bluecoat Arts Centre School Lane ⓣ0151/709 5297, ⓦwww.bluecoatartscentre.com. Eclectic mix of events – drama, dance, poetry, comedy, music and art exhibitions.

Everyman Theatre and Playhouse Hope St ⓣ0151/709 4776, ⓦwww.everymanplayhouse.com. Presents everything from Shakespeare to Jarman, as well as concerts, exhibitions, dance and musical performances.

Liverpool Empire Lime St ⓣ08706/063536, ⓦwww.liverpool-empire.co.uk. The city's largest theatre, a venue for touring West End shows, opera, ballet and music. The Beatles' first major gig was here in 1962.

Philharmonic Hall Hope St ⓣ0151/709 3789, ⓦwww.liverpoolphil.com. Home of the Royal Liverpool Philharmonic Orchestra, and with a full programme of other concerts. Shows classic films once a month.

Picturehouse at FACT Wood St ⓣ0151/707 4460, ⓦwww.picturehouses.co.uk. The city's only independent cinema screens, with a great programme of new films, re-runs, festivals and a Saturday morning kids' club. Movies also shown in The Box, a full-size screen with 25 two-seater settees for that private showing experience. Cheaper tickets weekdays before 6pm, and cheapest Tues to Thurs before 4pm.

Royal Court Theatre Roe St ⓣ0151/709 4321, ⓦwww.royalcourttheatre.net. Art Deco theatre and concert hall, which sees regular pop and rock concerts among other events.

Unity Theatre Hope Place ⓣ0151/709 4988, ⓦwww.unitytheatreliverpool.co.uk. This place puts on the city's most adventurous range of contemporary works.

Listings

Airport ⓣ0151/288 4000, ⓦwww.liverpooljohnlennonairport.com.

Banks and exchange ATMs are ubiquitous. American Express, 54 Lord St ⓣ0870/600 1060; Thomas Cook, 75 Church St ⓣ0151/552 1340. You can also change money at the two tourist offices, the main post office (see below) and at the airport.

Books Most of the bookshops are along Bold Street: Dillons at no. 14, Waterstones at no. 52 and the more radical News from Nowhere at no. 112.

Buses Merseytravel ⓣ0151/236 7676, National Express ⓣ08705/808080.

Car rental Avis ⓣ0151/709 4737; easyRentacar ⓣ09063/333333; Europcar ⓣ0151/709 7563; Hertz ⓣ0151/486 7444.

Ferries Isle of Man Steam-Packet Company for ferries/Sea Cats to Isle of Man ⓣ08705/523523, ⓦwww.seacat.co.uk; Mersey Ferries ⓣ0151/330 1444, ⓦwww.merseyferries.co.uk.

Hospital Royal Liverpool University Hospital, Prescot Street ⓣ0151/706 2000.

Internet Planet Electra, 36 London Rd (daily 10am–6pm); Caffe Latte.net, 4 South Hunter St (Mon–Fri 9am–9pm, Sat & Sun 9am–5.30pm).

Laundry Liver Launderette, 80 & 170 Aigburth Rd & 104 Prescot Rd.

Pharmacy Boots, Clayton Sq Shopping Centre ⓣ0151/709 4711; Moss Pharmacy, 68–70 London Rd ⓣ0151/709 5271 (daily until 11pm).

Police Canning Place ⓣ0151/777 4545.

Post office City-centre office at The Lyceum, 1 Bold St (Mon–Sat 8.30am–6pm).

Taxis Mersey Cabs ⓣ0151/298 2222; Davy Liver ⓣ0151/709 4646.

Travel agent Discounted and student tickets from STA Travel, 78 Bold St ⓣ0151/707 1123.

Blackpool

Shamelessly brash **BLACKPOOL** is the archetypal British seaside resort, its "Golden Mile" of piers, fortune-tellers, amusement arcades, tram and donkey rides, fish-and-chip shops, candyfloss stalls, fun pubs and bingo halls making no concessions to anything but low-brow fun-seeking of the finest kind. From ukelele-strumming George Formby and his "little stick of Blackpool rock" to today's predatory, half-dressed gangs of stag and hen parties, few visitors, then or now, are in any doubt about the point of a holiday here. There are seven miles of wide sandy beach backed by an unbroken chain of hotels and guest houses, attracting sixteen million people each year. If you want a bit more isolation than those numbers allow, come in winter when there's nothing more bracing than a lonely tramp along the windswept sands – "bracing", of course, as Paul Theroux points out, being "the northern euphemism for stinging cold".

Wealthy visitors were already summer holidaying in Blackpool at the end of the eighteenth century, and while it took a day to get there from Manchester by carriage and two days from Yorkshire, the town remained a select destination. It was the coming of the railway in 1846 that made Blackpool what it is today: within thirty years, there were piers, promenades and theatres for the thousands who descended. The Winter Gardens, with its barrel-vaulted ballroom, the Baroque Grand Theatre on Church Street, Blackpool's own "Eiffel Tower" on the seafront and other refined diversions were built to cater to the tastes of the first influx, but it was the Central Pier's "open air dancing for the working classes" that heralded the crucial change of accent. Suddenly Blackpool was favoured destination for the "Wakes Weeks", when whole Lancashire mill towns descended for their annual seven days' holiday.

Attention to the accents tells you that Lancashire, Yorkshire and Scotland still provide the bulk of the resort's visitors, who show no signs of drying up. Where other British holiday resorts have suffered from the rivalry of cheap foreign packages, Blackpool has simply gone from strength to strength by shrewdly providing exactly what its visitors want. Underneath the populist veneer there's a sophisticated marketing approach, which balances ever more elaborate rides and attractions with well-grounded traditional entertainment. The best example of this is the way the town has cleverly extended its season: when other resorts begin to close up for the winter, Blackpool's main season is just beginning, as over half a million light bulbs are used to create **the Illuminations** which decorate the promenade from the beginning of September to early November. The first static display took place in 1912, was re-created periodically between the wars and has been an annual event since 1949, "switched on" each year by publicity-hungry TV and pop stars. Lately, Blackpool has been looking to extend its attractions further, with plans laid to build a series of casino-resorts, entertainment complexes and leisure parks. Development is expected to take up to twenty years and cost around £1 billion, though the masterplan shies away from the inevitable comparisons with Las Vegas – laser shows, glass domes and resort-style hotels might all follow, but they will complement, not supplant, the town's Victorian heritage.

Arrival and information

Blackpool's main train station is **Blackpool North** (direct trains from Manchester and Preston), half a dozen blocks up Talbot Road from North Pier. A few steps down Talbot Road, towards the sea, stands the combined National Express and local **bus station**; town buses run from here direct to the Pleasure Beach, though it's more fun to walk down to the front, take a tram and get your bearings. Alternatively, some trains from Preston also run to **Blackpool South**, near the Pleasure Beach. There are **car parks** signposted all over town (including on Albert Road, Talbot Road, Bank Street and Central Drive), and it's best to use them since on-street parking is only short-term. Blackpool's **airport** – which handles regular flights to and from London Stansted, Isle of Man, Belfast and Dublin – lies two miles south of the centre; there are buses from the bus station or it's a £5 taxi ride. The main **tourist office** at 1 Clifton St (Mon–Sat 9am–5pm, Wed from 9.30am; Ⓣ01253/478222, Ⓦwww.blackpooltourism.com) is on the corner of Talbot Road; a second office sits on the promenade opposite Blackpool Tower (summer only: Mon–Sat 9.15am–5pm, Wed from 9.30am, Sun 10.15–4.15pm). You can pick up maps and hefty accommodation brochures; they also sell Travel Cards (one-day £4.95; three-day £12.75; five-day £16.25; seven-day £17.25) for use on all local buses and trams. Local **transport information** is available from Blackpool Transport (Ⓣ01253/473000, Ⓦwww.blackpooltransport.com). **Taxi ranks** are on Market Street, Corporation Street, Church Street, Talbot Square, Clifton Street and the Promenade.

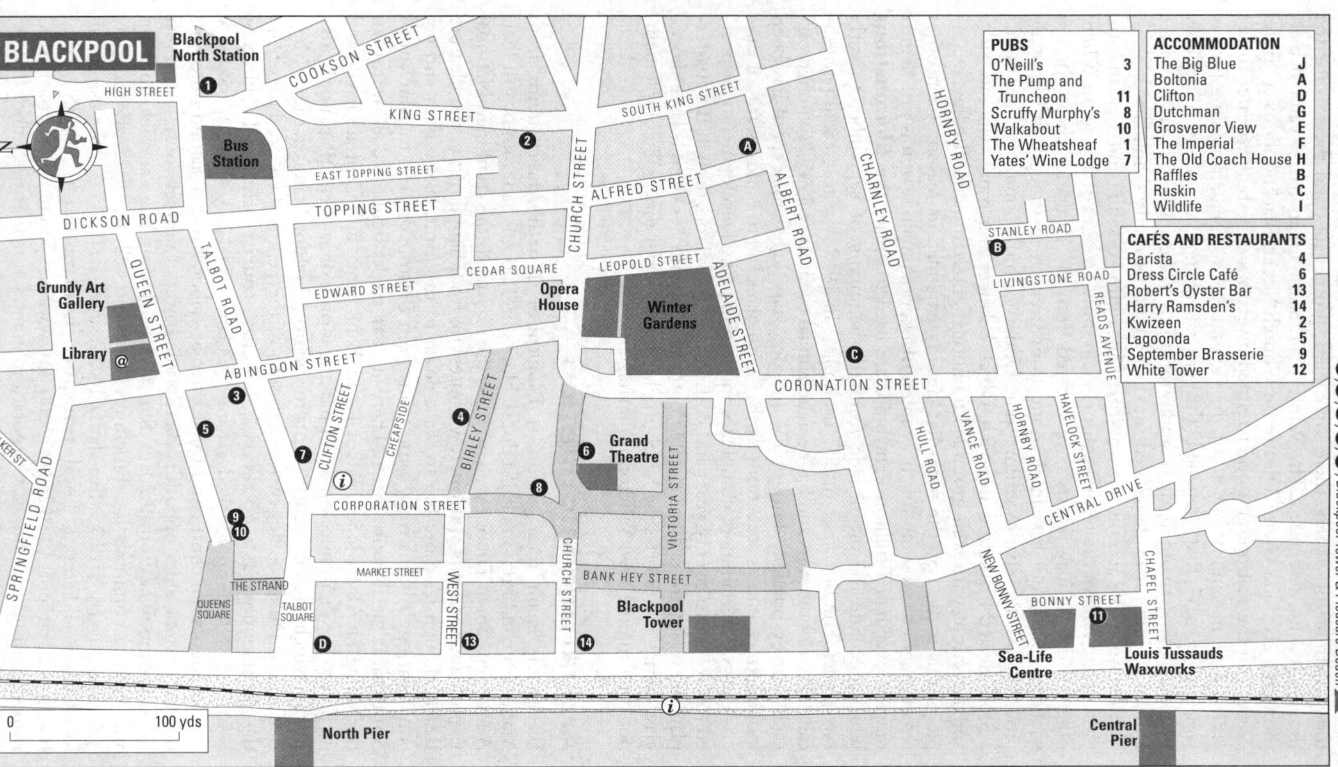
BLACKPOOL
Blackpool North Station
Bus Station
Grundy Art Gallery
Library
Opera House
Winter Gardens
Grand Theatre
Blackpool Tower
Sea-Life Centre
Louis Tussauds Waxworks
North Pier
Central Pier
HIGH STREET
COOKSON STREET
KING STREET
SOUTH KING STREET
EAST TOPPING STREET
TOPPING STREET
DICKSON ROAD
CHURCH STREET
ALFRED STREET
ALBERT ROAD
CHARNLEY ROAD
HORNBY ROAD
STANLEY ROAD
LIVINGSTONE ROAD
READS AVENUE
CEDAR SQUARE
LEOPOLD STREET
ADELAIDE STREET
EDWARD STREET
QUEEN STREET
TALBOT ROAD
ABINGDON STREET
CORONATION STREET
CLIFTON STREET
CHEAPSIDE
BIRLEY STREET
CORPORATION STREET
VICTORIA STREET
HULL ROAD
VANCE ROAD
HAVELOCK STREET
CENTRAL DRIVE
NEW BONNY STREET
BONNY STREET
CHAPEL STREET
BANK HEY STREET
MARKET STREET
WEST STREET
THE STRAND
QUEENS SQUARE
TALBOT SQUARE
WALKER ST
SPRINGFIELD ROAD
N
0
100 yds
E & F
G, H, I, J, 12, Blackpool Tower & Pleasure Beach
PUBS
O'Neill's 3
The Pump and Truncheon 11
Scruffy Murphy's 8
Walkabout 10
The Wheatsheaf 1
Yates' Wine Lodge 7
ACCOMMODATION
The Big Blue J
Boltonia A
Clifton D
Dutchman G
Grosvenor View E
The Imperial F
The Old Coach House H
Raffles B
Ruskin C
Wildlife I
CAFÉS AND RESTAURANTS
Barista 4
Dress Circle Café 6
Robert's Oyster Bar 13
Harry Ramsden's 14
Kwizeen 2
Lagoonda 5
September Brasserie 9
White Tower 12

Accommodation

Bed-and-breakfast prices are generally low (from £15 per person, even less on a room-only basis or out of season), but rise at weekends and during the Illuminations. In peak season, it's simply a matter of looking for vacancy signs or asking the tourist office for help – anything cheap between North and Central piers is guaranteed to be noisy; for more peace and quiet (an unusual request in Blackpool, it has to be said), look for places along the more restful North Shore, beyond North Pier.

The Big Blue Ocean Boulevard, Blackpool Pleasure Beach ⓣ0845/367 3333, ⓦwww.bigbluehotel.com. The shape of things to come in Blackpool – family suites with DVDs, games consoles and separate children's area, plus smart furnishings and a gym. Rates are room-only, and rise slightly during the Illuminations. It's next to the south entrance to the Pleasure Beach. ❹

Boltonia 124–126 Albert Rd ⓣ01253/620248, ⓦwww.boltoniahotel.co.uk. The choices on Albert Road, between the Tower and Central Pier, mark a qualitative step up from your basic Blackpool boarding houses. The *Boltonia* is not far from the Winter Gardens, on a corner plot which lets lots of light into the rooms – all have en-suite showers, though the superior rooms are a bit more spacious and have large TVs. Parking available. ❷

Clifton Talbot Square ⓣ01253/621481, ⓕ01253/627345. On the North Pier prom, this traditional beauty – a Grade 2 listed building – has fine sea views from many rooms, though decor could do with a touch up here and there. Rooms are often a good deal cheaper than the posted prices; check for special offers. ❻

Dutchman 269 The Promenade ⓣ01253/404812, ⓦwww.dutchmanhotel.com. A great budget seafront choice between Central and South piers. The small, cheery rooms have showers, and though those at the front get traffic noise, you do wake up with a view of the sea. There's a bar and café too (and it's probably the only Blackpool B&B to offer a cream-cheese bagel for breakfast). Two-night minimum stay at weekends. ❷

Grosvenor View 7–9 King Edward Ave ⓣ01253/352851. Along North Shore, a mile or so from the action, the grid west of Warbreck Hill Road has hundreds of options. Rooms in this detached property are larger and better equipped than most – and you're in the care of an award-winning landlady. Parking available. ❷

The Imperial North Promenade ⓣ01253/623971, ⓦwww.paramount-hotels.co.uk. The politicians' conference favourite, a four-star hotel with excellent sea-facing rooms, pool and gym, the famous oak-panelled *No. 10 Bar*, *Palm Court* restaurant, and parking. It's a short tram ride away from the Tower and the rest of the sights. ❼

The Old Coach House 50 Dean St ⓣ01253/349195, ⓦwww.theoldcoachhouse.freeserve.co.uk. Historic survivor of 1851, this detached Tudor-style villa near the Pleasure Beach and South Prom offers a rare Blackpool commodity – peace and quiet. Eleven bedrooms, with crisp decor, king-sized beds and high-spec bathrooms, plus warm service, good breakfasts, bistro-style restaurant (set dinner £20) and parking. Conservatory and courtyard garden provide a nice place for a drink, and there's even an outdoor spa (fizz supplied on request). ❺

Raffles 73–77 Hornby Rd ⓣ01253/294713, ⓦwww.raffleshotelblackpool.co.uk. Nice place back from Central Pier and away from the bustle, with seventeen well-kept rooms, bar, and traditional tearooms attached. Some parking available. Winter rates are an especially good deal. ❹

Ruskin Albert Rd ⓣ01253/624063, ⓦwww.ruskinhotel.com. At the prom end of Albert Road, the *Ruskin* exudes repro-Victorian style and offers rather smart rooms with decent bathrooms, all individually decorated. Bar and brasserie, and parking available. ❺

Wildlife 39 Woodfield Rd ⓣ01253/346143. Ideal for anyone wanting a vegan guest house, this non-smoking, animal-friendly place is just off the promenade, between Central and South piers. Twelve simple rooms with showers and toilets – and a picture wall of adopted animals that the owner sponsors. No credit cards. ❶

The Town

With seven miles of beach – the tide ebb is half a mile, leaving plenty of sand at low tide – and accompanying promenade, you'll want to jump on and off the electric **trams** if you plan to get up and down much between the piers.

South Pier to North Pier – between which lies most of what there is to see and do – costs £1.10, though Travel Cards are available, too (see p.821). Most of the town-centre shops, bars and cafés lie between Central and North piers.

Blackpool Pleasure Beach

The major event in town is **Blackpool Pleasure Beach** on the South Promenade (March–Easter Sat & Sun 10am–8pm; Easter–June Mon–Fri 2–8pm, Sat & Sun 10am–10pm; July to Nov 5 daily 10am–11pm; hours can vary, call ⓣ0870/444 5566, ⓦwww.blackpoolpleasurebeach.com), just south of South Pier – visited by over seven million people each year. Entrance to the amusement park is free, but you'll have to fork out for the superb array of "white knuckle" rides including "The Big One", the world's fastest roller coaster (85mph), which involves a terrifying near-vertical drop from 235ft. As if this isn't bad enough, the "Ice Blast" whooshes you up a 200-foot steel tower at 80mph and then drops you back down in free-fall; while "Valhalla" is claimed to be the biggest "dark ride" (ie very scary) ever built. After these, the Pleasure Beach's wonderful array of antique wooden rollercoasters – "woodies" to aficionados – seems like kids' stuff, but each is unique. The original "Big Dipper" was invented at Blackpool in 1923 and still thrills; the "Wild Mouse" (1958) and, best of all, the "Grand National" (1935) – whose 3300-foot twin track races you against a parallel car – are both equally, excitingly, rattly. Before each one sets off, the public-service announcement intones "Please do not wave your hands in the air" – when any self-respecting woodie rider knows that's exactly what you have to do. Individual rides cost from £1 to £5, but if you're not leaving until you've been on everything – a sensible course of action – buy an unlimited ride wristband (£26, usually cheaper in the off-season).

The seafront and the tower

Across the road from the Pleasure Beach, the **Sandcastle** (June–Oct daily 10am–5.30pm; Nov–May Sat & Sun only 10am–4.30pm; £5.40, £4.40 after 2pm; ⓦwww.blackpool-sandcastle.co.uk) is the only place you are likely to want to swim. With every aquatic diversion kept at a constant 29°C it can be a welcome respite from the biting sea air.

Jump a tram for the ride up to **Central Pier** with its 108-feet-high revolving Big Wheel. The **Sea-Life Centre** (July & Aug Mon–Thurs & Sun 10am–6pm, Fri & Sat 10am–10pm; Sept–June daily 10am–6pm; £7.50; ⓦwww.sealife.co.uk) nearby is one of the country's best, with eight-foot sharks looming at you as you march through a glass tunnel and a very large, lurking Giant Pacific octopus. For a taste of what Blackpool attractions used to be like, you could then hit **Louis Tussauds Waxworks**, 87–89 Central Promenade (daily 10am–10pm; £6) – these days, more Posh and Becks than Churchill and Margaret Thatcher, but still with its "highly educational" adults-only anatomy section.

Blackpool's elegant cast-iron **piers** also strike a traditional note. They're covered with arcades and amusements, while much of what passes for evening family entertainment – TV comics and variety shows – takes place in the various pier theatres. Between Central and North piers stands the 518-feet **Blackpool Tower** (June–Oct daily 10am–11pm; Nov–May daily 10am–6pm; £11.50; ⓦwww.theblackpooltower.co.uk), erected in 1894 when it was thought that the northwest really ought not to be outdone by Paris. It provides the skyline's sole touch of grace, but paying the hefty entrance fee is the only way to ride up to the top (where there's a postbox) for the stunning view and an unnerving walk on the see-through glass floor. The all-day ticket covers all the other tower attractions, including a visit to the Edwardian ballroom, with

Blackpool – behind the scenes

There's an alternative Blackpool behind the resort's facade – one of history, heritage and (whisper it softly) even culture. The following walk takes around an hour, though more if you stop for refreshments in everywhere mentioned.

Start at the **Mitre** pub (bottom of West St, across from the North Pier), where for the price of a pint you can examine the collected black-and-white photos of Victorian and Edwardian Blackpool. **Robert's Oyster Bar** (92 The Promenade) next door is a rare survivor of the period, while down the prom and then up Victoria Street leads directly to the **Winter Gardens** (Coronation Street), which opened to fanfares in 1878. There used to be an adjacent **Great Wheel** – 230 feet high – that carried 900 people at a time, though it was demolished in the 1920s. The other associated period pieces all survive, however, notably the Frank Matcham-designed ballroom in the Winter Gardens (scene of party political conferences over the decades), the **Opera House**, and his splendid **Grand Theatre** around the corner (Church Street). The Gardens house a fairly motley set of cafés, shops and amusements these days, but it's worth taking a peek at the extraordinary Spanish Hall Suite and the ornate Victoria Bar.

From in front of the Opera House, follow Abingdon Street to Queen Street and the porticoed Central Library, next to which the **Grundy Art Gallery** (Mon–Sat 10am–5pm; free) might tempt you in to see its Victorian oils and watercolours, old photos, contemporary art and special exhibitions. Walking down Queen Street to the promenade you reach **North Pier**, the first pier to be opened (1863) on the Blackpool seafront and now a listed building. At this point, let chance and the trams dictate the final part of the tour – Blackpool, incidentally, had the world's first permanent electric street **tramway** (1885). Head northbound and you can get off at the *Imperial Hotel* (North Promenade), whose wood-panelled **No. 10 Bar** really is worth a look, covered with photographs and mementoes of every British prime minister since Lloyd George. Or, if the southbound tram arrives first, stay on as far as Central Pier until you see **McDonald's** (corner of Chapel St), which only has one photograph on display, but a most extraordinary one – it's hard to say who looks more surprised, the staff on duty one day in October 2002 or their unexpected customers, Bill Clinton and Kevin Spacey.

its Wurlitzer organ performances, tea dances and big band evenings, plus the world's largest indoor adventure playground. From the very early days, there's been a Moorish-inspired **circus** (shows also included in the entry ticket; up to three daily performances) between the tower's legs, which still functions, though in the spirit of the times it's now animal-free.

If you've seen and been on everything mentioned so far you'll have been here for days, spent a fortune and thoroughly enjoyed yourself. These, it has to be said, are just the A-list attractions – indefatigable holiday-makers also take in Blackpool's zoo and model village on East Park Drive, the summer circus at the Pleasure Beach, or any one of a number of pleasure flights, go-kart rinks, donkey rides, children's play areas, ten-pin bowling alleys, games arcades or other jollifications.

Eating

Eating out revolves around the typical British seaside fare of fish and chips, available all over town. Given the sheer volume of customers, other restaurants don't have to try too hard: you'll have no trouble finding cheap roasts, pizzas, Chinese or Indian food, but might struggle if you're seeking a bit more sophistication.

Cafés

Barista 24 Birley St. Seattle-style coffee house, with grilled sandwiches, muffins and croissants. Closes 5.30pm.

Dress Circle Café Grand Theatre, Church St. Dine in the ornate bar to show tunes – the food's inexpensive, concentrating on things like a daily roast, steak, scampi and lasagne. Closes 5.30pm.

Robert's Oyster Bar 92 The Promenade. Glorious, wood-panelled, 130-year-old café where you can buy oysters, cockles and mussels, or seafood platters, then wash them down with a Guinness from the *Mitre* pub around the corner. Closes 5pm in winter.

Restaurants

Harry Ramsden's 60–63 The Promenade, corner of Church St ⓣ01253/294386. The celebrated Yorkshire chippie chain has the town's pre-eminent (and priciest) sit-down fish and chips – there's a takeaway counter too. Meet "Harry's Challenge" (eating a giant cod or haddock plus trimmings) and you get a free pud and certificate. Moderate.

Kwizeen 47 King St ⓣ01253/290045. Anglo-Med bistro, with a bargain two-course weekday lunch (£5.95) and a seasonally changing menu. Closed Sun. Moderate.

Lagoonda 37 Queen St ⓣ01253/293837. Party-time Afro-Caribbean restaurant with surprisingly good food and service given that the staff have to spend their time negotiating the limbo bar. Choose from jerk or ginger pork, stuffed plantain, fruity curry and other such dishes. Moderate.

September Brasserie 15–17 Queen St ⓣ01253/623282. The restaurant with the best reputation in town – set prices for two- and three-course meals with plenty of choice, the menu ranging from locally potted shrimps to king prawn tempura. Local meat and vegetarian selection too. Closed Sun, & Mon lunch. Moderate.

White Tower Ocean Blvd, Blackpool Pleasure Beach ⓣ01253/346710. Blackpool's posh night out and the closest the town gets to Vegas – a lounge-style restaurant with prom views (great for the Illuminations), snappy service and pricey Modern British food. Closed Mon, & Sat lunch. Expensive.

Drinking, nightlife and entertainment

If you like your **nightlife** late, loud and libidinous, summertime Blackpool has few English peers. In all the pubs and clubs, young men can expect to have their attire and demeanour given the once-over by the hired hulks at the door; "girls" and "ladies" can expect free drinks and entry and a lot of largely good-natured amorous jousting. *Yates' Wine Lodge* has two popular branches, in Talbot Square and between Central and South piers where you can sip an amontillado sherry or champagne on draught. There's also the huge *Walkabout* Australian bar on Queen Street; and a plethora of Irish theme bars, notably *O'Neill's* on the corner of Talbot Road and Abingdon Street, *Finn's* in the *Clifton Hotel* on Talbot Square and *Scruffy Murphy's*, 32 Corporation St. *The Wheatsheaf* on Talbot Road, opposite Blackpool North Station, features real ales from local breweries, an open fire and beat-era memorabilia, and *The Pump and Truncheon*, 13 Bonny St, behind the Sea Life Centre, is also a real-ale pub.

For **dancing**, local opinion favours *Blue*, on Corporation Street, near the Grand Theatre, or *The Syndicate* on Church Street (the UK's biggest club), which features star DJs. *Bar Red* on Church Street, next to the Winter Gardens, is the pre-club party venue. *Funny Girls*, a transvestite-run bar at 9 The Strand (ⓣ01253/624901), has nightly shows that attract long (gay and straight) queues. Otherwise, entertainment is based very heavily on family shows, musicals, veteran TV comedians, crooners and stage spectaculars put on at a variety of end-of-pier and Pleasure Beach theatres or historic venues such as the **Grand Theatre** (ⓣ01253/290190, ⓦwww.blackpoolgrand.co.uk), **Winter Gardens** (ⓣ01253/292029, ⓦwww.blackpoollive.co.uk) and **Opera House** (ⓣ01253/292029), all on Church Street.

Preston and around

With the siren draws of the Lakes, the Peak District and the Yorkshire Dales so close, the rest of Lancashire often gets bypassed in the rush to the surrounding national parks, and more's the pity. It's true, the old cotton towns of north and east Lancashire might not be first on everyone's must-see list, but in **Preston,** 25 miles northwest of Manchester, the county has one of England's oldest towns, containing two fine museums and some appealing Georgian and Victorian remnants. North of the town, rural Lancashire is at its most bucolic in the villages of the **Ribble Valley**, particularly in the **Forest of Bowland**, whose gateway is the small market town of **Clitheroe**. Here, you'll find country walks and old inns easily the measure of any across the county borders, with the bonus of far less tourists with which to share them.

Preston

Strategically placed on the banks of the River Ribble, **PRESTON** (possibly a contraction of "Priest's Town") was already an important market town in Anglo-Saxon times and received its royal charter in 1179 – origin of the famous Preston Guild celebrations, which since 1542 have taken place every twenty years (the next in 2012). The town was attacked by Robert the Bruce, changed hands in the Civil War and saw action during the Jacobite rebellions, while Charles Dickens gathered material here for *Hard Times*, his coruscating attack on the factory system. True, there's little to show for such a long history save the nickname, "Proud Preston", but as the administrative and commercial centre of Lancashire, it's a useful shopping and service centre.

Some handsome Victorian public buildings do survive, most notably the majestic Greek-Revival-style **Harris Museum and Art Gallery** (Mon–Sat 10am–5pm; free), in the central Market Square. It's a fine building in its own right, purpose-built in 1893 and boasting, among other things, a monumental pediment outside and rotunda café (open until 4pm) inside, from where you can ponder the classical friezes and sculptures. The permanent collection focuses on fine art (particularly British landscape and portraiture, and contemporary photography) and decorative art, while temporary exhibitions often explore links with the town's significant Asian population. Scout around long enough and you'll encounter exhibits as diverse as a collection of delicate Victorian scent bottles and the skeleton of an Ice Age elk, the latter in the self-explanatory "Story of Preston" section. On either side of the Harris lies the modern shopping area, converging on Fishergate, the main street through town: the Victorian **Miller Arcade** (facing Fishergate) and outdoor and indoor **markets** (up Market Street; closed Sun) are the main draw. For a change in emphasis, cross Fishergate to explore the handsome Georgian development of **Winckley Square**, once home to the town's richest cotton magnates. Lancashire's favourite chef, Paul Heathcote, has a brasserie, *Simply Heathcotes*, here. Beyond the square, the ground drops away to the River Ribble and **Avenham Park**, one of the country's best examples of a landscaped Victorian park, with slopes steep enough for traditional egg-rolling every Easter.

If you needed any more incentive to stop it would be to make your way to the ground of Preston North End – one of Britain's oldest football clubs and winners of the first Football League championship – for the marvellous **National Football Museum**, Sir Tom Finney Way, Deepdale Stadium (Tues–Sat 10am–5pm, midweek matchday 10am–7.30pm, Sun 11am–5pm; free; Ⓦwww.nationalfootballmuseum.com). On one level, this is simply an unparalleled collection of football memorabilia: those who know about such things will relish the chance to see items as diverse as the Geoff Hurst crossbar from the 1966 World Cup or the neck-brace worn by legendary Manchester City goalkeeper Bert Trautman, who broke his neck (yet played on) in the 1956 FA Cup Final. But you really don't have to know anything about football to enjoy the museum, since "the true story of the world's greatest game" is backed by fascinating print, film and sound material on football's origins, its social importance, the experience of fans through the ages, and other relevant themes. Plus there are some great interactive exhibits – including do-it-yourself television punditry and table football with a video replay of your goals – and a good café.

For the football museum, it's a ten-minute ride on bus #19 from Preston **bus station**, right in the centre of town. The **train station**, on the west coast main line, has regular services to Lancaster, Manchester and Blackpool; a bus (every 20min, free with valid train ticket) connects the train station to the town centre and the bus station; otherwise, just follow Fishergate into the centre, a ten-minute walk. The **tourist office** is in the Guild Hall, on Lancaster Road (Mon–Sat 10am–5.30pm; ⓣ01772/253731, ⓦwww.visitpreston.com), just round the corner from the Harris Museum.

The mill towns of north and east Lancashire

Tourists rarely stray into the old, unsung mill towns of **north and east Lancashire**, reasoning perhaps that they are unlikely to offer much in the way of cultural promise or light-hearted diversion. There's something in that view, though to look solely at their unremarkable town centres and archetypal rows of housing is to miss the historical point. In the eighteenth and nineteenth centuries, the great cotton-weaving centres of **Bolton**, **Bury**, **Rochdale**, **Burnley** and **Blackburn** changed the way the world worked, with Lancashire innovation – Kay's flying shuttle, Hargreaves' spinning jenny, Arkwright's water frame – transforming cottage industries into hugely profitable mechanized production lines. Millions of tons of raw cotton flowed in to the Liverpool docks, to be turned into yarn and calico in an ever increasing number of Lancashire mills. The towns themselves acquired their character in one swift burst of expansion, as houses were thrown up to accommodate the weavers. The result was rarely pretty, but then it wasn't supposed to be – J.B. Priestley correctly identified the cotton towns as places "meant to work in and not really to live in". That was probably still true in the 1930s, when Priestley toured Britain, but today, with cotton long gone and contemporary prosperity underpinned by the engineering, technology and service industries, there's a more appealing air to the towns. Even so, although they might be thoroughly decent places to live, it's still hard to propose any serious tourist investigation of the region – although anyone with a keen eye for Victorian industrial and civic architecture will relish the surviving mill buildings (mostly converted to other uses these days) and proud, local town halls, museums and galleries.

The Ribble Valley

When the nineteenth-century Lancashire cotton weavers enjoyed a rare break from their industry they took to the bucolic retreats of the **Ribble Valley**, north of Preston, which cuts through the heart of northern Lancashire to the River Ribble's source in the Yorkshire Dales. In stark contrast to the conurbations to the south, the valley parades a stream of small market towns and isolated villages set among verdant fields and rolling hills. Much of the northwestern part of the region is occupied by thinly populated grouse moorland known as the **Forest of Bowland** – the name "forest" is used in its traditional sense of "a royal hunting ground", and much of the land still belongs to the Crown. What few trees do grow here are clustered in the valleys, which are accessible only by unclassified roads that follow former cattle droving tracks. **Public transport** is limited to the train service from Manchester and Blackburn, or buses from Preston, to the market town of **Clitheroe** on the forest's southern fringes; from there, buses run out to Dunsop Bridge, Newton and **Slaidburn** (with connections on to Settle in Yorkshire), the three tiny villages in the heart of the region. Hikers can follow the course of the river from its source to the estuary along the seventy-mile **Ribble Way**, which passes through Clitheroe: route guides are available from local bookshops and tourist offices.

Clitheroe

A tidy little market town on the banks of the River Ribble, **CLITHEROE** is best seen from the terrace of its empty **Norman keep** which towers above the Ribble Valley floor. From here, the small centre is laid out before you and, if there's little else specific to see – save a **Castle Museum** (11am–4.30pm: Easter–Oct daily; Nov–Dec & Feb weekends only; March–Easter closed Thurs & Fri; £1.65) in the extensive grounds – you can at least spend an hour or two browsing around the shops and old pubs. There's been a **market** in town since the thirteenth century: the current affair is held off King Street every Tuesday, Thursday and Saturday.

One obvious target is Pendle Hill, a couple of miles to the east, where the ten **Pendle Witches** allegedly held the diabolic rites that led to their hanging in 1612. The evidence against them came mainly from one small child, but nonetheless a considerable mythology has grown up around the witches, whose memory is perpetuated by a hilltop gathering each Halloween. The Clitheroe tourist office can provide a self-drive leaflet guiding you around the locality. With a car, you could also run out to the ruined Cistercian abbey at Whalley (a few miles south of Clitheroe) or the Roman museum at Ribchester (southwest).

You can sort out transport connections at the **bus and rail interchange** at the train station; a **Ribble Valley Day Ranger** ticket (£3, available on board any bus) is the best local deal. Ribble Way walkers might be glad of the town's accommodation options – full details from the **tourist office**, at 14 Market Place (Mon–Sat 9am–5pm; ⓣ01200/425566, ⓦwww.ribblevalley.gov.uk) – but you're unlikely to stop otherwise. The best place for a coffee and a light **meal** is the *Exchange Coffee Company*, 24 Wellgate (closed Sun), where the smell of roasted coffee wafts through the old house and up the stairs into the café. Pedal Power on Waddington Road (ⓣ01200/422066) can sort you out with a **mountain bike** for in-depth exploration of the Forest of Bowland or nearby Gisburn Forest.

The Forest of Bowland

Heading northwest from Clitheroe on the B6478 brings you to the **Forest of Bowland** just beyond Waddington, with a short run over the fells to **NEWTON**, a village centred on the *Parkers Arms* pub. It's two miles west of here to **DUNSOP BRIDGE**, a duck-riddled riverside hamlet from where an old drover's track (now a very minor road) known as the Trough of Bowland begins its twenty-mile slog across the tops to Lancaster. Those in the know make their way the couple of miles south from here to the splendid *Inn at*

Whitewell (Ⓣ01200/448222; ❻), which serves fabulous food in its restaurant (reservations essential) and also has a welcoming, old-fashioned bar serving meals.

Keep to the B road past Newton and it's a couple of miles northeast to **SLAIDBURN**, the most substantial and attractive of the forest's settlements. Hoary stone cottages fronted by a strip of aged cobbles set the tone – a truly ancient **inn**, the *Hark to Bounty* (Ⓣ01200/446246, Ⓦwww.hark-to-bounty.co.uk; ❸), and a popular **youth hostel** (Ⓣ0870/770 6034, Ⓔslaidburn@yha.org.uk; £10.25; closed Nov–Easter), itself a former inn, complete the picture. Both stand opposite each other in the centre of the village; the *Hark to Bounty* is known for its good bar food. For snacks, drinks and meals there's also the *Riverbank Tearooms*, with some outside seating (daily until 5pm).

Lancaster and around

LANCASTER, Lancashire's county town, dates back at least as far as the Roman occupation, though only the scant remains of a bath-house and traces of the fort wall survive from that period. A Saxon church was later built within the ruined Roman walls as Lancaster became a strategic trading centre, and by medieval times ships were using the River Lune and the coastal routes to Cumbria. A castle on the heights above the river defended the town from attack and provided a focus for the dispensing of regional justice. It was here that the Pendle Witches were tried in 1612, before being hanged on the heights outside town. Lancaster became an important port on the slave triangle, and it's the legacy of predominantly Georgian buildings from that time that gives the town its character, particularly in the leafy areas around the castle. It's no surprise that many people choose to spend a night here on the way to the Lakes or Dales to the north. If the lure of the beach becomes too strong, it's an easy side-trip the few miles west to the resort of **Morecambe** and to neighbouring **Heysham village** and its ancient churches.

Arrival, information and tours

Lancaster is a regular stop on the West Coast rail line from London to Carlisle and Scotland; there are also hourly trains from Manchester and even more frequently from Preston. From either the **train station** on Meeting House Lane, or the combined local **bus** and National Express station on Cable Street in town, it's a five-minute walk to the **tourist office** at 29 Castle Hill (March–Sept Mon–Sat 10am–5pm, Tues closes at 4pm; Oct–Feb Mon–Sat 10am–4pm; Ⓣ01524/32878, Ⓦwww.lancaster.gov.uk), in front of the castle. You can change money at the office, book accommodation, and check on space on the **Old Calendar Walks** – seasonal, "olde-worlde" strolls (£3.50) through the city streets with costumed guides. Annual **events and festivals** include an Easter maritime festival, the Worldbeat weekend for global music and crafts (Aug), Georgian festival (Aug bank holiday), and spectacular Bonfire Night celebrations (Saturday nearest Nov 5).

Accommodation

The tourist office can help you find somewhere to stay if our choices are full, and many of the town's pubs also offer accommodation. However, there's no local youth hostel and campsites are all a drive away from town.

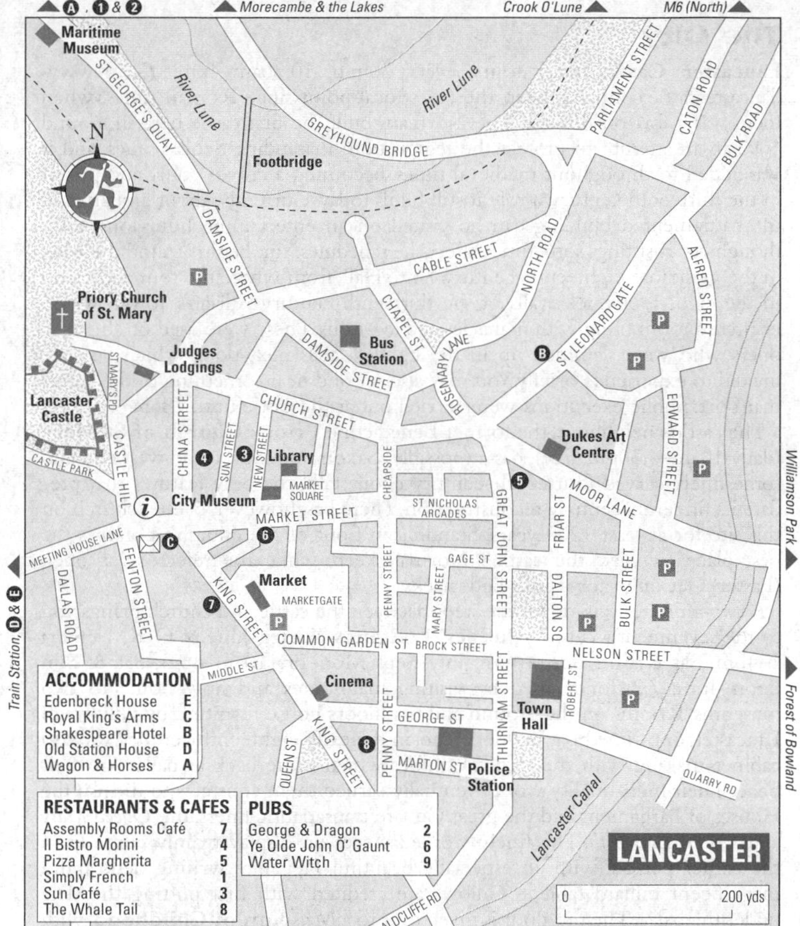

Edenbreck House Sunnyside Lane ☎01524/32464. For peace and quiet head for this large Victorian house ten minutes' walk out of the centre, set in its own grounds at the end of Ashfield Avenue, off Meeting House Lane. Just three en-suite rooms, so call ahead. No credit cards. ❷

Old Station House 25 Meeting House Lane ☎01524/381060. By the train station, providing amiable, non-smoking accommodation, this place has two doubles and a twin available, each with shower or private bathroom. The biggest room sports a brass bedstead. Parking available. No credit cards. ❸

Royal King's Arms Market St ☎01524/32451, ⓦwww.bookmenzies.com. Lancaster's best-sited hotel, opposite the castle, has fifty prettily furnished rooms with smart bathrooms, plus a bar and brasserie. Ask for a castle view. Rates are negotiable during the week, and always a little lower at the weekend (when breakfast is included in the price). ❻

Shakespeare 96 St Leonardsgate ☎01524/841041. Hard-working hosts maintain eight cosy rooms in this popular town-house hotel on a central street near several long-stay car parks. Rooms, of assorted shape and size, are en suite and non-smoking. Advance reservations advised. No credit cards. ❸

Wagon & Horses 27 St George's Quay ☎01524/846094. Pleasant rooms above a riverside pub, just past the Maritime Museum. No credit cards. ❷

The City

Lancaster Castle (daily tours, every 30min, 10.30am–4pm; £4; ⓦwww.lancastercastle.com) has been the city's focal point since Roman times, when there was a fort on this site. The Normans built the first castle here in around 1093 in an attempt to protect the region from marauding Scots armies, and it was added to throughout medieval times, becoming a crown court and prison in the thirteenth century, a role it still fulfils today. Currently, about a quarter of the battlemented building can be visited on an entertaining hour-long tour, though court sittings sometimes affect the schedules. You begin around the back in the grandiose eighteenth-century Shire Hall, from where the tour moves on to the eight-foot-thick walls of the thirteenth-century Adrian's Tower, which encircle a room hung with manacles and leg-irons. These were used on the prisoners who were slammed up in the lightless cells next door, which you are invited to experience briefly. You may also see and hear something of the hangman's art: public executions were carried out at the castle until 1865.

The castle's neighbour, the former Benedictine **Priory Church of St Mary** (daily 10am–4.30pm; free), has a (possibly) Saxon doorway at the west end and some finely carved fourteenth-century choir stalls, the only features that predate its fifteenth-century reconstruction. There has, however, been a church on this site for at least 1200 years. Standing in front of the church's porch is the best place to view the castle's Norman keep, while the refectory is open (Easter–Oct only) for drinks and snacks.

A two-minute walk down the steps between the castle and church brings you to the seventeenth-century **Judges' Lodgings** (Easter–June & Oct Mon–Fri 1–4pm, Sat & Sun noon–4pm; July–Sept Mon–Fri 10am–4pm, Sat & Sun noon–4pm; £2), once used by visiting magistrates and now home to two museums. Rooms on the ground and first floors house furniture by Gillows of Lancaster, one-time boat builders who, in the early eighteenth century, took to cabinet-making with the tropical timber which came back as ballast in their boats. Their high-quality work eventually earned them contracts to furnish the Houses of Parliament and the great Cunard transatlantic liners, the *Queen Mary* and *Queen Elizabeth*. The finely worked pieces on display mainly come from the earlier period, with an especially beautiful Regency writing desk and a magnificent billiard table – Gillows are credited with first putting the slate under the baize. The top floor is given over to a **Museum of Childhood**, with memory-jogging displays of toys and games, and a period (1900) schoolroom.

Continuing down the hill and left onto Damside Street, you arrive on the banks of the **River Lune** – which lent Lancaster its name – whose navigable lengths inspired the growth of the port. The river was first bridged in Roman times: the latest span, an eye-catching steel suspension bridge for pedestrians, follows the line of the medieval wooden, later stone, bridge. The top floor of one of the eighteenth-century warehouses here is taken up by part of the **Maritime Museum**, St George's Quay (daily: Easter–Oct 11am–5pm; Nov–Easter 12.30–4pm; £2), entered through the Old Custom House on the riverside. The museum's ample coverage of life on the sea and inland waterways of Lancashire is complemented by the **City Museum** on Market Square back in town (Mon–Sat 10am–5pm; free). Based in the former Town Hall, five minutes' walk southeast of the Judges' Lodgings, this explores the city's history from Neolithic to Georgian times.

For a panorama of the town, Morecambe Bay and the Cumbrian fells, take a bus from the bus station (or a steep 25-minute walk up Moor Lane) to **Williamson Park** (Easter–Oct daily 10am–5pm; Nov–Easter Mon–Fri

11am–4pm, Sat & Sun 10am–4pm; free), Lancaster's highest point. The grounds were laid out among old stone quarries by cotton workers, put out of work by the cotton famine caused by the American Civil War. Funded by local statesman and lino magnate Lord Ashton, the park's centrepiece is the 220-foot-high **Ashton Memorial** (same hours as park; free), a Baroque folly raised by his son in memory of his second wife. The views are pretty fine from here, and there's a small art gallery on the upper level, while the grounds also contain a **butterfly house and bird garden** (same hours as park; £3.50). The *Pavilion Tea Room* (daily: June–Sept 10am–5pm; Oct–May closes 4pm) at the memorial is a nice spot. The other local excursion is to the **Crook O'Lune**, a beauty spot made famous by J.M.W. Turner. It's four miles northeast of the city, reached by a path/cycle-way along the River Lune (part of the River Lune Millennium Park), and there's a picnic site, snack bar and public art works at the other end.

John Ruskin fans, meanwhile, won't want to miss the **Ruskin Library**, out at Lancaster University (Mon–Sat 11am–4pm, Sun 1–4pm; free; ⓦwww.lancs.ac.uk/users/ruskinlib), where a unique selection of pictures, manuscripts, books and photographs relating to the great man are shown in a series of changing exhibitions; buses run up every half an hour from the bus station.

Eating, drinking and entertainment

There's a fair selection of **cafés and restaurants** in town to suit most budgets, and a waterside **pub** or two for a tipple. For anything more cultural, the main destination is **Dukes** on Moor Lane (ⓣ01524/598500, ⓦwww.dukes-lancaster.org), the city's main arts centre, with cinema, theatre (including open-air performances in Williamson Park in summer) and other events.

Cafés

Assembly Rooms Café King St. Home-cooked café food amid the craft, antique, clothes and accessories stalls in the Georgian assembly rooms. Closed Sun & Mon.

The Whale Tail 78a Penny St. Veggie and wholefood café, tucked up a yard on the first floor, serving good breakfasts, tasty dips, salads, burgers, sandwiches and baked potatoes. Closes 5pm, 3pm on Sun.

Restaurants

Il Bistro Morini 26 Sun St ⓣ01524/846252. The best Italian in town, with a veggie-friendly Mediterranean menu. Only the steaks push the cost up, otherwise it's a reasonably priced place for a smart night out. Best to book in advance. Closed Sun. Moderate.

Pizza Margherita 2 Moor Lane ⓣ01524/36333. Friendly pizza place, with sixteen choices on the menu (and Lancashire cheese on a couple of them), plus a few pastas and some salad-type starters. You can fill up for around £10. Inexpensive.

Simply French 27 St George's Quay ⓣ01524/843199. Riverside brasserie in a converted warehouse close to the Maritime Museum. The early bird menu (before 6.30pm) is a good deal (mains for £6); dinner might be pan-seared fish or fillet steak, or classics like snails or sautéed frogs' legs. Closed Mon, also Tues & Wed lunch. Moderate.

Sun Café 25 Sun St ⓣ01524/845599. The contemporary bistro cooking is the draw in this stylish café/restaurant, but you might equally come for a sandwich and a glass of wine, Sunday brunch with the papers, the live jazz, or even the contemporary art gallery. Closed Sun evening. Inexpensive to Moderate.

Pubs

George & Dragon St George's Quay. For a stroll along the river and a quiet drink, either here or the *Wagon & Horses* up the road are the best pubs.

Water Witch Aldcliffe Rd (across the canal bridge). Canalside pub named after an old canal packet boat. A youthful crowd munches burgers, shoots pool and hogs the canal-side tables, but there's posh pub food too and an impressive range of real ales and continental lagers.

Ye Olde John O'Gaunt 53 Market St, near the City Museum. Terrific city-centre local with home-cooked food, a large range of whiskies and vodkas, special beers, tea and coffee on request, live trad jazz and R&B, plus a small beer garden.

Morecambe

Although the name **MORECAMBE**, meaning "Great Bay", dates from Celtic times, the seaside town five miles west of Lancaster only took it in the nineteenth century when it rapidly expanded from a small fishing village into a full-blown resort. The catalyst, as with Blackpool, was the arrival of the railway, which not only brought in the northern mill workers on holiday, but also enabled the quick transport of the bay's shrimps and mussels to the towns they had come from. Across the bay, Grange-over-Sands was always the more refined resort and with Blackpool to the south hoovering up the rest of the local demand for bucket-and-spade holidays, Morecambe went into decline after the war. There's been plenty of recent regeneration – notably the restored Stone Jetty, an arts centre and revamped amusements and attractions – but the sweep of the bay is still the major attraction, with the lakeland fells visible beyond and the local sunsets a renowned phenomenon. The **Stone Jetty**, all that remains of the former harbour, has been remodelled by sculptors and stonemasons and now features bird sculptures, games and motifs – recognizing Morecambe Bay as Britain's most important wintering site for wildfowl and wading birds (two-night guided birdwatching breaks are based in the town; ask at the tourist office). A little way along the prom stands the most popular statue of all, of one of Britain's most treasured comedians – Eric Bartholomew, who took the stage name **Eric Morecambe** when he met his comedy partner, Ernie Wise. He appears here in famous Bring-Me-Sunshine prancing mode.

Regular buses or trains from Lancaster make the ten-minute trip to Morecambe: from the **bus** or **train stations**, on either side of Central Drive, it's five minutes' walk to the Stone Jetty. The **tourist office** is just back from here in the Old Station Buildings on the Central Promenade (Mon–Sat 9.30am–5pm, Sun 10am–4pm; ⓣ01524/582808), and can provide information about seasonal **guided walks** taking in the town's Art Deco heritage. The tourist office also operates a room-booking service for local **guesthouses and hotels** and Morecambe is certainly a lot quieter a place to spend the night than Blackpool. Most places are ranged along the front, and – at the budget end of the market at least – are resolutely old-fashioned in style. If you are going to stay, you'll find it worth your while to pay for the sweeping views from the front rooms of the nicely refurbished *Clarendon Hotel*, Marine Rd West (ⓣ01524/410180, ⓦwww.mitchellshotels.co.uk; ❻) – rates are at the bottom end of the range and include breakfast. The **Platform arts centre** (ⓣ01524/582803) shares the same building as the tourist office.

Heysham

The main historic interest on this side of Morecambe Bay is at **HEYSHAM**, three miles southwest of Morecambe and best approached on foot, along the promenade from the resort. Largely known for its ferry port (services to Belfast and the Isle of Man) and unsightly nuclear power station, Heysham's hidden gem is the shoreside **Heysham Village**, centred on a group of charming seventeenth-century cottages and barns, one of which is now the local **Heritage Centre** (April–Sept daily 11am–4pm; Oct–March Sat & Sun only 12.30–3pm; free). Settlement here can be traced back to prehistoric times, though proudest relic is the well-preserved Viking hog's-back tombstone in Saxon **St Peter's Church**, set in a romantic churchyard below the headland. Just up the lane, on the headland itself, the earlier ruins of **St Patrick's Chapel** occupy a superb vantage-point over the bay and to the lakeland hills beyond. Views aside, the singular interest here is the series of rough-cut stone graves by the chapel, possibly dating from the eighth or ninth centuries. Once you've seen these, all that remains is to step back into one of the village tearooms for a glass of (non-alcoholic) nettle beer, a local speciality dating from the Victorian era.

The Isle of Man

The **Isle of Man**, almost equidistant from Ireland, England, Wales and Scotland, is one of the most beautiful spots in Britain, a mountainous, cliff-fringed island just thirty-three miles by thirteen, into which are shoehorned austere moorlands and wooded glens, sandy beaches, fine castles, beguiling narrow-gauge railways and scores of standing stones and Celtic crosses. It takes some effort to reach, and the weather is hardly reliable, factors that have seen tourist numbers fall since its Victorian heyday, when the island developed as rapidly as the other northwestern coastal resorts. This means, though, that the Isle of Man has been spared the worst excesses of the British tourist trade: there's peace and quiet in abundance, walks around the unspoilt hundred-mile coastline, picket fences and picnic spots, rural villages straight out of a 1950s' picture-book, steam trains and cream teas – a yesteryear ensemble if ever there was one.

The capital, **Douglas**, is atypical of an island that prides itself on its Celtic and Norse heritage, and it's the vestiges of the distant past – the castles at the former capital **Castletown** and the west coast port of **Peel** – that make the most obvious destinations. Elsewhere, **Port Erin** has one of the island's best beaches, while to the north **Laxey** is an attractive proposition for its huge waterwheel and the meandering train ride to the barren summit of **Snaefell**, the island's highest peak. From Snaefell's summit you get an idea of the range

Walking on the Isle of Man

Quite apart from the local walking opportunities that the glens, coastline and hills offer, there are a number of established day **hikes** and **long-distance walks**. OS Landranger map 95 covers the entire island, while the free small guide *Walks on the Isle of Man*, available from Douglas tourist office, spells out all the options and indicates what you're likely to see en route at any particular time of the year.

Short sections of **disused railway line** provide some of the gentlest introductions to the scenery: notably the Heritage Trail (10 miles), from the Quarterbridge in Douglas to Peel, and the route from Peel north to Ramsey, via Kirk Michael (16 miles). A good route to combine with an outward journey or return by steam train is the **Port Erin to Castletown** (12 miles) hike along the cliff tops and beaches, with a possible detour to Cregneash village. From the summit of **Snaefell**, various descents are possible, the easiest of which is the direct route back down the Laxey Valley to Laxey.

There are two main long-distance footpaths, the shortest being the 28-mile **Millennium Way**, from Castle Rushen in Castletown to Ramsey, following the old medieval "Royal Way". It splits into three day hikes (though serious hikers do it in one day), with the second half of the walk, from Baldwin to Ramsey, across the most remote terrain. The greatest challenge, however, is the round-island **Raad ny Foillan (Road of the Gull)**, a well-signposted (white gull on a blue background) 100-mile coastal walk which takes most people around five days to complete. The path follows the coast wherever possible, and only on the northern stretch – north and west of Ramsey – are accommodation and other facilities sparse.

Guided walking holidays are offered by Legs of Man, based at *St Heliers Hotel*, Central Promenade, Douglas ⓣ01624/624355, costing £300–350 per week, including bed, breakfast, evening meal and transfers.

of the Manx scenery, the finest parts of which are to be found in the seventeen officially designated National Glens, most of them linked by the **Raad Ny Foillan** (Road of the Gull) coastal footpath, which passes several of the island's numerous hill forts, Viking ship burials and Celtic crosses.

Although the landscapes are wonderful, the island's main tourist draw is the **TT (Tourist Trophy) motorcycle races** (held in the two weeks after the late-May bank holiday), a frenzy of speed and burning rubber that's shattered the island's peace annually since 1907. Thousands of bikers swamp the place to watch a nonstop parade of maniacs hurtling round the roads on a 37-mile circuit at speeds averaging 126mph. This is only the most famous of a summer-long list of **rallies and races** on the island's roads, from the Manx Rally, International Rally and Manx Classic to the Manx Kart Grand Prix, when go-carts buzz through the streets of Peel. If you want to stay on the island at these times (exact dates available from the Isle of Man tourist office), you must book your accommodation well in advance.

Some history

The island may have already been populated when it became a separate land mass at the end of the last Ice Age around 8000 BC, but the earliest substantial human traces are Mesolithic flint workings from about 6000 BC, predating the Neolithic farming settlements by around three millennia. St Patrick is said to have come here in the fifth century AD bringing Christianity, which struggled for a while when the **Vikings** established garrisons here in the eleventh century, though they converted while they reigned as **Kings of Mann** – the name derived from that of the island's ancient sea-god, Manannan Mac Lir (Son of the Sea). The Scots under Alexander wrested power from the Norsemen in 1275, the beginning of an ultimately unsuccessful 130-year struggle with the English for control of the island. During the English **Civil War**, James Stanley, Seventh Earl of Derby and Lord of Man, raised an army to support Charles II, but in his absence a local militia offered the island to Cromwell, provided the traditional rights of the islanders – long infringed upon by English overlords – were maintained. It was a shortlived insurrection: with the restoration of the monarchy, the leaders of the militia were executed and the island returned to Crown control.

The **distinct identity** of the island remained intact, however, and many true Manx inhabitants, who comprise a shade under fifty percent of the island's 76,000 population, insist that the Isle of Man is not part of England, nor even of the UK. Indeed, although a Crown dependency, the island has its own government, **Tynwald**, arguably the world's oldest democratic parliament, which has run continuously since 979 AD. Tynwald consists of two chambers, the 24-member House of Keys (directly elected every five years) and the nine-member Legislative Council (elected by the House of Keys). To further complicate matters, the island maintains a unique associate status in the EU, neither contributing nor receiving funds but enjoying the same trading rights. The island has its own sterling currency, worth the same as the mainland currency; its own laws, though they generally follow Westminster's; an independent postal service; and a Gaelic-based language which nearly died out but is once again being taught in schools and is most visible on dual-language road signs throughout the island. The island, of course, also produces its own tailless version of the domestic cat, as well as famously good kippers and queenies (scallops).

For most of its history, crofting and fishing, interspersed with a good bit of smuggling, have formed the basis of the economy. The first regular steamship service from England commenced in 1819, and **tourism** began to flourish during the late-Victorian and Edwardian eras with the influx of northwestern

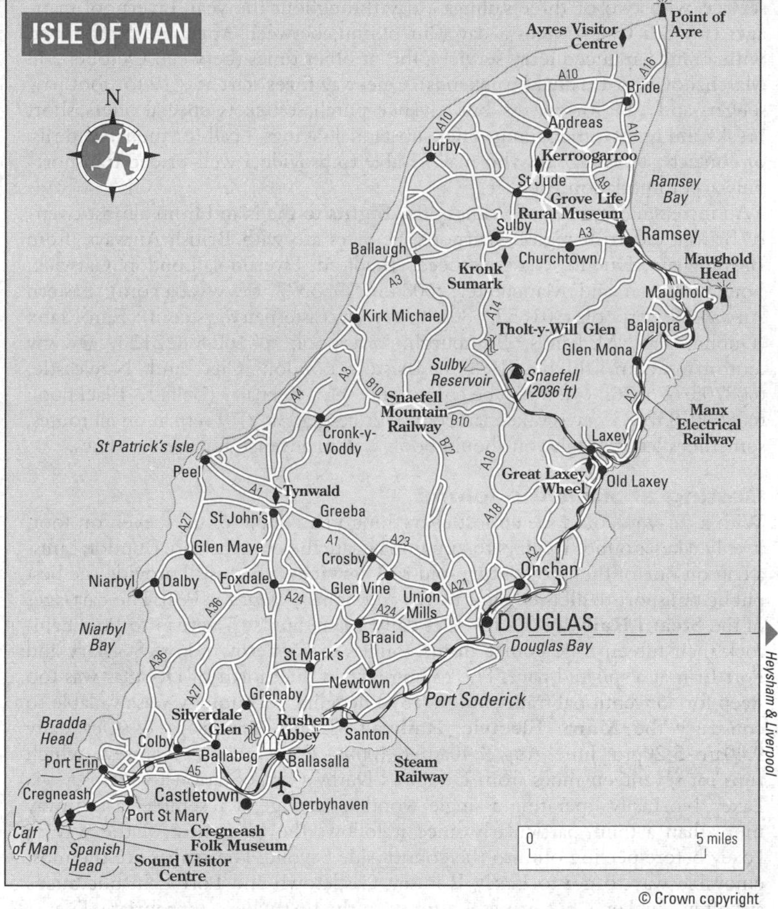

© Crown copyright

factory workers. At its height – at the turn of the twentieth century – tourism was bringing in half a million visitors a year, but in recent times the real money-spinner has been the **offshore finance industry**, exploiting the island's low income tax and absence of capital gains tax and death duties. More than fifty banks have been established on the island since 1991, whole streets in Douglas, the capital, are taken up by consultancies and the island is dotted with the houses and swanky cars of tax exiles. Given its financial expertise, the Isle of Man is also playing a major role in the development of **e-banking and e-commerce**, while the low-tax island has provided incentives for the **filming** of an increasing number of movies.

Getting to the island

Most visitors from England arrive at Douglas, the main port, on **ferries** or the quicker **Sea Cats**, both run by the Isle of Man Steam Packet Company (Ⓣ08705/523523, Ⓦwww.seacat.co.uk), from either Heysham (near Lancaster) or Liverpool. Heysham (Sea Cat 2hr, ferry 3hr 30min) has the most frequent service, with two or three sailings a day throughout the year. Liverpool manages two Sea Cat services a day (2hr 30min) between April and September, with a much-reduced ferry service (4hr) at other times (between October and March, down to 1 daily at weekends). One-way **fares** start at £19 for foot passengers and £89 for drivers, but advance-purchase tickets, special offers, short breaks and night-time sailings offer substantial savings – call for the latest deals, or contact a travel agent, who may be able to provide a well-priced transport-plus-accommodation package.

An increasing number of airlines offer **flights** to the island from almost twenty British and Irish regional airports. Services are with British Airways (from Birmingham, Dublin, Glasgow, Leeds Bradford, Liverpool, London Gatwick, London Luton and Manchester; ⓣ0845/773 3377, ⓦwww.ba.com); Eastern Airways (Liverpool; ⓣ01652/680600, ⓦwww.easternairways.com); EuroManx (Dublin, East Midlands, Edinburgh, Liverpool; ⓣ01624/822123, ⓦwww.euromanx.com); Flybe (Belfast, Bristol, London City and Newcastle; ⓣ08705/676676, ⓦwww.flybe.com); and Fly Keenair (Belfast, Blackpool; ⓣ08000/837783, ⓦwww.keenair.co.uk). Prices start at £79 return on all routes, sometimes less, though you should book well in advance for the best fares.

Getting around the island

With a car you could see almost everything in a couple of days; even on foot, it only takes around five days to circumnavigate the entire island. But don't miss a trip on one of the two century-old **rail services** which still provide the best public transport to all the major towns and sights except for Peel. The carriages of the **Steam Railway** (Easter–Oct daily 10am–5pm; £7 return to Port Erin) rock their fifteen-mile course from Douglas to Castletown, Port St Mary and Port Erin at a spirited pace. The rolling terrain due north of Douglas was too steep for conventional trains, but by 1893 fledgling technology was available to construct the **Manx Electric Railway** (Easter–May, Sept & Oct daily 9.40am–5.20pm; June–Aug 9.40am–6.40pm; £6 return to Ramsey) which runs for seventeen miles from Douglas's Derby Castle Station to Ramsey via Laxey. Normally operating a single wooden carriage, it resembles a tramway more than a train, particularly since it follows the road most of the way to Laxey before peeling off into the countryside beyond. The **trains** are the most enjoyable way to get to Laxey, Ramsey, Castletown and Port Erin but **buses** are often quicker – bus routes are given in the text where appropriate. There's also the Snaefell Mountain Railway from Laxey to the top of the island's highest mountain, Snaefell; see p.843 for details.

The "**Island Explorer**" ticket gives one (£8), three (£18), five (£26) or seven (£32) days' unlimited travel on all bus services, plus steam and electric train routes, the trip to Snaefell and horse-tram rides in Douglas. Tickets are available from the Travel Shop (see p.839), main train and tram stations, and the tourist office in Douglas.

Outside race times, the roads are a joy to **drive** – there's relatively little traffic, even in summer, and on the TT stretches, the straights and gentle curves tempt you all too easily into Michael Schümacher mode, encouraged by the fact that there's no speed limit on the Isle of Man outside the towns and villages (though in these the limit is often reduced to 20mph).

Douglas

DOUGLAS, heart of the offshore finance industry, also has the vast majority of the island's hotels and best restaurants, and it makes as good a base as any, since all roads lead here. A mere market town as late as 1850, with one pier and an undeveloped seafront, Douglas was a product of Victorian mass tourism and displays many similarities to Blackpool, just across the water: five-storey terraces back the two-mile-long curve of the promenade and its tram tracks, and the town even makes an attempt to emulate the illuminations. However, where once half a million people a year sported on the sands, package tourism to hotter climates has long since burst the bubble. As long as you put aside thoughts of Blackpool-style state-of-the-art entertainment, you can still have a thoroughly enjoyable time here, but it's likely to consist largely of pulling up a candy-striped deckchair and enjoying the extensive sands, with a ride on the horse-drawn tram thrown in for variety. There's an excellent museum and truly dramatic bay views from the promenade, but if you just see Douglas you won't have seen the best of the island.

Arrival, orientation and information

All flights arrive at **Ronaldsway Airport** at Ballasalla, around ten miles south of Douglas, close to Castletown. Buses (every 30min–1hr, 7am–11pm) connect the airport with Douglas as well as Castletown/Port St Mary. A taxi costs around £16 to Douglas, £20 to Peel.

Ferries and Sea Cats dock by the **Sea Terminal** at the southern end of the Douglas waterfront. Fifty yards beyond the forecourt taxi rank, the Lord Street **bus terminal** is the hub of the island's dozen or so bus routes; the **Travel Shop** here (Mon 10am–12.30pm & 1.30–5.45pm, Tues 8am–12.30pm & 1.30–4pm, Wed–Fri 8am–5.45pm, Sat 8am–12.30pm & 1.30–5.45pm; ⓣ01624/662525) has timetable information and sells Island Explorer **travel tickets** for buses and trains – see "Getting around the island" opposite for details.

North Quay runs 300yd west from the bus terminal alongside the river and fishing port to Douglas Station, the northern terminus of the **steam railway** to Port Erin. The waterfront (progressively Loch, Central and Queen's promenades) runs two miles north to Derby Castle Station for the **electric railway** to Laxey and Ramsey – take the horse-drawn tram along the promenade or bus #24, #24a, #26 or #26a from North Quay.

The **tourist office** is in the Sea Terminal building (mid-May to Sept daily 9.15am–7pm; April to mid-May & Oct daily 9am–5pm; Nov–March Mon–Thurs 9am–5.30pm, Fri 9am–5pm, Sat 9.30am–12.30pm); ⓣ01624/686766). There's a smaller office at the airport, open to meet flight arrivals. The main **websites** for information are ⓦwww.gov.im, ⓦwww.isleofman.com, and ⓦwww.visitisleofman.com. The twelve heritage sites and museums are run under the umbrella of Manx National Heritage (ⓦwww.storyofmann.com). They all have individual admission charges, though a **4 Site Pass** (£10, available from any attraction) will save you some money. English Heritage members get half-price admission to all the sites during their first year of membership, and free entry in subsequent years.

Accommodation

B&Bs are packed in along Douglas's front and up the roads immediately off Harris Promenade, particularly along Broadway, Castle Mona Avenue, Empress Drive and Empire Terrace. Prices start at as little as £35 for a double (in admittedly small rooms) and a sea-view room can be had for £50. Note that many places demand a two-night minimum stay in the summer. If you're prepared to spend a bit more money – and many businesspeople are, so book ahead – then again, comparative bargains abound. In particular, there's an increasing number of rather splendid boutique-style **hotels** in renovated seafront buildings, with significantly higher prices. The **campsites** listed below are the ones nearest to Douglas, but for a full list of rural sites contact the tourist office.

B&Bs, guest houses and hotels

Admiral House Loch Promenade ⓣ01624/629551, ⓦwww.admiralhouse.com. At the ferry terminal end of the prom, this lovingly restored, club-like retreat features very comfortable rooms, adorned in bold colours and equipped with elegant bathrooms. There's a café-bar and Italian restaurant too. ❺

Bentlea 8 The Esplanade ⓣ01624/673879. Old-style promenade guest house with a little patio at the front. No frills, but you can't beat the price, and two singles and a double at the front have sea views. No credit cards. ❶

Blossoms 4 The Esplanade ⓣ01624/673360. One of the better choices at the cheaper end of the market, *Blossoms* has a few sea-view rooms, which tend to go early. No credit cards. ❶

Claremont 18–19 Loch Promenade ⓣ01624/698800, ⓦwww.sleepwellhotels.com. Sympathetically renovated promenade hotel with a good bar and restaurant. Rooms have all the latest gadgets, including voicemail, DVD and Internet hook-ups, while executive suite upgrades get you a separate lounge area. ❺

Cubbon House 48 Loch Promenade ⓣ01624/670799. Hiding its smart en-suite rooms behind an old-fashioned holiday hotel facade, this is an unpretentious and good-value place, with comfortable beds and quiet rooms at the rear. ❸

Dreem Ard Ballanard Rd, 2 miles west of the centre ⓣ01624/621491. Tranquil, out-of-town B&B with three en-suite rooms, including a family room with a separate lounge area (plus single bed), and large garden suite with its own dressing room and sitting area. No credit cards. ❸

Regency Queen's Promenade ⓣ01624/680680, ⓦwww.regency.iom-1.net. A contemporary facelift has retained the Victorian leaded windows and decorative oak panelling in the public rooms while kitting out guest quarters in style. Popular with businesspeople, it also makes a comfortable touring base. Similar rooms also available in the associated *Hotel Penta* further down the prom (book through the *Regency*), plus three two-person apartments. Breakfast not included. ❺, apartments ❻

Sefton Harris Promenade ⓣ01624/645500, ⓦwww.seftonhotel.co.im. Next to the Gaiety Theatre, this has sleek, spacious rooms offering a sea view or a balcony over the impressive internal water garden. It's the only four-star hotel in Douglas, with facilities to match, including pool, gym, Internet access, bike rental, bar and restaurant. Weekend rates are £10 cheaper per room, and book online and you save yourself another fiver. ❻

St Heliers Hotel Central Promenade ⓣ01624/624355. Reasonably priced guest house on the front with a friendly welcome and a variety of simply furnished rooms, some with tiled shower-and-loo, and a few with sea views. It's used as the base for Legs of Man guided walking holidays, so you can expect hearty breakfasts and comfortable beds. No credit cards. ❷

Welbeck Hotel Mona Drive, off Central Promenade ⓣ01624/675663, ⓦwww.welbeckhotel.com. Mid-sized family-run hotel 100yd up the hill off the seafront – some rooms have a sea view though. Accommodation is nicely decorated (modern furniture and coordinated colours), with a bit more space available in deluxe rooms as well as six two-person self-catering apartments (breakfast not included in the apartments). Rooms and apartments ❺

Campsites

Glendhoo International Campsite ⓣ01624/621254. In a sheltered valley, two miles north at the Cronk ny Mona crossroads on the A18. Closed Oct–Easter.

Glenlough Farm ⓣ01624/851326. Three miles west at Union Mills on the Peel road. Closed Oct–April.

Grandstand ⓣ01624/621132. Closest to Douglas, this backs onto Noble's Park Grandstand on Glencrutchery Road, a mile north of the tourist office. Closed Oct–May and during TT and Manx Grand Prix races.

The Town

Douglas's seafront vista has changed little since Victorian times, and is still trodden by heavy-footed carthorses pulling **trams** (May–Sept, from 9am; Island Explorer ticket valid). On Harris Promenade the opulent **Gaiety Theatre**, fronted by a stained-glass canopy, is one of the nine theatres designed by Frank Matcham, which include the Grand in Blackpool (see p.823). The lush interior, paintings, decorated stage backdrop and understage machinery have been restored with precision, and hour-and-a-half-long tours of the theatre take place each Saturday at 10.30am (Easter–Sept only; £4; information and box office ☎01624/625001).

The town is at its oldest, and most interesting, in the streets near the **harbour**, where an attempt has been made to preserve Douglas's "historic quayside". There's not much to it, save a few old pubs and the odd teetering building, and you're soon pushed up Victoria Street, past the Manx Legislative Building, to the **Manx Museum**, on the corner of Kingswood Grove and Crellin's Hill (Mon–Sat 10am–5pm; free). The museum makes a good start for anyone wanting to get to grips with Manx culture and heritage before setting off around the island, kicking off with a National Gallery of Manx painters – from Alfred James Collister and his friend Archibald Knox to the contemporary abstract artist Bryan Kneale. Other rooms provide an absorbing synopsis of the island's history, packed with Neolithic standing stones, Celtic grave markers and other artefacts, notably some excellent displays relating to Viking burials and runic crosses. Much of the current understanding of Manx culture was pieced together from digs at Peel Castle in the 1980s, which turned up a cache of silver coins minted in Dublin in 1030, and evidence of a pagan sacrifice, in the form of a woman's severed scalp, on display next to the trove. More recent activities get the full treatment, too, with collections of smutty postcards from the 1930s, displays about the TT races and information boards explaining the capital's financial wheeling and dealing.

Eating and drinking

Douglas has the best choice of **cafés and restaurants** on the island, with plenty of inexpensive places to grab a bite to eat as well as some more sophisticated dining options. Manx-brewed beer is on sale at most **pubs** and brews such as "Old Bushy Tail" soon revive flagging spirits, while for a more fashionable night out, the **bar scene** in Douglas is ever improving.

Cafés and café-bars

C'est La Vie 28 Victoria St. Good-looking café-bar that's well-known for its globally inspired food – bangers and mash to spicy Indonesian noodles. A busy lunchtime spot, though they serve food until 9pm.

Greens Douglas Station, North Quay. Vegetarian café in the ticket office serving drinks and snacks until 5pm, with hot lunches and a veggie buffet from noon to 2.30pm.

Spill the Beans 1 Market Hill. Douglas' best coffee house, with a choice of brews plus muffins, croissants, cakes and pastries. Closes at 5pm, and all Sun.

Restaurants

Café Tanroagan 9 Ridgeway St ☎07624/472411. The best fish and seafood on the island, in a relaxed, contemporary restaurant with the kitchen open to view. Visiting film crews and actors all make a beeline here, for fish straight off the boat given either an assured Mediterranean twist or served simply grilled, steamed or poached. Reservations essential. Closed Sat lunch & all Sun. Expensive.

Highlander Inn Main Rd, A1, Greeba, 5 miles west of Douglas ☎01624/852609. A popular night out is this family-run restaurant offering an imaginative menu and a real fire. Reservations advised. Closed Tues. Moderate.

Paparazzi 26 Loch Promenade ☎01624/673222. Locals like this large pizzeria-trattoria with Sicilian beer and a few more unusual specialities alongside the traditional pizzas, pastas and Italian dishes. Moderate.

Scotts Bistro 7 John St ☎01624/623764. Near the old town hall, this is housed in Douglas's oldest (seventeenth-century) building and has queenies (scallops) in garlic sauce and Manx trout on its bistro menu. Courtyard for summer dining. Closed Sun. Moderate.

Pubs and bars

Bar George Hill St. A fashionable haunt housed in a converted Sunday School.

British Hotel North Quay. Harbourside pub that's been given a going-over inside but retains some character.

Colours *Hilton Hotel*, Central Promenade. Outdoor sea-view tables make for a nice coffee stop, while it's more of a party venue at night.

Fiesta Havana 7–17 Wellington St. For drinks and cocktails, Latin American food, salsa nights and club sounds, this is the place; open until 3am Fri and Sat.

Rovers Return 11 Church St. Cosy old local around the corner from *Scotts Bistro*, where you can try the local Manx beers.

Listings

Airport Ronaldsway Airport, flight enquiries ⓣ01624/821600, ⓦwww.iom-airport.com.

Banks ATMs at Barclays, Victoria St; NatWest, Prospect Hill; Lloyds-TSB, Prospect Hill; HSBC, Ridegeway St; Isle of Man Bank, Sea Terminal.

Bicycle rental Eurocycles, 8a Victoria Rd, off Broadway ⓣ01624/624909. Closed Sun.

Buses All bus enquiries ⓣ01624/662525.

Car rental Most outfits have offices at the airport or can arrange to deliver cars to the Sea Terminal. Contact: Athol, Athol Garage, Peel Rd and at the airport ⓣ01624/822481, ⓦwww.athol.co.im; Isle of Man Rent-a-Car, at the airport and deliveries to your hotel or Sea Terminal ⓣ01624/825855; Mylchreests, at the airport and deliveries to Sea Terminal ⓣ08000/190355.

Cruises Seasonal cruises, from Villier steps, Douglas promenade, to Port Soderick or Laxey on the *MV Karina*. Departures daily April–Sept, weather permitting; tickets £10; call ⓣ01624/861724 or ⓣ07624/493592.

Ferries and Sea Cats Isle of Man Steam Packet Company ⓣ01624/661661, ⓦwww.seacat.co.uk.

Hospital Noble's Hospital, Strang ⓣ01624/650000.

Internet Feegan's Lounge, 22 Duke St, off Victoria St (Mon–Fri 9am–6pm, Sat 9am–5pm).

Pharmacies Boots, 14 Strand St; John Atkinson, 2 Granville St.

Police Douglas Police Station, Glencrutchery Rd ⓣ01624/631212.

Post office Main post office is at 6 Regent St ⓣ01624/686141.

Telephones Using a UK-registered mobile phone in the Isle of Man incurs international call rates for making and receiving calls. Pay-as-you-go phones may not permit calls from the Isle of Man either.

Trains Steam Railway enquiries ⓣ01624/673623; Electric Railway and Snaefell Mountain Railway enquiries ⓣ01624/663366.

Laxey

Filling a narrow valley, the straggling village of **LAXEY**, seven miles north of Douglas, spills down from its train station to a small harbour and long, pebbly beach, squeezed between two bulky headlands. The Manx Electric Railway from Douglas drops you at the station used by the Snaefell Mountain Railway (see p.843). Shops and a couple of cafés here attempt to divert the crowds who disembark and then head inland and uphill to Laxey's pride, the **"Lady Isabella" Great Laxey Wheel** (Easter–Oct daily 10am–5pm; £3), smartly painted in red and white. With a diameter of over 72ft it's said to be the largest working waterwheel in the world. Until 1929 the wheel was used to pump water from the local lead mines which, with their silver-rich ore, were a major money-spinner. The mechanism and its relation to the mine are all well explained and you can stroll around the various buildings and bits of machinery before climbing to the top of the wheel for a fine view. **Laxey Woollen Mills**, over on Glen Road (Mon–Sat 10am–5pm; free), is also still in operation and you can see weaving taking place there most days. Otherwise Laxey is at its best down in **Old Laxey**, around the harbour, half a mile below the station, where large car parks attest to the popularity of the beach and river.

Half a mile out of town (follow the A2 to Ramsey) a sign points you up a side street to **King Orry's Grave**, named for the heroic eleventh-century Manx king who created the first Kingdom Of Mann. Would that it were any such thing, historical evidence of him being slight, though the two grave sites on show – one either side of the road – are interesting enough. It's thought that they're five-thousand-year-old stone chambered tombs, built by Neolithic

Outdoor activities

The island's glorious countryside encourages all sorts of outdoor activities, from farm-based horse or quad-bike rides to clambering up waterfalls in a wetsuit. Individuals and families are welcome at all the places listed below, but it's essential to make bookings in advance. Bring along clothes and trainers you don't mind getting dirty/wet.

Abbeylands Equestrian Centre Lower Sulby Farm, Scollag Rd, Onchan ⓣ01624/676717; closed Fri afternoon. Off-road pony trekking, riding and jumping lessons, for all levels of ability, from £15.

Gemini Charter Boat ⓣ01624/832761 or 07624/483328. Fishing trips, and bird- or seal-watching trips out of Port St Mary, all year, weather permitting. From £5 an hour per person, plus £4 for rod hire.

Quad Bike Trail Rides Ballacraine Farm, A1 road, St John's ⓣ01624/801219. An hour and a half's exhilarating quad-bike ride on farmland and open moorside; full instruction and protective clothing provided; £35 per person, includes a huge farmhouse tea afterwards.

The Venture Centre Lewaigue Farm, Maughold ⓣ01624/814240, ⓦwww.adventure-centre.co.uk. Canoeing, sea-kayaking, abseiling, gorge-climbing, powerboat training, sailing and archery, from around £30 a session, though prices vary according to numbers and activities. Half-, full- or multi-day activities provided; also self-catering bunkhouse accommodation available on site.

farmers under cairns, the earth of these now long worn away and leaving just a small arc of standing stones.

Hourly **buses** #3 and #3A run to Laxey from Douglas; the #3B and #3C run directly to Old Laxey four times a day (not Sun). The *Mines Tavern*, by the station, has some shaded outdoor seats and serves **meals** (lunch and dinner), while *Brown's* on the fantastically named Ham and Egg Terrace (by the wheel car park) is the place for grills and fry-ups or some Manx kippers and bread and butter. Down at the harbour, **drinking** is done at the *Shore Hotel*, a nice pub by the bridge, which brews its own bitter, and there's the *Mona Lisa* (ⓣ01624/862488; dinner only; closed Sun & Mon) just opposite, over the bridge, a popular Italian pizzeria-trattoria.

Snaefell, Tholt-y-Will Glen and Sulby Glen

Every thirty minutes, the tramcars of the **Snaefell Mountain Railway** (Easter–Oct daily 10.30am–3.30pm; £6 return, £7.50 from Douglas) begin their thirty-minute wind from Laxey through increasingly denuded moorland to the island's highest point, the top of **Snaefell** (2036ft) – the Vikings' "Snow Mountain" – from where you can see England, Wales, Scotland and Ireland on a clear day. The four-and-a-half miles of track were built in seven months over the winter of 1895 by two hundred men; one gang worked down from the summit, the other up from Laxey, an unimaginable effort in bitter conditions. At the summit, most people are content to pop into the inelegant café and bar and then soak up the views for the few minutes until the return journey. But with a decent map and a clear day, you could walk back instead, following trails down the mountain to Laxey, Sulby Glen or the Peel–Ramsey road.

The road route up, the A18 from Douglas or Ramsey, also makes for a great ride, since it forms part of the TT course. Where the A18 and A14 (Snaefell–Sulby) meet, just below the summit, there's an isolated railway halt where drivers and hikers can pick up the mountain railway for a truncated ride to the summit and back. Three miles below the summit, down the A14, which sweeps past **Sulby Reservoir**, the road drops into **Tholt-y-Will Glen**, one of the island's more picturesque corners, with its gushing river and walks through the verdant plantations.

The A14 continues north to join the A3 Ramsey road, along a fine route – above the river – through **Sulby Glen**, with bracken-clad hills flanking the road. At the junction, the *Sulby Glen Hotel* (ⓣ01624/897240, ⓦwww.sulbyglenhotel.com; ❸) has Manx beer and bistro meals (no food served Sun and Mon nights). A signposted turn, just before the A3, cuts east to **Cronk Sumark**, a Celtic hill-top fort close to a large picnic area.

Maughold, Ramsey and the north

The Manx Electric Railway trains stop within a mile and a half of **MAUGHOLD**, seven miles northeast of Laxey, a tiny hamlet just inland from the cliff-side lighthouse at **Maughold Head**. It's an isolated spot which only adds to the attraction of Maughold's parish church, in whose grounds is maintained an outstanding collection of early Christian and Norse **carved crosses** – 44 pieces, dating from the sixth to the thirteenth century, and ranging from fragments of runic carving to a six-foot-high rectangular slab. Look inside the church, too, at the old parish cross, fourteenth century in date and sporting the earliest known picture of the Three Legs of Mann apart from that on the twelfth-century Sword of State. Bus #16 comes direct to Maughold from Ramsey, four or five times a day (not Sun).

RAMSEY marks the northern terminus of the Electric Railway, 45 minutes beyond Laxey. The Victorian tourist boom left behind the island's only iron pier and a solitary grand terrace along the front, but the bulk of the town, by the harbour – once more important than that in Douglas – is a dispiriting swatch of build-by-numbers modernity. The beach really isn't worth hanging around for and the only sight, the **Grove Rural Life Museum** (Easter–Sept daily 10am–5pm; £3), is a mile north on the A9. This, once the summer home of a Merseyside shipping magnet, is crammed with Victorian country-house furniture, and there's a very nice café too.

You'll really need a car to see any more of the island beyond Ramsey. Due north at the end of the A16 is the **Point of Ayre** lighthouse, at the northeastern tip of the island, built in 1818. There's a car park here, where you could leave your vehicle and walk west along the coastal footpath the two miles to the **Ayres Visitor Centre** (end of May–Sept Wed–Sun & bank hol Mon 2–5pm; free), which acts as an interpretation centre for the surrounding Ayres National Nature Reserve. It's an important coastal habitat of lichen heath, dune grassland and marsh, with common sightings of tern, oystercatchers, cormorants and ringed plovers. Offshore, you might be lucky enough to see porpoises and seals. You can drive directly to the visitor centre and nature reserve, but it means doubling back from the lighthouse to Bride and then looking for the signposted narrow lane a mile or so to the west. If you're not in a hurry, it's also a nice idea to seek out the unfinished Civil War fort at **Kerroogarroo**. This is just to the south of Andreas off the A17; a signpost points you through the fields to the banks and ramparts, hastily constructed in the 1640s but now completely grass-grown and very peaceful.

For **accommodation** in the north, *Hillcrest House* on May Hill (ⓣ01624/817215, ⓦwww.HillcrestHouse.co.uk; ❸; no credit cards), five minutes' walk from the centre of Ramsey, makes an excellent base. The lovely non-smoking Victorian home is furnished with period pieces, from paintings to quilts; there are three individually styled bedrooms (either en-suite or with private bathroom), and breakfast is sensational – using organic ingredients to conjour up freshly squeezed fruit and veg juices, pancakes, Welsh rarebit and other delights, accompanied by homemade bread, preserves, yoghurt and museli.

St John's

The trans-island A1 (and hourly bus #5 or #6 from Douglas) follows a deep twelve-mile-long furrow between the northern and southern ranges from Douglas to Peel. A hill at the crossroads settlement of **ST JOHN'S**, nine miles along it, is the original site of **Tynwald**, the ancient Manx government, which derives its name from the Norse *Thing Völlr*, meaning "Assembly Field". Nowadays the word refers to the Douglas-based House of Keys and Legislative Council, but acts passed in the capital only become law once they have been proclaimed here on July 5 (ancient Midsummer's Day) in an annual open-air parliament that also hears the grievances of the islanders. Tynwald's four-tiered grass mound – made from soil collected from each of the island's parishes – stands at the other end of a processional path from the stone **St John's Church**, which traditionally doubled as the courthouse. Early accounts of the ceremony indicate that the king sat at the top of the mound, facing east and brandishing his sword; the barons to his side, judges in front of him, and the representatives of the Keys, clergy and squires on the terraces below – with the rabble kept outside the enclosure. Until the nineteenth century the local people arrived with their livestock and stayed a week or more – in true Viking fashion – to thrash out local issues, play sports, make marriages and hold a fair. Now Tynwald Day begins with a service in the chapel, followed by a procession to the mound where the offices of state are carried out, after which a fair and concerts begin.

Peel

The main settlement on the west coast, **PEEL** immediately captivates, with its fine castle rising across the harbour and a popular sandy beach running the length of its eastern promenade. It's a town of some antiquity and its enduring appeal is as one of the most "Manx" of all the island's towns, a character that is manifested in various ways – from an age-old Tuesday market in the marketplace above the harbour to the line of wood-smoke-belching kipper factories along the harbourside.

Archeological evidence indicates that **St Patrick's Isle**, which guards the harbour, has had a significant population since Mesolithic times. What probably started out as a flint-working village on a naturally protected spot gained significance with the foundation of a monastery in the seventh or eighth century, parts of which remain inside the ramparts of the red sandstone **Peel Castle** (Easter–Oct daily 10am–5pm; £3). The Vikings built the first fortifications and the site became the residence of the Kings of Mann until 1220, when they moved to Castle Rushen in Castletown. The English continued strengthening the fortress, eventually completing a fifteen-foot curtain wall around the islet. Only this is in good repair, leaving the huge ward dotted with miscellaneous remains, including the Gothic vaults of St Germain's Cathedral, whose fourteenth-century crypt was later used as a prison. An annual Shakespeare festival (July) and concerts take place within the castle walls, while below the ramparts on the west side there's a tiny sand beach.

It's a fifteen-minute walk from the town around the river harbour and over the bridge to the castle. On the way, you'll have passed the excellent harbourside House of Mannannan **heritage centre** (daily 10am–5pm; £5, combined ticket with Peel Castle £7) named after the island's ancient sea god. You should allow at least two hours to get around the museum, which concentrates strongly on participatory exhibits – whether it's listening to Celtic legends in a replica roundhouse, examining the contents and occupants of a life-sized Viking ship, walking through a kipper factory or steering a steamer. There are dozens of other diversions throughout, illuminating the island's history and culture by way of dioramas, video presentations, hands-on exhibits and re-created street and domestic scenes – all in all, an essential counterpoint to Douglas's Manx Museum. Finally, past the museum, by the bridge, **Moore's** (Mon–Sat 10am–5pm; tours at 2pm & 3.30pm, £2) is a traditional curing yard where you can see how Manx kippers are smoked before buying some to take home.

Practicalities

The most regular **bus** service to Peel is the hourly #5 or #6 from Douglas; this service continues to Ramsey via Kirk Michael and Sulby. The much less frequent #8 (not Sun) connects Peel to Port Erin, via St John's and Castletown. There's central **accommodation** at the Georgian *Merchant's House*, 18 Castle St (☎01624/842541; no credit cards; ❷), with just three rooms and small discounts for longer stays. Or for sea views you could try one of the old-fashioned guest houses at the end of Marine Parade, such as *Fernleigh* (☎01624/842435; no credit cards; ❶). The *Peel Camping Park*, on Derby Rd (☎01624/842341; closed mid-Sept to mid-May), is signposted about half a mile out on the Douglas road.

When it comes to **eating**, if you're looking for something more than the seafront cafés and fish-and-chip shops, then head for the pub opposite the House of Mannannan: the *Creek Inn* (☎01624/842216; Ⓦwww.creekinn.co.im/) serves a delicious array of specials, from seafood platters to scallops mornay, inside or out, lunch and dinner. Self-catering apartments are also available here to rent, year-round (❷). Locals also like the *Marine Hotel*, a pub on the seafront, with bar meals and a bistro.

Glen Maye, Niarbyl and Dalby

Three miles south of Peel, down the A27, you can park by the road and walk down through **Glen Maye** to the beach, a nice walk with the prospect of lunch afterwards back at the *Waterfall Hotel*, by the car park. Two miles further south of Peel, off the A27, just after Dalby, a minor road runs down to the grassy car park above **Niarbyl**, a little headland of jutting rock, framed by clear water and steep banks and fronted by a flat pebbled beach, above which sits a picture-perfect thatched cottage. Scenes from the movie *Waking Ned* were filmed here. On clear days, the Calf of Man (see p.848) is visible in the distance; on even better days, seals can be seen on the rocks. South of the headland, the moorland road (A27, then A36) is one of the most dramatic on the island, forming a high-level switchback route to Port Erin, providing sweeping views both southwest across the cliffs and southeast across the plain to Castletown.

Back at the A27 turn-off for Niarbyl, at **Dalby**, *Ballacallin House Hotel* (☎01624/841100; ❺) is a traditional country inn with comfortable en-suite rooms, welcoming service and famed sunset views. There's good food – Manx goat's cheese tart followed by lamb shank or sea bass, for example – very moderately priced, served either in the lounge bar or restaurant.

Port Erin

Plans for the southern branch of the steam railway beyond Castletown included the speculative construction of the new resort of **PORT ERIN**, at the southwestern tip of the island, an hour and a quarter's ride from Douglas. The aspect certainly demanded a resort: a wide, fine sand beach backing a deeply indented bay sits beneath green hills, which climb to the tower-topped headland of Bradda Head to the northwest.

A century on, an arm of holiday apartments stretches out towards the headland, while the far side of town is marked by the breakwater and small harbour. Families relish the beach and nearby coves, and the timewarped atmosphere, which appears to have altered little in forty years. The town's elegant red-brick train station is still here, with one of its engine sheds converted into a small **railway museum** (Easter–Oct daily 10am–5pm; £1). For a stretch of the legs, head up the promenade past the golf club to the entrance of **Bradda Glen**, where you can follow the path out along the headland to Bradda Head.

Practicalities

The **train station** is on Station Road, a couple of hundred yards above and back from the beach. **Buses** #1 and #2 from Douglas/Castletown, and #8 from Peel/St John's, stop on Bridson Street, across Station Road and opposite the *Cherry Orchard* hotel.

For **accommodation**, the best B&B is *Rowany Cottier* (Ⓣ01624/832287; no credit cards; ❸), a detached, non-smoking house overlooking the bay, opposite the entrance to Bradda Glen. The *Falcon's Nest*, back down the promenade at the seafront end of Station Road (Ⓣ01624/834077, Ⓦwww.falconsnesthotel.co.uk; ❺), has reasonable hotel rooms and offers better deals if you book by the week. Or check on space at the nearby *Balmoral Hotel* (Ⓣ01624/833126; ❸), also at the bottom of the promenade. The nicest rooms, though, are at the *Cherry Orchard* on Bridson Street (Ⓣ01624/833811, Ⓦwww.cherry-orchard.com; ❻), a couple of hundred yards back from the promenade, which has a range of self-catering or serviced **apartments** sleeping up to six people. These are available by the night, and guests also have the use of a pool, Jacuzzi, gym, sauna, restaurant and bar.

There are a couple of beachfront **cafés** serving the usual daytime snacks and meals, or call into the *Whistlestop Café* at the train station for a light lunch or afternoon tea. Come the evening, your choice is between bistro **meals** at the *Bay Hotel* down by the beach; bar meals or the restaurant in the *Falcon's Nest*; or the restaurant at the *Cherry Orchard*, which also has a popular Sunday buffet lunch.

Port St Mary and around

Two miles east of Port Erin, the fishing harbour still dominates little **PORT ST MARY**, with its houses strung out in a chain above the busy dockside. The best beach is away to the northeast, reached from the harbour along a well-worked Victorian path that clings to the bay's rocky edge.

From Port St Mary, a minor road runs out along the Meayll peninsula towards Cregneash, the oldest village on the island, part of which now forms the **Cregneash Village Folk Museum** (Easter–Oct daily 10am–5pm; £3), a picturesque cluster of nineteenth-century thatched crofts. This was a real Gaelic-speaking village until well into the twentieth century, though the advent of postwar tourism turned it into a tourist attraction. It's now peopled at weekends with spinners, weavers, turners and smiths dressed in period costumes; there's a café, an information centre with introductory video, demonstrations of thatching and dry-stone walling, and a chance to walk through the seasonal crops in the field and watch the horses at work. The local views are stunning and it's only a short walk south to **The Chasms**, a headland of gaping rock cliffs swarming with gulls and razorbills.

The footpath continues around **Spanish Head**, the island's southern tip, to **The Sound Visitor Centre** (daily 10am–5pm; free), which also marks the end of the road from Port St Mary. There's a café, with windows looking out across The Sound, where basking sharks and grey seals can sometimes be spotted. Across the narrows lies the **Calf of Man**, a small islet now preserved as a bird sanctuary. Boat trips run out here, departing either from the pier at Port Erin (April–Oct daily; £10; usually at 10.15am, 11.30am and 1.30pm, weather permitting; ⓣ01624/832339) or from Port St Mary (year-round, weather permitting; £10; ⓣ01624/832761 or ⓣ07624/483328). It's best to call in advance in either case for information. From the visitor centre, the **coastal footpath** continues to Port Erin, a six-mile loop in all from Port St Mary and considered one of the best short walks on the island. The Steam Railway connects the two small towns (and runs back to Douglas), so it's an easy day's walking.

Practicalities

Regular **steam trains** run to Port Erin or back to Douglas from Port St Mary, with the station a ten-minute walk from the harbour along High Street, Bay View Road and Station Road; hourly **buses** from the harbour serve the same places. Nicest **accommodation** is at *Aaron House*, The Promenade (ⓣ01624/835702; ❹), a lovingly re-created Victorian experience combining brass beds, hot-water bottles and clawfoot bathtubs with doilies and cake in the parlour, sepia photographs and dried flowers. You'll be well looked after – splendid breakfasts, chocolate biscuits on the tea tray, plump towels in a basket by the bathroom door – and there are superb bay views from the windows.

For tasty home-cooked pub **meals**, you can't beat *The Albert* on Athol Street (no food Sun night or Mon; ⓣ01624/832118), by the harbour – it's a nice place for a pint of Manx beer, though you should book for evening meals at the weekend. Otherwise, just across the road, there's *The Port* (ⓣ01624/832064; dinner only; closed Sun & Mon), a pricey but locally renowned bistro with fresh fish specials daily.

Castletown and around

From the twelfth century until 1869, **CASTLETOWN** was the island's capital, but then the influx of tourists and the increase in trade required a bigger harbour and Douglas took over. So much the better for Castletown, which is a much more pleasant place than it might otherwise have been. Its sleepy harbour and low-roofed cottages are all dominated by **Castle Rushen** (Easter–Oct daily 10am–5pm; £4.25), one of the most complete and compact medieval castles in Britain. Formerly home to the island's legislature and still the site of the investiture of new lieutenant-governors, the present structure was probably started in the thirteenth century, its limestone walls well under way by the time the last Viking monarch, Magnus, died here in 1256. The heavy defences, comprising three concentric rings of stone-clad ramparts, fosses and a complex series of doors and portcullises, must have made entry a forbidding objective. Today, a mannequin archer guards access to displays on the castle's history, a prelude to five floors of rooms furnished in medieval and seventeenth-century styles, the most evocative being the tapestry-draped banqueting hall. The rooms may seem unending, but it's worth pressing on to the rooftop viewpoint to admire the town below, its somnolent streets centred on a dinky **Market Square** with an unfinished memorial column – the "candlestick" – commemorating a nineteenth-century governor.

Across Market Square and down Castle Street in tiny Parliament Square you'll find the **Old House of Keys**. Built in 1821, this was the site of the Manx parliament, the Keys, until 1874 when it was moved to Douglas. The frock-coated Secretary of the House meets you at the door and shows you into the restored debating chamber, where visitors are included in a highly entertaining participatory session of the House, guided by a hologram Speaker. Here, you'll be asked to vote on weighty historical Manx matters, such as women's suffrage or local taxation, risking withering asides from the Speaker ("there's a radical in the House!") if you go against the prevailing orthodoxy. The visits are conducted on the hour (Easter–Oct daily 10am–noon & 2–5pm; £3) and advance tickets are available from the **Old Grammar School** on nearby Quay Lane, which was the former capital's first church, built around 1200, and used as a school from 1570. There's not a lot to see here, save a few information boards, but it does house a handy **tourist office** (Easter–Oct daily 10am–5pm). Below the castle, boats and yachts bob about in the harbour, while something of the island's maritime heritage can be gleaned from the little **Nautical Museum** on Bridge Street (Easter–Oct daily 10am–5pm; £3), just across the harbour footbridge. You can find out about smuggling and sailmaking here, while displays include an armed eighteenth-century yacht ("The Peggy").

Practicalities

The **steam train station** is five minutes' walk from the centre of Castletown, out along Victoria Road from the harbour; **buses** #8 (from Peel/Port Erin) and #1 (from Douglas) stop in the main square. The only central **accommodation** is the *George Hotel* in the square (ⓣ01624/822533; ❷), where there are eleven en-suite rooms above the pub and parking around the back; breakfast is £5.50 extra. Best place for **food** is *The Garrison*, across from the hotel at 5 Castle St (ⓣ01624/824885; closes Sun at 5pm), a tapas bar with a sunny courtyard that serves coffee and snacks from 9.30am and meals from noon until 9.30pm. The *Castle Arms*, on the quayside, also serves food, including a Thai menu on Friday and Saturday nights. Out of town, at **Santon**, about 5 miles northeast of Castletown, the *Mount Murray Hotel and Country Club* (ⓣ01624/661111, ⓦwww.mountmurray.com; ❼) is the highest-rated rural hotel on the island, with its own golf-course, pool and health club. Weekend rates can be a good deal.

Rushen Abbey and Port Soderick

The island's most important medieval religious site, **Rushen Abbey** (Easter–Oct daily 10am–5pm; £3), lies two miles north of Castletown at Ballasalla ("place of the willows"). A Cistercian foundation of 1134, it was abandoned by its "White Monks" in the 1540s and in more recent times the site was used as a school and later a hotel, with tea dances held in the abbey grounds. The excavated remains themselves – low walls, grass-covered banks and a sole church tower from the fifteenth century – would hold only specialist appeal were it not for the excellent interpretation centre, which explains much about daily life in a Cistercian abbey. It's particularly good for children, who can learn about church architecture, illuminated manuscripts and archeology through a series of fun hands-on experiments and activities. The **Silverburn Trail** runs from Castletown to the abbey, and there are pleasant walks in the surrounding area too, including a crossing of the fourteenth-century packhorse bridge known as the **Monks' Bridge**, just upstream of the abbey gardens. Ballasalla is also a stop on the Steam Railway, with the abbey a few minutes' walk from the village. The *Whitestone* on Station Road serves **pub food** seven days a week.

If you're in no hurry to get back to Douglas, you could also stop off at *Port Soderick*, halfway along the train route between Castletown and Douglas, where you can walk down the glen to a cliff-backed bay with a stony beach and the nicely sited *Anchor Inn*.

Travel details

Buses

For information on all local and national bus services, contact Traveline ⓣ0870/608 2608, ⓦwww.traveline.org.uk.

Blackpool to: London (4–6 daily; 6hr); Manchester (every 2hr; 1hr 50min); Preston (every 2hr; 40min).

Chester to: Liverpool (every 20min; 1hr 20min).

Lancaster to: Carlisle (4–5 daily; 1hr 10min); Kendal (hourly; 1hr); Leeds (1 daily; 3hr); London (2–3 daily; 5hr 30min); Manchester (2 daily; 2hr); Windermere (hourly; 1hr 45min).

Liverpool to: Blackpool (1 daily; 2hr); Chester (hourly; 1hr); Leeds (hourly: 2hr 40min); London (5 daily; 4hr); Manchester (hourly; 1hr); Preston (2 daily; 1hr).

Manchester to: Birmingham (6 daily; 3hr); Blackpool (5 daily; 1hr 40min); Leeds (6 daily; 2hr); Liverpool (hourly; 40min); London (every 1–2hr; 4hr 30min–6hr 45min); Newcastle (6 daily; 5hr); Sheffield (4 daily; 2hr 40min).

Trains

For information on all local and national rail services, contact National Rail Enquiries ⓣ08457/484950, ⓦwww.rail.co.uk.

Blackpool to: Manchester (hourly; 1hr 10min); Preston (hourly; 30min).

Chester to: Birmingham (5 daily; 2hr); Knutsford (hourly; 50min); Liverpool (2 hourly; 45min); London (3 daily; 3hr 30min); Manchester (2 hourly; 1hr–1hr 20min); Northwich (hourly; 30min).

Lancaster to: Barrow-in-Furness (hourly; 1hr); Carlisle (every 30–60min; 1hr); Heysham (2–3 daily; 30min); Manchester (every 30–60min; 1hr); Morecambe (every 30min–60min; 10min); Preston (every 20–30min; 20min).

Liverpool to: Birmingham (hourly; 1hr 40min); Chester (2 hourly; 45min); Leeds (hourly; 2hr); London (hourly; 2hr 40min); Manchester (hourly; 50min); Newcastle (8 daily; 4–5hr); Oxford (12 daily; 3–4hr); Preston (14 daily; 1hr 5min); Sheffield (hourly; 1hr 45min); York (hourly; 2hr 20min).

Manchester to: Barrow-in-Furness (Mon–Sat 7 daily, Sun 3 daily; 2hr 15min); Birmingham (hourly; 1hr 30min); Blackpool (hourly; 1hr 10min); Buxton (hourly; 50min); Carlisle (8 daily; 1hr 50min); Chester (every 30min; 1hr–1hr 20min); Lancaster (hourly; 1hr); Leeds (hourly; 1hr); Liverpool (every 30min; 50min); London (hourly; 2hr 40min); Newcastle (10 daily; 3hr); Northwich (hourly; 30min); Oxenholme (4–6 daily; 40min–1hr 10min); Penrith (2–4 daily; 2hr); Preston (every 20min; 55min); Sheffield (hourly; 1hr); York (hourly; 1hr 35min).

11

Cumbria and the Lakes

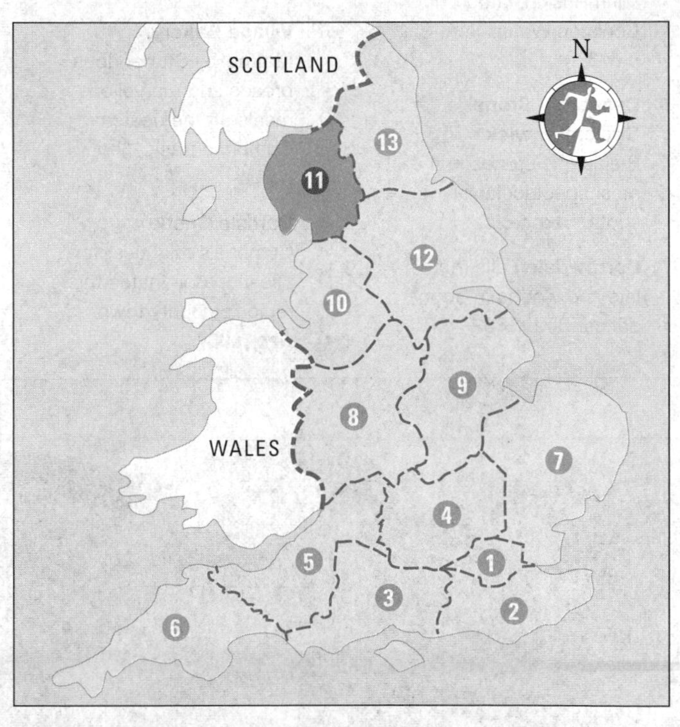

CHAPTER 11 **Highlights**

* **Windermere** England's largest lake never disappoints. See p.862
* **Old Dungeon Ghyll, Langdale** Cosy rooms, stone-flagged floors, open fires and real ale. See p.868
* **Brantwood** The home of John Ruskin, sited on Coniston Water. See p.873
* **Castlerigg Stone Circle, Keswick** Prehistoric stones in the most spectacular of spots. See p.880
* **Borrowdale** Falls, hamlets and woods in abundance. See p.882
* **Church of St Mary and St Michael, Cartmel** Magnificent reminder of the wealth of the medieval Church. See p.892
* **The Rum Story, Whitehaven** West Cumbria's most intriguing museum attraction. See p.899
* **Village Bakery, Melmerby** Stupendous breads and marvellous meals off the beaten Cumbrian track. See p.904
* **Carlisle Castle** Cumbria's mightiest fortification dominates the region's county town. See p.907

△ Castlerigg Stone Circle

11

Cumbria and the Lakes

The **Lake District** is England's most hyped scenic area, and for good reasons. Within an area a mere thirty miles across, sixteen major lakes are squeezed between the steeply pitched faces of the country's highest mountains, an almost alpine landscape that's augmented by waterfalls and picturesque stone-built villages packed into the valleys. Most of what people refer to as the Lake District – or simply the Lakes – lies within the **Lake District National Park**. This, in turn, falls entirely within the north-western county of **Cumbria**, formed in 1974 from the historic counties of Cumberland and Westmorland, and the northern part of Lancashire. Consequently Cumbria contains more than just its lakes, stretching south and west to the **coast**, and north to its county town of **Carlisle**, a place that bears traces of a pedigree that stretches back beyond the construction of Hadrian's Wall. To the east, **Penrith** and the **Eden Valley** separate the lakes from the near wilderness of the northern Pennines.

The heart of the region is **Scafell**, a volcanic dome that had already been weathered into its present shape before the last Ice Age, when glaciers flowed off its flanks to gouge their characteristic U-shaped valleys. As the ice withdrew, terminal moraines of sediment dammed the meltwater, so that the main lakes now radiate like immense spokes from the hub of Scafell. Human interaction has also played a significant part in the shaping of the Lake District. Before Neolithic peoples began to colonize the region around five thousand years ago, most of the now bare uplands were forested with pine and birch, while the valleys were blanketed with thickets of oak and alder. As these first settlers learned to shape flints into axes, they began to clear the upland forests, a process accelerated by the road-building Romans. An even greater impact was made by the Norse Vikings in the ninth and tenth centuries, who farmed the land extensively and left their mark on the local dialect: a mountain here is referred to as a "fell", a waterfall is a "force", streams are "becks", a mountain lake is a "tarn", while the suffix "-thwaite" indicates a clearing. In later centuries grazing flocks of sheep cropped the hills of their wild flowers, while charcoal-making and the mining of copper and graphite further altered the contours and vegetation.

The region remained a land apart for centuries, its features – rugged and isolated – mirrored in the characteristics of its inhabitants. Daniel Defoe thought

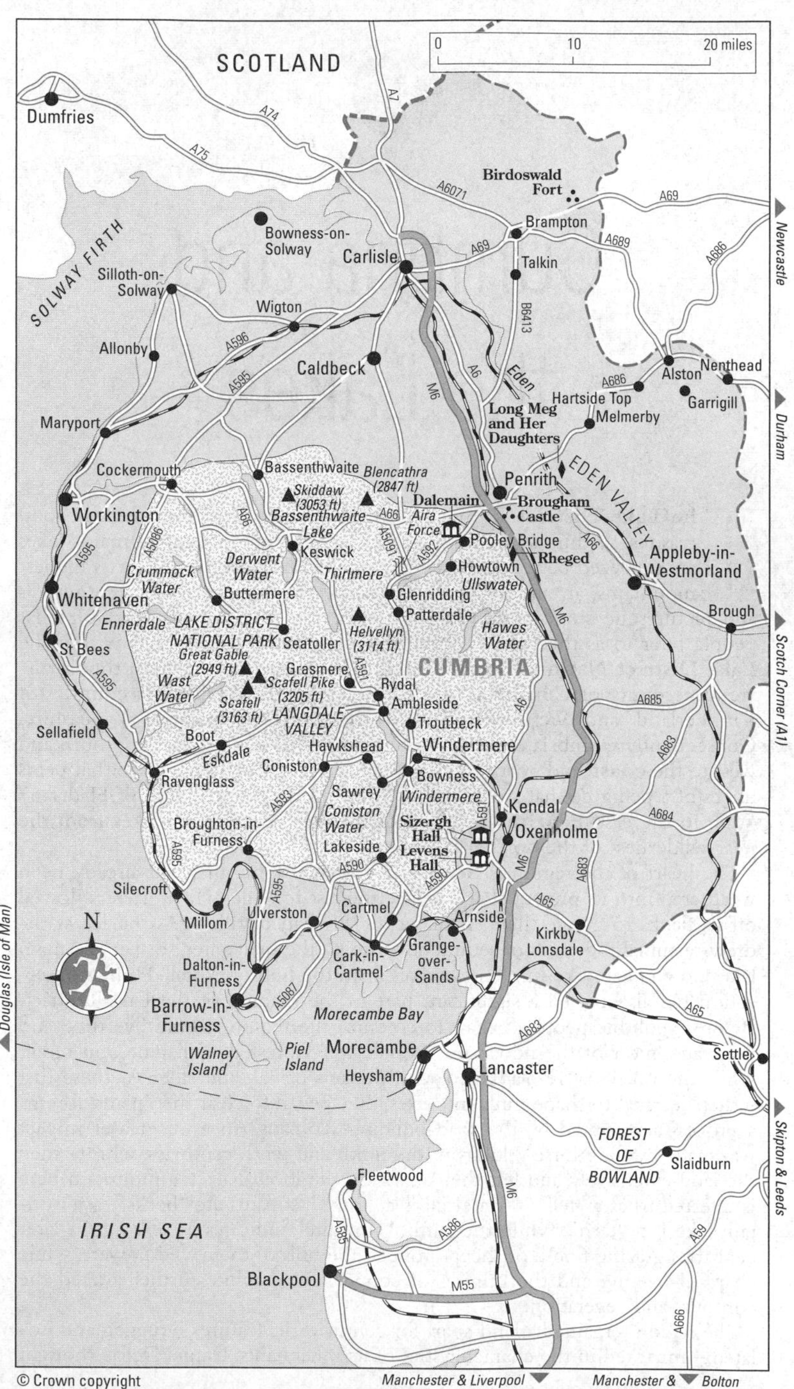
SCOTLAND
0
10
20 miles
Dumfries
A74
A75
A7
A6071
Birdoswald Fort
A69
Brampton
A689
A686
Newcastle
SOLWAY FIRTH
Bowness-on-Solway
Carlisle
Talkin
Silloth-on-Solway
Wigton
B6413
Allonby
A596
Caldbeck
Eden
A595
A6
M6
Alston
Nenthead
Hartside Top
Garrigill
Durham
Melmerby
Maryport
Long Meg and Her Daughters
EDEN VALLEY
Cockermouth
Bassenthwaite
Blencathra (2847 ft)
Penrith
Skiddaw (3053 ft)
Dalemain
Brougham Castle
Workington
Bassenthwaite Lake
A66
Aira Force
Pooley Bridge
A5086
A5091
A592
Rheged
Keswick
Appleby-in-Westmorland
Derwent Water
Howtown
Crummock Water
Thirlmere
Ullswater
Whitehaven
Buttermere
Glenridding
Helvellyn (3114 ft)
Brough
Ennerdale
LAKE DISTRICT NATIONAL PARK
Seatoller
Patterdale
Hawes Water
Scotch Corner (A1)
St Bees
Great Gable (2949 ft)
Grasmere
A591
CUMBRIA
Wast Water
Scafell Pike (3205 ft)
Rydal
Scafell (3163 ft)
LANGDALE VALLEY
Ambleside
A685
Sellafield
Troutbeck
Boot
Hawkshead
Windermere
A683
Eskdale
Coniston
Bowness
Ravenglass
Sawrey
Windermere
Kendal
A593
Coniston Water
Sizergh Hall
A684
Broughton-in-Furness
Oxenholme
Levens Hall
Lakeside
A590
Silecroft
A65
Cartmel
Arnside
Millom
Ulverston
Kirkby Lonsdale
N
Grange-over-Sands
Dalton-in-Furness
Cark-in-Cartmel
Douglas (Isle of Man)
Barrow-in-Furness
A5087
Morecambe Bay
Walney Island
Piel Island
Morecambe
Settle
Heysham
Lancaster
FOREST OF BOWLAND
Slaidburn
Skipton & Leeds
Fleetwood
IRISH SEA
A585
A586
A59
Blackpool
M55
A666
Manchester & Liverpool
Manchester & Bolton

it "eminent only for being the wildest, most barren and frightful of any that I have passed over" – and, as he went on to point out, he'd been to Wales so he knew what he was talking about. Two factors spurred the first waves of **tourism**: the reappraisal of landscape brought about by such painters as Constable and the writings of Wordsworth and his contemporaries, and the outbreak of the French Revolution and its subsequent turmoil, which put paid to the idea of the continental Grand Tour. At the same time, as the war pushed food prices higher, farmers began to reclaim the hillsides, a tendency sanctioned by the General Enclosure Act of 1801. Most of the characteristic drystone walls were built at this time, a development that alarmed Wordsworth, who wrote in his *Guide to the Lakes* that he desired "a sort of national property, in which every man has a right and interest who has an eye to perceive and a heart to enjoy." His wish finally came to fruition in 1951 when the government designated 880 square miles of the Lake District as England's largest national park.

On any scale, the **National Park** has been wildly successful, attracting millions of visitors every year to its famous lakes and picturesque villages. This, of course, has come at some price, mainly in terms of traffic and environmental pressure, which a forward-thinking integrated transport strategy is attempting to alleviate. There's always been a severe contrast, too, between the touristed villages of the Lakes and the old industrial towns of coastal **West Cumbria**, which have struggled in the past to attract visitors and investment. However, regeneration has been dramatic in recent years, with the reviving fortunes of places such as Whitehaven, Maryport and Barrow-in-Furness providing keen incentives to stray from the Lakes.

Regional transport

National Express **coaches** connect London and Manchester with Windermere, Ambleside, Grasmere and Keswick. **Trains** leave the West Coast main line at **Oxenholme**, north of Lancaster, for the branch line service to Kendal and Windermere. The only other places directly accessible by train are Penrith, further north on the West Coast line, and the towns along the Cumbrian coast, between Grange-over-Sands and Maryport. A **Lakes Ranger** (one day, £10) gives unlimited train travel between Lancaster, the Cumbrian coast and Windermere, plus free bus travel south of Keswick and a Windermere cruise. Of the lakes themselves, Windermere, Coniston Water, Derwent Water and Ullswater have useful **cruise and ferry** services – the summer-season **Cross Lakes Shuttle** (£11 return) integrates boats and buses in a combined timetable that connects Windermere with Coniston.

Stagecoach is Cumbria's biggest **local bus** operator. Their **Explorer Tickets** (one-day £7.50, four-day £17, seven-day £25) are valid on the entire network and can be bought on the bus, while other combination tickets (picked out in the text) offer a variety of good deals. The two main bus services are the #555 (Kendal–Windermere–Ambleside–Grasmere–Keswick, with connections to Lancaster and Carlisle) and the open-top #599 (Kendal–Windermere–Bowness–Ambleside–Grasmere), but all routes are all spelled out in detail in the free *Lakeland Explorer* timetable or the *Getting Around Cumbria and the Lake District* timetable book, produced twice a year by Cumbria County Council; both are available from tourist offices and other outlets throughout the region. **Traveline** (daily 7am–8pm; ⓣ0870/608 2608, ⓦwww.traveline.org.uk) can advise about all the region's bus, coach, rail and ferry services. Finally, the **YHA** operates a shuttle-bus service from Ambleside YHA to the Hawkshead, Coniston, Elterwater, Langdale and Grasmere hostels (Easter–Oct; £2.50 a journey; information on ⓣ0870/770 5672).

The Lake District

Although the **Lake District** might appear too popular for its own good, tourist numbers are concentrated in fairly specific areas, and it's relatively easy to escape the crowds even on the busiest of days. Given a week you could see most of the famous settlements and lakes – a circuit taking in the towns of Ambleside, Windermere and Bowness, all on **Windermere**, the Wordsworth houses and sites in pretty villages such as **Hawkshead** and **Grasmere**, and the more dramatic northern scenery near **Keswick** and **Ullswater** would give you a fair sample of the whole. But it's away from the crowds that the Lakes really begin to pay dividends, so aim if you can to steer by central valleys such as **Langdale** and **Eskdale**, and the lesser visited lakes of **Wast Water** and **Buttermere**. Of course, it's only when you start to walk and climb around the Lakes that you can really say you've explored the region. Four peaks top out at over 3000ft – including **Scafell Pike**, the highest in England – but there are literally hundreds of other mountains, crags and fells to roam.

High summer isn't the ideal **time to visit** the Lakes – April, May, September and October are the best months, as the crowds are thinner, the sights are still open and the high walks unlikely to be snowbound. During the summer school holidays, **accommodation** – including abundant B&Bs, excellent country guest houses and 26 youth hostels – can be stretched to capacity, though you'll always find something, somewhere. **Campsites** are widely scattered about the entire region, or you could check out the Lake District

Walking in the Lake District

An almost unchartable network of **paths** connect the lakes themselves, track the broken knife-edge ridges of the fells and mountains or weave easier courses around the flanks and onto the tops. Some of the most celebrated walks form circuits or **"horseshoe" routes** around various peaks and valleys. Of the long-distance paths, Wainwright's Coast-to-Coast, which starts in St Bees, near Whitehaven, spends its first few sections in the northern Lakes; while the Dales Way finishes in Windermere; but the only true Lake District hike is the seventy-mile **Cumbria Way** between Ulverston and Carlisle.

The various walks detailed in this chapter are largely aimed at the moderate walker with half a day or so on their hands, and require no real experience. Even so, you should always be properly equipped: wear strong-soled, supportive shoes or boots, carry water, and take a map (and know how to use it). Bad weather can move in quickly, even in the height of summer, so before starting out you should check the **weather forecast** – many hotels and outdoor shops post a daily forecast – or call ⓣ017687/75757 (24-hour line).

The best general **map** of the area is the Ordnance Survey inch-to-the-mile (1:63,360) Touring Map and Guide 3, with hill shading and illustrated text on the back. Essential for **walking** are the 1:50,000 OS Landranger maps 89, 90, 96 and 97, or, better, the yellow 1:25,000 OS Outdoor Leisure series, which cover the whole Lake District. Many shops and tourist offices also sell local walk leaflets, and regional trail and hiking guides, of which Wainwright's (see p.858) are the best known.

Long-distance hikers and cyclists following the Coast-to-Coast, Sea-to-Sea, Cumbria Way and Dales Way routes, all of which cut through the region, can call on the **door-to-door baggage services** of Coast to Coast Packhorse (ⓣ017683/42028, ⓦwww.cumbria.com/packhorse) or Sherpa Van (ⓣ0871/520 0124, ⓦwww.sherpavan.com). Typically, you'll pay around £5 per bag per day, for it to be delivered to your next overnight accommodation.

National Park Authority's **camping barn** network – ask for a brochure at tourist offices.

For more **information** about all aspects of the National Park, visit Ⓦwww.lake-district.gov.uk; while the official site of the Cumbria Tourist Board is Ⓦwww.golakes.co.uk. All the background information you could possibly want on **outdoors sports and activities** can be found on Ⓦwww.lakedistrictoutdoors.co.uk.

Kendal and around

The limestone-grey town of **KENDAL** might be billed as the "Gateway to the Lakes", but it's nearly ten miles from Windermere – the true start of the lakes – and has more in common with the market towns to the east. It's a pleasant stop, though, cut through by an attractive river and boasting two of Cumbria's grandest stately homes – **Sizergh Castle** and **Levens Hall** – both within easy reach of the town.

Arrival, information and accommodation

Kendal's **train station** is the first stop on the Windermere branch line, just five minutes from the **Oxenholme** main-line station. By catching bus #41 or #41A to the town hall from Oxenholme (Mon–Sat; every 20min) you can avoid the wait for the connecting train. Otherwise, head across the river and up Stramongate and Finkle Street to reach Highgate, a ten-minute walk. All buses (including National Express services) stop at the **bus station** on Blackhall Road (off Stramongate). The **tourist office** (July & Aug Mon–Sat 9am–6pm, Sun 10am–5pm; Sept–June Mon–Sat 9am–5pm, Sun 10am–4pm; Jan & Feb closed Sun; Ⓣ01539/725758, Ⓦwww.kendaltown.org) is in the town hall on Highgate. You can book space here on the weekly informative summer guided walks around town (July & Aug usually Wed; £2.50). There's **Internet** access at Kendal library on Stricklandgate (closed Sun) and at *Dot Café*, inside the Westmorland Shopping Centre. Kirkland Books, 68 Kirkland, has a terrific selection of secondhand and antiquarian **books**, especially strong on local interest and walking.

Best local **B&B** is the very relaxed *Lakeland Natural Vegetarian Guesthouse* at Low Slack, Queen's Road (Ⓣ01539/733011, Ⓦwww.lakelandnatural.co.uk; ❹), which backs onto woods five minutes' walk west of the centre – breakfasts incorporate homemade muffins, organic yoghurt and fresh fruit salad. Alternatively, look along Milnthorpe Road, a few minutes' south of the centre – walk straight down Highgate and Kirkland – where several places cluster together, including *The Headlands*, 53 Milnthorpe Rd (Ⓣ01539/732464; ❷), with a selection of rooms, a small bar and a free pick-up service from the bus or train stations. There's a **youth hostel** at 118 Highgate (Ⓣ0870/770 5982, Ⓔkendal@yha.org.uk; dorm beds £14; closed 1–2 days of the week Oct–Easter), which is attached to The Brewery arts centre (see below), while the most convenient **campsite** is *Ashes Lane* at Staveley, four miles northwest of town, off the Windermere Road (Ⓣ01539/821119; closed mid-Jan to mid-March), reached by bus #555 from the bus station.

The Town

The largest of the southern Cumbrian towns, Kendal offers rewarding rambles around the "yards" and "ginnels" which make an engaging maze on both sides of Highgate and Stricklandgate, the main streets. The old **Market Place** has long since succumbed to development, with the market hall now converted to the Westmorland Shopping Centre, but traditional stalls still do business outside every Wednesday and Saturday. Strolling around will take you down to the riverside walk and past restored almshouses, mullioned shopfronts and trade signs, including the pipe-smoking Turk outside the snuff factory on Lowther Street. The "Kendal green" cotton cloth, actually yellow wool, was worn by English archers and earned Kendal a mention in Shakespeare's *Henry IV*, but today the town's most visible product is **Kendal Mintcake**, an energy-giving solid block of sugar and peppermint oil that has been hoisted to the top of the world's highest mountains.

The **Kendal Museum**, on Station Road (Mon–Sat: Easter–Oct 10.30am–5pm; Nov, Dec & mid-Feb–Easter 10.30am–4pm; £3.50; Ⓦwww.kendalmuseum.org.uk), holds the district's natural history and archeological finds, as well as plenty of well-presented displays relating to the town's history. These are bolstered by the preserved office, pen-and-ink drawings and personal effects of **Alfred Wainwright** (1907–91), Kendal's former borough treasurer (and honorary clerk at the museum). Born in Blackburn, Lancashire, his lifelong love of the lakes began with his first visit in 1930. Wainwright moved to Kendal in 1941, and by 1952, dissatisfied with the accuracy of existing maps of the paths and ancient tracks across the fells, he embarked on what became a series of highly personal walking guides, painstakingly handwritten with mapped routes and delicately drawn views. They have been hugely popular guidebooks ever since, which many treat as gospel in their attempts to "bag" ascents of the 214 fells he recorded. Wainwright died in 1991, having given away most of his considerable earnings to animal-rescue charities, and his ashes were scattered on his favourite fell – Haystacks in Buttermere.

The other two museums are in the Georgian **Abbot Hall** (Ⓦwww.abbothall.org.uk) and its stable block, by the river to the south. The main hall houses the **Art Gallery** (Mon–Sat: Easter–Oct 10.30am–5pm; Nov, Dec & mid-Feb–Easter 10.30am–4pm; £3.75), where cherubic portraits by society painter George Romney line the walls. Temporary exhibitions of modern art take place upstairs, and there are also displays of furniture designed and built by the incomparable Gillows of Lancaster. Across the way, the former stables contain the **Museum of Lakeland Life and Industry** (Mon–Sat: Easter–Oct 10.30am–5pm; Nov, Dec & mid-Feb–Easter 10.30am–4pm; £2.75, joint admission with Art Gallery £4.50; Ⓦwww.lakelandmuseum.org.uk). Here, reconstructed seventeenth-, eighteenth- and nineteenth-century house interiors stand alongside workshops which exhibit rural trades and crafts, from spinning and weaving to tanning – medieval Kendal was on the main north–south cattle-trade routes and leather production was once an important local industry. In addition, there's a mock-up study of Arthur Ransome, author of the children's classic *Swallows and Amazons*, while John Cunliffe, creator of Postman Pat, whose adventures are set just north of Kendal, gets similar treatment.

Just behind Abbott Hall, the wide aisles of the Early English **parish church** house a number of family chapels, including that of the Parr family, who once owned **Kendal Castle**, on a hillock to the east across the river. First erected in the early thirteenth century, it's claimed as the birthplace of Catherine Parr, Henry VIII's sixth wife, but the story is probably apocryphal – she was born in 1512, at which time the building – now a ruin – was already in an advanced state of decay.

Eating, drinking and entertainment

Kendal certainly doesn't lack decent **cafés**, starting with the *1657 Chocolate House*, off Finkle Street on Branthwaite Brow, an olde-worlde spot which sells hot chocolate (in dozens of guises) and cakes. There's also a good café at the Abbot Hall Art Gallery. For inexpensive veggie wholefood lunches and riverside seating, visit the *Waterside Café* on Gulfs Road, by the river at the bottom of Lowther Street. Best **restaurant** is the highly regarded *Moon*, 129 Highgate (Ⓣ01539/729254; dinner only, closed Mon & Tues), an easy-going contemporary bistro using locally sourced ingredients, or eat Thai at the *Chiang Thai*, 54 Stramongate (Ⓣ01539/720387; dinner only, closed Mon), which is more moderately priced.

For evening entertainment, the **Brewery Arts Centre**, on Highgate (Ⓣ01539/725133, Ⓦwww.breweryarts.co.uk), is the town's central focus. Its *Green Room Restaurant* and lively *Vats Bar* serve light lunches and pizzas, pastas and stir-fries for dinner; the centre also has two cinema screens, a theatre and concert hall. There's live music throughout the year and a renowned annual **jazz and blues festival** each November. Several characterful **pubs** beckon, too, including the *Ring o' Bells* by the church, and the *Bridge Hotel*, a classic old local at the bottom of Stramongate.

Sizergh Castle

Three miles to the south of Kendal stands **Sizergh Castle** (Easter–Oct Mon–Thurs & Sun 1.30–5.30pm; gardens same days 12.30–5.30pm; £5, gardens only £2.50; NT), tucked away off the A591 amid acres of parkland and reached on bus #555. Home of the Strickland family for eight centuries, Sizergh is more of a grand manor house than a castle, but owes its epithet to the fourteenth-century peel tower (which you'll often see spelt "pele" in the north) at its core, one of the best examples of the towers built throughout the region as safe havens during the protracted border raids of the Middle Ages. Like much of the rest of the house, the Great Hall underwent significant changes in Elizabethan times, when extensions were added to the house and most of its rooms were panelled in oak, with their ceilings layered in elaborate plasterwork. Each room is hung with portraits of the family and their royal acquaintances and stocked with exquisite furniture, including an extraordinary bedstead made from a pew that once stood in Kendal parish church. Little has changed in the Banqueting Hall since the fourteenth century, save for the loss of an upper storey and the addition of a partition at the east end, added to provide more private sleeping quarters for the heads of the family.

Levens Hall

Two miles south of Sizergh, just of the A590 and on the #555 bus route, **Levens Hall** (Easter to mid-Oct Mon–Thurs & Sun noon–5pm; gardens same days 10am–5pm; £7, gardens only £5.50; Ⓦwww.levenshall.co.uk), also built around an early peel tower, is more uniform in style than Sizergh, since the bulk of it was built or refurbished in classic Elizabethan style between 1570 and 1640 by James Bellingham. The house did not stay in the Bellingham family; a descendant lost the whole estate in a hedonistic spate of gambling, and it was later bought by the privy purse to James II and ancestor of the present owners, the Bagots.

The main entrance opens into the spacious Great Hall, its panelled walls lined with coats of arms; to the left of the hall are the large and small drawing rooms. The other end of the Great Hall leads to the most splendid apartment, the dining room, panelled not with oak but with goat's leather, printed with a deep green floral design – one goat was needed for every forty or so squares. Upstairs, the bedrooms offer glimpses of the beautifully trimmed **topiary gardens** below, where yews in the shape of pyramids, peacocks and top hats stand between blooming bedding plants. There's also a steam engine collection and café.

Windermere town and Brockhole

WINDERMERE town was all but non-existent until 1847 when a railway terminal was built here, making England's longest lake (after which the town is named) an easily accessible resort. Most of the guest houses and amenities built for the Victorians still stand, and Windermere remains the transport hub for the southern lakes, but there's precious little else to keep you in the slate-grey streets. Instead, all the traffic pours a mile down hill to Windermere's older twin town, Bowness; buses leave Windermere train station every twenty minutes for the ten-minute run down to the lakeside piers.

It's understandable to want to rush straight to Bowness and the lake, but you should certainly make time for the **Lake District Visitor Centre at Brockhole** (Easter–Oct daily 10am–5pm; grounds & gardens open all year; free, parking £3), a fine mansion set in landscaped grounds on the shores of the lake, three miles northwest of Windermere. It's the headquarters and main information point for the Lake District National Park, and besides the permanent natural history and geological displays, the centre hosts a full programme of guided walks, children's activities, garden tours, special exhibitions, lectures and film shows. The bookshop is one of the best in the region for local guides and maps, and there's a café with an outdoor terrace overlooking the lake. The #555 and #559 **buses** between Windermere and Ambleside run past the visitor centre, or you can get there by Windermere Lake Cruises **launch** from Waterhead, Ambleside or from Bowness (see box on p.863).

Practicalities

Windermere is a major **bus terminus**, with National Express and all local services stopping outside Windermere **train station**. With a Bus & Boat ticket (£6) you can travel from Windermere to Bowness and Ambleside on the open-top #599 and return by boat down the lake. A hundred yards away from the station at the top of Victoria Street stands the **tourist office** (daily: July & Aug 9am–7.30pm; rest of the year 9am–6pm; ⓣ015394/46499), which has money-exchange and room-booking services; you can also change money inside Windermere's **post office** on Crescent Road. There's free **Internet** access at the library, in the park off Broad Street. For **bike rental**, contact Country Lanes, The Railway Station, Windermere (ⓣ015394/44544, ⓦwww.countrylanes.co.uk), which provides route maps for local rides. Mountain Goat, near the tourist office on Victoria Street (ⓣ015394/45161, ⓦwww.mountain-goat.com) offers **minibus tours** (half-day from £14, full-day £26) that get off the beaten track, departing daily from Windermere and other lakeland towns.

Windermere doesn't have the waterside advantages of Bowness, but it does have a lot more **accommodation** – good places to look for B&Bs are on High Street and neighbouring Victoria Street, with other concentrations on College Road, Oak and Broad streets. There's a good backpackers' **hostel** in Windermere itself – the nearest YHA is at Troutbeck (p.864) – but for **camping** you'll have to head down to Bowness.

Eating and drinking is generally better done down in Bowness, but it is worth seeking out the *Miller Howe Café* inside Lakeland Ltd, behind the train station, which serves up superior snacks, sandwiches and daily specials. At night, a favoured local spot is the *Lamplighter Bar* at the *Oakthorpe Hotel* on High Street, where bistro meals (gammon, fresh fish, rack of lamb) are provided at value-for-money prices. *Jambo* on Victoria Street (ⓣ015394/43429; dinner only, closed Mon Nov–Easter) is a moderately priced Modern British place with a Mediterranean flavour. The *Queen's* on Victoria Street is the main **pub**

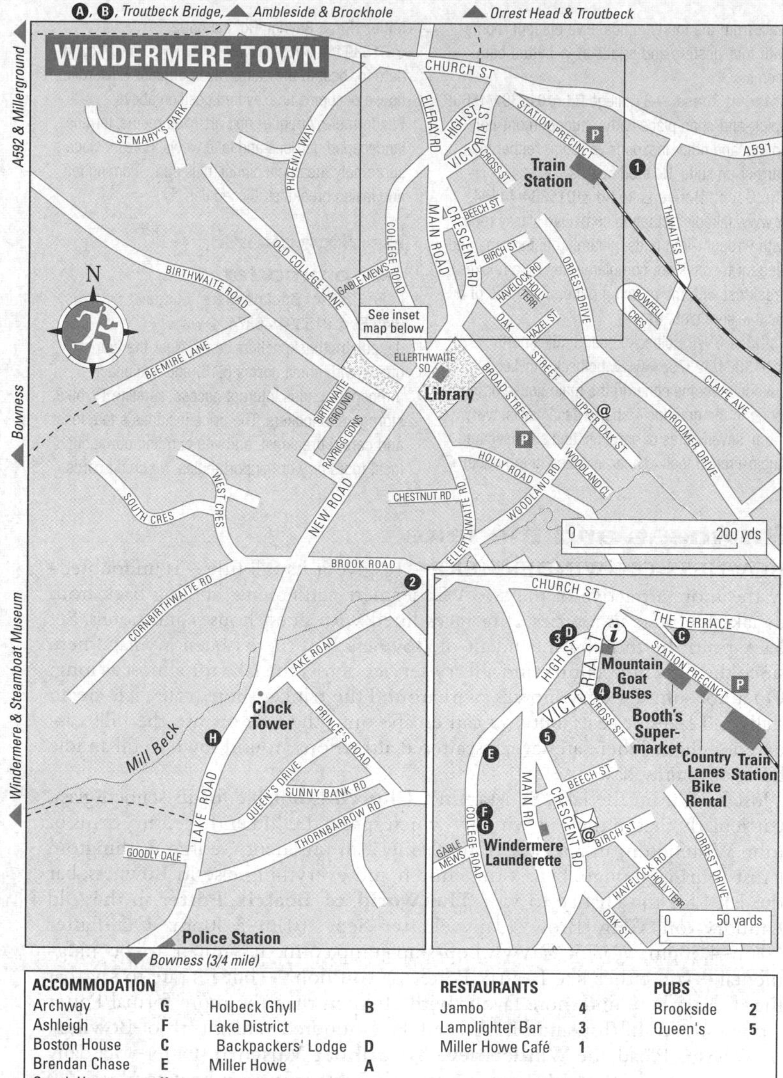

in town, with inexpensive meals and cask ale, though the *Brookside*, on Lake Road, is the nicer, quieter choice.

B&Bs, guest houses and hotels

Archway 13 College Rd ⓣ015394/45613, ⓦwww.communiken.com/archway. Victorian house known for its breakfasts, with specials such as pancakes, kippers and homemade yoghurt and granola. No credit cards. ❸

Ashleigh 11 College Rd ⓣ015394/42292, ⓦwww.ashleighhouse.com. Smart non-smoking house whose tasteful rooms have been furnished in welcoming country pine. No credit cards. ❷

Boston House The Terrace ⓣ015394/43654, ⓦwww.bostonhouse.co.uk. Beautifully restored non-smoking Victorian Gothic house, a minute's walk from the tourist office. Five elegant rooms with four-posters and bright-as-a-button bathrooms. ❺

Brendan Chase 1–3 College Rd ⓣ015394/45638. Spick-and-span place with a budget room-only option, and other inexpensive rooms, either standard or en suite. No credit cards. ❶

The Coach House Lake Rd ⓣ015394/44494, ⓦwww.lakedistrictbandb.com. Five classy rooms with wrought-iron beds, gleaming bathrooms and elegant touches are complemented by a relaxed breakfast with the morning papers, and use of a local leisure club. ❹

Holbeck Ghyll Holbeck Lane, 3 miles north ⓣ015394/32375, ⓦwww.holbeck-ghyll.co.uk. Luxurious rooms either in the main house or in the lodge in the grounds – sherry decanter in every room, seven acres of gardens, and sophisticated Anglo-French food (dinner included in the price). ❾

Miller Howe Rayrigg Rd, the A592 ⓣ015394/42536, ⓦwww.millerhowe.com. A candidate for best in the Lakes, this gorgeous Edwardian house occupies an elevated position above Windermere. Antique- and art-filled rooms, terraces, landscaped gardens and lake views. Rates include a supremely theatrical dinner, plus early morning tea and lavish breakfast. Closed Jan. ❾

Backpackers' accommodation

Lake District Backpackers' Lodge High St ⓣ015394/46374, ⓦwww.lakedistrictbackpackers.co.uk. Near the tourist office, with small dorms (£13) and a laidback atmosphere, plus Internet access, satellite TV, bike storage and lockers. The price includes a tea, toast and cereal breakfast, and you can find out about local tours or work opportunities. No credit cards.

Bowness and the lake

BOWNESS-ON-WINDERMERE – to give it its full title – is undoubtedly the more attractive of the two Windermere settlements, spilling back from its lakeside piers in a series of terraces lined with guest houses and hotels. Set back from the thumbprint indent of Bowness Bay, there's been a village here since the fifteenth century and a ferry service across the lake for almost as long. On a hot summer's day, crowds swirl around the trinket shops, cafés, ice-cream stalls and lakeside seats, but you can escape onto the lake or into the hills easily enough, and there are several scattered attractions around town to fill an idle hour or a rainy day.

Just back from the lake, **St Martin's Church** is notable for its stained glass, particularly that in the east window which sports the fifteenth-century arms of John Washington, an ancestor of first American president George Washington. Most tourists, though, bypass the church and everything else in Bowness, bar the lake, for the chance to visit **The World of Beatrix Potter** in the Old Laundry on Crag Brow (daily: Easter–Sept 10am–5.30pm; Oct–Easter 10am–4.30pm; £3.75; ⓦwww.hop-skip-jump.com). It's unfair to be judgmental – you either like Beatrix Potter or you don't – but it's safe to say that the displays here find more favour with children than the more formal Potter attractions at Hill Top and Hawkshead. Five hundred yards north of Bowness, on Rayrigg Road, the **Windermere Steamboat Museum** (Easter–Oct daily 10am–5pm; £3.50, steam-launch cruises £5; ⓦwww.steamboat.co.uk) has as its star exhibit the 1850 *Dolly*, claimed to be the world's oldest mechanically driven boat, and extremely well preserved after spending 65 years in the mud at the bottom of Ullswater. In addition, an Arthur Ransome exhibition reveals the inspiration behind the boats *Swallow* and *Amazon*, and most days there are steam launch **cruises** (£5) on the lake aboard one of the museum's gleaming specimens.

The lake itself – simply **Windermere** (from the Norse, "Vinandr's Lake", and thus never "*Lake* Windermere") – is the heavyweight of Lake District waters, at ten and a half miles long, a mile wide in parts and a shade over two hundred feet deep. The only settlements are at Bowness and Ambleside, which means that the views from the water tend towards the magnificent: north to the cen-

Windermere cruises

Windermere Lake Cruises (ⓣ015394/31188, ⓦwww.windermere-lakecruises.co.uk) operates services to Lakeside at the southern tip (£4.40 one-way, £6.60 return) or to the Lake District Visitor Centre at Brockhole and Waterhead (for Ambleside) at the northern end (£4.30 one-way, £6.40 return). There's also a direct hourly service from Ambleside to Brockhole (£5 return) and a shuttle service between Bowness pier and Sawrey (£1.60 one-way, £2.80 return), saving pedestrians the walk down to the car ferry. A 24-hour **Freedom-of-the-Lake** ticket costs £11.50. Services on all routes are frequent between Easter and October (every 30min–1hr at peak times), but much reduced during the winter.

The company also operates an enjoyable 45-minute circular **cruise around the islands** (departs several times daily from Bowness; £5), a summer evening **wine cruise** (mid-May to mid-Aug; £6.60), and a two-hour evening **buffet cruise** with jazz band (mid-May to mid-Aug every Wed; £19.95); timings for the latter two trips change frequently, so call to check. There are also combination boat tickets available for the Lakeside and Haverthwaite Railway and the Aquarium of the Lakes – information is available from the pier-side ticket office.

tral fells, or south along a wooded shoreline that is mostly under the protection of the National Trust. As Wordsworth's *Guide to the Lakes* had it, "None of the other Lakes unfold so many fresh beauties."

Rowing boats are available for rent by the lakeside piers, while Windermere Lake Cruises (see box above) operates modern cruisers and vintage steamers throughout the year. The traditional **ferry service** is the chain-guided contraption across the water from Ferry Nab on the Bowness side to Ferry House, Sawrey (Mon–Sat 7am–10pm, Sun 9am–10pm; departures every 20min; 40p; cars £2), providing access to Beatrix Potter's former home at Hill Top and to Hawkshead beyond. The ferry pier is a ten-minute walk south of the cruise piers, through the parkland of Cockshott Point.

Practicalities

The **bus** from Windermere train station stops at the lakeside piers, with the **Bowness Bay Information Centre** nearby on Glebe Road (Easter–Oct daily 9.30am–5pm, July & Aug until 6pm; Nov–Easter Fri–Sun 10am–4pm; ⓣ015394/42895). Crag Brow and then Lake Road is the main thoroughfare up from the lake towards Windermere, on and off which you'll find much of the accommodation, cafés and restaurants. T2, 4 Windermere Bank, on Lake Road, is the local **Internet** outlet.

Accommodation is plentiful, though note that most places with even a glimpse of the water set their prices accordingly. The nicest **café** is *2 Eggcups*, 6a Ash St, which serves the best sandwich in Bowness, plus other blackboard specials. Budget pizza and pasta is on offer at *Rastelli's*, Lake Road (ⓣ015394/44227; dinner only, closed Wed), while the *Porthole*, 3 Ash St (ⓣ015394/42793; closed Tues and mid-Dec to mid-Feb), is the most respected quality **restaurant**, serving regional Anglo-Italian cuisine in a seventeenth-century cottage – lunch is available Thursday, Friday and Sunday, otherwise it's dinner only. For a **drink**, you can't beat the *Hole in't Wall* **pub**, the town's oldest hostelry, on Falbarrow Road behind Bowness church; cosy in winter when the fires are lit, and pleasant in summer when you can sit outside. For sunset drinks with a lake view, the terrace of *The Olde England* hotel beckons. *The Royalty* on Lake Road (ⓣ015394/43364) is that rare lakeland beast, a **cinema**, with a repertory programme alongside the more commercial screenings.

B&Bs, guest houses and hotels

Above The Bay 5 Brackenfield ⓣ015394/88658, ⓦwww.abovethebay.co.uk. An elevated house in a residential area, just off the Kendal road, a little way south of the centre. Three spacious rooms open onto a private terrace with stunning lake views. No credit cards. ❸

Gilpin Lodge Crook Rd ⓣ015394/88818, ⓦwww.gilpin-lodge.co.uk. A country-house retreat a couple of miles east on the Kendal road (B5284). Fourteen elegant rooms, individually styled, some with four-posters, others with whirlpool baths or private patios, and rates include an excellent dinner. ❾

Laurel Cottage St Martin's Square ⓣ015394/45594, ⓦwww.laurelcottage-bnb.co.uk. Pretty rooms with low ceilings in a seventeenth-century cottage, or more space – for a few extra pounds – in the adjacent Victorian building. No credit cards. ❸

Montclare House Crag Brow ⓣ015394/42723. Simple B&B accommodation that's about the best value in Bowness. No credit cards. ❷

New Hall Bank Fallbarrow Rd ⓣ015394/43558, ⓦwww.newhallbank.com. Detached Victorian house with a lake view and a central location (a few yards from the *Hole in't Wall* pub), whose room views get better the higher you go. ❺

Old England Church St ⓣ015394/42444, ⓦwww.heritage-hotels.com. A relaxed grande-dame hotel opposite the church, with heated outdoor pool and terraced lakeside gardens. Prices drop in winter. ❼

Campsite

Braithwaite Fold Glebe Rd ⓣ015394/42177. Closest site to the lakeshore for tents, near the ferry to Sawrey, half a mile from Bowness; closed Nov–March.

Around Bowness

A mile and a half south of Bowness, there's the rare chance to visit a house designed by one of the major exponents of the Arts and Crafts Movement. Mackay Hugh Baillie Scott's **Blackwell** (mid-Feb to Dec daily 10am–5pm, closes 4pm in winter; £4.50; ⓦwww.blackwell.org.uk) was built in 1900 as a lakeside holiday home for Edward Holt, of the Manchester brewing family, and selected rooms of its restored interior can be viewed. Lakeland motifs (particularly trees, flowers, birds and berries) are visible in virtually every nook and cranny, from the stonework to the stained glass, and you'll also have the chance to see changing exhibitions of Arts and Crafts furniture and other contemporary pieces. There's a tea room and gardens too, though no bus – the walk from Bowness is about 25 minutes.

From Bowness piers, cruises (see p.863) head south down the lake the five or so miles to **Lakeside**, on Windermere's quieter southern reaches and the terminus of the **Lakeside and Haverthwaite Railway** (Easter–Oct 6–7 daily; £4.30 return; ⓣ015395/31594), whose steam-powered engines chuff along four miles of track through the forests of Backbarrow Gorge. The boat arrivals at Lakeside connect with train departures throughout the day, and you can buy a joint boat-and-train ticket (£10.50 return) at Bowness if you fancy the extended tour. Also on the quay at Lakeside is the **Aquarium of the Lakes** (daily: April–Sept 9am–6pm; Oct–May 9am–5pm; £5.95; ⓦwww.aquariumofthelakes.co.uk), an entertaining natural history exhibit centred on the fish and animals found in and along a lakeland river, including a pair of captive otters and a walk-through-tunnel aquarium. Again, there's a joint ticket available with the boat ride from Bowness (£11.30 return).

Troutbeck

Troutbeck Bridge, a mile northwest of Windermere along the A591, heralds the start of a gentle valley below Wansfell, where you'll find Windermere's local **youth hostel**, High Cross at Bridge Lane (ⓣ0870/770 6094, ⓔwindermere@yha.org.uk; dorm beds £11.50; weekends only in Dec), almost a mile uphill from the bridge. A YHA shuttle-bus service (£2) operates to the hostel from

Windermere train station (meeting arriving trains) and from Ambleside youth hostel, or there's a fine cross-country walking route (3 miles; 1hr 30min) via **Orrest Head** (784ft), whose summit gives a 360° panorama from the Yorkshire fells to the Langdales and Troutbeck Valley – the path branches off the main road a hundred yards south of Windermere train station, by the *Windermere Hotel* on the A591.

TROUTBECK's main attraction lies at the southern end of the village, a little further up the minor valley road from the hostel. **Townend** (Easter–Oct Tues–Fri & Sun 1–5pm; £3; NT) has been preserved as a seventeenth-century yeoman-farmer's house, complete with original furniture and decorative woodwork. There's not much more to the village itself than a road crossing at the village green, but it marks the starting point for the five-hour walk along **High Street**, a nine-mile range running north to Brougham near Penrith. The course of a Roman road follows the ridge, probably once linking the forts at Brougham and Galava in Waterhead.

Troutbeck's **inn**, the *Mortal Man* (Ⓣ015394/33193, Ⓦwww.themortalman.co.uk; ❺, ❻ with dinner; closed mid-Nov to mid-Feb), has terrific valley views from its rooms and beer garden. Cheaper B&Bs in the village offer less exalted lodgings – Windermere and Ambleside tourist offices can help – while Troutbeck's other old inn, the *Queen's Head*, down on the main A592 (Ⓣ015394/32174, Ⓦwww.queensheadhotel.com; ❺; two-night minimum stay at weekends), serves very good food. The *Queen's Head* is a stop on the summer weekend #517 bus route from Bowness and Windermere.

Ambleside

Five miles northwest of Windermere, **AMBLESIDE** is at the heart of the southern lakes region, making it a first-class base for walkers. The town centre consists of a cluster of grey-green stone houses, shops and B&Bs hugging a circular one-way system, which loops round just south of the narrow gully of stony Stock Ghyll. The rest of town lies a mile south at **Waterhead** (referred to as Ambleside on ferry timetables), a harbour on the shores of Windermere that's filled with ducks, swans and rowing boats and overlooked by the landscaped gardens of several plush hotels. There are quieter shores a few minutes' walk further south for picnics or, if the weather's good, a bracing dip in the lake.

In Ambleside itself, spare a few minutes for the mural of the rush-bearing ceremony in **St Mary's Church**, whose spire is visible from all over town. For some background on Ambleside's history, stroll a couple of minutes along Rydal Road to the **Ambleside Armitt Museum** (daily 10am–5pm; £2.50; Ⓦwww.armitt.com), whose collection catalogues the very distinct contribution to lakeland society made by John Ruskin, Beatrix Potter and longtime Ambleside resident, writer Harriet Martineau. Finally, soccer fans shouldn't miss the **Homes of Football** (daily 10am–5pm, until 7pm in July and Aug; free; Ⓦwww.homesoffootball.co.uk), 100 Lake Rd. The gallery of soccer photographer Stuart Clarke, it's a permanent archive of over 60,000 images of the country's stadiums and fans, and is quite irresistible.

Practicalities

Walking up to Ambleside proper from the ferry piers at Waterhead takes about fifteen minutes. The town is at the hub of most major routes across the National Park; **buses** (including National Express) all stop on Kelsick Road, opposite the library. The **tourist office** is just up the road, in Central Buildings on Market Cross (daily 9am–5.30pm; Ⓣ015394/32582); for **online information**, consult Ⓦwww.ambleside.u-k.org, a useful community website. You can

Walks from Ambleside

The Rothay Valley north of Ambleside is largely taken up by the fast A591, which means that Rydal Water and Rydal Mount – the closest attractions – are best seen by bus or on the circular walk from Grasmere (see p.869). Where Ambleside scores is in its proximity to the fells immediately east and west of town, and a couple of good **walks** are possible straight from the town centre.

The first walk heads west past Ambleside church, through Rothay Park and down to the footbridge across the river. From here you tack past Brow Head Farm, following the path to Lily Tarn and then striking up and northwest across **Loughrigg Fell** (1099ft). Dropping down to Loughrigg Terrace (2hr) overlooking Grasmere, you can then join the Grasmere circular walk at this point, before cutting south at Rydal on the A591 and following the minor road back along the River Rothay to Ambleside – a total of 6 miles (4hr).

The walk over **Wansfell** to **Troutbeck** and back (6 miles; around 4hr) has more extensive views and is a little tougher. Stock Ghyll Lane runs up the left bank of the tumbling stream to one of the more attractive waterfalls in the region, **Stock Ghyll Force**. The path then rises steeply to **Wansfell Pike** (1581ft) and down into Troutbeck village, with the *Mortal Man* inn a short detour to the left. Head south down the minor road through the village, towards Townend, just before which a track leads west onto the flanks of Wansfell and around past the viewpoint at **Jenkin Crag** back to Ambleside.

change money at the **post office** in Market Place. For **bike rental**, try Biketreks on Compston Road (☎015394/31505), or Ghyllside Cycles on The Slack (☎015394/33592, Ⓦwww.ghyllside.co.uk). Ambleside is a good place to pick up **walking gear and climbing equipment** – classic old stores like F.W. Tyson (Market Place) and Wilf Nicholson (Market Cross) complement specialists such as The Climber's Shop (Compston Corner) and large retailers including the YHA Adventure Shop (Compston Road).

Accommodation

Lake Road, running between Waterhead and Ambleside, is lined with **B&Bs**, while other options are scattered all over town, with particular concentrations on central Church Street and Compston Road.

B&Bs, guest houses and hotels

3 Cambridge Villas Church St ☎015394/32307. The well-kept house hides a variety of agreeably furnished rooms. No credit cards. ❷

Brantfell Rothay Rd ☎015394/32239, Ⓦwww.brantfell.co.uk. Solid Victorian house on the edge of town, which offers guests use of a nearby pool and leisure club. ❸

Compston House Compston Rd ☎015394/32305, Ⓦwww.compstonhouse.co.uk. There's a New York welcome in this traditional lakeland house, with American-style themed rooms and breakfasts of pancakes and maple syrup if you wish. ❸

Grey Friar Lodge Clappersgate ☎015394/33158, Ⓦwww.cumbria-hotels.co.uk. A mile southwest of town, the lodge – an old vicarage – makes the most of its commanding position over the River Brathay. Closed mid-Dec to mid-Feb. ❺

Linda's B&B Shirland, Compston Rd ☎015394/32999. The cheapest rates in town. Guests can use the kitchen, while two of the rooms (all share a bathroom) can sleep three or four. No credit cards. ❶

Mill Cottage Rydal Rd ☎015394/34830. Housed in a sixteenth-century mill building, with a riverside café underneath. ❷

Hostels

Ambleside Backpackers Old Lake Rd ☎015394/32340, Ⓦwww.englishlakesbackpackers.co.uk. Midway between lake and town, this independent backpackers' hostel is a secluded property with a decent kitchen, free breakfasts of tea, toast and cereal, a barbecue area and mountain bikes for rent. Dorm beds cost £13.75.

Ambleside YHA Waterhead, A591, 1 mile south

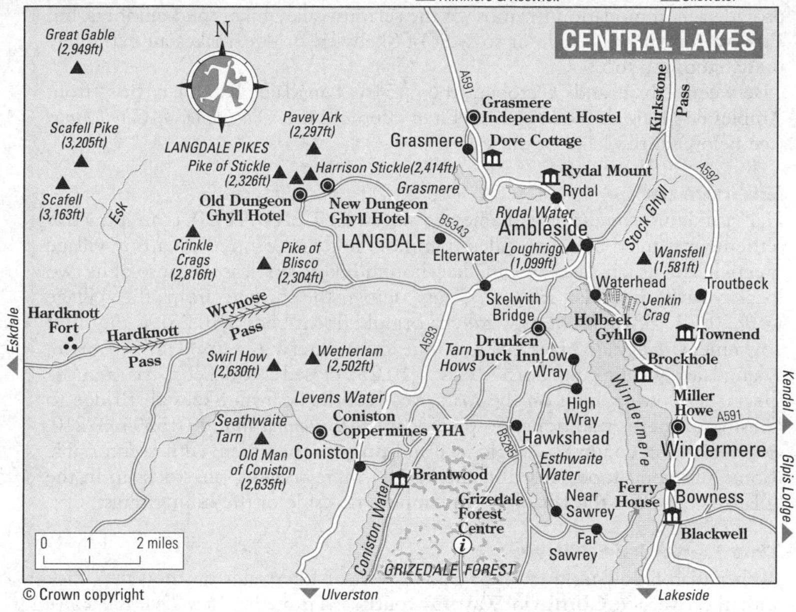

© Crown copyright

ⓣ0870/770 5672, ⓔambleside@yha.org.uk. The YHA's flagship regional hostel, a huge lakeside affair with dorms (£14), doubles (1) and family rooms, bike rental, Internet access and various other useful services; the drawbacks are that it's a fifteen-minute walk from Ambleside itself, and is often filled to capacity with school parties.

Campsite

Low Wray National Trust Campsite Wray, three miles south of town ⓣ015394/32810. Nearest campsite to Ambleside, by the lake – an hourly bus on the Ambleside to Hawkshead/Coniston route passes within a mile. Closed Nov–Easter.

Eating and drinking

Cafés and restaurants are easily found in Ambleside, and there are lots of **pubs**, including beer-lovers' and climbers' favourite, the *Golden Rule*, on Smithy Brow by Stock Ghyll.

Apple Pie Rydal Rd ⓣ015394/33679. Busy daytime café with patio seating and a range of dishes from homemade pies to BLTs. Inexpensive.

Glass House Rydal Rd ⓣ015394/32137. Renovated, split-level fulling mill with waterwheel, which serves accomplished Mediterranean/Modern British cooking. Closed Tues in winter. Expensive.

Lucy's on a Plate Church St ⓣ015394/31191. Enjoyable bistro offering a daily-changing menu with tons of choice. *Lucy 4*, 2 St Mary's Lane, just over the way, is its tapas offshoot. Moderate.

Pippins 10 Lake Rd ⓣ015394/31338. Great for all-day breakfasts, burgers and night-time pizzas. Inexpensive.

Zeffirelli's Compston Rd ⓣ015394/33845. Specializes in vegetarian food, either in the daytime *Garden Café* or upstairs in the restaurant (closed Mon–Fri lunch) for pizzas and pasta – there's also a two-course dinner with cinema-ticket special. Moderate.

Langdale

Three miles west of Ambleside along the A593, Skelwith Bridge marks the start of **Great Langdale**, a U-shaped glacial valley overlooked by the prominent rocky summits of the **Langdale Pikes**, the most popular of the central Lakeland fells. A couple of classic inns and campsites further along the B5343 provide accommodation for most of the serious valley hikers and climbers, but **Elterwater** village, a mile or so west of Skelwith Bridge, makes an extremely pretty stopover, too.

Between April and October, the #516 Langdale Rambler **bus** from Ambleside's Kelsick Road runs to Elterwater and the *Old Dungeon Ghyll Hotel* (see below) at the head of the valley.

Elterwater

Half a mile northwest of its namesake water, **ELTERWATER** is an attractive settlement fringed by sheep-filled common land and centred on a tiny village green. It sees its fair share of Langdale-bound hikers, not least because of its two local **youth hostels**: *Elterwater*, just across the bridge from the village (ⓣ0870/770 5816, ⓔelterwater@yha.org.uk; dorm beds £10.25), is the most convenient; *Langdale High Close*, a mile from Elterwater (ⓣ0870/770 5908, ⓔlangdale@yha.org.uk; dorm beds £10.25; closed Nov–Feb), has a more spectacular setting, high on the road over Red Bank from Skelwith Bridge to Grasmere. There's traditional hospitality at the *Britannia Inn* (ⓣ015394/37210, ⓦwww.britinn.co.uk; ❺), an old lakeland **pub** on the green, with comfortable rooms and good food served in the bar. If you're moving on, stock up in the village shop, as it's the last place for supplies this side of the hiking trails.

The Langdale Pikes

Rather than following the minor B5343 west of Elterwater up the valley, stick with the riverside **Cumbria Way footpath** as far as the *New Dungeon Ghyll Hotel*, three miles from Elterwater. A path indicated by the "Stickle Ghyll" sign follows the beck straight up to **Stickle Tarn**, around to the right then left up to Pavey Ark. Two more adventurous routes to the top of **Pavey Ark** (2297ft) can be easily seen on the crags above Stickle Tarn: **Jack's Rake** trail ascends the face right to left, and is the hardest commonly used route in the Lake District, requiring a head for heights and steady footing. From near its base, an easier route rises to the right. It is fairly easy from then on to **Harrison Stickle** (2414ft), down to the stream forming the headwaters of Dungeon Ghyll and slowly up to **Pike of Stickle** (2326ft). Backtracking a short distance, a path leads to the right almost parallel with Dungeon Ghyll, back to the start (4 miles; 2400ft ascent; 4hr).

The traditional **accommodation** for anyone visiting the valley is the peerless *Old Dungeon Ghyll Hotel* (ⓣ015394/37272, ⓦwww.odg.co.uk; ❺, ❼ with

A circular walk from Grasmere

One of the Lakes' easier circuits is the trip **around Grasmere and Rydal Water** from Grasmere village, a shade over four miles. It can be completed in two hours or so, though as it passes Wordsworth haunts Rydal Mount and Dove Cottage, it could be turned into an all-day sightseeing venture.

From the tourist office in Grasmere, follow Red Bank Road along the western edge of the lake, climbing up a track through Redbank Woods after a mile (signposted "Loughrigg Terrace and YHA"). Signposts soon lead you out onto **Loughrigg Terrace** itself, where tremendous views of the lake unfold. The terrace skirts Loughrigg Fell as it heads east and then you switch ridges to follow that above **Rydal Water**, where you'll pass the dripping, water-filled maw of **Rydal Cave**, a disused slate quarry. Rounding the eastern edge of Rydal, you cross and climb off the A591, past the church, to **Rydal Mount**, above which a bridleway (the so-called "Coffin Trail") runs back above the northern shore of Rydal Water, via **White Moss Tarn** (look out for butterflies). The path emerges at Dove Cottage, on the outskirts of Grasmere.

dinner), superbly isolated at the end of the B5343, seven miles northeast of Ambleside; it offers great three-course dinners in its restaurant (£19.50, book in advance) and also has a stone-flagged hikers' bar with roaring range and filling food. In the evening, the bar fills up with refugees from the nearby *Great Langdale* **campsite** (Ⓣ015394/37668). A mile or so back down the road, the comfortable rooms at the *New Dungeon Ghyll Hotel* (Ⓣ015394/37213, Ⓦwww.dungeon-ghyll.com; ❻) feature dramatic fell views. You can also eat here, or at the adjacent *Sticklebarn Tavern* (Ⓣ015394/37356), which has big breakfasts served every day and inexpensive bar meals available year-round, as well as some very popular **bunk-barn accommodation** (£10 per night).

Grasmere and around

Four miles northwest of Ambleside, the village of **GRASMERE** consists of an intimate cluster of grey-stone houses on the old packhorse road that runs beside the babbling River Rothay. It's an eminently pleasing ensemble, set back from one of the most alluring of the region's small lakes, but it loses some of its charm in summer thanks to the hordes who descend on the trail of the village's most famous former resident, **William Wordsworth** (1770–1850). The poet, his wife Mary, sister Dorothy and other members of his family are buried beneath the yews in **St Oswald's churchyard**, around which the river makes a sinuous curl. Inside the church you can admire the unique twin naves, split by a solid arched partition. At the rear entrance to the churchyard stands **Sarah Nelson's Gingerbread Shop** (Mon–Sat 9.30am–5.30pm, Sun 12.30–5.30pm), converted from the schoolhouse where Wordsworth once taught, and issuing delicious smells throughout the day.

Practicalities

Grasmere is on the main #555 and #599 **bus** routes, which both stop on the village green. The Lakes Day Rider bus ticket (£5.50) allows unlimited travel between Windermere, Bowness or Ambleside and the Wordsworth houses and Grasmere. The **tourist office** (Easter–Oct daily 9.30am–5pm; Nov–Easter Fri, Sat & Sun 10am–3.30pm; Ⓣ015394/35245), five minutes away from the green down Langdale Road, is tucked in by the main car park on Red Bank Road at the southern end of the village. Note that there's no bank in Grasmere, though there is an **ATM** inside the post office on Red Lion Square.

Of the many **tearooms and cafés**, picnic fixings are best from *Newby's Deli & Bakery* in Red Lion Square (underneath the *Harwood Hotel*), while just a step across the road, *Baldry's* (closed Tues–Thurs in winter) offers homemade cakes, puddings, pies and quiches. The *Jumble Room Café* on Langdale Road (Ⓣ015394/35188; closed Mon & Tues) is a funky, reasonably priced **café-restaurant** with an organic touch to its ethnically diverse menu; or there's the *Dove Cottage Tea Rooms and Restaurant*, at Town End near Dove Cottage, open during the day for tearoom favourites and at night (Ⓣ015394/35268; closed Mon May–Oct, plus Tues & Sun rest of year) for fashionable, moderately priced dinners. The only real **pub** in the village is the *Red Lion Inn*, whose public bar is called the *Lamb Inn*. Otherwise, you'll need to walk out to the *Traveller's Rest*, half a mile north along the A591, a popular place for real ale and bar meals.

Accommodation

Bed and breakfast **accommodation** can be hard to come by in summer, so book well in advance, but Grasmere does have three very popular youth hostels. There's no campsite, however.

Writers in the Lake District

William Wordsworth was not the first to praise the Lake District – Thomas Gray wrote appreciatively of his visit in 1769 – but it is Wordsworth that dominates its literary landscape, not solely through his poetry but also through his still-useful *Guide to the Lakes* (1810). Born in Cockermouth in 1770, he was sent to school in Hawkshead before a stint at Cambridge, a year in France and two in Somerset. In 1799 he returned to the Lake District, settling in the Grasmere district, where he spent the last two-thirds of his life with his sister Dorothy, who not only transcribed his poems but was an accomplished diarist as well.

Wordsworth and fellow poets **Samuel Taylor Coleridge** and **Robert Southey** formed a clique that became known as the "Lake Poets", a label based more on their fluctuating friendships and their shared passion for the region than on any common subject matter in their writings. A fourth member of the Cumbrian literary elite was the critic and essayist **Thomas De Quincey**, chiefly known today for his *Confessions of an English Opium-Eater*. One of the first to fully appreciate the revolutionary nature of Wordsworth's and Coleridge's collaborative *Lyrical Ballads*, De Quincey became a long-term guest of the Wordsworths' in 1807, taking over Dove Cottage from them in 1809. He stayed there until 1820, but it was only in the 1830s that he started writing his *Lake Reminiscences*, offending Wordsworth and Coleridge in the process.

Meanwhile, after short spells at Allan Bank and The Vicarage, both in Grasmere, the Wordsworths made Rydal Mount their home, supported largely by William's position as Distributor of Stamps for Westmorland and his later stipend as Poet Laureate. After his death in 1850, William's body was interred in St Oswald's churchyard in Grasmere, to be joined five years later by Dorothy and by his wife Mary four years after that.

Inspired by Wordsworth's writings and by the terrain itself, the social philosopher and art critic **John Ruskin** also made the Lake District his home, settling at Brantwood, outside Coniston, in 1872. His letters and watercolours reflect a deep love of the area, also demonstrated by his unsuccessful fight to prevent the damming of Thirlmere. Much of Ruskin's feeling for the countryside permeated through to two other literary immigrants, **Arthur Ransome**, also a Coniston resident and writer of the children's classic *Swallows and Amazons*, and **Beatrix Potter**, whose favourite Lakeland spots feature in her children's stories. Potter, in fact, is the only serious lakeland rival to Wordsworthian dominance, with her former home at Hill Top in Near Sawrey, her husband's office in Hawkshead and a museum in Bowness all packed with international visitors throughout the year. Whatever you think of her work, every visitor to the Lakes has at least some cause to be grateful to Beatrix Potter, who donated several parcels of land to the National Trust.

Other famous Lake District literary names number **Sir Hugh Walpole**, who lived at Derwentwater and set his Herries novels in Borrowdale; **Harriet Martineau**, who lived in Ambleside for thirty years and received most of literary England in her drawing room; poet **Norman Nicholson** from Millom on the Cumbrian coast; and writer and broadcaster **Melvyn Bragg**, born in Wigton.

B&Bs, guest houses and hotels

Banerigg House One mile south of Grasmere on A591 ⓣ015394/35204. Non-smoking lakeside property fifteen minutes' walk from town, with mostly en-suite rooms offering lake views (though no TVs). Guests are free to take boats out onto the water. No credit cards. ③

Harwood Red Lion Square ⓣ015394/35248, ⓦwww.harwoodhotel.co.uk. Genial, non-smoking family-run hotel with eight rooms. Walkers welcome. Two-night minimum stay at weekends. ③

How Foot Lodge Town End ⓣ015394/35366, ⓦwww.howfoot.co.uk. A spacious Victorian villa, just yards from Dove Cottage, with six non-smoking rooms, one with its own sun lounge. Closed Jan. ③

Lancrigg Vegetarian Country House Hotel Easedale Rd ⓣ015394/35317, ⓦwww.lancrigg.co.uk. Relaxed gourmet vegetarian retreat half a mile northwest of the village, occupying a secluded country house. A dozen variously sized rooms, plus an inventive four-course dinner included in the price, though B&B is available at £20 less than the full rates. ❽

Nab Cottage Rydal ⓣ015394/35311. Both De Quincey and Hartley Coleridge lived in this oak-beamed farmhouse, two miles south of Grasmere. It's now a language school, but offers B&B when space is available – usually *not* between June and September, but call to check. No credit cards. ❷

Red Lion Red Lion Square ⓣ015394/35456, ⓦwww.hotelgrasmere.uk.com. Sympathetically renovated eighteenth-century coaching inn right in the centre, with views over the village and fells. ❻

Titteringdales Pye Lane ⓣ015394/35439. Cosy detached house five minutes' walk from the centre, with fell views from its dining room. No single-night advance reservations. ❷

White Moss House Rydal Water, one mile south on the A591 ⓣ015394/35295, ⓦwww.whitemoss.com. Once owned by Wordsworth, the ivy-clad house has antique-filled rooms in the main house and two more in a cottage suite. It's a glorious spot, and the food (dinner included in room rate) is wonderful. Closed Dec & Jan. ❽

Wordsworth Hotel College St ⓣ015394/35592, ⓦwww.grasmere-hotels.co.uk/wordsworth. The plum choice in the village itself – relaxed, attractive and comfortable, with a heated pool, conservatory and terrace. ❼

Hostels

Butterlip How Easedale Rd ⓣ0870/770 5836, ⓔgrasmere@yha.org.uk. Closest YHA hostel to the centre, 150yd north of the green in a well-equipped lakeland house with grounds. Closed Mon–Thurs in winter. Dorm beds £13.

Grasmere Independent Hostel Broadrayne Farm ⓣ015394/35055, ⓦwww.grasmerehostel.co.uk. Just north of town on the A591, past the *Travellers' Rest* pub. Rooms here sleep three to six people (£12.50 per bed) and are all en-suite, while other facilities include a full kitchen and laundry, sauna, and common room with valley views.

Thorney How ⓣ0870/770 5836, ⓔgrasmere@yha.org.uk. Grasmere's smaller, simpler YHA hostel, a characterful former farmhouse, is just under a mile further along the unlit road past Butterlip How. Closed Nov–Easter. Dorm beds £10.25

Dove Cottage

On Grasmere's southeastern outskirts, on the main A591, stands **Dove Cottage** (daily 9.30am–5.30pm; closed mid-Jan to mid-Feb; £5.80; ⓦwww.wordsworth.org.uk), home to William and Dorothy Wordsworth from 1799 to 1808 and where Wordsworth wrote some of his best poetry. Guides bursting with anecdotes lead you around rooms that reflect Wordsworth's guiding principle of "plain living but high thinking" and are little changed now but for the addition of electricity and internal plumbing. This maxim, however, was only temporary, as Wordsworth was raised in comfortable surroundings and returned to a relatively high standard of living when he moved to Rydal Mount. Most of the furniture in the cottage belonged to the Wordsworths, while in the upper rooms are various other possessions, including a pair of William's ice skates. In good weather, the garden is open for visits as well (same hours as cottage). In the adjacent museum are more paintings, manuscripts and personal effects once belonging to the Wordsworths (most poignantly Mary's wedding ring), plus mementoes of Southey, Coleridge and Thomas De Quincey.

Rydal Mount

Another mile and a half southeast along the A591 from Grasmere, the hamlet of **RYDAL** consists of an inn, a few houses and **Rydal Mount** (March–Oct daily 9.30am–5pm; Nov–Feb daily except Tues 10am–4pm, closed for three weeks in Jan; £4.50, gardens only £2; ⓦwww.rydalmount.co.uk), home of William Wordsworth from 1813 until his death in 1850. Parts of the house have been redecorated, but furniture and portraits give a good sense of its former occupants: in the drawing room and library is the only known portrait of Dorothy, while memorabilia includes William's black leather sofa, his ink stand and despatch box. For many, the highlight is the **garden**, which has been preserved as Wordsworth designed it, complete with terraces where he used to declaim his poetry. Buses #555 and #599 pass the house on the way to Grasmere from Windermere and Ambleside.

Coniston

At five miles long and half a mile across at its widest point, **Coniston Water** is not one of the most immediately imposing of the lakes, yet it has a quiet beauty which sets it apart from the more popular destinations. The nineteenth-century art critic and social reformer John Ruskin made the lake his home, and today his isolated house, **Brantwood**, on the northeastern shore, provides the most obvious target for a day-trip. However, the plain village of **Coniston**, to the west, grows on visitors after a while, especially those who base themselves here for some of the central Lakes' most rewarding walking. Some come here, too, on the *Swallows and Amazons* trail. **Arthur Ransome** was a frequent visitor, his memories and experiences providing much of the detail in his famous children's books.

In the mid-1960s, the glass-like surface of Coniston Water attracted the attention of national hero **Donald Campbell**, who in 1955 had set a world water-speed record of 202mph on Ullswater, bumping it up to 276mph nine years later in Australia. On January 4, 1967, he set out to better his own mark on Coniston Water, but just as his jet-powered *Bluebird* hit an estimated 320mph, a patch of turbulence sent it into a somersault. Campbell was killed immediately and his body and boat lay undisturbed at the bottom of the lake until both were retrieved in 2001.

Coniston village

A memorial seat and plaque to Donald Campbell decorates the green in the slate-grey village of **CONISTON** (a derivation of "King's Town"), hunkered below the craggy and copper-mine-riddled bulk of **The Old Man of Coniston** (see box opposite). **Campbell's grave** is nearby, in the new cemetery behind the *Crown Hotel*: before the memorial service in September 2001, his blue coffin (the colour of his boat, *Bluebird*) was taken through the village by horsedrawn carriage. Having studied this and **Ruskin's grave**, which lies in St Andrew's original churchyard beneath a beautifully worked Celtic cross, you've seen all that Coniston has to offer, save for the excellent **Ruskin Museum** on Yewdale Road (Easter to mid-Nov daily 10am–5.30pm; mid-Nov to Easter Wed–Sun 10am–3.30pm; £3.50; Ⓦwww.ruskinmuseum.com), which combines local history and geology exhibits with a fascinating look at Ruskin's life and work through his watercolours, manuscripts and personal memorabilia. The museum is also the place to track the latest developments in the reconstruction of Campbell's *Bluebird*, which will eventually be displayed here in a purpose-built Campbell Gallery. For now, photographs of Campbell, his funeral and the recovery of the craft are on display, along with related mementoes.

Coniston Water

Coniston Water is hidden out of sight, half a mile southeast of the village. Here, the *Bluebird Café* sells ices and drinks, while the adjacent **Coniston Boating Centre** (Ⓣ015394/41366) can provide the wherewithal for fooling around on the water – rowing boats, sailing dinghies, canoes, electric launches and motorboats. From the nearby pier, the sumptuously upholstered **Steam Yacht Gondola** (Ⓣ015394/63856, Ⓦwww.nationaltrust.org.uk/gondola), built in 1859, leaves on the hour (Easter–Oct 11am–4pm, not 1pm; £5 round

The Old Man of Coniston

The walk from Coniston village to the top of the **Old Man of Coniston** (2628ft) is one of the Cumbrian classics, tiring but not overly difficult. Staying at *Coniston Coppermines* hostel (see p.874) gives you an early start; otherwise, from the bridge in the village, follow the path to the *Coppermines* hostel up past the *Sun Hotel* (see p.874). At Church Beck, with the hostel in the distance ahead, a sign on the gated bridge puts you on the path, with the stream to your right. The path gradually swings to the left, taking a steep and twisting route through abandoned quarry works and their detritus, including several fallen heavy-duty pulley systems. Cairns keep you on the right route, up past a gorgeous glassy tarn, and then there's a final scramble to the massive cairn at the summit (under 2hr for most walkers). The views from here are tremendous – to the Cumbrian coast, and across to Langdale, Windermere and Coniston itself.

trip) for Ruskin's Brantwood. The wooden **Coniston Launch** (Easter–Oct hourly; Nov–Easter up to 4 daily depending on the weather; ⓣ015394/36216, ⓦwww.conistonlaunch.co.uk) operates a year-round service to Brantwood on two routes, north (£3.80 return) or south (£5.80) around the lake. Special cruises (Easter–Oct; call for times) concentrate on the various sites associated with *Swallows and Amazons* (£7.50) and Donald Campbell (£6.50), or show you the lake at breakfast time (£12, breakfast included) or in the evening (£8).

Brantwood

Nestling among trees on a hillside above the eastern shore of Coniston Water, **Brantwood** (mid-March to mid-Nov daily 11am–5.30pm; mid-Nov to mid-March Wed–Sun 11am–4.30pm; house & gardens £4.75, gardens only £3; ⓦwww.brantwood.org.uk), two and a half miles by road from Coniston, was where art critic and moralist John Ruskin lived from 1872 until his death in 1900. If you combine Brantwood with the Gondola or the Coniston Launch, you get a 50p discount on entry.

Champion of J.M.W. Turner and the Pre-Raphaelites and proponent of the supremacy of Gothic architecture, Ruskin insisted upon the indivisibility of ethics and aesthetics, and was appalled by the conditions in which the captains of industry made their labourers work and live, while expecting him to applaud their patronage of the arts. "There is no wealth but life," he wrote in his study of capitalist economics, *Unto the Last*, elaborating with the observation: "that country is richest which nourishes the greatest number of noble and happy human beings." A twenty-minute video expands on his philosophy and whets the appetite for rooms full of his watercolours, doing justice to a man who greatly influenced such disparate figures as Proust, Tolstoy, Frank Lloyd Wright and Gandhi. Nonetheless, not all of Ruskin's projects were a success, partly because of his refusal to compromise his principles. A London teashop, established to provide employment for a former servant, failed since Ruskin refused to advertise; meanwhile, his street-cleaning and road-building schemes, designed to instil a respect for the dignity of manual labour into his students (including Arnold Toynbee and Oscar Wilde), simply accrued ridicule.

Ruskin bought Brantwood in 1871, sight unseen, from engraver and Radical William James Linton, complaining when he saw it that it was "a mere shed". The views captivated him, however, and Ruskin spent the next twenty years adding to the house and laying out its gardens. His **study** – hung with hand-made paper to his own design – and **dining room** boast superlative lake views, bettered only by those from the **Turret Room** where he used to sit in later life in his bathchair, itself on display downstairs, along with his mahogany desk and Blue John wine goblet, among other memorabilia. Various other exhibition rooms and galleries display Ruskin-related arts and crafts, while the *Jumping Jenny Tearooms* – named after Ruskin's boat – has outdoor terrace seating for meals and drinks. There's also a well-stocked bookshop full of information on the Pre-Raphaelites and the Arts and Crafts Movement.

Practicalities

Buses – principally the #505 from Ambleside and Hawkshead and the #12 from Ulverston – stop on the main road through Coniston village, though some of the services also run down to the ferry pier at the lake. A Ruskin Explorer ticket (£10.40) gets you return bus travel between Bowness and Coniston, plus use of the Coniston Launch and free entry to Ruskin's house – buy the ticket on the bus. The **tourist office** (Easter–Oct daily 9.30am–5.30pm; Nov–Easter Fri–Sun 10am–3.30pm; ⓣ015394/41533) is right in the centre on Ruskin Avenue. You can **rent bikes** from Summitreks on Yewdale Road (ⓣ015394/41212, ⓦwww.summitreks.co.uk), which also organizes adventurous days out on water and land. There's no **ATM** in Coniston, so you'll have to get your cash in Ambleside before setting out.

Eating opportunities outside the pubs are limited, but in any case you shouldn't look much further than the *Sun Hotel*, whose cosy bar has filling meals and real ales as well as photographs and newspaper accounts of the famous Campbell crash. The *Sun* is also the cheeriest place for a **drink**, though the *Black Bull* in the centre brews its own Bluebird beer. For sandwiches, homemade pies, all-day breakfasts and **Internet** access, visit the *Village Pantry* on Yewdale Road.

Accommodation

B&Bs are plentiful in and around Coniston, and all the pubs have **rooms** available too. The **hostels** are popular with walkers, especially *Coniston Coppermines*, so book early if you need a budget bed. The closest **campsite** is *Coniston Hall* (ⓣ015394/41223; closed Nov–Easter), a mile south of town by the lake at Haws Bank; booking is essential.

B&Bs, guest houses and hotels

Bank Ground Farm Coniston Water, east side ⓣ015394/41264, ⓦwww.bankground.com. On the lakeshore just north of Brantwood, *Swallows and Amazons* fans won't want to miss out on a night spent here; it was the model for Holly Howe Farm in the book, and also featured in the 1970s' film. ❸, lake view ❹

Beech Tree Guesthouse Yewdale Rd ⓣ015394/41717. Friendly vegetarian place 150yd north of the village on the Ambleside road. No credit cards. ❷

Lakeland House Tilberthwaite Ave ⓣ015394/41303, ⓦwww.lakelandhouse.com. Opposite the Campbell memorial, this is a friendly place, accustomed to walkers and their ways and with an attached café. No credit cards. ❷

Shepherds Villa Tilberthwaite Ave ⓣ015394/41337. One of the village's most popular B&Bs, with a decent sense of space, an approachable owner and ten comfortable rooms, some en suite. ❷

Sun Hotel ⓣ015394/41248, ⓦwww.thesunconiston.com. Coniston's best pub rooms are at this fine old inn, 200yd uphill from the bridge in the centre of the village. Minimum two-night stay at weekends. ❺

Thwaite Cottage Waterhead, half a mile from Coniston on the Hawkshead road ⓣ015394/41367, ⓦwww.thwaitcot.freeserve.co.uk. Slate-flagged, seventeenth-century cottage with a couple of acres of gardens, and three peaceful rooms with oak beams and panelled walls. No credit cards. ❸

Hostels

Coniston Coppermines ⓣ0870/770 5772, ⓔcoppermines@yha.org.uk. Peaceful, dramatic mountain setting a steep mile or so from the village. Dorms cost £10.25; closed Nov–March, & Sun & Mon in April, May, Sept & Oct.

Coniston Holly How Ambleside Rd ⓣ0870/770 5770, ⓔconistonhh@yha.org.uk. Closest hostel to the village (just a few minutes' walk north), and popular with families. Dorms beds cost £10.25; limited weekend opening outside summer holiday period. Closed Nov to mid-Jan.

Hawkshead and around

Greystone **HAWKSHEAD**, between Coniston and Ambleside, wears its beauty well, its patchwork of cottages and cobbles backed by woods and fells and barely affected by twentieth-century intrusions. This is partly due to the enlightened policy of banning traffic in the centre – huge car parks at the village edge take the strain, and when the crowds of day-trippers leave, Hawkshead regains its natural tranquillity.

The Vikings were the first to settle the land here, the village probably founded by and named for one Haukr, a Norse warrior. It was an important wool market at the time Wordsworth was studying at **Hawkshead Grammar School** (Easter–Oct Mon–Sat 10am–12.30pm & 1.30–5pm, Sun 1–5pm; £2), founded in 1585, whose entrance lies opposite the tourist office. The school closed in 1909, but the interior has been preserved – pride of place is given to the desk on which William carved his signature. While there he attended the fifteenth-century **Church of St Michael** above the school, which harks back to Norman designs in its rounded pillars and patterned arches. Its chief interest is in the 26 pithy psalms and biblical extracts illuminated with cherubs and flowers, painted on the walls during the seventeenth and eighteenth centuries.

From its knoll the churchyard gives a good view over the village's twin central squares, and of Main Street, housing the **Beatrix Potter Gallery** (Easter–Oct Mon–Wed, Sat & Sun 10.30am–4.30pm; £3, joint ticket with Hill Top £7; NT), occupying rooms once used by her solicitor husband. With their timed-entry tickets, fans get bustled into rooms full of Potter's original illustrations, though the less devoted might find displays on her life as keen naturalist, conservationist and early supporter of the National Trust more diverting – Potter bequeathed her farms and land in the Lake District to the Trust on her death.

Practicalities

The main **bus service** to Hawkshead is the #505 between Windermere, Bowness, Ambleside and Coniston; on reaching Hawkshead it loops down to Hill Top and back for the Beatrix Potter house at Near Sawrey. The **tourist office** is at the main car park (Easter–Oct daily 9.30am–5.30pm; Nov–Easter Fri, Sat & Sun 10am–3.30pm; ⓣ015394/36525) and can change money and book you on local guided walks.

Accommodation

Book a long way ahead if you want to **stay** in Hawkshead during the peak summer season. The tourist office can help with finding accommodation if the places listed below are full.

B&Bs, guest houses and hotels

Ann Tyson's Cottage Wordsworth St ⓣ015394/36405, ⓦwww.anntysons.co.uk. Some contend that Wordsworth briefly boarded here, and today there are B&B rooms in the barn conversion or two cottages to rent. ❸

Ivy House Main St ⓣ015394/36204, ⓦwww.ivyhousehotel.com. The eighteenth-century elegance here makes for a pleasantly characterful base. Six rooms in the main house, five more in the lodge behind. Rates include dinner, but you can get B&B only, on request, for around £20 less than the posted rates. ❻

King's Arms Market Square ⓣ015394/36372, ⓦwww.kingsarmshawkshead.co.uk. Bags of character in this old inn, with nine rooms retaining their oak beams and idiosyncratic proportions (bathrooms are up-to-date, though). ❺

Queen's Head Main St ⓣ015394/36271, ⓦwww.queensheadhotel.co.uk. Guest rooms here have been thoroughly modernized; family rooms sleep three or four. ❺

Yewfield Hawkshead Hill, 2 miles west off B5285 ⓣ015394/36765, ⓦwww.yewfield.co.uk. Vegetarian guest house set amongst organic vegetable gardens. The house is a Victorian Gothic beauty and breakfast is a real treat. Closed mid-Nov to Jan. ❸

Hostel

Esthwaite Lodge YHA ⓣ0870/770 5836, ⓔhawkshead@yha.org.uk. A mile to the south down the Newby Bridge road, housed in a Regency mansion. Good-sized family rooms (❷) available, otherwise dorm beds cost £11.50. Closed Nov–Jan, plus other days in winter.

Campsites

Croft Caravan and Campsite North Lonsdale Rd ⓣ015394/36374, ⓦwww.hawkshead-croft.com. Busy site, right by the village, with bike rental available. Closed Nov to mid-March.

Hawkshead Hall Farm Half a mile north of the village on the Ambleside road ⓣ015394/36221. An inexpensive tap-and-toilet affair. Closed Dec–Feb.

Eating and drinking

Apart from the daytime cafés and small local supermarket, Hawkshead's **pubs** provide the main eating options. Both the *King's Arms* and *Queen's Head* have bar meals as well as a more formal restaurant, and the *King's Arms* has a snug little bar with a fire and a fine beer selection. Of the **tearooms**, *Whig's* on The Square (closed Thurs, and all Jan) serves its eponymous speciality baked rolls, while the fifteenth-century *Minstrels' Gallery* on the main square has an espresso machine – ask here, too, about renting cottages in the area.

Grizedale Forest

If the weather looks promising, time is well spent among the remarkable sculptures in **Grizedale Forest**, southwest of Hawkshead, which drapes over the Furness Fells separating Coniston Water from Windermere. Access to the forest is easiest from Hawkshead, from where there's a summer-season minibus shuttle (part of the Cross Lakes Shuttle service) to **Grizedale Forest Centre** (daily: March–Nov 10am–5pm; Dec–Feb 10am–4pm; free, all-day parking £3; ⓣ01229/860010, ⓦwww.nwefd.co.uk), three miles southwest of Hawkshead. Grizedale Mountain Bikes at the centre (daily 9am–5pm; ⓣ01229/860369) has **mountain bikes** available to rent – there are miles of bike trails to explore – or just head out on foot along ten miles of the **Silurian Way**, which links the majority of the eighty-odd stone and wood sculptures scattered among the trees. Since 1977, artists have been invited to come here, often for six months at a time, to create a sculptural response to their surroundings using natural materials. Some of the resulting works are startling, as you round a bend to find a hundred-foot-long wave of bent logs or a dry-stone wall slaloming the conifers. More adventurous still is the forest high-ropes course known as **Go Ape** (April–Oct daily, advance bookings required on ⓣ0870/444 5562; £14.50; minimum age 10), which has you frolicking under supervision in the tree canopy for a couple of hours.

Hill Top

It's two miles from Hawkshead, down the eastern side of Esthwaite Water on the B5285 to the pretty twin hamlets of Near and Far Sawrey, the first the site of Beatrix Potter's beloved **Hill Top** (Easter–Oct Mon–Wed, Sat & Sun 10.30am–4.30pm; £4.50, joint ticket with Beatrix Potter Gallery £7; NT). A Londoner by birth, Potter bought the farmhouse here with the proceeds from her first book, *The Tale of Peter Rabbit*, and retained it as her study long after she moved out following her marriage in 1913. Its furnishings and contents have been kept as they were during her occupancy – a condition of Potter's will – and the small house is always busy with visitors; so much so that numbers are often limited. In summer, expect to have to queue. From April to October, you can travel to Hill Top directly from Bowness on a combined "boat-and-goat" **ferry-and-minibus service** (10am–4.30pm every 40min; ⓣ015394/45161, ⓦwww.mountain-goat.com), which runs on from Hill Top to Hawkshead and back. In the village, the *Tower Bank Arms* is the place to muse on your next move; it serves good sandwiches, homemade pies and local sausages.

Tarn Hows

A minor road off the Hawkshead–Coniston B5285 winds the couple of miles northwest to the highly popular **Tarn Hows**, a body of water surrounded by spruce and pine and circled by paths and picnic spots. The land was donated by Beatrix Potter in 1930 – one of several such grants – since when the National Trust has carefully maintained it. It takes an hour to walk around the tarn, during which you can ponder on the fact that this miniature idyll is in fact almost entirely artificial – the original owners enlarged two small tarns to make the one you see today, planted and landscaped the surroundings and dug the footpaths. It's now a Site of Special Scientific Interest, so keep an eye out for some of the Lakes' (and England's) few surviving native red squirrels.

A free National Trust Tarn Hows **bus service** runs between Hawkshead and Coniston on Sundays between Easter and the end of October. Otherwise, you'll have to pay to use the designated car park – or, of course, walk the two miles up from Coniston or Hawkshead on country paths and lanes. Drivers have the option of following the signs north to Ambleside along the minor road, reaching the *Drunken Duck Inn* (ⓣ015394/36347, ⓦwww.drunkenduckinn.co.uk; ❻) after three miles, at the Barngates crossroads. There's a cheery welcome, stylish rooms, deservedly popular food and their own-brewed beer.

Keswick and Derwent Water

Standing on the shores of Derwent Water at the junction of the main north–south and east–west routes through the Lake District, **KESWICK** makes a good base for exploring delightful Borrowdale – the start of many walking routes to the central peaks around Scafell Pike – or Skiddaw and Blencathra, which loom over the town. There's plenty of accommodation and some good cafés aimed at walkers, while several bus routes radiate from the town, getting you to the start of even the most challenging hikes. For those not up to a day on the fells, Keswick remains a popular place throughout the year, with a big enough population (around five thousand) to warrant a bevy of local museums and sights.

Arrival, information and accommodation

All **buses**, including National Express services, use the terminal behind Lakes Foodstore, off Main Street. The **tourist office** is in the Moot Hall on Market Square (daily: April–Oct 9.30am–5.30pm; Nov–March 9.30am–4.30pm; ⓣ017687/72645, ⓦwww.keswick.org). George Fisher, at 2 Borrowdale Rd (ⓣ017687/772178), is one of the most celebrated **outdoors stores** on the Lakes, with a full range of equipment and maps, a daily weather information service and café. For **bike rental**, try Keswick Mountain Bikes on Southey Hill (ⓣ017687/775202, ⓦwww.keswickmountainbikes.co.uk). **Guided walks** – from lakeside rambles to mountain climbs – depart daily (Easter–Oct 10.15am; £5) from the Moot Hall; just turn up with a packed lunch. There's

Walks from Keswick

All sorts of major **walks** start from Keswick and the surrounding villages, including tough climbs up Blencathra and the celebrated Coledale Horseshoe, an all-day circuit which takes in up to eleven summits. However, moderate walkers keen to spend just half a day or so on the fells can settle for either of the walks detailed below – you'll still need to carry decent maps and be properly equipped.

Rising sharply through coniferous forests above Keswick, the walk up **Latrigg Fell** (4–6 miles; 900ft ascent; 2–3hr) gives splendid views across Derwent Water to Borrowdale and the high fells. Follow Station Road past the Keswick town youth hostel and museum and, as it bends around to the right to become Brundholme Road/Briar Rigg, look for the right turn up Spooney Green Lane across the A66. From here skirt the west flank of Latrigg before zigzagging to the summit from the north. Return either directly down the southern gully or follow the longer eastern ridge to Brundholme, returning through Brundholme wood or along the railway path.

More demanding, but the easiest of the region's true mountain walks, is the hike up **Skiddaw** (5 miles; 3000ft ascent; 5hr), a smooth mound of splintery slate. Follow the walk above, skirting the west flank of Latrigg, but continue straight ahead when the path branches right to the Latrigg summit. It is pretty much a steady walk (with a possible diversion up Little Man along the way) before reaching a false summit and finally the 3054-foot High Man.

Internet access at U-Compute, above the post office at 48 Main St (daily 9am–5.30pm, sometimes later in summer; ⓣ017687/775127).

You should have no trouble finding **accommodation**, and competition at the lower end of the market keeps the prices keen. B&Bs cluster along Bank and Stanger streets, near the post office, and around Southey, Blencathra and Eskin streets, in the grid near the start of the A591 Penrith road. Smarter places line the street known as The Heads, overlooking Hope Park, a couple of minutes' south of the centre on the way to the lake.

B&Bs, guest houses and hotels

Bluestones 7 Southey St ⓣ017687/774237. Well-kept guest house used to walkers, with a variety of rooms (some sleeping three or four), plus big breakfasts and on-street parking. ❷

Bridgedale Guesthouse 101 Main St ⓣ017687/773914. Keswick's most amenable landlady makes her rooms suit all requirements – whether you're looking for an early breakfast, packed lunch, a room-only deal, en-suite room, cycle storage or discount for a longer stay, you'll find it here. Just around the corner from the bus station; mention *Rough Guides* for a discount. No credit cards. ❶–❷

Derwentwater Hotel Portinscale, off the A66 ⓣ017687/772538, ⓦwww.derwentwater-hotel.co.uk. Superior lakeside retreat, two miles west of Keswick, with comfortable rooms – some deluxe, with lounges and sweeping views – a conservatory and locally renowned restaurant. Two-night rates covering dinner, bed and breakfast are a good deal. ❼

Fitz House 47 Brundholme Terrace, Station Rd ⓣ017687/774488, ⓦwww.fitzhouse.co.uk. Stylish Victorian villa overlooking the park, glowing with restored pine, lovely furnishings and artwork. Sit in the conservatory and sip a sundowner (corkscrew provided). Two-night minimum weekend stay. ❷

George Hotel St John's Street ⓣ017687/772076, ⓦwww.georgehotelkeswick.co.uk. Keswick's oldest coaching inn, with bags of character downstairs and fully modernized rooms up. The food is good, either eaten in the bar or more formal restaurant. Parking available. ❹

Greystones Ambleside Rd ⓣ017687/773108, ⓦwww.greystones.tv. Non-smoking Victorian terraced house close to the centre at the end of St John's St. En-suite rooms with fell views and TVs, and parking available. ❸

Highfield Hotel The Heads ⓣ017687/772508, ⓦwww.highfieldkeswick.co.uk. Beautifully restored hotel whose stylish "feature rooms" include two turret rooms and a converted chapel. There's also garden seating, parking and an inventive restaurant (dinner included in the price). ❻, ❼ for feature rooms.

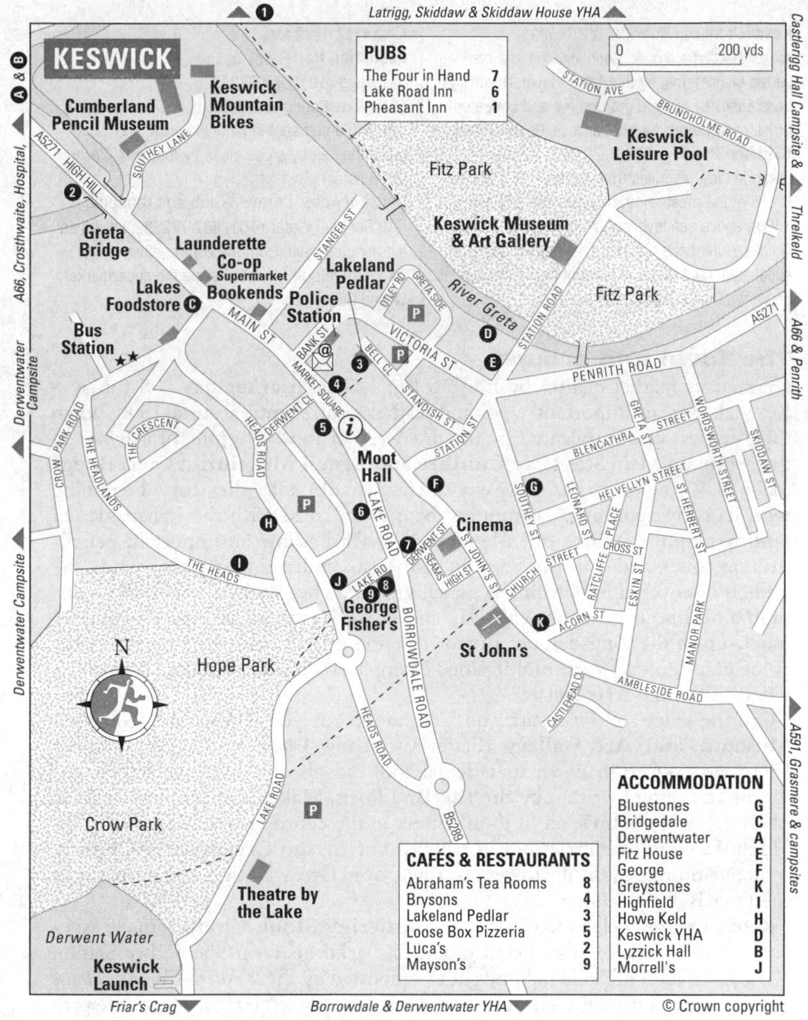

Howe Keld 5–7 The Heads ⓣ017687/772417, ⓦwww.howekeld.co.uk. Welcoming, non-smoking, guest house with a reputation for great breakfasts (vegetarian specialities included) and cosy rooms. Parking available. 3

Lyzzick Hall Under Skiddaw, A591 ⓣ017687/772277, ⓦwww.lyzzickhall.co.uk. A couple of miles northwest of town, this is a relaxed country-house hotel set in its own grounds, with an indoor pool and very good restaurant. 6, 7 with dinner.

Morrels 34 Lake Rd ⓣ017687/772666, ⓦwww.morrels.co.uk. Good-value restaurant-with-rooms operation, with the sleeping quarters decked out in vibrant colours, and a lovely bar and restaurant downstairs with good Modern British food (residents get ten percent off dinner). 4

Youth hostels

Derwentwater Barrow House, Borrowdale ⓣ0870/770 5792, ⓔderwentwater@yha.org.uk. Based in an old mansion with fifteen acres of grounds sloping down to the lake, a couple of miles south of Keswick along the B5289. Closed Nov & Dec, and open weekends only in Jan. Dorm beds £11.50.

Keswick Station Rd ⓣ0870/770 5894, ⓔkeswick@yha.org.uk. Good location in a converted woollen mill by the river in town. Dorm beds cost £11.50, you get free tea and coffee on arrival, and there's Internet access. Open all year.
Skiddaw House ⓣ0780/120 7401. On the Cumbria Way, six miles from Keswick by path, this is one of the most remote buildings in England, 1500ft above sea level and with no motor vehicle access. Bunk beds (£8), log fires and limited food supplies (though there is draught beer from a local brewery). Closed Oct to mid-May.

Campsites

Castlerigg Hall Rakefoot Lane, off the A591, Castlerigg ⓣ017687/772437, ⓦwww.castlerigg.co.uk. Out-of-town campsite, a mile and a half southeast of Keswick; you can reach the nearby stone circle by footpath. Closed Nov–Easter.
Derwentwater Caravan Club and Camping Site Derwent Water ⓣ017687/772392. Less than ten minutes' walk from the centre, down by the lake; turn left off Main St beside the supermarket. Closed Dec & Jan.

The Town and around

Granted its market charter by Edward I in 1276 – **market day** is Saturday – Keswick was an important wool and leather centre until around 1500, when these trades were supplanted by the discovery of local graphite. Northwest of the centre up Main Street, the **Cumberland Pencil Museum** at Greta Bridge (daily 9.30am–4pm; £2.50; ⓦwww.pencils.co.uk) tells the story, beginning with its early application as moulds for cannon balls. With the Italian idea of putting graphite into wooden holders, Keswick became an important pencil-making town, and remained one until the late eighteenth century, when the French discovered how to make pencil graphite cheaply by binding the common amorphous graphite with clay, and broke Keswick's monopoly. Inside, a mock-up of the long-defunct Borrowdale mine leads through a potted history of graphite use, with multifarious examples of the finished product and a video of the modern process.

On the edge of Fitz Park, on Station Road, you'll find the **Keswick Museum and Art Gallery** (Easter–Oct daily 10am–4pm; £1), a quirky Victorian collection of ancient dental tools, fossils and some prized manuscripts and letters written by the Lakeland Poets. Make time, too, for a couple of churches: **St John's**, on St John's Street in the centre, where the novelist Sir Hugh Walpole (of Herries novels fame) is buried; and **Crosthwaite Church**, a fifteen-minute walk northwest of town over Greta Bridge, resting place of the poet Robert Southey.

Keswick's most celebrated landmark, **Castlerigg Stone Circle**, is made especially resonant by its magnificent mountain backdrop. From the end of Station Road, take the Threlkeld rail line path (signposted by the *Keswick Country House Hotel*) for half a mile, then turn onto the minor road to the right where the path runs under the road – the site's a mile further on atop a sweeping plateau. Thirty-eight hunks of Borrowdale volcanic stone, the largest almost eight feet tall, form a circle a hundred feet in diameter; another ten blocks delineate a rectangular enclosure within. The array probably had an astronomical or time-keeping function when it was erected four or five thousand years ago. Back on the rail path, you can easily continue all the way to **Threlkeld** itself, three miles from town, on a delightful riverside walk with the promise of a drink in one of Threlkeld's old pubs at the end. Keener hikers use Threlkeld as the starting point for the gut-busting climb up **Blencathra** (2847ft), whose five great ridges loom above the A66: you'll need to be well prepared to tackle this.

Eating, drinking and entertainment

Many of Keswick's **cafés** and **restaurants** cater to a walking crowd, which means large portions and few airs. As well as those listed below, meals at the

George Hotel and *Morrel's* (see pp.878 & 879) are locally renowned. Several of the **pubs** also have meals worth investigating, while there's a fair amount of entertainment in Keswick throughout the year: a **cinema** on St John's Street which hosts an annual film festival (times vary), the **jazz festival** each May, **beer festival** in June, and traditional country shows in the locality during the summer. The **Theatre by the Lake** on Lake Road (ⓣ017687/774411, ⓦwww.theatrebythelake.com) hosts a full programme of drama, concerts, exhibitions, readings and talks.

Cafés

Abraham's Tea Rooms George Fisher's, 2 Borrowdale Rd. The top-floor tearoom in the outdoor store comes to your aid with warming mugs of *glühwein*, homemade soups, big breakfasts and daily specials. No credit cards.

Brysons 42 Main St. Top-notch bakery and tearooms with breakfasts, traditional main dishes and cream teas. No credit cards.

Lakeland Pedlar Henderson's Yard, Bell Close, off Main St. Keswick's best café serves inventive veggie food – from breakfast burritos to veg crumble – and the coffee's great too. Open evenings July & Aug.

Restaurants

Loose Box Pizzeria King's Arms Courtyard, Main St ⓣ017687/72083. Popular pizza-and-pasta joint – the house special is *spaghetti rustica* (tomato, garlic, chilli and prawns). Moderate.

Luca's Greta Bridge ⓣ017687/774621. Classic pastas and pizzas, and pricier main meals (such as monkfish wrapped in pancetta) in a riverside Italian bistro; closed Mon. Expensive.

Mayson's 33 Lake Rd ⓣ017687/774104. Licensed, self-service restaurant serving lasagne, moussaka, pies, curries and stir-fries (until 9pm in summer). No credit cards. Inexpensive.

Pubs

The Four in Hand Lake Rd, opposite George Fisher's. Popular pub for its food – grilled Cumberland ham and eggs, local trout and other lakeland specialities.

Lake Road Inn Lake Rd. Intimate Jenning's pub known for its good-value food, particularly the homemade pies and Borrowdale trout.

Pheasant Inn Crosthwaite Rd. A 10min walk out of town (up the road on the west side of the park) is rewarded by a drink in Keswick's nicest local.

Around Derwent Water

On any reasonably decent day, the best move in Keswick is down to the shores of **Derwent Water**, five minutes' walk south of the centre along Lake Road and through the pedestrian underpass. It's among the most attractive of the lakes, ringed by crags and studded with islets, and is most easily seen by hopping on the **Keswick Launch** (Easter–Nov daily 10am–6pm, until 8pm in July & Aug; Dec–Easter Sat & Sun 10am–6pm; £5.40 round-trip, 85p per stage; ⓣ017687/772263, ⓦwww.keswick-launch.co.uk), which runs right around the lake calling at several points en route. There's also an enjoyable one-hour evening cruise (£6) from May Day bank holiday until mid-September; phone or pop down during the day to reserve a place.

Departures are frequent enough to combine a cruise with a lakeside walk; or you can make the entire lake loop on foot from Keswick on the **Derwent Water Circuit** (around 10 miles; 3–4hr), outlined in a leaflet available from the tourist office. The closest and most popular hike is to **Friars' Crag**, from where medieval pilgrims left for St Herbert's Island in the middle of the lake to seek the hermit's blessing. Ruskin's childhood visit to Friars' Crag inspired "intense joy, mingled with awe", feelings likely to be duplicated if you return to Keswick via the 530-foot **Castlehead** view point – a three-mile round-trip in all. Other ports of call as you make your way around Derwent Water on foot or by launch include the dry-stone **Ashness Bridge** and **Lodore Falls** (see "Borrowdale", overleaf, for both). Best climb is up **Cat Bells** (launch to Hawes End), a renowned vantage point (1481ft) above the lake's western shore – allow two and a half hours for the scramble to the top and a return along the wooded lake shore.

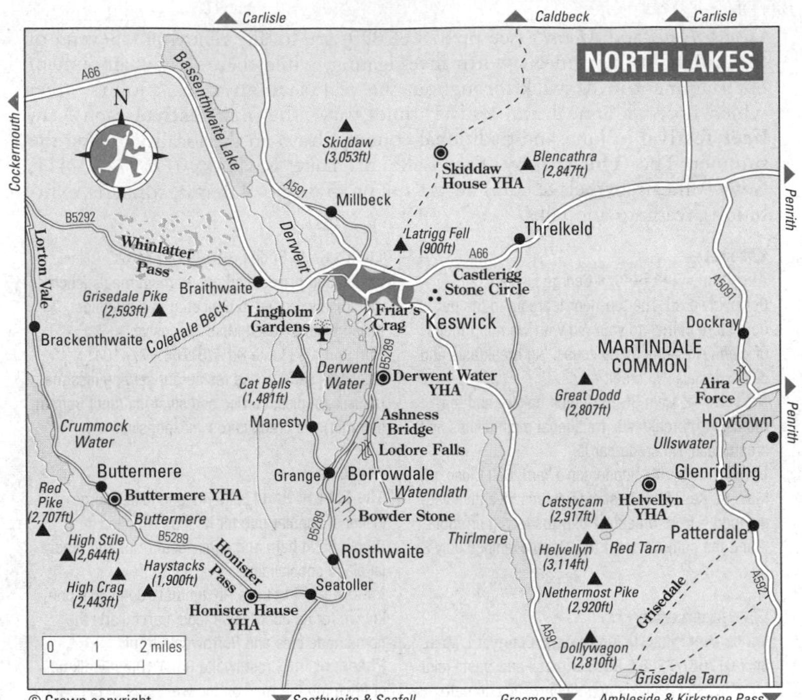

Borrowdale and Scafell

It is difficult to overstate the beauty of **Borrowdale**, with its river flats and yew trees, lying at the head of Derwent Water and overshadowed by the peaks of Scafell and Scafell Pike, the highest in England. Climbs up these, as well as up Great Gable, one of the finest-looking mountains in England, start from the head of the valley, accessible on the #77/77A and #79 **buses** from Keswick.

Just before the *Derwentwater* youth hostel, a narrow road branches left for a steep climb to the photogenic **Ashness Bridge**. The minor road ends two miles further south at **Watendlath**, an idyllic little tarn and tearooms which can be hopelessly overrun at times in summer – the National Trust's free Watendlath Wanderer bus runs here every couple of hours from Keswick on summer Sundays, via Ashness. A path from Watendlath continues on to Rosthwaite, a mile and a half southwest – an easy hour's walk.

Back on the B5289, a signposted path heads to the **Lodore Falls**. This diversion is only really worth it after sustained wet weather, when you'll be able to appreciate Robert Southey's magnificent, alliterative evocation of the falls in *The Cataract of Lodore*: "Collecting, projecting, receding and speeding, and shocking and rocking, and darting and parting", and so on, for line after memorable line.

Further south, there's a slight detour across an old packhorse bridge to **GRANGE**, a peaceful riverside hamlet peered down upon by Borrowdale's forested crags. A very minor road (and the Cumbria Way) meanders up the west side of Derwent Water from here to Keswick, with a diversion at Manesty to climb Cat Bells (see above). At Grange, it's under a mile south to the 1900-ton **Bowder Stone**, a house-sized lump of rock scaled by way of a wooden ladder and worn to a shine on top by thousands of pairs of feet. Controversy surrounds the origin of the rock: some say it came from the fells above, others contend it was brought by the last Ice Age from Scotland.

Shaded paths through the wood, and the B5289, lead in around a mile to the straggling hamlet of **ROSTHWAITE**. As well as two or three B&Bs, there are comfortable **rooms** at the hiker-friendly *Royal Oak Hotel* (ⓣ017687/777214, ⓦwww.royaloakhotel.co.uk; ❺, includes dinner) and the smarter, neighbouring *Scafell Hotel* (ⓣ017687/777208, ⓦwww.scafell.co.uk; ❺, ❼ with dinner). Tea and scones served in the *Royal Oak*'s firelit sitting room are a treat. For a more substantial **meal**, the *Scafell Hotel*'s attached *Riverside Inn* – the only local pub – serves popular bar food, while the set dinner in either hotel's restaurant is a good deal, too. At the general store – the only one in the valley – you'll be able to put together a basic picnic. A nice **youth hostel**, *Borrowdale Longthwaite* (ⓣ0870/770 5706, ⓔborrowdale@yha.org.uk; dorm beds £11.50; closed Jan–March), is a mile south of Rosthwaite, on the riverside footpath to Seatoller; while across the river, on the eastern side of the B5289, is the *Chapel House Farm* **campsite** (ⓣ017687/777602).

Another mile on, **SEATOLLER** and the **Seatoller Barn National Park Information Centre** (Easter–Nov daily 10am–5pm; limited weekend opening in winter; ⓣ017687/777294) marks the end of the #79 bus route from Keswick. There are regular events, craft displays, talks and walks based at the information centre; there's also a car park and a few slate-roofed houses clustered around a café and outdoors store. *Seatoller House* (ⓣ017687/777218, ⓦwww.seatollerhouse.co.uk; ❹, ❻ with dinner; no dinner Tues, closed Dec–Feb) has rooms in an atmospheric seventeenth-century farmhouse right by the road. It's the base for good-humoured "hare and hounds" hunts a couple of times each year, stalking people rather than foxes across the local fells.

There's also an informal **campsite** in a small field by the beck along the minor road south to **SEATHWAITE**, twenty minutes' walk away. This is a popular base for walks up the likes of Great Gable and Scafell Pike: the trout farm at the foot of the valley has a fine **café** (Easter–Sept daily 10am–6.30pm), serving fresh grilled trout or sandwiches, as well as another informal and basic campsite (no phone) used extensively by Great Gable climbers.

Scafell, Scafell Pike and Great Gable

In good weather, the minor road to Seathwaite is lined with parked cars by 9am as hikers take to the paths for the rugged climbs up the three major peaks of Scafell, Scafell Pike and Great Gable. Technically, the climbs are not too difficult, though, as always, you should be well prepared and reasonably fit.

The summit of **Scafell Pike** (3205ft), the highest point in England, is close to the second-highest point in the Lakes, **Scafell** (3163ft), and an eight-mile, six-hour, loop walk taking in both leaves Seathwaite via Stockley Bridge to the south, branching up Styhead Ghyll to **Styhead Tarn**. This is as far as many get, and on those all-too-rare glorious summer days the tarn is a fine place for a picnic. A direct, but very steep, approach to **Great Gable** (2949ft) is also possible from Styhead Tarn, though most people cut west at Seathwaite campsite up Sourmilk Ghyll and approach via **Green Gable** (2628ft), also an eight-mile, six-hour return walk. However, the easiest Great Gable climb is actually from Honister Pass.

Honister Pass

Overlooked by the steep Borrowdale Fells, the B5289 cuts west at Seatoller, up and over the dramatic **Honister Pass**. Slate quarrying was well established here by the mid-eighteenth century, and though full commercial quarrying ceased in 1986, you can't miss the vicious scars of the old workings. To get an idea of what slate mining entailed in the nineteenth century, you can don a hard hat and lamp to descend the **Honister Slate Mine** (tours daily March–Oct; ⓣ017687/777230, ⓦwww.honister-slate-mine.co.uk; £7), at the top of the pass. Bus #77/77A comes this way, making the initial, and steep, mile-and-a-quarter grind from Borrowdale to the car park at the top of Honister Pass, by the *Honister Hause* **youth hostel** (ⓣ0870/770 5870, ⓔhonister@yha.org.uk; dorm beds £10.25; closed mid-Nov to Easter). Great Gable climbers start from here and follow a path (6 miles; 4hr) past Grey Knotts and Brandreth to Green Gable, before rounding Great Gable and returning along an almost parallel path to the west.

Buttermere, Crummock Water and Loweswater

From Honister Pass, the B5289 follows Gatesgarthdale Beck for three miles and makes a dramatic descent into the **Buttermere Valley** by *Gatesgarth Farm* **campsite and B&B** (ⓣ017687/770256; no credit cards; ❷), then runs another mile beside the lake – past more camping and rooms at *Dalegarth* (ⓣ017687/770233; ❷; closed Nov–March) – to the **youth hostel** (ⓣ0870/770 5736, ⓔbuttermere@yha.org.uk; dorm beds £11.50; Sept–Easter closed certain days of the week) just before **BUTTERMERE** village. The village has two hotels: the *Bridge Hotel* (ⓣ017687/770252, ⓦwww.bridge-hotel.com; ❼, includes dinner) and the smaller *Fish Hotel* (ⓣ017687/770253; ❹) – both serve reasonable meals, while the *Bridge* has a popular bar complete with traditional flagstones. There's also simple **camping** right by the lake at *Syke Farm* (ⓣ01768/770222; closed Nov–March). To get to Buttermere directly from Keswick, take the #77/77A bus.

The village itself – set between the two expanses of Buttermere and neighbouring **Crummock Water** – makes a good walking base, with a particularly easy two-mile hike out along Crummock Water's southwestern edge to the 125-foot **Scale Force** falls. The four-mile, **round-lake** stroll circling Buttermere itself shouldn't take more than a couple of hours; you can always detour up Scarth Gap to Haystacks if you want more of a climb and some views. The much longer classic walkers' circuit (8 miles; 6hr 30min) climbs from the village up **Red Pike** and then runs along the ridge, via High Stile, High Crag and Haystacks, before descending Scarth Gap or Warnscale Bottom back to the lake.

The scenery flattens out as the road heads north from Crummock Water and into the pastoral **Lorton Vale**, with Cockermouth just a few miles beyond. A minor road south just beyond Brackenthwaite leads directly to minuscule **Loweswater**, one of the less frequented lakes, around which there's a gentle, four-mile (2hr) walk. En route, you'll pass the *Kirkstile Inn* (ⓣ01900/85219, ⓦwww.kirkstile.com; ❹), a welcoming sixteenth-century place with bistro-style meals available in the cosy bar or restaurant, and a relaxed beer garden.

Wast Water and Eskdale

Great Gable and Scafell stand as a formidable last-gasp boundary between the mountains of the central lakes and the gentler land to the southwest, which smoothes out its wrinkles as it descends to the Cumbrian coast. **Wast Water**, which points its slender finger towards the pass between both ranges, remains one of the most isolated of the region's lakes; at its southern end, forested valleys fall away into **Eskdale**, perhaps the prettiest of the unsung Lakeland

Valleys. **Public transport** is very limited; in fact, there's none to Wast Water, which makes it one to savour if you fancy getting right off the beaten track. Eskdale is accessed either by the Ravenglass and Eskdale Railway (see p.897), which drops you right in the heart of superb walking country around the hamlet of Boot; or by the east–west minor road route between the coast, via Eskdale Green and Little Langdale, just west of Skelwith Bridge.

Wast Water

The awesome sight of the peaks crowding slim, deep **Wast Water** impresses most visitors who venture to this remote lake. The highest slopes in England frame the northern shores, while on the wild southeastern banks rise the impassable screes which separate the lake from Eskdale to the south. The only road winds from the main coastal A595, through remote settlements, before meeting the lake at its southwestern tip, at the *Wasdale Hall* **youth hostel** (ⓣ0870/770 6082, ⓔwastwater@yha.org.uk; dorm beds £10.25; Sept–Easter closed 1–2 days a week), a country house set in its own lakeside grounds.

The minor road then hugs the shore of the lake, ending four miles away at **Wasdale Head**, a Shangri-la-like clearing between the mountain ranges, where you'll find the marvellous *Wasdale Head Inn* (ⓣ019467/26229, ⓦwww.wasdale.com; ❻), one of the most celebrated of all lakeland inns, with legendary breakfasts, a great public bar and hearty four-course dinners. Nearby, there's **B&B**, friendly advice and packed lunches from hiker-friendly *Lingmell House* (ⓣ019467/26261, ⓦwww.lingmellhouse.com; no credit cards; ❸; closed Jan), on the track to the church, or **camping** at the National Trust's *Wasdale Head* campsite (ⓣ019467/26220; closed Nov–March). Scafell Pike and Great Gable are both popular hiking targets from here, as is the route over the pass into Borrowdale. Hikers can also head south, via Wasdale Head Hall Farm and Burnmoor Tarn, over the fells into Eskdale (5 miles; 3hr).

Eskdale

The attractive rural ride by road or train through **Eskdale** from the west begins to peter out as you approach Dalegarth Station (terminus of the Ravenglass and Eskdale Railway), just beyond which nestles the dead-end hamlet of **BOOT**. The few stone houses cowering beneath the fells mark the last remnant of civilization before the road turns serious. Three miles beyond Boot and 800 feet up, the remains of granaries, bath houses and the commandant's quarters for **Hardknott Roman Fort** (always open; free access) command a strategic and panoramic position. After negotiating the appalling, narrow switchbacks of **Hardknott Pass**, the road drops to Cockley Beck, before making the equally alarming ascent of **Wrynose Pass**; at the col, the **Three Shire Stone** marks the old boundary of Cumberland, Westmorland and Lancashire. Beyond, it's a seven-mile descent past the foot of the Langdale

A riverside walk from Eskdale

An easy riverside walk (2 miles; 1hr) starts 200yd east of Dalegarth Station down a track to St Catherine's Church opposite the road to Boot. In low water you can cross the river below the church by stepping stones; you turn right, then left, up a path beside a stream to Stanley Ghyll Waterfall. Returning along the path beside the stream, a branch on the left leads back to Dalegarth Station via a bridge over a swimming hole. If you don't cross the stepping stones, you can take a path following the right bank to Doctor Bridge where you can cross and double back for Stanley Ghyll or continue to the road and the *Woolpack Inn*.

Valley to Ambleside – by the time you reach the *Three Shires* pub in Little Langdale you'll need a stiff drink.

Boot has a fair smattering of **accommodation and services**, which makes it the obvious base for extended walks in the valley, though there are B&Bs and the occasional pub in nearby hamlets such as Eskdale Green and Santon Bridge, back down the valley. The nearest place to Dalegarth Station is *Brook House Inn* (Ⓣ019467/23288, Ⓦwww.brookhouseinn.co.uk; ❹), which serves meals in its *Poachers Bar* and has a separate restaurant, too. In Boot itself, the *Burnmoor Inn* (Ⓣ019467/23224, Ⓦwww.burnmoor.co.uk; ❸) is the traditional hikers' choice, with hearty Cumbrian food – there's *glühwein* available in the bar and a peaceful beer garden.

Further up the road past the turn-off to Boot, it's 500yd to *Hollins Farm* **campsite** (Ⓣ019467/23253), and another three-quarters of a mile to the *Woolpack Inn* (Ⓣ019467/23230; ❸–❹), which as well as **rooms** has a purpose-built **bunkhouse** (£16.50 including breakfast). This is also a hikers' favourite, serving filling food, and doubling as a common starting point for the **Woolpack Round** (16 miles; 8–10hr), a tough circuit topping the two highest mountains in England and several others which aren't much lower. It is not easy going and a certain amount of scrambling is required, but the views and the varied terrain make this one of the finest lakeland walks. Another 400yd beyond the pub you'll find Eskdale **youth hostel** (Ⓣ0870/770 5824, Ⓔeskdale@yha.org.uk; dorm beds £10.25; closed Nov–Feb).

Cockermouth

The farming community of **COCKERMOUTH**, midway between the coast and Keswick at the confluence of the Cocker and Derwent rivers, is yet another station on the Wordsworth trail: the **Wordsworth House** on Main Street (Easter–May & Sept Mon–Fri 10.30am–4.30pm; June–Aug Mon–Sat 10.30am–4.30pm; £3.50; NT) is where William and Dorothy were born and spent their first few years. The terracotta-hued eighteenth-century building was nearly replaced by a bus station in the 1930s, but was saved and given to the National Trust who have furnished it with imports from their vaults. Some of the original features remain and there are occasional Wordsworthian relics – a chest of drawers here, a pair of candlesticks there – but despite the best endeavours of the enthusiastic staff it's disappointingly lifeless. The kitchen has been put to good use as a café, but on a warm day the walled garden beside the river is more pleasurable than the house.

There's certainly no shortage of rainy day attractions ranged along Main Street – including museums of printing, toys and models, and motoring – while if you follow your nose, you're likely to stumble upon **Jennings Brewery**, on Brewery Lane near the river. The hour-and-a-half-long Jenning's Brewery Tour (£4.50; booking advisable; Ⓣ08451/297190; Ⓦwww.jenningsbrewery.co.uk) culminates with a tasting. Check also to see what's on inside **Castlegate House** (Mon–Wed, Fri & Sat 10.30am–5pm, Sun 2–5pm; free; Ⓦwww.castlegatehouse.co.uk), a Georgian mansion on Castlegate, opposite the entrance to Cockermouth Castle – itself a private residence and closed to the public. The house supports a changing programme of contemporary art displays, specializing in the work of some very accomplished local artists. Finally, there's entertainment to be had at the **Lakeland Sheep and Wool Centre** (daily 10am–6pm; Ⓣ01900/822673, Ⓦwww.sheep-woolcentre.co.uk), a mile south of town on the Egremont road, where indoor sheepdog trials, sheep-shearing displays and related exhibits introduce visitors to the complexities of country life. The sheepdog show costs £4 (March–Oct Mon–Thurs & Sun, call for current times), but access to the visitor centre, shop and café is free.

Practicalities

All **buses**, including National Express services, stop on Main Street, from where you follow the signs east to the **tourist office** in the Town Hall, off Market Place (April–June & Oct Mon–Sat 9.30am–4.30pm; July–Sept Mon–Sat 9.30am–5pm, Sun 10am–2pm; Nov–March Mon–Fri 9.30am–4pm, Sat 10am–2pm; ⓣ01900/822634). For **online information**, visit ⓦwww.cockermouth.org.uk.

Most appealing **B&B** is *Pumpkin House*, 3 Challoner St (ⓣ01900/828269, ⓦwww.lakesnw.co.uk/pumpkinhouse; no credit cards; ❷), a vegetarian-friendly place where you can also get a packed lunch for the fells or an evening meal. The *Trout Hotel* on Crown Street (ⓣ01900/823591, ⓦwww.trouthotel.co.uk; ❼), by the river, is the top choice, and there are also modern, en-suite rooms available in the *Shepherd's Hotel*, out at the Lakeland Sheep and Wool Centre (ⓣ01900/822673, ⓦwww.shepherdshotel.co.uk; ❸). Ten minutes' walk south along Station Road, Fern Bank brings you to the Double Mills **youth hostel** (ⓣ0870/770 5768; dorm beds £9; closed Nov–Easter), set in a seventeenth-century watermill.

All the **pubs** along Main Street compete to sell bar meals at rock-bottom prices, though best choice by far is *The Bitter End* on Kirkgate, housing Cumbria's smallest brewery. Of the **cafés**, the *Norham Coffee House*, 73 Main St (closed Sun), trades on its history – formerly the home of John Christian, grandfather of Mutiny on the Bounty's Fletcher Christian. *Over The Top*, 36 Kirkgate (ⓣ01900/827016; closed Sun–Tues), caters for veggies and meat-eaters with an eclectic menu of home-cooked dishes from around the world; it's open during the day and for dinner, and also has **Internet** access. *The Cockatoo*, 16 Market Place (ⓣ01900/826205; closed Mon, Tues & Sun eve), is a friendly place, with simple lunches and more elaborate dinners such as steaks or spiced lamb, halibut or mushroom stroganoff. The *Quince & Medlar*, 12 Castlegate (ⓣ01900/823579; dinner only; closed Sun & Mon), meanwhile, serves gourmet vegetarian dishes in a wood-panelled Georgian house. **Market day** in Cockermouth is Monday.

Ullswater

Wordsworth declared **Ullswater** "the happiest combination of beauty and grandeur, which any of the Lakes affords" – a judgement that still holds good. At over seven miles long, Ullswater is the second longest lake in Cumbria and much of its appeal derives from its serpentine shape, a result of the complex geology of this area: the glacier that formed the trench in which the lake now lies had to cut across a couple of geological boundaries, from granite in the south, through a band of Skiddaw slate, to softer sandstone and limestone in the north.

The main **public transport to Ullswater** is the #108 bus service (Easter–Oct) from Penrith, which runs via Pooley Bridge, Aira Force and Glenridding to Patterdale. On summer weekends, the #517 Kirkstone Rambler bus continues south over the Kirkstone Pass to Bowness.

Patterdale and Glenridding

The chief lakeside settlements, Patterdale and Glenridding, are less than a mile apart at the southern tip of Ullswater, each with a smattering of cafés and B&B

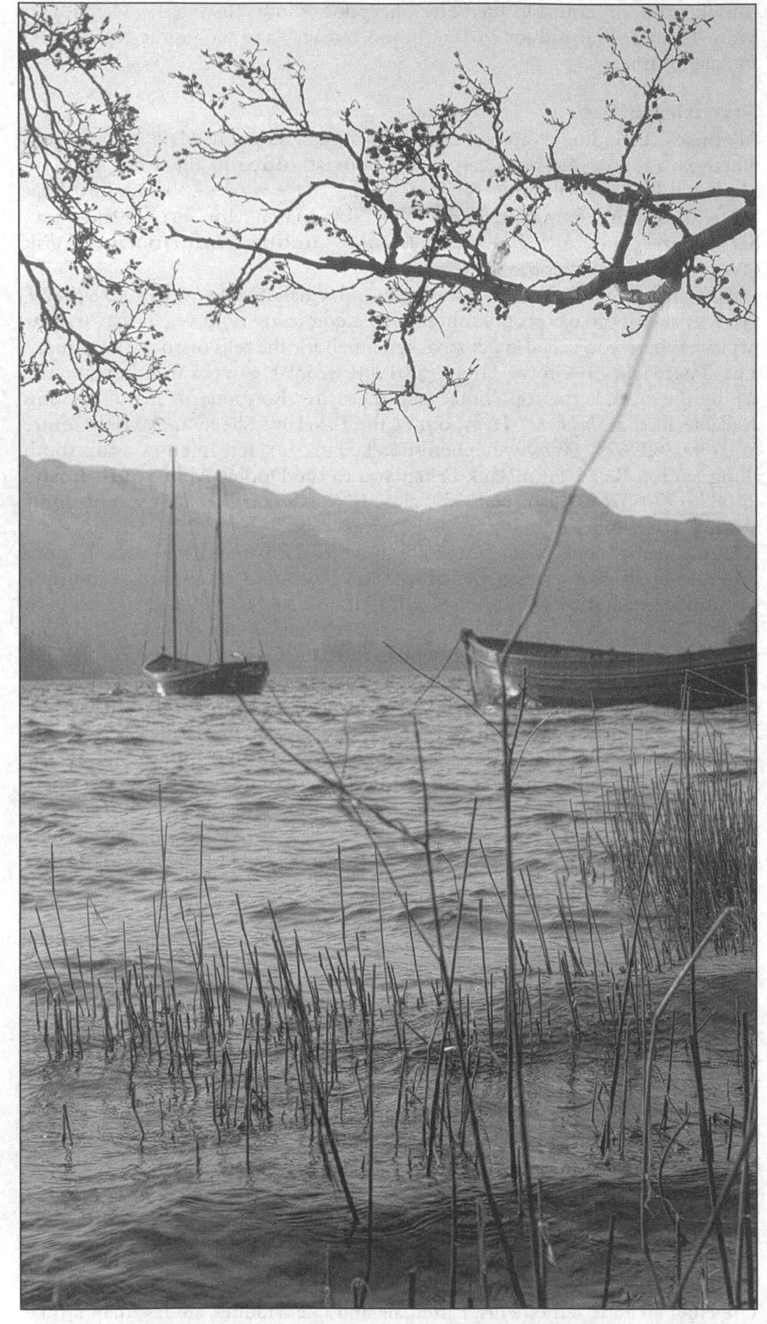

△ Ullswater

but not otherwise notable except as a base for one of the most popular scrambling routes in the country – up the considerable heights of Helvellyn.

GLENRIDDING features several inexpensive B&Bs such as *Fairlight Guest House* (Ⓣ017684/82397; ❷), by the hamlet's main car park, which has its own café. However, it's at the *Inn on the Lake* (Ⓣ017684/82444, Ⓦwww.innonthelakeullswater.com; ❻–❼) that you really begin to appreciate Ullswater's charms; its *Ramblers Bar* is *the* place for a beer and a bar meal. Similarly sited is the *Glenridding Hotel* (Ⓣ017684/82228, Ⓦwww.glenridding-hotel.co.uk; ❼), this time complete with indoor pool, bar, restaurant and coffee shop with Internet access. *Gillside Caravan & Camping* (Ⓣ01768/482346, Ⓦwww.gillsidecaravanandcampingsite.co.uk; closed Nov–Feb) is half a mile away up the valley behind the helpful **tourist office** (Easter–Oct daily 9am–6pm; Nov–Easter Fri–Sun 9.30am–3.30pm; Ⓣ017684/82414) in the main car park. You can get a bite to eat at *Fellbites*, opposite the tourist office, a **café** with a menu ranging from sandwiches and filled jacket potatoes to local sausage or lamb with mash. Climbers wanting an early start on Helvellyn stay at the Helvellyn **youth hostel** (Ⓣ0870/770 6110, Ⓔhelvellyn@yha.org.uk; dorm beds £10.25; closed certain days of the week except in July & Aug), a mile and a half up the valley track from Glenridding. Even if you're not staying here – or climbing Helvellyn – it's a nice **walk up the valley** to the hostel following Glenridding Beck, which sits amid lead mine workings abandoned in the 1960s.

In **PATTERDALE**, the cheapest and most popular place to stay is the rustic **youth hostel** (Ⓣ0870/770 5986, Ⓔpatterdale@yha.org.uk; dorm beds £11.50; closed certain days of the week except Sept–March), just south of the hamlet on the A592, which serves good food and has Internet access. Nearby *Ullswater View* (Ⓣ017684/82175, Ⓦwww.ullswater-view.co.uk; ❸; closed mid-Nov to Dec) is an attractive non-smoking guest house with private gardens. Patterdale's only **pub**, the *White Lion* (Ⓣ017684/82214; ❸), has a few rooms available and decent beer – sizzling steak platters are the speciality here. There's **camping** at *Side Farm* (Ⓣ017684/82338; closed Nov–Easter) – the track to the farm is across from the church, with the campsite on the eastern shore of the lake. The only other service is a small post office/village **shop** opposite the pub.

Around the lake

On busy summer days the A592 up the western side of the lake is packed with traffic, all looking for space in one of the few designated car parks. Busiest is usually that below **Gowbarrow Park**, three miles north of Glenridding, where the A5091 meets the A592; the hillside still blazes green and gold in spring, as it was doing when the Wordsworths visited; it's thought that Dorothy's recollections of the visit in her diary inspired William to write his famous "Daffodils" poem. The car park at Gowbarrow is also the start of an easy, brief walk up to **Aira Force**, a bush-cloaked seventy-foot fall that's spectacular in spate and can be viewed from bridges spanning the top and bottom of the drop. There's a tearoom (closed Nov–Easter) at the Aira Force car park.

It's best, if you have time, to get out on the lake itself, traversed by the **Ullswater Steamer** (Ⓣ017684/82229, Ⓦwww.ullswater-steamers.co.uk), which has year-round services from Glenridding to Howtown, halfway up the lake's eastern side (£3.90 one-way; 35min), and from Howtown to Pooley Bridge, at the northern end of the lake (£3.90; 20min). Alternatively, you can buy a ticket between Glenridding and Pooley Bridge that effectively makes a two-hour, round-the-lake cruise (£8.80). There's a bar on board the steamer.

Ullswater walks

While Helvellyn (see below) dominates the southwest side of Ullswater, the fells flanking the east side of the lake offer some invigorating hikes, too.

Using the Ullswater Steamer to travel from Glenridding to **Howtown**, the easiest walk back (5 miles; 3hr) follows the shore of Ullswater around Hallin Fell (or over, climbing 263ft) to **Sandwick**, then crosses fields before rejoining the shore at **Long Crag** for the final two miles to the south end of the lake at Patterdale.

A considerably more strenuous route (8 miles; 4–5hr) from Howtown cuts past the *Howtown Hotel* and then heads up lovely **Fusedale**, at the head of which there's a sharp and unrelenting climb up to the **High Street**, a broad-backed ridge that was once a Roman road. Once on top the path is clearly visible for miles, and following the ridge south you meet the highest point, **High Raise** (2632ft) – 2hr from Howtown – where there's a cairn and glorious views. The route then runs south and west, via the stone outcrops of **Satura Crag**, past **Angle Tarn** and finally down to the A592, just shy of Patterdale's pub and post office.

Either of these walks can be combined with an initial stretch **between Pooley Bridge and Howtown**. The most popular haul (7 miles; 3–4hr) leaves Pooley Bridge pier, heads through the village and follows the road up to **Roehead**. A path then runs up to the **Stone Circle** on the Roman road and down the side of the fell, south of Sharrow Bay, to Howtown pier.

HOWTOWN is tucked into a little clearing at the foot of beautiful Fusedale, where the *Howtown Hotel* makes a great spot for lunch or a drink in the pocket-sized hikers' bar around the back. A minor road from here hugs the eastern shore of the lake the four miles to **POOLEY BRIDGE**, passing the incomparable *Sharrow Bay* (Ⓣ017684/86301, Ⓦwww.sharrow-bay.com; ⑨ with dinner) on the way, one of England's finest hotel-restaurants. Pooley Bridge itself has more basic pleasures. It's a cute retreat – packed to distraction in summer – with a church and three **pubs**, most notably the eighteenth-century *Sun Inn*.

Climbing Helvellyn

The climb to the summit of **Helvellyn** (3114ft), the most popular of the four 3000-foot mountains in Cumbria, is challenging enough for most visitors, who tend to make a day-long circuit from either Glenridding or Patterdale. On summer weekends and bank holidays the car parks below and paths above are full by 10am, but the variety of routes up and down at least offers a chance of escaping the crowds. You might, anyway, want to avoid the most frequently chosen approach via the infamous **Striding Edge**, an alarming, undulating rocky ridge offering the most direct access to the summit. With **Red Tarn** – the highest Lake District tarn – a dizzying drop below, purists negotiate the very ridge top of Striding Edge; slightly safer, but no less precipitous tracks follow the line of the ridge, just off the crest. However you get across (and some refuse to go any further when push comes to shove) there's a final, sheer, hands-and-feet scramble to the flat **summit** (2hr 30min from Ullswater). As rockside memorials (and the occasional hovering rescue helicopter) attest, people do get into trouble on Striding Edge: if you're at all nervous of heights you'll find it a challenge to say the least; in poor weather, it's madness even to contemplate it.

The good news is that once you're up the various descents all seem like child's play. The classic return is to the northeast via the less demanding **Swirral Edge**, where a route leads down to Red Tarn, then follows the beck to the disused slate quarry workings and the dramatically sited **Helvellyn youth hostel**, a mile and a half from Glenridding. Another route, of equal duration, climbs back up to **Catstycam** and drops down the northern ridge path into Keppel Cove, where you cross the dam and continue to the hostel. Either of these Helvellyn approaches and descents makes for around a seven-mile (5–6hr) walk.

Northwest from the summit, a path (2.5 miles; 1hr 30min) runs down to **Thirlmere reservoir** (a straight up-and-down route which provides the easiest walk to Helvellyn's summit). Bus #555 between Keswick and Grasmere/Ambleside runs along Thirlmere's eastern shore, stopping outside the *King's Head* at Thirlspot. Most enjoyable of all, though, is the path south from Helvellyn, following the flat ridge past **Nethermost Pike and Dollywagon Pike**. After Dollywagon Pike, there's a long scree scramble down to **Grisedale Tarn** and then the gentlest of descents down **Grisedale Valley**, past Ruthwaite Lodge hut, alongside the babbling beck, emerging on the Patterdale–Glenridding road – a good six hours all told for the entire circuit.

The Cumbrian coast

South and west of the national park, the **Cumbrian coast** attracts much less attention than the spectacular scenery inland, but it would be a mistake to write it off. It splits into two distinct sections, the most accessible being the **Furness peninsulas** area (Ⓦ www.lake-district-peninsulas.co.uk), just a few miles from Windermere's lakeside, where varied attractions include the genteel resort of **Grange-over-Sands**, the monastic priory at **Cartmel**, and enjoyable market towns such as **Ulverston** and **Broughton-in-Furness**. Parts of this region share nearby Lancashire's industrial heritage and in the ship-building port of **Barrow-in-Furness** it's possible to see a slow revival that's only just starting to pay dividends in terms of tourism – though the dramatic ruins of nearby **Furness Abbey** have been attracting visitors for almost two hundred years.

The **Cumbrian coast** itself is generally judged to begin at **Silecroft** near Millom and stretches for more than sixty miles to the small resort of **Silloth**, on the shores of the Solway Firth. In between lie isolated beaches and the headland of **St Bees** as well as the delights of the **Ravenglass and Eskdale Railway** and the attractive Georgian port of **Whitehaven**.

Grange-over-Sands

Before the coming of the railways, the main route to the Lake District was the "road across the sands" from near Lancaster to **GRANGE-OVER-SANDS**, travellers being led by monks from Cartmel Priory and then, from the sixteenth century, by a royally appointed guide. The tradition continues today with one guide left, who leads the way around the slip sands and hidden channels which claimed so many lives between the fourteenth and nineteenth centuries. The eight-mile walk takes the best part of a day and departures are usually every other week between May and October. Further details are available from the Grange **tourist office**, which is located in Victoria Hall on Main Street (daily: Easter–Oct 10am–5pm; Nov–Easter 10am–4pm; Ⓣ 015395/34026, Ⓦ www.grange-over-sands.com), 400yd left from the **train station** and National Express stop.

After tramping along the mile-long esplanade with its fine views of the marshy bay, you've just about covered all Grange has got to offer, other than the walk to the top of **Hampsfell** (750ft; 3hr; 4 miles). On a clear day the view from the crinkled limestone summit is spectacular; a well-marked pointer on the roof of a nineteenth-century hospice will help you identify peaks as far away as Skiddaw.

Cartmel

Sheltered several miles inland from Morecambe Bay, **CARTMEL** grew up around its twelfth-century Augustinian priory and is still dominated by the proud **Church of St Mary and St Michael** (daily: June–Sept 9am–5.30pm; Oct–May 9am–3.30pm; tours Easter–Oct Wed 11am & 2pm; free), the only substantial remnant to survive the Dissolution. A diagonally crowned tower is the most distinctive feature outside, while the light and spacious Norman-transitional interior climaxes at a splendid chancel, illuminated by the 45-foot-high **East Window**. You can spend a good half-hour scanning the immaculate misericords and numerous tombs, chief among them the **Harrington Tomb** in the Town Choir, to the south of the chancel – the weathered figure is that of John Harrington, who rebuilt this section in 1340. The choir went on to act as the parish church when the rest of the building was abandoned following the Reformation, the nave only regaining its cover in the 1620s, thanks to the munificence of local landowner George Preston. Another patron of the church was one Rowland Briggs, who paid for a shelf on a pier near the north door and for a supply of bread to be distributed from it every Sunday in perpetuity "to the most indigent housekeepers of this Parish".

Everything else in the village is modest in scale, centred on the attractive **market square**, beyond the church, with its Elizabethan cobbles, water pump and fish slabs. Given Cartmel's rather twee attraction, you'll not be surprised to find a couple of antique shops, though better browsing is done at Peter Bain Smith's **bookshop** on the square – with a huge selection of local books and guides – and at the **Cartmel Village Shop**, known to aficionados for the quality of its sticky toffee pudding. The **racecourse** – with a delightful setting by the River Eea – also deserves a look even if the races (held on the last weekend in May and August) aren't in action.

Practicalities

Trains stop at Cark-in-Cartmel, two miles southwest of the village proper; **buses** from there or from Grange-over-Sands train station run to the village. Alternatively, an hour-long walk across the low hills from Grange up Grange Fell Road and across the breast of Hampsfell into the pastoral Eea Valley makes a more interesting approach. There's no tourist office, but the local **website**, ⓦwww.cartmelvillage.com, can fill you in on history, sights, events and businesses.

The only time you'll need to book **accommodation** well in advance is during race weeks. On Market Square, *Market Cross Cottage* (ⓣ015395/36143, ⓔburgess@marketcross.freeserve.co.uk; no credit cards; ❸) is a cosy, seventeenth-century B&B with an oak-beamed tearoom downstairs (tearoom closed Mon). Up a notch, the celebrated *Cavendish Arms* on Cavendish Street (ⓣ015395/36240, ⓦwww.thecavendisharms.co.uk; ❹), just off the square, is a sixteenth-century inn which retains many of its original features. Top spot is *L'Enclume*, also on Cavendish Street (ⓣ015395/36362, ⓦwww.lenclume.co.uk; ❽; closed first 2 weeks of Jan), an exclusive gourmet restaurant with rooms – the sort of place that includes helicopter landing directions for its guests. For a stay in one of its delightful estate **cottages**, contact *Longlands at Cartmel*, at the base of Hampsfell just a mile north of the village (ⓣ015395/36475, ⓦwww.cartmel.com); guests get free use of a nearby pool, spa and sauna.

The village **pubs** form the basis of the evening's eating and entertainment. The *King's Arms* (Ⓣ015395/36220; ❸) on the square has attractive rooms, outdoor tables and bar **meals**, with daily chalk-board specials that ring the changes. The *Cavendish*, though, is the real winner, the oldest and most characterful of the pubs, sitting on the site of a monastic guest house and offering good (if pricey) food.

Holker Hall

One of Cumbria's most interesting and well-presented country estates, **Holker Hall** (Easter–Oct Mon–Fri & Sun 10am–6pm; last admission 4.30pm; hall, gardens, grounds & motor museum £8.75; various cheaper combination tickets also available; Ⓦwww.holker-hall.co.uk) lies just over a mile north of Cark-in-Cartmel Station. The vast, sandstone hall, which is made up of a pleasing combination of Victorian, Elizabethan and older styles, overlooks acres of beautifully designed gardens, woods and nature trails. Only the **New Wing** of the house, rebuilt following a fire in 1871, is open to the public, displaying silk wall coverings, Louis XV furniture and a bedroom where Queen Mary slept in 1937. Its opulent rooms are still in use by the Cavendish family, who've owned the hall since the late seventeenth century, but you can wander freely around them. The real showpieces are the cantilevered staircase and the library, which is stocked with more than 3000 leather-bound books, some of whose spines are fakes, constructed to hide electric light switches added later.

The 25-acre **gardens** incorporate a variety of water features, including a limestone cascade and fountain, while next to the house, the **Lakeland Motor Museum** (Easter–Oct Mon–Fri & Sun 10.30am–4.45pm) displays more than a hundred vehicles, from 1880s tricycles and wartime ambulances to funky 1920s bubble cars and 1980s MGs. A special exhibition concentrates on the speed-freak Campbells – Sir Malcolm and son Donald.

There's also an annual **garden and countryside festival** held over three days at the end of May/beginning of June, when the garden's floral displays are at their best, backed by a whole host of craft displays and musical events.

Ulverston

The railway line winds westwards to **ULVERSTON**, a close-knit market town which formerly prospered on the cotton, tanning and iron-ore industries. It's an attractive place, enhanced by its dappled grey limestone cottages and a jumble of cobbled alleys and traditional shops zigzagging off the central **Market Place**. Stalls are still set up here and in the surrounding streets every Thursday and Saturday; on other days (not Wed or Sun), the **market hall** on New Market Street is the centre of commercial life.

The first thing you'll notice on the approach to Ulverston is what looks like a lighthouse high on a hill to the north of town. This is the **Hoad Monument**, built in 1850 to honour locally born Sir John Barrow, a former secretary of the admiralty. It's open on summer Sundays and public holidays (if the flag's flying) and the walk to the top grants fine views of the bay and fells. However, Ulverston's most famous son is Stan Laurel (born Arthur Stanley Jefferson), the whimpering, head-scratching half of the comic duo, celebrated in a mind-boggling collection of memorabilia at the **Laurel and Hardy Museum** (Feb–Dec daily 10am–4.30pm; £2; Ⓦwww.laurel-and-hardy-museum.co.uk), up an alley at 4c Upper Brook St, near Market Place. The copy of Stan's birth certificate (16 June 1890, in Foundry Cottages, Ulverston) lists his father's occupation as "comedian" – young Arthur Stanley could hardly have become anything else.

The eccentric showcase of hats, beer bottles, photos, models, puppets, press cuttings and props is mixed with copies of letters from the pair: one from Stan, in retirement in Santa Monica (where he's buried), complains that, since his incapacitating stroke, he can't pursue his favourite sport – shark fishing. There's also a Twenties-style cinema, with almost constant screenings of the duo's films. It's also worth checking to see what's on at the **Lanternhouse**, on The Ellers (exhibitions, when on, Wed–Sat 11am–4pm; free; ⓦwww.welfare-state.org), just off the A590 at the bottom of Market Street and across Tank Square (a traffic roundabout). A group of multimedia artists known as Welfare State International occupy this award-winning conversion of an old school, presenting imaginative exhibitions relating to the "celebratory arts".

The other main attraction is the **Lakes Glass Centre**, at Oubas Hill on the A590, behind Booths supermarket (ⓦwww.lakesglasscentre.co.uk), where you can watch the crystal-making process from blowing to painstaking carving (Mon–Fri 10am–4pm, Sat & Sun 10am–5pm; £2); there's also a factory shop on site and a café.

Practicalities

Ulverston **train station**, serving the Cumbrian coast railway, is only a few minutes' walk from the town centre – head down Prince's Street and turn right at the main road for County Square. **Buses** arrive on nearby Victoria Road from Cartmel, Grange-over-Sands, Barrow, Coniston, Bowness, Windermere and Kendal. The **tourist office** is in Coronation Hall on County Square (Mon–Sat 9am–5pm; ⓣ01229/587120, ⓦwww.ulverston.net). The 70-mile **Cumbria Way** long-distance footpath from Ulverston to Carlisle starts from The Gill, at the top of Upper Brook Street – a waymarker spire marks the start. **Bike rental** is available from Gill Cycles, on The Gill (ⓣ01229/581116).

Pick of the **B&Bs** is *Dyker Bank* (ⓣ01229/582423; no credit cards; ❷), a Georgian house very near the station at 2 Springfield Rd, while for something a little grander, *Trinity House Hotel*, 200yd downhill from the station, on the corner of Prince's Street and the main A590 (ⓣ01229/588889 ⓦwww.traininghotel.co.uk; ❹, weekend room-only rate ❷), has spacious rooms in a handsome old building – the staff here are all under training for the local hospitality industry, so the prices for rooms and food are very competitive. There's also a great *Walker's Hostel* on Oubas Hill (ⓣ01229/585588, ⓦwww.walkershostel.freeserve.co.uk; no credit cards; £13; closed Nov & Dec), fifteen minutes' walk from the centre on the A590 near Canal Head, at the foot of the Hoad Monument: there are thirty beds in small rooms (you won't have to share with strangers), with vegetarian breakfasts (included) and evening meals available (£7). **Cafés** include the funky *Hot Mango*, 27 King St, or the Buddhist-run (and organic vegetarian) *Peace Café* at 5 Cavendish St (closed Sun & Mon), which has **Internet** access (as does the library, on King's Road). Most of the **pubs** serve food, too, best being the *Farmers Arms* in Market Place, which has some outdoor tables. Or try *King's*, 15–17 Queen St (ⓣ01229/588947), a good-value café-bar with sandwiches, light lunches, tapas and a la carte meals.

Out of town, drivers can follow the A590 briefly and turn off at the signpost for **Canal Foot**, running through an industrial estate to reach the beautifully sited *Bay Horse* (ⓣ01229/583972, ⓦwww.thebayhorsehotel.co.uk; ❽ including dinner), by the last lock on the Ulverston canal. You can also walk here in around half an hour from the town centre, along the canal. The cooking is celebrated far and wide, and even if you can't run to lunch or dinner in the waterside conservatory, you can have a beer or a bar lunch (not Mon) at one of the outdoor tables.

Barrow-in-Furness and around

With shipyard cranes piercing the skyline, the distinctly industrial feel of **BARROW-IN-FURNESS** has been the town's hallmark since it grew up around a booming iron industry in the mid-nineteenth century. Steelworks and shipbuilding followed, making Barrow one of England's busiest ports, and the town still makes a handsome living from orders for military hardware. Yet even Barrow's most enthusiastic supporters could hardly claim the town as attractive: recession in the 1980s emptied many of the proud Victorian buildings and left the centre rough at the edges. However, there's been a significant amount of town-centre regeneration in recent years, while some of the older buildings still retain the capacity to surprise – the splendid sandstone Gothic Town Hall for one.

For visitors, the best move is straight to the **Dock Museum** (Easter–Oct Tues–Fri 10am–5pm, Sat & Sun 11am–5pm; Nov–Easter Wed–Fri 10.30am–4pm, Sat & Sun 11am–4.30pm; last admission 45min before closing; free; Ⓦ www.dockmuseum.org.uk), on North Road, half a mile from the centre; it's signposted from all over town. Located in the dried-out graving dock where ships were once repaired, the museum tells the history of Barrow – which is also the history of modern shipbuilding. The creation of the Furness railway in 1846 to carry iron ore to the coast led to Barrow's growth from a village of less than two hundred people to a thriving port within 25 years. Steel-making and shipbuilding went hand in hand, and boomed between the wars. Later, as the steelworks declined (the last one finally closed in 1983) and the Cold War intensified, the emphasis shifted to submarine building – today, nuclear subs are constructed in the town's Devonshire Dock Hall. Even if the history leaves you cold, the museum exhibits (on the shipbuilding process, local railways, iron- and steel-making) are well presented, while a series of family events every summer add focus to a visit.

Few lake-bound tourists stay the night, though Barrow's **tourist office**, located in the theatre-arts centre, Forum 28, opposite the town hall on Duke Street (Mon–Wed & Fri 9.30am–5pm, Thurs 10.30am–5pm, Sat 10am–4pm; Ⓣ 01229/894784, Ⓦ www.barrowbc.gov.uk), can help with accommodation if necessary. You can also get information here on visiting the nearby nature reserves on **Walney Island**, a six-mile strip of land accessed from Barrow's Jubilee Bridge.

Furness Abbey

Furness Abbey (April–Sept daily 10am–6pm; Oct daily 10am–5pm; Nov–March Wed–Sun 10am–4pm; £3; EH), a set of roofless sandstone arcades and pillars hidden in a wooded vale – the so-called "Valley of Deadly Nightshade" – lies a mile and a half out of Barrow on the Ulverston road (local buses to Dalton-in-Furness and Ulverston pass close by). Now one of Cumbria's finest ruins, it was once the most powerful abbey in the northwest, possessing much of southern Cumbria as well as land in Ireland and the Isle of Man. Founded in 1124, the abbey's industry was remarkably diverse – it owned sheep on the local fells, controlled fishing rights, produced grain and leather, smelted iron, dug peat for fuel and manufactured salt. By the fourteenth century it had become such a prize that the Scots raided it twice, though it survived until April 1536, when Henry VIII chose it to be the first of the large abbeys to be dissolved; the abbot and 29 of his monks, who had hitherto resisted (and indeed, had encouraged the locals to resist Dissolution – a treasonable offence), were pensioned off for the sum of two pounds each.

The abbey has been a popular tourist diversion since the early nineteenth century, when a train station was built to bring in visitors – among them Wordsworth, who was very taken with the "mouldering pile". Borrow a portable tape-player from the reception desk to get the best out of the site since there are no maps or explanatory signs. The transepts stand virtually at their original height, while the massive slabs of stone-ribbed vaulting, richly embellished arcades and intricately carved *sedilia* in the presbytery are the equal of any of Yorkshire's far busier abbey ruins. A small **museum** houses some of the best carvings, including rare examples of effigies of armed knights with closed helmets and – as medieval custom dictated – crossed legs. Only seven others have ever been found intact. The *Abbey Tavern* at the entrance serves drinks at tables scattered about some of the ruined outbuildings.

Piel Island

The attacks by the Scots goaded Furness Abbey into protecting itself with Piel Castle on **Piel Island**, now in ruins but once guarding the approaches south of the town. This is reached from Roa Island, three miles southeast of Barrow down the A5087 (bus #11; not Sun); turn off at Rampside (signposted "Lifeboat station"). At **ROA**, which has a pub and a small café, you can debate the prospects of the weather- and tide-dependent **ferry** (Easter–Sept daily 11am–5pm; Oct–Easter on request; £1.50 each way; ⓣ01229/835809 or mobile 07799/761306) across to Piel Island. Apart from the ruins of a massive keep and the lifeboat station, it's the island's only commercial building, the *Ship Inn*, which draws people over here. This serves bar meals and allows camping.

Dalton and Broughton-in-Furness

North of Barrow, the A590 runs the four miles to the straggling town of **DALTON-IN-FURNESS**, old enough to have been mentioned in the Domesday Book but retaining little of interest today save the surviving fourteenth-century keep of **Dalton Castle** (Easter–Sept 2–5pm; free) at the top of the old market square. If you've stopped for this, you may as well walk past the keep to the churchyard of **St Mary's**, where the eighteenth-century artist George Romney is buried. Fairly regular buses run up to Dalton from Barrow (and on to Ulverston).

Whatever you feel about zoos, you're likely to be positively surprised by the **South Lakes Animal Park** (daily: Easter–Sept 10am–5pm; Oct–Easter 10am–dusk; £7.50, £5.50 Nov–Feb; ⓣ01229/466086, ⓦwww.wildanimalpark.co.uk), half a mile or so outside Dalton. An award-winning "conservation" zoo, it relies on ditches and trenches (not cages) for the most part to contain its animals and is split into separate habitat areas, ranging from the Australian bush to a tropical rainforest. It's quite something to encounter free-roaming kangaroos in rural Cumbria. Call for feeding times to see the park at its best – the tiger-feeding (encouraging them to climb and jump for their meal) is unique in Europe. There's a Zoo Bus Link from Dalton train station between June and August, while in school summer holidays you can get here directly by bus (Tues & Thurs only) from Bowness and Windermere – and if you keep your bus ticket, you'll get £1 off the entrance fee.

Beyond Dalton, it's ten miles up the A595 to the small market town of **BROUGHTON-IN-FURNESS** which, unlike its near namesake, has retained much of its Georgian beauty. Tall houses surround a charming square, complete with obelisk, stone fish slabs and stocks. From the square, follow Church Street to the edge of town and you'll reach **St Mary Magdalene**, originally twelfth-century, though much restored in the nineteenth century. Nestling in the Duddon Valley, the town makes a handy local walking or touring base (Coniston is only eight miles away) and the **tourist office** in the old Town Hall on the square (Easter–Oct Mon–Fri 10am–4pm, Sat 9am–4pm, Sun 9am–1pm; ⓣ01229/716115, ⓦwww.broughton-in-furness.co.uk) can help with accommodation. There's **B&B** at *Annan House*, attached to the *Square Café* (ⓣ01229/716388, ⓦwww.thesquarecafe.co.uk; no credit cards; ❷) on the square, which also has a pleasant tearooms. Alternatively, there are **pub** rooms at the *Manor Arms*, The Square (ⓣ01229/716286; ❷), where you can have breakfast served in your room.

Along the coast to St Bees

Road (A595) and rail routes follow the **Cumbrian coast** from Broughton-in-Furness to **St Bees**, with diversions to a series of small villages and lengthy beaches that, for the most part, live a quiet existence outside the short summer season. The first decent stretch of sand is at **Silecroft**, a few miles northwest of Millom; the Cumbria Coastal Way runs along the back of the beach and there's a train station back in Silecroft village. However, **Ravenglass** is the principal stop before the headland of St Bees – a sleepy little estuary village overshadowed by the nearby nuclear reprocessing plant, **Sellafield**.

Ravenglass and the Ravenglass and Eskdale Railway

The single main street of **RAVENGLASS**, fifteen miles or so up the coast, preserves a row of characterful nineteenth-century cottages facing out across the mud flats and dunes. Despite appearances, the village dates back to the arrival of the Romans, who established a supply post here in the first century AD for the northern legions manning Hadrian's Wall. Look for the sign to the "Roman Bath House", just past the station: 500yd up a single-track lane lie the fairly extensive remains of a fort which survived in Ravenglass until the fourth century.

Ravenglass Station is the starting point for the **Ravenglass & Eskdale Railway** (Easter week & May–Oct daily; rest of year Sat & Sun; £7.80 return; ⓣ01229/717171, ⓦwww.ravenglass-railway.co.uk), known affectionately as La'al Ratty. Opened in 1875 to carry ore from the Eskdale mines to the coastal railway, the tiny train, running on a 15-inch gauge track, takes forty minutes to wind its way through seven miles of forests and fields between the fell sides of the Eskdale Valley to Dalegarth Station. Take your bike up on the train and you can cycle back from Dalegarth down the traffic-free **Eskdale Trail** (8.5 miles); a route guide is available from stations at either end and from local tourist offices. The other stations on the line are popular starting points for walks on and up into the central lakeland peaks, and consequently the railway makes for a fine approach to Eskdale itself (see p.885).

From the first stop, **Muncaster Mill**, there's a path south through the woods to **Muncaster Castle** (ⓣ01229/717614, ⓦwww.muncaster.co.uk), built around a medieval tower and which now hosts a variety of attractions. Apart from the rooms of the castle itself (Mon–Fri & Sun noon–5pm; £2.10), there are also spectacular **gardens**, as well as an **owl centre** and **meadowvole maze** (both daily 10.30am–6pm, closing at dusk in winter; £5.70), where you'll learn about the Muncaster voles, follow the hiking trails, and see kestrel displays or wild herons feeding.

There are B&Bs in Ravenglass, but the best **accommodation** hereabouts is at Muncaster Castle, where rooms (see above for contact details; ❷, en suite ❸) in the converted stable block offer a comfortable night.

Sellafield

The main blot on the Cumbrian coast looms large after Ravenglass, namely British Nuclear Fuels' (BNFL) Sellafield nuclear reprocessing plant, sited midway between Ravenglass and Whitehaven. It's a significant local employer – thousands of jobs currently depend on BNFL's presence in Cumbria – which enjoys high-level bipartisan political support, given that nuclear power currently supplies something like thirty percent of the country's electricity needs. At the Sellafield Visitors' Centre (daily 10am–6pm; free; Ⓦwww.bnfl.com), the interactive exhibits on electricity generation and the role of nuclear power were commissioned from London's Science Museum, whose independent stance allows you to make up your own mind about the pros and cons of nuclear power. As you might imagine, it's a complex and controversial subject. Critics question the entire reprocessing system at Sellafield and elsewhere, pointing to the lethal maritime and atmospheric discharges (virtually all European radioactive pollution comes from reprocessing) and the manifest dangers of waste transportation.

It's easiest to visit with your own transport – there's free parking at the visitor centre. You can arrive by train, getting off at Sellafield Station (request stop, infrequent weekend service), but then you'll need to walk ten minutes up to the main gate, from where transport on to the centre will be arranged.

St Bees

The close-knit central streets in the coastal village of **ST BEES** give it the feel of a retirement colony. It's a suitably elderly settlement, with a nunnery established here as early as the seventh century, succeeded by **St Bees Priory**, just north of today's train station, in the twelfth century. This was slightly damaged in the Dissolution, but retains huge Norman arches above its entrance porch; it also houses a small exhibition of Celtic crosses and headstones in the nave. The long sands lie a few hundred yards west of the village, while the steep, sandstone cliffs of **St Bees Head** to the north are good for windy walks and birdwatching. The headland's lighthouse marks the start of Wainwright's 190-mile **Coast-to-Coast Walk** to Robin Hood's Bay.

St Bees is on the Cumbrian coast train line and lies just five miles south of Whitehaven, from where there's a regular bus service. **Accommodation** needs advance reservations in high season, though at other times of the year there should be no problem finding somewhere to stay. *Fairladies Barn*, Main Street (Ⓣ01946/822178, Ⓦwww.fairladiesbarn.co.uk; no credit cards; ❸), is an attractive, converted seventeenth-century sandstone barn; while the *Queen's Hotel*, also on Main Street (Ⓣ01946/822287; ❸), is a nice old pub with a beer garden. Not far from either, *Fleatham House*, High House Road (Ⓣ01946/822341, Ⓦwww.fleathamhouse.com; ❺), is a lovely retreat set in its own grounds. There are only six rooms, with tea served on arrival, dinner available in the restaurant, and pick-ups on request from the train station.

Whitehaven

Some fine Georgian houses mark out the centre of **WHITEHAVEN**, one of the few grid-planned towns in England. The economic expansion that forced this planning was as much due to the booming slave trade as to the more widely recognized coal traffic. Whitehaven spent a brief period during the eighteenth century as Britain's third-busiest port (after London and Bristol), making it a prime target for an abortive raid led by Scottish-born American lieutenant **John Paul Jones**. Disgusted with the slave trade he witnessed while ship's mate in America, Jones returned to the port of his apprenticeship to rebel, but, let down by a drunk and potentially mutinous crew, he damaged only one of the two hundred boats in dock and his mini-crusade fell flat. All this and more is explained in **The Beacon** (Easter–Oct Tues–Sun 10am–5.30pm; Nov–Easter 10am–4.30pm; £4.25), an enterprising heritage centre on the harbour. Resembling a squat lighthouse, and with an interactive Met Office weather gallery on the top floor, The Beacon entertainingly covers the town history, from slaving to smuggling, with a special emphasis on the local characters who have shaped the town. The **harbour** itself sits at the heart of a renaissance project which has spruced up the quayside and provided new promenades, sculptures and heritage trails. The Crow's Nest, a 120-feet-high tower, lit at night, is the dramatic centrepiece of the marina. The whole waterfront comes alive during the annual **maritime festival** in June.

For all the changes round the harbour, it's Whitehaven's Georgian streets and neatly painted houses that make it one of Cumbria's most distinguished towns. There's a **market** held here every Thursday and Saturday, which adds a bit of colour. Otherwise, stroll up Lowther Street to the **Rum Story** (daily: April–Sept 10am–5pm; Oct–March 10am–4pm; £4.50; Ⓦwww.rumstory.co.uk), housed in the eighteenth-century shop, courtyard and warehouses of the Jefferson's rum family. This is another place you could easily spend an hour or so, discovering Whitehaven's links with the Caribbean and learning all about rum, the Navy, temperance and the hideousness of the slaves' Middle Passage, amongst other matters. Across Lowther Street is the seventeenth-century church of **St Nicholas**, though all that stands is its tower (containing a café). The rest succumbed to a fire in 1971, but there's a lovely garden now surrounding the former nave. Also on Lowther Street, don't miss Michael Moon's secondhand **bookshop** at no. 19 (closed Sun), a bookworm's treasure trove.

On the cliffs above Whitehaven, you can get to grips with the industry which set the town on its way at the **Haig Colliery Mining Museum**, Solway Road, Kells (Mon & Thurs–Sun 11am–5pm; free; Ⓦwww.haigpit.com). This was Cumbria's last deep-coal mine (closed in 1986), and you can view the restored winding engines and learn about the dreadful living and working conditions that, in part at least, funded the elegant Georgian town below. A walking tour (ask at the museum; £3) shows visitors the ruins of the early eighteenth-century Saltom Pit, the world's first undersea pit.

Practicalities

Trains follow the coastal route south to Barrow and north via Maryport to Carlisle. From the station you can walk around the harbour to The Beacon in less than ten minutes; the **bus station** is just across Tesco's car park from the train station. The helpful **tourist office** is in the Market Hall on Market Place (Easter–Oct Mon–Sat 9.30am–5pm, plus July & Aug Sun 11am–3pm; Nov–Easter Mon–Sat 10am–4.30pm; Ⓣ01946/852939, Ⓦwww.copelandbc.gov.uk), just back from the harbour.

For **accommodation**, the best central B&B is the very comfortable *Corcickle Guest House*, 1 Corcickle (Ⓣ01946/692073, Ⓔcorcickle@tinyworld.co.uk; no credit cards; ❷), five minutes' walk from the centre – keep on up Lowther Street, past Safeway and *McDonald's* to find the row of Georgian town houses. North of town at Moresby, *Moresby Hall* (Ⓣ01946/696317; ❺) – medieval in origin – also provides B&B, this time in an attractive Grade I listed building with walled gardens, and sea and fell views. Dinner is available here, and there are also two cottages to rent.

For **meals**, the *Courtyard Café* in the Rum Story serves wraps, sandwiches, baked potatoes and snacks under a glass roof. For something a bit more modish, there's *Zest Harbourside* on West Strand, a waterside café-bar doing mix-and-match tapas-style bowls and dishes of things. The sister restaurant, *Zest*, on Low Road (ⓣ01946/692848; dinner only Wed–Sat), is three-quarters of a mile out of the centre (on the B5349 Whitehaven–St Bees road), for moderately priced Modern British cuisine. You can get a decent pint in the *John Paul Jones Tavern*, on Duke Street, a modern **pub** that delivers a nod to the father of the American Navy by modelling its interior on that of a sailing ship.

Maryport to Silloth

North of Whitehaven it's undistinguished country for the most part, at least until you're past Workington. Historic **Maryport**, fifteen miles from Whitehaven, is on the Cumbrian coast rail line, and there's a regular bus service out here from Cockermouth (not Sun) and Carlisle. Thirteen miles to the north, **Silloth** is the Solway Firth's nicest small resort, reachable via buses (not Sun) from Maryport and Carlisle, just 21 miles away.

Maryport

MARYPORT sports splendid views of the Solway Firth and the Scottish hills across the water, and boasts a history going back to Roman times. That's taken care of in the excellent **Senhouse Roman Museum** (July–Oct daily 10am–5pm; April–June Tues & Thurs–Sun 10am–5pm; Nov–March Fri–Sun 10.30am–4pm; £2.50; ⓦwww.senhousemuseum.co.uk), high on a hill above the harbour, ten minutes' walk from the centre of town. It's a fascinating exhibition, based around the largest collection of Roman altars found at a single site in Britain, whose inscriptions and carvings shed much light on the fort and settlement of Roman Aluana. Recent surveys have shown the Roman town here to be considerably larger than originally thought, with a civilian population of several hundred. A wooden watchtower provides views over the site and along the coastline below, from where it's thought that Roman freighters unloaded supplies for the fort.

Maryport's modern history dates from its eighteenth-century heyday as an industrial port – the town is named after the wife, Mary, of local lord and entrepreneur Humphrey Senhouse. The most appealing part of town is the harbour and marina, now smartly landscaped and featuring the **Lake District Coast Aquarium** (daily: March–Oct 10am–5pm; Nov–Feb 11am–4pm; £4.25; ⓦwww.lakedistrict-coastaquarium.co.uk), on the South Quay, with its underwater Cumbrian world and fish-feeding sessions. The streets behind the harbour are slowly reviving, but still show evidence of Maryport's long decline since the Great Depression of the 1930s: local coal-mining reduced drastically in the 1950s, the port closed for business in the 1960s and was then silted up for the best part of twenty years until the recent regeneration. For a glimpse of better days, walk uphill to **Fleming Square** (on the way to the Roman museum), whose surviving cobbles are still surrounded by Georgian houses. It's also pleasant to stroll out along the promenade and get down on the beach when the tide's out.

It's a ten-minute walk from the **train station** to the harbour, down the main Senhouse Street, at the bottom of which is the **tourist office** (Easter–Oct Mon–Thurs 10am–5pm, Fri–Sun 10am–1pm & 2–5pm; Nov–Easter Mon–Sat 10am–1pm & 2–4.30pm; ⓣ01900/813738); it shares the premises, an old inn, with the town's small maritime and local history museum. As for eating or bedding down for the night, you're better off heading back to Whitehaven.

North to Silloth

Five miles further up the coast, the B5300 road runs right through **ALLONBY**, a former weaving village with a long shingle-and-sand beach, and the *Ship Inn*, where Dickens once slept. Both beach and road continue north as far as **SILLOTH-ON-SOLWAY**, another eight miles away and the Solway Firth's nicest spot, though its pleasures are all modest – a Victorian resort with wide cobbled streets, a large seafront green and promenade, and wildlife-rich local salt marshes and dunes. The name, incidentally, is a corruption of the "sea-lathes", or seaside grain silos, established by Cistercian monks who farmed the area in medieval times. For more on the history, visit the **Solway Coast Discovery Centre** on Liddell Street (daily 10am–4.30pm; £2.50), which also has a café.

There's a **tourist office** at 10 Criffel St, by the green (Easter–Oct Mon–Fri 10am–4.30pm, Sat 10am–1pm & 2–4.30pm, Sun 2–4.30pm; Nov–Easter Mon & Thurs 11am–3pm, Fri–Sun noon–3.30pm; ⓣ016973/31944), where you can debate the possibility of a room and pick up a leaflet on local walks.

East Cumbria: the Eden Valley and Penrith

The Lake District might end abruptly with the market town and transport hub of **Penrith**, ten miles northeast of Ullswater, but Cumbria doesn't. To the east, the **Eden Valley** splits the Pennines from the Lake District fells, and boasts a succession of hardy market towns, prime among which is the former county town of **Appleby-in-Westmorland**. This lies on the magnificent **Settle to Carlisle railway**, connecting Cumbria with the Yorkshire Dales (see p.952). The other great local feat of engineering – the M6, following the main London–Penrith–Glasgow rail line – misses the best of the valley, yet remains one of the most attractive sections of motorway in the country. Northeast of Penrith, the A686 leads you imperceptibly from Cumbria into Teesdale, via the high town of **Alston**, providing a superb if lonely approach to Hexham and Hadrian's Wall.

Penrith and around

Once a thriving market town on the main north–south trading route, **PENRITH** today suffers from undue comparisons with the improbably pretty settlements of the nearby Lakes. The brisk streets, filled with no-nonsense shops and shoppers, have more in common with the towns of the North Pennines than the stone villages of south Cumbria, and even the local building materials emphasize the geographic shift. Its deep-red buildings were erected from the same rust-red sandstone used to construct **Penrith Castle** (daily: June–Sept 8am–9pm; Oct–May 8am–4.30pm; free) in the fourteenth century, as a bastion against raids from the north; it's now a romantic, crumbling ruin, opposite the train station. Traditionally, warnings of attack came from the north side of town, from the site of the beacon tower on **Beacon Hill**, from where you'll get good views of the surroundings. To get there, head up Fell Lane, from Meeting House Lane, beyond the bus station (it takes around an hour, there and back). The town itself is at its best in the narrow streets, arcades and alleys off **Market Square**, and around **St Andrew's** churchyard, whose so-called "Giant's Grave" is actually a collection of pre-Norman crosses and "hogsback" tombstones.

Practicalities

Trains from Manchester, London, Glasgow and Edinburgh pull into Penrith Station, five minutes' walk south of Market Square and Middlegate. The **bus station** is on Albert Street, behind Middlegate, and has regular services to Patterdale, Keswick, Cockermouth, Carlisle and Alston. The **tourist office** on Middlegate (April–July & Sept Mon–Sat 9.30am–5pm, Sun 1–4.45pm; Aug Mon–Sat 9.30am–6pm, Sun 1–5.45pm; Oct–March Mon–Fri 10am–4pm, Sat 10.30–4pm; ⓣ01768/867466, ⓦwww.visiteden.co.uk) shares its seventeenth-century schoolhouse premises with a small local museum; staff can help you find **accommodation**. The bulk of the B&Bs line Victoria Road, the continuation of King Street running south from Market Square: *Victoria Guest House*, at no. 3 (ⓣ01768/863823, ⓦwww.vicguesthouse.co.uk; no credit cards; ❷), and *Blue Swallow*, at no. 11 (ⓣ01768/866335, ⓦwww.blueswallow.co.uk; no credit cards; ❷), are the two most convenient choices. The *George Hotel*, on Devonshire Street by Market Square (ⓣ01768/862696, ⓦwww.georgehotelpenrith.co.uk; ❺), is a central old coaching inn with attractive prices, cosy wood-panelled lounges and a decent bar. Or try *The Limes* at Redhills (ⓣ01768/863343; ❸), one and a half miles west of town, a comfortable Victorian house in a rural setting.

For **food**, the fantastically stocked J. & J. Graham's deli-grocery in Market Square can't be beaten. Otherwise, there's inexpensive tapas at *Costa's*, 9 Queen St (ⓣ01768/895550), or elegant dining at *Passepartout*, 51 Castlegate (ⓣ01768/865852; dinner only, closed Mon). *Ruhm*, 15 Victoria Rd, combines a gallery displaying art and ceramics with a cheery continental café. Penrith is the regional **arts and music** hub, and Eden Arts (ⓣ01768/899444, ⓦwww.edenarts.co.uk) can provide full details of events in and around town. **Edenfest**, a three-day music festival, takes place every summer (usually Aug) in the Deer Park, off the A6 at Brougham, while one of the more unusual shows is **Potfest in the Pens**, an annual exhibition of ceramics in the sheep and cattle auctions mart, just outside town.

Around Penrith

Several attractions lie close to town, the nearest being **Brougham Castle** (daily: April–Sept 10am–6pm; Oct 10am–5pm; £2.50; EH), a mile and a half south of Penrith by the River Eamont. Passed down through the influential Clifford family, the castle overlaps the site of a Roman fort and contains a collection of tombstones commemorating Britons who adopted Roman customs and the Latin language.

Slightly further out, three miles southwest of town, reached from either the A66 or A592, is **Dalemain** (Easter to mid-Oct Mon–Thurs & Sun 10.30am–5pm; £5.50; gardens only £3.50; ⓦwww.dalemain.com). This country house, set in ample grounds, started life in the twelfth century as a fortified tower, but has subsequently been added to by every generation, culminating with a Georgian facade grafted onto a largely Elizabethan house. There's the usual run of imposing public rooms, while the medieval courtyard and Elizabethan great barn doubled as the grim schoolroom and dormitory of Lowood School in the TV adaptation of Charlotte Brontë's Jane Eyre.

However, top local attraction is undoubtedly **Rheged** (daily 10am–5.30pm; ⓦwww.rheged.com; free) at Redhills on the A66, a couple of minutes' drive from the M6 (junction 40); bus #X4/X5/X50 between Penrith and Keswick stops outside. Billed as Britain's largest earth-covered building, it takes its name from the ancient kingdom of Cumbria and features a spectacular atrium-lit underground visitor centre, which fills you in on the region's culture and history by way of exhibitions, local art and craft displays and family activities. There's also a giant-format cinema screen showing *Rheged: The Movie*, documenting a Cumbrian journey through time (£5.50); as well as the separate **National Mountaineering Exhibition** (same times; £5.50; Ⓦwww.mountain-exhibition.co.uk), presenting an entertaining history of mountain-climbers and climbing, from the Lake District to Everest. Three other big-screen presentations – *Everest, The Movie*; *The Living Sea*; and *Mysteries of Egypt* – also play here several times daily (all £5.50), adding up to five separate attractions, for which there are discounted combo tickets available (£9.50 to £19.50); it's wise to buy movie tickets on arrival to be sure of a viewing.

Appleby-in-Westmorland

One-time county town of Westmorland, **APPLEBY-IN-WESTMORLAND** is protected on three sides by a loop in the River Eden. The fourth was defended by the now privately owned **Appleby Castle** (Easter–Sept daily 10am–6pm; £5), whose Norman keep was restored by Lady Anne Clifford, who, after her father's death in 1605, spent 45 years trying to claim her rightful inheritance. Opening hours at the castle are a bit erratic, and it's closed throughout the winter, but the entrance fee lets you see the keep, moat and children's animal playground, and there are walks through the 25-acre grounds. Lady Anne also founded the lovely **almshouses** on Boroughgate, the town's backbone, which runs from High Cross, former site of the cheese market outside the castle, to Low Cross, previously a butter market but now home of the general Saturday market. **St Lawrence's Church**, at Low Cross, holds the tombs of Lady Anne Clifford and her mother. The tourist office (see below) can give you a map and a short walk guide, which takes you around all the local points of interest.

The town is usually peaceful, but changes its character completely in June when the **Appleby Horse Fair** takes over nearby Gallows' Hill, as it has done since 1750. Britain's most important gypsy gathering, it draws hundreds of chrome-plated caravans and more traditional horse-drawn "bow-tops", as well as the vehicles of tinkers, New-Age travellers and sightseers. Historically, the main day of the fair was the second Wednesday of June (the official day for horse trading), but today most of the action (including road racing, hair-raising stunts and fortune-telling) and trading takes place between the previous Sunday and the Tuesday, culminating on the Tuesday evening with trotting races at Holme Farm field. The whole week gets the full support of the local council but only some of the residents, many complaining about the disruption and the boisterous revelry.

Practicalities

The **Settle to Carlisle railway** is the best way to get to Appleby, although **bus services** from Penrith are frequent enough. The **tourist office**, in the Moot Hall on Boroughgate (April–Oct Mon–Sat 9.30am–5pm, Sun noon–4pm; Nov–March Mon–Thurs 10am–noon, Fri & Sat 10am–3pm; Ⓣ017683/51177, Ⓦwww.applebytown.org.uk), is ten minutes' walk from the station.

During the horse fair, **accommodation** is scarce; if you're planning to visit at this time, book well in advance. There's a clutch of places on Bongate, 500yd from town, over the river from Low Cross, then south along the Brough road: *Old Hall Farm* (Ⓣ017683/51773; no credit cards; ❷), signposted off the road, is a very friendly place, while the *Royal Oak*, further out on Bongate

(Ⓣ017683/51463, Ⓦwww.mortal-man-inns.co.uk; ❺) has some comfortable rooms in an aged inn. The top hotel in town is the *Tufton Arms* on Market Square (Ⓣ017683/51593; ❻). The closest **campsite** is the *Wild Rose* (with swimming pool) three miles south at Ormside (Ⓣ017683/51077); a similar distance to the north, the quiet hamlet of Dufton has the nearest **youth hostel** (Ⓣ0870/770 5800, Ⓔdufton@yha.org.uk; dorm beds £10.25; closed Wed year-round, plus Tues in April, May, Sept & Oct, & Nov–Easter).

There is no shortage of places to eat, and the old **pubs** tend to be the most atmospheric places: the *Tufton Arms* dishes up generous bar meals and has a more formal restaurant where you can tuck into fell-bred Cumbrian lamb and other joys. The *Royal Oak*, meanwhile, is renowned for its Cumberland sausages. Otherwise *Lady Anne's Pantry*, 9 Bridge St (closed Sun in winter), is a good **café**, and there's tea and cakes too in the Courtyard Gallery, 32 Boroughgate (closed Mon), an arts and crafts store in an ancient granary. The *Stag Inn* at Dufton (where the hostel is) is an enjoyable country inn with a beer garden, and it's worth the five-mile drive south to **Sandford** to the *Sandford Arms* for its excellent bar meals and more formal restaurant.

Northeast to Alston

The main routes north from Penrith are the M6 and the rail line to Carlisle, but if you're heading for Hadrian's Wall the A686 provides an alternative transmoor route, via **Alston**. Various bus services follow the route, many passing through Alston from Penrith, with onward services to Teesdale, Durham and Newcastle. Having your own transport gives you the opportunity to make a couple of detours along the way, with the first diversion to the prehistoric stone circle known as **Long Meg and her Daughters**. Standing outside a ring of stones nearly 400ft in diameter, Long Meg is the tallest stone at 18ft and has a profile like the face of an austere old lady. The stone family, said by some to be a coven of witches turned to stone by a magician, is just outside Little Salkeld, off the A686, six miles north of Penrith and just over a mile's walk from Langwathby on the Settle to Carlisle railway.

Back on the main road, at **MELMERBY**, make a point of stopping at the *Village Bakery* (daily until 5pm), whose proprietor's enthusiasm for his wood-fired brick oven has sparked interest in such matters in some of the most fashionable restaurants in the country. Wonderful, inexpensive breakfasts, lunches and teas are served.

Having covered an initial stretch of smooth vales and aromatic pine woods, the road then winds steeply up the bracken-strewn slopes of **Hartside Top**. Its 1900-feet-high bulk marks the western edge of the Pennines and has a welcome café at its summit (closed Nov–March).

Alston

Seven miles beyond Hartside Top, **ALSTON** commands the head of the South Tyne Valley. It no longer has a market to back up its claim to being the highest market town in England, but still has its market cross, beside the cobbled curve of the steep main road, Front Street, which is lined with cottages, shops, a tearoom or two and several cosy pubs. Alston's parish **church of St Augustine**, at the bottom of the street, is of some interest for the history of the Derwentwater Clock inside. It belonged to the local landowner and Jacobite rebel James Radcliffe who was beheaded for treason in 1716, followed 48 years later by his brother Charles Radcliffe – the last traitor to be decapitated – after which his heirs bequeathed the clock to the church. The town's Congregational Church, on The Butts, 100yd (signposted) down a lane from the market cross, is now **Gossipgate Gallery** (Easter–Oct Wed–Sat 10am–5pm, Sun 11am–5pm; Nov, Dec & mid-Feb to Easter Sat & Sun 11am–4.30pm), specializing in local arts and crafts; there's a nice coffee shop inside.

The town's also of note for the narrow-gauge **South Tynedale Railway** (Easter week, July & Aug daily; rest of the year Sat & Sun only; £5 return, day-ticket £12.50; ⓣ01434/382828, ⓦwww.strps.org.uk), whose steam engines follow the route of an old coal-carrying branch of the Carlisle to Newcastle line. The line runs for around three miles to Kirkhaugh on the Pennine Way (60min round-trip from Alston), a handy starting point for the twelve-mile walk north to Greenhead on Hadrian's Wall.

The South Tynedale **train station** lies just down the Hexham road, five minutes' walk from the centre, where the **tourist office** is inside the Town Hall at the bottom of Front Street (Easter–Oct Mon–Sat 10am–5pm, Sun 10am–4pm; Nov–Easter Mon & Wed–Sat 11am–2.30pm; ⓣ01434/382244, ⓦwww.alstonmoor.com). Vegetarian *Nentholme Guest House*, on The Butts next to Gossipgate Gallery (ⓣ01434/381523, ⓦwww.nentholme.co.uk; no credit cards; ❸), is one of the best **B&Bs**; there are also rooms at the *Angel Inn* on Front Street (ⓣ01434/381363; no credit cards; ❷), a nice old seventeenth-century pub serving bar meals (not Tues). Alston's **youth hostel** (ⓣ0870/770 5668, ⓔalston@yha.org.uk; dorm beds £10.25; closed Nov–Easter, and Wed & Thurs in April, May, Sept & Oct) is just five minutes' walk south of the centre (signposted off the Penrith road as you approach town). You can **camp** centrally at *Tyne Willows* (ⓣ01434/382515; closed Nov–Easter), by the train station behind the Texaco garage.

There are other good accommodation and eating possibilities out of town. A couple of miles east on the **Nenthead** road, the *Lovelady Shield Country House* (ⓣ0871/288 1345, ⓦwww.lovelady.co.uk; ❽ including dinner) is a beautiful Georgian establishment that serves excellent food. Or you can drive the four miles southeast to **Garrigill** (also on the Pennine Way from Alston), a cute hamlet set around a green, where the *George & Dragon* has flagstoned floors, a roaring fire, real ale and bar meals. Nearby *Ivy House* (ⓣ01434/382501, ⓦwww.garrigill.com; ❷) has B&B rooms and offers **llama trekking** (from £16) to nearby Thortergill Force.

Carlisle and around

The county capital of Cumbria and its only city, **CARLISLE** is also the repository of much of the region's history, its strategic location having been fought over for more than 2000 years. The original Celtic settlement was superseded by a Roman town, whose first fort was raised here in 72 AD. Carlisle thrived during the construction of Hadrian's Wall and then, long after the Romans had gone, the Saxon settlement was repeatedly fought over by the Danes and the Scots – the latter losing it eventually to the Normans. The struggle with the Scots defined the very nature of Carlisle as a border city: William Wallace was repelled in 1297 and Robert the Bruce eighteen years later, but Bonnie Prince Charlie's troops took Carlisle in 1745 after a six-day siege, holding it for only six weeks before surrendering to the Duke of Cumberland, who bombarded the city with cannon dragged from Whitehaven.

It's not surprising, then, that Carlisle still trumpets itself as the "great border city", and it's well worth taking a day or two to explore its compact centre and

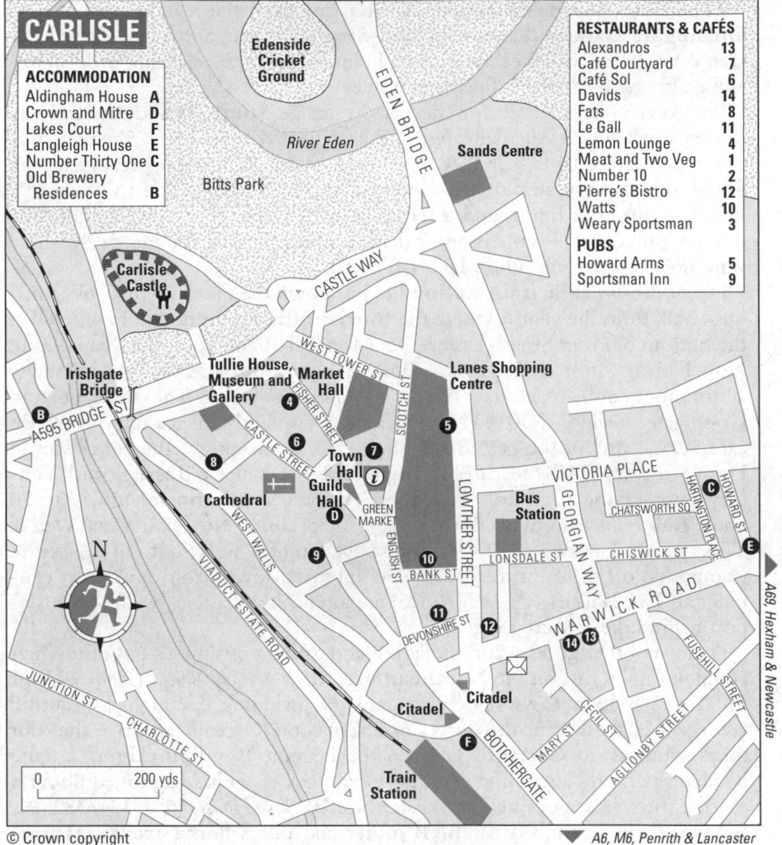

visit the trio of top-class sights: **cathedral**, **castle** and **Tullie House Museum**. If you've a couple of days to spare you can tour the locality: nearby **Talkin Tarn**, the ruins of **Lancercost Priory** and the only surviving bit of Hadrian's Wall in Cumbria, at **Birdoswald Fort**, are all worth a stop. Heading on, Edinburgh is under two hours north, while Carlisle also is terminus of the historic Settle to Carlisle Railway.

Arrival, information and accommodation

From either the **train station** (just off Botchergate, outside the Citadel) or the **bus station** (off Lowther Street, parallel to English Street), it's a five-minute walk to the **tourist office** in the Old Town Hall on Green Market (June–Aug Mon–Sat 9.30am–5.30pm, Sun 10.30am–4pm; March–May, Sept–Oct Mon–Sat 9.30am–5pm, Sun 10.30am–4pm; Nov–Feb Mon–Sat 10am–4pm; ⓣ01228/625600, ⓦwww.historic-carlisle.org.uk). You can book accommodation here, pick up a map and access the **Internet**. Ask, too, about the **guided tours** in summer (usually £3), which highlight varying aspects of the city – medieval and modern Carlisle, say, or a tour of sights associated with Woodrow Wilson, 28th president of the United States, whose mother was born in Carlisle.

Most of the budget **accommodation** is east of the tourist office, concentrated in a conservation area in the streets between Victoria Place and Warwick Road.

B&Bs, guest houses and hotels

Aldingham House 1 Eden Mount, Stanwix ⓣ01228/522554, ⓦwww.aldinghamhouse.co.uk. Superior B&B accommodation in a refined town house, a 10min walk from the centre over Eden Bridge. Three large, luxuriously appointed rooms with glorious beds, crisp linen, thick towels and superb bathrooms, plus a delightful lounge and garden, and memorable breakfasts – Aga-cooked local sausages and bacon, pancakes and fruit smoothies. ❺

Crown and Mitre English St, Green Market ⓣ01228/525491, ⓦwww.crownandmitre-hotel-carlisle.com. Refurbished Edwardian hotel in an excellent central location, with parking, indoor pool and whirlpool spa. Reduced weekend rates available on request. ❻

Lakes Court Hotel Court Square ⓣ01228/531951, ⓦwww.lakescourthotel.co.uk. Right by the train station, with smart and spacious rooms in a renovated Victorian building. Superior rooms offer a bit more space for your money, and weekend rates typically knock off about ten percent. ❺

Langleigh House 6 Howard Place ⓣ01228/530440, ⓦwww.langleighhouse.co.uk. Modest, but nicely presented, town house B&B with eight rooms, including a family room that sleeps four. Parking. No credit cards. ❷

Number Thirty One 31 Howard Place ⓣ01228/597080, ⓦwww.number31.freeservers.com. Grand Victorian house offering comfort in three well-appointed rooms named after their colour schemes, blue, green or yellow. Dinner (£20) is by arrangement. ❺

Youth hostel

Old Brewery Residences Bridge Lane, Caldewgate ⓣ0870/770 5752, ⓔdee.carruthers@unn.ac.uk. Summer-only (July & Aug) YHA accommodation, just west of the town centre (take the A595, and it's on the right past the castle), in university halls of residence. Dorm beds £14.

The City

Directly opposite the train station stands the **Citadel**, its twin drum towers and battlemented gatehouses framing the main thoroughfare of English Street. The original Citadel was erected on the orders of Henry VIII as he revamped the city defences – today's is a nineteenth-century pastiche, housing council offices, but effective nonetheless as a symbolic entrance to the city centre. English Street is pedestrianized as far as the expansive **Green Market** square, formerly heart of the medieval city, though a huge fire in 1392 destroyed its buildings and layout. The Lanes shopping centre on the east side of the square – its "alleys" lit through a cast-iron-and-glass roof – stands where the medieval city's lanes once ran. Otherwise, the only historic survivors are the **market cross** (1682), the Elizabethan former **Town Hall** behind it, which now houses the tourist office and, at the southern end of Fisher Street, the timber-framed **Guildhall** (1405). Although much restored, the Guildhall contains a small museum (Easter–Sept Tues–Sun noon–4.30pm; free) of guild and civic artefacts – Carlisle's eight historical trade guilds each had a meeting room in the hall.

The rest of the sights lie up Castle Street, which runs between Green Market and the castle itself. It's only a few steps along to **Carlisle Cathedral** (Mon–Sat 7.30am–6.15pm, Sun 7.30am–5pm; £2 donation requested), founded in 1122 but embracing a considerably older heritage. Christianity was established in sixth-century Carlisle by St Kentigern (often known as St Mungo), who became the first bishop and patron saint of Glasgow. The cathedral's sandstone bulk has endured the ravages of time and siege: Parliamentarian troops during the Civil War destroyed all but two powerful arches of the original eight bays of the Norman nave, but there's still much to admire in the ornate fifteenth-century choir stalls and the glorious **East Window**, which features some of the finest pieces of fourteenth-century stained glass in the country (although two-thirds of it is a faithful nineteenth-century restoration). In the northwest corner of the nave, steps lead down to the **Treasury**, containing glittering chalices and communion sets, and Henry VIII's charter of the foundation of the Dean and Chapter in 1541. Opposite the main entrance, the reconstructed **Fratry**, or monastic building, houses the cathedral library, while its undercroft doubles as the *Prior's Kitchen*, a daytime café (Mon–Sat 10am–4pm) aptly using space that was once the monks' dining hall.

For more on Carlisle's history, head for the **Tullie House Museum and Art Gallery** (Mon–Sat 10am–5pm, Sun noon–5pm; Nov–March closes at 4pm; £5.20; Ⓦwww.tulliehouse.co.uk), reached up Castle Street or through the cathedral grounds, via Abbey Street. This takes a highly imaginative approach to Carlisle's turbulent past, with special emphasis put on life on the edge of the Roman Empire – climbing a reconstruction of part of Hadrian's Wall, you learn about catapults and stone-throwers, while other sections elaborate on domestic life, work and burial practices. There's also plenty on the Jacobite siege of 1745, as well as a dramatic attempt to convey the intensity of the feuds between the "Reivers" – border families who, from the fourteenth to the seventeenth century, lived beyond the jurisdiction of the Scottish and English authorities in the so-called "Debatable Lands". The Rotunda provides castle views from its exterior deck, while down in the underground Millennium Gallery are innovative displays devoted to local geology, archeology and architecture, contrasted with a glass "Whispering Wall" in which are embedded recordings of stories and tales by the locals themselves. There's also free entrance to the **art gallery** at Tullie House, which has a selection of pre-Raphaelite paintings and stages changing exhibitions of contemporary arts and crafts. Meanwhile the adjacent **Tullie Old House** (also free) contains assorted paintings, china and other exhibits, including a diverting Gallery of Childhood. The café here is pleasant, too, with terrace seating overlooking the gardens.

A public walkway from outside Tullie House, or the eye-catching Irishgate Bridge – incorporating design elements from the city's former medieval Irish Gate – cross Castle Way to **Carlisle Castle** (daily: Easter–Oct 9.30am–6pm; Nov–Easter 10am–4pm; £3.50; EH). This was originally built by William Rufus on the site of a Celtic hillfort, though having now clocked up over nine hundred years of continuous military use, the castle has undergone considerable changes. These are most evident in its outer bailey, which is filled with fairly modern buildings named after battles from the Napoleonic Wars and World War I. Apart from the gatehouse, with its reconstructed warden's quarters, it's the **inner bailey** surrounding the keep that's the real draw. It was here, in 1568, that Elizabeth I kept Mary Queen of Scots as her "guest". There's a **Military Museum** located in the former armoury, but much more interesting are the excellent displays in the **Keep**, and the elegant heraldic carvings made by prisoners in a second-floor alcove. The castle was recaptured from Bonnie Prince Charlie's troops in 1745, but the story of "the licking stone" in the dungeon providing moisture for the parched Scottish prisoners is probably apocryphal. More credible is the claim that they were the first to sing "You'll take the high road and I'll take the low road", referring to their poor prospects of returning to Scotland alive. **Guided tours** of the castle (Easter–Oct daily; ask at the entrance; an extra £1.60) help bring the history to life. Don't leave without climbing to the battlements for a view of the Carlisle rooftops.

Eating, drinking and entertainment

Carlisle and its surroundings has a good selection of **cafés** and **restaurants** – better, in fact, than anywhere else in Cumbria, so if you're staying the night you'll be able to treat yourself. Decent **pubs** in the centre include the *Howard Arms*, 107 Lowther St, extravagantly tiled on the outside and with nice little snug rooms and real ale inside; and the *Sportsman Inn* on Heads Lane (at the back of Marks and Spencer), a cosy old local – one of the oldest in the city – backing on to St Cuthbert's churchyard. For a drive out to the country, head for the *Near Boot* at Tarraby, a mile and a half east of Carlisle, which serves Cumbrian real ales and good pub food. Cultural **entertainment** revolves around the concerts, plays, performances, talks, exhibitions and workshops at Tullie House or the associated Stanwix Arts Theatre on Brampton Road (box office ⓣ01228/534664).

Cafés and café-bars

Café Courtyard Treasury Court. Enter through the gates on Scotch or Fisher streets to find this hidden-away café, a really nice place to sit out when the sun shines. Sandwiches, salads and light meals form the mainstay of the menu.

Café Sol Castle St, opposite the cathedral. Funky little café-bar serving good-value breakfasts, gourmet sandwiches and *panini* melts. At weekends you can drink here until midnight.

Fats 48 Abbey St. Where the students do their socializing – a stripped-down, contemporary café-bar near the cathedral serving sandwiches and *nachos*.

Le Gall Devonshire St. Café-bar with a brasserie-diner style menu, popular for a late-night drink or Sunday brunch.

Watts Victorian Coffee Shop 11 Bank St. Traditional coffee-house with a wide range of roasted beans and a couple of outdoor tables.

Restaurants

Alexandros 68 Warwick Rd ⓣ01228/592227. Country Greek specialities, from dips, salads and stuffed vegetables to chargrilled meats and seafood. Meze platters provide a good mix of dishes, and there's a budget two-course lunch deal. Closed all Sun, plus Mon lunch. Moderate.

Davids 62 Warwick Rd ⓣ01228/523578. Formal Modern British restaurant that fuses flavours to great effect, drawing on Asian and Mediterranean ingredients for its seasonally changing offerings. Lunch is cheaper and set mid-week menus provide good value for money. Dinner only, closed Sun & Mon. Expensive.

The Lemon Lounge 18 Fisher St ⓣ01228/546363. Easy-going cellar bistro with a sun-trap outdoor terrace, where you can roam the gastronomic world – tapas and dips, Thai green curry, Mediterranean salads, burgers or even a local "tattie pot". It's inexpensive at lunch; prices rise slightly at night. Moderate.

Meat and Two Veg Laughingstock, Crosby, 4 miles east of Carlisle ⓣ01228/573111. There's nothing jokey about the food here, which is refined contemporary British (menu changes monthly) served in a minimalist setting, but the name reflects the laidback atmosphere and warm service. Garden seating in summer for fantastic Pennine views. Dinner only, closed Sun & Mon. Expensive.

Number 10 10 Eden Mount ⓣ01228/524183. Very agreeable town-house restaurant that many rate as the best in the city, serving a seasonally changing Modern English menu. The welcoming service makes for a highly relaxed night out. Dinner only, closed Sun & Mon. Expensive.

Pierre's Bistro 6a Lowther St ⓣ01228/515111. Classic bistro dishes – grilled goats' cheese, mussels, lamb with rosemary, salmon en croute etc. Prices drop dramatically at lunchtime, when three courses are just £6, while Thursday night usually sees Mexican specials. Closed Sun & Mon, and Tues lunch. Moderate.

The Weary Sportsman Castle Carrock, Brampton, 8 miles east of Carlisle ⓣ01228/670230, ⓦwww.weary-sportsman-inn.com. The inn with the "wow" factor – traditional eighteenth-century on the outside, utterly contemporary inside, with a sleek designer bar and conservatory, and fashionable food, from steak and ale pie to chilli prawns with Thai spices. No lunch Mon. Moderate.

Around Carlisle

Eight miles east of Carlisle, the market town of **BRAMPTON** is at the centre of several outlying attractions that can make a fine day's tour from the city.

Two miles south of Brampton, on the B6413 (Castle Carrock road), **Talkin Tarn** is the city's traditional bolthole, a pretty lake set within 120 acres of farm and woodland. There's a shop and tearoom here, with bike rental, and many locals come out in the summer to sail, kayak or fish. At nearby Talkin village, the *Blacksmith's Arms* on the green make a good lunch or drinks stop.

A similar distance to the northeast of Brampton (just north of the A69, at Low Row), the highly attractive ruins of **Lanercost Priory** (Easter–Sept daily 10am–6pm; Oct daily 10am–5pm; £2.50; EH), occupy a lovely spot in deep countryside. The Augustinian priory dates from 1166 – though carved stones found here date back to Roman times – and you can view the remains of a medieval undercroft and the Prior's Tower, with its brick fireplace and ovens *in situ*. The adjacent priory church (daily 9am–dusk) is still used as the district's parish church; the nearby *Abbey Bridge Inn* is the local hostelry.

A little further east, signposted from the A69 five miles beyond Brampton and fifteen from Carlisle – **Birdoswald Fort** (March–Nov daily 10am–5.30pm; £3; half-price for EH members; Ⓦwww.birdoswaldromanfort.org.uk) is the area's real highlight. One of sixteen forts along Hadrian's Wall, it has all tiers of the Roman structure intact, the defences comprising an earth ditch, a large section of masonry wall, and the trench and mound foundations behind. The east gateway, in particular, is one of the best preserved on the wall, while a drill hall and other buildings have been excavated. An informative visitor centre fleshes out the historic background, and then you can walk the third of a mile to the nearby **Harrow's Scar Milecastle** for some spectacular views. There's a tearoom and picnic area at the fort, while the fort's residential study centre is available to overnight hikers and others as a summer-only **youth hostel** (Ⓣ0870/770 6124, Ⓔgreenhead@yha.org.uk; dorm beds £11.50), open mid-July to first week of September only.

The **Hadrian's Wall Bus** (see p.1086) leaves Carlisle three times daily in summer (June to mid-Sept, plus Sun in April, May & Oct), calling at Brampton (20min), Lanercost (30min) and Birdoswald (40min), before running on to the the rest of the Hadrian's Wall sights. The rest of the year, the #685 from Carlisle runs to Brampton and Gilsland (the latter a two-mile walk from Birdoswald).

Travel details

Buses

For information on all local and national bus services, contact Traveline Ⓣ0870/608 2608, Ⓦwww.traveline.org.uk.

Carlisle to: Appleby (1 daily; 1hr 15min); Keswick (4 daily; 1hr 30min); Lancaster (4 daily; 1hr 10min); London (3 daily; 5hr 30min); Manchester (2 daily; 2hr 30min); Newcastle (hourly; 2hr 30min); Whitehaven (hourly; 1hr 30min); Windermere/Bowness (3 daily; 2hr 20min).

Kendal to: Ambleside (hourly; 40min); Cartmel (7 daily; 1hr); Grasmere (hourly; 1hr); Keswick (hourly; 1hr 30min); Lancaster (hourly; 1hr); Windermere/Bowness (hourly; 30min).

Keswick to: Ambleside (hourly; 1hr); Buttermere (2 daily; 30min); Carlisle (4 daily; 1hr 30min); Cockermouth (7 daily; 35min); Grasmere (hourly; 40min); Kendal (hourly; 1hr 30min); Manchester (1–3 daily; 3hr); Seatoller (9 daily; 30min); Whitehaven (5 daily; 1hr 30min); Windermere (hourly; 1hr).

Windermere to: Ambleside (up to 3 hourly; 15min); Carlisle (3 daily; 2hr 20min); Grasmere (hourly; 30min); Kendal (hourly; 30min); Keswick (hourly; 1hr); Lancaster (hourly; 1hr 45min); Manchester (3 daily; 3hr).

Trains

For information on all local and national rail services, contact National Rail Enquiries Ⓣ08457/484950, Ⓦwww.rail.co.uk.

Appleby-in-Westmorland to: Carlisle (6 daily; 40min).
Carlisle to: Appleby (6 daily; 40min); Barrow-in-Furness (5 daily; 2hr 20min); Edinburgh (8 daily; 1hr 40min); Lancaster (every 30–60min; 1hr); Leeds (Mon–Sat 8 daily, 3 on Sun; 2hr 40min); London (8 daily; 4hr 20min); Manchester (2 daily; 2hr 30min); Maryport (hourly; 40min); Newcastle (hourly; 1hr 20min–1hr 40min); Preston (21 daily; 1hr 20min–1hr 40min); Whitehaven (hourly; 1hr 10min).
Oxenholme (Lake District) to: Birmingham (6 daily; 2hr 30min–3hr); Carlisle (14 daily; 40–50min); London (5 daily; 3hr 30min–5hr); Manchester (1–5 daily; 1hr 40min); Penrith (14 daily; 30min); Preston (hourly; 30–40 min).
Windermere to: Kendal (hourly; 15min); Oxenholme (hourly; 20min).

12

Yorkshire

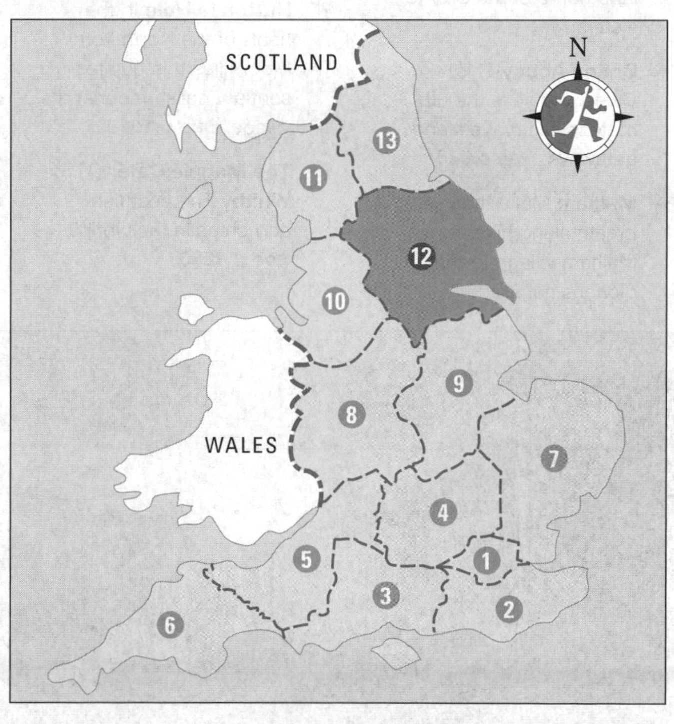

12 YORKSHIRE

CHAPTER 12

Highlights

* **National Museum of Photography, Film and Television, Bradford** The north's most hands-on museum has all there is to know about film, photography and TV. See p.934

* **Haworth** Bleak moorland home of the Brontë sisters. See p.937

* **Bolton Abbey** This Dales' village is the ultimate in luxury weekend getaways. See p.946

* **Malham** Make the breathtaking hike from Malham village to the glorious natural amphitheatre of Malham Cove. See p.950

* **York** From historic York Minster to the award-winning National Railway Museum, there's never a dull day in the north's most compelling city. See pp.976–993

* **Hutton le Hole** In the heart of the North York Moors lies this quintessential English moorland village. See p.1010

* **The Magpie Café, Whitby** The best fish and chips in the world? See p.1030

△ Malham

12

Yorkshire

Few visitors pass through **Yorkshire**, England's largest county, without spending time in history-soaked **York**, for centuries England's second city until the Industrial Revolution created new centres of power and influence. Famed primarily for its minster, the city is a comprehensive, if somewhat over-restored, ensemble of tiny medieval alleys, castle ruins, tucked-away churches, riverside gardens and top-notch museums. York's mixture of medieval, Georgian and Victorian architecture is mirrored in miniature in the prosperous north and east of the county by towns such as **Beverley**, centred on another soaring minster; **Richmond**, banked under a crag-bound castle; and **Ripon**, gathered around its honey-stoned cathedral. **Knaresborough** shares similar attributes, but is overshadowed by the faded gentility of neighbouring **Harrogate**, a spa town geared these days towards the conference trade rather than health-seeking visitors. The Yorkshire coast, too, retains something of the grandeur of the days when its towns were the first to promote themselves as resorts: places such as **Bridlington** and **Scarborough** boomed in the nineteenth century and again in the postwar period, though these days they're living on past glories. Instead, it's in characterful places such as **Whitby** and **Robin Hood's Bay** – much smaller resorts with unspoiled historic centres – that the best of the coast is to be found.

The engine of growth during the Industrial Revolution was not in the north of the county, but in the south and west. By the nineteenth century, Leeds, Bradford, Sheffield and their satellites were the world's mightiest producers of **textiles** (an industry first nurtured by the monastic houses of the moors and dales) and of **steel**. Ruthless economic logic devastated the area in the last century, leaving only disused textile mills, abandoned steel- and heavy-engineering works, and great soot-covered civic buildings in cities battered by depression. However, a new vigour has infused South and West Yorkshire during the last decade, and the city-centre transformations of **Leeds** and **Sheffield** in particular have been remarkable. Both are now making open play for tourists with a series of high-profile attractions, while **Bradford** and its **National Museum of Photography, Film and Television** waylays people on their way to **Haworth**, birthplace of the Brontë sisters.

During even the worst of times, broad swathes of moorland survived above the slum- and factory-choked valleys, and it can come as a surprise to discover the amount of open countryside on Leeds' and Bradford's doorsteps. The **Yorkshire Dales**, to the northwest, form a lovely patchwork of stone-built villages, limestone hills, serene valleys and majestic heights. The whole area is covered by tracks, long-distance paths and old drove roads, most of them waymarked by the Yorkshire Dales National Park, which runs information centres

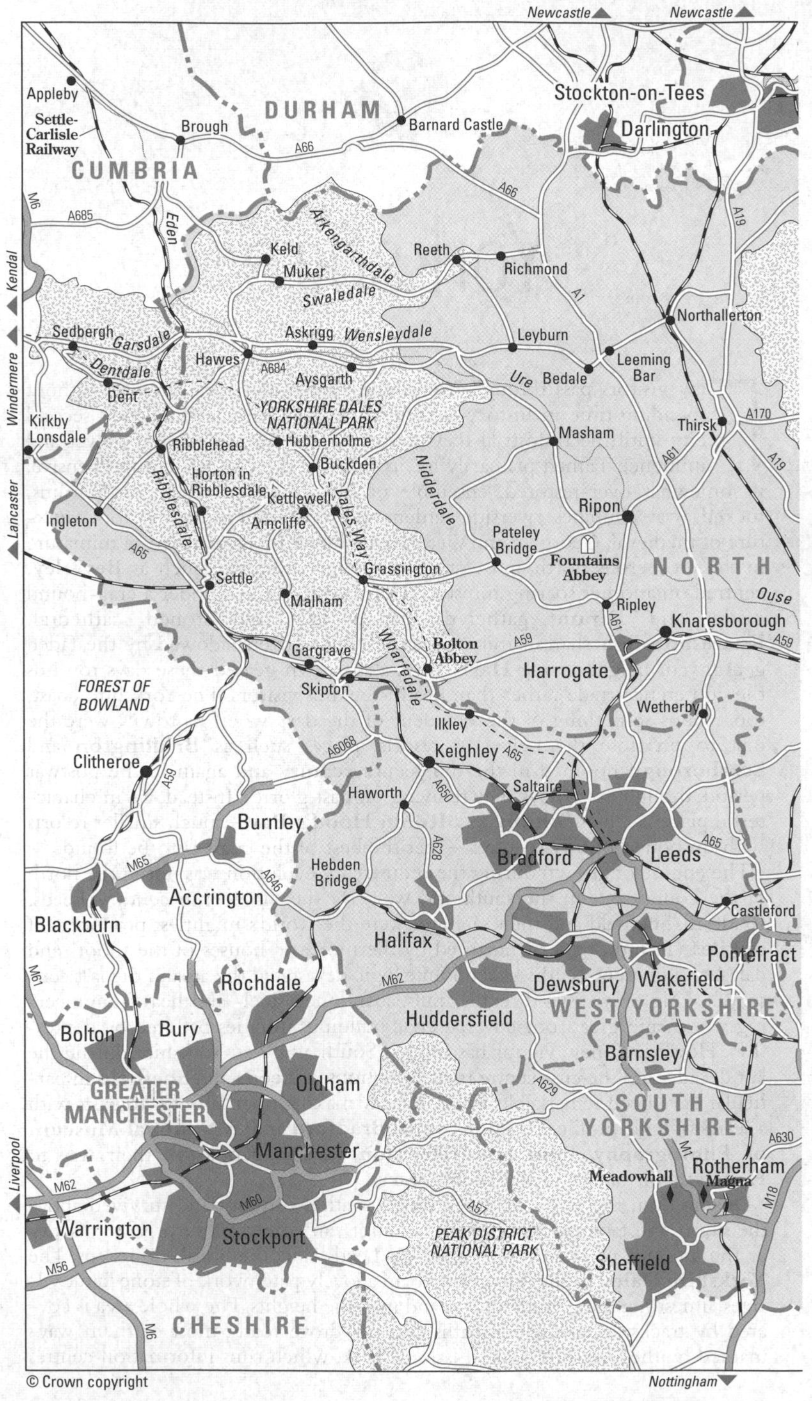
Newcastle
Newcastle
Appleby
Settle-Carlisle Railway
DURHAM
Stockton-on-Tees
Darlington
Brough
Barnard Castle
A66
CUMBRIA
M6
A685
Eden
Arkengarthdale
Keld
Muker
Swaledale
Reeth
Richmond
A1
A19
Kendal
Windermere
Sedbergh
Garsdale
Dentdale
Dent
Askrigg
Wensleydale
Hawes
A684
Aysgarth
Leyburn
Northallerton
Leeming Bar
Bedale
Ure
YORKSHIRE DALES NATIONAL PARK
Kirkby Lonsdale
Ribblehead
Hubberholme
Buckden
Masham
Thirsk
A170
Lancaster
Horton in Ribblesdale
Ribblesdale
Kettlewell
Dales Way
Arncliffe
Nidderdale
A61
Ripon
Ingleton
A65
Pateley Bridge
Fountains Abbey
NORTH
Grassington
Settle
Malham
Ripley
Ouse
Knaresborough
A59
Wharfedale
Bolton Abbey
Gargrave
Harrogate
FOREST OF BOWLAND
Skipton
Ilkley
Wetherby
A6068
Keighley
Clitheroe
A650
Saltaire
Haworth
A628
Burnley
Bradford
Leeds
M65
Hebden Bridge
A646
Accrington
Castleford
Blackburn
Halifax
Pontefract
M61
Rochdale
M62
Dewsbury
Wakefield
WEST YORKSHIRE
Huddersfield
Bolton
Bury
Barnsley
GREATER MANCHESTER
Oldham
A629
SOUTH YORKSHIRE
Liverpool
Manchester
M1
A630
Rotherham
Meadowhall
Magna
M18
M60
A57
Warrington
Stockport
PEAK DISTRICT NATIONAL PARK
Sheffield
M56
CHESHIRE
Nottingham

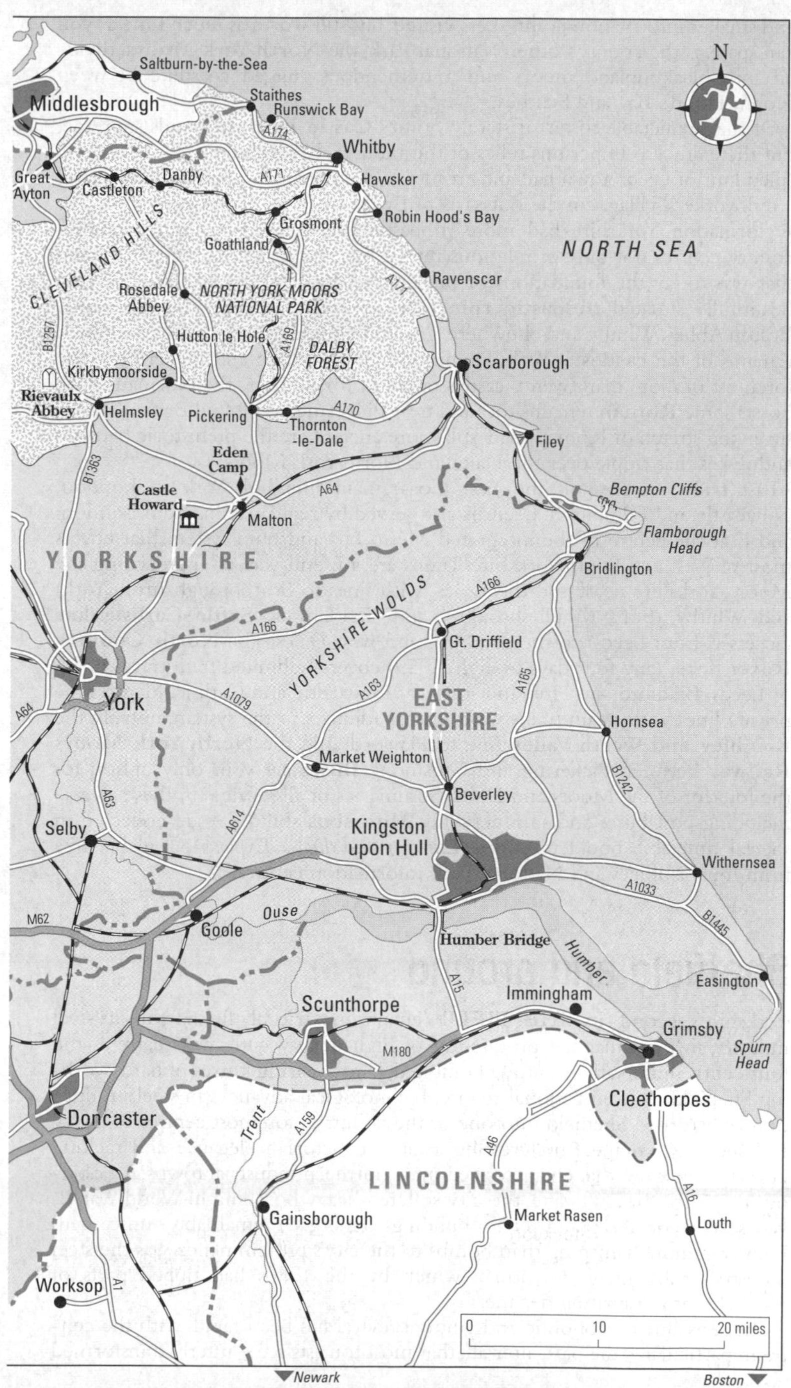

12

YORKSHIRE

and smaller information points. Less visited, but still worth as much time as you can spare, is the county's other National Park, the **North York Moors**, divided into bleak upland moors and a tremendous rugged coastline between Robin Hood's Bay and Staithes.

Of the predictable roster of stately homes **Castle Howard** stands supreme, but there are also imperious relics of the Industrial Revolution, from the civic splendour of Leeds' town hall and arcades to the Italianate pastiche of **Saltaire**, a millworkers' village on the outskirts of Bradford. In an earlier age, before the Reformation, Yorkshire had more monastic houses than any other English county, centres not only of religious retreat but also of a commercial acumen that was to lay the foundations of the region's great woollen industry. Many beautifully situated **monastic ruins** survive today at Fountains, Rievaulx, Bolton Abbey, Whitby and elsewhere, graceful counterpoints to the more solid remains of the **castles** at York, Richmond, Scarborough and Pickering – the foremost of more than twenty castles raised in Yorkshire by the Normans. York boasts some **Roman** remains too, and near Pickering you'll find Britain's finest surviving stretch of Roman road; still more ancient are the prehistoric barrows and dykes that ripple over the Dales and North York Moors.

Fast **train** services on the East Coast main line link York to London, Newcastle and Edinburgh. Leeds is also served by regular trains from London, and is at the centre of the integrated Metro bus and train system that covers most of West and South Yorkshire. Trains are a useful way of approaching the Moors, Yorkshire coast and the Dales, with lines to Scarborough (from York) and Whitby (from Middlesbrough), and the famous **Settle–Carlisle** line (accessed from Leeds) to the southern and west Dales. The **North Country Rover** ticket (any four days in eight; £59) covers unlimited train travel north of Leeds, Bradford and Hull and south of Newcastle and Carlisle. Picturesque private lines with steam trains make useful adjuncts to the system, notably the **Keighley and Worth Valley** line to Haworth and the **North York Moors Railway** between Pickering and Grosmont. **Buses** are your only option for the interior of the Moors and Dales. Summaries of all services in these areas – including post buses and summer-only **Moorsbus** shuttles – are collected in special timetable booklets (*Moors Explorer* and *Dales Explorer*), available free from tourist offices and National Park information centres.

Sheffield and around

Yorkshire's second city, **SHEFFIELD** remains inextricably linked with its steel industry, in particular the production of high-quality cutlery. As early as the fourteenth century, the carefully fashioned, hard-wearing knives of hard-working Sheffield enjoyed national repute. Technological advances in steel production later turned Sheffield into one of the country's foremost centres of heavy and specialist engineering, creating a city of Victorian elegance and racking poverty, a mixture that characterized most northern industrial towns. An obvious target for the Luftwaffe, the city suffered heavy bombing in World War II, yet several of its grand civic buildings emerged remarkably unscathed. However, more damaging than bombs to the city's pre-eminence was the steel industry's subsequent downturn, which by the 1980s had tipped parts of Sheffield into dispiriting decline.

The subsequent economic and cultural revival has been rapid, with the centre in particular – the part, after all, that most tourists see – utterly transformed by flagship architectural projects, from gardens to galleries. As an emerging city-break destination, Sheffield can't fail to surprise, and with the Peak District so close (over a third of the city lies within the boundary of the Peak District, see pp.686–707), it's easy to escape for the day. A glut of sports facilities (including the Ski Village, Europe's largest artificial ski resort) backs Sheffield's claim to be considered "National City of Sport". Meanwhile, the city's two universities and large student population (around 45,000) lend the alternative shopping, café and nightlife scene a welcome edge.

Steel, of course, still underpins much of what Sheffield is about. The city that gave the world *The Full Monty* – the black comedy about five former steel workers carving out a new career as a striptease act – also boasts **Meadowhall** shopping centre, located in an old steel works and billed as Europe's most successful mall. Museum collections tend to hone in the region's industrial heritage, which is complemented by the startling science-and-adventure exhibits at **Magna** built on a disused steel works at nearby **Rotherham**, the former coal and iron town a few miles northeast of the city.

Arrival, information and accommodation

Sheffield's **train station** is on the eastern edge of the city centre, by Sheffield Hallam University, with the bus and coach station, known as **Sheffield Interchange**, about two hundred yards to the north on Pond Street. Pay-and-display **parking** is signposted throughout the city from the ring road. You'll find the **tourist office** on Tudor Square (Mon–Thurs 10am–4pm, Fri 10.30am–4pm, Sat 9.30am–4pm; ⓣ0114/221 1900, ⓦwww.sheffieldcity.co.uk) easily enough, just five minutes' walk from the stations, near the Winter Gardens, and well equipped with brochures, maps and guides to the city.

Sheffield city centre is easy to make your way around on foot, and you only need public transport to reach a couple of the outlying museums, the Botanical Gardens and Meadowhall. Most local **buses** depart from the High Street, while the sleek, cheap **Supertram** system connects the city centre with Meadowhall (northeast), Middlewood (northwest) and Halfway (southeast). For fare and timetable information, visit the **Travel Information Centre** at the Interchange (Mon–Fri 8am–5.30pm, Sat 8.30am–5pm, Sun 9am–5pm). A one-day TravelMaster Pass (£4.95) gives unlimited travel on buses, trains and trams throughout South Yorkshire.

Sheffield has a fair amount of mid-range central **accommodation** – even so, the tourist office's free room-booking service can come in handy (ⓣ0114/201 1011), especially if you're looking for cheaper B&Bs on the outskirts. There's no youth hostel, though the university has accommodation available during the summer vacation.

Hotels and guest houses

Hotel Bristol Blonk St ⓣ0114/220 4000, ⓦwww.hotel-bristol.co.uk. Breezy, informal business hotel near the river, quays and markets. All rooms are en suite and stylishly kitted out, with TV/video, modem point and extra fold-down sofa bed. Parking. ❺

Cutlers George St ⓣ0114/273 9939, ⓦwww.cutlershotel.co.uk. Handily located city-centre inn, close to the theatres, with budget en-suite rooms, bistro and bar. Weekend rates shave around £10 off the price of a double/twin room. ❹

Hilton Victoria Quays, Furnival Rd ⓣ0114/252 5500, ⓦwww.hilton.com. Four-star hotel that makes superb use of its revitalized canalside site, with a range of leisure facilities. The standard mid-week rate is room only; special and weekend deals (two-night minimum) bring the price down considerably and usually include breakfast. ❺

Houseboat Hotels Victoria Quays ⓣ0114/244 4136 or 07974/590264, ⓦwww.houseboathotels.com. Something a little bit different – two moored houseboats, available by the night, very nicely styled, both with en-suite bathrooms, kitchens, TV and video. Tea and coffee is provided, continental breakfast can be arranged (£3 extra), parking is included, and there's use of the *Hilton*'s leisure centre. They're rented exclusively, for two people ❹ or four people ❺

Novotel 50 Arundel Gate ⓣ0114/278 1781, ⓦwww.novotel.com. Sleek business lodgings by the Winter Gardens – worth considering since there's a pool. ❺

Travel Inn Metro Angel St ⓣ0870/238 3324, ⓦwww.travelinn.co.uk. Few frills in this standard chain hotel, but you can't beat the price for convenient room-only accommodation. ❸

Westbourne House 25 Westbourne Rd, Broomhill ⓣ0114/266 0109, ⓦwww.westbournehousehotel.com. Victorian town house, a mile out of the centre (and 5min from the Botanical Gardens, or 10min from the bars and restaurants of Ecclesall Rd), with individually furnished, non-smoking rooms. ❺

Whitley Hall Elliott Lane, Grenoside, 4 miles north ⓣ0114/245 4444, ⓦwww.whitleyhall.com. Country house hotel with Elizabethan roots, accessible from the motorways or the city centre (A61 out of Sheffield; call for directions). Rooms are traditionally furnished (some four-posters, next price category up), and there's a restaurant. ❻

University accommodation

University of Sheffield ⓣ0114/222 6059, ⓦwww.sheffield.ac.uk. Variety of single rooms from around £15 per person – either with wash-basin or en-suite facilities – in the various student halls of residence. Available mid-June to mid-Sept only; small discount for stays of more than three nights. Essential to call in advance.

The City

New-look Sheffield is at its best around the landmark **Town Hall**, at the junction of Pinstone and Surrey streets. Completed in 1897, it's topped by the figure of Vulcan, the Roman god of fire and metalworking, and the facade sports a fine frieze depicting traditional Sheffield industries. The adjacent **Peace Gardens** feature a wide terrace (with outdoor café) above the lawns, monumental goblet cascades, and central water jets that whoosh up intermittently to send children giddy with delight. Rising to the east, a minute's walk away, is the main symbol of the city regeneration, the **Winter Gardens** (daily 8am–6pm; free), an arched steel-and-wood glasshouse almost 200 feet long and over 60 feet high. It's a stunning public space, filled with plants and shrubs – the central Norfolk pines will eventually touch the roof.

Sheffield's **Millennium Galleries** (Mon–Sat 10am–5pm, Sun 11am–5pm; free, visiting exhibitions £4; ⓦwww.sheffieldgalleries.org.uk) back on to the gardens and provide pedestrian access down to Arundel Gate, the station and the Cultural Industries Quarter. As well as visiting exhibitions, loaned by London's Victoria and Albert Museum among others, there are two permanent displays here, both specific to Sheffield and its heritage. In the **Metalworks Gallery** you can discover why the eighteenth-century city's natural endowments (a fast water supply, forests for charcoal, and gritstone deposits) ensured the rapid development of the cutlery industry. Not surprisingly, the gallery contains the most extensive collection of Sheffield cutlery in the world, and sixteenth-century knives and designer cleavers gleam from the display cases. There's also the highly diverting **Ruskin Gallery**, based on the collection founded by John Ruskin in 1875 to improve the working people of Sheffield. Their education must have been wonderfully eclectic if the collection is anything to go by – a library of classic nineteenth-century texts ("the working man's Bodleian") is complemented by an intriguing selection of watercolours, sketches, minerals, paintings, casts and medieval illuminated manuscripts.

An exit from the Millennium Galleries leads across Surrey Street to the **Graves Art Gallery** (Mon–Sat 10am–5pm; free), located on the top floor of the City Library. This leans most heavily towards nineteenth- and twentieth-century British artists, including Turner, Nash, Gwen John and the Pre-Raphaelites, but it holds some Impressionist works too, plus the odd Cezanne,

Gaugin, Miro, Picasso and Klee. To the side of the library, opposite the Winter Gardens, **Tudor Square** is another intelligently landscaped space, with the tourist office at one end and Sheffield's renowned **theatres** at the other.

The rest of central Sheffield divides into neat areas, touted rather grandly as quarters. Southeast of the Winter Gardens, clubs and galleries exist alongside arts and media businesses in the **Cultural Industries Quarter**. This contains the one high-profile casualty of the city redevelopment, namely the four giant stainless-steel drums on Paternoster Row that housed the now defunct National Centre for Popular Music. The unique building is currently owned by Sheffield Hallam University and will, in future, possibly house their student union or become a Cultural Studies Centre. However, the quarter still draws a local crowd to the **Showroom** cinema-and-bar complex across the road, and to the renowned **Site Gallery**, just up the road on Brown Street (Tues–Fri 11am–6pm, Sat 11am–5.30pm; free; ⓦwww.sitegallery.org), which specializes in photography and multimedia exhibitions.

North of the stations, near the River Don, **Castlegate** and its traditional **markets** are still undergoing redevelopment, while the spruced-up warehouses and cobbled towpaths in the neighbouring canal basin, **Victoria Quays**, house high-tech businesses, designer shops, several hotels and leisure facilities. Closer to the Town Hall, at the end of Fargate, the city's **Cathedral of St Peter and St Paul** retains elements of its fifteenth-century origins, though it's been restored on many occasions. Across from here on Church Street sits the **Cutler's Hall** of 1832, an imposing reminder of Sheffield's traditions. The Company of Cutlers was first established in 1624 to regulate the affairs of the cutlery industry, and this is the third hall on the site. Its silver collection is unrivalled, though viewing is by appointment only (ⓣ0114/272 8456; minimum group charge applies). South of the Town Hall, the pedestrianized **Moor Quarter** draws in shoppers, though it's the nearby **Devonshire Quarter**, centred on Division Street, that is the trendiest shopping area. At The Forum by Devonshire Green, thirty-odd retail outlets flog club- and skate-wear, retro clothing, music, applied art and baubles, while the café-bar here is a popular hang-out spot.

Other attractions are all on the city outskirts. A mile or so west, the **Mappin Art Gallery** in Weston Park and adjacent **City Museum** are currently under longterm restoration (due to re-open in 2005), though you could still make a case for coming out this side of the city to visit the lovely **Botanical Gardens** (Mon–Fri 8am–dusk, Sat & Sun 10am–dusk; free), where there are nineteen acres of Victorian landscaping, some impressively restored glass pavilions and a café-bar. There are two entrances – one on Clarkehouse Road (bus #50 or #59 from High St), the other on Thompson Road (buses #81–86 from High St). Closer in, fifteen minutes' walk north of the cathedral, the **Kelham Island Museum** on Alma Street (Mon–Thurs 10am–4pm, Sun 11am–4.45pm; £3.50), reveals the breadth of the city's industrial output, where exhibits range from a colossal twelve-thousand horsepower steam engine to a silver-plated penny-farthing made for the tsar of Russia. Many of the old machines are still working, arranged in period workshops where craftspeople demonstrate some of the finer points of cutlery production.

Rotherham: Magna

About six miles northeast of Sheffield, across the M1, **ROTHERHAM** sees itself as just as much a gateway to Yorkshire as its bigger neighbour. The town centre has been improved over recent years, and locals (and architectural arbiter Nikolaus Pevsner) point to its churches as its proudest feature. Certainly, the medieval parish church is particularly fine, while in the Chapel of Our Lady on Rotherham Bridge, the town has one of only four surviving examples in England of a medieval bridge chantry. For most visitors to the region, however, these pale in comparison with **Magna** (daily 10am–5pm; £8; Ⓦwww.magnatrust.org.uk), the UK's first science adventure centre, housed in the building of a former steel works on Sheffield Road (A6178), Templeborough, just off the M1 a mile from the Meadowhall shopping complex. You can get there on bus #69 from either Sheffield or Rotherham Interchanges, or it's a ten-minute taxi ride from Meadowhall's Supertram station. Signs from the M1 (junctions 33 or 34) direct drivers straight there.

The massive building offers four gadget-packed, themed **pavilions** around the four basic elements of earth, air, fire and water. You are invited to experience over a hundred interactive exhibits, including handling a mechanical digger, blasting a rock face, firing a water cannon, or investigating a twister. Although most of the centre is aimed at children, the half-hourly Big Melt will have everyone gripping onto the railings. An original arc furnace is used in a bone-shaking light and sound show, showing the moment when metal is transformed into white molten steel. For a recovery stop you can chill out in O2, an inflatable restaurant designed by Per Lindstrand, Richard Branson's balloon manufacturer.

Eating and drinking

Sheffield has plenty of great **café-bars** and good-value **restaurants**, all pretty adept at making a play for the student pound. The **pubs** listed below are those with a bit of character and staying power, but for the best insight into what makes Sheffield tick as a party destination take a night-time walk along **Division Street** and **West Street** where competing theme and retro bars go in and out of fashion. Students also frequent the bars and pubs of Broomhill and Ecclesall Road, but neither area is particularly central.

Cafés and café-bars

Azure Millennium Galleries, Arundel Gate. Stylish café-bar with a sunny roadside terrace under the galleries.

Blue Moon Café 2 St James St. Relax in the skylit dining room, next to the cathedral, and tuck into homemade vegetarian/vegan food, including pies, burritos, a cold-counter selection and organic beers. The noticeboard is a great source of information on what is happening in the city. Closes 8pm; closed Sun.

Eat Crucible Theatre, Tudor Sq, 55 Norfolk St. Everything from sandwiches and salads to sharing platters and bistro classics, with most things priced between £5 and £9. Food until 7.30pm; closed Mon.

The Forum 127–129 Division St. Long the mainstay of the Devonshire Quarter, the *Forum* has a great menu and laid-back clientele. A sun-terrace overlooks the green. Closed Sun.

Jules & Giovanna 1 Brown St. Lovely little deli-café by the Site Gallery, serving good coffee, Mediterranean snacks, panini, wraps, pastas and breakfast. Closes 5pm; closed Sun.

Lion's Lair 31 Burgess St. Former city-centre rocker-boozer turned bar-restaurant, a favourite with uptown types for good food.

Showroom 7 Paternoster Row. Part of the independent cinema complex, the relaxed *Showroom* has a café-restaurant on one side serving contemporary meals (pasta, stir-fries, grills), and a great bar on the other with a long see-and-be-seen window. Check out their week-night film-and-food offers.

Takapuna 52–54 West St. The cool crowd has moved out west to stylish *Takapuna*, for eating, greeting and drinking, with DJs and club nights an added incentive.

Twenty Two A 22a Norfolk Row. With a few outdoor tables on a cobbled backstreet, this little café is a nice find for breakfast, inventive sandwiches or more substantial meals like *mee goreng* (fried noodles) or sesame prawns. Closes 5pm; closed Sun.

Restaurants

Blue Room Brasserie 798 Chesterfield Rd, Woodseats ⓣ0114/255 2004. Treat yourself at this Modern British brasserie, south of the centre, that combines flavours and ingredients from around the world. Closed Sun dinner, & all Mon. Expensive.

Nonna's 539–541 Eccleshall Rd ⓣ0114/268 6166. Where the Sheffield beautiful hang out, a combination Italian café, wine-bar and restaurant with a great reputation. Moderate.

Pizza Volante 255 Glossop Rd ⓣ0114/273 9056. Rumbustious pasta and pizza place that's a hit with locals and students looking for quality on a budget. Inexpensive to Moderate.

Slammers 625 Eccleshall Rd ⓣ0114/268 0999. Seafood (and pretty much only seafood) is what's on offer in Sheffield's buzziest restaurant, with seared scallops, Thai crab cakes, salt-and-pepper squid, mussels, monkfish, lobster and other delights offered as starters or mains. Bring your own wine allowed Mon–Wed, but fully licensed. Expensive.

Trippet's Wine Bar 89 Trippets Lane ⓣ0114/278 0198. There's always a nice atmosphere in this unstuffy wine bar behind West Street. The bistro food is popular and there's live jazz and blues on occasion. Moderate.

Vietnamese Noodle Bar 200–202 London Rd ⓣ0114/258 3608. BYO place that's hugely popular for cheap Oriental eats – it pays to book ahead. Inexpensive.

Pubs

Bath Hotel 66 Victoria St. Timeless Victorian classic off Glossop Rd – no frills, but well-kept real ale and handsome original features.

Devonshire Cat 49 Wellington St, Devonshire Green. A big pub where the beer is the point, the whole point and nothing but the point. There's a beer menu on every table and good cheap food with drinks matched to every selection. For a bit more tradition, take a walk out (15min from the centre) to the *Fat Cat* 23 Alma St, the *Devonshire Cat*'s cosier, older sister, also famed for its umpteen real ales and imported bottles.

Frog & Parrot 94 Division St. A boisterous pub with big windows onto the Division Street scene, lots of beers (including the hellishly strong *Roger & Out*) and a good jukebox. Decent mix of locals and students.

Rutland Arms 86 Brown St. Victorian pub with one of the city's nicest beer gardens, just a minute from the *Showroom* cinema.

The Washington 79 Fitzwilliam St. A favoured muso's hangout, just two minutes across the green from Division St.

Nightlife, music and the arts

Friday's *Sheffield Telegraph* lists the week's performances, events, concerts and films. Also look out for the highly useful and entertaining *Dirty Stop Out's Guide* (£2.50; ⓦwww.dirtystopoutsguide.co.uk), a comprehensive tell-it-like-it-is listings and reviews booklet, available at the tourist office.

Clubs and live music venues

The Boardwalk 39 Snig Hill ⓣ0114/279 9090, ⓦwww.theboardwalklive.co.uk. Popular venue for indie bands, rock, folk and comedy.

The Casbah 1 Wellington St ⓣ0114/275 6077. As in "Rock the . . .", which tells you what to expect – a stroll down punk/rock memory lane with an older crowd reliving their youth.

Dempsey's 1 Hereford St ⓣ0114/275 4616. Bar and club with the most reliable gay scene in the city.

Gatecrasher One 112 Arundel St ⓣ0114/276 6777. Formerly *The Republic*, this highly successful club housed in an old steel and engineering works has relaunched itself as flagship of the Gatecrasher clubbing brand.

The Last Laugh *Lescar Hotel*, 303 Sharrowvale Rd ⓣ0114/267 9787, ⓦwww.grinreaper.co.uk. Yorkshire's longest-running comedy club. Local and visiting comedians on Thurs at 9pm.

Leadmill 6–7 Leadmill Rd ⓣ0114/221 2828, ⓦwww.leadmill.co.uk. In the Cultural Industries Quarter, this place hosts live bands and DJs most nights of the week.

Sheffield Hallam University Nelson Mandela Building, Pond St ⓣ0114/253 4122. Hosts regular gigs and club nights.

University of Sheffield Students' Union Western Bank ⓣ0114/222 8777. Regular indie/rock gigs and a varied programme of club nights, including the city's biggest gay/lesbian night, *Climax*.

Theatre, cinema and concerts

Crucible, Lyceum & Studio Tudor Sq ⓣ0114/249 6000, ⓦwww.sheffieldtheatres.co.uk. Sheffield's theatres put on a full programme of theatre, dance, comedy and concerts. The Crucible also hosts the annual Music in the Round festival of chamber music (May), and the Sheffield Children's Festival (late June or July), whose events are performed entirely by children.

Sheffield City Hall Barker's Pool ☎0114/278 9789, Ⓦwww.sheffieldcityhall.com. Year-round programme of classical music, opera, mainstream concerts, comedy and club nights. Expected to be closed for refurbishment from mid-2004 for a year.

The Showroom 7 Paternoster Row ☎0114/275 7727, Ⓦwww.showroom.org.uk. The biggest independent cinema outside London.

Listings

Hospital Royal Hallamshire Hospital, Glossop Rd ☎0114/271 1900.
Internet Havana Internet Café 32–34 Division St. Also free access at the City Library.
Police West Bar ☎0114/220 2020.
Post office The Co-op, Castle House, Angel St.
Sports Sheffield Ski Village, Vale Rd (☎0114/276 9459, Ⓦwww.sheffieldskivillage.co.uk), is Europe's largest all-season ski resort, for skiing, boarding and snow-blading, plus bar and bistro. There's an Olympic-sized pool, plus leisure pool and slides at Ponds Forge, Sheaf St (☎0114/223 3413, Ⓦwww.ponds-forge.co.uk). Or visit The Foundry, 45 Mowbray St (☎0114/279 6331, Ⓦwww.foundryclimbing.com), a terrific indoor climbing centre.
Transport Online timetables and ticket information from the South Yorkshire Passenger Transport Executive Ⓦwww.sypte.co.uk. For Supertram services call ☎0114/272 8282.

Leeds and around

Yorkshire's commercial capital, and one of the fastest-growing cities in the country, **LEEDS** has undergone a radical transformation in recent years. There's still a true northern grit to its character, and in many of its dilapidated suburbs, but the grime has been removed from the Victorian centre and the city is revelling in its renaissance as a financial, administrative and cultural boomtown. An early market town, wool was traded here in medieval times by the monks of nearby Kirkstall Abbey. By the eighteenth century, the advent of canals and technical innovations such as the harnessing of steam power turned what had been a cottage industry into a dynamic large-scale economy. Leeds quickly boomed beyond its capacity to support its burgeoning population, and while the textile barons prospered, the city acquired a reputation for grimness that proved hard to shake off. In 1847 Charles Dickens described Leeds as "the beastliest place, one of the noisiest I know", an observation that many visitors might have applied to the city until comparatively recently.

Now, however, improved communications, a major clean-up and urban rejuvenation schemes have been the making of modern Leeds. The most obvious manifestation of change has been the advent of late-opening cafés, bars, clubs and eclectic restaurants, and the arrival of the swanky department store, Harvey Nichols. It's also long been the region's **cultural** centre, home to Opera North, the noted West Yorkshire Playhouse and a triennial international piano competition that ranks among the world's top musical events. Museums start with the hugely impressive **Royal Armouries**, which hold the national arms and armour collection, while the **City Art Gallery** has one of the best collections of British twentieth-century art outside London. **Leeds Industrial Museum** and **Abbey House Museum** take care of the city's historical legacy; while further from the city you might try to see one of the country's great Georgian piles, **Harewood House**.

Arrival, transport and information

National and local Metro trains use **Leeds Station** off City Square on the southern flank of the city centre, which also houses the Gateway Yorkshire

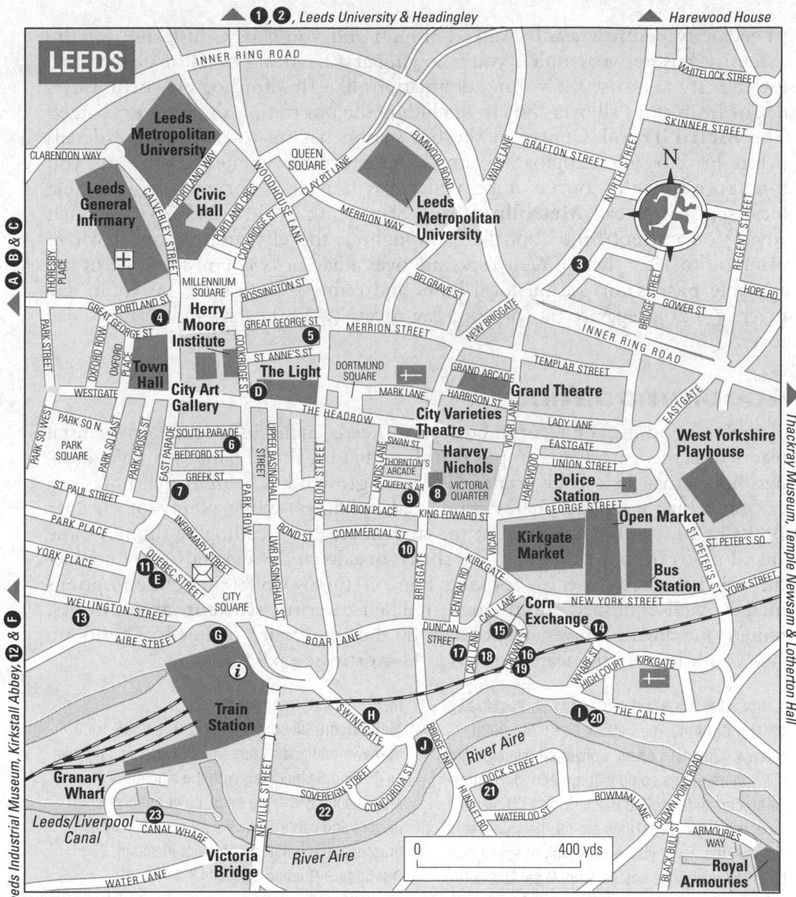

ACCOMMODATION		CAFÉS & RESTAURANTS				PUBS	
Avalon Guest House	A	Appetite	13	Harry Ramsden's	12	Duck & Drake	14
Fairbairn House	B	Bibi's	7	Leodis	22	The Ship	9
42 The Calls	I	Brasserie 44	20	Norman	17	Victoria	4
Glengarth	C	Brodericks	15	Oporto	18	Whitelocks	10
Holiday Inn Express	F	Bryan's	1	Pool Court at 42	20		
Malmaison	J	The Courtyard	5	Salvo's	2		
Quebecs	E	Cuban Heels	19	Simply Heathcotes	23		
The Queen's	G	Dimitri's	21	Souz le Nez en Ville	11		
Radisson SAS	D	Espresso Bar	8	Tampopo	6		
Travelodge	H	Fourth Floor Café	8	Townhouse	16		
		Hansa's	3				

tourist office in the Arcade (Mon 10am–5.30pm, Tues–Sat 9.30am–5.30pm, Sun 10am–4pm; ⊕0113/242 5242, ⓦwww.leeds.gov.uk), stuffed with leaflets and information about Leeds and the rest of Yorkshire. The **bus station** occupies a site to the east, behind Kirkgate Market, on St Peter's Street, close to the West Yorkshire Playhouse. Drivers will eventually be fed onto the City Centre Loop road and though **parking** in the myriad signposted pay-and-display car parks is expensive, it's better than driving around all day looking for free on-street space.

Leeds city centre is easily walked around and you'll have little use for the extensive bus network unless you're staying at a far-flung B&B or planning to use the city as a base for visiting destinations like Bradford or Haworth. Buses depart from stops all over the city, including the bus station on St Peter's Street. The **Metro Travel Centre** at the bus station has up-to-date service details (Mon–Fri 8.30am–5.30pm, Sat 9am–4.30pm; ⓦwww.wymetro.com), and you can also ask in the tourist office, which has timetables for every conceivable local service; or call **Metroline** (daily 8am–8pm; ⓣ0113/245 7676), which advises on current routes and fares throughout the city and region. If you're planning to see a slice of West Yorkshire over a day or two, consider one of the available **passes** for use on local buses and trains – there's the bus/train day rover (£4.50), separate bus or train day rovers (£3.80 each) and a family day rover (£6).

Accommodation

There's a good mix of accommodation in Leeds, including some fairly central places near the university campus that shouldn't break the bank, as well as business hotels that do a steady trade. The recent growth has been in stylish designer hotels, many located in revamped old buildings, while plenty of cheaper B&Bs lie out to the northwest in the student area of Headingley, though these are all a bus or taxi ride away. For **short breaks** and weekends away contact the tourist office's special booking line on ⓣ0800/808050. Other options include well-equipped rooms in shared self-catering **student apartments**, rented out during university holidays by the University of Leeds. There's no city youth hostel; the nearest one is at Haworth (see p.940).

Guest houses and hotels

42 The Calls 42 The Calls ⓣ0113/244 0099, ⓦwww.42thecalls.co.uk. Converted riverside grain mill, where rooms come with great beds, sharp bathrooms, filter coffee machine and CD player, though the cheapest rates are for the smallest "studio" rooms; anything with a bit of space will be in the next price category up. Breakfast not included. Weekend rates, when available, drop the price to around £99 a night. ❼

Avalon Guest House 132 Woodsley Rd ⓣ0113/243 2545. Decent budget B&B near the university in a large Victorian house. Rooms have TVs; some of the cheaper ones share a bathroom. ❷

Fairbairn House 71–75 Clarendon Rd ⓣ0113/343 6633. Victorian house owned by the university. Quiet setting and good value. ❷

Glengarth Hotel 162 Woodsley Rd ⓣ0113/245 7940. Homely B&B with good rates and a variety of single and double rooms; the cheapest don't have en-suite facilities. No credit cards. ❷

Holiday Inn Express Cavendish St ⓣ0113/242 6200, ⓦwww.ichotelsgroup.com. On the western edge of the centre, but only a 15min walk from the shops, bars and restaurants. The one-size-fits-all room rate includes continental breakfast (and weekend rates can knock another tenner off), and there's limited free parking. ❹

Malmaison Sovereign Quay ⓣ0113/398 1000, ⓦwww.malmaison.com. Classy waterside premises (behind Swinegate), with the signature Malmaison style – big beds, power showers, CD players and cable TV in the rooms, plus stylish brasserie and bar. Breakfast not included. ❼

Quebecs 9 Quebec St ⓣ0113/244 8989, ⓦwww.theetongroup.com. A boutique makeover for the former Leeds and County Liberal Club, with oak panelling and stained glass in the entrance hall to the chic rooms with plumped pillows and Victorian clawfoot bathtubs. Its five-star comforts aren't that bad a deal either, with weekend rates from £99. ❼

The Queen's City Square ⓣ0113/243 1323, ⓦwww.paramount-hotels.co.uk. Refurbished four-star Art Deco landmark, right in front of the station, with piano bar, restaurant and free car parking. Rates are fairly flexible – even during the week you can sometimes get a room from £70 (the code below is the official rate), while weekend prices include breakfast. ❼

Radisson SAS No.1 The Light, The Headrow ⓣ0113/236 6000, ⓦwww.radissonsas.com. The Grade II listed former HQ of the Leeds Permanent Building Society now exudes contemporary style within the SAS brand. Snazzy rooms and suites reflect high-tech, Art Deco or modern Italian design, culminating in the original panelling and stained glass of the Presidential Boadroom Suite. Breakfast not normally included, though it is with weekend rates (from £110), while deals booked through the website can sometimes get you a room for as low as £75. ❽

Travelodge Blayds Court, off Swinegate ☎0870/191 1655 or 08700/850950, ⓦwww.travelodge.co.uk. Reasonable centrally located accommodation from this chain. Set price per room, breakfast not included. ❸

Student accommodation

Clarence Dock Holiday Apartments Clarence Dock ☎0113/233 6100. Student apartments near the Royal Armouries, available mid-July to the beginning of September. Single en-suite rooms (£25 per person per night for the first night, or £30 for two nights and £15 a night thereafter) in shared five-bed flats. Parking available.

The City

Leeds city centre splits itself into three reasonably distinct areas, starting with the **universities** on the heights to the northwest, arranged around some pleasant green swathes but framed by the more brutal excrescences of Sixties' planning. The city's revitalized commercial life is most apparent in the packed pedestrianized streets south of **The Headrow**, where the Victorian and Edwardian buildings, arcades and markets glitter with brand names and designer labels, while down along the **Leeds–Liverpool Canal** and **River Aire** a kind of post-industrial chic has infused the converted warehouses and railway arches. If you want some purpose to your wanderings, take one of the themed **guided walks** that depart from the tourist office (dates and times vary; £2.50), concentrating on things like Leeds' traditional pubs, local heroes and heroines, or eccentrics.

City Square to The Headrow

Opposite the train station, a prancing statue of Edward, the Black Prince, welcomes you to **City Square**, a smartened-up space that still retains its bronze nymph gas lamps. It's a short walk to the top of East Parade where you can't miss **Leeds Town Hall**, one of the finest expressions of nineteenth-century civic pride in the country. The masterpiece of local architect Cuthbert Broderick, it's a classical colossus of great skill, colonnaded on all sides, guarded by white lions and topped by a perky clocktower and sculptures embodying Industry, Art, Music and Science. Venture at least as far as the *Victoria Tearooms* (Mon–Fri 10am–4pm) – the entrance is on Calverley Street – for a cup of tea with a nice view. Further up Calverley Street, to the side of the Town Hall, the city's turn-of-the-twenty-first-century contribution is **Millennium Square**, handsome enough in its landscaped, contemporary way, but not a patch on nearby **Park Square**. This graceful Georgian ensemble, southwest of the Town Hall, is a peaceful place for a sit-down among the rose bushes, where you can contemplate the flanking bulk of St Paul's House (1878), a red-brick neo-Gothic former warehouse and cloth-cutting workshop – there's now a bar in the ground floor.

East from the Town Hall and you're on **The Headrow**, the city's central spine, with the Art Gallery (see below) the major draw. At the junction with Cookridge Street, more redevelopment has seen the former headquarters of the Leeds Permanent Building Society and adjacent buildings emerge as **The Light**, a shopping, cinema, health club, hotel and bar-restaurant complex on four levels.

City Art Gallery and Henry Moore Institute

Leeds' **City Art Gallery** (Mon–Sat 10am–5pm, Wed 10am–8pm, Sun 1–5pm; free; ⓦwww.leeds.gov.uk/artgallery) on The Headrow comprises one of the best arrays outside London of twentieth-century British art. Changing selections from the permanent collection of nineteenth- and twentieth-century art and sculpture are presented, with an understandable bias towards pieces by Henry Moore and Barbara Hepworth, both former students at the Leeds School of Art; Moore's *Reclining Woman* lounges at the top of the steps outside the gallery. There's Victorian painting and sculpture on the ground floor, with notable chunks of work by local landscapist John Atkinson Grimshaw, while the upper floor merges French Impressionists with the English artists they influenced. Prime amongst these was the founder of the Camden Town Group, Walter Sickert, and his younger disciples Spencer Frederick Gore and Harold Gilman; later artists such as Matthew Smith, Stanley Spencer and Wyndham Lewis are also represented. In addition, there are some outstanding pieces by names with greater recognition – busts by Jacob Epstein, paintings by L.S. Lowry, a David Hockney etching here, a Francis Bacon snarl there. The café (Mon–Sat 10am–4pm, Sun 1–4pm) is a quiet place to unwind, and there's direct access to the **Craft Centre and Design Gallery** below (Tues–Fri 10am–5pm, Sat 10am–4pm; free), where changing displays of contemporary jewellery, ceramics and applied art are on show.

From the City Art Gallery, a slender bridge connects to the adjacent **Henry Moore Institute** (daily 10am–5.30pm, Wed until 9pm; free; ⓦwww.henry-moore-fdn.co.uk), which has its own entrance on The Headrow. Housed in a former Victorian merchant's warehouse, now faced in black marble, the Institute is devoted to showcasing temporary exhibitions of sculpture from all periods and nationalities, and not, as you might imagine, pieces by the masterful Moore himself.

Briggate and the markets

Most visitors, it has to be said, make a beeline for the brimming, shop-filled arcades on either side of pedestrianized **Briggate**. These nineteenth-century palaces of marble, mahogany, stained glass and mosaics have been magnificently restored and perhaps the most splendidly decorated of all is the light-flooded **Victoria Quarter**, with Harvey Nichols as its designer lodestone. The famous sales here start on the day after Boxing Day and the last Wednesday in June, and you can always revive yourself in the fashionable *Espresso Bar* or *Fourth Floor Café-Bar*.

Across Vicar Lane, **Kirkgate Market** (closed Wed afternoon & Sun) is the largest market in the north of England. Housed in a superb Edwardian building, it's a descendant of the medieval woollen markets that were instrumental in making Leeds the early focus of the region's textile industry. The **open market** behind here (Tues, Fri & Sat), incidentally, is where Michael Marks set up stall in 1884 with the slogan "don't ask the price, it's a penny" – an enterprise that blossomed into the present-day retail giant Marks & Spencer.

Visible at the bottom of the street, on the corner of Vicar Lane and Duncan Street, the elliptical, domed **Corn Exchange** (open daily) was built in 1863, also by Cuthbert Broderick, whose design leaned heavily on his studies of Paris's corn exchange. This listed building is now a hip market for jewellery, retro clothes, furnishings, music and other bits and bobs – extra craft stores open up at weekends. Behind here, under the railway arches on Assembley Street and along Call Lane, Leeds' **Exchange Quarter** flexes its fashionable muscles in a series of hip cafés and restaurants, many housed in beautifully restored buildings.

Granary Wharf to the Royal Armouries

The biggest transformation in Leeds has been along the **Leeds–Liverpool**

Canal and **River Aire**, formerly a stagnant relic of industrial decline. New businesses, sought-after balconied apartments and trendy restaurants line both sides, while a slew of attractions stretch along a mile or so of the waterside, connected by a pleasant footpath. At **Granary Wharf**, a couple of minutes' walk from the train station, stores, restaurants and craft shops fill the extensive cobbled, vaulted arches (the "Dark Arches"), while every weekend (and bank holiday) a market with stalls, bands and entertainers spills out onto the canal basin.

Further east along the river, on the south side, beckons the glass turret and gun-metal grey bulk of the **Royal Armouries** (daily 10am–5pm; free; Ⓦwww.armouries.org.uk). Purpose-built to house the arms and armour collection from the Tower of London, it's a hugely adventurous museum that requires a leap of faith – discard the notion that all you'll see are casefuls of weapons, and you're in for a treat. Themed galleries cover concepts such as "War" and "Hunting", with displays – ranging from gun emplacements to Mughal Indian elephant armour – backed up by intelligent commentary, video exhibits and documentary evidence. Interpretations and demonstrations take place throughout the day (you're handed a schedule on entering), so you might learn smallsword techniques from a Georgian swordsmaster or sixteenth-century javelin skills in the outdoor Tiltyard. There are even crossbow and simulated gun ranges on the top floor (£2 charge), so you're unlikely to be bored. It's an easy ten-minute walk along the river to the museum from the centre, or bus #752 runs from Eastgate to Clarence Dock (where there's parking outside the museum).

Eating, drinking and nightlife

Eating out in Leeds has been transformed in recent years, with a plethora of conversions of warehouses and grain mills into up-to-the-minute **restaurants and brasseries**. Michelin stars are not unknown, but there's a down-to-earth approach to prices, with even the fanciest places offering special lunch or early-bird deals. It's all a long way from when the big name in local cooking was *Harry Ramsden's*, a byword for "proper" fish and chips, but now franchised all over England and even as far away as Hong Kong – the original restaurant is in Guiseley, northwest of the city. Along with its restaurants, Leeds rivals Manchester in the number of late-opening, continental-style **café-bars** which dot the centre and exploit the city's relaxed licensing laws to the full. Many put tables out year round, and most serve good food too. The best of the city's **pubs** are the ornate, spruced-up Victorian ale-houses in which Leeds specializes, and when these close you can move on to one of the city's DJ bars or **clubs**, many of which have a nationwide reputation – not least because Leeds lets you dance until 5 or 6am most weekends.

For information about **what's on**, the *Yorkshire Evening Post* is your best bet, or pick up a copy of the fortnightly *Leeds Guide* (£1.70) for listings and features on the city. Best **website** is Ⓦwww.itchyleeds.co.uk, which is really useful for insightful club, bar and entertainment listings and all sorts of local information.

Cafés and café-bars

Appetite City Central, 2 Wellington St. City deli and sandwich bar, with seats outside, a big old fireplace inside, and a menu of panini, salads and lunchboxes. Closed Sun.

Brodericks Corn Exchange, Call Lane. See-and-be-seen café in the bowels of the Corn Exchange with a couple of sofas for shopping breaks. Serves English and international breakfasts and lunches.

The Courtyard 25–37 Cookridge St. Huge, airy café-bar that gets a bit too packed at night, but slip in during the day for snacks, coffee and drinks in the brick-paved courtyard (heated in winter). Fresh and funky club sounds until 2am at weekends.

Cuban Heels The Arches, 28–30 Assembley St. A salsa café under the railway arches, opposite the Corn Exchange. Good *bocadillos* (grilled sandwiches), Tex-Mex food, bottled beers and cool sounds, then pop next door where *Fudge* offers funk and soul until 2am.

Espresso Bar Harvey Nichols, Victoria Quarter, Briggate. Domain of the high-fashion shopper, the arcade espresso bar is a pleasant, if overpriced, place to muse on exactly how much those shoes will set you back.

Norman 36 Call Lane. The industrial-chic background of scuffed floor and cast-iron girders is lightened by sinuous lights, and red plastic tables and chairs. Add the juice bar, the Asian noodle-curry-and-satay menu, the club nights and Monday Latin jazz, and you've got one of the city's more unique spots. The "Daily Norman" deal (all Mon & Tues–Fri noon–3pm) provides a meal and a beer for a fiver.

Townhouse Assembley St. Café-bar grill and restaurant, serving fashionable food, all-day drinks, cocktails, and with weekend club nights. There's a fairly brisk circuit between here and the *Pitcher & Piano*, and other local hangouts.

Restaurants

Bibi's Minerva House, 16 Greek St ☎0113/243 0905. Classic old-time Italian, busy at lunch and weekends, with a full range of pizzas and pastas alongside pricier mainstream meat and fish concoctions. Moderate.

Brasserie 44 44 The Calls ☎0113/234 3232. Informal but trendy Modern British brasserie, with some temptingly priced lunch and early-bird deals, serving everything from Whitby cod to Middle Eastern meze. Closed Sat lunch & Sun. Expensive.

Bryan's 9 Weetwood Lane, Headingley ☎0113/278 5679. The local rival to *Harry Ramsden's* – order the haddock and chips and judge for yourself. Inexpensive.

Dimitri's Simpson's Fold, 20 Dock St ☎0113/246 0339. Plenty of choice in this Greek-Mediterranean tapas-style diner, where you can pick and mix dishes and flavours. The platters make for a big meal, and it's a good destination for veggies. Inexpensive.

Fourth Floor Café Harvey Nichols, Victoria Quarter, Briggate ☎0113/204 8000. Light lunches, souped-up British classics (grilled steak, fish and chips, bangers and mash) and exotic flavours (Thai spices are common) at dinner. And great views over the rooftops of central Leeds. Closed Mon–Wed eve & all Sun. Moderate (lunch) to Expensive (dinner).

Hansa's 72–74 North St ☎0113/244 4408. This Gujarati vegetarian restaurant serves aromatic Indian food with choice of Indian, vegetarian or organic wines. The philosophy of the place matches the food – take time to look through the beautiful menu full of maps, quotes and thoughts. Inexpensive.

Harry Ramsden's White Cross, Otley Rd, Guiseley ☎01943/874641. If you feel like making the pilgrimage (best done in a taxi) then expect to wait in line at the original *Harry Ramsden's* fish-and-chip restaurant. It's well worth the effort. Moderate.

Leodis Victoria Mill, Sovereign St ☎0113/242 1010. Former mill with a handsome rescued cast-iron and wood interior, serving Anglo-French brasserie classics. There's a summer waterside terrace. Closed Sat lunch & all Sun. Expensive.

Oporto 31–33 Call Lane ☎0113/245 4444. Funky Exchange Quarter bistro-bar where the flavours mix and match: gourmet doorstop sandwiches, homemade burgers and risottos during the day, Asian-influenced Modern British meals at night. Lunch Moderate, dinner Expensive.

Pool Court at 42 42–44 The Calls ☎0113/244 4242. This is the sharp end of the business – cutting-edge Modern British cuisine with a seasonally changing menu, and featuring a sought-after balcony overlooking the river. Closed Sat lunch & Sun. Very Expensive.

Salvo's 115 Otley Rd, Headingley ☎0113/275 5017. Pizza in Leeds to a local means *Salvo's*, though there's a big, classic Italian menu as well. You may have to queue. Closed Sun. Moderate.

Simply Heathcotes Canal Wharf, Water Lane ☎0113/244 6611. A tiny spot of gourmet Lancashire in Yorkshire's grittiest city, Paul Heathcote's latest brasserie outpost adds black pudding and Goosnargh duck to the impeccably Modern British menu. Very stylish, with a great interior and canal views. Lunch Moderate, dinner Expensive.

Souz le Nez en Ville Basement, Quebec House, 9 Quebec St ☎0113/244 0108. Housed in the splendid red-brick building of the former Liberal Club, this basement wine bar/restaurant is particularly strong on fish – there are always half a dozen special starters and mains, plus a wide bistro-style menu. Closed Sun. Expensive.

Tampopo 15 South Parade ☎0113/245 1816. Best of the central noodle bars, this is the place to sort out your *ramen* from your *pho*. There's nothing much over £7 or £8 and though it's an in-and-out kind of place, it doesn't feel like a production line. Inexpensive.

Pubs

Duck & Drake 43 Kirkgate, by the railway bridge. Real-ale pub with a changing selection, and local bands performing for free two or three nights a week.

The Ship Ship Inn Yard, off Briggate. Less well known than *Whitelocks* but almost as appealing, and serving lunchtime snacks. The yard tables – crammed into a space about three feet wide – take the city's obsession with continental outdoor ways to extremes.

Victoria Great George St. Ornate Victorian "family and commercial hotel", restored to its former glory, with proper pub food and a period feel.

Whitelocks Turk's Head Yard, off Briggate. Leeds' oldest and most atmospheric pub (tucked up an alley) retains its traditional decor, though you'll be hard pushed to see any of it at peak times. Good beer choice.

DJ bars, clubs and live music

Atrium 6–9 The Grand Arcade ⓣ0113/242 6116. Relaxed and laidback vibe upstairs and a funky basement club for the diehard clubbers. Friday night is for salsa/Latino sounds.

Cockpit Bridge House, Swinegate ⓣ0113/244 1573, ⓦwww.thecockpit.co.uk. The city's best live music venue. Regular live bands, plus assorted club nights, including the especially popular gay night "Poptastic" on Thursdays.

Creation 55 Cookridge St ⓣ0113/242 7272, ⓦwww.creation-leeds.co.uk. Hosts high-profile live bands as well as regular club nights, chart to cheese, with the 70s night Love Train each Friday.

Dr Wu 35 Call Lane ⓣ0113/242 7629. DJs, live bands, singer-songwriters and open-mike nights provide the entertainment from 7pm onwards.

The Elbow Room 64 Call Lane ⓣ0113/245 7011, ⓦwww.theelbowroom.co.uk. Funk and food, and a place to play pool.

Fibre 168 Lower Briggate ⓣ0113/234 1304, ⓦwww.barfibre.com. Leeds' coolest gay café-bar with contemporary food served from noon until 7pm, outside balcony, cocktail bar, DJs most nights and dancing until midnight, 2am at weekends. It's the pre-club bar for Leeds' most dramatic club night, Federation (first Sat of month) at the Blank Canvas, Dark Arches, Granary Wharf.

Hifi 2 Central Rd ⓣ0113/242 7353, ⓦwww.thehificlub.co.uk. Smart and stylish, ultra-fashionable Exchange Quarter club, playing everything from Stax and Motown to hip-hop or drum 'n' bass. There's live jazz funk most weeks, while Friday's funk, soul and rare grooves night gets the local vote.

Milo 10–12 Call Lane ⓣ0113/245 7101. Unpretentious bar with DJs most evenings, ringing the changes from old soul and reggae to electronica.

Mint Club 8 Harrison St ⓣ0113/244 3168, ⓦwww.themintclubleeds.co.uk. Up-to-the-minute beats (there's a "no-cheese" policy), and the best chill-out space in the city.

Rehab 2 Waterloo House, Assembley St ⓣ0113/223 7644. Where it's currently at in Leeds – including Friday night's Sleaze, the legendary Basics house night every Saturday and cutting-edge DJs at all times.

The Wardrobe St Peter's Sq ⓣ0113/383 8800, ⓦwww.the-wardrobe.co.uk. Self-styled "café, bar, kitchen, club" with live jazz and soul acts, and DJs playing the best funk, soul, jazz and hip-hop.

The Warehouse 19–21 Somers St ⓣ0113/246 8287. One of the biggest clubs in the city, with house, garage and techno sounds bringing in clubbers from all over the country. Saturday's glam funky house party keeps going until 9am.

Arts, festivals and entertainment

The city supports an enterprising arts scene, not just confined to the showpiece theatres and halls listed below. **Opera North** (ⓦwww.operanorth.co.uk) gives a free performance each summer at Temple Newsam (see p.933), as does the **Northern Ballet Theatre** – details from the tourist office. Temple Newsam hosts concerts and events, from plays to rock gigs, while at Kirkstall Abbey every summer there's a Shakespeare Festival (ⓦwww.openairshakespeare.com) with open-air productions of the Bard's works. Roundhay Park is the other large outdoor venue for concerts, while **Millennium Square** hosts gigs, festivals, markets and other events, including the annual Ice Cube, a temporary outdoor ice rink and café (mid-Jan to end-Feb). An international **film festival** is held in the city each October (programmes from the tourist office), and August heralds another festival in the **West Indian Carnival** (only beaten in size by Notting Hill).

Venues

City Varieties Swan St, Briggate ⓣ08456/441881, ⓦwww.cityvarieties.co.uk. One of the country's last surviving music halls, though it's less music-hall fare these days and more tribute bands, comedians and cabaret – great building and bar though.

Grand Theatre and Opera House 46 New Briggate ⓣ0113/222 6222, ⓦwww.leeds.gov.uk/grandtheatre. The regular base of Opera North and Northern Ballet, also puts on a full range of theatrical productions.

Hyde Park Picture House Brudenell Rd, Headingley ⓣ0113/275 2045, ⓦwww.leeds.gov.uk/hydepark. The place to come for classic cinema with independent and art-house shows alongside more mainstream films; take bus #56, #57 or #63 from the city centre.

Leeds Town Hall The Headrow ⓣ0113/224 3801, ⓦwww.leedsconcertseason.com. Supports an annual international concert season of great distinction and is the venue for Leeds' internationally renowned piano competition.

Ster Century Cinema The Light, The Headrow ⓣ0870/240 3696, ⓦwww.stercentury.co.uk. The only cinema in Leeds' city centre, with13 screens showing mainstream releases.

West Yorkshire Playhouse Quarry Hill Mount ⓣ0113/213 7700, ⓦwww.wyplayhouse.com. The city's most innovative playhouse has two theatres and hosts a wide range of productions and premieres of local works.

Listings

Hospital Leeds General Infirmary, Great George St ⓣ0113/243 2799.

Internet Internet Exchange, 29 Boar Lane ⓣ0113/242 1093. There's free access at the Central Library, Calverley St ⓣ0113/247 8274 (call for hours).

Pharmacy Boots, Leeds Station Concourse ⓣ0113/242 1713, and 49 Merrion Centre ⓣ0113/242 8194.

Police Millgarth Police Station, Millgarth St ⓣ0845/606 0606.

Post office Main Post Office, City Square.

Sports and swimming Leeds United play at Elland Rd ⓣ0845/121 1992, ⓦwww.leedsunited.com, and there are usually some tickets on general sale. Yorkshire County Cricket Club, Headingley ⓣ08000/326644, is the place to see county and international cricket. Leeds International Pool, Westgate ⓣ0113/214 5000, is the best, most central place for a swim.

Taxis Taxis are available 24hr at the train station, outside the bus station, and on New Briggate.

Out of the city

The nearest of the outlying sights is the **Thackray Museum** on Beckett Street (daily 10am–5pm, last admission 3pm; £4.90; ⓦwww.thackraymuseum.org), next to the well-known St James' Hospital ("Jimmy's" from the TV series). Sited in a former workhouse, it's a mile east of the city centre, with buses #4, #22, #42, #49, #50 and #88 all running past. Essentially a medical history museum, it's a hugely popular and entertaining place – ghoulish too at times when it delves into topics like surgery before anaesthetics, and the workings of the human intestine. Needless to say, kids love it.

For Leeds' industrial past, visit the vast **Leeds Industrial Museum**, two miles west of the centre off Canal Road (Tues–Sat 10am–5pm, Sun 1–5pm; £2; ⓦwww.leeds.gov.uk/armleymills), which runs between Armley and Kirkstall Road – take bus #5a, #14, #66 or #67. There's been a mill on the site since at least the seventeenth century, and the present building was one of the world's largest woollen mills until its closure in 1969. Displays recount the whole story of Leeds' industrial history, with plenty of working machinery, together with a definitive account of how cloth was made, starting from the fleece off the sheep's back to great rolls of finished cloth. An informative Printing Gallery is devoted to the story of the city's printing trade.

You should also see the ruins of **Kirkstall Abbey** (dawn to dusk; free), the city's most important medieval relic. Built between 1152 and 1182 by Cistercian monks from Fountains Abbey, it was the site of 400 years of monastic life before being surrendered to Henry VIII in 1539. The abbey lies about three miles northwest of the city centre on Abbey Road; take bus #732, #733, #734, #735 or #736. Despite the urban huddle close at hand, the site's still evocatively bucolic, with plenty of signed footpaths around, and the cloisters in particular are a nice spot to while away some quiet time. The former gatehouse now provides the setting for the **Abbey House Museum** (Tues–Fri & Sun 10am–5pm, Sat noon–5pm; £3). Two floors dedicated to Victorian Leeds take a look into the city's industrial past and a dedicated children's section is popular with kids.

Four miles east of the city, the Tudor-Jacobean house of **Temple Newsam** (April–Oct Tues–Sun 10.30am–5pm; Nov–March Tues–Sun 10.30am–4pm; £3) contains many of the paintings and much of the decorative art owned by Leeds City Art Gallery, including one of the largest collections of Chippendale furniture in the country. The house has recently been restored, and new displays installed, though many still come out solely for the splendid park, walled gardens and estate grounds (daily 10am–dusk; free), laid out by Capability Brown in 1762. There are over 1500 acres on the estate, which also contains Europe's largest rare-breeds farm (closed Mon; £3). There's an hourly Sunday bus service to the house; otherwise, parking costs £1.50. Further east still, about thirteen miles from Leeds, the rest of the city's art collection is housed in **Lotherton Hall** (Tues–Sat 10am–5pm, Sun 1–5pm; closed Jan & Feb; £2), off the B1217 near Aberford. Once the home of a local industrialist, it's been endowed with fine gardens, a deer park and bird garden, with everything from vultures to wallabies on view. Buses #64 and #64a run to the village, from where it's a twenty-minute walk to the hall (there are direct buses on summer Sundays).

Stately **Harewood House**, seven miles north of Leeds (Easter–Oct daily 11am–4.30pm, grounds & bird garden 10am–6pm; Nov–Easter Sat & Sun only; £9.50, grounds & bird garden only £6.75, plus £1 extra on Sun and bank hols; ⓦ www.harewood.org), was designed and decorated by one of the greatest architectural teams ever assembled. Conceived in 1759 by York architect John Carr, the building was finished by Robert Adam, the furniture made by Thomas Chippendale and the landscaped gardens laid out by Capability Brown. To cap it all, a sweeping terrace designed by Sir Charles Barry (architect of the Houses of Parliament) overlooks the garden. Georgian purists might lament some of the later Victorian additions but the ensemble is still outstanding, and is further enhanced by paintings by Turner, Gainsborough, Reynolds, El Greco and a whole host of Italian masters. One of the more unusual features outside is the **Bird Garden**, four acres of aviaries caging over 150 species – the penguins get fed at 2pm. There are frequent buses to Harewood from Leeds (including the #36, every 20min, 30min on Sun), and if you come on the bus, you'll get a fifty-percent discount on admission (keep your bus ticket). The house is near the junction of the A659 and the A61 Leeds to Harrogate road, and parking is free.

Bradford and around

Lost in its smoky valley among the Pennine hills ... Bruddersford is generally held to be an ugly city ... but it always seemed to me to have the kind of ugliness that could not only be tolerated but often enjoyed.

J.B. Priestley, Bright Day, 1940.

Priestley was writing about a thinly disguised **BRADFORD**, his home town, and the sentiment – from a writer who championed Bradford at every possible opportunity – though typically blunt, is not unduly harsh. Even today's civic authority seems content to accept the judgement: the quotation, after all, is emblazoned on the plinth of the statue of the city's favourite, if most cantankerous, son. For first and foremost, Bradford has always been a working town, booming in tandem with the Industrial Revolution, when it changed in decades from a rural seat of woollen manufacture to a polluted metropolis. In its Victorian heyday it was the world's biggest producer of worsted cloth, its skyline etched black with mill chimneys, and its hills clogged with some of the foulest back-to-back houses of any northern city. Contemporary Bradford is valiantly rinsing away its associations with urban decrepitude, and a few spruced-up buildings and the rejuvenation of the late-Victorian woollen warehouse quarter, Little Germany, signify an attempt to beautify the city centre, but in truth the city doesn't have the architectural heritage or the cultural interest to detain you long. Although there are the unexpected pleasures of the **National Museum of Photography, Film and Television** and the nearby model village of **Saltaire**, with its David Hockney Gallery, you couldn't make out a case for seeing much else. Most visitors hang around at least long enough to sample one of Bradford's famous **curry houses**, but with Haworth the indisputable local draw, and York and the heart of the Yorkshire Dales only an hour away, few stay longer.

The City

The focal point of the city centre is **Centenary Square**, commemorating not the founding of the original town – the "broad ford" was known before the arrival of the Romans – but the hundredth anniversary of the granting of its city charter by Queen Victoria in 1897; Elizabeth II turned up to snip the ribbon. The **City Hall** behind shouts its Victorian credentials; the Gothic extension at the back was the work of Richard Norman Shaw, architect of, among other things, the more fantastical Northumbrian country house of Cragside. The City Hall's original architects, local boys Lockwood and Mawson, also provided Bradford with **St George's Hall**, a Neoclassical extravaganza on Bridge Street still in use as a concert hall. Edwardian audiences later flocked to the minaret-topped **Alhambra Theatre**, across Princes Way, again splendidly restored and boasting a full programme of events.

Just across from here, on the rise, is the superb **National Museum of Photography, Film and Television** (Tues–Sun & public holidays 10am–6pm; free; Ⓦwww.nmpft.org.uk), one of the most visited national museums outside London, which wraps itself around one of Britain's largest cinema screens, whose daily **IMAX** and 3D film screenings (£5.95; Ⓦwww.imaxnorth.co.uk) are billed as "so real you'll think you're there". When you arrive it's as well to buy your cinema ticket for a later showing since this is one of the most popular attractions. There's also a ground-floor café/restaurant, *Intermission* (open until 6pm), and a shop stuffed full of movie posters, videos, and related knick-knacks. The museum's ground floor kicks off with the Kodak Gallery, a museum-within-a-museum which houses the contents of Kodak's private collection and traces the story of popular photography. Like the floors that follow, it's crammed with memorabilia and hundreds of cameras, but also contains the world's biggest lens and other superlatives. Successive exhibitions are devoted to every nuance of film and television, including state-of-the-art topics like digital imaging and computer animation, and detours into advertising and news-gathering. The place is a revelation to anyone with any technical or professional interest, and in the unlikely event that the endless gizmos don't appeal there are all sorts of nostalgic nuggets to grab the attention.

Back across Centenary Square, a walk past the Venetian-Gothic **Wool Exchange** building on Market Street – designed by Lockwood and Mawson – provides ample evidence of the wealth of nineteenth-century Bradford. The building has been splendidly restored and is now almost entirely taken up by a *Waterstone's*, its main hall stacked with books and overlooked by a statue of Richard Cobden, the statesman and economist who led the 1838–46 campaign against the restrictive Corn Laws. Over to the east, north of Leeds Road, the tight grid of streets that is **Little Germany** retains an enclave of warehouse and office buildings in which transplanted German and Jewish merchants once plied their wool trade. The buildings have enticed in new businesses and community ventures, and at the **Design Exchange**, 34 Peckover St (Mon–Fri 9am–5pm; free), the temporary art and design exhibitions are usually worth a peek. A sign on the building next door (no. 36) highlights the site of the inaugural conference of the independent Labour Party in 1893. On the other side of the city centre, a former mill and home of the society of dyes and colourists now houses the **Colour Museum** (Tues–Sat 10am–4pm; £2), on Providence Street, where an interactive display shows how colours and textiles have been made and applied over the centuries.

For further insights into what once made the city tick, visit the **Bradford Industrial Museum** (Tues–Sat 10am–5pm, Sun noon–5pm; free) in the old Victorian Moorside Mills, on Moorside Road in Eccleshill, three miles northeast of the centre. Exhibitions and special events document the city's industrial heritage, alongside working textile machinery, surviving examples of the former workers' cottages, historic transport collection and working shire horses, who haul around a selection of trams and buses. Buses #608 and #609 from Bank Street run here, stopping on Moorside Road, or take #612 from the Interchange.

Practicalities

Trains and buses both arrive at **Bradford Interchange** off Bridge Street, a little to the south of the city-centre grid. There's also a much smaller station at **Forster Square**, across the city, for trains to Keighley. The **tourist office** (Mon–Sat 9am–5.30pm; ⓣ01274/433678, ⓦwww.visitbradford.com), located in Centenary Square's City Hall, is three minutes' signposted walk from the Interchange or five minutes from Forster Square. **Guided walks** (alternate Saturdays, late April to Aug; £2.50) show you more of the city's history and might persuade you to stay – in which case the tourist office can provide local **accommodation** details.

Bradford's large Asian population has made the city famous for its **curry houses**. The *Kashmir*, 27 Morley St (ⓣ01274/726513; open until 3am) – two minutes up the road that runs between the Alhambra and the National Museum – claims to be Bradford's first curry house and, though it's been upgraded in parts, it still sports formica tables in the basement and rock-bottom prices: like many others in town it's unlicensed, though you can take your own booze. At the *Mumtaz*, 386–400 Great Horton Rd (ⓣ01274/571861; no alcohol allowed), the food is sold by weight – a half-pound dish feeds two and the sweet lassi is legendary. It may be a twenty-minute walk up towards the university, but you won't be disappointed. Further afield, a short drive away up Great Horton Road, past the university, more excellent curries are to be found at the *The Bharat*, 496–502 Great Horton Rd (ⓣ01274/521200), while out east on the Leeds Road in Thornbury, again a drive away, *Akbar's*, 1276–1278 Leeds Rd (ⓣ01274/773311), is a buzzing balti house whose huge naan breads are draped over a hook placed on the table so you can tear off strips at will.

For more information on the scene, consult the comprehensive **Bradford Curry Guide** (Ⓦhttp://website.lineone.net/~bradfordcurryguide), which reviews and grades around seventy local curry restaurants.

For post-curry entertainment, the **Pictureville** cinema at the National Museum of Photography, Film and Television has a year-round repertory programme and hosts three major annual **festivals**: the Bradford Film Festival (March), Bite the Mango, the Black and Asian Film-Makers' Festival (June), and the Animation Festival (Nov).

Saltaire

Three miles out of Bradford towards Keighley, along the A650 to the north, no one should pass up the chance to drop in on **SALTAIRE**, a model industrial village and textile mill built by the industrialist Sir Titus Salt. You can catch trains to Saltaire Station (right by Salt's Mill; see below) from Bradford Forster Square, or take bus #679 from the Interchange, which stops in Saltaire village. Buses #662–665, also from the Interchange, drop you at the top of Victoria Road from where it's a half-mile walk to Salt's Mill. Drivers should follow the signs to Keighley (along the A650) from the city centre and then look for the signs to Saltaire and the car parks.

The village (still lived in today) is a perfectly preserved 25-acre realization of one man's vision of an industrial utopia. Having built his fortune on the innovative use of alpaca and mohair, Salt found that by 1850 his factory was too small to meet demand for his new textiles. While economic imperatives demanded a new factory, Salt's spell as mayor of Bradford during a cholera epidemic had also stirred his Congregationalist conscience. "Cholera," he said, "is God's voice to people," adding that he had been confronted with "disclosures too frequently made of immorality and vice prevalent among a large class of the population". Saltaire was built between 1851 and 1876, modelled on buildings of the Italian Renaissance, a period evoked because it was perceived as an era when cultural and social advancement were a direct consequence of the commercial acumen of textile barons. It was built, moreover, in open countryside – impossible to imagine now from the urban surroundings – so that Salt's employees would reap the benefits of the unpolluted, uplifting fresh air.

Salt's Mill, built to emulate an Italian palazzo and larger than St Paul's Cathedral in London, was the biggest factory in the world when it opened in 1853 (on Salt's 50th birthday). Its 1200 looms produced over 30,000 yards of cloth a day, and the mill was surrounded by schools, hospitals, a train station, parks, baths and wash-houses, plus 45 almshouses and around 850 homes. The style and size of each dwelling was designed to reflect the place of the head of that family in the factory hierarchy, one example – for all Salt's philanthropic vigour – of his rigid adherence to the prevailing class orthodoxy. Nor was Salt in any doubt of his own position in the scheme of things: of the village's 22 streets, for example, all – bar Victoria and Albert streets – were named after members of his family. Further to the master's whim, the church was the first public building to be finished and was strategically placed directly outside the factory gates. Most tellingly of all, the village contained not a single pub.

Salt's Mill remains the fulcrum of the village, its several floors now housing art, craft and furniture shops, and a craft centre. But its enterprising centrepiece is the **1853 Gallery** (daily 10am–6pm; free; Ⓦwww.saltsmill.org.uk), an entire floor of the old spinning shed given over to the world's largest retrospective collection of the works of Bradford-born David Hockney. Changing exhibitions cover all phases of the artist's career, from his student days through his

Californian-swimming-pool period and up to his more recent experiments with faxes, Xerox machines and Polaroids. *Salt's Diner* on the same floor has a Hockney-designed logo, menu and crockery, and serves Mediterranean-inspired meals amid the original cast-iron pillars.

To enjoy the area further, take the short signposted walk, across the Leeds–Liverpool Canal and River Aire at the bottom of Victoria Road, and through the bluebell woods, to **Shipley Glen**, where there's a Victorian **funicular tramway** (Easter week, May–Oct & Dec Sat & Sun only, Nov Sat only; 60p return; Ⓦwww.glentramway.co.uk) up to the family pleasure grounds and funfair. Or there's a **waterbus** service along the canal between Saltaire and Shipley, allowing you to cruise the waterway at leisure and make the return journey to Bradford by train from the station at Shipley (Easter–Oct; timetable and fare information on Ⓣ01274/595914). Finally, Saltaire's **tourist office**, 2 Victoria Rd (daily 10am–5pm; Ⓣ01274/774993, Ⓦwww.visitsaltaire.com), is housed in one of the original shops and offers hour-long guided walks of the village throughout the year.

Haworth

Of English literary shrines, probably only Stratford sees more visitors than the quarter of a million who swarm annually into the village of **HAWORTH** to tramp the cobbles once trodden by the Brontë sisters. Quite why the sheltered life of the Brontës should exert such a powerful fascination is a puzzle, though the contrast of their pinched provincial existences with the brooding moors and tumultuous passions of *Wuthering Heights* may well form part of the answer. Whatever the reasons, during the summer the village's steep, cobbled Main Street is lost under huge crowds, herded by multilingual signs around the various stations on the Brontë trail.

Of these, the **Brontë Parsonage Museum**, at the top of the main street (April–Sept daily 10am–5.30pm; Oct–March daily 11am–5pm; £4.80, Ⓦwww.bronte.info), is the obvious focus, a modest Georgian house bought by Patrick Brontë in 1820 to bring up his family. After the tragic early loss of his wife and two eldest daughters, the surviving four children – Anne, Emily, Charlotte and their dissipated brother, Branwell – spent most of their short lives in the place, which is furnished as it was in their day, and filled with the sisters' pictures, books, manuscripts and personal treasures. You can see the sofa on which Emily is said to have died in 1848, aged just 28, for example, and the footstool on which she sat outside on fine days writing *Wuthering Heights*. In Charlotte's

The Keighley and Worth Valley Railway

The **Keighley and Worth Valley Railway** runs steam trains (Easter week, school holidays, July & Aug daily; rest of the year Sat & Sun) along a five-mile stretch of track between Keighley and Oxenhope, stopping at Haworth en route. The restored stations are a delight, with sections of the line etched into the memory of those who recall the film of E. Nesbit's *The Railway Children*, which was shot here in 1970. Valley footpaths run between the stations at Oakworth, Haworth and Oxenhope, allowing you to make a day of your reminiscences. Regular trains from Leeds or Bradford's Forster Square run to Keighley, where you change onto the branch line for the **steam services** (day rover ticket £10; recorded information Ⓣ01535/647777, Ⓦwww.kwvr.co.uk).

room are displayed her tiny shoes and wedding clothes, while other rooms contain mementoes of the rest of the family, including a copy of Branwell's portrait of his three sisters which hangs on the staircase. An exhibition room tells the family history in exhaustive detail, bolstered by personal letters, childhood writings, sketches, diaries, documents and other interesting archive material.

Not surprisingly, it can all be a bit of a scrum inside the house, though it's scarcely any less crowded at the other stops. The bluff **parish church** in front

The Brontës at Haworth

Patrick Prunty or Bronty (it's unclear which) was born in Ireland and became a schoolmaster at the age of 16. He later won a place at St John's, Cambridge, where he changed his name to **Brontë**, perhaps influenced by naval hero Lord Nelson, who was made the Duke of Brontë. Later ordained, the Reverend Brontë, and his Cornish wife Maria, took up a living at Thornton, just outside Bradford, where the four youngest of their six children – Maria, Elizabeth, Charlotte, Branwell, Emily and Anne – were born between 1816 and 1820. The house, at 72–74 Market St, still stands. Later that year, the Brontë family moved into the draughty **parsonage** in nearby Haworth.

It could hardly be called an auspicious start to life in a new home. Mrs Brontë died within the year and her sister was despatched to help look after the children. The four oldest girls were sent away to school, but withdrawn after first Maria, then Elizabeth, died after falling ill. The surviving daughters, and the cosseted Branwell, were kept at home, where they amused themselves by making up convoluted stories and writing miniature books. As they successively came of age, the girls took up short-lived jobs as governesses at various local schools; Charlotte and Emily even spent a year in Brussels, learning French. **Branwell**, meanwhile, was already sowing the dissolute seeds of his disappointing future: he acquired an interest and certain talent for art, but failed to apply to study at the Royal Academy, got into debt, and then spent two years as a junior stationmaster near Halifax but was later dismissed in disgrace. He then took a tutor's job but was dismissed again after developing what was darkly referred to as an "unwise passion" for his employer's wife. He retreated to Haworth, made himself overly familiar with the beer in the *Black Bull* and began experimenting with drugs.

Charlotte's, Emily's and Anne's continuing attempts to amuse themselves with their writings led to the private publication, in 1846, of a series of poems, paid for using part of a legacy from their aunt. They used the (male) pseudonyms Currer, Ellis and Acton Bell – corresponding to their own initials – and though few copies of the collection were ever sold, the little volume acted as a catalyst. Keeping the pseudonym, **Charlotte** wrote a novel the same year, which was rejected by various publishers; but her *Jane Eyre*, submitted in 1847, was an instant success. **Emily**'s *Wuthering Heights* and **Anne**'s *Agnes Grey* received similar acclaim the same year; Anne's second novel, the better-known *Tenant of Wildfell Hall*, was published in 1848. As far as the public was concerned, the brilliant Bell brothers were a publishing sensation.

But the next two years destroyed the family, as it was ravaged by consumption. First Branwell, who had sunk ever deeper into addictive misery and ill health, died in September 1848, followed by Emily in December of that year, and Anne in May of the following year. Charlotte lived on for another six years, writing two more novels – *Shirley* (1849) and *Villette* (1853) – and becoming something of a literary figure once she had revealed her identity, making friends with fellow author Elizabeth Gaskell, who later wrote Charlotte's biography. Charlotte finally **married** Reverend Brontë's curate, Arthur Bell Nicholls, who moved into the parsonage, but she died after nine months of marriage in the early stages of pregnancy. The Reverend Brontë lived on until 1861 – the entire family, except Anne (who is buried in Scarborough), lies in the **Brontë vault** in the village church, next to the house.

of the parsonage – substantially rebuilt since the Brontës lived here – contains the family vault; Charlotte was married here in 1854. At the **Sunday School**, between the parsonage and the church, Charlotte, Anne and even Branwell did weekly teaching stints; Branwell, however, was undoubtedly more at home in the **Black Bull**, a pub within staggering distance of the parsonage near the top of Main Street. He got his opium at the pharmacist's over the road (now a lace shop).

Local walks

A century and a half of academic sleuthing has pinned down many of the local houses and locations the sisters incorporated into their work. However, more than any other locale, it's the wild moorland surrounding Haworth that best captures the Brontë spirit. If you've come this far you should try some of the well-signed and much-travelled **walks**, many described by the sisters themselves, particularly those to the spots which are popularly – but in most cases wrongly – said to have been the inspiration for various locations in the novels. A leaflet available from the tourist office describes the routes.

The most popular walk runs to **Brontë Falls** and **Bridge**, reached via West Lane and a track from the village, and to **Top Withens**, a mile beyond, a ruin fancifully thought to be the model for Wuthering Heights (allow 3hr for the round trip). A plaque here bluntly points out that "the buildings, even when complete, bore no resemblance to the house she [Emily] described". The moorland setting, however, beautifully evokes the flavour of the book, and to enjoy it further you could walk on another two and a half miles to **Ponden Hall**, perhaps the Thrushcross Grange of *Wuthering Heights* (this section of path, incidentally, forms part of the Pennine Way).

Practicalities

Haworth is eight miles northwest of Bradford. To get there by bus, take the #662 from Bradford Interchange to Keighley (every 10min), and change there for the #663, #664 or #665 (every 20min), which drop at various points in the streets immediately below the cobbled Main Street. On Sundays, only the #663 and #665 operate (every 30min). However, the nicest way of getting here is by **train**, using the steam trains of the **Keighley and Worth Valley Railway** (see box on p.937); the station is half a mile from the upper village – cross the footbridge from the station and follow Butt Lane up the side of the park to the bottom of Main Street. Steep **Main Street** and its continuation, **West Lane**, form one long run of gift and teashops, cafés and guest houses, with the busy Haworth **tourist office** at the top at 2–4 West Lane (daily 9.30am–5.30pm; closes at 5pm Oct–March; ⓣ01535/642329, ⓦwww.visithaworth.com).

If you want to stay, you'll need to book ahead at most times of the year – even in winter special events (like the Christmas fair) fill the available **accommodation** at the drop of a hat. There's any number of teashops and **cafés** along Main Street, and the **pubs** serve bar meals. The *Fleece Inn* near the bottom of Main Street, is the place for cask ales, or try the *Black Bull*, near the tourist office, where you can join Branwell's ghost. *Aitches* guest house has a **restaurant** that serves meals to residents (Tues–Thurs), and is open to the public on Friday and Saturday evenings – the proprietor-chef trained with French maestro Paul Bocuse, and dinner will cost you around £20 plus drinks. Otherwise, *Weaver's* (Tues–Sat dinner only, plus Sun lunch) is the place – good modern northern cuisine using local ingredients from around £25 a head. It's essential to book ahead.

Guest houses and hotels

Aitches 11 West Lane ⓣ01535/642501, ⓦwww.aitches.co.uk. This place offers a few comfortable, cottage-style, en-suite rooms, and attached restaurant. ❸

Apothecary 86 Main St ⓣ01535/643642. Traditional guest house opposite the church, whose breakfast room and attached café have splendid views. ❷

Moorfield Guest House 80 West Lane ⓣ01535/643689, ⓦwww.moorfieldgh.demon.co.uk. Victorian house 5min walk from the village centre that makes the most of its elevated position above the valley. ❷

Old White Lion Main St ⓣ01535/642313, ⓦwww.oldwhitelionhotel.com. Old coaching inn at the top of Main St, offering pub-style accommodation and an oak-panelled lounge and bar. ❹

Weaver's 15 West Lane ⓣ01535/643822, ⓦwww.weaversmallhotel.co.uk. A renowned restaurant-with-rooms operation housed in a converted row of weavers' cottages. ❺

Youth hostel

Haworth YHA Longlands Hall ⓣ0870/770 5858, ⓔhaworth@yha.org.uk. Dorm beds (£10.25) in the mansion of a Victorian mill owner, overlooking the village a mile from the centre at Longlands Drive, Lees Lane, off the Keighley road. The Bradford buses stop on the main road nearby. Weekends only Nov to mid-Dec, closed mid-Dec to Jan.

The Yorkshire Dales

The **Yorkshire Dales** – "dales" from the Viking word *dalr* (valley) – form a lovely and varied upland area of limestone hills and pastoral valleys at the heart of the Pennines, wedged between the Lake District to the west and the North York Moors to the east. Protected as a National Park, the region is crammed with opportunities for outdoor activities, from several long-distance footpaths and a specially designated circular cycle way, to a host of centres geared up for caving and other more specialist pursuits.

Most approaches are from the industrial towns to the south, via the superbly engineered **Settle to Carlisle Railway**, or along the main A65 road from towns such as **Skipton**, **Settle** and **Ingleton**. This makes southern dales like **Wharfedale** the most visited, while neighbouring **Malhamdale** is also immensely popular, thanks to the fascinating scenery squeezed into its narrow confines around **Malham**, perhaps the single most visited village in the region. **Ribblesdale**, approached from Settle, is more sombre, its villages popular with hikers intent on tackling the Dales' famous **Three Peaks** – the mountains of Pen-y-ghent, Ingleborough and Whernside. To the northwest lies the more remote **Dentdale**, one of the least known but most beautiful of the valleys. Moving north, there are two parallel dales, **Wensleydale** and **Swaledale**, the latter pushing Dentdale as the most rewarding overall target. Both flow east, with Swaledale's lower stretches encompassing **Richmond**, an appealing historic town with a terrific castle. Finally, outside the National Park boundary, to the east, is **Nidderdale**, relatively under visited, but whose beautiful upper reaches stand comparison with its more famous neighbours.

Public transport throughout the Dales is surprisingly good, though bus services are limited in winter and to the more remote valleys. However, countless special summer Sunday and bank holiday services (usually between May and Sept, peaking in school holidays) connect almost everywhere. Pick up the invaluable, free *Dales Explorer* **timetable** (ⓦwww.dalesbus.org), published twice a year and available from tourist offices and from the **National Park information centres** at Grassington, Aysgarth Falls, Malham, Reeth, Hawes and Clapham. The information centres can also help with accommodation, sell excellent walk and trail leaflets, and organize year-round hikes and events, from nature trails to photography workshops. In addition, there are numerous

National Park **information points** in shops, post offices and cafés throughout the region, which tend to open during local business hours throughout the year (usually Mon–Fri 9am–5pm).

For any kind of serious hiking, you'll need the OS Outdoor Leisure **maps** #2, #10 and #30. The **Pennine Way** cuts right through the heart of the Dales, and the region is crossed by the Coast-to-Coast Walk, but the principal local route is the **Dales Way**, an 84-mile footpath from Ilkley to Bowness on Windermere in the Lake District, which takes around a week to walk. Colin Speakman's *Dales Way* guidebook (Dalesman Press) or Aurum Press/Ordnance Survey's *The Dales Way* guidebooks are useful. An alternative route is the less-walked, seventy-mile **Ribble Way** from the estuary of the River Ribble, between Lytham St Anne's and Preston in Lancashire, to Ribblehead in Ribblesdale; there's a National Park guidebook to the route.

Skipton

SKIPTON, southernmost town of the Dales, rightly belongs to Airedale, but almost any trip to the southern dales is going to pass through here, particularly if you want to see Wharfedale, five miles to the east. Apart from practical advantages, however, the town's worth a few hours in its own right, particularly on one of its four weekly **market** days (Mon, Wed, Fri & Sat), when the streets and pubs are filled with what seems like half the Dales population, milling around and determined to enjoy themselves. Similarly lively Christmas markets in December are an enjoyable feature, too.

Sceptone, or "Sheeptown", was a settlement long before the arrival of the battling Normans, whose **Castle**, located at the top of the High Street (March–Sept Mon–Sat 10am–6pm, Sun noon–6pm; Oct–Feb Mon–Sat 10am–4pm, Sun noon–4pm; £4.80; ⓦ www.skiptoncastle.co.uk), provided the basis for the present fortress, among England's best preserved, thanks mainly to the efforts of Lady Anne Clifford, who rebuilt much of her family seat between 1650 and 1675 following the pillage of the Civil War. The castle withstood a three-and-a-half-year Parliamentary siege – at one point it was the last remaining Royalist stronghold in the north – and when its surrender was finally negotiated, the Royal garrison marched out through the gates "with colours flying, trumpets sounding, drums beating". Little survives in the way of furniture or fittings, but starting with the proud battlements – emblazoned with the Clifford cry, *Desormais* ("Henceforth"!) – the castle very much looks the part. A self-guided tour leads you through the original Norman gateway into the beautiful Conduit Court, whose yew tree was supposedly planted by Lady Anne. Beyond lie the banqueting hall, spacious kitchens and storerooms (giving a clue as to how the castle withstood such a long siege), bedchambers and six towers with their slit windows.

Lady Anne also displayed her restorative skills on the **Church of the Holy Trinity**, which stands in front of the castle at the top of the High Street (summer daily 9am–4.30pm; winter daily 9am–dusk; £1 donation requested), and has a fine bossed fifteenth-century roof, beautiful chancel screen (dating from 1533) and a twelfth-century font crowned with a towering wooden Jacobean cover. The church retains a medieval anchorite's cell, a rare find in England, let alone Yorkshire.

Down the High Street, on the first floor of the town hall, drop into the entertaining **Craven Museum** (April–Sept Mon & Wed–Sat 10am–5pm, Sun 2–5pm; Oct–March Mon & Wed–Fri 1.30–5pm, Sat 10am–4pm; free), which provides a brief introduction to the geology, flora, fauna, folk history and

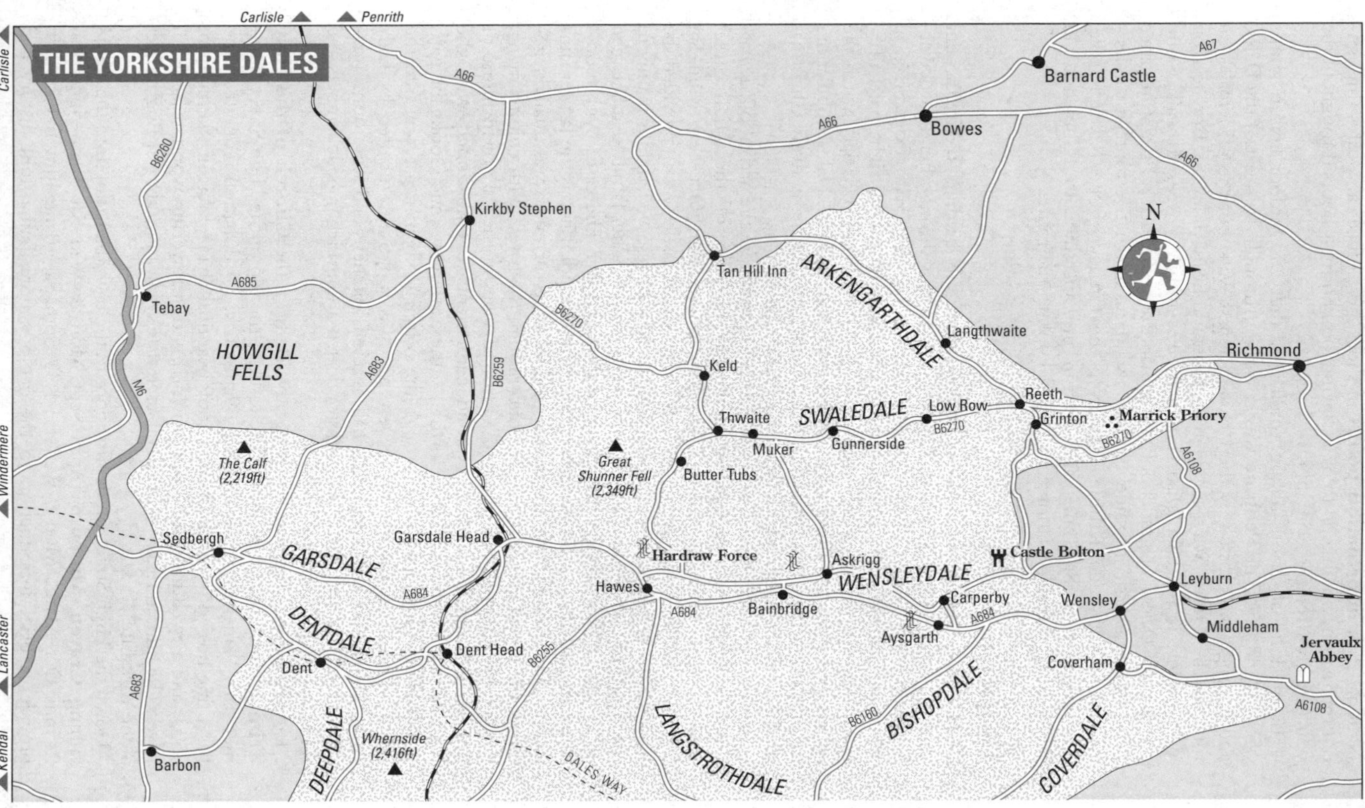
THE YORKSHIRE DALES
Carlisle
Penrith
A1
Leeming Bar & Northallerton
Masham
Windermere
Lancaster
Kendal
N
Barnard Castle
Bowes
Richmond
Kirkby Stephen
Tan Hill Inn
Tebay
Langthwaite
Keld
Reeth
Grinton
Marrick Priory
Low Row
Thwaite
Muker
Gunnerside
Butter Tubs
Great Shunner Fell (2,349ft)
The Calf (2,219ft)
Whernside (2,416ft)
Sedbergh
Garsdale Head
Hardraw Force
Askrigg
Castle Bolton
Hawes
Bainbridge
Carperby
Aysgarth
Wensley
Leyburn
Middleham
Jervaulx Abbey
Coverham
Dent Head
Dent
Barbon
HOWGILL FELLS
ARKENGARTHDALE
SWALEDALE
WENSLEYDALE
GARSDALE
DENTDALE
DEEPDALE
LANGSTROTHDALE
BISHOPDALE
COVERDALE
DALES WAY
A66
A67
A685
A683
A684
A6108
B6260
B6259
B6270
B6255
B6160
M6

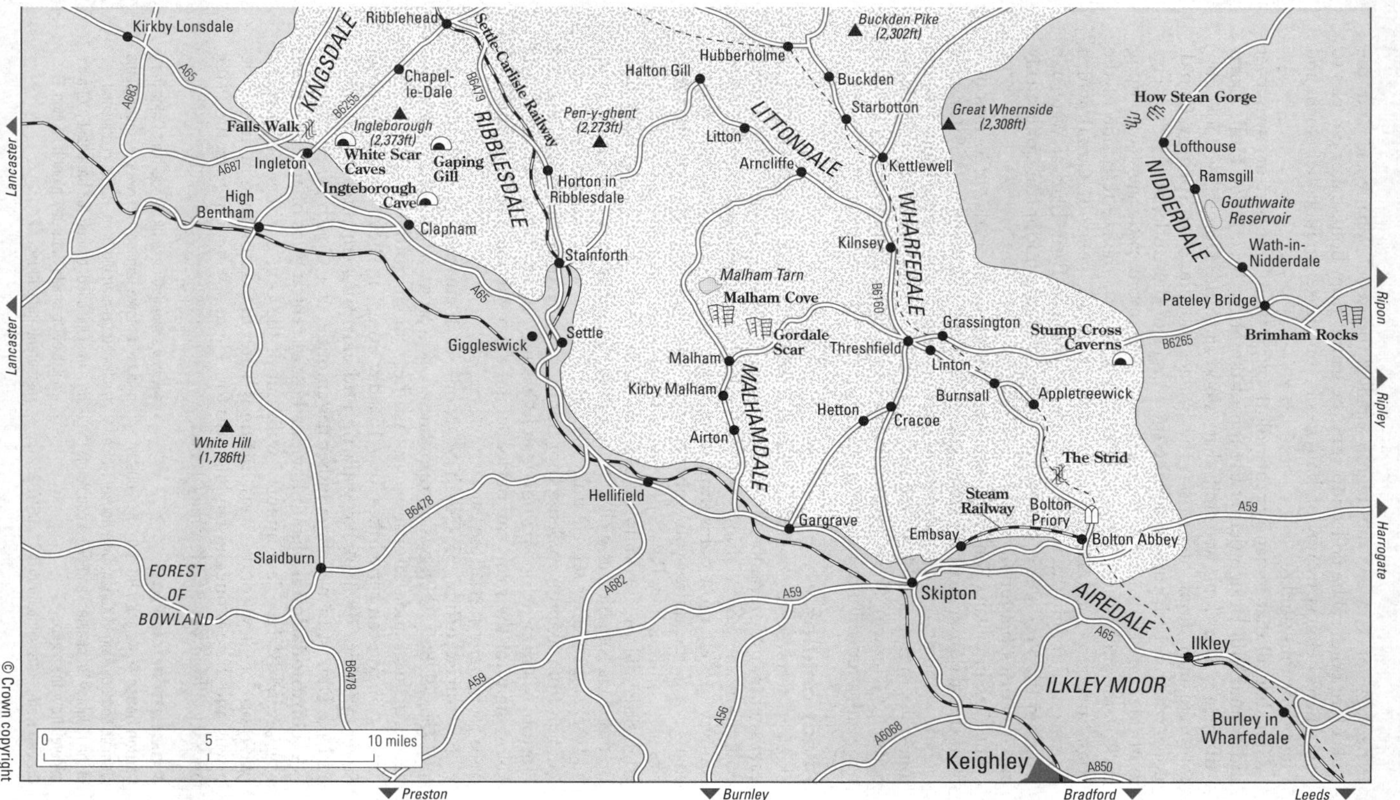
Ripon
Ripley
Harrogate
Leeds
Bradford
Burnley
Preston
Lancaster
Lancaster
Kirkby Lonsdale
A65
A683
Ribblehead
KINGSDALE
Chapel-le-Dale
B6255
B6479
Settle-Carlisle Railway
RIBBLESDALE
Falls Walk
Ingleborough (2,373ft)
White Scar Caves
Gaping Gill
Ingleton
A687
Ingteborough Cave
High Bentham
Clapham
Pen-y-ghent (2,273ft)
Horton in Ribblesdale
Stainforth
A65
Giggleswick
Settle
White Hill (1,786ft)
Hellifield
B6478
Slaidburn
FOREST OF BOWLAND
A682
A59
B6478
A59
A56
Buckden Pike (2,302ft)
Hubberholme
Buckden
Starbotton
Halton Gill
Litton
LITTONDALE
Arncliffe
Kettlewell
Great Whernside (2,308ft)
WHARFEDALE
Kilnsey
B6160
Malham Tarn
Malham Cove
Gordale Scar
Malham
MALHAMDALE
Kirby Malham
Airton
Threshfield
Grassington
Linton
Hetton
Cracoe
Burnsall
Appletreewick
Gargrave
Stump Cross Caverns
B6265
The Strid
Steam Railway
Bolton Priory
Embsay
Bolton Abbey
Skipton
A59
AIREDALE
A65
Ilkley
ILKLEY MOOR
A6068
Keighley
A850
Burley in Wharfedale
How Stean Gorge
Lofthouse
NIDDERDALE
Ramsgill
Gouthwaite Reservoir
Wath-in-Nidderdale
Pateley Bridge
Brimham Rocks
0
5
10 miles

archeology of Craven, the region cradled between Wharfedale and the Lancashire border. The collection runs the gamut from boneshaker bicycles to policemen's helmets, by way of flints, fossils, snuff boxes, grandfather clocks and a hippopotamus skull.

After that, all that remains is to stroll through the oldest part of town, over and around Mill Bridge (left at the top of the High Street). The **High Corn Mill** here is a working watermill that's stood since the Domesday Book, now converted into shops. Steps from the bridge lead down to **Springs Canal**, along which a path runs under the sheer walls of the castle, bears left over a footbridge and then returns on high ground for more castle views, emerging back at the mill twenty minutes later. The alleys on the western side of the High Street emerge onto the banks of the **Leeds–Liverpool Canal**, which runs right through the centre of Skipton. Pennine Boat Trips at Waterside Court (Ⓣ01756/790829), next to the George Fisher outdoor store, offers daily **canal cruises** (Easter–Oct; £4).

The Yorkshire Dales Railway Society runs an impressive range of locomotives from the station at **Embsay**, two miles east of the town on the A59 (up to 5 daily in summer; rest of year runs at least on Sun; 11am–4pm). Trains run the four miles to Bolton Abbey Station (call Ⓣ01756/795189 or 710614 for information; £6 return). There are hourly buses from Skipton to Embsay (the #214; not Sun), a ten-minute ride away.

Practicalities

Skipton receives direct **trains** from Leeds, Bradford, Keighley, Carlisle, Lancaster and Morecambe. The station is on Broughton Road, a ten-minute walk from the centre. Note that if you're heading for the Settle–Carlisle Railway (p.952), most trains from Skipton are direct – you shouldn't need to change at Settle unless you want to break your journey. The **bus station** is closer in, on Keighley Road, just shy of Devonshire Place at the bottom of the High Street. There are National Express coaches from London, and buses from Bradford via Keighley, as well as from Leeds, Ilkley, Harrogate and York; a useful weekend summer service links the Lake District with Skipton. Local services run from Skipton to Settle (not Sun) for connections on to Ingleton and Horton; Malham (Mon–Fri only); and Grassington (not Sun). Drivers should follow signs for the main **car parks** behind the town hall (off High Street) or on Coach Street nearer the canal.

The **tourist office**, 35 Coach St (Mon–Sat 10am–5pm, Sun 11am–3pm; Ⓣ01756/792809, Ⓦwww.skiptononline.co.uk), offers a friendly service and details of local and seasonal events. Ask here about **guided walks** of town (from £3). You can **rent bikes** for £15 a day from The Bicycle Shop on Water Street (Ⓣ01756/794386). For **walking and camping supplies**, the celebrated Lake District firm George Fisher has an outlet at 1 Coach St.

Accommodation is plentiful, with a host of central pubs offering rooms, as well several B&Bs a few minutes' walk out of the centre, either on Gargrave (west) or Keighley (south) roads. **Eating** is better in Skipton than in most Dales towns, and there is one outstanding **pub** too. There's even a **cinema**, the *Plaza*, on Sackville Street off Keighley Road.

Accommodation

Carlton House 46 Keighley Rd Ⓣ01756/700921. A small, non-smoking Victorian town house, typical of the Keighley Rd choices, and just a couple of minutes from the centre. ❷

Craven Heifer Grassington Rd Ⓣ01756/792521, Ⓦwww.cravenheifer.co.uk. Stone-built Dales inn, a mile out of town (2min drive), with en-suite rooms fashioned from an old barn. Buffet continental breakfast included, though full breakfast (£6) also available. No single Saturday-night bookings. Bar, restaurant and parking. ❷

Dalesgate Lodge 69 Gargrave Rd ☎01756/790672, ⓔdalesgatelodge@hotmail.com. Three en-suite doubles and one twin room available in this friendly, family-run, non-smoking B&B. Three-night winter stays (Oct–March) are a real bargain, knocking fifty percent off the regular price. Parking. No credit cards. ❷

Unicorn Hotel Devonshire Place, Keighley Rd ☎01756/794146, ⓦwww.unicorn.hotel.8k.com. Resolutely old-fashioned hotel, right in the centre. Most of the rooms are pretty spacious, and there's a pay-and-display car park over the road. ❸

Woolly Sheep Inn 38 Sheep St ☎01756/700966. A restored seventeenth-century inn at the bottom of the High Street with nine pine-furnished rooms. Some are a bit tight on space, but very comfortable nonetheless with decent beds, good showers, and cafetieres supplied. Downstairs in the public bar there are Timothy Taylor's beers and meals served daily, lunch and dinner. Parking available. ❸

Cafés

Café Jaca 8 High St. Contemporary café – at the top, by the church – serving assorted grilled sandwiches, drinks, cakes and a range of hot brasserie-style dishes. Closed Tues.

Coffee House Coach St Car Park. Known for its coffee, but also the place for warm, filled herb baguettes, stuffed ciabattas, toasted bagels, homemade soups and the like. Closed Sun.

Restaurants

Aagrah Devonshire Place, off Keighley Rd ☎01756/790807. It might be decked out like a snake-charmer's boudoir, but it has a loyal local following for its fresh, tasty Indian dishes. Dinner only. Inexpensive.

Bizzie Lizzies 36 Swadford St ☎01756/701131. The town's award-winning fish-and-chip shop, with the restaurant side of the operation (dining over the canal) open until 9pm every night. Inexpensive.

Le Caveau 86 High St ☎01756/794274. Skipton's top spot, an Anglo-Med cellar restaurant with lunchtime specials and a seasonal menu. Good for fish, with maybe a Rocquefort salad and a summer fruit terrine either side. Closed Sun & Mon. Expensive.

Pub

The Narrow Boat 38 Victoria St. All you want from a pub – not just varied cask ales and a multitude of Belgian and German beers, but good, inexpensive food (lunch daily, dinner until 8pm, not Fri or Sat) that ranges from Cumberland sausage and mash to grilled salmon fillet. Add a no-smoking ground floor, no piped music, and jazz and quiz nights, and it's the recipe for coming for one drink and staying put.

Wharfedale

The lower reaches of **Wharfedale** extend way to the east, embracing towns as distant as Wetherby before joining the Ouse south of York, but for most people the dale really starts just south and east of Skipton, with **Ilkley** and **Bolton Abbey**, and then continues north in a broad, pastoral swathe scattered with villages as picture-perfect as any in northern England. **Grassington** is the main village, a popular walking centre, packed to capacity in summer; smaller hamlets in Upper Wharfedale, like **Kettlewell** and **Buckden**, make less frenetic bases. Upland roads lead from the head of the valley up minor dales to cross the watershed into Wensleydale, though the most attractive itinerary would take you up lonely Littondale to **Arncliffe**, a village almost too good to be true, and then over the tops to either Malham or Ribblesdale.

Throughout the year, **buses** run roughly hourly (not Sun) to Grassington from Skipton (via Cracoe and Threshfield), and then half a dozen times a day on up the B6160 to Kettlewell, Starbotton and Buckden. This is augmented by the special #800/805/806 weekend services (Sun all year, plus extra summer services on Sat & Sun) from Leeds, Bradford and Ilkley, running through Wharfedale and travelling on to Wensleydale.

Ilkley

Approaching Wharfedale from Leeds and the southeast, along the A65, it's a gentle climb to the approaching moorland, with barely a hint of the coming grandeur even by the time you reach the small, stone town of **ILKLEY**, gamely claiming to be the gateway to the Dales. It's really no such thing, though it was once a spa town of some repute and still boasts a handsome centre of Victorian buildings and landscaped gardens. Its history can be traced right back to the Romans, who built the fort of Olicana here in 79 AD, the foundations of which lie under the grassy knoll behind All Saints parish church on Church Street. Sundry Roman relics and other local finds are displayed in the adjacent, sixteenth-century **Manor House Museum** (Wed–Sat 11am–5pm, Sun 1–4pm; free).

To the south, encroaching upon the very town, broods **Ilkley Moor**, littered with ancient stone circles and weathered rocks – and, if the more lurid tales are to be believed, site of numerous UFO appearances and alien abductions. In the words of a round known to many Yorkshire schoolchildren, the windswept moor is also where "tha's been a-courtin' Mary Jane, on Ilkley Moor baht-'at [without a hat]" – a foolish sartorial omission since, according to the round, you'll catch your death of cold, die, be buried, eaten by worms, which are eaten by ducks, which are eaten by people, until "then we shall all 'ave etten thee". With hat firmly in place you can follow the numerous tracks which cut across the highest part of the moor, seeking out Bronze Age stone circles like the Twelve Apostles or the weathered rocks known as the Cow and the Calf, before heading south to Keighley, six miles away.

The **bus** and **train stations** are next to each other on Station Road. Aside from regular train and bus connections with Leeds/Bradford, the #X84 bus runs every twenty minutes between Leeds and Ilkley (and hourly onto Skipton), and there's a summer Sunday service from Ilkley to Bolton Abbey. Opposite the station in the Town Hall is the **tourist office** (Mon–Sat 9.30am–5.30pm; ☎01943/602319), outside which is pinned a local accommodation list. You're unlikely to stay, but you might find time to eat. There's a branch of the Harrogate tea-and-cake stalwart *Betty's* at 32 The Grove; while *Bart'at*, 7 Cunliffe Rd, behind *Betty's*, is an ale and wine bar with good brasserie food (not Tues & Sun night; ☎01943/608888). Ilkley's annual **literature festival** (Sept/Oct) attracts top names to its events and readings.

Bolton Abbey and the Strid

BOLTON ABBEY, five miles east of Skipton, is the name of a whole village rather than an abbey, a confusion compounded by the fact that the place's main monastic ruin is known as **Bolton Priory** (daily 9am to dusk; free). The priory formed part of an Augustinian community founded at nearby Embsay by Cecily de Romille in 1135, and was moved here in the 1150s by her daughter, Alice, to commemorate the drowning of her son in the Strid (see below). Turner painted the site, and Ruskin described it as the most beautiful in England, though the priory is now mostly ruined, a consequence of the Dissolution; only the nave, which was incorporated into the village church in 1170, has survived in almost its original state. A £10 bribe sent by the last prior to Thomas Cromwell, Henry VIII's lieutenant, unsurprisingly failed to change the course of history.

The priory is also the starting point for several highly popular riverside walks, including a section of the **Dales Way** footpath that follows the river's west bank to take in Bolton Woods and the **Strid** (from "stride"), an extraordinary piece of white water two miles north of the abbey, where softer rock has allowed the river to funnel into a cleft just a few feet wide. Numerous people have drowned trying to make the leap (the river here is 30ft deep), and the quite obvious dangers are underlined by the lifebelts hung nearby. Beyond the

Strid, the path – a designated nature trail – emerges at **Barden Bridge**, four miles from the priory, where the fortified **Barden Tower** was another little restoration job for Lady Anne Clifford; there's a tearoom here. You can then return to Bolton Abbey either by doubling back the same way, or by taking the country lanes and tracks on the other (east) bank, perhaps incorporating a lovely short detour past the becks and waterfalls of the **Valley of Desolation** midway between Barden and Bolton.

To get here without your own transport, you're reliant upon the weekend-only #800/805/806 bus service, or a taxi from Skipton – the journey will set you back around £8 each way. Embsay and Bolton Abbey Steam Railway is a mile and a half from the priory ruins, and there's a signposted footpath. Drivers have to stump up £4 to park in one of the estate **car parks**. There's local **information** from the estate office (ⓣ01756/718009, ⓦwww.boltonabbey.com) and an information point at **Cavendish Pavilion**, a mile north of the priory, where there's also a riverside restaurant and café (April–Oct daily; Nov–March weekends only). *Bolton Abbey Tea Cottage*, next to the priory, offers traditional afternoon teas; it's a bit over-priced but worth it if the weather allows you to sit in the garden and admire the views.

At Bolton Abbey the main **hotel** is the sumptuous *Devonshire Arms* (ⓣ01756/710441, ⓦwww.thedevonshirearms.co.uk; ⑨), just south of the village, owned by the duke and duchess of Devonshire and furnished with antiques from their ancestral pile at Chatsworth; there's a brasserie and bar open to the public too. The sister hotel, the *Devonshire Fell*, at Burnsall (see "Grassington", p.947), is a cheaper choice, though considerably easier on the pocket all round are two **B&Bs**, one at *Hesketh Farm*, a mile west of the village (ⓣ01756/710541; no credit cards; ❶), the other at *Holme House Farm*, a quarter of a mile south of Barden, overlooking the river (ⓣ01756/720661; no credit cards; ❶; closed Nov–March). Skipton tourist office has details of several other local farmhouse B&Bs. *Barden Bunk Barn*, right by the tower and just 300yd off the Dales Way (ⓣ01756/720330; £8, groups only at weekends), is a useful bunkhouse stop for long-distance hikers.

Grassington and around

You should follow the Dales Way up the River Wharfe at least as far as **GRASSINGTON**, the dale's popular main village, located nine miles from Bolton Abbey. It has a good Georgian centre, albeit one tempered by dollops of fake rusticity, and the surroundings are at their best by the river, where the shallow Linton Falls thunder after rain; a waterside path leads a mile upstream to the Grass Wood nature reserve. Back in the village, the cobbled **Market Square** is home to several inns and a small local museum. Traditional rural pursuits, as well as music and arts events, are celebrated in both the annual **Grassington Festival**, held every June, and the Christmas market, held on December Saturdays in the village square.

The **National Park information centre** on Hebden Road (April–Oct daily 10am–5pm; Nov–March Wed & Fri–Sun 10am–4pm; ⓣ01756/752774), across from the **bus stop**, books accommodation and provides wide-ranging information. You might grab a one-hour parking space in the Market Square; otherwise, there's a huge pay-and-display **car park** at the information centre. For **hiking and camping** gear, visit The Mountaineer, in Pletts Barn on Garrs Lane (ⓣ01756/752266), up past the *Black Horse* pub. Grassington also has the bulk of the dale's **services** – a bank with ATM, small supermarket and post office.

In summer you should book **accommodation** in advance. There's a fair amount in the village, but even so, at busy times you may have to look further afield – no hardship since Grassington is surrounded by tiny scenic villages, all connected by minor country roads and footpaths (both Burnsall and Appletreewick are on the Dales Way). The nearest hostels are at Malham (7 miles) or Kettlewell (8 miles).

Hotels, inns and B&Bs

Ashfield House Summers Fold, Grassington ⓣ01756/752584, ⓦwww.ashfieldhouse.co.uk. Lovely seventeenth-century house, 50yd off the square (behind the *Devonshire Hotel*), boasting a walled garden, good breakfasts and some special weekend deals. Dinner available too (£17). Closed Dec & Jan. ❺

Devonshire Arms Cracoe, 2 miles south of Grassington ⓣ01756/730237. Not to be confused with the Duke and Duchess' luxury pad, this country pub (with parking outside) has simple but comfortable rooms. They do bar meals too, but you're only a mile's walk from the gourmet experience of the *Angel* at Hetton (see "Eating and drinking" below). ❸

Devonshire Fell Burnsall, 3 miles southeast of Grassington ⓣ01756/729000, ⓦwww.devonshirefell.co.uk. Ten bedrooms and two suites here have been given the designer treatment – although this is a country house retreat, it's definitely not "country" in feel. Views are either of garden and village or fells and river, while a classy bar and bistro complete the experience. Guests can use Bolton Abbey's *Devonshire Arms'* leisure facilities. Weekend two-night minimum. ❼

Devonshire Hotel Main St, Grassington ⓣ01756/752525, ⓕ01756/753748. The old inn on the square has plenty of character, well-priced rooms, a cosy bar, open fire and real ales. ❹

Grassington Lodge 8 Wood Lane, Grassington ⓣ01756/752518, ⓦwww.grassingtonlodge.co.uk. Relax in the Wades' quiet village house, where all seven en-suite rooms, furnished in country pine, have a really airy feel. The top two, in the eaves, have the most space, while the house bathroom has a bath for walkers wanting to soak away the day's rigours. There's parking, and a holiday cottage available. No credit cards. ❹

Kirkfield Hebden Rd, Grassington ⓣ01756/752385. A detached house with dale views, set in its own grounds, 100yd from the National Park Centre. Parking available. No credit cards. ❷

Red Lion Burnsall, 3 miles southeast of Grassington ⓣ01756/720204, ⓦwww.redlion.co.uk. A real old country inn, with log fires, oak beams, a cosy bar, and river views from its comfortable, traditionally furnished rooms. Inventive meals (in the bar or restaurant) use local ingredients and there's great beer. ❼

Campsites

Bell Bank Skirethorns Lane, Threshfield ⓣ01756/752321. Nearest campsite to Grassington, a little over a mile to the west – milk and eggs are available to buy. Closed Nov–Easter.

Mason's Ainhams Farm, Appletreewick ⓣ01756/720236. Farm camping, 4 miles southeast of Grassington. Closed Nov–Easter.

Eating and drinking

Angel Inn Hetton, 4 miles southwest of Grassington ⓣ01756/730263. Gastro-pub par excellence, with renowned Modern British food served either in the bar-brasserie (lunch & dinner) or more formal restaurant (Mon–Sat dinner & Sun lunch) – best to book for either if you want to eat. The menu's seasonal but there's always locally sourced meat and great fish. Expensive.

Dales Kitchen 51 Main St, Grassington ⓣ01756/753208. This place serves traditional tearoom dishes during the day – rarebits, Yorkshire ham, Cumberland sausage, and homemade fruitcake with Wensleydale cheese. Inexpensive.

Fountaine Inn Linton, 1 mile southwest of Grassington ⓣ01756/752210. The old pub on the green makes a nice target for a walk across the river from Grassington. Real ales, sandwiches and more elaborate bar meals served daily. Inexpensive.

Old Hall Inn Threshfield, 1 mile west of Grassington ⓣ01756/752441. Stone-flagged inn with great food: expect to have to wait for a table before tucking into the likes of grilled salmon, local steaks and sausages. Closed Mon lunch. Moderate.

Kilnsey and Littondale

Wharfedale's scenery above Grassington grows still more impressive, starting a mile north with a tract of ancient woodland, **Grass Wood**, and followed two miles later by **Kilnsey Crag**, a dramatic, glacially carved overhang which attracts its fair share of climbers. Information on the crag and its surroundings can be gleaned from the **National Park information point** at Kilnsey Park on the southern edge of **KILNSEY** village. There's a **trout farm** in the park (daily 9am–5.30pm or dusk if earlier), which aside from its fishing (rods available to rent) provides a whole host of children's activities as well as a café; the deli-shop is worth a visit if you're self-catering, selling everything from eggs and honey to game and gravadlax.

Just beyond Kilnsey Crag, a minor road branches off left into **Littondale**, an empty, pristine dale with stunning scenery and views, especially at Hesleden Bergh, around six miles up the dale, where a road climbs south over the moors – with Pen-y-ghent looming to the west – to Stainforth in Ribblesdale. **ARNCLIFFE**, halfway up the dale, is as idyllic a village as you'll find, with a pub on the village green that attracts walkers from far and wide. The minor moorland road south to Malham from Arncliffe can be treacherous in winter; check the weather reports before setting off. *Raikes Cottage*, just out of Arncliffe on the Malham road, is a nice riverside tearoom (weekends only in winter).

On foot, the ideal way to see the dale is to follow the valley-floor footpath from Arncliffe to **LITTON** (2–3 miles), where the ancient and unspoilt *Queen's Arms* (Ⓣ01756/770208; ❸) could serve as a base for climbing Pen-y-ghent; a steep track also cuts north across the fells to Buckden.

Kettlewell

The landscapes in the last six miles of Wharfedale and its continuation, **Langstrothdale**, hardly suffer by comparison with Littondale, a large proportion of their moors and valleys forming part of the National Trust's vast Upper Wharfedale Estate. **KETTLEWELL** (Norse for "bubbling spring"), three miles north of Kilnsey, is the main centre for the upper dale, a far more attractive proposition for a weekend's walking or relaxing than Grassington, with an informal **National Park information point** in the Over and Under outdoor shop, a campsite (Ⓣ01756/760886) just to the north at Fold Farm, and **youth hostel** (Ⓣ0870/770 5896, Ⓔkettlewell@yha.org.uk; £10.25; closed Sun April–June, Sept & Oct, & closed other days during winter) in the centre of the village. There's plenty of other local **accommodation**: the *Racehorses* (Ⓣ01756/760233; ❹), on the bridge, is an eighteenth-century hotel with twelve en-suite rooms and views of the River Wharfe; or there's *Chestnut Cottage* by the stream (Ⓣ01756/760804; no credit cards; ❷). The village **pubs**, the *Bluebell* and the *King's Head*, are both cosy places for a drink.

Starbotton, Buckden and Hubberholme

It's lovely country north of Kettlewell, accessed either via the dale's single lonely road (B6160) or the Dales Way path, both of which push to the dale's upper limit. At **STARBOTTON**, two miles away, the *Fox & Hounds* (closed Mon & all Jan) has ancient flagged floors, a huge fire and popular food. There's also a great pub in **BUCKDEN**, another couple of miles to the north, the *Buck Inn* (Ⓣ01756/760228; ❺), which has good food and beer. For information on Buckden's other half-dozen cheaper B&B options (many on outlying farms), contact the **National Park information point** at the village's Riverside Gallery. Beyond Buckden, the road winds up and down Bishopdale the ten miles or so to Aysgarth in Wensleydale.

A mile upstream, the river flows through Langstrothdale to **HUBBERHOLME** and the stone-flagged, whitewashed *George* (Ⓣ01756/760223; ❸), the favourite pub of archetypal Yorkshireman J.B. Priestley, who revelled in visiting a hamlet he thought "one of the smallest and pleasantest places in the world". He's buried in the churchyard of the small chapel of St Michael and

All Angels, over the stone bridge from the pub. There's a year-round bunkhouse barn in Hubberholme at *Grange Farm* (☎01756/760259; £8, groups only at weekends), just five minutes' walk from the pub on the route back to Buckden. The Dales Way marches on up the valley, with the next halt over in Dent (see p.957), a superb cross-dales hike.

Malhamdale

A few miles west of Wharfedale lies **Malhamdale**, the uppermost reaches of Airedale and one of the National Park's most heavily visited regions, thanks to its three outstanding natural features: Malham Cove, Malham Tarn and Gordale Scar. It is classic limestone country, dominated by a mighty escarpment topped by a fractured pavement, and cut through with sheer walls, tumbling waterfalls and dry valleys – in short, a place to feed the soul while exercising the body. Unfortunately for those seeking solitude, all three main attractions are within easy hiking distance of **Malham village**, so any walking you do locally is likely to be in company, with the Pennine Way further adding to the column of walkers processing through the area. Local **information** is available on a useful website, Ⓦwww.malhamdale.com.

The approach by **public transport** is on the #210 bus from Skipton (not weekends) or the summer Sunday #820 from Grassington, a thirty- to sixty-minute ride depending on the service. You may simply choose to **walk** in across country: Malham is only around six miles from Gargrave (a station on the Skipton–Settle train line, and on the Pennine Way) to the south, and a similar distance from Settle to the west – a particularly fine approach – or from Grassington in the east.

Malham village

Unless you're here off-season, some idea of what to expect in **MALHAM** comes at the vast peripheral car park, likely to be packed solid with hikers and day-trippers. The village is home to barely a couple of hundred people, who inhabit the huddled stone houses on either side of a bubbling river, but this microscopic gem attracts perhaps half a million visitors a year. Provided you're prepared to do some walking you can escape the worst of the crowds, and something of the village's off-peak charm can be enjoyed in the evening when most of the trippers have gone home. If, however, you're planning on staying, note that competition is stiff for rooms. Something of the village's tradition can be seen every year at the **Malham Show** (August bank holiday Saturday), an agricultural country fair that draws thousands of visitors.

Unless you already have maps and accommodation sorted out, your first stop should be the **National Park information centre** on the southern edge of the village (Easter–Oct daily 10am–5pm; Nov–Easter Fri–Sun 10am–4pm; ☎01729/830363). In summer, you'll need to book ahead to get a bed at the **youth hostel** (☎01729/830321, Ⓔmalham@yha.org.uk; £11.50; closed Sun–Wed Nov–Jan). However, there's also a centrally heated **bunkhouse barn** at *Hill Top Farm* (☎01729/830320; £8, groups only at weekends), immediately north of the National Park information centre, and several good village **B&Bs**, among them *Beck Hall* (☎01729/830332, Ⓦwww.beckhallmalham.com; ❸), set in its own streamside gardens a couple of hundred yards from the fork in the village centre; the excellent *Miresfield Farm* (☎01729/830414; ❸), on the edge of the village near the information centre; or comfortable *Riverhouse Hotel* (☎01729/830315, Ⓦwww.riverhousehotel.co.uk; ❸), on the road through the village. There are pub rooms at the welcoming *Buck Inn*

(Ⓣ01729/830317; ❸), almost next door. You can **camp** under Gordale Scar at *Gordale Scar House Campsite* (Ⓣ01729/830333; closed Nov–March). There's a tearoom or two in the village, and a basic shop. Meals are served in the **pubs**, notably at the *Buck Inn*, with a popular walkers' back bar, but also at the fancier *Lister Arms* (Ⓣ01729/830330, Ⓦwww.listerarms.co.uk; ❸) over the bridge, which has a good range of beers.

Malham Cove, Malham Tarn and Gordale Scar

Appearing in spectacular fashion a mile north of Malham, **Malham Cove** is a white-walled limestone amphitheatre rising three hundred feet above its surroundings. Like Gordale Scar's ramparts to the east, it was formed by a shear along the Mid-Craven Fault, a geological tear that runs 22 miles from Wharfedale to Kirkby Lonsdale in Cumbria. A broad track leads to the cove, passing some of England's most visible prehistoric field banks en route. Fewer people make the breath-sapping haul to the top, where the rewards are fine views and the famous **limestone pavement**, an expanse of clints (slabs) and grykes (clefts) created by water seeping through weaker lines in the limestone rock. Unusual plants and ferns such as dog's mercury and hart's tongue shelter in the crevices, making this a favoured spot for botanists.

A simple walk over the moors, either via the Pennine Way or the more interesting dry valley to the west, abruptly brings **Malham Tarn** into sight, a lake created by an impervious layer of glacial debris. This, too, is an area of outstanding natural interest, its numerous waterfowl protected by a nature reserve on the west bank, visible from a nature trail which forms part of the Pennine Way on the east bank. Meanwhile, at **Gordale Scar** (also easily approached direct from Malham village), the cliffs are if anything more spectacular than at Malham Cove, complemented by a deep ravine to the rear caused by the collapse of a cavern roof. A little to the south of the scar, off the road, lies **Janet's Foss**, a peach of a waterfall set amidst green-damp rocks and overarching trees.

There's a classic circuit which takes in cove, tarn and scar in a clockwise **walk from Malham** (8 miles; 3hr 30min), the only problem being at Gordale Scar, where it may be difficult to scramble down the stream-cut gorge after heavy rain for the last leg back to Malham. If you don't want to see the tarn and open moorland, the walk is easily cut short by taking a waymarked track from the northern edge of the pavement, above Malham Cove, down to Gordale Bridge and thus on to Gordale Scar (5 miles; 2hr 30min). From Gordale Scar you could simply follow the Gordale lane back into the village, though the longer path via Janet's Foss, along the beck and across the fields, is more agreeable.

Ribblesdale

The scenery of **Ribblesdale**, to the west of Malhamdale, is more dour and brooding than the bucolic valleys to the east. It's entered from Settle, starting point of the superbly engineered **Settle–Carlisle Railway**, among the most scenic rail routes in the country (see box p.952). After Stainforth, close to one of the more noted of the Dales' many waterfalls (or "forces"), the valley's only village of any size is **Horton in Ribblesdale**, a focus not only for the Ribble Way and Pennine Way, but also where most people start the **Three Peaks Walk**, an arduous hike around the Dales' highest peaks.

Settle is the **transport** junction for Ribblesdale, with daily **trains** heading north through Horton to Carlisle and south to Skipton, Keighley and Leeds; a limited service operates on Sundays. The hourly #580/581 **bus** (not Sun) connects Skipton with Settle, from where it runs three or four times daily (not

Sun) north through Stainforth to Horton but no further, and northwest via Giggleswick and Clapham to Ingleton in the western Dales. There's also the summer Sunday and bank holiday bus #807 from Skipton to Settle, Horton and Ribblehead, continuing on to Wensleydale and Richmond. Coming from Malham, you could **walk** the six miles along an old pack road via Kirkby Fell and the grandiose cliffs of Attermire Scar.

Settle

Nestled under the wooded knoll of Castleberg, **SETTLE** is well placed for upper Ribblesdale and a pleasant enough base if you haven't the time to find a more intimate overnight stop within the National Park. The village has a typical seventeenth-century market square, top-heavy with tearooms but still sporting its split-level arcaded shambles, which once housed butchers' shops.

The Settle to Carlisle Railway

In the six years between 1869 and 1875, when the 72-mile **Settle to Carlisle** line opened, herculean efforts were made by thousands of navvies to blast a route through the unforgiving Dales mountainsides. Living in squalid shanty towns by the sides of the track, and even in the newly opened railway tunnels themselves, six thousand men built twenty viaducts and bored fourteen tunnels in a feat of Victorian engineering that has few equals in Britain. Over two hundred of the workers died, some of smallpox and other diseases, others in horrific accidents; many now lie buried in the village churches that line the route.

The railway itself was an immediate success, forming a popular route to Scotland and later used as a freight and troop carrier during World War II. By the 1970s, though, services had been severely reduced as British Rail "rationalized" its operations and in 1983 it was announced that the line was to close. After a vociferous campaign, local groups kept the line open and as tourist interest has picked up, the route seems set to have an assured future, at least in the medium term. Stations have been restored to their nineteenth-century glory and special steam train services sometimes operate.

The attraction in riding the line is the chance to experience what the operators – with no hint of hype – dub **"England's most scenic railway"**. From Settle, the drag up Ribblesdale brings ever more spectacular views – between Horton and Ribblehead the line climbs two hundred feet in five miles, before crossing the famous 24-arched Ribblehead viaduct. The station at Dent Head is the highest, and bleakest, main-line station in England. Further on, the route heads through Ais Gill, 1100ft above sea level, before it finally drops into the gentler Eden Valley and on to Carlisle.

The journey from Settle to Carlisle takes just under an hour and forty minutes, so it's easy to make a **return trip** (£16.40 for adult day return) along the whole length of the line if you wish. Two **rover tickets** are also available: for three consecutive days (£30) or three days in seven (£35).

There are connections to Settle from Skipton (20min) and Leeds (1hr); full **timetable** details are available from National Rail Enquiries, ⓣ08457/484950, or from the website, ⓦwww.settle-carlisle.co.uk. If you only have time for a short trip, the best section is that between Settle and Garsdale (30min), though note that you'll typically have a very short or very long wait for the return train. It's best to combine a trip with a **hike**. You can access the Pennine Way or Coast-to-Coast walk from the line; use it to link places like Settle, Dent and Ingleton in a loop walk; or sign up for one of the **free guided walks** from stations along the route, organized by the Friends of the Settle–Carlisle Line (leaflets available at stations or email ⓔwalksinfo@settle-carlisle.co.uk for details).

Other than on Tuesdays, when the **market** is in full swing, there's not much to see in the few streets behind the square. Aim instead for the **Watershed Mill Visitor Centre**, on Langliffe Road (Mon–Sat 10am–5pm, Sun 11am–5pm; free), north of the centre by the river on the Horton road. The early nineteenth-century cotton mill has been transformed into a shopping centre selling Dales goods; there are craft demonstrations throughout the year and a coffee shop.

All other local diversions involve a good walk. The shortest is the ten-minute climb up through the woods to the top of **Castleberg** for views over the town. The **Ribble Way** footpath, which passes through town, continues to Stainforth (see p.953), or there's the four-mile round-trip hike northeast to **Victoria Cave**, a gaping maw in the Mid-Craven Fault in which archeologists found the bones of prehistoric hyenas and elephants.

The **tourist office** in the town hall on Cheapside, just off Market Place (daily 9.30am–4.30pm; ⓣ01729/825192), is the place to seek out onward routes and hiking itineraries; local walks are all detailed in leaflets. The **train station** is less than five signposted minutes' walk from Market Place, down Station Road. As for accommodation, two comfortable old town **inns**, the *Royal Oak* on Market Place (ⓣ01729/822561; ❸), and the *Golden Lion*, just off Market Place along Duke Street (ⓣ01729/822203, ⓦwww.goldenlionhotel.net; ❸), are the most atmospheric places to stay. There's **B&B** at the Georgian *Liverpool Guest House* on Chapel Square (ⓣ01729/822247; no credit cards; ❷), while the *Oast Guest House*, 5 Penyghent View, Church Street, on the Giggleswick road (ⓣ01729/822989, ⓦwww.oastguesthouse.co.uk; no credit cards; ❷), caters for vegetarians, vegans and others with special diets – all the food is homemade and locally sourced. The nearest hostel and campsite is at Stainforth.

Both the inns serve reasonable **food** and decent beer. The *Royal Oak* gets the nod by virtue of its extraordinary carved oak-panelled bar and dining room. The *Little House*, a Modern English restaurant on Duke Street (ⓣ01729/823963; dinner only, not Tues), next to the police station, is moderately priced and changes its menu monthly to fit the season. Or there's a BYO curry house, the *Ruchee* (ⓣ01729/823393; dinner only), on Duke Street by the Station Road car park. During the day, however, it's hard to see anyone resisting the lure of *Ye Olde Naked Man Café* (closed Wed), serving breakfasts, proper coffee and good homemade food; a former undertakers, the café's name refers to the old adage that "you bring now't into the world and you take now't out".

Stainforth

STAINFORTH, two miles north of Settle, makes a good base for walks in the lower part of the Ribble Valley. There are several B&Bs; a **pub**, the *Craven Heifer* (ⓣ01729/822599; ❸); a **youth hostel** (ⓣ0870/770 6046, ⓔstainforth@yha.org.uk; £11.50; open most weekends and daily in school holidays), located in an old Georgian country house set in extensive grounds about a quarter of mile south of the village; and a **campsite** at *Knight Stainforth Hall*, Little Stainforth (ⓣ01729/822200). Stone-built *Husbands Barn* (ⓣ01729/822240; ❸; closed Jan & Feb) is a farm B&B south of the village on the main road, near the youth hostel.

The nicest route to the village is by the **footpath from Settle**, part of the Ribble Way, which runs gently alongside the river, reaching Stainforth Force waterfall in around an hour, the village itself ten minutes later. The path starts in Settle just across the bridge to Giggleswick and, though poorly signposted, is easy to follow. **Stainforth Force** is hardly in the Niagara league, but there's some splashing around to be done in the shallow pools, and you might like to peer over the seventeenth-century **Stainforth Bridge**, a packhorse bridge just a stone's throw away. The best of the area's short walks climbs up to another waterfall, **Catrigg Force**, a mile east of the village, easily reached by an unsurfaced lane.

Horton in Ribblesdale and the Three Peaks

The noted walking centre of **HORTON IN RIBBLESDALE** dates from Norman times – its church, St Oswald's, retains its original proportions in the fine nave – but the village gained a new lease of life in the nineteenth century when the arrival of the Settle–Carlisle Railway allowed it to expand its age-old quarrying operations. Mine workings old and new slightly spoil the west side of the village, but it's of no consequence whatsoever for some of the Dales' finest hiking opportunities. Walks west of the village can be planned to hike up over vast tracts of limestone pavement, scars, gills, potholes, becks and dry valleys, while old "green roads" (shepherd's trackways) provide plenty of scope for gentle pottering.

The village is most convenient for the ascent of sphinx-shaped **Pen-y-ghent** (3–4hr round trip), arguably the most dramatic of the three summits, just to the east on the Pennine Way; the other peaks are more easily climbed from Ingleton, Chapel-le-Dale or Dentdale. The celebrated **Pen-y-ghent Café** in the village is a **National Park information point** (Mon & Wed–Fri 9am–6pm, Sat & Sun 8am–6pm; ⓣ01729/860333) and an unofficial headquarters for the famous **Three Peaks Walk**, a twenty-five-mile, twelve-hour circuit of Pen-y-ghent (2273ft), Whernside (2416ft) and Ingleborough (2373ft). The last Sunday of April sees lunatics running over the three peaks in the gruelling "Three Peaks Race" – what takes normal people the best part of a day to walk takes the winner under three hours. As well as providing huge mugs of tea and coffee, warming platefuls of food, maps, guides and weather reports, the *Pen-y-ghent Café* operates a "safety service" for walkers, enabling anyone undertaking a long hike (including the Three Peaks) to register in and out (not Tues or Fri).

Horton straggles along an L-shaped mile of the Settle–Ribblehead road (B6479), with the **train station** at the northern end and the church at the southern end. In between are the café, a post office/store and a campsite. **Accommodation** in Horton is much in demand and should be booked in advance. B&Bs include the *Willows* (ⓣ01729/860373; no credit cards; ❷), left out of the station and a little way up the Ribblehead road, and the *Knoll* (ⓣ01729/860283; no credit cards; ❷), by the post office. The *Crown Hotel* (ⓣ01729/860209, ⓦwww.crown-hotel.co.uk; ❷), by the bridge, is a popular walkers' haunt with plain but cosy rooms and good bar food served until 8.30pm. The *Golden Lion* (ⓣ01729/860206), at the other end of the road by the church, has both B&B rooms (❷) and bunk-room beds (£8; breakfast and packed lunches available). There's also a grassy tents-only **campsite** at *Holme Farm* (ⓣ01729/860281), near the church.

Ribblehead

However you get there – walk, cycle, drive or take a train – you shouldn't miss a trip to the head of the valley, where the **Ribblehead Viaduct** cuts a superb profile, backed by some of the most uncompromising moors in the entire National Park. It's a wonderfully bleak spot, the viaduct towering a hundred feet overhead, supporting the railway line which then disappears into the 2629 yards of the Blea Tunnel, no less dramatic a feat of engineering. You can access the Dales, Ribble and Pennine Ways from points east of the line, or walk from Ribblehead Station the five miles down the windswept B6255 towards Ingleton, past White Scar Caves. Should you miss the last train, **rooms and food** are at hand in the *Station Inn* (℡01524/241274), right by the rail bridge, which serves pub grub daily and has rooms (❷) and a **bunkhouse** with small kitchen (£8; individuals should call in advance to check on space). There's nothing else near the station, and the next stop on the line is at Dent, similarly isolated, so it pays to study timetables carefully.

The western Dales

The **western Dales** is a term of convenience for a couple of tiny dales running north from **Ingleton**, a village perfectly poised for walks up **Ingleborough** and **Whernside**, and for **Dentdale**, one of the loveliest valleys in the National Park. (Much of this region has been hived off into Cumbria, to the disgust of its erstwhile Yorkshire population.) Ingleton has the most accommodation, but **Dent** is by far the best target for a quiet night's retreat, with a cobbled centre barely altered in centuries. Meanwhile, just outside the park and county boundary to the west, the interesting market town of **Kirby Lonsdale** also beckons, not least to see its graceful medieval bridge spanning the River Lune.

Ingleton is linked by **bus** to Kirby Lonsdale, Clapham, Settle (for Skipton) and Horton, and the Settle–Carlisle Railway offers access to upper Dentdale and Garsdale, with fine walks possible virtually off the station platforms.

Clapham and its caves

CLAPHAM, a seductive little village at the southern foot of Ingleborough, is the starting point for the short half-hour walk on the nature trail through Clapdale Woods to **Ingleborough Cave** (March–Oct daily 10am–5pm; Nov–Feb Sat & Sun 10.30am–dusk; £4.50; Ⓦwww.ingleboroughcave.co.uk), the Pennines' oldest show cave. The trail footpath – the only access – was laid out with numerous exotic trees and flora, most brought to Britain by Reginald Farrer, a scion of the family which owns Ingleborough Hall and the surrounding estate. Farrer was one of the fathers of alpine botany and his obsession was such that on returning from expeditions he would refuse to greet friends or family until his specimens were safely potted and planted. Follow the footpath beyond the cave, and after a little over a mile you reach **Gaping Gill**, 365ft deep and 450ft long, probably the most famous of the Dales' many potholes. There's normally no public access, though the local caving club winches down intrepid visitors on some days every August. Carry on another two miles northwest from the ghyll and the summit of Ingleborough looms – a more interesting approach than the haul up from Ingleton.

Clapham is equidistant from Settle and Ingleton, just off the A65, around four miles from either; its **train station** (on the Leeds/Skipton–Lancaster line) offers another entry to the Dales, but lies over a mile south of the village. There's a post office, general store, and a café or two, plus a couple of places offering rooms, as well as the *Flying Horseshoe* pub by the station.

Ingleton

INGLETON caters for a fair share of tourists, cavers and climbers, but while the straggling slate-grey village is pleasant enough there's little specific to see, save a substantially rebuilt Norman church. The village sits upon a ridge at the confluence of two streams, the Twiss and the Doe, whose beautifully wooded valleys are easily the area's best features. The four-and-a-half mile **Falls' Walk** (daily 9am–dusk; entrance fee £3, parking – including fee – £6; Ⓦwww.ingletonwaterfallswalk.co.uk) is the main local attraction, a lovely circular walk up the tree-hung Twiss Valley, past viewing points over the Pecca Falls and Thornton Force, turning east at Ray Bridge to reach the head of the Doe at Beezley Farm (refreshments available), where a signed path takes you back down the Doe Valley to Ingleton by way of Beezley, Rival and Snow falls. The walk entrance is through the car park, beyond the small bridge in Ingleton. Reckon on at least two and a half hours to complete the circuit, and take care in wet weather.

More serious hikers tackle **Ingleborough** (2373ft), one of the Three Peaks, whose flat plateau is reached by a slightly laborious route to the east (3 miles; 2hr 30min). There are splendid views from here on a clear day, and for anyone fit, equipped and experienced enough the option arises to move on to **Whernside** (2416ft) to the north, the third peak and Yorkshire's highest point.

The Inglesport **hiking store** on Main Street (Ⓣ015242/41146, Ⓦwww.inglesport.com) in the village is the place for maps, equipment and weather forecasts. Otherwise, various leaflets and town maps are available from Ingleton's **tourist office** in the community centre car park, just off Main Street (April–Oct daily 10am–4pm; Ⓣ015242/41049), and there's useful local information on the **community website** Ⓦwww.ingleton.co.uk. The main **bus stop** is outside the tourist office.

The **youth hostel** (Ⓣ0870/770 5880, Ⓔingleton@yha.org.uk; £11.50; closed certain days of the week Sept–Feb) is an old stone house in its own gardens, located centrally in a lane between the market square and the swimming pool. There are a dozen local **B&Bs and guest houses**, starting with the no-smoking *Bridge End*, the handsome old mill owner's house on Mill Lane (Ⓣ015242/41413; ❷), close to the Falls Walk entrance. Most of the rest lie along Main Street, five minutes' walk south of the tourist office. *Ingleborough View* (Ⓣ015242/41523; no credit cards; ❷) has a patio overlooking the river, or try nearby *Riverside Lodge* (Ⓣ015242/41359, Ⓔinfo@riversideingleton.co.uk; ❸), which has rooms in the main house or adjacent converted coach house, while breakfast is served in the valley-view conservatory. Below the village, on the A65, *Thorngarth* (Ⓣ015242/41295, Ⓦwww.thorngarth.com; ❸) also has some grand views. You can **camp** at *Stackstead Farm*, a mile south off the minor road to High Bentham (Ⓣ015242/41386, Ⓔenquiries@stackstead-farm.co.uk), which has tent space and a **bunkhouse barn** (£10, groups only at weekends).

Ingleton has its fair share of **services** – bank, shops, bakers and grocery stores – making it a good place to stock up for the hiking to come, but it fails to make much impact when it comes to **eating**. The *Inglesport Café* on the first floor of the store on Main Street (daily 9am–6pm) at least knows what its customers want – hearty soups and chips with everything. In the evening there's *La Tavernetta*, 23 Main St (Ⓣ015242/42465) for inexpensive Italian meals and pizza. None of the **pubs** in the village is up to much, though with your own transport you can drive three miles down the A65 towards Clapham to the *Goat Gap* (Ⓣ015242/41230, Ⓦwww.goatgap.demon.co.uk; ❺), a seventeenth-century **inn** with traditionally furnished rooms and a restaurant with decent food. You can pitch a tent here too.

White Scar Caves and Chapel-le-Dale

Just one and a half miles out of Ingleton on the Ribblehead/Hawes road (B6255) is the entrance to the **White Scar Caves** (daily 10am–5pm; £6.50;

Ⓣ015242/41244, Ⓦwww.whitescarcave.co.uk), the longest show cave in England. Don't be put off by the steep price – it's worth every penny for the eighty-minute tour of dank underground chambers, contorted cave formations and glistening stalactites. The system was discovered in 1923 by a student, one Christopher Long, who crawled into a fissure in the hillside pushing a candle wedged in a bowler hat ahead of him to light his way. Within two years a tunnel had been blasted out to accommodate visitors – it's now lined with steel-grid walkways along which you edge, the thundering of the internal waterfall becoming ever louder the further in you venture. The 200,000-year-old Battlefield Cavern, only open to the public since 1990, is a remarkable 330 feet long and 100 feet high, and to get this far you've had to negotiate natural features like the "Squeeze" (where the walkway between two rock faces is little over a foot wide) and the "Gorilla Walk" (several hundred yards where you need to hunch your way along a low-roofed tunnel). With water underfoot for the entire trip, the caves are most impressive after heavy rain when the water level rises rapidly – on occasion tours are suspended (so if in doubt, call to check). **Tours** run every hour or so, and there's a café on site.

Three miles further up the road, a path strikes southeast from the hamlet of **CHAPEL-LE-DALE** for the **Souther Scales Nature Reserve**, a fine limestone pavement with associated flowers and ferns. The summit of Ingleborough is less than two miles beyond. A mile or so up the main road from Chapel-le-Dale, call in at the flagstoned *Hill Inn* (Ⓣ015242/41256; ❹), one of the lonelier pubs in England, but worth the diversion for the cosily restored interior, good beers and posh pub food.

Dentdale and around

Any rail or road route to **Dentdale** has plenty of scenic rewards, but the most breathtaking is the minor-road route from Ingleton up Kingsdale and down Deepdale, with the vast whalebacks of Gragareth and Whernside rising to each side of the windswept little road. As you might expect, there's next to nothing to do locally except walk or revel in the scenery, but there are few better spots to do either, with **DENT** village an unbeatable base. When travel writers turn out clichés like "stepping back in time", they mean to describe places like this – the main road gives way to grassy cobbles, while the huddled stone cottages sport blooming window-boxes trailing over ancient lintels, and have tiny windows to keep in the warmth. In the seventeenth and eighteenth centuries, Dent supported a flourishing hand-knitting industry, later ruined by mechanization. These days, the hill-farming community supplements its income through tourism and craft ventures, most notably the independent Dent Brewery, a little way up the dale.

You can stay at either of the village's two **pubs**, the *Sun Inn* (Ⓣ01539/625208, Ⓔthesun@dentbrewery.co.uk; ❶) and the *George & Dragon* (Ⓣ01539/625256, Ⓔthedragon@dentbrewery.co.uk; ❸), which are virtually next to each other in the centre. The *Sun* is the nicer, truly welcoming to walkers and with a great traditional feel; that said, the en-suite rooms at the *George & Dragon* are been modernized and are more comfortable. There are a handful of other **B&B** possibilities, most notably the *White House* (Ⓣ01539/625041; ❷; closed Nov–Easter), with a couple of rooms in a pretty stone cottage, and *Stone Close Guest House* (Ⓣ01539/625231, Ⓔheather@stoneclose.com; ❷), which has a good café (10.30am–5.30pm; Nov–Easter weekends only) doubling as a National Park **information point**. If you ask around, you'll also find B&B in local private houses, while there's a **campsite** on the western edge of the village, at *High Laning Farm* (Ⓣ01539/625239). Both the pubs serve bar **meals** and Dent Brewery beers, nicest at the *Sun* where you can eat and drink in front of a log fire. The only other facilities in the village are a post office, small store and half a dozen craft shops.

Confusion – and not a few sore feet – is caused by Dent's **train station** (on the Settle–Carlisle line) not being in Dent at all, but four miles to the east. A Wednesday and Saturday bus service runs between the station, Dent, Sedburgh and Kendal in the Lakes. If you get stuck, the hamlet of **Cowgill**, half a mile below the station, has the *Sportsman's Inn* (Ⓣ01539/625282; ❷) to hand. Dentdale **youth hostel** (Ⓣ0870/770 5790, Ⓔdentdale@yha.org.uk; £11.50; closed: Sun Easter–Aug, Sun & Mon Sept & Oct, and all Dec & Jan; weekends only Nov & Feb) is a couple of miles south of here down the Dales Way. Family rooms are available and it serves evening meals.

Kirkby Lonsdale

Close to the point where Yorkshire, Cumbria and Lancashire meet, the flint and limestone houses of quaint **KIRKBY LONSDALE** sit on a rise above the River Lune. It's a prosperous-looking place, Georgian in character though dating back to early medieval times – the original stone market cross still stands in Horsemarket, while the market itself continues today (every Thursday) in nearby Market Square. Ten minutes' walk south of town on the A683, the three-arched **Devil's Bridge** dates from the same period and once formed the main route into Yorkshire from the Lakes. There's parking by the bridge and a path from here follows the river to the base of a steep flight of steps that re-enters the town behind St Mary's Church at a point called **Ruskin's View**. Turner painted the famous view of the Lune Valley from here but it was John Ruskin who, with typical overstatement, declared that, "I do not know in all my own country, still less in France or Italy, a place more naturally divine."

Technically Kirkby Lonsdale is in Cumbria, but that doesn't stop it from being a very handy base for the western Yorkshire Dales, with either Dent (no public transport) or Ingleton only around eight miles away. The #567 **bus** from Ingleton runs here four times daily (not Sun), a fifteen-minute ride. The local **tourist office** is at 24 Main St (March–Oct daily 9.30am–5pm; Nov–Feb Thurs–Sun 10am–1pm & 2–5pm; Ⓣ015242/71437, Ⓦwww.kirkbylonsdale.co.uk) and has maps and guides for local walks. **Accommodation** is plentiful, with a grander air than usual in these parts. The *Snooty Fox* on Main St (Ⓣ015242/71308, Ⓦwww.mortal-man-inns.co.uk; ❸) is a local favourite, a country inn with flair, serving good Mediterranean-inspired food. Or there's the *Sun Hotel*, 6 Market St (Ⓣ015242/71965; ❹), which backs onto the churchyard, equally venerable and with a contemporary brasserie. For a family-run atmosphere, the *Orange Tree Hotel* on Fairbank (Ⓣ015242/71716, Ⓦwww.theorangetreehotel.co.uk; ❹) provides half a dozen smart rooms in a converted pub. **Cafés and restaurants** are thick on the ground, typified by the likes of *Avanti*, 57 Main St (Ⓣ015242/73500), a fashionable deli-bar-restaurant, and *Courtyard*, 2 Mill Brow (Ⓣ015242/71779), a cellar-style wine bar, brasserie and evening pizzeria.

Wensleydale

Best known of the Dales, if only for its cheese, **Wensleydale** is the largest, least varied and most serene of the National Park's dales. Known in medieval times as Yoredale, after its river (the Ure), the dale takes its present name from an easterly village, and while there are towns to detain you – including one of the area's biggest in Hawes, to the west – it's Wensleydale's rural attractions that linger longest in the mind. Many will be familiar to devotees of the **James Herriott** books and TV series, set and filmed in the dale; elsewhere, there are several well-known waterfalls – notably **Aysgarth Falls** – and, as the dale opens into the Vale of York, a variety of historic buildings that range from **castles** at Bolton and Middleham to **abbeys** at Jervaulx and Coverham.

The dale is traversed by the National Park's only east–west **main road** (the A684), and linked by high moor roads to virtually all the park's other dales of note. Although the scenery is less spectacular than in other valleys, hiking possibilities are as plentiful as elsewhere, with the **Pennine Way** crossing the valley at Hawes. Year-round **public transport** is provided by a combination of post and service buses (#156 and #157) from Hawes on varied routes via Bainbridge, Askrigg, Aysgarth and Castle Bolton to Leyburn (for Richmond); and the #159 between Masham, Leyburn and Richmond. There are also summer weekend and bank holiday services connecting Hawes to Wharfedale (#800/801/805/806), Hawes to Masham and Ripon (#803), Hawes to Richmond or Ribblesdale (#807), and Leyburn and Masham to Ripon (#802). There's also a once-daily bus from **Garsdale Head Station** on the Settle–Carlisle Railway to Hawes, but only on schooldays and Tuesdays.

Hawes

HAWES – from the Anglo-Saxon *haus*, a mountain pass – is head of Wensleydale in all respects: it's the chief town, main hiking centre, and home to its tourism, cheese and rope-making industries. Hawes also claims to be Yorkshire's highest market town, and received its market charter in 1699; the weekly **Tuesday market** – crammed with farmers and market traders – is still going strong. If you haven't yet bought any cheese, the groaning stalls will doubtless persuade you otherwise. The cheese trail invariably leads to the **Wensleydale Creamery** on Gayle Lane (Mon–Sat 9am–5pm, Sun 10am–4.30pm; £2; Ⓦ www.wensleydale.co.uk), a few hundred yards (signposted) south of the centre. The first cheese in Wensleydale was made by medieval Cistercian monks from ewes' milk, and after the Dissolution local farmers made a version from cows' milk which, by the 1840s, was being marketed as "Wensleydale" cheese. The Creamery's "Cheese Experience" tours tell you all this and more, with plenty of opportunity to see the stuff being made, to sample and purchase in the shop, or tuck in at the *Buttery* restaurant.

All three of Wensleydale's industries come together in the **Dales Countryside Museum** (daily 10am–5pm; £3), housed in Station Yard's former train station and warehouses, on the Aysgarth side of town. The comprehensive and well-presented collection, garnered by Dales chroniclers Marie and Joan Ingilby, embraces lead-mining, farming, peat-cutting, knitting (hand-knitted hosiery was a speciality) and all manner of rustic minutiae. Alongside it, in a long shed, the **Hawes Ropemakers Museum** (July–Oct Mon–Fri 9am–5.30pm, Sat 10am–5.30pm; Nov–June Mon–Fri 9am–5.30pm; free) presents popular demonstrations of traditional rope-making. Over the road, the **Wensleydale Pottery** (Mon–Sat 10am–5.30pm) also presents handware made on the premises.

Another local attraction is a mile and a half out of town to the north, where people cough up the £1 toll at the *Green Dragon* pub to walk to **Hardraw Force**. It's about all the fall is worth for much of the year, for although this is the highest above-ground waterfall in the country (Gaping Gill and other potholes have longer underground drops) there's often barely a trickle dribbling over the edge. A summer brass-band recital (second Sun in Sept) in the natural amphitheatre of Hardraw Scar makes for a more surreal attraction.

Services and accommodation in Hawes are gathered together along and just off the main A684, which runs through town. The **National Park information centre** shares the same building as the Dales Countryside Museum (daily 10am–5pm; ⓣ01969/667450). A comprehensive local **website**, ⓦwww.wensleydale.org, lists attractions and businesses in the region. **Buses** stop in Market Place except for the special summer-only services, which pull up outside the museum, and the post buses, which depart from outside the post office (over the road from the information centre car park).

Accommodation is plentiful in local B&Bs, while all the pubs on and around the market square – the *Board*, *Crown*, *Fountain*, *Bull's Head* and *White Hart* – have rooms, too, so you shouldn't be stuck for choice. **Tearooms and cafés** cluster around Market Place, and include the first-floor *Wensleydale Pantry*, opposite the *Crown* on the main road through town. *Beckindales*, by the Ropemakers Museum, has a more contemporary air and an outdoor terrace. Traditional English meals – game a speciality – are served in the *Cocketts Hotel* **restaurant**, though Hawes' best dining experience is at *Herriot's Hotel*, whose restaurant (no lunch Wed & Thurs) features a wide-ranging continental menu.

B&Bs, guest houses and hotels

Cocketts Market Place ⓣ01969/667312, ⓦwww.cocketts.co.uk. The smartest choice in town, offering eight traditionally decorated en-suite rooms (two of them with four-poster beds) in a seventeenth-century building. ❹

Green Dragon 1.5 miles north of Hawes ⓣ01969/667392, ⓦwww.greendragoninn.fsnet.co.uk. Country inn with rural views set in its own grounds, offering hotel rooms or self-catering apartments. Homecooked food, real ales and live folk/rock/blues/R&B every Sat. ❸

Herriot's Main St ⓣ01969/667536, ⓦwww.herriotshotel.com. Small hotel with restaurant, just off Market Place, where a couple of the rooms have fell views. ❹

Laburnum House The Holme ⓣ01969/667717, ⓦwww.stayatlaburnumhouse.co.uk. At the turn-off from the main road to the museum, this tearoom/B&B has four simple rooms available, plus self-catering in a converted coach house. No credit cards. ❷

Rose & Crown Bainbridge, 5 miles east of Hawes ⓣ01969/650225. Fifteenth-century coaching inn with restaurant and bar, overlooking an emerald village green. Nightly at 9pm from Holyrood (late Sept) to Shrove Tuesday, a horn (hanging in the hall when not in use) is blown three times on the green – a tradition dating to Norman times when it was used to guide travellers through the dense woodland that once encircled the village. ❹

Steppe Haugh Guest House Town Head ⓣ01969/667645, ⓦwww.steppehaugh.co.uk. Non-smoking seventeenth-century cottage with cosy rooms, a few minutes' walk from the centre. No credit cards. ❸

Youth hostel and campsite

Bainbridge Ings ⓣ01969/667354, ⓦwww.bainbridge-ings.co.uk. Half a mile east (10min walk) of the centre, just off the A684 (Aysgarth road). Milk and eggs available.

Hawes YHA Lancaster Terrace ⓣ0870/770 5854, ⓔhawes@yah.org.uk. Modern hostel on the edge of town, at the junction of the main A684 and B6255. Some twin and family rooms available (❶), otherwise dorm beds cost £10.25. Sept–March closed certain days of the week.

Askrigg

The mantle of "Herriot country" lies heavy on **ASKRIGG**, six miles east of Hawes, as the TV series *All Creatures Great and Small* was filmed in and around the village. There is, however, little to see or do, though the pubs and Georgian houses have their charms, and you might stroll to a couple of nearby falls, **Whitfield Force** and **Mill Gill Force**, both a mile or so to the west of the village. To the east, there are well-signed paths along high ground via Carperby to Aysgarth or Castle Bolton, around a five-mile hike to either.

The market at Askrigg has its origins in medieval times, and predates that of Hawes – notice the bull-ring set outside the church here, a relic of bull-baiting days. There's an **information point** in the village shop in the Market Place, while local **B&Bs** include the *Apothecary's House* (☎01969/650626; no credit cards; ❷) opposite the church. For a rural retreat, you can't beat *Helm Country House* (☎01969/650443, Ⓦwww.helmyorkshire.com; ❹), a seventeenth-century farmhouse a mile west with magnificent views, open fires, oak beams and a cast-iron Aga oven – dinner is served in the stone-flagged dining room. The *King's Arms* in the village has stills from the *All Creatures* TV series, and it's a cosy old haunt with wood panelling, good beer and bar meals.

Aysgarth and around

The ribbon-village of **AYSGARTH**, straggling along and off the A684, is the vortex that sucks in Wensleydale's largest number of visitors, courtesy of the twin Aysgarth Falls, half a mile below the village (there's a path through the fields), where water crashes down a series of limestone steps – impressive in full spate. A marked nature trail runs through the surrounding woodlands and there's a big car park and excellent **information centre** on the north bank (Easter–Oct daily 10am–5pm; Nov–Easter Fri, Sat & Sun 10am–4pm; ☎01969/663424). The **Upper Falls** and picnic grounds lie just back from here, by the bridge and church; the more spectacular **Lower Falls** are a half-mile stroll to the east through shaded woodland. Don't leave without calling at the church of **St Andrew**, worth a look for its carved pews and one of Yorkshire's finest rood screens, dating from 1500 and possibly removed from nearby Jervaulx Abbey.

Aysgarth has a superb aspect, with glorious views across the valley from several points, a setting spoiled only by the fast A684 through the village. The only **pub**, the *George & Dragon* (☎01969/663358; ❺), has pleasant en-suite rooms (cheaper out of season) and a bar-meal menu with plenty of choice. *Field House* at East End (☎01969/663556; ❸; closed Dec–Feb) is a Georgian property with a couple of spacious **B&B** rooms, just a short walk along a footpath from the falls. Also down by the falls, you'll find the well-regarded **youth hostel** (☎0870/770 5678, Ⓔaysgarth@yha.org.uk; £10.25; under refurbishment, call for opening details), and there's a **campsite**, *Westholme Caravan Park* (☎01969/663268; closed Nov–Easter), half a mile east on the A684.

Castle Bolton

There's a superb **circular walk** northeast from Aysgarth via Castle Bolton (6 miles; 4hr), a route detailed in a National Park pamphlet available from the information centres in Hawes or Aysgarth – or you can simply drive to the castle in about ten minutes. The walk starts at the falls themselves and climbs up through Thoresby, with the foursquare battlements of **Castle Bolton** (March–Nov daily 10am–5pm; restricted winter opening, call for details; ☎01969/623981, Ⓦwww.boltoncastle.co.uk; £4) themselves a magnetic lure from miles away across the fields. Built in 1379 by Richard le Scrope, Lord Chancellor to Richard II, it's a massive defensive structure in which Mary, Queen of Scots was imprisoned for six months in 1568. The Great Hall, a few adjacent rooms, and the castle gardens have been restored, and there's also a café (free to enter) that's a welcome spot if you've just trudged up from Aysgarth. There's **bike rental** at the castle from Wensleydale Bikehire (☎01969/623981, Ⓦwww.wensleydalebikehire.co.uk). The only other facility hereabouts is the village post office, housed in what could pass for Goldilocks' cottage; the nearest **pub** is just over a mile to the east, the *King's Arms* at Redmire.

Wensley and Leyburn

A few miles east of Aysgarth, Wensleydale broadens into a low-hilled pastoral valley, the border of the National Park marking the end of classic Dales scenery and the start of the Vale of York's more mundane flats. **WENSLEY** is a beguiling place wound around a dinky village square. The church of the **Holy Trinity** ranks as one of the Dales' finest, founded in the thirteenth century but with fabric dating from the five centuries that followed, the most impressive being an extravagant box pew and a sixteenth-century rood screen removed from Richmond's Easby Abbey.

The market town of **LEYBURN** – a couple of miles east of Wensley and eleven miles southwest of Richmond – occupies almost the last piece of straggling high ground on the valley's north edge, a handsome place set around three open squares, replete with buildings from its eighteenth-century heyday. Market day is Friday, when Market Place puts out its fruit, veg, hard goods and bric-a-brac stalls; this is where the local **buses** stop. Trains have returned to Wensleydale too, with the re-opening of the **Wensleydale Railway** (Ⓣ01677/425805 or 08454/505474; £8 day rover) between Leyburn and Leeming Bar, 12 miles to the east (on the A1), closed since the 1950s. It's hoped to open the line through to nearby Northallerton in the future, though for now there are bus transfers there on market day (Wednesday). There's a **tourist office** just off Market Place at 4 Central Chambers on Railway Street (April–Oct daily 9.30am–5.30pm; Nov–March Mon–Sat 9.30am–4.30pm; Ⓣ01969/623069), which has details of local **accommodation**. Market Place has a range of tearooms and coffee houses, or you could plump for the *Golden Lion*, a traditional inn on Market Place (Ⓣ01969/622161, Ⓦwww.thegoldenlion.co.uk; ❹). For decent Masham beer, visit the *Sandpiper Inn*, a little seventeeth-century **pub** on the road at the bottom of Market Place.

Middleham and Jervaulx Abbey

Two miles southeast of Leyburn, the tiny town of **MIDDLEHAM** is approached over an impressive early-nineteenth-century castellated bridge – a morning bus (not Sun) comes this way from Leyburn. A well-to-do place set around a sloping cobbled square, it's dominated by the imposing ruins of **Middleham Castle** (April–Sept daily 10am–6pm; Oct daily 10am–5pm, Nov & Dec daily 10am–4pm; Jan–March Wed–Sun 10am–4pm; £3; EH). Built by the Normans to guard the route from Skipton to Richmond, it gained added historical resonance when it passed by marriage to the future Richard III in 1471 and became his favourite home; his son, Edward, died here. The keep is one of England's largest, despite being badly damaged after Richard's defeat at Bosworth Field.

Castle aside, Middleham captivates for at least long enough to have a coffee in one of its pubs or tearooms. Racehorses clip-clopping through the centre are a common sight, with over five hundred trained locally at more than a dozen stables – on Good Friday each year there's free access to all the racing stables. There are a few rather nice **accommodation** possibilities, including *Domus*, a seventeenth-century house overlooking Market Place (Ⓣ01969/623497; ❸), and *Castle Keep* on nearby Castle Hill (Ⓣ01969/623665; ❸), whose guest rooms are above a little daytime tearoom. Otherwise, several **pubs** vie for custom around the square – the *White Swan*, *Black Swan*, *Richard III* and *Black Bull* all have rooms available; the best food is at the *White Swan*.

Wensleydale all but peters out with the overgrown and privately owned ruins of **Jervaulx Abbey** (daily dawn–dusk; £2), four miles southeast of Middleham on the A6108 road to Ripon. Founded in 1156, it is the least prepossessing of the great trio of Cistercian abbeys completed by Fountains and Rievaulx, but makes an enjoyable stop for a ramble amid the bramble-covered stones. A conservatory-style tearoom over the road (closed Nov–Feb) has snacks and lunches.

Masham

If you're a beer fan, the handsome market town of **MASHAM** (pronounced Mass'm, without the 'h'), another four miles along the road, is an essential point of pilgrimage. It's home to **Theakston's** brewery (tours: April–Oct daily 10.30am–5.30pm; at other times, call ⓣ01765/684333; £4.50, ⓦwww.theakstons.co.uk), sited here since 1827, where you can learn the arcane intricacies of the brewer's art and become familiar with the legendary Old Peculier (sic) ale. The tour-price includes a free pint and there's a visitor centre and bar on site. Following Theakston's huge marketing success, one of the family brewing team left to set up the **Black Sheep Brewery**, also based in Masham and offering tours (daily 11am–4pm, but call for availability; £4.50; ⓣ01765/680101, ⓦwww.blacksheepbrewery.com). To many, Black Sheep bitter is even better than Theakston's. Both breweries are just a few minutes' signposted walk out of the centre.

Masham is one of the most attractive small towns in Yorkshire, with a huge central market place (market days are Wed & Sat) and a smattering of fine local shops. **Buses** from the Market Place depart several times a day for Ripon or Richmond (not Sun), and on summer Sundays a service runs to Hawes or Leeds and Bradford. There's no more agreeable **accommodation** – here, or for many miles around – than *Swinton Park* (ⓦwww.swintonpark.com; ➐), a stunning stately home with elegant rooms that overlook the sweeping grounds and curving river. It's a hugely enjoyable experience, and informal despite its pedigree, with the only sound the clack of croquet balls from the lawns. There are comfortable public areas, a snooker room, bar and good restaurant (lunch £16, dinner, £32). You're also only a gentle mile's stroll from Masham, where the *King's Head*, 42 Market Place (ⓣ01765/689295), is the best place to eat in town, more restaurant than pub. There's also a bistro inside the Black Sheep Brewery (open when the brewery's open and also for dinner Wed–Sat). The beer's good at any of the pubs, though at its best in the *White Bear*, the brewery pub attached to Theakston's, which is very popular for bar meals.

Swaledale

Narrow and steep-sided in its upper reaches, **Swaledale** emerges rocky and rugged in its central tract, which takes in the remote villages of **Keld**, **Thwaite** and **Muker**, before more typically pastoral scenery cuts in at the main village of **Reeth**. Unless you're hiking, it's Reeth that provides the best overnight stop, with the best choice of accommodation in the dale. From Richmond, **bus** #30 (not Sun) runs up the valley along the B6270 as far as Keld. The only other public transport access is with the summer-only #801 (Sat, from Leeds/Bradford and Wharfedale) to Keld, or the #803 (Sun, from Hawes) to Muker and Reeth.

Keld, Thwaite, Muker and around

KELD, eight miles north of Hawes, and eleven from Kirkby Stephen, is at the crossroads of the Pennine Way and the Coast-to-Coast path, making it an ideal hiking centre. No more than a straggle of hardy buildings, it's surrounded by relics of the lead-mining industry that once brought a prosperity of sorts to much of the valley (though at a price – the average life expectancy of a nineteenth-century Swaledale miner was 46 years). Here you'll also see the incredible profusion of ancient field barns, or laithes, for which the dale is renowned, the legacy of a system of husbandry that dates back to Norse times. Keld's busy **youth hostel** is *Keld Lodge*, an old shooting lodge near the telephone kiosk (ⓣ0870/770 5888, ⓔkeld@yha.org.uk; £10.25; closed Nov–Feb and certain days in winter). There's also a **campsite** at *Park Lodge* (ⓣ01748/886274; closed Oct–Easter), but no pub, nor any other facilities, apart from the odd, isolated B&B.

The shortest local walk is to **Kisdon Force**, a triple-stacked waterfall and its wooded gorge half a mile east of Keld, though the best is the hike southeast along the River Swale to Muker, below the circular bulk of Kisdon hill (2–3 miles; 1hr 30min). The valley road cuts round Kisdon to the south, following part of the so-called **Corpse Way**, a lane used by those paying their last respects when the nearest church was ten miles away at Grinton – footpaths follow its still obvious route down the valley.

North and west of Keld, the upper reaches of Swaledale are wild indeed, with an atmosphere bordering on desolate even in summer. The Pennine Way shadows the very minor Stonesdale road for the three or four miles across **Stonesdale Moor** to the splendid *Tan Hill Inn* (ⓣ01833/628246; ❷). Reputedly the highest pub in Britain (1732ft above sea level), the wind blows hard year-round up here, and in winter snow drifts up to the windows – but there's an open fire lit daily in the stone-flagged interior, good beer and bar meals, and camping outside for the truly dedicated.

THWAITE, another Norse-founded settlement, is the first hamlet south of Keld, just a two-mile walk away. Some of the loveliest scenery follows beyond the little village of **MUKER** (the name derives from the Norse for "meadow"), a mile or so to the east, distinguished by tiny side-valleys such as Oxnop Beck, south of Oxnop. Muker has a National Park **information point** in the village store, which has details of local B&Bs. There are also a couple of teashops and a nice **pub**, the *Farmers Arms*, serving good food.

Beyond Muker, there's not much to tempt you away from the riverside, save perhaps for the **Gunnerside Gill**, a little valley which contains the best of the area's old lead mines. These are all easily seen on a circular six-mile walk from **GUNNERSIDE** itself, and are covered in a special trail leaflet available from the village post office's National Park information point. Further east at **LOW ROW**, there's an organic farm and visitor centre at **Hazel Brow** (Easter–Sept daily 11am–6pm; £4; ⓦwww.hazelbrow.co.uk), which has lots of demonstrations, activities, tours and play areas. The hamlet's *Punch Bowl Inn* (ⓣ01748/886233; closed Mon Nov–Feb) offers B&B (❸), a bunkroom (£15 with your own sleeping bag, otherwise £17.50, includes breakfast) and basic bar meals, and fine valley views from the pub tables.

Reeth and around

A couple of miles east lies **REETH**, set in a dramatic moorland bowl. It's the dale's main village and market centre – market day is Friday – and its desirable cottages are gathered around a triangular green. Reeth has the biggest range of facilities in the whole dale, including a petrol station, a post office and the only bank, and it also boasts several craft workshops making everything from cabinets to guitars. The National Park **information centre** on the green (daily 10am–5pm; ⓣ01748/884059) has local maps and brochures.

Some cottages around the green post **B&B** signs in their windows, or walk a minute down the Grinton road at the edge of the village to *2 Bridge Terrace* (ⓣ01748/884572; no credit cards; ❶; closed Dec–Feb), which offers a particularly good breakfast made from local ingredients. The three central **pubs** also have rooms, most notably the *King's Arms* (Ⓣ01748/884259, Ⓦwww.thekingsarms.com; ❹; weekend 2-night minimum), on the green. The *Arkleside Hotel* (Ⓣ01748/884200, Ⓦwww.arklesidehotel.co.uk; ❺), just off the top of the green, was converted from a row of old miners' cottages and is a very cosy place to stay; or there's the *Burgoyne Hotel* (Ⓦwww.theburgoyne.co.uk; ❻), lording it over the top of the green, for superior old-fashioned comforts. Some of the cottages around the green double as **cafés**, and bar meals are served in the pubs – it's nice to sit outside the *Black Bull* or *King's Arms* in the sun. For picnic supplies there's Reeth Bakery, known for its great chocolate cake. More formal dinners are available at the *Arkleside* and *Burgoyne* hotels (around £25).

To escape Reeth's crowds, walk or drive three miles east to **Marrick Priory**, a ruined twelfth-century Benedictine nunnery set among trees on the north bank of the Swale. A mile further east, approached from the B6270 road, are the tower and ruined nave of **Ellerton Priory**, a fifteenth-century Cistercian foundation. There are also numerous paths across the fields on the south side of the river, letting you complete a circular walk from Reeth via **GRINTON**, whose attractive bridge, church and riverside inn, *The Bridge*, are just a mile away by road. The local **youth hostel**, *Grinton Lodge* (Ⓣ0870/770 5844, Ⓔgrinton@yha.org.uk; £11.50; winter closed 1–2 days a week), is housed in a former shooting lodge spectacularly sited in the hills above, ten minutes' walk from Grinton. You can rent mountain bikes here (book in advance), and the hostel can provide route details for local rides.

Many people come to this area to make a television-inspired pilgrimage up **Arkengarthdale** to **Langthwaite**, three miles to the northwest, a cute village used in the opening credits of *All Creatures Great and Small*; a handful of local B&Bs and the atmospheric *Red Lion* pub soak up the passing trade there.

Richmond

Although marginalized on the National Park's northeasternmost borders, **RICHMOND** is the Dales' single most tempting historical town, thanks mainly to its magnificent castle, whose extensive walls and colossal keep cling to a precipice above the River Swale. Indeed, the entire town is an absolute gem, centred on a huge cobbled market square backed onto by hidden alleys and gardens housing mainly Georgian buildings of great refinement. The town itself is much older, having been dubbed *Riche-Mont* ("noble hill") by the Normans who first built a castle here in 1071. That heritage is also celebrated in local street names such as Frenchgate and Lombard's Wynd (a "wynd" being a narrow alley).

There's no better place to start than **Richmond Castle** (daily: April–Oct 10am–6pm; Nov–March 10am–4pm; £3; EH), reached by signposted alleys from the market square. Originally built by Alan Rufus, first Norman Earl of Richmond, it retains many features from its earliest incarnation, principally the gatehouse, curtain wall and Scolland's Hall, the oldest Norman great hall in the country. There are prodigious views from the splendidly preserved fortified keep, which is over a hundred feet high, and from the Great Court, now an open lawn which ends in a sheer fall to the river below. Outside the main entrance a Georgian terrace, the **Castle Walk**, wraps around the skirts of the castle, offering more views of the river and hills beyond.

Most of medieval Richmond sprouted around the castle, but much of the town now radiates from the vast **Market Place**, with the Market Hall alongside (markets on Tues, Thurs, Fri & Sat). It's difficult to get a good view of things now the square is overwhelmed by traffic, but the Victorian and Georgian buildings that border the square still have some appeal. The most unusual structure is the defunct **Holy Trinity Church**, built in 1135 and now serving as the **Green Howards Museum** (April–Oct Mon–Sat 9.30am–4.30pm; Nov, Dec & March Mon–Fri 10am–4pm; closed Jan & Feb; £2.50). This honours North Yorkshire's Green Howards regiment, and contains a lot more than just uniforms and medals. The **Richmondshire Museum**, reached down Ryder's Wynd, off King Street on the northern side of the square (Easter–Oct daily 10.30am–4.30pm; £1.50), has displays relating to lead-mining and local crafts, and contains a brick-by-brick reconstruction of a local fifteenth-century "cruck" house, built using a curved timber frame.

The keenest interest of all, however, is in the town's **Theatre Royal**, dating from 1788, making it one of England's oldest extant theatres. Unassuming from the outside, the theatre's tiny interior is one of England's finest pieces of Georgian architecture. Built by one Samuel Butler – an actor-manager who owned several regional theatres in the north, and third husband of the splendidly named actress Tryphosa Brockell – the theatre hosted the greats of eighteenth-century theatre, Edmund Kean among them, before packed houses of over 400 people, each person paying a shilling a time. The theatre is open for both performances (box office ⓣ01748/823021) and tours, while a museum at the rear gives an insight into eighteenth-century theatrical life, allowing visitors to have a go at scene-shifting, use the thunderbox prop or try on the various masks and costumes. The theatre has been under refurbishment; museum hours and tours details are available on ⓣ01748/823710.

Below the castle, the **River Swale** cuts a pastoral swathe through the surrounding countryside, with the banks immediately east of town popular for picnics. A lovely signposted walk runs along the north bank out to the beautifully situated church of St Agatha and adjacent **Easby Abbey** (dawn to dusk; free; EH), whose golden stone walls stand a mile southeast of the town centre. Founded in 1152 by Premonstratensian canons – the so-called White Monks – the abbey is now ruined, the greatest damage having been caused in 1346 when the English army was billeted here on its way to the battle of Neville's Cross. However, the evocative remains are extensive, and in places – notably the thirteenth-century refectory – still remarkably intact. You can vary your return to town by crossing the bridge a little further down from the abbey and walking back along the old railway track.

Practicalities

Buses all stop in the Market Place; there are regular services into Wensleydale and Swaledale, to Barnard Castle in County Durham, and to Darlington, just ten miles to the northeast, which is on the main East Coast train line. There's free two-hour **parking** in Market Place (pick up a disc from local shops), or aim for the pay-and-display Nunn's Close car park on Hurgill Road, off Victoria Road. The **tourist office**, at Friary Gardens, Victoria Road (summer daily 9.30am–5.30pm; winter Mon–Sat 9.30am–4.30pm; ⓣ01748/850252, ⓦwww.richmond.org.uk), is helpful in finding accommodation, and also organizes **guided walking tours** around the town in summer (free, donations welcome).

Accommodation is plentiful, with central Frenchgate in particular boasting small B&Bs and guest houses in historic buildings, while the pubs around Market Place all have rooms too. As for **eating**, apart from the places listed below, you could book for *Restaurant on the Green* or dine at the *King's Head* (see "Accommodation" opposite for both). On the whole, Richmond's **pubs** –

there are half a dozen around the market square alone – are nothing special, though the *Black Lion* on Finkle Street has its moments while the *Unicorn*, on Georgian tree-lined Newbiggin (at the end of Finkle St), is a quieter spot.

Accommodation

Frenchgate Hotel 59–61 Frenchgate ⓣ01748/822087, ⓦwww.frenchgatehotel.com. Georgian town house with brightly furnished rooms – twins, doubles and singles – a beamed lounge, patio garden, bar and restaurant. Parking available. ❺

King's Head Hotel Market Place ⓣ01748/850220, ⓦwww.kingsheadrichmond.co.uk. The town's principal hotel, with traditionally furnished rooms, plus lounge and log fire. Bar meals available, or eat in the restaurant for around £20 (excluding drinks). Parking available. ❻

Restaurant on the Green 5–7 Bridge St ⓣ01748/826229. Seventeenth-century house in a quiet spot, below the castle, near the river, with just a couple of nice B&B rooms available. A good place for dinner too (Fri & Sat dinner only), though you'll need to book – bistro food at moderate prices. ❷

West End Guest House 45 Reeth Rd ⓣ01748/824783, ⓦwww.stayatwestend.com. Ten minutes' walk out of the centre (along and beyond Victoria Road), this gets consistently good reports. The tranquil gardens also contain four self-catering cottages. No credit cards. ❸

Willance House 24 Frenchgate ⓣ01748/824467. Characterful seventeenth-century cottage with three rooms. No credit cards. ❷

Cafés and restaurants

Frenchgate Café 29 Frenchgate ⓣ01748/824949. Open from 10am for coffee and breakfast, followed by pasta, stir-fry and baked potato lunches, and bistro-style dinners – the evening menu is posted daily at 6pm, and has fish and veggie options alongside the chicken and lamb. Closed Mon. Inexpensive to Moderate.

Latino's 2 Trinity Church Sq ⓣ01748/825008. Italian restaurant and pizzeria, next to Holy Trinity Church on the square. Dinner only, closed Sun & Mon. Moderate.

A Taste of Thailand 15 King St ⓣ01748/829696. Just as it says, with a menu to satisfy most. You can bring your own wine too. Moderate.

Nidderdale

Nidderdale, the easternmost dale, is probably the least known of the Yorkshire Dales, stretching for around twenty miles from the source of the River Nidd on Great Whernside to the village of **Ripley** in the lower dale, just four miles from Harrogate. The main approach is along the east–west B6265 between Grassington in Wharfedale and Ripon, with the only available route north being along the wild road from **Pateley Bridge**, the dale's main village, to Masham and, ultimately, Wensleydale. The **bus** service is pretty much restricted to the regular #24 service from Harrogate to Pateley Bridge, though there are summer Sunday services up to How Stean Gorge or on to Grassington; another summer Sunday service runs between Bradford/Leeds and Ripon via Pateley Bridge and Brimham Rocks. A long-distance footpath, the **Nidderdale Way**, runs in a circular 53-mile loop around the dale from Hampsthwaite village car park, three miles northwest of Harrogate. Dalesman Publishing produces a guide, *The Nidderdale Way*, and the route is indicated on OS maps 99 and 104. There's useful information on the local **website** ⓦwww.nidderdale.co.uk.

Ripley

The lower dale is a patchwork of farming land, its first obvious distraction coming at **RIPLEY** (bus #36 from Ripon or Harrogate). This is an impeccably kept village whose bizarre appearance is due to a whim of the Ingilby family, who between 1827 and 1854 rebuilt it in the manner of an Alsace-Lorraine village, for no other reason than they liked the style. (The project was financed by selling an outlying farm on the Ingilby estate, now Harrogate's town centre.) Summer crowds pile in for the cobbled square, original stocks and the twee cottages and shops, not to mention the Ingilby house, parkland and **castle** (Jan–May & Sept–Dec Tues, Thurs, Sat & Sun 10.30am–3pm; June–Aug daily 10.30am–3pm; gardens daily 9am–5pm or dusk; castle & gardens £6, gardens only £3.50; Ⓦwww.ripleycastle.co.uk), with its museum of armour, weapons, furniture and suchlike. You don't have to pay to patronize the excellent deli and separate café outside the castle walls. Opposite the castle's fifteenth-century gatehouse, look in on **All Saints' Church**, whose stonework bears the indentations of musket balls, damage said to have been caused by the execution of Royalist soldiers after the Battle of Marston Moor. The graveyard also contains the "Kneeling" or "Weeping" cross, a stone with eight niches to receive the bowed heads of kneeling penitents. It's believed to be the only one of its kind in the country.

The highly attractive *Boar's Head* (Ⓣ01423/771888, Ⓦwww.boarsheadripley.co.uk; ❼), opposite the village stocks, has pricey rooms, but there's a lovely bar and beer garden, and a high-class restaurant.

Pateley Bridge and around

The little town of **PATELEY BRIDGE** serves as the dale's focus, housing the **tourist office** at 18 High St (Easter–Oct daily 10am–5pm; Ⓣ01423/711147) and acting as a base for campers, cavers and visitors of every kind. Its **Nidderdale Museum** (Easter–Oct daily 1.30–4.30pm; Aug daily 10.30am–4.30pm; Nov–Easter Sat & Sun 1.30–4.30pm; £2), in the old council offices opposite the church on the edge of the village, provides a run-through of dale life in days gone by, with a re-created village shop, office and house interior to poke around. After that, you could stroll the **Panorama Walk** (2 miles; 1hr), signposted from the top of the High Street, or refuel in one of the tearooms, pubs and restaurants along the High Street. Several local guest houses and hotels provide **accommodation**, one of the nicest places being the *Sportsmans Arms* (Ⓣ01423/711306; ❺), a couple of miles out off the Nidderdale road at Wath-in-Nidderdale – there's really good food served here too.

Five miles west of the village on the Grassington road lie the **Stump Cross Caverns** (April–Oct daily 10am–6pm; Nov–March Sat & Sun 11am–4pm; £4.85), one of England's premier show caves, complete with massive stalagmites.

About the same distance east of the village, signposted off the B6265, are the extraordinary **Brimham Rocks**, nearly four hundred acres of strangely eroded millstone grit outcrops scattered over one-thousand-foot high moors. The land at Brimham was once part of the wealthy Fountains Abbey estate (see p.970), whose monks grazed their sheep between the weatherbeaten tors. Today, it's all under the protection of the National Trust, which maintains the paths between the rocks and safeguards the nesting jackdaws. It costs £2.50 to park your car, and after a clamber on the rocks, you can follow the path up to the **information centre** at Brimham House (April, May & Oct Sat & Sun 11am–5pm; June–Sept daily 11am–5pm; free). Views from the terrace here are superlative, stretching over the Vale of York, with York Minster visible on clear days. A refreshment kiosk (Sat & Sun only in winter) serves drinks and cakes.

Upper Nidderdale

North of Pateley Bridge, above the **Gouthwaite Reservoir**, Nidderdale closes in and the scenery is superb. Part of the reservoir is a restricted-access nature reserve, but plenty of geese, waders and waterfowl can be seen all year round from the surrounding roads and tracks. At **Ramsgill**, at the northern end of the reservoir, the *Yorke Arms* (Ⓣ01423/755243, Ⓦwww.yorke-arms.co.uk; ❾ includes dinner; closed 2 weeks in Jan) is a renowned restaurant-with-rooms operation. You can just pop in for lunch and, as it was an old pub, the beer is pretty good too.

A couple of miles further up the road in the upper valley, seven miles from Pateley Bridge, the **How Stean Gorge** (Jan & Feb Wed–Sun 10am–5pm; March–Sept daily 10am–6pm; Oct–Dec daily 10am–5pm; £3) is a terrific ice-gouged ravine of surging waters and overhanging rocks. Take a torch and you can explore Tom Taylor's Cave, a dark, narrow squeeze through an underground cavern. There's summer **camping** (☎01423/755666) behind the gorge café.

Ripon

The unassuming market town of **RIPON**, eleven miles north of Harrogate, is centred upon its relatively small but vital **Cathedral** (daily 7.30am–6.30pm; donation requested), which can trace its ancestry back to its foundation by St Wilfrid in 672; the original crypt is still extant below the central tower. The rest of the building was destroyed by the Danes in the ninth century, then a second church fell foul of the Normans, part of whose replacement remains, though the bulk of the present building dates from the reign of Archbishop Roger of York (1154–81). Despite a rather plain exterior, there's plenty that pleases here, from the subtle, twin-towered, thirteenth-century west front to the choir's misericords, full of painted figures of miserable clergymen, executed by the same team that carved the impressive stalls at Beverley (see p.997).

The town's other focus is its **Market Place**, "...the finest and most beautiful square...in England", according to Defoe, linked by Kirkgate to the cathedral; market day is Thursday. A ninety-foot obelisk built in 1780 dominates the square, a blustering conceit in stone, raised by William Aislabie to celebrate his sixty years as the local MP. At its apex stands a horned weather vane, an allusion to the "Blowing of the Wakeman's Horn", a ceremony – now something of a tourist attraction – which may date from 886, when Alfred the Great reputedly granted Ripon a charter and an ox's horn was presented for the setting of the town's watch. The last official Wakeman died in 1637 – his half-timbered **Wakeman's House** stands on the square – but the horn is still blown nightly at 9pm in the square's four corners and outside the house of the incumbent mayor.

Three restored buildings show a different side of Ripon's heritage, under the banner of the Yorkshire Law and Order Museums (all open April–Oct daily: July, Aug & school hols 11am–4pm, other times 1–4pm; combined ticket £4). At the **Prison and Police Museum** (£2.50), on St Marygate behind the cathedral, the old cells serve as the backdrop for an informative exhibition on policing since Anglo-Saxon times. Cases were heard at the 1830s **Courthouse** on Minster Road (£1), with guilty prisoners packed off to the cells or, in the early days at least, even transported to Australia. Law-abiding locals often fared little better, with the "undeserving" poor incarcerated in the nearby **Ripon Workhouse**, on Allhallowgate (£1.50), for such heinous crimes as being unable to pay their bills.

Practicalities

The **bus station** (regular services from Masham, Harrogate, Knaresborough and Leeds) is dead central, just off the Market Place, while the town's **tourist office** is on Minster Road opposite the cathedral (July & Aug Mon–Sat 10am–6pm, Sun 10am–1pm; April–June & Sept Mon–Sat closes 5/5.30pm,

Sun 10am–1pm; Oct Mon–Sat closes 4pm & closed Sun; Nov–March Tues–Sat 10am–1pm & 1.30–4.30pm; ⓣ01765/604625, ⓦwww.riponcity.info). Ripon is the nearest base from which to visit Newby Hall and Fountains Abbey (see below) and local **accommodation** options include *Bishopton Grove House*, Bishopton (ⓣ01765/600888; no credit cards; ❶), a Georgian house in a peaceful corner of the town; and the *Unicorn Hotel*, Market Place (ⓣ01765/602202, ⓦwww.unicorn-hotel.co.uk; ❹), an old coaching inn and central Ripon's finest. The *Ripon Spa Hotel*, on Park Street (ⓣ01765/602172, ⓦwww.stemsys.co.uk/spa; ❻), set in its own grounds five minutes' walk from the centre, has a good restaurant and pleasant bar. Otherwise, there are several small cafés and **restaurants** along Kirkgate across from the cathedral. *The Warehouse*, down a side yard called Court Terrace, is a popular lunch stop for quiche, salad platters, soup and sandwich, or there's *Cibo*, 25 Kirkgate (ⓣ01765/602722), an unpretentious Italian place, open daily for lunch and dinner.

Newby Hall

One of England's most splendid Queen Anne houses, **Newby Hall** (April–Sept Tues–Sun noon–5pm, gardens open from 11am; £7; gardens only £5.50; ⓦwww.newbyhall.com), stands just five miles southeast of the Ripon near Skelton, south of the B6265. Completely overhauled by Robert Adam for his patron William Weddell, it contains some outstanding decorative plasterwork, and is further adorned by lashings of Chippendale furniture and rich eighteenth-century tapestries. The grounds and gardens, too, are a delight, with parts sectioned off for the entertainment of kids – there's an adventure playground, miniature railway and paddling pool, as well as a tearoom and picnic area.

Fountains Abbey and Studley Royal

It's tantalizing to imagine how the English landscape might have appeared had Henry VIII not dissolved the monasteries, with all the artistic ruin precipitated by that act. **Fountains Abbey**, four miles southwest of Ripon off the B6265, gives a good idea of what might have been, and is the one ruin amongst Yorkshire's many monastic fragments you should make a point of seeing. Linked to it are the elegant water gardens of **Studley Royal**, landscaped in the eighteenth century to form a setting for the abbey, but only reunited as a single 680-acre estate in 1983. The estate is owned by the National Trust, which organizes an ambitious range of activities and events – from opera and firework displays to **free guided tours** (April–Oct daily; call ⓣ01765/608888 for details).

Getting there by **public transport** is not as easy as it might be. There are regular buses to Ripon from Harrogate and York (amongst other places), but the onward service to the abbey is patchy in summer (Sundays and bank holidays only), paltry in winter. Ring Ripon tourist office or the abbey for the latest.

The Abbey

Beautifully set in a narrow, wooded valley, **Fountains Abbey** (April–Sept daily 10am–6pm; Oct–March daily 10am–4pm; last admission 1hr before closing; £5 including Studley Royal and Fountains Hall; NT) was founded in 1133 by thirteen dissident Benedictine monks from the wealthy abbey of St Mary's in York. Their enterprise may well have been encouraged by the success of

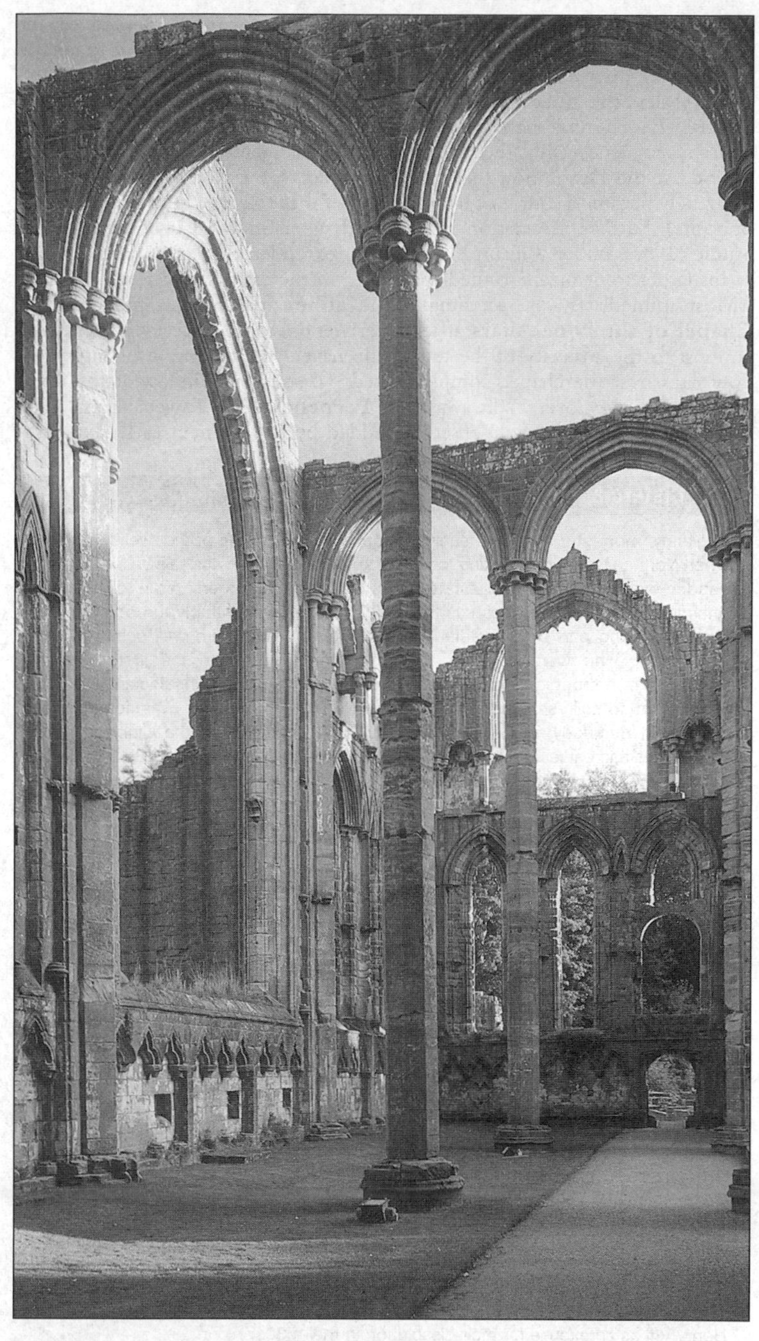

△ Fountains Abbey

Rievaulx, founded a year earlier, and they were formally adopted by the Cistercians two years later (see box below). Within a hundred years, Fountains had become the wealthiest Cistercian foundation in England and it was to this century that the three main phases of the abbey's structural development belong: the church's nave and transepts, the domestic buildings, and the church's east end. Only the church's domineering tower belongs to a later period. At the Dissolution the abbey was sold to Sir Richard Gresham, and ultimately became a source of building stone for the nearby Fountains Hall (see opposite). Further desecration was avoided when in 1768 it became part of Studley Royal under William Aislabie, who extended the landscaping exploits of his father to bring the ruined abbey within the estate's orbit.

Most immediately eye-catching is the **abbey church**, in particular the **Chapel of the Nine Altars** at its eastern end, whose delicacy is in marked contrast to the austerity of the rest of the nave. A great sixty-foot-high window rises over the chapel, complemented by a similar window at the nave's western doorway, over 370ft away. The **Perpendicular Tower**, almost 180ft high, looms over the whole ensemble, added by the eminent early-sixteenth-

The Cistercians

England's **monastic tradition** received a boost in the middle of the twelfth century when Norman landlords, seeking to secure spiritual salvation and raise a bit of cash, handed over portions of their estates to various religious orders, often to dissident offshoots of the Benedictines such as the **Cistercians**. Inevitably the poorest and least promising part of an estate, these parcels of land were well suited to the Cistercians, who were bent on removing themselves from the world and a Benedictine orthodoxy which in their eyes had become insufficiently strict. Committed to toil, self-sufficiency and prayer, the movement was founded at Cîteaux in Burgundy, in reaction to the arrogant affluence of the Cluniacs, who themselves had earlier reacted against the same perceived fault in the Benedictines. Fountains found itself in the vanguard of the movement, founded just five years after Waverley, the first Cistercian foundation in England.

Dressed in rough **habits** of undyed sheeps' wool, the so-called "White Monks" lived a frugal and mostly silent existence. Besides this core of priest-monks common to all Benedictine communities, whose obligatory presence at choir seven times daily, starting with matins at 2.30am, left little time for work outside the cloister, the Cistercians uniquely had a second tier of lay brethren known as **conversi**, or "bearded ones". At Fountains, around forty monks were complemented by two hundred such *conversi*. At Rievaulx the imbalance was equally marked, its community comprising over 500 *conversi* and only 150 monks. Not ordained, and with fewer religious demands, the new recruits – often skilled farmers and masons – could venture far from the mother house, returning only for major festivals and feast days. They were organized into **granges** (farms) to run flocks of sheep, drain land (hence Yorkshire's many "Friar's Ditches"), clear pasture, mine stone, lead or iron – even, in a couple of cases, to run a stud farm and sea-fishing business. Fountains' holdings in the Craven area of the Dales alone totalled over a million acres.

The Cistercians' success prompted the Augustinians (Kirkham and Guisborough) and Benedictines (York and Whitby) to promote similar economic ventures though within a hundred years much of their early vigour had been lost, partly as a result of an economic downturn which followed the Black Death. Granges were broken into smaller units and leased to a new class of tenant farmer, as the Cistercians joined the older orders in living off rents rather than actively developing their own estates. The resulting greed and complacency of the monasteries was ultimately used by Henry VIII as an excuse for their dissolution in the 1530s.

century Abbot Marmaduke Huby, who presided over perhaps the abbey's greatest period of prosperity. Equally grandiose in scale is the undercroft of the **Lay Brothers' Dormitory** off the cloister, a stunningly vaulted space over 300ft long that was used to store the monastery's annual harvest of fleeces. Its sheer size gives some idea of the abbey's entrepreneurial scope, some thirteen tons of wool a year being turned over, most of it sold to Venetian and Florentine merchants who toured the monasteries. The monks soon became speculators, buying wool from local farmers to sell in addition to their own production.

The size of the lay buildings – including a substantial **Lay Brothers' Infirmary** – gives an idea of the number of lay brothers at the abbey. All are considerably larger than the corresponding monks' buildings, of which the most prepossessing are the **Chapter House** and **Refectory** – notice the huge fireplace of the tiny **Warming Room** alongside the refectory, the only heated space in the entire complex. Outside the abbey perimeter, between the gatehouse and the bridge, are the Abbey Mill and **Fountains Hall** (same times; NT), the latter a fine example of early-seventeenth-century domestic architecture.

Studley Royal

A bucolic riverside walk, marked from the visitor centre car park, takes you from Fountains Hall through the abbey to a series of ponds and ornamental gardens, harbingers of **Studley Royal** (same times as the abbey; NT), which can also be entered via the village of Studley Roger, where there's a separate car park. This lush medley of lawns, lake, woodland and **Deer Park** (daily dawn to dusk; free) was laid out in 1720 by John Aislabie, MP for Ripon and Chancellor of the Exchequer until his involvement with the South Sea Company – one of the great financial scandals of the century – led to his resignation. There are some scintillating views of the abbey from the gardens, though it's the cascades and water gardens, fed by canals from the Skell, which command most attention, framed by several small temples positioned for their aesthetic effect. Just within the park stands the 1871 **Church of St Mary** (April–Sept daily 1–5pm; free), neatly approached by an avenue of limes that frame the distant towers of Ripon Cathedral. Organ recitals are held here most weekends (May–Sept). You could easily spend an afternoon whiling away time in the gardens: the full circuit, from visitor centre to abbey and gardens and then back, is a good couple of miles' walk.

Harrogate

HARROGATE – the very picture of genteel Yorkshire respectability – owes its airy, planned appearance and early prosperity to the discovery of Tewit Well in 1571. This was the first of over eighty ferrous and sulphurous springs that, by the nineteenth century, were to turn the town into one of the country's leading spas. By the mid-twentieth century, however, taking the waters had become a less popular pastime, and since the early 1970s Harrogate has instead concentrated on hosting conferences, exhibitions and festivals. Monuments to its past splendours still stand dotted around town and, despite the jarring efforts of contemporary architects, Harrogate manages to retain its essential Victorian and Edwardian character. Much of its appeal lies in the splendid parks and gardens – "England's floral town" keeps admirable pace with the changing seasons, and if you pick up a "Floral Trail" leaflet from the tourist office you'll be guided around the best of the current blooms.

Harrogate's spa heritage begins with the **Royal Baths Assembly Rooms**, built in 1897, where you can still take a Turkish bath in the plush, tiled Victorian surroundings (call ⓣ01423/556746 for hours; from £10.50 a session); the public entrance is on Parliament Street. The contemporaneous **Royal Hall**, built as a concert hall, stands across the way at the corner of Ripon Road and King's Road, while just around the corner from the Assembly Rooms stands the **Royal Pump Room**, built 1842, in Crown Place, over the sulphur well that feeds the Royal Baths. The **museum** here (April–Oct Mon–Sat 10am–5pm, Sun 2–5pm; Nov–March Mon–Sat 10am–4pm, Sun 2–4pm; £2.50) re-creates something of the town's health-fixated past and also lets you sample the water; free hour-long **guided walks** leave here several times a week between July and October (information from the tourist office). The town's earliest surviving spa building, the old Promenade Room of 1806, is just 100yd from the Pump Room on Swan Road – now housing the **Mercer Art Gallery** (Tues–Sat 10am–5pm, Sun 2–5pm; free), which hosts regularly changing fine-art exhibitions.

Harrogate deserves much credit for the preservation of its green spaces, most prominent of which is **The Stray**, a jealously guarded green belt that curves around the south of the town centre. To the southwest, the 120-acre **Valley Gardens** are the venue for the annual Spring Flower Show and Sunday band concerts in summer, while many visitors also make for the **Harlow Carr Botanical Gardens** (daily 9am–6pm or dusk if earlier; £4.50; ⓦwww.rhs.org.uk), the main showpiece of the Northern Horticultural Society. These lie one and a half miles out, on the town's western edge; take the B6162 Otley road, or walk beyond the Valley Gardens, through the Pine Woods. Although laid out with a scientific purpose – breeding fruit and vegetable stock suited to northern climates – the gardens are a year-round floral extravaganza, with especially wonderful rose displays. A specialist **Museum of Gardening** in the grounds (included in the gardens entry fee) gathers together gardening tools and historical material, while the *Garden Room Café-Bar* and a refreshment kiosk (closed Oct–March) provide meals and drinks – or you can bring your own picnic.

Practicalities

National Express buses and all local and regional bus services (from Knaresborough, York, Skipton, Pateley Bridge, Ripon and Leeds) use the **bus station** on Station Parade. The **train station** (for services from Leeds and York) is on the same street, just a few minutes from all the central sights. There's limited-hours **parking** along and around West Park, on the way into town, and there are central car parks on Oxford Street and near the train station. Harrogate's **tourist office** (April–Sept Mon–Sat 9am–6pm, Sun 10am–1pm; Oct–March Mon–Sat 9am–5pm; ⓣ01423/537300, ⓦwww.harrogate.gov.uk) is in the Royal Baths on Crescent Road.

There are scores of **accommodation** options, starting with the B&Bs on King's Road and Franklin Road, north of the centre. Side streets like Studley Road, off King's Road beyond the conference centre, are quieter. You shouldn't have any problem finding somewhere to stay, other than during one of Harrogate's many festivals. Of these the most famous are the **flower shows** (second weeks of April and Sept), but there's also the **Great Yorkshire Show** (second week in July), the Northern Antiques Fair (second half of Sept), and various book fairs, music festivals and craft shows.

Accommodation

Alexander Guest House 88 Franklin Rd ⓣ01423/503348. Recommended Victorian-era, non-smoking guest house on a residential street, under 10min walk from the centre. No credit cards. ❸

Cavendish Hotel 3 Valley Drive ⓣ01423/509637. A comfortable, friendly place, whose best rooms (all en suite) overlook the Valley Gardens. ❸

Cutlers on the Stray 19 West Park ⓣ01423/524471, ⓦwww.cutlers-web.co.uk. Former coaching inn, now contemporary brasserie with rooms (some with views across the green expanse of The Stray). Warm Mediterranean colours, stylish decor, sharp little bathrooms and CD players provide a comfortable night. Parking available. ❻

Fountains Hotel 27 King's Rd ⓣ01423/530483, ⓦwww.fountains.fsworld.co.uk. Family-run house just a minute or two from the conference centre. Non-smoking rooms have trim little bathrooms (some with bath as well as shower); it's quieter at the side, where the rooms look over a shady copse. Parking available. ❸

Hotel du Vin Prospect Place ⓣ01423/856800, ⓦwww.hotelduvin.com. Fashionable town house hotel and bistro overlooking The Stray, with variously sized boutique-style rooms (four of them "loft suites") featuring trademark big beds and bathrooms. Breakfast available (£9.50–13.50), and meals in summer served in the walled garden. Parking available. ❻

Old Swan Hotel Swan Rd ⓣ01423/500055, ⓦwww.oldswanhotel.com. Large ivy-clad hotel set in its own grounds, much rebuilt in Victorian times. Agatha Christie hid out here during her disappearance in 1926; today's comforts are suitably country-house in style if a tad tired. There's a terrace, gardens and conservatory, while D, B & B rates aren't a bad deal. Parking available. ❼

Rudding Park Hotel Rudding Park, Follifoot ⓣ01423/871350, ⓦwww.ruddingpark.com. Stylish country-house hotel located three miles southeast of town (down the A661). Terrifically relaxing with a fine bar and brasserie, and attached gardens and golf course. Parking available. ❽

Ruskin Hotel 1 Swan Rd ⓣ01423/502045, ⓦwww.ruskinhotel.co.uk. Appealing Victorian villa with seven characterful, spacious en-suite rooms (one a four-poster), terraced bar and charming garden. Parking available. ❻

Restaurants and pubs

Betty's 1 Parliament St ⓣ01423/502746. Very much a Harrogate institution, established by a Swiss emigrant in the 1920s. The cakes and tarts are to die for (takeaway available), but full meals are also served – Alpine maccaroni or *rösti*, say, or a full menu of seasonal specialities. Closes at 9pm. Inexpensive.

Courtyard 1 Montpellier Mews ⓣ01423/530708. Fashionable food – such as Thai-spiced fishcakes and seared sea bass – served in a good-looking mews restaurant. Lighter lunches are good value. Closed Sun. Expensive.

Drum and Monkey 5 Montpellier Gardens ⓣ01423/502650. Long-standing fish and seafood restaurant, a firm favourite with locals and out-of-towners alike. Choose the best of the daily catch grilled, or go cheaper (poached trout, fish brochette) or more expensive (seafood platter with garlic butter). Closed Sun. Moderate to Expensive.

Old Bell Tavern 6 Royal Parade ⓣ01423/507930. Period tavern that's serious about its drinks, with a dozen guest beers and a good bottled beer/wine list. Treat it as a pub – it's the best in town – or come to eat, since there are bar meals and sandwiches served daily (lunchtime and 6–7pm) and a non-smoking brasserie upstairs dispensing Mediterranean vegetable tart, braised lamb shank and stuffed filo parcels. Moderate.

Orchid 28 Swan Rd ⓣ01423/560425. Wok-wielding chefs conjour up specialities from all corners of Southeast Asia, which means dishes from tempura to Shanghai noodles. There's *dim sum* at lunch, and sushi and sashimi every Tuesday. Closed Mon & Sat lunch. Moderate.

Salsa Posada 4 Mayfield Grove ⓣ01423/565151. Funky Mexican restaurant with good-natured staff churning out reasonably authentic nachos, burritos, fajitas and the rest. Dinner only. Moderate.

Knaresborough

A four-mile hop east from Harrogate, **KNARESBOROUGH** rises spectacularly above the River Nidd's limestone gorge, its old town houses, pubs, shops and gardens clustered together on the wooded northern bank, with the river itself crossed by two bridges ("High" and "Low") and an eye-opener of a rail viaduct. The rocky crag above the town is crowned by the stump of a **Castle**

(Easter–Sept daily 10.30am–5pm; £2.50) dating back to Norman times. Built on the site of Roman and Anglo-Saxon fortifications, it's now little more than a fourteenth-century keep in landscaped grounds, thanks to Cromwell's wrecking tactics during the Civil War. It was here that Henry II's knights fled after the murder of Thomas à Becket in Canterbury Cathedral; here, too, that Richard II was held before being removed to Pontefract, where he was murdered in 1400. In Castle Yard, close to the castle entrance, stands the **Old Court House Museum** (same hours & ticket as castle), with an original Tudor court and displays on local history and the Civil War; you're also allowed into the spooky **sallyport**, the old escape tunnel from the castle.

These historic sites aside, there's not much to the town, but it's a very appealing place nonetheless, with a central **Market Place** (markets every Wednesday) claiming the oldest pharmacist's shop in England, in business since 1720. There's also a pub named after local boy "Blind Jack" (John) Metcalfe, the celebrated eighteenth-century civil engineer, who, despite his lack of sight, managed to build roads and bridges all over Britain. Below town, the enjoyable **riverside** is the other focus, with wooded walks along both banks.

The town's two novelty acts are to be found on the west side of the river. **Mother Shipton's Cave** (daily: March–Oct 9.30am–5.45pm; Nov & Feb 10am–4.45pm; closed Dec & Jan; £4.95; ⓦwww.mothershipton.co.uk) was home to a sixteenth-century soothsayer who predicted the defeat of the Armada, the Great Fire of London, world wars, cars, planes, iron ships – falling short, however, in the most important oracular chestnut of them all, predicting the End of the World: "The world to an end will come," she prophesied, "in eighteen hundred and eighty one." Close by is the **Petrifying Well**, where dripping, lime-soaked waters coat everyday objects – gloves, hats, coats, toys – in a brownish veneer that sets rock-hard in a few weeks. Both cave and well are contained within a riverside estate, reached along a fine eighteenth-century wooded "Long Walk", studded with picnic areas; the main entrance is just over the High Bridge, north of the town, which you can reach by walking along the river from below the castle.

Regular **trains** and **buses** (every 10min) from Harrogate are frequent enough to make Knaresborough an easy side trip. Signs point you to the **tourist office** at 9 Castle Courtyard, around the back of Market Place (Easter–Oct Mon–Sat 10am–5.30pm, July & Aug until 6pm, Sun 10am–1pm; ⓣ01423/866886), from where free **guided walks** depart on Tuesday afternoons in summer (July–Sept).

York

YORK is the north's most compelling city, a place whose history, said George VI, "is the history of England". This is perhaps overstating things a little, but it reflects the significance of a metropolis that until the Industrial Revolution was second only to London in population and importance, not only at the heart of the country's religious life, but also a key player in some of the major events that have shaped the nation. These days a more provincial air hangs over the city, except in summer when York feels like a heritage site for the benefit of tourists. That said, no trip to this part of the country is complete without a visit to York, and the city's former importance has made it easy to get to, with plenty of road and rail connections. Heavy tourist traffic has also produced plenty of accommodation, with the emphasis on small B&B places in quiet residential districts near the city centre. And if you want more than museums and monuments, York's university and colleges provide the spur for a reasonably healthy nightlife.

The city is well placed for any number of **day-trips**: the coast is only an hour away by car or train (longer by bus), while Harrogate, Knaresborough and Ripon are all easily accessible, too. However, if you've only time for one day-trip, it should probably be to **Castle Howard**, the gem amongst English stately homes. There's a different kind of nostalgia at work at nearby **Eden Camp** – a World War II museum occupying buildings that once housed German prisoners-of-war.

A brief history of York

The **Romans** chose York's swampy position, at the confluence of two minor rivers, as the site of a military camp during their campaigns against the Brigantes in 71 AD, and in time this fortress became a city – **Eboracum**, capital of the empire's northern European territories and one of its most important administrative centres. The base for Hadrian's northern campaigns, it was also ruled for three years by Septimius Severus, one of two emperors to die in the city. The other, Constantine Chlorus, was the father of Constantine the Great, first Christian emperor and founder of Constantinople; at Chlorus' death, his son was proclaimed Roman Emperor here – the only occasion an emperor was enthroned in Britain.

Much fought over after the decline of Rome, the city emerged as a **Saxon** vassal, Eoforwic, and later became the fulcrum of Christianity in northern England. It was here, on Easter Day in 627, that Bishop Paulinus, on a mission to establish the Roman Church, baptized King Edwin of Northumbria in a small timber chapel built for the purpose. Six years later the church became the first minster and Paulinus the first archbishop of York. In 867 the city fell to the **Danes**, who renamed it **Jorvik**, and later made it the capital of eastern England (Danelaw), following a treaty in 886 between Alfred the Great and Guthrum the Dane. Later Viking raids culminated in the decisive **Battle of Stamford Bridge** (1066) six miles east of the city, where English King Harold defeated Norse King Harald – a Pyrrhic victory in the event, for his weakened army was defeated by the Normans just a few days later at the Battle of Hastings, with well-known consequences for all concerned. In York, aside from the physical remains left by the Vikings on show in several of the museums, the very street names tell of their profound influence – the suffix "-gate" is derived from an old Norse word for street.

The **Normans** devastated much of York's hinterland in their infamous "Harrying of the North", building two castles astride the Ouse in the city itself. Stone walls were thrown up during the thirteenth century, when the city became a favoured Plantagenet retreat and commercial capital of the north, its importance reflected in the new title of Duke of York, bestowed ever since on the monarch's second son. The 48 **York Mystery Plays**, one of only four surviving such cycles, date from this era, created by the powerful guilds that rose with the city's woollen industry.

Although Henry VIII's Dissolution of the Monasteries took its toll on a city crammed with religious houses, York remained strongly wedded to the Catholic cause, and the most famous of the Gunpowder Plot conspirators, **Guy Fawkes**, was born here. During the **Civil War** Charles I established his court in the city, which was strongly pro-Royalist, inviting a Parliamentarian siege that was eventually lifted by Prince Rupert of the Rhine, a nephew of the King. Rupert's troops, however, were routed by Cromwell and Sir Thomas

Fairfax at the **Battle of Marston Moor** in 1644, another seminal battle in England's history, which took place just six miles west of York. It's said that only the fact that Fairfax was a local man saved York from destruction.

The city's eighteenth-century history was marked by its emergence as a social centre for Yorkshire's landed elite. Whilst the Industrial Revolution largely passed it by, the arrival of the **railways** brought renewed prosperity, thanks to the enterprise of pioneering "Railway King" George Hudson, lord mayor during the 1830s and 1840s. The railway is still a major employer, as is the confectionery industry, in the shape of companies such as Terry Suchard and Nestlé, together with the proceeds from new service and bioscience industries – not forgetting, of course, the income from four million annual tourists.

Arrival, information, transport and tours

Trains arrive at **York Station**, just outside the city walls on the west side of the River Ouse, a 750-yard walk from the historic core. There are information and accommodation centres at the station and a luggage-storage office. Long-haul National Express **buses** and most other regional bus services drop off and pick up on Rougier Street, 200yd north of the train station, just before Lendal Bridge, though National Express services call at the train station, too. Arriving by car you'd be advised to park in one of the **car parks** on the roads shadowing the city walls: in the north, Gillygate and Clarence Street are closest to the Minster; Piccadilly and Tower Street in the southeast are convenient for Clifford's Tower and the Castle Museum; and there are also car parks on Queen Street near the train station.

Information

There's a useful **tourist office** at the train station (April–Oct Mon–Sat 9am–6pm, Sun 9.30am–4.30pm; Nov–March Mon–Sat 9am–5pm, Sun 10am–4pm), though the main office is over Lendal Bridge, 200yd west of the Minster in the De Grey Rooms, on Exhibition Square (April–Oct Mon–Sat 9am–6pm, Sun 10am–5pm; Nov–March Mon–Sat 9am–5pm, Sun 10am–4pm). Each office shares the same telephone number and useful website (ⓣ01904/621756, ⓦwww.visityork.org), can provide maps and leaflets on every conceivable tour and attraction, and has an accommodation service (see opposite). Also check out the York City Council website, ⓦwww.york.gov.uk, for details of the major sites, museums, galleries and much else.

City transport

Walking is the best way to acquaint yourself with the city, and often the only way to get from A to B, given the confused historic layout of pedestrianized streets, alleys and yards. City **bus routes** are operated by First York (ⓣ01904/622992), though visitors are unlikely to get much use out of their FirstDay (£2.10) or FirstWeek rover tickets (£10), available on board the buses. Consider renting a bike instead, as York is one of the country's most bike-friendly cities, with over forty miles of cycle lanes and paths – there's a rental outfit listed on p.993.

Tours

York is probably tour capital of Britain, the streets clogged by double-decker buses, costumed guides and carefully shepherded sightseers. Doing it yourself is, frankly, the most enjoyable way, though if time is limited, or you fancy some of the more inventive options, there's plenty of choice. The tourist office push-es the various **bus tours** (from around £8 per person), but much more interesting are the various **guided walks** on offer, from evening ghost walks to historical tours, many led by the York Association of Voluntary Guides (Ⓣ01904/640780, Ⓦwww.york.touristguides.btinternet.co.uk). They offer a free, two-hour guided tour throughout the year (daily at 10.15am), plus additional tours in summer (April, Sept & Oct at 2.15pm; June–Aug at 2.15pm & 6.45pm), departing from outside the Art Gallery in Exhibition Square; just turn up. It's also pleasant to get out on the river, and several operators offer **cruises**, including YorkBoat (Ⓣ01904/628324, Ⓦwww.yorkboat.co.uk), sailing daily from King's Staith and Lendal Bridge (Feb–Nov; cruises from £6, £6.50/7.50 in the evening).

Accommodation

York is a busy tourist town, with the range of **accommodation** you'd expect, from countless cheap B&Bs to a clutch of luxury hotels. The main B&B concentrations are in the sidestreets off **Bootham and Clifton** (immediately west of Exhibition Square), as well as in the **Mount** area (turn right out of the station and head down Blossom Street. Booking's definitely a good idea from June to August, and bear in mind that many places aren't keen on single-night stays in summer. If you're stuck for a bed, make straight for the tourist offices, who'll **book you a room**. They also put out an accommodation list if you want to hunt on your own, and there's a useful board of places posted in the station office window. Or consider the rooms at the various **budget chains**, like *Travelodge*, *Holiday Inn Express*, *Ramada*, *Novotel*, *Quality Hotel*, and so on, which all have hotels in York. In a reversal of policy in most cities, larger hotels here tend to charge slightly less during the week than at weekends.

Hotels and B&Bs

23 St Mary's 23 St Mary's, Bootham Ⓣ01904/622738. Very pleasant and amiable family-house hotel just west of St Mary's Abbey and gardens. All rooms are en suite; parking available. ❹

Abbey 14 Earlsborough Terrace, Marygate Ⓣ01904/627782, Ⓦwww.bedandbreakfastyork.co.uk. Riverside terraced guest house in a great location with bright, pretty rooms, two of which, overlooking the river, are en suite. Parking. ❸

Arnot House 17 Grosvenor Terrace, Bootham Ⓣ01904/641966, Ⓦwww.arnothouseyork.co.uk. Victorian family house preserving many of its original features, offering four well-furnished and no-smoking en-suite rooms with distant views of the Minster. Vegetarian breakfasts on request. ❸

The Bar Convent 17 Blossom St Ⓣ01904/643238, Ⓦwww.bar-convent.org.uk. Grand Georgian building next to Micklegate Bar, housing a museum and café as well as eleven single rooms (£26 each), six twins and a double; one of the twins and the double is en suite, otherwise there are separate bathrooms and access to a self-catering kitchen and guest lounge. Pay-and-display parking over the road. Continental breakfast included. ❷

Bootham Bar 4 High Petergate Ⓣ01904/658516. Petite town house rooms in an eighteenth-century building, just 100yd from the Minster. All are en suite except for three basic singles (£25) in the attic, which share a bathroom. Parking available. ❹

City 68 Monkgate Ⓣ01904/622483, Ⓦwww.cityguesthouse.co.uk. Central, non-smoking, family-run guest house with budget rates, not far from the Minster. All rooms (six doubles/twins and just one single) have en-suite showers and there's a useful car park. ❸

Clifton Bridge Water End, Clifton Ⓣ01904/610510, Ⓦwww.cliftonbridgehotel.co.uk. A mile northwest of the Minster beyond Bootham, but close to a riverside walk to the city centre. Of the fourteen rooms, three on the ground floor are wheelchair accessible, and there's a larger family room, too. Nicely situated in its own grounds, with parking available. ❺

Dairy 3 Scarcroft Rd Ⓣ01904/639367, Ⓦwww.dairyguesthouse.co.uk. Charming Victorian house half a mile south of the station, retaining its pine doors, cast-iron fireplaces, stained glass and pretty courtyard. Five cottage-style rooms available, and a choice of healthily cooked (no frying)

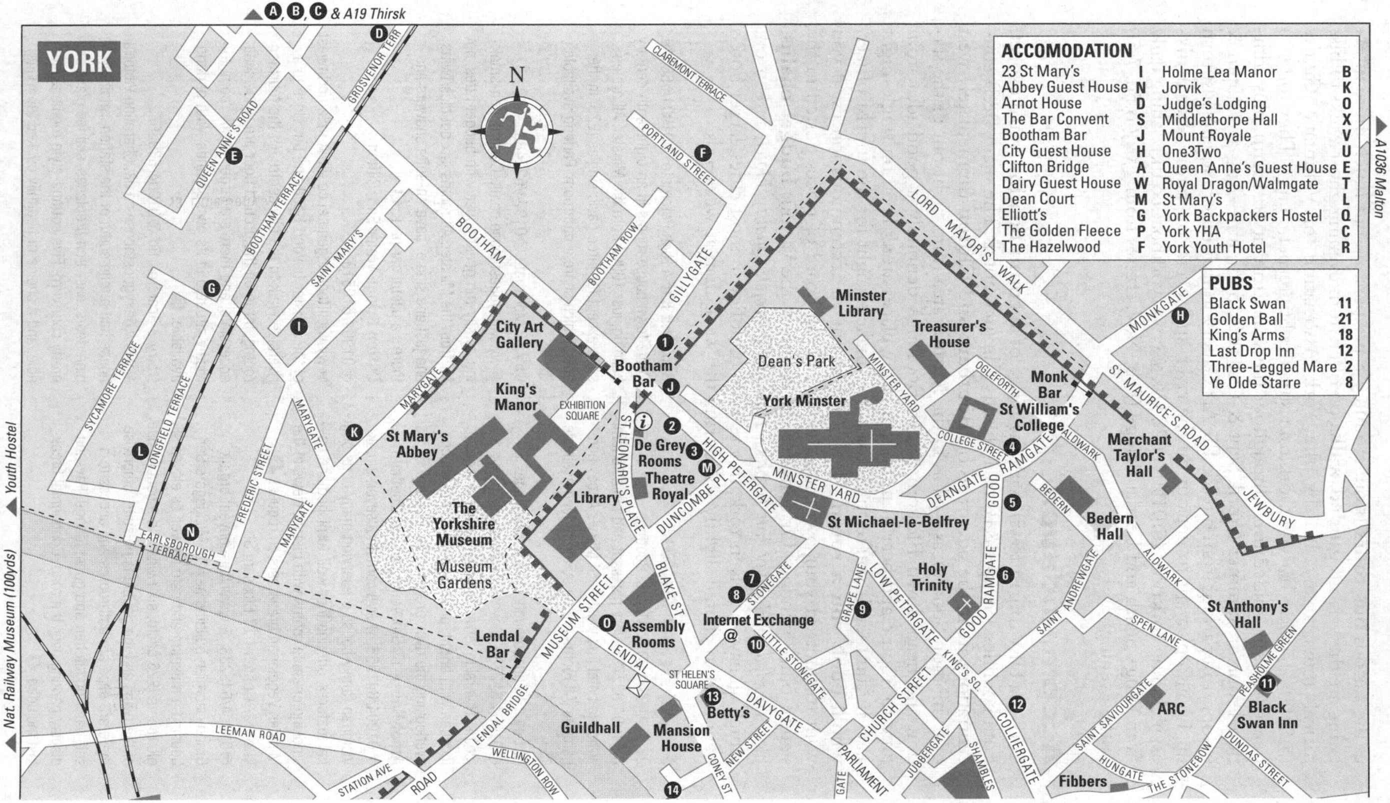

YORK

ACCOMODATION

23 St Mary's	I	Holme Lea Manor	B
Abbey Guest House	N	Jorvik	K
Arnot House	D	Judge's Lodging	O
The Bar Convent	S	Middlethorpe Hall	X
Bootham Bar	J	Mount Royale	V
City Guest House	H	One3Two	U
Clifton Bridge	A	Queen Anne's Guest House	E
Dairy Guest House	W	Royal Dragon/Walmgate	T
Dean Court	M	St Mary's	L
Elliott's	G	York Backpackers Hostel	Q
The Golden Fleece	P	York YHA	C
The Hazelwood	F	York Youth Hotel	R

PUBS

Black Swan	11
Golden Ball	21
King's Arms	18
Last Drop Inn	12
Three-Legged Mare	2
Ye Olde Starre	8

A, B, C & A19 Thirsk
A1036 Malton
Youth Hostel
Nat. Railway Museum (100yds)
N
Grosvenor Terr
Queen Anne's Road
Bootham Terrace
Saint Mary's
Sycamore Terrace
Longfield Terrace
Frederic Street
Marygate
Earlsborough Terrace
Leeman Road
Station Ave
Road
Lendal Bridge
Wellington Row
Bootham
Bootham Row
Claremont Terrace
Portland Street
Gillygate
Lord Mayor's Walk
Monkgate
St Maurice's Road
Jewbury
City Art Gallery
King's Manor
Exhibition Square
St Mary's Abbey
The Yorkshire Museum
Museum Gardens
Lendal Bar
Museum Street
Library
St Leonard's Place
Bootham Bar
De Grey Rooms
Theatre Royal
Duncombe Pl
High Petergate
Minster Library
Dean's Park
York Minster
Minster Yard
Treasurer's House
Ogleforth
College Street
Monk Bar
St William's College
Merchant Taylor's Hall
Aldwark
Bedern
Bedern Hall
Deangate
Goodramgate
St Michael-le-Belfrey
Holy Trinity
Low Petergate
Grape Lane
Stonegate
Little Stonegate
Internet Exchange
Assembly Rooms
Blake St
Lendal
St Helen's Square
Betty's
Davygate
Guildhall
Mansion House
New Street
Coney St
Church Street
King's Sq.
Parliament
Jubbergate
Shambles
Colliergate
Saint Andrewgate
Spen Lane
St Anthony's Hall
Peasholme Green
Black Swan Inn
ARC
Saint Saviourgate
Hungate
The Stonebow
Dundas Street
Fibbers
Gate

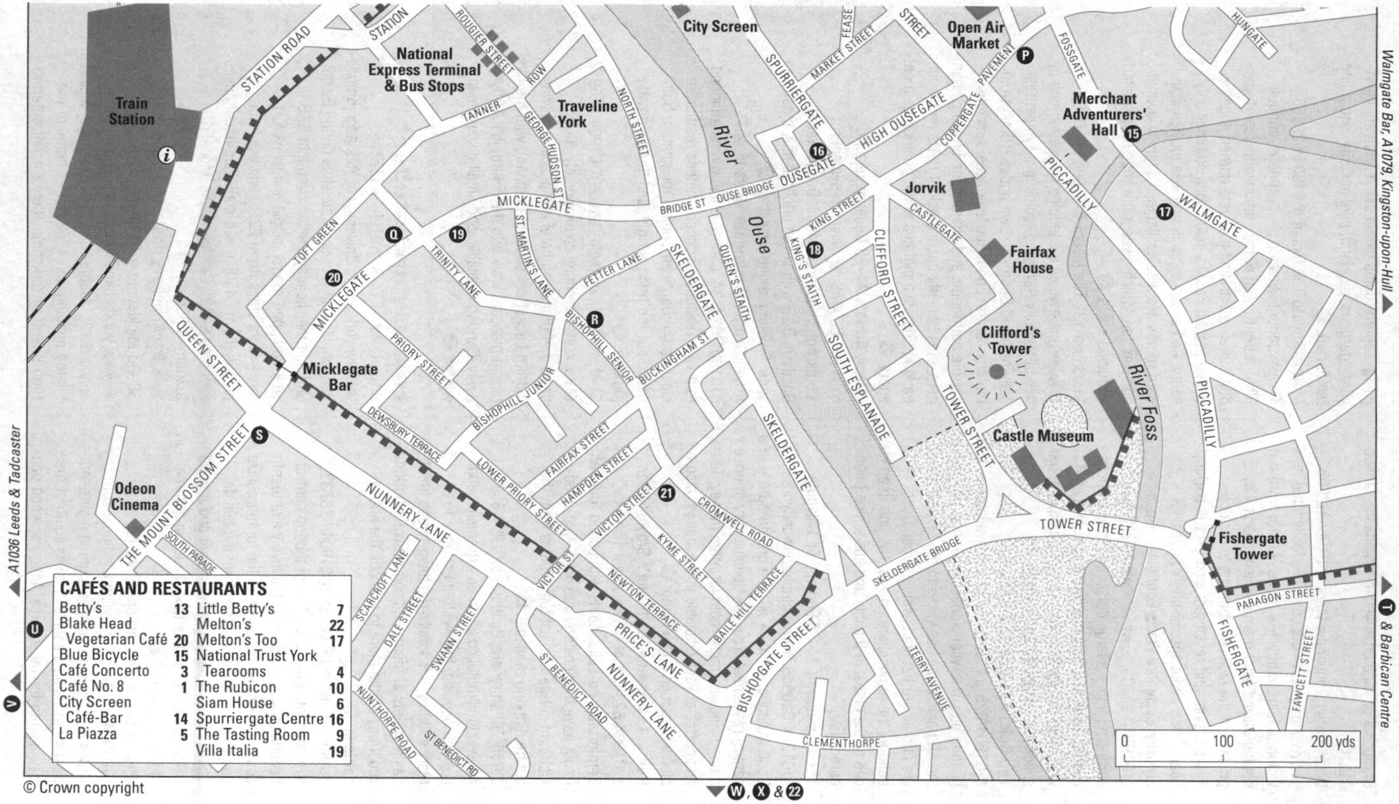

Walmgate Bar, A1079, Kingston-upon-Hull

T & Barbican Centre

A1036 Leeds & Tadcaster

W, X & 22

CAFÉS AND RESTAURANTS

Betty's	13	Little Betty's	7
Blake Head Vegetarian Café	20	Melton's	22
Blue Bicycle	15	Melton's Too	17
Café Concerto	3	National Trust York Tearooms	4
Café No. 8	1	The Rubicon	10
City Screen Café-Bar	14	Siam House	6
La Piazza	5	Spurriergate Centre	16
		The Tasting Room	9
		Villa Italia	19

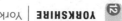

Train Station
National Express Terminal & Bus Stops
Traveline York
City Screen
Open Air Market
Merchant Adventurers' Hall
Jorvik
Fairfax House
Clifford's Tower
Castle Museum
Fishergate Tower
Micklegate Bar
Odeon Cinema
River Ouse
River Foss
Station Road
Station
Rougier Street
Row
Tanner
George Hudson St
North Street
Spurriergate
Market Street
Fease
Street
Pavement
Fossgate
Hungate
High Ousegate
Coppergate
Ousegate
Ouse Bridge
Bridge St
Micklegate
Piccadilly
Walmgate
Castlegate
King Street
King's Staith
Clifford Street
South Esplanade
Tower Street
Skeldergate
Queen's Staith
Toft Green
Trinity Lane
St. Martin's Lane
Fetter Lane
Bishophill Senior
Buckingham St
Bishophill Junior
Priory Street
Dewsbury Terrace
Queen Street
The Mount
Blossom Street
South Parade
Nunnery Lane
Lower Priory Street
Fairfax Street
Hampden Street
Victor Street
Victor St
Kyme Street
Cromwell Road
Newton Terrace
Baile Hill Terrace
Price's Lane
Bishopgate Street
Skeldergate Bridge
Terry Avenue
Clementhorpe
St Benedict Road
Scarcroft Lane
Dale Street
Swann Street
Nunthorpe Road
St Benedict Rd
Paragon Street
Fishergate
Fawcett Street
0 100 200 yds

traditional or vegetarian/vegan breakfasts. Closed Jan. ❹

Dean Court Duncombe Place ⓣ01904/625082, ⓦwww.deancourt-york.co.uk. Perfectly sited neo-Victorian hotel with views of the Minster from the double-glazed front rooms, which means it's pricey, but the facilities come up to scratch. There's a bar and restaurant, and garage parking nearby. Ask about special-break prices. ❼

Elliott's Sycamore Place, Bootham Terrace ⓣ01904/623333, ⓦwww.elliottshotel.co.uk. A surprising find – a large detached Victorian house tucked away in a peaceful and convenient spot, with eight comfortable rooms, big breakfasts, bar snacks, a restaurant and parking. ❹

The Golden Fleece 16 Pavement ⓣ01904/625171. Just four rooms available in this historic pub, but what a collection – one overlooks the Shambles, one has views to the Minster towers and all are haunted (well, maybe). Decor is antique, the atmosphere unique. The pub itself is one of the oldest in the city and has a nice beer garen. ❺

The Hazelwood 24–25 Portland St, Gillygate ⓣ01904/626548, ⓦwww.thehazelwoodyork.com. Good variety of rooms – all with private bath – in a central residential area. The doubles vary in price a bit, giving you more room for more money. Tea and coffee always available in the lounge; also a pleasant garden and parking. ❺

Holme Lea Manor 18 St Peter's Grove, Clifton ⓣ01904/623529, ⓦwww.holmelea.co.uk. Comfortable en-suite rooms with period touches (most have four-posters) in a quiet, tree-lined Victorian cul-de-sac just ten minutes from the centre. Parking available. ❹

Jorvik 52 Marygate, Bootham ⓣ01904/653511, ⓦwww.jorvikhotel.co.uk. In an extremely good position opposite the western entrance to St Mary's Abbey, this family-run town-house hotel has a variety of rooms and some private parking – you'll pay a little more to overlook the abbey gardens. ❹

Judge's Lodging 9 Lendal ⓣ01904/638733, ⓔjudgeshotel@aol.com. One of the top central, historic choices, located in the lovely eighteenth-century Georgian residence of the former assize court judges, a few minutes from the Minster. There's secure parking, a restaurant and a good cellar bar, plus some outdoor tables in summer for al fresco drinking. ❼

Middlethorpe Hall Bishopsthorpe Rd ⓣ01904/641241, ⓦwww.middlethorpe.com. York's most celebrated spot, a grand eighteenth-century mansion a couple of miles south of the city, next to the racecourse. Antiques, wood panelling, superb rooms (some set in a private courtyard), gardens, parkland, pool and spa, and a fine restaurant. ❽

Mount Royale The Mount ⓣ01904/628856, ⓦwww.mountroyale.co.uk. Luxurious, antique-filled retreat south of the station with superb garden-suites set around a private garden, together with a heated outdoor pool (open summer only), sauna and steam room. Some less exalted standard rooms are also available. It's family-owned and run, too, which gives it the edge over similarly endowed spots. ❻

One3Two 132 The Mount ⓣ01904/600060, ⓦwww.one3two.co.uk. Indulge yourself in one of five beautifully furnished rooms in a sympathetically restored Georgian town house, 10min from the city centre. Enormous teak beds, spacious marble bathrooms and champagne breakfast hampers, plus honesty bar, a stack of DVDs and limited parking. Stay five nights and the price drops a category. ❼

Queen Anne's 24–26 Queen Anne's Rd ⓣ01904/629389, ⓦwww.s-h-systems.co.uk/hotels/queenann.html. Budget-rated Bootham B&B with seven bright rooms, mostly en suite. Private parking available. ❷

Royal Dragon/Walmgate 16 Barbican Rd ⓣ01904/623134. Clean, simple rooms attached to a very reasonably priced Chinese restaurant close to the Barbican Centre. You share a bathroom, but the price is right, and there's private parking. ❷

St Mary's 17 Longfield Terrace ⓣ01904/626972, ⓦwww.stmaryshotel.co.uk. Homely, flower-draped, no-smoking hotel in a peaceful railway-cutting backstreet south of Bootham, with the river (and a pleasant walk into the centre) just 100yd away. Parking available, and small discounts in winter. ❸

Hostels and student halls

University of York ⓣ01904/432222, ⓦwww.york.ac.uk. University of York accommodation available at four separate sites during Easter and summer holidays, either overnight B&B in well-equipped rooms (single and twins ❸), or three-night stays (from £250) and week-long breaks (from £450) in self-contained flats/houses (sleeping 6–12). Call for details (Mon–Fri 9.30am–4.30pm).

York Backpackers Hostel Micklegate House, 88–90 Micklegate ⓣ01904/627720, ⓦwww.yorkbackpackers.mcmail.com. Dorm space (£13), doubles and family rooms in a Grade I listed building, the 1752 former home of the High Sheriff of Yorkshire. There's a self-catering kitchen, laundry, Internet access, TV and games room, café and licensed cellar bar. Prices include breakfast. ❷

York YHA Water End, Clifton ⓣ0870/770 6102, ⓔyork@yha.org.uk. Large Victorian mansion 20min walk along Bootham from the tourist office and then a left turn at Clifton Green; or follow the riverside footpath west from the station. Beds are mostly in four-bedded dorms (£16.50), though private rooms also available with TV, towels and kettle; book well in advance for these. Facilities include a café (with licence for alcohol with meals), Internet access, large garden (for volleyball and croquet) and parking. ❶

York Youth Hotel 11–13 Bishophill Senior ⓣ01904/625904, ⓦwww.yorkyouthhotel.demon.co.uk. Centrally located, on the west side of the river, off Micklegate, and attracting a mixed international crowd. Variously priced 4-, 8- and 20-bed dorms available (£11–16), plus single and twin rooms. Also a kitchen, laundry, games room, TV lounge and Internet access. Breakfast available Sun only (£2–3.50). ❶

The City

Take a look at one of the maps dotted around the city centre and you're confronted with a baffling and intimidating prospect. If the city council and tourist office are to be believed, there are around sixty churches, museums and historic buildings crammed within York's walls. In fact the tally of things you really want to see is surprisingly limited, with most sights within easy walking distance of one another. Even so, it's hard to get round everything in less than two days, and equally difficult to stick to any rigid itinerary. The **Minster** is the obvious place to start, followed by the cluster of buildings that circle it; then you might cut south to the **Shambles**, central to the city's old centre and pedestrianized grid, or walk around **the walls** from the Minster to Exhibition Square and Museum Street for the **City Art Gallery**, **Yorkshire Museum** and **St Mary's Abbey**, evocative ruins surrounded by the city's loveliest gardens. Thereafter you could walk through the main shopping streets to take in the **Merchant Adventurers' Hall**, most striking of the city's smaller medieval buildings, then deal with **Clifford's Tower** and the nearby **Jorvik Viking Centre** and **Castle Museum**. Lastly, be sure to leave time to take in the **National Railway Museum**, a superb museum whose appeal goes way beyond railway memorabilia.

York Minster

York Minster (daily: June–Sept 7am–8.30pm; Oct–May 7am–6pm; £4.50, Minster and all its attractions £6; ⓦwww.yorkminster.org) ranks as one of the country's most important sights. Seat of the archbishop of York, it is Britain's largest Gothic building and home to countless treasures, not least of which is the world's largest medieval stained-glass window and an estimated half of all the medieval stained glass in England. Samuel Johnson, visiting in 1773, was overwhelmed, but not, of course, lost for words, thinking it "an edifice of loftiness and elegance equal to the highest hopes of architecture". In addition to the main body of the church, any complete tour of the building, which took 250 years to complete, should also include the foundations, crypt, chapter house and an ascent of the great central tower. Once inside, be sure to pick up the Welcome to York Minster leaflet, a detailed account of the building. Voluntary guides are also on hand (at the reception desk by the entrance) to offer free tours of the interior.

In its earliest incarnation, the Minster was probably the wooden chapel used to baptize King Edwin of Northumbria in 627. After its stone successors were destroyed by the Danes, the first significant foundations were laid around 1080 by the first Norman archbishop, Thomas of Bayeux. Subsequent incumbents, notably Archbishop Roger (1154–81), added to the building, and it was from the germ of this Norman church that the present structure emerged. The oldest surviving fabric, in the south transept, dates from 1220 and the reign of Archbishop Walter de Grey, who also began work on a new north transept in 1260. A new chapter house, in the Decorated style, appeared in 1300, and a new nave in the same style was completed in 1338. The Perpendicular choir was realized in 1450 and the western towers in 1472. In 1480, the thirteenth-century central tower, which had collapsed in 1407, was rebuilt, thereby bringing the Minster to more or less its present state.

In the 1960s, in the course of investigating subsidence that had begun to affect the building, it was found that the 20,000-ton, 234-foot central tower was resting on only a shallow bed of loose stones, a discovery which prompted a £2-million project that was to involve packing the foundations with thousands of tons of concrete and over six miles of reinforced steel rods. That wasn't the end of the church's troubles, though. In 1984 lightning struck the Minster, unleashing a disastrous fire that raged through the south transept, destroying the timber-framed central vault and all but two of its extraordinary roof bosses.

The windows

Nothing else in the Minster can match the magnificence of the stained glass in the nave and transepts. The **West Window** (1338) contains distinctive heart-shaped upper tracery (the "Heart of Yorkshire"), whilst in the nave's north aisle, the second bay window (1155) contains slivers of the oldest stained glass in the country. In the fifth bay, notice the window showing St Peter attended by pilgrims (1312), with the funeral of a monkey among the fascinating details in its lower scenes. Moving down to the crossing, the north transept's **Five Sisters Window** is named after the five fifty-foot lancets, each glazed with thirteenth-century grisaille, a distinctive frosted, silvery-grey glass. Opposite, the south transept contains a sixteenth-century, 17,000-piece **Rose Window**, commemorating the 1486 marriage of Henry VII and Elizabeth of York, an alliance which marked the end of the Wars of the Roses.

The greatest of the church's 128 windows, however, is the majestic **East Window** (1405), at 78ft by 31ft the world's largest area of medieval stained glass in a single window. Its themes are the beginning and the end of the world, the upper panels showing scenes from the Old Testament, the lower sections mainly episodes from the book of Revelation. Notice also the glass of the transeptal bays, midway down the south wall of the choir, with their scenes from the lives of saints Cuthbert and William of York. The tombs of William, a twelfth-century archbishop of York, and of Cuthbert, ordained bishop in 685, stood near the high altar until the Reformation, and were credited with numerous miracles.

The rest of the interior

Before leaving the main body of the interior, give some time to the north transept's 400-year-old wooden clock with its oak knights, and the stone **choir screen**, knotted with incredibly intricate carvings and decorated with life-size figures of English monarchs from William I to Henry VI – all except the latter carved in the last quarter of the fifteenth century. Most of the choir dates from restorations following a fire in 1829. The painted **stone shields** round much of the nave and choir are those of Edward II and the barons who in 1309–10 held a parliament in York. Amongst the many tombs, those of most interest are the monument in the south transept to Walter de Grey, a beautiful grey-green canopy protecting a recumbent stone figure, and the tomb of the 10-year-old William, second son of Edward III, in the choir aisle.

The foundations, or **undercroft** (Mon–Sat 9am–5.15pm, Sun 12.30–5.15pm; £2.50), have been turned into a museum, fitted into a space excavated during the restorations in the 1960s. Fragments of the Roman fort which once stood on this site have been uncovered, as well as capitals, sculpture and fabric from the present Minster and its Norman predecessor. Amongst precious church relics in the adjoining **treasury** are silver plate found in Walter de Grey's tomb and the eleventh-century *Horn of Ulf*, presented to the Minster by a relative of the tide-turning King Canute. There's also access from the undercroft to the **crypt**, the spot that transmits the most powerful sense of antiquity, as it contains portions of Archbishop Roger's choir and sections of the 1080 church, including pillars with fine Romanesque capitals. The font stands over the supposed site of Paulinus's timber chapel, while a small illuminated doorway opens onto the base of a pillar belonging to the guardhouse of the original Roman camp.

Access to the undercroft, treasury and crypt is from the south transept, also the entrance to the **central tower** (£2.50), which you can climb for rooftop views over the city. Finally pop into the **Chapter House**, an architectural novelty whose buttressed octagonal walls remove the need for a central pillar, otherwise a common feature of this type of building.

Around the Minster

Past the Minster's west front a gateway leads into **Dean's Park**, a quiet green oasis bordered by a seven-arched fragment of arcade from the Norman archbishop's palace and by **York Minster Library** (Mon–Fri 9am–5pm; free), housed in the thirteenth-century chapel of the same palace. Among its more interesting exhibits is the baptismal entry for Guy Fawkes (April 16, 1570), removed from **St Michael-le-Belfrey** on High Petergate (open for Sunday services only), immediately south of the Minster. The church was built in 1536 and is bursting with seventeenth-century brasses and stained glass.

Walk through Dean's Park with the Minster on your right, then through the gate at the top to reach the **Treasurer's House** in Chapter House Street (Easter–Oct Mon–Thurs, Sat & Sun 11am–4.30pm; £4; NT), a glorious seventeenth-century town house that stands on the site of houses used by the Minster's treasurers until the Dissolution. Now owned by the National Trust, it offers exhibitions and videos that trace the site's changing fortunes, together with the paintings and furniture of industrialist Frank Green, who lived here from 1897 to 1930. His collection adorns the various period rooms – including an authentically kitted-out eighteenth-century kitchen and medieval hall – and there's also a walled garden and nice café on site, too.

Just around the corner in College Street stands **St William's College**, an eye-catching half-timbered building studded with oriel windows, initially dedicated to the great-grandson of William the Conqueror (first archbishop of York) and built in its present guise in 1467 for the Minster's chantry priests. During Charles I's three-year residence it served time as the Royal Mint and the king's printing press. These days it serves as a visitor centre for the Minster and a conference hall and banqueting centre, though three of the medieval rooms are open for viewing provided they're not in use.

The walls

Although much restored, the city's superb **walls** date mainly from the fourteenth century, though fragments of Norman work survive, particularly in the gates (or "bars"), whilst the northern sections still follow the line of the Roman ramparts. The only break in the walls is east of Monk Bar, where the city was first protected by the marshes of the River Foss and later by the deliberately flooded area known as King's Pool.

Monk Bar at the northern end of Goodramgate is as good a point of access as any, tallest of the city's four main gates and host to a small **Richard III Museum** (daily: March–Oct 9am–5pm; Nov–Feb 9.30am–4pm; £2; Ⓦwww.richardiiimuseum.co.uk), where you're invited to decide on the guilt or innocence of England's most maligned king. For just a taste of the walls' best section – with great views of the Minster and swathes of idyllic-looking gardens – take the ten-minute stroll west from Monk Bar to Exhibition Square (see p.987) and **Bootham Bar**, the only gate on the site of a Roman gateway and marking the traditional northern entrance to the city. A stroll round the walls' entire two-and-a-half-mile length will take you past the southwestern **Micklegate Bar**, long considered the most important of the gates since it, in turn, marked the start of the road to London. It was built to a Norman design reputedly using ancient stone coffins as building stone, and was later used to exhibit the heads of executed criminals and rebels. The engaging **Micklegate Bar Museum** (daily 9am–5pm; £2) occupies a surviving fortified tower and tells the story by way of old lithographs, models, paintings and the odd gruesome skull. **Walmgate Bar** in the east is the best preserved and has traditionally been the city's strongest bar. It was unsuccessfully undermined by the Roundheads during the Civil War, its present slight sag said to be a consequence of that episode.

Goodramgate and the Shambles

East of Goodramgate, in a labyrinth of quiet residential streets centred on Aldwark, a series of good-looking historic buildings are clustered. **Bedern Hall**, a medieval lodging and refectory for the Minster's priests, and the plain-faced **St Anthony's Hall** can be walked past pretty quickly, though the half-timbered **Black Swan Inn** down on Peasholme Green beckons for a drink, while the **Merchant Taylors' Hall** (April–Oct Tues only 10am–4pm; free) is a similar picture of late-medieval perfection. The Merchant Taylors' guild took upon itself the job of establishing a weaving workhouse to prevent "laytering and ydleness of vacabunds and poor follc"; a small upstairs museum explains their good work. At the south end of Goodramgate, **Our Lady's Row**, the oldest houses in the city (1316), stands hard against **Holy Trinity** (March–Oct Tues–Sat 9.30am–5pm; Nov–April Tues–Sat 9.30am–4pm; free), a much altered fifteenth-century church known for its east window, jumbled box pews and saddle-back tower, an unusual feature in English churches.

The Shambles, off King's Square at the southern end of Goodramgate, could be taken as the epitome of medieval York, though the crowds and self-conscious quaintness take the edge off what would otherwise be a perfect medieval thoroughfare. Flagstoned, almost impossibly narrow and lined with perilously leaning timber-framed houses, it was the home of York's butchers, its erstwhile stench and squalor now difficult to imagine, though old meat hooks still adorn the odd house. At no. 35, there's a **shrine** (closed to the public) to Margaret Clitherow, the Catholic wife of a butcher, martyred in 1586 for allegedly sheltering priests; she was pressed to death with rocks piled on top of a board on the city's Ouse Bridge. Newgate **market** (daily 8am–5pm) lies off the Shambles, together with the core of the city's shopping streets; **Parliament Street** sees a couple of outdoor markets a year, usually in high summer and a month before Christmas.

Exhibition Square

Exhibition Square, outside Bootham Bar, holds the city's main tourist office in the De Grey Rooms, opposite which stands the **York Art Gallery** (daily 10am–5pm; free), housing an extensive collection of early Italian, British and northern European paintings. It's fun to pick out the smattering of York scenes, which include L.S. Lowry's take on Clifford's Tower. Otherwise, the gallery puts on a year-round series of excellent special exhibitions, and is noted for its collections of British studio pottery – particularly that of Bernard Leach – and twentieth-century British painters, including Gwen John, Stanley Spencer and Walter Sickert.

Left of the gallery as you face it stands **King's Manor**, founded in 1270 and enlarged in 1490 to provide lodgings for the abbot of nearby St Mary's Abbey. After the Dissolution it was ceded to the lord president of the Council of the North, effectively making it northern England's royal headquarters: Henry VIII, James I and Charles I all stayed here. It's now owned by the university, but the courtyard is open if you want a peek inside, while a café serves morning coffee and afternoon tea.

The Yorkshire Museum and St Mary's Abbey

South of Exhibition Square on Museum Street stands the entrance to the **Yorkshire Museum** (daily 10am–5pm; £4), which lies within the beautifully laid-out grounds of St Mary's Abbey, itself now in ruins. It's one of York's better museums, with changing temporary exhibitions aimed largely at kids, but otherwise strong on archeological remains which it presents in a series of rooms examining the Roman presence in the city – grave effects, cooking utensils in a reconstructed Roman kitchen, glassware, farming equipment and jewellery all illustrate the sophistication of life in the provincial capital of "Lower Britain". There are impressive displays of Viking and Anglo-Saxon artefacts, too, though chief exhibit is the fifteenth-century Middleham Jewel, found in 1985 – a diamond-shaped jewel with an oblong sapphire, claimed as the finest piece of Gothic jewellery in England.

Part of the museum basement incorporates the fireplace and chapter house of **St Mary's Abbey** (dawn to dusk; free), whose ruins lie around the Museum Gardens, the abbey's former grounds. Founded around 1080, the abbey later became an important Benedictine foundation, additionally significant as it was from here that disenchanted monks fled to found Fountains Abbey. The fact that the abbey controlled the city's brothels at the time can hardly have helped the Benedictine cause. The church (1259) and gatehouse are both reasonably well preserved, but this is really a spot to come for time out from the sightseeing. For a good extended stroll drop down to the river at Lendal Bridge for a quiet walk to Water End Bridge.

Lendal and St Helen's Square

The street called **Lendal** cuts down from Museum Street to **St Helen's Square** – marking the entrance to the Roman city – and the York institution that is **Betty's** tearooms, where you're close to a clutch of impressive historic buildings. The Georgian **Mansion House** (1725), in St Helen's Square, is the private home of the city's mayor, and is consequently open only to guided tours by prior arrangement (call ☎01904/552013). However, you can visit the 600-year-old **Guildhall** (May–Oct Mon–Fri 9am–5pm, Sat 10am–5pm, Sun 2–5pm; Nov–April Mon–Fri 9am–5pm; free) behind, which was almost totally destroyed by bombing in 1942, but has since been restored to a near identical replica of its original, timber-roofed state, though only one of the fourteen magnificent Victorian stained-glass windows remains. Back up Blake Street from the square, have a look inside the **Grand Assembly Rooms**, built between 1732 and 1736 by the third earl of Burlington. An epicentre of chic during York's eighteenth-century social heyday, the building attempted to emulate London's grander salons; its 52-columned Central Hall is a tribute to the Egyptian Hall of the capital's Mansion House. The rooms are now occupied by a restaurant (open daily from noon), so for the price of a meal you can lounge around the ornate marbled interior, taking the opportunity to search the rotunda's mural of Roman York, in which Burlington had himself painted as Constantine the Great.

Back at St Helen's Square, **Stonegate** leads northeast towards the Minster, a street as ancient as the city itself. Originally the Via Praetoria of Roman York, it's now paved with thick flags of York stone, which were once carried along here to build the Minster, hence the street name. Guy Fawkes' parents lived on Stonegate (there's a plaque opposite *Mulberry Hall*) and its Tudor houses retain their considerable charm – an alley at no. 52a leads to the scant remains of a twelfth-century Norman stone house, a rarity in England.

South to Jorvik

Coney Street, Davygate, Parliament Street and all the alleys and streets off and in between heave shoulder-to-shoulder most of the year with shoppers. There's not much to stop for until you reach the entrance to the **Merchant Adventurers' Hall**, off Fossgate (Easter–Sept Mon–Thurs 9am–5pm, Fri & Sat 9am–3pm, Sun noon–4pm; Oct–Easter Mon–Sat 9am–3pm; £2), where the overpowering whiff of wood polish prepares you for one of the finest medieval timber-framed halls in Europe. The beautiful building was raised by the city's most powerful guild, dealers in wool from the Wolds, woollens from the Dales and lead from the Pennines, commodities that were traded for exotica from far and wide. An icon brought back from Russia gives some idea of the organization's commercial scope. Antique fairs are held in the undercroft most Saturdays throughout the year.

Fairfax House, on nearby Castlegate (Mon–Thurs & Sat 11am–5pm, Sun 1.30–5pm; guided tours only on Fri at 11am & 2pm; closed Jan & Feb; £4.50; Ⓦ www.fairfaxhouse.co.uk), celebrates the wealth of a later period. This elegant Georgian town house was restored to house the collection of fine arts left by Noel Terry, scion of one of the city's chocolate dynasties. The bulk of the collection consists of eighteenth-century furniture and clocks, though seasonal exhibitions showcase other arts, while every December the popular "Keeping of Christmas" exhibition recreates a Georgian Christmas in the house.

Around the corner, in the Coppergate shopping centre, the crowds descend upon the city's blockbuster Viking exhibit – **Jorvik** (daily: April–Oct 10am–5pm; Nov–March 10am–4pm; £7.20; Ⓦ www.vikingjorvik.com). This multi-million-pound affair flies visitors back in "time capsules" to the tenth-century city of York, presenting not just the sights but the sounds and even the smells of a riverside Viking settlement, complete with costumed villagers, street scenes and panoramic views of the re-created city. This was a period when York was expanding rapidly, and most of the sites (blacksmiths' to bedrooms) and artefacts (leather shoes to wooden combs) were discovered during the 1976 excavations of Coppergate's real Viking settlement, now lost beneath the shopping centre outside; Jorvik shows how they were found and how they were used. Not surprisingly, it's a hugely popular exhibit, and great for children. Lines form early, but you can avoid queuing by pre-booking your entrance ticket online (though this costs £1 more).

It's worth noting that the museum organizes York's annual **Viking Festival** every February when themed events take place throughout the city – details from the Festival Office at the centre. You may also want to move on to the associated Archeological Resource Centre, or **ARC**, housed in the medieval church of St Saviour, St Savioursgate (during school terms Mon–Fri 10am–3.30pm, school holidays Mon–Sat 11am–3pm; £4.50, joint ticket with Jorvik £10.20), close to the Shambles, a hands-on archeology centre – the only one of its kind in the country – where you can grapple with everything from old bones to computers to build up a picture of Viking and Roman life.

York Castle and the Castle Museum

Despite the rich architectural heritage elsewhere in the city, there's precious little left of **York Castle**, one of two established by William the Conqueror. Only the perilously leaning **Clifford's Tower** (daily: Easter–June & Sept 10am–6pm; July & Aug 10am–7.30pm; Oct 10am–5pm; Nov–Easter 10am–4pm or dusk; £2.50; EH) remains, as evocative a piece of military engineering as you could wish for: a stark and isolated stone keep built on one of William's mottes between 1245 and 1262. The old Norman keep was destroyed in 1190 during one of the city's more shameful historical episodes, when 150 Jews were put inside the tower for their own protection during an outburst of anti-Semitic rioting. The move did little to appease the mob, however, and faced with starvation or slaughter the Jews committed mass suicide by setting the tower on fire.

Immediately east of the tower lies the excellent **Castle Museum** (daily 9.30am–5pm; £6), a remarkable collection founded by a Dr Kirk of Pickering, who in the 1920s realized that many of the everyday items used in rural areas were in danger of disappearing. He took the unusual step of accepting bric-a-brac from his patients in lieu of fees. When the pile of miscellanea grew too large for his own home it was housed in the city's old Debtors' Prison and Female Prison, the former, incidentally, where the famous highwayman Dick Turpin spent his last night on earth. A whole range of early craft, folk and agricultural ephemera is complemented by costumes, militaria, workshops, two entire reconstructed streets and special exhibitions on subjects as diverse as chocolate, burials and fire engines. In particular, look for the lovely corridor of old hearths and fireplaces, Kirk's fetishistic collections of truncheons and biscuit moulds – surely unsurpassed – and some magnificently archaic televisions and washing machines. The military displays, the rambling dungeons and period rooms are all well worth seeing, too. Pride of place is given to a dazzling Viking helmet, discovered during the Coppergate excavations and the only one of its kind ever found.

The National Railway Museum

The **National Railway Museum** on Leeman Road (daily 10am–6pm; free; Ⓦwww.nrm.org.uk), ten minutes' walk (600yd) from the station, is a must if you have even the slightest interest in railways, history, engineering or Victoriana. It was the first national museum to open outside London and contains a stunning collection. The Great Hall alone features some fifty restored locomotives dating from 1829 onwards, among them the Mallard, at 126mph the world's fastest steam engine; its record-speed run wrecked the engine, and it had to be towed back to base. By way of complete contrast, there's a Japanese bullet train also on display which, despite its sleek lines, has a similar average running speed – it's the first locomotive built and run outside Britain to enter the national collection. The Station Hall, a former goods station, complete with tracks and platforms, holds the major permanent exhibitions, where you can

George Hudson

It would be hard to find a better caricature of a Victorian business baron than the portly and bewhiskered "Railway King" **George Hudson** (1800–71), a perfect symbol of the fortitude and failings of Victorian capitalism. Starting out as he meant to go on, Hudson was sent away from home at the age of 15. Soon afterwards he became apprenticed to a York draper, married the boss's daughter and then quickly inherited the business when his father-in-law was found drowned in the Ouse in mysterious circumstances. Another £30,000 came his way from a great-uncle in 1827, Hudson having spent many days at his relative's deathbed, during which time the will was altered in his favour. The windfall was ploughed into North Midland Railway shares, the basis of his subsequent empire, and a stepping stone to a career in local politics which saw him become councillor, alderman and ultimately – in 1837 – Lord Mayor of York.

He seized the main chance in 1833, as the rail network crept closer to York, offering local landowners huge tranches of cut-price shares to allow the railways to cross their land. With the gentry in his pockets his business boomed, and by 1844 he controlled 1016 miles of track – the largest network under single ownership until rail nationalization – and was elected MP for Sunderland a year later. In one typical move he managed to buy the Whitby and Pickering Railway in 1845 for £80,000, £25,000 less than it had cost to build.

Hudson's empire continued to expand, but only by paying artificially high dividends to his shareholders. When his stocks, which had made countless paper fortunes, failed to go on rising, nemesis was just round the corner. Investigations and law suits brought by disgruntled investors revealed untold dubious business deals and in 1849 Hudson was forced to resign the directorship of his six companies. A ruined man, he was committed to York's Debtors' Prison, able to afford only one meal a day, before being rescued by a small pension offered by a hard core of loyal shareholders. York, for its part, chose to forget the undoubted wealth Hudson's railways had brought the city, shunning its former hero until 1968, when a street and offices near the station were given his name.

see the plush splendour of the royal carriages ("Palaces on Wheels") and the bleak segregation of classes in the Victorian coaches. Take a walk through the 1938 dining car and then take a break on the platform at the Brief Encounter café. Dotted around the hall is a welter of miscellaneous memorabilia: posters, models, paintings and period photographs, even a lock of George Stephenson's hair. A separate wing, "The Works", provides access to the engineering workshop where conservation work is undertaken; to a walk-round backstage warehouse area, showcasing the museum's reserve collection; and to a track-and-signal viewing area which has been established over the East Coast main line.

Eating and drinking

It's impossible to walk more than about 50yd in central York without coming across either a pub, teashop, café or restaurant – Defoe put it down to the "abundance of good company . . . and good families", though these days it's the tourist and student pound which fires the commercial engines. In keeping with much else in the city, many establishments are relentlessly and self-consciously old-fashioned, though there are some real highlights – truly historic **pubs**, the remarkable *Betty's*, the ultimate **teashop** experience, and a scattering of well-regarded **restaurants**. There's a sense of solid Yorkshire worth in most establishments and provided you pick and choose carefully, you can avoid much of the tourist-aimed dross that passes for budget eating and drinking. The **coffee**

and café-bar scene has flourished too, with the main chain-names (Starbucks, Coffee Republic, Bar 38, Pitcher & Piano) all represented, alongside some honourable independents.

Tearooms, cafés and café-bars

Betty's 6–8 St Helen's Square. If there are tea-shops in heaven they'll be like *Betty's*. It's a York institution, with an Art Nouveau cladding and a permanent queue waiting for seats, despite the relatively high prices. There are a dozen or so fish and meat hot dishes, some extraordinary puddings, and a shop where you can buy fine-grade teas and coffees, and some of the teashop staples – like pikelets and Yorkshire fat rascals. Daily 9am–9pm.

Blake Head Vegetarian Café 104 Micklegate. Bookstore-café with patio for freshly baked cakes, pâtés, quiche, brunch, salads and soups – a favoured student hangout. Mon–Sat 9.30am–5pm, Sun 10am–5pm.

Café Concerto 27 High Petergate. A good all-rounder in the heart of the city that's café by day (wraps, pasta and *croque monsieur* for example) and bistro by night (lamb shank to tuna steak). Always a relaxed atmosphere. Daily 10am–10pm.

Café No. 8 8 Gillygate. Caesar salads, inventive ciabatta sarnies and cool sounds in this funky little café-bar, just outside Bootham Bar. There's a summer garden too, and dinner served Fri & Sat. Mon–Fri 11am–3pm, Thurs & Fri also 5–11pm, Sat 11am–11pm, Sun 11am–5pm.

City Screen Café-Bar 13–17 Coney St. York's independent cinema has a splendid riverside café-bar, serving food until 9pm and boasting a whole host of events and evenings – from stand-up comedy and afternoon jazz to poetry evenings and once-a-month film quizzes. Daily 11am–11pm.

Little Betty's 46 Stonegate. Owned by *Betty's* and in the same league; over 100 years old, it's the picture of a classic tearooms, also serving more substantial dishes like fish and chips, bangers and mash or an all-day grilled breakfast. Daily 9am–5.30pm.

Melton's Too 25 Walmgate. Exposed brickwork, cushions scattered on armchairs and the daily papers set the tone for this relaxed café-bar and bistro. Drop in for coffee, superior tapas, pasta, Thai green curries (a house speciality), salads, steaks and more. Mon–Sat 10.30am–10.30pm, Sun 10.30am–9.30pm.

National Trust York Tearooms 30 Goodramgate. A slickly run place just 200yd from the Minster, serving snacks and light meals. Choose from the likes of scrambled eggs and smoked ham, BLTs and omelettes, and maybe sample one of Yorkshire's noted "fruit wines". Mon–Sat 10am–5pm.

Spurriergate Centre St Michael's Church, Spurriergate. Quiche, salads and baked potatoes served in the impressive interior of twelfth-century St Michael's. Mon–Fri 10am–4.30pm, Sat 9.30am–5pm.

Restaurants

Blue Bicycle 34 Fossgate ⓣ01904/673990. York's most relaxed gourmet experience, with a seasonally changing menu that doesn't shy away from innovation. The confident cooking comes at a price, but York's *beau monde* is happy to pay it. Reservations advised. Expensive.

Melton's 7 Scarcroft Rd ⓣ01904/634341. Long the *Good Food Guide* standard-bearer in York, you're assured of simple, classy cooking, including very good fish dishes, and imaginative vegetarian food – Tuesdays (veggie) and Thursdays (fish) have the best non-meat choices. Set lunch and early-bird deals too. Closed Mon lunch & Sun dinner. Reservations advised. Expensive.

La Piazza 45 Goodramgate ⓣ01904/642641. Authentic Italian coffee bar out front, courtyard restaurant out back, tucked into a nice Tudor building. Proper pizzas, Italian pop music and friendly family staff. Moderate.

The Rubicon 5–7 Little Stonegate ⓣ01904/676076. Contemporary style and vegetarian world flavours, so there's moussaka and veggie lasagne but also Thai red curry and cinnamon couscous on offer. The menu turns less snacky after 5pm, and early-bird dinner offers are a good deal; organic wines and beers available. Moderate.

Siam House 63a Goodramgate ⓣ01904/624677. This prettily furnished Thai restaurant rarely disappoints – the menu is huge enough to cater for any tastes, and with things like sweetcorn fritters and whole steamed red snapper authenticity is assured. Lunch for £6.95 is good value. Closed Sun lunch. Moderate.

The Tasting Room 13 Swinegate Court East, off Grape Lane ⓣ01904/627879. Plenty of choice in this informal café/restaurant, from a light lunch menu (omelettes, pasta, oak-smoked salmon salad) to more elaborate meals in the evening – seared tuna and green olive mash or cumin-spiced lamb are typical. Closed Sun & Mon. Lunch Inexpensive, dinner Moderate.

Villa Italia 69 Micklegate ⓣ01904/670501. York's premier Italian shows its class away from the short (and inexpensive) pizza menu, where delights on offer include things like Sardinian fish stew, garlic-and-lime-marinated tuna or roast duck with rosemary and celery. Closed Sun. Expensive.

Pubs

Black Swan Peasholme Green. York's oldest (sixteenth-century) pub and a Grade II listed building with some superb stone flagging and wood panelling. The beer's not bad either – you can get the local York Brewery stuff here – and it's also home of the city's folk club (see below).

Golden Ball Cromwell Rd, Bishophill. Perhaps the city centre's nicest and most archetypal "local", with an attractive beer garden tucked away at the back. It's just two minutes from the river, on the west side.

King's Arms King's Staithe. Close to the Ouse Bridge, this pub has a fine riverside setting with outdoor tables – and accordingly gets very busy in summer (and very wet in the winter when it's prone to flooding).

Last Drop Inn 27 Colliergate. A friendly, bare-boards pub with York Brewery beers, inexpensive food and live music some nights.

Three-Legged Mare 15 High Petergate. York Brewery's cosy outlet for its own quality beer and definitely a pub for grown-ups – no juke box, no video games and no kids.

Ye Olde Starre 40 Stonegate. Vies with the *Black Swan* for historic precedence, but although there's good beer, a beer garden and plenty of atmosphere it's usually too crowded for prolonged enjoyment.

Nightlife, culture and entertainment

There are healthy helpings of live music, culture and nightlife in York, much of it detailed in the local *Evening Press* (and on their useful website, ⓦwww.thisisyork.co.uk). Most bigger bands bypass the city in favour of Leeds, though the Barbican Centre pulls in its fair share of major mainstream artists. **Clubbing** is a bit of a disaster in York – you know, with names like *Toffs* and *Ziggy's*, that the northern club revolution has yet to hit the city – but *The Gallery* on Clifford Street can usually be relied upon, or head on out to Clifton Moor Retail Park to *Ikon* and *Diva*.

Cultural entertainment is wide and varied, with the city supporting theatres, cinemas and regular classical music recitals, often in its churches and York Minster itself. The annual **Early Music Festival**, held in July, is perhaps the best of its kind in Britain, with dozens of events spread over ten days – details are available on ⓣ01904/658338, ⓦwww.ncem.co.uk, or from the tourist office. The famous **York Mystery Plays** have traditionally been held every four years, though funding and organizational problems have taken their toll – the next performances are now not envisaged until 2010.

Cinema, theatre and the arts

Cinema City Screen 13–17 Coney St ⓣ01904/541155, ⓦwww.picturehouses.co.uk. The choice for art-house cinema, with a riverside café-bar. Mainstream screens at the Odeon, Blossom St ⓣ01904/623287, info line ⓣ0870/505 0007, and Warner Village multiplex out of town at Clifton Moor ⓣ0870/240 6020, ⓦwww.warnervillage.co.uk.

Grand Opera House Cumberland St, at Clifford St ⓣ01904/671818. Musicals, ballet and family entertainment in all its guises.

Theatre Royal St Leonard's Place ⓣ01904/623568, ⓦwww.theatre-royal-york.co.uk. Musicals, pantos and mainstream theatre, as well as a café-bar.

Live music venues

Barbican Centre Barbican Rd ⓣ01904/656688. Country, rock, folk and MOR stalwarts all appear here sooner or later.

Black Swan Peasholme Green ⓣ01904/632922, ⓦwww.freeweb.telco4u.net/blackswanfolk. Regular folk nights with a full range of quality bands and singer-songwriters, plus jazz jam sessions once or twice a week.

Fibbers Stonebow House, Stonebow ⓣ01904/466148, ⓦwww.fibbers.co.uk. Indie and guitar-pop bands (local and national) play most nights of the week at this inventive venue. There's a café-bar too.

Listings

Banks and exchange Most main banks are in and around St Helen's Square. American Express, 6 Stonegate; Thomas Cook, 4 Nessgate, and inside HSBC, 13 Parliament St. You can also change money at the tourist offices; in Marks and Spencer, 9 Pavement; and at Lunn Poly, 14 Low Ousegate.

Bike rental Bob Trotter, 13–15 Lord Mayor's Walk, at Monkgate ⓣ01904/622868, ⓦwww.bobtrottercycles.com. Rates from £10 per day, plus a deposit.

Bookshop Biggest selection in the city is at Borders, 1–5 Davygate, where there's also a café.

Bus information Traveline York, 20 George Hudson St (office Mon–Fri 8.30am–5pm; telephone enquiries Mon–Sat 8am–8pm, Sun 8am–2pm; ⓣ01904/551400) can advise about all local and regional bus (and train) information. Or call National Express ⓣ08705/808080; East Yorkshire ⓣ01482/222222 (for Hull, Beverley and Bridlington); or Yorkshire Coastliner ⓣ01653/692556 (for Leeds, Castle Howard, Pickering, Scarborough and Whitby).

Car rental Avis ⓣ01904/610460; Budget ⓣ01904/644919; Europcar ⓣ01904/656161; Hertz ⓣ01904/612586; Practical ⓣ01904/624277.

Hospital York District Hospital, Wigginton Road (24hr emergency number ⓣ01904/631313); bus #1, #2 or #3. Also York Walk-in Centre, 31 Monkgate (ⓣ01904/674557) offers care, advice and treatment without an appointment.

Internet Internet Exchange, 13 Stonegate ⓣ01904/638808; Gateway, 26 Swinegate ⓣ01904/646446; access also available at the youth hostels.

Pharmacy Boots, Coney St ⓣ01904/653657.

Police Fulford Rd ⓣ01904/631321.

Post office The main office is at 22 Lendal ⓣ01904/617285.

Racing York Racecourse ⓣ01904/620911, ⓦwww.yorkracecourse.co.uk. One of Britain's finest, York Racecourse has regular meetings during the May–Sept season, including the John Smith's Cup, the highlight of the annual calendar each July.

Taxis Ranks at Rougier Street, Duncombe Place, Exhibition Square, and the train station; or call Station Taxis ⓣ01904/623332; Castle Taxis ⓣ01904/611511.

Castle Howard

Immersed in the deep countryside of the Howardian Hills, fifteen miles north-east of York off the A64, **Castle Howard** (mid-Feb to Oct daily 11am–5pm; gardens open at 10am; £9; grounds only £6; ⓦwww.castlehoward.co.uk) is the seat of one of England's leading aristocratic families and among the country's grandest stately homes. Since providing the setting for the television version of *Brideshead Revisited*, the house's car parks have been packed every weekend, but fitting it into a public transport itinerary is something of a problem. In summer there are two Yorkshire Coastliner buses a day (one on Sun) from York, Malton or Pickering, but daily bus tours from York can bring you out and back, too, or take the train to Malton (regular services on the York–Scarborough line) and then a taxi the five miles from the station to the house.

The colossal main house was designed by **Sir John Vanbrugh** in 1699 and was almost forty years in the making – remarkable enough, were it not for the fact that Vanbrugh was, at the start of the commission at least, best known as a playwright. He had no formal architectural training and seems to have been chosen by Charles Howard, third Earl of Carlisle, for whom the house was built, purely on the strength of his membership of the same London gentlemen's club. Shrewdly, Vanbrugh recognized his limitations and called upon the assistance of Nicholas Hawksmoor, who had a major part in the house's structural design – the pair later worked successfully together on Blenheim Palace. If Hawksmoor's guiding hand can be seen throughout, Vanbrugh's influence is clear in the very theatricality of the building, notably in the palatial **Great Hall**. This was gutted by fire in the 1940s, but has subsequently been restored from old etchings and photographs to something approaching its original state. The rest of the house is full of furniture by Sheraton and Chippendale, paintings by the likes of Gainsborough, Veronese, Rubens and Van Dyck, and room after room of decorative excess – all trinkety objets d'art, gaudy friezes and monumental pilasters.

Vanbrugh soon turned his attention to the estate's thousand-acre **grounds** where he could indulge his playful inclinations to excess, and the formal gardens, clipped parkland, towers, obelisks and blunt sandstone follies stretch in all directions, sloping gently to a large artifical lake. He completed the **Temple of the Four Winds** before his death in 1726, leaving Hawskmoor to design the Howard family **Mausoleum**, which is taller than the house itself. Take a look, too, at the fine **stables** which have been converted into the Costume and Regalia Gallery, Britain's largest private collection of period clothes. There are **cafés** here, one in the main house and another by the lake, as well as a children's playground, nature trails, plant centre, gift shop and very popular camping and caravan park (Ⓣ01653/648316)

Eden Camp

Further along the A64 from the Castle Howard turn-off, **Eden Camp** (daily 10am–5pm, last admission 4pm; £4; Ⓦwww.edencamp.co.uk), a World War II museum sited within a former POW camp, makes for another good day out from York. It's eighteen miles northeast of the city at Malton, at the junction of the A169 to Pickering. Originally built in 1942 to house Italian and, later, German POWs captured in the North Africa campaigns, the barracks and buildings have been re-equipped to tell the story of what it dubs "The People's War". Walk-through exhibits and tableaux deal with topics such as rationing, air raids, evacuees, the Home Guard, the Land Army, munitions and the various branches of the services. Most visitors need around three hours to get around everything.

Hull, the Humber and the East Yorkshire coast

Generations of Yorkshire folk, born and bred in the historic **East Riding**, were outraged to wake up one morning and find themselves part of "Humberside", just one of the notorious local government conveniences created by the 1974 bastardization of the English counties. Consequently, there was almost universal rejoicing when the Lincolnshire adjuncts from across the **River Humber** were dropped in 1996 and places like **Hull** could once again revel in their Yorkshire ancestry. The region's character has been shaped by a strong seafaring tradition, boosted by Hull's advantageous position on the Humber estuary. Beyond Hull, up the **East Yorkshire coast**, lonely beaches, wild foreshores and forgotten seafront villages draw curious tourists keen to get off the beaten track. The bucket-and-spade resorts of **Bridlington** and **Filey** are the traditional seaside draws, while the cliffs of **Flamborough Head** provide one of the best places in Britain for birdwatching. Inland, this part of the country boasts historic **Beverley**, with its marvellous Minster, plonked among the flatlands which stretch northwards from Hull to meet the **Yorkshire Wolds**, a crescent-shaped ridge of hills that falls to the sea at Flamborough.

Beverley can be easily reached by **bus** from Hull or York, while there are direct **trains** from London to Hull. Hull is also linked to Doncaster by the main London–York train line; a branch line links Hull and Beverley with

Bridlington, Filey and Scarborough, further up the coast. Drivers approaching from Lincolnshire and the south will cross the famous **Humber Bridge**, an immense single-span suspension bridge opened in 1981; a viewing area allows you to stop and gasp.

Hull

HULL – officially Kingston upon Hull – has a maritime pre-eminence that dates back to 1299, when it was laid out as a seaport by Edward I. It quickly became England's leading harbour, and was still a vital garrison when the gates were closed against Charles I in 1642, the first serious act of rebellion of what was to become the English Civil War. Daniel Defoe visited the town several times in the early eighteenth century, part of the travels that were later to spawn his encyclopedic *Tour Through the Whole Island of Britain*; despite thinking it "second rate", he remembered Hull well enough to have Robinson Crusoe set sail from here on his fateful voyage. Fishing and seafaring have always been important here, and today's city maintains a firm grip on its heritage while bolstering its attractions for visitors – the dramatic aquarium known as The Deep joins a superior set of free local museums and a revived Old Town area that provide scope for a good couple of day's worth of sightseeing. There must be something, too, in the adage that fish is good for the brain, when you consider Hull's roll-call of artistic luminaries – poets (Andrew Marvell, Stevie Smith), dramatists (Alan Plater, John Godber) and actors (John Alderton, Tom Courtenay). Her most famous adopted son, the poet and university librarian Philip Larkin, was being typically curmudgeonly when he wrote, "I wish I could think of just one nice thing to tell you about Hull, oh yes … *it's very nice and flat for cycling*". This is too harsh – museums aside, he might have mentioned the city's excellent historic pubs or the various festivals and fairs that Hull arranges with great flair. The biggest regular event is Hull Fair, a colossal travelling funfair running for eight days in early October; the most discrete is the Hull Literature Festival, which runs for two weeks in November.

The City

The central **Princes Dock** sets the tone for Hull's modern refurbishment, the once abandoned waters now lined by landscaped brick promenades and café-bars, and overlooked by **Princes Quay**, a multi-tiered, glass-spangled shopping centre, with the **marina** beyond.

First stop for the maritime legacy should be the exhaustively detailed **Maritime Museum** (Mon–Sat 10am–5pm, Sun 1.30–4.30pm; free), housed in the Neoclassical headquarters of the former Town Docks Offices on Queen Victoria Square, immediately north of Princes Quay. The main boost to the town's coffers in the eighteenth and nineteenth centuries was whaling, and the museum tells the story well, displaying gruesome whaling equipment, such as a blubber pot cauldron, alongside model ships, old photographs, Inuit relics and a whale skeleton. Hull whalers pursued the right whale in their thousands, so known because it was the "right" whale to catch for commercial purposes. There are displays about whale species and conservation, examples of the maritime art of "scrimshandering" – the ornate carving of whale bone and walrus tusk by bored sailors – and yet more rooms detailing trawling methods, and Hull's long relationship with the Humber.

Leave Queen Victoria Square by pedestrianized Whitefriargate and, after about 200yd, turn right down Trinity House Lane for **Holy Trinity** (April–Sept

Mon–Fri 11am–3pm, Sat 9.30am–noon; Oct–March Tues–Fri 11am–2pm, Sat 9.30am–noon; free), among the most pleasing parish churches in the country, notable for its brick transepts and chancel. It's the third church to be built on this site, the last in the eighteenth century, though parts of the building date back to the original thirteenth-century foundation. The surrounding area is traditionally home to Hull's market traders: there's the indoor **Trinity Market** (Mon–Sat 7.30am–5pm) across from the church and an **open market** next to it (Tues, Fri & Sat 9am–4pm). Close by on South Church Side is one of Hull's most revered relics – the **Old Grammar School**, a red-brick edifice built in 1583 which for 120 years doubled as the town's Merchant Adventurers' Hall. The building now incorporates an educational resource centre called **Hands On History** (Sat 10am–5pm, Sun 1.30–4.30pm; during school holidays also Mon–Fri 10am–5pm; free), which is aimed at schoolchildren, though anyone can pop in to have a scout around its displays and archives.

Two blocks east, over towards the River Hull, you reach the **High Street**, whose crop of former merchants' houses and narrow cobbled alleys have seen it designated an "Old Town" conservation area and **Museums Quarter** (all attractions Mon–Sat 10am–5pm, Sun 1.30–4.30pm; free). At its northern end stands **Wilberforce House**, the former home of William and containing some fascinating exhibits on slavery and its abolition to which cause he dedicated much of his life. Next door is **Streetlife**, devoted to the history of transport in the region and centred on a 1930s street scene of reconstructed shops, railway goods yard, and cycle and motor works. This is as much about social as transport history, with the smells of a nineteenth-century coaching yard, recorded conversations on a Hull Tram, or the rules of bicycle polo vying for your attention. If this is good, then the adjacent **Hull and East Riding Museum** is even better, with the sort of inventive displays that might just inspire a long-dormant interest in history and archeology. A life-size mammoth and a walk-through Iron Age village set you up for the showpiece attractions, namely vivid displays of Celtic burials, medieval battles and spectacular Roman mosaics retrieved from the East Yorkshire countryside. Dredged from a river, meanwhile, came the Hasholme boat, an oak cargo boat 41 feet long and 2300 years old – now confined within the see-through walls of "Boatlab" where you can see it dripping under a constant protective spray of water and wax. Last on the agenda is the **Arctic Corsair** (March–Oct Wed & Sat 10am–4pm, Sun 1.30–4pm; £2), a reconditioned trawler from the 1960s, moored on the River Hull around the back of Wilberforce House and offering guided tours of the cramped interior.

Protruding from a promontory overlooking the River Humber looms **The Deep** (daily 10am–6pm, last entry 5pm; £6.50; Ⓦwww.thedeep.co.uk), ten minutes' walk from the old town across a pedestrian footbridge that spans the River Hull. Its educational displays and videos wrap around an immense thirty-foot-deep, 2.3-million-gallon viewing tank filled with sharks, rays, octopuses and any number of other deep-sea denizens. You see into the tank at every level on the ramped walk down – while diverting off to a deep-sea research station or the ice-cold Polar Gallery – and then return by underwater lift. It's very slick, and very entertaining, with a café overlooking the Humber estuary and picnic benches outside on the promenade, from where porpoises are occasionally sighted.

Practicalities

The **train station** is on the west side of town, on the main drag of Ferensway, with the **bus station** just to the north. Drivers might as well aim straight for the **car park** in the Princes Quay shopping centre, signposted on every road into town. **Ferries** from Rotterdam and Zeebrugge arrive at the ferry port on the eastern edge of Hull, and from there buses run into the centre; bus times coincide with ferry arrivals (and departures) and the journey takes ten minutes. The main **tourist office** is on Paragon Street at Queen Victoria Square (Mon–Sat 10am–5pm, Sun 11–3pm; Ⓣ01482/223559, Ⓦwww.hullcc.gov.uk). They co-ordinate richly anecdotal **guided tours** around the old town (April–Oct Mon–Sat at 2pm, Sun 11am; £2.50) departing from their office, or you can pick up one of the self-guided trail leaflets and do it yourself. The Hull Ghost Walk (March–Oct Mon at 7pm; £3) departs from the Old Grammar School.

Hull is busiest during the week, though there's a fair choice of **accommodation** on offer. The tourist office can help – and through them you can get special weekend hotel rates (from around £25 per person per night) by calling Ⓣ01482/615744. Amongst several reasonably central B&Bs, one especially good choice is the *Clyde House Hotel*, 13 John St (Ⓣ01482/214981; ❷), five minutes' walk north of Princes Quay, near Hull New Theatre. Many of the central hotels are a pretty good deal, too, with decent rooms and rates at the the *Quality Hotel Royal*, 170 Ferensway (Ⓣ01482/325087; ❸), right by the station; *Comfort Inn*, just south of the train station at 11 Anlaby Rd (Ⓣ01482/323299, Ⓦwww.choicehotels.com; ❸); and the *Hotel Ibis*, Osborne St, Ferensway (Ⓣ01482/387500, Ⓦwww.ibishotel.com; ❷), over the road. Best of the lot is the *Holiday Inn Hull Marina* on Castle Street overlooking the marina (Ⓣ0870/400 9043; ❺), which has an indoor pool, gym and sauna.

Café-bars around Princes Quay and the marina provide sightseeing pitstops – *McCoy's* in Colonial Chambers, Princes Dock Street, serves wraps, sandwiches and pasta on three floors. Or there's *Studio 101/2* (closed Sun), opposite Holy Trinity Church on King Street, for tasty veggie specials. **Restaurants** include *Cerutti's* (Ⓣ01482/328501; closed Sat lunch & Sun), down at the end of the east side of the marina at 10 Nelson St, which leads the way in local seafood. *Venn*, 21 Scale Lane (Ⓣ01482/224004), in the old town, is a contemporary brasserie-restaurant with fine Modern British food. And there's real value-for-money at *Mimosa*, 406–408 Beverley Rd (Ⓣ01482/474748), a friendly Turkish restaurant with an open charcoal grill – it's around a mile and a half out of the centre, though very regular buses run up Beverley Road from the stations.

Hull has dozens of **pubs**, the best of which are picked out in a "Hull Ale Trail" leaflet available from the tourist office. *Ye Olde White Harte*, 25 Silver St, has a pleasant courtyard and a history going back to the seventeenth century, while around the corner is the equally venerable *George*, found on the curiously named street The Land of Green Ginger. *Green Bricks*, 9 Humber Dock St, offers real ales from its prize waterside location, and, further along the marina at the corner of Nelson Street, there's the *Minerva*, with cosy nooks, outdoor tables and cheap food. *Ye Olde Black Boy*, 150 High St, also specializes in real ales – and offers cider and fruit wines too. The excellent **Hull Truck Theatre Company**, on Spring Street (Ⓣ01482/323638, Ⓦwww.hulltruck.co.uk), is where, among others, many of the plays of award-winning John Godber first see light of day.

Beverley

BEVERLEY, nine miles north of Hull, ranks as one of northern England's premier towns, its minster the superior of many an English cathedral, its tangle of old streets, cobbled lanes and elegant Georgian and Victorian terraces the very picture of a traditional market town. Over 350 buildings are listed as possessing historical or architectural merit, and though you could see its first-rank offerings in a morning, this is one of a handful of places in this part of the world where you might want to stay.

Approaches to the town are dominated by the twin towers of **Beverley Minster** (March–Oct Mon–Sat 9am–5pm; Nov–Feb Mon–Sat 9am–4pm; plus Sun year round, depending on services, but usually noon–4.30pm; donation requested; Ⓦ www.beverleyminster.co.uk), visible for miles across the wolds and flatlands. Initiated as a modest chapel, the minster became a monastery under John of Beverley. Trained at Whitby and later ordained bishop of York, he was buried here in 721 and canonized in 1037 – his body lies under the crossing at the top of the nave. Fires and the collapse of the central tower in 1213 paved the way for two centuries of rebuilding, funded by bequests from pilgrims paying homage to the saint, and the result was one of the finest Gothic creations in the country. The **west front**, which crowned the work in 1420, is widely considered without equal, its survival due in large part to Baroque architect Nicholas Hawksmoor, who restored much of the church in the eighteenth century. Similar outstanding work awaits in the interior, most notably the fourteenth-century **Percy Tomb** on the north side of the altar, its sumptuously carved canopy one of the masterpieces of medieval European ecclesiastical art. Nearby stands the **Fridstol**, a Saxon "sanctuary chair" dating from Athelstan's reign (924–39), which provided safe haven for men on the run. Athelstan himself is said to have deposited a dagger on the altar in 934, vowing to return to Beverley if he defeated the Vikings and Scots in battle, which he duly did, carrying the banner of St John before him. Other incidental carving throughout the church is magnificent, particularly the 68 misericords of the oak **choir** (1520–24), one of the largest and most accomplished in England. Much of the decorative work here and elsewhere is on a musical theme. Beverley had a renowned guild of itinerant minstrels, which provided funds in the sixteenth century for the carvings on the transept aisle capitals, where you'll be able to pick out players of lutes, bagpipes, horns and tambourines.

Cobbled Highgate runs from the minster through town, along the pedestrianized shopping streets of Butcher Row and Toll Gavel and past the main Market Square, to Beverley's other great church, **St Mary's** (April–Sept Mon–Fri 9.15am–noon & 1.30–5.30pm, Sat 10am–5.30pm, Sun 2–5pm; Oct–March Mon–Fri 9.15am–noon & 1–4.15pm; free), a chapel once attached to the minster. On the corner of Hengate and North Bar Within, it nestles alongside the **North Bar**, sole survivor of the town's five medieval gates. The church is a tantalizing amalgam of styles, from the south porch's Norman arch to the thirteenth-century chancel and fifteenth-century Perpendicular elements of the tower and nave. Inside, the chancel's painted panelled ceiling (1445) contains portraits of English kings from Sigebert (623–37) to Henry VI, from about the same time as the eye-catching rood screen and misericords. Amidst the carvings, the favourite novelty is the so-called "Pilgrim's Rabbit", said to have been the inspiration for the White Rabbit in Lewis Carroll's *Alice in Wonderland*.

Practicalities

Beverley's **train station** is beside Station Square, just a couple of minutes' walk from the minster. The **bus station** is at the junction of Walkergate and Sow Hill Road, with the main street just a minute's walk away. The **tourist office** is at 34 Butcher Row in the main shopping area (June–Aug Mon–Fri 9.30am–5.15pm, Sat 10am–4.45pm, Sun 10am–2pm; Sept–May closed Sun; Ⓣ 01482/391672).

There's plenty of local **accommodation**, including a recommended guest house, the *Eastgate*, 7 Eastgate (Ⓣ01482/868464; no credit cards; ❷), a few minutes' from the minster, which also has cheaper rooms available that share bathroom facilities. *Number One*, 1 Woodlands (Ⓣ01482/862752, Ⓦwww.number-one-bedandbreakfast-beverley.co.uk; no credit cards; ❷), is a smaller B&B in a quiet Victorian house two minutes' walk from the market place. Among the hotels, the top town-centre choice is the *Beverley Arms*, North Bar Within (Ⓣ01482/869241, Ⓦwww.regalhotels.co.uk; ❻), though there are several other less expensive choices. Most of the pubs have rooms too: try the *Windmill Inn*, 53 Lairgate (Ⓣ01482/862817; ❷), which has a dozen rooms. The **youth hostel** (Ⓣ0870/770 5696, Ⓔbeverleyfriary@yha.org.uk; £10.25; closed Nov–Easter, and closed Sun & Mon) occupies one of the town's finer buildings, a restored Dominican friary that was mentioned in the Canterbury Tales. It's located in Friar's Lane, off Eastgate, just a hundred yards southeast of the minster.

For **food**, *Courts*, 1 Sow Hill Rd, is the place for good coffee, bagels and gourmet sandwiches, while *Cerutti 2*, in Station Square (Ⓣ01482/866700; closed Sun), is a sister brasserie to that in Hull and serves fresh fish. Otherwise, there's a full complement of tearooms and cafés, or you can eat in the **pubs** – the celebrated *White Horse* on Hengate, near St Mary's, is a thoroughly atmospheric traditional drinking den with folk music nights. The **Beverley and East Riding Folk Festival** takes place each June, featuring an international roster of music, song, dance and comedy, while if you fancy a day at the races, contact **Beverley Races** (Ⓣ01482/867488, Ⓦwww.beverley-racecourse.co.uk).

The East Yorkshire coast

The **East Yorkshire coast** curves south in a gentle arc from the mighty cliffs of Flamborough Head to Spurn Head, a finger-thin isthmus formed by the constant erosion and shifting currents that scour much of England's eastern shores. Between the two lie a handful of tranquil villages and miles of windswept dunes and mudflats, noted bird sanctuaries, and superbly lonely retreats accessible to anyone prepared to cycle or walk the paths and lanes that fan out amidst the dunes. **Buses** run out to a few points, mostly from Hull, Beverley and Bridlington, but you'll need your own transport to make the most of the region. However, the two main resorts, **Bridlington** and **Filey**, are linked by the regular **train** service between Hull and Scarborough. There's also an hourly bus service between Bridlington, Filey and Scarborough.

Hikers also converge on Filey from a couple of **long-distance footpaths**. The **Wolds Way** links the resort to the River Humber by way of a 79-mile path through the gently rolling chalk hills to Hessle, in the shadow of the Humber Bridge, west of Hull. More challenging still, Filey is the traditional end of the 110-mile moor-and-coast **Cleveland Way**, which loops from Helmsley to Saltburn and then heads south down the coast. Leaflets and information on the hikes are available from Filey's tourist office, and there are useful trail guides to both, published by Aurum Press.

Spurn Head

Few parts of the British coast are as dangerous as **Spurn Head**, a hook-shaped sand and pebble promontory that hardly suggests the imminence of maritime catastrophe, but whose lifeboat station is the only one in Britain permanently staffed by a professional crew. Access is via the village of **Easington** (at the end of the B1445), beyond which a four-mile toll road runs through a Yorkshire

Wildlife Trust nature reserve known for its seals, butterflies, dunal flora and seabirds – this is one of the best spots in the country to observe spring and autumn bird migrations. Sheltered from the sea by the loop of Sunk Head are the **Sunk Island Sands**, at the mouth of the Humber and a birdwatchers' haven.

Bridlington

The southernmost major resort on the Yorkshire coast, **BRIDLINGTON** has maintained its harbour for almost a thousand years, though for much of that time it remained a small-scale place of little consequence: Defoe noted it only because of its use to the eighteenth-century coastal coal ships who sought shelter here in bad weather. Like many coastal stations, it flourished in Edwardian times as a resort, but has spent recent decades in the same decline as other English bucket-and-spade holiday destinations. Renovations have smartened up the seafront promenade, which looks down upon the town's best asset – its sweeping sandy **beach**. It's an out-and-out family resort, which means plenty of candy-floss, amusement arcades, rides, boat trips and other diversions – a paddle in the sea and fish and chips eaten on the milling harbourfront are traditional pursuits. The historic core of town is a mile inland, where in largely Georgian Bridlington Old Town the **Bayle Museum** (May–Sept Mon–Fri 10am–4pm; £1) presents local history in a building that once served as the gateway to a fourteenth-century priory. The **tourist office** is close to the harbour at 25 Prince St (Easter–Oct daily 9.30am–5.30pm; Nov–Easter Mon–Sat 9.30am–5.30pm, Sun 11am–4pm; ☎01262/673474); they might be able to persuade you to stay, and have full lists of local accommodation.

Flamborough Head and Bempton Cliffs

Around fourteen miles of precipitous four-hundred-foot cliffs gird **Flamborough Head**, just to the northeast of Bridlington. The best of the seascapes are visible on the peninsula's north side, accessible by road from **FLAMBOROUGH** village. The lighthouse beyond is closed to the public, the latest in a line of warning beacons here that date back to the seventeenth century, but which, in earlier times at least, manifestly failed to do their job: between 1770 and 1806, 174 ships went down in the hazardous waters off the headland. Ancient tumuli ripple over much of the headland, while the tip of the peninsula is almost cut off by **Danes' Dyke**, a two-mile wooded ditch that runs from Cat Nab in the north to Sewerby Rocks in the south. Some believe it was a formal boundary built during the Viking invasions, though the chances are that it's an earthwork of pre-Roman vintage.

To see the best of Flamborough Head's coastline, try to walk at least part of the signposted Heritage Coast path, a grassy cliff-top track that negotiates most of the headland. One good place to join it is **BEMPTON**, two miles north of Bridlington. From Bempton, you can follow the path all the way round to Flamborough Head or curtail by cutting up paths to Flamborough village. The *Seabirds*, at the junction of the roads to the two villages, is a nice pub with a good line in fresh-fish bar meals.

Also of great appeal is the RSPB sanctuary at **Bempton Cliffs**, reached along a quiet lane from Bempton. The cliffs are the best single place to see the area's thousands of cliff-nesting birds; parking costs £3. This is the only mainland gannetry in England and you'll see gannets diving from fifty feet in the air to catch mackerel and herring. Bempton also boasts the second-largest puffin colony in the country, with several thousand returning to the cliffs between March and August – they spend the winter on the open seas. Late March and

April is the best time to see the puffins, when they display before nesting in the cliff's deep crevices, but the **Visitor Centre** (March–Nov daily 10am–5pm; Dec & Feb weekends only 9.30am–4pm; ⓣ01262/851179) can advise on other breeds' activities and rent you a pair of binoculars (£2.50). Other birds here in numbers include kittiwakes, guillemots, razorbills and the largest colony of fulmars in England. Not surprisingly, an egg-collecting industry once thrived here, the eggs' albumen being used in the tanneries of Leeds – you can still see the pulleys used by the local "climmers", as they were called. RSPB puffin and seabird **cruises** (mid-May to Sept, various times, usually on Sat & Sun; £9; ⓣ01662/850959) are a spectacular way to see the Bempton and Flamborough Head cliffs. They last three to four hours and depart from Bridlington.

Filey

FILEY, half a dozen miles further north up the coast, is at the very edge of the Yorkshire Wolds (and technically in North Yorkshire). It has a good deal more class as a resort than Bridlington, retaining many of its Edwardian features, including some splendid panoramic gardens. It, too, claims miles of wide sandy beach, stretching most of the way south to Flamborough Head and north the mile or so to the jutting rocks of **Filey Brigg**, where a nature trail wends for a couple of miles through the surroundings. If you're going to clamber around on the Brigg, check the tide tables first at the tourist office since people do get caught unawares by the incoming waters. **Bus** and **train** stations are just west of the centre on Station Avenue; there's a **car park** just behind the bus station. Walk down Station Avenue and Murray Street to **Filey Visitor Centre** on John Street (May–Sept daily 10am–5.30pm; Oct–April Sat & Sun 10am–4.30pm; ⓣ01723/518000). You'll find a clutch of standard **B&Bs** on Rutland Street, off West Avenue, which runs from the church in the centre of town. A few pricier **hotels** sit amongst the holiday flats down on the beachfront. *Downcliffe House* (ⓣ01723/513310; ❺) is the pick of them, with a sea-view restaurant with outdoor terrace serving a decent menu of fresh fish.

The North York Moors

Virtually the whole of the **North York Moors**, from the Hambleton and Cleveland hills in the west to the cliff-edged coastline to the east, is protected by one of the country's finest National Parks. The moors are lonely, heather-covered, flat-topped hills cut by deep, steep-sided valleys, and views here stretch for miles, interrupted only by giant cultivated forests, pale shadows of the woodland that covered the region before it was cleared by Neolithic and later peoples. Barrows and ancient forts provide memorials of these early settlers, mingling on the high moorland with the **Roman remains** of Wades Causeway, the battered stone crosses of the first Christian inhabitants and the ruins of great monastic houses such as Rievaulx.

Two pivotal market towns in the park's southern reaches provide the main approaches: **Helmsley**, best starting point for any exploration of the western and central moors, and **Pickering** (actually just outside the National Park), for the eastern moors and northern Esk Valley. The central moors offer the best walking and the most noted landscapes, with **Hutton le Hole** perhaps the most picture-perfect village in the region. Any exploration of the district should also include: the religious ruins of **Rievaulx Abbey** and possibly

Byland Abbey or Mount Grace Priory; the views from **Sutton Bank** or from the windows of the trains of the North York Moors Railway; the gentle landscapes of the **Esk Valley**, blessed with its own small train line; and any one of countless deep-rural pubs, isolated hamlets or woodland walks. Popular long-distance paths cross the park, notably the Cleveland Way, which follows the coast and northern moors, and the Lyke Wake Walk, both of which are covered in more detail in the following section.

Help and information is available from a number of **National Park information centres**, where you can pick up local trail guides and accommodation listings – most also organize special events and guided walks throughout the year. The seasonal *Moors Visitor* newspaper details local attractions, while the best hiking **maps** are the Ordnance Survey Outdoor Leisure maps #26 and #27.

The main southern artery linking the western, central and eastern divisions is the A170, which runs from Thirsk, through Helmsley and Pickering to Scarborough. Two trans-moor roads, the Helmsley–Stokesley B1257 (west side) and the Pickering–Whitby A169 (east), offer access into the very heart of the moors, with minor (often extremely minor) roads and tracks branching off in all directions: in winter, check the forecast first before setting off on any minor route, since this part of the country is always one of the first to be cut off in bad weather.

The steam trains of the **North York Moors Railway** run between Pickering and Grosmont (even more popular since being used as the *Hogwarts Express* in the *Harry Potter* films). At Grosmont you can connect with the regular trains on the Esk Valley line, running either six miles east to Whitby and the coast, or west through scintillating countryside to more remote settlements (and ultimately to Middlesbrough). The main **bus** approaches to the moors are from Scarborough and York to Helmsley and Pickering, though beyond these towns local services are limited. You'll need the free *Moors Explorer* booklet, a summary of all rail and bus routes on and around the moors, available from tourist offices and park information centres. There are also special summer **Moorsbus** services, running between points not usually served by public transport; see the box on p.1004 for more details.

The western moors

The **western moors** are marked on their western edge by the scarp of the **Hambleton Hills** – crowned by the Cleveland Way – and the A19 road between York, **Thirsk** (just outside the park, but a useful gateway) and Middlesbrough. To the east they are closed by Ryedale, one of the region's more bucolic valleys, and the B1257 from **Helmsley**, by far the area's nicest town and its best base for explorations. Most outings are likely to centre less on the scenery – except for the walks and staggering views from **Sutton Bank** on the A170 – than on a cluster of historic buildings, of which the most prepossessing is **Rievaulx Abbey**, easily seen from Helmsley. It's closely followed by **Mount Grace Priory**, to the north of Thirsk, and then by Shandy Hall, Byland Abbey and Newburgh Priory at the pretty village of **Coxwold**, grouped conveniently close together on a minor road loop from Thirsk to Helmsley.

Thirsk

The small market town of **THIRSK**, 23 miles north of York, made the most of its strategic crossroads position on the ancient drove road between Scotland

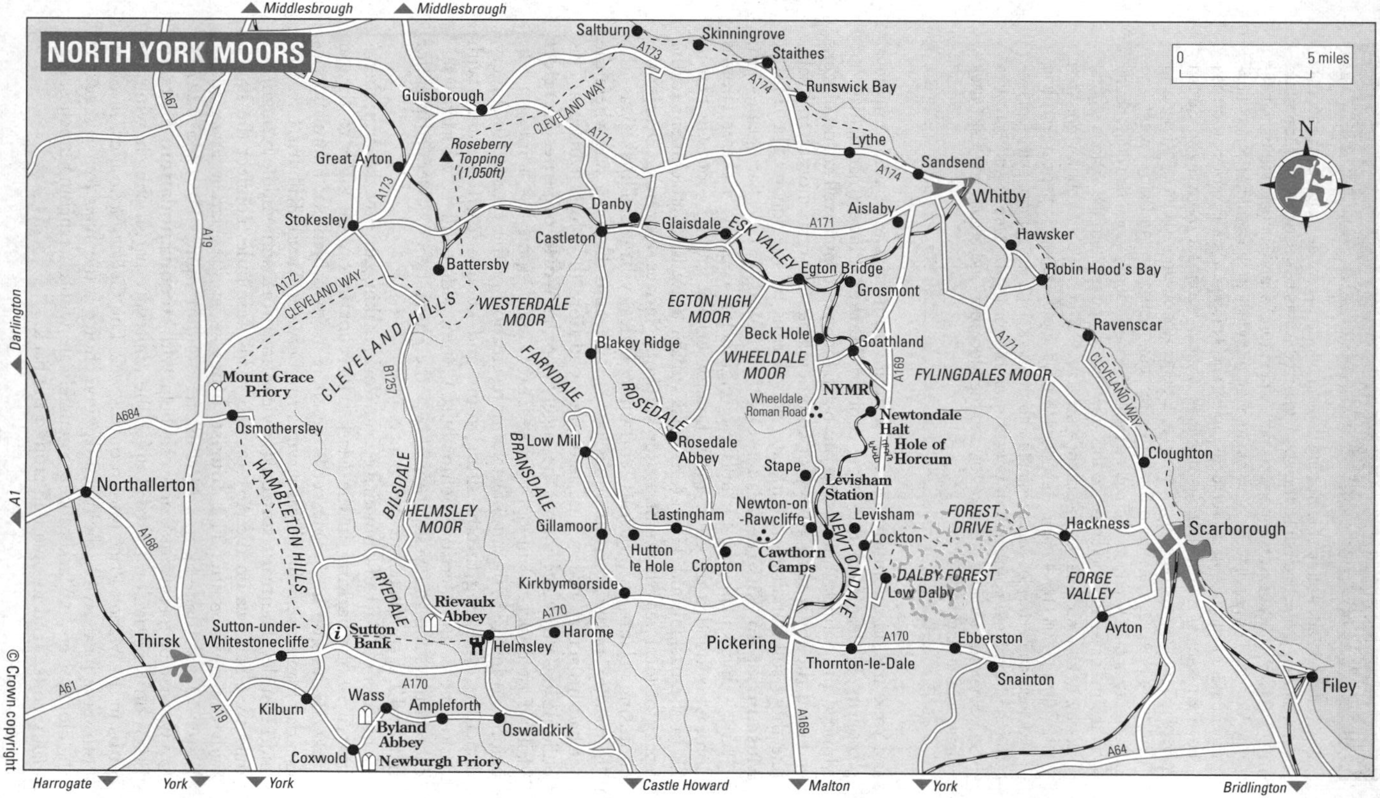

NORTH YORK MOORS

0 5 miles
N

Middlesbrough
Middlesbrough
Saltburn
Skinningrove
Staithes
Runswick Bay
Guisborough
CLEVELAND WAY
A173
A174
A171
A67
Roseberry Topping (1,050ft)
Great Ayton
Lythe
Sandsend
Whitby
A174
Aislaby
A171
Stokesley
A173
Danby
Glaisdale
ESK VALLEY
Castleton
A19
Hawsker
Battersby
Egton Bridge
Robin Hood's Bay
Grosmont
A172
CLEVELAND WAY
WESTERDALE MOOR
EGTON HIGH MOOR
Darlington
Ravenscar
CLEVELAND HILLS
Blakey Ridge
Beck Hole
Goathland
A171
FARNDALE
WHEELDALE MOOR
A169
FYLINGDALES MOOR
B1257
ROSEDALE
CLEVELAND WAY
Mount Grace Priory
NYMR
A684
Wheeldale Roman Road
Newtondale Halt
Osmothersley
Low Mill
Rosedale Abbey
Hole of Horcum
HAMBLETON HILLS
BRANSDALE
Cloughton
BILSDALE
Stape
Levisham Station
Northallerton
A1
HELMSLEY MOOR
Lastingham
Newton-on -Rawcliffe
Levisham
FOREST DRIVE
Gillamoor
Hackness
Scarborough
A168
Hutton le Hole
Cropton
Cawthorn Camps
NEWTONDALE
Lockton
DALBY FOREST
Low Dalby
FORGE VALLEY
Kirkbymoorside
RYEDALE
Rievaulx Abbey
A170
Sutton-under-Whitestonecliffe
Sutton Bank
Harome
Pickering
A170
Ebberston
Ayton
Thirsk
Helmsley
Thornton-le-Dale
A61
A170
Snainton
Filey
Kilburn
Wass
Ampleforth
A19
Byland Abbey
Oswaldkirk
A169
A64
Coxwold
Newburgh Priory

Harrogate
York
York
Castle Howard
Malton
York
Bridlington

The Moorsbus

The National Park Authority is making sterling efforts to reduce traffic congestion in the region by promoting public transport, in particular its bus service, the **Moorsbus** (Ⓣ01845/597426, Ⓦwww.moorsbus.net), which runs every Sunday and bank holiday Monday from April to the end of October, and daily in the summer school holidays (late July to late Aug). All local tourist and National Park information offices have timetables, but the various **services** basically connect Helmsley to Sutton Bank, Osmotherley, Rievaulx, Coxwold, Byland Abbey and Kilburn; Pickering to Hutton le Hole, Castleton and Danby, to Rosedale Abbey and to Dalby Forest; and Helmsley and Pickering to each other. Departures are usually four times daily (hourly on the main routes), and timed so that day-trips are possible to the various sights; all-day **tickets** cost £3. Long-distance services (£5) from Scarborough (1hr), York (1hr 10min), Hull (1hr 40min), Beverley (1hr), Darlington (2hr), Hartlepool (2hr) and Middlesbrough (1hr) let you commute into the park for a day's moorland sightseeing; and there are **combination tickets** available for the Moorsbus and Yorkshire Coastliner bus services (1 day, £10), and the Moorsbus and NYMR and Esk Valley train lines (1 day, £14).

and York and on the historic east–west route from dales to coast. Its medieval prosperity is clear from the large, cobbled **Market Place** (market days are Monday and Saturday), now overrun by traffic, while later well-to-do citizens endowed the town with a bevy of commendable Georgian houses and halls, like those still standing on Kirkgate, which runs off the square. The **Thirsk Museum** at 16 Kirkgate (Easter–Oct Mon–Wed, Fri & Sat 10am–4pm; £1.50) – incidentally, the birthplace of eighteenth-century cricketer Thomas Lord, who founded the eponymous London cricket ground – does its best to fill in the background. However, Thirsk's main draw is its attachment to the legacy of local vet Alf Wight, better known as **James Herriott**. Despite the confusing claims of various Yorkshire Dales villages, Thirsk was the "Darrowby" of the Herriott books, not least because the town was where the vet had his actual surgery, just across the road from the Thirsk Museum. This building at 23 Kirkgate is now the hugely popular **World of James Herriott** (daily: Easter–Oct 10am–6pm; Nov–Easter 11am–4pm, last admission 1hr before closing; £4.70), an entertaining re-creation of the vet's 1940s surgery, dispensary, operating theatre, sitting room and kitchen, each crammed with period pieces and Herriott memorabilia. Countryside exhibits, veterinary science displays and an investigation of how the Herriott books were adapted for film and TV complete the experience.

Thirsk is only a half-hour drive from York, making an easy day-trip; there's free two-hour **parking** in the Market Place or follow the signs to the car parks. **Buses** stop in the Market Place: there are two National Express services a day from York, while local services run between Thirsk, Kilburn, Coxwold and Helmsley. The **train station** (services from York and Middlesbrough) is a mile west of town on the A61 (Ripon road); minibuses connect the station with the town centre. The **tourist office** is at 49 Market Place (daily: Easter–Oct 10am–5pm; Nov–Easter 11am–4pm; Ⓣ01845/522755, Ⓦwww.hambleton.gov.uk), and can help with **accommodation**. There are B&Bs on Kirkgate, on the road up to the impressive parish church, while the **pubs** in the Market Place offer rooms as well. The *Golden Fleece* and *Three Tuns* both serve meals, while the nicest daytime choice is the *Yorks Tearooms*, next to the clocktower on Market Place, a genteel café with enterprising lunches, speciality coffees and its own deli around the back.

Osmotherley

Eleven miles north of Thirsk, the little village of **OSMOTHERLEY** huddles around its green, proud of its ancient market cross and curious adjacent stone table from on top of which it's said John Wesley preached during one of his sermon tours. Having seen agriculture and industry come and go, the pretty settlement now gets by as a hiking centre, since it's a key stop on the Cleveland Way as well as starting point for the infamous Lyke Wake Walk (see box below). Its proximity to Mount Grace Priory is another reason to stop by – it's around a two-mile walk from the village, via Chapel Wood Farm, with a short detour to the nearby **Lady Chapel** on the way there or back. A more strenuous local hike involves following the Cleveland Way beyond the farm to the 982-foot summit of Scarth Wood Moor and then down to Cod Beck Reservoir (3 miles; 1hr 30min).

There's a popular **youth hostel** at Cote Ghyll (Ⓣ0870/770 5982, Ⓔosmotherley@yha.org.uk; £10.25; closed Nov–Feb), half a mile north of the village, and an adjacent campsite too – you should really book in advance. For more comfort make straight for the *Three Tuns* (Ⓣ01609/883301; ④) on the village green, a renovated **pub** brimming with awards and serving classy meals. A couple of teashops and cottage B&Bs complete the picture.

Mount Grace Priory

The fourteenth-century **Mount Grace Priory** (Easter–Oct daily 10am–6pm; Nov–March Wed–Sun 10am–1pm & 2–4pm; £3.20; NT & EH), the most important of England's nine Carthusian ruins and the only one in Yorkshire, provides a striking contrast to its more grandiose and worldly Cistercian counterparts. The Carthusians took a vow of silence and lived, ate and prayed alone in their two-storey cells, each separated from its neighbour by a privy, small garden and high walls. The incumbents were given their meals through a hatch, specially angled to prevent the monks from seeing their waiters. The foundations of the cells are still clearly visible, together with one that has been recon-

The Lyke Wake Walk

One of England's more macho long-distance paths, the **Lyke Wake Walk** was founded in 1955 as a light-hearted idea: anyone who completed the 42-mile walk in less than 24 hours became a member of the Lyke Wake Club and qualified for a badge in the shape of a coffin. As word spread it became something of a cult, the net result being deeply eroded paths and mountains of litter – to the extent that the National Park authority now discourages large groups. The path isn't marked on most maps for the same reason. Although still the most popular walk on the moors, it has recently become less choked with groups, and is complemented by another trans-moors route, Wainwright's similarly controversial Coast to Coast walk.

The Lyke Wake starts at **Osmotherley**, eleven miles north of Thirsk, and shadows the Cleveland Way for a while along the northern edge of the Cleveland Hills before reaching **Ravenscar**, south of Robin Hood's Bay, by way of Fylingdales and the notorious descent and ascent at Jugger Howes. It links numerous prehistoric sites, following the age-old tracks of monks, miners and smugglers. The path's name, incidentally, comes from a dialect poem, the *Lyke Wake Dirge*, the story of a journey across one of the "burial routes" that linked the moors' ancient burial mounds. It recalls the ancient practice of waking (keeping vigil) over a dead body (the lyke). Provided you're completely fit, used to long-distance walking, have been in training and have back-up, first-timers can complete the walk in around sixteen hours – some people have *run* it in less than five, though they are, of course, completely insane.

structed to suggest its original layout and the monks' way of life. Other substantial remains include the ruins of the gatehouse and the walls and tower of the priory church, which divides the site's two main courtyards. Road access to the priory is straight up the busy A19 from Thirsk, eleven miles to the south; it's reached off a signposted minor road just after the Osmotherley turn-off.

Sutton Bank and Kilburn

The main A170 road enters the National Park from Thirsk as it climbs five hundred feet in half a mile to **Sutton Bank** (960ft), a phenomenal viewpoint whose panorama extends across the Vale of York to the Pennines on the far horizon. At the top of the climb stands a huge car park and a North York Moors National Park **Visitor Centre** (Easter–Oct daily 10am–5pm; Nov, Dec & March daily 11am–4pm; Jan & Feb Sat & Sun 11am–4pm; ⓣ01845/597426, ⓦwww.moors.uk.net), full of background on the short waymarked walks you can make from here, and with a café too.

To the south of the A170, the marked **White Horse Nature Trail** (2–3 miles; 1hr 30min) skirts the crags of Roulston Scar, passing the Yorkshire Gliding Club en route to the **Kilburn White Horse**, northern England's only turf-cut figure, at 314 feet long and 228 feet high. Unlike its ancient southern counterparts, it's a rather sham affair cut by a local schoolmaster in 1857 and only white because it's covered in imported chalk chippings. You could make a real walk of it by dropping a couple of miles down to **KILBURN** village – a minor road also runs from the A170, passing the White Horse – synonymous with woodcarving since the days of "Mouse Man" Robert Thompson (1876–1955), whose woodcarvings are marked by his distinctive mouse motif and can be found in York Minster and Westminster Abbey. There's a showroom and viewing gallery (closed weekends) at Robert Thompson's craftworks in the village, while the attached **Mouseman Visitor Centre** (ⓣ01347/869102, ⓦwww.robertthompsons.co.uk) has woodworking demonstrations and other displays. The village's *Forresters Arms* – a good place to recuperate – also sports locally made furniture.

Coxwold

The first serious diversion off the A170 is **COXWOLD**, as attractive a little village as they come. The majority of its many visitors come to pay homage to the novelist **Laurence Sterne**, who is buried by the south wall (close to the porch) in the churchyard of **St Michael's**, where he was vicar from 1760 until his death in 1768; the gravestone is badly damaged, though the one that marked the place of his original grave in London (see box opposite) hangs in the porch, complete with an inscription by enthusiastic eighteenth-century masons who admired him. The church, with its odd octagonal tower, is worth closer scrutiny – particularly the three-decker pulpit and medieval stained glass – before heading for **Shandy Hall**, 150yd further up the road past the church (May–Sept Wed 2–4.30pm, Sun 2.30–4.30pm; gardens May–Sept Mon–Fri & Sun 2–4.30pm; house & gardens £4.50, gardens only £2.50), Sterne's home, now a museum crammed with literary memorabilia. It was here that he wrote *A Sentimental Journey through France and Italy* and the wonderfully eccentric *The Life and Opinions of Tristram Shandy, Gentleman*, which prompted Samuel Johnson loftily and misguidedly to declare "nothing odd will last".

Of the village's many lovely, ivy-covered stone buildings, the *Fauconberg Arms* (ⓣ01347/868214, ⓦwww.fauconbergarms.co.uk; ❹), a superb old **inn** on Main Street, has the most to recommend it, with a cosy bar serving good food, a more formal restaurant and pleasant rooms.

The mysterious corpse of Laurence Sterne

Irish-born **Laurence Sterne** (1713–68) took Holy Orders after receiving his Cambridge degree, married in 1741 and by 1760 was living in Coxwold, officiating at St Michael's Church. The first two volumes of his great novel, the rambling and brilliant *Tristram Shandy*, published in 1760, catapulted him to fame and he became a controversial figure in literary London. Further volumes of *Tristram Shandy* enhanced his reputation, and Sterne began to travel in the 1760s, partly in an attempt to improve his poor health. His sojourn in France and Italy provided material for *A Sentimental Journey* (1768), but the journey proved too much for him and he died of pleurisy in London, where he was buried. Immediate rumours surfaced that Sterne's body had been unknowingly appropriated by body-snatchers and sold to doctors for medical experimentation – a story given credence when Sterne's body was finally exhumed from its London graveyard in 1969 for reburial in Coxwold. Various bones and no fewer than five skulls were uncovered in the grave, one of which – after comparison with contemporary busts – is thought to have been Sterne's. Presumably, the eighteenth-century doctors who illegally bought the body were horrified to learn of its identity and hurriedly reburied it in its grave together with other human bits and pieces they had lying around. Sterne – or at least part of him – now lies at rest in Coxwold churchyard.

The pub is named for the viscount who married Mary, daughter of Oliver Cromwell, whom he brought to live in **Newburgh Priory**, half a mile south of the village (April–June Wed & Sun 2–6pm; also Easter & May bank hols 2.30–4.45pm; £5, grounds only £2.50). Raised on the site of an Augustinian monastery founded in 1150, the house is famous for reputedly containing a tomb with the headless body of Oliver Cromwell. The story claims that Mary brought her father's body here after it was exhumed from Westminster Abbey in readiness to be "executed" at Tyburn in revenge for Cromwell's part in the Civil War. Resourceful Mary is supposed to have exchanged Oliver's corpse with that of some ordinary Joe, but it's not quite clear how this tale can be made to tally with the fact that Oliver's body had been mummified before its burial, and thus would have been expected to resemble the recently deceased leader.

Buses run from Thirsk to Coxwold (and on to Helmsley) on Mondays, Fridays and Saturdays, and the Moorsbus runs here daily from Thirsk and Helmsley in summer. By car, turn off the A170 after Sutton-under-Whitestonecliffe, five miles east of Thirsk, or come south down the A19 and follow the signs through the country lanes – either approach lets you take in Kilburn and the White Horse on the way to or from Coxwold.

Byland Abbey

Laurence Sterne talked of "A delicious Walk of Romance" from Coxwold to twelfth-century **Byland Abbey** (June–Sept daily 10am–1pm & 2–6pm; Oct–May closed Tues & Wed; £2; EH), a mile and a half northeast of the village; the summer Moorsbus runs here. His description captures the appeal of the ruins – seen from the distance as a mere finger of stone – which, though larger in ground area than the Cistercian houses at Fountains and Rievaulx, are far less well preserved, leaving the haunting location and stark west front as the abbey's most memorable aspects. Other colossal but skeletal remains include the lay brothers' "lane", a rare example of the corridor which kept abbey servants at a remove from the cloister and the ordained monks. Equally unusual are some fine thirteenth-century green-and-yellow tiled floors, seen to best effect in the south transept chapels. The *Abbey Inn* (closed Sun eve & Mon), opposite the priory entrance, serves coffee and meals.

Helmsley

One of the moors' most appealing towns, **HELMSLEY** makes a perfect base for visiting the western moors and Rievaulx Abbey. Local life revolves around a large cobbled market square (market day is Friday), dominated by a vaunting monument to the second earl of Feversham, whose family was responsible for rebuilding most of the village in the nineteenth century. The old **market cross** marks the start of the 110-mile Cleveland Way (see box opposite), and the town hall on the western edge of the square houses the tourist office and National Park information centre.

Close to the square, on the village's western fringe, is **Helmsley Castle** (April–Sept daily 10am–6pm; Oct daily 10am–5pm; Nov–March Wed–Sun 10am–1pm & 2–4pm; £2.60; EH), its unique twelfth-century D-shaped keep ringed by massive earthworks. After a three-month siege during the Civil War it was "slighted" by Sir Thomas Fairfax, the Parliamentary commander, and much of its stone was plundered by townspeople for local houses.

To the southwest of the town, overlooking a wooded meander of the Rye, stands the Fevershams' country seat, **Duncombe Park** (April–Oct Mon–Thurs & Sun: house, tours 12.30–3.30pm; garden, parkland & visitor centre 11am–5.30pm; house, gardens & parkland £6, gardens £3, parkland £2; Ⓦwww.duncombepark.com), built for the Fevershams' ancestor Sir Thomas Duncombe in 1713. The building is by gentleman-architect William Wakefield, though he was probably influenced by Vanbrugh who was working on Castle Howard at about the same time. The grounds are perhaps more appealing than the house (which was extensively rebuilt after a fire in 1879), boasting swathes of landscaped gardens, which include Britain's tallest ash and lime trees, and a brace of artfully sited temples. Keen gardeners will also want to visit the **Helmsley Walled Garden**, within the Duncombe Park Estate (April–Oct daily 10.30am–5pm; Nov–March Fri–Sun noon–4pm; £2.50), whose five carefully tended acres are slowly emerging from a wholesale renovation after years of neglect.

Practicalities

Helmsley is connected by **bus** to Pickering and Scarborough, Malton, York and Thirsk, which makes it a fairly handy base. It's also a hub for the Moorsbus (see box, p.1004). There's a useful **tourist office** in the town hall on Market Place (Easter–Oct daily 9.30am–5pm; Nov–Easter Fri–Sun 10am–4pm; Ⓣ01439/770173, Ⓦwww.ryedale.gov.uk), which sells local trail leaflets and has information on the two **long-distance footpaths**: the Cleveland Way and the Ebor Way, the latter a gentle seventy-mile route to Ilkley that links with the Dales Way.

Talk to the tourist office if you want local B&B **accommodation** as space fills fast, though a good starting point is *Stilworth House*, behind the tourist office at 1 Church St (Ⓣ01439/771072; no credit cards; ❸). Of the places ringing Market Place, the best mid-range hotel is the *Crown* (Ⓣ01439/770297; ❺), a comfortable, old-fashioned (in the best sense), family-run inn serving very good-value evening meals. Finest of all is the *Black Swan* (Ⓣ0870/400 8112; ❼), a gorgeous Elizabethan-Georgian hybrid with splendid gardens and some good off-season deals. There's also the classy *Feversham Arms*, behind the church at 1 High St (Ⓣ01439/770766; ❼), which combines hip styling with comfort

The Cleveland Way

The 110-mile **Cleveland Way**, one of England's premier long-distance National Trails, starts at Helmsley in the North York Moors and follows a route that embraces both the northern rim of the moors and Cleveland Hills and the cliff scenery of the North Yorkshire coast. The path hits the sea at Saltburn and then runs south, terminating at Filey, south of Scarborough – though an unofficial "Missing Link" joins Scarborough to Helmsley, through the Tabular Hills, thus completing a circular walk. Most people complete the Cleveland Way in around nine or ten days, though it's easy to walk short stages instead, particularly on the **coastal section**, where towns, villages and services are closer together. The outstanding high-cliff sections are (from south to north): Hayburn Wyke to Robin Hood's Bay (7 miles); Robin Hood's Bay to Whitby (6 miles); Sandsend to Runswick Bay to Staithes (7 miles); and Staithes to Skinningrove, the section with the highest cliffs (5 miles).

The **Cleveland Way Project** (The Old Vicarage, Bondgate, Helmsley, YO6 5BP; Ⓣ01439/770657) produces an annual *Accommodation and Information Guide*. Local information offices in Helmsley, Whitby, Sutton Bank, Scarborough and Filey can also advise you. As well as B&Bs, hotels and campsites en route, there are **youth hostels** at Helmsley, Osmotherley, Whitby, Robin Hood's Bay and Scarborough – all should be booked well in advance.

You'll need the OS Outdoor Leisure **maps** #26 and #27 and Landranger sheet #101, though the *National Trail Guide: Cleveland Way* by Ian Sampson (Aurum Press) and *Walking the Cleveland Way and The Missing Link* by Malcolm Boyes (Cicerone Press) cover the ground in detail, too.

in its spacious rooms and brasserie – there's a pool, gym, tennis court and terrace here, too. The purpose-built **youth hostel** (Ⓣ0870/770 5860, Ⓔhelmsley@yha.org.uk; £10.25; closed Nov–Easter, and closed Sun & Mon Sept & Oct) is a few hundred yards east of Market Place – follow Bondgate to Carlton Road and turn left.

Market day in Helmsley is Friday. The old **pubs** in the Market Place – the *Royal Oak* and the *Feathers* – are both atmospheric places for a drink and a bite to eat. The *Black Swan* is the place for drinks in its panelled bar, afternoon teas and good, if pricey, lunches and dinners. Hunters, at 13 Borogate, just by the Market Place, is an overstuffed **deli**, excellent for putting together a picnic. Borogate itself has several fine little **shops** in ancient houses, including a working smithy and a good second-hand bookshop in the old fire station. **Helmsley Arts Centre** in the Old Meeting House, off Bridge St (Ⓣ01439/771700, Ⓦwww.helmsleyarts.co.uk), has a full programme of theatre, film, music and other events.

For a drive out into the country, and a fine meal, you can't do better than the invariably packed *Star Inn* (Ⓣ01439/770397, Ⓦwww.thestaratharome.co.uk; no food Sun eve & Mon; ❼) at **Harome**, a thatched pub a couple of miles south of the A170, where Michelin-rated food awaits. Should you use to make a night of it, eight very nice rooms in the adjacent lodge are individually furnished, some with spa baths, a couple with a private garden, and one with its own snooker table.

Rievaulx Abbey

From Helmsley you can easily hike across country to **Rievaulx Abbey** (daily: April–Sept 10am–6pm; Oct 10am–5pm; Nov–March 10am–4pm; £3.80; EH), once one of England's greatest Cistercian abbeys, and these days the most heavily visited historic building on the moors. The signposted path follows the opening two miles of the Cleveland Way, plus a mile's diversion off the Way, and takes around an hour and a half – a trail leaflet is available from the tourist office in Helmsley. If you don't fancy the walk, take the summer-only Moorsbus, which runs a shuttle service out here.

Founded in 1132, the abbey became the mother church of the Cistercians in England (see box on p.972), quickly developing from a series of rough shelters on the deeply wooded banks of the River Rye to become a flourishing community with interests in fishing, mining, agriculture and the woollen industry, the latter supported by a chain of associated moorland farms. At its height, 140 monks and up to 500 lay brothers lived and worked at the abbey, though numbers fell dramatically once the Black Death (1348–49) had done its worst. The end came with the Dissolution, when many of the walls were razed and the roof lead stripped – the beautiful ruins, however, still suggest the abbey's former splendour. They are at their best in the triple-arched nave, oriented from north to south instead of the conventional west–east axis because of the valley's sloping site. The Chapter House retains an original shrine to the first abbot, William. A **visitor centre** mounts exhibitions pertaining to the ruins and to monastic life in the valley.

Rievaulx Terrace

Although they form some sort of ensemble with the abbey, there's no access between the ruins and **Rievaulx Terrace and Temples** (Easter–Oct daily 10.30am–6pm; £3.30; NT), a site entered from the B1257, a couple of miles northwest of Helmsley. This pleasing half-mile stretch of grass-covered terraces and woodland was laid out as part of Duncombe Park in the 1750s, and as with Studley Royal at Fountains Abbey, the terrace was engineered partly to enhance the views of the abbey. The resulting panorama over the ruins and the valley below is superb, and this makes a great spot for a picnic or simply for strolls along the lawns and woodland trail. Tuscan and Ionic temples lie at opposing ends of the terrace, the latter with a fine painted ceiling, excellent furniture and a permanent exhibition on eighteenth-century English landscape design.

The central moors

The highest and wildest terrain in the North York Moors is in the **central moors**, bounded by Ryedale in the west and by **Rosedale** in the east. Purple swathes of summer heather carpet the tops, where ancient crosses and standing stones provide hints of the moorland's distant past. Stunning villages such as **Hutton le Hole** and **Lastingham** give way to higher, isolated valleys, connected by steep minor roads and rough tracks – it's the one part of the National Park where having your own transport is vital if you don't want to hang around too long. The Moorsbus connects most destinations, but really this is an area for walking and taking in the scenery.

Hutton le Hole

Lying eight miles northeast of Helmsley, one of Yorkshire's quaintest villages, **HUTTON LE HOLE**, has become so great a tourist attraction that you'll have to come off-season to get much pleasure from its tidy gardens, its stream-crossed village green and the sight of sheep wandering freely through the lanes. On warm summer days, the stream banks are covered with splashing picnickers. Apart from the sheer photogenic quality of the place, the big draw is the **Ryedale Folk Museum** (Easter–Oct daily 10am–5.30pm; £3.25; ⓦwww.ryedalefolkmuseum.co.uk), an ever-expanding set of displays over a two-acre site. Local life is documented from the era of prehistoric flint tools, through Romano-British artefacts and pottery, to a series of reconstructed buildings, notably a sixteenth-century house, a glass furnace, a crofter's cottage and a nineteenth-century blacksmith's shop. Special events and displays throughout the season mean there's always something going on.

The museum also houses a **National Park information centre** (same hours as museum; ⓣ01751/417367), where you can buy leaflets detailing local hikes. The nearby car park fills very quickly in summer as walkers disperse from the village. **Accommodation** is zealously fought for, too: try *Moorlands* (ⓣ01751/417548, ⓦwww.moorlandshouse.com; ④), a hospitable Georgian house with streamside garden (and self-catering cottage also available); the *Barn Hotel* (ⓣ01751/417311; ④), on the through road just down from the museum; or the Georgian *Hammer and Hand* (ⓣ01751/417300; ③), a comfortable period B&B on the village green next to the pub; or fall back on the mercy of the information centre, which holds lists of other local B&Bs. *Moorlands* and the *Hammer and Hand* serve evening meals (£15/18), while the *Forge Tea Shop* (closed weekdays Nov–Feb) – a renowned stop for tea and cakes – completes the set. If you stay the night you'll have plenty of time to become acquainted with the *Crown*, the friendly local pub.

Lastingham

About a mile and a half east of Hutton le Hole is **LASTINGHAM**, its rose-fronted stone cottages gathered in a dell near its bubbling beck. Here stands **St Mary's** (daily 9am–dusk), a superb little church, built over Lastingham Abbey, a Benedictine house founded in 654 by monks Cedd and Chad from Lindisfarne, both of whom were later canonized. The monastery was destroyed by the Danes and then partly rebuilt by monks from Whitby, who left in 1087 to found St Mary's in York without finishing their work here. The present church, however, preserves the early Norman crypt, one of Yorkshire's great ecclesiastical treasures. Burial place of St Cedd, the crypt was once a sacred point of pilgrimage. Today its heavy vaults and carved columns still shelter the head of an eighth-century Anglo-Saxon cross, a Viking "hogback" tombstone and the original doorposts of the Saxon monastery.

The hamlet is tiny, with just one cosy **pub**, the *Blacksmith's Arms* opposite the church.

Farndale

Farndale is entered from the south by a minor road from **Gillamoor**, a little to the west of Hutton le Hole. Further up the vale the country lanes are packed in spring with tourists here to see the area's wild daffodils, protected by the two-thousand-acre **Farndale nature reserve**. The Moorsbus runs a special "Daffodil" service every Sunday in April and over Easter, shuttling visitors from Hutton le Hole. The flowers grow in several parts of the dale, but the best area is north of **Low Mill**, where roads from Gillamoor and Hutton le Hole meet, about four miles north of the latter. Take the path beside the car park (signposted "High Mill") over the bridge and follow the track alongside the somnolent River Dove. As well as the thousands of daffodils, notice the alder trees, whose Gaelic name, *ferna*, may well have given Farndale its name. At High Mill, *Poppy's Pantry* (closed Wed) can serve you a refreshing glass of homemade lemonade in the garden, just beyond which, at **Church Houses**, you regain the road (and find the tiny, stone *Feversham Arms*). Turn right on the road here for about three-quarters of a mile and you can follow the route back south to Low Mill via High Wold House (just over 3 miles; 2hr–2hr 30min).

Rosedale and Blakey Ridge

Rosedale, just a couple of miles east of Farndale, is slightly wilder and steeper than the latter, and has a good network of wild upland roads ranging over its moors, which are densely studded with prehistoric tumuli and ancient stone crosses, including **Ralph Cross**, which stands sentinel at the isolated crossroads at the top of the dale.

The largest of its communities, trim and tidy **ROSEDALE ABBEY**, four miles northeast of Hutton le Hole, preserves only a few fragments of the Cistercian priory (1158) that gave it its name, most of them incorporated into **St Lawrence's** parish church. It's hard to believe now, but in the last century the village had a population of over five thousand, most employed in the ironstone workings whose remnants lie scattered all over the lonely high moors round about. The first mine opened in 1851, some three million tons of ore being excavated between 1856 and 1885. Horse-drawn wagons dragged the stone by pack road to Pickering until the opening of a remarkable moorland railway which connected with the main Esk Valley line at Battersby to carry ore north to the ironworks of Teesside.

You can pick up the still clearly distinct line, now a panoramic footpath, at several points near the high road on Blakey Ridge, on the west of the dale, but for a fine circular walk join it at **Hill Cottages**, one and half miles northwest of Rosedale Abbey, and follow it all the way round the head of the valley, returning either via Dale Head Farm, the valley bottom and Thorgill, or the broad track that runs south down Blakey Ridge above Thorgill (10 miles; 3hr 30min).

Rosedale village itself gets packed on summer weekends and it can be tough finding a parking space on the grass verges. A fair proportion of visitors are here to sit outside the *Milburn Arms* (Ⓣ01751/417312, Ⓦwww.milburnarms.co.uk; ❺; closed Jan), overlooking the small green, which makes a peaceful base: its **rooms** have views over the hills and there's a beer garden out front. Otherwise, there are teas and snacks to be had in the *Abbey Tearooms* (closed Wed & Nov–Easter), and a popular **campsite** at *Rosedale Caravan Park* (Ⓣ01751/417272) down by the river. There's a good restaurant and bar meals, too, at the *Blacksmiths' Inn* (Ⓣ01751/417331, Ⓦwww.blacksmithsinn-rosedale.co.uk; ❺) at **Hartoft End**, a couple of miles south of Rosedale Abbey. Also a couple of miles out (call for directions), in peaceful surroundings, the *Orange Tree* (Ⓣ01751/417219, Ⓦwww.theorangetree.com) at Rosedale East offers "relaxation therapy" weekends throughout the year – walks, massages, treatments and homecooked food from £159 for two nights (Friday to Sunday).

North of Rosedale Abbey is the *Lion Inn* (Ⓣ01751/417320, Ⓦwww.lionblakey.co.uk; ❸) on **Blakey Ridge**, a couple of miles south of the junction with the Hutton le Hole–Castleton road (along which the Moorsbus travels). A truly windswept local, with a sixteenth-century core, the inn has fairly standard bar meals, but good beer and an unbeatable location for an isolated night's stay – though come Sunday lunchtime the car park soon fills up. Some make the slight detour from the Lyke Wake Walk, since the pub roughly marks the halfway spot.

Pickering and the eastern moors

The biggest centre for miles around, **Pickering** takes for itself the title "Gateway to the Moors", which is pushing it a bit, though it's certainly a handy place to stay if you're touring the villages and dales of the **eastern moors**. Its undoubted big pull, and biggest plus if you're using public transport, is the

North Yorkshire Moors Railway (NYMR; see box on p.1014), which provides a beautiful way of travelling up (and walking from) **Newtondale**, the Moors' most immediately spectacular dale, and of connecting with the Esk Valley line in Esk Dale and, ultimately, Whitby and the Yorkshire coast. Otherwise, you could make use of the Moorsbus services, which radiate from Pickering, and there are regular bus services to and from Helmsley, Scarborough, York and Leeds.

Few people pay much attention to the countryside east of Pickering, which consists for the most part of apparently unending ranks of conifers and characterless moorland. **Dalby Forest**, however, the most accessible of the woodlands, is redeemed by a superb forest drive and a large number of specially marked trails. Villages are few and far between, though in **Thornton-le-Dale** the region has a high-ranking contender for prettiest village in Yorkshire. By far the best itinerary here is to see Thornton-le-Dale and then drive or bike through Dalby Forest to rejoin the main A170 Pickering–Scarborough road at one of several points just outside Scarborough. Without your own transport you're stuck as far as touring around is concerned, though there is a Moorsbus service into the forest from Pickering.

Pickering

A thriving market town at the junction of the A170 and the transmoor A169 (Whitby road), **PICKERING** rather fancies itself, yet a couple of hours is enough to show you its charms, certainly if you've already seen the best of the North York Moors to the west. Its most attractive feature is its motte and bailey **Castle** on the hill north of the Market Place (Easter–Sept daily 10am–6pm; Oct daily 10am–5pm; Nov–March Wed–Sun 10am–4pm; £2.60; EH), reputedly used by every English monarch up to 1400 as a base for hunting in nearby Blandsby Park. Eight monarchs certainly put up here, including Edward II after his trouncing by the Scots at the Battle of Byland Abbey in 1322, and possibly a ninth, Richard II, was kept here as a prisoner shortly before his murder in Pontefract. The ruins are in pretty good shape, with much of the walls, keep and original towers intact, and some good views over the town and countryside. A simple chapel in the grounds dates back to 1227 and is dedicated to St Nicholas, the fourth-century Bishop of Myra – Santa Claus by any other name.

Buses stop outside the library and **tourist office** on The Ropery, (Easter–Oct Mon–Sat 9.30am–5pm, Sun 9.30am–4pm; Nov–Easter Mon–Sat 10am–4.30pm; ⓣ01751/473791, ⓦwww.ryedale.gov.uk) opposite Safeway in the centre of town; the **NYMR train station** is less than five minutes' signposted walk away. If you haven't made an **accommodation** reservation in summer, you may as well call at the tourist office first to see what's still available. Tree-lined Eastgate (the Scarborough road) has the tastefully presented *Eden House* at no. 120 (ⓣ01751/472289, ⓦwww.edenhousebandb.co.uk; no credit cards; ❸), and there are more modest places on the same road. *Bramwood*, 19 Hallgarth (ⓣ01751/474066; ❸), lies through a gateway off the Whitby road, a lovely eighteenth-century house with walled garden; it also has two cottages to rent by the week. A couple of the **pubs** have rooms, top choice easily being the *White Swan*, on Market Place (ⓣ01751/472288, ⓦwww.white-swan.co.uk; ❻), whose dozen non-smoking bedrooms are fashionably turned out and have good bathrooms. There are cafés and tearooms throughout town, and a couple of Indian **restaurants**, though it's the *White Swan* that's most serious about its cooking – fine Modern British food at moderate prices, lunch and dinner. **Market** day in town is Monday.

The North Yorkshire Moors Railway

The volunteer-run **North Yorkshire Moors Railway** (NYMR) connects **Pickering** with the Esk Valley (Middlesbrough–Whitby) line at **Grosmont**, 18 miles to the north. The line was completed by George Stephenson in 1835, just ten years after the opening of the Stockton and Darlington Railway, making it one of the earliest lines in the country. Even by the standards of later projects it was a remarkable feat of engineering, navigating 1-in-15 gradients and using thousands of tons of brushwood and heather-stuffed sheepskins to provide bedding for the track through the dale's extensive bogs. For twelve years carriages were pulled by horse, with steam locomotives only arriving in 1847. The line closed in 1965 and was formally reopened in 1973.

Scheduled **services** operate between mid-March and early November (plus Christmas specials), with trains running hourly to three times daily depending on the time of year. For **advance bookings and information**, call ⓣ01751/472508 (Mon–Fri 9am–5pm, Sat & Sun 10am–2.30pm); for the talking timetables call ⓣ01751/473535; or check the website at ⓦwww.nymr.demon.co.uk. A day-return **ticket** for the whole line costs £12. Part of the line's attraction, of course, are the **steam trains**, though be warned that diesels are pulled into service when the fire risk in the forests is high.

The nearest **youth hostel** is a simple affair at the Old School, Lockton (ⓣ0870/770 5938; £8; closed Oct–Easter), five miles northeast off the A169 – about two miles' cross-country walk from the NYMR station at Levisham (see below), or ask to be dropped at the turn-off by the Whitby bus. The local **campsite** is *Upper Carr* (ⓣ01751/473115, ⓦwww.uppercarr.demon.co.uk; closed Nov–Feb), a mile and half south of town on the Malton Road. It also has on-site chalets available (❷).

Walks from the North Yorkshire Moors Railway

Most people make a full return journey for the superb scenery of the roadless **Newtondale**, but if you want to combine some walking with the train rides, stop en route at one of the minor stations.

The first is Levisham, perfect for walks to the village of **LEVISHAM**, a mile and a half to the east, where the *Horseshoe Inn* (ⓣ01751/460240; no credit cards; ❹) is a favourite target, especially for Sunday lunch, with rooms available too. A steep winding road continues another mile beyond Levisham, down across the beck and then up to **LOCKTON**, where there's a youth hostel and a path due north to the **Hole of Horcum**, a bizarre natural hollow gouged by the glacial meltwaters that carved out Newtondale. The paths run back to Levisham Station from here, and the entire seven-mile circuit is one of the Moors' best short walks – take the short detour halfway round to the *Saltersgate Inn*, on the A169, which has good-value food (and a fire that hasn't been allowed to go out for a couple of centuries).

The second train stop, **Newtondale Halt**, is only a couple of miles north-west of the Hole of Horcum, or you can head off through the extensive woods of **Cropton Forest** to the west on trails specially marked by the Forestry Commission – some forest scenes in the first *Harry Potter* movie were filmed here. At Stape – three miles southwest through the forest – you're just two miles south of the best-preserved stretch of Roman road in Europe, **Wheeldale Roman Road**, a mile of Wade's Causeway that ran from York to bases on the coast: the remains show a twenty-foot-wide stretch of sand and gravel studded by sandstone slabs and edged with kerbs and ditches. It's sign-posted off the untarred road from Stape to Goathland (the third stop on the railway line), perhaps the wildest and most adventurous north–south route over the moors – though anyone equipped with a decent map will also be able to find their way to the Roman road direct by track from Newtondale Halt, again around a three-mile walk.

Thornton-le-Dale

THORNTON-LE-DALE, two miles east of Pickering, hangs onto its considerable charm despite the main A170 Scarborough road scything through its centre. Most of the houses, pubs and shops are fairly alluring, none more so than the thatched cottage near the parish church, which features in so many ads, magazine covers, chocolate boxes and calendars that it's been described as the most photographed house in Britain. There are too many cafés, gift shops and other people around for most tastes, but the old market cross, stocks and various stream-side strolls are well worth half an hour if you can get here off-season.

Various local **B&Bs** might entice too, while both the **pubs** – the *New Inn* and *Buck Inn* – also have rooms. Tearooms and bar meals aside, food in the village isn't up to much. Consider instead the four-mile diversion to the east, along the A170, to the village of **Ebberston**, where the *Grapes* pub serves home-cooked meals.

Dalby Forest

Minor roads from Thornton-le-Dale and from the A169 (Whitby road) lead into the monumental expanse of **Dalby Forest**: drivers pay a toll (£4; road closed 9pm–7am) to join the start of a nine-mile forest drive that emerges close to Hackness, just four miles from Scarborough. It's best to make first for the **visitor centre** (April & Oct daily 10am–4pm; May, June & Sept daily 10am–5pm; July & Aug daily 10am–5.30pm; winter hours restricted, call for information; ⓣ01751/460295, ⓦwww.forestry.gov.uk) at **Low Dalby**, which has information not only on the forest, one of the first to be planted after the foundation of the Forestry Commission in 1919, but also on wildlife, picnic spots and the range of marked trails scattered around the woods, varying in length from one to sixteen miles. A kiosk here (closed Nov–Easter) sells drinks, snacks and ices. The Moorsbus calls at the centre in summer.

The best hikes are from a car park about three miles north of Low Dalby at Low Staindale, which include the Cross Cliff View Walk and the marvellous one-and-a-half mile (1hr) **Bridestones Trail** – a trail leaflet is available for the latter walk, which is of added interest for the bridestones themselves, great sandstone tors rising out of the heather that have been eroded into unearthly shapes. Similarly named outcrops are found all over the moors, and may be named for their connections with ancient fertility rites, or derive from a Norse word meaning "brink", or "boundary" stones. Another extremely popular walk or drive – trail leaflet available – takes in the **Forge Valley**, a deep-cut gorge scoured by glacial meltwaters during the last Ice Age. Start the walk (4 miles; 2hr–2hr 30min) from the Green Gate car park at the vale's northern end, three miles south of Hackness.

The Esk Valley

The northernmost reaches of the National Park are crossed by the east–west **Esk Valley**, whose pretty river flows into the sea at Whitby. It's a part of the North York Moors overlooked by many visitors – partly, one suspects, because its very attractions, at least in the eastern stretches, are its valley characteristics: there's not much moorland tramping to be done until you reach **Danby**, one of the finest of all moorland villages. Access is easy, either by road from Whitby via the A169 through Sleights, or more attractively by **train**: the North York Moors Railway connects at **Grosmont**, where you're on the **Esk Valley line**, which runs between Middlesbrough and Whitby, stopping at **Great Ayton**, the childhood home of explorer James Cook.

Grosmont to Danby

GROSMONT, little more than a level-crossing, station and a couple of tearooms, sees plenty of summer traffic. Walkers pile off the trains to head north up the appealing rail and riverside path to Goathland (see opposite), three miles away, but if you're sticking with the train wait until the next stop west at **EGTON BRIDGE**. It's similarly tiny but has the bonus of a beautifully sited riverside pub, the *Horseshoe* (ⓣ01947/895245; ❷), with a spacious beer garden and terrific food. Half a mile north, up the steep road from the station, there's a second pub, the *Wheatsheaf*, at **EGTON** itself, also serving fine meals in its restaurant. Don't confuse the other pub here, also a *Horseshoe*, with the one down by the river.

Further west, the scenery becomes tinged by the looming moors until, at the isolated stone village of **DANBY**, you're once again within striking distance of some excellent walks, all detailed on trail leaflets available from the **Moors Centre** (Easter–Oct daily 10am–5pm; Nov, Dec & March daily 11am–4pm; Jan & Feb Sat & Sun 11am–4pm; ⓣ01439/772737, ⓦwww.moors.uk.net). The centre, a converted sixteenth-century farmhouse and former shooting lodge, also houses exhibitions about the local flora and fauna as well as a good tearoom. Whitby tourist office (ⓣ01947/602674) can help with accommodation in local farmhouse B&Bs scattered up the sheep-laden side dales, and there's certainly much to be said for a quiet night away from the crowds. There's a **pub**, the *Duke of Wellington*, while the *Stonehouse Bakery & Tea Shop* is great for daytime snacks, serving olive bread or ciabatta sandwiches alongside coffee, scrumptious peanut brittle and other treats. A mile out of the village at **Ainthorpe**, the *Fox & Hounds* (ⓣ01287/660218, ⓦwww.foxandhounds-ainthorpe.com; ❹) looks out over the moors, its refurbished rooms and tasty home-cooked food both good reasons to stop.

Great Ayton

On reaching **GREAT AYTON**, the North York Moors gives way to the **Cleveland Hills**, whose scattered peaks provide the buffer between the rural east of the region and the encroaching industry of Teesside to the west. The town makes a handsome enough stop, with the River Leven flowing through the middle connecting the pretty High Green and Low Green at either end of the long High Street. It's Great Ayton's **Captain Cook** connections, though, that draw most visitors: the town was the boyhood home of James Cook between 1736 (when he was 8) and 1745. The young Cook lived at Aireyholme Farm (no public access) on the outskirts of town, though after James left to go to sea his father built a family **cottage** on Bridge Street, which was later dismantled and shipped to Melbourne, Australia in 1934; its site is marked by an obelisk of Australian granite near Low Green. Other Cook-related sights include **All Saints' Church**, also at Low Green, which the family attended and where Cook's mother Grace is buried; Cook's school, now the **Schoolroom Museum** at 101 High St (Easter–Oct daily 1–4pm; July & Aug from 11am; £2); and a **sculpture** of a youthful Cook on High Green which depicts him – bare-chested, long-locked – in Leonardo DiCaprio mode. For an afternoon's leg-stretching, a waymarked path runs northeast out of Great Ayton, past Aireyholme Farm and up to the summit of **Roseberry Topping** (1050ft), the queerly shaped conical peak visible from all over the locality –

beacons were lit on top of here during the threat by the Spanish Armada. It's a reasonably stiff climb, followed by a tramp across Easby Moor to the south to the fifty-foot-high **Cook Monument** (1827) for more amazing views, before circling back to Great Ayton.

The Esk Valley **train station** lies half a mile northeast of town. **Buses** from Middlesbrough and Guisborough stop on the High Green, just back from which, in the car park, is the **tourist office** (Easter–Oct Mon–Sat 10am–4pm, Sun 1–4pm; ⓣ01642/722835, ⓦwww.hambleton.gov.uk), which has all the relevant Cook brochures and trail guides. Great Ayton has two nice **pubs**: the *Buck* at Low Green by the river and the *Royal Oak* on High Green.

Beck Hole and Goathland

South of Grosmont, train, footpath and beck climb out of the Esk Valley towards Goathland. Only on foot will you be able to stop at **BECK HOLE**, after a couple of miles, an idyllic bridgeside hamlet focused on the *Birch Hall Inn*, one of the finest rural pubs in all England – tiny to the point of claustrophobic, still doubling as a sweet shop and store as it has for a century, and serving great slabs of sandwiches with local ham and home-baked pies.

A gentle path from the hamlet runs the mile through the fields up to **GOATHLAND**, another highly attractive village, this time set in open moorland beneath the great expanses of Wheeldale and Goathland moors. If it seems oddly familiar – and if it seems unduly crowded – it's because it's widely known as "Aidensfield", the fictional village at the centre of the *Heartbeat* TV series. Pub, shop, garage and houses are all roped in to appear in most episodes: the large car parks tell of its popularity on the tourbus circuit. Outside summer weekends, when it's packed to distraction, Goathland can still be a joy to wander, with signposts pointing you to the local sight, the **Mallyan Spout**, a seventy-foot-high waterfall. This lies half a mile or so from the imposing, stone *Mallyan Spout Hotel* on the common (ⓣ01947/896486; ❺), itself the best place to stay, and certainly the best place to eat and drink; there are bar meals and a recommended restaurant. Plenty of other local **B&Bs** offer cheaper rooms, or you might like the idea of the *NYMR Camping Coach* (ⓣ01751/472508, ⓦwww.nymr.demon.co.uk; £350–600 per week, includes NYMR train pass), a converted, self-catering railway carriage parked right at Goathland Station.

The North Yorkshire coast

A bracing change after the flattened seascapes of East Anglia and much of East Yorkshire, the **North Yorkshire coast** is the southernmost stretch of a cliff-edged shore that stretches almost unbroken to the Scottish border. **Scarborough** is the biggest town and resort, and the terminus for bus and rail links from York and beyond. Like many places hereabouts it has tempting sands, though the vagaries of the northern climate and the chilly North Sea waters mean that you'll probably do little more than admire them from afar. Cute **Robin Hood's Bay** is the most popular of the many Yorkshire villages, with fishing and smuggling traditions, while bluff **Staithes** – a fishing harbour on the far edge of North Yorkshire – has yet to tip over into full-blown tourist mode. **Whitby**, in between the two, is the best stopover, its fine sands and resort facilities tempered by its abbey ruins, cobbled streets, Georgian buildings and maritime heritage – more than any other local place Whitby celebrates Captain Cook as one of its own. Heading to virtually any of the smaller coastal hamlets will bring you to similar-looking but far quieter spots, and for those who want to sample the most dizzying cliff-tops, the **Cleveland Way** provides a marked path along virtually the entire length of the coast.

Hourly **buses** (fewer on Sun) run along the A171 between Scarborough and Whitby, and a similarly frequent service operates to Robin Hood's Bay, and north between Whitby and Staithes. The Yorkshire Coastliner service connects Leeds and York with Scarborough (hourly) or Whitby (2–5 daily). You can also reach Scarborough direct by **train** from York or Hull, and Whitby from Middlesbrough.

Scarborough

The oldest resort in the country, **SCARBOROUGH** first attracted early-seventeenth-century visitors to its newly discovered mineral springs. By the 1730s, the more enterprising spa-goers were also venturing onto the sweeping local sands and dipping themselves in the bracing North Sea, popularizing the racy pastime of sea-bathing. Still fashionable in Victorian times – to whom it was "the Queen of the Watering Places" – Scarborough saw its biggest transformation after World War II, when it (and many other resorts) became a holiday haven for workers from the industrial heartlands. In the 1950s, three million visitors a year thronged the beaches, rode on the donkeys and paddled in the rock pools, enjoying the full-blooded facilities of a town that, in a memorable phrase of Paul Theroux's, "had the same ample contours as its landladies". The age of air travel changed the holiday demographics of all English resorts, but although numbers are down since its heyday, you wouldn't necessarily know it on a hot summer's day when there are long queues outside the seafront fish-and-chip shops and ice-cream stalls. All the traditional ingredients of a beach resort are here in force, from superb, clean sands, kitsch amusement arcades and Kiss-Me-Quick hats to the more refined pleasures of its tight-knit old-town streets and a genteel round of quiet parks and gardens.

Arrival, information and accommodation

The **train station** is at the top of town facing Westborough; **buses** pull up outside or in the surrounding streets, though the National Express services (direct from London) stop in the car park behind the station. Scarborough's **tourist office** is in Pavilion House, Valley Bridge Rd (daily: May–Sept 9.30am–6pm; Oct–April 10am–4.30pm; ⓣ01723/373333, ⓦwww.discoveryorkshirecoast.com), just over the road from the station, diagonally opposite the landmark Stephen Joseph Theatre. To reach the harbour and castle, walk straight down Westborough, Newborough and Eastborough, through the main shopping streets.

It's a fair hike from one end of Scarborough to the other; ease the strain by taking one of the open-top **seafront buses** (April–Sept daily from 9.30am, March weekends only; £1), which run throughout the season from the *Corner Café* in North Bay to the Spa Complex in South Bay.

Scarborough is crammed with inexpensive **hotels and guest houses**. In high season, if you arrive without a reservation, you'd do best to head straight for the tourist office and let them find something; at other times it's worth looking around for the best deals, since off-season prices often drop considerably. Happy hunting grounds include North Bay's Queen's Parade, where most of the guest houses have sweeping bay views and parking; to be closer to the castle head up its continuation, Blenheim Terrace, where a score more options await. The cheapest places in town are those without the sea views – try along central Aberdeen Walk (off Westborough), or on North Marine Road and Trafalgar Square, behind Queen's Parade. Above South Bay, hotels tend to be pricier, though there's a clutch of B&Bs along and around West Street.

Hotels and guest houses

Crown Esplanade ⓣ01723/357426, ⓦwww.chariethotels.co.uk. Built in 1847 in a Regency terrace above South Bay, the *Crown* makes the most of its period features, views and genteel feel. There's a gym, pool and brasserie. D,B&B rates offer the best deal. ❻

Interludes 32 Princess St ⓣ01723/360513, ⓦwww.interludeshotel.co.uk. Quiet, non-smoking, Georgian town house in the old-town streets behind the harbour. Bay views from the upper floors, and theatre bills, stage photographs, antiques, fresh flowers and traditional English decor throughout; call for details of Stephen Joseph Theatre breaks. It's a gay-friendly place, though all (except children) are welcome. ❸

Paragon 123 Queen's Parade ⓣ01723/372676, ⓦwww.paragon-hotel.demon.co.uk. Traditional, family-run B&B (some rooms with sea views), where an above-average breakfast lifts the spirits. Parking available. ❸

Red Lea Prince of Wales Terrace ⓣ01723/362431, ⓦwww.redleahotel.co.uk. Part of a stylish terrace above South Bay, boasting sea-view rooms and a small indoor pool. ❺

Riviera St Nicholas Cliff ⓣ01723/372277, ⓦwww.rivierahotel.scarborough.co.uk. Restored Victorian hotel opposite the *Grand* (down Bar St, off Westborough) with super bay views and comfortable en-suite rooms. ❹

Whiteley 99 Queen's Parade ⓣ01723/373514, ⓔwhiteleyhotel@bigfoot.com. Formerly a Victorian merchant's house (its best facade facing North Marine Road, around the back), this is one of the best Queen's Parade options with good-value en-suite rooms (a few pounds extra for a sea view). Parking available. ❷

Windmill Mill St, off Victoria Rd ⓣ01723/372735, ⓦwww.windmill-hotel.co.uk. Eighteenth-century windmill sited incongruously in the town centre with its country-style en-suite rooms (upper-floor ones with veranda) ranged around a cobbled courtyard; you take breakfast inside the mill dining room. Two family rooms available, plus two self-catering flats within the windmill tower. Parking. ❸

Wrea Head Country House Hotel Barmoor Lane, Scalby, 2 miles north of town ⓣ01723/378211, ⓦwww.englishrosehotels.co.uk. Peaceful country house outside Scarborough where traditionally furnished rooms (lush fabrics, canopied beds) all come with glorious rural views – the seaside bustle seems an age away. The room rate includes dinner. ❼

Youth hostel and campsites

Scalby Close Park Burniston Rd, 2 miles north of town ⓣ01723/365908. Tents and caravans. Closed Nov–Easter.

Scalby Manor Caravan Park Burniston Rd, 2 miles north of town ⓣ01723/366212. There are tent spaces at this huge site, handy for the North Bay. Closed Nov–Easter.

Scarborough YHA Burniston Rd, Scalby Mills, 2 miles north of town ⓣ0870/770 6022, ⓔscarborough@yha.org.uk. Occupies a converted watermill, off the A165, 10min walk from the Sea Life Centre and the sea; the Cleveland Way passes close by. Dorm beds cost £10.25; closed Sun & Mon in Sept & Oct, and closed Nov–Easter.

The Town

There's no better place to acquaint yourself with the local layout than from the walls of **Scarborough Castle** (daily: April–Sept 10am–6pm; Oct 10am–5pm; Nov–March 10am–4pm; £3; EH), mounted on a jutting headland between two golden-sanded bays east of the town centre. Bronze and Iron Age relics have been found on the wooded castle crag, together with fragments of a fourth-century Roman signalling station, Saxon and Norman chapels and a Viking camp, reputedly built by a Viking with the nickname of *Scardi* (or "hare-lip"), from which the town's name derives. The present castle consists mainly of a three-storey keep dating from the twelfth century, and a thirteenth-century barbican and raking buttressed walls that trace the cliff edge. Although besieged many times, the fortifications were never taken by assault, its only fall coming in the Civil War when the Parliamentarians starved the garrison into surrender. It took a further pounding from an infamous German naval bombardment of the town in 1914. As you leave the castle, drop into the **Church of St Mary** (1180), immediately below on Castle Road, whose graveyard contains the tomb of Anne Brontë, who died here in 1849.

The town museums are clustered around Valley Road, south of the train station; an "Annual Pass" (£3; valid for a year) gets you into each of them. The Victorian **Wood End** on The Crescent (June–Sept Tues–Sun 10am–5pm; Oct–May Wed, Sat & Sun 11am–4pm) was the holiday home of the Sitwell family of writers and aesthetes. There's a fine conservatory and various natural history collections, while in the adjacent **Art Gallery** (June–Sept Tues–Sun 10am–5pm; Oct–May Thurs, Fri & Sat 11am–4pm) you'll find changing art exhibitions. The nearby **Rotunda Museum** on Vernon Road (June–Sept Tues–Sun 10am–5pm; Oct–April Tues, Sat & Sun 11am–4pm; £2), housed in a circular Georgian rotunda of great refinement, holds the local archeological and historic finds, including Gristhorpe Man, a 3500-year-old local found buried with his grave goods in a hollowed oak trunk; there's also a diverting exhibition on the famous **Scarborough Fair**, first granted a charter by Henry III in 1253. After this, the chief distraction is the unexpected concentration of Pre-Raphaelite art in the **Church of St-Martin-on-the-Hill** (1863) further south on Albion Road. The Victorian-Gothic pile has a roof by William Morris, a triptych by Burne-Jones, a pulpit with four printed panels by Rossetti, stained glass by Morris, Burne-Jones and Ford Madox Brown, and an east wall whose tracery provides the frames for angels by Morris and *The Adoration of the Magi* by Burne-Jones.

The bays

Most of what passes for family entertainment takes place on the **North Bay** – massive water slides at Atlantis, the kids' amusements at Kinderland, and the miniature North Bay Railway (daily Easter–Sept), which runs up to the most educational of the lot, the **Sea Life Centre**, with its pools of flounders, rock-pool habitats and fishy exhibits. The most enjoyable **amusements and rides** are the old-fashioned ones on the harbour, under the castle, where creaky dodgems and shooting galleries compete for custom. From the harbourside here you'll be able to take one of the short **cruises and speedboat trips** that shoot off throughout the day in the summer; or look over the *Hatherleigh*, a deep-sea trawler permanently moored on the Lighthouse Pier.

The **South Bay** is more refined, backed by the pleasant Valley Gardens and the Italianate meanderings of the South Cliff Gardens, and topped by an esplanade from which a **hydraulic lift** (daily 10am–4pm, till 10pm July & Aug) putters down to the beach. Here, Scarborough's Regency and Victorian glories are still evident in hotels like the *Crown* and, most impressively of all, the **Grand Hotel** built in 1867 by Cuthbert Broderick, the shaper of central Leeds. Its six million bricks and fifty-two chimneys dominate the cliff top, an ensemble that drew high praise from architectural arbiter Nikolaus Pevsner, who thought it a "high Victorian gesture of assertion and confidence". For years now it's been operated as a pack-'em-in-cheap lodging house, which means no one will stop you if you stroll in through the still-grand interior, buy a drink at the bar and head out onto the gargantuan, neglected terrace from which the views of town, beach and castle are magnificent.

Eating, drinking and entertainment

Cafés, **fish-and-chip shops** and **tearooms** are thick on the ground: those down by the harbour are of variable quality and popularity, serving up fried food as fast as the punters can get it down. There's a more discerning selection when it comes to **restaurants**, not least because the town has a fair-sized Italian population – including the descendants of several POWs who were held at Malton's Eden Camp and settled in Scarborough after the war.

Virtually every street too has a **pub**, though few pass muster as the sort of place you might want to spend the entire evening – the best are picked out below. Finally, whatever the posters and advertising suggest, the cultural heart of Scarborough is not the Spa Complex or Futurist Theatre and their end-of-pier summer shows, but the renowned **Stephen Joseph Theatre**, a real North Yorkshire gem.

Cafés and restaurants

Bonnet 38–40 Huntriss Row, off Westborough. The Victorian-styled pedestrianized street has several coffee shops worth investigating: this one also opens for dinner (Wed–Sat until 9.30pm).

Café Italia 36 St Nicholas Cliff. Utterly charming, microscopic Italian coffee bar next to the *Grand*, where genuine coffee, focaccia slices and ice cream keep a battery of regulars happy. Closes 5pm.

Florio's 37 Aberdeen Walk, off Westborough ⓣ01723/351124. Cheery pasta-and-pizza restaurant, popular with families and parties, open evenings only. Moderate.

Gianni's 13 Victoria Rd ⓣ01723/507388. The most immediately welcoming of the town's Italian restaurants, housed in a Scarborough town house. The good-natured staff bustle up and down stairs, delivering quality pizzas, pastas and quaffable wine by the carafe. Moderate.

The Golden Grid 4 Sandside ⓣ01723/360922. The harbourside's choicest fish-and-chip establishment, "catering for the promenader since 1883". Offers grilled fish, a fruits-de-mer platter and a wine list alongside the standard crispy-battered fry-up. Closed Mon–Thurs dinner in winter. Inexpensive–Moderate.

Il Castello 34–36 Castle Rd ⓣ01723/377312. The town's best pizzas, and some inventive home-made pastas and other Italian dishes, at slightly higher prices than usual. Closed Mon & Tues. Moderate.

Lanterna 33 Queen St ⓣ01723/363616. Long-established, special-night-out destination, featuring traditional, seasonal Italian cooking in quiet, formal surroundings. Closed Sun. Expensive.

Peppers 11 York Place ⓣ01723/500642. Latin American flavours enhance an inviting menu, where specialities range from a grilled red mullet and roast pepper salad to tuna steak with a *salsa romesco*. Dinner only; closed Sun. Expensive.

Stephen Joseph Theatre Restaurant Westborough ⓣ01723/356655. Fashionable food in the theatre restaurant – sandwiches, pastas, fishcakes, noodles and salads at lunch, and seasonally changing Modern Brit dinners. Lunch Mon–Sat, dinner Thurs–Sat. Moderate.

Pubs

The Alma 1 Alma Parade, at the top of Westborough. A thoroughly decent local, just right for a quiet pint.

The Highlander 15–16 Esplanade, next to the *Crown*. A traditional lounge bar with beer garden. Its owner has a collection of over a thousand bottles of whisky – drams from around fifty of them are for sale.

Hole in the Wall 26 Vernon Rd. Cosy, real-ale haunt with beer-knowledgeable staff and good food (served noon–2pm).

Theatre

Stephen Joseph Theatre Westborough ⓣ01723/370541, ⓦwww.sjt.uk.com. Housed in a former Art Deco cinema, this premieres every new play of local playwright Alan Ayckbourn and promotes strong seasons of theatre and film; a good café/restaurant and bar is open daily except Sunday.

Hayburn Wyke and Ravenscar

At **Hayburn Wyke**, a tiny and tranquil bay mostly owned by the National Trust, Hayburn Beck runs through scrub and woodland before tumbling onto the rocky beach in a small waterfall. The waters have carved away layers of the surrounding boulder clay, making this a good spot to forage for fossils. The Cleveland Way cuts through from Scarborough, six miles to the south, but road access takes you only as far as the *Hayburn Wyke Hotel*, half a mile back from the beach, an arrangement which keeps the bay area and the adjoining 34-acre nature reserve remarkably unspoilt.

A back-lane drive, or a four-mile hike – one of the Cleveland Way's more exhilarating passages – over the five-hundred-foot ramparts of Beast Cliff, brings you to the village of **RAVENSCAR**, six hundred feet above the sea in the lee of tumuli-spotted Stoupe Brow (871ft). Views to the north around the sweep of Robin Hood's Bay are superb, particularly from the mock-battlemented *Raven Hall Hotel* (ⓣ01723/870353, ⓦwww.ravenhall.co.uk; ❼), constructed on the site of an old Roman signal station and used as a hideaway for George III when his bouts of madness kept him from the public gaze. There's a small charge for non-patrons to wander the hotel's panoramic cliff-edge terraces or to use the Yorkshire coast's most precariously sited and windswept swimming pool. The hotel marks the end of the Lyke Wake Walk (see p.1005), so it's not uncommon to see hikers celebrating with a beer in front of the open fire.

Close by is a National Trust **Coastal Centre** (Easter–Sept daily 10.30am–5pm; ⓣ01723/870138), which has displays on the village's dead-end streets and isolated houses, part of an 1895 scheme to create "another Scarborough", an enterprise foiled by the cliffs' unstable geology. The most detailed exhibits, however, relate to the area's alum mines. Quarries dot the Old Peak cliffs and the ridges of Stoupe Brow, where alum was mined between 1640 and 1862, the mineral being used in the leather and textile industry to fix dyes, and in the manufacture of candles and parchment. The industry declined in the nineteenth century, as chemical byproducts of the iron and steel foundries came to replace alum in many of the processes in which it had been used. The last mine closed in 1871, and a marked trail from the centre takes you past re-excavated workings.

Robin Hood's Bay

Although known as Robbyn Huddes Bay as early as Tudor times, there's nothing except half-remembered myth to link **ROBIN HOOD'S BAY** with Sherwood's legendary bowman – locals anyway prefer the old name, Bay Town or simply Bay. Among the best-known and most heavily visited spot on the coast, the village fully lives up to its reputation, with narrow streets and pink-tiled cottages toppling down the cliff-edge site, evoking the romance of a time when this was both a hard-bitten fishing community and smugglers' den *par excellence.* So packed together are the houses, legend has it that ill-gotten booty could be passed up the hill from cottage to cottage without the pursuing king's men being any the wiser.

From the upper village, lined with Victorian villas, now mostly B&Bs, it's a very steep walk down the hill to the harbour. Here, Bay is little more than a couple of narrow streets lined with gift shops and cafés, and a slipway that leads down to the curving, rocky shoreline. The **Old Coastguard Station** (June–Sept daily 10am–5pm; Oct–May weekends only; free; ⓣ01947/885900) has been turned into a visitor centre with displays relating to the area's geology and sealife. When the tide is out, the massive rock beds below are exposed, split by a geological fault line and studded with fossil remains. There's an easy circular walk (2.5 miles) to **Boggle Hole** and its youth hostel, a mile south, returning inland via South House Farm and the path along the old Scarborough–Whitby railway line (see "Hawsker" opposite). Back in the old village, a rash of second-hand bookshops has appeared, the biggest and best being The Old Chapel, in the old hillside Wesleyan Chapel. Author **Leo Walmsley** (1892–1966), who spent his childhood in Bay, was educated in the chapel's schoolroom and later wrote several novels of seaside life coloured by his experiences. One, *Three Fevers*, was filmed in Robin Hood's Bay and

Whitby as *Turn of the Tide* (1935), the first feature by the newly formed J. Arthur Rank organization.

Practicalities

The main approach, the B1447, comes in from the north off the A171, and drivers will have to leave their car in one of two **car parks** in the upper part of the village. **Buses** from Scarborough or Whitby, seven miles north, drop you here too. Whitby has the nearest train station, and the nearest tourist office; **walkers**, along the coastal Cleveland Way, can make Whitby to Robin Hood's Bay in around three hours.

Accommodation is plentiful, but often in short supply during high season. Many people see the village as a day-trip from Whitby, and you can check on Bay accommodation in the tourist office there, or simply stroll the streets of the lower, old part of the village to see if any of the small cottage **B&Bs** has got vacancies. *York House* on King St (ⓣ01947/880088, ⓦwww.robinhoodsbay.uk.com; ❷) is typical of what's on offer, a cosy Georgian house close to the harbour. There are also three good **pubs** in the lower village, two of which have rooms: the tiny *Laurel*, on Main Street (ⓣ01947/880400; ❶; two-night minimum), whose small self-catering flat sleeps two; and the *Bay Hotel*, right on the harbour (ⓣ01947/880278; ❸), which is the traditional start or end of the Coast-to-Coast Walk. As well as a score of guest houses in the upper village, there's the late-Victorian *Victoria Hotel*, Station Rd (ⓣ01947/880205; ❹), at the top of the hill, with fine views from some of its rooms, and a cliff-top beer garden.

You'll probably end up **eating** in the pubs – food at the *Bay Hotel* is the best – though the *Old Chapel* bookshop has a vegetarian café and great coastal views from its terrace tables; while Bay Fisheries, a wet-fish shop next to the *Laurel*, serves crab sandwiches to take away. The other pub, the eighteenth-century *Dolphin* in King Street, is the oldest in the village, and has folk nights every Friday.

Boggle Hole's **youth hostel** is one of Yorkshire's most popular, a former mill located in a wooded ravine about a mile south of Robin Hood's Bay at Mill Beck (ⓣ0870/770 5704, ⓔbogglehole@yha.org.uk; £10.25). Note that a torch is essential after dark, and that you can't access the hostel along the beach once the tide is up.

Hawsker

The twenty-mile Whitby to Scarborough railway line was a victim of the 1960s' cuts, though its length has been preserved as a bridleway that makes an alternative route to the Cleveland Way. The best section is undoubtedly that between Whitby and Ravenscar via Robin Hood's Bay, boasting huge views of the tumbling cliffs and sparkling sea. A couple of miles northwest of Robin Hood's Bay at **HAWSKER**, on the A171, Trailways (ⓣ01947/820207, ⓦwww.trailways.fsnet.co.uk) is a bike-rental outfit based in the old Hawsker train station, perfectly placed for day-trips along the largely flat railway line in either direction. They'll deliver or pick up from local addresses (including *Boggle Hole* youth hostel); there's also a refreshments kiosk at the station, and a small campsite and bunkhouse (call for details).

Whitby

If there's one essential stop on the North Yorkshire coast it's **WHITBY**, whose historical associations, atmospheric ruins, fishing harbour and intrinsic charm make it many people's favourite northern resort. The seventh-century abbey here made Whitby one of the key foundations of the early Christian period, and a centre of great learning, though little interfered with the fishing community that scraped together a living on the harbour banks of the River Esk below. For a thousand years, the local herring boats landed their catch until the great whaling boom of the eighteenth century transformed the fortunes of the town. Melville's *Moby Dick* makes much of Whitby whalers such as William Scoresby, while James Cook took his first seafaring steps from the town in 1746, on his way to becoming a national hero. All four of Captain Cook's ships of discovery – the *Endeavour*, *Resolution*, *Adventure* and *Discovery* – were built in Whitby, and a stunning replica *Endeavour* moors in the harbour most summers for guided visits (schedule available at ⓦwww.barkendeavour.com.au).

Bram Stoker and Dracula

For a moment or two I could see nothing, as the shadow of a cloud obscured St Mary's Church. Then as the cloud passed I could see the ruins of the Abbey coming into view; and as the edge of a narrow band of light as sharp as a sword-cut moved along, the church and churchyard became gradually visible... [It] seemed to me as though something dark stood behind the seat where the white figure shone, and bent over it. What it was, whether man or beast, I could not tell.

Dracula, Bram Stoker

It was, of course, the figure of the voracious Count, feasting upon the blood of Lucy. Her friend Mina Murray – despite "flying along the fish-market to the bridge" and "toiling" up the endless steps to the Abbey – failed to save her. The story of Dracula is well known, but it's this exact attention to the geographical detail of Whitby – little changed since Stoker first wrote the words – which has proved a huge attraction to visitors on the Dracula trail.

Bram Stoker was born in Dublin in 1847 and wrote his first stories while working in the Irish civil service. A meeting with Sir Henry Irving in 1877 led him to quit his job and move to London, where he became Irving's manager and close friend. Forgettable adventure novels followed, until in 1890, on holiday in Whitby, Stoker began to become interested in writing a story of vampires and the undead, already popularized in "Gothic" novels earlier that century. Using first-hand observation of a town he knew well – he stayed at a house on the West Cliff, now marked by a plaque – Stoker built a story which mixed real locations, legend, myth and historical fact: the grounding of Count Dracula's ship on Tate Hill Sands was based on an actual event reported in the local papers. The novel was published in 1897 and became synonymous with Stoker's name; it's been filmed, with varying degrees of faithfulness, dozens of times since, though no film version has yet used Whitby as a backdrop.

With many of the early chapters recognizably set in Whitby, it's hardly surprising that the town has cashed in on its **Dracula Trail**. The various sites – Tate Hill Sands, the abbey, church and steps, the graveyard, Stoker's house – can all be visited, while down on the harbourside the Dracula Experience attempts to pull in punters to its rather lame horror-show antics. Keen interest has also been sparked amongst the **Goth** fraternity, who now come to town en masse a couple of times a year (usually in late spring and around Halloween) for a vampire's ball, concerts and readings; at these times the streets are overrun with pasty-faced characters in Regency dress, wedding gowns, top hats and capes, meeting and greeting at their unofficial headquarters, the otherwise sedate *Elsinore* pub on Flowergate. A kind of truce has been called with the authorities at St Mary's Church, who understandably objected to the more lurid goings-on in the churchyard at midnight; these have largely been curtailed and now there's even a special Goths service held at the church.

Hemmed in by steep cliffs and divided by the River Esk, the town splits into two distinct halves joined by a swing bridge: the **old town** to the east, centred on a curving cobbled street of great character, and the newer (though mostly eighteenth- and nineteenth-century) town across the bridge, generally known as **West Cliff**, which is home to the quayside, most of the hotels and shops, and the few arcades, amusements and souvenir stalls that have been allowed to proliferate. Virtually everything you want to see is in or above the old town on the east side, principally the glorious Abbey ruins and St Mary's Church, and the Captain Cook Memorial Museum, though the town museum on the west side shouldn't be missed by anyone with a nostalgic bent.

Walkers should note that two of the best parts of the Cleveland Way depart from Whitby: southeast to Robin Hood's Bay (six miles) and northwest to Staithes (eleven miles), both along thrilling high-cliff sections.

Arrival and information

Trains on the Esk Valley line to Whitby from Middlesbrough, via Danby and Grosmont (for connections for the North Yorkshire Moors Railway), arrive at the station in Station Square, a couple of hundred yards south of the bridge to the old town. Most local buses leave from the adjacent **bus station**, though the Yorkshire Coastliner services (from Leeds, York and Pickering) and National Express buses (from London and York) sometimes stop around the corner on Langborne Road, just down from the tourist office. There's a **Travel Centre** (ⓣ01947/602146) in the train station, for all local transport enquiries.

Whitby's **tourist office** (daily: May–Sept 9.30am–6pm; Oct–April 10am–12.30pm & 1–4.30pm; ⓣ01947/602674, ⓦwww.discoveryorkshirecoast.com, ⓦwww.visitwhitby.com) is a right turn outside the train station to the corner of Langborne Road and New Quay Road, and will book accommodation.

Accommodation

The main **B&B** concentrations are on West Cliff, in the streets stretching back from the elegant Royal Crescent. Across the river in the old town, several pubs have rooms, while if you're prepared to travel a couple of miles out of Whitby you can find some pleasant inns and hotels in relaxed country surroundings. For superior **holiday cottages** in town, contact Shoreline Cottages (ⓣ0113/289 3539, ⓦwww.shoreline-cottages.com) or Coast Cottages (ⓣ01947/821390, ⓦwww.coastcottages.co.uk).

Hotels, B&Bs and guest houses

Beehive Newholm ⓣ01947/602703. Isolated country pub in a hamlet a couple of miles inland, reached on the Sandsend road, with a roaring log fire in winter and sunny space outside in summer. ❸

Bramblewick 3 Havelock Place ⓣ01947/604504, ⓦwww.bramblewick.co.uk. Rather grand Victorian house which retains its original fireplaces and wrought-iron balconies. The old attic rooms at the top have the best views. Two-night minimum stay. ❷

Duke of York Church St ⓣ01947/600324. At the bottom of the 199 steps, this popular pub has en-suite rooms overlooking the harbour, and is only a few steps from the harbour beach. ❷

Dunsley Hall Dunsley ⓣ01947/893437. Quite the grandest retreat in the locality, this stately oak-panelled pile has all the trimmings, including a pool, sauna and leisure club, a good restaurant and very cosy bar. It's a couple of miles inland (west) of town. ❼

Estbek House Sandsend ⓣ01947/893424, ⓦwww.fastfix.com/estbek. Georgian house with five rooms, restaurant and tea garden, overlooking the stream at Sandsend, a couple of miles from Whitby, just yards from the beach and next to a good pub. ❹

Middle Earth 26 Church St ⓣ01947/606014. A nice pub with rooms, decent beer and outdoor seats overlooking the marina. It's the other way down Church St from the 199 steps, back past the bridge and along the river. No credit cards. ❷

Number Five 5 Havelock Place ⓣ01947/606361. Amiable West Cliff B&B that provides a good breakfast (veggie options available) and has a laid-back atmosphere. There are four doubles and a couple of singles, each with small but smart shower rooms. No credit cards. ❷

Shepherd's Purse 95 Church St ⓣ01947/820228. Popular wholefood shop and restaurant with its best rooms (with brass bedsteads and pine furniture) set around a galleried courtyard. The two pricier doubles on the upper level are nicest; one has its own balcony. Vegetarian breakfast available. ❸

White Horse & Griffin 87 Church St ⓣ01947/604857, ⓦwww.whitehorseandgriffin.co.uk. Easily the most atmospheric place to stay in the old town – a welcoming eighteenth-century coaching inn with stylishly decorated en-suite rooms (some have antique panelling, others a rooftop view), open fires and a good restaurant. Ask about their country house B&B at nearby Sandsend or the old-town self-catering cottages. ❹

White Linen 24 Bagdale ⓣ01947/603635. Superior B&B in a restored Georgian house, not far from the train station. Beds and, of course, linen are top-notch. Limited parking available. ❹

Hostels

Harbour Grange Spital Bridge, Church St ⓣ01947/600817, ⓦwww.whitbybackpackers.co.uk. Non-smoking backpackers on the eastern side of the river with 24 beds in five small dorms (£9–10, plus £1 for bedding if you don't have your own). Self-catering kitchen and lounge; curfew at 11.30pm.

Whitby Backpackers 28 Hudson St ⓣ01947/601794, ⓦwww.thewhitbybackpackers.co.uk. Easy-going and immaculatey clean, this West Cliff hostel has 19 beds (from £10) in a variety of rooms, including a couple of twin/double rooms and en-suite family rooms (both ❶). There's a kitchen and lounge, lovely garden, free tea and coffee, and no curfew. Closed Jan & Feb.

Whitby YHA East Cliff ⓣ0870/770 6088, ⓔwhitby@yha.org.uk. A converted stable a stone's throw from the abbey, with superb views over the town. One room sleeps two (❶), otherwise beds (£10.25) in variously sized dorms – book well in advance. Self-catering kitchen, evening meal available. Open weekends only Nov–March.

The old town

Cobbled **Church Street** is the old town's main thoroughfare, barely changed in aspect since the eighteenth century, though now lined with tearooms and gift shops, many selling jewellery and ornaments made from **jet**. This hard, black natural carbon, found locally, was worn first by the Romans but received its greatest boost after being shown at the Great Exhibition of 1851, after which it was popularized as mourning wear. In nineteenth-century Whitby, the industry employed over a thousand people, many working in factories around Church Street; now just a handful of workshops remain. Parallel **Sandgate** has more of the same, the two streets meeting at the small marketplace where souvenirs and trinkets are sold; there's a famer's market here every Thursday. Off either side, impossibly skinny alleys ("yards") – once gated, to keep out thieves – lead to quiet courtyards and flower-decked cottages.

Whitby, understandably, likes to make a fuss of Captain Cook who served an apprenticeship here from 1746–49 under John Walker, a Quaker shipowner. The **Captain Cook Memorial Museum** (Easter–Oct daily 9.45am–5pm; March Sat & Sun 11am–3pm; £3; ⓦwww.cookmuseumwhitby.co.uk), housed in Walker's rickety old house in Grape Lane (on the east side of the swing bridge), contains an impressive amount of memorabilia, including ships' models, letters and paintings by artists seconded to Cook's voyages. The 18-year-old Cook assisted on the coal runs between Newcastle and London, learning his seafaring skills in flat-bottomed craft called "cats". Designed for inshore and river work their specifications were to prove perfect for Cook's later surveys of the South Sea Islands and the Australian coast. When he wasn't at sea, Cook, together with the other apprentices, slept in Walker's attic.

At the north end of Church Street, you climb the famous **199 steps** of the Church Stairs – now paved, but originally a wide wooden staircase built for

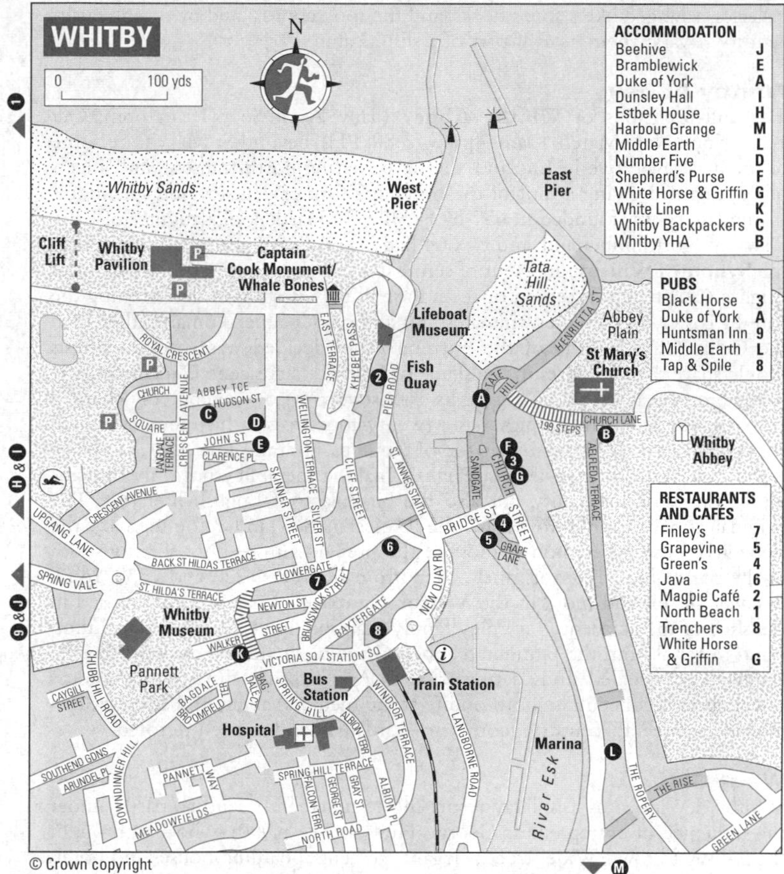

pallbearers carrying coffins to the church of St Mary above. Having made the climb, you've followed in the fictional footsteps of Bram Stoker's **Dracula**, who in the eponymous novel (see box p.1024) takes the form of a large dog that bounds up the steps after the wreck of the ship bearing his coffin. In the precarious cliffside graveyard he claimed Lucy as his victim, taking refuge in the grave of a suicide victim, which he then used as a base for his nocturnal forays. On wild and windswept nights the atmosphere up here is still suitably ghoulish; during the day, the views over the harbour and town are magnificent, while a little searching reveals the grave of William Scoresby Snr, master whaler, and inventor of the crow's nest.

The bizarre parish church of **St Mary** at the top of the steps, loftily removed from the town it served, is an architectural dog's dinner dating back to 1110, boasting a Norman chancel arch, a profusion of eighteenth-century panelling, box pews unequalled in England and a triple-decker pulpit – note the built-in ear trumpets, added for the benefit of a nineteenth-century rector's deaf wife. The Cholmley family pew, in particular, almost obscuring the chancel, is superb, a capricious confection of twisting wooden columns. Notice also the galleries, arranged like a ship's decks, and the roof, constructed by seventeenth-century naval carpenters as if part of a ship's cabin.

Whitby Abbey

The cliff-top ruins of **Whitby Abbey** (daily: April–Sept 10am–6pm; Oct 10am–5pm, Nov–March 10am–4pm; £3.80; EH), beyond St Mary's, are some of the most evocative in England, the nave, soaring north transept and lancets of the east end giving a hint of the building's former delicacy and splendour. Its monastery was founded in 657 by St Hilda of Hartlepool, daughter of King Oswy of Northumberland, and by 664 had become important enough to host the **Synod of Whitby**, an event of seminal importance in the development of English Christianity. It settled once and for all the question of determining the date of Easter, and adopted the rites and authority of the Roman rather than the Celtic Church. One of the burning issues decided was whether priests should shave their tonsures in the shape of a ring or a crescent. **Caedmon**, one of the brothers at the abbey during its earliest years who was reputedly charged with looking after Hilda's pigs, has a twenty-foot cross to his memory which stands in front of St Mary's, at the top of the steps. His nine-line *Song of Creation* is the earliest surviving poem in English, making the abbey not only the cradle of English Christianity, but also the birthplace of English literature. The original abbey was destroyed by the Danes in 867 and refounded by the Benedictines in 1078, though most of the present ruins – built slightly south of the site of the Saxon original – date from between 1220 and 1539. You'll discover all this and more in the **Visitor Centre** (hours as above), housed in the shell of the adjacent Cholmley family mansion, built after the Dissolution using material from the plundered abbey. Ongoing archeological work on the headland has yielded finds dating back to Anglo-Saxon times, while audio-visual displays concentrate both on life at the medieval abbey and at the house, whose seventeenth-century geometric "hard" garden has been restored.

West Cliff

Whitby developed as a holiday resort in the nineteenth century, partly under the influence of entrepreneur George Hudson (see p.990), who had brought the railway to town. Wide streets, elegant crescents, boarding houses and hotels were laid on the heights of **West Cliff**, across the harbour from the old town, topped by a whalebone arch, commemorating Whitby's former industry, and a statue of Captain Cook. The small **harbour front** below, along Pier Road, sports an active fish market and a run of arcades and chip shops, leading to the twin, pincered piers and lighthouses: when the tide's out, the broad, clean sands to the west stretch for three miles to **Sandsend** (where the beer garden of the *Hart Inn* makes a tempting target).

More matters maritime are explored in the **Whitby Lifeboat Museum** (irregular hours; donation requested), on Pier Road, the best museum of its kind in the country. Whitby lifeboat crews over the years have won more RNLI gold medals for gallantry than any other crew in Britain; you'd envy none of them the job, particularly after seeing one exhibit, the last RNLI hand-rowed boat, a flimsy-looking craft used until well into the twentieth century. A more recent lifeboat now carries passengers out of the harbour on short **cruises**, leaving from near the bandstand most summer days.

Final port of call should be the gloriously eccentric **Whitby Museum** in Pannett Park (May–Sept Mon–Sat 9.30am–5.30pm, Sun 2–5pm; Oct–April Tues 10am–1pm, Wed–Sat 10am–4pm, Sun 2–4pm; £2.50), up the hill from the train station. There's more Cook memorabilia, including various ethnic

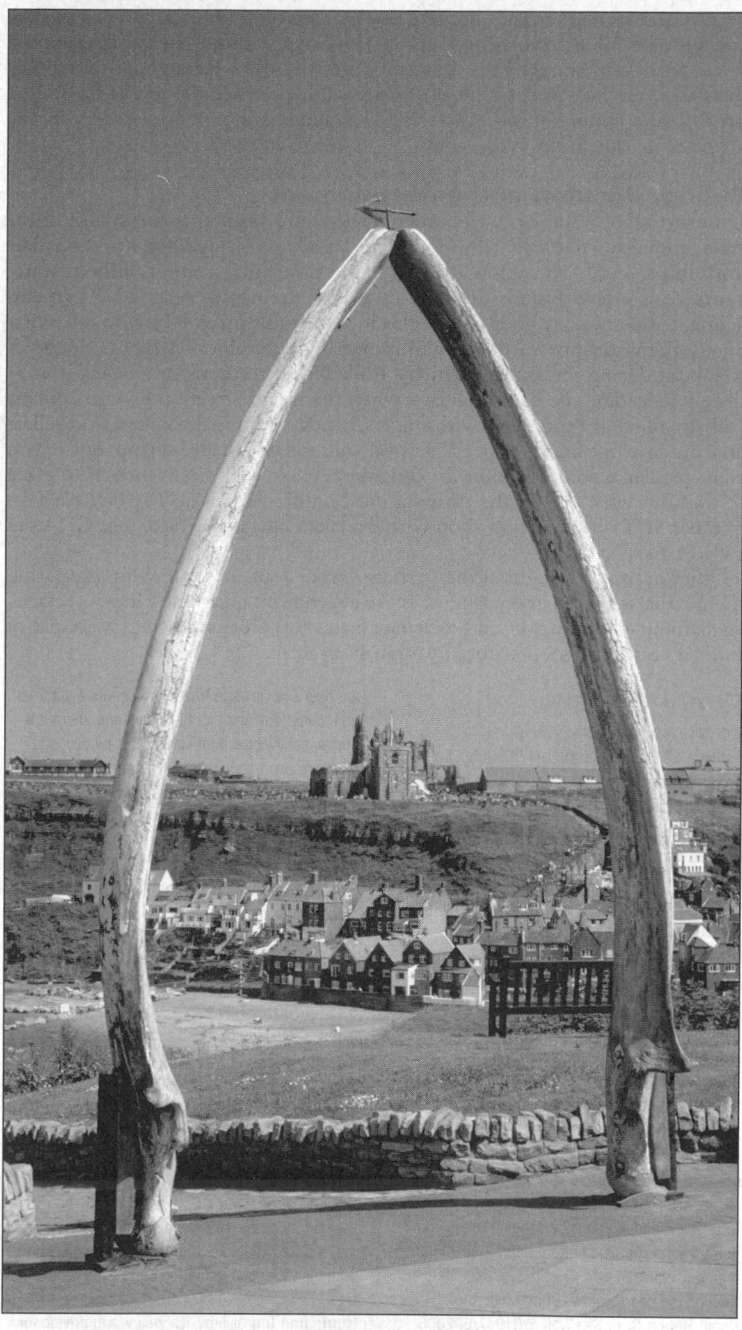

△ Whalebone arch

objects and stuffed animals brought back as souvenirs by his crew, as well as casefuls of exhibits devoted to Whitby's seafaring tradition, its whaling industry in particular. Some of the best and largest fossils of Jurassic period reptiles unearthed on the east coast are also preserved here, while the rest of the museum is a fine jumble of local material, all carefully annotated in spidery handwriting and on clunky typed cards.

Eating, drinking and entertainment

Unsurprisingly, Whitby is well known for its freshly caught fish. A multitude of cafés around town – especially along Pier Road and Bridge Street – serve **fish and chips**, bread and tea for around £4; the same thing in most of the **restaurants** costs a few pounds more. Whitby is at the centre of the local **music scene**, with especially good folk nights in some of its **pubs** – English folk's first family, the Waterson/Carthys, are from nearby Robin Hood's Bay. It all comes to a head during the annual **Whitby Folk Week** in August (the week immediately preceding the bank holiday), when the town's streets, pubs and concert halls are filled day and night with singers, bands, traditional dancers, storytellers and music workshops. A special festival campsite is usually set up, but if you want regular accommodation for this week, book well in advance. Best place to find out what's on in the thriving local music scene is at *The Port Hole*, 16 Skinner St, a fair trade craft shop with excellent attached world/folk CD store called Folk Devils.

Other festivals throughout the year also make a splash, some with a seafaring theme; the **Regatta** every August is a weekend of fairground rides, spectacular harbourside fireworks and boat races; and the **Goths** descend a couple of times a year for a good-natured vampiric vacation.

Café-bars and restaurants

Finley's 22 Flowergate ⓣ01947/606660. Easy-going café-bar with deep sofas, playing soulful tunes and dishing up gourmet sandwiches, *nachos*, pasta, fish cakes and the like. Inexpensive.

Grapevine 2 Grape Lane ⓣ01947/820275. Tiny, funky, dinner-only place serving tapas-style meals, from creamy butter-bean stew to Spanish chicken. Closed Sun & Mon. Inexpensive.

Green's 13 Bridge St ⓣ01947/600284. Whitby's best and most relaxed restaurant, where chef Rob Green produces stylish meals – using local fish, lamb and game – with contemporary flavours. Reservations essential. Expensive.

Java 2 Flowergate ⓣ01947/821973. From early till late, seven days a week, this place offers cappuccino, latte, all-day breakfasts, grilled sandwiches and the daily papers. Inexpensive.

Magpie Café 14 Pier Rd ⓣ01947/602058. The traditional fish-and-chip choice in town for over forty years, and with a wide-ranging menu if you don't want something battered and fried. In summer you'll have to wait in long queues to get through the doors. Closes 9pm. Moderate.

North Beach Café Sea Wall ⓣ01947/602066. The roof-terrace of the Art Deco beach café has the best sea views in town, and serves a summer grill menu (day and night). Downstairs, there are drinks, sandwiches and light meals by day, and Mediterranean-style fish and meat mains at dinner; an open fire keeps things cosy in winter (when it's open during the day and on selected evenings). Moderate.

Trenchers New Quay Rd ⓣ01947/603212. Highly rated fish-and-chip restaurant, near the tourist office, with snappy service and mountainous portions – nearly always a queue in summer. Closes 9pm & all Nov–March. Moderate.

White Horse & Griffin 87 Church St, ⓣ01947/604857. Well-cooked local fish and game, served in cosy bistro surroundings. Expensive.

Pubs and live music

Black Horse 91 Church St. Idiosyncratic old-town "heritage" pub with a tiny front bar and good Tetley's beer.

Duke of York Church St. Classic Whitby pub, at the bottom of the 199 steps, with harbour views and a mixed clientele of tourists and locals who come for the good-value food and occasional music.

Huntsman Inn Aislaby. It's well worth driving (or cabbing) out the couple of miles to Aislaby for the

home-cooked pub food here – steaks a speciality.
Middle Earth 26 Church St. Regular music nights at this local, down by the marina – outdoor seats provide harbour views.

Tap & Spile New Quay Rd. The town's real-ale haunt, with a changing selection of guest beers and live music nearly every night.

Staithes

Beyond the beach at Sandsend, a fine coastal walk through pretty Runswick Bay leads in around four hours to the fishing village of **STAITHES**; road access is along the A174. At first sight, it's an improbably beautiful grouping of huddled stone houses around a small harbour, backed by the severe outcrop of Cowbar Nab, a sheer cliff face which protects the northern flank of the village. There's much less tourism here than in Robin Hood's Bay, which means few if any gift shops and only a smattering of cafés and B&Bs. Any time spent here, especially out of season, soon reveals its gruffer side – crumbling houses on either side of the beck, the fierce winter wind whistling down the cobbled main street, and the tenacious last gasp of a declining fishing fleet which once employed 300 men in 120 boats. Storms and floods have battered Staithes for centuries: the *Cod and Lobster*, the pub on the harbour, has been rebuilt three times and is shuttered against the wind, while the draper's shop in which James Cook first worked before moving to Whitby collapsed completely in 1745 – its rebuilt successor is now marked by a plaque. Cook is remembered in the **Captain Cook and Staithes Heritage Centre**, on the High Street (daily 10am–5.30pm; £2.50), which re-creates an eighteenth-century street among other interesting exhibits. Other than this, you'll have to content yourself with pottering about the rocks near the harbour – there's no beach to speak of – or clambering the nearby cliffs for spectacular views; at **Boulby**, a mile and a half's trudge up the coastal path (45min), you're walking on the highest cliff (670ft) on England's east coast. You may also be interested to learn that the coast between Whitby and Staithes has some of the best **surf** waves in Britain and there's quite a local community dedicated to riding them – details and gear from Zero Gravity (ⓣ01947/820660), Whitby's surfshop at 14 Flowergate.

Practicalities

The road into Staithes, off the A174, puts drivers into a **car park** at the top of the hill leading down into the old village; don't ignore the signs and drive down, since there's nowhere to park, and it's hard work turning round again. There's no tourist office, though ⓦwww.staithes-holidays.co.uk is a useful website.

You could stay at one of the B&Bs in the houses at the top of the village, but better **accommodation** is available down below, either at *Brooklyn* (ⓣ01947/841396; ❷), a comfortable B&B in a former sea captain's house on Brown's Terrace – just off the steep road down, on the right – or at the *Endeavour Restaurant* (ⓣ01947/840825, ⓦwww.endeavour-restaurant.co.uk; ❹). The latter, incidentally, is the best place to eat for miles around, with superb (but pricey) fresh fish meals (dinner only; closed Sun & Mon, except bank holidays). The *Black Lion* (ⓣ01947/841132; ❷) in the village has functional bedrooms, cosy fires and a decent bar menu. There's **camping** back up the road out of the village at *Staithes Caravan Park*, Warp Mill (ⓣ01947/840291; closed Nov–Feb).

Alternatively, drive the three miles south (back towards Whitby) to **Runswick Bay**, a tiny little one-pub-village-and-beach, where the *Cliffemount Hotel* (ⓣ01947/840103, ⓦwww.cliffemounthotel.co.uk;) glories in its elevated position. It has a good sea-facing restaurant too, specializing in locally caught seafood.

Travel details

Buses

Details of minor and seasonal local bus services are frequently given in the text. It's essential to pick up either the Dales Explorer or Moors Explorer timetable booklets from a local tourist office if visiting those parts of the county. For details of the Moorsbus in the North York Moors National Park see p.1004. For information on all other local and national bus services, contact Traveline ⓣ0870/608 2608 (daily 7am–9pm), ⓦwww.traveline.org.uk.

Harrogate to: Knaresborough (every 10min; 15min); Leeds (every 30–60min; 40min); Pateley Bridge (hourly; 50min); Ripon (every 30min; 30min); York (hourly; 1hr 15min).

Helmsley to: Pickering (hourly; 40min); Scarborough (hourly; 1hr 30min); York (3 daily; 1hr 30min).

Pickering to: Helmsley (3–7 daily; 40min); Scarborough (hourly; 1hr); Whitby (5 daily; 1hr); York (hourly; 1hr 20min).

Richmond to: Masham (Mon–Sat hourly; 50min); Ripon (Mon–Sat hourly; 1hr 15min).

Scarborough to: Bridlington (hourly; 1hr 15min); Filey (hourly; 30min); Helmsley (hourly; 1hr 30min); Hull (1 daily; 2hr); Leeds (hourly; 3hr); Pickering (hourly; 1hr); Robin Hood's Bay (hourly; 45min); Whitby (hourly; 1hr); York (hourly; 1hr 45min).

Skipton to: Grassington (Mon–Sat hourly; 30min); Malham (4 daily; 35min); Settle (Mon–Sat hourly; 40min).

Whitby to: Robin Hood's Bay (hourly; 25min); Staithes (hourly; 30min); York (4–5 daily; 2hr).

York to: Beverley (4 daily; 1hr 15min); Harrogate (hourly; 1hr 15min); Hull (5 daily; 1hr 30min); Pickering (hourly; 1hr 15min); Whitby (4–5 daily; 2hr).

Trains

Main routes and services are given below. For more detailed information about specific lines, turn to the following pages: Settle to Carlisle Railway p.952; North Yorkshire Moors Railway p.1014; Keighley and Worth Valley Railway p.937.

Harrogate to: Knaresborough (every 30min; 15min); Leeds (every 30min; 45min); York (hourly; 30min).

Hull to: Beverley (Mon–Sat hourly, Sun 4 daily; 15min); Leeds (hourly; 1hr); London (3–4 daily; 2hr 45min); Scarborough (every 2hr; 1hr 30min); York (10 daily; 1hr 15min).

Knaresborough to: Harrogate (every 30min; 15min); Leeds (every 30min; 45min); York (hourly; 30min).

Leeds to: Birmingham (10 daily; 2hr); Bradford (every 15min; 20min); Carlisle (3–9 daily; 2hr 40min); Harrogate (every 30min; 45min); Hull (hourly; 1hr); Knaresborough (every 30min; 45min); Lancaster (3 daily; 2hr); Liverpool (hourly; 2hr); London (every 30min; 2hr); Manchester (every 30min; 35min); Scarborough (every 30–60min; 1hr 15min); Settle (3–8 daily; 1hr); Sheffield (every 30min; 45min–1hr 15min); Skipton (hourly; 40min); York (every 30min; 40min).

Pickering to: Grosmont (April–Oct 5–8 daily, plus limited winter service; 1hr).

Scarborough to: Hull (every 2hr; 1hr 30min); Leeds (hourly; 1hr 15min); York (every 30–60min; 45min).

Sheffield to: Leeds (every 30min; 45min–1hr 15min); London (every 45min; 2hr 30min); York (hourly; 1hr 20min).

Whitby to: Danby (4–5 daily; 35min); Egton Bridge (4–5 daily; 20min); Great Ayton (4–5 daily; 1hr 10min); Grosmont (4–5 daily; 15min); Middlesbrough (4–5 daily; 1hr 30min).

York to: Birmingham (10 daily; 2hr 40min); Bristol (10 daily; 4hr); Bradford (every 45min; 1hr); Durham (every 30min; 40min); Edinburgh (hourly; 2hr); Exeter (5 daily; 5hr); Harrogate (hourly; 30min); Hull (hourly; 1hr 15min); Leeds (every 30min; 40min); London (every 30min; 2hr); Manchester (hourly; 1hr 45min); Newcastle (every 30min; 1hr); Penzance (4 daily; 7hr 30min); Scarborough (8–15 daily; 45min); Sheffield (hourly; 1hr 20min).

13

The Northeast

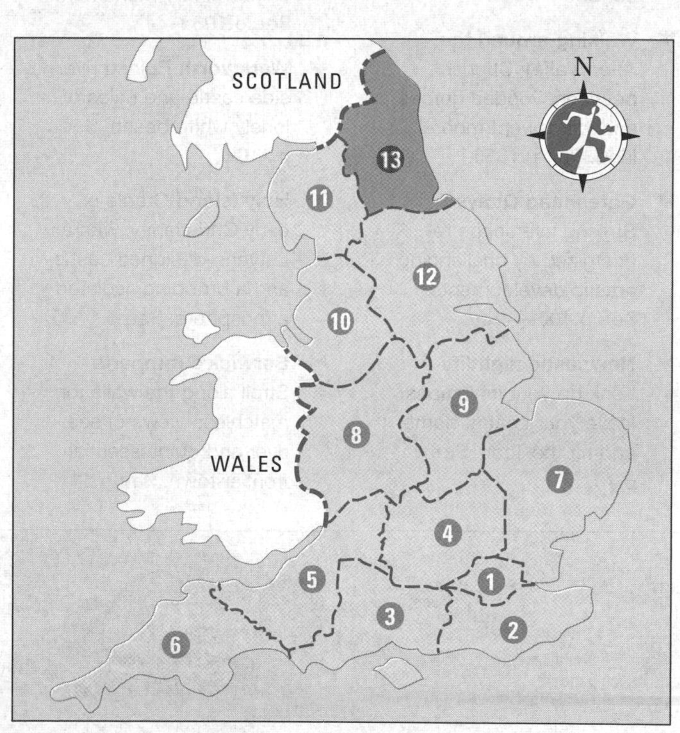

CHAPTER 13

Highlights

* **Durham Cathedral** Awe-inspiring Romanesque church towering above the River Wear. See p.1042

* **Beamish Museum** The northeast's industrial past poignantly re-created. See p.1047

* **Walking around the Allen Valley** Choose between wooded gorges and windswept moorland. See p.1055

* **Gateshead Quays** Striking riverscape re-energized by challenging artistic developments. See p.1069

* **Newcastle nightlife** Lock up your inhibitions, leave your coat at home and hit the Toon. See p.1073

* **Bede's World** Fascinating evocation of the life and times of one of Europe's greatest scholars. See p.1079

* **Hadrian's Wall** Put your walking boots on to make the most of this extraordinary monument. See p.1084

* **Warkworth** Ruined riverside castle and miles of lonely white beach. See p.1102

* **Holy Island** Cradle of early Christianity, with a Lutyens-designed castle and a brooding, isolated atmosphere. See p.1109

* **Berwick's ramparts** Stroll along the walls for matchless views of sea, river and quintessential frontier town. See p.1112

△ Hadrian's Wall

13

The Northeast

For England's northeastern region – in particular the counties of **Northumberland** and **Durham** – the period between the Roman invasion and the 1603 union of the English and Scottish crowns was one of almost incessant turbulence. To mark the empire's limit and to contain the troublesome tribes of the far north, **Hadrian's Wall** was built along the 76 miles between the North Sea and the west coast, an extraordinary military structure that is now one of the country's most evocative ruins. When the Romans departed, the northeast was divided into unstable Saxon principalities until order was restored by the kings of Northumbria, who dominated the region from 600 until the 870s. It was they who nourished the region's early Christian tradition, which achieved its finest flowering with the creation of the **Lindisfarne Gospels** on what is now known as Holy Island. The monks abandoned their island at the end of the ninth century, in advance of the Vikings' destruction of the Northumbrian kingdom, and only after the Norman Conquest did the northeast again become part of a greater England. The Norman kings and their successors repeatedly attempted to subdue Scotland, passing effective regional control to powerful local lords, whose authority is recalled by a sequence of formidable **fortresses** dotted along the Northumbrian coast.

Long after the northeast had ceased to be a critical military zone, its character and appearance were transformed by the **Industrial Revolution**. Coal had been mined here for hundreds of years, but exploitation only began in earnest towards the end of the eighteenth century, when two main coalfields were established – one dominating County Durham from the Pennines to the sea, the other stretching north along the Northumberland coast from the Tyne. The world's first railway, the Darlington and Stockton line, was opened in 1825 to move coal to the nearest port for export, while local coal and ore also fuelled the foundries that supplied the shipbuilding and heavy-engineering companies of Tyneside.

Most visitors from the south dodge the industrial areas, bypassing the towns along the **Tees Valley** – Darlington, Stockton, Middlesbrough and Hartlepool – on the way to **Durham**, the region's biggest historical attraction. It's a handsome university city, dominated by Durham Cathedral, the magnificent twelfth-century church of the Prince Bishops of Durham, who once ruled the whole of the county. From Durham it's a short hop to **Newcastle upon Tyne**, distinguished by some fine Victorian buildings, the revitalized Quayside, and a vibrant cultural scene and nightlife. North, past the old colliery villages, the **Northumberland coast** boasts some superb castles – most impressively at

Edinburgh
Berwick-upon-Tweed
0 5 10 miles
N
Norham Castle
Tweed
A697
B6354
Holy Island
SCOTLAND
Coldstream
A698
Etal Castle
Beal
Waren Mill
Cornhill-on-Tweed
Ford
Farne Islands
Branxton
Bamburgh
Edinburgh
Tweed
A697
B6525
Belford
Seahouses
Beadnell
Kirk Yetholm
Wooler
Newton-by-the-Sea
A1
Chillingham Castle
Embleton
The Cheviot (2,674ft)
Dunstanburgh Castle
Craster
B1340
A68
A697
Alnwick
Alnmouth
A1
THE CHEVIOT HILLS
Warkworth
Byrness
Amble
Cragside
NORTHUMBERLAND NATIONAL PARK
Rothbury
REDESDALE
Brinkburn Priory
A697
Kielder
KIELDER FOREST PARK
Otterburn
NORTH SEA
Falstone
Kielder Water
Ashington
Stannersburn
Greenhaugh
Cambo
Wallington
Morpeth
Bellingham
Bedlington
A189
Blyth
N. Tyne
NORTHUMBERLAND
A68
Belsay
A1
Seaton Delaval

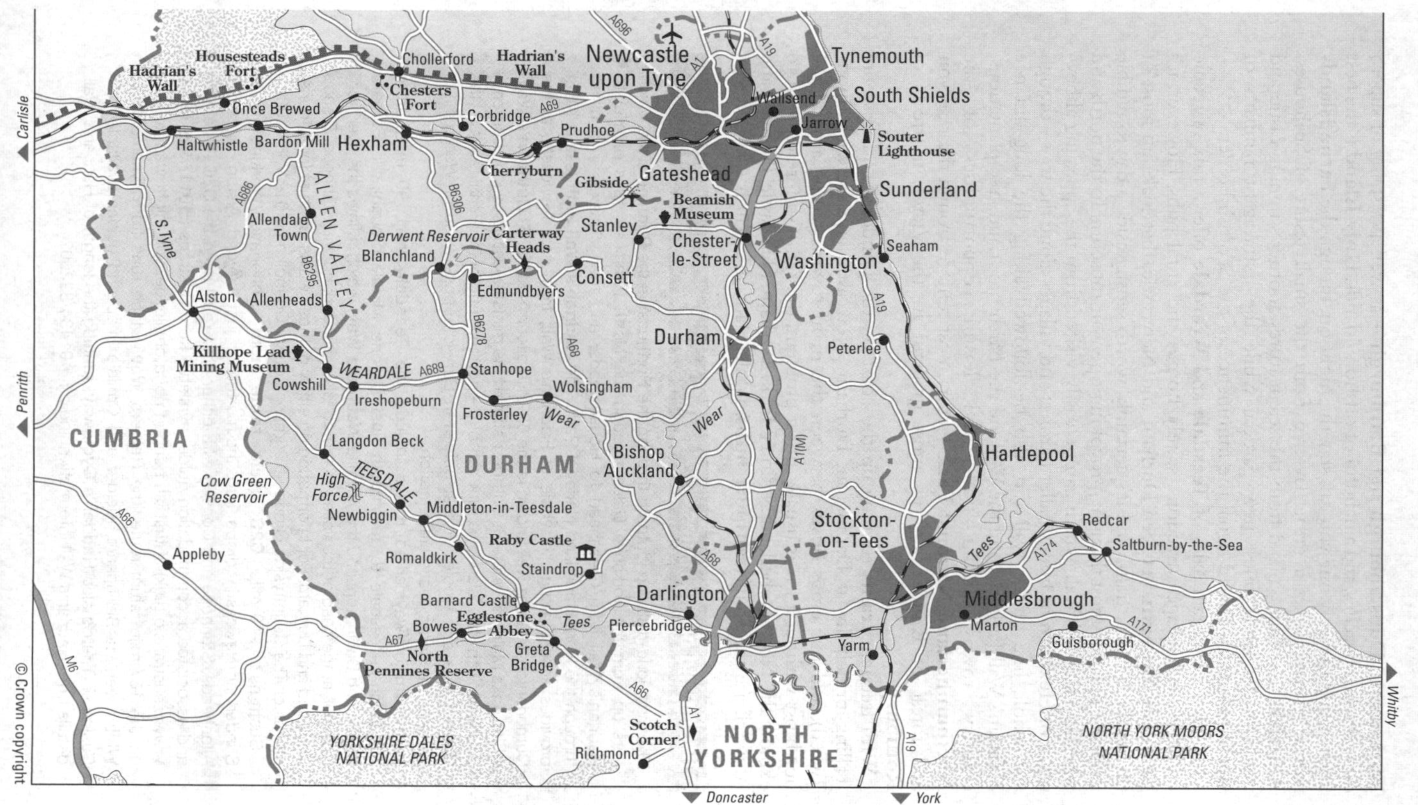
Newcastle upon Tyne
Tynemouth
South Shields
Wallsend
Jarrow
Souter Lighthouse
Gateshead
Sunderland
Beamish Museum
Stanley
Chester-le-Street
Washington
Seaham
Hadrian's Wall
Housesteads Fort
Chollerford
Chesters Fort
Once Brewed
Corbridge
Prudhoe
Haltwhistle
Bardon Mill
Hexham
Cherryburn
Gibside
ALLEN VALLEY
Allendale Town
S.Tyne
Derwent Reservoir
Carterway Heads
Blanchland
Consett
Edmundbyers
Alston
Allenheads
Durham
Peterlee
Killhope Lead Mining Museum
WEARDALE
Stanhope
Wolsingham
Cowshill
Ireshopeburn
Frosterley
Wear
CUMBRIA
Langdon Beck
DURHAM
Bishop Auckland
A1(M)
Hartlepool
Cow Green Reservoir
High Force
TEESDALE
Middleton-in-Teesdale
Newbiggin
Stockton-on-Tees
Redcar
Saltburn-by-the-Sea
Raby Castle
Romaldkirk
Staindrop
Appleby
Darlington
Middlesbrough
Barnard Castle
Egglestone Abbey
Tees
Piercebridge
Marton
Bowes
Greta Bridge
Yarm
Guisborough
North Pennines Reserve
Scotch Corner
Richmond
NORTH YORKSHIRE
YORKSHIRE DALES NATIONAL PARK
NORTH YORK MOORS NATIONAL PARK
A696
A1
A19
A69
A686
B6306
B6295
B6278
A68
A689
A66
A67
A174
A171
M6
Carlisle
Penrith
Doncaster
York
Whitby

Warkworth, **Dunstanburgh** and **Bamburgh** – as well as a string of superb dune-backed beaches, and a handful of offshore islands. **Holy Island** is the best known, and the only one you can stay the night on, though the **Farne Islands** nature reserve makes a great day-trip from the small resort of Seahouses. **Alnwick**, four miles inland from the sea, features another stunning castle and northern England's finest new garden, while the extravagant ramparts of **Berwick-upon-Tweed** signal the imminence of the Scottish border.

Inland, the Durham dales of **Teesdale** and **Weardale** offer a mix of scenic countryside, heritage attractions, stately homes and rural pubs. However, it's **Beamish Museum**, between Durham and Newcastle, that soaks up most of the regional visitor traffic and it's certainly worth setting aside a day to ramble around England's most thought-provoking open-air museum. To the north and west lies Hadrian's Wall, which can be easily visited from the appealing abbey-town of **Hexham** or from smaller hamlets and villages along the way – though the whole line of the Wall can also be followed along the long-distance Hadrian's Wall Path. Beyond the Wall are the harsh moorland, tree plantations, country towns, hiking trails and leisure opportunities of the **Northumberland National Park** – at its most remote around the reservoir and forest of **Kielder** and its most graceful in the Victorian streets of **Rothbury**.

With frequent **trains** running up the coast on the London–Scotland route (calling principally at Darlington, Durham, Newcastle and Berwick-upon-Tweed), and numerous **buses** between the main towns, getting around the northeast without a car is usually not a problem, though it's more difficult to explore the Northumberland National Park. Durham, Newcastle, Hexham and Alnwick are the main **transport hubs**, while Hadrian's Wall has its own bus

Hiking and biking routes

The main long-distance footpath through the Northeast is the **Pennine Way**, which cuts up from the Yorkshire Dales through the North Pennines, runs parallel to Hadrian's Wall from Greenhead to Housesteads, and then climaxes in a climb through the Northumberland National Park. The **Hadrian's Wall Path** (see p.1086) provides access along the whole of Hadrian's Wall, from near Newcastle to the Cumbrian coast. Less well known is the 63-mile pilgrim's route, **St Cuthbert's Way**, which links Melrose, where St Cuthbert started his ministry just across the border in Scotland, with Holy Island, via Kirk Yetholm – northern end of the Pennine Way – the Cheviot Hills and Wooler. Tourist offices in Berwick-upon-Tweed or Wooler have route and accommodation information.

Other major waymarked routes include the **Teesdale Way**, 90 miles from Middleton-in-Teesdale to Teesmouth (just beyond Middlesbrough), via Barnard Castle and Darlington; and the 78-mile **Weardale Way**, which follows the river from Cowshill at the head of the valley to the coast at Sunderland, via Stanhope, Bishop Auckland and Durham. For information on either of these walks, contact local tourist offices or The Countryside Group at Durham County Council on ⓣ0191/383 4082.

Sustrans's 140-mile **C2C cycle route** from Whitehaven/Workington to Sunderland/Newcastle drops into the northeast just beyond Alston and links Allenheads, Stanhope and Consett with either city. You'll need the C2C route map and associated accommodation guide, available from Sustrans (ⓣ0117/929 0888, ⓦwww.sustrans.org.uk). If that isn't enough of a challenge, you might want to take on the 187-mile return route, the **Reivers Way**, which runs from Tynemouth to Whitehaven via Bellingham, Kielder and Carlisle (map and guides available from Sustrans). There's also **Hadrian's Cycleway**, running the length of Hadrian's Wall, details from Hadrian's Wall information line on ⓣ01434/322002.

service (see p.1086). For more transport information see Travel details, p.1114 or log onto Nexus, the local transport website, which has a useful journey planner option (ⓦwww.nexus.org.uk). The **Northeast Explorer Pass** (1-day; £5.75), valid after 9am on weekdays and all day at weekends, gives unlimited travel on local buses from Berwick-upon-Tweed as far south as Scarborough in North Yorkshire or west to Carlisle – buy it on board any bus. Useful **train passes** include the Northeast Regional Rover (7 days; £73) and the wide-ranging North Country Rover (any 4 days out of 8; £61.50), which is valid as far south as Leeds and Hull and west as far as Preston. You'll find the *Northumberland Public Transport Guide* (£1) very useful – it's sold at most local tourist offices.

If there are two or more of you, it's well worth getting hold of a Northumbria Tourist Board **Powerpass** (£2) from any of the region's tourist offices, which gives two-for-the-price-of-one entry to many attractions, including Beamish, Bede's World and Segedunum.

Durham

The view from **DURHAM** train station is one of the finest in northern England – a panoramic prospect of Durham Cathedral, its towers dominating the skyline from the top of a steep sandstone bluff within a narrow bend of the River Wear. This dramatic site has been the resting place of St Cuthbert since 995, when his body was moved here from nearby Chester-le-Street, over one hundred years after his fellow monks had fled from Lindisfarne in fear of the Vikings, carrying his coffin with them. Cuthbert's hallowed remains made Durham a place of pilgrimage for both the Saxons and the Normans, who began work on the present cathedral at the end of the eleventh century. In the meantime, William the Conqueror, aware of the defensive possibilities of the site, had built a castle that was to be the precursor of ever more elaborate fortifications.

Subsequently, the bishops of Durham were granted extensive powers to control the troublesome northern marches of the kingdom, ruling as semi-independent **Prince Bishops**, with their own army, mint and courts of law. The first, William de Carileph, laid the foundation stone of the new cathedral in 1093; his successors provided glorious chapels and treasures that owed as much to the Prince Bishops' confident sense of self-worth as to their devotion to God. The bishops were at the peak of their power in the fourteenth century, but thereafter the office went into decline, especially in the wake of the Reformation, yet they clung to the vestiges of their authority until 1836, when they ceded them to the Crown. They abandoned Durham Castle for their palace in Bishop Auckland and transferred their old home to the fledgling **Durham University**, England's third oldest seat of learning after Oxford and Cambridge. And so matters rest today, cathedral and university monopolizing a city centre that remains an island of privilege in what is otherwise a moderately sized, working-class town at the heart of the old Durham coalfield.

Arrival, information and tours

From either Durham **train station,** or the **bus station** on North Road, it's about ten minutes' walk to the city centre, across the river. The "Cathedral" **bus** (#40) links train and bus stations with the Market Place (for the tourist office) and the cathedral (every 20min; 50p for all-day ticket). Arriving by car, park in

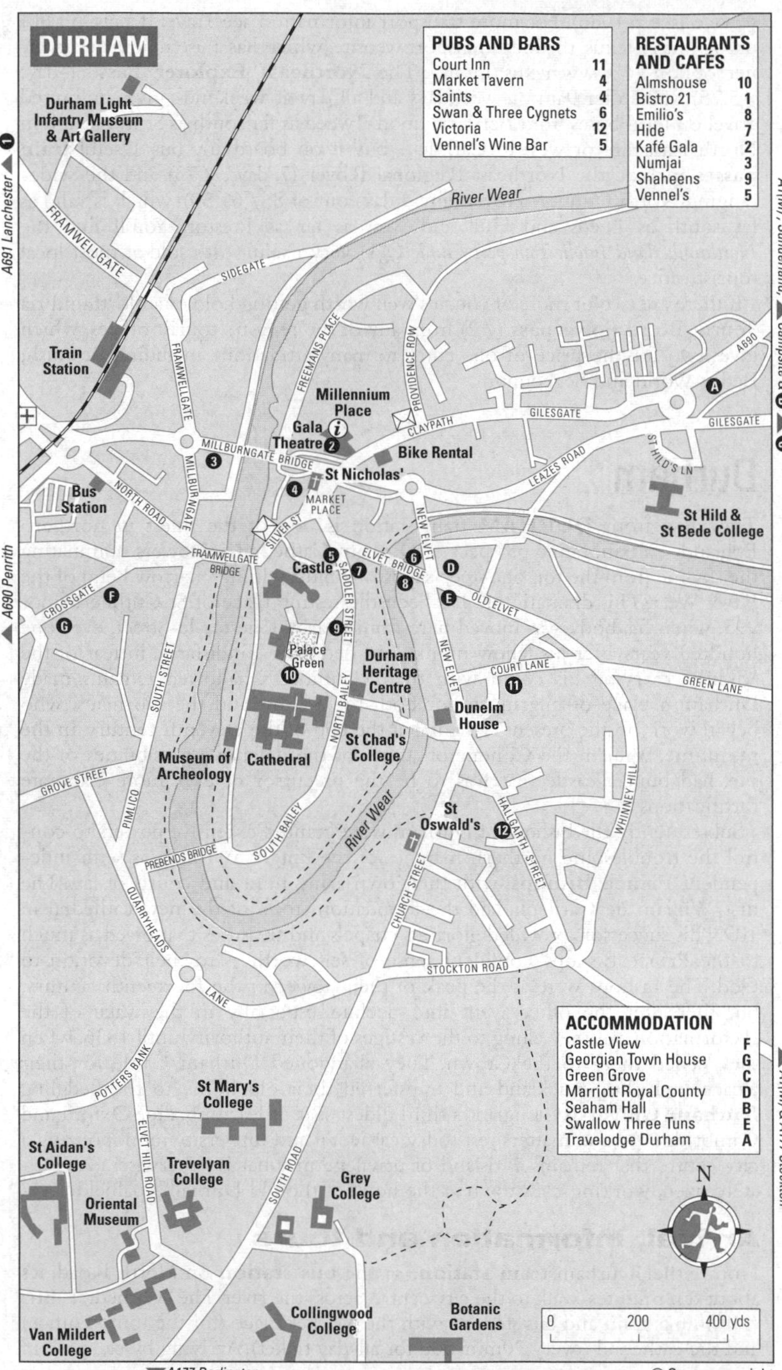
DURHAM
PUBS AND BARS
Court Inn 11
Market Tavern 4
Saints 4
Swan & Three Cygnets 6
Victoria 12
Vennel's Wine Bar 5
RESTAURANTS AND CAFÉS
Almshouse 10
Bistro 21 1
Emilio's 8
Hide 7
Kafé Gala 2
Numjai 3
Shaheens 9
Vennel's 5
ACCOMMODATION
Castle View F
Georgian Town House G
Green Grove C
Marriott Royal County D
Seaham Hall B
Swallow Three Tuns E
Travelodge Durham A
Durham Light Infantry Museum & Art Gallery
A691 Lanchester
A690 Penrith
A1(M), Sunderland, Campsite & B, C
A1(M) & A177 Stockton
A177 Darlington
River Wear
Framwellgate
Sidegate
Freemans Place
Providence Row
Train Station
Millennium Place
Gala Theatre
Claypath
Gilesgate
A690
St Hild's Ln
Leazes Road
Millburngate Bridge
Bike Rental
St Nicholas'
Market Place
Silver St
Millburngate
North Road
Bus Station
Framwellgate Bridge
Castle
Elvet Bridge
New Elvet
Old Elvet
St Hild & St Bede College
Crossgate
Saddler Street
Palace Green
Durham Heritage Centre
Court Lane
Green Lane
South Street
North Bailey
Dunelm House
St Chad's College
Museum of Archeology
Cathedral
Grove Street
Pimlico
South Bailey
St Oswald's
Hallgarth Street
Whinney Hill
Prebends Bridge
Quarryheads
Church Street
Stockton Road
Lane
Potters Bank
St Mary's College
Elvet Hill Road
South Road
St Aidan's College
Trevelyan College
Grey College
Oriental Museum
Collingwood College
Botanic Gardens
Van Mildert College
0 200 400 yds
N

one of the designated **car parks**, signposted as you enter town, as on-street parking is difficult to find; and note that the peninsula road (to the castle and cathedral) is a toll road (Mon–Sat 10am–4pm; £2).

The **tourist office** (Ⓣ0191/384 3720, Ⓦwww.durhamtourism.co.uk) will book accommodation, and provide a free map and what's-on listings. It's located at **Millennium Place**, off Claypath, a development which also incorporates a cinema showing a forty-minute large-format film presentation on Durham (twice daily; £2.50), plus theatre, public library, bar and café.

You can **walk** around the whole of the city centre very easily, and a couple of outlying attractions can be reached by local bus. Ask at the tourist office about their **guided walks** (£2), if you'd like a little more historical direction to your ramblings. To get out onto the river, either rent a **rowing boat** (£2.50/person; 1hr) from Brown's Boathouse, Elvet Bridge, or take a **cruise** aboard the *Prince Bishop* (Ⓣ0191/386 9525; £4.50; 1hr), which has regular summer departures, again from Elvet Bridge.

Accommodation

Durham has a few central guest houses and B&Bs, while a wide variety of private bedrooms is also offered at the colleges of **Durham University** (Christmas, Easter and July–Sept), all within walking distance of the centre; the tourist office has a full list, or call the Conference and Tourism Office for a brochure (Ⓣ0800/289970, Ⓦwww.dur.ac.uk/conference_tourism). Prices are from £20 per person, or £30 in en-suite rooms, breakfast included. Of the dozen colleges, University College has rooms inside the castle, St Chad's and St John's are by the cathedral, while the college of St Hild and St Bede is set in beautiful grounds overlooking the cathedral.

Guest houses and hotels

Castle View Guest House 4 Crossgate Ⓣ0191/386 8852. Pretty town house, on a cobbled terrace next to St Margaret's Church, with en-suite bathrooms, a garden and, of course, great castle views. ❸

Georgian Town House 10 Crossgate Ⓣ0191/386 8070, Ⓦwww.thegeorgiantownhouse.co.uk. Boasting more character than most, this place serves up good breakfasts and has some rooms with cathedral views. No credit cards. ❹

Green Grove 99 Gilesgate Ⓣ0191/384 4361. Suburban B&B, a 20min walk from the centre, with a mix of standard and en-suite rooms. No credit cards. ❷

Marriott Royal County Old Elvet Ⓣ0191/386 6821, Ⓦwww.marriotthotels.com. Durham's top hotel, perfectly located for a city break, has its own riverside leisure centre with indoor swimming pool, sauna and solarium. Very comfortable rooms with plump beds, plus restaurant, brasserie, bar and parking. Breakfast not included except when booked as special/weekend rate. ❼

Seaham Hall Lord Byron's Walk, Seaham, ten miles northeast of Durham Ⓣ0191/516 1400, Ⓦwww.seaham-hall.com. Hip, holistic spa hotel that makes a great coastal base for city sightseeing – Durham is a 20min drive away. Luxurious, contemporary rooms (you even get a "pillow menu"), breakfast in bed as standard, and full spa facilities, plus cliff top grounds, beaches and coastal walks nearby. ❽

Swallow Three Tuns New Elvet Ⓣ0191/386 4326, Ⓦwww.swallowhotels.com. A former sixteenth-century coaching inn with a bar, restaurant and parking, plus access to the *Royal County*'s leisure centre. Weekend rates knock around £20 off the standard room rate. ❻

Travelodge Durham Station Rd, Gilesgate Ⓣ08700/850950, Ⓦwww.travelodge.co.uk. Motel-style accommodation on the edge of town, nothing fancy but a good deal for families as there's just one rate for all the rooms (breakfast not included).

Campsite

Grange Camping and Caravan Site Meadow Lane, Carrville Ⓣ0191/384 4778. By the junction of the A1(M) and the A690, two miles northeast of the city; take bus #220 or #222 for Sunderland from the bus station. Hot showers and laundry facilities.

The City

Surrounded on three sides by the River Wear, Durham's surprisingly compact centre is readily approached by two road bridges that lead from the western, modern part of town across the river to the spur containing castle and cathedral. The commercial heart of this "old town" area is the triangular **Market Place**, inappropriately dominated by an equestrian statue of the third marquis of Londonderry, a much-hated nineteenth-century colliery owner – in the words of John Doyle, a pitman from Horden: "His Lordship reached three score and ten/A very fine performance when/One thinks how many did him scorn/And wished him dead 'ere he was born."

Flanking the square are the **Guildhall** and **St Nicholas' Church**, both now modernized beyond distinction. The Victorian **Market Hall**, buried in the vaults of the buildings that line the west side of the square (closed Sun), hosts a lively outdoor market every Saturday, as well as farmers' markets, held on the third Thursday of the month, and other special events.

The Cathedral

From Market Place, it's a five-minute walk up cobbled Saddler Street to majestic **Durham Cathedral**, facing the castle across the manicured Palace Green (July–Sept Mon–Sat 9.30am–8pm, Sun 12.30–8pm; Oct–June Mon–Sat 9.30am–6.15pm, Sun 12.30–5pm; guided tours Easter–Sept Sat at 11am & 2.30pm, plus July & Aug Sat 6.15pm, Sun 5pm; access sometimes restricted, call ⓣ0191/386 4266 to check; £3 suggested donation; tours £3.50; ⓦwww.durhamcathedral.co.uk). Standing on the site of an early wooden Saxon cathedral, built to house the remains of St Cuthbert, the present cathedral – the work of French master masons – was completed in 1133, and has survived the centuries pretty much intact, a supreme example of the Norman-Romanesque style. Visiting in 1773, Samuel Johnson captured its overpowering essence well: "it rather awes than pleases, as it strikes with a kind of gigantick dignity, and aspires to no other praise than that of rocky solidity and indeterminate duration".

The awe-inspiring **nave**, completed in 1128, used pointed arches for the first time in England, raising the vaulted ceiling to new and dizzying heights. The weight of the stone is borne by massive pillars, their heaviness relieved by striking Moorish-influenced geometric patterns – chevrons, diamonds and vertical fluting. Most of the cathedral's early fixtures and fittings were destroyed by Cromwell's Scottish prisoners, who were deposited inside the church after the battle of Dunbar in 1650. The Scots did not, however, damage the gaudily painted, sixteenth-century **Prior Castell's clock**, which now hangs in the south transept, because it sported their emblem, the thistle. A door here gives access to the **tower** (Mon–Sat 10am–4pm; £2) and from the top there are gut-wrenching views of the city. Separated from the nave by a Victorian marble screen is the **choir**, where the dark-stained Restoration stalls are overshadowed by the vainglorious **bishop's throne**, reputedly the highest in medieval Christendom, built on the orders of the fourteenth-century Bishop Hatfield, whose militaristic alabaster tombstone lies just below. Beyond, the **Chapel of the Nine Altars** dates from the thirteenth century, its Early English stonework distinguished by its delicacy of detail. Here, and around the adjoining **Shrine of St Cuthbert**, much of the stonework is Frosterley marble, each dark shaft bearing its own fancy pattern of fossils. Cuthbert himself lies beneath a plain marble slab, his presence and shrine having gained a reputation over the centuries for their curative powers. The legend was given credence in 1104, when the saint's body was exhumed for reburial here, and was found to be completely uncorrupted, more

△ Sanctuary knocker, Durham Cathedral

than four hundred years after his death on Lindisfarne. Almost certainly, this was the result of his fellow monks having (unintentionally) preserved the body by laying it in sand containing salt crystals – though to medieval eyes, here was testament enough to the saint's potency.

Back near the entrance, stuck on the edge of the ravine at the west end of the church, the **Galilee Chapel** was begun in the 1170s, its light and exotic decoration in imitation of the Great Mosque of Córdoba, a contrast to the forcefulness of the nave. Subdivided by twelve slender columns, each surrounded by a medley of geometric patterns, the chapel contains the simple tombstone of the **Venerable Bede**, the Northumbrian monk credited with being England's first historian. Bede died at the monastery of Jarrow in 735, and his remains were first transferred to the cathedral in 1020.

An ancient wooden doorway opposite the main entrance leads into the spacious **cloisters**, which are flanked by what remains of the monastic buildings. These include the **monks' dormitory** (Mon–Sat 10am–3.30pm, Sun 12.30–3.15pm; 80p) and the **Treasures of St Cuthbert** exhibition in the undercroft (Mon–Sat 10am–4.30pm, Sun 2–4.30pm; £2), where you can see some striking relics of St Cuthbert, including the reassembled fragments of his delicately carved oak coffin, a beautiful gold pectoral cross and a silver-plated portable altar. The cathedral's original twelfth-century lion-head Sanctuary Knocker is displayed here (there's a replica on the main door), while a computer terminal gives you a virtual opportunity to see the major illustrated pages of the Lindisfarne Gospels. There's also a splendid facsimile copy of the Gospels (the originals are in the British Library in London), whose pages are turned at regular intervals. Also in the undercroft is the cathedral café, while next door in the impressively converted monastic kitchen is the bookshop.

The Castle

Across Palace Green from the cathedral, **Durham Castle** (Easter & July–Sept daily 10am–12.30pm & 2–4pm; rest of the year Mon, Wed, Sat & Sun 2–4pm; £3; ⓣ191/374 3800, ⓦwww.durhamcastle.com) lost its medieval appearance long ago during refurbishments arranged by a succession of prince bishops, but the university went further by renovating the old keep as a hall of residence. It's only possible to visit the castle on a 45-minute guided tour, highlights of which include rapid visits to the fifteenth-century kitchen, a climb up the enormous hanging staircase and the jog down to the Norman chapel, notable for its lively Romanesque carved capitals. In the Great Hall, your guide will suggest that the miniature suits of armour above the musicians' gallery were issued to young boys by Cromwell, who sent them into battle ahead of his regular troops as a human shield. Treat this tale with caution – it may be Royalist propaganda. The castle is sometimes closed for functions during its regular opening hours, so it's best to call ahead to check.

The rest of the city

Below the castle and the cathedral are the wooded banks of the **River Wear**, where a pleasant footpath runs right round the peninsula. It takes about thirty minutes to complete the circuit, passing a succession of elegant bridges with fine vantage points over town and cathedral. **Framwellgate Bridge** originally dates from the twelfth century, though it was widened to its present proportions in the mid-nineteenth century. Just along from here, on the riverbank, the university's **Museum of Archeology** (April–Oct daily 11am–4pm; Nov–March Mon & Fri–Sun 11.30am–3.30pm; £1) occupies an old stone fulling mill, its displays a mixture of permanent archeological relics and temporary exhibitions. Eighteenth-century **Prebends Bridge** boasts celebrated views of the cathedral, and the path then continues round to the handsome **Elvet Bridge**, again widened far beyond its medieval course, though still retaining traces of both its erstwhile bridge-houses and the chapel, St Andrew's, which once stood at its eastern end.

The alternative route from Prebends to Elvet Bridge is along **South Bailey** and **North Bailey**, a cobbled thoroughfare lined by well-worn Georgian houses, many of them occupied by university college buildings. The church of St Mary-le-Bow, on North Bailey, immediately below the cathedral, now does duty as the **Durham Heritage Centre** (April, May & Oct Sat & Sun 2–4.30pm; June daily 2–4.30pm; July–Sept daily 11am–4.30pm; £1.20), a pot-pourri of audiovisual displays, dioramas, temporary exhibitions and activities such as brass rubbing.

The university's **Oriental Museum** (Mon–Fri 10am–5pm, Sat & Sun noon–5pm; £1.50; Ⓦwww.dur.ac.uk/oriental.museum) is set among college buildings a couple of miles south of the city centre on Elvet Hill Road (take bus #5 or #6 to South Rd). Highlights of its wide-ranging collection include outstanding displays of Chinese ceramics and Arabic calligraphy, a magnificent Chinese bed and Japanese wood-block prints, complemented by temporary exhibitions and events such as wood-block workshops, oriental games days and bazaars. After the museum, you may as well continue on foot to the nearby **Botanic Garden** (daily: March–Oct 10am–5pm; Nov–Feb 11am–4pm; £1.50), whose glasshouses, café and visitor centre are set in eighteen acres of diverse woodland, grassland and gardens near Collingwood College; buses run back to the centre from either Elvet Hill Road or South Road.

North of the centre, a ten-minute walk from the train station takes you to the **Durham Light Infantry Museum and Art Gallery**, at Aykley Heads (daily: April–Oct 10am–5pm; Nov–March 10am–4pm; £2.50; Ⓦwww.durham.gov.uk/dli). Downstairs, it tells the story of World War I, in which 12,000 men of the DLI died, through moving testimonies and wide-ranging artefacts, including a tribute to the soldiers, often suffering from shell shock, who were shot for cowardice; the less compelling first floor traces the history of the regiment through World War II to its last parade in 1968. The art gallery plays host to an indefinable variety of temporary exhibitions.

Eating, drinking and entertainment

Durham is not a city for gourmets, with only a few town-centre **restaurants** that really cut the mustard. However, as a student and tourist haven it has plenty of cafés, tearooms and budget eateries, and you don't have to look far for inexpensive pizza, pasta or bar meals. Durham's **pubs** blow hot and cold, depending on whether or not the students are in town, though there are a few reliable standbys. Regular **classical concerts** are held at various venues around the city, including the cathedral, while Durham is lucky enough to have two **arts-centre venues**, namely the DLI Museum and Art Gallery and the Gala Theatre, which between them host a full annual programme of music, theatre, dance, comedy and cinema.

Annual events and **festivals** come thick and fast in the summer. June sees the university's **arts week**, and in the same month the **Durham Regatta** packs the riverbanks and river. Over the first weekend in July, the **Durham Summer Festival** encompasses all manner of musical entertainments, as well as historical re-enactments on Palace Green; on the following Saturday, the **Miners' Gala** – when the traditional lodge banners are paraded through the streets – has been revived as a celebration of the international labour movement. For further details of all events, consult the tourist office.

Cafés

Almshouse Palace Green. This place conjures up inventive bistro meals for around £5–6 in a historic building in the shadow of the cathedral. In summer (May–Aug) open until 8pm.

Kafé Gala Millennium Place. Drinks, muffins and light meals with sunny courtyard seating at Millennium Place. Open until 9pm.

Vennel's Saddler's Yard, Saddler St. Named after the skinny alley or "vennel" where it stands – it's signposted near the junction with Elvet Bridge – this place serves drinks, sandwiches, salads, quiche and pastas in its hidden sixteenth-century courtyard. Closes 5pm, though upstairs bar open after 7pm (see "Bars and pubs" below).

Restaurants

Bistro 21 Aykley Heads ⓣ0191/384 4354. Excellent Modern British cuisine and service in a converted farmhouse north of the centre, ten minutes' walk from the DLI Museum and Art Gallery; there's courtyard seating in summer and good-value set menus at lunchtime. Closed Sun. Expensive.

Emilio's 96 Elvet Bridge ⓣ0191/384 0096. A smart refurbishment of an eleventh-century chapel, this is the city's Italian of choice. Happy hour pizza and pasta deals are a steal. Closed Sun lunch. Moderate.

Hide 39 Saddler St ⓣ0191/384 1999. The best of the café-bars with foodie pretensions, *Hide* serves a mean gourmet pizza or brunch-style menu during the day, with prices rising at night for a funky Modern British tour of world cuisine. It's a buzzy place, with the music cranked up high. Inexpensive to Moderate.

Numjai 19 Millburngate Centre ⓣ0191/386 2020. Top-notch, authentic Thai restaurant that dishes up plenty of seafood and veggie options, accompanied by great views of the cathedral. Expensive.

Shaheens 48 North Bailey ⓣ0191/386 0960. The place to head for the best curry in town. Closed Mon. Moderate.

Bars and pubs

Court Inn Court Lane. Best pub dining in town, a favourite with students and locals, with a classic pub menu (how can you not admire a "gourmet selection" of egg, beans and chips?), plus dip-and-share tapas and some intriguing blackboard specials.

Market Tavern Market Place. Bleary-eyed old socialists will want to make time for a quick pint in the place where the influential Durham Miners' Association was founded in 1871.

Saints Market Vaults, Back Silver St. Student vaults bar, below Millburngate bridge, with real ales, drinks deals, and budget meals and grills – busy and boisterous at weekends.

Swan & Three Cygnets Elvet Bridge. Town and gown converge in this popular riverside pub with cheap Sam Smith's ale, budget sandwiches and a full-to-the-brim outdoor terrace.

Victoria 86 Hallgarth St. Once, all pubs were like this, which will either appeal or appal – half-a-dozen well-kept ales, no food, no music, and closed between 2 and 6pm (7pm on Sun). A quiet, welcoming local that retains its Victorian feel and decor.

Vennel's Wine Bar Saddler's Yard, Saddler St. "Durham's bohemian retreat", or so they claim – a nice, evening-only hangout with cool tunes and a decent range of wines by the glass.

Live music and arts venues

DLI Museum and Art Gallery Aykley Heads ⓣ0191/384 2214, ⓦwww.durham.gov.uk/dli. Slightly out-of-town venue, putting on lunchtime recitals, special exhibitions, summertime brass band concerts, ceilidhs and other events.

Durham Students' Union Dunelm House, New Elvet ⓣ0191/374 2000. Student venue with gigs during term time, and regular rock, jazz and comedy.

Gala Theatre and Cinema Millennium Place ⓣ0191/332 4041, ⓦwww.galadurham.co.uk. Live music of all kinds is offered here, plus theatre, cinema (outdoor classic movies in summer), and Comedy Store gigs on the first Sun of every month.

Listings

Banks and exchange ATMs are ubiquitous; there's currency exchange at the post office.

Bike rental Cycle Force 2000, 87 Claypath ⓣ0191/384 0319. Open 7 days a week.

Hospital University Hospital, North Rd ⓣ0191/333 2333.

Internet Free access at the City Library, Millennium Place.

Pharmacy Boots, 2–5 Market Place.

Police HQ, Aykley Heads ⓣ0191/386 4929; also on New Elvet ⓣ0191/386 4222.

Post office Silver St (Mon–Fri 9.30am–5pm).

The rest of County Durham

In the 1910s, **County Durham** produced 41 million tons of coal each year, raised from three hundred pits by 170,000 miners. This was the heyday of an industry that since the 1830s had transformed the county's landscape, spawning scores of pit villages that matted the rolling hills from the Pennines to the North Sea, and from Newcastle to Stockton-on-Tees. The miners' union, waging a long struggle against serf-like pay and conditions, achieved a gradual improvement of the miners' lot, but could not prevent the slow decline of the Durham coalfield from the 1920s: just 127 mines were left when the industry was nationalized in 1947, only 34 in 1969, and today not a single pit remains. As a consequence, the old colliery villages have lost their sense of purpose and structure, some becoming godforsaken terraces in the middle of nowhere, others being swallowed up by neighbouring towns. For a taste of the old days, most people troop off to the reconstructed colliery village (and much more) at the open-air **Beamish Museum**, north of Durham.

County Durham's other obvious tourist attractions are to the west of the coalfield. There's **Raby Castle**, a stately home to the east of the market town of **Barnard Castle**, itself the setting for the opulent art collection of the **Bowes Museum**. Further west lie the Pennine valleys of **Teesdale** and **Weardale**, whose upper reaches boast some enjoyable moorland scenery, most dramatically at Teesdale's **High Force** waterfall, which adjoins the Pennine Way. These two dales are best toured in a clockwise direction, beginning at Barnard Castle and travelling up Teesdale to Langdon Beck and on to Alston in Cumbria, where you can cross over to Weardale and take the road back down the valley through Stanhope and into Bishop Auckland. Another option is to leave Weardale at Stanhope for the ten-mile trip north across the moors to the delightful stone village of **Blanchland**, tucked away in the valley of the Derwent River across the border in Northumberland.

Getting around County Durham by bus and train presents few problems. A comprehensive range of services links all the major towns and villages, although the bus network does peter out as you travel up the dales. Many services are also greatly reduced, or nonexistent, during the winter months. For a **public transport information** pack contact Durham County Council (ⓣ0191/383 3337). If you want to get further off the beaten track, contact the Council's Environment Department (ⓣ0191/383 4144) for details of its year-round programme of **guided walks**. These range from rural rambles to industrial heritage trails, and most cost just £2; for more information contact Durham's tourist office, or any of the local tourist offices detailed below.

Beamish Museum

The open-air **Beamish Museum** (Easter–Oct 10am–5pm; Nov & Dec daily 10am–4pm; Jan–Easter Tues–Thurs, Sat & Sun 10am–4pm; last admission 3pm; admission £12, £4 in winter; ⓣ0191/370 4000, ⓦwww.beamish.org.uk) spreads out over 300 acres beside the A693, about ten miles north of Durham. It's the one County Durham attraction you really shouldn't miss, as popular with tourists as it is with local people, who come to chew the fat with the costumed guides, many of whom are recruited for their real-life experience. The collier who takes you down the drift mine may once have been a miner, and some of the blokes driving the steam engine used to work for British Rail, adding a touch of authenticity and sadness to the proceedings, as these industries have deteriorated in tandem with the boom in heritage museums like this one.

Buildings from all over the region have been reassembled in six main sections, linked by restored trams and buses and all painstakingly kitted out with period furnishings and fittings. Costumed shopkeepers, workers and householders can answer your questions, and you can walk through many of the buildings and workshops to find out about daily life a century or two ago. Four of the sections show life in 1913, before the upheavals brought about by World War I: a pint-sized **colliery village**, complete with drift mine (regular tours throughout the day), old stone winding house, cottages, Methodist chapel and school; a **farm** inhabited by breeds of livestock that were popular in the period; a **train station** and goods shed; and a large-scale re-creation of a market **town**, its High Street lined by shops, bank, pub, dentist's surgery, newspaper office, garage, stables, sweet factory and solicitor's office. Two areas date to 1825, at the beginning of the northeast's industrial development: a **manor house**, with horse yard, formal gardens, vegetable plots and orchards; and the **Pockerley Waggonway**, where you can ride behind a replica of George Stephenson's *Locomotion*, the first passenger-carrying steam train in the world, which ran from Darlington to Stockton (see p.1060). There's a great deal to see and what with the summertime Victorian funfair, the *Sun Inn* pub and café in the town, and picnic areas, most people make a day of it – reckon on at least four hours to get round the lot in summer, two in winter when only the town and train station are usually open. Call ahead to check on this, or on the concerts and **special events** held throughout the summer, from craft displays to whippet racing.

To **get there**, drivers should follow signs to the museum off the A1(M) Chester-le-Street exit, then follow the signs along the A693 to Stanley. By **bus**, take the #720 from Durham bus station (hourly) or the #709 from Newcastle's Eldon Square (hourly), which drop you close to the main entrance. There are also regular services from Sunderland Park Lane. In summer, hang on to your bus ticket and you'll get a discount on entrance to the museum.

Bishop Auckland

Eleven miles southwest of Durham city, **BISHOP AUCKLAND** has been the country home of the bishops of Durham since the twelfth century and their official residence for more than a hundred years. Their palace, the gracious **Auckland Castle** (Easter–Sept Sun & Mon 2–5pm; £4; Ⓦ www.auckland-castle.co.uk), standing in eight-hundred-acre grounds, is approached through an imposing gatehouse just off the town's large Market Place. The palace has been extensively remodelled since its medieval incarnation, redesigned to satisfy the whims of such occupants as the seventeenth-century Bishop Cosin who refurbished the original banqueting hall to create today's splendid marble and limestone chapel. Here, the stained-glass windows relate the stories of early Christian saints familiar throughout the northeast, especially Cuthbert, Bede and Aidan. The other rooms are rather sparse, though – for the moment at least – there's an outstanding exception in the long dining room, with its thirteen paintings of Jacob and his sons by Zurbarán, commissioned in the 1640s for a monastery in South America. However, the Church of England has decided to sell its most valuable set of paintings, though it's possible they could yet be saved for the nation. After you've seen the castle you can stroll into the adjacent **Bishop's**

Deer Park (daily dawn–dusk; free), where an eighteenth-century deer house survives.

The town itself plays second fiddle to the castle, though don't leave until you've followed the mile-long lane from behind the Town Hall (signposted by the *Sportsman Inn*) to the remains of **Binchester Roman Fort** (Easter & May–Sept daily 11am–5pm; £1.60). Only a small portion of the ten-acre site – Roman Vinovia – has been excavated (with most of the finds displayed in the Bowes Museum at Barnard Castle), but a stretch of cobbled Dere Street has been uncovered (a fortified supply route stretching from York to Corbridge on Hadrian's Wall) and, more remarkably, so has the country's best example of a **hypocaust**, built to warm the private bath suite of the garrison's commanding officer.

The fort was abandoned in the fifth century and many of its stones, stamped with the inscription of the cavalry regiment stationed here, found their way to the hamlet of **ESCOMB**, two miles west of Bishop Auckland (bus #86 from town), where they were used to build a seventh-century **Saxon church** (daily: summer 9am–8pm; rest of year 9am–4pm; free). Now surrounded by modern houses, the church (key at 22 Saxon Green if closed) has a striking steep-roofed nave, only sixty by twenty feet. Opposite, you can get a bar meal at the sixteenth-century *Saxon Inn*.

Practicalities

Bishop Auckland is linked by **train** to Darlington, Middlesbrough and Saltburn and by regular **buses** to Weardale, Barnard Castle, Durham, Newcastle and Darlington. Buses drop you centrally, near Market Place, where the Town Hall, library (free Internet access) and **tourist office** share the same premises (April–Sept Mon–Fri 10am–5pm, Sat 9am–4pm Sun 1–4pm; Oct–March closed Sun; ⓣ01388/602610).

A mile east of town, along the A688 (Spennymoor/Durham road), there's courtyard **accommodation**, a bar and restaurant at the *Park Head Hotel*, at New Coundon (ⓣ01388/661727, ⓦwww.parkheadhotel.com; ❹). A mile further up, just off the A688 in Binchester is *Five Gables Guest House*, in the former colliery manager's house (ⓣ01388/608204, ⓦwww.fivegables.co.uk; ❸), which offers cosy en-suite B&B. The best **restaurant** hereabouts is the *Fox & Hounds* in Newfield (ⓣ01388/662787; closed Sun dinner & all Mon), a gastro-pub two miles beyond *Five Gables*. It's known for its Modern British food (good on fish, game, vegetarian dishes and desserts); turn left at the *Queen's Head* in Newfield and it's the last cottage on the left.

Raby Castle

The A688 between Bishop Auckland and Barnard Castle provides access to the splendid, sprawling battlements of **Raby Castle** (May & Sept Wed & Sun 1–5pm; June–Aug Mon–Fri & Sun 1–5pm; gardens same days 11am–5.30pm; castle & gardens £6, gardens only £4; ⓦwww.rabycastle.com), roughly halfway between the two towns. The castle mostly dates from the fourteenth century, reflecting the power of the Neville family, who ruled the local roost until 1569. It was then that Charles Neville helped plan the "Rising of the North", the abortive attempt to replace Elizabeth I with Mary Queen of Scots. The revolt was a dismal failure, and Neville's estates were confiscated, with Raby subsequently passing to the Vane family in 1626. The Vanes held on to the castle despite some difficult times: the second owner, Sir Henry, a leading Puritan and briefly the governor of Massachusetts at the tender age of 23, was imprisoned by Cromwell for his criticism of the overzealous Protectorate, and then executed on the orders of Charles II for treason in 1662.

The Vanes, now the Lords Barnard, still live in the castle, the **interior** of which was extensively renovated in the eighteenth and nineteenth centuries, though the medieval kitchen remains intact. Raby's focal point is the first-floor Baron's Hall, still of cathedral-like dimensions in spite of the floor being raised ten feet in 1787 to let carriages pass through the neo-Gothic entrance below. Also of note are the Palladian library and the octagonal drawing room, unchanged since its completion in the 1840s. The whole castle is stuffed with antiques, from the usual oligarchic family portraits and ranks of Meissen porcelain, to paintings by artists such as Joshua Reynolds and Luca Giordano.

Outside in the two-hundred-acre **deer park** are the walled **gardens**, where peaches, apricots and pineapples once flourished under the careful gaze of forty Victorian gardeners. Heated cavity walls and curtains protected the trees from frost – above the last remaining apricot tree you can still see the hooks for the curtain rail. The castle's coach houses contain a collection of horse-drawn carriages, admission to which is included with a ticket to the castle or gardens. A tearoom in the former stables has seats in the old horse stalls.

Barnard Castle and around

Fifteen miles southwest of Bishop Auckland, the skeletal remains of **Barnard Castle** (April–Sept daily 10am–6pm; Oct daily 10am–5pm; Nov–March Wed–Sun 10am–4pm; often closed 1–2pm for lunch; £2.60; EH), poking out from a cliff high above the River Tees, overlook the town that grew up in its shadow. First fortified in the eleventh century, the castle was long a stronghold of the Balliols, a Norman family interminably embroiled in the struggle for the Scottish crown. It was one of this clan, Bernard, who built the circular tower, which survives to this day, an impressive thirteenth-century fortification just to the right of the later Round Tower, where a beautiful oriel window carries the emblematic boar of Richard III, one of the subsequent owners. By the seventeenth century the castle had outlived its usefulness and the Vanes quarried its stone to repair their premises at Raby.

The **town**, however, continued to thrive as a market centre and it's quite pleasant to potter around the wide, well-kept streets of what the locals call "Barney". Wednesday is market day, while further down from Market Place, St Mary's Church, founded in the twelfth century, and the circular, colonnaded Market Cross building (used, variously, as a butter market and jail) make up the official sights.

Castle aside, the prime attraction is the grand French-style chateau that constitutes the **Bowes Museum** (daily 11am–5pm; £6; Ⓦwww.bowesmuseum.org.uk), half a mile east of the centre, signposted along Newgate. Begun in 1869, the chateau was commissioned by John and Josephine Bowes, a local businessman and MP and his French actress wife, who spent much of their time in Paris collecting the ostentatious treasures and antiques. They shipped the whole lot back to County Durham and, in an early show of arts patronage, turned the house into a museum for the enlightenment of the Teesdale public (though neither lived to see its formal opening in 1892). It's a hugely rewarding collection, ranging from furniture, paintings, tapestries and ceramics to incidental curiosities, notably a late eighteenth-century mechanical silver swan in the lobby which still performs daily at 2pm, preening to a brief forty-second melodic burst. Among the paintings, you'll find one of the most important Spanish collections in the UK, including El Greco's *The Tears of St Peter* and a couple of

Goyas, plus works by Boudin, Tiepolo and Canaletto; elsewhere, there's varied interest in the French decorative and religious art, English period furniture, and an excellent toy collection – whose nineteenth-century lead soldiers were made possible by the new industry in nearby Stanhope. There's a café, too, and a stroll in the grounds on a nice day is no bad thing – there are 23 acres of parkland here, with various marked routes along a "Tree Trail".

Practicalities

Buses stop on either side of central Galgate – once the road out to the town gallows, hence the name. The **tourist office** is on Flatts Road, at the end of Galgate by the castle (April–Oct daily 10am–6pm; Nov–March Mon–Sat 11am–4pm; ⓣ01833/690909). Among several convenient **B&Bs** along the upper reaches of Galgate, the welcoming *Homelands*, 85 Galgate (ⓣ01833/638757, ⓦwww.homelandsguesthouse.co.uk; no credit cards; ❸), offers pretty bedrooms and good breakfasts, while the similar *Marwood House*, opposite at no. 98 (ⓣ01833/637493, ⓦwww.kilgarriff.demon.co.uk; no credit cards; ❷), provides a small fitness room and sauna for guests to work off the effects of the home-cooked dinners (on request, £12). The *Old Well Inn*, 21 The Bank (ⓣ01833/690130, ⓦwww.oldwellinn.co.uk; ❹), originally a Tudor coaching inn, has huge en-suite rooms and weekend half-board deals. The town is ringed by **campsites**, including a Camping and Caravanning Club site with plenty of facilities on Dockenflatts Lane at Lartington, two miles west of the centre (ⓣ01833/630228; closed Nov–Feb; bus #95 towards Middleton).

Stables, in Horsemarket between Galgate and the Market Place (part of the Hayloft indoor craft market), provides inexpensive **café** meals and all-day breakfasts, while the *Market Place Teashop*, 29 Market Place (closed Sun Oct–March), is a traditional tearoom with daily special meals on a blackboard. Barney's top **restaurant** is *Blagraves House* at 30–32 The Bank (ⓣ01833/637668; closed Sun & Mon), a sixteenth-century former inn sporting low-beamed ceilings and large open fires, with set menus (£16.95) that change monthly. For a quiet **drink**, try the *Old Well Inn*, which has a beer garden backing onto the castle walls.

Egglestone Abbey, Rokeby Park and the North Pennines Reserve

From the town centre, it's a pleasant mile-and-a-half walk from the castle, southeast (downriver) through the fields above the banks of the Tees, to the glorious shattered ruins of **Egglestone Abbey** (dawn–dusk; free), a minor Premonstratensian foundation dating from 1195 (this and other short hikes from the town centre are covered by leaflets available from the tourist office). Turner painted here on one of his three visits to Teesdale, and also at nearby **Rokeby Park** (June–Aug Mon & Tues 2–5pm; £5), a Palladian country house where Walter Scott wrote his ballad *Rokeby*. The house is noted for its extensive collection of eighteenth-century needlework pictures. You can get to the hall directly on bus #79 from Barnard Castle, which also runs to Abbey Bridge End, for Egglestone Abbey.

In the other direction, the moorland A66 heads west from Barnard Castle into Cumbria, towards Appleby. Three miles west of Bowes, you could call in at the Otter Trust's excellent **North Pennines Reserve** (Easter–Oct daily 10.30am–6pm; £4.50; ⓦwww.ottertrust.org.uk) at Vale House Farm, on the south side of the A66. A small valley of the River Greta cuts through the 230-acre farmland, and hides let you glimpse the wildlife; the otters are fed at noon and 3pm.

Charles Dickens and the Yorkshire schools

The precociously talented, 26-year-old **Charles Dickens**, already a hugely successful author with his *Pickwick Papers* and *Oliver Twist*, produced his third novel in serial form in 1838. *Nicholas Nickleby* presented the usual panoply of comic and grotesque figures, none more so than Wackford Squeers, the "villainous", one-eyed headmaster of Dotheboys Hall who, memorably, "appeared ill at ease in his clothes, and as if he were in a perpetual state of astonishment at finding himself so respectable". As throughout his career, Dickens did his homework assiduously. On a trip north in early 1838 he visited various of the so-called "Yorkshire Schools" in the area around Barnard Castle – established, more often than not, by unscrupulous businessmen who cared little for their charges. In these schools, illegitimate or awkward children, or simply those of unsuspecting parents, were destined for years of neglect, abuse or worse. Dickens stayed at the *King's Head* (now the *Charles Dickens*) on Market Place in **Barnard Castle**, spied on a local watchmaker's shop (giving him the idea for *Master Humphrey's Clock*) and visited nearby **Bowes**, whose Bowes Academy was run by the notorious William Shaw, earlier prosecuted for neglect of his schoolboys, several of whom had gone blind in his care. Dickens took careful note and modelled Squeers on Shaw and Dotheboys Hall on Bowes' school; along with others in the locality it closed in the wake of the success of the novel, with parents and authorities finally moved to action. The school building – "a long cold-looking house" – still stands at the west end of the village; Shaw is buried in the churchyard. As is the way with notoriety, several teachers soon claimed to be the original Wackford Squeers and Dickens himself, in print at least, remained vague about his identity, claiming in the novel's preface that Squeers was "representative of a class, and not of an individual". This was perhaps just as well, since the same preface reveals the reactions of those who believed themselves to be so slighted: one gentleman, according to Dickens, proposed coming to London "for the express purpose of committing an assault and battery upon his traducer".

Teesdale

Extending twenty-odd miles northwest from Barnard Castle, **Teesdale** begins calmly enough, though the pastoral landscapes of its lower reaches are soon replaced by wilder Pennine scenery. There's a regular bus service as far as **Middleton-in-Teesdale**, the valley's main settlement, with infrequent (Tues, Wed, Fri & Sat) services on to the spectacular **High Force** waterfall and **Langdon Beck** (for the youth hostel). However, your own transport makes Teesdale an easy day's sightseeing from Barnard Castle.

Middleton-in-Teesdale and Romaldkirk

MIDDLETON-IN-TEESDALE was once the archetypal "company town", owned lock, stock and barrel by the Quaker-run London Lead Company, which began mining here in 1753. The firm built substantial stone cottages for their workforce, who in return were obliged to observe a host of regulations, such as sending their children to Sunday school and keeping off the booze. Not that the Quakers were over-mindful of working conditions: lead miners here, as elsewhere, suffered bronchial complaints brought on by the contaminated air in the mines, illnesses compounded by long hours and an early start – "washer-boys", who sorted the lead ore from the rock for ten hours a day and more, began at 8 years old. A heritage centre – known as Meet the Middletons – based around the life and work of a mining family, is scheduled to open in 2004. The **tourist office** in the central Market Place (daily 10am–1pm & 2–5pm, closes 4pm in winter; ☎01833/641001) can tell you more about this and provide details of local **accommodation**. The best B&B is at *Cornforth & Cornforth*, a genial continental café at 16 Market Place (☎01833/640300, ⓔcornjohnviv@aol.com; ❷) – three brightly painted, country-style, en-suite rooms with little fridges (organic milk provided), daytime meals in the café (closed Mon & Wed), and dinner (£10) by arrangement. Heading the other way up Market Place, past the tourist office, the *Teesdale Hotel* (☎01833/640264; ❸) is a seventeenth-century coaching inn, with spick-and-span en-suite accommodation and a bar menu.

Three miles back down the road towards Barnard Castle, **ROMALDKIRK** encompasses an impressive church, and no less than three village greens (one with its old stocks still intact). The *Rose & Crown* (☎01833/650213, ⓦwww.rose-and-crown.co.uk; ❻) here, an ivy-clad eighteenth-century inn, has very comfortable rooms and highly accomplished Modern British cooking in the bar or restaurant (prices moderate to expensive).

Up the valley to Langdon Beck

Past Middleton, the countryside becomes harsher and the Tees more vigorous as the B6277 travels the three miles on to **Bowlees Visitor Centre** (April–Sept daily 10.30am–5pm; Oct–March Sat & Sun 10.30am–4pm; 50p), site of a small wildlife display and the halt for the short walk to the rapids of **Low Force**. A mile further up the road is the altogether more compelling **High Force**, a seventy-foot cascade that rumbles over an outcrop of the Whin Sill, a black dolerite ridge that pokes up in various parts of northern England. The waterfall is on private Raby land, and visitors must pay £1 to view the falls and £1.50 to use the nearby car park, by the B6277. From the road, it's a ten-minute walk through the woods to the viewing point, where daredevil visitors clamber on the rocks above the gushing waters – after rain, it's a thunderously impressive sight. You can avoid the entrance fee by walking up from Low Force on the opposite bank of the river along the Pennine Way, but the view of the falls isn't as spectacular. Back by the car park, the *High Force Hotel* (☎01833/622222, ⓦwww.highforcehotel.com; ❸) brews its own beer (a Teesdale Bitter and the stronger, award-winning, Cauldron Snout) to accompany the bar meals.

The Pennine Way continues the six miles upstream to **Cauldron Snout**, near the source of the Tees, where the river rolls two 200ft down a dolerite stairway as it leaves **Cow Green Reservoir**. It's also possible to reach the reservoir by car: turn off the main road at **Langdon Beck** – about a mile north of the stone-built **youth hostel** on the B6277 at Forest-in-Teesdale (☎0870/770 5910, ⓔlangdonbeck@yha.org.uk; £10.25; closed Nov to mid-Feb) – and follow the three-mile-long lane to the car park, a mile's walk from the Snout. The B6277, meanwhile, climbs ever higher as it leaves Teesdale, peaking at just under 2000ft before dropping into Cumbria.

Weardale

Seeing the dramatic high-dale scenery of **Weardale** by public transport can be a frustrating business. Bus #101 runs roughly hourly between Bishop Auckland and **Stanhope**, the main village, with less frequent extensions up the valley to Cowshill; however, to get the bus to take you to the fascinating lead-mining museum at **Killhope**, two miles further on, you'll have to ask the driver (or arrange it in advance with the bus company; ☎01388/528235) – and don't forget to request a pick-up for the way back. Otherwise, your only hope is the #X21 from Newcastle to Stanhope (Sat only). It's better on foot, as the

Weardale Way runs the length of the valley, kicking off with an interesting eleven-mile loop at its western end linking Cowshill, Killhope and Allenheads, with the option of a brief scramble up 2200-feet Killhope Law for towering views over the dale and beyond. From Cowshill, the looping thirty-mile **Leadmining Trail** runs over the tops to Edmundbyers and back, or can be split into three day-hikes (a leaflet pack is available from local tourist information centres). With your own transport, you can cut between the two valleys, Teesdale and Weardale, on one of the minor moorland roads, branching off at Egglestone, Newbiggin or Langdon Beck. The account below runs west to east, starting at the Alston (p.904) end.

Killhope and Ireshopeburn

Lead and iron-ore mining flourished in and around Weardale from the 1840s to the 1880s, leaving today's landscape scarred with old workings. One of the bigger mines, situated about three miles west of Cowshill, up at the head of the valley and a chilly 1500 feet above sea level, has been turned into the **Killhope Lead Mining Museum** (April–July & Sept daily 10.30am–5pm; Aug until 5.30pm; Oct Sat & Sun 10.30am–5pm; £3.40, £5 including mine visit; Ⓦwww.durham.gov.uk/killhope), where all sorts of industrial debris lies scattered across a large open-air site, including a restored 34-foot-high waterwheel, built to power the crushing apparatus. It still turns, using six thousand gallons of water per minute from a string of diverted streams. You can also try your hand as a washerboy on the old washing floor – if you're prepared to compete with the schoolkids – while descending Park Level Mine with hard-hat and lamp gives you a taste of the miserable mining life. Incidentally, if you're intending to take a trip on the South Tynedale railway, at nearby Alston, buy a combined ticket at the mine.

At Cowshill (the *Cowshill Hotel* here does bar meals), there's a turning north onto the B6295 for Allendale, while two miles further east down the main road, tiny **IRESHOPEBURN** is the home of the **Weardale Museum** (Easter, May–July & Sept Wed–Sun 2–5pm; Aug daily 2–5pm; £1.50), an excellent small folk museum with displays on lead mining, the railways and Methodism, the faith of the majority of Durham's lead miners; entry to the museum also allows you access to the adjacent **High House Chapel**, the oldest Methodist chapel in the world in continuous use, built in 1760 just eight years after John Wesley's first visit to the region.

Stanhope

About nine miles downstream from Ireshopeburn lies **STANHOPE**, an elongated village that makes a useful base for hikes on the moors, made more appealing in summer by its open-air heated swimming pool (mid-May to mid-Sept; £2). It has a castle (closed to the public), built for a local MP in 1798, whose walled gardens now house the **Durham Dales Centre** – on the main road through Stanhope – in which you'll find the **tourist office** (Easter–Oct daily 10am–5pm; Nov–Easter Mon–Fri 10am–4pm, Sat & Sun 11am–4pm; Ⓣ01388/527650). This can provide information about local walks, including the enjoyable five-mile circuit from the town centre, up through the woods of **Stanhope Dene** and across open moorlands past old lead mines and quarries. Before you go, take a quick look at the 250-million-year-old **fossilized tree trunk** in the grounds of St Thomas' Church, on the main road through town, close to the Durham Dales Centre; there's a café at the centre. **Accommodation** is available in several local B&Bs, but you may not want to pass up the chance to stay at *Stanhope Old Hall* (Ⓣ01388/528451; ❹), a twelfth-century fortified hunting lodge of the Prince Bishops of Durham. It's on the main road just west of the town centre, opposite the swimming pool – there's a coffee shop here too, or make do with a cosy drink in front of a huge open fire.

North across the moors

Two minor roads branch **north from Weardale**, over the border into Northumberland, heading towards Hexham and Hadrian's Wall and crossing some of the most glorious, isolated moorland in the north of England. With your own transport, it's well worth forsaking the main roads to follow either of these routes, to Allendale or Blanchland. **By bus**, there are two routes into the area, but they don't meet up: the #688 runs from Hexham to Allendale and Allenheads, but no further, between five and nine times a day; while the #773 heads west from Consett (which is itself linked by hourly bus with Newcastle) to Edmundbyers and Blanchland (not Sun).

The Allen Valley

The B6295 climbs out of Weardale and drops into the **Allen Valley**, where heather-covered moorland shelters small settlements that once made their living from lead mining. The River Allen itself can be extremely beautiful at times, widening as it tumbles north to join the River Tyne just east of Bardon Mill. It was from this valley that painter John Martin (see p.1071) drew much of his inspiration, and the dramatic surroundings are still easily viewed today from a series of river walks (see box below) accessible from either of the main settlements.

At **ALLENHEADS**, at the top of the valley, twelve miles from Stanhope, handsome stone buildings stand close to the river. The **Heritage Centre** (Easter–Sept daily 10am–5pm; £1) details the village's erstwhile industry, and incorporates an early Armstrong hydraulic engine used for driving the sawmill and a blacksmith's workshop, while a short nature trail guides you through the

Walks in and around the Allen Valley

The **Allen Valley** offers some of the finest walking in the region. There are all manner of circular walks that can be undertaken from Allendale Town, the best base hereabouts, most of which involve pottering up or down the banks of the river. A very good path takes you all the way from Allendale **south to Allenheads** (around nine miles one way), leaving or crossing the river on occasion, though connoisseurs rate higher the northern section, **from Allendale Town to the River Tyne** (eight miles one way), much of it National Trust land with waymarked side trails through ancient woodland. This is at its most dramatic when passing through the beautiful, tree-clad **Allen Gorge**, watched over by Staward Peel, a medieval fortified tower-house; there's road access at **Plankey Mill**, around which the river becomes full of splashing families on summer weekends. Where the Allen flows into the Tyne, you're only a mile or so east of the train station at **Bardon Mill** and only another hour and a half's cross-country walk from **Hadrian's Wall** at Housesteads, enabling you to move on east or west by train, bus or on foot.

Alternatively, back at Allendale Town, there are glorious moorland routes east across **Hexhamshire Common**, descending either to Hexham itself (via Dipton Mill and its pub; or, three miles further east, to Corbridge. Both towns are easily reached in a day from Allendale. From Allenheads, after a bit of initial clambering north or south, the cross-moorland routes east are to Blanchland (see p.1056), a tiring day's walk but eminently worthwhile; or you can loop south to Cowshill and Killhope.

woodland around the East Allen River. Pop into the village's *Allenheads Inn* (Ⓣ01434/685200, Ⓦwww.theallenheadsinn.co.uk; ❷), stuffed with every conceivable piece of junk-shop arcana. Lunch and dinner are served, and the owners also rent out the adjacent six-person stone cottage.

ALLENDALE TOWN, another four miles north, also goes about its quiet, rural way, and claims to be at the exact centre of the British Isles. This is a peaceful place to stay, with a small supermarket, a post office and several friendly pubs and small hotels, all centred on the main market square. The best **accommodation** is at the welcoming *King's Head* (Ⓣ01434/683681; ❸), right in the square, which has nice rooms, home-cooked meals, and Jennings' beers. B&B is also on offer in the *Allendale Tea Rooms* (Ⓣ01434/683575; no credit cards; ❷), opposite the hotel. Allendale's major curiosity is the **New Year's Eve** "tar barrels" ceremony, when a huge, spluttering bonfire is lit in the square around which the locals parade with barrels – more like trays – of burning pitch balanced on their heads to usher in the new year.

Blanchland

The other trans-moorland route is the B6278 which cuts north from Weardale at Stanhope for ten extraordinarily wild miles to tiny **BLANCHLAND**, a handful of ancient, lichen-stained stone cottages huddled round an L-shaped square that was once the outer court of a twelve-man Premonstratensian abbey, founded in the twelfth century. The village has been preserved and protected since 1721, when Lord Crewe, the childless bishop of Durham, bequeathed his estate to trustees on condition that they rebuilt the old conventual buildings, as Blanchland had slowly fallen into disrepair after the abbey's dissolution. The original trustees obliged and their successors have allowed but the faintest whiff of subsequent centuries to intrude, their last concession being the construction of a pint-sized shelter in celebration of Queen Victoria's Diamond Jubilee.

Consequently, the village bears many reminders of its monastic past, from the sturdy gatehouse that now accommodates the post office to the L-shaped parish church. But it's the *Lord Crewe Arms Hotel* (Ⓣ01434/675251, Ⓦwww.crewearms.freeserve.co.uk; ❼) that steals the show. Once the abbot's lodge, the hotel's nooks and crannies have all sorts of surprises, an enticing mixture of medieval and eighteenth-century Gothic features, including the dark vaulted basements, two big fireplaces left over from the canons' kitchen and a priest's hideaway stuck inside the chimney. It's a superb place to stay – check out the good-value half-board deals – with lavish rooms and a delightful garden-cum-cloister. The restaurant serves table d'hôte dinners for around £30, or there are cheaper meals in the fine public bar in the undercroft.

East of Blanchland

Beyond Blanchland, drivers will probably be keen to get to Hexham by the most direct route along the B6306, but consider taking a detour east to the main A68 and driving past the Derwent Reservoir. At the attractive village of **EDMUNDBYERS**, where B6306 meets B6278, is a (heavily restored) twelfth-century church and a simple youth hostel (Ⓣ0870/770 5810, Ⓔedmundbyers@yha.org.uk; £9; closed Tues except July & Aug, & closed Nov–Easter) in seventeenth-century Low House, just half a mile from the reservoir. You can camp at the hostel, too, and there are a couple of local B&Bs and a **pub** with rooms if you crave more comfort. Two miles further east, at the junction with the A68, at Carterway Heads, the *Manor House Inn* (Ⓣ01207/255268; ❹) has en-suite rooms overlooking the reservoir and posh pub food at around £15 a head, though there's a cheaper lunchtime sandwich menu too.

The Tees Valley: Darlington to the coast

The **River Tees**, along with the Tyne further north, was one of the great engines of British economic power in the late nineteenth century. That it's so far off the contemporary tourist map as to be invisible is hardly the fault of towns whose livelihood largely disappeared once iron- and steel-making and shipbuilding became things of the past in England. But once there were rich pickings here, in places such as **Darlington**, twenty miles south of Durham city, where the first public passenger-carrying steam train, George Stephenson's *Locomotion*, made its inaugural run and is now on permanent display. The line ran first to **Stockton-on-Tees** and was then extended to ports at **Middlesbrough** and **Hartlepool**, to enable ever-increasing amounts of Durham coal to be unloaded and exported. Iron from the local Cleveland Hills supported a shipbuilding industry, which in Hartlepool at least had been flourishing since the eighteenth century.

In truth, few people are going to stop at any of these towns. For those that do, Darlington is the most surprisingly attractive, and you'd have to be hard-hearted not to derive some pleasure from Hartlepool's historic quay. Drivers will find navigating the swirling ring roads and bypasses something of a trial, but it's worth bearing in mind the route east as one possible approach to North Yorkshire. Once out on the coast at the Victorian resort of **Saltburn**, or inland beyond Guisborough, you're very quickly in the heart of the North York Moors. **Public transport** links are good, too, with regular services connecting the bus and train stations of all the towns in the area. In particular, note the **Esk Valley train line** from Middlesbrough to Whitby, which runs via Grosmont, northern terminal point of the North Yorkshire Moors Railway.

Darlington and around

DARLINGTON hit the big time in 1825, when George Stephenson's *Locomotion* hurtled from here to nearby Stockton-on-Tees, with the inventor at the controls and flag-carrying horsemen riding ahead to warn of the onrushing train, at the terrifying speed of fifteen miles per hour. This novel form of transport soon proved popular with passengers, an unlooked-for bonus for Edward Pease, the line's instigator: he had simply wanted a fast and economical way to transport coal from the Durham pits to the docks at Stockton. Subsequently, Darlington grew into a rail-engineering centre, and didn't look back till the pruning of the network and the closure of the works in 1966.

It's little surprise, then, that all signs in town point to the **Darlington Railway Centre and Museum** (daily 10am–5pm; £2.10; Ⓦ www.drcm.org.uk), housed in Darlington's North Road Station, which was completed in 1842; it's a twenty-minute walk up Northgate from the central Market Place. The museum's pride and joy is the original *Locomotion*, actually built in Newcastle, which continued in service until 1841 – other locally made engines superseded it, and some of these are on show, too. The museum comes to life on Saturdays when you can watch enthusiasts at work building a new Pacific locomotive in the refurbished Darlington Locomotive Works (11am–4pm; same ticket), and on the occasional days, including a September festival and "Santa Special" days in December, when an engine hauls visitors up a quarter-mile stretch of track next door.

The origins of the rest of Darlington lie deep in Saxon times, following which it enjoyed a long history as an agricultural centre and staging post on the Great North Road. The monks carrying St Cuthbert's body from Ripon to Durham stopped here, the saint lending his name to the graceful central, riverside church of **St Cuthbert** (Easter–Sept Mon–Sat 11am–2pm; Oct–Easter Fri 11am–1pm), where the needle-like spire and decorative turrets herald the delicate Early English stonework inside. One of England's largest market squares spreads beyond the church up to the restored Victorian covered **market** (Mon–Sat 8am–5pm, with a large outdoor market Mon & Sat), next to the clocktower, both designed by Alfred Waterhouse, the architect responsible for Manchester's grandiose town hall and London's Natural History Museum. The surrounding buildings are all solidly nineteenth-century, too, many paid for by the town's hardworking Quaker industrialists (of whom Pease was a leading light), who doubtless would have frowned upon the current civic authority's attempts to humanize the town centre. The pedestrianized **Market Place** has been given back to the people and while it may not be Rome, you can sip a cappuccino at one of several cafés and pubs that spill tables outside at the first hint of sunshine.

Practicalities

Darlington's **train station** is on the main line from London to Scotland (via Durham and Newcastle) and there are also services to Middlesbrough, Saltburn and Bishop Auckland. From the station, walk up Victoria Road to the roundabout and turn right down Feethams for the central Market Place. You'll pass the Town Hall on Feethams, opposite which most **buses** stop.

The town's **tourist office** on the south side of Market Place at 13 Horsemarket (Mon–Fri 9am–5pm, Sat 10am–4pm; ⓣ01325/388666, ⓦwww.visitdarlington.net) can help with **accommodation**. Cheap and basic board (no-frills rooms, separate bathrooms, no breakfast) is available at the town's Arts Centre (ⓣ01325/483271; ❶), in Vane Terrace, less than ten minutes' walk west of the centre, where guests can use the centre's bars and lunchtime bistro – follow Duke Street from central Skinnergate. Other options include the *Balmoral Guest House*, a grand Victorian town house at 63 Woodland Rd, five minutes' walk northwest of the centre (ⓣ01325/461908, ⓦwww.balmoral-darlington.co.uk; ❷), and the *New Grange Hotel*, a smartly refurbished, 200-year-old mansion just southwest of the town centre on Southend Avenue (ⓣ01325/365858, ⓦwww.thenewgrangehotel.com; ❺).

There are several **cafés** on and around Market Place, while the *Hole in the Wall* pub here serves spicy Thai meals (Mon–Sat lunch & Thurs–Sat dinner) for under a tenner. Best central **restaurant** is *Joe Rigatoni's* (ⓣ01325/464642), a busy Italian place on the corner of Grange and Coniscliffe roads, just up from Market Place. For **drinking**, first port of call should be *Number Twenty 2*, 22 Coniscliffe Rd, a self-professed "alehouse" with guest beers on tap, wine by the glass and gastro-pub-style lunches (not Sun). You might also favour *The Old Yard*, 98 Bondgate, where not only is the ale real but there's also a full, inexpensive tapas menu (Spanish and Greek). For entertainment, check out the highly enterprising **Arts Centre** (Vane Terrace) and its affiliated **Civic Theatre** (Parkgate, between the Market Place and the train station), which together offer a full, year-round programme of theatre, movies, comedy, exhibitions and live music (bookings on ⓣ01325/486555, ⓦwww.darlington-arts.co.uk).

Piercebridge

Five miles west of Darlington, off the A67, the remains of a **Roman fort** (free access) are visible at the small village of **PIERCEBRIDGE**, on the River Tees. The site was first occupied in 70 AD and soon became a major strategic river crossing on the fortified Dere Street supply route; defensive ditches and sections of the fort wall are clearly visible, while various foundations have been identified as the remains of guard rooms, a temple and a row of houses. Amble out here late in the day and Piercebridge can make a decent overnight stop, provided you book ahead for the highly attractive eighteenth-century *George Hotel* (Ⓣ01325/374576; ❺), whose en-suite rooms and restaurant look across the gentle banks of the river. Buses run this way from Darlington or Barnard Castle.

Middlesbrough

MIDDLESBROUGH, Teesside's largest town, fifteen miles east of Darlington, is entirely a product of the early industrial age, with nineteenth-century iron and steel barons throwing up factories and housing almost as fast as they could ship their products out of the docks. What was a hamlet at the turn of the nineteenth century was a thriving industrial town of 100,000 people by the turn of the twentieth – "a vast dingy conjuring trick" to J.B. Priestley's mind. When iron and steel declined in importance and the local shipbuilding industry collapsed (the last shipyard closed in 1986), Middlesbrough took to the chemical industry, whose expansive, belching plants still surround the outskirts, making for an unsightly, forbidding approach to the town. Add to this a contemporary renaissance in light engineering and it seems that, compared to many of its neighbours, Middlesbrough can boast relative success in keeping its economic head above water. For visitors, however, none of these enterprises lend themselves easily to the celebration of industrial heritage so much in evidence further west, in the coalfields. The modern town centre is unremarkable in every way and only a pair of bridges recall earlier engineering feats. The **Transporter Bridge** (1911), at Ferry Road just north of the centre, its central section carting cars and pedestrians across the Tees towards Hartlepool (Mon–Sat 5am–11.05pm, Sun 2–11.05pm; cars 80p, pedestrians 30p), is the sole working example left in the country and now sports its own small **visitor centre** (June–Sept Thurs–Sun noon–5pm; Oct–May Sat & Sun noon–4pm; 50p), where you can find out how it operates. Further southwest, the **Newport Bridge** (1934) was the first vertical lift bridge built in England.

The town prefers to trumpet its position as "Gateway to Captain Cook Country", fair enough given that he was born a mile and a half south of the centre in Marton in 1728. Here, the **Captain Cook Birthplace Museum** in Stewart Park (Tues–Sun: Easter–Oct 10am–5.30pm; Nov–Easter 9am–3.30pm; £2.40) covers the life and times of Britain's greatest seaman and explorer, Captain James Cook, and does it very well by way of good interpretative and interactive displays. As well as displays of artefacts brought back from the South Seas on Cook's three main eighteenth-century voyages, touch-screen terminals provide contemporary testimony by his botanist Sir Joseph Banks, while a series of short films fill in the background about Cook's life and a sailor's lot at sea. Buses run from the bus station every fifteen minutes or so to Marton – ask the driver for the stop – and while you're in the park you may as well call in at nearby **St Cuthbert's Church** on Stokesley Road, where Cook was baptized. For more on the captain and the local area, see Ⓦwww.captaincook.org.uk.

The **Dorman Museum** (Tues, Wed & Fri–Sun 10am–5.30pm, Thurs 11am–6.30pm; free), on Linthorpe Road, is the other main reason to delay your onward journey from Middlesbrough. As a museum of the town's history, it incorporates some eye-catching pieces, including the early eighteenth-century Acklam Lordship map, showing views of the hamlet in 1716. There's also an excellent collection of Linthorpe pottery – richly glazed, unusually shaped ceramics from a late-nineteenth-century workshop designed to combat local unemployment. But the museum pursues other interests too, from the social history of twentieth-century women to the evolution of life on earth, combined with a discovery centre for children and adults, revolving around the science and use of water.

Practicalities

From Middlesbrough **train station** (direct services from Darlington, Manchester, Leeds, York and Newcastle), it's just a short walk up Albert Road to the main Corporation Road. Turn right for the **bus station** – five minutes further up on its continuation, Newport Road – and carry straight on for the **tourist office**, 99 Albert Rd (Mon–Thurs 9am–5pm, Fri 9am–4.30pm, Sat 9am–1.30pm; ⓣ01642/358086, ⓦwww.middlesbrough.gov.uk). Linthorpe Road, for the museum, runs south off Corporation Road, parallel to and west of Albert Road. For **accommodation** in the area, there are highly agreeable lodgings at *Judges Country House Hotel* at Kirklevington Hall, eight miles southwest of Middlesbrough and a mile south of Yarm on the A67 (ⓣ01642/789000, ⓦwww.judgeshotel.co.uk; ❽). Formerly the lodgings of circuit judges on duty in Teesside, this grand country house boasts beautiful gardens and woodlands, a fine restaurant and attentive staff – and good half-board deals at weekends. The eccentrically decorated *Purple Onion*, 80 Corporation Rd (ⓣ01642/222250), is the best **restaurant** in Middlesbrough, serving bitingly trendy food at middling-to-high prices; book at the weekends.

Stockton-on-Tees and Yarm

To complete the Captain Cook trail through this part of the country, you'll need to hop across the river from Middlesbrough to **STOCKTON-ON-TEES**. Tied up at Castlegate Quay is a detailed full-sized replica of **HM Bark Endeavour**, the converted collier in which Cook set sail in 1768 on his first scientific and surveying expedition to Tahiti, New Zealand and Australia. The ship's taken over by youth groups for part of the week, but from Sundays to Wednesdays (April–Oct 11am–5pm; £3) enthusiastic and knowledgeable volunteer guides recount the rigours of life on board during this hazardous voyage.

If all these tall tales of the high seas give you a taste for the water, you might be tempted by a **cruise** from the same quay aboard the Teesside Princess (ⓣ01642/608038, ⓦwww.princessrivercruises.co.uk), which potters upstream to Yarm and back in three and half hours. Sailings (May–Sept Tues–Sun 10.15am & 2pm; Oct–April Wed, Sat & Sun 10.15am & 2pm; £6 return) are timed to allow you to lunch in **YARM**, an affluent former market town which has preserved its good looks and supports a decent restaurant or two, as well as an attractive riverside pub, the *Blue Bell*.

Stockton's **train station** (similar services to Middlesbrough's but less frequent) is five minute's walk northwest of the High Street, where numerous **buses** from Middlesbrough will drop you. Off the east side of the High Street in Theatre Yard is the **tourist office** (Mon–Sat 9am–5pm; ⓣ01642/393936), with the river and Castlegate Quay just beyond.

Hartlepool

If there's one Teesside town trying hard to reinvent itself it's **HARTLEPOOL**, ten miles north of Middlesbrough, England's third-largest port in the nineteenth century and once a noted shipbuilding centre. After years in the doldrums, its image has been transformed by the renaissance of its once decaying dockland area, now spruced up as the popular **Hartlepool Historic Quay** off Marina Way (daily 10am–5pm; last admission 2hr before closing; £5.50). The entrance fee gets you on to the bustling eighteenth-century quayside where active attractions based around press gangs, the Royal Navy, seaport life and fighting ships stir the senses. There are also period shops, a replica eighteenth-century maritime pub, games and play area, coffee shop and market, while a separate fee is charged if you want to take a guided tour of **HMS Trincomalee** (daily: April–Oct 10.30am–5pm; Nov–March 10.30am–4pm; £3.50), a navy training ship built in 1817 and now berthed here. On the edge of the quay in the entertaining **Museum of Hartlepool** at Jackson Dock (daily 10am–5pm; free), you can climb the port's original lighthouse, board a restored paddle steamer and trace the town's history, including its most notorious episode, which to this day earns Hartlepudlians the nickname "monkey hangers": legend has it that when a French ship sank off the coast during the Napoleonic Wars, the locals mistook the sole survivor, a monkey, for a Frenchman, and tried and hanged it as a spy. The story subsequently turned full circle, with the election in 2002 of Hartlepool's first directly elected mayor, the independent candidate Stuart Drummond – previously known in town as H'Angus the Monkey, the official mascot for the football team, Hartlepool United.

In the town centre, ten minutes' walk south of the quay, the restored nineteenth-century Christ Church, on Church Square, houses Hartlepool's accomplished **Art Gallery** (Tues–Sat 10am–5.30pm, Sun 2–5pm; free) and the **tourist office** (same hours; ⓣ01429/869706, ⓦwww.destinationhartlepool.com), which can help if you're seduced into staying.

Saltburn

On the coast to the south of the Tees estuary, it's not a difficult decision to bypass the kiss-me-quick tackiness of Redcar in favour of **SALTBURN**, twelve miles east of Middlesbrough, a graceful Victorian resort in a dramatic setting overlooking extensive sands and mottled red sea cliffs. Soon after the railway arrived in 1861 to ferry Teessiders out to the sea on high days and holidays, Saltburn became a rather fashionable spa town boasting all the necessary accoutrements: hydraulic **inclined tramway**, complete with stained-glass windows, that connects upper town to pier and promenade; ornate **Italian Gardens** in the more bucolic Valley Gardens that run beneath the eastern side of town, linked to the beach by a **miniature railway**, and prominent hotels, some of which continue to flourish today. Modern attractions include the **Smugglers Heritage Centre** (April–Oct daily 10am–6pm, last tour 5.30pm; £1.95), a vivid audio-visual re-creation of Saltburn's darker past, set in fishermen's cottages to the east of the pier. Three dimly lit and cramped rooms of a 200-year-old tavern are once again populated by rowdy, swashbuckling seamen and buxom barmaids in an atmospheric retelling of the adventures of the smugglers' gangs, or "free traders", who made themselves popular with locals by sneaking vast quantities of tea, coffee, fine silks, lace and other such illicit cargoes ashore. Afterwards, don't forget to have a **drink** at the *Ship Inn*, the original smugglers' haunt next door. Steps from the beach behind the *Ship Inn* lead up the cliff to join the coastal section of the **Cleveland Way**, the path that starts deep in the North York Moors at Helmsley. It hits the coast at Saltburn, from where it's nine miles across the high cliffs to the next stop at Staithes in Yorkshire, and 54 miles in total to the end of the path at Filey.

There are regular **train** services to Saltburn from Newcastle, Durham and Bishop Auckland, via Darlington and Middlesbrough, while frequent **buses** from Middlesbrough bus station (with connections from Newcastle) stop in the parade outside the train station. If you want to stay in summer, it's best to call first at the **tourist office** in the railway station buildings (Easter–Sept Mon–Sat 9am–5pm; Oct–Easter Tues–Sat 9am–5pm; ⓣ01287/622422, ⓦwww.redcar-cleveland.gov.uk) and find out about **accommodation** vacancies. For surroundings in keeping with the town, the *Rushpool Hall Hotel* in Saltburn Valley (ⓣ01287/624111, ⓦwww.rushpoolhall.com; ❼) is a nineteenth-century country house set in extensive grounds about a mile south of the centre off Saltburn Lane, whose turrets, grand staircase and elegant public rooms are straight out of an Agatha Christie whodunnit. If your wallet won't stretch that far, *The Rose Garden*, just west of the station at 20 Hilda Place (ⓣ01287/622947, ⓦwww.therosegarden.co.uk; ❷), offers comfortable bedrooms and good breakfasts, including vegetarian options. *Virgo's*, just down from the station at 7 Dundas St East (closed Sun) is the best **café** in town.

Newcastle upon Tyne

At first glance **NEWCASTLE UPON TYNE** – virtual capital of the area between Yorkshire and Scotland – may appear to be just another northern industrial conurbation, but the banks of the Tyne have been settled for nearly two thousand years and the city consequently has a greater breadth of attractions than many of its rivals. The Romans were the first to bridge the river here, and the "new castle" appeared as long ago as 1080. In the seventeenth century a regional monopoly on coal export brought wealth and power to Newcastle and – as well as giving a new expression to the English language – engendered its other great industry, shipbuilding. At one time, 25 percent of the world's shipping was built here, and the first steam train and steam turbine also emerged from local factories. In its nineteenth-century heyday, Newcastle's engineers and builders gave the city an elegance that has survived today in the impressive buildings of Grainger Town – indeed, only London and Bath have more listed classical buildings.

Industrial decline hit Newcastle early, as highlighted by the Jarrow Crusade of 1936 (see p.1079), but there's been an extraordinary revival over the last decade as the city has shed its dowdy provincial coat to emerge as a vibrant European arts and nightlife destination. The pre-eminent artistic symbol of this renewal is Antony Gormley's **Angel of the North**, a magnificent steel sculpture the size of a jumbo jet that welcomes anyone approaching from the south by rail or road. Newcastle's city centre has been transformed, particularly along the banks of the River Tyne, whose famous series of bridges acts as a backdrop to the ever-developing cultural and entertainment scene. Both Newcastle and Gateshead sides of the river have seen dramatic change – indeed, these days visitors are encouraged to think of the city not as Newcastle upon Tyne but as "Newcastle Gateshead". On **Gateshead Quays** are the BALTIC contemporary arts centre and Norman Foster's Sage music centre, while Newcastle's **Quayside** is scene of much of the city's contemporary nightlife, rivalling the traditional knees-up antics of the notorious Bigg Market. Add to these the lure of some impressive museums and galleries, including the unique Life Science Centre and the best traditional art gallery in the Northeast, the Laing, and there's a case for taking whatever time you were going to spend in the city and doubling it.

Newcastle's inhabitants, known as **Geordies**, have a partisan pride in their city, which finds its most evident expression in fanatical support for the **Newcastle United** football team (the "Magpies"). With the stadium firmly anchored in the heart of the city, and every other young (and not so young) supporter wearing the familiar black-and-white shirt, it's difficult to overstate the team's importance.

Arrival

Coming to Newcastle by train gives a fantastic view of the city's trademark bridges across the steep Tyne Valley. **Central Station**, on Neville Street, is a five-minute walk from the city centre or Quayside, and has a useful tourist office and Metro station. National Express services arrive at the **coach station** on St James's Boulevard, not far from Central Station, while most regional **bus** services use the **Haymarket** bus station on Percy Street on the north side of the centre (Haymarket Metro). Many other city and local bus services arrive at and depart from the underground bus station a hundred yards down the same street in **Eldon Square Shopping Centre**.

Newcastle's **airport**, six miles north of the city, is linked by Metro to Central Station (5.50am–11.10pm, every 7–15min; 20min; £1.80) and beyond. Alternatively, take a taxi into the centre (around £12). **Ferry arrivals** from Scandinavia and Holland dock at Royal Quays, North Shields, seven miles east of the city. Connecting bus services run you into the centre, stopping at Central Station, while a taxi will cost around £10.

For all **departure details** and enquiry numbers, see "Listings", p.1076.

Information, city transport and tours

There are **tourist offices** at 132 Grainger St (Mon–Wed & Fri 9.30am–5.30pm, Thurs 9.30am–7.30pm, Sat 9am–5pm, Sun 10am–4pm; Oct–May closed Sun; ⓣ0191/277 8000, ⓦwww.visitnewcastlegateshead.com); in Central Station (Mon–Fri 9.30am–5pm, Sat 9am–5pm; same contact details); and at Gateshead Quays in St Mary's Church, Oakwellgate (Mon–Fri 9am–5pm, Sat & Sun 10am–4pm; ⓣ0191/477 5380). All hand out useful maps and city guides, and have various brochures and booklets available, including self-guided walking-tour "heritage trails".

You can walk around the whole of central Newcastle easily enough, but for journeys further afield you'll need to get to grips with the conurbation's cheap and efficient rail system, the **Metro** (daily 5.15am–11.30pm, services every 3–15min). The landmark Grey's Monument marks the city centre and the site of **Monument**, the main interchange for the Metro's two lines: the green line for South Shields, Jarrow, Gateshead, Jesmond and the airport; and the yellow line for Wallsend, Tynemouth and Whitley Bay, plus a southern branch to Gateshead and Sunderland. The most useful discount pass is the Metro Day Saver for unlimited rides (£3 after 9am Mon, Tues, Thurs & Fri, all day Sat & Sun; £2 after 9.30am Wed; or £1.50 after 6.30pm any day), available from ticket machines at every station. For all public transport enquiries, call **Nexus Traveline** (ⓣ0870/608 2608), log onto the Nexus website (ⓦwww.nexus.org.uk), which has a useful journey planner option, or visit the Nexus Travelshops at Haymarket, Monument or Gateshead Metro stations.

To get out on the Tyne, sign up for one of Tyne River Cruises' three-hour **sightseeing cruises** (£10; ⓣ0191/296 6740, ⓦwww.tyneleisureline.co.uk). These depart most weekends throughout the year, and Tuesdays and Thursdays in summer, from Newcastle's Quayside. The local public transport authority

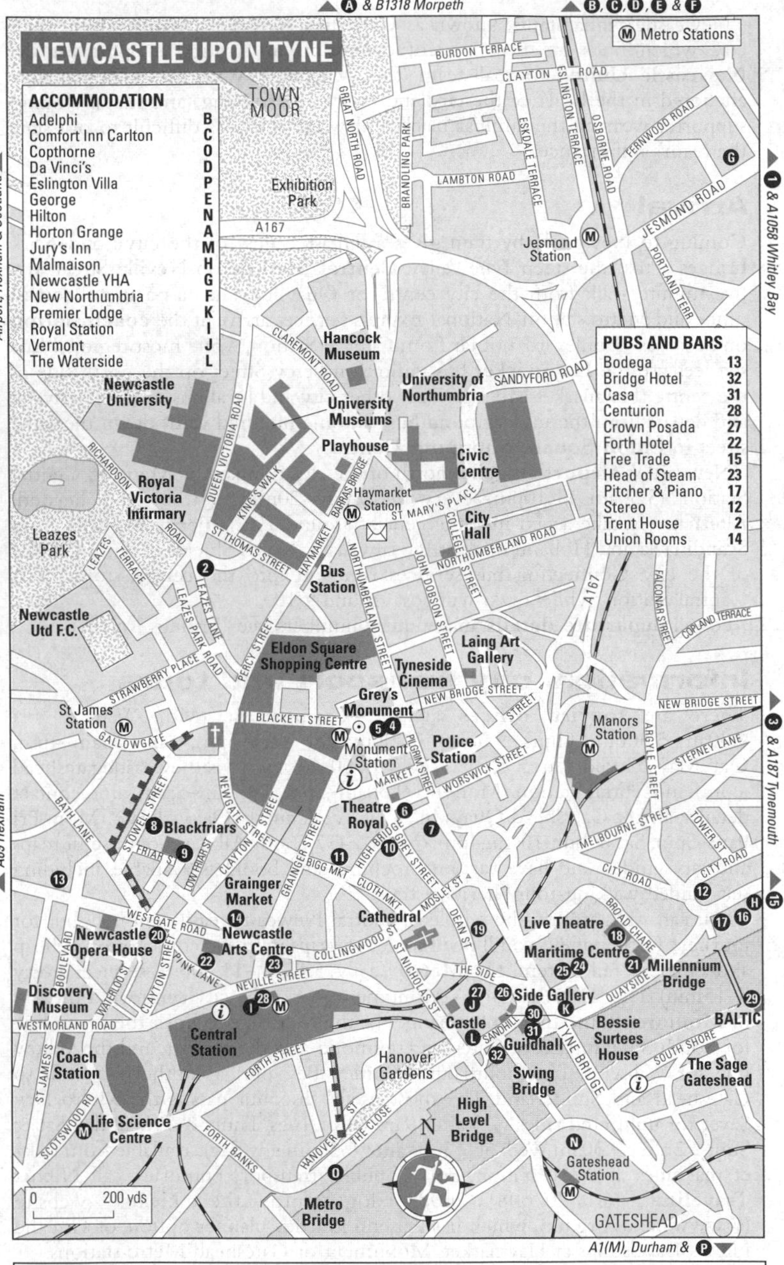

RESTAURANTS

Barn @ The Biscuit Factory	3
Big Mussel	26
Blackfriars	9
Blakes Coffee House	10
Café 21	25
Café Live	18
Fisherman's Lodge	1
Heartbreak Soup	21
Intermezzo	4
La Tasca	16
Leela's	19
Mangos	8
Pani's	6
Paradiso	7
Riverside Café-Bar	29
Rooftop & Riverside	29
Rupali	11
Salsa Club	20
Tyneside Coffee Rooms	5
Uno's	30
Vujon	24

also operates summer afternoon cruises (Sun & Wed, £6–12) from South Shields, at the mouth of the river (details from Nexus). Guided, themed **walking tours** of the city centre (June–Sept daily; £2) are arranged by the Grainger Street tourist office. There's also a hop-on, hop-off, open-top **sightseeing bus**, which departs from Central Station (Easter–Sept daily 10am–4pm, until 5pm in Aug, departures every 30–60min; £5; Ⓦ www.city-sightseeing.com).

Accommodation

Budget chains offer plenty of good-value rooms in the city centre and down by the Quayside, while the biggest concentration of small hotels and guest houses is a mile north of the centre in Jesmond, along and off Osborne Road: take bus #30B, #31B or #80 from Central Station or Haymarket. You shouldn't have difficulty finding a bed, though business visitors make weekdays busier than weekends for most of the year. Consequently, many hotels offer discounts for Friday- and Saturday-night stays, especially at the upper end of the scale where savings can be considerable. Save yourself time and effort by using the free **room-booking service** available at the tourist offices to personal callers.

Hotels and guest houses

Adelphi Hotel 63 Fern Ave, off Osborne Rd, Jesmond Ⓣ0191/281 3109. Five minutes off the main road, in a quiet residential street, this cheery family-run B&B offers a variety of acceptable rooms. Most are en suite (with shower cubicles), though two share a large bathroom, and some are big enough to sleep three. ❸

Comfort Inn Carlton 82–86 Osborne Rd, Jesmond Ⓣ0191/281 3361. Decent-value motel-style rooms, with everything you need (ironing board, hair-drier, satellite TV) for a comfortable night. There's a bar and restaurant, and deck seating out front for those balmy Newcastle evenings. ❺

Copthorne The Close, Quayside Ⓣ0191/222 0333, Ⓦ www.millenniumhotels.com. Superbly located on the riverside, this stylish four-star hotel has Tyne views from most of its well-appointed rooms. Modems and voicemail come as standard, while "connoisseur" upgrades offer late check-outs and free continental breakfast. Breakfast not included except for weekend packages. ❽, weekend ❼

Da Vinci's 73 Osborne Rd, Jesmond Ⓣ0191/281 5284, Ⓦ www.davincis.co.uk. Nothing flash, but the sixteen well-priced rooms, most of them fairly large and light, are a popular Jesmond choice. And there's the bonus of a classy Italian restaurant on the premises. ❹

Eslington Villa 8 Station Rd, Low Fell, Gateshead Ⓣ0191/487 6017, Ⓕ0191/420 0667. On the south side of Gateshead overlooking the Team Valley trading estate and only practicable with your own transport, this small, quiet hotel has huge, stylishly decorated rooms, well-tended gardens and a top-class restaurant. Dinner, bed and breakfast deal usually available for around £130 double. ❺

George 88 Osborne Rd, Jesmond Ⓣ0191/281 4442, Ⓦ www.thegeorgehotel.org. Victorian town-house hotel with a dozen of the city's least expensive en-suite rooms, including good rates for families. Renovations have smartened the place up a bit, and there's a patio, restaurant and bar with open fire. ❷

Hilton Newcastle Gateshead Bottle Bank, Gateshead Quays Ⓣ08705/515151, Ⓦ www.hilton.co.uk. Newest arrival on the Gateshead side is the four-star *Hilton*, near the Tyne Bridge, with terrific views, pool, gym, health club, bar and restaurant. ❽, weekend ❼

Horton Grange 2 miles north of Dinnington Ⓣ01661/860686, Ⓦ www.horton-grange.co.uk. Relaxed and welcoming country-house hotel with an excellent conservatory restaurant, five miles north of the city centre off the A1(M). ❻

Jury's Inn Scotswood Rd Ⓣ0191/201 4400, Ⓦ www.bookajurysinn.com. Three-star budget accommodation close to the Life Science Centre and Central Station. Fixed-rate rooms accommodate up to three adults or a family, there's a pub and restaurant on site, and 24hr reception. Seventh-floor rooms have city (though not river) views. ❹

Malmaison Quayside Ⓣ0191/245 5000, Ⓦ www.malmaison.com. Chic lodgings in the former Co-op building, right on the Quayside. Rooms come with great beds, CD players, power showers, cable TV and modems. Jazzy sounds, crushed velvet sofas, brasserie, bar and gym round off the facilities. ❼

New Northumbria 61–69 Osborne Rd, Jesmond Ⓣ0191/281 4961, Ⓦ www.newnorthumbriahotel.co.uk. Contemporary boutique-style lodgings offering spacious rooms (some with sofa and chair), big beds, warm decor, and lovely panelled bathrooms with power showers. Café-bar and restaurant attached, with garden seating. ❺

Premier Lodge Quayside ⓣ0870/990 6530, ⓦwww.premierlodge.com. An unbeatable location for this no-frills chain: in the nineteenth-century Exchange Buildings under the Tyne Bridge. One price for all bedrooms, so singles lose out and families gain. Be sure to ask for a room with a river view. ❸

Royal Station Neville St ⓣ0191/232 0781, ⓦwww.royalstationhotel.com. The city's original Victorian station hotel in a great central location, opened in 1858 by Victoria herself. It's been fully refurbished, and has an indoor pool, Jacuzzi and gym, while rooms are often available at discounted rates. Breakfast not included. ❻, weekend ❺

Vermont Castle Garth ⓣ0191/233 1010, ⓦwww.vermont-hotel.com. High-class twelve-storey business hotel, with reception next to the castle and its lowest floor giving onto the Quayside. Good views and facilities, including in-room modem ports and a fitness centre, three bars and a restaurant. ❽, weekend ❼

The Waterside 48–52 Sandhill ⓣ0191/230 0111, ⓦwww.watersidehotel.com. Small, luxury hotel in a listed building right in the centre of the Quayside night-time action. Rooms are decently equipped, if a bit on the small side, and it has its own bar. Breakfast not included. ❺

Hostel and university accommodation

Newcastle YHA 107 Jesmond Rd ⓣ0870/770 5972, ⓔnewcastle@yha.org.uk. Popular town-house hostel with sixty beds (£11.50), including five twin rooms (❶), near Jesmond Metro station – reserve in advance in summer. Breakfast and cheap evening meals served, though no laundry facilities. Closed Christmas to mid-Jan.

University of Newcastle ⓣ0191/222 6296. Hundreds of rooms available at various locations, singles and twins, during Easter holidays and from July to September. From £22 per person.

University of Northumbria ⓣ0191/227 4024. Call for details of single rooms available in diverse student halls of residence during Easter holidays and from July to September. From £22.50 per person.

The City

The city splits into several distinct areas, though it's only a matter of minutes to walk between them. Castle and cathedral occupy the heights immediately above the River Tyne, whose Newcastle and Gateshead quaysides now form the biggest single attraction in the city. North of the cathedral lies Grainger Town, the city-centre district of listed Victorian buildings that is at its most dramatic along Grey Street. West of here is Chinatown and the two big draws of the Discovery Museum and Life Science Centre; east is the renowned Laing Gallery; and north the university museums and open parkland known as Town Moor.

Castle and Cathedral

Anyone arriving by train from the north will get a sneak preview of the **Castle** (daily: April–Sept 9.30am–5.30pm; Oct–March Tues–Sun 9.30am–4.30pm; £1.50), as the rail line splits the keep from its gatehouse, the Black Gate, on St Nicholas' Street. A wooden fort was built here over an Anglo-Saxon cemetery – which itself had been dug into the site of the Roman fort of Pons Aelius – by Robert Curthose, illegitimate eldest son of William the Conqueror, but the present keep dates from the twelfth century and is everything a castle should be: thick, square and labyrinthine. Staircases and rooms, including a bare Norman chapel, lie off a draughty Great Hall, where displays relate to the Civil War siege of 1644 by a Scottish army supporting the Parliamentarian cause; a small museum room shows various archeological finds. Down in the garrison room, prisoners were incarcerated during the sixteenth to eighteenth centuries, while locals rushed to its deep shelter in World War II to sit out German bombing. There's also a great view from the rooftop over the river and city. Little remains of the outer fortifications except the Black Gate, which was added in 1247–50, and is topped by a seventeenth-century house.

Further along St Nicholas' Street stands the **Cathedral** (Mon–Fri 7am–6pm, Sat 8.30am–4pm, Sun 7.30am–noon & 4–7pm; guided tours Easter–Sept Wed 11am; free), dating mainly from the fourteenth and fifteenth centuries and remarkable chiefly for its tower – erected in 1470, it is topped with a crown-like structure of turrets and arches supporting a lantern. Inside, behind the high altar, is one of the largest funerary brasses in England; it was commissioned by Roger Thornton, the Dick Whittington of Newcastle, who arrived in the city penniless and died its richest merchant in 1430. The brass is etched with near life-size figures of Thornton and his wife. Much of the interior was given a neo-Gothic remodelling in the late nineteenth century under Sir George Gilbert Scott – the ornate reredos, depicting various Northumbrian saints, is from this period, as is the font canopy with its intricate pinnacles.

Along the River Tyne

From between the castle and the cathedral a road known simply as The Side – formerly the main road out of the city – descends to Newcastle's **Quayside** where the first bridges across the Tyne stood. There have been fixed river crossings here since Roman times and today the Tyne is spanned by seven bridges in close proximity, the most prominent being the looming **Tyne Bridge** of 1928, symbol of the city, which bears a striking resemblance to the roughly contemporaneous Sydney Harbour Bridge – not surprising really, as both were built by Dorman Long of Middlesbrough. To the west of it, road and rail lines cross the river on the **High Level Bridge**, built by Robert Stephenson in 1849 – Queen Victoria was one of the first passengers across, promoting the railway revolution. Further west, under the bridge and up the steep steps to Hanover Street, a section of the old encircling medieval city wall survives, and the river views from the adjacent **Hanover Gardens** are magnificent.

Protected by the towering castle, the Quayside became the commercial heart of the city and in the sixteenth and seventeenth centuries its half-timbered houses were the homes of Newcastle's wealthiest merchants. One is **Bessie Surtees' House**, at 41–44 Sandhill (Mon–Fri 10am–4pm; free), the residence of an eighteenth-century woman who scandalously eloped to Scotland with her beau; all ended well and the groom in question went on to become Lord Eldon, Chancellor of England. Three rooms, decorated with elaborate panelling and plaster ceilings, are open to the public. While you're here, it's well worth checking out the **Side Gallery**, just round the corner at 9 The Side (Tues–Sat 10am–5pm, Sun 11am–3pm; free; Ⓦwww.amber-online.com), which hosts temporary exhibitions of documentary photography (changing every six weeks or so) from all over the world.

Directly opposite Bessie Surtees' House is the **Guildhall**, rebuilt many times since its foundation in 1316, where court sessions were held; John Wesley preached here in 1742 and had to be rescued from a volatile crowd by a hefty fishwife. On Sundays a busy morning **market** spreads around the nearby hydraulic **Swing Bridge**, which was erected in 1876 by Lord Armstrong to replace the old Tyne Bridge, so that larger vessels could reach his shipyards upriver.

Beyond the Tyne Bridge, the modern-day regeneration of the Quayside is in full swing. Riverside apartments, a landscaped promenade, public sculpture and pedestrianized squares have paved the way for a series of fashionable new bars and restaurants, centred on the supremely graceful **Millennium Bridge**, the world's first tilting span, which is designed to pivot to allow ships to pass. This revolutionary structure has sorely exercised the imaginations of commentators, who have compared it variously to a lyre, shark's teeth and a warped tennis

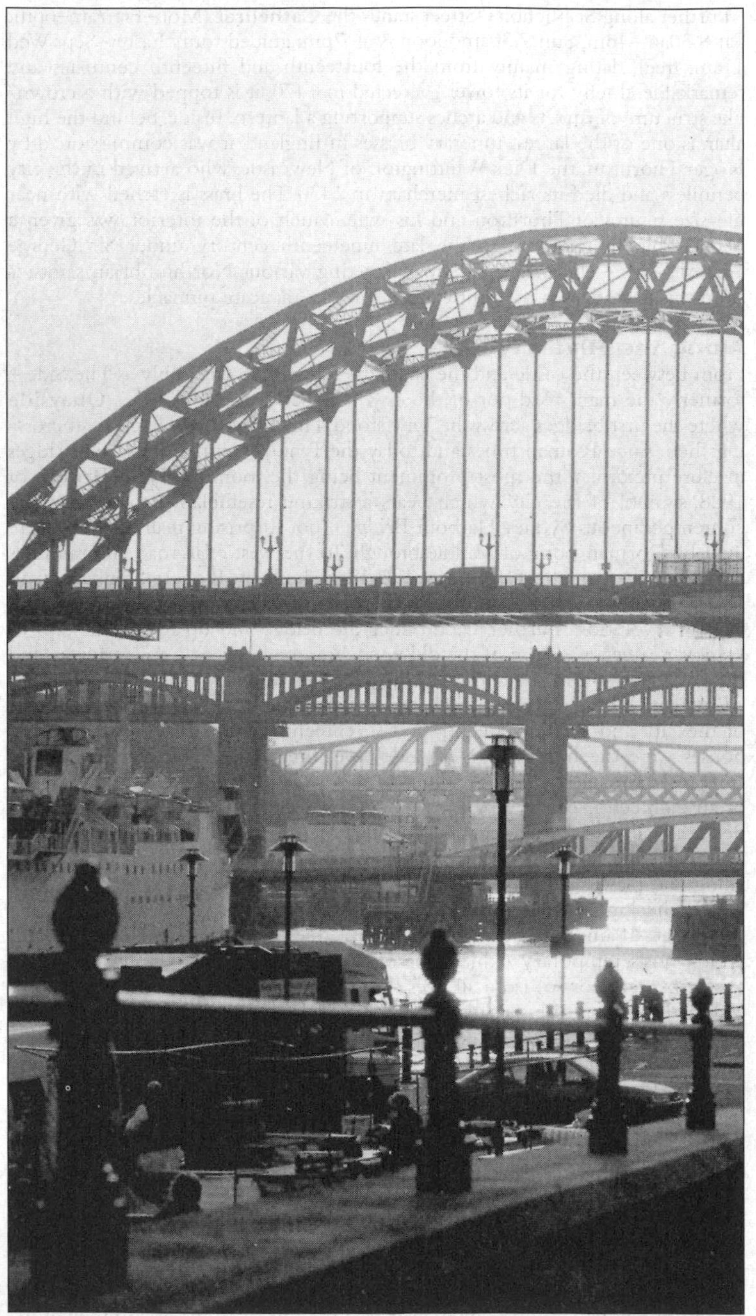

△ The Tyne Bridges, Newcastle

racket, though locals, who chose the design in a public vote, have settled on the "blinking eye".

The bridge allows pedestrians and cyclists to cross the Tyne to the **Gateshead Quays**, either to complete a mile-long circuit of the riverfronts via the Swing Bridge, or to visit **BALTIC**, the dramatic Centre for Contemporary Art (Mon–Wed & Sat 10am–7pm, Thurs 10am–8pm, Sun 10am–5pm; free; Ⓦwww.balticmill.com), fashioned from a brick flour mill built in the 1940s. This has been converted into a huge visual "art factory", second only in scale to London's Tate Modern. There's no permanent collection here, though the galleries display a robust series of specially commissioned or invited art exhibitions – Antony Gormley has already had a huge solo exhibition and the centre is scheduled to hold more ambitious international art shows as well as local community projects and other displays. Alongside the galleries, the BALTIC accommodates artists' studios, education workshops, an art performance space and cinema, plus a café-bar and two restaurants, one at river level with an outdoor terrace, the other on the roof with uninterrupted views of the Newcastle skyline.

The BALTIC has been joined on the Gateshead side by **The Sage Gateshead** (Ⓦwww.thesagegateshead.org), a billowing steel, aluminium and glass structure that's home to the Northern Sinfonia and Folkworks, an organization promoting British and international traditional music. It already promotes a full concert programme at venues around the region, but the inaugural 2005 season will see The Sage's main concert hall and studio space in use, along with a public concourse offering marvellous river and city views, a café-bar and bistro.

Grainger Town and the city centre

By the mid-nineteenth century, Newcastle's centre of balance had shifted away from the river, uphill to the rapidly expanding Victorian town. In a few short years, businessmen-builders and architects such as Richard Grainger, Thomas Oliver and John Dobson fashioned what Nikolaus Pevsner later thought to be the best-designed Victorian town in England, with classical facades of stone lining splendid new streets, most notably **Grey Street** – "that descending, subtle curve", as John Betjeman described it. The street takes its name from the Northumberland dynasty of political heavyweights whose most illustrious member was the second Earl Grey, prime minister from 1830 to 1834. In the middle of his term in office he carried the Reform Bill through parliament, an act commemorated by **Grey's Monument** at the top of the street.

Cleaning and restoration has rescued many of Newcastle's finer buildings: J.B. Priestley, visiting in the 1930s, thought that the city "might almost have been carved out of coal", so black was its stone. Today, Grey Street shows off much of its Victorian elegance, best exemplified by the **Theatre Royal**, halfway down. Other streets fell to the municipal butchers in the 1960s and 1970s – Eldon Square, once a model of Victorian balance, now a shopping centre, a case in point – though not all was lost: **Grainger Market** (Mon–Sat 8am–5pm) near Grey's Monument, Europe's largest undercover market when built in the 1830s, maintains its style; while John Dobson's **Central Station**, facing Neville Street, trumpeted the confidence of the Railway Age with its soaring interior spaces and curved ironwork.

West of here, behind Gallowgate, is the most complete stretch of the old **city walls**, leading down to Westgate Road. Once encircling the whole of medieval Newcastle, built six to ten feet thick and 25 feet high in parts, they remained in place until the sixteenth century, after which time many sections were plundered for building stone. Several towers remained in use by the city guilds as meeting houses and here, at the "West Walls", alongside Stowell Street, one, the

Morden Tower, gained prestige as the haunt of poets such as Allen Ginsberg, Basil Bunting and Tom Pickard. Through the arch, the outer defensive ditch has been restored. Stowell Street, incidentally, is Newcastle's **Chinatown**, lined with restaurants and supermarkets. Across Stowell Street from the tower, at Friar's Green, is the tranquil courtyard of **Blackfriars**, a thirteenth-century stone monastery with ruined cloistered grounds, now lovingly restored to house a crafts centre and restaurant.

Discovery Museum

On the south side of Westgate Road, the **Discovery Museum** in Blandford Square (Mon–Sat 10am–5pm, Sun 2–5pm; free; Ⓦwww.twmuseums.org.uk) puts into context the city's history in a series of extremely impressive displays housed in the former headquarters of the Co-operative Wholesale Society. You are confronted on arrival by the hundred-foot-long *Turbinia*, the world's first steam-turbine-powered ship, built by the brilliant but unconventional and occasionally absent-minded local engineer, Charles Parsons: having resorted to gate-crashing the naval review at Spithead aboard the *Turbinia* to bring her to the military establishment's attention, Parsons was obliged to add a lookout post towards the front of the ship as he'd built the bridge behind the funnel. Galleries on three floors surround the *Turbinia*, with standout attractions including the "Newcastle Story", a walk through the city's past with tales from animated characters along the way, and the interactive "Science Maze" which focuses on Newcastle's pioneering inventors (including one Joseph Swan who, according to locals at least, beat Edison to the invention of the light bulb). There's plenty for children (and adults) to participate in, particularly in the "Science Maze" but also in the "Tyne Story" galleries, where the role of the river in the development of the city is investigated. From the café above the gallery, a stunning display of ship models can be viewed, alongside a forty-foot-long model of the River Tyne and a working model of the swing bridge. Elsewhere in the museum, there are walk-through fashion galleries, displaying some of the 8000 costume items in the collection, and old favourites like the talking regimental horse and barking drill sergeant in "The Soldier's Life" exhibition.

Life Science Centre

Heading back towards the Central Station along Westmorland Street, you can't miss the sleek, contemporary lines of the **International Centre for Life**, whose buildings reach around the sweeping expanse of Times Square. This ambitious "science village" project combines bioscience and genetics centres with the **Life Science Centre** (Mon–Sat 10am–6pm, Sun 11am–6pm, last admission 4pm; £6.95; Ⓦwww.lifesciencecentre.co.uk), which aims to convey the scientific secrets of life using the latest entertainment technology. The emphasis is squarely on learning through having fun, though you probably don't have to undergo the white-knuckle "Crazy Motion Ride", the world's longest motion simulator, to learn that "life is a rollercoaster" – or that you don't like rollercoasters. Imaginative and humorous computer games include "Cell Wars", wherein you're invited to help Professor Pukestopper zap bacteria, while more obviously didactic purposes are served by "Jack's Story", an arresting 3D film showing a baby developing from embryo to birth, and "Choices", which invites you to explore the ethical issues surrounding genetic research. The centre is always adding new attractions, from science experiments to virtual reality experiences, and children find the whole thing enormously rewarding – expect to spend a good three hours here, if not more, with the *Times Square Café* on hand to provide a break.

Laing Gallery

Newcastle's – indeed, the northeast's – premier art collection is the **Laing Gallery** on New Bridge St (Mon–Sat 10am–5pm, Sun 2–5pm; free; Ⓦ www.twmuseums.org.uk), off John Dobson Street, behind the library. It's a splendidly organized museum, in which local pottery, glassware, costume and sculpture play their part, while on permanent display is a sweep through British art from Reynolds to John Hoyland, with a smattering of Pre-Raphaelites, so admired by English industrial barons.

The real treat here is the lashings of **John Martin** (1789–1854), a self-taught Northumberland painter with a penchant for massive biblical and mythical scenes. He came from a rather dysfunctional family – his elder brother wore a tortoiseshell hat, another brother set fire to York Minster – and with the benefit of twenty-first-century psychological hindsight, it's easy to imagine what demons drove him in his work. Early studies are inoffensive topographical works of castles and landscapes, but the dramatic northeastern scenery was soon to influence him strangely. In *The Bard* (1817), depicting Thomas Gray's poem of the same name, the last surviving Welsh bard – resembling a biblical Charlton Heston on drugs – curses the English troops before jumping to his death from crags Martin conjured from his visits to the Allen Gorge. Much later, in *The Destruction of Sodom and Gomorrah* (1852), blazing buildings and violent colours were presumably influenced by the Tyne's industrial furnaces. Whatever you think of Martin's work – and it certainly provokes extreme reactions – it's hard not to be moved by a paranoiac who was convinced equally of his own genius and of everyone else's opposition to his talent.

Martin's histrionics aside, the other must-see in the gallery is the **Art on Tyneside** exhibition, which romps through the history of art and applied art in the region since the seventeenth century with considerable gusto. There's portraiture and landscapes of the city through the ages, as well as digressions on eighteenth-century coffee houses, clothes and materials, glassware and wood engraving – the latter, most famously, by Thomas Bewick (see p.1078), whose pastoral works were inspired by the surrounding countryside. The exhibition also covers Sixties pop artists Richard Hamilton and Victor Pasmore, both of whom taught at Newcastle University, and the architectural developments in the 1980s, including analysis of the award-winning Byker Wall project, on the outskirts of the city centre, pioneered by Ralph Erskine.

Temporary exhibitions and a permanent children's gallery designed for the under-5s round off matters, and there's a good café too. Outside the Laing's front door don't miss a stroll over the notorious **Blue Carpet** – a public art installation whose tiles fold back on themselves to form unusual benches, lit from underneath.

The university museums, Hancock Museum and Town Moor

Newcastle University, opposite Haymarket Metro, contains a knot of fine museums and galleries, located off King's Walk: the **Museum of Antiquities** (Mon–Sat 10am–5pm; free) makes a good place to get to grips with the history of Hadrian's Wall, with a fascinating scale model of the whole length of the wall; the small **Shefton Museum of Greek Art and Archeology** (Mon–Fri 10am–4pm; free) contains a valuable collection of armour, sculpture and pottery; while the celebrated **Hatton Gallery** (Mon–Fri 10am–5.30pm, Sat 10am–4.30pm; free), attached to the Fine Art Department, features a collection of African sculpture, the only surviving example of Kurt Schwitters' Merzbau (a sort of architectural collage) and a wide variety of temporary exhibitions.

Also attached to the university is the **Hancock Museum** on Barras Bridge (Mon–Sat 10am–5pm, Sun 2–5pm; £4.50; Ⓦwww.twmuseums.org.uk). Based on an eighteenth-century natural history collection, it's grown to immense dimensions – with more than 150,000 insect specimens alone – and presents engaging displays on subjects as diverse as the history of life and ancient Egypt, as well as hosting annual blockbuster exhibitions.

Beyond the University of Newcastle, through the landscaped **Exhibition Park**, you reach the **Town Moor**, 1200 acres of common land where freemen of the city, including former US president Jimmy Carter, are entitled to graze their cattle. It's the site of the annual "Hoppings" in the last week of June, a huge week-long fair of rides, stalls and other attractions which keeps the cows awake until well after dark.

Eating

Newcastle's tastes have moved a long way from the traditional gargantuan bread rolls called "stottie cakes" – you're more likely to find them drizzled with olive oil and stuffed with Parma ham and chargrilled vegetables these days. At the budget end of the market Italian, Indian and Chinese food dominates the scene, while at the top end of the scale the city has attracted some inventive chefs. For Chinese food, check out Stowell Street in Chinatown where you'll find cheap all-you-can-eat buffets as well as more refined Cantonese restaurants. If you're counting the pennies, aim to eat early – many city-centre restaurants offer **early bird/happy hour** deals before 7pm, while others serve **set lunches** at often ludicrously low prices.

Cafés and café-bars

Blakes Coffee House 53 Grey St. Friendly and hugely popular haunt serving sandwiches, salads and daily specials. Daytime only.

Intermezzo 10–12 Pilgrim St. Café-bar (open daily until 11pm) attached to the Tyneside Cinema, with Italian pastries, sandwiches, pizza slices and salads. Drinks are good too, whether it's great coffee, juices and shakes, or the cocktails it's known for.

Pani's 61–65 High Bridge St, off Grey St. Just up a side street below the Theatre Royal, this Italian coffee and sandwich bar has a loyal clientele, who come during the day for stuffed sandwiches, *antipasti*, pasta and salads or at night (open until 10pm) for the same authentic cheap eats. Closed Sun.

Paradiso 1 Market Lane. Hidden down an alley off Pilgrim Street, a mellow café-bar-restaurant with great food (Thai-style mussels to handmade pasta), amiable staff, indoor booths and a sundeck. Sunday brunch is a memorable experience, while the *Popolo* lounge bar downstairs mops up post-diners and drinkers. Closes Sun at 7pm.

Riverside Café-Bar BALTIC, South Shore Rd, Gateshead. The BALTIC's ground-floor café-bar is a handy spot for a coffee and gourmet sandwich (food served until 7pm), and makes a relaxed target for a post-dinner drink, too.

Tyneside Coffee Rooms Tyneside Cinema, 10–12 Pilgrim St. Coffee, light meals and art-house movie talk in the Art Deco cinema café. Closes 9pm and all Sun.

Restaurants

Barn @ The Biscuit Factory Stoddart St ⓣ0191/230 3338. Superbly creative cooking in the contemporary surroundings of the old biscuit factory-now-art gallery. Everything on the menu tantalizes, from smoked paprika-dusted cod to balsamic-vinegar ice cream, and the service is as sharp as the cuisine. Café menu served at lunchtime, a la carte at dinner. It's a bit of a way out; take a taxi. Closed Sun dinner. Expensive.

Big Mussel 15 The Side ⓣ0191/232 1057. Mussels, chips and mayo served seven ways for a tenner, though there are other fish and seafood choices on the menu. A £6 lunch and "clock saver" dinner (5.30–7pm) provide value for money too. Moderate.

Blackfriars Friar St ⓣ0191/261 5945. Hard to think of a more atmospheric location for a restaurant than this stylishly updated twelfth-century former monks' refectory. The food trips around the world with confidence, from liver and mash to Thai curry. Set lunches are a good deal, while prices rise at night. Sunday brunch comes with live jazz. Closed Sun dinner and all Mon. Moderate –Expensive.

Café 21 21 Queen St ☎0191/222 0755. Stylish Parisian-influenced bistro with a classic menu – confit of duck, smoked haddock with bubble and squeak, steak with herb butter – and good service. Blackboard specials ring the seasonal changes, and the set lunches are a bargain for the quality. Closed Sun. Expensive.

Café Live Live Theatre, 27 Broad Chare ☎0191/232 1331. Coffee, drinks and sandwiches (gourmet and classic) downstairs in the espresso bar, and a restaurant upstairs (courtesy of the *Café 21* people) with a wider, pricier Mediterranean menu – though the set lunches and pre-theatre deals are some of the best in town. Closes Mon at 5pm and all Sun. Moderate.

Fisherman's Lodge Jesmond Dene ☎0191/281 3281. Still the benchmark for gourmet restaurants in the region, this classy, formal place in landscaped parkland, two miles from the centre, offers well-received modern and traditional British cuisine. Excellent seafood and vegetarian choices. Closed Sat lunch & all Sun. Very Expensive.

Heartbreak Soup Baltic Chambers, 77 Quayside ☎0191/222 1701. Good-value global food – jerk pork, crab risotto or Catalan-style chicken – in colour-splashed surroundings down by the river. Dinner only, closed Sun. Moderate.

La Tasca 106 Quayside ☎0191/230 4006. A veritable tapas barn, near the Millennium Bridge, with Spanish tiling and cast-iron candelabras. The food's not bad, though the place really comes into its own in summer when you can sit out on the terrace, grazing, chatting and drinking. Moderate.

Leela's 20 Dean St ☎0191/230 1261. A rare treat among the flock-wallpaper curry houses, *Leela's* serves high-quality South Indian cuisine, with plenty of vegetarian options, including a great *masala dosa*. Closed Sun. Expensive.

Mangos 43 Stowell St ☎0191/232 6522. A bit more stylish and a bit more authentic than most Chinatown eateries, *Mangos* offers traditional and new-wave Cantonese dishes, from *dim sum* to sizzling plate specials. Sunday is the day for *congee* (rice porridge) with thousand-year-old eggs, and they serve meals every night until 2am. Moderate.

Rooftop & Riverside Restaurants BALTIC, South Shore Rd, Gateshead ☎0191/440 4949. The cheaper *Riverside* has a popular outdoor terrace and serves sandwiches and light meals until 4pm and a bistro menu in the evening. Up at the *Rooftop*, tables (at least for dinner) are hard to come by without a reservation, but the food is well regarded and the views sublime. Rooftop closed Sun dinner. Moderate to Expensive.

Rupali 6 Bigg Market ☎0191/232 8629. Budget Indian restaurant owned by the self-styled Lord of Harpole, spiced up with special student offers and challenges – eat a plate of the hottest curry on the menu and you get it for free. Inexpensive.

Salsa Club 89 Westgate Rd ☎0191/221 1022. A cosy, bare-boards place with people dropping in for a coffee, sandwich and tapas or hunkering down over the combo platters, which offer a choice of fourteen salsas. There's San Mig on draft and DJs some nights. Closed Sun lunch. Inexpensive.

Uno's 18 Sandhill ☎0191/261 5264. There are loads of budget Italian places in town but none quite so adept at delivering good food at decent prices (come weekdays before 7pm, or Saturdays before 5pm, and pizzas or pastas are a staggering £2.45). The party (and price) picks up at night, when this can prove to be a loud, packed, but fun place to eat. Moderate.

Vujon 29 Queen St ☎0191/221 0601. The city's classiest Indian restaurant with dishes a cut above the ordinary, from Rajastani-style rack of lamb to *bhuna*-style salmon. You pay for the experience but it's worth it. Moderate.

Drinking and nightlife

Newcastle's boisterous nightlife centres on the pubs and clubs in the older parts of town: between Grainger Street and the cathedral in the area called the **Bigg Market** – spiritual home of Sid the Sexist and the Fat Slags from *Viz* magazine – and around the **Quayside**, where the bars tend to be slightly more sophisticated. If you want to get away from the mayhem, make a bolt for Westgate Road and Pink Lane, while in Jesmond, there's a thriving strip of café-bars along Osborne Road – none particularly worth going out of your way for but handy for a night out if that's where you're staying. The grandiosely named "**Gay Quarter**" of mostly mixed gay and lesbian bars and clubs centres on the International Centre for Life, spreading out to Waterloo Street and Westmorland and Scotswood roads – the scene is chronicled exhaustively in *The Crack*, the city's free monthly listings magazine

There's not a great deal of point listing all the Bigg Market or Quayside **pubs** and **bars** – everyone swans in and out of each in the biggest (and largely good-natured) cattle market in Western Europe. But try and make time for one or two of the places listed below, each of which has its own particular attraction. Expect to queue to get into the more popular places, and to have someone scrutinize your clothes as you attempt to gain entry – jeans and trainers are best avoided. As with restaurants, **happy hour** is a big deal in Newcastle – early-doors drinking is positively encouraged. Top brew is, of course, **Newcastle Brown** – an ale known locally as "Dog" – produced in this city since 1927.

Pubs and bars

Bodega 125 Westgate Rd. Restored Edwardian gin palace with a good beer selection, cheap food and a student crowd that packs in to watch the soccer on TV.

Bridge Hotel Castle Sq, St Nicholas St. Right opposite the castle, by the High Level Bridge, this Victorian pub has a great view of the Tyne from its beer garden. It's a real ale place, too.

Casa 58 Sandhill, next to the Guildhall. One of the bars of the moment, but with enough style for the popularity to last – and enough space to cater for it, whether on the comfy sofas or in the elegant riverside conservatory.

Centurion Central Station, Neville St. The station's former first-class waiting rooms, now revived as an extraordinary bar, brasserie and deli. Victorian tiling, sculpted fireplace, soaring ceiling and impressive mural – and draft Newcastle Brown Ale.

Crown Posada 31 The Side. Local beers and guest ales in a small but highly attractive wood-and-glass-panelled Victorian pub down by the Quayside.

Forth Hotel Pink Lane. A modern refit hasn't dulled the atmosphere at this honest city-centre boozer and there's still a fine juke box, a lively, varied crowd, good lunchtime food and a decent range of wines by the glass.

Free Trade St Lawrence Rd. Walk along the Newcastle Quayside past the Millennium Bridge and look for the shabby pub on the hill, where you are invited to "drink beer, smoke tabs" with the city's pub *cognoscenti*. Cask beer from local microbreweries, a great juke box and superb river views from the windows and beer garden.

Head of Steam 2 Neville St. In a modern building opposite the *Royal Station Hotel* (but a whole lot better-looking inside), this relaxed drinking den has a big range of real ales, imported bottles, good sounds and big sofas. Live gigs every night in the basement from 8pm.

Pitcher & Piano 108 Quayside. The riverfront's most spectacular bar – sinuous roof, huge plate-glass walls, by the Millennium Bridge – is a great place to drink.

Stereo Sandgate, Quayside. Sharp designer style, plus an outdoor deck with Millennium Bridge views.

Trent House 1–2 Leazes Lane. Many people's favourite pub, run by the WHQ people (see "Clubs" below), which means the jukebox is great. Good beer too, not to mention a surviving Space Invaders machine.

Union Rooms 48 Westgate Rd. Huge former gentlemen's club complete with porter's lodge and imposing central staircase, now offering cheap beer and sandwiches to the masses; large parts smoke-free, music-free throughout.

Clubs

Baja Beach Club Hillgate Quay, Gateshead ⓣ0191/477 6205. Hugely popular club with a beach-party theme – little more than an excuse for bikini-clad dancers and "tub girls". Closed Sun.

The Cooperage 32 The Close, Quayside ⓣ0191/233 2941. Quayside pub, originally a sixteenth-century house, just along from the Tyne Bridge, with a good range of guest beers. The club upstairs hosts indie, funk, African and dance nights, local bands and monthly salsa sessions.

Foundation 57–59 Melbourne St ⓣ0191/261 8985. Stylish venue hosting club nights (Mon & Wed–Sat), with *Shindig* (ⓦwww.shindiguk.com) the long-running Saturday special.

Tuxedo Princess Hillgate Quay, Gateshead ⓣ0191/477 8899. Floating nightclub, on the south side of the river below the Tyne Bridge, serving up scantily clad dancers and seven different styles of music in seven bars to a raucous 18–25-year-old set. Closed Sun.

World Headquarters Carliol Square ⓣ07775/848 358, ⓦwww.theworldheadquarters.com. Newcastle's mellowest bar and club, playing funk, soul and hip-hop every Friday and Saturday, plus regular DJ slots.

Live music

There's live music most nights in the city, with *The Crack* (monthly; free; available in shops, pubs and bars) the best way to find out about gigs, clubs and other entertainments. You should also check programmes at the various arts centres and all-round venues for gigs (see "Arts, culture and festivals" below).

Club and pub venues

Black Swan Newcastle Arts Centre, 69 Westgate Rd ☎0191/261 9959. Cellar bar with live music up to five nights a week – rock, folk, world and jazz – and a Friday-night salsa session that is a real hit. Late bar until 2am.

The Cluny 36 Lime St, Ouseburn ☎0191/230 4474. The best small venue in the city is out in the eastern sticks (20min walk from Quayside if you know where you're going; otherwise take a taxi), with gigs almost every night from 7.30pm, real ales and a nice bar courtesy of the *Head of Steam*, and good food until 9pm.

Jazz Café 23 Pink Lane ☎0191/232 6505. Intimate jazz club with a late licence, near the station. Live music from 8pm; salsa nights Thurs–Sat. Closed Sun.

Trillians Rock Bar Princess Square ☎0191/232 1619, ⓦwww.trilliansrockbar.com. Pub venue for local and national rock acts.

Tyneside Irish Centre 43–49 Gallowgate ☎0191/261 0384. Regular Irish folk gigs and dances and the main venue for the Tyneside Irish Festival in October.

Stadium venue

Newcastle Telewest Arena Arena Way ☎0191/401 8000, ⓦwww.telewestarena.co.uk. City-centre stadium which attracts all the big pop and rock names, but it's a lifeless venue, better suited to the ice hockey and basketball that is also played here.

Arts, culture and festivals

There's a varied theatrical and cultural life in the city and its surroundings, from the offerings at the splendid Victorian Theatre Royal and Newcastle Opera House to those of smaller contemporary **theatre** companies and local **arts centres**. The Sage and City Hall are the main classical music **concert venues**, but you'll also find performances throughout the year at Newcastle University's King's Hall, and in St Nicholas' Cathedral and St Mary's Catholic Cathedral and other atmospheric churches around town. There's a full **festival calendar** (details from the tourist office), with particular emphasis on outdoor concerts and sports – in October, Europe's biggest half-marathon, the Great North Run, sees 50,000 competitors running across the Tyne Bridge. Undoubted highlight is the New Year's Eve celebration on the Quayside, an exuberantly good-natured rival to the traditional gatherings in London.

Arts centres

BALTIC South Shore Rd, Gateshead ☎0191/478 1810, ⓦwww.balticmill.com. As well as the galleries here, there's a full programme of events – studio sessions and classes, films, artists' talks, community projects, dance and concerts.

Buddle Arts Centre 258 Station Rd, Wallsend ☎0191/200 7132. Friendly community arts centre with a fine range of events and concerts, and easy to reach (yellow line Wallsend Metro) from central Newcastle.

Customs House Mill Dam, South Shields ☎0191/454 1234. Arts centre on the banks of the Tyne hosting gigs, films and theatre. There's also a bar and a restaurant. South Shields Metro.

Newcastle Arts Centre 69 Westgate Rd ☎0191/261 5618, ⓦwww.newcastle-arts-centre.co.uk. Art gallery, workshops, and concert, drama and club venue.

Concert venues

Caedmon Hall Gateshead Central Library, Prince Consort Rd, Gateshead ☎0191/477 3478, ⓦwww.gateshead.gov.uk. Hugely varied programme of dance, world and folk music, African, jazz and classical.

City Hall Northumberland Rd ☎0191/261 2606, ⓦwww.newcastle.gov.uk/cityhall. The city centre's main concert venue, hosting orchestras from around the world, as well as mainstream rock, pop and comedy acts.

Newcastle Opera House 111 Westgate Rd ☎0191/232 0899, ⓦwww.newcastleoperahouse.com. Beautifully restored Victorian theatre with a wide range of shows, comedy and gigs.

The Sage Gateshead South Shore Rd, Gateshead Quays ☎0191/443 4555, ⓦwww.thesagegateshead.org. Stunning international music centre, home of the Northern Sinfonia and

Folkworks, hosting a full annual programme of classical, folk, world and jazz music.

Cinema

Odeon @ The Gate Newgate St ⓣ0870/505 0007. Twelve-screen mainstream city-centre cinema in the leisure/retail experience that is The Gate, which means bars, restaurants and shops to occupy you before or after the movies.
Tyneside Cinema 10 Pilgrim St ⓣ0191/232 1507, ⓦwww.tynecine.org. The city's premier art-house cinema, with a wide-ranging international programme.

Theatre, dance and comedy

The Hyena Leazes Lane ⓣ0191/232 6030. Stand-up comedy with visiting national and international acts every Thurs, Fri and Sat night from 7.30pm.
Live Theatre 27 Broad Chare ⓣ0191/232 1232, ⓦwww.live.org.uk. Enterprising theatre company with regular productions promoting local actors and writers (Lee Hall gave his boy-ballet movie, *Billy Elliot*, its first reading here). Also has exhibitions and occasional club nights, plus fine live blues, reggae, country, soul and roots at its regular *Jumpin' Hot Club*.
Newcastle Playhouse Barras Bridge ⓣ0191/230 5151. Home of Newcastle's own Northern Stage company (ⓦwww.northernstage.com) and co-host of the annual RSC season in Nov. The Gulbenkian Studio here hosts small-scale theatre, dance and recitals. Good café-bar (closed Sun).
Theatre Royal Grey St ⓣ0870/905 5060, ⓦwww.theatre-royal-newcastle.co.uk. Drama, opera, dance, musicals and comedy; also co-host of the annual RSC season in Nov.

Listings

Airport 24hr enquiry line ⓣ0191/286 0966, ⓦwww.newcastleairport.com.
Banks and exchanges Banks are concentrated around Grey and Northumberland streets. There's a bureau de change at the airport, in the main post office and in Thomas Cook travel agency (see below).
Books Waterstone's, 104 Grey St; Blackwells, Grand Hotel Buildings, 141 Percy St.
Car rental Avis ⓣ0191/232 5283 and at the airport ⓣ0191/214 0116; Europcar ⓣ0191/261 0833 and at the airport ⓣ0191/286 5070; Hertz ⓣ0191/232 5313 and at the airport ⓣ0191/286 6748.
Ferries North Shields ferry terminal at Royal Quays, seven miles east of the city, has sailings to Scandinavia and Amsterdam. Contact Fjord Line (for Bergen, Haugesund and Stavanger; ⓣ0191/296 1313, ⓦwww.fjordline.com) or DFDS (Gothenberg, Kristiansand and Amsterdam; ⓣ08705/333000, ⓦwww.dfdsseaways.co.uk). Buses leave from Central Station to the terminal before each sailing.
Football Newcastle United play at St James' Park (ticket office ⓣ0191/261 1571, ⓦwww.nufc.co.uk) in front of the country's most fanatical supporters. You're unlikely to get a ticket for the big matches against major rivals, but seats do go on general sale for some games. If you can get in, you're in for a treat – just don't wear anything red (the colour of arch-rivals Sunderland).
Hospital Royal Victoria Infirmary, Queen Victoria Rd ⓣ0191/232 5131, behind the university, just 400yd from Haymarket bus station.
Internet Internet Exchange, 26–30 Market St (Mon–Fri 9.30am–8pm, Sat 10am–8pm, Sun 11am–6pm). There's free access at the Library and at the Live Wires Centre in the Discovery Museum.
Pharmacies The handiest central pharmacy is Boots, Monument Mall, Grey St ⓣ0191/232 4423.
Police Corner of Market and Pilgrim streets ⓣ0191/214 6555.
Post office St Mary's Place, near the Civic Centre, at Haymarket.
Taxis There are ranks all over the centre, including those at Haymarket, Bigg Market, and outside Central Station. Weekend nights are the most difficult times to hail a cab; the queues at the Bigg Market ranks can be horrendous. Call Noda Taxis (ⓣ0191/222 1888 or 232 7777) at Central Station for advance bookings.
Travel agents STA, 9 St Mary's Place ⓣ0191/233 2111 and University of Northumbria, 2 Sandyford Rd ⓣ0870/160 6070; Thomas Cook, 79 Grainger St ⓣ0191/232 5809; Trailfinders, 7–9 Ridley Place ⓣ0191/261 2345.

Around Newcastle

The Metro network connects most of the day-trip destinations along the Tyne, and a Metro Day Saver ticket (see p.1063) enables you to get the best out of the local transport system. In addition to the Metro, the ticket is valid for most buses in the county of Tyne and Wear, and the ferry between North and South Shields. Note also that Beamish Museum, just across the border in County Durham (see p.1047), is within easy reach of Newcastle.

Along the Tyne

The Metro runs east along both banks of the **River Tyne**, connecting Newcastle with several historic attractions, and with the sandy beaches at Tynemouth and Whitley Bay – the beaches are fine if you just want to see the sea, though anyone intending to head further north up the Northumberland coast will find there's no comparison. It's worth noting that to make a round trip of it, you can cross the river between North Shields and South Shields on the **Shields Ferry** (Mon–Sat 7am–10.50pm, Sun 10.30am–5.30pm; every 15–30min; 7min; £1 one-way). There are Metro stations on either side, a ten-minute walk (or connecting bus) from North Shields Ferry Station and five minutes' walk from the South Shields ferry.

Wallsend and Segedunum

As the name tells you, **WALLSEND**, four miles east of Newcastle, was the last outpost of Hadrian's great border defence. **Segedunum**, the "strong fort" a couple of minutes' signposted walk from the Metro station here (daily: April–Oct 10am–5pm; Nov–March 10am–3.30pm; £3.50; Ⓦwww.twmuseums.org.uk), has been admirably developed as one of the prime attractions along the Wall. A range of activities and events takes place year-round (including summer re-enactments of Roman drill and equipment) and, besides the extensive excavations, the grounds contain a fully reconstructed bathhouse, complete with steaming pools and colourful frescoes, and a rebuilt section of the Wall itself. The cleverly conceived museum combines excavated finds with interactive computer displays to give a strong flavour of life at the fort, as well as bringing the history of the site up to the present day with displays on coalmining and shipbuilding. To complete the picture, climb the 110-foot tower for a spectacular overview of the remains and the adjacent ship-repair yards. The "wall's end" itself is visible at the edge of the site, close to the river and Swan Hunter shipyard, and it's from here that the **Hadrian's Wall Path** (see p.1086) runs for 84 miles to Bowness on Solway in Cumbria; you can get your walk "passport" stamped inside the museum.

Tynemouth

Pressing on through North Shields brings you to the coast at **TYNEMOUTH**, a pleasant village perched on the promontory between sea and river. Long considered a strategically important site, on the cliff top stand the striking ruins of the **Benedictine priory** (April–Sept daily 10am–6pm; Oct daily 10am–5pm; Nov–March Wed–Sun 10am–1pm & 2–4pm; £2.50; EH), later fortified with a castle, where early kings of Northumbria were buried. A church was first built here in the seventh century, but the oldest visible features, such as the beautiful chancel, are Norman. Biggest contemporary attraction, though, is the **Blue Reef Aquarium** on Grand Parade (daily 10am–6pm; £4.95; Ⓦwww.bluereefaquarium.co.uk), which pulls in the punters with its tropical ocean tank with underwater tunnel, but retains a sense of its place in the world with North Sea and Northumberland coast habitat displays. There are talks, tours and feeds throughout the day.

Gibside and Cherryburn

Upriver on the south bank of the Tyne, one of the finest landscaped gardens in the North is a quick, six-mile hop from the centre of Newcastle (bus #611 from Central Station, then a half-mile signposted walk from the village of Rowlands Gill). The grounds of **Gibside** (Tues–Sun: April–Oct 10am–6pm; Nov–March 10am–4pm; £3.50; NT) represent a very rare survival of mid-eighteenth-century park design, combining striking formal vistas with naturalistic woodland. Created by coal baron George Bowes between 1729 and 1760, the estate went into decline as early as 1885 after the death of his great-grandson John Bowes (founder of the Bowes Museum at Barnard Castle, see p.1050), but the National Trust have been slowly attempting to restore the original design. A series of hour-long trails will take you past the atmospheric shell of the earlier Jacobean mansion, an orangery and walled garden, the 130-foot Column to Liberty (erected to reaffirm Bowes' loyalty to George II after the Jacobite uprising of 1745), and along the east bank of the River Derwent near its confluence with the Tyne. Back towards the entrance and tearoom stands the most striking and complete architectural remnant, the **chapel** (April–Oct Tues–Sun 11am–4.30pm). Inspired by Palladio's Villa Rotonda in the Veneto in northeastern Italy, this elegantly symmetrical building features an array of delicate carvings under its portico, but is dominated by one of the grandest pulpits you're ever likely to see – a triple-decker mahogany affair decked out in velvet with a grand inlaid sounding board. Gibside hosts a full annual programme of walks, lectures, concerts, children's activities and other events – call the booking office on ☎01670/773939 for details.

If you have your own transport (otherwise bus #602 from Newcastle Central Station towards Hexham), it's worth pressing on another five miles west along the A695 from here to **Cherryburn** (Easter–Oct Mon & Thurs–Sun 1–5.30pm; £3; NT), the birthplace museum of **Thomas Bewick**, England's greatest engraver (1735–1828). Still offering beautiful views of the rolling landscape which inspired Bewick, the simple cottage contains well-thought-out displays that tell the story of his far-reaching legacy, including examples of contemporary use of his engravings, from "Nature Notes" in *The Times* to Californian wine labels. Sunday is the big day here, with demonstrations of printing and bookbinding, and live folk music in the garden.

Jarrow

JARROW, five miles east of Newcastle, and south of the Tyne, has been ingrained on the national consciousness since the 1936 march (see box opposite), though the town made a mark much earlier, as the seventh-century St Paul's church and monastery was one of the region's early cradles of Christianity. The first Saxon church here was built in 681 AD by monks from St Peter's at Monkwearmouth, a few miles southeast of here, and its monastic buildings soon attracted a reputation for scholastic learning. It was here that the **Venerable Bede** (673–735 AD) came to live as a boy, growing to become one of Europe's greatest scholars and England's first historian – his *History of the English Church and People*, describing the struggles of the island's early Christians, was completed at Jarrow in 731. His other writings were many and varied – poetry, scientific works on chronology and the calendar, lives of St Cuthbert, historical and geographical treatises – and his influence was immense, prompting a European-wide revival in monastic learning. Yet astonishingly Bede rarely left the monastery, and

The Jarrow Crusade

Jarrow provides the perfect example of what happens to a company town when its company closes. It owed its growth in the nineteenth century to the success of the steelworks and shipyard owned by local MP Charles Palmer. Producer of the world's first oil tanker, the Jarrow production line was a phenomenal organization, employing at its zenith some ten thousand men. However, demand for steel and ships went into decline after World War I, and eighty percent of the workforce had been laid off by 1934, the year Palmers was sold off and broken up. From the consequent despair was born the Jarrow Crusade.

On October 5, 1936, led by the town's radical MP Ellen Wilkinson, two hundred men left Jarrow to walk the 290 miles to London under the "**Jarrow Crusade**" banner. Supported by all the town's politicians, the protesters gathered sympathy and support all along the road to the capital, becoming the most potent image of the hardships of 1930s Britain. Some charitable aid was forthcoming after the marchers presented their petition to Parliament, but real recovery only came about through the rearmament of Britain in the build-up to World War II. Palmers was resurrected at nearby Hebburn, and struggled through a series of takeovers into the 1970s, by which time the local economy was on the brink of a state nearly as bad as that of the 1930s. In 1986, with unemployment on Tyneside reaching 32 percent, the 50th anniversary of the Jarrow Crusade was marked by another march on the seat of government. The hardships of the 1930s were instrumental in the creation of the Welfare State; the hardships of the 1980s were all but ignored.

probably never travelled further than York, relying on visitors and friends for much of his information. After he died in 735, St Paul's soon became a site of pilgrimage, though church and monastery were later sacked by Viking raiding parties. Even after Bede's bones had been appropriated by a relic-collecting Durham priest in 1020 (they were eventually interred in Durham Cathedral), Jarrow remained high in the clerical consciousness, with monks eager to study at the monastery where Bede had once lived. The monastery was revived in 1074 and continued in existence until the Reformation.

The years have been kind to **St Paul's** (Mon–Sat 10am–4.30pm, Sun 2.30–4.30pm), a tranquil stone church framed by the industrial clutter of the Tyneside docks beyond. The original seventh-century dedication stone (dated 23 April, 685 AD, the earliest in England) can be seen inside, set in the arch above the chancel. Outside are the bare ruins of the buildings, cloister and burial ground of the **monastery**. Most of the standing walls and ruins date from the later eleventh-century re-foundation.

Access to the church and monastery ruins is free, although they stand within the wider development that is **Bede's World** (April–Oct Mon–Sat 10am–5.30pm, Sun noon–5.30pm; Nov–March Mon–Sat 10am–4.30pm, Sun noon–4.30pm; £4.50; Ⓦwww.bedesworld.co.uk), a fascinating exploration of early medieval Northumbria, centred on a museum and an Anglo-Saxon farm site. The multi-media **museum**, housed in a beautiful Mediterranean-style edifice and dotted with striking sculptures and other artworks, traces the development of Northumbria and England through the use of extracts from Bede's writings, set alongside archeological finds and vivid re-creations of monastic life. After this you can take a turn through Gyrwe, the eleven-acre demonstration **farm** which features reconstructed timber buildings from the early Christian period, as well as demonstrating contemporary agricultural methods. Kids can feed the goats and throughout the summer there are craft demonstrations, themed feasts and other activities. Over at the Georgian **Jarrow Hall** there's a monastic herb garden and an excellent **café**. Allow at least a couple of hours for church, museums and farm.

St Paul's and Bede's World are at Church Bank in Jarrow, a signposted fifteen-minute walk through an industrial estate from **Bede Metro station**. Alternatively, buses #526 or #527 run roughly every 30 minutes from Neville Street (Central Station) in Newcastle or Jarrow Metro station, and stop in front of the church. Drivers will find the site a little way off the A185, at the south end of the Tyne tunnel; follow the signs at the A185/A19 roundabout junction.

South Shields and the South Tyneside coast

Beyond Jarrow, it's impossible to miss the fact that South Tyneside is officially designated **Catherine Cookson Country**: the prolific author was born in **SOUTH SHIELDS**, the small but distinctive town which guards the south side of the entrance to the Tyne. Although her childhood homes have since been demolished, South Shields **tourist office**, at the museum and art gallery on Ocean Road, a five-minute walk from the Metro station (Easter–Sept Mon–Sat 10am–1pm & 2–5.30pm, Sun 1–5pm; Oct–Easter Mon–Sat 10am–1pm & 2–5pm; ⓣ0191/454 6612, ⓦwww.s-tyneside-mbc.gov.uk), can provide details of the "Catherine Cookson Trail" – plaques, sites and buildings associated with her life and novels, which romanticize the grittier industrial corners of South Tyneside.

Of more general interest is **Arbeia Roman Fort** (Easter–Sept Mon–Sat 10am–5.30pm, Sun 1–5pm; Oct–Easter Mon–Sat 10am–4pm; free; ⓦwww.twmuseums.org.uk), on Baring Street, off River Drive, five minutes' signposted walk north from the tourist office. Built in 120–160 AD as a supply depot for Hadrian's Wall, the fort encloses substantial granaries, where you can usually watch archeologists and stonemasons at work, and a museum containing the most complete Roman ring-mail shirt found in Britain. Fine views of the site and across towards the sister fort of Segedunum (see p.1077) can be had from the stone reconstruction of the huge west gate, and you can also poke around the commanding officer's house, with richly decorated living rooms off a central courtyard, and the dark, cramped barracks next door, all rebuilt using authentic Roman construction methods. If you have kids in tow, be sure to take them into **Time Quest** (Mon–Fri 10am–3pm during school terms, 11am–4pm in the holidays; Easter–Oct also Sat 10am–5pm, Sun 1–5pm; £1.50, children 80p), where they can have a go at being archeologists, digging for finds in a gravel pit, doing Roman weaving and making mosaics.

The A183 runs south down the coast from South Shields towards Sunderland, with a nice sandy beach at **Marsden Bay** – and the *Tavistock* seafood restaurant and bistro (ⓣ0191/455 6060; restaurant closed Sun & Mon) in the cave at Marsden Grotto. Just beyond, near Lizard Point, five miles north of Sunderland, you'll pass **Souter Lighthouse** (Easter–Oct Mon–Thurs, Sat & Sun 11am–5pm; £3; NT), opened in 1871 and the first lighthouse in the world to use electric light. Volunteer guides will talk you through the still-operable engine room and the re-created living room and bedrooms of one of the keeper's houses, and, of course, escort you up the light tower, from where on the clearest of days you'll be able to glimpse Flamborough Head, over fifty miles away in Yorkshire.

North of Newcastle: the stately homes

North of the city, a bevy of stately homes vie for attention. You could see any of them as half-day trips out of Newcastle by bus, though those with their own transport have the best of things. You can visit **Seaton Delaval** en route to the

Northumberland coast, or **Belsay** and **Wallington** before heading into the Northumberland National Park.

Seaton Delaval Hall

One of Vanbrugh's great Baroque houses, **Seaton Delaval Hall** (June–Sept Wed & Sun 2–6pm; £4), lies eleven miles northeast of Newcastle in fine gardens, its gloomy north facade looking over the bleak terrain towards the port of Blyth. Fire badly damaged the hall in 1822, a century after it was built, but subsequent restorations have done ample justice to the sombre grandeur of a building that exemplifies the architect's desire to create country houses with "something of the castle air". An unusual ice house, dating from the early nineteenth century, has been restored and there's also a small tearoom. Public transport is by the #363 (hourly) or #364 (hourly; not Sun) **bus** from Haymarket, a 35-minute ride to Seaton Delaval Avenue head, which drops you at the main gates to the hall.

Belsay Hall

Belsay Hall, Castle and Gardens (daily: April–Sept 10am–6pm; Oct 10am–5pm; Nov–March 10am–4pm; £4.50; EH), fourteen miles northwest of Newcastle, were inherited in 1795 by Sir Charles Monck, who eleven years later decided to build a brand new hall here after his return from a honeymoon-cum-Grand-Tour of Europe. Inspired by the Neoclassical buildings of Berlin and the classical architecture of Athens, Sir Charles planned a majestic Doric house, an austere one-hundred-foot-square sandstone block raised on a podium of three steps. Built between 1807 and 1817, the **Hall** has now been impressively restored, though the equally severe interior, with the bedrooms and state rooms surrounding a multi-columned hall, is devoid of furnishings and fittings – instead, special exhibitions often adorn the main reception rooms.

To the west lie the **gardens**, where a footpath threads through the trim formality of the winter gardens to reach the magical **Quarry Gardens**. Here, in the shelter of the sandstone quarry used for the building of the Hall, lush exotic vegetation cascades over exposed rock faces, planned by Sir Charles as a Romantic antidote to the severity of the house. The track also leads to the substantial remains of the medieval **castle**, its battlements punctuated by four formidable corner turrets. **Belsay village**, on the main road about a mile from the Hall, is readily reached by **bus** from Newcastle: the #808 from Eldon Square (not Sun), or #508 from Haymarket (summer Sun only). There's a tearoom at the Hall and, just off the main road near the village, the *Blacksmith's Coffee Shop* (closed Mon, except bank holidays), which makes its own scones.

Wallington House

Eight miles northwest of Belsay lies the tiny village of **Cambo**; the summer Sunday #508 service (twice a day) links the two. Just outside the village stands **Wallington House** (admission and ticket information on ⓣ01670/773600; NT), an ostentatious mansion rebuilt by Sir Walter Blackett, the coal- and lead-mine owner, in the 1740s. The house re-opens after repairs in 2004, with the Rococo plasterwork and William Bell Scott's Pre-Raphaelite murals of scenes from Northumbrian history on display. There are diverse attractions for kids, including the dolls' house collection and museum of curiosities, while a tearoom and shop rounds off the facilities. There's a separate charge (£4.30) if you only want to see the **grounds** (daily dawn–dusk), with their lawns, woods and lakes, and incorporating beautiful **walled gardens** (daily: April–Sept 10am–7pm; Oct 10am–6pm; Nov–March 10am–4pm), which shelter conservatories, fountains and a huge variety of plants.

Wearside

There's been a long rivalry between Newcastle and Sunderland, twelve miles to the southeast: both cities outraged about being lumped together in the municipal appellation Tyne *and* Wear; both Geordies (from Newcastle) or Mackems (from Sunderland) indignant at being taken for the other by know-nothing southerners; with supporters of both passionately followed football teams cock-a-hoop at the old enemy's misfortunes. To an outsider it can seem at times to be a bewildering argument over nothing at all, but whisper in **Wearside** at your peril the obviously superior charms of Newcastle as a city. Yet **Sunderland** and the River Wear do have their attractions, and in the adjacent new town of **Washington** stands one of the more intriguing historic sites of the northeast.

Sunderland

SUNDERLAND, bisected by the River Wear and elevated in 1992 to the ranks of Britain's cities, shares Newcastle's long history, river setting and industrial heritage but cannot match its architectural splendour. Formed from three medieval villages flanking the Wear, it was one of the wealthiest towns in England by 1500, and later supported the Parliamentary cause in the Civil War. The twentieth century made and broke the town: from being the largest shipbuilding centre in the world, supporting a dozen shipyards, Sunderland slumped after ferocious bombing during World War II. Depression and recession did the rest. However, the city centre has seen a revival of late and now has a couple of visitor attractions to rival anything in nearby Newcastle.

The City

First stop should be the **Sunderland Museum** (Mon 10am–4pm, Tues–Sat 10am–5pm, Sun 2–5pm; free; Ⓦwww.twmuseums.org.uk), straight down Fawcett Street from the tourist office, at the junction with Borough Road, which does a very good, multimedia job of telling the city's history. Highlights include the elegantly intricate model ships in "Launched on Wearside", which relates how Sunderland ships were once sent around the world – a trade, incidentally, which gave the city inhabitants their "Mackem" nickname, derived from a stage in the shipbuilding process. In "Coal", which deals movingly with the local coal-mining industry, the roll call of closed collieries is sobering – one of the last to go, Wearmouth, has since been reclaimed as the site of Sunderland Football Club's ground, the Stadium Of Light. The attached **Winter Gardens**, housed in an impressive steel and glass hot-house, replaces the original Victorian glasshouses bombed by the Germans in 1941. Exotic trees and palms, sound effects, hot and cold zones, and a fern gully help to give the gardens that faraway tropical feeling.

The main interest in Sunderland lies across the River Wear, whose landscaped **Riverside** is actually the oldest settled part of the city. You can walk here easily enough, up Fawcett Street and then Bridge Street from the centre and across the Victorian Wearmouth Bridge (around 20min). Along the north bank of the river, in front of the university campus buildings, the early Christian **Church of St Peter** (Easter–Oct daily 2–4pm), built in 674 AD, is the elder sibling of St Paul's Church at Jarrow (see p.1079). The tower and west wall are original Saxon features and the church displays fragments of the oldest stained glass in the country, the work of seventh-century European craftsmen. Walk from the church down to the waterside to find the city's extraordinary

National Glass Centre (daily 10am–5pm; £5; Ⓦwww.nationalglasscentre.com), which tells the story of British glass and glass-making – a traditional industry in Sunderland since the seventh century, when workshops turned out stained glass for the north's monastic houses and churches. There's plenty to get your teeth into, not least an expansive gallery that entertainingly explains the history and multifarious uses of glass. Regular tours throughout the day (£5) include a glass-making demonstration in the on-site workshop, or you can simply browse for free in the exhibition galleries and glass shop.

Further north, out in the beach resort of **Roker** (bus #E1, #E3 or #19 from the bus station), the **Church of St Andrew's** on Park Avenue (Mon–Fri 9.30–11.30am) is known as "the cathedral of the Arts and Crafts Movement". The nave echoes the upturned hull of a ship, while the sanctuary has a beautiful painting depicting the heavens, with an electric light fitting at the centre of the sun. The tapestries and carpets are from the William Morris workshop and, like the church, they date from the early 1900s. It's a mile or so north up the coast from Roker to the twin resort of **Seaburn**, again with a goodish stretch of sand, and beyond that you could follow a waymarked trail along dramatic cliff tops all the way to South Shields in three hours.

The fifteen-mile **River Wear Trail** follows the course of the river upstream from Sunderland, through Washington. The trail starts in town on the south side of the Wearmouth Bridge, the first stretch running through Festival Park before entering the green Wear Valley. A few miles to the west, and visible from every road in the vicinity, the hilltop **Penshaw Monument** draws admiring glances – a nineteenth-century pseudo-Greek temple, 100 feet long and 70 feet high, erected in honour of John George Lambton, the first earl of Durham.

Practicalities

The main stop for **Metros** from Newcastle is in the central **train station** opposite the Bridges Shopping Centre, but get off at the previous stop, St Peter's, to walk along the north side of the river to the National Glass Centre or St Peter's Church. The **tourist office** is behind the central station on the main shopping drag, at 50 Fawcett St (Mon–Sat 9am–5pm, Sun 10am–4pm; Ⓣ0191/553 2000, Ⓦwww.sunderland.gov.uk). All buses use the **Park Lane Bus Station** (also on the Metro), a five-minute walk south of the train station.

For daytime food in the city centre, *21 John Street* (at that address) is a relaxed, airy Italian **café** offering everything from made-to-order sandwiches to pasta and more substantial dishes. There's also *Eden* café-brasserie in the museum, where you can take your cappuccino and muffin out on to the wonderful terrace overlooking the lake in Mowbray Park. The best town-centre **restaurant** is *Tavistock Place*, 11 Tavistock Place (Ⓣ0191/514 5000; closed Sun), round the corner from the museum, dishing up cosmopolitan cuisine at moderate prices. Alternatively, head for the fine *Throwing Stones* restaurant in the National Glass Centre (Ⓣ0191/565 3939; lunch daily, dinner Fri & Sat), where a sandwich or stuffed-tortilla lunch can be had for around a fiver. There's a pricier, contemporary British menu, too, all accompanied by riverside views.

Washington

Five miles west of Sunderland, the River Wear keeps to the south of the new town of **WASHINGTON**, focus of much of the area's contemporary investment and manufacture. Split into planned, numbered districts and organized on American lines, it's not an obvious stop, although the original **old village** has been zealously preserved as a conservation area and boasts a couple of pubs and tearooms.

Just off the village green, past the leafy churchyard on The Avenue, stands the ancestral home of the family that spawned the first **US president**. The "de Wessyngtons" – later the Washingtons – originally came over with William the Conqueror, and by 1183 were based at the **Old Hall** (April–Oct Mon–Wed & Sun 11am–5pm; £3; NT), where they lived until 1613. Carefully preserved as a Jacobean showpiece, the echoing, stone-flagged house has a fine kitchen, Great Hall and garden, and some exemplary wood panelling, and although none of the furniture is original to the Washington family, it is contemporaneous. A breezy video tells the life of George Washington and plenty of memorabilia pads things out – a notable John Singleton Copley portrait, commemorative spoons and coins, and even the silver spade with which President Jimmy Carter planted a tree during his 1977 visit. Every Fourth of July, the raising of the US flag at the house heralds Independence Day celebrations and entry to the Old Hall is free for the occasion. Washington himself probably knew little of his family's northeast English origins – the Old Hall had passed into other hands well before the future president's great-grandfather emigrated to Virginia in 1656, an exile after the English Civil War. Yet it seems too much of a coincidence that the old Washington family coat-of-arms (three stars and three horizontal red-and-white stripes) found its echo more than a century later in the earliest version of the new country's Stars and Stripes.

The other main attraction in the area is the **Washington Wildfowl and Wetlands Centre** (daily: April–Oct 9.30am–5pm; Nov–March 9.30am–4pm; £5.50, Ⓦwww.wwt.org.uk), east of town and north of the River Wear in District 15, its hundred acres designed by Sir Peter Scott and home to swans, geese, ducks, herons and flamingos. Its trails, hides, play areas, visitor information centre and children's activities make for an enjoyable day out. It's signposted off most local roads, four miles from the A1(M), or see below for public transport.

For Washington village and the Old Hall, the best service is on the #185 bus from Sunderland Park Lane Bus Station (not Sun). The Wildfowl Centre is reached on the #56A from Newcastle's Market Street (not Sun) or the #X4 from either Newcastle's Eldon Square or Sunderland Park Lane (not Sun). All these buses (and many others from Newcastle or Sunderland) call or terminate at **Washington Galleries Bus Station**, from where you'll be able to reach either site. Most buses prefixed with a "W" run to Washington village from the Galleries.

Hadrian's Wall and Hexham

Some of the great monuments of antiquity are hard to take in at a glance. You need a guide, a knowledgable person to explain the significance of dilapidated stonework. The Wall is an exception. You can see exactly what the Romans were up to.

John Hillaby, *Journey Through Britain*, 1970.

In 55 and 54 BC, Julius Caesar launched two swift invasions of southeast England from his base in Gaul, his success proving that Britain lay within the Roman grasp. The full-scale assault began under Claudius in 43 AD and, within forty years, Roman troops had reached the Firth of Tay in modern Scotland.

In 83 AD, the Roman governor Agricola ventured farther north, but Rome subsequently transferred part of his army to the Danube, and the remaining legions withdrew to the frontier which was marked by the **Stanegate**, a military roadway linking Carlisle and Corbridge.

Emperor Hadrian, who toured Roman Britain in 122 AD, found this informal arrangement unsatisfactory. His imperial policy was quite straightforward – he wanted the empire to live at peace within stable frontiers, most of which were defined by geographical features. In northern Britain, however, there was no natural barrier and so Hadrian decided to create his own by constructing a 76-mile **wall** from the Tyne to the Solway Firth – "to separate the Romans from the barbarians", according to his biographer. It was not intended to be an impenetrable fortification, but rather a base for patrols that could push out into hostile territory and a barrier to inhibit movement. Built up to a height of fifteen feet in places, it was punctuated by **milecastles**, which served as gates, depots and mini-barracks, and by observation **turrets**, two of which were stood between each pair of milecastles. Before the Wall was even completed, major modifications were made: the bulk of the garrison had initially been stationed along the Stanegate, but they were now moved into the Wall, occupying a chain of new **forts**, which straddled the Wall at six- to nine-mile intervals. These new arrangements concentrated the Wall's garrison in a handful of key points and brought them nearer the enemy, making it possible to respond quickly to any threat. Simultaneously, a military zone was defined by the digging of a broad ditch, or **vallum**, on the south side of the Wall, crossed by causeways to each of the forts, turning them into the main points of access and rendering the milecastles, in this respect, largely redundant. The revised structure remained in operation until the late fourth century AD, though centralized Roman rule in Britain had broken down by then.

Most of Hadrian's Wall disappeared centuries ago, yet walking its length remains a popular pastime, made easier now there's an official waymarked **Hadrian's Wall Path** (see p.1086); even if you're not up to tramping the entire course of the Wall, it's well worth walking at least one section to get an idea of the whole enterprise. Approached from Newcastle along the valley of the Tyne, via the Roman museum and site at **Corbridge**, the prosperous-looking market town of **Hexham** makes a good base. Most visitors stick to the best-preserved portions of the Wall, which are concentrated between the hamlet of **Chollerford**, three miles north of Hexham, and **Haltwhistle**, sixteen miles to the west. It's here, especially between Housesteads and Steel Rigg, that the Wall is at its most beautiful, as it clings to the edge of the Whin Sill, a precipitous line of dolerite crags towering above the austere Northumberland National Park moorland. Scattered along this section are a variety of key archeological sites and museums, notably **Chesters Roman Fort and Museum** near Chollerford, the remains of **Housesteads Fort** and that of **Vindolanda**, and the milecastle remains at **Cawfields**, north of Haltwhistle.

Visiting the Wall

Corbridge, Hexham and Haltwhistle have the best choice of **accommodation** along the Wall, augmented by plenty of B&Bs in the dramatic countryside between Hexham and Greenhead, and **youth hostels** at Once Brewed, Greenhead and Acomb (near Hexham). Drivers use the A69 (Hexham to Carlisle) to flit between major towns, though it's the narrower B6318 – the Military Road built with huge amounts of stone from the Wall by General Wade after the second Jacobite uprising – that actually follows the line of the Wall from Chollerford to Greenhead.

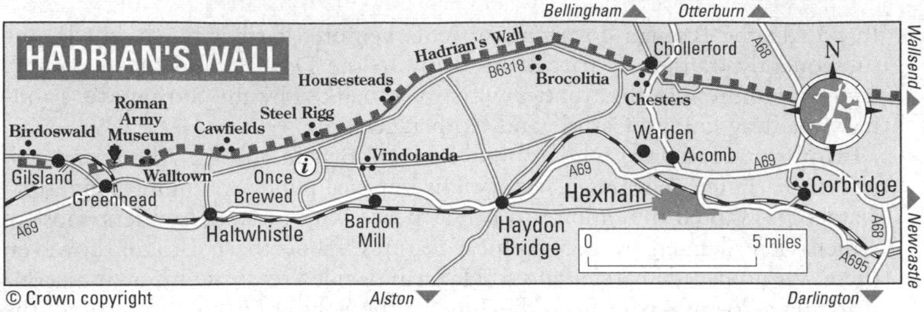

A special **Hadrian's Wall bus**, the cutely tagged #AD122, runs from Wallsend and Newcastle to Corbridge, Hexham, and all the wall sites and villages, and then on to Carlisle and Bowness-on-Solway (the end of the Hadrian's Wall Path). This operates between Easter and October, up to four to five times a day in each direction in high summer (Sun only in April and October); a typical one-way ticket, from Hexham to Vindolanda, costs £2.30, though Day Rover tickets (£6 one day, £10 three days) offer better value. There's also a year-round service on the #685 bus between Newcastle and Carlisle, and other local services from Carlisle and Hexham, which provide access to various points on the Wall. The nearest **train** stations are on the Newcastle–Carlisle line at Corbridge, Hexham, Haydon Bridge, Bardon Mill and Haltwhistle. Hexham, Bardon Mill and Haltwhistle will leave you a fair walk to Chesters, Vindolanda/Once Brewed and Cawfields/Greenhead respectively, or you can connect at Hexham or Haltwhistle with the bus services described above. The best place to **park and ride** is at Once Brewed visitor centre, where there's all-day parking and a bus stop for the Hadrian's Wall bus.

Holders of Northeast Explorer and Stagecoach Cumberland Explorer bus **passes** get free travel on the Hadrian's Wall bus. There's also a Hadrian's Wall Rail Rover Ticket (£12.50, available from train stations), valid for two days in any three-day period (after 9am weekdays), covering travel on the Newcastle–Carlisle train line, the #AD122 and the Tyne & Wear Metro; and a Tyne Valley Day Ranger (£11), a one-day pass for train travel between Whitehaven, Carlisle and Sunderland, plus the #AD122 (after 9am weekdays).

The Hadrian's Wall Path

The **Hadrian's Wall Path**, an 84-mile waymarked National Trail, runs from Wallsend in the east to Bowness-on-Solway in the west, shadowing the line of the Wall, with over forty other linear or circular walks accessible en route. You could walk the main route in four days, but that's allowing little or no time to explore the archeological sites, remains, towns and villages on the way, so a week is a more realistic timescale. To prove you made it, a "path passport" is available, which you get stamped at six locations along the way. Contact the Hadrian's Wall information line (see p.1087) at Haltwhistle tourist office for an official free **walking and accommodation guide**; there's also the *Hadrian's Wall Path: National Trail Guide* (Aurum Press), which details the route in exhaustive detail. Accommodation en route is not abundant – at least not on the Wall itself – so it's essential to book ahead and be prepared to be flexible. You may have to spend some nights a few miles from the end of your day's walk, though the Hadrian's Wall bus service is a boon in this respect. The best time to do the walk is between May and October, as the wet winter months are not only heavier going but also contribute to erosion and archeological damage. For the same reason, keep off the Wall itself at all times.

You can pick up a comprehensive Hadrian's Wall **public transport timetable** from Newcastle, Hexham, Carlisle and Haltwhistle tourist offices, and the Once Brewed Visitor Centre. Or contact the **Hadrian's Wall information line** on ⓣ01434/322002, ⓦwww.hadrians-wall.org.

Corbridge

CORBRIDGE is a quiet and well-heeled commuter town overlooking the River Tyne from the top of a steep ridge. This spur of land was first settled by the Saxons, and their handiwork survives in parts of the **Church of St Andrew**, on the central Market Place, but it's the adjacent **Vicar's Pele** that catches the eye, an unusually well-preserved fortified tower-house dating to the fourteenth century. Other buildings are less striking but form a handsome ensemble of tawny-coloured stone houses.

One mile to the west of the Market Place, accessible either by road or along the riverside footpath, lies **Corbridge Roman Site** (Easter–Sept daily 10am–6pm; Oct daily 10am–5pm; Nov–March Wed–Sun 10am–1pm & 2–4pm; £3.10; EH), the location of the garrison town of Corstopitum. This is the oldest fortified site in the region, first established as a supply base for the Roman advance into Scotland in 80 AD (and thus predating the Wall itself). It remained in regular military use until the end of the second century, after which it became surrounded by a fast-developing town – most of the visible archeological remains date from this period, when Corstopitum served as the nerve centre of Hadrian's Wall, guarding the bridge at the intersection of Stanegate and Dere Street. The extensive, clearly labelled remains provide an insight into the layout of the civilian town, showing the foundations of temples, public baths, garrison headquarters, workshops and houses as well as the best-preserved Roman granaries in Britain – huge, buttressed buildings with a ventilation system enabling the grain to be stored for long periods.

The site **museum** boasts a good selection of Roman artefacts, from domestic items and imported ceramics to vivid temple friezes. The celebrated *Lion and Stag* fountainhead – the so-called "Corbridge Lion" – gets pride of place; to the Romans, the lion and its prey symbolized the triumph of life over death.

Practicalities

The **train station** is half a mile outside town, across the river; from here it's an easy walk into the centre, with the *Angel Inn* on Main Street one of the first places you reach having crossed the bridge. Outside the inn is one place that **buses** stop; you might also be dropped near the post office on Hill Street, around the corner. Corbridge **tourist office** is also on Hill Street, at the library (mid-May to Sept Mon–Sat 10am–1pm & 2–6pm, Sun 1–5pm; Easter to mid-May & Oct Mon–Sat 10am–1pm & 2–5pm, Sun 1–5pm; ⓣ01434/632815).

There's plenty of **accommodation** in and around Corbridge, with a few B&Bs by the train station and a wider choice in the centre of town. The *Riverside Guest House* on Main Street (ⓣ01434/632942, ⓦwww.theriversideguesthouse.co.uk; ❸) is a comfortable eighteenth-century house with fine views of the Tyne; a few rooms without private shower are a category cheaper. Or there's spacious, tastefully decorated *Clive House*, in the former schoolhouse just east of here on Appletree Lane (ⓣ01434/632617; ❸). You'll need to book in advance for the *Angel Inn* on Main Street (ⓣ01434/632119, ⓦwww.theangelofcorbridge.co.uk; ❺, ❼ with dinner), which has had a contemporary makeover – this is now also the best place to eat in town, with classy lunches and dinners served daily.

Several **cafés**, sandwich shops and delis can provide the wherewithal for a picnic on the riverbanks, while *Al Ponte*, just up from the bridge at 18 Front St (☎01434/634214), offers a wide selection of traditional and regional Italian dishes, and good lunch deals. Otherwise, there's the *Valley* (☎01434/633434; dinner only, closed Sun), a high-quality Indian **restaurant** by the station on Station Road. The *Dyvels*, 20yd from here, is a nice, small local **pub** with bar meals (not Mon) and a beer garden. Or there's the *Wheatsheaf*, on Watling Street in town, an attractive seventeenth-century former farmhouse with a couple of Roman stones in the stableyard.

Hexham

In 671, on a bluff above the Tyne, four miles west of Corbridge, St Wilfrid founded a Benedictine monastery whose church was, according to contemporary accounts, the finest to be seen north of the Alps. Unfortunately, its gold and silver proved irresistible to the Vikings, who savaged the place in 876, but the church was rebuilt in the eleventh century as part of an Augustinian priory, and the town of **HEXHAM**, governed by the Archbishop of York, grew up in its shadow. It's a handsome market town of some interest – indeed, it's the only significant stop between Newcastle and Carlisle – and however keen you are to reach the Wall, you'd do well to give Hexham a night or even make it your base.

Arrival, information and accommodation

Hexham's **train station** sits on the northeastern edge of the town centre, a ten-minute walk from the abbey; the **tourist office** is halfway between the two, in the main Wentworth **car park**, near the Safeway superstore (Easter to mid-May & Oct Mon–Sat 9am–5pm, Sun 10am–5pm; mid-May to Sept Mon–Sat 9am–6pm, Sun 10am–5pm; Nov to Easter Mon–Sat 9am–5pm; ☎01434/652220, ⓦwww.tynedale.gov.uk). The **bus station** is off Priestpopple, a few minutes' stroll east of the abbey. There's free **Internet** access in the library, inside Queen's Hall on Beaumont Street. **Accommodation** is usually pretty easy to come by, though the tourist office can make other suggestions if our choices are full.

Guest houses and hotels

Beaumont Beaumont St ☎01434/602331, ⓦwww.beaumont-hotel.co.uk. Old-fashioned family-run hotel with spacious doubles overlooking the abbey; breakfast isn't included, though there are special weekend dinner, bed and breakfast deals (two-night minimum). ❺

Kitty Frisk House Corbridge Rd ☎01434/601533, ⓦwww.kittyfriskhouse.co.uk. Welcoming Edwardian retreat, half a mile from the centre down the Corbridge road (past the hospital) in a residential area. No credit cards. ❸

Royal Priestpopple ☎01434/602270, ⓦwww.hexham-royal-hotel.co.uk. Restored coaching house near the bus station, topped by a gleaming gold dome and offering a dozen modern-styled en-suite rooms, a cosy, oak-panelled bar and good discounts for stays of two nights or more. ❹

Topsy Turvy 9 Leazes Lane ☎01434/603152. Bright and breezy central B&B. No credit cards. ❷

West Close House Hextol Terrace, off B6305, Allendale Rd ☎01434/603307. Quiet, secluded and very friendly, with a delightful garden and wholefood continental breakfasts alongside the usual fry-ups. No credit cards. ❸

Youth hostel

Acomb YHA Main St, Acomb ☎0870/770 5664. Small, simple, 36-bed hostel (£8 per night) occupying converted stable buildings in the village of Acomb, two miles from Hexham – take bus #880 or #882, which pass Hexham train station. Closed Nov & Dec, and Mon & Tues April–June, Sept & Oct; weekends only Jan–March.

Campsites

Fallowfield Dene Caravan Park Acomb ☎01434/603553. A tranquil place with laundry facilities. See hostel above for transport details. Closed Nov–March.

Riverside Leisure Campsite Tyne Green Rd ⓣ01434/604705. Beside the River Tyne, half a mile north of the abbey. Closed Nov–Feb.

The Town

The stately exterior of **Hexham Abbey** (daily: May–Sept 9am–7pm; Oct–April 9am–5pm; free), properly the Priory Church of St Andrew, still dominates the west side of the Market Place. Entry is through the south transept, where there's a bruised but impressive first-century tombstone honouring Flavinus, a standard-bearer in the Roman cavalry, who's shown riding down his bearded enemy. The memorial lies at the foot of the broad, well-worn steps of the canons' **night stair**, one of the few such staircases – providing access from the monastery to the church – to have survived the Dissolution. Beyond, most of the high-arched nave dates from an Edwardian restoration and it's here that you gain access to the **crypt**, a Saxon structure made out of old Roman stones, where pilgrims once viewed the abbey's reliquaries. The nave's architect also used Roman stonework, sticking various sculptural fragments in the walls, many of which he had unearthed during the rebuilding. At the end of the nave is the splendid sixteenth-century **rood screen**, whose complex tracery envelops the portraits of local bishops. Behind the screen, the chancel displays the inconsequential-looking **frith stool**, an eighth-century stone chair that was once believed to have been used by St Wilfrid, rendering it holy enough to serve as the medieval sanctuary stool. Nearby, close to the high altar, there are four panels from a fifteenth-century **Dance of Death**, a grim, darkly varnished painting.

The rest of Hexham's large and irregularly shaped **Market Place** (main market day is Tuesday) is peppered with remains of its medieval past. The massive walls of the fourteenth-century **Moot Hall** were built to serve as the gatehouse to "The Hall", a well-protected enclosure that was garrisoned against the Scots. Nearby, the archbishops also built their own prison, a formidable fortified tower dating from 1330 and constructed using stones plundered from the Roman ruins at Corbridge. Now, as the **Old Gaol**, this accommodates the **Border History Museum** (April–Oct daily 10am–4.30pm; Feb, March & Nov Mon, Tues & Sat 10am–4.30pm; £2), which provides information and displays concerning the border-raiding Reivers as well as the building's use as a prison – a function it abandoned in 1824.

Down by Hexham Bridge, behind the railway line, a short trail runs through the riverside **Tyne Green Country Park**, a couple of miles upstream to **Warden**, the scenic spot where the North Tyne (from Kielder Water) and South Tyne (from the Pennines) rivers join. The *Boatside Inn* at Warden has bar meals and outdoor tables, and the walk there and back is very pleasant on a summer's evening.

Eating, drinking and entertainment

There are several **coffee shops** and **tearooms** in town open during the day, of which *Mrs Miggins*, on St Mary's Wynd, just off Beaumont Street by Queen's Hall, is among the best, serving inexpensive homemade meals and snacks. Off the Market Place, the *Hexham Tans*, 11 St Mary's Chare, is a homely vegetarian café (closed Sun & Mon).

There are four Indian and a couple of Italian **restaurants** in town, but the only place that really stands out is *Danielle's*, an unpretentious bistro at 12 Eastgate (ⓣ01434/601122; closed Sun & Mon). If you don't mind heading out of town – driving or walking – you can try one of the local **country pubs** instead; the tourist office will point you in the right direction. On Dipton Mill Road, two miles south of the centre (45min walk), *Dipton Mill Inn* serves wholesome bar meals (until 8.30pm) and own-brewed beer, in a lovely streamside setting. Or a similar distance to the northeast is the *Rat* at Anick (pronounced Ay-nick), on a glorious hillside location, with sweeping views, a pretty garden and fine food.

The main focus of entertainment in town is the **Queen's Hall Arts Centre** on Beaumont Street (ⓣ01434/652477), which puts on a year-round programme of theatre, dance, music and art exhibitions; it also has a café that stays open late on performance evenings. The centre has information about the **Hexham Gathering**, a folk festival held at various venues at the end of May, and the **Hexham Abbey Festival**, which presents mostly classical music concerts in the abbey in mid-September. There's often live music at various town-centre **pubs**, none of which, otherwise, are particularly enticing. For just a drink, the *Tap & Spile* on the corner of Battle Hill and Eastgate is the most welcoming, with a full range of guest beers.

Chollerford and Chesters Roman Fort

At **CHOLLERFORD**, around four miles north of Hexham, a bridge crosses the North Tyne River, overlooked by the swanky *Swallow George Hotel* (ⓣ01434/681611, ⓦwww.georgehotel-chollerford.com; ❼), whose renowned restaurant has a fine garden and river views; there's a heated indoor pool too.

Two thousand years ago, the main river crossing was a little way downstream, half a mile west of present-day Chollerford, where **Chesters Roman Fort** (daily: Easter–Sept 10am–6pm; Oct 10am–5pm; Nov–Easter 10am–4pm; £3.10; EH), otherwise known as *Cilurnum*, was built to guard the erstwhile Roman bridge over the river, its six-acre plot accommodating a cavalry regiment roughly five hundred strong. Enough remains of the original structure to pick out the design of the fort, and each section has been clearly labelled, but the highlight is down by the river where the vestibule, changing room and steam range of the garrison's **bath house** are still visible, along with the furnace and the latrines. The **museum** at the entrance has an excellent collection of Roman stonework, most of which was retrieved by the Victorian antiquarian John Clayton, who spent years attempting to preserve the Wall. In particular, look out for Juno (now headless) in a delicately pleated dress standing on a cow, one of the finest pieces of statuary found along the Wall.

Next door to the site is the beautiful **Chesters Walled Garden** (April–Oct daily 10am–5pm; Nov–March variable hours, call ⓣ01434/681483; £2), which shelters a fragrant display of herbs, including national collections of thyme and marjoram and a Roman herb section. If you've got your own transport (it's not worth the walk), head another three miles west from Chesters along the B6318 to Carrawburgh, the site of **Brocolitia Fort** (dawn–dusk; free) and its late third-century temple, part of a mysterious cult that spread throughout the empire dedicated to Mithras, the Persian god of sun and light.

Housesteads to Cawfields

Overlooking the bleak Northumbrian moors from the top of the Whin Sill, **Housesteads Roman Fort** (daily: Easter–Sept 10am–6pm; Oct 10am–5pm; Nov–Easter 10am–4pm; £3.10; EH & NT), eight miles west of Chesters, has long been the most popular site on the Wall. The fort was built in the second phase of the Hadrianic construction and is of standard design but for one enforced modification – forts were supposed to straddle the line of the Wall, but here the original stonework tracked along the very edge of the cliff, so Housesteads was built on the steeply sloping ridge to the south. Access is via the tiny **museum**, from where you stroll across to the south gate, beside which lie the remains of the civilian settlement that was dependent on the one thousand infantrymen stationed within. Inside the perimeter, look out for the distinctive cubicles of the barrack blocks, the courtyard plan of the commanding officer's house and the tooth-like stone supports of the granaries.

You don't need to pay for entrance to Housesteads if you simply intend to walk west along the Wall from here. The three-mile hike past the lovely wooded **Crag Lough** to **Steel Rigg** (car park) offers the most fantastic views, especially when you spy the course of the Wall as it threads over the crags ahead. Leaving the Wall at Steel Rigg, it's roughly half a mile south to the main road (B6318) and the visitor centre at **Once Brewed**, where there's also a youth hostel, pub and access road to the Vindolanda excavations (see p.1092). Otherwise, wall-walkers can continue another three miles west from Steel Rigg to **Cawfields** (free access). This was the site of a temporary Roman camp that again pre-dated the Wall, and there are also the remains of another milecastle, this one perched on one of the most rugged crags on this section. There's a car park and picnic site at Cawfields, while if you make your way the mile or so south to the main B6318 you'll find the splendid *Milecastle Inn*, a pub that specializes in home-cooked pies.

Practicalities

The very informative **Once Brewed National Park Visitor Centre** (June–Aug daily 9.30am–5.30pm; mid-March to May, Sept & Oct daily 9.30am–5pm; much reduced hours in winter, usually Sat & Sun only, call for details; ☎01434/344396) has exhibitions and information on both the Wall and the National Park. There are also refreshments for sale and free **Internet** access. The side road beyond the centre continues for half a mile down to Vindolanda and then runs on to the A69, where you can turn left for Haydon Bridge and Hexham or right for Haltwhistle.

By far the best local **restaurant** is the *General Havelock Inn* on the A69 in Haydon Bridge (☎01434/684376), serving fine modern European cuisine either in the bar (closed Mon), in the grand rear restaurant (closed Sun eve & Mon), or in the garden on the banks of the river. Bar meals are very reasonably priced, and there are set lunch deals in the restaurant for around £15; otherwise, expect to pay around £25–30 a head.

Accommodation

Gibbs Hill Farm Once Brewed ☎01434/344030. Working farm with attractive, en-suite rooms and great views of the Wall, two miles north of Steel Rigg. Closed Nov–Feb. ❷

Hadrian's Wall Camping and Caravan Site 2 miles north of Melkridge, just south of B6318 ☎01434/320495. Friendly, family-run site just half a mile from the Wall, with tent space, showers, washing machine and dryer, and bike storage; breakfast available. Open all year.

Langley Castle A686, 2 miles south of Haydon Bridge ☎01434/688888, Ⓦwww.langleycastle.com. You don't get many chances to spend the night in a genuine medieval castle – nor many chances to spend this kind of money in Northumberland. The cheaper rooms are in the grounds, looking on to the castle, but all are spacious, modernized and comfortable, some with four-posters, saunas and spa baths. There's also an atmospheric restaurant, cocktail bar, lounge and gardens. ❼, castle rooms ❾

Once Brewed YHA Military Rd, B6318, Once Brewed ☎0870/770 5980, Ⓔoncebrewed@yha.org.uk. Next to the visitor centre, providing walking leaflets, packed lunches, cheap three-course dinners (£5.10), kitchen and lounge. Dorms (£11.50) are small (mostly four-bed), modern facilities. Closed Dec & Jan, and Sun Feb, March & Nov.

Twice Brewed Inn Military Rd, B6318 ☎01434/344534, Ⓦwww.twicebrewedinn.co.uk. Friendly pub, 50yd up from Once Brewed visitor centre and hostel, with simple rooms (mainly standard, though en suite available, in next price category), food served all day until 8.30pm, beer garden, local beers on tap and Internet access. Closed Jan. ❶

Vallum Lodge Military Rd, B6318 ☎01434/344248. A comfortable small hotel with good home cooking, a mile or so west down the main road from the visitor centre. Closed Nov–Feb. ❸

Vindolanda

The excavated garrison fort of **Vindolanda** actually predates the Wall itself – as do several of the forts hereabouts – though most of what you see today dates from the second to third century AD, when the fort was a thriving metropolis of five hundred soldiers with its own civilian settlement attached. The site (daily: May & June 10am–6pm; July & Aug 10am–6.30pm; April & Sept 10am–5.30pm; March & Oct 10am–5pm; Nov, Dec & Feb 10am–4pm; £4.10, Ⓦwww.vindolanda.com) is operated by the private Vindolanda Trust, which has done an excellent job of imaginatively presenting its finds. Note that the trust also administers the Roman Army Museum at Greenhead; if you're visiting both sites, request a discounted joint-admission ticket (£6).

The ongoing **excavations** at Vindolanda are spread over a wide area, with civilian houses, inn, guest quarters, administrative building, commander's house and main gates all clearly visible. Full-scale re-creations give an idea of what the Wall would have looked like: a stone turret and wall section, alongside a timber milecastle and a bit of turf wall to replicate the original appearance of the western third of the Wall, where limestone was in short supply.

The path through the excavations then descends to what's termed the **open-air museum**, where you can walk into reconstructions of a shrine of the water nymphs, a shop and a house, all with lively sound commentaries. Beyond lies the café, shop and **museum**, the latter housing the largest collection of Roman leather items ever discovered on a single site – dozens of shoes, belts, even a pair of baby boots – which were preserved in the black silt of waterlogged ditches. The most intriguing sections are concerned with the excavated hoard of **writing tablets**, now in the British Museum (see p.91). Between 1973 and 1992, two hundred significant texts were discovered on the site, dealing with subjects as diverse as clerical filing systems and children's schoolwork. Then, in 1993, final excavations from a bonfire site revealed more tablets, apparently discarded when the garrison received orders in 103–104 AD to move to the Danube to participate in Emperor Trajan's Second Dacian War. The writings depict graphically the realities of military life in Northumberland, under the prefecture of Flavius Cerialis: soldiers' requests for more beer, birthday party invitations, court reports on banishments for unspecified wrongdoings, even letters from home containing gifts of underwear for freezing frontline grunts.

Haltwhistle

There's not much to the small town of **HALTWHISTLE**, and it's a couple of miles off the Wall itself, but it makes a useful overnight stop, features the only full set of amenities (ATMs, supermarket, shops and cafés) this side of Hexham, and has a lively **market** each Thursday. The town also claims to be the very centre of Britain, something you could debate with the **tourist office** (Easter to mid-May & Oct Mon–Sat 9.30am–1pm & 2–5pm, Sun 1–5pm; mid-May to Sept Mon–Sat 9.30am–1pm & 2–5.30pm, Sun 1–5pm; Nov to Easter Mon, Tues & Thurs–Sat 10am–noon & 1–3.30pm; ☎01434/322002) in the train station, at the western edge of town, close to the A69. From here, walk up to Westgate, which becomes Main Street. **Mountain bikes** can be rented from Edens Lawn petrol station on the eastern edge of town (☎01434/320443).

The best **hotel**, the *Centre of Britain* (Ⓣ01434/322422, Ⓦwww.centre-of-britain.org.uk; ❸–❺), is on Main Street, right in the centre of town. Built around a fifteenth-century peel tower are a variety of tasteful bedrooms (some with spa bath and sauna) and lounges with wooden beams and stone fireplaces. The town also has a good selection of **B&Bs**, including the attractive, ivy-covered *Hall Meadows*, on Main Street (Ⓣ01434/321021; no credit cards; ❷) close to the *Centre of Britain*. Or there's *Ashcroft* in an elegant former vicarage on Lantys Lonnen (Ⓣ01434/320213, Ⓦwww.ashcroftguesthouse.co.uk; ❸) – a turn off Main Street just after the *Centre of Britain* – that has nice rooms and colourful terraced gardens. Two or three of the pubs along Main Street also offer accommodation. The local **campsite** is in Burnfoot Park (Ⓣ01434/320106; closed Nov–Feb), beside the Tyne on the southeast edge of town.

There are several **tearooms** along and around Main Street, while a couple of miles south of town, the *Wallace Arms* at Rowfoot, near Featherstone, is a nice place for a **pub** meal and a country walk.

Roman Army Museum and Greenhead

A further four-mile trek west from Cawfields takes you past the remains of **Great Chesters Fort** before reaching a spectacular section of the Wall, known as the **Walltown Crags**, where a turret from a signal system predating the Wall still survives. The views from here are marvellous. Adjacent to the crags, at Carvoran, you can call into the Vindolanda Trust's **Roman Army Museum** (daily: May & June 10am–6pm; July & Aug 10am–6.30pm; April & Sept 10am–5.30pm; March & Oct 10am–5pm; early Nov & late Feb 10am–4pm; £3.30; joint ticket with Vindolanda £6), which tells you everything there is to know about life in the Roman army by way of exhibits, dioramas, reconstructions and games. There's also a virtual-reality aerial "flight" along the Wall.

Push on just a mile southwest, and you're soon in minuscule **GREENHEAD**, where the **youth hostel** (Ⓣ0870/770 5842, Ⓔgreenhead@yha.org.uk; £10.25; closed Nov–Easter) is located in a converted Methodist chapel. *Holmhead Guest House* (Ⓣ016977/47402, Ⓦwww.bandbhadrianswall.com; ❸), an old stone farmhouse sporting exposed beams, and partly built with stones taken from the Wall itself, is up a track behind the hostel. There are only four rooms, and guests should reserve in advance for the excellent set-menu dinner (£20) using local ingredients. There are also two **camping** spaces here, and a small bunk barn (£8 per person), handy for Wall walkers. The hamlet is where the **Pennine Way** cuts east, following the Wall as far as Housesteads before bearing north again. Heading west, the next section of Hadrian's Wall worth exploring is at Birdoswald, in Cumbria, a four-mile walk or ten-minute ride on the bus; there's overnight hostel accommodation here in summer (see p.910).

Northumberland National Park

Northwest Northumberland, the great triangular chunk of land between Hadrian's Wall and the coastal plain, is dominated by the wide-skied landscapes of the **Northumberland National Park** (Ⓦwww.northumberland-national-park.org.uk), whose four hundred windswept square miles rise to the Cheviot Hills on the Scottish border. These uplands are interrupted by great slabs of forest, mostly the conifer plantations of the Forestry Commission, and a string of river valleys, of which Coquetdale, Tynedale and Redesdale are the longest. Remote from lowland law and order, these dales were once the homelands of the **Border Reivers**, turbulent clans who ruled the local roost from the thirteenth to the sixteenth century. The Reivers took advantage of the struggles between England and Scotland to engage in endless cross-border rustling and general brigandage, activities recalled by the ruined **bastles** (fortified farmhouses) and **peels** (defensive tower-houses) that lie dotted across the landscape.

To attempt a tour of the region by bus – there aren't any trains – is a time-consuming business. Most services go up or down the valleys, with few crossing the hills between them. The most popular hiking trail is the **Pennine Way**, which, entering the National Park at Hadrian's Wall, cuts up through Bellingham on its way to **The Cheviot**, the park's highest peak at 2674ft, finishing at Kirk Yetholm, over the border in Scotland. As an introduction, it's hard to beat the lovely moorland scenery of the fifteen-mile stretch from Housesteads at Hadrian's Wall to **Bellingham**, a pleasant town on the banks of the North Tyne. Bellingham is also on the road to **Kielder Water**, a massive pine-surrounded reservoir, water-sports centre and nature reserve. Further north, **Rothbury**, in Coquetdale, is close to both the Simonside Hills and **Cragside**, the nineteenth-century country home of Lord Armstrong, whilst at **Wooler**, footpaths lead into the Cheviot Hills. Beyond Wooler, a succession of battle sites and **castles** attest to the erstwhile military significance of this border region; notable among them are idiosyncratically restored **Chillingham**, which is home to an equally unusual herd of wild cattle, and the weatherbeaten pink ruins of **Norham**, in an inspiring location on the banks of the Tweed.

Bellingham

The stone terraces of **BELLINGHAM** (pronounced Bellinjum) slope up from the banks of the Tyne on the eastern edge of the Northumberland National Park. There's nothing outstanding about the place, but it is a restful spot set in splendid rural surroundings, and it does contain the medieval **Church of St Cuthbert**, which has an unusual stone-vaulted roof – designed (successfully) to prevent raiding Border Reivers from burning the church to the ground. The volunteer-run **Heritage Centre** just east of the village centre on Woodburn Road (May–Sept Mon & Fri–Sun 10.30am–4.30pm; £1) has more on this turbulent period. For a local stroll, follow the two-and-a-half-mile round-trip trail through the woods to **Hareshaw Linn**, a charming waterfall with a thirty-foot drop.

Buses from Hexham and Otterburn (also direct from Newcastle's Eldon Square on summer Wed, Sun & bank holidays) stop in the centre on Market Place, a few hundred yards down from the tourist office. There are onward services to Kielder or Otterburn most days. The helpful **tourist office** on Main Street (Easter–Oct Mon–Sat 9.30am–1pm & 2–5pm, Sun 1–5pm; Nov–Easter Mon–Fri 2–5pm; ⓣ01434/220616) is housed in Bellingham's former Poor House building and is well stocked with local information.

Despite its size, the village's proximity to the park and its location on the Pennine Way means that there's a fair choice of **accommodation**. You may still want to book ahead in summer, particularly if you're coinciding with the last Saturday in August, when the Bellingham Show, the big agricultural event of the year, is staged. The **youth hostel** (ⓣ0870/770 5694; £9; closed Nov–Easter, & closed Sun & Mon April–June, Sept & Oct) has simple self-catering facilities 600yd from the centre of the village on Woodburn Road (signposted from Main Street). All other lodgings are within a hundred yards or so of each other, including the modern, en-suite rooms at *Lyndale Guest House* (ⓣ01434/220361, ⓦwww.lyndaleguesthouse.co.uk; ❸), just past the *Rose & Crown* pub. Bellingham's **pubs** – the *Rose & Crown*, the *Black Bull* and the *Cheviot* – all have a few rooms, too; those at the *Cheviot* (ⓣ01434/220696; ❸) are the nicest.

Swankiest choice in Bellingham is *Riverdale Hall Hotel* (ⓣ01434/220254, ⓦwww.riverdalehall.demon.co.uk; ❺), a nineteenth-century country house on the village's western edge, with an indoor swimming pool and extensive grounds. The local **campsite** is at Demesne Farm (ⓣ01434/220258; closed Nov–Feb), right in the centre near the police station. Bellingham has a bank with an ATM, small supermarket and a couple of **cafés**, though otherwise you're dependent on the bar meals served at the pubs.

Bastles on the Tarset

The constant cross-border skirmishing of the late medieval period had an immediate effect on the rural vernacular architecture of the northeast. Lonely farmhouses were fortified in an attempt to ward off attacks, and the area west of Bellingham is rich in the remains of these so-called **bastle houses**. The best preserved lies seven miles northwest of the village, beyond Greenhaugh, where the late-sixteenth-century **Black Middens Bastle House** (free access; EH) sits above the waters of Tarset Burn. From a distance, it looks like any other ruined, roofless, stone farmhouse; indeed, close up, it looks like any other ruined, roofless, stone farmhouse, albeit one with extremely thick walls, strategic, narrow upper-floor windows and low surrounding walls. The main door and living quarters were on the upper floor, reached by an exterior staircase, which made it more difficult for attackers to batter their way in. From here, you can continue up the marked trail along the **Tarset Valley**, passing several more ruined bastles, though none as evocatively placed as Black Middens.

The hamlet of **GREENHAUGH** has the only facilities hereabouts in the shape of the rustic *Holly Bush Inn* (ⓣ01434/240391; ❷), a squat, 200-year-old cottage that offers B&B, bar meals and real ales, and also doubles as the post office.

Kielder Water and Forest

Further west, the road from Bellingham follows the North Tyne River and skirts the forested edge of **Kielder Water** (ⓦwww.kielder.org), passing the assorted visitor centres, waterside parks, picnic areas and anchorages that fringe its southern shore. First stop is the Visitor Centre at **Tower Knowe** (daily: July & Aug 9am–6pm; April–June, Sept & Oct 10am–5pm; ⓣ0870/240 3549), eight miles from Bellingham, with a café and an exhibition on the history of the valley and lake.

Another four miles west, at **Leaplish**, the waterside park (daily: April & Oct 9am–6pm; May–Sept 9am–11pm; Nov–March call to check times on ⓣ0870/240 3549), bar and restaurant are the focus of most of Kielder's outdoor activities: water sports and fishing are on offer, and there's a heated indoor pool and sauna. The **Bird of Prey Centre** here (March–Oct daily 10.30am–5pm; £3.50) lays on flying displays, falconry courses and winter hawk walks. A ten-mile, hour-and-a-half's cruise on the **Osprey ferry** (Easter–Oct 5 daily; £5) is always a pleasure; departures are from the piers at either Tower Knowe or Leaplish.

Five miles from Leaplish at the top of the reservoir and just three miles from the Scottish border, **KIELDER VILLAGE** is dominated by Kielder Castle, built in 1775 as the hunting lodge of the Duke of Northumberland and now the **Forest Park Visitor Centre** (Easter–Oct daily 10am–5pm; Nov & Dec Sat & Sun 11am–4pm; ⓣ01434/250209), whose free exhibitions praise the work of the Forestry Commission as well as focusing on the birds of the area. Visitor centre facilities are rounded off by a gift shop and restaurant.

The castle is surrounded by the **Kielder Forest Park**, comprising several million spruce trees, criss-crossed by trails and home to red squirrels, deer and countless birds. Several easy and clearly marked footpaths, dotted with arresting modern sculptures, lead from the castle into the forest – try the "Duke's Trail" through Ravenshill Wood, a slice of ancient and semi-natural woodland. There's **mountain-bike rental** available from Kielder Bikes (Ⓣ01434/250392) at the castle, with thirteen waymarked trails and two off-road routes through the forest to choose from.

Practicalities

On Sundays and bank holidays from the end of May to mid-October, the **Kielder Bus** (day rover ticket £5) runs once daily in the morning from Gateshead Metro, Newcastle Central Station and Newcastle Haymarket to Kielder Castle, and then provides a shuttle service to Kielder attractions before returning to the city in the late-afternoon. At other times, you're dependent on the local bus **from Bellingham** which calls at Tower Knowe, Leaplish and Kielder, and less regularly at Stannersburn and Falstone. The twice-daily post bus from Hexham follows a similar route past Bellingham, though it takes a lot longer to complete the journey. You'll pass a couple of small villages with pubs on the way, while **facilities** in Kielder village include a general store, garage, tearoom and pub.

As well as the **accommodation** options listed below, there are several B&Bs in Kielder village and the surrounding area – the Tower Knowe and Kielder visitor centres can assist. The **Kielder Campsite** (Ⓣ01434/250291; closed Oct–Easter) is in Kielder village, about half a mile north of the castle on the banks of the Tyne.

Accommodation

Blackcock Inn Falstone, 1 mile north of Stannersburn Ⓣ01434/240200. Small inn located in a riverside hamlet. You can eat here, or at the tearooms in the former village school. ❸

Kielder YHA Butteryhaugh, Kielder village Ⓣ0870/770 5898, Ⓔkielder@yha.org.uk. Well-equipped activity-based hostel, with some two- and three-bedded rooms plus small dorms (£10.25). It has a self-catering kitchen, and a restaurant offering breakfast and three-course dinners. Closed Nov–Easter.

Leaplish Waterside Park Information Ⓣ0870/240 3549, reservations through Hoseasons Ⓣ0870/333 2000. An old fishing lodge on the side of the reservoir has been converted to provide bunk-barn accommodation (dorms £10–12) and three en-suite rooms (double £25, family £40), plus a drying room, kitchen, laundry and showers. It also has well-equipped lodges available, £230–620 per week depending on season (cheaper 3-day stays available all year).

Pheasant Inn Stannersburn Ⓣ01434/240382, Ⓔthepheasantinn@kielderwater.demon.co.uk. On the road in from Bellingham, a couple of miles before the water, this early-seventeenth-century inn has eight comfortable rooms in a modern extension and decent meals served in the bar or restaurant. ❹

Redesdale

From Bellingham, it's a fifteen-mile trek north along the Pennine Way to Byrness in **Redesdale**, which can also be reached direct from Kielder Castle via a rough, eleven-mile forestry road that snakes through the pine-clad hills of the northeast portion of the Kielder Forest Park. Set beside the main A68 road, **BYRNESS** is a tiny village, but walkers can take refuge at the simple **youth hostel** at 7 Otterburn Green (Ⓣ0870/770 5740; £8; closed Oct–Easter).

Redesdale has only one settlement of any size, **OTTERBURN**, ten miles southeast of Byrness down the A68. It's an undistinguished place today, surrounded by heather-clad, sheep-laden countryside, with little except the name of the local pub, the *Percy Arms*, to recall its most notable hour. It was at Otterburn in August 1388 that an English army led by Sir Henry Percy ("Hotspur") was defeated by the Scots under James, Earl of Douglas. Douglas was killed in battle, as were 1800 English troops, while Hotspur was taken prisoner – a chain of events later made the subject of the medieval ballad of *Chevy Chase*. The supposed battle site is about a mile northwest of the village, off the A68, marked by a stone cross set in a little pinewood – though you may as well pick virtually any large field in the vicinity, since historians not only dispute its exact location, but also argue about the site of the Scottish base camp and even the exact date of the battle itself.

From Byrness and Otterburn there are two to four **buses** a day to Newcastle (or north through the borders to Edinburgh) as well as less regular services to Bellingham (from where buses run to Hexham and Kielder). After Byrness comes Northumberland's longest uninterrupted stretch of the Pennine Way, the 27-mile haul to the end of the hike at Kirk Yetholm (see p.1100), though you can detour to Wooler (see p.1099). Local information is available inside the **Otterburn Mill** (Mon–Sat 9am–5pm, Sun 10am–4pm), which, though it no longer produces textiles, sells them and maintains a small museum, including a restored nineteenth-century water turbine and Europe's only remaining tenterhooks, used for stretching and drying newly woven cloth. There's a garden **café** at the mill, or you can get more substantial **bar meals** at the *Percy Arms*, round the corner on Main St, or the *Redesdale Arms*, an old coaching inn on the A68, three miles west of the village.

Rothbury and around

ROTHBURY, straddling the River Coquet eighteen miles northeast of Otterburn, prospered as a late Victorian resort because it gave ready access to the forests, burns and ridges of the Simonside Hills. In the centre, where the High Street widens to form a broad triangle, there are hints of past pretensions in the assertive facades overlooking the **Rothbury Cross**, erected in 1902. Rothbury remains a popular spot for walkers, and the **Tourist Information and National Park Visitor Centre**, near the cross on Church Street (April–Oct daily 10am–5pm; June–Aug until 6pm; Nov–March Sat & Sun 10am–5pm; ⓣ01669/620887, ⓦwww.visit-rothbury.co.uk), offers exhibitions related to the National Park and can provide advice on local **trails**, several of which begin in the Simonside Hills car park, a couple of miles southwest of town. The most appealing is the five-mile round trip along the Simonside ridge, with panoramic views out over Coquetdale. The town also has a renowned **traditional music festival** each July, bringing folkies and fans into town from all over the region for Northumbrian pipe music, dancing and story-telling.

Practicalities

Buses from Morpeth (with connections from Newcastle) stop at the bottom of Rothbury's High Street, outside the *Queen's Head*. There are several convenient **B&Bs**, including *Katerina's Guest House* up the High Street (ⓣ01669/620691, ⓦwww.katerinasguesthouse.co.uk; ❸), where all the en-suite rooms boast four-poster beds and TVs; and the comfortable, Georgian *Orchard Guest House*, further up the same street (ⓣ01669/620684, ⓦwww.orchardguesthouse.co.uk; ❸). Otherwise, it's worth heading out of town to *Silverton Lodge*, a comfortably refurbished Victorian schoolhouse with excellent views of the surrounding countryside on Silverton Lane

(T 01669/620144, W www.silvertonlodge.co.uk; 3), about ten minutes' walk from the centre, up the main street. Most of the places to **eat and drink** – two or three cafés, a deli and a couple of pubs – are strung out along the High Street. There's **Internet** access at Rothbury Computer Services, opposite the *Queens' Head*.

Cragside

Victorian Rothbury was dominated by Sir William, later the first **Lord Armstrong**, the immensely wealthy nineteenth-century arms manufacturer, shipbuilder and engineer who built his country home at **Cragside** (Easter–Sept Tues–Sun 1–5.30pm, Oct until 4.30pm; £7.20, gardens only £4.80; NT), on the steep, forested slopes of Debdon Burn, a mile to the east of the village. He hired Richard Norman Shaw, one of the period's top architects, and work continued until the mid-1880s, culminating in a grandiose, and utterly romantic, Tudor-style mansion, whose black and white timber-framed gables and upper storeys are entirely out of place in the Northumbrian countryside. The interior is stuffed with Armstrong's furnishings and fittings, heavy dark pieces enlivened by his art collection and by the William Morris stained glass in the library and the dining-room inglenook. Later extensions catered for Armstrong's numerous hobbies and diversions – his natural history and shell collection was placed in the gallery, a billiard room was added, while the marble-decked drawing room was completed in time for the visit of the Prince and Princess of Wales in 1884. Doubtless, they were too well brought up to comment on Shaw's "masterpiece", the spectacularly hideous Renaissance-style marble chimneypiece, which uses ten tons of the stuff to overly sentimental effect. House **tours** are usually available on Friday and Sunday mornings.

Armstrong was an avid innovator, fascinated by hydraulic engineering and by hydroelectric power. At Cragside he could indulge himself, damming the Debdon Burn to power several domestic appliances, such as the spit and the dumb waiter in the massive kitchen, as well as heating his personal Turkish-style plunge bath and steam room. In 1880, after several false starts, he also managed to supply Cragside with electricity, making this the first house in the world to be lit by hydroelectric power. The remains of the original system – including the powerhouse and pumping station – are still visible in the **grounds**, which, together with the splendid **formal gardens**, have longer opening hours (Easter–Oct Tues–Sun 10.30am–7pm or dusk; Nov to mid-Dec Wed–Sun 11am–4pm).

Given the hefty admission price you'll probably want to make a day of it, and that's easily done, especially if you come clutching a picnic. Shaded, signposted trails run up hill and down dale through the grounds, past banks of bluebells and rhododendrons; the tallest tree in England (a 191-foot Douglas fir) pierces the pine grove. Over at the visitor centre there's a **café/restaurant**, and an explanatory video and other displays in the adjacent Armstrong Energy Centre.

Brinkburn Priory

From Rothbury the B6344 runs four miles southeast through pretty **Coquetdale**, following the course of the river, to reach the splendid sight of **Brinkburn Priory** (April–Sept daily 10am–6pm; Oct daily 10am–5pm; £2; EH), nestling in a loop of the Coquet. Founded as an Augustinian priory in 1135, its church – the only surviving building – was built fifty years later and it's this that provides the focus of interest today. Thoroughly but sympathetically restored in the nineteenth century, it's a superb example of northern Transitional architecture, featuring a fine Norman doorway and an echoing nave, empty save for a remarkable series of enormous contemporary wooden religious sculptures by Durham sculptor Fenwick Lawson. English Heritage is also responsible for the rambling manor house adjacent to the church. Built around 1810, but incorporating parts of the earlier monastic buildings, it was rebuilt by the great Newcastle architect John Dobson in the 1830s, and last lived in during the 1950s. It's now a rather forlorn ruin, though essential maintenance work has arrested its decline and the public is free to wander its beautifully proportioned halls.

Wooler and around

Stone-terraced **WOOLER**, a grey one-street market town twenty miles north of Rothbury, was wholly rebuilt after a calamitous fire in the 1860s, though its hillside setting high above Harthope Burn and its proximity to the **Cheviot Hills** do much to lift the spirits. Local walks provide an introduction to the range, with a particular favourite being the one-mile hike to the top of Humbleton Hill, site of a battle in 1402 in which Hotspur inflicted heavy casualties on forces of the Douglas clan. But to get into the heart of the Cheviots you'll have to tackle the trek to The Cheviot itself (see below), seven miles to the southwest. Wooler is also a staging-post on **St Cuthbert's Way**, the trans-Cheviot route, which runs west from the town to Kirk Yetholm and beyond or northeast to Holy Island.

Frequent buses link Wooler with Berwick-upon-Tweed and Alnwick, the two nearest towns, and the **bus station** is set back off the High Street. At the other end of the High Street, off Burnhouse Road (by the free **car park**), you'll find the **tourist office** in the Cheviot Centre at Padgepool Place (Easter–Oct Mon–Sat 10am–1.30pm & 2–5pm, Sun 10am–1.30pm & 2–6pm; ⓣ01668/282123), which can provide walking information, including a leaflet on country hikes of between five and nine miles around the town, accessible by local bus.

The High Street pubs all offer **accommodation**, and there are a couple of good central B&Bs. *Tilldale House*, 34 High St (ⓣ01668/281450, ⓔtilldalehouse@freezone.co.uk/; ❷), has spacious en-suite rooms and serves evening meals; while *Winton House*, just off the High Street at 39 Glendale Rd (ⓣ01668/281362, ⓦwww.wintonhouse.ntb.org.uk; no credit cards; ❷; closed Dec–Feb), is a stone-built Edwardian house with garden, owned by a friendly couple who can give information on local walks and provide a packed lunch, too. For a bit more luxury, try the *Tankerville Arms* on Cottage Rd (ⓣ01668/281581, ⓦwww.tankervillehotel.co.uk; ❺), a seventeenth-century coaching inn just off the A697 below town, which has a good restaurant overlooking the attractive garden and a wide range of bar meals. Wooler also has a comfortable **youth hostel** – the most northerly in England – at 30 Cheviot St (ⓣ0870/770 6100; £10.25; closed Nov–Feb & closed various days March–June, Sept & Oct), a five-minute walk up the hill from the bus station, as well as a **campsite**, Highburn House on Burnhouse Road (ⓣ01668/281344; closed Nov–Feb), just north of town, about half a mile from the bus station.

To the Cheviot and Kirk Yetholm: the end of the Pennine Way

It's a fair hike from Wooler up the Harthope Valley to **The Cheviot**, which at 2674ft is the highest point in the Cheviot Hills. Starting out from Wooler youth hostel, count on four hours up, a little less back. It helps if you can drive, or catch a lift, to Hawsen Burn, the nearest navigable point, which still leaves you two hours walking there and back – your reward, an utterly bleak spot with views, on a clear day, to the coast, the castles at Bamburgh and Dunstanburgh, and over to Holy Island.

If you're properly equipped, and prepared for a long day's walking, on the west side of the peak you can join the **Pennine Way** at Scotsman's cairn. Here, you're about seven miles south of the trail end at the Scottish village of **KIRK YETHOLM**, where there's a **youth hostel** (ⓣ0870/155 3255; £9.50; closed Oct–March), down a lane off the village green, and several **B&Bs**. At this point, you're just over the border and just out of the National Park; it's fourteen miles east by road back to Wooler.

Chillingham

Six miles southeast of Wooler, and served by bus #470 towards Alnwick, the eccentricities of **Chillingham Castle** (Easter–Sept daily except Sat 1–5pm; £5; ⓦwww.chillingham-castle.com) provide a refreshing counterpoint to the high-minded tidiness of National Trust-restored stately homes. Starting from an eleventh-century tower, the castle was augmented at regular intervals until 1873, though it keeps the essential structure of its mid-fourteenth-century incarnation, a grand, heavily walled courtyard with four impressive corner towers. For fifty years from 1933, however, Chillingham was largely left to the elements, until the present owner set about restoring it in his own individualistic way: bedrooms, living rooms and even a grisly torture chamber are stuffed and decorated with all manner of historical flotsam to give an idea of how the place would have looked through the ages, while chatty guides in each room tell tall tales of the castle and its visitors. In the **grounds** (open from noon), which were designed by Sir Jeffrey Wyatville, nineteenth-century landscaper of Windsor Castle, you can look around a small Elizabethan topiary garden, with its intricately clipped hedges of box and yew, and take a mile-long walk through the woods to the lake. Several self-catering **apartments** within the castle, including the Elizabethan Long Gallery, are available, either by the night (ⓣ01668/215359; breakfast not included, ⑥) or by the week.

In 1220, the adjoining 365 acres of parkland were enclosed to protect the local wild cattle for hunting and food. And so the **Chillingham Wild Cattle**, a fierce, primeval herd with white coats, black muzzles and black tips to their horns, have remained to this day, cut off from mixing with domesticated breeds. It's possible to visit these unique relics, whose numbers vary between forty and sixty, but only in the company of a warden and from a safe distance – bring binoculars if you can – as the animals are potentially dangerous and need to be protected from outside infection (April–Oct Mon & Wed–Sat 10am–noon & 2–5pm, Sun 2–5pm; £3; ⓣ01668/215250, ⓦwww.chillingham-wildcattle.org.uk). The visit takes about an hour and a half.

North to Berwick

North of Wooler, the B6525 leads straight to Berwick-upon-Tweed, but if you're in no hurry you'd do well to meander northwestwards up the A697 towards Coldstream, a route which allows you a glimpse into the precarious fourteenth- to sixteenth-century history of the border region. You're soon into rich, flat farmland, watered by the tributaries of the River Tweed, which marks the border with Scotland at this point. The views behind you are of the Cheviots, while detours off the main roads put you on country lanes presided over here and there by stately mansions with gatehouses.

Ford, Etal, Branxton and Crookham

Eight miles north of Wooler, head east off the A697 a short way along the B6354 to reach the village of **FORD**. The fourteenth-century castle isn't open to the public, but you can stay in the grounds: the *Estate House* (Ⓣ01890/820668, Ⓦwww.theestatehouse.supanet.com; ❸) is a delightful retreat serving a good breakfast and evening meals with a vegetarian slant (£14). While here, you could take a look inside the former school, now **Lady Waterford Hall** (Easter–Oct daily 10.30am–12.30pm & 1.30–5.30pm; £1.75), which features pictures and murals by Louisa Anne, Marchioness of Waterford, a pupil of Ruskin.

Three miles further up the B6354 lies **ETAL** (pronounced "Eetle"), whose **castle** (daily: April–Sept 10am–6pm; Oct 10am–5pm; £3; EH) can be visited. Built in 1340 on the banks of the quiet River Till, only the well-preserved central keep and gatehouse still stand, but they make a handsome sight, especially when taken in conjunction with the pretty little village itself. The *Black Bull* here is the only thatched pub in Northumberland, and serves sandwiches and bar meals. If you've got children in tow, it's worth knowing that from Heatherslaw Mill, halfway back down the road to Ford, the narrow-gauge **Heatherslaw Light Railway** (hourly service, Easter–Oct daily 11am–3pm; extra trains during school holidays; £5 return) runs up the banks of the River Till to the foot of Etal Castle; the return journey takes about forty minutes. The railway's *Granary Café* keeps body and soul together, and **bikes** can be rented (Ⓣ01890/820338) for further exploration of the area's rolling countryside.

Back on the A697 just beyond Crookham, a minor road leads a mile or so west to the hamlet of **BRANXTON**, just above which, on the slopes of Branxton Hill, is the site of the English victory at the **Battle of Flodden** (1513). It was one of the most decisive of sixteenth-century conflicts: up to ten thousand Scots died in battle, including James IV – fighting at the head of his troops – and most of the contemporary Scottish nobility. The bodies were dumped in pits in Branxton churchyard, their passing now remembered by a simple granite memorial on the hill inscribed "To the brave of both nations". You can stay in **CROOKHAM**, where the atmospheric *Coach House* (Ⓣ01890/820293, Ⓦwww.coachhousecrookham.com; ❹) has a range of rooms in converted farm buildings sporting exposed beams. Guests are pampered with tasty homemade breakfasts and dinners (£20). The *Blue Bell* in the village serves bar meals.

The border and Norham Castle

The A697 runs four miles west of Branxton to reach the **border**, marked by Cornhill-on-Tweed on the English side and Coldstream in Scotland across the River Tweed. There's little point lingering in either with Berwick so close, but save time for the ruins of **Norham Castle** (April–Sept daily 10am–6pm; £2; EH), overlooking the tumbling Tweed, just six miles or so to the northeast (signposted off the A698). Its surviving pink sandstone walls and foursquare keep, celebrated in paint by J.M.W. Turner and in verse in Sir Walter Scott's *Marmion*, stand out above the flat farming country, the trees lining the green-grassed ramparts stripped bare by the winds in winter and providing a leafy curtain in summer. It was considered one of the strongest of the border castles, but James IV of Scotland nevertheless engineered its capture before meeting his nemesis at Flodden Field.

The Northumberland coast

The low-lying **Northumberland coast**, stretching 64 miles north from Newcastle to the Scottish border, boasts many of the region's principal attractions, but first you have to clear the disfigured landscape of the old Northumbrian coalfield, which extends up as far north as the port of Amble. In its heyday at the beginning of the twentieth century this area employed a quarter of Britain's colliers, but all bar one of the mines closed years ago. Attempts have been made to clean up parts of this coast and its hinterland: at Ashington, once a huge pit village (birthplace of the footballing Charlton brothers and the great Jackie Milburn), a country park has been created from a former slag heap, while the marina at Amble and the prospect of summer jaunts to offshore Coquet Island and its nature reserve provide some relief.

Beyond Amble, however, you emerge into a pastoral, gently wooded landscape that spreads over the thirty-odd miles to Berwick-upon-Tweed. On the way there's a succession of mighty fortresses, beginning with **Warkworth Castle** and **Alnwick Castle**, former and present strongholds of the Percys, the county's biggest landowners. Further along, there's the formidable fastness of **Bamburgh** and then, last of all, the magnificent Elizabethan ramparts surrounding **Berwick-upon-Tweed**. In between you'll find splendid sandy beaches – notably at Warkworth, Bamburgh and the tiny seaside resort of **Alnmouth** – as well as the site of the Lindisfarne monastery on **Holy Island** and the seabird and nature reserve of the **Farne Islands**, reached by boat from Seahouses.

An excellent network of **bus** services makes it easy to travel up and down the coast, and the main London to Edinburgh **train** line passes through Alnmouth and Berwick – though very few fast services stop at the former. Only Holy Island is tricky to reach by public transport, an infrequent bus from Berwick-upon-Tweed being the sole connection. **By car**, the A1 from Alnwick (and, before that, from Newcastle) provides the fastest route to Berwick, though it runs well inland of the major coastal attractions. For these, the B1340 from Alnwick and its offshoots – often signposted "Coastal Route" – is the one to follow.

Warkworth

WARKWORTH, a coastal hamlet set in a loop of the River Coquet a couple of miles from Amble, is best seen from the north, from where the grey stone terraces of the long main street slope up towards the commanding remains of **Warkworth Castle** (daily: April–Sept 10am–6pm; Oct 10am–5pm; Nov–March 10am–1pm & 2–4pm; £3; EH), which perch on top of an immense grassy mound at the far end of the village. Enough remains of the outer wall to give a clear impression of the layout of the medieval bailey, but – apart from the well-preserved gatehouse through which the site is entered – nothing catches your attention as much as the keep. Mostly built in the fourteenth century, this three-storeyed structure, with its polygonal turrets and high central tower, has a honeycomb-like interior, a fine example of the designs developed by the castle-builders of Plantagenet England. It was here that most of the Percy family, earls of Northumberland, chose to live throughout the fourteenth and fifteenth centuries.

The main street sweeps down into the attractive village, flattening out at Dial Place before curving right to cross the River Coquet; just over the bridges – a modern affair flanked by a splendid medieval turreted span – a signposted quarter-mile lane leads to the **beach**, which stretches for five miles from Amble to Alnmouth. Back in Dial Place stands the **Church of St Lawrence**, whose many Norman features include the impressive ribbed vaulting of the chancel. From the churchyard (or, further up, from below the castle), a delightful path heads the half-mile inland along the peaceful right bank of the Coquet to the little boat that shuttles visitors across to **Warkworth Hermitage** (April–Sept Wed & Sun 11am–5pm; £2; EH), a series of simple rooms and a claustrophobic chapel that were hewn out of the cliff above the river sometime in the fourteenth century, but abandoned by 1567. The last resident hermit, one George Lancaster, was charged by the sixth earl of Northumberland to pray for his noble family, for which lonesome duty he received around £15 a year and a barrel of fish every Sunday.

Practicalities

Warkworth is on the route of the **bus service** linking Alnwick, Alnmouth and Newcastle, while other local services run to and from Alnwick and Amble. Buses stop in Dial Place, near the church. There are several **B&Bs** just on the other side of the Coquet bridges and handy for the beach, including *North Cottage* (☎01665/711263; ❷) and *Beck'n'Call* (☎01665/711653; ❷). The top spot is the splendid *Sun Hotel*, 6 Castle Terrace (☎01665/711259, ⓦwww.rytonpark-sun.co.uk; ❺), which commands fine views from its perch between the castle and the river. Good rooms are also available down the hill at the *Hermitage Inn* (☎01665/711258; ❸), a cosy place with well-kept beers, bar meals and more interesting a la carte dishes including local cod and salmon. At the *Greenhouse*, opposite on the corner of Dial Place (closed Tues & Sun eves), coffee and cakes, salmon kebabs, cassoulet, and other bistro favourites are served on stripped pine tables. Over the road, the *Mason's Arms* has traditional **pub** food and a beer garden.

Alnmouth

It's just three miles north from Warkworth to the seaside resort of **ALNMOUTH**, whose narrow, mostly nineteenth-century centre is strikingly situated on a steep spur of land between the sea and the estuary of the Aln. It's a lovely setting, and there's a wide sandy beach and rolling dunes. Alnmouth was a busy and prosperous port up until 1806, when the sea, driven by a freakish gale, broke through to the river and changed its course, moving the estuary from the south to the north side of Church Hill and rendering the original harbour useless. Alnmouth never really recovered, though it has been a low-key holiday spot since Victorian times, as attested by the elegant seaside villas at the south end of town. Many come for the golf: the village's splendid nine-hole course, right on the coast, was built in 1869 (it's claimed to be the second oldest in the country) and dune-strollers really do have to heed the "Danger – Flying Golf Balls" signs which adorn Marine Road.

The resort is a convenient interlude on the journey up or down the coast. There are local **bus services** from Alnwick and Warkworth, while the regular Newcastle to Alnwick bus also passes through Alnmouth and calls at its **train station** at Hipsburn, a mile and a half west of the centre.

Most of the **accommodation** lies along or just off the main Northumberland Street. Best central B&B is *The Grange* opposite the church (☎01665/830401, ⓔenquiries@thegrange-alnmouth.com; no credit cards; ❹), a reclusive stone house with walled gardens, overlooking the river. This also has two distinctive **cottages to rent**, the Old Watchtower (originally the harbourmaster's office) and a converted Coach House. A few yards further down Northumberland Street, at no. 56, the friendly *Beaches* (Ⓣ01665/830443, Ⓦwww.beachesbyo.co.uk; no credit cards; ❸) has a variety of highly individual en-suite rooms attached to a good **restaurant** (Tues–Sat dinner only), where meals of local cod, Northumbrian game casserole and the like go for around £15 a head; you can take your own wine. Otherwise, there are a couple of **coffee houses** along the main street, while meals are also served in the bar-lounges and dining rooms of the main street **pubs**.

Alnwick

The unassuming town of **ALNWICK** (pronounced "Annick"), thirty miles north of Newcastle and four miles inland from Alnmouth, is renowned for its castle and gardens – seat of the dukes of Northumberland – which overlook the River Aln immediately to the north of the town centre. You'll need a full day to do these justice while, as the biggest town between Hadrian's Wall and the Scottish border, Alnwick itself warrants an overnight stop in any case. It's an appealing market town of cobbled streets and Georgian houses, centred on the old cross in Market Place, site of weekly markets (Thursdays and Saturdays) since the thirteenth century (and a farmers' market on the last Friday of the month). Other than catching the market in full swing, the best time to visit is during the week-long **Alnwick Fair**, a medieval re-enactment which starts on the last Sunday in June and features a costumed procession, craft fair, concerts and other entertainment.

Arrival, information and accommodation

Drivers should park in the **car park** around the back of the castle and gardens on Greenwell Road, a right turn just before the Bondgate arch as you come in from the A1. Alnwick is a hub for much of the coastal and inland transport, and there are regular bus services to and from Alnmouth, Warkworth and Newcastle, as well as inland to Wooler and up the coast to Craster, Seahouses and Bamburgh. Alnwick **bus station** is on Clayport Street, a couple of minutes' walk west of the Market Place, where you'll find the **tourist office**, in the arcaded Shambles (Easter–Sept Mon–Fri 9am–6pm, Sat 9am–5pm, Sun 10am–4pm; Oct–March Mon–Fri 9am–5pm, Sat 10am–4pm; Ⓣ01665/510665, Ⓦwww.alnwick.gov.uk).

Several **accommodation** options cluster round the gatehouse at the end of Bondgate. Inside the gate, the welcoming *Tower Restaurant & Accommodation*, 10 Bondgate Within (Ⓣ01665/603888, Ⓦwww.tower-alnwick.co.uk; ❺, stands out for its bright, tasteful, en-suite rooms of varying sizes and hearty breakfasts; there's parking around the back. Among other places beyond the gate, you'll easily find *Bondgate House Hotel* at 20 Bondgate Without (Ⓣ01665/602025; ❸). Alnwick's main hotel is the *White Swan*, on Bondgate Within (Ⓣ01665/602109, Ⓦwww.macdonaldhotels.co.uk; ❼), where you might want to pop in at least for coffee – there's a comfortable lounge, while the hotel's fine panelled dining room was swiped from an old ocean liner, the *Olympic*, the twin of the *Titanic*. If you'd prefer to stay in the countryside, consider the *Masons' Arms* at **Rennington** (Ⓣ01665/577275, Ⓦwww.masonsarms.net; ❹), four miles northeast of town on the Seahouses (B1340) road, an old coaching inn with good bar food, as well as six en-suite bedrooms with private sitting rooms. You can **camp** at Alnwick Rugby Club in Greensfield Park (Ⓣ01665/510109; closed Oct–March), a little way south of the centre but walkable.

Alnwick Castle, gardens and Hulne Park

The Percys – who were raised to the dukedom of Northumberland in 1750 – have owned **Alnwick Castle** (Easter–Oct daily 11am–5pm; £7.50; joint ticket with gardens £10; Ⓦ www.alnwickcastle.com) since 1309, when Henry de Percy reinforced the original Norman keep and remodelled its curtain wall. His successor, another Henry, built the imposing barbican and connecting gatehouse. In the eighteenth century, the castle was badly in need of a refit, so the first duke had the interior refurbished by Robert Adam in an extravagant Gothic style – which in turn was supplanted by the gaudy Italianate decoration preferred by the fourth duke in the 1850s. As you enter, look up to the sturdy battlements, which sport a number of stone soldiers – a piece of eighteenth-century flummery replacing the figurines of medieval times, set up there to ward off the evil eye.

There's plenty to see inside, though the **interior** is not to everyone's taste and it can be crowded at times – not least with families on the *Harry Potter* film trail, since the castle doubled as Hogwarts School. The most lavish decoration is in the red drawing room, where the rich polygonal panels of the ceiling bear down on damask-covered walls and some magnificent ebony cabinets rescued from Versailles during the French Revolution. Each room displays part of the duke's extensive collection of paintings, including pieces by Canaletto, Titian, Tintoretto, Van Dyck and Turner. Three of the perimeter towers contain **museum** collections – the Regimental Museum of the Royal Northumberland Fusiliers in the Abbot's Tower, early British and Roman finds in the Postern Tower, and an exhibition dedicated to the Percy Tenantry Volunteers, a private force raised by the second duke during the Napoleonic Wars, in the Constable's Tower – but the bucolic garden walks and Capability Brown-designed **grounds** are a more profitable use of time once you've seen the main rooms.

Signs lead you out of the grounds for the short walk to **Alnwick Garden** (daily 10am–dusk; £4, joint admission with castle £10; Ⓦ www.alnwickgarden.com), which is still to be established fully but already draws crowds to marvel at its sheer scale. At its heart is the computerized Grand Cascade, which shoots water jets in a regular synchronized display, while the rose garden is a particular favourite with many, sporting its own variety, the "Alnwick Castle". Superior ices, teas and snacks are available, while each month brings seasonal garden highlights that volunteers are happy to explain.

From outside the castle, it's a few minutes' walk north along Bailiffgate and then Ratten Row to the gates of **Hulne Park**, a substantial tract of hilly woodland to the northwest of Alnwick. Deep inside the park, a three-mile hike from the entrance, are the rusticated remains of **Hulne Priory**, a thirteenth-century Carmelite monastery built above the north bank of the River Aln. It's a lovely, peaceful spot and, although the greystone ruins are slight, they are enlivened by several whimsically carved stone monks, modern sculptures which have the place pretty much to themselves. The duke owns the park, and access is controlled – pedestrians and cyclists only, from 11am to sunset in summer.

The rest of town

Once you've dealt with the castle and gardens, the main sight in town is the **Bailiffgate Museum**, 14 Bailiffgate (Easter–Oct daily 10am–5pm, Nov–Easter Tues–Sun 10am–4pm; £2.20, Ⓦ www.bailiffgatemuseum.co.uk), housed in the former church of St Mary, just around the corner from the castle's main entrance. This tells the history of the town and its trades in an entertaining fashion, mixing archive film and traditional music with buttons to press, armour to try on and a coal seam to crawl through. The principal remains of the medieval town walls are on view at the **gatehouses** on Pottergate and Bondgate, while you can't miss the grandiose **Percy Tenantry Column** just to the southeast of the centre along Bondgate Without. This 75-foot-high column, surmounted by the Percy lion, was built by the tenants of the second duke in 1816 after he had reduced their rents by 25 percent. As it turned out, their humble gratitude was somewhat premature. The third duke promptly bumped the rents up again and locals wryly renamed their monument the "Farmers' Folly". A little further on, housed in the Victorian train station, **Barter Books** (Ⓦwww.barterbooks.co.uk), one of the largest second-hand bookshops in England, is worth a call.

Eating, drinking and entertainment

There are traditional **cafés** and coffee shops throughout town, but the nicest is the *Grapevine Café*, just up from the tourist office on the corner of Market Place, serving *panini*, salads and drinks until 10pm (Sun until 5pm). For more of a **restaurant** experience, there's *Bibbi's*, 14 Bondgate Within (Ⓣ01665/602607; closed lunch Mon–Wed) – up a side alley next to the *White Swan Hotel* – a Modern British café/restaurant with a tempting menu. The pine-furnished *Tower Restaurant* next door serves everything from breakfast to licensed meals, but closes at 8pm. In the other direction, heading towards the castle, *Benvenuti* on Narrowgate (Ⓣ01665/604465; closed Sun) is a reliable, traditional Italian occupying an atmospheric eighteenth-century town house. Check to see what's on at the **Alnwick Playhouse**, just through the arch on Bondgate Without (Ⓣ01665/510785, Ⓦwww.alnwickplayhouse.co.uk), a venue for theatre, music and film throughout the year, and also host to concerts during the town's annual **International Music Festival** every August and the **Alnwick Northumbrian Gathering** of traditional music in November.

Craster and Dunstanburgh Castle

Heading northeast out of Alnwick along the B1340, it's a six-mile hop to the region's kipper capital, the tiny fishing village of **CRASTER**, perched above its minuscule harbour. There's not a great deal to make you stop long, but you can buy wonderful kippers here at Robson's factory and have a pot of tea in the *Bark Pots*. Even better is the *Jolly Fisherman*, the **pub** above the harbour, with sea views from its back window and garden and famously good crabmeat, whisky and cream soup, crab sandwiches and kipper pate.

Most spectacularly, however, the village provides access to **Dunstanburgh Castle** (April–Sept daily 10am–6pm; Oct daily 10am–5pm; Nov–March Wed–Sun 10am–4pm; £2.20; NT & EH), whose shattered medieval ruins occupy a magnificent promontory about thirty minutes' windy walk up the coast – there's a car park in Craster. Originally built in the fourteenth century, parts of the surrounding walls survive – offering heart-stopping views down to the crashing sea below – though the dominant feature is the massive keep-gatehouse, which stands out from miles around on the bare coastal spur. Mel Gibson's *Hamlet* used the walls and keep to impressive effect.

Half a dozen **buses** a day run to Craster from Alnwick, a half-hour journey; the service continues to Seahouses and Bamburgh. There's a small **tourist office** in the village car park (Easter–Oct daily 9.30–4.30pm; Nov–Easter Sat & Sun 10am–4pm; Ⓣ01665/576007).

Embleton, Newton-by-the-Sea and Beadnell

EMBLETON, on the other side of the promontory from Dunstanburgh Castle, has a fine sandy beach, windswept and deserted in winter, busier in summer though rarely overly so. A couple of pubs here, and in similarly attractive **NEWTON-BY-THE-SEA**, next beachside hamlet north, make good lunch stops. Newton's *The Ship* is the pick of the bunch, on a square of old cottages, just yards from the beach and serving fresh crab and salmon dishes and a range of real ales. **BEADNELL**, too, has a pub and fine beaches, which offer the best windsurfing on the northeast's coast – boards can be rented from the Outdoor Trust shed (£10/hr, £30/day; ⓣ01668/213289; closed Oct–March), along with kayaks, bodyboards and sailing dinghies. The excellent *Beach Court* on Harbour Rd (ⓣ01665/720225, ⓦwww.beachcourt.com) is a distinctive guest house right next to the shore, with sea views and three lovely suites (❹, ❺ & ❼) – the most expensive of which is a "turret" suite with its own observatory. Tourist offices in Alnwick, Craster and Seahouses can arrange other local B&B accommodation, and the #501 bus from Alnwick passes through Embleton, Newton and Beadnell.

Seahouses and the Farne Islands

From Beadnell, it's three miles north to **SEAHOUSES**, a desultory fishing-port-cum-resort that's the embarkation point for boat trips to the windswept and treeless **Farne Islands**, a rocky archipelago lying a few miles offshore. Owned by the National Trust and maintained as a nature reserve, the Farnes are the summer home of many species of migrating seabirds, especially puffins, guillemots, terns, eider ducks and kittiwakes, and home to the only grey seal colony on the English coastline. To protect the wildlife, only two of the islands are open to visitors: **Inner Farne** (April–Sept daily; landing fee £4.50 May–July, £3.50 at other times) and **Staple Island** (same months & prices). The crossing can be rough, but the islands have a wild beauty that makes it all worthwhile, and on Inner Farne you can also visit a tiny, restored fourteenth-century chapel built in honour of St Cuthbert, who spent much of his life and died here.

Weather permitting, several boat owners operate daily **excursions**, usually starting at around 10am: Billy Shiel (ⓣ01665/720308, ⓦwww.farne-islands.com), the best of the bunch, runs a varied programme, from two-and-a-half-hour **cruises** round either island (£10), to all-day trips landing at both (£20). Note that if you land on the islands, you'll have to pay the separate NT landing fee (members free); wear an old hat to protect you from the bird droppings. For more information, contact the **National Trust Shop**, 16 Main St, Seahouses (ⓣ01665/721099), across from the *Olde Ship* (see below).

Practicalities

It's unlikely you'd choose to stay the night in Seahouses, and there are regular **buses** to both Alnwick and Berwick-upon-Tweed, but, if you've returned from the Farnes late in the day, you may not want to go any further. Seahouses has a range of reasonably priced **B&Bs** – details from the **tourist office** (daily: April–Oct 10am–5pm; ⓣ01665/720884, ⓦwww.seahouses.org), in the Seafield Road car park above the harbour.

The *Olde Ship*, overlooking the harbour at 9 Main St (ⓣ01665/720200, ⓦwww.seahouses.co.uk; ❺), quite apart from its pleasant rooms, is a great place to drink, full of nautical bits and pieces and serving good **food**. There's also a whole host of fish-and-chip restaurants. If you want to take some of the local catch home, the *Fisherman's Kitchen,* 2 South St, sells smoked kippers and salmon from its traditional **smokehouse**.

Bamburgh

Flanking a triangular green in the lee of its castle, three miles north of Seahouses, the tiny village of **BAMBURGH** is only a five-minute walk from two splendid sandy beaches, backed by rolling, tufted dunes. From the sands – in fact from everywhere – **Bamburgh Castle** (April–Oct daily 11am–5pm; £5; Ⓦwww.bamburghcastle.com) is a spectacular sight, its elongated battlements crowning a formidable basalt crag high above the beach. This beautiful spot was first fortified by the Celts, but its heyday was as an Anglo-Saxon stronghold, one-time capital of Northumbria and the protector of the preserved head and hand of St Oswald, the seventh-century king who invited St Aidan over from Iona to convert his subjects. To the Normans, however, Bamburgh was just one of many border fortresses administered by second-rank vassals: as an eleventh-century monastic chronicler expressed it, "renowned formerly for the magnificent splendour of her high estate, [Bamburgh] has been burdened with tribute and reduced to the condition of a handmaiden."

Nonetheless, rotted by seaspray and buffeted by winter storms, Bamburgh Castle struggled on until 1894, when it was bought by Lord Armstrong, who demolished most of the structure to replace it with a cumbersome hybrid castle-mansion. The focal point of the new building was the King's Hall, a teak-ceilinged affair of colossal dimensions, whose main redeeming feature is an exquisite collection of Fabergé stone animal carvings. In the ground floor of the keep, the stone-vaulted ceiling maintains its Norman appearance, making a suitable arena for a display of fetters and man-traps. There's some interest, too, in a display in the former laundry building, where exhibits trace Armstrong's career as inventor, shipbuilder and arms manufacturer, a neat counterpoint to the displays at Cragside.

Bamburgh is also the home of the **Grace Darling Museum** (Easter–Oct Mon–Sat 10am–5pm, Sun noon–5pm; donation requested), which celebrates the daring sea rescue accomplished by Grace and her lighthouseman father, William, in September, 1838. It began when a gale dashed the steamship *Forfarshire* against the rocks of the Farne Islands. Nine passengers struggled onto a reef, where they were subsequently saved by the Darlings, who left the safety of the lighthouse to row out to them. *The Times* trumpeted Grace's bravery, offers of marriage and requests for locks of her hair streamed into the Darlings' lighthouse home and for the rest of her brief life Grace was plagued by unwanted visitors – she died of tuberculosis aged 26 in 1842. The museum details the rescue and displays the fragile boat the Darlings used; in the churchyard of thirteenth-century **St Aidan's** opposite is the pompous Gothic Revival memorial that covers Grace's body.

Practicalities

A regular **bus** service links Alnwick and Berwick-upon-Tweed with Bamburgh, stopping on Front Street by the green. There's a public **car park** on the road below the castle and another at the castle itself for visitors. It's relatively easy to find **accommodation**, though booking ahead in summer is wise. At the top of the village green, the *Victoria Hotel* (Ⓣ01668/214431, Ⓦwww.victoriahotel.net; ⑥) has been tastefully refurbished, and operates a brasserie with a Modern-British menu, a pleasant conservatory and a few outdoor tables where you can get a cappuccino. *The Greenhouse*, a few doors down at 5 Front St (Ⓣ01668/214513, Ⓦwww.thegreenhouseguesthouse.co.uk; ❸) has en-suite rooms and serves daytime meals (not Tues), or further down the green there's the *Lord Crewe Arms Hotel*, Front St (Ⓣ01668/214243; ❻, winter ❺; closed Jan, weekends only Dec & Feb), a comfortable old inn with oak beams, open fires, public bar and restaurant. Other moderate B&Bs are found on Lucker Road, beyond the top of the village green. **Eating and drinking** is best done at the places mentioned above – the *Victoria* is classiest – though there are also a couple of tearooms, a small deli, a butcher's selling homemade pies, and a bucket-and-spade general store.

Romantic big-spenders should head out of town to **Waren Mill**, a couple of miles to the west on the B1342, where the *Waren House Hotel* (Ⓣ01668/214581, Ⓦwww.warenhousehotel.co.uk; ❼) is set in its own grounds on the edge of Budle Bay, overlooking Holy Island. Eating well here is no trouble whatsoever. At the other end of the scale, *Waren Caravan Park* (Ⓣ01668/214366; closed Nov–March) has the closest **camping** to Bamburgh; take the local #501 bus to Waren Mill.

Holy Island

There's something rather menacing about the approach to **Holy Island**, past the barnacle-encrusted marker poles that line the causeway. The danger of drowning is real enough if you ignore the safe crossing times posted at the start of the three-mile trip across the tidal flats. (The island is cut off for about five hours every day, so to avoid a tedious delay it's best to consult the **tide timetables** at one of the region's tourist offices or in the local newspapers.) Once on the island, the ancient remains of the priory and the brooding castle conjure yet more fantasies, not all pleasant. Small (just one and a half miles by one), sandy, flat and bare, it's easy to picture the furious Viking hordes sweeping across Holy Island, giving no quarter to the monks at this quiet outpost of early Christianity. Today's sole village is plain in the extreme, which doesn't deter summer day-trippers from clogging the car parks as soon as the causeway is open. But Holy Island has a distinctive and isolated atmosphere, especially out of season. Give the place time and, if you can, stay overnight, when you'll be able to see the historic remains without hundreds of others cluttering the views.

Once known as **Lindisfarne**, Holy Island has an illustrious history. It was here that St Aidan of Iona founded a monastery at the invitation of King Oswald of Northumbria in 634. The monks quickly evangelized the northeast and established a reputation for scholarship and artistry, the latter exemplified by the **Lindisfarne Gospels**, the apotheosis of Celtic religious art, now kept in the British Library. The monastery had sixteen bishops in all, the most celebrated being **St Cuthbert**, who only accepted the job after Ecgfrith, another Northumbrian king, pleaded with him. But Cuthbert never settled here and, within two years, he was back in his hermit's cell on the Farne Islands, where he died in 687. His colleagues rowed the body back to Lindisfarne, which became a place of pilgrimage until 875, when the monks abandoned the island in fear of marauding Vikings, taking Cuthbert's remains with them. In 1082 Lindisfarne, renamed Holy Island, was colonized by Benedictines from Durham, but the monastery was a shadow of its former self, a minor religious house with only a handful of attendant monks, the last of whom was evicted at the Dissolution.

The island

There's not much to the **village**, just a couple of streets radiating out from a small green and church cross, everything within a five-minute walk of everything else. If you've arrived by car, you'll have to **park** in one of the large signposted carparks – keep an eye on the time and tide if you're not intending to stay.

Just off the green, the pinkish sandstone ruins of **Lindisfarne Priory** (daily: Easter–Sept 10am–6pm; Oct 10am–5pm; Nov–Easter 10am–4pm; £3; EH) are from the Benedictine foundation. Enough survives to provide a clear impression of the original structure, notably the tight Romanesque arches of the nave and the gravity-defying stonework of the central tower's last remaining arch. Behind lie the scant remains of the monastic buildings while adjacent is the mostly thirteenth-century **Church of St Mary the Virgin**, whose delightful churchyard overlooks the ruins. The **museum** (same times as priory; entrance included in priory fee) features a collection of incised stones that constitute all that remains of the first monastery. The finest of them is a round-headed tombstone showing armed Northumbrians on one side, and kneeling figures before the Cross on the other – presumably a propagandist's view of the beneficial effects of Christianity. The priory, incidentally, marks the end of **St Cuthbert's Way**, the 63-mile cross-border hiking route from Melrose in Scotland, where St Cuthbert started his ministry.

The **Lindisfarne Heritage Centre** (daily 10am–5.30pm, though times may vary according to the tides; £2.50; Ⓦwww.lindisfarne-heritage-centre.org), occupying a former coaching inn on the main street, holds computer terminals giving you a virtual opportunity to see the major illustrated pages of the Lindisfarne Gospels and details the wildlife as well as the former living and working conditions on the island. Everyone then decants into **St Aidan's Winery**, just up from the green, sole producer of Lindisfarne Mead, a sickly concoction on sale all over the northeast. You can sample the mead before you buy, which – given its rather challenging taste – seems a misguided marketing ploy.

Stuck on a small pyramid of rock half a mile away from the village, past the dock and along the seashore, **Lindisfarne Castle** (Easter–Oct Mon–Thurs, Sat & Sun, hours vary according to tide but always include noon–3pm; £4.20; NT) was built in the middle of the sixteenth century to protect the island's harbour from the Scots. It was, however, merely a decaying shell when Edward Hudson, the founder of *Country Life* magazine, stumbled across it in 1901. Hudson bought the castle and turned it into a holiday home to designs by Edwin Lutyens, who used the irregular levels of the building to create the L-shaped living quarters that survive today. Lutyens kept the austere spirit of the castle alive in the great fireplaces, stone walls, columns and rounded arches that dominate the main rooms.

The historic sites are all that most people bother with, but a **walk** around the island's perimeter is a fine way to spend a couple of hours. From the grass banks above the harbour, there are views across to the two nineteenth-century obelisks, built on the distant sandbanks as navigational aids – boats line them up with the church tower to steer their way in. Most of the northwestern portion of the island is maintained as a **nature reserve**: from a bird hide you can spot terns and plovers, and then plod through the dunes and grasses to your heart's content. The island even supports a seal colony, though sightings by visitors are rare – legend rather touchingly has it that the seals kept vigil with St Cuthbert as he prayed at the water's edge of his new domain.

Practicalities

The #477 **bus** from Berwick-upon-Tweed to Holy Island is something of a law unto itself given the interfering tides, but basically service is daily in August and twice weekly (Wed & Sat) the rest of the year. Departure times (and sometimes days) vary with the tides, and the journey takes thirty minutes; local tourist offices can provide the latest details. Throughout the year, you can also ask to be dropped off by the Berwick–Newcastle buses at Beal, though from here you face a four-mile walk to the island. Phone the island's **taxi service** if you can't face the hike (ⓣ01289/389236).

The island is short on **accommodation** and you should make an advance booking, whenever you visit. Two good places are the *Open Gate*, on Marygate (ⓣ01289/389222; ❸), which offers comfortable rooms in a sixteenth-century listed building; or the cheaper, and very friendly, *Castlereigh* (ⓣ01289/389218; ❷; closed Nov–Feb), just by the green. Among the **pubs**, best is the *Ship* on Marygate (ⓣ01289/389311; ❷; closed Jan). **Camping** isn't allowed anywhere on the island. Options for **eating and drinking** are limited to a couple of tea rooms and the hostelries, of which the *Ship* is the pick, with a garden and a cosy panelled bar, good-value meals and well-kept real ales.

Berwick-upon-Tweed

Before the union of the English and Scottish crowns in 1603, **BERWICK-UPON-TWEED**, twelve miles north of Holy Island, was the quintessential frontier town, changing hands no fewer than fourteen times between 1174 and 1482, when the Scots finally ceded the stronghold to the English. Interminable cross-border warfare ruined Berwick's economy, turning the prosperous Scottish port of the thirteenth century into an impoverished garrison town, which the English forcibly cut off from its natural trading hinterland up the River Tweed. By the late sixteenth century, Berwick's fortifications were in a dreadful state of repair and Elizabeth I, apprehensive of the resurgent alliance between France and Scotland, had the place rebuilt in line with the latest principles of military architecture. The new design recognized the technological development of artillery, which had rendered the traditional high stone wall obsolete. Consequently, Berwick's ramparts – one and a half miles long and still in pristine condition – are no more than twenty feet high but incredibly thick: a facing of ashlared stone protects ten to twelve feet of rubble, which, in turn, backs up against a vast quantity of earth.

The ramparts are now the town's major attraction, and you'll want to stop at least long enough to take a walk around the walls. A set of interesting local museums, and the town's attractive riverside location, warrant a night's stay, especially as Berwick is a useful staging post between England and Scotland. It's not a large place – with a modern population of around 12,000 – but there's a fair choice of accommodation and services.

Arrival, information and tours

From Berwick **train station** it's about ten minutes' walk down Castlegate and Marygate to the town centre. Most regional **buses** stop closer in on Golden Square (where Castlegate meets Marygate), on the approach to the Royal Tweed Bridge, though some may also stop in front of the station. Drivers should use the main **car parks**, just outside the walls off Castlegate, and down below the quay walls at the bottom of Sandgate.

The helpful **tourist office** at 106 Marygate (Easter–Oct Mon–Sat 10am–5pm, Sun 11am–3pm; Nov–Easter Mon–Sat 10am–4pm; ⓣ01289/330733, ⓦwww.berwickonline.org.uk, ⓦwww.exploreberwick.co.uk) can book you on to informative one-hour **walking tours** of town (Easter–Oct Mon–Fri, 4 daily; £3). For local **bike rental**, contact Tweed Cycles, 17a Bridge St (☎01289/331476) – you can get details of a scenic route to Holy Island (24 miles return) either here or from the tourist office. There's free **Internet** access in the library, behind the tourist office on the corner of Walkergate and Chapel Street.

Accommodation

Berwick has plenty of **accommodation** and the tourist office offers a room-booking service – local hotels and B&Bs post pictures and adverts inside the office. If our choices are full, you'll find others ranged along Church Street and Ravensdowne (off Woolmarket, the continuation of Marygate); or head north up Castlegate, past the station, to North Road. Other concentrations are found in **Tweedmouth**, just on the other side of the bridge (10min walk), or near the beach at **Spittal** (bus from Golden Square). There are plenty of local **campsites**, though only *Marshalls Meadows Farm*, off the A1, two miles north (☎01289/307375; closed Nov–Feb) has space for tents.

Berwick Backpackers 56–58 Bridge St ☎01289/331481. Town house backpackers with a six-bed dorm (£10), one single (£12) and three cheap twins/doubles (❶), all with en-suite facilities. Also a kitchen, Internet access, cycle storage and bike rental for guests. No credit cards.

Clovelly House 58 West St ☎01289/302337, ⓦwww.clovelly53.freeserve.co.uk. Traditional guest house, centrally located on a steep cobbled street. No credit cards. ❷

Dervaig Guest House 1 North Rd ☎01289/307378, ⓦwww.dervaig-guesthouse.co.uk. Spacious, well-appointed rooms, a large walled garden and parking, 5min walk from the centre. ❸

King's Arms Hide Hill ☎01289/307454, ⓦwww.kings-arms-hotel.com. The best central hotel, one of the myriad English coaching inns in which Charles Dickens is supposed to have slept and lectured. Bedrooms are being upgraded and downstairs there's a contemporary café, Italian restaurant and summer dining in the walled garden. ❻

No.1 Sallyport Bridge St ☎01289/308827, ⓦwww.1sallyport-bedandbreakfast.com. Berwick's most luxurious B&B, with three sensational rooms in a seventeenth-century house next to the city walls (by the Bridge Street Bookshop). Master bedroom, suite (sleeps four) or "Manhattan loft" (with widescreen TV and DVD) are all elegantly furnished and breakfast is terrific; rustic French suppers (BYO wine) available on request. Reservations essential. ❺

Old Vicarage Guest House 24 Church Rd, Tweedmouth ☎01289/306909, ⓦwww.oldvicarageberwick.co.uk. The finest choice in Tweedmouth, a delightful Victorian villa with a range of rooms, some sharing bathrooms; book ahead as it's popular. No credit cards. ❷

Whyteside House 46 Castlegate ☎01289/331019. Victorian splendour at the top end of Castlegate – the house retains many original features, including the oak panelling, rooms are spacious and nicely furnished, and there's private parking. No credit cards. ❸

The Town

Berwick's **walls** – protected by ditches on three sides and the Tweed on the fourth – are strengthened by immense bastions, whose arrowhead-shape ensured that every part of the wall could be covered by fire. Begun in 1558, the defences were completed after eleven years at a cost of £128,000, more than Elizabeth paid for all her other fortifications put together. And, as it turned out, it was all a waste of time and money: the French didn't attack and, once England and Scotland were united, Berwick was stuck with a white elephant. Today, the easy mile circuit along the top of the walls and ramparts (say an hour) offers a succession of fine views out to sea, across the Tweed and over the orange-tiled rooftops of a town that's distinguished by its elegant **Georgian mansions**. These, dating from Berwick's resurgence as a seaport between 1750 and 1820, are the town's most attractive feature, with the tapering **Lions' House**, on Windmill Hill, and the daintily decorated facades of **Quay Walls**, beside the river, of particular note. The three bridges spanning the Tweed are worth a second look, too – the huge arches of the **Royal Border Railway Bridge**, built in the manner of a Roman aqueduct by Robert Stephenson in the 1840s, contrasting with the desultory concrete of the **Royal Tweed**, completed in 1928, and the modest seventeenth-century **Berwick Bridge**. This last was opened in 1624 and cost £15,000 to build, an enormous sum partly financed by James VI of Scotland, who is said to have been none too impressed with its rickety wooden predecessor which he crossed on his way to be crowned James I of England in 1603.

Within the ramparts, the Berwick skyline is punctured by the stumpy spire of the eighteenth-century **Town Hall** (Easter–Oct Mon–Fri tours at 10.30am & 2pm; £1.50) at the bottom of Marygate, right at the heart of the compact centre. This retains its original jailhouse on the upper floor, now housing the **Cell Block Museum**, entertaining tours of which dwell on tales of crime and punishment in Berwick. Unruly visitors can spend a reflective minute or two locked in the condemned cell. From here, it's a couple of minutes' walk along Church Street to **Holy Trinity Church**, one of the few churches built during the Commonwealth, the absence of a tower supposedly reflecting the wishes of Cromwell, who found them irreligious.

Opposite the church, the finely proportioned **Barracks** (Easter–Sept daily 10am–6pm; Oct daily 10am–4pm; Nov–Easter Wed–Sun 10am–4pm; £3; EH) date from the early eighteenth century and were in use until 1964, when the King's Own Scottish Borderers regiment decamped. Inside, there's a regimental museum, as well as the *By Beat of Drum* exhibition, which in a series of picture boards and dioramas traces the life of the British infantryman from the sixteenth to the nineteenth century. These are of rather specialist interest, though most will warm to the temporary exhibitions of contemporary art in the **Gymnasium Gallery** and the superior borough museum and art gallery, sited in the **Clock Block**. Geared up for school parties, the museum features imaginative dioramas, recordings and displays of local traditional life, even a model of a local clergyman haranguing visitors from his pulpit. Upstairs is the kernel of the gallery's fine and applied art collection, the gift of the shipping magnate William Burrell, who lived near Berwick in his retirement. Highlights include examples of ceramic Oriental jars displayed under glass floor panels in a sinuous, walk-in dragon, plus Roman glassware, church sculpture, and several Chinese bronzes.

Eating, drinking and entertainment

Berwick has plenty of daytime **cafés and tearooms**, including one on the ground floor of the historic Town Hall, though fine **restaurant** dining is a bit limited. In 1799 there were 59 **pubs** and three coaching inns in town – today only one really stands out from the crowd, though between that and the local **arts centre** you should be able to spend quite a happy evening.

Cafés and restaurants

Café 52 50–52 Bridge St ☎01289/306796. Fresh and funky café-bistro with coffee and ciabatta sandwiches during the day, and a Mediterranean menu (grilled goat's cheese, seared tuna, etc) served until 10pm. Closed Sun eve and all Mon. Moderate.

Foxton's 26 Hide Hill ☎01289/303939. Bar-brasserie serving an inexpensive daytime menu of sandwiches, light meals and traditional main courses, and a more varied menu in the evening. Closed Sun. Moderate.

Queen's Head 6 Sandgate ☎01289/307852. Old Berwick inn that's gone for the gastro-pub look and menu – Craster crab with sweet chilli, rack of Northumbrian lamb, or ostrich fillet are typical dishes. Expensive.

Royal Garden 35 Marygate ☎01289/331411. Chinese restaurant whose menu raises it above the ordinary – tofu, *char siu*, oyster dishes included. Flavours have been anglicized, but it's an enjoyable night out. Moderate.

Drinking and entertainment

Barrels Ale House 59–61 Bridge St ☎01289/308013, ⓦwww.thebarrelsalehouse.com. Chilled-out independent pub at the foot of the Berwick Bridge, with guest beers, tapas lunches (Wed–Sun) and an interesting programme of live music and DJs in the basement.

The Maltings Eastern Lane ☎01289/330999, ⓦwww.maltingsberwick.co.uk. Berwick's arts centre with a year-round programme of music, theatre, comedy, film and dance, and river views from its licensed café.

Travel details

Buses

For more information on all local and national bus services, contact Traveline ☎0870/608 2608, ⓦwww.traveline.org.uk.

Alnwick to: Bamburgh (4–6 daily; 1hr 5min); Berwick-upon-Tweed (3 daily; 2hr).

Bamburgh to: Alnwick (4–6 daily; 1hr 5min); Craster (4–5 daily; 30–40min); Seahouses (Mon–Sat 9 daily, Sun 4; 10min).

Barnard Castle to: Bishop Auckland (Mon–Sat 9 daily, Sun 6; 50min); Darlington (hourly; 35min); Middleton-in-Teesdale (hourly; 35min); Raby Castle (9 daily; 15min).

Berwick-upon-Tweed to: Holy Island (Aug 2 daily, rest of the year 2 weekly; 30min); Newcastle (Mon–Sat 6 daily, Sun 3; 2hr 30min); Wooler (Mon–Sat 4–7 daily; 50min).

Bishop Auckland to: Barnard Castle (Mon–Sat 9 daily, Sun 6; 50min); Cowshill (Mon–Sat 7 daily, Sun 4; 1hr 10min); Darlington (Mon–Sat hourly; 35min); Newcastle (hourly; 1hr 15min); Stanhope (Mon–Sat 7 daily, Sun 4; 45min); Sunderland (Mon–Sat 4 daily; 2hr).

Darlington to: Barnard Castle (hourly; 35min); Bishop Auckland (Mon–Sat hourly; 35min); Carlisle (1 daily; 3hr); Durham (every 30min; 1hr); Middleton-in-Teesdale (Mon–Sat 9 daily, Sun 3; 1hr 20min); Newcastle (every 30min; 2hr).

Durham to: Barnard Castle (1 daily; 1hr); Beamish (May–Sept 1–3 daily; 25min); Bishop Auckland (every 30min; 30min); Darlington (every 30min; 1hr); Newcastle (hourly; 1hr); Stanhope (June–Sept 1–2 weekly; 45min); Sunderland (every 15–30min; 50min).

Haltwhistle to: Alston (Mon–Sat 4–5 daily; 45min); Hexham (hourly; 45min).

Hexham to: Allendale (Mon–Sat 4–6 daily; 25min); Allenheads Mon–Sat 4–6 daily; 45min); Bellingham (Mon–Sat 5 daily; 40min); Haltwhistle (hourly; 40min).

Middlesbrough to: Newcastle (hourly; 1hr); Saltburn (hourly; 40min).

Newcastle to: Alnmouth (hourly; 1hr 30min); Alnwick (Mon–Sat 6 daily, Sun 3; 1hr 15min); Bamburgh (3 daily; 2hr 30min); Barnard Castle (1 daily; 1hr 25min); Berwick-upon-Tweed (Mon–Sat 6 daily, Sun 3; 3hr); Carlisle (hourly; 2hr); Craster (3 daily; 1hr 50min); Darlington (every 30min; 2hr); Durham (hourly; 1hr); Hexham (every 30min; 1hr 15min); Leeds (10 daily; 3hr); Middlesbrough (hourly; 1hr); Otterburn (2 daily; 2hr); Rothbury (Mon–Sat 7 daily, Sun 2; 1hr 15min); Seahouses (3 daily; 2hr 10min); Warkworth (hourly; 1hr 20min); Wooler (Mon–Fri 1–2 daily, Sat 4 (2hr 15min).

Wooler to: Alnwick (Mon–Sat 4 daily; 45min); Berwick-upon-Tweed (Mon–Sat 4–7 daily; 50min).

Trains

For information on all local and national rail services, contact National Rail Enquiries ☎08457/484950, ⓦwww.rail.co.uk.

Darlington to: Bishop Auckland (every 1–2hr; 30min); Durham (every 30min; 20min); Newcastle (every 30min; 35min).

Durham to: Darlington (every 30min; 20min); London (hourly; 3hr); Newcastle (every 30min; 15min); York (hourly; 50min).

Hexham to: Carlisle (hourly; 1hr); Haltwhistle (hourly; 20min); Newcastle (hourly; 40min).

Middlesbrough to: Durham (hourly; 50min); Grosmont, for North York Moors Railway (see p.1014: Mon–Sat 4 daily; 1hr); Newcastle (hourly; 1hr 10min); Saltburn (hourly; 40min); Whitby (Mon–Sat 4 daily; 1hr 30min).

Newcastle to: Alnmouth (Mon–Sat 9–10 daily, Sun 3 daily; 30min); Berwick-upon-Tweed (hourly; 45min); Carlisle (hourly; 1hr 30min); Corbridge (hourly; 40min); Darlington (every 30min; 35min); Durham (every 30min; 15min); Edinburgh (hourly; 1hr 30min); Haltwhistle (hourly; 1hr); Hexham (hourly; 40min); London (hourly; 2hr 45min–3hr 30min); York (hourly; 1hr).

Contexts

Contexts

History

England's history is long and fascinating, and events within this small nation have had an influence far outweighing the country's modest size. What follows is therefore a necessarily brief introduction to a complex subject. For more detailed coverage see *The Rough Guide History of England* and "Books", p.1152.

Stone and Bronze Age England

England has been inhabited for the best part of half a million years, though the earliest archeological evidence of human life dates from about **250,000 BC**. These meagre remains, found near Swanscombe, east of London across the Thames from Tilbury, belong to one of the migrant communities whose comings and goings were dictated by the fluctuations of the several Ice Ages. Renewed glaciation then created a longer break and the next traces – mainly roughly worked flint implements – were left around **40,000 BC** by cave-dwellers at Creswell Crags in Derbyshire, Kent's Cavern near Torquay and Cheddar Cave in Somerset. The last spell of intense cold began about 17,000 years ago, and it was the final thawing of this **last Ice Age** around 5000 BC that caused the British Isles to separate from the European mainland.

The sea barrier did nothing to stop further migrations of nomadic hunters, drawn by the rich forests that covered ancient Britain. In about 3500 BC a new wave of colonists arrived from the continent, probably via Ireland, bringing with them a **Neolithic culture** based on farming and the rearing of livestock. These tribes were the first to make some impact on the environment, clearing forests, enclosing fields, constructing defensive ditches around their villages and digging mines to obtain flint used for tools and weapons. Fragments of Neolithic pottery have been found near Peterborough and at Windmill Hill, near Avebury in Wiltshire, but the most profuse relics of this culture are their graves, usually stone-chambered, turf-covered mounds (called **long barrows**). These are scattered throughout the country – the most impressive ones are at Belas Knap and Rodmarton in Gloucestershire and at Wayland's Smithy in Berkshire.

The transition from the Neolithic to the **Bronze Age** began around 2000 BC, with the immigration from northern Europe of the so-called **Beaker People** – named from the distinctive cups found at their burial sites. Originating in the Iberian peninsula and bringing with them bronze-workers from the Rhineland, these newcomers had a comparatively well-organized social structure with an established aristocracy and they quickly intermixed with the native tribes. Many of England's stone circles were completed at this time, including **Avebury** and **Stonehenge** in Wiltshire, while many others belong entirely to the Bronze Age – for example, the Hurlers and the Nine Maidens on Cornwall's Bodmin Moor. Large numbers of earthwork forts were also built in this period, suggesting endemic tribal warfare, but none were able to withstand the Celtic invaders who, spreading from a homeland in central Europe, began sweeping over England around 600 BC.

The Celts and the Romans

Highly skilled in battle, the **Celts** soon displaced the local inhabitants all over England, establishing a sophisticated farming economy and a social hierarchy that was dominated by a druidic priesthood. Familiar with Mediterranean artefacts through their far-flung trade routes, they introduced superior methods of metal-working that favoured iron rather than bronze, from which they forged not just weapons but also coins and ornamental works, thus creating the first recognizable English art. The principal Celtic contribution to the landscape was a network of hillforts and other defensive works stretching over the entire country, the greatest of them at **Maiden Castle** in Dorset, a site first fortified almost 2500 years earlier.

Maiden Castle was also one of the first Celtic fortifications to fall to the **Roman** legions in 43 AD. Coming at the end of a long period of commercial probing, the Roman invasion had begun hesitantly, with small cross-Channel incursions led by **Julius Caesar** in 55 and 54 BC. Britain's rumoured mineral wealth was a primary motive, but the immediate spur to the eventual conquest that came nearly a century later was anti-Roman collaboration between the British Celts and their fiercely independent cousins in France. The sub-text was that the **Emperor Claudius**, who led the invasion, owed his power to the army and needed a military triumph. The death of the king of southeast England, Cunobelin – Shakespeare's Cymbeline – presented Claudius with a golden opportunity and in **August 43 AD** a substantial Roman force landed in Kent, from where it fanned out, soon establishing a base along the estuary of the Thames. Joined by a menagerie of elephants and camels for the major battle of the campaign, the Romans soon reached Camulodunum (Colchester) – the most important city – and within four years were dug in on the frontier of south Wales.

Some determined resistance did occur, notably from the Catuvellauni chief, **Caractacus**, who conducted a guerrilla campaign from Wales until he was captured in about 50 AD. This was, however, nothing compared with the revolt of the East Anglian Iceni, under their queen **Boudicca** (or Boadicea) in 60 AD. The Iceni sacked Camulodunum and Verulamium (St Albans), and even reached the undefended new port of Londinium (London), but the Romans rallied and exacted a terrible revenge. In the event, the rebellion turned to be an isolated act of resistance, and it would seem that most of the southern tribes were content – or at least resigned – to their absorption into the empire. In the next decades, the Romans extended their control, subduing Wales and the north of England by 80 AD. They did not, however, manage to conquer Scotland and eventually gave up – as signified by the construction of **Hadrian's Wall** in 130 AD. Running from the Tyne to the Solway, the wall marked the northern limit of the Roman Empire, and stands today as the most impressive remnant of the Roman occupation.

The written history of England begins with the Romans, whose rule lasted nearly four centuries. For the first time, the country emerged as a clearly identifiable entity with a defined political structure. Peace also brought prosperity. Commerce flourished and cities prospered, including the most northerly Roman town of Eboracum (York), the garrison of Isca Dumnoniorum (Exeter), the leisure resort of Aquae Sulis (Bath), and of course **Londinium**, which immediately assumed a pivotal role in the commercial and administrative life of the colony. Although Latin became the language of the Romano-British ruling elite, local traditions were allowed to coexist with imported customs, so that Celtic gods were often worshipped at the same time as Roman ones, and sometimes merged with them. Perhaps the most important legacy of the Roman occupation, however, was the introduction of **Christianity** from the third century on, becoming firmly entrenched after its official recognition by the Emperor Constantine in 313.

Anglo-Saxon England and the Danes

As early as the reign of Constantine, Roman England was being **raided** by Germanic Saxon pirates, and by the middle of the fourth century – with the Romans on the run – Picts from Scotland and Scots from northern Ireland were harrying inland areas in the north and west. As economic life declined and rural areas became depopulated, individual military leaders began to usurp local authority. Indeed, by the start of the fifth century England had become irrevocably detached from what remained of the Roman Empire and within fifty years the **Saxons** had begun settling England themselves. This marked the start of a gradual conquest that culminated in the defeat of the native Britons in 577 at the **Battle of Dyrham** (near Bath) and, despite the despairing efforts of such semi-mythical figures as King Arthur, the last independent Britons were driven deep into Cumbria, Wales and the southwest. The Saxons all but eliminated Romano-British culture and by the end of the sixth century the rest of England was divided into the Anglo-Saxon kingdoms of Northumbria, Mercia, East Anglia, Kent and Wessex. So complete was the Anglo-Saxon domination of England, through conquest and intermarriage, that some ninety percent of English place names today have an Anglo-Saxon derivation. Only in the westerly extremities of the country did the ancient Celtic traditions survive, as untouched by the new invaders as they had been by the Romans. Here also, Christian worship was kept alive, though the countrywide revival of Christianity was driven mainly by the arrival of **St Augustine**, who was despatched by Pope Gregory I and landed on the Kent coast in 597, accompanied by forty monks.

The missionaries were received by Ethelbert, the overlord of all the English south of the River Humber, whose marriage to a Christian princess from France made him sympathetic to Augustine's message. **Ethelbert** gave Augustine permission to found a monastery at Canterbury (on the site of the present cathedral), where the king himself was then baptized, followed by ten thousand of his subjects at a grand Christmas ceremony. Despite some reversals in the years that followed, the Christianization of England proceeded quickly, so that by the middle of the seventh century all of the Anglo-Saxon kings had at least nominally adopted the faith. Tensions and clashes between the Augustinian missionaries and the Celtic monks inevitably arose, to be resolved by the **Synod of Whitby** in 663, when it was agreed that the English Church should follow the rule of Rome, thereby ensuring a realignment with the European cultural mainstream.

The central English region of **Mercia** became the dominant Anglo-Saxon kingdom in the eighth century under kings Ethelbald and Offa. The latter was responsible for the greatest public work of the Anglo-Saxon period, **Offa's Dyke**, an earthwork marking the border with Wales from the River Dee to the River Severn. Yet, after Offa's death, **Wessex** gained the upper hand, and by 825 the Wessex kings had conquered or taken allegiance from all the other English kingdoms. Their triumph was, however, short-lived. Carried here by their remarkable long boats, the **Vikings** – in this case mostly **Danes** – had started to raid the east coast towards the end of the eighth century, one notable casualty being the great monastery of Lindisfarne, which was razed in 793. Emboldened by their success, these raids grew in size and then – prompted by land shortages in Scandinavia – turned into a migration. In 865, a substantial Danish army landed in East Anglia, and within six years they had conquered Northumbria, Mercia and East Anglia. The Danes then set their sights on Wessex, whose new king was the formidable and exceptionally talented **Alfred the Great**. Despite the odds, Alfred successfully resisted the Danes and eventually the two warring parties signed a truce, which fixed an uneasy border between Wessex and Danish territory – the **Danelaw** – to the north. Ensconced in northern England and what is today the East Midlands, the Danes soon succumbed to Christianity and internal warfare, while Alfred modernized his kingdom and strengthened its defences.

Alfred died in 899, but his successor, **Edward the Elder**, capitalized on his efforts, establishing Saxon supremacy over the Danelaw to become the de facto overlord of all England. The relative calm continued under Edward's son, **Athelstan**, who extended his overlordship over much of Scotland and Wales, and his son, **Edgar**, who became the first ruler to be crowned **king of England** in 973. However, this was but a lull in the Viking storm. Returning in force, the Vikings milked Edgar's son **Ethelred the Unready** ("lacking counsel") for all the money they could, but the ransom (the Danegeld) paid brought only temporary relief and, in 1016, Ethelred hot-footed it to Normandy, leaving the Danes in command.

The first Danish king of England was **Canute**, a shrewd and gifted ruler, but his two disreputable sons quickly dismantled his carefully constructed Anglo-Scandinavian empire. Thereafter, the Saxons regained the initiative, restoring Ethelred's son, **Edward the Confessor**, to the throne in 1042. It was a poor choice. Edward was more suited to be a priest than a king and he allowed power to drift into the hands of his most powerful subject, Godwin, Earl of Wessex, and his son Harold. On Edward's death, the Witan – a sort of council of elders – confirmed **Harold** as king, ignoring several rival claims including that of William, Duke of Normandy. William's claim was a curious affair, but he always insisted – however improbable it may seem – that the childless Edward the Confessor had promised him his crown. Unluckily for Harold, his two main rivals struck at the same time. First up was his alienated brother **Tostig** and his ally King Harald of Norway, a giant of a man reliably reckoned to be seven feet tall. They landed with a Viking army in Yorkshire and Harold hurriedly marched north to meet them. Harold won a crushing victory at the battle of Stamford Bridge, but then he heard that William of Normandy had invaded the south. Rashly, Harold did not take time to muster more men, but dashed south, where William famously routed the Saxons – and killed Harold – at the **Battle of Hastings** in 1066. On Christmas Day, William the Conqueror was installed as king in Westminster Abbey.

The Normans and the Plantagenets

Making little attempt to reach any understanding with his new subjects, **William I** imposed a Norman aristocracy, reinforcing his rule with a series of strongholds, the grandest of which was the Tower of London. Initially, there was some resistance, but William crushed these sporadic rebellions with great brutality – Yorkshire and the north were ravished and the fenland resistance of Hereward the Wake was brought to a savage end. Nonetheless, perhaps the single most effective controlling measure was the compilation of the **Domesday Book** between 1085 and 1086. Recording land ownership, type of cultivation, the number of inhabitants and their social status, it afforded William an unprecedented body of information about his subjects, providing the framework for the administration of taxation, the judicial structure and feudal obligations.

In 1087, William died to be succeeded by his son **William Rufus**, an ineffectual ruler but a notable benefactor of religious foundations. Rufus died in mysterious circumstances – killed by an unknown assailant's arrow while hunting in the New Forest – and the throne passed to **Henry I**, William I's youngest son. Henry spent much of his time struggling with his unruly barons, but at least he proved to be more conciliatory in his dealings with the Saxons, even marrying into one of their leading families. On his death in 1135, William I's grandson Stephen of Blois contested the accession of Henry's daughter Mathilda and the result was a long-winded civil war. Matters were eventually resolved when both factions accepted Mathilda's son as **Henry II**, the first of the **Plantagenets**, so-called after this branch of the family. Energetic and far-sighted, Henry kept his barons firmly in check and instigated profound administrative reforms, including the introduction of trial by jury. Neither was England Henry's only concern, his inheritance bequeathing him great chunks of France. This territorial entanglement was to create all sorts of problems for his successors, but Henry was brought low by his attempt to subordinate church to crown. This went terribly awry in 1170, when Henry sanctioned the murder in Canterbury Cathedral of his erstwhile drinking companion **Thomas à Becket**, whose canonization just three years later created an enduring Europe-wide cult.

The last years of Henry's reign were riven by quarrels with his sons, the eldest of whom, **Richard I** (or Lionheart), spent most of his ten-year reign crusading in the Holy Land. Neglected, England fell prey to the scheming of Richard's brother **John**, the villain of the Robin Hood tales, who became king in his own right after Richard died of a battle wound in 1199. But John's inability to hold on to his French possessions and his rumbling dispute with the Vatican alienated the English barons, who eventually forced him to consent to a charter guaranteeing their rights and privileges, the **Magna Carta**, which was signed in 1215 at Runnymede, on the Thames.

The power struggle with the barons continued into the reign of **Henry III**, who was defeated by their leader Simon de Montfort at Lewes in 1264, when both Henry and Prince Edward were taken prisoner. Edward escaped and promptly routed the barons' army at the battle of Evesham in 1265, killing de Montfort in the process. This was something of a watershed and Henry's successor, **Edward I**, who inherited the throne in 1272, was much more in control of his kingdom. Edward was also a great law-maker, but he became obsessed by military matters, spending years subduing Wales and imposing English jurisdiction over Scotland. Fortunately for the Scots – it was too late for Wales – the next king of England, **Edward II**, proved to be completely hopeless and in 1314 Robert the Bruce inflicted a huge defeat on his guileless army at the battle of **Bannockburn**. This reverse spelt the beginning of the end for Edward, who was subsequently murdered by his wife Isabella and her lover Roger Mortimer in 1327.

Edward III began by sorting out the Scottish imbroglio before getting stuck into his main preoccupation – his (essentially specious) claim to the throne of France. Starting in 1337, the resultant **Hundred Years War** kicked off with several famous English victories, principally Crécy in 1346 and Poitiers in 1356, but was interrupted by the outbreak of the **Black Death** in 1349. The plague claimed about one and a half million English souls – some one third of the population – and the scarcity of labour that followed gave the peasantry more economic clout than they had ever had before. Predictably, the landowners attempted to restrict the concomitant rise in wages, but thereby provoked the widespread rioting that culminated in the **Peasants' Revolt** of 1381. The rebels marched on London under the delusion that they could appeal to the king – now **Richard II** – for fair treatment, but they soon learnt otherwise. The king did indeed meet a rebel deputation in person, but his aristocratic bodyguards took the opportunity to kill the peasants' leader, **Wat Tyler**, the prelude to the enforced dispersal of the crowds and mass slaughter.

Running parallel with this social unrest were the clerical reforms demanded by the scholar **John Wycliffe**, whose acolytes made the first translation of the Bible into English in 1380. Another sign of the elevation of the common language was the success enjoyed by **Geoffrey Chaucer** (c.1345–1400), a wine merchant's son, whose *Canterbury Tales* was the first major work written in the vernacular and one of the first English books to be printed.

The houses of Lancaster and York

In 1399, the weak and indecisive Richard II was overthrown by **Henry IV**, the first of the **Lancastrian** kings. Henry died in 1413 to be succeeded by his son, the bellicose **Henry V**, who promptly renewed the Hundred Years War with vigour. Henry famously defeated the French at the battle of **Agincourt**, a comprehensive victory that forced the French king to acknowledge Henry as his heir in the Treaty of Troyes of 1420. However, Henry died just two years later and his son, **Henry VI** – or rather his regents – all too easily succumbed to a French counter-attack inspired by **Joan of Arc**; by 1454, only Calais was left in English hands.

It was soon obvious that Henry VI was mentally unstable, and consequently, as Henry drifted in and out of insanity, so two aristocratic factions attempted to squeeze control. These two factions were the Yorkists, whose emblem was the white rose, and the Lancastrians, represented by the red rose – hence the **Wars of the Roses**. At first, the Lancastrians had the better of things, but the Yorkist **Edward IV** seized the crown in 1461. Imprudently, Edward then attempted to shrug off his most powerful backer, Richard Neville, Earl of Warwick – aka "Warwick the Kingmaker" – and Warwick returned the favour by switching sides. Edward was driven into exile and Henry VI returned for a second term as king – but not for long. In 1471, Edward IV was back again, Warwick was killed and Henry was captured – and subsequently dispatched – when the Yorkists crushed the Lancastrians at the battle of Tewkesbury.

Edward IV proved to be a precursor of the great Tudor princes, licentious, cruel and despotic, but also a patron of Renaissance learning. In 1483, his 12-year-old son succeeded as **Edward V**, but his reign was cut short after only two months, when he and his younger brother were murdered in the Tower of London – probably by their uncle, the Duke of Gloucester, who was crowned **Richard III**. Richard was famously toppled at Bosworth Field in 1485 by Henry Tudor, Earl of Richmond, who took the throne as **Henry VII**.

The Tudors

The opening of the **Tudor** period brought radical transformations. A Lancastrian through his mother's line, **Henry VII** promptly reconciled the Yorkists by marrying Edward IV's daughter Elizabeth, thereby ending the Wars of the Roses at a stroke. It was a shrewd gambit and others followed. Henry married his daughter off to James IV of Scotland and his son to Catherine, the daughter of Ferdinand and Isabella of Spain – and by these means England began to assume the status of a major European power. There were economic stirrings too, with the burgeoning wool and cloth trades spawning an increasingly prosperous merchant class.

Henry's son, **Henry VIII** is best remembered for his separation of the English Church from Rome and his establishment of an independent Protestant church – the **Church of England**. This is not without its ironies. Henry was not a Protestant himself and such was his early orthodoxy that the pope even gave him the title "Defender of the Faith" for a pamphlet he wrote attacking Luther's treatises. In fact, the schism between Henry and the pope was triggered not by doctrinal issues but by the failure of his wife **Catherine of Aragon** – widow of his elder brother – to provide Henry with male offspring. Failing to obtain a decree of nullity from Pope Clement VII, he dismissed his long-time chancellor Thomas Wolsey and turned instead to Thomas Cromwell, who helped make the English Church recognize Henry as its head. One of the consequences was the **Dissolution of the Monasteries**, which conveniently gave both king and nobles the chance to get their hands on valuable monastic property. The Dissolution was done in two stages in the late 1530s, though Henry was briefly delayed by the **Pilgrimage of Grace**, a widespread rebellion that began in Louth, in Lincolnshire, and spread across the north buoyed up by pro-Catholic sentiment.

In his later years Henry became a corpulent, syphilitic wreck, six times married but at last furnished with an heir, **Edward VI**, who was only 9 years old when he ascended the throne in 1547. His short reign saw Protestantism established on a firm footing, with churches stripped of their images and Catholic services banned, yet on Edward's death most of the country readily accepted his half-sister **Mary**, daughter of Catherine of Aragon and a fervent Catholic, as queen. She returned England to the papacy and married the future Philip II of Spain, forging an alliance whose immediate consequence was war with France and the loss of Calais, the last of England's French possessions. The marriage was unpopular and so was Mary's foolish decision to begin persecuting Protestants, executing the leading lights of the English Reformation, Hugh Latimer, Nicholas Ridley and Thomas Cranmer, the archbishop of Canterbury who was largely responsible for the first **English prayer book**, published in 1549.

When she came to the throne in 1558 on the death of her half-sister, **Elizabeth I** looked very vulnerable. The country was divided by religion - Catholic against Protestant – and threatened from abroad by Philip II of Spain, the most powerful man in Europe. Famously, Elizabeth eschewed marriage and, although a Protestant herself, steered a delicate course between the two religious groupings. Her prudence rested well with the English merchant class, who were becoming the greatest power in the land, its members mostly opposed to foreign military entanglements. An exception was, however, made for the piratical activities of the great English seafarers of the day, sea captains like Walter Raleigh, Martin Frobisher, John Hawkins and Francis Drake, who made a for-

Chronology of English monarchs

House of Wessex
Egbert 802–39
Ethelwulf 839–55
Ethelbald 855–60
Ethelbert 860–66
Ethelred I 866–71
Alfred the Great 871–99
Edward the Elder 899–924
Athelstan 924–39
Edmund I 939–46
Eadred 946–55
Eadwig 955–59
Edgar 959–75
Edward the Martyr 975–78
Ethelred II (Ethelred the Unready) 978–1016
Edmund II (Edmund Ironside) 1016

House of Skjoldung
Canute 1016–35
Harold I 1035–40
Harthacanute 1040–42

House of Wessex
Edward the Confessor 1042–66
Harold II 1066

House of Normandy
William I (William the Conqueror) 1066–87
William II (William Rufus) 1087–1100
Henry I 1100–35
Stephen 1135–54

House of Plantagenet
Henry II 1154–89
Richard I (Richard the Lionheart) 1189–99
John 1199–1216
Henry III 1216–72
Edward I 1272–1307
Edward II 1307–27
Edward III 1327–77
Richard II 1377–99

House of Lancaster
Henry IV 1399–1413
Henry V 1413–22
Henry VI 1422–61 & 1470

House of York
Edward IV 1461–70 & 1471–83
Edward V 1483
Richard III 1483–85

House of Tudor
Henry VII 1485–1509
Henry VIII 1509–47
Edward VI 1547–53
Mary I 1553–58
Elizabeth I 1558–1603

House of Stuart
James I 1603–25
Charles I 1625–49
Commonwealth and Protectorate 1649–60
Charles II 1660–85
James II 1685–88
William III and Mary II 1688–94
William III 1694–1702
Anne 1702–14

House of Hanover
George I 1714–27
George II 1727–60
George III 1760–1820
George IV 1820–30
William IV 1830–37
Victoria 1837–1901

House of Saxe-Coburg
Edward VII 1901–10

House of Windsor
George V 1910–36
Edward VIII 1936
George VI 1936–52
Elizabeth II 1952–

tune raiding Spain's American colonies. Inevitably, Philip II's irritation took a warlike turn, but the **Spanish Armada** he sent in 1588 was defeated, thereby establishing England as a major European sea power. Elizabeth's reign also saw the efflorescence of a specifically English Renaissance – **William Shakespeare** (1564–1616) is the obvious name – the only blot being the queen's reluctant execution of her cousin and rival **Mary Queen of Scots** in 1587.

The early Stuarts and the Commonwealth

Elizabeth was succeeded by the son of Mary Queen of Scots, James VI of Scotland, who became **James I** of England in 1603, thereby uniting the English and Scottish crowns. James quickly moved to end hostilities with Spain and adopted a policy of toleration to the country's Catholics. Inevitably, both initiatives offended many Protestants, whose worst fears were confirmed in 1605 when **Guy Fawkes** and a group of Catholic conspirators were discovered preparing to blow up king and Parliament in the so-called **Gunpowder Plot**. During the ensuing hue and cry, many Catholics met an untimely end and Fawkes himself was hung, drawn and quartered. These goings-on convinced many Protestants that the English state was irredeemably corrupt and some of the more dedicated **Puritans** fixed their eyes on establishing a "New Jerusalem" in North America after commercial and secular interests founded the first permanent **colony in North America** in Virginia in 1608. Twelve years later, the Pilgrim Fathers landed in New England, establishing a colony that would absorb about a hundred thousand Puritan immigrants by the middle of the century.

Meanwhile, James was busy alienating his landed gentry. He clung to an absolutist vision of the monarchy – the divine right of kings – that was totally out of step with the Protestant leanings of the majority of his subjects and he also relied heavily on court favourites, especially the much reviled George Villiers, Duke of Buckingham. It was a recipe for disaster, but it was to be his successor, **Charles I**, who reaped the whirlwind. Charles inherited James's dislike of the Protestants and liking for absolutism, ruling without Parliament from 1629 to 1640. But he over-stepped himself when he tried to impose a new Anglican prayer book on the Scots, who rose in revolt, forcing Charles to recall Parliament to raise the money for an army. This was Parliament's chance and they were not going to let it slip. The **Long Parliament** as it became known impeached several of Charles's allies – most notably Archbishop Laud, who was left out to dry by the king and ultimately executed – and compiled its grievances in the Grand Remonstrance of 1641.

Facing the concerted hostility of Parliament, the king withdrew to Nottingham where he raised his standard, the opening act of the **Civil War**. The Royalist forces ("Cavaliers") were initially successful, winning the battle of Edgehill, but afterwards the Parliamentarian army ("Roundheads") was completely overhauled by **Oliver Cromwell**. The New Model Army Cromwell created was something quite unique: singing psalms as they went into battle and urged on by preachers and "agitators", this was an army of believers whose ideological commitment to the Parliamentary cause made it truly formidable. Cromwell's revamped army cut its teeth at the battle of Naseby and thereafter simply brushed the Royalists aside. Attempting to muddy the political waters, Charles surrendered himself to the Scots, but they finally handed him over to the English Parliament, by whom – after prolonged negotiations, endless royal shenanigans and more fighting – he was ultimately executed in January 1649.

For the next eleven years England was a **Commonwealth** – at first a true republic, then, after 1653, a **Protectorate** with Cromwell as the Lord Protector and commander in chief. Cromwell reformed the government, secured advantageous commercial treaties with foreign nations and used his New Model Army to put the fear of God into his various enemies. The turmoil of the Civil War and the pre-eminence of the army unleashed a furious legal, theological and political debate in every corner of the country. This milieu spawned a host of leftist sects, the most notable of whom were the **Levellers**, who demanded wholesale constitutional reform, and the more radical **Diggers**, who proposed common ownership of all land. **Nonconformist** religious groups also flourished, prominent among them the pacifist **Quakers**, led by the much persecuted George Fox (1624–91), and the **Dissenters**, to whom the most famous writers of the day, John Milton (1608–74) and John Bunyan (1628–88), both belonged.

Cromwell died in 1658 to be succeeded by his son **Richard**, who ruled briefly and ineffectually and, while the leftists squabbled among themselves, more conservative Protestants, led by General Monk, moved to restore the monarchy. Charles II, the exiled son of the previous king, entered London in triumph in May 1660.

The Restoration and the later Stuarts

A Stuart was back on the English throne, but **Charles II** had few absolutist illusions – the terms of the **Restoration** were closely negotiated and included a general amnesty for all those who had fought against the Stuarts, with the exception of the regicides (those who had signed Charles I's death warrant). Nonetheless, there was a sea-change in public life with the re-establishment of a royal court, a new exuberance in art, literature and theatre, and the foundation of the **Royal Society**, whose scientific endeavours were furthered by Isaac Newton (1642–1727). The low points of Charles's reign were the **Great Plague** of 1665 and the 1666 **Great Fire of London**, though the London that rose from the ashes was an architectural showcase for Christopher Wren (1632–1723) and his fellow classicists. Politically, there were still underlying tensions between the monarchy and Parliament, but the latter was more concerned with the struggle between the **Whigs** and **Tories**, political factions representing, respectively, the low-church gentry and the high-church aristocracy. There was a degree of religious toleration too, but its brittleness was all too apparent in the anti-Catholic riots of 1678.

James II, the brother of Charles II, came to the throne in 1685. He was a Catholic, which made the bulk of his subjects uneasy, but there was still an indifferent response when the Protestant **Duke of Monmouth**, the favourite among Charles II's illegitimate sons, raised a rebellion in the West Country. Monmouth was defeated at Sedgemoor, in Somerset, in July 1685, and was beheaded for his pains; his followers received summary treatment at the hands of the notorious Judge Jeffreys in the aptly named **Bloody Assizes**. However, if James felt secure he was mistaken. A foolish man, James showed all the traditional weaknesses of his family, from his enthusiasm for the divine right of kings to an over-reliance on sycophantic favourites. Even worse, as far as the Protestants were concerned, he built up a massive standing army, officered it with Roman Catholics and proposed a **Declaration of Indulgence**, removing anti-Catholic restrictions. When James's queen gave him a son, securing a Catholic succession, the most powerful Protestants in the land begged **William of Orange**, the Dutch husband of Mary, the Protestant daughter of James II, to save them from Catholic tyranny – and that was precisely what he did. William landed in Devon and, as James's forces simply melted away, he speedily took control of London in the **Glorious Revolution** of 1688. This was the final postscript to the Civil War – although it was another three years before James's and his Jacobite forces were finally defeated in Ireland.

William and Mary were made joint sovereigns after they agreed a **Bill of Rights** defining the limitations of the monarchy's power and the rights of its subjects. This, together with the **Act of Settlement of 1701** – among other things, barring Catholics or anyone married to one from succession to the English throne – made Britain a **constitutional monarchy**, in which the roles of legislature and executive were separate and interdependent. The model was broadly consistent with that outlined by the philosopher and political thinker John Locke (1632–1704), whose essentially Whig doctrines of toleration and social contract were gradually embraced as the new orthodoxy.

Ruling alone after Mary's death in 1694, William regarded England as a prop in his defence of Holland against France, a stance that defined England's political alignment in Europe for the next sixty years. In the reign of **Anne**, second daughter of James II, English armies won a string of remarkable victories on the continent, beginning with the Duke of Marlborough's triumph at Blenheim in 1704, followed the next year by the capture of Gibraltar, establishing a British presence in the Mediterranean. These military escapades were part of the Europe-wide **War of the Spanish Succession**, which rumbled on until the Treaty of Utrecht in 1713 – a treaty which all but settled the European balance of power for the rest of the eighteenth century. Otherwise Anne's reign was distinguished mainly for the 1707 **Act of Union**, uniting the English and Scottish parliaments.

With none of her children surviving into adulthood, Anne was the last of the Stuarts and, when she died in 1714, the succession passed – in accordance with the terms of the Act of Settlement – to the Duke of Hanover, a non-English-speaking, Protestant German who became George I of England.

The Hanoverians

As power leaked away from the monarchy into the hands of the Whig oligarchy – many Tories having been discredited for suspected Jacobite sympathies – the king ceased to attend Cabinet meetings, his place being taken by his chief minister. Most prominent of these ministers was **Robert Walpole**, regarded as England's **first prime minister**. To all intents and purposes, Walpole governed the country from 1721 to 1742, a tranquil period politically, with the country standing aloof from foreign affrays. The financial world, however, was prey to a mania for speculation and of numerous fraudulent or ill-conceived financial ventures, the most dramatic was the fiasco of the South Sea Company, which in 1720 sold shares in its monopoly of trade in the Pacific and along the east coast of South America. The "**bubble**" burst when the shareholders took fright at the extent of their own investments and the value of the shares dropped through the floor at breakneck speed, reducing many to penury and almost bringing down Walpole and his government.

Peace ended in the reign of **George II**, when England declared war on Spain in 1739 at the start of yet another dynastic squabble, the eight-year War of the Austrian Succession. Then, in 1745, the country was invaded by the **Young Pretender**, **Charles Stuart**, in the second and most dangerous of the Jacobite rebellions (the first had failed dismally in 1715). So-called Bonnie Prince Charlie and his Highland army managed to reach Derby, just 120 miles from London, creating pandemonium in the capital, but their lines of supply were over-extended and they were obliged to retreat north. It all ended in Jacobite tears, when a Hanoverian army under the brutal Duke of Cumberland caught up with them and hacked them to pieces at Culloden, in Scotland. Otherwise, the **Seven Years War** harvested England yet more overseas territory in India and Canada at the expense of France and, in 1768, **Captain James Cook** sailed to New Zealand and Australia, thereby netting another chunk of the globe.

In 1760, **George III** succeeded his father. The early years of his sixty-year reign saw a revived struggle between king and Parliament, enlivened by the intervention of John Wilkes, first of a long and increasingly vociferous line of parliamentary radicals. The contest was exacerbated by the deteriorating relationship with the thirteen colonies of North America, a situation brought to a head by the **American Declaration of Independence** and Britain's subsequent defeat in the Revolutionary War. Chastened by this disaster, Britain chose not to interfere in the momentous events taking place across the Channel, where France, long its most consistent foe, was convulsed by revolution. Out of the turmoil emerged the most daunting of enemies, **Napoleon**, whose stunning military progress was interrupted by Nelson at **Trafalgar** in 1805 and finally stopped ten years later by the Duke of Wellington at **Waterloo**.

The Industrial Revolution

England's triumph over Napoleon was underpinned by its financial strength, which was itself born of the **Industrial Revolution**, the switch from an agricultural to a manufacturing economy that completely changed the country over a hundred years. The earliest mechanized production lines were in the Lancashire **cotton mills**, where cotton-spinning was transformed from a cottage industry into a highly productive factory-based system. Initially, river water powered the mills, but the technology changed after James Watt patented his **steam engine** in 1781. Watt's engines needed **coal**, which made it convenient to locate mills and factories near coal mines, a tendency that was accelerated as **ironworks** took up coal as a smelting fuel, vastly increasing the output from their furnaces. Accordingly, there was a shift of population towards the Midlands and north of England, where the great coal reserves were located, and as the industrial economy boomed and diversified, so these regions' towns mushroomed at an extraordinary rate. There were steel towns like Sheffield, huge cotton warehouses in Manchester, ceramics in Stoke-on-Trent and vast dock facilities in Liverpool, where raw materials from India and the Americas came in and manufactured goods went out. Commerce and industry were also served by improving transport facilities, such as the building of a network of **canals** in the wake of the success of the Bridgewater Canal in 1765, which linked coal mines at Worsley with Manchester and the River Mersey. But the great leap forward came with the arrival of the **railway**, heralded by the Stockton–Darlington line in 1825, followed five years later by the Liverpool–Manchester railway, courtesy of George Stephenson's *Rocket*.

Boosted by a vast influx of Jewish, Irish, French and Dutch workers, the country's population rose from about seven and a half million at the beginning of George III's reign to more than fourteen million at its end. Immigration was, however, of less demographic importance than the slowing-down of the death-rate due to improvements in medical science. As the factories and their attendant towns expanded, so the rural settlements of England suffered, inspiring the elegiac pastoral yearnings of Samuel Taylor Coleridge and William Wordsworth, the first great names of the **Romantic** movement. Later Romantic poets such as Percy Bysshe Shelley and Lord Byron took a more socially engaged position, inveighing against social injustices that were aggravated by the expenses of the Napoleonic Wars and their aftermath, when many returning soldiers found their jobs had been taken by machines. Discontent emerged in demands for parliamentary reform, and in 1819 demonstrators in Manchester – the most important of the industrial boom towns still unrepresented in Parliament – were hacked down by troops in what became known as the **Peterloo Massacre.**

The following year a weak, blind and insane George III finally died and was succeeded by his son **George IV**. One of the hallmarks of the new reign was a greater degree of religious toleration with Catholics and Nonconformists now permitted to enter Parliament. Furthermore, after years of struggle, workers' associations were legalized, and a civilian police force was created, largely the work of **Robert Peel**, a reforming Tory. More far-reaching changes came under **William IV**, with the passing of the **Reform Act** of 1832, whereby the principle of popular representation was acknowledged (though most adult males still had no vote); two years later, the revised **Poor Law** alleviated the condition of the destitute. Significant sections of the middle classes wanted far swifter democratic reform, as was expressed in public indignation over the **Tolpuddle Martyrs** – the Dorset labourers transported to Australia in 1834 for joining an agricultural trade union – and support for **Chartism**, a working-class movement demanding universal male suffrage. Poverty and injustice were the dominant theme of the novels of **Charles Dickens** (1812–70) and the preoccupation of the paternalistic reform movements that were a feature of the nineteenth century. This social concern had been anticipated in the previous century by the Methodism of John Wesley (1703–91) and the anti-slavery campaign promoted by evangelical Christians such as the Quakers and William Wilberforce. As a result of their efforts, slavery was banned in Britain in 1772 and throughout the colonies in 1833 – putting an end to what had been a major factor in the prosperity of ports such as Bristol and Liverpool.

Victorian England

In 1837 William IV was succeeded by his niece **Victoria**, whose long reign witnessed the zenith of British power. For much of the period, the economy boomed and typically the cloth manufacturers could boast that they supplied the domestic market before breakfast, the rest of the world thereafter. The British shipping fleet was easily the mightiest in the world and underpinned an empire on which "The sun never set" with Victoria herself becoming the symbol of both the nation's success and the imperial ideal. There were extraordinary intellectual achievements too – as typified by the publication of Charles Darwin's **On the Origin of Species** in 1859 – and the country came to see itself as both a civilizing agent and, on occasion, the hand of (a very Protestant) God on earth. Britain's industrial and commercial prowess was best embodied by the great engineering feats of Isambard Kingdom Brunel and by the **Great Exhibition** of 1851, a display of manufacturing achievements from all over the world.

With trade at the forefront of the agenda, much of the political debate crystallized into a conflict between the **Free Traders** – represented by an alliance of the Peelites and the Whigs, forming the Liberal Party – and the **Protectionists** under Bentinck and **Disraeli**, guiding light of the Tories. During the last third of the century, Parliament was dominated by the duel between Disraeli and the Liberal leader **Gladstone**. Although it was Disraeli who eventually passed the Second Reform Bill in 1867, further extending the electoral franchise, it was Gladstone who had first proposed it, and it was Gladstone's first ministry of 1868–74 that passed some of the century's most far-reaching legislation, including compulsory education, the full legalization of trade unions and an Irish Land Act.

There were foreign entanglements, too. In 1854 troops were sent to protect the Turkish empire against the Russians in the **Crimea**, an inglorious debacle whose horrors were relayed to the public by the first ever press coverage of a military campaign and by the revelations of a shocked Florence Nightingale. The potential fragility of Britain's empire was exposed by the Indian Mutiny of 1857, but the imperial status quo was eventually restored and Victoria took the title Empress of India after 1876. Thereafter, the British army was flattered by a series of minor wars against poorly armed Asian and African opponents, but promptly came unstuck when it faced the Dutch settlers of South Africa in the **Boer War** (1899–1902). The British ultimately fought their way to victory, but the discreditable conduct of the war prompted a military shake-up at home that was to be of significance in the coming European war.

From World War I to World War II

Victoria died in 1901, to be succeeded by her son, **Edward VII**, whose leisurely life could be seen as the epitome of the complacent era to which he gave his name. This complacency came to an end on August 4, 1914, when the Liberal government, honouring the Entente Cordiale signed with France in 1904, declared war on Germany. Hundreds of thousands volunteered for the army, but their enthusiastic nationalism was not enough to easily win **World War I**, which dragged on for four years and cost millions of lives. Britain and her allies eventually prevailed, but the number of dead beggared belief, undermining the English majority's respect for the ruling class, whose generals had shown a particularly potent combination of incompetence and indifference to the plight of their men. Many looked admiringly at the Soviet Union, where the communists had rid themselves of the Tsar and seized control in 1917.

At the war's end in 1918 the political fabric of England was changed dramatically when the sheer weight of public opinion pushed Parliament into extending the **vote** to all men over 21 and to women over 30. This tardy liberalization of women's rights owed much to the efforts of the radical **Suffragettes**, led by Emmeline Pankhurst and her daughters Sylvia and Christabel, but the process was only completed in 1929 when women were at last granted the vote at 21, on equal terms with men.

During this period, the **Labour Party** supplanted the Liberals as the main force on the left wing of British politics, its strength built on an alliance between the working-class trade unions and middle-class radicals. Labour formed its first government in 1923 under Ramsay MacDonald, but following the publication of the **Zinoviev Letter**, a forged document that seemed to prove Soviet encouragement of British socialist subversion, the Conservatives were returned with a large majority. In 1926, the tensions that had been building up since the end of the war – produced by a severe decline in manufacturing and attendant mass unemployment – erupted in the **General Strike**. Spreading instantly from the coal mines to the railways, the newspapers and the iron and steel industries, the strike lasted nine days and involved half a million workers, provoking the government into draconian action – the army was called in, and the strike was broken. The economic situation deteriorated even further after the crash of the New York Stock Exchange in 1929, which precipitated a worldwide depression. Unemployment reached over 2.8 million in 1931, generating a series of mass demonstrations that reached a peak with the **Jarrow March** from the Northeast to London in 1936. The same year, economist John Maynard Keynes argued in his *General Theory of Employment, Interest and Money* for a greater degree of state intervention in the management of the economy, though the whole question was soon overshadowed by international events.

Abroad, the structure of the British Empire had undergone profound changes since World War I. The status of Ireland had been partly resolved following the electoral gains of the nationalist Sinn Fein in 1918. Their success led to the establishment of the Irish Free State in 1922, though (and this was to cause endless problems thereafter) the six counties of the mainly Protestant North chose to "contract out". Four years later, the **Imperial Conference** recognized the autonomy of the British dominions, an agreement formalized in the 1931 Statute of Westminster, whereby each dominion was given an equal footing in a Commonwealth of Nations, though each still recognized the British monarch. The royal family itself was shaken in 1936 by the **abdication of Edward VIII**, following his decision to marry a twice-divorced American, Wallis Simpson. Although the succession passed smoothly to his brother **George VI**, the scandal further reduced the standing of the royals.

Non-intervention in both the Spanish Civil War and the Sino-Japanese War was paralleled by a policy of appeasement towards **Adolf Hitler**, who began to rearm Germany in earnest in the mid-1930s. This policy was epitomized by the antics of Prime Minister Neville Chamberlain, who returned from meeting Hitler and Mussolini at Munich in 1938 with an assurance of good intentions that he took at face value. Consequently, when **World War II** broke out in September 1939, Britain was seriously unprepared. In May 1940 the discredited Chamberlain stepped down in favour of a national coalition government headed by the charismatic **Winston Churchill**, whose bulldog persistence and heroic speeches provided the inspiration needed in the backs-against-the-wall mood of the time. Partly through Churchill's manoeuvrings, the United States became a supplier of foodstuffs and munitions to Britain and this, combined with the US breaking trade links with Japan in June (in protest at their attacks on China), may have helped precipitate the Japanese bombing of Pearl Harbour on December 7, 1941. Once attacked, the US immediately joined the war, declaring against both Japan and Germany, and its intervention, combined with the heroic efforts of the Soviet Red Army, swung the military balance. In terms of the number of casualties, World War II was not as calamitous as World War I, but its impact upon the civilian population of Britain was much greater. In its first wave of **bombing** on the UK, the Luftwaffe caused massive damage to industrial and supply centres such as London, Coventry, Manchester, Liverpool, Southampton and Plymouth. In later raids, intended to shatter morale rather than factories and docks, the cathedral cities of Canterbury, Exeter, Bath, Norwich and York all took a battering too. At the end of the fighting, nearly one in three of all the houses in the nation had been destroyed or damaged, nearly a quarter of a million members of the British armed forces had lost their lives and over 58,000 civilians were dead.

Postwar England

The end of the war in 1945 was quickly followed by a general election. Hungry for change (and demobilization), the electorate replaced Churchill with the Labour Party under **Clement Attlee**, who, with a large parliamentary majority, set about a radical programme to **nationalize** the coal, gas, electricity, iron and steel industries, as well as the inland transport services. Building on the plans for a social security system presented in Sir William Beveridge's report of 1943, the **National Insurance Act** and the **National Health Service Act** were both passed early in the Labour administration, giving birth to what became known as the **welfare state**. But despite substantial American aid, the huge problems of rebuilding the economy made austerity the keynote, with the rationing of food and fuel remaining in force long after 1945.

In April 1949, Britain, the United States, Canada, France and the Benelux countries signed the **North Atlantic Treaty** as a counterbalance to Soviet power in Eastern Europe, thereby defining the country's postwar international commitments. Yet confusion regarding Britain's post-imperial role was shown up by the **Suez Crisis** of 1956, when Anglo-French and Israeli forces invaded Egypt to secure control of the Suez Canal, only to be hastily recalled following international (American) condemnation. Revealing severe limitations on the country's capacity for independent action, the Suez incident resulted in the resignation of the Conservative prime minister Anthony Eden, who was replaced by the more pragmatic **Harold Macmillan**. Nonetheless, Macmillan maintained a nuclear policy that suggested a continued desire for an international role, and nuclear testing went on against a background of widespread marches under the auspices of the Campaign for Nuclear Disarmament.

The 1960s, dominated by the Labour premiership of **Harold Wilson**, saw a boom in consumer spending, some pioneering social legislation (primarily on the legalization of homosexuality and abortion), and a corresponding cultural upswing, with London becoming the hippest city on the planet. The good times lasted barely a decade. Though Tory prime minister Edward Heath led Britain into the brave new world of the **European Economic Community** (ECC), the 1970s were a decade of recession and industrial strife. A succession of public-sector strikes and mis-timed decisions by James Callaghan's Labour government handed the 1979 general election to the Conservatives and

Margaret Thatcher, who four years earlier had ousted Heath to become the first woman to lead a major political party in Britain.

Thatcher went on to win three general elections, steering the UK into a period of ever greater social polarization. While taxation policies and easy credit fuelled a consumer boom for the professional classes, the erosion of manufacturing industry and the weakening of the welfare state impoverished a great swathe of the population. However, Thatcher won an increased majority in the 1983 election, largely thanks to the successful recapture of the **Falkland Islands**, a remote British dependency in the south Atlantic, retrieved from the occupying Argentine army in 1982. Her electoral domination was also assisted by the fragmentation of the Labour opposition, from which the short-lived Social Democratic Party had split in panic at what it perceived as the radicalization of the party.

Social and political tensions surfaced in sporadic urban rioting and the year-long **miners' strike** (1984–85) against colliery closures, a bitter industrial dispute in which the police were given unprecedented powers to restrict the movement of citizens, while the media perpetrated some immensely misleading coverage of events. The violence in Northern Ireland also intensified, and in 1984 the bombing campaign of the IRA came close to killing the entire Cabinet when they blew up the Brighton hotel where the Conservatives were staying during their annual conference.

The 1990s to today

The divisive politics of Thatcherism reached their apogee with the introduction of the **Poll Tax**, a disastrous scheme that led ultimately to Thatcher's overthrow by colleagues who feared annihilation should she lead them into another general election. The beneficiary was **John Major**, a notably uninspiring figure who nonetheless managed to win the Conservatives a fourth term of office in 1992, albeit with a much reduced Parliamentary majority. While his government presided over a steady growth in economic performance, they gained little credit amid allegations of mismanagement, incompetence and feckless leadership. They were also engulfed by endless tales of Tory "sleaze", with revelations of extramarital affairs, cover-ups and financial deceit gleefully blazed by the British press. The Conservatives were also ideologically split over Europe. One part of the party was pro the European Union (formerly the EEC), the other – a vocal right-wing group of **Eurosceptics** – insisted Britain should keep a safe distance from the EU in general and the proposed common currency – the euro – in particular.

If the Conservative government was in deep trouble in the early 1990s then so was the **Royal Family**, whose credibility fissured with the break-up of the marriage of Prince Charles and Diana. Revelations about the cruel treatment of Diana by both the prince and his family badly damaged the royals' reputation and suddenly the institution itself seemed an anachronism, its members stiff, old-fashioned and dim-witted. By contrast, **Diana**, who was formally divorced from Charles in 1994, appeared warm-hearted and glamorous, so much so that her death in a car accident in Paris in 1997 may actually have saved the royal family as an institution. In the short term, Diana's death had a profound impact on the British, who joined in a media-orchestrated exercise in public grieving unprecedented in modern times.

Meanwhile, the **Labour Party**, which had been wracked by factionalism in the 1980s, regrouped under Neil Kinnock and then John Smith, but the two never reaped the political rewards. These dropped into the lap of a new and dynamic young leader, **Tony Blair**, who pushed the party away from traditional left-wing socialism. Blair's mantle of idealistic, media-friendly populism worked to devastating effect, sweeping the Labour Party to power in the **general election of May 1997** on a wave of genuine popular optimism. There were immediate rewards in enhanced relations with Europe and progress in the Irish peace talks, and Blair's electoral touch was soon repeated in Labour-sponsored **devolution referenda**, whose results semi-detached Scotland and Wales from their larger neighbour. There was also much Labourite tub-thumping about the need to improve **public services**, but Blair only set about the task in earnest after the **general election of June 2001**, which Labour won with another parliamentary landslide. This second victory was, however, qualitatively different from the first. There remained little of the optimism of before and voter turnout was lower than any time since World War II. Government "**spin**" was blamed, as was the electorate's belief that public services were not improving despite Blair's grand words.

Spin and internal dissent overshadowed the government's genuine achievements – introduction of a minimum wage, reform of the House of Lords – but did little to bolster the ailing Conservative Party, leaving Blair streets ahead of his political rivals in the opinion polls when the hijacked planes hit New York's World Trade Centre on **September 11, 2001**. Blair rushed to support President Bush, joining in the attack on Afghanistan and then, much to the horror of many in the Labour Party, sending British forces into **Iraq** alongside the Americans in 2003. Saddam Hussein was deposed with relative ease, but neither Bush nor Blair seemed to have a coherent exit strategy, and back home Blair's government was widely seen as having spun Britain into the war by exaggerating the danger Hussein presented. With no **WMDs** (Weapons of Mass Destruction) so far found and the Conservatives and Liberal Democrats gaining ground in the opinion polls, British politics is the most balanced it's been in a decade, and Blair's government faces considerable challenges if it's to regain the popular appeal it once had.

Monuments and buildings

If England sometimes seems like a historic theme park, crammed full of **monuments** and **buildings** recalling a fascinating past, then it's because physical evidence of its long history is so easily accessible. Despite the best efforts of Victorian modernizers, wars and twentieth-century town planners, every corner of the country has some landmark worthy of attention, whether it be a Neolithic burial site or a Postmodern addition to a world-famous gallery.

Prehistoric England

The oldest traces of building in England date from the **fourth millennium BC**, when **Neolithic** peoples, who practised rudimentary agriculture, succeeded the hunter-gatherers, who had inhabited cave-dwellings and hide-covered camps. The remains of round stone huts have been excavated on Carn Brea, outside Redruth in Cornwall, but the major surviving habitations are entrenched sites found throughout southern England. These consist of concentric rings of ditches and banks, with the largest being at Windmill Hill in Wiltshire. Neolithic peoples were also responsible for the numerous **long barrows** (burial mounds) that lie dotted all over England. These featureless, pear-shaped hummocks of earth are concentrated along the southern chalk downs from Sussex to Dorset, with others sprinkled around Lincolnshire, Yorkshire and the Cotswolds, where the barrows are noteworthy for holding stone chambers for collective family burials.

One of the largest and most elaborate Neolithic burial sites is **Woodhenge**, on Salisbury Plain, comprising a network of banks and ditches enclosing no fewer than six concentric ovals of wooden posts, arranged along the axis of the midsummer sunrise. Woodhenge is also near the most famous of all English prehistoric monuments, **Stonehenge**, a remarkable megalithic stone circle started around 3000 BC and subsequently added to over the next thousand years by the early Bronze Age Beaker People. Stonehenge probably had an astronomical and sacred significance, as did **Avebury**, on the other side of Salisbury Plain, which is even more extensive than Stonehenge, though neither as massive nor as well preserved. The size and complexity of both imply a highly organized communal effort, though they were undoubtedly embellished over the centuries – in much the same way as medieval cathedrals. Less grandiose **stone circles and rows** survive up and down the country, from Castlerigg, near Keswick in the Lake District, to the Hurlers of Cornwall's Bodmin Moor. **Hut circles** on the moors of the West Country bear testimony to the presence of later Bronze Age peoples; Grimspound, on Dartmoor, is one of the best examples – dating from around 1200 BC, its round stone houses with beehive roofs are ringed by a protective wall.

The Celtic and Roman periods

Around 700 BC, **Celtic** invaders brought the Iron Age to the British Isles. Their chief contribution to the English landscape was a series of **hilltop forts** and other defensive works, often adapted from earlier constructions. At their simplest, these strongholds consisted of a circular earthwork within which the inhabitants dwelt in timber-built round huts – a good example is Castle Dore, near Fowey in Cornwall. At **Maiden Castle**, in Dorset, a town was enclosed within a multiple system of ramparts, a formidable enlargement of what had been a modest and much more ancient hillfort. The best preserved of all Iron Age villages, however, is the stronghold of **Chysauster**, near Zennor in Cornwall, consisting of stone houses arranged in pairs, each with a courtyard and garden plot. The settlement was inhabited until well into the Roman era, preserved thanks to its distance from the most westerly Roman outpost.

The **Romans** imposed order and peace, the prerequisites for the construction of those **public buildings** that appeared in every part of the empire. There were several types, including amphitheatres, like the one in Chester, theatres as in York, and baths, the most famous of which was at Bath. No Roman temples remain standing, but Colchester and St Albans have revealed impressive remains, as befits two of Roman Britain's principal towns. Other important settlements – for example London, Gloucester, Leicester and Lincoln – were all planned according to the classic chessboard pattern favoured by the Romans, but have yielded little, the Roman remains obliterated by later occupants. In general terms, the architecture of Roman Britain was, as one might anticipate, thoroughly provincial – and not a patch on that of Rome – but nonetheless it certainly proclaimed imperial power and wealth. A prime example is the palace at **Fishbourne** in West Sussex, built around 75 AD, probably for a Romanized British chieftain. Fishbourne's columned entrance prefaces an interior whose decorative details were as carefully elaborated as the ground plan, with lavish use of mosaics, a feature also exemplified by private houses excavated at St Albans and Cirencester. Most of the great Roman villas reached their peak of comfort and artistic excellence during the first half of the fourth century, when even relatively modest farmhouses were equipped with central heating.

Anglo-Saxon England

The **Anglo-Saxons** who followed the Romans had little interest in their predecessors' architectural achievements and certainly didn't try to emulate them. Initially, the newcomers stuck to mud, wattle and thatch before moving on to **timber**, a specialization in which the English were to excel throughout the Middle Ages, though the perishability of timber has meant that little remains from this period. What fragments have survived were the product of the new Christian ideology, expressed in **stone-built churches** that were the chief medium of architectural innovation until the Reformation. But even stone churches were vulnerable to the Vikings and those that did survive were subject to constant modifications and accretions. Such was the case with two of the earliest English churches, both in **Canterbury** – St Peter and St Paul, dating from 597, and the town's first cathedral, erected about five years later. In general terms, Anglo-Saxon churches were modelled on churches in Rome, with round apses at the eastern end, unlike the more Celtic-inspired square ends that can, for example, be seen at the church of St Lawrence, in Bradford-on-Avon, Wiltshire, or in the seventh-century Christian revival churches of **Northumbria**. In the latter case, the ascetic Celtic tradition of the Scottish and Irish monks who led the movement did not encourage refined architecture, and the three churches built by Benedict Biscop in County Durham – Monkwearmouth, Escomb and the Venerable Bede's own church at Jarrow – are small and roughly built. The most impressive of all Saxon churches, however, lies in the Midlands, at **Brixworth** in Northamptonshire, erected around 670, and distinguished by the systematic use of arches.

In the eighth and ninth centuries, the Vikings despoiled the richest of the country's churches and pretty much put a stop to new construction work. However, a revival came with the installation of Dunstan as bishop of Glastonbury around 940, which led to the foundation of monasteries all over the country, much of the work being undertaken by churchmen who had spent time in the great European monasteries. Yet, far from showing the influence of continental styles, the sparse remains demonstrate instead a penchant for quirky decoration – for example the spiral columns in the crypt at Repton, Derbyshire.

The Normans

England's architectural insularity faded away in the early eleventh century. Continental influences wafted across the Channel and when Edward the Confessor rebuilt **Westminster Abbey** (1050–65) he employed the Romanesque style in imitation of the great French abbey churches of Caen and Jumièges. Edward's work disappeared centuries ago, but in any case this was the last fling of the Anglo-Saxon dice as the **Normans** of William the Conqueror seized control of the country in 1066. To subdue his new subjects, William built dozens of **castles**. The earliest types followed a "motte and bailey" design, consisting of a central tower (or keep) placed on a mound (the motte), and encircled by one or more courts (the baileys). Most were built of wood until the time of Henry II, though some of the more important sites were stone-constructed from the beginning, including **Rochester** and **Colchester** castles and the **White Tower** at the **Tower of London**, which was itself the most formidable of all the Norman strongholds. **Dover Castle** (1168–85), built by Henry II, introduced the refinement of a double row of outer walls with towers at intervals, a design probably influenced by the fortresses encountered by Crusaders in the Holy Land.

Once the country had been secured, the Normans set about transforming the English Church, filling its key positions with imported clergy, all of whom proved keen to introduce the lofty architectural conceptions then current in mainland Europe. Many of the major churches of the country – for example at **Canterbury**, **York**, **St Albans**, **Winchester**, **Worcester** and **Ely** – were rebuilt along Norman lines, with cruciform ground plans and massive cylindrical columns topped by semicircular arches. The finest Norman church was **Durham Cathedral**, begun in 1093 and boasting Europe's first example of large-scale ribbed vaulting. The cathedral also had spectacular zigzag and diamond patterns on its colossal piers, a strong and immediately influential contrast to the austerity of the first generation of Norman churches. Furthermore, an increasing love of decoration was evident in the elaborately carved capitals and blind arcading in Canterbury Cathedral and the beakhead moulding in Lincoln Cathedral. Neither were the Normans idle when it came to the country's parish churches, though the newly intricate ornamental features on dozens of these often owe more to the creative vigour of the Anglo-Saxon masons than they do to the influence of the Normans.

In common with the rest of Europe, the twelfth century brought a dramatic increase in the wealth and power of England's **monastic houses**, a process that had actually begun with the Benedictines before the Conquest. The **Cistercians** were responsible for some of the most splendid foundations, establishing an especially grand group of self-sufficient monasteries in Yorkshire – **Fountains**, **Rievaulx** and **Jervaulx**. These all featured examples of the pointed arch, an idea imported from northern France, where it may have been introduced by Crusaders returning from the Middle East. The reforming Cistercians favoured a plain style, but the native penchant for decoration gradually infiltrated their buildings – for instance at Kirkstall Abbey (c.1152), near Leeds – while other orders had a preference for greater elaboration from the very beginning. Amongst the latter was the **Cluniac** order, whose extravagantly ornate west front of Norfolk's Castle Acre priory (1140–50) is typical.

Incidentally, it's characteristic of the English Church that **bishoprics** were often given to the heads of monastic houses. Thus, many English cathedrals were also monastic churches, which explains the prevalence of **cloisters**, **chapter houses** and other monastic structures within the precincts of English cathedrals.

The Transitional and Early English Styles

Profuse carved decoration and pointed arches were distinctive elements in the evolution of a **Transitional style** from the middle of the twelfth century. This represented a shift away from purely Romanesque forms. The **pointed arch** permitted a far greater flexibility in the relation of the height of a building to its span than had the round arch. It also allowed the introduction of highly scientific systems of vaulting and buttressing, which in turn led to a significant increase of window area in the walls between the buttresses, since these walls no longer had to carry the main weight of the roof. Improvements in masonry techniques also meant that walls could be reduced in thickness, and the cylindrical columns of the Normans replaced by more slender piers.

In England, the first phase of **Gothic** architecture began in earnest in the last quarter of the twelfth century, when Gothic motifs were used at Roche Abbey and **Byland**, both in Yorkshire. However, it was the French-designed **choir** at **Canterbury Cathedral**, built 1175–84, which really established the new style, though admittedly the Gothic themes were somewhat compromised here by being grafted onto the remains of the earlier Anglo-Norman building. This first phase of English Gothic, lasting through most of the thirteenth century, is known as **Early English** (or Pointed or Lancet), and was given its full expression in what is regarded as the first truly Gothic cathedral in England, **Wells**, largely completed in 1190.

Begun shortly afterwards, **Lincoln Cathedral** takes the process of vertical emphasis further, substituting Wells' three-tier nave, which was subdivided horizontally, with wall-shafts that soar all the way to the ceiling. The decoration was also more profuse than anything anywhere in France, never mind England. The influence of Lincoln remained strong in English architecture, though it was resisted by the builders of **Salisbury Cathedral**, which is one of the most homogeneous of the Early English churches, most of it being built in the comparatively short period 1220–65.

A transitional phase in the evolution of Gothic architecture is represented by the **rebuilding of Westminster Abbey** in 1220, when the abbey became the most French of English churches. There was a French influence at work in the flying buttresses that were added to support its greater height, and in the lavish use of **window tracery**, whereby geometric patterns were created by subdividing each window with moulded ribs (or mullions), a device first seen at Reims in 1211.

The Decorated and Perpendicular styles

The development of complicated tracery is one of the chief characteristics of the **Decorated** style, ushered in by Westminster Abbey and by the Angel Choir at Lincoln and the nave of Lichfield, both designed in the late 1250s. The fully blown Decorated style emerged around the end of the thirteenth century and the beginning of the fourteenth, when the cathedral at **Exeter** was almost completely rebuilt, with a dense exuberance of rib vaulting and multiple moulding on the arches and piers. **York Minster**, rebuilt from 1225 and the largest of all English Gothic churches, introduced another innovation associated with this period – **lierne vaulting**, whereby a subsidiary, mainly ornamental, rib is added to the roof complex. Intricately carved roof bosses and capitals are other common features of Decorated Gothic, as is the use of the organic **ogee curve** – ie a curve with a double bend in it. One-off experiments are also characteristic of this period, the most striking examples being the octagonal lantern tower at **Ely** (1320s), and the rebuilding of **Bristol** cathedral (1298–1330), which shows many of the features of the continental hall-church type of design, in which the nave and aisles are roughly the same height.

The style that came to prevail in the second half of the fourteenth century, the severe **Perpendicular**, was the first post-Conquest architecture that was unique to England. This insularity was due partly to the loss of almost all the English possessions in France by the end of the Hundred Years War, and partly to the Black Death, which had depleted the number of craftsmen capable of the elaborate carvings and mouldings characteristic of the Decorated style. Whereas France had progressed to an emphatically curvilinear or "Flamboyant" style, the emphasis in England was on rectilinear design, anticipated in the rebuilding of **Gloucester Cathedral** (1337–57). Here the cloister features the first fully developed **fan vault** while the massive east window is a good example of the new window design, in which the maximization of light is paramount and the tracery organized in vertical compartments. Edward II's tomb – the focal point of Gloucester Cathedral – also exemplifies the wave of **memorial building** during the Perpendicular period.

The chantry tombs at **Winchester Cathedral** and **Tewkesbury Abbey** are resplendent monuments from this period, as is the tomb of the Black Prince in **Canterbury Cathedral**, where the Norman nave was rebuilt after 1379, though it was the addition of the Bell Harry Tower and tracery in the aisle windows that injected the most strongly Perpendicular elements. Henry Yevele, who was responsible for this work at Canterbury, and his contemporary at Winchester, William Wynford, were forerunners of the modern architect, reflecting the gradual elevation of the master-mason into an overall creative and supervisory role.

The turmoil of the Wars of the Roses meant that few new "prestige" buildings were commissioned in the half-century after 1425, though parish churches eagerly embraced the new style, most notably in East Anglia, Somerset and the Cotswolds. The restoration of strong government saw a resurgence of royal patronage and the realization of a triad of major architectural projects in **St George's Chapel**, Windsor, **King's College Chapel**, Cambridge, and **Henry VII's Chapel** in Westminster Abbey, all completed in the reign of Henry VII. By now, walls had become panelled screens filled mostly with stained glass, with the weight transmitted from stone ribs onto bold buttresses that were usually capped with tall pinnacles. King's College developed fan vaulting into an element that extended over the whole nave and harmonized with the windows and wall panelling, but it was the densely sculptured Henry VII's Chapel that took such vaulting to the limit, the complexity heightened by a lavish use of decorative pendants – a rare element in English design.

The Renaissance

Perpendicular motifs remained prominent throughout the Tudor era, with the impact of **Renaissance** architecture confined initially to small decorative features. Such were the terracotta busts of Roman emperors at the otherwise conventionally Tudor **Hampton Court Palace**, to which Henry VIII added a Great Hall with a superb hammer-beam roof similar to that in Westminster Hall (1397–99), albeit here embellished with Italianate details.

The dissemination of the latest ideas in design and decoration came about chiefly through commissions from high-ranking courtiers and statesmen. These notables flamboyantly demonstrated their acquaintance with the sophisticated classical canons in such mansions as **Burghley House**, Lincolnshire (1552–87), and **Longleat**, Wiltshire (1568–80), projects which mingled the Gothic and the Renaissance while also heralding a taste for landscaped parklands in preference to enclosed courtyards. (With Henry VIII's Dissolution of the Monasteries some twenty to thirty percent of England's land was suddenly released into private hands.) The mason at Longleat, Robert Smythson, was probably also the designer of **Hardwick Hall** in Derbyshire (1591–96), celebrated in local rhyme as "Hardwick Hall, more glass than wall" – words which sum up the predilection for huge glazed areas displayed in Elizabethan great houses.

Hatfield House in Hertfordshire, rebuilt 1607–11 by the chief minister of Elizabeth and James I, Robert Cecil, represents a bridge between Elizabethan and Jacobean architecture, which is characterized by a greater infusion of classical ideas. Classicism at this time, however, was considered primarily decorative, as exemplified in the Tower of the Five Orders (1613–18) at the **Bodleian Library** in Oxford, where the Classical Orders as defined by Vitruvius were applied as appendages to a building with mullioned windows, battlements and pinnacles. The unadulterated spirit of the Renaissance did not find full expression in England until **Inigo Jones** (1573–1652) began to apply the lessons learned from his visits to Italy, and in particular from his familiarity with Palladio's rules of proportion and symmetry, as laid out in the Quattro Libri dell'Architettura, published in 1570. Appointed Royal Surveyor to James I in 1615 (a position he held also under Charles I), Jones changed the direction of English architecture with only a handful of works, in which he brilliantly adapted Palladian ideals to English requirements. Three of his most prominent projects were built in London: the **Banqueting House** in Whitehall (1619–22), the first truly classical building to be completed in England since Roman times; the **Queen's House** at Greenwich (1617–35); and **St Paul's Church**, Covent Garden (1630s), the focal point of the first planned city square in England.

Wren and Baroque

Despite Jones's promulgation of classical architecture, the Gothic endured into the seventeenth century, especially in Oxford, where Christ Church was given a magnificent fan-vaulted staircase hall as late as 1640. Oxford's first classical construction, the **Sheldonian Theatre**, was also the first building designed by the artistic heir of Inigo Jones, **Christopher Wren** (1632–1723), who established himself as a brilliant mathematician and astronomer before turning to architecture shortly after the Restoration of 1660. As far as is known, Wren never visited Italy (though he met Bernini, the greatest architect of the day, in Paris), and his work was never so wholeheartedly Italianate as that of Inigo Jones, the influences of French and Dutch architecture contributing to an eclectic style that mingled orthodox classicism with **Baroque** inventiveness.

Wren's work in Oxford was quickly followed by Pembroke College Chapel, Cambridge, but the bulk of his achievement is to be seen in London, where the **Great Fire of 1666** led to a commission for the building of 51 churches. The most striking of these buildings display a remarkable elegance and harmony within the constraints of very cramped sites; they include **St Bride** in Fleet Street, **St Mary-le-Bow** in Cheapside, **St Vedast** in Foster Lane, and, perhaps the finest of all, the domed **St Stephen Walbrook** alongside Mansion House – all of which were rebuilt after partial destruction in World War II. Most monumental of all was Wren's rebuilding of **St Paul's Cathedral** (1675–1710), which was built in a cruciform shape very different from his original radical design, though its principal feature – the massive central dome – was retained.

As Surveyor-General, Wren also rebuilt, extended or altered several royal palaces, including the south and east wings of **Hampton Court** (1689–1700). Other secular works include **Chelsea Hospital** (1682–92), **Trinity College Library**, Cambridge (1676–84), the **Tom Tower of Christ Church**, Oxford (1681–82) – a rare work in the Gothic mode – and, grandest of all, **Greenwich Hospital** (1694–98), a magnificent foil to the Queen's House built by Inigo Jones, and to Wren's own Royal Observatory (1675).

Work at Greenwich Hospital was continued by Wren's only major pupil, **Nicholas Hawksmoor** (1661–1736), whose distinctively muscular form of the Baroque style is seen to best effect in his London churches. Most of these are in the East End with the best being **St George-in-the-East** (1715–23) and **Christ Church**, Spitalfields (1723–29). His exercises in Gothic pastiche included the western towers of **Westminster Abbey** (1734) and **All Souls**

College, Oxford (1716–35), while the mausoleum at **Castle Howard** in Yorkshire (1729) shows close affinities with the Roman Baroque.

The third great English architect of the Baroque era was **John Vanbrugh** (1664–1726), who was famed as a dramatist but lacked any architectural training when he was commissioned by the Earl of Carlisle to design a new country seat at **Castle Howard** (1699–1726). More flamboyant than either Hawksmoor or Wren – both of whom he worked with – Vanbrugh went on to design numerous other grandiose houses, of which the outstanding examples are the gargantuan **Blenheim Palace** (1705–20), the culminating point of English Baroque, and the fortress-like **Seaton Delaval**, not far from Newcastle upon Tyne (1720–28), a building which harks back to the architecture of medieval England.

Gibbs and Palladianism

In the field of church architecture, the most influential architect of the eighteenth century was **James Gibbs** (1682–1754), whose masterpiece, **St Martin-in-the-Fields** in London (1722–26), with its steeple sprouting above a pedimented portico, was widely imitated as a model of how to combine the classical with the Gothic. Gibbs was barred from royal commissions on account of his Catholic and Jacobite sympathies, but he worked at the two universities, designing Cambridge's **Senate House** (1722–30) and the **Fellows' Building** at King's College (1723–49), and Oxford's **Radcliffe Camera** (1737–49), a beautifully sited construction drawing heavily on Gibbs's knowledge of Roman styles. Gibbs was one of the very few architects of his generation to have studied in Italy, which had been cut off by war, but this situation changed when the Treaty of Utrecht (1713) opened up Europe to English aristocrats on the Grand Tour, as the self-educating long holiday on the continent became known. For architecture in England, the immediate result was a rebirth of the **Palladianism** introduced by Inigo Jones a century before, an orthodoxy that was to dominate secular architecture in eighteenth-century England.

The movement was championed by a Whig elite led by **Lord Burlington** (1694–1753), an enthusiastic patron of the arts whose own masterpiece was **Chiswick House** in London (1725), a domed villa closely modelled on Palladio's Villa Rotonda. Burlington collaborated with the decorator, garden designer and architect **William Kent** (1685–1748) in such stately piles as **Holkham Hall** in Norfolk (1734), whose imposing portico and ordered composition typify the break with Baroque dramatics. The third chief player in the return to Renaissance simplicity was **Colen Campbell** (1673–1729), author of the influential Vitruvius Britannicus (1715), a compilation of designs from which architects freely borrowed. Campbell worked closely with Burlington on such works as **Burlington House** in London (1718–19), though his best achievements were two country homes, Houghton Hall, Norfolk (1722), and Mereworth Castle, Kent (1723).

The Palladian idiom was further disseminated by such men as **John Wood** (1704–54), designer of Liverpool Town Hall (1749–54) but better known for the work he did in his native **Bath**, helping to transform the city into a paragon of town planning. His showpieces there are **Queen Square** (1729–36) and the **Circus** (1754), the latter completed by his son, **John Wood the Younger** (1728–81), who went on to design Bath's **Royal Crescent**

(1767–74). The embellishment of Georgian Bath was furthered also by **Robert Adam** (1728–92), a Palladian who designed the town's **Pulteney Bridge** (1769–74). Adam's forte, however, was in the field of domestic architecture, especially in the designing of decorative interiors, where he showed himself to be the most versatile and refined architect of his day. His elaborate concoctions are best displayed in **Syon House** (1762–69) and **Osterley Park** (1761–80), both on the western outskirts of London, and **Kenwood** (1767–79) on the edge of Hampstead Heath, all epitomizing his scrupulous attention to detail as well as his dexterity at large-scale planning. Adam's chief rival was the more fastidious **William Chambers** (1723–96), whose masterpiece, **Somerset House** on London's Aldwych (1776–98), is an academic counterpoint to Adam's dashing originality.

Adam and Chambers competed in a highly active market whose chief patrons regarded themselves as belonging to the most cultivated class in the island's history. Undoubtedly they were among the wealthiest, spending vast sums of money not just on their houses but also on the grounds in which these houses stood. **Landscape gardening** was the quintessential English contribution to European culture in the eighteenth century, and its greatest exponent was **Capability Brown** (1716–83) – so-called because of his custom of assessing the "capabilities" of a landscape. All over England, Brown and his acolytes modified the estates of the landed gentry into "Picturesque" landscapes, an idealization of nature along the lines of the paintings of Poussin and Lorrain, often enhancing the view with a romantic "ruin" or some exotic structure such as a Chinese pagoda or Indian temple.

The nineteenth century

The greatest architect of the late eighteenth and early nineteenth centuries was **John Nash** (1752–1835), whose Picturesque country houses, built in collaboration with the landscapist Humphry Repton (1752–1818), represented just one part of his diverse repertoire. In this versatility Nash was typical of his time, though he is associated above all with the style favoured during the **Regency** of his friend and patron the Prince of Wales (afterwards George IV), a decorous style that owed much to Chambers and Adam, making plentiful use of stucco. His strangest and best-known building was also a commission from the Prince – the orientalized Gothic palace known as the **Brighton Pavilion**. A prolific worker, Nash was responsible for much of the present-day appearance of such **resorts** as Brighton, Weymouth, Cheltenham, Clifton and Tunbridge Wells, as well as numerous parts of central **London**, including the **Haymarket Theatre** (1820), the church of **All Souls**, Langham Place (1822–25), **Clarence House** (1825) and **Carlton House Terrace** (1827). He also planned the layout of **Regent's Park** and **Regent's Street** in London (from 1811), and remodelled **Buckingham Palace** (1826–30), a project that foundered at the death of his patron.

Nash's contemporary, **Sir John Soane** (1753–1837), was more of an inventive antiquarian, his pared-down classical experiments presenting a serious-minded contrast to Nash's extrovert creations. Very little remains of his greatest masterpiece, the **Bank of England** (1788–1833), but his idiosyncratic style is well illustrated by two other buildings in London – his own home on **Lincoln's Inn Fields** (1812–13) and **Dulwich Art Gallery** (1811–14).

Classicism was, however, soon challenged. As early as 1753, the connoisseur Horace Walpole built an ornate villa, **Strawberry Hill** near Twickenham, in an ornate Gothic style. Nash and other exponents of the Picturesque also dabbled in the Gothic, as a passion for romance and medievalism gained ground in literary and intellectual circles. In 1818, when Parliament voted a million pounds for the construction of new Anglican churches, the **Gothic Revival** got properly under way – two-thirds of the churches built under this Act were in a Gothic or near-Gothic style. Many public buildings continued to draw on Renaissance, Greek or Roman influences – notably the town halls of Birmingham and Leeds (1832–50 & 1853–58) and the British Museum (1823–52) – but the pre-eminence of neo-Gothic was confirmed when the Houses of Parliament were rebuilt in that style after the fire of 1834. The contract was given to **Charles Barry** (1795–1860), the designer of the classical Reform Club, but his collaborator, **Augustus Welby Pugin** (1812–52), was to become the unswerving apostle of the neo-Gothic. Nonetheless, it wasn't all one-way traffic: the eminent architect **George Gilbert Scott** (1811–78) submitted a Gothic design for the new government offices (now the Foreign Office) in **Whitehall** (1855–72), but was told to go back to the drawing board and prepare an Italian Renaissance design instead. On the other hand, Scott was able to give rein to his personal tastes in the extravaganzas of **St Pancras Station** (1868–74) and the **Albert Memorial** (1863–72), both based on his preferred Flemish and north Italian Gothic models. When the first English cathedral to be consecrated outside London since the Middle Ages was built at Truro (1880–1910), the approved design was a scholarly exercise in French-influenced Gothic; yet when it came to commissioning the Catholic **Westminster Cathedral** (1895–1903), the design chosen was neo-Byzantine.

This architectural stew was further enriched by a string of engineer-architects, who employed cast iron and other industrial materials in works as diverse as Isambard Kingdom Brunel's **Clifton Suspension Bridge** in Bristol (1829–64) and Joseph Paxton's glass and iron **Crystal Palace** (1851), which was subsequently transferred from London's Hyde Park to the suburb of Sydenham, where it burned down in 1936. The potential of iron and glass was similarly exploited in **Newcastle Central Station** (1846–55), the first of a generation of monumental railway stations incorporating classical motifs and rib-vaulted iron roofs.

John Ruskin (1819–1900) and his disciple **William Morris** (1834–96), leader of the Arts and Crafts Movement, rejected these industrial technologies in favour of traditional materials – such as brick, stone and timber – worked in traditional ways. Morris was not an architect himself, but he did plan the interior of his own home, the **Red House** in Bexley, Kent (1854), from designs by Philip Webb (1831–1915). Unusually, Morris took responsibility for every aspect of the work, as did **Richard Norman Shaw** (1831–1912), whose red-brick, heavily gabled constructions were widely imitated in central London. His best work is displayed in Swan House, Chelsea (1875), Albert Hall Mansions, Kensington (1879) – one of England's earliest apartment blocks – and in Bedford Park, west London (1877), the first of the capital's "garden suburbs".

Another architect to fall under the sway of the Arts and Crafts Movement was **Charles Voysey** (1851–1941), whose clean-cut cottages and houses eschewed all ostentation, depending instead on the meticulous and subtle use of local materials for their effect. The originality of Voysey's work and that of his contemporaries M.H. Baillie Scott (1865–1945) and Ernest Newton (1856–1922) was later debased by scores of speculative suburban builders, though not before their refreshingly simple style had found recognition first in Germany and then across the rest of Europe.

The twentieth century to the present

At the turn of the twentieth century, English architecture was rooted in a nostalgic aesthetic that was typified by **Edwin Lutyens** (1869–1944). Most of Lutyens's early works were country houses in the Arts and Crafts style, but later he moved onto virtuoso classicized structures, such as the elegant Baroque of what he himself termed "Wrenaissance" and a more sober neo-Georgianism that helped initiate a widespread Georgian Revival. However, perhaps his most striking achievements in England are the one-off **Castle Drogo** on Dartmoor (1910–30), the last of the great country houses, and the **Cenotaph** on London's Whitehall (1918), a masterpiece of stripped-down monumentalism.

The revivalist tendency prevailed throughout the early decades of the century, but an awareness of more radical architectural trends surfaced in isolated projects in the 1930s. One of these was **Senate House** in London's Bloomsbury (1932), designed by **Charles Holden** (1875–1960), who was also responsible for some of London's Underground stations, notably **Arnos Grove** (1932). Perhaps the most successful applications of the austere International Modern style were achieved by the **Tecton group**, led by the Russian immigrant Lubetkin, whose **Penguin Pool** in London Zoo (1934) is a witty demonstration of the plastic possibilities of concrete.

Yet general acceptance of modern style had to wait for the reforming atmosphere of the years immediately following World War II, and in particular for the 1951 **Festival of Britain** on London's South Bank, which showcased the latest technological marvels. Many of the festival pavilions were designed by **Basil Spence** (1907–76), whose best-known work was the replacement of the bombed **Coventry Cathedral**, incorporating defiantly modernist detail into a neo-Gothic structure (1951–59). The only architectural remnant of the Festival of Britain is the **Royal Festival Hall** (1949–51), an immensely practicable and handsome structure. The site was later augmented by the addition of the far less attractive **National Theatre** (1967–77) by **Denys Lasdun** (1914–2001), a Tecton architect who remained true to the principles of the group.

The massive postwar rebuilding programme was conditioned by an acute housing crisis and severe financial constraints, so the emphasis was on the utilization of prefabricated technologies to get as many units built as quickly and as cheaply as possible, with little overall planning or consideration for the environment. The unpopularity of the ubiquitous tower blocks was aggravated by the insensitivity shown by speculative developers, who were given almost free rein in the construction of office buildings and shopping centres throughout the country – Plymouth and Southampton have especially hideous examples.

Some of the more interesting architecture of the 1960s was created at the new "red-brick" universities, notable examples being Spence's **Sussex University** at Brighton (1961) and Lasdun's **University of East Anglia** at Norwich (1963). Among a younger generation who designed some of their first works for the universities were **James Stirling** (1926–92) and **Norman Foster** (b. 1935), architects who, along with **Richard Rogers** (b. 1933), initially found greater scope working abroad than in Britain. That said, Stirling's Postmodern extension for London's Tate Gallery (1989) was one of the more controversial projects of the period, and Rogers' Lloyd's Building (1978–86) in London is a bold hi-tech display along the lines of his Pompidou Centre in Paris. Factory sites provided Foster with several English contracts, though the building which first raised his profile was his glass-tent terminal at London's **Stansted Airport** (1991).

A major, and not particularly helpful, influence on recent British architecture has come not from an architect but from Prince Charles, who, posing as the voice of common sense, has campaigned against architectural modernism. The most obvious repercussion was in regard to the **Sainsbury Wing** (1991) at London's National Gallery, a commission that was eventually handed to Postmodernist supremos Robert Venturi and Denise Scott-Brown, who produced a safe pastiche of Neoclassicism. One architect whose works found critical acclaim – without royal blessing – is **Michael Hopkins**, who rose to prominence with his eye-catching Mound Stand for the Lord's Cricket Ground, followed by a delicate balancing act at the **Glyndebourne Opera House** (1994) and his **Inland Revenue Headquarters** in Nottingham (1995), while his latest work, **Portcullis House** in London (2001), proved more controversial.

The century finished with a rush to regenerate inner-city brownfield sites. Rogers' **Millennium Dome** (1999), in a rundown part of Greenwich, was heavily criticized – though more for its content than the space itself – while a Foster-dominated London scene produced the Millennium Bridge and **British Museum Great Court** (both 2000), the Greater London Assembly (2002) and the Swiss Re skyscraper (2003) in the City, nicknamed the "Erotic Gherkin". Most spectacular of all London's redevelopments, however, was the transformation of Giles Gilbert Scott's South Bank power station into the world's largest modern art gallery, **Tate Modern** (2000), by Herzog & de Meuron.

Not to be outdone by the capital, the resurgence of formerly industrial cities saw such eye-catching developments as Gateshead's **BALTIC** arts centre (Ellis Williams Architects, 2002), Manchester's **Imperial War Museum North** (Libeskind, 2002) and the demolition of Birmingham's much-derided Bullring and its replacement by a collection of buildings dominated by Future Systems' shimmering organic **Selfridge's** department store (2003).

Wildlife

Almost every part of England has a history of human settlement, a history that has had a profound effect on the country's wildlife, bequeathing a patchwork of woodland, heathland, meadowland and a miscellany of other habitats. An inventory of England's wildlife could run for hundreds of pages, and there are plenty of specialized publications for those who want to get to grips with the subject. What follows is a necessarily brief overview of the species to be found in England.

Wild flowers

It may seem paradoxical, but it was the traditional use of old habitats that created England's wealth of wild flowers. Chalk grassland, the habitat of yellow vetches, pinkish restharrow, blue bellflower and many wild orchids, is a typical example. This abundance of wild flowers is due partly to the lime in the soil, and partly to its impoverishment by centuries of **grazing** by sheep or rabbits – the poor soil prevents ranker plants from elbowing out the flowers, and any that do take root are quickly cropped short by the animals. The reason that many downland flanks are today developing patches of coarse grass and scrub is that grazing has ceased.

The artificial **fertilization** of downland and meadowland, by encouraging the growth of grasses, wipes out wild flowers almost as effectively as spraying a herbicide. Communities of pepper saxifrage, great burnet and adder's-tongue fern are all good indicators of old meadowland, but a consequence of modern high-tech farming is that many of the modest downland and meadowland flowers are now rare on farmland and are more likely to be observed on **roadside verges**. Indeed, the latter sometimes constitute a record of the botany lost from the ploughed and planted field on the other side of the fence. Sadly, these displaced species have no security here, their cramped populations being too small to guarantee survival after harsh summers or insect attacks. Hardly at risk, however, are the cow parsleys – in the plural since their massed ranks disguise a succession of different species. Originally growing in woodland glades, **cow parsleys** are now typical of English country lanes, and once again their presence is largely determined by human interference – ie by the intensity of trimming.

It's a similar story with **woodland flowers**, whose growth is encouraged by traditional **coppicing**, which regularly opens up the soil to the sun. Indeed the typical thick carpet of **bluebells** is as much due to coppicing as to the mild Atlantic climate, and masses of bluebells can often indicate an old wood, especially if backed by early purple orchids and wood anemones. **Snowdrop** woods are often indicative of the former presence of a monastery – a European flower with a natural range that ends in Normandy, the snowdrop was grown here to celebrate Candlemas in February, and quickly spread beyond the monastery walls. Of course, soil conditions and other natural factors are extremely influential too, resulting in different types of flower being found in different types of woodland. Thus some **beech woods** are famous for their white or purplish **helleborines** and other orchids; **ash woods**, which grow on limestone, are known for **lily of the valley** and the dusky red **bloody cranesbill**.

Ancient **ploughland** was distinguished by blue cornflower and yellow corn marigold, but only **poppies** seem able to survive modern farming. **Heathers** are characteristic of the bleak moorlands, where – in the very wet areas – you might also find the delicate flowers of **cranberry**, the brilliant yellow **bog asphodel** and the insect-trapping **sundew**. The higher zones of the Lake District and Pennine hills might be as colourful as the Alpine slopes were it not for centuries of hard grazing, but white **mountain avens**, dusky **saxifrage** and pink **moss campion** can still be found on rock faces out of the reach of sheep. On **heathland**, but not moorland, heathers are often accompanied by yellow **broom** and **gorse**; but both share yellow **tormentil**, pink **lousewort** and dainty blue **harebell**.

English **wetland** and **water** plants have evolved from land-growing species, a kinship that's evident from the close resemblance of the white **water crowfoots** and the buttercups – only the **water lilies** have no surviving relatives on dry land. Among the most attractive wild flowers of these habitats are the gold **kingcup** – popular with Victorian botanists and thus often found in the vicinity of granges and rectories – and the **bogbean**, with its creamy pink-fringed petals. Pollution and disturbance are major threats to wetland plants, as is evident on the Norfolk Broads, where holiday craft have eradicated plants from all but a few lagoons.

Communities of wild flowers manage to flourish even in the seemingly harsh conditions of the **seashore**, none of them more colourful than the blue-tinted **sea holly** and the yellow **horned-poppy**, which grow out on the bare sand. A host of flowers grows on the back shore, where the sand is harder and broken shells add lime to the ground, while on the edges of salt marshes you'll come across **sea lavender**, **sea aster** and **thrift**, among a variety of other species.

Birds

The destruction of the countryside has had a severe impact on England's 130 resident **bird species** – even the ubiquitous blackbird perhaps totals only three million pairs, and these numbers can plummet in a harsh winter. **Seabirds** such as gannets, gulls, fulmars and cormorants safe on their offshore bolt holes are virtually the only species unaffected by increasing urbanization. Nonetheless, an extraordinary variety of birds still thrives on mainland England.

Some birds are uniquely adapted for life with certain trees – such as the crossbill, which has a beak that has evolved to prise open fir cones – but in general, **woodland birds** select their habitat according to the profile of the wood rather than the actual species of tree it contains. Thus an acre of dense oak wood may hold more than a dozen types of songbird, while in the more open beech wood only the **wood warbler** is likely to nest. The **nightingale**, found only in the south of England, prefers the low bushy growth of recently coppiced woods, which it abandons seven years after the cut – another example of the link between land use and wildlife.

Over the centuries some species have become typical of the **farmed countryside**, such as the **rook**, **linnet**, **bunting** and the **barn owl**, which was encouraged to nest in barns as a rat catcher – often a hole was left in a side wall for the bird to enter. A recent arrival is the **collared dove**, which first nested in England in 1955, and is partial to the spills of grain from barley farms. The

pheasant, originally raised and released for sport, now breeds wild in large numbers.

Game birds are a case apart, however, and their control can be an influence on the countryside. Shooting woods are often landscaped to steer pheasants into the line of fire, while belts of weed are now being left around fields to sustain **partridges**. The August **grouse** shoot has an effect on moorland, as large areas of heather are burnt to encourage fresh green growth to feed the birds.

Numerous species are adapted to specific environments, such as the **freshwater** birds, which split into two general groups – the **dipper** and a few other species that like the rushing upland streams, and the larger group that includes the "diving" and "dabbling" **ducks** found on lowland waters.

Birds that are found in every type of habitat are the opportunistic **scavengers** such as the **crow**, which is now so widespread that its "natural" home is not known. Persecution is sometimes a key factor in the distribution of scavengers and **raptors**. For instance, a couple of hundred years of shotguns and gamekeeping have forced the **golden eagle** back to one or two pairs in the Lake District, whilst the once common **red kite** has been pushed out to Wales. Similarly, peregrines, the bane of pigeon-racers' lives, are now found only on remote moors and sea cliffs and even **buzzards** are far from numerous.

Migrants are a key feature of English birdlife. **Swifts**, **swallows** and **martins** are easy to spot at the start of the summer, and of course the **cuckoo** has a distinctive call, as does the **chiffchaff**, an even earlier arrival from the south, with an unmistakable song that gives it its name. Many birds retreat from the cold of the Arctic to winter here, common examples including the **brent goose**, **barnacle goose**, **whooper swan** and **Bewick's swan**. Just as many species stop off on longer winter journeys to rest and feed, with English estuaries often safeguarding European stocks – the Dee for example regularly feeds hundred-thousand-strong flocks of **grey plover**, **oystercatcher** and numerous other waders.

Migration can also be a relatively local affair, however. The **curlew**, a wader with a particularly plaintive cry, nests on the moors of the Pennines and elsewhere but in winter flies down to the seashore. The **kingfisher** similarly forsakes the frozen streams for the coast. Non-migratory birds are surprisingly mobile in winter too, when hedgerow blackbirds often fly far afield in search of food and even blue tits, which might seem to have a range not much bigger than a back garden, may well fly daily miles across a county.

Mammals

Most of England's **mammals** are originally **woodland** species that moved in when the wild wood became established. There have been some changes since then, of course: the wolf and bear have gone, as has the beaver, which has left just a memory of its presence in the name of Beverley and a few other town names. The wildcat has left England for Scotland, but the **pine marten** is just about holding on, thanks to the massive spread of conifer plantations.

There have been changes of habitat too: the **red deer**, for example, forced out of the woodlands by coppicing, is now found wild on open upland such as the Lake District, the herds seen in forests and parks being semi-domesticated. The **fallow deer** was brought over by the Romans and became a favourite target for the baronial hunt. The native **roe deer**, hunted almost to extinction two hundred years ago, was reintroduced, and is now the deer most often seen in the open countryside, although like all deer species they are shy and usually active only around dawn and dusk. **Sika deer**, slightly smaller than red deer, were introduced in the seventeenth century, while the pig-like **muntjac** and small **Chinese water deer** are more recent arrivals, descended from wildlife park escapees. Other mammalian oddities are the goats living wild in the Lake District, the semi-wild ponies of the New Forest and Dartmoor, the wild boar that occasionally harass walkers in the southeast and, most bizarrely, the wallabies that bounce around the Peak District.

Badgers link the woodlands and more open terrain, preferring to dig their burrows (or setts) among trees, though their foraging trails run out into the fields where they dig for young rabbits and earthworms. The sett entrance is a wide, clean hole – if you see a sizeable burrow littered with food remnants, the odds are that you're looking at a **fox**'s "earth". Badgers and foxes are generally regarded as nocturnal, but it's likely that their predilection for the dark is a result of contact with humans – foxes are often active during daylight hours in areas where they feel safe and badgers forage by day in quiet places such as remote coastal valleys. However, the **dormouse** – a species recognized by its squirrel-like tail – is a truly nocturnal animal, and one of the few true indigenous hibernators. It is typical of hazel coppice, building its nest from the bark of the honeysuckle that is usually found growing here – peeled stems can be the clue to its presence. In built-up areas, in addition to **foxes** and **hedgehogs**, **bats** are a familiar sight at dusk. Contrary to myth, they rarely nest in belfries (with their sensitive hearing, the bells would drive them mad), preferring the warm roof-spaces and cladding of modern houses.

The **grey squirrel**, one of the most familiar English "wild" animals, is in fact an interloper from North America and one that has virtually ousted the native red squirrel – though there's evidence that a strain of super-resilient red is fighting back in the Merseyside area. **Hares** are native – the brown hare found in the lowlands, the grey in some Pennine areas – but the **rabbit** was introduced in Norman times to be raised for its meat and fur. Having escaped and bred relentlessly, the rabbit has for centuries been a natural lawnmower, helping to create the fine sward of the chalk downlands and other grasslands.

Rabbits are preyed on by **stoats** and **weasels**, which also prey on **mice**, **voles** and **shrews**. These similar small species may share some larders, but generally do not compete with each other for food: bank voles, for example, eat seeds, field voles eat grass, and the sharp-nosed shrew has a mainly insect diet and is almost ceaselessly active, needing to eat its own weight every day. Like the blue cornflower, the **harvest mouse** has fled the modern arable fields, now making its nest high amongst the waterway reedbeds. Of the purely wetland species, the **water rat** (in fact a vole) is widespread and the otter is making a comeback in a few areas, despite water pollution and disturbance to its nesting "holts". The otter also has a serious competitor in the **mink**, a species that escaped from fur farms but is well equipped to survive in the wild, being capable of swimming after fish and climbing up to birds' nests.

On the coast, **common seals** haul out on the mud flats of the Wash to give birth in June, whereas **grey seals** are more common on rocky coasts, where they give birth in noisy "rookeries" in December. Only decades ago, almost every seaside resort used to boast its own **porpoises** or **dolphins**; such semi-resident animals have largely disappeared from the bays, although visitors are sometimes seen, and the occasional whale might swim up one of the larger estuaries.

Reptiles, fish and insects

For the **adder** (England's only venomous species) and **grass snake**, abandoned railway cuttings offer a palatable replacement for more natural habitats – the latter is especially fond of wet places. Things are more difficult for the **smooth snake**, which is totally reliant on fragmented heathland and is therefore now comparatively rare – the same is true of the **sand lizard**. The **common lizard** has fared better. The clearance of field ponds means that springtime frog spawn is harder to find – the modern **frog** stronghold is in fact the garden pond. **Common toads** rely more on ancestral breeding ponds, to which they travel miles: some local conservation groups even organize toad patrols at key road crossings. The scuttling **natterjack toad** is also rare, restricted to a few sand dunes and similar sites. **Newts** are most obvious in spring – like the other amphibians they tend to spend most of the year hidden away on land.

The most natural of the **fish** populations are those of the classic game fish, the native **brown trout** and **salmon**, the first still plentiful in the downland streams of the south and the mountain streams of the north, the latter migratory and nowadays only common in the tumbling northern rivers. England's coarse fish – all freshwater species unrelated to the salmon family – have widely interbred with specimens raised in reservoirs and farms for sport; similarly the American rainbow trout, once found only in commercial pens, has escaped to breed wild in some areas. That other famed migrator, the **eel**, is still caught in numbers in the Somerset levels and in the East Anglian fens.

There are over three thousand different species of **beetle** in England – but few are noticed apart from the sizeable **may bug** and **stag beetle**, both most common near old semi-natural oak woods in the south. Bees, flies, gnats and wasps are of course very widespread, as are the dazzling **mayflies** and **dragonflies**, to be found on England's cleaner bodies of water. Many species of **butterfly** are fairly widespread in scrubby places, with the gorgeous **peacock butterfly** often seen in gardens. Deserted railway cuttings are a stronghold of some of the commoner **browns** and **skippers**. Generally, though, butterflies are choosy about the plants on which they lay their eggs, which means that many species are closely linked with very specific habitats. The **Adonis** and **chalkhill blues** need the low-growing horsehoe vetch of old downland, while the **fritillaries** need the violets of old oak woodland and the most exotic of all, the **swallowtail**, relies on a relative of cow parsley that grows in the Norfolk Broads, and is thus rarely seen elsewhere. However, some swallowtails may fly in from France during the summer, when the migrant **clouded yellow** often arrives in large numbers along the south coast.

Books

Most of the books listed below are in print and in paperback – those that are out of print (o/p) should be easy to track down in second-hand book shops. Finally, while we recommend all those we've listed below, we do have our favourites: we've indicated those that we particularly recommend with a ★.

Travel and journals

★ **Bill Bryson** *Notes from a Small Island*. Bryson's best-selling and highly amusing account of his farewell journey round Britain.

William Cobbett *Rural Rides.* First published in 1830, Cobbett's account of his various fact-finding tours bemoaned the death of the old rural England and its customs, while decrying both the growth of cities and the iniquities suffered by the exploited urban poor.

★ **Nick Danziger** *Danziger's Britain*. A well-timed journey through the "other Britain" of council estates and poverty. Captures the mood of the underclass created by Thatcher and sets a tall order for the present Blairite administration.

Daniel Defoe *Tour through the Whole Island of Great Britain* (o/p). Classic travelogue, opening a window onto Britain in the 1720s.

John Hillaby *Journey Through Britain*. An account of an epic 1100-mile walk from Lands End to John O'Groats encapsulates much of the state of the country (and countryside) in the late 1960s.

Charles Jennings *Up North*. A provocative, but very readable account of a journey round the north of England, by a self-confessed southerner.

Samuel Pepys *The Diary of Samuel Pepys*. Pepys kept a voluminous diary from 1660 until 1669, recording the fall of the Commonwealth, the Restoration, the Great Plague and the Great Fire, as well as describing the daily life of the nation's capital.

J.B. Priestley *English Journey*. Quirky account of Bradford-born author's travels around England in the 1930s.

Jonathan Raban *Coasting*. Trip around the coast of England, with the occasional trip ashore in order to make supercilious remarks about the locals.

Paul Theroux *The Kingdom by the Sea*. Thoroughly bad-tempered critique of a depressed and drizzly nation.

Dorothy Wordsworth *The Grasmere Journals*. Engaging diaries of William's sister, with whom he shared Dove Cottage in the Lake District.

History, society and politics

G. N. Garmonsway (ed) *Anglo-Saxon Chronicle*. Everyman have published a bargain basement 295-page edition of the monk-compiled *Chronicle* for the last thirty years.

Julian Barnes *Letters from London: 1990–1995*. Social and cultural commentary from this *New Yorker* column, covering the fall of Thatcher and the emergence of Blair.

★ **Asa Briggs** *Social History of England.* Immensely accessible overview of English life from Roman times to the 1980s.

Beatrix Campbell *Diana, Princess of Wales: How sexual politics shook the monarchy.* A little hastily written perhaps, but still the most penetrating insight into the life and times of Diana – and the appalling callousness of her in-laws. Read this and you'll never want Charles to be king (if you ever did).

★ **Alan Clark** *Diaries.* Candid, conceited and often cutting insight into the heart of Thatcher's government by this controversial former minister. Easily the most interesting of the barrow loads of political memoirs churned out in the 1980s and 1990s.

Linda Colley *Britons: Forging the Nation 1707-1837.* Successful and immaculately researched book that offers all sorts of fresh insights into eighteenth-century Britain and the evolution of a national identity.

Norman Davies *The Isles.* Chunky but immaculately written tome that covers the history of the British Isles. Its strength is in its explorations of changing national identities and its willingness to tie its subject in with mainland/mainstream Europe.

Friedrich Engels *The Condition of the Working Class in England.* Portrait of life in England's hellish industrial towns, written in 1844 when Engels was only 24.

Gretchen Gerzina *Black England.* An interesting study of the role of black people in Britain's history.

Mark Girouard *Life in the English Country House.* Fascinating documentation of day-to-day existence of the landed gentry; packed with the sort of facts that get left out by tour guides.

Christopher Hill *The English Revolution; The World Turned Upside-Down.* Britain's foremost Marxist historian, Hill is without doubt the most interesting writer on the Civil War and Commonwealth period.

★ **Eric Hobsbawm** *Industry and Empire.* Ostensibly an economic history of Britain from 1750 to the late 1960s charting Britain's rise and fall as a world power, Hobsbawm's great skill lies in detailed analysis of the effects on ordinary people.

W.G. Hoskins *The Making of the English Landscape.* Absorbing account of the changing English countryside from pre-Roman times to the present day.

Will Hutton *The State We're In.* One of the most influential books to be published in the last decade offered both an incisive analysis of British society and a virtual manifesto for an incoming Labour government.

Arthur Marwick *British Society since 1945.* Readable social history, taking you up to the late 1980s.

Brian Moynahan *The British Century.* A lavish coffee-table book telling the story of the twentieth century in black-and-white photographs.

★ **George Orwell** *The Road to Wigan Pier; Down and Out in Paris and London. Wigan Pier* depicts the effects of the Great Depression on the industrial communities of Lancashire and Yorkshire; *Down and Out* is Orwell's tramp's-eye view of the world, written with first-hand experience – the London section is particularly harrowing.

Jeremy Paxman *The English: A portrait of a People.* Paxman is a well-known British TV interviewer and newsman, renowned for his penetrating questions and acerbic style. This well-received book explores the character of the English as he sees it – from attitudes to sex and sport to the emotionalism of Princess Diana's funeral – and the ways it is in flux.

Sheila Rowbotham *Hidden from History*. An uncompromising account of the last 300 years of women's oppression in Britain alongside a cogent analysis of the ways in which key female figures have been written out of history.

W.A. Speck *A Concise History of Britain*. Straightforward political history from 1707 to 1975.

★ **A.J.P. Taylor** *English History 1914–45*. Thought-provoking survey from Britain's finest populist historian.

★ **E.P. Thompson** *The Making of the English Working Class*. A seminal text – essential reading for anyone who wants to understand the fabric of English society.

G.M. Trevelyan *English Social History*. A "history of people with the politics left out" in Trevelyan's own words – liberal social history from Chaucer to 1901.

Venerable Bede *Ecclesiastical History of the English People*. First-ever English history, written in seventh-century Northumbria.

Regional guides

Paul Bailey (ed) *Oxford Book of London* (o/p). Typically authoritative Oxford anthology of writings, observations and opinions about the capital.

Andrew Davies *The People's Guide to London* (o/p). An alternative history of central London and its landmarks, focusing on the ordinary people involved.

Christopher Hibbert (ed) *Pimlico County History Guides* (o/p). An informative series giving a detailed history of selected English counties. Those covered include Bedfordshire, Cambridgeshire, Dorset, Lincolnshire, Norfolk, Oxfordshire, Somerset (with Bath and Bristol), Suffolk and Sussex.

Daphne du Maurier *Vanishing Cornwall*. Good overall account of Cornwall from an author who lived most of her life there.

Simon Jenkins *England's Thousand Best Churches*. Jenkins is a well-known UK journalist and this superb book describes the pick of England's churches in lucid detail. Hanily divided up into counties with a star system to indicate the best of the best. Also available is *England's Thousand Best Houses*, which is just as good.

Jan Morris *Oxford*. Adulatory but inspiring collection on Oxford by the famous travel writer and cityphile.

Alan Myers *Myers's Literary Guide: Writers in the North East*. Exhaustive account of the Northeast's literary heritage, including details of any writer who ever spent any time in the region.

Pathfinder Walks Series of practical guides with maps and route descriptions to popular outdoor spots such as the Yorkshire Dales, Chilterns, Cornwall and Cotswolds.

W. G. Sebald *Rings of Saturn*. Hard to categorise, this intriguing book is a heady mix of novel, travel, memoir and rumination. The travel focuses on East Anglian coast walk and there are several plum historical accounts of those that have lived there, including Joseph Conrad.

★ **A. Wainwright** *A Coast to Coast Walk*. Beautiful palm-sized guide by acclaimed English hiker and Lake District expert. Printed from his handwritten notes and sketched maps. Also in the series are seven authoritative books covering a variety of walks and climbs in the Lake District.

Ben Weinreb and Christopher Hibbert *The London Encyclopaedia*. More than a thousand pages of concisely presented and well-illustrated information on London past and present – the most fascinating single book on the capital.

Gilbert White *Natural History of Selborne*. Masterpiece of nature writing, observing the seasons in a Hampshire village.

Which? *Good Bed & Breakfast Guide*. Thoroughly researched, annually updated book describing in detail several hundred of the UK's prime B&Bs. Which? also publish a comparable *Best Hotels* and *Best Country Pubs*. All are the best of their sort on the market.

Art, architecture and archeology

John Betjeman *Ghastly Good Taste, Or, A Depressing Story of the Rise and Fall of English Architecture*. Classy – and classic – one-hundred page justification of its title written by one of England's shrewdest poet-commentators. First published in 1970.

Nicholas Best and Jason Hawkes *Historic Britain from the Air*. Beautiful aerial photos illustrate this geographical overview of Britain from Roman times to the aftermath of the Blitz.

Richard Bisgrove *The National Trust Book of the English Garden* (o/p). Excellent socio-cultural-botanical history, making the best introduction to the subject.

Robert Harbison *Shell Guide to English Parish Churches* (o/p). Refreshingly opinionated and lushly illustrated survey of some of England's finest buildings.

Samantha Hardingham *London: A guide to recent architecture* A handy pocket-sized book detailing the best of the capital's modern buildings.

Andrew Hayes *Archaeology of the British Isles* (o/p). Useful introduction to the subject from Stone Age caves to early medieval settlements.

Thomas Packenham *Meetings With Remarkable Trees*. Unusual but intriguing large-format picture book about the author's favourite sixty trees, delving into their character as much as the botany.

Nikolaus Pevsner *The Englishness of English Art*. Wide-ranging romp through English art concentrating on Hogarth, Reynolds, Blake and Constable, including a section on the Perpendicular style and landscape gardening.

Pevsner and others *The Buildings of England*. Magisterial series, at least one volume per county, covering just about every inhabitable structure in the country. This project was initially a one-man show, but later authors have revised Pevsner's text, inserting newer buildings but generally respecting the founder's personal tone.

T.W. Potter *Roman Britain*. Generously illustrated account of Roman occupation written by the British Museum's own curators.

Literary classics

Jane Austen *Pride and Prejudice*; *Sense and Sensibility*; *Emma*; *Persuasion*. All-time classics on manners, society and the pursuit of the happy ever after; all laced with bathos and ironic plot twists.

R.D. Blackmore *Lorna Doone*. Blackmore's swashbuckling, melodramatic romance, set on Exmoor, has done more for West Country tourism than anything else since.

James Boswell *The Life of Samuel Johnson*. England's most famous man of letters and pioneer dictionary-maker has his engagingly low-life Scottish biographer to thank for the longevity of his reputation.

Charlotte Brontë *Jane Eyre*. Deep and harrowing and quietly feminist story of a much put-upon governess.

Emily Brontë *Wuthering Heights*. The ultimate bodice-ripper, complete with volcanic passions, craggy landscapes, ghostly presences and gloomy villagers.

John Bunyan *Pilgrim's Progress*. Simple, allegorical tale of hero Christian's struggle to achieve salvation.

Samuel Butler *The Way of All Flesh*. Popular Edwardian novel debunking orthodox Victorian pieties, partly set in Nottinghamshire.

★ **Geoffrey Chaucer** *Canterbury Tales*. Fourteenth-century collection of bawdy verse tales told during a pilgrimage to Becket's shrine at Canterbury and translated into modern English blank verse.

Daniel Defoe *Journal of a Plague Year*. An account of the Great Plague seen through the eyes of an East End saddler and written some sixty years after the event.

Charles Dickens *Bleak House*; *David Copperfield*; *Little Dorritt*; *Oliver Twist*; *Hard Times*. Many of Dickens' novels are set in London, including *Bleak House*, *Oliver Twist* and *Little Dorritt*, which contain some of his most trenchant pieces of social analysis; *Hard Times*, however, is set in a Lancashire mill town, while *David Copperfield* draws on Dickens' own unhappy experiences as a boy, with much of the action taking place in Kent and Norfolk.

George Eliot *Scenes of Clerical Life*; *Middlemarch*; *Mill on the Floss*. Eliot (real name Mary Ann Evans) wrote mostly about the county of her birth, Warwickshire, setting for the three depressing tales from her fictional debut, *Scenes of Clerical Life*. *Middlemarch* is a gargantuan portrayal of English provincial life prior to the Reform Act of 1832, while *Mill on the Floss* is based on her own childhood experiences.

Henry Fielding *Tom Jones*. Mock-epic comic novel detailing the exploits of its lusty orphan-hero, set in Somerset and London.

Elizabeth Gaskell *Sylvia's Lovers*; *Mary Barton*. *Sylvia's Lovers* is set in a Whitby (Monkshaven in the novel) beset by press gangs, while *Mary Barton* takes place in Manchester and has strong Chartist undertones.

Thomas Hardy *Far from the Madding Crowd*; *The Mayor of Casterbridge*; *Tess of the D'Urbervilles*; *Jude the Obscure*. Hardy's novels contain some famously evocative descriptions of his native Dorset, but at the time of their publication it was Hardy's defiance of conventional pieties that attracted most attention: *Tess*, in which the heroine has a baby out of wedlock and commits murder, shocked his contemporaries, while his bleakest novel, the Oxford-set *Jude the Obscure*, provoked such a violent response that Hardy gave up novel-writing altogether.

Jerome K. Jerome *Three Men in a Boat*. Light-hearted accident-prone paddle on the River Thames.

Rudyard Kipling *Stalky & Co*. Nine stories about a mischievous trio of schoolboys, drawn from Kipling's experiences of public school in Devon.

Sir Thomas Malory *La Morte d'Arthur*. Fifteenth-century tales of King Arthur and the Knights of the Round Table, written while the author was in London's Newgate Prison.

Thomas De Quincey *Confessions of an English Opium Eater*. Tripping out with the most famous literary drug-taker after Coleridge – *Fear and Loathing in Las Vegas* it isn't, but neither is this a simple cautionary tale.

William Shakespeare *Complete Works*. The entire output at a bargain price. For individual plays, you can't beat the Arden Shakespeare series, each volume containing illuminating notes and good introductory essays.

Lawrence Sterne *Tristram Shandy*. Anarchic, picaresque eighteenth-century ramblings based on life in a small English village, and full of bizarre textual devices – like an all-black page in mourning for one of the characters.

William Makepeace Thackeray *Vanity Fair*. A sceptical but compassionate overview of English capitalist society by one of the leading realists of the mid-nineteenth century.

Anthony Trollope *Barchester Towers*. The "Barsetshire" novels, of which Barchester Towers is the best known, are set in and around a fictional version of Salisbury.

Izaak Walton *Compleat Angler*. Light-hearted, seventeenth-century fishing guide set on London's River Lea, sprinkled with poems and songs, which has gone through more reprints than any other comparable book in the English language.

Modern works

Peter Ackroyd *English Music*. A typical Ackroyd novel, constructing parallels between interwar London and distant epochs to conjure a kaleidoscopic vision of English culture. His other novels, such as *Chatterton*, *Hawksmoor* and *The House of Doctor Dee*, are variations on his preoccupation with the English psyche's darker depths.

Kingsley Amis *Lucky Jim*. Difficult to believe that an establishment figure like Amis was once one of the "Angry Young Men" of the 1950s. *Lucky Jim*, the novel that made him famous, is hilariously funny in the opinion of many.

Martin Amis *London Fields*. "Ferociously witty, scabrously scatological and balefully satirical" observation of low-life London, or pretentious drivel from literary London's favourite bad boy, depending on your viewpoint.

Kate Atkinson *Behind the Scenes At the Museum*. Amusing, lucid and highly engaging saga about an extended Yorkshire family.

Arnold Bennett *Anna of the Five Towns*; *Clayhanger* trilogy. Bennett's first novel, *Anna* is the story of a miser's daughter and, like the later *Clayhanger* trilogy, is set in the Potteries.

★ **Joseph Conrad** *The Secret Agent*. Spy story based on the 1906 anarchist bombing of Greenwich Observatory, exposing the hypocrisies of both the police and anarchists.

Helen Fielding *Bridget Jones's Diary*. Originating as a newspaper column, Fielding's fictional account of contemporary female "neuroses" proved to be the literary phenomenon of the late 1990s, spawning a host of lesser imitators.

Ford Madox Ford *Parade's End*. One of the great unread masterpieces of English literature, this evocation of the passing of old Tory England in the aftermath of World War I is superb.

E.M. Forster *Howard's End*. Bourgeois angst in Hertfordshire and Shropshire; the best book by one of the country's best-loved modern novelists.

John Fowles *The Collector*; *The French Lieutenant's Woman*; *Daniel Martin*. The

Collector, Fowles' first novel, is a psychological thriller in which the heroine is kidnapped by a psychotic pools-winner, the story being told once by each protagonist. *The French Lieutenant's Woman*, set in Lyme Regis on the Dorset coast, is a tricksy neo-Victorian novel with a famous DIY ending. *Daniel Martin* is a dense, realistic novel set in postwar Britain.

Stella Gibbons *Cold Comfort Farm*. Merciless parody of primitivist rural fiction of the type popularized by the likes of Mary Webb.

William Golding *The Spire*. Atmospheric novel centred on the building of a cathedral spire, taking place in a thinly disguised medieval Salisbury.

Robert Graves *Goodbye to All That*. Horrific and wryly humorous memoirs of boarding school and World War I trenches, followed by postwar trauma and life in Wales, Oxford and Egypt.

★ **Graham Greene** *Brighton Rock*; *The Human Factor*; *The Heart of the Matter*. Three of the best from the prolific Greene: *Brighton Rock* is a melancholic thriller with heavy Catholic overtones, set in the criminal underworld of a seaside resort; *The Human Factor*, written some forty years later, probes the underworld of London's spies; while *The Heart of the Matter* is a searching and very English novel that noses round the Anglo-Catholic mind.

Nick Hornby *Fever Pitch*; *High Fidelity*. Hornby made his name with *Fever Pitch*, an autobiographical account of his obsession with Arsenal FC from teenage years to 30-something. *High Fidelity* is a fictionalized account of another obsession – records and record collecting – and examines the modern male and his foibles with caustic incision.

A.E. Housman *A Shropshire Lad*. Collection of bucolic and love poems, popular for their lyrical gloom and idealized vision of the English countryside.

D.H. Lawrence *Sons and Lovers*; *The Rainbow*; *Women in Love*; *Selected Short Stories*. Before he got his funny ideas about sex and became all messianic, Lawrence wrote magnificent prose on daily working-class life in Nottinghamshire's pit villages – or rather his vision of it. His interpretation never went down well with the locals and even now his name can raise a snarl or two. Lawrence's early short stories contain some of his finest writing, as does *Sons and Lovers*, a fraught, autobiographical novel. With *The Rainbow* and *Women in Love*, his other two major novels, the loopy sub-Nietzschean theorizing slowly gains the upper hand.

Laurie Lee *Cider with Rosie*. Reminiscences of adolescent bucolic frolics in the Cotswolds during the 1920s.

★ **Ian McEwan** *Atonement*. McEwan's ninth novel and possibly his most masterful, tracing the course of three lives from a sweltering country garden in 1935 to seeking absolution in the new century.

Somerset Maugham *Liza of Lambeth* (o/p); *Of Human Bondage*. Maugham considered himself a "second-rater" but these books are packed with vivid local colour: *Liza of Lambeth* is a depiction of Cockney low-life; *Of Human Bondage* is set in Whitstable and Canterbury and based on Maugham's own experiences as an orphan.

Daphne du Maurier *Frenchman's Creek*; *Jamaica Inn*; *Rebecca*. Nail-biting, swashbuckling romantic novels set in the author's adopted home of Cornwall.

Alan Sillitoe *Saturday Night and Sunday Morning*. Gritty account of factory life and sexual shenanigans in Nottingham in the late 1950s.

★ **Zadie Smith** *White Teeth* Startling popular, episodic and very humourous tale of three families – one Indian, one white, one mixed race – in London and Oxford from the 1940s until today.

David Storey *This Sporting Life*; *Saville*. Storey's first novel, *This Sporting Life,* is a grimly realistic portrayal of a Rugby League player in the north of England. *Saville,* which won him the Booker Prize, revolves around his favourite themes of mid-life crisis and loss of class identity.

Graham Swift *Waterland*; *Last Orders*. *Waterland* is a family saga set in East Anglia's fenlands – excellent on the history and appeal of this superficially drab landscape. Booker Prize-winning *Last Orders* reminisces with four old folk on a trip to the south coast to scatter a friend's ashes.

Adam Thorpe *Ulverton*. Imaginative re-creation of life in a small town in southwest England over the course of three centuries.

Evelyn Waugh *Sword of Honour* trilogy; *Brideshead Revisited*. The trilogy is essentially a lightweight remake of Ford's *Parade's End*, albeit laced with some of Waugh's funniest set-pieces. The best-selling *Brideshead Revisited* is possibly his least likeable work, rank with snobbery, nostalgia and money-worship.

★ **Virginia Woolf** *Orlando*; *Mrs Dalloway*. Woolf's lover, Vita Sackville-West, is the model for *Orlando*, whose life spans four centuries and both genders. *Mrs Dalloway*, which relates the thoughts of a London society hostess and a shell-shocked war veteran, sees Woolf's "stream of consciousness" style in full flow.

Anthologies

English Mystery Plays Peter Happe (ed). These simple Christian tales were produced annually in Chester, York, Wakefield and other great English towns, and are often revived even now.

Four English Comedies J.M. Morrell (ed). Laugh a minute from Congreve, Jonson, Goldsmith and Sheridan.

Landmarks of Modern British Drama Roger Cornish and Violet Ketels (eds; o/p). The 1960s volume features plays by Wesker, Osborne, Pinter and Orton; the 1970s volume covers the likes of Ayckbourn, Brenton, Stoppard and Caryl Churchill.

Literature of Renaissance England Hollander and Kermode (eds). Spenser's *Faerie Queene*, a bit of Marlowe, Shakespeare's Sonnets, Donne, Jonson and Milton.

Modern British Literature Hollander and Kermode (eds). Weighted towards the classic writers of the late nineteenth and early twentieth centuries – Hardy, Conrad, Lawrence and so on.

★ **The New Penguin Book of English Verse** Paul Keegan (ed). Seven hundred years of English poetry, listed chronologically rather than by author – a simple innovation, but startlingly effective.

The New Poetry Hulse, Kennedy and Morley (eds). Over fifty poets, all born since World War II.

The Restoration and the Eighteenth Century Martin Price (ed). From Dryden, Swift and Pope to Sterne.

Victorian Prose and Poetry Trilling and Bloom (eds). Carlyle, Ruskin, Tennyson, Rossetti and Wilde's *Ballad of Reading Gaol.*

Film

For much of its history the British **film industry** has largely been an English affair, with its major studios (Ealing, Pinewood and Shepperton) not far from central London and its stars drawn from the ranks of the capital's stage. However, unlike the Hollywood star system, the English film industry tended and still significantly relies on strong ensemble playing. While Ealing's films were a by-word for social comedy, other significant elements have included the Hammer horror series (usually featuring Christopher Lee and Peter Cushing), costume dramas typified by the Gainsborough company's productions and the James Bond films, while the Carry On series kept a generation of comedy actors in work long past their sell-by date. In the 1960s, English films developed a justifiable reputation for social realism, which has been maintained in more recent times by directors such as Ken Loach and Mike Leigh.

Today's film industry is in a healthier state than perhaps at any point since the 1930s with a diversity and vitality that reflects the dominance of independent productions. Some film fans might argue that the influence of television means that many such productions are essentially small-screen ventures, but within the last ten years a host of English pictures – *The Full Monty* and *Shakespeare in Love* are just two examples – have enjoyed great success internationally.

The films listed below are all set in England. They are not exclusively greats – though some rank amongst the best movies ever made – but all depict a particular aspect of English life, whether reflecting the experience of immigrant communities, exploring the country's history, or depicting its richly varied landscapes.

The 1930s and 1940s

Brief Encounter (David Lean, 1945). Extra-marital attraction at a railway station is the theme of this mysteriously popular classic. Noel Coward is responsible for the clipped dialogue, Rachmaninov for the weepy score, Trevor Howard keeps his upper lip stiff and Celia Johnson wears an improbable hat.

Brighton Rock (John Boulting, 1947). A fine adaptation of Graham Greene's novel, featuring a young, genuinely scary Richard Attenborough as the psychopathic hood Pinkie, who marries a witness to one of his crimes to ensure her silence. Beautiful cinematography and good performances, with a real sense of *film noir* menace.

A Canterbury Tale (Michael Powell and Emeric Pressburger, 1944). Set in a wartime Kent village, where a plucky land girl, a small-town GI and a sardonic English sergeant are billeted. Overseen by a mysterious local magistrate, they make their own pilgrimage to Canterbury, the cathedral glowing high over bomb-damaged streets. A mystical vision of English history is fused with bucolic images of rural life, a restrained exploration of the characters' personal suffering underlying a truly magical masterpiece.

Fires Were Started (Humphrey Jennings, 1943). One of the best films to come out of the documentary tradition, this is the story of the experiences of a group of firemen through one night of bombing during the Blitz. The use of real firemen as performers rather than professional actors, and the avoidance of formulaic heroics, gives the film great power as an account of the courage of ordinary people who fought, often uncelebrated, on the home front.

Great Expectations (David Lean 1946). Early film by one of England's finest directors – *Lawrence of Arabia, Bridge on the River Kwai* – this superb rendition of the Dickens novel features magnificent performances by John Mills (as Pip) and Finlay Currie (as Abel Magwitch). The scene in the graveyard is nothing short of wonderful.

Henry V (Laurence Olivier, 1944). Featuring glowing Technicolor backdrops, this wonderful piece of wartime propaganda is emphatically "theatrical", the action spiralling out from the Globe Theatre itself. Olivier is a brilliantly charismatic king, the pre-battle scene where he goes disguised amongst his men being delicately muted and atmospheric.

Jane Eyre (Robert Stevenson, 1943). Joan Fontaine does a fine job of portraying Jane, and Orson Welles is a suavely sardonic Rochester – the scene where he is thrown from his horse in the mist hits the perfect melodramatic pitch. With the unlikely tagline"A Love Story Every Woman Would Die a Thousand Deaths to Live!", it briefly features a young Elizabeth Taylor as dying Helen Burns.

Kind Hearts and Coronets (Robert Hamer, 1949). As with the best of the Ealing movies, this is a totally savage comedy on the cruel absurdities of the British class system. With increasing ingenuity, Dennis Price's suave and ruthless anti-hero murders his way through the d'Ascoyne clan (all brilliantly played by Alec Guinness) to claim the family title.

The Life and Death of Colonel Blimp (Michael Powell and Emeric Pressburger, 1943). An epic celebration of the oft-ridiculed romantic spirit of the English, personified by the wonderful Roger Livesey. We follow him through the actual and emotional duels of his youth, against his equally dashing German foe, to crusty old age in World War II. A daring and visually stunning story of love and friendship, it was hated by Churchill for supposedly being unpatriotic, which is surely recommendation enough.

A Matter of Life and Death (Michael Powell and Emeric Pressburger, 1946). Remarkable fantasy, opening with David Niven's airman miraculously surviving a fall from his stricken bomber. There follows a tussle between the monochrome bureaucracy of Heaven, who seek to reclaim him, and his fast-evolving Earth-bound love affair. Great performances and beautiful Technicolor images in another of Powell and Pressburger's enchanting romances.

The Private Life of Henry VIII (Alexander Korda, 1933). The film which catalysed a boom in British film-making – thanks to the success of the gargantuan Charles Laughton in the title role – has little now to commend it other than some superb cinematography and Laughton's own sometimes grotesque performance.

Rebecca (Alfred Hitchcock, 1940). Hitchcock does Du Maurier: Laurence Olivier is wonderfully enigmatic as Maxim de Winter, and Joan Fontaine glows as his meek second wife, living in the shadow of her mysterious predecessor. Perfectly paced and beautifully shot, Hitch's first Hollywood picture is a true classic.

The Thirty-Nine Steps (Alfred Hitchcock, 1935). Hitchcock's best-loved British movie, full of wit and bold acts of derring-do. Robert Donat stars as innocent Richard Hannay, inadvertently caught up in a mysterious spy ring and forced to flee both the spies and the agents of Scotland Yard. In a typically perverse Hitchcock touch, he spends a generous amount of time handcuffed to Madeleine Carroll, fleeing across the Scottish countryside, before the action returns to London for the film's great music-hall conclusion.

The Wicked Lady (Leslie Arliss, 1945). One of the best of Gainsborough Studios' series of escapist romances, this features a magnificently amoral and headstrong Margaret Lockwood, wooed into a criminal double life by James Mason's quintessentially dashing highwayman. Its opulent re-creation of eighteenth-century England is terribly appealing, as are the tempestuous entanglements of its two wayward stars.

1950 to 1970

Billy Liar! (John Schlesinger, 1963). Tom Courtenay is stuck in a dire job as an undertaker's clerk in a northern town, and spends his time creating extravagant fantasies. His life is lit up by the appearance of Julie Christie, who holds out the glamour and promise of swinging London. Touching and amusing.

Carry On Screaming (Gerald Thomas, 1966). One of the better efforts from the Carry On crew, with most of the usual suspects (Kenneth Williams, Charles Hawtrey, Joan Sims) hamming it up in a Hammer Horror spoof and serving up a few scares along with the usual single-entendre jokes.

Dracula (Terence Fisher, 1958). Classic Hammer Horror flick, loosely based on Bram Stoker's original book and pairing Christopher Lee as the blood-sucking count with Peter Cushing's vampire-staking Van Helsing.

Far From the Madding Crowd (John Schlesinger, 1967). A largely successful and imaginative adaptation of Hardy's doom-laden tale of the desires and ambitions of wilful Bathsheba Everdene. Julie Christie is a radiant and spirited Bathsheba, Terence Stamp flashes his blade to dynamic effect, Alan Bates is quietly charismatic as dependable Gabriel Oak, and the West Country setting is sparsely beautiful.

If... (Lindsay Anderson, 1968). The stifling world of the English public school as a rather inadequate microcosm of society. Malcolm McDowell plays our iconoclastic hero, leading his little cell in revolution against the arbitrary discipline and cruelty of the school hierarchy. Although beautifully shot and well realized in its own caricatural terms, it seems dated now and rather too narrowly of its time.

I'm Alright Jack (John and Roy Boulting, 1959). The best of The Boulting Brothers' comic explorations of English social mores explores the class system in the context of industrial unrest. Peter Sellers is on top form as the shop steward, while management is represented by a hapless Ian Carmichael (brought in to cause disruption through his own ineptitude) who, naturally, falls in love with Sellers' daughter.

Kes (Kenneth Loach, 1969). This is the unforgettable story of a neglected Yorkshire schoolboy who finds solace and liberation in training his kestrel. As a still pertinent commentary on poverty and an impoverished school system, it's bleak but idealistic, and pale and pinched David Bradley who plays Billy Casper is hugely affecting.

The Ladykillers (Alexander Mackendrick, 1955). Alec Guinness is fabulously toothy and malevolent as "Professor Marcus", a murderous conman who lodges with a sweet little old lady, Mrs Wilberforce. The professor and his ragbag of criminal accomplices – their sinister intent a hilarious counterpoint to Mrs Wilberforce's genteel tea parties – try to pass themselves off as musicians, while, thanks to her innocent interventions, the body count inexorably mounts.

A Man For All Seasons (Fred Zinnemann, 1966). Sir Thomas More versus Henry VIII: one of British history's great moral confrontations made skilfully tedious by this film's stage-bound, talky origins in Robert Bolt's play. Despite muted, atmospheric visuals and a heavenly host of theatrical talent (including a cheering appearance by Orson Welles as Cardinal Wolsey), nothing can save this from paralysing dullness.

Night and the City (Jules Dassin, 1950). Great *film noir*, with Richard Widmark as an anxious nightclub hustler on the run. Gripping and convincingly sleazy, the London streetscapes have an expressionist edge of horror.

Performance (Nicolas Roeg/Donald Cammell, 1970). Credited with precipitating James Fox's breakdown and subsequent retirement from the movies, this shape-shifting tale of gangsters and pop culture is the best account of the hedonistic end to Britain's psychedelic 1960s. Well known for its strange drug-hazed second half, the film is also brilliantly funny in parts and should be cherished for its hilarious destruction of the myth of Kray-style criminals.

Saturday Night and Sunday Morning (Karel Reisz, 1960). Reisz's monochrome captured all the grit and dead-end grind of Albert Finney's work in a Nottingham bicycle factory and his attempts to find spice and romance in the city's pubs and on its canal banks.

This Sporting Life (Lindsay Anderson, 1963). One of the key British films of the 1960s, *This Sporting Life* tells the story of a northern miner turned star player for his local rugby team. The young Richard Harris gives a great performance as the inarticulate anti-hero, able only to express himself through physical violence, and the film is one of the best examples of the gritty "kitchen sink" genre it helped to usher in.

The War Game (Peter Watkins, 1965). Watkins' astonishing documentary approach to the effects of a Russian nuclear attack on southeast England, using both local people and various official "talking heads", shocked its commissioner, the BBC, into refusing to show it; hardly surprising, since its overall effect was to question our trust in authority. Much-dated in comparison to modern computer-driven special effects, it still retains the power to alarm.

The 1970s and 1980s

Akenfield (Peter Hall, 1974). A powerfully involving evocation of English rural life whose ingredients include glowing cinematography and Michael Tippett's wonderful music. Past and present are skilfully contrasted, but the heart of the film lies in its sometimes ecstatic, but also harsh, rendering of the past.

Babylon (Franco Rosso, 1980). A moving account of black working-class London life. We follow the experiences of young Blue through a series of encounters that reveal the insidious forces of racism at work in Britain. Good performances and a great reggae soundtrack: an all too rare example of Black Britain taking centre stage in British movies.

Chariots of Fire (Hugh Hudson, 1981). This hugely successful movie prompted writer Colin Welland to bombastically – and optimistically – proclaim, "The British are coming." Based around the 1924 Olympics, it tells the true story of Scottish missionary Eric Liddell (Ian Charleson) and repressed Cambridge student Harold Abrahams (Ben Cross). Oscar-winning and overblown, it is distinguished only by Charleson's quiet performance, and some great locations.

A Clockwork Orange (Stanley Kubrick, 1971). Famously banned in the UK by director Kubrick, this is a genuinely disturbing if now slightly dated depiction of violence and society's reaction to it, in which young droog Alex – played with charm and menace by Malcolm McDowell – finds himself first the perpetrator and then the victim, to a rousing soundtrack of Beethoven classics.

Comrades (Bill Douglas, 1986). In 1830s England, a group of farm workers decide to stand up to the exploitative tactics of the local landowner, and find themselves prosecuted and transported to Australia. Based on the true story of the Tolpuddle Martyrs, this combines political education (the founding of the modern union movement) with a moving and visually stunning celebration of working lives.

Distant Voices, Still Lives (Terence Davies, 1988). Beautifully realized autobiographical tale of growing up in Forties and Fifties Liverpool. The mesmeric pace is punctuated by astonishing moments of drama, and the whole is a very moving account of how a family survives and triumphs, in small ways, against the odds.

Frenzy (Alfred Hitchcock, 1972). Hitchcock comes back to Blighty in top form, with the story of a man on the run, under suspicion for the vicious "neck tie" murders carried out in Covent Garden. Trademark sly black humour combines with a disturbing exploration of sexual immaturity.

Get Carter (Mike Hodges, 1971). Although not the masterpiece some claim, this is still one of the most vivid and interesting British gangster movies, featuring a monumentally evil outing for Michael Caine as the eponymous villain, returning to his native Newcastle to avenge his brother's death. Great use of its northeast locations and a fine turn by playwright John Osborne as the local godfather don't quite, however, compensate for its now faintly ridiculous misogyny.

Hope and Glory (John Boorman, 1987). A glorious autobiographical feature about the Blitz seen through the eyes of 9-year-old Bill, who revels in the liberating chaos of bombsite playgrounds, tumbling barrage balloons and shrapnel collections. His older sister's unfettered romps with a Canadian soldier and the adults' privation and occasional despair are an additional source of amusement for Bill and his tiny sister.

The Last of England (Derek Jarman, 1987). Derek Jarman was a genuine maverick presence in Eighties Britain; this is his most abstract account of the state of the nation. Composed of apparently unrelated shots of decaying London landscapes, rent boys and references to emblematic national events such as the Falklands War, this may not be to all tastes, but it is a fitting testament to a unique talent in British film making.

Letter to Brezhnev (Chris Bernard, 1986). Frank Clarke's screenplay about chicken factories,

Russian sailors, drink, love and idealism proved a marvellous vehicle for his larger-than-life sister, Margi, and the more considered Alexandra Pigg.

The Long Good Friday (John MacKenzie, 1979). Despite a maniacal turn from Bob Hoskins as the East End gang boss threatened by powerful, mysterious new arrivals, this is not all it's cracked up to be. Its vision of East End villains seems self-indulgent and dated, and the plodding TV visual style doesn't help to raise the level.

Made in Britain (Alan Clarke, 1982). One of Alan Clarke's series of savage dissections of Eighties Britain, featuring a 17-year-old Tim Roth as skinhead Trevor on a downbeat odyssey of job-centre visits, drug-taking and racist explosions. The energy of the central performance delivers a film of real force, and a very powerful indictment of Thatcher's Britain.

The Madness of King George (Nicholas Hytner, 1994). Adapted from an Alan Bennett play, this eighteenth-century royal romp has an irritating staginess, with the king's loopy antics played against a cartoon-like court and an England apparently devoid of real people.

Mona Lisa (Neil Jordan, 1986). This fine London-based thriller has powerful performances from Bob Hoskins, Michael Caine and then-newcomer Cathy Tyson, the latter playing a high-class prostitute who recruits Hoskins to help find her lost friend. This takes him, and us, on a nightmarish exploration of the dark side of Eighties London, lightened only slightly by an utterly convincing, poignant love story, as Bob begins to fall for his beautiful employer.

My Beautiful Laundrette (Stephen Frears, 1985). A slice of Thatcher's Britain, with a young Asian, Omar, on the make, opening a ritzy laundrette. His lover, Johnny (Daniel Day-Lewis), is an ex-National Front glamour boy, angry and inarticulate when forced by the acquisitive Omar into a menial role in the laundrette. The racial, sexual and class dynamics of their relationship are closely observed, and mirror the tensions engendered by the Asian presence in a hostile London.

Withnail and I (Bruce Robinson, 1986). Richard E. Grant is superb as the raddled, drunken Withnail, an out-of-work actor with a penchant for drinking lighter fluid. Paul McGann is the "I" of the title – a bemused and beautiful spectator of Withnail's wild excesses, as they abandon an astonishingly grotty London flat for the wilds of a remote cottage, and the attentions of Withnail's randy uncle Monty. A rare look at the Sixties that avoids nostalgia, and opts instead for emotional truth.

The 1990s to the present

Bend It like Beckham (Gurinder Chadha, 2003). Immensely successful film focusing on the coming of age of a football-loving Punjabi girl in a suburb of London. Both socially acute and comic.

Bhaji on the Beach (Gurinder Chadha, 1993). An Asian women's group takes a day-trip to Blackpool in this issue-laden but enjoyable picture. A lot of fun is had contrasting the seamier side of British life with the mores of the Asian aunties, though the male characters are cartoon villains all.

Billy Elliot (Stephen Daldry, 2000). Set against the depressing backdrop of the turbulent miners' strike of 1984, this ultimately feel-good film tells the story of a young boy (Jamie

Bell), torn between his unexpected love of dance and the disintegration of his family.

Brassed Off (Mark Herman, 1996). A pacy film about British working-class life that eschews pathos, opting instead for uncompromising anger, underscored by robust black humour. With the imminent demise of the town's coal pit, the future for the Grimley Colliery Brass Band looks hopeless. Danny (Pete Postlethwaite) valiantly attempts to keep the band alive as the emotional lives of the musicians collapse.

Bridget Jones's Diary (Sharon Maguire, 2001). American Renée Zellweger put on a plummy English accent and several pounds to play the lead in this *Pride and Prejudice* for the new millennium. Ably assisted by deliciously nasty love-interest Hugh Grant, the film stands out as one of the better British romantic comedies of the last few years.

Calendar Girls (Nigel Cole, 2003). A group of middle-aged North Yorkshire ladies pose naked for their Women's Institute calendar in the hope of raising money for cancer research – and succeed beyond their wildest dreams. Based on a true story, unfortunately the film wasn't quite as big a hit as the calendar was.

Dirty, Pretty Things (Stephen Frears, 2003). A tumbling mix of melodrama, social criticism and black comedy, this forceful, thought-provoking film explores the world of Britain's illegal migrants.

East is East (Damien O'Donnell, 1999). Seventies Salford is the setting for this lively comedy, with a Pakistani chip-shop owner struggling to keep control of his seven children as they rail against the strictures of Islam and arranged marriages. Inventively made, and with some pleasing performances.

Elizabeth (Shekahar Kapur, 1998). Charismatic Cate Blanchett is, thankfully, the still heart of this history-lite and madly over-blown production, where all political and emotional nuance is lost in an orgy of decapitations, swirling cloaks and stagy thunderstorms.

Enigma (Michael Apted, 2001). This blockbuster, scripted by playwright Tom Stoppard, is a fictional tale depicting Britain's war-time efforts to crack the Germans' Enigma encrypting machine, with Kate Winslet excelling amongst a generally fine cast.

Four Weddings and a Funeral (Mike Newell, 1994). Standard rom-com that used an American actress and gags based on English eccentricities to pull in big audiences worldwide. Unrepresentative of contemporary England with its Hugh Grant-led cast of middle-class whites, it still manages some very funny – and quite moving – set-pieces.

The Full Monty (Peter Cattaneo, 1997). Six Sheffield ex-steel workers throw caution to the wind and become male strippers, their boast being that all will be revealed: the "full monty". Unpromising physical specimens all, they score an unlikely hit with the local lasses. The film was itself an unlikely hit worldwide: the theme of manhood in crisis is sensitively explored, and the long-awaited striptease is a joy to behold.

Gosford Park (Robert Altman, 2001). Astutely observed upstairs-downstairs murder mystery set in class-ridden 1930s England. The multi-layered plot is typical of the director while the who's who of great British actors is led by the superb Maggie Smith – and only let down by Stephen Fry's bumbling police inspector who looks like he's wandered in from an entirely different film.

Harry Potter and the Philosopher's Stone (Chris Colombus, 2001). Though this overly-faithful-to–the-original-book adaptation crams in too much and feels rushed, this film about hero Harry's first year at wizards' school did wonders for the English tourist industry with its use of places such as Alnwick Castle as locations. The second outing, *Harry Potter and the Chamber of Secrets* proved better-paced and more darkly enjoyable.

Howards End (James Ivory, 1991). E.M. Forster's tale of the forward-thinking Schlegel sisters, and their relationship with the conventional, domineering Wilcoxes. One of many immaculate British costume dramas, with precise performances from Vanessa Redgrave, Helena Bonham Carter and, most notably, Emma Thompson as Margaret Schlegel.

Little Voice (Mark Herman, 1998). Entertaining screen adaptation of Jim Cartwright's hit play about reclusive "Little Voice" (Jane Horrocks), who comes miraculously to life only on stage, brilliantly impersonating Fifties stars such as Marilyn Monroe. It features a great performance from Michael Caine as the impossibly seedy agent who seeks to exploit her bizarre talent, and offers a great glimpse of seaside England, with all its eccentric charm.

Lock, Stock and Two Smoking Barrels (Guy Ritchie, 1998). Four lads attempt to pay off gambling debts by making a drug deal in this over-stylized and rather shallow picture, which, though it has a modern setting, pays dubious homage to the London of the Kray twins. However, the suits are sharp, the production is slick and football's hardman turned actor Vinnie Jones turns in a surprisingly solid debut performance.

Nil by Mouth (Gary Oldman, 1997). With strong performances by Ray Winstone (Ray) as a boorish south Londoner and Kathy Burke (Valery) as his battered wife, this brave and bleak realist picture depicts Ray as a victim of his own violence, as well as the devastatingly vulnerable Valery. Brace yourself.

Notting Hill (Roger Michell, 1999). After their huge hit with *Four Weddings,* writer Richard Curtis and actor Hugh Grant returned with more middle-class jollity. Grant reprises his bumbling floppy-haired Englishman role and falls for a glamorous American (Julia Roberts) – again. Spanning a year in the life of Notting Hill, it perversely fails to feature the event for which this part of London is best known: the biggest and best street carnival in Europe.

Orlando (Sally Potter, 1992). Although modest in budget terms, this is a vivid and visually beautiful adaptation of Virginia Woolf's novel, following its hero/heroine through 400 years of British history. Tilda Swinton is perfectly cast as the androgynous immortal, and choice moments spanning Elizabethan England to the present day (through the Civil War and Victoria's reign, for example) are perfectly and mysteriously realized.

The Remains of the Day (James Ivory, 1993). Kazuo Ishiguro's masterly study of social and personal repression translates beautifully to the big screen. Anthony Hopkins is the overly decorous butler who gradually becomes aware of his master's fascist connections, Emma Thompson the housekeeper who struggles to bring his real, deeply suppressed feelings to the surface.

Richard III (Richard Loncraine, 1995). A splendid film version of a renowned National Theatre production, which brilliantly transposed the action to a fascist state in the 1930s. The infernal political machinations of a snarling Ian McKellen as Richard are heightened by Nazi associations, and the style of the period imbues the film with the requisite glamour, as does languorously drugged Kristin Scott-Thomas as Lady Anne.

Secrets and Lies (Mike Leigh, 1995). Much-loved Mike Leigh slice-of-life drama, with wonderful Timothy Spall at the head of a spectacularly dysfunctional London family. His sister Cynthia (Brenda Blethyn), her heart of gold buried in boozy, cloying unhappiness, is reunited with the black daughter she gave up for adoption at birth. Over-long improvised sequences and a depiction of suburban vulgarity which comes close to parody, are lifted by stunning ensemble performances and sustained by the simple strength of its central tenet: that secrets and lies in a family will only cause unnecessary pain.

Sense and Sensibility (Ang Lee, 1995). Jane Austen's sprightly essay on the merits of well-modified behaviour is nicely realized by Lee, and neatly scripted by Emma Thompson. Thompson and Kate Winslet are charming as the downtrodden Dashwood sisters: Winslet is a brilliantly over-wrought, romantic Marianne, while Thompson turns in another perfect performance as prudent Elinor.

Shakespeare in Love (John Madden, 1998). An irresistible homage to life, love and Shakespeare has an energetic Joseph Fiennes as the quill-chewing bard and Gwyneth Paltrow as his sparky love interest. Sharply scripted by Tom Stoppard, it skips a dainty line between parody and over-reverence, and has fun sending up the British fondness for cameos, with Rupert Everett as melancholy Kit Marlowe, off on a one-way trip for a drink in Deptford.

Glossaries

Architectural terms

Aisle Clear space parallel to the nave, usually with lower ceiling than the nave.

Altar Table at which the Eucharist is celebrated, at the east end of the church. (When church is not aligned to the geographical east, the altar end is still referred to as the "east" end.)

Ambulatory Passage behind the chancel.

Apse The curved or polygonal east end of a church.

Arcade Row of arches on top of columns or piers, supporting a wall.

Bailey Area enclosed by castle walls.

Barbican Defensive structure built in front of main gate.

Barrel vault Continuous rounded vault, like a semi-cylinder.

Boss A decorative carving at the meeting point of the lines of a vault.

Box pew Form of church seating in which each row is enclosed by high, thin wooden panels.

Broach spire Octagonal spire rising straight out of a square tower.

Buttress Stone support for a wall; some buttresses are wholly attached to the wall, others take the form of an outer support with a connecting half-arch, known as a "flying buttress".

Capital Upper section of a column, usually carved.

Chancel Section of the church where the altar is located.

Chantry Small chapel in which masses were said for the soul of the person who financed its construction; none built after the reign of Henry VIII.

Choir Area in which the church service is conducted; next to or same as chancel.

Clerestory Upper storey of nave, containing a line of windows.

Coffering Regular recessed spaces set into a ceiling.

Crenellations Battlements with square indentations.

Decorated Middle Gothic style; about 1280–1380.

Dogtooth Form of early Gothic decorative stonework, looking like raised "X"s.

Early English First phase of Gothic architecture in England, about 1150–1280.

Fan vault Late Gothic form of vaulting, in which the area between walls and ceiling is covered with stone ribs in the shape of an open fan.

Finial Any decorated tip of an architectural feature.

Flushwork Kind of surface decoration in which tablets of white stone alternate with pieces of flint; very common in East Anglia.

Gargoyle Grotesque exterior carving, usually a decorative form of water spout.

Hammer beam Type of ceiling in which horizontal brackets support vertical struts that connect to the roof timbers.

Keep Main structure of a castle.

Lady Chapel Chapel dedicated to the Virgin, often found at the east end of major churches.

Lancet Tall, narrow and plain window.

Lantern Upper part of a dome or tower, often glazed.

Misericord Carved ledge below a tip-up seat, usually in choir stalls, as support when occupant stands.

Motte Mound on which a castle keep stands.

Mullion Vertical post between the panes of a window.

Nave The main part of the church to the west of the crossing.

Ogee Double curve; distinctive feature of Decorated style.

Oriel Projecting window.

Palladian Seventeenth- and eighteenth-century classical style adhering to the principles of Andrea Palladio.

Pediment Triangular space above a window or doorway.

Perpendicular Late Gothic style, about 1380–1550.

Pilaster Flat column set against a wall.

Reredos Painted or carved panel behind an altar.

Rood screen Wooden screen supporting a crucifix (or rood), separating the choir from the nave; few survived the Reformation.

Rose window Large circular window, divided into vaguely petal-shaped sections.

Stalls Seating for clergy in the choir area of a church.

Tracery Pattern formed by narrow bands of stone in a window or on a wall surface.

Transept Section of the main body of the church at right angles to the choir and nave.

Triforium Arcade above the nave or transept in a church.

Tympanum Panel over a doorway, often carved in medieval churches.

Vault Arched ceiling.

English slang expressions

Bill Restaurant check

Biscuit Cookie or cracker

Bonnet Car hood

Boot Car trunk

Brummies People born in Birmingham

Caravan Trailer

Car park Parking lot

Cheap Inexpensive

Chemist Pharmacist

Chips French fries

Coach Bus

Crisps Potato chips

Dual carriageway Divided highway

Dustbin Trash can

First floor Second floor

Fiver Five pounds (money)

Flat Apartment

Fortnight Two weeks

Geordie Person from Newcastle upon Tyne

Ground floor First floor

High Street Main Street

Hire Rent

Jam Jelly

Jelly Jell-O

Jumble sale Yard sale

Jumper Sweater

Lay-by Road shoulder

Leaflet Pamphlet

Lift Elevator

Lorry Truck

Motorway Highway

Off-licence Liquor store

Pants Underwear

Petrol Gasoline

Pudding Dessert

Queue Line

Return ticket Round-trip ticket

Roundabout Rotary interchange

Scouser Person from Liverpool

Single carriageway Non-divided highway

Single ticket One-way ticket

Snug Small, intimate section of a pub

Stalls Orchestra seats
Stone Fourteen pounds (weight)
Subway Pedestrian passageway
Sweets Candy
Tap Faucet
Tenner Ten pounds (money)
Tights Pantyhose
Torch Flashlight
Trainers Sneakers
Trousers Pants
Tube/Underground Subway (train)
Vest Undershirt

Index

and small print

Index

Map entries are in colour

C

F

G

H

I

M

N

INDEX

O

P

Q

R

S

INDEX

INDEX

Y

Z

INDEX

A Rough Guide to Rough Guides

In the summer of 1981, Mark Ellingham, a recent graduate from Bristol University, was travelling round Greece and couldn't find a guidebook that really met his needs. On the one hand there were the student guides, insistent on saving every last cent, and on the other the heavyweight cultural tomes whose authors seemed to have spent more time in a research library than lounging away the afternoon at a taverna or on the beach.

In a bid to avoid getting a job, Mark and a small group of writers set about creating their own guidebook. It was a guide to Greece that aimed to combine a journalistic approach to description with a thoroughly practical approach to travellers' needs – a guide that would incorporate culture, history and contemporary insights with a critical edge, together with up-to-date, value-for-money listings. Back in London, Mark and the team finished their Rough Guide, as they called it, and talked Routledge into publishing the book.

That first *Rough Guide to Greece*, published in 1982, was a student scheme that became a publishing phenomenon. The immediate success of the book – with numerous reprints and a Thomas Cook prize shortlisting – spawned a series that rapidly covered dozens of destinations. Rough Guides had a ready market among low-budget backpackers, but soon also acquired a much broader and older readership that relished Rough Guides' wit and inquisitiveness as much as their enthusiastic, critical approach. Everyone wants value for money, but not at any price.

Rough Guides soon began supplementing the "rougher" information about hostels and low-budget listings with the kind of detail on restaurants and quality hotels that independent-minded visitors on any budget might expect, whether on business in New York or trekking in Thailand.

These days the guides – distributed worldwide by the Penguin group – offer recommendations from shoestring to luxury and cover more than 200 destinations around the globe, including almost every country in the Americas and Europe, more than half of Africa and most of Asia and Australasia. Our ever-growing team of authors and photographers is spread all over the world, particularly in Europe, the USA and Australia.

In 1994, we published the *Rough Guide to World Music* and *Rough Guide to Classical Music*; and a year later the *Rough Guide to the Internet*. All three books have become benchmark titles in their fields – which encouraged us to expand into other areas of publishing, mainly around popular culture. Rough Guides now publish:

- Travel guides to more than 200 worldwide destinations
- Dictionary phrasebooks to 22 major languages
- History guides ranging from Ireland to Islam
- Maps printed on rip-proof and waterproof Polyart™ paper
- Music guides running the gamut from Opera to Elvis
- Restaurant guides to London, New York and San Francisco
- Reference books on topics as diverse as the Weather and Shakespeare
- Sports guides from Formula 1 to Man Utd
- Pop culture books from Lord of the Rings to Cult TV
- World Music CDs in association with World Music Network.

Visit **www.roughguides.com** to see our latest publications.

Rough Guide credits

Text editor: Clifton Wilkinson, Polly Thomas, Claire Saunders and Alison Murchie
Layout: Andy Hilliard and Katie Pringle
Cartography: Katie Lloyd-Jones
Picture research: Mark Thomas
Proofreader: Jo Mead

Editorial: **London** Martin Dunford, Kate Berens, Helena Smith, Geoff Howard, Ruth Blackmore, Gavin Thomas, Richard Lim, Lucy Ratcliffe, Clifton Wilkinson, Fran Sandham, Sally Schafer, Alexander Mark Rogers, Karoline Densley, Andy Turner, Ella O'Donnell, Andrew Lockett, Joe Staines, Duncan Clark, Peter Buckley, Matthew Milton; **New York** Andrew Rosenberg, Richard Koss, Yuki Takagaki, Hunter Slaton, Chris Barsanti, Thomas Kohnstamm, Steven Horak
Design & Layout: London Helen Prior, Dan May, Diana Jarvis; **Delhi** Madhulita Mohapatra, Umesh Aggarwal, Ajay Verma

Production: Julia Bovis, John McKay, Sophie Hewat
Cartography: **London** Maxine Repath, Ed Wright, Katie Lloyd-Jones; **Delhi** Manish Chandra, Rajesh Chhibber, Jai Prakesh Mishra, Ashutosh Bharti, Rajesh Mishra, Animesh Pathak
Cover art direction: Louise Boulton
Picture research: Sharon Martins, Mark Thomas, Jj Luck
Online: New York Jennifer Gold, Cree Lawson, Suzanne Welles; **Delhi** Manik Chauhan, Amarjyoti Dutta, Narender Kumar
Marketing & Publicity: **London** Richard Trillo, Niki Smith, David Wearn, Chloë Roberts, Demelza Dallow; **New York** Geoff Colquitt, David Wechsler, Megan Kennedy
Finance: Gary Singh
Manager India: Punita Singh
Series editor: Mark Ellingham
PA to Managing Director: Julie Sanderson
Managing Director: Kevin Fitzgerald

Publishing Information

This sixth edition published March 2004 by
Rough Guides Ltd,
80 Strand, London WC2R 0RL.
345 Hudson St, 4th Floor,
New York, NY 10014, USA.
Distributed by the Penguin Group
Penguin Books Ltd,
80 Strand, London WC2R 0RL
Penguin Putnam, Inc.
375 Hudson Street, NY 10014, USA
Penguin Books Australia Ltd,
487 Maroondah Highway, PO Box 257,
Ringwood, Victoria 3134, Australia
Penguin Books Canada Ltd,
10 Alcorn Avenue, Toronto, Ontario,
Canada M4V 1E4
Penguin Books (NZ) Ltd,
182–190 Wairau Road, Auckland 10,
New Zealand
Typeset in Bembo and Helvetica to an original design by Henry Iles.

Printed in Italy by LegoPrint S.p.A

1216pp includes index
A catalogue record for this book is available from the British Library
ISBN 1-84353-249-2

1 3 5 7 9 8 6 4 2

Help us update

We've gone to a lot of effort to ensure that the sixth edition of **The Rough Guide to England** is accurate and up-to-date. However, things change – places get "discovered", opening hours are notoriously fickle, restaurants and rooms raise prices or lower standards. If you feel we've got it wrong or left something out, we'd like to know, and if you can remember the address, the price, the time, the phone number, so much the better.

We'll credit all contributions, and send a copy of the next edition (or any other Rough Guide if you prefer) for the best letters. Everyone who writes to us and isn't already a subscriber will receive a copy of our full-colour thrice-yearly newsletter. Please mark letters: **"Rough Guide England Update"** and send to: Rough Guides, 80 Strand, London WC2R 0RL, or Rough Guides, 4th Floor, 345 Hudson St, New York, NY 10014. Or send an email to **mail@roughguides.com**

Have your questions answered and tell others about your trip at **www.roughguides.atinfopop.com**

Acknowledgements

The **authors** would like to thank English Heritage, the National Trust, the Youth Hostels Association and all the regional tourist offices and local development agencies for their advice and assistance. They would also like to thank Margaret Ross at Stanfords Map and Travel Bookshop for map information.

Robert Andrews would like to acknowledge the brilliant contributions of Bea Uhart and Kate Hughes, the incisive editing of Clifton Wilkinson, and the Universal Muse that inspires the cosmic act (thanks Mum).

Jules Brown would like to thank Lesley Wragge, Mike Chadwick, John Lally, Dave Holroyde, Joan Turnbull, Diane Green, Anna Young, Susan Wear, Maria Manion, Lorna Southron, Barbara Macniven, Suzi Williams, Neil Anderson, Melanie Clarkson and Daphne Cain for their practical help and guidance; to Mark Mulrooney, Ian Little, Mark Murray, Mark Batey and the spirit of the ethereal Trai for pub visits far and wide; to Katie, for her love, patience and support; and to Fox, who thinks a chewed book is an improved book.

Phil Lee would like to thank Dave and Lorna Robson for their help with Shrewsbury; Gerard Heelan for his assistance with Buxton; Salford Quays marketing for their attentive help in the Northwest and the kind endeavours of Velimir Ilic of the Birmingham Marketing Partnership. Finally, a word of appreciation to my diligent editor, Clifton Wilkinson.

Clifton Wilkinson would like to thank Polly, Alison and Claire for their much-appreciated help with the book, and all at Autumn Rise for their knowledge of Newcastle's nightlife.

Readers' letters

Thanks to the following who have written into Rough Guides with helpful comments: Sarah Anslow, William Baldwin, Heather Barback, Jayne Becker, Aaron Behaparks, Tim Blood, Ruth Bonington, Janet Boorman, Jason Borthwick, Mandi Brooker, Robert Carding, Richard Chandler, Dani Church, Kim Coates, Joe Cowley, Barry Cox, Diane Cromie, Pete Daly, Roman Dubowski, Ann Feltham, Kathy Field, Shirley Foguenl, David Gothard, Paul Gray, Chris Green, A. R. Handleby, Chris Heaps, Kevin B. Hubbard, Michael Jordan, Steven Kajganich, Fanny Lee, Jan Leech, Johanna Kweizl, L. Levens, Maggie Le Mare, Fritha Lewin, Holly Lincoln, Pam Martin, Kalba Meadows, Bri Miles, Gilda Misur, Duncan Neish, Craig Newcombe, Irene Nichols, Martin Pepperfell, Alan Reid, Dyana & Mel Rodriguez, Margaret Rollason, Edith Rose, Janet Shipperlee, Ellie Sparks, Christopher Stocks, Geoff Taylor, Dominic Thompson, Claire Veares, Pat Walker, James Ward, Eva Weber, Janet Young, Robert Zieminski, Olivia Zurkinden

Photo credits

Cover credits

Main front: Bodiam Castle © Getty
Small front top picture: Angel of the North © Getty
Small front lower picture: Stonehenge © Neil Setchfield
Back top picture: Castle Howard © Joe Cornish
Back lower picture: Durdle Door © Getty

Colour introduction

Brighton Pier © Sean Evison/Travel Ink
Yorkshire Dales © Ellen Rooney/Axiom
Big Ben clock face © Mark Thomas
Shaftesbury, Dorset © English Tourism Council
Football badges © Liam Bailey/Photofusion
Beachy Head Lighthouse, Sussex © Edmund Nagele
The Angel of the North © English Tourism Council
Standing Stones, Cornwall © Edmund Nagele
Notting Hill pub © Alberto Arzoz/Axiom
Stone Signpost © Greg Balfour Evans
Weather vane © Robert Harding
Deckchairs on Blackpool Beach © Chris Parker/Axiom

Things not to miss
Bath © Dave Young/Axiom
North York Moors Railway © David Toase/Travel Ink
Tate Gallery, St Ives © C Wormald/Trip
Scafell Pike, Cumbria © Jim Gibson/Travel Ink
Prince of Wales pub, Cheltenham Spa © Edmund Nagele
Surfing © B Slater/Trip
Royal Pavilion, Brighton © Chris Parker/Axiom
Notting Hill Carnival © Greg Balfour Evans
Royal Albert Hall © Nigel Francis/Robert Harding
Avebury Stone Circle © E James/Trip
Tea at the Ritz © G Adam Woolfit/Robert Harding
Tate Modern © Greg Balfour Evans
Riding on Dartmoor © Kim Sayer/Dorling Kindersley Picture Library
Hay-on-Wye © Dave G. Houser/ Corbis
Oxford from the air © Edmund Nagele
Blackpool illuminations © Edmund Nagele
Glastonbury © Mick Hutson/ Referns
Newcastle nightlife © Graeham Peacock
York Minster © Axiom
Eden Project © R Westlake/Trip
Punting on the River Cam © Neil Setchfield
Canterbury Cathedral © Edmund Nagele
Bonfire Night © David Simson/ Greg Evans Picture Library
Lizard Point © Edmund Nagele
Fish and Chips © Simon Reddy/Travel Ink
Ely Cathedral © Neil Setchfield
Appleby Horse Fair © Richard Turpin/Aspect Picture Library
WOMAD Festival © Angela Hampton/Travel Ink
The Peak District © Corbis
Lake Windermere © Jules Brown
Isle of Man TT races poster © Swim Ink/Corbis
Durdle Door, Dorset © A Tovy/Trip
Alnwick Castle © Simon Harris/Robert Harding
A Day at the Races © Historical Picture Archive/ Corbis
Curry © Clive Streeter/Patrick Mcleavy/ DK Picture Library
Wimbledon © Trevor Creighton/Travel Ink
Hadrian's Wall © Corbis

Black and whites
The British Museum © Mark Thomas
Trafalgar Square © C, Bowman/Axiom
The London Eye © Mark Thomas
Brighton Pier © H Rogers/Trip
The White Cliffs of Dover © Kevin Schafer/Corbis
Ferris Wheel, Brighton © H Rogers/Trip
New Forest © A Tovy/Trip
Cowes Week,Isle of Wight © F Torrance/Trip
All Souls College, Oxford © Ronald Badkin/Travel Ink
RadcliffeCamera, Oxford © Tony Page/Travel Ink
Royal Crescent, Bath © English Tourist Council
Glastonbury Tor © P. Craven
Clovelly Harbour, Devon © Edmund Nagele
Surfing, Bude beach © Adam Woolfitt/Robert Harding
Southwold beach, Suffolk © Fraser Hall/Robert Harding
Flatford Mill, Suffolk © Andrew Milliken/Travel Ink
Windmill © Dorling Kindersley Picture Library
Hassop Hall © Phil Lee
Selfridges Building, Birmingham © John James/Alamy
Hardwick Hall © Phil Lee
Lincoln Cathedral © Peter Murphy/Travel Ink
Blackpool Tower and Beach © David Toase/Travel Ink
Imperial War Museum North © Architectural Images/Alamy
Castlerigg Stone Circle © C. Bowman/Robert Harding
Ullswater, the Lake District © Neil Dyson/Robert Harding
Malham Cove © Bill Broadhurst
Fountains Abbey © DK Images
Whalebone arch, Whitby © Paul Ridsdale/Lesley Garland Picture Library/Alamy
Hadrian's Wall, Northumberland © Adam Woolfitt/Robet Harding
The Sanctuary Knocker, Durham Cathedral © Mark Thomas
Tyne Bridges © Mark Thomas

Rough Guides travel...

UK & Ireland
Britain
Devon & Cornwall
Dublin
Edinburgh
England
Ireland
Lake District
London
London mini guide
London Restaurants
London & SE England, Walks in
Scotland
Scottish Highlands & Islands
Wales

Europe
Algarve
Amsterdam
Andalucía
Austria
Baltic States
Barcelona
Belgium & Luxembourg
Berlin
Brittany & Normandy
Bruges & Ghent
Brussels
Budapest
Bulgaria
Copenhagen
Corfu
Corsica
Costa Brava
Crete
Croatia
Cyprus
Czech & Slovak Republics
Dodecanese & East Aegean
Dordogne & The Lot
Europe
First-Time Europe
Florence
France
Germany
Greece
Greek Islands
Hungary
Ibiza & Formentera
Iceland
Ionian Islands
Italy
Languedoc & Roussillon
Lisbon
The Loire
Madeira
Madrid
Mallorca
Malta & Gozo
Menorca
Moscow
Netherlands
Norway
Paris
Paris Mini Guide
Poland
Portugal
Prague
Provence & the Côte d'Azur
Pyrenees
Romania
Rome
Sardinia
Scandinavia
Sicily
Slovenia
Spain
St Petersburg
Sweden
Switzerland
Tenerife & La Gomera
Turkey
Tuscany & Umbria
Venice & The Veneto
Vienna

Asia
Bali & Lombok
Bangkok
Beijing
Cambodia
China
First-Time Asia
Goa
Hong Kong & Macau
India
Indonesia
Japan
Laos
Malaysia, Singapore & Brunei
Nepal
Philippines
Singapore
South India
Southeast Asia
Thailand
Thailand Beaches & Islands
Tokyo
Vietnam

Australasia
Australia
Gay & Lesbian Australia
Melbourne
New Zealand
Sydney

North America
Alaska
Baltic States
Big Island of Hawaii
Boston
California
Canada
Chicago
Florida
Grand Canyon
Hawaii
Honolulu
Las Vegas
Los Angeles
Maui
Miami & the Florida Keys
Montréal
New England
New Orleans
New York City
New York City Mini Guide
New York Restaurants
Pacific Northwest
Rocky Mountains
San Francisco
San Francisco Restaurants
Seattle
Skiing & Snowboarding in North America
Southwest USA
Toronto
USA
Vancouver
Washington DC
Yosemite

Caribbean & Latin America
Antigua & Barbuda
Argentina
Bahamas
Barbados
Belize
Bolivia
Brazil
Caribbean
Central America
Chile
Costa Rica
Cuba
Dominican Republic
Ecuador
First-Time Latin America
Guatemala
Jamaica
Maya World
Mexico
Peru
St Lucia
South America
Trinidad & Tobago

Rough Guides are available from good bookstores worldwide. New titles are published every month. Check www.roughguides.com for the latest news.

...music & reference

Africa & Middle East
Cape Town
Egypt
The Gambia
Jerusalem
Jordan
Kenya
Morocco
South Africa, Lesotho & Swaziland
Syria
Tanzania
Tunisia
West Africa
Zanzibar
Zimbabwe

Travel Theme guides
First-Time Around the World
First-Time Asia
First-Time Europe
First-Time Latin America
Gay & Lesbian Australia
Skiing & Snowboarding in North America
Travel Online
Travel Health
Walks in London & SE England
Women Travel

Restaurant guides
French Hotels & Restaurants
London
New York
San Francisco

Maps
Algarve
Amsterdam
Andalucia & Costa del Sol
Argentina
Athens
Australia
Baja California
Barcelona
Boston
Brittany
Brussels
Chicago
Crete
Croatia
Cuba
Cyprus
Czech Republic
Dominican Republic
Dublin
Egypt
Florence & Siena
Frankfurt
Greece
Guatemala & Belize
Iceland
Ireland
Lisbon
London
Los Angeles
Mexico
Miami & Key West
Morocco
New York City
New Zealand
Northern Spain
Paris
Portugal
Prague
Rome
San Francisco
Sicily
South Africa
Sri Lanka
Tenerife
Thailand
Toronto
Trinidad & Tobago
Tuscany
Venice
Washington DC
Yucatán Peninsula

Dictionary Phrasebooks
Czech
Dutch
Egyptian Arabic
European
French
German
Greek
Hindi & Urdu
Hungarian
Indonesian
Italian
Japanese
Mandarin Chinese
Mexican Spanish
Polish
Portuguese
Russian
Spanish
Swahili
Thai
Turkish
Vietnamese

Music Guides
The Beatles
Cult Pop
Classical Music
Country Music
Cuban Music
Drum'n'bass
Elvis
House
Irish Music
Jazz
Music USA
Opera
Reggae
Rock
Techno
World Music (2 vols)

100 Essential CDs series
Country
Latin
Opera
Rock
Soul
World Music

History Guides
China
Egypt
England
France
Greece
India
Ireland
Islam
Italy
Spain
USA

Reference Guides
Books for Teenagers
Children's Books, 0–5
Children's Books, 5–11
Cult Football
Cult Movies
Cult TV
Digital Stuff
Formula 1
The Internet
Internet Radio
James Bond
Lord of the Rings
Man Utd
Personal Computers
Pregnancy & Birth
Shopping Online
Travel Health
Travel Online
Unexplained Phenomena
The Universe
Videogaming
Weather
Website Directory

Also! More than 120 Rough Guide music CDs are available from all good book and record stores. Listen in at www.worldmusic.net

NOTES

NOTES

NOTES

NOTES

NOTES

NOTES

NOTES

NOTES

NOTES

NOTES

NOTES

NOTES